dev.	development	GDP	Gross Domestic Product	LNG	liquefied natural gas
dwt	dead weight tonnage	GNP	Gross National Product	m	million/metres
ECU	European Currency Unit	HEP	hydroelectric power	mi	miles
EEC/EC/EU	European Union	in	inches	NGO	Non-Governmental Organization
EMS	European Monetary System	kg	kilograms	NIC	Newly Industrialized Country
est	estimated	km	kilometres	PC	personal computer
°F	degrees Fahrenheit		square kilometre	sq	square
ft	feet			TV	television
g			ours	VCR	video cassette recorder

RESC

 Electr
year in ...... .ours (kwh),
and total available capacity (kw)

 Oil production: barrels pe.
(b/d); total oil reserves in
billion barrels (bbl)

 Estimated livestock resou.

 Main mineral resources

 Fish catch per year

 .Media censorship assessment

 Cable TV availability

ENVIRONMENT

 Protected land as percentage of
total land area

 Trend indicators:
increase/no variation/
decrease in the importance of
environmental issues as a
national concern

SIGNATORY TO THE FOLLOWING TREATIES

 International Tropical Timber
Agreement (ITTA) *Geneva, 1983*

 Convention on the International
Trade in Endangered Species of
Wild Fauna and Flora (CITES)
Washington DC, 1973

United Nations Convention on
the Law of the Sea (UNCLOS)
Montego Bay, Jamaica, 1982

Protocol on Substances that
Deplete the Ozone Layer
(Montreal Protocol)
Montreal, 1987

CRIME

 Total prison population (where
available)

 Crime trend indicators:
increase/no variation/
decrease over previous year

EDUCATION

 Literacy rate (percentage of
total population)

HEALTH

 Doctor/population ratio

 Major causes of death

WEALTH

 Sample blue collar/managerial
wage rates (in local currency)

MAP SYMBOLS AND LETTERING

ADMINISTRATION

International border
Disputed border (*de facto*)
Disputed border (territorial claim)
Undefined border
Cease-fire line
Internal administrative border

COMMUNICATIONS

International airport
Motorway/Highway
Major road
Secondary road
Unsurfaced road, track
Rail
Canal
Tunnel
Mountain pass

HYDROGRAPHY

Major river
Minor river
Seasonal river
Lake
Seasonal lake
Wetland
Salt lake
Salt pan
Waterfall
Dam/reservoir

OTHER SYMBOLS

▲ Highest point in country
▲ High point
Site of interest (mentioned in text)

LETTERING

ECUADOR Country name

DUBLIN Capital city

San Francisco } Cities and towns (type is graded according
Dover } to population size and map scale)

QUEBEC Administrative division

LANGUEDOC Regional name

HIMALAYAS
Lake Baikal
Congo
Mt Fiji } Physical and hydrographic features
Baffin Bay
SULU SEA

THE DORLING KINDERSLEY

WORLD

REFERENCE

ATLAS

THE DORLING KINDERSLEY

WORLD

REFERENCE

ATLAS

DORLING KINDERSLEY
London   New York   Stuttgart

A DORLING KINDERSLEY BOOK

MANAGING EDITOR
Ian Castello-Cortes

MANAGING ART EDITOR
Philip Lord

PROJECT EDITORS
Catherine Day, Jo Edwards, Jane Oliver

PROJECT DESIGNERS
Martin Biddulph, Karen Gregory

EDITORS
Alastair Dougall, Ailsa Heritage, Susan Turner
Chris Whitwell, Elizabeth Wyse

DESIGNERS
Scott David, Yahya El-Droubie,
Rhonda Fisher, Nicola Liddiard

PROJECT CARTOGRAPHERS
John Plumer, Julie Turner,
James Mills-Hicks
Caroline Bowie, Ruth Duxbury

CARTOGRAPHERS
James Anderson, Roger Bullen, Tony Chambers,
Clare Ellam, Julia Lunn, Michael Martin,
Peter Winfield, Claudine Zante

ADDITIONAL EDITORIAL ASSISTANCE
Debra Clapson, Caroline Lucas
Crispian Martin St. Valery
Laura Porter
Donna Rispoli, Sally Wood
Nicholas Kynaston

ADDITIONAL DESIGN ASSISTANCE
Paul Bayliss, Carol Ann Davis,
Adam Dobney, Kenny Laurenson

PICTURE RESEARCH
Sarah Moule

READERS
Jane Bruton, Reg Grant, Ann Kramer, Lesley Riley

INDEX GAZETTEER
Jayne Parsons, Margaret Hynes, Barbara Nash, Janet Smy

EDITORIAL DIRECTION
Andrew Heritage, Louise Cavanagh

ART DIRECTOR
Chez Picthall

PRODUCTION
Hilary Stephens

First published in Great Britain in 1994
by Dorling Kindersley Limited,
9 Henrietta Street, London, WC2E 8PS

A CIP catalogue record for this book is available from the British Library.

ISBN: 0-7513-0130-2

Reproduction by Colourscan (Singapore) and Face Creative Services (London)
Text film output by Lyledale T/A Elements (London)
Printed and bound by New Interlitho (Italy)

FOREWORD

THIS ATLAS is presented to the public in the full knowledge that the world is in a state of continual flux. Political fashions and personalities come and go, while the ebb and flow of peoples and ideas across the face of the planet create constant shifts in the cultural landscape. All the material assembled for this Atlas has been researched from the most up-to-date and authoritative sources; our team of consultants and contributors, designers, editors and cartographers have endeavoured not only to explain the meaning of this material, to place it in a useful and clear context, but also to present it in a way which has a lasting value and relevance, regardless of the turmoil of daily events. The Atlas is thus intended not so much as a 'snapshot' of the state of the world today, but rather a detailed portrait in which the underlying features and characteristics of its subject are brought to life.

The publishers would like to thank the many consultants and contributors whose diligence, perseverance and attention to detail made this book possible.

GENERAL CONSULTANTS
Anthony Goldstone, Senior Editor Asia-Pacific, *The Economist* Intelligence Unit, London
Professor Jack Spence, Director of Studies, The Royal Institute of International Affairs, London

REGIONAL CONSULTANTS

ASIA
Anthony Goldstone, London

USA
Michael Elliot, Diplomatic Editor, *Newsweek*, Washington DC

AFRICA
James Hammill, Lecturer in African Politics, University of Leicester
Kaye Whiteman, Editor-in-Chief, *West Africa Magazine*, London

EUROPE
John Ardagh, London
Rory Clarke, Senior Editor Europe, *The Economist* Intelligence Unit, London
Charles Powell, Centre for European Studies, St Antony's College, Oxford

RUSSIA AND CIS
Martin Macauley, Senior Lecturer, School of Slavonic and East European Studies, University of London

MIDDLE EAST
John Whelan, Ex Editor-in-Chief, *Middle East Economic Digest*

CENTRAL AND SOUTH AMERICA
Nick Caistor, Producer, Latin American Section, BBC World Service

PACIFIC
Jim Boutilier, Professor in History, Royal Roads Military College, Victoria, Canada

CARIBBEAN
Canute James, *The Financial Times*, Kingston, Jamaica

CONTRIBUTORS

Janice Bell, School of Slavonic and East European Studies, University of London
Gerry Bourke, Asia Correspondent, *The Guardian*, Islamabad
Vincent Cable, Director, International Economics Programme
P K Clark, MA, Former Chief Map Research Officer, Ministry of Defence
Ken Davies, Senior Editor, *The Economist* Intelligence Unit, London
Roger Dunn, Analyst, Control Risks Group, London
Aisan Foster-Carter, Senior Lecturer in Sociology, University of Leeds
Professor Murray Forsyth, Centre for Federal Studies, University of Leicester
Natasha Franklin, School of Slavonic and East European Studies, London
Adam Hannestad, *Blomberg Business News*, Copenhagen
Peter Holden, *The Economist* Research Department, London
Tim Jones, Knight Ritter, Brussels
Angella Johnstone, Home Affairs Correspondent, *The Guardian*, London
Oliver Keserü, International Chamber of Commerce, Paris
Robert Macdonald, *The Economist* Intelligence Unit
William Mader, Former Europe Bureau Chief, *Time Magazine*, Washington DC
Professor Brian Matthews, Institute of Commonwealth Studies, London
Nick Middleton, Oriel College, Oxford
Professor Mya Maung, Department of Finance, Boston College, Massachusetts
Judith Nordby, Leeds University
Simon Orme, London

Professor Richard Overy, Department of History, King's College, London
Steve Percy, East Asia Service, BBC World Service
Douglas Rimmer, Honorary Senior Research Fellow, Centre for West African Studies, University of Birmingham
Ian Rodger, *The Financial Times*, Zürich
The Royal Institute of International Affairs, London
Struan Simpson, St. James Research, London
Julie Smith, Brasenose College, Oxford
Michiel Van Kuyen, Erasmus University, Rotterdam
Steven Whitefield, Pembroke College, Oxford
Georgina Wilde, Regional Director, Asia-Pacific, *The Economist* Intelligence Unit, London
H P Willmott, Visiting Professor, Dept. of Military Strategy & Operations, The National War College, Washington DC
Andrew Wilson, Sydney Sussex College, Cambridge
Tom Wingfield, *Reuters*, Bangkok
The World Conservation Monitoring Centre, Cambridge

Database research:
CIRCA Research and Reference Information Limited, Cambridge, UK
Roger East, Rosemary Payne, John Coggins, Tanya Joseph, Stephen Lewis, Frances Nicholson, Jolyon Pontin, Darren Sagar, Farzana Shaikh

5

CONTENTS

Overseas Territories & Dependencies

3
Global Issues

4
Index ~ Gazetteer

======= End Papers =======
Key to Symbols, Icons and
Abbreviations used in the Atlas

HOW THE ATLAS WORKS

T HE DORLING KINDERSLEY WORLD REFERENCE ATLAS is divided into the four main sections detailed below. Each section has four main elements: maps, charts, icons and text. The opposite page explains how each of these are used in the book. The central section of the book is the Nations of the World which includes detailed mapping and encyclopedic information for every one of the world's 191 countries as defined by the UN.

The political reference map of the world includes an inset map of the world's time zones

1 THE WORLD TODAY: Ten double-page spreads examine the world and its continents. Regional maps highlight major physical features, with additional data about the continent's physical and political geography listed in the fact box. Introductory texts offer a concise view of each continent – its physical geography, people and resources, while illuminating cross-sections offer a different perspective.

A further eight double-page spreads are devoted to The Formation of the Modern World, which surveys world history over the last 500 years focusing on key dates and periods, starting with The Age of Discovery: 1492.

One of eight historical world maps

2 THE NATIONS OF THE WORLD: 580 pages of information broken down on a nation-by-nation basis, and listed alphabetically. For a detailed explanation of how this section works, refer to opposite page.

National coverage is presented across one, two, three or four double-page spreads

The eight continental and regional maps provide a detailed overview of the physical and political geography of each part of the world

3 GLOBAL ISSUES: 18 pages of double-page spreads which examine major issues in the modern world, presented thematically on a global map supplemented by regional examples, diagrams, text and captions.

4 INDEX – GAZETTEER: 77 pages of index list all the names shown on the national maps. Cross-references are made to alternative place-name forms and spellings. This section also includes a listing of international organizations.

One of the nine Global Issues double-page spreads, which combines a world map with diagrams, illustrations and informative text

THE NATIONS OF THE WORLD

THE NATIONS OF THE WORLD is the largest section in the Atlas. Countries are arranged alphabetically for ease of reference. Each nation is mapped, has an introductory Country Profile Reference Panel and is analyzed under 18 consistent subject headings. See following pages for a complete listing.

The Atlas is designed so that every country entry is structured in the same way. The title headings are always arranged in the same sequence and all the information is comparable from one country to another.

This makes it very easy to find exactly what you want to read about in a particular country section. It also makes comparisons between countries much easier.

In addition to the explanations and definitions provided overleaf, both endpapers carry a detailed key to the icons, map symbols and abbreviations used in this section of the Atlas.

— BUSINESS AND LAND USE MAPS —

The world's 70 largest countries are also provided with business and land use maps to reflect the more complex nature of their economies. These give an instant idea of where major business sectors are located and the nature of the nation's agriculture.

DENMARK : MAJOR BUSINESSES

RUSSIAN FEDERATION : LAND USE

— NATIONAL FLAGS —

The national flag of each country is shown in colour and in its correct geometric proportions.

— LOCATOR MAPS —

The locator maps are always found next to the country name. They provide both a world and regional location for each country.

— COUNTRY MAPS —

Each country is mapped in considerable detail. The maps show the national boundaries and neighbouring countries, the major physical features, main road and rail infrastructure and populated and administrative centres. A key provides a breakdown of land height (in metres and feet) and of populated places.

UKRAINE
Total Area : 603 700 sq. km (233 090 sq. miles)

POPULATION
 over 1 000 000
 over 500 000
over 100 000
over 50 000
over 10 000

LAND HEIGHT
2000m/6562ft
1000m/3281ft
500m/1640ft
200m/656ft
Sea Level

— REGIONAL MAPS —

Regional maps are featured for 13 of the world's leading countries. The regions or cities are chosen to reflect national differences or because they are of particular economic importance. Each map has a full explanatory text.

CHARTS

Charts are used to show each country's climate, social make-up and the economy. All countries have a standard set of charts.

The top 70 countries have additional charts. This chart, for example, provides a guide to the country's economic performance.

This sort of chart can be found in the Defence, Education and Health sections. It shows how much major countries spend on each, as a proportion of Gross National Product.

ICONS

Icons are a key feature of the book. The design of the icon gives an indication of the information being represented.

Icons are of three types. The icons appearing under the title give a ready reference to the political, economic and social status of the country.

Icons under section headings appear for all countries.

Grouped icons are mostly found in the world's top 70 countries.

Trend icons show whether the trend of their subject matter is increasing, decreasing or level.

TEXT

Denmark is a constitutional monarchy and a multiparty democracy. The associated territories of Greenland and the Faroe Islands have home rule.

MAIN POLITICAL ISSUES
Relations with the EU
In recent years, Denmark's left-of-centre parties have been suspicious of any EU moves for closer ties between the air caused by the ratification of the Maastricht Treaty in 1992. The Treaty was approved by parliament but rejected in a referendum. The population objected to proposals for a

The text in the Atlas is intended to be highly accessible so that essential information can always be found quickly.

The larger countries are presented across more pages and thus have more text, reflecting their greater complexity. Longer text entries have, however, been broken down by introducing sub-headings to guide the reader to the subject of interest.

The text for larger countries also has extra features, including, for example, more detailed profiles of political and economic systems.

KEY TO CHARTS AND ICONS

Icons and trend indicators vary. Not all variations are shown in the key below, but where they do occur the symbols have been 'stacked'.

COUNTRY PROFILE REFERENCE PANEL

These icons are coloured yellow when the information is applicable.

 Date of independence, or date current borders set.

 Democratic system of election in use.

 Convertible national currency.

 International aid status: donor/receiver/neither.

 Net energy importer/exporter.

 Compulsory military service.

 Death penalty currently in use.

 Welfare provision: full social security/ health benefits only/ unemployment benefits only.

CLIMATE

 Statistics are given for the the national capital. They represent maximum summer and minimum winter averages.

COMMUNICATIONS

 The country's principal international airport with annual passenger numbers.

 Total size of national merchant or cargo fleet.

THE TRANSPORT NETWORK

National communications infrastructure given in kilometres and miles.

 Extent of national road network

 Extent of motorways or major national highways

 Extent of commercial rail network

 Extent of inland waterways navigable by commercial craft

TOURISM

 Number of visitors per year, including business travellers.

 Indicators showing trend in recent visitor numbers (up/level/down).

 The state of each nation's tourism is explained, with reasons given when there is no significant tourist industry. The chart shows the percentage of total visitors by country of origin.

PEOPLE

 Main languages spoken, in descending order of importance.

 Population density. This is an average over the whole country.

 The pie chart proportions show the religious affiliations of those who profess a belief.

 This pie chart illustrates the ethnic origin of the country's population.

 This graph represents the proportion of the population living in urban areas (grey) and rural areas (green).

 This chart shows the breakdown of the population by age groupings over a 40-year period, providing an interesting insight into the nation's demography.

POLITICS

 Date of next election. Where the situation is not clear, 'uncertain' is used.

 Name of head of state. In many cases this is a nominal position and does not indicate that this is the nation's most powerful person.

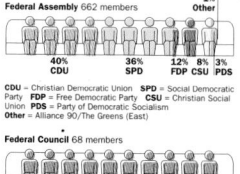 A graphic representation of the political make-up of the nation's government, based on each party's showing at the last election. Where there are two houses, the most important elected body is shown first.

WORLD AFFAIRS

 Abbreviations in the flag symbols indicate a nation's membership of international organizations. United Nations and World Bank membership is assumed. Grey flags signify no additional membership of international organizations. The main issues which dominate each nation's politics are outlined in the text.

AID

 The amount of net international aid donations or receipts is given in US$. Undisclosed military aid is not included.

 Symbols indicate whether aid payments or receipts are rising, level or declining.

DEFENCE

 The defence budget, the nation's annual expenditure (in US$) on arms and military personnel.

 Symbols indicate if the trend in defence spending is rising, level or declining.

Spending on arms is shown as a proportion of Gross Domestic Product (GDP). The general state of the country's defences and the status of the military is discussed in the text.

THE ARMED FORCES

Icons represent the main branches of the national armed forces.

 Army: equipment and personnel

 Navy: equipment and personnel

 Airforce: equipment and personnel

 Nuclear capability: armaments

ECONOMICS

 Gross National Product (GNP) – the total value of goods and services produced by a country.

 Average exchange rate against the US$ over the last year. Some currencies are too volatile for a useful figure to be given.

❏ World GNP Ranking	24th
❏ GNP per Capita	$24,388
❏ Balance of Payments	$2.2bn
❏ Inflation	5.6%
❏ Unemployment	10.6%

The score cards are intended to give a broad picture of the country's economy. Gross National Product (GNP) includes income from investments and businesses held abroad. Balance of payments is the difference between a country's payments to and receipts from abroad.

 This graph shows year-on-year variations in GDP and consumer prices.

 This pie chart gives a broad picture of the nation's principal import trading partners.

This pie chart gives a broad picture of the nation's principal export trading partners.

RESOURCES

 Electricity generation is expressed in kilowatt hours (kwh) per year, and total available capacity (kw).

 Oil produced in barrels per day (b/d). Refining capacity, oil reserves and other fossil fuels are given where applicable.

 Estimated livestock resources.

 Main mineral reserves are listed in descending order of economic importance.

 Fish catch per year (where appropriate).

Percentages of the different energy sources used for the generation of electricity are represented graphically. An account of the nation's resource base is given in the text.

ENVIRONMENT

 Percentage of land which is protected or conserved by law. Protection is often only theoretical.

 Symbols indicate a trend in the importance of environmental issues as a national concern.

ENVIRONMENTAL TREATIES
National signatory to international environmental treaties.

 ITTA: timber

 CITES: endangered species

 UNCLOS: marine dumping

 Montreal Protocol: CFC emissions

MEDIA

 An assessment of political censorship in national media.

PUBLISHING AND BROADCAST MEDIA
National broadcast and print media, by size and ownership.

 Main national newspapers

 Television stations: state-owned/independent

 Radio: state-owned/independent

 Satellite TV availability

 Cable TV availability

CRIME

 Prison population statistics (where available).

 Symbols show general trend in crime figures.

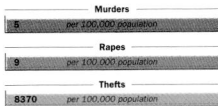

This section records official crime figures only. Reported statistics are normally lower than the actual figures.

CHRONOLOGY

Beginning at a significant date in the recent history of the nation, the outline chronology continues through to the present day.

EDUCATION

 Literacy icon. A person who is able to read and write a short statement about his or her everyday life is defined by UNESCO as literate. Literacy percentages are given for each country.

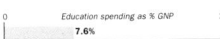

The state's total budget for education is shown as a proportion of its Gross National Product (GNP).

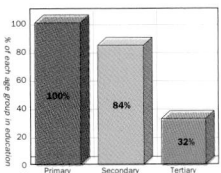 This graph shows the percentages of each age group in education. Primary is up to age 11; secondary is age 11–16/18; tertiary is further education, beyond school level.

HEALTH

 Ratio of doctors per head of population is given as a national average.

 Major causes of death are listed.

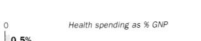

Health spending is shown as a proportion of the Gross National Product (GNP).

WEALTH

 This section highlights wealth disparities by contrasting sample blue-collar and managerial salaries. Earnings are shown in local currency.

 This graph shows the comparative ownership of consumer goods. Figures may reflect access to, rather than ability to purchase, high-value consumer durables.

WORLD RANKING

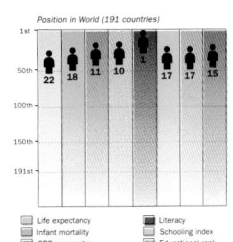

The World Ranking is based on the UN Human Development Index. Expert consultants have advised on various indicators, covering a range of financial, medical, educational and social fields.

1

THE WORLD TODAY

THE POLITICAL WORLD

THE PHYSICAL WORLD

• NORTH AMERICA • SOUTH AMERICA • EUROPE • AFRICA
• WEST ASIA • NORTH ASIA • SOUTH ASIA
• AUSTRALASIA & OCEANIA

THE FORMATION OF THE MODERN WORLD

• THE WORLD IN 1492 • THE AGE OF DISCOVERY 1492-1648

• THE AGE OF EXPANSION 1648-1789

• THE AGE OF REVOLUTION 1789-1830

• THE AGE OF EMPIRE 1830-1914

• THE AGE OF GLOBAL WAR 1914-1945

• THE MODERN AGE 1945-1994

THE POLITICAL WORLD

IN TODAY'S RAPIDLY EVOLVING WORLD, a political perspective on international boundaries is more important than ever before. The world currently comprises 191 independent states – more than at any previous time – and 58 dependencies. Antarctica is the only land area on the earth's surface which is not part of and does not belong to any one country.

A massive transformation has taken place since 1950, when the world comprised only 82 countries. In the decades following the Second World War, many states came into being as they achieved independence from their former colonial rulers. Most recently, the break-up of the Soviet Union in 1991 swelled the ranks of independent states. Generally, a worldwide trend towards fragmentation has been seen as nationalist aims have come to the fore. Civil wars are currently being waged in many parts of the world, including Yugoslavia, Angola, Rwanda, Liberia, Indonesia, Afghanistan and Yemen. Within the former Soviet Union itself instability continues, notably in the fighting between Azerbaijan and Armenia over Nagorno Karabakh and in the conflict within Georgia.

The Russian Federation is the world's largest state; Vatican City is the smallest. In 1993, Eritrea became the most recent addition to the world map.

THE WORLD POLITICAL MAP

ABBREVIATIONS
B-H   Bosnia and Herzegovina
DOM. REP.   Dominican Republic
LIECH.   Liechtenstein
LUX.   Luxembourg
NETH.   Netherlands
RUSSIAN FED.   Russian Federation
SWITZ.   Switzerland
U.A.E.   United Arab Emirates
YUGO.   Yugoslavia

POLITICAL STATUS
Eg MEXICO: independent state
Eg COOK ISLANDS (to NZ): Self-
governing dependent territory, with
parent state indicated
Eg *Azores (to Portugal)*: Non self-
governing dependent territory, with
parent state indicated

TIME ZONES

The World is divided into 24 time zones, which are measured in relation to 12 noon Greenwich Mean Time (GMT), on the Greenwich Meridian (0º). The time zones do not follow a regular pattern, but are adapted to regional administrative boundaries.

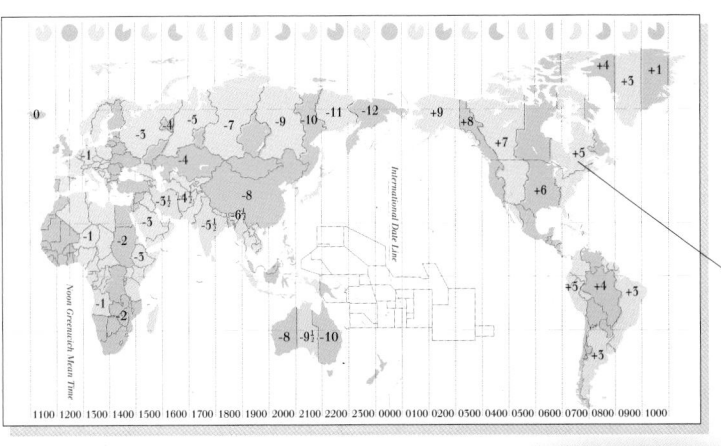

The world's 24 time zones. Numbers on the map indicate the number of hours which must be added or subtracted, as appropriate, in that time zone to reach GMT. Thus, east coast USA (+5) is 5 hours behind GMT.

GREENLAND
(to Denmark)

Arctic Circle

Alaska
(to US)

CANADA

Aleutian Is (to US)

P A C I F I C

O C E A N

ST PIERRE & MIQUELON
(to France)

A T L A N T I C

O C E A N

UNITED STATES
OF AMERICA

BERMUDA
(to UK)

PUERTO RICO (to US)
VIRGIN IS (to US)
BRIT. VIRGIN IS (to UK)
ANGUILLA (to UK)
ST KITTS & NEVIS
ANTIGUA & BARBUDA
MONTSERRAT (to UK)
GUADELOUPE (to France)
DOMINICA
MARTINIQUE (to France)
ST LUCIA
BARBADOS
ST VINCENT & THE GRENADINES

MIDWAY
ISLANDS (to US)

Guadalupe
(to Mexico)

MEXICO

CAYMAN IS
(to UK)

BAHAMAS

TURKS &
CAICOS IS
(to UK)

Tropic of Cancer

Hawaii
(to US)

Revillagigedo Islands
(to Mexico)

CUBA

HAITI

DOM.
REP.

NAVASSA I. (to US)

ND

JOHNSTON ATOLL
(to US)

BELIZE
GUATEMALA
EL SALVADOR

JAMAICA
HONDURAS
NICARAGUA

Caribbean Sea

LL
S

KINGMAN REEF (to US)
PALMYRA ATOLL (US)

CLIPPERTON ISLAND
(to French Polynesia)

COSTA RICA
PANAMA

GRENADA
TRINIDAD & TOBAGO

BAKER & HOWLAND
IS (to US)
JARVIS I (to US)

VENEZUELA

SURINAM

FRENCH GUIANA (to France)

KIRIBATI

ARUBA (to Netherlands)
NETHERLANDS ANTILLES (to Netherlands)

COLOMBIA

Equator

UVALU

TOKELAU
(to NZ)

Galapagos Is
(to Ecuador)

ECUADOR

Fernando de Noronha
(to Brazil)

WESTERN
SAMOA
WALLIS &
FUTUNA
(to France)

AMERICAN
SAMOA
(to US)

COOK
ISLANDS
(to NZ)

P A C I F I C

O C E A N

PERU

B R A Z I L

FIJI

TONGA

NIUE
(to NZ)

FRENCH POLYNESIA
(to France)

PITCAIRN
ISLANDS
(to UK)

BOLIVIA

Trinidade
(to Brazil)

PARAGUAY

Tropic of Capricorn

K ISLAND
stralia)

Kermadec Islands
(to NZ)

Easter Island
(to Chile)

San Felix Island (to Chile)

Sala y Gomez
(to Chile)

San Ambrosio Island
(to Chile)

URUGUAY

A T L A N T I C

NEW ZEALAND

Chatham Islands (to NZ)

Juan Fernandez Islands
(to Chile)

CHILE

ARGENTINA

O C E A N

Bounty Islands (to NZ)

Antipodes Islands (to NZ)

lands (to NZ)

'I Island
NZ)

FALKLAND ISLAND
(to UK)

SOUTH GEORGIA & SOUTH
SANDWICH ISLANDS (to UK)

South Shetland
Islands (to UK)

South Orkney
Islands (to UK)

THE PHYSICAL WORLD

Svalbard
Franz Joseph Zemlya
Savernaya Zamlya
Novaya Zemlya
Kara Sea
Laptev Sea
Novos Ostova
Greenland Sea
Barents Sea
Kirebet Chen
Denmark Strait
Norwegian Sea
Lapland
Scandinavia
Ural Mts
West Siberian Plain
Ob'
Yenisey
Central Siberian Plateau
Lena
Siberia
Iceland
North Sea
British Isles
Baltic Sea
North European Plain
EUROPE
Volga
ASIA
See Okh
Lake Baikal
Bay of Biscay
Alps
Carpathian Mts
Ukraine
Caucasus
Aral Sea
Lake Balkhash
Altai Mts
Sak
Manchurian Plain
Pyrenees
Iberia
Danube
Black Sea
Anatolia
Caspian Sea
Tien Shan
Gobi
Hokk
Sea of Japan
Mediterranean Sea
Balkans
Pamirs
Hindu Kush
Kunlun Shan
Huang He (Yellow River)
Jang Chiang (Yangtze)
Japan
Hons
Atlas Mts
Zagros Mts
Iranian Plateau
Plateau of Tibet
Himalayas
Yellow Sea
Kyūshū
Maderia
Canary Is
Indus
Thar Desert
Ganges
East China Sea
Ryukyu Is
Ja
Tr
Cape Verde Is
Sahara
Ahaggar
Tibesti
AFRICA
Sahel
Niger
Lake Chad
Nile
Red Sea
Arabian Peninsula
Arabian Basin
Deccan
Taiwan
Philippine Sea
Mar
M
Ethiopian Highlands
Horn of Africa
Arabian Basin
Arabian Sea
Bay of Bengal
Indochina Peninsula
South China Sea
Philippine Trench
Marianas
Adamawa Highlands
Sri Lanka
ATLANTIC OCEAN
Gulf of Guinea
Congo
Congo Basin
Lake Victoria
Great Rift Valley
Somali Basin
Malay Peninsula
Borneo
East Indies
Bismarck Archipelago
Lake Tanganyika
Seychelles
INDIAN OCEAN
Sumara
Java Sea
Java
New Guinea
Mid Atlantic Ridge
Angola Basin
Lake Nyasa
Zambezi
Ninetyeast Ridge
Java Trench
Timor Sea
Arafura Sea
Great Barrier Reef
Gre
Madagascar
Mauritius
Reunion
Great Sandy Desert
AUSTRALIA
Namib Desert
Kalahari Desert
Drakensberg
Mozambique Channel
South Indian Ridge
Great Victoria Desert
Nullarbor Plain
Darling
Cape Basin
Cape of Good Hope
Southwest Indian Ridge
Bass
Tasmani
South Georgia
Kerguelen
South Sandwich Islands
Australian Antarctic Basin
Enderby Plain
Dronning Maud Land
ANTARCTICA
Wilkes Le

ARCTIC OCEAN

Limit of permanent pack ice

Ellesmere Island

Queen
Elizbeth
Islands

Greenland

*Greenland
Sea*

erian Sea

Chukchi Sea

Beaufort Sea

Baffin Bay

Baffin Island

Arctic Circle

Brooks Range

Yukon

Mackenzie

Great Bear
Lake

Great Slave
Lake

Canadian Shield

Hudson
Bay

*Ungava
Peninsula*

*Labrador
Sea*

Iceland

Bering Straits

Bering Sea

Aleutian Basin

*Gulf of
Alaska*

Coast Mountains

Rocky Mountains

Coast Ranges

Lake
Winnipeg

NORTH AMERICA

Great Lakes

Appalachian Mountains

North America
Basin

*Grand
Bank*

Mid Atlantic Ridge

Aleutian Islands

Aleutian Trench

Vancouver I

Great Plains

Missouri

Mississippi

ATLANTIC

OCEAN

Azores

ench

Emperor Seamount Chain

Mendocino Fracture Zone

Murray Fracture Zone

Baja California

Gulf of
Mexico

*Yucatán
Peninsula*

West Indies

Greater Antilles

*Caribbean
Sea*

*Lesser
Antilles*

Tropic of Cancer

Hawaiian Islands

Sierra Madre

Guatemala Trench

*Pacific
untains*

PACIFIC

OCEAN

*P
o
l
y
n
e
s
i
a*

*Galapagos
Islands*

*Guiana
Highlands*

Amazon

Amazon Basin

Equator

ronesia

Gilbert Is

Line Islands

Phoenix Is

SOUTH
AMERICA

Mato Grosso

*Brazilian
Highlands*

Brazilian
Basin

lands

Fiji

Tonga

Cook Is

*Tuamotu
Islands*

Peru Basin

Tonga Trench

*A
n
d
e
s*

Peru-Chile Trench

Paraná

Tropic of Capricorn

East Pacific Ridge

Southwest

Pacific

Basin

Pampas

Patagonia

*Argentine
Basin*

*Tristan
da Cunha*

Kermadec Trench

*North
Island*

*New
Zealand*

Falkland Is

*Tierra
del Fuego*

South Georgia

Mid Atlantic Ridge

an

*mpbell
ateau*

Cape
Horn

Drake Passage

*Antarctic
Peninsula*

Antarctic Circle

*Bellinghausen
Sea*

Weddell Sea

Ross Sea

Byrd Land

Ronne Ice Shelf

ANTARCTICA

Ross Ice Shelf

Scale : 1:32 500 000

0   250   500 km

ICELAND

Denmark Strait

GREENLAND
(Danish province)

NUUK

Davis Strait

Baffin
Bay

Baffin Island

Ellesmere I.

North Pole

Queen Elizabeth Islands

Devon I.

Melville I.
Bathurst I.
Cornwallis I.
Somerset I.
Prince
of Wales
I.

Banks I.

Victoria I.

A   R   C   T   I   C

O   C   E   A   N

Beaufort
Sea

Inuvik

Brooks Range

ALASKA
(to US)

Fairbanks

Denali
6194m
Anchorage

Alaska Range

Yukon

Dawson

YUKON
TERRITORY

Mackenzie Mts

NORTHWEST
TERRITORIES

Yellowknife

Great
Bear
Lake

Great Slave
Lake

Churchill

Hudson Strait

Péninsula
D'ungava

Hudson
Bay

James
Bay

NEWFOUNDLAND

Labrador

Sept Iles

St John's

Newfoundland

ST PIERRE &
MIQUELON
(to France)

PRINCE
EDWARD I.

Halifax

NOVA SCOTIA

NEW
BRUNSWICK

MAINE

NEW
HAMPSHIRE

MASSACHUSETTS
Boston
RHODE ISLAND
CONNECTICUT

VERMONT

QUEBEC

Labrador City

Québec

Montréal

OTTAWA

Toronto

L. Ontario

New York

Philadelphia

NEW
YORK

Buffalo

PENNSYLVANIA

Pittsburgh

Cleveland

OHIO

L. Erie

Detroit

L. Huron

MICHIGAN

L. Michigan

Sault Saint
Marie

L. Superior

Great Lakes

ONTARIO

Thunder
Bay

C   A   N   A   D   A

MANITOBA

Lake
Winnipeg

Winnipeg

SASKATCHEWAN

Saskatoon

Regina

Medicine Hat

Calgary

ALBERTA

Edmonton
Athabasca
Athabasca L.

BRITISH
COLUMBIA

Coast Mountains

R   o   c   k   y   M   o   u   n   t   a   i   n   s

P   r   a   i   r   i   e   s

MINNESOTA

St Paul
Minneapolis

WISCONSIN

Milwaukee
Chicago

Mississippi

IOWA

ILLINOIS

NORTH DAKOTA

SOUTH DAKOTA

Omaha

NEBRASKA

Kansas City

Missouri

MONTANA

Great
Plains

WYOMING

Denver

COLORADO

U   N   I   T   E   D   S   T   A   T   E   S

IDAHO

Boise

Snake

Salt Lake
City

UTAH

Great
Basin

NEVADA

Reno

Las
Vegas

Death
Valley

Sierra Nevada

WASHINGTON

Spokane

Seattle

Portland

OREGON

Cascade Range

Columbia R.

Great
Basin

Vancouver

Vancouver I.

Queen
Charlotte Is

Alexander
Archipelago

Juneau

Gulf
of
Alaska

Kodiak I.

Alaska Peninsula

Unimak

Unalaska

Atka

Aleutian Islands

Attu

Bering
Sea

St Lawrence I.

Bering Strait

Arctic Circle

RUSSIAN
FEDERATION

Sacramento
San Francisco

CALIFORNI

Los Angeles

P   A   C   I   F   I

POPULATION

| over 5 000 000 |
| over 1 000 000 |
| over 500 000 |
| over 100 000 |
| over 50 000 |
| under 50 000 |

LAND HEIGHT

4000m/13 124ft
3000m/9845ft
2000m/6562ft
1000m/3281ft
200m/656ft
Sea Level

Line of cross-section

Arctic Circle

NORTH AMERICA

North America's climate is as varied as its topography: much of Canada is snowbound or clothed in forest, its sparse population congregating along the US border. Along the continent's western flank are the spectacular Rocky Mountains. To the east lie the older, wooded Appalachians. Between these are the Great Plains – grazed by herds of livestock or sown with cereals. These plains were once home to tribes of native Americans, supplanted by incoming white settlers. America's population and industry are concentrated in the temperate northeast, while the drier south and west are rural and thinly populated. North America is rich in minerals and oil. Mexico is the world's largest Spanish-speaking nation. Central America and the Caribbean contain some 30 countries and numerous small islands. The climate is tropical and prone to storms, the landscape mountainous and volcanic.

CONTINENTAL FACTS

PHYSICAL FEATURES

LARGEST LAKE: Lake Superior, Canada/USA 83,270 sq km (32,140 square miles)

LONGEST RIVER: Mississippi-Missouri, USA 619 km (3740 miles)

HIGHEST POINT: Denali (formerly Mt McKinley), Alaska, USA 6194 m (20,322 ft)

LOWEST POINT: Death Valley, California, USA 86 m (282 ft) below sea level

POLITICAL FEATURES

TOTAL POPULATION: 435.9 million

LARGEST CITY WITH POPULATION: Mexico City, Mexico 20.2 million

COUNTRY WITH HIGHEST POPULATION DENSITY: Barbados 598 people per sq km

LARGEST COUNTRY: Canada 9,976,139 sq km (3,851,817 square miles)

SMALLEST COUNTRY: Grenada 340 sq km (131 square miles)

CROSS-SECTION THROUGH NORTH AMERICA: 43°N, 126°W–65°W

SOUTH AMERICA

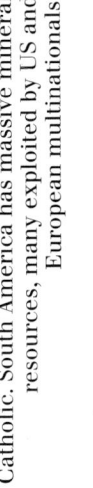

THE WORLD'S fourth largest continent includes one of its most important resources – the Amazonian rainforest. It is a major source of oxygen and includes half of all known living species, while the Amazon – the world's second longest river – contains one fifth of the world's fresh water. The Andes mountain chain reaches down South America's western flank, sheltering the prairies of the Gran Chaco, the Pampas and the wastes of the far south. Most South Americans are *mestizo* – of mixed European and Amerindian descent and live in the coastal regions. Spanish is the most widely-spoken language, and over 90% of South Americans are Roman Catholic. South America has massive mineral resources, many exploited by US and European multinationals.

ATLANTIC OCEAN

Equator

Fernando de Noronha

Cabo de São Roque

João Pessoa
Recife
Olinda
Maceió
Aracaju

Fortaleza

Salvador

São Luís
Teresina

B R A Z I L

Represa de Sobradinho

São Francisco

Brazilian Highlands

Belém
Imperatriz

Tocantins

BRASÍLIA
Goiânia

Araguaia

Planalto de Mato Grosso

Xingu

Tapajós

Amazon

Madeira

Manaus

Guaporé

BOLIVIA

Mamoré

Santa Cruz

Sucre

Cordillera Oriental

Cordillera

LA PAZ
Oruro

Lake Titicaca

Arequipa

PERU

A n d e s

LIMA

Trujillo

Marañón

Ucayali

ECUADOR

Guayaquil
Gulf of Guayaquil

QUITO

Napo

Putumayo

Caquetá

COLOMBIA

BOGOTÁ

Cali

Medellín

Montería

Barranquilla

Magdalena

Cauca

Cúcuta

Maracaibo

Lago de Maracaibo

ARUBA (to Neth.)

NETHERLANDS ANTILLES (to Neth.)

Valencia

CARACAS

Turmero

VENEZUELA

Apure

Arauca

Orinoco

Meta

Guaviare

PANAMA

Caribbean Sea

Lesser Antilles

TRINIDAD & TOBAGO

Morawhanna

Charity

GEORGETOWN

Bartica
Linden

New Amsterdam

Essequibo

Salto del Angel

Caroní

Branco

Negro

Japurá

Juruá

Purús

Guiana Highlands

GUYANA

SURINAM

PARAMARIBO
New Amsterdam
Totness
Brokopondo

FRENCH GUIANA (to France)

CAYENNE

St-Laurent-du-Maroni

PACIFIC

Equator

Amazon

Madeira

Paraguay

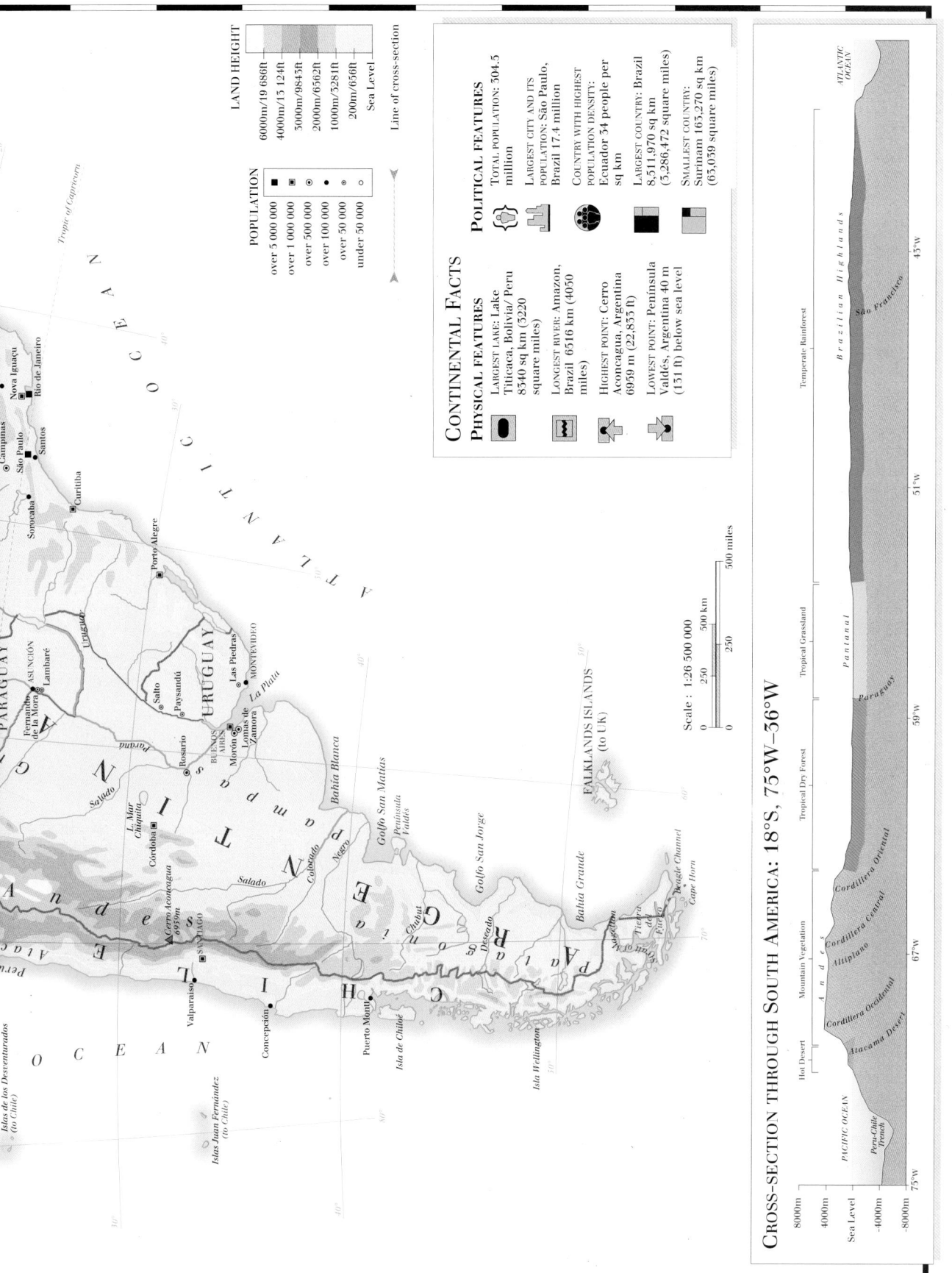

LAND HEIGHT

6000m/19 686ft
4000m/15 124ft
3000m/9845ft
2000m/6562ft
1000m/3281ft
200m/656ft
Sea Level

Line of cross-section

POPULATION

over 5 000 000
over 1 000 000
over 500 000
over 100 000
over 50 000
under 50 000

CONTINENTAL FACTS

PHYSICAL FEATURES

LARGEST LAKE: Lake Titicaca, Bolivia/ Peru 8340 sq km (3220 square miles)

LONGEST RIVER: Amazon, Brazil 6516 km (4050 miles)

HIGHEST POINT: Cerro Aconcagua, Argentina 6959 m (22,835 ft)

LOWEST POINT: Península Valdés, Argentina 40 m (151 ft) below sea level

POLITICAL FEATURES

TOTAL POPULATION: 304.5 million

LARGEST CITY AND ITS POPULATION: São Paulo, Brazil 17.4 million

COUNTRY WITH HIGHEST POPULATION DENSITY: Ecuador 54 people per sq km

LARGEST COUNTRY: Brazil 8,511,970 sq km (5,286,472 square miles)

SMALLEST COUNTRY: Surinam 165,270 sq km (65,059 square miles)

Scale: 1:26 500 000

0   250   500 km
0   250   500 miles

CROSS-SECTION THROUGH SOUTH AMERICA: 18°S, 75°W–36°W

8000m
4000m
Sea Level
-4000m
-8000m

Hot Desert | Mountain Vegetation | Tropical Dry Forest | Tropical Grassland | Temperate Rainforest

PACIFIC OCEAN
Peru-Chile Trench
Atacama Desert
Cordillera Occidental
Altiplano
Cordillera Central
Cordillera Oriental
Andes
Pantanal
Paraguay
São Francisco
Brazilian Highlands
ATLANTIC OCEAN

75°W   67°W   59°W   51°W   45°W

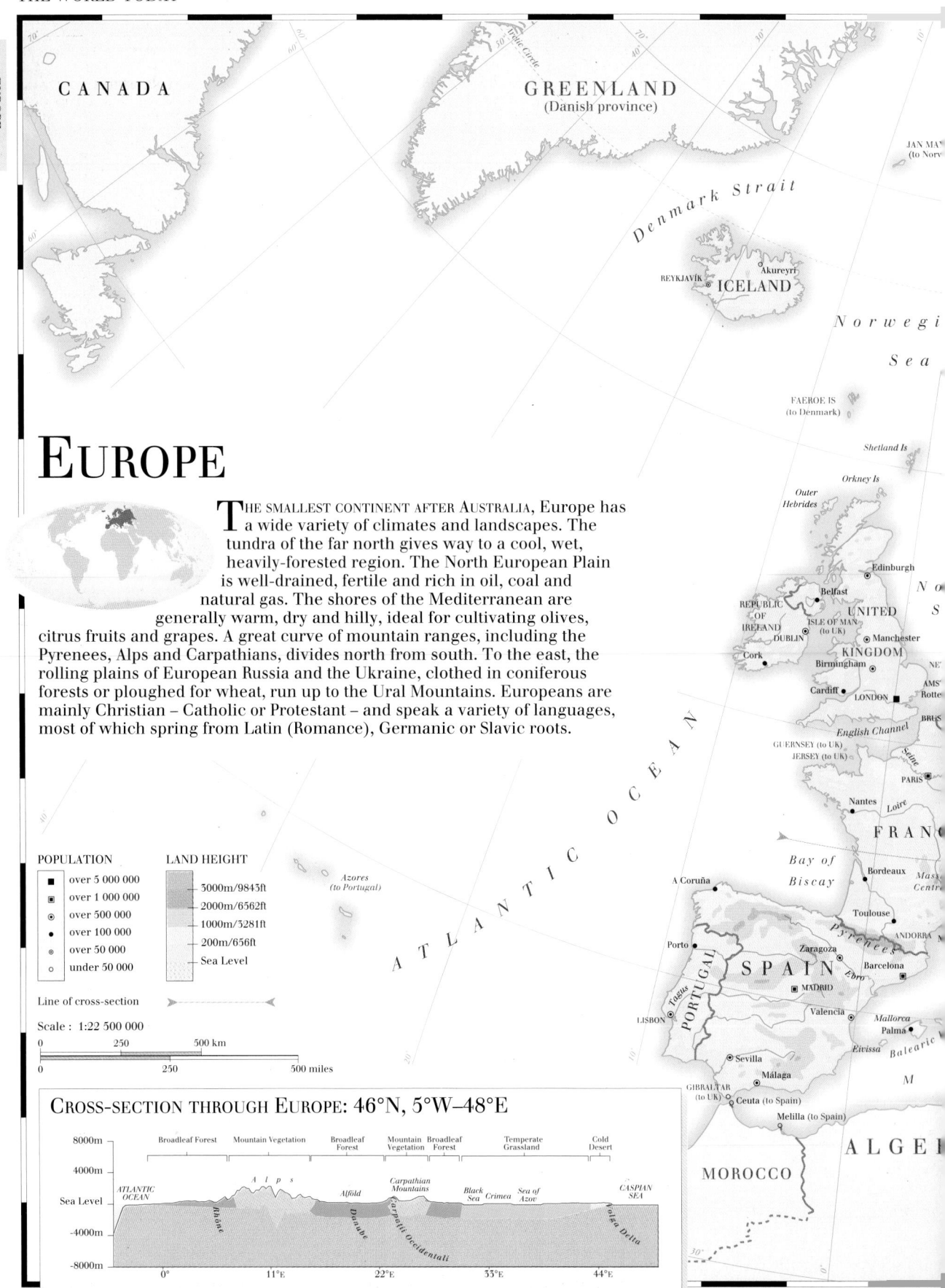

CANADA

GREENLAND
(Danish province)

JAN MA
(to Norv

Denmark Strait

Akureyri
REYKJAVÍK ICELAND

Norwegi

Sea

FAEROE IS
(to Denmark)

Shetland Is

Orkney Is

Outer
Hebrides

EUROPE

THE SMALLEST CONTINENT AFTER AUSTRALIA, Europe has a wide variety of climates and landscapes. The tundra of the far north gives way to a cool, wet, heavily-forested region. The North European Plain is well-drained, fertile and rich in oil, coal and natural gas. The shores of the Mediterranean are generally warm, dry and hilly, ideal for cultivating olives, citrus fruits and grapes. A great curve of mountain ranges, including the Pyrenees, Alps and Carpathians, divides north from south. To the east, the rolling plains of European Russia and the Ukraine, clothed in coniferous forests or ploughed for wheat, run up to the Ural Mountains. Europeans are mainly Christian – Catholic or Protestant – and speak a variety of languages, most of which spring from Latin (Romance), Germanic or Slavic roots.

Edinburgh

Belfast

REPUBLIC
OF
IRELAND
DUBLIN

UNITED
ISLE OF MAN
(to UK)   Manchester
KINGDOM

Cork

Birmingham

Cardiff   LONDON

NE

AMS
Rotte

BRE

GUERNSEY (to UK)
JERSEY (to UK)

English Channel

Seine

PARIS

Nantes   Loire

FRAN

Bay of
Biscay

Bordeaux

Mass
Centr

POPULATION

- ■ over 5 000 000
- ▣ over 1 000 000
- ◉ over 500 000
- ● over 100 000
- ◉ over 50 000
- ○ under 50 000

LAND HEIGHT

- 3000m/9843ft
- 2000m/6562ft
- 1000m/3281ft
- 200m/656ft
- Sea Level

Line of cross-section

Scale : 1:22 500 000

0   250   500 km

0   250   500 miles

ATLANTIC OCEAN

Azores
(to Portugal)

A Coruña

Toulouse

Pyrenees

ANDORRA

Porto

PORTUGAL

SPAIN

Zaragoza

Barcelona

Ebro

MADRID

Valencia

Mallorca
Palma

LISBON

Tagus

Eivissa

Balearic

Sevilla

Málaga

M

GIBRALTAR
(to UK)   Ceuta (to Spain)

Melilla (to Spain)

ALGE

MOROCCO

CROSS-SECTION THROUGH EUROPE: 46°N, 5°W–48°E

| Broadleaf Forest | Mountain Vegetation | Broadleaf Forest | Mountain Vegetation | Broadleaf Forest | Temperate Grassland | Cold Desert |

8000m

4000m

Alps

Carpathian
Mountains

Sea Level
ATLANTIC
OCEAN

Rhône

Alföld

Black
Sea   Crimea

Sea of
Azov

CASPIAN
SEA

Danube

Carpatii Occidentali

Volga Delta

-4000m

-8000m

0°   11°E   22°E   33°E   44°E

EUROPE

CONTINENTAL FACTS

PHYSICAL FEATURES

LARGEST LAKE: Ladoga, European Russia 18,390 sq km (7,100 square miles)

LONGEST RIVER: Volga, European Russia 3,688 km (2,290 miles)

HIGHEST POINT: El' brus, Caucasus Mts, European Russia 5,642 m (18,510 ft)

LOWEST POINT: Volga Delta, Caspian Sea, European Russia 28 m (92 ft) below sea level

POLITICAL FEATURES

TOTAL POPULATION: 692.126 million

COUNTRY WITH HIGHEST POPULATION DENSITY: Monaco 15,321 people per sq km

LARGEST CITY AND ITS POPULATION: Moscow, European Russia 8.8 million

LARGEST COUNTRY: European Russia 3,955,818 sq km (1,527,341 square miles)

SMALLEST COUNTRY: Vatican City, Italy 0.44 sq km (0.17 square miles)

SVALBARD (to Norway)

Novaya Zemlya

Barents Sea

Karskoye More

Arctic Circle

Pechora

Tromsø

Murmansk

Arkhangel'sk

Severnaya Dvina

RUSSIAN

Ufa

Kemi

Onezhskoye Ozero

Ladozhskoye Ozero

FEDERATION

KAZAKHSTAN

SWEDEN

NORWAY

FINLAND

Vaasa

Tampere

Turku

HELSINKI

Gulf of Bothnia

St Petersburg

Kazan'

Yaroslavl'

Nizhniy Novgorod

Orenburg

Samara

Ural

Uppsala

Örebro

STOCKHOLM

Åland

TALLINN

Tartu

EUROPEAN RUSSIA

MOSCOW

OSLO

Vänern

ESTONIA

RIGA

Vättern

Kristiansand

Göteborg

Gotland

LATVIA

Volga

Saratov

Daugavpils

Tula

Voronezh

LITHUANIA

Orsha

DENMARK

Malmö

COPENHAGEN

KALININGRAD (to Russian Fed.)

VILNIUS

MINSK

Gdańsk

BELORUSSIA

Homyel'

Don

GERMANY

Hamburg

Elbe

BERLIN

Wisła

WARSAW

Łódź

POLAND

Kharkiv

Volgograd

Astrakhan'

Kraków

Dnieper

Donets'k

Volga Delta

Frankfurt am Main

PRAGUE

CZECH REPUBLIC

UKRAINE

Dnipropetrovs'k

Rostov-na-Donu

Caspian Sea

SLOVAKIA

Dniester

Makhachkala

Strasbourg

BRATISLAVA

Miskolc

MOLDOVA

CHIŞINĂU

Sea of Azov

Krasnodar

Carpathian Mts

Iaşi

Odesa

München

VIENNA

BUDAPEST

Crimea

El'brus 5642m

Caucasus

GEORGIA

LIECHTENSTEIN

Salzburg

HUNGARY

Carpaţii Occidentali

TBILISI

AZERBAIJAN

AUSTRIA

Alföld

ROMANIA

Braşov

ARMENIA

SWITZERLAND

LJUBLJANA

SLOVENIA

ZAGREB

Timişoara

Novi Sad

BUCHAREST

Milano

CROATIA

Varna

Po

BOSNIA & HERZEGOVINA

BELGRADE

Danube

ITALY

SAN MARINO

SARAJEVO

YUGOSLAVIA

BULGARIA

Trabzon

Split

Podgorica

SOFIA

Black Sea

MONACO

Appennino

Adriatic Sea

SKOPJE

Plovdiv

Istanbul

ANKARA

ROME

VATICAN CITY

TIRANA

MACEDONIA

Thessaloníki

Bursa

IRAN

Napoli

ALBANIA

Kırıkkale

Tyrrhenian Sea

Lárisa

GREECE

Gaziantep

Sardinia

ATHENS

Pátra

Aegean Sea

Konya

Adana

SYRIA

IRAQ

Cágliari

İzmir

TURKEY

Palermo

Ionian Sea

Irákleio

NICOSIA

Sicily

Crete

LEBANON

CYPRUS

MALTA

ISRAEL

TUNISIA

Mediterranean Sea

LIBYA

EGYPT

SEYCHELLES

VICTORIA

INDIAN

OCEAN

Equator

Gulf of Aden

SAUDI
ARABIA

YEMEN

Horn of Africa

SOMALIA

MOGADISHU

Kismaayo

DJIBOUTI
DJIBOUTI

Hargeysa

Dire Dawa
Lac Assat
ADDIS ABABA

Mombasa

ERITREA

ASMARA

Ethiopian
Highlands

ETHIOPIA

KENYA

Kilimanjaro
5895m

Zanzibar
Dar es Salaam

NAIROBI

DODOMA

Red Sea

Nubian
Desert

Port Sudan

Blue Nile

Juba

UGANDA

Mwale

KAMPALA

Kisumu

L.
Victoria

Mwanza

TANZAN

Aswan

Buheiret
Nāsir

KHARTOUM

White Nile

KIGALI

RWANDA

BURUNDI

Great Rift Vo

SYRIA

JORDAN

LEBANON
CYPRUS
ISRAEL

Nile

EGYPT

El Obeid

SUDAN

BUJUMBURA

L. Tanganyika

TURKEY

Alexandria

CAIRO

Sudd

Kisangani

Black Sea

GREECE

Mediterranean Sea

Benghazi

Abéché

CENTRAL
AFRICAN REPUBLIC

Congo (Zaire)

ZAIRE

Mbuji-Mayi

Kananga

LIBYA

Sabhā

CHAD

N'DJAMENA

L. Chad

BANGUI

BRAZZAVILLE
KINSHASA

Azaou Strip

Adamawa
Highlands

LUANDA

ITALY

TUNIS

Sfax

TUNISIA

TRIPOLI

MALTA

CAMEROON

YAOUNDE

CONGO

GABON

CABINDA
(to Angola)

Pointe-Noire

Ahaggar

Constantine

ALGIERS

NIGER

Agadez

NIGERIA

Kano

Douala

MALABO

LIBREVILLE

EQUATORIAL
GUINEA

Principe GUINEA
Bata

SÃO TOMÉ

SÃO TOMÉ
& PRÍNCIPE

ABUJA

Port Harcourt

FRANCE

SPAIN

GIBRALTAR (to UK)
Tanger
Ceuta (to Spain)

Oran
Melilla (to Spain)

ALGERIA

MALI

NIAMEY

Ibadan
Lagos

PORTO-
NOVO

LOMÉ

Gulf of
Guinea

PORTUGAL

Fez

RABAT
Casablanca

Marrakech

MOROCCO

Atlas Mts

Niger

OUAGADOUGOU

BURKINA

BENIN

TOGO

ACCRA

GHANA

Sahara

Lake
Volta

ATLAN

Islas Canarias
(to Spain)

Laâyoune

WESTERN
SAHARA
(Occupied by
Morocco)

MAURITANIA

NOUAKCHOTT

YAMOUSSOUKRO

IVORY
COAST

Abidjan

Tropic of Cancer

Nouâdhibou

SENEGAL

DAKAR

BAMAKO

GUINEA

SIERRA
LEONE

LIBERIA

MONROVIA

FREETOWN

CONAKRY

BISSAU

GAMBIA
BANJUL
GUINEA-BISSAU

ATLANTIC OCEAN

ASCENSION
(to St Helena)

Equator

Tropic of Cancer

AFRICA

AFRICA IS THE SECOND LARGEST CONTINENT after Asia. It is dominated by the Sahara in the north and the Great Rift Valley in the east. The Mediterranean climate of the extreme north and south enables cultivation of grapes and other fruit. A belt of tropical rainforest lies along the Equator, while Africa's great tropical grasslands provide grazing for herds of wild animals and domestic livestock. The centre and south of the continent are rich in minerals. The Nile, which sustained prehistoric communities. The centre and south of the continent are rich in minerals. Almost one tenth of the world's population lives in Africa – a wide variety of peoples with their own distinctive languages and cultures. Although Islam and Christianity are widespread, many Africans adhere to their own local customs and religious beliefs.

LAND HEIGHT

	4000m/13 124ft
	3000m/9843ft
	2000m/6562ft
	1000m/3281ft
	200m/656ft
	Sea Level

POPULATION

■	over 5 000 000
▣	over 1 000 000
◉	over 500 000
●	over 100 000
◎	over 50 000
○	under 50 000

▸ Line of cross-section

CONTINENTAL FACTS

PHYSICAL FEATURES

LARGEST LAKE: Lake Victoria 68,880 sq km (26,560 square miles)

LONGEST RIVER: Nile, Uganda/ Sudan/ Egypt 6695 km (4160 miles)

HIGHEST POINT: Kilimanjaro, Tanzania 5895 m (19,341 ft)

LOWEST POINT: Lac' Assal, Djibouti 156 m (512 ft) below sea level

POLITICAL FEATURES

TOTAL POPULATION: 681.7 million

LARGEST CITY AND POPULATION: Cairo, Egypt, 9 million

COUNTRY WITH HIGHEST POPULATION DENSITY: Mauritius 553 people per sq km

LARGEST COUNTRY: Sudan 2,505,810 sq km (967,495 square miles)

SMALLEST COUNTRY: Seychelles 280 sq km (108 square miles)

Scale : 1:36 000 000

0   500   1000 km
0   500   1000 miles

CROSS-SECTION THROUGH AFRICA 7°N, 15°W–55°E

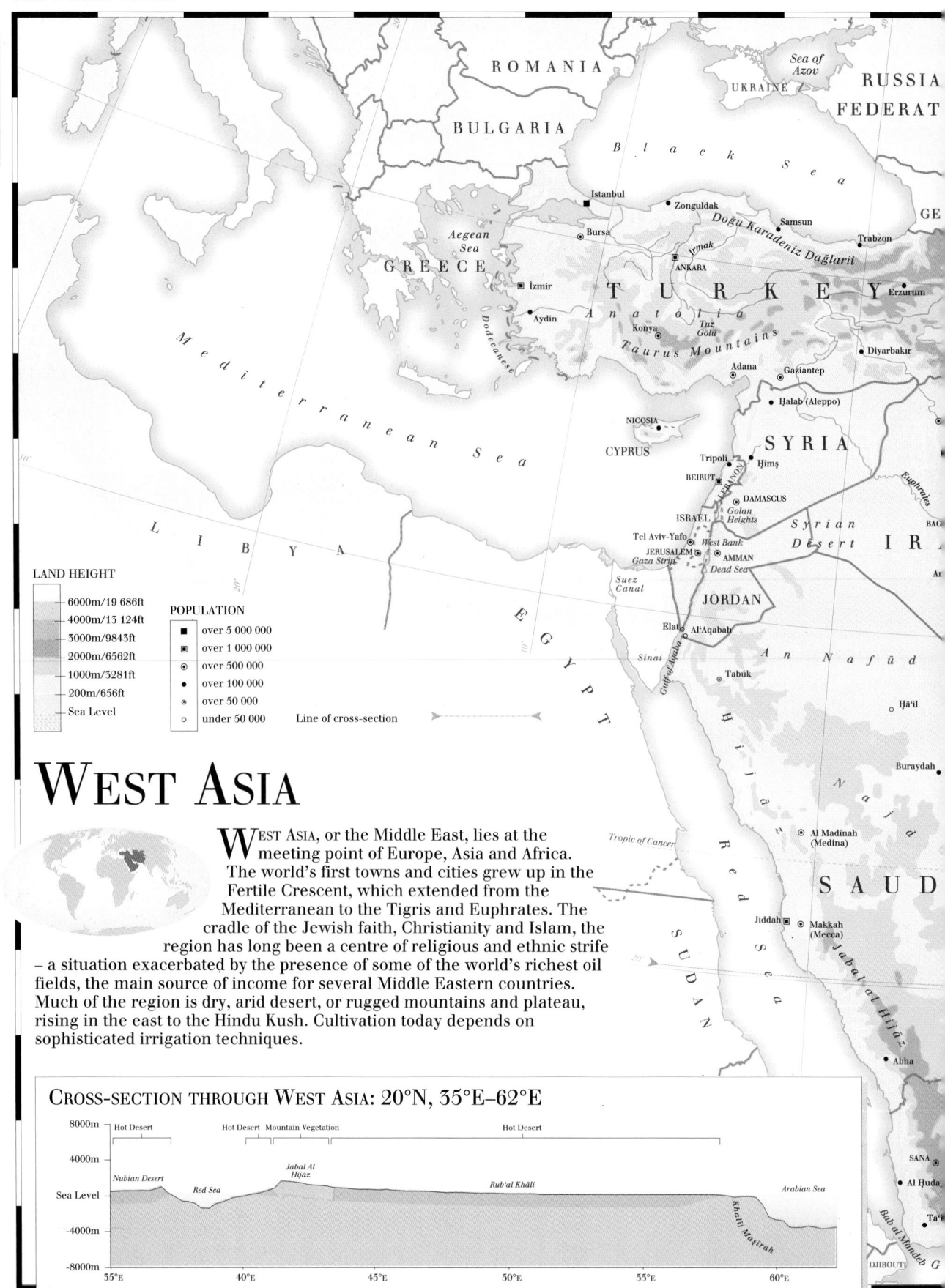

LAND HEIGHT

6000m/19 686ft
4000m/13 124ft
3000m/9843ft
2000m/6562ft
1000m/3281ft
200m/656ft
Sea Level

POPULATION

■ over 5 000 000
▣ over 1 000 000
◉ over 500 000
● over 100 000
◎ over 50 000
○ under 50 000

Line of cross-section

WEST ASIA

WEST ASIA, or the Middle East, lies at the meeting point of Europe, Asia and Africa. The world's first towns and cities grew up in the Fertile Crescent, which extended from the Mediterranean to the Tigris and Euphrates. The cradle of the Jewish faith, Christianity and Islam, the region has long been a centre of religious and ethnic strife – a situation exacerbated by the presence of some of the world's richest oil fields, the main source of income for several Middle Eastern countries. Much of the region is dry, arid desert, or rugged mountains and plateau, rising in the east to the Hindu Kush. Cultivation today depends on sophisticated irrigation techniques.

CROSS-SECTION THROUGH WEST ASIA: 20°N, 35°E–62°E

8000m
4000m
Sea Level
-4000m
-8000m

Hot Desert   Hot Desert   Mountain Vegetation   Hot Desert

Nubian Desert   Red Sea   Jabal Al Hijāz   Rub'al Khāli   Arabian Sea

Khalīj Maṣīrah

35°E   40°E   45°E   50°E   55°E   60°E

K A Z A K H S T A N

Aral Sea

Kyzyl Kum

Karakol
BISHKEK
Ozero Issyk-Kul'

Kirghiz Range

TASHKENT
KYRGYZSTAN

U Z B E K I S T A N

Namangan
Osh
Naryn

Dashkhovuz
Urgench

Ozero Aydarkul'

Khudzhand

C H I N A

Caspian Sea

ERBAIJAN
BAKU
Krasnovodsk
Nebîtdag

Karakumy

Samarkand
Karshi

TAJIKISTAN
DUSHANBE

Pamirs

K2
8611m

Länkäran

Chardzhev
Amu

Kulyab
Khorog

Karakoram Range
Indus

T U R K M E N I S T A N

Khrebet Kopetdag
ASHGABAT

Kurgan-Tyube

Rasht

Mary

Mazār-e-Sharīf
Baghlān

Hindu Kush

Gorgān

Mashhad

ISLĀMĀBĀD
Peshāwar
Rāwalpindi

Reshteh-ye Kuhhā ye Alborz

Jalālābād

Gujrānwāla

TEHRĀN
Herāt
KĀBUL

Chenáb

Hamadān
Qom

A F G H A N I S T A N

Lahore

Bākhtarān

Dasht-e-Kavir

Faisalābad

I R A N

Plateau of Iran

Esfahān

Kandahār

Multān

Ahvāz
Ābādān

Hāmūn-e Şāberī

Zagros Mountains

Helmand

Kermān

Quetta

KUWAIT CITY

Shīrāz

Zāhedān

Indus

Thar Desert

VAIT

P A K I S T A N

Sukkur

I N D I A

Bandar-e 'Abbās

Persian Gulf

MANAMA
BAHRAIN

Strait of Hormuz

Hyderābād

Al Hufūf
DOHA
QATAR

Dubai
Sharjah

Gulf of Oman
Suhār

PH
ABU DHABI

Tropic of Cancer

Ḩaraḑ

Karāchi

UNITED ARAB EMIRATES

MUSCAT

A r a b i a n

Ar Rustāq
Nazwá
Şūr

S e a

RABIA

Scale : 1:17 500 000

0   250   500 km

0   250   500 miles

al Khāli

O M A N

Khalīj Maşīrah

MEN

Şalālah

I N D I A N   O C E A N

Hadhramaut

Mukallā

den

Socotra (to Yemen)

CONTINENTAL FACTS

PHYSICAL FEATURES

LARGEST LAKE: Caspian Sea 371,000 sq km (143,205 square miles)

LONGEST RIVER: Euphrates, Syria/ Iraq 2815 km (1750 miles)

HIGHEST POINT: K2, Kashmir, India/ Pakistan 8611m (28,252 ft)

LOWEST POINT: Dead Sea, Israel/Jordan 392 m (1286 ft) below sea level

POLITICAL FEATURES

TOTAL POPULATION: 390.5 million

LARGEST CITY AND ITS POPULATION: Istanbul, Turkey 6.5 million

COUNTRY WITH HIGHEST POPULATION DENSITY: Bahrain 723 people per sq km

LARGEST COUNTRY: Saudi Arabia 2,149,690 sq km (830,001 square miles)

SMALLEST COUNTRY: Bahrain 680 sq km (263 square miles)

NORTH ASIA

CONTINENTAL FACTS

PHYSICAL FEATURES

LARGEST LAKE: Aral Sea, Asiatic Russia 66,500 sq km (25,700 square miles)

LONGEST RIVER: Chang Jiang (Yangtze), China 6380 km (3965 miles)

HIGHEST POINT: Xixabangma Feng, China 8012 m (26,286 ft)

LOWEST POINT: Turpan Hami (Turfan Basin), China 154 m (505 ft) below sea level

POLITICAL FEATURES

TOTAL POPULATION: 1446 million

LARGEST CITY AND ITS POPULATION: Tokyo, Japan 18.1 million

COUNTRY WITH HIGHEST POPULATION DENSITY: Taiwan 575 people per sq km

LARGEST COUNTRY: Asiatic Russia 13,119,582 sq km (5,065,471 square miles)

SMALLEST COUNTRY: Taiwan 36,179 sq km (13,969 square miles)

POPULATION

over 5 000 000	■
over 1 000 000	▣
over 500 000	◉
over 100 000	•
over 50 000	⊙
under 50 000	○

LAND HEIGHT

6000m/19 686ft	
4000m/13 124ft	
3000m/9843ft	
2000m/6562ft	
1000m/3281ft	
200m/656ft	
Sea Level	

▷————————◁ Line of cross-section

Scale : 1:31 000 000

0   250   500 km

0   250   500 miles

NORTH ASIA

THE URAL MOUNTAINS form a huge natural boundary between European and Asian Russia. East of the Urals, vast areas of windswept grassland – the steppes – stretch as far as the Pacific Ocean. Much of Siberia is a frozen wilderness, covered by pine forests, but rich in oil and precious stones. To the south, the deserts of Kazakhstan merge with the Tien Shan range. The Central Asian r epublics lie along the ancient Silk Road between Asia and Europe, where traditional nomadic lifestyles are being replaced by agriculture and mineral prospecting. Tibet lies on a remote plateau, the world's highest region. In Mongolia, the world's largest landlocked country, people still depend on herding. One fifth of the world's population lives in China, the majority along the coast and in the warm, fertile river valleys. China remains a predominantly rural country, but has extensive reserves of coal and iron ore. Japan's four main islands are mountainous, heavily forested, and have few raw materials, most of the large population living along the coastal fringes.

CROSS-SECTION THROUGH NORTH ASIA: 38°N, 52°E–145°E

Cold Desert | Mountain Vegetation | Cold Desert | Mountain Vegetation | Cold Desert | Broadleaf Forest

8000m
4000m
Sea Level
-4000m
-8000m

Caspian Sea · Karakumy · Khrebet Kopetdag · Pamirs · Taklimakan Shamo · Altun Shan · Qaidam Pendi · Qilian Shan · Huang He · Yellow Sea · Korean Peninsula · Sea of Japan · Honshū (Japan) · PACIFIC OCEAN · Japan Trench

52°E   71°E   90°E   109°E   128°E

SOUTH ASIA

DOMINATED IN THE NORTH by the Himalayas, the highest mountain range in the world, India is isolated from the rest of Asia, forming a densely populated subcontinent. Its climate and topography range from the mountains of Kashmir in the north to coral beaches in the south. It is the birthplace of Hinduism, Buddhism and Sikhism. Much of mainland South East Asia is mountainous and forested, the people living in the river valleys and fertile coastal plains. Tropical rainforests, rich in species, cover much of the region. Indonesia forms a huge arc of some 13,000 volcanic islands. The Philippines, the region's only Christian country, comprises over 7000 mountainous islands.

CROSS-SECTION THROUGH SOUTH ASIA: 28°N, 60°E–124°E

Cold Desert   Hot Desert   Monsoon Forest   Mountain Vegetation   Temperate Rainforest

8000m
Sandy Desert   Thar Desert   Everest Himalayas
4000m
Sea Level   Indus   Ganges   Brahmaputra   Hengduan Shan   Chang Jiang   Dalou Shan   Nanzia Shan   East China Sea
-4000m
-8000m
60°E   73°E   86°E   99°E   112°E

CONTINENTAL FACTS

PHYSICAL FEATURES

LARGEST LAKE: Tônlé Sap, Cambodia 2850 sq km (100 square miles)

LONGEST RIVER: Mekong, China/ Vietnam 4425 km (2750 miles)

HIGHEST POINT: Mount Everest, Nepal 8848 m (29,030 ft)

LOWEST POINT: About half of Bangladesh lies between sea level and 8 m (25 ft)

POLITICAL FEATURES

TOTAL POPULATION: 1500.3 million

LARGEST CITY AND ITS POPULATION: Calcutta, India 11.8 million

COUNTRY WITH HIGHEST POPULATION DENSITY: Singapore 4295 people per sq km

LARGEST COUNTRY: India 3,287,590 sq km (1,269,339 square miles)

SMALLEST COUNTRY: Maldives 300 sq km (116 square miles)

POPULATION

over 5 000 000
over 1 000 000
over 500 000
over 100 000
over 50 000
under 50 000

LAND HEIGHT

6000m/19 686ft
4000m/13 124ft
3000m/9843ft
2000m/6562ft
1000m/3281ft
200m/656ft
Sea Level

Line of cross-section

Scale : 1:25 000 000

0   250   500 km

0   250   500 miles

Yellow Sea

JAPAN

East China Sea

TAIWAN   *Tropic of Cancer*

HONG KONG (to UK)

MACAO (to Portugal)

Hai Phong

Gulf of Tongking

PARACEL IS (Disputed)

Hue

Da Nang

Pakxé

VIETNAM

South China Sea

ODIA

Quy Nhon

mpông

am

Nha Trang

Hô Chi Minh

My Tho

SPRATLY IS (Disputed)

Nansei Shotō

Luzon

Baguio

Cabanatuan City

MANILA

Philippine Sea

Mindoro

PHILIPPINES

Samar

Panay

Iloilo   Tacloban

Bacolod   Cebu

Palawan

Negros

Butuan

Cagayan de Oro

Sulu Sea

Mindanao

Zaamboanga   Davao

PACIFIC OCEAN

BANDAR SERI BEGAWAN

Sandakan

Sabah

BRUNEI

Miri

Celebes Sea

LAYSIA

Keputauan Natuna (to Indonesia)

Sarawak

Borneo

Kuching   *Rajang*

ru

GAPORE   Pontianak

Kapuas

Kalimantan

Samarinda

Balikpapan

Barito

Banjarmasin

Selat Makasar

Palu

Sulawesi

Ujungpandang

Manado

Halmahera

Sorong

Moluccas

Seram

Buru   Ambon

Jayapura

Irian Jaya

pegunungan Maoke

New Guinea

PAPUA NEW GUINEA

N   D   O   N   E   S   I   A

Pulau Bangka

lembang

Pulau Belitung

Java Sea

Banda Sea

Tanjungkarang-Telukbetung

JAKARTA

Bandung

Java

Semarang

Malang   Surabaya

Denpasar

N u s a   T e n g g a r a

Flores

Sumba

Kupang

Timor

Arafura Sea

Merauke

Equator

CHRISTMAS I. (to Australia)

ASHMORE & CARTIER IS (to Australia)

Timor Sea

A   U   S   T   R   A   L   I   A

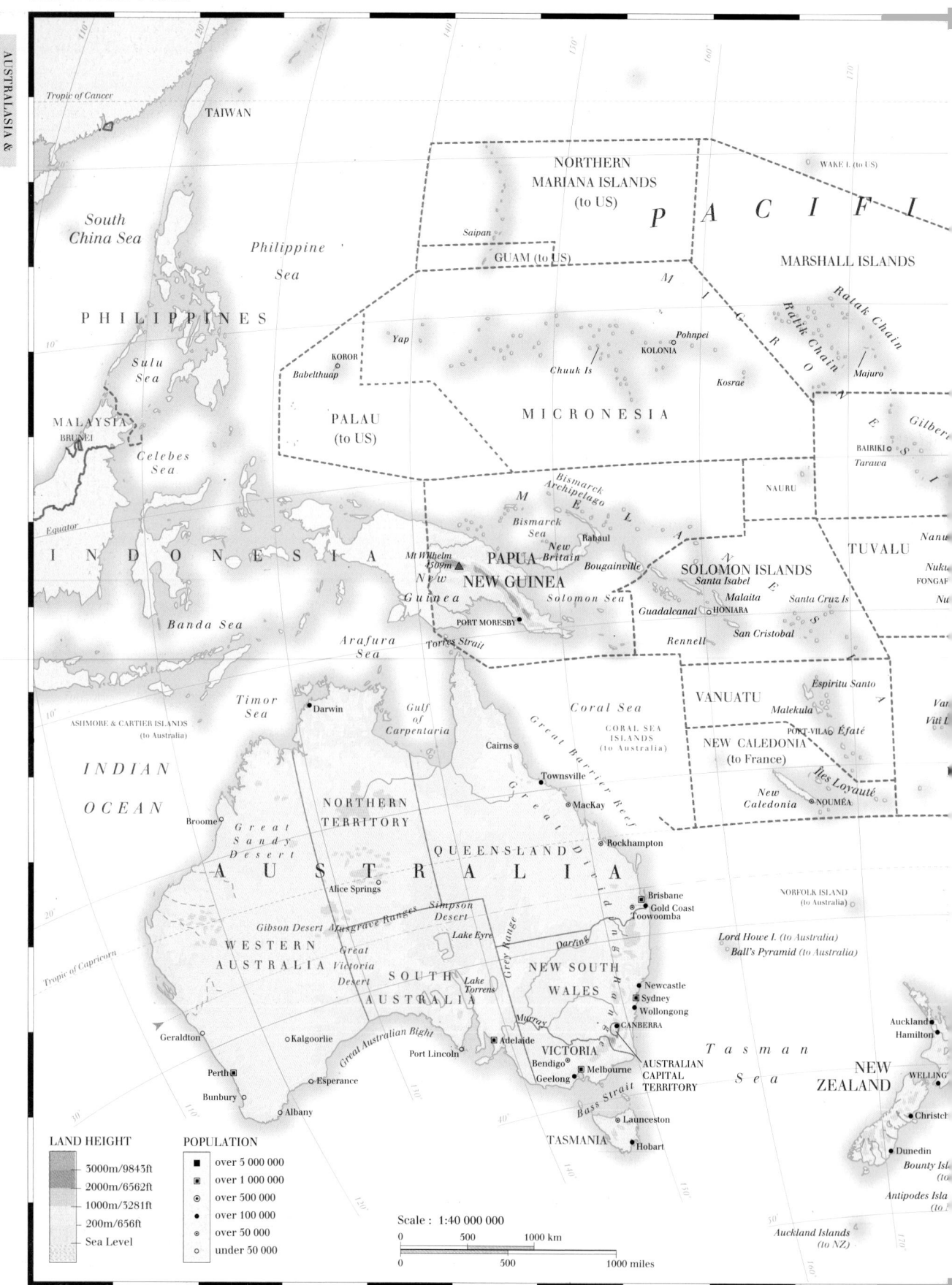

TAIWAN

*South
China Sea*

*Philippine
Sea*

NORTHERN
MARIANA ISLANDS
(to US)

WAKE I. (to US)

P A C I F I

Saipan

GUAM (to US)

MARSHALL ISLANDS

Ratak Chain

Ralik Chain

PHILIPPINES

*Sulu
Sea*

Yap

KOROR

Babelthuap

Pohnpei
KOLONIA

Chuuk Is

Kosrae

Majuro

MALAYSIA
BRUNEI

*Celebes
Sea*

PALAU
(to US)

M I C R O N E S I A

NAURU

BAIRIKI
Tarawa

Gilber

TUVALU

Nanu

Nuku
FONGAF

Nu

Equator

I N D O N E S I A

*Bismarck
Archipelago*

M

*Bismarck
Sea*

Rabaul

*New
Britain*

Mt Wilhelm
4509m ▲

PAPUA

*New
Guinea*

NEW GUINEA

Bougainville

SOLOMON ISLANDS
Santa Isabel

Malaita
HONIARA

Santa Cruz Is

PORT MORESBY

Banda Sea

*Arafura
Sea*

Torres Strait

Solomon Sea

Guadalcanal

Rennell

San Cristobal

Espíritu Santo

Var

Viti I

*Timor
Sea*

• Darwin

*Gulf
of
Carpentaria*

Coral Sea

CORAL SEA
ISLANDS
(to Australia)

VANUATU

Malekula

PORT-VILA ⊙ *Éfaté*

ASHMORE & CARTIER ISLANDS
(to Australia)

*I N D I A N

O C E A N*

Cairns •

Great Barrier Reef

Townsville •

NORTHERN
TERRITORY

NEW CALEDONIA
(to France)

Îles Loyauté

*New
Caledonia*

⊙ NOUMÉA

Broome ⊙

*Great
Sandy
Desert*

• MacKay

QUEENSLAND

A U S T R A L I A

Alice Springs •

*Simpson
Desert*

Rockhampton •

NORFOLK ISLAND
(to Australia)

Tropic of Capricorn

WESTERN
AUSTRALIA

Gibson Desert *Musgrave Ranges*

*Great
Victoria
Desert*

Lake Eyre

SOUTH
AUSTRALIA

*Lake
Torrens*

Brisbane ■
⊡ Gold Coast
Toowoomba

Darling

NEW SOUTH
WALES

Newcastle •
■ Sydney
• Wollongong

⊙ CANBERRA

Lord Howe I. (to Australia)
Ball's Pyramid (to Australia)

T a s m a n

Geraldton ⊙

Kalgoorlie ⊙

Great Australian Bight

Port Lincoln ⊙

⊡ Adelaide

VICTORIA

Bendigo ⊙
Geelong ⊙ ⊙ Melbourne

AUSTRALIAN
CAPITAL
TERRITORY

Auckland ■
Hamilton •

S e a

NEW
ZEALAND

WELLING

Perth ⊡

Bunbury ⊙

Esperance ⊙

⊙ Albany

Murray

Bass Strait

• Launceston

TASMANIA

• Hobart

Christch

• Dunedin

*Bounty Isl
(to*

*Antipodes Isla
(to*

*Auckland Islands
(to NZ)*

LAND HEIGHT

	3000m/9843ft
	2000m/6562ft
	1000m/3281ft
	200m/656ft
	Sea Level

POPULATION

■	over 5 000 000
⊡	over 1 000 000
⊙	over 500 000
•	over 100 000
⊙	over 50 000
○	under 50 000

Scale : 1:40 000 000

0 — 500 — 1000 km

0 — 500 — 1000 miles

AUSTRALASIA & OCEANIA

OCEANIA EMBRACES THE WORLD'S smallest continent, Australia, large island groups such as New Zealand, Papua New Guinea and Fiji, and the myriad volcanic and coral islands scattered across the Pacific Ocean, consisting of three main groups, Micronesia, Melanesia and Polynesia. Australia, flat and dry, is sparsely populated, most people living along the coastal lowlands, especially in the southeast. The continent's first settlers, the Aboriginal peoples, retain some of their original lands in the interior, but later European and Asian settlers form most of the population. Owing to its isolation from other continents, Australia's flora and fauna have evolved many unique species. The continent is rich in minerals, such as gold, uranium and iron ore, which are the basis of Australia's prosperity. Mountainous Papua New Guinea is covered in tropical rainforest, while New Zealand is temperate, rugged and volcanic in the north. The peoples of Oceania colonized the Pacific by AD1500, and the many insular farming and fishing communities have developed distinctive cultures, the Maoris of New Zealand being among the most notable.

Map labels

Tropic of Cancer
HAWAII (to US)
Honolulu
JOHNSTON ATOLL (to US)
OCEAN
KINGMAN REEF (to US)
PALMYRA ATOLL (to US)
Teraina
Tabuaeran
Kiritimati
JARVIS ISLAND (to US)
R & HOWLAND IS
KIRIBATI
Phoenix Islands
Equator
Starbuck Island
Caroline Island
Flint Island
TOKELAU (to NZ)
Penrhyn
Rakahanga
Manihiki
Suwarrow
Northern Cook Islands
Îles Marquises
WESTERN SAMOA
AMERICAN SAMOA (to US)
Savai'i
Upolu
APIA
PAGO PAGO
TONGA
NIUE (to NZ)
COOK ISLANDS (to NZ)
Palmerston
Vava'u Group
Îles de la Société
PAPEETE
Tahiti
Îles Tuamotu
NUKU'ALOFA
Tongatapu Group
Southern Cook Islands
Rarotonga
Mangaia
FRENCH POLYNESIA (to France)
Îles Australes
Îles Gambier
PITCAIRN ISLANDS (to UK)
Îlots de Bass
PACIFIC OCEAN
Line of cross-section

CONTINENTAL FACTS

PHYSICAL FEATURES

- LARGEST LAKE: Lake Eyre, Australia 9583 sq km (3700 square miles)
- LONGEST RIVER: Murray-Darling, Australia 3750 km (2330 miles)
- HIGHEST POINT: Mt Wilhelm, Papua New Guinea 4509 m (14,794 ft)
- LOWEST POINT: Lake Eyre, Australia 16 m (52 ft) below sea level

POLITICAL FEATURES

- TOTAL POPULATION: 27.5 million
- LARGEST CITY AND ITS POPULATION: Sydney, Australia 3.7 million
- COUNTRY WITH HIGHEST POPULATION DENSITY: Nauru 429 people per sq km
- LARGEST COUNTRY: Australia 7,686,850 sq km (2,967,893 square miles)
- SMALLEST COUNTRY: Nauru 21 sq km (8 square miles)

CROSS-SECTION THROUGH AUSTRALIA: 27°S, 112°–160°E

Hot Desert — Tropical Grassland — Mediterranean-type Vegetation

4000m
Sea Level
-4000m
-8000m

INDIAN OCEAN
Great Victoria Desert
Musgrave Ranges
Lake Eyre
Simpson Desert
Grey Range
Great Dividing Range
PACIFIC OCEAN
Lord Howe Rise
New Caledonia
South Fiji Basin

112°E   125°E   138°E   151°E   164°E

THE FORMATION OF THE MODERN WORLD

T HE WORLD AS WE KNOW IT today, like all of the species that inhabit it, is the product of many thousands of years of evolution. The political and cultural map of the globe bears the hallmark of many varied courses of human development the world over. Nevertheless, much of the modern human geography of the planet can be traced to developments in the relatively recent past. The following pages chart the rise and fall of the various states and empires of the

early modern and modern ages. Beginning with the first great achievement of European exploration, the discovery of the Americas in 1492, the maps show the way in which various European and Asian powers expanded their cultural and political influence and control down to the present day. This process left indelible cultural imprints in the form of language, religion, education and systems of government on every part of the planet.

MAJOR MIGRATIONS SINCE 1500

KEY
- Europeans
- Russians
- Africans
- East Asians
- South Asians

LANGUAGES OF THE WORLD

Arabic
Chinese
English
French
Portuguese
Russian
Spanish
Hindi
Others

NAHUATL
MAYA
QUECHUA
AYMARA
AFRIKAANS

ATLANTIC OCEAN

GERMANIC
SLAVIC
TURKIC
PERSIAN
BERBER
AMHARIC
BANTU
MONGOL
UIGHUR
MONGOL
KOREAN
JAPANESE
TIBETAN
AUSTRO-ASIATIC
AUSTRONESIAN
FILIPINO, CEBUANO

PACIFIC OCEAN

INDIAN OCEAN

SIBERIA
JAPAN to the Americas
CHINA
SOUTH ASIA
PACIFIC OCEAN
EAST INDIES
INDIAN OCEAN
AUSTRALIA
NEW ZEALAND

LANGUAGES OF THE WORLD

There are over 3000 languages or 'speech communities' in the world today; some are spoken by many millions, some by only dozens. Many people speak more than one language. The diffusion of the major languages throughout the world during the modern era has seen the emergence of a few dominant languages (shown on the map). In many areas, the language of a colonial power has been maintained either as an official language or has become the *lingua franca* of the region. The largest single language, encompassing many dialects, is Chinese, with over 1000 million speakers; Hindi (400 million) and Arabic (200 million) are the next largest first languages. The most successful colonial languages were English (estimated at up to 1,500 million, including those using English as a second language), French (200 million) and Spanish (270 million). While the latter is now estimated to be the world's fastest growing language, owing to Latin America's burgeoning population growth, both English and French are spoken in a wide variety of patois, pidgins and creoles, thus achieving unique levels of cultural penetration.

MAJOR MIGRATIONS SINCE 1500

The last five hundred years have witnessed a dramatic redistribution of the world's population, which occurred in a series of waves. The first of these involved, from the 16th–18th centuries, the mass trans-shipment of captive peoples from sub-Saharan Africa to supply the slave markets of West Asia and to work newly-founded European plantations in the Americas. The rapidly growing populations of Europe and Asia encouraged a heavy flow of migration. The Cantonese from southern China spread throughout South East Asia, while from the 16th century millions of Europeans emigrated to the 'New Worlds' of the Americas and, later, Australasia. This European diaspora reached a peak at the end of the 19th century. Then, as the colonial empires coalesced in the early years of the 20th century, there was a final wave of global movement within them, when South and East Asians migrated to fill labour markets and exploit opportunities in Africa and the Americas. While homogenous societies have developed in North America and Australia, many diverse ethnic communities remain scattered across the world.

THE WORLD IN 1492

WHEN CHRISTOPHER COLUMBUS sailed west from Europe, seeking a quicker route to Asia, he launched a process of discovery that was eventually to bring the disparate regions of the world into closer contact, to form the global map we know today. The largest political entity in the world at that time was the Chinese Ming empire. Culturally, the Islamic faith had forged a bond of religious unity which extended in a broad swathe from South East Asia to the Atlantic coast of North Africa. Europe was a mêlée of rival monarchies; sub-Saharan Africa a patchwork of trading kingdoms; the Americas, a separate world of rich tribal cultures, with empires established only in Central America and the central Andes.

GLOBAL STATES AND TERRITORIES

KEY

	Chinese
	Ottoman
	Russian
○	Portuguese
◉	Spanish
○	English
	French
	Danish (Union of Kalmar)
1415	Date of acquisition

An illuminated Aztec codex records tribute payments from subject tribes.

GREENLAND   Arctic Ocean

ICELAND to Denmark 1580
NORWAY SWEDEN
R (MU

SCOTLAND DENMARK
THE PALE 1169 ENGLAND
IRELAND HOLY ROMAN EMPIRE POLAND-LITHUANIA
VENICE HUNGARY
EUROPE FRANCE
PAPAL STATES OTTOMAN E
PORTUGAL SPAIN NAPLES
AZORES 1459
Ceuta 1415
MADEIRA 1418 Mediterranea
MAM EM
CANARY IS 1478
S a h a r a
A F R I C A
TEKRUR KANEM BORNU E
SONGHAY DARF
MALI WADAI
YORUBA STATES HAUSALAND
AKAN BENIN
FERNANDO PO I. 1472
KONGO
ZI

Bering Strait
Hudson Bay
Rocky Mountains
NORTH AMERICA
CENTRAL AMERICA
Gulf of Mexico
West Indies
MAYA STATES
Caribbean Sea
AZTEC EMPIRE
ATLANTIC OCEAN
PACIFIC OCEAN
SOUTH AMERICA
INCA EMPIRE
Andes
ATLANTIC OCEAN

THE AMERICAS

The New World discovered by Columbus was inhabited by a string of small tribal societies, and by two large native empires, the Aztec civilization of Mexico, and the Inca empire of Peru. Both were of recent origin, established by warrior tribes in the 12th–14th centuries. They reached their fullest extent as the first European explorers arrived. Aztec rule extended over much of modern Mexico. The Incas spread their rule south into present-day Chile and Argentina, and north into Ecuador.

Christopher Columbus, an Italian navigator employed by the Spanish crown to find a westward route to Asia, discovered instead the Americas. Within 50 years one third of the New World was under Spanish control.

EUROPE

Though Christian Europe later transformed the exploration and settlement of the world, the Europe from which Columbus sailed was an unstable, violent continent, threatened by invaders from Asia to the east, and from the Ottoman Empire to the south. Civil wars and dynastic conflict resulted in shifting frontiers and small, militarily weak states. Only France, united by the late 15th century, Spain, a single monarchy from the 1490s, Portugal and England were close to their modern forms.

The Portuguese caravel, buoyant, sturdy and lateen-rigged, was an ideal ocean-going vessel.

EAST ASIA

The most powerful state in the world in 1492 was Ming China. Set up in 1386 after the collapse of Mongol power, the Ming dynasty ruled an area from Manchuria in the north to the borders of Vietnam in the south. Based on a traditional structure of bureaucratic control, the Ming emperors controlled their vast empire from Peking (Beijing), from where they launched punitive wars against the Mongols and Japanese pirates along the coast. Chinese culture and trade spread throughout East and South East Asia, and Chinese navigators reached the Red Sea and the East African coast.

Chinese junks plied the China seas, and traded as far as the East Indies, Ceylon and East Africa.

OCEANIA

The ethnic, political and religious map of South East Asia was largely in place by the late 15th century. The largest state was the vast Srivijayan Hindu-Buddhist Empire, which spanned the East Indian archipelago. Muslim traders were already incorporating this rich region into an Indian Ocean trading empire. Further east, the scattered island groups of the Pacific were being successively colonized by waves of Melanesian colonists.

The outrigger canoe was the vehicle of Pacific colonization.

Arab dhows built a trading network around the Indian Ocean.

MIDDLE EAST AND AFRICA

After centuries of invasion from the Christian West and Asian nomadic empires, the Middle Eastern world stabilized around a revival of the Ottoman Empire. Vassal states extended across North Africa to Morocco, which linked the trading kingdoms of sub-Saharan Africa with the markets of Asia. The great cities of the Middle East surpassed those of Europe in wealth and learning.

The magnetic compass, in use since the 13th century, was a primary navigational tool for the first ocean-going explorers, although early compasses were not always reliable, and ships often went astray. Accurate navigation only came later with the invention of the chronometer.

Map labels

Bering Strait
Siberia
ASIA
Gobi
Aral Sea
UZBEKH KHANATE
Sea of Japan
JAPAN
KOREA
MURID PERSIA
Himalayas
NEPAL
SULTANATE OF DELHI
TIBET
MING EMPIRE
Persian Gulf
Arabian Sea
AVA
LAOS
Bay of Bengal
PEGU
ANNAM
SIAM
CAMBODIA
South China Sea
YEMEN
VIJAYANAGAR
PACIFIC OCEAN
Ceylon
Micronesia
INDIAN OCEAN
SRIVIJAYAN EMPIRE
East Indies
Melanesia
Madagascar
AUSTRALIA
NEW ZEALAND

THE AGE OF DISCOVERY: 1492-1648

THE FIRST STATE to take advantage of the new age of exploration was Spain. By the middle of the 16th century, under the Emperor Charles V, Spain was established as the foremost European colonial power, and one of the richest and most powerful kingdoms in Europe. Spanish rule was extended over the whole of Central America, much of South America, Florida and the Caribbean; in Asia, Spanish rule was established in the Philippines. Spain led the way in establishing European settler colonies overseas. By the middle of the 17th century, British, Dutch and French colonists began to challenge Spanish dominance in the Americas and East Asia, while pirates around the world plundered Spain's wealthy merchant convoys.

GLOBAL STATES AND TERRITORIES

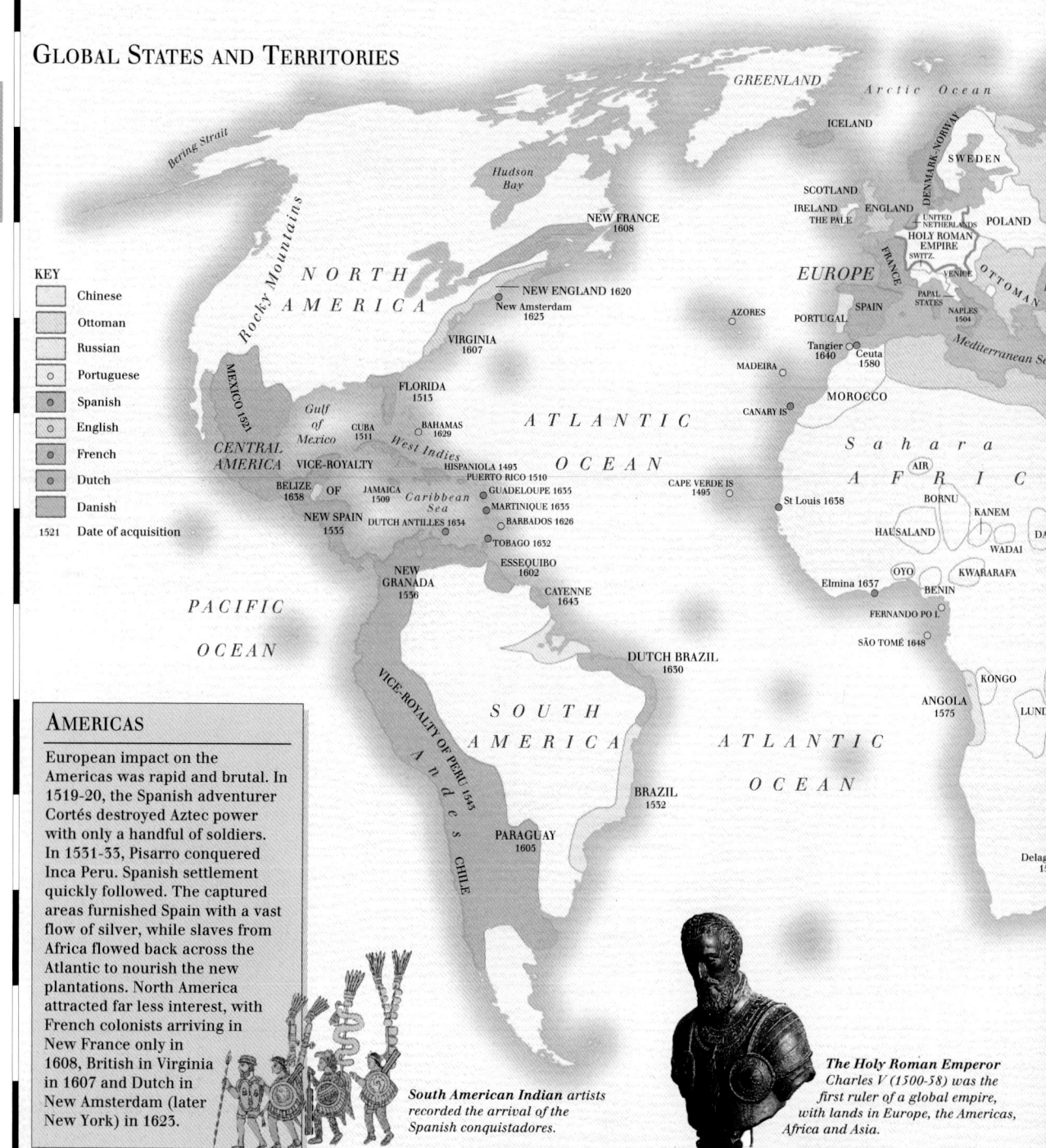

KEY

	Chinese
	Ottoman
	Russian
○	Portuguese
◉	Spanish
○	English
◉	French
◉	Dutch
	Danish
1521	Date of acquisition

GREENLAND
Arctic Ocean
ICELAND
DENMARK-NORWAY
SWEDEN
SCOTLAND
IRELAND ENGLAND
THE PALE
UNITED NETHERLANDS POLAND
HOLY ROMAN EMPIRE
SWITZ.
EUROPE
FRANCE
VENICE OTTOMAN E.
PAPAL STATES
PORTUGAL SPAIN
NAPLES 1504
AZORES
Mediterranean Sea
Tangier 1640 Ceuta 1580
MADEIRA
MOROCCO
CANARY IS
Sahara
AFRIC
CAPE VERDE IS 1495
St Louis 1638
AIR
BORNU
KANEM
HAUSALAND
WADAI
DA
OYO KWARARAFA
Elmina 1637 BENIN
FERNANDO PO I.
SÃO TOMÉ 1648
KONGO
ANGOLA 1575
LUND
ATLANTIC OCEAN
Delago 15

Bering Strait
Hudson Bay
NORTH AMERICA
Rocky Mountains
NEW FRANCE 1608
NEW ENGLAND 1620
New Amsterdam 1623
VIRGINIA 1607
FLORIDA 1513
MEXICO 1521
Gulf of Mexico
CUBA 1511
BAHAMAS 1629
ATLANTIC OCEAN
CENTRAL AMERICA
VICE-ROYALTY
West Indies
HISPANIOLA 1493
PUERTO RICO 1510
BELIZE 1638 OF
JAMAICA 1509
Caribbean Sea
GUADELOUPE 1635
MARTINIQUE 1635
NEW SPAIN 1555
DUTCH ANTILLES 1634
BARBADOS 1626
TOBAGO 1632
ESSEQUIBO 1602
NEW GRANADA 1556
CAYENNE 1643
PACIFIC OCEAN
VICE-ROYALTY OF PERU 1545
Andes
CHILE
SOUTH AMERICA
DUTCH BRAZIL 1630
ATLANTIC OCEAN
BRAZIL 1552
PARAGUAY 1605

AMERICAS

European impact on the Americas was rapid and brutal. In 1519-20, the Spanish adventurer Cortés destroyed Aztec power with only a handful of soldiers. In 1531-33, Pisarro conquered Inca Peru. Spanish settlement quickly followed. The captured areas furnished Spain with a vast flow of silver, while slaves from Africa flowed back across the Atlantic to nourish the new plantations. North America attracted far less interest, with French colonists arriving in New France only in 1608, British in Virginia in 1607 and Dutch in New Amsterdam (later New York) in 1623.

South American Indian artists recorded the arrival of the Spanish conquistadores.

The Holy Roman Emperor *Charles V (1500-58) was the first ruler of a global empire, with lands in Europe, the Americas, Africa and Asia.*

EUROPE

For more than a century after Martin Luther inspired the Protestant Reformation in the 1520s, Europe was torn by religious wars. Scandinavia, England and Scotland adopted the new church but elsewhere bitter civil conflicts led to the prolonged warfare and persecution known as the Thirty Years War. This ended in 1648; it destroyed wide areas of Central Europe and decimated the German population, but resulted in a religious settlement which carried down to the 20th century. The Dutch Republic and northern Germany became Protestant while southern Germany, Poland and southwest Europe remained Catholic.

Printing, using movable type, was a key development in the dissemination of ideas, knowledge and commerce in early modern Europe.

ASIA

In 1480, the small principality of Muscovy (Moscow) threw off Mongol control, and proceeded to expand Muscovite power over the whole of the area from the Arctic Ocean to the Caspian Sea. In the 1550s, the conquest of Kazan brought Russian power to the Urals, and over the next century it spread across Siberia reaching the Pacific coast by 1649. Much of the area remained uninhabited, but to the south this new empire jostled uneasily with a string of Central Asian Muslim khanates, and with the newly-established Manchurian Ch'ing dynasty, which wrested control of China from the Ming in 1644.

European navigators and surveyors produced accurate maps and charts of their voyages.

The Indian Mughal ruler Shahjahan (1592-1648), builder of the Taj Mahal.

SOUTH ASIA AND OCEANIA

The Portuguese and the Spanish were the first European powers to open trade with the powerful Asian states of Mughal India and Ch'ing China, the Spanish opening trans-Pacific routes between Central America, the Philippines and China. But the establishment of the Dutch and British East India companies in the early 17th century announced the advent of two new maritime powers.

West African trading kingdoms produced artefacts such as this bronze Portuguese soldier from Benin.

AFRICA AND THE MIDDLE EAST

While Europe was divided by the Reformation, Islam experienced a remarkable resurgence in the 16th century. The revival of the Ottoman Empire brought Islamic rule over much of southeast Europe. Islam spread along trade routes to sub-Saharan Africa. In east Africa, it spread south along the coast. Further east, Muslim rulers established new imperial states in Persia (Iran) and India.

The sextant allowed navigators to take accurate measurements of heavenly bodies in relation to the horizon, thus allowing latitude to be calculated correctly. Early sextants had to be hand-held and were often used on shore rather than on board ship.

Map labels

RUSSIAN EMPIRE
Siberia
Bering Strait
KAZAKHSTAN
Aral Sea
KHWARIZM
KHOKAND KHANATE
KASHGAR KHANATE
UZBEKISTAN
A S I A
SAFAVID PERSIA
Persian Gulf
Himalayas
TIBET
NEPAL
MUGHAL EMPIRE
MANCHU (CH'ING) EMPIRE
Sea of Japan
JAPAN
KOREA
Deshima 1641
PACIFIC OCEAN
OMAN 1508
Diu 1555
Daman 1559
Surat 1608
Bombay 1534
Hooghly 1640
BURMA
ARAKAN
Bay of Bengal
LAOS
ANNAM
Macao 1557
FORMOSA 1624
Arabian Sea
Goa 1510
Masulipatam 1611
Madras 1639
SIAM
South China Sea
PHILIPPINES from 1565
CEYLON 1505
Galle 1640
Malacca 1641
MOLUCCAS from 1605
Micronesia
Melanesia
INDIAN OCEAN
Batavia 1619
Makassar 1607
East Indies
1610
TIMOR 1618
PORTUGUESE AFRICA 1505
ETHIOPIA
Madagascar
AUSTRALIA
NEW ZEALAND

THE AGE OF EXPANSION: 1648-1789

THE YEARS FROM the middle of the 17th century to the end of the 18th century saw a massive consolidation of European discovery and exploration, which took the form of colonial settlement and political expansion. This period also witnessed the beginning of a sharp rise in European population and in its economic strength, accompanied by rapid developments in the arts and sciences. All these factors powered European expansion – a process that would bring European culture to every part of the globe, gradually filling in the world map, and bringing it into often fatal contact with less robust indigenous cultures. By the last quarter of the 18th century, with Europe poised on the brink of political turmoil, only Africa and Australasia remained largely unmolested by European attentions.

GLOBAL STATES AND TERRITORIES

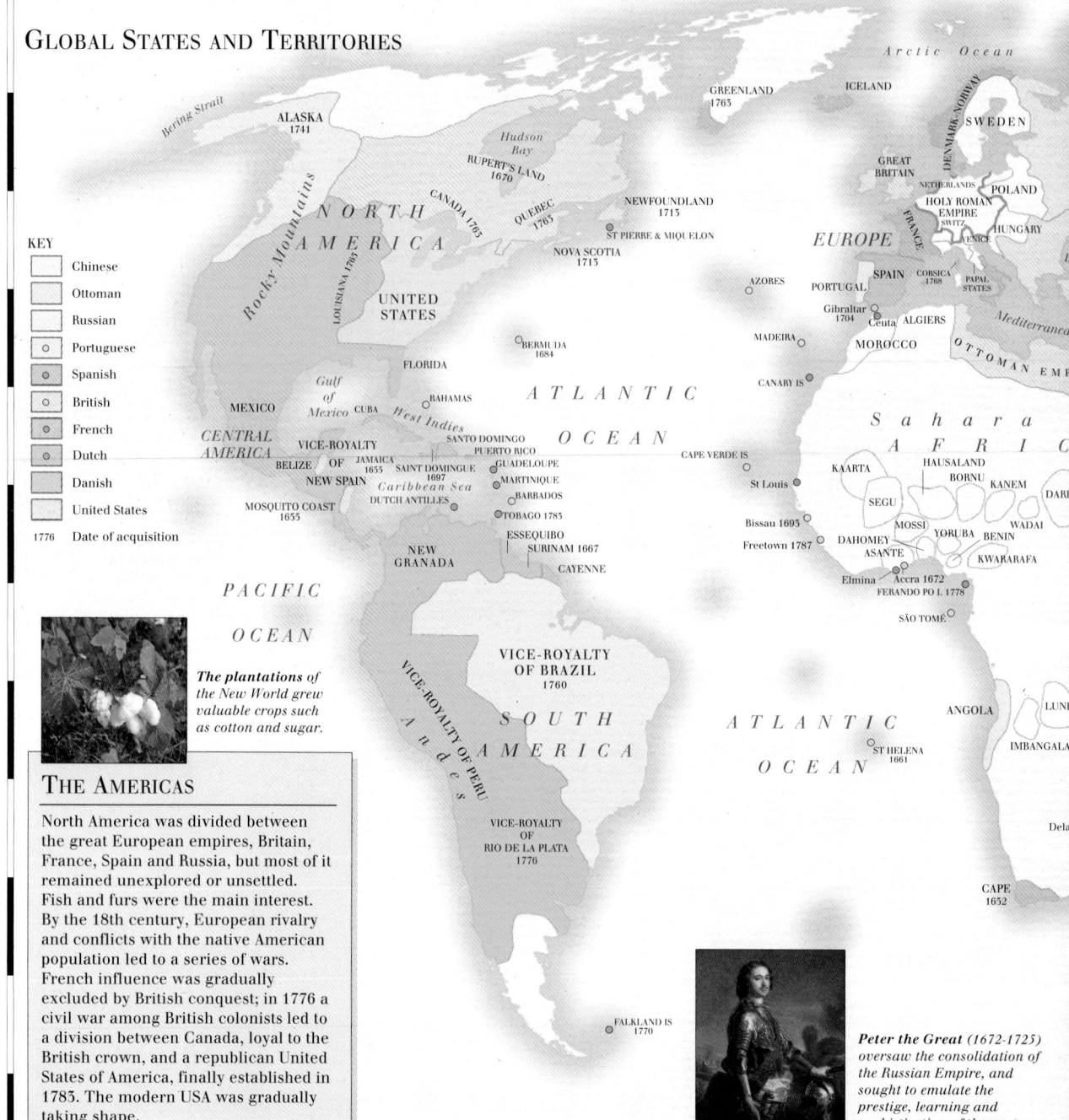

KEY

	Chinese
	Ottoman
	Russian
○	Portuguese
○	Spanish
○	British
○	French
○	Dutch
	Danish
	United States
1776	Date of acquisition

Arctic Ocean

GREENLAND 1765 · ICELAND

DENMARK-NORWAY · SWEDEN

ALASKA 1741

Bering Strait

Hudson Bay

RUPERT'S LAND 1670

GREAT BRITAIN · NETHERLANDS · POLAND

Rocky Mountains

CANADA 1763

QUEBEC 1763

NEWFOUNDLAND 1713

ST PIERRE & MIQUELON

HOLY ROMAN EMPIRE · SWITZ · HUNGARY

NORTH AMERICA

NOVA SCOTIA 1713

EUROPE

FRANCE · VENICE

LOUISIANA 1763

UNITED STATES

AZORES · PORTUGAL · SPAIN · CORSICA 1768 · PAPAL STATES

Gibraltar 1704 · Ceuta · ALGIERS

Mediterranean

BERMUDA 1684

MADEIRA · MOROCCO

OTTOMAN EMP.

FLORIDA

CANARY IS

Gulf of Mexico · CUBA · BAHAMAS

Sahara

ATLANTIC OCEAN

MEXICO

West Indies

AFRICA

CENTRAL AMERICA · VICE-ROYALTY · SANTO DOMINGO · PUERTO RICO

CAPE VERDE IS

KAARTA · HAUSALAND · BORNU · KANEM · DARF

BELIZE · OF · JAMAICA 1655 · SAINT DOMINGUE 1697 · GUADELOUPE · MARTINIQUE

St Louis

NEW SPAIN · *Caribbean Sea* · BARBADOS

SEGU · MOSSI · YORUBA · BENIN · WADAI

DUTCH ANTILLES

TOBAGO 1785

Bissau 1695

MOSQUITO COAST 1655

ESSEQUIBO

SURINAM 1667

Freetown 1787 · DAHOMEY · ASANTE · KWARARAFA

NEW GRANADA

CAYENNE

Elmina · Accra 1672 · FERANDO PO I. 1778

PACIFIC OCEAN

SÃO TOMÉ

VICE-ROYALTY OF BRAZIL 1760

VICE-ROYALTY OF PERU

Andes

SOUTH AMERICA

ANGOLA · LUND

ATLANTIC OCEAN

ST HELENA 1661

IMBANGALA

VICE-ROYALTY OF RIO DE LA PLATA 1776

Dela

CAPE 1652

FALKLAND IS 1770

The plantations of the New World grew valuable crops such as cotton and sugar.

THE AMERICAS

North America was divided between the great European empires, Britain, France, Spain and Russia, but most of it remained unexplored or unsettled. Fish and furs were the main interest. By the 18th century, European rivalry and conflicts with the native American population led to a series of wars. French influence was gradually excluded by British conquest; in 1776 a civil war among British colonists led to a division between Canada, loyal to the British crown, and a republican United States of America, finally established in 1783. The modern USA was gradually taking shape.

Peter the Great (1672-1725) oversaw the consolidation of the Russian Empire, and sought to emulate the prestige, learning and sophistication of the western European monarchies.

EUROPE

After the crisis of the Thirty Years War, Europe began to develop a more settled state system as successful dynastic houses imposed more centralized rule. The Habsburgs acquired control over Hungary and much of Central Europe. Russia's frontiers pushed into Poland and the Ukraine. The French Bourbon monarchy became the most powerful in Europe. Its material wealth and culture made it a rival to the older empires of Asia. French became the common language of educated Europeans and French philosophy led to the intellectual 'enlightenment'.

Isaac Newton (1642-1727), the leading scientist of Europe's Age of Reason.

ASIA

The Ch'ing Dynasty forged the shape of modern China. By 1658 the whole of southern China was under Manchu control. Formosa (Taiwan) was occupied in 1683, outer Mongolia in 1697. A protectorate was established over Tibet in 1751. Over the course of this expansion, the population of China trebled and the economy boomed through trade in tea, porcelain and silk with Russia and the West. Manchu China was powerful enough to resist incursions by the European empires, avoiding the fate of the crumbling Mughal Empire in India, where Britain and France competed for trade and territory.

Dutch and British East Indiamen carried the vast European trade with Asia.

Maori New Zealand was one of the few indigenous cultures to remain untouched by European contact until the 19th century.

OCEANIA

South East Asia and Oceania was an area of small, warring kingdoms, increasingly prey to the ambitions of European traders, first Spanish and Portuguese, then Dutch and British. Yet, by the late 18th century, there was still little formal colonization. Though first discovered by Tasman in 1692, most of Australasia was still unexplored and unsettled, except for a number of small penal colonies set up by the British in New South Wales (1788) and Tasmania (1804).

AFRICA

During the 17th and 18th centuries Africa was regarded by the rest of the world as a source of two things: gold and slaves. Some 13.5 million slaves were shipped in the 1700s, from the west coast and from Portuguese Angola. African dealers sold to European middlemen, who in turn sold on the surviving slaves. In northern and northeastern Africa, Arab slavers traded with the Ottoman Empire. But the rest of Africa remained isolated from the outside world.

African slavers marched their human cargo from the interior to the coast for transhipment.

Harrison's chronometer, invented in 1762, allowed navigators to measure time accurately, and thus calculate longitude correctly. This greatly reduced the risk of shipwreck and heralded the beginning of accurate mapping of the world.

Map labels

SSIAN EMPIRE

Bering Strait

ZAKHSTAN
Aral Sea
A S I A
MONGOLIA 1697
KHOKAND
SINKIANG 1760
TURKESTAN
PERSIA
AFGHANISTAN
M A N C H U (CH'ING) EMPIRE
Himalayas
TIBET 1751
NEPAL
BALUCHISTAN
BENGAL 1757
Sea of Japan
JAPAN
KOREA
Deshima
PACIFIC OCEAN
rsian Gulf
Surat
Diu
MARATHA CONFEDERACY
Daman
Bombay 1661
BURMA
Chandernagore 1688
Bay of Bengal
FORMOSA 1683
Macao
Arabian Sea
Goa
NORTHERN CIRCARS 1756
SIAM
ANNAM
South China Sea
PHILIPPINES
MARIANAS 1668
Mahé 1725
MADRAS 1789
ANDAMAN IS 1789
Karikal 1758
Pondicherry 1674
CAROLINE IS 1686
PIA
Galle
CEYLON 1658
Penang 1786
MALAYA
Micronesia
I N D I A N O C E A N
MOLUCCAS
Melanesia
GUESE FRICA
CHAGOS IS 1784
DUTCH EAST INDIES
TIMOR
RÉUNION 1662
ort Dauphin 1766
A U S T R A L I A
LORD HOWE I. 1788
NEW SOUTH WALES 1788
NEW ZEALAND

THE AGE OF REVOLUTION: 1789-1830

IN 1789 ROYAL POWER was shattered by the French Revolution. The collapse of the most powerful monarchy in Europe reverberated worldwide. The revolutions in France and America ushered in the idea of the modern nation state, and of popular representative government. Revolutionary outbreaks occurred elsewhere in Europe, and overseas colonies in Latin America won their independence. At the same time, an industrial revolution was taking place in Europe, transforming the old trading economy into a manufacturing base which would require a global supply of raw materials and a global market to fuel it. The revolutionary years thus marked the beginning of the modern political and economic world order.

GLOBAL STATES AND TERRITORIES

KEY

- Chinese
- Ottoman
- Russian
- Portuguese
- Spanish
- British
- French
- Dutch
- Danish
- United States

1790   Date of acquisition

[1820]   Date of independence

THE AMERICAS

The fledgling United States of America began to expand rapidly, purchasing the Midwest territories from France in 1803, and taking Florida from Spain in 1819. Revolutionary fervour both here and in Europe weakened the control of France, Spain and Portugal throughout Latin America. From 1810 there followed 20 years of violent revolt, with native armies fighting their European masters and each other. The new states were prey to political violence and instability, but they never again came under European rule.

Simón Bolívar (1783-1830), led armies of liberation in Peru, Bolivia and Venezuela.

Napoleon Bonaparte (1769-1821) began his career as a French Revolutionary commander. By 1804 he had become emperor of much of mainland Europe.

EUROPE

Under the Revolutionary general, Napoleon Bonaparte, France conquered a large part of Europe and destroyed the old feudal order. Napoleon helped to shape the new nation states that emerged in 19th-century Europe – Belgium, Italy and Germany. He gave much of Europe its modern legal code and systems of education and local government.

Steam-powered engines transformed the European industrial economy.

ASIA

The principal colonial power in Asia was Russia, whose consolidation of its empire in northern and central Asia continued throughout the 19th century. But now the Dutch began to extend their control of the East Indies, while a bitter struggle between the British and the French was conducted in and around the Indian Ocean. France was gradually forced to concede many of its footholds in India, where the British East India Company rapidly extended its interests by a mixture of diplomacy and military force. But the elusive key to Asia's largest markets remained the slumbering giant of Ch'ing China, whose Manchu rulers, like those of Japan, remained unimpressed by European overtures.

The spices of the East Indies, such as pepper, were among the most highly valued traded commodities from Asia.

James Cook (1728-1779) charted much of the Pacific between 1768 and 1779.

OCEANIA

Though Portuguese and Dutch explorers had confirmed the existence of Australasia in the 16th and 17th centuries, it was not until the voyages of Captain Cook in the 1770s that the geography of the Pacific was established, and the fertile eastern coast of Australia was explored and charted. Over the next 30 years, small settlements were established around the coast; by 1829, Britain had brought the whole continent under the British flag.

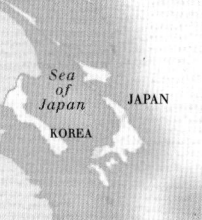

Map labels

USSIAN EMPIRE

Bering Strait

A S I A

Aral Sea

MONGOLIA

MANCHU (CH'ING) CHINA

TIBET (Chinese protectorate from 1750)

Himalayas

NEPAL BHUTAN

ERSIA

AFGHAN-ISTAN

Persian Gulf

OMAN

Diu Daman

Arabian Sea Goa

INDIA

Mahé Pondicherry

LACCADIVE IS 1791

Karikal

Ceylon

BURMA

ANNAM

SIAM

TENASSERIM 1826

ANDAMAN IS

Bay of Bengal

Macao FORMOSA

Sea of Japan JAPAN

KOREA

PACIFIC OCEAN

South China Sea

PHILIPPINES

MARIANAS

CAROLINE IS

Micronesia

Melanesia

MALAYA
Malacca 1824

SINGAPORE 1819

MALDIVE IS 1815

BIA

3AR (an)

SEYCHELLES 1794

CHAGOS IS

New Guinea

DUTCH EAST INDIES

Timor

I N D I A N O C E A N

IGUESE A

HOVA KINGDOM

RÉUNION

MAURITIUS 1810

WESTERN AUSTRALIA 1829

NEW SOUTH WALES

A U S T R A L I A

LORD HOWE I.

NEW ZEALAND

CHATHAM IS 1791

TASMANIA (Van Diemen's Land)

AUCKLAND IS 1806

MACQUARIE IS 1811

The first European migrants to Africa settled in Cape Colony.

AFRICA

The northern regions of Africa were part of the vast Islamic Ottoman Empire; from here Islam spread south to West Africa and the Horn of Africa. Holy wars (or *jihads*) late in the 18th and early 19th centuries completed the conversion to Islam of much of Saharan and sub-Saharan Africa. In the south, large tribal kingdoms flourished, in the Congo basin, Zimbabwe and southern Africa.

The development during the European industrial revolution of mechanized manufacturing plant and machinery, such as power looms, gave Europe effective control of a booming global trade in raw materials and mass-manufactured commodities.

THE AGE OF EMPIRE: 1830-1914

THE NINETEENTH CENTURY was dominated by the spread of modern industry and transport, and the expansion of European trade and influence worldwide. Industry made Europe rich and powerful; its capital cities were monuments to the self-confidence of the new European age. Railways and steam ships revolutionized communications, bringing a stream of industrial goods, technical know-how, and European settlers across America, Africa and Asia. Modern industry and weapons brought Europe to the summit of global influence. In these developments lay the origins of the division of the world into rich and poor regions; a developed, prosperous north, an under-developed, dependent south.

GLOBAL STATES AND TERRITORIES

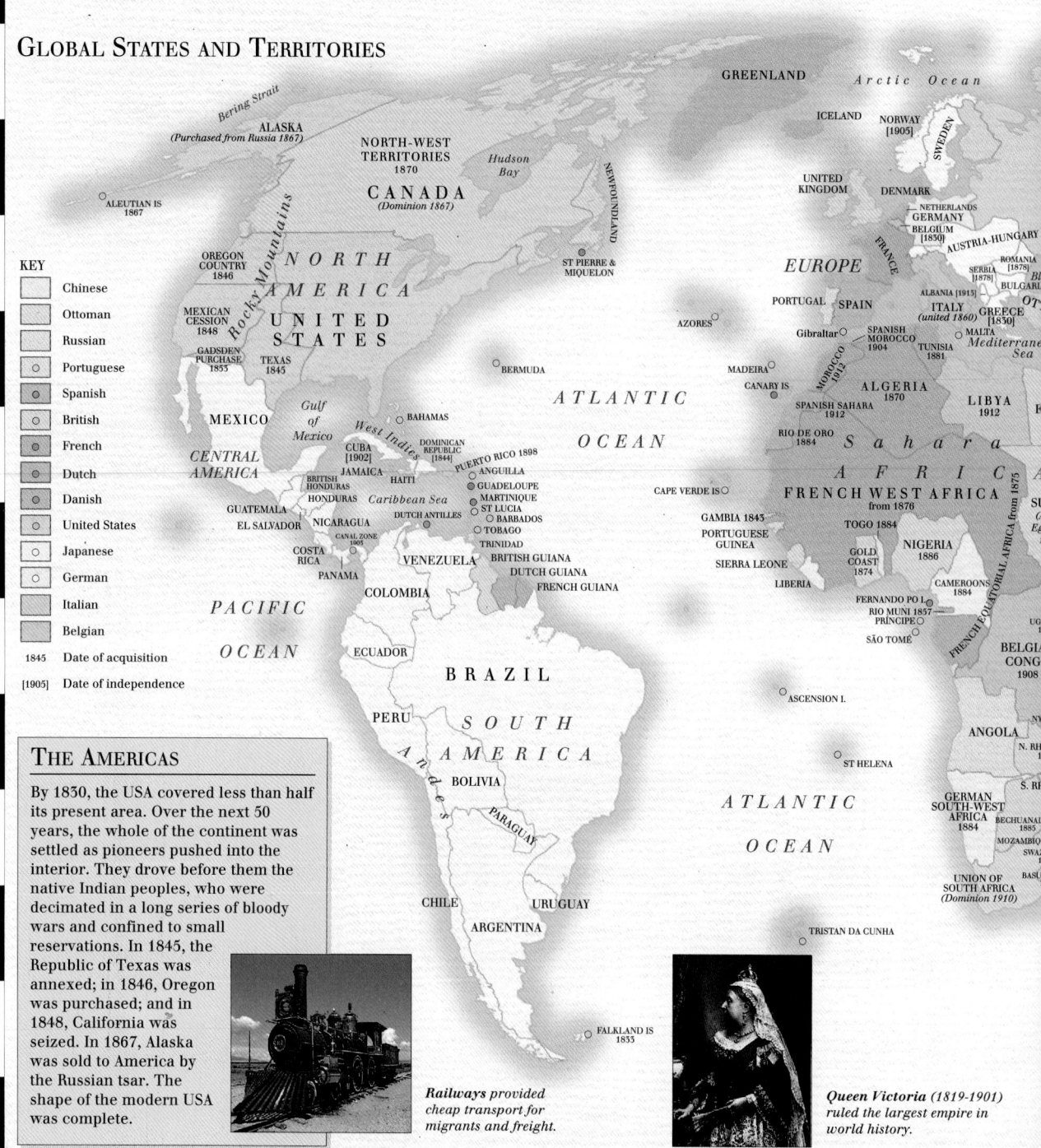

KEY

- Chinese
- Ottoman
- Russian
- Portuguese
- Spanish
- British
- French
- Dutch
- Danish
- United States
- Japanese
- German
- Italian
- Belgian

1845 Date of acquisition

[1905] Date of independence

GREENLAND

Arctic Ocean

ICELAND — NORWAY [1905] — SWEDEN

UNITED KINGDOM — DENMARK

NETHERLANDS
GERMANY
BELGIUM [1830]
AUSTRIA-HUNGARY

EUROPE

FRANCE

ROMANIA [1878]
SERBIA [1878]
ALBANIA [1913]
BULGARIA

PORTUGAL SPAIN

ITALY (united 1860)
GREECE [1830]

AZORES

Gibraltar
SPANISH MOROCCO 1904
MALTA
TUNISIA 1881
Mediterranean Sea

MADEIRA
CANARY IS
MOROCCO 1912
ALGERIA 1870
LIBYA 1912

SPANISH SAHARA 1912
Sahara

RIO DE ORO 1884
A F R I C A

CAPE VERDE IS
FRENCH WEST AFRICA from 1876

GAMBIA 1843
TOGO 1884
NIGERIA 1886

PORTUGUESE GUINEA
GOLD COAST 1874

SIERRA LEONE
LIBERIA

FERNANDO PO I.
RIO MUNI 1857
PRÍNCIPE

CAMEROONS 1884

SÃO TOMÉ

FRENCH EQUATORIAL AFRICA from 1875

BELGIAN CONGO 1908

Bering Strait

ALASKA
(Purchased from Russia 1867)

NORTH-WEST TERRITORIES 1870

Hudson Bay

NEWFOUNDLAND

ALEUTIAN IS 1867

Rocky Mountains

CANADA
(Dominion 1867)

OREGON COUNTRY 1846

N O R T H

A M E R I C A

MEXICAN CESSION 1848

UNITED STATES

GADSDEN PURCHASE 1853
TEXAS 1845

ST PIERRE & MIQUELON

BERMUDA

A T L A N T I C

O C E A N

MEXICO

Gulf of Mexico

BAHAMAS

West Indies

CENTRAL AMERICA

CUBA [1902]
DOMINICAN REPUBLIC [1844]

PUERTO RICO 1898
ANGUILLA

JAMAICA

BRITISH HONDURAS
HONDURAS

HAITI

GUADELOUPE
MARTINIQUE
ST LUCIA
BARBADOS
TOBAGO

Caribbean Sea

GUATEMALA
EL SALVADOR NICARAGUA
CANAL ZONE 1903

DUTCH ANTILLES

TRINIDAD

COSTA RICA
PANAMA

VENEZUELA

BRITISH GUIANA
DUTCH GUIANA
FRENCH GUIANA

COLOMBIA

PACIFIC

OCEAN

ECUADOR

B R A Z I L

PERU

S O U T H

A M E R I C A

Andes

BOLIVIA

PARAGUAY

ASCENSION I.

ST HELENA

A T L A N T I C

O C E A N

TRISTAN DA CUNHA

ANGOLA

N. RH.

S. RH.

GERMAN SOUTH-WEST AFRICA 1884
BECHUANAI 1885

MOZAMBIQU
SWAZI
BASU

UNION OF SOUTH AFRICA
(Dominion 1910)

CHILE
URUGUAY

ARGENTINA

FALKLAND IS 1835

THE AMERICAS

By 1830, the USA covered less than half its present area. Over the next 50 years, the whole of the continent was settled as pioneers pushed into the interior. They drove before them the native Indian peoples, who were decimated in a long series of bloody wars and confined to small reservations. In 1845, the Republic of Texas was annexed; in 1846, Oregon was purchased; and in 1848, California was seized. In 1867, Alaska was sold to America by the Russian tsar. The shape of the modern USA was complete.

Railways provided cheap transport for migrants and freight.

Queen Victoria (1819-1901) ruled the largest empire in world history.

THE WORLD 1830-1914

EUROPE

In the 19th century, Europe was transformed into an industrial economy. In the new industrial cities, pressure developed for liberal reforms and parliamentary politics. Nationalists created new states in Germany, Italy, Greece, Serbia and Belgium. While the modern map of Europe gradually began to take shape, European imperialist brought still further areas of the world under their control.

Sailing ships carried most oceanic trade until 1900.

ASIA

Building on colonial interests that stretched back into the 18th century, Britain and France transformed the political world of South Asia. Britain extended its rule in India and, in 1885, Burma was brought under British control. The Vietnamese and Chinese Empires were pressured by Europeans anxious to trade and to spread Christianity: the Ch'ing Empire conceded areas of influence; the Vietnamese Empire resisted and was brought by force under French domination. By the 1890s the whole of southern Asia except for Siam was dominated by Europe, which created the modern state structure of the region.

The Japanese emperor Mutsuhito (1852-1912) opened Japan to Western trade and influence.

The colonization of Australia and New Zealand was based on sheep farming.

OCEANIA

During the 19th century, Australia and New Zealand remained closely tied to the British homeland. British settlers came to farm and later to prospect for gold and other valuable minerals. In 1840, New Zealand came under British rule and the native Maoris were forced off the land. Not until 1872 was the continent of Australia traversed, and not until 1901 was a single state, the Commonwealth of Australia, proclaimed.

Quinine – the cure for malaria.

New medicines made the colonization of Africa possible.

AFRICA

The political structure of independent Africa was torn up by encroaching European empires. As native societies reacted violently to European intrusion, so European military and political power was increased to secure European interests. In 1884, in Berlin, the European powers divided Africa between them. The 'Partition of Africa' established many states' modern frontiers.

The first machine gun, invented by Gatling in 1862.

The European imperial powers maintained control of their often far-flung colonies by military superiority. Native forces were rarely a match for the large, highly trained armies, powerful navies and technically advanced weaponry which the Europeans had at their disposal.

Map labels

RUSSIAN EMPIRE

Bering Strait

KAZAKHSTAN 1854
Aral Sea
TURKESTAN 1895
BUKHARA 1868
TURKMENISTAN 1884
AFGHANISTAN
PERSIA
Persian Gulf

MONGOLIA (autonomous 1912)
MANCHURIA
A S I A
TIBET [1912]
Himalayas
NEPAL   BHUTAN
BURMA
CHINA

AMUR 1858
1853
SAKHALIN 1905
USSURI 1860
KURILE IS 1875
Sea of Japan
Port Arthur 1905
Weihaiwei 1898
Tsingtao 1898
KOREA 1905
JAPAN
RYUKYU IS 1874

PACIFIC OCEAN

Chandernagore
INDIA
Diu
Daman
Arabian Sea
Goa
Mahé
Pondicherry
Karikal
LACCADIVE IS
CEYLON
NICOBAR IS 1869
MALDIVE IS

FRENCH INDO-CHINA 1887
SIAM
ANDAMAN IS
MALAYA
SARAWAK 1888
BRITISH NORTH BORNEO 1881

Macao
Hong Kong 1841
FORMOSA 1895
South China Sea
PHILIPPINES 1898

Bay of Bengal

MARIANAS 1899
GUAM 1898
CAROLINE IS 1899
Micronesia

HADHRAMAUT 1888
Aden 1839
SOCOTRA 1886
FRENCH SOMALILAND 1884

SEYCHELLES
CHAGOS IS

DUTCH EAST INDIES
NEW GUINEA
PAPUA 1906
TIMOR

BISMARCK ARCHIPELAGO 1884
NAURU 1888
SOLOMON IS 1893
Melanesia

INDIAN OCEAN

CHRISTMAS I. 1888
COCOS IS 1857

COMORO IS 1886

MAURITIUS
RÉUNION

NEW CALEDONIA 1853

AUSTRALIA (Commonwealth 1901)

LORD HOWE I.

NEW ZEALAND 1840 (Dominion 1907)

CHATHAM IS

TASMANIA

AUCKLAND IS
MACQUARIE IS

THE AGE OF GLOBAL WAR: 1914-45

IN 1914, IMPERIAL AND MILITARY rivalry in Europe provoked the first of two world wars, the largest and most destructive wars in human history. At the end of the first war, in 1918, the old international order was dead. The Russian Empire collapsed in revolution and was transformed by a communist minority into the Soviet Union. The German, Habsburg and Ottoman empires were dismembered. A fragile peace ensued but the old equilibrium was gone. The rise of strident nationalism in Germany, Japan and Italy destroyed the peace once again in 1939. The second war cost the lives of 50 million people and ravaged Europe and Asia. At its end, in 1945, the USA and the Soviet Union had emerged as the new superpowers.

GLOBAL STATES AND TERRITORIES

KEY

	Chinese
○	USSR
○	Portuguese
○	Spanish
○	British/Commonwealth
○	French
○	Dutch
○	Danish
○	United States
	Belgian
1945	Date of acquisition
[1922]	Date of independence
⬭	Axis occupied territories 1942

The Model T Ford, manufactured on the world's first assembly lines.

THE AMERICAS

In 1917, the USA entered the war against Germany with the aim of restoring world peace and the spread of democracy. After the Great Crash in 1929, American prosperity was destroyed and in the 1930s the USA, impoverished and disarmed, sat on the sidelines as the world plunged again into war. However, in 1941, the Japanese attacked American territories in the Pacific: the American economy recovered and the USA became the leading military power. By 1945 America dominated the western world.

The four founders of communism.

46

EUROPE

Both world wars had their origins in Europe. In 1914 Britain, France and Russia combined to defeat Germany, with US help. In 1918 new nation states were established in Eastern Europe. But, by 1939, revived German nationalism started a second world war; much of Western Europe came under a German 'New Order' until the Soviet Union, Britain and the USA developed sufficient military strength to reconquer Europe and defeat Germany.

World War II was decided by mechanical and industrial superiority.

ASIA

The collapse of the Chinese Empire in 1911, followed in 1917 by the disappearance of the Russian Empire, produced instability across Asia. Full-scale war broke out between Japan and China in 1937, with Japan trying to conquer China. The Soviet Union was the victim of German aggression from 1941. Both Japan and Germany were held at bay by communist forces which eventually succeeded in imposing stable politics on Asia. By 1945, the Soviet Union had reconquered its lost territories and dominated Eastern Europe. In China, communist armies filled the vacuum left by the Japanese defeat.

Mahatma Gandhi (1869-1948) led India to independence through peaceful non-co-operation and protest.

OCEANIA

For the only time in its history, Australia was faced with the very real prospect of invasion. In the Second World War, Japanese armies reached the island of New Guinea, and bombed towns in northern Australia. Japanese submarines attacked Sydney harbour. The Battle of the Coral Sea, in May 1942, saved Australia, but it took almost three years to clear Japanese forces from the South Pacific, where they hung on grimly to the rich oil and mineral resources they had captured.

Japan promoted itself as the liberator of Asia from the chains of European colonialism.

Haile Selassie (1892-1975), ruler of Ethiopia, the only independent empire in Africa.

MIDDLE EAST

In 1918, the Turkish Empire disappeared after 400 years of Ottoman rule. The modern map of North Africa and the Middle East was carved out of its ruins by the victors of the First World War. After the Second World War, the foundation was laid for a new state of Israel, following the genocide of Europe's Jews by Nazi Germany. This led to conflict between native Arabs and Jewish migrants.

The conquest of the air was the most important technological achievement of the period. It added a devastating dimension to warfare, in the form of bombing, while transforming civil transport.

A German Zeppelin airship of the 1930s.

THE MODERN AGE: 1945-94

THE WARTIME ALLIANCE between the USA and the Soviet Union turned sour in efforts to reconstruct Europe and the Far East. The world became divided into two hostile camps; liberal-capitalism on the one hand, communism on the other. The two sides fought a 'Cold War', each trying to contain and subvert the other. The main conflicts of the war occurred over small issues – Korea (1950-53), Cuba (1962), Vietnam (1954-75). Larger wars were avoided because of the nuclear deterrent. With the crumbling of communist power in Russia and Eastern Europe, the stalemate of the Cold War was replaced by a less stable international order, dominated by economic uncertainty and revived nationalism.

GLOBAL STATES AND TERRITORIES

KEY

○	Portuguese
◉	Spanish
○	British
◉	French
◉	Dutch
	Danish
○	US
[1972]	Date of independence

US President John F Kennedy (1917-63) personified American post-war optimism.

THE AMERICAS

After 1945 the USA became a global power, using its vast economic and military strength to secure its trading and political interests in Europe, the Middle East and Asia. American popular culture followed in its wake; 'Americanization' replaced European influence. After decades of political oppression and poverty, the states of Latin America, encouraged by US pressure on human rights, moved closer to democracy from the 1970s. But Latin America remained economically unstable, with high population growth, chronic inflation and international debt, and powerful criminal organizations producing Latin America's fastest growing export, drugs.

In 1985, the Soviet leader Mikhail Gorbachev launched a programme of economic and political reform which brought Soviet communism to an end.

The Berlin Wall, symbol of the Cold War division of Europe, was demolished in 1989.

EUROPE

In 1945, Europe lay in ruins, but during the next 30 years, Western Europe experienced a long economic boom, restoring widespread prosperity and political stability. It progressed towards economic and political unity under the EC. In Eastern Europe development was overshadowed by Soviet communism until its collapse. As democracies many new nations now face an uncertain future.

ASIA

In southern Asia, popular nationalist movements came to power in India, Burma, Malaya and Indonesia; in China and Indo-China, power passed to native communist movements whose roots went back to the 1920s. After 1949, China under Mao Zedong became, with its vast population and large military forces, a second communist superpower. But the success story of modern Asia has been Japan. Defeated in 1945, its economy and cities laid waste by bombing, Japan began a programme of economic rebuilding with American aid. By the 1980s Japan had emerged as one of the world's largest manufacturing economies.

Chinese communism, based on the mobilization of peasants and workers, has nevertheless recognized the need for economic reforms.

A treaty banning the testing of nuclear bombs in the Pacific was signed in 1986.

OCEANIA

The post-war economies of Japan, USA and Australia had by the 1990s created a new industrial and trading network around the Pacific Rim. Cheap labour and low overheads drew younger states – South Korea, Taiwan, Singapore, Indonesia – into the system and much of the world's manufacturing is now concentrated there, creating a consequent shift in the balance of the global economy.

Gamal Abdel Nasser (1918-70) of Egypt, galvanized the Arab states to resist the West.

AFRICA AND THE MIDDLE EAST

The colonial powers, weakened by war, faced an irresistible wave of demands for self-determination. Between 1958 and 1975, 41 African countries gained independence, leaving only South Africa in white hands until 1994. In North Africa and throughout the Middle East a new form of anti-imperialism emerged in the 1970s in the form of Islamic fundamentalism.

From the 1950s to the 1970s, superpower rivalry focused on space exploration. The Soviets put the first man in space in 1961, and the Americans landed on the moon in 1969. Since then both manned and unmanned missions have become almost everyday events.

Map labels

RUSSIAN FEDERATION

Bering Strait

KAZAKHSTAN [1991]
Aral Sea
UZBEKISTAN [1991]
KYRGYZSTAN [1991]
TURKMENISTAN [1991]
TAJIKISTAN [1991]
MONGOLIA
ASIA
CHINA
IRAN
AFGHANISTAN
TIBET (to China 1950)
Himalayas
PAKISTAN [1947]
NEPAL
BHUTAN
N. KOREA [1953]
Sea of Japan
JAPAN
SOUTH KOREA
RYUKYU IS (to Japan)
UNITED ARAB EMIRATES (formed 1971)
QATAR
BANGLADESH [1971] (formerly E. Pakistan)
Macao
BURMA [1948]
NORTH VIETNAM [1954]
TAIWAN [1949]
Hong Kong
Persian Gulf
SAUDI ARABIA
[1995]
NORTH YEMEN
Yemen united [1990]
SOUTH YEMEN
INDIA [1947]
Bay of Bengal
LAOS [1954]
Vietnam united 1976
Arabian Sea
SOCOTRA (to S. Yemen)
DJIBOUTI [1977]
THAILAND
CAMBODIA [1954]
SOUTH VIETNAM [1954]
PACIFIC OCEAN
PHILIPPINES [1946]
MARIANAS
GUAM
South China Sea
ETHIOPIA [1960]
LACCADIVE IS (to India)
ANDAMAN IS (to India)
NICOBAR IS (to India)
MALAYA [1957]
BRUNEI [1984]
MALAYSIA (formed 1963)
MICRONESIA [1991]
SOMALIA [1960]
CEYLON [1948] (Sri Lanka 1972)
MALDIVE IS [1965]
SINGAPORE [1965]
BISMARCK ARCHIPELAGO (to P N G)
NAURU [1968]
KENYA [1964]
SEYCHELLES [1976]
CHAGOS IS
INDONESIA [1949]
PAPUA NEW GUINEA [1975]
SOLOMON IS [1978]
Melanesia
COMOROS [1975]
MOZAMBIQUE
INDIAN OCEAN
CHRISTMAS I. (to Australia)
COCOS IS (to Australia)
E. TIMOR (to Indonesia)
MADAGASCAR [1960]
RÉUNION
MAURITIUS [1968]
NEW CALEDONIA
AUSTRALIA
LORD HOWE I. (to Australia)
NEW ZEALAND
CHATHAM IS (to N Z)
AUCKLAND IS (to N Z)
MACQUARIE IS (to Australia)

2

THE NATIONS OF THE WORLD

OF THE
WORLD

The Nations of the World
• Afghanistan ~ Zimbabwe
Overseas Territories & Dependencies

A

AFGHANISTAN

OFFICIAL NAME: Islamic State of Afghanistan   **CAPITAL:** Kābul
POPULATION: 16.5 million   **CURRENCY:** Afghani   **OFFICIAL LANGUAGES:** Persian and Pashtu

LAND-LOCKED IN southwestern Asia, Afghanistan is surrounded by Iran, Pakistan, China, Tajikistan and Turkmenistan. Approximately three quarters of its territory is inaccessible terrain. Afghanistan effectively has no government, other than a fragile power-sharing arrangement between *mujahideen* leaders, whose factions have been fighting each other since the departure of Soviet invasion forces in 1989. Agriculture is the main economic activity, but less than two thirds of farmland is cultivated. Since the April 1992 handover of power to the *mujahideen*, women have returned to wearing the veil in public.

The Band-i-Amir River, in the Hindu Kush. Afghanistan is mountainous and arid. Many Afghans are nomadic sheep farmers.

CLIMATE

WEATHER CHART

Afghanistan has a harsh continental climate and the severity of winter is accentuated by high altitudes. It has the widest temperature range in the world with lows of –50°C and highs of +53°C.

COMMUNICATIONS

Kābul International

Has no fleet

THE TRANSPORT NETWORK

19,200 km (11,930 miles)	None
25 km (16 miles)	1200 km (746 miles)

The repair and reconstruction of war-damaged roads and the provision of a minimum of facilities to allow air traffic to function safely are the present priorities. Road rebuilding is usually carried out by local communities. However, neighbouring Pakistan has undertaken to rebuild a number of key routes, including the Kābul–Torkam link, which will benefit its own trade with central Asia.

Obtaining and securing key supply routes is a crucial factor in intra-*mujahideen* feuding. The *Hezb-i-Islami* has recently increased its stranglehold on the main eastern artery out of Kābul, and is also seeking to control the Salang Highway, the northern route out of the capital. Much of Afghanistan's outlying territory is sown with land-mines.

TOURISM

 War zone. Very few tourists

 No increase in past year

MAIN OVERSEAS ARRIVALS

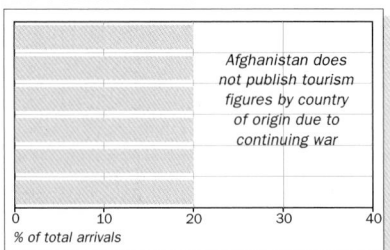

Afghanistan does not publish tourism figures by country of origin due to continuing war

% of total arrivals

Afghanistan is a war zone. There are virtually no visitors apart from occasional UN and aid agency personnel, and journalists. Few hotels or restaurants are open in Kābul. Travel is extremely dangerous due to mines as well as bandit activity. *Air Ariana*, the Afghan national airline, no longer flies from Kābul, but from Dushanbe in neighbouring Tajikistan.

The lack of a formal economy means that Afghanistan gets few visits from businessmen, and any expatriates who were previously in Kābul have left.

PEOPLE

Persian, Pashtu, Dari, Uzbek, Turkmen

26 people per km²

THE URBAN/RURAL POPULATION SPLIT

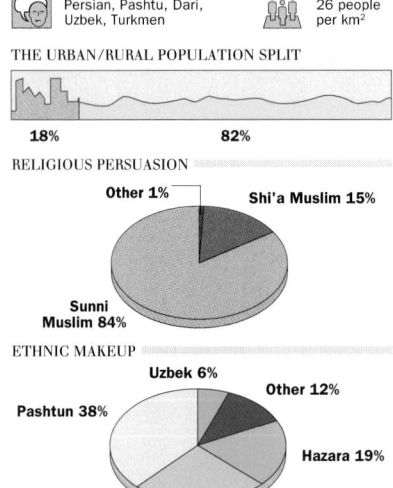

18%   82%

RELIGIOUS PERSUASION

Other 1%
Shi'a Muslim 15%
Sunni Muslim 84%

ETHNIC MAKEUP

Uzbek 6%
Other 12%
Pashtun 38%
Hazara 19%
Tajik 25%

The Pashtuns are the largest ethnic group and traditional rulers of Afghanistan, making up 38% of the population; the main minorities are Tajiks, Hazaras and Uzbeks. It is these ethnic divisions which have largely, though not exclusively, determined the intra-*mujahideen* feuding that has plagued the country since April 1992. Assaults on Kābul by

the *Hezb-i-Islami* group represent an attempt by the Pashtuns to retake control of the capital, which is now under the precarious control of a Tajik–Uzbek alliance. The *Hezb-i-Islami* group's main rivals are the predominantly Tajik *Jamiat-i-Islami*.

Some two million of the country's population were killed as a result of the 1979–1989 war, which followed invasion by the Soviet Union. As many again were maimed. A further six million were forced to flee to neighbouring Pakistan and Iran; most have not yet been able to return. Women in Afghanistan have few rights in what is rapidly becoming a male-dominated Islamic fundamentalist society. They are officially discouraged from working and are largely confined to the home.

POPULATION AGE BREAKDOWN

	0–14	15–64			65+
65+	2.1%	2.2%	2.5%	2.8%	2.7%
15–64	55.4%	54.9%	54.5%	55.2%	54.6%
0–14	42.5%	42.9%	43%	42%	42.7%
	1960	1970	1980	1990	2000

A

POLITICS

 Uncertain   President Burhanuddin Rabbani

THE STATE OF THE PARTIES

House of Representatives 234 members

Following the downfall of Najibullah's regime in April 1992, both houses were dissolved and an interim *mujahideen* legislature formed

Senate 192 members

Afghanistan is now technically ruled by a multiparty *mujahideen* cabinet, under the authority of the prime minister.

MAIN POLITICAL ISSUES

Elections

According to the March 7th 1993 Islamabad peace accord, elections were to be held by the end of the year. However, they are still awaited as the civil war continues.

Control of Kābul

Kābul is at present in the hands of the *Jamiat-i-Islami*. Afghanistan's nominal prime minister and leader of the *Hezb-i-Islami* Hekmatyar, is still unable to enter the capital.

PROFILE

The political system has all but collapsed in Afghanistan. All the key players have their own private armies and make their influence felt militarily. The country has been under the control of rival *mujahideen* factions since April 1992, when President Najibullah, who had held power since the withdrawal of Soviet forces in 1989, stepped down.

The main *mujahideen* leaders met in Islamabad in March 1993 and agreed a basis for government of the country until elections could be held and a constitution formulated. However, two of the most powerful warlords, Rashid Dostam and Ahmad Shah Massoud, the defence minister, were not included in the power-sharing arrangement. President Rabbani, leader of the *Jamiat-i-Islami*, was confirmed as president and Golboddin Hekmatyar, head of the rival *Hezb-i-Islami*, became prime minister.

There is little chance that this government will be able to function viably in present conditions. Even convening the cabinet is problematic, and takes place, at the prime minister's insistence, in a fortified base at Charasaib, south of Kābul.

Burhanuddin Rabbani, president since 1992.

Prime Minister Hekmatyar, the Pashtun leader.

WORLD AFFAIRS

 ADB   CP   ESCAP   IBRD   IDB

At the end of 1992, 60,000 refugees, who opposed the neo-communist government in Dushanbe, fled from southern Tajikistan into Afghanistan. Northern Afghanistan faces cross-border bombardments by CIS forces based in Tajikistan. An estimated 3500 CIS troops are stationed there in an attempt to stem the flow of weapons and militants from Afghanistan to Islamic groups in Tajikistan. Relations with Pakistan, which has attempted to broker a peace, are important. It has pledged to provide over-land transit facilities for fruit exports to India, and also to consider the provision of port facilities for land-locked Afghanistan.

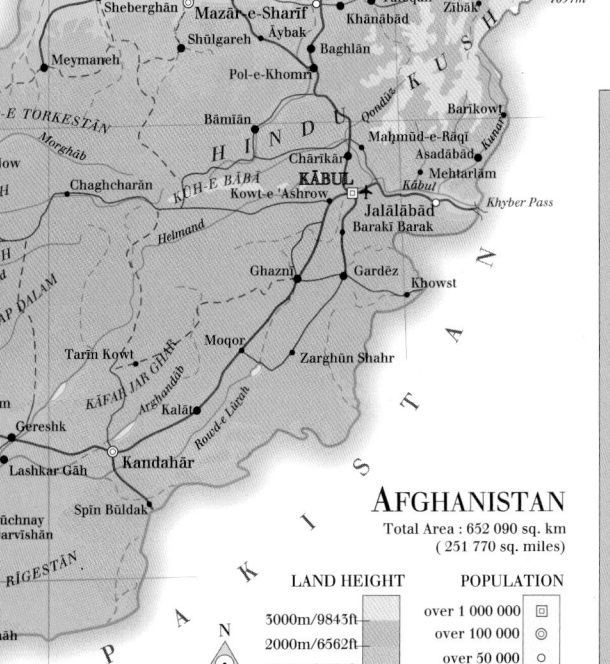

AFGHANISTAN

Total Area : 652 090 sq. km
(251 770 sq. miles)

LAND HEIGHT		POPULATION	
3000m/9843ft		over 1 000 000	▣
2000m/6562ft		over 100 000	◎
1000m/3281ft		over 50 000	○
500m/1640ft		over 10 000	●
200m/656ft		under 10 000	·

0   100 km
0   100 miles

CHRONOLOGY

The foundations of an Afghan state of Pashtun peoples were laid in the mid-18th century, when Durrani Ahmad Shah became paramount chief of the Abdali Pashtun peoples.

❏ **1838–1842** First Anglo-Afghan war. Britain fails in attempt to install Shah Shura on throne.
❏ **1878** Second British invasion of Afghan territory.
❏ **1879** Under Treaty of Gandmak signed with Amir Yaqub Ali Khan, various Afghan areas annexed by Britain. Yaqub Ali Khan later exiled. New treaty signed with Amir Abdul Rahman, establishing the Durand line, a contentious boundary between Afghanistan and Pakistan.
❏ **1919** Declaration of Afghan independence as an autonomous state backed at Paris Peace Conference. Britain briefly declares war on Afghanistan.

➪

A

CHRONOLOGY *continued*

- ❑ **1921** Treaty of friendship with Russia signed.
- ❑ **1933** Muhammed Zahir Shar in power.
- ❑ **1936** Mutual trade agreement signed with USSR.
- ❑ **1950** Pakistan closes its border with Afghanistan.
- ❑ **1953** Mohammed Daud Khan prime minister. Links with USSR developed.
- ❑ **1963** Daud resigns after king rejects his proposals for democratic reforms.
- ❑ **1965** Elections held, but monarchy still retains power. Marxist Party of Afghanistan (PDPA) formed and banned. PDPA splits into the *Parcham* and *Khalq* factions.
- ❑ **1973** Daud mounts a successful coup, abolishes monarchy and declares republic. *Mujahideen* rebellion begins. Thousands of refugees flee into Pakistan.
- ❑ **1978** Opposition to Daud from PDPA culminates in *Saur* revolution. Revolutionary Council under Mohammad Taraki takes power. Daud assassinated.
- ❑ **1979** Taraki ousted. Hafizullah Amin takes power. Amin killed in December coup backed by USSR. 80,000 Soviet Army troops invade Afghanistan. Worldwide protests. *Mujahideen* rebellion stepped up into full-scale guerrilla war, with US backing.
- ❑ **1980** Babrak Karmal, leader of *Parcham* PDPA, flown in by USSR from eastern Europe and installed as head of Marxist regime. Fighting escalates.
- ❑ **1986** Najibullah replaces Karmal as General Secretary of the Party.
- ❑ **1989** Soviet Army withdraws. *Mujahideen* control limited to rural areas. Najibullah remains in power.
- ❑ **1991** Russia and USA stop arms supplies to competing factions.
- ❑ **1992** Najibullah hands over power to *mujahideen* factions. Pakistan stops supplying arms to its *mujahideen* groups.
- ❑ **1993** Civil war continues.

AID

 $521m (receipts)   The trend is up

The main official aid is emergency humanitarian assistance from the UN. Saudi Arabia, Iran and Pakistan have promised modest grants. Large-scale funding for reconstruction is conditional on the restoration of peace. Individual *mujahideen* factions receive aid from Islamic states, Muslim organizations and wealthy benefactors.

DEFENCE

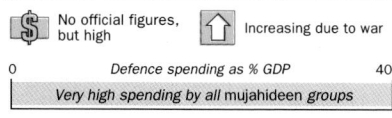

💲 No official figures, but high

⬆ Increasing due to war

0   *Defence spending as % GDP*   40

Very high spending by all mujahideen groups

AFGHAN ARMED FORCES

🚙	1200 main battle tanks (T-54/T-55/T-62)	40,000 personnel
🚢	None	
✈	233 combat aircraft (80 Su-7,-17,-22/ 30 Mig-23/80 Mig-21F)	5000 personnel
🚀	None	

In 1991, the US–Russian agreement to suspend military supplies to the Afghan groups marked the end of the superpowers' active involvement in Afghanistan. The Kābul communists, in particular, had been almost totally dependent on Moscow for arms, even after the Soviet withdrawal in 1989. In practice, Afghanistan has no formal defence arrangements. Ahmad Shah Massoud, who holds much of Kābul, is the current defence minister. He controls the *Jamiat-i-Islami,* a leading Tajik *mujahideen* grouping. They have enough ex-Soviet arms stockpiled to last several years. Weapons dumps in no-man's-land on the border with Pakistan supply Golboddin Hekmatyar, the nominal prime minister.

Afghanistan still has around 300–400 of the 1000 *Stinger* missiles given by the USA to the *mujahideen* in the 1980s. The USA, worried that they may be used against civilian airliners, is offering $100,000 each to buy them back. To date, none has been returned.

ECONOMICS

🏢 $2.7bn (est)   💲 1689.76 afghanis

SCORE CARD

- ❑ WORLD GNP RANKING........................130th
- ❑ GNP PER CAPITA $164
- ❑ BALANCE OF PAYMENTS.................–$143.3m
- ❑ INFLATION ....*The formal economy*
- ❑ UNEMPLOYMENT........................*has collapsed*

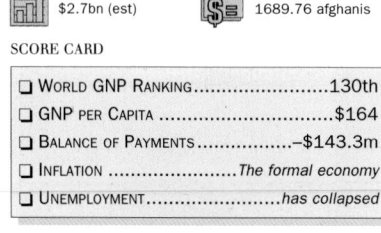

EXPORTS

Germany* 5%   UK 5%
India 6%
Pakistan 8%
CIS* 58%
Other 18%

IMPORTS

Germany* 4%   Singapore 5%
Japan 14%
CIS* 47%
Other 30%

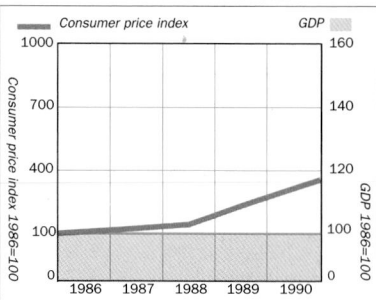

ECONOMIC PERFORMANCE INDICATOR

Consumer price index   GDP

(Consumer price index 1986=100; GDP 1986=100; years 1986, 1987, 1988, 1989, 1990)

STRENGTHS

Very few, apart from illicit opium trade. Agriculture, still the largest sector, accounted for 45% of GDP in 1986–1987.

WEAKNESSES

The economy has collapsed. No end to factional fighting in sight. Damage to agriculture, with knock-on effect on industry. Inaccessible terrain and severed communications links.

PROFILE

Following ten years of war between the Soviet-backed Kābul government and *mujahideen* rebels and subsequent *mujahideen* in-fighting, Afghanistan is one of the poorest and least developed countries in the world. Estimates suggest $4 billion is needed to rebuild the country and that 80% of its infrastructure has been destroyed. Agricultural activity has fallen back from pre-1979 levels; the Soviets' 'scorched earth' policy laid waste large areas and much of the rural population fled to the cities. Many farmers are now turning back to opium production. Afghanistan is regarded by the UN as the world's largest opium producer. However, most profits are made by Pakistani middlemen.

*A **mujahideen** **guerrilla**, a member of just one of the many factions vying for power in Afghanistan, guards a pass east of Kābul.*

RESOURCES

 1.1bn kwh (capacity 494,000 kw)

 Not an oil producer and has no refineries

12.5m sheep, 1.6m cattle, 1.3m asses, 400,000 horses

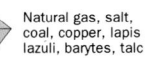 Natural gas, salt, coal, copper, lapis lazuli, barytes, talc

ELECTRICITY GENERATION

Hydro 68% (764m kwh)

Thermal 32% (364m kwh)

Nuclear 0%

Other 0%

0 20 40 60 80 100
% of total generation by type

Natural gas and coal are Afghanistan's most important strategic resources. Restoring the power generation system, which has suffered widespread deterioration and destruction, is a government priority. The construction of dams on the Kunar and Laghman rivers is being considered. Coal production has fallen from pre-war levels and mines are also in urgent need of rehabilitation. Western technology is needed to rebuild the gas industry.

AFGHANISTAN : LAND USE

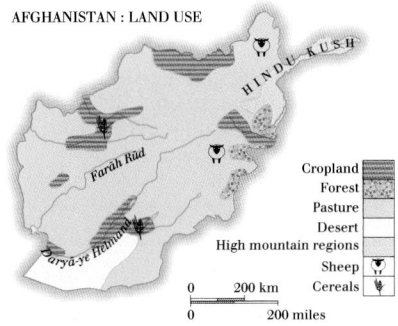

HINDU KUSH

Farāh Rūd

Daryā-ye Helmand

Cropland
Forest
Pasture
Desert
High mountain regions
Sheep
Cereals

0   200 km
0   200 miles

ENVIRONMENT

 0.3% (0.2% partially protected)

 Civil war prevents any initiatives

ENVIRONMENTAL TREATIES

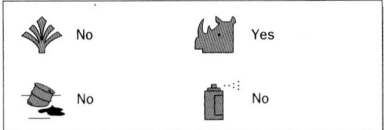

No   Yes

No   No

Environmental priorities are low given Afghanistan's anarchic civil war conditions. However, the country's relative lack of industry, even in Kābul, means that industrial pollution is minimal. The biggest problem facing Afghanistan is land-mines – over ten million have been laid – and the UN estimates it will take 100 years to make the country safe for civilians.

MEDIA

 Information is regulated by individual factions in the areas which they control

PUBLISHING AND BROADCAST MEDIA

There are 4 daily newspapers, including *Hewad* and the *Kābul New Times*

1 state-owned service

2 state-owned, plus independent services

Arabsat 1C

None

Most of the *mujahideen* factions run their own newspapers and radio stations, which follow the party line and denigrate rivals. The BBC, which broadcasts in Pashtu and Dari, is more popular than Radio Free Afghanistan, especially for its soap operas. These convey information on issues such as health care and the disposal of land-mines.

CRIME

 Afghanistan does not publish prison figures

Levels of all crimes remain very high

CRIME RATES

No statistics for murders, rapes and thefts are published due to the war situation

Fear of looting in Kābul is stifling economic activity. Gun law operates in most parts of Afghanistan. Herāt, ruled by Amir Ishmail Khan, is an exception – not even the Amir needs a bodyguard.

EDUCATION

 29%

0   Education spending as % GNP   25

1.8%

THE EDUCATION SYSTEM

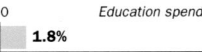

100
80
60
40
20
0

% of each age group in education

24% Primary
8% Secondary
2% Tertiary

The education system has been destroyed by the war, and as a result illiteracy rates are high. However, some schools have responded to a mid-1993 government directive and reopened. Kābul University has been closed since the fall of the Najibullah regime.

HEALTH

 1 per 5148 people

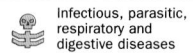 Infectious, parasitic, respiratory and digestive diseases

0   Health spending as % GNP   25

3%

The health service has collapsed completely and almost all medical professionals have left the country. Infant and maternal mortality rates are among the highest in the world, and life expectancy the lowest, at 42 years. Parasitic diseases and infections are a particular problem. The UN has organized a well-water chlorination programme, following an outbreak of cholera in Kābul. The admission of women to hospital is strongly discouraged under increasingly prevalent Islamic laws of modesty.

WEALTH

 Faction leaders and arms dealers are the wealthiest groups

CONSUMER GOODS OWNERSHIP

1000
750
500
250
0

Per 1000 population

TVs limited to an elite

VCR and PC ownership limited to a small elite

2   2

The vast majority of Afghans live in conditions of extreme poverty. The country does not have the resources to feed its people at present – a situation likely to be exacerbated by the return of refugees from neighbouring Pakistan and Iran – and is likely to be heavily dependent on outside assistance for its rehabilitation. However, a number of *mujahideen* leaders have accumulated personal fortunes during the war. These derive in part from the substantial foreign aid that was once available and, in some cases, from the trafficking of opium.

WORLD RANKING

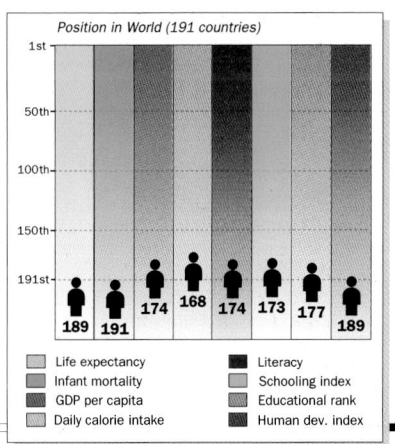

Position in World (191 countries)

1st
50th
100th
150th
191st

189 191 174 168 174 173 177 189

Life expectancy
Infant mortality
GDP per capita
Daily calorie intake
Literacy
Schooling index
Educational rank
Human dev. index

ALBANIA

OFFICIAL NAME: Republic of Albania **CAPITAL:** Tirana
POPULATION: 3.3 million **CURRENCY:** New Lek **OFFICIAL LANGUAGE:** Albanian

LYING AT THE southeastern end of the Adriatic Sea, opposite the heel of Italy, Albania is a mountainous country vulnerable to earthquakes. It achieved *de facto* independence from Turkey in 1913 and became a one-party communist state in 1944. Albania held its first multiparty elections in 1991. Its return to the international community has been delayed by its support for the ethnic Albanian insurrection in the Kosovo region of Serbia.

CLIMATE

WEATHER CHART

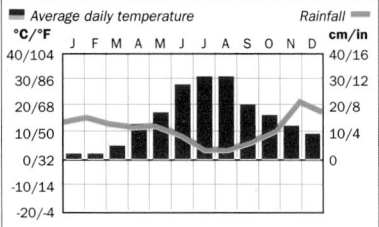

The coastal climate is Mediterranean, but rather wet in winter. Heavy rain or snow falls in winter in the mountains.

COMMUNICATIONS

 Tirana Rinas   20 ships 85,500 dwt

THE TRANSPORT NETWORK

16,700 km (10,377 miles) | None
684 km (425 miles) | 43 km (28 miles)

Albania has Europe's least developed transport network and lowest ratio of cars to population. Private cars were first allowed in 1991. The horse and cart is the main means of transport.

TOURISM

 Albania receives fewer than 100,000 visitors a year 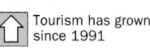 Tourism has grown since 1991

MAIN OVERSEAS ARRIVALS

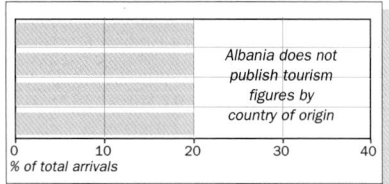

Albania does not publish tourism figures by country of origin

% of total arrivals

Tourism during the communist era was limited to small organized groups. The government has now begun to exploit Albania's scenic beauty.

PEOPLE

 Albanian, Greek   111 people per km²

THE URBAN/RURAL POPULATION SPLIT

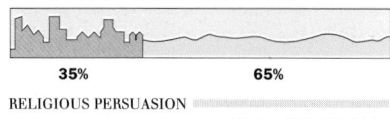

35% | 65%

RELIGIOUS PERSUASION

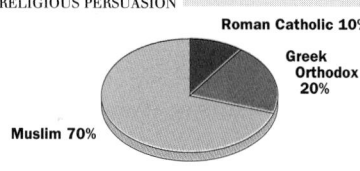

Roman Catholic 10%
Greek Orthodox 20%
Muslim 70%

Official statistics admitted the existence of ethnic minorities in Albania only in 1989. The Greek minority strongly contests these statistics, which state that 98% of the population are Albanian. Located mainly in the south and identifying with Athens rather than Tirana, the Greeks claim to make up 10% of the population. They suffer considerable discrimination. Many have sought refuge in northern Greece, but tensions between the two states have also led to a number of these refugees being sent back to Albania.

Under communism, Albania was the only officially atheist state in the world. Many Albanians maintained their beliefs in private – 70% are Muslim. Religious worship is now permitted and mosques have reopened. Society is traditional and male-dominated. The extended family remains strong.

City of a thousand windows. Berat was preserved as a museum city whilst a new town was built further down the valley.

POLITICS

1996   President Sali Berisha

THE STATE OF THE PARTIES

People's Assembly 140 members

2% Other
66% DPA | 27% SPA | 5% SDP

DPA = Democratic Party of Albania **SPA** = Socialist Party of Albania **SDP** = Social Democratic Party
Other = Union for Human Rights, Albanian Republican Party

Albania was dominated for more than 40 years by communist ruler Enver Hoxha, who died in 1985. At first, it seemed to resist the tide of change that swept through eastern Europe in 1989. However, by 1990, it became apparent that an upheaval in the one-party communist state could be delayed but not resisted. An increase in popular demonstrations gave reformers within the Party the upper hand and hardliners were forced to concede changes. A mass exodus of Albanians towards the end of 1991 finally persuaded Ramiz Alia, Enver Hoxha's successor, to call multiparty elections. These were held in 1992 and saw victory for the centre-right DPA-led coalition. The Greek minority was forbidden to field candidates. The main issue in politics is the creation of a Western-style liberal economic state.

WORLD AFFAIRS

 CSCE   ECE   EBRD

The conflict in the region of Kosovo in Serbia dominates foreign policy. Rich in minerals and 90% ethnically Albanian, Kosovo was an autonomous republic in former Yugoslavia. In 1989, it was forcibly integrated into Serbia. Persecution of Albanians by Serbs has increased tension in the region. Tirana is now suspected of supporting armed resistance groups in Kosovo.

AID

 $190m (receipts)   Aid receipts have risen since 1991

The West replaced the Soviet Union as the main source of aid to Albania after 1991. Initially, most was humanitarian food aid. The largest proportion came from Italy, which wished to prevent a potential flood of economic migrants to its shores. Aid is now directed at infrastructure modernization projects.

DEFENCE

 $103.2m

Down 36% in 1991

Officer ranks were re-established in the Albanian armed forces in 1991. The ability of the under-resourced army to defend Albania's borders has been questioned. Albanians perform 18 months of mandatory military service.

ECONOMICS

 $4.1bn

 109.81 lekë

SCORE CARD

❏ WORLD GNP RANKING........................115th
❏ GNP PER CAPITA $1250
❏ BALANCE OF PAYMENTS.................$−113.9m
❏ INFLATION 35.5%
❏ UNEMPLOYMENT................................9.1%

STRENGTHS

Europe's highest growth rate in 1993. Growth in agricultural output. Oil and gas reserves.

ALBANIA

Total Area : 28 750 sq. km (11 100 sq. miles)

POPULATION

◎ over 100 000
○ over 50 000
● over 10 000
• under 10 000

LAND HEIGHT

2000m/6562ft
1000m/3281ft
500m/1640ft
200m/656ft
Sea Level

WEAKNESSES

Rudimentary infrastructure. Low level of technical skills. Regional instability has discouraged foreign investment.

EXPORTS

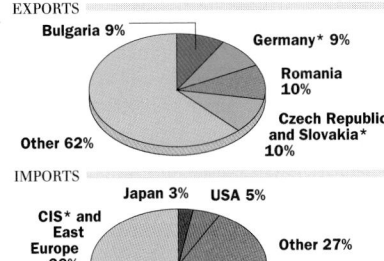

Bulgaria 9%
Germany* 9%
Romania 10%
Czech Republic and Slovakia* 10%
Other 62%

IMPORTS

Japan 3%   USA 5%
CIS* and East Europe 36%
Other 27%
EU 29%

RESOURCES

 4.1bn kwh (capacity 780,000 kw)

 25,700 b/d (reserves 165,000,000 bbl)

5m poultry, 1.5m sheep, 1.2m goats

Chromium, oil, coal, natural gas, copper, nickel

Albania needs huge capital investment to develop its minerals and to create a modern electricity supply system.

ENVIRONMENT

 1.6% (0.8% partially protected)

There is no money for environmental protection measures

Industry, which is underdeveloped, has little impact on the environment. Years of shortages in the economy mean that most materials are recycled.

MEDIA

Since the fall of communism there has been no official censorship

PUBLISHING AND BROADCAST MEDIA

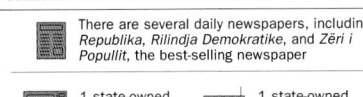

There are several daily newspapers, including *Republika*, *Rilindja Demokratike*, and *Zëri i Popullit*, the best-selling newspaper

1 state-owned service

1 state-owned service

The leading paper, *Zëri i Popullit*, is run by the SPA. Journalists opposing the government can suffer intimidation.

CRIME

 1640 prisoners

 Crime levels are rising sharply

Most crimes are on the increase; tourists in Tirana are targets for mugging. Cannabis is widely grown.

CHRONOLOGY

Albania gained independence for the first time in its history in 1913.

❏ **1924–1939** Ahmet Zogu, crowned King Zog in 1928, in power.
❏ **1939–1943** Occupied by Italy.
❏ **1944** Communist state; led by Enver Hoxha until 1985.
❏ **1948–1961** Pro-Soviet period.
❏ **1961–1978** Pro-Chinese period.
❏ **1981** Prime minister, Mehmet Shehu, shot dead.
❏ **1991** Democratic multiparty state.

EDUCATION

 85%

The system is derived from the Soviet, Chinese and Italian models. Albania has four universities.

HEALTH

 1 per 574 people

 Heart, respiratory and digestive diseases, cancers

The health service is rudimentary and dependent on Western aid for most drugs and medical supplies.

WEALTH

 Demand for imported luxury goods has increased

CONSUMER GOODS OWNERSHIP

Cars limited to an elite
VCR and PC ownership is limited to a small elite
83
3

Wealth is limited to a small, slowly expanding group of private-sector entrepreneurs.

WORLD RANKING

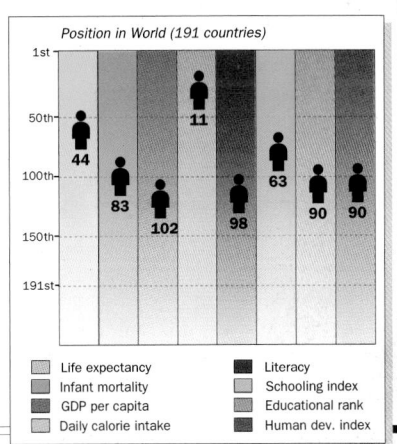

Position in World (191 countries)

44
83
102
11
98
63
90
90

Life expectancy
Infant mortality
GDP per capita
Daily calorie intake
Literacy
Schooling index
Educational rank
Human dev. index

A

ALGERIA

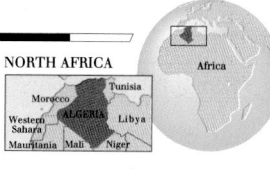

NORTH AFRICA

OFFICIAL NAME: Democratic and Popular Republic of Algeria   **CAPITAL:** Algiers
POPULATION: 26.4 million   **CURRENCY:** Algerian dinar   **OFFICIAL LANGUAGE:** Arabic

AFRICA'S SECOND LARGEST COUNTRY, Algeria shares borders with Morocco, Mauritania, Mali, Niger, Libya and Tunisia. Algeria won independence from France in 1962. Today, the military-dominated government faces a severe challenge from Islamic fundamentalists. A founder-member of OPEC, Algeria has significant oil and gas reserves. The country also has one of the youngest populations, and highest birth rates, in North Africa.

CLIMATE

WEATHER CHART

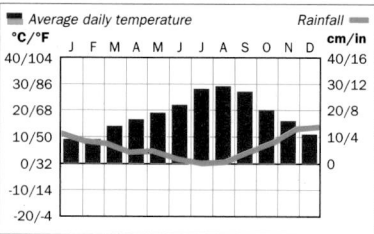

Coastal areas have a warm, temperate climate. The area to the south of the Atlas Mountains is hot desert.

COMMUNICATIONS

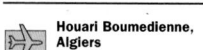

Houari Boumedienne, Algiers
3.68m passengers

78 ships
1.08m dwt

THE TRANSPORT NETWORK

| 82,000 km (50,954 miles) | None |
| 4146 km (2576 miles) | None |

There are five international airports. Rail is the quickest way to travel between the main urban centres.

TOURISM

 1.14m visitors   Down 6% in 1990

MAIN OVERSEAS ARRIVALS

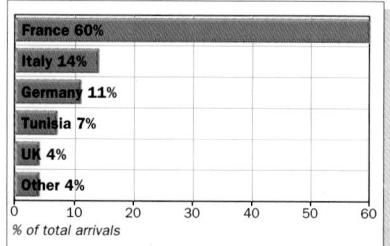

| France 60% |
| Italy 14% |
| Germany 11% |
| Tunisia 7% |
| UK 4% |
| Other 4% |

0   10   20   30   40   50   60
% of total arrivals

The once-popular desert safaris are now rare. Tourists are a target for militant Islamic groups.

PEOPLE

 Arabic, Berber (Kabyle, Shawia, Tamashek), French

11 people per km²

THE URBAN/RURAL POPULATION SPLIT

52%   48%

RELIGIOUS PERSUASION

Other 1%

Sunni
Muslim 99%

ETHNIC MAKEUP

European 1%

Arab and
Berber 99%

Algeria's population is predominantly Arab, under 30 years of age and urban; about 20% are Berber. More than 85% speak Arabic, the official language, and 99% are Sunni Muslim. Of the million or so French who settled in Algeria before independence, only about 6000 remain. Most Berbers consider the mountainous Kabylia region their homeland. If the struggle between Islamic fundamentalists and the government intensifies, Kabylia may seek independence. As in the rest of North Africa, the mosque is an important provider of social and medical services.

POPULATION AGE BREAKDOWN

%	0–14	15–64	65+
	3.9%	4.1%	3.9%	3.6%	3.3%
	52.4%	47.5%	49.6%	52.8%	57.4%
	43.7%	48.4%	46.5%	43.6%	39.3%
	1960	1970	1980	1990	2000

POLITICS

 1996   President Ali Kafi

THE STATE OF THE PARTIES

National People's Assembly 430 members

The National People's Assembly was dissolved in 1992, following the first round of elections

Algeria is currently ruled by the military under a state of emergency. Elections have been promised in 1996.

MAIN POLITICAL ISSUES

Islamic fundamentalism

Nearly 3000 Algerians have died in the past two years from political violence. The country's new *mujahideen* (holy warriors) are engaged in what they see as a second war of liberation, under the leadership of the Islamic Salvation Front (FIS). They wish to establish a theocracy along Iranian lines. The FIS has had considerable success at the polls. In the 1991 general election it took 188 of the 228 seats contested. However, the army declared a state of emergency and scrapped the second round of voting, in order to stop the FIS from taking power.

The market economy

In 1988, President Bendjedid's administration decided to embark on a series of market reforms, designed to introduce competition into Algeria's large state-run economy. The policy was encouraged by the World Bank and the IMF and included tough austerity measures. The suggestion that the policy showed how Algeria was falling under US and Western influence partly accounted for Islamic fundamentalists' strong showing in the 1991 polls. Since the army takeover in 1991, the policy has been put on hold.

PROFILE

Until 1988, Algeria was a regime in the Soviet model. With the collapse of the Soviet Union, Algeria's ageing ruling elite adopted IMF privatization policies. The process was vigorously opposed by Islamic fundamentalists. An army clampdown in 1991 prevented the fundamentalists seizing power, but, apart from vague promises of elections, the future looks unclear. The fundamentalists have established a parallel organization to the state's, based on the mosque. In practice they control most areas outside Algiers.

WORLD AFFAIRS

AL OPEC NAM AMU AFESD

Algeria's struggle for independence from France lasted from 1954 until 1962. Throughout the 1960s and 1970s, Algeria's success in rejecting a colonial power made it a champion for the developing world. It had a leading voice within the UN, the Arab League and the Organization for African Unity. However, relations with the West remained essentially stable. Algeria was increasingly seen by the diplomatic community as a useful bridge between the West and Iran.

In 1981, Algerian diplomats helped to secure the release of American hostages held in Teheran during the last days of US President Carter's term of office. Algeria also attempted to act in a mediating role during the 1980–1988 Iran–Iraq War.

Algeria's influence overseas has diminished as the country has become increasingly unstable politically. Throughout the 1990s, the government has been under severe pressure from the Islamic fundamentalist FIS. A victory for the FIS in Algeria would greatly encourage Islamic militants in neighbouring Morocco and Tunisia, and further undermine Egypt's embattled government.

European governments are also concerned that an FIS takeover could trigger a wave of refugees seeking entry into France, Spain and Italy.

AID

 $310m (receipts)   Up 43% in 1991

As a major oil producer, Algeria receives only small quantities of aid. During the 1980s, its economy became dependent on eastern European manufactures, which were swapped for oil. The collapse of this trade in the 1990s led Algeria to turn to the West for loans. Oil revenues encouraged the West to offer export credits. The IMF provided loans to help Algeria meet payments on its massive $127-billion debt on condition that the government move towards a market-orientated economy. However, these sources are now threatened by Algeria's growing political instability.

ALGERIA

Total Area :
2 381 740 sq. km
(919 590 sq. miles)

POPULATION

over 500 000	◉
over 100 000	◎
over 50 000	○
over 10 000	●

LAND HEIGHT

2000m/6562ft	
1000m/3281ft	
500m/1640ft	
200m/656ft	
Sea Level	

Saharan town, showing the wide range of Algeria's scenery, from lush, irrigated gardens near water sources to barren sand dunes beyond. 80% of Algeria is desert.

Former president, Bendjedid Chadli, head of state from 1979 to 1992.

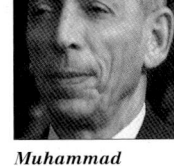

Muhammad Boudiaf, head of state assassinated in 1992.

MEDITERRANEAN SEA

ALGIERS
Boufarik
Mostaganem
Mohammadia
Oran
Chlef
Médéa
Blida
Tizi Ouzou
Béjaïa
Jijel
Skikda
Annaba
Kabylia Mts
Sétif
Constantine
Guelma
Souk Ahras
Relizane
Bordj Bou Arreridj
Barika
Khenchela
Tébessa
Sidi Bel Abbès
Mascara
Aïn Oussera
Batna
Tlemcen
Saïda
Tiaret
Biskra
Chott ech Chergui
Djelfa
Mecheria
Ouled Djellal
Chott Melrhir
Laghouat
Djamâa
Hauts Plateaux
El Oued
Touggourt
Ghardaïa
Ouargla
Béchar
GRAND ERG OCCIDENTAL
GRAND ERG ORIENTAL
El Goléa
HAMADA DU DRA
PLATEAU DU TADEMAÏT
In Aménas
Tindouf
WESTERN SAHARA
MAURITANIA
ERG CHECH
In Salah
Reggane
Sebkha Mekerrhane
Tassili n Ajjer
Sebkha Azzel Matti
TANEZROUFT
Djanet
▲ Tahat 2918m
HAGGAR
Tamanrasset
Tassili ta-n-Ahaggar
MOROCCO
MALI
NIGER
TUNISIA
LIBYA

0   200 km
0   200 miles

N

A

CHRONOLOGY

The conquest of Algeria by France began in 1830. By 1900, French settlers occupied most of the best land. In 1954, war was declared on the colonial administration by the National Liberation Front (FLN).

❑ **1962** Cease-fire reached, followed by declaration of independence and founding of Algerian republic.

❑ **1965** Military junta topples government of Ahmed Ben Bella. Revolutionary council set up, under Col Boumedienne.

❑ **1966** Judiciary 'Algerianized'. Tribunals try 'economic crimes'.

❑ **1971** Oil industry nationalized. Boumedienne continues with land reform, a national health service and 'socialist' management.

❑ **1976** National Charter establishes a socialist state.

❑ **1978** Col Boumedienne dies of natural causes.

❑ **1979** Bendjedid Chadli sworn in as president.

❑ **1980** Ben Bella released after 15 years' detention. Agreement signed with France, whereby latter gives incentives for return home of 800,000 Algerian immigrants.

❑ **1981** Algeria helps to negotiate release of American hostages from the US embassy in Teheran, Iran.

❑ **1985** The two most popular Kabyle (Berber) singers are given 3-year jail sentences for opposing regime.

❑ **1987** Government introduces limited liberalization by giving private enterprise more freedom. Algeria signs co-operation agreement with Soviet Union.

❑ **1988** Violence directed at ruling party. State of emergency. Algeria negotiates release of Kuwaiti hostages held on aircraft by Shi'a gunmen. The hijackers escape unpunished.

❑ **1989** Constitutional reforms, which diminish power of FLN. New political parties are founded, including the Islamic Salvation Front (FIS). The Arab Maghreb Union is established by the leaders of Algeria, Libya, Morocco and Tunisia.

❑ **1990** Political exiles permitted to return home. FIS wins municipal elections.

❑ **1991** FIS leaders Abassi Madani and Ali Belhadj arrested. FIS wins large majority in National Assembly.

❑ **1992** Bendjedid overthrown by military. Second round of elections scrapped. President Boudiaf assassinated. Succeeded by Ali Kafi. FIS leaders Abassi Madani and Ali Belhadj given 12 years in jail.

❑ **1994** Political violence led by Armed Islamic Group.

DEFENCE

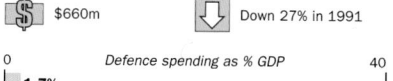

💲 $660m   ⬇ Down 27% in 1991

0   *Defence spending as % GDP*   40

| 1.7% |

The National Liberation Army (NLA), equipped with Russian weapons, is the dominant power in politics. There are fears that parts of the army will forge an alliance with Muslim militants. The extreme rebel Armed Islamic Group, which has split from the FIS, is led by former army officers.

ALGERIAN ARMED FORCES

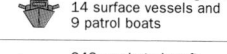

	960 main battle tanks (330 T–54,–55/ 330 T–62/300 T–72)	120,000 personnel
	2 submarines, 3 frigates, 14 surface vessels and 9 patrol boats	7000 personnel
	242 combat aircraft (30 MiG–17/10 Su–24/ 17 MiG-23BN,-23MF)	12,000 personnel
	None	

ECONOMICS

📊 $43.2bn   💲 23.82 dinars

SCORE CARD

❑ WORLD GNP RANKING..........................43rd
❑ GNP PER CAPITA $1640
❑ BALANCE OF PAYMENTS $1.6bn
❑ INFLATION 32%
❑ UNEMPLOYMENT...............................25%

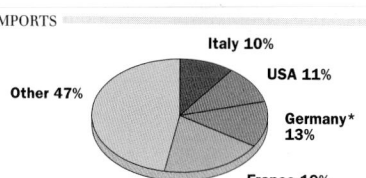

EXPORTS

Other 33%
Netherlands 11%
Italy 17%
France 20%
USA 19%

IMPORTS

Other 47%
Italy 10%
USA 11%
Germany* 13%
France 19%

STRENGTHS
Oil and gas. Recent collaboration with Western oil companies should see improvements in productivity. Natural gas is supplied to Europe.

WEAKNESSES
Oil revenues yet to recover from the 1986 collapse in world prices. Political turmoil threatens many new projects and has led to an exodus of European and non-expatriate workers important to the economy. Lack of skilled labour coupled with high unemployment. Limited agriculture. Shortages of basic foodstuffs. A thriving black market.

PROFILE
Under the pro-Soviet National Liberation Front, the Algerian economy was dominated by centralized socialist planning. In the late 1980s, the economic collapse of the Soviet Union led to a change in policy, and Algeria began moving towards a market economy. However, these reforms were frozen following the military takeover

ECONOMIC PERFORMANCE INDICATOR

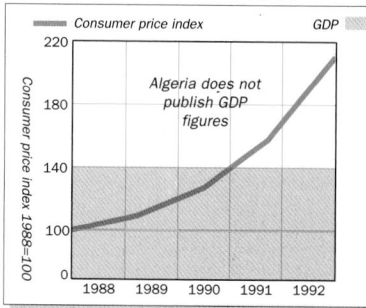

Consumer price index   GDP

Algeria does not publish GDP figures

Consumer price index 1988=100

1988 1989 1990 1991 1992

in 1991. The army still favours a centrally planned economy and, as a result, the state still retains control of the vast majority of the economy's most productive sectors.

Only in the oil industry has private investment been encouraged. A number of Western oil companies have signed exploration contracts with Algiers since it has accepted more competitive production-sharing agreements. However, Western investment levels are likely to remain small as long as the political situation is unstable. Algeria is now importing more than half its grain, and long food lines are routine in the capital.

ALGERIA : MAJOR BUSINESSES

Constantine
Algiers
Oran
Annaba
Hassi R'Mel
Hassi Messaoud

⚓ Oil/gas
✳ Textiles
◇ Iron & steel
⚙ Heavy engineering
▩ Light engineering
⚗ Chemicals/petrochemicals
🗄 Food processing

0   200 km
0   200 miles

RESOURCES

15.9bn kwh (capacity 4.66m kw)

782,700 b/d (reserves 9,200,000,000 bbl)

12.5m sheep, 3.6m goats, 1.4m cattle, 300,000 asses

Oil, natural gas, iron, phosphates, lead, zinc, silver, copper, tungsten

ELECTRICITY GENERATION

Hydro 1% (135m kwh)	
Thermal 99% (15.9bn kwh)	
Nuclear 0%	
Other 0%	

0   20   40   60   80   100
% of total generation by type

Crude oil and natural gas, Algeria's main resources, were first produced in the 1950s. Algeria also has diverse minerals, including iron ore, zinc, silver, copper ore and phosphates. In the 1960s and 1970s, Algeria sought to become a manufacturing country, with investments in building materials, refined products and steel; none of these sectors is competitive on world markets. Although agriculture employs one quarter of Algeria's workforce, its importance to the economy is diminishing. State forests cover some 2% of Algeria's land. Most are brushwood, but some areas include cork oak trees, Aleppo pine, evergreen oak and cedar. Algeria has a large fishing fleet. Sardines, anchovies, tuna-fish and shellfish are the major species caught commercially.

ENVIRONMENT

5% (0.1% partially protected)

Desertification owing to pressure on land

ENVIRONMENTAL TREATIES

No   No

Yes   No

Since most of Algeria is desert or semi-desert, over 90% of the population is forced to live on the remaining 20% of land. The desert is moving northwards. Vegetation has been stripped for use as firewood and animal fodder, leaving fragile soils exposed which then require expensive specialist care to conserve them. Water purification techniques are below standard and rivers are being increasingly contaminated by untreated sewage, industrial effluent and wastes from petroleum refining.

MEDIA

 The media is under government control

PUBLISHING AND BROADCAST MEDIA

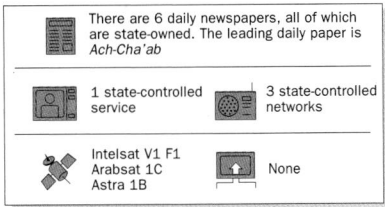

There are 6 daily newspapers, all of which are state-owned. The leading daily paper is *Ach-Cha'ab*

1 state-controlled service

3 state-controlled networks

Intelsat V1 F1 Arabsat 1C Astra 1B

None

Newspapers, TV and radio are state-controlled and permit no criticism of government actions. TV is broadcast in Arabic, French and Kabyle (Berber), but Algeria has only about 1.6 million sets. The six daily newspapers have a combined circulation of 1.4 million. However, distribution is limited outside the main cities.

CRIME

Algeria does not publish prison figures

Crime levels rising sharply

CRIME RATES

Algeria does not publish official statistics for murders, rapes or thefts

Political violence kills about 15 Algerians every day. Foreigners, Jews and Christians are singled out by the radical Armed Islamic Group, many of whom are teenagers. Human rights activists allege that pro-government death squads roam the cities and rural areas seeking out suspected Islamic militants and their relatives.

EDUCATION

 57%

0   *Education spending as % GNP*   25
9.4%

THE EDUCATION SYSTEM

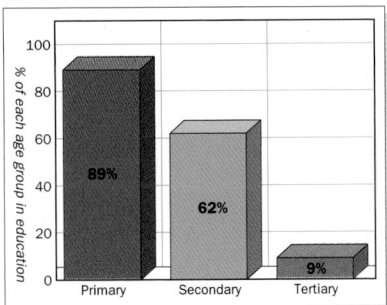

89%   62%   9%
Primary   Secondary   Tertiary

Over three quarters of the school-age population receive a formal education. The literacy rate is 57%. Since 1973, the curriculum has been Arabized and the teaching of French has diminished. Ten universities and seven polytechnics provide higher education to some 175,000 students.

ALGERIA : LAND USE

SAHARA

Forest
Pasture
Cropland
Desert
Sheep
Potatoes
Dates

0   200 km
0   200 miles

HEALTH

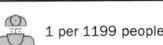

1 per 1199 people

Respiratory, heart and cerebrovascular diseases, malaria

0   *Health spending as % GNP*   25
1.2%

Primary health care is rudimentary outside main cities. The infant mortality rate is 5.5%, comfortably below the North African average of 7.3%. Life expectancy is just above the average for the region, at 66 years for men and 68 for women.

WEALTH

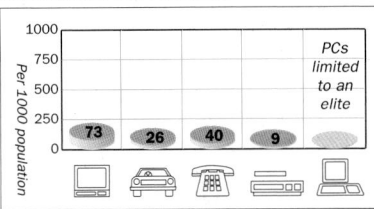

Waiter, 2282 dinars per month; doctor, 5802 dinars per month

CONSUMER GOODS OWNERSHIP

1000
750
500
250
0
Per 1000 population

PCs limited to an elite

73   26   40   9

There is great disparity in wealth between the political elite and the rest of the population. Those connected to the military are the wealthiest group. Most Algerians have had to contend with soaring prices for basic necessities.

WORLD RANKING

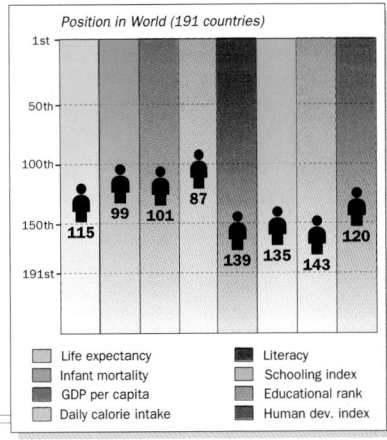

Position in World (191 countries)

1st
50th
100th
150th
191st

115   99   101   87   139   135   143   120

Life expectancy   Literacy
Infant mortality   Schooling index
GDP per capita   Educational rank
Daily calorie intake   Human dev. index

ANDORRA

OFFICIAL NAME: Principality of Andorra **CAPITAL:** Andorra la Vella
POPULATION: 58,000 **CURRENCY:** French franc and Spanish peseta **OFFICIAL LANGUAGE:** Catalan

A TINY, LAND-LOCKED principality between France and Spain, Andorra lies high in the eastern Pyrenees. From the 13th century, French and Spanish co-princes (today the President of France and the Bishop of Urgel) have governed Andorra. In December 1993, the principality held its first full elections. Andorra's spectacular scenery, alpine climate and duty-free shopping have made tourism, especially skiing, its main source of income.

Andorra's outstanding mountain scenery attracts 500,000 skiers a year.

CLIMATE

WEATHER CHART

Springs are cool and wet; summers are dry and warm. Snowfalls in December and January lay the ground for good skiing up to March. Andorra's climate supports an abundance of wild flowers.

COMMUNICATIONS

None

Has no fleet

THE TRANSPORT NETWORK

220 km
(124 miles)   None

None   None

The road from France to Spain climbs to 2704 m through one of the most dramatic mountain passes in Europe. During the summer months, the sheer number of day-trippers often brings traffic to a standstill around Andorra la Vella.

TOURISM

12m visitors

Up 20% between 1990 and 1992

MAIN OVERSEAS ARRIVALS

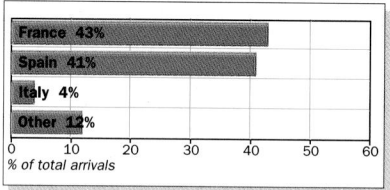

France 43%
Spain 41%
Italy 4%
Other 12%

% of total arrivals

Most tourists visit Andorra to ski or shop. However, the traditional trade in day-trippers from France and Spain, coming to shop in the many tax-free designer-label boutiques is threatened by EU regulations seeking to end Andorra's beneficial tax regime. Five ski resorts receive over 500,000 visitors a year. In summer they cater for mountain hikers; Andorra's wild flowers attract many, but there is also much for the bird-watcher to see. Hunting of wild boar is popular and the goat-like chamois can be hunted under special licence.

PEOPLE

Spanish, Catalan, French, Portuguese

111 people per km²

THE URBAN/RURAL POPULATION SPLIT

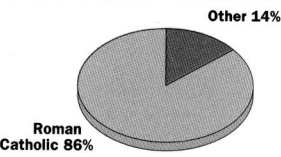

95%   5%

RELIGIOUS PERSUASION

Other 14%

Roman Catholic 86%

Immigration is strictly monitored and restricted by quota to French and Spanish nationals intending to work in Andorra. Divorce is illegal.

POLITICS

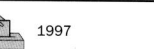 1997

Co-Princes François Mitterrand and Joan Martí Alanis

THE STATE OF THE PARTIES

General Council of the Valleys 28 members

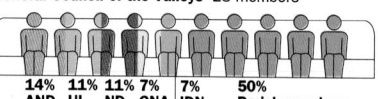

14%   11%   11% 7%   7%   50%
AND   UL   ND   CNA IDN Parish members

AND = National Democratic Grouping **UL** = Liberal Union
ND = New Democracy **CNA** = National Andorran Coalition
IDN = New Democratic Initiative

14 members are elected on a national list and 14 are elected in 7 dual-member parishes

Until recently, Andorra was a semi-feudal state. But, in March 1993, a referendum approved democratic measures which legalized political parties and the right to strike, and altered relations with the co-princes. Following elections in December 1993, an AND-led coalition government was formed.

ANDORRA

Total Area : 468 sq. km
(181 sq. miles)

N

POPULATION

over 10 000 ●
under 10 000 ·

LAND HEIGHT

2000m/6562ft
1500m/4921ft
1000m/3281ft
above 800m

0   5 km
0   5 miles

WORLD AFFAIRS

Andorra's limited membership of world bodies reflects its ambiguous status; it is still not recognized by Japan. The main concern is the future of free trade with Spain, following the advent of the EU internal market.

AID

 Andorra has no aid receipts or donations Not applicable

The principality of Andorra neither receives nor provides aid, and has no plans to do so.

DEFENCE

 Andorra has no defence budget Not applicable

Andorra has no defence budget; protection is provided by France and Spain. The French intervention of 1933 was the last military action on Andorran soil.

ECONOMICS

 $895m 5.90 francs 142.93 pesetas

SCORE CARD

❏ WORLD GNP RANKING	158th
❏ GNP PER CAPITA	$15,430
❏ BALANCE OF PAYMENTS	Included in Spanish total
❏ INFLATION	Not applicable
❏ UNEMPLOYMENT	0%

STRENGTHS
Tourism, the basis of the economy. Strict banking secrecy laws make Andorra an important tax haven; low consumer taxes have also encouraged a healthy luxury retail sector. Farming: cereals, potatoes and tobacco are the major products.

WEAKNESSES
France and Spain effectively decide economic policy. There is a dependence on imported food and raw materials.

EXPORTS

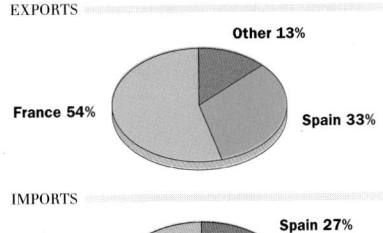

Other 13%
France 54%
Spain 33%

IMPORTS

Spain 27%
France 42%
Other 31%

RESOURCES

 115m kwh

5600 sheep, 1700 cattle

 Not an oil producer and has no refineries

None

Water is a major resource, hydro-power providing most domestic energy needs. However, Andorra has to import twice as much electricity as it produces, and there are plans to increase capacity. A third of the country is designated forest.

ENVIRONMENT

 None

 Desire for larger tourist revenues conflicts with nature conservation

Twelve million tourists a year have had an inevitably adverse impact over time on a country of 52,000 people. Concern is growing, at the moment chiefly amongst NGOs, about the scarring of Andorra's alpine landscape by hotel and ski developments, as well as about the future of its unique mountain flora. Hunting, notably of the Pyrenean chamois and the wild boar, is still a significant tourist attraction. However, restrictions are gradually being introduced to preserve certain animal species.

MEDIA

 No political censorship since 1993

PUBLISHING AND BROADCAST MEDIA

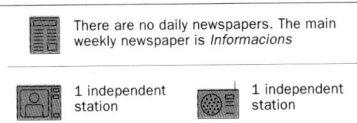

There are no daily newspapers. The main weekly newspaper is *Informacions*

1 independent station

1 independent station

Andorra receives most Spanish and French TV broadcasts. A private TV company in Spain broadcasts one hour a day of programmes designed specifically for Andorra.

CRIME

 Andorra does not publish prison figures

 Ten times more car theft in 1990 than 1987

Tourists are natural targets for thieves, most of whom are not Andorran. Thefts of expensive cars for resale in France and Spain are on the increase.
Andorra has two criminal courts – the *Tribunals de Corts*.

EDUCATION

 99%

There are 18 schools in Andorra, most of which teach in Spanish and French. Instruction in Catalan is available, but only in the primary schools and one secondary school.

CHRONOLOGY

Since 1278, Andorra has been autonomous, ruled by French and Spanish co-princes.

- ❏ **1933** Andorran revolt against extension of the franchise put down by French.
- ❏ **1970** Women get the vote.
- ❏ **1982** First constitution enshrines popular sovereignty.
- ❏ **1983** General Council votes in favour of income tax.
- ❏ **1984** Government resigns over attempt to introduce indirect taxes.
- ❏ **1991** EC Customs Union comes into effect.
- ❏ **1992** Political demonstrations demanding constitutional reform. Government resigns.
- ❏ **1993** Referendum approves new constitution. Democratic elections.

HEALTH

 1 per 467 people

 Heart and cerebrovascular diseases

Andorra has one public and one private hospital. Hot springs at les Escaldes are popular with rheumatism sufferers.

WEALTH

 Experienced waiter, 170,000 pesetas per month; primary school teacher, 220,000 pesetas per month

CONSUMER GOODS OWNERSHIP

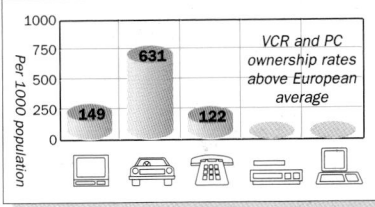

VCR and PC ownership rates above European average

149   631   122

Per 1000 population

Hotel owners are the wealthiest group in Andorran society; many choose to live across the border in Spain.

WORLD RANKING

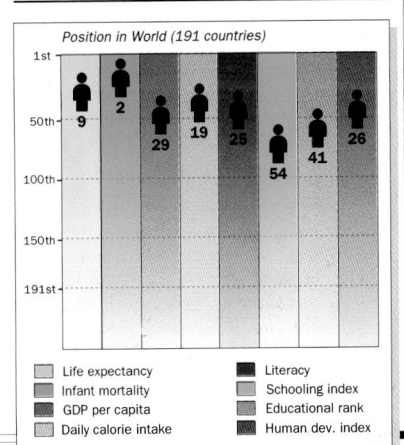

Position in World (191 countries)

9   2   29   19   25   54   41   26

- Life expectancy
- Infant mortality
- GDP per capita
- Daily calorie intake
- Literacy
- Schooling index
- Educational rank
- Human dev. index

A

ANGOLA

OFFICIAL NAME: People's Republic of Angola **CAPITAL:** Luanda
POPULATION: 9.9 million **CURRENCY:** New kwanza **OFFICIAL LANGUAGE:** Portuguese

AN OIL-RICH COUNTRY in southwest Africa, Angola has been in a state of almost permanent civil war since 1975 when the colonial power, Portugal, left. For many years it was a key Cold War frontier in Africa, with the West supporting UNITA against the Soviet-backed MPLA. Elections in 1992 confirmed the MPLA in power. In 1993, UNITA decided to resume the war.

CLIMATE

WEATHER CHART

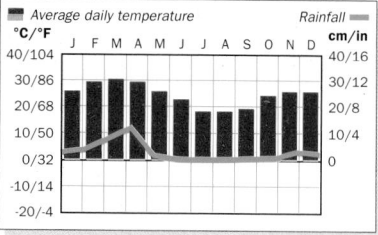

The climate varies from temperate to tropical. Rainfall decreases from north to south. The Benguela Current makes the coast unusually cool and dry.

COMMUNICATIONS

 Luanda International
1.33m passengers

 29 ships
112,500 dwt

THE TRANSPORT NETWORK

 72,400 km (44,992 miles) according to most recent figures. Much has been destroyed during civil war.

 3189 km (1981 miles) according to most recent figures. Much has been destroyed during civil war.

The war has destroyed Angola's transport infrastructure. This has contributed to mass starvation as relief supplies are unable to reach affected areas. Air travel is the safest means of transport, although still risky due to UNITA's use of advanced ground-to-air missiles. The war has led to a collapse in port traffic: Namibe handled 6 million tons in 1973, but just 171,000 tons by 1985. The resumption of war in 1993 halted a $340-million road and bridge repair programme.

TOURISM

 Angola is a war zone. There are no tourists.

 Not applicable

Most overseas visitors are Western journalists, or employees of the big oil multinationals in Cabinda. Angola, a disease-ridden war zone, where up to 500,000 people have died since October 1992, attracts no tourists.

PEOPLE

 Portuguese, Umbundu, Kimbundu, Kongo

 8 people per km²

THE URBAN/RURAL POPULATION SPLIT

28% 72%

ETHNIC MAKEUP

Ovimbundu 37%
Bakongo 13%
Other 25%
Kimbundu 25%

Ethnic tensions in Angola are few. UNITA has cast itself as the sole representative of the Ovimbundu in order to attack the mainly urban-based and largely Kimbundu MPLA. Religion has undergone a revival since the 1980s as the MPLA has now abandoned its Marxist philosophy. For most Angolans life is simply a day-to-day battle for survival.

Angola's capital, Luanda. *Founded in 1575 by the Portuguese, it became a transshipment point for slaves en route to Brazil.*

POLITICS

 1996

 President José Eduardo dos Santos

THE STATE OF THE PARTIES

National Assembly 233 members

4% Other

59% MPLA 32% UNITA 3% PRS 2% FNLA

MPLA = People's Movement for the Liberation of Angola
UNITA = National Union for the Total Independence of Angola
PRS = Social Renewal Party **FNLA** = National Front for the Liberation of Angola **Other** = Democratic Liberal Party

Angola is dominated by two main groups, the MPLA and UNITA. In 1991, the MPLA, in power since 1975, decided to abandon Marxist one-party rule and embraced market-capitalism. In 1992, democratic elections were held. These were unexpectedly lost by Jonas Savimbi's UNITA, which decided to reopen the civil war. Questions were raised about the fairness of the elections, but the EU, UN and other observers thought they broadly represented voters' wishes. Numerous peace efforts culminated in a failed conference in Lusaka, Zambia, in 1994.

ANGOL
Total Area : 1 246 700 sq.
(481 551 sq. mi

POPULATION

over 1 000 000
over 100 000
over 50 000
over 10 000
under 10 000

LAND HEIG

2000m/6562ft
1000m/3281ft
500m/1640ft
200m/656ft
Sea Level

0   200 km
0   200 miles

WORLD AFFAIRS

Angola was one of the key Cold War frontiers in Africa, with Soviet advisers and Cuban troops supporting the MPLA, and South Africa and the USA backing UNITA forces. In 1991, the USA, USSR and Portugal brokered a peace agreement under a UN mandate. UNITA forces did not disarm as agreed and were in a stronger position when they resumed the civil war after losing the elections in 1992. MPLA forces, however, with access to the $3.5 billion-a-year oil revenues, began rearming in 1993.

AID

 $250m, excluding military aid to both MPLA and UNITA

 Up 10% in 1993

In the 1980s, the Soviet Union was the main donor, with over $4 billion in military aid to the MPLA government. At least three million Angolans are dependent on the most basic form of aid – food. Distribution in conditions of war is the major problem. Portugal, the EU and Brazil are the major donors.

DEFENCE

 Precise figures n/av, but largest proportion of budget

Rose again in 1993, after 1992 fall

In the 1980s conflict with South African-backed UNITA, the Cuban units proved most effective within the 100,000-strong MPLA army. The MPLA army was hastily re-formed in 1993 in response to the resumption of war by UNITA. Oil wealth allows the MPLA access to the world arms market. Brazil is a major supplier, particularly of missiles.

ECONOMICS

$6.2bn

6611.20 new kwanza

SCORE CARD

❏ WORLD GNP RANKING	103rd
❏ GNP PER CAPITA	$625
❏ BALANCE OF PAYMENTS	$–511m
❏ INFLATION	92.2%
❏ UNEMPLOYMENT	18.9%

STRENGTHS
Oil sector, which is currently protected from the worst effects of war, earns Angola $3.5 billion a year. Some of the richest mineral deposits in Africa.

WEAKNESSES
Civil war. The oil sector remains a key UNITA war target. Lack of skilled manpower.

EXPORTS

Netherlands 5%
Spain 5%
Other 46%
Netherlands Antilles 6%
Bahamas 16%
USA 22%

IMPORTS

Brazil 5%
Portugal 5%
Other 75%
France 6%
USA 9%

RESOURCES

 1.8bn kwh (capacity 620,000 kw)

 535,300 b/d (reserves 1,500,000,000 bbl)

 3m cattle, 485,000 pigs, 270,000 sheep, 5000 asses

 Oil, diamonds, iron, copper, lead, zinc, gold, manganese

Cabinda is the main oil-producing region. Angola has some of the richest alluvial diamond deposits in the world.

ENVIRONMENT

 2% (1% partially protected)

 War makes any ecological initiatives impossible

The 1990 drought threatened three million Angolans with famine. Other ecological issues do not feature at all.

MEDIA

 The constitution recognizes freedom of speech. Minor criticisms are tolerated in practice

PUBLISHING AND BROADCAST MEDIA

There is 1 daily newspaper, *O Jornal de Angola*

1 state-owned service

1 state-owned, also independent services

The *Voice of the Black Cockerel*, UNITA's powerful propaganda radio station in the south, covers most of Angola.

CRIME

 Most prisoners are simply killed

Dramatic increase due to war

Murder, theft, corruption and diamond smuggling are commonplace in war-torn Angola. All areas outside main cities are effectively controlled by armed gangs. Both the MPLA and UNITA have poor human rights records.

EDUCATION

 42%

The system has all but collapsed in most areas, although the university in Luanda still functions.

CHRONOLOGY

The Portuguese first established forts along the coast of present day Angola in 1482.

- ❏ **1956** Marxist MPLA founded.
- ❏ **1961** FNLA begins intense guerrilla liberation struggle.
- ❏ **1975** Independence from Portugal. Civil war between Soviet and Cuban-backed MPLA and US and South African-backed UNITA.
- ❏ **1979** José Eduardo dos Santos (MPLA) becomes president.
- ❏ **1991** UN-brokered peace.
- ❏ **1992** Elections won by MPLA.
- ❏ **1993** UNITA reopens civil war.

HEALTH

 1 per 13,489 people

 Malaria, diarrheal and respiratory diseases, severe malnutrition

The system is in a state of collapse, unable to cope with the three million at risk of famine and the estimated 10,000 war wounded a day. Angola has the highest infant mortality rate and the greatest number of amputees (caused by exploding mines) in the world.

WEALTH

 Formal employment has effectively collapsed in Angola

CONSUMER GOODS OWNERSHIP

VCR and PC ownership is limited to a small elite
6   14   4

Higher-ranking state officials enjoy luxuries, such as private MPLA shops and access to cars. Much of the rest of the population is struggling to survive.

WORLD RANKING

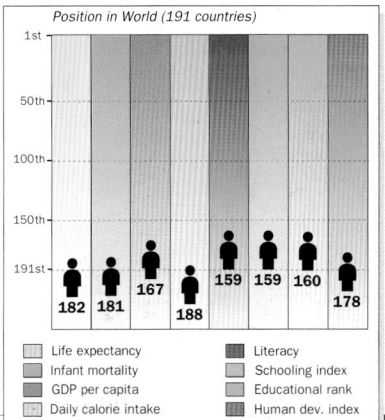
Position in World (191 countries)
182 181 167 188 159 159 160 178

Life expectancy
Infant mortality
GDP per capita
Daily calorie intake
Literacy
Schooling index
Educational rank
Human dev. index

A

ANTARCTICA

OFFICIAL NAME: Antarctica **CAPITAL:** *None*
POPULATION: 4000 **CURRENCY:** *None* **OFFICIAL LANGUAGE:** *None*

ANTARCTICA

THE FIFTH LARGEST CONTINENT, Antarctica is almost entirely covered by ice over 2 km thick. The area sustains a varied wildlife, including seals, whales and penguins. The Antarctic Treaty, which came into force in 1961, provides for international governance of Antarctica. To gain Consultative Status, countries have to set up an active programme of scientific research in the continent. Several countries support the proposal that Antarctica should become a world park and a sanctuary for whales.

CLIMATE

WEATHER CHART

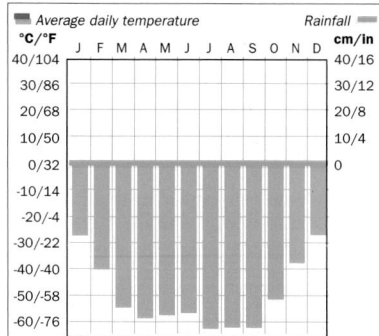

Antarctica is the windiest as well as the coldest continent. Powerful winds create a narrow storm belt around the continent, which brings cloud, fog and severe blizzards. Icebergs, which tend to be slab-shaped, barricade more than 90% of the coastline. Antarctica contains over 80% of the world's fresh water in the form of ice. The blood of polar fish contains anti-freeze agents.

COMMUNICATIONS

Airstrips to some stations

Has no fleet

Ships are the main mode of transport to Antarctica. They are also used for marine research projects. Air traffic from Chile is growing, and France and the UK are building new airstrips. Most planes have to be equipped with skis.

Antarctic Peninsula

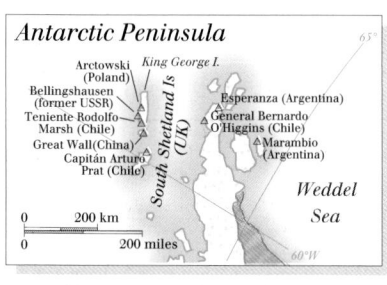

TOURISM

3000 visitors

Small increase from year to year

Tourism is mainly by cruise-ship to the Antarctic Peninsula, Ross Sea and the sub-Antarctic islands. In 1983, the Chileans began flights to King George Island, where an 80-bed hotel has been built. Main attractions are the wildlife, skiing and visits to scientific stations and historic huts. The growth of tourism has disrupted scientific programmes and official regulation of tourism is now essential.

PEOPLE

English, Spanish, French, Norwegian, Chinese, Polish, Russian, German, Japanese

0 people per km²

ETHNIC MAKEUP

Antarctica has a transient population of Americans, English, French, Norwegians, Argentinians, Chileans, Chinese, Russians, Poles and Japanese. Most are involved in research. Few stay more than two years

Antarctica has no indigenous population. The people who live in the continent are scientists and logistical staff working at the 40 permanent, and as many as 100 temporary, research stations. Most stations are too far apart for direct contact between different nationalities. A few Chilean settler families are resident on King George Island.

ANTARCTICA

Total Area : 13 900 000 sq. km (5 366 790 sq. miles)

TERRITORIAL CLAIMS

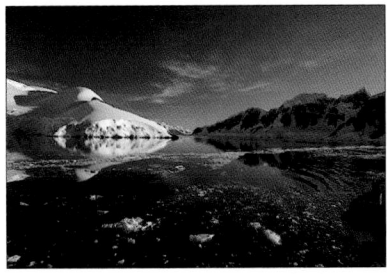

Neumayer Channel, Antarctica. *Many states are pressing for the whole of Antarctica to be protected as an international park.*

POLITICS

 Not applicable

 Consultative Parties to Antarctic Treaty

THE STATE OF THE PARTIES

The Antarctic Treaty of 1959 was signed by 12 nations and acceded to by 29. Consultative meetings are held annually to discuss scientific, environmental and political matters

There are 26 signatories to the Antarctic Treaty and 14 nations with observer status. There are territorial claims by Australia, France, New Zealand and Norway, and overlapping claims in the Antarctic Peninsula by Argentina, Chile and the UK. Other states do not recognize these claims. Of main concern is the adoption of a protocol to ban mining. Most member states have agreed to this. Further protection of the environment is proposed by monitoring all scientific activities, and prosecuting any country whose research would lead to detrimental global change.

WORLD AFFAIRS

Rivalries exist between nations wishing to preserve Antarctica as a world park and those pursuing territorial claims.

AID

 Each country's research is government-funded

 Subject to individual government budgets

Scientific programmes in the Antarctic are almost entirely funded by government agencies in the home countries. Some funding is sometimes provided by scientific institutions and universities.

DEFENCE

 No defence force

 Not applicable

Under the Antarctic Treaty, Antarctica can be used only for peaceful purposes. Any military personnel present perform purely scientific or logistical roles.

ECONOMICS

 Not applicable

 Antarctica has no currency

Research is government-funded and therefore subject to cuts. The exploitation of marine stocks provides no income to Antarctica.

RESOURCES

 Each station has its own generator

 Not an oil producer and has no refineries

 Included in national fish catch totals

 Minerals

Antarctica's main resources are its marine stocks, including fin fish, squids, krill, seals and whales. In 1989, France and Australia joined environmental groups in demanding a ban on potential mineral activities, and campaigning for Antarctica to be declared a world park. Chile and Argentina, in particular, see this as a threat to possible territorial claims. Use of alternative energy sources to fossil fuels are being encouraged, such as solar power and wind generators.

ENVIRONMENT

 0.02%

 1994 Antarctic whale sanctuary established

Antarctica is one of the last great wildernesses on Earth. Its layer of ice, 4000 m thick in places, has taken thousands of years to form. Its ecosystem is so fragile that even a footprint will leave its mark for years. Several species are unique to the continent, including King penguins. A major ecological concern in Antarctica is overfishing, particularly of krill, cod and squid. Also of concern is the depletion of the ozone layer over Antarctica which may have adverse effects on phytoplankton, the foundation of the food chain for marine life. In 1994, the IWC agreed to a French proposal to create an Antarctic whale sanctuary. Together with the Indian Ocean sanctuary, this will protect the feeding grounds of 90% of the world's whales.

MEDIA

 There are no daily newspapers produced in Antarctica. Any papers would have to be brought in from the home countries

A few bases publish news-sheets for local consumption. Local radio stations are found at some of the larger bases.

CRIME

 There are no prisons in Antarctica

 Crime is negligible

Crime is negligible. Each person in Antarctica is subject to their national laws. Occasional petty theft from stations is linked to visits from tourists.

CHRONOLOGY

The Russian explorer, Thaddeus von Bellinghausen, was the first to sight Antarctica, in 1820. The South Pole was first reached by the Norwegian, Roald Amundsen, in December 1911.

- ❑ **1912** UK team of five, led by Scott, find they have been beaten to the Pole. All perish on return journey.
- ❑ **1957–1958** International Geophysical Year. Aims to explore Antarctic region scientifically.
- ❑ **1959** Antarctic Treaty. Signed by 12 countries. Territorial claims frozen. Area to be used only for peaceful purposes.
- ❑ **1978** Convention for the Conservation of Antarctic Seals. Limits number of seals killed.

EDUCATION

 100%

Schoolhouses exist on the Chilean base, Villa Las Estrellas, and the Argentinian base, Esperanza. Teaching is geared to the relevant national system. Some researchers' studies contribute to higher degrees.

Antarctic-based research has resulted in a number of scientific breakthroughs, including the discovery of ozone depletion.

HEALTH

 1 medical officer per station

 Deaths are extremely rare in Antarctica

There is no central health system. Each station has its own medical officer who treats mostly minor complaints. Disease is rare as all personnel are medically screened. The problems usually associated with polar conditions, such as frost bite and snow blindness, are very rare. Serious illness cannot be treated locally, and patients have to be evacuated.

WEALTH

 Most Antarctic researchers draw salaries equivalent to their earnings at home

Wealth disparities reflect the different levels of funding received by each national base. The US bases are the best-funded. Most stations have a TV and video recorder. Telephone systems operate only within stations. PCs are supplied for scientific research. There are no cars.

WORLD RANKING

The UN Human Development Index conditions are not applicable to Antarctica

ANTIGUA & BARBUDA

OFFICIAL NAME: Antigua and Barbuda **CAPITAL:** St John's
POPULATION: 64,000 **CURRENCY:** East Caribbean dollar **OFFICIAL LANGUAGE:** English

LOCATED BETWEEN the Atlantic and the Caribbean, Antigua, one of the Windward Islands, was in turn a Spanish, French and British colony. British influence is still strong, and most clearly revealed in the Antiguans' passion for cricket. Antigua has two remote dependencies: Barbuda, 48 km to the northeast, sporting a magnificent beach; and Redonda, 40 km southwest, an uninhabited rock with its own king.

CLIMATE

WEATHER CHART

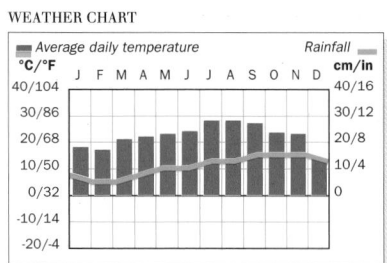

Antigua is less humid than other Caribbean islands. Year-round trade winds moderate the heat.

COMMUNICATIONS

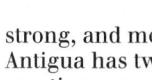

V C Bird International, St John's
727,292 passengers

310 ships
1.21m dwt

THE TRANSPORT NETWORK

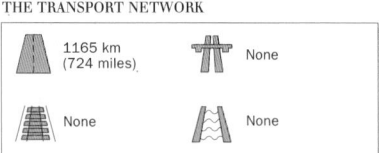

1165 km (724 miles)	None
None	None

Encouraging tourism lies behind two recent projects: the improvement of the international airport and an extended pier at St John's to take cruise ships.

TOURISM

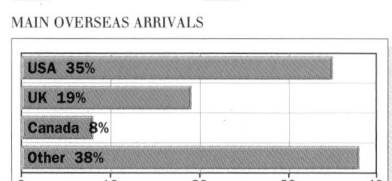

209,902 visitors

Up 7% in 1992

MAIN OVERSEAS ARRIVALS

USA 35%	
UK 19%	
Canada 8%	
Other 38%	

% of total arrivals

Antigua is increasingly popular with US cruise-ship tourists and the yachting rich who attend the annual Sailing Week. The 18th-century Nelson's Dockyard at St John's is a major attraction.

PEOPLE

English, English patois

145 people per km²

THE URBAN/RURAL POPULATION SPLIT

31%   69%

RELIGIOUS PERSUASION

Other 3%   Roman Catholic 10%
Anglican 45%   Other Protestant 42%

Most of Antigua's population is descended from Africans, brought over between the 16th and 19th centuries. There are, in addition, a few Europeans and South Asians. Racial tensions are few. Life is based around the extended family. Since the 1960s, the status of women has risen as a result of their greater access to education and many are now entering the legal, financial and medical professions. Unemployment is low and wealth disparities are small.

ANTIGUA & BARBUDA

Total Area : 440 sq. km (170 sq. miles)

POLITICS

 1999   HM Queen Elizabeth II

THE STATE OF THE PARTIES

House of Representatives 17 members

65% **ALP**   29% **UPP**   6% **Other**

ALP = Antigua Labour Party **UPP** = United Progressive Party
BPM = Barbuda People's Movement

Senate 17 members

11 members chosen by the prime minister, 4 by the leader of the opposition, 1 by the governor-general and 1 by the Barbuda Council

Antigua's multiparty democracy has been dominated for the past 30 years by the Bird family. Vere Bird Sr, prime minister and ALP leader, indicated his intention of retiring in 1993. His two sons, Vere Jr and Lester, were arguing over the succession, but Vere Jr was banned from office after being accused of involvement in gun-running. Lester Bird, therefore, took over on his father's retirement in December 1993. He went on to win the general elections in March the following year.

POPULATION
over 10 000 ●
under 10 000 •

LAND HEIGHT
200m/656ft
Sea Level

A

WORLD AFFAIRS

Antigua backs US policy in the Caribbean, supporting both the US invasion of Grenada in 1983 and economic sanctions against Cuba.

AID

 $7m (receipts)　 Up 75% in 1991

Donors, which include the USA, UK and France, have expressed concern that project development aid may have been misused by the Bird regime. The EU gives aid under the Lomé Convention.

DEFENCE

 $1.4m　 Slight increase in 1992

The USA and UK are the main suppliers of equipment and training to the small army and coastguard. The army is not involved in politics. Two military bases on Antigua are leased to the USA.

ECONOMICS

 $355m　 2.70 East Caribbean dollars

SCORE CARD

- WORLD GNP RANKING........................169th
- GNP PER CAPITA $5550
- BALANCE OF PAYMENTS..................$−59.5m
- INFLATION 7.7%
- UNEMPLOYMENT.....................................5%

STRENGTHS

Tourism is a growing business. The extension of the pier at St John's will encourage more cruise-ship trade. Sailing Week has proved a great success, attracting world-class competition every April.

WEAKNESSES

Very little diversification makes Antigua vulnerable to downturns in the world tourism market.

EXPORTS

IMPORTS

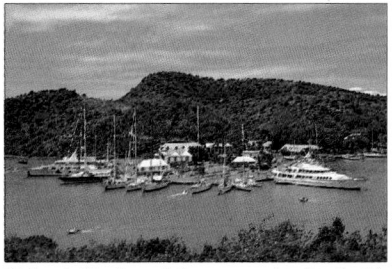

Nelson's Dockyard. Luxury yachts fitted with 20th-century, state-of-the-art gadgetry contrast with the 18th-century St John's harbour.

RESOURCES

 95m kwh (capacity 30,000 kw)　 Not an oil producer and has no refineries

 18,000 cattle, 13,000 sheep, 13,000 goats　 None

Antigua has no strategic or commodity resources and has to import almost all its energy requirements.

ENVIRONMENT

 9%　 Continuing state failure to control hotel development

Uncontrolled sewage disposal from beach-front hotels causes problems. In the 1990 McKinnon Swamp incident, untreated hotel effluent killed valuable inshore fish stocks. Antigua's mangrove systems are also threatened by hotel developments.

MEDIA

 Laws forbid political interference with the media, but the opposition press still faces suppression

PUBLISHING AND BROADCAST MEDIA

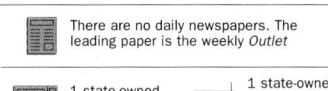

There are no daily newspapers. The leading paper is the weekly *Outlet*

1 state-owned service

1 state-owned, 2 independent services

There are no independent newspapers in Antigua and Barbuda. Three of the weekly newspapers are published by political parties; the fourth is funded by the government.

CRIME

 Antigua and Barbuda does not publish prison figures　 There are no particularly dangerous areas on the islands

Murder is rare on Antigua and Barbuda. Rape, armed robbery and burglary are the main local concerns.

EDUCATION

 90%

Education is based on the British selective 11-plus system. Students go on to the University of the West Indies, or to study in the UK and the USA.

CHRONOLOGY

In 1667, Antigua became a British colony. Barbuda, formerly owned by the British Codrington family, was annexed in 1860.

- 1941 USA builds military bases.
- 1951 Universal adult suffrage introduced.
- 1972 Sugar industry, unable to compete with neighbouring states, closed down.
- 1981 Independence from Britain; opposed by Barbudan secessionist movement.
- 1983 Supports US invasion of Grenada.
- 1990 Vere Bird Jr banned for life from government office.

HEALTH

 1 per 1606 people　 Heart and respiratory diseases, cancers

By Caribbean standards, Antigua and Barbuda's health system is extremely efficient, with easy access to the state-run clinics and hospitals.

WEALTH

 Minimum wage, 4 East Caribbean dollars per hour

CONSUMER GOODS OWNERSHIP

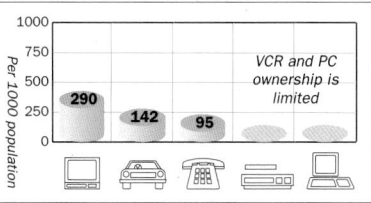

Antigua is fairly socially mobile. Wealthier Antiguans are involved in the tourist industry; Japanese cars, BMWs and satellite dishes are their favoured status symbols.

WORLD RANKING

A

ARGENTINA

OFFICIAL NAME: Argentine Republic **CAPITAL:** Buenos Aires
POPULATION: 33.1 million **CURRENCY:** Argentine peso **OFFICIAL LANGUAGE:** Spanish

OCCUPYING MOST OF THE SOUTHERN half of South America, Argentina extends 3460 km from Bolivia to Cape Horn. The Andes mountains in the west run north–south, forming a natural border with Chile. To the east they slope down to the fertile central pampas, the region known as Entre Rios. Agriculture, especially beef, wheat and fruit, and energy resources are Argentina's main sources of wealth. Politics in Argentina has been characterized in the past by periods of military rule. In 1983, however, Argentina returned to multiparty democracy.

Herding cattle in the northeast, near Corrientes. Beef, Argentina's first source of wealth, remains a major export.

CLIMATE

WEATHER CHART

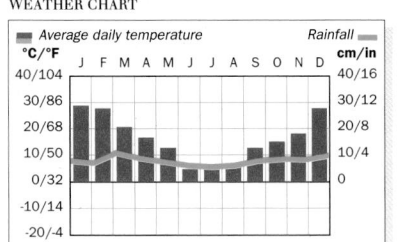

The northeast is near-tropical. The Andes are semi-arid in the north and snowy in the south. The western lowlands are desert, whilst the pampas have a mild climate with heavy summer rains.

COMMUNICATIONS

Ezeiza Intl, Buenos Aires
2.6m passengers

68 ships
1.01m dwt

THE TRANSPORT NETWORK

211,369 km (131,364 miles)	378 km (235 miles)
34,509 km (21,441 miles)	11,000 km (6835 miles)

The government is seeking to privatize as much of the transport network as possible. The state airline, *Aerolíneas Argentinas*, has been successfully sold off to the Spanish national carrier, *Iberia*. Argentina's antiquated rail system will be harder to sell, even in the proposed regional sections, which will end the notion of a national railway. In 1993, virtually the whole system was temporarily closed down, threatening 20,000 jobs.

Private investment is also being sought for new toll roads and for a massive plan to link Buenos Aires to Uruguay and Brazil with a tunnel under the River Plate. Road deaths remain a major problem; Argentina has one of the worst fatality rates in the world.

TOURISM

3.03m visitors

Up 6% in 1992

MAIN OVERSEAS ARRIVALS

Uruguay	32%
Chile	19%
Brazil	11%
Paraguay	9%
Bolivia	3%
Other	26%

% of total arrivals

Although tourism is a significant export earner, Argentina is still on the fringe of the world tourism market as 80% of foreign visitors come from adjoining countries, attracted mainly by Buenos Aires' city life and the ski resorts. The resort of Mar del Plata on the coast and the ski stations in the Córdoba highlands have become mass tourism destinations. Wealthy Argentinians, however, are abandoning these in favour of foreign trips. The rash of privatization plans includes the very popular state-run casinos.

PEOPLE

Spanish, Italian, Amerindian languages

12 people per km²

THE URBAN/RURAL POPULATION SPLIT

86% 14%

RELIGIOUS PERSUASION

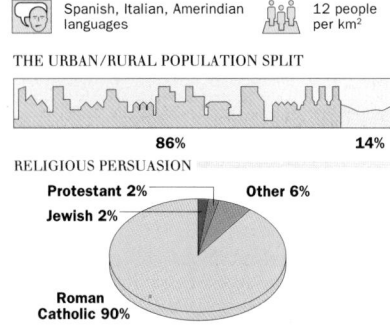

Protestant 2% Other 6%
Jewish 2%
Roman Catholic 90%

ETHNIC MAKEUP

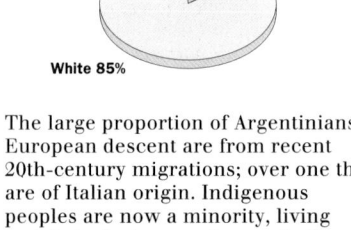

Other 15%
White 85%

The large proportion of Argentinians of European descent are from recent 20th-century migrations; over one third are of Italian origin. Indigenous peoples are now a minority, living mainly in Andean regions or in the *Gran Chaco*. Over 85% of Argentinians are urban dwellers, with 40% living in the capital, Buenos Aires. In general,

POPULATION AGE BREAKDOWN

% of population by age group	0–14	15–64	65+

	1960	1970	1980	1990	2000
65+	5.5%	7%	8.2%	9.1%	9.8%
15–64	63.7%	63.6%	61.7%	61%	63%
0–14	30.8%	29.4%	30.1%	29.9%	27.2%

there is little ethnic tension. Bolivian and Paraguayan immigrants remain the poorest groups.

Catholicism and the extended family remain strong in Argentina and social and religious reunions are common. The family also forms the basis of many successful businesses.

Women have a higher profile than in most Latin American states. Argentinian women were enfranchised before their French counterparts received the vote. Today, many enter the professions and rise to positions of influence in service businesses such as the media. The exception is politics. Eva Perón, who inspired the musical *Evita*, did help to push women into a more active political role in the 1940s and 1950s, but this trend was reversed under military rule.

POLITICS

 Lower House 1995
Upper House 1995

 President Carlos
Saúl Menem

Argentina is a multiparty democracy; the president is head of state.

MAIN POLITICAL ISSUES

Maintaining economic stability
Carlos Menem's radical privatization policies and his vigorous cutting back of the state sector succeeded in reducing inflation from a high of over 7000% to 18% by 1992. A new currency, the peso, introduced in 1992, has maintained parity with the dollar. The central aim of policy now is to maintain growth, keeping a tight rein on inflation, and encouraging foreign investment.

Carlos Menem's re-election
Until 1993, Argentina's constitution prevented presidents from standing for consecutive terms. President Menem called an election in 1994 to allow him to change the constitution so that he could stand again. The issue sharply divided the electorate. Menem's supporters wished to secure his free-market policies. His opponents feared Menem could turn into a second Perón, running a *de facto* civilian dictatorship.

The role of the military
Following the military's fall from power in 1983, officers were tried during Alfonsín's administration for the murder of thousands of 'suspects'. Carlos Menem decided to pardon the officers, but the issue continues to generate controversy. Many remain suspicious of the military's political power behind the scenes.

THE STATE OF THE PARTIES

Chamber of Deputies 257 members

| 50% PJ | 32% UCR | 16% Other | 2% US |

PJ = Justicialist Party (Peronists) UCR = Radical Civic Union
US = Socialist Union MPN = Neuquen Popular Movement
Other = Democratic Progression Party, Movement for Dignity and Independence, Union of the Democratic Centre, Republican Power

Senate 48 members

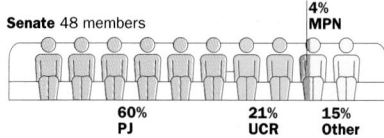

| 60% PJ | 21% UCR | 15% Other | 4% MPN |

PROFILE
The Peronists have been the dominant civilian political force in Argentina since the 1940s. The party was founded on mass working-class and left-wing intellectual support. It has often been at loggerheads with the military, which in practice represents the right and which mounted coups in 1955, 1966 and 1976. The UCR tends to stay in opposition, except when the electorate wishes to register a protest vote, as in 1983. Carlos Menem won elections in 1989 on a populist, left-wing platform. However, he switched tack quickly, steering the Peronists towards right-wing, free-market policies, and in the process gained the support of conservatives.

ARGENTINA

Total Area : 2 766 890 sq. km
(1 068 296 sq. miles)

POPULATION		LAND HEIGHT	
over 1 000 000	▣	4000m/13124ft	
over 500 000	◉	2000m/6562ft	
over 100 000	◎	1000m/3281ft	
over 50 000	○	200m/656ft	
over 10 000	●	Sea Level	

N

0   200 km
0   200 miles

Carlos Menem, Justicialist Party (Peronist) leader; president since 1989.

Domingo Cavallo, finance minister and architect of radical privatization.

WORLD AFFAIRS

 OAS   Mercsr   GATT   RG   LAES

Argentina's claim to the Falkland Islands (known in Latin America as the Islas Malvinas) remains at the top of its foreign policy agenda. Following the failure to take the islands from the UK by military action in 1982–1983, the claim is now being pursued through diplomatic channels. Relations between the two states, however, have improved to the point where Argentinian and British troops are serving side-by-side in UN operations in Cyprus.

Argentina is keen to move closer to the USA, which had traditionally been treated with suspicion by the Peronists. The main reason for the change in policy is Argentina's move away, under the Menem administration, from state-run businesses to American-style free-market economics, and the need to attract US investment. Trade relations with Brazil, Uruguay and Paraguay are also being pursued vigorously. The four states are aiming to achieve a tariff-free common market by 1995.

Argentina is actively promoting itself as a member of the 'first world'. Making its forces available to the UN is part of this strategy, as is the current suggestion of a South Atlantic Defence Alliance with South Africa.

A

AID

 Minimal receipts

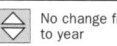 No change from year to year

Receipts, other than restructured loan arrangements with international bodies, are negligible. IMF loans from the 1980s are now regularly serviced.

CHRONOLOGY

The Spanish first established settlements in the Andean foothills in 1543. The indigenous Indians, who had stopped any Inca advance into their territory, also prevented the Spaniards from settling in the east until the 1590s.

❏ **1816** United Provinces of Río de la Plata declare independence; 70 years of civil war follow between central government unitarists and provincial federalists.
❏ **1835–1852** Dictatorship of Juan Manuel Rosas.
❏ **1853** Federal system set up.
❏ **1857** Europeans start settling the pampas; six million by 1930. Most land is held by an oligarchy of 200 families.
❏ **1877** First refrigerated ship starts frozen beef trade to Europe.
❏ **1878–1883** War against the Pampas Indians almost exterminates them.
❏ **1916** Hipólito Yrigoyen wins first democratic presidential elections.
❏ **1930** Military coup upsets republican constitution.
❏ **1943** New military coup. Juan Perón organizes trade unions.
❏ **1946** General Juan Perón elected president, with backing of the military and organized labour.
❏ **1952** Eva Perón, wife of Juan Perón and charismatic champion of workers' welfare, dies of leukemia.
❏ **1955** Military coup ousts Perón. Inflation, strikes, unemployment.
❏ **1973** Perón returns from exile in Madrid and is re-elected president.
❏ **1974** Perón dies; succeeded by his third wife 'Isabelita', who is unable to control either left-wing Peronist or urban guerrilla violence.
❏ **1976** Military junta under General Videla seizes power. Political parties are banned. Brutal repression of Dirty War sees 'disappearance' of over 10,000 'left-wing suspects'.
❏ **1981** General Galtieri president.
❏ **1982** Galtieri orders invasion of Falkland Islands. UK retakes them.
❏ **1983** Pro-human rights candidate Raúl Alfonsín (UCR) becomes president in free multiparty elections. Hyperinflation.
❏ **1989** Carlos Menem (Peronist) wins presidency.
❏ **1992** Inflation down to 18%.

DEFENCE

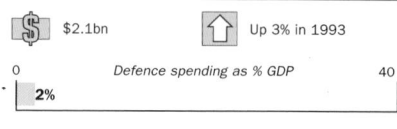

$2.1bn   Up 3% in 1993

0   *Defence spending as % GDP*   40
2%

ARGENTINIAN ARMED FORCES

266 main battle tanks (M-4 *Sherman*/TAM)	35,000 personnel
4 submarines and 13 surface vessels	20,000 personnel
174 combat aircraft (4 *Canberra* B-62/ 20 *Mirage* IIIC)	10,000 personnel
None	

Despite the military's fall from power in 1983, its influence remains strong; Carlos Menem has felt obliged to grant amnesties to officers found guilty of human rights abuses during the military dictatorship.

Argentina has a well-developed arms industry, much of it built up with Israeli assistance. France was a major source of weapons – the role of *Mirage* fighters and *Exocet* missiles was well publicized during the Falklands war. Recently, the air force has been buying US fighter aircraft. Argentina, despite having signed the Nuclear Non-Proliferation Treaty, is suspected of being close to achieving an independent nuclear capability.

ECONOMICS

 $224.5bn

 1.00 Argentine pesos

SCORE CARD

❏ WORLD GNP RANKING 18th
❏ GNP PER CAPITA $6800
❏ BALANCE OF PAYMENTS .... $–8.5bn
❏ INFLATION 18%
❏ UNEMPLOYMENT 7.3%

EXPORTS

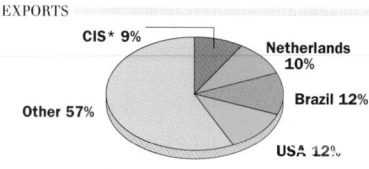

CIS* 9%
Netherlands 10%
Other 57%
Brazil 12%
USA 12%

IMPORTS

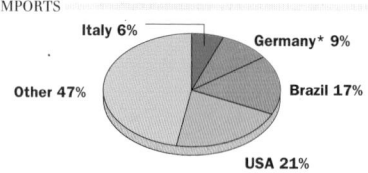

Italy 6%
Germany* 9%
Other 47%
Brazil 17%
USA 21%

STRENGTHS

Argentina manages an export surplus in most years. A rich and varied agricultural base, powerful agribusiness (mainly beef, wheat, fruit and wine), a wealth of energy resources and a skilled labour force are major strengths. The Menem government's economic reforms, in particular currency stabilization and the reduction in inflation, are starting to make Argentina more attractive to overseas investors.

WEAKNESSES

The recent history of hyperinflation still casts doubts over the longevity of low inflation. Despite Menem's successes in privatizing state-owned industries, many major businesses are still under highly inefficient central control. A long history of political instability remains a deterrent to some investors.

ECONOMIC PERFORMANCE INDICATOR

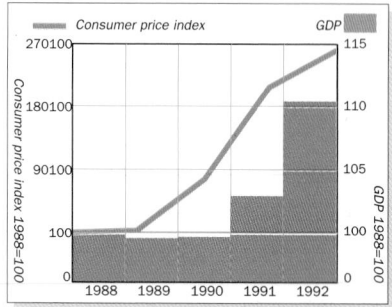

Consumer price index   GDP

(Consumer price index 1988=100; GDP 1988=100)
1988 1989 1990 1991 1992

PROFILE

Hyperinflation during the 1980s made economic planning in Argentina impossible. The Menem government was the first to tackle the problem head-on, by imposing wage freezes, refusing to print money to finance deficits and introducing a new stable currency, the peso. Inflation has since dropped dramatically. The Menem administration is now reversing Perón's major legacy, nationalization.

ARGENTINA : MAJOR BUSINESSES

Salta
San Salvador de Jujuy
Corrientes
Córdoba
Santa Fé
Mendoza
Buenos Aires
Viedma

Wine
Textiles
Agribusiness
Metals
Oranges
Tobacco
Vehicle assembly
Light engineering
Cattle/Meat packing
Heavy engineering

0   400 km
0   400 miles   * significant multinational ownership

RESOURCES

50.9bn kwh (capacity 17.1m kw)

551,000 b/d (reserves 1,569,987,000 bbl)

50m cattle, 29m sheep, 4m pigs, 3m horses

Oil, natural gas, coal, iron, zinc, lead, tin, uranium, silver

ELECTRICITY GENERATION

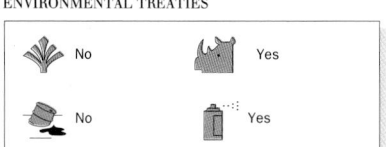

Hydro 36% (18.1bn kwh)

Thermal 50% (28.5bn kwh)

Nuclear 14% (7.3bn kwh)

Other 0%

% of total generation by type

Only one third of Argentina has been properly surveyed for oil and other mineral resources. Important known

ARGENTINA : LAND USE

Cropland
Pasture
Forest
Wetlands
High mountain regions
Wheat - cash crop
Cattle

0   400 km
0   400 miles

oil and gas reserves are still under-exploited. The Menem government sees privatization as a way of developing the energy sector. Argentina is among the world's leading exporters of beef, wheat and fruit.

HEALTH

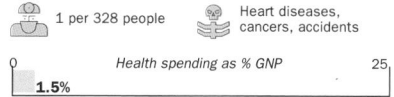

1 per 328 people

Heart diseases, cancers, accidents

0   *Health spending as % GNP*   25

1.5%

Health care in Argentina is nationwide and Argentina has proportionately more doctors than the USA. Doctors charge, but most Argentinians are covered by insurance policies. High-technology equipment is concentrated in private Buenos Aires hospitals. The recent Worker's Health Plan system was introduced by the Menem administration and designed to improve care for the poor.

WEALTH

Chambermaid, 800 Argentine pesos per month; company director, 5000 Argentine pesos per month

CONSUMER GOODS OWNERSHIP

Higher than South American average

219   135   115   59

Per 1000 population

Considerable social mobility can still be achieved in Argentina. The wealthy travel in private jets to their *estancias* (country estates), holiday in Europe and the USA, and play polo and rugby. Argentina is a major market for designer labels – Rolex watches, BMW cars and Italian fashion are particularly favoured. Middle-income groups travel to resorts such as Punta del Este in Uruguay or Copacabana in Brazil, and enjoy the European-style life of Buenos Aires, which boasts a world-class opera house. The standard of living of the underclass, most of whom are from poor rural interior provinces and trying to find work in Buenos Aires, has been falling since Menem took power.

ENVIRONMENT

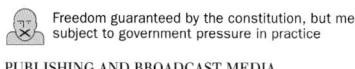

3% (2% partially protected)

Increasing general interest in environmental issues

ENVIRONMENTAL TREATIES

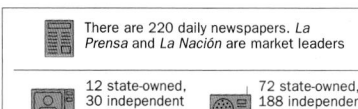

No   Yes

No   Yes

Nuclear power was encouraged by the military, which covered up leaks and accidents from the two main plants – Atocha I and II. Otherwise, the main concerns are the extreme pollution of rivers in Buenos Aires, the 50% depletion of the ozone layer in southern regions and the illegal export of rare birds, particularly from the north.

Environmental issues are of increasing interest to the electorate, but have yet to make a political impact. In 1993, however, residents in Tierra del Fuego succeeded in diverting an oil pipeline to save a colony of penguins.

CRIME

27,720 prisoners

Most crime is on the increase

CRIME RATES

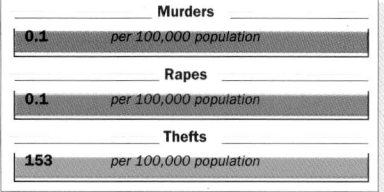

Murders
0.1   *per 100,000 population*

Rapes
0.1   *per 100,000 population*

Thefts
153   *per 100,000 population*

Buenos Aires remains one of the safest cities in Latin America, apart from the shanty town areas, where crime is rising. Drugs-money laundering is also a growing problem. The army has still not recovered respect following the human rights abuses of the 1970s.

EDUCATION

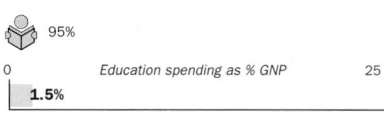

95%

0   *Education spending as % GNP*   25

1.5%

THE EDUCATION SYSTEM

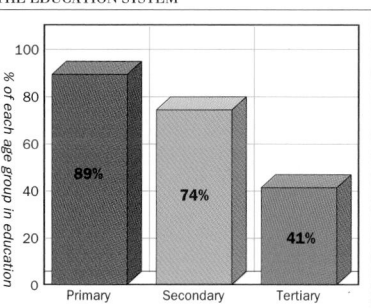

% of each age group in education

89%   74%   41%

Primary   Secondary   Tertiary

Schooling is effectively a mix of the French and US systems. Schools in the interior have the highest drop-out rate. Argentina has a strong tertiary sector, with most students attending free state universities.

MEDIA

Freedom guaranteed by the constitution, but media subject to government pressure in practice

PUBLISHING AND BROADCAST MEDIA

There are 220 daily newspapers. *La Prensa* and *La Nación* are market leaders

12 state-owned, 30 independent stations

72 state-owned, 188 independent stations

CNN is available in Corrientes and Buenos Aires

None

The press in Argentina was only truly free under the UCR (1983–1989). Many journalists were killed in the late 1970s for expressing their political beliefs. The Menem administration is once again applying pressure on the media, withdrawing state advertising from newspapers critical of its policies.

WORLD RANKING

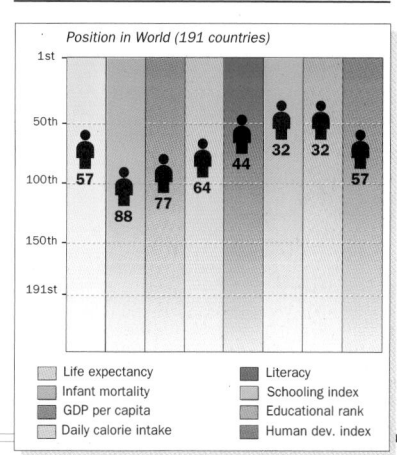

Position in World (191 countries)

1st
50th
100th
150th
191st

57   88   77   64   44   32   32   57

Life expectancy
Infant mortality
GDP per capita
Daily calorie intake
Literacy
Schooling index
Educational rank
Human dev. index

A

ARMENIA

OFFICIAL NAME: Republic of Armenia **CAPITAL:** Yerevan
POPULATION: 3.5 million **CURRENCY:** Dram **OFFICIAL LANGUAGE:** Armenian

EUROPE

Europe

LAND-LOCKED IN THE Lesser Caucasus Mountains, Armenia is the smallest of the former USSR's republics and was the first to adopt Christianity as its state religion. It is bordered by Muslim states to the south, east and west. Keen to develop links with the CIS, Armenia has kept to a path of radical economic reform including privatization. War with Azerbaijan over the enclave of Nagorno Karabakh has dominated national life since 1988.

Landscape near Yerevan. Armenia's very dry climate results in expanses of semi-desert. Its famous vineyards flourish in sheltered areas.

CLIMATE

WEATHER CHART

Armenia has a continental climate, with little rainfall in the lowlands. Winters can be very cold.

COMMUNICATIONS

  Yerevan Intl   Has no fleet

THE TRANSPORT NETWORK

10,200 km (6338 miles)		None
820 km (510 miles)		None

Public transport has been badly hit by the war-induced fuel crisis and the main road to Georgia is cut because it crosses Azerbaijani territory. The vital Aras bridge to Iran reopened in 1992.

TOURISM

 Very few, due to war with Azerbaijan   Similar levels from year to year

MAIN OVERSEAS ARRIVALS

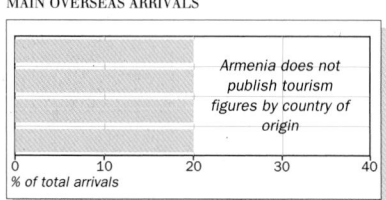

Armenia does not publish tourism figures by country of origin

0   10   20   30   40
% of total arrivals

War has discouraged visitors. Ancient churches and the cellar vaults of the cognac-producing regions are Armenia's chief attractions.

PEOPLE

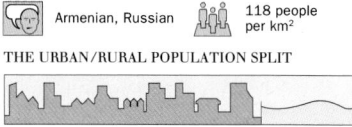

Armenian, Russian   118 people per km²

THE URBAN/RURAL POPULATION SPLIT

68%   **32%**

ETHNIC MAKEUP

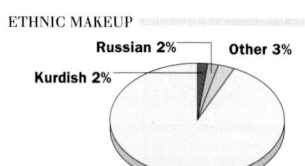

Russian 2%   Other 3%
Kurdish 2%
Armenian 93%

Minority nationalities are well integrated in the Armenian population. Very strong contacts are maintained with the large number of Armenian emigrants, estimated at some nine million in the USA, France and Syria. 100,000 Armenians who lived in Azerbaijan have been forced to return home since the outbreak of war.

POLITICS

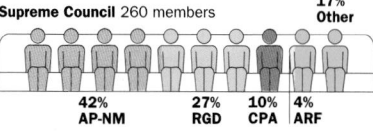

Uncertain   President Levon Ter-Petrosyan

THE STATE OF THE PARTIES

Supreme Council 260 members   **17% Other**

42% AP-NM **27% RGD** **10% CPA** **4% ARF**

AP-NM = Armenian Pan-National Movement
RGD = Republican Group of Deputies **CPA** = Communist Party of Armenia **ARF** = Armenian Revolutionary Federation

Armenia has been a multiparty democracy since 1991. The president's party, the AP-NM, has had problems passing legislation against the seven parliamentary opposition parties, but has managed to maintain the path of radical economic reform. The post of prime minister is currently occupied by Bagratyan, a young radical economist. A referendum on a new constitution was due to be held in 1994 to decide whether Armenia should be a presidential or parliamentary republic. The war with Azerbaijan, over the issue of whether the Armenian enclave of Nagorno Karabakh inside Azerbaijan should become part of Armenia, dominates politics. Some nationalist-orientated opposition parties, including the ARF, advocate recognition of an independent Nagorno Karabakh.

GEORGIA

Noyemberyan
Tashir Alaverdi
Ashots'k' Step'anavan
Amasia Vanadzor Ijevan
Gyumri Spitak Berd
Akhuryan Dilijan Artsvashen
Maralik Art'ik Aparan
T'alin *Aragats Lerr 4090m* Sevan
Tsaghkahovit Ch'arents'avan Hrazdan
Ashtarak Kamo Sevana Lich
Baghramyan Ejmiadzin Nor SHAKI-DAG
Hachn
YEREVAN Martuni Vardenis
Hoktemberyan Aras Masis Artashat
Vedi
Ararat
Yeghegnadzor Jermuk
Vayk' Arp'a
Sisian Goris
K'ajaran Kapan
Aras
Meghri

ARMENIA

Total Area : 29 000 sq. km
(11 505 sq. miles)

POPULATION

▣ over 1 000 000   LAND HEIGHT
◉ over 100 000
○ over 50 000   3000m/9843ft
● over 10 000   2000m/6562ft
• under 10 000   1000m/3281ft
500m/1640ft

N

0   50 km

0

WORLD AFFAIRS

The war with Azerbaijan dominates the agenda. Efforts to improve traditionally sour relations with Turkey have failed following Armenia's military successes in Nagorno Karabakh. Relations with Iran have cooled as Azerbaijan has developed closer ties with Tehran. Moscow is less supportive of Armenia since Azerbaijan rejoined the CIS.

AID

 No figures available as most aid is *ad hoc*   The trend in receipts is up

Most funds have come from Armenians living abroad. Armenia is seeking aid from the EU to restart the Medzamor nuclear power plant, closed since 1989.

DEFENCE

 $147.1m   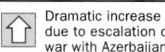 Dramatic increase due to escalation of war with Azerbaijan

The success of the armed forces in the war with Azerbaijan has increased their political profile and their independence from civilian control. In 1993, peace overtures to the Azeris by Armenia's President Ter-Petrosyan were ignored by the army, which mounted a further offensive into Nagorno Karabakh.

ECONOMICS

 $7.2bn   370 dram

SCORE CARD

❏ WORLD GNP RANKING	92nd
❏ GNP PER CAPITA	$2100
❏ BALANCE OF PAYMENTS	$–8m
❏ INFLATION	100.3%
❏ UNEMPLOYMENT	7.5%

STRENGTHS
Strong ties with Armenian emigrants. Major deposits of rare metals, as yet unexploited. Well-developed machine-building and manufacturing – includes textiles and bottling of mineral water.

WEAKNESSES
Dependent on imported energy, raw materials and semi-finished goods. Gas pipeline through Azerbaijani-controlled region of Georgia often sabotaged.

EXPORTS

Kazakhstan 11%
Ukraine 12%
Other 16%
Russia 61%

IMPORTS

Belorussia 7%
Ukraine 19%
Other 44%
Russia 30%

RESOURCES

 9.5bn kwh   Minimal oil production

 6.7m poultry, 686,500 sheep, 428,900 cattle   Coal, oil, natural gas, rare metals

Armenia has negligible energy resources, but viable deposits of rare metals have been found. Arable land is scarce, producing mainly vegetables and grapes. Abundant sources of mineral water have given rise to a large bottling industry.

ENVIRONMENT

 7.4%   War: all environmental measures on hold

The Medzamor nuclear power station was declared unsafe after the 1988 earthquake. It may be reactivated owing to the energy crisis, despite opposition from environmental groups. HEP generation near Lake Sevan has seriously reduced the lake's water level.

MEDIA

 Criticism of the government is not tolerated in practice

PUBLISHING AND BROADCAST MEDIA

There are 45 national newspapers, including *Golos Armenii*, *Hayastan* and *Avangard*

1 state-controlled service   1 state-controlled service

There are many independent journals and newspapers, but government control of the paper industry gives it an effective censorship weapon.

CRIME

 Armenia does not publish prison figures   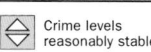 Crime levels reasonably stable

Armenia's legal system survived within the Soviet system. Crime levels are lower than those of other ex-Soviet states. Amnesty International gives Armenia a clean bill of health.

EDUCATION

 Highest literacy rate of the ex-Soviet republics

The education system, previously conforming to that of the USSR, now emphasizes Armenian history and culture. 14% of the population have received higher education.

CHRONOLOGY

Armenia lost its autonomy in the 14th century. In 1639, Turkey took the west and Persia the east; Persia ceded its part to Russia in 1828.

- ❏ **1877–1878** Massacre of Armenians during Russo-Turkish war.
- ❏ **1915** Ottomans force 1.75 million Turkish Armenians into desert exile; most die.
- ❏ **1917–1918** Russian Armenia's brief anti-Bolshevik alliance with Georgia and Azerbaijan.
- ❏ **1920** Independence. Turkish attack; Bolsheviks counter-invade.
- ❏ **1922** Becomes a Soviet republic.
- ❏ **1988** Earthquake kills 25,000.
- ❏ **1990** Declares Nagorno Karabakh (in Azerbaijan) part of Armenia.
- ❏ **1991** Independence from USSR.

HEALTH

 1 per 233 people   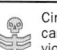 Circulatory diseases, cancers, accidents, violence

Hospitals are suffering from the erratic electricity supply, while the breakdown in sewerage and other services has led to a rise in hepatitis and tuberculosis.

WEALTH

 Around 70% of the Armenian population live in poverty, as defined by the UN

CONSUMER GOODS OWNERSHIP

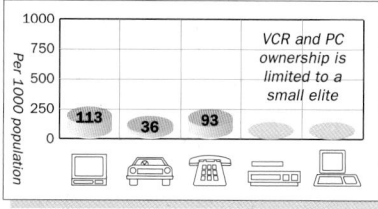

VCR and PC ownership is limited to a small elite

113   36   93

The richest Armenians are those living in the USA and France. The many refugees from Baku are the poorest.

WORLD RANKING

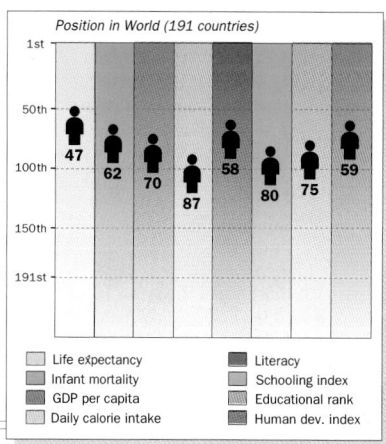

Position in World (191 countries)

47   62   70   87   58   80   75   59

Life expectancy | Literacy
Infant mortality | Schooling index
GDP per capita | Educational rank
Daily calorie intake | Human dev. index

A

AUSTRALIA

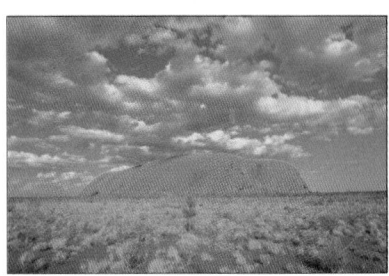

OFFICIAL NAME: Commonwealth of Australia CAPITAL: Canberra
POPULATION: 17.6 million CURRENCY: Australian dollar OFFICIAL LANGUAGE: English OVERSEAS TERRITORIES: 6

THE WORLD'S SIXTH LARGEST COUNTRY, Australia is an island continent located between the Indian and Pacific oceans. Its six states and the Northern Territory have a variety of landscapes, including tropical rainforests, the deserts of the arid 'red centre', snow-capped mountains, rolling tracts of pastoral land and magnificent beaches. Famous natural features include Uluru (Ayers Rock) and the Great Barrier Reef. Most Australians live on the coast. All the state capitals, with the exception of Canberra, are coastal cities. The strip down the length of the eastern seaboard is the country's richest and most populous area. In 2000, Sydney will host the millennium Olympics.

Uluru (Ayers Rock), Northern Territory.
The renaming of Ayers Rock reflects growing Aboriginal influence in Australia.

CLIMATE

WEATHER CHART

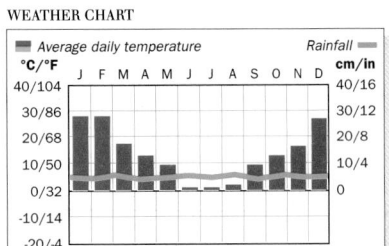

The interior, west and south are arid or semi-arid and very hot in summer; central desert temperatures can reach 50°C. The north, around Darwin and Cape York Peninsula, is hot all year and humid during the summer monsoon. Only the east and southeast within 400 km of the coast, and the southwest around Perth are temperate. It is in these areas that most Australians live.

COMMUNICATIONS

Kingsford Smith, Sydney
11.23m passengers

125 ships
3.56m dwt

THE TRANSPORT NETWORK

852,986 km (530,020 miles)	787 km (489 miles)
40,116 km (24,927 miles)	8368 km (5200 miles)

Air transport is well developed and vital to Australia's sparsely populated centre and west. Sydney suffers from air congestion; a third runway is being added to Kingsford Smith airport and Sydney West airport is due to open in 1998. A high-speed train linking Sydney, Canberra and Melbourne is under discussion. Most freight in Australia travels in massive trucks known as 'road trains'. Improvements in urban transport are a priority, particularly in Sydney, in the run-up to the 2000 Olympic Games.

TOURISM

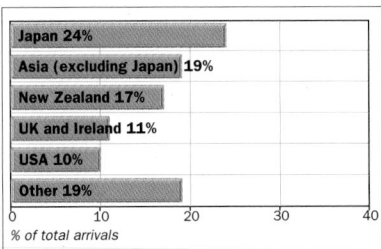

2.6m visitors

Up 10% in 1992

MAIN OVERSEAS ARRIVALS

Japan 24%
Asia (excluding Japan) 19%
New Zealand 17%
UK and Ireland 11%
USA 10%
Other 19%

% of total arrivals

Tourism is now Australia's largest single foreign exchange earner, accounting for 10% of the total. Faster, cheaper air travel and highly successful government marketing campaigns draw tourists in increasing numbers, especially from Asia, which has been the focus of Australia's strategy to develop tourism's rich potential. The Japanese are now the largest single group of visitors, although many also come from Europe, North America and New Zealand. While Japanese tourists stay a shorter time – on average eight nights – they tend to spend more than other nationalities.

The country's attractions include wildlife, swimming and surfing off Pacific and Indian Ocean beaches, skin-diving along the Great Barrier Reef and skiing in the Australian Alps. Aboriginal culture and the town of Alice Springs are among the outback's attractions. The far north has tropical resorts; the northwest pearl-fishing. The vineyards of the south and southeast attract many visitors, as do the cultural life of Melbourne and Sydney and the arts festivals held in state capitals. Sydney's hosting of the Olympic Games in 2000 will give the city a massive economic boost.

Growth, while still strong, is slowing from the phenomenal boom seen in the mid-1980s, when tourist arrivals rose by almost 200% in five years. One result of this is that the rush to invest has left many hotels, especially those at the luxury end of the market, struggling in the 1990s.

AUSTRALIA

Total Area : 7 686 850 sq. km (2 967 893 sq. miles)

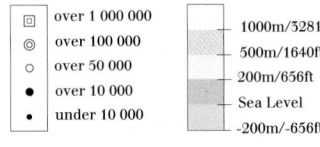

POPULATION

- over 1 000 000
- over 100 000
- over 50 000
- over 10 000
- under 10 000

LAND HEIGHT

- 1000m/3281ft
- 500m/1640ft
- 200m/656ft
- Sea Level
- -200m/-656ft

PEOPLE

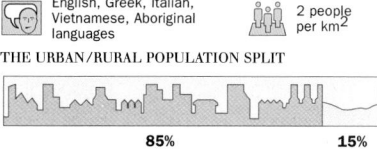

English, Greek, Italian, Vietnamese, Aboriginal languages

2 people per km²

THE URBAN/RURAL POPULATION SPLIT

85%   15%

The first settlers arrived in Australia almost 100,000 years ago. Their modern descendants, the Aborigines, today make up less than 1% of the population. European settlement began in 1788 and was dominated by British and Irish immigrants – some of whom were convicts – until the gold rushes of the 1850s. Immigrants of other nationalities – including many Chinese – arrived to prospect for gold, then settled in the cities, especially Melbourne and Sydney. When the new federal government was installed in 1901, one of its first acts was to prevent further Chinese immigration. The act set out the 'White Australia' policy, which conditioned attitudes to immigration for almost 70 years.

A massive immigration drive after the Second World War brought many more British settlers to Australia in the 1950s. Further government initiatives to 'populate or perish' saw the arrival of large numbers of Italians and Greeks.

From the late 1960s, the 'White Australia' policy was progressively wound down. It was officially ended during the 1972–1975 Whitlam administration. Ever since, up to 50% of immigrants each year have come from Asia, transforming Australia from an almost exclusively European enclave into a multicultural society, in which immigrant groups are encouraged to maintain connections with their own cultures and languages.

Aborigines are the exception in an otherwise integrated society. Numbering around 250,000, they remain marginalized economically and socially and still face considerable discrimination. Until the mid-1960s, they were not considered Australian citizens and were denied the vote, full social benefits and inclusion in the census. Aboriginal land had been occupied by settlers on the basis that it was *terra nullius* that belonged to no-one. Since the 1970s, Aborigines have made an increasingly organized stand over land rights and abuse of their civil rights. Government attempts to address the land rights issue initially foundered in the face of opposition by powerful mining companies and several state governments. However, the 1992 'Mabo Judgement', rescinding the concept of *terra nullius*, may pave the way to a settlement of Aborigines' grievances.

During the 1950s and 1960s, Catholic–Protestant differences were a strong enough force to cause a rift in the Australian Labor Party (ALP). However, a subsequent policy encouraging mixed denomination schooling, coupled with a decline in religious observance, has largely neutralized the issue.

RELIGIOUS PERSUASION

Anglican 26%
Other 24%
Roman Catholic 26%
Other Christian 24%

ETHNIC MAKEUP

Aboriginal and other 1%   Asian 4%
Caucasian 95%

POPULATION AGE BREAK DOWN

% of population by age group	0–14	15–64	65+		
65+	8.5%	8.3%	9.6%	10.9%	11.7%
15–64	61.4%	62.9%	65.1%	67%	67.7%
0–14	30.1%	28.8%	25.3%	22.1%	20.6%
	1960	1970	1980	1990	2000

(Map of Australia with labelled regions and cities)

PAPUA NEW GUINEA

ARAFURA SEA

Torres Strait
Bamaga   Cape York

Melville Island
Wessel Islands

Darwin

ARNHEM LAND

Gulf of Carpentaria

Groote Eylandt

CAPE YORK PENINSULA

Sir Edward Pellew Group

Wellesley Islands

Mitchell

Cairns

BARKLY TABLELAND

TANAMI DESERT

NORTHERN TERRITORY

Mount Isa

Flinders

GREAT BARRIER REEF

CORAL SEA

Townsville

Hughenden

Mackay

Macdonnell Ranges
Alice Springs

Winton

Longreach

Emerald   Rockhampton

QUEENSLAND

GREAT ARTESIAN BASIN

Uluru (Ayers Rock)

SIMPSON DESERT

Birdsville

Cooper Creek

Bundaberg
Fraser I.
Maryborough
Gympie

Charleville

SOUTH AUSTRALIA

Lake Eyre

Cunnamulla

Toowoomba
Ipswich   Brisbane
Gold Coast
Lismore

VICTORIA DESERT

Lake Torrens

Lake Frome

Darling

Bourke

Moree
Armidale
Grafton
Coffs Harbour

GREAT DIVIDING RANGE

Penong

Lake Gairdner

Broken Hill

NEW SOUTH WALES

Tamworth
Dubbo

Port Macquarie
Taree
Maitland

t Australian Bight

Whyalla
Port Pirie

Lachlan

Orange
Newcastle
Gosford

Eyre Peninsula
Port Lincoln

Port Augusta
Elizabeth
Adelaide

Mildura

Murrumbidgee
Griffith

Bathurst
Lithgow
Goulburn
Sydney
Wollongong

Kangaroo I.

Lacepede Bay

Murray

Wagga Wagga

Albury

Queanbeyan
CANBERRA

Mount Kosciusko 2228m

AUST. CAPITAL TERRITORY

SOUTH PACIFIC OCEAN

VICTORIA

Shepparton

Horsham
Bendigo
Wangaratta
AUSTRALIAN ALPS

Mount Gambier
Ballarat
Melbourne
Traralgon
Geelong
Morwell
Sale
Cape Howe

TASMAN SEA

Warrnambool

Bass Strait
King I.

Furneaux Group
Flinders I.

Burnie
Ulverstone
Devonport
Launceston

Hobart

400 km
400 miles

N

CHRONOLOGY

Dutch, Portuguese, French and – decisively – British incursions throughout the 17th and 18th centuries signalled the end of 40,000 years of Aboriginal occupancy. Governor Arthur Phillip raised the Union Jack at Sydney Cove on 26 January 1788.

❑ **1901** Inauguration of the Commonwealth of Australia.
❑ **1915** At the outbreak of First World War, Australian government calls for volunteers to Australian Imperial Force (AIF).
❑ **1915** Australian troops suffer heavy casualties at Gallipoli.
❑ **1929** Industrial upheaval and financial collapse: 'The Great Depression'.
❑ **1939** Prime Minister Menzies announces Australia will follow Britain into war with Germany.
❑ **1941** John Curtin becomes prime minister.
❑ **1942** Fall of Singapore to Japanese army. Japanese invasion of Australia seems imminent. Curtin turns to USA for help.
❑ **1950** Australian troops committed to UN–US Korean War against North Korean communists.
❑ **1962** Menzies government commits Australian aid to war in Vietnam.
❑ **1966** Australia adopts decimal currency.
❑ **1972** Election of Gough Whitlam government. Aid to South Vietnam ceases.
❑ **1975** Whitlam government dismissed by Governor-General Sir John Kerr. Malcolm Fraser forms Liberal–National Party coalition government.
❑ **1983** Fraser government defeated. Bob Hawke, having become leader of the Labor Party on the eve of the election, becomes prime minister.
❑ **1985** Corporate boom followed by deepening recession, termed 'the recession we had to have' by Treasurer Paul Keating.
❑ **1992** Paul Keating defeats Hawke in vote to become prime minister. He announces 'Turning towards Asia' policy and places republican debate at top of political agenda. Australian High Court's 'Mabo Judgement' on Aboriginal land title rescinds concept of *terra nullius*.
❑ **1993** March, against most predictions, Keating ALP government re-elected. Prime Minister Keating visits UK and outlines republican timetable to Queen Elizabeth II.

POLITICS

 1996   HM Queen Elizabeth II

THE STATE OF THE PARTIES

House of Representatives 148 members

| 54% ALP | 33% LP | 11% NP | 2% Other |

ALP = Australian Labor Party **LP** = Liberal Party
NP = National Party **AD** Australian Democrats
Other = Western Australia Green Party

Senate 82 members

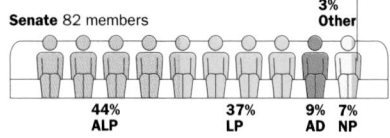

| 44% ALP | 37% LP | 9% AD | 7% NP | 3% Other |

Australia is a parliamentary democracy on the British model. There are six state governments, all but one (Queensland) bicameral. The Northern Territory became self-governing in 1978.

MAIN POLITICAL ISSUES

Aboriginal rights
In 1992, in what became known as the 'Mabo Judgement', the High Court decided in favour of Eddie Mabo of Murray Island in the Torres Strait, who had claimed title to land his family had occupied before white settlement. The judgement could have a considerable impact on mining and agricultural interests. Western Australia is fighting the judgement. Prime Minister Keating has suggested a compromise, offering Aborigines compensation for land used by mining companies, as well as an unspecified 'social justice package'. Australians generally support the judgement hoping that it will bury the conscience-pricking question of Aboriginal land rights.

Unemployment
Running at over 10%, unemployment was expected to be the issue that would sink Prime Minister Keating's ALP government in the 1993 election. A skilful campaign helped to bring the ALP back to power. For most Australians, however, unemployment remains a central concern. Now that the economy is showing signs of emerging from recession, there are hopes that the unemployment figures will begin to fall. Much new investment, however, is in high-tech, low-labour industries and commentators fear that unemployment will remain at around 10% for a number of years.

The Republic
Despite international press coverage, the republican issue is not of major importance to most Australians. The government is currently playing down the debate in order to avoid inflaming monarchist groups. A government-appointed consultative group explored the limits of the proposed republican constitution; many had hoped that a reconciliation with Aborigines would be included. However, the group recommended a simple replacement of the British monarch as head of state with an elected president. The Keating administration is hoping that the successful bid to hold the 2000 Olympics in Sydney and the republican issue will help to win it a fourth term in 1996.

PROFILE

The Labor (ALP), Liberal and National parties have dominated Australian politics since 1945. The Liberal and National parties are to the right of the political spectrum and work together in coalition. They broadly represent big business and agricultural interests. The ALP has managed to remain in power by attracting former traditional coalition supporters by, for example, adopting free-market policies. This has also brought a blurring of the differences between parties. However, policies that clearly distinguish the ALP from its opponents, such as its stance on the republican issue, could help it to win again in 1996.

Vineyards in South Australia. Wine-growing has been one of Australia's greatest agricultural success stories in recent years.

Labor leader and Prime Minister Paul Keating, won the election of 1993.

Alexander Downer, became opposition leader in 1994.

Brian Howe, deputy prime minister and minister for housing.

WORLD AFFAIRS

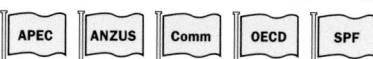

Australia's international focus has shifted from Europe and the USA towards Asia. Geopolitically it is in an ambiguous position. Having lost its place as a major trading partner for the UK when the latter joined the EEC, Australia has found that it is still regarded as a European outsider by the Asian nations with which it wishes to foster closer links. Australia has taken practical steps to redefine its role. It was the main backer of the 1989 Asia Pacific Economic Co-operation forum (APEC), an attempt to create a multilateral regional trading bloc, similar to the EU and NAFTA. After a faltering start, APEC began to get results. It was the first group to have China, Taiwan and Hong Kong sitting around the same table. The USA was a strong supporter, seeing APEC as a means of promoting free-market economics in Asia. Japan gave APEC its backing and now sees no conflict in belonging to APEC and leading ASEAN, the other key economic grouping. Australia's ambition is for APEC to become the leading association in the region.

Relations with the USA are tense on questions of trade. Australia objects to subsidized US wheat undercutting its own in Asia, particularly in the key Chinese market. It now sees the EU and USA as its main competitors in booming South East Asian economies.

However, on security issues Australia still supports the West. Against much public opposition, it sent troops to the 1991 Gulf War. Its commitment to the Pacific region also remains strong. The end of the Cold War, however, has meant that this is now expressed in terms of development aid rather than defence arrangements.

Within the Pacific region, fishing is a major issue. There have been a number of minor skirmishes with Indonesian and Japanese long-line fishing boats. Australia objects to this form of fishing as it kills large numbers of dolphins, and employs anti-submarine patrols to regulate the industry.

AID

 $1,384m donations   Up 1% in 1993

Australia spends 0.36% of its GNP on aid programmes. Most is spent in the Asia–Pacific region. Particular areas of focus are non-governmental organizations and HIV/AIDS programmes. By far the greatest recipient, with $335 million, is Papua New Guinea, where Australian companies such as Broken Hill Proprietary have major mining operations.

DEFENCE

 $7.3bn   Up 3% in 1992

0	Defence spending as % GDP	40

2.4%

Strategic ties with the USA remain an important element of defence policy. Australia has defence arrangements with the Philippines, Brunei and Thailand among others. Expenditure is designed to keep Australia self-reliant in defence and to encourage the participation of industry.

AUSTRALIAN ARMED FORCES

🪖	103 main battle tanks (103 *Leopard* 1A3)	30,300 personnel
🚢	5 submarines, 8 frigates, 3 destroyers and 19 patrol boats	15,300 personnel
✈	157 combat aircraft (22 F-111C/ 52 F-18A,-18B)	22,300 personnel
	None	

ECONOMICS

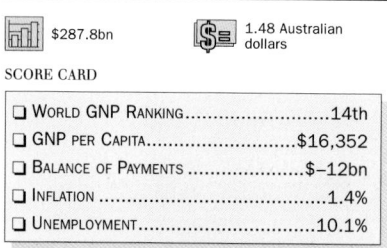 $287.8bn   1.48 Australian dollars

SCORE CARD

❑ WORLD GNP RANKING	14th
❑ GNP PER CAPITA	$16,352
❑ BALANCE OF PAYMENTS	$-12bn
❑ INFLATION	1.4%
❑ UNEMPLOYMENT	10.1%

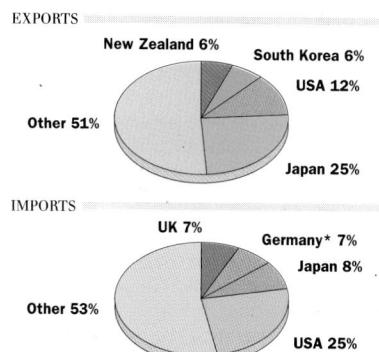

EXPORTS

New Zealand 6%
South Korea 6%
USA 12%
Japan 25%
Other 51%

IMPORTS

UK 7%
Germany* 7%
Japan 8%
USA 25%
Other 53%

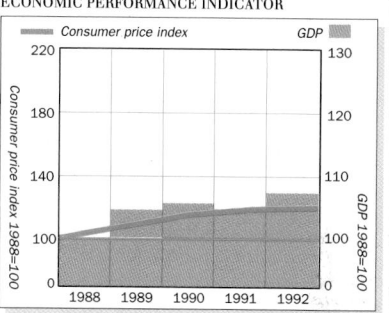

ECONOMIC PERFORMANCE INDICATOR

Consumer price index   GDP

Consumer price index 1988=100 / GDP 1988=100

1988 1989 1990 1991 1992

STRENGTHS

Efficient agricultural and mining industries. Vast mineral deposits. Highly profitable tourist industry with huge untapped potential. Successful investor in booming South East Asian economies, such as Vietnam.

WEAKNESSES

May suffer from EU and NAFTA protectionist policies. Political instability in some export markets in South East Asia could dent exports. Competition from Asian economies with lower wage rates and poorer working conditions. Balance of payments deficit. Unemployment likely to remain high.

PROFILE

Australia's companies are concentrating on the growing Asian market. From accounting for 25% of exports in 1960, Asia now accounts for 60% of Australia's trade. Japan remains its most important trading partner.

In order to compete in Asia, Australia's economy has been undergoing massive structural adjustment. The ALP government has slowly been removing the tariffs that made Australia one of the most heavily protected economies within the OECD. Higher unemployment and the collapse of many businesses accompanied the change. In 1994, however, strong growth was seen.

AUSTRALIA : MAJOR BUSINESSES

🚗 Vehicle manufacture
⚙ Heavy enginnering
Bauxite mining
Coal mining
Gold mining
Electronics
Computers
Metallurgy
Brewing
Chemicals

Nhulunbuy
Weipa
Tennant Creek
Brisbane
Perth
Kalgoorlie
Sydney
Canberra
Adelaide
Melbourne
Hobart

0   200 km
0   200 miles   * significant multinational ownership

RESOURCES

- 151bn kwh (capacity 33.9m kw)
- 533,100 b/d (reserves 1,767,900,000 bbl)
- 165m sheep, 22.4m cattle, 2.7m pigs
- Coal, iron, bauxite, zinc, lead, copper, nickel, opals, gold

ELECTRICITY GENERATION

| Hydro 10% (14.8bn kwh) |
| Thermal 90% (139.8bn kwh) |
| Nuclear 0% |
| Other 0% |

0   20   40   60   80   100
% of total generation by type

Australia has one of the world's most important mining industries. It is a world leader in exports of coal, iron ore, gold, bauxite and copper. Minerals account for 9.4% of Australia's GDP and 53% of all its merchandise export earnings. Since the first discoveries of coal in 1798, mineral production in Australia has risen every year. In the decade to 1992 it doubled. Even further growth is expected in the late 1990s. Eighty major new mining projects are already planned, worth some $33 billion. Minerals' share of the total economy will continue to grow into the next century. The industry has benefited from Australia's location. Most increases in production go to the booming economies of South East Asia.

While minerals underpin much of Australia's wealth, there is growing concern at the environmental cost of extraction. The 'Mabo Judgement' of 1992 could also restrict the industry's operations. Many mining companies are concerned that Aborigines could lay claim to land holding valuable minerals. In 1993, Comalco threatened to halt expansion plans worth over $1 billion if Aboriginal claims over its bauxite leases were upheld. While the state found in Comalco's favour, a proper legal framework for the industry in the light of the 'Mabo Judgement' has yet to be established.

AUSTRALIA : LAND USE

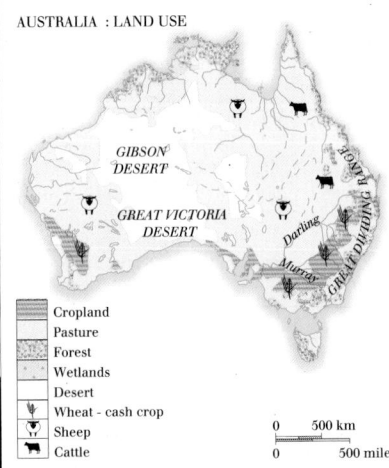

GIBSON DESERT

GREAT VICTORIA DESERT

GREAT DIVIDING RANGE

Darling

Murray

- Cropland
- Pasture
- Forest
- Wetlands
- Desert
- Wheat - cash crop
- Sheep
- Cattle

0   500 km
0   500 miles

Green Island, on the Great Barrier Reef Marine Park in the far north of Queensland. The reef stretches 2000 km down the coast.

ENVIRONMENT

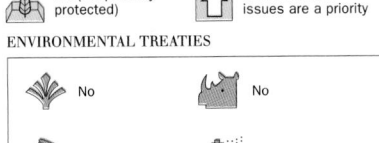

- 6% (2% partially protected)
- Environmental issues are a priority

ENVIRONMENTAL TREATIES

- No
- No
- Yes
- Yes

Australia's voters are among the most environmentally conscious in the industrialized world. Green issues are dominated by the Australian Conservation Foundation (ACF) and the more radical Greenpeace. The ACF has concentrated on developing links with industry in co-operative conservation programmes. Its endorsement of the ALP in 1993 helped to keep the party in power. The ACF has also been behind stricter laws to protect endangered species. Its major success, however, has been in persuading the government to adopt a nationwide policy making environmental concerns a key part of any planning decision.

MEDIA

 The press is free from government control

PUBLISHING AND BROADCAST MEDIA

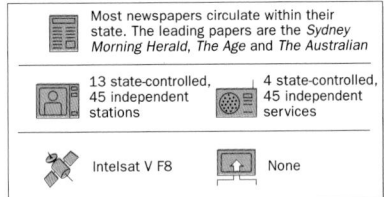

	Most newspapers circulate within their state. The leading papers are the *Sydney Morning Herald*, *The Age* and *The Australian*
13 state-controlled, 45 independent stations	4 state-controlled, 45 independent services
Intelsat V F8	None

The Australian press is firmly in the grip of press 'barons' such as Rupert Murdoch, Kerry Packer and Conrad Black. In 1992, the ALP decided to begin deregulating media industries by auctioning satellite pay-TV. Public-sector broadcasting remains dominated by the politically neutral Australian Broadcasting Corporation (ABC), which receives complaints about its coverage from both main parties.

CRIME

- 12,557 prisoners
- Significant increase in all types of crime

CRIME RATES

Murders	
2	per 100,000 population

Rapes	
15	per 100,000 population

Thefts	
3577	per 100,000 population

Crime in Australia is on the increase. In the 1980s, the number of recorded crimes rose by about 70%. Most crimes are committed in towns and cities.

Each state has its own police force and court system. Federal courts deal with disputes between states. The High Court and Family Court both have national jurisdiction. Since the 1970s, the legal system has been placing greater emphasis on the rights of the individual. The deaths of a number of Aborigines in custody have, however, led to calls for their greater protection.

Rising drug-related offences are a major concern. Australia is active in drug control throughout South East Asia.

EDUCATION

100%

0   Education spending as % GNP   25
     3.8%

THE EDUCATION SYSTEM

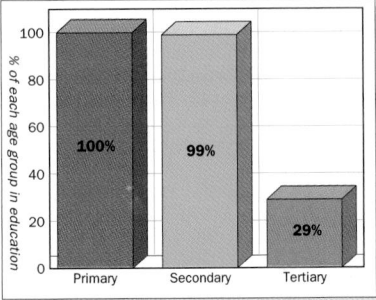

100
80
60
40
20
0

% of each age group in education

Primary: 100%
Secondary: 99%
Tertiary: 29%

Education in Australia is a state responsibility except in Canberra, where it is funded by the federal government. State education departments run the government schools and set the policies for educational practice and standards for all schools. Non-government schools, run by religious and other groups, exist in all states. Special provision is made for inaccessible outback areas. Schooling is compulsory from age 5–6 to age 15–16 in all states. Universities are independent of state control and are funded by the federal government. In 1990, education accounted for over 13% of government expenditure.

REGIONS
SYDNEY

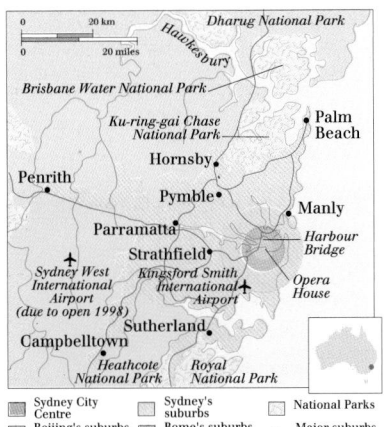

SYDNEY IS Australia's largest and most famous city. Its success in winning the bid to host the 2000 Olympics will further raise its global profile. Since 1932, it has had one of the world's most recognizable structures – the Harbour Bridge, which spans Sydney's stunning harbour. In 1973, its new Opera House also became an instantly recognizable landmark. Sydney has the world's largest suburban area, a conurbation so vast that the city is twice as large as Beijing and six times the size of Rome.

As Australia changes its focus towards Asia, so Sydney will gain in importance as one of the key cities of the Pacific Rim.

Legend:
- Sydney City Centre
- Beijing's suburbs (to scale)
- Sydney's suburbs
- Rome's suburbs (to scale)
- National Parks
- Major suburbs

QUEENSLAND

THE CLOSEST Australian state to the booming economies of South East Asia, Queensland's economy has been expanding. In recent years it has experienced a net migration from the southern states. Tourism has been a major beneficiary of closer links with Japan. Cairns in particular has seen rapid growth as the gateway to the Great Barrier Reef. Stretching for over 2000 km along the Queensland coast, it is the largest marine park in the world. Composed mostly of coral polyps, it is also the largest living organism on earth. Clear waters, sponges, algae and 1500 species of fish make the reef a superb snorkelling and diving location.

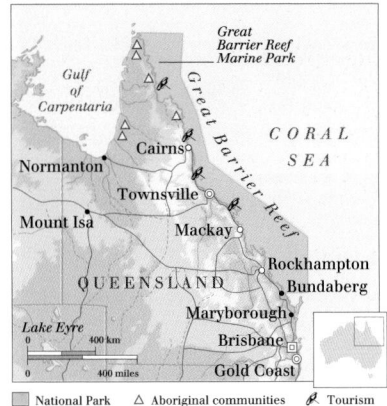

Legend:
- National Park
- △ Aboriginal communities
- Tourism

WESTERN AUSTRALIA

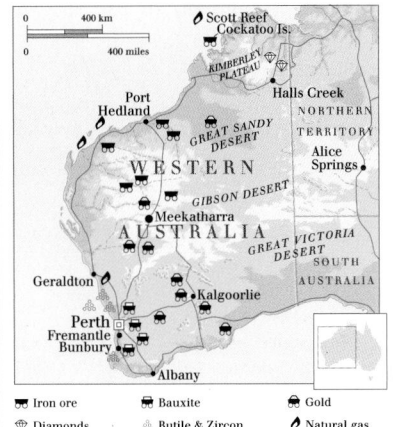

Legend:
- Iron ore
- Diamonds
- Bauxite
- Rutile & Zircon
- Gold
- Natural gas

OCCUPYING one third of the Australian continent, and with a greater land area than western Europe, Western Australia exports twice as much per capita as the national average. Its main economic strength is its mineral resources. The state produces 11% of the world's iron ore, 60% of Australia's gold, and is a major supplier of bauxite to the West. The northwest shelf includes one of the world's major deposits of natural gas and the largest known diamond deposits, accounting for one third of global production.

Perth is the state capital. Australia's most isolated city, it is 4000 km from the eastern seaboard; it is quicker and cheaper to fly to Hong Kong from Perth than to Sydney. With a population of just over one million, Perth is Australia's fourth largest city. The success of minerals industries has also made it the fastest-growing. The booming economy has brought high-rise steel and glass office blocks, which have transformed the Perth skyline.

HEALTH

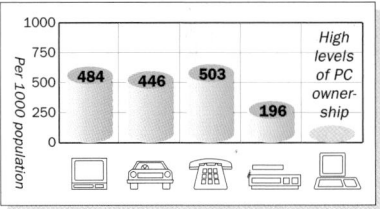

1 per 426 people | Heart, cerebrovascular and respiratory diseases, cancers

Health spending as % GNP — 0 to 25 — **2.9%**

Australia's extensive public health service has standards as high as any in the world. Hospital waiting lists are short. Outback areas are served by the efficient Royal Flying Doctor Service. While vigilance continues in the areas of hygiene, nutrition and general living standards, Australian health authorities have targeted Aboriginal health, heart disease, injury prevention, personal fitness and the prevention of cancers – particularly lung, cervical, breast and skin cancers – as contemporary priorities. Life expectancy is 79 years for women and 73 for men.

WEALTH

Industrial worker, 20,000–23,000 Australian dollars; industrial project engineer, 45,000–50,000 Australian dollars

CONSUMER GOODS OWNERSHIP

Per 1000 population: 484, 446, 503, 196 — High levels of PC ownership

Australians enjoy reasonable equality of wealth. A large proportion of families own two cars and have relatively high disposable incomes. A benign climate helps most to live comfortably. However, high unemployment during the 1990s' recession has widened the gap between rich and poor, and Australia has slipped down the world standard of living list in recent years. The incidence of homelessness, critical poverty and child neglect due to poverty have increased slightly.

WORLD RANKING

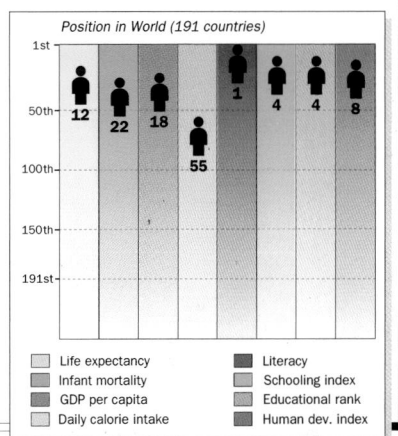

Position in World (191 countries): 12, 22, 18, 55, 1, 4, 4, 8

Legend:
- Life expectancy
- Infant mortality
- GDP per capita
- Daily calorie intake
- Literacy
- Schooling index
- Educational rank
- Human dev. index

A

AUSTRIA

OFFICIAL NAME: Republic of Austria **CAPITAL:** Vienna
POPULATION: 7.8 million **CURRENCY:** Austrian schilling **OFFICIAL LANGUAGE:** German

L YING IN THE HEART of Europe, Austria is dominated by the European Alps in the west of the country, while fertile plains make up its eastern half. Created in 1920, after the collapse of the Habsburg empire, Austria was absorbed into Hitler's Germany in 1938. It gained independence again in 1955 after the departure of the last Soviet troops from the Allied Occupation Force. Austria's economy encompasses successful high-tech sectors, a tourist industry which attracts the wealthier end of the market and a strong agricultural base. In 1994, Austria applied to join the EU.

CLIMATE

WEATHER CHART

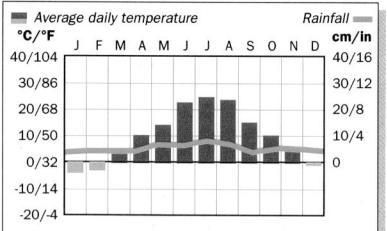

Austria has a temperate continental climate. Alpine areas experience colder temperatures and higher precipitation.

COMMUNICATIONS

 Wien–Schwechat, Vienna
5.5m passengers

 26 ships
208,500 dwt

THE TRANSPORT NETWORK

107,651 km (66,894 miles)	1447 km (899 miles)
5624 km (3495 miles)	446 km (277 miles)

Austria's central geographical position has encouraged the development of a sophisticated communications and transport network.

The Tirol is situated in the heart of Austria's Alps. It is the most mountainous region of all and attracts both winter and summer visitors.

AUSTRIA

Total Area : 83 850 sq. km (32 375 sq. miles)

LAND HEIGHT
- 3000m/9843ft
- 2000m/6562ft
- 1000m/3281ft
- 500m/1640ft
- 200m/656ft
- Sea Level

POPULATION
- ⊡ over 1 000 000
- ◉ over 500 000
- ◎ over 100 000
- ○ over 50 000
- ● over 10 000

TOURISM

 19.1m visitors   Up 1% in 1991

MAIN OVERSEAS ARRIVALS

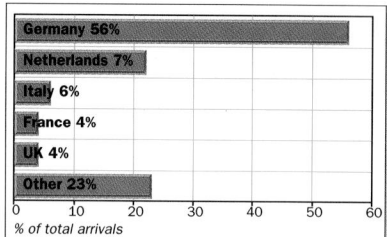

Germany 56%
Netherlands 7%
Italy 6%
France 4%
UK 4%
Other 23%

% of total arrivals

The earnings of the Austrian tourist industry amount to more than 14% of GDP. The well-developed Alpine skiing and winter sports resorts account for almost one third of the country's total tourist earnings. Many resorts, such as St Anton and Kitzbühel, cater for the top end of the market. In the summer season, which peaks in July and August, tourists visit the scenic Tirol and the lakes around Bad Ischl. Vienna and Salzburg, the country's second city, are major attractions. The latter is internationally famous for its summer music festival and as the birthplace of Mozart.

PEOPLE

 German, Croatian, Slovene   94 people per km²

THE URBAN/RURAL POPULATION SPLIT

58%   42%

RELIGION PERSUASION

Protestant 6%
Other 9%
Roman Catholic 85%

ETHNIC MAKEUP

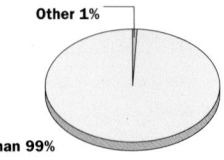

Other 1%
German 99%

Austrian society is homogeneous. Almost 99% of Austrians are German speakers. However, Austrians like to consider themselves ethnically distinct from Germans. Minorities are few; there are a small number of ethnic Slovenes, Croats and Hungarians in the south and east. These minorities have been supplemented by large numbers of immigrants from eastern Europe and refugees from the conflict in former Yugoslavia. The result has been a perceptible increase in ethnic tension, particularly as the downturn in the economy has led some Austrians to claim that migrants are taking jobs from the local population.

The nuclear family is the norm in Austria. It is common for both parents to work. While sexual equality is enshrined in the constitution, in practice society is still strongly patriarchal. Compared to the rest of Europe, few women enter politics.

Young Austrians tend to live in their parental home until they marry. In part, this reflects the long time taken to complete university degrees, and the fact that students do not receive maintenance grants. Austrians marry at a younger age than the European average. Nominally a Catholic country, Austria has a less conservative society than some German states.

POPULATION AGE BREAKDOWN

%	■ 0–14		15–64		□ 65+
12%	14.1%	15.4%	15%	15.7%
65.9%	61.6%	64.2%	67.7%	67.6%
22.1%	24.3%	20.4%	17.3%	16.7%
1960	1970	1980	1990	2000

POLITICS

 1994   President Thomas Klestil

THE STATE OF THE PARTIES

National Council 183 members

44%   33%   18% 5%
SPÖ   ÖVP   FPÖ GAL

SPÖ Social Democratic Party of Austria **ÖVP** = Austrian People's Party **FPÖ** = Freedom Party of Austria **GAL** = Green Alternative List

Federal Council 64 members

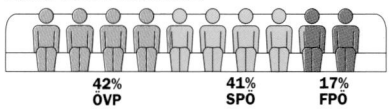

42%   41%   17%
ÖVP   SPÖ   FPÖ

Austria is a federal, multiparty democracy. The chancellor (premier) holds real executive power.

MAIN POLITICAL ISSUES

Entry into the EU

Austria's population remains divided over its entry into the EU. Although Austrians are likely to reap benefits, such as lower food prices and greater consumer choice, there are fears that joining the EU may result in a loss of national identity and independence. The agricultural and environmentalist lobbies have expressed doubts about joining – likely reforms to the EU agricultural policy could endanger the livelihood of up to half of Austria's farmers. Environmentalists fear the increase in heavy goods lorries and transit traffic that will accompany membership. Austrians are also concerned that joining the union will threaten their traditional neutral stance.

Economic decline

The economy has become a major issue in recent years. After stability in the 1970s and 1980s, industry has been exposed to recession in the neighbouring countries of eastern Europe and Germany. As a result, export orders have fallen and unemployment has increased. In particular, the traditional methods of protectionism and subsidies have failed to work and this has been followed by growing social and political tension.

PROFILE

A coalition headed by the SPÖ, with the ÖVP as the junior partner, has governed Austria since the 1950s. The left-of-centre consensus is beginning to show signs of strain as the ÖVP is losing many of its working-class voters to the right-wing FPÖ. The main reason is the decline in the economy and the perception that immigrant labour is taking jobs from Austrians. The FPÖ's anti-EU stance has also attracted support. Local government is run by the nine provincial assemblies. Vienna is dominated by the SPÖ. The FPÖ has control of the province of Carinthia.

Dr Thomas Klestil, *the ÖVP candidate, became Austria's president in 1992.*

Franz Vranitzky. *Elected chancellor in 1990, he leads an SPÖ-ÖVP coalition.*

WORLD AFFAIRS

 EFTA   CE   OECD   HG   NAM

While Austria wants to be seen as independent of German influence, it cannot avoid the fact that Germany is its main trading partner and the most powerful state in the region. Relations with Germany are therefore Austria's major concern. However, there is a conscious policy to create a diplomatic distance from Berlin. Austria is keen to maintain its direct line to Washington. The fact that Austria supplies much of the US army's small arms helps to cement this relationship.

Keeping a distance from Germany will probably mean that once Austria has joined the EU it will align itself with the Scandinavian countries. Austria will also support the early entry to the EU of east European states. Austria has been exploiting its geo-political position to increase its influence in the region, and remains an important trading partner of many ex-COMECON states. Austria's constitution bans its forces from serving abroad. It has, however, been a critic of the failure by the UN and EU to stop the conflict in former Yugoslavia.

AID

 $548m (donations)   Small reduction in 1993

Austria is a major donor of aid to eastern Europe. Much aid is aimed at stemming a large influx of economic refugees from the former communist states. Aid donations to former Yugoslavia are likely to increase once peace is achieved. Austria was a major exporter to the region and will be seeking a key role in reconstruction.

A

CHRONOLOGY

Austria came under the control of the Habsburgs in 1273. In 1867, the Dual Monarchy of Austria-Hungary was formed under Habsburg rule. Defeat in the First World War led to the abdication of the last Habsburg emperor, Charles, in 1918.

- ❑ **1920** Republic of Austria formed after break-up of Habsburg Empire.
- ❑ **1934** Chancellor Dollfuss dismisses parliament and starts imprisoning Social Democrats, Communists and National Socialist Party (NAZI) members. NAZIs attempt coup.
- ❑ **1938** The Anschluss – Austria forcibly incorporated into Germany.
- ❑ **1945** End of German rule. Austria occupied by Russian, British, US and French forces. Provisional government under Karl Renner, veteran of First World War peace negotiations. Elections result in People's Party (ÖVP) and Social Democratic Party (SPÖ) coalition. Remains in power for most of the post-war period.
- ❑ **1950** Attempted coup by Communist Party fails. Marshall aid helps economic recovery. USSR resists calls from France, USA and UK for independent Austria.
- ❑ **1955** Soviet troops finally withdrawn. USSR recognizes Austria as a sovereign state.
- ❑ **1971** First single-party government formed by SPÖ under Federal Chancellor Bruno Kreisky. Although a minority administration, the ÖVP's political strength grows throughout the 1970s.
- ❑ **1983** Socialists regain power by forming a government with the Freedom Party (FPÖ).
- ❑ **1986** Dr Kurt Waldheim, former UN secretary-general, elected president, despite war crimes allegations. Franz Vranitsky, Federal Chancellor. Nationalist Jörg Haider succeeds more moderate Norbert Steger as FPÖ leader. SPÖ pulls out of government due to FPÖ's swing to right. Elections produce stalemate. Return to 'grand coalition' between SPÖ and ÖVP.
- ❑ **1990** ÖVP loses 17 seats in parliamentary elections.
- ❑ **1992** Thomas Klestil (ÖVP) elected president, replacing controversial Kurt Waldheim. Elections confirm some traditional ÖVP supporters defecting to FPÖ.
- ❑ **1993** FPÖ splits into two. Breakaway Liberal Forum takes over 5 FPÖ seats. Liberal Forum voices opposition to FPÖ's nationalism.

DEFENCE

 $1.7bn

⬆ Up 1% in 1992

```
0          Defence spending as % GDP          40
 1%
```

Under the terms of the 1955 State Treaty, which granted Austria its full independence, the country has taken a neutral stance. Despite the small size of its own defence forces, Austria's arms industry is thriving and provides most of the hardware needed to maintain the army. It also exports arms to the USA.

AUSTRIAN ARMED FORCES

🛡	159 main battle tanks (159 M–60A3)	46,000 personnel
🚢	None	
✈	54 combat aircraft (30 SAAB 105 Oe/ 24 J–350e)	6000 personnel
🚀	None	

ECONOMICS

 $157.5bn

 11.91 Austrian schillings

SCORE CARD

- ❑ WORLD GNP RANKING...........................23rd
- ❑ GNP PER CAPITA $20,192
- ❑ BALANCE OF PAYMENTS....................$–703m
- ❑ INFLATION 4.1%
- ❑ UNEMPLOYMENT................................3.5%

EXPORTS

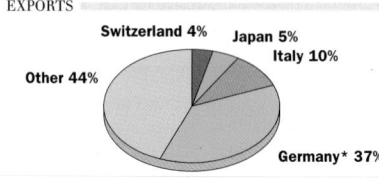

Switzerland 4% Japan 5% Italy 10% Other 44% Germany* 37%

IMPORTS

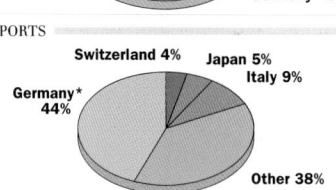

Switzerland 4% Japan 5% Italy 9% Germany* 44% Other 38%

STRENGTHS

Large manufacturing base. Strong chemical and petrochemical industries. Electrical engineering sector, textiles and wood processing industries. Highly-skilled labour force. Tourism an important foreign currency earner.

WEAKNESSES

Lacks natural resources. Reliant on imported raw materials, particularly oil and gas. High levels of subsidies to state-owned industry. Weak and over-regulated banking system.

PROFILE

Austria's industrial and high-tech sector is highly developed and contributes around 25% to GDP. Some services, notably tourism, are highly sophisticated and profitable. However, the Austrian economy suffers from a weak banking sector. This is due in part to the high level of state subsidies to industry, which has in turn meant that there has been little demand for flexible private finance.

ECONOMIC PERFORMANCE INDICATOR

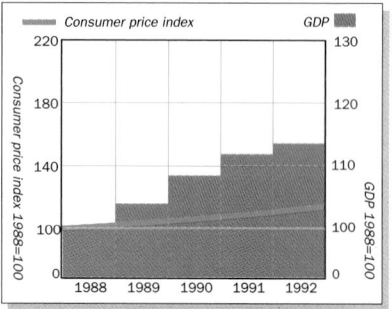

Consumer price index ——— GDP ▓

The banking system is likely to suffer the stiffest competition when Austria joins the EU. Austrian banks have begun to merge in preparation for the challenge. There will, however, be benefits from EU membership. Prices for many products, particularly food and books, will fall. The Austrian labour market will see an influx of immigrant labour more willing to accept flexible working arrangements and lower wages. There will probably be an increase in foreign investment, as more multinationals locate their headquarters for east European operations in Austria.

AUSTRIA : MAJOR BUSINESSES

❄	Textiles
🜍	Chemicals
△	Metallurgy
🗲	Electronics
⬙	Iron & steel
✐	Pharmaceuticals
❀	Light engineering
✿	Heavy engineering

0   100 km
0   100 miles

RESOURCES

50bn kwh (capacity 16.8m kw)

24,800 b/d (reserves 93,200,000 bbl)

13.1m chickens, 3.7m pigs, 2.6m cattle

Iron, coal, magnesite, zinc, lead

ELECTRICITY GENERATION

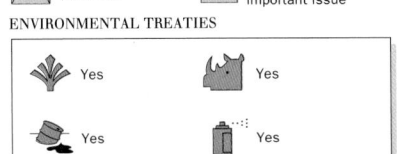

Hydro 64% (34.5bn kwh)
Thermal 36% (17.9bn kwh)
Nuclear 0%
Other 0%

% of total generation by type

Austria has few resources. It lacks significant oil, coal and gas deposits and has to import over $2.7 billion-worth of energy every year. Russia remains one of Austria's main energy suppliers. Gas is provided via pipelines running through the Czech and Slovak republics. Oil is imported up the Danube. Russia and Germany are the major suppliers of iron ore and raw steel for Austria's industry.

ENVIRONMENT

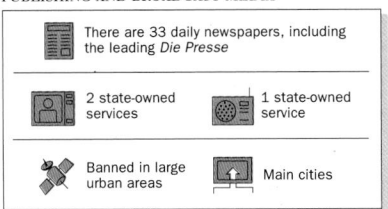

25% partially protected

Environment is an increasingly important issue

ENVIRONMENTAL TREATIES

Yes

Yes

Yes

Yes

Environmental awareness is high. Domestic waste has to be separated for recycling; heavy fines exist for those who fail to observe the regulations. Car emissions are increasingly controlled. New cars in Austria have catalytic converters and most drivers use lead-free petrol. The safety of nuclear reactors in Slovakia is a major concern.

MEDIA

 Media is, for the most part, independent of the government. It is relatively conservative

PUBLISHING AND BROADCAST MEDIA

There are 33 daily newspapers, including the leading *Die Presse*

2 state-owned services

1 state-owned service

Banned in large urban areas

Main cities

TV and radio are more tightly controlled than the press. They are controlled by *Österreichischer Rundfunk* (ORF), under a politically-appointed general director. Cable TV is carefully licensed by ORF, to prevent it taking viewers away from existing stations. Satellite dishes are banned in main cities. Some unlicensed radio stations broadcast from neighbouring states.

AUSTRIA : LAND USE

Cropland
Pasture
Forest
High mountain regions
Pigs
Cattle
Wheat

0   100 km
0   100 miles

CRIME

5862 prisoners

Up 8% in 1990

CRIME RATES

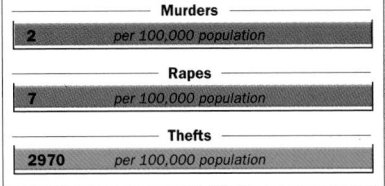

Murders	
2	per 100,000 population

Rapes	
7	per 100,000 population

Thefts	
2970	per 100,000 population

Austria's crime rate is below Europe's average. However, the number of burglaries is rising. The arrival of the Russian mafia in Vienna has led to an increase in money laundering.

EDUCATION

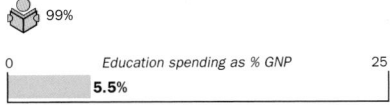

99%

0   *Education spending as % GNP*   25

5.5%

THE EDUCATION SYSTEM

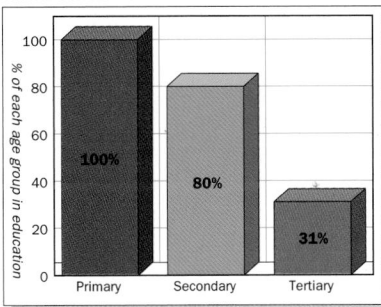

% of each age group in education

Primary 100%
Secondary 80%
Tertiary 31%

Children are streamed into two types of school according to their ability. Those in a *Gymnasium* (11–18) are entitled to enter university. However, children in a *Hauptschule* (11–15) are not. The universities are oversubscribed, with students taking six years or more to finish their basic degrees.

HEALTH

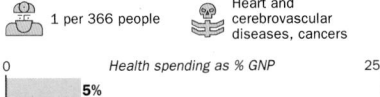

1 per 366 people

Heart and cerebrovascular diseases, cancers

0   *Health spending as % GNP*   25

5%

Austria has relatively high levels of spending on health. The ability of the state to continue to maintain the current level of service is being questioned. Many patients choose to use the expanding private health sector to avoid waiting lists for operations.

WEALTH

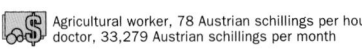

Agricultural worker, 78 Austrian schillings per hour; doctor, 33,279 Austrian schillings per month

CONSUMER GOODS OWNERSHIP

Per 1000 population

475   387   413   181

High levels of PC ownership

Despite having had a centrist government for most of the last four decades, Austria has retained its traditional social divisions. Inherited wealth is still respected above earned wealth, and social mobility is rather less than in neighbouring Germany. Austrians have the highest savings rate of any country in the OECD. Limited amounts are invested in stocks and shares, government bonds or property. Austria's financial markets are restrictive. Strict rules govern the amount of speculation permitted on the Vienna stock exchange and also limit gains and losses to 5% of the amount invested. Government bonds offer low rates of interest and the property market is weak. Viennese tend to rent rather than buy their apartments. The poorest group are the refugees from the conflict in the former Yugoslavia.

WORLD RANKING

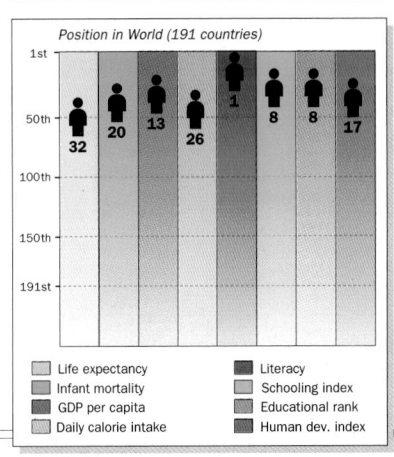

Position in World (191 countries)

1st
50th
100th
150th
191st

32   20   13   26   1   8   8   17

Life expectancy
Infant mortality
GDP per capita
Daily calorie intake
Literacy
Schooling index
Educational rank
Human dev. index

A

AZERBAIJAN

OFFICIAL NAME: Republic of Azerbaijan **CAPITAL:** Baku
POPULATION: 7.3 million **CURRENCY:** Manat **OFFICIAL LANGUAGE:** Azerbaijani

1991

SITUATED ON THE WESTERN COAST of the Caspian Sea, Azerbaijan was the first Soviet republic to declare independence, in 1991. The issue of the disputed enclave of Nagorno Karabakh, which Armenia seeks to annex, led to full-scale war in 1993 and has since dominated all other concerns in Azeri life. The war and an estimated 500,000 refugees have added to the problems of Azerbaijan's troubled economy. Its oil wealth, however, gives it long-term potential.

Landscape typical of the Lesser Caucasus mountains near Qazax in the extreme northwest of Azerbaijan.

CLIMATE

WEATHER CHART

Bitterly cold Azeri winters have become a life-or-death issue for the thousands of war refugees.

COMMUNICATIONS

 Baku   Has no fleet

THE TRANSPORT NETWORK

30,400 km (18,890 miles)		None
2040 km (1268 miles)		None

Improving links with Iran and Turkey to the south, rather than with Moscow, is the focus of transport spending.

TOURISM

 The only visitors are on business   No change from year to year

MAIN OVERSEAS ARRIVALS

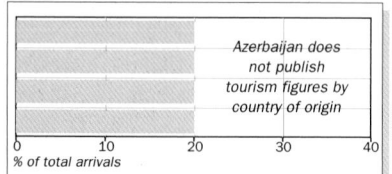

Azerbaijan does not publish tourism figures by country of origin

% of total arrivals

Because of the war over Nagorno Karabakh, and strong anti-Western feelings (Azerbaijan interprets the West as taking the Armenian side in the conflict), there is only a tiny trickle of visitors, most of them on business.

PEOPLE

Azerbaijani, Russian   82 people per km²

THE URBAN/RURAL POPULATION SPLIT

53%   47%

ETHNIC MAKEUP

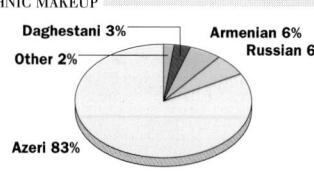

Daghestani 3%
Other 2%
Armenian 6%
Russian 6%
Azeri 83%

At the last census, held in 1989, Azeris made up 83% of the population. Today the proportion is even greater – thousands of Armenians, Jews and Russians have left as a result of rising nationalism amongst Azeris. Racial hostility against those that remain is increasing. Women, once prominent within the ruling party, have lost their position in political life, and their general status is also declining. The once effective social security system has collapsed.

POLITICS

Uncertain   President Heydar Aliev

THE STATE OF THE PARTIES

National Assembly 360 members

80% CPA   20% Other

CPA = Communist Party of Azerbaijan **Other** = Popular Front of Azerbaijan (PFA), National Independence Party, Musvat Party, Dozkurt Party

The 1988 decision by Nagorno Karabakh's Armenian-dominated council to unite the enclave with the Armenian republic brought to a head decades of ethnic tension between Armenians and Azeris. Armenian separatists were soon engaged in an escalating war in which thousands were killed and hundreds of thousands made homeless. In 1993, Armenian troops invaded to aid the separatists; over 20% of Azerbaijan's territory is now under Armenian control.

AZERBAIJAN

Total Area : 86 600 sq. km (33 436 sq. miles)

POPULATION

⊡ over 1 000 000
◉ over 100 000
○ over 50 000
● over 10 000
• under 10 000

LAND HEIGHT

4000m/13 124ft
3000m/9843ft
2000m/6562ft
1000m/3281ft
500m/1640ft
200m/656ft
Sea Level

A

WORLD AFFAIRS

Russia's withdrawal of troops in 1993 ended the chances of a CIS-brokered settlement of the war with Armenia. Armenia, ignoring threats from Iran (which has an Azeri minority of 15 million), has since gained the upper hand. Azeri forces have received some help from Afghan *mujahideen*.

AID

 Mostly military. No figures published   Military aid is rising

Azerbaijan has been receiving covert military aid from Iran and Turkey, both vying for influence in Baku.

DEFENCE

 $1.6bn   Rising sharply as the conflict with Armenia has escalated

The 30,000-strong Azeri army has performed badly in the war with Armenia. Russia withdrew the last of its 62,000 troops in 1993.

ECONOMICS

 $12.1bn   Manat. Not convertible

SCORE CARD

❏ WORLD GNP RANKING	70th
❏ GNP PER CAPITA	$1660
❏ BALANCE OF PAYMENTS	$499m
❏ INFLATION	1350% (est)
❏ UNEMPLOYMENT	No figures, but well over 50%

STRENGTHS
Oil and natural gas have considerable potential; a $7 billion oil deal has now been struck. The wine industry is efficient by regional standards.

WEAKNESSES
Years of antiquated practices in the oil industry are reflected in poor production efficiency. The war in Nagorno Karabakh remains an enormous drain on state resources.

EXPORTS

IMPORTS

RESOURCES

 Azerbaijan does not publish energy statistics   240,000 b/d (reserves 1,300,000,000 bbl)

 5.3m sheep and goats, 1.9m cattle   Iron, bauxite, copper, lead, zinc, limestone, salt, oil, gas

The USSR did little to modernize Azerbaijan's oil fields, preferring to concentrate on Siberia; Azeri oil production fell from 8% of the USSR's total in 1965 to 0.6% by 1988. Major Western investment is now needed.

ENVIRONMENT

 2.1%   Environmental issues are not yet receiving state attention

Under the Soviet regime there was relatively unchecked oil pollution into the Caspian Sea and an overuse of pesticides in agriculture. Azeris are now far more conscious of the need to protect their environment.

MEDIA

 No press comment critical of the government is tolerated

PUBLISHING AND BROADCAST MEDIA

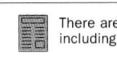 There are 151 newspapers published, including 133 in Azerbaijani

 1 state-controlled service   1 state-controlled service

The return of the Communists has ended the brief period of press freedom. All comment is now vetted.

CRIME

 Azerbaijan does not publish prison figures   Still relatively low, but rising

The judicial system returned to political control in 1993. Levels of crime outside Nagorno Karabakh are relatively low. Within the enclave, however, there are frequent reports of human rights abuses by members of the armed forces.

EDUCATION

 Over 90%

The return of the Communists has ended the Democrats' Western-influenced education policy, particularly in the teaching of history, economics and politics. Baku, the main university, has an international reputation for Oriental studies.

HEALTH

 1 per 257 people   Heart, cerebrovascular and respiratory diseases, cancers

The already basic health system in Azerbaijan effectively collapsed as a result of shortages caused by the war.

CHRONOLOGY

Under consecutive Persian, Ottoman and Russian influence, Azerbaijan, one of the world's major oil producers in 1900, was established as an independent state in 1917.

- ❏ **1920** Soviet Red Army invades. Soviet republic established.
- ❏ **1922** Incorporated in Transcaucasian Soviet Federative Socialist Republic (TSFSR).
- ❏ **1930** Forced collectivization of agriculture. Peasant uprisings.
- ❏ **1936** TSFSR disbanded. Azerbaijan a full union republic (ASSR).
- ❏ **1945** Failed attempt to annex Azeri region of Iran.
- ❏ **1985** President Gorbachev makes tackling corruption in CPA a priority.
- ❏ **1988** Nagorno Karabakh council requests unification with Armenia. Outbreaks of ethnic violence.
- ❏ **1990** Nagorno Karabakh tries to secede. Riots in Baku. PFA takes control. Soviet troops move in.
- ❏ **1991** Independence from Moscow.
- ❏ **1993** Internal ethnic conflict over enclave of Nagorno Karabakh escalates into war with Armenia.

WEALTH

 A majority of Azeris live close to the breadline

CONSUMER GOODS OWNERSHIP

The old Communist Party executives, once more in control of the state economy, are the wealthiest group.

WORLD RANKING

BAHAMAS

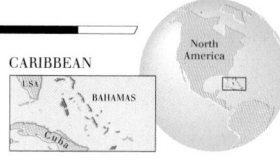

CARIBBEAN

OFFICIAL NAME: The Commonwealth of the Bahamas   **CAPITAL:** Nassau
POPULATION: 300,000   **CURRENCY:** Bahamian dollar   **OFFICIAL LANGUAGE:** English

L OCATED OFF THE FLORIDA COAST in the western Atlantic, the Bahamas comprises an archipelago of some 700 islands and 2400 cays, of which 30 are inhabited. One of the first trans-Atlantic tourist destinations, the Bahamas today is also a major offshore financial centre. It has one of the world's largest open-registry fleets, but only 0.2% of the total tonnage is owned by Bahamian nationals.

CLIMATE

WEATHER CHART

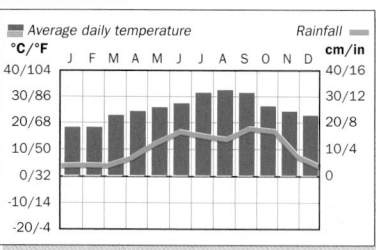

Average daily temperature   *Rainfall*

The whole of the Bahamas chain has a typically subtropical climate with consistently mild winters. Hurricanes may occur from July to December.

COMMUNICATIONS

Freeport International
1.23m passengers

914 ships
32.51m dwt

THE TRANSPORT NETWORK

2400 km
(1491 miles)

None

None

None

Getting around 700 islands spread over 260,000 square km is a major problem. There are plans to increase the number of ferry and seaplane services.

TOURISM

1.56m visitors

Up 1% in 1990

MAIN OVERSEAS ARRIVALS

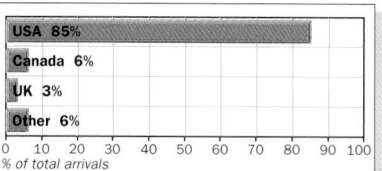

USA 85%	
Canada 6%	
UK 3%	
Other 6%	

0   10   20   30   40   50   60   70   80   90   100
% of total arrivals

The casinos and beaches are major attractions. Charters from the USA, which arrive in the afternoon, allowing visitors to play the casinos and return home the next morning, are increasingly popular. The Bahamas is also one of the Caribbean's major cruise-ship centres.

PEOPLE

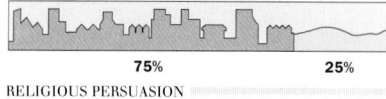

English, English Creole, French Creole

18 people per km²

THE URBAN/RURAL POPULATION SPLIT

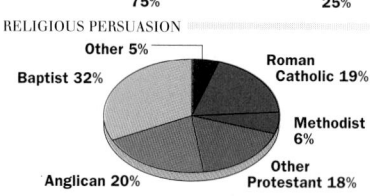

75%   25%

RELIGIOUS PERSUASION

Other 5%
Roman Catholic 19%
Baptist 32%
Methodist 6%
Other Protestant 18%
Anglican 20%

Africans first came to the Bahamas as slaves in the 16th century; their descendants now constitute most of the population. The nuclear family is the norm, although absentee fathers are fairly common, especially in outlying fishing communities. More women are going into the professions.

POLITICS

1997

HM Queen Elizabeth II

THE STATE OF THE PARTIES

House of Assembly 49 members

67%
FNM

33%
PLP

FNM = Free National Movement   **PLP** = Progressive Liberal Party

Senate 16 members

9 members chosen by the prime minister, 4 by the leader of the opposition and 3 by the prime minister after consultation with the leader of the opposition

The 1992 election defeat of Lynden Pindling, the result of increasing numbers of allegations of narcotics corruption against senior government members, ended a period of 25 years of continuous rule by his PLP. Pindling was instrumental in steering the Bahamas to independence, ending the domination of the white elite 'Bay Street Boys' in Bahamian politics and bringing blacks into the political process for the first time. The new administration, under Hubert Ingraham, has concentrated on tightening up ministerial accountability in government. However, enquiries into the Pindling administration will probably take several years to complete.

Map

Straits of Florida
ATLANTIC
West End
Freeport   Grand Bahama I.
Little Abaco
Abaco I.
Marsh Harbour
Hope Town
Northwest Providence Channel
Great Abaco
Bimini Is
Berry Is
Northeast Providence Channel
Spanish Wells
Current   Governor's
Nicholls Town
NASSAU
New Providence
Eleuthera I.
Rock Sound
Andros Town
Andros I.
Tongue of the Ocean
Exuma Cays
Cat I.
The Bight
San Salvador
George Town
Great Exuma I.
Cockburn Town
Rum Cay
Exuma Sound
Double Headed Shot Cays
Cay Sal
Anguilla Cays
Long I.
Clarence Town
Samana Cay
Ragged Island Range
Crooked Island Passage
Crooked I.
Plana Cays
Acklins I.
Mayaguana Passage
Mayaguana
The Carlton
Caicos Passage
Little Inagua
Great Inagua
Matthew Town   Lake Rosa

BAHAMAS

Total Area: 13 880 sq. km (5359 sq. miles)

POPULATION   LAND HEIGHT

 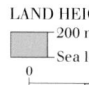

over 100 000
over 10 000
under 10 000

200 m/656ft
Sea level

0   100 km
0   100 miles

B

WORLD AFFAIRS

Dealing with Haitian refugees and repairing relations with the USA, following the narcotics scandals of the 1980s, in which several government ministers were allegedly implicated, are the main issues.

AID

 $3m (receipts)   No change in 1991

One of the healthiest economies in the Caribbean, the Bahamas receives negligible aid. The USA is the principal donor, mainly providing soft loans.

DEFENCE

 $66.96m (including police spending)   Up 5% in 1992

The UK is the main trainer of and supplier for the 900-strong defence force and coastguard. Intercepting narcotics smugglers and Haitian refugees are the main activities.

ECONOMICS

 $3bn   1.00 Bahamian dollars

SCORE CARD

❏ WORLD GNP RANKING	124th
❏ GNP PER CAPITA	$10,000
❏ BALANCE OF PAYMENTS	$–113m
❏ INFLATION	6.1%
❏ UNEMPLOYMENT	11.7%

STRENGTHS
A major international financial services sector, including banking and insurance, which has benefited from political uncertainty in Hong Kong. Tourism and ship registration are also major businesses.

WEAKNESSES
Growing competition in financial services from the Cayman Islands and Bermuda.

EXPORTS

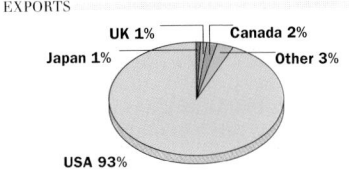
UK 1% Canada 2% Japan 1% Other 3% USA 93%

IMPORTS

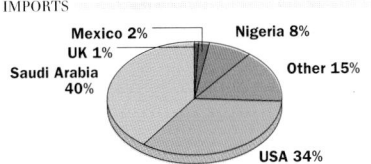
Mexico 2% Nigeria 8% UK 1% Saudi Arabia 40% Other 15% USA 34%

Archetypal island paradise. *Its natural beauty belies the fact that six tourists per inhabitant visit the Bahamas every year.*

RESOURCES

 950m kwh (capacity 400,000 kw)   Not an oil producer and has no refineries

 1m chickens, 40,000 sheep, 20,000 pigs   Salt, aragonite

The Bahamas has no strategic resources and all its energy requirements have to be imported.

ENVIRONMENT

 9%   Plans to increase numbers of protected sites

As in other Caribbean states, hotel overdevelopment is a major cause for concern. Environmental groups have also pointed out the potential for accidents posed by the Bahamas' enormous oil storage depots.

MEDIA

 No restrictions on political reporting

PUBLISHING AND BROADCAST MEDIA

There are 3 daily newspapers, the *Nassau Guardian*, the *Tribune* and the *Freeport News*

1 limited state-owned service   1 state-owned service

The state-owned TV channel faces very stiff competition from Florida-based US broadcasters.

CRIME

 3789 prisoners   Up 8% in 1990

The Bahamas was a key transshipment point for US-bound Colombian cocaine during the 1980s. Today, drugs-related crimes such as muggings in tourist resorts and contract killings by competing gangs are increasing.

EDUCATION

 95%

Education follows the standard pattern of other Caribbean states, with a British 11-plus selective system. Students go on to the University of the West Indies.

CHRONOLOGY

Once an English pirate base, the Bahamas, which gained its first parliament in 1729, became a formal British colony in 1783.

❏ **1920–1933** US prohibition laws turn the Bahamas into a prosperous bootlegging centre.
❏ **1959** Introduction of male suffrage.
❏ **1962** Women gain the vote.
❏ **1973** Independence.
❏ **1976** The Bahamas becomes flag of convenience for merchant fleets.
❏ **1983** Narcotics smuggling scandals involving the Bahamian government.

HEALTH

 1 per 809 people   Heart diseases, cancers, nutritional disorders, accidents

The Bahamian health service combines state and private systems. Access to care in the outlying islands is difficult, relying on unscheduled inter-island or privately-owned boats.

WEALTH

 Hotel cook, 13,000 Bahamian dollars per year; professional nurse, 15,000-27,500 Bahamian dollars per year

CONSUMER GOODS OWNERSHIP

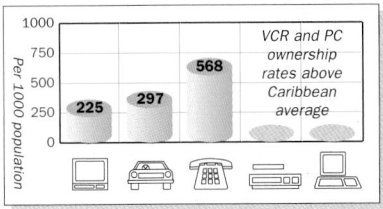
225 297 568 VCR and PC ownership rates above Caribbean average

There are marked wealth disparities between urban professionals working in the financial sector and poor fishermen from the outlying islands. Haitian refugees, who have no legal status, are the poorest group.

WORLD RANKING

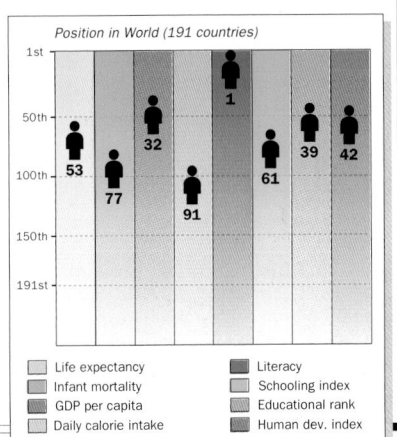
Position in World (191 countries)
53 77 32 1 91 61 39 42
Life expectancy, Infant mortality, GDP per capita, Daily calorie intake, Literacy, Schooling index, Educational rank, Human dev. index

BAHRAIN

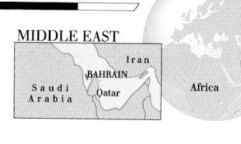

OFFICIAL NAME: State of Bahrain   **CAPITAL:** Manama
POPULATION: 500,000 · **CURRENCY:** Bahrain dinar   **OFFICIAL LANGUAGE:** Arabic

BAHRAIN IS AN ARCHIPELAGO of 33 islands between the Qatar peninsula and the Saudi Arabian mainland. Only three of the islands are inhabited. Bahrain Island is connected to Saudi Arabia's eastern province by a road causeway opened in 1986. Bahrain was the first Gulf emirate to export oil; its reserves are now almost depleted. Services such as offshore banking, insurance and tourism are major employment sectors for skilled Bahrainis.

CLIMATE

WEATHER CHART

Temperatures soar to 40ºC from June to September. Between December and March the weather is pleasantly warm.

COMMUNICATIONS

 Bahrain International, Muharraq
1.87m passengers

 15 ships
158,700 dwt

THE TRANSPORT NETWORK

2614 km (1624 miles)		None
None		None

Saudi Arabia paid for the 25-km-long causeway linking it with Bahrain; the four-lane road was completed in 1986.

TOURISM

 1.4m visitors

 Tourist levels have risen since 1991

MAIN OVERSEAS ARRIVALS

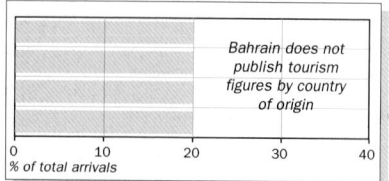

Bahrain does not publish tourism figures by country of origin

% of total arrivals

Bahrain's liberal lifestyle is reflected in Manama's bars and nightlife. Since the causeway opened in 1986, there has been a boom in weekend tourists from Saudi Arabia and other Gulf states. Bahrain is a business convention centre.

PEOPLE

 Arabic

723 people per km²

THE URBAN/RURAL POPULATION SPLIT

83%   17%

ETHNIC MAKEUP

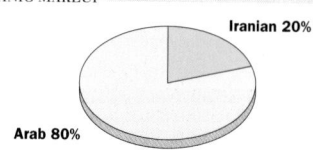

Iranian 20%

Arab 80%

The key division in Bahrain is between Sunni and Shi'a Muslims, 30% and 70% of the population respectively. The ruling class is Sunni and they hold the best jobs in business and the bureaucracy. Shi'a Muslims tend to do menial work and have a lower standard of living. Tension between the two groups can spill over into violence, particularly during religious festivals.

Bahrain has a smaller expatriate population than many other Arab countries. The ruling Al-Khalifa family has responded to declining oil reserves by diversifying the economy to provide service industry jobs for Bahrainis.

Bahrain is the most liberal of the Gulf states. Women have access to education and the professions and are not obliged to wear the veil. Arranged marriages, however, remain common.

The Grand Mosque, Manama. *It is the largest building in Bahrain and can accommodate 7000 people.*

POLITICS

 Not applicable

 Amir Sheikh Isa bin Sulman Al-Khalifa

THE STATE OF THE PARTIES

Bahrain is an absolute monarchy, ruled by the Amir through an appointed cabinet

The Al-Khalifa family has dominated Bahraini politics since 1783. Politics is effectively autocratic and political dissent is not tolerated. Bahrain is one of the few Gulf states with political prisoners. Opponents of the regime – usually Shi'a fundamentalists – are frequently exiled and have their passports cancelled. Iran has sought to encourage fundamentalists in Bahrain by distributing cassettes of Iranian mullahs' sermons preaching revolution. Radio broadcasts from Teheran also reach Bahrain. Whilst there is considerable Shi'a discontent at their low social status, there are few channels by which this can be expressed or organized.

The current Amir, Sheikh Isa bin Sulman Al-Khalifa, is a liberal in economic policy, encouraging private enterprise. Politically he is cautious of introducing democracy. An attempt at representative government in 1973 was suspended in 1975 on the grounds that it provoked instability. The fear that democracy will be used by fundamentalists to gain power, as in Algeria, makes any real liberalization of politics unlikely.

WORLD AFFAIRS

 AL   OAPEC   NAM   ESCWA   AFESD

Bahrain holds to a staunchly independent line in foreign policy. It maintains good relations with the USA, the main guarantor of its security, yet has also called for relations with Iraq to be restored. Despite objecting to Bahrain's liberal social attitudes, Saudi Arabia finds the Al-Khalifas useful allies against Gulf fundamentalists.

AID

 $101m (receipts)

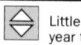 Little change from year to year

Bahrain receives moderate levels of aid, but takes the lion's share of the offshore oil field shared with Saudi Arabia, effectively a subsidy from the latter.

B

DEFENCE

 $236.8m   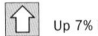 Up 7% in 1992

The 6150-strong defence force includes a small but well-equipped air force. Bahrain has traditionally maintained close relations with the USA. US airbases on Bahrain were used in the 1990-1991 Gulf War. The small navy is hard pressed to patrol the 33-island archipelago.

ECONOMICS

 $3.1bn   0.38 Bahrain dinars

SCORE CARD

- ❏ WORLD GNP RANKING........................118th
- ❏ GNP PER CAPITA $6200
- ❏ BALANCE OF PAYMENTS.................$−738.3m
- ❏ INFLATION 2%
- ❏ UNEMPLOYMENT......................................8%

STRENGTHS
Oil. Arab world's major offshore banking sector. Lack of restrictions encourages inward investment. Tourism.

WEAKNESSES
Depleted oil reserves and insufficient diversification could lead to future drop in currently high living standards. High levels of government borrowing.

EXPORTS

USA 3%   Japan 3%
United Arab Emirates 3%   Saudi Arabia 5%
Other 86%

IMPORTS

Japan 6%   USA 7%
Saudi Arabia 42%   UK 11%
Other 34%

RESOURCES

 3.5bn kwh (capacity 1.04m kw)   38,200 b/d (reserves 69,584,000 bbl)

 16,000 goats, 8000 sheep, 6000 cattle   Oil, natural gas

Bahrain remains dependent on its oil and gas production. Production of crude oil declined however, from 65,000 b/d in the 1970s to 38,200 b/d in 1994. Reserves will probably run out by 2010. As oil has declined, so gas has assumed greater importance. Most is used to supply local industries, particularly the aluminium plant established in 1972.

BAHRAIN

Total Area : 680 sq. km (263 sq. miles)

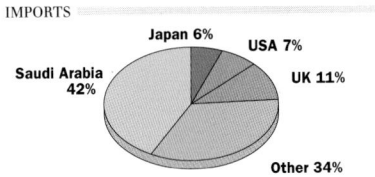

Persian Gulf

Jazīrat al Muḥarraq   Samāhīj
Al Busaytin   Qalālī
Al Muḥarraq   Arād   Al Ḥidd
Bārbār   Karrānah Sanābis
Ad Dirāz   MANAMA
Al Budayyi   As Sahlah   Jidd
Al Muḥammadīyah   al Ḥadīyah   Ḥalṣ   Al Jufayr
Jiddah   Banī   Jamrah   Sār
Madīnat ʿĪsá   Jazīrat an Nabīh aṣ Ṣalīḥ
ʿAlī   Al Qaryah
Al Jasrah   Khamījīyah   Marqūbān
Al Hamalah   Ar Rifā ʿal   Ar Rifā ʿash   Wādiyān
Umm an Naʿsān   Gharbī   Sharqī   Sitrah
Karzakkān   Dumistān   Al Maʿāmīr
Madīnat Hamad   An Nuwaydirāt
Al Mālikīyah

Gulf of Bahrain

Awalī
Az Zallāq   Askar
Ra's Abū Jarjūr
Ra's Ḥayyān
Ra's Abu al Matwj   Jabal ad Dukhān 134m
Ra's Nawmah
Ra's al Jazā'ir   Ra's al Qurayn
Ra's al Mumma qlah
Ḥadd al Jamal
26°10'
26°
25°50'
50°40'

N

POPULATION
- ◎ over 100 000
- ○ over 50 000
- • over 10 000
- • under 10 000

LAND HEIGHT
- 100m/328ft
- Sea Level

0   10 km
0   10 miles

ENVIRONMENT

 None   Environmental issues not a priority

Local marine life, particularly the dugong, is vulnerable to upstream oil pollution from the Gulf.

MEDIA

 The information ministry is relatively liberal. However, the press is still semi-controlled

PUBLISHING AND BROADCAST MEDIA

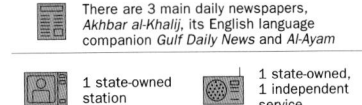
There are 3 main daily newspapers, *Akhbar al-Khalij*, its English language companion *Gulf Daily News* and *Al-Ayam*

1 state-owned station   1 state-owned, 1 independent service

Bahrain has the most liberal information policy in the Gulf. CNN and BBC satellite TV are freely available.

CRIME

 Bahrain does not publish prison figures   Down 57% in 1990

Crime is minimal and theft and muggings rare. Suspected political dissidents are monitored by the police.

CHRONOLOGY

Bahrain has been ruled since 1783 by the Al-Khalifa family.

- ❏ **1971** Independence from Britain.
- ❏ **1981** Founder-member of GCC. December, abortive coup backed by Iran. Bahrain gives backing to Iraq in Iran–Iraq war.
- ❏ **1991** Bahrain backs UN in expelling Iraq from Kuwait.
- ❏ **1992** Bahrain calls for Iraq to be admitted to the GCC.

EDUCATION

 77%

Female literacy rates are well above the Gulf average. Lack of funding has held up plans for a university.

HEALTH

 1 per 713 people   Circulatory diseases, perinatal deaths, injury, poisonings

The health service is extensive and run to world-class standards. Bahraini nationals receive free treatment. Some go abroad for advanced care.

WEALTH

 Agricultural worker, 196 dinars per month; oil engineer, 698 dinars per month

CONSUMER GOODS OWNERSHIP

High levels of PC owner-ship

402   182   282   200

Beneficiaries of the Amir's extensive patronage are the wealthiest group. Shi'a Muslims are the poorest.

WORLD RANKING

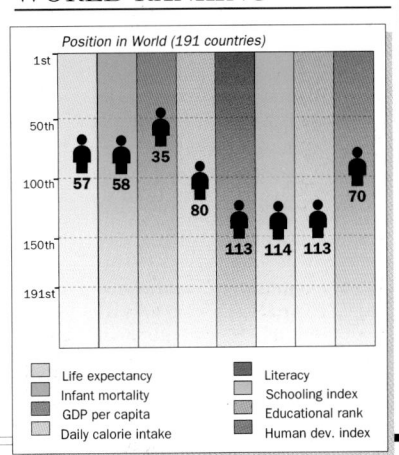

Position in World (191 countries)

1st
50th
100th
150th
191st

57   58   35   80   113   114   113   70

- Life expectancy
- Infant mortality
- GDP per capita
- Daily calorie intake
- Literacy
- Schooling index
- Educational rank
- Human dev. index

BANGLADESH

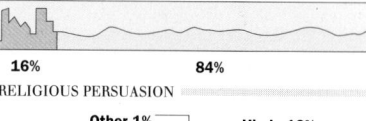

OFFICIAL NAME: People's Republic of Bangladesh   **CAPITAL:** Dhaka
POPULATION: 119.3 million   **CURRENCY:** Taka   **OFFICIAL LANGUAGE:** Bengali

BANGLADESH LIES AT the north of the Bay of Bengal and shares borders with India and Burma. Most of the country is composed of fertile alluvial plains; the north and northeast is mountainous, as is the Chittagong region. Since its secession from Pakistan in 1971, Bangladesh has had a troubled history of political instability, with periods of emergency rule. Effective democracy was restored in 1991. Bangladesh's major economic sectors are jute production, textiles and agriculture. Its climate can wreak havoc. In 1991, a massive cyclone killed more than 140,000 people.

CLIMATE

WEATHER CHART

During the monsoon, the water level normally rises 6 m above sea level, flooding two thirds of the country. The floods are made much worse when the Ganges, Jamuna and Meghna rivers, which converge in a huge delta in Bangladesh, are swollen by the melting of the Himalayan snows, and heavy rain, in India. Cyclones regularly build up in the Bay of Bengal, with sometimes devastating effect on the flat coastal region.

COMMUNICATIONS

Zia International, Dhaka
1.19m passengers

172 ships
532,600 dwt

THE TRANSPORT NETWORK

6240 km
(3877 miles)

None

2792 km
(1735 miles)

8433 km
(5240 miles)

Most transport in Bangladesh is by water, although government transport policy is now concentrating on developing road and rail links. A major bridge is currently being built across the Jamuna River, which bisects Bangladesh from north to south. The $500-million project has suffered numerous delays and is now due to be completed in 1996. Bangladesh's two major ports, Mungla and Chittagong, are being upgraded to take advanced container ships.

Begum Khaleda Zia, *prime minister since February 1991.*

Gen Ershad, *president from 1983 to 1990.*

TOURISM

110,475 visitors

Down 2% in 1992

MAIN OVERSEAS ARRIVALS

India 32%	
Pakistan 13%	
UK 9%	
USA 7%	
Japan 5%	
Other 34%	

% of total arrivals

Tourist earnings and numbers have been falling since the mid-1980s. Most visitors are Indian businessmen or Bangladeshis who live overseas returning to see their relatives. The mogul architecture in Dhaka and the Pala dynasty (7th–10th centuries) city of Sonargaon are major attractions.

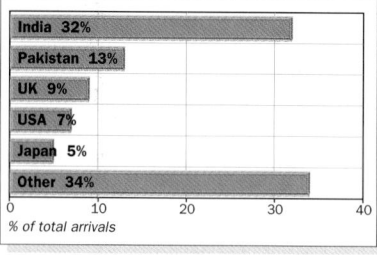

Traders on the Meghna River, *which flows into the Padma. Bangladesh's flood-plains are among the most fertile in the world.*

PEOPLE

Bengali, Urdu, Chakma, Marma (Magh), Garo, Khasi, Santhali, Tripuri, Mro

754 people per km²

THE URBAN/RURAL POPULATION SPLIT

16%   84%

RELIGIOUS PERSUASION

Other 1%
Hindu 16%
Muslim 83%

ETHNIC MAKEUP

Other 2%
Bengali 98%

Bangladesh is one of the most densely populated countries in the world, despite the fact that 84% of the population are rural. As in India, there is considerable Muslim–Hindu tension; the destruction of the Ayodhya mosque in northern India in 1992 incited violence in Bangladesh.

The only genuinely ethnic-based conflict occurs in the Chittagong Hill Tracts in the southeast, where 12 tribes – mostly Buddhists – demanding autonomy have been waging a low-level guerrilla war since 1974. The south of the country is also having to cope with an influx of refugees fleeing neighbouring Burma.

Although about 55% of Bangladeshis, rural and urban, still live below the poverty line, there has been an improvement in living standards over the past decade.

The textile trade, by providing an independent income, has been one factor in the growing emancipation of Bangladeshi women. They are now included in official employment statistics and are the main customers of the most successful rural bank. Women lead both the government and opposition.

POPULATION AGE BREAKDOWN

% of population by age group	0–14	15–64			65+
	3.7%	3.5%	3.4%	2.9%	3%
	55.4%	51.1%	50.4%	53.2%	58.2%
	40.9%	45.4%	46.2%	43.9%	38.8%
	1960	1970	1980	1990	2000

POLITICS

 1996   President Abdur Rahman Biswas

THE STATE OF THE PARTIES

National Assembly 330 members

46% BNP · 30% AL · 12% NP · 12% Other

BNP = Bangladesh National Party **AL** = Awami League
NP = National Party **Other** = Islamic Party of Bangladesh, Bangladesh Communist Party

Bangladesh returned to multiparty democracy in 1991, following a period of military rule.

MAIN POLITICAL ISSUES

The State sector
Bangladesh is coming under increasing pressure from multilateral lending institutions, which account for the vast majority of the country's capital inflows, to cut costs in the state sector. Simultaneously, state sector workers are demanding wage increases in line with inflation.

BANGLADESH

Total Area : 143 998 sq. km (55 598 sq. miles)

POPULATION
- over 1 000 000
- over 500 000
- over 100 000
- over 50 000
- over 10 000

LAND HEIGHT
- 500m/1640ft
- 200m/656ft
- Sea Level

0 100 km
0 100 miles

The Chittagong Hill Tracts insurgency
Buddhist Mongol groups have been waging a low-level guerrilla war since 1974, when their demands for partial autonomy and restrictions on Bengali settlers in the region were rebuffed. State policy seems to be to contain rather than eradicate the conflict.

Golam Azam
Golam Azam, leader of the Islamic Party, has been in custody since 1990, accused of atrocities and siding with Pakistan during the war of independence. Hindu groups in Bangladesh are pushing for a dramatic trial; any moves to try him risk inflaming Muslim passions.

PROFILE
Between 1975 and 1990 the military was in power in Bangladesh. The overthrow of President Ershad in 1990 saw a return to multiparty politics; the army remains poised, however, to intervene in the event of a breakdown in law and order. Bangladesh's first woman prime minister, Begum Khaleda Zia, head of the ruling BNP, was elected in February 1991. A change from a presidential to a prime-ministerial system of government followed. Intense factionalism within the Awami League – which steered Bangladesh to independence in 1971 – weakens its ability to challenge the BNP.

WORLD AFFAIRS

Bangladesh concentrates mostly on maintaining good relations with the West, the main source of essential aid. Relations with Pakistan have slowly been improving since the low point of 1971. Pakistan finally agreed in 1991 to repatriate the 250,000 pro-Pakistani Bihari Muslims languishing in Bangladeshi refugee camps since 1971. Relations with India are strained. The effects of the Indian construction of the Farakka Dam across the Ganges have deprived Bangladeshi farmers of water for irrigation. The failure of Delhi to curb guerrilla groups operating out of India into the Chittagong region has also soured relations.

AID

 $1.6bn (receipts) 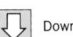 Down 20% in 1991

Aid disbursements to Bangladesh each year are over 1000 times greater than the annual value of foreign investment in the country. Aid also finances more than 90% of state capital spending. The Bangladesh Development Aid Consortium meets annually to discuss aid spending under the auspices of the World Bank. One result of the level of aid is that Bangladesh has fallen into one of the traps of an aid-dependent economy: the large middle class has a vested interest in perpetuating a system which provides its members with lucrative contracts and access to external resources.

CHRONOLOGY
British rule in India began in Bengal (now Bangladesh), when Robert Clive, army head of the East India Company, defeated the ruler of Bengal at Plassey in 1765.

❏ **1905** Muslims persuade British rulers to partition state of Bengal, to create a Muslim-dominated East Bengal.
❏ **1906** Muslim League established in Dhaka.
❏ **1912** Partition of 1905 reversed.
❏ **1947** British withdrawal from India. Partition plans establish a largely Muslim state of East (present-day Bangladesh) and West Pakistan, separated by 1600 km of Indian, and largely Hindu, territory. The capital of the new, bisected state established at Islamabad in West Pakistan.
❏ **1949** Awami League founded to campaign for autonomy from West Pakistan.

B

CHRONOLOGY *continued*

- ❏ **1968** General Yahya Khan heads government in Islamabad.
- ❏ **1970** Elections give Awami League, under Sheikh Mujibur Rahman, clear majority. Rioting and guerrilla warfare following Yahya Khan's refusal to convene assembly. The year ends with the worst recorded storms in Bangladesh's history – between 200,000 and 500,000 dead.
- ❏ **1971** Civil War, as Sheikh Mujibur and Awami League declare unilateral independence. Ten million Bangladeshis flee to India. Pakistani troops defeated in 12 days by *Mukhti Bahini* – the Bengal Liberation Army.
- ❏ **1972** Sheikh Mujibur prime minister. Nationalization programme for the utilities and tea, jute and textiles industries introduced. Bangladesh achieves international recognition and joins Commonwealth. Pakistan withdraws in protest.
- ❏ **1974** Severe floods damage rice crop; famine and inflation exacerbate rising discontent.
- ❏ **1975** Sheikh Mujibur assassinated. Military coups end with General Zia Rahman taking power. Institution of single-party state.
- ❏ **1976** Banning of trade union federations.
- ❏ **1977** General Zia assumes presidency. Islam adopted as first principle of the constitution.
- ❏ **1981** General Zia assassinated.
- ❏ **1982** General Ershad takes over.
- ❏ **1983** Democratic elections restored by Ershad; marred by government intimidation and violence. Ershad assumes presidency.
- ❏ **1986** Elections, again affected by intimidation and violence. Awami League and BNP fail to unseat Ershad.
- ❏ **1987** Proposed bill to allow military to stand for parliament causes anti-government strikes and demonstrations, supported by trade unionists and student groups. Thousands detained; Ershad announces state of emergency.
- ❏ **1988** Islam becomes constitutional state religion.
- ❏ **1990** Ershad resigns following renewed campaign of demonstrations and strikes. Bangladeshis working in Kuwait suffer significant loss of earnings as a result of Gulf War.
- ❏ **1991** Elections won by BNP, headed by Begum Khaleda Zia, who becomes prime minister. Ershad imprisoned. Role of the president reduced to that of titular head of state.

DEFENCE

 $303.31m

 Down 6% in 1991

0   *Defence spending as % GDP*   40

1.3%

The military, which dominated politics between 1975 and 1990, continues to wield considerable influence behind the scenes. The defence budget accounts for 7.5% of state spending (1.3% of GDP). The army, at 93,000 personnel, is relatively small. China is the major source of weapons.

BANGLADESHI ARMED FORCES

50 main battle tanks (T-59/T-54/T-55)		93,000 personnel
4 frigates and 35 patrol boats		7500 personnel
85 combat aircraft (17 J-7M/16 MiG-21MF/ 2 MiG-21U)		6500 personnel
None		

ECONOMICS

 $23.4bn   39.00 taka

SCORE CARD

- ❏ WORLD GNP RANKING.........................60th
- ❏ GNP PER CAPITA $200
- ❏ BALANCE OF PAYMENTS $182.3m
- ❏ INFLATION 7.2%
- ❏ UNEMPLOYMENT................................30%

ECONOMIC PERFORMANCE INDICATOR

EXPORTS

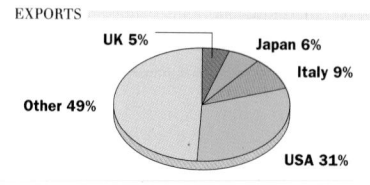

UK 5%   Japan 6%   Italy 9%   Other 49%   USA 31%

IMPORTS

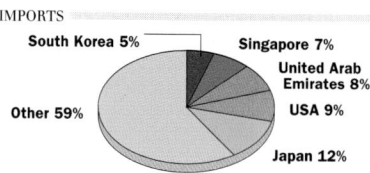

South Korea 5%   Singapore 7%   United Arab Emirates 8%   USA 9%   Japan 12%   Other 59%

STRENGTHS

Jute is the major industry: Bangladesh accounts for 80% of world jute fibre exports. Low wages ensure a competitive and expanding textile industry, which constitutes one third of the small manufacturing sector.

WEAKNESSES

The agricultural sector, which employs 68% of Bangladeshis, is vulnerable to the violent and unpredictable climate.

PROFILE

Government ministers like to portray Bangladesh as an emerging NIC, but its economy is still overwhelmingly dependent on agriculture and large aid inflows. Agriculture, which provides the major export, jute, is productive; Bangladesh's soils, fed by the Ganges, Jamuna and Meghna rivers, are highly fertile. However, the effects of the weather can be devastating, frequently destroying a whole year's crop. Agricultural wages are among the lowest in the world.

The state sector, which owns large, inefficient and massively loss-making companies (such as the Bangladesh Jute Mills Corporation), is in difficulty. The World Bank, which channels most aid into the country, wishes to see loss-making concerns cut their workforces or close down.

Textiles and garments are perhaps the healthiest sectors. Economic zones (Export Processing Zones) with special concessions have attracted foreign investment, as well as helping to promote a small indigenous electronics industry. Bangladesh receives generous textile import quotas from the EU and NAFTA, but its economy is so weak that it fails to reach them.

BANGLADESH : MAJOR BUSINESSES

Bogra   Mymensingh   Dhaka   Nawábganj   Khulna   Chittagong

- Brewing
- Tobacco
- Cotton milling
- Jute processing
- Light engineering

0   100 km
0   100 miles

RESOURCES

 8bn kwh (capacity 2.52m kw)

 Not an oil producer; refines 31,200 b/cd

 23.2m cattle, 1.2m sheep, 45,000 horses

 Salt, oil, natural gas, limestone

ELECTRICITY GENERATION

Hydro 11% (884m kwh)
Thermal 89% (7.2bn kwh)
Nuclear 0%
Other 0%

% of total generation by type

Bangladesh is the world's major jute producer, accounting for 80% of world jute fibre exports and about 50% of world jute manufactures exports. Natural gas from the Bay of Bengal, exploited by the state-owned Bangladesh Oil, Gas and Minerals Corporation, came on stream in 1988; production had increased to 5 billion cubic metres by 1991. Reserves are estimated at 200 years.

BANGLADESH : LAND USE

Cropland
Wetlands
Forest
Rice
Jute - cash crop

0   100 km
0   100 miles

ENVIRONMENT

 0.7% partially protected

 Protection measures being incorporated into donor programmes

ENVIRONMENTAL TREATIES

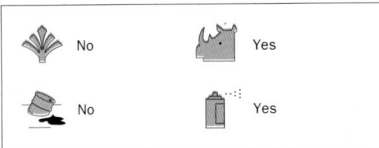

No   Yes
No   Yes

Bangladesh's climate, which results in huge death tolls and frequently destroys a whole season's crops, dwarfs all other environmental problems. Bangladesh is too poor to finance environmental initiatives.

MEDIA

 After many years of censorship, political intervention in the media was greatly reduced in 1990

PUBLISHING AND BROADCAST MEDIA

There are 59 daily newspapers. *Dainik Ittefaq* has the highest circulation

1 state-controlled service

1 state-controlled service

Palapa B2-P

None

Since the fall of President Ershad at the end of 1990, the press has enjoyed almost total political independence. Of the daily newspapers, the 11 English-language titles tend to appeal primarily to the urban elite. Amongst political weeklies, the most respected is called *Holiday* (the owners bought it as a travel magazine and decided not to change the name). Over 70% of TV programmes are produced locally; about one third are in black and white.

CRIME

 31,192 prisoners

 Up 6% in 1990

CRIME RATES

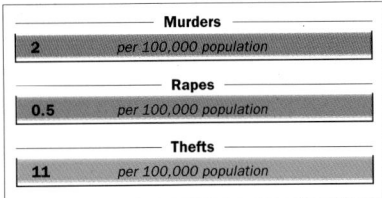

Murders
2   per 100,000 population

Rapes
0.5   per 100,000 population

Thefts
11   per 100,000 population

Rising levels of political and religious violence led the new government of 1991 to introduce a controversial anti-terrorism law, which offered swift (and many thought careless) justice with heavy penalties, including death. The Special Powers Act, which was used by Ershad to detain political opponents, is still in force. Deaths in Bangladeshi prisons are common and the army's human rights record, especially that of the paramilitary Bangladesh Rifles in the Chittagong Hills, has also been questioned by Amnesty International.

EDUCATION

 35%

0   Education spending as % GNP   25
2.2%

THE EDUCATION SYSTEM

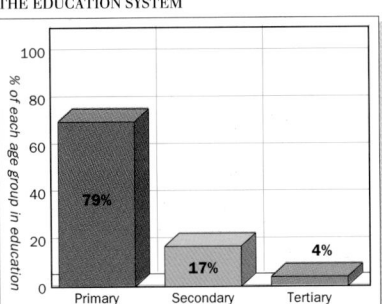

% of each age group in education

Primary 79%
Secondary 17%
Tertiary 4%

Education in almost all sectors of Bangladeshi society is poorly addressed, with the resultant low literacy figure. The seven universities, with an enrolment of just 50,000, are often forced to close owing to political violence on campus.

HEALTH

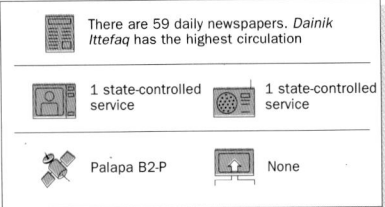 1 per 6129 people

Parasitic, diarrheal and communicable diseases

0   Health spending as % GNP   25
0.6%

Although primary health care in rural areas has improved over the last decade, Bangladesh's health problems remain severe and are exacerbated by a shortage of medical staff and facilities. The priority given to birth control programmes has helped to reduce the population growth rate by 23% over the last 15 years, from 2.6% to 2% a year.

WEALTH

Machine cloth weaver, 950 taka per month; natural gas engineer, 2850 taka per month

CONSUMER GOODS OWNERSHIP

Per 1000 population

VCR and PC ownership is limited to a small elite

4   0.4   19

Average incomes are very low, but wealth disparities are not quite as marked as in India or Pakistan. State officials tend to be among the better-off.

WORLD RANKING

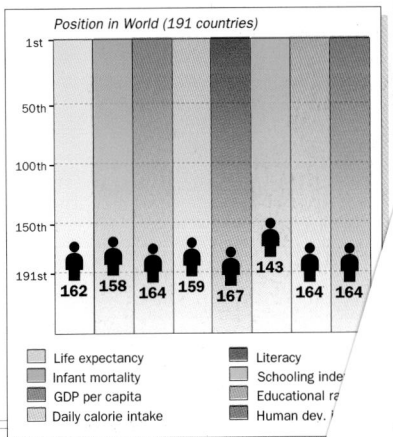

Position in World (191 countries)

1st
50th
100th
150th
191st

162 158 164 159 167 143 164 164

Life expectancy
Infant mortality
GDP per capita
Daily calorie intake
Literacy
Schooling inde
Educational ra
Human dev.

BARBADOS

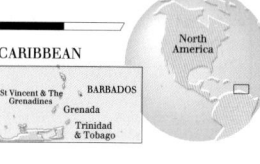

CARIBBEAN

OFFICIAL NAME: Barbados   **CAPITAL:** Bridgetown
CURRENCY: Barbados dollar   **POPULATION:** 300,000   **OFFICIAL LANGUAGE:** English

SITUATED TO THE NORTHEAST of Trinidad, Barbados is the most easterly of the West Indian Windward Islands. In the 16th century, the Portuguese became the first Europeans to reach the island, which was inhabited by Arawak Indians. However, Barbados was not colonized until the 1620s, when British settlers arrived. Popularly referred to by its neighbours as 'little England', Barbados still retains a strong British influence.

CLIMATE

WEATHER CHART

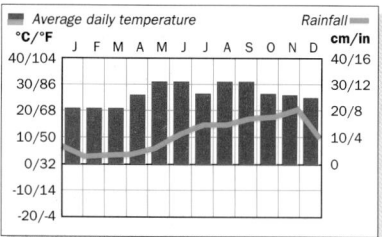

Barbados has a moderate tropical climate and is sunnier and drier than its more mountainous Caribbean neighbours. Hurricanes may occur in the rainy season.

COMMUNICATIONS

 Grantley Adams International, Bridgetown 1.21m passengers

 3 ships 79,900 dwt

THE TRANSPORT NETWORK

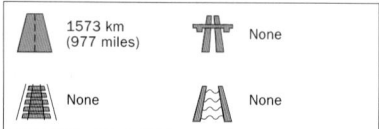

1573 km (977 miles)		None
None		None

Recent major construction projects have included the resurfacing of the runway at the international airport and the expansion of piers at Bridgetown's port. Upgrading the island's dense road network is a priority. Bus routes cover most of the island.

House of Assembly, Trafalgar Square, Bridgetown. Barbados's parliament, the third oldest in the Commonwealth, dates from 1639.

TOURISM

 394,222 visitors   Down 6% in 1991

MAIN OVERSEAS ARRIVALS

USA 33%
UK 22%
Canada 13%
Other 32%

% of total arrivals

The airport runway has been improved in an effort to encourage tourists. Visitors come mainly from North America and Europe. Cruise-ship traffic is on the increase.

PEOPLE

 Bajan (Barbadian English), English

 598 people per km²

THE URBAN/RURAL POPULATION SPLIT

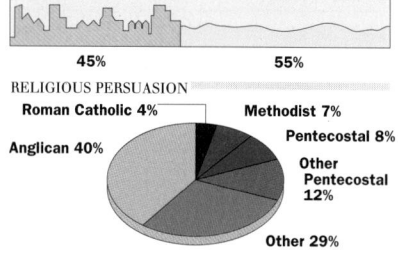

45%   55%

RELIGIOUS PERSUASION

Roman Catholic 4%   Methodist 7%
Anglican 40%   Pentecostal 8%
Other Pentecostal 12%
Other 29%

Most Bajans are the descendants of Africans brought to the island between the 16th and 19th centuries; there are also small groups of South Asians and of Europeans, mainly expatriate Britons, many of whom take up residence on retirement. There is some latent tension between the white community, which controls most of the economy, and the majority black population, although this rarely spills over into violence. Increasing social mobility has allowed many black Bajans to move into the professions and the civil service. Barbados enjoys a higher standard of living than most Caribbean countries.

POLITICS

 1996   HM Queen Elizabeth II

THE STATE OF THE PARTIES

House of Assembly 28 members

64% DLP   36% BLP

DLP = Democratic Labour Party   BLP = Barbados Labour Party

Senate 21 members

12 members chosen by the prime minister, 2 by the leader of the opposition and 7 by the governor-general

Barbados is a multiparty democracy. The main power brokers are a primarily European, affluent elite, who finance the parties and exert an indirect influence on government policy. The main political issue is the government's handling of the economy. Prime Minister Erskine Sandiford's state salary freezes and tax increases went some way to alleviating the country's budgetary problem, but increased opposition at home.

WORLD AFFAIRS

 Comm   Caricom   OAS   GATT   NAM

Barbados is a strong supporter of US policy in the region, and was a staging post for the 1983 invasion of Grenada.

AID

 $4m (receipts)   Up 33% in 1991

Barbados receives the bulk of its aid from the USA, EU and UK, mainly in the form of development project loans and balance of payments support.

DEFENCE

 $10.6m   Up 14% in 1990

The 1000-strong Barbadian army and the constabulary benefit from financial support and training from the US and UK governments, which also supply equipment. The country is the headquarters of the Regional Security System, established in 1982 by the Windward and Leeward Islands, a body which acts as a multinational security force for its members.

B

ECONOMICS

 $1.7bn   2.01 Barbados dollars

SCORE CARD

❑ WORLD GNP RANKING	142nd
❑ GNP PER CAPITA	$5700
❑ BALANCE OF PAYMENTS	$−29.9m
❑ INFLATION	5.5%
❑ UNEMPLOYMENT	17.1%

STRENGTHS
Well-developed tourism based on climate and accessibility. Sugar industries. Information processing and financial services are important new growth sectors.

WEAKNESSES
Narrow economic base, vulnerable to downturns in tourism, failures of sugar harvest and the threatened liberalization of the sugar market. Relatively high manufacturing costs.

EXPORTS

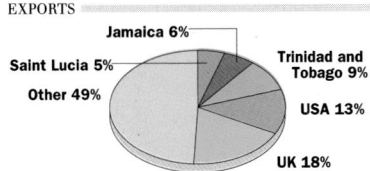

Jamaica 6%
Saint Lucia 5%
Other 49%
Trinidad and Tobago 9%
USA 13%
UK 18%

IMPORTS

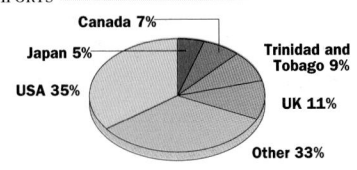

Canada 7%
Japan 5%
USA 35%
Trinidad and Tobago 9%
UK 11%
Other 33%

BARBADOS

Total Area : 430 sq. km (166 sq. miles)

Checker Hall
Speightstown • Boscobelle
Rose Hill
Belleplaine
Lower Carlton
Endeavour
Mt Hillaby 340m ▲
Bathsheba
Holetown
Surinam
Welchman Hall
Pothouse
Cave Hill •
Valley
Ellerton
Wellhouse
Church Village
Black Rock
Station Hill
Brereton
Marchfield
Mount Friendship
The Crane
BRIDGETOWN
St Patricks
St. Martins
Hastings
Providence
Grantley Adams Intl Airport
Worthing
Oistins • Scarborough

ATLANTIC OCEAN
ATLANTIC OCEAN

13°15'
13°10'
13°05'
59°35'
59°30'

N

0   5 km
0   5 miles

POPULATION
over 10 000   ●
under 10 000   •

LAND HEIGHT
200m/656ft
Sea Level

RESOURCES

 468m kwh (capacity 140,000 kw)

1246 b/d (reserves 5,892,000 bbl)

 1m chickens, 56,000 sheep, 49,000 pigs

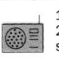 Oil, natural gas

Barbados has few strategic resources. The domestic petroleum industry provides about one third of the country's energy requirements.

ENVIRONMENT

 1%

 The only mangrove swamp on Barbados is still unprotected

Oil slicks created by waste dumped from passing ships is polluting the encircling reef and adversely affecting the life cycle of the flying fish, Barbados' main fish stock.

MEDIA

Freedom of expression guaranteed by the constitution. Defamation law restrictive to investigative journalism

PUBLISHING AND BROADCAST MEDIA

There are 2 daily newspapers, the *Barbados Advocate* and the *Daily Nation*

1 state-owned service

1 state-owned, 2 independent services

There is no political interference in the media in Barbados. The two daily newspapers are privately owned, as are two of the radio stations.

CRIME

260 prisoners   Up 6% in 1990

Compared with other Caribbean islands, Barbados still has a low crime rate. There are no 'no-go' areas on the island. However, armed bank robberies, murders and attacks on tourists are all on the increase.

EDUCATION

99%

Barbados prides itself on its education system, which is considered the best in the English-speaking Caribbean. It hosts one of the campuses of the University of the West Indies.

CHRONOLOGY

Colonized by the British in 1627, Barbados grew rich in the 18th century from sugar produced using slave labour.

❑ **1951** Universal adult suffrage introduced.

❑ **1961** Full internal self-government. The DLP, led by Errol Barrow, comes to power.

❑ **1966** Full independence from Britain.

❑ **1983** Supports and provides a base for the US invasion of Grenada.

HEALTH

 1 per 1167 people   Heart and digestive diseases, cancers

The health system is based on subsidized government-run clinics and hospitals, supplemented by more expensive private clinics and private doctors. Facilities are within easy reach of all Bajans.

WEALTH

 Plantation field worker, 4 Barbados dollars per hour; oil refinery foreman, 564 Barbados dollars per week (minimum)

CONSUMER GOODS OWNERSHIP

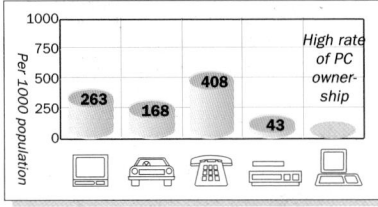

High rate of PC ownership

263   168   408   43

Per 1000 population

There is a significant disparity between most Bajans and a small affluent group, usually of European origin, which owns and controls business and industry. Among the latter, status symbols include yachts and exclusive club membership.

WORLD RANKING

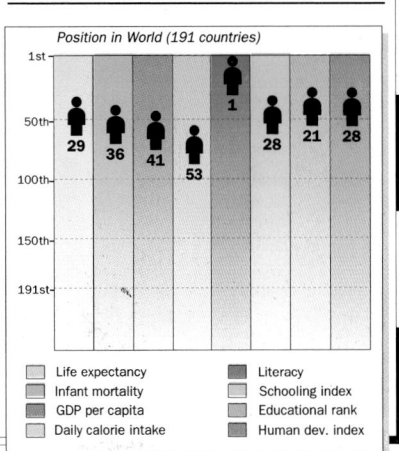

Position in World (191 countries)

1st
50th
100th
150th
191st

29   36   41   53   1   28   21   28

Life expectancy
Infant mortality
GDP per capita
Daily calorie intake
Literacy
Schooling index
Educational rank
Human dev. index

BELGIUM

OFFICIAL NAME: Kingdom of Belgium **CAPITAL:** Brussels
POPULATION: 10 million **CURRENCY:** Belgian franc **OFFICIAL LANGUAGE:** Dutch, French and German

B

LOCATED BETWEEN GERMANY, France and the Netherlands, Belgium has a short coastline on the North Sea. The south includes the forested Ardennes region while the north is dissected by canals. Belgium has been fought over many times in its history. It was occupied by Germany in both World Wars. Long–standing tensions have existed between the majority Flemish and minority French-speakers since the 1830s. These are now being defused by Belgium's move to a federal political structure and the national consensus on the benefits of EU membership.

CLIMATE

WEATHER CHART

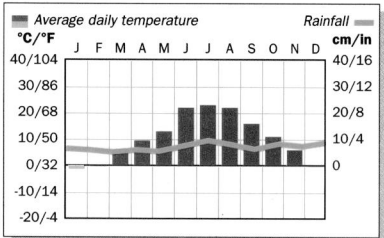

Belgium has a typical maritime climate and is influenced by the Gulf Stream. Temperatures are mild with heavy cloud cover and much rain. The west coast climate can be disrupted by widely fluctuating weather conditions, caused by cyclonic disturbances. Summers tend to be short.

COMMUNICATIONS

 Zaventem International, Brussels
6.87m passengers

 27 ships
47,100 dwt

THE TRANSPORT NETWORK

 128,345 km (79,750 miles)

1631 km (1013 miles)

 8408 km (5224 miles)

1528 km (949 miles)

Belgium can be crossed within four hours by car or train, and access to Germany, the Netherlands and beyond is easy. Belgium's motorway network is extensive and so well lit that, along with the Great Wall of China, it is the most distinctive sight from orbit. Although the railway system has been reduced since 1970, it is still one of the world's densest networks. The opening of the Channel Tunnel will improve Brussels's link with London and Paris. Once the TGV line is opened in 1997, it will be possible to reach London in 2 hours and 10 minutes and Paris in 3 hours. Antwerp, an old Hanseatic city, is Europe's second largest port.

TOURISM

 9.9m bed-nights.
Belgium does not record visitor numbers

Up 12% in 1991

MAIN OVERSEAS ARRIVALS

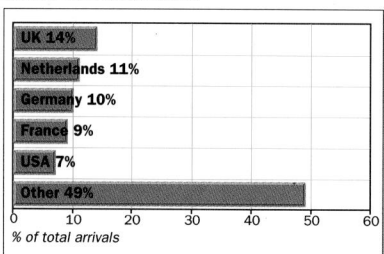

Belgium's main attractions are its historic cities and museums of Flemish art. Bruges, the capital of west Flanders, is often called the 'Venice of the North'. With unspoiled Renaissance architecture and a complex canal system, it has become a favoured destination for British weekend trippers and Japanese honeymooners. In Brussels the famous 'Grand Place', a cluster of Gothic, Renaissance and Baroque buildings in a cobbled square, survived bombing during the Second World War. Much of the rest of the old city centre, however, was destroyed. Belgium has 15 resorts on its 62 km coastline, with a single tramline running its entire length. Forests in the Ardennes to the south attract hikers.

Ardennes, southeast Belgium, is famous for its forests, cuisine and lakes. Rivers, like the Meuse and Semois, dissect the countryside.

PEOPLE

 Flemish, French, German

321 people per km²

THE URBAN/RURAL POPULATION SPLIT

97%   3%

RELIGIOUS PERSUASION

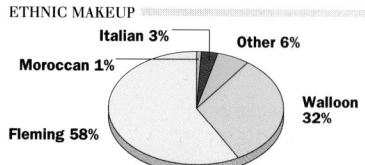

Other (including Protestant) 25%

Roman Catholic 75%

ETHNIC MAKEUP

Italian 3%   Other 6%
Moroccan 1%
Walloon 32%
Fleming 58%

Belgian history has been marked by the divisions between its Flemish and French-speaking communities. Flemish speakers, who are a majority, are concentrated in Flanders. Wallonia is French-speaking and Brussels is 85% francophone. French-speakers were in the ascendancy for many years as they controlled the profitable coal and steel industries in Wallonia. Their greater economic wealth was reinforced by a constitution which gave them political control. Tensions between French-speakers and Flemings occasionally erupted into violence. However, in the past two decades, the position of the two communities has been reversed. Wallonia's industries have declined and Flanders is now the wealthier region. In order to contain tensions, Belgium began to change in 1980, from being the most centralist to the most federal state in Europe; both communities now have their own governments and control most of their own affairs.

Belgium has a sizeable immigrant population. Women gained the vote in 1948. They earn, on average, 25% less than their male counterparts.

POPULATION AGE BREAKDOWN

% of population by age group	0–14	15–64	65+		
65+	12%	13.4%	14.3%	14.9%	16.5%
15–64	64.5%	63%	65.6%	67.2%	66.2%
0–14	23.5%	23.6%	20.1%	17.9%	17.3%
	1960	1970	1980	1990	2000

EUROPE

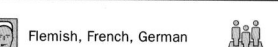

B

BELGIUM

Total Area : 33 100 sq. km
(12 780 sq. miles)

POPULATION

⊙ over 500 000
◎ over 100 000
○ over 50 000
● over 10 000

LAND HEIGHT

500m/1640ft
200m/656ft
Sea Level

0 — 40 km
0 — 40 miles

[Map of Belgium showing cities including Zeebrugge, Oostende, Brugge, Maldegem, Sint-Niklaas, Antwerpen, Ekeren, Beveren, Schoten, Brasschaat, Turnhout, Geel, Lier, Lokeren, Deinze, Gent, Roeselare, Waregem, Aalst, Grimbergen, Mechelen, Beringen, Maasmechelen, Genk, Hasselt, Aarschot, Vilvoorde, Leuven, Sint-Truiden, Kortrijk, Ieper, Menen, Ninove, Dilbeek, BRUSSELS, Tienen, Herstal, Mouscron, Braine-l'Alleud, Liège, Seraing, Verviers, Tournai, La Louvière, Andenne, Esneux, Mons, Courcelles, Namur, Ciney, Malmédy, Binche, Charleroi, Châtelet, Marche-en-Famenne, Dinant, Walcourt, Couvin, Bastogne, Arlon. Surrounding countries: NORTH SEA, NETHERLANDS, FRANCE, GERMANY, LUXEMBOURG. Regions: FLANDERS, KEMPEN, ARDENNES, HESBAYE, HAUTES FAGNES. Rivers: Scheldt, Rupel, Leie, Dender, Senne, Sambre, Meuse, Ourthe, Amblève, Lesse. Botrange ▲694m.]

POLITICS

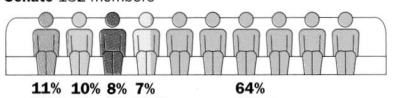

1995   HM King Albert II

THE STATE OF THE PARTIES

Chamber of Representatives 212 members

18% CVP	17% PS	13% SP	12% PVV	9% PRL	31% Other

CVP = Christian People's Party **PS** = Socialist Party (French-speaking) **SP** = Socialist Party (Flemish-speaking)
PVV = Freedom and Progress Party **PRL** = Liberal Reform Party

Senate 182 members

11% CVP	10% PS	8% SP	7% PVV	64% Other

106 members are directly elected, 50 elected by provincial councils and 25 co-opted by the elected members and the heir to the throne

Until 1970, Belgium was a unitary state. Tensions between language groups led to four waves of federalist reforms from 1980, which culminated in the St Michel Accords of 1993, confirming the state as a federal monarchy.

MAIN POLITICAL ISSUES

Language
Tensions between the two language groups are receding. However, the divisions remain strong. Each community has its own Socialist Party (the PS in Wallonia, the SP in Flanders) and the Christian Democrats are split into the francophone PSC and Flemish CVP. Under the premiership of Jean-Luc Dehaene the four parties have worked in an uneasy coalition.

Debt
Belgium's debt is now greater than its national income. The question of how to deal with it dominates and defines most political debate. Dehaene pushed through unpopular tax-raising budgets in 1993. However, many Flemings, who feel they are subsidizing Wallonia's costs, want the debt to be regionalized.

PROFILE

Belgian politics is defined by language. Apart from this, a high degree of consensus exists over the benefits of EU membership and monetary union. In recent years, there has been an increase in support for the racist *Vlaams Blok*, which objects to Belgium's Turkish and Moroccan minorities. *Vlaams Blok* captured 25% of Antwerp's vote in 1991.

The current government is a left-of-centre coalition, composed of the Socialist and Christian Democrat parties from the Flemish and French-speaking communities. Although the coalition has a majority in parliament, it had difficulty in securing the necessary two thirds majority for the constitutional reform enacted in the St Michel Accords. These gave the three regional governments, Flanders, Wallonia and Brussels, significant powers under a federal government. Most of the population sees this as the best system to cope with the country's diversities.

King Baudouin died in 1993. He was succeeded by King Albert II.

Jean-Luc Dehaene, premier and leader of the Christian People's Party (CVP).

WORLD AFFAIRS

EU   NATO   OECD   Benelux   WEU

Belgium's key concern is its leading role in the EU. It is a keen supporter of economic and monetary union. During its EU presidency in 1993, it tried to accelerate the Maastricht process by setting the ground rules for a future European Central Bank. The EU is also seen as an anchor for its own federalist structure; many fear that without it Belgium could split into two.

Belgium often contributes troops to UN operations. Belgian soldiers have served in Bosnia and Somalia. The Belgian community in Rwanda had to be evacuated in 1994 after ten Belgian UN troops were murdered during ethnic violence.

AID

 $831m (donations)   Down 7% in 1991

In 1993, overseas aid accounted for about 0.7% of budgetary spending. Between 1987 and 1993, most of the aid programme was spent on education and agricultural projects in Africa. The former colonies of Burundi and Rwanda were the major beneficiaries.

CHRONOLOGY

Formerly ruled by the French dukes of Burgundy, Belgium became a Habsburg possession in 1477. It passed to the Austrian Habsburgs in 1700. Napoleon ended Austrian rule of the Low Countries in 1797.

- ❑ **1814–1815** Congress of Vienna; European powers decide to merge Belgium with the Netherlands under King William I of Orange.
- ❑ **1830** Revolt against Dutch. Provisional government declares independence.
- ❑ **1831** European powers place Leopold Saxe Coburg as King.
- ❑ **1865** Leopold II crowned King.
- ❑ **1885** After agreement by European powers, King Leopold given Congo basin as colony.
- ❑ **1908** King Leopold allows brutality in Congo basin. Parliament takes over control of its administration.
- ❑ **1914** German armies invade. Leopold II declares war on Germany. Germans occupy Belgium until 1918.
- ❑ **1921** Belgo–Luxembourg Economic Union formed. Luxembourg locks its currency to the Belgian franc.
- ❑ **1932** Flemish language accorded equal official status with French.
- ❑ **1936** Belgium declares neutrality.
- ❑ **1940** King Leopold III capitulates to Hitler. Belgium occupied until 1944.
- ❑ **1948** Forms customs union with Luxembourg and the Netherlands (BENELUX).
- ❑ **1950** King wins referendum but rumours over his collaboration in War persist. Abdicates in favour of his son, Baudouin.
- ❑ **1957** Signs Treaty of Rome with France, Germany, Italy, the Netherlands and Luxembourg.
- ❑ **1958** Treaty of Rome members form the EEC.
- ❑ **1992** Culmination of reforms transforming Belgium into federal state. Greater powers for regions and city governments.
- ❑ **1992** Christian-Democrat–Socialist government led by Jean-Luc Dehaene takes over federal government.
- ❑ **1993** Death of King Baudouin. Succeeded by Albert II. Belgian EU presidency advances moves towards monetary union agreed at Maastricht in 1992.
- ❑ **1994** French-speaking Socialist Party, dominant in Wallonia, racked by political scandal after allegations of corruption and murder. Wallonia's premier, Guy Spittaels, and federal deputy premier, Guy Coeme, resign.

DEFENCE

💲 $3bn

⬇ Down 1% in 1992

0   *Defence spending as % GDP*   40

1.5%

BELGIAN ARMED FORCES

🛡	359 main battle tanks (334 *Leopard* 1/25 M–41)	54,000 personnel
⚓	4 frigates	4400 personnel
✈	122 combat aircraft (F–16A,–16B)	17,300 personnel
	None	

Belgium spends less on defence than the NATO average and over the next decade the defence budget will fall further. In 1994, as part of Belgium's programme to reduce government debt, all three military services were targeted for cuts. The government abolished conscription and cut troop levels from 75,000 to 40,000. The defence budget of around $4.5 billion was frozen for five years.

Spending on paratroopers and transport planes has increased, however. The aim is to allow Belgian forces to fulfil their role in NATO's new rapid reaction forces. It will also make Belgian forces more useful to the UN's worldwide operations.

ECONOMICS

📊 $192bn

💲 34.10 Belgian francs

SCORE CARD

- ❑ WORLD GNP RANKING..........................21st
- ❑ GNP PER CAPITA $19,200
- ❑ BALANCE OF PAYMENTS $4.7m
- ❑ INFLATION 3%
- ❑ UNEMPLOYMENT................................8.1%

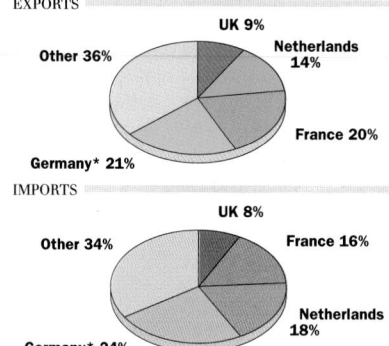

EXPORTS

UK 9%
Other 36%
Netherlands 14%
France 20%
Germany* 21%

IMPORTS

UK 8%
Other 34%
France 16%
Netherlands 18%
Germany* 24%

STRENGTHS

One of world's most efficient producers of metal products and textiles. Flanders is a world leader in new high-tech industries. Successful chemicals industry. Highly-educated and motivated multilingual workforce: estimates suggest productivity is 20% above that of Germany. Location makes Belgium an attractive location for US multinationals. Good sea outlets and access to Rhine inland waterway from Antwerp and Ghent.

WEAKNESSES

Highest public debt in the EU at 122% of GDP; costs 10% of public income per year to service. Rising unemployment. Large numbers of workers retire early resulting in high state pension bill. Larger bureaucracy than European average.

ECONOMIC PERFORMANCE INDICATOR

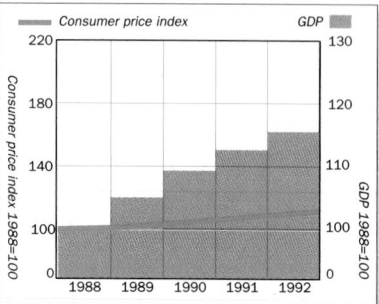

— Consumer price index   GDP ▨

PROFILE

The Belgian economy went into recession with the rest of Europe in the early 1990s. Falling tax revenues coincided with rising unemployment, particularly in Wallonia, and a larger social security bill. In 1993, the Dehaene government introduced a scheme which encouraged work-sharing as a way of combating unemployment. Belgium aims to meet the criteria for European Monetary Union (EMU) by 1996.

BELGIUM : MAJOR BUSINESSES

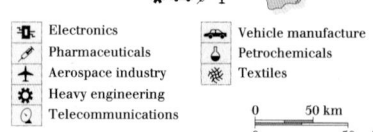

🔌 Electronics		🚗 Vehicle manufacture
✎ Pharmaceuticals		🛢 Petrochemicals
✈ Aerospace industry		✷ Textiles
✿ Heavy engineering		
🖂 Telecommunications		

0   50 km
0   50 miles

B

RESOURCES

70.2bn kwh (capacity 14.14m kw)

30.7m chickens, 6.4m pigs, 3m cattle

 Not an oil producer; refines 607,000 b/cd

 Coal, natural gas, shale, marble, sandstone, dolomite

ELECTRICITY GENERATION

Hydro 0.2% (266m kwh)

Thermal 39% (27.2bn kwh)

Nuclear 60.8% (42.7bn kwh)

Other 0%

0　20　40　60　80　100
% of total generation by type

Belgium has few natural resources and depends largely on the export of goods and services. The once-rich coal mines of Wallonia are almost depleted. There is some deciduous and conifer forestry in the Ardennes region.

BELGIUM : LAND USE

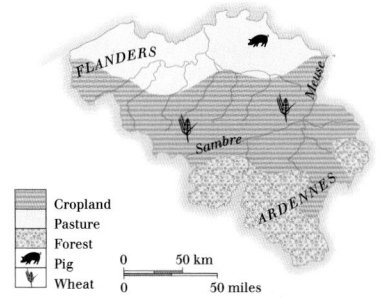

Cropland
Pasture
Forest
Pig
Wheat

0　50 km
0　50 miles

ENVIRONMENT

 2% partially protected

 Government may introduce a green tax to help environment

ENVIRONMENTAL TREATIES

Yes

Yes

No

Yes

The regional government of Flanders is concerned about the pollution of its groundwater supplies through acid rain, heavy metals, fertilizers and pesticides. It is operating an environmental management plan to meet prescribed standards. Wallonia has initiated strict laws to prevent the illegal tipping of waste, and is also governing air quality and emissions. The population's growing awareness of environmental issues is reflected in the rise of the Green Party.

MEDIA

 Censorship is banned under the constitution. All types of media tend to be divided by language

PUBLISHING AND BROADCAST MEDIA

There are 33 daily newspapers; 18 in French, 14 in Dutch and 1 in German

3 state-owned, 2 independent services

3 state-owned, over 75 local stations

A mix of European satellite channels

Extensive use throughout the country

Newspapers tend to be regional and divided by language. Circulation is low, with the most widely read newspaper having a circulation of just 300,000. Over 80% of Belgians have cable TV, receiving as many as 30 channels from all over Europe. Commercial TV only began in 1989, with the Flemish *Station VTM* showing imported English-language programmes and gameshows.

CRIME

 6450 prisoners

Up 5% in 1990

CRIME RATES

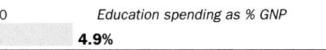

Murders
2 | per 100,000 population

Rapes
6 | per 100,000 population

Thefts
2618 | per 100,000 population

Belgium's crime level is low compared with surrounding countries, though car theft has become more common. The majority of convicted offences are for minor assaults and theft.

EDUCATION

 100%

0　Education spending as % GNP　25
4.9%

THE EDUCATION SYSTEM

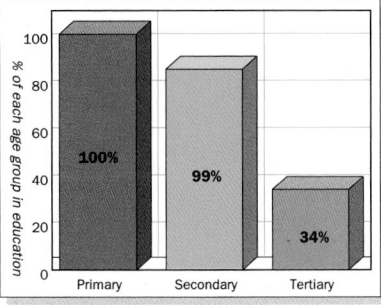

100% Primary
99% Secondary
34% Tertiary

% of each age group in education

In 1959, parents were given the choice between secular and religious schooling. Since 1989, the system has been administered by the governments of the two main language groups. Education in Flanders is in Dutch whilst Wallonia teaches in French. All universities are split by language.

HEALTH

 1 per 309 people

 Heart and respiratory diseases, cancers, accidents

0　Health spending as % GNP　25
0.9%

The quality of health care in Belgium is among the best in the world. Belgium is a world leader in fertility treatment and heart and lung transplants. Treatment is not free, but Belgians hold insurance enabling them to claim back up to 75% of their costs. Car accidents are second only to heart disease as a cause of death; 62,000 accidents resulted in personal injury in 1990. In 1993, there were 1600 registered AIDS patients.

WEALTH

 Baker, 305 Belgian francs per hour; bank employee, 43,009 Belgian francs per month

CONSUMER GOODS OWNERSHIP

447　398　516　162　19
Per 1000 population

Despite high levels of state debt and the run down of its traditional industries, Belgium remains one of the richest countries in Europe. GDP per head, at $16,351, is lower than Germany, but higher than the UK or Italy. The figure, however, masks considerable regional differences. Flanders, where most high-tech businesses are located, has an unemployment rate of 6%, whilst in Wallonia it is 11%; 25% of under 25s in Wallonia are unemployed. The presence of highly-paid EU and international bank employees has made Brussels a distinctly wealthy city. In contrast to the state, Belgians are privately great savers. In 1993, they saved, on average, 20% of their income.

WORLD RANKING

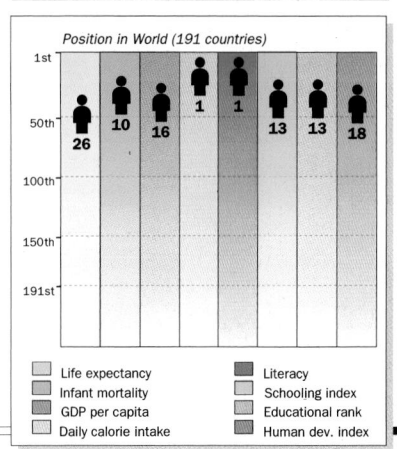

Position in World (191 countries)

26　10　16　1　1　13　13　18

Life expectancy
Infant mortality
GDP per capita
Daily calorie intake
Literacy
Schooling index
Educational rank
Human dev. index

BELIZE

B

OFFICIAL NAME: Belize **CAPITAL:** Belmopan
POPULATION: 194,000 **CURRENCY:** Belizean dollar **OFFICIAL LANGUAGE:** English

CENTRAL AMERICA

FORMERLY CALLED BRITISH HONDURAS, Belize was the last Central American country to gain its independence, in 1981. It lies on the eastern shore of the Yucatan peninsula and shares a border with Mexico along the River Hondo. Belize is Central America's least populous country, and almost one half of its land area is still forested. Its swampy coastal plains are protected from flooding by the world's second largest barrier reef.

Small fish market in Belize City. More than 500 tonnes of Caribbean spiny lobster, the main inshore species, are caught every year.

CLIMATE

WEATHER CHART

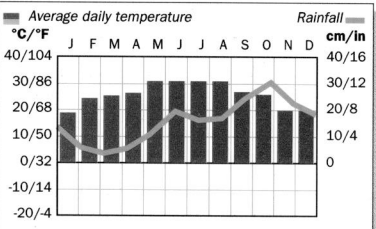

Conditions are hot and humid throughout the year. Coastal regions are affected by hurricanes.

COMMUNICATIONS

Philip S W Goldson, Belize City
272,000 passengers

27 ships
48,300 dwt

THE TRANSPORT NETWORK

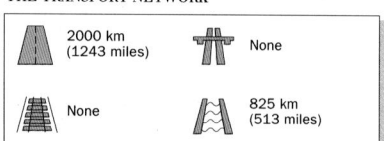

2000 km (1243 miles)	None
None	825 km (513 miles)

Rising prosperity has led to an increase in road traffic, although traffic lights have yet to be installed. Work to increase the passenger capacity of the airport at Belize City was completed in 1981.

TOURISM

221,826 visitors

Up 1% in 1990

MAIN OVERSEAS ARRIVALS

USA 37%	
UK 5%	
Canada 3%	
Other 55%	

% of total arrivals

Governments before 1983 sought to limit tourism. However, eco-tourism is now encouraged.

PEOPLE

English Creole, Spanish, English, Maya, Garifuna (Carib)

9 people per km²

THE URBAN/RURAL POPULATION SPLIT

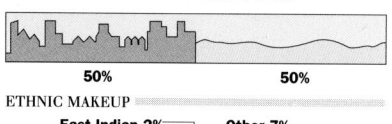

50%   50%

ETHNIC MAKEUP

East Indian 2%
Other 7%
Garifuna 8%
Creole 40%
Maya 10%
Mestizo (European-Indian) 33%

40% of the population can trace their roots back to Africans brought over in the 17th century; the rest is composed of Maya groups, black Caribs (Garifuna), and immigrants from Mexico, the Middle East and India. Belize has a few self-contained communities of Swiss-descended Mennonites.

POLITICS

1998

HM Queen Elizabeth II

House of Representatives 29 members

55% UDP   **45% PUP**

UDP = United Democratic Party **PUP** = People's United Party

Senate 8 members

The members of the Senate are appointed by the governor-general

The desire for independence dominated politics until the 1980s.
It was the PUP, under George Price, that negotiated this with the British in 1981.
During the 1984–1989 UDP administration, the maintenance of a pro-US line and fears of communism in the region were the main concerns. The UDP won power back from the PUP in 1994 and today the state of the economy is the key issue. In the absence of any major ideological or policy distinctions between the PUP and UDP, which are both centrist, elections are fought mostly on candidates' records and personalities.

BELIZE

Total Area : 22 960 sq. km (8865 sq. miles)

POPULATION
● over 10 000
• under 10 000

LAND HEIGHT
1000m/3281ft
500m/1640ft
200m/656ft
Sea Level

N

0   50 km
0   50 miles

B

WORLD AFFAIRS

At the end of 1993, Guatemala officially recognized Belize as an independent state, thus ending a long period of uncertainty and fear of invasion.

AID

 $28m (receipts)   Up 33% in 1991

Belize is one of the highest per capita recipients of US aid; since the staunchly pro-US UDP administration, Belize has been seen as a useful anti-communist buttress in the region.

DEFENCE

 $9.68m   Down 3% in 1990

The 555-strong Belize Defence Force includes two female platoons and is trained by the UK, the USA and Canada. As a result of Guatemala dropping its territorial claim, Britain withdrew its military garrison in 1994.

ECONOMICS

 $389m   2.00 Belizean dollars

SCORE CARD

❑ WORLD GNP RANKING	166th
❑ GNP PER CAPITA	$1970
❑ BALANCE OF PAYMENTS	$–36.5m
❑ INFLATION	2.4%
❑ UNEMPLOYMENT	12%

STRENGTHS
Sugar, textile manufacture, citrus fruits, bananas and cocoa. Small foreign debt, 90% of which is held by multilateral institutions on favourable concessionary terms.

WEAKNESSES
Heavy reliance on imports of processed foods. The economy's small size makes Belize vulnerable to even slight changes in external trading conditions.

EXPORTS
IMPORTS

RESOURCES

105m kwh (capacity 20,000 kw). Not an oil producer and has no refineries. 51,000 cattle, 25,000 pigs, 5000 horses, 4000 mules. None

Exploration for oil and gas, largely by US companies, is currently under way in the Corozal basin region.

ENVIRONMENT

 5% partially protected   Little protection for unique ecosystems

Belize's low population density, relative poverty and lack of industry have kept its dense tropical forests intact. It is still home to many endangered wild animals, including jaguars, tapirs and rare tropical birds.

MEDIA

 Journalists have occasionally been detained for criticizing the government

PUBLISHING AND BROADCAST MEDIA

 There are no daily newspapers. The leading papers are the weekly *Belize Times* and the *People's Pulse*

 1 state-owned service   1 state-owned service

Belize has not suffered the degree of press interference experienced in neighbouring states, but the government remains sensitive to even minor criticisms. In 1989, the PUP, newly returned to power, fulfilled its manifesto commitment by establishing a broadcasting corporation modelled on the British BBC, and by revoking the restrictive law of criminal libel. *Amandala* is the most politically independent newspaper, as well as the best for sports coverage.

CRIME

 89 prisoners   Increase in gun-related crime

Belize was one of Latin America's major exporters of marijuana to the USA until the US Drug Enforcement Agency destroyed the plantations. It is now an increasingly important transshipment point for Colombian cocaine to the USA. The result is that narcotics-related crime in Belize City has risen sharply since the 1980s.

EDUCATION

 93%

Belize's schools are administered by its three main religious denominations: Roman Catholics, Anglicans and Methodists. University College of Belize maintains close links with the University of Michigan in the USA.

CHRONOLOGY

Originally part of the Maya heartland, between 1798 and 1981 Belize was effectively a British colony.

❑ **1919** Demands for more political rights by black Belizeans returning from First World War.
❑ **1936** New constitution with limited franchise.
❑ **1950** PUP formed. Voting age for women reduced from 30 to 21.
❑ **1954** Full adult suffrage.
❑ **1972** Guatemala threatens invasion. Britain sends troops.
❑ **1980** UN passes unopposed – except by Guatemala – resolution calling for independence.
❑ **1981** Full independence.

HEALTH

 1 per 1956 people   Respiratory, heart and cerebrovascular diseases

Around 75% of Belizeans have access to government health services, which include seven hospitals and numerous mobile clinics. Sanitation and water supplies are being improved; 62% of homes in Belmopan now have both.

WEALTH

 Skilled labourer, 700 Belizean dollars per month; general manager, 4600 Belizean dollars per month

CONSUMER GOODS OWNERSHIP

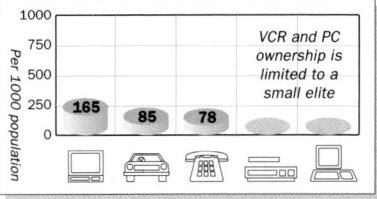

Wealth is more evenly distributed than in the rest of Central America. The drug trade is still a source of wealth.

WORLD RANKING

BELORUSSIA (BELARUS)

OFFICIAL NAME: Republic of Belarus **CAPITAL:** Minsk
POPULATION: 10.3 million **CURRENCY:** Belorussian rouble **OFFICIAL LANGUAGE:** Belorussian

B

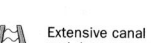

FORMERLY KNOWN AS White Russia, Belorussia is bordered by Lithuania and Latvia in the northwest, Ukraine in the south, and Poland and Russia in the west and east. The land-locked country, which reluctantly became independent of Moscow in 1991, has few resources other than agriculture. The Chernobyl nuclear disaster in neighbouring Ukraine in 1986 has had many profound and lasting effects on the environment. The health of Belorussians has suffered severely and many areas are still contaminated.

CLIMATE

WEATHER CHART

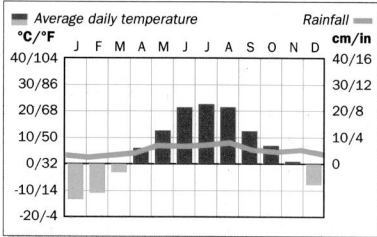

Belorussia has a continental climate. Temperatures in winter drop well below freezing, while in summer fairly high temperatures are reached.

Much of southern Belorussia is marshy and sparsely populated. It includes the vast Pripet Marshes and the Dnieper lowlands.

COMMUNICATIONS

Minsk International

Has no fleet

THE TRANSPORT NETWORK

	265,600 km (165,036 miles)		None
	5590 km (3474 miles)		Extensive canal and river systems

Belorussia has no direct access to the sea, but is close to the Baltic ports. Railway communications are good.

TOURISM

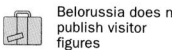

Belorussia does not publish visitor figures

No significant change from year to year

MAIN OVERSEAS ARRIVALS

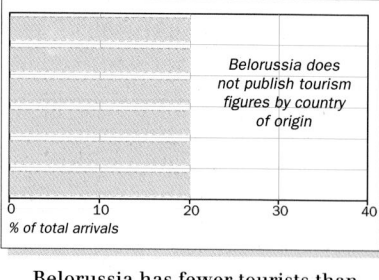

Belorussia does not publish tourism figures by country of origin

% of total arrivals

Belorussia has fewer tourists than its Slav and Baltic neighbours. Many of its historic buildings were destroyed during the Second World War. Minsk was completely flattened and is now characterized by Stalinist and high-rise buildings. There are few assets on which to build a tourist industry.

BELORUSSIA

Total Area : 207 600 sq. km
(80 154 sq. miles)

POPULATION

over 1 000 000	⊡
over 500 000	◉
over 100 000	◎
over 50 000	○
over 10 000	●
under 10 000	·

LAND HEIGHT

200m/656ft

100m/328ft

LATVIA

RUSSIAN FEDERATION

LITHUANIA

POLAND

UKRAINE

Braslaw
Navapolatsk
Polatsk
Drissa
Vitsyebsk
Drysa
Pastavy
Hlybokaye
Lyepyel'
Byahoml'
Western Dvina
Smarhon'
Vilyeyka
Plyeshchanitsy
Orsha
Ashmyany
Maladzyechna
Horki
Zhodzina
Barysaw
Lida
MINSK
Byerazino
Mahilyow
Krychaw
Hrodna
Hora Dzyarzhynskaya 345m
Byerazina
Cherikaw
Navahrudak
Bykhaw
Kastsyukovichy
Neman
Vawkavysk
Nyasvizh
Shyshchytsy
Asipovichy
Babruysk
Sozh
Baranavichy
Slutsk
Rahachow
Slonim
Zhlobin
Ivatsevichy
Salihorsk
Pruzhany
Svyetlahorsk
Byaroza
Tsna
Ptsich
Homyel'
Yasyel'da
Rechytsa
Dobrush
Brest
Kobryn
Luninyets
Pinsk
PRIPET MARSHES
Pripet
Davyd-Haradok
Mazyr
Kalinkavichy
Dnieper
Ubarts'
Yel'sk
Khoyniki

N

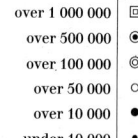

0 50 km
0 50 miles

PEOPLE

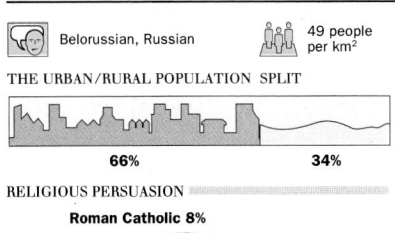

Belorussian, Russian

49 people per km²

THE URBAN/RURAL POPULATION SPLIT

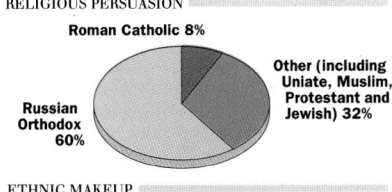

66%   34%

RELIGIOUS PERSUASION

Roman Catholic 8%

Other (including Uniate, Muslim, Protestant and Jewish) 32%

Russian Orthodox 60%

ETHNIC MAKEUP

Ukranian 3%   Polish 4%

Other 2%   Russian 13%

Belorussian 78%

Only 2 per cent of the population is non-Slav and there is little ethnic tension. According to a law passed in September 1992, the entire population has an automatic right to Belorussian citizenship. Only 11% of the population, most of whom live in the countryside, are fluent in Belorussian. Attempts by Chairman Shushkevich to boost the popularity of the official language proved unsuccessful.

POPULATION AGE BREAKDOWN

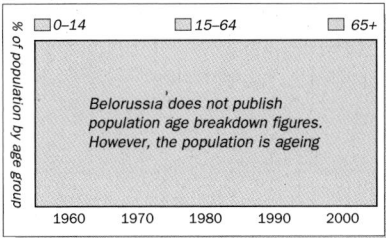

% of population by age group

☐ 0–14   ☐ 15–64   ☐ 65+

Belorussia does not publish population age breakdown figures. However, the population is ageing

1960   1970   1980   1990   2000

POLITICS

  1994

  Parliamentary chairman: Mechislau Grib

THE STATE OF THE PARTIES

Supreme Soviet 360 members

92% PKB   8% BPF

PKB = Communist Party of Belorussia **BPF** = Belorussian Popular Front. Under the 1994 constitution, the Supreme Soviet is to be replaced by a new 260-member assembly

Under the 1994 consitution, Belorussia is a multiparty democracy headed by a directly-elected president.

MAIN POLITICAL ISSUES

Relationship with Russia
Belorussia's relationship with Russia is the key political issue. Mechislau Grib, the parliamentary chairman, is strongly pro-Russian. Under his leadership, Belorussia has agreed a monetary union that effectively gives Moscow control of Belorussia's economic policy. In return, Russia will take on Belorussia's $1.5 billion debt. Belorussia also hopes for Russian economic support.

The environment
The 1986 Chernobyl nuclear disaster continues to cast a shadow over life in Belorussia. The devastating effects of the accident are still being revealed in higher incidences of leukaemia and cancers. Much of Belorussia's land and farm produce is still tainted with fallout radiation. The clean-up operation is slow and laborious and will take decades. It is a major drain on state finances. In 1993, 17% of government spending was set aside for this purpose.

PROFILE
Following independence in 1991, Belorussia was the slowest of the ex-Soviet states to implement political reform and a post-soviet consitution was not adopted until March 1994. The current parliament was elected in 1990 and is therefore predominantly composed of communist deputies. The pro-democracy BPF has only 8% of the seats. Much of the real power lies in the hands of the prime minister, the conservative Vyacheslau Kebich. However, with the replacement in 1993 of the moderate Shushkevich by the conservative Mechislau Grib as parliamentary chairman, the reformers now have even less influence than in 1991. The current broad trend is a return to pre-independence politics.

The policy of seeking a closer rapprochement with Russia reflects this. Monetary union in 1993 could well lead to Belorussia eventually joining a unitary Russian state. Much depends on events in Moscow. The Belorussian leadership is banking on the reformers there losing ground to the conservatives, who are more likely to provide Belorussia with economic aid.

Vyacheslau Kebich, *conservative prime minister of the Council of Ministers.*   ***Chairman Stanislau Shushkevich,*** *ousted in a no-confidence vote in 1993.*

WORLD AFFAIRS

 CIS   CSCE   CE   ECE

Relations with Russia are paramount. Numerous bilateral agreements have been signed since 1991. These ties are being strengthened now that the pro-Russian communist, Mechislav Grib, has become parliamentary chairman. However, relations could sour if the reformers in Moscow gain power. Many in Russia are opposed to closer links with Belorussia, believing it represents a drain on Moscow's resources for little strategic gain.

The good relations with the West developed by ex-Chairman Shushkevich have cooled. However, Belorussia retains its Most Favoured Nation (MFN) trading status with the USA.

AID

  Receipts undisclosed   Rising, particularly from Russia

In 1993, the World Bank and IMF granted Belorussia its first loans, on condition that the government carries out economic reforms. Under this package, $98 million was promised by the IMF and $120 million by the World Bank. The anti-reform stance of the current administration makes it unlikely that Belorussia will receive the full package.

The EU has extended some credits to Belorussia to assist in the conversion of the defence industry to non-military production. Belorussia still requires aid to combat the effects of radiation pollution in the wake of the Chernobyl nuclear accident of 1986. Some help is being provided through the western-sponsored Know-How Fund.

CHRONOLOGY

After forming part of medieval Kievan Rus, Belorussia experienced rule by three of its neighbours – Poland, Lithuania and Russia – before incorporation into the USSR.

- ❏ **1917** Nationalists and socialists try to gain autonomy within Russia.
- ❏ **1918** Belorussian Bolsheviks stage coup. Independence as Belorussian Soviet Socialist Republic.
- ❏ **1919** Invaded by Poland.
- ❏ **1920** Minsk retaken by Red Army. Eastern Belorussia re-established as Soviet Socialist Republic (BSSR).
- ❏ **1921** Treaty of Riga – western Belorussia incorporated into Poland. New Economic Policy applied.
- ❏ **1922** BSSR merges with Russian Federation to form USSR.
- ❏ **1929** Stalin implements collectivization of agriculture.

- ❏ **1939** Western Belorussia reincorporated into USSR when Soviet Red Army invades Poland.
- ❏ **1941–1944** Belorussia under German occupation during Second World War.
- ❏ **1945** Belorussia a-founding member of the UN along with Ukraine and USSR.
- ❏ **1965** KT Mazurau, leader of Communist Party of Belorussia (PKB), becomes first deputy chairperson of USSR's Council of Ministers.
- ❏ **1986** April, accident at Chernobyl nuclear power plant. Belorussia affected by 70% of plant's radioactive fallout. December, Belorussian intellectuals petition Soviet leader Mikhail Gorbachev over dangers of 'linguistic extinction' of Belorussian language.
- ❏ **1988** Archaeologist Zianon Pazniak reveals evidence of mass executions (over 300,000) by Soviet military between 1937 and 1941 in Kurapaty wood near Minsk. Popular outrage fuels formation of nationalist Belorussian Popular Front (BPF), with Pazniak as president. PKB authorities crush demonstration.
- ❏ **1989** Belorussian adopted as republic's official language.
- ❏ **1990** PKB prevents BPF participating in March elections to Supreme Soviet. BPF members join other opposition groups in Belorussian Democratic Bloc (BDB). BDB wins 25% of seats. July, CPB bows to opposition pressure and issues Declaration of the State Sovereignty of BSSR.
- ❏ **1991** March, 83% vote in referendum to preserve union with USSR. April, strikes against PKB and its economic policies. August, independence declared. Republic of Belarus adopted as official name. Stanislau Shushkevich elected chairman of Supreme Soviet. December, Belorussia, Russia and Ukraine establish CIS.
- ❏ **1992** Supreme Soviet announces Soviet nuclear weapons must be cleared from Belorussia by 1999. Help promised from USA.
- ❏ **1993** January, national army comes into existence. Ratification of START-1 and nuclear non-proliferation treaties by Belorussian parliament.
- ❏ **1994** Shushkevich ousted from post as chairman of Supreme Soviet. Replaced by pro-Russian former communist, Mechislau Grib. Monetary union (re-entry into rouble zone) agreed with Russia.

DEFENCE

💲 $660m   ⬇ Down 30% in 1993

0	*Defence spending as % GDP*	40
2.6%		

BELORUSSIAN ARMED FORCES

🚂	1850 main battle tanks (1520 T–72/310 T–62/ 20 T–54)	95,000 personnel
🚢	None	
✈	502 combat aircraft (Su–25/MiG–29)	20,000 personnel
🚀	54 SS–25 ICBM missiles (under Russian control)	

Under ex-Chairman Shushkevich, Belorussia was committed to a policy of neutrality. By mid-1993 all tactical nuclear weapons were removed and Belorussia announced its aim of removing its strategic nuclear weapons by 1995. Shushkevich also refused to sign the CIS Collective Security Pact, believing an independent army was essential to Belorussia's sovereignty.

Under Grib, stronger military ties with Moscow are being established and Belorussia is now bearing some of the costs of Russian troops stationed on its territory. However, Belorussia's large defence industry is hoping that the arrangement will mean an increase in orders from Russia.

ECONOMICS

📊 $32.1bn   💱 1906.00 Belorussian roubles

SCORE CARD

- ❏ WORLD GNP RANKING..........................53rd
- ❏ GNP PER CAPITA $3117
- ❏ BALANCE OF PAYMENTS ....Deficit
- ❏ INFLATION 1100%
- ❏ UNEMPLOYMENT..................................1.2%

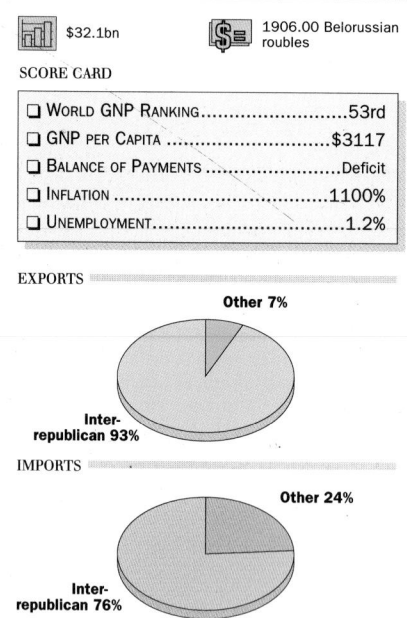

EXPORTS

Other 7%

Inter-republican 93%

IMPORTS

Other 24%

Inter-republican 76%

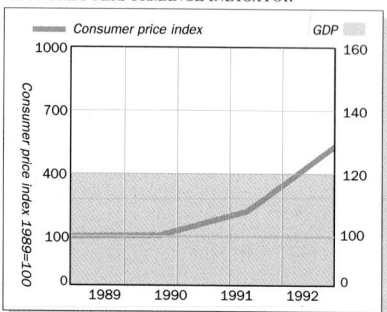

ECONOMIC PERFORMANCE INDICATOR

— Consumer price index   GDP ▓

STRENGTHS

Low unemployment rate: just over 1% of labour force (approximately 50,000). Better economic prospects than other CIS states. Monetary union with Russia aids currency stability. Potential of forestry and agriculture.

WEAKNESSES

Decision not to pursue economic reform will keep increasingly inefficient industries in business. Few natural resources. Dependence on Russia for energy. Clean-up costs of Chernobyl drain government finances.

PROFILE

Following independence, Belorussia adopted a slower pace of economic reform than the other ex-Soviet states. Chairman Shushkevich was thwarted

in his attempts to move more quickly to a market economy by the largely conservative parliament. Grib's accession to its chairmanship has frozen moves towards privatization. He wishes to see a return to the Soviet-style direction of all economic enterprises from the centre. Traditional industries will continue to receive heavy subsidies. The small, pro-reform opposition fears the failure to reform will leave Belorussia impoverished.

BELORUSSIA : MAJOR BUSINESSES

🔧 Micro electronics		✳ Textiles	
⚓ Shipbuilding		⚗ Chemicals	
✿ Heavy engineering		🖥 Computers	
📖 Food processsing		🌲 Saw milling	
🚗 Vehicle assembly			
🏭 Manufacturing		0 100 km	
🖥 Consumer goods		0 100 miles	

* significant multinational ownership

RESOURCES

37.6bn kwh (capacity 8.03m kw)

6.4m cattle, 4.7m pigs, 380,000 sheep

 Produces very small quantities of oil

 Natural gas, coal, rock salts

ELECTRICITY GENERATION

Electricity is supplied by thermal power stations burning coal, oil, gas or peat

% of total generation by type

Belorussia has no significant strategic resources and is heavily dependent on the Russian Federation for fuel and energy supplies. Small quantities of oil and natural gas exist close to the Polish border.

BELORUSSIA : LAND USE

Cropland
Forest
Pasture
Wetlands
Flax - cash crop
Cereals
Cattle

BYELRUSKAYA HRADA

Pripet

Dniepr

0   100 km
0   100 miles

ENVIRONMENT

 1.1%

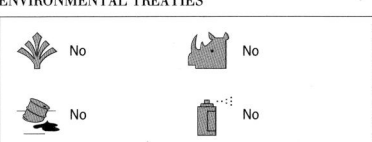 Inadequate funds to deal with Chernobyl clean-up

ENVIRONMENTAL TREATIES

	No		No
	No		No

In 1986 a massive leak from Ukraine's Chernobyl nuclear reactor sent a huge cloud of radiation into Belorussia. 70% of the fallout fell on 40% of the country, including the capital Minsk; 2.3 million people were immediately affected. The government at the time kept the leak secret. Farmland, forests and water were all contaminated, including underwater streams feeding rivers in eastern Poland.

Cases of leukaemia and cancer are continuing to increase. Some areas in the fallout zone are still being farmed. Unscrupulous dealers are suspected of selling meat meant for destruction. A clean-up programme is under way, swallowing 17% of government finances each year. Belorussia is seeking substantial Western aid to cope with the problem.

MEDIA

 High level of state censorship

PUBLISHING AND BROADCAST MEDIA

There are 216 newspapers, of which almost two thirds are published in Belorussian

1 state-run service

1 state-run service

Intelsat V1 F1

None

The media are under central government control and are largely dependent on state subsidies. The one independent TV station was closed down in 1992.

CRIME

 Belorussia does not publish prison figures

 Rising

CRIME RATES

The rates of all categories of crime have increased since independence

As elsewhere in the former Soviet Union, economic hardship (although unemployment stands at only just over 1%) and a general breakdown in law and order have resulted in a significant rise in crime. The murder rate increased by nearly 50% and muggings by nearly 60% in the first half of 1993. Belorussia has become a transshipment point for illegal drugs destined for western Europe, while locally-produced opium supplies the internal market.

EDUCATION

 100%

0   *Education spending as % GNP*   25

7.9%

THE EDUCATION SYSTEM

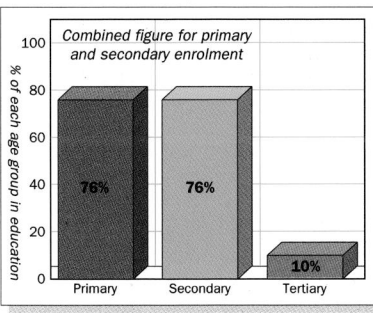

Combined figure for primary and secondary enrolment

% of each age group in education

76%   76%   10%

Primary   Secondary   Tertiary

Russian remains the main language of instruction in both secondary and tertiary establishments, despite attempts by Shushkevich to promote Belorussian. University education is of a fairly high standard.

HEALTH

 1 per 246 people

 Circulatory diseases, cancers, accidents, violence

0   *Health spending as % GNP*   25

Insufficient to cope with abnormal circumstances

Belorussia's good health service has been placed under enormous strain as a result of the Chernobyl nuclear disaster. The number of cancer and leukaemia cases is currently 10,000 above the previous annual average. More wards and specialist units have had to be built. Under the Know-How Fund, many Belorussian doctors are being trained in the latest bone-marrow techniques in Europe and the USA.

WEALTH

 Inflation is eroding the value of most salaries

CONSUMER GOODS OWNERSHIP

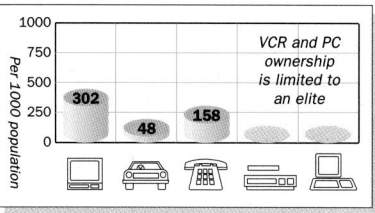

Per 1000 population

VCR and PC ownership is limited to an elite

302   48   158

The deteriorating economic situation has resulted in an overall drop in living standards. High inflation has particularly affected people on fixed incomes. Wealth is concentrated in the hands of a small, communist elite, which has been opposed to any market mechanisms. Now that they have the upper hand in parliament, they will strengthen their grip on the state's resources. Belorussia is unlikely to see the expansion of entrepreneurial activity to be found in Poland or Russia. However, the state's commitment to low unemployment will mean that the extreme social deprivation to be found in other ex-USSR states should be avoided.

WORLD RANKING

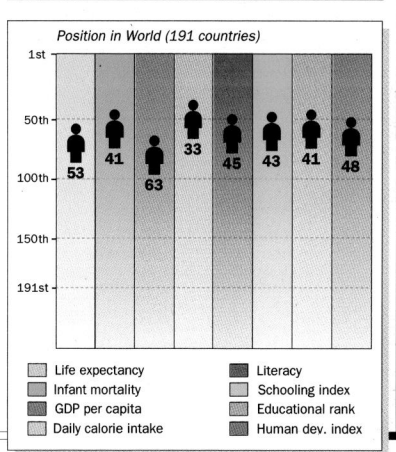

Position in World (191 countries)

1st
50th
100th
150th
191st

53   41   63   33   45   43   41   48

Life expectancy		Literacy
Infant mortality		Schooling index
GDP per capita		Educational rank
Daily calorie intake		Human dev. index

BENIN

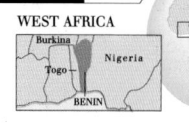

WEST AFRICA

OFFICIAL NAME: Republic of Benin   **CAPITAL:** Porto-Novo
POPULATION: 4.9 million   **CURRENCY:** CFA franc   **OFFICIAL LANGUAGE:** French

BENIN STRETCHES NORTH from the West African coast, with a 100 km shoreline on the Bight of Benin. Formerly the kingdom of Dahomey, Benin became a French protectorate and then a part of colonial French West Africa. It gained independence in 1960. In 1990, Benin became one of the pioneers of African multipartyism, ending 17 years of one-party Marxist-Leninist rule. Benin's economy is based on a well-diversified agricultural sector.

CLIMATE

WEATHER CHART

There are two rainy seasons. The hot, dusty *harmattan* wind characterizes the December to February dry season.

COMMUNICATIONS

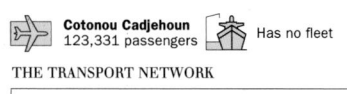

Cotonou Cadjehoun
123,331 passengers   Has no fleet

THE TRANSPORT NETWORK

| 7445 km (4626 miles) | None |
| 635 km (395 miles) | None |

The joint Benin–Niger railway runs only as far as Parakou. Air travel through Cotonou is increasing rapidly.

TOURISM

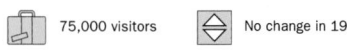

75,000 visitors   No change in 1989

MAIN OVERSEAS ARRIVALS

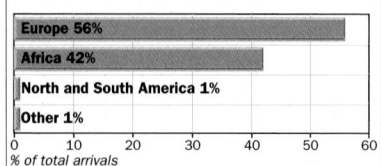

Europe 56%
Africa 42%
North and South America 1%
Other 1%

% of total arrivals

Tourism is not well-developed, although there are plans to develop package tourism. There is some safari tourism in the north, particularly in the Atakora Mountains. Benin is popular as a weekend break for visitors to Nigeria.

PEOPLE

Fon, Bariba, Yoruba, Adja, Houeda, Somba, French

41 people per km²

THE URBAN/RURAL POPULATION SPLIT

38%   62%

RELIGIOUS PERSUASION

Christian 15%
Muslim 15%
Indigenous beliefs 70%

Benin is politically dominated by the southern Fon people. There is some north–south tension, partly because the south is more developed, and partly reflecting a Muslim-Christian divide. Women hold positions of power in the retail trade.

BENIN

Total Area : 112 620 sq. km (43 480 sq. miles)

POPULATION

◎ over 500 000
○ over 100 000
● over 50 000
• over 10 000

LAND HEIGHT

500m/1640ft
200m/656ft
Sea Level

0   100 km
0   100 miles

POLITICS

1996   President Nicéphore Soglo

THE STATE OF THE PARTIES

National Assembly 64 members

| 19% Coalition | 14% PNDD/ PRD | 13% PSD/ UNSP | 11% RND | 43% Other |

Coalition (composed of: UDFP = Democratic Union of the Forces of Progress, MDPS = Movement for Democracy and Social Progress, ULD = Union for Liberty and Development)
PNDD = National Party for Democracy and Development
PRD = Party of Democratic Renewal   **PSD** = Social Democratic Party   **UNSP** = National Union for Solidarity and Progress   **RND** = National Rally for Democracy

Benin has been at the forefront of African democratization. This process began at the National Conference of 1990, when General Kerekou agreed to hold multiparty elections after years of military one-party rule. Following elections in 1991, Kerekou became the first of the African one-party leaders to hand over power peacefully. Nicéphore Soglo, a former official of the World Bank and nephew of General Soglo who ruled from 1965 to 1967, took over the presidency. The former ruling party failed to gain any seats in the new parliament. The main political parties in Benin are regionally based and depend on the leadership of individuals influential in local communities. Soglo does not have an automatic majority in parliament, but depends on an alliance with Houngbedji, an arch-opponent. As Soglo moves towards the 1996 elections, indications are that the struggle will be tough. The main political issue is the effect on the economy of Soglo's World Bank-style deregulation. The reforms he has introduced have to date failed to reduce the economic hardships of the late 1980s.

WORLD AFFAIRS

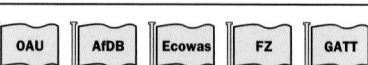

| OAU | AfDB | Ecowas | FZ | GATT |

Benin is largely dominated by its giant neighbour, Nigeria, by far the most powerful state in the region. President Soglo was recently chairman of ECOWAS and supports regional integration with neighbouring countries. Continuing good relations with France, the main source of aid, is critical.

AID

 $256m (receipts)   Down 6% in 1991

Benin's poverty is such that the maintenance of aid is at the top of the political agenda. France, the main protector of Benin's independence since 1960, is the major aid donor. Other donors include the World Bank and IMF, the EU, Germany, Belgium, the Netherlands, Spain and the USA. Almost all development finance comes from aid, and some has been used to finance debt-servicing. There is the usual problem of finding suitable projects, although Benin has a large, well-educated (if top-heavy) civil service, making implementation easier than in many parts of Africa.

DEFENCE

 $25.71m   Up 26% in 1992

The 3800-strong army is actively involved in the attempt to curb smuggling on the border with Nigeria. In 1989, the army was employed internally against rioters.

ECONOMICS

 $2.1bn   295.23 CFA francs

SCORE CARD

- ❑ WORLD GNP RANKING........................137th
- ❑ GNP PER CAPITA $430
- ❑ BALANCE OF PAYMENTS...................$–107m
- ❑ INFLATION 1%
- ❑ UNEMPLOYMENT....Widespread underemployment

STRENGTHS
Agriculture-based economy, with good product diversification. President Soglo's World Bank expertise. New-found political stability.

WEAKNESSES
Combined problems of smuggling and over-valued CFA make it almost impossible to estimate income. Top-heavy civil service owing to return of civil servants from other AOF countries.

EXPORTS

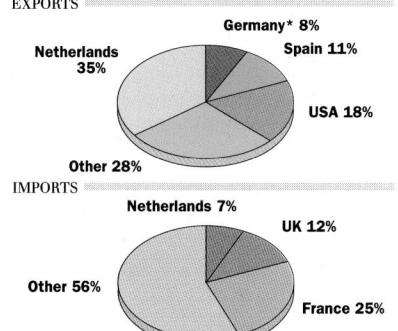

Germany* 8%
Netherlands 35%
Spain 11%
USA 18%
Other 28%

IMPORTS

Netherlands 7%
UK 12%
Other 56%
France 25%

Flat landscape near Cotonou, *characteristic of Benin's coastal region. Numerous lagoons lie behind its short, 100-km coastline.*

RESOURCES

5m kwh (capacity 15,000 kw) Reserves of 19,900,000 bbl

 932,000 cattle, 890,000 sheep, 680,000 pigs   Oil, limestone, marble, gold

Since 1988 most electricity – which previously had to be imported from Ghana – is generated by the Nangbeto Dam on the River Mono.

ENVIRONMENT

 7% 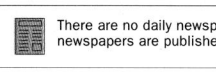 New, environmentally aware rural development ministry

Desertification in the north is the major problem. Benin has been used in the past as a dumping ground for toxic waste.

MEDIA

 Although freedom of expression is guaranteed under the constitution, the press is quick to defend its rights

PUBLISHING AND BROADCAST MEDIA

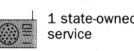

There are no daily newspapers; most newspapers are published fortnightly

1 state-owned service 1 state-owned service

The newly independent press faces economic difficulties. The fortnightly *La Gazette du Golfe* has failed in its attempt to build a regional market.

CRIME

 Benin does not publish prison figures   Little significant change from year to year

Benin is relatively free of serious crime, though armed robbery is an increasing problem. There is also a very high level of smuggling, especially along the border with Nigeria.

EDUCATION

 23%

More is spent on education than on defence, and this is reinforced by Benin's active intellectual community, the 'Latin Quarter of Africa'. The university at Abomey-Calavi is rated highly in medicine and law.

HEALTH

 1 per 16,025 people   Communicable and diarrheal diseases, malaria

Outside major towns, health services are scarce. Benin trains many doctors, but more of them work in France than in Benin.

WEALTH

 Railway ticket clerk, 35,000 CFA francs per month; oil industry engineer, 323,000 CFA francs per month

CONSUMER GOODS OWNERSHIP

VCR and PC ownership is limited to a small elite

5 8 4

Substantial differences in wealth reflect the strongly hierarchical nature of society, especially in the south. French cars are considered status symbols.

WORLD RANKING

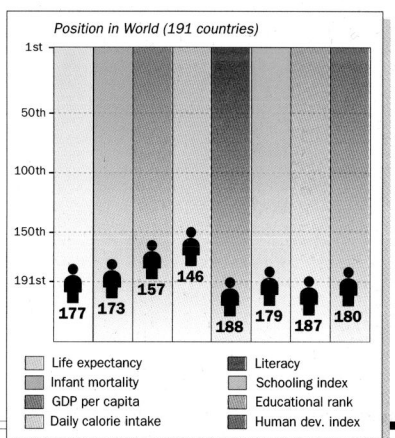

Position in World (191 countries)

177 173 157 146 188 179 187 180

- ☐ Life expectancy
- ☐ Infant mortality
- ☐ GDP per capita
- ☐ Daily calorie intake
- ■ Literacy
- ☐ Schooling index
- ☐ Educational rank
- ■ Human dev. index

BHUTAN

SOUTH ASIA

OFFICIAL NAME: Kingdom of Bhutan   **CAPITAL:** Thimpu
POPULATION: 1.6 million   **CURRENCY:** Ngultrum   **OFFICIAL LANGUAGE:** Dzongkha

PERCHED IN THE HIMALAYAS between India and China, Bhutan is 70% forested. The land rises from the low, tropical southern strip, through the fertile central valleys, to the high Himalayas, inhabited by semi-nomadic yak herders. A formal Buddhist state where power is shared by the king and government, Bhutan began modernizing in the 1960s, but has chosen to do so gradually and remains largely closed to the outside world.

CLIMATE

WEATHER CHART

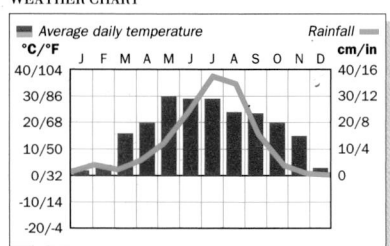

The south is tropical, the north alpine, cold and harsh. The central valleys are warmer in the east than in the west. The summer monsoon affects all parts.

COMMUNICATIONS

Paro International
19,939 passengers

Has no fleet

THE TRANSPORT NETWORK

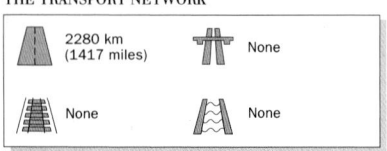

2280 km (1417 miles)	None
None	None

The main surfaced road runs east–west across central Bhutan. Two others run south into India. Only the national airline, Druk Air, flies into Bhutan.

BHUTAN

Total Area :
47 000 sq. km (18 147 sq. miles)

LAND HEIGHT

- 6000m/19686ft
- 4000m/13124ft
- 2000m/6562ft
- 1000m/3281ft
- 500m/1640ft
- 200m/656ft
- Sea Level

POPULATION

- ● over 10 000
- • under 10 000

TOURISM

 1480 visitors   Up 4% in 1990

MAIN OVERSEAS ARRIVALS

USA 30%	
Germany 19%	
UK 11%	
Other 40%	

% of total arrivals

The government's policy of allowing tourism to expand only very slowly aims to protect Bhutan's cultural values and natural environment. Most monasteries are closed to foreigners. First steps to privatize the industry were taken in 1991.

Less than 10% of Bhutan is arable, but its fertility allows almost any crop to grow. The diversity of wild plant species inspired its old name: Southern Valleys of the Medicinal Herbs.

PEOPLE

Dzongkha, Nepali, Assamese

32 people per km²

THE URBAN/RURAL POPULATION SPLIT

5%   95%

RELIGIOUS PERSUASION

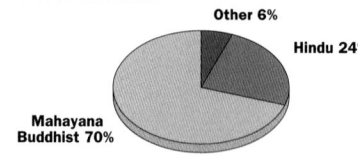

Other 6%

Hindu 24%

Mahayana Buddhist 70%

The majority of the population, the Drukpa peoples, originated from Tibet and are devoutly Buddhist. Twenty-five per cent are Hindu Nepalese who settled in the south from 1910 to 1950. Bhutan has 20 languages. Dzongkha, the language of western Bhutan, native to just 16% of people, was made the official language in 1988 and Nepali was banned. Many southerners have been deported as illegal immigrants, creating fierce ethnic tension.

POLITICS

 Not applicable

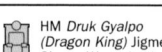 HM *Druk Gyalpo (Dragon King)* Jigme Singye Wangchuck

THE STATE OF THE PARTIES

Bhutan is an absolute monarchy, ruled by the King together with the Council of Ministers, the National Assembly and the head of Bhutan's Buddhist monks

The present King is following his father's plans to modernize Bhutan. Until 1961, the country was run on feudal lines and closed to the outside world. The Drukpa-dominated government's policy of instilling a new sense of national identity has alienated the ethnic Nepalese in the south. It has also led directly to the foundation of the Bhutan People's Party. Banned in Bhutan, it has its headquarters in Kathmandu, Nepal.

WORLD AFFAIRS

    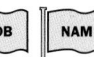

Bhutan's closest relations are with India. It also maintains cordial links with China and negotiations to settle the China–Bhutan border have been progressing since 1984. Relations with Nepal are cool owing to the Bhutan government's policy of sidelining its own ethnic Nepalese population.

AID

 $64m (receipts)　 Up 33% in 1991

Bhutan relies on foreign aid for about half of its annual budget. The largest single donor is India.

DEFENCE

 Small army; India effectively guarantees security　 Little change

Bhutan's 5000-strong army, under the King's command, is trained by Indian military instructors. India provides *de facto* protection and would act to defend Bhutan against attack.

ECONOMICS

 $260m　 31.39 ngultrum

SCORE CARD

❏ WORLD GNP RANKING	172nd
❏ GNP PER CAPITA	$163
❏ BALANCE OF PAYMENTS	$9.4m
❏ INFLATION	8.6%
❏ UNEMPLOYMENT	Low rate

STRENGTHS

New development of cash crops for Asian markets (cardamom, apples, oranges, apricots). Hardwoods in south, especially teak, but exploitation so far tightly controlled. Large hydroelectric potential.

WEAKNESSES

Dependence on Indian workers for many public sector jobs from road-building to teaching. 90% of population dependent on agriculture. Just 6% of land cultivated – expansion difficult because of steep mountain slopes. Very little industry. Few mineral resources.

EXPORTS

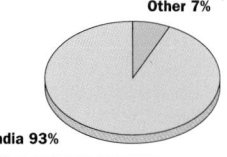

Other 7%
India 93%

IMPORTS

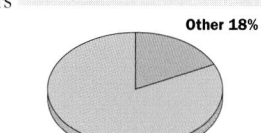

Other 18%
India 82%

RESOURCES

 1.6bn kwh (capacity 350,000 kw)　 Not an oil producer and has no refineries

 2000 pigs, 1000 cattle, 1000 horses　 Talc, gypsum, coal, limestone, slate, dolomite

Bhutan's forests remain largely intact and logging is severely controlled. Hydroelectric potential is considerable, but few dams have been built. Power is sold to India from the Chhukha Dam, bringing in substantial foreign earnings.

ENVIRONMENT

 19% (18% partially protected)　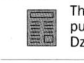 State is encouraging community tree–replanting projects

Bhutan's forests stabilize the steep mountainsides and supply 97% of all fuel needs. Road-building, which began in the 1960s, is the biggest cause of deforestation, which has led to topsoil erosion. The high northern pastures are at risk from overgrazing by yaks. Traditional Buddhist values instilling respect for nature and forbidding the killing of animals are still observed.

MEDIA

 All media are controlled by the government

PUBLISHING AND BROADCAST MEDIA

	There are no daily newspapers. *Kuensel* is published weekly by the government in Dzongkha, English and Nepalese
	No TV service
	1 state-owned service

Bhutan has never had a TV service. TV is banned on the grounds that it would dilute Bhutanese values.

CRIME

 Bhutan does not publish prison figures　 Little variation from year to year

There is little violent crime and levels of theft are low. In 1991, *Driglam namzha*, an ancient code of conduct including the requirement to wear traditional dress, was revived, with fines or imprisonment for non-compliance.

EDUCATION

38%

Education is free, but not compulsory – 5% of children attend secondary school. Teaching is in English and Dzongkha. There are no universities.

CHRONOLOGY

The Drukpa, originally from Tibet, united Bhutan in 1656. It lost the Duars Strip to British India in 1865.

❏ **1907** Monarchy established.
❏ **1953** National Assembly set up with some curbs on royal power.
❏ **1960** Breaks relations with China after Chinese annexation of Tibet.
❏ **1964** First surfaced road finished.
❏ **1968** King forms first cabinet.
❏ **1971** Joins UN.
❏ **1978** New links with China.
❏ **1990** Southern Bhutanese start violent campaign for minority rights. Modest privatization plans.

HEALTH

 1 per 9700 people　 Diarrheal, respiratory diseases, tuberculosis malaria, infant deaths

Free clinics, and Thimpu's hospital, provide basic health care. Progress is being made in child immunization, and monks have recently been persuaded to teach hygiene. Infant mortality is high at 13.3% of live births. Bhutanese, Tibetan and Chinese traditional medicines are widely practised.

WEALTH

 Over 80% of people farm their own plots of land and herd cattle and yaks. Most live a subsistence existence

CONSUMER GOODS OWNERSHIP

WORLD RANKING

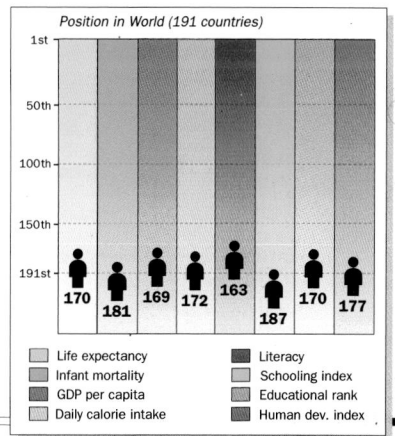

Most people are poor, but starvation is unknown. There is a small middle class of public employees and shop-owners.

111

BOLIVIA

OFFICIAL NAME: Republic of Bolivia   **CAPITAL:** La Paz
POPULATION: 7.8 million   **CURRENCY:** Boliviano   **OFFICIAL LANGUAGES:** Spanish, Quechua and Aymara

BOLIVIA LIES LAND-LOCKED high in central South America. Over half of the population lives on the *altiplano*, the windswept plateau 3500 m above sea level that sits between two ranges of the Andes Mountains. La Paz is the highest capital city in the world. Bolivia also has the world's highest golf course and ski run. The lowland regions in the east are tropical, sparsely populated and underdeveloped, although Santa Cruz, the main city, is growing fast. Bolivia remains one of the poorest nations in South America.

CLIMATE

WEATHER CHART

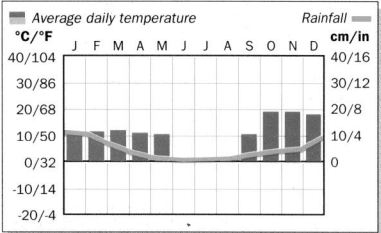

The Andean *altiplano* has an extreme tropical highland climate with frosts at night in winter. Annual rainfall in the west is only 25 cm. The hot eastern lowlands receive most rain in summer.

COMMUNICATIONS

 El Alto, La Paz

1 ship
15,800 dwt

THE TRANSPORT NETWORK

40,897 km (25,412 miles)		Pan-American Highway
3652 km (2269 miles)		14,000 km (8699 miles)

Land-locked Bolivia is badly connected. Obtaining port facilities on the Pacific coast and developing a Pacific–Atlantic railway system, linking Bolivia with both seaboards, are major long-term aims.

Copacabana on the shores of Lake Titicaca. *The town lies on a large headland owned by Bolivia on the Peruvian side of the lake.*

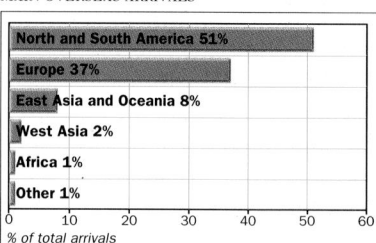

Potato harvest on the altiplano. *The government is encouraging migration to the more fertile lands in the east.*

TOURISM

194,000 visitors   Up 16% in 1989

MAIN OVERSEAS ARRIVALS

North and South America 51%	
Europe 37%	
East Asia and Oceania 8%	
West Asia 2%	
Africa 1%	
Other 1%	

% of total arrivals

Foreign tourists are attracted mostly by the traditional festivals, especially the carnival in February or March, the variety of Bolivia's scenery, and its Spanish colonial architecture. Major attractions include the Silver Mountain at Potosí, and Lake Titicaca, the highest navigable lake in the world, covering an area of 8970 km². Recent political stability has encouraged some growth in tourism. The industry's potential is limited, however, by Bolivia's isolation, the rugged, inaccessible terrain and the limited infrastructure.

BOLIVIA

Total Area : 1 098 580 sq. km
(424 162 sq. miles)

POPULATION

over 500 000	◉
over 100 000	◎
over 50 000	○
over 10 000	●
under 10 000	·

LAND HEIGHT

4000m/9843ft	
2000m/6562ft	
1000m/3281ft	
500m/1640ft	
200m/656ft	
	Sea Level

B

PEOPLE

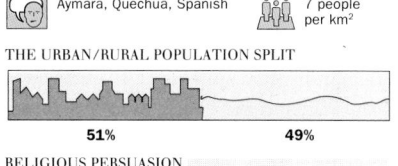

Aymara, Quechua, Spanish

7 people per km²

THE URBAN/RURAL POPULATION SPLIT

51%   49%

RELIGIOUS PERSUASION

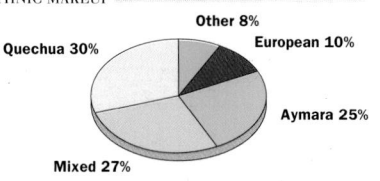

Other 5%

Roman Catholic 95%

ETHNIC MAKEUP

Other 8%

Quechua 30%

European 10%

Aymara 25%

Mixed 27%

Two thirds of Bolivia's population are indigenous, yet these groups suffer discrimination at most levels of society. The Aymara and Quechua lead an almost parallel existence and do not take part in the political process or the formal economy, which remain under the control of a few wealthy city families who established their position during Spanish colonial rule. Most Bolivians are poor and many are subsistence farmers or miners. In recent years, the state has been encouraging people to settle in the Santa Cruz region. In addition to Bolivians from the *altiplano*, Asians, South Africans and a few Mennonite communities have migrated there.

Family life tends to be close-knit; Roman Catholic influence and extended family ties among indigenous groups remain strong. Women have low status in Bolivia, particularly in Aymara and Quechua communities.

POPULATION AGE BREAKDOWN

% of population by age group	■ 0–14	■ 15–64	□ 65+		
	3.2%	3.3%	3.4%	3.6%	4.2%
	53.9%	53.8%	53.4%	55%	57.7%
	42.9%	42.9%	43.2%	41.4%	38.1%
	1960	1970	1980	1990	2000

POLITICS

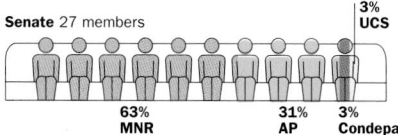

Lower House 1997
Upper House 1997

President Gonzalo Sánchez de Lozada

THE STATE OF THE PARTIES

Chamber of Deputies 130 members

8% Other

40% MNR   27% AP   15% UCS   10% Condepa

MNR = National Revolutionary Movement **AP** = Patriotic Accord (composed of: **ADN** = Democratic Nationalist Action, **MIR** = Movement of the Revolutionary Left) **UCS** = Civic Solidarity Union **Condepa** = Conscience of the Fatherland

Senate 27 members

3% UCS

63% MNR   31% AP   3% Condepa

Bolivia is a multiparty democracy.

MAIN POLITICAL ISSUES

Privatization

Sánchez de Lozada's government is continuing the privatization and free market economic policies of its predecessors, including the sale of 150 state-owned companies, and the privatization of the mining industry through joint ventures.

Cocaine

Cocaine barons are highly influential in Bolivia, the world's second largest exporter, after Colombia, of refined cocaine. The government is trying to trim the drug barons' power by encouraging new cash crops to replace coca, but with limited success. Cocaine has become a significant, though illegal, foreign exchange earner for Bolivia.

PROFILE

Between independence from Spain in 1825 and the early 1980s, Bolivia experienced, on average, more than one armed coup a year. The cycle ended in 1982 when, unable to control a general strike, the military agreed to return power to a national congress. Full elections were delayed until 1985.

Behind the scenes, the military and the cocaine barons continue to enjoy influence. The latter, whose profits underpin the whole economy, are frequently implicated in political corruption scandals. They are also the main backers of Max Fernández, the leader of the populist Civic Solidarity Union (UCS), who almost won the presidential elections in June 1993. The pattern of politics remains one of similar parties competing for power in unstable coalitions. The miners' union, the COB, is no longer a political force and will be weakened further by the privatization of the mines.

The congressional elections of 1993 brought the right-wing MNR to power, replacing a left-wing coalition. Policies have changed little, however, and prospects for Bolivia's poor and underemployed remain bleak.

WORLD AFFAIRS

AG   OAS   LAES   ECLAC   Opanal

B

Bolivia's main foreign policy concern is its attempt to negotiate an outlet to the Pacific with Peru and Chile. Relations with the USA are complicated. The USA is Bolivia's main source of aid, a key part of the national economy. Aid payments have, however, been made conditional on Bolivia taking measures to destroy the cocaine producing and trafficking industry, itself a major buttress of the Bolivian economy. The result to date has been a balancing act. Military attacks on the cocaine barons have kept US aid flowing, yet Bolivia remains the world's second largest producer of refined cocaine.

Bolivia is strengthening its regional links, particularly with Argentina and Brazil. It is a strong supporter of the idea of a South American common market. As one of the most isolated and poorest economies in South America, it would be the major beneficiary of a tariff-free zone in the Andean region.

Left-wing MIR leader and president until 1993, Jaime Paz Zamora.

President Gonzalo Sánchez de Lozada, MNR leader, took power in 1993.

CHRONOLOGY

The Aymara civilization was conquered by the Incas in the late 1400s. Fifty years later, the Incas were defeated by the *conquistadores* and Upper Peru, as it became, was governed by Spain from Lima.

❏ **1545** Cerro Rico, the Silver Mountain, discovered at Potosí. Provides Spain with vast wealth.
❏ **1776** Upper Peru becomes part of Viceroyalty of Río de la Plata centred on Buenos Aires.
❏ **1809** Simón Bolívar inspires first revolutionary uprisings in Latin America at Chuquisaca (Sucre), La Paz and Cochabamba, but they fail.
❏ **1824** Spaniards suffer final defeat by Bolívar's general, José de Sucre.
❏ **1825** Independence.
❏ **1836–1839** Union with Peru fails under presidency of Andrés de Santa Cruz. Internal disorder ensues as wealthy local *caudillos* vie for power.

➪

B

CHRONOLOGY *continued*

- ❑ **1864–1871** Mariano Melgarejo's ruthless rule. Three Indian revolts at seizure of ancestral lands.
- ❑ **1879–1883** War of the Pacific. Peru helps Bolivia against Chile, which had invaded nitrate-rich Atacama province. Chile wins. Bolivia is left land-locked.
- ❑ **1880–1930** Period of stable Liberal–Conservative governments. Exports from revived mining industry bring prosperity.
- ❑ **1903** Rubber-rich Acre province ceded to Brazil after conflict.
- ❑ **1914** Republican Party founded.
- ❑ **1920** Indian rebellion.
- ❑ **1923** Miners bloodily suppressed.
- ❑ **1932–1935** Chaco War with Paraguay. Bolivia loses three quarters of Chaco. Rise of radicalism and labour movement.
- ❑ **1951** Víctor Paz Estenssoro of NMR elected president. Military coup.
- ❑ **1952** Revolution. Paz Estenssoro and NMR brought back. Land reforms improve Indians' status. Education reforms, universal suffrage, nationalization of tin mines.
- ❑ **1964** Military takes over in coup.
- ❑ **1967** Che Guevara killed while trying to mobilize Bolivian workers.
- ❑ **1969–1979** Military regimes rule with increasing severity. 1979 coup fails. Interim civilian rule.
- ❑ **1980** Indecisive elections. Military takes over again.
- ❑ **1982** President-elect Dr Siles Zuazo finally heads leftist civilian MIR government. Inflation 24,000%.
- ❑ **1985** Paz Estenssoro's MNR wins elections. Austerity measures. Annual inflation down to 20%.
- ❑ **1986** Tin market collapses. 21,000 miners sacked.
- ❑ **1988** Anti-narcotics body set up.
- ❑ **1989** MIR takes power in close-run elections. President Paz Zamora makes pact with 1970s dictator Gen Hugo Bánzer, head of ADN.
- ❑ **1990** 1.6m hectares of rainforest recognized as Indian territory.
- ❑ **1992** Strikes halt plans to privatize mining industry.
- ❑ **1993** MNR voted back to power.

AID

 $473m (receipts)   Down 7% in 1991

Large amounts of aid come from the USA, but depend on Bolivia making efforts to eradicate coca farms. Smaller amounts are provided by West European countries. Particularly impoverished rural areas receive project aid from Western NGOs, charities and religious organizations. Corruption and inefficiency, however, hinder the implementation of many projects.

DEFENCE

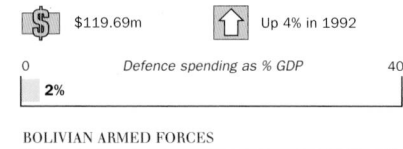

💲 $119.69m   ⬆ Up 4% in 1992

0   *Defence spending as % GDP*   40
2%

BOLIVIAN ARMED FORCES

🛡	36 light tanks (36 SK-105 *Keurassier*)	23,000 personnel
⚓	10 patrol boats	4500 personnel
✈	50 combat aircraft (12 AT-33N/4 F-86F)	4000 personnel
🚀	None	

The military has not actively interfered in politics for over a decade – a record for Bolivia. The army is the main focus of defence spending, with weaponry bought almost entirely from the USA. The Bolivian navy consists mainly of gunboats on Lake Titicaca, which borders Peru, and on the Pilcomayo River. The army has worked with US forces against the cocaine business, although many US advisers have suggested that by-passing the Bolivian armed forces would make the operation more effective. The main, but unrealizable, ambition of the military is to recapture territory that would allow Bolivia access to the Pacific. Military service lasts for one year.

ECONOMICS

📊 5.1bn   💲 4.47 bolivianos

SCORE CARD

- ❑ WORLD GNP RANKING......................112th
- ❑ GNP PER CAPITA $655
- ❑ BALANCE OF PAYMENTS.................$–553.3m
- ❑ INFLATION 10%
- ❑ UNEMPLOYMENT ....Over 50%

ECONOMIC PERFORMANCE INDICATOR

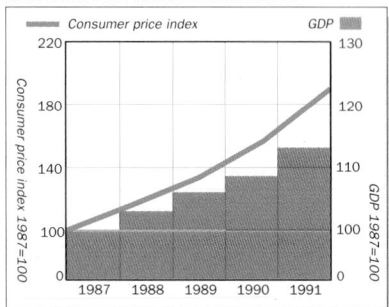

EXPORTS

Belgium and Luxembourg 8%
Other 31%
UK 14%
USA 19%
Argentina 28%

IMPORTS

Japan 10%
Other 34%
Argentina 11%
Brazil 21%
USA 24%

STRENGTHS

Mineral riches: gold, silver, zinc and tin. Newly-discovered oil and natural gas deposits.

WEAKNESSES

Bolivia's extreme poverty has created political instability. Although inflation has been reduced to around 10% annually, a history of hyperinflation – a severe problem until the late 1980s – still deters investors.

PROFILE

Traditionally, the state has used earnings from the public-owned mining sector to control the economy. Since 1985, however, successive governments have sold off state-owned companies and encouraged joint ventures and private investment in an attempt not only to modernize mining and other state sectors, but also to bring inflation under control and curb foreign debt. Bolivia's medium-term economic prospects have been boosted by the recent discovery of oil and gas fields, which should add a useful foreign exchange earner to the economy. However, there is little prospect of developing a significant industrial base. Overseas investors remain deterred by Bolivia's political instability, the social problems of extreme poverty, and the influence of cocaine barons.

BOLIVIA : MAJOR BUSINESSES

Riberalta
Cochabamba
Santa Cruz
La Paz
Oruro
Potosí

Textiles
Saw milling
Food processing
Pharmaceuticals
Tin mining
Narcotics
Agribusiness

0   200 km
0   200 miles

RESOURCES

 1.9bn kwh (capacity 740,000 kw)

 21,300 b/d (reserves 112,136,000 bbl)

 12m sheep, 5m cattle, 2m pigs, 630,000 asses

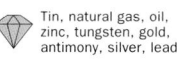 Tin, natural gas, oil, zinc, tungsten, gold, antimony, silver, lead

ELECTRICITY GENERATION

Hydro 66% (1.3bn kwh)
Thermal 34% (670m kwh)
Nuclear 0%
Other 0%

% of total generation by type

Bolivia is the world's largest tin producer. The government is keen to allow foreign companies to prospect for more oil, and to increase sales of natural gas to Brazil and Argentina.

BOLIVIA : LAND USE

Cropland
Pasture
Forest
Wetlands
High mountain regions
Coca - cash crop
Sugar cane
Cattle

0   200 km
0   200 miles

ENVIRONMENT

 9% (5% partially protected)

 No effective controls on exports of rare species

ENVIRONMENTAL TREATIES

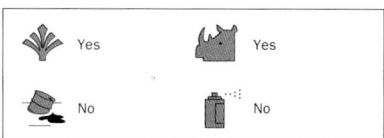

Yes   Yes
No   No

Deforestation is Bolivia's major ecological problem. Land clearances are occurring at the record rate of 200,000 hectares a year. This is one of the world's highest annual depletion rates. Much of the cleared land is turned over to cattle ranching or the growing of coca. The overuse of pesticides and fertilizers in the coca business is also a concern. The industry is effectively uncontrolled and rivers in Amazonia have high pollution levels.

Pollution problems are compounded by waste chemicals used in minerals industries. Mercury, used in the extraction of silver, has been found in dangerous quantities in river systems.

MEDIA

 Little formal censorship, but local journalists rarely comment on the drugs business for fear of reprisals

PUBLISHING AND BROADCAST MEDIA

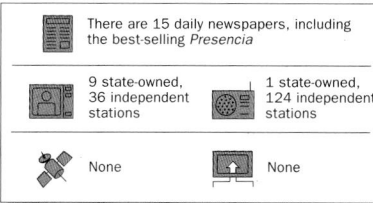

There are 15 daily newspapers, including the best-selling *Presencia*

9 state-owned, 36 independent stations

1 state-owned, 124 independent stations

None

None

Bolivia has the largest number of TV stations in South America. Political parties and cocaine barons frequently exert pressure on the media.

CRIME

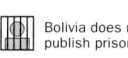 Bolivia does not publish prison figures

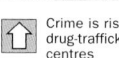 Crime is rising in drug-trafficking centres

CRIME RATES

General crime levels are relatively low in urban areas. Bolivians are concerned about the increase in violence associated with the drugs trade

Violent crime is centred on the drug-trafficking towns in the eastern lowlands, particularly Santa Cruz. However, the main cities are much safer for tourists, and have lower crime rates than cities in neighbouring Peru, for example. The Bolivian police and army have a reputation for mistreating poor farmers and miners.

EDUCATION

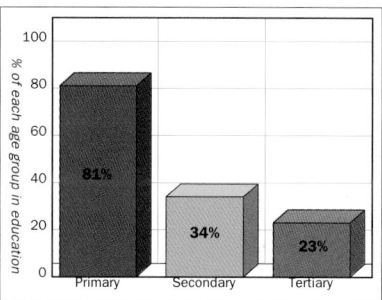 63%

0   Education spending as % GNP   25
2.3%

THE EDUCATION SYSTEM

Primary 81%
Secondary 34%
Tertiary 23%

% of each age group in education

Education is based on a combination of the French and US systems. Although the majority of the population speaks indigenous languages, most teaching is in Spanish. Bolivia has one of the lowest literacy rates on the continent. Only the 51% of the population who live in towns receive schooling.

HEALTH

 1 per 2100 people

 Influenza, tuberculosis, other communicable diseases, malaria

0   Health spending as % GNP   25
0.4%

Bolivia has one of the lowest numbers of doctors per capita in Latin America. Only half the children under one year old are immunized, and diseases that are preventable by vaccination are a major cause of death. Approximately half of the population of Bolivia has safe drinking water. Rural areas are barely served by medicine.

WEALTH

 Miner, 695 bolivianos per month; aircraft engine mechanic, 3086 bolivianos per month

CONSUMER GOODS OWNERSHIP

VCR and PC ownership is limited to a small elite

Per 1000 population

98   5   29

There is little social mobility in Bolivia; the main routes for advancement are the armed forces or the cocaine business. Generally, the indigenous peoples who form the rural poor are the worst-off. The Andean highlands are extremely poor; economic growth is concentrated in the fertile, tropical, eastern lowlands, where the population density is lowest.

The small number of wealthy Bolivians holiday in Brazil or Miami. German luxury goods, and Mercedes cars in particular, are popular among Bolivians and the small German immigrant population. A recent reduction in tariff barriers has resulted in an increase in the import and sale of electronic goods.

WORLD RANKING

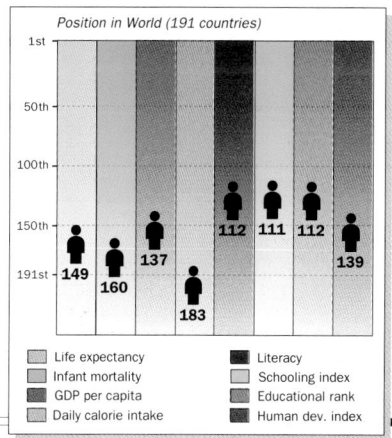

Position in World (191 countries)

149   160   137   183   112   111   112   139

Life expectancy
Infant mortality
GDP per capita
Daily calorie intake
Literacy
Schooling index
Educational rank
Human dev. index

BOSNIA & HERZEGOVINA

OFFICIAL NAME: The Republic of Bosnia and Herzegovina **CAPITAL:** Sarajevo
POPULATION: 4.2 million **CURRENCY:** Bosnian dinar **OFFICIAL LANGUAGE:** Serbo-Croatian

A MOUNTAINOUS COUNTRY with a few kilometres of coast on the Adriatic Sea, Bosnia is bordered by Croatia, Serbia and Montenegro. Between 1943 and 1990, the Yugoslavian regime largely prevented conflict between Muslims, Croats and Serbs by allowing cultural freedom. Since April 1992, however, the three main ethnic populations of the dissolved Yugoslavia have fought over Bosnia. Tens of thousands have died and many historic cities have been destroyed.

CLIMATE

WEATHER CHART

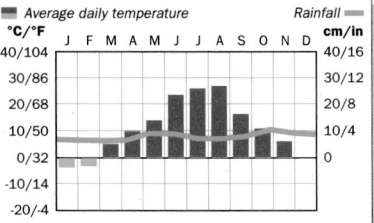

Bosnia has a continental climate with warm summers and bitterly cold winters, often with snow.

COMMUNICATIONS

  Sarajevo Intl   Has no fleet

THE TRANSPORT NETWORK

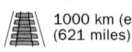 21,168 km (13,154 miles)		None
1000 km (est) (621 miles)		None

War has severely damaged the communications network, resulting in wrecked bridges, roads and railways. The capital, Sarajevo, was formerly the focus for all national and international communications networks.

TOURISM

 None   No tourism likely until peace settlement

MAIN OVERSEAS ARRIVALS

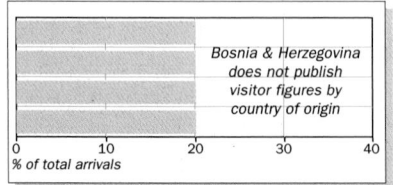

Bosnia & Herzegovina does not publish visitor figures by country of origin

% of total arrivals

Despite having hosted the 1984 Winter Olympics, Bosnia has not developed the infrastructure for a tourist industry.

PEOPLE

 Serbo-Croatian   82 people per km²

THE URBAN/RURAL POPULATION SPLIT

36%   64%

RELIGIOUS PERSUASION

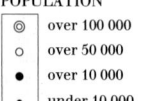

Protestant 4%
Other 10%
Orthodox Catholic 31%
Roman Catholic 15%
Slavic Muslim 40%

Before the war, the population was 44% ethnic Bosnian (mostly Muslim), 31% Serb, 17% Croat and 8% originally from other parts of former Yugoslavia. Intermarriage was common and ethnic violence rare. Society was largely secular and materialistic. In the aftermath of secession, cultural differences became a basis for dividing society in order to lay claim to other ethnic groups' wealth.

POLITICS

Uncertain   President Dr Alija Izetbegovic

THE STATE OF THE PARTIES

National Assembly 240 members

36% PDA   30% SDP   18% CDU–BH   5% ARF   8% DP   2% Others

PDA = Party of Democratic Action **SDP** = Serbian Democratic Party **CDU–BH** = Croatian Democratic Union of Bosnia and Herzegovina **DP** = Socialist Democratic Party **ARF** = Alliance of Reform Forces

The Serbian and Croatian parties have withdrawn from the National Assembly since the outbreak of civil war

The electoral defeat of the Yugoslavian Communist Party in 1990 resulted in a coalition of the Muslim PDA, the Serbian SDP and the Croatian CDU–BH. Disputes soon broke out between Serbs and Croats. Backed by the Serb-dominated Yugoslav People's Army, Bosnian Serb territories declared autonomy and allegiance to Serbia. The PDA and CDU–BH then declared Bosnia a sovereign state. Civil war broke out between the three groups in 1992. The Serbs, led by Radovan Karadzic, are the strongest force, and have received most international blame. In 1993, an uneasy truce was reached between the SDP and CDU–BH. Conflict between the PDA and SDP continues. In 1994, the UN tried to contain the fighting by declaring key Muslim towns 'safe areas' and by sponsoring peace talks.

BOSNIA & HERZEGOVINA

Total Area : 51 130 sq. km (19 741 sq. miles)

POPULATION
◎ over 100 000
○ over 50 000
● over 10 000
• under 10 000

LAND HEIGHT
2000m/6562ft
1000m/3281ft
500m/1640ft
200m/656ft
Sea Level

B

WORLD AFFAIRS

The UN failed to end war with the 1992 Vance-Owen plan for three autonomous communities. NATO threats of air strikes and Russian diplomatic pressure on the Serbs may be the best hope for peace.

AID

 $696m (receipts) in first six months of 1994

 Likely to need increasing amounts of aid

Humanitarian aid has been crucial to the survival of many Bosnians, with the UN playing a vital role in distributing relief. Its Inter-Agency Appeal raised $696 million for the first half of 1994, chiefly for Bosnian Muslim refugees, but also for those in Serbia, Montenegro, Macedonia and Croatia.

DEFENCE

 Almost all state spending is on arms

 No likely change until peace

It has been estimated that the Muslim government controls 60,000 lightly armed troops and 120,000 reservists. The 'Serbian Republic of Bosnia' has 80,000 troops, backed by heavy weapons, and the Croats 50,000.

ECONOMICS

 $4bn (pre-war)

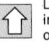 751.22 Bosnian dinars

SCORE CARD

☐ WORLD GNP RANKING........................116th
☐ GNP PER CAPITA ....*The formal*
☐ BALANCE OF PAYMENTS ....*economy now*
☐ INFLATION..............................*operates under*
☐ UNEMPLOYMENT ....*war conditions*

STRENGTHS
Before 1991, Bosnia possessed five of former Yugoslavia's largest companies. Retail outlets were mostly privately operated and there was a sizeable small-business sector. Rising unemployment was the one economic problem. The country has the potential to become a thriving market economy, with a solid manufacturing base.

WEAKNESSES
Enormous foreign investment is needed to repair war damage to infrastructure and the industrial sector.

EXPORTS/IMPORTS

Bosnia & Herzegovina has no significant exports.
Most imports are in the form of UN aid and arms from the international market.
Oil imports are probably from the Middle East

RESOURCES

 Output down by 85% owing to war

 Not an oil producer

 11.5m poultry, 1.4m sheep, 884,000 cattle, 608,000 pigs

 Coal, lignite, iron, bauxite, cement

Bosnia's land is not well suited to agriculture, but has mineral deposits, forests and hydroelectric potential.

ENVIRONMENT

 None owing to war

 No initiatives possible

Apart from war damage, Bosnia faces the effects of industrial pollution incurred during the communist regime.

MEDIA

 Censorship imposed owing to war

PUBLISHING AND BROADCAST MEDIA

 There are two daily newspapers. *Oslobodjenje (Liberation)* has appeared every day since the start of war

 3 state-run, some independent services

 3 state-run, some independent services

Between secession and war, Bosnia had an independent press with no censorship. The Muslim government has since engaged US PR firms to shape media coverage of the war.

CRIME

 Bosnia does not publish prison figures

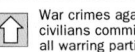 War crimes against civilians committed by all warring parties

All sides in the civil war have been implicated in human rights abuses, in particular the 'ethnic cleansing' of towns and villages, whereby entire populations are forced to evacuate their homes to avoid murder, rape and torture. Army officers have been accused of exploiting their power by running mafia-style operations.

EDUCATION

 93%

Formerly obligatory for eight years, education at all levels has been disrupted or suspended by the war.

The Muslim town of Mostar. *Its 16th-century bridge at a strategic river crossing and much of the old town have been destroyed by war.*

CHRONOLOGY

Following the defeat in 1943 of the Nazi-backed Croat Ustasa regime by communist partisans led by Tito, Bosnia Herzegovina became one of Yugoslavia's six republics.

☐ **1990** Nationalists defeat communists in multiparty elections. PDA leader Dr Alija Izetbegovic president.
☐ **1991** Serbs declare 'Autonomous regions'. Parliament announces republican sovereignty.
☐ **1992** EC and USA recognize Bosnia. Serbs announce 'Serbian Republic'. Civil war between Muslims, Croats and Serbs begins. UN sends troops to guard aid convoys.
☐ **1994** NATO threat of air strikes on Serbs attacking UN 'safe areas'.

HEALTH

 War has led to an exodus of doctors

 Cholera and diphtheria epidemics, violence, deaths from war-stress

War has placed an enormous strain on an underfunded service. Thousands have died for want of basic treatment.

WEALTH

 Most salaries have been eroded by hyperinflation. By 1993, one million people had been displaced by the war and one million had fled Bosnia

CONSUMER GOODS OWNERSHIP

The only people currently acquiring wealth in Bosnia are those involved in profiteering and extortion.

WORLD RANKING

BOTSWANA

B

OFFICIAL NAME: Republic of Botswana   **CAPITAL:** Gaborone
POPULATION: 1.3 million   **CURRENCY:** Pula   **OFFICIAL LANGUAGE:** English

ARID AND LAND-LOCKED, Botswana's central plateau separates the populous eastern grasslands from the Kalahari Desert and swamps of the Okavango Delta in the west. Botswana is a multiparty democracy, but the Botswana Democratic Party has won every election since independence. Diamonds provide Botswana with a prosperous economy, but rain is an even more precious resource, honoured in the name of the currency, *pula*.

The Okavango Delta. Plans to draw water from it for irrigation were shelved in 1991 in the interests of wildlife conservation.

CLIMATE

WEATHER CHART

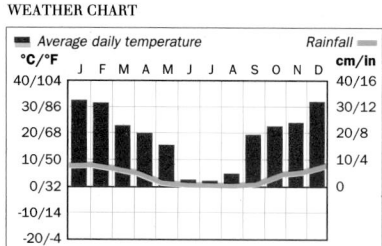

Botswana's subtropical climate is dry and prone to drought. Rainfall declines from 64 cm in the north to under 10 cm in the Kalahari Desert in the west.

COMMUNICATIONS

Sir Seretse Khama Intl, Gaborone
168,000 passengers — Has no fleet

THE TRANSPORT NETWORK

13,500 km (8388 miles)		None
887 km (551 miles)		None

The completion of the trans-Kalahari road to Namibia in 1996 will reduce Botswana's dependence on South African ports. Upgrading domestic road and rail networks is a priority.

TOURISM

844,295 visitors   Up 22% in 1990

MAIN OVERSEAS ARRIVALS

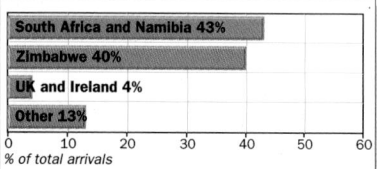

South Africa and Namibia 43%
Zimbabwe 40%
UK and Ireland 4%
Other 13%
0 10 20 30 40 50 60
% of total arrivals

Tourism is aimed at wealthy wildlife enthusiasts and focuses on safaris, especially to the Okavango Delta.

PEOPLE

Tswana, English, Shona, San, Khoikhoi, Ndebele | 2 people per km²

THE URBAN/RURAL POPULATION SPLIT

28%   72%

ETHNIC MAKEUP

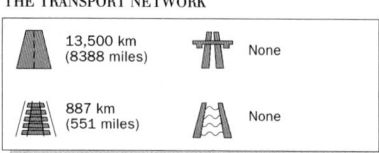

White 1%   —   Kalanga, Basarwa, Kgalagadi 4%

Tswana 95%

Botswana's stability reflects its ethnic homogeneity and the continuing importance of traditional forms of authority, notably the village *kgotla*, or parliament. The Tswana make up 95% of the population, with the Bamangwato forming the largest Tswana group. Botswana's first inhabitants, the San, or Kalahari Bushmen, have been marginalized. Whites dominate the professions.

POLITICS

1994 | President Ketumile Joni Masire

THE STATE OF THE PARTIES

National Assembly 34 members

91%   9%
BDP   BNF

BDP = Botswana Democratic Party   **BNF** = Botswana National Front

House of Chiefs 15 members

Comprises the chiefs of the 8 principal tribes, 4 sub-chiefs and 3 members elected by the other members of the House

Formally a multiparty democracy, Botswana has been ruled by a single elected party, the BDP, since independence. In 1991, opposition parties, led by the BNF, formed the Botswana People's Progressive Front (BPPF) to fight the 1994 elections. The Front's chances of victory depend on its ability to break the BDP's control of the majority rural vote. This seems unlikely. Popular dissatisfaction with the BDP has so far been mainly urban based.

BOTSWANA

Total Area : 581 750 sq. km
(224 600 sq. miles)

POPULATION

over 100 000   ◎
over 50 000   ○
over 10 000   ●
under 10 000   ·

LAND HEIGHT

1000m/3281ft
500m/1640ft

WORLD AFFAIRS

Having been at the receiving end of South African destabilization during the 1980s, Botswana's main concern is the republic's progress to democracy and the possible spillover effects of any breakdown in the process. Potential South African domination of the SADC is another fear. Relations with the UK and USA are important internationally.

AID

 $135m (receipts)   Down 9% in 1991

Botswana's political and economic record has made it a favoured aid recipient, notably from the EU, UK, USA and World Bank. Environmental projects trying to balance wildlife needs with rural development are the priority; 90% of EU aid is environment linked. Transport is also an aid target.

DEFENCE

 $130.9m   Up 19% in 1990

The Botswana Defence Force budget has increased steadily since 1987. This reflects concern over South Africa and ties between army chiefs and the BDP.

ECONOMICS

 $3.6bn   2.54 pula

SCORE CARD

❏ WORLD GNP RANKING	119th
❏ GNP PER CAPITA	$2769
❏ BALANCE OF PAYMENTS	$47.4m
❏ INFLATION	15%
❏ UNEMPLOYMENT	25%

STRENGTHS
Diamonds: transformed Botswana from subsistence to middle-income economy in 25 years; world's third largest producer. High economic growth, averaging 11.3% a year in 1980s. Prudent economic management. Large financial reserves. Copper, nickel, beef.

WEAKNESSES
Overdependence on diamonds (80% of export earnings; 50% of GNP). Weak agriculture and industry. Small population, water shortages and drought add to diversification problems. Adverse impact of beef industry on environment. High transport costs to coast.

EXPORTS

IMPORTS

RESOURCES

 Energy derived from fuelwood and coal   Not an oil producer and has no refineries

 2.5m cattle, 286,000 sheep, 151,000 asses   Diamonds, copper, coal, nickel, soda ash

Diamonds are mined by the 50% state-owned Debswana. Large coal deposits are the basis of power grid expansion. Water is Botswana's scarcest resource.

ENVIRONMENT

 17% (2% partially protected)   National Conservation Strategy regarded among world's best

Botswana is trying to reduce conflict between rural development and the environment by helping communities to earn a living from wildlife protection.

MEDIA

 There is no overt censorship

PUBLISHING AND BROADCAST MEDIA

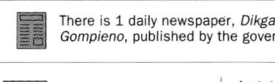 There is 1 daily newspaper, *Dikgang Tsa Gompieno*, published by the government

 No TV service   1 state-owned service

The government bias of the one daily paper and radio is offset in the many weekly and other journals. The 20,000 TVs receive South African stations.

CRIME

 Botswana does not publish prison figures   Rising slowly

Crime levels are generally low. Official corruption, diamond smuggling and robbery are the main concerns. Human rights are generally respected.

EDUCATION

 74%

Education is not compulsory. Primary education is free. Enrolment drops from 90% to under 40% at secondary level. Adult literacy projects are well funded.

CHRONOLOGY

From 1600, Tswana migrations slowly displaced San people. In 1895, at local request, the UK set up the Bechuanaland Protectorate to pre-empt annexation by South Africa.

- ❏ **1965** BDP wins first general election, led by Sir Seretse Khama, and then all subsequent general elections.
- ❏ **1966** Independence; Khama president until his death.
- ❏ **1980** Vice-President Quett (later Ketumile) Masire president.
- ❏ **1985–1986** South African raids.
- ❏ **1991** Opposition parties form BPPF to jointly contest 1994 elections.
- ❏ **1992** Strikes. Corruption scandals. Vice President Mmusi resigns.
- ❏ **1993** Scandals continue; more resignations of senior BDP figures.

HEALTH

 1 per 7185 people   Tuberculosis, heart diseases, pneumonia

The emphasis is on expanding primary health care services. The drought early warning system includes a national nutritional surveillance programme.

WEALTH

 80% of the population live in rural areas and those with cattle are better off

CONSUMER GOODS OWNERSHIP

At $2769, GNP per capita is among Africa's highest, but most people are poor. Wealth belongs to the urban elite.

WORLD RANKING

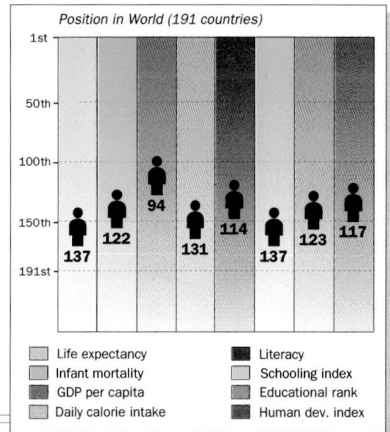

BRAZIL

OFFICIAL NAME: Federative Republic of Brazil   **CAPITAL:** Brasília
POPULATION: 153.2 million   **CURRENCY:** Real   **OFFICIAL LANGUAGE:** Portuguese

SOUTH AMERICA

THE LARGEST COUNTRY in South America, Brazil became independent of Portugal in 1822. Today, it is renowned as the site of the world's largest tropical rainforest, the threat to which led to the UN's first international environmental conference being held at Rio de Janeiro in 1992. Covering one third of Brazil's total land area, the rainforest grows around the massive Amazon River and its delta. Apart from the basin of the River Plate to the south, the rest of the country consists of highlands. The mountainous north is part forested and part desert. Brazil is the world's leading coffee producer and also has rich reserves of gold, diamonds, oil and iron ore. Cattle-ranching is an expanding industry. The city of São Paulo is the world's second biggest conurbation, with 17 million inhabitants.

BRAZIL

Total Area : 8 511 970 sq. km
(3 286 472 sq. miles)

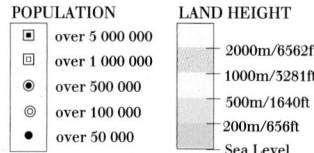

POPULATION	
▣	over 5 000 000
▨	over 1 000 000
◉	over 500 000
◎	over 100 000
●	over 50 000

LAND HEIGHT

- 2000m/6562ft
- 1000m/3281ft
- 500m/1640ft
- 200m/656ft
- Sea Level

CLIMATE

WEATHER CHART

- ■ Average daily temperature
- Rainfall

Brazil's share of the Amazon basin, occupying half of the country, has a model equatorial climate. The 150–200 cm of rain are spread throughout the year, although some periods are rather wetter than others according to region. Temperatures are high, with almost no seasonal variation, but scarcely ever rise above 38°C.

The Brazilian plateau, which occupies most of the rest of the country, has far greater temperature ranges. Rain falls mainly between October and April. However, the northeast, the least productive region of Brazil, is very dry and in recent years has been suffering from severe drought, which has compounded its problems. The southern states have hot summers and cool winters, when frost may occur.

COMMUNICATIONS

 Guarulhos Intl, São Paulo
5.78m passengers

277 ships
8.5m dwt

THE TRANSPORT NETWORK

1.67m km (1.04m miles)	Trans-Amazonian Highway 5000 km (3109 miles)
30,129 km (18,721 miles)	50,000 km (31,069 miles)

A vast road network is being built to link the main centres of Brazil. The antiquated railways are increasingly unreliable. São Paulo's metro is being extended to cope with the city's rapidly expanding population.

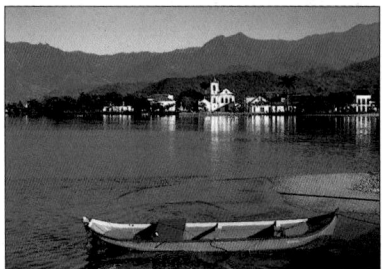

Parati, in Rio state, was one of Brazil's major gold exporting ports in the 17th century. Its colonial architecture is well preserved.

TOURISM

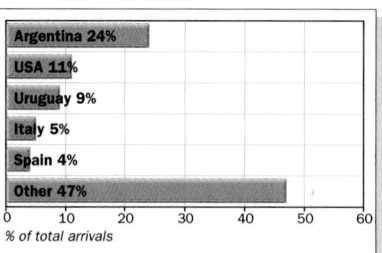

1.08m visitors   Down 23% in 1990

MAIN OVERSEAS ARRIVALS

- Argentina 24%
- USA 11%
- Uruguay 9%
- Italy 5%
- Spain 4%
- Other 47%

% of total arrivals

Its 2000 km of Atlantic beaches, the folklore and music of the northeast coast and the annual *Mardi Gras* carnival in Rio de Janeiro, are Brazil's major attractions. However, the increasingly affluent and international audience now controls the carnival.

The largely Afro-Brazilian residents of Rio's *favelas*, or shanty towns, can often no longer afford to take part in the parades that originate in their culture.

Brazil has targeted eco-tourism as a major growth area. Foreign investment in tourist facilities in Amazonia is being encouraged by the government. But Brazilians show little interest in eco-tourism, preferring to visit Amazonia for the duty-free shopping zone in Manaus.

Brazil is still a relatively cheap destination for European and American tourists. Despite this, visitor numbers are declining, falling from 0.5% to 0.1% of the world market since 1970. Many visitors have been put off by the negative publicity generated by the conditions in the shanty towns and by Brazil's past human rights record.

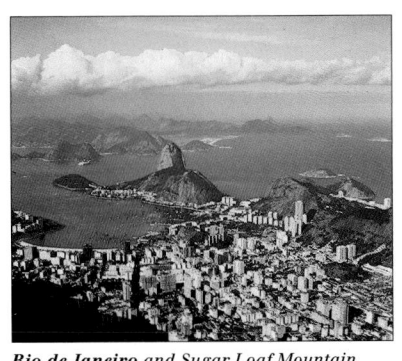

Rio de Janeiro and Sugar Loaf Mountain seen from Corcovado (Hunchback) Peak. With a population of 11 million, the Rio conurbation is Brazil's largest after São Paulo.

PEOPLE

Portuguese, German, Italian, Spanish, Polish, Japanese, Amerindian languages

18 people per km²

THE URBAN/RURAL POPULATION SPLIT

75%   25%

RELIGIOUS PERSUASION

Other 10%

Roman Catholic 90%

ETHNIC MAKEUP

Black 6%

Other (including Portuguese, Italian, German and Amerindian) 56%

Mixed 38%

POPULATION AGE BREAKDOWN

% of population by age group	0–14	15–64	65+

	1960	1970	1980	1990	2000
65+	2.9%	3.4%	4%	4.7%	5.6%
15–64	53.5%	54.3%	58.3%	60.6%	65.3%
0–14	43.6%	42.3%	37.7%	34.7%	29.1%

Brazil's population is highly diverse. It includes indigenous Indian groups who have had little contact with the outside world, as well as the descendants of both its Portuguese colonizers and the Africans brought to work the sugar plantations in the 17th century. More recent immigrant groups include both Italians and Japanese. Amerindians suffer prejudice from most other peoples in Brazil. Since 1900, 87 Amerindian groups have become extinct as a result of disease, starvation or the forceful taking of their land by miners, settlers and loggers. The Amerindian population today is estimated at just 220,000. Migrants from the poor northeast suffer considerable discrimination in Brazil's larger cities.

Brazil is a profoundly Catholic country with a traditional emphasis on the family. In the urban areas, however, family structures are under pressure. Migrants from the northeast often leave their families behind.

Women in Brazil have had the vote since 1934, but are still discriminated against in jobs and politics. A ministry for women has been established with the aim of defending and promoting their interests.

CHRONOLOGY

The first Portuguese, Pedro Alvares Cabral, arrived in Brazil in 1500. By the time Spain took control of the region, in 1580, it was a thriving colony drawing its wealth from sugar plantations in the northeast, worked by imported Africans, or Amerindians captured from further and further inland.

❑ **1637–1654** Dutch control sugar-growing areas.
❑ **1763** Rio becomes capital.
❑ **1788** *Inconfidência* rebellion, led by Tiradentes, fails.
❑ **1807** French invade Portugal. King João VI flees to Brazil with British naval escort. In return, Brazil's ports opened to foreign trade.
❑ **1821** King returns to Portugal. Son Pedro made regent of Brazil.
❑ **1822** Pedro declares independence and is made Emperor of Brazil.
❑ **1828** Brazil loses Uruguay.
❑ **1831** Military revolt after war with Argentina (1825–1828). Emperor abdicates. Five-year-old son succeeds him as Pedro II.
❑ **1835–1845** Rio Grande secedes.
❑ **1865–1870** Brazil wins war of Triple Alliance with Argentina and Uruguay against Paraguay.
❑ **1888** Pedro II abolishes slavery; landowners and military turn against him.
❑ **1889** First Republic established. Emperor goes into exile in Paris. Increasing prosperity as result of international demand for coffee.
❑ **1891** Federal constitution established.
❑ **1914–1918** First World War hits coffee exports.
❑ **1920s** Working class and intellectual movements call for end to oligarchical rule.
❑ **1930** Coffee prices collapse. Revolt led by Dr Getúlio Vargas, the 'Father of the Poor', who becomes president. Fast industrial growth.
❑ **1937** Vargas' position as benevolent dictator formalized in 'New State', based on fascist model. ⇨

B

POLITICS

Lower House 1994
Upper House 1994

President Itamar
Augusto Cantiero Franco

THE STATE OF THE PARTIES

Chamber of Deputies 503 members

| 22% PMDB | 18% PFL | 9% PDT | 8% PRN | 8% PDS | 35% Other |

PMDB = Party of the Brazilian Democratic Movement
PFL = Liberal Front Party **PDT** = Democratic Labour Party
PRN = National Reconstruction Party **PDS** = Social Democratic Party

Federal Senate 81 members

3 members are elected by each of the 26 states and the Federal District

Brazil is a democratic federal republic with 27 regional parliaments and a national congress. In 1993, Brazilians voted to retain directly elected presidents.

MAIN POLITICAL ISSUES

Controlling inflation
The military regime's difficulties with the economy were the main reason for its withdrawal from politics in 1988. Tackling hyperinflation, which is currently running at over 40% a month, remains the main concern of the civilian government.

Redrafting the constitution
The 1988 constitution, detailing promises for a better future, has proved to be unworkable in practice. The state cannot afford its social security, health and pension commitments. The proliferation of local governments, designed to check federal power, has led to a duplication of functions and is very expensive. The aim now is to develop a shorter and clearer constitution. Reformists want provisions to curb tax evasion and to allow greater foreign investment in state-owned enterprises such as oil. Many also want to see changes in the electoral system in order to curb the increasing involvement of small parties in government.

Eradicating corruption
Former President Collor de Mello's 1992 impeachment for fraud underlines the depth of the problem of corruption in Brazil. Many are now demanding an end to parliamentary immunity: under the current system, elected officials cannot be prosecuted unless they have been suspended from office by a two-thirds vote.

PROFILE
Brazil's young democracy is characterized by a weak party system,

Fernando Cardoso, ex-finance minister and a presidential candidate in 1994.

Luís Ignacio da Silva, 'Lula', leader of the left-wing Workers' Party.

President Itamar Franco, who took office in December 1992.

centred around personalities rather than parties. Parties do not have set ideological programmes, but tend to form *ad hoc* coalitions to get legislation through congress. The preponderance of small parties adds to the problems.

Politics has been further rocked by recent corruption scandals. Itamar Franco, who became president after Collor de Mello had been impeached for alleged fraud, was himself under investigation in 1993.

The dissatisfaction with the centre-right has been a boost to the left. However, a victory for the left, led by the influential Luís da Silva – who came second to Collor de Mello in the 1989 presidential elections – could provoke another military intervention. This was a factor limiting the left's popular support in the run-up to the 1994 elections; Brazilians do not want a return to military rule.

The military, in power between 1964 and 1985, was responsible for human rights abuses, particularly against Amazon Indians. Its economic mismanagement left Brazil with a legacy of huge debts and inefficient state industries.

Coffee plantation, *São Paulo state. Coffee was introduced into Brazil in the early 18th century. It is declining in importance and now accounts for less than 4% of export revenues.*

WORLD AFFAIRS

Brazil's main foreign policy concern is the formation of MERCOSUR, a common market with Argentina, Paraguay and Uruguay, which will create an additional market of over 40 million for Brazil's relatively efficient producers. A successful outcome to negotiations with Chile and Peru for a Pacific port outlet would further boost Brazil's exports.

Beyond Latin America, relations with the USA and Japan, Brazil's main creditors, are critical. Rescheduling debt, much of it incurred during the military regime, is essential to curb Brazil's inflation problem.

The 1992 Rio Earth Summit was a major boost to Brazil's international image. However, cases of continuing exploitation of Amazon Indian groups have recently come to light.

AID

 189m (receipts)   Down 9% in 1993

Brazil's main aid donors are the USA and the EU. As well as official aid, much comes from NGOs, mainly for environmental and housing projects. Large aid donations were promised by the states attending the Rio Summit in 1992; little has materialized.

DEFENCE

$2.1bn   Down 8% in 1992

0	Defence spending as % GDP	40
0.9%		

BRAZILIAN ARMED FORCES

	520 light tanks (150 M-3/80 X-1A)	196,000 personnel
	5 submarines, 19 surface vessels and 30 patrol boats	50,000 personnel
	307 combat aircraft (14 F-103E/4 F-103D)	50,700 personnel
	None	

Although it withdrew from direct participation in government in 1985, Brazil's military remains a powerful force in national political life. In 1989, it played a behind-the-scenes role in ensuring Collor de Mello's election. It controls the far north for national security reasons. Brazil has a large arms industry. Exports to Iraq, a major market, were hit by a UN embargo in 1991 following the Gulf War. Plans to develop nuclear weapons have now been abandoned by the military.

ECONOMICS

$2.7bn   The real was introduced in 1994

SCORE CARD

- ☐ WORLD GNP RANKING..........................11th
- ☐ GNP PER CAPITA..............................$2680
- ☐ BALANCE OF PAYMENTS ....$-3788m
- ☐ INFLATION ....Over 40% a month
- ☐ UNEMPLOYMENT.................................3.9%

EXPORTS

Germany* 5%
Japan 7%
Netherlands 8%
Other 57%
USA 23%

IMPORTS

Iraq 7%
Argentina 7%
Germany* 8%
Other 55%
USA 23%

STRENGTHS

Local industry is well developed, making Brazil dominant in the region. Immense natural resources: the world's largest producer of coffee and soya beans and one of the largest sugar and orange juice exporters. Large deposits of gold, silver and iron. One of world's most important steel producers.

WEAKNESSES

Hyperinflation – currently over 40% a month. Corruption among politicians and officials, as well as in business, has created mistrust and an unwillingness by overseas investors to make long-term commitments. Lack of any coherent economic planning in the early 1990s.

PROFILE

Brazil has one of the world's major economies, but also one of the hardest to manage. During the 1960s and 1970s, GDP expanded by an average of 11% a year. The economy underwent major diversification and industrialization, and today Brazil is a significant producer of cars and computers. However, profligate spending during this period left Brazil saddled with a huge debt burden of over $116 billion, which dominated economic affairs in the 1980s.

Although economic reform, initiated by the Collor de Mello administration in 1990, has enabled Brazil to reschedule its debts, the country still faces major problems. The most important is inflation, which was running at over 40% a month in 1994. Inflation is also aggravating wealth disparities between rich and poor –

ECONOMIC PERFORMANCE INDICATOR

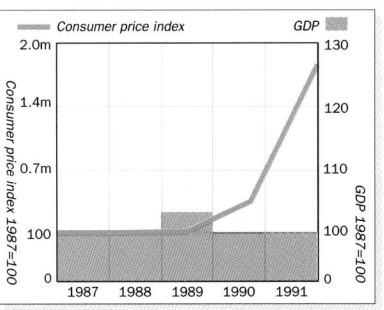

already the greatest in the world. Despite its vast natural and economic resources, Brazil still has 32 million of its people living below the breadline and has not begun to tackle the problem of homeless street children in Rio, São Paulo and other large cities.

Before his impeachment, President Collor announced a sweeping privatization programme as the first step in economic reform. For it to succeed, Brazil needs to attract high levels of foreign investment, but the country's political and economic instability frightens off many companies. Corruption scandals add to the lack of trust among potential investors and intensify the feeling of many that Brazil is only paying lip service to change.

The private sector is highly efficient and has succeeded in working around Brazil's bureaucracy. The array of regulations aimed at protecting Brazil's workers, for example, have led many employers to invest in machinery instead, with resulting increases in productivity.

In sharp contrast to its regulation of industry, however, the state has imposed few controls on the loggers and gold prospectors in Amazonia.

BRAZIL : MAJOR BUSINESSES

Manaus
Belém
Amazon
Recife
Brazilia
Salvador
Belo Horizonte
Rio de Janeiro
São Paulo
Porto Alegre

- 🏦 Banking
- 🖥 Computers
- ▯ Publishing
- ▮ Electronics
- Saw milling
- Sugar cane refining
- Vehicle assembly
- Coffee processing

0	1000 km
0	1000 miles

* significant multinational ownership

B

RESOURCES

 222.2bn kwh (capacity 52.9m kw)

 625,700 b/d (reserves 3,030,000,000 bbl)

186.8m cattle, 31.7m pigs, 20.5m sheep

 Iron, manganese, coal, bauxite, nickel, oil, tin, silver, diamonds, gold

ELECTRICITY GENERATION

Hydro 93% (207.2bn kwh)	
Thermal 6% (12.7bn kwh)	
Nuclear 1% (2.2bn kwh)	
Other 0%	

0   20   40   60   80   100
% of total generation by type

Under the military, Brazil had big ambitions for nuclear power, and commissioned several power stations from former West Germany. Energy from these has been more expensive than expected. Hydro-power has been more successful, accounting for 90% of electricity generation. A 2200 km pipeline from the Bolivian gas fields to Brazil's industrial south has been proposed, but Brazil is unable to finance the multi-billion dollar project from public funds; its constitution prevents private ownership of energy assets. Ethanol is being made from sugar in an attempt to reduce petrol imports. Within the agricultural sector, Brazil is the world's largest producer of both coffee and soya beans.

BRAZIL : LAND USE
- Cropland
- Forest
- Pasture
- Cattle
- Coffee - cash crop
- Oranges

0   1000 km
0   1000 miles

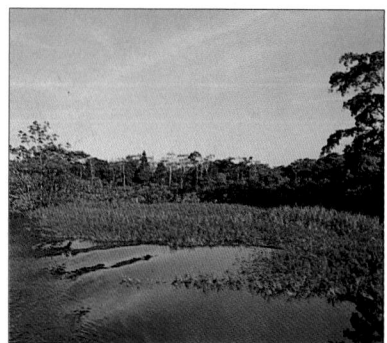

Equatorial vegetation near Manaus in the centre of Amazonas state. The brown waters of the Rio Solimões and the black waters of the Rio Negro meet near Manaus.

ENVIRONMENT

 3% (1% partially protected)

Use of alcohol fuels for cars is reducing urban pollution

ENVIRONMENTAL TREATIES

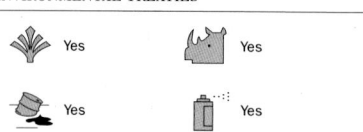

	Yes		Yes
	Yes		Yes

In 1992, the UN held its first Earth Summit in Rio, partly to highlight the destruction of the Amazon rainforest.

The Amazon rainforest contains an estimated 90% of all of the world's plants and animals and is the most complex ecosystem known. However, the demands of agriculture are leading to its destruction at a rate of 4 km² per hour, or 35,000 km² per year. As a result of such massive clearances, usually for conversion to cattle pasture, vital genetic diversity is being lost.

Brazil faces other environmental problems. Open-cast bauxite mining is polluting rivers and threatening the livelihoods of indigenous Amerindians. In the cities, widespread industrial pollution and untreated sewage are major problems.

MEDIA

 There has officially been freedom from censorship since the military withdrew from politics in 1985

PUBLISHING AND BROADCAST MEDIA

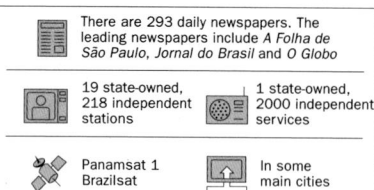

There are 293 daily newspapers. The leading newspapers include *A Folha de São Paulo*, *Jornal do Brasil* and *O Globo*

19 state-owned, 218 independent stations

1 state-owned, 2000 independent services

Panamsat 1 Brazilsat

In some main cities

Although there is now no official censorship, TV and radio operating licences are awarded as political favours and state advertising is so extensive it cannot fail to influence editorial policy. Media ownership is also highly concentrated. The *Globo* group, Brazil's only nationwide broadcasting company, was able to exclude the left from news reports and debates during the 1989 presidential elections, thus securing the victory of Collor de Mello.

CRIME

 87,053 prisoners

The rate is sharply up. More street children are being murdered

CRIME RATES

Murders	
2	per 100,000 population

Rapes	
3	per 100,000 population

Murders	
	High levels of theft

Urban life in Brazil can be violent. The incidence of armed robbery and drugs-related crime is rising. Human rights abuses by the police are frequently reported. Death squads, uncontrolled by the government, target street children in particular, especially in Rio, São Paulo and Recife. Since 1985, the rate of street child murders has been rising. However, international condemnation of the crimes has led to action in some areas.

In the countryside, violent land disputes are common. Landless workers are repeatedly displaced and indigenous peoples driven from land to which the government has, in theory, guaranteed their rights. In Roraima state, the discovery of large gold deposits has led to the homelands of Brazil's largest tribe, the Yanomani, being invaded by thousands of gun-toting prospectors, *garimpeiros*. The government halted their activities during the 1992 Earth Summit in Rio.

EDUCATION

 80%

0   Education spending as % GNP   25

3.7%

THE EDUCATION SYSTEM

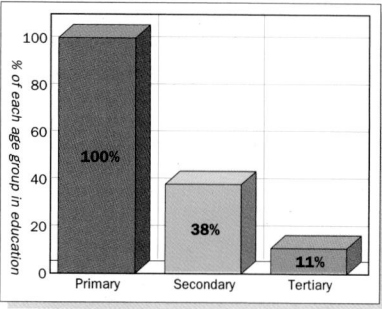

% of each age group in education

Primary	Secondary	Tertiary
100%	38%	11%

Education follows the French system with a *bachillerato* (*baccalauréat*) at the end of secondary schooling. State schools enjoyed a good reputation until the 1950s, but have declined since then. Most middle-class parents now send their children to private schools. The wealthy send theirs to Switzerland or France. Millions of the poor receive little education – especially those living in the northeast and Amazonia, and the urban poor. Brazil's three million street children have no schooling at all. Public degree courses work on credits, as in the USA. Of Brazil's 95 universities, 55 are administered by the state. São Paulo University is the most prestigious.

REGIONS
NORDESTE

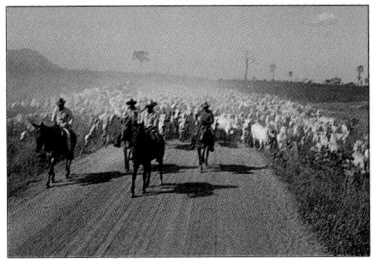

Cattle ranchers in Pará state, where land reform is a major political issue.

NORDESTE, the northeast of Brazil, comprises nine states and is the country's most traditional region, but also its most backward. It was settled by the Portuguese, who brought Africans to work the sugar plantations. In the region's interior, the land is still divided into large ranches owned by a few families. This, and several years of drought that have made the land even more barren, have led to the emigration of millions of subsistence farmers to the more prosperous cities of the south, where they encounter great prejudice. The big landowners still hold a great deal of political power nationally, being heavily represented in the Congress, where they regularly obstruct attempts at land reform.

PANTANAL

THE PANTANAL, situated in the centre-west of Brazil, bordering Paraguay and Bolivia, is the largest area of wetlands in the world. Flooded for seven months a year, it has some of the most diverse wildlife on the continent, with many thousands of species of birds, caymans (a type of alligator) and many varieties of snake. The inhabitants, or *pantaneros*, are indigenous groups who have adapted their way of life, which includes raising cattle and horses, to the regular flooding. The Pantanal is a great attraction for tourists and scientists who study wildlife behaviour. As with many regions in Brazil, it is now coming under pressure from cattle ranchers and those who want to turn the area over to agriculture. However, its special climatic conditions act as a protection from any massive exploitation of its resources.

| National Park | Wetlands | Wildlife tourism |

ESTADO DE SÃO PAULO

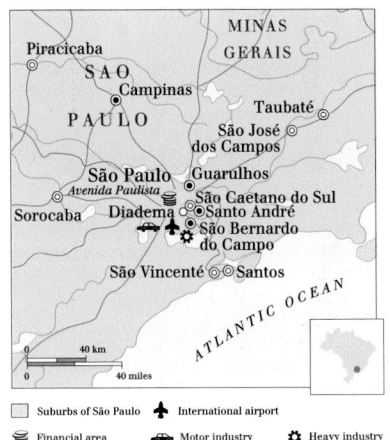

| Suburbs of São Paulo | International airport |
| Financial area | Motor industry | Heavy industry |

SÃO PAULO STATE, with almost 34 million inhabitants, is among the world's 20 most powerful economies.

At its centre lies the city of São Paulo, which has over 10 million inhabitants and is the fastest growing city on the continent. Its population is mixed, including the *nordestinos* who have come in search of work, and a large Italo-Brazilian community who first helped the city to industrialize. The city is also home to almost two million Japanese descendants, the largest Japanese community outside Japan. The area of Avenida Paulista, once the home of coffee barons and São Paulo's wealthy citizens, is now Brazil's largest financial centre. The urban area around São Paulo is the nucleus of Brazilian heavy industry, particularly the car and large-scale engineering industries. On the coast of São Paulo state is Brazil's largest port, Santos, which exports most of the country's coffee, as well as machinery and other heavy goods.

HEALTH

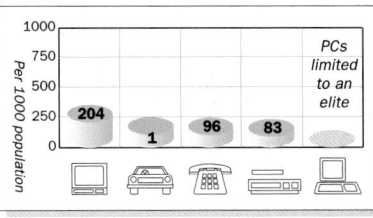

1 per 852 people | Heart diseases, external causes, cancers

0 — Health spending as % GNP — 25
1.7%

The public health system is limited. Less than 20% of hospitals are state-run and private care is very expensive. The World Bank has criticized the under-financing of preventive health care. On average, only 15% of the health budget is allocated to child health, immunization and other preventive programmes. Reported malaria cases tripled between 1980 and 1990; 90% are in Amazonia, mainly in settler towns. Leprosy and parasitic skin infections are also becoming more common, again often affecting settlers.

WEALTH

Due to the high inflation rate, salaries have to be reviewed every month

CONSUMER GOODS OWNERSHIP

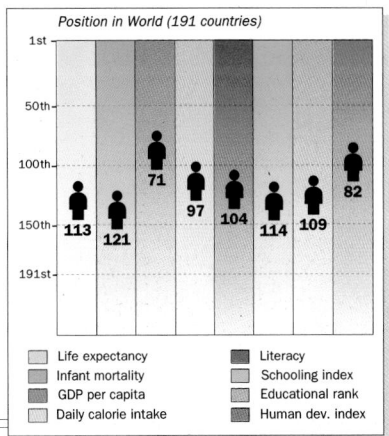

Per 1000 population: 204, 1, 96, 83

PCs limited to an elite

Brazil's large wealth disparities have been growing during the last decade. Relatively low levels of unemployment conceal large-scale underemployment, and the UN classifies over 50% of the population as suffering poverty. The large number of poor rural migrants to the cities live in the *favelas*, or shanty towns. *Favelas* are now also appearing in the countryside. The wealthy like to drive European cars, holiday in Paris or ski in Switzerland, where most of them keep their money to avoid scrutiny and interference in their accounts by the government.

WORLD RANKING

Position in World (191 countries)

1st
50th
100th — 71
150th — 113 121 97 104 114 109 82
191st

Life expectancy	Literacy
Infant mortality	Schooling index
GDP per capita	Educational rank
Daily calorie intake	Human dev. index

BRUNEI

OFFICIAL NAME: The Sultanate of Brunei **CAPITAL:** Bandar Seri Begawan
CURRENCY: Brunei dollar **POPULATION:** 300,000 **OFFICIAL LANGUAGE:** Malay

LYING ON THE NORTHWESTERN coast of the island
of Borneo, Brunei is divided in two by a strip of the
surrounding Malaysian state of Sarawak. The interior is mostly rainforest.
Independent from the UK since 1984, Brunei is ruled by decree of the
Sultan. It is undergoing increasing Islamicization. Oil and gas reserves
have brought one of the world's highest standards of living.

CLIMATE

WEATHER CHART

 Average daily temperature   Rainfall

Just 480 km north of the equator,
Brunei has a six-month rainy season
with extremely high humidity.

COMMUNICATIONS

Brunei International,
Bandar Seri Begawan   10 ships
342,700 dwt

THE TRANSPORT NETWORK

2199 km (1366 miles)		None
19 km (12 miles)		209 km (130 miles)

Interest-free loans for civil servants,
subsidized petrol and limited
public transport account for
the high rates of car
ownership.

TOURISM

305,522 visitors   Up 57% in 1992

MAIN OVERSEAS ARRIVALS

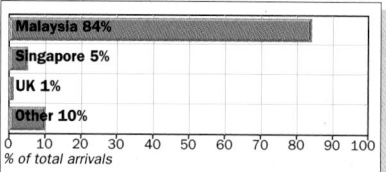

Malaysia 84%
Singapore 5%
UK 1%
Other 10%
% of total arrivals

Although keen to protect Bruneians
from Western influence, the
government wants to develop quality
tourism as part of its diversification
programme. Promoted as the 'Gateway
to Borneo', Brunei's rainforests could
be developed for eco-tourism. A former
attraction was the Churchill Museum,
founded by the late Sultan. This has
now been superseded by the Museum
of Royal Regalia.

PEOPLE

Malay, English, Chinese   35 people per km²

THE URBAN/RURAL POPULATION SPLIT

81%   19%

ETHNIC MAKEUP

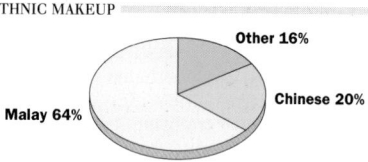
Other 16%
Chinese 20%
Malay 64%

Malays benefit from positive
discrimination; many in the Chinese
community are either stateless or hold
British protected person passports.
Amongst indigenous groups, the Murut
and Dusuns are favoured over the Ibans.
Women, less restricted than in some
Muslim states, are obliged to wear
headscarves but not the veil. Many hold
influential posts in the civil service.

POLITICS

Not applicable   HM Sultan Haji
Hassannal Bolkiah
Mu'izzadin Waddaulah

THE STATE OF THE PARTIES

Council of Cabinet Ministers

Brunei is an absolute monarchy. The Council of Cabinet
Ministers is chosen by the Sultan. Political parties were
banned in 1988

Since a failed rebellion in 1962, a state
of emergency has been in force and the
Sultan has ruled by decree. Hopes for
democracy were dashed when political
parties were banned in 1988. In 1990,
'Malay Muslim Monarchy' was
introduced, promoting Islamic values
as the state ideology. This further
alienated the large Chinese and
expatriate communities. Power is
closely tied to the royal family. Two of
the Sultan's brothers hold the finance
and foreign affairs portfolios; the
Sultan himself looks after defence.

WORLD AFFAIRS

 ASEAN Comm ESCAP IDB NAM

Brunei claims part of the Spratly
Islands. Political exiles opposed to the
government and based in Malaysia are
a main concern. Relations with Britain,
the ex-colonial power, are good.

Map

SOUTH CHINA SEA

Perkemahan Berakas
Pekan Muara
Pulau Muara Besar
Kampong Jerudong
Kampong Paring
BRUNEI BAY
Kampong Parit
BANDAR SERI BEGAWAN
Kampong Bunut
Kampong Labu
Tutong
Kampong Kuala Abang
Bangar
Kampong Lumut
Kampong Benutan
Pekan Seria
Kuala Belait
Badas
Kampong Batang Duri
Kampong Bukit Sawat
Kampong Kuala Balai Kampong Tanajor
Kampong Labi
Bukit Pagon 1618m
Kampong Teraja
Kampong Sukang
MALAYSIA (SARAWAK)

N
0   20 km
0   20 miles

BRUNEI
Total Area :
5770 sq. km
(2228 sq. miles)

POPULATION
○ over 50 000
● over 10 000
• under 10 000

LAND HEIGHT
1500m/4921ft
1000m/3281ft
500m/1640ft
200m/656ft
Sea Level

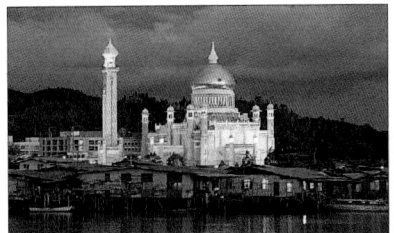

The Sultan spent $450 million building the world's largest palace at Bandar Seri Begawan.

AID

 Ad hoc handouts of around $150,000

 Increase or decrease depends on Sultan's decision

Aid spending is largely *ad hoc*. It has included donations to the Contras in Nicaragua, the Bosnian Muslims and the homeless of New York.

DEFENCE

 $233m

 Up 21% in 1988

As well as being head of the 4500-strong armed forces, the Sultan has a personal bodyguard of 2000 UK-trained Gurkhas. The UK and Singapore are close defence allies.

ECONOMICS

 $9bn (est)

 1.61 Brunei dollars

SCORE CARD

- ❑ WORLD GNP RANKING..........................83rd
- ❑ GNP PER CAPITA............................$30,000
- ❑ BALANCE OF PAYMENTS $1.1bn
- ❑ INFLATION ....–5.1%
- ❑ UNEMPLOYMENT...................................6%

STRENGTHS

25 years of known oil reserves; 40 years of gas. Earnings from massive overseas investments, mainly in the USA and Europe, now exceed oil and gas revenues.

WEAKNESSES

Single-product economy. Failure of diversification programmes could lead to problems in the future.

EXPORTS

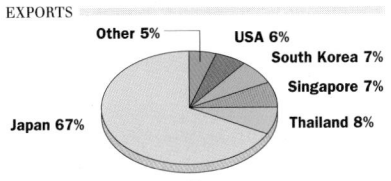

Other 5% | USA 6% | South Korea 7% | Singapore 7% | Thailand 8% | Japan 67%

IMPORTS

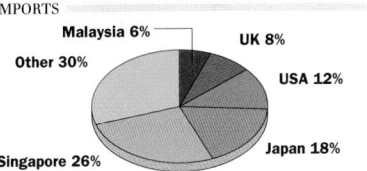

Malaysia 6% | UK 8% | Other 30% | USA 12% | Singapore 26% | Japan 18%

RESOURCES

1.2bn kwh (capacity 380,000 kw)

165,400 b/d (reserves 1,350,000,000 bbl)

25,000 pigs, 10,000 buffaloes

Oil, natural gas

Oil and gas are the major resources, accounting for 0.5% and 9% of world production respectively. Energy policy now focuses on regulating output in order to conserve stocks.

ENVIRONMENT

 14% (5% partially protected)

Little impetus behind legislation to protect forests

The Forest Strategic Plan aims to protect Brunei's forests (which account for 80% of its land area), but has yet to make specific areas of responsibility clear. The result is that rainforest is still under threat. Brunei's mangrove swamps, the largest in Borneo, remain unprotected.

MEDIA

 Extensive censorship, including foreign papers. Pictures deemed lewd or blasphemous by Religious Affairs Ministry are blacked out

PUBLISHING AND BROADCAST MEDIA

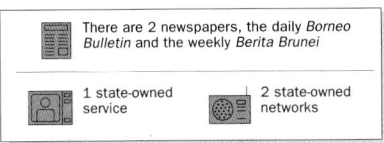

There are 2 newspapers, the daily *Borneo Bulletin* and the weekly *Berita Brunei*

1 state-owned service

2 state-owned networks

The state effectively controls all media. Brunei TV has recently increased its religious programming.

CRIME

 Brunei does not publish prison figures

 Theft up 191% between 1985 and 1990

Crime levels are low. Most crime involves petty theft or is linked to alcohol and drugs (both banned). A stolen car often makes TV news headlines. The state of emergency gives the government the power to detain without charge or trial for indefinitely renewable two-year periods.

EDUCATION

 85%

Free schooling is available to all the population, with the exception of stateless Chinese, who do not qualify. The University of Brunei Darussalam is undergoing Islamicization.

HEALTH

 1 per 1456 people

Heart diseases, cancers

The health service is free, although for major surgery Bruneians tend to travel to Singapore.

CHRONOLOGY

Under British control since 1841, Brunei became a formal British Protectorate in 1888.

- ❑ **1929** Oil extraction begins.
- ❑ **1941–1945** Occupied by Japan.
- ❑ **1959** First constitution enshrines Islam as state religion. Internal self-government.
- ❑ **1962** Pro-democracy rebellion crushed with help of British Gurkhas. State of emergency announced: Sultan rules by decree.
- ❑ **1984** Independence from Britain. Brunei joins ASEAN.
- ❑ **1990** Ideology of 'Malay Muslim Monarchy' introduced.
- ❑ **1991** Imports of alcohol banned.
- ❑ **1992** Joins Non-Aligned Movement.

WEALTH

 Average manufacturing wage, 3.5 Brunei dollars per hour

CONSUMER GOODS OWNERSHIP

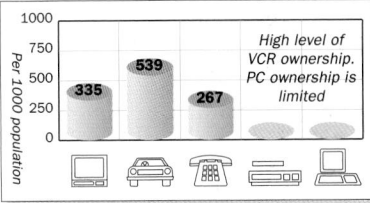

High level of VCR ownership. PC ownership is limited

335 | 539 | 267

The wealthy in Brunei are those close to the Sultan, the world's richest man according to *Forbes* magazine. A high general standard of living keeps discontent to a minimum. Promotion within the civil service and universal education allow some social mobility amongst Malays. Bruneians are major consumers of high-tech hi-fi and video equipment, label watches and Western designer clothes. Telephone lines, however, are difficult to install. Only the Sultan may ride in a Rolls Royce.

WORLD RANKING

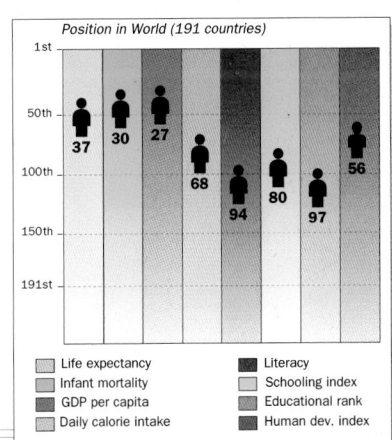

Position in World (191 countries)

37 | 30 | 27 | 68 | 94 | 80 | 97 | 56

Life expectancy | Literacy
Infant mortality | Schooling index
GDP per capita | Educational rank
Daily calorie intake | Human dev. index

BULGARIA

OFFICIAL NAME: Republic of Bulgaria **CAPITAL:** Sofia
POPULATION: 9 million **CURRENCY:** Lev **OFFICIAL LANGUAGE:** Bulgarian

EUROPE

LOCATED IN SOUTHEASTERN EUROPE, Bulgaria is a mainly mountainous country. The River Danube forms the northern border, while the popular resorts of the Black Sea lie to the east. The most populated areas are around Sofia in the west, Plovdiv in the southeast, and along the Danube plain. Bulgaria was ruled by the Turks from 1396 until 1878. It became an independent kingdom in 1908, and was under communist rule from 1947 to 1989, the last 35 of those years under the leadership of Todor Zhivkov. The 1990s brought political instability as the country moved towards democracy.

Rila Monastery in the Rila Mountains. It is famous for its 1200 National Revival Period frescoes dating from the mid-19th century.

CLIMATE

WEATHER CHART

The central valley and the lowlands have warm summers and cold, snowy winters, but hot or cold winds from Russia can bring spells of more extreme weather. The hotter summers on the Black Sea coast have encouraged the growth of tourist resorts. Snow may lie on the high mountain peaks until June.

COMMUNICATIONS

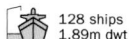

Sofia International

128 ships
1.89m dwt

THE TRANSPORT NETWORK

36,934 km (22,950 miles)	266 km (165 miles)
4299 km (2617 miles)	470 km (292 miles)

The railways are an integral part of the freight transport system, but have become unsafe through lack of investment. North–south routes were intentionally left undeveloped under the Warsaw Pact. Ferries are used for most cross-Danube traffic – in 1989 there was only one bridge. Urban transport is also lacking. Construction of an underground railway for Sofia began in 1979. The first section has yet to be completed.

TOURISM

8.22m visitors

Down 1% in 1989

MAIN OVERSEAS ARRIVALS

Romania	20%
Former Yugoslavia	13%
CIS	6%
Greece	5%
Hungary	3%
Other	53%

% of total arrivals

Under communism, Bulgaria's tourist industry catered for the East European mass market, which accounted for about two thirds of visitors. In 1993, tourism showed unprecedented growth as the country found new popularity with Western visitors, attracted by low prices for sea and sun package holidays. Bulgaria is privatizing the industry, hoping to attract more up-market tourism by emphasizing its heritage.

BULGARIA

Total Area : 110 910 sq. km
(42 822 sq. miles)

POPULATION

over 1 000 000
over 100 000
over 50 000
over 10 000

LAND HEIGHT

2000m/6562ft
1000m/3281ft
500m/1640ft
200m/656ft
Sea Level

B

PEOPLE

 Bulgarian, Turkish, Macedonian, Romany, Armenian, Russian

 81 people per km²

THE URBAN/RURAL POPULATION SPLIT

68%   32%

RELIGIOUS PERSUASION

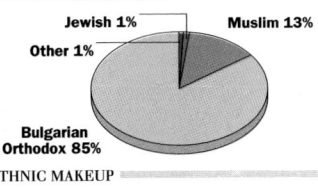

Jewish 1%   Muslim 13%
Other 1%
Bulgarian Orthodox 85%

ETHNIC MAKEUP

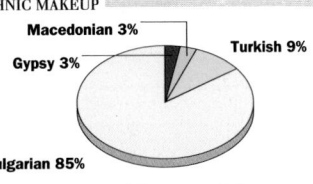

Macedonian 3%   Turkish 9%
Gypsy 3%
Bulgarian 85%

The government has sought to assimilate separate ethnic groups, thereby suppressing cultural identities. During the 1970s, Bulgarian Muslims, or *Pomaks*, had been forced to change Muslim names to Bulgarian ones. Bulgarian Turks were targeted in the 1980s. Despite the granting of linguistic and religious freedom in 1989, there was a mass exodus of ethnic Turks, when 300,000, or 40%, left for Turkey. Their farming skills have traditionally made an important contribution to the agricultural sector. Recent privatization programmes left many Turks landless and provoked new emigration. Now that the Turkish party, the MRF, holds the balance of power in parliament, however, conditions for the community should improve. The Gypsy minority still has no such protection and suffers discrimination at all levels. Women, particularly Turks, have equal right in theory but rarely in practice.

POPULATION AGE BREAKDOWN

	■ 0–14	■ 15–64	□ 65+		
% of population by age group	7.5%	9.6%	11.9%	13%	15.6%
	66.4%	67.6%	66%	66.6%	65.3%
	26.1%	22.8%	22.1%	20.4%	19.1%
	1960	1970	1980	1990	2000

POLITICS

 1995

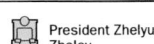 President Zhelyu Zhelev

THE STATE OF THE PARTIES

National Assembly 240 members

46% UDF   44% BSP   10% MRF

UDF = Union of Democratic Forces **BSP** = Bulgarian Socialist Party **MRF** = Movement for Rights and Freedoms

Bulgaria is a multiparty democracy.

MAIN POLITICAL ISSUES

Weak coalition government
The delicate balance of power in parliament is resulting in weak government. Stalemate and no-confidence votes brought down governments in 1990, 1991 and 1992. Since losing its majority in parliament, the UDF, itself suffering internal division, has attempted to discredit both Prime Minister Berov's BSP–MRF coalition and the president through accusations of 'creeping recommunism'. The Turkish-backed MRF holds the balance of power, but its electoral position will be reduced by the emigration to Turkey of many of its supporters.

Political trials
After several years' delay, former communist officials are being prosecuted for abuses under the former regime. Ex-autocrat Todor Zhivkov has been sentenced to seven years' imprisonment, pending appeal. Parliament has decided temporarily to block access to the State Security archives. Even the suggestion of collaboration was sufficient to force the resignation of the UDF chair; open files would be much too destabilizing.

PROFILE
In practice, Bulgaria is in a period of transition to a full democracy. The BSP, mostly former communists, are back in power and are resisting political and economic change. The result is one of the slowest privatization programmes in eastern Europe; the old communist web of patronage and influence is still in place. The MRF, which represents the Turks, has been willing to collaborate with their former oppressors as this has allowed them to reverse laws restricting the Turkish community.

Zhelyu Zhelev, a founder-member of the UDF, and president since 1990.

Lyuben Berov, prime minister and minister of foreign affairs.

WORLD AFFAIRS

 CE CSCE ECE NACC

Although maintaining good relations with Turkey is as important now as it was under communism, Bulgaria's new aims are to raise its profile in international organizations and gain greater trading access to the EU. Bulgaria has sent peace-keepers to Cambodia and has been conscientious in adhering to UN sanctions against former Yugoslavia, despite the costs of lost trade. Trade with former Soviet countries continues to supply important raw materials and spare parts.

AID

 $192.8m   Down 49% in 1992

Aid, mainly from the IMF, World Bank, EU and EBRD, is granted mostly for infrastructure works. In 1993, IMF agreements were suspended because of a growing budget deficit. The absence of a modern banking and financial services industry hinders development. Western donors have agreed to reduce commercial bank debt by one half.

CHRONOLOGY

Bulgaria was part of the Ottoman empire for five centuries until its independence in 1908. Under King Ferdinand, it took sides with Germany during the First World War, and subsequently lost valuable territory to Greece and Serbia. Under King Boris, Bulgaria once again sided with Germany in the Second World War.

❑ **1943** King Boris dies.
❑ **1944** Allies fire-bomb Sofia. Soviet Army invades. Anti-fascist Fatherland Front coalition (FF), including Agrarian Party and Bulgarian Communist Party (BCP), takes power in bloodless coup. Kimon Georgiev prime minister.
❑ **1946** September, referendum abolishes monarchy. Republic proclaimed. October, Grand National Assembly elections result in BCP majority. Communist leader Georgi Dmitrov prime minister.
❑ **1947** Prime Minister Dmitrov discredits Agrarian Party leader Nikola Petkov. Petkov arrested and sentenced to death. Dmitrov government receives international recognition. Soviet-style constitution adopted; Bulgaria becomes a one-party state. Country renamed the People's Republic of Bulgaria. Nationalization of the economy begins. ⇨

DEFENCE

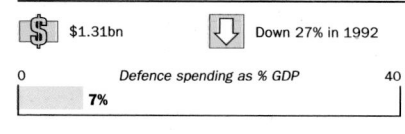

$1.31bn   Down 27% in 1992

Defence spending as % GDP   0 — 40
7%

BULGARIAN ARMED FORCES

	2100 main battle tanks (1200 T-55/590 T-34)	75,000 personnel
	3 submarines, 2 frigates and 27 patrol boats	10,000 personnel
	259 combat aircraft (39 Su-25/18 Mig-23)	22,000 personnel
	None	

Economic difficulties have meant that Bulgaria has had to trim its defence spending. Moves to reorganize the army have caused serious disaffection in officer ranks. The government's defence priority is to ensure that Bulgaria can maintain national security without its old Soviet backing. It is therefore seeking new alliances. If the conflict in former Yugoslavia were to spread south, Bulgaria would probably join an anti-Serbian alliance. It also needs to decide whether to run down or expand the large arms industry of the communist era. Its main products were missiles, sub-machine guns, Kalashnikov rifles, ammunition and electronic equipment.

ECONOMICS

$11bn   26.80 leva

SCORE CARD

- WORLD GNP RANKING...........................75th
- GNP PER CAPITA $1300
- BALANCE OF PAYMENTS....................$–780m
- INFLATION 80%
- UNEMPLOYMENT...................................12%

ECONOMIC PERFORMANCE INDICATOR

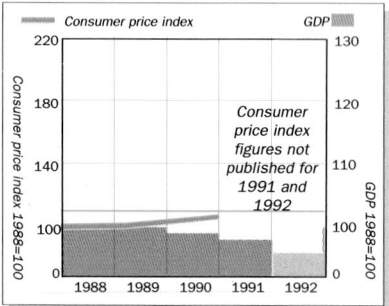

Consumer price index —— GDP

Consumer price index figures not published for 1991 and 1992

1988 1989 1990 1991 1992

EXPORTS

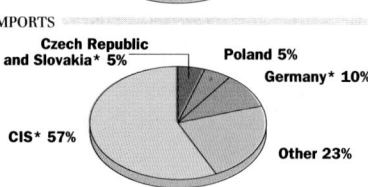

Czech Republic and Slovakia* 4%   Romania 4%
Libya 4%
Other 24%
CIS* 64%

IMPORTS

Czech Republic and Slovakia* 5%   Poland 5%
Germany* 10%
CIS* 57%
Other 23%

firms to own companies outright. Investment is still negligible. Trade has shifted towards the EU, which by 1992 accounted for a third of foreign trade. The former Soviet Union's share fell from 75% of all foreign trade in 1989 to just over 25% in 1992. Considerable potential exists for trade with Russia and Ukraine. Bulgaria specialized in producing information technology for COMECON countries; it now seeks expansion into Western markets.

STRENGTHS

Coal and natural gas. Good agricultural production, especially grapes for well-developed wine industry, and tobacco. Strong expertise in computer software.

WEAKNESSES

Outdated equipment and outstanding debt throughout industry. Dependence on Russia for machinery and spare parts for existing factories. Location prevents easy access to rest of Europe.

PROFILE

Restructuring the economy is linked to privatization – a process that has been delayed for political and technical reasons. In 1980, joint ventures were allowed. This permitted the party elite to transfer valuable assets to companies that they or their families owned. In 1992, new legislation allowed foreign

BULGARIA : MAJOR BUSINESSES

Pleven   Ruse   Shumen
Pernik
Varna
Burgas
Zagora
Plovdiv
Sofia

- Wine
- Steel
- Textiles
- Shipbuilding
- Leather tanning
- Food processing
- Metal processing
- Vehicle assembly
- Heavy engineering
- Tobacco
- Computers
- Oil refining

0   200 km
0   200 miles

RESOURCES

41.3bn kwh (capacity 9.98m kw)

8.6m sheep, 4.1m pigs, 1.6m cattle, 329,000 asses

Reserves of 15,000,000 bbl; refines 300,000 b/cd

Coal, iron, copper, lead, zinc, oil, natural gas

ELECTRICITY GENERATION

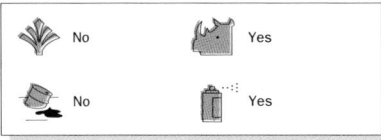

Hydro 6% (2.3bn kwh)

Thermal 64% (26.5bn kwh)

Nuclear 30% (12.5bn kwh)

Other 0%

% of total generation by type

Bulgaria has modest oil reserves and somewhat larger ones of coal and natural gas, but still has to import about 70% of its primary energy needs, much of it from the former Soviet Union. Unreliability of supplies in the past led to frequent winter power cuts. These have largely disappeared as decreased production in heavy industry and improved domestic supply from nuclear sources have lowered import demand. Bulgaria is partly reliant on nuclear power. Two of the four reactors at Kozloduy were upgraded after criticisms over safety measures, and a new plant is being planned. The first generator at the Chaira Dam came into service in 1993 to boost hydroelectric supplies. Bulgaria must soon decide how many of its 14 coal mines to close – ten are unprofitable.

BULGARIA : LAND USE

Cropland
Pasture
Forest
Sheep
Cereals
Tobacco

ENVIRONMENT

 2%

 Several grassroots environmental pressure groups

ENVIRONMENTAL TREATIES

No

Yes

No

Yes

Serious environmental degradation in the 1980s resulted from the state's unwillingness to enforce existing environmental laws, and led to the foundation of the party *Ecoglasnost* in 1989. It has been active in circulating information on pollution, health and nuclear waste dump locations and in bringing polluters to court. Bulgaria's main environmental problems are deforestation and air pollution. The spontaneous formation of regional environmental pressure groups indicates the severity of pollution problems.

MEDIA

 Nominally free press since 1989

PUBLISHING AND BROADCAST MEDIA

There are 14 daily newspapers, including *Demokratsiya, Duma, Zemya* and *Trud*

1 state-owned service

1 state-owned service

Arabsat 1C Intelsat V1 F1

None

The media was liberalized in 1989 and at present a wide range of dailies are published. No paper is completely independent as each is linked to some party or interest. The *Bulgarian Business News* and *24 Chasa* are among the most influential, owned by a former communist entrepreneur and supported by the First Private Bank.

CRIME

 9000 prisoners

 Rising

CRIME RATES

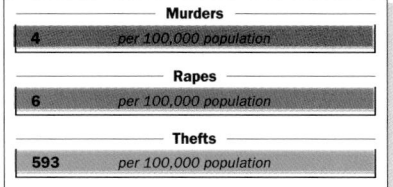

Murders

4 per 100,000 population

Rapes

6 per 100,000 population

Thefts

593 per 100,000 population

Police have been attempting to combat the increase in robberies and muggings. Tourists in the major holiday resorts are targets for muggers. In Sofia, the rise in organized crime is of growing concern. Violations of the Turkish minority's human rights are now a sensitive political issue.

EDUCATION

 96%

0   Education spending as % GNP   25

 5.5%

THE EDUCATION SYSTEM

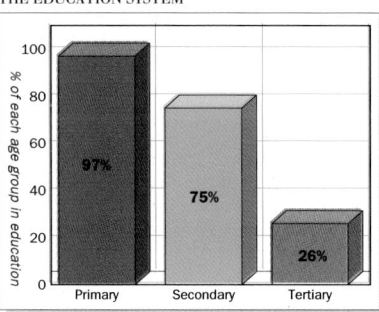

% of each age group in education

97% Primary

75% Secondary

26% Tertiary

Bulgaria is changing its educational system from a Soviet-inspired to a European-style model. Teaching standards are lowest in the rural and Turkish communities.

HEALTH

 1 per 324 people

Heart and cerebrovascular diseases, cancers

0   Health spending as % GNP   25

3.2%

Although hospital facilities have kept pace with population growth, the emigration of many doctors and nurses has lowered the standard of care. Shortages of medicines are widespread.

WEALTH

 Disparities in wealth are considerable

CONSUMER GOODS OWNERSHIP

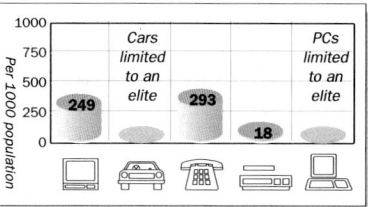

Per 1000 population

Cars limited to an elite

PCs limited to an elite

249   293   18

The former Communist party elite is still the richest group; Turks and Gypsies are the poorest.

WORLD RANKING

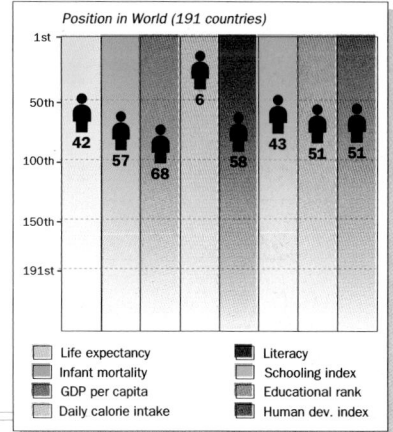

Position in World (191 countries)

1st

50th

100th

150th

191st

42   57   68   6   58   43   51   51

Life expectancy

Infant mortality

GDP per capita

Daily calorie intake

Literacy

Schooling index

Educational rank

Human dev. index

BURKINA

OFFICIAL NAME: Burkina   **CAPITAL:** Ouagadougou
POPULATION: 9.5 million   **CURRENCY:** CFA franc   **OFFICIAL LANGUAGE:** French

LAND-LOCKED IN WEST AFRICA, Burkina (formerly Upper Volta) gained independence from France in 1960. The majority of Burkina lies in the arid fringe of the Sahara known as the Sahel. Ruled by military dictators for much of its post-independence history, Burkina became a multiparty state in 1991. However, much power still rests with President Blaise Compaoré. Burkina's economy remains largely based on agriculture.

CLIMATE

WEATHER CHART

The tropical climate comprises two seasons – unreliable rains from June to October, and a long, dry season.

COMMUNICATIONS

Ouagadougou Intl
186,673 passengers

Has no fleet

THE TRANSPORT NETWORK

| 13,134 km (8161 miles) | None |
| 622 km (386 miles) | None |

The railway to the port of Abidjan in the Ivory Coast provides the main commercial route to the sea. Roads through Benin, Togo and Ghana provide alternative access.

TOURISM

 106,144 visitors   Up 4% in 1991

MAIN OVERSEAS ARRIVALS

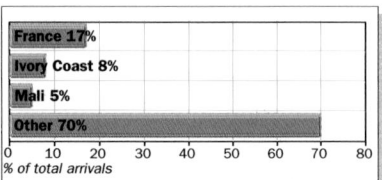

France 17%
Ivory Coast 8%
Mali 5%
Other 70%

% of total arrivals

Some potential exists for safari tourism and the cities offer an attractive mix of colonial and African architecture. Big game hunting is allowed in some areas.

PEOPLE

Mossi, Fulani, French, Tuareg, Dyula, Songhai

33 people per km²

THE URBAN/RURAL POPULATION SPLIT

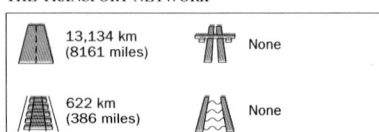

9%   91%

RELIGIOUS PERSUASION

Christian (mainly Roman Catholic) 10%
Muslim 25%
Indigenous beliefs 65%

No ethnic group is dominant in Burkina, although the Mossi people who live in the area of their old empire around Ouagadougou have always played an important role in government. Burkina's first president, Maurice Yameogo, and the present leader, Blaise Compaoré, are both Mossi. The people from the west are much more ethnically mixed.

The extended family is important and reaches from the villages into the towns and cities. Extreme poverty has led to a strong sense of egalitarianism within society. The lack of women in public life belies their real power and influence, particularly within the traditional framework of the extended family. However, most women are still denied access to education and senior professional positions.

Camel ploughing. *Burkina's poor soils and frequent droughts lead many young men to emigrate seasonally in search of work.*

POLITICS

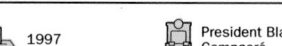 1997   President Blaise Compaoré

THE STATE OF THE PARTIES

Assembly of Popular Deputies 107 members   6% Other

73% ODP/MT   11% CNPP–PSD   6% RDA   4% ADF

OPT/MT = Organization for Popular Democracy/Labour Movement   **CNPP–PSD** = National Convention of Progressive Patriots – Social Democratic Party   **RDA** = African Democratic Assembly   **ADF** = Alliance for Democracy and Federation

A multiparty democracy in theory, Burkina is still dominated in practice by the former military dictator, Blaise Compaoré. He has been in power since the assassination in 1987 of Capt Thomas Sankara, Compaoré's former leader. Several of Compaoré's close military colleagues have also since been murdered.

Compaoré's grip on power in Burkina appears to be solid. In the National Assembly, the ODP/MT alliance offers total support. Most opposition leaders are still living in exile and real opposition within Burkina remains underground. Compaoré's military background also gives him the support of the army. Whilst the military no longer holds ministerial posts – a measure which helps Burkina maintain its democratic image – it remains influential behind the scenes.

There are signs, however, that a small group within the ODP/MT will push for greater democracy once Compaoré retires from office.

WORLD AFFAIRS

 OAU   Ecowas   FZ   GATT   AfDB

Burkina's land-locked position means good relations with countries to the south are a major foreign policy concern. However, Compaoré's relationship with other ECOWAS states is deteriorating over the war in Liberia.

AID

 $409m (receipts)   Up 22% in 1991

External aid, mostly from France and the EU, is important to Burkina's economy. The large number of NGOs has caused organizational problems; there is often difficulty in finding suitable projects for all the prospective donors.

B

BURKINA

Total Area : 274 200 sq. km
(105 870 sq. miles)

POPULATION

◎	over 100 000
○	over 50 000
●	over 10 000
•	under 10 000

LAND HEIGHT

- 500m/1640ft
- 200m/656ft
- Sea Level

DEFENCE

 $108.1m   Up 41% in 1991

The army's main role has been maintaining internal security. Burkina is reliant on France for most equipment and training.

ECONOMICS

$2.9bn   295.23 CFA francs

SCORE CARD

❑ WORLD GNP RANKING	126th
❑ GNP PER CAPITA	$305
❑ BALANCE OF PAYMENTS	$−167m
❑ INFLATION	4.6%
❑ UNEMPLOYMENT	16%

STRENGTHS

Significant remittances from plantation workers in Ghana and the Ivory Coast – $100 million a year between 1980 and 1985. Low debt burden. Ability to attract foreign aid. Cotton growing. Gold is now leading non-agricultural export.

WEAKNESSES

Land-locked. Few economically-viable natural resources. Prone to drought. Despite the benefits of foreign earnings, seasonal emigration has meant a decline in rural productivity.

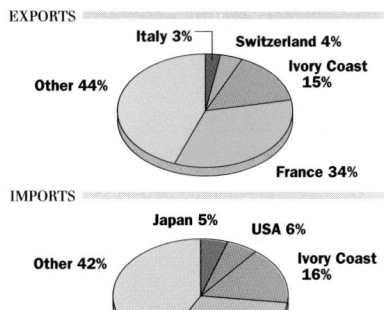

EXPORTS

Italy 3%
Switzerland 4%
Ivory Coast 15%
Other 44%
France 34%

IMPORTS

Japan 5%
USA 6%
Ivory Coast 16%
Other 42%
France 31%

RESOURCES

155m kwh (capacity 59,000 kw)   Not an oil producer and has no refineries

3m sheep, 2.8m cattle, 496,000 pigs   Gold, antimony, marble, manganese, silver, zinc

Burkina has considerable mineral wealth, including large manganese and silver deposits. However, the only metal ore being exploited is gold. Three dams to produce hydroelectric power will reduce dependence on thermal energy.

ENVIRONMENT

10% (8% partially protected)   Droughts of 1973 and 1983 have aggravated desertification

Like other countries on the southern rim of the Sahara, desertification is the major ecological issue. The rate of tree cutting for fuel is on the increase.

MEDIA

 In spite of press freedom guarantees in the 1991 constitution, political censorship still exists in practice

PUBLISHING AND BROADCAST MEDIA

There are 3 daily newspapers, *Sidwaya*, *Kibare* and *Observateur Paalga*

1 state-owned service   1 state-owned, 2 independent services

Limited press freedom since 1991 has seen the growth of a number of small independent newspapers funded by opposition parties.

CRIME

 Burkina does not publish prison figures   General crime levels are rising

Crime levels have traditionally been low. However, the urbanization of society and the increase in political violence have seen levels increase.

EDUCATION

 18%

Education is based on the French system. Recently, practical subjects have received more emphasis.

HEALTH

 1 per 29,914 people   Malaria, diarrheal and respiratory diseases

The focus of Burkina's health spending is on primary health care and vaccination.

WEALTH

 Shop assistant, 30,250 CFA francs per month; dentist, 100,000 CFA francs per month

CONSUMER GOODS OWNERSHIP

VCR and PC ownership is limited to a small elite

5   1   2

Burkina is a country of extreme, almost universal poverty. Displays of wealth are rare.

WORLD RANKING

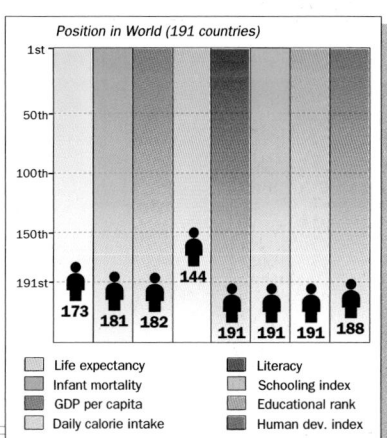

Position in World (191 countries)

173   181   182   144   191   191   191   188

- Life expectancy
- Infant mortality
- GDP per capita
- Daily calorie intake
- Literacy
- Schooling index
- Educational rank
- Human dev. index

133

BURMA (MYANMAR)

SOUTH EAST ASIA

OFFICIAL NAME: Union of Myanmar **CAPITAL:** Rangoon (Yangon)
POPULATION: 43.7 million **CURRENCY:** Kyat **OFFICIAL LANGUAGE:** Burmese (Myanmar)

FORMING THE EASTERN shores of the Bay of Bengal and the Andaman Sea in South East Asia, Burma is mountainous in the north, while the once-forested, fertile Irrawaddy basin occupies most of the country. Burma gained independence from British colonial control in 1948 and has recently suffered widespread political repression and ethnic conflict. In 1990, the National League for Democracy (NLD) gained a majority in free elections but was prevented from taking power by the military. Rich in natural resources, which include fisheries and teak forests, Burma's economy remains mostly agricultural.

Transporting timber on the Irrawaddy River near Mandalay. Burma once had the world's largest reserves of teak.

CLIMATE

WEATHER CHART

The tropical climate has three seasons: the wet season, when rainfall in the Irrawaddy delta and Tenasserim peninsula can reach 500 cm; summer, when northern Burma experiences 50°C and 100% humidity; and winter, when it is rarely cooler than 15°C except in the northern mountains.

COMMUNICATIONS

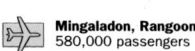

Mingaladon, Rangoon
580,000 passengers

72 ships
1.33m dwt

THE TRANSPORT NETWORK

23,463 km
(14,579 miles)

None

4508 km
(2801 miles)

3200 km
(1988 miles)

Most current construction projects are linked to the booming China–Burma border trade, the majority of which was legalized in 1989. Old bridges and roads (including the famous Burma, Ledo and Silk Roads, all key routes into China) are being renewed and new ones built with Chinese aid. Although it will be easier to distribute key products, including opium, the motives for their construction are military as well as commercial. The state has recently relaxed its monopoly of transport: since 1988, private bus companies have been given licences to operate. Air and rail routes, however, remain under government control.

TOURISM

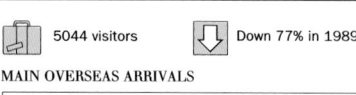
5044 visitors   Down 77% in 1989

MAIN OVERSEAS ARRIVALS

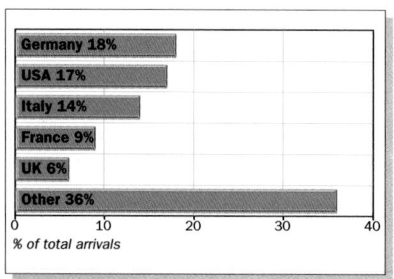

Germany 18%
USA 17%
Italy 14%
France 9%
UK 6%
Other 36%

% of total arrivals

From 1962 until 1988, tourists were limited to one-week stays. Burma has recently adopted an open-door policy, designed to attract foreign exchange. Old hotels are now being renovated and new ones built in joint ventures with private companies. Much of the finance comes from Japan, Singapore, South Korea and Hong Kong. China is also helping to build an international airport at Mandalay. Since 1990, the junta has been face-lifting historic monuments and relocating 'unsightly' villages away from temples at Pagan, Mandalay, Sagaing and Amarapura.

PEOPLE

Burmese, Karen, Shan, Chin, Kachin, Mon, Palaung, Wa

62 people per km²

THE URBAN/RURAL POPULATION SPLIT

25%   75%

RELIGIOUS PERSUASION

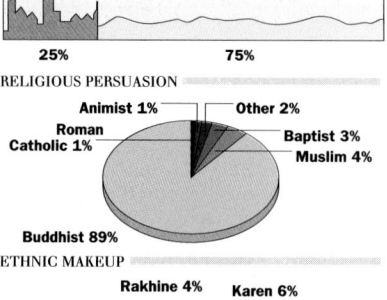

Animist 1% Other 2%
Roman Catholic 1%
Baptist 3%
Muslim 4%
Buddhist 89%

ETHNIC MAKEUP

Rakhine 4%   Karen 6%
Shan 9%
Other 13%
Burman (Bamah) 68%

Burma suffers from considerable ethnic tension, between the Burman majority and the smaller ethnic groups. At independence, the Shans, Karens, Kachins, Mons, Karennis and Chins all demanded their own state within a federation but were refused by the central government. All groups have kept their demands alive with low-level guerrilla activity against the state; in 1988 they united in a common cause against the military dictatorship, but several groups have recently signed peace treaties with the government.

A savage history, mainly of Burman repression of smaller groups, still plays a large part in the mistrust felt by the minorities for the Burman. Each group maintains a distinct cultural identity. Whilst the Burman claim racial purity, in fact many of them are of mixed blood, or ethnically Chinese.

Family life in Burma is still based around the extended family. Women have a prominent role, with access to education. Many run or own businesses in their own right. However, top jobs in government are still held almost exclusively by men.

POPULATION AGE BREAKDOWN

% of population by age group	0–14	15–64	65+		
65+	3.4%	3.7%	4%	4%	4.4%
15–64	55.5%	54.9%	56.4%	58.1%	58.8%
0–14	41.1%	41.4%	39.6%	37.9%	36.8%
	1960	1970	1980	1990	2000

POLITICS

Uncertain   General Than Shwe

THE STATE OF THE PARTIES
Constituent Assembly 485 members

The National League for Democracy (NLD) won 81% of seats in the Assembly in elections in 1990. However, they were prevented from taking power by the State Law and Order Restoration Council (SLORC)

Burma has been ruled by the military-backed SLORC dictatorship since 1988.

MAIN POLITICAL ISSUES

Restoring democracy
The military rules Burma with little regard to human rights. Opposition is not tolerated and torture and killings are commonplace. Ethnic rebel groups (with 30,000 armed members) have joined forces with democrats to oppose the regime. The focal point of opposition is Aung San Suu Kyi, kept under house arrest but effectively protected by the publicity she has generated in the West.

Refugees
Dislocated by the policies of the military regime, around one million refugees are stranded along Burma's borders with Bangladesh, Thailand, China and India.

PROFILE
Demands for a return to democracy culminated in the student-led political uprisings of 1987–1988. The military seized power in September 1988, ostensibly to maintain order until multiparty elections could be held. Instead, the State Law and Order Restoration Council (SLORC) was formed and all state bodies were abolished. Elections were held in 1990 and won by

Aung San Suu Kyi, figurehead of the pro-democracy movement.

General Ne Win, Burma's leader 1964–1988

BURMA

Total Area : 676 550 sq. km
(261 200 sq. miles)

▲ *Hkakabo Razi 5881m*

POPULATION

▣	over 1 000 000
◉	over 500 000
◎	over 100 000
○	over 50 000
●	over 10 000
•	under 10 000

LAND HEIGHT

4000m/13 124ft
2000m/6562ft
1000m/3281ft
500m/1640ft
200m/656ft
Sea Level

the NLD. However, the SLORC failed to relinquish power and pro-democracy opposition was brutally crushed. Ethnic rebel forces and opposition groups united to form the parallel Democratic Alliance of Burma government in Manerplaw.

WORLD AFFAIRS

CP   ESCAP   GATT   ADB

Burma's key relationship is with China. The latter has consistently backed the SLORC military regime and is a major supplier of weapons to the 350,000-strong Burmese army. The relationship is symbiotic, allowing China access to the Indian Ocean and giving it great influence over a regime partly dependent on its support. Burma's neighbours regard the arrangement as one which is seriously destabilizing the whole of the Asia–Pacific region.

Western governments have been active in the UN and EU in condemning the human rights abuses of the regime, and in 1991 Aung San Suu Kyi received the Nobel Peace Prize. In practice, however, they maintain an ambiguous relationship with the SLORC regime. Economic ties are growing stronger, particularly between the SLORC-owned state enterprises and Western multinationals. The latter are well represented in the increasingly profitable Burmese offshore oil and gas drilling industries.

CHRONOLOGY

From the 11th century, Burma's many ethnic groups came under the rule of three Tibeto-Burman dynasties, interspersed with periods of rule by the Mongols and the Mon. The Third Dynasty came into conflict with the British in India, sparking the Anglo-Burmese Wars of 1824, 1852 and 1885.

❏ **1886** Burma becomes a province of British India.
❏ **1906** Young Men's Buddhist Association founded to maintain cultural identity under British colonial influence.
❏ **1930–1931** Economic depression and slump in rice prices provokes uprising led by monk Saya San.
❏ **1937** Separation from India.
❏ **1942** Japan invades, receiving help from Burmese Independence Army (BIA) under 'Thirty Comrades' previously trained in Japan.
❏ **1945** BIA swaps sides and, supported by Anti-Fascist People's Freedom League (AFPFL) led by Aung San, helps Allies reoccupy country.
❏ **1947** UK agrees to Burmese independence. Aung San wins elections, but is assassinated. ⇨

B

135

B

CHRONOLOGY *continued*

- **1948** Independence under new prime minister, U Nu, who initiates socialist policies. Revolts by ethnic separatists and communists, notably Karen liberation struggle.
- **1958** Ruling AFPFL splits into two. Shan liberation struggle begins.
- **1960** U Nu's faction wins elections.
- **1961** Kachin rebellion begins.
- **1962** Military coup led by Gen Ne Win. 'New Order' policy of 'Buddhist Socialism' – isolation from outside world. Mining and other industries nationalized. Free trade prohibited.
- **1964** Ne Win makes Socialist Programme Party sole legal party.
- **1976** Social unrest. Attempted military coup. 40% of country now held by ethnic liberation groups.
- **1982** Non-indigenous people barred from public office.
- **1987** UN labels Burma a 'least-developed nation'. Ne Win accepts need to review economic policy.
- **1988** Student riots. Ne Win resigns. Martial law. More riots; 3000–4000 dead. Students and monks take control of many towns. NLD founded to form an alternative government by ex-premier U Nu, Aung San Suu Kyi, daughter of Gen Aung San, and others. Gen Saw Maung leads military coup. Students flee cities. SLORC takes power. National Democratic Front of ethnic resistance groups forms Democratic Alliance of Burma to include 11 more groups.
- **1989** Army arrests NLD leaders and steps up anti-rebel activity.
- **1990** Elections permitted. NLD wins 81% of seats. SLORC, however, remains in power. More NLD leaders arrested.
- **1991** Aung San Suu Kyi, under house arrest, awarded Nobel Peace Prize. NLD expels her as result of SLORC pressure. Many parties deregistered.
- **1992** Gen Than Shwe takes over as SLORC leader.

AID

Undisclosed military and soft loan receipts from China

On the increase, mostly from China

In 1988, Western nations, the World Bank and certain UN agencies such as the UNDP halted bilateral aid. The UN has, however, continued funding some development projects through its Drug Control Programme and the World Health Organization. The largest bilateral donor is now China, which in 1990 struck an arms deal worth $1.4 billion and recently agreed a 50 million yuan interest-free loan.

DEFENCE

$1.3bn

Up 19% between 1990 and 1992

0   Defence spending as % GDP   40

4.8%

BURMESE ARMED FORCES

	56 main battle tanks (26 *Comet*/30 Ch T-69II)	350,000 personnel
	60 patrol boats (1 Yan Taing Aung/ 1 Yan Gyi Aung)	13,500 personnel
	37 combat aircraft (10 F-7/2 FT-7/15 PC-7)	9000 personnel
	None	

The SLORC has steadily obtained modern weapons and military technology from around the world, primarily from China, but also from France, Germany, Sweden and former Yugoslavia. In the five years to 1993, the army expanded by 20% to 350,000 men.

Since 1988, the army has waged dry-season campaigns against minority groups every year except 1993. It has successfully put down most Mon and Karen insurgent campaigns and has destroyed their bases in southeastern Burma. Its 1989 assault on Muslim minorities in the Arakan region of western Burma resulted in 300,000 seeking refuge in Bangladesh.

ECONOMICS

$37.7bn   6.41 kyats

SCORE CARD

- ❑ WORLD GNP RANKING..........................49th
- ❑ GNP PER CAPITA $863
- ❑ BALANCE OF PAYMENTS ....£–418m
- ❑ INFLATION ....Very high on black market
- ❑ UNEMPLOYMENT ....Widespread underemployment

EXPORTS

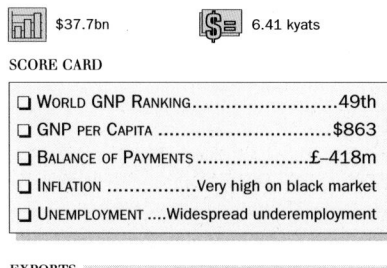

EU 7%
China 9%
Other 44%
India 17%
South East Asia 23%

IMPORTS

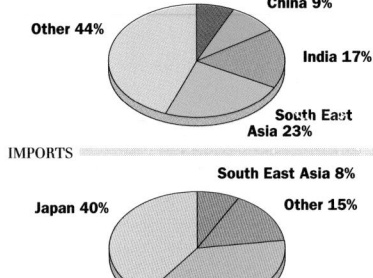

South East Asia 8%
Other 15%
Japan 40%
EU 37%

STRENGTHS

Very rich in natural resources: fertile soil, rich fisheries, timber including diminishing teak reserves, gems, offshore natural gas and oil.

WEAKNESSES

Shortage of skilled labour, managers and technicians. Rudimentary financial systems and institutions. Nationwide black market. Huge external debt. Dependence on imported manufactures.

PROFILE

Burma's economy is agriculture-based and functions mainly on a cash and barter system. Its key industries are controlled by 20 military-run state enterprises. Every aspect of economic life is permeated by a black market, on which prices are rocketing – a reaction to official price controls.

ECONOMIC PERFORMANCE INDICATOR

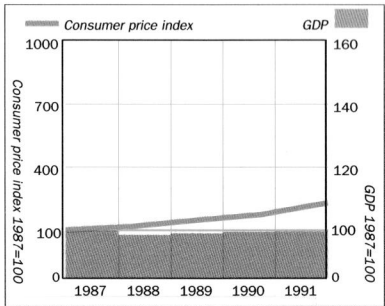

Consumer price index   GDP

Since 1989, the SLORC's open-door market-economy policy has brought a flood of foreign investment in oil and gas (by Western companies) and forestry, tourism and mining (by Asian companies). The recent boom in trade with China has turned less-developed Upper Burma into a thriving business centre full of Chinese goods and foreign visitors. The junta is concentrating on developing the northeastern border states – the area which produces 200 tonnes of heroin a year, 60% of the world total. Few plans exist for the manufacturing sector, however, and an almost total dependence on imports will continue.

BURMA : MAJOR BUSINESSES

- 🏠 Real estate
- Defence
- Jade
- Teak industries
- Trading centre
- Gas
- Oil
- Fish processing
- Manufacturing
- Opium

0   200 km
0   200 miles

B

RESOURCES

 2.6bn kwh (capacity 1.12m kw)

 Foreign companies are currently prospecting for oil

 9m cattle, 2.4m pigs, 269,000 sheep

 Oil, natural gas, tin, antimony, zinc, copper, tungsten, lead, coal

ELECTRICITY GENERATION

Hydro 48% (1.2bn kwh)
Thermal 52% (1.4bn kwh)
Nuclear 0%
Other 0%

% of total generation by type

Burma is the world's largest teak exporter. It is also a major producer of pearls, rubies and other gems. Foreign capital is funding exploration for natural gas and oil in the Tenasserim peninsula. However, Burma suffers from energy shortages.

BURMA : LAND USE

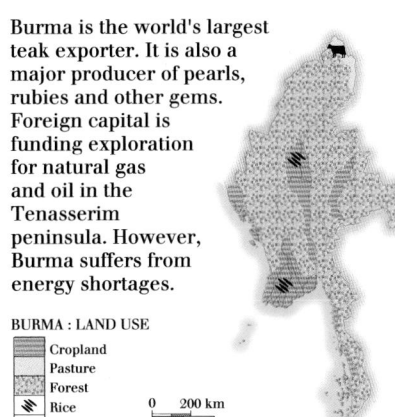

- Cropland
- Pasture
- Forest
- Rice
- Cattle

0　200 km
0　200 miles

ENVIRONMENT

 0.3%

New logging rights for Chinese companies

ENVIRONMENTAL TREATIES

No　No
No　No

Deforestation is a major problem and has increased since the 1988 coup. Chinese companies have been given unrestricted logging concessions.

MEDIA

 No press freedom since 1962. All private periodicals and books have to be registered with, and approved by, the Ministry of Information

PUBLISHING AND BROADCAST MEDIA

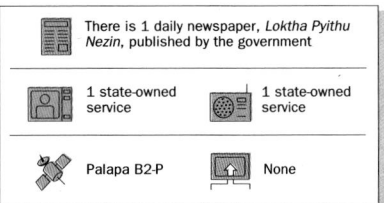

There is 1 daily newspaper, *Loktha Pyithu Nezin*, published by the government

1 state-owned service

1 state-owned service

Palapa B2-P

None

Political dissent of any kind is a criminal offence. An underground pro-democracy press produces anti-government material.

CRIME

 Burma does not publish prison figures

Down 1% in 1990

CRIME RATES

Murders
5　per 100,000 population

Rapes
2　per 100,000 population

Thefts
56　per 100,000 population

Levels of robbery, murder, bribery, corruption, embezzlement and black marketeering are high, compared to similar totalitarian regimes. The state is guilty of illegal activity. The UN reports regularly on human rights abuses against civilians, and the murder of innocent civilians including children, women, Buddhist monks, students, minorities and political dissidents.

There is a nominal civilian judicial system in Burma, but in practice all judges and lawyers are appointed by the junta and all legal functions executed by the SLORC. The most common charge is that of sedition against the state or the army under the 1975 'Law to Protect the State from Destructionists'. Among the SLORC's frequent arbitrary 'notices' is the Order 2/88 prohibiting assemblies of more than five persons. Most detainees have no legal rights of representation and are either jailed, used as forced labour or put under house arrest without public trial. Amnesty International is banned.

EDUCATION

 81%

0　Education spending as % GNP　25
2.2%

THE EDUCATION SYSTEM

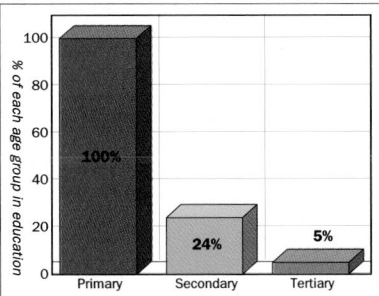

% of each age group in education

100%　Primary
24%　Secondary
5%　Tertiary

The education system provides ten years of schooling. There are two universities, three medical schools and one technical institute. There is a general shortage of qualified teachers. Most foreign teachers, doctors and engineers have left or are in jail.

HEALTH

 1 per 3354 people

 Malaria, fevers, heart and diarrheal diseases

0　Health spending as % GNP　25
0.6%

Leprosy, although it affects relatively few people compared with other diseases, has a higher prevalence in Burma than in the rest of Asia. There has been an increase in the incidence of malaria in the last few years. The growing number of AIDS cases is largely due to migrant prostitution across the Thai–Burmese border.

WEALTH

 Forestry worker, 475 kyats per month; technical education secondary teacher, 1000 kyats per month

CONSUMER GOODS OWNERSHIP

Per 1000 population

VCR and PC ownership is limited to a small elite

2　2　2

The state monopoly of the production and distribution of goods by rationing under General Ne Win's administration led to an increase in corruption and the rise of a nationwide black market, with huge disparities between official and unofficial prices. Only the military elite and their supporters could afford to live well. The situation has not changed significantly since 1988. Giant military enterprises grouped under a Defence Services holding company, whose capital amounts to 10% of GDP, now reap wealth and distribute privileges for a minority. Nevertheless, traditional social and economic mobility still exist. Climbing the socio-economic ladder is mainly a matter of loyalty to the military. Dissidents forced out of their jobs and hill tribes are the poorest groups.

WORLD RANKING

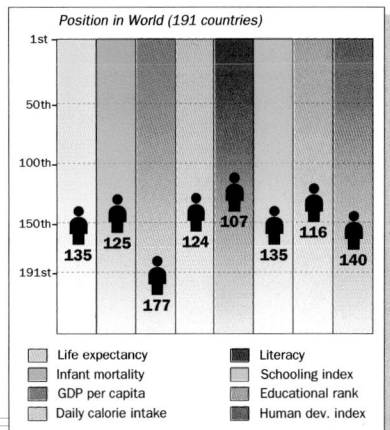

Position in World (191 countries)

1st
50th
100th
150th
191st

135　125　124　107　116　140
177

- Life expectancy
- Infant mortality
- GDP per capita
- Daily calorie intake
- Literacy
- Schooling index
- Educational rank
- Human dev. index

BURUNDI

CENTRAL AFRICA

OFFICIAL NAME: Republic of Burundi **CAPITAL:** Bujumbura
POPULATION: 5.8 million **CURRENCY:** Burundi franc **OFFICIAL LANGUAGE:** French and Kirundi

LAND-LOCKED BURUNDI lies just south of the equator on the Nile–Congo watershed. Lake Tanganyika forms part of its border with Zaire. Ethnic tension between the Hutu majority and the dominant Tutsi minority remains the main factor in politics. In October 1993, this spilled over into violence as the Tutsi-dominated army mounted a coup that resulted in the assassination of the country's first-ever Hutu president.

Pig farming and fish ponds. The majority of Burundi's population depends on subsistence farming.

CLIMATE

WEATHER CHART

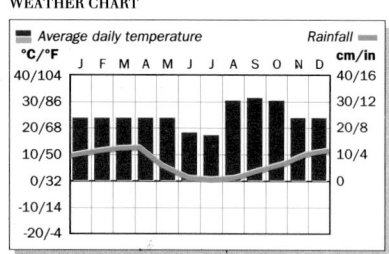

Burundi is temperate with high humidity, much cloud and frequent heavy rain. The highlands have frost.

COMMUNICATIONS

 Bujumbura International 70,000 passengers   Has no fleet

THE TRANSPORT NETWORK

6285 km (3905 miles) — None — None — Lake Tanganyika

The dense road network has been rehabilitated. There are plans to build a railway linking Burundi with Rwanda, Uganda and Tanzania.

TOURISM

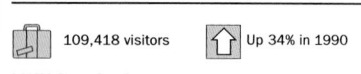 109,418 visitors — Up 34% in 1990

MAIN OVERSEAS ARRIVALS

Central Africa 47%
Europe 38%
Central Asia 8%
Other 7%
% of total arrivals

A lack of basic infrastructure and violent ethnic strife deter tourists. The industry has limited potential as Burundi lacks its neighbours' spectacular scenery and big game parks.

PEOPLE

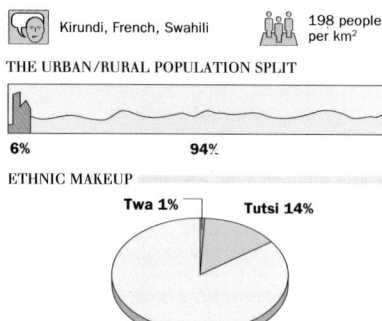

Kirundi, French, Swahili — 198 people per km²

THE URBAN/RURAL POPULATION SPLIT

6%   94%

ETHNIC MAKEUP

Twa 1% Tutsi 14% Hutu 85%

Burundi's history has been marked by violent ethnic conflict between the majority Hutu and the Tutsi, who control the army. Large-scale massacres have occurred repeatedly over the past two decades. Over 120,000 people, mostly Hutu, have been killed in ethnic conflict since October 1992. The Twa pygmies do not suffer similar repression. Most Burundians are subsistence farmers. The capacity of women to work determines their marriageability. 78% of Burundians are Roman Catholic.

BURUNDI
Total Area : 27 830 sq. km (10 750 sq. miles)

LAND HEIGHT
2000m/6562ft
1000m/3281ft
500m/1640ft

POPULATION
over 100 000
over 50 000
over 10 000
under 10 000

POLITICS

1998 — Interim president Synvestre Ntibantunganya

THE STATE OF THE PARTIES
National Assembly 81 members

80% FRODEBU   20% UPRONA

FRODEBU = Front for Democracy in Burundi
UPRONA = Union for National Progress

Politics in Burundi remains sharply divided along ethnic lines, with the minority Tutsi seeking to control the majority Hutu population.

From 1966, the Tutsi UPRONA was the only legal party. Tutsi dominated the civil service, judiciary and the army. The latter engaged in occasional mass slaughter of Hutu. In 1990, President Buyoya, a Tutsi, called for greater unity between the two groups, leading to hopes that Hutu could be brought into the political process. His report was approved by referendum and opposition parties were legalized. Burundi's first free presidential elections were held in June 1993. They were won by Melchior Ndadaye, a Hutu and leader of FRODEBU. Tutsi fears of Hutu dominance led to a coup in October and the assassination of Ndadaye. Thousands of Hutu were killed by the army; 150,000 fled into Rwanda and Zaire. In 1994, Burundi's new president and the Rwandan president died when their aircraft was shot down in Rwanda as they were returning from ethnic peace talks.

B

WORLD AFFAIRS

In 1994, Burundi asked for UN military intervention to prevent further ethnic violence; the request was declined.

AID

 $253m (receipts)   Food aid rising sharply to meet risk of famine

The crisis of 1993–1994 led one million Burundians to flee their homes and miss two planting seasons. In 1994, 970,000 were dependent on UN food aid.

DEFENCE

 $32.05m   Up 1% in 1988

The army is run by Tutsi. In line with the political changes taking place in Burundi, President Ndadaye proposed bringing Hutu into officer ranks. Tutsi resistance to this move was a major factor behind the October 1993 coup. The army has threatened to become a Tutsi militia.

ECONOMICS

 $1.1bn   247.94 Burundi francs

SCORE CARD

- ❏ WORLD GNP RANKING.......................155th
- ❏ GNP PER CAPITA $189
- ❏ BALANCE OF PAYMENTS.....................$–75m
- ❏ INFLATION 4.7%
- ❏ UNEMPLOYMENT....Widespread underemployment

STRENGTHS
Small quantities of gold and tungsten. Potential of massive nickel reserves and oil in Lake Tanganyika.

WEAKNESSES
Failure of democratic process to stem ethnic strife. Overwhelmingly agricultural economy (91% of labour force) under pressure from high birth rate. Little prospect of political stability.

EXPORTS

Japan 5%
Finland 21%
Other 47%
Germany* 27%

IMPORTS

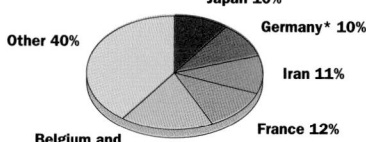

Japan 10%
Germany* 10%
Other 40%
Iran 11%
France 12%
Belgium and Luxembourg 17%

RESOURCES

 106m kwh (capacity 43,000 kw)   Not an oil producer and has no refineries

420,000 cattle, 400,000 sheep, 84,000 pigs   Gold, tungsten, nickel, vanadium, oil

Burundi has around 5% of the world's nickel reserves. Extraction, however, is not economically viable. There are also deposits of gold and vanadium. Surveys in the 1980s detected oil reserves below Lake Tanganyika but production has yet to begin. Burundi imports petrol from Iran and electricity from Zaire. However, once the HEP plants at Mugera and Rwegura are operational, they will meet most domestic electricity requirements.

ENVIRONMENT

 3% partially protected   Serious deforestation and soil impoverishment

Only 2% of Burundi is forest and even this is now under pressure from one of Africa's highest birth rates. Burundi suffers from the problems associated with deforestation, particularly soil erosion. Some soils are also being exhausted from over-use. Several tree planting programmes have been introduced. UNESCO is also running ecological education initiatives at village level aimed at women farmers.

MEDIA

 The media is state-controlled. General thaw in censorship since 1992 constitution in theory. Media has been regularly liberalized

PUBLISHING AND BROADCAST MEDIA

 There is 1 daily newspaper, *Le Renouveau du Burundi*, published by the government

 1 state-owned service   1 state-owned service

Le Renouveau du Burundi and the Roman Catholic *Burundi Chrétien* are the most influential newspapers. Colour TV transmission began in 1985.

CRIME

 Burundi does not publish prison figures   Down 53% in 1990

Burundi has an appalling human rights record. There have been frequent massacres of Hutu by the Tutsi-dominated army. The worst pogroms occurred in 1972, 1988, 1993 and 1994.

EDUCATION

 50%

Primary schooling begins at seven years of age and is compulsory, though further schooling is not. There are 76 primary school children per teacher. The one university is located in the capital.

HEALTH

 1 per 18,365 people   Communicable infections, parasitic diseases

2.1 million people have no access to health services. Only 7% of women use contraception; on average, women have seven children. 38% of the population have access to safe drinking water.

WEALTH

 Bus conductor, 63 Burundi francs per hour; bank accountant, 1100 Burundi francs per hour

CONSUMER GOODS OWNERSHIP

VCR and PC ownership is limited to a small elite

Wealth is concentrated within the Tutsi political and business elite. Most Burundians live a subsistence existence.

WORLD RANKING

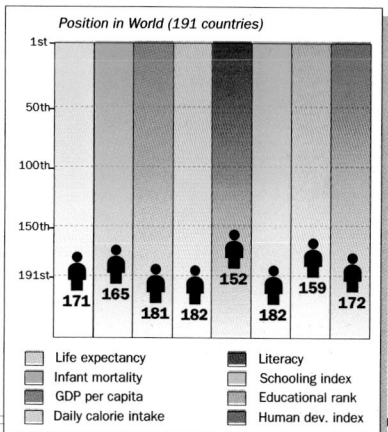

Position in World (191 countries)

- ☐ Life expectancy
- ☐ Infant mortality
- ☐ GDP per capita
- ☐ Daily calorie intake
- ■ Literacy
- ☐ Schooling index
- ☐ Educational rank
- ■ Human dev. index

CAMBODIA

SOUTH EAST ASIA

OFFICIAL NAME: State of Cambodia   **CAPITAL:** Phnom Penh
POPULATION: 8.8 million   **CURRENCY:** Riel   **OFFICIAL LANGUAGE:** Khmer

C

LOCATED IN THE INDOCHINESE PENINSULA in South East Asia, Cambodia has a coastline on the Gulf of Thailand and shares borders with Thailand, Laos and Vietnam. Its main topographical feature is the Tônlé Sap, or Great Lake, which drains into the Mekong River. Over three quarters of Cambodia is forested, with mangroves lining the coast. Rice is the principal crop. Cambodia has emerged from two decades of civil war and invasion from Vietnam. The UN's biggest-ever peace-keeping operation resulted in free elections in 1993.

PEOPLE

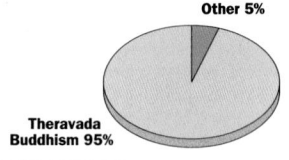 Khmer, French, Chinese, Vietnamese, Cham   45 people per km²

THE URBAN/RURAL POPULATION SPLIT

12%   88%

RELIGIOUS PERSUASION

Other 5%

Theravada Buddhism 95%

ETHNIC MAKEUP

Vietnamese 1%   Chinese 4%
Other 1%

Khmer 94%

CLIMATE

WEATHER CHART

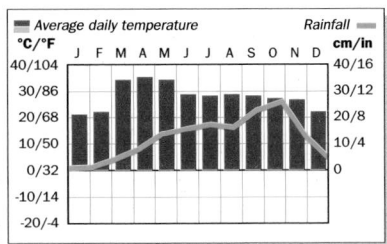

Cambodia has a more varied climate than neighbouring Vietnam. Low-lying regions have moderate rainfall and the most consistent yearly temperatures. The wettest areas are the hillsides facing the Gulf of Thailand. The dry season lasts from December to April and is characterized by high temperatures and an average eight hours of sunshine a day. During the rainy season, Cambodia experiences high humidity and sultry heat. From May to September, winds are southeasterly, whilst from October to April they are north or northeasterly.

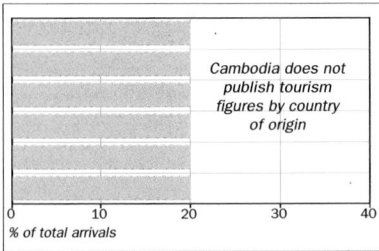

Angkor Wat stands in the ruins of the ancient city of Angkor, once the capital of the Khmer empire. It is now one of Cambodia's leading tourist attractions.

TOURISM

 10,000 (est)   Significant increase since 1990

MAIN OVERSEAS ARRIVALS

Cambodia does not publish tourism figures by country of origin

0   10   20   30   40
% of total arrivals

Cambodia, the centre of the Khmer empire between 800 and 1400 AD, has some of the most impressive temples in South East Asia. The most famous is the extraordinary site at Angkor Wat, near Siĕmréab. During the war it was controlled by the Khmer Rouge, who threatened any visitors with attack. Visitors are now allowed in small numbers; 3000 visited the site in 1993.

Once basic infrastructure is in place and the political situation has stabilized, Cambodia has considerable tourism potential. It currently attracts adventurous, independent travellers. Tourists are occasionally kidnapped.

COMMUNICATIONS

 Pochentong, Phnom Penh   1 ship 1500 dwt

THE TRANSPORT NETWORK

13,351 km (8296 miles)   None

550 km (342 miles)   3700 km (2299 miles)

The civil war led to a near-collapse of Cambodia's road and rail system. Some parts of the network are still subject to attack by Khmer Rouge bandits. International aid is now being used to rehabilitate key routes, such as Highways 3 and 5, and to rebuild the Chroy Changba Bridge out of Phnom Penh. The bicycle and rickshaw are the main form of urban transport.

Cambodian society underwent one of the 20th century's most horrific programmes of social transformation between 1975 and 1979 under Pol Pot's Khmer Rouge regime. Over one million Cambodians, or one in eight, died from warfare, starvation, overwork or execution. Half a million more went into exile in Thailand. The Pol Pot regime's reforms led to the scrapping of money, possessions and hierarchy. Only peasants, soldiers of the revolution and some industrial workers were allowed to retain their pre-revolution status. Boys and girls of 13 and 14 were taken from their homes, indoctrinated in the tenets of revolution and allowed to kill those perceived to be guilty of bourgeois crimes. Violence at all levels was sanctioned in the name of revolution.

Pol Pot's regime ended with the Vietnamese invasion of 1979. Most professionals who had survived emigrated. The effects of revolution and subsequent civil war are still felt and reflected in the world's highest rate of orphans and widows.

POPULATION AGE BREAKDOWN

	0–14	15–64	65+		
65+	2.7%	2.8%	2.5%	2.9%	3.5%
15–64	54.8%	54%	64.6%	62.2%	57.9%
0–14	42.5%	43.2%	32.9%	34.9%	38.6%
	1960	1970	1980	1990	2000

POLITICS

Uncertain

President Prince
Norodom Sihanouk

THE STATE OF THE PARTIES

National Assembly 120 members

1%
NLMK

48%
FUNCINPEC

43%
CPP

8%
BLDP

FUNCINPEC = United National Front for an Independent,
Neutral, Peaceful and Co-operative Cambodia   CPP =
Cambodian People's Party   BLDP = Buddhist Liberal
Democratic Party   NLMK = National Liberation Movement of
Kampuchea

Cambodia held free multiparty
elections under UN supervision in 1993.

MAIN POLITICAL ISSUES

Fledgling democracy

The UN's Cambodia operation, the
biggest in the organization's history,
introduced a degree of stability to
Cambodia's political system. Some
22,000 troops provided the conditions
for free elections held in 1993. Whether
or not competing political factions can
be contained within the newly-
established democratic framework
remains the key political question.

The Khmer Rouge

The Khmer Rouge decided not to take
part in the elections of 1993, resuming
instead the armed struggle in areas of
central and western Cambodia. The
group is demanding membership of a
government of national reconciliation,
but is unwilling to see its troops
merged with a national army.

PROFILE

In 1975, the US-installed government
was overthrown by the Marxist Khmer
Rouge under Pol Pot. Pol Pot was in
turn overthrown, following the
Vietnamese invasion in 1979. The
invasion united Cambodia's three main
factions – the Khmer Rouge, FUNCINPEC
and the Khmer Peoples' National
Liberation Front (KPNLF) – in common
cause against the Vietnamese. The
coalition was recognized by the UN
as the government of Democratic
Kampuchea. Vietnam's decision to
leave in 1989 led to peace talks in Paris
and the signing of the October 1991
Paris Accords. The Paris Accords
mandated the UN's UNTAC operation to
steer the country to free democratic
elections. The task involved imposing
the ceasefire agreed, repatriating
370,000 refugees and overseeing
the election campaign. Following
FUNCINPEC's victory in the elections,
Prince Sihanouk proposed a coalition
government of national reconciliation.
The Khmer Rouge refused to join as
they wanted a greater part in the
government than their election results
warranted. In 1994 they continued
armed resistance.

*Saloth Sar, who
assumed the name
Pol Pot, still leads the
Khmer Rouge.*

*Prince Norodom
Sihanouk. He
abdicated kingship to
enter politics in 1955.*

WORLD AFFAIRS

ADP   CP   ESCAP   NAM

During the years of civil war that
followed the Vietnamese invasion, the
Phnom Penh government suffered the
same isolation that was imposed on
Vietnam. Recognized by few countries
outside the Soviet bloc, it became an
international pariah. The resistance
movement that included the Khmer
Rouge was allotted Cambodia's seat at
the UN and gained the backing of an
anti-Soviet, anti-Vietnamese alliance
that included the USA and China.

Cambodia's new constitution talks of
making the country once again a non-
aligned 'island of peace'. While China
and Thailand have disavowed their
former support for the Khmer Rouge,
the Thai military still provides arms,
personnel and sanctuary for its troops,
and China has supported King
Sihanouk's call to bring the Khmer
Rouge into the ruling coalition. By
contrast, the USA has threatened to
withdraw aid to the government if the
Khmer Rouge is allowed to join the
coalition. The government has to date
been reluctant to fuel the historic
animosity that exists with Vietnam.

AID

 $62m (receipts)

 Up 48% in 1991

Aid is the single most important part of
the Cambodian economy. It provides
around 70% of government revenues.
The coalition government has
benefited from large aid commitments
from a Japanese-led consortium.
However, disbursing aid is difficult.

CAMBODIA

Total Area : 181 040 sq. km (69 000 sq. miles)

POPULATION	
⊙	over 500 000
○	over 50 000
●	over 10 000
•	under 10 000

LAND HEIGHT	
	1000m/3281ft
	500m/1640ft
	200m/656ft
	Sea Level

C

CHRONOLOGY

A former French protectorate, Cambodia gained independence in 1953 as a constitutional monarchy with Norodom Sihanouk as king.

- ❑ **1955** Sihanouk abdicates to pursue political career.
- ❑ **1970** Right-wing coup led by Prime Minister Lon Nol deposes Sihanouk. Exiled Sihanouk forms Royal Government of National Union of Cambodia (GRUNC), backed by formerly hostile communist Khmer Rouge. Lon Nol proclaims Khmer Republic.
- ❑ **1974** GRUNC forces capture Phnom Penh. Prince Sihanouk head of state, Khmer Rouge assumes power. Hundreds of thousands die during radical social programme.
- ❑ **1976** Country renamed Democratic Kampuchea. Elections. Sihanouk resigns; GRUNC dissolved. Khieu Samphan head of state; Pol Pot prime minister.
- ❑ **1977** Regime called the Communist Party of Kampuchea (CPK), led by Pol Pot.
- ❑ **1978** Vietnam invades, supported by Cambodian communists opposed to Pol Pot.
- ❑ **1979** Vietnamese capture Phnom Penh. CPK ousted by Kampuchean People's Revolutionary Party (KPRP), led by Pen Sovan. Khmer Rouge starts guerrilla war. Pol Pot held responsible for three million deaths and sentenced to death in absence. Vietnamese and DK (mostly Khmer Rouge) forces begin conflict on Thai border.
- ❑ **1980** Heng Samrin KPRP leader.
- ❑ **1982** Government-in-exile formed, including Khmer Rouge and Khmer People's National Liberation Front, headed by Prince Sihanouk; recognized by UN.
- ❑ **1988** Vietnam announces troop withdrawals. Khmer Rouge offensive. Khmer Rouge refuses to take part in peace talks.
- ❑ **1989** Vietnamese troops withdraw. Khmer Rouge forces make gains.
- ❑ **1990** UN Security Council approves plan for UN-monitored ceasefire and elections. Cambodian factions form Supreme National Council (SNC) but no agreement reached.
- ❑ **1991** SNC agree on elections. Factions sign accord. Sihanouk head of State of Cambodia. Khmer Rouge officials flee after attacks.
- ❑ **1992** Clashes between Cambodian troops and Khmer Rouge. UN ceasefire repeatedly violated.
- ❑ **1993** UN-supervised elections go ahead. UN peace operation leaves.
- ❑ **1994** Khmer Rouge refuses to join peace process.

DEFENCE

$58.1m   up 36% in 1992

0   *Defence spending as % GDP*   40
Proportion is increasing

CAMBODIAN ARMED FORCES

🔫	150 main battle tanks (150 T-54,-55,-59)	80,000 personnel
🚢	12 patrol boats (2 Sov *Turya* PFI)	4000 personnel
✈	17 combat aircraft (17 MiG-21)	1000 personnel
	None	

The current government's defence priority is unifying the command structures of the three armies of the main coalition partners. This is essential to contain the continuing Khmer Rouge struggle. The Khmer Rouge have so far rejected the terms of a 'national reconciliation' advanced by the government.

Despite the fact that the coalition's three armies (the Cambodian People's Armed Forces, FUNCINPEC's Armée Nationale Sihanoukiste and the KPNLF's Khmer People's National Liberation Armed Forces) number over 150,000 men, they are meeting strong resistance from the Khmer Rouge's estimated 10,000 troops. After some initial victories, the government's forces suffered a series of defeats at the hands of the Khmer Rouge in the west of the country in mid-1994. In part, this reflected low morale among coalition forces who are poorly paid and have suffered heavily from disease.

ECONOMICS

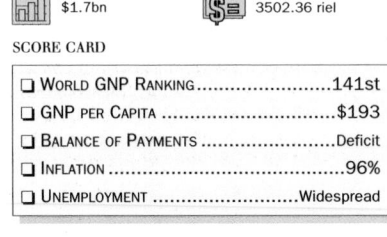

$1.7bn   3502.36 riel

SCORE CARD

- ❑ WORLD GNP RANKING 141st
- ❑ GNP PER CAPITA $193
- ❑ BALANCE OF PAYMENTS ....Deficit
- ❑ INFLATION 96%
- ❑ UNEMPLOYMENT ....Widespread

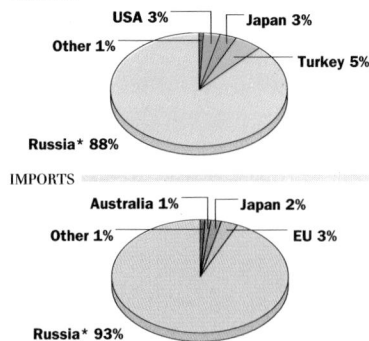

EXPORTS
USA 3%   Japan 3%
Other 1%
Turkey 5%
Russia* 88%

IMPORTS
Australia 1%   Japan 2%
Other 1%
EU 3%
Russia* 93%

STRENGTHS
Currently very few as economy is still recovering from civil war. Considerable future potential. Given the right conditions, Cambodia could achieve self-sufficiency in rice. Gems, especially sapphires. Possible offshore oil wealth. Timber trade to Thailand.

WEAKNESSES
Tiny tax base makes economic reform hard to implement. Dependence on overseas aid; corruption at most levels of government limits its effectiveness. Loss of skilled workers as result of Khmer Rouge anti-bourgeois atrocities in the 1970s.

ECONOMIC PERFORMANCE INDICATOR

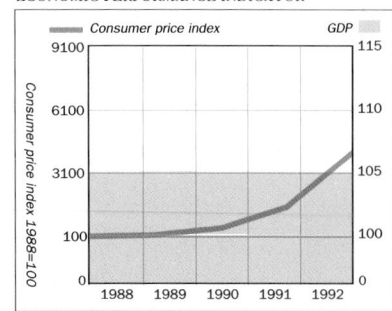

Consumer price index   GDP

PROFILE
Cambodia's economy was devastated during the Pol Pot years. The Vietnamese attempted some reconstruction based on central planning, then switched to policies encouraging the private sector. The presence of the UN encouraged some limited development.

CAMBODIA : MAJOR BUSINESSES

Bătdâmbâng
Mémót
Ta Khmau
Kâmpôt
Phnom Penh

🐄 Rubber
✳ Textiles
⚗ Fertilizers
⛏ Gold mining

0   200 km
0   200 miles

C

RESOURCES

70m kwh (capacity 35,000 kw)

Not an oil producer and has no refineries

2.1m cattle, 1.6m pigs, 750,000 buffaloes

Salt, phosphates

Tropical rainforest timber, particularly teak and rosewood, is Cambodia's most important resource. Most forests are located in the north and west.

ELECTRICITY GENERATION

Hydro 43% (30m kwh)

Thermal 57% (40m kwh)

Nuclear 0%

Other 0%

% of total generation by type

CAMBODIA : LAND USE

Tonlé Sap
Tonlé Sap
Mekong

0   200 km
0   200 miles

Cropland
Pasture
Wetland
Forest
Cattle
Rice
Rubber - cash crop

ENVIRONMENT

 None

 Enforcement of any initiatives is impossible

ENVIRONMENTAL TREATIES

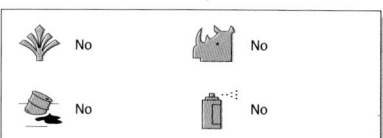

No

No

No

No

Deforestation is one of the most serious problems facing Cambodia. Timber, one of the country's most valuable assets, was sold in huge quantities by all Cambodian factions to finance their war efforts. According to the UN, in 1992 alone, more than 250,000 hectares of forest were cleared. This provided over one million cubic metres of timber. A moratorium on logging was declared at the end of 1992, but was largely ignored. In many parts of the country logging is impossible to police and, at current rates, estimates suggest that what remains of Cambodia's forests will be cut down by 2000. The environmental consequences – topsoil erosion and increased risk of flooding – are enormous and will hold back Cambodia's reconstruction.

MEDIA

 There are plans to impose censorship

Since the UN-sponsored elections, the press has flourished in Cambodia. Over 40 Khmer-language papers are now on sale. Criticism of the government, on issues such as corruption, is voiced openly. However, the coalition is planning new censorship laws.

CRIME

Cambodia does not publish prison figures

Civilian crime rates are now fairly stable

CRIME RATES

Violence is increasing as more areas come under renewed attack by the Khmer Rouge

The UN-sponsored peace process and the successful elections in 1993 led to a dramatic drop in crime in Cambodia. Many areas are experiencing the first period of stability in two decades.

The exceptions are areas controlled by the Khmer Rouge, mostly in the west of the country. The regions around Pailĭn and Bătdâmbâng are particularly dangerous. Khmer Rouge guerrillas carry out frequent terror missions against villages. Police stations are particular targets. An estimated 40,000 civilians were displaced by the Khmer Rouge's May 1994 onslaughts. Western aid agencies have removed their personnel from Bătdâmbâng and Banthey Meanchey. The lack of adequate policing has also led to a rise in banditry in these regions.

EDUCATION

 35%

0   Education spending as % GNP   25

Sufficient to send 80% of children to primary school

THE EDUCATION SYSTEM

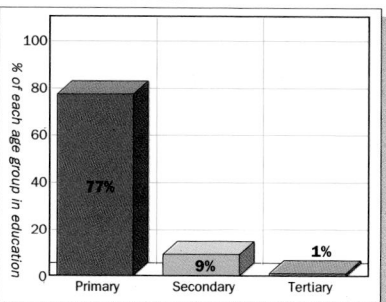

% of each age group in education

77%
9%
1%

Primary   Secondary   Tertiary

Only 5000 of Cambodia's 20,000 teachers survived the Pol Pot period. The Vietnamese-installed government trained or retrained about 40,000.

PUBLISHING AND BROADCAST MEDIA

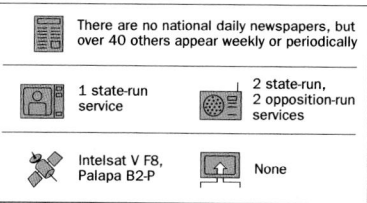

There are no national daily newspapers, but over 40 others appear weekly or periodically

1 state-run service

2 state-run, 2 opposition-run services

Intelsat V F8, Palapa B2-P

None

HEALTH

 1 per 27,000 people

Circulatory and infectious diseases, cancers

0   Health spending as % GNP   25

Insufficient to provide comprehensive primary care

The Cambodian health system was effectively destroyed by the Khmer's period in power. Only 50 doctors survived the Pol Pot period. In the immediate aftermath of the Vietnamese invasion, Cambodia's health indicators were among the worst in the world. Over 25% of babies were dying before their first birthday.

Conditions have since improved. However, infant mortality remains high and malaria and cholera are endemic.

WEALTH

 Most Cambodians live a subistence existence

CONSUMER GOODS OWNERSHIP

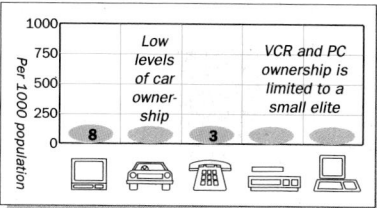

Per 1000 population

Low levels of car ownership

VCR and PC ownership is limited to a small elite

8

3

The opening up of the country's economy has led to an influx of capital. The benefits of new investment, however, are limited to those in power.

WORLD RANKING

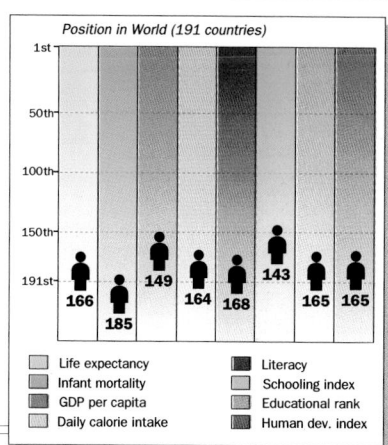

Position in World (191 countries)

1st
50th
100th
150th
191st

166
185
149
164
168
143
165
165

Life expectancy
Infant mortality
GDP per capita
Daily calorie intake
Literacy
Schooling index
Educational rank
Human dev. index

CAMEROON

OFFICIAL NAME: Republic of Cameroon **CAPITAL:** Yaoundé
POPULATION: 12.2 million **CURRENCY:** CFA franc **OFFICIAL LANGUAGES:** French and English

C

LOCATED ON THE CENTRAL WEST AFRICAN coast, over half of Cameroon is forested, with equatorial rainforest to the south, and evergreen forest and wooded savanna north of the Sanaga River. Most cities are located in the south, although there are densely populated areas around Mount Cameroon, a dormant volcano. For 30 years Cameroon was effectively a one-party state. Democratic elections in 1992 returned the former ruling party to power.

*Savanna landscape at **Mindif Pic** in Cameroon's far north. From here, the land slopes down to the hot, arid Lake Chad basin.*

CLIMATE

WEATHER CHART

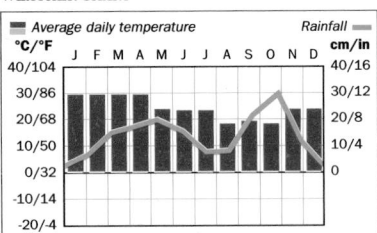

Climate varies from the equatorial south with 500 cm of rain a year to the drought-beset Sahel of the far north.

COMMUNICATIONS

Douala International
436,000 passengers

2 ships
33,500 dwt

THE TRANSPORT NETWORK

52,214 km (32,444 miles)		Trans-African Highway
1104 km (686 miles)		2090 km (1299 miles)

Major projects are the east–west Trans-African Highway and realigning the Douala–Nkongamba railway.

TOURISM

 100,000 visitors   Up 15% in 1990

MAIN OVERSEAS ARRIVALS

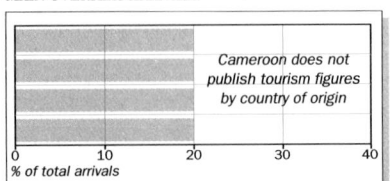

Cameroon does not publish tourism figures by country of origin

0   10   20   30   40
% of total arrivals

In 1989, the first tourism minister was appointed to boost the still small industry. Some package tours visit the northern game parks. A new airport near Yaoundé will replace the present one. Beaches near Kribi have a few hotels.

PEOPLE

 Fang, Bulu, Yaundé, Duala, Mbum, Fulani, Pidgin English, French, English

 25 people per km²

THE URBAN/RURAL POPULATION SPLIT

41%   59%

RELIGIOUS PERSUASION

Muslim 16%

Indigenous beliefs 51%

Christian 33%

Cameroon is ethnically diverse – there are 230 groups although no single group is dominant. The largest is the Bamileke of the centre southwest, but this group has never held political power. When President Ahidjo, a northern Fulani, retired, he was replaced by Paul Biya of the southeastern Bulu-Beti group. The north–south enmity which affects many other West African states is also present in Cameroon, albeit diminished by the great diversity of peoples. There is tension between competing groups of the south. There are sizeable groups of French-speaking and English-speaking peoples.

POLITICS

 1997   President Paul Biya

THE STATE OF THE PARTIES

National Assembly 180 members

| 49% RDPC | 38% UNDP | 10% UPC | 3% MDR |

RDPC = Cameroon People's Democratic Movement
UNDP = National Union for Democracy and Progress
UPC = Union of Peoples of Cameroon
MDR = Movement for the Defence of the Republic

Despite ruthless use of the security forces during demonstrations for change in 1990, multiparty elections were held in 1992. They were won by the ruling RDPC. The following presidential elections were won by Paul Biya, although the results have been disputed; the Social Democratic Front (SDF) of John Fru Ndi claims to have defeated Biya. Despite being the most important opposition group, the SDF boycotted the parliamentary elections.

CAMEROON

Total Area : 475 440 sq. km
(183 570 sq. miles)

POPULATION

over 1 000 000	▣
over 500 000	◉
over 100 000	◎
over 50 000	○
over 10 000	●
under 10 000	•

LAND HEIGHT

2000m/6562ft	
1000m/3281ft	
500m/1640ft	
200m/656ft	
Sea Level	

C

WORLD AFFAIRS

OAU ECA GATT FZ NAM

Cameroon's most important relationship is with France, which gives considerable support. Restoring democratic credentials, damaged in the presidential elections, is also a priority. Cameroon has to carefully balance relations between mainly French-owned and US-owned oil companies.

AID

 $501m (receipts)   Up 16% in 1991

France is by far the most important donor, even having twice paid Cameroon's back debts to the IMF to avoid its being blacklisted. However, IMF aid is now virtually frozen because of Cameroon's poor economic performance. Cameroon can no longer afford any of its development projects.

DEFENCE

 $190.9m   Up 34% in 1990

The military has been an active force in supporting the regime and maintaining order in the face of democratic protests since before independence. The 6600-man army is equipped mainly from France. There is a 4000-man gendarmerie and Cameroon still has a strong political police, the CENER.

ECONOMICS

 $9.8bn   295.23 CFA francs

SCORE CARD

- ❏ WORLD GNP RANKING..........................79th
- ❏ GNP PER CAPITA $805
- ❏ BALANCE OF PAYMENTS...................$–792m
- ❏ INFLATION ....–2.2%
- ❏ UNEMPLOYMENT....Widespread underemployment

STRENGTHS
Moderate oil reserves. Very diversified agricultural economy (timber, cocoa, coffee, rubber) and food self-sufficiency preserved through oil boom. Historical liberalism. Private sector in relatively good state. 95% of electricity is HEP.

WEAKNESSES
Massive fuel smuggling from Nigeria affects refinery profits. Inflated civil service. Growing national debt owing to failure to adjust to fall in oil revenues.

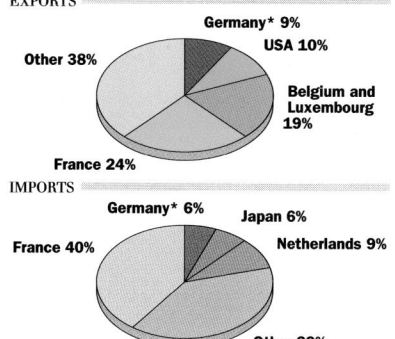

EXPORTS

- Germany* 9%
- USA 10%
- Belgium and Luxembourg 19%
- France 24%
- Other 38%

IMPORTS

- Germany* 6%
- Japan 6%
- Netherlands 9%
- France 40%
- Other 39%

RESOURCES

 2.7bn kwh (capacity 627,000 kw)

 140,400 b/d (reserves 400,000,000 bbl)

 4.6m cattle, 3.2m sheep, 1.3m pigs, 39,000 asses

 Oil, tin, limestone, natural gas, bauxite, iron, uranium, gold

New oil discoveries may bolster declining extraction rates. In spite of large bauxite deposits, much is imported for the Edea smelter, which takes 50% of national electricity output.

ENVIRONMENT

 4% (2% partially protected)

 Environmental forests ministry ineffective

Conservation groups and official nature reserves are attempting to curb commercial timber felling. National parks are celebrated for their flora.

MEDIA

 Press censorship eased in 1990, but it is still fairly severe

PUBLISHING AND BROADCAST MEDIA

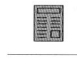 There are 2 daily newspapers, *Le Tribune du Cameroun* and *La Détente*

 1 state-owned service   1 state-owned service

Press censorship has been more severe in the French-speaking areas than in the English-speaking areas. Journalists are still wary of challenging authority.

CRIME

 Cameroon does not publish prison figures

 No figures published, but the trend is up

Armed robbery and burglary in Douala and Yaoundé are rising fast. The CENER political police are known to use torture.

EDUCATION

 54%

The French-speaking majority has failed in its attempt to take over the bilingual system. In 1991, two new single-language universities were created.

CHRONOLOGY

One of the great trading emporia of West Africa, Cameroon was divided between the French and British in 1919, after 30 years of German rule.

- ❏ **1955** Revolt; French kill 10,000.
- ❏ **1960** French sector independent.
- ❏ **1961** British southern sector votes to join Cameroon; northern joins Nigeria. Federal system set up. Lasts 11 years – centralized 1972.
- ❏ **1966** One-party state.
- ❏ **1982** Ahidjo dies. Paul Biya succeeds as president.
- ❏ **1983–1984** Coup attempts. Heavy casualties; 50 plotters executed.
- ❏ **1990** Demonstrations and strikes; declaration of multiparty state.
- ❏ **1991** Annexes nine Nigerian villages.
- ❏ **1992** Multiparty elections.

HEALTH

 1 per 13,237 people

Malaria, diarrheal and respiratory diseases

The sharp fall in government provision and financing means that more people are using the private health sector or traditional practitioners.

WEALTH

Wealth disparities are marked

CONSUMER GOODS OWNERSHIP

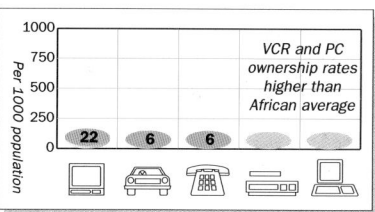

VCR and PC ownership rates higher than African average

22   6   6

The biggest African importer of French champagne in the oil boom, Cameroon still has a small but very wealthy sector.

WORLD RANKING

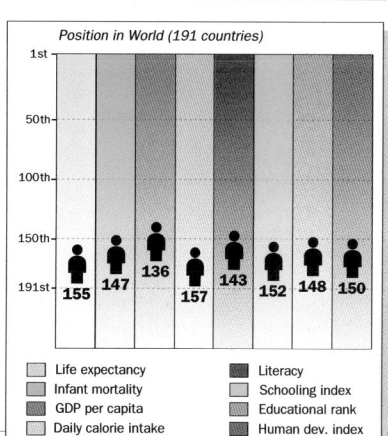

Position in World (191 countries)

- Life expectancy — 155
- Infant mortality — 147
- GDP per capita — 136
- Daily calorie intake — 157
- Literacy — 143
- Schooling index — 152
- Educational rank — 148
- Human dev. index — 150

CANADA

OFFICIAL NAME: Canada **CAPITAL:** Ottawa **POPULATION:** 28.2 million
CURRENCY: Canadian dollar **OFFICIAL LANGUAGES:** English, French

S TRETCHING FROM CAPE COLOMBIA on Ellesmere Island in the north to Middle Island in Lake Erie in the south, Canada is the world's second largest country. It stretches across five time zones and is divided into ten provinces and two territories. The interior lowlands around Hudson Bay make up 80% of Canada's land area and include the vast Canadian Shield. West of the shield, the plains of Saskatchewan and Manitoba include vast prairie lands. The St Lawrence River and Great Lakes lowlands are the most populous areas. Canada's main rivers – the St Lawrence, Yukon, Mackenzie and Fraser – are among the world's 40 largest. In recent years, the continued political relationship of French-speaking Québec with the the rest of the country has been the key constitutional issue.

CANADA

Total Area : 9 976 140 sq. km (3 851 788 sq. miles)

CLIMATE

WEATHER CHART

Canada's climate ranges from polar and sub-polar in the north, to cool in the south. Winters in the interior are colder and longer than on the coast, with temperatures well below freezing and deep snow; summers are hotter. The Pacific Coast around Vancouver has the warmest winters; temperatures rarely fall below zero.

COMMUNICATIONS

Lester B Pearson International, Toronto 10.25m passengers

155 ships 515,800 dwt

THE TRANSPORT NETWORK

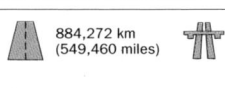

884,272 km (549,460 miles)

Trans-Canada Highway

194,000 km (120,546 miles)

3000 km (1864 miles)

Canada's size means the emergence of a national economy has depended on the development of an efficient system of transport. The Trans-Canada Highway and two trans-continental rail systems are the focus of road and rail networks which reach into the far north. Air services are well-developed and expanding. However, easy access to the cheap water transport of the Great Lakes–Saint Lawrence Seaway system has helped Ontario and Québec retain their dominance of the economy.

TOURISM

 15m visitors

 Up 1% in 1990

MAIN OVERSEAS ARRIVALS

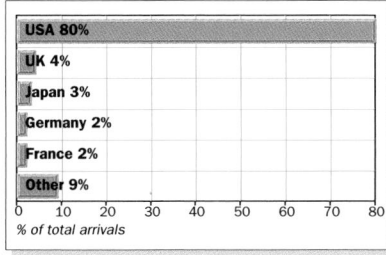

USA 80%
UK 4%
Japan 3%
Germany 2%
France 2%
Other 9%

% of total arrivals

The majority of tourists still come from the USA, despite efforts to attract more European visitors with campaigns emphasizing Canada's unpolluted natural beauty. An increasing number of tourists are Japanese, many on visits to *Anne of Green Gables'* Prince Edward Island home.

PEOPLE

English, French, Chinese, Italian, German, Ukranian, Portuguese, Inuktitut, Cree

3 people per km²

THE URBAN/RURAL POPULATION SPLIT

77%   23%

RELIGIOUS PERSUASION

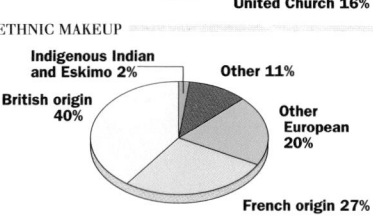

Roman Catholic 46%
Anglican 10%
Other 28%
United Church 16%

ETHNIC MAKEUP

Indigenous Indian and Eskimo 2%
British origin 40%
Other 11%
Other European 20%
French origin 27%

Relations between French-speaking Québécois and the English-speaking majority in Canada have been the dominant ethnic issue of the past 25 years. The Québécois feel distinct from the rest of Canada; their wish to preserve their culture and language from further anglicization has been reflected in the growth of secessionism. Support for pro-separatist parties has increased in the 1990s, mainly because of the failure of the provinces to deal with Québec's demand to be recognized as a 'distinct society'. However, any referendum on the issue is still likely to produce a 'no' vote, as it did in

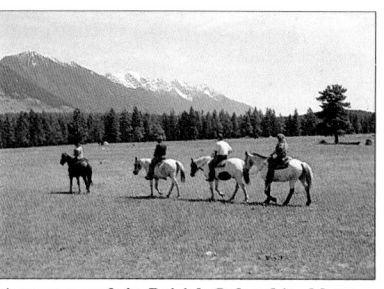

A guest ranch in British Columbia. Many tourists are attracted by Canada's wide choice of outdoor pursuits.

POPULATION AGE BREAKDOWN

% of population by age group	■ 0–14	■ 15–64	□ 65+

	1960	1970	1980	1990	2000
65+	7.5%	7.9%	9.5%	11.4%	12.7%
15–64	58.9%	61.9%	67.5%	67.7%	68.6%
0–14	33.6%	30.2%	23%	20.9%	18.7%

1980 – ending the violent separatism which had characterized the 1970s.

More than 65% of the population still lives in the 5% of Canada taken up by the Great Lakes–St Lawrence lowlands. However, Canada's ethnic mix has changed significantly in the past 20 years due to a move from a restrictive immigration policy to one which welcomes those with money or skills. Significant numbers of Asians have moved to Canada. The government promotes a policy which encourages each group to maintain its own culture. Canada is now officially a 'Community of communities'.

Canada has a long tradition of state welfare more akin to Scandinavia than the USA. Unemployment provision and health care, supported by high taxes, are still generous, despite recent cutbacks. The government has sought to end inequalities. Measures include the 'pay-equity' laws which aim to specify pay rates for jobs done mainly by women – like receptionists – equivalent to similar skill jobs for men. Women are well-represented at most levels of business and government.

Indigenous Canadians account for less than 2% of the population. There are some 38,000 Innuit and 630,000 Canadians of indigenous Indian descent. The majority live in the north, in the Northwest and Yukon Territories. They are disadvantaged, with higher school drop-out and criminality rates than average. In 1992, the Innuit successfully settled their longstanding land claim, paving the way for other indigenous groups. In 1999, the Innuit Nunavut area will become a territory, and the first part of Canada to be governed by indigenous Canadians in modern history.

CHRONOLOGY

Peopled for centuries by indigenous Innuits and Indians, Canada began to experience extensive European settlement following the landing of the English expedition led by John Cabot in 1497 and the French landing of Jacques Cartier in 1534.

- ❏ **1754** French and Indian War between Britain and France. France forced to relinquish St Lawrence and Québec settlements to Britain.
- ❏ **1774** Act of Québec recognizes Roman Catholicism, French language, culture and traditions.
- ❏ **1775–1783** American War of Independence. Canada becomes refuge for loyalists to British Crown.
- ❏ **1846** Oregon Treaty confirms present borders with USA.
- ❏ **1885** Transcontinental railroad completed.
- ❏ **1897** Klondike gold rush begins.
- ❏ **1914–1918** Canadian troops fight in First World War.
- ❏ **1926** Commonwealth Conference. Principle of equal status with London in deciding foreign policy accepted.
- ❏ **1930s** Canada experiences economic depression.
- ❏ **1936** Reciprocity Treaty with the USA lays foundations for increased economic links.
- ❏ **1939–1945** Canadian troops fight in Second World War.
- ❏ **1949** Founder member of NATO. Newfoundland joins Federation.
- ❏ **1951** Canadian troops fight in Korean War.
- ❏ **1968** Liberal Party under Pierre Trudeau in power. Québec Party (PQ) formed to demand complete separation from federal government.
- ❏ **1970s** Québec secessionist movement grows, accompanied by terrorist bombings and murders.
- ❏ **1976** PQ wins Québec elections.
- ❏ **1976** French made official language in Québec.
- ❏ **1980** Separation of Québec rejected at referendum. Pierre Trudeau prime minister again.
- ❏ **1982** UK transfers all powers relating to Canada in British law.
- ❏ **1984** Trudeau resigns. Elections won by Brian Mulroney and Conservatives.
- ❏ **1987** Meech Lake Accord.
- ❏ **1989** Canadian–USA Free Trade Agreement (NAFTA).
- ❏ **1992** Charlottetown Agreement rejected at referendum. Canada, Mexico and USA finalize terms for NAFTA.
- ❏ **1994** NAFTA takes effect.

POLITICS

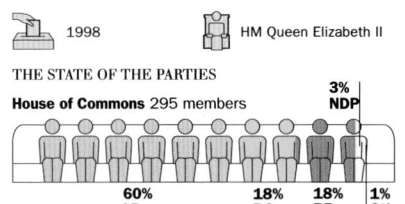 1998   HM Queen Elizabeth II

THE STATE OF THE PARTIES

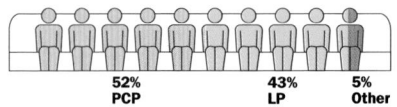

House of Commons 295 members

3% NDP · 60% LP · 18% BQ · 18% RP · 1% Other

LP = Liberal Party **BQ** = Québec Bloc **RP** = Reform Party
NDP = New Democratic Party **PCP** = Progressive Conservative Party

Senate 98 members

52% PCP · 43% LP · 5% Other

The Senate's members are nominated

Canada is a federal multiparty democracy.

MAIN POLITICAL ISSUES

The unity of the state
Canada has been struggling to find a place for francophone Québec and its separatist tendencies almost since the foundation of the state. The issue rose to prominence again in 1976 when the separatist Québec Party (PQ) won power at the 1976 federal elections. The PQ at first advocated independence then economic association. However, its proposals were rejected in a referendum in 1980 by 59.5% to 40.5%. In 1990, a constitutional agreement, the Meech Lake Accord, recognized Québec as a distinct society within the Canadian Federation. The Accord also granted additional powers to other federal states. However, it was not ratified as Newfoundland objected to its provisions. In 1992, another proposal, the Charlottetown Agreement, was put to referendum. This recognized Québec as a distinct society and granted the province a guaranteed 25% of seats in the National Assembly. This was turned down both in Québec and at national level. Opinion polls suggest that a majority of Canadians have latterly lost enthusiasm for too much federalism. In 1993, Mr Robert Bourassa, the then Québec premier, declared that Québec's aspirations could best be met without cutting all ties with Ottawa.

NAFTA
The proposed North American Free Trade Agreement (NAFTA) dominated the Canadian elections of 1988. Many are still opposed to the agreement. There are fears that Canadian workers may suffer from competition from Mexico. Tensions between Canadian and US trades unions have also risen as Canadian workers have been forced to accept more flexible US working practices. Many sectors of business,

The Niagara Falls are situated between Lakes Erie and Ontario on the Canada–US border. The Horseshoe Falls, in Canada, are 49 m high and 790 m across.

particularly grains, oilseeds, textiles, oil and gas and engineering services, have benefited from NAFTA.

PROFILE
Until recently, Canadian politics was dominated by three main parties. The PCP and LP had few ideological differences. The NDP advocated greater government intervention. Only the PCP and LP had held office. The NDP gained influence when voters registered a mid-term protest.

Major political changes were seen in 1993. Brian Mulroney, the leader of the PCP, resigned in the wake of economic recession, the unpopularity of a new sales tax and the failure of the Charlottetown Agreement. He was replaced by Kim Campbell as PCP leader. However, in elections in October 1993, nine years of PCP rule were brought to an end by a landslide LP victory. The PCP held onto only 2 of its 157 seats whilst the NDP managed to hold 8 out of 44 seats. The change represented a rejection of mainstream politics by the electorate who voted in favour of parties representing strong regional interests.

Kim Campbell, Canada's first woman premier.

Brian Mulroney resigned as PCP leader in 1992.

Robert Bourassa, premier of Québec until 1994.

C

WORLD AFFAIRS

Canada's most important relationship is with the USA, its main trading partner. There are tensions in the relationship, however. Canada has not managed to reach agreement on restricting pollution from US border plants, which have been responsible for much of the acid rain affecting Canada's forests. A US–Canadian commission recommended a $5 billion programme, but did not suggest sources of funding. Minor maritime waters disputes exist with the USA over stretches of the Northwest Passage; the USA recognizes Canadian claims over the islands, but not the waters. A dispute with France over the boundary of waters around St Pierre et Miquelon, the French-controlled islands off Newfoundland's coast, was settled in 1993. Until 1993, Canada's trade with Mexico was just 1.6% of that with the USA. However, as trade increases under NAFTA, so relations will become more important.

AID

 $2.6bn (donations) Up 5% in 1990

Canada's aid budget has been one of the first areas of government spending to be earmarked for cuts. Whilst most Canadians support aid – Canada gives twice as much per capita as the USA – the issue is not politicized to the point where cuts have been reversed.

First to suffer have been the large number of NGOs which the Canadian International Development Agency (CIDA) supports. The regional focus of aid has shifted from traditional areas, such as francophone West Africa, to South East Asia. This reflects the growing importance of Canada's Asian minority trade links; Pacific trade is now 65% greater than that across the Atlantic. Aid now aims to provide know-how skills, rather than funding for large-scale development projects.

DEFENCE

 $10.4bn Down 10% in 1992

0	*Defence spending as % GDP*	40
1.9%		

CANADIAN ARMED FORCES

	114 main battle tanks (*Leopard* C–1)	22,000 personnel
	14 frigates, 3 submarines 4 destroyers and 12 patrol boats	17,000 personnel
	198 combat aircraft (CF–18/CF–5)	22,400 personnel
	None	

Canada co-operates with the USA in the defence of North America. However, in response to the end of the Cold War in Europe, Canada withdrew its forces stationed there in 1992. As in other NATO states, defence spending has been cut significantly. Even so, many Canadians would like to see it cut even further. The focus of defence planning is now the creation of rapid reaction forces. In 1993 and 1994, Canadian troops were deployed in UN peace-keeping operations in Somalia and in former Yugoslavia.

ECONOMICS

 $569bn 1.32 Canadian dollars

SCORE CARD

❏ WORLD GNP RANKING	7th
❏ GNP PER CAPITA	$20,758
❏ BALANCE OF PAYMENTS	$–23.7bn
❏ INFLATION	1.3%
❏ UNEMPLOYMENT	10.3%

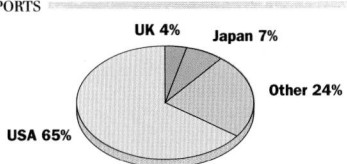

EXPORTS

UK 2% Japan 6% Other 16% USA 76%

IMPORTS

UK 4% Japan 7% Other 24% USA 65%

STRENGTHS

A broad and rich resource base. Provides exports, raw materials for manufacturing sector and massive cheap energy, notably HEP; also large oil and gas reserves. Agriculture and forestry contribute 3% of GDP; mining 4%. Successful manufacturing sector, contributes 17% of GDP; notably forestry products, transport equipment, and chemicals. Free access to huge US and Mexican markets through NAFTA.

WEAKNESSES

Increasingly uncompetitive; higher taxes, more regulations, lower productivity relative to most competitors. Political uncertainty over future of Federation dents business confidence. High federal and provincial budget deficits; slow recovery from early 1990s recession.

CANADA : MAJOR BUSINESSES

Symbol	Industry	Symbol	Industry
✈	Aerospace industry		
🚗	Vehicle manufacture	▦	Electronics
♣	Timber industries	✿	Engineering
♥	Pulp & paper	△	Chemicals
▯	Food processing	◬	Metallurgy
◨	Fish processing	⚲	Oil & gas

ECONOMIC PERFORMANCE INDICATOR

Consumer price index   GDP

PROFILE

Canada's enormous resource base has delivered one of the OECD's highest standards of living since 1945. After the mid-1980s, however, its manufactured exports faced increasing competition, while prices for its primary exports fell. From 1980–1988, real growth averaged 3.5% a year. After 1989 it stagnated, while budget deficits rose – forcing restructuring at both federal and provincial level. Many of Canada's welfare programmes were cut back; the defence budget was sharply reduced. The end result was a sharp drop in inflation from 4% to 1.3%, the lowest in the G7, and a resumption of growth after 1993. Another motivation for the changes was Canada's membership of NAFTA. Its firms have had to become more competitive to maintain exports. Most have been successful, but better productivity and a shift to high-tech has left unemployment at around 10%.

St John's

Edmonton

Halifax

Vancouver

Calgary Regina Québec

Winnipeg ThunderBay Montréal

0 500 km
0 500 miles

Toronto

C

RESOURCES

 482bn kwh (capacity 104.14 m kw)

 12.2m cattle, 10.8m pigs, 729,000 sheep

1.6m b/d (reserves 5,291,630,000 bbl)

Zinc, uranium, asbestos, nickel, potash, gypsum

ELECTRICITY GENERATION

Hydro 62% (296.7bn kwh)

Thermal 23% (112.2bn kwh)

Nuclear 15% (72.9bn kwh)

Other 0%

% of total generation by type

Canada is a country of enormous natural resources. It is the world's largest exporter of forest products and a top exporter of fish, furs and wheat. Minerals have played a key role in Canada's transformation into an urban–industrial economy. Alberta, British Columbia, Québec and Saskatchewan are the principal mining regions. Ontario and the Northwest (NWT) and Yukon Territories are also significant producers. Canada is the world's largest producer of zinc and uranium; the second largest of

nickel, asbestos, potash and gypsum. Oil and gas are exploited in Alberta, off the Atlantic coast and in the NWT – huge additional reserves are thought to exist in the high Arctic. Most exports go to the USA. Canada is also one of the world's top hydroelectricity producers.

CANADA : LAND USE

Cropland / Forest / Pasture / Tundra / High mountain regions / Wheat / Cattle

0   1000 km
0   1000 miles

ENVIRONMENT

 5% (2% partially protected)

State policies framed with sustainable development in mind

ENVIRONMENTAL TREATIES

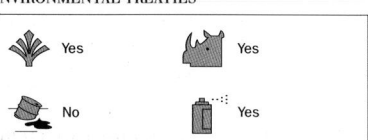

Yes / Yes / No / Yes

With a population of 28.2 million living in the world's second largest country, Canada does not suffer from the environmental pressures of more populated states. It is justly renowned for vast tracts of wild countryside untroubled by industrial pollution or pollution caused by intensive farming methods.

Canadians have tighter pollution controls than neighbouring USA. However, Canada's rate of carbon-dioxide emissions is higher, at 4.1 tonnes per person per year, than the Soviet Union's (3.4), Japan's (2.1) or France's (1.7). Per capita production of hazardous waste is also higher than the European average. Environmental measures are now concentrating on bringing both measures up to the world's highest standards.

A particular concern to Canadians has been damage to the ozone layer caused by CFCs. Canada followed the US lead in 1978 by banning the use of CFCs for aerosols. In 1987, Montreal was the site of the international agreement to cut CFC use by half by the year 2000.

MEDIA

 No political censorship

PUBLISHING AND BROADCAST MEDIA

There are 110 daily newspapers, including the Globe and Mail, the Toronto Star, Le Journal de Montréal and La Presse

1 state-owned, 2 independent services

1 state-owned, also independent services

Galaxy 5

67% of homes are connected to a cable network

Two of the three national TV networks are run by the Canadian Broadcasting Corporation (CBC), one channel in English the other in French. Canadian TV is renowned for its news and sports coverage. Over three quarters of the country can receive broadcasts from the USA. Most cities now have cable TV which usually offers at least one multi-lingual or ethnic channel. La Presse is the leading French-language daily.

Autumn in the tundra in northern Canada. Trees such as the black spruce are subject to the effects of acid rain originating in the USA's northern industrial regions.

CRIME

 31,302 prisoners

 No significant change

CRIME RATES

Murders	
6	per 100,000 population

Rapes	
30	per 100,000 population

Thefts	
5039	per 100,000 population

Crime rates in Canada are much lower than in the USA. Canadians ascribe this to their far tighter gun control laws. In 1993, the regulations were made even stricter. Another factor has been the careful efforts to maintain the inner cities as crime-free zones. The ghetto problems of US inner cities have largely been avoided. However, Canada does have a rising drugs problem. Youth crime is also growing, with over 22% of federal charges being laid against youths between the ages of 12 and 17. in 1991. However only 0.04% of youth charges were murder-related.

EDUCATION

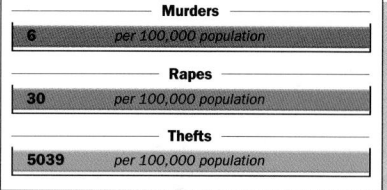 99%

0   Education spending as % GNP   25
7%

THE EDUCATION SYSTEM

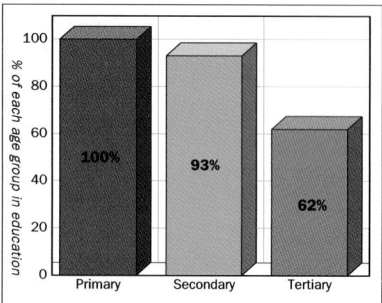

Primary 100% / Secondary 93% / Tertiary 62%

Education policy is a responsibility of the provinces. The period of free compulsory school attendance varies, but is a minimum of nine years. The prime medium of instruction is English in all provinces except francophone Québec. However, in several other provinces, French-speaking students are entitled to be taught in French.

Canada has 69 universities and 203 other higher education institutions. Over 75% of secondary level students go on to some form of higher education – the highest proportion in the industrialized world. The emphasis placed on education is also reflected in the fact that Canada's total education expenditure as a percentage of GDP also tops the league at over 7%.

REGIONS
QUÉBEC

Aerospace industry   Hi-tech industry   Food processing
Hydro-electric power   Pharmaceuticals

ALMOST ALL 6.9 MILLION Québécois live in the south of the province; 50% in Greater Montreal. The northern forests generate 20% of the world's pulp and paper. Québec is also the world's fourth largest hydro-power producer. Secession has long been an issue for the francophone majority. However, support for separatist parties in the early 1990s reflected discontent with traditional parties as much as a wish to go it alone. Separation could be costly, notably in jobs. 90% of exports go to the USA and the rest of Canada. To keep these NAFTA markets, Québec would have to embrace free trade. At present, it is highly protectionist.

TORONTO

TORONTO is Canada's largest, fastest growing and most polyglot city. As the destination for 50% of immigrants and most of Canada's internal migrants, it is expected to almost double in size to five million by 2000. One in six housing-starts in Canada during the late 1980s were in Toronto. Like Ontario as a whole, it has a broad industrial base and excellent public services. Toronto is also the country's leading financial and services centre – a role it took from Montreal during the secession fears of the late 1970s. Like Montreal, it was hard hit by recession in the early 1990s. Unemployment rose and the city government had to impose unpopular budget cuts.

Park or open land   Financial area   Expressway
Government area   Chinatown   Major sites

NORTHWEST TERRITORIES

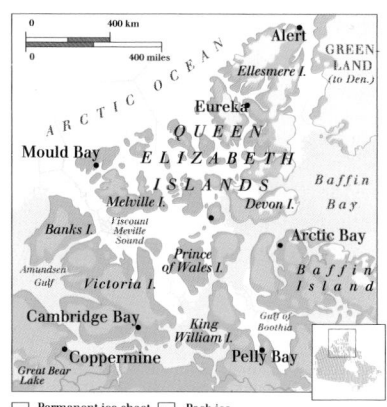

Permanent ice sheet   Pack ice

THE NORTHWEST TERRITORIES covers 3.4 million km², or one third of Canada. However, its population is tiny – just 57,650 people. Over 60% are of indigenous descent, mostly Innuit, but also Dene and Métis Indians. The incomer minority work mainly in the mining industry, which has grown rapidly since the discovery of gold in the 1930s. Zinc is the top export, but oil and gas and many other minerals are extracted. There are growing concerns about the effects of mining on the NWT's environment, but the main casualties have been the Innuit. They have largely given up their nomadic, hunting lifestyle and today are Canada's most marginalized and poorest people. However, the 1992 settlement of Innuit land claims in the high Arctic holds out hope of a better future. They have won title to 350,000 km² of land and now have a say in how it is developed. In 1999, the area will become the self-governing Nunavut Territory, making the Innuit the first indigenous North Americans to gain self-determination.

HEALTH

1 per 452 people   Heart and respiratory diseases, cancers, accidents

0   *Health spending as % GNP*   25
8.6%

Canada's state health service, funded by a national insurance scheme, covers the whole population. However, about 25% use private health facilities. The government is under pressure to cut the budget deficit whilst facing a higher health bill. Rising costs are the result of an ageing population and more expensive treatments. Surveys show, though, that most Canadians want to retain the present system.

WEALTH

Similar wage levels to the USA

CONSUMER GOODS OWNERSHIP

Per 1000 population: 626, 493, 780, 220

High levels of PC ownership

Despite the strains caused by recession during the early 1990s – including a rise in unemployment to 11% – life for most Canadians remains very good. In fact, the UN ranks Canada as one of the best countries in the world in which to live. In its 1993 overall assessment of human development indicators, like income, education and life expectancy, Canada came in second behind Japan.

However, disadvantaged groups do exist, in particular among indigenous Canadians. Unemployment, poor housing and mortality rates for Indians and Innuits are well above those for other Canadians; the Innuit suicide rate is three times higher. Those who live on reserves are the poorest group.

WORLD RANKING

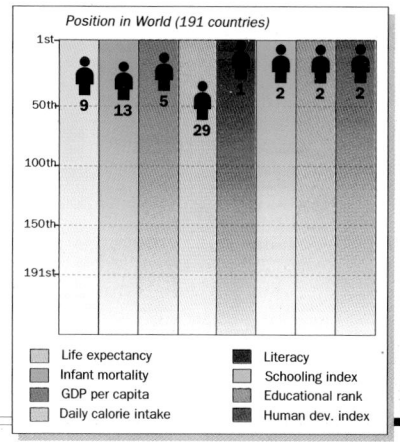

Position in World (191 countries)

1st, 50th, 100th, 150th, 191st

9, 13, 5, 29, 1, 2, 2, 2

Life expectancy   Literacy
Infant mortality   Schooling index
GDP per capita   Educational rank
Daily calorie intake   Human dev. index

CAPE VERDE

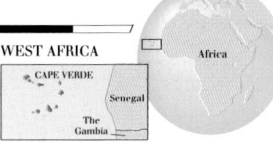

OFFICIAL NAME: Republic of Cape Verde **CAPITAL:** Cidade de Praia
POPULATION: 400,000 **CURRENCY:** Cape Verde escudo **OFFICIAL LANGUAGE:** Portuguese

C

T HE CAPE VERDE ARCHIPELAGO off the west coast of Africa became independent of its colonial ruler, Portugal, in 1975. Following a period of single-party socialist rule, Cape Verde held its first multiparty elections in 1991. Most of the islands are mountainous and volcanic; the low-lying islands of Sal, Boa Vista and Maio have agricultural potential, though they are prone to debilitating droughts. Around 50% of the population lives on São Tiago.

CLIMATE

WEATHER CHART

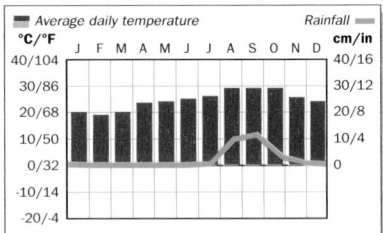

Cape Verde has a very dry climate, subject to droughts that sometimes last for years at a time.

COMMUNICATIONS

Amilcar Cabral, Sal Island
156,000 passengers

17 ships
25,900 dwt

THE TRANSPORT NETWORK

2250 km (1398 miles)		None	
None		None	

Cape Verde has a strategic position on international sea and air routes, which it is beginning to exploit.

TOURISM

156,000 visitors

Down 5% in 1991

MAIN OVERSEAS ARRIVALS

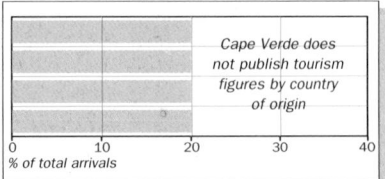

Cape Verde does not publish tourism figures by country of origin

% of total arrivals

Tourism has not been a government priority and is on a modest scale. The islands of São Tiago, Santo Antão, Fogo and Brava have tourist potential, offering a combination of mountain scenery and extensive beaches.

PEOPLE

Portuguese Creole, Portuguese

99 people per km²

THE URBAN/RURAL POPULATION SPLIT

29%   71%

ETHNIC MAKEUP

Other 1%

African 28%

Creole (*mestiço*) 71%

The majority of the population is Portuguese-African *mestiço*; the remainder is largely African, descended either from slaves or from more recent immigrants from the mainland. The Creolization of the culture has led to a relative lack of ethnic tension, though there is some bad feeling between islands. African traditions of the extended family and the Catholic Church have helped to ensure the vitality of family life. Women's role in public affairs is not prominent, in part due to the conservative Catholic influence.

POLITICS

1996

President António Mascarenhas Monteiro

THE STATE OF THE PARTIES

National People's Assembly 79 members

71% MPD   29% PAICV

MPD = Movement for Democracy
PAICV = African Party for the Independence of Cape Verde

Cape Verde experienced a peaceful transition to multipartyism in 1991, when elections brought the MPD to power. Although there had previously been a decade of single-party rule under the PAICV, it had in fact operated a liberal system in which opposition and dissent were tolerated. The large number of Cape Verdeans living abroad, who had remained in contact with the islands, helped to smooth the process as democracy was already widely understood and favoured.

The main issue for the government now, apart from preserving the present political consensus, is that of economic survival, particularly in periods of drought. An ideological debate continues over the extent of the successes and failures of the PAICV's period of rule.

WORLD AFFAIRS

OAU   Ecowas   AfDB   ECA   ACP

Cape Verde aims to diversify its international contacts in order to secure aid, while maintaining good relations with the former colonial power, Portugal, although it is not a major donor. Within the region, Cape Verde seeks to restore normal relations with Guinea-Bissau, after withdrawing from a proposed union in 1980, and is developing contacts with other mainland nations, such as Senegal.

Chã da Igreja · Vila Maria Pia
Santo Antão · Ribeira Grande
· Janela
Tarrafal
São Pedro · Mindelo · Calhau
São Vicente · Santa Luzia
Ilhéu Branco · Ribeira Funda
Ilhéu Raso · Barril · Vila de Brava
· Castiliano
· Preguiça
São Nicolau

Sal
Palmeira · Pedra Lume
· Santa Maria

Derrubado
Sal Rei · Gata
Boa Vista
· João Barrosa
· Curral Velho

A T L A N T I C

O C E A N

0   100 km
0   100 miles

N

Maio
Tarrafal · Santo Antonio
Ribeira · Santiago
da Barça · Maior · Maio
Ilhéus do Rombo
Fogo · Fajãzinha
Santiago
(São Tiago)
Furna · Picodo Cano 2829m
Fajã · São · Cova · Cidade
Filipe · Figueira · Velha
Brava · PRAIA

CAPE VERDE

Total Area : 4030 sq. km (1556 sq. miles)

LAND HEIGHT

2000m/6562ft	
1000m/3281ft	
500m/1640ft	
200m/656ft	
Sea Level	

POPULATION

over 50 000	○
over 10 000	●
under 10 000	●

AID

 $79m (receipts)

 Fairly constant from year to year

The most important donor is the EU, which has provided substantial food aid in the wake of recent droughts, as well as funding aid programmes. The World Bank is also a major source, as are the Netherlands, Sweden, Germany, France and Italy. Aid donations finance almost all development in Cape Verde, which is one of the least industrialized countries in the world.

DEFENCE

 $3.5m

 Fairly constant from year to year

After independence, small armed forces were established, consisting of a 1000-strong army, a navy of 200 and an air force of 100. These forces have never been called upon to play a political role; their main duties are to curb smuggling and to protect territorial waters against illegal fishing.

ECONOMICS

 $353m

 74.01 Cape Verde escudos

SCORE CARD

❑ WORLD GNP RANKING	170th
❑ GNP PER CAPITA	$890
❑ BALANCE OF PAYMENTS	$–40.46m
❑ INFLATION	14.3%
❑ UNEMPLOYMENT	25%

STRENGTHS
Strategic geographical position, off the westernmost tip of Africa, close to the mid-Atlantic where Africa is nearest to Latin America. This has military and economic advantages, including shipping maintenance and air travel. Low debt servicing costs.

WEAKNESSES
Permanent threat of drought and problem of water supply, despite desalination plants. Lack of agricultural land and dependency on food aid. Difficulties of communications between islands.

EXPORTS

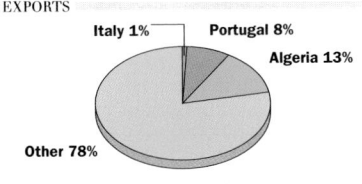

Italy 1% Portugal 8% Algeria 13% Other 78%

IMPORTS

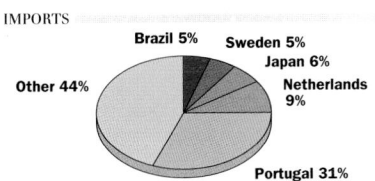

Brazil 5% Sweden 5% Japan 6% Netherlands 9% Other 44% Portugal 31%

Portuguese colonial-style architecture on Fogo, one of the larger islands. The volcano in its centre is the highest point in Cape Verde.

RESOURCES

 36m kwh (capacity 7000 kw)

 Not an oil producer and has no refineries

 86,000 pigs, 19,000 cattle, 11,000 asses

 Salt, pozzolana

Cape Verde has no known strategic resources. With no oil and no possibility of hydroelectric power, it depends on imported petroleum for energy. However, experimental projects have been carried out to investigate the potential of windmills, wave power and biogas.

ENVIRONMENT

 None

 Introduction of reforestation programmes

Cape Verde has recently suffered several years of persistent drought, which has affected food production and reduced livestock herds. It is a very active member of CILSS, which struggles against drought in the Sahel region. One initiative has involved reforestation, undertaken in an attempt to encourage rainfall.

MEDIA

 Since multipartyism, virtually no censorship

PUBLISHING AND BROADCAST MEDIA

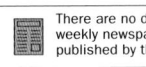 There are no daily newspapers. The only weekly newspaper is *Voz do Povo*, published by the government

 1 state-owned service

 1 state-owned service

For economic reasons, the press is limited to some extent, as it was under single-party rule. An experimental TV station was forced to close in the late 1980s, but French assistance has allowed both TV and radio to start broadcasting again.

CRIME

 Cape Verde does not publish prison figures

 Little change from year to year

Crime is not a serious problem, even in urban centres, though smuggling is fairly widespread.

CHRONOLOGY

Cape Verde was a Portuguese colony from 1462 until 1975, and was ruled jointly with Guinea-Bissau.

❑ **1961** Joint struggle for liberation of Cape Verde and Guinea-Bissau (then Portuguese Guinea) begins.
❑ **1974** Guinea-Bissau independent.
❑ **1975** Independence, but with view to union with Guinea-Bissau.
❑ **1981** New constitution formalizes final split from Guinea-Bissau.
❑ **1990** Multipartyism legalized.

EDUCATION

 66%

At independence, education became a priority after years of neglect. 80% of children now attend primary school.

HEALTH

 1 per 7660 people

Diarrheal, cerebrovascular and respiratory diseases

Health care has improved since the colonial period, yet there are still only 50 doctors in the whole archipelago.

WEALTH

 Most Cape Verdeans lead a subsistence existence

CONSUMER GOODS OWNERSHIP

VCR and PC ownership is limited to a small elite

14 5 162

Compared with the 90% of the population in primary production, the small business class in Praia is well-off.

WORLD RANKING

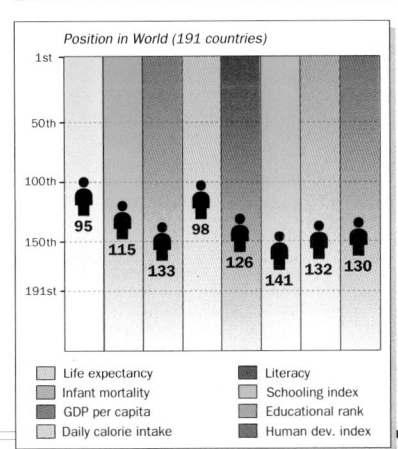

Position in World (191 countries)

95 115 133 98 126 141 132 130

Life expectancy
Infant mortality
GDP per capita
Daily calorie intake
Literacy
Schooling index
Educational rank
Human dev. index

CENTRAL AFRICAN REPUBLIC

OFFICIAL NAME: Central African Republic   **CAPITAL:** Bangui
POPULATION: 3.2 million   **CURRENCY:** CFA franc   **OFFICIAL LANGUAGE:** French

C

L AND-LOCKED AT THE WESTERN end of the Sahel, the Central African Republic (CAR) is a low plateau stretching north from one of Africa's great rivers, the Ubangi, which forms its border with Zaire. Most of the population lives in the equatorial, rainforested south. The arid north sustains less than 2% of the population. Emperor Bokassa's 14-year rule from 1965 to 1979 was followed by military dictatorship. Democracy was restored in 1993.

CLIMATE

WEATHER CHART

The south is equatorial, the north has a savanna-type climate, and the far north lies within the Sahel.

COMMUNICATIONS

THE TRANSPORT NETWORK

24,438 km (15,185 miles)	Trans-African Highway
None	800 km (497 miles)

The CAR has a limited transport system, with great dependence on the river link to Brazzaville, Congo, and rail from there to Pointe-Noire and Zaire's ports.

TOURISM

 6000 visitors   No change in 1992

MAIN OVERSEAS ARRIVALS

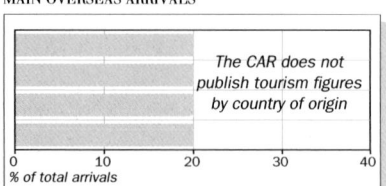

The CAR does not publish tourism figures by country of origin

% of total arrivals

Tourist promotion is small-scale, but since 1979 there has been a modest increase in national park safaris. Plans for a new runway in Bangui will permit air charters, chiefly from France.

PEOPLE

 Sango, Banda, Gbaya, French   5 people per km²

THE URBAN/RURAL POPULATION SPLIT

47%   53%

ETHNIC MAKEUP

Other 8%
Baya 34%
Sara 10%
Mandjia 21%
Banda 27%

Although the Baya and the Banda are the largest ethnic groups, the *lingua franca* is Sango. This is spoken by the southern riverine minorities, who provided the political leaders from independence (Presidents Dacko and Kolingba and Emperor Bokassa), until President Patasse, who comes from the interior. Resentment against the river peoples occasionally flares up, but ethnic diversity minimizes polarization. Women, as in other non-Muslim African countries, have considerable power. Elizabeth Domitien was prime minister from 1975–1976 and Ruth Rolland ran for president in 1993.

POLITICS

 Uncertain   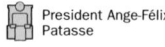 President Ange-Félix Patasse

THE STATE OF THE PARTIES

National Assembly 85 members

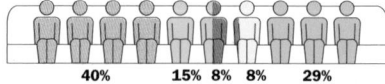

40% MLPC   15% RDC   8% FPP   8% PLD   29% Other

MLPC = Central African People's Liberation Party
RDC = Central African Democratic Rally   **FPP** = Patriotic Front for Progress (part of the CFD = Consultative Group of Democratic Forces)   **PLD** = Liberal Democratic Party

Economic and Regional Council

One half of the members are chosen by the president and the other half are elected by the National Assembly

WORLD AFFAIRS

OAU   AfDB   GATT   ECA   NAM

Apart from keeping up the momentum of its improving political image in international life, the CAR is anxious to continue good relations with France, whose financial help will be needed for some time, and with Cameroon and Congo – its main outlets to the sea. Otherwise, containing any spill-over from the civil war in Chad and insulating itself from the problems in Sudan and Zaire are priorities.

AID

 $174m (receipts)   Down 29% in 1991

Almost all development projects are funded from external aid. France, as the former colonial power, provides two thirds of the total. The EU (notably Belgium, Italy and Germany), Japan and, since 1989, the USA and Israel, are major donors. Help from the IMF and World Bank, although currently in a 'pause', is probable given the CAR's bankruptcy.

DEFENCE

 $21.98m   Up 18% in 1988

The 6200-strong armed forces (3500 army and 2700 gendarmerie) are the subject of major spending and are very well equipped, mostly with French hardware. The French also provide important economic military aid and officers to fill key posts. The French base at Bouar, closed under Bokassa, has been reopened.

The return to democratic elections in 1993 after Gen Kolingba's single-party rule brought in Ange-Félix Patasse as president. He was Bokassa's prime minister in the 1970s, but was jailed for dissent and subsequently went into exile in Paris. His party, the MLPC, is the most important in the new parliament, but can govern only in coalition with others, notably the CFD grouping led by Abel Goumba, a veteran opposition figure. Balancing coalitions can be a problem in the CAR – it was the confusion of alliances in Dacko's government which led to Kolingba's coup in 1981. Grave economic problems, which have left civil servants unpaid, are the major political concern.

CENTRAL AFRICAN REPUBLIC

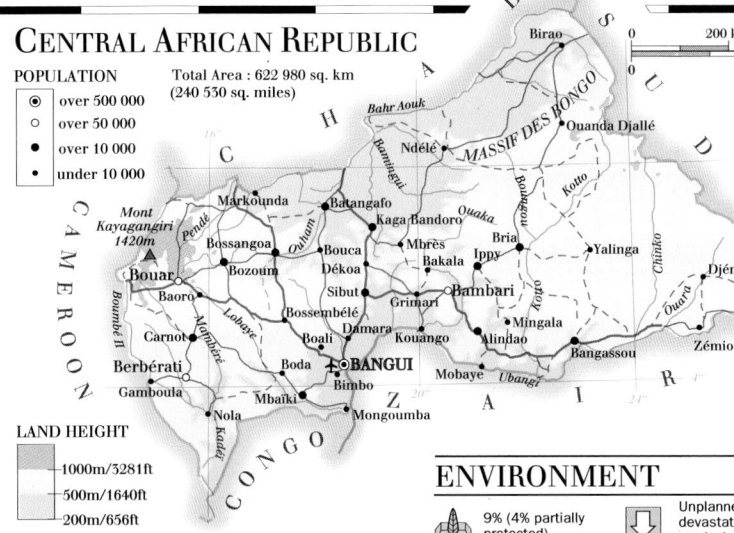

POPULATION

Total Area : 622 980 sq. km (240 550 sq. miles)

⊙ over 500 000
○ over 50 000
● over 10 000
· under 10 000

LAND HEIGHT

1000m/3281ft
500m/1640ft
200m/656ft

ECONOMICS

$1.3bn   295.23 CFA francs

SCORE CARD

❏ WORLD GNP RANKING	148th
❏ GNP PER CAPITA	$405
❏ BALANCE OF PAYMENTS	$–47.7m
❏ INFLATION	6.1%
❏ UNEMPLOYMENT	Widespread underemployment

STRENGTHS

Self-sufficiency in food. Some diversity of export earnings (iron, cotton, timber, diamonds, coffee). Transit zone in central Africa. Trans-African Highway and waterways.

WEAKNESSES

Land-locked. Poor infrastructure. Not enough trained people to run economy.

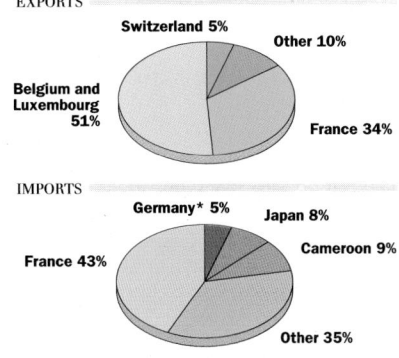

EXPORTS

Switzerland 5%
Other 10%
Belgium and Luxembourg 51%
France 34%

IMPORTS

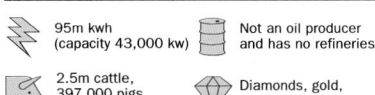

Germany* 5%
Japan 8%
France 43%
Cameroon 9%
Other 35%

RESOURCES

95m kwh (capacity 43,000 kw)

Not an oil producer and has no refineries

2.5m cattle, 397,000 pigs, 130,000 sheep

Diamonds, gold, uranium

Cotton is one of the few major exports, but mineral resources are of potential importance.

ENVIRONMENT

 9% (4% partially protected)

 Unplanned devastation of tropical rainforest

There has been an attempt to impose a conservationist forest policy. Hunting of elephants was banned only in 1985; numbers fell from 80,000 in the mid-1970s to 13,000 in 1987.

MEDIA

Although an opposition press has developed, censorship can still be imposed

PUBLISHING AND BROADCAST MEDIA

There is 1 daily newspaper, *E Le Songo*

1 state-owned service

1 state-owned service

An opposition press has developed with multipartyism, but is inhibited by lack of resources and journalists. The Catholic Church maintained some independent media under Bokassa.

CRIME

 CAR does not publish prison figures

Down 48% in 1989

Human rights abuses have decreased drastically since the excesses of the Bokassa years. The level of criminality is low and increasing urban robbery is regarded as the chief problem. The Muslims form too small a minority to influence the French-style legal system.

Baskets of cotton, *Meme village. Cotton is one of the Central African Republic's most significant export crops.*

C

EDUCATION

 38%

Schooling, on the French model, is compulsory, but in practice is only received by 59% of 6–14 year olds.

HEALTH

 1 per 16,788 people

 Communicable and parasitic diseases, malnutrition

Colonial neglect and post-colonial maladministration have resulted in a poorly-developed health system.

WEALTH

 Bricklayer, 35,000 CFA francs per month; physiotherapist, 82,000 CFA francs per month

CONSUMER GOODS OWNERSHIP

VCR and PC ownership is limited to a small elite

3   15   5

For the politico-military elite, which only arose after colonial days, Paris is the choice destination and style leader.

WORLD RANKING

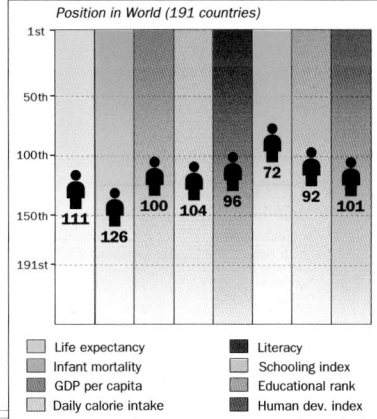

Position in World (191 countries)

1st
50th
100th
150th
191st

111   126   100   104   96   72   92   101

Life expectancy	Literacy
Infant mortality	Schooling index
GDP per capita	Educational rank
Daily calorie intake	Human dev. index

CHAD

CENTRAL AFRICA

Africa

OFFICIAL NAME: Republic of Chad   **CAPITAL:** N'Djamena   **POPULATION:** 5.8 million
CURRENCY: CFA franc   **OFFICIAL LANGUAGE:** French

C

LAND-LOCKED IN north central Africa, Chad has had a turbulent history since independence from France in 1960. Intermittent periods of civil war involving French and Libyan troops followed a military coup in 1975. In 1990, a transitional government was established to oversee the change to multipartyism. Chad remains one of the poorest countries in Africa. The tropical, cotton-producing south is the most populous region. The north is semi-arid desert.

POLITICS

 1995   President Idriss Deby

THE STATE OF THE PARTIES

Higher Transitional Council 57 members

Multiparty elections were scheduled for 1994

Following an invasion from Sudan, where he had been in exile since a previous coup attempt, Idriss Deby overthrew President Hissène Habré in 1990. He promised to bring multipartyism to Chad, and legalized political parties in 1992, the first time they had been allowed since the early 1960s. However, the transitional process has been subject to delays. Continuing instability has prevented progress on the drawing up of the constitution and the holding of presidential and parliamentary elections. Some opponents question whether President Deby and his backers, the Zaghawa tribesmen, want to give up power at all. France has been intervening to support the fragile government. Meanwhile, the issue of economic recovery has been put on hold.

CLIMATE

WEATHER CHART

There are three distinct zones: the tropical south, the central semi-arid Sahelian belt and the desert north.

COMMUNICATIONS

 N'Djamena International 7760 passengers   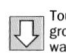 Has no fleet

THE TRANSPORT NETWORK

40,000 km (24,855 miles)

None

None

2000 km (1243 miles)

Chad has a limited transport infrastructure. The nearest rail links are in Nigeria and Cameroon.

TOURISM

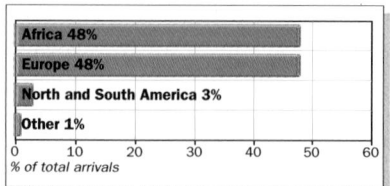

29,000 visitors   Tourism has failed to grow since the civil war ended

MAIN OVERSEAS ARRIVALS

Africa 48%	
Europe 48%	
North and South America 3%	
Other 1%	

% of total arrivals

Tourism is now virtually non-existent. The national parks and game reserves are the main potential attractions. The prehistoric rockpainting of the Tibesti plateau and the Muslim cities of central Chad attract the adventurous.

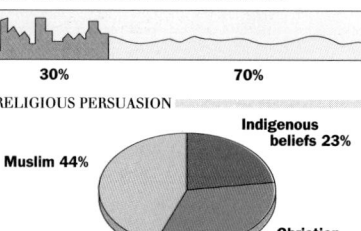

Watering hole at Oum Hadjer, a village on the Batha watercourse in central Chad, 145 km east of Ati.

PEOPLE

 French, Sara, Arabic, Maba   4 people per km²

THE URBAN/RURAL POPULATION SPLIT

30%   **70%**

RELIGIOUS PERSUASION

Indigenous beliefs 23%

Muslim 44%

Christian 33%

About half the population, mainly the Sara-speaking and related peoples, is concentrated in the south in one fifth of the national territory. Most of the rest are located in the central sultanates. The northern third of Chad has a population of only 100,000 people, mainly nomadic Muslim Toubeu.

CHAD

Total Area : 1 284 000 sq. km (495 752 sq. miles)

POPULATION

⊙ over 500 000
◎ over 100 000
○ over 50 000
● over 10 000
. under 10 000

LAND HEIGHT

3000m/9843ft
2000m/6562ft
1000m/3281ft
500m/1640ft
200m/656ft
100m/328ft

N

200 km

200 miles

WORLD AFFAIRS

Chad has to balance relations with France and Libya, both of whom have been important influences.

AID

 $262m (receipts)   Down 14% in 1991

France is by far the major donor. Other sources include Libya, the EU, USA, IMF, and Arab funds, especially OPEC. Without assistance to cover civil servants' pay over recent years, the administration would have collapsed.

DEFENCE

 $57.99m   Down 26% in 1989

On seizing power, Deby swelled the existing army to 50,000 with irregulars from Darfur in Sudan. The policy has now been reversed and Chad plans to reduce its army to 25,000. France provides military aid.

ECONOMICS

 $1.3bn   295.23 CFA francs

SCORE CARD

- ❏ WORLD GNP RANKING........................149th
- ❏ GNP PER CAPITA $180
- ❏ BALANCE OF PAYMENTS..................$–91.7m
- ❏ INFLATION 2.2%
- ❏ UNEMPLOYMENT....Widespread underemployment

STRENGTHS

Revenues from recent discovery of large oil deposits could transform Chad's poor financial position. Cotton industry; potential for other agriculture in south. Strategic trading location in heart of Africa.

WEAKNESSES

Underdevelopment and poverty. Lack of transport infrastructure an obstacle to development. Frequent droughts.

EXPORTS

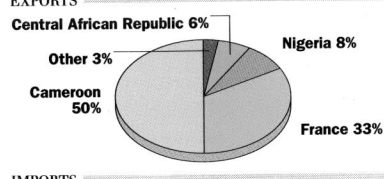

Central African Republic 6%
Other 3%
Cameroon 50%
Nigeria 8%
France 33%

IMPORTS

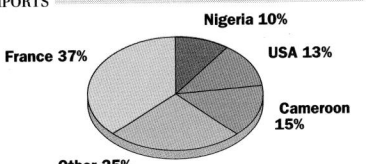

Nigeria 10%
France 37%
USA 13%
Cameroon 15%
Other 25%

RESOURCES

 82m kwh (capacity 31,000 kw)

4.2m cattle, 1.9m sheep, 239,000 asses

Not an oil producer and has no refineries

Natron, uranium oil, kaolin

A consortium of ESSO, Shell and ELF has discovered large oil reserves in the south, mostly near Doba, which could make Chad a major African producer. Natron, found north of Lake Chad, is the only mineral currently exploited. Uranium exists in the Aozou strip.

ENVIRONMENT

 0.3% Extensive destruction of habitats due to civil war

The worst single environmental crisis Chad has had to face in recent years was the drought of 1983, which coincided with intensified fighting in the civil war. Most recent governments have not regarded the preservation of the environment as a political priority. Chad has yet to establish an environmental protection ministry.

MEDIA

 The government claims to support press freedom, but interference in editorial decisions has been reported

PUBLISHING AND BROADCAST MEDIA

 There is 1 daily newspaper, *Info-Tchad*, a daily bulletin produced by the government news agency

 1 state-owned service   1 state-owned service

Since Deby came to power, the press has opened up and a number of outspoken independent publications have appeared. The best known is the weekly *N'Djamena-Hebdo*, produced by Saleh Kebzabo, a well-known journalist who was briefly a member of the transitional government.

CRIME

 Chad does not publish prison figures   Crime is rising

Armed robbery and vandalism are problems, as well as traditional crime such as smuggling. In N'Djamena and the south, the activities of a bandit group known as *les enturbannés*, 'the turbanned ones', from President Deby's army, are widely feared.

EDUCATION

 30%

Education is based on the French model, although there are Koranic schools in the north. Recently, World Bank aid has been directed at primary schooling. The literacy rate is among the lowest in Africa.

CHRONOLOGY

Chad gradually came under Arab domination. The French overthrew the last Arab ruler in 1900.

- ❏ **1960** Independence. N'Garta Tombalbaye's one-party state.
- ❏ **1966** Northern-based rebels start Libyan-backed insurgency.
- ❏ **1973** Libyans invade Aozou strip.
- ❏ **1975** Coup. Gen Malloum comes to power. Receives French support.
- ❏ **1979–1982** Civil war between Christian south and Muslim north.
- ❏ **1980** Goukouni Weddeye in power.
- ❏ **1982** Hissène Habré (northerner) defeats Goukouni. France transfers military support to Habré.
- ❏ **1987** Libyans pushed out of Chad.
- ❏ **1990** Idriss Deby invades from exile in Sudan. Defeats Habré.

HEALTH

 1 per 47,640 people   Diarrheal, parasitic and communicable diseases

There are only nine city hospitals. Of the 283 smaller health centres, half are run by religious groups or charities.

WEALTH

 Butcher, 17,571 CFA francs per month; central government official, 76,487 CFA francs per month

CONSUMER GOODS OWNERSHIP

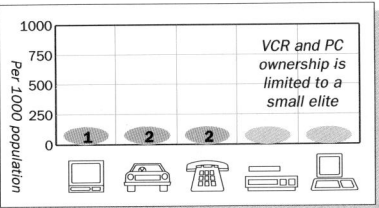

VCR and PC ownership is limited to a small elite

1 2 2

Poverty is almost universal; the middle class is very small. Individuals have been known to achieve wealth – Habré looted the treasury when he left power.

WORLD RANKING

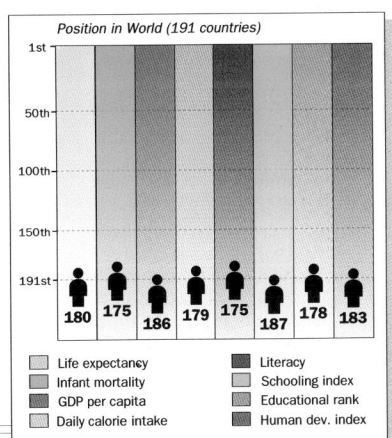

Position in World (191 countries)

180 175 186 179 175 187 178 183

- ☐ Life expectancy
- ☐ Infant mortality
- ☐ GDP per capita
- ☐ Daily calorie intake
- ☐ Literacy
- ☐ Schooling index
- ☐ Educational rank
- ☐ Human dev. index

CHILE

OFFICIAL NAME: Republic of Chile   **CAPITAL:** Santiago
POPULATION: 13.6 million   **CURRENCY:** Chilean peso   **OFFICIAL LANGUAGE:** Spanish

CHILE EXTENDS IN A NARROW RIBBON 4350 km down the Pacific coast of South America. The plains of the central pampa lie between a coastal range and the Andes; most of the population lives in the fertile heartland around Santiago. Glaciers are a prominent feature of the southern Andes, as are fjords, lakes and deep sea channels. In 1989, Chile returned to elected civilian rule, following a popular rejection of the Pinochet dictatorship. Today, the world's largest copper producer is enjoying economic growth which has averaged 5% a year.

General Pinochet, *a dictatorial president rejected by popular referendum in 1988.*

President Eduardo Frei. *He took office following elections in 1993.*

CLIMATE

WEATHER CHART

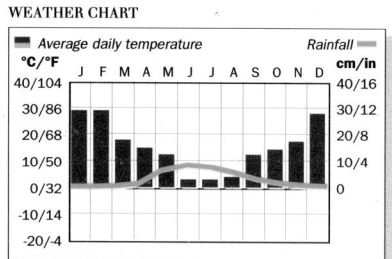

Chile has an immensely varied climate. The north, which includes the world's driest desert, the Atacama, is frequently cloudy and cool for its latitude. The central regions have an almost Mediterranean climate, with changeable winters and hot, dry summers. The higher reaches of the Andes have a typically alpine climate, with glaciers and year-round snow. The south is the wettest region.

COMMUNICATIONS

 Comodoro Arturo Merino Benítez, Santiago 1.95m passengers

 51 ships 735,900 dwt

THE TRANSPORT NETWORK

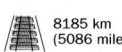 79,130 km (49,170 miles)

Pan-American Highway 3455 km (2146 miles)

 8185 km (5086 miles)

725 km (451 miles)

Chile's unusual shape, 4350 km long and nowhere more than 180 km wide, makes air travel indispensable. Internal air routes are well developed; some, including flights to the Juan Fernández Islands, are served by air taxis. The Pan-American Highway is Chile's only arterial road, crossing the Peruvian border and running down, via the capital Santiago, to Puerto Montt. Santiago is notorious in Latin America for its severe congestion. It has one of the highest taxi and bus densities in the world.

TOURISM

 950,000 visitors   Up 19% in 1990

MAIN OVERSEAS ARRIVALS

Argentina 51%
Peru 10%
USA 7%
Bolivia 6%
Brazil 6%
Other 20%

% of total arrivals

The Pinochet years saw a dramatic decline in tourists from the USA and West Europe. The number of visitors from neighbouring Latin American states remained fairly constant; South Americans with a closer knowledge of Chile's political culture were aware that much of the violence was state-directed and aimed at Chileans, not tourists. Since 1988, tourists have returned and Chile has been making more of its stunning Andean scenery, its immensely long coastline and a number of exceptional sites, including Chuquicamata, the world's largest copper mine, the Elqui Valley wine-growing region, and the spectacular glaciers and fjords of southern Chile. Easter Island in the Pacific is another major attraction.

Peaks in the Paine range, southern Chile. *Fjords, glaciers and a myriad islands typify Chile's very wet, wild and stormy south.*

PEOPLE

 Spanish, Amerindian languages

 17 people per km²

THE URBAN/RURAL POPULATION SPLIT

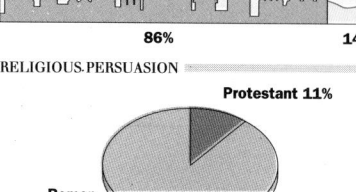

86%   14%

RELIGIOUS PERSUASION

Protestant 11%
Roman Catholic 89%

ETHNIC MAKEUP

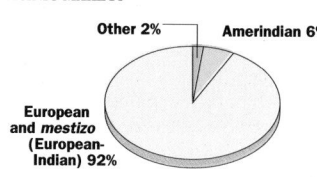

Other 2%   Amerindian 6%
European and *mestizo* (European-Indian) 92%

Chile is highly urbanized, with 86% of the population living in towns. Most people are of mixed Spanish-Indian descent. The estimated 800,000 Mapuche Indians live almost exclusively in the south. Santiago is home to one third of the population. Large slum areas known as *callampas*, or mushrooms, have grown up around Santiago, and water and air pollution are major problems. Many Chileans, especially those in small enterprises, live on subsistence wages. Over 25% of working women are employed in domestic service.

POPULATION AGE BREAKDOWN

%	0–14	15–64			65+
	4.3%	4.7%	5.1%	5.6%	6%
	58.9%	55.9%	55.8%	61%	63.4%
	36.8%	39.4%	39.1%	33.4%	30.6%
	1950	1960	1970	1980	1990

% of population by age group

C

CHILE

Total Area :
756 950 sq. km
(292 258 sq. miles)

POPULATION

▣	over 1 000 000
◉	over 100 000
○	over 50 000
●	over 10 000
·	under 10 000

LAND HEIGHT

4000m/13124ft	
2000m/6562ft	
1000m/3281ft	
200m/656ft	
Sea Level	

N

0   300 km
0   300 miles

POLITICS

Lower House 1997
Upper House 1997

President Eduardo Frei
Ruiz-Tagle

THE STATE OF THE PARTIES

Chamber of Deputies 120 members

31% PDC	24% RN	13% PS	13% PPD	13% UDI	6% Other

PDC = Christian Democratic Party   **RN** = National Renewal
PS = Socialist Party of Chile   **PPD** = Party for Democracy
UDI = Independent Democratic Union   **Other** = Radical Party

Senate 46 members

28% PDC	24% RN	9% PS	39% Other

38 members elected and 8 chosen by the outgoing
government and the Supreme Court

After 12 years of military rule under
Pinochet, Chile returned to multiparty
democracy in 1989.

MAIN POLITICAL ISSUES

Human rights abuse trials

The 1989–1993 Aylwin administration
resisted popular pressure to try known
members of the death squads which
operated during the Pinochet regime.
It argued that 1988 marked a time for
national reconciliation, but knew that
the army, still headed by Pinochet, would
not tolerate any human rights trials.

Poverty

Opposition groups point out that
the promised 'trickle down' effect of
Pinochet's Chicago School economic
policies has not reached Chile's poor.
Many believe that the present Frei
administration cannot deliver improved
conditions for the poor and maintain
Pinochet's economic policies.

PROFILE

In 1988, Chile voted for political
change, effectively rejecting the system
instituted by the military dictator,
Pinochet, for a return to Chile's
once-strong democratic traditions.

Pinochet seized power in a chaotic
situation. The socialist Allende
government had been attempting
the wholesale nationalization of the
Chilean economy. His nationalization
of the largely US-owned copper mines
led the CIA – which had a specific
budget to overthrow the
democratically-elected Allende –
to back the Pinochet coup.

In 1973, the military stormed the
presidential palace; it is now accepted
that Allende committed suicide during
the attack. Subsequently, thousands
of Chileans were killed by the
military, an estimated 3000 people
'disappeared' and 80,000 political
prisoners were taken.

Pinochet's politics – largely based on a
notion of the nation state modelled on
Franco's Spain – replaced democratic
traditions and conflict. His economic
policy reversed Allende's, and was
one of the first experiments in the free-
market Chicago School of monetarism
which was later to be influential in
the West, particularly in the UK under
Margaret Thatcher.

Although opposition to the regime
was brutally suppressed by DINA, the
secret police, it also had considerable
support – particularly amongst Chile's
business and middle classes, which
prospered. Opposition came from the
Church, an embarrassment to Pinochet,
who saw himself as a champion
of Catholicism, and the urban poor.

In 1988, Pinochet, seeking
popular legitimacy, held a plebiscite
which, given the military's control
over the country, he expected to win.
Contrary to his expectations, the vote
turned not on his economic record but
on whether Chile wished to continue
living under a military dictatorship.
On a turnout of 93%, 55% voted for
democracy and 43% for the *status
quo*. Pinochet stepped down, but
remained head of the army. Patricio
Aylwin won the presidential elections
held in 1989.

During Aylwin's presidency, Chilean
politics became more stable, in part
the result of a cross-party consensus
on economic policy. The economy
continued to grow and social measures,
which marginally increased protection
for workers, gave Aylwin the support
of the trade unions.

In elections at the end of 1993,
Eduardo Frei of the PDC was elected
president. He has pledged to
continue the economic and social
policies of his predecessor, and
is governing a broad coalition of
centre-left parties. The armed forces,
however, remain strong in politics;
they, not the president, appoint
their own chief.

CHRONOLOGY

The Spanish first attempted the
conquest of Chile against the fierce
indigenous Araucanian people in
1535. Santiago was founded in 1541.
Chile was subject to Spanish rule
until independence in 1818.

❏ **1817–1818** Bernardo O'Higgins
leads the republican Army of the
Andes in victories against royalist
forces at the battles of Chacabuco
and Maipú.

❏ **1879–1883** War of the Pacific with
Bolivia and Peru. Chile gains
valuable nitrate regions. ⇨

C

CHRONOLOGY *continued*

- ❏ **1891–1924** Parliamentary republic ends with growing political chaos.
- ❏ **1936–1946** Communist, Radical and Socialist parties form influential Popular Front coalition.
- ❏ **1943** Chile backs USA in Second World War.
- ❏ **1946–1964** Right-wing Chilean presidents follow US McCarthy policy and marginalize the left.
- ❏ **1964–1970** Social reforms of PDC government alienate the right.
- ❏ **1970** Salvador Allende elected. Rapid Marxist reforms bring economic chaos.
- ❏ **1973** Allende dies in military coup. Brutal dictatorship of Gen Pinochet. Economy prospers.
- ❏ **1988** Referendum votes 'no' to Pinochet continuing as president.
- ❏ **1989** Democracy peacefully restored; Pinochet steps down after Aylwin election victory.
- ❏ **1990** Mapuche set up council to fight for recognition of land titles granted by Allende government.

WORLD AFFAIRS

OAS | LAES | ECLAC | GATT | RG

Chile's most important relationship remains with its main trading partner, the USA, which supplies 95% of materials for the critical copper industry. The relationship has not always been easy. Under Allende, the USA actively worked against the government, fearing that the spread of socialism would jeopardize its investments in Chile and the rest of Latin America. Pinochet's human rights record eventually became an embarrassment to the Reagan administration, which qualified its backing for him. Present relations are good; the Frei government concurs with US economic and regional policy in Latin America.

Chile's territorial dispute with Argentina over islands in the Beagle Channel, which almost led to war in 1978, was finally settled in 1984 with Vatican mediation. Chile was awarded 12 islands including Picton, Nueva and Lennox. International arbitration is still deciding ownership of the Laguna del Desierto region. Border disputes also continue with Bolivia and Peru.

AID

 $120m (receipts)　 Up 18% in 1991

The majority of aid is in the form of debts rescheduled by the World Bank at the instigation of the USA.

DEFENCE

$1bn　　Up 24% in 1991

0 ——— *Defence spending as % GDP* ——— 40

3.2%

CHILEAN ARMED FORCES

🛡	171 main battle tanks (M-51/AMX-30)	54,000 personnel
🚢	4 submarines and 20 surface vessels	25,000 personnel
✈	106 combat aircraft (17 F-71/16 F-5/ 15 *Mirage* 50)	12,800 personnel
	None	

The military, and in particular the army, enjoyed preferential treatment under Pinochet. Its success in taking power in 1973 was a reflection of its cohesive command structure rather than of any right-wing ideological conviction. Pinochet exercised enormous influence in his position as commander-in-chief, but during his period in office worked with civilian rather than military advisers. The army retains considerable passive influence; the recent Aylwin government decided not to press human rights charges over atrocities committed during the Pinochet years. Much of its equipment is supplied by Chile's own CARDOENS munitions factories.

ECONOMICS

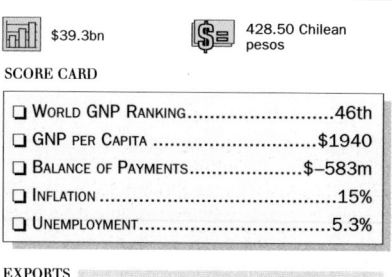

$39.3bn　　**428.50 Chilean pesos**

SCORE CARD

- ❏ WORLD GNP RANKING..........................46th
- ❏ GNP PER CAPITA $1940
- ❏ BALANCE OF PAYMENTS...................$–583m
- ❏ INFLATION 15%
- ❏ UNEMPLOYMENT................................5.3%

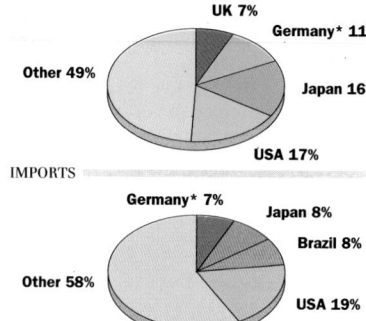

EXPORTS

UK 7% / Germany* 11% / Japan 16% / USA 17% / Other 49%

IMPORTS

Germany* 7% / Japan 8% / Brazil 8% / USA 19% / Other 58%

STRENGTHS
The world's biggest copper producer. Political stability and free market policies of the Aylwin government led to a massive inflow of investment, which has kept the economy growing at 5% a year since 1991. Continuing sell-off of the state sector – ruthlessly cut by Pinochet to leave it small and efficient – will attract further investment.

WEAKNESSES
Dependence on the USA as its largest single trading partner makes Chile vulnerable to changes in US trade policy. Copper revenues are vulnerable to shifts in world market prices.

PROFILE
Chile's economy has been a battle-ground for competing ideologies. Under Allende, socialist policies brought huge

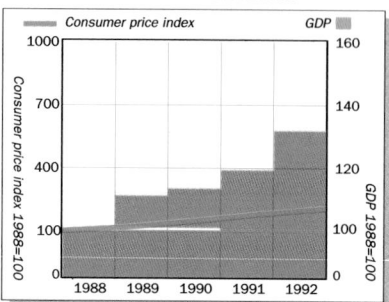

ECONOMIC PERFORMANCE INDICATOR

Consumer price index / GDP

Consumer price index 1988=100 / GDP 1988=100

1988 1989 1990 1991 1992

corporations into the state sector. The Pinochet dictatorship which overthrew him introduced radical monetarist policies. Drastic cutting of the state sector and the selling-off of state enterprises at below market value led to large profits for investors and speculators. Tough economic measures, irrespective of the social consequences, reduced Chile's inflation rate from 400% to 15%.

The Aylwin and Frei governments have continued the market-led approach to the economy with some success. In particular, exports are continuing to rise, helping to finance the capital goods imports which are vital to the modernization of Chile's industrial sector.

CHILE : MAJOR BUSINESSES

- ⚓ Oil
- ❚ Oil refining
- ⛏ Copper mining
- 🏭 Manufacturing
- ✎ Pharmaceuticals
- ✿ Heavy engineering
- ⌐ Fish processing
- ◐ Agribusiness

Iquique / Chuqui / Vina del Ma / Santiago / Teniente / Talcahuano / Concepción / Punta Arenas / Straits Magel

0 ——— 300 km
0 ——— 300 miles

C

RESOURCES

18.4bn kwh (capacity 4.1m kw)

14,700 b/d (reserves 300,000,000 bbl)

6.6m sheep, 3.3m cattle, 1.4m pigs, 500,000 horses

Copper, gold, silver, iron, molybdenum, iodine

ELECTRICITY GENERATION

Hydro 49% (9.1bn kwh)

Thermal 51% (9.3bn kwh)

Nuclear 0%

Other 0%

0   20   40   60   80   100
% of total generation by type

Chile is the world's most important copper producer. The state-owned industry was established in 1968 as a joint venture with US companies, but was fully nationalized under Allende. It accounts for 35% of Chile's GNP. New investments in gold mining will bring Chile into the world's top ten producers. It also leads the world in fishmeal production and has a flourishing wine industry.

CHILE : LAND USE

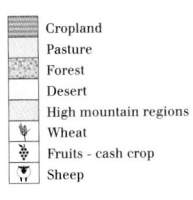

Cropland
Pasture
Forest
Desert
High mountain regions
Wheat
Fruits - cash crop
Sheep

0   300 km
0   300 miles

ATACAMA DESERT

ENVIRONMENT

18% (7% partially protected)

Felling of endangered *araucaria* pines recently banned

ENVIRONMENTAL TREATIES

No   Yes
No   Yes

Environmental concerns do not rank highly on the political agenda. Pinochet's constitution enshrined the right to live in a pollution-free environment, but bad smogs still cover Santiago, due in part to diesel fumes from the city's 14,500 buses. The chief concern is logging in the south by Japanese and other foreign companies. The huge growth of the salmon industry, which fences off sea lakes, is resulting in dolphins losing their natural habitats.

MEDIA

 Many of the army's powers over the press imposed during the Pinochet regime have yet to be repealed

PUBLISHING AND BROADCAST MEDIA

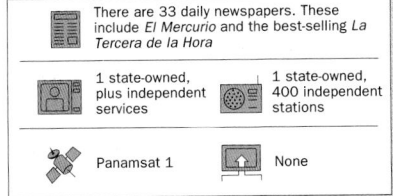

There are 33 daily newspapers. These include *El Mercurio* and the best-selling *La Tercera de la Hora*

1 state-owned, plus independent services

1 state-owned, 400 independent stations

Panamsat 1   None

The media was brutally controlled by Pinochet; journalists 'disappeared' in the early years of the regime. It is now relatively free, but journalists can still be tried under military justice for slander or abuse of the armed forces.

CRIME

 2176 prisoners   Up 2% in 1990

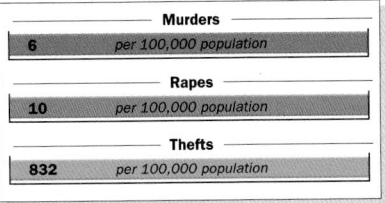

Murders
6   per 100,000 population

Rapes
10   per 100,000 population

Thefts
832   per 100,000 population

The judiciary is still not independent and is not pursuing the human rights cases from the Pinochet regime, in spite of the discovery in 1991 of the mass graves of victims of the DINA (secret police). Mapuche leaders were among those who 'disappeared'.

EDUCATION

 93%

0   Education spending as % GNP   25
3.6%

THE EDUCATION SYSTEM

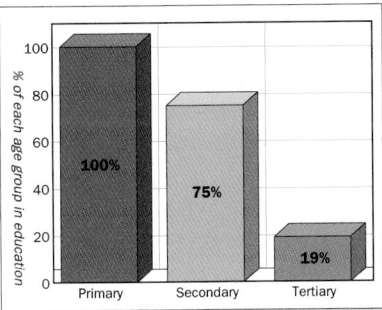

% of each age group in education

100%   Primary
75%   Secondary
19%   Tertiary

Recent years have seen many new private universities operating for profit and offering vocational courses. Environmental issues and human rights now appear on school curricula.

HEALTH

1 per 2383 people

Heart diseases, cancers (notably of the stomach), accidents

0   Health spending as % GNP   25
2%

The public health service covers 80% of the population, but medical personnel are mostly concentrated in urban areas. Pollution in Santiago is so bad that it is noticeably affecting its inhabitants' health.

WEALTH

 Live-in maid, 80,000 Chilean pesos per month; company secretary, 1m Chilean pesos per month

CONSUMER GOODS OWNERSHIP

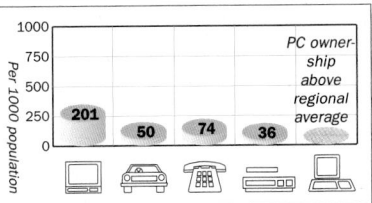

1000
750
500
250
0

Per 1000 population

PC ownership above regional average

201   50   74   36

Chile's traditionally large middle class did well under Pinochet and the economic policies of the Chicago School. The wealthiest sections benefited considerably from the sale of state assets at 40% to 50% of their true market value. Five years into the regime, wealth had become highly concentrated, with just nine economic conglomerates controlling the assets of the top 250 businesses, 82% of banking and 64% of all financial loans. The regime's artificially high domestic interest rates enabled those with access to international finance to earn an estimated $800 million between 1977 and 1980, simply by borrowing abroad and lending at home. These groups have retained their position.

The poor, by contrast, are 15% worse off than in 1970, with an estimated four million living just above the UN poverty line and one million below it.

WORLD RANKING

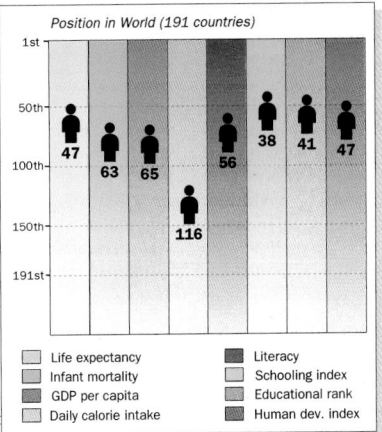

Position in World (191 countries)

1st
50th
100th
150th
191st

47   63   65   116   56   38   41   47

Life expectancy   Literacy
Infant mortality   Schooling index
GDP per capita   Educational rank
Daily calorie intake   Human dev. index

CHINA

C

OFFICIAL NAME: People's Republic of China   CAPITAL: Beijing
POPULATION: 1.2 billion   CURRENCY: Yuan   OFFICIAL LANGUAGE: Mandarin

COVERING A VAST AREA of eastern Asia, China is bordered by 14 countries; to the east it has a long Pacific coastline. Two thirds of China is uplands. The southwestern mountains include the Tibetan Plateau. In the northwest, the Tien Shan Mountains separate the Tarim and Dzungarian basins. The low-lying east is home to two thirds of the population. From the founding of the Communist People's Republic in 1949, until his death in 1976, China was dominated by Mao Zedong. Under Mao, China became an industrial and nuclear power, but also experienced the disasters of the 1950s Great Leap Forward and the 1960s Cultural Revolution. Today, China is rapidly moving towards a market-orientated economy. However, as the 1989 Tiananmen Square massacre tragically underlined, political reform is not on the agenda of China's ageing leadership.

Li river valley. Irrigation farming helps Chinese farmers feed 20% of the world's people, using only 7% of the world's farmland.

CLIMATE

WEATHER CHART

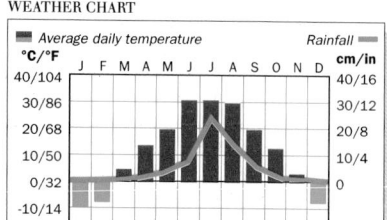

China is divided into two main climatic regions. The north and west are semi-arid or arid, with extreme temperature variations. The south and southeast are warmer and more humid, with year-round rainfall.

Winter temperatures vary with latitude and are warmest on the sub-tropical southeast coast, where they average about 16°C. Summer temperatures are more uniform, rising above 21°C throughout China. On the southeast coast, the July average is about 30°C. In the north and west, temperate summers contrast with harsh winters. In northern Manchuria, rivers freeze for five months and temperatures can fall to –25°C. In the deserts of Xinjiang province, temperatures range from –11°C in winter to 33°C in summer.

Summer and autumn are China's wettest seasons. Only the south and east have wet winters. The winter monsoon, which brings cold, dry air from Siberia, affects the rest of China. Moisture-laden winds from the Pacific during the summer monsoon bring rains to most of the country.

Droughts and floods are frequent. The 1960–1962 drought contributed to the famine which killed millions during the Great Leap Forward.

CHINA

Total Area : 9 396 960 sq. km
(3 628 166 sq. miles)

POPULATION

- ◉ over 5 000 000
- ◻ over 1 000 000
- ◉ over 500 000
- ◎ over 100 000
- ○ over 50 000
- ● over 10 000

⌐⌐ Great Wall of China

LAND HEIGHT

- 6000m/19686ft
- 4000m/13124ft
- 3000m/9843ft
- 2000m/6562ft
- 1000m/3281ft
- 500m/1640ft
- 200m/656ft
- Sea Level

0   400 km
0   400 miles

C

TOURISM

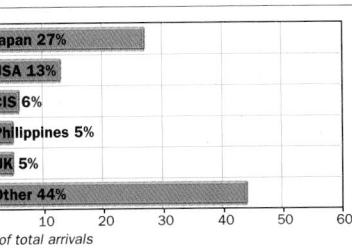

4m visitors — Up 20% in 1990

MAIN OVERSEAS ARRIVALS

Japan 27%	
USA 13%	
CIS 6%	
Philippines 5%	
UK 5%	
Other 44%	

0 10 20 30 40 50 60
% of total arrivals

Most visitors to China are overseas Chinese or business travellers, but an increasing number of tourists are also coming. The easing of restrictions since the 1980s has led to the rapid growth of all kinds of tourism, from luxury tours to back-packing. Most of China is now open to visitors. The Great Wall, the Forbidden City in Beijing and the terracotta warriors at Xi'an remain among the top attractions. The Chinese government has also begun to open up Tibet to tourists. Hong Kong is a major entry point for many visitors.

COMMUNICATIONS

 Capital International Central, Beijing

 1577 ships
20.41 m dwt

THE TRANSPORT NETWORK

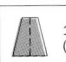	1.1m km (683,507 miles)		None
	54,000 km (33,554 miles)		109,800 km (68,226 miles)

Roads and railways have been extended since 1949 to provide a basic national network. The aim now is to modernize and expand the transport system to support the push for economic growth. Additions to the railway system – all provinces but Tibet are connected to the system – have been concentrated in the west. However, the railways, especially in the east, are still badly congested. The priority is to develop new lines, and to double-track and electrify the main routes from Beijing to Shanghai and Guangzhou, and between Zhejiang and Hunan provinces. In 1992, a rail link with Kazakhstan was reopened.

The leading ports, including Shanghai and Tianjin, are being steadily improved and the congestion problems of the 1980s have eased. Hong Kong has the best natural harbour and handles 40% of China's exports. The inland waterway system, which was allowed to fall into a state of disrepair, is now being upgraded. Water transport now accounts for about 33% of internal freight traffic. The Chang Jiang is navigable by ships of over 1000 tons for more than 1000 km from the coast.

Many small airlines have sprung up since the state monopoly ended in 1988. Air transport is growing rapidly, like private car ownership, as wealth increases. However, the bicycle is still the ubiquitous mode of personal transport in China.

Li River, Guangxi, China's most beautiful region. Its spectacular mountain scenery has encouraged large-scale tourist development.

C

PEOPLE

 Mandarin, Wu, Cantonese, Hsiang, Min, Hakka, Kan

 121 people per km²

THE URBAN/RURAL POPULATION SPLIT

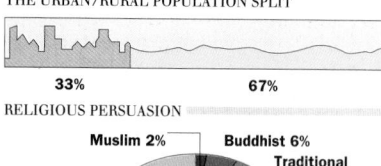

33%   **67%**

RELIGIOUS PERSUASION

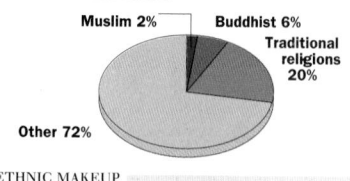

Muslim 2%   Buddhist 6%
Traditional religions 20%
Other 72%

ETHNIC MAKEUP

Hui 1%   Other 5%
Zhaung 1%
Han 93%

About 93% of China's population of nearly 1.2 billion are Han Chinese. The remaining 92 million belong to one of 55 minority nationalities, or recognized ethnic groups. The minorities have disproportionate political significance because many, like the Mongolians, Tibetans, or Muslim Uygurs in Xinjiang, live in strategic border areas.

The policy of resettling Han Chinese in remote regions is deeply resented and has led to uprisings in Xinjiang and Tibet, all ruthlessly suppressed. Han Chinese are now a majority in Xinjiang and Nei Mongol Zizhiqu. Tibet, however, is gaining international support for its call for true autonomy.

The government has relaxed family planning controls for minorities, after some small groups were brought near to extinction by the one-child policy adopted in 1979. Most Han Chinese still face strict controls. Even so, the population will top 1.3 billion by 2000.

Chinese society is patriarchal in practice and several generations tend to live together. However, economic change is putting pressure on family life and breaking down the social controls of the Mao era. Divorce and unemployment are rising; materialism has replaced the puritanism of the past. A resurgence of religious belief is another response to the uncertainties of life in today's China.

POPULATION AGE BREAKDOWN

	0–14	15–64	65+		
% of population by age group					
65+	4.8%	4.3%	4.7%	5.8%	7%
15–64	56.3%	56%	59.8%	67.7%	66.4%
0–14	38.9%	39.7%	35.5%	26.5%	26.6%
	1960	1970	1980	1990	2000

POLITICS

 1998

 President Jiang Zemin

THE STATE OF THE PARTIES

National People's Congress 2938 members

The members of the National People's Congress are elected by the provinces, municipalities and autonomous regions under the government, and by the armed forces. The Communist Party of China (CCP) has effective political control

China is a single-party state, dominated by the Communist Party (CCP), the world's largest political party. The National People's Congress, indirectly elected every five years, is theoretically the supreme organ of state power. It appoints the president and executive State Council, headed by the prime minister. The real focus of power, however, is the 22-member Politburo of the CCP and, in particular, its Standing Committee of six.

MAIN POLITICAL ISSUES

Reform and the authority of the CCP
Since the death of Mao Zedong in 1976, China has embarked on a process of economic reform which has led to divisions between reformers and conservatives within the CCP. Both sides want to secure the dominance of the party and avoid political reform. The reformers, headed by Deng Xiaoping, China's paramount leader, believe only a fast-track move to a 'socialist market economy' will save the CCP. They look to South Korea and Taiwan as countries which have achieved high growth without political reform. The conservatives recognize the need for economic change, but want it to be slow and controlled by the centre.

The pro-democracy protests of 1989, culminating in the Tiananmen Square massacre, enabled the conservatives under premier Li Peng to gain the upper hand for a while. Several leading reformers were demoted. Deng moved to restore the balance between the two groups. The growing unpopularity of Li Peng and the rise of reformers such as Vice-Premier Zhu Rongji suggest the reformers are again in the ascendant.

Nanjing Donglu (Nanking Road), in central Shanghai, is one of China's most famous shopping streets. With a population of nearly eight million, Shanghai is China's largest city.

Economic reform does, however, pose a real threat to the CCP's authority. The 22 provinces, particularly those in the southeast, are acting increasingly independently of Beijing. At a popular level, party authority is being challenged by growing rural discontent over widening wealth differentials.

The succession
China's leaders are predominantly in their late 80s, so the succession is an immediate issue. Deng has tried to strengthen the hand of the reformers, overseeing the election of younger reform-orientated members to the Politburo at the CCP's 14th National Congress in 1992. China's new leaders will come from here. But, as there is no formal structure for the transfer of power, who eventually comes to the fore will depend on which of the gerontocracy dies first and on the outcome of complex power brokering.

PROFILE

Politics is dominated by the last of the 'Immortals' who took part with Mao Zedong in the 1934–1935 Long March. Deng Xiaoping, the architect of China's economic reforms and its paramount leader, has no official post. He is the most prominent of the Immortals, but has to work hard behind the scenes forming alliances to promote his ideas and followers. The succession and the effects of economic change are a challenge to the 52-million-strong CCP, but it faces no real opposition as yet.

Deng Xiaoping, China's paramount leader, although he holds no official post.

Jiang Zemin, CCP leader and China's president since Deng resigned the post.

Premier Li Peng, urging economic reform, but keeping conservative values.

Zhu Rongji, vice-premier, reformer and a protégé of Deng Xiaoping.

WORLD AFFAIRS

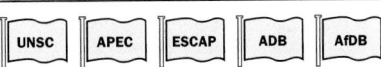

The push for economic modernization is a key determinant of China's foreign policy. Investment, technology and trade, rather than ideology, now tend to condition its relationships. The other, often interlinked factor, is China's desire to secure regional stability.

China has moved quickly to establish diplomatic links with the states of the former Soviet Union, and a vigorous trade is developing across China's northern border. On the Korean peninsula, China has acted to restrain North Korea while deepening ties with Seoul. Relations with Vietnam have been normalized and links with Japan are growing, despite China's suspicions about Tokyo's intentions towards ASEAN. Towards Taiwan, China is currently pursuing a 'one country, two systems' approach as a basis for reunification.

Relations with the West are still overcast by the 1989 Tiananmen Square massacre. Relations with the USA, a major export market, are particularly tense. Beijing resents the need to have China's Most Favoured Nation (MFN) status confirmed each year by Washington, and considers as unacceptable US attempts to link MFN to progress on human rights. Relations with the UK are dominated by Hong Kong, and have been strained by London's plans to increase democracy in the colony before handing it back to China in 1997.

AID

 $2.2bn (receipts)   Up 2% in 1991

Aid was an important part of Chinese diplomacy in the 1970s. Most went to Africa, but other communist and South East Asian states were also recipients. Aid flows outward have almost dried up since the late 1970s, as the economic reform process has turned China itself into a major aid recipient. Japan is the biggest bilateral donor to China, but the potential of the Chinese market means most developed states provide aid. A significant proportion of aid funding is used to finance high-tech imports. The 1989 Tiananmen Square massacre led to a temporary suspension of aid disbursements by the West.

DEFENCE

$6.8bn   Up 11% in 1992

Defence spending as % GDP
0   40
1.6%

CHINESE ARMED FORCES

8000 main battle tanks (T-54/T-59/T-69)	2.3m personnel
46 submarines, 37 frigates, 17 destroyers and 860 patrol boats	260,000 personnel
4970 combat aircraft (500 Q-5/400 J-5/3000 J-6,-B,-D,-E/500 J-7)	470,000 personnel
ICBM (2 CSS-4/6 CSS-3) IRBM (60 CSS-2) SSBN (12 CSS-N-3)	

China's armed services are grouped in the People's Liberation Army (PLA). It has about three million troops – one third conscripts, two thirds in the army. The PLA has close links with the CCP. From 1967, when it restored order after the chaos of the Cultural Revolution, to 1989, when it fired on civilians in Tiananmen Square, the PLA has been used to ensure the party's dominance. It is still used to suppress dissent in Tibet, but elements within the military are thought to want a less political role. The army, in particular, is modernizing, reducing numbers and improving training. China has a large weapons industry, including nuclear weapons, and is a significant arms exporter.

ECONOMICS

 $433bn   5.76 yuan

SCORE CARD

❑ WORLD GNP RANKING	10th
❑ GNP PER CAPITA	$361
❑ BALANCE OF PAYMENTS	$6.4bn
❑ INFLATION	5.8%
❑ UNEMPLOYMENT	Widespread underemployment

STRENGTHS

A domestic market of 1.2 billion. Self-sufficiency in food. Mineral reserves. Increasingly diversified industrial sector. Economic reforms which led to growth averaging 10% a year in 1980s, rapid rise in exports. Low wage costs.

ECONOMIC PERFORMANCE INDICATOR

EXPORTS

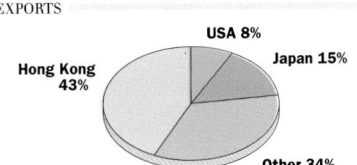

USA 8%
Japan 15%
Hong Kong 43%
Other 34%

IMPORTS

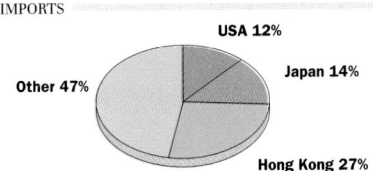

USA 12%
Japan 14%
Other 47%
Hong Kong 27%

WEAKNESSES

Population growth and unemployment. Unevenly distributed resources. Poor transport system. Political reluctance to reform areas such as price control, investment allocation, state industries.

CHINA : MAJOR BUSINESSES

♠	Oil
✳	Textiles
♨	Chemicals
▯	Computers
▮	Electronics
⌂	Iron & steel
✿	Engineering
⌨	Consumer goods
◉	Research & development

0   1000 km
0   1000 miles

* significant multinational ownership

PROFILE

China's shift from a centrally planned to a market-orientated economy has steamed ahead since the 1980s, notably in the south, where liberalization has gone furthest. However, growth had to be curbed twice in the 1980s and also in 1992 because of high inflation. China is in danger of remaining in this stop-go cycle unless reforms are extended to reduce price controls and subsidies. At a national level, this would be politically difficult, exacerbating problems in the poorer north and west. In the south, however, some provinces are using the greater autonomy brought by reform to implement changes, including decontrol of rice prices.

C

REGIONS

BEIJING

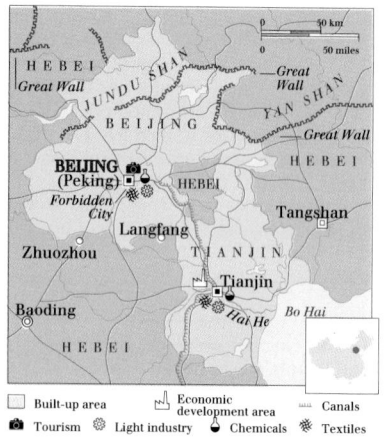

Built-up area
Economic development area
Canals
Tourism
Light industry
Chemicals
Textiles

WITH A COMBINED population of almost 19 million, the cities of Beijing and Tianjin have the status of provinces. Beijing is China's capital and the focus of politics. Together with its port of Tianjin, 140 km away, it also forms a powerful industrial and commercial nexus which has attracted much foreign investment since 1980.

Both cities are leading producers of textiles, chemicals and light industrial goods. Beijing is also China's top tourist destination. Almost two million visitors a year come to see the old imperial capital and its Forbidden City.

In 1992, Beijing attracted over $18 billion in foreign investment, mainly into high-tech and specialized

manufacturing industries. Foreign companies like its improved infrastructure and living conditions, and its educated and relatively affluent workforce. However, frequent power cuts and rising land and labour costs are starting to reduce its attractions.

Tianjin, and especially its economic development area (TEDA), are benefiting. Costs are lower and city officials are less constrained than their Beijing counterparts by the watchful eye of central government. Tianjin is rapidly developing into China's leading gateway city. It has the country's largest container port and its largest air cargo centre.

THE SOUTHEAST

THE SOUTHEASTERN COAST, especially Guangdong province, is the exemplar of modern market-orientated China. It was in Guangdong, and neighbouring Fujian province, that the first Special Economic Zones were set up in 1980 to attract foreign investors. The target was the 30 million overseas Chinese, particularly those living in Hong Kong and Taiwan, who have their ancestral home in the two provinces.

Hong Kong and, to a lesser extent, Taiwan, have been responsible for over half of all recent foreign investment into China. Most has been concentrated in Guangdong – notably the Pearl River delta to the south – which has become a centre of export-orientated light industry.

Growth has been spectacular and income levels in Guangdong are now ten times the national average. The province has many millionaires and its residents have quickly acquired the consumer aspirations of their Hong Kong counterparts.

China's paramount leader, Deng Xiaoping, has set Guangdong the target of becoming Asia's largest industrial region within 20 years. However, explosive growth has also brought problems which threaten to undermine future development. Prime among these are rising wage and land costs, and escalating housing and power shortages. They are forcing out many of the low-cost industries which formed the basis of Guangdong's early growth and are deterring high-tech companies.

Special Economic Zones
Stock exchange - opened 1990

SHANGHAI

Canals
Steelworks
Financial centre
Wheat
Major ports
Rice
Tea

SHANGHAI AND ITS SATELLITE cities in Jiangsu and Zhejiang provinces form China's economic heartland.

Shanghai, a city state of 12.5 million, is China's largest and most densely populated urban area. It was a focus of foreign settlement in the 19th century and of revolutionary activity in the 20th. In 1921, the Chinese Communist Party was founded there, and it was the base for the 1960s Cultural Revolution.

Despite relative stagnation after 1949, Shanghai remains China's foremost industrial and commercial city, and its leading financial centre and port. With important political friends such as Vice-Premier Zhu Rongji and CCP Secretary-General Jiang Zemin, both former mayors, to promote its interests, it is beginning to undergo a revival which could restore it to its status as one of Asia's greatest cities.

Shanghai is popular with foreign firms which like its workers, who are China's best educated and most highly skilled. Overcrowding in the city centre

means, however, that most future investment is likely to take place in Shanghai's new development area, across the Chang Jiang estuary.

Jiangsu and Zhejiang provinces are also gearing up for a major investment drive. In 1992, foreign investment approvals for the two totalled nearly $13 billion (those for Guangdong are $18 billion). However, Jiangsu already has a larger industrial output than any other province. And, notwithstanding Guangdong's recent growth, it is still the country's leading producer of light industrial goods. Its capital, Nanjing, is benefiting from rising costs and infrastructure problems in the southeast, as are Shanghai's other satellite cities – Nantong, Ningbo, Hangzhou and Suzhou. The Chang Jiang delta is expected to become the major focus for foreign investors.

REGIONS

THE NORTHEAST

Coalfields

Cereals

Oil reserves

Rice

Iron ore

Soyabeans

Called Dongbei by the Chinese, the northeast is a vast region of 800,000 km². It was once the territory of the Manchus, founders of China's last dynasty. Today, it comprises Liaoning, Jilin and Heilongjiang provinces.

Except for Liaoning, the region is quite sparsely populated, mainly by the descendants of recent migrants. The fertile Manchurian plain makes the northeast a leading producer of grains and soya beans. It also has rich mineral resources. Heilongjiang has China's largest oilfield, at Daqing. Large coal and iron ore reserves have helped make Liaoning China's second largest producer of heavy industrial goods.

Growth in the northeast lagged behind most of China during the 1980s, due mainly to the dominance of state industry. However, there are signs of change, notably in Liaoning and Jilin, where the non-state sector has more than doubled since 1992. Growth is encouraged by the region's strategic location. Trade across the northern border with Russia is expanding rapidly. Liaoning borders the Korean peninsula. South Korean firms are beginning to invest in a large way, primarily in the port of Dalian. Proximity has also helped make Dalian the preferred target of Japanese investment in China. By 1993, 125 Japanese companies were operating in the city.

CENTRAL CHINA

This region focuses on the inland provinces of Henan, Hubei, Hunan and Sichuan. It also includes Anhui and Jiangxi provinces to the east, and Shaanxi and Shanxi to the west.

Traversed by the Chang Jiang and Huang He rivers, central China is the country's agricultural heartland. Henan, Hubei, Hunan and Sichuan are the leading producers of rice and wheat. Minerals, including coal, oil and tungsten, are also important to the region,

Sichuan is China's most populous province, with 10% of the population. Under the leadership of Zhao Ziyang, later China's premier, Sichuan was the testing ground in the late 1970s for the shift from communal to

individual farm production which marked the start of the present era of reform. It has also had success in developing rural enterprises to absorb surplus farm labour. Around 25% of the population is now employed by these.

Sichuan and most other central provinces have a significant industrial base, but have not benefited as much as was hoped from China's 'open door' foreign investment policy. This in part reflects their distance from the country's economic hub on the eastern seaboard. The government is now pushing the development of Hubei's capital, Wuhan, as the gateway to central China. A centre of industry since the 19th century, Wuhan is the major inland port on the Chang Yiang.

Coalfields

Spring wheat

Oilfields

Rice

Tungsten

Tea

TIBET

Monasteries

Vast, high and mountainous, Tibet has features in common with the other provinces and regions of western China – Xinjiang, Qinghai, Gansu, Ningxia and Nei Mongol Zizhiqu. All are sparsely populated and ethnic minorities make up a significant percentage of the population. Tibet has China's lowest population density. Despite strongly resented Han Chinese immigration, Tibetans are still just in a majority.

Another common feature is opposition to Beijing's centralist policies. Although part of the Manchu empire from the 18th century until 1911, Tibet exercised full control over most of its affairs under the rule of the Dalai Lama, spiritual head of Tibetan Buddhism. In 1950, China invaded Tibet, and ruthlessly crushed the 1959 independence uprising. The Dalai Lama fled to India and established a government in exile. In 1965, Tibet was made a region of China. Opponents of Chinese rule were imprisoned or executed. Clashes between nationalists and Chinese troops in 1987 led to a renewed clampdown on Tibetans.

C

CHRONOLOGY

China has the world's oldest continuous civilization. Its recorded history begins 4000 years ago with the Shang dynasty, founded in the north in 1766 BC. Succeeding dynasties expanded China's boundaries; it reached its greatest extent under the Manchu (Qing) dynasty in the 18th century. Chinese isolationism frustrated Europe's attempts to expand into the empire until the 19th century, when China had fallen behind the industrializing West. For the previous 3000 years, it had been one of the world's most advanced nations.

❑ **1839–1860** Opium Wars with Britain. China defeated; forced to open ports to foreigners.
❑ **1850–1873** Internal rebellions against Manchu empire.
❑ **1895** Defeat by Japan in war over Korean peninsula.
❑ **1900** Boxer Rebellion to expel all foreigners suppressed.
❑ **1911** Manchu empire overthrown by nationalists led by Sun Yat-sen. Republic of China declared.
❑ **1912** Sun Yat-sen creates National People's Party (Guomindang).
❑ **1916** Nationalists factionalize. Sun Yat-sen sets up government in Guangdong. Rest of China under control of rival warlords.
❑ **1921** Communist Party of China (CCP) founded in Shanghai.
❑ **1923** CCP joins Soviet-backed Guomindang to fight warlords.
❑ **1925** Chiang Kai-shek becomes Guomindang leader on death of Sun Yat-sen.
❑ **1927** Chiang turns on CCP. CCP leaders, including Mao Zedong, escape to rural south.
❑ **1930–1934** Mao formulates strategy of peasant-led revolution.
❑ **1931** Japan invades Manchuria.
❑ **1934** Chiang forces CCP out of its southern bases. Start of 12,000 km Long March.
❑ **1935** Long March ends in Yanan, Shaanxi province. Mao becomes CCP leader.
❑ **1936** Chiang agrees to joint offensive with CCP against Japan.
❑ **1937–1945** War against Japan; CCP Red Army in north, Guomindang in south. Japan defeated.
❑ **1945–1949** War between Red Army and Guomindang. US-backed Guomindang retreats to Taiwan.
❑ **1949** 1 October, Mao proclaims People's Republic of China.
❑ **1950** Invasion of Tibet. Mutual assistance treaty with USSR.
❑ **1950–1958** Land reform; culminates in setting up of communes. First five-year plan (1953-1958) fails. ➪

RESOURCES

618bn kwh (capacity 98.6m kw)

2.8m b/d (reserves 24,000,000,000 bbl)

349.2m pigs, 110.6m sheep, 74.8m cattle

Coal, natural gas, salt, iron, molybdenum, titanium, tungsten

ELECTRICITY GENERATION

Hydro 18% (110.5bn kwh)	
Thermal 82% (507.5bn kwh)	
Nuclear 0%	
Other 0%	

0   20   40   60   80   100
% of total generation by type

China has commercial deposits of most minerals and probably the world's largest reserves of about 17, including molybdenum, titanium and tungsten, in which it dominates the world market.

China is the world's largest coal producer, with an output of over 1.1 billion tonnes a year used mainly for power generation. Reserves are estimated at around 800 billion tonnes, primarily in the Shaanxi and Sichuan basins.

Power generation is lagging well behind demand and China could become an energy importer, despite plans to develop other energy sources. China's first two nuclear plants opened in the early 1990s. The world's largest

ENVIRONMENT

 3% partially protected

 Economic growth has precedence over ecological concerns

ENVIRONMENTAL TREATIES

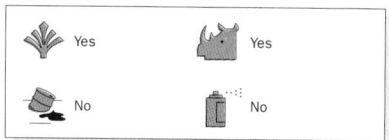

Yes

Yes

No

No

Climate and geology mean that natural disasters are quite frequent in China. However, their impact is often made worse by human actions. Poor building standards helped push the death toll in the 1976 Tangshan earthquake to over 500,000. The economic policies of the 1950s turned drought into a famine, which is estimated to have killed up to 100 million between 1959 and 1961.

Economic growth is the priority of China's leaders, who tend to view Western pressure for environmental controls with suspicion. As a result, industrial pollution and environmental degradation, already widespread, are increasing. However, the environment appears to be a growing concern among educated Chinese. In 1992, they campaigned, albeit unsuccessfully, to stop the Three Gorges hydroelectric scheme which will lead to large-scale loss of wildlife habitats and could increase the risk of earthquakes.

hydro-power station, known as the 'Three Gorges' scheme, is being built at Santoup'ing on the Chang Jiang. The scheme has raised controversy over its proposed benefits and costs.

Oil is also a problem. Exports, once a top foreign exchange earner, are falling as onshore fields are depleted. Offshore exploration has proved disappointing. Hopes for the future now centre on the Tarim basin in the far west, which Western oil companies say could have Middle East-size reserves.

CHINA : LAND USE

Cropland
Forest
Pasture
Wetlands
Desert
High mountain regions
Sheep
Tea
Rice

0   200 km
0   200 miles

MEDIA

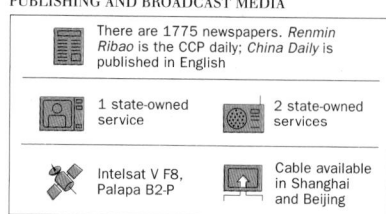 The government still attempts to enforce tight censorship, often by withdrawal of licences

PUBLISHING AND BROADCAST MEDIA

There are 1775 newspapers. *Renmin Ribao* is the CCP daily; *China Daily* is published in English

1 state-owned service

2 state-owned services

Intelsat V F8, Palapa B2-P

Cable available in Shanghai and Beijing

For China's leaders, one less welcome result of a more open, market-orientated economy has been people's increasing access to non-official sources of information. TV ownership is rising with living standards. Many sets, especially in the populous south and east, are tuned to Hong Kong stations. The growing number of satellite-dish owners have an even wider choice.

These changes have undermined but not ended censorship. Recent efforts to control satellite-dish ownership have had limited success, but the printed media remain on a tight rein. Papers considered undesirable have their licences removed in periodic clean-ups. Millions still buy, but few now read, the CCP-owned *Renmin Ribao* (People's Daily) with its editorials defending revolutionary purity.

CHRONOLOGY *continued*

- **1958** 'Great Leap Forward' to boost production fails; contributes to millions of deaths during 1959–1961 famine. Mao resigns as CCP chairman; succeeded by Lui Saoqi.
- **1960** Sino-Soviet split.
- **1961–1965** More pragmatic economic approach led by Lui and Deng Xiaoping.
- **1966** Cultural Revolution initiated by Mao to restore his supreme power. Youthful Red Guards encouraged to attack all authority. Revolutionary Committee formed, including Mao's wife Jiang Qing. Mao rules with Military Commission under Lin Biao and State Council under premier Zhou Enlai.
- **1967** Army intervenes to restore some order amid countrywide chaos. Lui and Deng purged from party.
- **1969** Mao regains chairmanship of CCP. Lin Biao designated his successor, but quickly comes under attack from Mao.
- **1971** Lin dies in plane crash.
- **1972** US President Nixon visits. More open foreign policy initiated by Zhou Enlai, a moderating force during Cultural Revolution.
- **1973** Jiang Qing, Zhang Chunquio and other 'Gang of Four' members elected to Politburo. Deng Xiaoping rehabilitated as vice-premier.
- **1976** January, death of Zhou Enlai. April, mass demonstration of support for Zhou and moderates. Mao strips Deng of posts, confirms Hua Guo Feng as new premier. September, Mao dies. October, Gang of Four arrested.
- **1977** Deng regains party posts, begins to extend his power base.
- **1978** Decade of reform and economic modernization launched. Open door policy to foreign investment; farmers allowed to farm for profit.
- **1980** Deng emerges as China's paramount leader. Economic reform gathers pace; but hopes for political change suppressed.
- **1983–1984** Conservative elderly leaders attempt to slow pace of economic reform under Deng. Several subsequently forced to step down from Politburo.
- **1984** Industrial reforms announced; less successful than earlier agricultural changes.
- **1989** Demonstrations in Tiananmen Square demanding greater openness in government. Crushed by army; between 1000 and 5000 dead. Beijing under martial law.
- **1992** Trials of pro-democracy activists continue. Plans for socialist market economy accelerated.

CRIME

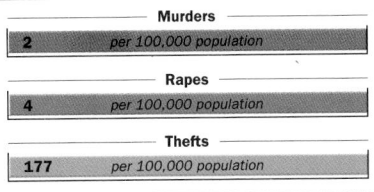

1.3m prisoners   Up 10% in 1990

CRIME RATES

Murders	
2	per 100,000 population

Rapes	
4	per 100,000 population

Thefts	
177	per 100,000 population

China's legal system is a mix of custom and statute, and has a local reputation for arbitrariness. Economic reform and the breakdown of former social controls have been paralleled by a rise in corruption and violent crime. Many new economic crimes have been made capital offences, but with little effect.

China has a poor human rights record and still holds thousands of political prisoners. The 1989 massacre in Tiananmen Square brought human rights to the fore in China's relations with the USA and EU. Detainees are now occasionally being released. The Red Cross is negotiating with China to allow access to political prisoners.

EDUCATION

 73%

0	Education spending as % GNP	25
2.4%		

THE EDUCATION SYSTEM

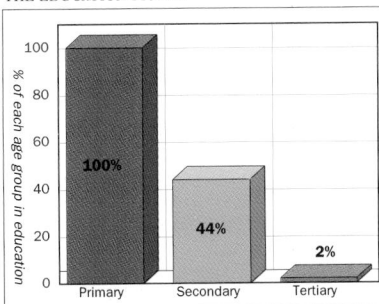

Despite the expansion of education since 1949, illiteracy and semi-literacy are still quite widespread. In part, this is due to the Cultural Revolution which left a generation with little education. It also reflects lower rural attendance and attitudes to women. In 1990, 38% of women and 16% of men were illiterate. To raise skill levels, the government has set a target of nine years of education for all. School attendance fell when fees were introduced in the 1980s, but is now nearing 90%. Higher education, which is also fee-paying, attracts only 2% of 20–24 year-olds. Today, however, selection is based on academic rather than political criteria.

HEALTH

 1 per 1077 people   Cardiovascular and diarrheal diseases, cancers, tuberculosis

0	Health spending as % GNP	25
1.3%		

Health care is one of China's successes. Combining traditional and Western medicine, it is based on an extensive primary care network – including paramedic 'barefoot doctors' – which extends to the remotest regions. Life expectancy is now on a par with many richer nations, at an average of 70 years. However, economic reform could reduce access. Fees are rising and fewer people are covered by the free care that goes with state employment.

WEALTH

Garment cutter, 215 yuan per month; doctor, 216 yuan per month

CONSUMER GOODS OWNERSHIP

Economic change has led to improved living standards, seen in the growing demand for consumer goods, but also widening wealth disparities. The burgeoning small-business class and employees of companies with foreign investment have benefited most. They mainly live in the east, especially the southeast, which is home to a number of millionaires. The main losers are the 150 million 'surplus' agricultural workers, many of whom have migrated to the cities in search of jobs. The majority of Chinese are still farmers. They initially benefited from reform, but their living standards are now threatened by rising production costs.

WORLD RANKING

COLOMBIA

OFFICIAL NAME: Republic of Colombia **CAPITAL:** Bogotá
POPULATION: 33.4 million **CURRENCY:** Colombian peso **OFFICIAL LANGUAGE:** Spanish

C

LYING IN NORTHWEST SOUTH AMERICA, Colombia has coastlines on both the Caribbean and the Pacific. The east of the country is densely forested and sparsely populated, and separated from the western coastal plains by the Andes Mountains. The Andes divide into three ranges (*cordilleras*) in Colombia. The eastern range is divided from the two western ranges by the densely-populated Magdalena river valley. The Colombian lowlands are very wet, hot and fertile, supporting two harvests and allowing many crops to be planted at any time of year. A multiparty democracy since 1957, Colombia is noted for its coffee, emeralds and gold.

CLIMATE

WEATHER CHART

Most of Colombia is wet and the hot Pacific coastal areas receive up to 500 cm of rain a year. The Caribbean coast is a little drier. The Andes have three climatic regions: the *tierra caliente* (hot lowlands), *tierra templada* (temperate uplands), and *tierra fría* (cold highlands). A feature of the last is year-round spring-like conditions such as those found in Bogotá. The equatorial east has two wet seasons.

COMMUNICATIONS

 Eldorado, Bogotá
4.66m passengers
 48 ships
385,300 dwt

THE TRANSPORT NETWORK

 129,177 km
(80,267 miles)
 Caribbean Trunk Highway

 2532 km
(1573 miles)
 14,300 km
(8886 miles)

Roads in the north are in reasonable condition. Those in the south and east tend to be rutted and badly affected by the frequent rains. Colombia's antiquated railway system, which currently has few fast intercity services, is due to be privatized.

Rivers are an important means of transport in Colombia; the Magdalena, Orinoco, Atrato and Amazon river systems are all extensively navigable. Plans exist to connect Colombia to the Pan-American Highway.

TOURISM

 812,796 visitors   Up 11% in 1990

MAIN OVERSEAS ARRIVALS

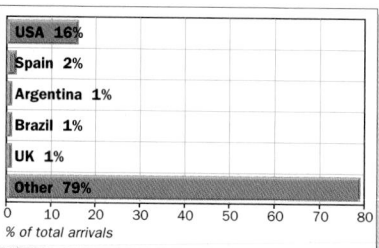

Tourism in Colombia is largely limited to the beaches of the Caribbean coast. Cartagena, Barranquilla and Santa Marta are the main resorts. Cartagena has also been developed as a major Latin American conference centre.

Expansion of the tourist business has been limited by Colombia's political instability and the prevalence of narcotics-related crime. The well-publicized activities of drugs cartels in Medellín and Cali, and instances of kidnappings in Bogotá, are major deterrents.

Limited infrastructure makes many regions of Colombia, particularly Amazonia to the east of the Andes, almost inaccessible. The Atlantic coast is also barely exploited.

Simón Bolívar and Cristóbal Colón, twin peaks with a height of over 5800 metres in the heart of the Colombian Andes.

PEOPLE

 Spanish, Amerindian languages, English Creole   29 people per km²

THE URBAN/RURAL POPULATION SPLIT

70%   30%

RELIGIOUS PERSUASION

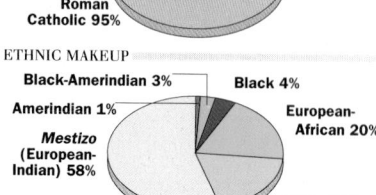
Other 5%
Roman Catholic 95%

ETHNIC MAKEUP

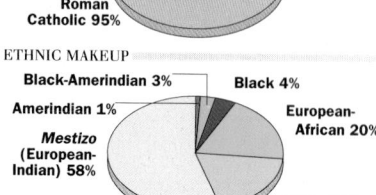
Black-Amerindian 3%   Black 4%
Amerindian 1%   European-African 20%
Mestizo (European-Indian) 58%
White 20%

The majority of Colombians are people of mixed blood. An estimated 450,000 indigenous Amerindians are largely concentrated in the southwest and Amazonia, although some communities have scattered throughout the country. A small black population lives along both coasts, and especially in Chocó, Colombia's poorest region. Blacks are the most unrepresented group.

Some progress has been made in giving Amerindians a greater political voice. In 1991, constitutional reforms reserved two seats in the Senate for indigenous representatives, and Amerindian pressure groups are increasingly active. However, harassment by land-owners and drugs traffickers in Amazonia continues. Very few investigations into suspected human rights violations against Amerindians have led to prosecutions.

Women in Colombia have a higher profile than in much of the rest of Latin America. Many are prominent in the professions, though few reach the top in politics. The traditional extended Catholic family is still the norm in Colombia. Regional identity is strong.

POPULATION AGE BREAKDOWN

% of population by age group	0–14	15–64	65+		
65+	3.2%	3.3%	3.7%	4.1%	4.7%
15–64	52.2%	50.7%	55.5%	59.8%	64.9%
0–14	44.6%	46%	40.8%	36.1%	30.4%
	1960	1970	1980	1990	2000

C

POLITICS

 Lower House 1998
Upper House 1998
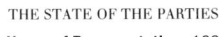 President Carlos
Angel César Gaviria
Trujillo

Colombia is a presidential democracy. Presidents may not serve two consecutive terms.

MAIN POLITICAL ISSUES

Guerrillas and drugs cartels

Guerrilla activity is a major problem in Colombia, causing instability which makes many regions ungovernable. In 1991, the Gaviria administration persuaded two of Colombia's four main guerrilla groups to accept an amnesty. The Armed Revolutionary Force of Colombia (FARC) – communist guerrillas who turned down the plan – are now the main problem.

Gaviria also declared war on the drug cartels of Medellín and Cali. In 1991, Pablo Escobar, leader of the Medellín cartel and one of the country's most powerful men, was captured. He was later shot dead by police after escaping jail. The issue now is whether to keep up the war or try to reach a political compromise with the drug barons.

THE STATE OF THE PARTIES

House of Representatives 163 members

50% PL   27% CMNS   23% Other

PL = Liberal Party **CMNS** = Conservative Movement of the National Salvation Party   **NDF** = New Democratic Force
ADM–19 = Democratic Alliance

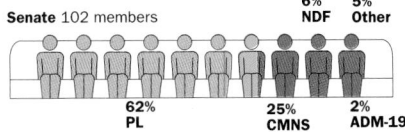

Senate 102 members

62% PL   25% CMNS   6% NDF 5% Other 2% ADM-19

The economy

Colombia is privatizing state assets. It aims to encourage more overseas investment in its uncompetitive nationalized industries.

PROFILE

The Conservatives (PSC) and the Liberals (PL), have shared power in Colombia for the past 40 years. Both have large numbers of followers. However, guerrilla groups, all with different ideologies, and drugs cartels continue to disrupt the political process. A new generation of Liberal politicians, including César Gaviria, are looking towards the USA for funds in their attempts to make Colombia more stable.

***Carlos Angel César Gaviria Trujillo,** president from 1991 to 1994.*

***Pablo Escobar,** cocaine king and leader of the Medellín cartel until 1993.*

WORLD AFFAIRS

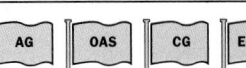 AG OAS CG ECLAC GATT

Colombia's most important foreign relations are with the USA, the major market for its exports and also its main source of aid. However, the relationship is not without its difficulties. The USA has intervened directly to attack the drugs business in Colombia, making this a condition of aid. Colombia, however, disagrees with many US tactics and has refused US demands that drugs traffickers be extradited for trial in the USA.

Relations with neighbouring states are fairly stable. A border dispute with Venezuela, Colombia's traditional enemy, is yet to be resolved, but the issue is unlikely to lead to conflict. In 1991, Nicaragua accepted Colombia's sovereignty over the San Andrés and Providencia islands.

AID

 $123m (receipts)   Up 40% in 1991

Apart from US military aid to help fight the drugs cartels, Colombia's aid receipts are mostly spent on education. Improving primary education in rural areas is a priority.

COLOMBIA

Total Area : 1 138 910 sq. km
(439 733 sq. miles)

POPULATION

- ▣ over 1 000 000
- ◉ over 500 000
- ◎ over 100 000
- ○ over 50 000
- ● over 10 000
- · under 10 000

LAND HEIGHT

- 3000m/9843ft
- 2000m/6562ft
- 1000m/3281ft
- 500m/1640ft
- Sea Level

0   200 km
0   200 miles

CHRONOLOGY

In 1525, Spain began the conquest of Colombia, which became its chief source of gold.

❏ **1819** Simón Bolívar defeats Spanish at Boyacá. Republic of Gran Colombia formed with Venezuela, Ecuador and Panama.
❏ **1830** Venezuela and Ecuador split away during revolts and civil wars.
❏ **1849** Conservative and Liberal parties established, the former with centralist and the latter with federalist tendencies.
❏ **1861–1886** Liberals hold monopoly on power.
❏ **1886–1930** Conservative rule.

- **1899–1903** Liberal 'War of 1000 Days' revolt fails. 120,000 die.
- **1903** Panama secedes, but is not recognized by Colombia until 1921.
- **1930** Liberal President Olaya Herrera elected by coalition in first peaceful change of power.
- **1946** Conservatives take over.
- **1948** Shooting of Liberal mayor of Bogotá and riot known as *El Bogotazo* sparks civil war, *La Violencia*, to 1957; 300,000 killed.
- **1953–1957** Military dictatorship of Rojas Pinilla.
- **1958** Conservatives and Liberals agree to alternate government in a National Front until 1974. Other parties banned.
- **1965** Left-wing guerrilla National Liberation Army and Maoist Popular Liberation Army founded.
- **1966** Pro-Soviet FARC guerrilla group formed.
- **1968** Constitutional reform allows new parties, but two-party parity continues. Guerrilla groups proliferate from now on.
- **1971** M-19 emerges as armed left-wing guerrilla group.
- **1984** Minister of Justice assassinated for attempting to enforce anti-drugs campaign.
- **1985** M-19 guerrillas blast way into Ministry of Justice; 11 judges and 90 others killed. Patriotic Union (UP) party formed.
- **1986** Liberal Virgilio Barco Vargas wins presidential elections, so ending power-sharing. UP wins 10 seats in parliament. Right-wing paramilitary start murder campaign against UP politicians. Violence by both left-wing groups and death squads run by drugs cartels continues.
- **1989** M-19 reaches peace agreement with government, including the granting of a full pardon. Becomes legal party.
- **1990** UP and Liberal presidential candidates murdered during general and presidential elections. Liberal César Gaviria elected on anti-drugs platform.
- **1991** New constitution legalizes divorce and prohibits extradition of Colombian nationals. Indigenous peoples' democratic rights guaranteed, but territorial claims not addressed.
- **1992** Six armed anti-terrorism units set up to combat rising violence.
- **1992** Medellín drugs cartel leader, Pablo Escobar, captured. Escapes.
- **1993** Pablo Escobar dies in shoot-out with police.

DEFENCE

$1.2bn   Up 65% in 1991

0   *Education spending as % GNP*   25
2.9%

COLOMBIAN ARMED FORCES

12 light tanks	120,000 personnel	
2 submarines, 5 frigates and 26 patrol boats	12,000 personnel	
68 combat aircraft (15 *Mirage* 5/13 *Kfir*)	7000 personnel	
None		

The Colombian military is powerful but remains a background force, leaving the politicians to run the country. Its main concern is combating the guerrilla groups and drugs barons in Amazonia. The power of drugs money has, however, led to some corruption in army ranks and dented the effectiveness of campaigns. Drugs barons have their own armed forces, which are often better equipped than the state's.

Colombia participates in the joint Latin American Defence Force. The largest proportion of defence spending goes on the army. Most arms are bought from the USA, although France supplies the Colombian Air Force.

ECONOMICS

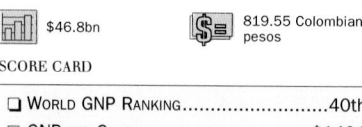

$46.8bn   819.55 Colombian pesos

SCORE CARD

- ❏ WORLD GNP RANKING.........................40th
- ❏ GNP PER CAPITA $1401
- ❏ BALANCE OF PAYMENTS $848m
- ❏ INFLATION 27%
- ❏ UNEMPLOYMENT ......Officially 10%; probably 30%

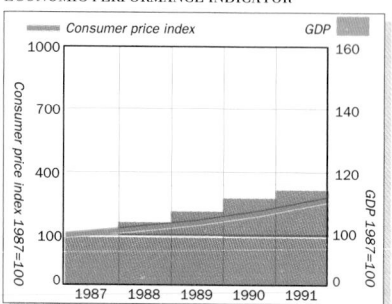

ECONOMIC PERFORMANCE INDICATOR

Consumer price index   GDP

EXPORTS
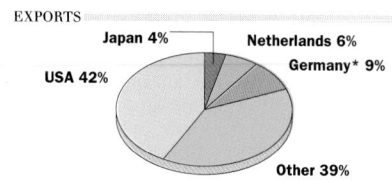
Japan 4%   Netherlands 6%
USA 42%   Germany* 9%
Other 39%

IMPORTS
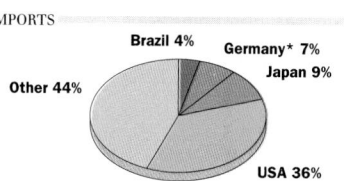
Brazil 4%   Germany* 7%
Other 44%   Japan 9%
USA 36%

STRENGTHS
Substantial oil and coal deposits plus well-developed hydroelectric power makes Colombia almost self-sufficient in energy. Healthy and diversified export sector – especially coffee and coal. Light manufactures. Worldwide market for cocaine still growing.

WEAKNESSES
Drugs-related violence and corruption discourages foreign investors. Industries serving local markets uncompetitive owing to decades of protection. High unemployment rate, officially 10% but, in reality, probably nearer 30%.

PROFILE
Of all the Latin American economies, Colombia's is probably the closest to the US model. The state has traditionally played a relatively minor role and

Colombia has a successful private export sector. A programme of privatization is reducing the state's involvement further; the railways, telephone company and banks are all being sold off.

Regional disparities remain marked. Most wealth is centred in the Bogotá, Medellín and Cali regions. Rural areas are largely underdeveloped. The main obstacle to growth is the instability caused by the drugs business. Given stability and investment, Colombia's potential for growth is considerable.

COLOMBIA : MAJOR BUSINESSES

Pulp and paper
Narcotics
Steel
Chemicals
Vehicle assembly
Food processing
Textiles
Oil

0   200 km
0   200 miles
* significant multinational ownership

RESOURCES

36,000m kwh (capacity 9.41m kw)

435,800 b/d (reserves 1,935,200 bbl)

24.6m cattle, 2.7m sheep, 2.6m pigs, 2m horses

Oil, natural gas, coal, nickel, emeralds, gold

ELECTRICITY GENERATION

Hydro 76% (27.2bn kwh)
Thermal 24% (8.8bn kwh)
Nuclear 0%
Other 0%

0 20 40 60 80 100
% of total generation by type

Recent discoveries have made Colombia self-sufficient in oil. Coal surpluses are exported mainly to the UK and USA. Gold reserves are significant. Colombia also produces 60% of the world's emeralds.

COLOMBIA : LAND USE

- Cropland
- Pasture
- Forest
- High mountain regions
- Coffee - cash crop
- Cattle

0 200 km
0 200 miles

ENVIRONMENT

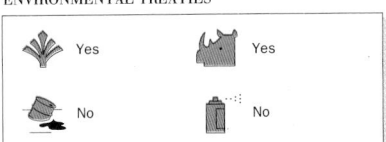

8%

Rising pollution levels in the Magdalena River

ENVIRONMENTAL TREATIES

Yes

Yes

No

No

Cattle-ranching, logging and coca growing have caused extensive soil degradation and loss of bird habitat.

MEDIA

In theory the press is free, but in practice there is some political censorship. Journalists tend to avoid criticizing drugs cartels

PUBLISHING AND BROADCAST MEDIA

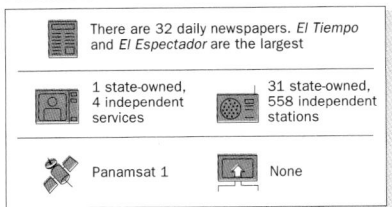

There are 32 daily newspapers. *El Tiempo* and *El Espectador* are the largest

1 state-owned, 4 independent services

31 state-owned, 558 independent stations

Panamsat 1

None

The independent press is small. The main papers are owned by corporations whose interests they promote.

CRIME

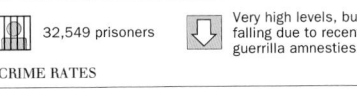

32,549 prisoners

Very high levels, but falling due to recent guerrilla amnesties

CRIME RATES

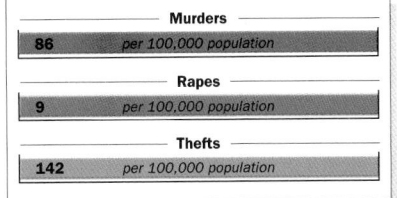

Murders
86 per 100,000 population

Rapes
9 per 100,000 population

Thefts
142 per 100,000 population

Colombia is the most violent society in Latin America and one of the most violent in the world. Its judicial police reported 28,237 murders in 1992. Homicide is the main cause of death among young men in cities; overall it is the most common cause of death after cancer. Most of the violence is

EDUCATION

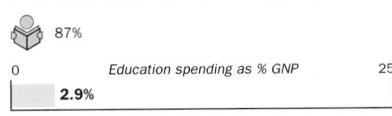

87%

0 Education spending as % GNP 25
2.9%

THE EDUCATION SYSTEM

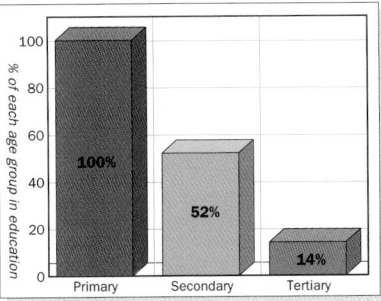

% of each age group in education

Primary 100%
Secondary 52%
Tertiary 14%

Colombia's education system is a mixture of the French and US models, with a *baccalauréat* exam at the end of secondary schooling. Educational provision in rural areas is uneven and increasing numbers of schools are being closed. The public universities (the main ones are in Bogotá, Medellín and Cali) are occasionally disrupted by political strikes and violence.

HEALTH

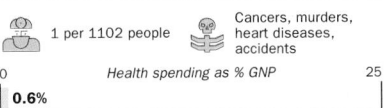

1 per 1102 people

Cancers, murders, heart diseases, accidents

0 Health spending as % GNP 25
0.6%

Only 16% of Colombians benefit from any social security system, rather fewer than in most neighbouring states. Rural areas have little health provision, as most doctors work in the larger cities. A polio vaccination campaign has largely eradicated the virus, except in coastal regions.

drugs-related and Cali and Medellín are the most dangerous cities. The frequency of urban armed robbery makes residents extremely security conscious. Wealthier Colombians employ several security guards.

The army and police have used intimidation and torture in the fight against both guerrillas and drugs traffickers, but have themselves also been accused of participating in the trade. A relatively new phenomenon is that of 'social cleansing', the murder of street children and beggars by organized armed gangs. Some gangs in Bogotá are funded by local businesses.

Colombia's extensive gem deposits attract large numbers of illegal miners and smugglers. Around 15,000 were estimated to be active in Boyacá department in 1993.

WEALTH

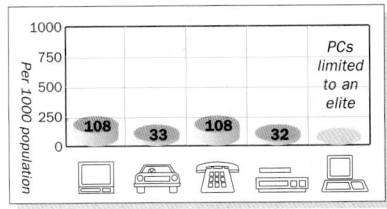

School teacher, 150,000 pesos per month; Senior engineer, 500,000 pesos per month

CONSUMER GOODS OWNERSHIP

1000
750
500
250
0

Per 1000 population

108 33 108 32

PCs limited to an elite

There is little social mobility in Colombia; the historically wealthy Spanish families still dominate political and business life. The rich favour BMWs or jeeps, weekend in Miami or Colombia's Caribbean islands, shop in Paris and Rome, and go to the USA for medical treatment. Their children are educated overseas. The rural poor are mostly landless. The inhabitants of the shanty towns of Cali, Barranquilla, Cartagena and Buenaventura are the poorest groups in Colombian society.

WORLD RANKING

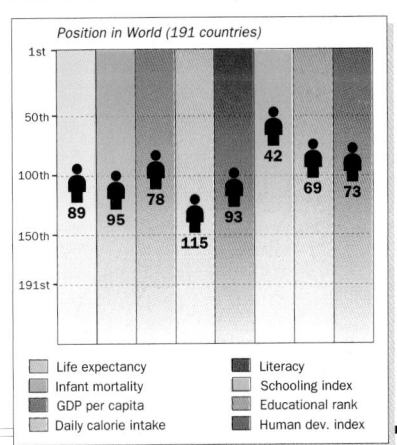

Position in World (191 countries)

1st
50th
100th
150th
191st

89 95 78 115 93 42 69 73

- Life expectancy
- Infant mortality
- GDP per capita
- Daily calorie intake
- Literacy
- Schooling index
- Educational rank
- Human dev. index

COMOROS

C

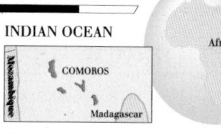

INDIAN OCEAN

COMOROS

Madagascar

Africa

OFFICIAL NAME: Federal Islamic Republic of the Comoros   **CAPITAL:** Moroni
POPULATION: 600,000   **CURRENCY:** Comoros franc   **OFFICIAL LANGUAGES:** Arabic and French

THE ARCHIPELAGO republic of the Comoros lies between Mozambique and Madagascar and consists of three main islands and a number of islets. The region is poor, with most of the population engaged in subsistence farming. In 1975, the Comoros, with the exception of the island of Mayotte, became independent of France. Since then instability has plagued the political process, and there have been several coups and counter-coups.

Moroni, the capital, on Njazidja. The Comoros islands are highly fertile and heavily forested. Many are ringed by coral reefs.

CLIMATE

WEATHER CHART

The islands are tropical; it is hot and humid on the coasts and cooler higher up, notably on Mount Kartala.

COMMUNICATIONS

 Moroni-Hahaya, Njazidja

3 ships 2300 dwt

THE TRANSPORT NETWORK

750 km (466 miles)		None
None		None

Recent projects have included development of the port at Moroni and upgrading the international airport.

TOURISM

 8000 visitors

No significant change from year to year

MAIN OVERSEAS ARRIVALS

| France 63% |
| South Africa 5% |
| UK 2% |
| Other 30% |

0 10 20 30 40 50 60 70 80
% of total arrivals

In 1988, Sun International of South Africa joined a major project to build four hotels designed to attract 12,000 visitors a year from South Africa, France and Italy. Mauritius and the Seychelles provide tough competition.

PEOPLE

 Arabic, Comoran, French

322 people per km²

THE URBAN/RURAL POPULATION SPLIT

28%   **72%**

RELIGIOUS PERSUASION

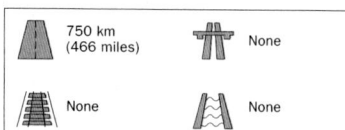

Roman Catholic 14%

Muslim 86%

The Comoros has absorbed a diversity of Polynesians, Africans, Indonesians, Persians and Arabs over its history; in addition, there have also been Portuguese, Dutch, French and Indian immigrants. However, some sections of the community have retained their individual character; Mwali and Mayotte are still primarily African. Ethnic tension is rare, partly owing to the unifying force of the predominant religion, Islam.

POLITICS

1997   Saïd Mohamed Djohar

THE STATE OF THE PARTIES

Federal Assembly 42 members

57%   **43%**
RDR   **UNDC**

RDR = Union for Democracy and Renovation
UNDC = National Union for Democratic Comoros

Senate 15 members

Five members chosen from each island by an electoral college

The Comoros has begun a transition from one-party rule to a democratic system, although the precise form is still to be established.

In 1989, President Djohar came to power. He committed himself to working towards a new constitution but political instability has continued. In 1990, 1991 and 1992, for example, there were a further three attempted coups. These difficulties have had an adverse effect on the economy. There have been calls for the presidential guard, involved in some of the coups, to be brought under constitutional control.

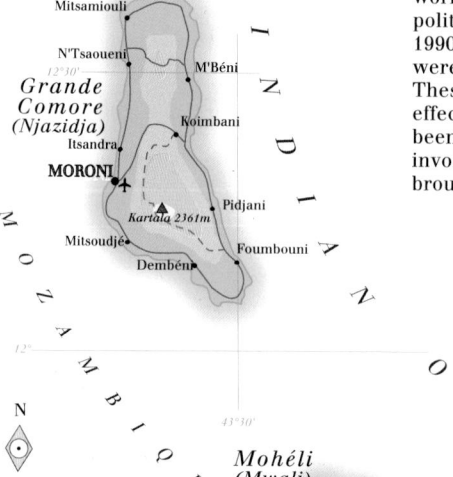

Mitsamiouli

N'Tsaoueni   M'Béni
Grande
Comore
(Njazidja)   Koimbani
          Itsandra
MORONI
          Pidjani
Kartala 2361m
Mitsoudjé   Foumbouni
          Dembéni

N

0   20 km
0   20 miles

Mohéli
(Mwali)   Fomboni
          Hoani
          Itsamia
          Moihani

I N D I A N

O C E A N

M O Z A M B I Q U E

C H A N N E L

COMOROS

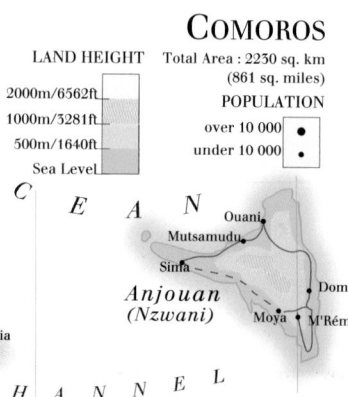

LAND HEIGHT

2000m/6562ft
1000m/3281ft
500m/1640ft
Sea Level

Total Area : 2230 sq. km (861 sq. miles)
POPULATION
over 10 000
under 10 000

Ouani
Mutsamudu
Sima
Anjouan
(Nzwani)   Domor
          Moya   M'Réma

WORLD AFFAIRS

The Comoros has a close relationship with France, its main benefactor. More recently, an economic link has been developed with South Africa, which used the islands for sanctions-busting purposes. In 1985, the Comoros became the fourth member of the Indian Ocean Commission (IOC), with the Seychelles, Mauritius and Madagascar.

AID

 $43m (receipts)   Little change from year to year

Foreign aid, mainly from France, accounts for over 40% of GDP, but even so has been insufficient to install the infrastructure necessary for economic development. Because of its Islamic links, the Comoros benefits from some Arab aid, as well as some from the EU, the World Bank and OPEC.

DEFENCE

 $3.1m   Little change from year to year

The influence of the military is small beyond the presidential guard, financed by France and South Africa, which has been involved in coups.

ECONOMICS

 $262m   276.26 Comoros francs

SCORE CARD

❏ World GNP Ranking	171st
❏ GNP per Capita	$440
❏ Balance of Payments	$–14.1m
❏ Inflation	2.5%
❏ Unemployment	16%

Strengths
Vanilla, ylang-ylang and cloves are the main cash crops. Tourism is a potential growth area.

Weaknesses
Underdevelopment of agriculture; most production is at a subsistence level using traditional techniques. Over 50% of food requirements are imported. Lack of basic infrastructure, especially electricity and transport.

EXPORTS

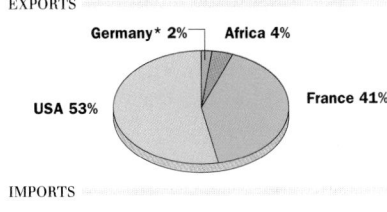

Germany* 2%   Africa 4%
USA 53%   France 41%

IMPORTS

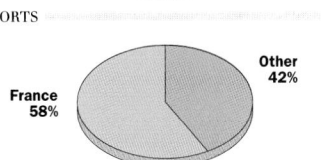

France 58%   Other 42%

RESOURCES

 16m kwh (capacity 5000 kw)   Not an oil producer and has no refineries

 47,000 cattle, 13,000 sheep, 4000 asses   None

The Comoros has no strategic resources. An HEP plant is under construction on Nzwani, but there is no prospect of moving away from imports for the bulk of fuel requirements.

ENVIRONMENT

 None   The Comoros is too poor for any major initiatives

The environment is not a major priority in the Comoros; natural disasters, such as the volcanic eruption in 1977 which left 20,000 homeless, are of more immediate concern. The government is promoting tourism and recognizes the long-term commercial value of imposing environmental controls on new developments.

MEDIA

 The press had little political independence after the 1990 coup attempt, but since then, the situation has slowly been improving

PUBLISHING AND BROADCAST MEDIA

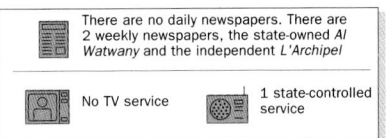

There are no daily newspapers. There are 2 weekly newspapers, the state-owned *Al Watwany* and the independent *L'Archipel*

No TV service   1 state-controlled service

There is currently a shift towards liberalization. The French government has announced that it will fund the establishment of a TV station.

CRIME

 The Comoros does not publish prison figures   The general trend is up

Although the judiciary can arbitrate where the government is accused of malpractice, some members of opposition groups have been arrested and imprisoned on political grounds.

EDUCATION

 48%

The education system does not extend beyond secondary level. Schools are equipped to teach only basic literacy, hygiene and agricultural techniques. Pupil-teacher ratios are high.

CHRONOLOGY

The Comoros was ruled by matrilineally-inherited sultanates until shortly before becoming a French protectorate in 1886.

- ❏ **1912** Proclaimed a French colony.
- ❏ **1961** Internal self-government.
- ❏ **1975** July, independence. Mayotte votes to remain French. August, President Abdallah overthrown in coup.
- ❏ **1978** Mercenaries led by Bob Denard restore Abdallah to power.
- ❏ **1989** Abdallah assassinated. Saïd Mohamed Djohar named interim president.
- ❏ **1990** Djohar elected president.
- ❏ **1992** September, pro-Abdallah coup is put down. November, first multiparty elections are chaotic and boycotted by UDZIMA and UNDC.

HEALTH

 1 per 12,237 people   Malaria, infectious intestinal and bacterial diseases

Health care is rudimentary; loans have been used to construct two maternity clinics and renovate 30 health centres.

WEALTH

 Virtually the whole population live close to the poverty line

CONSUMER GOODS OWNERSHIP

VCR and PC ownership is limited to a small elite

1   2   7

Wealth is concentrated among the political and business elite; most of the population lives at subsistence level.

WORLD RANKING

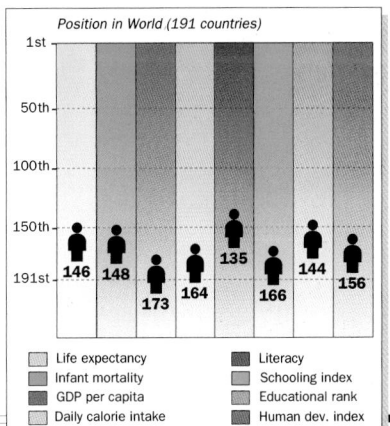

Position in World (191 countries)

146 148 173 164 135 166 144 156

- ☐ Life expectancy
- ☐ Infant mortality
- ☐ GDP per capita
- ☐ Daily calorie intake
- ☐ Literacy
- ☐ Schooling index
- ☐ Educational rank
- ☐ Human dev. index

C

CONGO

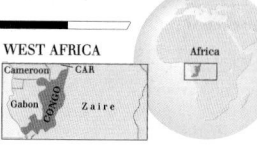

WEST AFRICA

OFFICIAL NAME: The Republic of the Congo **CAPITAL:** Brazzaville
POPULATION: 2.4 million **CURRENCY:** CFA franc **OFFICIAL LANGUAGE:** French

C

S TRADDLING THE EQUATOR in west central Africa, the area now covered by the Congo was first inhabited by Bantu-speaking peoples in the 15th century. In the 1880s it became a French colony, achieving independence in 1960. Rich in oil reserves, the Congo is now emerging from two decades of Marxist-Leninist rule.

CLIMATE

WEATHER CHART

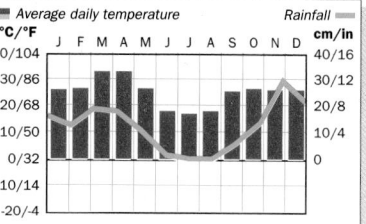

In most years there are two wet seasons and two dry seasons. Rainfall is heaviest in the coastal regions south of the equator.

COMMUNICATIONS

Brazzaville International   Has no fleet

THE TRANSPORT NETWORK

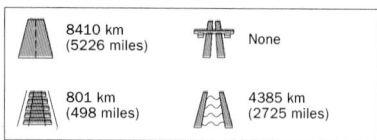

8410 km (5226 miles)	None
801 km (498 miles)	4385 km (2725 miles)

The Congo aims to maintain its entrepôt position linking the Central African Republic, Chad and Cameroon with the Atlantic coast. The Congo Ocean Railway runs from Brazzaville to the major port of Pointe-Noire.

TOURISM

39,000 visitors   Little change from year to year

MAIN OVERSEAS ARRIVALS

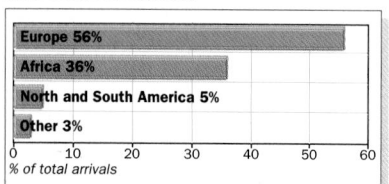

| Europe 56% |
| Africa 36% |
| North and South America 5% |
| Other 3% |

% of total arrivals

The Marxist-Leninist regime did not seek to develop tourism, and visitors, mostly on safaris and business-related trips, are still rare.

The Loufoulakari Falls, near Brazzaville. Swamps and mangroves border many of the rivers in the Congo's northern region.

PEOPLE

  Kongo, Teke, Lingala, French   7 people per km²

THE URBAN/RURAL POPULATION SPLIT

41%   59%

ETHNIC MAKEUP

Other 3%   Mbochi 12%
Bakongo 48%
Teke 17%
Sangha 20%

The Congo is one of the most tribally conscious countries in Africa. The main tensions are between the Bakongo, who live in the north, and the Mbochi, concentrated in the more prosperous south. Since the 1950s, women have achieved considerable emancipation.

POLITICS

Lower House 1998   President Pascal
Upper House 1998   Lissouba

THE STATE OF THE PARTIES

National Assembly 125 members

| 38% UPADS | 22% MCDDI | 12% CLP | 8% RDPS | 20% Other |

UPADS = Pan-African Union for Social Democracy
MCDDI = Congolese Movement for Democracy and Integral Development **CLP** = Congolese Labour Party **RDPS** = Rally for Democratic and Social Progress **RDD** = Rally for Democracy and Development

Senate 60 members

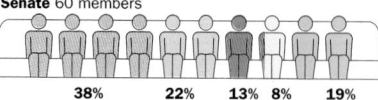

| 38% UPADS | 22% MCDDI | 13% RDD | 8% RDPS | 19% Other |

In 1990, the Congo renounced Marxism. A multiparty constitution was introduced, and legislative and presidential elections were held in 1992. Parties were deadlocked and, in June 1993, President Lissouba called new elections. The results were disputed, but Lissouba's UPADS party won rerun elections.

CONGO

Total Area :
342 000 sq. km
(132 040 sq. miles)

N

0   100 km
0   100 miles

POPULATION

over 500 000
over 50 000
over 10 000
over 10 000
under 10 000

LAND HEIGHT

500m/1640ft
200m/656ft
Sea Level

C

WORLD AFFAIRS

Carefully balancing its relations with France and the USA is a priority. Both wish to gain control of the oil industry.

AID

 $133m (receipts)   Down 38% in 1991

Before 1990, the USSR, Cuba and China were the major donors. Most aid now comes from France. High levels of 1970s debt mean that, despite its oil, the Congo remains dependent on aid.

DEFENCE

 $100.5m   Fairly stable from year to year

The army backed democratization in 1991, but made sure that its own relatively large numbers (10,000) and budgets were maintained. Although small, the airforce is well equipped, with 20 MiG-17s and 12 MiG-21s.

ECONOMICS

 $2.6bn   295.23 CFA francs

SCORE CARD
- ❏ WORLD GNP RANKING.......................133rd
- ❏ GNP PER CAPITA $1010
- ❏ BALANCE OF PAYMENTS...................$–210m
- ❏ INFLATION ....–5%
- ❏ UNEMPLOYMENT....Widespread underemployment

STRENGTHS
Oil has increased in importance, now providing 90% of export revenues compared with 5% in 1970. Significant timber supplies. Skilled and well-trained workforce helps sustain substantial industrial base in the capital and Pointe-Noire.

WEAKNESSES
$4 billion debt by the late 1980s. Top-heavy bureaucracy inherited from Marxist years. Over-dependence on oil.

EXPORTS

Italy 9%
Other 12%
USA 54%
Spain 12%
France 13%

IMPORTS

USA 5% Italy 5%
Spain 6%
France 53%
Other 31%

The Congo is keen to maintain the ties developed during the 1970s and 1980s with what was then the communist world. Relations with eastern Europe, the former Soviet Union, Cuba and particularly China remain strong.

RESOURCES

 398m kwh (capacity 149,000 kw)   185,100 b/d (reserves 830,000,000 bbl)

104,000 sheep, 62,000 cattle, 44,000 pigs   Oil, natural gas, bauxite, iron

Oil is by far the Congo's most important resource. Natural gas reserves have yet to be exploited; the oil industry currently flares excess gas. Bauxite and iron ore reserves are not large enough to be profitably mined and phosphate production was abandoned in 1977. Chinese aid has helped build two hydroelectric dams, on the Bouenza and Djoué rivers. A third is currently being built on the Léfini at Imboulou.

ENVIRONMENT

 4% partially protected   Still no effective controls on deforestation

There is increasing concern at the uncontrolled exploitation of tropical timber. The Congo has also been used in the past as a dumping ground for dangerous toxic waste from the West.

MEDIA

In theory all censorship restrictions have been lifted. However, occasional acts of censorship and press intimidation are still reported

PUBLISHING AND BROADCAST MEDIA

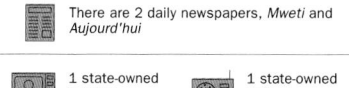
There are 2 daily newspapers, *Mweti* and *Aujourd'hui*

1 state-owned service   1 state-owned service

During the Second World War, *Radio Brazzaville* was a vital organ of De Gaulle's Free French. Satellite links will mean *Canal France Internationale* TV will soon be available.

CRIME

 The Congo does not publish prison figures   Fairly constant in last 5 years

Armed robbery and smuggling are the major problems. The state's human rights record has improved since the Marxist-Leninist secret police years.

EDUCATION

 57%

Originally pioneered by French Catholic missions, schools are still subject to inspection from Paris.

CHRONOLOGY

The kingdoms of Teke and Loango were incorporated as the Middle Congo (part of French Equatorial Africa) between 1880 and 1885.

- ❏ **1960** Independence. Former priest Fulbert Youlou president.
- ❏ **1964** Marxist-Leninist National Revolution Movement (MNR) becomes only legal party.
- ❏ **1977** President Ngoumbi assassinated. Martial law declared; Yhompi-Opango head of state.
- ❏ **1979** Col Denis Sassou-Nguesso president.
- ❏ **1990** Return to multiparty democracy.
- ❏ **1992** Elections. Pascal Lissouba (former geneticist) president.
- ❏ **1993** In elections, Lissouba's UPADS party gains majority.

HEALTH

 1 per 4334 people   Diarrheal, parasitic and respiratory diseases, malaria

The health service, established by French military doctors at the turn of the century, is considered effective.

WEALTH

 Wage rates among the Congo's middle class are higher than in most African countries

CONSUMER GOODS OWNERSHIP

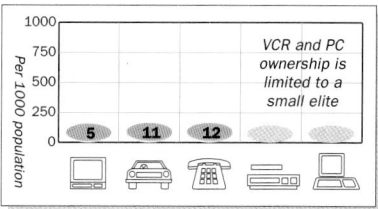

VCR and PC ownership is limited to a small elite

5 11 12

Oil has sustained an active and confident middle class. French label products are seen as status symbols.

WORLD RANKING

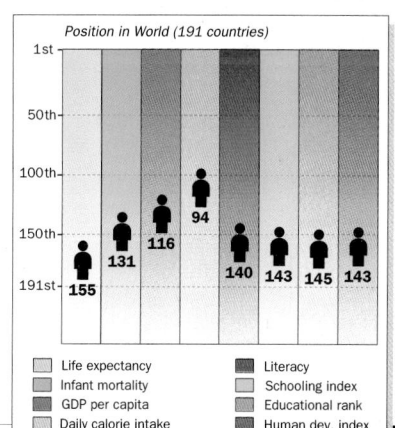

Position in World (191 countries)

155 131 116 94 140 143 145 143

- ▢ Life expectancy
- ▢ Infant mortality
- ▢ GDP per capita
- ▢ Daily calorie intake
- ▢ Literacy
- ▢ Schooling index
- ▢ Educational rank
- ▢ Human dev. index

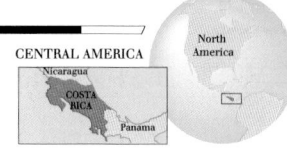

COSTA RICA

OFFICIAL NAME: The Republic of Costa Rica **CAPITAL:** San José
POPULATION: 3.2 million **CURRENCY:** Costa Rican colón **OFFICIAL LANGUAGE:** Spanish

C

LOCATED IN CENTRAL AMERICA between Nicaragua and Panama, Costa Rica gained independence from Spain in 1821. From 1948 until the end of the 1980s, it was the most developed welfare state in Central America. Costa Rica is a multiparty democracy gradually moving towards a two-party system. Coffee and bananas are the major exports. Its constitution is the only one in the world to forbid national armies; its own was abolished in 1949.

CLIMATE

WEATHER CHART

The Atlantic coast has heavy rainfall, whilst the Pacific coast is much drier. The central uplands are temperate.

COMMUNICATIONS

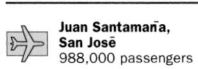

Juan Santamaña, San José — 988,000 passengers

4 ships 2700 dwt

THE TRANSPORT NETWORK

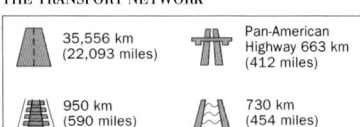

35,556 km (22,093 miles)

Pan-American Highway 663 km (412 miles)

950 km (590 miles)

730 km (454 miles)

The government is reviving the 'Jungle Train' railway line for tourists. The rest of the network has closed.

TOURISM

988,000 visitors

Up 13% in 1990

MAIN OVERSEAS ARRIVALS

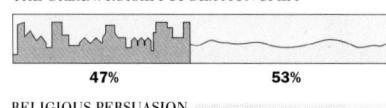

USA 34%
Nicaragua 15%
Panama 11%
Other 40%

% of total arrivals

Well-organized government promotions and a reputation for being the only violence-free country in Central America have helped to increase tourist numbers considerably in recent years. Costa Rica attracts many birdwatchers.

PEOPLE

 Spanish, English Creole, Bribri, Cabecar

 63 people per km²

THE URBAN/RURAL POPULATION SPLIT

47% 53%

RELIGIOUS PERSUASION

Other 5%

Roman Catholic 95%

The majority of the population is *mestizo* of Spanish origin. One third of people in the Puerto Limón area are black and often English-speaking. There are only about 5000 indigenous Indians.

POLITICS

 1998

 President José María Figueres

THE STATE OF THE PARTIES

Legislative Assembly 57 members

49% PLN   44% PUSC   7% Other

PLN = National Liberation Party **PUSC** = Social Christian Unity Party **Other** = General Union Party, Popular Front, Farmers of Cartaginesa Action

Employees of Costa Rica's extensive bureaucracy tend to belong to one of the two main parties – the PUSC or the PLN. This strengthens the parties' grip on power. Former president Luis Alberto Monge of the PLN, the Calderón family which supports the PUSC, and the major banana and coffee families are powerful behind the scenes, forming coalitions and shaping policies. The USA exercises a very powerful influence on politics. The PLN held power from 1982 until 1990, when Rafael Calderón was elected president. The general elections saw five parties, including the Communist Party, almost disappear from the political scene, and confirmed Costa Rica's movement towards a PUSC–PLN two-party state. These two parties competed, on the basis of similar economic policies, in the 1994 elections which were won by President José María Figueres of the PLN.

WORLD AFFAIRS

 AG OAS CACM   LAES   ECLAC

Costa Rica has always emphasized its neutrality in foreign affairs, but it has very strong ties with the USA. The protection of export prices for coffee and bananas is a major concern. Costa Rica has long-term aspirations to join NAFTA.

Pineapple plantation near Buenos Aires, crossed by the Pan-American Highway which runs for 663 km through Costa Rica.

COSTA RICA

Total Area : 51 100 sq. km (19 730 sq. miles)

POPULATION

over 100 000
over 50 000
over 10 000
under 10 000

LAND HEIGHT

3000m/9843ft
2000m/6562ft
1000m/3281ft
500m/1640ft
200m/656ft
Sea level

0   50 km
0   50 miles

C

AID

 $173m (receipts)   Down 24% in 1991

Costa Rica received $150 million of aid a year throughout the 1980s, principally from the USA. However, this was sharply reduced in 1990 after the signing of peace agreements in the region's war-torn countries. The USA sees Costa Rica as a useful base against potential left-wing insurgencies in neighbouring El Salvador, Guatemala and Nicaragua.

DEFENCE

 No armed forces; anti-terrorist and security force exist   Not applicable

The last period of violence was the 1948 civil war, from which Costa Rica emerged as a neutral, demilitarized modern state. The 7500-strong National Guard, together with an anti-terrorist battalion of 750 men, are the only security forces, and have little political influence. Spending on security is the lowest in the region. Costa Rica's defence aim is to maintain a neutral line by keeping out of any Central American conflicts.

ECONOMICS

 $6.3bn   147.30 colones

SCORE CARD

❏ WORLD GNP RANKING	101st
❏ GNP PER CAPITA	$1969
❏ BALANCE OF PAYMENTS	$−432m
❏ INFLATION	29.3%
❏ UNEMPLOYMENT	5.5%

STRENGTHS

Traditional coffee industry still creates largest export revenues. Tourism continuing to grow because of political stability. Government privatization programme has lowered costs and encouraged competition.

WEAKNESSES

Main exports of coffee, beef and especially bananas have been hit by

EXPORTS

Guatemala 4% Italy 5%
USA 39% Germany* 14%
Other 38%

IMPORTS

Guatemala 4% Mexico 6%
Japan 7%
USA 40% Venezuela 8%
Other 35%

falling international prices. Drop of 15% in banana exports due to EU quotas on non-Caribbean bananas. Dependent on imported oil. National economy too small to provide rapid growth; need for regional economic integration.

RESOURCES

 3.6bn kwh (capacity 933,000 kw) Not an oil producer; refines 15,000 b/cd

 1.7m cattle, 223,000 pigs, 114,000 horses Bauxite, gold, silver, manganese, mercury

Costa Rica has large bauxite deposits at Boruca – aluminium smelting is an important industry. Small quantities of gold, silver, manganese and mercury are also mined. Self-sufficiency in energy is being pursued through the development of hydroelectric power. Forests cover 34% of the country.

ENVIRONMENT

 12% (3% partially protected) Monteverde Cloud Forest is an example of a well-run reserve

The remaining rainforests are slowly being cut down to make way for commercial agriculture. The government, however, is beginning to protect land by designating national parks. Eco-tourism is being encouraged, as is the sensitive exploitation of natural resources.

MEDIA

 Journalists are supposed to join *Colegio*, a state-run trade union, effectively run by the government

PUBLISHING AND BROADCAST MEDIA

There are 4 daily newspapers, *La Nación*, *La República*, *La Prensa Libre* and *Extra*

1 state-owned, 4 independent stations State-owned and independent stations

There are four private TV stations providing round-the-clock programming direct from the USA.

CRIME

 Costa Rica does not publish prison figures   Up 3% in 1990

Costa Rica is the least violent Central American country. Crime is mostly petty theft, although there is concern over increasing drug trafficking. Its human rights record is better than that of neighbouring states. The police show some hostility towards refugees, mostly from Nicaragua and El Salvador.

CHRONOLOGY

Costa Rica, ruled since the 16th century by Spain, gained independence in 1821.

❏ **1948** Disputed elections lead to civil war; ended by Social Democratic Party (later known as the PLN) forming provisional government under José Ferrer.
❏ **1949** Ferrer abolishes army.
❏ **1987** Central American Peace Plan initiated by President Arias.

EDUCATION

 93%

Schooling is based on the French system. The regional University of Central America is based in Costa Rica.

HEALTH

 1 per 1205 people   Heart diseases, stomach cancer, perinatal deaths

The public health system is one of the most developed in Latin America. The private system is noted as a regional centre for plastic surgery.

WEALTH

 Agricultural worker, 16,661 colones per month; construction worker, 23,319 colones per month

CONSUMER GOODS OWNERSHIP

VCR and PC ownership is limited to a small elite

136 50 143

The plantation-owning families are the wealthiest group; the blacks on the Caribbean coast are the poorest.

WORLD RANKING

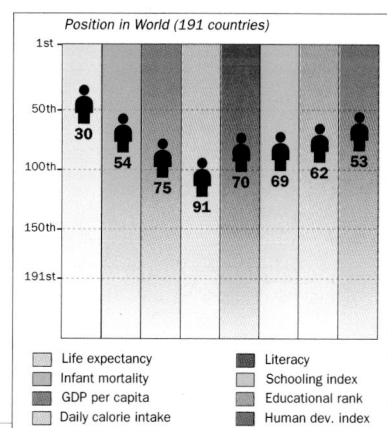

Position in World (191 countries)

30 54 75 91 70 69 62 53

❏ Life expectancy ❏ Literacy
❏ Infant mortality ❏ Schooling index
❏ GDP per capita ❏ Educational rank
❏ Daily calorie intake ❏ Human dev. index

CROATIA

OFFICIAL NAME: Republic of Croatia **CAPITAL:** Zagreb
POPULATION: 4.8 million **CURRENCY:** Kuna **OFFICIAL LANGUAGE:** Croatian

C

LOCATED TO THE SOUTH OF Slovenia and west of Serbia, Croatia includes the historic regions of Istra, Dalmatia and Slavonia. Croatia's Adriatic coastline is vitally important for tourism and shipping, which have been major contributors to the economy. Since the dissolution of the Federal Republic of Yugoslavia, Croatia has been involved in warfare in Bosnia and Herzegovina and in defending its own territory. One third of Croatia is held by Serbian troops.

CLIMATE

WEATHER CHART

Northern Croatia has a temperate continental climate. Its Adriatic coast has a Mediterranean climate.

COMMUNICATIONS

 Pleso International, Zagreb   85 ships 184,000 dwt

THE TRANSPORT NETWORK

27,378 km (17,012 miles)	302 km (188 miles)
2425 km (1507 miles)	Islands are linked to the mainland by ferries

Communications in Serb-dominated Krajina and Slavonia were badly affected by fighting in 1991–1992. In 1993, Croats regained control of the Maslenica Bridge, a vital link between northern Croatia and Dalmatia.

TOURISM

 630,000 visitors in 1991   Modest increase in tourist arrivals in Istra and the north

MAIN OVERSEAS ARRIVALS

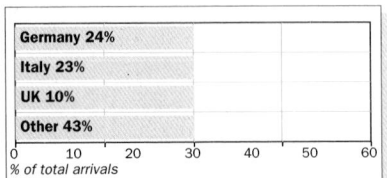

Germany 24%	
Italy 23%	
UK 10%	
Other 43%	

% of total arrivals

Croatia's seaside resorts, particularly in northern Istra, are leading a modest recovery of the tourist industry.

PEOPLE

 Croatian   81 people per km²

THE URBAN/RURAL POPULATION SPLIT

51%   49%

RELIGIOUS PERSUASION

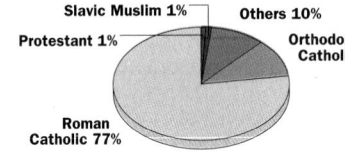

Slavic Muslim 1%   Others 10%
Protestant 1%   Orthodox Catholic 11%
Roman Catholic 77%

Croats make up 80% of the population, Serbs 12%. In 1990, the Serbs, alienated by Croatian nationalism, pressed for autonomy in the areas where they formed a majority, notably Krajina, Baranja, Western Srem and Slavonia. Independence brought the Serb-dominated federal army (JNA) into Croatia, in defence of the Serbs. Conflict erupted in 1992, particularly in Slavonia in eastern Croatia. The 1993 UN-brokered ceasefire saw the JNA withdraw, but the peace was broken by a Croat attack on Serb-held Krajina in late 1993.

POLITICS

 1996   President Dr Franjo Tudjman

THE STATE OF THE PARTIES

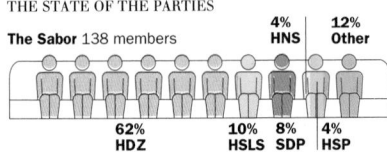

The Sabor 138 members   4% HNS   12% Other

62% HDZ   10% HSLS   8% SDP   4% HSP

HDZ = Christian Democratic Union **HSLS** = Croatian Social Liberal Party **SDP** = Party of Democratic Change **HNS** = Croatian National Party **HSP** = Croatian Party of Rights **Others** = Croatian Peasant Party, Serbian National Party, Independents, Regional Parties

With the break-up of former Yugoslavia, the Croatian independence movement was led by the right-wing Croatian Democratic Union (HDZ)

WORLD AFFAIRS

Croatia's major concern is with the Serb-held area of Krajina, which represents 30% of Croatia, as recognized by the UN. It also contains key infrastructure links between Zagreb and Dalmatia. The HDZ and the EU have stated that any peace agreement on the former Yugoslavia must include a satisfactory settlement of the Krajina problem.

The creation in March 1994 of a bi-national Muslim-Croat federation in Bosnia was widely recognized as a major foreign policy success for President Franjo Tudjman.

AID

 $500m (est)   Aid levels have increased markedly since 1991

Croatia has been a major target of UNHCR and bilateral humanitarian aid. It has an estimated 526,000 refugees from Bosnia and Serb-held areas in Croatia. The main UNHCR warehouses are in Zagreb, Split and Rijeka.

DEFENCE

 Government spends one third of budget on defence   Defence spending up 30% in 1992

Croatia has about 95,000 army, 4000 navy and 4000 air force personnel. In addition, the Croat Defence Association (HOS) has about 10,000 armed men in Bosnia. The army tried unsuccessfully to recapture Serb-held Krajina in September 1993. The air force is suspected of breaking the UN-imposed 'No-Fly' zone in Bosnia.

under Franjo Tudjman. Multiparty elections in 1992 consolidated the HDZ's hold on power. It gained a majority in parliament and Tudjman was elected president. The main political issues remain the status of Serb-held territory in Croatia, and the status of Croats in Bosnia. The agreement to form a Croat and Muslim federation in Bosnia signifies a major policy change by Serbia, with the emphasis now on a political, rather than a military, approach. The HDZ has also begun to address the issue of autonomy for Serbs in Croatia. In early 1994, the Russians were attempting to arrange a ceasefire between Croatian armed forces and the Serbian stronghold of Kradjina.

ECONOMICS

 8.3bn   6130.46 kuna

SCORE CARD

- ❏ WORLD GNP RANKING.........................88th
- ❏ GNP PER CAPITA $1789
- ❏ BALANCE OF PAYMENTS...................$−536m
- ❏ INFLATION 122.6%
- ❏ UNEMPLOYMENT..................................17%

STRENGTHS

Tourism recovering in safe areas. Exports to the West growing. Economy well placed to expand in peacetime.

WEAKNESSES

Economic reform held up by outdated infrastructure. Costs of repairing war damage. Refugees an economic strain.

EXPORTS/IMPORTS

> *Before the conflict, Croatia's main trading partners were the former Yugoslavian republics, Italy and Germany*

***Dubrovnik, Dalmatia.** This historic city on the Adriatic coast was shelled and besieged by the Yugoslav federal army in 1991.*

RESOURCES

 8531bn kwh

 17.1m poultry, 1.6m pigs, 829,000 cattle

Oil production affected by loss of some fields to Serbia

Coal, bauxite, iron, oil, china clay, natural gas

Croatia generates half its energy needs from thermal and half from hydroelectric sources. It has few minerals, although it does have oil and gas fields. The rich fishing grounds of the Adriatic are a major resource.

ENVIRONMENT

 6%   Environmental issues not yet a priority following war

Croatia was the first Yugoslav republic to create reserves in order to protect endangered and unique wetlands.

MEDIA

 The government has extended its influence over the media. The HDZ effectively controls Hina, the national news agency

PUBLISHING AND BROADCAST MEDIA

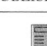 There are 9 daily newspapers, published locally, including *Vercenji List* in Zagreb and *Slobodna Dalmacija* in Split

 1 state-controlled service   1 state-controlled service

Inconsistencies in the official media line in war reporting led to enforced guidelines for presenting information.

CRIME

Croatia does not publish prison figures   Crime has risen since Independence

The Croat militia in Bosnia, the HOS, is suspected of involvement in 'ethnic cleansing'. The UN has accused all sides in Bosnia of human rights abuses.

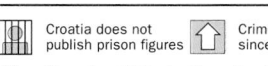

CROATIA

Total Area : 56 540 sq. km
(21 830 sq. miles)

LAND HEIGHT

1000m/3281ft
500m/1640ft
200m/656ft
Sea Level

POPULATION

over 500 000 ⊙
over 100 000 ◎
over 50 000 ○
over 10 000 ●
under 10 000 ·

CHRONOLOGY

In 1089, Croatia became a vassal of Hungary and then the Habsburgs.

- ❏ **1918–1941** Part of Yugoslavia. Growing Serb-Croat resentment.
- ❏ **1941–1945** Germans install Croat Fascist state. Many Serbs Killed.
- ❏ **1945–1991** Croatia a constituent republic in the Yugoslav federation. Nationalism suppressed by state.
- ❏ **1990** HDZ wins republic elections and calls for Croat independence.

EDUCATION

 93%

Croatia has a well-developed education system. It has four universities, at Zagreb, Rijeka, Osijek and Split.

HEALTH

 1 per 436 people   Cerebrovascular and heart diseases, cancers

Most Croats are covered by a health insurance scheme. However, coping with refugees and war casualties poses an extra strain on already scarce funds.

WEALTH

 Standards of living are falling under the government's austerity programme

CONSUMER GOODS OWNERSHIP

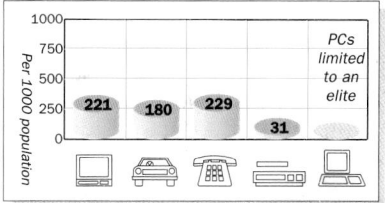

The net monthly wage in Croatia is equal to $149. Many Croatians are finding it difficult to meet basic needs.

WORLD RANKING

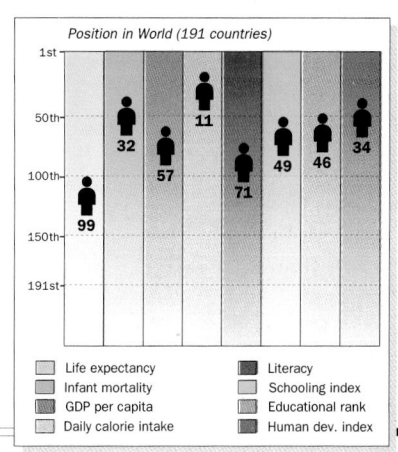

CUBA

OFFICIAL NAME: Republic of Cuba CAPITAL: Havana
POPULATION: 10.8 million CURRENCY: Cuban peso OFFICIAL LANGUAGE: Spanish

THE CARIBBEAN'S LARGEST ISLAND, Cuba has widely cultivated lowlands, which fall between three mountainous areas. The fertile soil of the lowlands supports the sugar cane, rice and coffee plantations. Sugar, the country's major export, is suffering from depressed world prices. A former Spanish colony, Cuba is the only communist state in the Caribbean. Since the collapse of communism in the Soviet Union, the USA sees Cuba as less of a threat, in marked contrast to 1962, when the Soviet nuclear missiles on the island brought the two superpowers close to war. Cuba is still subject to US sanctions and unable to afford oil imports.

Valle de Viñales, Pinar del Río province.
Cuba's undulating countryside is ideal for growing the main export crop, sugar.

CLIMATE

WEATHER CHART

Cuba's subtropical climate is hot all year round and very hot in the summer. Rainfall is heaviest in the mountains, which receive up to 250 cm a year. Generally, the north is wetter than the south; the Guantánamo area receives only 20 cm of rainfall annually. In winter, the west is sometimes affected by cold air from the USA, but only for a day or two at a time.

COMMUNICATIONS

José Martí, Havana
1.2m passengers

85 ships
711,300 dwt

THE TRANSPORT NETWORK

34,000 km (21,127 miles)	575 km (357 miles)
14,519 km (9022 miles)	240 km (149 miles)

Public transport has been extremely cheap in Cuba, although fuel shortages have made it increasingly erratic and unreliable. Cubans rely mostly on traditional black bicycles, which are imported by the thousand from China. Havana owes much of its charm to the number of 40-year-old Chevrolets and Oldsmobiles still being driven around. Although this is another result of sanctions, it keeps the many inventive local spare-parts workshops in business.

TOURISM

424,041 visitors

Up 25% in 1991

MAIN OVERSEAS ARRIVALS

Canada	19%
Germany	15%
Mexico	11%
Spain	9%
Italy	5%
Other	41%

% of total arrivals

Cuba, once a playground for wealthy Americans, reduced tourism after 1959 as being unfit for a socialist society. Recently the policy has changed. Although most tourist arrivals are from Canada, Germany, Mexico and Spain, some are Americans going via these destinations to skirt the US trade embargo – the Cuban authorities do not stamp US passport holders. About 2000 affluent Latin American 'health-tourists' visit Cuba annually for low-cost, advanced surgery, or to stay at sanatoria.

Guanabo, 25 km east of Havana, is a low-key holiday resort favoured by Cubans. The most modern cars in Cuba are imported, along with computers, in exchange for sugar in a special trading deal with Japan.

CUBA

Total Area : 110 860 sq. km
(42 803 sq. miles)

POPULATION

▣	over 1 000 000
◉	over 500 000
◎	over 100 000
○	over 50 000
●	over 10 000
•	under 10 000

LAND HEIGHT

1000m/3281ft
500m/1640ft
200m/656ft
Sea Level

PEOPLE

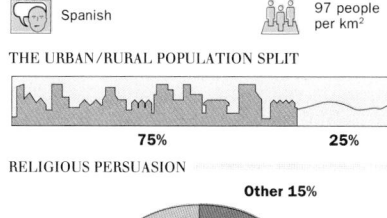

Spanish

97 people per km²

THE URBAN/RURAL POPULATION SPLIT

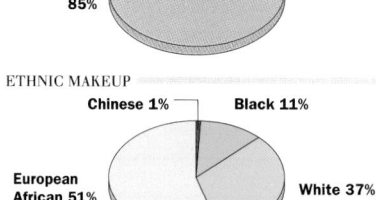

75%   25%

RELIGIOUS PERSUASION

Other 15%

Roman Catholic 85%

ETHNIC MAKEUP

Chinese 1%   Black 11%

European African 51%   White 37%

Ethnic tension in Cuba is minimal. About 70% of Cubans are of Spanish descent, mainly from the settlers who began arriving in Cuba in the 16th century, but also from the more recent influx of exiles from Franco's Spain. The black population is descended from the slaves and migrants from Cuba's neighbouring states, in particular Jamaica.

Living standards in Cuba have fallen dramatically since the collapse of the East European communist bloc, previously its main trading partner. In 1991, further rationing was introduced for most basic foodstuffs; yet in Havana, exotic goods are easily available in the many exclusive dollar stores.

An increasing number of women are playing prominent roles in politics, the professions and the armed forces. Child-care facilities are freely available and there is a law requiring men to share equally in housework and child-rearing if a wife is working in 'social production'; the state, however, does not check how well this law is observed.

POPULATION AGE BREAKDOWN

%	0–14	15–64		65+	
	5%	6.1%	7.6%	8.5%	9.4%
	60.8%	56.9%	60.7%	68.8%	67.2%
	34.2%	37%	31.7%	22.7%	23.4%
	1960	1970	1980	1990	2000

% of population by age group

POLITICS

 1998

 President Fidel Castro Ruz

THE STATE OF THE PARTIES

National Assembly of People's Power 589 members

100% PCC

PCC = Cuban Communist Party

Fidel Castro has led Cuba since 1959 and was the founder of the one-party communist system, formalized in the 1976 constitution.

MAIN POLITICAL ISSUES

The succession
Castro has stated his wish to retire from the Council of State when his current term ends in 1998. Contenders for the leadership include his brother Raúl, current defence minister, Roberto Robaina, the foreign minister, and economic guru Carlos Lage. Castro, who has said that the Communist Party must be invigorated with younger minds, is thought to favour Robaina.

The economy
Cuba chose not to go down the capitalist route when its main patron and supplier, the former USSR, ended aid in 1991. The socialist economy remains in place, although it is increasingly short of supplies and subject to the disabling effects of the US trade embargo.

PROFILE
Cuban politics has always been dominated by the perceived US threat. The Party has reacted to the collapse of the USSR by strengthening its dominance, as illustrated by the 1992 imposition of death sentences on several Cuban dissidents. As the USA has tightened economic sanctions, as the surest way to end Castro's rule, so Castro has increased his powers. Constitutional changes in 1992 gave the president the right to declare a state of emergency and to take full command of the military.

Raúl Castro, brother of Fidel and the Minister of Defence.

Fidel Castro, Cuba's leader since 1959. The USA is keen to oust his regime.

Moa
Baracoa
El Salvador
Guantánamo
GUANTANAMO BAY (to US)
Windward Passage

WORLD AFFAIRS

(OAS)   NAM   GATT   LAES   IAEA

Since the 1962 stand-off, when Cuba accepted Russian missiles targeted at US cities, Cuba has been considered a danger by the USA and has been subject to diplomatic isolation from countries which support US policies in the Caribbean. The end of aid from Moscow after 1991, following the collapse of the USSR, made conditions in Cuba increasingly difficult. The USA increased pressure on the Castro administration by tightening the rules of the trade embargo, including an effective ban on ships docking in the USA which had been in a Cuban port. Cuba has mustered support in the UN, as well as EU backing, for a lifting of the US embargo, but without effect. The USA has vetoed any UN debate, and will not abandon its stand until Cuba adopts a multiparty democracy.

Iran and the Russian Federation now take most of Cuba's sugar, in exchange for badly needed oil supplies. Iran is now one of Cuba's few supporters worldwide. Trade between the two countries has grown as the Moscow alliance declines in importance.

AID

 $42m (receipts)

 Up 45% in 1991

Cuba claims to receive no aid, but does receive donations from Spain. Sweden used to be an important donor, but withheld aid payments in 1993 in response to human rights violations by the Castro regime.

CHRONOLOGY

Originally inhabited by the Arawak people, Cuba was claimed by Columbus for Spain in 1492. Development of the sugar industry from the 18th century, using imported slave labour, made Cuba the world's third largest producer by 1860.

- ❑ **1868** End of the slave trade.
- ❑ **1868–1878** Ten Years' War for independence from Spain.
- ❑ **1895** Second war of independence. Thousands die in Spanish concentration camps.
- ❑ **1898** USA declares war on Spain in support of Cuban rebels to protect strong American financial interests in Cuba.
- ❑ **1899** USA takes Cuba and installs military interim government.
- ❑ **1901** USA is granted intervention rights and military bases, including Guantanamo Bay naval base.

⇨

C

CHRONOLOGY *continued*

- ❏ **1902** Tomás Estrada Palma takes over as first Cuban president. USA leaves Cuba, but intervenes in 1906–1909 and 1919–1924.
- ❏ **1909** Liberal presidency of José Miguel Goméz. Economy prospers; US investment in tourism, gambling and sugar.
- ❏ **1925–1933** Dictatorship of President Gerardo Machado.
- ❏ **1933** Years of guerrilla activity end in revolution. Sergeant Fulgencio Batista takes over and leads military dictatorship.
- ❏ **1955** Fidel Castro exiled after two years imprisonment for subversion.
- ❏ **1956–1958** Castro returns to lead a guerrilla war in the Sierra Maestra.
- ❏ **1959** Batista flees. Castro takes over, his brother, Raúl, is deputy, Che Guevara third in rank. Wholesale nationalizations; Cuba reorganized on Soviet model.
- ❏ **1961** USA breaks off relations. US-backed, anti-Castro Cubans attempt invasion at Bay of Pigs. Fail. Cuba declares itself Marxist-Leninist.
- ❏ **1962** US economic and political blockade. Missile crisis: May, Khrushchev agrees to defend Cuba; 14 October, US spy planes see nuclear missile on site; 22 October, Kennedy orders seizure of weapons on Soviet ships in 'quarantine zone'. USA prepares for war; 28 October, Khrushchev orders return of weapons; 20 November, USA lifts 'quarantine'.
- ❏ **1965** Che Guevara resigns to pursue foreign liberation wars. One-party state formalized.
- ❏ **1972** Cuba joins COMECON.
- ❏ **1976** New socialist constitution. Cuban troops in Angola until 1991.
- ❏ **1977** Sends troops to Ethiopia.
- ❏ **1980** 125,000 Cubans, including 'undesirables' (criminals or people with learning disabilities) flee to USA.
- ❏ **1982** USA tightens sanctions and bans flights and tourism to Cuba.
- ❏ **1983** US invasion of Grenada. Cuba involved in clashes with US forces.
- ❏ **1984** Agreement with USA on Cuban emigration and repatriation of 'undesirables' is short-lived.
- ❏ **1986** Many government changes, but Soviet-style *glasnost* rejected.
- ❏ **1987** Cubans riot in US jails at new repatriation accord.
- ❏ **1988** UN's second veto of US attempt to accuse Cuba of human rights violations. Diplomatic relations established with EC.
- ❏ **1989** Senior military men executed for arms and drugs smuggling.
- ❏ **1991** Preferential trade agreement with USSR ends. Severe rationing.
- ❏ **1992** USA tightens blockade.
- ❏ **1993** All ex-Soviet military leave.

DEFENCE

💲 $1.2bn   ⬇ Down 15% in 1991

0   *Defence spending as % GDP*   40

4.5%

CUBAN ARMED FORCES

🛡	1700 main battle tanks (T-54/T-55/T-62)	145,000 personnel
🚢	3 submarines, 3 frigates and 28 patrol boats	12,000 personnel
✈	162 combat aircraft (146 MiG); also 200+ SAM launchers	7000 personnel
	None	

From 1959 to the 1980s, Cuba's efficient military was one of the achievements of the revolution. Under Castro's brother, Raúl, it succeeded in repelling the US-sponsored Bay of Pigs invasion in 1961, and saw effective action in Africa in the 1970s, preventing South Africa from taking control of Angola, and Somalia from occupying the Ogaden region. Today, with communist regimes collapsed around the world, it has lost much of its prestige. Russia is still the main supplier of arms and spares, but now has to be paid in increasingly scarce hard currency. In an effort to save money, compulsory military service has been cut from three years to two.

ECONOMICS

📊 $20.9bn   💱 0.76 Cuban pesos

SCORE CARD

- ❏ WORLD GNP RANKING..........................64th
- ❏ GNP PER CAPITA $1935
- ❏ BALANCE OF PAYMENTS ....In deficit
- ❏ INFLATION ....High
- ❏ UNEMPLOYMENT.....................................6%

EXPORTS

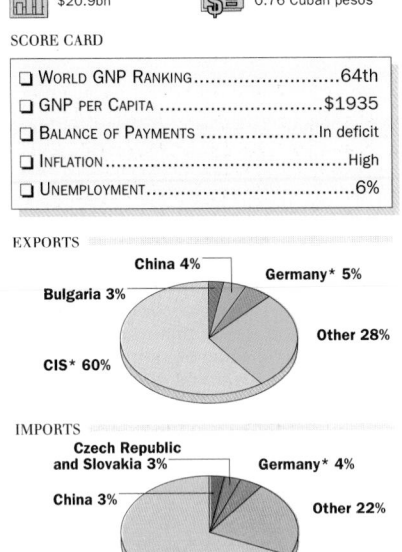

China 4%   Germany* 5%
Bulgaria 3%
Other 28%
CIS* 60%

IMPORTS

Czech Republic and Slovakia 3%   Germany* 4%
China 3%
Other 22%
CIS* 68%

ECONOMIC PERFORMANCE INDICATOR

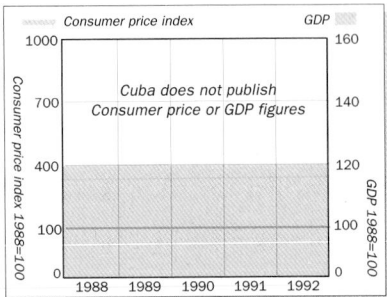

Consumer price index ▒▒▒ GDP
1000 — 160
700 — 140
Cuba does not publish Consumer price or GDP figures
400 — 120
100 — 100
0 — 0
1988 1989 1990 1991 1992

STRENGTHS

A relatively broad base compared with other Caribbean states. Sugar is the main product, followed by nickel, citrus fruits, tobacco and, increasingly, tourism.

WEAKNESSES

US trade embargo robs Cuba of a major market and investment capital; Cuba was once second only to Venezuela in US overseas investment in Latin America. Non-convertible currency an increasing liability as Russia demands payment for oil in dollars. Loss of ex-communist states as trading partners.

PROFILE

Since 1959, the nationalized economy has oscillated between concentration on sugar and attempts at industrialization. Following a brief experiment in market liberalization, the Castro regime went back to total state-control in 1986 – although some moves towards a free market were made in 1993. Since then, the economy has been in recession and is suffering from an acute shortage of fuel, spare parts for the sugar industry and chemicals. Foreign capital is increasingly hard to come by, although Castro is beginning to allow some foreign investment in hotels and tourism. The government is also selling its first oil concessions to foreign companies. The USA is now relying on the regime to collapse with the economy. It is, therefore, unlikely to lift its trade embargo unless Cubans adopt a multiparty democracy and reject Castro.

CUBA : MAJOR BUSINESSES

Havana
Matahambre   Cardenas Bay
Ciego de Avila
Cienfuegos
Pinar del Rio
Isla de la Juventud
Santiago de Cuba

🛢 Oil refining   ⛏ Nickel mining
🏭 Manufacturing   🍊 Citrus fruits
🍬 Sugar cane refining   🚬 Cigars
💊 Pharmaceuticals   ⛽ Oil

0   100 km
0   100 miles

RESOURCES

16.2bn kwh
(capacity 4m kw)

15,000 b/d
(reserves
100,000,000 bbl)

4.9m cattle,
1.9m pigs,
630,000 horses

Iron, nickel, cobalt,
chromite, gold,
manganese, oil

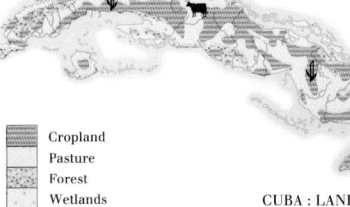

Cropland
Pasture
Forest
Wetlands
Sugar cane - cash crop
Cattle

CUBA : LAND USE
0　　　100 km
0　　　100 miles

ELECTRICITY GENERATION

Hydro 0.5% (85m kwh)
Thermal 99.5% (16.2bn kwh)
Nuclear 0%
Other 0%

% of total generation by type

ENVIRONMENT

6% (2% partially
protected)

Deforestation rate
remains lowest in
Latin America

ENVIRONMENTAL TREATIES

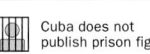

No
Yes
Yes
No

Before the revolution, Cuba had no
environmental protection laws at all.
At that time, only 14% of its forest
cover remained, but a strong drive to
replant has raised the tree cover level
to 18%. There is concern about a
nuclear reactor under construction
at Juraguá.

MEDIA

Government censorship; demand for more
outspoken media is growing

PUBLISHING AND BROADCAST MEDIA

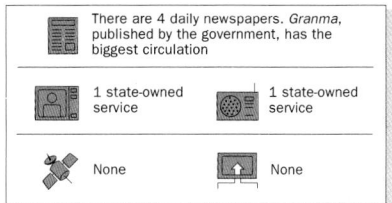

There are 4 daily newspapers. *Granma*,
published by the government, has the
biggest circulation

1 state-owned
service

1 state-owned
service

None

None

The Cuban media is state controlled.
Two Florida-based stations, *Radio
Martí* and *TV Martí*, financed by the US
government, make anti-Castro
broadcasts.

Cuba's major resource is its sugar.
Production is the fifth largest in
the world and helps to determine
international prices. The island also
has the world's fourth largest nickel
deposits, but lack of investment capital
means they are under-exploited and
inefficiently worked. Energy policy is
aimed at encouraging foreign companies,
through profit-sharing agreements,
to exploit Cuba's known oil
reserves. A Russian-built
nuclear reactor was due
to be completed in 1995.

CRIME

Cuba does not
publish prison figures

Crime is rising

CRIME RATES

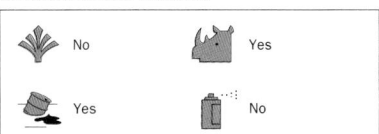

*Cuba does not publish official statistics for
murders, rapes or thefts*

Cuba has a low crime rate. Murders
are rare and there are few unsafe
areas on the island. Political dissent,
however, is not tolerated and human
rights abuses by the military and
police are frequently reported.
Occasionally Cuba opens its jails.
Petty criminals often flee to the USA as
refugees. The Revolutionary Summary
Tribunal deals with serious political
crimes, as defined by the communist
constitution.

EDUCATION

94%

0　　　*Education spending as % GNP*　　　25
6.6%

THE EDUCATION SYSTEM

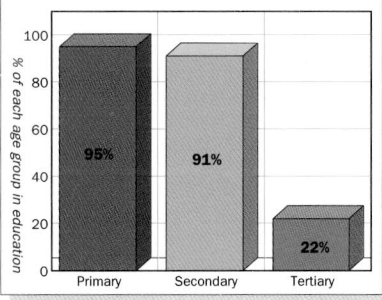

% of each age group in education

Primary 95%
Secondary 91%
Tertiary 22%

Education in Cuba combines academic
with manual work, in line with Marxist-
Leninist principles. The high priority
given to education under Castro, which
is reflected in the high literacy rate, is
now being promoted to attract foreign
investment in high-tech industries,
particularly biotechnology.

HEALTH

1 per 333 people

Heart disease,
cancers, nutritional
disorders

0　　　*Health spending as % GNP*　　　25
3%

Life-expectancy in Cuba is 76 years, the
highest in Latin America, which is a
reflection of its efficient, countrywide
health service. The US blockade has led
to shortages of hospital equipment and
raw materials for drugs. The latter are
normally supplied by Havana's sizeable
pharmaceuticals industry. Cuba's
advanced eye surgery techniques
attract patients from overseas.

WEALTH

Factory worker, 220 Cuban pesos per month;
engineer, 300 Cuban pesos per month

CONSUMER GOODS OWNERSHIP

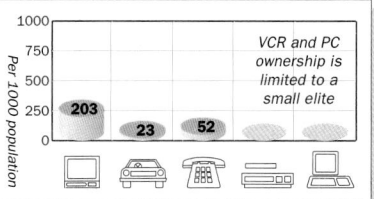

Per 1000 population

203　　23　　52

*VCR and PC
ownership is
limited to a
small elite*

Under Batista, Cuba had huge wealth
disparities, and was a playground for
the rich. The 1959 revolution
succeeded in reducing these, partly by
taking over all businesses, from oil
companies to barbers' shops, and partly
by prescribing not only minimum but
also maximum wages. Economic
regulations have varied since then; for
a brief period in 1985, different wage
rates were allowed in an attempt to
provide incentives for hard workers,
but this decision was reversed in 1986.
In the same year, a purge of old party
hands on the grounds of corruption
revealed the relatively high standard of
living enjoyed by a few government
officials. Generally, however, wealth is
fairly evenly distributed.

WORLD RANKING

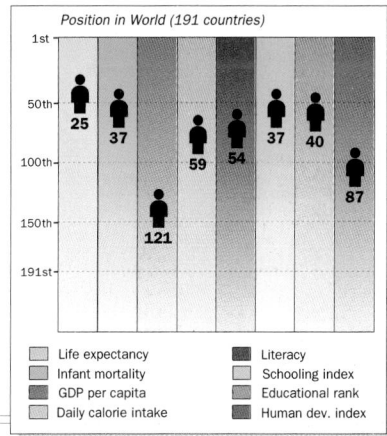

Position in World (191 countries)

1st
50th — 25　37　59　54　37　40
100th — 121　87
150th
191st

Life expectancy
Infant mortality
GDP per capita
Daily calorie intake
Literacy
Schooling index
Educational rank
Human dev. index

C

CYPRUS

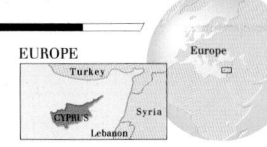

OFFICIAL NAME: Republic of Cyprus   **CAPITAL:** Nicosia   **POPULATION:** 708,000
CURRENCY: Cyprus pound (Turkish lira)   **OFFICIAL LANGUAGES:** Greek (Turkish)

C

THE ISLAND OF CYPRUS, which rises from a central plateau to a high point at Mount Olympus, lies south of Turkey in the eastern Mediterranean. Cyprus was partitioned in 1974, following an invasion by Turkish troops. The south of the island is the Greek Cypriot Republic of Cyprus (Cyprus); the self-proclaimed Turkish Republic of Northern Cyprus (TRNC) is recognized only by Turkey.

CLIMATE

WEATHER CHART

The climate is typically Mediterranean: summers are hot and dry and winters mild, though there is mountain snow.

COMMUNICATIONS

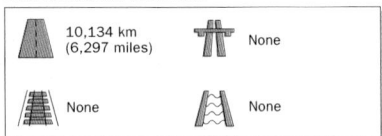

Larnaka
2.48m passengers

1384 ships
35.55m dwt

THE TRANSPORT NETWORK

10,134 km (6,297 miles)	None
None	None

Travel between the two zones is impeded. The south regards the airport at Ercan as an illegal point of entry.

TOURISM

 1.56m visitors   Up 13% in 1990

MAIN OVERSEAS ARRIVALS

UK 49%
Sweden 7%
Finland 5%
Other 39%

% of total arrivals

Tourism in southern Cyprus expanded rapidly during the 1980s, as new resorts were built replacing those lost to the north. Tourism in the north is now growing. The Akamas peninsula is being promoted for eco-tourists, who may stay in restored village houses.

PEOPLE

 Greek, Turkish   76 people per km²

THE URBAN/RURAL POPULATION SPLIT

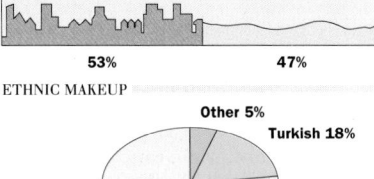

53%   47%

ETHNIC MAKEUP

Other 5%
Turkish 18%
Greek 77%

Cyprus's Greek majority, who make up 77% of the population, are Christian. The 18% Turkish minority are Muslims. Some are the descendants of Turks who settled on the island from the 16th century, under the rule of the Ottoman Empire. Turkish Cypriots have been isolated following the 1974 partitioning, since when they have officially been recognized only by Turkey, which has resettled thousands of mainland Turks on the island. Both communities have suffered great upheavals: in 1974, 180,000 Greek Cypriots were forced to flee to the south, while 100,000 Turkish Cypriots fled in the other direction. Wage levels are on average four times higher in the south, where eastern European contract labour is brought in to staff the hotel industry. Unemployment levels in the north, meanwhile, are rising.

The 2nd-century theatre at the ruined city of Curium, 14 km west of Limassol. Curium was a flourishing Mycenaean colony before 1100 BC.

POLITICS

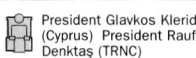

1996 (Cyprus)
1995 (TRNC)

President Glavkos Klerides (Cyprus) President Rauf Denktaş (TRNC)

THE STATE OF THE PARTIES

House of Representatives (Cyprus) 56 members

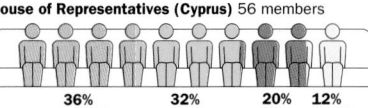

36% DR/LP	32% AKEL	20% DP	12% EDEK

DR/LP = Democratic Rally/Liberal Party   **AKEL** = Progressive Party of the Working People (Communist Party)
DP = Democratic Party   **EDEK** = Cyprus National Democratic Union (Socialist Party)

Legislative Assembly (TRNC) 50 members

68% UBP	28% DMP	4% Other

UBP = National Unity Party   **DMP** = Democratic Struggle Party (composed of: CTP = Republican Turkish Party, TKP = Communal Liberation Party, YDP = New Dawn Party)

The UN-backed proposal of a two-zoned federation for Cyprus is supported by both the Greek and Turkish governments, eager to solve the dispute. Under this plan, each community would have its own territory but share a number of government functions and ministries. TRNC president Rauf Denktaş, mindful of the Greek Cypriots' suppression of the Turks prior to 1974, is unwilling to accept a plan that does not ensure full sovereignty and political equality for Turks. Greek Cypriots, in turn, fear the plan would lead to domination of their affairs by the small Turkish minority, who would be able to veto all government decisions.

WORLD AFFAIRS

 Comm   CSCE   ECE   GATT   OIC

The permanent presence of 2000 UN troops since 1974 manning the 'Green Line' – only the Middle East and Kashmir have longer-standing peace-keeping forces – is estimated to cost in excess of $100 million a year. Cyprus's 1990 application for EU membership is a source of contention.

AID

 $34m (receipts)   No change in 1991

Cyprus receives aid from the international agencies, as well as the EU and countries such as the UK. The TRNC is dependent on aid from Turkey of more than $60 million a year.

CYPRUS

Total Area : 9251 sq. km
(3572 sq. miles)

CHRONOLOGY

Cyprus came, in turn, under the domination of Egypt, Greece, the Byzantines, the Ottomans and Britain.

- ❏ **1960** Independence from Britain.
- ❏ **1963** Following constitutional violation by Greeks, Turkish Cypriots abandon parliament.
- ❏ **1974** President Makarios overthrown in coup supported by Greek military junta. Turkey invades. Partition.

DEFENCE

 $284.5m

 Down 6% in 1991

In addition to UN forces, there are Greek Cypriot, Turkish Cypriot, Greek and Turkish troops posted along the buffer zone that divides the island. Both the 8000-strong Greek Cypriot and 4000-strong Turkish Cypriot armies rely heavily on conscripts.

ECONOMICS

 $6.1bn

 0.52 Cyprus pounds
14922.00 Turkish liras

SCORE CARD

❏ WORLD GNP RANKING	104th
❏ GNP PER CAPITA	$8615
❏ BALANCE OF PAYMENTS	$241.7m
❏ INFLATION	6%
❏ UNEMPLOYMENT	3%

STRENGTHS

Tourism, the basis of the economy. Manufacturing sector and provision of services to Middle Eastern countries.

WEAKNESSES

Tourism damaged by effects of Gulf crisis. Economic stagnation and lack of foreign investment in TRNC. Collapse of Asil Nadir's manufacturing empire – employer of 12% of Turkish Cypriots.

EXPORTS

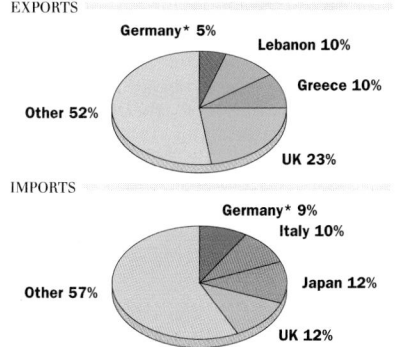

Germany* 5%
Lebanon 10%
Greece 10%
Other 52%
UK 23%

IMPORTS

Germany* 9%
Italy 10%
Other 57%
Japan 12%
UK 12%

RESOURCES

 1.98m kwh (capacity 471,000 kw)

 Not an oil producer; refines 18,600 b/cd

 300,000 sheep, 284,000 pigs, 46,000 cattle

 Asbestos, gypsum, iron, bentonite, copper

Cyprus has continued to supply electricity to the TRNC, although it has not been paid for this. A petrol refinery has been built in a project involving the Greek Cypriot government, BP, Mobil and a local company.

ENVIRONMENT

 0.2% partially protected

Increasing environmental awareness

The protection of the 155 km² Akamas peninsula from the threat of development by landholders, including the Orthodox Church, is a major project. This new national park is home to an unusual variety of plant and bird life, and contains the bay where the rare green turtle breeds.

MEDIA

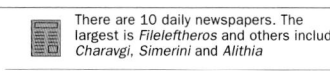 Freedom of speech is guaranteed in both Cyprus and the TRNC

PUBLISHING AND BROADCAST MEDIA

 There are 10 daily newspapers. The largest is *Fileleftheros* and others include *Charavgi*, *Simerini* and *Alithia*

1 state-controlled, 1 independent service

1 state-controlled, 9 independent stations

Cyprus' press is lively and tends to be highly politicized. The radio and TV services for British troops based in Cyprus are also popular.

CRIME

 219 prisoners

 Down 1% in 1990

Crime is not a major problem in Cyprus or the TRNC, where the population is generally law-abiding. Ethnic tensions are largely kept in check by the division of the island. There have been isolated cases of Palestinian-linked terrorism.

EDUCATION

 94%

Education is free and compulsory up to the age of 12 (15 in the TRNC). Many Greek Cypriots go to university abroad.

HEALTH

 1 per 484 people

 Heart diseases, accidents, cancers

Health care is more advanced in the south; sophisticated surgery is carried out at Nicosia General Hospital.

WEALTH

 Wages in the south are 4 times those in the north

CONSUMER GOODS OWNERSHIP

High levels of PC ownership

Income per capita in the south is higher than in mainland Greece, and is comparable to that of Spain.

WORLD RANKING

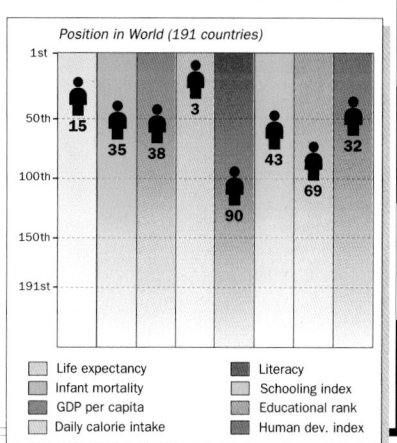

Position in World (191 countries)

Life expectancy	Literacy
Infant mortality	Schooling index
GDP per capita	Educational rank
Daily calorie intake	Human dev. index

CZECH REPUBLIC

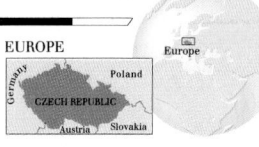

OFFICIAL NAME: Czech Republic   **CAPITAL:** Prague
POPULATION: 10.3 million   **CURRENCY:** Czech koruna   **OFFICIAL LANGUAGE:** Czech

C

L AND-LOCKED IN eastern Europe, the Czech Republic comprises the territories of Bohemia and Moravia and was formerly part of Czechoslovakia. In 1989, Czechoslovakia's 'Velvet Revolution' led to the fall of the communist regime. Free elections followed in 1990. In 1993, the Czech Republic and Slovakia peacefully dissolved their federal union to become two independent states.

CLIMATE

WEATHER CHART

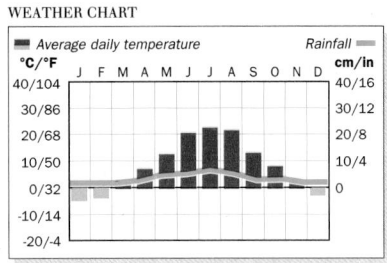

The Czech climate is more moderate than that of Slovakia, though easterly winds bring low temperatures in winter.

COMMUNICATIONS

🛫 **Ruzyně, Prague**   18 ships 443,155 dwt

THE TRANSPORT NETWORK

55,530 km (34,506 miles)	366 km (227 miles)
9439 km (5865 miles)	303 km (188 miles)

New rail links and motorways to Germany are planned. Customs barriers have been installed on the border with Slovakia.

TOURISM

🧳 50m visitors   ⬆ Rising in 1993

MAIN OVERSEAS ARRIVALS

Germany 43%
Austria 8%
Italy 7%
Other 42%

0   10   20   30   40   50   60
% of total arrivals

Revenues from the expansion of tourism have kept the Czech economy flush with hard currency. In 1992, 50 million tourists and day-trippers visited the country, the majority of them Germans, bringing in around $1.2 billion. Prague, which rivals Paris as the most beautiful capital in Europe, is visited by most tourists. Skiing and spa towns are the other main attractions.

CZECH REPUBLIC

Total Area : 78 370 sq. km (30 260 sq. miles)

LAND HEIGHT

1000m/3281ft
500m/1640ft
200m/656ft
150m/492ft

POPULATION

over 1 000 000
over 500 000
over 100 000
over 50 000
over 10 000
10 000

PEOPLE

Czech, Slovak, Hungarian   122 people per km²

THE URBAN/RURAL POPULATION SPLIT

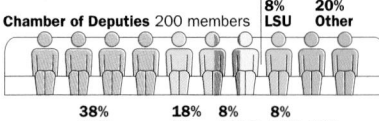

77%   23%

RELIGIOUS PERSUASION

Orthodox Catholic 2%
Protestant 20%
Roman Catholic 50%
Other 28%

Czechs make up 85% and Moravians 14% of the population. The 300,000 Slovaks left in the country after partition now form the largest ethnic minority. Ethnic tensions are few, but there is some resentment against Romanian immigrants. A new commercial elite is emerging alongside ex-communist entrepreneurs. Divorce rates are high.

POLITICS

 1996   President Václav Havel

THE STATE OF THE PARTIES

Chamber of Deputies 200 members   8% LSU   20% Other

38% CDP   18% LB   8% CSDP   8% CDU–CPP

CDP = Civic Democratic Party   **LB** = Left Bloc
CSDP = Czechoslovak Social Democratic Party
LSU = Liberal Social Union   **CDU–CPP** = Christian Democratic Union – Czechoslovak People's Party   **Other** = Association for the Republic – Czechoslovak Republican Party, Civic Democratic Alliance, Movement for Autonomous Democracy – Society for Moravia and Silesia

Senate 81 members

Members are elected for 6 years by universal adult suffrage

In 1990, the Civic Forum coalition of opposition groups won free elections and dissident playwright Václav Havel became president. By 1991, the Civic Forum had splintered and Václav Klaus's CDP emerged as the dominant party. Klaus was a major force behind the split from Slovakia in 1993. The main division in politics now is between the radical privatizers and those who want a more gradual transition to a market-led economy.

C

WORLD AFFAIRS

Good relations with Germany are a priority. However, the issue of property restitution for Germans ejected from the republic in 1945 is a source of friction. Germany has implied that the matter must be resolved before it will back Czech membership of the EU. The Czech Republic has downgraded relations with its V4 neighbours.

AID

 The Czech Republic is an aid recipient   Aid donations are increasing steadily

Aid, mainly from the IMF and the EU, is crucial for modernizing infrastructure such as telecommunications.

DEFENCE

 $804m (est)   Spending is decreasing as cuts are implemented

The split with Slovakia left an army too large and expensive for the new Czech state. In 1994, plans to cut the military by 20,000 were approved. Professional soldiers with a communist past will be the first to go. The Czech Republic has a strong armaments and explosives industry. It is now seeking markets beyond the former Warsaw Pact.

ECONOMICS

 25.7bn (est)   29.96 Czech koruny

SCORE CARD

- ❑ WORLD GNP RANKING.........................59th
- ❑ GNP PER CAPITA $2495
- ❑ BALANCE OF PAYMENTS..............$500m (est)
- ❑ INFLATION 17%
- ❑ UNEMPLOYMENT..................................2.6%

STRENGTHS
Skilled industrial labour force. Good industrial base. Speed of privatization of state industries. Attractive to German investors, including Volkswagen. Draw of Prague as tourist centre.

WEAKNESSES
Lack of diversification in sectors likely to attract overseas investment. Some reluctance to face costs of restructuring. Rising unemployment.

EXPORTS

IMPORTS

RESOURCES

 Nuclear power generates 29% of electricity output 4.9m cattle, 7m pigs, 1m sheep   Not an oil producer   Copper, lead, zinc, coal

Copper, lead, zinc and coal are the chief resources. The government is aiming to phase out the worst-polluting coal-fired power stations. A 2000-MW Soviet-designed nuclear power station at Temelin is due to come on stream in the late 1990s.

ENVIRONMENT

 6%   Public awareness of environmental problems is rising

High pollution levels from the power, chemical and cement industries are the main environmental problem.

MEDIA

 No official censorship

PUBLISHING AND BROADCAST MEDIA

There are 9 daily newspapers. *Mladá Fronta Dnes* has the largest circulation. 2 state-owned services. Several networks

Since the fall of communism, the Czech media has grown rapidly. Political debates are well covered in the press.

CRIME

 8002 prisoners   The crime rate has tripled since 1989

The republic is a major transit point for Turkish drugs destined for Germany. Drug trading, not possession, is illegal.

EDUCATION

 99%

Schooling has reverted to the pre-1945 system. Charles University in Prague was founded in the 13th century.

HEALTH

 1 per 270 people   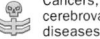 Cancers, heart and cerebrovascular diseases, accidents

In the worst polluted towns, infant mortality reached levels found in the developing world. Wealthy Czechs travel to Germany for complex operations.

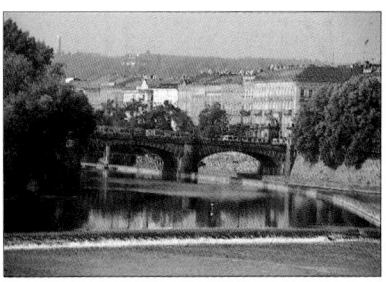
The Vltava River in Prague. Over 50 million tourists, mainly from Europe and the USA, now visit Prague each year.

CHRONOLOGY

Following the collapse of the Austro-Hungarian empire in 1918, the Republic of Czechoslovakia was established.

- ❑ **1968** 'Prague Spring'. Invasion by Warsaw Pact countries.
- ❑ **1989** Beginning of the 'Velvet Revolution'. Demonstrations in main cities. Majority of non-communists in parliament.
- ❑ **1990** Free legislative elections.
- ❑ **1993** Split into the Czech Republic and Slovakia.

WEALTH

 Entrepreneurs in the private sector have rapidly acquired wealth

CONSUMER GOODS OWNERSHIP

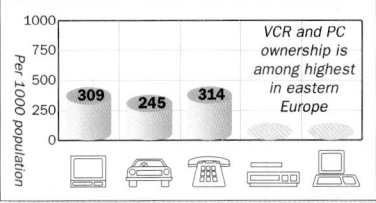

A new entrepreneurial class has emerged since 1989. Almost all Czechs have shares in privatized enterprises.

WORLD RANKING

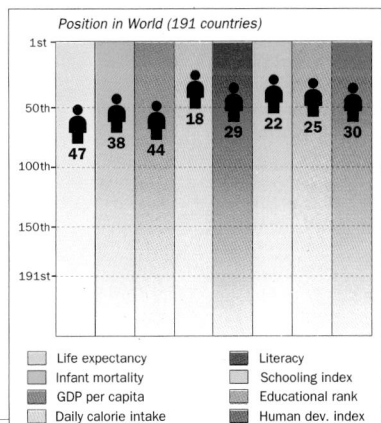

DENMARK

OFFICIAL NAME: Kingdom of Denmark   **CAPITAL:** Copenhagen   **POPULATION:** 5.2 million
CURRENCY: Danish kroner   **OFFICIAL LANGUAGE:** Danish   **OVERSEAS TERRITORIES:** 2

D

THE MOST SOUTHERLY COUNTRY in Scandinavia, Denmark occupies the Jutland peninsula, the islands of Sjælland, Fyn, Lolland and Falster, and over 400 smaller islands. Its terrain is among the flattest in the world. The Faroe Islands and Greenland in the North Atlantic are self-governing associated territories. Politically, Denmark is stable, despite a preponderance of minority governments since 1945. It possesses a long liberal tradition and was one of the first countries to establish a welfare system, in the 1930s.

TOURISM

51.4 m bed-nights. Denmark does not record visitor numbers

Up 13% in 1992

MAIN OVERSEAS ARRIVALS

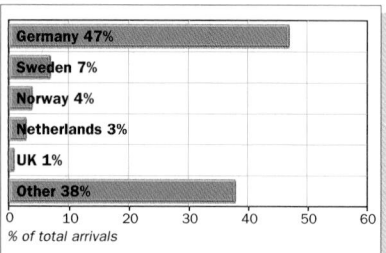

Germany 47%
Sweden 7%
Norway 4%
Netherlands 3%
UK 1%
Other 38%

% of total arrivals

Denmark is a popular destination for Scandinavian, German and Dutch tourists. The principal attractions are Copenhagen – with its Tivoli Gardens and fine 18th-century architecture – Legoland, the countryside and seaside resorts. Greenland attracts wildlife tourists.

CLIMATE

WEATHER CHART

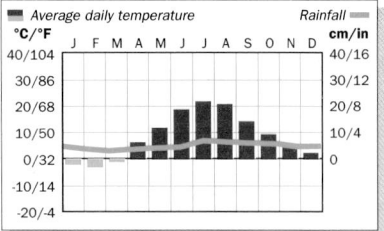

Denmark's temperate, damp climate is one of the keys to its agricultural success. The Faroes are windy, foggy and cool. Greenland's climate ranges north–south from arctic to sub-arctic.

The island of Fyn, like the rest of Denmark, is flat and depends on coastal defences to prevent flooding by the sea.

COMMUNICATIONS

Kastrup, Copenhagen
9.27m passengers

499 ships
6.74m dwt

THE TRANSPORT NETWORK

71,063 km (44,158 miles)

650 km (404 miles)

523 km (325 miles)

417 km (259 miles)

Denmark maintains an extensive, well-integrated transport network, with bus, rail and ferry services linking the whole kingdom. State-owned companies predominate, although plans to privatize parts of the ferry and rail systems have been mooted. Denmark wishes to reduce the subsidies paid to transport, a major part of public spending. A few private companies, supported by state grants, operate in the Faroes and Greenland.

Major new construction projects focus on bridge and tunnel links. The much-postponed Storebælt project to connect Denmark's main islands, Fyn and Sjælland, is now due to be completed in 1995. Tunnel and bridge projects are also being discussed with Sweden and Germany.

DENMARK

Total Area : 43 070 sq. km (16 629 sq. miles)

POPULATION

over 1 000 000
over 100 000
over 10 000
under 10 000

LAND HEIGHT

175m/574ft
Sea Level
Ferry link

D

PEOPLE

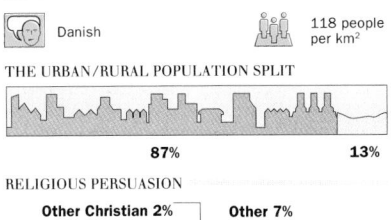

Danish

118 people per km²

THE URBAN/RURAL POPULATION SPLIT

87%   13%

RELIGIOUS PERSUASION

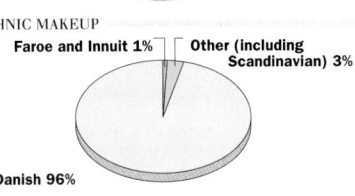

Other Christian 2%   Other 7%

Evangelical Lutheran 91%

ETHNIC MAKEUP

Faroe and Innuit 1%   Other (including Scandinavian) 3%

Danish 96%

Danish society is homogeneous. Out of a population of 5.2 million, just 200,000 are foreign citizens, mainly from other Scandinavian or EU states. The most visible minority groups are the Inuit, Greenland's indigenous inhabitants, and the Turkish community. Rising unemployment has engendered some ethnic tension, although racially-motivated attacks are still rare.

Denmark has undergone profound social changes over the last 20 years. The role of women has been transformed. Helped by Denmark's extensive social and educational provision, 76% of women now work in part-time or full-time jobs. Denmark provides the best state child-support in Europe. Almost 50% of children under two, and 67% of three to six-year-olds are in day nurseries, compared with under 30% in the 1970s.

Less than half the population lives in a nuclear family, partly due to the high divorce rate. Marriage is also becoming less common; almost 40% of children are brought up by unmarried couples or single parents. Cohabitating couples now have the same legal rights as those who are married. In 1990, Denmark became the first country to allow registered partnerships between homosexual couples, effectively granting them the same legal married status as heterosexuals.

POPULATION AGE BREAKDOWN

%	▨ 0–14	▨ 15–64		☐ 65+	
15.5%	10.6%	12.3%	14.4%	15.4%	15.5%
	64.2%	64.4%	64.8%	67.6%	68.2%
	25.2%	23.3%	20.8%	17%	16.3%
	1960	1970	1980	1990	2000

of population by age group

POLITICS

 1994

 HM Queen Margrethe II

THE STATE OF THE PARTIES

Parliament 179 members

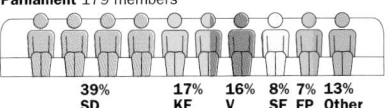

| 39% SD | 17% KF | 16% V | 8% SF | 7% FP | 13% Other |

SD = Social Democratic Party   KF = Conservative People's Party   **V** = Liberal Party   **SF** = Socialist People's Party   **FP** = Progress Party   **Other** = Centre Democrats, Radical Liberals, Christian People's Party

Denmark is a constitutional monarchy and a multiparty democracy. The associated territories of Greenland and the Faroe Islands have home rule.

MAIN POLITICAL ISSUES

Relations with the EU

In recent years, Denmark's left-of-centre parties have been suspicious of any EU moves for closer ties between member states. This was highlighted by the stir caused by the ratification of the Maastricht Treaty in 1992. The Treaty was approved by parliament but rejected in a referendum. The people objected to proposals for a monetary union, a common defence force and voting rights for European citizens living in Denmark. The result threatened the Treaty and embarrassed the government. Later that year, at an EU summit meeting, Denmark was exempted from clauses on monetary union, defence and European citizenship. A new referendum was held in 1993 and the Treaty approved, leaving the way clear for other countries, such as the UK, to ratify it.

Immigration

In what many saw as a vindication for Danish liberal traditions, Prime Minister Poul Schlüter was forced to resign in 1993 over the 'Tamilgate'

WORLD AFFAIRS

 EU   NATO   CSCE   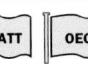 GATT   OECD

Relations with the rest of Europe are the most important foreign policy concern, notably the issue of a common European defence policy. Denmark is limiting its defence relations to NATO. However, it is giving priority to promoting economic ties with Norway, Sweden and Finland and is promoting their entry into the EU. Links with former Eastern Bloc states, especially those on the Baltic, are being fostered. In part, this is a way of influencing their governments to reduce pollution.

Internationally, Denmark has a long history of involvement with the developing world, particularly aid programmes in Africa.

Uffe Ellemann-Jensen, charismatic Liberal opposition leader.

Poul Schlüter, resigned as premier over Tamil refugees immigration issue.

affair. A judicial enquiry ruled that he had falsely denied in parliament that immigration officials were hindering the entry of the families of Tamil workers resident in Denmark. However, the issue of how many refugees Denmark should take from the world's trouble spots, and how they should be integrated into society, continues to be a point of national debate.

PROFILE

Denmark's intricate electoral system ensures that parliament truly reflects voters' wishes, but also tends to lead to minority governments. SD governments were predominant until 1982. A decade of Conservative-Liberal rule under Prime Minister Poul Schlüter followed. In 1993 the SD regained power. However, the conservative coalition under Liberal leader Uffe Ellemann-Jensen has since been making ground in opposition.

Policy differences between the two main political groups are few, although arguments exist about the best way of reducing the tax burden without cutting the large budget for the comprehensive Danish social security system.

CHRONOLOGY

Founded in the 10th century, Denmark is Europe's oldest monarchy. It was the dominant Baltic power until the 17th century, when it was eclipsed by Sweden.

❑ **1815** Denmark forced to cede Norway to Swedish rule.

❑ **1849** First democratic constitution.

❑ **1864** Denmark forced to cede provinces of Schleswig and Holstein after losing war with Prussia.

❑ **1914–1918** Denmark neutral in First World War.

❑ **1915** Universal adult suffrage introduced. Rise of Social Democratic Party (SD).

❑ **1920** Northern Schleswig votes to return to Danish rule.

D

AID

 $1.2bn (donations)   Up 2% in 1991

In GNP terms, Denmark is one of the world's leading aid donors, contributing an average 1% of its national income. It supports both economic and social development projects and policy reforms. Aid is an important political issue; the current debate is over its use as a tool to promote democracy.

Denmark provides aid to Asia and Latin America, but its closest ties are with Africa. Tanzania is the largest single aid recipient. Denmark has also provided considerable support to the other south African SADC states.

DEFENCE

 $2.6bn   Down 1% in 1992

0	*Defence spending as % GDP*	40

2%

DANISH ARMED FORCES

Denmark was neutral until 1945. Apart from its NATO commitments, defence has a low priority. Spending accounts for 2% of GDP. Its troops have joined UN forces on peace-keeping duties in former Yugoslavia. 10,000 of the army's troops are conscripts. Denmark does not have plans to join the WEU forces.

ECONOMICS

 $122bn   6.79 Danish kroner

SCORE CARD

- ❏ WORLD GNP RANKING...........................26th
- ❏ GNP PER CAPITA $24,388
- ❏ BALANCE OF PAYMENTS $4.6bn
- ❏ INFLATION 2.1%
- ❏ UNEMPLOYMENT................................9.5%

EXPORTS

IMPORTS

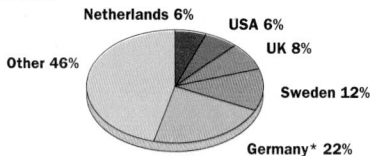

STRENGTHS
Successful high-tech, high-profit manufacturing industries. Low inflation and moderate budget deficit. Large gas and oil reserves. Skilled population. Large balance of payments surplus.

WEAKNESSES
Rising budget deficit and heavy tax burden. High unemployment, currently around 11%. Low GDP growth; 1.3% in 1992. Frequent minority governments.

PROFILE
Denmark's mix of a large state sector and a private sector has been successful. At $24,388, GNP per capita is one of the highest among the OECD countries.

During the 1980s, the advent of a minority conservative government and the prospect of the wider European market led to a number of major policy changes. A stable exchange rate policy was introduced and tighter budget controls were aimed at reducing inflation and reversing the balance of payments deficit. Real GNP per capita

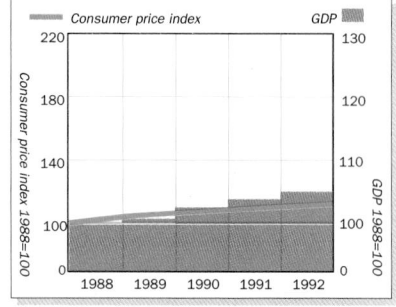

ECONOMIC PERFORMANCE INDICATOR

grew by 2.1% a year from 1981–1991. The balance of payments went into surplus and inflation was cut to 2%. Denmark refused to join the EMU, but was one of the few countries able to meet the convergence criteria.

After 1991, the recession in Europe led to slower growth. Denmark is expected to weather the recession better than many of its EU neighbours, but high unemployment is a problem. The government wants to impose budgetary constraint and tax cuts to restore growth. However, any attempts to reduce generous welfare provisions will meet with strong opposition.

DENMARK : MAJOR BUSINESSES

RESOURCES

25.7bn kwh (capacity 9.13m kw)

156,900 b/d (reserves 729,618,000 bbl)

9.1m pigs, 2.2m cattle, 86,000 sheep

Natural gas, oil

ELECTRICITY GENERATION

Hydro 0%

Thermal 98% (25.1bn kwh)

Nuclear 0%

Other 2% (604m kwh)

% of total generation by type

Although a net oil exporter since 1993, Denmark is still an overall importer of energy. The expansion of North Sea

oil and gas output should balance import and export costs by 1997. Agriculture is highly efficient.

DENMARK : LAND USE

Cropland
Forest
Pasture
Pigs
Cereals

ENVIRONMENT

10% (9% partially protected)

Very strict laws in Greenland to protect polar ecosystems

ENVIRONMENTAL TREATIES

Yes   Yes

No   Yes

The environment is of popular and governmental concern. Denmark's regulations, including those aimed at reducing ozone-destroying emissions and water pollution, are probably the strictest in Europe. Fears that they may be eroded has been a key element in Danish ambivalence towards the EU. In 1993, Denmark was successful in persuading the EU to locate the Environmental Agency in Copenhagen. It hopes to extend its own standards to the rest of Europe.

MEDIA

Media censorship is forbidden by the constitution

PUBLISHING AND BROADCAST MEDIA

There are 49 daily newspapers, including *BT*, *Politiken*, *Ekstra Bladet* and *Berlingske Tidende*

1 state-owned, 30 independent services

1 state-owned, 300 independent services

Thor, Astra 1B, Intelsat V1 F1

The cable network is growing

The media has a long history of political independence, and objectivity is prized. Most of the press has a political viewpoint, but expression of this is largely limited to editorials. The tone of both TV and the press is serious; Denmark does not have a scandal-mongering tabloid press as found in the USA, UK and Germany. Invasion of privacy laws are strict.

CRIME

3469 prisoners

Down 2% in 1990

CRIME RATES

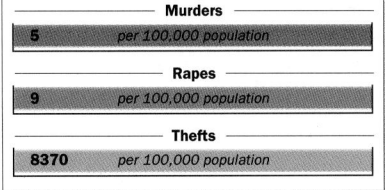

Murders

5   *per 100,000 population*

Rapes

9   *per 100,000 population*

Thefts

8370   *per 100,000 population*

The main concern is that mafia-style organized crime could be imported from eastern Europe. Computer hacking and drug trafficking are also problems.

EDUCATION

100%

0   *Education spending as % GNP*   25

7.6%

THE EDUCATION SYSTEM

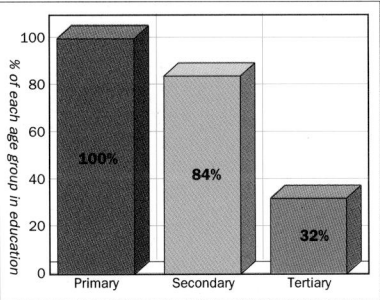

% of each age group in education

100%   84%   32%

Primary   Secondary   Tertiary

The average educational level is high, in part reflecting the need for a skilled workforce. Formal schooling begins at age seven and is mandatory for nine years. However, most children receive pre-school education and over 90% of pupils go on at the age of 16 to further academic or vocational training.

HEALTH

1 per 375 people

Heart diseases, cancers, accidents

0   *Health spending as % GNP*   25

0.5%

Denmark was one of the first countries to introduce a state social welfare system. The national health service, which still provides free treatment for almost everything, is the main reason for Denmark's high taxes. Any attempts to reduce expenditure will meet with strong opposition. Repeated surveys show that most Danes prefer their system to those based on private health insurance.

WEALTH

Dairy product processor, 120 Danish kroner per hour; airline pilot, 27,671 Danish kroner per month

CONSUMER GOODS OWNERSHIP

Per 1000 population

528   313   856   204   26

Most Danes are comfortably off. Income distribution is more even than in many Western countries and social mobility is high. Free higher education has made access to the professions more a question of ability than family wealth or connections. Many of Denmark's top industrialists have made their fortunes within the last 30 years. However, wealth is still quite concentrated. The richest 10% of Danes control almost two thirds of national assets.

The social security system means that Denmark suffers little from social deprivation. The most disadvantaged groups are refugees and recent immigrants.

WORLD RANKING

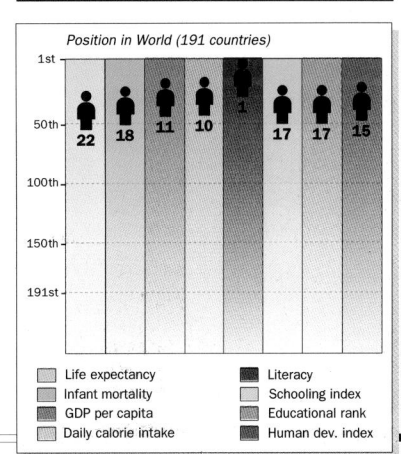

Position in World (191 countries)

1st
50th   22   18   11   10   1   17   17   15
100th
150th
191st

Life expectancy   Literacy
Infant mortality   Schooling index
GDP per capita   Educational rank
Daily calorie intake   Human dev. index

DJIBOUTI

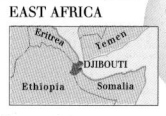

EAST AFRICA

OFFICIAL NAME: Republic of Djibouti **CAPITAL:** Djibouti
POPULATION: 500,000 **CURRENCY:** Djibouti franc **OFFICIAL LANGUAGES:** Arabic and French

D

A CITY STATE with a desert hinterland, Djibouti lies in northeast Africa on the strait joining the Red Sea and the Indian Ocean. Known from 1967 as the French Territory of the Afars and Issas, Djibouti became independent in 1977. Its economy relies on the port, the railway to Addis Ababa, and French aid. A guerrilla war erupted in 1991 as a result of tension between the country's two major ethnic groups – the Issas in the south and the Afars in the north.

CLIMATE

WEATHER CHART

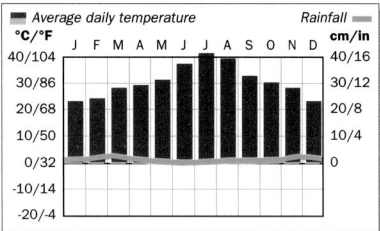

Despite extremely low rainfall, the monsoon season is characterized by very humid conditions. Even locals find the June to August heat unbearable.

COMMUNICATIONS

Ambouli Intl, Djibouti   2 ships
2300 dwt

THE TRANSPORT NETWORK

| 3067 km (1906 miles) | None |
| 100 km (62 miles) | None |

The key to Djibouti's livelihood is its port, created by the French in the 19th century and now a modern container facility. The railway to Addis Ababa is one of Ethiopia's key links to the sea.

TOURISM

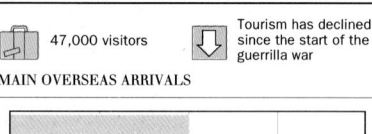 47,000 visitors   Tourism has declined since the start of the guerrilla war

MAIN OVERSEAS ARRIVALS

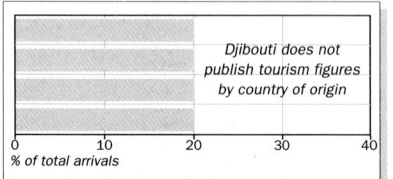

Djibouti does not publish tourism figures by country of origin

% of total arrivals

Most visitors are passing through on their way to Ethiopia, or coming to see relatives working in the port.

 Nomadic Djiboutian village, close to Balho near the Ethiopian border.

PEOPLE

 Somali, Afar, French, Arabic   17 people per km²

THE URBAN/RURAL POPULATION SPLIT

81%   19%

ETHNIC MAKEUP

Other 5%
Afar 35%
Issa 60%

The two main tribes are the Afars and Issas; tension between these groups developed into a guerrilla war in 1991. The population was swelled in 1992 by 20,000 Somali refugees. The rural people are mostly nomadic.

POPULATION

◎ over 100 000
• under 10 000

LAND HEIGHT

1000m/3281ft
500m/1640ft
200m/656ft
Sea Level
-200m/656ft

POLITICS

 1997   President Hassan Gouled Aptidon

THE STATE OF THE PARTIES

National Assembly 65 members

100% RPP

RPP = People's Progress Party

Since independence, politics has been dominated by President Aptidon, an Issa, and a carefully chosen group of Issa and Afar politicians. Behind the scenes, French backing is essential to the ruling group. Afar fears of Issa domination erupted in 1991, when the Afar guerrilla group FRUD took control of much of the country against a background of similar ethnic conflicts in neighbouring states. The French intervened militarily to keep Aptidon in power, but forced him to hold elections in 1992. These were won by the RPP, on a turnout of only 49%. The expected parliamentary reforms did not follow, to the displeasure of the French. The country remains divided between RPP-controlled and FRUD-controlled areas.

DJIBOUTI

Total Area : 23 200 sq. km
(8958 sq. miles)

WORLD AFFAIRS

Relations with France, which wants to see faster moves to reform, have soured. Djibouti, Ethiopia and Eritrea all wish to contain Afar militancy; the ethnic group crosses national borders and has demanded its own state.

AID

 $120m (receipts)   French defence-related aid has increased

France is the major donor, effectively financing one third of government expenditure. Djibouti has also received aid from Saudi Arabia and Kuwait.

DEFENCE

 Estimated to be 50% of government expenditure in 1992   Large increase in 1992 to finance anti-FRUD operations

Djibouti's armed forces were increased five-fold in 1992 to an estimated 12,000 personnel, mostly army, to counteract FRUD guerrilla activity. There is a 3800-strong French garrison.

ECONOMICS

 $480m   177.76 Djibouti francs

SCORE CARD

- ❏ WORLD GNP RANKING 162nd
- ❏ GNP PER CAPITA $960
- ❏ BALANCE OF PAYMENTS..................$–43.8m
- ❏ INFLATION 3.2%
- ❏ UNEMPLOYMENT....................................40%

STRENGTHS

Free port in key Red Sea location; made large profits from 1991 Gulf War and from 1992 US and UN intervention in Somalia. Development as container transshipment port continuing.

WEAKNESSES

Dependence on French aid and garrison. Civil war has delayed planned Saudi investment. Other ports on Red Sea now providing stiff competition.

EXPORTS

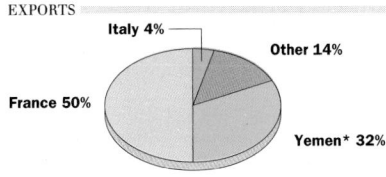

Italy 4%
Other 14%
France 50%
Yemen* 32%

IMPORTS

Italy 5%
Japan 5%
USA 3%
Ethiopia 11%
Other 45%
France 31%

RESOURCES

 175m kwh (capacity 38,000 kw)   Not an oil producer and has no refineries

 415,000 sheep, 72,000 cattle, 58,000 camels   Gypsum, mica, amethyst, sulphur

The few mineral resources are scarcely exploited. Geothermal energy is being developed and natural gas has recently been found. The war has delayed attempts to develop underground water supplies for agriculture.

ENVIRONMENT

 0.4%   Minimal industry presents no ecological threat

The concentration of business around Djibouti port means the inland desert areas are not threatened. Ecological issues are not a national concern.

MEDIA

 The press was freed from restrictions in 1992, but with little effect; most is still state-owned

PUBLISHING AND BROADCAST MEDIA

There are no daily newspapers. The only weekly, *La Nation de Djibouti*, is published by the government

1 state-owned service

1 state-owned service

Djibouti is a member of the Arab Satellite Communications Organization. It has two earth stations for radio, TV and telecommunications.

CRIME

 Djibouti does not publish prison figures   Crime has risen dramatically in northern areas

Crime is difficult to define in a guerrilla war. The government has accused FRUD of atrocities, but its own human rights record has been criticized by Amnesty International. Livestock smuggling across the Red Sea is a problem.

EDUCATION

 48%

Schooling is mostly in French, although there has been a growing emphasis on Islamic teaching, particularly as Saudi Arabia has declared an interest in providing aid for education. Djibouti does not provide university education.

HEALTH

 1 per 5604 people   Respiratory and heart diseases

AIDS is a growing problem in Djibouti port, with its large prostitute population. Estimates suggested 3500 HIV-positive cases in 1992, as against government figures of 1600. Small French-financed hospitals cater for the urban elite.

CHRONOLOGY

Formerly the Islamic state of Adal, the French made Djibouti the capital of French Somaliland in 1896.

- ❏ **1917** Railway from Addis Ababa reaches Djibouti port.
- ❏ **1946** Given French Overseas Territory status.
- ❏ **1977** Independence. Hassan Gouled Aptidon president.
- ❏ **1981** One-party state declared.
- ❏ **1989** Violence erupts between Afar and Issa groups.
- ❏ **1991** FRUD opposition formed. Launches armed insurrection.

WEALTH

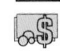 Minimum wage, 15,860 Djibouti francs per month; senior manager (not expatriate), 700,000 Djibouti francs per month

CONSUMER GOODS OWNERSHIP

VCR and PC ownership is limited to a small elite

55   18   23

As in many African states, wealth is concentrated among those closest to government. Djiboutians working in the port also do well, although much port labour is expatriate. The war has had little effect on port life, as it is almost completely isolated from the rest of the country. The nomads of the interior are the poorest group.

Trade in the mild narcotic *qat*, grown in Ethiopia and shipped through Djibouti, is highly lucrative. The state is now taking its share of the profits, granting export licences to only a few favoured traders. In Djibouti, as in Yemen and Somalia, *qat* chewing is an age-old, if expensive, social ritual.

WORLD RANKING

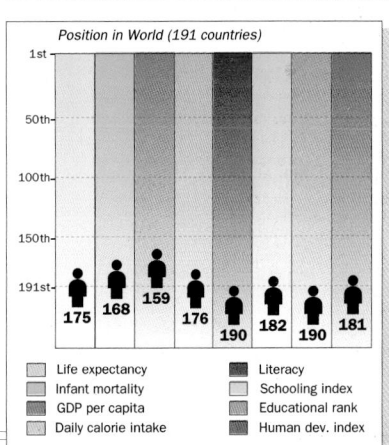

Position in World (191 countries)

1st
50th
100th
150th
191st

175   168   159   176   190   182   190   181

- Life expectancy
- Infant mortality
- GDP per capita
- Daily calorie intake
- Literacy
- Schooling index
- Educational rank
- Human dev. index

D

DOMINICA

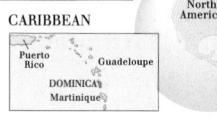

OFFICIAL NAME: Commonwealth of Dominica **CAPITAL:** Roseau
POPULATION: 83,000 **CURRENCY:** East Caribbean dollar **OFFICIAL LANGUAGE:** English

D

DOMINICA IS RENOWNED as the Caribbean island that resisted European colonization until the 18th century, when it was controlled first by the French, then, from 1759, by the British. Known as the 'Nature Island' due to its spectacular, lush and abundant flora and fauna, which are protected by extensive national parks, Dominica is the most mountainous of the Lesser Antilles. Located between Guadeloupe and Martinique in the West Indian Windward Islands group, its volcanic origin has given it very fertile soils and the second largest boiling lake in the world.

CLIMATE

WEATHER CHART

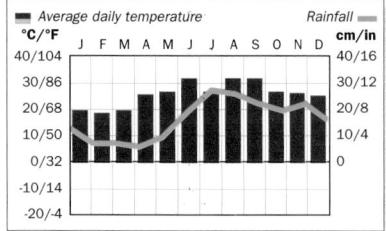

Part of the Windward Islands group in the eastern Caribbean, Dominica is subject to constant trade winds. The rainy season is in the summer, and tropical depressions and hurricanes are likely between June and November. Short, thundery showers in the late afternoon and evening are common all year round.

COMMUNICATIONS

Canefield, Roseau
108,179 passengers

2 ships
1600 dwt

THE TRANSPORT NETWORK

750 km
(466 miles)

None

None

None

The two airports can take only small propeller aircraft. Improving the road system is now a priority.

TOURISM

55,211 visitors

Up 5% in 1991

MAIN OVERSEAS ARRIVALS

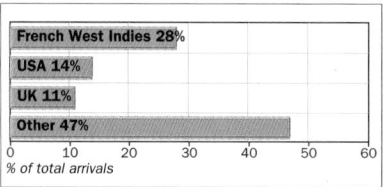

French West Indies 28%	
USA 14%	
UK 11%	
Other 47%	

% of total arrivals

The lack of an airport able to take commercial jetliners (visitors arrive on connecting flights from Barbados or Antigua) has made Dominica less accessible to mass-market tourism than its neighbours. Eco-tourism is growing, with visitors coming to view the national parks with their rare indigenous birds, hot springs and sulphur pools.

PEOPLE

French Creole, English

133 people per km²

THE URBAN/RURAL POPULATION SPLIT

41%   59%

RELIGIOUS PERSUASION

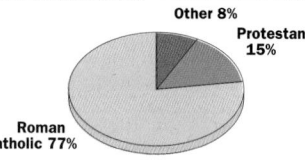

Other 8%
Protestant 15%
Roman Catholic 77%

The majority of Dominicans are descendants of Africans brought over to work the banana plantations.
Family life is based on the extended family and in rural areas is often matriarchal.

POLITICS

 1995

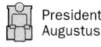 President Clarence Augustus Seignoret

THE STATE OF THE PARTIES

House of Assembly 30 members

49%
DFP

27%
DUWP

24%
LPD

DFP = Dominica Freedom Party **DUWP** = Dominica United Workers' Party **LPD** = Labour Party of Dominica

Dominica's electoral system is based on the British model. Politicians tend to come from the professional classes – usually young lawyers and doctors. Occasionally the larger farmers, who provide most party funding, stand for elections. The DFP, led by Dame Eugenia Charles, has held power since 1980. The dominant political issue is the proposal that Dominica join with the three other islands of the Windward group to form a political and economic union, leading to a single state. The government broadly supports the proposal, but any change will be subject to a referendum.

WORLD AFFAIRS

| Comm | OAS | Caricom | ACP | ECLAC |

A disagreement with Latin American states over banana exports to the EU is the dominant issue. Dominica wishes to maintain its preferential market share and has threatened to leave the Organization of American States.

DOMINICA

Total Area : 750 sq. km
(290 sq. miles)

LAND HEIGHT

1000m/3281ft
500m/1640ft
200m/656ft
Sea Level

POPULATION
over 10 000
under 10 000

0   10 km
0   10 miles

Guadeloupe Passage

Pennville
Clifton
Guillet
Vieille Case
Thibaud
Belmanier
Bense Calibishie
Larieu
Portsmouth
Prince Rupert Bay
Dos D'Ane
Glanvillia
Wesley
Dublanc
Morne Diablotins 1447m
Marigot
Bataka
NORTHERN FOREST RESERVE
Melville Hall
Colihaut
Coulibistri
Salibia
Gaulette
Morne Raquette
Salisbury
Layou
Castle Bruce
St Joseph
Good Hope
Saint Sauveur
Mahaut
Petite Soufrière
Massacre
Morne Trois Pitons
Morne Aux Frégates
Rosalie
Canefield Airport
Roger
Trafalgar
Laudat
La Plaine
ROSEAU
Charlotte Ville
Giraudel
Boetica
Loubiere
Bellevue
Chopin
Pichelin
Délices
Pointe Michel
Petite Savane
Soufrière
Tête Morne
Berekua
Fond St. Jean
Scotts Head Village
Martinique Passage

ATLANTIC OCEAN
CARIBBEAN SEA

D

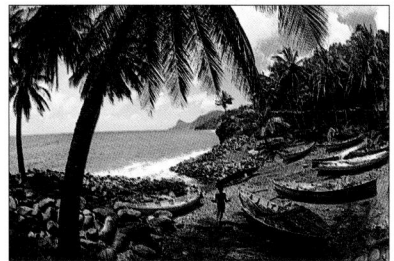

Inshore fishing boats, which mostly supply the domestic market, on a typical Dominican beach.

AID

 $15m (receipts)   A favoured recipient of aid in the region

The generous US aid of the 1980s was a response to Dominica's support for American foreign policy in the region. The EU and UK are also major donors.

DEFENCE

 Dominican Defence Force officially disbanded in 1981   Not applicable

Dominica has no armed forces, but it does participate in the US-sponsored Regional Security System.

ECONOMICS

 $181m   2.70 East Caribbean dollars

SCORE CARD

- ❏ WORLD GNP RANKING 181st
- ❏ GNP PER CAPITA $2200
- ❏ BALANCE OF PAYMENTS ....$−26.3m
- ❏ INFLATION 6.1%
- ❏ UNEMPLOYMENT...................................10%

STRENGTHS

Bananas have proved a useful foreign currency earner, though this sector is now threatened.

WEAKNESSES

Dependence on preferential access to US and EU markets for its banana crop (70% of export earnings) highlighted by US moves to deregulate the banana trade. Dominica cannot compete with cheaper Latin American fruit.

EXPORTS

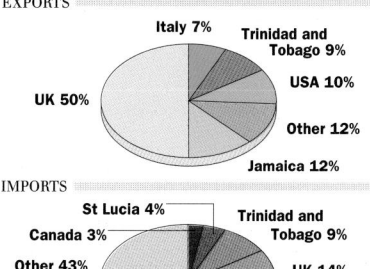

Italy 7%, Trinidad and Tobago 9%, USA 10%, Other 12%, Jamaica 12%, UK 50%

IMPORTS

St Lucia 4%, Canada 3%, Other 43%, Trinidad and Tobago 9%, UK 14%, USA 27%

RESOURCES

 30m kwh (capacity 8000 kw)   Not an oil producer and has no refineries

 9000 cattle, 7000 sheep, 5000 pigs   None

Dominica has no natural resources and has to import almost all its energy. The development of hydroelectric power at Morne Trois Pitons has been proposed.

ENVIRONMENT

 9%   Hydro-power plans threaten Morne Trois Pitons National Park

The expansion of both agriculture and timber harvesting is threatening Dominica's rainforest; already there is more land under cultivation than planned by the government. Tourism does not currently pose a threat, but this could change if the government succeeds in raising funds to expand the airports to take jets. Two species of parrot – the *Amazonia imperialis* and the Red Necked – are threatened, despite conservation orders. Turtles living on coral reefs off the island will soon be protected.

MEDIA

 No government restrictions

PUBLISHING AND BROADCAST MEDIA

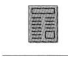 There are no daily newspapers. The dominant newspaper is the bi-weekly *New Chronicle*, which takes a centre-left editorial stance

 No TV service   1 state-owned station

Local franchises, offering cable TV with selected US networks, serve one third of the island. Broadcasts from other Caribbean states can also be received. Dominica has one cinema.

CRIME

 Dominica does not publish prison figures   Up 62% between 1983 and 1986

Dominica has a lower crime rate than most of its Caribbean neighbours. Burglary and armed robbery are the major concerns; murders are rare. Justice is based on British common law and administered by the Eastern Caribbean Supreme Court, which is based in St Lucia.

EDUCATION

 94%

Education is based on the British system, and retains the selective 11-plus exam for entrance to high school. Students go on to the University of the West Indies or, increasingly, to colleges in the USA and the UK.

CHRONOLOGY

Colonized first by the French, Dominica came under British control in 1759.

- ❏ **1951** Universal suffrage.
- ❏ **1975** Morne Trois Pitons national park established.
- ❏ **1978** Independence from UK. Patrick John first prime minister.
- ❏ **1980** Eugenia Charles, the Caribbean's first woman prime minister, elected.
- ❏ **1981** Two coup attempts, backed by Patrick John, foiled.
- ❏ **1991** First meeting with Grenada, St Lucia, and St Vincent and the Grenadines on constitution for political union.

HEALTH

 1 per 2623 people   Heart and respiratory diseases, cancers

There are 44 health centres, but difficult communications hamper emergency hospital access for people living in the interior.

WEALTH

 Agricultural field hand, 2 East Caribbean dollars per hour; office manager, 9 East Caribbean dollars per hour

CONSUMER GOODS OWNERSHIP

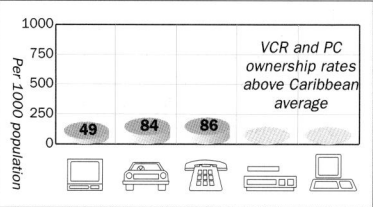

VCR and PC ownership rates above Caribbean average. 49, 84, 86

Wealth disparities are not as marked as on the larger Caribbean islands. Dominica now has access to US cable shopping networks. New Japanese cars are particularly favoured.

WORLD RANKING

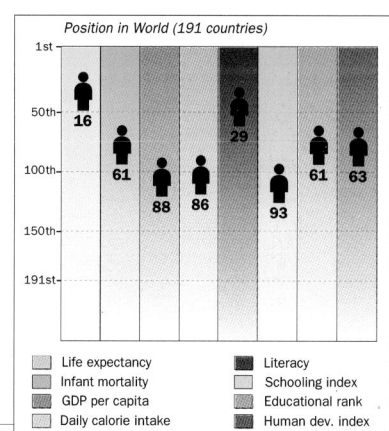

Position in World (191 countries): 16, 61, 88, 86, 29, 93, 61, 63

Life expectancy, Infant mortality, GDP per capita, Daily calorie intake, Literacy, Schooling index, Educational rank, Human dev. index

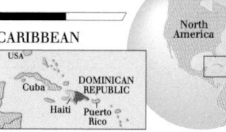

CARIBBEAN

DOMINICAN REPUBLIC

D

OFFICIAL NAME: Dominican Republic **CAPITAL:** Santo Domingo
POPULATION: 7.5 million **CURRENCY:** Dominican Republic peso **OFFICIAL LANGUAGE:** Spanish

THE LARGEST TOURIST DESTINATION in the Caribbean, greatly favoured by Germans and Italians, the Dominican Republic lies 970 km southeast of Florida. Once ruled by Spain, it occupies the eastern two thirds of the island of Hispaniola and boasts both the highest point (Pico Duarte, 3175 m) and the lowest point (Lake Enriquillo, 44 m below sea level) in the West Indies. Frequent coups and a strong US influence mark its recent history.

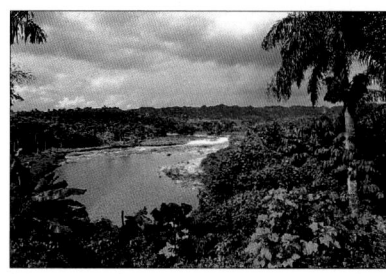

View south from Pico Duarte along the fertile banks of the Río Yaque del Norte.

CLIMATE

WEATHER CHART

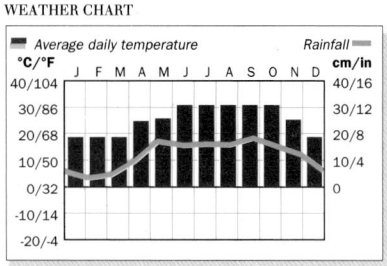

The trade winds blow all year round, providing relief from the tropical heat. The hurricane season runs from June until November.

COMMUNICATIONS

Aeropuerto Intl de las Américas, Santo Domingo
1.79m passengers

12 ships
12,500 dwt

THE TRANSPORT NETWORK

12,000 km (7457 miles)		None
1746 km (1085 miles)		None

Transport is mainly by road; railways are used for transporting sugar cane and ores. Improvements to Santo Domingo's airport, aimed at increasing tourism, were completed in 1992.

TOURISM

1.53m visitors

Up 10% in 1990

MAIN OVERSEAS ARRIVALS

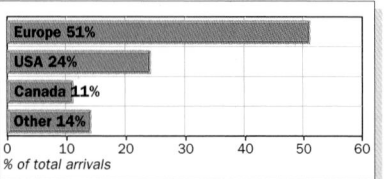

The Dominican Republic has good beaches and a hotel capacity of 30,000 rooms, the highest in the Caribbean.

PEOPLE

Spanish, French Creole

149 people per km²

THE URBAN/RURAL POPULATION SPLIT

60%   40%

RELIGIOUS PERSUASION

Other 5%

Roman Catholic 95%

The white population, primarily the descendants of Spanish settlers, still owns most of the land. The mixed race majority – about 73% – controls much of the republic's commerce, and forms the bulk of the professional middle classes. Blacks, the descendants of Africans, are mainly small-scale farmers and often the victims of latent racism, especially in business. Women in the black community work the farms; in the white and mixed race communities women are starting to appear in the professions.

POLITICS

1994

President Sr Joaquín Balaguer Ricardo

THE STATE OF THE PARTIES

Chamber of Deputies 120 members

43% PRSC   41% PLD   16% Other

PRSC = Christian Socialist Reform Party **PLD** = Dominican Liberation Party Other = Dominican Revolutionary Party, Independent Revolutionary Party

Senate 30 members

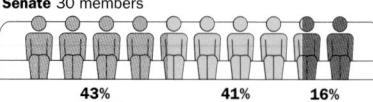

43% PRSC   41% PLD   16% Other

Affluent white landowners and the military hold power behind the scenes; the landowners fund the major political parties, while the military makes clear its support for preferred candidates. There is little political choice between the main parties; all are centre-right. Two octogenarians continue to dominate politics – Balaguer of the PRSC and Bosch of the PLD. Cutbacks in government spending are causing popular disaffection.

DOMINICAN REPUBLIC

Total Area : 48 730 sq. km (18 815 sq. miles)

POPULATION

over 1 000 000
over 100 000
over 50 000
over 10 000
under 10 000

LAND HEIGHT

2000m/6562ft
1000m/3281ft
500m/1640ft
200m/656ft
Sea Level

0   50 km

WORLD AFFAIRS

 Caricom ECLAC GATT Lomé OAS

The Dominican Republic's main concerns are whether to join Caribbean or Central and South American economic organizations. It has uneasy relations with its neighbour, Haiti.

AID

 $66m (receipts)   Down 34% in 1991

Substantial foreign aid is received from the USA and, more recently, from the EU under the Lomé Convention.

DEFENCE

 $35m   Up 4% in 1991

The 25,000-strong military, apart from its interest in domestic politics, concentrates on preventing illegal immigration from Haiti. The main equipment supplier is the USA.

ECONOMICS

 $7.5bn   12.48 Dominican Republic pesos

SCORE CARD

❑ WORLD GNP RANKING	90th
❑ GNP PER CAPITA	$1000
❑ BALANCE OF PAYMENTS	$–58.4m
❑ INFLATION	4.6%
❑ UNEMPLOYMENT	30%

STRENGTHS

Dramatic growth in tourism in recent years. Mining – mainly of nickel and gold – and sugar are major sectors. Tobacco – most is sold to the USA. Large hidden economy based on transshipment of narcotics to the USA.

WEAKNESSES

Major sectors severely affected by current low world prices and cutbacks in US import quotas. Failure to diversify, and loan repayments, are long-term problems.

EXPORTS

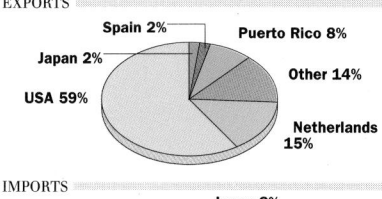

Spain 2%
Japan 2%
USA 59%
Puerto Rico 8%
Other 14%
Netherlands 15%

IMPORTS

Japan 8%
Mexico 9%
USA 38%
Venezuela 10%
Other 35%

RESOURCES

 5.3bn kwh (capacity 1.45m kw)   Not an oil producer; refines 15,000 b/cd

 21,800 tonnes   Ferro-nickel, gold, silver

The government is investing $450 million in two new dams to produce HEP as power cuts are almost a daily occurrence. Attempts at oil prospecting have not been successful. Under the terms of the San José Agreement, almost 2 million tonnes of oil is bought annually from Venezuela and Mexico at preferential terms (20% of the cost is converted into loans).

ENVIRONMENT

 20% (10% partially protected)   Inadequate legislation has not halted deforestation

The government is lax about enforcing existing laws protecting diminishing forests. Legislation is often conflicting: a 1931 hunting law effectively nullifies recent wildlife protection measures.

MEDIA

 No overt censorship laws, though many instances of newspapers caving in to state pressure

PUBLISHING AND BROADCAST MEDIA

 There are 12 daily newspapers, including *Listín Diario*, *Ultima Hora* and *El Nacional*

 1 state-owned, 6 independent stations   10 state-owned, 140 independent stations

Both Mexican and US TV broadcasts can be received easily in the Dominican Republic.

CRIME

 Dominican Republic does not publish prison figures   Rape down 70% between 1985 and 1988

Recent increases in violent crime are mainly the result of drug traffickers fighting for territory. The USA has accused government officials of complicity in the narcotics trade.

EDUCATION

 83%

Most schools operate a curriculum aimed at preparing pupils for graduate studies in the USA. However, wealthier Dominicans send their children to universities in Spain.

HEALTH

 1 per 937 people   Infectious and parasitic diseases

Wealthy Dominicans fly to Cuba rather than Florida for medical treatment. The poor rely on a rudimentary public service.

CHRONOLOGY

The 1697 Franco-Spanish partition of Hispaniola left Spain with the eastern two thirds of the island, today the Dominican Republic.

- ❑ **1865** Independence from Spain.
- ❑ **1930–1961** Gen Molina dictator.
- ❑ **1962** Bosch Gaviño president.
- ❑ **1965** Civil war. US intervention.
- ❑ **1966–1978** Balaguer president.
- ❑ **1978–1982** Guzmán president; commits suicide in 1982.
- ❑ **1982–1986** Blanco president.
- ❑ **1986** Balaguer re-elected president.
- ❑ **1992** Opposition to Columbus celebrations brutally crushed.

WEALTH

 Clothing worker, 333 Dominican Republic pesos per month; oil refinery worker, 2594 Dominican Republic pesos per month

CONSUMER GOODS OWNERSHIP

VCR and PC ownership is limited to a small elite

82   21   26

Per 1000 population

There are great disparities between rich and poor. Generations of governments have promised to close the gap, with few results. The most socially-mobile group in the last 20 years has been of mixed race, and has come to dominate the expanding professional sector. Black Dominicans remain at the bottom of the social ladder, accounting for the major proportion of small farmers. The old Spanish families are still the wealthiest, retaining their grip on the valuable estates; their younger members spend weekends at Puerto Plata, or on shopping trips to Miami.

WORLD RANKING

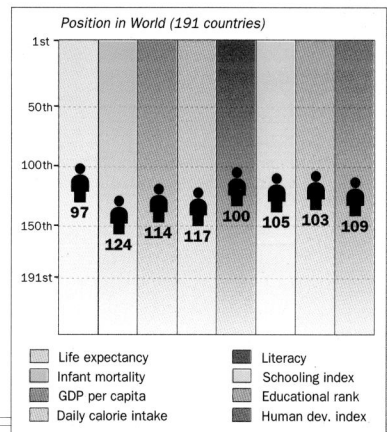

Position in World (191 countries)

97 124 114 117 100 105 103 109

- Life expectancy
- Infant mortality
- GDP per capita
- Daily calorie intake
- Literacy
- Schooling index
- Educational rank
- Human dev. index

ECUADOR

OFFICIAL NAME: Republic of Ecuador **CAPITAL:** Quito
POPULATION: 11.1 million **CURRENCY:** Sucre **OFFICIAL LANGUAGE:** Spanish

SOUTH AMERICA

E

ONCE PART OF the Inca heartland, Ecuador lies on the western coast of South America. It was ruled by Spain from 1533, when the last Inca emperor was executed, until independence in 1830. Most Ecuadorians live either in the lowland Costa region or in the Andean Sierra. The Amazonian Indians are now successfully pressing for their land rights to be recognized. Oil deposits have boosted the economy in recent years.

CLIMATE

WEATHER CHART

Climate varies from hot equatorial in the Amazon forests, to dry heat in the south and 'perpetual spring' in Quito.

COMMUNICATIONS

Mariscal Sucre, Quito
1.71m passengers

55 ships
480,600 dwt

THE TRANSPORT NETWORK

37,636 km (23,386 miles)		Pan-American Highway
965 km (600 miles)		1500 km (932 miles)

Ecuador's extensive road network and antiquated rail system suffer from regular flooding.

TOURISM

 306,000 visitors   Down 12% in 1989

MAIN OVERSEAS ARRIVALS

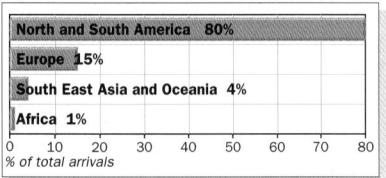

| North and South America 80% |
| Europe 15% |
| South East Asia and Oceania 4% |
| Africa 1% |

0   10   20   30   40   50   60   70   80
% of total arrivals

Tourism is well developed. Quito, once the capital of the Inca empire, is having its Spanish imperial buildings, including 86 churches, restored. Access to the Galápagos is restricted to 40,000 visitors a year.

PEOPLE

Spanish, Quechua, other Amerindian languages

34 people per km²

THE URBAN/RURAL POPULATION SPLIT

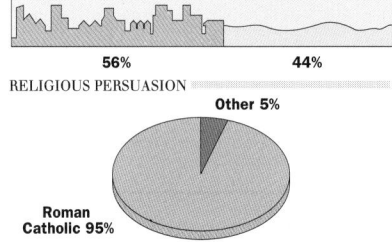

56%   44%

RELIGIOUS PERSUASION

Other 5%

Roman Catholic 95%

Over half of the population is of Indian-Spanish extraction (*mestizo*). The Indians, who make up about 25% of the population, are currently pressing for Ecuador to be described as a pluri-national state, where different communities of Indians are recognized as distinct nationalities. Their case has been backed by the Catholic Church. The result is a strong and largely unified Indian movement.

POLITICS

1994

President Sixto Durán Ballén

THE STATE OF THE PARTIES

National Congress 77 members

| 32% PSC | 14% PRE | 10% MPD | 9% ID | 35% Other |

PSC = Social Christian Party **PRE** = Ecuadorian Republican Party **MPD** = Popular Democratic Movement **ID** = Democratic Left **Other** = Ecuadorian Conservative Party, United Republican Party, Popular Democratic Party

After years of social democracy, Ecuador followed the rest of Latin America in 1992 and voted for a right-wing, privatizing government dedicated to tackling inflation, which until 1993 had hovered at around 50% for over a decade. The major parties are fairly evenly balanced in terms of political power, and coalition arrangements on specific items of policy are not uncommon. The military still has considerable political influence as well as large shareholdings in business.

WORLD AFFAIRS

| OAS | RG | LAES | NAM | AG |

Keeping preferential access to the US and EU markets for bananas is a major concern. Ecuador is developing free trade agreements with its neighbours.

ECUADOR

Total Area : 283 560 sq. km (109 483 sq. miles)

POPULATION

☐	over 1 000 000
◉	over 500 000
◎	over 100 000
○	over 50 000
●	over 10 000
·	under 10 000

LAND HEIGHT

4000m/13124ft
2000m/6562ft
500m/1640ft
Sea Level

Galapagos Islands
I. Darwin
I. Wolf
I. Pinta
I. Marchena
I. Genovesa
I. Fernandina
I. Santiago
I. Santa Cruz
I. Isabela
I. San Cristóbal
I. Santa María   Puerto Baquerizo Moreno
I. Española

San Lorenzo
Esmeraldas
Tulcán
San Miguel
Puerto El Carr de Putumayo
Otavalo
Ibarra
Nueva Loja
Cayambe
Aguarico
Napo
QUITO
Santo Domingo de los Colorados
Caráquez
Chone
Cotopaxi
Tena
Nuev Rocaf
Curaray
Manta   Calceta
Velasco Ibarra
Latacunga
Ambato
Baños
Puyo
Portoviejo
Balzar
Chimborazo 6310 m
Guaranda
Riobamba
Jipijapa
Vinces
Daule
Babahoyo
Pastaza
Salinas
Milagro
La Libertad
Guayaquil   Eloy Alfaro
Alausí
Macas
Isla Puna
Cuenca
Azogues
Machala
Sigsig
Pasaje
Santa Rosa
Loja
Zamora
Macará

N

0   100 km
0   100 miles

Quito is the highest *capital in the world after La Paz in Bolivia. It lies in an Andean valley, lined by 30 volcanoes.*

AID

 $220m (receipts)   Up 42% in 1991

Aid is mostly from the USA and EU, and is essential in tackling Ecuador's $3.2-billion debt. The Galápagos receive generous grants from UNESCO.

DEFENCE

 $260.92m   Up 41% in 1991

The 58,000-strong military is trained by the USA. Drugs gangs are the major concern. Since a brief period of military rule in the mid-1970s, the army has not been directly involved in politics.

ECONOMICS

 $12bn   1900.78 sucres

SCORE CARD

❏ WORLD GNP RANKING	71st
❏ GNP PER CAPITA	$1010
❏ BALANCE OF PAYMENT	$–6m
❏ INFLATION	60.2%
❏ UNEMPLOYMENT	7.9%

STRENGTHS

Net oil exporter. World's biggest banana producer. Fishing industry. Hopes for Andean free trade accords.

WEAKNESSES

Agricultural land has relatively low productivity. Banana crop vulnerable to new EU import regimes.

EXPORTS

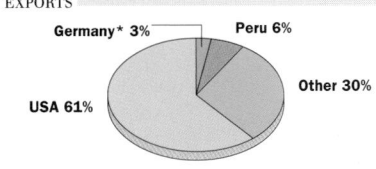

Germany* 3%   Peru 6%
Other 30%
USA 61%

IMPORTS

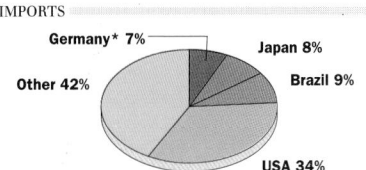

Germany* 7%   Japan 8%
Brazil 9%
Other 42%
USA 34%

RESOURCES

 6.3bn kwh (capacity 1.66m kw)   312,600 b/d (reserves 1,599,793 bbl)

 4.2m cattle, 4.2m pigs, 1.3m sheep, 460,000 horses   Oil, natural gas, gold, silver, copper, zinc

The government is encouraging faster oil exploration and higher output. Ecuador left OPEC in 1992. Over-fishing is threatening mackerel and squid stocks.

ENVIRONMENT

  6%   Area of arid land has increased by 32% in 25 years

The invasion of oil drillers to new areas of Amazonia could spell the end of the Waorani nomads, who have to date successfully avoided all contact with outsiders. In the offshore territory of the Galápagos islands, the growth in legal and illegal tourism has upset the islands' delicate ecosystems; the land iguana has become sterile and black coral is being stolen in quantity for souvenirs.

MEDIA

 Freedom of speech is guaranteed

PUBLISHING AND BROADCAST MEDIA

 There are 36 daily newspapers. The most popular are *El Universo* and *El Comercio*

 3 national independent networks   1 state-owned, 32 independent networks

Ecuador's press is largely independent and free of censorship. It is highly regionalized, based either in the Quito region, or around Guayaquil on the coast. The latter is also a centre for commercial radio stations.

CRIME

 Ecuador does not publish prison figures   Up 1% in 1986

Unlike its neighbours, Ecuador has not suffered from instability caused by left-wing guerrilla action. Minor groups, such as *Alfaro Vive, ¡Carajo!*, have joined the legal political process. Ecuador is classified by the USA as a 'transit country' for drugs, and received $6.2 million of anti-drugs aid in 1992. Several aircraft have also been donated to help combat trafficking.

EDUCATION

 86%

Around 25% of Ecuadorians – a total of 300,000 students – receive higher education at 16 universities. In schools, teaching is often in Indian languages. Programmes have been launched to combat the relatively high levels of adult illiteracy in the countryside.

CHRONOLOGY

Alternating republican and military governments ruled Ecuador from independence in 1830 to 1978.

❏ **1941** War as Peru invades part of mineral-rich El Oro Province; Rio Protocol awards it to Peru in 1942.
❏ **1948–1960** Prosperity from bananas.
❏ **1972** Oil production starts.
❏ **1979** Return to democracy.
❏ **1983** Economic crisis grows: oil prices fall; floods destroy railway.
❏ **1987** President Febres kidnapped briefly by army in protest at his 'Andean Thatcherism' experiment.
❏ **1990** Indians demand land reform.
❏ **1992** Indians granted title to 1 million hectares in Amazonia.

E

HEALTH

 1 per 939 people   Intestinal infectious diseases, pneumonia, accidents, murders

Health care services are now being brought to poor urban districts, but are still unavailable in many rural areas. Between 1987 and 1990, 469 outpatient centres opened. Malaria and stomach cancer are significant health problems.

WEALTH

 Junior company executive, 400,000 sucres per month; chauffeur, 200,000 sucres per month

CONSUMER GOODS OWNERSHIP

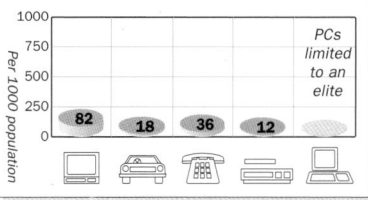

82   18   36   12   PCs limited to an elite

During the 1980s, income per capita dropped by 7.5%. An estimated 60% of the population live in poverty.

WORLD RANKING

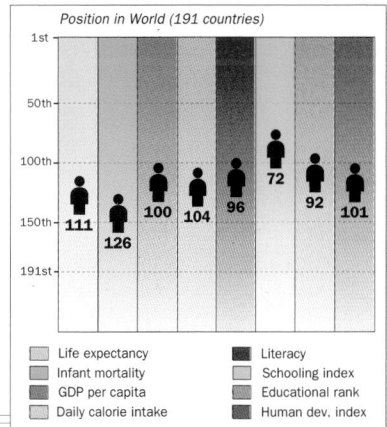

Position in World (191 countries)

Life expectancy	Literacy
Infant mortality	Schooling index
GDP per capita	Educational rank
Daily calorie intake	Human dev. index

EGYPT

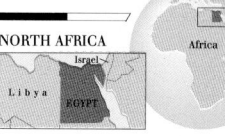

NORTH AFRICA

OFFICIAL NAME: Arab Republic of Egypt   **CAPITAL:** Cairo
POPULATION: 54.8 million   **CURRENCY:** Egyptian pound   **OFFICIAL LANGUAGE:** Arabic

E

OCCUPYING THE NORTHEAST CORNER of Africa, Egypt is bisected by the highly fertile Nile valley which separates its arid western desert from the smaller semi-arid eastern desert. Egypt's 1979 peace treaty with Israel brought security, the return of the Sinai and large injections of US aid. Its essentially pro-Western military-backed regime is now being challenged by an increasingly influential Islamic fundamentalist movement.

18th-Dynasty Temple of Queen Hatshepsut *dating from the Middle Kingdom, c 1480 BC. It is at Deir el-Bahri on the west bank of the Nile opposite Thebes, Egypt's capital at the time.*

CLIMATE

WEATHER CHART

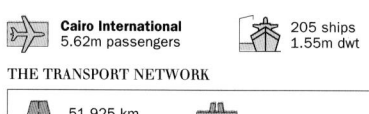

Summers are very hot, especially in the south, but winters are cooler. The only significant rain falls in winter along the Mediterranean coast.

COMMUNICATIONS

Cairo International
5.62m passengers

205 ships
1.55m dwt

THE TRANSPORT NETWORK

51,925 km
(32,265 miles)

None

5110 km
(3175 miles)

Suez Canal
173 km
(107 miles)

Egypt's cities are linked by adequate roads, but railways are the main transport arteries. The Suez Canal is a vital international shipping lane. Cairo's metro opened in 1987.

TOURISM

2.6m visitors

Down 19% in 1993 following terrorist attacks on tourists

MAIN OVERSEAS ARRIVALS

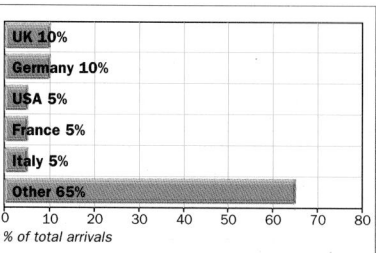

Egypt's wealth of antiquities from its ancient civilizations have made it a key tourist destination since the 1880s. Today, it also offers Nile cruises and some of the world's best subaqua diving, notably at the coral reefs near Hurghada on the Red Sea.

In the 1990s, however, the industry went into sharp decline. Islamic fundamentalists began attacking Western tourists. Their aim was to pressure the government into moving the state more towards Islam. The result has been a sharp decline in the number of visitors from 3.2 million in 1992 to 2.6 million in 1993, and a major dent in foreign exchange earnings. The business convention trade has been particularly affected.

EGYPT

Total Area : 1 001 450 sq. km
(386 660 sq. miles)

POPULATION

over 5 000 000
over 1 000 000
over 500 000
over 100 000
over 50 000
over 10 000
under 10 000

LAND HEIGHT

2000m/6562ft
1000m/3281ft
500m/1640ft
200m/656ft
Sea Level
-200m/-656ft

0   200 km

0   200 miles

PEOPLE

 Arabic, French, English, Berber   53 people per km²

THE URBAN/RURAL POPULATION SPLIT

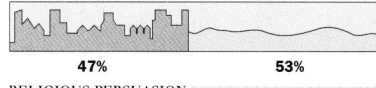

47%   53%

RELIGIOUS PERSUASION

Other 6%

Muslim (mainly Sunni) 94 %

ETHNIC MAKEUP

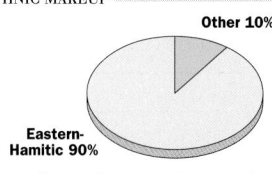

Other 10%

Eastern-Hamitic 90%

Egypt has a long tradition of ethnic and religious tolerance. Most Egyptians speak Arabic, though many also have French or English as a second language. There are Berber-speaking communities in the western oases. Small colonies of Greeks and Armenians live in the larger towns. Islam is the dominant religion, followed by Coptic Christianity. While many Jews left Egypt after the creation of Israel in 1948, a small Jewish community remains in Cairo.

Cairo is Africa's most populous city, and a key social question in Egypt is the high birth rate. Aware of the demands this puts on the country's resources, economy and social services, in 1985 the government set up the National Population Council, which made birth control readily available. Since then, the birth rate has dropped by 10% but Egypt's population is still growing at a rate that will see it double in 30 years. The growing influence of Islamic fundamentalists, who are opposed to contraception, could see the rate accelerate once more.

Egyptian women have traditionally been among the most liberated in the Arab world, playing a full part in the education system, politics and the economy. The steady rise of Islamic fundamentalism, however, threatens their position, particularly in rural areas.

POPULATION AGE BREAKDOWN

%	0–14	15–64		65+
3.3%	4.3%	4%	3.9%	4.4%
54.2%	54.3%	56.5%	56.7%	61%
42.5%	41.4%	39.5%	39.4%	34.6%
1960	1970	1980	1990	2000

POLITICS

 1995   President Muhammad Hosni Mubarak

THE STATE OF THE PARTIES

People's Assembly 454 members

77% NDP   1% NPUP   22% Other

NDP = National Democratic Party
NPUP = National Progressive Unionist Party

Egypt is a multiparty system in theory. In practice, the ruling NDP, backed by the military, runs a one-party state.

MAIN POLITICAL ISSUES

Islamic fundamentalism
The NDP government is engaged in a struggle against Islamic terrorist groups who are seeking to turn Egypt into a Muslim theocracy along Iranian lines. Extremists have perpetrated numerous outrages, including attacks on police and tourists. The fundamentalist message, with promises of improved conditions, has proved attractive to both urban and rural poor. The mosques are also growing in prestige as they increasingly provide education and health services that parallel the state's. The NDP's response has been to introduce draconian measures to counter the terrorist threat, while allowing religious organizations to pursue their social programmes. As long as the NDP retains the support of the army, its position is unlikely to be seriously threatened.

The state of emergency
The ruling NDP party has enforced a national state of emergency since the assassination of President Sadat by Islamic terrorists in 1981. It continues to resist demands for democratic and electoral reforms. As a result, the main conservative and socialist opposition parties boycotted the last elections in 1990. An influential strand of liberal opinion in Egypt claims the ban on religion-based political parties fuels violent protest. There have also been calls for reports of human rights abuses to be investigated.

Hosni Mubarak, *president since the assassination of Anwar Sadat in 1981.*

Dr Atif Sidki, *prime minister and minister for international co-operation since 1986.*

PROFILE

Egypt has been politically stable since the Second World War. Since the death of President Nasser in 1970, it has had just four presidents. Although Anwar Sadat was assassinated in 1981, he was immediately replaced by a man in the same mould, President Hosni Mubarak, who has been in power ever since. The NDP retains a tight grip on the political process through its use of the state of emergency. It has close links with the military (both Sadat and Mubarak were fighter pilots) and with Egypt's massive bureaucracy.

Under Nasser, Egypt promoted Arab socialism, influenced by the Soviet model. Since Sadat, the economy has been liberalized and private enterprise encouraged. However, no parallel liberalization has occurred in politics – one reason for the growing success of Islamic fundamentalists.

WORLD AFFAIRS

 AL   OAU   OAPEC   ACC   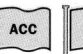 CAEU

Following the 1979 peace treaty with Israel, Egypt has developed closer relations with the USA. Its political and military support for the US-led reaction to Iraq's invasion of Kuwait in 1990 was critical to the success of Operation Desert Storm in 1991. By having the backing of the most powerful state in the region, the Gulf states were able to avoid the charge that they were simply acting at the bidding of the USA. Egypt received massive economic reward from Saudi Arabia for its participation.

Relations with Iran are tense. Iran actively supports the Islamic groups operating against the NDP government, and characterizes Egypt as a corrupt state under US influence. Egypt is concerned that the international boycott and air exclusion zones imposed on Iraq are simply allowing Iran to extend its power in the Middle East.

Egypt's diplomatic service is the Arab world's largest and many Egyptians serve on international bodies. UN Secretary General Boutros Boutros Ghali is an ex-Minister of State for Egypt. Cairo hosts the headquarters of the Arab League.

AID

 $4.6bn (receipts)   Falling since massive Saudi injection of aid in 1991

Since the Camp David peace accords of 1978, Egypt has received massive levels of US military aid; the aim was for Egypt to achieve parity with Israel in aid receipts. By 1991, this had almost been achieved.

E

CHRONOLOGY

Egypt's centuries-old Ottoman occupation ended in 1914 when the country came under British rule. It became fully independent in 1936. Army officers led by Lt-Col Nasser seized power in 1952.

❑ **1953** Political parties dissolved, monarchy abolished. Republic proclaimed with General Neguib as president.

❑ **1954** UK agrees to withdraw troops from Suez Canal in 1956. Nasser deposes Neguib to become president.

❑ **1956** Suez Crisis. British troops withdraw from Canal. UK and USA refuse to help finance Aswân Dam. Nasser orders nationalization of Suez Canal Company to raise revenue for the dam. Israeli, British and French forces invade, but withdraw after pressure from UN and USA.

❑ **1957** Suez Canal reopens after UN salvage fleet clears blockade.

❑ **1958** Egypt merges with Syria as United Arab Republic.

❑ **1960** Soviets begin work on the Aswân Dam.

❑ **1961** Syria breaks away from union with Egypt.

❑ **1967** Six Day War with Israel results in loss of Sinai.

❑ **1970** Nasser dies of heart attack. Succeeded by Anwar Sadat.

❑ **1971** Readopts the name Egypt. Islam becomes state religion.

❑ **1972** Soviet military advisers dismissed from Egypt.

❑ **1974–1975** USA brokers partial Israeli withdrawal from Sinai.

❑ **1977** Sadat visits Jerusalem for first-ever meeting with Israeli prime minister.

❑ **1978** Camp David accords brokered by US President Carter, signed by Egypt and Israel.

❑ **1979** Egypt and Israel sign peace treaty. Egypt is shunned by most Arab states.

❑ **1981** Sadat assassinated by Islamic extremists. Succeeded by Hosni Mubarak.

❑ **1982** Last Israeli troops leave Sinai.

❑ **1986** President Mubarak meets Israeli Prime Minister Shimon Peres to discuss Middle East peace.

❑ **1989** Saudi Arabia's King Fahd visits Cairo, symbolizing Egypt's rehabilitation in Arab world. After 12-year rift, Egypt and Syria resume diplomatic relations.

❑ **1990** Egypt participates in UN operation to liberate Kuwait.

❑ **1991** Damascus declaration provides for a defence pact among Egypt, Syria and Gulf co-operation countries against Iraq.

DEFENCE

💲 $2.5bn   ⬆ Up 11% in 1992

0   *Defence spending as % GDP*   40
7.5%

EGYPTIAN ARMED FORCES

🛡	3090 main battle tanks (1040 T-54,-55/600 T-62/ 1450 M-60)	290,000 personnel
⚓	4 submarines, 1 destroyer, 4 frigates and 39 patrol boats	20,000 personnel
✈	492 combat aircraft (14 *Alpha Jet*/33 F-4E/ 33 F-16A/40 F-16C)	30,000 personnel
☢	None	

Egypt's armed forces, the largest in the Arab world, are battle-hardened from successive wars with Israel and from participation in Operation Desert Storm to liberate Kuwait in 1991. Over 500,000 reservists augment the regular troops.

After the 1978 Camp David accords with Israel, Egypt stopped buying Soviet weapons and aircraft in favour of Western suppliers. Co-operation with the USA has reaped dividends in the form of more sophisticated defence equipment and improved training. Egypt has a small arms industry and sells light weapons, notably a version of the AK-47 assault rifle, to other developing countries.

ECONOMICS

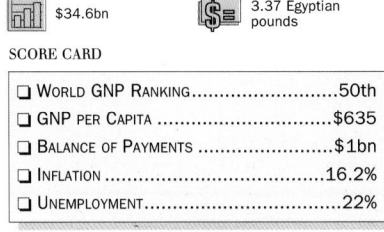

📊 $34.6bn   💲 3.37 Egyptian pounds

SCORE CARD

❑ WORLD GNP RANKING	50th
❑ GNP PER CAPITA	$635
❑ BALANCE OF PAYMENTS	$1bn
❑ INFLATION	16.2%
❑ UNEMPLOYMENT	22%

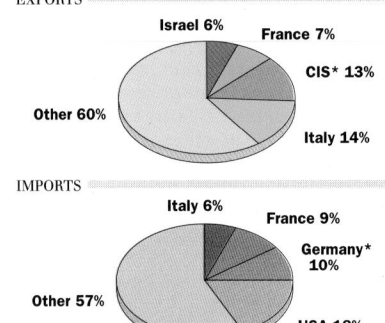

EXPORTS

Israel 6%   France 7%
CIS* 13%
Other 60%
Italy 14%

IMPORTS

Italy 6%   France 9%
Germany* 10%
Other 57%
USA 18%

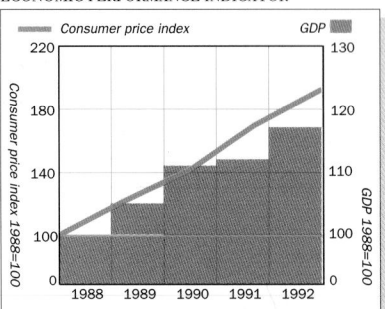

ECONOMIC PERFORMANCE INDICATOR

Consumer price index ▬▬   GDP ▨

Consumer price index 1988=100
GDP 1988=100
220 / 130
180 / 120
140 / 110
100 / 100
1988 1989 1990 1991 1992

STRENGTHS

Oil and gas revenues. Tourist industry. Remittances from Egyptians working overseas. Suez Canal tolls. Agricultural produce, especially cotton. Light industry and manufacturing.

WEAKNESSES

Reduction in remittances from Egyptians working overseas owing to Gulf States' recession. Dependence on imported technology. High birth rate.

PROFILE

Under President Nasser, Egypt followed an economic policy inspired by the Soviet model. Rigid and highly centralized, it gave Egypt one of the largest public sectors of all developing countries. Economic restrictions were first relaxed in 1974. President Sadat's open-door policy allowed joint ventures

with foreign partners for the first time, although the business classes were the only ones to profit. Most Egyptians suffered from new austerity measures.

Under President Mubarak, economic reform has quickened and policies are more sensitive to the high levels of unemployment and poverty. Priorities now are to reduce import dependence by encouraging manufacturing, and to sustain economic growth to keep up with the increase in population.

EGYPT : MAJOR BUSINESSES

Alexandria   Cairo
Suez
El Minya   Ḥelwân
Asyut
Aswân

🌀	Cement	✿	Heavy engineering
	Iron & steel	🚗	Vehicle manufacture
	Food processing	⚗	Chemicals
	Consumer goods	✾	Textiles
	Electronics		

0   200 km
0   200 miles

* significant multinational ownership

E

E

RESOURCES

39.5bn kwh (capacity 11.7m kw)

880,900 b/d (reserves 6,200,000,000 bbl)

4m sheep, 3.4m cattle, 2m asses, 190,000 camels

Natural gas, oil, phosphates, manganese, uranium

ELECTRICITY GENERATION

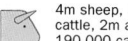

Hydro 20% (8.1bn kwh)

Thermal 80% (31.5bn kwh)

Nuclear 0%

Other 0%

% of total generation by type

Oil and gas are Egypt's most valuable resources. Most of the oil comes from its western desert, the Red Sea, Sinai and Upper Egypt. Oil multinationals are involved in new explorations, but Egypt is not as profitable a source as more competitive oil-rich countries, such as Algeria and Yemen. 55% of Egypt's oil production is consumed locally.

Most electricity is derived from hydroelectric power and coal. The massive Aswân Dam provides the bulk of hydroelectricity. Built between 1960 and 1970, the dam has a generating capacity of 10 billion kwh. By 1974, revenue from it had covered construction costs.

EGYPT : LAND USE

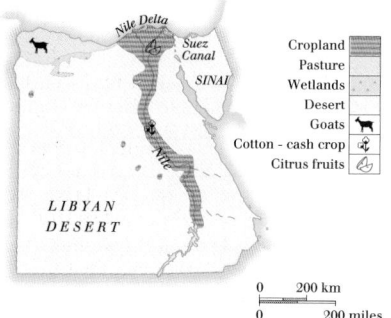

Cropland
Pasture
Wetlands
Desert
Goats
Cotton - cash crop
Citrus fruits

ENVIRONMENT

0.8% (0.7% partially protected)

Population control and water are prime concerns

ENVIRONMENTAL TREATIES

Yes   Yes
Yes   Yes

Most of Egypt suffers from a chronic lack of water. The Nile is the only perennial source and is increasingly saline due to the Aswân Dam. The main cities suffer heavy industrial pollution, and environmental controls are few. In Cairo, the recent completion of a sewerage system has improved sanitary conditions.

MEDIA

 Free press in theory, but government restrictions in practice

Long regarded as a centre of Arab liberal journalism, Egypt is increasingly under siege from Islamic political dogma. Even the leading liberal newspaper *Al Ahram* has altered its coverage. TV now gives more airtime to Islamic sermons and less to secular or Western opinions.

CRIME

 Egypt does not publish prison figures   Up 11% in 1990

CRIME RATES

Murders
2   per 100,000 population

Rapes
0.01   per 100,000 population

Thefts
58   per 100,000 population

Terrorist attacks have tarnished Egypt's reputation as a law-abiding country; street crime and muggings were previously rare. Inter-community violence – particularly attacks by Muslims on Christians and *vice versa* – has recently become more common. Islamic fundamentalist extremists have also been attacking Western tourists as part of their campaign against the government. Under the state of emergency, the Egyptian police have considerable powers. There have been reports of human rights abuses.

EDUCATION

  48%

0   Education spending as % GNP   25
6.8%

THE EDUCATION SYSTEM

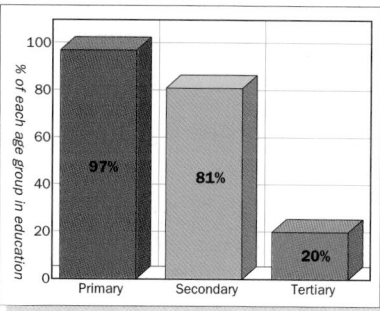

Primary 97%   Secondary 81%   Tertiary 20%

Education is free. Most Egyptians attend primary school to the age of 11, but few complete secondary education, even though it is in theory compulsory until 15 years of age. The literacy rate is 62% for men and 34% for women. Egypt has 13 universities.

PUBLISHING AND BROADCAST MEDIA

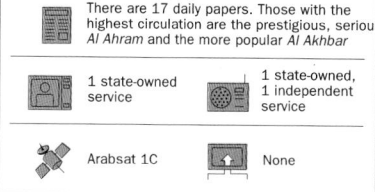

There are 17 daily papers. Those with the highest circulation are the prestigious, serious *Al Ahram* and the more popular *Al Akhbar*

1 state-owned service

1 state-owned, 1 independent service

Arabsat 1C

None

HEALTH

 1 per 5092 people   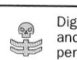 Digestive, respiratory and heart diseases, perinatal deaths

0   Health spending as % GNP   25
1.1%

Health care is rudimentary – there is only one hospital bed for every 500 people. Patient–doctor ratios are among the lowest in the Arab world. Islamic medical centres based on the mosque organization are spreading and replacing the state system.

WEALTH

 Wealth heavily concentrated in Cairo

CONSUMER GOODS OWNERSHIP

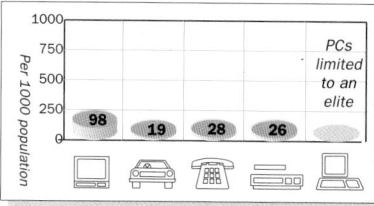

PCs limited to an elite

98   19   28   26

Wealth disparities are highly marked in Egypt. The largely urban Coptic Christian community is the group with the highest standard of living. Most Egyptians are subsistence farmers. The return of many unemployed workers from the Gulf states has further depressed conditions in the countryside.

WORLD RANKING

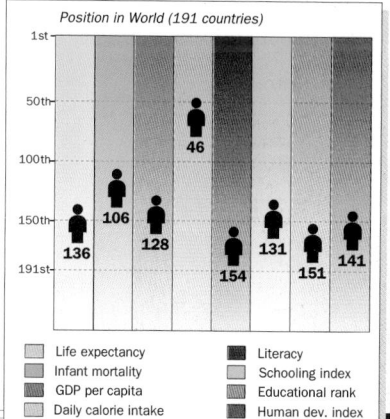

Position in World (191 countries)

46   106   128   136   154   131   151   141

Life expectancy
Infant mortality
GDP per capita
Daily calorie intake
Literacy
Schooling index
Educational rank
Human dev. index

EL SALVADOR

OFFICIAL NAME: Republic of El Salvador **CAPITAL:** San Salvador
POPULATION: 5.4 million **CURRENCY:** Colón **OFFICIAL LANGUAGE:** Spanish

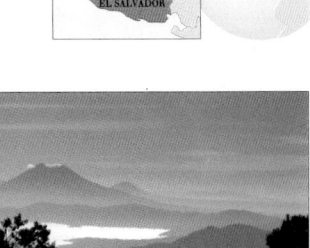

THE SMALLEST AND MOST densely populated Central American republic, El Salvador won full independence in 1856. Located on the Pacific coast, it lies within a seismic zone. Between 1979 and 1991, El Salvador was ravaged by a civil war between US-backed right-wing governments and left-wing FMLN guerrillas. Since the UN-brokered peace agreement, the country has been concentrating on rebuilding its shattered economy.

View over the capital, San Salvador. It lies in a depression in the southern and higher of El Salvador's two mountain ranges, which is punctuated by more than 20 volcanoes.

CLIMATE

WEATHER CHART

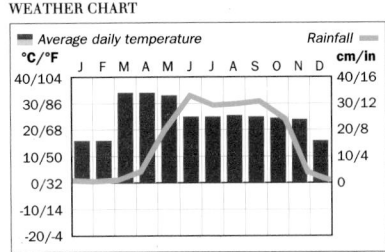

The tropical coastal *tierra caliente* is very hot, with seasonal rains. The low hills are cooler at night; the higher *tierra templada* is drier and also cooler.

COMMUNICATIONS

 Cuscatlan, San Salvador
537,961 passengers
 Has no fleet

THE TRANSPORT NETWORK

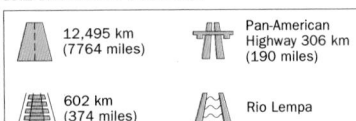

Infrastructure was badly affected by the civil war. Roads and bridges, natural FMLN targets, are gradually being repaired.

TOURISM

 314,482 visitors
 Up 58% in 1992

MAIN OVERSEAS ARRIVALS

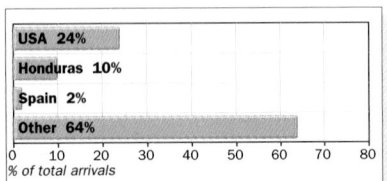

The civil war effectively ended tourism. Peace has brought a few visitors back to the unspoilt beach resorts of El Salvador's Costa del Sol.

PEOPLE

 Spanish   261 people per km²

THE URBAN/RURAL POPULATION SPLIT

44%   56%

RELIGIOUS PERSUASION

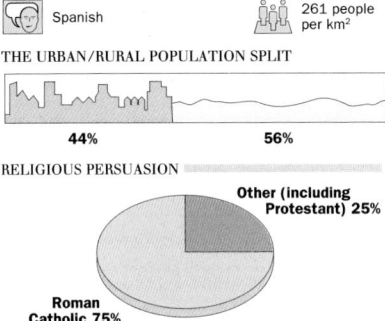

Other (including Protestant) 25%

Roman Catholic 75%

Salvadoreans are largely a *mestizo* people with few ethnic tensions. The civil war was fought over economic disparities, which still exist.

POLITICS

 1997   President Armando Caldéron Sol

THE STATE OF THE PARTIES

Legislative Assembly 84 members

3% Other

46% ARENA   25% FMLN   21% PDC   5% PCN

ARENA = National Republican Alliance **FMLN** = Farabundo Martí Liberation Front **PDC** = Christian Democratic Party **PCN** = National Conciliation Party **Other** = Democratic Convergence, National United Movement

El Salvador has traditionally been dominated by two main parties, the centrist PDC and right-wing ARENA. The latter represents the interests of the 14 main coffee-growing families. However in the 1994 elections, the left-wing FMLN, whose guerrillas at one time controlled one third of El Salvadorean territory, won 25% of the vote. The elections marked the return of the left and centre-left to the formal political system for the first time in 60 years. Apart from the huge task of rebuilding the shattered economy, the major problem is resettling the estimated 500,000 war refugees.

WORLD AFFAIRS

 OAS   CACM Opanal   LAES   BCIE

During the 1980s, El Salvador was renowned internationally for abuses of human rights by military death squads, allegedly controlled by ex-ARENA leader, Roberto D'Aubuisson. El Salvador's attempt to defend its record at the UN failed.

Today, conditions have improved and El Salvador is talking of integration with its neighbours, reflecting US policy for the region. Dependence on US aid means that the US ambassador remains one of the most influential figures in El Salvador's external and internal affairs.

AID

 $290m (receipts)   Down 17% in 1991

The USA has long been the main aid donor. During the civil war, around 75% of aid was spent on arms for fighting FMLN guerrilla forces. The focus is now to secure peace and achieve national reconciliation by funding rebuilding and refugee resettlement programmes. The World Bank and Inter-American Development Fund have also directed hundreds of millions of dollars into El Salvador.

DEFENCE

$145m   Up 3% in 1992

Between 1979 and 1991, the military fought an unrestricted war against the FMLN. Human rights were effectively suspended and governments that opposed the military overthrown. Its main backers were the USA, which supplied over $1 billion-worth of arms, and Israel. The peace treaty includes plans to reduce the size of the army and establish a civilian police force.

E

ECONOMICS

 $6.4bn

 8.68 colones

SCORE CARD

- ❏ WORLD GNP RANKING..........................99th
- ❏ GNP PER CAPITA $1185
- ❏ BALANCE OF PAYMENTS....................$−195m
- ❏ INFLATION 11.9%
- ❏ UNEMPLOYMENT................................7.5%

STRENGTHS
Very few. El Salvador requires massive injections of aid to survive.

WEAKNESSES
Civil war caused $2 billion-worth of damage. Over-dependence on coffee, which accounts for 90% of exports. Rural areas desperately poor, with rising numbers of landless rural poor.

EXPORTS

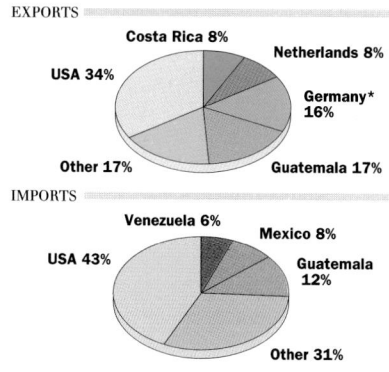

Costa Rica 8%
Netherlands 8%
USA 34%
Germany* 16%
Other 17%
Guatemala 17%

IMPORTS

Venezuela 6%
Mexico 8%
USA 43%
Guatemala 12%
Other 31%

RESOURCES

2.3bn kwh (capacity 740,000 kw)

Not an oil producer; refines 15,100 b/cd

1m cattle, 450,000 pigs, 93,000 horses

Salt, limestone, gypsum

El Salvador has no significant resources. The restoration of the electricity system is a priority.

ENVIRONMENT

 1% (0.2% partially protected)

20,235 hectares set aside for conservation

Most of the rainforest has been cut down for agriculture, leading to topsoil erosion and desertification. Pesticide poisoning of land is a major problem.

MEDIA

 Total censorship by the military during the civil war. The 4 independent TV stations have one owner

PUBLISHING AND BROADCAST MEDIA

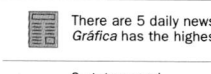

There are 5 daily newspapers. *La Prensa Gráfica* has the highest circulation

2 state-owned, 4 independent stations

1 state-owned, 75 independent stations

Many opposition journalists were murdered during the civil war. The FMLN is now able to publish its views.

CRIME

 El Salvador does not publish prison figures

Falling since 1991, but still high by regional standards

The legal system was largely bypassed by the military during the civil war. It operated the paramilitary death squads responsible for over 50,000 murders. Political violence is still relatively high. The peace terms of 1991 called for an overhaul of the politically-appointed legal system.

EDUCATION

73%

Education is based on the US system. Provision is limited in rural areas. During the civil war, state universities were closed and occupied by the military. The government, however, encouraged the establishment of private universities, now increasingly popular among the middle classes.

CHRONOLOGY

El Salvador was Spanish until 1821. Part of the United Provinces of Central America from 1823–1839, it became fully independent in 1856.

- ❏ **1932** Army crushes popular insurrection led by Farabundo Martí.
- ❏ **1944–1979** Army effectively rules through PCN.
- ❏ **1979** Reformist officers overthrow PCN government. Fail to curb rising army-backed political violence.
- ❏ **1981** Left-wing Farabundo Martí National Liberation Movement (FMLN) launches civil war.
- ❏ **1991** UN-brokered peace. FMLN recognized as a political party.
- ❏ **1992** Peace achieved.

HEALTH

 1 per 2641 people

Accidents, violence, circulatory diseases, infections

Health spending almost halved during the civil war. Only the military hospitals are now adequately supplied.

WEALTH

 Machine assembler, 1772 colones per month; insurance agent, 6510 colones per month

CONSUMER GOODS OWNERSHIP

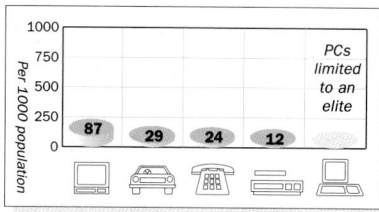

PCs limited to an elite

87 29 24 12

El Salvador has considerable wealth disparities, with 20% owning 70% of national wealth. The rich favour bullet-proof cars and tend to own second homes in Los Angeles or Miami.

WORLD RANKING

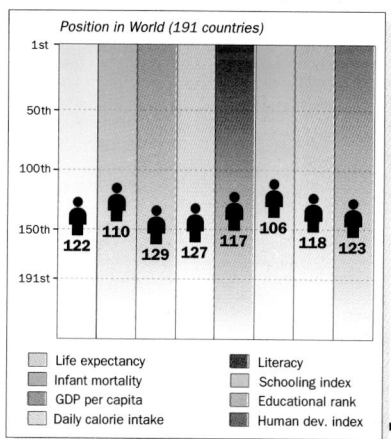

Position in World (191 countries)

122 110 129 127 117 106 118 123

- ▢ Life expectancy
- ▢ Infant mortality
- ▢ GDP per capita
- ▢ Daily calorie intake
- ▢ Literacy
- ▢ Schooling index
- ▢ Educational rank
- ▢ Human dev. index

E

EL SALVADOR

Total Area : 21 040 sq. km (8124 sq. miles)

POPULATION
- over 500 000 ⊙
- over 100 000 ◎
- over 50 000 ○
- over 10 000 ○
- under 10 000 •

LAND HEIGHT
- 2000m/6562ft
- 1000m/3281ft
- 500m/1640ft
- 200m/656ft
- Sea Level

EQUATORIAL GUINEA

WEST AFRICA
EQUATORIAL GUINEA
Cameroon
Gabon
Congo

Africa

OFFICIAL NAME: Republic of Equatorial Guinea **CAPITAL:** Malabo
POPULATION: 400,000 **CURRENCY:** CFA franc **OFFICIAL LANGUAGE:** Spanish

E

COMPRISING FIVE ISLANDS and the territory of Río Muni on the west coast of Africa, Equatorial Guinea lies just north of the equator. Mangrove swamps border the mainland coast. The republic gained its independence in 1968 after 190 years of Spanish rule. Multipartyism was accepted in 1991, but observers questioned the fairness of parliamentary elections in 1993.

Bioko, formerly Fernando Po. Although the volcanic land is very fertile, cocoa production fell by 90% during the Macías years.

CLIMATE

WEATHER CHART

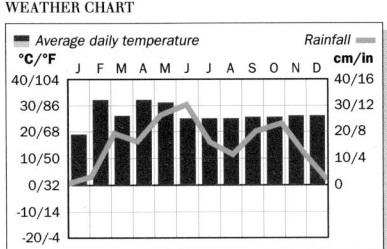

The island of Bioko is extremely wet and humid, with an annual rainfall of 200 cm, while the mainland is only marginally drier and cooler.

COMMUNICATIONS

 Malabo

 2 ships
6700 dwt

THE TRANSPORT NETWORK

2628 km (1633 miles)	None
None	None

Apart from once or twice-weekly *Iberia* flights, all airlinks are through neighbouring countries. The Chinese financed the Ncue-Mongomo Highway project in the 1980s.

TOURISM

 A few independent visitors

 Numbers are unlikely to increase

MAIN OVERSEAS ARRIVALS

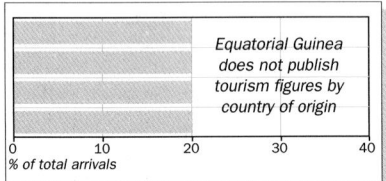

Equatorial Guinea does not publish tourism figures by country of origin

% of total arrivals

Equatorial Guinea is still very much a destination for the adventurous independent tourist only, despite the potential attraction of Malabo's spectacular scenery and beaches.

PEOPLE

 Spanish, Fang, Bubi

 14 people per km²

THE URBAN/RURAL POPULATION SPLIT

29%   71%

RELIGIOUS PERSUASION

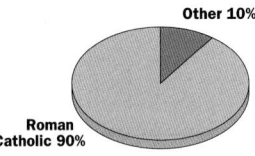

Other 10%

Roman Catholic 90%

The mainland has a majority of Fang, a people who also inhabit Cameroon and northern Gabon. Bioko is populated by a majority of Bubi and a minority of Creoles, known as *Fernandinos*. The Macías dictatorship consolidated the power of the Fang, especially the Mongomo clan, from which both Macías and his successor Obiang come. The extended family is strong and maintained its solidarity despite disruptive social pressure during the Macías dictatorship.

EQUATORIAL GUINEA

Bioko **MALABO**
Pico de Basilé 3008m
Basacato del Este
Luba Riaba
Bococo San Antonio de Ureca
Punta Santiago
Bight of Biafra

Total Area : 28 050 sq. km (10 830 sq. miles)

POPULATION
over 10 000
under 10 000

LAND HEIGHT
2000m/6562ft
1000m/3281ft
500m/1640ft
200m/656ft
Sea Level

0   50 km
0   50 miles

ATLANTIC OCEAN
Gulf of Guinea
CAMEROON
Yengue Ntem Ayamiken Mikomeseng Ebebiyin
Bata Niefang Ncue Añisoc
Cabo Dos Puntas Mbini
Bolondo Río
Mbini Senye Nkumekie Mbini Mongomo
Nume Muni
Etembue Evinayong
Cabo San Juan Kogo Nsok
Acalayong Utamboni Akurenan
Isla de Corisco
G A B O N

POLITICS

 1998

 President Brig-Gen Teodoro Obiang Nguema Mbasogo

THE STATE OF THE PARTIES

National Assembly 80 members

UDS 6%
PDGE 85%
CSDP 8%
PL 1%

PDGE = Democratic Party of Equatorial Guinea
CSDP = People's Social Democratic Convention
UDS = Social Democratic Union **PL** = Liberal Party

Despite officially being a multiparty state since 1991, some of the several exiled political parties have not yet found it safe to return – opposition leaders who publicize themselves tend to be arrested. The ruling PDGE was set up in 1987 by Teodoro Obiang Nguema Mbasogo, nephew of the dictator Francisco Macías Nguema, whom he overthrew in 1979. It replaced Macías' even more notional party, the National Workers' Party (PUNT), which in 1970 had forced a merger of the parties existing before independence. The PDGE benefits from heavy government patronage, receiving 3% of all salaries.

The movement towards multipartyism – which was initiated in 1988 following the first elections for 20 years – has been marked by instability. This appears likely to continue following the controversy surrounding the fairness of elections at the end of 1993. Local observers believe that the country may be vulnerable to a coup.

WORLD AFFAIRS

 OAS   OAU   AfDB   FZ   ECA

After a period of extreme isolation under the Macías dictatorship, Equatorial Guinea is seeking to rebuild links, especially its relationship with Spain, traditionally a haven for political dissenters. In 1989, Madrid was the base used by exiled opposition groups forming a coalition to press for democracy. Joining the Franc Zone in 1988 did not bring the expected benefits. Spain is suspicious of French commercial ambitions in the country.

AID

 $174m (receipts)   Up 71% in 1991

Equatorial Guinea is underdeveloped and aid is vital to get such projects as there are off the ground. Planning and implementation, however, have proved difficult owing to the lack of skilled labour, inefficiencies and instances of corruption.

The EU, especially France, Italy and Spain, the World Bank, IMF and Arab funds are all important sources of aid. The Chinese have also provided project aid to Equatorial Guinea.

DEFENCE

Equatorial Guinea does not release budget figures   Not applicable

The main concern for the 1300-man military and paramilitary force is internal security. Morocco has provided a 360-strong presidential guard since the early 1980s to guarantee Obiang's security. Nigeria, Cameroon and Gabon have interests in maintaining the autonomy of the Malabo and Río Muni regions.

ECONOMICS

 $149m   295.23 CFA francs

SCORE CARD

- ❏ WORLD GNP RANKING........................183rd
- ❏ GNP PER CAPITA $380
- ❏ BALANCE OF PAYMENTS $4.5m
- ❏ INFLATION ....–0.3%
- ❏ UNEMPLOYMENT ....Little formal employment

STRENGTHS
Fertile soils. Large tropical timber reserves. Cocoa and coffee. Extensive territorial waters, with potential for fisheries. Oil and natural gas reserves yet to be fully exploited.

WEAKNESSES
Lasting effects of economic regression under the Macías dictatorship. Maladministration and ideological

RESOURCES

 1.8m kwh (capacity 5000 kw)   Reserves of 3,600,000 bbl

35,000 sheep, 5000 pigs, 5000 cattle   Oil, natural gas

Offshore and mainland oil and gas reserves have yet to be fully exploited, but companies such as ELF, BP and AGIP are drilling. Bata is served by a 3.2 MW hydro-power station built by the Chinese in 1983.

ENVIRONMENT

 None   Government has no environmental protection expertise

The government has failed to take any serious measures to stop timber companies depleting the rainforest.

MEDIA

 Censorship is liable to be arbitrarily and suddenly imposed

PUBLISHING AND BROADCAST MEDIA

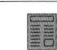 There is no regular daily press. The formerly daily newspaper *Poto Poto* now appears irregularly

 1 state-owned service   1 state-owned service

There has been very little sign of press liberalization, despite the adoption of multipartyism. Political parties produce a few tracts and broadsheets.

CRIME

 Equatorial Guinea does not publish prison figures   No measurable change from year to year

Levels of recorded crime are relatively low, although much does not get reported. Many human rights abuses still occur.

EXPORTS

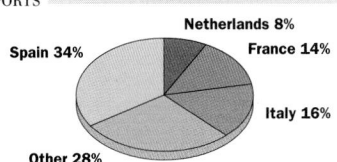

Netherlands 11%
Italy 12%
Spain 44%
Other 14%
Germany* 19%

IMPORTS

Netherlands 8%
Spain 34%
France 14%
Italy 16%
Other 28%

attacks on the educated have restricted growth; during the Macías period, cocoa production slumped by 90%. Lack of a coherent, trained administration. Continuing problems with communications.

CHRONOLOGY

Equatorial Guinea remained a backwater of Spanish colonialism until development began after 1939.

- ❏ **1968** Independence. President Macías launches reign of terror. Puts own family in all top jobs.
- ❏ **1972** Attempt to stop mass exodus: people forbidden to leave country.
- ❏ **1979** Coup puts nephew in power with Spanish approval.
- ❏ **1991** Multiparty constitution.

E

EDUCATION

 50%

Education declined in the Macías years, when attendance rates fell from 90% to 55%. It has now been declared the State's first priority.

HEALTH

 1 per 61,000 people   Diarrheal and respiratory diseases, malaria

Life expectancy has risen from 37 years in 1960 to 47 in 1990. Restoring basic health care is a priority.

WEALTH

 Most of the population leads a subsistence existence; a minority has formal employment

CONSUMER GOODS OWNERSHIP

VCR and PC ownership is limited to a small elite

9   13   5

What wealth there is tends to be concentrated in the ruling clan. There is also a relic of Spanish plutocracy.

WORLD RANKING

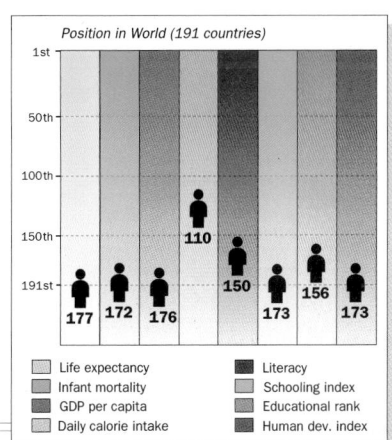

Position in World (191 countries)

1st
50th
100th
110
150th
150
156
191st
177   172   176   173   173

- ◻ Life expectancy
- ◻ Infant mortality
- ◻ GDP per capita
- ◻ Daily calorie intake
- ◼ Literacy
- ◻ Schooling index
- ◻ Educational rank
- ◼ Human dev. index

ERITREA

OFFICIAL NAME: State of Eritrea   **CAPITAL:** Asmara
POPULATION: 3.5 million   **CURRENCY:** Egyptian pound   **OFFICIAL LANGUAGES:** Tigrinya and Arabic

L YING ON THE SHORES of the Red Sea, Eritrea's landscape is dominated by rugged mountains, bush and the Danakil Desert. The country effectively seceded from Ethiopia in 1991, after a 30-year war for independence that left much of its infrastructure in ruins. A failure of the harvest in 1993 compounded the new state's problems, placing 400,000 at risk of famine. The transitional government is due to hold multiparty democratic elections in 1997.

CLIMATE

WEATHER CHART

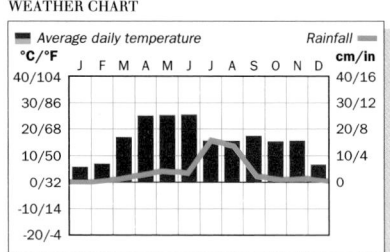

Eritrea's harvest is dependent on rainfall in September. Droughts from July onwards are common.

COMMUNICATIONS

 Yohannes IV, Asmara   Has no fleet

THE TRANSPORT NETWORK

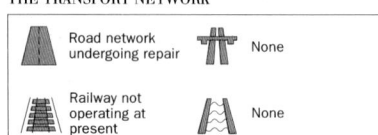

Road network undergoing repair	None
Railway not operating at present	None

All transport systems require massive investment. Eritrea will benefit as a transit point for land-locked neighbours.

TOURISM

Visitors limited to aid workers and business people

Government is encouraging the tourist sector

MAIN OVERSEAS ARRIVALS

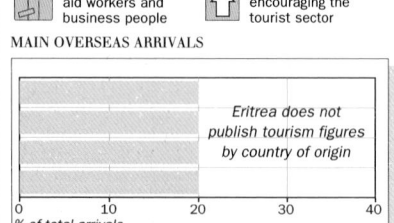

Eritrea does not publish tourism figures by country of origin

0   10   20   30   40
% of total arrivals

There is very little tourism; most visitors are aid workers or on business. Planners are keen to develop coastal resorts for the regional Arab market. However, the task of clearing beaches of mines will take several years.

PEOPLE

Tigrinya, Tigre, Afar, Arabic, Bilen, Kunama, Nara, Saho, Hadareb

28 people per km²

THE URBAN/RURAL POPULATION SPLIT

20%   80%

RELIGIOUS PERSUASION

Other (including Animist) 10%
Christian 45%
Muslim 45%

Tigrinya-speakers form the largest of Eritrea's nine main ethnic groups. A strong sense of nationhood has been forged by the 30-year war against Ethiopia. Women played an important role in the war. From 1973, 30,000 fought alongside men, some in positions of command. Their claim to equal rights is likely to be enshrined in the new constitution. Over 80% of the people are subsistence farmers. Few live beyond the age of 45.

ERITREA

Total Area : 93 680 sq. km (36 170 sq. miles)

LAND HEIGHT

2000m/6562ft
1000m/3281ft
500m/1640ft
200m/656ft
Sea Level
-200m/-656ft

POPULATION

◎ over 100 000
○ over 50 000
● over 10 000
• under 10 000

N

0   100 km
0   100 miles

POLITICS

1997   Interim President Issaias Afwerki

THE STATE OF THE PARTIES

Provisional Government of Eritrea

The transitional government will be in place until 1997

Eritrea became a region of Ethiopia as a result of European power politics. Formerly an Italian colony, it came under British mandate in 1941. In 1952, London handed the region to Addis Ababa. The long struggle for independence began in the same year. The Eritrean People's Liberation Front (EPLF) finally drove out Ethiopian troops in 1991. A referendum held in May 1993 resulted in 99.8% of voters on a 98.2% turnout voting 'yes' to independence.

The country is currently being run by a core of EPLF leaders who conducted the military campaign. Led by Issaias Afwerki, they plan to dissolve the EPLF and to hold multiparty elections in 1997. A new constitution is planned that will forbid parties based on religious or ethnic affiliations. Issaias, a Christian, has also been careful to include Muslims in his transitional cabinet.

WORLD AFFAIRS

 OAU   WFP

Eritrea's secession was significant for African politics. It marked the first major redrawing of the national borders established by Africa's colonizers. The OAU fears that other African secessionist movements will be encouraged by Eritrea's success. For Eritrea, however, the main concern is attracting Western aid for reconstruction. Relations with Ethiopia's new government, which also fought the Mengistu regime, are good. The EPLF has promised land-locked Ethiopia access to the ports of Assab and Massawa.

AID

 $147m   Rising; mostly emergency food aid

Eritrea's economy is almost entirely aid-dependent. Food aid, on which 75% of the population survive, is the most pressing need. The failure of the harvest in 1993, which placed 400,000 at risk of starvation, led to the UN pledging a further 225,000 tons of food. Western donors have been less generous with aid for the $2 billion reconstruction costs. Compared with Somalia, Eritrea's aid receipts are tiny.

DEFENCE

 Army unpaid at present   Demobilization of troops after independence

The 100,000-strong army (30,000 of whom are women) is currently being demobilized. As with the rest of the people, troops are being reintegrated into the national economy on 'food for work' schemes. In return for repairing the damage wrought by war on the environment and to the infrastructure, they receive basic rations.

ECONOMICS

 $393m (est)   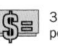 3.37 Egyptian pounds

SCORE CARD

- ❏ WORLD GNP RANKING.......................165th
- ❏ GNP PER CAPITA $120
- ❏ BALANCE OF PAYMENTS ....Deficit
- ❏ INFLATION 12%
- ❏ UNEMPLOYMENT....Widespread underemployment

STRENGTHS
Strategically important position on Red Sea. Potential for developing a mining industry and for foreign earnings from oil exports. Government commitment to reducing dependence on food aid. Potential for tourism on Red Sea coast.

WEAKNESSES
Lack of basic information and equipment. Coherent economic policy still being formulated. Not an aid priority for Western donors. Legacy of disruption and destruction from civil war. Port of Massawa heavily bombed. Most of population living at subsistence level. Susceptibility to drought and famine. Expense of repatriating and supporting the 750,000 who fled abroad as refugees and now wish to return.

EXPORTS/IMPORTS

Eritrea does not yet publish export or import figures

RESOURCES

 Electricity supply is prone to surges   Not an oil producer; oil refinery at Assab

 Livestock includes sheep, goats, cattle and camels   Copper, potash, gold, iron, silver, zinc, oil, silica, granite, marble

Eritrea has substantial copper reserves, and lesser ones of silver, zinc and gold. High-quality silica, granite and marble deposits could be exploited. Onshore and offshore oil deposits are believed to exist. Concessionary exploration deals with Western companies have yet to be established.

ENVIRONMENT

 None at present   New government conscious of conservation needs

Deforestation and soil erosion are major problems. The Ethiopian army uprooted trees to destroy the cover they provided for Eritrean soldiers. Since 1991, 22 million seedlings have been grown in a replanting scheme. The Red Sea coast is a conservation priority.

MEDIA

 Most of the media is controlled by the government

PUBLISHING AND BROADCAST MEDIA

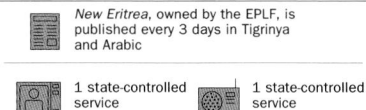

New Eritrea, owned by the EPLF, is published every 3 days in Tigrinya and Arabic

1 state-controlled service   1 state-controlled service

The media is largely controlled by the EPLF who run both the radio and TV services. Independent newspapers are not encouraged.

CRIME

 Eritrea does not publish prison figures   Crime levels remain low

Crime has not been a problem since independence. The judiciary and police answer to the EPLF. There are a number of political prisoners.

EDUCATION

 20%

Very few schools functioned during the war. There is one university. In an attempt to reduce potential ethnic tension, all children above the age of 11 are being taught in English.

HEALTH

 1 per 48,000 people   Malaria. Potential risk of famine

The risk of famine overrides normal health concerns. Eritreans built their own hospitals during the war with Ethiopia. Health provision is basic.

Seasonal river beds carry rain from the Ethiopian highlands into Eritrea, providing essential irrigation for agriculture.

E

CHRONOLOGY

British military rule replaced Italian colonial authority in 1941.

- ❏ **1952** Eritrea incorporated in Ethiopia.
- ❏ **1961** EPLF begins armed struggle.
- ❏ **1987** EPLF refuses offer of autonomy; fighting intensifies.
- ❏ **1991** EPLF takes control of Asmara. New EPRDF government in Addis Ababa effectively agrees to Eritrean secession.

WEALTH

 Demobilized soldier in Asmara, $325 per month; the 1 million refugees who fled to neighbouring countries are destitute

CONSUMER GOODS OWNERSHIP

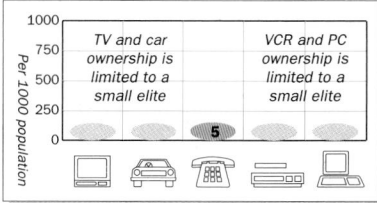

TV and car ownership is limited to a small elite. VCR and PC ownership is limited to a small elite. 5

Over 80% of people are subsistence farmers. A few of the 150,000 refugees who fled to Arab and Western countries have built up some personal savings.

WORLD RANKING

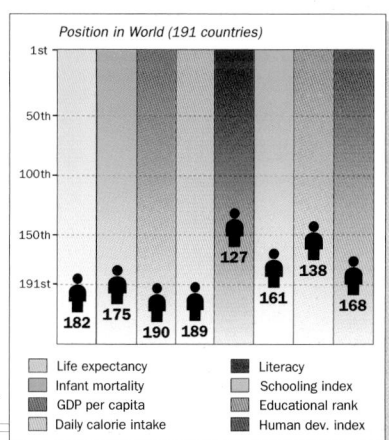

Position in World (191 countries)

182 175 190 189 127 161 138 168

- Life expectancy
- Infant mortality
- GDP per capita
- Daily calorie intake
- Literacy
- Schooling index
- Educational rank
- Human dev. index

ESTONIA

OFFICIAL NAME: Republic of Estonia   **CAPITAL:** Tallinn
POPULATION: 1.6 million   **CURRENCY:** Kroon   **OFFICIAL LANGUAGE:** Estonian

E

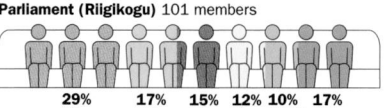

EUROPE

T RADITIONALLY the most Western-orientated of the Baltic states, Estonia is bordered by Latvia and the Russian Federation. Its terrain is flat, boggy and partly wooded, and includes more than 1500 islands. Estonia formally regained its independence as a multiparty democracy in 1991. In contrast to the peoples of the other Baltic states, Latvia and Lithuania, Estonians are Finno-Ugric and their language is similar to Finnish.

CLIMATE

WEATHER CHART

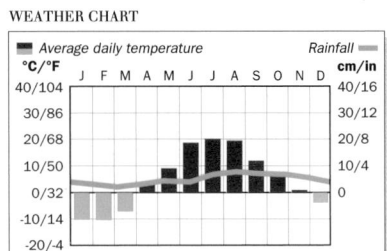

Estonia's coastal location gives it wet springs and cool summers. Winters are cold as the Baltic freezes.

COMMUNICATIONS

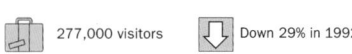

Tallinn Ulemiste

102 ships
587,800 dwt

THE TRANSPORT NETWORK

30,200 km (18,766 miles)		None
1030 km (640 miles)		None

The transport system is in need of modernization. Tallinn airport is currently being upgraded.

TOURISM

277,000 visitors   Down 29% in 1992

MAIN OVERSEAS ARRIVALS

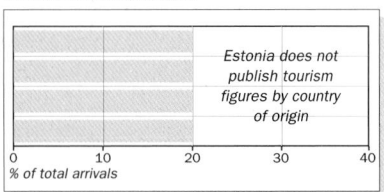

Estonia does not publish tourism figures by country of origin

% of total arrivals

Estonia is a popular destination for Scandinavians, in particular Finns. Tallinn's medieval centre is a major attraction. The capital is also an important Baltic yachting centre, with many summer regattas.

PEOPLE

Estonian, Russian

35 people per km²

THE URBAN/RURAL POPULATION SPLIT

71%   29%

ETHNIC MAKEUP

Other 8%
Russian 30%
Estonian 62%

Under Moscow's rule, Estonia underwent a process of enforced Sovietization. The immigration of a large Russian workforce, many attracted by Estonia's higher living standards, reduced the proportion of Estonians from 90% to 62% of the population. Since 1991, Estonians have been reasserting their dominance. Non-Estonian Russian speakers are finding it harder to get jobs, and several thousand have left. Estonians are predominantly Protestant. Families are small; divorce rates are high.

POLITICS

 1996   President Lennart Meri

THE STATE OF THE PARTIES

Parliament (Riigikogu) 101 members

29% FP	17% SH	15% PF	12% M	10% ENIP	17% Other

FP = Fatherland Party   **SH** = Secure Home
PF = Popular Front   **M** = Moderates   **ENIP** = Estonian National Independence Party   **Other** = Estonian Citizen, Independent Royalists

Since 1992, Estonian politics has been dominated by a coalition led by the conservative, nationalist FP. President Meri and Prime Minister Maart Laar are both FP members. Other ministers come from the Moderates alliance and the ENIP. The proliferation of parties and factions within parliament makes it hard to pass legislation. The status of Russians is a major issue. A 1993 proposal to classify all non-ethnic Estonians as foreigners was passed in parliament, but vetoed at the last minute by the president under international pressure. The coalition government remains committed to market-led economic reform and is privatizing former Soviet enterprises.

ESTONIA

Total Area :
45 125 sq. km
(17 423 sq. miles)

LAND HEIGHT

200m/565ft
Sea Level

POPULATION

⊙ over 500 000
◎ over 100 000
○ over 50 000
● over 10 000
• under 10 000

WORLD AFFAIRS

Estonia wants to secure the return of territories ceded to Russia in the Soviet period. It is keen to obtain greater access to EU markets and to develop its links with Germany. Relations with Finland are particularly good. The government has been criticized by the international community for its treatment of the ethnic Russian minority; the prospect of a Russian intervention is Estonia's main fear.

AID

 Estonia does not publish aid receipts   Probably rising

Finland, Sweden, Germany, the EU and the IMF are major sources of aid, which is spent on infrastructure projects.

DEFENCE

 Army set up; navy and air force planned.   Increasing

Estonia is eager to build up its military forces. The continuing presence of 8000 Russian troops is seen as a potential threat to security. Estonia is also seeking to develop a closer relationship with NATO under the Partnership of Peace programme.

ECONOMICS

 $6.1bn   13.86 kroons

SCORE CARD

❑ WORLD GNP RANKING	105th
❑ GNP PER CAPITA	$3820
❑ BALANCE OF PAYMENTS	$113m
❑ INFLATION	3%
❑ UNEMPLOYMENT	1%

STRENGTHS
Oil shale and phosphorite reserves. Light industrial sector. Own stable currency, the kroon. Reduced dependence on Russia. Growing links with Finland and Germany.

WEAKNESSES
Antiquated industrial infrastructure in urgent need of investment. Poor raw materials base. Dependence on imported energy supplies.

EXPORTS

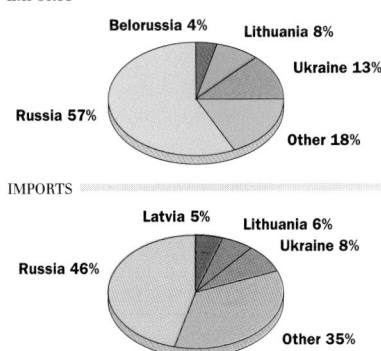

Belorussia 4%   Lithuania 8%
Ukraine 13%
Russia 57%
Other 18%

IMPORTS

Latvia 5%   Lithuania 6%
Ukraine 8%
Russia 46%
Other 35%

RESOURCES

 Oil shale used to generate electricity   Oil figures not published

 6.8m poultry, 1.1m pigs, 806,000 cattle   Oil shale, phosphorite

The chief resources are oil shale and phosphorite. The latter is processed to make phosphates for agricultural use.

ENVIRONMENT

 8%   Northern coniferous forests are suffering from acid rain

Environmental issues are prominent. Protests against Soviet plans to expand phosphorite mining in the northeast, the most polluted area, were part of the late 1980s independence movement.

MEDIA

 Little censorship for Estonians; Russian access to the media is decreasing

PUBLISHING AND BROADCAST MEDIA

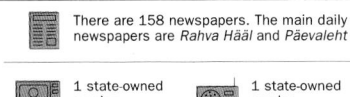
There are 158 newspapers. The main daily newspapers are *Rahva Hääl* and *Päevaleht*

1 state-owned service   1 state-owned service

The media are mostly pro-government. The number of Russian language programmes is declining. Estonians have been able to receive Finnish satellite TV for some years.

CRIME

 Estonia does not publish prison figures   Fairly constant from year to year

Robbery and drugs are the main crime problems. Generally, however, crime levels are still relatively low.

EDUCATION

 Figures not published, but among highest of ex-Soviet republics

Education is becoming increasingly Westernized. Six higher-education establishments have 26,000 students.

HEALTH

 1 per 217 people   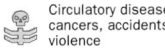 Circulatory diseases, cancers, accidents, violence

The health system, improved since the collapse of communism, is better than that of most former Soviet republics.

The Russian Orthodox convent of Pühtitsa at Kuremäe in Estonia's marshy north. Most of the population is Evangelical Lutheran.

E

CHRONOLOGY

After first Swedish and then Russian rule, Estonia enjoyed a brief period of independence from 1921 until its incorporation into the Soviet Union, in 1940.

❑ **1945–1953** Sovietization; cultural repression, deportations.
❑ **1986–1989** Growing independence movement, helped by *glasnost*.
❑ **1990** Unilateral declaration of independence.
❑ **1991** Independence recognized by Russia.
❑ **1992** Multiparty elections.

WEALTH

 Traders are the wealthiest group

CONSUMER GOODS OWNERSHIP

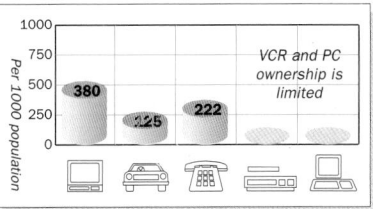

VCR and PC ownership is limited

380   225   222

Growing Western economic ties have maintained Estonia's traditionally high standard of living.

WORLD RANKING

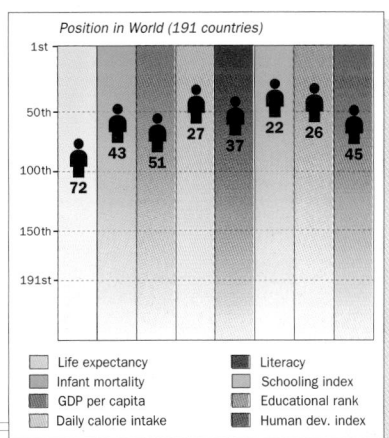

Position in World (191 countries)

72   43   51   27   37   22   26   45

Life expectancy
Infant mortality
GDP per capita
Daily calorie intake
Literacy
Schooling index
Educational rank
Human dev. index

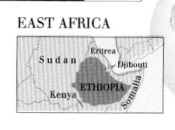

ETHIOPIA

OFFICIAL NAME: Ethiopia *(formal name as yet undetermined)* **CAPITAL:** Addis Ababa
POPULATION: 53 million **CURRENCY:** Ethiopian birr **OFFICIAL LANGUAGE:** Amharic

L OCATED IN NORTHEAST AFRICA, Ethiopia reverted
to its historical land-locked status in 1993, when
Eritrea, its coastal province on the Red Sea, regained its independence.
Ethiopia is mountainous except for the desert lowlands in the northeast
and southeast and is subject to devastating droughts and famines. Civil
war began in the 1960s and ended in 1991 with the defeat of the military
dictatorship that had ruled since 1974. Since then, a transitional
government has been taking steps to establish a free-market, multiparty
democracy. The proposed system is intended to give Ethiopia's ethnic
groups proper representation. Farming reforms and good rains have
halved Ethiopia's need for food aid.

PEOPLE

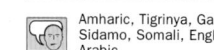 Amharic, Tigrinya, Galla, Sidamo, Somali, English, Arabic   40 people per km²

THE URBAN/RURAL POPULATION SPLIT

13%   87%

RELIGIOUS PERSUASION

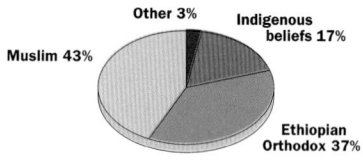

Other 3%
Indigenous beliefs 17%
Muslim 43%
Ethiopian Orthodox 37%

ETHNIC MAKEUP

Sidamo 9%
Oromo 40%
Other 19%
Amhara and Tigrean 32%

CLIMATE

WEATHER CHART

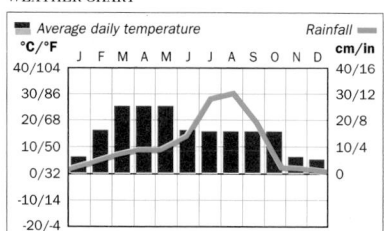

In general, the climate is moderate,
except in the lowlands of the Danakil
Desert and the Ogaden, which are hot
all year round and can suffer severe
drought. The highlands are warm,
with night frost and snowfalls in the
mountains. The single rainy season
in the west brings twice as much
rain as do the two wet seasons in
the east. During these cloudy periods,
thunderstorms occur almost daily.

COMMUNICATIONS

 Bole Intl, Addis Ababa 480,000 passengers   20 ships 87,000 dwt

THE TRANSPORT NETWORK

 39,482 km (24,534 miles)   Trans-East Africa Highway

 681 km (423 miles)   None

The single railway links Addis Ababa
with Djibouti and the only all-weather
roads are those between main business
centres. Repairing war damage is a
priority, with efforts concentrated on
the roads through Eritrea to the Red
Sea ports of Assab and Massawa. As
ownership of motor vehicles of any
kind is rare, pack donkeys and donkey
carts are widely used, especially in
the highlands.

TOURISM

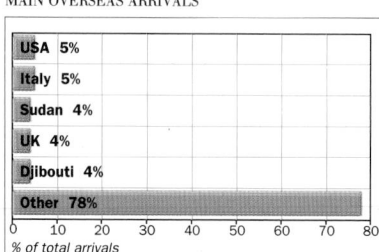 83,213 visitors   Up 2% in 1992

MAIN OVERSEAS ARRIVALS

USA	5%
Italy	5%
Sudan	4%
UK	4%
Djibouti	4%
Other	78%

% of total arrivals (scale 0–80)

Tourism has always been on a small
scale, although since 1991 there has
been a moderate increase in the
number of visitors. By 1994, the need
for permits to travel within the country
had been abolished. Several new hotels
are being built. Most tourists go to
Ethiopia on expensive organized tours,
and Lake Gonder with its spectacular
scenery is a popular destination.
Ethiopia's ancient forts, churches
and cities such as Āksum, the royal
capital of the first Ethiopian kingdom,
are now accessible. Some safari tours
operate to the five national parks.

*Lalibela, 120 km northwest of Desē in
Ethiopia's central highlands. An important
pilgrimage centre, it is famous for its ten
12th-century Christian churches.*

There are 76 nationalities in Ethiopia
speaking 286 languages. Oromos form
the largest group, followed by Amharas
and Tigreans.

Civil war was sparked by fighting
between different ethnic groups, but
they later united in opposition to the
Mengistu regime's centralist policies.
Ethnic tensions are still near the
surface, in spite of the new federal
structure, and there have been
reports of boundary disputes in several
regions. The Oromos withdrew from
the Tigrean-dominated government
in 1992. Opposition to the transitional
government has also been voiced
by disaffected Amharas, who had
held the reins of power for the last
century, and by the Orthodox Church.
Amnesty International has also
expressed concern at the arrest
of Amharan leaders.

No discrimination is shown towards
minorities. Most of the small Jewish
population was evacuated to Israel
in 1991. The participation of women
in rural organizations is increasing,
reflecting the key role women
played in the war.

POPULATION AGE BREAKDOWN

% of population by age group	0–14	15–64	65+

	1960	1970	1980	1990	2000
65+	2.5%	2.5%	2.6%	2.9%	2.8%
15–64	53%	53%	52.9%	51.3%	50.6%
0–14	44.5%	44.5%	44.5%	45.8%	46.6%

E

ETHIOPIA

Total Area :
1 221 900 sq. km
(471 775 sq. miles)

POPULATION

over 1 000 000	▣
over 100 000	◎
over 50 000	○
over 10 000	●
under 10 000	·

LAND HEIGHT

4000m/13 124ft	
3000m/9843ft	
2000m/6562ft	
1000m/3281ft	
500m/1640ft	
200m/656ft	
Sea Level	
-200m/656ft	

0   200 km
0   200 miles

WORLD AFFAIRS

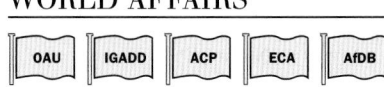

Land-locked Ethiopia is anxious to maintain cordial relations with Eritrea, in order to retain access to the Red Sea. These have been partly cemented in a number of recent bilateral accords, which allow for the harmonization of economic policy and the free movement of peoples.

Ethiopia has been active in regional diplomacy. It has made numerous attempts at brokering peace in Somalia. President Zenawi has played a key role by hosting several Somali reconciliation conferences in Addis Ababa.

During the Mengistu regime, Ethiopia's liberation movements supported dissidents in neighbouring Sudan and Somalia. However, the transitional government now has an official policy of not interfering in its neighbours' affairs, in order to reduce regional tensions. Links with the USA, the main bilateral aid donor, and Israel have been strengthened.

POLITICS

 1994

 President Meles Zenawi

THE STATE OF THE PARTIES

Council of Representatives 84 members

A transitional government is in place. Constitutional elections were to be held in 1994, with legislative elections to follow

Since the collapse of the military dictatorship of Mengistu Haile Mariam in 1991, Ethiopia has been ruled by a transitional government.

MAIN POLITICAL ISSUE

Ethnic representation
The transitional government plans to establish Ethiopia as a democratic ethnic federation of autonomous regions, representing different ethnic groups. Electoral constituencies will each have 100,000 voters, and parliamentary candidates must speak the language of the area they represent. Former members of Mengistu's communist-inspired Workers' Party of Ethiopia are barred from taking part.

PROFILE
The current government was set up in 1991 by the Ethiopian People's

Revolutionary Democratic Front (EPRDF), the strongest of the liberation groups that fought Mengistu's Marxist regime and the one chiefly responsible for winning the civil war. The presidency is held by Meles Zenawi, leader of the Tigrean People's Liberation Front, the largest group within the EPRDF. There is growing opposition to the dominance of Tigreans by the Oromos and Amharas, the next largest groups, notably since January 1994, when the government granted itself a second extension to its caretaker period in office. The regions are largely administered by members of the clan-dominated local liberation movements, which helped to overthrow the Mengistu regime.

***President Meles Zenawi**, leader of the* EPRDF, *which ousted the Mengistu regime.*

***Mengistu Haile Mariam**, who ran Ethiopia on Soviet lines from 1977–1991.*

CHRONOLOGY

After repelling a devastating Muslim invasion in 1523, Ethiopia developed as an isolated empire until Egyptian and Sudanese incursions in the 1850s led to its renewed political power under Emperor Theodor. His successor, Menelik II, doubled the empire southwards and eastwards.

❑ **1896** Italian invasion of Tigre defeated. Europeans recognize Ethiopia's independence.
❑ **1913** Menelik II dies.
❑ **1916** His son, Lij Iyasu, deposed for his conversion to Islam and proposed alliance with Turkey. Menelik's daughter, Zauditu, becomes empress with Ras Tafari as regent.
❑ **1925** Joins League of Nations.
❑ **1930** Zauditu dies. Ras Tafari crowned Emperor Haile Selassie.
❑ **1936** Italians occupy Ethiopia. Europe fails to react.
❑ **1941** Allies oust Italians and restore Haile Selassie, who sets up a constitution, parliament and cabinet, but retains personal power and the feudal system.
❑ **1952** Eritrea, formerly ruled first by the Italians then by the British, federated to Ethiopia. ⇨

E

E

- **1962** Unitary state created; Eritrea fully absorbed.
- **1972–1974** Famine kills 200,000.
- **1974** Strikes and army mutinies at Haile Selassie's autocratic rule and country's economic decline. Dergue (Military Committee) stages coup.
- **1975** Becomes socialist state. Nationalizations, worker co-operatives and health reforms.
- **1977** Col Mengistu Haile Mariam takes over. Somali invasion of the Ogaden defeated with Soviet and Cuban help.
- **1978–1979** Thousands of political opponents killed or imprisoned.
- **1984** Workers' Party of Ethiopia (WPE) set up on Soviet model. Live Aid concert raises funds to relieve famine caused by war and three years' drought. One million die.
- **1986** Eritrean rebels now control the whole northeastern coast.
- **1987** People's Democratic Republic of Ethiopia declared with Mengistu as president. New serious drought.
- **1988** Eritrean and Tigrean People's Liberation Fronts (EPLF and TPLF) begin new offensives. Mengistu's budget is for 'Everything to the War Front'. Ethiopia agrees not to interfere in Somali factional fighting and resumes diplomatic relations severed in 1977.
- **1989** Military coup attempt fails. TPLF in control of most of Tigre. TPLF and Ethiopian People's Revolutionary Movement form alliance – the EPRDF.
- **1990** WPE renamed Ethiopian Democratic Unity Party and opened to non-Marxists. Moves towards market economy begin. Distribution of food aid for victims of new famine hampered by both government and rebel forces.
- **1991** Mengistu flees country in face of big advances by EPRDF and EPLF. EPRDF enters Addis Ababa and sets up provisional government, dividing country into 14 semi-autonomous regions and promising representation for all ethnic groups. However, fighting continues between the mainly Tigrean EPRDF troops and various opposing groups. EPLF enters Asmara, the Eritrean capital, and sets up government.
- **1992** Regional elections – malpractice by all sides and boycotts by opposition groups. EPRDF gets 90% of votes. Fighting in southeast stops aid delivery to 600,000 Somali refugees who arrived in 1991–1992.
- **1993** Eritrean independence recognized.

AID

 $1.1bn (receipts)   Up 8% in 1991

The World Food Programme and the EU are the largest sources of assistance, while the USA has taken over from Italy and the former Soviet Union as the major bilateral donor. Aid per capita is low by regional standards.

However, long-term development assistance and balance of payments support look set to continue their recent growth. Aid is now playing an increasingly important part in the economy. The emphasis is shifting from food aid towards credit for infrastructure development.

DEFENCE

 $1.31bn   Up 42% in 1990

0   *Defence spending as % GDP*   40
21.4%

Ethiopia has no formal military alliances. A key issue is improving government control of the many ethnic and clan-based militias. Plans exist to create a national army representing all ethnic groups. Much of the Mengistu regime's $6-billion arms debt to the former USSR is unpaid.

ETHIOPIAN ARMED FORCES

350 main battle tanks (T-54/T-55/T-62)	100,000 (est)
Has no navy	None
38 combat aircraft (20 MiG-21MF/ 18 MiG-23BN)	Included under army
None	

ECONOMICS

 $6.6bn   4.92 Ethiopian birr

SCORE CARD

- WORLD GNP RANKING...........................97th
- GNP PER CAPITA $125
- BALANCE OF PAYMENTS $41m
- INFLATION 7.7%
- UNEMPLOYMENT....Widespread underemployment

EXPORTS

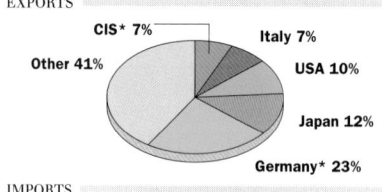

CIS* 7% Italy 7%
Other 41% USA 10%
Japan 12%
Germany* 23%

IMPORTS

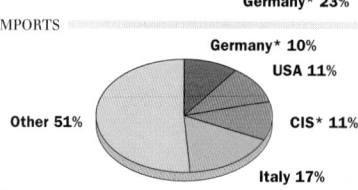

Germany* 10%
USA 11%
Other 51% CIS* 11%
Italy 17%

STRENGTHS

Peace and greater flows of economic aid. Dismantling of total state control. Coffee production.

WEAKNESSES

Overwhelming dependence on agriculture – engages 75% of population, accounts for 80% of exports. Periodic serious droughts. War-damaged infrastructure. Massive displacement of population by war and drought. Small industrial base. Lack of skilled workers. Legacy of Mengistu regime's disastrous experiment in a centrally-planned economy.

ECONOMIC PERFORMANCE INDICATOR

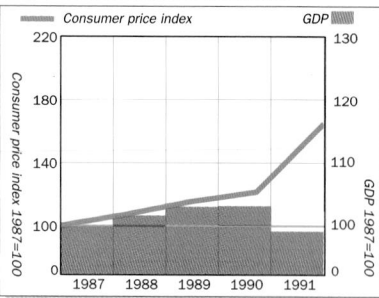

Consumer price index   GDP

PROFILE

Since the end of the civil war, Ethiopia has begun moving towards a market economy by encouraging foreign investment and reforming land tenure. Economic decline was reversed in 1993 as agricultural and industrial output grew. The latter was fuelled by the purchase of parts and raw materials funded by foreign aid. Ethiopia is the world's second poorest nation.

ETHIOPIA : MAJOR BUSINESSES

Light engineering
Coffee processing
Food processing
Publishing
Textiles

Gonder
Addis Ababa
Dirē Dawa
Nazrēt
Jīma
Yirga 'Alem

0   250 km
0   250 miles

RESOURCES

906m kwh (capacity 400,000 kw)

Not an oil producer; refines 18,000 b/cd

29m cattle, 24m sheep, 5m asses, 3m horses

Oil, gold, platinum, copper, potash

ELECTRICITY GENERATION

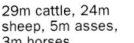

Hydro 80% (722m kwh)
Thermal 13% (118m kwh)
Nuclear 0%
Other 7% (66m kwh)

0   20   40   60   80   100
% of total generation by type

Manpower and financial constraints have prevented a systematic survey of mineral resources. At present, mining contributes less than 1% of GDP. Ethiopia has great potential for hydroelectric power which, in the long run, could offset a domestic reliance on fuelwood and also slow massive deforestation and soil erosion. Current exploration for oil and gas has revealed reserves in the Ogaden, but exploitation has not begun. When Eritrea seceded in 1993, Ethiopia lost other substantial oil reserves and many oil concessions.

ETHIOPIA : LAND USE
Cropland
Forest
Pasture
Cattle
Coffee - cash crop
Cereals

0   250 km
0   250 miles

ENVIRONMENT

2.5%

Soil erosion due to deforestation is the biggest problem

ENVIRONMENTAL TREATIES

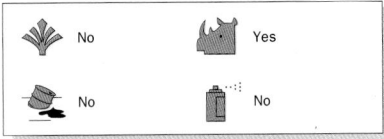

No

Yes

No

No

Deforestation for fuelwood and the resultant rapid soil erosion, particularly in the highlands, are serious problems. Forest cover has fallen from 40% in 1900 to only 2% today. Shortage of wood means that dung is increasingly being used for fuel. Its fertilizer value is put at $123 million a year, enough to increase annual grain harvests by up to 1.5 million tonnes. Local projects include terracing hillsides to prevent soil and water run-off – 36,000 km of terraces were built in Tigray in 1992.

MEDIA

There is now considerable freedom of expression compared with the blanket censorship of the Mengistu years

The government remains uneasy about the post-Mengistu independent press, which has become prolific and critical. Legal action has been taken to silence several publications. A recent proliferation of pornographic magazines has also resulted in closures and government clamp-downs.

PUBLISHING AND BROADCAST MEDIA

There are 3 daily newspapers, *Addis Zemen*, *Ethiopian Herald* and *Hibret*, all published by the government

1 state-owned service

1 state-owned, also independent services

Arabsat 1C Palapa B2-P

None

CRIME

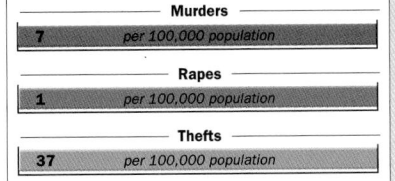

13,585 prisoners

Down 2% in 1988

CRIME RATES

Murders
7   per 100,000 population

Rapes
1   per 100,000 population

Thefts
37   per 100,000 population

EDUCATION

71%

0   *Education spending as % GNP*   25
4.4%

THE EDUCATION SYSTEM

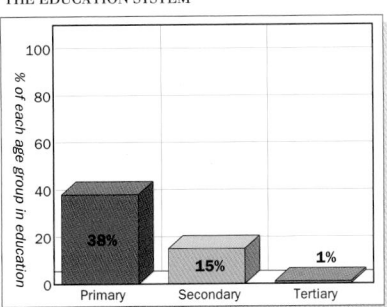

100
80
60
40
20
0
% of each age group in education

38% Primary
15% Secondary
1% Tertiary

The education system was severely disrupted during the civil war. Addis Ababa University has been a centre of political activity, usually anti-EPRDF, and is subject to periodic closures and the dismissal of its leading academics.

HEALTH

1 per 38,359 people

Diarrheal and respiratory diseases, tuberculosis, malaria

0   *Health spending as % GNP*   25
1.2%

Only about half of the population lives within 12 km of a health unit. Hospital building, distribution of resources to rural areas, outpatient visits and referrals are all very slow. Skin and eye diseases are common. Church hospitals are of a reasonably high standard.

A number of human rights abuses by the transitional government have been documented by the independent Ethiopian Human Rights Council. These include detention without trial, 'disappearances' and extra-judicial killings. There is some concern over indiscipline among EPRDF forces, who provide a *de facto* police force in many regions. In many rural areas traditional clan justice has replaced the state system.

WEALTH

Most Ethiopians lead a subsistence existence

CONSUMER GOODS OWNERSHIP

1000
750
500
250
0
Per 1000 population

VCR and PC ownership is limited to a small elite

2   1   3

There is very little wealth in Ethiopia. The central plateau is historically the richest region. Average incomes fell by 8.5% in 1991, while prices rose by 25%. Corruption among public employees is rising again, owing to pressures on incomes. Ethiopian culture places more value on maintaining traditional social structures than on individual ambition.

WORLD RANKING

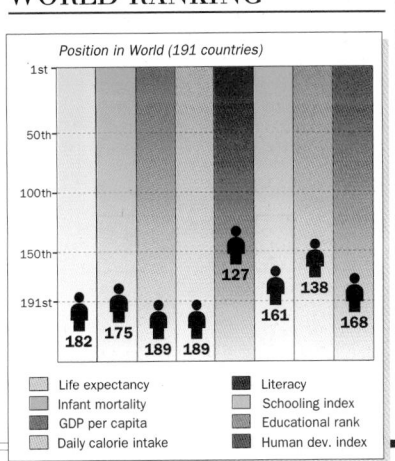

Position in World (191 countries)
1st
50th
100th
150th
191st

127
138
161
168
182   175   189   189

Life expectancy
Infant mortality
GDP per capita
Daily calorie intake

Literacy
Schooling index
Educational rank
Human dev. index

E

FIJI

OFFICIAL NAME: Republic of Fiji CAPITAL: Suva

POPULATION: 700,000 CURRENCY: Fiji dollar OFFICIAL LANGUAGE: English

FIJI IS A VOLCANIC ARCHIPELAGO in the southern Pacific Ocean, comprising two large islands and 880 smaller islets. From 1874 to 1970, Fiji was a British colony. The British introduced Indian workers to the islands and by 1946 their descendants, the Indo-Fijians, outnumbered the Native Fijian population. In 1987, Native Fijians overthrew the democratically-elected government. After the coups, thousands of Indo-Fijians left the country.

CLIMATE

WEATHER CHART

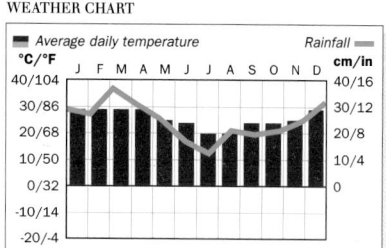

The eastern sides of the main islands are wettest, having more than twice the annual rainfall of the western flanks. Fiji lies in a cyclone path.

COMMUNICATIONS

Nadi International
785,000 passengers

25 ships
62,900 dwt

THE TRANSPORT NETWORK

4821 km (2996 miles)	None
595 km (370 miles)	122 km (76 miles)

On the axis of Australian–US west coast air routes, Fiji is well served by international flights. It is promoting an increase in Pacific shipping routes.

TOURISM

 278,534 visitors   Up 7% in 1992

MAIN OVERSEAS ARRIVALS

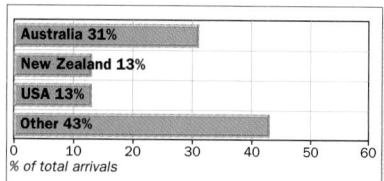

| Australia 31% |
| New Zealand 13% |
| USA 13% |
| Other 43% |

0 10 20 30 40 50 60
% of total arrivals

Tourists – mainly from Australia, New Zealand and west coast USA – are returning, after a 76% drop in numbers following the 1987 coups.

PEOPLE

Fijian, English, Hindi, Urdu, Tamil, Telugu

44 people per km²

THE URBAN/RURAL POPULATION SPLIT

39% **61%**

RELIGIOUS PERSUASION

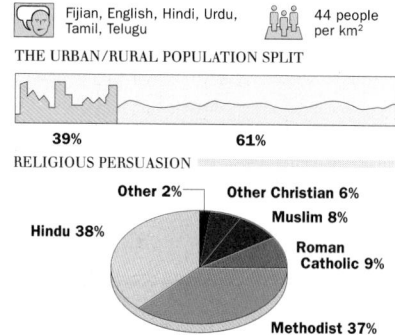

Other 2%
Hindu 38%
Other Christian 6%
Muslim 8%
Roman Catholic 9%
Methodist 37%

The exodus of Indo-Fijians after the 1987 coups left Native Fijians in the majority for the first time since 1946. There are tensions between urban and rural Native Fijians. Women, who head 12% of households, are lobbying for more rights. They cannot obtain loans without a husband's or father's consent, while children born of marriages to non-Fijian men are denied full citizenship.

POLITICS

1999

President Ratu Sir Kamisese Mara

THE STATE OF THE PARTIES

House of Representatives 70 members

7% FA   4% Other

44% SVT   **29% NFP**   **10% FLP**   **6% GVP**

SVT = Fijian Political Party   NFP = National Federation Party   FLP = Fiji Labour Party   FA = Fijian Association   GVP = General Voters' Party   Other = All Nationals Congress

Senate 34 members

24 members are chosen by the Great Council of Chiefs, 9 by the president and 1 by the Rotuma Island Council

The 1987 coups were justified as defending the land rights of Native Fijians. In practice, they were a move by Native Fijian chiefs to secure their power, which was being threatened both by the growing Indo-Fijian urban class, and by the increasingly Westernized younger Native Fijians. The 1990 constitution, enshrining Native Fijian supremacy, makes any future Indo-Fijian challenge to the current *status quo* unlikely.

FIJI

Total Area : 18 270 sq. km (7054 sq. miles)

POPULATION

over 50 000 ○
over 10 000 ●
under 10 000 ●

LAND HEIGHT

1000m/3281ft
500m/1640ft
Sea Level

F

WORLD AFFAIRS

ESCAP · ACP · ADP · SPC · SPF

Fiji is still working to repair its international reputation following the coups of 1987, the subsequent discriminatory constitution and its expulsion from the Commonwealth.

AID

 $45m (receipts)

 Fairly stable in recent years

Fiji is one of the world's highest per capita aid recipients. Australia, Japan and the EU are the main donors.

DEFENCE

 $27m

 Up 4% in 1991

Of the 5000-strong, almost entirely Native-Fijian military, 1200 are assigned to UN duties and have served in Lebanon and Afghanistan.

ECONOMICS

 $1.5bn

 1.57 Fiji dollars

SCORE CARD

❏ World GNP Ranking	146th
❏ GNP per Capita	$1770
❏ Balance of Payments	$46m
❏ Inflation	5.6%
❏ Unemployment	5.9%

STRENGTHS
Relatively well-diversified economy, with a growing tourist industry. Location on Pacific air routes an impetus to tourism; the many regional and international organizations located in Suva also bring benefits.

WEAKNESSES
Privileged access to key world markets now threatened by the new GATT arrangements. Major exports – sugar, copra and gold – subject to large fluctuations in world prices.

EXPORTS

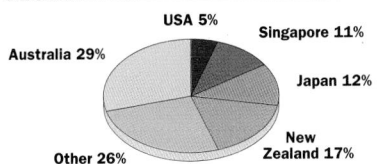

USA 6%   Australia 6%
New Zealand 7%
UK 39%
Malaysia 8%
Other 34%

IMPORTS

USA 5%   Singapore 11%
Australia 29%
Japan 12%
New Zealand 17%
Other 26%

Cane field on the west side of Viti Levu, between Nadi and Lautoka. Sugar accounts for about one third of Fiji's exports.

RESOURCES

 435m kwh (capacity 200,000 kw)

 Not an oil producer and has no refineries

 32,800 tonnes

Gold, silver

The varied terrain allows diversified agriculture. There are minerals and hydroelectric potential, which is partly developed in the Monasavu project.

ENVIRONMENT

 0.3%

 Overuse of fertilizers

The government is environmentally aware; Fiji is downwind of France's Pacific nuclear test sites. Tourism is damaging the coral reefs.

MEDIA

 Under newly introduced restrictions, no aspersions may be cast on the Fijian leadership

PUBLISHING AND BROADCAST MEDIA

 There are 2 English-language dailies, the *Fiji Times* and the *Fiji Sun*. *Nai Lalakai* and *Shanti Dut* are the Fijian and Indian weeklies

 1 state-owned service

 5 state-controlled, 2 independent stations

Newspapers and video tapes are the major source of information on the islands. Radios keep the many Fijians who are away from home in touch with news from their villages.

CRIME

 859 men 19 women

 Down 3% between 1985 and 1990

Theft and drink-related violence top the crime list. Fiji also has one of the world's highest *crime passionel* rates.

EDUCATION

 87%

Education, originally modelled on the British system, is now mostly run by local committees and is increasingly racially segregated. Attendance, though high, is not compulsory.

CHRONOLOGY

The British decision to import Indian sugar workers between 1879 and 1916, many of whom settled, dramatically changed Fijian society.

❏ **1970** Independence from Britain.
❏ **1972–1987** Alliance Party maintains Native and Indo-Fijian balance.
❏ **1987** Indo-Fijian majority coalition wins power. Two coups led by Maj-Gen Rabuka secure minority Native Fijian supremacy. Fiji ejected from Commonwealth.
❏ **1989** Mass Indo-Fijian emigration.
❏ **1990** Constitution discriminating against Indo-Fijians introduced.
❏ **1992** Elections. Rabuka's Fijian Political Party secures power.

HEALTH

 1 per 2224 people

 Cerebrovascular and heart diseases, cancers, accidents

People living in rural areas and on the outlying islands are served by 95 nursing stations. Fiji is free of almost all tropical diseases, including malaria.

WEALTH

 Agricultural worker, 12 Fiji dollars per day; construction worker, 14 Fiji dollars per day

CONSUMER GOODS OWNERSHIP

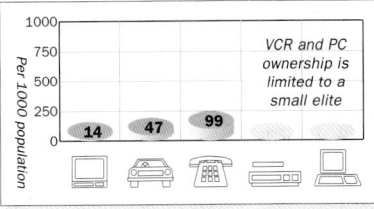

VCR and PC ownership is limited to a small elite

Per 1000 population: 14, 47, 99

Ostentatious displays of wealth are rare; prestige derives from family and landholdings. The professional middle class, while still dominated by Indo-Fijians, is becoming more mixed.

WORLD RANKING

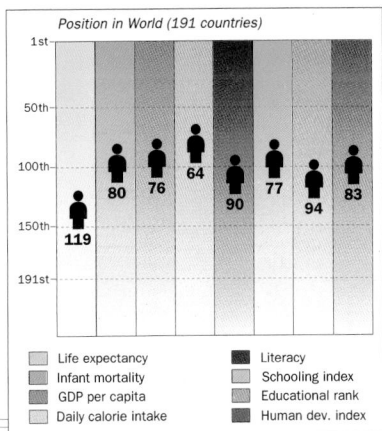

Position in World (191 countries)

119, 80, 76, 64, 90, 77, 94, 83

☐ Life expectancy
☐ Infant mortality
☐ GDP per capita
☐ Daily calorie intake
■ Literacy
☐ Schooling index
☐ Educational rank
■ Human dev. index

FINLAND

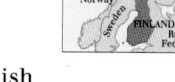
EUROPE

OFFICIAL NAME: Republic of Finland   CAPITAL: Helsinki
POPULATION: 5 million   CURRENCY: Markka   OFFICIAL LANGUAGES: Finnish and Swedish

F

 1917

BORDERED TO THE north and west by Norway and Sweden, and to the east by Russia, Finland is a low-lying country of forests and over 60,000 lakes. Politics are based on consensus and the country has been stable despite successive short-lived coalitions. Finland was ruled by Russia until 1917, and subsequently accepted a close relationship with the Soviet Union as the price of maintaining its independence. It intends to join the EU in 1995. Living standards are high, but the country is recovering from a recession which, in 1990, ended a decade of record growth.

CLIMATE

WEATHER CHART

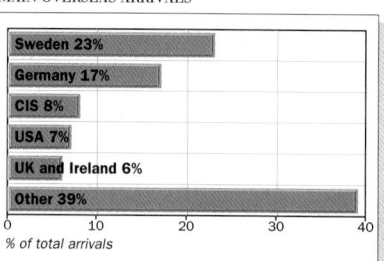

North of the Arctic Circle the climate is extreme. Temperatures fall to –30°C in the six-month winter and rise to 27°C during the 73 days of summer midnight sun. In the south, summers are mild and short, winters are cold. The annual average temperature in Helsinki is 5°C.

COMMUNICATIONS

 Helsinki-Vantaa,
5.51m passengers
 121 ships
1.02m dwt

THE TRANSPORT NETWORK

 133,631 km
(83,037 miles)
 249 km
(155 miles)

 5884 km
(3656 miles)
 6100 km
(3790 miles)

Finland has a well-integrated transport system. The railway connects with the Swedish and Russian networks. There are also frequent air services to most neighbouring states. At present, links with the Baltic countries are being improved. Internal air travel is also important, particularly north of the Arctic Circle.

With over 60,000 lakes and rivers, Finland has Europe's largest inland waterway system. Although it still carries freight, its use today is mainly recreational. Finland's international ports handle around 60 million tons a year. Kotka is the chief port for exports. Helsinki, with its five specialized harbours, handles most imports.

TOURISM

🧳 2.24m visitors   ⬆ Up 2% in 1992

MAIN OVERSEAS ARRIVALS

Sweden 23%	
Germany 17%	
CIS 8%	
USA 7%	
UK and Ireland 6%	
Other 39%	

% of total arrivals (0, 10, 20, 30, 40)

The scenery of the southern lakes and the vast forests of its Arctic north are Finland's main attractions. Helsinki is an important cultural centre and hosts an annual arts festival. Its opera house has an international reputation and the capital has many first-class restaurants. Most tourists try a sauna, a Finnish invention, and the local vodka, which is reputedly among the world's finest.

Visitors come mostly from other Nordic countries and Germany. Since 1990, there has been an increase in visitors from the Baltic States and Russia. The depreciation of the markka since 1992 has helped to boost visitor numbers.

A summer's night at Lake Kilpisjärvi, 'The Way of the Four Winds', which lies at the point where Finland, Sweden and Norway meet.

PEOPLE

 Finnish, Swedish, Lappish   👥 15 people per km²

THE URBAN/RURAL POPULATION SPLIT

60%   40%

RELIGIOUS PERSUASION

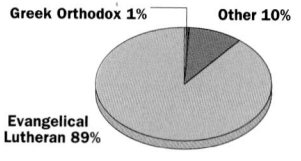

Greek Orthodox 1%   Other 10%
Evangelical Lutheran 89%

ETHNIC MAKEUP

Other (including Sami) 1%

Finn 99%

Most Finns are of Scandinavian-Baltic extraction. Finnish belongs to the small Finno-Ugric linguistic group and is a legacy of the country's earliest invaders from Asia. Although they were later ousted by the ancestors of today's Finns, their language was retained. Lappish, also a Finno-Ugric language, is spoken by the small Sami (Lapp) population, who live above the Arctic Circle. Around 6% of the population live in the Åland Islands in the southwest and speak Swedish.

More than 50% of Finns live in the five southernmost districts around Helsinki. Families tend to be close-knit, although divorce rates are high. The sauna is an integral part of everyday life; there are 1.5 million saunas among five million Finns.

Finnish women have a long tradition of political and economic participation. They were the first in Europe to get the vote, in 1906, and the first in the world able to stand for parliament. Almost 50% of women now work outside the home. Both the governor of the central bank and the defence minister are women.

POPULATION AGE BREAKDOWN

% of population by age group	■ 0–14	■ 15–64	□ 65+
65+	7.2%	9.2%	12%	13.2%	14.4%
15–64	62.4%	66.2%	67.7%	67.5%	68.1%
0–14	30.4%	24.6%	20.3%	19.3%	17.5%
	1960	1970	1980	1990	2000

POLITICS

 1995

 President Martti Ahtisaari

Finland's constitution combines parliamentary government with a strong presidency. The external territory of the Åland Islands has internal self-government.

MAIN POLITICAL ISSUES

EU membership

Finland is due to join the EU in 1995, pending a national referendum. The EU is a less contentious issue than in other Nordic countries. Many Finns support entry as a way of identifying with western Europe. However, a 'yes' vote is not certain. The small but influential farming community is hostile to membership because it poses a threat to farm subsidies. This opposition could widen if further public spending cuts, in particular welfare cuts, are required to meet the economic criteria for membership.

THE STATE OF THE PARTIES

Parliament 200 members

| 27% KESK | 24% SDP | 20% KOK | 10% V | 6% SFP | 13% Other |

KESK = Finnish Centre Party **SDP** = Finnish Social Democratic Party **KOK** = National Coalition Party **V** = Left-wing Alliance **SFP** = Swedish People's Party **Other** = Green Union, Finnish Christian Union, Finnish Rural Party

President Martti Ahtisaari, who won the 1994 presidential election.

Prime Minister Esko Aho, leader of the KESK–KOK coalition.

F

WORLD AFFAIRS

 EEA   CSCE   OECD   GATT 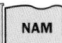 NAM

After carefully balancing its relations with the Soviet Union and the West during the Cold War, Finland has now decided that its national interest lies within western Europe. It is due to join the EU in 1995 and is also considering participation in the WEU. However, the government is also keen not to alienate Russia and will continue to pursue some form of special relationship with Moscow.

AID

 $930m (donations)   Up 10% in 1991

Finland is one of the few donor countries to have achieved the UN target of allocating 0.7% of GDP to aid. The main recipients are countries in South East Asia and Africa.

Unemployment

The victory of SDP candidate Martti Ahtisaari in the 1994 presidential election was a sign of discontent with the conservative KESK–KOK coalition led by Prime Minister Esko Aho. Its handling of the recession resulted in record unemployment levels and welfare cuts. It also strained the traditional consensus approach to politics in Finland. Elections due in 1995 are expected to return an SDP-led coalition.

PROFILE

Proportional representation has led to government by coalition, usually dominated by the SDP or KESK. The emphasis on consensus has favoured stability, but also results in slow decision-making. The parties tend to agree on aims, but not the means of achieving them.

CHRONOLOGY

Finland's history has been closely linked with the competing interests of Sweden and Russia.

❑ **1323** Treaty of Pähkinäsaari. Finland part of Swedish Kingdom.
❑ **1809** Treaty of Fredrikhamn, Sweden cedes Finland to Russia. Finland becomes a Grand Duchy enjoying considerable autonomy.
❑ **1812** Helsinki becomes capital.
❑ **1863** Finnish becomes an official language alongside Swedish.
❑ **1865** Grand Duchy acquires its own monetary system.
❑ **1879** Conscription law lays the foundation for a Finnish army.
❑ **1899** Tsar Nicholas II begins process of Russification. Labour Party founded.
❑ **1900** Gradual imposition of Russian as the official language begins.
❑ **1901** Finnish army disbanded, Finns ordered into Russian units. Disobedience campaign prevents men being drafted into the army. ➪

FINLAND

Total Area :
338 130 sq. km
(130 552 sq. miles)

POPULATION

⊚ over 100 000
○ over 50 000
• over 10 000

LAND HEIGHT

500m/1640ft
200m/656ft
Sea Level

F

DEFENCE

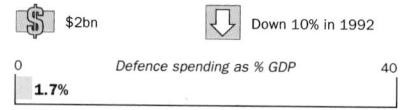

💲 $2bn   ⬇ Down 10% in 1992

0   Defence spending as % GDP   40

1.7%

The Finnish military is small, with 32,800 troops, but there are also 700,000 active reservists and a large border guard force. Russia's instability has reinforced concern about border security, the top defence issue. Finland is reconsidering its neutrality and may opt for participation in the WEU.

FINNISH ARMED FORCES

🔫	123 main battle tanks (60 T–55/63 T–72)	27,300 personnel
🚢	23 patrol boats	2500 personnel
✈	116 combat aircraft (MiG 21bis/Hawk Mk51/ J–35)	3000 personnel
	None	

ECONOMICS

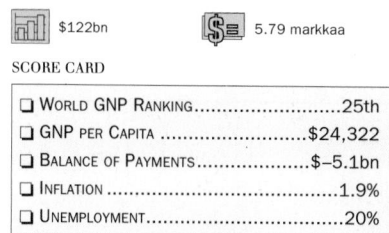

📊 $122bn   💲 5.79 markkaa

SCORE CARD

❑ WORLD GNP RANKING	25th
❑ GNP PER CAPITA	$24,322
❑ BALANCE OF PAYMENTS	$–5.1bn
❑ INFLATION	1.9%
❑ UNEMPLOYMENT	20%

ECONOMIC PERFORMANCE INDICATOR

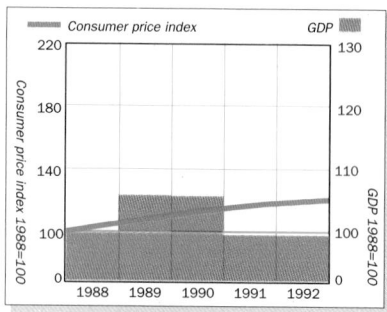

Consumer price index —— | GDP ▨

EXPORTS

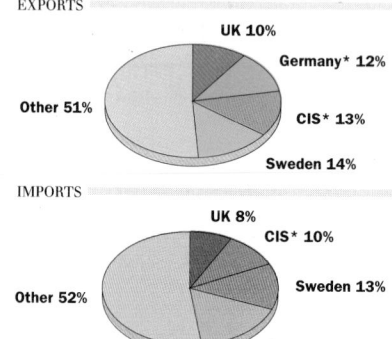

UK 10%
Germany* 12%
CIS* 13%
Sweden 14%
Other 51%

IMPORTS

UK 8%
CIS* 10%
Sweden 13%
Germany* 17%
Other 52%

STRENGTHS

Industry is export and quality orientated. Large high-tech sector. World leader in pulp and paper. Exports quick to recover from recession. Low inflation, now less than 2% a year. Improved foreign investment incentives. Gateway to Russian and Baltic economies.

WEAKNESSES

Severe recession following 1980s fast growth; real GDP declined 15% during 1991–1993. High level of public sector and foreign debt, the latter 22% of GDP. Highest unemployment rate in western Europe, up from 3.5% in 1990 to 20% in 1993. Small domestic market and peripheral position in Europe.

PROFILE

Finland is a market economy and still a wealthy one, although just emerging from its worst recession in 60 years. The boom years of the 1980s, when GDP expanded by almost 4% a year, came to an abrupt end in 1990. The collapse of the former Soviet Union, which had taken 28% of Finland's exports, was largely responsible for the downturn. A rapid rise in unemployment and business failures pushed up government spending. The floating of the markka in 1992 and austerity measures, including welfare benefit cuts, higher taxes and wage restraints, improved Finland's competitiveness. Exports have largely recovered. However, full recovery will take longer and unemployment is likely to stay above 15% for some years. With private investment at a ten-year low and the pressure of EU membership looming, the economy will take time to recover.

FINLAND : MAJOR BUSINESSES

🚢	Shipbuilding
	Electronics
⚙	Light engineering
✿	Heavy engineering
⚡	Electrometallurgy
	Pulp & paper
	Agribusiness
	Ceramics
	Chemicals
✳	Textiles
■	Retail

Oulu

Vaasa

Tampere

Pori

Rauma

Turku

Lahti

Helsinki

Jyväskylä

Lappeenranta

0   100 km
0   100 miles

RESOURCES

54.5bn kwh (capacity 13.2m kw)

Not an oil producer; refines 200,000 b/cd

1.4m cattle, 1.3m pigs, 59,000 sheep

Gold, copper, zinc, iron, lead, silver

ELECTRICITY GENERATION

Hydro 20% (10.9bn kwh)

Thermal 45% (24.4bn kwh)

Nuclear 35% (19.2bn kwh)

Other 0%

% of total generation by type

Finland's trees are its prime natural resource. Commercial forests cover 65% of the land and wood products account for 40% of exports. Finland has no oil, but has significant hydroelectric resources. Industry's high energy demands are met chiefly by thermal and nuclear power. A fifth nuclear power station is planned. Oil import costs have risen since 1990, when the collapse of the USSR ended a 42-year agreement on the exchange of Finnish manufactures for Soviet oil.

FINLAND : LAND USE

Cropland
Forest
Pasture
Reindeer
Barley

0   100 km
0   100 miles

ENVIRONMENT

2% (1% partially protected)

Very high degree of ecological consciousness

ENVIRONMENTAL TREATIES

Yes

Yes

No

Yes

Finland has strict laws on industrial emissions. Energy efficiency is a priority; over 40% of homes are connected to district heating systems. Growing public concern about nuclear safety has led to opposition to the planned fifth nuclear plant and to proposals for the greater use of waste materials in energy generation. The government is funding nuclear safety programmes in Russia. Rising levels of pollution in the Baltic are of concern.

MEDIA

 There is no censorship of the media

PUBLISHING AND BROADCAST MEDIA

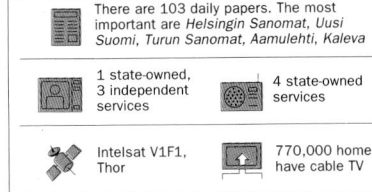

There are 103 daily papers. The most important are *Helsingin Sanomat, Uusi Suomi, Turun Sanomat, Aamulehti, Kaleva*

1 state-owned, 3 independent services

4 state-owned services

Intelsat V1F1, Thor

770,000 homes have cable TV

Nine out of ten Finns take a daily paper, the world's third highest circulation to population ratio. Regional papers dominate; the only national is *Helsingin Sanomat*. There is no censorship, but the press shows restraint in criticizing the government.

CRIME

3106 prisoners

Up 9% in 1990

CRIME RATES

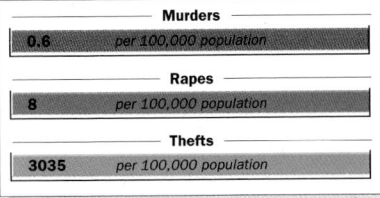

Murders
0.6   per 100,000 population

Rapes
8   per 100,000 population

Thefts
3035   per 100,000 population

The jump in unemployment, from 3.5% in 1990 to 20% in 1993, is one cause of rising crime. There is concern about links with organized crime in Russia.

EDUCATION

100%

0   Education spending as % GNP   25
5.8%

THE EDUCATION SYSTEM

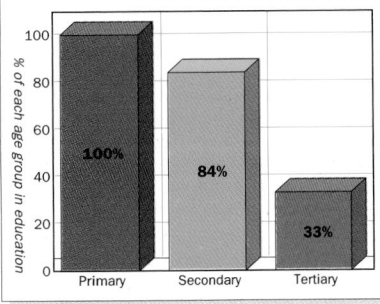

100%   Primary
84%   Secondary
33%   Tertiary

% of each age group in education

Compulsory education lasts from 7 to 16 years of age. Almost all children receive pre-school education and go on to three years of upper secondary education. Tough examinations mean that only 35% of entrants qualify to attend one of the 20 universities.

HEALTH

1 per 430 people

Cerebrovascular and heart diseases, cancers, suicides

0   Health spending as % GNP   25
2.5%

Spending on Finland's well-developed health care system accounts for about 10% of the state budget. Every Finn is legally guaranteed access to a local health centre staffed by up to four doctors, as well as nurses and a midwife. National health insurance covers most non-hospital medical costs and hospital fees are moderate.

F

WEALTH

Paper machine operator, 58 markkaa per hour; general physician, 16,900 markkaa per month

CONSUMER GOODS OWNERSHIP

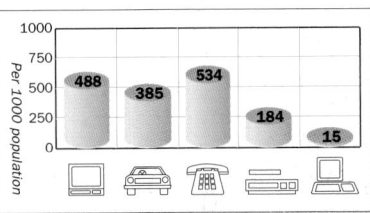

488   385   534   184   15

Per 1000 population

Income disparities are more marked in Finland than in the rest of Scandinavia. However, the economic boom and labour shortages of the 1980s led to a sharp rise in all living standards. Personal consumption reached Swedish levels and many families were able to take two holidays a year. Social security benefits were extended.

Since the recession began in 1990, this improvement has been reversed. Wealth disparities have also widened. Cuts in budgetary expenditure have resulted in a decline in social security benefits paid to the unemployed. Those in work have had to accept lower pay rises and higher taxes. Average real disposable income has dropped by more than 7% since 1991. Estonian immigrants form the poorest group.

WORLD RANKING

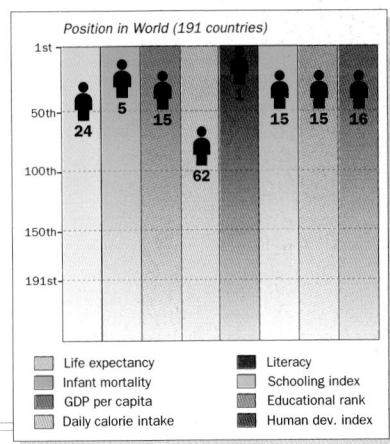

Position in World (191 countries)

1st
50th
100th
150th
191st

24   5   15   62   15   15   16

Life expectancy
Infant mortality
GDP per capita
Daily calorie intake
Literacy
Schooling index
Educational rank
Human dev. index

FRANCE

OFFICIAL NAME: The French Republic   **CAPITAL:** Paris   **POPULATION:** 57.2 million
CURRENCY: Franc   **OFFICIAL LANGUAGE:** French   **OVERSEAS TERRITORIES:** 10

F

STRADDLING WESTERN EUROPE from the English Channel to the Mediterranean, France was Europe's first modern republic and possessed a colonial empire second only to Britain's. Today it is one of the world's major industrial powers and its fourth largest exporter. Industry is the leading economic sector, but the agricultural lobby remains powerful – French farmers are willing to mount the barricades in defence of their interests. Today, France's focus is very much towards Europe. Together with Germany it was a founder member of the European Economic Community. Following the 1992 referendum, it endorsed the Maastricht proposals which created the European Union. Paris, its capital, is generally considered one of the world's most beautiful cities. It has been home to some of the 20th century's most influential artists, writers and film-makers.

Le Plessis-Bourré, Loire Valley. The region *is famous for its many chateaux, which attract thousands of visitors every year.*

CLIMATE

WEATHER CHART

Average daily temperature   Rainfall

France has, in broad terms, three climates – Atlantic, Continental and Mediterranean. The northwest, in particular Brittany, is mild but damp. The east has hot summers and stormy winters. Summers in the south are dry and hot, and forest fires are common.

COMMUNICATIONS

Charles de Gaulle, Paris
22.5m passengers

210 ships
5.56m dwt

THE TRANSPORT NETWORK

| 804,450 km (499,861 miles) | 6680 km (4151 miles) |
| 34,421 km (21,388 miles) | 8500 km (5282 miles) |

Once pioneers of aviation and co-builders of Concorde, the French today lead the world in high-speed train technology, with the TGV (*Train à Grande Vitesse*). The first TGV line, opened in 1983, does the 459-km Paris to Lyon journey in two hours – faster, door-to-door, than air travel. TGV lines have since been built to the north and west as well as to the Channel Tunnel, which opened in 1994. It was the French, rather more than the British, who pressed for the tunnel to be built.

TOURISM

53.2m visitors   Up 6% in 1990

MAIN OVERSEAS ARRIVALS

Germany 23%
UK 14%
Belgium 14%
Italy 11%
Spain 6%
Other 32%

% of total arrivals

France is one of the world's leading tourist destinations. It is top of the list for the Germans and the British, and is the most popular European destination for the Japanese. The majority of French people prefer to spend their holidays in their own country, rather than travelling abroad.

Paris is the most visited European city. Its attractions include the Eiffel Tower, Nôtre Dame cathedral, the Pompidou Centre and the Louvre, the world's largest and most popular museum.

Modern tourism was all but invented on the Côte d'Azur, when crowned heads and grandees flocked to new fashionable resorts, such as Nice, at the end of the 19th century. Today, tourism outside Paris still focuses on the south but is more populist, including camping holidays and package tours. Cannes is the venue for the world's leading film festival, as well as a growing business convention trade.

In 1992, EuroDisney opened east of Paris. However, it has not proved as popular with the public as traditional French cultural attractions, losing millions of dollars in its first year.

EUROPE

Europe

FRANCE

Total Area :
551 500 sq. km
(212 930 sq. miles)

POPULATION

over 1 000 000
over 100 000
over 50 000
over 10 000

LAND HEIGHT

3000m/9843ft
2000m/6562ft
1000m/3281ft
500m/1640ft
200m/656ft
Sea Level

N

0   100 km
0   100 miles

PEOPLE

French, Provençal, German, Breton, Catalan, Basque

104 people per km²

The French, despite their strong national identity, are a great mix of peoples. Bretons, Normans, Flemmings, Alsatians, Savoyards, Provençaux, Basques and Corsicans still maintain their traditions, although today local languages are little spoken. France has 4.5 million people of foreign origin, nearly 40% of whom originate from southern Europe, as well as the largest Jewish community in Europe outside Russia, numbering over 700,000.

From 1945 until the mid-1980s, France suffered relatively little from racism. Many Muslim

THE URBAN/RURAL POPULATION SPLIT

74% 26%

POPULATION AGE BREAKDOWN

% of population by age group	0–14	15–64	65+

	1960	1970	1980	1990	2000
65+	11.6%	12.9%	14%	13.8%	15.4%
15–64	62%	62.3%	63.7%	66.1%	65.2%
0–14	26.4%	24.8%	22.3%	20.1%	19.4%

RELIGIOUS PERSUASION

Muslim 1% Protestant 2%
Jewish 1% Other 6%
Roman Catholic 90%

ETHNIC MAKEUP

German 2% Other 2%
Breton 1% North African 3%
French 92%

immigrants from North Africa settled in cities such as Paris and Marseilles, becoming well-integrated into the workforce. Rising unemployment over the past decade has, however, led to a rise in intolerance, reflected in the 14% vote received by the racist National Front (FN). Many large anti-racist rallies have been held to counter FN propaganda and the majority of French wish to maintain a strong liberal tradition. However, many North Africans have come to feel threatened. Black migrants from France's present-day overseas departments do not face the same problems. As full French citizens they are well-integrated.

The Catholic Church, once the dominant conservative force in French society, has lost much of its influence since the 1950s. Abortion and birth control were both legalized in the 1970s despite strong opposition from the Church. Up to 50% of couples now live together before marriage and common-law marriage is legally recognized. Women and men now have identical legal rights, although women did not get the vote until 1945. Today, women are well represented in the professions. Edith Cresson served as France's first woman prime minister from 1991 to 1992.

CHRONOLOGY

The French Revolution of 1789 overthrew a monarchy that had lasted for more than 1300 years. It ushered in a period of alternating republicanism, Napoleonic imperialism and monarchism, ending in 1870 when the founding of the Third Republic established France firmly in the republican tradition.

❑ **1914–1918** 1.4 million Frenchmen killed in the First World War.

❑ **1918–1939** Economic recession and political instability; 44 governments and 20 prime ministers.

❑ **1940** Capitulation to Germany. Marshal Pétain heads puppet Vichy regime. General de Gaulle founds 'Free French' government in London.

❑ **1944** Liberation of France.

❑ **1946–1958** Fourth Republic. Political instability; 26 governments. Nationalizations. France takes leading role in EEC formation.

❑ **1958** Fifth Republic founded. De Gaulle becomes president. Political stability enhanced by increased presidential powers.

❑ **1960** Most French colonies gain independence; retain close links with France in French Community.

❑ **1962** Algerian independence after bitter war with France.

❑ **1966** France withdraws from NATO military command.

❑ **1968** General strike and riots over education policy and low wages. National Assembly dissolved; Gaullist victory in June elections.

❑ **1969** De Gaulle resigns after defeat in referendum on regional reform; replaced by Georges Pompidou.

❑ **1974** Valéry Giscard d'Estaing becomes president after death of Pompidou. Centre-right coalition.

❑ **1981** PS victory in elections; François Mitterrand president.

❑ **1983–1986** Differences over approach to economic recession cause dissension in left-wing coalition. PCF withdraws support.

❑ **1986** *Cohabitation* between socialist president and right-wing government after elections return right-wing coalition led by Jacques Chirac, who challenges presidential powers. Privatization programme introduced.

❑ **1988** Mitterrand wins second term. PS-led coalition returns.

❑ **1989** Start of spate of scandals particularly involving PS politicians.

❑ **1991** Michel Rocard resigns as prime minister. Edith Cresson becomes first woman prime minister.

❑ **1993** Centre-right coalition under Edouard Balladur wins elections.

POLITICS

Lower House 1998
Upper House 1995

President François Mitterrand

THE STATE OF THE PARTIES

National Assembly 577 members

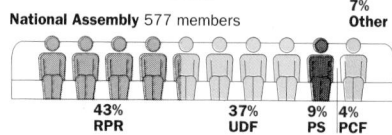

| 43% RPR | 37% UDF | 9% PS | 4% PCF | 7% Other |

RPR = Rally for the Republic **UDF** = Union for French Democracy **PS** = Socialist Party **PCF** = French Communist Party **GRR** = Rally for the Republic Group **GS** = Socialist Group **GUCDP** = Central Union of Progressive Democrats Group **GURI** = Union of Republicans and Independents Group **GGD** = Democratic Left Group **Other** = Left Radical Movement, Communist Party

Senate 321 members

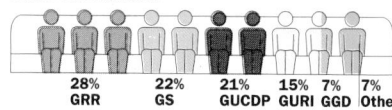

| 28% GRR | 22% GS | 21% GUCDP | 15% GURI | 7% GGD | 7% Other |

France is a multiparty democracy where the president rules in tandem with a prime minister and government chosen by the *Assemblée Nationale*. The two are elected separately and serve, respectively, seven and five-year terms. This occasionally results in periods of *cohabitation,* where the president and *Assemblée* are of opposite political persuasions. Presidents tend to look after foreign policy and defence issues, while the *Assemblée* focuses on domestic and economic policy.

MAIN POLITICAL ISSUES

The presidential system
The experience since 1986 of periods of *cohabitation* between Socialist President Mitterrand and a right-wing government has effectively weakened the power of the presidential office. Many are convinced that presidential and *Assemblée* terms should in future run concurrently and for the same number of years.

Racism
The problem of rising unemployment has led to the growth of racist parties, such as Jean Marie Le Pen's National Front (FN), which are threatening many of France's democratic traditions. None of the major parties has yet provided policies to combat the problem.

Reviving a strong opposition
Political scandals since 1989 have badly dented the reputation of the Socialist Party (PS), which took a knock at the polls in 1993. The French political system requires an effective opposition voice and this is currently lacking.

European integration
Before German reunification in 1990, there was a clear consensus in France on the benefits of European integration. Since then, however, support for union has cooled. Only 51% voted in favour of the Maastricht Treaty proposals at the 1992 referendum. France's withdrawal from the EU's Exchange Rate Mechanism (ERM) the following year reduced support further.

PROFILE
Between 1959 and 1981, France was governed by a right-of-centre coalition, firstly under the presidency of General de Gaulle, then Georges Pompidou and Valéry Giscard d'Estaing. The election in 1981 of François Mitterrand brought the left, including the French Communist Party (PCF), to the fore. The PS-led government nationalized many of France's most famous businesses, including the chemical company Rhône Poulenc. Local government was decentralized. However, the failure of its reflationary economic policy forced the PS to change course in 1983.

This was the most important turning point in French politics since 1958. The PS became a social democratic party, adopting the monetarist policies then in vogue. All the major French parties have since moved towards the political centre, and broad agreement now exists on economic policy.

The fortunes of the far left have continued to decline. In 1945, the PCF had 25% of the vote. Today it is nearer 7%, mainly because workers no longer believe Marxism will help raise their living standards. Unemployment, however, has increased support for the far right. Some workers have switched allegiance to Jean Marie Le Pen's racist FN. The FN's share of the vote rarely rises above 14%, but it has had a disproportionate political impact, partly because of Le Pen's ability to attract publicity. One impact of the FN's rise has been that all the main parties now support tougher immigration laws.

François Mitterrand, president of France since 1981.

Jacques Chirac, RPR leader and mayor of Paris.

Edouard Balladur, former finance minister, became prime minister in 1993.

F

WORLD AFFAIRS

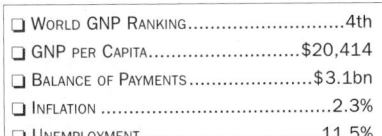

French foreign policy has followed two, apparently contradictory, strands since the Second World War – maintenance of a strongly independent line and furtherance of French interests within a united Europe. France's effective leadership of the EU meant that, until recently, it could combine the two. However, the reunification of Germany and its subsequent increased influence in the EU have led many to question the wisdom of the 'what is good for Europe is good for France' policy. This shift in attitudes was seen in the Maastricht referendum, when only 51% voted for the treaty.

The keystone of foreign policy remains the containment of German power in Europe through political and monetary union, whilst resisting moves towards a supranational European state. France supports broadening the EU to include Scandinavia, but opposes the entry of East European states that would naturally fall within Germany's sphere of influence.

France also seeks to combat US influence in both foreign affairs and culture. It left NATO's military command in 1966, maintains an independent nuclear deterrent and provides a balance to US influence in the Middle East and Africa.

AID

 $6.5bn (donations)   Down 30% in 1991

France is one of the world's major aid donors. Its motives are not simply commercial; it also wishes to maintain the influence of the French language, particularly in West Africa, which has been the main aid recipient. *Médecins sans Frontières* reflects a long French tradition of NGO aid agencies.

DEFENCE

$34.9bn   Up 1% in 1992

0	Defence spending as % GDP	40
2.8%		

FRENCH ARMED FORCES

1343 main battle tanks (AMX-30)	260,900 personnel	
2 carriers, 17 submarines, 1 cruiser, 4 destroyers and 34 frigates	64,900 personnel	
808 combat aircraft (Mirage F-1B,-1C,-1CR/ Jaguar/Alpha Jet)	91,700 personnel	
64 SLBM in 4 SSBN, 18 IRBM (SSBS S-3D/TN-61), 24 Pluton SSM launchers		

ECONOMICS

$1167.7bn   5.90 francs

SCORE CARD

❑ WORLD GNP RANKING	4th
❑ GNP PER CAPITA	$20,414
❑ BALANCE OF PAYMENTS	$3.1bn
❑ INFLATION	2.3%
❑ UNEMPLOYMENT	11.5%

EXPORTS

Belgium and Luxembourg 9%
UK 9%
Italy 11%
Other 54%
Germany* 17%

IMPORTS

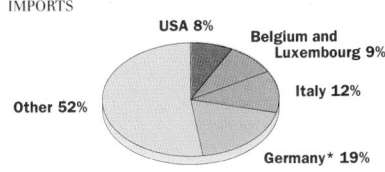

USA 8%
Belgium and Luxembourg 9%
Italy 12%
Other 52%
Germany* 19%

STRENGTHS

Heavy engineering, reflected in the success of the TGV and nuclear industries. Specialization in key fields such as motor cars (Renault and Citroën) and telecommunications (Alcatel). Luxury goods: France is world leader in cosmetics, perfumes and quality wines. Defence sector a major exporter, particularly of Dassault *Mirage* jets and *Exocet* missiles. French technocratic traditions mean that, unlike the USA or UK, top graduates are attracted into engineering. Most agriculture well-modernized. Docile trade unions; only 12% of the French workforce is unionized.

WEAKNESSES

High unemployment, currently running at over 11%. Many sectors of industry still failing to compete due to outmoded

France was a founder member of NATO, but left its military command structure in 1966 because of US domination of the alliance. France is isolated in its support for an EU-based defence force. As a result, its defence policy is still effectively defined by NATO.

The French military has historically been very strong. The influence of the army, however, is now much diminished due to the debacles of 1940 and of the 1962 Algerian war. Most young French are anti-militarist.

France has one of the world's largest defence industries, producing its own tanks, *Mirage* jets and the new *Rafale* fighter. Much of this production is exported, often controversially.

ECONOMIC PERFORMANCE INDICATOR

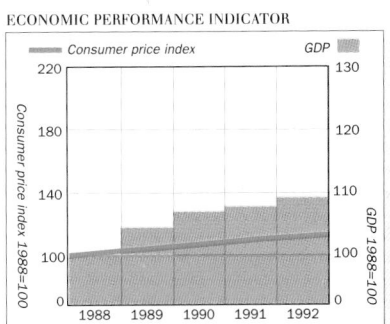

Consumer price index   GDP

working practices, particularly in machine tools, electric consumer durables and some textiles. Some major high-tech industries, such as telecommunications, partly run to further national pride, rather than on a strictly commercial basis. Despite agricultural modernization, there are still many small farms.

PROFILE

Compared to Germany and Britain, France was slow to industrialize. The 1950s and 1960s saw major changes. Protectionist France started competing in world markets and modernizing its industry with considerable success. By the 1980s, France was among the world's top three exporters.

France has a long tradition of state-ownership. Between 1938 and 1945 the railways, Air France, Renault, the coal, electricity and gas industries, large insurance companies and banks were nationalized. Between 1986 and 1988, a right-of centre government reversed the policy. But even after the massive sell-offs, much of the economy remains under state control. France is the EU's largest agricultural producer and its farmers are a powerful political lobby.

FRANCE : MAJOR BUSINESSES

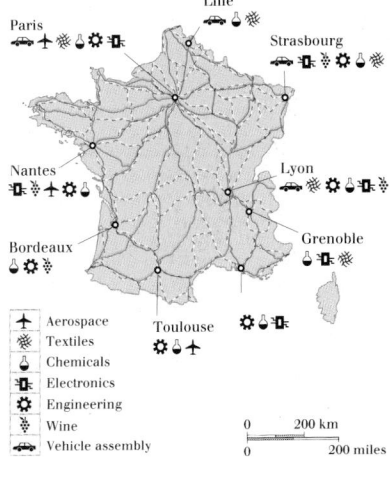

✈ Aerospace	
※ Textiles	
⚗ Chemicals	
⎍ Electronics	
✿ Engineering	
⚱ Wine	
🚗 Vehicle assembly	

0	200 km
0	200 miles

F

F

RESOURCES

419bn kwh (capacity 103m kw)

57,000 b/d (reserves 177,434,000 bbl)

21.8m cattle, 12.4m pigs, 11.9m sheep, 269,000 asses

Coal, natural gas, iron, zinc

ELECTRICITY GENERATION

Hydro 14% (57.4bn kwh)

Thermal 11% (48.2bn kwh)

Nuclear 75% (314.1bn kwh)

Other 0%

0   20   40   60   80   100
% of total generation by type

France is the world's most committed user of nuclear energy, which provides 75% of its electricity requirements. The policy reflects a desire for national energy self-sufficiency. Coal, once plentiful in the north and Lorraine, is now mostly exhausted, as are the gas fields off the southwest coast.

FRANCE : LAND USE

Forest
Pasture
Cropland
High mountain regions
Cattle
Sugarbeet
Vineyards

CORSICA

0   200 km
0   200 miles

ENVIRONMENT

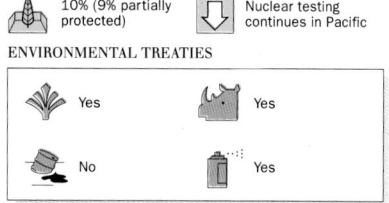

10% (9% partially protected)

Nuclear testing continues in Pacific

ENVIRONMENTAL TREATIES

Yes

Yes

No

Yes

French 'green' consciousness, in the past lower than that of Germans or Britons, has been rising. The Seine has been cleaned up, the size of buildings on the south coast is now controlled and, in Paris, air pollution is carefully monitored. The state policy of backing big projects (*gigantisme*), such as the Grande Motte tourist complex in Languedoc, has been reversed. The exception is nuclear policy. France's testing programme in the Pacific continues despite strong opposition.

REGIONS
THE NORD-PAS DE CALAIS REGION

Channel Tunnel   Disused coal fields   Former steel area

THE NORD-PAS DE CALAIS region has suffered mixed fortunes since the 1970s. Once a French industrial heartland, with Lille its foremost city, the region shed jobs and businesses at an alarming rate during the 1970s as traditional coalfields were worked out and the steel industry proved to be less competitive than its overseas rivals. By 1979, unemployment was 30% above the national average.

The arrival of the Channel Tunnel project dramatically changed the prospects for the region. French railways (SNCF) built a TGV line to connect Paris to both London and Brussels in less than three hours, providing a new focus for the region.

PARIS

SINCE THE 1960S, the regeneration of Paris has been inextricably linked to national prestige. In 1961, the *Schéma Directeur* sought to solve congestion by creating five new towns within a 40-km radius of the centre. Meanwhile, government set out to make Paris the architectural, scientific and cultural envy of the world. The high-tech Pompidou arts centre (1977) set the tone. Under Mitterrand the process accelerated, resulting in numerous *Grands Projets*, such as the Arab World Institute, the Villette science centre, the remodelling of the Louvre museum (including I M Pei's glass pyramid entrance) and a massive new opera house at La Bastille.

Major tourist sites   Sites built or renovated since 1985
Park or open land   14e Number of arrondissement

LANGUEDOC

Cultural tourism   Tourism   Rhône-Montpellier canal
Fruit orchards   Hi-tech industry   Vineyards

LANGUEDOC has benefited from several initiatives in recent years. The Rhône-Montpellier canal system, Europe's biggest post-war irrigation network designed to improve yields, led to the replacement of much vine land with fruit orchards, but was not as wealth-creating as had been hoped due to cuts in EU fruit quotas.

Languedoc was also the subject of the biggest state-sponsored tourist development in history. Built to a master plan by architect George Candillis, a pupil of Le Corbusier, 280,000 new tourist beds were provided in massive resort complexes along a previously undeveloped mosquito-ridden coast. Visitor numbers have risen from 500,000 in 1965 to around four million today.

In the 1980s, Languedoc became France's leading high-tech region. IBM established its largest French manufacturing plant in Montpellier, bringing in its wake many 'sun-belt' companies. The new industries have also been a great boost to the town's university, the largest in the region.

F

MEDIA

 The media has been free of state control since the 1980s

PUBLISHING AND BROADCAST MEDIA

There are 82 daily newspapers, including the Parisian *Le Monde* and *Le Figaro*. *Ouest-France* has the highest circulation

2 state-owned, 4 independent networks

1 state-owned network

Intelsat V1 F1 Astra 1B

Extensive in all main cities

Formerly controlled and censored by the state and very timid, TV and radio were freed from direct state influence by the PS government in the 1980s. *TF1*, the primary TV network, is now privately owned and financed by advertising revenue. *France 2* is still owned by the state but is now fairly autonomous. In sharp contrast to its very strong cinema tradition, France has a weak TV service and standards are low, with many bought-in US soaps.

Le Monde and *Libération* are the leading daily newspapers. *Le Canard Enchaîné* is the most influential satirical weekly.

CRIME

 46,423 prisoners

Up 6% in 1990

CRIME RATES

Murders	
4	per 100,000 population

Rapes	
8	per 100,000 population

Thefts	
4018	per 100,000 population

The French legal system is based on Roman law codified by Napoleon. The *juge d'instruction* is arguably the most important figure, a magistrate who has considerable powers in examining witnesses and assessing evidence. The press are not restricted by *sub judice* rules in reporting trials and can speak freely of suspects as though already proven guilty.

Petty crime and crimes of violence have risen sharply in recent years. Public concern about the rising crime rate helped return the right – with a law and order platform – to power in 1993. Drug trafficking through Marseilles remains a problem.

HEALTH

 1 per 381 people

Liver, heart and cerebrovascular diseases, cancers

0	Health spending as % GNP	25
	9.2%	

The French national health system is not entirely free. Patients pay the full cost of treatment to their physicians and are then reimbursed for 70% to 80% of the cost by an insurance company paid by the social services. Health awareness has recently risen, and the French still consume more medicines per capita than any other nation. However, the 1992 law banning smoking in public places is widely infringed. Alcoholism remains a problem, and cirrhosis of the liver is still the most common cause of death.

WEALTH

 Waiter, 11,000 francs per month; senior manager, 50,000 francs per month

CONSUMER GOODS OWNERSHIP

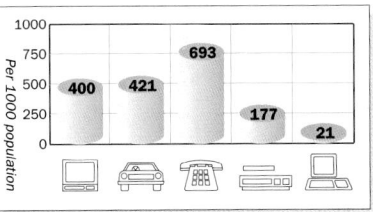

Wealth and income disparities in France are higher than in most OECD countries. The Socialists narrowed the gap a little with the introduction of the legal minimum wage (*le SMIC*). Most tax is indirect – a result of a long French tradition of income-tax evasion – which hits the poor and rich equally.

France has a fairly rigid class structure, although social mobility is increasing. The wealthy favour expensive French, German and British cars, and take exotic holidays to the Himalayas, the Andes and Polynesia.

EDUCATION

 99%

0	Education spending as % GNP	25
	5.3%	

THE EDUCATION SYSTEM

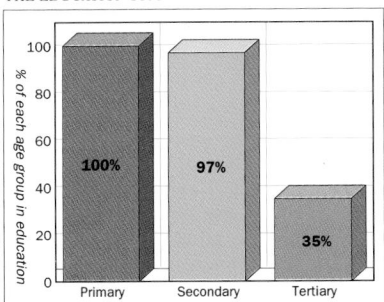

French education remains centralized, despite some relaxation of the system brought about by the student riots of 1968. The education ministry organizes the curriculum, exams and staffing, and most schools have little autonomous control over their affairs. Catholic Church schools, which account for 17% of the school population, are the exception. These are fee-paying but also receive large state subsidies. However, despite their relative independence, they are still obliged to follow the national curriculum.

The focus in teaching remains the acquisition of a broad range of knowledge, and classes are highly disciplined. French children tend to be better informed than their counterparts in other West European countries.

France has over 70 universities – 13 in Paris – and higher education bodies with 1.2 million students. Entry is not competitive, but based on passing the secondary-level exam, the *baccalauréat*. Most students attend their local university. The universities have not been given the funds or staff to cope with the huge increase in student numbers in recent years. The 150 *Grandes Écoles* are outside the university system and have just a few hundred carefully selected students each. The most influential tertiary institutions, they open the door to the top civil service and professional jobs.

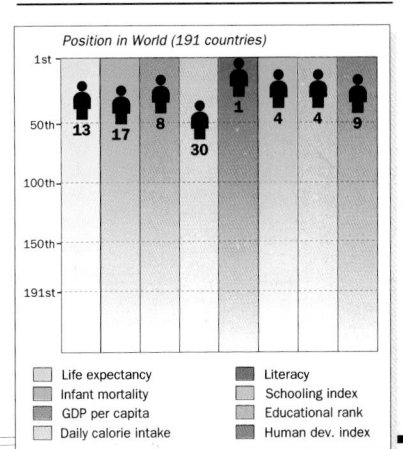

The Massif Central, Auvergne. The Massif's lonely granite plateaux and extinct volcanoes are France's oldest rock formations.

WORLD RANKING

Position in World (191 countries)

Life expectancy — 13
Infant mortality — 17
GDP per capita — 8
Daily calorie intake — 30
Literacy — 1
Schooling index — 4
Educational rank — 4
Human dev. index — 9

GABON

OFFICIAL NAME: The Gabonese Republic   CAPITAL: Libreville
POPULATION: 1.2 million   CURRENCY: CFA franc   OFFICIAL LANGUAGE: French

WEST AFRICA

Africa

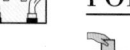

AN EQUATORIAL COUNTRY on the west coast of Africa, Gabon's major economic activity is oil. Only a small area of Gabon is cultivated and more than two thirds constitutes one of the world's finest virgin rainforests. Gabon became independent of France in 1960. A single-party state from 1968, it returned to multiparty democracy in 1990. Gabon's population is small and the government is encouraging its increase.

POLITICS

 1996

President Omar
(Albert-Bernard) Bongo

THE STATE OF THE PARTIES

National Assembly 120 members

| 55% | 16% | 14% | 15% |
| PDG | PGP | RNB | Other |

PDG = Gabonese Democratic Party   **PGP** = Gabonese Progress Party   **RNB** = National Rally of Lumberjacks   **Other** = Association for Socialism in Gabon, Gabonese Socialist Union

Gabon has had a multiparty constitution since 1990, when a national conference paved the way for elections. The elections confirmed in power the only constitutional party of the previous 20 years – Omar Bongo's PDG. In part this was due to the divided opposition, which comprised over 30 distinct parties. In 1993, the opposition learned from the mistakes of 1990 and agreed to back only one candidate to challenge Bongo in the presidential elections. Bongo was re-elected, but doubts were expressed about the fairness of the elections and future prospects for the democratic process in Gabon.

CLIMATE

WEATHER CHART

Gabon's climate is heavily equatorial, with very little distinction between seasons. The cold Benguela current lowers coastal temperatures.

COMMUNICATIONS

 Léon M'Ba
611,000 passengers

 7 ships
27,600 dwt

THE TRANSPORT NETWORK

| 7535 km (4682 miles) | None |
| 650 km (404 miles) | 1600 km (994 miles) |

The Trans-Gabon Railway completed in 1986, from Owendo port near Libreville to Massoukou, is the key transport link. Air transport is well developed and most big companies have airstrips.

TOURISM

 108,000 visitors

 Down 5% in 1990

MAIN OVERSEAS ARRIVALS

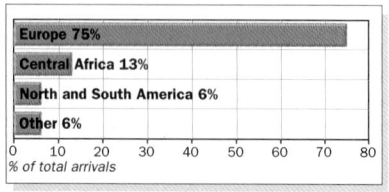

| Europe 75% |
| Central Africa 13% |
| North and South America 6% |
| Other 6% |

0 10 20 30 40 50 60 70 80
% of total arrivals

Despite Libreville's many hotels, Gabon has little tourism, in part a reflection of its lack of good beaches.

PEOPLE

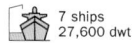 Fang, French, Punu, Sira, Nzebi, Mpongwe

5 people per km²

THE URBAN/RURAL POPULATION SPLIT

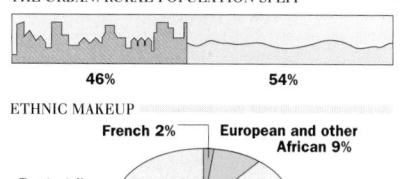

46%   54%

ETHNIC MAKEUP

French 2%   European and other African 9%

Bantu tribes (including Fang and Bareke) 89%

The largest ethnic group in Gabon is the Fang, who live mainly in the north, but they have yet to gain control of government. President Omar Bongo, from a sub-group of the minority Bateke in the southeast, has artfully united the common interests of other ethnic groups to keep the Fang from power. The Myene group around Port-Gentil consider themselves to be the aristocrats of Gabonese society owing to their long-standing ex-colonial contacts. Oil wealth has led to the growth of a distinct bourgeoisie.

WORLD AFFAIRS

 OAU | OPEC | AfDB | GATT | FZ

Gabon still maintains close links with France, although US companies are also making inroads into Gabon's oil-rich economy. In regional terms, Gabon remains influential in francophone Africa, although relations further afield, particularly with OPEC (Gabon was president in 1993), are also important.

GABON

Total Area : 267 670 sq. km (103 347 sq. miles)

POPULATION

over 100 000 ◎
over 10 000 ●
under 10 000 ·

LAND HEIGHT

500m/1640ft
200m/656ft
Sea Level

0   100 km
0   100 miles

G

G

AID

 $142m (receipts)   Up 8% in 1991

France is by far the major aid donor, providing two thirds of total receipts. For a middle income country with one of the highest GNPs per capita in the developing world, Gabon has benefited from considerable aid. Its indebtedness is the result of excessive borrowing encouraged by Western banks in the 1970s. Much aid goes to servicing this debt.

DEFENCE

 $145.8m   Down 5% in 1989

President Bongo's background in the military is reflected in Gabon's large defence budget and prestige weaponry, which includes French *Mirage* jets. Even the presidential guard has its own fleet of 12 aircraft. France guarantees Gabon's security and keeps an 800-strong garrison in Libreville; this last intervened in 1964 to suppress an attempted coup.

ECONOMICS

 $5.4bn   295.23 CFA francs

SCORE CARD

❏ World GNP Ranking	....111th
❏ GNP per Capita	....$4500
❏ Balance of Payments	....$105m
❏ Inflation	....2%
❏ Unemployment	High underemployment

STRENGTHS

Oil and a relatively small population give Gabon a high per capita GNP. Other abundant resources – including some of the world's best tropical hardwoods – are just beginning to be tapped.

WEAKNESSES

Large debt burden incurred in the 1970s. Continuing dependence on French technical assistance.

EXPORTS

Canada 4% UK 4%
Spain 7%
France 33%
USA 19%
Other 33%

IMPORTS

Germany* 6% Japan 6%
France 46% USA 10%
Other 32%

RESOURCES

 915m kwh (capacity 279,000 kw) 297,100 b/d (reserves 730,000,000 bbl)

159,000 pigs, 157,000 sheep, 27,000 cattle Oil, manganese, uranium, gold, iron, natural gas

Oil is the major export earner. Gabon also has large deposits of uranium and over 100 years' reserves of manganese. The unexploited iron ore deposits at Bélinga are the world's largest.

ENVIRONMENT

 4% partially protected   Adoption of EU-funded pilot conservation project

The Trans-Gabon Railway has sliced through one of the world's finest virgin rainforests and has opened the interior to indiscriminate exploitation of rare woods such as oleoirme. Gabon abandoned plans for nuclear power following the 1986 Chernobyl disaster.

MEDIA

 No restrictions

PUBLISHING AND BROADCAST MEDIA

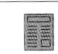 There are 2 daily newspapers, *L'Union* and *Gabon-Matin*

 1 state-owned service   1 state-owned service

The media has become much more diverse since 1990 and Gabon now has an opposition press and *La Griffe*, a satirical weekly. *L'Union*, the state paper, carries occasional contributions from Omar Bongo, the president.

CRIME

 Gabon does not publish prison figures   Up 15% in 1990

Urban crime rates (Gabon is one of Africa's most urbanized nations) have been growing. Gabon's human rights record has improved in the last five years.

Albert Schweitzer Hospital, Lambaréné, on the lower Ogooué River. Schweitzer won a Nobel Prize for his pioneering work in Africa.

CHRONOLOGY

Gabon became a French colony in 1886, administered as part of French Equatorial Africa.

- ❏ **1960** Independence. Léon M'ba president.
- ❏ **1964** Military coup. French intervene to reinstate M'ba.
- ❏ **1967** Albert-Bernard (later Omar) Bongo president.
- ❏ **1968** Single-party state instituted.
- ❏ **1990** Multiparty democracy. Omar Bongo's PDG wins elections.

EDUCATION

 61%

Education follows the French system. Libreville University, founded in the 1970s, now has over 2500 students.

HEALTH

 1 per 2000 people   Heart and diarrheal diseases, pneumonia, accidents

Oil revenues have allowed substantial investment in the health service which is now among the best in Africa.

WEALTH

 Cabinet-maker, 86,000 CFA francs per month; electricity industry office clerk, 204,000 CFA francs per month

CONSUMER GOODS OWNERSHIP

VCR and PC ownership is above the African average

36 14 13

Oil wealth has led to the growth of an affluent bourgeoisie. Menial jobs are done by immigrant workers.

WORLD RANKING

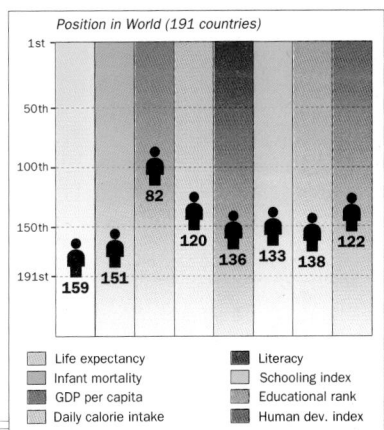

Position in World (191 countries)

159 151 82 120 136 133 138 122

- Life expectancy
- Infant mortality
- GDP per capita
- Daily calorie intake
- Literacy
- Schooling index
- Educational rank
- Human dev. index

GAMBIA

WEST AFRICA / Africa

OFFICIAL NAME: Republic of The Gambia CAPITAL: Banjul
POPULATION: 901,000 CURRENCY: Dalasi OFFICIAL LANGUAGE: English

A NARROW COUNTRY, on the western coast of Africa, the Gambia is remarkable among African countries in having practised democratic politics since independence. Agriculture accounts for 65% of its GDP. Yet, more Gambians are leaving rural areas for the towns, where average incomes are four times higher. Its position as an enclave within Senegal seems likely to endure following the failure of an experiment in federation in the 1980s.

G

CLIMATE

WEATHER CHART

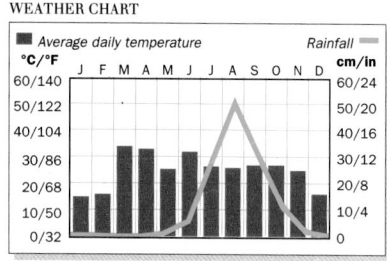

The subtropical and sunny dry season is punctuated by intermittent hot *harmattan* winds.

COMMUNICATIONS

 Yundum Intl, Banjul 220,156 passengers   Has no fleet

THE TRANSPORT NETWORK

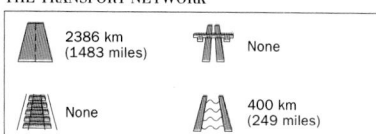

2386 km (1483 miles)	None
None	400 km (249 miles)

The River Gambia carries more traffic than the roads – ships of up to 3000 tonnes can reach Georgetown. Yundum airport was upgraded by NASA in 1989 for US space shuttle emergency landings.

TOURISM

 101,419 visitors   Up 18% in 1990

MAIN OVERSEAS ARRIVALS

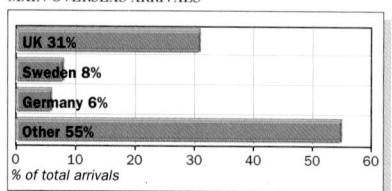

UK 31%
Sweden 8%
Germany 6%
Other 55%

% of total arrivals

The successful tourist industry offers sunshine, beaches and resort hotel life. Most visitors are North Europeans escaping winter.

PEOPLE

Mandinka, Fulani, Wolof, Diola, Soninke, English 80 people per km²

THE URBAN/RURAL POPULATION SPLIT

23%   77%

ETHNIC MAKEUP

Jola 7%
Mandinka 41%
Serahuli 7%
Wolof 13%
Fulani 14%
Other 18%

If there is any ethnic tension in the Gambia, it comes from minority resentment of the Mandinka's domination of politics. The ruling PPP has, however, sought to distribute political offices fairly according to ethnic origins. The Creole community, known as the Aku, is small but socially prominent. In the early years of the tourist industry, the presence of North Europeans created some tension in a country that is essentially Muslim. About 85% of Gambians follow Islam although there is no official state religion. There is a yearly influx of seasonal immigrants, who come from Senegal, Guinea and Mali to grow groundnuts. The Gambia is still a very poor country, with 80% of the labour force engaged in agriculture. As elsewhere in West Africa, women are active as traders.

Fishing village. Overfishing in the waters off the Gambia and Senegal, mainly by distant nations, is a growing problem.

POLITICS

 1997   President Sir Dawda Kairaba Jawara

THE STATE OF THE PARTIES

House of Representatives 150 members

50% PPP 12% NCP 4% GPP 34% Other

PPP = People's Progressive Party **NCP** = National Convention Party **GPP** = Gambia People's Party

Despite the fact that the ruling PPP has been in power since 1962, the Gambia has never been a single-party state. The PPP is strongly backed by traditional rulers, especially in the Mandinka areas. The main opposition party, the NCP, is also Mandinka-led, but depends on minority parties for support. Politics in the Gambia has, since 1962, been dominated by President Jawara, leader of the PPP. When he expressed a wish to retire in 1992, there were widespread calls for him to stay in office. He went on to secure a fourth term with 58% of the vote, as opposed to 22% won by his main rival, Sherif Mustapha Dibba of the NCP. The 1981 junior officers' putsch, which was put down only with Senegal's help, indicated that the Gambia's renowned stability could be vulnerable. Any hint of a new instability would be liable to draw in both Senegal and Nigeria, which now has considerable influence over the Gambian army.

WORLD AFFAIRS

Ecowas Comm ECA AfDB ACP

Relations with Senegal are crucial, especially since the collapse in 1989 of the Senegambian federation, which had been set up under pressure from the Senegalese after the putsch of 1981. Outside West Africa, ties remain chiefly with the Commonwealth; good relations with the UK, a major aid donor, are important.

AID

 $94m (receipts)   The trend is up

The Gambia's relative stability has enabled it to attract aid easily, notably from the World Bank, IMF, AfDB, the UK and Saudi Arabia. Italy and the Netherlands have given aid for health, and Japan for ferry services.

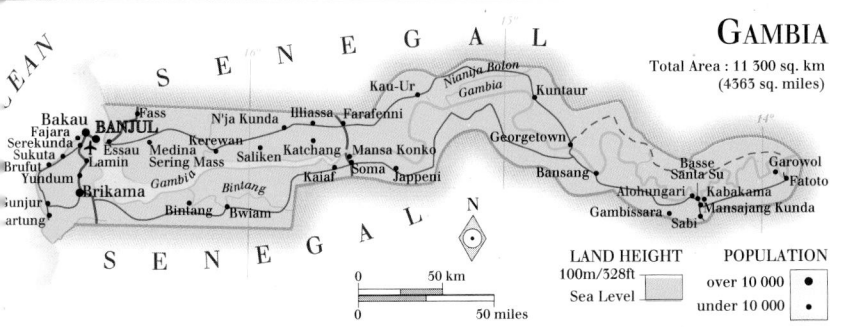

GAMBIA

Total Area : 11 300 sq. km
(4363 sq. miles)

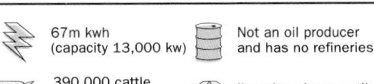

LAND HEIGHT
100m/328ft
Sea Level

POPULATION
over 10 000 •
under 10 000 ·

DEFENCE

 $3m

 No significant change from year to year

The Gambia National Army, with one infantry battalion, takes about half of the defence budget; the rest finances the 600-strong gendarmerie. Most arms are bought from the UK, although supplies are now increasingly coming from Nigeria too. A defence pact with Senegal collapsed with the federation in 1989.

ECONOMICS

 $229m

 8.76 dalasi

SCORE CARD

❑ WORLD GNP RANKING	171st
❑ GNP PER CAPITA	$260
❑ BALANCE OF PAYMENTS	$33.93m
❑ INFLATION	14.1%
❑ UNEMPLOYMENT	Widespread underemployment

STRENGTHS

Low tariffs make the Gambia a focus of regional trade. Natural deep-water harbour at Banjul, one of the finest on the West African coast. Well-managed economy, favourably viewed by donors.

WEAKNESSES

Small size of country, and hence small size of market, sometimes inhibits investment. Smuggling, which deprives government of significant revenues. Lack of resources and little diversification in agriculture.

EXPORTS

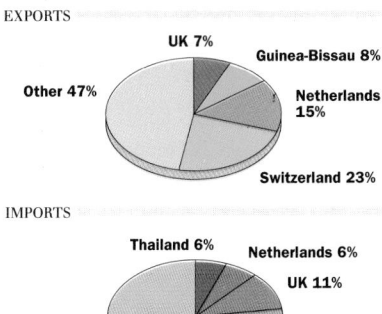

UK 7%
Guinea-Bissau 8%
Other 47%
Netherlands 15%
Switzerland 23%

IMPORTS

Thailand 6%
Netherlands 6%
UK 11%
Other 63%
France 14%

RESOURCES

 67m kwh (capacity 13,000 kw)

 Not an oil producer and has no refineries

 390,000 cattle, 166,000 sheep, 11,000 pigs

Ilmenite, zircon, rutile, kaolin, tin

The River Gambia is one of Africa's few good waterways, but is underused as it is separated from its natural hinterland by the Gambia–Senegal border. Irrigation is at present provided by a single dam; plans for further dams for power generation have met with opposition. Most mineral deposits have yet to be exploited.

ENVIRONMENT

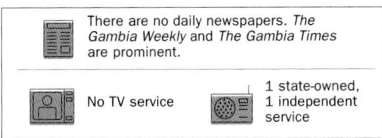 2%

Increasing awareness of environment by tourism ministry

The impact of tourism on the country's environment and overfishing in Gambian waters are major concerns.

MEDIA

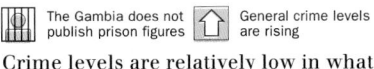 Very little censorship. Personal criticism of the president is tolerated.

PUBLISHING AND BROADCAST MEDIA

There are no daily newspapers. *The Gambia Weekly* and *The Gambia Times* are prominent.

No TV service

1 state-owned, 1 independent service

The Gambian press is editorially independent. In 1988, *The Torch* carried allegations of corruption, which led to the dismissal of two ministers.

CRIME

 The Gambia does not publish prison figures

General crime levels are rising

Crime levels are relatively low in what is a peaceful society compared to many other states in the region.

EDUCATION

 27%

The literacy rate is low for the level of school enrolment – 75% in primary and 20% in secondary schools. Tertiary education is limited to teacher training.

G

HEALTH

 1 per 9900 people

 Malaria, tuberculosis, parasitic diseases

Most people have access to basic medicines, but these are no longer free. Advanced medical care in the public sector is limited. A quarter of state doctors work in the main hospital.

WEALTH

 The majority of the population is poor. Rising educational opportunites should result in greater social mobility.

CONSUMER GOODS OWNERSHIP

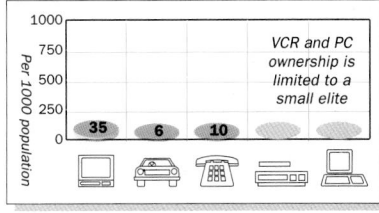

VCR and PC ownership is limited to a small elite

35   6   10

Public service and the professions have made some comfortably off, but great wealth is not a feature of Gambian life. Unemployed young men in Banjul are regarded as the underclass.

WORLD RANKING

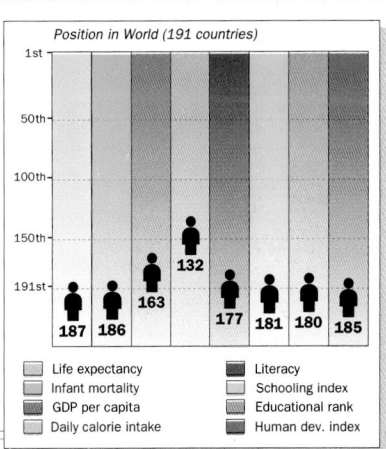

Position in World (191 countries)

187 186 163 132 177 181 180 185

☐ Life expectancy	☐ Literacy
☐ Infant mortality	☐ Schooling index
☐ GDP per capita	☐ Educational rank
☐ Daily calorie intake	☐ Human dev. index

GEORGIA

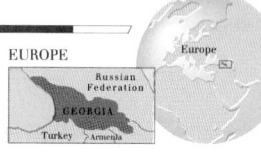

OFFICIAL NAME: Republic of Georgia   CAPITAL: Tbilisi
POPULATION: 5.5 million   CURRENCY: Coupon   OFFICIAL LANGUAGE: Georgian

G

SITUATED ON THE EASTERN coast of the Black Sea, Georgia is largely mountainous. Its coastline stretches from Abkhazia in the north to Ajaria in the south. Georgia was one of the first republics to demand independence from Moscow, but has been plagued over recent years by civil war and ethnic disputes in Abkhazia and South Ossetia. The birthplace of Stalin, Georgia is primarily agricultural and is famous for its wine.

CLIMATE

WEATHER CHART

Georgia's climate is continental inland and subtropical along the coast, where grapes, citrus fruit and tea are grown.

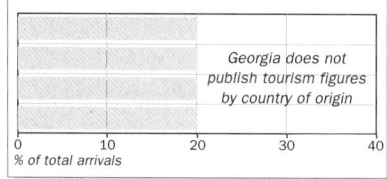

Tbilisi, Georgia's capital since the 5th century AD. Its buildings rise in steep terraces from both banks of the River Kura.

COMMUNICATIONS

Novo Alexeyevka, Tbilisi

47 ships
1.01m dwt

THE TRANSPORT NETWORK

35,100 km (21,811 miles)		None
1570 km (976 miles)		None

Civil war has caused the near collapse of the transport system. The autonomous republic of Ajaria maintains good communications with Turkey.

TOURISM

Flourishing Black Sea tourist trade before civil war

Sharp fall since start of civil war

MAIN OVERSEAS ARRIVALS

Georgia does not publish tourism figures by country of origin

0   10   20   30   40
% of total arrivals

The volatility of the current political situation has discouraged tourism, although Georgia was previously a popular destination.

PEOPLE

Georgian, Russian

78 people per km²

THE URBAN/RURAL POPULATION SPLIT

56%   44%

ETHNIC MAKEUP

Ossetian 3%   Azeri 5%
Armenian 9%
Other 14%
Georgian 69%

Georgia is a paternalistic society, with strong family and cultural traditions. The proportion of Georgians, who currently make up 69% of the population, is gradually increasing. Minority groups include Armenians, Russians, Azeris, Ossetians, Greeks and Abkhazians.

POLITICS

Uncertain

Chairman Eduard Shevardnadze

THE STATE OF THE PARTIES

Supreme Soviet 235 members

12% PB   6% UB   5% GP   63% Other
8% 11OC   6% NDPG

PB = Peace Bloc   11OC = 11 October Coalition   UB = Unity Bloc   NDPG = National Democratic Party of Georgia   GP = Green Party

Politics in Georgia is in a state of flux. An uneasy truce has followed the 1990–1993 civil war between the supporters of ex-president Zviad Gamsakhurdia, who committed suicide while under fire at the end of 1993, and troops loyal to the government. Russian military intervention on the government's side brought the fighting to an end.
In Abkhazia, another civil war is being fought as ethnic Abkhazians attempt to secede from Georgia. Georgians are being expelled from the region. Party groupings within the Supreme Soviet are unstable.

GEORGIA

Total Area :
69 700 sq. km
(26 911 sq. miles)

POPULATION

◎ over 100 000
○ over 50 000
● over 10 000
· under 10 000

LAND HEIGHT

3000m/9843ft
2000m/6562ft
1000m/3281ft
500m/1640ft
200m/656ft
Sea Level

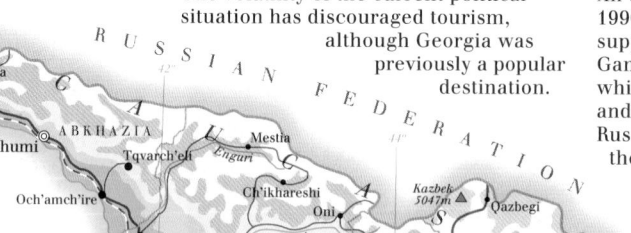

0   50 km
0   50 miles

WORLD AFFAIRS

Georgia joined the CIS in 1993 in order to secure Russian military support against Gamsakhurdia.

AID

 Undisclosed receipts

 No obvious increase

Georgia has yet to achieve the economic and political stability that will secure IMF aid.

DEFENCE

 $333.3m (est)

 Sharp increase in spending owing to civil war

Georgia's military strength has been boosted by the presence of Russian troops in the country since it joined the CIS in October 1993. The Abkhazian conflict now dominates the agenda for the Georgian army. Training for the government security forces is provided by the CIA.

ECONOMICS

 $9bn

 700,000 coupons

SCORE CARD

- ❑ World GNP Ranking 82nd
- ❑ GNP per Capita $1636
- ❑ Balance of Payment ....The formal
- ❑ Inflation ....economy has
- ❑ Unemployment ....collapsed

STRENGTHS
Potential gateway to West for Azeri oil through pipelines over Georgian territory. Ports on the Black Sea, such as Bat'umi in Ajaria.

WEAKNESSES
Breakdown of economy due to war and severance of links with other ex-Soviet republics. Hyperinflation following introduction of coupon as parallel currency to rouble. Influence of powerful economic mafias.

EXPORTS

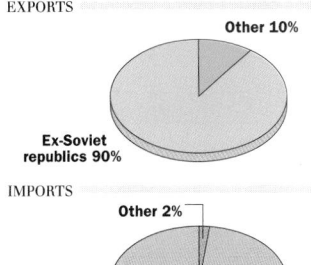

Other 10%

Ex-Soviet republics 90%

IMPORTS

Other 2%

Ex-Soviet republics 98%

RESOURCES

 14.2bn kwh (capacity 4.9m kw)

 Not an oil producer and has no refineries

 24m poultry, 1.8m sheep, 1.4m cattle, 1m pigs

Manganese, coal, oil, natural gas, zinc, cobalt, vanadium

Known oil reserves are as yet undeveloped and Georgia is dependent on Russia for much of its petrol and electricity supply. Cobalt and vanadium are being mined, although only in small quantities which are not easy to sell on the world market. Georgia is a predominantly agricultural country and food processing and wine production are the major industries.

ENVIRONMENT

 3%

 No resources for environmental initiatives

Pollution of the Black Sea is a major concern. The protection of upland pastures and hill farms from soil erosion is another key issue.

MEDIA

 Government censorship is widespread

PUBLISHING AND BROADCAST MEDIA

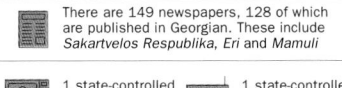

There are 149 newspapers, 128 of which are published in Georgian. These include *Sakartvelos Respublika*, *Eri* and *Mamuli*

1 state-controlled network

1 state-controlled network

There is little press freedom as the media survive on government subsidies. All TV broadcasting is controlled by the state.

CRIME

 Georgia does not publish prison figures

 Levels of all crime, especially organized crime, are rising

Organized crime under the control of mafia-style groups has flourished since independence in 1991. The judicial system currently favours Shevardnadze and his supporters.

EDUCATION

 100%

All levels of education are now seriously underfunded. The University of Tbilisi was formerly of a high standard, with a particular reputation for the arts and economics.

HEALTH

 1 per 170 people

Circulatory and respiratory diseases, cancers, accidents

The health system was limited under the Soviet Union. Internal strife and a lack of resources have prevented any recent investment.

CHRONOLOGY

A Russian protectorate from 1763, Georgia was absorbed into the Russian empire in 1801. It was established as an independent state under a Menshevik socialist government in 1918.

- ❑ **1879** Stalin born in Gori.
- ❑ **1920** Recognized as an independent state by Soviet Russia.
- ❑ **1921** Soviet Red Army invades. Effectively part of USSR.
- ❑ **1922** Incorporated into the Transcaucasian Soviet Federative Socialist Republic (TSFSR).
- ❑ **1936** TSFSR dissolved.
- ❑ **1978** Public protests at threat to replace Georgian with Russian as official language.
- ❑ **1989** Pro-independence riots in Tbilisi put down by Soviet troops.
- ❑ **1990** Declares sovereignty. Shevardnadze resigns as Soviet foreign minister.
- ❑ **1991** Independence. Gamsakhurdia elected president.
- ❑ **1992** Gamsakhurdia flees Tbilisi. Shevardnadze elected chairman of Supreme Soviet and State Council.

G

WEALTH

 Wealth is concentrated in Tbilisi

CONSUMER GOODS OWNERSHIP

TV ownership is limited

Telephone, VCR and PC ownership is limited to an elite

At least 80% of the population live in poverty. There is a small wealthy and extravagant elite.

WORLD RANKING

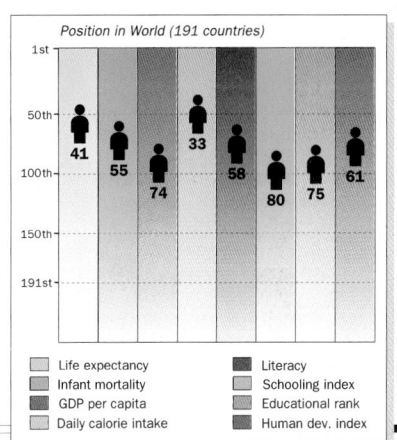

Life expectancy	Literacy
Infant mortality	Schooling index
GDP per capita	Educational rank
Daily calorie intake	Human dev. index

GERMANY

EUROPE

Europe

Netherlands   Denmark
Belgium   GERMANY   Poland
Luxembourg   Czech
France   Switz.   Austria   Rep.

OFFICIAL NAME: Federal Republic of Germany   **CAPITAL:** Berlin

POPULATION: 80.3 million   **CURRENCY:** Deutsche Mark   **OFFICIAL LANGUAGE:** German

1990

G

WITH COASTLINES on both the Baltic and North Seas, Germany is bordered by nine states. The north is characterized by plains and rolling hills; the south by more mountainous terrain. The most populous country in Europe after Russia, Germany is also its foremost industrial power and, after Japan, the world's second biggest exporter. United in the 1870s, it was divided following the defeat of the Nazi regime in 1945. The western two thirds became a free-market democracy aligned with the West; the east became a communist-ruled state in the Soviet bloc. The collapse of the East German regime in 1989 paved the way for political reunification in 1990. Social and economic unification remain elusive, however. The tensions created by the wealth differences between the east and the west dominate politics and have been exacerbated by the recent recession.

GERMANY

Total Area : 356 910 sq. km
(137 800 sq. miles)

POPULATION

▣	over 1 000 000
◉	over 500 000
◎	over 100 000
○	over 10 000

0   100 km

0   100 miles

N

LAND HEIGHT

2000m/6562ft
1000m/3281ft
500m/1640ft
200m/656ft
Sea Level

CLIMATE

WEATHER CHART

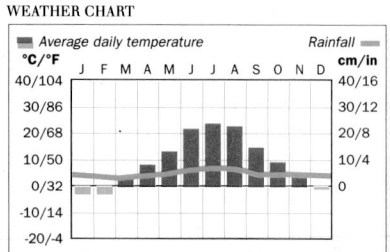

Germany has a broad climatic range. The upper Rhine Valley is very mild and suitable for wine-making. The Bayrische Alpen, the Harz Mountains and the Black Forest are by contrast cold, with heavy falls of snow in winter.

COMMUNICATIONS

✈ Frankfurt/Main International
28.7m passengers

🚢 720 ships
6.21m dwt

THE TRANSPORT NETWORK

🛣 621,297 km (386,055 miles)	🛤 8822 km (5482 miles)
� 42,000 km (26,098 miles)	〜 6700 km (4163 miles)

Germany virtually invented the modern motorway with its 1930s *Autobahnen*, built by the Nazis primarily for military purposes. Today, the country has Europe's most elaborate motorway network. Most *Autobahnen* do not have a speed limit, a contrast to the very strict speed restrictions and slow Trabant cars of former East Germany. German railways are mostly state-owned and efficient. Its ICE lost the high-speed train race to the French TGV. Germany is now planning a 350 km per hour MAGLEV train.

TOURISM

🧳 45m visitors

⬇ Down 24% in 1992

MAIN OVERSEAS ARRIVALS

Austria 21%	
Spain 16%	
Italy 14%	
Hungary 8%	
Switzerland 8%	
Other 33%	

% of total arrivals

Northerly beaches and a colder climate make Germany less of a tourist draw than France or Italy. Skiing in the Bayrische Alpen, the historic castles of the Rhine Valley, the Black Forest and, for a significant number of visitors, Germany's excellent beer, are all major attractions. Even before reunification, Berlin attracted many tourists with its rich cultural life and its Wall separating the West from the communist East. As the capital of reunified Germany, it is now receiving a major face-lift.

The Stillach Valley, Allgäu Alps, *Bavaria. Germany's forests, which are found mainly in its mountain regions, are suffering badly from the effects of acid rain.*

PEOPLE

German, Sorbian

217 people per km²

THE URBAN/RURAL POPULATION SPLIT

86% 14%

RELIGIOUS PERSUASION

Other 18%
Protestant 45%
Roman Catholic 37%

ETHNIC MAKEUP

Turkish 2% Other 3%
Other European 3%
German 92%

Germans share a common language, but they speak it with a variety of dialects, reflecting a strong sense of regionalism. Some German-speaking peoples live in neighbouring Austria, France and Switzerland, but most now live in Germany. The north is still largely Protestant, while the south and southwest, particularly Bayern (Bavaria), have strong Catholic traditions. Other traditional differences between northern and southern Germans – the Prussian reputation for authoritarianism, the Bavarian for jollity – are waning, however, and most now share a common culture.

A large immigrant population, some five million people, provided much of the labour on which former West Germany's economic recovery was built. Known as *Gastarbeiter* (guest workers), they cannot easily claim full German nationality and so do not have equal rights. The 1.6 million Turks are the largest single group.

Germany's once liberal asylum laws were tightened in 1993, in response to the domestic tension created by high unemployment in the east and the huge influx of 'economic' refugees from Russia, Romania and Poland following the collapse of communism. Another result of unemployment and disappointed expectations, particularly among young Germans, has been the growing support for right-wing parties and a rise in racial attacks.

Family ties in Germany are little different from those in the USA or UK. Millions of couples live together in common-law arrangements, and while this is frowned upon by the Catholic Church, it is largely in rural districts in Bayern that traditional habits are still observed. The birth rate is one of Europe's lowest and the population would be falling were it not for the influx of immigrants since the 1950s.

Women have full rights under the law and play a bigger role in politics than in most other European countries. In 1990, they formed one fifth of the *Bundestag* (Parliament). However, they are less well represented in top jobs in business and industry. Germany has a tradition of strong feminism. Abortion remains a charged issue, with laws varying from region to region. After unification, women in former East Germany wanted to keep their right to abortion on demand. However, they were overruled by the constitutional court, after strong Catholic lobbying.

Despite their liberal reputation, Germans retain their formal social habits. Clear distinctions are drawn between acquaintances and good friends. Compared with the rest of Europe, there is little use of first names and many Germans generally use the formal *Sie* rather than the more familiar *du* as a form of address.

G

CHRONOLOGY

The Frankish Empire reached its peak under Charlemagne, crowned Holy Roman Emperor in 800. From 1273 until the 19th century, German history was tied to that of Austria's Habsburg dynasty.

❑ **1815** German Confederation under nominal Austrian leadership.
❑ **1834** Zollverein Customs Union leads to economic convergence of 18 states, including Prussia, and reflects unification aspirations.
❑ **1862** Otto von Bismarck appointed Prussian chancellor.
❑ **1864–1870** Prussian defeats of Danes, Austrians and French; north German states brought under Prussian control.
❑ **1871** South German states join new German Empire; William I of Prussia declared emperor. France cedes Alsace and Lorraine.
❑ **1870s** Rapid industrialization. Bismarck's social legislation.
❑ **1890** Kaiser Wilhelm II accedes with aspirations for German world role; Bismarck sacked.

POPULATION AGE BREAKDOWN

	0–14	15–64		65+
11.5%	13.7%	15.6%	14.6%	15.4%
67.2%	63.1%	65.9%	68.7%	67.7%
21.3%	23.2%	18.5%	16.7%	16.9%
1960	1970	1980	1990	2000

G

***The Messeturm,** Frankfurt, the tallest office building in Europe. Frankfurt is Germany's financial services centre and home to many of its leading companies.*

POLITICS

 Lower House 1994   President Richard von Weizsäcker

THE STATE OF THE PARTIES

Federal Assembly 662 members

| 40% CDU | 36% SPD | 12% FDP | 8% CSU | 3% PDS | 1% Other |

CDU = Christian Democratic Union   SPD = Social Democratic Party   FDP = Free Democratic Party   CSU = Christian Social Union   PDS = Party of Democratic Socialism
Other = Alliance 90/The Greens (East)

Federal Council 68 members

Between 3 and 6 members represent each of 16 states (*Länder*)

Germany is a federal democratic republic of 16 states, or *Länder*. The government is led by the chancellor, who is elected by the *Bundestag* (Federal Assembly). The president's role is largely ceremonial. The 'Basic Law' of West Germany, drawn up in 1948, became the 1990 constitution of reunified Germany.

MAIN POLITICAL ISSUES

Reunification
Although, in 1989, 85% of Germans voted for reunification, the general rejoicing at the fall of the Berlin Wall at the end of that year has soured as the true costs of the process have become clear. Unemployment in the east has risen to 30% with the collapse of inefficient industries. In the west, taxes have gone up to pay the costs of privatization as well as a growing social security bill. However, long-term German policy remains to raise east German living standards up to the west German average.

The recession
Germans, used to constant growth since the 1950s, have been shocked by the recession that began in 1991. For the first time in living memory, car firms such as Volkswagen have been laying off workers. The recession has been doubly painful because it has coincided with the enormous and unexpected costs of reunification.

Nationalism
The problems of unemployment have led to anti-immigrant attacks and an increase in support for far-right parties. Some young Germans have felt resentment that foreigners hold jobs. Turks have come in for particular vilification and were the subjects of the Rostock attack in 1992. The problem of racism is no worse than in many other European states, but is more sensitive given Germany's history.

PROFILE
Germany's politics remains strongly democratic and essentially stable. It has a long tradition of federative association. Before unification in 1871, Germany was a mass of separate principalities, kingdoms and city states. This tradition was in many ways maintained by Bismarck in his unification constitution; some of the *Länder* even retained their own monarchies until 1918. The 1933–1945 Nazi period, during which the federal system was abolished, was very much a hiatus. The Allies re-established the system in West Germany in 1945; in the east, the *Länder* were restored after reunification in 1990.

In many ways, the *Länder* are at the heart of German political life. Each *Land* has its own elected parliament and is able to raise many of its own taxes and run its own investment policies. The decentralized nature of German politics continues down to city level and below. German cities have larger budgets than their European counterparts and city mayors wield considerable power. By general consensus the system works well, delivering efficient and commercially astute democratic government.

Nationally, a conservative CDU–CSU coalition dominated the *Bundestag* from 1949 to 1969, followed by an SPD–FPD coalition, with Willy Brandt and Helmut Kohl as chancellors, from 1969 to 1982. Since then, a conservative government has again been in power, led by Chancellor Helmut Kohl. The two coalitions have little to distinguish them. Their economic policies, based on low inflation, stable growth and an independent central bank, are almost identical. All parties still support the *Sozialmarktwirtschaft*, the social market economy, on which West Germany's prosperity was built.

Dr Helmut Kohl, *Federal Chancellor and CDU chairman.*   ***Dr Klaus Kinkel,*** *took over as foreign minister in 1992.*

Hans-Dietrich Genscher, *foreign minister 1974–1992.*

WORLD AFFAIRS

Before reunification, Germany played only a modest part in international politics. The focus of West Germany was the creation of the EU and the policy of *Ostpolitik* – improving relations with

Moscow, which had 400,000 troops stationed in East Germany.

Since 1990, the emphasis has changed and a united Germany is beginning to voice a foreign policy which reflects its position as the most powerful country in Europe. It is still a leading proponent of unity. France

remains its closest ally within the EU, although the relationship has cooled a little since 1990.

Germany's focus, however, has shifted eastward. It is the biggest investor in all the ex-COMECON economies, bringing the region once again under German influence.

AID

 $6.9bn (donations) ⬆ Up 5% in 1991

Unlike the USA, the UK and France, Germany's aid programmes are not directly motivated by its desire for political influence in the world's poorer regions. Most are multilateral, although there is also a strong tradition of direct aid. Much comes directly from Church organizations such as the Protestant *Brot für die Welt*. Many German volunteers and missionaries work overseas on aid programmes.

DEFENCE

 $31bn ⬇ Down 4% in 1992

0   *Defence spending as % GDP*   40
1.9%

The German army, the *Bundeswehr*, is the largest in Europe. 200,000 US and British NATO troops remain stationed in western Germany. With France, Germany has been developing the Eurocorps, a joint army of 50,000. The constitution still forbids *Bundeswehr* activity beyond the NATO area.

GERMAN ARMED FORCES

🛡	7090 main battle tanks (2084 *Leopard* 1A1/ 2083 *Leopard* 2/T-54,-55)	316,000 personnel
🚢	22 submarines, 6 destroyers, 8 frigates and 43 patrol boats	35,200 personnel
✈	653 combat aircraft (230 F-4/236 *Tornado*/ 20 MiG-29/163 *Alpha*)	95,800 personnel
🚀	None	

G

ECONOMICS

 $1690bn   1.65 Deutsche Marks

SCORE CARD

- ❑ WORLD GNP RANKING............................3rd
- ❑ GNP PER CAPITA.............................$21,046
- ❑ BALANCE OF PAYMENTS ....$–30.2bn
- ❑ INFLATION 3.4%
- ❑ UNEMPLOYMENT................................4.7%

EXPORTS

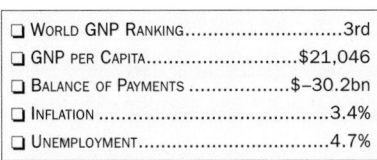

France 4%, Poland 6%, Netherlands 4%, CIS* 52%, Other 34%

IMPORTS

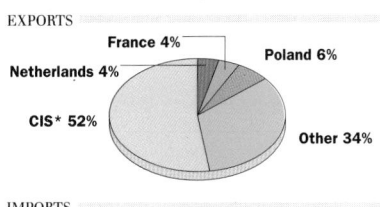

Netherlands 5%, Poland 7%, Other 49%, CIS* 39%

ECONOMIC PERFORMANCE INDICATOR

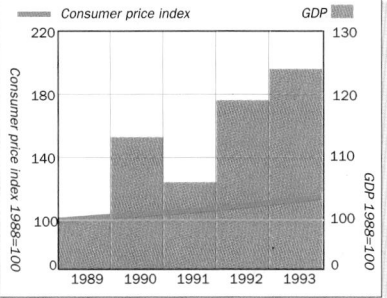

Consumer price index / GDP (1988=100), 1989–1993

Traditionally harmonious labour relations under pressure in recent years. Growing competition from increasingly efficient, low-wage Asian economies.

PROFILE

West Germany's post-war economic recovery from a war-shattered state to become the world's third strongest economy was remarkable. US aid played its part, but equally important was the thinking behind the *Sozialmarktwirtschaft,* or social market economy. This charged the state with providing welfare and ensuring workers' rights, whilst leaving the economy largely in private hands.

Germany has developed little of the co-ordinated state and regional planning found in France. All the major banks and businesses are in private hands. One exception is Volkswagen, which is partly state-owned. The central bank, which sets interest rates and is responsible for controlling inflation, also has a large measure of independence from the government.

GERMANY : MAJOR BUSINESSES

Kiel, Hamburg, Berlin, Ruhr Valley, Dresden, Frankfurt am Main, Nürnberg, München, Stuttgart

◊ Optics
⚬ Shipbuilding
⚗ Chemicals
⚡ Electronics
✿ Engineering
⊛ Research & development
🚗 Vehicle assembly

0   200 km
0   200 miles

The greatest challenge for Germany remains rebuilding the east. The state privatization agency, the *Treuhand,* has now sold off 8000 of the formerly East German state-owned concerns.

Friedrichstrasse, East Berlin. *Berlin was redesignated Germany's capital city in 1991. Redevelopment of its centre has been planned.*

STRENGTHS

Europe's major industrial power and, until now, most successful economy. Very efficient industry benefits from Germany's low inflation environment. German workers and managers live up to their reputation for hard work, thoroughness and discipline. Strongest sectors are cars, heavy engineering, electronics and chemicals; all have massive export success.

WEAKNESSES

The east: costs of incorporating out-of-date and massively inefficient ex-communist economy underestimated.

G

RESOURCES

572bn kwh (capacity 123m kw)

66,500 b/d (reserves 449,814,000 bbl)

35.1m pigs, 20.4m cattle, 4.1m sheep, 477,000 horses

Coal, natural gas, copper, salt, potash, tin, nickel

ELECTRICITY GENERATION

Hydro 3% (19.5bn kwh)

Thermal 68% (389.7bn kwh)

Nuclear 29% (162.8bn kwh)

Other 0%

0   20   40   60   80   100
% of total generation by type

Germany has relatively few natural resources. It imports over 50% of its energy needs. Coal, the basis of its industrialization, has diminished in importance, accounting for less than

ENVIRONMENT

16% partially protected

Successful energy conservation programme

ENVIRONMENTAL TREATIES

Yes

Yes

No

Yes

Germans are among the world's most environmentally conscious people. Led by the Green Party, which emerged as a powerful political force in the 1980s, environmental campaigns have had a major influence on the policies of all the major parties. The Greens have won only a few seats in the *Bundestag*, but are far more heavily represented in *Land* parliaments and local councils.

Germany has some of the strictest pollution controls in the world, adding extra costs to businesses and forcing them to become even more efficient. Germans recycle 42% of their waste paper, reprocess 70% of their used tyres, and sort 50% of their glass according to colour, to aid recycling.

Apart from the nuclear debate, which has been vigorously fought and won by the Greens, the main concern is Germany's forests. Acid rain from car fumes and industrial pollution was suspected to be killing trees in all parts of the country. Official estimates in 1986 suggesting that up to 50% of trees were sick or dying resulted in Germany becoming the first European country to insist that new cars be fitted with catalytic converters.

The east had particular problems, including the highest per capita rate of sulphur emissions in the world. These have been reduced by the shut-down of industrial plants, and the fact that the noxious Trabant cars are quickly being replaced with Western ones.

20% of energy today, compared with 51% 30 years ago. Unlike France, the former West Germany did not invest heavily in nuclear power; the accident at Chernobyl in the Ukraine strengthened the anti-nuclear lobby's case. In the east, all the Soviet-built stations have been shut down. Germany's energy conservation programme is generally considered the most successful in Europe.

GERMANY : LAND USE

Cropland
Forest
Pasture
Vineyards
Pigs
Cattle

0   200 km
0   200 miles

MEDIA

No political censorship

PUBLISHING AND BROADCAST MEDIA

There are 400 daily newspapers, including the *Frankfurter Allgemeine Zeitung*, the *Süddeutsche Zeitung* and *Die Welt*

2 state-controlled, 2 independent networks

3 state-controlled networks

Intelsat V1 F1 Astra 1B

Extensive in all main cities

German TV is carefully supervised by the political parties to ensure a balance of views. The main channels, ARD and ZDF, have a reputation for safe programming, but the arrival of satellite and cable TV and competition has begun to make TV more lively. Newspapers are mostly regional and serious. An exception is *Bild Zeitung*, the right-wing, sensationalist tabloid, which sells four million copies daily.

Neuschwanstein Castle in Bavaria, one of Germany's major tourist attractions. It was built for the eccentric King Ludwig II.

EDUCATION

99%

0   Education spending as % GNP   25
4.5%

THE EDUCATION SYSTEM

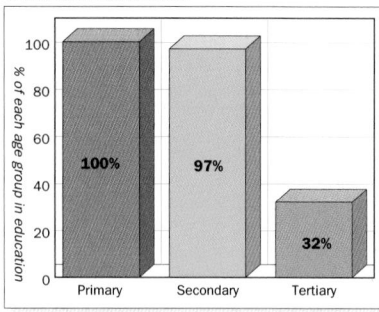

100%   97%   32%

Primary   Secondary   Tertiary

% of each age group in education

Education in Germany is run by the separate *Länder*. They co-ordinate their teaching policies, but have full autonomy within their own borders. The German approach to education stresses academic efficiency and discipline, with few sporting or cultural activities.

Those who wish to go to university attend the upper-secondary *Gymnasien* to prepare for the essential *Abitur* exam. Since this was made easier, thousands more have exercised their right to attend university, leading to strains on resources. Students frequently take eight years or more to complete degrees. Research is done as much by firms, such as Siemens, as by universities.

CRIME

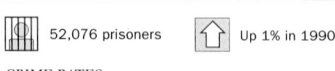

52,076 prisoners

Up 1% in 1990

CRIME RATES

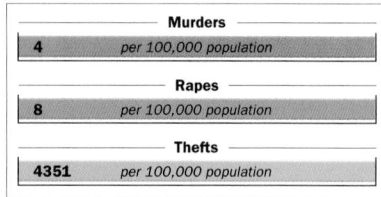

Murders	
4	per 100,000 population

Rapes	
8	per 100,000 population

Thefts	
4351	per 100,000 population

Crime rates in Germany are lower than in most other European countries. This is largely the result of a genuine respect for the law, coupled with a strong police force. Recently, however, rising unemployment has led to an increase in petty theft and a wave of violence, notably against immigrants.

German politics, once with an enviably clean reputation, has suffered several corruption scandals. Civil service corruption remains rare. People convicted under environmental laws will face ten-year jail sentences.

REGIONS

BERLIN

Reichstag
Konraße
Halle
Charlottenburg
Alexander Platz
Spree
National Gallery
Brandenburg
Tor
Berlin Museum
Tiergarten
Potsdamer Platz
Sowjetisches
Ehrenmal
Rathaus
Treptower Park

0   2 km
0   2 miles

━━ Motorways   ⌒⌒ Location of Berlin Wall (pre 1989)
☐ Park or open land   ⊙ Major tourist sites

THE PROCESS OF REBUILDING Berlin as the capital of Germany began after reunification in 1990. The planning is being undertaken by an international team of architects led by Norman Foster. Much of the city was destroyed during the war. In the Cold War years, it was split into US, UK, French and Soviet occupation zones. The first three were separated from the fourth by the notorious Berlin Wall. Many people were shot trying to cross the Wall to the western sector, which itself was an enclave within East Germany. In 1989, the almost spontaneous demolition of the Berlin Wall became a potent symbol of German reunification.

BADEN-WÜRTTEMBERG

BADEN-WÜRTTEMBERG has a long industrial tradition. It was here that Benz and Daimler invented the motor car. Its capital, Stuttgart, remains home to both Porsche and Daimler-Benz, as well as to Bosch and IBM's main European plants.

Baden-Württemberg is also a centre for medium-sized precision manufacturing firms. It has emerged as a centre of excellence for new technologies, including robotics and molecular industries. Lothar Späth, prime minister from 1978–1991, was largely responsible for initiatives to establish 30 new research institutes and 10 science parks, encouraging links between Stuttgart University and local industry.

Stuttgart
Porsche
Bosch
Rosenstein-Park
Neckar
Kräherwald
Mittlerer
Schoßgarten
Oberer
Schoßgarten
Rot- und
Schwarzwild
Rathaus
IBM
Daimler-
Benz
Dürrbach
Silberwald
Stuttgart
Unitversity

0   2 km
0   2 miles

━━ Motorways   ☐ Park or open land   ⊙ Major tourist sites
🚗 Motor industry   💻 Hi-tech industry   ⚡ Electronics industry

BAYERN

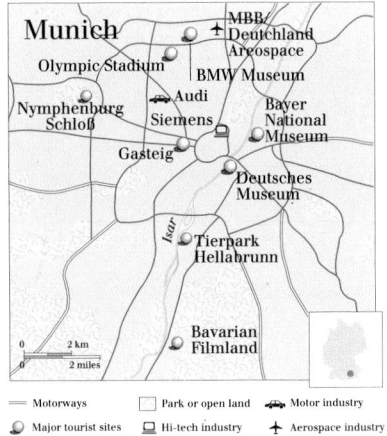

Munich
MBB/
Deutchland
Aerospace
Olympic Stadium
BMW Museum
Nymphenburg
Schloß
Audi
Siemens
Bayer
National
Museum
Gasteig
Deutsches
Museum
Isar
Tierpark
Hellabrunn
Bavarian
Filmland

0   2 km
0   2 miles

━━ Motorways   ☐ Park or open land   🚗 Motor industry
⊙ Major tourist sites   💻 Hi-tech industry   ✈ Aerospace industry

THE LARGEST of the *Länder*, Bayern (Bavaria) has a reputation for conservatism. It was one of the

Länder to maintain its monarchy until 1918. Catholicism is stronger here than elsewhere in Germany. Liberal social and sexual habits, acceptable in most other regions, are still frowned upon in Bayern's rural districts. In its heavily agricultural economy, small farms have suffered as the subsidies provided by the EU have become less generous.

Other parts of its economy are doing well and it has been developing new high-tech industries. It is often referred to, along with Baden-Württemberg, as Germany's sunbelt. Its major firms – BMW, Siemens and Audi – have also been growing.

Munich, Bayern's capital, is the centre for the German fashion, film and advertising industries, and is a centre for the arts. Its now multi-purpose arts centre, the *Gasteig*, opened in 1985.

HEALTH

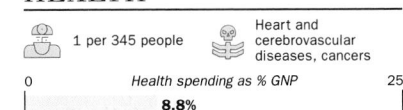

1 per 345 people

Heart and cerebrovascular diseases, cancers

0   *Health spending as % GNP*   25
8.8%

The German social security system, first pioneered by Bismarck, is one of the most comprehensive in the world. Health insurance is compulsory and employer and employee contributions are high. Although most hospitals are run by the *Länder*, some are still owned by Germany's wealthy churches.

Germans are increasingly health-conscious, paying great attention to diet. Millions go on cures every year to the country's 200-plus spas. In the east, many are still suffering from lung diseases caused by pollution.

WEALTH

Car mechanic, 18 Deutsche Marks per hour; government official, 8314 Deutsche Marks per month

CONSUMER GOODS OWNERSHIP

Per 1000 population

1000
750
500
250
0

552   374   575   207   26

The effects of the Nazi period, which discredited many of Germany's ruling class, and the destruction of the property of millions of families in the war, account for the relatively classless nature of German society. Status is now more closely linked to wealth than to birth. In the west, disparities are less than in most of Europe; workers are generally well-paid and social security is generous. East German wages, however, are still pegged well below western rates, and there are a disproportionate number of unemployed living on welfare benefit.

WORLD RANKING

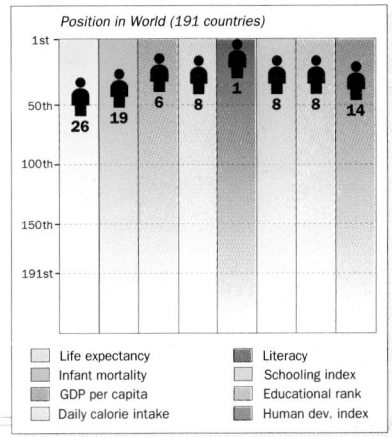

Position in World (191 countries)

1st
50th
100th
150th
191st

26   19   6   8   1   8   8   14

☐ Life expectancy   ▨ Literacy
☐ Infant mortality   ☐ Schooling index
☐ GDP per capita   ☐ Educational rank
☐ Daily calorie intake   ☐ Human dev. index

G

GHANA

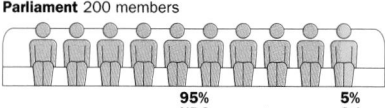

WEST AFRICA

OFFICIAL NAME: Republic of Ghana **CAPITAL:** Accra
POPULATION: 16 million **CURRENCY:** Cedi **OFFICIAL LANGUAGE:** English

T HE HEARTLAND OF THE ancient Ashanti kingdom, modern Ghana is a union of the former British colony of the Gold Coast and the British-administered part of the UN Trust Territory of Togoland. Ghana gained independence in 1957, the first British colony to do so. Its recent history has been one of intermittent military rule; the embracing of multiparty democracy in 1992 confirmed former military leader Jerry Rawlings in power.

CLIMATE

WEATHER CHART

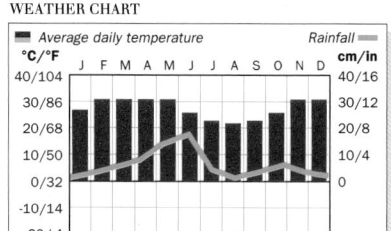

Southern Ghana has two rainy seasons: from April to July and September to November. The drier north has just one, from April to September.

COMMUNICATIONS

Kotoka Intl, Accra
467,000 passengers

11 ships
83,400 dwt

THE TRANSPORT NETWORK

28,300 km (17,585 miles)		None
953 km (592 miles)		155 km (96 miles)

In 1983, work began to restore Ghana's roads, which had fallen into disrepair in the 1960s and 1970s; the network is now improving.

TOURISM

172,462 visitors

Up 18% in 1991

MAIN OVERSEAS ARRIVALS

UK 10%
Ivory Coast 10%
USA 8%
Other 72%

0 10 20 30 40 50 60 70 80
% of total arrivals

Tourism is still small-scale; most visitors come from Africa, the UK and the USA. Good beaches and old coastal forts are major attractions.

PEOPLE

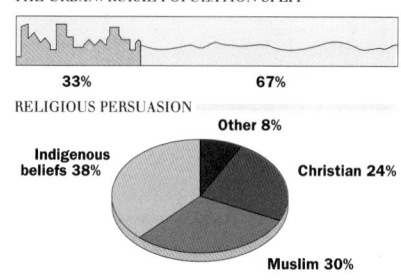

Twi, Fanti, Ewe, Ga, Adangbe, Gurma, Dagomba (Dagbani)

63 people per km²

THE URBAN/RURAL POPULATION SPLIT

33%   67%

RELIGIOUS PERSUASION

Other 8%
Indigenous beliefs 38%
Christian 24%
Muslim 30%

Ghana contains various cultural-linguistic groups. The largest is the Akan, who include the Ashanti and Fanti peoples. Other important groups are the Mole-Dagbani in the north, Ga-Adangbe around Accra and Ewe in the southeast. There are few tribal tensions. Family ties are strong.

POLITICS

Uncertain

President Jerry Rawlings

THE STATE OF THE PARTIES

Parliament 200 members

95% NDC   5% Other

NDC = National Democratic Congress (closely linked to the former PNDC) **Other** = National Convention Party, Independent Party, Egle Party

Ghana's return to multiparty rule in 1992 marked the effective legitimization of the military government which had previously resisted the call for greater democracy. Jerry Rawlings, a flight-lieutenant of Ewe-Scottish descent and one of the great survivors of African politics, staged coups in 1979 and 1981, and led the 1981–1992 Provisional National Defence Council military government. Rawlings emerged as a late candidate for the NDC and won 58% of the vote in the 1992 presidential elections. Opposition parties claimed malpractice and refused to contest the parliamentary elections the following month. The NDC swept the board. Opposition is still effectively outside parliament; the difference is that since 1992 political dissent is accepted.

WORLD AFFAIRS

Ecowas OAU Comm NAM GATT

Good relations with the West, which provides the bulk of Ghana's military and development aid, are a priority. Ghana has played a significant part in UN peacekeeping operations. After Nigeria, it is also the main contributor to the ECOWAS forces (ECOMOG) stationed in war-torn Liberia since 1990. In 1993, the Ghanaian government called unsuccessfully for ECOWAS to intervene to suppress civil unrest in Togo.

GHANA

Total Area : 238 540 sq. km (92 100 sq. miles)

LAND HEIGHT

500m/1640ft
200m/656ft
Sea Level

POPULATION

over 500 000
over 100 000
over 50 000
over 10 000
under 10 000

0 100 km
0 100 miles

G

AID

 $724m (receipts)   Up 45% in 1991

In 1983, the PNDC began a largely successful economic recovery programme backed by World Bank and IMF aid. Between 1984 and 1989, Ghana received $3.5 billion, the third largest recipient of World Bank aid after India and China.

DEFENCE

 $45.39m   Up 32% in 1990

In 1966, 1972, 1979 and 1981, the military mounted successful coups. There have also been frequent unsuccessful coups, many mounted by disaffected officers against both military and civilian governments. Outside Ghana, the army has been deployed mainly in UN and ECOWAS operations.

ECONOMICS

 $6.8bn   783.68 cedis

SCORE CARD

❑ World GNP Ranking	96th
❑ GNP per Capita	$425
❑ Balance of Payments	$−377.8m
❑ Inflation	18.1%
❑ Unemployment	0.5%

STRENGTHS
Cocoa, the main export crop, is cheap to produce and accounts for 15% of the world total. 1993 gold exports totalled 1 million fine ounces; the main source is the Ashanti goldfields. Bauxite – with some processed alumina – is a major export. Since 1983, economic recovery policies have raised GNP 5% a year.

WEAKNESSES
High budget deficits and debt repayments; the cedi was devalued in 1983 and has since tended to float downwards. Foreign investors generally invest solely in gold mining. Many loss-making state enterprises.

EXPORTS
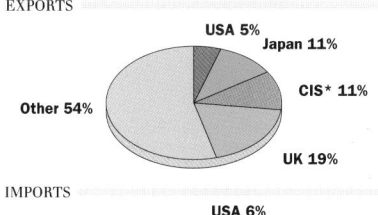
USA 5%
Japan 11%
CIS* 11%
Other 54%
UK 19%

IMPORTS
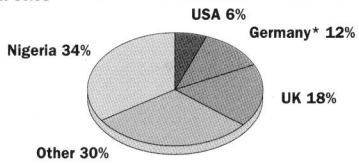
USA 6%
Germany* 12%
Nigeria 34%
UK 18%
Other 30%

Dixcove harbour, *close to Ghana's most southerly cape. The majority of Ghanaians lead a traditional subsistence existence.*

RESOURCES

 5.3bn kwh (capacity 1.12m kw)   Reserves of 500,000 bbl; refines 26,600 b/cd

 2.2m sheep, 1.1m cattle, 559,000 pigs, 10,000 asses   Gold, diamonds, bauxite, manganese

Over the last ten years, gold production has expanded; in 1993, gold was the major export. Diamonds, bauxite and manganese are also exported. Surplus hydro-power from the Volta Dam, completed in the early 1960s, is exported to Togo and Benin.

ENVIRONMENT

 5%   Very low public awareness of ecological issues

Cutting of wood for fuel, timber and farming has destroyed 70% of forests. Mining has devastated the surrounding land and caused serious pollution.

MEDIA

 Self-censorship by press. Overt criticism of government is not tolerated

PUBLISHING AND BROADCAST MEDIA

 There are 3 daily newspapers, the *Ghanaian Times,* the *People's Daily Graphic* and the *Evening News*

 1 state-controlled service   1 state-controlled service

New independent weeklies reflect the increase in private press ownership. Radio and TV tend to follow government reporting guidelines.

CRIME

 Ghana does not publish prison figures   Up 4% in 1990

The judiciary has little independence and the government often resorts to *ad hoc* 'people's tribunals'. Corruption is less of a problem than in recent years.

EDUCATION

 60%

All sectors of the education system are over-subscribed. There are a few high-quality boarding schools and four universities.

 (G marker)

CHRONOLOGY

Finding the Ashanti uncompliant with their demands, the British sacked Kumasi, their capital, in 1874 and created the Gold Coast colony.

❑ **1957** Independence under authoritarian Kwame Nkrumah.
❑ **1964** Single-party state.
❑ **1966** Economy founders. Bloodless army coup.
❑ **1972–1979** Corrupt 'kleptocracy' of Gen Acheampong. Executed 1979.
❑ **1979** Flt-Lt Jerry Rawlings' coup. Civilian Dr Limann wins elections.
❑ **1981** Rawlings takes power again.
❑ **1992** Rawlings' NDC wins elections – boycott by four opposition parties.

HEALTH

 1 per 12,523 people   Malaria, diarrheal diseases, tuberculosis

The health of most of the population has benefited more from improvements in public hygiene than improvements in medical care.

WEALTH

 The many Ghanaians who emigrated in search of better jobs remit $300 million a year – a substantial contribution to Ghana's economy

CONSUMER GOODS OWNERSHIP

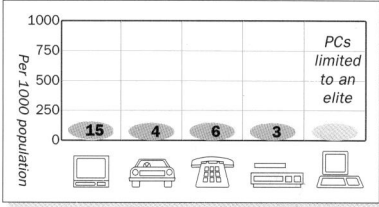
PCs limited to an elite
15   4   6   3

Political uncertainty brought few opportunities for advancement and many Ghanaians emigrated, but the situation is now improving. The key disparity is still between the poorer north and richer, more urban, south.

WORLD RANKING

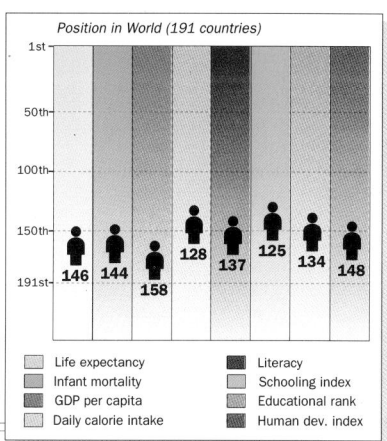
Position in World (191 countries)
146   144   158   128   137   125   134   148

▢ Life expectancy	▢ Literacy
▢ Infant mortality	▢ Schooling index
▢ GDP per capita	▢ Educational rank
▢ Daily calorie intake	▢ Human dev. index

GREECE

OFFICIAL NAME: Hellenic Republic **CAPITAL:** Athens
POPULATION: 10.2 million **CURRENCY:** Drachma **OFFICIAL LANGUAGE:** Greek

THE SOUTHERNMOST NATION of the Balkans, Greece is surrounded by the Aegean, Ionian and Cretan seas. Its territory includes over 2000 islands. Three fifths of the mainland is mountainous and only one third of the land is cultivated. The country has a strong seafaring tradition and Greeks are the world's biggest ship owners. Greece is rich in minerals, including chromium, not found elsewhere in the EU. The key foreign policy concern is the Former Yugoslav Republic of Macedonia (FYRM); Greece fears its potential claim over the Greek province of Macedonia.

CLIMATE

WEATHER CHART

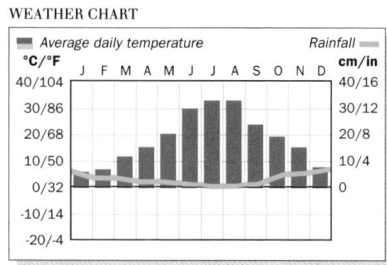

The climate varies from region to region. The northwest is alpine while parts of Crete border on the subtropical. The large central plain experiences high summer temperatures. Water is a problem as many rivers have been diverted underground by earthquakes.

COMMUNICATIONS

 Athinai, Athens 6.3m passengers
 1407 ships 46.35m dwt

THE TRANSPORT NETWORK

 38,938 km (24,196 miles)
 91 km (57 miles)
 2484 km (1544 miles)
 Corinth Canal

The easiest and cheapest method of transport between the islands and the mainland is by boat or Russian-built hovercraft. Greece has a total of 444 ports, of which 123 are large enough to handle passenger or freight traffic. Of the 37 civilian airports in Greece, two thirds are located on the islands and are also used by the military. Although the rail system is undeveloped, an inter-urban bus system and fleet of air-conditioned tourist pullmans offer a more extensive service. In general, Greece has a good, if increasingly congested, road network; the number of motor vehicles is three million and rising. Piraeus is the country's main port.

TOURISM

 8.2m visitors   Down 11% in 1991

MAIN OVERSEAS ARRIVALS

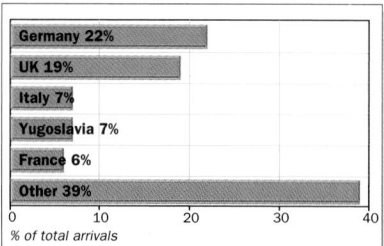

Tourism is a mainstay of the Greek economy and a major source of foreign exchange. Until recently, the government gave grants for hotel development. As a result, many third grade hotels were built, especially on Crete and Rhodes. Smaller islands also tried to encourage tourism, but few have reliable water supplies or enough sandy beaches to attract visitors. Recently, tourism has declined as many people have opted for cheaper holidays elsewhere. The break-up of former Yugoslavia has also deterred visitors. The Greek tourist industry is now trying to encourage visitors by upgrading its image to include sailing and conference tourism. Thessaloníki will be the European City of Culture in 1997.

Roman ruins, Dodona. *Classical sites such as this amphitheatre in northwestern Greece, have helped to make tourism one of Greece's most important industries.*

PEOPLE

Greek, Turkish, Macedonian, Albanian   78 people per km²

THE URBAN/RURAL POPULATION SPLIT

62%   38%

RELIGIOUS PERSUASION

Other 1%   Muslim 1%
Greek Orthodox 98%

ETHNIC MAKEUP

Other 2%
Greek 98%

Greece was for many centuries a largely agrarian and seafaring nation. The German occupation during the Second World War, and the civil war that followed, destroyed much of the fabric of rural life and there was rapid urbanization between the 1950s and the 1980s. There was also extensive emigration during the 1950s and 1960s to northern Europe, Australia, the USA, Canada and southern Africa. However, many people returned to Greece in the 1980s, putting pressure on the labour market. The socialist PASOK governments of 1981–1989 spent large sums, mostly from EU sources, on developing the infrastructure and business life of the rural regions with a view to halting emigration to the cities. The policy was mostly successful, but over half the population still lives in the capital, Athens, and the main northern city, Thessaloníki.

Christianity is the main religion; 98% of the population belong to the Greek Orthodox Church. Civil marriage and divorce only became legal in 1982. There are small minorities of Muslims, Catholics and Jews.

POPULATION AGE BREAKDOWN

% of population by age group	0–14	15–64	65+
1960	26.5%	65.2%	8.3%
1970	24.9%	64%	11.1%
1980	22.8%	64.1%	13.1%
1990	19.7%	66.6%	13.7%
2000	17.2%	65.9%	16.9%

POLITICS

1997

President Konstantinos
Karamanlis

THE STATE OF THE PARTIES

Parliament 300 members

**3%
KKE**

**57%
PASOK** **37%
ND** **3%
POLA**

PASOK = Panhellenic Socialist Movement **ND** = New
Democracy Party **POLA** = Political Spring
KKE = Communist Party of Greece

Greece is a multiparty democracy.
A military government was in power
between 1967–1974.

MAIN POLITICAL ISSUES

Terrorism
During the 1990s, left-wing groups,
notably November 17, attacked
'capitalist' targets. These included US
companies and individuals of the
conservative ND party. In 1990, a law
was passed forbidding the publishing of
alleged terrorists' views. This was
abolished in 1993, but in January 1994,

November 17 ended 13 months of
inaction by murdering a banker
involved with the privatization of the
state-owned *Ayet Iraklis* cement works.

Albanian refugees
Large numbers of Albanians of Greek
descent have been entering Greece
illegally since 1990. Willing to work or
very low wages, they have swelled
Greece's already thriving black
economy. In an attempt to stem the
tide, the government has embarked on
an aid programme in southern Albania.

PROFILE
After a financial scandal brought down
the PASOK government in 1989, the ND
party presented itself as the party of
fiscal probity. Its policies to reduce
inflation, balance the budget and curb
mounting debt, though relatively
successful, proved as unpopular as its
privatization plans. The 1993 elections
returned PASOK, and Andreas
Papandreou, to power. The
privatization programme

**President
Karamanlis,** *who
began a second – and
last – term in 1990.*

**Andreas
Papandreou,** *leader
of* PASOK *and prime
minister since 1993.*

has been cut back, however, and
economic realities have forced PASOK to
continue with many of the ND's policies.

G

WORLD AFFAIRS

EU   NATO   OECD   CSCE   GATT

Throughout the Cold War, Greece was
closely allied to the West, although
there are strong sympathies between
the Greeks, Russians and Serbs because
of their shared Orthodox heritage.
Greece withdrew from the military
command of NATO in 1974 in protest at
the failure of the Alliance to prevent
the Turkish invasion of Cyprus. It has
since rejoined under a formula to
negotiate with Turkey new command
and control arrangements over the
Aegean. These regional security issues,
however, remain unresolved.

AID

$35m (receipts)   Up 17% in 1990

Greece gives relatively little aid. It is,
however, a large net receiver of
regional development assistance
from the EU. Total EU aid could
reach $19 billion by the end of the
decade. In particular, it is a
major beneficiary of the EU's
structural and cohesion funds.
The allocation of cohesion
funds for Greece are
estimated to amount to
around $3.5 billion over
the 1993–1999 period.
Some of the money has
been used to reverse
the decline of
northeast Greece –
the EU's least-
developed region.
EU funds make
up 70% of a
$370 million
programme to
upgrade the
region's road
network and expand
its port facilities.

GREECE

Total Area : 131 990 sq. km
(50 961 sq. miles)

POPULATION
◉ over 1 000 000
◉ over 500 000
◎ over 100 000
○ over 50 000
• over 10 000

LAND HEIGHT
2000m/6562ft
1000m/3281ft
500m/1640ft
200m/656ft
Sea Level

0   100 km
0   100 miles

G

CHRONOLOGY

Greece was occupied by Nazi Germany between 1941 and 1944. After liberation by the Allies, communists and royalists fought a five-year civil war. This ended with communist defeat, and King Paul became the constitutional monarch.

❏ **1964** King Paul dies. Succeeded by son, King Constantine.
❏ **1967** Military coup. King in exile. Colonel Papadopoulos premier.
❏ **1973** Greece declared a republic, with Papadopoulos as president. Papadopoulos overthrown in military coup. Lt-Gen Ghizikis becomes president with Adamantios Androutsopoulos as prime minister.
❏ **1974** Greece leaves NATO in protest at Turkish occupation of northern Cyprus. Government falls. Constantinos Karamanlis becomes premier of Government of National Salvation. Karamanlis' ND party wins subsequent elections.
❏ **1975** Konstantinos Tsatsou becomes president.
❏ **1977** Elections. ND re-elected.
❏ **1980** Karamanlis president. Georgios Rallis prime minister. Greece rejoins NATO.
❏ **1981** Socialist PASOK party wins elections. Andreas Papandreou first-ever socialist premier. Greece full member of EC.
❏ **1985** Proposals to limit power of president. Karamanlis resigns. Christos Sartzetakis president. Greece and Albania re-open borders, closed since 1940.
❏ **1985–1989** Civil unrest caused by economic austerity programme.
❏ **1988** Cabinet implicated in financial scandal. Several leading members resign.
❏ **1989** Defence agreement with the USA. After inconclusive elections, Left coalition between communist KKE and EAR form government. Charilaos Florakis president. ND join Left coalition in government. Tzannis Tzannetakis premier for three months, then succeeded by Yannis Grivas. Further election inconclusive. All-party coalition. Xenofon Zolotas prime minister.
❏ **1990** Coalition government collapses. ND party wins protracted elections. Mitsotakis prime minister; Karamanlis president.
❏ **1990–1992** Strikes against economic, educational and social security reform.
❏ **1992** EC persuaded to withhold recognition of Republic of Macedonia (FYRM). Maastricht Treaty on European union ratified.
❏ **1993** PASOK win general election, Andreas Papandreou premier.

DEFENCE

 $4.3bn   ⬆ Up 17% in 1992

0   *Defence spending as % GDP*   40
5.9%

Greece spends a higher percentage of GDP on defence than any other NATO country. Its main concern is the perceived threat from Turkey. Greece is seeking full membership to the Western European Union, although this is being blocked because of disputes with Turkey.

GREEK ARMED FORCES

1879 main battle tanks (396 M–47/1220 M–48/154 AMX–30)	113,000 personnel
4 frigates, 10 submarines, 9 destroyers and 37 patrol boats	19,500 personnel
381 combat aircraft (F–4E/F–5A,-B/F–104G/F–16/F–4E)	26,800 personnel
None	

ECONOMICS

 $65.5bn   214.9 drachmae

SCORE CARD

❏ WORLD GNP RANKING..........................35th
❏ GNP PER CAPITA $6422
❏ BALANCE OF PAYMENTS......................$–1bn
❏ INFLATION 15.8%
❏ UNEMPLOYMENT................................8.9%

ECONOMIC PERFORMANCE INDICATOR

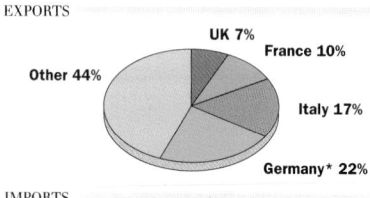

EXPORTS

UK 7%
France 10%
Other 44%
Italy 17%
Germany* 22%

IMPORTS

Netherlands 7%
France 8%
Other 48%
Italy 16%
Germany* 21%

STRENGTHS
One of the major tourist destinations in Europe. Efficient agricultural exporter. Shipping: the world's largest beneficially-owned fleet.

WEAKNESSES
High levels of public debt. High interest rates and bureaucratic banking system discourage private initiative. State involved in almost 70% of businesses. High levels of tax evasion. Black economy accounts for 30%–50% of GDP.

PROFILE
Greece took longer than most other northern European countries to recover from the Second World War owing to years of civil strife. It was not until the 1960s that any substantial investment occurred. The Colonels' dictatorship curbed inflationary pressures by the introduction of a wage freeze. When civilian government was restored in 1974, a spate of high wage settlements and the oil price shocks of 1973 and 1979 drove inflation

to above 20%, a level at which it hovered for some years. From 1982–1986, Greece's largest companies reported substantial losses. There was a modest return to profitability following the socialists' austerity programme of 1986–1987.

In general, the return on capital has persistently been a fraction of the rate of inflation. However, economic reforms in the late 1980s led to a resurgence of interest in the Stock Exchange, which also attracts investment from the black economy.

GREECE : MAJOR BUSINESSES

🌀	Cement
✹	Textiles
🝫	Chemicals
🖵	Electronics
🍶	Beverages
⬦	Iron & steel
🛳	Shipbuilding
◗	Pulp & paper
🍒	Fruit processing
✎	Pharmaceuticals
➘	Tobacco processing

0   200 km
0   200 miles

RESOURCES

 35bn kwh (capacity 8.5m kw)

 13,900 b/d (reserves 41,000,000 bbl)

10.4m sheep, 1.2m pigs, 731,000 cattle

Coal, iron, bauxite, oil, gas, marble, nickel, magnesite, chromium

ELECTRICITY GENERATION

Hydro 6% (2bn kwh)

Thermal 94% (33bn kwh)

Nuclear 0%

Other 0%

0 20 40 60 80 100

% of total generation by type

Greece has an oil and gas field off the coast of Thásos island. Reserves may be available in its eastern waters, ownership of which is contested by Turkey. Coal, iron and other mining contributes less than 2% to GDP. Greece is a leading producer of marble.

ENVIRONMENT

 0.8% (0.2% partially protected)

 Economic growth has precedence over ecological concerns

ENVIRONMENTAL TREATIES

Yes

No

No

Yes

Local fishing interests have formed a highly successful anti-pollution organization known as *Helmepa*. Athens is plagued with smog known as *nefos*, which is irritating to the eyes and throat. It is also highly damaging to Greece's ancient monuments. The Parthenon in Athens has suffered more erosion in the last two decades than in the previous 2000 years.

MEDIA

 The press are free from government interference, however, the state broadcasting services are under strong government control

PUBLISHING AND BROADCAST MEDIA

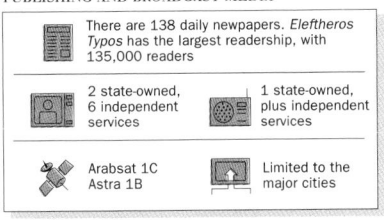

There are 138 daily newpapers. *Eleftheros Typos* has the largest readership, with 135,000 readers

2 state-owned, 6 independent services

1 state-owned, plus independent services

Arabsat 1C Astra 1B

Limited to the major cities

The state had a monopoly on radio and TV until 1989. Commercial broadcasting has made politicians far more answerable to the electorate than ever before. It has also had a cultural impact with the import of more foreign, particularly US, programming. There are eight legal TV networks and many pirate stations.

GREECE : LAND USE

RHODOPE MTS

PINDOS

AEGEAN ISLANDS

Cropland
Forest
Pasture
High mountain regions
Sheep
Fruit

0 100 km

0 100 miles

CRIME

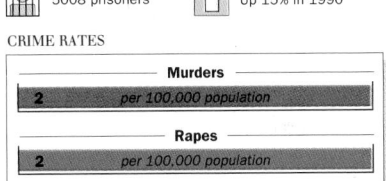 5008 prisoners

Up 15% in 1990

CRIME RATES

Murders

2 per 100,000 population

Rapes

2 per 100,000 population

Thefts

475 per 100,000 population

An influx of refugees from eastern Europe, North Africa and the Far East has seen an increase in violent crime. The terrorist group November 17 has assassinated wealthy citizens.

EDUCATION

 93%

0 Education spending as % GNP 25

2.7%

THE EDUCATION SYSTEM

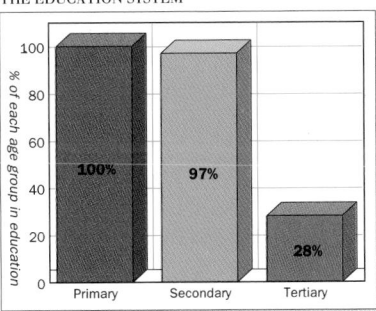

100% — Primary
97% — Secondary
28% — Tertiary

% of each age group in education

Teachers are poorly paid and qualifications are low. University places are limited and many students go abroad for tertiary education. Technical courses, funded by the EU, have increased since the 1990s.

HEALTH

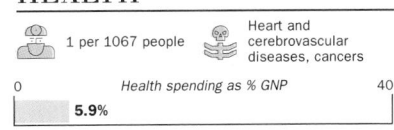 1 per 1067 people

Heart and cerebrovascular diseases, cancers

0 Health spending as % GNP 40

5.9%

The socialists (PASOK) introduced a National Health Service and a national pharmaceuticals industry. However, the service is short of staff and families have to perform many of the services normally expected of nurses. The New Democracy (ND) government tried to upgrade private medicine and incorporate its activities with those in state hospitals. Many Greeks requiring major surgery travel to Germany, Switzerland or the UK for treatment.

G

WEALTH

 Teacher, 120,000 drachmas a month; doctor, 230,000 drachmas a month

CONSUMER GOODS OWNERSHIP

1000
750
500
250
0

195 172 362 94 4

Per 1000 population

Greek society changed dramatically in the post-war period. Formerly a largely isolated agricultural community, rapid urbanization in the 1950s led to many former agricultural workers making fortunes. Many grabbed opportunities presented by the shipping industry. Among these were the prominent Niarchos and Onassis families.

The advent of the republic in 1973 reflected social changes which had occurred since the war. New wealth and success became more admired than aristocratic birth or prestige. Greece is now a socially mobile society. Living standards have improved throughout society since the 1950s.

WORLD RANKING

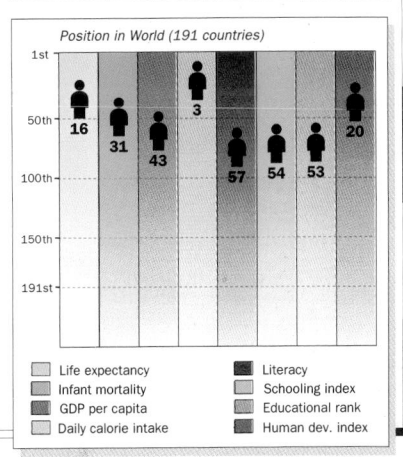

Position in World (191 countries)

1st
50th
100th
150th
191st

16 31 43 3 57 54 53 20

Life expectancy
Infant mortality
GDP per capita
Daily calorie intake
Literacy
Schooling index
Educational rank
Human dev. index

GRENADA

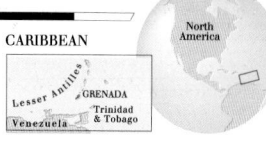

CARIBBEAN

OFFICIAL NAME: Grenada **CAPITAL:** St George's
POPULATION: 84,000 **CURRENCY:** East Caribbean dollar **OFFICIAL LANGUAGE:** English

THE MOST SOUTHERLY of the Windward Islands, Grenada also includes the islands of Carriacou and Petite Martinique. It is the world's second largest nutmeg producer. Grenada became a focus of attention in 1983 when the USA, with token backing from several Caribbean states, mounted an invasion to sever its growing links with Castro's Cuba. Grenada is discussing a political union with St Lucia, Dominica, and St Vincent and the Grenadines.

G

POLITICS

 1995 HM Queen Elizabeth II

THE STATE OF THE PARTIES

House of Representatives 15 members

| 47% NDC | 27% GULP | 13% TNP | 13% NNP |

NDC = National Democratic Congress GULP = Grenada United Labour Party TNP = The National Party NNP = New National Party

Senate 13 members

10 members chosen by the prime minister (3 after consulting various interests) and 3 by the leader of the opposition

The past 20 years have seen Grenada move towards a position of political isolation to that of being a fully-fledged democracy following US policy in the Caribbean. Former prime minister Sir Eric Gairy was as well known for his eccentric requests to the UN Security Council – he once asked it to investigate UFOs on the island – as for his intimidation of political opponents with organized gangs. Gairy was overthrown in 1979 in a civilian coup by the pro-Cuba Maurice Bishop, who was in turn overthrown and then executed by the army in 1983. This coup was the pretext for the US invasion in October of that year; the primary motive was to end Cuban influence in Grenada. Elected government was restored in 1984 and the USA provided large amounts of aid for reconstruction. Politics has since been centre-right and ideologically there is little to choose between the four main parties. The dominant political issue is the proposed federation between Grenada and its neighbours in the Windward Islands: St Lucia, Dominica, and St Vincent and the Grenadines. Nicholas Braithwaite, the prime minister and leader of the ruling NDC, supports the proposal for union.

CLIMATE

WEATHER CHART

Annual rainfall ranges from 150 cm on the coast to 300 cm in the mountains. Hurricanes occur in the rainy season.

COMMUNICATIONS

Point Salines, St George's 206,000 passengers
Has no fleet

THE TRANSPORT NETWORK

| 1127 km (700 miles) | None |
| None | None |

Mountain roads are frequently washed away in the rains. US aid helped to finance the international airport.

TOURISM

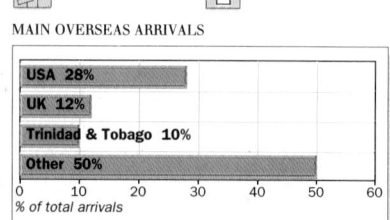

87,554 visitors Up 3% in 1992

MAIN OVERSEAS ARRIVALS

USA 28%
UK 12%
Trinidad & Tobago 10%
Other 50%
% of total arrivals

Tourism has developed since the restoration of democracy and the completion of the international airport in 1984. Large resort projects have caused serious beach erosion, in turn requiring costly coastal defences.

PEOPLE

English, English Creole
290 people per km²

THE URBAN/RURAL POPULATION SPLIT

15% 85%

RELIGIOUS PERSUASION

Other 15%
Anglican 17%
Roman Catholic 68%

Most Grenadians are descendants of Africans, brought over to work sugar plantations between the 16th and 19th centuries. Intermarriage between this group and the small numbers of Europeans and indigenous Indians has meant that there is little racial tension. As in other Caribbean states, extended families with absentee fathers are not uncommon.

GRENADA

Total Area : 340 sq. km (131 sq. miles)

WORLD AFFAIRS

The main issues are the proposed federation between Grenada and the rest of the Windward Islands group, and concern that the EU may remove preferential access for Grenadian bananas. Since 1983, Grenada has supported US policy in the Caribbean.

AID

 $17m (receipts)   Up 55% in 1991

The main aid sources are the UK, the EU and the USA. Cuba was a major donor before the 1983 invasion, helping to build the airport at Point Salines.

DEFENCE

 Minimal receipts   Defence spending is falling

The People's Revolutionary Army, created by Maurice Bishop in the wake of his 1979 coup, was replaced in 1983 by a paramilitary defence unit trained by the USA and the UK.

ECONOMICS

 $207m   2.70 East Caribbean dollars

SCORE CARD

❏ WORLD GNP RANKING	177th
❏ GNP PER CAPITA	$2465
❏ BALANCE OF PAYMENTS	$-39.1m
❏ INFLATION	2.5%
❏ UNEMPLOYMENT	30%

STRENGTHS
The world's second largest producer of nutmeg after Indonesia, with 23% of the world market. Other important sectors are tourism and bananas.

WEAKNESSES
Failure to revive world nutmeg cartel with Indonesia (collapsed in 1988). Labour productivity levels are the lowest in the East Caribbean.

EXPORTS
Trinidad and Tobago 9%
Other 28%
Germany* 17%
Netherlands 24%
UK 22%

IMPORTS
Japan 7%
Other 37%
Trinidad and Tobago 12%
UK 17%
USA 27%

RESOURCES

 51m kwh (capacity 9000 kw)   Not an oil producer and has no refineries

15,000 sheep, 11,000 pigs, 11,000 goats   None

Grenada has no strategic resources and has to import most of its energy. Its major asset is the nutmeg industry, which accounts for almost one quarter of total world production.

ENVIRONMENT

 None   National parks legislation still inadequate

The government has recently become aware of the potential value of eco-tourism, but has failed to protect some key environmental sites. The best remnant of rainforest, near Epping Forest, has not been included within an ecological protection zone.

MEDIA

 Freedom of expression guaranteed under the constitution. Little government censorship

PUBLISHING AND BROADCAST MEDIA

There are no daily newspapers. The *Grenadian Voice* and the *Grenada Guardian* are published weekly

1 state-owned service   1 state-owned station

The press in Grenada is privately owned and free from overt political interference.

CRIME

 Grenada does not publish prison figures   Down 53% between 1986 and 1989

Disaffected members of the disbanded People's Revolutionary Army were responsible for an increase in violent crime following the US invasion in 1983. The crime rate is now down to the Caribbean average.

EDUCATION

 90%

Education follows the former British selective 11-plus system. Most students go on to the University of the West Indies, or to college in the USA.

HEALTH

 1 per 1625 people   Heart diseases, cancers, nutritional disorders

After Maurice Bishop's takeover in 1979, Cuban physicians provided a basic health care system, which did not include any dental treatment. Subsidized state hospitals now cover most areas fairly efficiently, matching the Caribbean average.

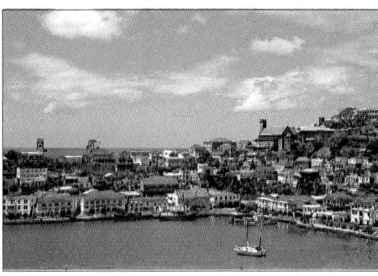

St George's Harbour. *The newest hotel developments are on the beaches to the south of the capital.*

CHRONOLOGY

A French colony from 1650, Grenada was captured by the British in 1762.

- ❏ **1951** Universal suffrage introduced.
- ❏ **1967** Internal self-government. Labour Party wins elections and campaigns for independence.
- ❏ **1974** Full independence from UK. Eric Gairy prime minister.
- ❏ **1979** Coup. Maurice Bishop prime minister. Growing links with Cuba.
- ❏ **1983** US invasion establishes pro-US administration.

WEALTH

 The disparities which existed between a few rich farmers and the majority of labourers have been reduced

CONSUMER GOODS OWNERSHIP

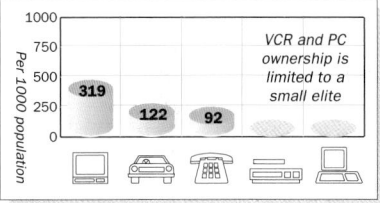

Wealth disparities on Grenada are less marked than in most Caribbean states. The wealthiest groups control the nutmeg trade.

WORLD RANKING

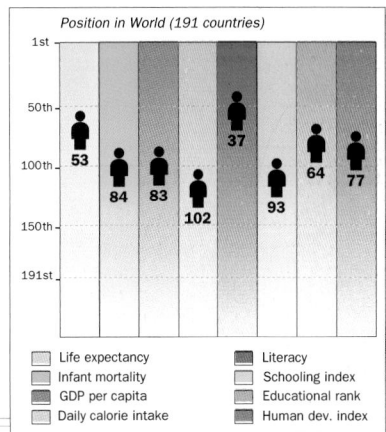

249

GUATEMALA

OFFICIAL NAME: Republic of Guatemala   **CAPITAL:** Guatemala City
POPULATION: 9.7 million   **CURRENCY:** Quetzal   **OFFICIAL LANGUAGE:** Spanish

L ARGEST AND MOST POPULOUS of the states of the Central American isthmus, Guatemala was home to the ancient Mayan civilization. Its fertile Pacific and Caribbean coastal lowlands give way to the highlands which dominate the country. Independent since 1838, Guatemala's history since 1954 has been one of military rule. Civilian rule returned in 1986, but 90% of people still live below the poverty line.

G

CLIMATE

WEATHER CHART

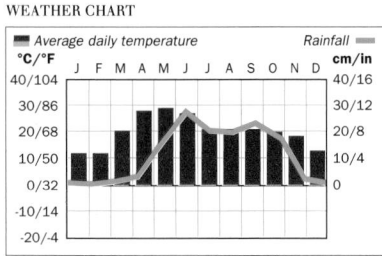

The climate varies with altitude. Daytime temperatures average 28°C in the tropical coastal regions and 20°C in the more temperate central highlands.

COMMUNICATIONS

La Aurora, Guatemala City
939,000 passengers — Has no fleet

THE TRANSPORT NETWORK

13,352 km (8296 miles)		None
884 km (549 miles)		990 km (615 miles)

Good roads link the towns, but volcanic ash surfaces elsewhere are difficult in the wet. There are almost 400 airstrips.

TOURISM

541,025 visitors — Up 6% in 1990

MAIN OVERSEAS ARRIVALS

USA 26%
El Salvador 22%
Honduras 9%
Other 43%
% of total arrivals

Almost destroyed by military excesses in the 1980s, tourism rapidly revived after the return to civilian rule and is now the third largest foreign exchange earner. Mayan ruins are top attractions.

PEOPLE

Quiché, Mam, Cakchiquel, Kekchí, Spanish — 85 people per km²

THE URBAN/RURAL POPULATION SPLIT

39% — 61%

ETHNIC MAKEUP

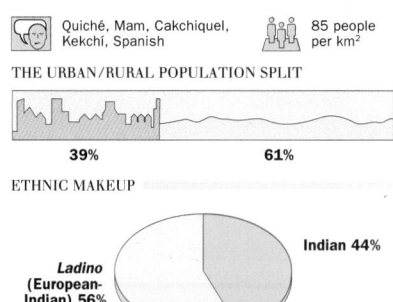

Indian 44%
Ladino (European-Indian) 56%

About 50% of Guatemalans are Indians, descendants of the founders of the Mayan civilization. Culture and language distinguish them from *ladino*, non-Indian, groups. *Ladinos* include a white elite, a large mixed-race group, and now also Indians who have rejected traditional dress and language to escape oppression and marginalization. Political power and 65% of land are in the hands of a few *ladino* families. Indians mainly live in the highlands, by subsistence farming. Women are legally as well as traditionally discriminated against.

GUATEMALA

Total Area : 108 890 sq. km (42 043 sq. miles)

POPULATION
- □ over 1 000 000
- ◉ over 100 000
- ○ over 50 000
- ● over 10 000

LAND HEIGHT
- 3000m/9843ft
- 2000m/6562ft
- 1000m/3281ft
- 500m/1640ft
- 200m/656ft
- Sea Level

POLITICS

1995 — President Ramiro de León Carpio

THE STATE OF THE PARTIES

National Congress 116 members — 6% Other

35% UCN — 24% PDCG — 16% MAS — 10% PAN — 9% Coal.

UCN = National Centre Union   PDCG = Christian Democratic Party of Guatemala   MAS = Solidarity and Action Movement   PAN = National Advancement Party   Coal. = Coalition (composed of Constitutional Democratic Party, Guatemalan Republican Front, National Unity Front)

In 1954, the military, with US-backing, toppled a democratic government pledged to land and social reforms. Its 32-year rule was based on the violent suppression of all opposition. The huge increase in death-squad murders and the scorched-earth campaigns against highland Indians from 1979 to 1984 led to the suspension of US support. International criticism and the wishes of moderate army factions helped bring back civilian rule in 1986. In 1993, the courts prevented President Serrano from imposing a new dictatorship. The former human rights ombudsman, Ramiro de León Carpio, was chosen to succeed him. However, he too remains dependent on military support to contain the rise in crime and continued guerrilla activity.

WORLD AFFAIRS

Relations with the USA are central, but strained by human rights issues – as they were from 1979–1984. Guatemala renounced its claim to Belize in 1986.

AID

 $85m (receipts)   Down 3% in 1991

The USA was the major donor in the 1980s, but human rights concerns and changing policy in the region have led to cuts in military and economic aid in the 1990s. Donors are pushing hard for IMF-backed trade liberalization.

DEFENCE

 $94.6m   Down 13% in 1993

In 1994, the army was put in charge of internal security after police failure to contain violence and crime. Indian-dominated URNG guerrillas have been the main armed opposition since the 1980s. Most arms come from the USA.

ECONOMICS

 $8.3bn   5.83 quetzales

SCORE CARD

- ❏ WORLD GNP RANKING..........................87th
- ❏ GNP PER CAPITA $856
- ❏ BALANCE OF PAYMENTS.................$–705.9m
- ❏ INFLATION 32.8%
- ❏ UNEMPLOYMENT...................................13%

STRENGTHS

Central America's largest economy. Agriculture key sector. Coffee, sugar, bananas, beef, cardamom top exports.

WEAKNESSES

Low GDP growth and investment. Widening trade deficit. Rising inflation. Extreme inequalities in land and wealth distribution limit the domestic market and agriculture modernization.

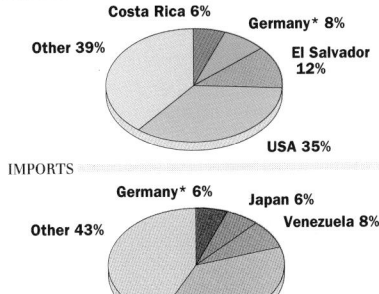

EXPORTS

Costa Rica 6%
Germany* 8%
Other 39%
El Salvador 12%
USA 35%

IMPORTS

Germany* 6%
Japan 6%
Venezuela 8%
Other 43%
USA 37%

North Acropolis, Tikal, Petén. *One of the largest lowland Mayan cities, Tikal was virtually abandoned by about AD 900.*

RESOURCES

 2.4bn kwh (capacity 700,000 kw)

 Reserves of 27,000,000 bbl; refines 16,000 b/cd

 2m cattle, 800,000 pigs, 660,000 sheep

 Oil, antimony, lead, tungsten, nickel, copper

Agriculture provides 25% of GDP and about 70% of export earnings. Guerrilla activity has hindered exploitation of oil reserves. Chixoy hydro-plant, which generates 65% of power, was closed by low rainfall in 1991–1992.

ENVIRONMENT

 8% (0.5% partially protected)

 Environmental laws have been enacted but had little effect

Guatemala means 'land of trees', but its rich biodiversity is endangered. Forest cover has been halved to 35% since 1954. The quetzal, the national bird, is one of 133 near-extinct species. Urban pollution and erosion are problems.

MEDIA

 The media is ostensibly free, but journalists are still subjected to beatings and death threats, despite the return to civilian rule

PUBLISHING AND BROADCAST MEDIA

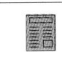 There are 8 daily newspapers, including *Prensa Libre, Siglo Veintiuno, El Gráfico* and the state *Diario de Centro América*

 1 state-owned, 4 independent stations

 5 state-owned, 140 independent stations

Intimidation, coupled with low pay, explain the lack of critical and investigative reporting of both human rights abuses and the government.

CRIME

 Guatemala does not publish prison figures

 All types of crime are increasing

A rapid escalation in violent crime is overshadowing concern, locally, about continuing human rights abuses.

EDUCATION

 48%

The capital takes 70% of an education budget of under 2% of GDP. As a result, Guatemala has 75% rural illiteracy, the worst record in Latin America.

CHRONOLOGY

Site of the Mayan civilization, Guatemala declared independence from Spain in 1821. It became fully independent in 1838, when the Central American Federation ended.

- ❏ **1954** US-backed coup topples reformist democratic government.
- ❏ **1966–1968** Counter-insurgency war; first use of 'disappearances' as a terror tactic in Latin America.
- ❏ **1978–1984** Highlands 'pacification'; thousands flee to Mexico and USA.
- ❏ **1986** President Cerezo of the PDCG becomes civilian president.
- ❏ **1991** President Serrano takes over.
- ❏ **1993** Fails in attempt at personal dictatorship. Flees country. Ramiro de León Carpio chosen as president.

HEALTH

 1 per 1370 people   Gastrointestinal and respiratory diseases

Mortality rates are the highest, while health spending is the lowest in Central America. 70% of funding goes to the capital, where 80% of doctors work. Most deaths are poverty linked.

WEALTH

 The majority of the population lives a subsistence existence

CONSUMER GOODS OWNERSHIP

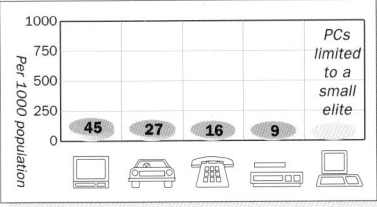

PCs limited to a small elite

45   27   16   9

Poverty has risen since 1980. 90% now live below the poverty line. The rich 10% control 45% of national wealth.

WORLD RANKING

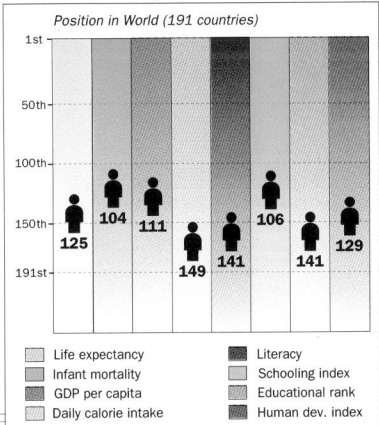

Position in World (191 countries)

125   104   111   149   141   106   141   129

- Life expectancy
- Infant mortality
- GDP per capita
- Daily calorie intake
- Literacy
- Schooling index
- Educational rank
- Human dev. index

GUINEA

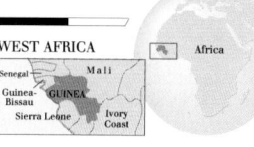

OFFICIAL NAME: Republic of Guinea   **CAPITAL:** Conakry
POPULATION: 6.1 million   **CURRENCY:** Guinea franc   **OFFICIAL LANGUAGE:** French

G

GUINEA LIES ON the western coast of Africa. Coastal plains and swamps in the west rise to densely-forested or savanna highlands before sloping down to the semi-desert of the north. Since 1984, the country has been under military rule; in 1993 presidential elections were allowed.

CLIMATE

WEATHER CHART

Guinea's climate is similar to that of Sierra Leone; the rainy season lasts from April to September.

COMMUNICATIONS

✈	**Conakry-Gbessia**	🚢	1 ship 100 dwt

THE TRANSPORT NETWORK

🛣	30,100 km (18,703 miles)	🛤	None
🚆	1038 km (645 miles)	⚓	1295 km (805 miles)

Major roads and rail lines are being rebuilt with World Bank and French aid. Much of the rail network is exclusively for the use of the bauxite industry.

A small mosque in Conakry. Muslims make up 85% of the population; 8% are Christian. The remainder follow traditional beliefs.

TOURISM

🧳	5600 visitors	⬆	Up 24% in 1991

MAIN OVERSEAS ARRIVALS

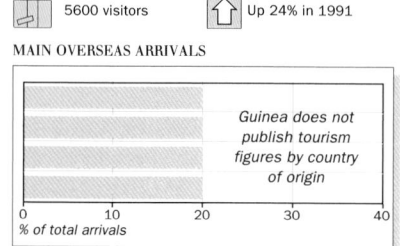

Guinea does not publish tourism figures by country of origin

Limited infrastructure means that Guinea cannot exploit the tourist potential of its beaches, scenery and rich culture.

PEOPLE

	Fulani, Malinke, Soussou, French		24 people per km²

THE URBAN/RURAL POPULATION SPLIT

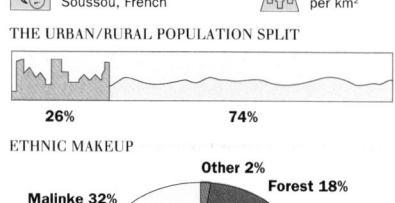

26%   74%

ETHNIC MAKEUP

Other 2%
Forest 18%
Malinke 32%
Soussou 18%
Fulani 30%

Guinea has a population of over six million people consisting of a number of ethnic groups. Since 1984, and the death of the Marxist dictator Sekou Touré, traditional rivalries have re-emerged. The largest ethnic group, the Malinke, lost the power they held under Touré, and have suffered reprisals. Today, the coastal peoples, including the Soussou, are dominant, benefiting from renewed rivalry between the two major groups – Malinke and Fulani, the latter based in the western highland region of Fouta Jallon.

Daily life in Guinea revolves around the extended family, which survived the climate of suspicion generated by paid informers under Touré. Women acquired influence within Touré's Marxist party, but a Muslim revival since 1984 has reversed this trend.

POLITICS

🗳 1994		President Gen Lansana Conté

THE STATE OF THE PARTIES

Transitional Committee for National Recovery 15 members

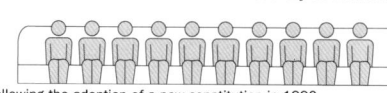

Following the adoption of a new constitution in 1990, parliamentary elections were scheduled to take place at the end of 1994

Politics in Guinea are in a state of flux. In 1984, Sekou Touré died, having headed the Marxist single-party regime of the Guinea Democratic Party (PDG) since 1958. This opened the way for the military to intervene, with promises of multiparty elections to come. In 1990, a referendum overwhelmingly approved the changes, but the military appointed a Transitional Committee to run the country. The tactic was to delay democratization for as long as possible.

When presidential elections were finally held at the end of 1993, the incumbent, Gen Lansana Conté, won with 52% of the votes. His closest rival, the Malinke leader Alpha Condé who had been in exile until 1992, received 20% of the votes. This was widely contested by opposition parties, which alleged the elections had been rigged. Serious violence broke out after the result was announced.

Guinea was dominated for so long by the PDG that the new parties tend to lack experience and effective organization. There is evidence that some oppression of opposition groups still exists.

WORLD AFFAIRS

Ecowas	OAU	FZ	AfDB	ECA

Guinea is an important financial backer of ECOWAS and contributes to its multinational force in neighbouring Liberia. A growing concern is balancing the interests of its two major aid donors, France and the USA.

AID

💲	$371m (receipts)	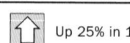	Up 25% in 1991

In 1969, the World Bank funded the Boké bauxite project, one of its most ambitious projects at that time. Western aid dried up during the Touré years but, since 1986, it has returned in full force, now financing more than 85% of all Guinea's development projects.

GUINEA

Total Area : 245 860 sq. km
(94 926 sq. miles)

POPULATION

⊙	over 500 000
○	over 50 000
•	over 10 000
·	under 10 000

LAND HEIGHT

1000m/3281ft
500m/1640ft
200m/656ft
Sea Level

DEFENCE

 $27m (est)   Rising owing to ECOMOG commitments

Defence forces consist of a 10,000-strong army and 7000-strong militia, which have been partly merged since the 1984 coup. China, North Korea and the Eastern bloc used to be the main arms procurement markets. Most weaponry is now supplied by France and the USA.

ECONOMICS

 $3.1bn   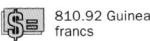 810.92 Guinea francs

SCORE CARD

❏ WORLD GNP RANKING	123rd
❏ GNP PER CAPITA	$480
❏ BALANCE OF PAYMENTS	$−291m
❏ INFLATION	22.7%
❏ UNEMPLOYMENT	Widespread underemployment

STRENGTHS

Wide range of natural resources, including bauxite, gold, diamonds. Major iron ore deposits at Mount Nimba. Good soil and climate lead to high cash-crop yields and allow Guinea the prospect of self-sufficiency in food.

WEAKNESSES

Years of confused state control under Touré make IMF and World Bank reforms hard to implement. Limited and antiquated infrastructure.

EXPORTS

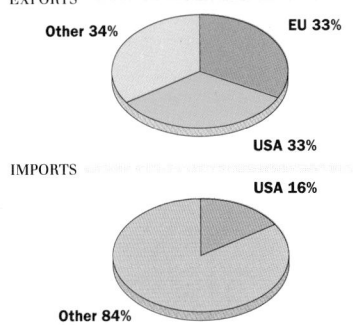

Other 34%   EU 33%
                   USA 33%

IMPORTS

USA 16%

Other 84%

RESOURCES

 518m kwh (capacity 176,000 kw)

 Not an oil producer and has no refineries

 1.8m cattle, 506,000 sheep, 33,000 pigs

 Bauxite, diamonds, gold, iron

Bauxite accounts for over 90% of export earnings. Guinea, with 30% of known world reserves, is the world's largest producer after Australia. Demand for electricity for bauxite processing is high. Aid from former Yugoslavia funded the dam on the Bafing River.

ENVIRONMENT

 0.7%   Droughts, as in 1973 and 1983, seriously affect savanna areas

Uncontrolled deforestation, particularly of rainforest areas, is the major long-term problem.

MEDIA

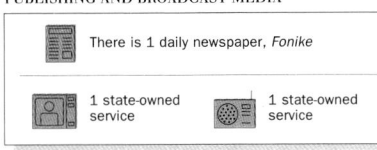 Although there has been a relaxation of strict censorship, political parties are still communicating through pamphlets

PUBLISHING AND BROADCAST MEDIA

There is 1 daily newspaper, *Fonike*

 1 state-owned service   1 state-owned service

For a country of almost six million, Guinea has a limited media. There has been a relaxation in censorship. *Horoya*, the main newspaper, is a weekly.

CRIME

Guinea does not publish prison figures   Down 16% in 1990

The state's human rights record has not improved since 1984 and there has been an increase in political violence. Diamond smuggling is commonplace.

CHRONOLOGY

France made Guinea a colony in 1890, strongly opposed by the Fulani Muslim empire of Fouta Djallon.

❏ **1958** Full independence under Sekou Touré. France ends support.
❏ **1970** Coup attempt by Portuguese-backed exiles fails.
❏ **1984** Touré dies. Army coup.
❏ **1990** Referendum on democracy.

EDUCATION

 24%

French was readopted as the main teaching language in 1984, after Touré's decolonizing teaching experiments.

HEALTH

 1 per 10,300 people   Malaria, diarrheal and respiratory diseases, tuberculosis

Health provision is very poor, reflected in an infant mortality rate of 144 per 1000 live births and an average life expectancy of 42.5 years.

WEALTH

 Manual worker, 150,000 Guinea francs per month; secretary, 300,000 Guinea francs per month

CONSUMER GOODS OWNERSHIP

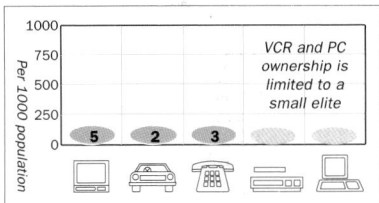

VCR and PC ownership is limited to a small elite

5   2   3

Poverty is endemic, but private enterprise has brought with it a new business class and some wealthy exiles. French and American tinned foods are highly favoured by the well-off.

WORLD RANKING

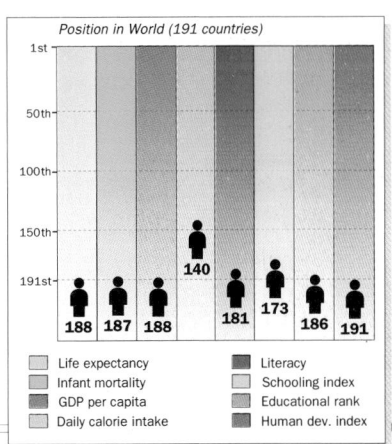

Position in World (191 countries)

188 187 188 140 181 173 186 191

▢ Life expectancy	▢ Literacy
▢ Infant mortality	▢ Schooling index
▢ GDP per capita	▢ Educational rank
▢ Daily calorie intake	▢ Human dev. index

GUINEA–BISSAU

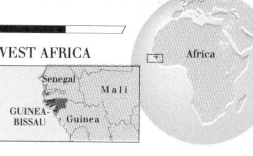

WEST AFRICA

OFFICIAL NAME: Republic of Guinea-Bissau **CAPITAL:** Bissau
POPULATION: 1 million **CURRENCY:** Guinea peso **OFFICIAL LANGUAGE:** Portuguese

G

LYING ON AFRICA'S west coast, Guinea-Bissau is bordered by Senegal to the north and Guinea to the south and east. Apart from savanna highlands in the northeast, the country is low-lying. In 1974, it was the first Portuguese colony to gain independence. The ruling PAIGC initiated a process of change to multiparty democracy in 1990, but free elections have yet to take place. Guinea-Bissau is one of the world's poorest countries.

CLIMATE

WEATHER CHART

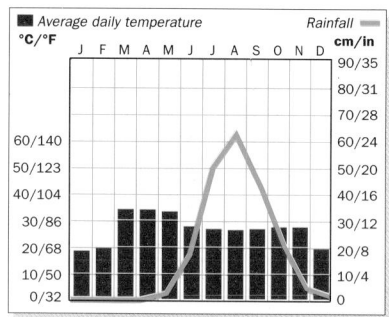

The climate is tropical. The north is affected by the Sahel, the wetter south by the Atlantic. Droughts can occur.

COMMUNICATIONS

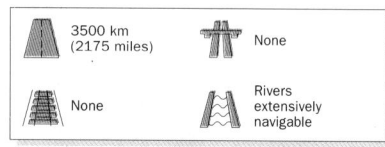

Bissalanca International, Bissau

THE TRANSPORT NETWORK

The many rivers, estuaries and islands mean water transport is as important as the roads. Both are being improved.

TOURISM

 A small number of visitors

 No significant change from year to year

MAIN OVERSEAS ARRIVALS

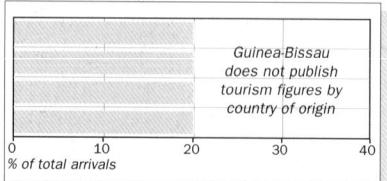

Guinea-Bissau does not publish tourism figures by country of origin

% of total arrivals

Guinea-Bissau's lack of tourist facilities means it remains a destination for only the most independent of travellers.

PEOPLE

 Portuguese Creole, Balante, Fulani, Malinke, Portuguese

28 people per km²

THE URBAN/RURAL POPULATION SPLIT

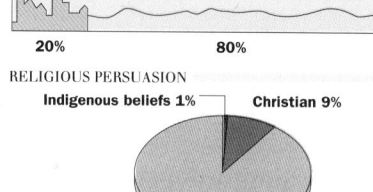

20% 80%

RELIGIOUS PERSUASION

Indigenous beliefs 1% Christian 9%

Muslim 90%

About 98% of Guinea-Bissau's people come from indigenous ethnic groups. The largest is the southern Balante, who form almost one third of the population. Mixed-race *mestiço* and European minorities make up just 2% of the population. Although small in number, the *mestiços* – many of whom derive from Cape Verde, Portugal's other former West African colony – still dominate the bureaucracy and the top ranks of the PAIGC. Resentment at this, especially among the Balante who provided most of the PAIGC troops in the independence war, was one cause of the 1980 coup. The majority of the population lives and works on small family farms, grouped in self-contained villages. The bulk of the urban population lives in the capital, Bissau.

POLITICS

1994 President Brig-Gen João Bernardo Vieira

THE STATE OF THE PARTIES

National People's Assembly 150 members

100% PAIGC

PAIGC = African Party for the Independence of Guinea-Bissau and Cape Verde

Council of State 15 members

Members are elected by the National People's Assembly from among their own number

Guinea-Bissau has been ruled by the PAIGC since independence in 1974. Since 1990, it has been moving slowly towards multiparty democracy. Elections, first due in 1992, have been repeatedly postponed. The delays reflect both the PAIGC's real fear of being voted out of power and the disunity of the 11 recognized opposition parties. When the elections are finally held, fragmentation of the vote means a clear winner is unlikely and continuing political instability is probable. This could create the conditions for a repeat of the 1993 attempted coup.

WORLD AFFAIRS

 OAU   Ecowas   ECA 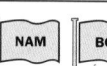 NAM BCP

Guinea-Bissau's foreign policy is non-aligned. It trades mainly with the West. Maritime border disputes have until recently soured relations with Senegal and Guinea. Casamance separatist bases in north Guinea-Bissau are a source of tension in relations with Senegal.

GUINEA-BISSAU

Total Area : 36 120 sq. km (13 940 sq. miles)

POPULATION

over 100 000
over 10 000
under 10 000

LAND HEIGHT

200m/656ft
Sea Level

AID

 $101m (receipts)   Down 14% in 1991

Portugal is Guinea-Bissau's largest aid donor. Balance of payments support is critical to the economy. Export earnings rarely top $20 million and import and debt service costs are over $100 million. Donors, however, have largely frozen support since 1991 because of Guinea-Bissau's World Bank arrears. Although now virtually bankrupt, the government has pushed ahead with economic reforms begun in the mid-1980s in the hope of restoring aid credits. The infrastructure, education and health care are the main targets of project aid.

DEFENCE

 $4.43m   Little change from year to year

The lower ranks of the 9200-strong armed forces are mainly Balante from the south. Resentment at their lack of promotion and the predominance of *mestiços* in the senior ranks was a cause of the 1980 coup. Troops serve with the UN in Angola and Mozambique.

ECONOMICS

 $219m   5003.38 Guinea pesos

SCORE CARD

- ❏ WORLD GNP RANKING.........................175th
- ❏ GNP PER CAPITA $219
- ❏ BALANCE OF PAYMENTS......................$–72m
- ❏ INFLATION 50%
- ❏ UNEMPLOYMENT...................................17%

STRENGTHS
Minimal at present, but good potential in fisheries and timber. Both are barely exploited. Offshore oil potential.

WEAKNESSES
Lack of sufficiency in rice staple. Few exports, mainly cashew nuts, groundnuts. Minimal industry. Lack of an entrepreneurial business class. High illiteracy. Poor state economic management.

EXPORTS

Netherlands 6%   Cape Verde 6%
Portugal 27%   Other 13%
Switzerland 23%
Spain 25%

IMPORTS

France 7%   Senegal 11%
Other 39%
CIS* 14%
Portugal 29%

Bafatá, the chief town in central Guinea-Bissau. It lies on the Gêba River and is also an important inland port.

RESOURCES

 17m kwh (capacity 7,000 kw)   Not an oil producer and has no refineries

 340,000 cattle, 290,000 pigs, 205,000 sheep   Bauxite, phosphate, oil

Fish and timber are the main natural resources, but local exploitation is only 10% of the sustainable levels of 250,000 tonnes and 100,000 tonnes a year. Guinea Bissau's considerable hydro-power potential is also under-exploited.

ENVIRONMENT

 None   Economic growth has precedence over ecological concerns

Drought and locust plagues are serious natural hazards. A small population and minimal industry mean there are few serious environmental problems.

MEDIA

 Censorship is still strong, but press freedom has increased markedly since 1991

PUBLISHING AND BROADCAST MEDIA

 There are 2 daily newspapers, *Voz da Guiné* and *Nô Printcha*, published by the government

1 state-owned service   1 state-owned service

Only one newspaper, *Baguerra*, and one magazine, *Expresso-Bissau*, are not state-owned. Portugal helps to fund the TV service, started in 1989.

CRIME

 Guinea-Bissau does not publish prison figures   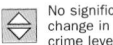 No significant change in crime levels

The death penalty was abolished in 1993. Reform of the legal system is in progress to make it more independent of the PAIGC. The government has been criticized for human rights abuses.

EDUCATION

 36%

Only 58% of children attend the rudimentary education service. Guinea-Bissau has no university.

CHRONOLOGY

The Portuguese explored the area in the 15th century. In 1879, Portuguese Guinea became a colony. A war of independence began in the 1960s, led by the PAIGC.

- ❏ **1974** Independence. PAIGC led by Luis Cabral takes power.
- ❏ **1980** Coup. João Vieira replaces Cabral.
- ❏ **1990** Vieira accepts principle of multiparty politics.
- ❏ **1991–1992** Opposition parties formed; election postponed.
- ❏ **1993** Coup attempt. Leading opposition figure João da Costa temporarily detained.

G

HEALTH

 1 per 7310 people   Parasitic, diarrheal and communicable diseases, malaria

Guinea-Bissau's health statistics are among the world's worst, due partly to the minimal medical facilities. Average life expectancy is just 42 years; infant mortality is 180 per 1000 live births; the maternal death rate almost one in 100.

WEALTH

 Most of the population lives in poverty

CONSUMER GOODS OWNERSHIP

TVs limited to an elite   VCR and PC ownership rates among lowest in world

Living conditions for the majority of people are extremely poor; over 70% are unable to meet their basic needs. The tiny elite is mainly *mestiço*.

WORLD RANKING

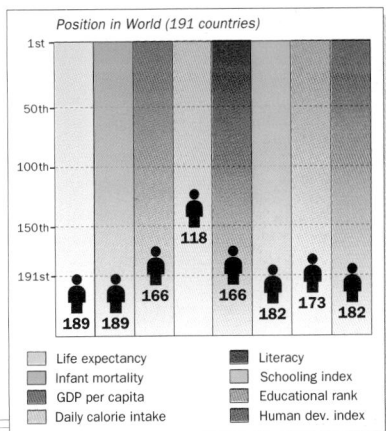

Position in World (191 countries)

- Life expectancy
- Infant mortality
- GDP per capita
- Daily calorie intake
- Literacy
- Schooling index
- Educational rank
- Human dev. index

GUYANA

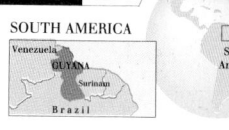

OFFICIAL NAME: Co-operative Republic of Guyana **CAPITAL:** Georgetown
POPULATION: 800,000 **CURRENCY:** Guyana dollar **OFFICIAL LANGUAGE:** English

G UYANA LIES ON the northeast coast of South
America, bordered by Venezuela, Brazil and
Surinam. Dense interior rainforest covers 85% of its
territory. Independence from Britain came in 1966. The export of four
key products, bauxite, gold, rice and sugar, sustains the economy. The
vast majority of Guyana's population lives on the narrow coastal plain,
which is partially reclaimed from the sea.

G

CLIMATE

WEATHER CHART

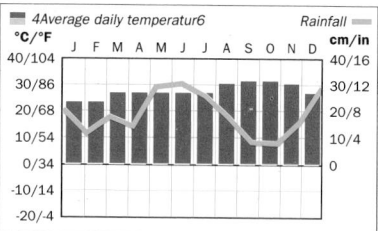

The lowlands are very humid with a
constant temperature. The highlands
are a little cooler, especially at night.

COMMUNICATIONS

Timehri Intl, Georgetown
270,500 passengers

11 ships
7600 dwt

THE TRANSPORT NETWORK

| 7665 km (4763 miles) | None |
| 88 km (55 miles) | 6000 km (3728 miles) |

Reliable travel into the interior is by air
or river; ferries link coastal roads. The
only international airport is Timehri.

TOURISM

74,881 visitors

Tourist numbers are
increasing slowly

MAIN OVERSEAS ARRIVALS

USA 46%
Caribbean 19%
Canada 19%
Other 16%
% of total arrivals

The government is keen to develop
eco-tourism using private investment.
Guyana means Land of Many Waters;
the Kaieteur Falls are among the world's
most impressive. Old Dutch wooden
architecture characterizes Georgetown.

*The arrivals hall at Georgetown's Timehri
International, Guyana's main airport, is
painted in traditional Guyanan style.*

PEOPLE

English Creole, Hindi, Tamil,
Amerindian languages,
English

4 people
per km²

THE URBAN/RURAL POPULATION SPLIT

35%   65%

ETHNIC MAKEUP

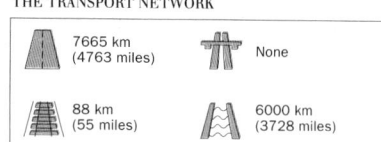

Chinese 2%   Amerindian 4%
South Asian 51%
Black and mixed 43%

Tension exists between
Afro-Guyanese, who are
descended from Africans
brought over between the
17th and 19th centuries, and
Indo-Guyanese, descendants
of South Asian labourers
brought from India in the
19th century. There were a
number of instances of
discrimination against Indo-
Guyanese during the PNC's rule.

GUYANA

Total Area : 214 970 sq. km (83 000 sq. miles)

POPULATION
◎ over 100 000
○ over 50 000
● over 10 000
• under 10 000

LAND HEIGHT
1000m/3281ft
500m/1640ft
200m/656ft
Sea Level

POLITICS

1997

President Cheddi Jagan

THE STATE OF THE PARTIES

National Assembly 65 members
1% TUF
50% PPP   48% PNC   1% WPA

PPP = People's Progressive Party **PNC** = People's National
Congress **WPA** = Working People's Alliance
TUF = The United Force

The main power brokers in Guyana's
multiparty democracy are the urban
businessmen and professionals who
fund the political parties. The 29-year
rule of the PNC was characterized by
favouritism towards the Afro-Guyanese.
This was reversed with the election of
the Indian-dominated PPP in 1992, in
what international observers – and
many Guyanese – saw as the first fair
election since independence. As leader
of the PPP, Cheddi Jagan's switch from
avowed Marxism in the 1970s to free-
market economics in the 1990s proved
a success with voters.

WORLD AFFAIRS

The main foreign policy concern is finding a definitive resolution to a long-standing border dispute with Venezuela, which claims the eastern two thirds of Guyana.

AID

 $106m (receipts)   No significant change from year to year

Most of Guyana's aid comes from the USA, EU and UK. Most aid has been in the form of development assistance and project loans.

DEFENCE

 $14.4m   Down 50% between 1986 and 1988

The security forces, which include a 2000-strong army, benefit from financial support and training provided by the US and UK governments.

ECONOMICS

 $233m   125.79 Guyana dollars

SCORE CARD

- ❏ WORLD GNP RANKING.........................174th
- ❏ GNP PER CAPITA $300
- ❏ BALANCE OF PAYMENTS.................$−116.1m
- ❏ INFLATION 56%
- ❏ UNEMPLOYMENT....Widespread underemployment

STRENGTHS
Widespread deregulation of the economy and introduction of floating exchange rate signal good economic prospects. Bauxite, gold, rice, sugar and diamond production. Sugar production has already increased. Overseas investment in rice and gold will see the further development of both sectors.

WEAKNESSES
Narrow economic base, vulnerable to price fluctuations of its main commodities. Dependence on imports.

EXPORTS

Japan 8%
Other 34%
Trinidad and Tobago 13%
USA 17%
UK 28%

IMPORTS

Netherlands 4%
Other 33%
UK 11%
USA 22%
Trinidad and Tobago 30%

RESOURCES

 220m kwh (capacity 110,000 kw)   Not an oil producer and has no refineries

 210,000 cattle, 185,000 pigs, 120,000 sheep   Bauxite, gold, diamonds

Gold and bauxite are the main strategic resources in Guyana. However several companies are prospecting offshore and onshore for oil, amid reports that commercially exploitable deposits have been located. Hydroelectric power plants are planned on the many rivers.

ENVIRONMENT

 0.05%   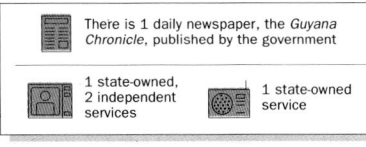 Some controls on logging

Of major concern is the disrepair of the 18th-century sea defence system. This threatens the urbanized coastline that lies below sea level. There is a growing logging industry, although this is being kept away from parks and rainforest reserves.

MEDIA

 A relaxation of government pressure on the media has been seen in recent years

PUBLISHING AND BROADCAST MEDIA

There is 1 daily newspaper, the *Guyana Chronicle*, published by the government

1 state-owned, 2 independent services

1 state-owned service

With the liberalization of the economy, which started with the Hoyte administration, there has been a relaxation of pressure on the media.

CRIME

 Guyana does not publish prison figures   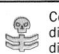 Up 7% in 1984

The poorer neighbourhoods of most major towns are considered unsafe to walk in by locals, especially at night. The smuggling of narcotics is an increasing problem.

EDUCATION

 96%

Education is based on the British system. Entry to high-schools is by 11-plus examination. Guyana has a state-financed university, although many students go to the USA or UK.

HEALTH

1 per 6809 people   Cerebrovascular, digestive and heart diseases

Around 95% of the population have access to Guyana's mainly state-run health service. The referral system is relatively good.

CHRONOLOGY

During the 17th and 18th centuries, the Dutch founded three colonies, Essequibo, Demerara and Berbice, in the region. In 1814, these came under British control, and were later combined to form the colony of British Guiana.

- ❏ **1953** First universal elections won by PPP under leadership of Dr Cheddi Jagan; parliament later suspended by Britain.
- ❏ **1957** Forbes Burnham founds PNC.
- ❏ **1964** PNC becomes leading force in coalition government.
- ❏ **1966** Independence from Britain.
- ❏ **1973** PPP boycotts parliament, accusing PNC of electoral fraud.
- ❏ **1985** Burnham dies. Replaced by Desmond Hoyte as PNC leader.
- ❏ **1989** Foreign aid suspended; renewed calls for reform.
- ❏ **1992** Fair elections won by PPP.

G

WEALTH

 Wealth is concentrated among a few Georgetown families

CONSUMER GOODS OWNERSHIP

Per 1000 population

VCR and PC ownership is limited to a small elite

31   43   41

Most Guyanese enjoy a relatively similar standard of living, although there are a few very affluent urban families whose wealth is derived from business and farming. Large air-conditioned four-wheel-drive vehicles and fine whiskies are the major status symbols. The poorest group are Amerindian subsistence farmers.

WORLD RANKING

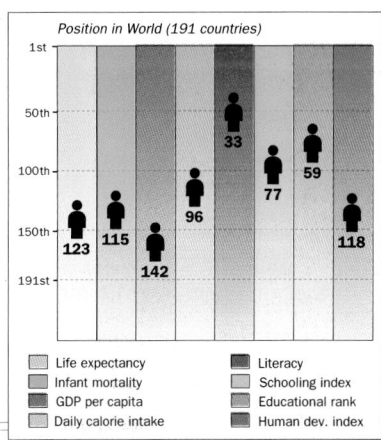

Position in World (191 countries)

123 115 142 96 77 33 59 118

- Life expectancy
- Infant mortality
- GDP per capita
- Daily calorie intake
- Literacy
- Schooling index
- Educational rank
- Human dev. index

HAITI

OFFICIAL NAME: Republic of Haiti   **CAPITAL:** Port-au-Prince   **POPULATION:** 6.8 million
CURRENCY: Gourde   **OFFICIAL LANGUAGES:** French and French Creole

CARIBBEAN

HAITI OCCUPIES the western third of the Caribbean island of Hispaniola. Formerly a Spanish colony, Haiti was the first Caribbean state to achieve independence, in 1804, and has been in a state of political chaos virtually ever since. Democracy did not materialize with the exile of the dictator Jean-Claude Duvalier in 1986. In 1991, an army coup overthrew the elected president, Father Jean-Bertrand Aristide, after nine months in office.

CLIMATE

WEATHER CHART

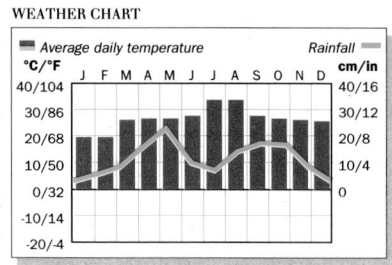

Haiti lies mostly in the rain shadow of the central mountains so is slightly less humid than average for the Caribbean.

COMMUNICATIONS

 Port-au-Prince
545,000 passengers

 Has no fleet

THE TRANSPORT NETWORK

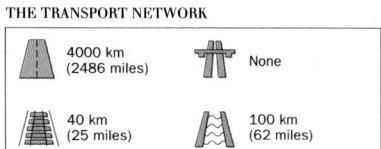

4000 km (2486 miles)	None
40 km (25 miles)	100 km (62 miles)

By regional standards, Haiti has a poor road system. Ferries provide the main transport to the southern peninsula.

TOURISM

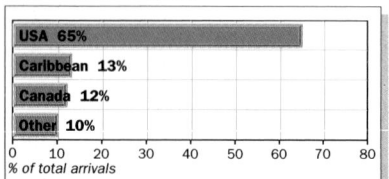 120,000 visitors   Down 2% in 1990

MAIN OVERSEAS ARRIVALS

USA	65%
Caribbean	13%
Canada	12%
Other	10%

% of total arrivals (scale 0 to 80)

Haiti's location, history and culture provided much of its attraction for tourists in the 1960s and 1970s. The resurgence of political instability and violence in the 1980s, however, led to the industry's near collapse.

PEOPLE

 French Creole, French

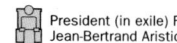 234 people per km²

THE URBAN/RURAL POPULATION SPLIT

28%   72%

RELIGIOUS PERSUASION

Other 4%
Other Protestant 6%
Baptist 10%
Roman Catholic 80%

Most Haitians are the descendants of Africans; a few have European roots, primarily French. The majority of the population lives in extreme poverty: Haiti is the poorest country in the Americas; Port-au-Prince has the worst slums in the Caribbean. Social tensions run high, and focus on class rather than race. The lack of political change, combined with repression and a collapsing economy, has led many to emigrate illegally to the USA, or across the border to the neighbouring Dominican Republic.

POLITICS

Uncertain

President (in exile) Fr Jean-Bertrand Aristide

THE STATE OF THE PARTIES

Chamber of Deputies 81 members

Haiti's politics are in a state of flux following the military coup of 1991 and exile of President Aristide

Senate 27 members

Haiti's politics have long been directly managed by the wealthy businessmen who live in palatial style above Port-au-Prince. It was this group, backed by the military, that supported the popularly detested Duvalier regime. It is this same group that, since the overthrow of 'Baby Doc' Duvalier in 1986, has financed regular coups to ensure that the 1987 democratic constitution cannot be implemented.

The military last intervened in 1991, following the 1990 election of Fr Jean-Bertrand Aristide on a populist platform. Aristide was exiled by the army and his supporters suppressed. The failure of the military to reinstate Aristide led the UN to impose sanctions. This move was answered by the assassination of Haiti's justice minister. In 1994, a blockade was mounted against Haiti, patrolled by US warships; Washington hinted it might consider military action to reinstate Aristide.

HAITI

Total Area : 27 750 sq. km
(10 714 sq. miles)

POPULATION	LAND HEIGHT
over 1 000 000	1000m/3281ft
over 500 000	500m/1640ft
over 10 000	200m/656ft
under 10 000	Sea Level

WORLD AFFAIRS

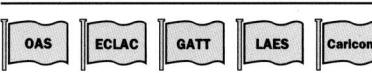

The main concerns of the military government are to circumvent economic sanctions and to persuade the OAS and UN not to intervene militarily to restore Jean-Bertrand Aristide.

AID

 Cut off since UN sanctions   Not applicable

Aid has been cut off since the military takeover. France, the USA and the UK used to be donors, but official corruption meant that most aid money was siphoned off to private bank accounts.

DEFENCE

 $29.4m   ⬆ Up 73% in 1991

The military has governed the country since the 1991 coup. Forces are concentrated in the capital; in rural areas, the military presence is represented by section chiefs of the *Tontons Macoutes,* who dispense rough justice.

ECONOMICS

 $2.6bn   11.98 gourdes

SCORE CARD

- ❏ WORLD GNP RANKING 132nd
- ❏ GNP PER CAPITA $370
- ❏ BALANCE OF PAYMENTS.................$–10.5m
- ❏ INFLATION 15.4%
- ❏ UNEMPLOYMENT....................................5.2%

STRENGTHS
Very few. Income from coffee and from Haitians living abroad. The military makes large profits from the transportation of narcotics to the USA.

WEAKNESSES
Political instability. Manufacturing collapsed following sanctions in 1991. Economic blockade in 1994.

EXPORTS

Belgium 9%
France 10%
Italy 12%
Other 13%
USA 56%

IMPORTS

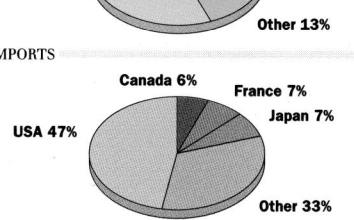

Canada 6%
France 7%
Japan 7%
USA 47%
Other 33%

Haiti: the poorest country in the Americas. In remote villages, most houses are made of earth and have no windows.

RESOURCES

 475m kwh (capacity 150,000 kw)   Not an oil producer and has no refineries

 1.6m cattle, 950,000 pigs, 432,000 horses   Marble, limestone, clay

Haiti has no strategic resources. Since the 1991 economic sanctions it has had to find unofficial sources of oil; much is imported from Europe.

ENVIRONMENT

 0.4%   Ecological initiatives hijacked for political purposes

The government is indifferent to Haiti's ecological problems. It is one of the most environmentally degraded countries in the world; one third of its soil is seriously eroded.

MEDIA

 Following 1991 coup most radio stations were shut down. Newspapers, almost exclusively in French, are not accessible to most Creoles

PUBLISHING AND BROADCAST MEDIA

 There are 5 daily newspapers, *Le Nouveau Monde, L'Union, Le Nouvelliste, Le Matin* and *Panorama*

 1 state-owned service   1 state-owned service

The military controls the media through intimidation; radio stations are frequently attacked and dissenting journalists tend to 'disappear'.

CRIME

 Haiti does not publish prison figures   Crime is rising

The authorities and security forces, particularly the *Attachés*, the private army of Haiti's renegade police chief, are a major source of crime, frequently terrorizing or murdering politicians and those opposed to military rule.

EDUCATION

 53%

Education, run by the state and the Roman Catholic and missionary churches, is based on the French system. The wealthy are often educated abroad.

CHRONOLOGY

In 1697, Spain ceded the west of Hispaniola to France. Ex-slave Toussaint l'Ouverture's rebellion in 1791 led to independence in 1804.

- ❏ **1915–1934** US occupation.
- ❏ **1957–1971** François, 'Papa Doc', Duvalier's brutal dictatorship.
- ❏ **1971** Son Jean-Claude, 'Baby Doc', takes over. Slight liberalization.
- ❏ **1986** Flees. Gen Namphy steps in.
- ❏ **1987** Elections abandoned until 1988 as a result of rioting.
- ❏ **1988** Namphy ousted in a coup by Lt-Gen Avril.
- ❏ **1990** Father Jean-Bertrand Aristide elected, but exiled in 1991 coup.

H

HEALTH

 1 per 6737 people   Malaria, other parasitic diseases, tuberculosis

Most Haitians cannot afford health care. In rural areas, help is often sought from voodoo priests.

WEALTH

 One million Haitians work as cheap labour in the Dominican Republic, many effectively as slaves on the state-owned sugar cane plantations

CONSUMER GOODS OWNERSHIP

VCR and PC ownership is limited to a small elite

5   4   9

Haiti's rigid class structure maintains extreme disparities of wealth between the mass of the population, who live in slums without running water or proper sanitation, and a few affluent families. These enjoy a luxurious way of life, and educate their children in France.

WORLD RANKING

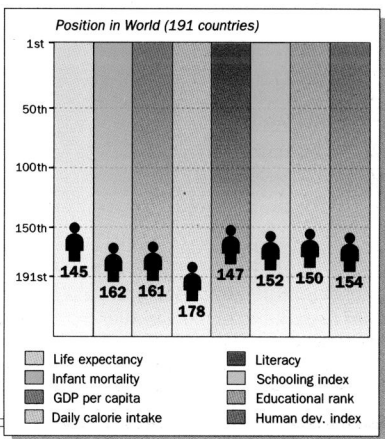

Position in World (191 countries)

145   162   161   178   147   152   150   154

Life expectancy	Literacy
Infant mortality	Schooling index
GDP per capita	Educational rank
Daily calorie intake	Human dev. index

HONDURAS

OFFICIAL NAME: Republic of Honduras **CAPITAL:** Tegucigalpa
POPULATION: 5.5 million **CURRENCY:** Lempira **OFFICIAL LANGUAGE:** Spanish

STRADDLING THE Central American isthmus,
Honduras has only a short Pacific coast. Its long
Caribbean shoreline includes the virtually uninhabited Mosquito Coast,
while most of the rest of the country is mountainous. Honduras declared
independence from Spain in 1821 and returned to civilian rule in 1981
after a succession of military governments. Honduras is one of the world's
leading banana producers, but is very poor and dependent on US aid.

CLIMATE

WEATHER CHART

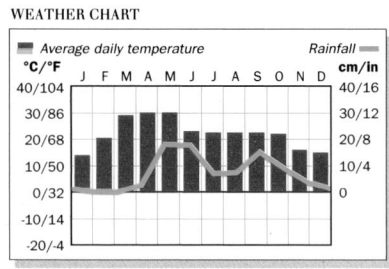

Honduras' Caribbean coast is
extremely hot. The central highlands
are much cooler.

COMMUNICATIONS

 Toncontín, Tegucigalpa
404,000 passengers

 572 ships
1.41m dwt

THE TRANSPORT NETWORK

11,371 km (7066 miles)	None
955 km (593 miles)	465 km (289 miles)

The government plans to close down
the remaining railways and improve
the road system with US aid.

TOURISM

 243,544 visitors   Up 8% in 1992

MAIN OVERSEAS ARRIVALS

USA 33%	
El Salvador 25%	
Guatemala 13%	
Other 29%	

0   10   20   30   40
% of total arrivals

Eco-tourism plans include building
hotels on the virgin coastline of the
Bay of Tela and lodges in the remote
region inland from the Mosquito Coast.
Jungle river rafting is a growing sport
among wealthy locals and foreigners.

PEOPLE

 Spanish, Black Carib, English Creole

46 people per km²

THE URBAN/RURAL POPULATION SPLIT

44%   56%

ETHNIC MAKEUP

Black 2% Amerindian 7%
White 1%
Mestizo (European-Indian) 90%

As in most of Central America, very
few pure indigenous groups remain.
There are an estimated 45,000 Miskito
Indians, and an English-speaking
black population on the Caribbean
coast. Poverty is the root cause of
social tension; whites still have the
best opportunities.

Honduras has one of the most
unequal societies in the region: 4%
of people own 60% of the land. Rural
poverty and strong Roman Catholicism
(93% are Roman Catholic) mean that
the family is a powerful unifying
force. Women's status is
low; many work in
domestic
service.

POLITICS

 1997   President Carlos Roberta Reina

THE STATE OF THE PARTIES

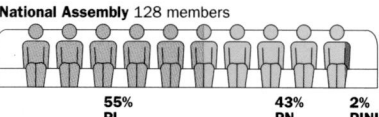

National Assembly 128 members

55% PL   43% PN   2% PINU

PL = Liberal Party **PN** = National Party **PINU** = Innovation and Unity Party

The main brokers in political power
today are the military, the US embassy
and the United Fruit Company, the
biggest banana producers in Honduras.

The military held power
intermittently from 1956 until 1981,
when, under pressure from US
President Jimmy Carter, it allowed a
return to multiparty democratic civilian
rule. Since then, the National and
Liberal parties have alternated in
power, although there are few real
ideological differences between them.
Presidents have tended to be weak
because they can serve only one
four-year term.

During the 1980s, US President
Ronald Reagan effectively converted
the country into a US 'aircraft carrier'
to counter a perceived communist
threat from El Salvador and Nicaragua.
The end of hostilities in these countries
has meant a reduction in US aid to
Honduras. The consequent shortage of
funds for development leaves the new
president with difficult problems.
Unemployment, agrarian reform and
improving the position of Honduras'
landless rural poor are
the main issues.

HONDURAS

Total Area : 112 090 sq. km
(43 278 sq. miles)

LAND HEIGHT	POPULATION
2000m/6562ft	over 500 000
1000m/3281ft	over 100 000
500m/1640ft	over 50 000
200m/656ft	over 10 000
Sea Level	under 10 000

WORLD AFFAIRS

OAS CACM LAES ECLAC BCIE

Honduras seeks to settle long-standing border disputes with El Salvador, to keep close ties with the USA and to achieve closer regional economic integration.

AID

 $275m (receipts) Down 39% in 1991

Peace in Central America has meant that Honduras is not of such strategic importance as it once was, and US aid has fallen.

DEFENCE

 $123.5m Up 3% in 1993

During the 1980s, the military repressed any internal dissent, joined manoeuvres with US troops based in Honduras and backed the Nicaraguan Contras. The air force is the largest in the region. Honduras' major supplier is the USA.

ECONOMICS

 $3.1bn 7.36 lempiras

SCORE CARD

- World GNP Ranking.......................121st
- GNP per Capita $570
- Balance of Payments....................$–134m
- Inflation 28.4%
- Unemployment ....High underemployment

STRENGTHS
Hardwoods. Unexploited mineral deposits. Bananas. Diversification into non-traditional, high-earning agriculture – flowers and fruit.

WEAKNESSES
Traditionally the poorest country in the region, now second to Nicaragua. Industry only 13% of GDP; industrial wages too low to spur development. Land reform has been halted. Decline in US investment.

EXPORTS

Belgium and Luxembourg 6%
Japan 8%
USA 42%
Germany* 10%
Other 34%

IMPORTS

Venezuela 6%
Mexico 7%
USA 40%
Japan 9%
Other 38%

***Tobacco field.** Tobacco accounts for 1% of export revenues. Honduras' biggest earners are bananas, almost 40%, and coffee, 20%.*

RESOURCES

 1.1bn kwh (capacity 290,000 kw)

 Not an oil producer; refines 14,000 b/cd

 728,000 pigs, 325,000 cattle, 170,000 horses

 Lead, zinc, silver, gold, copper, iron

Offshore oil exploration has begun in the north. An HEP dam at El Cajón now allows Honduras to export electricity.

ENVIRONMENT

 6% (1% partially protected)

 US company wants to exploit 1m hectares of rainforest for woodchip

Environmental groups are active, but have to face opposition from multinational commercial interests.

MEDIA

 Although the media is officially free, some journalists will accept bribes to misreport. Left-wing publications may receive death threats

PUBLISHING AND BROADCAST MEDIA

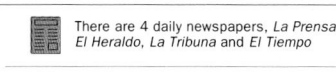

There are 4 daily newspapers, *La Prensa*, *El Heraldo*, *La Tribuna* and *El Tiempo*

9 independent stations

1 state-owned 280 independent stations

Honduras TV and radio is mostly US-sourced. As a result, local coverage remains limited.

CRIME

 Honduras does not publish prison figures

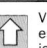 Violence in the cities, especially La Ceiba, is increasing

Drugs-related crime is a major problem in Honduras. Occasional human rights abuses by the military are reported.

EDUCATION

 73%

State-run education follows the US system, although the drop-out rate from secondary schools is high.

HEALTH

 1 per 1822 people

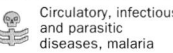 Circulatory, infectious and parasitic diseases, malaria

Only 66% of people have easy access to health services, although most infants receive basic care.

H

CHRONOLOGY

Honduras was a Spanish possession until 1821. In 1823, it joined the United Provinces of Central America with four neighbouring nations.

- **1838** Declares full independence.
- **1890s** US banana companies set up extensive plantations.
- **1932–1949** Dictatorship of Gen Tiburcio Carías Andino of PN.
- **1954** Elected PL president Dr Villeda Morales deposed.
- **1957** Villeda re-elected.
- **1963** Military coup.
- **1969** 13-day Football War with El Salvador sparked by World Cup.
- **1980** PL wins elections but Gen Alvarez holds real power. Military manoeuvres initiated with USA.
- **1982–1983** Alvarez arrests trades unionists; death squads operate.
- **1984** Return to democracy.
- **1988** 12,000 Contra rebels forced out of Nicaragua into Honduras.
- **1990** Contra troops leave.
- **1991** Free-trade zone agreed with El Salvador.

WEALTH

 Plantation worker, 175 lempiras per week; high school science teacher, 415 lempiras per week

CONSUMER GOODS OWNERSHIP

VCR and PC ownership is limited to a small elite

Per 1000 population

70 7 14

Two thirds of the rural population live in absolute poverty. The best chance of social mobility is to join the military. Salvadorean immigrants suffer low social status.

WORLD RANKING

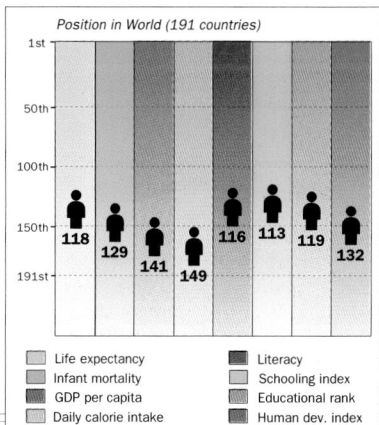

Position in World (191 countries)

1st
50th
100th
150th
191st

118 129 141 149 116 113 119 132

- Life expectancy
- Infant mortality
- GDP per capita
- Daily calorie intake
- Literacy
- Schooling index
- Educational rank
- Human dev. index

HONG KONG

OFFICIAL NAME: Hong Kong   **CAPITAL:** *None*   **POPULATION:** 5.9 million
CURRENCY: Hong Kong dollar   **OFFICIAL LANGUAGES:** English and Cantonese

H
ONG KONG COMPRISES Hong Kong Island, lying off the southeastern coast of China, Kowloon and the New Territories on the mainland, and adjacent islets. Its strategic position has made it one of the world's leading trade and financial centres. In 1997, Hong Kong will revert to China, when the UK's 99-year lease on the New Territories expires. Whether its fiercely capitalist system will survive under Beijing's rule is the dominant political issue.

CLIMATE

WEATHER CHART

Hong Kong's climate is subtropical; it feels hotter and more humid on the streets due to the number of people.

COMMUNICATIONS

Hong Kong Intl, Kai Tak
18.69m passengers

269 ships
12.01m dwt

THE TRANSPORT NETWORK

1529 km
(950 miles)

None

121 km
(75 miles)

None

The efficiency, cleanliness and safety of the underground Mass Transit Railway (MTR) is notable. A new airport at Chek Lap Kok is being built.

TOURISM

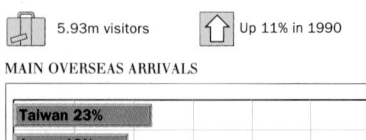

5.93m visitors

Up 11% in 1990

MAIN OVERSEAS ARRIVALS

Taiwan 23%
Japan 19%
USA 10%
Other 48%

0   10   20   30   40   50   60
% of total arrivals

The 'Manhattan of the Orient' attracts tourists with its shopping, its food and as a gateway to China and other parts of Asia. Tourism is now the third largest foreign exchange earner.

Hong Kong harbour and city skyline, looking across to the mainland, viewed from Victoria Peak on Hong Kong Island.

PEOPLE

Chinese (Cantonese and Mandarin), English

5914 people per km²

THE URBAN/RURAL POPULATION SPLIT

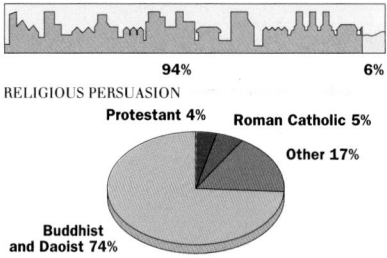

94%   6%

RELIGIOUS PERSUASION

Protestant 4%   Roman Catholic 5%
Other 17%
Buddhist and Daoist 74%

Ethnic tension is not a problem because of the homogeneity of the Han (Chinese) population, over 60% of whom were born in Hong Kong. Many wealthy citizens are planning to emigrate before 1997.

HONG KONG

Total Area : 1045 sq. km
(403 sq. miles)

Urban Areas

Harbour road tunnels

LAND HEIGHT

500m/1640ft
200m/656ft
Sea Level

N

0   20 km
0   20 miles

POLITICS

1995

HM Queen Elizabeth II

THE STATE OF THE PARTIES

Legislative Council 60 members

The United Democrats of Hong Kong (UDHK) won 12 of the 18 directly elected seats in the last elections in 1991. A further 21 members are elected to represent various professions and 21 are chosen by the governor.

At present a British Crown colony, Hong Kong will revert to Chinese sovereignty in 1997, when it will become a Special Administrative Region of China. The British and Chinese governments fundamentally disagree about the interpretation of the 1985 Sino-British agreement and the Basic Law (Hong Kong's post-1997 constitution). Britain wants to push Hong Kong further towards elective democracy. However, Governor Chris Patten's policy is being undermined by his failure to conclude a deal with China, which strongly opposes any change in the *status quo*. Talks stretching to 17 rounds have failed to resolve the dispute.

   Governor Patten's attempts to increase the number of elected members on the Legco (Legislative Council) have, however, speeded the formation of political parties. Prominent figures on the Hong Kong political scene include Martin Lee, leader of the UDHK, and his main rival, the leader of the Liberal Party, Allen Lee. In the 1995 Legco elections, pragmatism may lead to greater support for the Liberals, who are more acceptable to China.

WORLD AFFAIRS

As a Crown colony, Hong Kong's foreign policy is controlled by the UK. However, its diplomatic and economic links with other countries are extensive. The continuing Sino-British stand-off is the major issue.

AID

 Minimal aid donor
 Little variation from year to year

Hong Kong provides some aid to Vietnam to ease the repatriation of Vietnamese economic refugees.

DEFENCE

 UK responsible for weaponry
 Not applicable

Hong Kong bears the manpower cost of its 10,000-strong tri-national army, which is made up of Gurkhas, Hong Kong Chinese and UK personnel.

ECONOMICS

 $59.2bn
 7.73 Hong Kong dollars

SCORE CARD

- ☐ WORLD GNP RANKING...........................37th
- ☐ GNP PER CAPITA $10,320
- ☐ BALANCE OF PAYMENTS $673m
- ☐ INFLATION 7.2%
- ☐ UNEMPLOYMENT..................................1.8%

STRENGTHS
Natural harbour and role as hub of East and South East Asian trade. Position in time zone makes Hong Kong a key global financial market.

WEAKNESSES
Dependence on China for most resources. Sensitivity to price fluctuations on international markets. Dependence on trade, especially US–China trade. Continuing uncertainty about future under Chinese rule deters some investors.

EXPORTS

Germany* 7%
Other 44%
USA 24%
China 25%

IMPORTS

USA 8%
Other 39%
Japan 16%
China 37%

RESOURCES

28.9bn kwh (capacity 8.3m kw)

350,000 pigs, 1000 cattle, 1000 horses

Not an oil producer and has no refineries

Kaolin, feldspar

Hong Kong lacks strategic resources. Energy and water have to be imported from China. Coal is imported from the Guangdong province of China in return for the export of electricity by Hong Kong's China Light and Power Company.

ENVIRONMENT

 36% partially protected
 Few controls on pollution levels

Growth and urbanization have brought serious water and air pollution. The construction of the Daya Bay nuclear power station has been the focus of much public concern.

MEDIA

 Some self-censorship is reportedly being exercised in the run-up to 1997. Films that might be offensive to the Chinese are not allowed on TV

PUBLISHING AND BROADCAST MEDIA

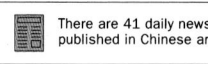 There are 41 daily newspapers, 31 published in Chinese and 2 in English

 1 state-controlled, 3 independent networks

1 state-controlled, 3 independent networks

The press is divided into pro-Chinese and independent camps. Satellite broadcasting to the whole of Asia is carried out by one of Hong Kong's largest conglomerates – Hutchvision Hong Kong, which opened five Star-TV channels in 1991.

CRIME

 12,095 prisoners
 Up 7% in 1990

Crime is rising and becoming more violent. This is partly due to growing links with organized crime and Triad activity in China. Corruption among the elite is increasingly an issue.

EDUCATION

 88%

Primary schools are oversubscribed and most can offer only two half-day sessions a week. There are three universities, where the emphasis is now on science and technology.

HEALTH

 1 per 927 people
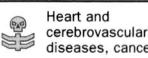 Heart and cerebrovascular diseases, cancers

Mother and child care, and emergency services, are free. Subsidies from the government keep charges for medical treatment and hospital care low.

CHRONOLOGY

Under the Treaty of Nanking in 1842, Hong Kong was ceded in perpetuity to Britain. The UK also acquired the Kowloon peninsula in 1860, and the New Territories, under a 99-year lease, in 1898.

- ☐ **1941–1945** Japanese occupation.
- ☐ **1981–1982** First wave of Vietnamese refugees arrive in Hong Kong.
- ☐ **1985** Sino-British Joint Declaration. China to regain Hong Kong sovereignty in 1997; its present social and economic systems to remain unchanged for 50 years.
- ☐ **1989** Large demonstrations following Tiananmen Square massacre in Beijing.
- ☐ **1992** Governor Chris Patten announces plans for democracy.

H

WEALTH

 Shoe sewer, 170 Hong Kong dollars per day; clerk of works, 11,738 Hong Kong dollars per month

CONSUMER GOODS OWNERSHIP

High levels of PC ownership

260
40
504
136

Per 1000 population

Social mobility is rapid, as exemplified by the rise to great wealth of families whose heads came to Hong Kong to escape communist China. Hong Kong consumers are highly status conscious and will pay over the odds for fashionable goods; attempts to curb car ownership by taxation have had little effect. Rich families have been able to buy citizenship overseas, allowing them to relocate, if necessary, in 1997.

WORLD RANKING

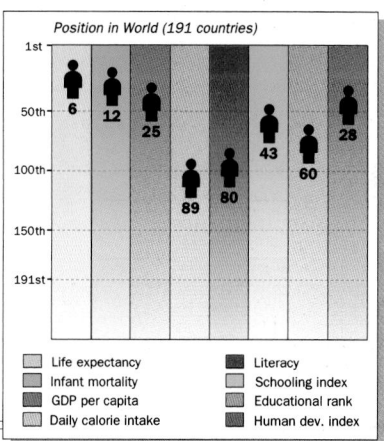

Position in World (191 countries)

6
12
25
89
80
43
60
28

- Life expectancy
- Infant mortality
- GDP per capita
- Daily calorie intake
- Literacy
- Schooling index
- Educational rank
- Human dev. index

HUNGARY

OFFICIAL NAME: Republic of Hungary   **CAPITAL:** Budapest
POPULATION: 10.5 million   **CURRENCY:** Forint   **OFFICIAL LANGUAGE:** Hungarian (Magyar)

L YING AT THE HEART of Central Europe, Hungary is land-locked and has borders with seven states. Historically, Hungary has been a cosmopolitan cultural centre, and during its years of market socialism was more prosperous and open to the West than the other Eastern Bloc countries. Hungary has changed its economic and political policies to develop closer ties with the EU. It now receives the lion's share of overseas investment in the former COMECON states. The treatment of the Hungarian minority in Romanian Transylvania is a major foreign policy concern.

H

TOURISM

 20.5m visitors   Up 42% in 1990

MAIN OVERSEAS ARRIVALS

Romania 31%
Poland 13%
Czech Republic and Slovakia 11%
Germany 10%
Serbia and Montenegro 9%
Other 26%

% of total arrivals

CLIMATE

WEATHER CHART

Average daily temperature   Rainfall

Hungary has a continental climate, with wet springs, late summers and cold, cloudy winters. There are no great differences of weather and climate within the country. Conditions in summer and winter may, however, differ from one year to the next. The transition between seasons tends to be sudden.

COMMUNICATIONS

Budapest Ferihegy
2.46m passengers

14 ships
133,000 dwt

THE TRANSPORT NETWORK

29,832 km
(18,537 miles)

351 km
(218 miles)

7765 km
(4825 miles)

1688 km
(1049 miles)

Freight travels mainly via the rail link from Budapest to the Austrian border. Most foreign investment is located along this corridor. Good roads link Hungary with Germany and Austria. The road system will be improved further once funds are available.

Tourism is an important source of hard currency earnings, which totalled $1.2 billion in 1993. Visitors come mainly from eastern Europe, Germany and Austria. Since 1989, Hungary has invested heavily in tourism. The number of travel agents and hotels has risen dramatically. Lake Balaton is the traditional summer destination. In the capital city, Budapest, the baths, some of which date from the Ottoman period, are among the most popular tourist attractions. Budapest is also promoting itself as an international business convention centre.

HUNGARY

Total Area : 93 030 sq. km
(35 919 sq. miles)

POPULATION

over 1 000 000
over 500 000
over 100 000
over 50 000
over 10 000

LAND HEIGHT

500m/1640ft
200m/656ft
80m/262ft

PEOPLE

 Hungarian

 112 people per km²

THE URBAN/RURAL POPULATION SPLIT

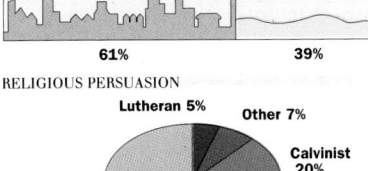

61%   **39%**

RELIGIOUS PERSUASION

Lutheran 5%   Other 7%

Calvinist 20%

Roman Catholic 68%

ETHNIC MAKEUP

Slovak 2%   Other 6%

German 2%

Hungarian 90%

Hungary is ethnically homogeneous. There are also small minorities of Germans, Slovaks, Gypsies, Serbs, Croats and Romanians. There is little ethnic tension at home, although there is considerable concern about the treatment of Hungarian minorities in neighbouring states. In terms of religion, the country is more diversified. A small Jewish community remains in Budapest. While there have been reports of isolated outbursts of anti-semitism, prevailing opinion in Hungary remains tolerant.

Hungary suffers from a severe housing shortage. Most family homes are overcrowded, a factor that may contribute to the high rate of stress-related health disorders. Since 1989, a bourgeois class which is benefiting from the market economy has emerged. Life for the unskilled and unemployed is tougher, however, than under communism. Hungary has the highest suicide rate in the world.

POPULATION AGE BREAKDOWN

	0–14		15–64		65+
% of population by age group	9%	11.6%	13.4%	13.4%	14.8%
	65.7%	67.6%	64.7%	66.7%	70.6%
	25.3%	20.8%	21.9%	19.9%	14.6%
	1960	1970	1980	1990	2000

POLITICS

 1994

 President Árpád Göncz

THE STATE OF THE PARTIES
National Assembly 386 members

54% HSP   **46% Other**

HSP = Hungarian Socialist Party (formerly HWSP = Hungarian Workers' Socialist Party) **Other** = Hungarian Democratic Forum, Alliance of Free Democrats, Independent Smallholders' Party, Federation of Young Democrats, Christian Democratic People's Party

Hungary has been a multiparty democracy since 1990.

MAIN POLITICAL ISSUES

The HSP's election promises
The clear victory of the ex-communists (the HSP) in the general elections of 1994 came as a surprise to most observers. The HSP promised voters a softer landing to the market economy, with greater social security and less unemployment. However, whether the HSP will be able to deliver its promises, given strict IMF guidelines on state spending, is now a key question.

Hungarian minorities abroad
Between 1989 and 1991, 50,000 ethnic Hungarians living abroad returned home. Many complained of poor treatment from nationalistic neighbouring states. The issue has achieved prominence, particularly as Hungarians are wary of the effects of any additional competition for jobs in a tight labour market.

PROFILE
The HDF government of József Antall was installed following the elections of 1990. Until his death in 1993, Antall was a symbol of stability in Hungarian democratic politics. However, party disintegrations and the lack of an economic upturn led to an increase in apathy and disillusionment among voters. In a 1993 poll, only 6% of Hungarians considered life to be better than under the communists.

In the May 1994 general election, voters rejected the MDF's Christian nationalist stance and voted ex-communists back into power. The victorious HSP, under Gyula Horn, pledged to work in coalition in order to ease the passage of economic and social reforms through parliament.

President Árpád Göncz *was elected in 1990 and is head of the armed forces.*

Gyula Horn, *ex-communist foreign minister and leader of the HSP.*

The Hungarian parliament buildings in Budapest, viewed across the Danube from the castle area of the city.

WORLD AFFAIRS

CE   CSCE   V4   GATT   HG

Hungary was disappointed with the rebuff dealt to its applications to join NATO and the WEU, being offered neither full nor associate status. However, it accepted the NATO Partnership for Peace proposal of 1993.

Hungary is an associate member of the EU, and has declared its intention to acquire full membership at the earliest opportunity. A treaty of co-operation and friendship has been signed with Russia, but relations have been strained by Hungary's open courting of the West.

The most problematic relations are with Romania. For centuries, the two nations have disputed the status of the Hungarian minority in Transylvania. Relations with Slovakia are also tense.

CHRONOLOGY

The region today occupied by Hungary was first settled by the Finno-Ugrian Magyar peoples from the 8th century. In the 16th and 17th centuries it came under Austrian domination, lasting until 1867, when Austria-Hungary was formed.

❑ **1918** Hungarian Republic created as successor state to Austria-Hungary.

❑ **1919** Béla Kún leads a short-lived communist government. Romania intervenes militarily and hands power to Admiral Horthy.

❑ **1938–1941** Hungary gains territory from Czechoslovakia, Yugoslavia and Romania in return for supporting Nazi Germany.

❑ **1941** Hungary drawn into Second World War on Axis side when Hitler attacks Soviet Union.

❑ **1944** Nazi Germany pre-empts Soviet advance on Hungary by invading. Deportation of Hungarian Jews and Gypsies to extermination camps begins. Soviet Red Army enters in October. Horthy forced to resign. ⇨

H

H

CHRONOLOGY *continued*

- ❑ **1945** Liberated by Red Army. Soviet-formed provisional government installed. Imre Nagy introduces land reform.
- ❑ **1947** Communists emerge as largest party in second post-war election.
- ❑ **1948** Forcible merger of Social Democrats with Communists to establish Hungarian Workers' Socialist Party (HWSP).
- ❑ **1949** New constitution; formally becomes People's Republic.
- ❑ **1950–1951** First Secretary Rákosi uses authoritarian powers to collectivize agriculture and industrialize the economy.
- ❑ **1953** Imre Nagy, Rákosi's rival, becomes premier and reduces political terror.
- ❑ **1955** Nagy deposed.
- ❑ **1956** Rákosi out. Student demonstrations demanding withdrawal of Soviet troops and Nagy's return become popular uprising. Nagy becomes premier; Kádár becomes First Secretary. Nagy announces Hungary will leave Warsaw Pact. Three days later, Soviet forces suppress protests. About 25,000 killed in resistance. Kádár becomes premier.
- ❑ **1958** Nagy executed following show trial.
- ❑ **1968** Kádár introduces New Economic Mechanism to bring market elements to socialism.
- ❑ **1986** Commemoration of the 1956 uprising broken up by police. Economists call for radical change. Democratic opposition demands Kádár's resignation.
- ❑ **1987** Party reformers establish HDF as a political movement.
- ❑ **1988** Federation of Young Democrats forms from independent student group. Kádár ousted. Environmental protests force suspension of plans for controversial Danube Dam.
- ❑ **1989** Parliament votes to allow independent political parties. Nagy rehabilitated and given full state funeral. First opposition candidate since 1947 elected in by-election. Round table talks between HWSP and opposition. Parliament approves holding of multiparty elections.
- ❑ **1990** Multiparty elections held. HDF wins decisively and Antall's government is sworn in. Speed of economic reform hotly debated.
- ❑ **1991** Warsaw Pact dissolved. Last Soviet troops leave.
- ❑ **1993** József Antall dies. Peter Boross elected prime minister.
- ❑ **1994** Hungary agrees to NATO Partnership for Peace initiative. HSP wins general election.

AID

 $1bn (receipts)   Aid is increasing

Hungary has received World Bank loans totalling $3.4 billion since 1982. The EU is also an important source of assistance. Hungary has credit lines with the World Bank's International Finance Corporation and the EBRD. Loans are mainly used for infrastructure and energy projects.

DEFENCE

 $1.2bn   ⬇ Down 6% in 1992

0	Defence spending as % GDP	40
2.3%		

Real defence spending has been halved from its 1989 level. Troop numbers have been slashed. Conventional arms and the military hierarchy have been updated to meet NATO standards. Hungary has been improving its rapid reaction forces with MiGs bought in debt-for-arms deals with Russia.

HUNGARIAN ARMED FORCES

🛡	1357 main battle tanks (T-34/T-55/T-54/T-72)	63,500 personnel
⚓	None	
✈	91 combat aircraft (MiG–21bis/MiG 23)	17,300 personnel
	None	

ECONOMICS

 $28.2bn   100.75 forint

SCORE CARD

- ❑ WORLD GNP RANKING..........................56th
- ❑ GNP PER CAPITA $2780
- ❑ BALANCE OF PAYMENTS.....................$–2bn
- ❑ INFLATION 22%
- ❑ UNEMPLOYMENT..................................15%

EXPORTS

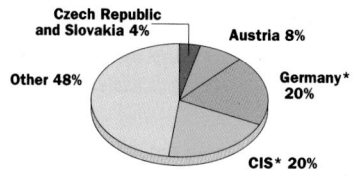

Czech Republic and Slovakia 4%
Austria 8%
Germany* 20%
Other 48%
CIS* 20%

IMPORTS

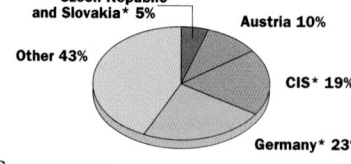

Czech Republic and Slovakia* 5%
Austria 10%
Other 43%
CIS* 19%
Germany* 23%

STRENGTHS

Openness to foreign direct investment. By 1990, Hungary had attracted half of the foreign investment coming to eastern Europe: $5 billion. Favourable tax regime, streamlined bureaucracy and new legislation permitting fully-owned subsidiaries help to attract international business.

WEAKNESSES

Continued lending by the banks to state-run and private firms regardless of creditworthiness has led to a crisis in the banking system. No plans to privatize banks. Downturn in overseas investment slowing privatization programme.

ECONOMIC PERFORMANCE INDICATOR

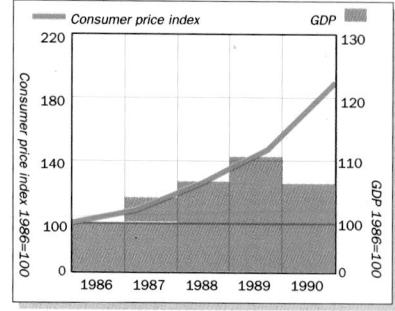

Consumer price index   GDP

PROFILE

The costs of Hungary's transition to a market economy have been higher than expected. The collapse of COMECON trade caused a reorientation of trade towards western Europe, and Hungary's economic recovery now depends largely upon trade with the EU. High tax rates make privatized assets less attractive to foreign investors.

HUNGARY : MAJOR BUSINESSES

Agribusiness		Heavy engineering	
Metallurgy		Light engineering	
Electronics		Pharmaceuticals	
Chemicals		Vehicle assembly	
Textiles		Computer software	

0 — 100 km
0 — 100 miles

* significant multinational ownership

RESOURCES

 28.4bn kwh (capacity 6.6m kw)

 34,700 b/d (reserves 146,956,000 bbl)

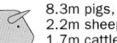 8.3m pigs, 2.2m sheep, 1.7m cattle

 Bauxite, coal, natural gas

ELECTRICITY GENERATION

Hydro 1% (178m kwh)

Thermal 51% (14.5bn kwh)

Nuclear 48% (13.7bn kwh)

Other 0%

0 20 40 60 80 100
% of total generation by type

Hungary has bauxite, coal and fertile farmlands. Electricity companies are currently being privatized. The state

ENVIRONMENT

 6% (5% partially protected)

Greater awareness of environmental problems

ENVIRONMENTAL TREATIES

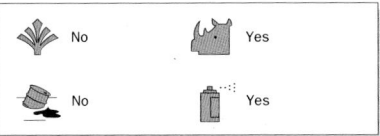

No

Yes

No

Yes

Hungary's oil reserves have a high sulphur content, which exacerbates the already serious air pollution in the industrial zones. It is estimated that 40% of Hungarians live in severely polluted areas.

Hungary's universities have an international reputation for their interdisciplinary approach to environmental science. The quality of data is high, but information has only recently become generally accessible.

MEDIA

 Little government censorship of the press

PUBLISHING AND BROADCAST MEDIA

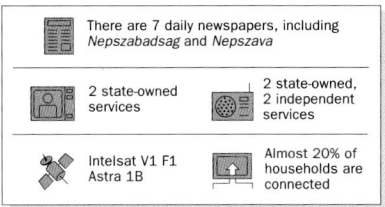

There are 7 daily newspapers, including *Nepszabadsag* and *Nepszava*

2 state-owned services

2 state-owned, 2 independent services

Intelsat V1 F1 Astra 1B

Almost 20% of households are connected

Following the end of official censorship in 1988–1989, the number of newspapers and magazines has soared. Some are foreign-owned; most are fiercely independent and critical of government policy. The TV broadcasting service is nominally independent, but in practice the state controls its news coverage. Public pressure to open frequencies to private local TV and radio networks is currently growing.

HUNGARY : LAND USE

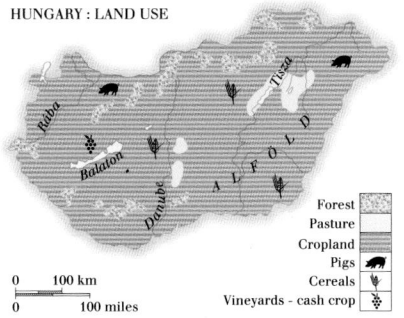

0 100 km
0 100 miles

Forest
Pasture
Cropland
Pigs
Cereals
Vineyards - cash crop

holding company will retain 50% of shares, with foreign companies acquiring controlling rights with 30% or more of shares.

CRIME

 12,373 prisoners

Up 54% in 1990

CRIME RATES

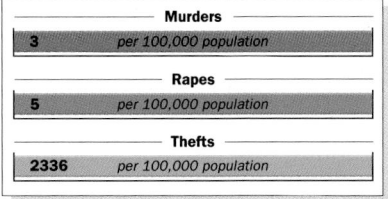

Murders

3 per 100,000 population

Rapes

5 per 100,000 population

Thefts

2336 per 100,000 population

There were 288 murders in 1993. A growing proportion of these were a settling of business scores. Organized crime is also rising, and Hungary has become a money-laundering centre.

EDUCATION

 99%

0 Education spending as % GNP 25
 6%

THE EDUCATION SYSTEM

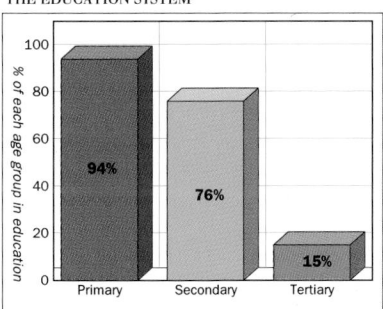

% of each age group in education

94% Primary
76% Secondary
15% Tertiary

Education is free and compulsory from the ages of six to 16. Bilingual schools are being established to provide education in the language of Hungary's ethnic minorities. There are 77 higher education institutions – including ten universities – from which over 20,000 students graduated in 1992.

HEALTH

 1 per 330 people

 Heart diseases, cancers, accidents, suicides

0 Health spending as % GNP 25
2.2%

Medical treatment in Hungary is free of charge to all patients, although there is a 15% charge towards the cost of prescriptions. The health service is currently underfunded and suffers from a lack of supplies. In order to jump waiting lists or to obtain better care, it is common for patients in the state health system to offer doctors gifts or bribes. The state provides sickness benefit at 75% of wages.

WEALTH

 Transport worker, 16,403 forint per month; teacher, 21,928 forint per month

CONSUMER GOODS OWNERSHIP

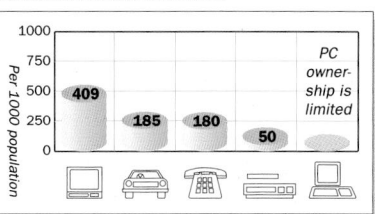

Per 1000 population

409 185 180 50

PC owner-ship is limited

Hungary currently enjoys a higher standard of living than the other ex-COMECON countries. Around 90% of households have refrigerators, washing machines and TVs. Demand for luxury goods is rising. In 1992, Hungary was the second biggest market after Germany for BMW cars.

Real wages fell less in Hungary than in other eastern European states. However, Hungarians have to work longer hours to pay for basic consumer goods than their western European counterparts. Per capita GDP is still lower than that in the poorest EU state. There is also a growing sense of inequality between those working in the state and private sectors.

WORLD RANKING

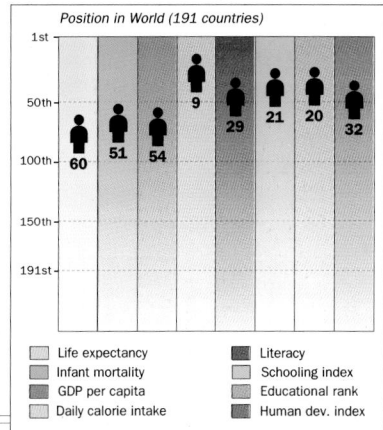

Position in World (191 countries)

1st
50th
100th
150th
191st

60 51 54 9 29 21 20 32

Life expectancy
Infant mortality
GDP per capita
Daily calorie intake
Literacy
Schooling index
Educational rank
Human dev. index

H

ICELAND

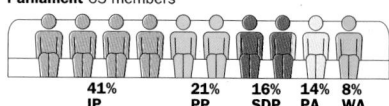

OFFICIAL NAME: Republic of Iceland **CAPITAL:** Reykjavík
POPULATION: 300,000 **CURRENCY:** New Icelandic króna **OFFICIAL LANGUAGE:** Icelandic

E UROPE'S WESTERNMOST COUNTRY, Iceland has a strategic location in the North Atlantic, just south of the Arctic Circle. Its position, on the rift where the North American and European continental plates are pulling apart, accounts for its 200 volcanoes and its numerous geysers and solfataras. Previously a Danish possession, Iceland became fully independent in 1944. Most settlements are along the coast, where ports remain ice-free in winter.

CLIMATE

WEATHER CHART

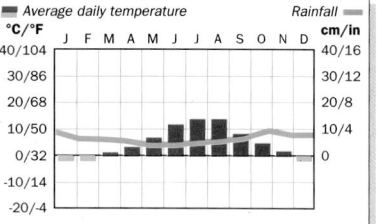

Iceland sits in the Gulf Stream. Winters are consequently mild. Summers are cool, with fine sunny days.

COMMUNICATIONS

Keflavik Intl, Reykjavik
557,000 passengers

18 ships
55,300 dwt

THE TRANSPORT NETWORK

11,387 km (7076 miles)		None	
None		None	

Icelanders rely entirely on cars, and ownership rates are among the world's highest. Most freight moves by sea. The only main road is the island ring road.

TOURISM

142,561 visitors   Down 1% in 1992

MAIN OVERSEAS ARRIVALS

Iceland is promoting itself, especially in Japan, as an upmarket destination for eco-tourists, attracted by its spectacular scenery, glaciers, green valleys, fjords and hot springs.

PEOPLE

Icelandic   3 people per km²

THE URBAN/RURAL POPULATION SPLIT

91%   9%

RELIGIOUS PERSUASION

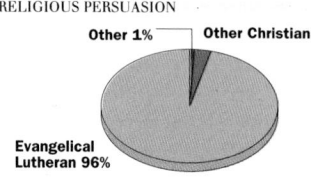

Other 1%   Other Christian 3%

Evangelical Lutheran 96%

Descended from Norwegians and Celts, Icelanders form an ethnically homogeneous society; there are only 4000 foreign residents. 96% of people follow the Evangelical Lutheran Church. Living standards are high and there are few social tensions. The predominant cultural influence is from the USA.

POLITICS

 1995   President Vigdís Finnbogadóttir

THE STATE OF THE PARTIES

Parliament 63 members

41% IP	21% PP	16% SDP	14% PA	8% WA

IP = Independence Party   **PP** = Progressive Party
SDP = Social Democratic Party   **PA** = People's Alliance
WA = Women's Alliance

From independence, Iceland was ruled by coalitions. However, in the 1980s the traditional four-party system began to splinter. In 1983, the WA was formed, and a general strike in 1984, in response to proposed tax increases, led a rebel group to leave the IP to form the Citizens' Party. By the 1991 elections, the latter had disappeared, and a new IP/SDP coalition promoted market-led reforms.

The main issues are the economic downturn and how best to manage Iceland's uneasy dependence on its major source of wealth: fish. Arguments over whether or not to join the EU were defused in 1992 with the successful negotiation of the EEA, giving Iceland access to the key EU market.

ICELAND

Total Area : 103 000 sq. km
(39 770 sq. miles)

POPULATION
- o over 50 000
- ● over 10 000
- · under 10 000

LAND HEIGHT
- 1000m/3281ft
- 500m/1640ft
- 200m/656ft
- Sea Level
- Ice Cap

WORLD AFFAIRS

 EFTA NATO NC CSCE OECD

Iceland has traditionally maintained an arm's length relationship with the EU and USA, while seeking to ensure access to both their markets. Its major disputes have been over the extension of its fishing waters. Agreements were ratified with the EEA in 1993, and with the International Whaling Commission over Iceland's wish to continue whaling.

AID

 $5.3m   No significant change

Aid donations are modest, and form a smaller proportion of the budget than in other Scandinavian states.

DEFENCE

 Coastguard of 130 personnel only   Not applicable

Iceland has no armed forces, but is a member of NATO. The USA has 3000 troops based at Keflavík.

ECONOMICS

 $5.9bn   71.57 new Icelandic krónur

SCORE CARD

❑ WORLD GNP RANKING	107th
❑ GNP PER CAPITA	$19,713
❑ BALANCE OF PAYMENTS	$–210m
❑ INFLATION	4.1%
❑ UNEMPLOYMENT	4.3%

STRENGTHS
High-tech fishing industry and exclusive access to prime fishing grounds place Iceland in an almost unique position to supply EU and US markets. Very cheap geothermal power.

WEAKNESSES
Dependence on fish for 75% export earnings. Attempts to diversify have been delayed by world recession.

EXPORTS

France 9%
USA 10%
Other 43%
Germany* 13%
UK 25%

IMPORTS

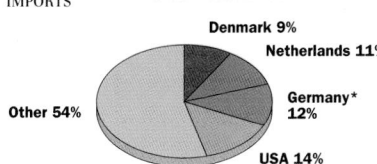

Denmark 9%
Netherlands 11%
Other 54%
Germany* 12%
USA 14%

Lava Towers, near Lake Mývatn in northern Iceland, a region of grassy lowlands. The centre consists of cold lava desert and glaciers.

RESOURCES

 4.6bn kwh (capacity 957,000 kw)   Not an oil producer and has no refineries

 700,000 sheep, 72,000 cattle, 56,000 horses   Diatomite

Iceland has virtually no minerals. All energy needs are met by geothermal and hydroelectric sources. It has implemented measures to try to restore its once abundant fish stocks.

ENVIRONMENT

 9% (7% partially protected)   Iceland has the largest bird sanctuary in Europe

Iceland has no nuclear or thermal power stations. The end of Soviet and US submarine operations in the Arctic Circle has removed an environmental threat. Believing that Minke whales eat valuable cod stocks, Iceland decided to resume whale hunting in 1992.

MEDIA

 Freedom of expression is guaranteed

PUBLISHING AND BROADCAST MEDIA

 There are six daily newspapers – most support the views of one political party. *Dagbladid-Vísir* has the largest circulation

 1 state-owned, 1 independent service   1 state-owned, 1 independent service

Iceland is renowned for having one of the highest per capita newspaper ciculations in the world.

CRIME

 89 prisoners   Crime rates are fairly stable

Crime rates are comparatively low. The rate of alcohol-related murders is higher than the European average.

EDUCATION

 100%

Icelanders buy more books per capita than any other nation. Education is state-run. 25% of school students go on to university at Reykjavík or Akureyri or to colleges in the USA.

CHRONOLOGY

Iceland was first settled in the 9th century by Norwegians. It was ruled by Denmark from 1380–1944. In 1918, it became fully self-governing.

- ❑ **1940–1945** Occupied by UK and, from 1941, USA.
- ❑ **1944** Independence as a republic.
- ❑ **1949** Founder-member of NATO.
- ❑ **1951** US air base built at Keflavík despite strong local opposition.
- ❑ **1972–1976** Extends fishing limits to 50 miles; two 'cod wars' with UK.
- ❑ **1975** Sets 200-mile fishing limit.
- ❑ **1980** Vigdís Finnbogadóttir elected; world's first woman head of state.
- ❑ **1985** Declares nuclear-free status.
- ❑ **1989** Bans whaling for two years.

HEALTH

 1 per 376 people   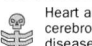 Heart and cerebrovascular diseases, cancers

The state health system is free to all Icelanders. Iceland has the lowest infant mortality rate, and one of the highest longevity rates, in the world.

WEALTH

 Meat packer, 387 new Icelandic krónur per hour; book keeper, 638 new Icelandic krónur per hour

CONSUMER GOODS OWNERSHIP

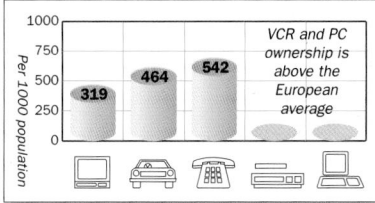

VCR and PC ownership is above the European average

Per 1000 population

319 464 542

Wealth distribution is comparatively even and social mobility is high. Domestic heating, from geothermal sources, is almost free.

WORLD RANKING

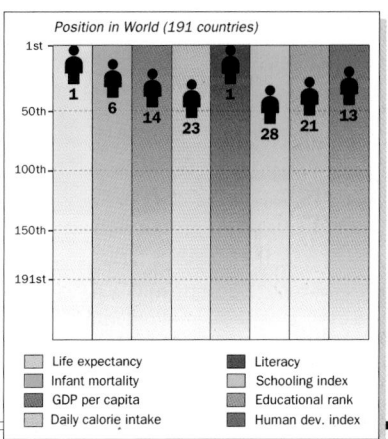

Position in World (191 countries)

1st
50th
100th
150th
191st

1 6 14 23 1 28 21 13

Life expectancy
Infant mortality
GDP per capita
Daily calorie intake

Literacy
Schooling index
Educational rank
Human dev. index

I

INDIA

OFFICIAL NAME: Republic of India   **CAPITAL:** New Delhi
POPULATION: 879.5 million   **CURRENCY:** Rupee   **OFFICIAL LANGUAGE:** Hindi and English

SOUTH ASIA

SEPARATED FROM THE REST of Asia by the Himalaya mountain range, India forms a subcontinent. Besides the Himalyas, there are two other main geographical regions, the Indo-Gangetic plain, which lies between the foothills of the Himalayas and the Vindhya Mountains, and the central-southern plateau. India is the world's largest democracy and second most populous country after China. The birth rate has recently been falling, but even at its current level India's population will probably overtake China's by 2030. After years of protectionism, India is opening up its economy to the outside world. The hope is that the free market will go some way to alleviating one of the country's major problems, poverty.

CLIMATE

WEATHER CHART

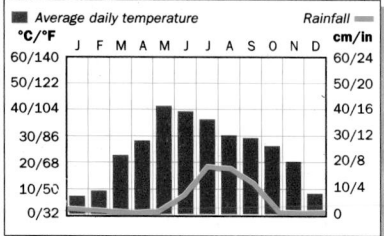

During the hot season, temperatures in the north can reach 40ºC. The monsoon breaks in June and peters out in September or October. In the cool season, average temperatures are 10ºC–15ºC in the north and the weather is mainly dry. However, the south has a less variable climate. Madras is always hot. Average temperatures range from 24ºC in January to 32ºC in May and June.

COMMUNICATIONS

 Bombay International
4.05m passengers

 347 ships
1m dwt

THE TRANSPORT NETWORK

 2.1m km
(1.3m miles)

 77 highways
totalling 34,058 km
(21,163 miles)

 62,000 km
(38,525 miles)

 19,145 km
(11,896 miles)

India's state-owned railway system spans all the major cities. Rail carries 40% of passenger traffic and 65% of freight. Some routes still use steam locomotives. Intercity highways are narrow, poorly maintained and congested. Scooter and cycle rickshaws are common in urban centres. Calcutta still has rickshaws pulled by hand.

INDIA

Total Area : 3 287 590 sq. km
(1 269 358 sq. miles)

POPULATION

■ over 5 000 000
▣ over 1 000 000
◉ over 500 000
◎ over 100 000
● over 10 000

LAND HEIGHT

5000m/16 405ft
4000m/13 124ft
3000m/9843ft
2000m/6562ft
1000m/3281ft
500m/1640ft
200m/656ft
Sea Level

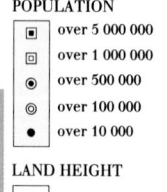

0   200 km
0   200 miles

A religious festival. Such festivals are a frequent occurrence and form an important part of Hindu culture.

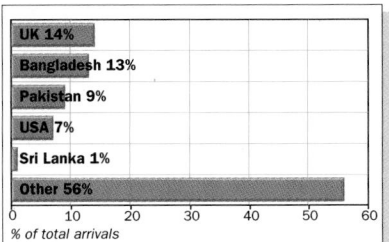

BAY OF
BENGAL

TOURISM

🧳 1.71m visitors   ⬇️ Down 2% in 1990

MAIN OVERSEAS ARRIVALS

	% of total arrivals
UK 14%	
Bangladesh 13%	
Pakistan 9%	
USA 7%	
Sri Lanka 1%	
Other 56%	

Tourism is India's sixth largest foreign exchange earner. More luxury hotels are now being built, and wildlife and adventure tourism are being developed. However, India still has only a small share of the world tourism market – 0.3% of the world's tourists and 1% of revenue – and is keen to expand this source of revenue and take in 2.5 million visitors by the late 1990s.

PEOPLE

  Hindi, Urdu, Bengali, Marathi, Telugu, Tamil, Bihari, Gujarati, Kanarese   👥 257 people per km²

THE URBAN/RURAL POPULATION SPLIT

27%   73%

RELIGIOUS PERSUASION

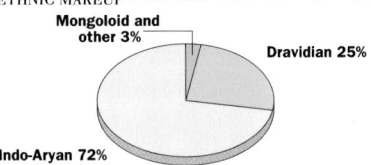

Sikh 2%   Christian 2%
Other 2%   Muslim 11%
Hindu 83%

ETHNIC MAKEUP

Mongoloid and other 3%   Dravidian 25%
Indo-Aryan 72%

The world's second most populous country, India is home to 16% of the global population. Despite a major birth control programme, population growth has come down only slightly from 2.1% a year in the mid-1980s to 2% in 1990–1991. Today, nationwide awareness campaigns aim to promote the idea of smaller families. India's planners consider the rise in the population the most significant brake on development. Cultural and religious pressures encourage large families, however, and the extended family is seen as an essential security for old age.

The fertile rice growing areas of the Gangetic plain and delta are very densely populated. The northern state of Uttar Pradesh has the largest population, at 139 million, followed by neighbouring Bihār and the western state of Mahārāshtra. Mahārāshtra is also the most urbanized state, with 55% of its people living in towns or cities. Elsewhere, most Indians live in rural areas, although poverty continues to drive many to the swelling cities.

Some 83% of the population are Hindus. Each Hindu belongs to one of thousands of castes and sub-castes. Hindus are born into their caste and caste determines whom they marry and their future status and occupation. Various attempts to reform the system have met with violent opposition.

POPULATION AGE BREAKDOWN

% of population by age group	▨ 0–14	▨ 15–64	☐ 65+		
65+	3.4%	3.7%	4%	4.5%	5.1%
15–64	56.8%	55.9%	57.5%	59%	60.4%
0–14	39.8%	40.4%	38.5%	36.5%	34.5%
	1960	1970	1980	1990	2000

CHRONOLOGY

The origins of an Indus valley civilization may be traced back to the third millennium BC. By the 3rd century BC, the Mauryan kingdom under Ashoka encompassed most of modern India. Following the Battle of Plassey in 1757, British rule – through the East India Company – was consolidated.

❏ **1885** Indian National Congress formed to press for political reform.
❏ **1919** Act of parliament for 'responsible government'.
❏ **1920–1922** Mahatma Gandhi's first civil disobedience campaign.
❏ **1930–1933** Further civil disobedience action.
❏ **1935** Government of India act.
❏ **1936** First elections under new constitution.
❏ **1942–1943** 'Quit India' movement.
❏ **1947** August, independence and partition into India and Pakistan. Jawarhalal Nehru becomes first prime minister.
❏ **1948** Assassination of Mahatma Gandhi. War with Pakistan over Kashmir. India becomes a republic.
❏ **1951–1952** First general election won by Congress party.
❏ **1957** Second elections won by Congress. First elected communist government anywhere installed in Kerala.
❏ **1960** Bombay divided into states of Gujarat and Maharashtra.
❏ **1962** Congress party re-elected. Brief border war with China.
❏ **1964** Death of Nehru. Lal Bahadur Shastri becomes prime minister.
❏ **1965** Second war with Pakistan over Kashmir.
❏ **1966** Shastri dies, Indira Gandhi (daughter of Jawarhalal Nehru) becomes prime minister.
❏ **1967** Congress again wins majority at elections. Opposition takes control of several states.
❏ **1969** Split of Congress party into two factions, the larger of which is led by Indira Gandhi.
❏ **1971** Indira Gandhi's Congress party wins elections. Friendship Treaty signed with USSR. Third war with Pakistan, over creation of Bangladesh; army occupies East Pakistan and recognizes it as independent state of Bangladesh.
❏ **1972** Simla Agreement signed with Pakistan.
❏ **1974** Explosion of first nuclear device in underground test.
❏ **1975–1977** Growing anti-government protest movement. Mass civil disobedience. State of emergency imposed. Many opposition leaders arrested. Elections postponed.

➭

I

I

CHRONOLOGY *continued*

- ❏ **1977** General election. Congress defeated and People's Party (JD) government comes to power, with Morarji Desai as prime minister.
- ❏ **1978** New political group, Congress (Indira) – Congress (I) – formally established. Conflict within JD.
- ❏ **1979** Desai resigns.
- ❏ **1980** Indira Gandhi's C(I) wins general election.
- ❏ **1984** Unrest in Punjab. Golden Temple of Amritsar, occupied by armed Sikhs, stormed by Indian army troops. Assassination of Indira Gandhi by members of her bodyguard. Her son Rajiv becomes prime minister.
- ❏ **1985** Assam and Punjab Accords.
- ❏ **1987** Former finance and defence minister V P Singh expelled from C(I) and becomes leader of opposition. Following signing of accord, Indian peace-keeping force stationed in northern Sri Lanka to combat Tamil terrorists.
- ❏ **1988** Punjab unrest continues. Golden Temple in Amritsar again stormed by army.
- ❏ **1989** Blockade of Nepal following disagreement on foreign policy and migration. Sri Lankan president Premadasa orders Indian troops to leave, but new accord postpones this. Right-wing Hindu party, the BJP, wins 86 seats in elections. Minority National Front government formed with V P Singh as prime minister.
- ❏ **1990** Withdrawal of peace-keeping troops stationed in Sri Lanka. BJP leader Lal Advani arrested. No-confidence motion in parliament; Chandra Shekhar prime minister of minority government.
- ❏ **1991** February, Rajiv Gandhi overthrows minority government. May, Rajiv Gandhi assassinated during polling in general elections. P V Narasimha Rao becomes prime minister in C(I) minority government. Programme of economic liberalization and reform introduced in attempt to solve huge economic problems, including balance of payments crisis. Government removes trade barriers and encourages foreign and private investment.
- ❏ **1992** Major financial scandal involving Bombay Stock Exchange. Demolition of the Babri Masjid mosque at Ayodhya by Hindu extremists. Resultant widespread violence leaves 1200 people dead.
- ❏ **1993** Resurgence of riots leaves over 500 dead in Bombay. Explosions rock Bombay Stock Exchange.

POLITICS

1996   President Shankar Dayal Sharma

THE STATE OF THE PARTIES

House of the People 545 members   **20% Other**

42% C(I)   22% BJP   10% JD   6% CPI-M

C (I) = Congress (I)   **BJP** = Indian People's Party
JD = People's Party   **CPI-M** = Communist Party of India – Marxist   **Other** = Communist Party of India, Telugu Nation

Council of States 245 members

41% C(I)   12% BJP   11% JD   7% CPI-M   29% Other

India is a multiparty democracy. The *Lok Sabha* (lower house) is directly elected by universal adult suffrage, while the *Rajya Sabha* (upper house) is indirectly elected by the state assemblies. Beyond Delhi, there are 25 states and seven union territories, each governed by a parliament and cabinet.

MAIN POLITICAL ISSUES

The 'rainbow coalition'

In the recent Uttar Pradesh state assembly election an alliance of the Samajwadi Party and the Bahujan Samaj Party secured the votes of Muslims, the lower castes and a grouping of 'untouchables' (also known as *Dalits* or *Harijans*) and swept into power. The forging of this so-called 'rainbow coalition' was made by promising to reserve government jobs for the lower castes. Significantly, the poor were seen to put their perceived interests above religious divisions. The win partly reflected circumstances peculiar to Uttar Pradesh, but opposition politicians nationwide see this as a way of defeating C(I) in other states.

Hindu militancy

Many observers have suggested the right-wing Hindu BJP could win the next general election. The rise of the BJP has been swift. Almost from nowhere it won 86 seats at the 1989 general election, and two years later, with its ally the *Shiv Sena*, took its tally to 123. It also formed the government in five states, including Uttar Pradesh. Most of its backing has come from the middle classes and prosperous trading and farming castes. However, voters are now beginning to question whether the BJP has defined policies other than the promotion of Hindu supremacy.

The free market

The opening up of the economy and the signing of the GATT agreement has led to large opposition-led demonstrations in Delhi and other parts of the country.

The opposition contends that GATT will undermine local production in sectors such as pharmaceuticals, and lead to higher prices, which will hit the poor hardest. Aware of the potential impact of this on their vote among the poor, the C(I) announced further spending for agricultural development to tackle rural poverty in the 1994 budget.

PROFILE

Prime Minister Narasimha Rao became leader of the C(I) following the assassination of Rajiv Gandhi. He was only the second leader of India's main party not to be related to the Nehru dynasty. In the state elections of 1993, he consolidated his rule by recapturing Madhya Pradesh and the Himalayan state of Himachal Pradesh. The wins also represented the first reversal since the early 1980s for the Hindu nationalist BJP. C(I) lost ground, however, in Rājasthān and Uttar Pradesh.

C(I) continues to be the most influential party in India. It traces its origins back to the 1930s, when it was an umbrella group, with a left-of-centre stance, fighting for independence. C(I) has retained its broad appeal and its members encompass businessmen as well as the poorer castes. It is the only party with a structure that allows it to organize on a national basis down to village level. Under Indira Gandhi, it adopted popular nationalization policies, yet also maintained close links with the urban capitalist elite. Rao has reshaped the party's philosophy, offering a 'new vision' of the market-led open economy. Coalitions have taken power from C(I), but they rarely manage to retain it for long. State communist governments are in power in Kerala, West Bengal and Andhra Pradesh.

P V Narasimha Rao, prime minister and leader of the ruling C(I).

President Shankar Dayal Sharma, who took office in July 1992.

Manmohan Singh, finance minister and architect of India's liberalization.

WORLD AFFAIRS

Delhi's overriding pre-occupation in foreign policy is the divided territory of Kashmir. Disputes with Pakistan sparked two bloody wars, in 1948 and 1965. Pakistan wishes to annex largely Muslim Kashmir, and believes it would receive the support of the Kashmiri population. India is unwilling to hold a referendum or to cede any territory. The USA sees Kashmir as a potential nuclear flashpoint. It is promoting a settlement on the basis that both states limit their nuclear arsenals. However, India will not discuss nuclear weapons. It regards the Nuclear Non-proliferation Treaty as an instance of first world discrimination. Indo-US relations have recently been strained following Washington's delivery of nearly 40 F-16 jets to Pakistan, in return for a cap on its nuclear programme. Relations with Beijing are now cordial.

AID

 $1.7bn (receipts)   Up 4% in 1991

India receives aid, but, unlike other countries in the region, is not dependent on it. Receipts have largely been spent on building infrastructure. The World Bank recently pulled out of the Narmada Dam project following a long campaign by environmentalists.

DEFENCE

 $6.8bn   Down 12% in 1992

0   Defence spending as % GDP   40
2.9%

INDIAN ARMED FORCES

	3800 main battle tanks (800 T–55/1300 T–72 1700 *Vijayanta*)	1.1m personnel
	2 carriers, 5 destroyers 21 frigates and 39 patrol boats	55,000 personnel
	674 combat aircraft (80 *Jaguar* IS/MiG–21 MiG–23/MiG–29)	110,000 personnel
	Nuclear capability	

India has an army of over one million men, making it the fourth largest in the world. Included in its arsenal is the recently displayed *Prithvi* missile. However, cuts in defence are forecast as the defence budget is squeezed. Much of India's foreign weaponry is outdated. Ageing MiG-21s, which form a central part of the air force, are unlikely to be replaced. India produces its own *Arjun* battle tank.

ECONOMICS

 $285bn   31.37 Indian rupees

SCORE CARD

❑ WORLD GNP RANKING	15th
❑ GNP PER CAPITA	$324
❑ BALANCE OF PAYMENTS	$–3bn
❑ INFLATION	9%
❑ UNEMPLOYMENT	Widespread underemployment

EXPORTS

IMPORTS

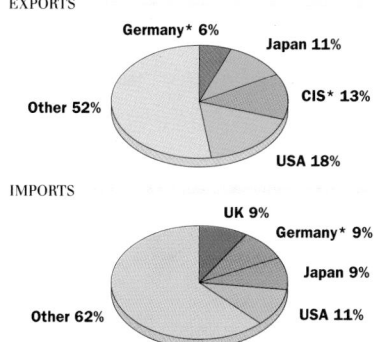

STRENGTHS

Massive home market of over 800 million people. Cheap labour. Some of the workforce possess skills for new high-tech industries such as software programming. Highly efficient textile sector and garment manufacturers. Growing competitiveness on world market reflected in high export growth – up 20% in 1993. Competition is encouraging firms to manufacture to international standards.

There has been a massive rise in foreign direct investment as the economy is opened up to foreign competition; $5 billion worth of investment has been approved by government since 1991, including $3 billion in 1993. Much of this will go into the power sector. Large multinationals, such as Coca-Cola and IBM, who left in 1977 rather than dilute their equity holdings, are returning.

WEAKNESSES

Inflation rate up to 9% in 1993. Budget deficit estimated to reach 7% for the year 1993–1994. Cuts in food and industrial subsidies aimed at reducing budget deficit have added to inflationary pressure. Analysts predict inflation may soon reach double figures, and could climb higher with poor monsoon rains. Poor roads, ports and telecommunications systems and power shortages are a brake on economic growth. Mass unemployment and underemployment; urban unemployed estimated to be 37 million.

PROFILE

India's economy is undergoing radical changes. From a highly protectionist

ECONOMIC PERFORMANCE INDICATOR

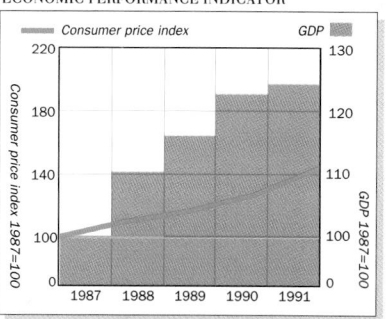

mixed economy, which succeeded in building the basis of a modern industrial state, India has converted to a free market economy and is entering the global marketplace. A series of wide-ranging reforms, from lowering trade barriers to attracting foreign investment, have been put firmly in place. Despite strong objections from opposition parties, India will soon ratify the GATT world trade agreement.

I

INDIA : MAJOR BUSINESSES

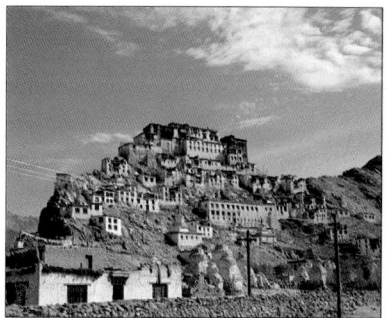

Hillside monastery in Ladakh, Kashmir, northern India. *The Ladakhi Buddhists maintain their traditional farming existence and are known for their friendliness.*

RESOURCES

 286bn kwh (capacity 75.9m kw)

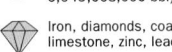 605,500 b/d (reserves 6,049,068,000 bbl)

195.5m cattle, 53.4m sheep, 10.3m pigs

Iron, diamonds, coal, limestone, zinc, lead

ELECTRICITY GENERATION

Hydro 23% (66.1bn kwh)
Thermal 75% (213.9bn kwh)
Nuclear 2% (6.1bn kwh)
Other 0%

0   20   40   60   80   100
% of total generation by type

ENVIRONMENT

4% (3% partially protected)

Forestry programmes are largely funded through foreign aid

ENVIRONMENTAL TREATIES

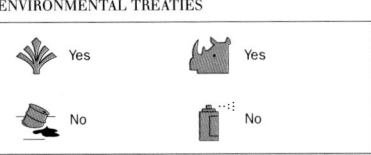

Yes   Yes

No   No

Deforestation is one of India's most pressing environmental problems. Unplanned industrial development and the pressure for more agricultural land have felled once lush tree cover and less than 11% of original forest cover remains. The effect has been a sharp rise in soil erosion, the silting up of dams, and landslides. India experienced its worst environmental accident in 1984, when an explosion at the Union Carbide plant in Bhopāl led to an escape of lethal gases. Over 2000 died.

MEDIA

 Some censorship of the press. Western TV soaps and films widely considered unsuitable

PUBLISHING AND BROADCAST MEDIA

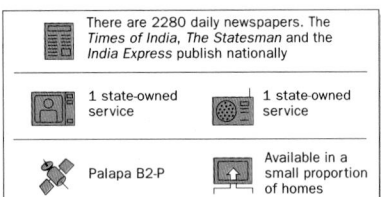

There are 2280 daily newspapers. The *Times of India*, *The Statesman* and the *India Express* publish nationally

1 state-owned service

1 state-owned service

Palapa B2-P

Available in a small proportion of homes

Satellite TV is increasingly popular in India. Services range from the BBC World Service to CNN, Hindi language Zee TV and MTV, and one state-run channel. In just two years, seven million households have acquired dishes. State-run terrestrial TV has suffered as a result. Critics fear a potential Western onslaught on Indian values. Recent newspaper launches include the *Asian Age*, which is simultaneously published in London by satellite and claims to be India's first truly international paper.

India's most significant mineral exports are iron ore and cut diamonds. There are, in addition, large coal reserves. The steel industry has recently been opened up in line with the free market reforms. Steel imports are now subject to lower duties, but the industry has so far withstood external competition, and exports have increased. However, production, which consumes up to twice as much energy as that used by some foreign competitors, is inefficient by international standards.

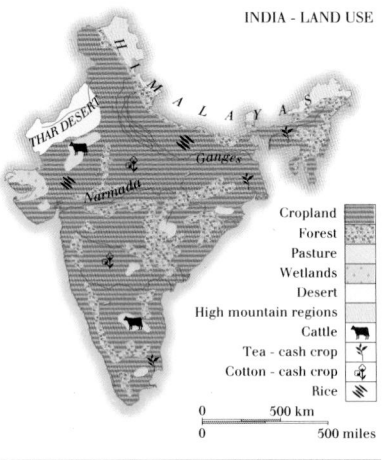

INDIA - LAND USE

Cropland
Forest
Pasture
Wetlands
Desert
High mountain regions
Cattle
Tea - cash crop
Cotton - cash crop
Rice

0   500 km
0   500 miles

CRIME

One of the lowest incarceration rates in the world

Crime rates rising significantly

CRIME RATES

Murders
4   per 100,000 population

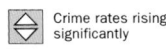
Rapes
1   per 100,000 population

Thefts
49   per 100,000 population

Violent crime is on the increase, particularly in the big cities. Theft has risen sharply as consumer spending increases.

Many violent criminal gangs operating in major cities such as Bombay have made vast profits from smuggling, prostitution, drugs, protection and extortion rackets, and forcibly taking land from the poor. Bombay's gangs have strong connections with Dubai and the Middle East; they are also said to have contacts among politicians and the police.

In large areas of central India and particularly in the region around Gwalior, *dacoits* still operate. Modelled on the *thugee* gangs of the 19th century, they are outlaws who live by highway robbery and terrorizing small rural communities.

The state is currently unable to meet the country's demand for electricity. Petroleum and coal are the main sources of energy generation; however, much of these are imported. In summer, cities face acute power shortages and frequent power cuts. Attempts have been made to improve the efficiency of existing stations, and the government is planning to increase capacity by another 31,000 MW by 1997. A scheme has also been launched to attract large-scale private investment in the industry.

EDUCATION

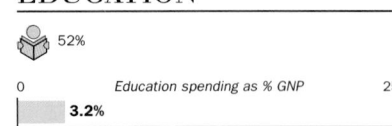 52%

0   Education spending as % GNP   25
3.2%

THE EDUCATION SYSTEM

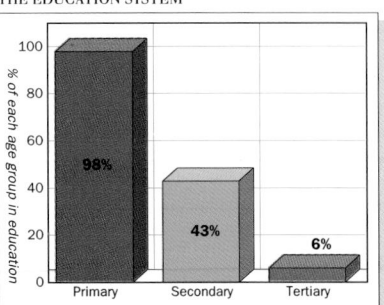

100
% of each age group in education
80
60
40
20
0

98%   Primary
43%   Secondary
6%   Tertiary

There is now a primary school in every village across the subcontinent. However, many children drop out of school to provide supplementary income for their families. There are 50 million students at secondary level, and some 10 million graduates from nearly 200 universities. Women make up 9% of those enrolled in higher education, a high percentage for a low-income economy. India has one of the largest pools of science graduates anywhere in the world. However, the 48% illiteracy rate among adults is a significant brake on development.

Maize cultivation in terraced fields in central India. In addition to rice, wheat, sorghum, maize, millet and barley are also important cereal crops.

REGIONS

WEST BENGAL

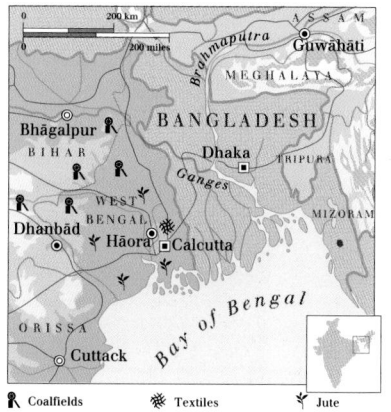

Coalfields   **Textiles**   **Jute**

WEST BENGAL is the only region in the world with a freely elected communist government. The communists have ruled the state since 1978. Once home to 80% of the country's industry, West Bengal then became synonymous with economic decline and stagnation. However, the government has now revolutionized its economic policy, welcoming once-hated multinationals in key sectors.

Calcutta, the capital of the British Raj until 1911, has been in slow decline ever since. Over 20% of the city's 12 million people live in appalling slum conditions. Mother Theresa runs her famous mission in the city.

KARNATAKA

BANGALORE, THE CAPITAL of Karnataka, has earned itself the name of the 'silicon plateau'. Reputed to be South Asia's fastest growing city, it is the home of a burgeoning electronics industry. A large pool of skilled engineering staff and comparatively low wage rates have attracted many foreign, particularly US, firms to the city.

The rich forest areas of Karnataka, particularly in the Western Ghats, include rare tracts of moist tropical deciduous forest. Vast acreages of eucalyptus trees have been planted, but most of these have been used for industrial purposes rather than to alleviate the fuelwood crisis faced by the rural poor.

Heavy industry exclusion zone   Heavy industry

Aerospace industry   Electronics   Textiles

BOMBAY

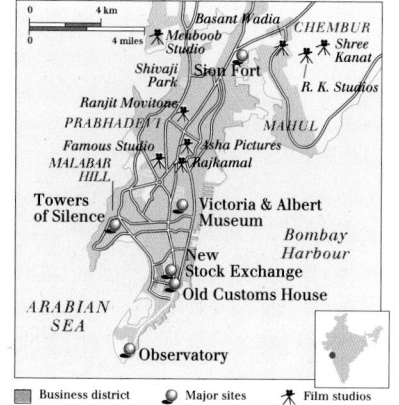

Business district   Major sites   Film studios

BOMBAY IS THE SYMBOL of 1990s India, with a reputation for making people rich, legally or illegally. Fast moving, cosmopolitan and rapidly expanding, it is the country's commercial capital. Central Bombay, a mixture of skyscrapers and English colonial architecture, boasts some of the highest real estate prices in the world. Dalal Street is home to the Bombay Stock Exchange, which was set up in 1875. One of the city's folk heroes is Harshad Mehta, who made a fortune selling stocks and shares in the early 1990s, before being exposed as the man behind India's biggest-ever financial fraud.

Bombay is the centre of India's film industry, which is the world's biggest producer of feature films. Indian films are exported to over 100 countries. The stars of what is known as 'Bollywood', India's Hollywood, live in the affluent Malabar Hills neighbourhood. Yet, beside this, there is also mass poverty. A 4.5 km sprawl of shanties known as Dharavi in central Bombay is reputed to be the world's biggest slum.

HEALTH

1 per 2400 people   Respiratory, nutritional and diarrheal diseases, malaria

0   *Health spending as % GNP*   25

0.8%

Malnutrition is common among the poor, and infant mortality stands at 90 per 1000 live births. Much of this is due to preventable diseases such as diarrhea. AIDS began to spread in the mid-1980s and is now accelerating. HIV infection rates among prostitutes have increased twentyfold in seven years. A five-year programme aimed at raising awareness and improving blood banks is being funded by the World Bank.

WEALTH

Field crop worker, 7–33 Indian rupees per day; office clerk, 380–875 Indian rupees per month

CONSUMER GOODS OWNERSHIP

Per 1000 population — 1000, 750, 500, 250, 0

27   3   6   4   PCs limited to an elite

According to the government, 240 million people (30% of the population), mostly in rural areas, were living below the poverty line in the late 1980s. Recent studies dispute whether this figure is rising or falling. Extremes of wealth, particularly with the opening up of the economy, are frequently seen alongside extremes of poverty. The middle class, who number some 150–200 million, have an exceedingly comfortable lifestyle, with servants and plush housing. Many of the slums in cities such as Bombay and Calcutta have five to nine people living in one room; few slum houses have sanitation. In Bombay alone, over 100,000 people live on the pavements.

WORLD RANKING

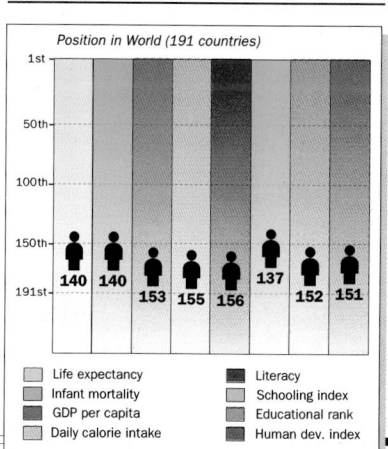

Position in World (191 countries)

1st, 50th, 100th, 150th, 191st

140   140   153   155   156   137   152   151

Life expectancy   Literacy
Infant mortality   Schooling index
GDP per capita   Educational rank
Daily calorie intake   Human dev. index

INDONESIA

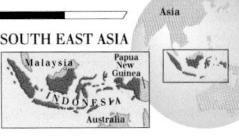

SOUTH EAST ASIA

OFFICIAL NAME: Republic of Indonesia   **CAPITAL:** Jakarta
POPULATION: 191.2 million   **CURRENCY:** Rupiah   **OFFICIAL LANGUAGE:** Bahasa Indonesia

THE WORLD'S LARGEST ARCHIPELAGO, Indonesia's myriad islands stretch 5000 km eastwards across the Pacific, from the Malay Peninsula to New Guinea. The main islands of Sumatra, Java, Kalimantan, Irian Jaya and Sulawesi are mountainous, volcanic and densely forested. Formerly the Dutch East Indies, Indonesia achieved independence in 1949. Politics has since been dominated by the military. Demands for greater autonomy on outlying islands and for liberation by East Timor, annexed in 1975, have been forcefully opposed.

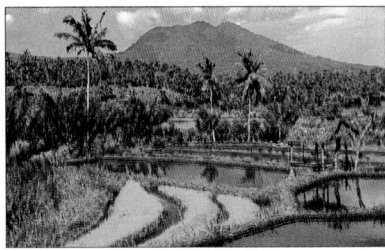

Rice terraces on Bali, one of Indonesia's 13,677 islands and its most popular tourist destination. Rice is the staple food crop.

CLIMATE

WEATHER CHART

Indonesia's climate is predominantly tropical monsoon. Variations relate mainly to differences in latitude and physical structure, but hilly areas are cooler overall. Rain falls throughout the year, often in thunderstorms, but there is a relatively dry season from June to September. December to March is the wettest period, except in the Moluccas, which receive the bulk of their rain between June and September. Rainfall averages between 150 cm and 400 cm a year.

COMMUNICATIONS

Sukarno-Hatta, Jakarta
7.53m passengers

810 ships
2.96m dwt

THE TRANSPORT NETWORK

214,030 km
(132,996 miles)

None

6708 km
(4168 miles)

21,579 km
(13,409 miles)

With 13,677 islands spread across nearly 5000 km and three time zones, communications are an obvious government priority. Indonesia was an early entrant into satellite communications and a countrywide, satellite-based telephone system is being installed.

Indonesia's road and shipping infrastructure is also being improved. Ports are being extended and motorway projects include the Jakarta–Bandung link. The toll roads around Jakarta are contracted to President Suharto's daughter, Siti.

TOURISM

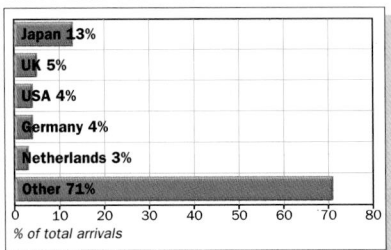

3.1m visitors

Up 20% in 1992

MAIN OVERSEAS ARRIVALS

Japan 13%	
UK 5%	
USA 4%	
Germany 4%	
Netherlands 3%	
Other 71%	

% of total arrivals

Tourism has taken off since the mid-1980s. The number of visitors increased by an average 24% a year between 1986 and 1992, to over three million. Bali, Java and Sumatra are the most popular destinations. The expansion has been underpinned by several factors, including a major investment in hotels and the opening of Bali to airlines other than the national carrier, *Garuda Indonesia.*

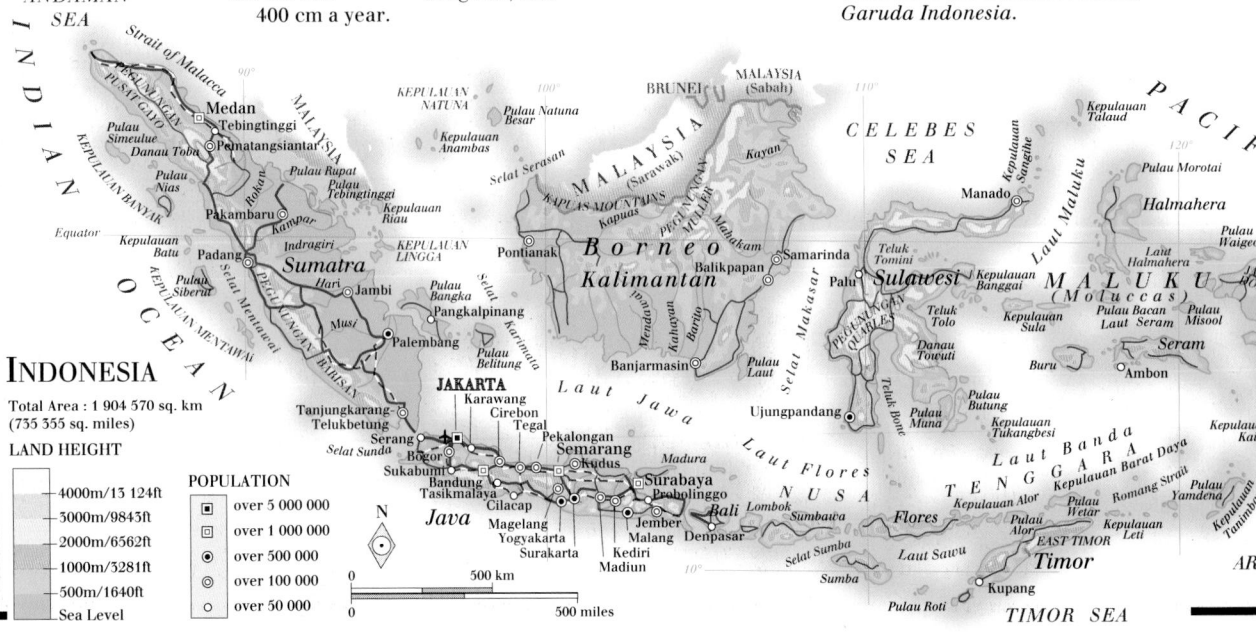

INDONESIA

Total Area : 1 904 570 sq. km
(735 355 sq. miles)

LAND HEIGHT

- 4000m/13 124ft
- 3000m/9843ft
- 2000m/6562ft
- 1000m/3281ft
- 500m/1640ft
- Sea Level

POPULATION

- ▣ over 5 000 000
- ▣ over 1 000 000
- ◉ over 500 000
- ◉ over 100 000
- ○ over 50 000

I

PEOPLE

Javanese, Madurese, Sundanese, Bahasa Indonesia, Dutch

94 people per km²

THE URBAN/RURAL POPULATION SPLIT

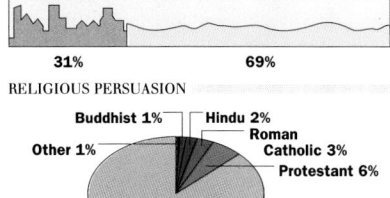

31%   69%

RELIGIOUS PERSUASION

Buddhist 1% | Hindu 2%
Roman Catholic 3%
Other 1%
Protestant 6%
Muslim 87%

ETHNIC MAKEUP

Madurese 8%
Malays 8%
Javanese 45%
Sundanese 14%
Other 25%

Indonesia's basic Melanesian–Malay ethnic division disguises a very diverse society. At least 250 languages or dialects are spoken. Urbanization and the national language, Bahasa Indonesia, have acted as unifying factors. The Javanese-dominated central government, however, has caused much resentment by attempting to suppress local culture and politics in order to create a national identity. The East Timoreans, the Aceh of northern Sumatra and the Papuans of Irian Jaya, denied autonomy, are all in conflict with the government.

Discrimination against the Chinese community, which has included a ban on Chinese script, has not undermined its dominance of big business.

The traditional extended family is breaking down in urban areas. There is legal sexual equality, and women are taking an increasingly active economic role – led by President Suharto's wife and daughter, both engaged in business.

POPULATION AGE BREAKDOWN

% of population by age group	0–14	15–64			65+
	3.3%	3.1%	3.3%	3.9%	5.1%
	56.6%	54.7%	55.7%	60.4%	63.6%
	40.1%	42.2%	41%	35.7%	31.3%
	1960	1970	1980	1990	2000

POLITICS

 1997
 President Gen Suharto

THE STATE OF THE PARTIES

House of Representatives 500 members

57% SG | 12% PPP | 11% PDI | 20% ABRI

SG = Joint Secretariat of Functional Groups **PPP** = United Development Party **PDI** = Indonesian Democratic Party **ABRI** = Indonesian Armed Forces (appointed members)

People's Consultative Assembly 1000 members

50% House of Representatives | 50% Others

500 members of House of Representatives and 500 further members, including delegates from regional assemblies and representatives of political organizations

Indonesia is a highly-controlled semi-democracy, headed by General Suharto, who was returned for his sixth consecutive term as president in 1993.

MAIN POLITICAL ISSUE

The succession
President Suharto will be almost 77 by the next elections, and is under pressure to ensure a peaceful transition. Vice-president Try Sutrisno appears to be the military's choice, but may not be Suharto's. A key factor in his decision is expected to be the protection of his children and their extensive economic interests.

PROFILE

Indonesia's elections are invariably won by the SG, a group representing farmers, fishermen and the professions, rather than a political party. The SG is dominated by President Suharto and the armed forces. There have been only two legal opposition parties since 1972, the Muslim-dominated United Development Party (PPP) and the Christian-orientated Indonesian Democratic Party (PDI). In practice, these operate as ineffective 'partners' of government. Opposition to the Javan political elite and its centralist politics has fuelled secessionist movements in Sumatra and Irian Jaya and a liberation movement on East Timor, annexed by Indonesia in 1975.

***General Suharto,** ex-army chief of staff. President since 1968.*

***Mrs Suharto,** influential in political and business circles.*

WORLD AFFAIRS

 ASEAN NAM OPEC GATT ADB

Indonesia's foreign policy under General Suharto has been one of non-alignment – it became NAM chairman in 1992 – tempered by the need to retain good relations with the West.

Foreign policy concerns include a continuing suspicion of China, despite the restoration of diplomatic ties in 1990. Indonesia has resolved its differences over the Timor Gap boundary with Australia, and relations have generally improved.

Internationally, the government is coming under pressure, particularly from the USA, to improve its human rights record.

AID

$1.9bn (receipts)   Up 7.5 in 1991

Indonesia relies on aid to cover its current account deficit. Japan accounts for 75% of bilateral aid; the World Bank for 58% of multilateral. Almost 30% of all aid is affected by 'leakage', including project delays and corruption.

CHRONOLOGY

On the trade route between India and China, the Indonesian archipelago, with its rich resources, has long attracted outside interest – Hindu, Buddhist, Islamic, then, from the 16th century, European. The Dutch were victors in the rivalry to exploit its strategic position, valuable spices and oil. Colonization began in the 17th century on Java. By 1910, the Dutch East Indies encompassed the whole of present-day Indonesia, except East Timor.

- **1901** Dutch introduce 'ethical policy' giving limited educational and administrative opportunities to indigenous population; encourages growth of intellectual class with nationalist aspirations.
- **1912** Sarekat Islam party formed.
- **1920** Indonesian Communist Party (PKI) formed; leads revolts in West Java, 1926; Sumatra, 1927.
- **1927** Indonesian National Party formed under Dr Sukarno.
- **1930s** Dutch repression.
- **1942–1945** Japanese occupation. Promise of autonomy in 'Greater East Asia'. Sukarno works with Japanese while promoting independence.
- **1945** August, three days after Japanese surrender, Sukarno declares Indonesia independent from the Netherlands.

I

CHRONOLOGY *continued*

- ❏ **1945–1949** Nationalist guerrilla war with Dutch – interspersed with negotiations – who refuse to recognize independence.
- ❏ **1949** December, independence. United States of Indonesia under President Sukarno: federation, giving limited self-government to regions. Irian Jaya stays under Dutch control until 1962.
- ❏ **1950** Federation dissolved. Unitary Republic of Indonesia.
- ❏ **1950–1957** Six governments, none able to address growing problems. Sukarno convinced country not ready for parliamentary democracy; introduces authoritarian 'guided democracy', then martial law.
- ❏ **1959** Sukarno extends presidential powers. Civilian legislature replaced by military. Extreme nationalist and pro-Chinese policies. A leader of the NAM.
- ❏ **1965** Corruption of Sukarno regime, inflation and breakdown of PKI–military alliance provoke abortive military coup. PKI implicated. Mass killing of alleged PKI supporters. PKI banned.
- ❏ **1966** Sukarno forced to hand over power to army chief-of-staff General Suharto. Temporary handover becomes permanent in following year.
- ❏ **1968** Gen Suharto becomes president. Declares 'New Order': real power passes from cabinet to small group of officers. Sukarno's anti-Western stance reversed; liberal economic policies introduced.
- ❏ **1971** First elections since 1955. Government-sponsored SG wins this and all succeeding elections. Opposition parties now passive partners of government.
- ❏ **1973** Suharto re-elected president; again in 1978, 1983 and 1988.
- ❏ **1975** Indonesia invades East Timor; incorporated as Indonesia's 27th province in 1976. Takeover not recognized by UN.
- ❏ **1984** Muslim protesters clash with troops in Jakarta. Start of resurgence of Islamic protest.
- ❏ **1985** Independence of East Timor declared by FRETILIN liberation front. Repressed by military.
- ❏ **1989** Growing discontent with authoritarian government; student protests, unrest in Java and Sumbawa. Demands for Suharto to retire. Low-key official response.
- ❏ **1991** New organizations, including Democratic Forum and League for Restoration of Democracy, allowed to form in response to growing demands for 'openness'.
- ❏ **1993** Suharto wins sixth term in office.

DEFENCE

$1.7bn   ⬆ Up 6% in 1992

Defence spending as % GDP
0   40
1.3%

INDONESIAN ARMED FORCES

🛡	155 light tanks (125 AMX-13/30 PT-76)	215,000 personnel
🚢	2 submarines, 3 frigates and 48 patrol boats	44,000 personnel
✈	18 combat aircraft (12 N-22 *Searchmaster* B/ 6 *Searchmaster* L)	1000 personnel
	None	

The constitution enshrines the military's political role, and it remains a key influence in Indonesia. The recent 'civilianization' of political parties, the bureaucracy and state companies has reduced the presence of the military in these areas, if not their influence. This was also apparent in the appointment of former supreme commander Try Sutrisno as vice-president, and thus a leading candidate to succeed Suharto. Defence spending is low by regional standards. However, 'off-budget funds' often supplement official allocations. The main defence issues are currently internal security and the perceived Chinese threat.

ECONOMICS

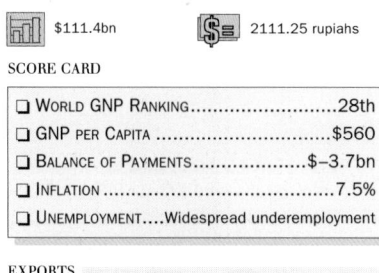

$111.4bn   2111.25 rupiahs

SCORE CARD

- ❏ WORLD GNP RANKING 28th
- ❏ GNP PER CAPITA $560
- ❏ BALANCE OF PAYMENTS....................$−3.7bn
- ❏ INFLATION 7.5%
- ❏ UNEMPLOYMENT....Widespread underemployment

ECONOMIC PERFORMANCE INDICATOR

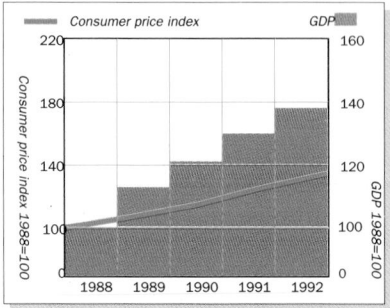

Consumer price index   GDP

EXPORTS

South Korea 5%   Singapore 7%
Japan 43%   USA 13%
Other 32%

IMPORTS

Singapore 6%   Germany* 7%
USA 12%
Other 51%
Japan 24%

STRENGTHS

Varied resources, especially energy. Expansion of manufacturing, including high-tech. Growth of nearly 7% a year. Cheap and plentiful labour.

WEAKNESSES

Red tape; corruption. State control of economy. Competition for investment from China and Vietnam. $85 billion debt burden.

PROFILE

For 25 years, the economy has grown by almost 7% a year, fuelled by foreign investment and oil. State-owned corporations play a significant role in the economy, which is protected against foreign competition. Non-oil exports, especially manufactures, are rapidly diversifying and expanding, but there is concern about the future. Oil revenues are set to decline and competition for investment from Vietnam and China is growing. However, the debt burden eats up 32% of export earnings. Government promises to cut red tape and privatize have yet to be fulfilled, reflecting conflict between advocates of deregulation and the 'technologists' who argue that, in the short term, industrialization is more important than profitable state concerns.

INDONESIA : MAJOR BUSINESSES

🔟	Rubber
⚙	Heavy engineering
◊	Gas
⚗	Chemicals
🌲	Timber industries
	Oil
	Oil refining
	Electronics
	Vehicle assembly
✈	Aerospace industry

0   500 km
0   500 miles

* significant multinational ownership

Medan   Balikpapan   Banjarmasin   Kendari   Sorong   Palembang   Jakarta   Bandung   Surabaya   Ujung Pandang

RESOURCES

 44.3bn kwh (capacity 11.48m kw)

 1.4m b/d (reserves 5,779,000,000 bbl)

 10.3m cattle, 6.6m pigs, 5.5m sheep

Oil, natural gas, tin, bauxite, nickel, copper, gold, coal

ELECTRICITY GENERATION

Hydro 20% (9bn kwh)
Thermal 79% (35.1bn kwh)
Nuclear 0%
Other 1% (210m kwh)

% of total generation by type

INDONESIA : LAND USE

Cropland, Forest, Pasture, Wetlands, Rice, Nutmeg - cash crop, Cattle

0 500 km
0 500 miles

Indonesia is rich in energy sources. Oil, which financed rapid industrialization, and liquefied natural gas – the country is the world's largest LNG exporter – are the main export earners. However, oil output is falling – down 6% in 1992 to 1.4m b/d. Combined with rapid growth in domestic energy demand, this could turn Indonesia into an oil importer in the next decade. The government is therefore encouraging the extension of exploration into remote regions. It is also considering developing geothermal and nuclear energy sources. Indonesia's other main resources are coal, bauxite and nickel, and agricultural products such as rubber and palm oil. With 75% of the land classified as forest, timber production is also significant.

ENVIRONMENT

 10% (3% partially protected)

 Few active restrictions on logging

ENVIRONMENTAL TREATIES

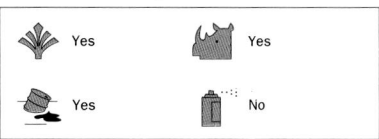

Yes | Yes
Yes | No

Environmental legislation is badly policed and often ignored. The worst problem relates to the protection of Indonesia's rich tropical forests, which are threatened by excessive logging. Some predict the forests could be gone in 30 years. Frequent oil spillages in the Malacca Strait are a major hazard.

MEDIA

 The Indonesian press is relatively free; criticism tends to be coded to avoid official censure

PUBLISHING AND BROADCAST MEDIA

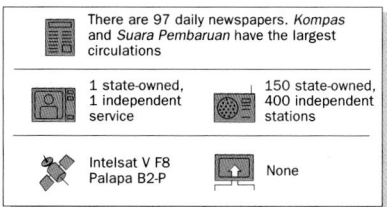

There are 97 daily newspapers. *Kompas* and *Suara Pembaruan* have the largest circulations

1 state-owned, 1 independent service | 150 state-owned, 400 independent stations

Intelsat V F8 Palapa B2-P | None

Media self-censorship encourages a rich rumour-mongering tradition. The daily *Kompas* and the weekly *Tempo* are outstanding among the printed media. President Suharto's children were quick to take advantage of the 1987 decision to open TV to the private sector.

CRIME

 35,000 prisoners (est) Down 6% in 1990

CRIME RATES

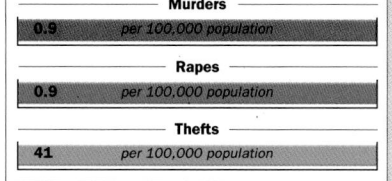

Murders — 0.9 per 100,000 population
Rapes — 0.9 per 100,000 population
Thefts — 41 per 100,000 population

Human rights agencies are concerned at the government's violent reaction to demands for autonomy.

EDUCATION

 77%

0 Education spending as % GNP 25
0.9%

THE EDUCATION SYSTEM

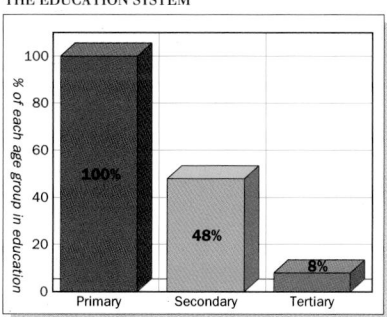

Primary 100%, Secondary 48%, Tertiary 8%

Primary education is compulsory. Secondary schooling is expanding, but is still limited in rural areas.

HEALTH

 1 per 7372 people | Lower respiratory and diarrheal diseases

0 Health spending as % GNP 25
0.5%

Hospitals are relatively few; about half are privately administered. However, the extensive network of clinics, down to village level, means access to health care is reasonable. As a result, health indicators have improved significantly over the past 20 years. The death rate declined from 20 per 1000 in 1965 to 9 per 1000 in 1990, helping to increase life expectancy to 62 years. Infant mortality more than halved, from 128 to 61 per 1000 live births, over the same period.

WEALTH

 Agricultural worker, 100,000 rupiahs per month; engineer, 1.5m rupiahs per month

CONSUMER GOODS OWNERSHIP

PCs are limited to an elite

55 | 7 | 5 | 8

Despite its oil wealth and the rapid industrialization and improvements in agricultural productivity of the past 30 years, Indonesia is still grouped among the low-income economies by the World Bank. Health and education have improved, but many Indonesians live in relative poverty, and those on the peripheral islands, notably Irian Jaya, northern Sumatra and East Timor, live in real poverty. This reflects both a concentration of wealth in the hands of a limited number of key political and business figures, and the concentration of development and investment on the main islands, particularly on Java.

WORLD RANKING

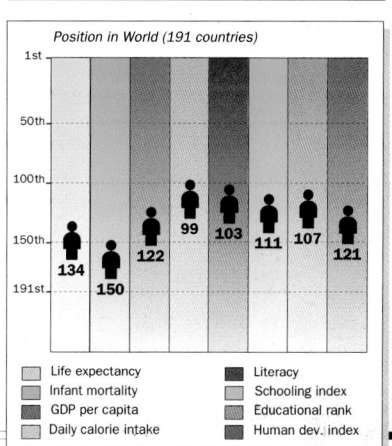

Position in World (191 countries)

134 | 150 | 122 | 99 | 103 | 111 | 107 | 121

Life expectancy, Infant mortality, GDP per capita, Daily calorie intake, Literacy, Schooling index, Educational rank, Human dev. index

279

IRAN

OFFICIAL NAME: Islamic Republic of Iran   **CAPITAL:** Tehran
POPULATION: 61.6 million   **CURRENCY:** Iranian rial   **OFFICIAL LANGUAGE:** Farsi

IRAN IS SURROUNDED by powerful neighbours, with republics of the former Soviet Union to the north, Afghanistan and Pakistan to the east and Iraq and Turkey to the west. The south faces the Persian Gulf and the Gulf of Oman. Since 1979, when a revolution led by Ayatollah Khomeini deposed the Shah, Iran has become the world's largest theocracy and the leading centre for militant Shi'a Islam. Iran's active support for Islamic fundamentalist movements has led to strained relations with Central Asian, Middle Eastern and North African nations, as well as the USA.

The Reshteh-ye Kuhhā-ye Alborz (Elburz Mountains). Their Caspian Sea slopes are rainy and forested; the southern slopes are dry.

CLIMATE

WEATHER CHART

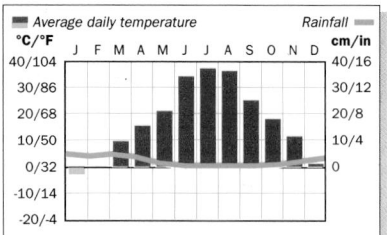

The area bordering the Caspian Sea is Iran's most temperate region. Most of the country has a desert climate.

COMMUNICATIONS

Mehrabad International, Tehran
1.16m passengers

184 ships
828,700 dwt

THE TRANSPORT NETWORK

139,368 km
(86,599 miles)

490 km
(304 miles)

4601 km
(2859 miles)

130 km
(81 miles)

Adequate roads link main towns, but rural areas are less well served. Most freight travels by rail. A ferry runs from Bandar-e 'Abbās to the UAE.

TOURISM

153,615 visitors

Up 72% in 1990

MAIN OVERSEAS ARRIVALS

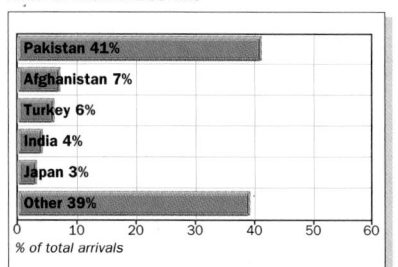

Iran's impressive historical heritage, mosques and bazaars formerly attracted sizeable numbers of tourists. This flow was cut off by the 1979 revolution. Since then, adverse publicity for the regime has deterred visitors, especially from the West. In the 1990s, however, the number of business people visiting Iran has risen as the regime shows clear signs of wishing to improve its international relations. Procedures at Tehran's Mehrabad airport have been greatly speeded up and the capital's hotels have undergone some restoration.

PEOPLE

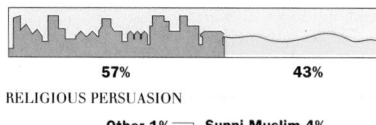

Farsi (Persian), Azerbaijani, Gilaki, Mazanderani, Kurdish, Baluchi, Arabic, Turkmen

33 people per km²

THE URBAN/RURAL POPULATION SPLIT

57%   43%

RELIGIOUS PERSUASION

Other 1%   Sunni Muslim 4%

Shi'a Muslim 95%

ETHNIC MAKEUP

Other 7%   Gilaki and Mazandarani 8%

Kurd 9%

Persian 51%

Azeri 25%

The population comprises several ethnic groups. The people of the north and centre – about half of all Iranians – speak Farsi (Persian), while a further 25% speak related languages, including Kurdish in the west and Baluchi in the southeast. About a quarter of the population speaks Turkic languages, primarily the Azeris in the northwest and the Turkmen in the northeast. Smaller groups, such as the Circassians and Georgians, are found in the northern provinces.

Until the 16th century, much of Iran followed the Sunni interpretation of Islam, but since then the Shi'a sect has been dominant. Religious minorities, accounting for just 1% of the population, include followers of the Bahai faith, who suffer discrimination, Zoroastrians, Christians and Jews.

Because of the religious idealism that inspires much of Iran's political decision-making, the regime has a remarkably liberal attitude to refugees of the Muslim faith. There are nearly three million Afghan refugees scattered through 24 provinces. In Khorosan province in the east, refugees account for 23% of the population, and near the Turkish border the figure rises to 50%. Many are young, resulting in intense competition with Iranians for jobs and consequent ethnic tensions.

One of the prime aims of the 1979 Islamic revolution was to reverse the policy of female emancipation, introduced during the Shah's rule. The revolution abruptly restricted the public role of women, limiting job prospects to the medical profession and teaching. A strict dress code was enforced, obliging women to wear the ankle-length *hijab* and keep their heads covered with a scarf. However, more liberal attitudes often prevail in private, especially in affluent homes.

POPULATION AGE BREAKDOWN

	0–14	15–64	65+
1960	44.8% / 51% / 4.2%		
1970	45.9% / 50.6% / 3.5%		
1980	44.4% / 52.2% / 3.4%		
1990	43.9% / 52.4% / 3.7%		
2000	38.6% / 57% / 4.4%		

I

POLITICS

 1996

 President Ali Akbar Hashemi Rafsanjani

THE STATE OF THE PARTIES

Consultative Assembly (*Majlis*) 270 members

All members are elected on a non-party basis

Iran is a theocracy. An uneasy relationship exists between the mullahs (their leader exercises supreme authority, in theory) and the secular authorities, headed by an elected president.

MAIN POLITICAL ISSUE

Mosque versus secular state

The precise division of power between the mullahs and the secular state remains ill-defined. Edicts contradicting secular policy are often issued. The result is a tussle over how to run a modern economy between the conservative clergy on the one hand,

***Ayatollah Khomeini**, architect of the revolution, who died in 1989.*

***President Rafsanjani**, Iran's secular leader since 1989.*

and members of the assembly (*Majlis*) and reformist politicians, led by President Rafsanjani, on the other.

The mullahs remain less concerned about the effects of stagnation than the secular authorities, believing that the people's adherence to religious values is more important than their economic or material welfare. President Rafsanjani has sought to modernize the economy gradually. However, with mullahs objecting to the use of borrowed money and the import of 'corrupt' Western technology, economic growth in Iran has become rather erratic.

PROFILE

Iran's religious revolution, which brought down the monarchy, was fuelled by an underprivileged people outraged at the corruption, repression and inequalities of the Shah's regime. Ayatollah Khomeini proved an effective leader of Iranian dissatisfaction. Iran's government is based on Khomeini's belief that it is the duty of the clergy, as the Prophet Mohammed's trustees on earth, to establish a just social system. Accordingly, the legislature, the executive and the judiciary may, in theory, be overruled by the religious leadership. President Rafsanjani's policies are constantly questioned by Ahmad Khomeini, son of the late Ayatollah, and by former ministers who believe in 'permanent revolution' and approve of international terrorism. The mullahs remain popular among many Iranians, limiting the secular state's policy-making freedom.

WORLD AFFAIRS

 OPEC   OIC   NAM   ESCAP   CP

Following the Khomeini revolution, Iran assumed international significance as the voice of militant Shi'a Islam. This was exemplified by the 1989 Salman Rushdie affair, in which Khomeini issued a *fatwa* (edict) demanding the death of the British novelist for blasphemy. Iran has attempted to foster revolution among the Shi'a minority in Saudi Arabia and has also extended its influence to the republics of the former Soviet Union, as well as to Sudan, Algeria, Egypt and Lebanon. The West views Iran's export of Islamic revolution with anxiety, but also sees the country as a buffer against Iraqi President Saddam Hussein's expansionist ambitions.

Iran's role in the Gulf has also caused controversy. Moderate Arab states were alarmed by the seizure of the islands of Abu Musa and the Tumbs from the UAE in 1970. Iran's main preoccupation, however, is Iraq, which allows *mujahideen* guerrillas to mount attacks on Iran from its territory.

IRAN

Total Area : 1 648 000 sq. km
(636 293 sq. miles)

POPULATION

- ▣ over 1 000 000
- ◉ over 500 000
- ◎ over 100 000
- ○ over 50 000

LAND HEIGHT

- 3000m/9843ft
- 2000m/6562ft
- 1000m/3281ft
- 500m/1640ft
- 200m/656ft
- Sea Level

N

0   200 km

0   200 miles

CHRONOLOGY

Iran (Persia) was ruled by the Shahs as an absolute monarchy until 1906 when the first constitution was approved. The Pahlavis took power in 1925 and changed the country's name to Iran in 1935.

- ❑ **1957** SAVAK, Shah's secret police, established to control opposition.
- ❑ **1964** Ayatollah Khomeini exiled for criticisms of secular state.
- ❑ **1971** Shah celebrates 2500th anniversary of Persian monarchy.
- ❑ **1975** Long-running dispute over access to Shatt Al Arab waterway settled with Iraq.
- ❑ **1977** Khomeini's son dies. Anti-Shah demonstrations during mourning.
- ❑ **1978** Riots and strikes. Khomeini exiled from Iraq to Paris.
- ❑ **1979** January, rising discontent; Shah goes into exile. February, Ayatollah Khomeini returns in triumph from exile in France. Islamic Revolutionary Council takes power. April, Iran declared Islamic republic. November, students seize 63 hostages at US Embassy in Tehran and demand Shah's return to face trial.
- ❑ **1980** Shah dies in exile. Start of eight-year Iran–Iraq war. Iraq invades, annulling 1975 Shatt Al Arab waterway agreement.
- ❑ **1981** US hostages released. Hojatoleslam Ali Khamenei elected president by huge majority.
- ❑ **1984** Iran captures part of marshlands around southern Iraqi island of Majnoun.
- ❑ **1985** Khamenei re-elected.
- ❑ **1986** UN Security Council blames Iraq for war with Iran.
- ❑ **1987** Around 275 Iranian pilgrims killed in riots in Mecca; relations with Saudi Arabia break down.
- ❑ **1988** July, *USS Vincennes* shoots down Iranian airliner; 290 killed. August, Iran–Iraq war ends with UN-arranged ceasefire.
- ❑ **1989** February, Khomeini issues *fatwa* condemning Salman Rushdie to death for blasphemy in his novel *The Satanic Verses*. June, Khomeini dies. President Ali Khamenei appointed Supreme Religious Leader. Hashemi Rafsanjani elected president.
- ❑ **1990** Earthquake hits northern provinces, killing 45,000 people. Gulf War – Iran remains neutral.
- ❑ **1991** Iranian diplomacy helps free Western hostages in Lebanon.
- ❑ **1992** *Majlis* elections result in two thirds support for president.
- ❑ **1993** *Fatwa* against Salman Rushdie reconfirmed. Rafsanjani re-elected president.

AID

 $81m (receipts) ⬆ Up 17% in 1991

As an oil exporter, Iran does not qualify for much aid. In addition, hardliners are opposed to Western aid – even in the face of disasters such as the 1990 earthquake. However, Iran receives some UN aid for its millions of refugees, who are mainly from Afghanistan, but also from Iraq, Sudan, Sri Lanka, Egypt, Palestine and India. Iran fosters the spread of Shi'a Islam by making donations for mosque building all over the world.

DEFENCE

 $4.3bn ⬆ Up 34% in 1991

Defence spending as % GDP — **7.1%**

With 528,000 men under arms, including the Revolutionary Guard Corps (*Pasdaran*), and battle experience from the war with Iraq, Iran represents a serious threat to neighbouring states. The *Pasdaran* form one third of personnel and often act as a paramilitary force to safeguard moral and behavioural standards set by the mullahs. They were used in mass frontal assaults in the war with Iraq.

IRANIAN ARMED FORCES

🚜	700 main battle tanks (T–54,–55/Ch T–59/T–62 T–72/*Chieftain* Mk3,-5)	305,000 personnel
🚢	3 destroyers, 5 frigates, 1 submarine and 33 patrol boats	18,000 personnel
✈	262 combat aircraft (60 F–4D,-E/60 F–5E,-F 60 F–14/30 MiG–29)	35,000 personnel
🚀	None	

The navy has been weakened by clashes with Iraq and the USA. Two years' military service is compulsory.

ECONOMICS

 $127.4bn 1750.00 Iranian rials

SCORE CARD

- ❑ WORLD GNP RANKING..........................24th
- ❑ GNP PER CAPITA $2068
- ❑ BALANCE OF PAYMENTS....................$–8.1bn
- ❑ INFLATION 22.9%
- ❑ UNEMPLOYMENT................................25%

EXPORTS

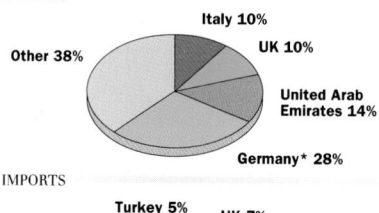

Italy 10%
UK 10%
United Arab Emirates 14%
Germany* 28%
Other 38%

IMPORTS

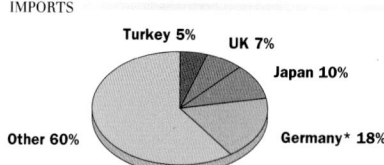

Turkey 5%
UK 7%
Japan 10%
Germany* 18%
Other 60%

STRENGTHS

OPEC's second-biggest oil producer. Potential for related industries and increased production of traditional exports: carpets, pistachio nuts and caviar.

WEAKNESSES

Theocratic government restricts contact with West, blocking acquisition of vital technology. Years of economic stagnation. High unemployment, inflation and foreign debts. Oil revenue vulnerable to market fluctuations.

ECONOMIC PERFORMANCE INDICATOR

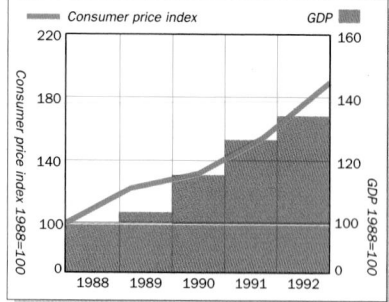

Consumer price index — GDP

PROFILE

Iran has few industries other than oil. The chronic shortage of foreign exchange and the costs of the long war with Iraq have accelerated a decline in living standards in the past decade.

IRAN : MAJOR BUSINESSES

Tehran, Mashad, Tabrīz, Qom, Eşfahān, Ahvāz, Kharg Island, Shirāz, Bandar -e Abbās', Kerman

- 🔘 Cement
- 🏵 Textiles
- 🛢 Oil refining
- ⚙ Engineering
- 🧶 Carpet weaving
- 🍾 Food processing
- ⚗ Petrochemicals/chemicals

0   400 km
0   400 miles

RESOURCES

56bn kwh (capacity 17.5m kw)

3.44m b/d (reserves 92,860,000,000 bbl)

34m sheep, 8m cattle, 1.7m asses

Iron, copper, lead, oil, zinc, chromite, coal, manganese, gypsum

ELECTRICITY GENERATION

Hydro 12% (6.6bn kwh)
Thermal 88% (49.4bn kwh)
Nuclear 0%
Other 0%

% of total generation by type

Iran has substantial oil reserves. It also has metal, coal and salt deposits, but these are relatively undeveloped. The agricultural sector is an important part of Iran's economy. Principal crops are wheat, barley, rice, sugar beet, tobacco and pistachio nuts.

Iran was once an opium exporter, but its cultivation and use has since been banned. The vodka industry has also been closed down. Enough wool is produced to supply the carpet weaving industry. Iran has insufficient livestock to supply the domestic meat market and has to import large quantities. The Caspian Sea fisheries are controlled by the state, which sells caviar for export.

IRAN : LAND USE

Cropland
Forest
Pasture
Wetlands
Desert
Sheep
Wheat
Tobacco

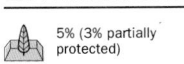

0　　　400 km
0　　　400 miles

ENVIRONMENT

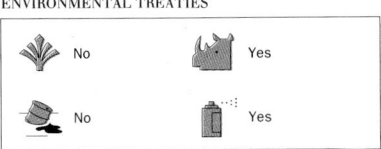

5% (3% partially protected)

Environmental protection is not of state concern

ENVIRONMENTAL TREATIES

No

Yes

No

Yes

War damage to southern Iran, especially at Bandar Khomeini, the tanker terminal at Kharg Island and the refinery at Ābādān, has caused significant environmental damage. Environmental issues are not of concern to the religious leadership.

MEDIA

Censorship was introduced by the stringent Press Law of 1979. Infringement is treated as a criminal offence

PUBLISHING AND BROADCAST MEDIA

Five of the 17 daily newspapers have national circulation. *Kayhan* and *Ettela'a*, controlled by the religious authorities, are the leaders

1 state-run service

1 state-run service

Reception of foreign satellite TV is banned

None

Press freedom has been curbed. Radio and TV are state-controlled and act as a mouthpiece for the revolution. The use of satellite dishes receiving Western programmes has recently been banned.

CRIME

Iran does not publish prison figures

Little change from year to year

CRIME RATES

Iran does not publish crime statistics. However, general crime rates are relatively low

Law and order is often enforced by revolutionary guards. A total of 109 offences carry the death penalty. Executions, of both men and women, are common for political 'crimes'. Religious minorities are persecuted.

Iran is repeatedly accused by Western governments of sponsoring international terrorism. Iran denies these charges.

EDUCATION

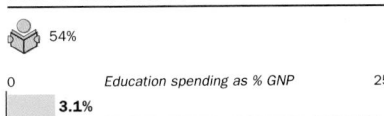

54%

0　　Education spending as % GNP　　25

3.1%

THE EDUCATION SYSTEM

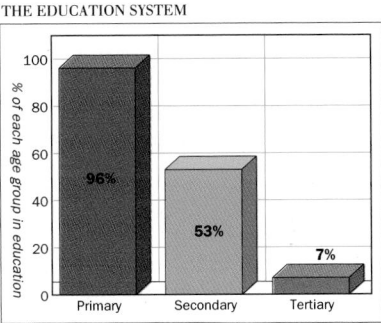

% of each age group in education

96% Primary
53% Secondary
7% Tertiary

Just over half the population is literate. Education in state primary schools and universities is free. Pupils pay small fees for secondary education. There are insufficient teachers to cope with rising student numbers. Most schools have been made single-sex since 1979.

HEALTH

1 per 2821 people

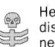

Heart and respiratory diseases, injuries, neonatal deaths

0　　Health spending as % GNP　　25

1.5%

Although an adequate system of primary health care exists in the cities, conditions in rural areas are basic. The major problem facing the nation's health is the fast-growing population. Under Khomeini, producing children became a political and religious duty. The government has now introduced sterilization and contraception programmes. Over 37% of children under seven are malnourished.

WEALTH

The acquisition of private wealth is discouraged

CONSUMER GOODS OWNERSHIP

Per 1000 population

66　35　41　13

PCs limited to a small elite

Since the 1979 revolution, living standards have declined markedly. A shortage of foreign exchange has stifled imports of consumer goods. Rationing, brought in during the war with Iraq, is still partly in force and smuggling from the Arab Gulf states is rife. One in four of the workforce is unemployed. Only one in 26 Iranians possess a telephone. Official figures for income per head do not relate to conditions on the ground. In reality, oil wealth fails to reach the economically deprived. Private business, on which Iran's former prosperity was based, is discouraged by the mullahs who have retained vital industries and services in public ownership.

WORLD RANKING

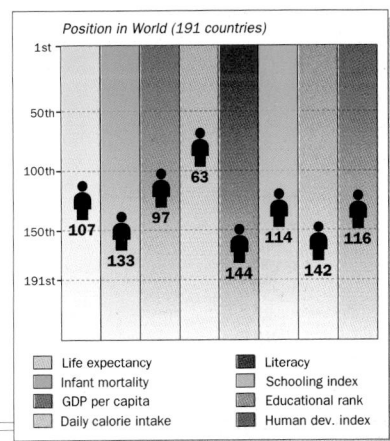

Position in World (191 countries)

1st
50th
100th
150th
191st

63
107　97
133　　144　114　142　116

Life expectancy
Infant mortality
GDP per capita
Daily calorie intake
Literacy
Schooling index
Educational rank
Human dev. index

I

IRAQ

OFFICIAL NAME: Republic of Iraq **CAPITAL:** Baghdad
POPULATION: 19.3 million **CURRENCY:** Iraqi dinar **OFFICIAL LANGUAGE:** Arabic

OIL-RICH IRAQ IS BISECTED by the River Euphrates and shares borders with Iran, Turkey, Syria, Jordan, Saudi Arabia and Kuwait. The fertile Euphrates Valley broadens into marshlands as it approaches the Gulf, but most of the country is desert or mountains. Iraq was the site of the ancient civilization of Babylon. Today, its borders encompass Shi'a Muslim holy shrines. Since the removal of the monarchy in 1958, Iraq has experienced considerable political turmoil. The current regime stays in power through repression.

Golden Mosque at Sāmarrā' on the Tigris. Among the extensive remains of its ancient city are those of the Great Mosque built in AD 847.

CLIMATE

WEATHER CHART

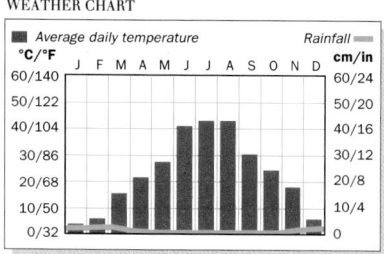

The weather is dry and rainfall is low and unreliable, except in the northeast. Iraq experiences a wide range of temperatures. The south has a desert climate, with hot, dry summers and mild winters. The summers are also dry in the north but in mountainous Iranian and Turkish border regions winters can be harsh, with frost and heavy falls of snow. Sudden hot spells are a unique feature of winter in the centre and north of the country.

COMMUNICATIONS

 Saddam International, Baghdad

 33 ships 136,870 dwt

THE TRANSPORT NETWORK

 25,479 km (15,822 miles)

 None

2032 km (1262 miles)

130 km (81 miles)

Adequate roads link main cities. Railways provide vital arteries for the movement of goods. The land route to the Gulf states via Kuwait is closed.

TOURISM

 747,000 visitors

 Down 27% in 1990

MAIN OVERSEAS ARRIVALS

West Asia 69%	
Africa 13%	
Europe 7%	*Pre 1991 Gulf War figures*
South Asia 4%	
South East Asia and Oceania 1%	
Other 6%	

0 10 20 30 40 50 60 70 80
% of total arrivals

The Shi'a holy shrines in the south attract thousands of pilgrims each year. Iraq is effectively closed to Western tourists, who once visited its many archaeological sites. In particular, the ruins of Babylon, and its fabled hanging gardens, were once a major tourist attraction. Westerners also used to journey to the marshlands close to the Shatt al 'Arab waterway. However, this area of ecological importance is now being drained as part of a campaign to suppress the Marsh Arabs.

IRAQ

Total Area : 438 320 sq. km (169 235 sq. miles)

POPULATION

- ▣ over 1 000 000
- ◉ over 500 000
- ◎ over 100 000
- ○ over 50 000
- • over 10 000

LAND HEIGHT

- 3000m/9843ft
- 2000m/6562ft
- 1000m/3281ft
- 500m/1640ft
- 200m/656ft
- Sea Level

PEOPLE

Arabic, Kurdish, Armenian, Assyrian

44 people per km²

THE URBAN/RURAL POPULATION SPLIT

71% 29%

RELIGIOUS PERSUASION

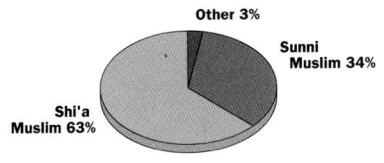

Other 3%
Sunni Muslim 34%
Shi'a Muslim 63%

ETHNIC MAKEUP

Persian 3%
Turkish 2%
Kurdish 16%
Arab 79%

In addition to the Arab and Kurdish populations, Iraq has a small number of minority groups, such as the Turks and Persians. Over 90% of the population is Muslim, while the rest comprises a variety of Christian sects. Since the creation of Israel, most Iraqi Jews have emigrated. The Arab Muslims are divided into Sunni and Shi'a sects. The Shi'a form the largest single religious group; however, Shi'a divines do not have as intimate a connection with the people as they do in Iran and their influence on government is limited.

Since the mid-1970s, many Iraqis have moved, or been forced to move, to the cities, where some 70% of the population now live.

In the marshes of the extreme south, communities of Marsh Arabs survive. In the wake of the 1991 Gulf War, some of these attempted a rebellion against the state, which is now draining the marshes in order to destroy both the people and their culture.

POPULATION AGE BREAKDOWN

%	0–14	15–64	65+		
	3%	2.7%	2.6%	2.4%	2.4%
	52.9%	50.9%	50.4%	51%	51.5%
	44.1%	46.4%	47%	46.6%	46.1%
	2000	1990	1980	1970	1960

(% of population by age group)

WORLD AFFAIRS

OPEC OAPEC AL ACC NAM

In 1990, Saddam Hussain embarked on a grand plan to show himself as the undisputed leader of the Arab world: the invasion of Kuwait. Saddam was counting on the West responding with sanctions rather than arms, and on Syria and Egypt not joining an Arab coalition to oppose him. A successful conclusion to the grand design would have placed Saddam in a position to control most of the oil supplies in the Gulf.

As a result of the Gulf War that followed, Iraq was economically and diplomatically isolated. Iraq was ousted from Kuwait, and sanctions were imposed. Relations with the West are now deadlocked. Iraq is effectively neutralized as a power in the region, but remains unwilling to allow UN inspection of its arsenal. No major Western state has restored diplomatic relations.

Relations with Iran are tense. Iranian guerrillas working against the regime in Tehran continue to use Iraq as a base for their operations.

I

POLITICS

Uncertain

President Saddam Hussain

THE STATE OF THE PARTIES

National Assembly 250 members

The National Assembly operates under the supervision of the Revolutionary Command Council. It is composed of Ba'athists and their supporters

Revolutionary Command Council

Members are appointed by the president

President Saddam Hussain has dominated Iraqi politics since overthrowing his predecessor in 1979. In theory, the highest state authority rests with the nine-member Revolutionary Command Council.

MAIN POLITICAL ISSUES

Kuwait

Iraq's invasion of Kuwait in 1990 led to UN sanctions being imposed; Iraq's overseas assets were also frozen. Despite its subsequent defeat by a US and Saudi-led coalition, the Iraqi leadership still maintains its claim to Kuwait, using it as a rallying call to unite the masses and divert attention from economic hardship. Iraq has repeatedly defied the UN's attempts to monitor its compliance with Security Council resolutions on the destruction of banned weapons. Sanctions have therefore remained in place. Numerous factories and businesses have closed as a result of the trade embargo.

Threats to the regime

Opposition is largely based outside the country and is united only in wishing to oust Saddam Hussain. The most significant groups are the Tehran-based Supreme Council for the Islamic Revolution in Iraq, which has strong backing in southern Iraq, and the Iraqi National Congress, an umbrella group with its headquarters in London.

The separatist Kurdish minority in the north of the country has been in almost continuous rebellion against Baghdad since 1962, but lacks sufficient external backing to pose a serious threat. Even Iraq's enemies do not wish to see the dismemberment of Iraq into component republics.

PROFILE

Iraq's regime – the most autocratic in the Arab world – is dominated by President Saddam Hussain and his lieutenants, mainly trusted members of his family. His cousin, Ali Hassan Al Majid, who was governor of Kuwait during the occupation, is responsible for atrocities against the Kurds.

Saddam Hussain has promoted his own extreme personality cult. In a

Tarek Aziz, deputy prime minister and mediator between Iraq and the UN.

Saddam Hussain, Iraq's dictatorial leader since he seized power in 1979.

typical political broadcast, his name is mentioned 30 to 50 times an hour. The streets of Baghdad grind to a halt whenever the president leaves his palace. The regime remains in force through terror and the backing of the military. A vast secret service and intelligence network ensure that opposition groups are not able to organize a challenge.

AID

$417m (receipts)

Humanitarian aid is rising

Before the Kuwait invasion, the regime received aid from various Gulf states to help pay for Iraq's war with Iran. Today, UN sanctions mean that any aid to Iraq has to be covert; humanitarian supplies are allowed, however.

CHRONOLOGY

Iraq became independent in 1932. In 1958, the Hashemite dynasty was overthrown when King Faisal died in a coup led by the military under Brigadier Kassem. He was initially supported by the Iraqi Ba'ath Party.

- ❑ **1961** Kurdish rebellion erupts in northern Iraq. Iraq claims sovereignty over Kuwait on the eve of Kuwait's independence.
- ❑ **1963** Kassem overthrown. Colonel Abd as-Salem Muhammad Aref takes power. Kuwait's sovereignty recognized.
- ❑ **1964** Ayatollah Khomeini, future leader of Iran, takes refuge at Najaf in Iraq.
- ❑ **1966** Aref is succeeded by his brother, Abd ar-Rahman.
- ❑ **1968** Ba'athists under Ahmad Hassan Al-Bakr take power.
- ❑ **1970** Revolutionary Command Council agrees manifesto on Kurdish autonomy with Kurdish leader Mulla Mustafa Barzani.
- ❑ **1972** Nationalization of Iraq Petroleum Company, owned by Western interests.
- ❑ **1973** Troops sent to fight on Syrian front against Israel.
- ❑ **1978** Iraq and Syria sign charter for economic and political union. Ayatollah Khomeini leaves Iraq for Paris.
- ❑ **1979** Saddam Hussein replaces President Al-Bakr, who is put under house arrest.
- ❑ **1980** War declared against Iran.
- ❑ **1982** President Saddam Hussein withdraws troops from Iran. Iran occupies parts of southern Iraq. Shi'a leader Mohammed Baqir Al-Hakim, exiled in Tehran, forms Supreme Council of the Islamic Revolution in Iraq.
- ❑ **1986** Armed excursion into Iran. Iraqi fighter kills 37 on *USS Stark*.
- ❑ **1988** Iraq and Iran agree cease fire. Iraqi troops alleged to be using chemical weapons in bomb attacks on Kurdish villages.
- ❑ **1990** British journalist Farzad Bazoft hanged for spying. Iraq and Iran restore diplomatic relations. Iraq invades Kuwait, annexing emirate as its 19th province. UN imposes trade sanctions.
- ❑ **1991** Western allies launch successful 100-hour campaign to liberate Kuwait. Shi'a rebellion in southern Iraq put down.
- ❑ **1992** USA, UK, France and Russia proclaim air exclusion zone over southern Iraq.
- ❑ **1993** Iraqi attempts to recover military equipment from Kuwait provoke Western air attacks.

DEFENCE

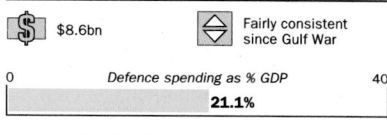

$ $8.6bn   ⬦ Fairly consistent since Gulf War

0   *Defence spending as % GDP*   40
21.1%

IRAQI ARMED FORCES

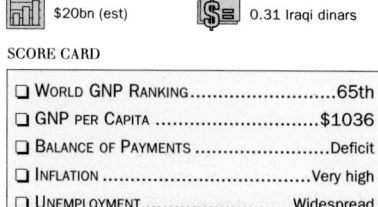

🪖	2300 main battle tanks (T–54,-55/Ch T–59/ T–62/T–72/M–60)	350,000 personnel
🚢	1 frigate and 10 patrol boats	1000 personnel
✈	310 combat aircraft (MiG–29/MiG–23/ MiG -27/*Mirage* F1EQ)	30,000 personnel
	None	

Iraq's defeat in the 100-hour US-backed UN ground campaign to free Kuwait led to the destruction of much of Iraq's arsenal. The high command has been restructured and many senior officers executed on suspicion of treason.

Iraq has now restored its defences, but lacks the high-tech weaponry that Kuwait and Saudi Arabia have acquired since the war from US and other Western suppliers. The army is large, but contains many poorly trained conscripts. The military is largely equipped with tanks and aircraft from the former Soviet Union and China. The air force, the most prestigious service, has some French *Mirage* fighters and US helicopters.

ECONOMICS

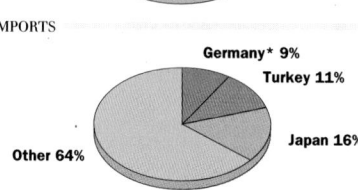

📊 $20bn (est)   💲 0.31 Iraqi dinars

SCORE CARD

- ❑ WORLD GNP RANKING............................65th
- ❑ GNP PER CAPITA $1036
- ❑ BALANCE OF PAYMENTS ....Deficit
- ❑ INFLATION ....Very high
- ❑ UNEMPLOYMENT ....Widespread

EXPORTS

United Arab Emirates 5%
Jordan 15%
Turkey 47%
Other 33%

IMPORTS

Germany* 9%
Turkey 11%
Japan 16%
Other 64%

STRENGTHS

Second largest crude oil and natural gas reserves in OPEC. Large labour force.

WEAKNESSES

Inability to sell oil on the international market; UN sanctions have halved Iraq's gross national product. Once-thriving agricultural sector devastated by war.

PROFILE

Before 1990, Iraq was the world's third largest oil supplier. Today, oil is being produced only for domestic consumption. Assuming an end to sanctions, however, the potential for Iraq's oil industry is massive.

Sanctions have hit Iraq hard, not least because oil sanctions are relatively easy to police and because there is currently a world oil glut. The

ECONOMIC PERFORMANCE INDICATOR

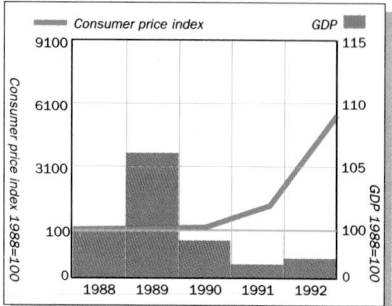

— Consumer price index   ■ GDP

diplomatic siege of Baghdad and the denial of Western assistance has also stifled initiatives in other sectors of the economy. Iraq was formerly rich in agriculture, but the sector was badly affected by war. Reforms to liberalize the economy have been promised, but centralized planning and state purchasing are still the norm. Participation in the thriving black market is dangerous: 42 traders were executed in 1992.

IRAQ : MAJOR BUSINESSES

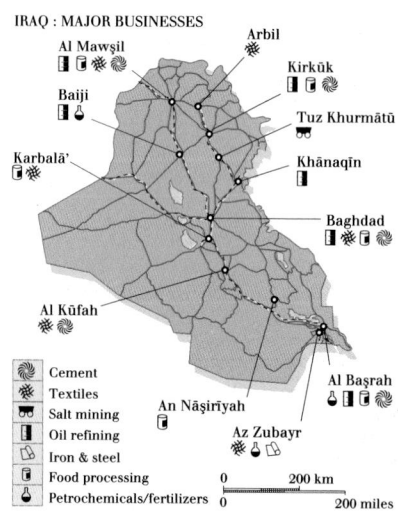

🌀 Cement
🌸 Textiles
⛏ Salt mining
🛢 Oil refining
🔧 Iron & steel
📦 Food processing
⚗ Petrochemicals/fertilizers

0   200 km
0   200 miles

RESOURCES

29.2bn kwh
(capacity 9m kw)

402,600 b/d
(reserves
100,000,000,000 bbl)

9.5m sheep,
1.7m cattle,
415,000 asses

Natural gas, sulphur

ELECTRICITY GENERATION

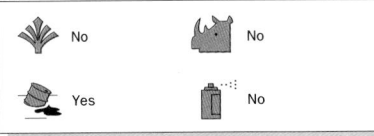

Hydro 2% (610m kwh)

Thermal 98% (28.6bn kwh)

Nuclear 0%

Other 0%

0   20   40   60   80   100
% of total generation by type

Iraq has huge reserves of oil and gas. The oil industry is controlled by the Iraqi National Oil Company. In 1990,

proven reserves were conservatively estimated at 100,000 million barrels – sufficient for 97 years' production at 1989 levels of 4.5 million b/d.

Total gas reserves, three quarters of which are associated with oil, are estimated at 2.69 billion cubic metres. Hydroelectic power is the main source of energy, though there is also a single oil-fired power station.

Before the invasion of Kuwait and subsequent war, Iraq was supplying 80% of the world's trade in dates. Production is now sharply down. Foods are now produced simply for domestic consumption. Iraq has, however, achieved a degree of self-sufficiency in crops such as wheat, rice and sugar.

IRAQ : LAND USE

Cropland
Forest
Pasture
Wetlands
Desert
Sheep
Wheat
Dates - cash crop

0   200 km
0   200 miles

ENVIRONMENT

 None

 Destruction of marshlands in south

ENVIRONMENTAL TREATIES

No

No

Yes

No

Wars with Iran and with the UN coalition over the Kuwait occupation led to massive environmental damage. Hundreds of thousands of landmines remain in the Kuwait border regions, posing lethal hazards to farmers, livestock and wild animals. The north has been affected by chemical weapons, used by the regime against the Kurds. In the south, an entire wetland ecosystem is being destroyed by an engineering programme aimed at draining the marshes for largely political reasons.

MEDIA

 Tight government censorship

PUBLISHING AND BROADCAST MEDIA

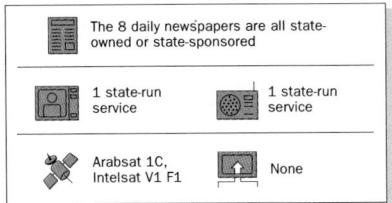

The 8 daily newspapers are all state-owned or state-sponsored

1 state-run service

1 state-run service

Arabsat 1C, Intelsat V1 F1

None

The Iraqi media is under strict state control, although rebel groups do circulate clandestine newspapers. Baghdad has four daily newspapers, one of which, the *Baghdad Times*, is in English. Members of Saddam's family control some newspapers. Foreign journalists are carefully vetted and their reports censored; those critical of the regime are refused future entry.

CRIME

 Iraq does not publish prison figures

Crime is rising sharply

CRIME RATES

Crime rates are high compared with neighbouring Arab states and Iran. Amnesty International has reported many cases of human rights abuses by the regime

Iraq was formerly a law-abiding society, but economic collapse has sent crime rates soaring, especially in cities. Theft has been made a capital offence – encouraging thieves to murder in order to escape detection.

EDUCATION

 60%

0   Education spending as % GNP   25
3.7%

THE EDUCATION SYSTEM

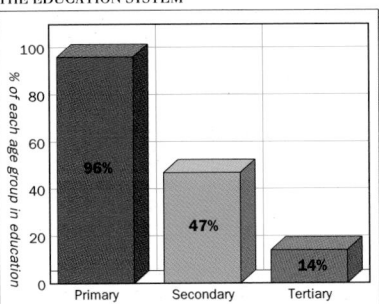

96% Primary
47% Secondary
14% Tertiary

% of each age group in education

Primary and secondary education are free and universal, except in remote rural areas. There are six universities. Academics from Iraq authorized the organized plunder of antiquities and university equipment from Kuwait during the 1990 occupation.

HEALTH

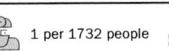 1 per 1732 people

Pneumonia, influenza, cancers, heart diseases

0   Health spending as % GNP   25
0.8%

Iraqi doctors claim that the welfare of children, the sick and the elderly has suffered because of the UN embargo. Child mortality is high and the standard of hospital equipment and facilities low.

WEALTH

 Few opportunities for enrichment

CONSUMER GOODS OWNERSHIP

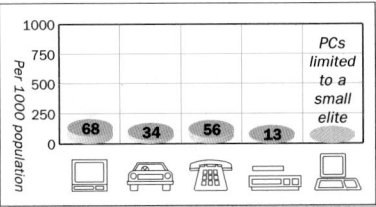

1000
750
500
250
0

Per 1000 population

68   34   56   13

PCs limited to a small elite

Many middle-class Iraqis and traders have taken advantage of the open border with Jordan to relocate from Baghdad to Amman.

WORLD RANKING

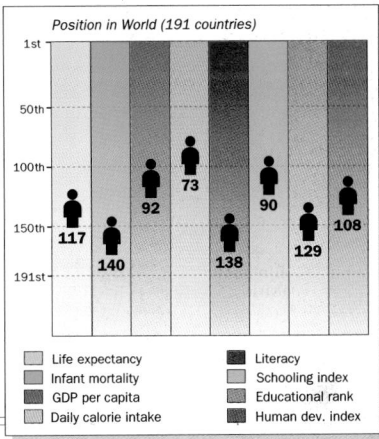

Position in World (191 countries)

1st
50th
100th
150th
191st

117   140   92   73   138   90   129   108

Life expectancy
Infant mortality
GDP per capita
Daily calorie intake
Literacy
Schooling index
Educational rank
Human dev. index

I

IRELAND

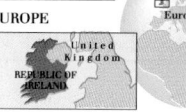

OFFICIAL NAME: Republic of Ireland   **CAPITAL:** Dublin   **POPULATION:** 3.5 million
CURRENCY: Irish pound   **OFFICIAL LANGUAGES:** Irish, English

LYING IN THE ATLANTIC OCEAN, off the west coast of Britain, the Irish Republic occupies about 85% of the island of Ireland. Surrounded by low coastal mountain ranges, the central basin is punctuated by lakes, undulating hills and peat bogs. Centuries of struggle against English colonialism led to the formation of the Irish Free State in 1921 and full sovereignty in 1937. The political reunification of the island remains a key aim of the Republic.

CLIMATE

WEATHER CHART

Moderated by the Gulf Stream, the Irish climate is mild, equable and wet. The mean annual temperature is 12°C.

COMMUNICATIONS

🛬 **Dublin International**   🚢 62 ships
189,400 dwt

THE TRANSPORT NETWORK

92,327 km (57,369 miles)		8 km (5 miles)	
1947 km (1210 miles)		429 km (267 miles)	

Over 40 road improvement projects are being funded by the EU. Dublin suffers from severe lorry congestion.

TOURISM

🧳 3.69m visitors   ⬆ Up 1% in 1991

MAIN OVERSEAS ARRIVALS

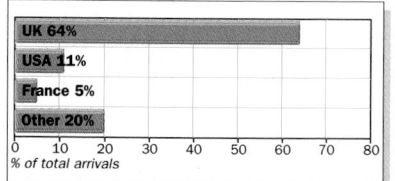

| UK 64% |
| USA 11% |
| France 5% |
| Other 20% |

0 10 20 30 40 50 60 70 80
% of total arrivals

Intensive promotional campaigns have helped Ireland widen its tourist base, notably in Germany and Scandinavia. Its attractions include its scenery and 'clean' environmental image, and its relaxed lifestyle.

PEOPLE

 English, Irish Gaelic   53 people per km²

THE URBAN/RURAL POPULATION SPLIT

46%   54%

RELIGIOUS PERSUASION

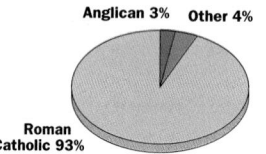

Anglican 3%   Other 4%

Roman Catholic 93%

The population is 95% ethnic Irish. The Catholic Church has a huge influence, opposing abortion and birth control. Many Irish still emigrate to find jobs.

POLITICS

🗳 1997   👤 President Mary Robinson

THE STATE OF THE PARTIES

House of Representatives 166 members   **4% Other**

41% FF   27% FG   20% LP   6% PD   2% DL

FF = Fianna Fáil (Soldiers of Destiny)   FG = Fine Gael (United Ireland Party)   LP = Labour Party   PD = Progressive Democrats   DL = Democratic Left

Senate 60 members

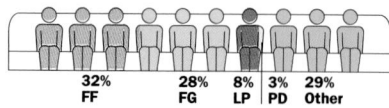

32% FF   28% FG   8% LP   3% PD   29% Other

In 1973, an FG–LP coalition took power, which saw the end of the FF as the traditional party of government – a role it had held since 1932. FF and FG–LP governments since have tended to be short-lived and, since 1989, the FF has needed PD support to govern. The 1994 'London Declaration' with the UK is part of renewed efforts to resolve Northern Ireland's future and end terrorism. In it, Dublin indicated its constitutional claim to the province could be reconsidered.

REPUBLIC OF IRELAND

Total Area :
70 280 sq. km
(27 135 sq. miles)

POPULATION

over 500 000	◉
over 100 000	◎
over 50 000	○
over 10 000	●
under 10 000	•

LAND HEIGHT

1000m/3281ft
500m/1640ft
200m/656ft
Sea Level

Map of Ireland showing provinces CONNAUGHT, LEINSTER, MUNSTER, ULSTER (Northern Ireland), and towns including Dublin, Cork, Limerick, Galway, Waterford, and surrounding seas: ATLANTIC OCEAN, IRISH SEA, CELTIC SEA, St George's Channel.

I

WORLD AFFAIRS

Northern Ireland is the dominant issue. Talks on its future are governed by the 1985 Anglo-Irish Agreement.

AID

 $72m (donations)   Up 26% in 1991

Africa is the main target of Irish aid. As one of the poorer European states, Ireland is a major recipient of EU aid.

DEFENCE

 $553m   Up 14% in 1991

Ireland is determined to maintain its traditional neutrality, notwithstanding provisions within the Maastricht Treaty for a common European defence policy.

ECONOMICS

 $37.7bn   0.71 Irish pounds

SCORE CARD

- ❏ WORLD GNP RANKING.........................48th
- ❏ GNP PER CAPITA $10,782
- ❏ BALANCE OF PAYMENTS $2.6bn
- ❏ INFLATION 3.1%
- ❏ UNEMPLOYMENT...............................15.4%

STRENGTHS
One of Europe's fastest-growing economies: real GDP rose 3.5% a year 1980–1990; slightly slower 1991–1993. Trade surplus. Low inflation. Efficient agriculture, food processing industries. Rapidly expanding high-tech sector; electronics account for 25% of exports. Large recipient of EU infrastructure funding. Highly educated workforce.

WEAKNESSES
Many key sectors owned by overseas multinationals. One of EU's highest unemployment rates: 15.4% overall; 28% youth unemployment. High interest rates slow investment.

EXPORTS

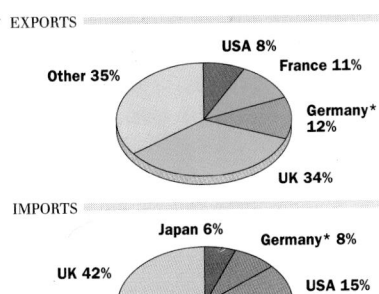

USA 8%
France 11%
Other 35%
Germany* 12%
UK 34%

IMPORTS

Japan 6%   Germany* 8%
UK 42%
USA 15%
Other 29%

RESOURCES

 14.5bn kwh (capacity 3.8m kw)   Not an oil producer; refines 56,000 b/cd

 5.6m cattle, 5m sheep, 961,000 pigs   Lead, zinc, natural gas, silver, coal

Oil has been found off the southern coast. Studies suggest this may be in commercially exploitable quantities.

ENVIRONMENT

 0.4% partially protected   Recent anti-pollution legislation

The main environmental concerns are over-exploitation of the country's peat bogs for fuel and the recent expansion of conifer plantations. While Ireland's levels of forest cover will increase in the next few years, most new planting is of conifers. Controls on pollution were extended in 1994 with the introduction of stringent new laws.

MEDIA

 There is no official censorship, but there can be self-censorship on moral issues

PUBLISHING AND BROADCAST MEDIA

 There are seven daily newspapers. These include the *Irish Times*, the *Irish Independent* and the *Irish Press*

 1 state-owned, 1 independent service   1 state-owned, 1 independent service

Censorship of media coverage of Sinn Féin was lifted in 1994. There is wide access to British papers, TV and radio.

CRIME

 1953 prisoners   Up 1% in 1990

Rural Ireland has the EU's lowest crime rate. Urban crime is growing and drugs are a problem in Dublin and Cork.

EDUCATION

 100%

The Catholic Church runs many schools. Trinity College, Dublin, is the most prestigious of four universities.

Clew Bay in County Mayo, on the western coast of Ireland, viewed from the slopes of neighbouring Croagh Patrick.

CHRONOLOGY

English colonization, which began in 1167, was reinforced after 1558 by oppressive anti-Catholic legislation and the settlement of Scottish Protestants in the north.

- ❏ **1845–1855** Famine. One million die, 1.5 million emigrate.
- ❏ **1919–1921** Anglo-Irish war after republican Sinn Féin proclaims Irish independence.
- ❏ **1921** Irish Free State set up; north opts to stay in UK.
- ❏ **1949** Ireland becomes a republic.
- ❏ **1973** FG–LP win elections. Ends 16 years continuous FF government.
- ❏ **1992** Financial scandals. Premier Charles Haughey, FF head, resigns.
- ❏ **1994** Irish–UK talks on Northern Ireland; London Declaration.

HEALTH

 1 per 633 people   Heart diseases, cancers

Free care is means tested. One third of the population relies on health care insurance. Ireland has the EU's lowest per capita consumption of alcohol.

WEALTH

 Fork lift truck driver, 285 Irish pounds per week; junior manager, 450 Irish pounds per week

CONSUMER GOODS OWNERSHIP

271   223   260   138   13

Per 1000 population

Living standards for those in jobs are rising steadily. Unemployment has, however, forced more onto welfare.

WORLD RANKING

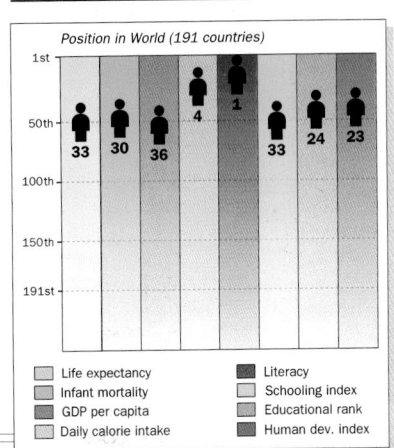

Position in World (191 countries)

33   30   36   4   1   33   24   23

- ☐ Life expectancy
- ☐ Infant mortality
- ☐ GDP per capita
- ☐ Daily calorie intake
- ☐ Literacy
- ☐ Schooling index
- ☐ Educational rank
- ☐ Human dev. index

I

ISRAEL

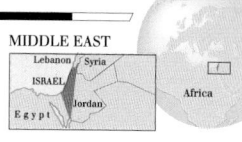

OFFICIAL NAME: State of Israel   CAPITAL: Jerusalem
POPULATION: 5.3 million   CURRENCY: New shekel   OFFICIAL LANGUAGE: Hebrew

CREATED AS A NEW STATE IN 1948 with the backing of the USA and other Allied powers, Israel is bordered by Egypt, Jordan, Syria and Lebanon. Its topography varies from the HaNegev desert in the south to the Dead Sea, the lowest point on the Earth's surface. Following wars with its Arab neighbours, Israel has unilaterally extended its original boundaries to control the West Bank, Gaza Strip, East Jerusalem and the Golan Heights.

CLIMATE

WEATHER CHART

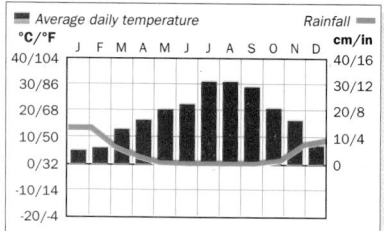

Summers are hot and dry. The wet season is between November and March, when the weather is mild.

COMMUNICATIONS

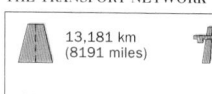 Ben-Gurion Intl, Tel Aviv-Yafo
3.5m passengers

 36 ships
820,000 dwt

THE TRANSPORT NETWORK

13,181 km (8191 miles)	None	
530 km (329 miles)	None	

Excellent roads link all Israeli towns. Railways are being extended, and there are three commercial ports.

TOURISM

 2.28m visitors

 Up 215% between 1990 and 1992

MAIN OVERSEAS ARRIVALS

USA 23%
France 11%
UK 11%
Germany 9%
Lebanon 4%
Other 42%

0   10   20   30   40   50   60
% of total arrivals

Jerusalem is the major tourist destination. Elat and the Dead Sea have been developed as beach resorts.

PEOPLE

 Hebrew, Arabic, Yiddish, German, Russian, Polish, Romanian, Persian

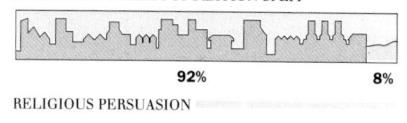 247 people per km²

THE URBAN/RURAL POPULATION SPLIT

92%   8%

RELIGIOUS PERSUASION

Christian 2%
Other 2%
Muslim (mainly Sunni) 14%
Jewish 82%

ETHNIC MAKEUP

Other (mostly Arab) 17%
Jewish 83%

Large numbers of Jewish immigrants settled in Palestine before Israel was founded in 1948. After the Second World War, there was a massive increase in immigration. Sephardic Jews from the Middle East and Mediterranean are now in the majority, but Ashkenazi Jews, mostly of central European origin, still dominate politics, business and social life. Thousands of Russian Jews have emigrated since 1989. Israel's Palestinian population totals some 800,000. While many take part in the democratic process, they remain sidelined in Israeli life. Those in occupied territories decline Israeli citizenship.

POPULATION AGE BREAKDOWN

	1960	1970	1980	1990	2000
65+	4.9%	6.7%	8.6%	8.8%	8.6%
15–64	59%	60.2%	58.2%	59.9%	63.3%
0–14	36.1%	33.1%	33.2%	31.3%	28.1%

POLITICS

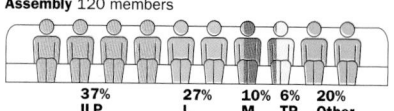 1996

President Gen Chaim Herzog

THE STATE OF THE PARTIES

Assembly 120 members

37% ILP   27% L   10% M   6% TP   20% Other

ILP = Israel Labour Party   L = Likud (Consolidation)
M = Meretz (composed of Ratz, Shinui, United Workers' Party)   TP = Tzomet Party   Other = Shas, National Religious Party, United Torah Judaism, Hadash, Moledet, Arab Democratic Party

Israel is a multiparty democracy. The prime minister and his cabinet wield executive power under the president.

MAIN POLITICAL ISSUES

Peace with the PLO
This complex issue is explained in detail on page 292.

Ethnic tensions
Rivalry between Sephardic and Ashkenazi Jews is likely to intensify, as the former, now in the majority, gain political power. Sephardic Jews already control many local councils. Russian Jewish immigrants are also demanding more representation in politics.

Religious militancy
Religious parties exert great influence in the Knesset. They seek support for religious institutions, including schools, and want changes in laws to enforce the proper observance of the Jewish faith in daily life.

PROFILE

Elected by proportional representation, Israeli governments tend to depend for survival on minor parties. The Labour coalition includes a religious party and also extreme-left, Arab-orientated parties. Political tensions are increased by confrontations between Orthodox and secular Jews, as well as between settlers and Arabs in the West Bank.

Yitzhak Rabin, prime minister of ruling Labour coalition since 1992.

Yasser Arafat, the militant-turned-moderate leader of the PLO.

WORLD AFFAIRS

 ECE   GATT   EBRD   OAS 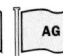 AG

Israel remains technically at war with all Arab states except Egypt. Regional stability may be improved by the 1993 peace accords. Links with Syria are unlikely to improve unless Israel withdraws from the Golan Heights.

AID

 $1.4bn (receipts)   Down 1% in 1991

Israel receives massive military and economic aid from the USA. Large *ad hoc* donations are also received from Jewish NGOs.

ISRAEL

Total Area : 20 700 sq. km (7992 sq. miles)

POPULATION

◎ over 100 000
○ over 50 000
● over 10 000

LAND HEIGHT

1000m/3281ft
500m/1640ft
200m/656ft
Sea Level
-200m/-656ft

DEFENCE

 $6.8bn   ⬆ Up 17% in 1992

0   Defence spending as % GDP   40
10%

The only Middle Eastern country with a nuclear deterrent, Israel has a small regular defence force which can be boosted by nearly 600,000 reservists. Equipped with some of the latest US technology, the forces' firepower is vastly superior to that of its Arab neighbours.

ISRAELI ARMED FORCES

	3890 main battle tanks (1080 Centurion/ 400 M-48A5/750 M-60)	134,000 personnel
	3 submarines and 61 patrol boats	10,000 personnel
	662 combat aircraft (112 F-4E/63 F-15/ 209 F-16/ 95 *Kfir* C2,-C7)	32,000 personnel
	Widely believed that Israel has a nuclear capacity with up to 100 warheads. Delivery via *Jericho 1* and *Jericho 2* missiles	

ECONOMICS

 $59.1bn   2.93 new shekels

STRENGTHS

Government commitment to economic reform. Huge potential of agriculture, manufacturing and industrial products. Important banking sector. Prospect of peace in region. Sizeable aid from US government and international Jewish organizations.

WEAKNESSES

High unemployment and inflation. Large defence budget. History of regional and internal instability inhibits foreign investment. No trade with Arab neighbours.

PROFILE

Progress in the peace negotiations with the PLO would be a huge boost to the economy. The government is seeking ways to reduce state spending, which accounts for two thirds of GNP. The state owns 90% of all land and controls over 20% of all industries and services. Public companies are being privatized and there are plans to end restrictive labour practices. Agriculture is highly specialized and profitable. The state is now aiming to boost the service sector.

Despite a world recession, Israel's economy has continued to expand in the 1990s. The engine of this continued

SCORE CARD

☐ WORLD GNP RANKING..........................38th
☐ GNP PER CAPITA $11,151
☐ BALANCE OF PAYMENTS $86m
☐ INFLATION 11.2%
☐ UNEMPLOYMENT.................................8.5%

EXPORTS

Belgium and Luxembourg 6%   Hong Kong 6%
Other 45%   UK 7%
                             Germany* 7%
                             USA 29%

IMPORTS

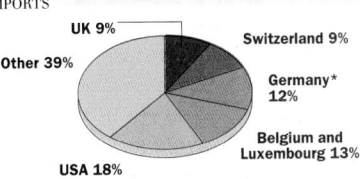

UK 9%   Switzerland 9%
Other 39%   Germany* 12%
                             Belgium and Luxembourg 13%
USA 18%

growth has been the mass immigration of Jews, many highly-educated, from the former Soviet Union. Although unemployment levels have risen as a result of immigration, new skills and contacts have also helped the Israeli economy towards sustained export-led growth.

ISRAEL : MAJOR BUSINESSES

Hefa
Tel Aviv-Yafo
Ashqelon
Be'ér Sheva'
Nazerat
Jerusalem

※ Textiles
🝕 Chemicals
💻 Computers
🗋 Food processing
✐ Pharmaceuticals
💻 Consumer goods

0   50 km
0   50 miles

ECONOMIC PERFORMANCE INDICATOR

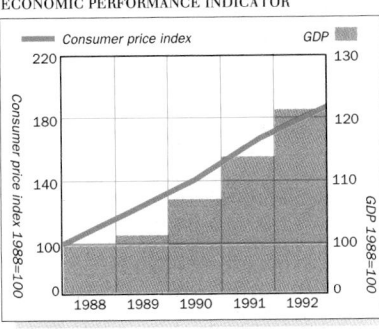

— Consumer price index   GDP ▨

Consumer price index 1988=100
220
180
140
100
0

GDP 1988=100
130
120
110
100
0

1988 1989 1990 1991 1992

I

THE WEST BANK & GAZA STRIP

OCCUPIED BY ISRAELI TROOPS in the Six Day War in 1967, the West Bank and Gaza Strip were administered by Israel until 1994. The West Bank, with a land area of 5900 sq km, has a population of 859,000, of whom 97% are Palestinian Arabs. Israeli settlers have encroached on much of the best land. The Gaza Strip covers only about 1000 sq km but has a population of almost 600,000 Palestinian Arabs. Both territories rely on agriculture and remittances from work in Israel. Following secret negotiations between Israel and the PLO in 1993, agreement was reached allowing limited autonomy for the Palestinians in Gaza and in an area around the town of Jericho.

HISTORY

Israeli settlement of the West Bank began soon after the area's conquest in 1967. The Gaza Strip, the most turbulent region, was not formally incorporated into Israel until 1973.

After Egypt's President Sadat visited Israel in 1977, progress on Palestinian autonomy seemed possible. The framework agreed at Camp David in 1978, however, failed to materialize and Israeli attitudes appeared to harden, with proposals for more Jewish settlements. By 1985, Israel had direct control of most of the West Bank. Attempts to bring peace to the region by allowing Palestinians an independent state were blocked by the PLO's refusal to recognize Israel's right to exist and Israel's refusal to negotiate with what it regarded as a terrorist group.

The frequency and violence of Arab anti-Israeli demonstrations in the Occupied Territories intensified, culminating, in January 1988, in an *intifada* (uprising) involving a strike by 120,000 Palestinians with jobs in Israel. The Israeli cabinet endorsed an 'iron fist' approach by the security forces, but was divided as to long-term solutions. That year, King Hussein of Jordan abandoned links

with the West Bank, allowing the PLO to declare an independent Palestinian state. The PLO also endorsed UN Resolution 242 and thus Israel's right to exist. However, only after the Rabin-led Labour coalition came to power in Israel in 1992 was progress made towards peace. At the same time, the Islamic militant group *Hamas*, opposed to any deal with Israel, was gaining support in the Occupied Territories.

KEY ISSUES

With the annexation of the West Bank and Gaza Strip, Israel was faced with the dilemma of whether to grant the Arab population citizenship or to exclude it from the democratic process. Although some right-wing Israeli leaders advocated retaining the territories, the growing power of *Hamas* demonstrated that incorporating the West Bank and Gaza into Israel was fraught with difficulty.

Much of the population in the West Bank and Gaza supports the PLO, although the organization's ranks are split. Hardliners disagree with PLO leader Yasser Arafat's moderate demands on Israel. The challenge for Israel is to maintain law and order and contain the extremists, while working to implement the 1993 Washington Accords. The problem for Arafat and his backers in the PLO is to keep a grip on the territories and to eclipse the influence of *Hamas*.

SETTLEMENT

By May 1994, only the first phase of the 1993 Accords had taken effect. The Palestinians gained home rule over the Gaza Strip and Jericho, with their control limited to home affairs such as education, utilities and policing.

Progress towards implementing the first stage of the peace plan was slow. Despite hopes that the first stage of Israeli withdrawal would start in 1993, deadlines passed without agreement until May 1994. Differences emerged over the authority of Palestinian law in the districts and the scale of a proposed

WEST BANK

Area under Palestinian control

■ Israeli settlement

□ Major settlement

0   25 km

0   25 miles

N

amnesty for Palestinian prisoners. A number of countries, including the UK and Russia, offered to train the Palestinian police forces, which are now handling internal security in Jericho and Gaza.

However, terrorist outrages, such as the 1994 murder of 50 Palestinians in a West Bank mosque by a Zionist fanatic, and reprisal bombings by Arab militants, pose a threat to a final settlement. There is now pressure on both the PLO and Israel to make further progress.

Bethlehem, *situated in the troubled West Bank, is just one of the many holy places that remain a principal attraction for visitors.*

GAZA STRIP

Area under Palestinian control

■ Israeli settlement

□ Urban areas

RESOURCES

20.7bn kwh (capacity 4.1m kw)

Not an oil producer; refines 221,000 b/cd

394,000 sheep, 13,000 pigs, 5000 asses, 2000 mules

Natural gas, potash, bromine, magnesium, salt, copper, gold

ELECTRICITY GENERATION

Hydro 0%

Thermal 100% (20.7bn kwh)

Nuclear 0%

Other 0%

0   20   40   60   80   100

% of total generation by type

The country's most valuable deposits of minerals are potash, bromine (of which Israel is the world's largest exporter) and other salts mined near the Dead Sea. Reserves of copper ore and gold were discovered in 1988. In the coastal plain, mixed farming, vineyards and citrus groves are plentiful. Former desert areas now have extensive irrigation systems supporting specialized agriculture.

Israel's most critical resource is water. Shortages have forced Israel to purchase water, transported in plastic bags, from Turkey.

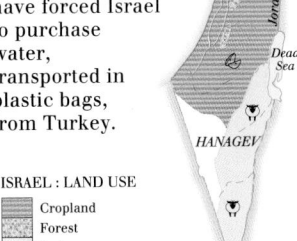

ISRAEL : LAND USE

- Cropland
- Forest
- Pasture
- Desert
- Sheep
- Citrus fruit - cash crop

0   50 km
0   50 miles

ENVIRONMENT

10% partially protected

Consistently high standards from year to year

The government declared 1993–1994 Environment Year. It aimed to promote recycling schemes, the clean-up of rivers and improvements in Israel's urban environment.

ENVIRONMENTAL TREATIES

No   Yes

No   No

MEDIA

Foreign journalists are monitored. The media is constrained by extensive military and security censorship and other administrative restrictions

PUBLISHING AND BROADCAST MEDIA

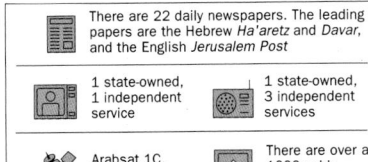

There are 22 daily newspapers. The leading papers are the Hebrew *Ha'aretz* and *Davar*, and the English *Jerusalem Post*

1 state-owned, 1 independent service

1 state-owned, 3 independent services

Arabsat 1C, Intelsat V1 F1

There are over a 1000 cable stations

The largely centrist to left-wing press has been at the forefront of support for the Arab-Israeli peace process.

CRIME

43,900 prisoners

Down 10% in 1990

CRIME RATES

Murders

2   *per 100,000 population*

Rapes

5   *per 100,000 population*

Thefts

2483   *per 100,000 population*

Terrorism by Arab, Islamic and Jewish extremists is the major problem. The army has been accused of abuses.

EDUCATION

97%

0   *Education spending as % GNP*   25

8.6%

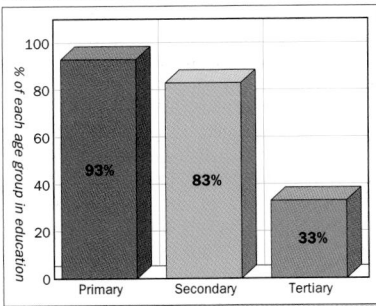

THE EDUCATION SYSTEM

% of each age group in education

100   80   60   40   20   0

93%   83%   33%

Primary   Secondary   Tertiary

Education is free and compulsory for all between five and 16. There are both secular and religious universities. Many students study in the USA.

HEALTH

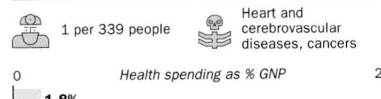

1 per 339 people

Heart and cerebrovascular diseases, cancers

0   *Health spending as % GNP*   25

1.8%

Primary health care reaches all communities. Israel's hospitals have pioneered many innovative treatments.

CHRONOLOGY

The creation of Israel in Palestine in 1948 realized the Zionist dream of a homeland for the Jewish people. However, the state was established in the face of bitter Arab opposition, leading to successive wars.

- ❑ **1967** The Six Day War with Arab states. Israel seizes the Gaza Strip, the Sinai Peninsula, the Golan Heights and the West Bank of the Jordan River. The UN Security Council adopts Resolution 242, the 'land for peace' formula, calling for Israeli withdrawal in return for right to live within secure borders.
- ❑ **1973** Egypt and Syria attack Israel and fight inconclusive 18-day war.
- ❑ **1977** Egypt's President Sadat's Jerusalem visit signals accord.
- ❑ **1979** Peace treaty signed with Egypt at Camp David, USA.
- ❑ **1982** Withdrawal from Sinai; invasion of Lebanon.
- ❑ **1993** Washington Accords signed with PLO: PLO recognition of Israel in return for autonomy for Palestinians in Gaza Strip and Jericho.
- ❑ **1994** First accords implemented.

I

WEALTH

Army officer, $1500 per month; social worker, $800 per month

CONSUMER GOODS OWNERSHIP

Per 1000 population

1000   750   500   250   0

266   159   465   88

PC ownership is high

Income per head is high, but taxation is heavy. Some Israelis live in communes and eschew personal material wealth.

WORLD RANKING

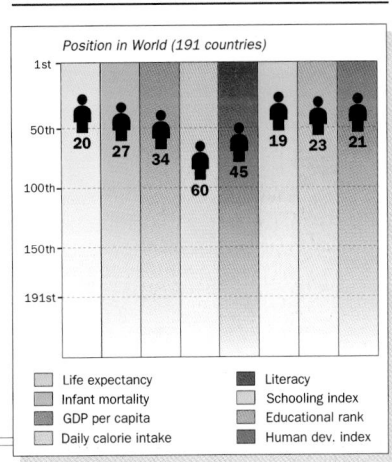

Position in World (191 countries)

1st   50th   100th   150th   191st

20   27   34   60   45   19   23   21

- Life expectancy
- Infant mortality
- GDP per capita
- Daily calorie intake
- Literacy
- Schooling index
- Educational rank
- Human dev. index

ITALY

OFFICIAL NAME: Italian Republic   **CAPITAL:** Rome
POPULATION: 57.8 million   **CURRENCY:** Italian lira   **OFFICIAL LANGUAGE:** Italian

LYING IN SOUTHERN EUROPE, Italy comprises the famous boot-shaped peninsula stretching 800 km into the Mediterranean and a number of islands – Sicily and Sardinia being the largest. The Alps form a natural boundary to the north, while the Appeninne Mountains run the length of the peninsula. The south is an area of seismic activity, epitomized by the volcanoes of Mounts Etna and Vesuvius. United under ancient Roman rule, Italy subsequently developed into a series of competing kingdoms and states which were not fully reunited until 1870. Italian politics was dominated by the Christian Democrats (CD) from 1945 to 1992 under a system of political patronage which extended through the judiciary, media and state businesses. Investigations into corruption from 1992 led to the demise of the CD in the elections of 1994.

CLIMATE

WEATHER CHART

Southern Italy has a Mediterranean climate; the north is more temperate. Summers are hot and dry, especially in the south. Temperatures range from around 24°C to over 27°C in Sardinia and Sicily. Southern winters are mild; northern ones are cooler and wetter. The mountains usually experience heavy snow. The Adriatic coast suffers from cold winds such as the *bora*.

COMMUNICATIONS

 Leonardo da Vinci (Fumicino), Rome 15.55m passengers

791 ships 10.13m dwt

THE TRANSPORT NETWORK

302,403 km (187,904 miles)	6091 km (3785 miles)
19,566 km (12,158 miles)	2400 km (1491 miles)

Many of Italy's key routes are congested. The trans-Appeninne *autostrada* (motorway) from Bologna to Florence is being doubled in size. A high speed train programme (*treno ad alta velocità* – TAV) is planned to link Turin, Milan, Venice, Bologna, Florence and Naples to Rome. Most of Italy's exports travel by road, via Switzerland and Austria. Only 16% goes by sea.

TOURISM

 20.28m visitors

 No change in 1992

MAIN OVERSEAS ARRIVALS

Germany 30%
France 10%
USA 9%
UK 6%
Austria 5%
Other 40%

% of total arrivals

Italy has been a tourist destination since the 16th century and probably invented the concept. Roman Popes consciously aimed to make their city the most beautiful in the world to attract travellers. In the 18th century, Italy was the focus of any Grand Tour. Today, its many unspoilt centres of Renaissance culture continue to make Italy one of the world's major tourism destinations. The industry accounts for 3% of Italy's GDP, and hotels and restaurants employ one million out of a working population of 21 million.

Most visitors travel to the northern half of the country, to cities such as Rome, Florence, Venice and Padova. Many are increasingly travelling to the northern lakes. Beach resorts such as Rimini attract a large, youthful crowd in summer. Italy is also growing in popularity as a skiing destination.

Fears have been expressed that tourism may be having a detrimental impact on Italy's environment. The pressure of visitors to Venice, in particular, is such that in summer one-way systems for pedestrians have to be introduced and day-trippers are often turned away.

Tuscan landscape. Chianti wine is produced in this region, where many northern Europeans own holiday homes.

ITALY

Total Area : 301 270 sq. km
(116 320 sq. miles)

PEOPLE

Italian, German, French, Rhaeto–Romanic, Sardinian

196 people per km²

POPULATION

over 1 000 000	⊡
over 500 000	⊙
over 100 000	⊚
over 50 000	○
over 10 000	●

LAND HEIGHT

3000m/9843ft	
2000m/6562ft	
1000m/3281ft	
500m/1640ft	
200m/656ft	
Sea Level	

THE URBAN/RURAL POPULATION SPLIT

69%   31%

RELIGIOUS PERSUASION

Roman Catholic 100%

ETHNIC MAKEUP

Other 2%

Italian 98%

Italy is a remarkably homogenous society. Most Italians are Roman Catholics and Italy has far fewer ethnic minorities than its EU neighbours. Most are fairly recent immigrants from Ethiopia, the Philippines and Egypt. In the 1980s, there was a sharp rise in illegal immigration from North and West Africa, and Turkey. In response to a growth in right-wing feeling, tighter visa controls were brought in. Residency was, however, extended to illegal migrants already in Italy. Immigration was an issue at elections in 1993 and a factor in the rise of the federalist Northern League.

Difficult economic conditions caused many Italians to emigrate in the 1950s and 1960s. There are now five million Italians living abroad. About half live in other EU countries, the rest mainly in the USA, South America and Australia. Most migrants then, as now, are from the poorer south – the *Mezzogiorno*. Within Italy, prejudice still exists in the north against southern Italians.

Italians do not have a strong sense of national identity – except when it comes to sport. State institutions are viewed as inefficient and corrupt. Allegiance is to Europe, the region or community, above all to the family. The extended family remains Italy's key social and economic support system. Most Italians live at home before marriage. Marriage rates are among the highest in Europe and divorce rates the lowest. Catholicism, however, has not stopped Italy having the lowest birth rate and one of the highest abortion rates in the EU.

Italians tend to dress well. Their preoccupation with style reflects the traditional importance of *bella figura* – image, cutting a dash – in Italian life as much as the high living standards which most now enjoy.

POPULATION AGE BREAKDOWN

% of population by age group	■ 0–14	■ 15–64	□ 65+		
	9.3%	10.9%	13.1%	14.3%	16.9%
	65.9%	64.6%	64.6%	69%	67.6%
	24.8%	24.5%	22.3%	16.7%	15.5%
	1960	1970	1980	1990	2000

CHRONOLOGY

Previously a collection of independent city states, dukedoms and monarchies, Italy became an independent unified nation in 1871.

❏ **1922** Mussolini asked to form government by King Victor Emmanuel III.
❏ **1928** One-party rule by Fascists.
❏ **1929** Lateran Treaties with Vatican recognize sovereignty of Holy See. Catholicism becomes state religion.
❏ **1936-1937** Axis formed with Nazi Germany. Ethiopia (Abyssinia) conquered.
❏ **1939** Albania annexed.
❏ **1940** Italy enters Second World War on German side, following fall of France.

I

0   100 km
0   100 miles

N

I

- **1943** Invaded by Allies. Mussolini imprisoned by Victor Emmanuel III. Armistice concluded with Allies. Italy declares war on Germany.
- **1944** Christian Democratic Party (DC) formed.
- **1945** Mussolini released. Establishes puppet regime in north. Subsequently executed by Italian partisans.
- **1946** Referendum votes in favour of Italy becoming a republic.
- **1947** Italy signs peace treaty with Allies. Cedes border areas to France and Yugoslavia, Dodecanese to Greece and gives up colonies.
- **1948** Elections. DC under De Gaspieri forms coalition with left-of-centre PSDI and PLI and PRI.
- **1949** Italy a founder member of NATO.
- **1950** Agreement with USA establishes US military bases on Italian soil.
- **1951** Joins European Iron and Steel Community.
- **1957** Founder member of European Community. Aided by EC funds and Marshall Aid, industrial growth accelerates.
- **1964** DC government under Aldo Moro forms coalition with PSI. Electoral support for DC falls to below 40%.
- **1969** Red Brigades, extreme left terrorist group, formed.
- **1972** Support for extreme right reaches post-war peak (9%). Rise in extreme left and right urban terrorism
- **1976** PCI support reaches a peak of 34% under Enrico Berlinguer's Eurocommunist philosophy.
- **1978** DC president Aldo Moro abducted and murdered by Red Brigades.
- **1980** Extreme right group plants bomb in Bologna railway station, killing 84 and wounding 200.
- **1983** Centre-left coalition formed under Bettino Craxi. Becomes longest serving Italian post-war government.
- **1987** Craxi government falls.
- **1990** Northern League (NL), a coalition of regionalist parties, attacks government's immigration policies and subsidies to southern Italy.
- **1992** Corruption scandal, involving the acceptance of bribes in return for public contracts, uncovered in Milan. Members of the government accused.
- **1994** General elections held. DC collapses. Unlikely coalition between Silvio Berlusconi's *Forza Italia*, and left and right-wing parties form government.

POLITICS

 Lower house 1997
Upper house 1997

 President Oscar Luigi Scalfaro

THE STATE OF THE PARTIES

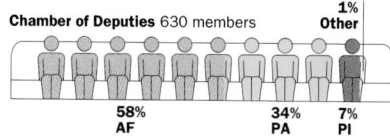

Chamber of Deputies 630 members

1%
Other

58%
AF

34%
PA

7%
PI

AF = Alliance for Freedom (composed of FI = Forza Italia, NL = Northern League, MSI/NA = National Alliance) **PA** = Progressive Alliance (composed of PDS = Democratic Party of the Left, RC = Reconstructed Communism, DA = Democratic Alliance, LR = La Rete, G = Green Party) **PI** = Pact for Italy (composed of PPI = Popular Party, SP = Segni Pact)

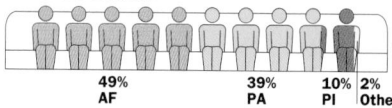

Senate 315 members

49%
AF

39%
PA

10%
PI

2%
Other

Italy is a multiparty democracy.

MAIN POLITICAL ISSUES

Corruption

The *Mani pulite*, 'Clean Hands', investigations, precipitated by the 1992 revelations of illegal party financing in Milan, have revealed a network of institutionalized corruption linking the traditional parties and business. By 1994, over 4500 people had been arrested, many of them top public figures. Several, like Carlo de Benedetti, head of one of Italy's most prestigious firms, Olivetti, have been imprisoned. The issue, which has destroyed the old political order, will remain prominent for some years owing to the enormous backlog of cases still to be tried. Silvio Berlusconi's *Forza Italia* has vowed to tackle the problem. Berlusconi himself was investigated in the early 1990s, but no charges were brought. To counter any

Giulio Andreotti, DC *leader and prime minister six times 1976-1992.*

Umberto Rossi, leader of the regionalist Northern League.

Silvio Berlusconi, leader of Forza Italia, *became prime minister in 1994.*

The church of Santa Maria della Salute marks the entrance to Venice. The city state managed to retain its independence until Napoleon Bonaparte's invasion of Italy.

conflicts of interest, a committee has been appointed to monitor the political links of his huge business empire.

Institutional Reform

Forza Italia has vowed to help the private sector by slashing red tape. The promise is popular as Italy's extreme bureaucratization encourages corruption. The new electoral system is also widely regarded as inadequate because, like the pure proportional representation system it replaced, it does not guarantee stable government.

PROFILE

In 1993, Italy experienced its worst political crisis since 1945. The dense network of institutionalized corruption being uncovered by the *Mani pulite* investigations had discredited a whole political class – in particular the Christian Democrats (CD) and Socialists (SP). Popular disgust was seen in the disastrous results for the CD and SP in municipal elections that year. Electoral reform by an interim government, after a positive referendum on the issue, meant that in the elections in March 1994, 75% of seats would be chosen by simple majority.

The left-wing alliance headed by the PDS, the reformed communists, initially seemed likely to win. However, in January 1994, millionaire businessman Silvio Berlusconi entered the race. His *Forza Italia* went into coalition with the secessionist NL and neo-fascist MSI/NA, to keep the left out. The PS and CD collapsed into factions. The CD was not only disgraced, it also lost the justification for its political dominance since 1945 – keeping from power Italy's once-large Communist Party.

Berlusconi's Freedom Alliance coalition won an electoral majority. Policy differences between the federal NL and centralist MSI/NA, which nearly split the alliance during the campaign, helped protract negotiations on a cabinet. But after 12 days, and for the first time since 1945, Italy had an avowedly right-wing government, including five MSI/NA neo-fascists.

WORLD AFFAIRS

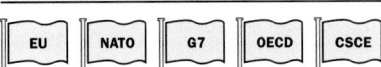

Since the Second World War, Italy has pursued a strongly Atlanticist foreign policy. Italy has also been one of the most committed members of the EU. Its strategic position in the central Mediterranean has made Italy a central member of NATO since its foundation in 1949. NATO's South European Command is based in Naples.

Since the end of the Cold War, Italy's major concern has been unrest in the Balkans. The fear that thousands of Bosnian war refugees would seek entry to Italy proved unfounded, however. The rise of Islamic fundamentalism in Algeria and the threat of a UN embargo against Libya are also of concern. Italy is highly dependent on the two North African states for its energy supplies.

AID

 $3.4bn (donations)   Down 1% in 1991

Italy has been targeting aid at the Balkan states and Albania. Its aim is to prevent a flood of economic migrants. Around 750 military personnel continue to operate relief in Albania; their stay has been extended indefinitely. Africa receives the bulk of development aid.

DEFENCE

 $21.2bn   Up 8% in 1992

0	*Defence spending as % GDP*	40
1.7%		

ITALIAN ARMED FORCES

🚂	1220 main battle tanks (300 M-60A1/920 *Leopard*)	230,000 personnel
⚓	1 carrier, 8 submarines, 1 cruiser, 3 destroyers and 24 frigates	48,000 personnel
✈	449 combat aircraft (80 *Tornado*/164 F-104S/ 99 G-91)	76,000 personnel
	None	

The breakup of the Soviet Union and civil war in parts of former Yugoslavia have refocused Italy's defence priorities. The 'New Model Defence' announced in 1992 will lead to a 23% reduction in all armed forces. The army is being remodelled for a rapid-intervention role for NATO's southern flank. The navy will be cut to fulfil Mediterranean coastal roles rather than maintaining its current ocean-going capabilities. An estimated 45% of Italy's weapons systems need to be replaced before the year 2000.

ECONOMICS

 $1134bn   1712 lire

SCORE CARD

❏ WORLD GNP RANKING	5th
❏ GNP PER CAPITA	$18,550
❏ BALANCE OF PAYMENTS	$–25.4bn
❏ INFLATION	7.1%
❏ UNEMPLOYMENT	10.4%

EXPORTS

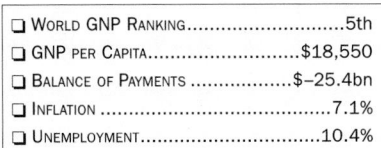

UK 8% · USA 8% · France 16% · Germany* 19% · Other 49%

IMPORTS

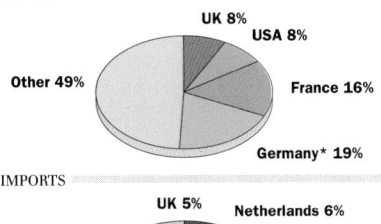

UK 5% · Netherlands 6% · France 12% · Germany* 22% · Other 52%

STRENGTHS

Highly competitive, innovative small to medium-size business sector. World leader in industrial and product design, textiles and household appliances. Several highly innovative firms include Fiat (cars), Montedison (plastics), Olivetti (computers), and Benetton (fashion). Strong tourism and agriculture sectors. Weak lira a boost to exports.

WEAKNESSES

Huge public deficit and government debt; over 100% of GDP. Large and inefficient public sector. Uneven wealth distribution: north Italy far richer than the south, which suffers from high unemployment and where organized crime deters investment. Relatively small companies could find competing in a free international market hard. Heavy dependence on imported energy.

PROFILE

Since the Second World War, Italy has developed from a mainly agricultural society into the world's fifth industrial power, with a GDP greater than the UK's. The economy is characterized by a large state sector, a mass of family-owned businesses, relatively high levels of protectionism and strong regional differences. Compared to the other G7 economies, Italy also has relatively few multinationals.

State businesses are run mainly by two holding companies, the Institute for Industrial Reconstruction (IRI) and the National Hydrocarbons Group (ENI). IRI owns major electronics, steel, telecommunications, engineering, shipbuilding and aerospace companies.

ECONOMIC PERFORMANCE INDICATOR

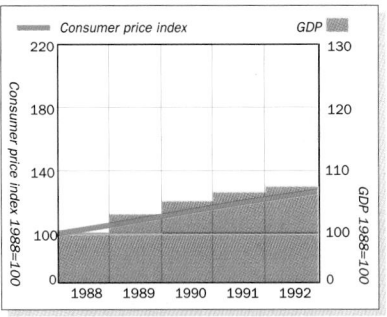

ENI is one of the world's top players in the energy and chemicals sectors.

Family-owned businesses are the backbone of Italy's private sector. They include Fiat, whose interests include aero-engines, telecommunications and bioengineering, as well as cars. Similar businesses tend to congregate together. This geographical specialization encourages local competition which has translated into national success.

The *Mezzogiorno* remains the exception. It has 35% of Italy's population, but contributes only 24% of GDP. State attempts to attract new investment have met with success in areas immediately south of Rome. Elsewhere, organized crime has deterred investors and siphoned off state funds. Industrial production has stagnated and unemployment soared. Anger at the misuse of state funds in the south has been a powerful factor in the growth of the Northern League with its demands for autonomy. One third of Italian tax revenue is generated in Italy's industrial heartland of Milan.

ITALY : MAJOR BUSINESSES

🌸	Textiles
🍶	Chemicals
👕	Garments
⚡	Electronics
🖊	Pharmaceuticals
🔦	Light engineering
⚙	Defence industries
🚗	Vehicle manufacture
✈	Aerospace industries

| 0 | 200 km |
| 0 | 200 miles |

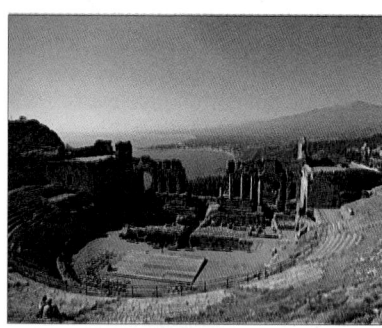

Remains of the Greek theatre at Taormina, eastern Sicily. It was rebuilt by the Romans in the 2nd century AD. Today, the theatre is the venue for an annual arts festival.

RESOURCES

 216.9bn kwh (capacity 56.5m kw)

84,200 b/d (reserves 746,977,000 bbl)

 11.6m sheep, 9.4m pigs, 8.7m cattle, 250,000 horses

Lignite, pyrites, fluorspar, barytes, bauxite, lead, zinc

ELECTRICITY GENERATION

Hydro 16% (35.1bn kwh)	
Thermal 82% (178.6bn kwh)	
Nuclear 0%	
Other 2% (3.2bn kwh)	

0   20   40   60   80   100
% of total generation by type

Italy has very few natural resources. It produces just 1% of its oil needs and is highly vulnerable to both fluctuations in world prices and political instability in its North African suppliers. It has reduced its exposure since 1973, when oil accounted for 71% of its needs. Even so, oil still accounts for 56% of energy consumption. Some power is generated from hydro and geothermal sources. Nuclear power was rejected in a 1987 referendum and development has effectively been abandoned. Italy's mineral assets are small and the sector contributes little to national wealth.

ITALY : LAND USE

Cropland	
Forest	
Pasture	
High mountain regions	
Vineyards	
Citrus fruits	
Cattle	

SARDEGNA

SICILIA

0   200 km
0   200 miles

ENVIRONMENT

 7% (6% partially protected)

Green issues not a priority for Berlusconi government

ENVIRONMENTAL TREATIES

Yes		Yes	
No		Yes	

Italy has extensive environmental legislation, but, compared to other EU states, has faced problems in enforcing directives. Under the Amato administration, new measures such as energy taxes and waste recycling laws were considered. However, the government of Silvio Berlusconi is expected to be less keen to introduce environmental laws which could restrict business competitiveness.

Pollution in cities such as Naples and Rome is a major concern. Bans on traffic for up to seven hours during windless days are not uncommon. Air pollution and acid rain have also been damaging forests; 10% of trees are affected. Concern has also been expressed at the hunting of migrant birds, a popular sport in Italy, and the use by some in the fishing industry of drift nets in the Ionian Sea. Sometimes up to 30 km long, these nets catch dolphins and turtles as well as fish. Under EU law, all drift nets over 2.5 km long are illegal.

MEDIA

 No censorship restrictions

PUBLISHING AND BROADCAST MEDIA

There are 99 daily newspapers. Only *Corriere della Serra* and *La Repubblica* have nationwide distribution			
3 state-controlled, 12 other national networks		3 state-controlled, 3000 commercial stations	
Astra 1-B Intelstat V1 F1		Most major cities	

Italy's media is dominated by a few conglomerates, notably the Fininvest Group owned by Prime Minister Silvio Berlusconi and Carlo de Benedetti's Ferruzzi group. It has traditionally been highly politicized. Until the exposures of the post-1992 corruption investigations brought reform, this was particularly true of the state TV RAI channels. Like the rest of the state sector, they were apportioned between the main parties: RAI 1 to the Christian Democrats, RAI 2 to the Socialists and RAI 3 to the former Communist Party. All the media reflect the Italian love of sport, especially football. *La Gazzetta dello Sport* has one of the largest circulations of the national dailies.

CRIME

 Italy does not publish prison figures

 Up 22% in 1990

CRIME RATES

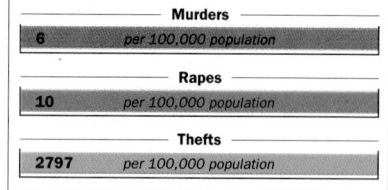

Murders	
6	per 100,000 population

Rapes	
10	per 100,000 population

Thefts	
2797	per 100,000 population

Organized crime remains Italy's most significant problem. The Mafias of Sicily, Naples and Calabria – the *Cosa Nostra*, *Camorra* and *'ndrangheta* – control wholesale agricultural markets and much of the drugs trade, bleed businesses of protection money and manipulate public works contracts and politics. Journalists and public officials delving too deeply into their activities are killed. Giovanni Falcone, the most successful anti-Mafia magistrate, was assassinated in Sicily in 1992. Estimates suggest Mafia businesses are worth $1 billion–$10 billion a year, on a par with US multinationals ITT and Exxon.

EDUCATION

 97%

0   Education spending as % GNP   25
5%

THE EDUCATION SYSTEM

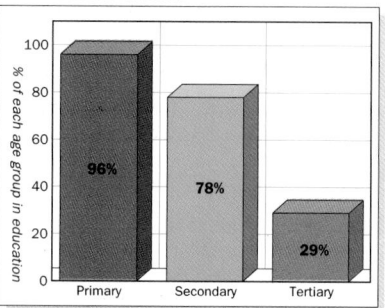

% of each age group in education

Primary 96%   Secondary 78%   Tertiary 29%

Italy's schooling is almost entirely state-run, apart from a few religious schools and elite private institutions. The pupil–teacher ratio is one of the best in Europe. In 1993, the school leaving age was raised from 14 to 16 years, bringing Italy in line with the rest of Europe. The intention was to cut the high drop-out rate in schools, which in Sicily is as high as 50%.

Universities in Italy are over-subscribed. Rome has 180,000 students, only 30% of whom gain a degree. Many Italian educationalists wish to restrict entry. Another concern is the fact that Italy devotes only 1.4% of its GNP to research, compared to the European average of 2.5%.

I

REGIONS

MILAN

Built-up area — **Park or open land** — **Old City**
Major sites — **Hi-tech industry** — **Electronics**
Motor industry — **Food processing** — **Fashion** — **Finance**

ITALY'S SECOND CITY is also its prime industrial and commercial centre. The focus of the fashion, finance and publishing industries, among others, Milan and its province contribute 12% of national GDP. Its inhabitants are among the wealthiest in Europe. Since the 1970s, there has been a shift from manufacturing towards the service and high-tech sectors which now employ 50% of the population. Many major firms have their head offices in Milan, but its economy depends on small, highly innovative businesses. The city's pride in its efficiency took a knock in 1992 when it became a focus of investigations into corruption in the awarding of public contracts.

TUSCANY

MIDWAY BETWEEN MILAN and Rome, Tuscany in many ways epitomizes Italy – certainly to the thousands of foreigners who have made it their home and the millions of tourists attracted by its beaches, hill towns and the artistic glories of its capital, Florence. It is also quintessentially Italian in that its economy depends on a myriad of small firms clustered around particular centres – such as Prato for textiles and Santa Croce for leather. Over the past 40 years, these family-run concerns have transformed Tuscany from a mainly agricultural society into a major industrial area and one of Italy's richest regions.

Etruscan/classical sites — **Renaissance sites**

CALABRIA

Areas of agricultural reform — **Areas of industrial reform** — **Tourism**
Vegetable oil — **Citrus fruits** — **Wine**

OCCUPYING THE FOOT of the Italian 'boot', Calabria is region of harsh mountains. It has poor soils, virtually no industry and Italy's highest rate of unemployment. The Calabrians are

Italy's poorest people, and among the poorest in Europe. To other Italians, the region is a world apart. Southern Calabria, home of the notorious 'ndrangheta Mafia, has Europe's highest murder rate. A few Mafia-dominated communities like Natile, San Luca and Plati have grown relatively wealthy extorting money from northern industrialists. The area is the kidnap capital of Italy. State development funds have been siphoned off by Mafia clans who control 90% of building and public works contracts. Investors, including state industries like IRI – used as pump primers in other parts of the south – have stayed away. Virtually abandoned by the state, which has made little attempt to control the 'ndrangheta, many Calabrians have emigrated. In the years after 1945, up to one third of Calabria's population emigrated to Australia.

HEALTH

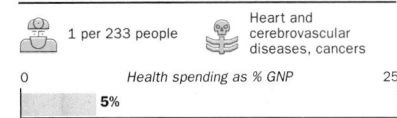

1 per 233 people — Heart and cerebrovascular diseases, cancers

Health spending as % GNP — 5%

Italy's current state-run health system was introduced in the 1970s. Standards vary as services are run by the regions, but few Italians rate their hospitals very highly. Initially free at point of use, charges were introduced in 1988. In addition to some dental and prescription costs, patients have to pay a daily hospital charge and a yearly health fee. AIDS patients are exempt.

WEALTH

Waiter, 1,533,871 Italian lire per month; journalist, 2,855,655 Italian lire per month

CONSUMER GOODS OWNERSHIP

Italians, particularly in the north, are today among the world's wealthiest people in terms of disposable income. This is a result not only of economic growth, but also of the structure of Italian society.

Many Italians have more than one job. The extended families in which most people still live often have access to more than one income. Few people have mortgages, and savings and tax avoidance levels are high.

The main exceptions are in parts of the south. In places like Calabria and Naples, where investment has been lowest and unemployment is highest, many people still live in poverty. For those who do not emigrate, organized crime is usually the only source of jobs.

WORLD RANKING

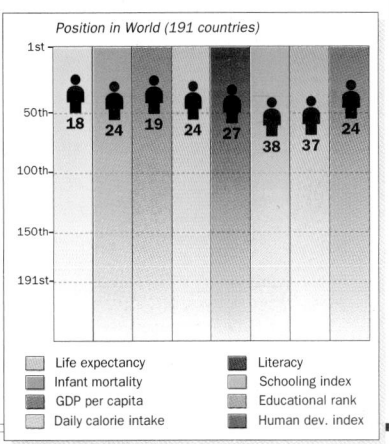

Life expectancy — Literacy
Infant mortality — Schooling index
GDP per capita — Educational rank
Daily calorie intake — Human dev. index

IVORY COAST

WEST AFRICA
Africa

OFFICIAL NAME: Republic of the Ivory Coast   **CAPITAL:** Yamoussoukro
POPULATION: 12.9 million   **CURRENCY:** CFA franc   **OFFICIAL LANGUAGE:** French

ONE OF THE LARGER of the West African coastal nations, the Ivory Coast remains under the powerful influence of its former colonial ruler, France; it is also called Côte d'Ivoire. Most of its population lives along the sandy coastal strip. The forested interior, apart from the capital, is sparsely populated. Between independence in 1960 and his death in 1993, the Ivory Coast was ruled by President Houphouët-Boigny.

CLIMATE

WEATHER CHART

The south's four seasons – two rainy and two dry – merge in the north into a single wet season with lower rainfall.

COMMUNICATIONS

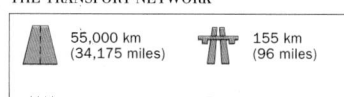
Abidjan–Port-Bouët
849,000 passengers
8 ships
93,300 dwt

THE TRANSPORT NETWORK

55,000 km (34,175 miles)	155 km (96 miles)
638 km (396 miles)	980 km (609 miles)

The relatively good transport system focuses on Abidjan, the premier port of francophone West Africa.

TOURISM

 178,000 visitors   Up 2% in 1988

MAIN OVERSEAS ARRIVALS

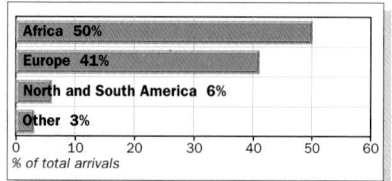
Africa 50%
Europe 41%
North and South America 6%
Other 3%
0   10   20   30   40   50   60
% of total arrivals

Ambitious plans for an 'African Riviera' east of Abidjan and the opening of an hotel by the French *Club Méditerranée* did not boost tourism as expected. The giant Christian basilica built at Yamoussoukro is a major attraction.

PEOPLE

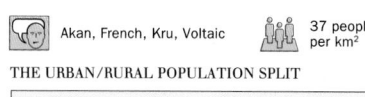
Akan, French, Kru, Voltaic
37 people per km²

THE URBAN/RURAL POPULATION SPLIT

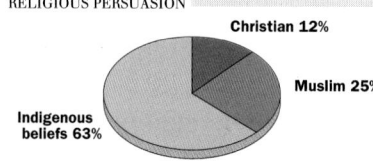
40%   60%

RELIGIOUS PERSUASION

Christian 12%
Muslim 25%
Indigenous beliefs 63%

Although there are more than 60 ethnic groups, the key ones are the Baoule in the centre, the Agri in the east, the Senufo in the north, the Dioula in the northwest and west, the Bété in the centre-west and the Dan–Yacouba in the west. Houphouët-Boigny promoted his own group, the Baoule, who number only 23% of the population. The succession of Konan Bedic, another Baoule, has annoyed many tribes, the Bété in particular. The extended family is an important force in the shanty towns of Abidjan and connects migrants with their villages. As a result of improved education, women now hold many top jobs.

IVORY COAST

Total Area : 322 463 sq. km
(124 503 sq. miles)

0   100 km
0   100 miles

POPULATION
☐ over 1 000 000
◎ over 100 000
○ over 50 000
● over 10 000
• under 10 000

LAND HEIGHT
1000m/3281ft
500m/1640ft
200m/656ft
Sea Level

POLITICS

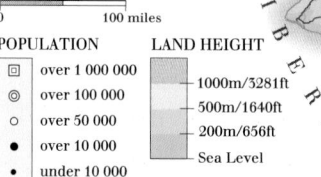 1995   President Konan Bedic

THE STATE OF THE PARTIES

National Assembly 175 members
2% Other
93% PDCI–RDA
5% FPI

PDCI–RDA = Democratic Party of the Ivory Coast – African Democratic Rally **FPI** = Ivorian People's Front
Other = Ivorian Labour Party

The death of President Houphouët-Boigny in 1993 threw the Ivory Coast's politics into turmoil. No clear successor had been identified by the man who had run the Ivory Coast since independence. Under his rule, the Democratic Party of the Ivory Coast (PDCI) developed a monopoly on patronage which permeated all ranks of the civil service, one reason for the opposition FPI's poor showing in the country's first multiparty elections in 1990. France (the main aid donor), the business community and party barons all maintained their influence under the rule of Houphouët-Boigny, who carefully balanced competing demands. The power vacuum that followed his death left all parties with an influence in politics in a state of uncertainty, at a time when the Ivory Coast had pressing economic problems to deal with. Fears were expressed that the army might decide to take a more prominent role in politics.

I

WORLD AFFAIRS

The Ivory Coast fears that the civil war in neighbouring Liberia could affect its own stability. However, its main concern is balancing the demands and interests of its creditors: the US-dominated World Bank on the one hand and France on the other. Within ECOWAS, the Ivory Coast's most important relationship is with Nigeria.

AID

 $633m (receipts)   Down 9% in 1991

France donates most overall aid. Structural adjustment loans from the World Bank have been particularly important in easing the acute debt problem. The Ivory Coast gives aid to poorer West African countries.

DEFENCE

 $185m   Fairly constant from year to year

Since independence, a defence accord has existed with France, the main supplier of equipment and trainer of officers for the 5500-strong army. The greatest security threat is along the border with war-torn Liberia.

ECONOMICS

 $8.7bn   295.23 CFA francs

SCORE CARD

- WORLD GNP RANKING..........................84th
- GNP PER CAPITA $675
- BALANCE OF PAYMENTS....................$–1.4bn
- INFLATION 1%
- UNEMPLOYMENT ..Lower than West African average

STRENGTHS
Diversified nature of the agricultural sector. Relatively good infrastructure. Benefits of early liberalism and attractiveness to investors.

WEAKNESSES
Major debt from over-borrowing for projects such as the Kossou Dam. Overproduction of some commodities. Political patronage system of the ruling party, which exploits farmers.

EXPORTS

UK 9%
USA 11%
Other 48%
France 15%
Netherlands 17%

IMPORTS

Italy 7%
UK 9%
Other 41%
Nigeria 11%
France 32%

concern is balancing the demands and interests of its creditors: the US-dominated World Bank on the one hand and France on the other. Within ECOWAS, the Ivory Coast's most important relationship is with Nigeria.

RESOURCES

 2.4bn kwh (capacity 1.17m kw)   Reserves of 100,000,000 bbl; refines 69,000 b/cd

 1m sheep, 1m cattle, 351,000 pigs, 1000 horses   Oil, diamonds

Oil reserves have failed to meet expectations; negotiations are under way on offshore gas development.

ENVIRONMENT

 6% (0.3% partially protected)   Ban on timber exports not yet in force

The government has committed itself to a ban on timber exports when the foreign payments situation improves.

MEDIA

 Despite reduction in censorship since 1990, the press is still subject to controls

PUBLISHING AND BROADCAST MEDIA

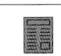 There are 2 daily newspapers, *Fraternité-Matin* and *Ivoir 'Soir*, both published by the government

 1 state-owned service   1 state-owned, 1 independent service

The heavy censorship of the past 30 years has now eased, but there is still a hesitancy to speak out politically.

EDUCATION

 54%

A high percentage of students fail the *baccalauréat*. As expenditure has been cut, student agitation has grown.

CRIME

 Ivory Coast does not publish prison figures   Down 52% in 1990

Crime levels are low in rural areas. However, armed robbery and violent crime are on the increase in Abidjan.

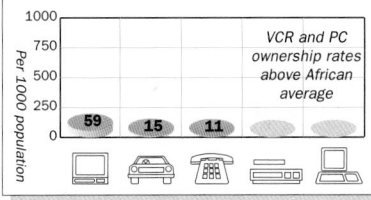

The basilica, Yamoussoukro. *Built in the new capital, President Houphouët-Boigny's birthplace, it is modelled on St Peter's, Rome.*

CHRONOLOGY

One of the great trading emporia of West Africa, the Ivory Coast was made a French colony in 1893. By 1918 the French had defeated the Malinke empire and the forest peoples of the interior.

- **1903–1935** Railway and roads built with forced labour.
- **1946** PDCI founded as sole party.
- **1948–1950** The Dark Years; arrests and deaths in anti-French activity.
- **1960** Félix Houphouët-Boigny declares independence.
- **1970** Oil production starts.
- **1990** First contested elections: Houphouët-Boigny and PDCI win.
- **1992** First black African state to open diplomatic links with South Africa.
- **1993** Houphouët-Boigny dies.

HEALTH

 1 per 15,950 people   Malaria, communicable diseases, neonatal deaths

Health improved notably in the 1980s, with many more paramedical workers. Infant mortality rates are high.

WEALTH

 Metalworking machine setter, 109,500–254,300 CFA francs per month; dentist, 154,000–422,500 CFA francs per month

CONSUMER GOODS OWNERSHIP

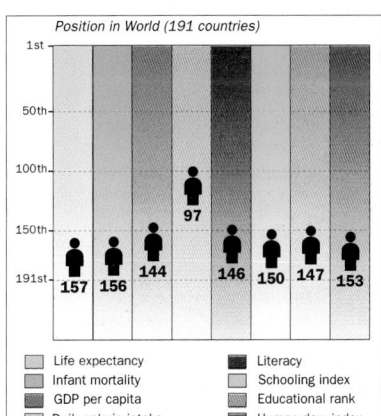

VCR and PC ownership rates above African average

59   15   11

A large bourgeoisie grew rich in the boom years. Urban living standards are better than in many African countries.

WORLD RANKING

Position in World (191 countries)

1st
50th
100th
150th
191st

97
157   156   144   146   150   147   153

- Life expectancy
- Infant mortality
- GDP per capita
- Daily calorie intake
- Literacy
- Schooling index
- Educational rank
- Human dev. index

JAMAICA

OFFICIAL NAME: Jamaica **CAPITAL:** Kingston
POPULATION: 2.5 million **CURRENCY:** Jamaican dollar **OFFICIAL LANGUAGE:** English

CARIBBEAN

FIRST COLONIZED BY THE SPANISH and then, from 1655, by the English, Jamaica is located in the Caribbean, south of Cuba. It was the first of the Caribbean island nations to become independent from colonial control in the post-war years, and remains an influential force in Caribbean politics. Jamaica is also influential on the world music scene; *reggae* and *ragga* (or *dancehall*) developed in the tough conditions of Kingston's poor districts.

CLIMATE

WEATHER CHART

Hurricanes are likely between June and November. The hills above Kingston are the coolest spot during hot summers.

COMMUNICATIONS

 Norman Manley International, Kingston
 4 ships 16,200 dwt

THE TRANSPORT NETWORK

18,200 km (11,309 miles) | None
339 km (211 miles) | None

Jamaica has a general shortage of buses and taxis. The airports at Kingston and Montego Bay have been improved recently.

TOURISM

 840,000 visitors | Up 18% in 1990

MAIN OVERSEAS ARRIVALS

USA 67%
Canada 14%
UK 10%
Other 9%
% of total arrivals

Tourism is a major industry in Jamaica. Most tourists stay in large, enclosed beach resorts. Ocho Rios and Montego Bay have the best beaches.

PEOPLE

 English Creole, English | 228 people per km²

THE URBAN/RURAL POPULATION SPLIT

52% | 48%

RELIGIOUS PERSUASION

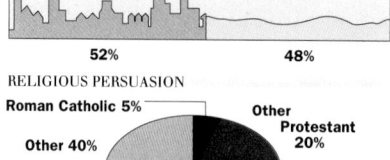
Roman Catholic 5%
Other Protestant 20%
Other 40%
Anglican 7%
Baptist 10%
Church of God 18%

Jamaica has a broad ethnic mix. Most Jamaicans are the descendants of Africans brought to the island between the 16th and 19th centuries, but there are also minorities of Europeans, Indians, Chinese and Arabs. Jamaica is also home to the Rastafarians, worshippers of the former Emperor of Ethiopia.

Most social tension is the result of the marked disparities of wealth. The Caribbean women's rights movement arrived first in Jamaica, and today many women hold senior positions in economic and political life.

Although life revolves around the family, absentee fathers are common. Many career women are single parents by choice. Life in the ghettos of Kingston is often violent and based largely on gun law. Kingston slums have their own patois.

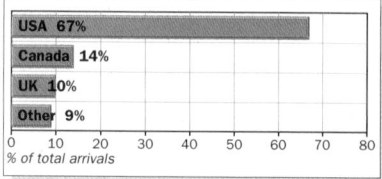
Bauxite mine and terminal, *Runway Bay. Bauxite – from which aluminium is made – is the main source of foreign income.*

POLITICS

1994 | HM Queen Elizabeth II

THE STATE OF THE PARTIES

House of Representatives 60 members
75% PNP | 25% JLP

PNP = People's National Party **JLP** = Jamaica Labour Party

Senate 21 members

13 members chosen by the prime minister and 8 by the leader of the opposition

Jamaica's political and economic life is dominated by a few long-established and wealthy families, who fund the parties. The country's political complexion changed markedly in the late 1980s, as the ideologies of the once socialist PNP and the conservative JLP converged towards a moderate free-market economic approach.

Violence during election time is a continuing problem. Despite strong denials, some politicians retain close connections with armed gangs who control the politically important slum areas of Kingston through intimidation. When threats fail, these gangs have been known to murder political opponents.

WORLD AFFAIRS

Comm | Caricom | OAS | GATT | NAM

The USA is the focus of foreign policy. Jamaica liaises with US agencies in anti-narcotics programmes.

AID

 $166m (receipts) | Down 61% in 1991

Most aid comes from the USA, the EU and the UK. It includes both project loans and balance of payments support.

DEFENCE

 $32.52m | Up 47% in 1990

Jamaica's 5500-strong defence force buys its arms from the USA, but is trained by the UK. Today, the defence force is used against narcotics smugglers and to break up violence during elections.

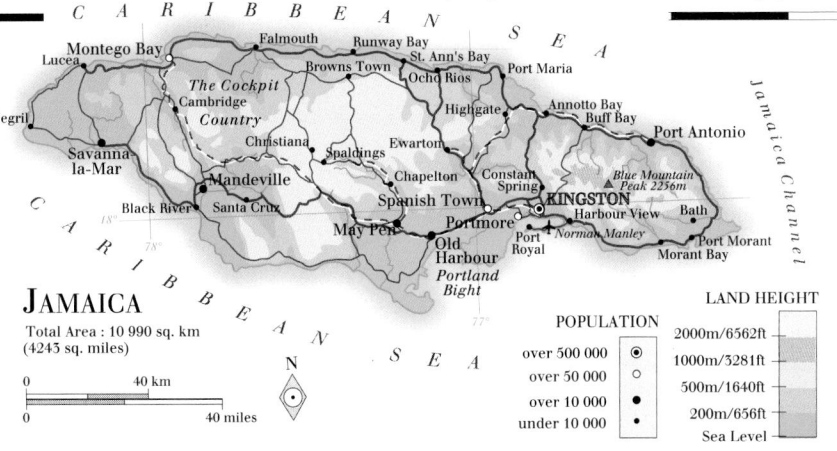

JAMAICA

Total Area : 10 990 sq. km
(4243 sq. miles)

 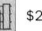

POPULATION
over 500 000	⊙
over 50 000	○
over 10 000	•
under 10 000	•

LAND HEIGHT
2000m/6562ft	
1000m/3281ft	
500m/1640ft	
200m/656ft	
Sea Level	

ECONOMICS

$2.8bn   28.46 Jamaican dollars

SCORE CARD
❑ WORLD GNP RANKING	128th
❑ GNP PER CAPITA	$1120
❑ BALANCE OF PAYMENTS	$–198m
❑ INFLATION	60.7%
❑ UNEMPLOYMENT	15.7%

STRENGTHS
A relatively broadly based economy. Mining and refining of bauxite for aluminium. Successful tourism industry. Agriculture, including sugar, bananas, rum and coffee. Light manufacturing and data processing for US companies are growing sectors.

WEAKNESSES
Most products are dependent on protected markets, which are under threat in both the USA and the EU.

EXPORTS
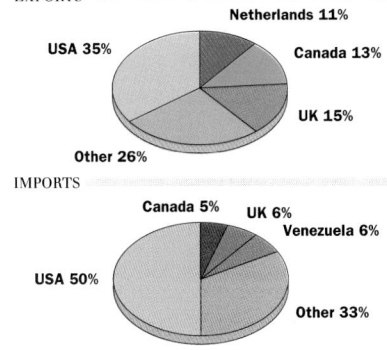

Netherlands 11%
USA 35%
Canada 13%
UK 15%
Other 26%

IMPORTS
Canada 5% UK 6%
Venezuela 6%
USA 50%
Other 33%

RESOURCES

 2.7bn kwh (capacity 730,000 kw)

 290,000 cattle, 240,000 pigs, 23,000 asses

 Not an oil producer; refines 32,000 b/cd

Bauxite, marble, gypsum, silica, clay

Jamaica is the world's third largest producer of bauxite, accounting for 11% of total global output.

ENVIRONMENT

 3%

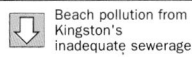 Beach pollution from Kingston's inadequate sewerage

Acidic dust from bauxite processing, the biggest heavy industry in Jamaica, is the major problem, and has led to the relocation of an entire village.

MEDIA

 Freedom of expression is guaranteed under the constitution

PUBLISHING AND BROADCAST MEDIA

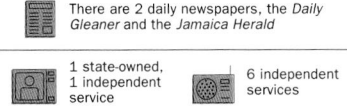

There are 2 daily newspapers, the *Daily Gleaner* and the *Jamaica Herald*

1 state-owned, 1 independent service

6 independent services

The government is in the process of loosening its hold on broadcasting. The Jamaican press is one of the most influential in the Caribbean.

CRIME

 4350 prisoners

 Down 19% in 1990

Armed crime is a major problem. Many murders are the result of armed robberies linked to narcotics gangs competing for territory. Much of the world crack trade is still controlled from Jamaica. Large areas of Kingston are ruled by *Dons*, gang leaders who administer their own violent justice. The armed police are also frequently accused of the peremptory shooting of suspects.

The British Privy Council is the last court of appeal; in 1993, 80 men on death row for more than 5 years were reprieved in a landmark decision.

EDUCATION

 98%

Education is based on the former British 11-plus selection system. Jamaica hosts the largest of the three campuses of the University of the West Indies.

HEALTH

 1 per 6687 people

 Cerebrovascular and heart diseases, cancers, diabetes

The once-efficient state health service is now seriously underfunded. There are fewer doctors and nurses than in the 1980s and hospitals generally have a shortage of drugs and rudimentary medical equipment.

WEALTH

 Miner, 1139 Jamaican dollars per week; metal manufacturing worker, 2840 Jamaican dollars per week

CONSUMER GOODS OWNERSHIP

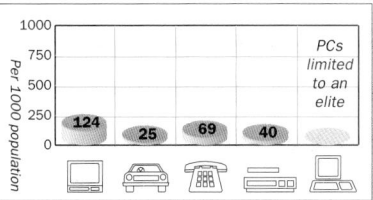

PCs limited to an elite

124 25 69 40

Wealth disparities are highly marked in Jamaica, although better education has seen an increase in the number of black Jamaicans taking more lucrative, white-collar jobs. The poorest in Jamaica, mostly migrants from rural areas, live in the slums of Kingston.

WORLD RANKING

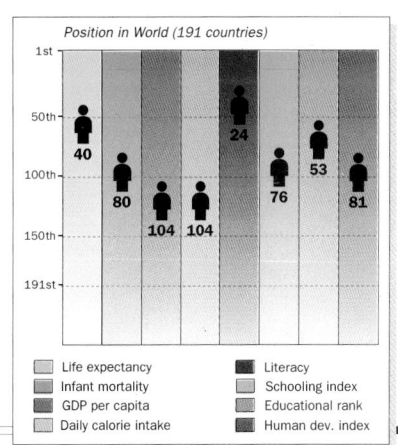

Position in World (191 countries)

1st
50th — 40, 24
100th — 80, 53
  104 104 76 81
150th
191st

- ☐ Life expectancy
- ☐ Infant mortality
- ☐ GDP per capita
- ☐ Daily calorie intake
- ☐ Literacy
- ☐ Schooling index
- ☐ Educational rank
- ☐ Human dev. index

J

JAPAN

OFFICIAL NAME: Japan **CAPITAL:** Tokyo **POPULATION:** 124 million
CURRENCY: Yen **OFFICIAL LANGUAGE:** Japanese

EAST ASIA

A CONSTITUTIONAL MONARCHY, with an emperor as head of state, Japan is located off the east Asian coast in the north Pacific. It comprises four principal islands, and over 3000 smaller islands. One chain of islands – the Kuriles in the north – is disputed with the Russian Federation. The terrain is mostly mountainous, with fertile coastal plains; over two thirds is woodland. The Pacific coast is vulnerable to *tsunamis* – tidal waves triggered by submarine earthquakes. Most cities are located by the sea; the Kanto plain around Tokyo, Kawasaki and Yokohama is the most populous and heavily industrialized. To the north, Hokkaido is the most rural of the main islands. Japan is the world's most powerful economy, with a current trade balance of over $100 billion per annum, and overseas investments of $240 billion.

Traditional paddy field in *Hokkaido. Rice farming is among the most protected sectors of the Japanese economy.*

CLIMATE

WEATHER CHART

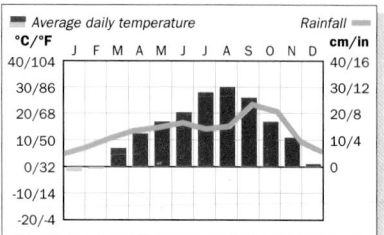

The Sea of Japan has a moderating influence on Japan's climate. Winters are less cold than on the Asian mainland. Japan also has much higher rainfall. Spring is perhaps the most pleasant season, with warm, sunny days, but without the sultry, oppressive heat and rainfall of the summer. The freak storms and floods of August 1992 were the worst for 120 years.

COMMUNICATIONS

Narita, Tokyo
32m passengers

3792 ships
36.34m dwt

THE TRANSPORT NETWORK

1.1m km
(683,507 miles)

Motorways
3900 km
(2423 miles)

27,327 km
(16,980 miles)

1770 km
(1099 miles)

Railways are the most important means of transport in Japan. The *Shinkansen*, known in the West as the bullet train, is the second fastest in the world. It is renowned as much for its reliability as its speed. The Tokyo–Chitose air route, with six million passengers a year, is the busiest in the world.

JAPAN

Total Area : 377 800 sq. km
(145 869 sq. miles)

POPULATION

- ◾ over 5 000 000
- ▣ over 1 000 000
- ◉ over 500 000
- ◎ over 100 000
- ○ over 50 000
- ● over 10 000

LAND HEIGHT

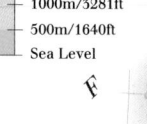

1500m/4921ft
1000m/3281ft
500m/1640ft
Sea Level

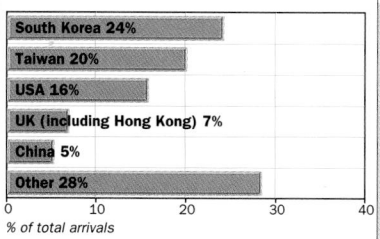

TOURISM

🧳 3.58m visitors   ⬆ Up 1% in 1993

MAIN OVERSEAS ARRIVALS

South Korea 24%	
Taiwan 20%	
USA 16%	
UK (including Hong Kong) 7%	
China 5%	
Other 28%	

% of total arrivals (0–40)

The high value of the yen makes Japan an expensive tourist destination. Attractions include the extraordinary variety of energetic high-tech urban living in Tokyo and Osaka. By contrast, rural areas such as Hokkaido are highly traditional.

A new trend in Japan is eco-tourism. Over three million people a year come to look at whales. Sightseeing boats leave from former whaling villages such as Ogata. The ancient imperial capital, Kyoto, remains the most popular tourist destination. Over 35 million people visit it every year.

High Street, Ginza District, Tokyo at night. Japan's well-policed cities are among the safest in the world.

PEOPLE

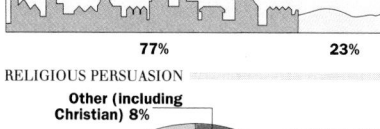

Japanese, Korean, Chinese   327 people per km²

THE URBAN/RURAL POPULATION SPLIT

77%   23%

RELIGIOUS PERSUASION
Other (including Christian) 8%
Buddhist 16%
Shinto and Buddhist 76%

ETHNIC MAKEUP
Other (mainly Korean) 1%
Japanese 99%

Japan is one of the most racially homogenous societies in the world. Its sense of order is reflected in the phenomenon of the lifetime employer. Many Japanese men define themselves by the company they work for rather than the job they do. An employer's influence stretches to commanding employees' social time, and even to encouraging and approving marriages.

Women mostly play a traditional role, running the home and supervising the all-important education of their children. They tend to work until the age of 26, when many will marry and continue to work part-time. Some Japanese women are, however, beginning to follow independent, long-term careers. More are entering the medical and legal professions. Japan saw its first female party leader – Takako Doi – in 1991.

There is little tradition of teenage rebellion in Japan. Whilst the young still tend to follow their parents' lifestyles, some are questioning established attitudes. They are less likely to want to work for the same company for life, and less willing to give up evenings and weekends to entertaining company clients.

Social form remains extremely important in Japanese society. Respect for elders and social and business superiors is still strong.

POPULATION AGE BREAKDOWN

% of population by age group	0–14	15–64	65+
1960	30%	64%	6%
1970	24%	69%	7%
1980	24%	67%	9%
1990	18%	70%	12%
2000	16%	68%	16%

CHRONOLOGY

Japan's tendency to limit its contacts with the outside world ended in 1853, when a US naval squadron coerced trading concessions from the last of the Tokugawa shoguns.

❑ **1868** Civil war. Tokugawa regime falls. Restoration of Meiji dynasty.
❑ **1869** Edo renamed Tokyo. Attempts to reverse increasing Western influence.
❑ **1872** Modernization along Western lines introduced: the 'Strong Army, Rich Country' programme. *Samurai* rank abolished. Japan's strong military tradition becomes state-directed.
❑ **1889** Constitution modelled on Bismarck's German constitution adopted.
❑ **1894–1895** War with China; ends in Japanese victory.
❑ **1904–1905** War with Russia; ends in Japanese victory. Formosa and Korea annexed.
❑ **1914** Japan joins First World War on Allied side. Sees limited naval action.
❑ **1919** Versailles peace conference gives Japan limited territorial gains in the Pacific.
❑ **1920** USA limits Japanese immigration.
❑ **1923** Yokohama earthquake kills 140,000.
❑ **1927** Japan enters period of radical nationalism, and introduces the notion of a 'co-prosperity sphere' in South East Asia under Japanese control. Interpreted in the USA as a threat to its Pacific interests.
❑ **1931** Manchuria invaded, placed under Japanese control and renamed Manchukuo.
❑ **1937** Japan launches full-scale invasion of China.
❑ **1938** All political parties placed under one common banner; Japan effectively ruled by militarists.
❑ **1939** Japan does not react to outbreak of war in Europe.
❑ **1940** Fall of France in Europe; Japan invades French Indo-China.
❑ **1941** July, Japan forces Vichy government in France to sanction take over of southern Indo-China. October, USA responds with a total trade embargo, including oil, and increases the strength of the US navy relative to the Japanese. December, Japan launches attack on US fleet at Pearl Harbour. British and Dutch possessions in the Pacific invaded.
❑ **1942** Japan loses decisive naval battle of the Coral Sea. USA begins naval campaign in the Pacific which leads to Japan's eventual defeat at sea.

J

J

- ❏ **1945** Huge US bombing campaign culminates in atomic bombing of Hiroshima and Nagasaki. Soviet Union declares war on Japan. Japanese Emperor surrenders, gives up his divine status, and Japan placed under US military government.
- ❏ **1945** US Gen MacArthur installed as supreme commander of Allied Powers in Japan.
- ❏ **1947** Japanese constitution, modelled on US, but retaining the emperor in ceremonial role, introduced.
- ❏ **1949** Elections. LDP in power.
- ❏ **1950** Korean War. US army contracts lead to quick expansion of Japanese economy.
- ❏ **1952** Treaty of San Francisco. Japan regains independence. Industrial production recovers to 15% above 1936 levels.
- ❏ **1960** Ikeda economic plan announced, with aim of doubling incomes in ten years.
- ❏ **1964** Tokyo Olympics. Bullet train (*Shinkansen*) inaugurated. Japan admitted to OECD.
- ❏ **1970** Osaka Expo confirms Japan as first rank economic power.
- ❏ **1973** Oil crisis. Economic growth cut. Government-led economic re-assessment decides to concentrate on high-tech industries.
- ❏ **1974** Ex-prime minister Sato receives Nobel prize for work on nuclear disarmament.
- ❏ **1979** Second oil crisis. Growth continues at 6% per year.
- ❏ **1982** Honda establishes first car factory in USA.
- ❏ **1983** Japanese banks account for 35% of international assets.
- ❏ **1986** Plaza Accords force upward valuation of the yen by 40%.
- ❏ **1988** Japan becomes world's largest aid donor and overseas investor.
- ❏ **1989** Death of Emperor Hirohito ends longest Japanese imperial reign. Recruit Co bribery scandal leads to resignation of Prime Minister Noburo Takeshita. Replaced by Sosuke Uno, forced to resign over sexual scandal. Tokyo stockmarket crash.
- ❏ **1990** General election. LDP gains majority in lower house.
- ❏ **1992** Sagawa Kyubin scandal forces resignation of LDP vice-president.
- ❏ **1993** July, LDP lose power in elections for first time in 38 years. Morihiro Hosokawa prime minister as head of seven-party coalition.
- ❏ **1994** Hokosawa forced to resign over bribery allegations. Tsutomu Hata prime minister.

POLITICS

 Lower House 1994
Upper House 1995

 Emperor Tsegu no Miya Akihito

THE STATE OF THE PARTIES

House of Representatives 512 members   **10% Shinseito**

| 43% LDP | 14% SDJP | 12% Komeito | 8% JNP | 13% Other |

LDP = Liberal Democratic Party   **SDJP** = Social Democratic Party of Japan   **Komeito** = Clean Government Party
Shinseito = Japan Renewal Party   **JNP** = Japan New Party
Other = Japan Communist Party, New Harbinger Party, Democratic Socialist Party and vacant seats

House of Councillors 252 members

| 43% LPD | 27% SDJP | 10% Komeito | 20% Other |

Japan is a multiparty democracy. The Emperor has a non-political role.

MAIN POLITICAL ISSUES

Reform
Japanese politics was dominated for 38 years by the ruling LDP. Politics was based on a close system of patronage, which linked big business, the bureaucracy and the LDP in a close arrangement. The fall of the LDP in the July 1993 elections was prompted by a popular desire for reform. Groups such as Ichiro Ozawa's *Kaishin* (Innovation) are now pressing for a more Western-style system of argumentative politics. Parties with specific programmes and policies are likely to emerge, replacing the LDP's patronage-based politics.

Tax reform
Prime Minister Tsutomu Hata's April 1994 cabinet established tax reform as one of its clearly defined policies. Hata's Japan Renewal Party wants to

Tsutomu Hata *became prime minister as head of a coalition in 1994.*

Eijiro Hata, *minister for international trade and industry.*

Koji Kakizawa, *foreign minister, ex-LDP, backed Tsutomu Hata in 1994.*

Emperor Tsegu no Miya Akihito. *He acceded in 1989 on the death of his father, Hirohito.*

raise the consumption tax to tap the resources of Japan's wealthy, retired population. He is opposed by the Social Democrats within the ruling coalition.

The role of the military
The Japanese constitution limits its army to a defence role. In a break with tradition, Japanese forces took part in the UN peace-keeping operation in Cambodia in 1993. The Japan Renewal Party is in favour of raising Japan's international profile by increasing its contributions to UN peace-keeping operations. Conservatives of both left and right feel that Japan has been well served by its pacifist stance and that it should stick to its traditional policy of total non-intervention.

PROFILE
In 1993, 38 years of LDP rule in Japan came to an end. Morihiro Hosokawa took over as prime minister, helped by the fact that he was not associated with the tainted world of Tokyo politics. He headed a fragile seven-party coalition.

A string of corruption scandals had led to the LDP's fall. Four LDP prime ministers – Takeshita, Uno, Kaifu, and Miyazawa – were forced to resign because they were implicated in scandals, or failed to stamp out corruption. Hosokawa's period in office was brief. He was accused of financial irregularities and resigned in 1994. However, Hosokawa did manage to pass laws on electoral reform, to apologize for Japan's war crimes and to begin the process of institutional deregulation. His popularity ranking in 1993 reached 70%, compared to the 10% who backed the LDP in its last months in power.

Tsutomu Hata took over in April 1994. He mostly continued Hosokawa's policies and retained his cabinet. However, politics could fragment again. Ichiro Ozawa had emerged as a strong challenger for the post of prime minister by mid-1994.

WORLD AFFAIRS

 G7   OECD   ASEAN   APEC   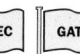 GATT

After years of limiting its role on the world stage to that of a minor power, rather than that of one of the world's most powerful economies, Japan is beginning to make its influence heard. Its eventual aim is a seat on the UN's Security Council. Tentative moves were made in 1993 with Japanese forces joining UN peace-keepers in Cambodia. The lobby that fears a resurgence of Japanese militarism is still strong, however, and wishes to avoid any foreign entanglements. In Asia, Japan is busy cultivating China, seeking to gain a prime position in the world's fastest growing market. Disputes over the Spratly Islands – China, Brunei and Vietnam also have claims – are a likely source of future tension.

AID

 $10bn (donations)   ⬆ Up 4% in 1994

Japan became the world's largest aid donor in 1991. Most aid is spent in Asia and the Pacific, particularly in the expanding economies of Thailand, Vietnam and Cambodia. Polynesian islands are beneficiaries of Japanese aid. Tokyo effectively supports their main livelihood, fishing.

DEFENCE

 $39.7bn   ⬆ Up 10% in 1993

| 0 | Defence spending as % GDP | 40 |
| 1% | | |

JAPANESE ARMED FORCES

	1200 main battle tanks (types -61,-74,-90)	156,000 personnel
	7 destroyers, 55 frigates 17 submarines and 8 patrol boats	44,000 personnel
	438 combat aircraft (F-1, F-4EJ, F-15J/DJ)	46,000 personnel
	None	

The defence establishment in Japan has not yet recovered from the effects of the 1941–1945 war. Any signs of military activity – even the UN peace-keeping duties which Japan undertook in Cambodia in 1993 – arouse fierce debate among pacifists. Japan's constitution forbids the use of troops abroad except in self-defence, and limits defence spending to 1% of GNP. However, Japan's economic success has allowed its armed forces to become relatively large in world terms.

ECONOMICS

 $3337.19bn   108.20 yen

ECONOMIC PERFORMANCE INDICATOR

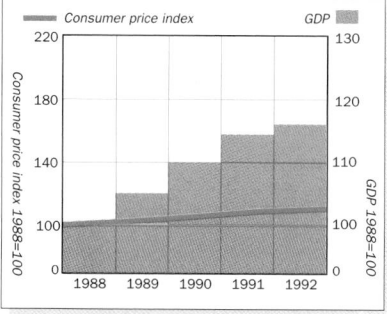

— Consumer price index   GDP ▉

STRENGTHS
The world's most competitive producer of high-tech electronic products and cars. Commitment to long-term research and development. Talent for developing ideas from EU and USA. Global spread of business, including plants in key markets of EU and USA. Revolutionary management and production techniques continue to lead the world. *Keiretsu* – vertically-integrated families of companies who agree to co-operate in business – keep non-Japanese companies out of Japanese markets.

WEAKNESSES
Heavy dependence on imported oil. Enormous, and rising, trade surplus encourages protectionism and anti-Japanese sentiment in EU and USA.

PROFILE
The Tokyo stock market crash in 1990, and particularly the collapse of the sky-high property market, ended a period of exponential growth in the Japanese economy. Industrial production fell by 8% in 1992, the sharpest drop since 1975. Corporate profits were also sharply down. The contraction in demand saw the flow of imports – particularly of European luxury products – stemmed.

However, through this slow-down, the economy continued to grow, at a rate of 2% a year. Companies did not shed great amounts of labour, and research and development spending went up. The government stepped in with a five-year economic plan ($60 billion in the first year) of infrastructure spending. The decline in imports saw Japan's trade surplus climb to $100 billion a year by 1993.

Policy is now shifting away from an almost total concentration on export-led growth, to stimulating the domestic economy. Japan is also aware that it has to relax its regulatory framework and allow in more imports, if relations with the USA

SCORE CARD

❏ WORLD GNP RANKING	2nd
❏ GNP PER CAPITA	$26,912
❏ BALANCE OF PAYMENTS	$117bn
❏ INFLATION	1.9%
❏ UNEMPLOYMENT	2.1%

and EU are not to be irreparably damaged.

Future growth is expected from new products, from wall-hung flat-screen TV sets, to digital video recorders and high-speed trains. Long overdue improvements to Japanese housing will further stimulate the home economy.

EXPORTS

IMPORTS

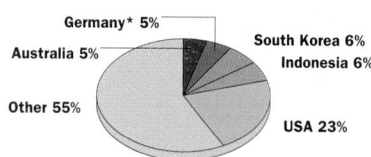

Japan's economic supremacy is likely to continue for some time. Analysts have predicted that, by 2010, Japanese GNP per capita could be over twice that of the USA.

JAPAN : MAJOR BUSINESSES

⊕ Research & development	♦ Brewing
⇄ Vehicle manufacture	❋ Textiles
✿ Heavy engineering	◊ Optics
⊟ Consumer goods	
◉ Shipbuilding	
▧ Iron & steel	
⊡ Electronics	
♨ Chemicals	

| 0 | 500 km |
| 0 | 300 miles |

J

RESOURCES

 857.3bn kwh (capacity 194.76 billion kw)

 17,000 b/d (reserves 59,850,000 bbl)

 11m pigs 4m cattle 27,000 sheep

 Limestone, sulphur, coal

ELECTRICITY GENERATION

Hydro 11% (95.8bn kwh)

Thermal 65% (557.4bn kwh)

Nuclear 24% (202.3bn kwh)

Other 0%

% of total generation by type

Japan has few commercially exploitable resources. Production costs make coal extraction uneconomical,

ENVIRONMENT

 6%

 Japan wishes to resume minke whale hunting

ENVIRONMENTAL TREATIES

Yes

Yes

Yes

Yes

Japanese governments have seen environmental issues as a way of making an impact on the world stage. First steps were taken in 1992 to set up an International Environmental Foundation, with a budget of $12 billion for grants to encourage environmentally friendly expansion in developing countries.

Respect for nature is deeply embedded in Japan's psyche, and reflected in a long history of highly sophisticated garden design. This attitude forms the bedrock of a vigorous grass-roots ecological movement, which has succeeded in preventing development at Tokyo's Narita airport for 20 years. It also continues effective opposition to nuclear expansion. Japan supports the hunting of minke whales. It argues that there are enough for this not to threaten the species.

Datsetsusan National Park, Hokkaido. Japan's northerly island is the least populous of the main group.

and Japan has become the world's largest coal importer. In an attempt to reduce dependence on imported fuels, Japan has developed alternative sources of energy. It is now the world's fourth biggest generator of nuclear power. However, environmentalists strongly oppose any expansion of this sector.

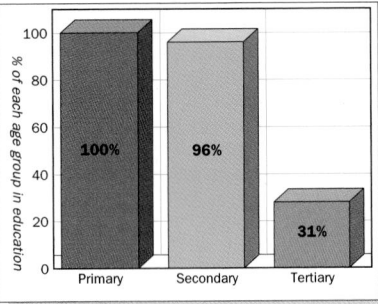

CHUGOKU-SANCHI

JAPAN : LAND USE

0   300 km
0   300 miles

Cropland
Forest
Pasture
Sheep
Fruits
Rice

MEDIA

 No political restrictions

PUBLISHING AND BROADCAST MEDIA

There are 125 daily newspapers. *Asahi Shimbun*, *Mainichi Shimbun*, and *Yomiuri Shimbun* are among the most popular

2 national, 70 other services

10 national, 123 other services

Superbird B Intelsat V F8

Available in all major cities

The Japanese are among the world's most avid newspaper readers. Most dailies carry serious news and are owned by large media groups who also have TV and cable interests. Weekly newspapers carry more tabloid journalism. The magazine market is huge. Over 36 billion magazines are sold in Japan every year. *Non Non*, a woman's magazine, is the best-selling title. Lifestyle magazines, encouraging the Japanese to make more use of their limited leisure time, are a growing sector of the market.

Japan is, in dollar terms, the world's second largest film maker after the USA. It is also Hollywood's major export market.

Japan has redefined much of the world's media. It invented the personal stereo and created the huge computer games market. In the past five years, this market has seen exponential growth. Nintendo, a leading games company, is one of the most profitable in Japan, rivalling long-established corporate giants such as Matsushita.

EDUCATION

 100%

0   *Education spending as % GNP*   25

5%

THE EDUCATION SYSTEM

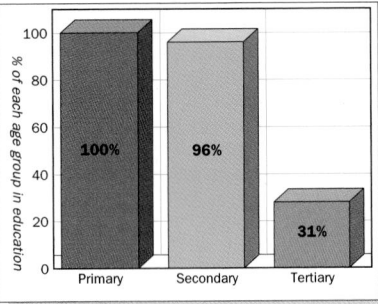

% of each age group in education

100% Primary
96% Secondary
31% Tertiary

One of the key dividing lines in Japanese society is between university graduates, who get the coveted white-collar jobs for life, and non-graduates. The latter have difficulty reaching management level. The result is that the Japanese education system is highly pressurized. Competition for university places is intense, and starts with the choice of kindergarten, which the Japanese attend from the age of four. Once at university, students tend to relax – the important thing is getting in. Tokyo, Kyoto, Waseda and Keio are the most prestigious universities. Their graduates have access to top civil service and business jobs. The system succeeds in producing a uniform, and thoroughly educated, workforce.

CRIME

 51,829 prisoners

 Up 2% in 1992

CRIME RATE

Murders
1   per 100,000 population

Rapes
1   per 100,000 population

Thefts
999   per 100,000 population

Japan has one of the lowest crime rates in the world. This is in part the result of an efficient police system. Cities are safe, with police kiosks at frequent intervals on street corners.

The major crime problem is fraud and the activities of the *kumi*, organized mafia-style syndicates whose members are known as *yakuza*. The authorities show little enthusiasm in challenging these groups, seeking to contain rather than eradicate their activities. *Kumi* are suspected of having connections with the extreme right in Japanese politics.

J

REGIONS

HOKKAIDO

National Park   ✈ Airports   ≋ Rice
🐂 Market gardening   Whisky distilling   Brewing

THE SECOND LARGEST and most northerly of the four main islands, Hokkaido is Japan's biggest and most productive farming region. Its open terrain and climate is similar to the US Midwest. US advisors established wheat production here in the 1860s, and Hokkaido now produces over half of Japan's cereal needs. German Americans, from Milwaukee, also established Japan's first brewery, which produces the world-famous *Sapporo* beer.

Recent government investment has encouraged high-tech industries on Hokkaido. Japan's first magnetic train (*maglev*) test track is being developed on the island.

TOKYO AND DISTRICT

THE IMMENSE concentration of Japanese wealth in Tokyo was reflected in 1988, when the value of one square mile of prime real estate in the capital was estimated to be greater than the whole of California. Unplanned expansion since 1945 has resulted in a large conurbation, merging Tokyo with neighbouring Yokohama and Kawasaki. During the 1980s, the demands on office space resulted in a rash of new office buildings, crammed into every available piece of land. The lack of vistas – Tokyo has few parks – gives Tokyo's architecture a rather uniform feeling. Notable exceptions to this include two office buildings by the French designer Philippe Starck.

Built-up area   Major sites   Electronics
🚗 Motor industry   Shipbuilding   Steelworks

KANSAI REGION

🚗 Motor industsry   Electronics

COMPRISING the six prefectures of Osaka, Hyogo, Kyoto, Shiga, Nara and Wakayama, Kansai has always had a strong regional identity. In recent years, support for a Kansai federation, with greater independence from Tokyo, has increased. Some 20 million people live here, producing 20% of Japan's textiles, 25% of its steel and 23% of its machine tools. Kansai's share of Japan's GNP exceeds the total GNP of Canada. Its industries have long been renowned for their creativity. Kansai developed the world's first desktop calculator and the first automatic ticket barrier. It is home to such world-famous companies as Matsushita, Sanyo and Sharp.

A healthy rivalry has grown up between Osaka – Kansai's main business city – and Tokyo. Osaka has sought to develop its own fashion and design industries in emulation of Tokyo. Kyoto, with its 1400 temples and shrines, remains Japan's favourite tourist destination. Kansai International, currently being built off Kobe, will be Japan's first 24-hour international airport.

HEALTH

👥 1 per 608 people   ☠ Heart disease, cancer

0   Health spending as % GNP   25
6.8%

Japan has a world-class health system, which has delivered some of the highest longevity and lowest infant mortality rates in the world. Most Japanese contribute towards health costs through a national insurance scheme, with premiums calculated on earnings. The poorest in society receive free treatment. Japan's rapidly ageing population presents a major future funding challenge.

WEALTH

💰 Factory manager, 596,665 yen per month; machine general worker, 339,524 yen per month

CONSUMER GOODS OWNERSHIP

Measured in consumer goods the Japanese are wealthy; highly restrictive city parking restrictions account for the low rates of car ownership. The yen's high value makes foreign holidays, for those who can afford to take time off, relatively inexpensive. However, living costs are high – a recent survey judged Tokyo more than twice as costly as New York – and mean that most Japanese live out and have a long, cramped journey into work. It is 18–25 years old girls who do best – receiving large cash donations from their doting fathers – by avoiding the pitfalls and living at home. As a group they are reputed to have the highest disposable income in Japan.

WORLD RANKING

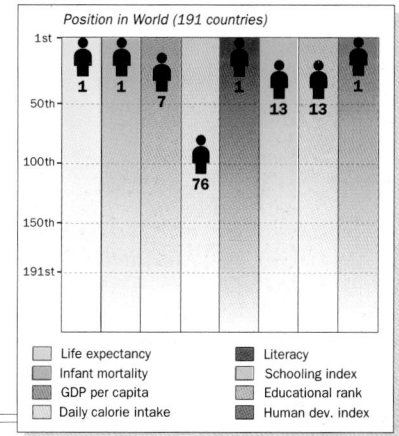

Life expectancy   Literacy
Infant mortality   Schooling index
GDP per capita   Educational rank
Daily calorie intake   Human dev. index

J

JORDAN

MIDDLE EAST

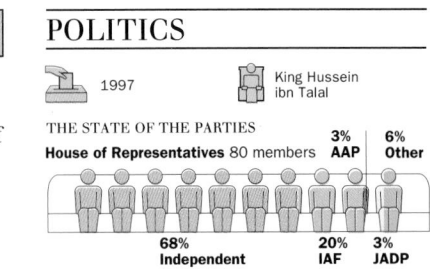

OFFICIAL NAME: Hashemite Kingdom of Jordan **CAPITAL:** Amman
POPULATION: 4.3 million **CURRENCY:** Jordanian dinar **OFFICIAL LANGUAGE:** Arabic

S HARING BORDERS WITH Iraq, Syria, Israel and
Saudi Arabia, Jordan has just 26 km of coastline on
the Gulf of 'Aqabah. Jordanian territory legally includes the West Bank of
the Jordan River and east Jerusalem, but Israel has occupied these areas
since 1967. Jordan ceded its claim to the West Bank to the PLO in 1988.
Phosphates and tourism associated with important historical sites such
as Petra are the mainstays of the economy.

POLITICS

1997 King Hussein ibn Talal

THE STATE OF THE PARTIES
House of Representatives 80 members 3% AAP 6% Other
68% Independent 20% IAF 3% JADP

Independent = Centrist (55%), Islamicist (8%) and Leftist
(5%) **IAF** = Islamic Action Front **JADP** = Jordan Arab
Democratic Party **AAP** = Al Ahd Party

Senate 30 members

The members of the Senate are appointed by the King

King Hussein, the longest reigning
Arab ruler, retains a strong grip on
government. In 1965, he eliminated any
doubts over the succession by naming
his technocrat brother, Hassan, as
Crown Prince. Hussein has sought to
promote a strong nationalism based
on Jordan's tribal structure. He is also
careful not to alienate Jordan's other
constituencies. In 1993, he responded
to calls for greater democracy by
agreeing to multiparty elections.
Contrary to expectations, gains were
not made by
fundamentalists.

CLIMATE

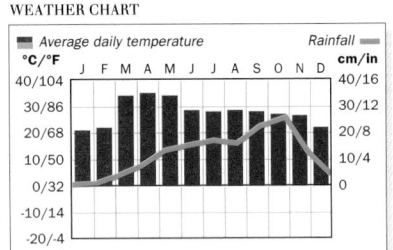

Summers are hot and dry, winters cool
and wet. Areas below sea level are very
hot in summer and warm in winter.

COMMUNICATIONS

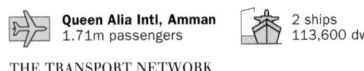
Queen Alia Intl, Amman 1.71m passengers 2 ships 113,600 dwt

THE TRANSPORT NETWORK
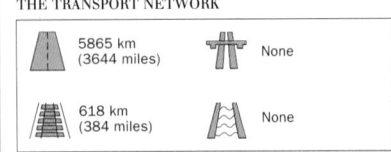
5865 km (3644 miles) None
618 km (384 miles) None

Adequate roads link main cities. A
railway links the port of Al 'Aqabah
with the Syrian capital, Damascus.

TOURISM

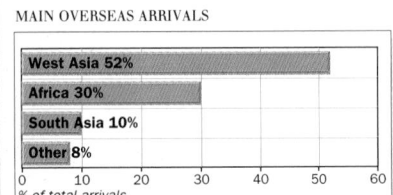
2.63m visitors Up 16% in 1990

MAIN OVERSEAS ARRIVALS

West Asia 52%
Africa 30%
South Asia 10%
Other 8%

% of total arrivals

Al 'Aqabah offers fine beaches, water
sports and subaqua diving, while the
ancient city of Petra attracts visitors
interested in Roman remains. Amman
is developing as a centre for Arabic
culture and the arts.

PEOPLE

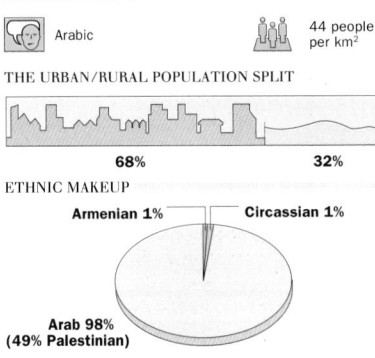
Arabic 44 people per km²

THE URBAN/RURAL POPULATION SPLIT
68% 32%

ETHNIC MAKEUP
Armenian 1% Circassian 1%
Arab 98% (49% Palestinian)

Jordan is a predominantly Muslim
country drawn from Bedouin roots,
with a Christian minority and a large
Palestinian population. The monarchy's
power base lies among the rural tribes,
which also provide the backbone of
the military.
National
identity is
strong.

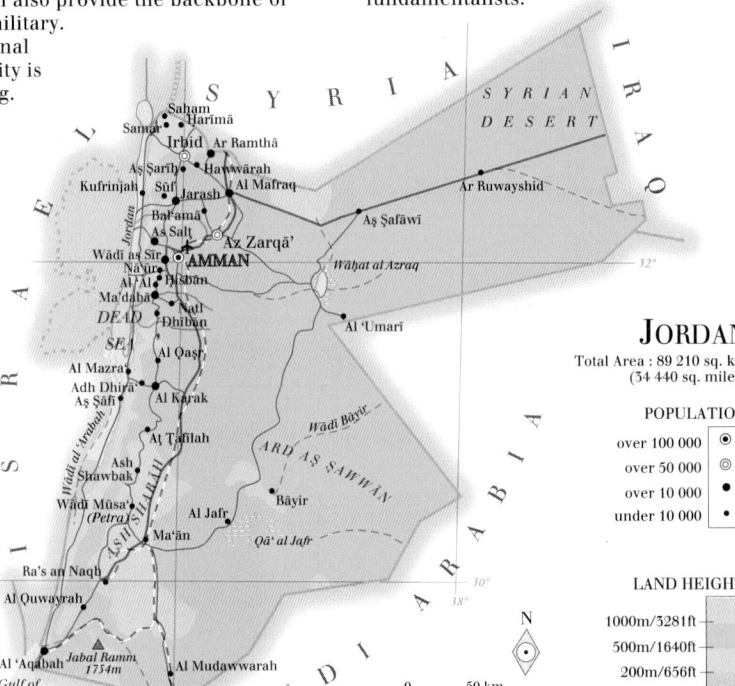

JORDAN
Total Area : 89 210 sq. km
(34 440 sq. miles)

POPULATION
over 100 000
over 50 000
over 10 000
under 10 000

LAND HEIGHT
1000m/3281ft
500m/1640ft
200m/656ft
Sea Level
-200m/-656ft

WORLD AFFAIRS

    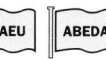

Jordan is a key player in Middle East politics. It is home to 1.7 million Palestinians. Its attitude towards the PLO has changed over the years. In 1986 it expelled the organization from Amman. However, Jordan's 1988 decision to rescind its claim to the Israeli-occupied West Bank in favour of the PLO proved decisive in bringing Israel and the PLO to the negotiating table. One result of the 1994 PLO–Israeli settlement was a settlement of Israeli-Jordanian disputes.

AID

 $668m (receipts)   Down 25% in 1991

The Gulf states and USA withdrew aid after Jordan backed Iraq in the Gulf war. US aid has now been restored.

DEFENCE

 $508.55m   Down 12% in 1992

Jordanian forces played no part in the 1991 Gulf War. The armed forces are loyal to the monarchy. They have a reputation for thorough training and professionalism. The forces are dependent on Western support for credit in purchasing advanced arms and equipment.

ECONOMICS

 $4.5bn   0.70 Jordanian dinars

SCORE CARD

- ❑ World GNP Ranking..........................114th
- ❑ GNP per Capita $1047
- ❑ Balance of Payments...................$−765m
- ❑ Inflation 6.6%
- ❑ Unemployment................................30%

STRENGTHS
Major exporter of phosphates and fresh foods to Gulf states. Skilled, educated and adaptable workforce.

WEAKNESSES
Reliant on imports to satisfy energy requirements. Unemployment owing to influx of Jordanians and Palestinians expelled from Kuwait. Tourism yet to recover from 1991 Gulf crisis.

EXPORTS

IMPORTS

RESOURCES

 3.7bn kwh (capacity 1m kw)   1000 b/d (reserves 4,000,000 bbl)

61m poultry, 1.3m sheep, 29,000 cattle Phosphates, potash

Oil deposits have been discovered. Phosphates, livestock and crops such as tomatoes, wheat, olives and vegetables are the main resources.

ENVIRONMENT

 1% partially protected   Government pursuing vigorous conservation programmes

Conservation is a government priority. Rare animals are protected and species that became extinct in the wild in the 1950s are being reintroduced into controlled environments.

MEDIA

 Widespread self-censorship of the press, in accordance with government guidelines

PUBLISHING AND BROADCAST MEDIA

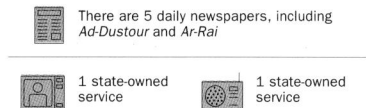
There are 5 daily newspapers, including *Ad-Dustour* and *Ar-Rai*

1 state-owned service   1 state-owned service

Radio and TV are controlled by the state. Private and publicly-owned newspapers follow the government line.

CRIME

 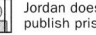 Jordan does not publish prison figures   Crime is rising

Jordan is largely peaceful. Crime levels are generally low, although theft in urban areas is rising.

EDUCATION

 80%

Men and women receive the same education. Jordanian teachers work all over the Middle East.

HEALTH

 1 per 842 people   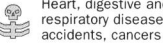 Heart, digestive and respiratory diseases, accidents, cancers

Health care is subsidized by the government. Hospitals are distributed throughout the country.

CHRONOLOGY

King Hussein succeeded to the throne in 1952 after his father was deposed owing to mental illness.

- ❑ **1958** Iraqi revolution ends Jordan's federation with Iraq.
- ❑ **1967** Israel seizes West Bank territories placed under Jordanian rule in 1949.
- ❑ **1988** King Hussein cedes claims to West Bank to PLO.
- ❑ **1993** Jordan signs protocol with Israel on future negotiations.

The King's Highway, seen from the castle at Al Karak. This strategic fortress was built by Crusader knights in the 12th century.

WEALTH

 The wealthiest are those closest to the King

CONSUMER GOODS OWNERSHIP

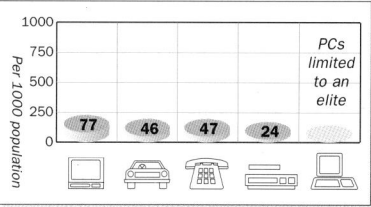

The wealthiest Jordanians are Amman-based entrepeneurs, bankers and engineers. Poverty is relatively rare.

WORLD RANKING

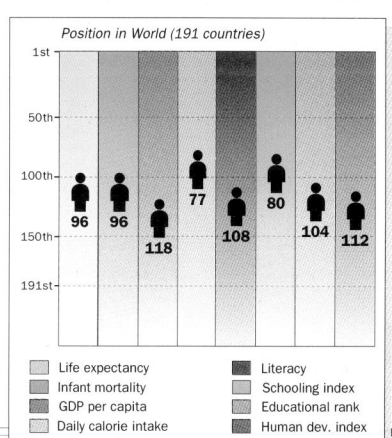

KAZAKHSTAN

OFFICIAL NAME: Republic of Kazakhstan **CAPITAL:** Alma-Ata
POPULATION: 17 million **CURRENCY:** Tenge **OFFICIAL LANGUAGE:** Kazakh

ASIA

THE SECOND LARGEST of the former Soviet republics, Kazakhstan extends almost 2000 km from the Caspian Sea in the west to the Altai Mountains in the east, and 1300 km north to south. It borders Russia to the north and China to the east. Kazakhstan was the last Soviet republic to declare its independence, in 1991. In 1994, elections confirmed the former-communist, Nursultan Nazarbayev, and his supporters in power. Kazakhstan is mineral-rich and has considerable economic potential. Many Western companies are seeking to exploit its natural resources.

The Altai Mountains, eastern Kazakhstan. *Subject to harsh continental winters, the Altai range is a cold, inhospitable place. Rivers carry meltwater down onto the vast steppe.*

CLIMATE

WEATHER CHART

Kazakhstan has a continental climate with large temperature variations between summer and winter. Average January temperatures range from –18ºC on the northern Kazakh steppe to –3ºC in the deserts 1300 km to the south. July temperatures average 19ºC and 30ºC respectively. As the Caspian Sea never freezes, winters are mildest on Kazakhstan's southwestern coast.

COMMUNICATIONS

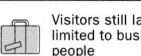 **Alma-Ata International**

Small Caspian Sea merchant fleet

THE TRANSPORT NETWORK

164,900 km (102,464 miles)	None
14,460 km (8985 miles)	Caspian Sea provides access to four countries

Transport networks focus on the north and east, the key economic areas. The railways link into the Russian system and most international flights go via Moscow. Extending the network and reducing dependence on Russia are priorities. There are now direct flights to Germany. A rail link with China was opened in 1992. Kazakhstan has asked Latvia for access to its Baltic ports.

TOURISM

Visitors still largely limited to business people

Increased since the break up of the USSR

MAIN OVERSEAS ARRIVALS

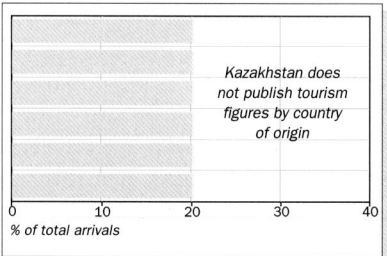

Kazakhstan does not publish tourism figures by country of origin

% of total arrivals

The number of visitors to Kazakhstan is increasing, but very few come solely as tourists. The majority are business travellers and a dense web of contacts with foreign companies has evolved. Of the Central Asian states, Kazakhstan has cultivated the closest links with the West. There is now a large community of foreign business people living in Alma-Ata.

KAZAKHSTAN

Total Area : 2 717 300 sq. km
(1 049 150 sq. miles)

POPULATION

over 500 000	⊙
over 100 000	◎
over 50 000	○
over 10 000	●
under 10 000	•

LAND HEIGHT

3000m/9843ft
2000m/6562ft
1000m/3281ft
500m/1640ft
200m/656ft
Sea Level
-200m/-656ft

0   200 km
0   200 miles

K

PEOPLE

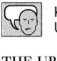 Kazakh, Russian, German, Uigur, Korean

 6 people per km²

THE URBAN/RURAL POPULATION SPLIT

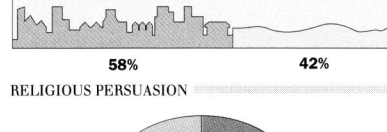

58%   **42%**

RELIGIOUS PERSUASION

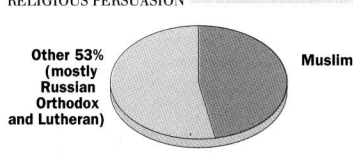

Other 53% (mostly Russian Orthodox and Lutheran)   Muslim 47%

ETHNIC MAKEUP

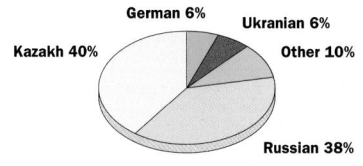

German 6%   Ukranian 6%
Kazakh 40%   Other 10%
                 Russian 38%

Kazakhstan's ethnic diversity is mainly a product of the forced settlement of Germans, Tatars and others during the Soviet era. Russian settlement began in the 19th century, but peaked after 1920. By 1959, ethnic Russians outnumbered Kazakhs. The balance

POPULATION AGE BREAKDOWN

% of population by age group

Kazakhstan has a high birth rate. However, the proportion of under-15s in the population, which was 31% in 1990, is now falling

1960   1970   1980   1990   2000

has recently been redressed by the immigration of ethnic Kazakhs from neighbouring states.

Ethnic tension has been less than in many former Soviet states, mainly due to President Nazarbayev, who has actively encouraged a multi-ethnic nationalism, and unifying causes like the anti-nuclear movement. However, there is potential for unrest from groups like the Kazakh nationalist *Azat*, which wants northern Kazakhstan incorporated into Russia.

Only a minority of Kazakhs retain their traditional nomadic life. However, their cultural traditions, commitment to Islam and loyalty to the three Hordes, or clan federations, remain strong.

POLITICS

  1998

 President Nursultan Nazarbayev

THE STATE OF THE PARTIES

Supreme Kenges 177 members

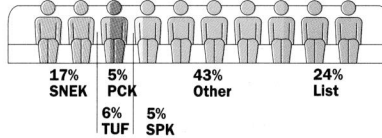

17% SNEK | 5% PCK | 43% Other | 24% List
6% TUF | 5% SPK

SNEK = Congress of People's Unity of Kazakhstan **TUF** = Trade Union Federation **PCK** = People's Congress of Kazakhstan **SPK** = Socialist Party of Kazakhstan **Other** = Peasant's Party, Republic Council of Women's Organizations **List** = President's List; 42 candidates elected from a list of politicians and businessmen drawn up by the president

The 1993 constitution vests legislative authority in the 177-member Supreme *Kenges* (or Soviet). The president, who must be fluent in Kazakh, has supreme executive power.

MAIN POLITICAL ISSUE

Ethnic relations

Kazakhstan's relative harmony is due to President Nazarbayev's successful efforts to balance Kazakh aspirations with the concerns of minorities, notably ethnic Russians. The constitution guarantees equal status to all groups while giving Kazakh linguistic preference. The formation of the People's Congress of Kazakhstan (PCK) as a Kazakh-dominated party to counter the Russian-dominated SPK, (former communists) went some way to satisfying nationalist demands.

The 1994 elections saw ethnic Kazakhs win 60% of the seats in parliament, despite forming only 40% of the population, raising ethnic Russian fears of under-representation.

PROFILE

Despite a democratic government, the president enjoys political dominance, and the patronage of the Kazakh clans is still important. Since coming to power in 1989, Nazarbayev has concentrated on reducing ethnic tension and on economic reform, reflecting his belief that growth is the best guarantor of stability. The impact of Nazarbayev's economic reforms has led to growing criticism of his government. He won a second term in early 1994, amid allegations of electoral tampering. The president's allies swept to victory in the parliamentary elections, confirming Nazarbayev's grip on power.

President Nursultan Nazarbayev, *who steered Kazakhstan to independence.*

Foreign Minister *Toleubai Suleimenov, the first professional diplomat in the post.*

WORLD AFFAIRS

CIS   CSCE

Maintaining close ties with other former Soviet republics is a priority. Kazakhstan is a leading supporter of the CIS. Relations with Russia, although strained at times by Moscow's concern over Kazakhstan's ethnic Russians, have been cemented by a 25-year co-operation treaty.

Another priority has been to develop international links and to attract foreign investment. Kazakhstan's rich mineral resources and relative ethnic stability have attracted investors from Europe, the USA and Asia. Ties with South Korea are growing particularly fast, partly reflecting President Nazarbayev's interest in South Korea's model of economic development. Relations with China remain strained, however, as Beijing has territorial claims to parts of eastern Kazakhstan.

AID

Sums undisclosed   Aid levels have risen since independence

Kazakhstan joined the IMF and World Bank in 1992, and is also a member of the EBRD. Both multilateral and bilateral aid tend to be directed at supporting economic reform and providing know-how and training. The government is seeking to link the dismantling of nuclear warheads to aid payments from the West.

CHRONOLOGY

Once part of the Mongol Empire, Kazakhstan was absorbed by the Russian Empire in the 19th century. Ethnic Russians began to settle on land used by nomadic Kazakhs. Russian settlement intensified after the 1917 revolution and Kazakhstan was subjected to intensive industrial and agricultural development.

❑ **1916** Rebellion against the Russian rule brutally repressed.

❑ **1917** Russian Revolution inspires civil war in Kazakhstan between Bolsheviks, anti-Bolsheviks and Kazakh nationalists.

❑ **1918** Kazakh nationalists set up autonomous republic.

❑ **1920** Bolsheviks take control. Kirghiz Autonomous Soviet Socialist Republic (ASSR) set up within Russian Soviet Federative Socialist Republic.

❑ **1925** Kirghiz ASSR renamed Kazakh ASSR.

❑ **1936** Kazakhstan becomes full union republic of the USSR as Kazakh SSR.

K

K

DEFENCE

$707m   Down 52% in 1993

0   *Defence spending as % GDP*   40
3.8%

KAZAKH ARMED FORCES

🛡	1200 main battle tanks	44,000 personnel
⚓	None	
✈	140 combat aircraft (MiG-23/MiG-27/Su-24)	Undisclosed
🚀	104 ICBM (SS-18 Satan) 40 Tu-95H (ALCM equipped) under Russian control	

Kazakhstan, as the largest of the five former Soviet Central Asian republics, has been seen as a potential guarantor of regional peace. However, the West is concerned about former Soviet nuclear warheads based in Kazakhstan. The government signed the Start I nuclear reduction treaty in 1991, but has yet to act on it. This reflects both a lack of finance, and efforts by Nazarbayev to use the weapons as a negotiating lever. In 1993, the USA agreed to provide $140 million in economic aid after Kazakhstan signed an agreement to dismantle some of its ICBMs. The government has plans to set up a national guard, mainly to protect the ruling elite. It will be trained by Russian troops.

ECONOMICS

$41.7bn   Tenge not convertible

SCORE CARD

❏ WORLD GNP RANKING	44th
❏ GNP PER CAPITA	$2455
❏ BALANCE OF PAYMENTS	Deficit
❏ INFLATION	84%
❏ UNEMPLOYMENT	Rising

EXPORTS

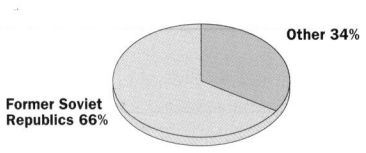

Other 34%

Former Soviet Republics 66%

IMPORTS

Imports are largely from the Russian Federation, followed by other CIS countries and China

STRENGTHS

Vast mineral resources, notably oil, gas, coal, gold, silver and uranium. Also bismuth and cadmium, used in electronics industry. Foreign investors attracted by early introduction of market reforms, liberal foreign investment laws and valuable resources. Joint ventures include modern processing industries and communications as well as the exploitation of oil and gas fields.

WEAKNESSES

Collapse of former Soviet economic and trading system. Heavy reliance on imported consumer goods. Departure from rouble zone, and rapid introduction of the tenge in 1993, increased economic instability. Inefficient industrial plants. Privatization limited to small-scale enterprises.

ECONOMIC PERFORMANCE INDICATOR

Consumer prices have risen sharply since 1991. GDP is likely to rise following new foreign investment

PROFILE

Under Nazarbayev, Kazakhstan has moved faster than other former Soviet republics to establish a market economy. It was the first to introduce free economic zones, investment incentives and privatization. Prices have been freed, foreign trade largely decontrolled and the tax system reformed. Despite these reforms, growth has been elusive. Unemployment and inflation have risen sharply, due in large part to the impact of the collapse of the wider Soviet economy.

However, by the end of 1993, $9 billion had already been committed in foreign direct investment, mainly in the energy sector. Outdated equipment and inadequate distribution networks mean that Kazakhstan, suprisingly, has to import energy. It hopes to become self-sufficient by 2000.

KAZAKHSTAN : MAJOR BUSINESSES

Petropavlovsk
Semipalatinsk
Aktyubinsk
Karaganda
Atyrau
Shymkent
Alma-ata

🛢 Oil
🏭 Steel
❄ Textiles
⚗ Chemicals
🛢 Oil refining
⚫ Coal mining
🏛 Food processing
⚙ Light engineering
💉 Pharmaceuticals

0   500 km
0   500 miles   * significant multinational ownership

RESOURCES

81.3bn kwh
(capacity 19.1m kw)

540,000 b/d
Massive new oil
reserves confirmed

34.2m sheep and
goats, 9.5m cattle,
2.6m pigs

Oil, gas, manganese,
gold, silver, coal, iron,
tungsten, chromite

ELECTRICITY GENERATION

> 80% of electricity
> generation is thermal
> (mainly from coal and
> gas); 5 HEP and 1
> nuclear installation
> supply the rest

% of total generation by type

Mining is the single most important
industry in Kazakhstan. Some of the
world's largest oil deposits are located
near the Caspian Sea. The US company
Chevron signed a deal to develop the
huge Tengiz oilfield in 1993. Kazakhstan
also holds vast iron ore reserves, has the
world's biggest chromium mine, and
one of the biggest goldfields. There are
plans to quadruple gold output by 1997.

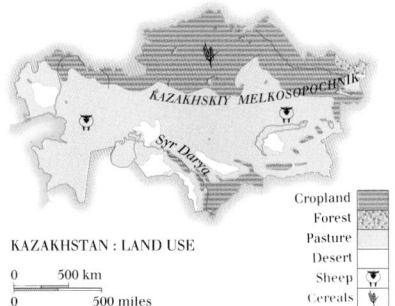

KAZAKHSTAN : LAND USE

Cropland	
Forest	
Pasture	
Desert	
Sheep	
Cereals	

0   500 km
0   500 miles

ENVIRONMENT

None

Western pressure
on government may
cause improvement

ENVIRONMENTAL TREATIES

No   No

No   No

The environmental damage caused by
intensive industrial and agricultural
development is a major concern. The
eastern cities are heavily polluted and
farmlands are being eroded. The Aral
Sea has been polluted by the overuse of
fertilizers and has shrunk by 40% owing
to the diversion of rivers for irrigation.

In 1991, environmental pressure
groups succeeded in ending 42 years of
nuclear testing at Semipalatinsk in the
northeast. The green lobby is now
pressing for tighter pollution controls.

MEDIA

Censorship exists. Neither direct criticism of the
president, nor the incitement of ethnic tension
is tolerated

PUBLISHING AND BROADCAST MEDIA

There are 6 principal daily newspapers and
over 500 other registered newspapers

1 state-owned
station

1 state-owned,
several private
stations

Arabsat 1C   None

The state-owned media competes with
a range of independent publications
and several privately owned radio
stations. However, the government's
continuing control of printing and
broadcasting facilities ensures that
criticism tends to be indirect. There are
over 400 registered newspapers, about
40% of them in Kazakh. Turkish state
TV broadcasts to Kazakhs by satellite.

CRIME

Kazakhstan does not
publish prison figures

Crime levels are
rising

CRIME RATES

> Theft is rising more sharply
> than other crime

Rural people are starting to grow drug
crops, mainly opium poppies, to offset
falling incomes. The government has
appealed for UN help to combat the
problem. General crime rates are low.

EDUCATION

Lower than ex-Soviet average

0   Education spending as % GNP   25

7.9%

THE EDUCATION SYSTEM

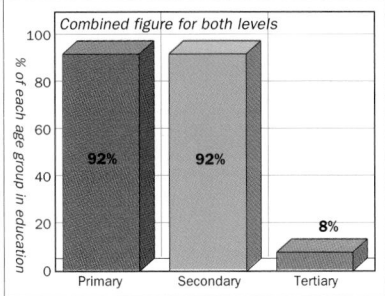

Combined figure for both levels

% of each age group in education

Primary 92%   Secondary 92%   Tertiary 8%

Education is based on the Soviet
model. Much teaching is still in Russian,
despite the adoption of Kazakh as the
state language. Kazakh textbooks and
Kazakh-speaking teachers are in short
supply. Literacy levels are relatively
low. There are 63 higher-education
institutions, and 53 medical schools.

HEALTH

1 per 245 people

Heart, cerebrovascular
and respiratory
diseases, cancers

0   Health spending as % GNP   25

5.8%

The health system is limited in terms
of both facilities and coverage. Rural
people have minimal access to clinics.
As a result, Kazakhstan has the highest
infant mortality rate in Central Asia.
The country's size means that extending
coverage, and improving the quality
of care will be costly. Attempts are
therefore being made to attract foreign
investment into the health sector. Many
doctors have emigrated to Russia.

WEALTH

The living standards of many Kazakhs has
declined since independence from the USSR

CONSUMER GOODS OWNERSHIP

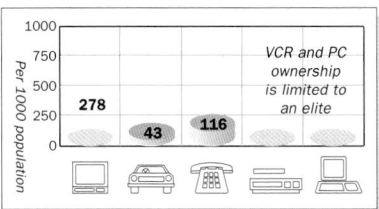

Per 1000 population

VCR and PC
ownership
is limited to
an elite

278   43   116

Life for the majority of Kazakhs
has always been hard, and has grown
even more difficult since 1989. Living
standards have deteriorated and
unemployment has climbed as a result
of market-orientated reforms within
Kazakhstan and the collapse of the
wider Soviet trading system on which
the country depended.

The rural population, the poorest
group, has been particularly badly
affected. The small wealthy elite is
made up mainly of former officials
within the CPK, many of whom have
benefited from privatization, or belong
to President Nazarbayev's clan. Foreign
nationals, and their hard currency,
are concentrated in the capital.

WORLD RANKING

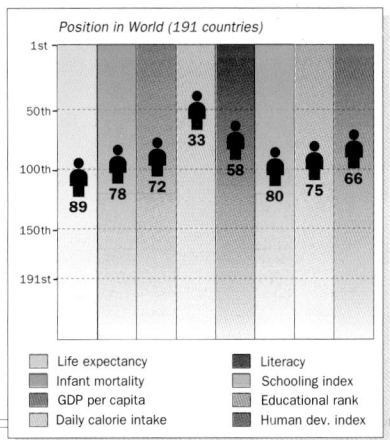

Position in World (191 countries)

1st
50th   33
100th   89   78   72   58   80   75   66
150th
191st

Life expectancy	Literacy
Infant mortality	Schooling index
GDP per capita	Educational rank
Daily calorie intake	Human dev. index

K

KENYA

OFFICIAL NAME: Republic of Kenya   CAPITAL: Nairobi
POPULATION: 25.2 million   CURRENCY: Kenya shilling   OFFICIAL LANGUAGE: Swahili

East Africa · Africa

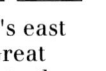

1963

KENYA STRADDLES THE EQUATOR on Africa's east coast. Its central plateau is bisected by the Great Rift Valley. The land to the north is desert, while to the east lies a fertile coastal belt. After gaining independence from Britain in 1963, politics was dominated by Jomo Kenyatta. He was succeeded in 1978 by President Moi, who easily survived a return to multiparty elections in 1992. Ethnic violence is now the main political issue. The economic mainstays are tourism and agriculture, notably coffee and tea. Very high population growth is a key constraint on economic growth.

Kenyatta Conference Centre, Nairobi. The modern skyline of the business centre contrasts sharply with the slums on the city's outskirts.

CLIMATE

WEATHER CHART

■ Average daily temperature   Rainfall ■
°C/°F   J F M A M J J A S O N D   cm/in
40/104   40/16
30/86   30/12
20/68   20/8
10/50   10/4
0/32   0
-10/14
-20/-4

The coast and Great Rift Valley are hot and humid, the plateau interior is temperate and the northeastern desert hot and dry. Rain generally falls from April to May and October to November.

COMMUNICATIONS

✈ **Jomo Kenyatta, Nairobi**
1.52m passengers

🚢 6 ships
9900 dwt

THE TRANSPORT NETWORK

54,700 km (33,990 miles)		None
2733 km (1698 miles)		Lake Victoria

Kenya's railway, ports and main airport are being upgraded, a reflection of the importance of tourism and Kenya's role as an outlet for land-locked neighbours.

Great Rift Valley, Kenya. This huge crack in the Earth's crust runs from the River Jordan right through Africa to the Zambezi River.

TOURISM

🧳 694,500 visitors

⬇ Down 3% in 1990

Tourism, which is mainly beach and safari orientated, is vital to the economy and a key foreign exchange earner. However, despite moving into the package holiday market during the 1980s, Kenya has seen visitor numbers decline since 1990. The main factors are world recession and the well-publicized murder of several tourists.

MAIN OVERSEAS ARRIVALS

Germany 18%
UK 15%
Tanzania 11%
USA 9%
Italy 6%
Other 41%

0   10   20   30   40   50   60
% of total arrivals

KENYA

Total Area :
580 370 sq. km
(224 081 sq. miles)

POPULATION

⊡ over 1 000 000
◉ over 500 000
◎ over 100 000
○ over 50 000
● over 10 000
· under 10 000

LAND HEIGHT

3000m/9843ft
2000m/6562ft
1000m/3281ft
500m/1640ft
200m/656ft
Sea Level

N

0   100 km
0   100 miles

SUDAN · ETHIOPIA · UGANDA · SOMALIA · TANZANIA · INDIAN OCEAN

ELEMI TRIANGLE

Lokitaung · Lake Rudolf (Lake Turkana) · Moyale · Daua · Lodwar · Turkwel · CHALBI DESERT · Marsabit · BOKHOL PLAIN · Wajir · BOJI PLAIN · Milgis · Kapenguria · Kitale · Maralal · Chandlers Falls · Ewaso Ngiro · Lorian Swamp · Bungoma · Kakamega · Tambach · Lake Baringo · Isiolo · Busia · Eldoret · Kabarnet · Nyahururu · Nanyuki · Meru · Tana · Garissa · Kisumu · Kapsabet · Londiani · Kirinyaga 5199m · Grand Falls · Winam Gulf · Nakuru · Nyeri · Embu · Masinga Reservoir · Rusinga I. · Kericho · Njoro · Murang'a · AGANGERABELL PLAIN · Mfanganu I. · Homa Bay · Elburgon · Naivasha · Thika · Kisii · Lake Naivasha · Lamu · Lake Victoria · Karungu Bay · Narok · NAIROBI · Kitui · NYIKA · Pate Isla · Manda Isla · LOITA HILLS · Machakos · YATTA PLATEAU · Ungama Bay · Lake Magadi · Magadi · Garsen · Namanga · NYIRI DESERT · Galana · Lugards Falls · Malindi · Oloitokitok · Vo · Kilifi · Taveta · Kwale · Mombasa · Athi

Equator

PEOPLE

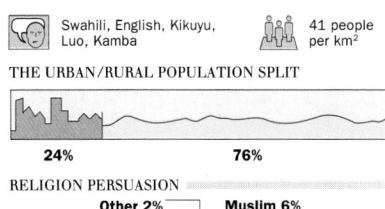

Swahili, English, Kikuyu, Luo, Kamba

41 people per km²

THE URBAN/RURAL POPULATION SPLIT

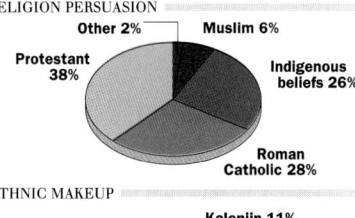

24%   76%

RELIGION PERSUASION

Other 2%   Muslim 6%
Protestant 38%
Indigenous beliefs 26%
Roman Catholic 28%

ETHNIC MAKEUP

Kalenjin 11%
Other 30%
Kamba 11%
Luo 13%
Kikuyu 21%
Luhya 14%

Kenya's ethnic diversity, with about 70 different groups, reflects its past as a focus of population movements. Asians, Europeans and Arabs form 1% of the population. The rural majority retains strong clan and extended family links, although these are being weakened by urban migration. Poverty and one of the world's highest population growth rates (3.5% a year) are the root causes of the land hunger which has recently been fuelling a surge in ethnic violence. Much is concentrated in western Kenya, where Kikuyu are the main targets of violent attacks by Kalenjin, Masai and Pokor groups. Over 300,000 Kikuyu have also been displaced from their villages by a form of organized ethnic cleansing known as *majimboism*.

POPULATION AGE BREAKDOWN

%	■ 0–14	▨ 15–64		□ 65+	
	4.1%	3.9%	3.4%	3%	2.9%
	50.3%	47.9%	46.5%	47.9%	50.9%
	45.6%	48.2%	50.1%	49.1%	46.2%
	1960	1970	1980	1990	2000

WORLD AFFAIRS

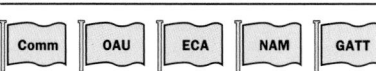

Comm   OAU   ECA   NAM   GATT

Relations with neighbouring states and with key Western donors, notably the USA, are Kenya's priorities. In 1991, human rights concerns were partly responsible for a suspension of aid. Payments were restored in 1993, but made subject to an improved record. The main regional concern is the resurrection, with Uganda and Tanzania, of the East African Community, an economic zone which collapsed in 1977. The northern border dispute with Sudan over the Elemi Triangle is unresolved. Kenya lays claim to this arid piece of land which has a concentration of Christian refugees fleeing Sudanese government repression. The conflict in Somalia has also spilt over into northeast Kenya.

POLITICS

 1997

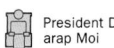 President Daniel arap Moi

THE STATE OF THE PARTIES

National Assembly 202 members   15% FORD-K   8% Other

51% KANU   15% FORD-A   11% DP

KANU = Kenya African National Union **FORD-A** = Forum for the Restoration of Democracy – Asili **FORD-K** = Forum for the Restoration of Democracy – Kenya **DP** = Democratic Party **Other** = Kenya Social Congress, Kenya National Congress

Kenya became a multiparty democracy in 1992 and has been led by President Daniel arap Moi since 1978.

MAIN POLITICAL ISSUE

Ethnic violence

The ethnic polarization of political parties in Kenya and rising poverty are fuelling ethnic violence. Determined to ensure KANU dominance, President Moi, a Kalenjin, is turning the party into an alliance of smaller ethnic groups opposed to the Kikuyu. The latter are the largest ethnic group, the main victims of violence and the main supporters of the opposition. Rift Valley, Nyanga and Western provinces – those with most seats in parliament – are foci of anti-Kikuyu ethnic cleansing.

PROFILE

Kenya's status following independence as a *de facto* one-party state was formalized in 1982. President Moi's subsequent efforts to entrench KANU's power further provoked demands at home for the introduction of multiparty politics, and condemnation abroad of human rights abuses. Forced in 1992 to concede free elections, Moi helped ensure KANU's victory by curtailing the campaign period. He has since been condemned again by the international community for manipulating ethnic conflict, part of his strategy to entrench KANU's power.

Opposition groups in Kenya remain divided, although popular pressure for reform is growing. Many are also critical of Moi's failure to improve the economy and to control corruption in the bureaucracy.

President Daniel arap Moi, Kenya's leader since 1978.

Oginga Odinga, veteran opposition leader died in 1994.

AID

 $873m (receipts)   Lifting of aid freeze in 1993

Kenya has been a major recipient of aid from donors – such as the UK, Japan, the EU, the World Bank and the IMF – who are keen to support its free-market approach. Little, however, has trickled down to the majority of the population, which continues to live in poverty. This is partly because of the high proportion of aid tied to construction projects and donor-country firms, and partly because of mismanagement and official corruption. Concern over both this and human rights abuses led to a freeze on aid from 1991 to 1993.

CHRONOLOGY

From the 10th century, Arab coastal settlers mixed with indigenous peoples in the region. Britain's need for a route to land-locked Uganda led to the formation in 1895 of the British East African Protectorate in the coastal region.

❑ **1900–1918** White settlement of interior; removal of local peoples from land.
❑ **1920** Interior becomes a British colony; coast remains protectorate.
❑ **1930** Jomo Kenyatta goes to UK; stays 14 years.
❑ **1944** Kenyan African Union (KAU) formed; Kenyatta returns to lead it.
❑ **1952–1956** *Mau Mau*, Kikuyu-led violent campaign to restore African lands. State of emergency. 13,000 people killed.
❑ **1953** KAU banned. Kenyatta jailed.
❑ **1960** State of emergency ends. Tom Mboya and Oginga Odinga form KANU.
❑ **1961** Kenyatta freed; takes up presidency of KANU.
❑ **1963** KANU wins elections. Kenyatta prime minister. Full independence declared.
❑ **1964** Republic of Kenya formed with Kenyatta as president and Odinga as vice-president.

➪

K

K

- ❏ **1966** Odinga defects to form Kenya People's Union (KPU).
- ❏ **1969** KANU is sole party to contest elections (also 1974). KANU Sec-Gen Tom Mboya assassinated. Unrest. KPU banned and Odinga arrested.
- ❏ **1978** Kenyatta dies. Vice-President Daniel arap Moi succeeds him.
- ❏ **1982** Kenya declared a one-party state. Opposition to Moi. Abortive air-force coup. Odinga rearrested.
- ❏ **1983** Election turnout under 50%.
- ❏ **1986** Open 'queue-voting' replaces secret ballot in first stage of general elections. Other measures to extend Moi's powers incite opposition.
- ❏ **1987** Government acts to suppress opposition groups. Political arrests and human rights abuses attract overseas criticism.
- ❏ **1988** Moi wins third term and extends his control over judiciary.
- ❏ **1989** Finance Minister George Saitoti replaces Vice-Pres J Karanja after corruption allegations. Political prisoners freed.
- ❏ **1990** Government implicated in deaths of Foreign Minister Robert Ouko and Anglican archbishop. Riots. Odinga and others form FORD, which is outlawed by government.
- ❏ **1991** Arrest of FORD leaders and attempts to stop pro-democracy demonstrations. Donors suspend aid. Moi agrees to introduce multiparty system. Ethnic violence on increase.
- ❏ **1992** FORD splits into factions led by ex-minister Kenneth Matiba and Odinga. Opposition weakness helps Moi win December elections.
- ❏ **1994** Odinga dies.

DEFENCE

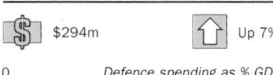 $294m   ⬆ Up 7% in 1989

0   *Defence spending as % GDP*   40
▮ **1.8%**

KENYAN ARMED FORCES

🛆	80 main battle tanks (80 *Vickers* Mk 3)	20,500 personnel
🚢	10 patrol boats (2 *Nyayo* PFM/ 4 *Otomat* II SSM)	1200 personnel
✈	40 combat aircraft (5 *Strikemaster* Mk 87/ 12 *Hawk* Mk 52)	2500 personnel
🚀	None	

Destabilization of the northeastern border by the Somali civil war is the main defence issue. The military plays little part in politics.

ECONOMICS

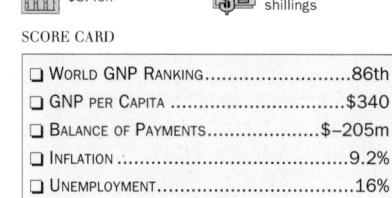

📊 $8.4bn   💲 68.10 Kenya shillings

SCORE CARD

❏ WORLD GNP RANKING	86th
❏ GNP PER CAPITA	$340
❏ BALANCE OF PAYMENTS	$−205m
❏ INFLATION	9.2%
❏ UNEMPLOYMENT	16%

EXPORTS

Uganda 9%
Germany* 12%
UK 20%
Other 59%

IMPORTS

Germany* 10%
United Arab Emirates 11%
Japan 12%
UK 19%
Other 48%

STRENGTHS

Tourism, which is the largest foreign exchange earner. Broad agricultural base, especially cash crops such as coffee and tea. East Africa's largest, most diversified manufacturing sector.

WEAKNESSES

Susceptibility of tourism, coffee and tea to fluctuating world prices. Poor recent GDP growth. High population growth of 3.5% a year. Land shortage, leading to subdivision of plots into uneconomical small units.

PROFILE

Kenya has been hailed as an example to the rest of Africa of the benefits of a mainly free-market economy. Government involvement has been relatively limited, and recently further reduced by privatization. Foreign investment has been encouraged, with some success. Tourism has developed into the leading foreign exchange earner over the past 20 years. Manufacturing now accounts for 21% of GDP, and is the most diversified sector in East Africa. However, it employs only 200,000 in formal jobs and needs to expand rapidly to provide more urban employment.

Economic growth was good by African standards during the 1980s, averaging over 4% a year. However, it was not good enough to compensate for one of the world's highest population growth rates. GDP per capita stagnated and too few jobs were created to make much impact on unemployment. The problem was exacerbated by urban migration and the yearly influx of thousands of school leavers onto the

labour market. For the majority of Kenyans, farming ever-smaller landholdings or earning a living in the informal sector, life has recently become harsher.

Other problems, including inflation, a heavy debt burden (now $7.5 billion), and growing dependence on balance of payments support came to a head in the early 1990s, when economic growth gave way to recession. Real GDP growth fell to 0.4% in 1992 and was negative in 1993. The rise in poverty-linked violence and political unrest hit tourism; earnings fell by 15% in 1992 and again in 1993. Agricultural and manufacturing output have both fallen in the past three years.

Partly as a response to pressure from donors, including the 1991–1993 freeze on balance of payments support, the government has implemented some economic liberalization measures. These include floating the Kenya shilling, raising interest rates and giving exporters direct access to their hard currency earnings. However, real growth is likely to remain elusive until Kenya overcomes two fundamental problems – the official corruption which drains vital resources, including foreign aid, and its high rate of population growth.

ECONOMIC PERFORMANCE INDICATOR

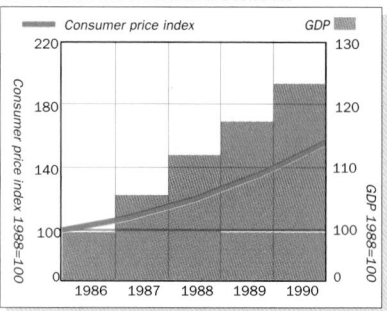

KENYA : MAJOR BUSINESSES

Eldoret, Nanyuki, Kisumu, Thika, Lake Victoria, Nakuru, Nairobi, Mombassa

Cement
Tobacco
Oil refining   Vehicle assembly
Electronics   Food processing
Steel   Agribusiness
Textiles   Chemicals

0   100 km
0   100 miles
* significant multinational ownership

RESOURCES

3bn kwh (capacity 723,000 kw)

Not an oil producer; refines 90,000 b/cd

13.5m cattle, 6.3m sheep, 100,000 pigs

Soda ash, fluorspar, limestone, rubies, gold, vermiculite

ELECTRICITY GENERATION

Hydro 83% (2.5bn kwh)

Thermal 6% (171m kwh)

Nuclear 0%

Other 11% (336m kwh)

% of total generation by type

Agriculture underpins Kenya's economy and is still the largest sector, accounting for 27% of GDP. Kenya's varied topography means tropical, subtropical and temperate crops may be grown. Coffee and tea, the main export crops, have been affected by falling world prices. Efforts to reduce dependence on these crops have led to the growth of a successful export-orientated horticultural industry.

Kenya has few mineral resources and mining accounts for only 0.2% of GDP. Hydroelectric and geothermal sources are being developed to reduce energy imports – currently 70% of total requirements. Oil exploration in the Great Rift Valley and the northeast has revealed deposits in Turkana District.

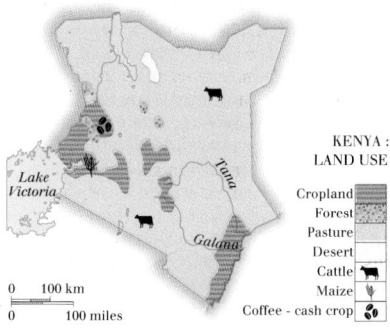

KENYA : LAND USE

Cropland, Forest, Pasture, Desert, Cattle, Maize, Coffee - cash crop

ENVIRONMENT

6%

Tourist numbers pose threat to safari park ecosystems

ENVIRONMENTAL TREATIES

No | Yes | Yes | Yes

The government recognizes the importance of wildlife conservation to the tourist industry, and recent elephant protection schemes have been a success. However, initiatives to set up national reserves are competing with agriculture for land. The effect of dams on the Tana River is another concern.

MEDIA

Criticism of the government is not tolerated in practice

PUBLISHING AND BROADCAST MEDIA

There are 5 daily newspapers. The *Daily Nation* has the largest circulation

2 state-controlled services | 1 state-controlled network

Intelsat V1 F1 | None

Government intolerance of criticism is long-standing and includes plays and novels as well as the media. Ngugi wa Thiongo, Kenya's most famous novelist, was exiled for his criticism of KANU.

CRIME

Kenya does not publish prison figures | Rising sharply

CRIME RATES

Murders: 4 per 100,000 population
Rapes: 2 per 100,000 population
Thefts: 42 per 100,000 population

Nairobi's high crime levels are spreading countrywide, as a result of worsening poverty, ethnic violence and rising banditry in the northeast. An increase in the use of guns underlies the rapid increase in violent crime.

EDUCATION

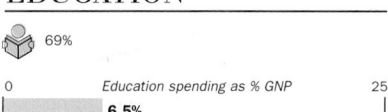

69%

Education spending as % GNP: 6.5%

THE EDUCATION SYSTEM

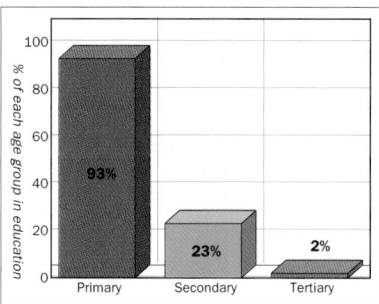

Primary 93%, Secondary 23%, Tertiary 2%

The education system is loosely based on the British model. Schooling is not compulsory, but free primary education means most children attend; the drop-out rate at secondary level is high. In higher education the emphasis is on vocational training.

HEALTH

1 per 6552 people

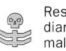

Respiratory and diarrheal diseases, malaria

Health spending as % GNP: 2%

The health system is a mix of state and private facilities, the latter mainly run by charities and missions. The state system has been hit by recession, worsening the already limited access of the rural majority. Poverty-related illnesses are increasing, particularly amongst children and women. HIV and AIDS are a growing problem among some sections of the community.

WEALTH

The majority of Kenya's rising number of poor live outside the formal economy

CONSUMER GOODS OWNERSHIP

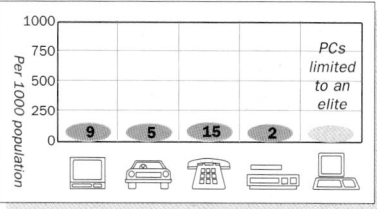

PCs limited to an elite

9, 5, 15, 2

Wealth disparities in Kenya are large and growing, exacerbated by land hunger and migration to the cities, where jobs are few and existence depends on the informal economy. The slum dwellers of Nairobi's Amarthi Valley are among Africa's poorest, worst-nourished people. Their lives contrast with those of the country's elite – top government officials with access to patronage; white Kenyans, who derive their wealth largely from agricultural estates; and the Asian business community. Amongst these groups, Mercedes and the latest four-wheel-drive cars are popular, as are designer-label clothes. Wealthy Kenyans often send their children abroad for higher education.

WORLD RANKING

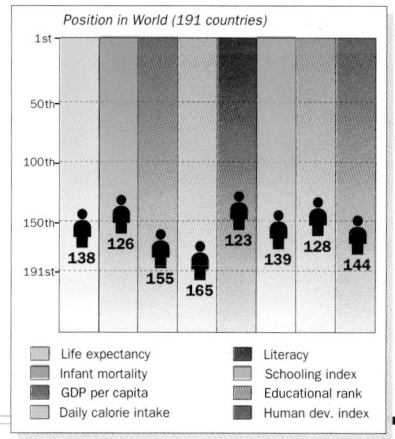

Position in World (191 countries)

138, 126, 155, 165, 123, 139, 128, 144

Life expectancy | Literacy
Infant mortality | Schooling index
GDP per capita | Educational rank
Daily calorie intake | Human dev. index

K

KIRIBATI

OFFICIAL NAME: Republic of Kiribati   CAPITAL: Bairiki
POPULATION: 73,000   CURRENCY: Australian dollar   OFFICIAL LANGUAGE: English

FORMERLY PART OF THE British colony of the Gilbert and Ellice Islands, the Gilberts became independent in 1979 and adopted the name Kiribati (pronounced Kiribass). British interest in the Gilberts rested solely on the exploitation of the phosphate deposits on Banaba; these ran out in 1980. In 1981, Kiribati won damages (but not the costs of litigation) from the British for decades of phosphate exploitation.

Banreaba Island, Tarawa atoll. None of the atolls is more than 8 m high except Banaba, the main source of phosphates.

CLIMATE

WEATHER CHART

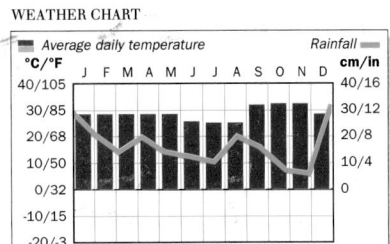

Kiribati's small land area in the vast Pacific means it often goes for months without rain. In the 1950s, a serious drought led to the resettlement of Gilbertese to the Solomon Islands.

COMMUNICATIONS

Bonriki Intl, Tarawa
51,000 passengers (est)

5 ships
2700 dwt

THE TRANSPORT NETWORK

640 km
(398 miles)

None

None

5 km
(3 miles)

Kiribati has a limited air link with Fiji. Small-scale shipping and good satellite communications also keep it in touch with the outside world.

TOURISM

3332 visitors

Up 21% in 1990

MAIN OVERSEAS ARRIVALS

USA 19%		
Australia 11%		
Japan 8%		
Other 62%		

0 10 20 30 40 50 60 70 80
% of total arrivals

Kiritimati, which has a weekly air service to Honolulu, has been singled out for tourist development.

PEOPLE

English, Micronesian dialect

89 people per km²

THE URBAN/RURAL POPULATION SPLIT

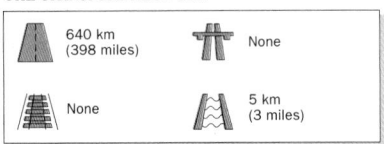

36%   64%

RELIGIOUS PERSUASION

Other 6%

Roman Catholic 53%

Protestant 41%

Locals still refer to themselves as Gilbertese. Apart from the inhabitants of Banaba, who employed anthropologists to establish their racial distinction, almost all Gilbertese are Micronesian. Tension with the Banabans is intense, but mostly fuelled by the historic value of Banaba's phosphate deposits. Most Gilbertese are poor. Many go to Nauru as guest workers, living in barrack-room conditions, or work as merchant shipping crew. Those who stay at home go through a circular migration from the outlying islands to Tarawa, returning to see relatives. Women play a prominent role, especially on outlying islands, where they run most of the farms.

POLITICS

1995

President Teato Teannaki

THE STATE OF THE PARTIES

House of Assembly 40 members

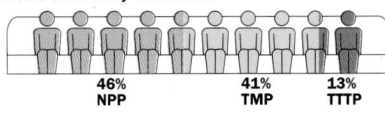

46%
NPP

41%
TMP

13%
TTTP

NPP = National Progressive Party   TMP = Te Maneaba Party
TTTP = Temauri Teraoi Ao TeTabomoa Party

The traditional chiefs still effectively rule Kiribati, through a party system on the British model. The main concern is the economy, which is extremely vulnerable to any fluctuations in world demand for coconuts. The overpopulation of Tarawa is the other major issue. Possible restrictions on travel to the island have been discussed. In part, the problem of migration is caused by the poverty and lack of opportunity on the outer islands. Plans for a wealth distribution programme to reduce migration exist, but they have yet to become policy. Ieremia Tabai has been the dominant political figure of the past decade.

KIRIBATI

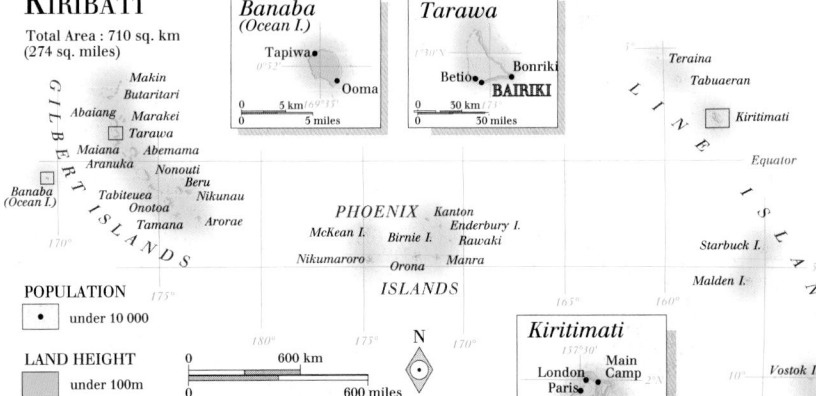

Total Area = 710 sq. km
(274 sq. miles)

POPULATION
• under 10 000

LAND HEIGHT
under 100m

WORLD AFFAIRS

In 1986, Kiribati was a signatory to a deal between the USA and a number of Pacific Island states that resulted in the USA paying $60 million, in return for access to Pacific fishing grounds. However, the USA has yet to sign the 1982 UN Law of the Sea accords; it objects to the sections defining the ownership of migratory species such as tuna. Kiribati used to play the USSR off against the USA. The USSR was happy to pay $1.5 million for fishing leases as it allowed it to spy on US nuclear testing on the neighbouring Kwajalein atoll in the Marshall Islands.

AID

 $22m (receipts)   Little change from year to year

Aid is mostly for small infrastructure projects. The causeway linking Tarawa to the airport on Bonriki, a nearby atoll, was built with Japanese aid.

DEFENCE

 Kiribati has no defence budget   Not applicable

Australia and New Zealand provide *de facto* protection, with regular anti-submarine patrols.

ECONOMICS

 $53m   1.47 Australian dollars

SCORE CARD

❏ WORLD GNP RANKING	189th
❏ GNP PER CAPITA	$730
❏ BALANCE OF PAYMENTS	$5.2m
❏ INFLATION	5.5%
❏ UNEMPLOYMENT	2.8%

STRENGTHS

Subsistence economy has survived, and Kiribati has no need to import food. Coconuts provide some export income: the EU is the biggest market. Fisheries have potential, but are hampered by US fisheries policy in the Pacific.

WEAKNESSES

Banaba's phosphate deposits ran out in 1980. Isolation, and large distances between islands. Almost no economic potential.

EXPORTS

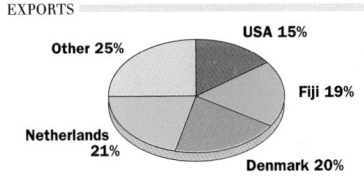

Other 25%
USA 15%
Fiji 19%
Netherlands 21%
Denmark 20%

IMPORTS

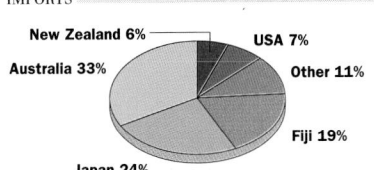

New Zealand 6%
Australia 33%
USA 7%
Other 11%
Fiji 19%
Japan 24%

RESOURCES

 7m kwh (capacity 2,000 kw)   Not an oil producer and has no refineries

 33,100 tonnes   Phosphate

Phosphate deposits on Banaba ran out in 1980. All energy supplies have to be imported. Underwater agriculture is being developed.

ENVIRONMENT

 39% (including marine and semi-protected areas)   Refusal to allow Western toxic waste dumping

Overpopulation on Tarawa is the cause of major problems. The coral reef, which protects Tarawa from the sea and which holds important inshore fish stocks in the lagoon, is threatened by untreated effluent. Approaches have been made by international – mainly US – companies seeking to dump industrial waste into the lagoons.

MEDIA

 No restrictions on political reporting

PUBLISHING AND BROADCAST MEDIA

There are no daily newspapers. There are 2 weekly newspapers, *Atoll Pioneer* and *Te Uekera*

No TV service   1 independent service

The main sources of news and information on Kiribati are *Pacific Islands Monthly* and *Islands' Business* magazines.

CRIME

 77 prisoners   Down 46% in 1990

Crime, apart from brawls resulting from drunkenness, is minimal. The judicial system is based on the British model.

EDUCATION

 90%

Education is British-inspired. The best students go to King George V School, and on to university in Fiji.

HEALTH

 1 per 3938 people   Heart diseases, diabetes

Most Gilbertese are healthy, thanks to the home-grown diet. Those on Tarawa are starting to import tinned food, due to a lack of agricultural land, and vitamin A deficiency is becoming a problem.

WEALTH

 The state is the only formal employer. Remittances from Gilbertese working in Nauru are an important source of national income

CONSUMER GOODS OWNERSHIP

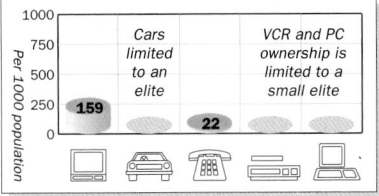

Cars limited to an elite
VCR and PC ownership is limited to a small elite
159
22

Life in Kiribati is modest. Civil servants in the capital, Bairiki, are the wealthiest group. There is a handful of cars on Tarawa, and these are confined to the single 18-mile stretch of road, from Tarawa to the airport. Most Gilbertese live by subsistence farming.

WORLD RANKING

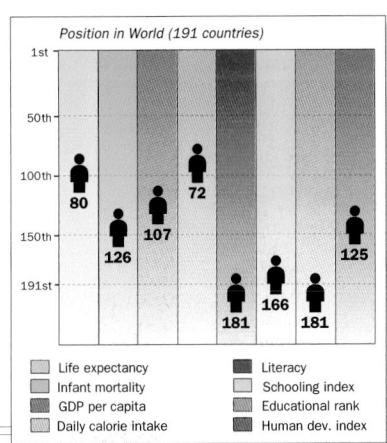

Position in World (191 countries)
80
126
107
72
181
166
181
125

Life expectancy — Literacy
Infant mortality — Schooling index
GDP per capita — Educational rank
Daily calorie intake — Human dev. index

K

KUWAIT

OFFICIAL NAME: State of Kuwait   CAPITAL: Kuwait City
POPULATION: 2.1 million   CURRENCY: Kuwaiti dinar   OFFICIAL LANGUAGE: Arabic

A T THE NORTHWEST EXTREME of the Persian Gulf, Kuwait is dwarfed by its neighbours Iraq, Iran and Saudi Arabia. The flat, almost featureless landscape conceals huge oil and gas reserves, which made Kuwait the world's first oil-rich state. In 1990, Iraq invaded, claiming Kuwait as its 19th province. A US-led alliance, under the aegis of the UN, expelled Iraqi forces following a short war in 1991. Since its liberation, Kuwait has built a wall separating its territory from Iraq.

Saffar Towers in the business centre of Kuwait City. The postwar cost of rebuilding Kuwait's economy is put at $25 billion.

CLIMATE

WEATHER CHART

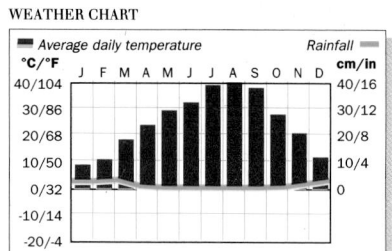

Summer temperatures can soar to over 40°C, but winters can be cold with frost at night.

COMMUNICATIONS

Kuwait International, Kuwait City
1.41m passengers

62 ships
3.79m dwt

THE TRANSPORT NETWORK

4273 km (2655 miles)	280 km (174 miles)
None	None

Kuwait has a system of radial motorways around the capital and good connecting roads to Saudi Arabia.

TOURISM

50,000 visitors

Down 44% in 1990

MAIN OVERSEAS ARRIVALS

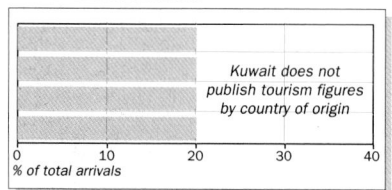

Kuwait does not publish tourism figures by country of origin

% of total arrivals

Most Western visitors to Kuwait go specifically to see relatives working in the oil industry. The limited tourism from neighbouring Arab states, notably Saudi Arabia, has not recovered since the 1990–1991 Gulf War.

PEOPLE

Arabic, English

112 people per km²

THE URBAN/RURAL POPULATION SPLIT

96%   4%

ETHNIC MAKEUP

Iranian 4%
Other 2%
South Asian 9%
Kuwaiti 50%
Other Arab 35%

Kuwait is a fundamentalist Sunni Muslim society. Women have considerable freedom, but are not allowed to vote.
Kuwait's oil wealth has drawn in thousands of workers from India, Pakistan and other Arab countries. Before the Iraqi invasion in 1990, Kuwait had the largest Palestinian population in the Arabian peninsula. The PLO's support for Iraq's invasion led to most Palestinians being driven out. After the war, Kuwaitis vowed never again to become a minority in their own country. In 1994, native Kuwaitis only just outnumbered resident foreign nationals.

KUWAIT

Total Area : 17 820 sq. km (6880 sq. miles)

POPULATION
◎ over 100 000
○ over 50 000
● over 10 000
• under 10 000

LAND HEIGHT
200m/656ft
Sea Level

0   25 km
0   25 miles

POLITICS

1996

Amir HH Sheikh Jaber al–Ahmad as–Sabah

THE STATE OF THE PARTIES

National Assembly 50 members

Political parties are not allowed. The members of the National Assembly are elected for a 4-year term by all literate Kuwaiti males over the age of 21, except servicemen and police

In 1992, Kuwait's ruler, Amir Sheikh Jaber, restored the National Assembly and allowed a general election to take place. The franchise was restricted to male Kuwaiti nationals. Islamic and independent candidates were elected, and six deputies with opposing views to those of the government were given cabinet posts in order to create a new sense of national unity.

K

WORLD AFFAIRS

Kuwait's strategic importance is as a major exporter of crude oil and natural gas. As such, it has always maintained very close links with the West. Since the war with Iraq, its foreign policy has become even more pro-Western. It therefore depends on its neighbour Saudi Arabia and on Western allies for its future security.

AID

 $1.7bn (donations)   Trend sharply upwards

The Kuwait Fund for Arab Economic Development continued to give aid even during the invasion crisis.

DEFENCE

 $9.3bn   Up 608% in 1991

Kuwait's 11,000-strong, partly volunteer army was easily overrun by vastly superior Iraqi forces in August 1990. Since the liberation, defence pacts have been signed with the USA, the UK, France and Russia. Kuwait is rearming fast, with weapons purchased from major Western suppliers.

ECONOMICS

 $32.8bn   0.30 Kuwaiti dinars

SCORE CARD

- WORLD GNP RANKING..........................51st
- GNP PER CAPITA $16,400
- BALANCE OF PAYMENTS $801m
- INFLATION 8%
- UNEMPLOYMENT..................................1.5%

STRENGTHS
Production of oil and gas has been restored to pre-invasion levels. Large overseas investments.

WEAKNESSES
Economy devastated by Iraqi scorched-earth policy, when oil installations were destroyed. Vulnerability to Iraqi attack deters Western industrial investment. Skilled labour, food and raw materials have to be imported.

EXPORTS

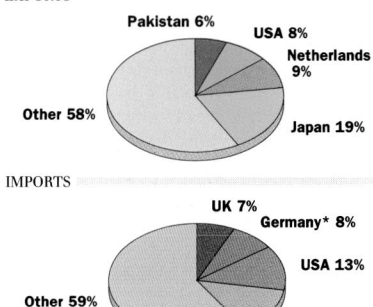

IMPORTS

RESOURCES

20.6bn kwh (capacity 6.8m kw)   1.03m b/d (reserves 94,000,000,000 bbl)
260,000 sheep, 24,000 cattle, 6000 camels   Oil, natural gas, salt

The oil industry is Kuwait's most profitable sector, accounting for over 80% of export earnings. It was badly hit as a result of the Gulf War, when large numbers of oil wells were deliberately fired, but with foreign assistance it has been quickly rehabilitated. Kuwait also possesses valuable reserves of natural gas.

ENVIRONMENT

 1.2% partially protected   Rapid clean-up in 1991 following end of Gulf War

The Iraqi invasion and the subsequent war caused an ecological disaster. Although the effects of this did not prove as grave as some observers first feared, marine life has been damaged and many thousands of acres of cultivated land have been obliterated. Millions of land-mines still litter Kuwait's border areas.

MEDIA

 There is officially no press censorship. However, the government acts swiftly against publishers who breach informal guidelines

PUBLISHING AND BROADCAST MEDIA

There are 7 daily newspapers, the largest of which is Al-Qabas

1 state-controlled service   3 state-controlled services

Radio and TV are state-controlled, but satellite TV is freely available. Press freedom exists in theory.

CRIME

 500 prisoners   Up 1% in 1988

Isolated acts of terrorism related to the war still occur. There have been reports of human rights abuses.

EDUCATION

73%

Kuwaiti citizens receive free education from nursery to university. Since liberation, more emphasis has been placed on technology in the curriculum.

CHRONOLOGY

Kuwait traces its independence to 1710, but was under British rule from the late 18th century until 1961. The government denies any historical link with Iraq.

- **1961** Independence from the UK. Iraqi claims against its sovereignty.
- **1976** The Amir suspends the National Assembly.
- **1990** Iraq invades Kuwait. The Amir flees to Saudi Arabia.
- **1991** Operation Desert Storm liberates Kuwait.
- **1992** National Assembly elections.

HEALTH

 1 per 675 people   Accidents, heart diseases, cancers, perinatal deaths

Despite theft of equipment during the Iraqi invasion, Kuwait has restored its Western-standard health care service. Nationals receive free treatment.

WEALTH

 Most Kuwaitis have total financial security

CONSUMER GOODS OWNERSHIP

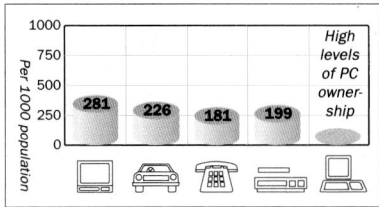

Kuwaitis enjoy high incomes and the government has repeatedly rescued citizens who have suffered stock market or other financial losses. School and university leavers are guaranteed jobs. Capital is easily transferred abroad and there are effectively no exchange controls.

WORLD RANKING

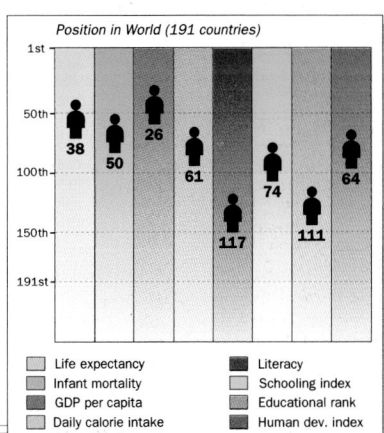

K

323

KYRGYZSTAN

OFFICIAL NAME: Kyrgyz Republic **CAPITAL:** Bishkek
POPULATION: 4.5 million **CURRENCY:** Som **OFFICIAL LANGUAGE:** Kyrgyz

CENTRAL ASIA

K

KYRGYZSTAN IS A SMALL and very mountainous nation in central Asia. It is the least urbanized of the ex-Soviet republics (the rural population is growing faster than the towns) and was amongst the last to develop its own cultural nationalism. Its moderate government is treading uncertainly between Kyrgyz nationalist pressures, and ensuring that the minority Russians are not alienated as they tend to possess the skills necessary to run a market-based economy.

CLIMATE

WEATHER CHART

Conditions vary from permanent snow and cold deserts at altitude to hot deserts in low regions. Intermediate slopes and valleys receive some rain.

COMMUNICATIONS

 Bishkek International   Has no fleet

THE TRANSPORT NETWORK

 28,400 km (17,647 miles)   None

 370 km (230 miles)   600 km (373 miles)

Kyrgyzstan does not have the funds to improve its poor mountain road network.

TOURISM

 Mainly business visitors   Little change from year to year

MAIN OVERSEAS ARRIVALS

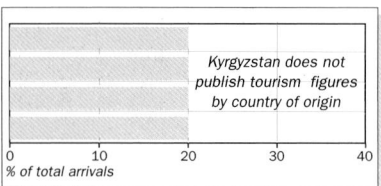

Kyrgyzstan does not publish tourism figures by country of origin

% of total arrivals

The tourist industry is undeveloped. Most visitors to Kyrgyzstan are people on business from Turkey and China in search of new contracts, or working on multilateral aid agency projects.

PEOPLE

 Kyrgyz, Russian   21 people per km²

THE URBAN/RURAL POPULATION SPLIT

38%   62%

ETHNIC MAKEUP

Kyrgyz 52%
Uzbek 13%
Other 14%
Russian 21%

Despite claims to the contrary, Kyrgyzstan suffers from a forceful nationalism similar to that in other ex-Soviet republics. There is considerable tension between the Kyrgyz and other minorities, particularly Uzbeks. The preference given to Kyrgyz in the political system and in particular in the land laws, which exclude all others from full title, has aggravated tensions. The trend in politics is towards greater Islamicization, which is linking religion and race issues more closely and adding pressure on 'foreigners', particularly Russians, to leave.

Current conditions differ radically from those in Soviet days, when the Russian community effectively ran the economy. It is only as recently as 1989 that the Kyrgyz resumed their position as the main ethnic group owing to their higher birth rate. The government is now trying to stem Russian emigration.

Loess landscape, Naryn valley. Kyrgyzstan is dominated by the ice-capped Tian Shan Mountains, but valleys are green and fertile.

POLITICS

 Uncertain   President Askar Akayev

THE STATE OF THE PARTIES

Supreme Soviet 350 members

Elections are scheduled for 1995, when it has been agreed that the current terms of the president and Supreme Soviet will expire, in accordance with the 1993 constitution

Kyrgyzstan has gone further than most ex-Soviet republics in embracing political change. As the first republic to denounce the attempted coup in Moscow in 1991, it swiftly banned all the activities of the Communist Party, which now no longer exists, even under another name.

Akayev, the academic picked as a reformist president by the Supreme Soviet in 1990, has since steered a precarious course aimed at trimming from official positions the number of more extreme nationalists. These are felt to threaten the presence of minorities, whose skills are needed for Kyrgyz reconstruction. Economic policy has embraced market-led reform theories, but with few tangible results.

Although the many nationalist parties have so far failed to form a united front against the government, the broad trend in politics is still towards greater nationalism.

Ethnic tension between Kyrgyz and Uzbeks has been rising since ethnic riots in 1990 in the city of Osh, home to a large number of the Uzbek minority.

WORLD AFFAIRS

 CIS   CSCE

Relations with Russia are good, though Kyrgyzstan is working to reduce its dependence on it. Turkey, the second country to establish a mission in Bishkek after the USA, is developing close links aimed at restraining Iranian fundamentalist influence in the region. Relations with Uzbekistan, which supports anti-democratic forces in Kyrgyzstan, are tense.

AID

 $300m (receipts)   Rising steadily

The USA, Germany, Turkey and Japan are the major bilateral donors. The IMF is funding economic restructuring.

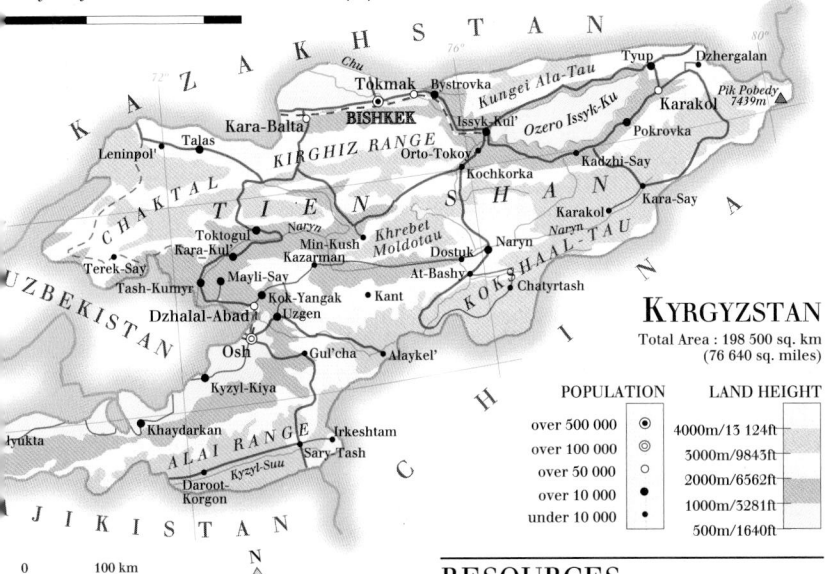

KYRGYZSTAN

Total Area : 198 500 sq. km
(76 640 sq. miles)

POPULATION		LAND HEIGHT
over 500 000	◉	4000m/13 124ft
over 100 000	◎	3000m/9843ft
over 50 000	○	2000m/6562ft
over 10 000	●	1000m/3281ft
under 10 000	•	500m/1640ft

CHRONOLOGY

The Kyrgyz first developed a recognizable ethnic consciousness in the late 18th century.

☐ **1860s** Expansion of Russian Empire into Kyrgyz lands.
☐ **1916** Kyrgyz resistance to call-up to Tsar's armies fighting Germany; 120,000 Kyrgyz die in uprisings.
☐ **1924** Incorporated in USSR.
☐ **1991** Independence from USSR.

EDUCATION

 Over 90%

Replacing Russian as the main teaching language is proving an enormous task. Russian is likely to survive at tertiary level as the Kyrgyz language lacks key technical and scientific terms.

HEALTH

 1 per 272 people — Respiratory, heart and cerebrovascular diseases, cancers

Kyrgyzstan had one of the Soviet Union's least developed public health systems. Infant mortality remains high.

WEALTH

Inflation is eroding the value of most salaries

CONSUMER GOODS OWNERSHIP

Luxury goods ownership limited to a small elite

The old Communist Party nomenklatura, using their contacts in trade, are still the wealthiest group.

WORLD RANKING

K

DEFENCE

 $47.1m — No significant change

The small army, composed of the Kyrgyz remnants of the former CIS force, is weak and not influential in politics. Recruitment to a 7000-strong National Guard was set up in 1992. Kyrgyzstan looks to its alliance with the CIS, particularly Russia, for its security.

ECONOMICS

 $6.9bn — 12.30 som

SCORE CARD

☐ WORLD GNP RANKING..........................95th
☐ GNP PER CAPITA $1533
☐ BALANCE OF PAYMENTS ....Deficit
☐ INFLATION 1500%
☐ UNEMPLOYMENT................................1.5%

STRENGTHS
Agricultural self-sufficiency. Minerals, especially gold and mercury for export. Large hydroelectric power potential.

WEAKNESSES
Agriculture-based economy. Economy still dominated by the state and the mentality of collective farming. Sharp economic decline since 1991 break-up of USSR, on which it depended totally for trade and supplies. Hyperinflation – high of 1500% a year at mid-1993.

EXPORTS/IMPORTS

Trade is overwhelmingly with the Russian Federation. A smaller proportion is with other states of the former Soviet Union

RESOURCES

 15m kwh (capacity 4.1m kw) — 3600 b/d
 10.5m sheep and goats, 1.2m cattle, 440,500 pigs — Coal, antimony, gas, oil, tin, mercury, iron uranium, zinc, gold

Kyrgyzstan has small quantities of commercially exploitable coal, oil and gas and great hydroelectric power potential. Energy policy, which relies on Western aid and technology, is primarily aimed at developing these further in order to reduce dependence on supplies from Russia, and eventually to achieve self-sufficiency in energy.

ENVIRONMENT

 1% — No funds for major initiatives

The major problem is the salination of the soil caused by excessive irrigation of cotton. Kyrgyzstan has a poor record in limiting industrial pollution.

MEDIA

 There is no censorship

PUBLISHING AND BROADCAST MEDIA

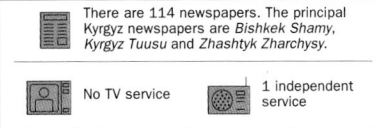
There are 114 newspapers. The principal Kyrgyz newspapers are *Bishkek Shamy, Kyrgyz Tuusu* and *Zhashtyk Zharchysy*.

No TV service — 1 independent service

TV programming is mostly from Russia. The Kyrgyz press is the most liberal in Central Asia.

CRIME

 Kyrgyzstan does not publish prison figures — 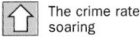 The crime rate is soaring

Outbreaks of violence are often the result of ethnic tensions. Economic decline is encouraging farmers to grow opium for the illegal drugs trade.

LAOS

SOUTH EAST ASIA

OFFICIAL NAME: Lao People's Democratic Republic
CAPITAL: Vientiane **POPULATION:** 4.3 million **CURRENCY:** Kip **OFFICIAL LANGUAGE:** Lao

LAOS IS A LAND-LOCKED country surrounded by Vietnam, Cambodia, Thailand, Burma and China. The Mekong River forms its main thoroughfare and feeds the fertile lowlands of the Mekong valley. Laos became independent of France in 1953. It was heavily bombed by US aircraft during the Vietnam War. The communist Lao People's Revolutionary Party (LPRP) has held power since 1975. The government began introducing market-orientated reforms in 1986. A transfer of power took place in 1992 following the death of party leader Kaysone Phomvihane.

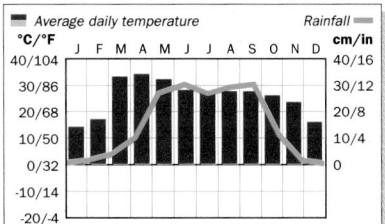

Farm in northeastern Laos. The only lowlands are along the Mekong River. Three quarters of Laotians are subsistence farmers.

CLIMATE

WEATHER CHART

The tropical southerly monsoon brings heavy rains from May to September. For the rest of the year Laos has dry northerly winds and sunny skies.

COMMUNICATIONS

Wattay, Vientiane
165,000 passengers

1 ship
1500 dwt

THE TRANSPORT NETWORK

| 13,971 km (8681 miles) | None |
| None | 4600 km (2858 miles) |

In 1994, a bridge was opened over the Mekong at Vientiane, creating the first road link between Thailand and Laos. Foreigners may enter Laos only via this route or by air to Vientiane. Other roads lead into Vietnam and Cambodia.

PEOPLE

Lao, Miao, Yao, Vietnamese, Chinese, French

17 people per km²

THE URBAN/RURAL POPULATION SPLIT

19%   81%

RELIGIOUS PERSUASION

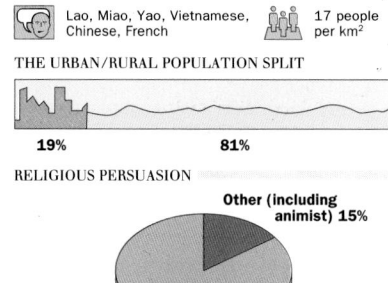

Other (including animist) 15%

Buddhist 85%

ETHNIC MAKEUP

Other 1%   Lao Soung 9%

Lao Loum 56%   Lao Theung 34%

There are more than 60 ethnic groups in Laos and this considerable diversity has hindered national integration. Society is broadly divided by altitude rather than by region.

The lowland Laotians (*Lao Loum*), who make up the majority of the population and are mostly ethnic Lao, reside in the river valleys along the Mekong River and practise wet rice agriculture. The upland Laotians (*Lao Theung*) live in the hills above the

POPULATION AGE BREAKDOWN

% of population by age group	0–14	15–64	65+
	2.4%	2.6%	2.8%	3%	3%
	55.5%	55.1%	55.2%	53.4%	52.6%
	42.1%	42.3%	42%	43.6%	44.4%
	1960	1970	1980	1990	2000

valleys and practise slash and burn agriculture. Efforts by the government in Vientiane to alter this traditional form of farming, which can destroy forests and watersheds, have been resisted by the people.

Similarly, the mountain-top Laotians (*Lao Soung*), who include the Hmong, Yao and Man groups, have resisted government efforts to introduce substitutes for traditional cash crops such as opium. The Hmong, in particular, are distanced from the Vientiane leadership. Tens of thousands fled to Thailand when the LPRP took power in 1975. Today, the government continues to face small pockets of Hmong resistance.

Two thirds of the population speak Lao and a large number of tribal dialects are also spoken. Buddhism is the main religion, but there are some Christians and animists.

TOURISM

 80,000 visitors

Increasing following opening of road link with Thailand

MAIN OVERSEAS ARRIVALS

Laos does not publish tourism figures by country of origin. Most tourists come to Laos on day trips from Thailand

0   10   20   30   40
% of total arrivals

Tourists were first allowed into Laos in 1989. The government is eschewing mass-market development, encouraging expensive package tours in small groups. Hotels are few, and travel outside the Vientiane area is difficult as passes must be obtained for each province. Thai entrepreneurs are funding some new hotels.

President Nouhak Phoumsavanh, who took office in November 1992.

General Khamtay Siphandon, prime minister and head of the armed forces.

L

POLITICS

Uncertain

President Nouhak
Phoumsavanh

THE STATE OF THE PARTIES

National Assembly 85 members

**100%
LPRP**

LPRP = Lao People's Revolutionary Party
Many candidates ran as independents, but all were
effectively approved by the LPRP

Laos is a communist, one-party
state under the direct control and
administration of the LPRP.

MAIN POLITICAL ISSUES

Political reform
Reforms are currently being introduced
to modernize key state functions. The
country's first written constitution was
adopted in 1991, and a modern legal
infrastructure has been introduced.

The LPRP has begun to relax its total
hold on power. The executive branch
of government appears to be asserting
its authority, although it still relies
on the Party for broad guidelines. The
legislative branch is also taking more
initiative and the National Assembly
is no longer simply a rubber stamp
for Party edicts.

Central control
Tensions continue to be felt between
the communist government in the
capital Vientiane and the rural areas,
where the rank and file of the LPRP
and the military have their roots.
There is particular resistance to
central attempts to alter traditional
farming methods.

PROFILE
Laos has been ruled by the same circle
of communist revolutionaries since
1975. They have proved to be one of
the world's most durable and closely
knit hierarchies.

The vacuum left by the death
of long-time Party leader, Kaysone
Phomvihane, in 1992 was quickly
filled by his protégés, who show
no sign of deviating from the path he
laid down. The military, the Party and
the executive branch remain closely
intertwined. Despite limited moves
towards political reform, the LPRP,
which is modelled on the Vietnam
Communist Party, continues
to dominate political
life at every level.

The long-standing
problem of corruption,
sometimes at high
levels, has become
a matter of concern
as Laos has opened
to foreign investors.
Concern that this
may lead to a loss
of faith has led
to government
crackdowns.

WORLD AFFAIRS

NAM   ADB   CP   ESCAP

Throughout the 1960s and 1970s,
Vietnam was Laos's most important
ally. In the 1980s, after many years of
political isolation, the party leadership
in Vientiane began to seek improved
relations with the outside world, the
West in particular. Closer ties with
Japan and rapprochement with both
Thailand and with former enemies,
the USA and France, were secured.
The motivation was mainly the need
for foreign aid.

Following the collapse of
communism in eastern Europe,
Laos turned to its northern neighbour,
China, for ideological support and to
counterbalance the growing influence
of Thailand. At the same time, the
government was careful not to
jeopardize links with Vietnam.

In July 1992, Laos acceded to the
Treaty of Amity and Concord of the
Association of South East Asian Nations
(ASEAN), marking a watershed in
relations with its former adversaries
in the region.

L

CHRONOLOGY

In the late 19th century France
established control over the three
small kingdoms of Champasak,
Louangphrabang and Vientiane.

❑ **1893** Franco-Siamese treaty
establishes French control over
all territory east of the Mekong.
❑ **1899** Creation of a unified Laos
under the French.
❑ **1941** Japanese seize power from
Vichy French in Indo-China.
❑ **1946** French rule resumed.
❑ **1950** Lao Patriotic Front, LPF, set
up to oppose French rule. Gains
support of newly-formed
communist Lao People's Party (LPP).
❑ **1953** Independence as a
constitutional monarchy backed by
France and the USA.
❑ **1963** LPF begins armed struggle
against royal government through
its armed wing, the *Pathet Lao*.
❑ **1964** US bombing of North
Vietnamese sanctuaries in Laos;
later escalated along the Ho Chi
Minh trail.
❑ **1973** LPRP (formerly known as
LPF) and royal government form
a coalition after withdrawal of US
forces from Indo-China.
❑ **1975** LPRP seizes power, abolishes
monarchy and proclaims Lao
People's Democratic Republic.
Premier Kaysone Phomvihane
adopts policies for 'socialist
transformation' of economy. ➪

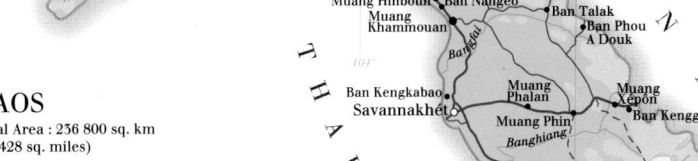

LAOS

Total Area : 236 800 sq. km
(91 428 sq. miles)

POPULATION

◎ over 100 000
○ over 50 000
● over 10 000
• under 10 000

LAND HEIGHT

2000m/6562ft
1000m/3281ft
500m/1640ft
75m/246ft

N

0   100 km

0   100 miles

CHRONOLOGY *continued*

- ❏ **1976** Kaysone begins a series of visits to USSR and eastern Europe.
- ❏ **1977** The Treaty of Friendship and Co-operation, providing for mutual assistance in national security, signed with Vietnam. Relations with China begin to cool.
- ❏ **1978** Resistance to collectivization. Series of natural disasters leads to rice shortages. After increasing internal dissent, the former King and Crown Prince are arrested and die in captivity. Almost 50,000 Laotians flee to Thailand.
- ❏ **1979** Softer economic line adopted and the speed of 'socialist transformation' slows.
- ❏ **1983** Thirty-two state officials are convicted of corruption and anti-state activities.
- ❏ **1986** Fourth Party Congress makes market-orientated reforms.
- ❏ **1988** Brief border war fought with Thailand. Diplomatic relations restored with China.
- ❏ **1989** National elections held. All candidates approved by LPRP. Rapprochement with Thailand.
- ❏ **1990** Counter-offensives against right-wing, largely Hmong, guerrilla bases located in the outer provinces. Most agricultural collectives and state farms disbanded. Arrest of three former government officials for promoting multiparty democracy.
- ❏ **1991** A constitution providing for a National Assembly, confirming the leading role of the LPRP and enshrining the right of private ownership, is promulgated. Kaysone steps down as prime minister and takes up post of president. Khamtay Siphandon becomes prime minister.
- ❏ **1992** Death of President Kaysone. Khamtay takes over as head of the LPRP. Laos accedes to the Treaty of Amity and Concord of the ASEAN countries.
- ❏ **1994** Thai–Laos bridge opens over Mekong – first ever direct road link between the two countries.

L

AID

 $131m (receipts)   Down 14% in 1991

Laos has one of the highest per capita aid inflows in the developing world. However, severe problems have been encountered in the implementation of aid programmes. In the 1980s, Laos was heavily dependent on the USSR and Vietnam for aid. Today, donors include the IMF, the World Bank, the Asian Development Bank, France, Sweden, Australia and Japan.

DEFENCE

 $18.94m   Increasing spending sourced from military-owned businesses

0	*Defence Spending as % GDP*	40
3.6%		

The armed forces are estimated by the West to number over 50,000 personnel. This total is further swelled by a paramilitary militia. Military service is compulsory for all Laotian males for 18 months.

The military and the ruling LPRP have close links. The prime minister, Khamtay Siphandon, has long been considered the army's chief supporter in the politburo and served as defence minister from 1975 to 1991. In 1977,

LAOTIAN ARMED FORCES

🪖	30 main battle tanks (T-54/T-55/T-34/T-38)	47,000 (est) personnel
🚤	50 patrol boats (8 PCI/4 LCM)	500 personnel
✈️	31 combat aircraft (29 MiG-21)	3500 personnel
	None	

Laos signed a treaty with Vietnam, providing for mutual assistance in the event of a threat to national security.

ECONOMICS

 $1.2bn   718.79 kips

SCORE CARD

❏ WORLD GNP RANKING	151st
❏ GNP PER CAPITA	$270
❏ BALANCE OF PAYMENTS	$–52m
❏ INFLATION	9.8%
❏ UNEMPLOYMENT	17%

EXPORTS

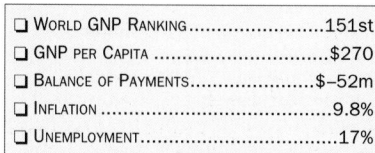

Japan 5%   France 10%   Germany 10%   Other 18%   Thailand 57%

IMPORTS

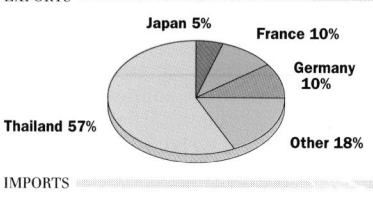

Italy 4%   China 8%   Japan 16%   Other 17%   Thailand 55%

ECONOMIC PERFORMANCE INDICATOR

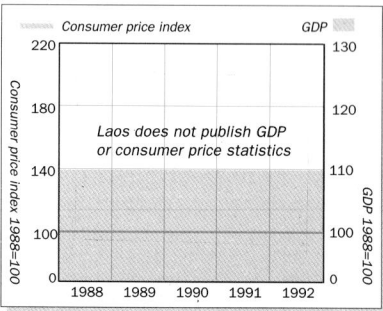

Laos does not publish GDP or consumer price statistics

STRENGTHS

Rising levels of overseas (mostly Thai) investment. Potential of garment manufacturing, mining, timber plantations, wood processing, tourism, banking and aviation. Minerals and possible oil and gas deposits.

WEAKNESSES

One of the world's 20 least-developed countries. Lack of technical expertise, a major constraint to further development. Imbalance in sources of foreign investment – most is Thai. Problems in targeting aid efficiently.

PROFILE

The LPRP began introducing market-orientated reforms in 1986. The collapse of the Soviet Union, and the subsequent loss of Soviet aid and markets in eastern Europe, speeded up this process in the early 1990s.

The reforms began by removing price controls on rice and other crops. This encouraged farmers to plant more and helped establish a degree of food self-sufficiency.

In recent years, the currency has been floated, interest rates eased and trade freed from restrictions. Laos has also opened its doors to foreign investment – the first country in Indo-China to do so. However, most foreign interest has been confined to sectors that offer quick returns, such as services, and natural resource exploitation such as logging and mining. A number of state-owned companies, including the highly profitable national brewery, have recently been privatized.

LAOS : MAJOR BUSINESSES

Ban Houayxay

Mekong

Pak Lay

Vientiane

Mekong

Timber industries   Precious stones   Gold mining   Textiles

0	200 km
0	200 miles

RESOURCES

 Significant hydroelectricity generation

 Not an oil producer and has no refineries

 1m pigs, 817,000 cattle, 43,000 horses

 Tin, gypsum, iron, copper, potash, lead, limestone, antimony

ELECTRICITY GENERATION

Hydro 95% (825m kwh)
Thermal 5% (45m kwh)
Nuclear 0%
Other 0%

0 20 40 60 80 100
% of total generation by type

Laos's most important agricultural resources are timber and coffee. The country is rich in minerals. Important deposits include tin and gypsum (which are also exported), iron ore, copper, potash, limestone, antimony, manganese, lead and salt. An increasing number of foreign companies have been awarded concessions to mine for gold and precious stones. Two oil and gas exploration agreements with oil multinationals were also negotiated between 1990 and 1991. Laos's principal source of electricity is hydroelectric power. Surpluses are exported to Thailand.

LAOS : LAND USE

Cropland
Forest
Pasture
Coffee - cash crop
Rice
Pigs

0   200 km
0   200 miles

ENVIRONMENT

 None

 Building of more HEP dams will further reduce forest cover

ENVIRONMENTAL TREATIES

No   No

No   No

Bombing and the use of defoliants in the Vietnam War did serious ecological damage. Slash and burn farming and illegal logging are destroying forests.

WEALTH

 Middle and high level state officials, $20–$40 per month; trishaw drivers in Vientiane can earn nearly five times that amount

CONSUMER GOODS OWNERSHIP

1000
750
500
250
0

Per 1000 population

VCR and PC ownership is limited to a small elite

5   4   20

There are large inequalities of wealth in Laos. A rapidly expanding group of Laotian entrepreneurs is profiting from the liberalization of the economy. The elite live in French-style villas. Mercedes are not uncommon in the capital and the number of motorcycles has doubled in the past two years.

Development is unevenly spread around the country. Many in the highlands and mountainous regions lead a subsistence existence, while farmers in the fertile Mekong valley are relatively well off. Most homes along the Mekong have TV sets which can receive broadcasts from Thai stations. Bribes are a key part of most bureaucrats' incomes.

MEDIA

 Tight government control of media

PUBLISHING AND BROADCAST MEDIA

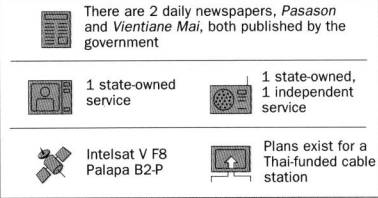

There are 2 daily newspapers, *Pasason* and *Vientiane Mai*, both published by the government

1 state-owned service

1 state-owned, 1 independent service

Intelsat V F8 Palapa B2-P

Plans exist for a Thai-funded cable station

Newspapers are owned and controlled by the LPRP. Revelations of corruption by state officials are not uncommon, but criticism of the party and its leaders remains taboo. In 1990, the illegal Radio Station of the Government for the Liberation of the Lao Nation began broadcasting anti-government propaganda for four hours per day.

EDUCATION

 50%

0   Education spending as % GNP   25
1.2%

THE EDUCATION SYSTEM

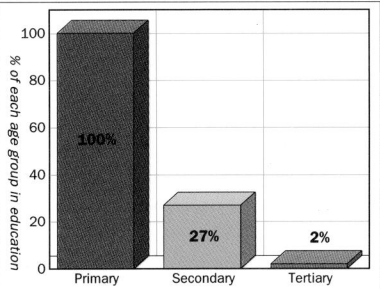

100
80
60
40
20
0

% of each age group in education

100%   27%   2%
Primary Secondary Tertiary

Literacy rates in Laos remain low, at 35% for women and 65% for men. However, adult education is currently being expanded and new schools are being built.

HEALTH

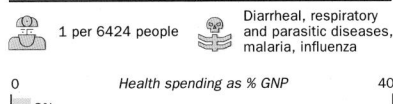 1 per 6424 people

Diarrheal, respiratory and parasitic diseases, malaria, influenza

0   Health spending as % GNP   40
2%

Poor sanitation and nutrition levels in most of rural Laos are reflected in the standard indicators of health and longevity. Infant mortality is over 10% and life expectancy is only 50 years. Malaria and haemorrhagic fever are on the increase.

CRIME

 Laos does not publish prison figures

 Rising overall, particularly corruption

CRIME RATES

Most crime is rising. However the trend in mountain regions is hard to establish

Laos is the world's third largest opium producer. Since 1990, attempts have been made to combat the production and trafficking of illegal drugs. The USA is providing funds to substitute cash crops for poppies in the mountainous northeastern provinces.

WORLD RANKING

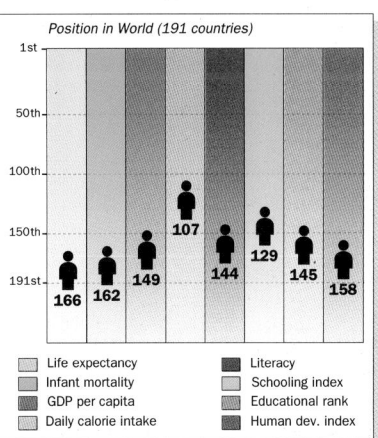

Position in World (191 countries)

1st
50th
100th
150th
191st

166 162 149 107 144 129 145 158

Life expectancy   Literacy
Infant mortality   Schooling index
GDP per capita   Educational rank
Daily calorie intake   Human dev. index

L

LATVIA

OFFICIAL NAME: Republic of Latvia **CAPITAL:** Riga
POPULATION: 2.7 million **CURRENCY:** Lats **OFFICIAL LANGUAGE:** Latvian

LYING BETWEEN Estonia and Lithuania, Latvia is situated on the eastern coast of the Baltic Sea. To the east it borders the Russian Federation and Belorussia. The whole country is a low-lying plain, which nowhere rises above 300 m. Latvia's independence was recognized by Moscow in 1991. Defence-related industries and agriculture play an important role in the economy. Only 52% of the population are ethnic Latvians.

CLIMATE

WEATHER CHART

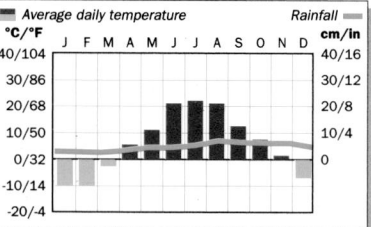

Latvia's coastal position means that the climate is temperate, with cold winters and cool summers.

COMMUNICATIONS

 Riga International   130 ships 1.34m dwt

THE TRANSPORT NETWORK

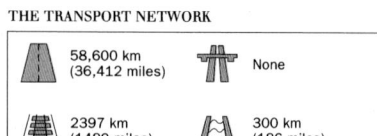

58,600 km (36,412 miles) — None
2397 km (1489 miles) — 300 km (186 miles)

The planned Finland–Poland road will run through Latvia. Ports are being upgraded, particularly Ventspils and Liepāja. The EBRD is spending 10 million ECU on improvements at Riga airport.

LATVIA

Total Area :
64 589 sq. km
(24 938 sq. miles)

POPULATION
⊙ over 500 000
◎ over 100 000
○ over 50 000
● over 10 000
• under 10 000

LAND HEIGHT
200m/656ft
Sea Level

The Russian Orthodox Cathedral in Riga. Used as a planetarium during the Soviet era, its interior is now being restored.

TOURISM

 370,000 visitors The number of visitors is increasing

MAIN OVERSEAS ARRIVALS

Germany 11%
Finland 8%
USA 6%
Other 75%

Riga is the main tourist destination, with many hotels and restaurants. Its medieval centre is being restored.

PEOPLE

Latvian, Russian 42 people per km²

THE URBAN/RURAL POPULATION SPLIT

71% 29%

ETHNIC MAKEUP
Other 5%
Ukrainian 4%
Belorussian 5%
Latvian 52%
Russian 34%

Latvians make up only 52% of the population, compared with 34% of Russians, and are a minority in the capital, Riga. Although some Latvians fear a potential cultural dilution, there is little tension between the various ethnic groups. Nevertheless, it is difficult for most ethnic Russians to become Latvian citizens. The status of women is on a par with that in western Europe. The divorce rate is high.

POLITICS

 1996 President Guntis Ulmanis

THE STATE OF THE PARTIES
Parliament (Saeima) 100 members

36% LW 15% LNNK 13% HLRNE 12% LZS 7% ER 17% Other

LW = Latvian Way **LNNK** = National Independence Movement of Latvia **HLRNE** = Harmony for Latvia and Rebirth for the National Economy **LZS** = Latvian Farmers' Union **ER** = Equal Rights **Other** = For the Fatherland and Freedom, Union of Christian Democrats, Democratic Centre Party

The LW has become the strongest branch of the Popular Front (PLF), the group formed in 1988 to lead the campaign for Latvian autonomy under the Gorbachev regime. The political situation is now beginning to stabilize after the factionalism that followed Latvia's independence. The question of citizenship remains contentious. Full rights are only granted to those with families resident before 1940. Two thirds of the Russian minority were thereby excluded from voting in recent general elections.

WORLD AFFAIRS

Latvia wishes to forge good relations with the EU, with the eventual aim of becoming a member. It is also keen to revive its pre-Soviet status as a country with close Western cultural and trading connections. Relations with Russia have recently cooled; Moscow's increasingly nationalistic foreign policy is the main cause.

AID

 Latvia does not publish aid receipts The trend is up

Aid to Latvia comes mainly from the World Bank, the IMF and the EU. Most of it goes towards improving the country's infrastructure.

DEFENCE

 $151.4m Rising now that some Russian troops have left

Building up the military is a priority. The withdrawal of Russian troops from Latvian territory is being urgently sought. Stationed ostensibly to secure the rights of ethnic Russians, they are seen as a threat to security. Latvia is also seeking closer links with Western forces and hopes to join NATO.

ECONOMICS

 $9.2bn 0.60 lati

SCORE CARD

❏ WORLD GNP RANKING	81st
❏ GNP PER CAPITA	$3410
❏ BALANCE OF PAYMENTS	50m
❏ INFLATION	7%
❏ UNEMPLOYMENT	5.6%

STRENGTHS
Well-developed industrial base, especially for defence-related industries. Numerous port facilities. Agricultural surplus.

WEAKNESSES
Lack of raw materials. Dependence on Russia for supplies of oil and natural gas. Slump in demand for Latvian exports from former Soviet and East European trading partners.

EXPORTS

IMPORTS

RESOURCES

 Electricity supplies are mainly imported   Not an oil producer and has no refineries

 12.2m poultry, 1.7m pigs, 1.5m cattle   Amber, dolomite, gravel, gypsum, limestone

Latvia has no strategic resources and is dependent on imports to meet its energy requirements. In 1991, these represented almost one third of total imports. Electricity supplies come chiefly from Lithuania and Estonia, while oil is imported from Russia and Lithuania. New infrastructure is being built to broaden the supply network.

ENVIRONMENT

 3%   Environmental issues' role in independence movement

Peat extraction – Latvia is 5% bog – has damaged the environment. Pollution of the Baltic Sea and general air and water quality are also of concern. Environmental awareness is strong. In the run-up to independence green issues had a high profile.

MEDIA

 Officially none. Russians have restricted access to the media

PUBLISHING AND BROADCAST MEDIA

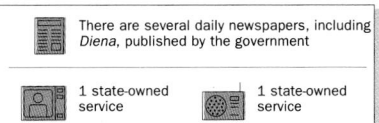

There are several daily newspapers, including *Diena*, published by the government

1 state-owned service   1 state-owned service

The press is now relatively free from state interference. Previously, the media was predominantly in Russian. Since 1991, the state, aiming to broaden the use of the official language, has actively promoted Latvian publications.

CRIME

 Latvia does not publish prison figures 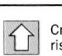 Crime levels are rising slightly

Levels of crime are lower than in other ex-Soviet republics. However, organized crime is a growing problem.

EDUCATION

 98%

Education in Latvia is now following the German model. There are 46,000 students in higher education.

CHRONOLOGY

Latvia was dominated by Germany and, briefly, Sweden before Russia completed its conquest in 1795.

- ❏ **1917** Supports Russian Bolshevik revolution. Declares independence.
- ❏ **1918–1920** Invaded by Bolsheviks in east and Germany in west.
- ❏ **1920** Gains independence.
- ❏ **1940** Soviet annexation.
- ❏ **1941** German occupation begins.
- ❏ **1944** Incorporated into the USSR.
- ❏ **1952** Armed resistance ends.
- ❏ **1987** Riga pro-independence rally.
- ❏ **1987** Latvian official language. PLF founded to group all reformists.
- ❏ **1989** PLF wins elections. Declaration of independence.
- ❏ **1991** Joins UN as independent state. Communist Party banned.

HEALTH

 1 per 201 people   Cerebrovascular and heart diseases, cancers, accidents

The state-run health system is beset by shortages of medicines and equipment. Standards have improved little since the demise of communism.

WEALTH

 Secretary, 30–40 lati per month; dentist, 80 lati per month

CONSUMER GOODS OWNERSHIP

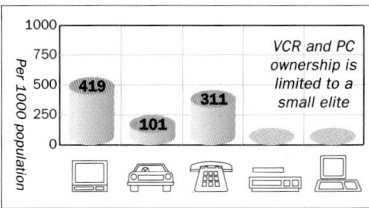

VCR and PC ownership is limited to a small elite

The old bureaucracy has retained its privileged status and contacts, and remains the wealthiest group.

WORLD RANKING

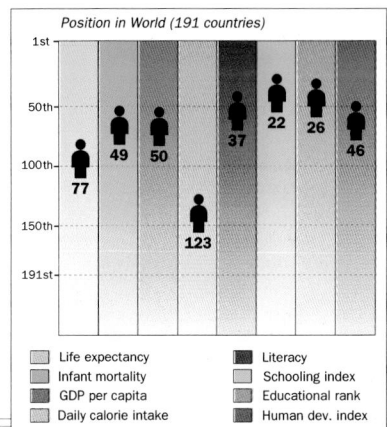

Position in World (191 countries)

Legend:
- Life expectancy
- Infant mortality
- GDP per capita
- Daily calorie intake
- Literacy
- Schooling index
- Educational rank
- Human dev. index

L

LEBANON

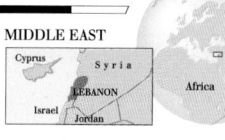

OFFICIAL NAME: Republic of Lebanon **CAPITAL:** Beirut
POPULATION: 2.8 million **CURRENCY:** Lebanese pound **OFFICIAL LANGUAGE:** Arabic

LEBANON IS DWARFED BY its two powerful neighbours, Syria and Israel. The country's coastal strip is fertile and the hinterland mountainous. Although in the minority, Maronite Christians have traditionally ruled Lebanon. A civil war between Muslim and Christian factional groups began in 1975 and threatened to lead to the break-up of the state. However, Saudi Arabia brokered a peace agreement in 1989. Elections were held in 1992.

POLITICS

1996 President Elias Hrawi

THE STATE OF THE PARTIES

National Assembly 128 members

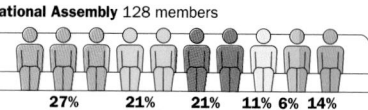

| 27% MC | 21% Su M | 21% Sh M | 11% GO | 6% D | 14% Other |

MC = Maronite Catholics **Su M** = Sunni Muslims
Sh M = Shi'a Muslims **GO** = Greek Orthodox
D = Druzes (religious sect linked to Islam)

The president must be a Maronite Christian and the prime minister a Sunni Muslim

Civil war broke out in Lebanon in 1975. The main cause was the breakdown in the Christian–Muslim consensus over the constitution, which gave Christians a disproportionate political voice. The presence of independent factions, each with its own grievances, added to the complexity of the war. Lebanon was close to fragmentation when the various factions agreed terms for peace at Taif, Saudi Arabia, in 1989. The settlement ended 16 years of civil war. It effectively gave the Muslims more power. The elections held in 1992 were the first for 20 years. Under Prime Minister Rafiq Al-Hariri, Lebanon has achieved relative stability.

CLIMATE

WEATHER CHART

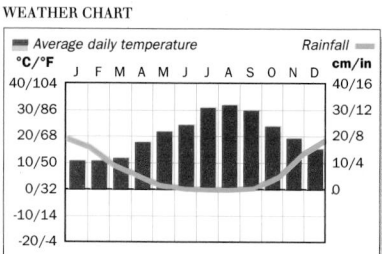

Winters are mild and summers hot, with high humidity on the coast. Snow falls on high ground in the winter.

COMMUNICATIONS

Beirut International, Kahldeh

139 ships 428,800 dwt

THE TRANSPORT NETWORK

| 7370 km (4579 miles) | None |
| 222 km (138 miles) | None |

The redevelopment of Beirut could see it regain its position as one of the Middle East's major entrepôts.

TOURISM

Lebanon still receives only a small number of visitors

The number of tourists is rising

MAIN OVERSEAS ARRIVALS

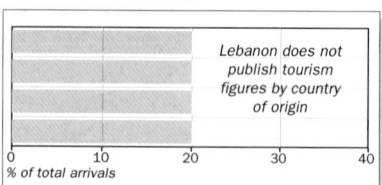

Lebanon does not publish tourism figures by country of origin

% of total arrivals

Once the playground of the Arab world where East met West, Beirut was devastated by the civil war, ruining its profitable tourist industry. Formerly, over two million people a year visited its fine beaches and historical sites.

PEOPLE

Arabic, French, Armenian, Assyrian

264 people per km²

THE URBAN/RURAL POPULATION SPLIT

84% 16%

RELIGIOUS PERSUASION

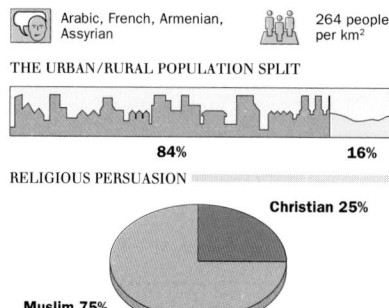

Christian 25%
Muslim 75%

The Lebanese population is fragmented religiously into sub-sects of Christians and Muslims, but retains a strong sense of national identity. There has been a large Palestinian refugee population in the country since 1948. Islamic fundamentalism is influential among poorer Shi'a Muslims.

LEBANON

Total Area : 10 400 sq. km (4015 sq. miles)

LAND HEIGHT

3000m/9843ft
2000m/6562ft
1000m/3281ft
500m/1640ft
200m/656ft
Sea Level

POPULATION

over 1 000 000
over 100 000
over 10 000
under 10 000

WORLD AFFAIRS

The civil war, hijackings, the Israeli invasion of 1982 and the Western hostage crisis brought Lebanon to the top of the international agenda in the 1980s. A 1989 Arab solution ended internal strife. More intractable is the Arab–Israeli dispute. The Iranian-backed *Hezbollah* militia, aided by Syria, and the Israeli-backed South Lebanon Army (SLA) still frequently clash in southern Lebanon.

AID

 $138m (receipts)   Up 3% in 1991

The government is seeking billions of dollars to rebuild the centre of Beirut and restore shattered infrastructure.

DEFENCE

 $173m   Up 15% in 1992

Under the terms of the Taif Agreement, 40,000 Syrian troops are stationed in Lebanon. Lebanon's own army has 21,000 troops. The south is controlled by the Israeli-backed South Lebanon Army. All the political factions maintain armed militias. A UN force attempts to police the border with Israel.

ECONOMICS

 $5.9bn   1835 Lebanese pounds

SCORE CARD

❏ WORLD GNP RANKING	106th
❏ GNP PER CAPITA	$2107
❏ BALANCE OF PAYMENTS	$–2246m
❏ INFLATION	100%
❏ UNEMPLOYMENT	50%

STRENGTHS

Peace will allow Lebanon to regain it's position as an Arab centre for banking and services. Potentially a major producer of wine and fruit.

WEAKNESSES

Dependent on imported oil and gas. Infrastructure – especially in Beirut – wrecked by civil war. Agriculture still at 40% of pre-war levels. High public debt and inflation.

EXPORTS

IMPORTS

RESOURCES

 4.7bn kwh (capacity 603,000 kw)

 210,000 sheep, 59,000 cattle, 49,000 pigs

Not an oil producer; refines 37,500 b/cd

Lignite, iron ore

Wine, cotton, fruit and vegetables are the main crops. Thermal power stations are fuelled by imported petroleum.

ENVIRONMENT

 0.3%   Initiatives will have to await reconstruction

Rebuilding Beirut's basic infrastructure and ridding the country of mines are the government's priorities.

MEDIA

 The press has greater freedom than in any other country in the Arab world

PUBLISHING AND BROADCAST MEDIA

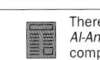 There are 40 daily newspapers, including *Al-Anwar*, *An-Nahar*, and its French companion, *L'Orient-Le Jour*

 1 state-owned service

 1 state-owned, 20 independent stations

Beirut could once again become a centre for Arab media. However, in 1994 private TV stations were banned.

CRIME

 Lebanon does not publish prison figures   Crime is sharply down since 1989

The kidnapping of hostages and the breakdown of law during the civil war made Beirut a dangerous city for Western visitors.

Politically motivated violence has recently declined, though the risk of urban terrorism remains. Rural areas untouched by the conflict have low levels of crime.

***The Corniche, Beirut,** due to be rebuilt by US consultant engineers and architects in a privately-financed scheme.*

CHRONOLOGY

Lebanon became independent, after 20 years of French mandate, in 1944.

❏ **1975** Civil war erupts, stirred by Palestinian guerrillas evacuated from Jordan in 1970.
❏ **1982** Israel invades Lebanon and lays siege to Beirut.
❏ **1989** Taif Agreement brokered in Saudi Arabia. Civil war ends.
❏ **1991** Lebanon and Syria conclude security agreement. Release of most Western hostages secured.

EDUCATION

 80%

Lebanon has the highest literacy rate in the Arab world. However, education was severely disrupted by the war.

HEALTH

 1 per 771 people   Heart diseases, infectious and parisitic diseases

An adequate system of primary health care exists. Hospital staffing is returning to pre-war levels.

WEALTH

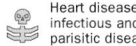 Minimum wage, 90 Lebanese pounds per month

CONSUMER GOODS OWNERSHIP

Average income per capita is low. A huge gulf exists between the poor and a small, massively rich elite.

WORLD RANKING

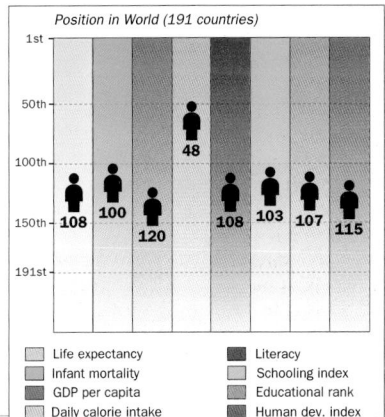

L

LESOTHO

OFFICIAL NAME: Kingdom of Lesotho **CAPITAL:** Maseru
POPULATION: 1.8 million **CURRENCY:** Loti **OFFICIAL LANGUAGE:** English and Sesotho

A MOUNTAINOUS AND land-locked country, Lesotho is entirely surrounded by South Africa. It is economically dependent on its larger neighbour, which provides all land transport links with the outside world. The completion of the Highlands Water Scheme should bring major energy export revenues. Democratic elections in 1993 ended a period of military rule. About 38% of the male labour force are migrant workers in South Africa.

CLIMATE

WEATHER CHART

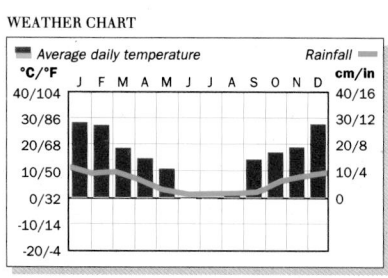

Drought is often followed by torrential rain storms. Snow is frequent in winter in the mountains.

COMMUNICATIONS

 Moshoeshoe Intl, Maseru
43,000 passengers **Has no fleet**

THE TRANSPORTATION NETWORK

2923 miles (4715 km)	None
1.2 miles (2 km)	None

Lesotho relies on South African road and rail outlets. New roads have been constructed to service the Highlands Water Scheme.

TOURISM

 169,000 visitors No change in 1989

MAIN OVERSEAS ARRIVALS

Africa 97%	
Europe 2%	
North and South America 0.5%	
South Asia 0.5%	

0 10 20 30 40 50 60 70 80 90 100
% of total arrivals

Tourism, largely based on Lesotho's spectacular mountain scenery, should benefit from South Africa's new political situation. Lakes created by Lesotho's HEP scheme will provide watersports.

PEOPLE

 English, Sesotho, Zulu   153 people per sq. mile

THE URBAN/RURAL POPULATION SPLIT

20%   80%

ETHNIC MAKEUP

Other 1%

Basotho 99%

The overwhelming majority of the population is Basotho, though there are also Europeans and some South Asians and Taiwanese. Ethnic homogeneity and a strong sense of national identity have tended to minimize ethnic tension. However, South Asian and Chinese shopkeepers, whose control of business is resented, came under attack in riots in 1991. The export of male contract labour to South African mines means that women head 72% of households; they also run farming, regarded by Lesotho men as 'women's work'.

POLITICS

1998   HM King Letsie III

THE STATE OF THE PARTIES

National Assembly 65 members

100%
BCP

BCP = Basotho Congress Party

Senate 33 members

22 members are principal Chiefs and 11 are chosen by the King

The armed forces have been the key political players in Lesotho since 1986, when, following a South African blockade, Chief Jonathan's Basotho National Party (BNP) government was deposed and a military council assumed power. Colonel Elias Ramaema took over as chairman of the military council in a bloodless coup in 1991 and shortly afterwards lifted the prohibition on political parties. Direct military rule ended in 1993, when free and peaceful general elections resulted in a sweeping victory for the BCP. However, a new constitutional clause gives the army precedence over the government in matters of national security, ensuring its continuing influence in politics.

The biggest single question dominating Lesotho politics is the future of the country itself as a sovereign state. Debate continues as to whether it should be integrated into a post-apartheid South Africa.

LESOTHO

Total Area : 30 350 sq. km (11 718 sq. miles)

POPULATION

⊚ over 100 000
• under 10 000

LAND HEIGHT

3000m/9843ft
2000m/6562ft
1000m/3281ft

SOUTHERN AFRICA   Africa

LESOTHO
South Africa

WORLD AFFAIRS

 Comm　OAU　SACU　SADC　GATT

Foreign policy is dominated by the nature of Lesotho's relationship with South Africa. Lesotho currently has duty-free access for most manufactured goods to the EU and preferential access to US and Scandinavian markets.

AID

 $123m (receipts)　Down 12% in 1991

Aid, over 50% of which comes from the Southern Africa Customs Union (SACU), is crucial to development, and accounts for 26% of Lesotho's GNP. Most is concentrated in land yield projects, with the aim of making Lesotho self-sufficient in food.

DEFENCE

 $179.3m　Increasing due to unrest

Many in the BCP are questioning the need for a 2000-strong army, which poses a potential coup threat.

ECONOMICS

 $1.1bn　3.40 maloti

SCORE CARD

❑ WORLD GNP RANKING	153rd
❑ GNP PER CAPITA	$470
❑ BALANCE OF PAYMENTS	$–70.3m
❑ INFLATION	13%
❑ UNEMPLOYMENT	35%

STRENGTHS

Membership of Southern African Customs Union. Highlands Water Scheme, which will be a major revenue earner and employer.

WEAKNESSES

Economic over-dependence on South Africa. Weak agricultural sector, although it is the principal occupation. Lack of industrial development.

EXPORTS

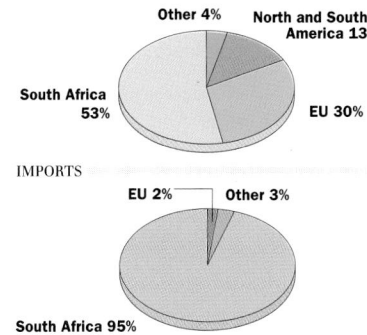

Other 4% / North and South America 13% / South Africa 53% / EU 30%

IMPORTS

EU 2% / Other 3% / South Africa 95%

***Landscape near Mohales Hoek** in Lesotho's lowest lands, which are over 1300 m above sea level. This spiral aloe grows only in Lesotho.*

RESOURCES

 Over 90% of energy imported from South Africa　 Not an oil producer and has no refineries

1m goats, 1m sheep, 530,000 cattle　Diamonds

The hugely ambitious Highlands Water hydroelectric scheme will supply all of Lesotho's energy requirements; it will also supply 63.3 cubic metres of water per second for South African use. Diamonds are mined in the northeast.

ENVIRONMENT

 0.2% partially protected　 Government sensitive to environmental questions

Lesotho's land is seriously eroded due to the climate and overgrazing. There is also concern over the effects of the Highlands Water Scheme. The project's pylons are, however, bird-friendly, and there are schemes to protect the Maluti mountain minnow in its reservoirs.

MEDIA

 Censorship has reduced since the previous military regime, under which the editor of the *Mirror* was deported to Kenya

PUBLISHING AND BROADCAST MEDIA

 There are no daily newspapers. *Leselinyana la Lesotho* and *Moeletsi oa Basotho* are popular religious periodicals

1 state-owned service　 1 state-owned service

The *Mirror* is the only independent paper in Lesotho. Radio and TV broadcasts are in Sesotho and English.

CRIME

 Lesotho does not publish prison figures　 Up 34% in 1986

Crime levels are much lower than in South Africa. Robbery and corruption are problems in urban areas.

EDUCATION

 74%

Lesotho has one of the highest literacy rates in Africa, and the highest female literacy rate – 84%.

CHRONOLOGY

King Moshoeshoe I created a strong kingdom, but sought British help after defeat by the Boers in 1843.

- ❑ **1884** British Crown colony.
- ❑ **1966** Independent kingdom.
- ❑ **1970** Chief Jonathan of BNP annuls elections and bans parties.
- ❑ **1974** BCP, which had in effect won the elections, attempts coup.
- ❑ **1986** Maj-Gen Lekhanya leads successful military coup.
- ❑ **1990** King disagrees with military council. Exiled. Son elected King.
- ❑ **1991** Col. Ramaema seizes power.
- ❑ **1993** Free elections – BCP wins.

HEALTH

 1 per 15,718 people　 Tuberculosis, parasitic diseases, nutritional disorders

Private health organizations and NGOs are responsible for about half of all health services and are regulated by the Ministry of Health. Although the government operates a flying-doctor service, the highlands are still not adequately covered. The main endemic disease is tuberculosis.

L

WEALTH

 Welder, 260 maloti per month; professional nurse, 531 maloti per month

CONSUMER GOODS OWNERSHIP

VCR and PC ownership is limited to a small elite

3　4　12

Social mobility is limited in Lesotho; the ruling elite keeps a tight control on power and wealth. Over 90% of the population live below the poverty line.

WORLD RANKING

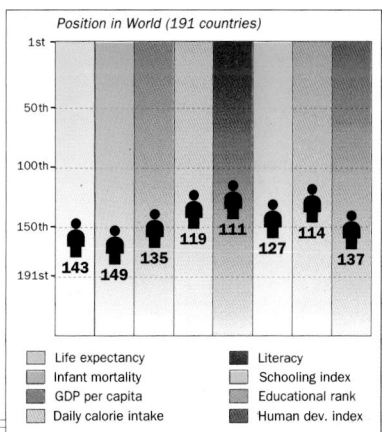

Position in World (191 countries)

143　149　135　119　111　127　114　137

Life expectancy / Infant mortality / GDP per capita / Daily calorie intake / Literacy / Schooling index / Educational rank / Human dev. index

LIBERIA

OFFICIAL NAME: The Republic of Liberia   **CAPITAL:** Monrovia
POPULATION: 2.8 million   **CURRENCY:** Liberian dollar   **OFFICIAL LANGUAGE:** English

NAMED AFTER PEOPLE LIBERATED from slavery who began returning from the USA in 1816, Liberia today is a war-torn country in a state of anarchy, with private armies competing for power. Facing the Atlantic in equatorial West Africa, most of its coastline is characterized by lagoons and mangrove swamps. Inland, a grassland plateau supports the limited agriculture (just 1% of land is arable). Liberia has the world's largest flag of convenience merchant fleet.

CLIMATE

WEATHER CHART

Except in the extreme southeast there is only one rainy season, from May to October. Temperatures are consistently high. During the October to March dry season when the dust-laden *harmattan* wind blows, they rise even higher inland.

COMMUNICATIONS

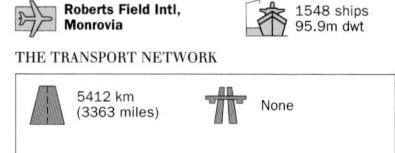

Roberts Field Intl, Monrovia

1548 ships
95.9m dwt

THE TRANSPORT NETWORK

5412 km (3363 miles)		None
490 km (304 miles)		None

Most roads in Liberia are unpaved. The 490-km railway was built to transport iron ore and carries little other traffic. Roberts Field airport was built by the USA during the Second World War.

TOURISM

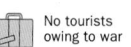

No tourists owing to war

Not applicable

MAIN OVERSEAS ARRIVALS

Liberia does not publish tourism figures by country of origin

% of total arrivals

Liberia is an anarchic war zone. Few tourists visited the country before the war, and tourism has now ceased.

PEOPLE

Kpelle, Vai, Bassa, Kru, Grebo, Kissi, Gola, Loma, English

23 people per km²

THE URBAN/RURAL POPULATION SPLIT

46%   54%

ETHNIC MAKEUP

Americo-Liberians 5%

Indigenous tribes (16 main groupings) 95%

A key distinction in Liberia has been between Americo-Liberians, the descendants of those freed from slavery (known as 'civilized persons'), and the majority indigenous 'tribals'. The latter were long held in contempt by the Americos, but intermarriage and political assimilation since 1944 have softened attitudes. Inter-tribal tension is now a more serious problem. Conflict erupted during the 1990 invasion, when Samuel Doe's Krahn tribe exacted retribution from the Gio and Mano groups.

POLITICS

Uncertain

Dr Amos Sawyer

THE STATE OF THE PARTIES

Interim Legislative Assembly

Liberia is in a state of chaos and its unelected parliament controls only the Monrovian region

Liberian politics effectively collapsed in 1990 into a chaotic, bloody and many-sided conflict, where the simple aim was the seizure of the spoils of office. The long period of Americo-Liberian rule had ended in 1980 when army sergeant Samuel Doe seized power. Doe executed the existing government and then succeeded in getting US backing. A series of armed invasions from neighbouring states followed, prompting ECOWAS to send a peace-keeping force (ECOMOG) in 1990. ECOMOG turned aside from its role as peace-keeper in 1993 and launched an offensive to capture territory from the most successful of the armed groups, the National Patriotic Front of Liberia (NPFL) led by Charles Taylor. A nominal government in Monrovia has been led by Amos Sawyer since 1991. Doe was captured and executed, by a faction of the NPFL led by Prince Johnson, in 1991.

LIBERIA

Total Area : 111 370 sq. km
43 000 sq. miles

POPULATION

◎ over 100 000
● over 10 000
• under 10 000

LAND HEIGHT

1000m/3281ft
500m/1640ft
200m/656ft
Sea Level

WORLD AFFAIRS

The USA was the main foreign influence in Liberia until the arrival of ECOMOG (the army formed by Liberia's neighbours in ECOWAS), backed chiefly by Nigeria and Ghana. Burkina Faso, Ivory Coast and Libya are suspected of backing the NPFL, the main group fighting with ECOMOG for control of the country. In 1993, the UN refused a request to become involved.

AID

 $115m (receipts)   Up 95% from 1989

International agencies stopped providing aid in 1986. The USA continued giving aid to the Doe regime until 1990, despite his apparent misuse of funds.

DEFENCE

 $37.62m   Up 34% in 1989

Most of the private armies now operating in Liberia, including the official Armed Forces of Liberia (AFL), live by extortion and intimidating local communities.

ECONOMICS

 $1.2 bn   1.00 Liberian dollars

SCORE CARD

- ❑ WORLD GNP RANKING 152nd
- ❑ GNP PER CAPITA $430
- ❑ BALANCE OF PAYMENTS ....*The formal*
- ❑ INFLATION ....*economy has*
- ❑ UNEMPLOYMENT ....*collapsed*

STRENGTHS
Very few. The Firestone rubber plantation and huge LAMCO iron ore mine are under the control of the NPFL. Tropical timber, but reserves declining.

WEAKNESSES
Little commercial activity. State of anarchy since 1990 has led to collapse of the economy.

EXPORTS

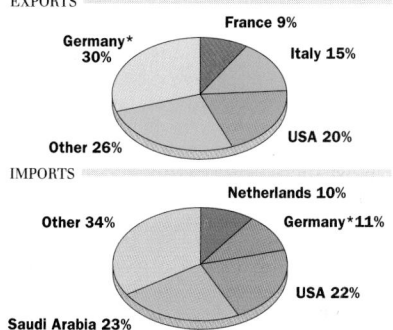

Germany* 30%
France 9%
Italy 15%
Other 26%
USA 20%

IMPORTS

Netherlands 10%
Other 34%
Germany* 11%
USA 22%
Saudi Arabia 23%

Village near Gbarnga. *The Kpelle, the largest of Liberia's 16 indigenous ethnic groups, are concentrated in this part of Liberia.*

RESOURCES

 565m kwh (capacity 0.33m kw)

 Not an oil producer; refines 15,000 b/cd

 240,000 sheep, 140,000 pigs, 42,000 cattle

Iron ore, diamonds, gold, barytes, kyanite, columbite, manganese

Liberia has an estimated one billion tons of iron ore reserves at Mount Nimba. Even if peaceful conditions existed, the current state of world demand would not justify exploitation.

ENVIRONMENT

 1%   Civil war makes environmental initiatives impossible

The NPFL, and other armed groups, have cut down tropical forests to finance their armies.

MEDIA

 Criticism of the government in the press was dangerous from 1980 until the fall of the Doe regime in 1991

PUBLISHING AND BROADCAST MEDIA

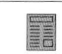 There are 2 daily newspapers, the independent *Daily Observer* and *The News,* published by the government

 1 state-owned service

 2 state-owned, 1 independent service

The Monrovia press has been freer since the fall of Doe, but distribution problems in a state of war lessen the impact of newspapers.

CRIME

 Liberia does not publish prison figures

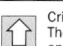 Crime is rampant. There are no enforcing agencies

Human rights have figured little in Liberian life, and since 1990 have disappeared altogether. The warring factions have regularly massacred civilians, press-ganged armies, and displaced thousands into seeking refuge in neighbouring states.

EDUCATION

 39%

Originally based on the US model, the education system has effectively collapsed during the civil war.

CHRONOLOGY

Between 1816 and 1892, 22,000 people liberated from slavery, most from the USA, resettled in Liberia.

- ❑ **1847** Established as an independent republic.
- ❑ **1926** US Firestone Rubber Company granted 405,000-hectare concession.
- ❑ **1930s** Interior brought under Monrovia's control.
- ❑ **1971** William Tolbert president.
- ❑ **1980** Coup. Tolbert assassinated by Master Sergeant Samuel Doe.
- ❑ **1990** Civil war grips whole country.
- ❑ **1991** Fall of Doe government.

HEALTH

 1 per 1625 people

Communicable, diarrheal, parasitic and heart diseases

Only the Americo-Liberian community had ready access to health care before the current state of war. Adequate care is now limited to the military.

WEALTH

 The underclass was composed of rural dwellers, but since the war started, it has encompassed most of the population

CONSUMER GOODS OWNERSHIP

VCR and PC ownership is limited to a small elite

18   1   9

Power and wealth have a very direct connection in Liberia. Both the Americo-Liberian regimes, and Doe who replaced them, saw the state as a source of plunder in the form of well-paid jobs and kick-backs from contracts. Current warring factions seek similar power.

WORLD RANKING

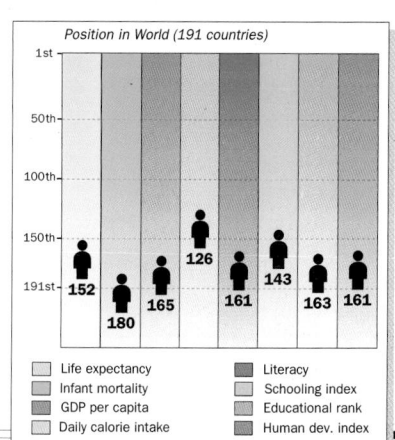

Position in World (191 countries)

152   180   165   126   161   143   163   161

- ❑ Life expectancy
- ❑ Infant mortality
- ❑ GDP per capita
- ❑ Daily calorie intake
- ❑ Literacy
- ❑ Schooling index
- ❑ Educational rank
- ❑ Human dev. index

L

LIBYA

OFFICIAL NAME: The Great Socialist People's Libyan Arab Jamahiriya
CAPITAL: Tripoli **POPULATION:** 4.9 million **CURRENCY:** Libyan dinar **OFFICIAL LANGUAGE:** Arabic

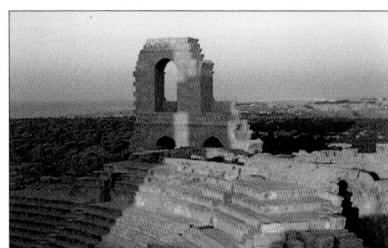

L IBYA IS SITUATED between Egypt and Algeria on the Mediterranean coast of North Africa, with Chad and Niger on its southern borders. Apart from the coastal strip and the mountains in the south, the country is desert or semi-desert. Libya's strategic position in North Africa and abundant oil and gas resources made it an important trading partner for European nations. However, it has been politically marginalized by the West for its past links with terrorist groups. Libya is also under UN sanctions for refusing to extradite two men suspected of the 1988 Lockerbie bombing.

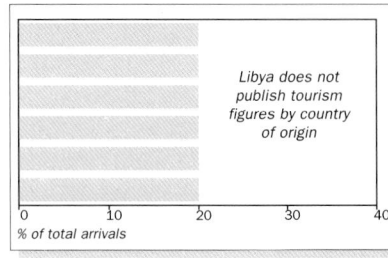

Roman amphitheatre, Sabrātah. *Libya's impressive Classical heritage testifies to its importance in ancient times.*

CLIMATE

WEATHER CHART

Average daily temperature | Rainfall

°C/°F — J F M A M J J A S O N D — cm/in
40/104 ... 40/16
30/86 ... 30/12
20/68 ... 20/8
10/50 ... 10/4
0/32 ... 0
-10/14
-20/4

The coastal region has a warm, temperate climate, with mild, wet winters and hot, dry summers.

COMMUNICATIONS

🛫 **Tripoli International**   🚢 42 ships
1.21m dwt

THE TRANSPORT NETWORK

| 32,500 km (20,195 miles) | None |
| None | None |

The National Coast Road runs 1825 km from the Tunisian to the Egyptian borders linking the principal urban centres. There are no railways, though some are planned. Owing to UN sanctions on international flights, the major transit point is through Tunisia.

Al Kufrah Oasis. *As 90% of Libya is arid rock and sand, oases provide essential agricultural land, besides being tourist attractions.*

TOURISM

🧳 120,000 visitors   ⬍ Little change from year to year

Libya possesses a rich Roman and Greek heritage, centred on the ancient Roman coastal towns of Labdah (Leptis Magna) and Sabrātah near Tripoli, and Shaḥḥāt (Cyrene) further east. There are fine beaches at Tripoli, which is also famous for its annual International Fair. However, UN sanctions on air links with Libya have effectively closed the country to Western tourists.

MAIN OVERSEAS ARRIVALS

Libya does not publish tourism figures by country of origin

0 — 10 — 20 — 30 — 40
% of total arrivals

PEOPLE

🗣 Arabic, Tuareg   👥 3 people per km²

THE URBAN/RURAL POPULATION SPLIT

70%   30%

RELIGIOUS PERSUASION

Other 3%
Sunni Muslim 97%

ETHNIC MAKEUP

Other 3%
Berber and Arab 97%

Ninety-seven per cent of Libyans are of Arab and Berber origin, split into many tribal groupings. They were artificially brought together when Libya was created in 1951 by the unification of the three historic provinces of Tripolitania, Cyrenaica and the Fazzān. The pro-Western monarchy, which was set up under King Idris, perpetuated the dominance of Cyrenaican tribes and the Sanusi religious order.

The revolution of 1969 brought to the

POPULATION AGE BREAKDOWN

% of population by age group	0–14	15–64	65+		
65+	4%	2.7%	2.2%	2.4%	2.9%
15–64	52.8%	52.4%	51.2%	51.8%	52.4%
0–14	43.2%	44.9%	46.6%	45.8%	44.7%
	1960	1970	1980	1990	2000

fore Arab nationalist Colonel Gaddafi, who embodied the character and aspirations of the rural Sirtica tribes from Fazzān: fierce independence, deep Islamic convictions, belief in a communal lifestyle and hatred for the urban rich. His revolution wiped out private enterprise and the middle-classes, banished European settlers and Jews, undermined the function of the religious Muslim establishment and imposed a form of popular democracy through the *jamahiriya* (state of the masses). However, resentment of the regime increased as it became clear that power now lay mainly with the Sirtica tribes, especially Gaddafi's own clan, the Qadhadhfa.

The years since the revolution have seen Libya change from being largely a nation of nomads and livestock herders to a society where 70% are city-dwellers.

POLITICS

 Not applicable

 Col Muammar al-Gaddafi

THE STATE OF THE PARTIES

General People's Congress 1112 members

The only authorized political party is the Arab Socialist Union (ASU), from which the members of the Congress are appointed.

Executive power is exercised by the General People's Committee. The General People's Congress elects the head of state, the Revolutionary Leader.

MAIN POLITICAL ISSUES

Repression
Dissidents, whether politicians, students or Islamic fundamentalists, have been violently suppressed, with public executions of alleged traitors and spies a routine occurrence. All political parties were banned in 1971. Opposition is based outside the country, notably in the Libyan Democratic Movement in Cairo, Egypt, and the National Front for the Salvation of Libya in Khartoum, Sudan.

The regime's public image
In the past few years, the regime has made a deliberate effort to improve its international image. Measures have included freeing some political prisoners, allowing exiles to visit the country and permitting foreign travel.

PROFILE
In 1977, a new form of direct democracy was promulgated, through which every adult was supposed to share in policy-making. Some 2000 People's Congresses have sought to take Libya back to the basics of a simple Bedouin way of life. In theory, their wishes are carried out by popular committees. In practice, however, ultimate control is in the hands of Colonel Gaddafi and his collaborators from the days of the 1969 revolution, a small clique linked to the Revolutionary Leader by personal ties or kinship. These include his deputy, Major Abdessalem Jalloud. Some sources report tensions between Gaddafi and Jalloud, with the latter becoming marginalized. Gaddafi now relies on members of his own tribal clan.

Colonel Gaddafi, Libya's leader since 1969, rejects all official titles.

Aby Zayd Omar Durdah, Secretary of the General People's Committee.

WORLD AFFAIRS

 AL OPEC OAU NAM AMU

Relations between the USA and Libya have been poor ever since 1985, when CIA attempts to undermine Gaddafi's regime were publicized in the USA. Libya's support for Palestinian and other terrorists led to increasing tension, which culminated in 1986 with US bombing raids on Gaddafi's own residence, and on military and civil targets. Libya's refusal in 1990 to hand over for trial in the West two men suspected of bombing a US airliner over Lockerbie, Scotland, resulted in UN sanctions: international air links were severed, a worldwide ban was placed on arms sales to Libya and cuts made in diplomatic missions. Libya was opposed to the 1993–1994 PLO–Israeli discussions on a future Palestinian state.

L

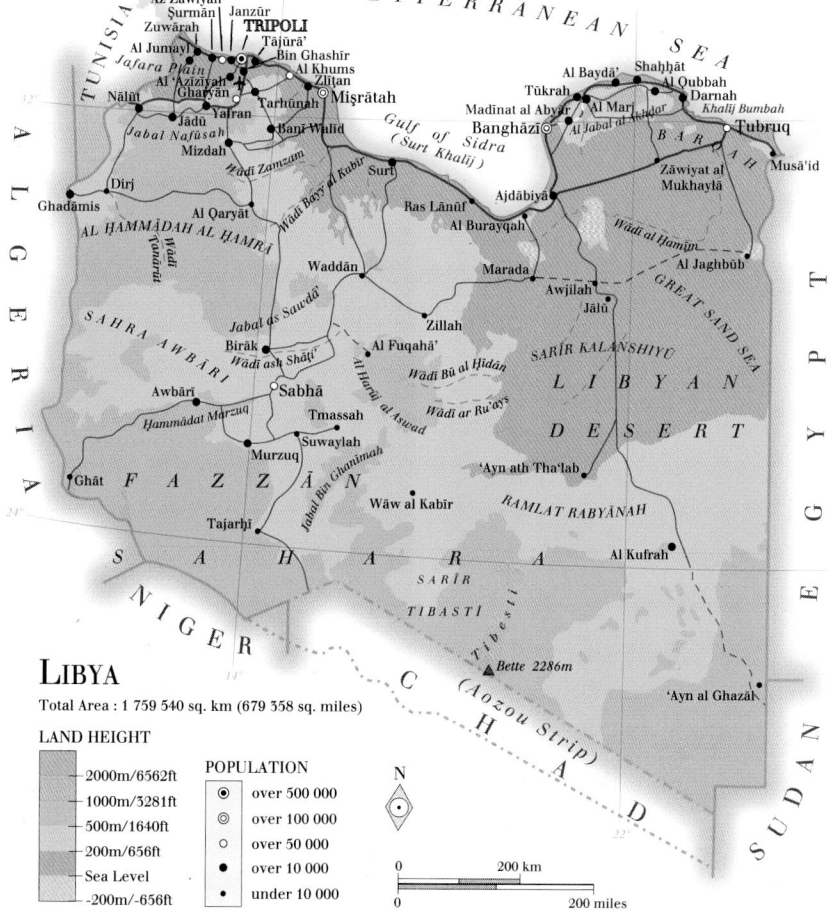

LIBYA

Total Area : 1 759 540 sq. km (679 358 sq. miles)

LAND HEIGHT

2000m/6562ft
1000m/3281ft
500m/1640ft
200m/656ft
Sea Level
-200m/-656ft

POPULATION
⊙ over 500 000
◉ over 100 000
○ over 50 000
● over 10 000
• under 10 000

N

0   200 km
0   200 miles

CHRONOLOGY

Italy occupied Libya and expelled the Turks in 1911. Britain and France agreed to a UN plan for an independent monarchy under King Idris in 1951.

❏ **1969** King Idris deposed in coup by Revolutionary Command Council led by Colonel Gaddafi. Tripoli Charter sets up revolutionary alliance with Egypt and Sudan.

❏ **1970** Remaining UK and US military establishments ordered out. Property belonging to Italians and Jews confiscated. Western oil company assets nationalized – a process completed in 1973.

❏ **1973** Libya forms abortive union with Egypt. Gaddafi launches Cultural Revolution – 1000 intellectuals arrested. Libya occupies Aozou Strip in Chad.

❏ **1974** Libya forms union of Libya and Tunisia.

❏ **1977** Frontier clashes with Egypt. Official name changed to The Great Socialist People's Libyan Arab Jamahiriya.
⇨

L

CHRONOLOGY *continued*

- **1979** Members of Revolution Command Council replaced by elected officials. Gaddafi remains Leader of the Revolution.
- **1980** Tunisia accuses Libya of involvement in guerrilla raid on Gafsa. Exiled journalist Mohammed Ramadan killed in London by Libyan agents.
- **1981** USA shoots down two Libyan aircraft over Gulf of Sirte.
- **1984** Commandos from rebel National Salvation Front attack Gaddafi's headquarters but fail to find him. Gunman at Libyan embassy in London kills British policewoman. Libya signs Oudja Accord with Morocco for an Arab Africa Federation.
- **1985** Libya expels 30,000 foreign workers. Tunisia cuts diplomatic links.
- **1986** US aircraft bomb Libya, including Gaddafi's residence, allegedly killing his adopted daughter. 101 people killed.
- **1988** Army and police abolished. Pan-Am airliner explodes over Lockerbie, Scotland. Allegations of Libyan complicity.
- **1989** Arab Maghreb Union established with Algeria, Morocco, Mauritania and Tunisia. Libya and Chad agree to end fighting in Aozou Strip.
- **1990** USA and Germany claim Libya is making mustard gas at a plant near Rabta, south of Tripoli.
- **1990** Libya expels Palestinian splinter group led by Abu Abbas.
- **1991** Opening of first branch of Great Man-Made River project.
- **1992** UN sanctions imposed as Libya fails to hand over Lockerbie suspects. Renewed 1993.

AID

 $20m (receipts)   Up 18% in 1990

As an oil exporting state, Libya fails to qualify for international aid, despite being a developing country. During the 1970s, Colonel Gaddafi aided several well-established African liberation movements, such as FROLINAT in Chad, and helped dissidents by training them in his Pan-African legion. He has also given finance to the PLO in the Middle East, the IRA in Northern Ireland, the Moros in the southern Philippines and the Basques, Corsicans and other ethnic causes in Europe. In recent years, Gaddafi's appetite for fomenting revolution abroad has ebbed, largely owing to the imposition of UN sanctions on Libya in 1992 and a lack of surplus resources.

DEFENCE

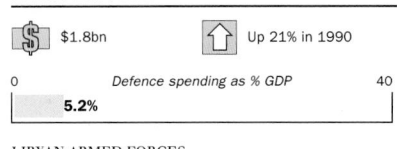

$1.8bn   Up 21% in 1990

0   *Defence spending as % GDP*   40
5.2%

LIBYAN ARMED FORCES

	2150 main battle tanks (1500 T-54,-55/ 350 T-62/300 T-72)	55,000 personnel
	6 submarines, 3 frigates and 45 patrol boats	8000 personnel
	409 combat aircraft (5 Tu-22,-20 MiG-23BN/ 8 MiG-23U/10 *Mirage* 5DD)	22,000 personnel
	None	

ECONOMICS

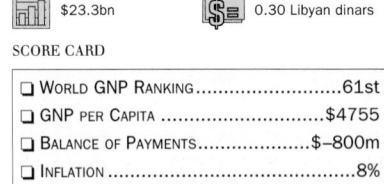

$23.3bn   0.30 Libyan dinars

SCORE CARD

- WORLD GNP RANKING...........................61st
- GNP PER CAPITA $4755
- BALANCE OF PAYMENTS....................$–800m
- INFLATION 8%
- UNEMPLOYMENT.....................................2%

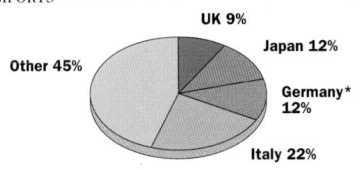

EXPORTS

Spain 7%
Germany* 7%
Italy 42%
Greece 8%
France 13%
Other 23%

IMPORTS

UK 9%
Japan 12%
Other 45%
Germany* 12%
Italy 22%

STRENGTHS
Oil and gas production. High investment in downstream industries – petrochemicals, refineries, fertilizers and aluminium smelting.

WEAKNESSES
Single-resource economy subject to oil-market fluctuations. Most food is imported. Reliance on foreign labour. Lack of water for agriculture. History of international unreliability.

PROFILE
Western oil companies had close business ties with Libya until the imposition of UN sanctions over the Lockerbie affair. If a diplomatic settlement is reached, co-operation will quickly resume. Gaddafi's most controversial economic project has been the Great Man-Made River.

The armed forces suffered a major blow in 1987 with the loss of thousands of men and equipment worth $1.4 billion in the Chad Civil War. Libya's southern border with Chad is still disputed and skirmishes occur, especially in the Aozou Strip. The armed forces were technically abolished in 1989 and replaced with 'the Armed People'. Colonel Gaddafi's attempts to depoliticize the armed forces have been largely ineffective and reports continue of dissent within the ranks. As a result of a total UN ban on arms sales to Libya, first enforced in 1992, Libya's forces are largely equipped with increasingly outdated, former Soviet bloc equipment.

ECONOMIC PERFORMANCE INDICATOR

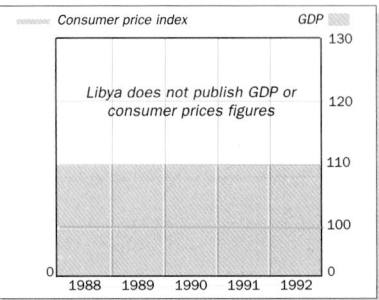

Consumer price index   GDP

Libya does not publish GDP or consumer prices figures

130
120
110
100
0

1988 1989 1990 1991 1992

Started in 1984 and engineered by European and Korean companies, this scheme will bring underground water from the Sahara to the coast. There, it will be utilized by industry and farming. Since the 1970s, there has been an ambitious programme of industrialization aimed largely at import substitution in sectors such as building materials and processed food.

LIBYA : MAJOR BUSINESSES

Mişrátah
Tripoli   Surt Basin   Al Burayqah
Bangházh
Ras Lanuf
Idri
Marada
Sarir
Ghát

- Oil
- Oil refining
- Gas refining
- Leather tanning
- Petrochemicals
- Light engineering
- Steel
- Textiles
- Salt production

0   400 km
0   400 miles

RESOURCES

19bn kwh (capacity 4.1m kw)

1.5bn b/d (reserves 22,800,000,000 bbl)

5.8m sheep, 193,000 camels, 240,000 cattle

Oil, natural gas, iron, potassium, gypsum, magnesium, sulphur

ELECTRICITY GENERATION

Hydro 0%

Thermal 100% (19bn kwh)

Nuclear 0%

Other 0%

0　20　40　60　80　100
% of total generation by type

With considerable crude oil reserves, Libya is likely to remain an oil exporting country well into the next century. Natural gas potential is more limited but, providing links are developed with other North African states, the future is assured. Libya also has reserves of iron ore, potassium, sulphur, magnesium and gypsum. With the Great Man-Made River project now on stream, the area of irrigated land has been increased, but 90% of Libya is desert. Animal husbandry is the basis of farming, but some cereal crops are grown, as well as dates, olives and citrus fruits. Cement production is sufficient to meet national demand and relies on local raw materials. Most other manufacturing inputs must be imported at considerable cost owing to UN sanctions.

LIBYAN DESERT

SAHARA

LIBYA : LAND USE

Cropland
Pasture
Desert
Sheep
Dates

0　400 km
0　400 miles

ENVIRONMENT

0.1% partially protected

Tapping desert water may shift rather than solve problems

ENVIRONMENTAL TREATIES

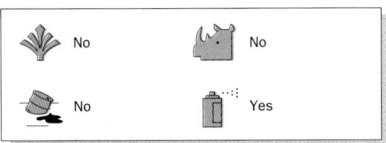

No

No

No

Yes

The UN Development Programme has described Libya as more than 90% 'wasteland'. Both nature and man have conspired against the environment. Apart from two coastal strips – the Jafara Plain and the Al Jabal al-Akhḍar in Cyrenaica – together with the Fazzān Oasis, most of Libya is desert. Much of the irrigated area is saline because of unwise use of naturally-occurring water from artesian wells. Seawater has penetrated the water table as far as 20 km inland near Tripoli.

MEDIA

The media is under strict government control

PUBLISHING AND BROADCAST MEDIA

There is 1 daily newspaper, *Al-Fajr al-Jadid*, published by the Jamahiriyah News Agency (JANA)

1 state-owned service

1 state-owned service

Arabsat 1C

None

Libya's press and TV are a mouthpiece for the leadership. The official news agency has voiced criticism of the wealthy elite for living in closed villas sprouting with satellite dishes. The only daily newspaper is published in Arabic and has a circulation of 40,000 readers. The TV station broadcasts mainly in Arabic, with some programmes in Italian, French and English.

CRIME

Libya does not publish prison figures

Down 2% in 1990

CRIME RATES

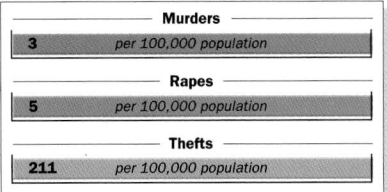

Murders
3　per 100,000 population

Rapes
5　per 100,000 population

Thefts
211　per 100,000 population

Policing is often in the hands of gangs appointed by Gaddafi's lieutenants to root out student protesters and other dissidents. Hit squads allegedly operate abroad against Libyan exiles.

EDUCATION

64%

0　Education spending as % GNP　25
10.1%

THE EDUCATION SYSTEM

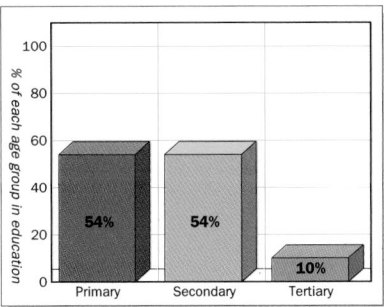

100
80
60
40
20
0

% of each age group in education

54%　Primary
54%　Secondary
10%　Tertiary

Some one million Libyans receive formal education. It is compulsory between the ages of 6 and 15, but varies in quality and is rudimentary in rural areas. There are universities, in Tripoli, Banghāzī and Sabhā. The literacy rate has improved from 39% in 1970 to 64% today.

HEALTH

1 per 687 people

Pneumonia, diarrheal diseases, accidents, cancers

0　Health spending as % GNP　25
3.2%

An adequate system of primary health care exists except in remote areas. Hospitals lack equipment.

WEALTH

Most Libyans have benefited little from oil wealth

CONSUMER GOODS OWNERSHIP

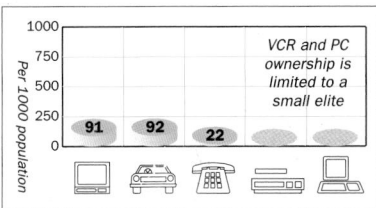

1000
750
500
250
0

Per 1000 population

VCR and PC ownership is limited to a small elite

91　92　22

There is widespread poverty after years of import constraints. The situation has worsened as imports have dwindled owing to UN sanctions. Consumer durables are the preserve of an elite.

WORLD RANKING

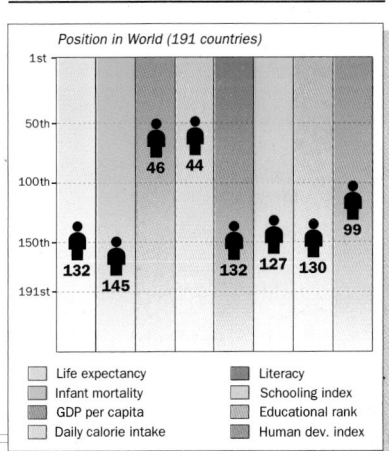

Position in World (191 countries)

1st
50th
100th
150th
191st

46　44

132　145　132　127　130　99

Life expectancy
Infant mortality
GDP per capita
Daily calorie intake

Literacy
Schooling index
Educational rank
Human dev. index

L

LIECHTENSTEIN

OFFICIAL NAME: Principality of Liechtenstein **CAPITAL:** Vaduz
POPULATION: 29,000 **CURRENCY:** Swiss franc **OFFICIAL LANGUAGE:** German

EUROPE

PERCHED IN THE ALPS between Switzerland and Austria, Liechtenstein is rare among small states in having both a thriving banking sector and a well-diversified manufacturing economy. It is closely allied to Switzerland, which handles its foreign relations and defence. Life in Liechtenstein is stable and conservative. Its banking secrecy laws and low taxes make it home to many overseas trusts, banks and investment companies.

CLIMATE

WEATHER CHART

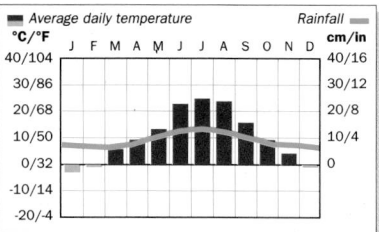

Climate varies with altitude. Excellent skiing conditions are the result of heavy settling snow from December to March. Summers are warm and dry.

COMMUNICATIONS

THE TRANSPORT NETWORK

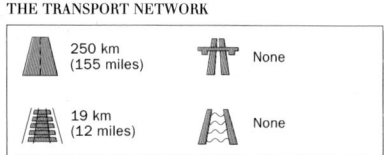

250 km (155 miles)	None	
19 km (12 miles)	None	

Public transport in Liechtenstein is mostly by the postal bus network. The single-track railway has few stops. Zurich, a two-hour drive away, is the nearest airport.

TOURISM

 71,990 visitors Up 1% in 1992

MAIN OVERSEAS ARRIVALS

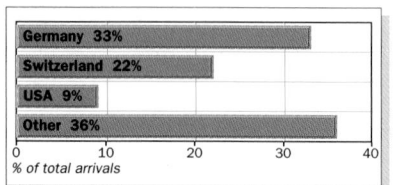

Germany	33%
Switzerland	22%
USA	9%
Other	36%

% of total arrivals

Liechtenstein's alpine scenery attracts skiers in the winter, and climbers and hikers in the summer.

PEOPLE

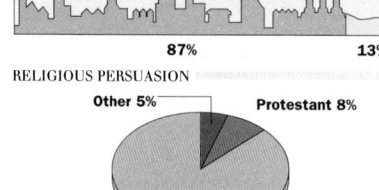

German, Alemannish dialect, Italian

175 people per km²

THE URBAN/RURAL POPULATION SPLIT

87%   13%

RELIGIOUS PERSUASION

Other 5%   Protestant 8%

Roman Catholic 87%

Liechtenstein's role as a financial centre accounts for the many foreign residents (over 35% of the population), of whom half are Swiss and the rest mostly German. The high standard of living results in few ethnic or social tensions. Family life is highly traditional; women received the vote only in 1984, after much controversy. A proposal the following year that equal rights for women be enshrined in the constitution was rejected in a referendum by a large majority.

POLITICS

 1997 Prince Hans-Adam II

THE STATE OF THE PARTIES

Landtag 25 members

51% VU   41% FBP   8% FL

VU = Patriotic Party **FBP** = Progressive Citizens' Party
FL = Free List

Historically, the VU and the FBP have alternated as coalition leaders. However, the VU has been the leading party since 1978, except for a few brief months in 1993. An increasing use has been made of referenda to decide policy issues, such as the 1992 proposal to reduce the voting age from 20 to 18, rejected by 56% of voters.

WORLD AFFAIRS

   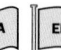

| CE | CSCE | EBRD | IAEA | EFTA |

Liechtenstein effectively gave up control of its external relations when it signed the 1924 Customs Union Treaty with Switzerland. This requires Swiss approval for any treaty arrangements between Liechtenstein and a third state. The country became a member of the UN only in 1990 and of EFTA in 1991. It is now renegotiating the Customs Union with Switzerland in order to gain entry to the EEA; a referendum on the issue was planned for 1994. Swiss rejection of EU membership in 1992 effectively ended this as a practical prospect for Liechtenstein.

AID

 Donor, but does not publish figures Not applicable

Although overseas aid donations are small and aid issues have little political importance, Liechtenstein has helped to fund shelter and reconstruction projects in former Yugoslavia and local development projects in Bulgaria.

LIECHTENSTEIN

Total Area : 160 sq. km (62 sq. miles)

POPULATION
under 10 000

LAND HEIGHT
2000m/6562ft
1500m/4921ft
1000m/3281ft
500m/1640ft
400m/1312ft

L

Alpine scenery near Vaduz. The state budget includes 2% allocated to restoring mountain vegetation and co-ordinating land use.

DEFENCE

 Police force of 56 men and 22 auxiliaries   Not applicable

There has been no standing army since 1868 and there is only a small police force. *De facto* protection is provided by Switzerland. In theory, any male under 60 is liable for military service during a national emergency, although this law has never been invoked.

ECONOMICS

 $900m (est)   1.49 Swiss francs

SCORE CARD

- ❏ WORLD GNP RANKING.......................157th
- ❏ GNP PER CAPITA $31,000
- ❏ BALANCE OF PAYMENTS ....Included in Swiss total
- ❏ INFLATION 5.4%
- ❏ UNEMPLOYMENT...............................0.1%

STRENGTHS

Stability and close association with Switzerland make Liechtenstein a favoured tax haven; its lack of EU membership makes the banking sector less vulnerable to future changes in EU banking laws. The economy is well-diversified; chemicals, furniture and the manufacture of ceramic dentures and precision instruments are all thriving sectors.

WEAKNESSES

Very few. Liechtenstein might suffer if the EU restricts imports from EFTA countries in future.

EXPORTS

EU 40% EFTA 22% Other 38%

IMPORTS

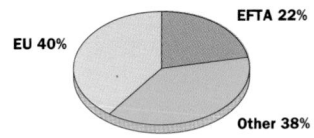
With a limited domestic market, Liechtenstein's industry is export-orientated. Liechtenstein has a customs union with Switzerland and does not publish separate import figures.

RESOURCES

 94% of energy requirements imported   Not an oil producer and has no refineries

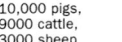 10,000 pigs, 9000 cattle, 3000 sheep   None

Liechtenstein has to import most of its energy. Almost all of its electricity comes from German power stations.

ENVIRONMENT

 38% partially protected   Greens won two seats in parliament in 1993

Protection of Liechtenstein's alpine scenery is high enough on the political agenda for one of the five councillors, or ministers, to have responsibility for the environment. As in Switzerland, the greatest worry is the effect of through traffic and high rates of car ownership. However, the 1988 experiment in providing free public bus transport proved a failure, as Liechtensteiners remained firmly wedded to their cars.

MEDIA

 No restrictions

PUBLISHING AND BROADCAST MEDIA

 There are 2 daily newspapers, *Liechtensteiner Vaterland* and *Liechtensteiner Volksblatt*

 No TV service   No radio service

The two newspapers, although free of formal state control, are both run by political parties: the *Vaterland* by the VU; the *Volksblatt* by the FBP. Both have circulations of about 8000.

CRIME

 Liechtenstein does not publish prison figures Crime does not pose any great problems

Crime is a minor problem, a result of the relatively even distribution of wealth and high average living standard. Liechtenstein has also taken great care to protect its tax-haven status by careful regulation of its financial sector. There have been no major scandals, such as the BCCI collapse which tainted the reputation of its main competitor, Luxembourg.

EDUCATION

100%

Education, modelled on the German system, includes two types of school at secondary level – the grammar-style *Gymnasium* and the *Realschule*. Liechtenstein has no university, students go on to colleges in Austria, Switzerland and Germany, and to business schools in the USA.

CHRONOLOGY

In 1719 Liechtenstein became an independent principality of the Holy Roman Empire.

- ❏ **1805** France, under Napoleon, controls Liechtenstein's affairs.
- ❏ **1919** Switzerland replaces Austria in representing Liechtenstein's interests abroad.
- ❏ **1920** Postal union established with Switzerland.
- ❏ **1924** Liechtenstein in joint customs union with Switzerland.

HEALTH

 1 per 948 people Heart and respiratory diseases, cancers

Although clinics and hospitals are few, the health system provides advanced care. Many Liechtensteiners have private health insurance arrangements, which also give them access to Swiss medical expertise. Rabies remains a significant problem.

WEALTH

 Experienced carpenter, 4700 Swiss francs per month; primary school teacher, 4800-7490 Swiss francs per month

CONSUMER GOODS OWNERSHIP

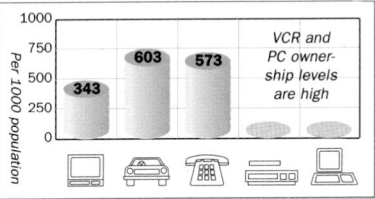

Most Liechtensteiners have a high standard of living, similar to that of the Swiss. Unlike other tax havens, such as Monaco, it does not attract the jet-set rich and private deposit accounts are not a key part of its banking business. The state welfare system is generous.

WORLD RANKING

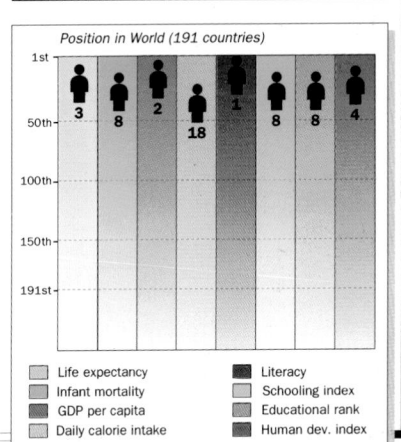

L

LITHUANIA

OFFICIAL NAME: Republic of Lithuania **CAPITAL:** Vilnius
POPULATION: 3.8 million **CURRENCY:** Litas **OFFICIAL LANGUAGE:** Lithuanian

L YING ON THE EASTERN coast of the Baltic Sea, Lithuania is bordered by Latvia, Belorussia, Poland and the Kaliningrad area of the Russian Federation. Its terrain is mostly flat with many lakes, moors and bogs. Now a multiparty democracy, Lithuania achieved independence from the former USSR in 1991. Industrial production and agriculture are the mainstays of the economy. Russia finally withdrew all its troops from Lithuania in 1993.

CLIMATE

WEATHER CHART

Lithuania's coastal position moderates an otherwise continental-type climate. Summers are cool.

COMMUNICATIONS

 Vilnius International
 69 ships 467,800 dwt

THE TRANSPORT NETWORK

44,177 km (27,450 miles)		None
3033 km (1885 miles)		River Neman

Lithuania has an efficient rail service. Plans exist to upgrade the Soviet-built road network and port facilities.

TOURISM

 Similar levels to Latvia and Estonia
 The trend is up

MAIN OVERSEAS ARRIVALS

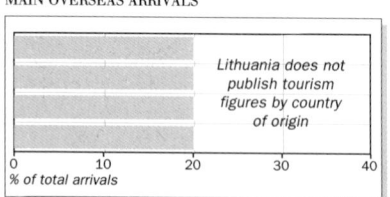

Lithuania does not publish tourism figures by country of origin

% of total arrivals

Tourism has expanded in recent years. Vilnius is well-preserved. Its historic centre survived German and Russian occupation. Trakai, the capital of the Grand Duchy in the 16th century, is also popular with visitors.

PEOPLE

 Lithuanian, Russian
 57 people per km²

THE URBAN/RURAL POPULATION SPLIT

69% 31%

ETHNIC MAKEUP

Belorussian 2% Polish 8%
Other 1% Russian 9%
Lithuanian 80%

The population is made up of an 80% majority of Lithuanians, together with small groups of Russians, Poles and Belorussians. Citizenship is not a political issue in Lithuania as it is in the other Baltic states. Ethnic relations are relatively good and inter-ethnic marriages are fairly common. Lithuania is strongly Catholic, in contrast to Protestant Latvia and Estonia. Divorce rates are high.

POLITICS

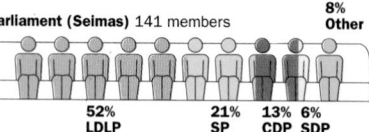

1996 President Algirdas Brazauskas

THE STATE OF THE PARTIES

Parliament (Seimas) 141 members

8% Other
52% LDLP 21% SP 13% CDP 6% SDP

LDLP = Lithuanian Democratic Labour Party **SP** = Sajudis Party **CDP** = Christian Democratic Party **SDP** = Social Democratic Party **Other** = Union of Lithuanian Political Prisoners and Refugees, Lithuanian Democratic Party

The elections of late 1992 saw a shift back to the pre-independence leadership, with the return to power of Algirdas Brazauskas and his ex-communist LDLP. This marked the end of a period of rule under the SP, led by Vytautas Landsbergis, which held office at independence in 1991. Landsbergis's leadership style had become increasingly nationalistic and autocratic, but the main reason for his defeat was a failure to tackle economic problems. Coping with the economic situation is a priority for the present government. The LDLP leadership, despite its communist past, is keenly pursuing free market and privatization policies.

Lithuania is the most politically stable of the three Baltic republics. In 1993, Russian troops left its territory, reducing fears of intervention from Moscow. Brazauskas's non-nationalist communist background has enhanced his support from the non-Lithuanian community.

LITHUANIA

Total Area :
65 200 sq. km
(25 174 sq. miles)

POPULATION

⊙ over 500 000
◎ over 100 000
○ over 50 000
● over 10 000
• under 10 000

LAND HEIGHT
—200m/656ft
—Sea Level

0 50 km
0 50 miles

L

WORLD AFFAIRS

The LDLP's communist background has eased relations with Russia. In 1993, Russia withdrew its troops from Lithuanian soil. Lithuania is keen to strengthen links with the EU.

AID

 Lithuania does not publish aid receipts   The trend is probably rising

Aid, mostly from the IMF and EU, is used for infrastructure projects and to promote private enterprise.

DEFENCE

 $588.2m   Rising now that Russian troops have left

Lithuania's security is in the hands of its army and a National Guard formed to patrol its frontiers. However, it would be unable to defend itself against Russian attack. Most of the Russian troops who left in 1993 were relocated in neighbouring Kaliningrad.

ECONOMICS

 $10.2bn   3.89 litas

SCORE CARD

- ❑ WORLD GNP RANKING..........................77th
- ❑ GNP PER CAPITA $2685
- ❑ BALANCE OF PAYMENTS ....Deficit
- ❑ INFLATION 176%
- ❑ UNEMPLOYMENT..................................0.5%

STRENGTHS
Occasional agricultural surpluses. Some exports of peat, amber, linen and light industrial goods.

WEAKNESSES
Poor raw material base. Need to import oil, natural gas and industrial products from Russia. Uncompetitive, outdated industry. Difficulty in attracting significant foreign investment. Economically the weakest Baltic state.

EXPORTS

IMPORTS

One of Lithuania's 3000 lakes. The entire country is low-lying. Its coast, fringed by sand dunes and pine forests, is famous for amber.

RESOURCES

 Nuclear power makes up 60% of electricity production   Not an oil producer and has no refineries

 2.7m pigs, 2.4m cattle, 78,600 sheep and goats   Sand, gravel, clay, limestone, gypsum

Lithuania has no strategic resources. Nuclear power is a major source of energy. Most of the country's oil still comes from Russia, as the supply infrastructure is in place. However, Lithuania is seeking other suppliers.

ENVIRONMENT

 2%   Pollution in Baltic Sea

The Ignalina nuclear plant, which came on stream in the mid-1980s, has experienced leakage problems. Water and air pollution levels are high. Lithuania's Baltic coast has been polluted by oil spillages.

MEDIA

 No restrictions on political reporting

PUBLISHING AND BROADCAST MEDIA

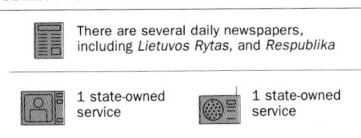 There are several daily newspapers, including *Lietuvos Rytas*, and *Respublika*

1 state-owned service   1 state-owned service

The mainstream media, Russian under communism, now publishes and broadcasts mainly in Lithuanian.

CRIME

 Lithuania does not publish prison figures   Crime levels are rising slightly

Levels of crime are low compared to other parts of the former USSR. Robbery is a growing problem.

EDUCATION

 Figures not published, but among highest of ex-Soviet republics

Teaching at all levels is in Lithuanian, making access to higher education harder for minorities. 8% of the population are graduates.

CHRONOLOGY

Russia annexed Lithuania in 1795. The suppression of rebellions in 1831 and 1863 failed to undermine its nationalist movement.

- ❑ **1915** Occupied by German troops.
- ❑ **1918** Independence declared.
- ❑ **1922** Lithuania proclaims itself a parliamentary democracy.
- ❑ **1926** Military coup leads to one-party rule.
- ❑ **1940** Annexed by Soviet Union.
- ❑ **1941–1944** Nazi occupation.
- ❑ **1945** Lithuania formally incorporated into USSR.
- ❑ **1989** Lithuanian Communist Party approves Lithuanian sovereignty. Past Soviet rule declared illegal.
- ❑ **1991** Achieves full independence.
- ❑ **1992** First multiparty elections.
- ❑ **1993** Russian troops withdraw.

HEALTH

 1 per 217 people   Circulatory and respiratory diseases, cancers, accidents

Reforms to Lithuania's health system began in 1990 and include the legalization of private medicine.

WEALTH

 Traders in Vilnius are the wealthiest group

CONSUMER GOODS OWNERSHIP

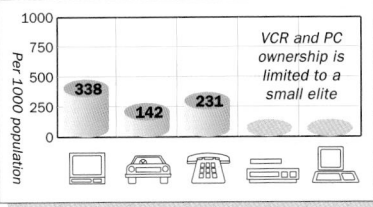

Western cars and designer goods are popular status symbols among an increasingly prosperous elite.

WORLD RANKING

L

LUXEMBOURG

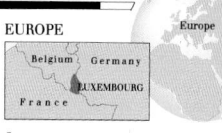
EUROPE

OFFICIAL NAME: Grand Duchy of Luxembourg   **CAPITAL:** Luxembourg
POPULATION: 400,000   **CURRENCY:** Luxembourg franc   **OFFICIAL LANGUAGE:** Letzeburgish

LUXEMBOURG SHARES BORDERS with the industrial regions of Germany, France and Belgium and has Europe's highest per capita income. Making up part of the plateau of the Ardennes, its countryside is undulating and forested. Its prosperity was once based on steel; before the Second World War it produced more per capita than the USA. Today, it is known as a tax haven and banking centre, and as the headquarters of key EU institutions.

CLIMATE

WEATHER CHART

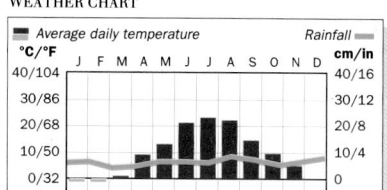

Average daily temperature   Rainfall
°C/°F   J F M A M J J A S O N D   cm/in

The south, where vines grow, is the warmest area. Winter is cold and snowy, especially in the Ardennes.

COMMUNICATIONS

Findel, Luxembourg-Ville
932,000 passengers

52 ships
2.61m dwt

THE TRANSPORT NETWORK

5091 km (3163 miles)	84 km (52 miles)
271 km (168 miles)	37 km (23 miles)

There is an excellent road network, though congestion is a problem. Rail and bus services are integrated.

TOURISM

861,284 visitors   Up 5% in 1991

MAIN OVERSEAS ARRIVALS

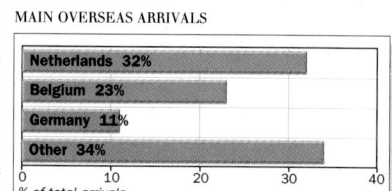

Netherlands 32%
Belgium 23%
Germany 11%
Other 34%

0   10   20   30   40
% of total arrivals

The mountains and forests, and 76 castles, many recently re-roofed, are the main attractions. The government has begun an initiative to teach foreign hotel workers the history, language and culture of the Duchy.

PEOPLE

Letzeburgish, German, French   155 people per km²

THE URBAN/RURAL POPULATION SPLIT

84%   16%

RELIGIOUS PERSUASION

Protestant and Jewish 3%
Roman Catholic 97%

Nearly a third of Luxembourg's residents and half of its workers are foreigners. Integration has been straightforward; most are fellow western Europeans and Catholics, mainly from Italy and Portugal. Life in Luxembourg is comfortable. Salaries are high, unemployment very low and social tensions few.

POLITICS

1994   HRH Grand Duke Jean d'Aviano

THE STATE OF THE PARTIES

Chamber of Deputies 60 members

37% PCS	30% POSL	18% PD	15% Other

PCS = Christian Social Party **POSL** = Luxembourg Socialist Workers' Party **PD** = Democratic Party **Other** = Five-Sixths Action Committee, Green Alternative Party, Luxembourg Communist Party

Council of State 21 members

The members of the Council of State are appointed for life by the Grand Duke

Luxembourg's politics have achieved remarkable consensus, and are characterized by coalitions and long-serving prime ministers. The main political issues are now economic – raising taxes and trimming spending to cope with the economic slow-down.

WORLD AFFAIRS

EU   Benelux   NATO   CSCE   GATT

Luxembourg has long been the keenest member of the EU. It was during its EU presidency that the Maastricht agreement for closer European union was brokered; Luxembourg was not only the first member state to meet all the economic, financial and legal requirements of union under Maastricht, but it also did so a year early. This commitment to the EU reflects the tremendous benefits Luxembourg has gained from membership. It is home to both the European Parliament and the Court of Justice, and its citizens enjoy the high, tax-free salaries that work in these organizations brings. In 1994, however, Luxembourg lost its bid for the European Central Bank to Frankfurt, Germany.

LUXEMBOURG

Total Area : 2586 sq. km (998 sq. miles)

0   10 km
0   10 miles

LAND HEIGHT
500m/1640ft
200m/656ft
Sea Level

POPULATION
over 50 000 ○
over 10 000 ●
under 10 000 ·

N

Buurgplaatz 559m
Clervaux
Wiltz
Ö Lac de la Haute Sûre
Vianden
Diekirch
Ettelbrück
Echternach
Redange
Mersch
Wasserbillig
Walferdange
Grevenmacher
Capellen
Mamer
Findel Airport
LUXEMBOURG
Hesperange
Pétange
Sanem
Remich
Differdange
Schifflange
Bettembourg
Esch-sur-Alzette
Kayl
Dudelange

B E L G I U M
G E R M A N Y
F R A N C E

Charlotte Bridge, Luxembourg.
The modern road system provides excellent communications with the rest of Europe.

AID

 $39m (donations) Up 56% in 1991

Luxembourg's aid donations, equal to only 0.35% of GNP, are largely directed towards sub-Saharan Africa.

DEFENCE

 $108m Up 7% in 1992

Luxembourg's army numbers 800 full-time soldiers. Spending is 1.2% of GDP and has risen slightly in recent years.

ECONOMICS

 $11 8bn 36.15 Luxembourg francs

SCORE CARD

☐ WORLD GNP RANKING	73rd
☐ GNP PER CAPITA	$28,730
☐ BALANCE OF PAYMENTS	Included in Belgian total
☐ INFLATION	2.1%
☐ UNEMPLOYMENT	1.3%

STRENGTHS
Site of EU institutions. Banking secrecy and expertise make the capital home to over 980 investment funds and 192 banks – more than in any other city in the world.

WEAKNESSES
International service industries account for 65% of GNP, making Luxembourg vulnerable to changing conditions overseas. Downturn in steel market.

EXPORTS

Netherlands 5%
France 17%
Other 31%
Belgium 17%
Germany* 30%

IMPORTS

Netherlands 4%
France 12%
Belgium 39%
Other 15%
Germany* 30%

RESOURCES

 1.4bn kwh (capacity 1.24m kw)

 Not an oil producer and has no refineries

 Cattle, deer, wild boar, sheep

 Iron, steel

Luxembourg can meet few of its own energy needs; it produces only a small amount of hydroelectricity. The steel industry accounts for 10% of GDP.

ENVIRONMENT

 None

 One of few nations active in transfrontier pollution control

Acid rain from European industry has affected about 19% of Luxembourg's trees and, in the worst cases, 30% of trees in mature stands. The Duchy is a member of an international committee on decreasing pollution of the Rhine.

MEDIA

 Freedom of expression is guaranteed by law

PUBLISHING AND BROADCAST MEDIA

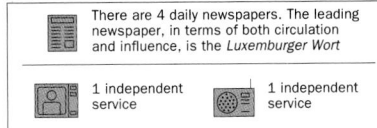

There are 4 daily newspapers. The leading newspaper, in terms of both circulation and influence, is the *Luxemburger Wort*

1 independent service

1 independent service

Broadcasting is dominated by RTL (*Radio-Television Luxembourg*), one of the largest media groups in Europe, which exports programmes in a variety of languages.

CRIME

 352 prisoners Up 4% in 1990

Luxembourg's stringent banking secrecy rules can provide a cover for both tax evasion and – as in the case of the collapsed BCCI bank, which was registered in Luxembourg – fraud.

EDUCATION

 100%

Teaching is mainly in German at primary and French at secondary level. Higher education is limited and many students go to universities in other European countries. Training given by Luxembourg banks is reputed to be the best in Europe.

HEALTH

 1 per 529 people 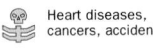 Heart diseases, cancers, accidents

There are no private commercial hospitals in Luxembourg; they are run either by the state or by nuns. The fees paid by patients are refunded from the *Caisse de Maladie* (state sickness fund).

CHRONOLOGY

Throughout its history, Luxembourg has been ruled by a succession of neighbouring European powers.

- ☐ **1890** Separates from Netherlands.
- ☐ **1912** End of Salic Law: Grand Duchess Marie accedes.
- ☐ **1919** Abortive republican coup.
- ☐ **1921** Economic union with Belgium. End of German ties.
- ☐ **1940–1944** Severe damage to infrastructure during resistance to German occupation.
- ☐ **1960** Benelux economic union, agreed 1948, comes into effect.
- ☐ **1970** Benelux customs union.
- ☐ **1989** Anti money-laundering laws.
- ☐ **1991** Luxembourg first country to ratify Maastricht Treaty.

WEALTH

 Junior salesperson, 10,000 Luxembourg francs per month; experienced sales representative, 500,000 Luxembourg francs per month

CONSUMER GOODS OWNERSHIP

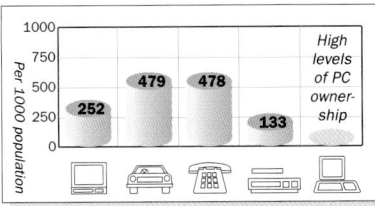

High levels of PC ownership

252 479 478 133

With the highest per capita income in the EU, Luxembourgers enjoy a comfortable lifestyle. In recent years, the government has been able to hand back 5% of GDP in tax relief, while simultaneously increasing public spending. Very low unemployment has led to the influx of a large number of foreign workers, mainly from other EU countries such as Portugal and Italy, to take less well-paid jobs. Financing the ageing population is likely to be a burden in the future.

WORLD RANKING

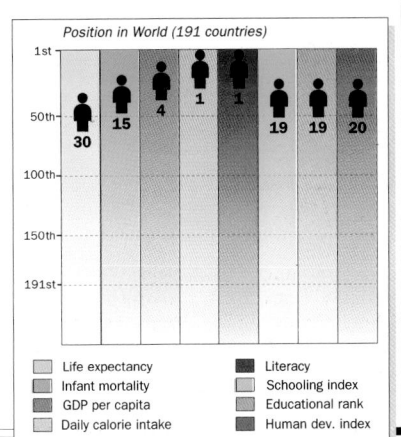

Position in World (191 countries)

30 15 4 1 1 19 19 20

■ Life expectancy	■ Literacy
■ Infant mortality	■ Schooling index
■ GDP per capita	■ Educational rank
■ Daily calorie intake	■ Human dev. index

L

MACEDONIA

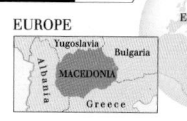

EUROPE

OFFICIAL NAME: *Former Yugoslav Republic of Macedonia*   **CAPITAL:** Skopje
POPULATION: 1.9 million   **CURRENCY:** Macedonian denar   **OFFICIAL LANGUAGE:** *None*

T HE FORMER YUGOSLAV Republic of Macedonia (FYRM) is land-locked in southeastern Europe. The economic blockade of Serbia and Montenegro has denied the FYRM two of its most important trading partners and crippled the economy. The Greek government is hostile to the FYRM because it suspects the country may try to absorb northern Greece – also called Macedonia – in a 'Greater Macedonia'.

A fisherman's hut on Lake Dojran, which lies on the border with Greece in southeastern Macedonia and is shared by the two countries.

CLIMATE

WEATHER CHART

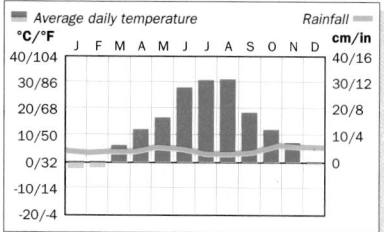

The FYRM has a continental climate, with dry autumns and wet springs. Winter snow supports skiing.

COMMUNICATIONS

 Skopje Intl   Has no fleet

THE TRANSPORT NETWORK

13,900 km (8637 miles)		None
1150 km (715 miles)		None

Germany has suspended the Munich–Athens rail link, the last service linking Skopje to western Europe.

TOURISM

 Small number of visitors only   Down, due to war in Yugoslavia and political tensions

MAIN OVERSEAS ARRIVALS

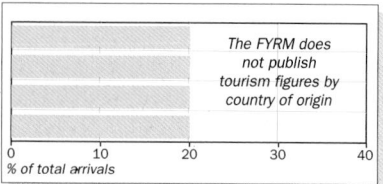

The FYRM does not publish tourism figures by country of origin

% of total arrivals

Tourism is a traditionally important income source. Lake resorts and skiing in the Šara mountains are among the attractions. However, regional political problems have reduced the number of tourists going to the FYRM.

PEOPLE

Macedonian, Serbo-Croatian   79 people per km²

THE URBAN/RURAL POPULATION SPLIT

54%   46%

ETHNIC MAKEUP

Turkish 4%   Other 7%
Serb 2%   Albanian 20%
Macedonian 67%

Around two thirds of the population are ethnically Slav Macedonians. Officially 20% are Albanian, although Albanians themselves claim they account for 40%. Unlike the more publicized tensions between Serbs and Albanians in Kosovo, Slav Macedonian–Albanian stress has so far been restrained. Most Macedonians are Eastern Orthodox, but there are also a substantial number of Slavic Muslims, whose ancestors converted to Islam during the Ottoman occupation. Ethnic Albanians are mostly Muslim. There are also Roman Catholic and Jewish groups.

POLITICS

 1994   President Kiro Gligorov

THE STATE OF THE PARTIES

National Assembly 120 members

| 31% VMRO–DPMNE | 26% SDAM | 21 % PDP–NDP | 16% LP | 6% Other |

VMRO–DPMNE = Macedonian Revolutionary Organization – Democratic Party for Macedonian National Unity
SDAM = Macedonian Social Democratic Alliance
PDP–NDP = Democratic Prosperity Party – National Democratic Party   **LP** = Liberal Party

Politics in the FYRM is fragmented along nationalist lines, and is heavily influenced by tensions in neighbouring states. Although the Slav Macedonian

WORLD AFFAIRS

Greece alone has refused to recognize the state under any name which includes a reference to Macedonia. In 1994, Greece barred the FYRM from access to the port of Thessaloníki.

AID

 Over $100m   Increasing levels of aid required for economic growth

The FYRM joined the World Bank in 1993 and a $40 million loan followed. The IDA has also extended $40 million in concessional lending. A $25 million grant from the Soros Foundation has boosted foreign exchange reserves.

DEFENCE

High, given regional tensions   Increasing to facilitate building up of army

The army is dominated by officers who resigned from the Yugoslav army in 1992. The USA has stationed 400 troops in the FYRM to deter Serbian expansionism.

and Albanian communities have acted with restraint, ethnic tensions are now growing. Ethnic Albanian parties are pursuing recognition as a constituent nation within the FYRM; a separatist paramilitary unit was recently detained. The Slav–Macedonian nationalist VMRO–DPMNE has been making inflammatory references to a 'Greater Macedonia'. The ruling coalition, headed by the ex-communist SDAM, attempts to steer a course between these competing forces. All political issues are overshadowed by the dispute with Greece over the state's name. Economic policy has changed little since independence and remains essentially communist.

M

ECONOMICS

 $2.2bn

751.22 Macedonian denars

STRENGTHS
Strong growth in private sector. 67,000 companies have been created since independence.

WEAKNESSES
Loss of supplies and markets under UN sanctions against Serbia has paralyzed international and domestic

EXPORTS/IMPORTS

Before the imposition of UN sanctions, Yugoslavia was the FYRM's main trading partner

SCORE CARD

☐ WORLD GNP RANKING	136th
☐ GNP PER CAPITA	$1158
☐ BALANCE OF PAYMENT	*No formal*
☐ INFLATION	*statistics*
☐ UNEMPLOYMENT	*published*

transactions; ex-Yugoslavia accounted for the majority of exports. Key trading link broken by Greeks' refusal to allow access to port at Thessaloníki.

RESOURCES

 Self-sufficient in electricity production

Not an oil producer

2.3m sheep, 287,000 cows, 179,000 pigs

Coal, copper, bauxite, iron, antimony, chromium, lead, zinc

Macedonia is self-sufficient in electricity production. Plants are thermal and fuelled by coal.

ENVIRONMENT

 6%

 Environmental concerns not a priority

City air pollution is a serious problem. The completion of a sewage works has reduced pollution in Lake Ohrid.

FORMER YUGOSLAV REPUBLIC OF MACEDONIA

Total Area : 25 715 sq. km (9929 sq. miles)

POPULATION	
◉	over 500 000
◎	over 100 000
○	over 50 000
●	over 10 000
•	under 10 000

LAND HEIGHT	
	2000m/6562ft
	1000m/3281ft
	500m/1640ft
	50m/164ft

MEDIA

 No censorship restrictions

PUBLISHING AND BROADCAST MEDIA

 Newspapers include the Albanian *Flaka e Vellazerimit* and the Turkish *Birlik*, both of which are funded by the government

 1 state-owned, 1 independent service

 1 state-owned, also independent services

The free and often critical press includes the influential *Nova Makedonija* and *Rilindja Demokratika*.

CRIME

 Macedonia does not publish prison figures

 Illegal labour market increasing rapidly

The local Albanian mafia controls the illegal trade in cigarettes, drugs, hard currencies and arms in Skopje.

EDUCATION

 93%

The education system is entirely under state control and there are no privately run schools.

CHRONOLOGY

Following the Balkan wars, Macedonia was partitioned between Greece and Serbia in 1912–1913.

- ☐ **1944** Tito establishes Republic of Macedonia and consolidates national identity, partly to counteract Bulgarian influence.
- ☐ **1945** Adoption of standardized Macedonian language.
- ☐ **1989** Communists concede multiparty elections.
- ☐ **1990** Nationalists victorious in multiparty elections.
- ☐ **1991** Independence declared. EC recognition delayed by Greeks.
- ☐ **1992** Referendum approves autonomy for Albanian-populated districts in western FYRM.

HEALTH

 1 per 523 people

 Heart and cerebrovascular diseases

In theory, the state guarantees universal health care, but effective and speedy treatment is increasingly only available in the private sector. Most pharmacies have also been privatized.

WEALTH

 The effects of war and and UN sanctions have contributed to a sizeable fall in living standards since 1991

CONSUMER GOODS OWNERSHIP

On average, basic food accounts for 40% of household expenditure. Most houses and flats are privately owned.

WORLD RANKING

M

MADAGASCAR

OFFICIAL NAME: Democratic Republic of Madagascar **CAPITAL:** Antananarivo
POPULATION: 12.8 million **CURRENCY:** Malagasy franc **OFFICIAL LANGUAGES:** Malagasy and French

LYING IN THE INDIAN Ocean, Madagascar is the world's fourth largest island. Its isolation means it is home to a host of unique wildlife and plants. To the east, the large central plateau drops precipitously through forested cliffs to the coast. On the west, gentler gradients give way to fertile plains. A former French colony, it became independent in 1960. After 18 years of radical socialism under Didier Ratsiraka, Madagascar is now a multiparty democracy struggling to rebuild an agriculturally-based economy.

POLITICS

1998   President Albert Zafy

THE STATE OF THE PARTIES

National Assembly 138 members

6% **Fi**

34% **CFV**   12% **MFM**   9% **LF**   8% **Fa**   31% **Other**

CFV = *Forces Vives* Coalition **MFM** = Movement for Proletarian Power (coalition) **LF** = *Leader-Familo*
Fa = *Famima* **Fi** = *Fihaonana*

Senate

Two thirds of members are selected by an electoral college and the remainder appointed by the president.

In 1993, 18 years of *de facto* one-party rule under Didier Ratsiraka ended when free elections were won by the *Forces Vives* (CFV) opposition coalition.

CLIMATE

WEATHER CHART

Madagascar is tropical and often hit by cyclones. The coastal lowlands are hot and humid. Rainfall averages 200 cm a year in the east, but under 80 cm in the southwest. The central plateau is cooler, with 100–150 cm of rain a year.

COMMUNICATIONS

Ivato, Antananarivo
340,000 passengers (est)

18 ships
46,300 dwt

THE TRANSPORT NETWORK

34,750 km (21,593 miles)		None
899 km (559 miles)		432 km (268 miles)

The extensive domestic air network is a response to the inadequacies of the road and rail systems. Many roads are impassable during the rains; the rail network is very limited. Toamasina port handles about 70% of total traffic.

PEOPLE

Malagasy, French

20 people per km²

THE URBAN/RURAL POPULATION SPLIT

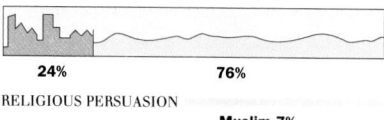

24%   76%

RELIGIOUS PERSUASION

Muslim 7%

Indigenous beliefs 52%   **Christian 41%**

The people of Madagascar, like their language, Malagasy, are essentially Malay–Indonesian in origin. Their ancestors migrated across the Indian Ocean in successive waves from the 1st century AD. Later migrants from the African mainland intermixed and provided the many African words in Malagasy. The main ethnic division is between the central plateau and *côtier* (coastal) peoples. Of more pronounced Malay extraction, the plateau Merina were Madagascar's historic rulers. They remain the social elite and largely run the government – to the resentment of the poorer *côtier* groups. Former president Didier Ratsiraka owed much of his political longevity to the fact that he is a *côtier*. The extended family is the focus of social life for the rural majority.

MADAGASCAR

Total Area : 587 040 sq. km (226 660 sq. miles)

N

POPULATION
- over 500 000
- over 100 000
- over 50 000
- over 10 000
- under 10 000

0   200 km
0   200 miles

LAND HEIGHT

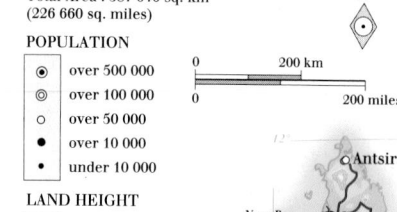

- 2000m/6562ft
- 1000m/3281ft
- 500m/1640ft
- 200m/656ft
- Sea Level

TOURISM

34,891 visitors

Down 34% in 1991

MAIN OVERSEAS ARRIVALS

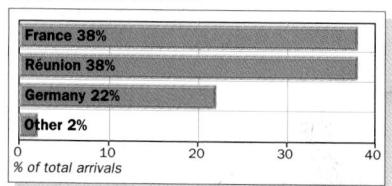

| France 38% |
| Réunion 38% |
| Germany 22% |
| Other 2% |

0   10   20   30   40
% of total arrivals

With 5000 km of tropical beaches and a unique flora and fauna, Madagascar has great tourism potential. However, while the sector is now an important foreign exchange earner, it is underdeveloped. After a marked decline in 1991, tourist arrivals were expected to reach a new peak of 57,000 in 1993.

WORLD AFFAIRS

    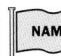
OAU | ECA | ACP | AfDB | NAM

Once-close ties with Moscow and North Korea have waned since the late 1980s, as Madagascar has improved relations with its main western trading partners, especially France and the USA. It has also increased regional links, re-establishing ties with South Africa and, in 1994, joining the east and southern Africa Preferential Trading Area (PTA).

AID

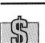 $557m (receipts)   Down 3% in 1991

France is the top bilateral donor. The main multilateral donors are the EU and the World Bank. Most aid is now tied to economic reforms.

DEFENCE

 $36.63m   Up 5% in 1991

A key political force, the army's priority is to maintain a stable, unitary state. In 1992, it acted against federalist *côtiers*.

ECONOMICS

 $2.85bn   1846.87 Malagasy francs

SCORE CARD

- ❏ WORLD GNP RANKING..........................127th
- ❏ GNP PER CAPITA $223
- ❏ BALANCE OF PAYMENTS....................$–182m
- ❏ INFLATION 12.7%
- ❏ UNEMPLOYMENT....Widespread underemployment

STRENGTHS

Varied agricultural base; vanilla, coffee and clove exports. Offshore oil and gas. Prawns. Tourism.

WEAKNESSES

Losing out to cheaper vanilla exporters. Vulnerability to drought. Government slow to reform economy by cutting central controls and budget deficit. Not self-sufficient in rice, the food staple.

EXPORTS

Japan 11%
Germany* 7%
Other 34%
USA 15%
France 33%

IMPORTS
CIS* 10%
USA 11%
Other 48%
France 31%

Tôlañaro (also known as Fort Dauphin), a port on the southeast coast. This was the area first settled by the French in the 16th century.

RESOURCES

 566m kwh (capacity 220,000 kw)
 Not an oil producer; refines 16,350 b/cd
10.2m cattle, 1.4m pigs, 700,000 sheep
 Chromite, graphite, beryl, mica, iron, bitumen, oil, gas

Madagascar is the world's largest vanilla exporter. Electricity is hydro-generated. Oil is imported, although offshore oil and gas have been found.

ENVIRONMENT

 2% (1% partially protected)
 Serious deforestation and soil erosion

Madagascar's environment is a unique resource; 80% of its plant and many animal species, such as the lemur, are found nowhere else. Aid donors are providing funds to fight deforestation.

MEDIA

 Censorship exists, but is limited

PUBLISHING AND BROADCAST MEDIA

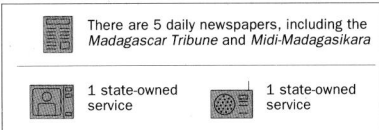
There are 5 daily newspapers, including the *Madagascar Tribune* and *Midi-Madagasikara*.
1 state-owned service
1 state-owned service

Even before the return of multiparty democracy in 1993, there was a flourishing opposition press, including the Catholic-sponsored *La Croix*.

CRIME

 33,280 prisoners   Crime is rising

Urban crime levels are starting to rise. The army has been criticized for human rights abuses, including the shooting of federalists in 1993.

EDUCATION

 80%

Primary education is universal. About 40% of children attend secondary school; 5% go on to higher education. Primary education is to become French-based instead of Malagasy-based.

CHRONOLOGY

Increasing European contacts after the 16th century culminated in the 1895 French invasion. Madagascar became a French colony and the Merina monarchy was abolished.

- ❏ **1947–1948** French troops kill thousands in nationalist uprisings.
- ❏ **1960** Independence.
- ❏ **1975** Didier Ratsiraka takes power with radical socialist policies.
- ❏ **1990** Political reforms allow parties other than ruling AREMA and official opposition FNDR.
- ❏ **1991** Opposition *Forces Vives* (CFV) coalition, led by Albert Zafy, set up. Mass strikes against regime.
- ❏ **1993** Ratsiraka and AREMA-FNDR coalition, named the MFM, defeated by Zafy and CFV in free elections.

HEALTH

 1 per 9939 people   Malaria, enteric and respiratory diseases

Private health care was legalized in 1993. State care is free but inadequate. Malaria is at epidemic levels. There are outbreaks of bubonic plague.

WEALTH

 Minimum wage in manufacturing, 22,000 Malagasy francs per month

CONSUMER GOODS OWNERSHIP

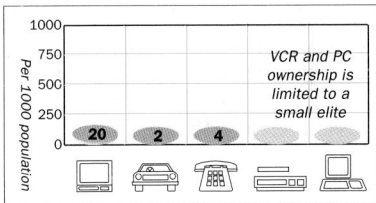
VCR and PC ownership is limited to a small elite
20   2   4

Most people are poor. However, central plateau dwellers are richer than the *côtier* farmers and fishermen.

WORLD RANKING

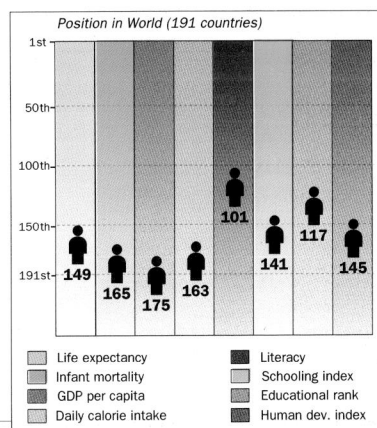
Position in World (191 countries)
149 | 165 | 175 | 163 | 101 | 141 | 117 | 145

Life expectancy | Literacy
Infant mortality | Schooling index
GDP per capita | Educational rank
Daily calorie intake | Human dev. index

M

MALAWI

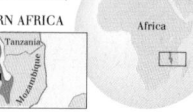

SOUTHERN AFRICA

OFFICIAL NAME: Republic of Malawi   **CAPITAL:** Lilongwe   **POPULATION:** 10.4 million
CURRENCY: Malawian kwacha   **OFFICIAL LANGUAGES:** Chewa and English

LAND-LOCKED IN southeast Africa, Malawi occupies a plateau bordering the Great Rift Valley. Lake Malawi, which is 568 km in length and takes up one fifth of the country, is among Africa's largest lakes and supports a sizeable fishing industry. Mount Mulanje is the highest mountain in East Africa. Politics in Malawi, a former British colony, is in a delicate transition period following three decades of one-party rule.

CLIMATE

WEATHER CHART

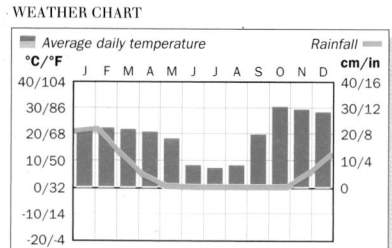

The south is hot and humid. The rest of Malawi is warm and very sunny in the dry season, but cooler in the highlands.

COMMUNICATIONS

 Kamuzu Intl, Lilongwe 232,000 passengers   Has no fleet

THE TRANSPORT NETWORK

12,215 km (7590 miles)	None
789 km (490 miles)	Lake Malawi, Shire River

Access from rural areas to the good main road system is limited. The Kamuzu Highway, a key north–south link, is currently being upgraded.

TOURISM

 117,069 visitors   Up 18% in 1989

MAIN OVERSEAS ARRIVALS

Zambia 29%
Zimbabwe 22%
Mozambique 11%
Other 38%

0   10   20   30   40
% of total arrivals

The waters of Lake Malawi, with its 500 species of fish, attract angling, wildlife and water-sports enthusiasts. The national parks and mountain lodges are also popular.

PEOPLE

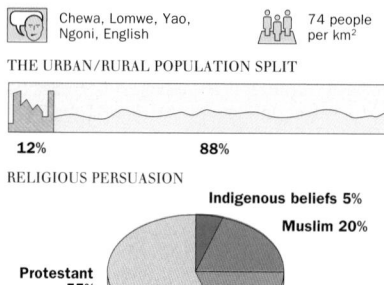

Chewa, Lomwe, Yao, Ngoni, English | 74 people per km²

THE URBAN/RURAL POPULATION SPLIT

12%   88%

RELIGIOUS PERSUASION

Indigenous beliefs 5%
Muslim 20%
Protestant 55%
Roman Catholic 20%

Ethnic tensions are few in Malawi as most of the population share a common Bantu origin. The main ethnic groupings are the Chewa, Yao, Chieoka, Tonga, Tumbuka, Ngoni and Nyanja. Ethnicity has not been exploited for political ends to the extent that it has in neighbouring states. However, in recent years tensions between the north and south have been rising. Northerners are increasingly disaffected at their lack of representation in politics and have become alienated from the ruling MCP.

Many of the Muslim Asians are involved in the retail trade. They have suffered some discrimination from the Banda regime. President Banda, a member of the Scottish Presbyterian Church, has promoted the expansion of Protestantism in Malawi.

Fruit and vegetable sellers on the Mozambican border. The south of the country is intensively cultivated.

POLITICS

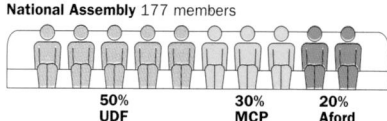

1999   President Bakili Muluzi

THE STATE OF THE PARTIES

National Assembly 177 members

50% UDF   30% MCP   20% Aford

UDF = United Democratic Front   **MCP** = Malawi Congress Party   **Aford** = Alliance for Democracy

Since independence in 1964 Malawi fell under the personalized rule of Dr Hastings Banda. Under a single-party regime, instituted in 1966, dissent was not tolerated and torture and imprisonment without trial were common. In 1992, international aid was suspended because of the regime's poor human rights record. A referendum was held in 1993 and Banda agreed to the introduction of multiparty politics.In May 1994, presidential and legislative elections were held. The United Democratic Front (UDF), which draws most of its support from the south, scored a dramatic victory in the parliamentary elections. The UDF leader, Bakili Muluzi, also won the presidential election, bringing to an end one of the world's longest dictatorships. President Maluzi, a wealthy businessman and a former secretary-general of the MCP, recruited a number of prominent MCP politicians to the UDF, one reason for the party's good showing in the central region – a traditional MCP stronghold.

WORLD AFFAIRS

   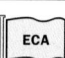

Comm   OAU   NAM   ECA   ACP

Malawi's principal concerns have been protecting its restored status as a recipient of Western aid and retaining a pragmatic relationship with South Africa. Malawi is the only black African country to have maintained full diplomatic relations with South Africa since 1967. One in ten Mozambicans fled to Malawi as refugees in the 1980s.

AID

 Aid suspended in 1992   Not applicable

In May 1992, all non-humanitarian aid was suspended, with democratic change a precondition for its resumption. This action proved significant in propelling Malawi to a referendum on democracy in 1993.

M

DEFENCE

 $22.02m

 Up 6% in 1989

The 10,800-strong military has lost confidence in the ruling party and is forcing the pace of democratization. In 1993, it took the step of disarming the Young Pioneers, in what looked like the first stages of a coup. Banda heads the 6000-strong paramilitary police force.

ECONOMICS

 $1.8bn

4.46 kwacha

SCORE CARD

- ❑ WORLD GNP RANKING.........................140th
- ❑ GNP PER CAPITA $200
- ❑ BALANCE OF PAYMENTS...................$–164m
- ❑ INFLATION 12.7%
- ❑ UNEMPLOYMENT....Widespread underemployment

STRENGTHS

Tobacco, accounting for 76% of foreign exchange earnings. Tea and sugar production. Unexploited reserves of bauxite, asbestos and coal.

WEAKNESSES

Agriculture, accounting for 80% of GDP, often hit by drought. Only 14% of GDP from industry. Small domestic market. Shortage of skilled personnel. Regional instability and refugee problem.

EXPORTS

Japan 12%
South Africa Customs Union 12%
Germany* 13%
UK 18%
Other 45%

IMPORTS

Japan 9%
UK 22%
South Africa Customs Union 32%
Other 37%

RESOURCES

 587m kwh (capacity 190,000 kw)

 1m cattle, 260,000 pigs, 200,000 sheep, 2000 asses

Not an oil producer and has no refineries

 Coal, limestone, gemstones

Malawi has few strategic resources. Three hydro-power plants account for 85% of electricity generating capacity, but only 3% of total energy use. Over 90% of energy needs are met from fuelwood as most Malawians do not have access to electricity. Malawi has reserves of bauxite and uranium, but not in commercially exploitable quantities. A deep-seam coal mine recently began production at Rumphi.

MALAWI

Total Area : 118 480 sq. km
(45 745 sq. miles)

POPULATION
- ◎ over 100 000
- ● over 10 000
- • under 10 000

LAND HEIGHT
- 2000m/6562ft
- 1000m/3281ft
- 500m/1640ft
- 200m/656ft
- Sea Level

0   100 km
0   100 miles

ENVIRONMENT

 11% (4% partially protected)

 Few environmental initiatives

Drought eclipses all other problems. Agricultural production fell by 25% in 1992 owing to its effects.

MEDIA

 Any hint of criticism in the media is outlawed by the government

PUBLISHING AND BROADCAST MEDIA

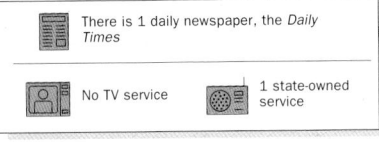

There is 1 daily newspaper, the *Daily Times*

No TV service

1 state-owned service

The authorities retain tight control over the press. Radio is effectively a mouthpiece for the government.

CRIME

 Malawi does not publish prison figures

 Up 3% in 1988

The Young Pioneers, the MCP's youth wing, have engaged in illegal violence. The proliferation of guns is contributing to an increase in armed robbery.

CHRONOLOGY

After strong Scottish missionary activity, Malawi came under British rule as Nyasaland in 1891.

- ❑ **1964** Independence under Dr Hastings Banda.
- ❑ **1966** One-party state.
- ❑ **1967** Only African country to recognize South Africa.
- ❑ **1992** Anti-government riots. Illegal pro-democracy groups unite.
- ❑ **1993** Referendum: 63% in favour of multipartyism.

EDUCATION

 52% males
31% females

Primary level education is widespread, with 73% of boys and 60% of girls attending school regularly.

HEALTH

 1 per 26,942 people

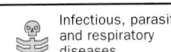 Infectious, parasitic and respiratory diseases

Access to health services is difficult and preventive care is viewed as a priority. Most doctors train abroad.

WEALTH

 Most Malawians lead a subsistence existence

CONSUMER GOODS OWNERSHIP

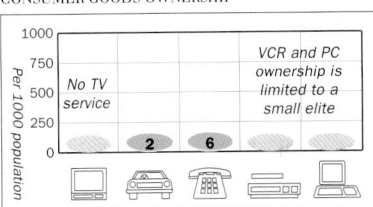

No TV service

VCR and PC ownership is limited to a small elite

2   6

The MCP elite is the richest group. Banda allegedly has links with the Press Group consortium, which has a $250-million annual turnover.

WORLD RANKING

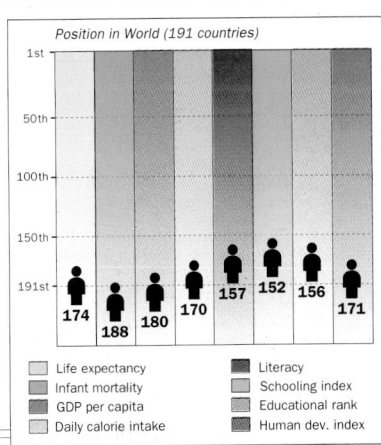

Position in World (191 countries)

174
188
180
170
157
152
156
171

- Life expectancy
- Infant mortality
- GDP per capita
- Daily calorie intake
- Literacy
- Schooling index
- Educational rank
- Human dev. index

M

MALAYSIA

OFFICIAL NAME: Malaysia **CAPITAL:** Kuala Lumpur
POPULATION: 18.8 million **CURRENCY:** Ringgit **OFFICIAL LANGUAGE:** Malay

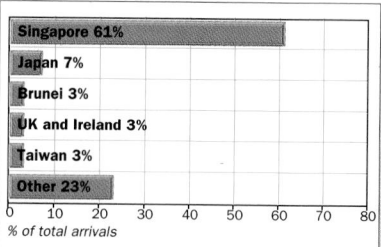

COMPRISING THE THREE separate territories of Malaya, Sarawak and Sabah, Malaysia stretches over 2000 km from Peninsular Malaysia to the northeastern end of the island of Borneo. It shares borders with Thailand, Indonesia and the enclave states of Singapore and Brunei. A central mountain chain divides Malaya, separating fertile western plains from a narrow eastern coastal belt. Sarawak and Sabah are characterized by swampy coastal plains rising to mountains on the border with Indonesia. Since 1987, Malaysia has been experiencing average economic growth rates of 8% a year.

CLIMATE

WEATHER CHART

The whole of Malaysia has an equatorial climate. The country has rainfall throughout the year; it falls on between 150 and 200 days almost everywhere. However, there are two distinct rainy seasons, when the heaviest rain falls – from March to May and from September to November. Coastal areas are also subject to the alternating southwest and northeast monsoon winds.

Tea plantation in the Cameron Highlands, in central-western Malaya. This region also contains one of Asia's most popular mountain resorts.

COMMUNICATIONS

 Subang Intl, Kuala Lumpur 4.46m passengers   310 ships 2.91m dwt

THE TRANSPORT NETWORK

| 40,174 km (24,963 miles) | None |
| 2075 km (1289 miles) | 3209 km (1994 miles) |

A major north–south highway is being built and in Kuala Lumpur a new mass transit system is being constructed to extend to its outer suburbs. Malaysia's 'national car', the Proton, has been a success; since 1985, national car ownership has tripled. Several ports are being updated to reduce Malaysia's current dependence on Singapore.

TOURISM

7.48m visitors Up 54% in 1990

MAIN OVERSEAS ARRIVALS

Singapore 61%	
Japan 7%	
Brunei 3%	
UK and Ireland 3%	
Taiwan 3%	
Other 23%	

% of total arrivals (0 10 20 30 40 50 60 70 80)

Malaysia is South East Asia's major tourist destination, with over seven million visitors a year. Most tourists come for the excellent tropical beaches on the east coast, to hike in the Cameron Highlands or to trek in the world's oldest rainforests in Borneo. There has recently been an increase in the international business convention trade.

By 1990, when the government ran the Visit Malaysia Year campaign, tourism had become Malaysia's third biggest foreign exchange earner. There is still untapped potential for growth. Over half of visitors to Malaysia are short-stay trippers from Singapore, and tourists' spending per day is less than half of that in Thailand. A second Visit Malaysia Year was launched in 1994, and a third is planned to coincide with the holding of the Commonwealth Games in Malaysia in 1998. Hotel capacity is currently growing at 10% a year and 70 new beach resorts are planned before 2000.

MALAYSIA

Total Area : 329 750 sq. km (127 317 sq. miles)

POPULATION

- ◉ over 500 000
- ◎ over 100 000
- ○ over 50 000
- ● over 10 000
- • under 10 000

LAND HEIGHT

- 2000m/6562ft
- 1000m/3281ft
- 500m/1640ft
- 200m/656ft
- Sea Level

M

PEOPLE

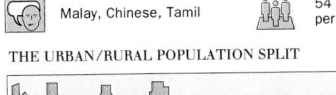
Malay, Chinese, Tamil

54 people per km²

THE URBAN/RURAL POPULATION SPLIT

43%   57%

RELIGION PERSUASION

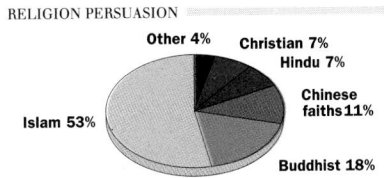
Other 4%
Christian 7%
Hindu 7%
Chinese faiths 11%
Islam 53%
Buddhist 18%

ETHNIC MAKEUP

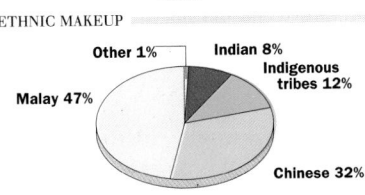
Other 1%
Indian 8%
Indigenous tribes 12%
Malay 47%
Chinese 32%

POPULATION AGE BREAKDOWN

% of population by age group	0–14	15–64			65+
65+	3.4%	3.4%	3.7%	3.7%	4.1%
15–64	51.3%	52%	56.9%	58.1%	60.7%
0–14	45.3%	44.6%	39.4%	38.2%	35.2%
	1960	1970	1980	1990	2000

The key distinction in Malaysian society is between the Muslim indigenous Malays and the Chinese. The Malays are the largest group, but the Chinese traditionally controlled most business activity. The New Economic Policy (NEP), introduced in the 1970s, emphasized a programme of positive discrimination in favour of Malays. Malays were favoured in education and jobs in the state and private sectors. Greater Islamicization was also promoted and women were encouraged to wear veils in the street. In states with a Christian government, such as Sabah, the presence of illegal Muslim immigrants from Indonesia and the Philippines was seen not simply as a source of useful cheap labour, but as a way of shifting the political balance further in favour of the Malays.

Considerable resentment was felt by both Chinese and Indian communities at the policy. The Chinese still control a large share of national wealth. However, they are increasingly uncertain of their status in society and are beginning to invest overseas.

POLITICS

1995

HM Sultan Azlan Shah

THE STATE OF THE PARTIES

House of Representatives 180 members

71% BN   11% DAP   8% PBS   4% PAS   4% S'46   2% Other

BN = National Front (coalition: principal party is UMNO = United Malays National Organization) **DAP** = Democratic Action Party **PBS** = Sabah United Party **S'46** = Spirit of '46 **PAS** = Pan-Malaysian Islamic Party

Senate 70 members

30 members elected – 2 from each of 13 State Legislative Assemblies and 2 Federal Territories – and 40 members chosen by the Head of State

Supreme power rests with the monarch, who acts on the advice of parliament. Opposition parties, whilst legal, are under tight control.

MAIN POLITICAL ISSUE

Malay superiority

While the current administration of Dr Mahathir has declared that it no longer wishes to discriminate positively in favour of Malays, the Chinese community is feeling increasingly isolated. They have accused the government of corruption and uncompetitive practices, declaring that Malays are still favoured in the placing of government contracts. In 1993, investment in the domestic economy by indigenous Chinese fell by an estimated 30%. The pro-Malay policy is also expressed in a more restrictive Islamic society, which further alienates the Chinese community.

PROFILE

Malaysia has been dominated by the UMNO since independence from Britain in 1947. In 1970, it introduced a policy of favouring Malays over the Chinese and other minorities. The party is heavily involved in business and controls a huge network of both political and economic patronage. The latter gives it and its Malay supporters a significant and growing control of the economy. The semblance of a working democracy is maintained by staged grass-roots political debate. An opposition exists, but its effectiveness is limited by the UMNO's policy of cutting funding to constituencies who vote against the party.

The success of the UMNO, and of its leader Dr Mahathir, has been to deliver consistent economic growth and prosperity. As long as this continues, few challengers will emerge to question Mahathir's pre-eminent position in Malay political life.

WORLD AFFAIRS

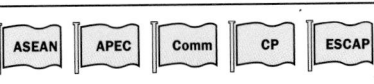
ASEAN   APEC   Comm   CP   ESCAP

Prime Minister Mahathir sees himself as one of the developing world's leading voices. He maintains a strongly anti-US line in his public speeches and has chastized the West for its failure to resolve the conflict in Bosnia. Singapore fears Mahathir's pro-Malay policies. Tensions are exacerbated by the fact that Singapore is dependent on Malaysia for water.

AID

$459m (receipts); also a donor

Little variation from year to year

Malaysia has received soft loans from the West for large infrastructure projects. In recent years, it has also made donations. It has given aid to Bosnian Muslims and offered to take Bosnian refugees. Technical assistance has been made available to Vietnam.

Dr Mahathir Mohamad, *prime minister since 1981.*

Sultan Azlan Shah, *supreme head of state since 1989.*

M

CHRONOLOGY

The former British protectorate of Malaya, made up of 11 states, gained independence in 1957. The federation of Malaysia, incorporating Singapore, Sarawak and Sabah, was founded in 1963.

- ❏ **1965** Singapore leaves federation, reducing Malaysian states to 13.
- ❏ **1970** Malay-Chinese ethnic tension results in resignation of Prime Minister Tunku Abdul Rahman. Tun Abdul Razak, new prime minister, creates national coalition, the BN.
- ❏ **1976–1978** Guerrilla attacks by banned Communist Party of Malaya (CPM), based in southern Thailand. Co-operation between Malaysian and Thai governments leads to eventual reduction in CPM activity.
- ❏ **1976** Tun Abdul Razak dies. Succeeded by his deputy, Dato' Hussein bin Onn.
- ❏ **1977** Unrest in Kelantan following expulsion of its Chief Minister from Pan-Malaysian Islamic Party (PAS). National emergency declared. PAS expelled from BN.
- ❏ **1978** Elections consolidate BN power. PAS marginalized. Flare-up of ethnic and religious tension over government rejection of Chinese university.
- ❏ **1978–1989** Unrestricted asylum given to Vietnamese refugees.
- ❏ **1981** Dr Mahathir Mohamad becomes prime minister.
- ❏ **1982** General elections return BN with increased majority.
- ❏ **1985** In Sabah state elections, BN defeated by PBS. Legality of PBS victory questioned.
- ❏ **1986** PBS wins new election and joins BN coalition. Dispute between Dr Mahathir and his deputy, Dakuk Musa, triggers general election. BN win, but criticism of leadership continues. Tensions increase between Malays and Chinese.
- ❏ **1987** 106 politicians from all parties suspected of Chinese sympathies detained without trial. Media censored.
- ❏ **1989** Disaffected UMNO members join PAS. Screening of Vietnamese refugees introduced. CPM sign peace agreement with Malaysian and Thai governments.
- ❏ **1990** General election. PBS leaves BN. BN wins with reduced majority.
- ❏ **1993** Assembly votes for reduction in powers, including loss of legal immunity, for the nine Sultans.
- ❏ **1994** Chief Minister of Sabah found guilty of corruption, but he and his PBS party returned in state election.

M

DEFENCE

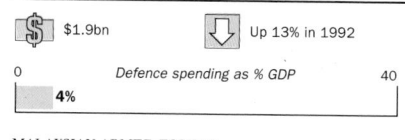

$1.9bn   Up 13% in 1992

Defence spending as % GDP
0 — 4% — 40

MALAYSIAN ARMED FORCES

🛡️	26 light tanks (26 *Scorpion* (90mm))	105,000 personnel
🚢	4 frigates and 37 patrol boats	10,500 personnel
✈️	69 combat aircraft (27 A-4PTM/6TA-4/ 13 F-5E/4 F-5F)	12,000 personnel
	None	

The military is entirely composed of Malays. Defence spending currently accounts for 4% of GDP. There are plans to raise it to 6%, in line with neighbouring Singapore. Malaysia is an important market for Western arms suppliers. The air force buys US equipment, although Malaysia has threatened to buy second-hand MiG fighters from Russia. In 1990, Malaysia expressed an interest in buying Tornado fighters from the UK. The main defence concerns are Singapore's large and highly mechanized army and growing Chinese influence in the South China Sea. Patrolling East and West Malaysia is a key function of the navy, which is large by regional standards.

ECONOMICS

📊 $55bn   💲 2.62 ringgits

SCORE CARD

- ❏ WORLD GNP RANKING..........................39th
- ❏ GNP PER CAPITA $2925
- ❏ BALANCE OF PAYMENTS...................$–1.7bn
- ❏ INFLATION 3.2%
- ❏ UNEMPLOYMENT ....Low rate

ECONOMIC PERFORMANCE INDICATOR

EXPORTS

South Korea 5% | Japan 15% | Other 40% | USA 17% | Singapore 23%

IMPORTS

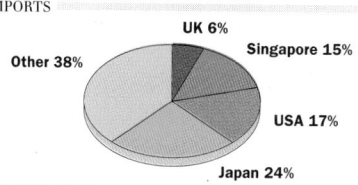

UK 6% | Singapore 15% | Other 38% | USA 17% | Japan 24%

STRENGTHS

Electronics: the world's biggest producer of disk drives. Proton car a national and international success. Heavy industries such as steel. Latex and rubber industries.

WEAKNESSES

Shortage of skilled labour. High interest rates deter private investors. High government budget spending. Competition from new NICs.

PROFILE

Growth in the economy took off in 1987. Since then, Malaysia has been expanding faster than any other South East Asian nation, at an average yearly rate of 8%. Much of the growth has been state-directed. In 1987, the government made a concerted push for foreign investment, which rose to a peak of 17.6 billion ringgits in 1990. The privatization of state assets was also stepped up. Goals have been set for full industrialization in a plan known as 'Vision 2020'.

MALAYSIA : MAJOR BUSINESSES

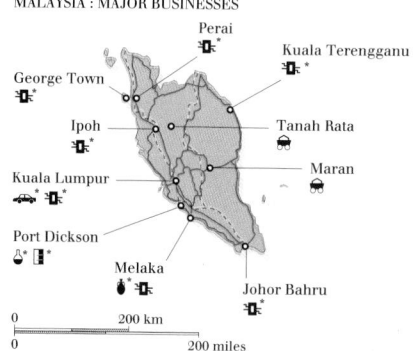

Perai | Kuala Terengganu | George Town | Ipoh | Tanah Rata | Kuala Lumpur | Maran | Port Dickson | Melaka | Johor Bahru

0 — 200 km
0 — 200 miles

Lutong

Palm oil
Tin mining
Electronics
Oil refining
Petrochemicals
Vehicle assembly

* significant multinational ownership

WORLD AFFAIRS

The Maldives is a long standing member of the Non-Aligned Movement. The government continues to support NAM and rejects the criticism that it does not have a role to play in the post-Cold War world. The Maldives' international standing was enhanced in 1990, when it hosted the fifth SARC summit meeting, held in Male'.

AID

 $28m (receipts)   Aid levels remain fairly constant

Aid has helped to finance development of port and airport facilities. Japan is the most important bilateral aid donor, contributing 25% of total assistance in 1991. Relief aid, principally from India, Pakistan and the USA, was given after the storms of 1991 which caused $30 million damage.

DEFENCE

 Paramilitary police force only   Not applicable

The British military presence ended in 1975, when troops were withdrawn from the staging post on Gan in the Addu atoll. The USSR's offer to lease the base was rejected, and it is now an industrial zone. The Maldives follows a policy of non-alignment.

ECONOMICS

 $101m $\boxed{\$}$ 11.95 rufiyaa

SCORE CARD

❏ WORLD GNP RANKING	185th
❏ GNP PER CAPITA	$455
❏ BALANCE OF PAYMENTS	$–38m
❏ INFLATION	11.4%
❏ UNEMPLOYMENT	2%

STRENGTHS
Growth of tourism. Fishing, especially tuna; mostly exported to the UK and Sri Lanka. Shipping. Clothing. Coconut production. Financial and commercial reforms as economy expands.

WEAKNESSES
Too dependent on fluctuating tourist industry. Growing trade deficit. Shortage of skilled labour. Small manufacturing base. Cottage industries employ 25% of workforce; little scope for expansion.

EXPORTS

UK 25%
Thailand 11%
Sri Lanka 19%
USA 23%
Other 22%

IMPORTS

UK 6%
Singapore 6%
Sri Lanka 8%
India 8%
Other 72%

RESOURCES

 29m kwh (capacity 5000 kw)   Not an oil producer and has no refineries

76,000 tonnes   None

Natural resources include abundant stocks of fish, particularly tuna. Fishing, still carried out by the traditional pole and line method to help conserve stocks, employs over 20% of the working population. Coconut production is also important. All oil products and virtually all staple foods are imported.

ENVIRONMENT

 None   Turtles are protected by law

It is believed global warming, climatic change and the rise of the sea level are threatening to submerge the islands which have an average height of just 1.6 m. A sea wall has been built around the capital island. Other environmental concerns are sewerage, waste disposal and the mining of coral for building.

MEDIA

 New libel laws are being implemented by the government against journalists

PUBLISHING AND BROADCAST MEDIA

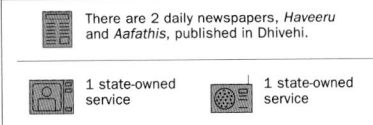

There are 2 daily newspapers, *Haveeru* and *Aafathis*, published in Dhivehi.

1 state-owned service

1 state-owned service

There is a marked degree of press censorship. In the past, journalists and satirists have been imprisoned. There are only two newspapers.

CRIME

 The Maldives does not publish prison figures   Up 3% in 1990

The Maldives is a strict Islamic society. Drugs crimes are heavily punished. Political prisoners are banished to outer islands. The judiciary and executive are closely linked.

CHRONOLOGY

The Maldives was a British protectorate from 1887 and gained its independence in 1965.

- ❏ **1932** First written constitution.
- ❏ **1968** Sultanate abolished. Declared a republic. Ibrahim Nasir elected as first president.
- ❏ **1988** Coup attempt. Suppressed by Indian troops sent over on request.
- ❏ **1993** President Gayoom re-elected for fourth five-year term.

EDUCATION

 91%

Primary education has been improved. Secondary education is less developed in the outer islands; the first school outside Male' was opened in 1992.

HEALTH

 1 per 5330 people   Infectious and parasitic diseases

There is a lack of general equipment and facilities. Health care is less developed on the outlying islands.

WEALTH

Private-sector secretary, 2868 rufiyaa per month; government minister, 5975 rufiyaa per month

CONSUMER GOODS OWNERSHIP

VCR and PC ownership is limited to a small elite

24   3   14

Great disparities exist between the people who live in Male' and those who live on the outer islands.

WORLD RANKING

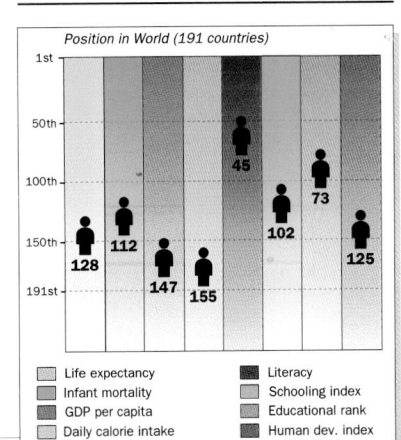

Position in World (191 countries)

128, 112, 147, 155, 45, 102, 73, 125

- ❏ Life expectancy
- ❏ Infant mortality
- ❏ GDP per capita
- ❏ Daily calorie intake
- ❏ Literacy
- ❏ Schooling index
- ❏ Educational rank
- ❏ Human dev. index

M

MALI

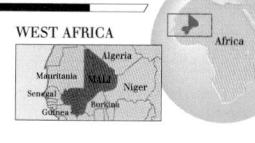

WEST AFRICA

OFFICIAL NAME: Republic of Mali   **CAPITAL:** Bamako
POPULATION: 9.8 million   **CURRENCY:** CFA franc   **OFFICIAL LANGUAGE:** French

MALI IS LAND-LOCKED in the heart of West Africa. Its mostly flat terrain comprises virtually uninhabited Saharan plains in the north and more fertile savanna land in the south, where most of the population lives. The River Niger irrigates the central and southwestern regions of the country. Following independence in 1960, Mali experienced a long period of largely single-party rule. It became a multiparty democracy in 1992.

CLIMATE

WEATHER CHART

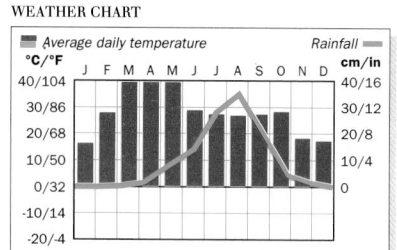

In the south, intensely hot, dry weather precedes the westerly rains. The northern half of Mali is almost rainless.

COMMUNICATIONS

🛪 **Bamako-Senou**   Has no fleet

THE TRANSPORT NETWORK

13,306 km (8268 miles)	None	
642 km (399 miles)	1815 km (1128 miles)	

Mali is linked by rail with the port of Dakar in Senegal, and by good roads to the port of Abidjan in Ivory Coast.

TOURISM

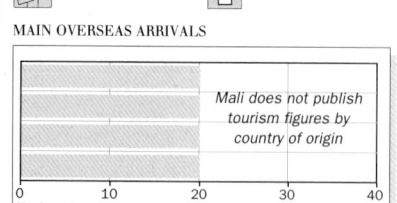

52,000 visitors   Up 2% in 1988

MAIN OVERSEAS ARRIVALS

Mali does not publish tourism figures by country of origin

0   10   20   30   40
% of total arrivals

Tourism is largely safari-orientated, although the historic cities of Djénné, Gao and Mopti, lying on the banks of the River Niger, also attract visitors. A national domestic airline began operating in 1990.

PEOPLE

Bambara, Fulani, Senufo, Soninke, French   7 people per km²

THE URBAN/RURAL POPULATION SPLIT

19%   81%

RELIGIOUS PERSUASION

Christian 1%   Indigenous beliefs 9%

Muslim 90%

Mali's most significant ethnic group, the Bambara, is also politically dominant. The Bambara speak the *lingua franca* of the River Niger, which is shared with other groups including the Malinke. The relationship betweeen the Bambara–Malinke majority and the Tuareg nomads of the Saharan north is tense and sometimes violent. As elsewhere in Africa, the extended family, often based on the village, is a vital social security system and link between the urban and rural poor. There are a few powerful women in Mali, but, in general, they have little status.

POLITICS

1997   President Alpha Oumar Konaré

THE STATE OF THE PARTIES

National Assembly 129 members   7% US–RDA   14% Other

66% ADEMA   8% CNID   5% PMD

ADEMA = Alliance for Democracy in Mali   **CNID** = National Committee for Democratic Initiative   **US–RDA** = Sudanese Union – African Democratic Rally   **PMD** = Popular Movement for the Development of West Africa   **Other** = Rally for Democracy and Progress, Union for Democracy and Development

The successful transition to multiparty politics in 1992 followed the overthrow in the previous year of Moussa Traoré, Mali's dictator for 23 years. The army's role was crucial in leading the coup, whilst Colonel Touré, who acted as interim president, was responsible for the swift return to civilian rule in less than a year. The change marks Mali's first experience of multipartyism. Maintaining good relations with the Tuaregs, after a peace agreement in 1991, is a key issue. However, the main challenge facing President Alpha Oumar Konaré's government is to alleviate poverty while placating the opposition, which feels that the luxury of multipartyism is something that Mali cannot afford. As Konaré's austerity measures begin to take effect, opposition to his policies is likely to increase.

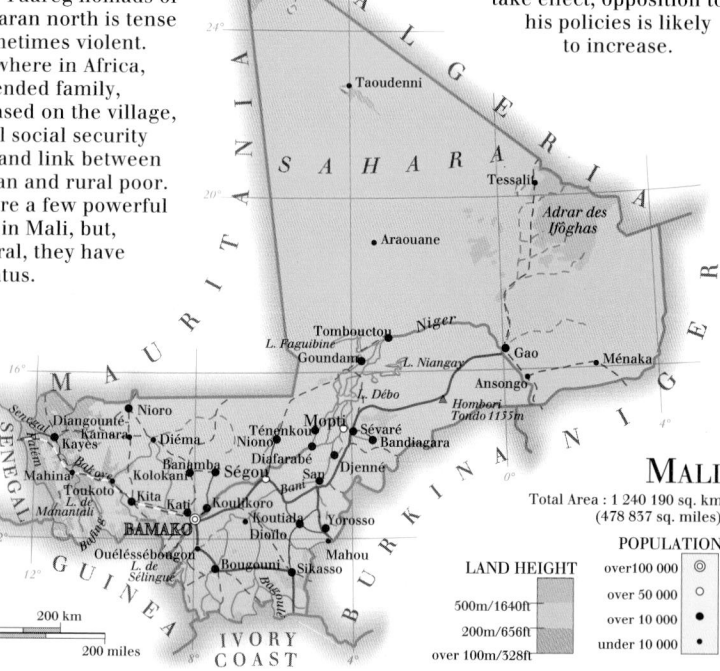

MALI

Total Area : 1 240 190 sq. km (478 837 sq. miles)

POPULATION

LAND HEIGHT

over 100 000
over 50 000
over 10 000
under 10 000

500m/1640ft
200m/656ft
over 100m/328ft

0   200 km
0   200 miles

M

WORLD AFFAIRS

 OAU Ecowas FZ ACP ECA

Mali concentrates on maintaining good relations with a wide variety of African neighbours, from the ECOWAS countries to its south, to its northern neighbours such as Algeria. Relations with Libya, which is suspected of fomenting Tuareg revolt, are tense. Good relations with Western aid-providers are crucial.

AID

 $455m (receipts)   Up 35% in 1991

Mali is highly dependent on foreign aid, which comes from France, the EU, China, a few Arab states, the USA and international lending institutions.

DEFENCE

 $63.82m   Up 4% in 1988

Mali has traditionally had a strong army. In 1985, the air force played an important role in the war with Burkina.

ECONOMICS

 $2.8bn   295.23 CFA francs

SCORE CARD

- ❏ WORLD GNP RANKING........................129th
- ❏ GNP PER CAPITA $285
- ❏ BALANCE OF PAYMENTS......................$–78m
- ❏ INFLATION ....–6.2%
- ❏ UNEMPLOYMENT....Widespread underemployment

STRENGTHS
Business opportunities arising from strategic location in heart of West Africa. Niger and Senegal rivers have irrigation and HEP potential.

WEAKNESSES
Serious poverty and underdevelopment. Land-locked status and vast size of country present considerable communications problems. Drought-prone climate.

EXPORTS

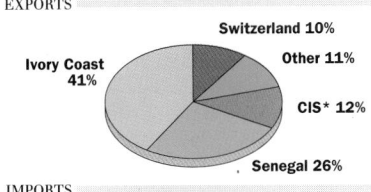

Switzerland 10%
Ivory Coast 41%
Other 11%
CIS* 12%
Senegal 26%

IMPORTS

Netherlands 7%
Senegal 8%
Other 44%
Ivory Coast 18%
France 23%

***Village near Bandiagara.** These low, broken hills typical of the east and southeast of Mali are the homeland of the Dogon people.*

RESOURCES

 214m kwh (capacity 90,000 kw)   Not an oil producer and has no refineries

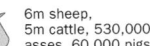 6m sheep, 5m cattle, 530,000 asses, 60,000 pigs   Gold, salt, marble, phosphate, limestone, iron, bauxite

Gold deposits are now being mined, and prospecting is under way for tungsten, diamonds and oil. The exploitation of other natural resources is hampered by Mali's poor infrastructure and land-locked situation. Almost all electricity is generated by hydroelectric power from the Selingue Dam on the Niger. When a second dam comes into operation, there should be a surplus.

ENVIRONMENT

 3% partially protected   New government takes environmental matters seriously

The 1983 drought destroyed herds and accelerated desertification and deforestation. The Selingue Dam seriously affects the levels of the Niger River, even in years of good rainfall.

MEDIA

 The constitution of 1992 guarantees freedom of expression. There are no restrictions on political reporting

PUBLISHING AND BROADCAST MEDIA

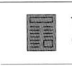 There is 1 daily newspaper, *L'Essor – La Voix du Peuple*, published by the government

 1 state-owned service   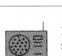 1 state-owned service

Even before the coup, previously rigid controls had begun to be relaxed. The militant campaigning of the privately-owned press in early 1991 was a significant factor in the overthrow of the Traoré regime.

CRIME

 Mali does not publish prison figures   Crime is rising slowly

Crime is not particularly prevalent compared with some other countries in the region, owing to strong family ties and the relative lack of urbanization. In towns, robbery, juvenile delinquency and smuggling are problems.

EDUCATION

 32%

Education in Mali is based on the French system. There are only 1000 students in higher education, a low figure for the region.

HEALTH

 1 per 22,835 people   Malaria, pneumonia, parasitic and diarrheal diseases

An estimated 50% of the health budget is spent on an area inhabited by just 10% of the population.

WEALTH

 Kindergarten teacher, 27,500 CFA francs per month; electrician, 101,500 CFA francs per month

CONSUMER GOODS OWNERSHIP

VCR and PC ownership is limited to a small elite

Per 1000 population: 39, 3, 2

Poverty is widespread. Malians disapprove of flaunted wealth and public ostentation is rare.

WORLD RANKING

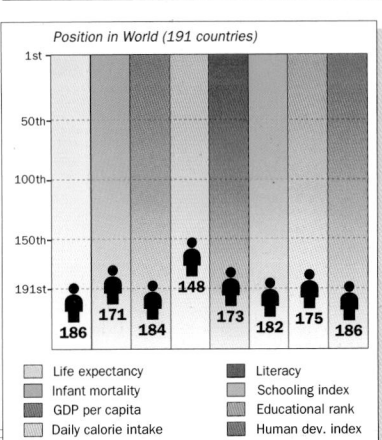

Position in World (191 countries)

186, 171, 184, 148, 173, 182, 175, 186

- Life expectancy
- Infant mortality
- GDP per capita
- Daily calorie intake
- Literacy
- Schooling index
- Educational rank
- Human dev. index

M

MALTA

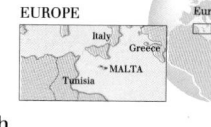

EUROPE

OFFICIAL NAME: Republic of Malta   **CAPITAL:** Valletta
POPULATION: 356,000   **CURRENCY:** Maltese lira   **OFFICIAL LANGUAGES:** Maltese and English

THE MALTESE ARCHIPELAGO is strategically located, lying midway between Europe and North Africa. Controlled throughout its history by successive colonial powers, Malta gained independence from the UK in 1964. The islands are mainly low-lying, with rocky coastlines; only Malta, Gozo and Kemmuna are inhabited. Tourism is Malta's chief source of income, with an influx of tourists each year over two times the islands' population.

CLIMATE

WEATHER CHART

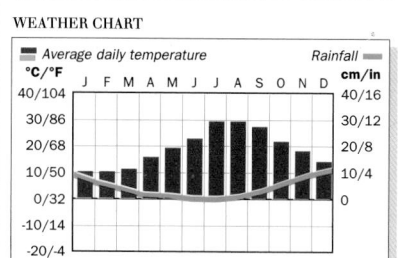

The climate is very similar to that of Greece – with at least six hours of sunshine a day, even in winter.

COMMUNICATIONS

 Luqa International
1.9m passengers

 837 ships
17.93m dwt

THE TRANSPORT NETWORK

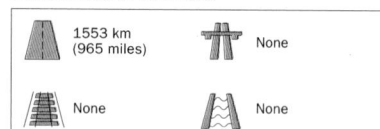

| 1553 km (965 miles) | None |
| None | None |

A new terminal with an annual capacity of 2.5 million passengers was recently opened at Luqa airport. The main external sea route is to Sicily. In summer, there is a five-minute helicopter link between the islands of Malta and Gozo, in addition to regular ferry and hovercraft services. There are regular buses on both islands.

Traditionally painted **luzzus** *at St Julian's harbour. The fish caught are now only for domestic and tourist consumption.*

TOURISM

871,675 visitors   Up 5% in 1990

MAIN OVERSEAS ARRIVALS

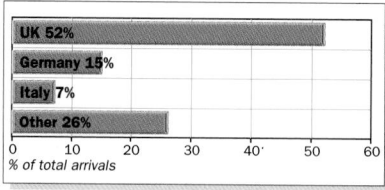

UK 52%
Germany 15%
Italy 7%
Other 26%

% of total arrivals

Tourism in Malta is a booming industry, accounting for 30% of GNP. In addition to Malta's beaches and scenery, the government is keen to promote the historical attractions of Mdina and Valletta. Development on the quieter island of Gozo is being limited to luxury-grade hotels.

PEOPLE

Maltese, English   1266 people per km²

THE URBAN/RURAL POPULATION SPLIT

87%   13%

RELIGIOUS PERSUASION

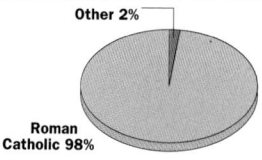

Other 2%

Roman Catholic 98%

Malta's population has been subject over the centuries to diverse Arabic, Sicilian, Norman, Spanish, English and Italian influences. Today, many young Maltese go abroad to find work, especially to the USA and Australia; opportunities for them on the islands are few.

The Maltese are staunch Roman Catholics, on a percentage basis more so than virtually any other nation. The remainder are mainly Anglicans, who are included within the diocese of Gibraltar. Divorce is illegal.

POLITICS

1997   President Censu (Vincent) Tabone

THE STATE OF THE PARTIES

House of Representatives 65 members

52% NP   48% MLP

NP = Nationalist Party   **MLP** Malta Labour Party

The Nationalists, led by Dr Fenech Adami, came to power in 1987 after 16 years of Labour rule. Adami's subsequent re-election to a second term of office in 1992 was largely due to a rise in living standards and economic growth. The Maltese were also reluctant to return to the divisive politics of the past.

Under Labour, politics was shaped by the leadership of the charismatic Dom Mintoff, who championed state control of industry and a strategy of international non-alignment. The Nationalists retained the non-aligned policy and wrote it into the constitution. In 1990, they succeeded in sealing a three-way accord between government, unions and businesses, under which wages are agreed in line with inflation.

The opposition is now led by Dr Alfred Sant, a leading Maltese writer and Harvard MBA, and Labour's traditional links with the unions have been diluted. The main current political issue is Malta's application for membership of the EU.

WORLD AFFAIRS

ECE   Comm   NAM   CSCE   CE

Malta is optimistic that it will gain entry into the EU; a formal application was made in 1990. All legislation is now drafted to EU regulations and old measures are being updated in accordance with them. Membership is expected to bring significant economic benefits; already, an estimated 75% of trade is with EU nations.

Closer links with Europe have to be balanced with Malta's traditional association with the Arab world and North Africa. Relations with Libya and the Gaddafi regime are good, though not as close as under the Labour government of Prime Minister Mintoff in the 1970s. However, a friendship treaty was recently signed between the two countries. Malta also maintains close commercial links with the CIS and China.

M

MALTA

Total Area : 320 sq. km
(124 sq. miles)

POPULATION   LAND HEIGHT

- over 10 000
- under 10 000

200m/656ft

Sea Level

AID

 $21m (receipts)

  Aid receipts remain constant

Malta receives economic assistance under an agreement with the EU. The UK is the main bilateral source of aid.

DEFENCE

 $27.7m

 Up 19% in 1992

The 1650-strong Maltese army, advised by the Libyans in the 1980s, now receives training and equipment from Italy, Germany and the UK.

ECONOMICS

$2.6bn   0.39 Maltese liri

SCORE CARD

- ❏ WORLD GNP RANKING........................131st
- ❏ GNP PER CAPITA $7298
- ❏ BALANCE OF PAYMENTS...................$−55.4m
- ❏ INFLATION 2.5%
- ❏ UNEMPLOYMENT...................................3.7%

STRENGTHS

Tourism and naval dockyards. Schemes to attract foreign high-tech industry. Offshore banking potential. Strategic position between Europe and Africa, on the main Mediterranean shipping lines.

WEAKNESSES

Lack of diversification at present. Cut-price competition from Africa and Asia in traditional textile industry. Need to import almost all requirements.

EXPORTS

IMPORTS

RESOURCES

 1.1bn kwh (capacity 250,000 kw)

 Not an oil producer and has no refineries

101,000 pigs, 21,000 cattle, 6000 sheep

Stone, sand

Electrical generating capacity is due to increase with the completion of a new 360 MW-capacity power station in 1997. Malta is dependent on desalination plants for most of its water supply. All oil has to be imported.

ENVIRONMENT

  None

 Controls on hotel developments

The main environmental concern is linked to the tourist industry. A lack of planning controls in the 1970s was responsible for unsightly beach developments. These are now tightly controlled, particularly on Gozo.

MEDIA

 Freedom of expression guaranteed under constitution

PUBLISHING AND BROADCAST MEDIA

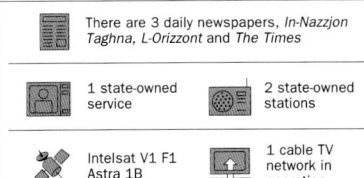

There are 3 daily newspapers, *In-Nazzjon Taghna*, *L-Orizzont* and *The Times*

1 state-owned service

2 state-owned stations

Intelsat V1 F1 Astra 1B

1 cable TV network in operation

The Maltese press is largely politically-orientated. Two of the three main press groups are affiliated to the NP and MLP; one is independent.

CRIME

 221 prisoners

 Up 3% in 1990

Crime rates are low compared to those on the European mainland. There has, however, been an increase in drugs transshipment and associated crimes.

CHRONOLOGY

Malta was dominated in turn by the Phoenicians, Carthaginians, Greeks and Romans; it later came under the rule of the Arabs, Norman Sicily, Spain, France and, finally, Britain.

- ❏ **1947** Internal self-government.
- ❏ **1964** Full independence from UK.
- ❏ **1971** MLP return to power, under Dom Mintoff.
- ❏ **1987** Nationalists, under Fenech Adami, in government.

EDUCATION

 96%

Spending on education is equal to 3.6% of GDP. There are 2500 full-time students at the University of Malta in Valletta.

HEALTH

 1 per 453 people

 Cerebrovascular and heart diseases, cancers, diabetes

Malta has six state-run hospitals. Around 7% of government expenditure is allocated to health services.

WEALTH

 Income per capita is below the European average

CONSUMER GOODS OWNERSHIP

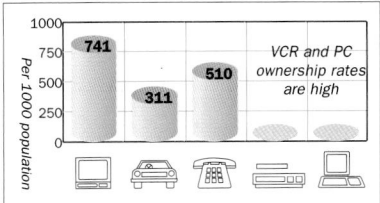

VCR and PC ownership rates are high

Remittances from Maltese working abroad are an important source of income for many island families.

WORLD RANKING

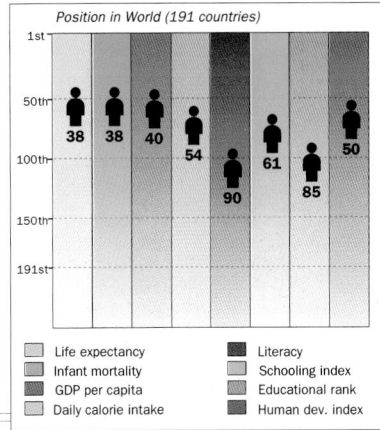

Position in World (191 countries)

Life expectancy
Infant mortality
GDP per capita
Daily calorie intake
Literacy
Schooling index
Educational rank
Human dev. index

M

363

MARSHALL ISLANDS

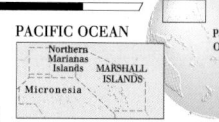

OFFICIAL NAME: Republic of the Marshall Islands **CAPITAL:** Majuro **POPULATION:** 48,000
CURRENCY: US dollar **OFFICIAL LANGUAGES:** English and Marshallese

THE MARSHALL ISLANDS comprise a group of 34 widely scattered atolls in the central Pacific Ocean. These include the largest atolls in the world, formed from low coral islands with sandy beaches. Formerly under US rule as part of the Trust Territory of the Pacific Islands, the islands became self-governing in 1979. The economy is almost entirely dependent on US aid and the rent paid by the USA for its missile base on Kwajalein atoll.

Ebeye Island in the Marshalls. Population pressures have led to the disappearance of most tree and grass cover on the island.

CLIMATE

WEATHER CHART

The climate is tropical oceanic. Temperatures show little seasonal variation, averaging around 30°C.

COMMUNICATIONS

✈ **Majuro Intl**   ⛴ Has no fleet

THE TRANSPORT NETWORK

Surfaced roads only on larger islands		None	
None		None	

The transport system is limited, although there is some inter-island shipping. Regular scheduled flights connect ten of the atolls.

TOURISM

🧳 7000 visitors   Little change from year to year

MAIN OVERSEAS ARRIVALS

The Marshall Islands does not publish tourism figures by country of origin

% of total arrivals

There are few hotels or amenities for tourists, though outlying islands have the potential of unspoilt beaches. Those who visit are mainly Japanese and American; many are war veterans.

PEOPLE

 Marshallese, English, Japanese, German   270 people per km²

THE URBAN/RURAL POPULATION SPLIT

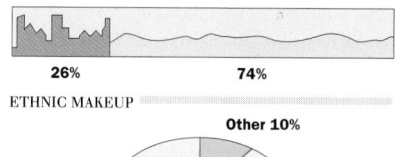

26%   **74%**

ETHNIC MAKEUP

Other 10%

Micronesian 90%

Of the 34 atolls making up the Marshall Islands, 24 are inhabited. Majuro, the capital and commercial centre, is home to almost half of the population, many of whom live in its overcrowded slums. The other main centre of population is Ebeye, where tensions are high due to poor living conditions. Most of Ebeye's inhabitants were forcefully relocated from Kwajalein in 1947 to make way for a US missile tracking, testing and interception base; many still travel back to Kwajalein daily to work at the base. Life on the outlying islands is still centred around subsistence agriculture and fishing. Society is traditionally matrilineal.

MARSHALL ISLANDS

Total Area : 181 sq. km (70 sq. miles)

LAND HEIGHT

■ 100m/328ft
— Sea Level

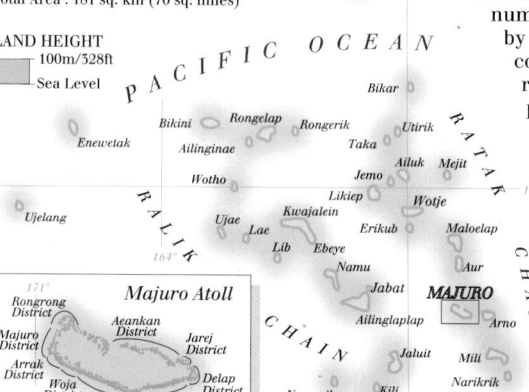

POLITICS

🗳 1995   👥 President Amata Kabua

THE STATE OF THE PARTIES

Parliament (Nitijela) 33 members

The 33 members are elected from 25 districts

Council of Chiefs 12 members

All 12 members are high chiefs

Politics is traditionally dominated by chiefs. President Amata Kabua, who has been in power since self-government began in 1979, is the islands' high chief. Members of his family hold several important government posts. There are two main political groupings, the ruling RMI and the opposition Ralik-Ratak Democratic Party. The main political issue is the islands' continuing inability to achieve financial self-sufficiency. Their economy is almost totally dependent on US aid. Discussion has centred recently on a number of projects proposed by foreign states, which could bring in additional revenue. These include a proposal for a plant to generate electricity by burning used tyres and a project to use toxic waste to build a causeway on Kwajalein. The likely environmental impact of such projects is an important issue.

M

WORLD AFFAIRS

From 1947 to 1979, the islands were controlled by the USA as part of the Trust Territory of the Pacific Islands, and US influence remains strong. Under the terms of the Compact of Free Association signed in 1983, the USA is to pay $1 billion in aid over 15 years. In return, the USA has gained control of Kwajalein at a fixed rent. In addition, no further claims for compensation by victims of US nuclear testing between 1946 and 1958 will be considered.

AID

 $39m from USA   Fairly constant from year to year

Aid from the USA accounts for around two thirds of the islands' revenue. Australia and Taiwan also provide some assistance.

DEFENCE

 USA responsible for defence   Not applicable

There is no defence force. All defence is provided by the USA under the Compact of Free Association. The USA does not have offensive weapons sited in the Marshalls, but its navy regularly patrols the region.

ECONOMICS

 $63m   US dollar

SCORE CARD

❏ WORLD GNP RANKING	188th
❏ GNP PER CAPITA	$1313
❏ BALANCE OF PAYMENTS	Deficit
❏ INFLATION	Volatile
❏ UNEMPLOYMENT	Widespread underemployment

STRENGTHS
Aid from the USA, on which the islands are almost totally dependent. Strategic refusal by US to allow them to become impoverished, so that no other foreign power can gain influence. Copra.

WEAKNESSES
Dependence on imports, which are 11 times greater than exports. All fuel has to be imported. Vulnerability to storm damage. Large state sector employing 75% of workers.

EXPORTS/IMPORTS

The Marshall Islands' main trading partners are the USA and Japan

RESOURCES

 Electricity is provided by small diesel generators   Not an oil producer and has no refineries

 200 tonnes   Phosphates

There are few known strategic resources. Exploratory tests have revealed some high-grade phosphate deposits, but not in economically viable quantities. Small diesel generators are used for electricity production.

ENVIRONMENT

 None   Plans for toxic waste dump

Between 1946 and 1958, Bikini and Enewetak atolls were the site of a series of US nuclear military tests. Islanders were exposed to radiation and both atolls were rendered uninhabitable. The residents of Enewetak were allowed to return in 1980, following some decontamination of the land. The USA has now paid out over $101 million to victims of nuclear testing. In recent years, the Marshall Islands have been proposed as a potential toxic waste dump by both the USA and Japan. Discussions have also taken place on creating landfill sites, to take US household refuse.

MEDIA

 The media is generally free of censorship

PUBLISHING AND BROADCAST MEDIA

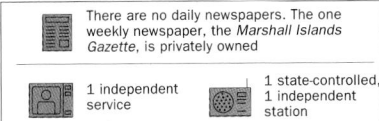

There are no daily newspapers. The one weekly newspaper, the *Marshall Islands Gazette*, is privately owned

1 independent service   1 state-controlled, 1 independent station

Radio is the main source of information in the Marshalls. There is also a subscription-only TV service. The US personnel stationed on Kwajalein have their own TV and radio stations.

CRIME

 The Marshalls does not publish prison figures   Little change from year to year

Crime levels are generally low; however, the rate is up on Ebeye. Outlying islands are crime-free.

EDUCATION

 91%

Education is based on the US model. The number of secondary school graduates exceeds the availability of suitable employment in the Marshall Islands. Many go on to university in the USA. Small church institutions in the USA often subsidize students.

CHRONOLOGY

Following a period under Spanish rule, the Marshall Islands became a German protectorate in 1885. Japan took possession of the islands at the outbreak of the First World War. They were transferred to US control in 1945.

- ❏ **1946** US government begins a programme of nuclear testing.
- ❏ **1947** UN Trust Territory of the Pacific established.
- ❏ **1961** Kwajalein becomes US army missile range, the target for ICBMs fired from California.
- ❏ **1979** Constitution approved in referendum. Government set up.
- ❏ **1986** Compact of Free Association with US operational.
- ❏ **1990** US control formally ended.

HEALTH

 1 per 2076 people   Respiratory, heart and diarrheal diseases

Medical facilities are rudimentary. Complex operations are performed in hospitals on Hawaii. Levels of malnutrition are high.

WEALTH

 Most Marshall Islanders live a subsistence existence

CONSUMER GOODS OWNERSHIP

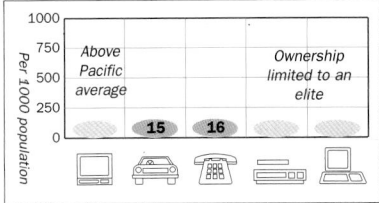

Wealth disparities are small. Very few citizens can afford luxuries such as air conditioning and cars.

WORLD RANKING

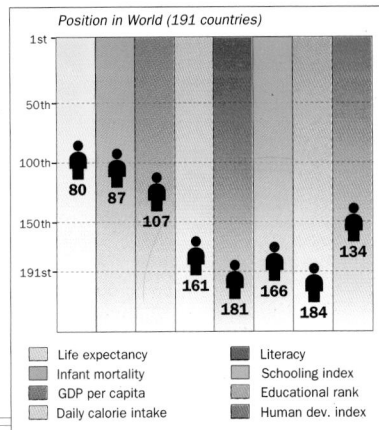

M

MAURITANIA

OFFICIAL NAME: Islamic Republic of Mauritania   **CAPITAL:** Nouakchott
POPULATION: 2.1 million   **CURRENCY:** Ouguiya   **OFFICIAL LANGUAGE:** French

NORTH AFRICA

LOCATED IN NORTHWEST AFRICA, Mauritania is a member of both the OAU and the Arab League. Formerly a French colony, the country has taken a strongly Arab direction since 1964; today, it is the Maures who control political life and dominate the minority black population. The Sahara extends across two thirds of Mauritania's territory. The only productive land is that drained by the Senegal River in the south and southwest.

CLIMATE

WEATHER CHART

The dusty Saharan *harmattan* wind often aggravates the very hot, dry conditions. Some rain falls in the south.

COMMUNICATIONS

 Nouakchott   2 ships 3000 dwt

THE TRANSPORT NETWORK

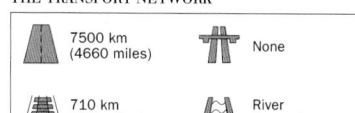

| 7500 km (4660 miles) | None |
| 710 km (441 miles) | River Senegal |

The transport system is limited and unevenly developed. There are two major roads, but shifting sands mean they require constant maintenance.

TOURISM

 12,000   No significant change from year to year

MAIN OVERSEAS ARRIVALS

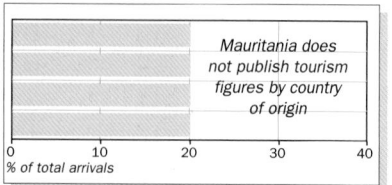
Mauritania does not publish tourism figures by country of origin

% of total arrivals

There are few tourists apart from desert safari enthusiasts. The more mountainous areas are especially dramatic, but access is difficult. Nouakchott has some hotels.

PEOPLE

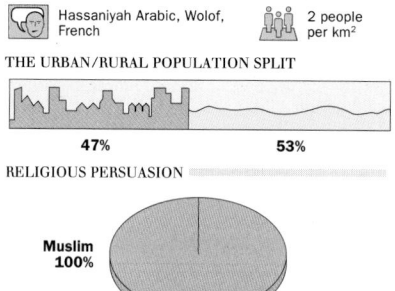
Hassaniyah Arabic, Wolof, French   2 people per km²

THE URBAN/RURAL POPULATION SPLIT

47%   53%

RELIGIOUS PERSUASION

Muslim 100%

The politically-dominant Maures make up about one third of the population. The black population is composed of the Havalin, the Senegalese peoples and the Tukolor, Peulh and Wolof groups. Ethnic tension centres on the oppression of blacks by Maures. The old black bourgeoisie has now been superseded by a Maurish class; tens of thousands of blacks are estimated to be in slavery. Ethnic tension came to a head in 1989, when 200,000 Maures fled from Senegal. There were attacks on Senegalese in Mauritania and many fled or were deported to refugee camps along the Senegal River.
    Family solidarity among nomads is particularly strong.

MAURITANIA

Total Area : 1 025 520 sq. km (395 953 sq. miles)

POPULATION
- ⊙ over 500 000
- ● over 10 000
- • under 10 000

LAND HEIGHT
- 500m/1640ft
- 200m/656ft
- Sea Level

POLITICS

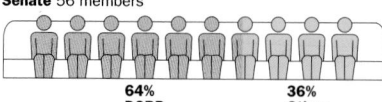
Lower House 1997   President Col Maaouya
Upper House 1998   Ould Sid'Ahmed Taya

THE STATE OF THE PARTIES

National Assembly 79 members

1% RDNU

85% DSRP   1% MPR   10% Other

DSRP = Democratic and Social Republican Party
MPR = Mauritanian Party for Renewal   **RDNU** = Rally for Democracy and National Unity
Senate 56 members

64% DSRP   36% Other

3 members are chosen to represent the interests of Mauritanians abroad

In 1991, partly because of pressure from Western aid donors, Mauritania officially returned to multiparty democracy. However, the 1992 presidential elections simply returned the incumbent military ruler, President Maaouya Ould Taya, to power. General elections were held but were boycotted by the opposition parties. These are mainly Maure-led; the blacks of the south support exiled parties, such as the Dakar-based liberation group, FLAM. The issue of ethnic relations is the central political problem, especially since a 1987 coup plot, which caused the blacks' base in the army to collapse.

M

WORLD AFFAIRS

OAU | AL | Ecowas | AMU | GATT

Mauritania has to maintain a delicate balance in relations with sub-Saharan Africa and the Arab world; as a result, it belongs to both ECOWAS and the Arab Maghreb Union. Relations with neighbouring Senegal have improved since the conflicts of 1989.

AID

 $208m (receipts)   Up 3% in 1991

France, Germany, the IMF, OPEC and Iraq are all donors. Most aid is used for development projects, such as the EU-funded Trans-Mauritanian Highway.

DEFENCE

 Mauritania does not publish defence budget figures   Not applicable

The 11,000-strong military is a strain on Mauritania's limited budget. Much arms procurement is still from France, but some is now from the Arab world.

ECONOMICS

 $1.1bn   122.98 ouguiyas

SCORE CARD

❏ WORLD GNP RANKING	154th
❏ GNP PER CAPITA	$530
❏ BALANCE OF PAYMENTS	$–125m
❏ INFLATION	9.8%
❏ UNEMPLOYMENT	21%

STRENGTHS

Iron from the Cominor mine at Zouérat. Largest gypsum deposits in the world. Copper, yet to be properly exploited. Offshore fishing among the best in West Africa.

WEAKNESSES

'Debt-distressed', with a debt of nearly $2 billion – a legacy of its move to leave the Franc Zone. Poor land – two thirds is desert. Very hot, dry climate.

EXPORTS
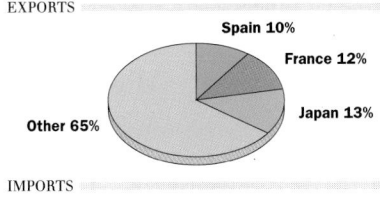
Spain 10%
France 12%
Japan 13%
Other 65%

IMPORTS

Senegal 8%
Spain 13%
Other 63%
France 16%

Mauritania's extreme aridity means that only 1% of the land is arable. Two thirds of the country is part of the Sahara desert; sparse vegetation over the rest supports some livestock.

RESOURCES

 140m kwh (capacity 110,000 kw)   Not an oil producer and has no refineries

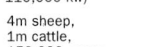 4m sheep, 1m cattle, 150,000 asses   Iron, gypsum, copper, gold, phosphates, yttrium

Iron, which in the 1960s brought economic profitability, continues to be exploited, despite low prices on the world market. Electricity generation has expanded rapidly since the late 1960s, from 38.4m kwh in 1967 to 245m kwh in 1989, reflecting the growing needs of the minerals industries. Phosphates have been found near the Senegal River.

ENVIRONMENT

 2% (0.2% partially protected)   Desertification is the major problem

The chief environmental problem in Mauritania is that of the encroaching Sahara desert, a situation worsened by the droughts of 1973 and 1983, which caused widespread loss of grazing land. The consequent exodus of people away from the land has led to Nouakchott's population increasing from 20,000 in 1960 to over 500,000 today.

MEDIA

 There are still instances of censorship

PUBLISHING AND BROADCAST MEDIA

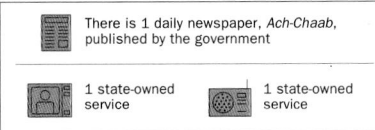
There is 1 daily newspaper, *Ach-Chaab*, published by the government

1 state-owned service   1 state-owned service

French-language press and radio is increasingly under pressure from militant Maures, who are eager to promote the use of Arabic.

CRIME

 Mauritania does not publish prison figures   Crime levels are stable

The main problems are smuggling and robbery. Levels of violence are lower than the West African average.

EDUCATION

 34%

Arabic has been compulsory in all schools since 1988, though this has met resistance from blacks. The University of Nouakchott has over 3000 students.

HEALTH

 1 per 9547 people   Diarrheal and respiratory diseases, influenza, tuberculosis

Historic regional inequalities persist and the best facilities are in the capital. The overall level of care is on a par with neighbouring states.

WEALTH

 Slavery officially became illegal in 1980, but much *de facto* slavery survives

CONSUMER GOODS OWNERSHIP

VCR and PC ownership is limited to a small elite
23   6   6

The ruling Maures form the wealthiest sector. Wealthy Maures travel to Mecca to perform the *haj* (Muslim pilgrimage).

WORLD RANKING

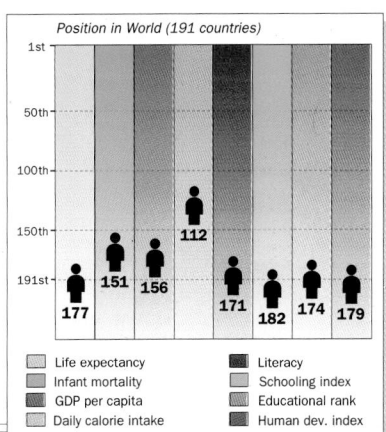
Position in World (191 countries)

177 | 151 | 156 | 112 | 171 | 182 | 174 | 179

- Life expectancy
- Infant mortality
- GDP per capita
- Daily calorie intake
- Literacy
- Schooling index
- Educational rank
- Human dev. index

M

MAURITIUS

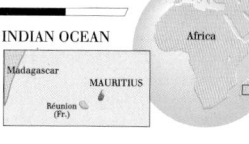

OFFICIAL NAME: Mauritius **CAPITAL:** Port Louis
POPULATION: 1.1 million **CURRENCY:** Mauritian rupee **OFFICIAL LANGUAGE:** English

THE ISLANDS THAT make up Mauritius lie in the Indian Ocean east of Madagascar. The principal island, from which the country takes its name, is of volcanic origin and surrounded by coral reefs. The outer islands, 500 km to the north, are Rodrigues, the Agalega Islands and the Cargados Carajos Shoals. Mauritius has enjoyed considerable economic success following recent industrial diversification and the expansion of its tourist industry.

CLIMATE

WEATHER CHART

The climate is subtropical and humid. December to March are the hottest and wettest months. Tropical cyclones are an occasional threat at this time.

COMMUNICATIONS

Sir Seewoosagur Ramgoolam Intl
870,000 passengers

8 ships
166,600 dwt

THE TRANSPORT NETWORK

1816 km
(1128 miles)

None

None

None

Roads are extensive, but often congested. Plans exist for a monorail link between Port Louis and Curepipe.

TOURISM

 870,000 visitors   Down 1% in 1991

MAIN OVERSEAS ARRIVALS

| Réunion 25% |
| France 18% |
| South Africa 14% |
| Other 43% |

% of total arrivals

Tourism has expanded rapidly in the past decade. Spectacular beaches, water sports and big game fishing are major attractions. However, many new hotels are usually only half full.

PEOPLE

French Creole, Hindi, Urdu, Tamil, Chinese, English, French

533 people per km²

THE URBAN/RURAL POPULATION SPLIT

41%   59%

RELIGIOUS PERSUASION

Protestant 2%   Other 3%
Muslim 17%
Hindu 52%
Roman Catholic 26%

The majority of the population are the descendants of indentured labourers brought over from India in the 19th century. Creoles make up 27% of the population, while 3% are of Chinese origin. The wealthiest group is the small minority of Mauritians of French descent, who control much of business, including the sugar cane industry.

POLITICS

1996   President Veerasamy Ringadoo

THE STATE OF THE PARTIES

National Assembly 71 members   MLP/PMS-D 5%

47% MSM   42% MMM   3% MTD   3% OPR

MSM = Mauritius Socialist Movement   **MMM** = Mauritius Militant Movement   **MLP/PMS-D** Mauritius Labour Party/ Mauritius Social Democratic Party   **MTD** = Democratic Labour Movement   **OPR** = Organization of the People of Rodrigues

Mauritius became a republic in 1992. Politics is characterized by coalition governments, and is largely based around personalities. There is little ideological difference between the main parties. Government is currently in the hands of an MSM–MMM coalition. The split in the MMM at the end of 1993, with one faction under the influential former finance minister, Paul Bérenger, defecting to the opposition, is a threat to political stability.

WORLD AFFAIRS

 Comm   OAU   ACP   ECA   GATT

Mauritius is a member of the Commonwealth, but it is also seeking to develop relations with French-speaking countries. In 1993, it hosted the fifth annual summit of francophone nations. Links with South Africa are also important.

RODRIGUES

Port Mathurin
Mont Limon 396m
Grand Montagne
Plaine Corail
Petite Butte
(continuation on same scale)

MAURITIUS

Total Area : 1860 sq. km (718 sq. miles)

LAND HEIGHT

500m/1640ft
200m/656ft
Sea Level

POPULATION

over 100 000
over 50 000
over 10 000
under 10 000

0   10 km
0   10 miles

M

AID

 $67m (receipts)   Down 25% in 1991

Aid is predominantly bilateral, with France and the UK as the main donors. Mauritius also receives aid from the EU, under the Lomé Convention, and other international organizations. A five-year conservation programme was initiated in 1990 with assistance from the World Bank. The Bank has also promised $53 million towards the development of Port Louis as a free port.

DEFENCE

 No defence forces; police unit maintains internal security   Not applicable

Mauritius has no defence forces. There is, however, a special police unit to ensure internal security. Expenditure on policing accounts for 1.4% of total government spending.

ECONOMICS

 $3bn   18.18 Mauritian rupees

SCORE CARD

- ❑ WORLD GNP RANKING.........................125th
- ❑ GNP PER CAPITA $2727
- ❑ BALANCE OF PAYMENTS.......................$–41m
- ❑ INFLATION 4.6%
- ❑ UNEMPLOYMENT ....Low

STRENGTHS

Economic growth averaging 6% a year over last decade. Sugar industry, which accounts for 30% of export earnings. Export Processing Zone (EPZ), especially for clothing manufacture. Tourism, the third largest foreign exchange earner. Highly educated workforce. Potential as offshore financial centre now being developed.

WEAKNESSES

Vulnerability to fluctuations in world prices for sugar. 75% of food requirements imported. Occasional cyclones mean few crops other than sugar can be grown. Remoteness. Lack of strategic resources.

EXPORTS

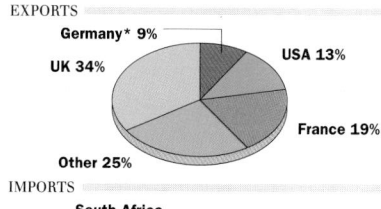

Germany* 9%
UK 34%
USA 13%
France 19%
Other 25%

IMPORTS

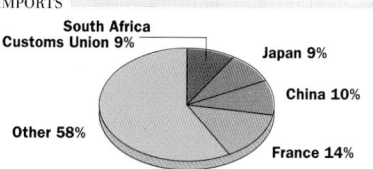

South Africa Customs Union 9%
Japan 9%
China 10%
France 14%
Other 58%

Villagers at a water source in the centre of Mauritius island. Mauritius' main rivers are used for hydro-power generation.

RESOURCES

 770m kwh (capacity 313,000 kw)   Not an oil producer and has no refineries

 34,000 cattle, 10,000 pigs, 7,000 sheep   None

Mauritius is heavily dependent on imported oil supplies. The government has put considerable investment into developing alternative energy schemes, including hydroelectric power generation. Power stations fuelled by bagasse (a by-product of the sugar industry) are now also in operation.

ENVIRONMENT

 2% (0.1% partially protected)   New government measures to restrict development

Rapid industrialization and unchecked hotel building have caused environmental problems. Coral reefs are under threat from both coral sand mining and the discharging of untreated sewage into the sea.

MEDIA

 Freedom of expression is guaranteed under the constitution. Foreign satellite TV broadcasts are subject to government approval

PUBLISHING AND BROADCAST MEDIA

 There are 8 daily newspapers. The *Sun*, *L'Express* and *Le Mauricien* have the largest circulations

2 independent stations   2 independent stations

Mauritius has an active press, subject to few regulations and with a wide readership. Newspapers are published in English, French, Creole, Hindi, Chinese and Tamil. However, opposition parties complain that TV and radio broadcasts are consistently biased towards the government.

CRIME

 2145 prisoners   Overall crime rates fairly constant from year to year

Crime rates on the main island are fairly low. There has been a small increase in thefts in the towns. Outlying islands are virtually crime-free.

EDUCATION

 83%

Educational provision is good and the literacy rate for Mauritians under the age of 30 is 95%. The University of Mauritius has 1800 students.

HEALTH

 1 per 1233 people   Circulatory and respiratory diseases, cancers

Free health care is universally available. There are 14 state hospitals and six private clinics.

WEALTH

 Sugar plantation worker, 13 Mauritian rupees per hour; journalist, 7045 Mauritian rupees per month

CONSUMER GOODS OWNERSHIP

VCR and PC ownership is limted

215   39   71

French-descended hotel and plantation owners are the wealthiest group. Government employees are well paid.

WORLD RANKING

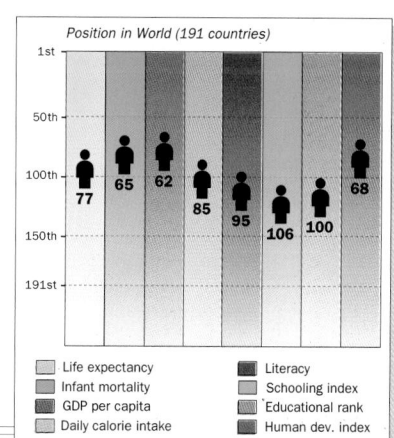

Position in World (191 countries)

77   65   62   85   95   106   100   68

Life expectancy / Infant mortality / GDP per capita / Daily calorie intake / Literacy / Schooling index / Educational rank / Human dev. index

M

MEXICO

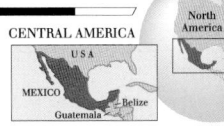

OFFICIAL NAME: United Mexican States **CAPITAL:** Mexico City
POPULATION: 88.2 million **CURRENCY:** Mexican new peso **OFFICIAL LANGUAGE:** Spanish

INCREASINGLY CONSIDERED a part of North rather than Central America, Mexico straddles the southern end of the continent. Coastal plains along its Pacific and Atlantic seaboards rise into an arid central plateau, which includes the world's biggest conurbation, Mexico City, built on the site of the Aztec capital, Tenochtitlán. Colonized by the Spanish for its silver mines, Mexico achieved independence in 1836. In the 'Epic Revolution' of 1910–1920, in which 250,000 died, much of modern Mexico's structure was established. In 1994, Mexico signed the North American Free Trade Agreement (NAFTA).

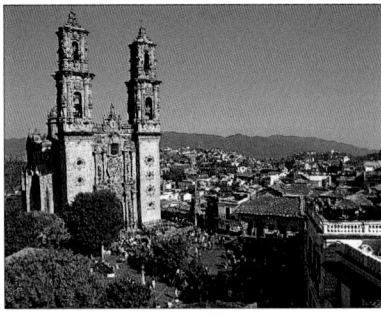

The cathedral of Santa Prisa at Taxco in Cuernavaca. It was built in Spanish chirrigueresque style in the 1740s.

CLIMATE

WEATHER CHART

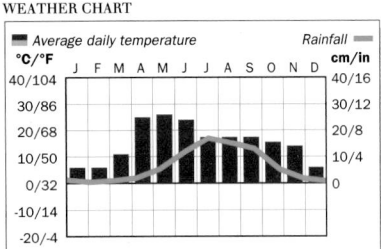

The plateau and high mountains are warm for much of the year. The Pacific coast has a tropical climate.

COMMUNICATIONS

 Benito Juárez International, Mexico City 3.83m passengers

79 ships 1.19m dwt

THE TRANSPORT NETWORK

237,057 km (147,300 miles)	3166 km (1967 miles)
20,366 km (12,655 miles)	2900 km (1802 miles)

The government has granted road building and operating concessions to private companies as part of its plans to upgrade the transport system. A $6-billion project to build four-lane motorways connecting major towns with beach resorts such as Acapulco and Puerto Vallarta is intended to increase tourism. The extensive rail network cannot be privatized without a change to the constitution.

TOURISM

6.7m visitors   Up 5% in 1993

MAIN OVERSEAS ARRIVALS

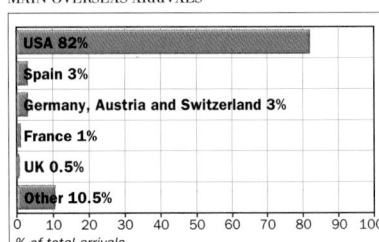

USA 82%
Spain 3%
Germany, Austria and Switzerland 3%
France 1%
UK 0.5%
Other 10.5%

0 10 20 30 40 50 60 70 80 90 100
% of total arrivals

Tourism is probably Mexico's largest employment sector. Visitors are drawn to excellent beach resorts like Acapulco on the Pacific, and the new resorts of the Peninsula de Yucatán on the Atlantic Coast. Mexico also has many Aztec and Maya World Heritage archaeological sites. Other major tourist attractions are the many Spanish colonial cities, like Morelia and Guadalajara, which have remained virtually intact since conquest. The government has made further tourism expansion a priority. A programme for improving the country's hotel infrastructure has been planned.

M

MEXICO

Total Area : 1 958 200 sq. km
(756 061 sq. miles)

LAND HEIGHT

- 3000m/9843ft
- 2000m/6562ft
- 1000m/3281ft
- 500m/1640ft
- 200m/656ft
- Sea Level

POPULATION

- ■ over 5 000 000
- ⊡ over 1 000 000
- ◉ over 500 000
- ◎ over 100 000
- ○ over 100 000

0   200 km
0   200 miles

PEOPLE

 Spanish, Nahuatl, Maya, Zapotec, Mixtec, Otomi, Totonac, Tzotzil, Tzeltal

 41 people per km²

THE URBAN/RURAL POPULATION SPLIT

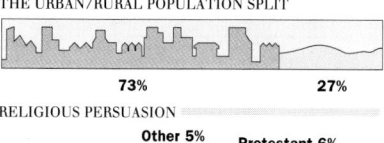

73%　　　27%

RELIGIOUS PERSUASION

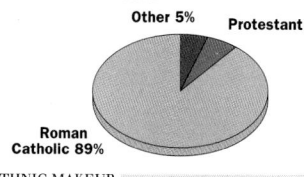

Other 5%　Protestant 6%

Roman Catholic 89%

ETHNIC MAKEUP

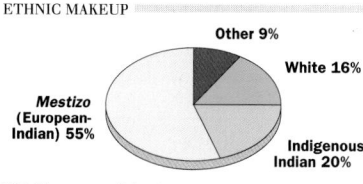

Other 9%

White 16%

Mestizo (European-Indian) 55%

Indigenous Indian 20%

Whilst most Mexicans are *mestizo*, it is Mexico's Indian culture which is promoted by the state. This obscures the fact that rural Indians are largely segregated from Hispanic society. The situation dates back to the Spanish colonial period and is accepted by both

POPULATION AGE BREAKDOWN

% of population by age group

	0–14	15–64		65+
	3.3%	3.4%	3.5%	3.8%	4.6%
	51.3%	49.7%	52.4%	59%	62.6%
	45.4%	46.9%	44.1%	37.2%	32.8%
	1960	1970	1980	1990	2000

groups. The small black community, which is concentrated mainly along the eastern coast, is well integrated.

Several hundred thousand refugees recently fled to Mexico to escape Central American civil wars. They were mainly housed in camps, which were set apart from Mexican society. They are now beginning to return home.

The most pressing problem in Mexico is poverty. The 1994 Chiapas *Zapatista* guerrilla rebellion was instigated by landless Indians who had little to lose by rebelling against the state.

As in much of Latin America, men retain their dominance in business and relatively few women take part in the political process.

POLITICS

 1994

 President Carlos Salinas de Gortari

THE STATE OF THE PARTIES

Federal Chamber of Deputies 500 members

64%	18%	8%	5%	3%	2%
PRI	PAN	PRD	PFCRN	PARM	Other

PRI = Institutional Revolutionary Party　**PAN** = National Action Party　**PRD** = Party of the Democratic Revolution
PFCRN = Cardenista National Reconstruction Party
PARM = Authentic Party of the Mexican Revolution

Senate 64 members

95%	3%	2%
PRI	PRD	PAN

Mexico is a multiparty democracy in name. In practice, the PRI retains power by tampering with elections. The PRI has its own intelligence service.

MAIN POLITICAL ISSUES

NAFTA
The North American Free Trade Agreement (NAFTA), signed with the USA and Canada, came into force in 1994; the transition to a tariff-free zone will take 15 years. US firms will be free to establish factories anywhere in Mexico. However, Mexican firms will no longer have the protection of high tariffs and will face tough competition from more desirable US products.

Land reform
For the first time since 1917, Mexicans are now able to buy private land. Many fear that agribusinesses will replace the state as the main landowner.

Poverty
Over 16% of Mexico's population are classified as living in 'extreme poverty'. The Chiapas rebellion of 1994 highlighted the poverty of many rural Indian communities.

PROFILE
The Institutional Revolutionary Party (PRI) dominates Mexican political life at every level. Since 1929, all the governments have been PRI, and all the presidents and almost all the state governors PRI members. The only real reins on PRI power are large private industrial groups, or multinationals operating in Mexico.

President Carlos Salinas de Gortari *has reinvigorated the* PRI, *the ruling party.*

Finance Minister *Pedro Aspe Armella, who is leading privatization policies.*

WORLD AFFAIRS

NAFTA | OAS | Opanal | ECLAC | GATT

Mexico's most important relationship is with the USA. The signing of the NAFTA pact has effectively bound together the economies of Mexico and the USA, and co-operation is likely to develop in other areas. The agreement should also bring more US-financed jobs to poorer regions, so reducing the large illegal migration of Mexicans to the USA every year. Most Mexicans support NAFTA; it is in the USA that there is opposition to the treaty, where workers fear losing jobs to Mexicans.

Relations with Central America could become difficult as a result. Many of Mexico's southern neighbours oppose the activities of the USA in the region. They were more comfortable with Mexico's previously independent line in foreign policy, which led it to recognize Castro's government in Cuba. Mexico's role as a mediator in Central America (it mediated in conflicts in El Salvador, Nicaragua and Guatemala) will, however, continue.

AID

 $183m (receipts)　 Up 31% in 1991

Mexico receives minimal aid, just $2 per capita a year. Some European and US NGOs provide assistance, particularly for literacy campaigns in poorer areas.

M

CHRONOLOGY

The Aztec kingdom of Montezuma II was defeated in war with the Spaniard, Hernán Cortés, in 1521. By 1546, the Spaniards had discovered major silver mines at Zacatecas. Mexico, then known as New Spain, became a key part of the Spanish colonial empire.

- ❏ **1808** Napoleon invades Spain.
- ❏ **1810** Fr Miguel Hidalgo leads abortive rising against Spanish.
- ❏ **1821** Spanish viceroy forced to leave by Agustín de Iturbide.
- ❏ **1822** Federal Republic established.
- ❏ **1823** Texas opened to US immigration.
- ❏ **1829** Spanish military expedition fails to regain control.
- ❏ **1836** The USA is the first country to recognize Mexico's independence. Spain then follows suit. Texas declares its independence from Mexico.
- ❏ **1846** War breaks out between Mexico and the USA.
- ❏ **1848** Treaty of Guadalupe Hidalgo. Mexico forced to cede almost half of its territory to the USA.

M

DEFENCE

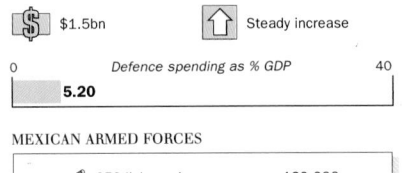

$1.5bn   Steady increase

Defence spending as % GDP   0 — 40

5.20

MEXICAN ARMED FORCES

350 light tanks	130,000 personnel
3 destroyers and 94 patrol boats	37,000 personnel
113 combat aircraft (9 F–5E)	8000 personnel
None	

The Mexican military has, on the whole, kept out of politics. Although large in regional terms, Mexico has no ambitions beyond its borders and the army acts to defend internal security. Most arms procurement is from the USA and France. Some members of the military are worried that the PRI's current privatization policies could target the military for cutbacks. In 1994, the role of controlling the border with the USA was handed over to the police.

The rebellion in Chiapas in 1994 was swiftly put down by the army, acting on PRI orders. Concern was expressed by Mexicans at the brutality of the action in which 100 *Zapatistas* died.

ECONOMICS

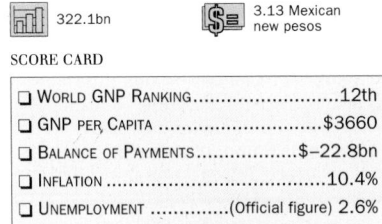

322.1bn   3.13 Mexican new pesos

SCORE CARD

- ❏ WORLD GNP RANKING.........................12th
- ❏ GNP PER CAPITA $3660
- ❏ BALANCE OF PAYMENTS.................$–22.8bn
- ❏ INFLATION 10.4%
- ❏ UNEMPLOYMENT ....(Official figure) 2.6%

ECONOMIC PERFORMANCE INDICATOR

EXPORTS

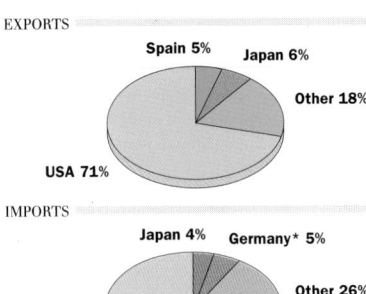

Spain 5%   Japan 6%   Other 18%   USA 71%

IMPORTS

Japan 4%   Germany* 5%   Other 26%   USA 65%

STRENGTHS

One of the world's largest oil producers, with substantial reserves. Extensive mineral resources – perhaps only 5% exploited to date. Inflation now under control. NAFTA agreement should boost the economy and aid stability.

WEAKNESSES

Population growth is outstripping job creation. Weak agriculture, with rural peoples lacking basic foodstuffs. Lack of development could turn Mexico into a cheap assembler of US products.

PROFILE

Traditionally the PRI ran almost every sector of the Mexican economy – around 160 major concerns. The debt crisis of the 1980s, however, forced a programme of privatization. To date,

banks, telecommunications and steel companies have been put up for sale.

Economic development in Mexico has been uneven, concentrated in Mexico City and the region up to the border with the USA. In the 1980s, US subsidiaries set up cheap assembly plants (*maquiladoras*) in towns close to the Río Grande which, despite slum-like living conditions, attracted a rush of migrants from the poor south. The government now hopes that one of the effects of NAFTA will be the spread of *maquiladoras* to poorer regions.

MEXICO : MAJOR BUSINESSES

Food processing   Petrochemicals
Vehicle assembly   Oil refining
  Computers
Tijuana   Silver mining
Ciudad Juárez   Electronics
Monterrey   Brewing
Reynosa   Textiles
Tampico
Durango   Minatitlán
Guadalajara
Salamanca   Mexico City

0 — 400 km
0 — 400 miles

* significant multinational ownership

RESOURCES

123bn kwh
(capacity 29.3m kw)

2.73m b/d
(reserves
51,298,000,000 bbl)

30.9m cattle,
16.2m pigs,
6.2m horses

Natural gas, silver,
copper, fluorite,
mercury, antimony

ELECTRICITY GENERATION

Hydro 21% (25.2bn kwh)

Thermal 73% (89.7bn kwh)

Nuclear 2% (2.9bn kwh)

Other 4% (4.7bn kwh)

0   20   40   60   80   100
% of total generation by type

Mexico is one of the largest oil exporters outside the OPEC cartel. Most oil production comes from offshore drilling platforms in the Gulf of Mexico. The industry is state-owned and state-run by PEMEX, the world's fifth largest oil company, employing 120,000. Whilst the state remains in control of the oil

MEXICO : LAND USE

Cropland
Forest
Pasture
Wetlands
Desert
Cotton - cash crop
Wheat
Cattle

0   400 km
0   400 miles

production industry (a change in the constitution is necessary to alter this), under NAFTA, US and Canadian companies will be able to break PEMEX's monopoly on supplying the domestic Mexican market. Despite its oil reserves, Mexico has embarked on a nuclear power programme. Its first plant was built at Laguna Verde.

ENVIRONMENT

5% (4% partially protected)

NAFTA's green measures might improve poor record

ENVIRONMENTAL TREATIES

No

Yes

Yes

Yes

Mexico's biggest ecological problem is probably the conurbation of Mexico City. Largely unplanned growth for its 20.2 million inhabitants and the absence of environmental controls on factories have contributed to perhaps the world's worst air quality levels.

Conditions along the Mexican border are a problem. *Maquiladora* have no environmental controls (making manufacturing there much cheaper than in the USA) and are usually surrounded by unsanitized slums. The few remaining tropical forests, in the southwest, are fast disappearing.

MEDIA

Free in practice, but power of government advertising a strong incentive against criticism. Several critical journalists have been murdered

PUBLISHING AND BROADCAST MEDIA

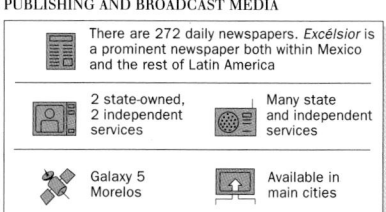

There are 272 daily newspapers. *Excélsior* is a prominent newspaper both within Mexico and the rest of Latin America

2 state-owned, 2 independent services

Many state and independent services

Galaxy 5 Morelos

Available in main cities

The state retains a tight grip on the media, frequently paying the press to run favourable front-page stories.

CRIME

Mexico does not publish prison figures

Down 2% in 1987

CRIME RATES

Mexico does not publish murder, theft or rape statistics

Northern Mexico is a centre for drugs transshipments to the USA. Guns are rife and minor incidents may end in shootings. Petty offences are usually settled by bribing the police. Mexico also has a relatively high rate of petty violence which accompanies crimes like robbery, car theft and burglary.

EDUCATION

87%

0   Education spending as % GNP   25
3.8%

THE EDUCATION SYSTEM

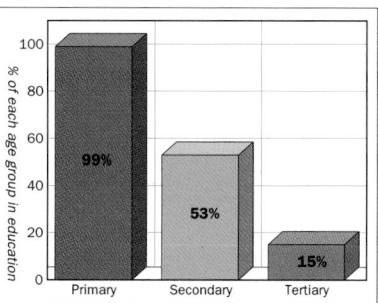

% of each age group in education

100
80
60
40
20
0

99%   Primary
53%   Secondary
15%   Tertiary

The system is a mixture of the French and US models. The public university system is well developed.

HEALTH

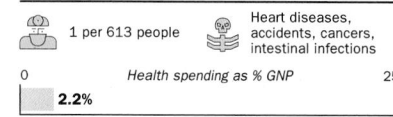
1 per 613 people

Heart diseases, accidents, cancers, intestinal infections

0   Health spending as % GNP   25
2.2%

Mexico's national health care system is rudimentary. Those in employment who pay social security receive slightly better care. Mexico has a good reputation for surgery and dentistry, but this is mostly in the private sector.

WEALTH

Plantation worker, 1746 Mexican new pesos per day; university science professor, 3516 Mexican new pesos per day

CONSUMER GOODS OWNERSHIP

Per 1000 population

1000
750
500
250
0

PCs limited to an elite

127   69   97   27

Mexico has enormous wealth disparities, from the twelve dollar-billionaires to the 16% living in extreme poverty. In the past, the wealthy did not generally pay taxes and often benefited from the large state machine. However, they now pay taxes. There is little social mobility; the old Spanish families retain their hold on government offices.

Rural Indians are probably the most disadvantaged group. In the last decade, poverty has forced them into city slums to work in factories or *maquiladora*. Conditions are so poor that there is a very high turnover in the workforce. Much of the problem resulted from Mexico's communal land laws, dating from the revolution in 1917. Without clear rights to title, the agricultural sector declined. The law was reversed in 1991 and this could result in improvements in productivity and social conditions in rural areas.

WORLD RANKING

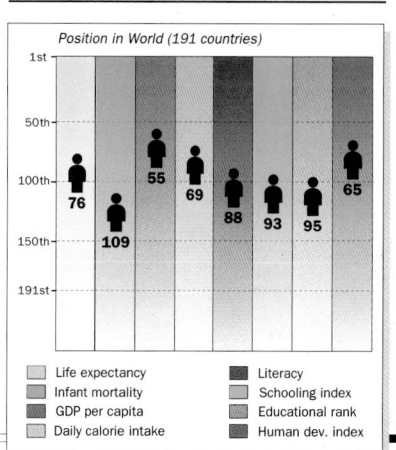
Position in World (191 countries)

1st
50th
100th
150th
191st

76   109   55   69   88   93   95   65

Life expectancy
Infant mortality
GDP per capita
Daily calorie intake
Literacy
Schooling index
Educational rank
Human dev. index

M

MICRONESIA

OFFICIAL NAME: Federated States of Micronesia **CAPITAL:** Kolonia
POPULATION: 101,000 **CURRENCY:** US dollar **OFFICIAL LANGUAGE:** English

THE FEDERATED STATES of Micronesia (FSM), situated in the Pacific Ocean, encompasses all the Caroline Islands except Belau. It is composed of four main island cluster states: Pohnpei, Kosrae, Chuuk and Yap. The islands are a mixture of high volcanic and low-lying coral types. Formerly a part of the US-administered Trust Territory of the Pacific Islands, the FSM has been independent since 1979. The islands continue to receive considerable aid from the USA, which supplements the fishing and copra-based economy.

CLIMATE

WEATHER CHART

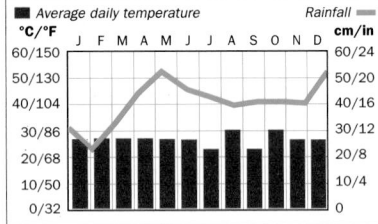

The islands are humid and fairly hot all year round, and the daily temperature range is small. Rainfall is abundant.

COMMUNICATIONS

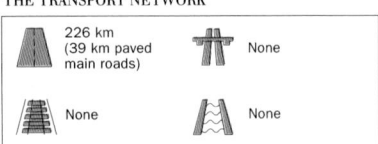

Chuuk | Has no fleet

THE TRANSPORT NETWORK

226 km (39 km paved main roads) | None
None | None

Fairly regular flights are available between the main islands. Local shipping is mainly used to transport bulk cargoes and copra.

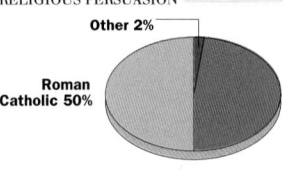

Micronesia, aerial view of rock islands.
Like many Pacific states, Micronesia fears rising sea levels as a result of global warming.

TOURISM

 20,475 visitors   No change in 1990

MAIN OVERSEAS ARRIVALS

Tourism is undeveloped. Chuuk's underwater war wreckage attracts visitors, and Kosrae has good beaches. The outlying islands remain unspoilt.

PEOPLE

Trukese, Pohnpeian, Mortlockese, Losrean, English | 158 people per km²

THE URBAN/RURAL POPULATION SPLIT

Most Micronesians live in small village communities

RELIGIOUS PERSUASION

Other 2%
Roman Catholic 50%
Protestant 48%

Increasing numbers of Melanesians, especially Filipino labourers, threaten to swamp the resident Micronesian population. Most islanders live without electricity or running water and many are effectively recipients of US welfare. Society is traditionally matrilineal on most of the islands.

POLITICS

1995 | President Bailey Olter

THE STATE OF THE PARTIES

Congress 14 members

There are no political parties. The 14 senators are elected as independents, 10 for 2 years and 4 at-large senators – 1 for each state – for 4 years.

The power of the traditional chiefs in politics is still very strong. Despite the existence of an elected house, it is generally accepted that the election candidates must be chiefs. Increasing Micronesia's economic independence is the key political issue. At present it is still heavily dependent on aid received from the USA under the Compact of Free Association, which is due for renegotiation in 2001.

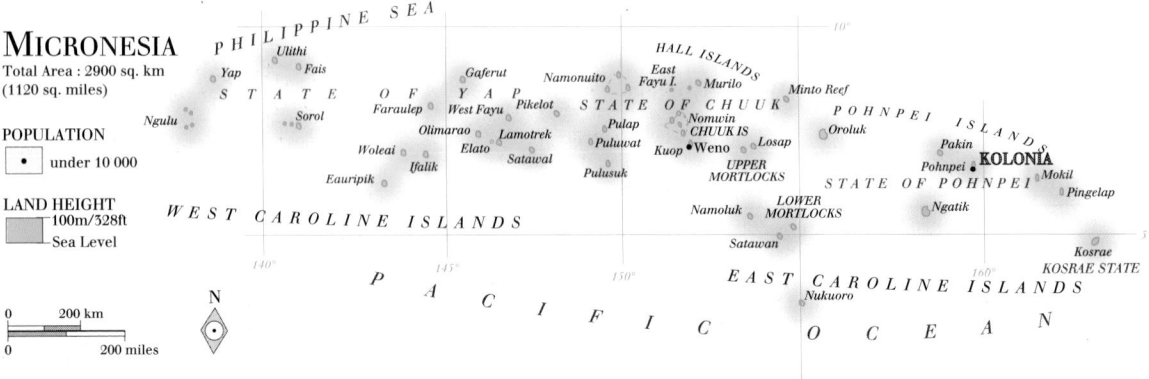

MICRONESIA

Total Area : 2900 sq. km (1120 sq. miles)

POPULATION
• under 10 000

LAND HEIGHT
100m/328ft
Sea Level

PHILIPPINE SEA

HALL ISLANDS

Yap Ulithi Fais Gaferut Namonuito East Fayu I. Murilo Minto Reef
STATE OF YAP Faraulep West Fayu Pikelot STATE OF CHUUK Nomwin POHNPEI ISLANDS
Ngulu Sorol Olimarao Lamotrek Pulap CHUUK IS Oroluk Pakin KOLONIA
Woleai Elato Satawal Puluwat Kuop • Weno Losap Pohnpei Mokil
Eauripik Ifalik Pulusuk UPPER MORTLOCKS STATE OF POHNPEI Pingelap
WEST CAROLINE ISLANDS Namoluk LOWER MORTLOCKS Ngatik

Satawan
Kosrae
KOSRAE STATE
PACIFIC EAST CAROLINE ISLANDS
Nukuoro
OCEAN

0 200 km
0 200 miles
N

Kapingamarangi

M

WORLD AFFAIRS

Micronesia's most important relationship is with the USA, which administered the islands until 1979 as part of the Trust Territory of the Pacific Islands. The Japanese are also important, especially economically;

some of the older generation still speak Japanese. Japan has provided funding for a project to widen the harbour on Yap. The FSM has developed a strong relationship with China. In 1992, President Bailey Olter made a state visit there, during which a treaty of co-operation was signed between the two countries.

AID

 12.6m (receipts)   Little change from year to year

The USA is the principal donor of aid, which funds hospitals, schools, food stamps and construction projects.

DEFENCE

 USA responsible for defence   Not applicable

Defence is entirely in the hands of the USA. Airstrips in the FSM were used by the USA in the Vietnam War.

ECONOMICS

 $99m   US dollar

SCORE CARD

- ❏ WORLD GNP RANKING........................186th
- ❏ GNP PER CAPITA $980
- ❏ BALANCE OF PAYMENTS..................$−54.5m
- ❏ INFLATION ....Volatile
- ❏ UNEMPLOYMENT ....High underemployment

STRENGTHS

Access to US economy, especially for garment manufacture through preferential trading rights. Construction industry is the largest private-sector activity. Tourism, fishing and copra production. US strategic interest in Micronesia and US budget subsidies.

WEAKNESSES

Dependence on USA for imports, especially for fuel. $30 million debt. Acute shortage of water limits development potential. High levels of underemployment.

EXPORTS

Other 8%
USA 15%
EU 77%

IMPORTS

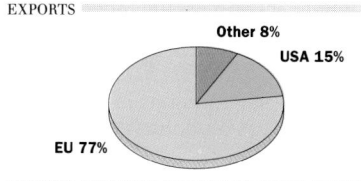

The majority of imports are from the USA

RESOURCES

 Most electricity is produced by small diesel generators   Not an oil producer and has no refineries

 3634 tonnes   None

The FSM is entirely dependent on external sources for its energy supply. Almost all electricity is produced by small diesel generators. The main resources are copra and valuable fish stocks, especially tuna.

ENVIRONMENT

 None   No funds for environmental initiatives

The FSM does not face pollution on the scale of that in the neighbouring Marshall Islands. However, Chuuk suffers serious droughts; rationing of water to one cup per person per day is occasionally introduced for short periods. In 1992, the US government used naval vessels to transport water from Guam to alleviate the problem.

MEDIA

 No political restrictions

PUBLISHING AND BROADCAST MEDIA

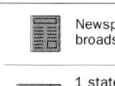 Newspapers are limited to small broadsheets

1 state-owned, 1 independent service   1 state-owned service

TV, which previously consisted of re-runs of US programmes, can now be received by satellite.

CRIME

 Micronesia does not publish prison figures   Little change from year to year

On Chuuk, assault, especially alcohol-related cases, is increasing. The outlying islands are crime-free.

EDUCATION

 Probably in the region of 65%

Education is compulsory between the ages of six and 14 years. The USA provides grants for some students to attend US universities.

CHRONOLOGY

The Caroline Islands were first colonized by the Spanish, but sold to Germany in 1899. Having formed an important Japanese base in the Second World War, the islands were transferred to US control in 1945.

- ❏ **1947** UN Trust Territory of the Pacific Islands established.
- ❏ **1967** Demands for increased local autonomy.
- ❏ **1977** US President Carter agrees to end trusteeship by 1981.
- ❏ **1979** Becomes independent Federated States of Micronesia.
- ❏ **1986** Compact of Free Association with USA implemented.
- ❏ **1990** Official termination of trusteeship agreement.
- ❏ **1991** Joins UN.

HEALTH

 1 per 2536 people   Heart, cerebrovascular and intestinal diseases

Basic health care is accessible to all, but outlying islands may not have access to qualified doctors. Diabetes and drug abuse are growing problems.

WEALTH

 Minimum wage on Pohnpei, $1.35 per hour

CONSUMER GOODS OWNERSHIP

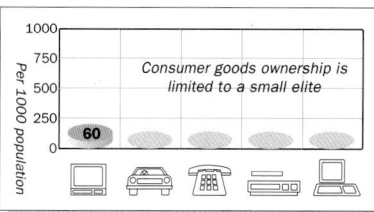

Consumer goods ownership is limited to a small elite

The gap between rich and poor is increasing as businessmen and local officials exploit US aid donations.

WORLD RANKING

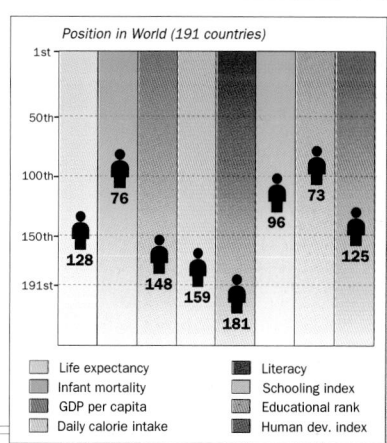

Position in World (191 countries)

MOLDAVIA

OFFICIAL NAME: Republic of Moldova **CAPITAL:** Chişinău
POPULATION: 4.4 million **CURRENCY:** Moldavian leu **OFFICIAL LANGUAGE:** Romanian

ONCE A PART OF ROMANIA, Moldavia was incorporated into the Soviet Union in 1940. Independence in 1991 brought with it the expectation that Moldavia would be reunited with Romania. At elections in 1993, however, Moldavians voted against the proposal. Moldavia is mostly undulating steppe country. It is the smallest and most densely populated of the ex-Soviet republics. Most of its population is engaged in intensive agriculture.

Agricultural landscape. Warm summers and even rainfall are ideal for cereal and fruit farming. Moldavia is famous for its wine.

CLIMATE

WEATHER CHART

Warm summers, mild winters and moderate rainfall give Moldavia an ideal climate for cultivation.

COMMUNICATIONS

 Chişinău International

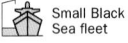 Small Black Sea fleet

THE TRANSPORT NETWORK

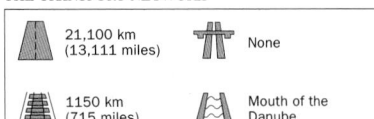

21,100 km (13,111 miles)	None
1150 km (715 miles)	Mouth of the Danube

Moldavia plans to build port facilities on the 900 m of the Danube River which are its international waters.

TOURISM

Businessmen make up the majority of visitors

Moldavia has seen no significant change in tourism arrivals

MAIN OVERSEAS ARRIVALS

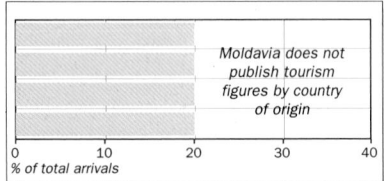

Moldavia does not publish tourism figures by country of origin

0 10 20 30 40
% of total arrivals

Few tourists visit Moldavia. However, its relatively well-developed infrastructure could allow some expansion of tourism in future. The vineyards and underground wine vault 'streets' are the main attractions.

PEOPLE

Romanian, Russian

130 people per km²

THE URBAN/RURAL POPULATION SPLIT

48% 52%

ETHNIC MAKEUP

Other 4% Gagauz 4%
Russian 13%
Ukrainian 14%
Moldavian 65%

Moldavians are of the same ethnic grouping as Romanians. The southern Gagauzi (Orthodox Christian Turks), and the population of mixed Russian-Moldavian-Ukrainian parentage on the eastern bank of the Dniester, declared themselves separate republics in 1990.

MOLDAVIA

Total Area : 33 700 sq. km (13 000 sq. miles)

POPULATION
⊙ over 500 000
◎ over 100 000
○ over 50 000
● over 10 000
• under 10 000

LAND HEIGHT
200m/656ft
80m/262ft

POLITICS

1998

President Mircea Ion Snegur

THE STATE OF THE PARTIES

Parliament 104 members

10% PIB
54% ADP
27% SP/YUM
9% CDPFA

ADP = Agrarian Democratic Party **SP/YUM** = Socialist Party and Yedinstvo Unity Movement **PIB** = Peasants and Intellectuals Party **CDPFA** = Christian Democratic People's Front Alliance

Moldavia declared itself a multiparty democracy in 1991, but initially kept the transitional administration appointed by the last Soviet in 1990. Elections were held in February 1993 and a new constitution was drafted. The first post-independence question was whether or not Moldavia should seek union with Romania. In March 1994, another election was held in which the Agrarian Democratic Party (ADP) emerged as the largest party in parliament. In a separate national plebiscite, held at the same time as the parliamentary elections, Moldavians rejected the idea of possible unification with Romania.

The secessionist republic of Transnistria (on the eastern bank of the Dniester) is seeking incorporation into the Ukraine, rather than Moldavia. Furthermore, the 153,000 Gagauzi minority are still hoping for independence.

WORLD AFFAIRS

Ties with nations in the Black Sea Economic Zone are being developed. Relations with Romania have been diluted now that reunification is no longer an issue. Links with Russia are now paramount. Economic pressure from Russia persuaded Moldavia to rejoin the CIS at the end of 1993. Russia still has troops stationed in Moldavia.

AID

 Moldavia is a net receiver of aid

 Aid receipts have risen since independence

The IMF and World Bank are supporting economic reforms. The EU, Romania, Turkey and Bulgaria are Moldavia's next most important aid providers.

DEFENCE

 $227.8m

 Down 74% in 1992

Moldavia began forming an army after independence and has signed military training agreements with Romania and Hungary. Former officers of the Soviet army are helping Transnistrian rebels.

ECONOMICS

 $9.5bn

 Moldavian leu not convertible

SCORE CARD

❏ WORLD GNP RANKING	80th
❏ GNP PER CAPITA	$2159
❏ BALANCE OF PAYMENTS	Deficit
❏ INFLATION	27%
❏ UNEMPLOYMENT	Widespread underemployment

STRENGTHS
Agriculture – notably wine, tobacco and cotton – and food processing. Light manufacturing. Good progress made in establishing markets for exports, and earning foreign exchange.

WEAKNESSES
Dependent on Russian raw materials and fuel. Most electricity imported. Isolated location and weak transport communications. Legacy of inefficient former Soviet state-run businesses. Shrinking economy as a result of privatization policies.

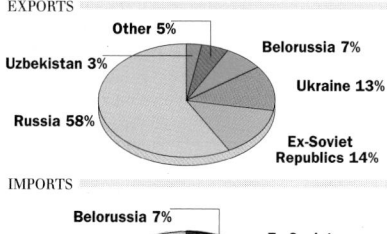

EXPORTS: Other 5%, Belorussia 7%, Ukraine 13%, Ex-Soviet Republics 14%, Russia 58%, Uzbekistan 3%

IMPORTS: Belorussia 7%, Ex-Soviet Republics 9%, Ukraine 13%, Other 23%, Russia 44%, Uzbekistan 4%

RESOURCES

 11.1bn kwh (capacity 3.1m kw); 23.6m poultry, 1.7m hogs, 1.2m sheep, 389,000 cattle

 Oil and gas reserves not exploited; Lignite, phosphate, gypsum, oil, natural gas

Moldavia has few mineral resources. It has to import all its fuel and most of its electricity.

ENVIRONMENT

 None

 Economic growth has precedence over ecological concerns

Northern Moldavia is still experiencing fallout from the Chernobyl nuclear accident in 1987. Over use of pesticides on tobacco farms is a serious problem.

MEDIA

 Media is relatively free from state control

PUBLISHING AND BROADCAST MEDIA

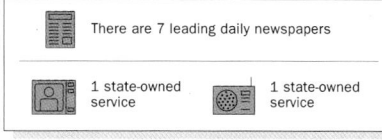

There are 7 leading daily newspapers; 1 state-owned service; 1 state-owned service

The press was privatized in 1993. The many new publications represent widely differing interest groups.

CRIME

 Moldavia does not publish prison figures

 Crime levels remain at a relatively low level

Moldavia still awaits a new legal system to accompany its constitution. Crime levels are generally low, but armed gangs have appeared in the south and west, and violence affects the two separatist republics.

EDUCATION

 96%

Haphazard attempts have been made to switch from a Soviet to a Romanian (French-inspired) system. Engineering is the largest university faculty.

HEALTH

 1 per 251 people

 Circulatory diseases, cancers, accidents

The centralized health service is poor by regional standards, with basic equipment and poorly-trained doctors.

WEALTH

 Increasing disparity in wealth between former-communist officials and the rest of the population

CONSUMER GOODS OWNERSHIP

TV ownership limited; VCR and PC ownership limited to small elite; 48; 122

Former Communist Party officials have benefited most from the advent of capitalism. Counterfeit Turkish Napoleon brandy and Marlboro cigarettes are highly favoured. The ethnic Gagauzi (Orthodox Christian Turks) form the poorest group.

WORLD RANKING

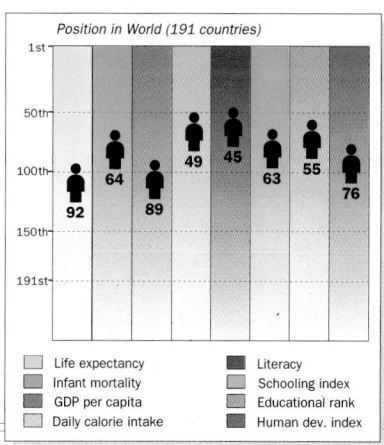

Position in World (191 countries): 92, 64, 89, 49, 45, 63, 55, 76

Life expectancy, Infant mortality, GDP per capita, Daily calorie intake, Literacy, Schooling index, Educational rank, Human dev. index

M

MONACO

OFFICIAL NAME: Principality of Monaco   **CAPITAL:** Monaco
POPULATION: 30,000   **CURRENCY:** French franc   **OFFICIAL LANGUAGE:** French

MONACO IS A TINY ENCLAVE on the Côte d'Azur in southeastern France. Its destiny changed radically in 1863 when Prince Charles III, after whom Monte Carlo is named, opened the casino. Today, Monaco is a lucrative banking and services centre, as well as a tourist destination. Prince Rainier's marriage to film star Grace Kelly, and some astute management of the economy, successfully transformed Monaco into a centre for the international jet-set. In 1962, the prince's absolute authority was abolished in a new, democratic constitution.

CLIMATE

WEATHER CHART

Summers are hot and dry; days with 12 hours of sunshine are not uncommon. Winters are mild and sunny.

COMMUNICATIONS

 None   Has no fleet

THE TRANSPORT NETWORK

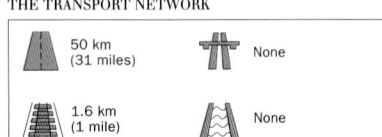

50 km (31 miles)	None	
1.6 km (1 mile)	None	

The 1.6 km of main-line track is run by French state railways. A helicopter shuttle links Fontvieille with Nice, the nearest airport. There are about 50 km of major roads. Monaco is an easy drive from northern Italy, the source of most of its private banking trade.

TOURISM

 245,592 visitors   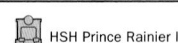 Up 3% in 1992

MAIN OVERSEAS ARRIVALS

Italy 34%
France 17%
USA 10%
Other 39%

% of total arrivals

A nation of less than 30,000 people, Monaco attracts huge numbers of tourists, mainly from France and Italy. Almost all are day-trippers, coming to gamble at the casino or to sample Monaco's high life. Just 245,000 of them stay the night, but efforts are being made to improve this by attracting business and holiday visitors. A new conference centre has opened and exhibition facilities are being built. Monaco is a long-time favourite destination of the rich, especially northern Italians. Spring is a key time for jet-set visitors, with several major social and sporting events: the Rose Ball (March), the Tennis Open (April) and the Grand Prix (May).

[Map of Monaco]

FRANCE

Lycée de l'Annonciade

Musée Nation
Larvotto

Centre de la Culture et d'Expositions

Monte-Carlo Sporting Club d'Eté

Casino

Hospitalier Grace

Railway Station   *La Condamine*   Centre de Congrès Monte-Carlo

Palais du Prince   *Port de Monaco*

Stade Louis II   *Port de Palais de Justice*   Ministère d'Etat

Cathédrale   **MONACO**

Fontvieille   Musée Océanographique

Heliport

MONACO
Total Area : 1.95 sq. km (0.75 sq. miles)

Places of Interest
Parks and Gardens
Grand Prix Circuit

0   500 m
0   656 ft

PEOPLE

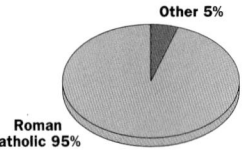

French, Italian, Monégasque, English   15,321 people per km²

THE URBAN/RURAL POPULATION SPLIT

100%

RELIGIOUS PERSUASION

Other 5%
Roman Catholic 95%

Less than one tenth of Monaco's residents are Monégasque. Over half are French, the rest Italian, American, British and Belgian. Monégasques enjoy considerable privileges, including housing subsidies to protect them from Monaco's high property prices, and the right of first refusal before a job can be offered to a foreigner. Women have equal status, but only acquired the vote in the constitutional changes of 1962.

POLITICS

1998   HSH Prince Rainier III

THE STATE OF THE PARTIES

National Council 18 members

83% LC   11% LM   6% Other

LC = Campora List   LM = Médecin List
There are no political parties, but candidates generally enter their names through an organization.

The Grimaldi princes (Rainier since 1949) have been hereditary rulers of Monaco for 700 years. The prince renounced absolute rule in the 1962 constitutional reforms. He still has considerable power and appoints the four-member executive. There are no political parties; National Council elections are based on personalities.

WORLD AFFAIRS

CSCE   IAEA   UN

Monaco's key concern is to protect both banking secrecy and the liberal tax regime from EU regulation. French citizens are banned from banking in Monaco, a 1962 decision enforced by President de Gaulle, who sent troops to the border.

M

Monte Carlo *with its luxury hotels and yacht harbour. The only space for new development is on land reclaimed from the sea.*

AID

 Monaco has no aid receipts or donations   Not applicable

Monaco neither receives nor gives aid, and the issue is not of concern to Monégasques.

DEFENCE

 France responsible for defence   Not applicable

Monaco has no armed forces and no defence budget. France, as the protecting power, bears responsibility for the defence of the Principality.

ECONOMICS

 $475m (est)   5.90 French francs

SCORE CARD

- ❏ WORLD GNP RANKING........................163rd
- ❏ GNP PER CAPITA $11,000
- ❏ BALANCE OF PAYMENTS ...Included in French total
- ❏ INFLATION ....Included in French total
- ❏ UNEMPLOYMENT.....................................0%

STRENGTHS
Banking secrecy laws and low tax rates attract over $10 billion of overseas deposits, particularly from Italy. Strong tourism sector, still fundamental to the economy. Services, including property management and overseas shipping companies' headquarters, as well as banking, account for 40% of economic turnover. Chemical, pharmaceutical, plastics, construction, electronics and printing industries.

WEAKNESSES
Banking secrecy makes Monaco vulnerable to money laundering. Some EU states wish to end Monaco's privileged tax and banking status. Lack of natural resources means Monaco is almost totally dependent on imports; lack of space could hinder growth. No agricultural land.

EXPORTS/IMPORTS

Monaco has a full customs union with France

RESOURCES

 Included within French total   Not an oil producer and has no refineries

 2 tonnes   None

Monaco has no strategic resources and imports all its energy from France. It has no agricultural land.

ENVIRONMENT

 None   ⬇ Environmental issues not paramount

Environmental questions do not feature highly in political life, except where they might affect profitability. The quality of the built environment around the harbour occasionally arouses local passions. The important populations of red coral are under threat from land reclamation and pollution.

MEDIA

 Freedom of expression guaranteed under constitution

PUBLISHING AND BROADCAST MEDIA

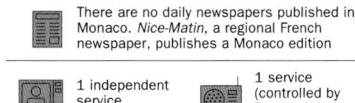 There are no daily newspapers published in Monaco. *Nice-Matin*, a regional French newspaper, publishes a Monaco edition

1 independent service   1 service (controlled by French state)

In addition to its domestic radio and TV, Monaco receives all the mainstream French and Italian channels.

CRIME

 Monaco does not publish prison figures   Up 8% in 1990

Monaco prides itself on its relatively low crime rates and the fact that, in contrast to northern Italy, it is quite safe for the rich to sport their furs and expensive jewellery in public.

EDUCATION

 99%

The education system is essentially the same as that of France, with students studying for the *baccalauréat* exam. Most go on to university in France, but then return to claim good jobs in Monaco. The Catholic Church exerts considerable influence and is still responsible for primary schooling.

HEALTH

 1 per 373 people   Heart and cerebrovascular diseases, cancers

Medical care is provided by a system of private health insurance. Doctors train in France. The Princess Grace Hospital can serve 60,000 people and thus caters for patients from outside Monaco.

WEALTH

 Owing to the high cost of living in Monaco, salaries have a premium of 5% over rates of pay in the neighbouring area of the Alpes-Maritimes, France

CONSUMER GOODS OWNERSHIP

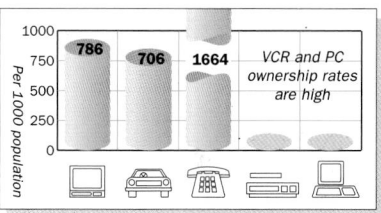

Monaco's image abroad has changed dramatically since Prince Rainier acceded in 1949. From being considered a simple gambling spot, it is now ranked as one of the world's most glamorous international jet-set destinations. In part, this was the result of Rainier's wedding to Grace Kelly, then a leading Hollywood star, which brought Monaco to the attention of US high society. More important was Rainier's work in turning Monaco into a major tax haven and an up-market resort, by making the most of its Mediterranean coastal location. Today, many tax exiles are resident, among them the Wall Street investment guru Bob Beckman.

WORLD RANKING

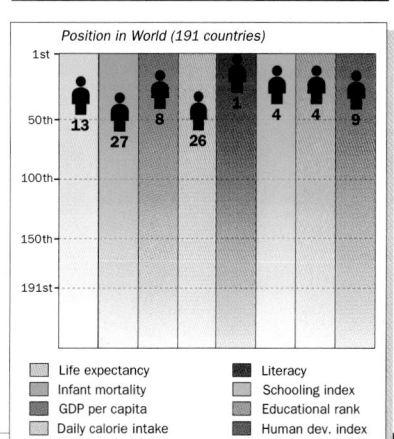

M

MONGOLIA

OFFICIAL NAME: Mongolia **CAPITAL:** Ulan Bator **POPULATION:** 2.2 million
CURRENCY: Tughrik **OFFICIAL LANGUAGE:** Khalkh Mongol

 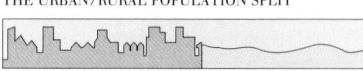

ASIA

LAND-LOCKED BETWEEN Russia and China, Mongolia rises from the semi-arid Gobi desert to mountainous steppe. Mongolia was unified by Ghenghis Khan in 1206 and became part of Manchu China in 1697. Independent in 1924, Mongolia became a communist state, and was officially aligned with the USSR from 1936. In 1990, it became the first Asian nation to abandon communist rule; nevertheless, in 1993, the former Communists were voted back into power.

CLIMATE

WEATHER CHART

Temperatures occasionally drop to –50°C but can rise to 41°C. Sudden cold periods in early spring, known as *zud*, can kill many young livestock.

COMMUNICATIONS

 Buyant-Ukhaa, Ulan Bator   Has no fleet

THE TRANSPORT NETWORK

3949 km (2454 miles)		None
1807 km (1123 miles)		397 km (247 miles)

The focus of state transport policy is shifting away from Moscow towards improved links with China and access to a Pacific port facility. Petrol shortages have meant a large increase in the use of draught-animals.

MONGOLIA

Total Area : 1 565 000 sq. km
(604 247 sq. miles)

0 ——— 400 km
0 ——— 400 miles

POPULATION
⊙ over 500 000
○ over 50 000
● over 10 000
• under 10 000

LAND HEIGHT
3000m/9843ft
2000m/6562ft
1000m/3281ft
above 500m

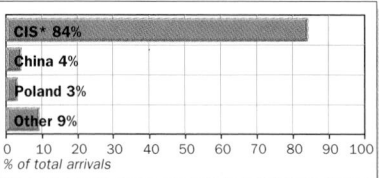
Traditional gers in the Gobi Desert.
Most Mongolians still choose to pursue a nomadic lifestyle, living in felt tents called gers.

TOURISM

 147,236 visitors   Tourism shrank after the USSR's collapse, but is now expanding.

MAIN OVERSEAS ARRIVALS

CIS* 84%	
China 4%	
Poland 3%	
Other 9%	

% of total arrivals

Tourism has expanded since the easing of visa restrictions in 1991. Under communism, all travel was arranged through the state agency, *Zhuuichin*, but private companies are now entering the market.

PEOPLE

 Khalkh Mongol, Turkic, Chinese, Russian   1.4 people per km²

THE URBAN/RURAL POPULATION SPLIT

52%   48%

ETHNIC MAKEUP

Russian 2%   Chinese 2%
Other 2%   Kazakh 4%
Khalkh Mongol 90%

Khalkh Mongols are the dominant ethnic group. The Kazakhs, who live in the northwest and speak a Turkic language, form the largest non-Mongol group. Since the collapse of the USSR, many Kazakhs have been emigrating to Kazakhstan. There is little indigenous ethnic tension, although there is considerable antagonism towards Chinese and Russian minorities.

POLITICS

 1997   President Punsalmaagiyn Ochirbat

THE STATE OF THE PARTIES

Great Hural 76 members

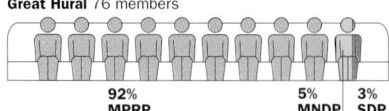

92% MPRP   5% MNDP   3% SDP

MPRP = Mongolian People's Revolutionary Party
MNDP = Mongolian National Democratic Party
SDP = Social Democratic Party

After over 50 years of Soviet-style communist rule the advent of democracy in 1990 revolutionized Mongolian politics. Communism was banned. Political activity now functions on a constituency system. The economic results of democratic reform have been less popular and are the dominant domestic issue. In 1992, the economy shrank by 16% and Mongolians began to look back to the guaranteed housing and jobs of the communist past. The 1993 elections saw the Democrats swept from power and the renamed communists (MPRP) returned with a large majority.

M

WORLD AFFAIRS

 ADB   GATT   NAM   ESCAP IBRD

Since 1990 Mongolia has tried to balance China's influence with that of Japan and other east Asian states. Mongolia is seeking to improve economic and political relations with China, but there is a fear of Chinese designs on its sovereignty. Mongolia is trying to ensure its security by joining international organizations.

AID

 $320m (receipts)   Up 113% in 1992

A large balance of payments deficit makes aid vital. The main donors are now the USA and Japan.

DEFENCE

 $130m   Up 9% between 1987 and 1992

The last Soviet forces left in 1992 after the collapse of communism in Russia. The Mongolian forces have been drastically reduced and have barely any equipment. Video surveillance is being used to monitor the Chinese border.

ECONOMICS

 $1.4bn   40.06 tughriks

SCORE CARD

- ❏ WORLD GNP RANKING........................144th
- ❏ GNP PER CAPITA $660
- ❏ BALANCE OF PAYMENTS ....$–640m
- ❏ INFLATION ....–1.3%
- ❏ UNEMPLOYMENT...............................2.4%

STRENGTHS
Coal and oil, though most remains untapped. Traditional farming economy still strong and supports the population efficiently in a harsh climate.

WEAKNESSES
Distance between centres. Limited infrastructure. Little manufacturing.

EXPORTS

Czech Republic and Slovakia* 5%

Bulgaria 3%

Other 14%

CIS* 78%

IMPORTS

Czech Republic and Slovakia* 4%

Germany* 4%

China 2%

Other 12%

CIS* 78%

RESOURCES

 3.6bn kwh (capacity 900,000 kw)

13m sheep, 2m cattle, 2m horses, 171,000 pigs

Contracts have recently been signed with oil prospectors

Oil, coal, copper, uranium, fluorspar, tungsten, tin, gold

Mongolia is rich in oil and many other minerals. Under communism, Mongolia's vast mineral resources were barely exploited, and prospecting has only recently begun in earnest. Known oil reserves indicate that Mongolia should meet most of its future domestic needs. Mongolia is establishing a uranium mining joint venture with Russia.

ENVIRONMENT

 4%

Traditional Buddhist values instil respect for nature

Industrial pollution around Ulan Bator is a concern; prevailing winds carry power station emissions over residential areas and there is a high incidence of chest diseases. The level of pollution in Lake Hövsgöl is also a serious problem.

MEDIA

 All restrictions on reporting have been removed

PUBLISHING AND BROADCAST MEDIA

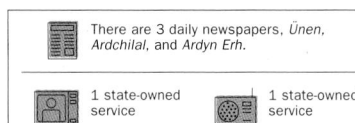

There are 3 daily newspapers, *Ünen*, *Ardchilal*, and *Ardyn Erh*.

1 state-owned service

1 state-owned service

Highly restricted under communism, Mongolia's press is now strongly outspoken; there are no slander or libel laws. However, limited supplies of ink and paper restrict publications. Fuel shortages are also a problem, making distribution into remote regions prohibitively expensive.

CRIME

 Mongolia does not publish prison figures

 Crime, especially theft, is rising.

Crime has risen rapidly since 1990, particularly organized crime and muggings by knife gangs. Ulan Bator is the most dangerous area, especially for foreigners; Russians, Chinese and dollar-carrying US tourists are the main targets.

EDUCATION

 89%

Education is modelled on the former Soviet system. The majority of teachers are women on low salaries. Private-sector schools emphasizing Mongol culture are beginning to open.

CHRONOLOGY

In the 17th century, the Manchus took control of Mongolia. It stayed in Chinese hands until 1911.

- ❏ **1911** Mongolian aristocracy, supported by Tsarist Russia, declares independence from China.
- ❏ **1919** China reoccupies Mongolia.
- ❏ **1921** White Russians, Chinese and communists struggle for control.
- ❏ **1924** Mongolia becomes an independent communist state.
- ❏ **1989–1990** Peaceful demonstrations in Ulan Bator demanding reform. Communists accede to request for multiparty democracy.

HEALTH

 1 per 357 people

 Heart, parasitic and respiratory diseases

Shortages of drugs and equipment have renewed interest in traditional Mongolian herbal medicine. As well as the state-run system, some Buddhist monasteries provide health care.

WEALTH

 Street cleaner, 4000 tughriks per month; hospital doctor, 8000 tughriks per month

CONSUMER GOODS OWNERSHIP

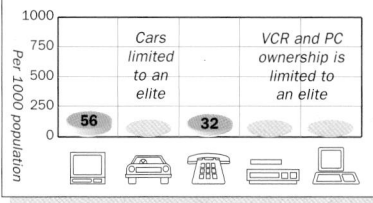

Cars limited to an elite

VCR and PC ownership is limited to an elite

Per 1000 population

56

32

The poorest Mongolians cannot even afford to buy bread. The wealthy are those with access to dollars, often spent on shopping expeditions to China. Russian cars are favoured as parts are readily available.

WORLD RANKING

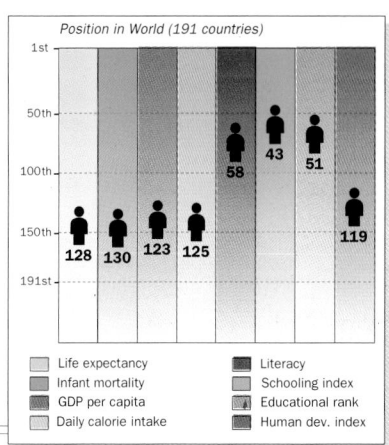

Position in World (191 countries)

1st

50th

100th

150th

191st

128 130 123 125 58 43 51 119

- ☐ Life expectancy
- ☐ Infant mortality
- ☐ GDP per capita
- ☐ Daily calorie intake
- ☐ Literacy
- ☐ Schooling index
- ☐ Educational rank
- ☐ Human dev. index

M

MOROCCO

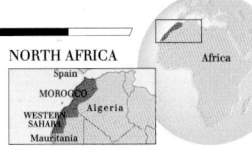

NORTH AFRICA

OFFICIAL NAME: Kingdom of Morocco   CAPITAL: Rabat
POPULATION: 26.3 million   CURRENCY: Moroccan dirham   OFFICIAL LANGUAGE: Arabic

MOROCCO IS SITUATED in northern Africa and bordered by Algeria and the Western Sahara, the future of which is to be determined by a UN-supervised referendum. Its northern regions have a Mediterranean climate, while the south comprises semi-arid desert. King Hassan's international prestige has given Morocco status out of proportion to its wealth. The main issues the country faces are the unresolved fate of the Western Sahara and the internal threat of Islamic militancy. Tourism, phosphate production and agriculture are key economic strengths.

TOURISM

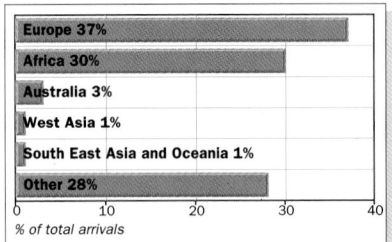

3.47m visitors   Up 22% in 1989

MAIN OVERSEAS ARRIVALS

Europe 37%
Africa 30%
Australia 3%
West Asia 1%
South East Asia and Oceania 1%
Other 28%

0   10   20   30   40
% of total arrivals

Tourism is vital to the economy. Good beaches abound; Agadir has 300 days of sunshine a year. Fès and Marrakech offer cultural interest, while the Atlas mountains attract walkers and skiers. Desert safaris are offered in the Sahara. Most Western tourists come from France, Germany and Spain.

CLIMATE

WEATHER CHART

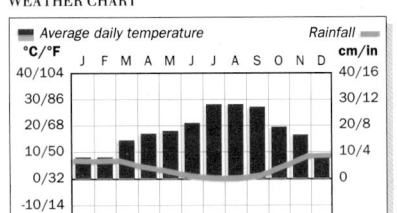

The climate ranges from warm and temperate in the north to semi-arid in the south, but temperatures are cooler in the mountains, especially in the high Atlas. During the summer, the effect of the *sirocco* and *chergui*, hot winds from the Sahara, are felt.

COMMUNICATIONS

Mohammed V, Casablanca   64 ships 483,700 dwt

THE TRANSPORT NETWORK

| 59,450 km (22,954 miles) | Rabat–Casablanca motorway |
| 1893 km (731 miles) | None |

Morocco has six international airports. A motorway links Rabat and Casablanca; however, roads tend to peter out in the rural areas. The railway service is cheap, although its routes are limited.

M

WESTERN SAHARA

[map of Western Sahara showing: Dawra, Al Haggounia, Jdiriya, Laâyoune, Lemsid, Saguia al Hamra, Semara, Boujdour, Boukra, Sebaiera, Guelta Zemmur, Ad Dakhla, Tagarzimat, Argoub, Fucht, Imilili, 550m, Guerguerat, Tichla, MOROCCO, ALGERIA, MAURITANIA, ATLANTIC OCEAN, 26°, 22°, 14°, 12°]

0   100 km
0   100 miles
N

[main map of Morocco showing cities: Tanger, Ceuta (to Spain), Tetouan, Larache, Chaouèn, Al Hoceima, Melilla (to Spain), Nador, Berkane, Oujda, Ksar el Kebir, Ouazzane, Taourirt, Jerada, Kénitra, RABAT, Salé, Sidi Kacem, Taza, Fès, Mohammedia, Casablanca, Meknès, Sefrou, El Jadida, Azrou, Settat, Khouribga, Khénifra, Safi, Oued Zem, Youssoufia, Beni Mellal, El Kelàa des Srarhna, Essaouira, Marrakech, Er Rachidia, Figuig, Jebel Toubkal 4165m, Boumalne Dadès, Ouarzazate, Agadir, Tiznit, Tan-Tan; features: Strait of Gibraltar, MEDITERRANEAN SEA, ATLANTIC OCEAN, RIF, Sebou, Moyen Atlas, HAUT ATLAS MOUNTAINS, ANTI ATLAS, Oum er Rbia, Tensift, Drâa, Moulouya, Ouarkziz, ALGERIA, WESTERN SAHARA]

MOROCCO

Total Area : 698 670 sq. km
(269 757 sq. miles)

POPULATION
over 1 000 000
over 500 000
over 100 000
over 50 000
over 10 000
under 10 000

LAND HEIGHT
3000m/9843ft
2000m/6562ft
1000m/3281ft
500m/1640ft
200m/656ft
Sea Level

0   100 km
0   100 miles
N

PEOPLE

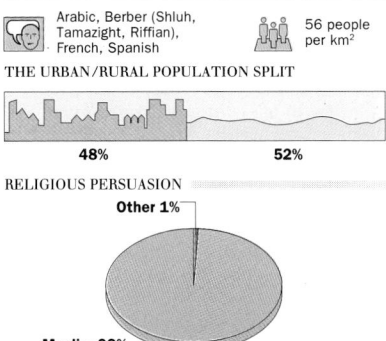

Arabic, Berber (Shluh, Tamazight, Riffian), French, Spanish

56 people per km²

THE URBAN/RURAL POPULATION SPLIT

48%　　　　**52%**

RELIGIOUS PERSUASION

Other 1%

Muslim 99%

ETHNIC MAKEUP

European 1%

Arab and Berber 99%

Morocco, the westernmost of the Maghreb states, is the last refuge for descendants of the original Berber inhabitants of northwest Africa. About 35% of Moroccans are Berber-speaking. They live mainly in mountain villages, while the Arab majority inhabit the lowlands. Before independence from France, 450,000 Europeans lived in Morocco; numbers have since greatly diminished. Some 45,000 Jews enjoy religious freedom and full civil rights – a role in society unique among Arab countries. Most people speak Arabic, and French is also spoken in urban areas. Sunni Muslim is the nominal religion of most of the population. King Hassan is the spiritual leader through his position as Commander of the Faithful. The emancipation of women was slow to take root in Morocco despite advances in education and increasing freedom of social intercourse between the sexes.

POPULATION AGE BREAKDOWN

% of population by age group	■ 0–14	■ 15–64	□ 65+		
	00%	4.2%	4.1%	3.6%	4%
	00%	48.2%	52.7%	55.9%	59.1%
	00%	47.6%	43.2%	40.5%	36.9%
	1960	1970	1980	1990	2000

The town of Boumaine-Dadès lies in the southern foothills of the Atlas Mountains. The region's outstanding scenery makes it one of Morocco's major tourist attractions.

WORLD AFFAIRS

AL　AMU　NAM　GATT　ECA

Morocco's important role in the quest for lasting peace in the Middle East was underlined by Israeli Prime Minister Yitzhak Rabin's visit to the capital Rabat following the signing of the 1993 peace accord with the Palestine Liberation Organization in Washington. King Hassan has a reputation as something of a maverick in Arab politics – he has negotiated with Israel but also heads the Jerusalem Committee of the Islamic Conference Organization – and his governments have adopted a pro-Western profile in international affairs. Morocco has also earned respect by protecting its own Jewish minority.

Despite international opposition, Morocco has occupied the former Spanish colony of Western Sahara since 1975, when King Hassan encouraged mass settlement by ordering the Green March of 350,000 people. Resistance by Polisario Front guerrillas, fighting for an independent Western Sahara, commenced in 1983 and continues, despite a UN-brokered peace plan. This rapidly foundered amid bitter disputes between the Moroccan government and the Polisario Front over voting rights to decide Western Sahara's political future.

In order to consolidate its claim on this phosphate-rich territory, Morocco has invested considerable sums to improve the Western Saharan infrastructure, employing troops to build roads and an airport in the capital, Laâyoune. An extensive programme of school and hospital building has also been undertaken.

POLITICS

 1999

 HM King Hassan II

THE STATE OF THE PARTIES

Chamber of Representatives 333 members

16%	16%	15%	15%	12%	26%
UC	USFP	MP	I	RNI	Other

UC = Constitutional Union　**USFP** = Socialist Union of Popular Force　**MP** = Popular Movement　**I** = Independence Party (*Istiqlal*)　**RNI** = National Assembly of Independents

Morocco is a constitutional monarchy with a single assembly, to which members are elected every six years.

Main Political Issues

The succession

King Hassan is only 64 and in good health, but the power of the monarchy is such that the succession is a major concern for the wealthy business and political elite. Crown Prince Sidi Mohammad will be the next head of state, but is a less dominating figure than his father and may wield less power. Most Moroccans accept that, for the next few years, the country has need of a strong, unifying force and, as a result, King Hassan is not challenged.

Islamic militancy

Mindful of the civil turmoil afflicting neighbouring Algeria, the government has cracked down on Islamic militants, banning all 13 known groups. However, support for Islamic fundamentalism is increasing, especially among university students, who fear Morocco is losing its identity as an Arab, Islamic country and becoming too influenced by Europe.

Profile

During his long reign, King Hassan has excelled at a policy of divide and rule where political parties are concerned. Although he now allows the majority party in the elected national assembly to choose most cabinet posts, he reserves the right to terminate parliament, and to appoint or dismiss the prime minister. After the 1993 elections, the centre-right emerged as the largest party. It turned down Hassan's invitation to form a government, whereupon the king himself appointed a non-party government of technocrats and politicians of liberal tendencies.

King Hassan II, who acceded to the throne on the death of his father in 1961.

Mohammed Karim Lamrani, prime minister for the fifth time in 1993.

AID

 $1.1bn (receipts)　 Up 5% in 1991

Saudi Arabia wrote off $2.7 billion of Moroccan debt after the Gulf War. The World Bank has given help to Morocco, but the country receives little aid.

M

M

CHRONOLOGY

Independence from France in 1956 was only the first step in ending colonial rule for the oldest kingdom in the Arab world, even though the present Alaoui dynasty has been in power for three centuries.

- ❏ **1956** France recognizes Moroccan independence under Sultan Mohammed Ibn Yousif. Morocco joins UN. Spain renounces control over its territories, except the enclaves of Ceuta, Melilla and Ifni and territories in the south.
- ❏ **1957** Sultan Mohammed king.
- ❏ **1961** Crown Prince Hassan becomes king on father's death.
- ❏ **1967** Morocco backs Arab cause in Six-Day War with Israel.
- ❏ **1969** Spain returns the enclave of Ifni to Morocco.
- ❏ **1971** Right-wing army officers stage abortive coup.
- ❏ **1972** King Hassan survives assassination attempt planned by defence minister and army chief.
- ❏ **1975** International Court of Justice grants self-determination to Western Saharan people. King Hassan orders Green March of 350,000 people. Moroccan forces seize Saharan capital.
- ❏ **1976** Morocco and Mauritania partition Western Sahara.
- ❏ **1979** Mauritania renounces claim to part of Western Sahara, which is added to Morocco's territory.
- ❏ **1984** King Hassan and Colonel Gaddafi of Libya sign Oujda Treaty as first step towards a Maghreb union. Morocco withdraws from OAU after criticism of its role in Western Sahara.
- ❏ **1985** Twenty-six members of left-wing Islamic Youth charged with treason. 14 sentenced to death.
- ❏ **1986** Morocco abrogates Oujda Treaty with Libya.
- ❏ **1987** Completion of defensive wall around Western Sahara.
- ❏ **1988** Morocco joins UN Human Rights Commission.
- ❏ **1989** Border treaty with Algeria ratified. Arab Maghreb Union (AMU) creates no-tariff zone between Morocco, Algeria, Tunisia, Libya and Mauritania. Hassan first AMU president.
- ❏ **1990** Morocco condemns Iraq's invasion of Kuwait.
- ❏ **1991** Morocco accepts UN plan for referendum in Western Sahara.
- ❏ **1992** New constitution allows members of the majority party in parliament to choose the cabinet.
- ❏ **1993** First general election for nine years. After major parties refuse his invitation, king appoints non-party government.

DEFENCE

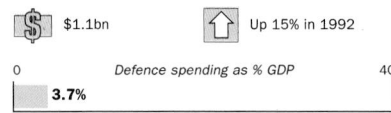

💲 $1.1bn	⬆ Up 15% in 1992

0   *Defence spending as % GDP*   40
3.7%

MOROCCAN ARMED FORCES

🛡	284 main battle tanks (224 M–48A5/ 60 M–60A1)	175,000 personnel
🚢	1 frigate, 4 surface vessels and 23 patrol boats	7000 personnel
✈	90 combat aircraft (15 F–5E/14 *Mirage* F-1EH/15 *Mirage* F–1CH)	13,500 personnel
🚀	None	

Morocco's long struggle in the Western Sahara against Polisario Front guerrillas has given the kingdom's forces a strong reputation. Moroccans have also fought as mercenaries in the Gulf. In the 1980s, Moroccan sappers constructed a 2500-km defensive wall to cordon off Western Sahara in an attempt to prevent incursions from Polisario guerrillas based in Algeria.

Morocco's pro-Western stance has allowed its forces access to sophisticated weapons and training from the West, particularly the USA – unlike neighbouring North African states, which are dependent on the former Soviet bloc.

The air force was formed in 1956 and flies US and European aircraft, notably *Mirage* interceptors. The navy uses Western-supplied ships, but is insignificant in regional terms.

Some 6% of national income is spent on defence – a relatively, but not prohibitively, high figure for a developing country. Military service is compulsory for 18 months.

ECONOMICS

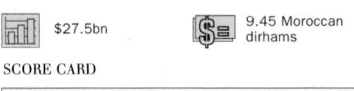

🏢 $27.5bn	💱 9.45 Moroccan dirhams

SCORE CARD

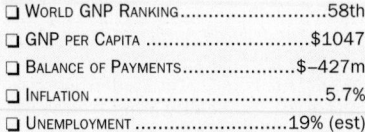

- ❏ WORLD GNP RANKING..........................58th
- ❏ GNP PER CAPITA $1047
- ❏ BALANCE OF PAYMENTS....................$–427m
- ❏ INFLATION 5.7%
- ❏ UNEMPLOYMENT ....19% (est)

EXPORTS

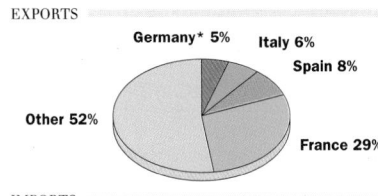

Germany* 5%   Italy 6%
Spain 8%
Other 52%
France 29%

IMPORTS

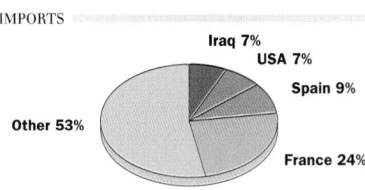

Iraq 7%
USA 7%
Spain 9%
Other 53%
France 24%

STRENGTHS

Pro-business policies and abundant labour attract foreign investment. Low inflation. Tourist industry, phosphates and agriculture all have great potential.

WEAKNESSES

High unemployment and population growth. Dirham not fully convertible. Droughts have hit agriculture. Cannabis production (30% of Europe's supply) complicates closer EU links.

PROFILE

The government has embarked on a privatization programme designed to attract investment – particularly from Europe. It raised $250 million (including $100 million from Spain) in 1993 and there are plans to sell companies worth a further $2 billion by 1995. These measures have been resisted by trade unions, which have organized strikes over rising prices and deteriorating working conditions.

ECONOMIC PERFORMANCE INDICATOR

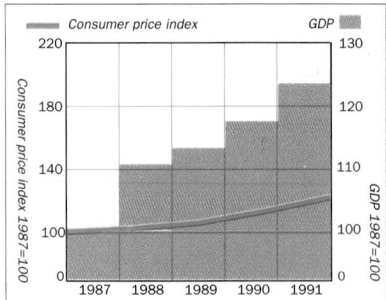

Consumer price index   GDP

Consumer price index 1987=100: 220, 180, 140, 100, 0
GDP 1987=100: 130, 120, 110, 100, 0
1987 1988 1989 1990 1991

MOROCCO : MAJOR BUSINESSES

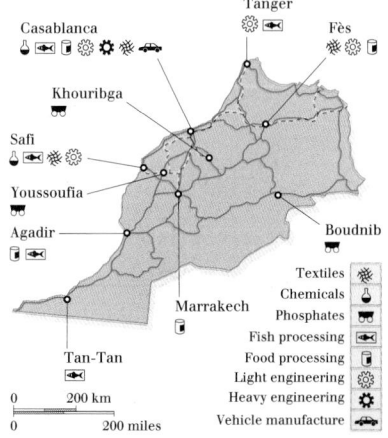

Tanger
Casablanca
Fès
Khouribga
Safi
Youssoufia
Agadir
Boudnib
Marrakech
Tan-Tan

Textiles
Chemicals
Phosphates
Fish processing
Food processing
Light engineering
Heavy engineering
Vehicle manufacture

0   200 km
0   200 miles

RESOURCES

 9.6bn kwh (capacity 2.36m kw)　 Not an oil producer; refines 154,600 b/cd

 17.5m sheep, 3.3m cattle, 918,000 asses　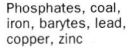 Phosphates, coal, iron, barytes, lead, copper, zinc

ELECTRICITY GENERATION

Hydro 13% (1.2bn kwh)
Thermal 87% (8.4bn kwh)
Nuclear 0%
Other 0%

% of total generation by type

Morocco possesses 75% of the world's phosphate reserves. Other minerals include anthracite and iron ore.

ENVIRONMENT

 0.8% (0.7% partially protected)　 Ecological issues are not a high priority

ENVIRONMENTAL TREATIES

Yes　　No
Yes　　No

Morocco's wealth of plant and animal life has suffered severely from long periods of drought, most recently in the early 1980s and early 1990s. The unplanned development of tourist resorts is posing a threat to fragile coastal ecosystems.

MEDIA

 Criticism of the king is not allowed

PUBLISHING AND BROADCAST MEDIA

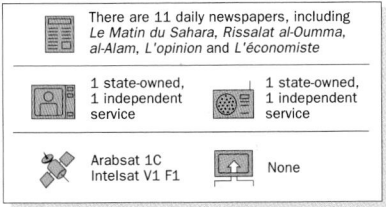

There are 11 daily newspapers, including *Le Matin du Sahara*, *Rissalat al-Oumma*, *al-Alam*, *L'opinion* and *L'économiste*

1 state-owned, 1 independent service　　1 state-owned, 1 independent service

Arabsat 1C Intelsat V1 F1　　None

The media is careful to avoid criticism of King Hassan, and the reporting of current affairs tends to be cautious. The sports pages, especially the football reports, are the most dynamic sections of the press – and may also contain implicit criticisms of the establishment. Newspapers are published both in Arabic and French. *L'economiste* supplies the most authoritative economic information. State-owned TV began transmissions in Arabic and French in 1962. Radio broadcasts are in Arabic, Berber, French, Spanish and English from Rabat and Tangier.

Forestry is carried out in the mountains. Crops include grain, fruit, peppers, tomatoes and cut flowers.

MOROCCO : LAND USE

Cropland
High mountain regions
Pasture
Forest
Desert
Sheep
Fruit
Wheat

0　200 km
0　200 miles

CRIME

 21,332 prisoners　 Up 26% in 1986

CRIME RATES

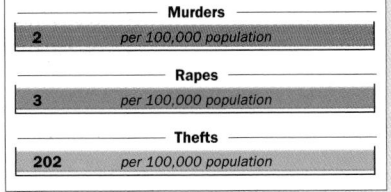

Murders
2　per 100,000 population

Rapes
3　per 100,000 population

Thefts
202　per 100,000 population

Urban crime is increasing, but muggings are rare. Apart from a 1990 strike that led to 40 deaths in Fès, Morocco has seen little civil unrest. Police watch Islamic militant activists.

EDUCATION

 50%

0　Education spending as % GNP　25
 7.3%

THE EDUCATION SYSTEM

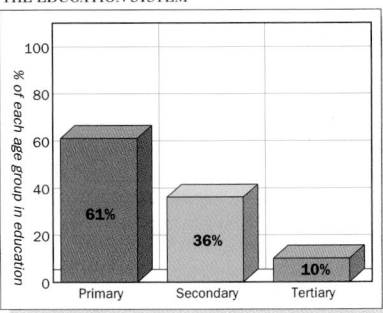

% of each age group in education

61% Primary
36% Secondary
10% Tertiary

Only 25% of Morocco's rural population is literate, as opposed to 60% in the cities. The literacy level and primary school enrolment rates are well below average for countries with similar living standards. There are six universities with a combined total of 100,000 students.

HEALTH

 1 per 4763 people　　Neonatal causes, cerebrovascular and heart diseases

0　Health spending as % GNP　25
1%

Despite recent progress, child mortality and nutritional standards for the poorest Moroccans remain well below average for countries with a similar standard of living. There is one doctor for every 4763 Moroccans and one hospital bed for every 1000 people. Outside the cities, primary health care is virtually non-existent, with the result that people depend on traditional remedies for illnesses.

WEALTH

 Factory foreman, 4950 Moroccan dirhams per month; executive engineer, 10,981 Moroccan dirhams per month

CONSUMER GOODS OWNERSHIP

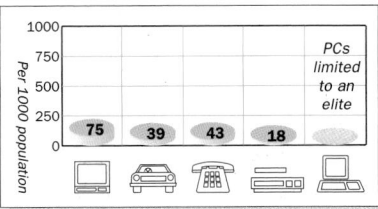

Per 1000 population

PCs limited to an elite

75　39　43　18

Income per head is considerably lower than in neighbouring Algeria and Tunisia. One in seven Moroccans live below the poverty line – an improvement on the 1985 figure, which was one in five. About 45% of the population live in rural areas and the rural-urban gap in wealth is considerable. Drought in the 1990s accelerated the urban drift.

Unrest has largely been avoided owing to Morocco's thriving informal sector. Apart from the illegal hashish trade and the smuggling of alcohol and Western goods, this provides jobs in clothes manufacturing, food processing, goods transport, and the hotel and building trades.

WORLD RANKING

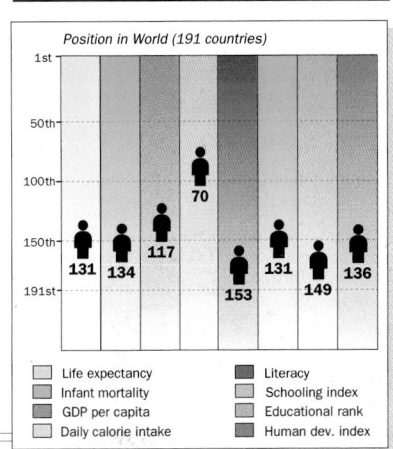

Position in World (191 countries)

1st
50th
100th　70
150th　131　134　117　　131　149　136
191st　　　　　153

Life expectancy　Literacy
Infant mortality　Schooling index
GDP per capita　Educational rank
Daily calorie intake　Human dev. index

M

MOZAMBIQUE

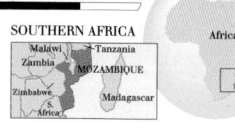

SOUTHERN AFRICA

OFFICIAL NAME: Republic of Mozambique **CAPITAL:** Maputo
POPULATION: 16.1 million **CURRENCY:** Metical **OFFICIAL LANGUAGE:** Portuguese

SITUATED ON THE SOUTHEAST African coast, Mozambique is bisected from east to west by the Zambezi River, which is dammed at Cahora Bassa. South of the Zambezi lies a semi-arid savanna lowland. The north-central delta provinces around Tete are the most fertile and it is here that the bulk of Mozambique's racially-mixed population lives. Since its independence in 1975 from Portugal, and the accession of the Marxist FRELIMO government, Mozambique has been in a state of civil war. It has depended on international food aid for ten years, and on several occasions the disruption of food supplies has led to mass starvation. The UN brokered a tenuous peace agreement in 1992.

CLIMATE

WEATHER CHART

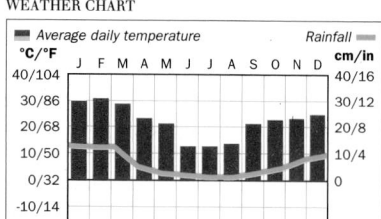

In theory, Mozambique has a rainy and a dry season. However, in the 1980s, frequent failure of the rains contributed to two disastrous famines: in 1982–1984 (when 100,000 died) and in 1986–1987. The coast south of Beira and the highlands adjoining Malawi and Zimbabwe are the wettest areas. The northern coast is dry because the moist trade winds are blocked by Madagascar. The Zambezi valley is the driest region.

COMMUNICATIONS

 Maputo Intl
409,000 passengers

 15 ships
24,100 dwt

THE TRANSPORT NETWORK

 26,095 km
(16,215 miles)

 None

3131 km
(1946 miles)

 3750 km
(2330 miles)

One of the biggest problems facing Mozambique is the estimated two million mines left over from the civil war, which prevent free access to many parts of the country. The hundreds of bridges destroyed in the war are slowly being rebuilt. Any major improvements to road and rail links will have to await a more stable political situation. Most of Mozambique's intercontinental trade continues to pass through South African ports.

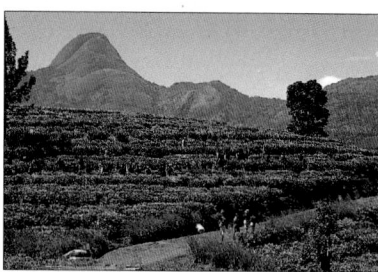

Tea picking. Other important cash crops are cashew nuts, cotton, sugar, copra and citrus fruits. Agriculture employs 85% of workers.

TOURISM

 Tourism has still not recovered after war

 No change due to effects of war

MAIN OVERSEAS ARRIVALS

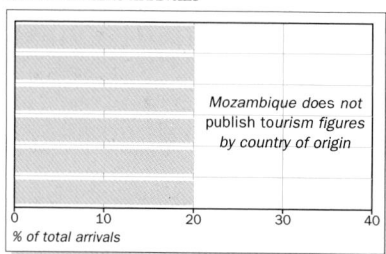

Mozambique does not publish tourism figures by country of origin

The tourist industry, which regularly used to attract around 300,000 South Africans and Rhodesians in the 1970s, has been destroyed by the war between the FRELIMO government and the Mozambique National Resistance (RENAMO) rebels. Travel outside the capital remains hazardous, and the city itself is subject to frequent power cuts and water shortages as a result of rebel activity. Tourist visas are also hard to obtain as the government regards any outsiders with suspicion.

Once political stability is achieved, however, Mozambique will be free to exploit its excellent beaches and game reserves, which include the Gorongosa Game Park.

PEOPLE

 Makua, Tsonga, Sena, Lomwe, Portuguese

20 people per km²

THE URBAN/RURAL POPULATION SPLIT

27%   73%

RELIGIOUS PERSUASION

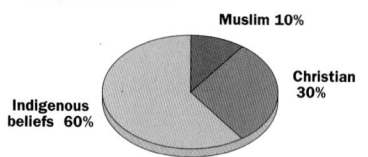

Muslim 10%

Christian 30%

Indigenous beliefs 60%

ETHNIC MAKEUP

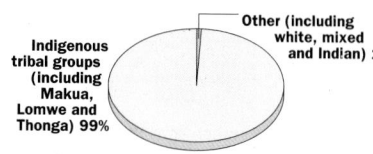

Other (including white, mixed and Indian) 1%

Indigenous tribal groups (including Makua, Lomwe and Thonga) 99%

Mozambique is racially very mixed. The tensions that exist in society, however, are not between the different groups but between northerners and southerners. The government has consistently been accused of favouring the south over the north and of including more southerners in its ministries; the greater economic success of the south adds to this tension. Anti-white feelings are growing as certain 'Africanist' groups are using the claim of excessive white influence in government as a means of gaining popular support.

Mozambican life is based around the extended family. In some provinces, notably Zambezia, Cabo Delgado and Tete, this is matriarchal. Polygamy is fairly widespread among those wealthy enough to take second wives. Under FRELIMO, women's rights have received particular attention. Women, who played an active part in FRELIMO armies, are now better protected by divorce, child-custody and husband-desertion laws. The Mozambican Women's Organization encourages participation in political life.

POPULATION AGE BREAKDOWN

	0–14		15–64		65+
	2.9%	3%	3.1%	3.3%	3.2%
	55.7%	53.9%	53.5%	52.3%	52.2%
	41.4%	43.1%	43.4%	44.4%	44.6%
	1960	1970	1980	1990	2000

M

POLITICS

 1994

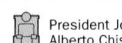 President Joaquim Alberto Chissano

THE STATE OF THE PARTIES

Assembly of the Republic 200–250 members

Politics in Mozambique is in a transitional phase. Elections are now scheduled for October 1994.

Mozambique is currently in a period of transition from single-party to multiparty democracy.

MAIN POLITICAL ISSUES

The peace process
The fragile UN-sponsored peace process, ending 15 years of civil war, is behind schedule. RENAMO's commitment remains in doubt, and in 1993 the UN had difficulty in securing the $260 million and the 7500 multinational forces required both to demobilize Mozambique's warring factions and to stage the first democratic elections.

Food relief
In 1993, the FRELIMO government and RENAMO rebels signed a humanitarian declaration ensuring the safe passage of UN food aid to the starving.

Reconstruction
Mozambique faces an enormous task in rebuilding a country ravaged by civil war, with its toll of 900,000 dead, one million refugees and an estimated 90% of the remaining population living below the poverty line.

PROFILE
Between 1977 and 1990, Mozambique was a one-party state ruled by the Soviet-backed FRELIMO, which had campaigned for independence from Portugal in the 1960s. The RENAMO rebel group, backed by Rhodesia and white South Africa, conducted a civil war to limit Soviet influence, under the guise of seeking democracy.

The changing international scene led to FRELIMO adopting a democratic constitution in 1990 and to RENAMO losing its international sponsors. The key questions now revolve around consolidating the peace process and moving the country to a full democracy. FRELIMO still retains much support in the country, while RENAMO wishes to receive some benefits from 15 years of struggle. New groups, such as the anti-white PALMO, COINMO and UNAMO, are also starting to emerge.

Joaquim Chissano, president since 1986, has pushed towards political pluralism.

RENAMO leader, Afonso Dhlakama, now turning from militarism to politics.

WORLD AFFAIRS

 OAU   SADC   ECA   FLS   AfDB

During the Cold War years, Mozambique was a key battleground in the conflict between Soviet-backed Marxism, and capitalism sponsored by the USA and South Africa. The result was a civil war, which devastated the country between 1977 and 1992.

A shift in the FRELIMO government's position had, however, already become apparent in the early 1980s, as Soviet aid levels became erratic. President Samora Machel then took steps towards a reconciliation with the West, which saw the USA lifting its ban on economic assistance in 1984 and Britain agreeing to provide military training for FRELIMO's forces in 1987. A peace accord was also signed with South Africa in 1984. Mozambique fulfilled its obligations by expelling the ANC, but South Africa did not and continued support for RENAMO until 1990.

The key concern now is the need to maintain the UN presence in the country to ensure the success of the peace process, given the fear that RENAMO, which is unlikely to do well at the polls, may choose to resume an armed struggle.

MOZAMBIQUE

Total Area : 801 590 sq. km
(309 493 sq. miles)

POPULATION

over 1 000 000	⊡
over 100 000	◎
over 50 000	○
over 10 000	●
under 10 000	·

LAND HEIGHT

2000m/6562ft	
1000m/3281ft	
500m/1640ft	
200m/656ft	
Sea Level	

CHRONOLOGY

The Portuguese tapped the local trade in slaves, gold and ivory in the 16th century and made Mozambique a colony in 1752. Large areas were run by private companies until 1929.

☐ **1962** FRELIMO founded.

☐ **1964** Starts war of liberation.

☐ **1975** Independence. Marxist FRELIMO leader Samora Machel is president. 230,000 of the 250,000 Portuguese leave, but destroy much transport and machinery.

☐ **1976** Resistance movement RENAMO set up inside Mozambique by Rhodesians.

☐ **1976–1980** Mozambique closes Rhodesian border, imposes economic sanctions, and supports Zimbabwean freedom fighters. Destructive reprisals by RENAMO. ⇨

M

CHRONOLOGY *continued*

- ❑ **1980** South Africa takes over backing of RENAMO.
- ❑ **1982** Zimbabwean troops arrive to guard Mutare–Beira oil pipeline and road–rail route.
- ❑ **1984** Nkomati Accord: South Africa agrees to stop support for RENAMO, and Mozambique for ANC. Ineffectual. Fighting continues.
- ❑ **1986** RENAMO declares war on Zimbabwe. Tanzania sends troops and military aid to FRELIMO. President Machel dies in mystery air crash in South Africa. Joaquim Chissano replaces him.
- ❑ **1988** Nkomati Accord reactivated. Mozambicans allowed back to work in South African mines.
- ❑ **1989** Civil war estimated to have killed 600,000 and caused 405,000 children to die of malnutrition. FRELIMO drops Marxism-Leninism.
- ❑ **1990** Multipartyism and free market economy written into new constitution. RENAMO fails to recognize it or keep ceasefire.
- ❑ **1992** Chissano and RENAMO's leader, Afonso Dhlakama, meet for first time for peace talks. Peace agreement signed in October.
- ❑ **1993** UN has difficulty raising international peace-keeping force.

AID

 $920m (receipts)   Down 2% in 1991

The economic situation left by the war has led Mozambique to launch a global campaign for assistance. Seven million Mozambicans are entirely dependent on food aid, and even the most basic economic activity relies on some form of aid. The main donor nations are Italy, the UK, the USA, Sweden, the Netherlands, Norway and, recently, South Africa – whose outlook has influenced Mozambique's turn towards a market economy. Debts from aid provided by the USSR in the late 1970s and early 1980s have been written off.

DEFENCE

 $114.44m   Up 1% in 1991

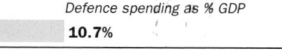

0   *Defence spending as % GDP*   40
10.7%

MOZAMBICAN ARMED FORCES

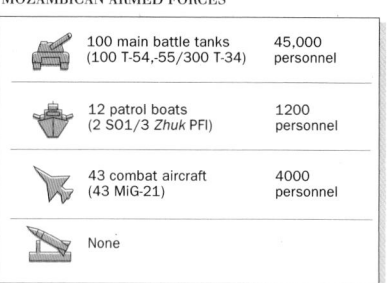

	100 main battle tanks (100 T-54,-55/300 T-34)	45,000 personnel
	12 patrol boats (2 SO1/3 *Zhuk* PFI)	1200 personnel
	43 combat aircraft (43 MiG-21)	4000 personnel
	None	

Not surprisingly, given the civil war between 1977 and 1992, the armed forces have had a dominant role in Mozambique's affairs, swallowing on average 40% of state income. Military figures have also been prominent in the FRELIMO government, holding the Foreign Affairs, Home Affairs and Transport portfolios. Since 1982, Zimbabwe has also deployed forces to secure the Beira railway and transport route against RENAMO attack.

The key issue now is demobilization, a prerequisite for elections to be held in 1994, and a crucial task if a return to civil war is to be avoided. Under the UN plan, RENAMO and FRELIMO forces would form a new national army of 30,000. However, its success remains in doubt given the historical animosity between the two sides. Also, there are fears that many RENAMO units have enjoyed too much autonomy to accept any central control.

ECONOMICS

 $844m   5279.01 meticais

SCORE CARD

- ❑ WORLD GNP RANKING.......................159th
- ❑ GNP PER CAPITA $80
- ❑ BALANCE OF PAYMENTS....................$–271m
- ❑ INFLATION 39.1%
- ❑ UNEMPLOYMENT................................50%

EXPORTS

- Spain 9%
- Germany* 12%
- Japan 12%
- USA 15%
- Other 52%

IMPORTS

- Portugal 8%
- France 6%
- South Africa Customs Union 12%
- CIS* 20%
- Other 54%

ECONOMIC PERFORMANCE INDICATOR

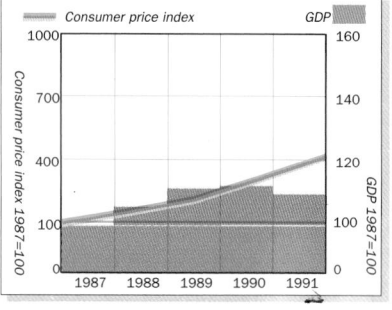

Consumer price index   GDP

(graph, Consumer price index 1987=100 on left axis 0–1000, GDP 1987=100 on right axis 0–160, years 1987 1988 1989 1990 1991)

STRENGTHS

Given the current war-ravaged conditions, Mozambique's economy has no strengths to speak of and is almost entirely dependent on foreign aid. Assuming peace prevails, Mozambique could develop the agricultural sector, which employs 85% of the workforce. The fisheries industry has great potential. Mozambique also has Africa's second largest harbour, Maputo. Modernized in 1989, it is well placed to service southern Africa's land-locked regions.

WEAKNESSES

Mozambique is susceptible to drought and cyclones. A war-shattered infrastructure has left the economy in a condition where overseas aid is essential to prevent at least half the population starving. Destroyed transport links make it impossible to exploit resources such as iron ore and bauxite. Skilled workers have sought employment in other countries; their absence will delay the return to normal economic activity. 70% of the workforce remains illiterate.

PROFILE

Mozambique's enormous problems are further exacerbated by the failure of the socialist model in industry and agriculture and, as with many eastern European economies, the need to learn from scratch the rules of private enterprise and the free market. Even if peaceful conditions can be assured, economic growth will still be extremely slow.

MOZAMBIQUE : MAJOR BUSINESSES

- Pemba
- Nacala
- Tete
- Quelimane
- Beira
- Maputo

- Textiles
- Fertilizers
- Coal mining
- Agribusiness
- Fish processing
- Food processing
- Manufacturing

0   200 km
0   200 miles   * significant multinational ownership

RESOURCES

485m kwh (capacity 2.36m kw)

Not an oil producer and has no refineries

1m cattle, 165,000 pigs, 120,000 sheep

Coal, iron, tantalite, bauxite, titanium, fluorspar, zirconium

ELECTRICITY GENERATION

Hydro 10% (50m kwh)

Thermal 90% (435m kwh)

Nuclear 0%

Other 0%

0   20   40   60   80   100

% of total generation by type

Mozambique's mineral reserves are modest and, due to the lack of useful transport links, currently unexploited.

ENVIRONMENT

None

Peace may ease environmental pressures

ENVIRONMENTAL TREATIES

No

Yes

No

No

The devastating effects of perennial floods followed by droughts are Mozambique's major concern. A three-year drought between 1982 and 1984 resulted in the deaths of 100,000 and left four million close to starvation. The drought was followed in 1984 by massive flooding, which left 50,000 homeless and destroyed much of the harvest. Other ecological concerns are some way down the political agenda in the aftermath of recent conflict. An estimated 50,000 elephants were slaughtered for ivory in order to help fund RENAMO's war effort.

MEDIA

The press is now theoretically free

PUBLISHING AND BROADCAST MEDIA

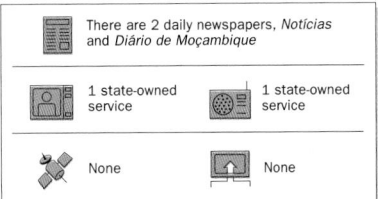

There are 2 daily newspapers, *Notícias* and *Diário de Moçambique*

1 state-owned service

1 state-owned service

None

None

The press, traditionally a FRELIMO publicity machine, was freed from restrictions by the terms of the 1990 constitution and will become more active during election periods. With only 40,000 TV sets in the whole of Mozambique, the political impact of television is minimal.

Fishing is the most important sector (shrimps accounted for 46% of all export revenue in 1988). The government is concentrating on restoring electricity supplies.

Forest
Pasture
Cropland
Cereals
Cattle

MOZAMBIQUE : LAND USE

0   200 km

0   200 miles

CRIME

Mozambique does not publish prison figures

Crime levels are very high and probably rising

CRIME RATES

Assessment of criminality impossible due to recent war

Mozambique is awash with weapons. Banditry, frequently carried out by gangs of former soldiers, is endemic. All areas outside the main urban centres are highly dangerous and road travel is particularly unsafe. Fraud and corruption linked to the misuse of food aid are also major problems.

EDUCATION

30%

0   Education spending as % GNP   25

Low due to recent war

THE EDUCATION SYSTEM

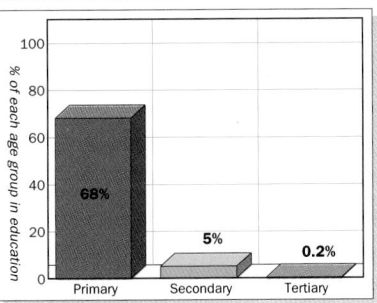

% of each age group in education

100
80
60
40
20
0

68% Primary
5% Secondary
0.2% Tertiary

Over 3000 schools closed between 1983 and 1990 as a direct result of the war. There were no private schools between 1977 and 1990. Students at Maputo University, which attracted many anti-apartheid academic exiles from South Africa, are obliged to spend time in public service in return for their education.

HEALTH

1 per 39,500 people

Tuberculosis, gastroenteric infections, pneumonia

0   Health spending as % GNP   25

1.7%

War casualties and almost anarchic conditions in the countryside are the major problems. 15% of the population cannot afford the drugs prescribed for them and attendance at health posts has declined. However, preventive medicines and ante-natal care are provided free. Doctors have to serve a mandatory two-year period in rural areas. In 1987, as part of the attempts at reconstruction, private clinics, which were previously banned as unsocialist, began to appear.

WEALTH

Agricultural labourer, 24,310 meticais per month (minimum); medical consultant, 146,000 meticais per month

CONSUMER GOODS OWNERSHIP

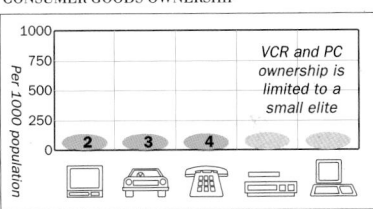

Per 1000 population

1000
750
500
250
0

VCR and PC ownership is limited to a small elite

2   3   4

Mozambique is one of the world's poorest countries. In 1991, GNP per capita was estimated at just $80. Society is hardly stratified as over 90% of the people live in similar breadline conditions. Measures linked to the provision of Western aid have made conditions tougher, raising the price of rice by 600%. Only the higher echelons of FRELIMO, RENAMO and the other political parties have luxuries such as cars, air-conditioning and brick-built apartments. The slow introduction of free-market reforms will, however, increase access to consumer goods in the longer term.

WORLD RANKING

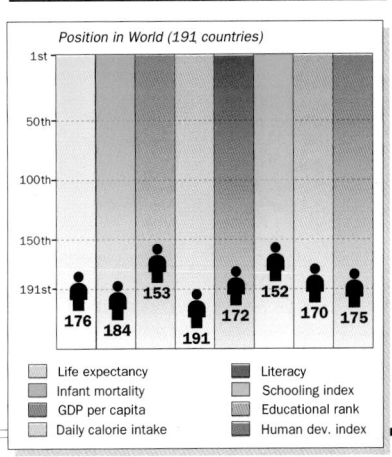

Position in World (191 countries)

1st
50th
100th
150th
191st

176   184   153   191   172   152   170   175

Life expectancy
Infant mortality
GDP per capita
Daily calorie intake

Literacy
Schooling index
Educational rank
Human dev. index

M

NAMIBIA

OFFICIAL NAME: The Republic of Namibia   **CAPITAL:** Windhoek
POPULATION: 1.5 million   **CURRENCY:** South African rand   **OFFICIAL LANGUAGE:** English

SOUTHERN AFRICA

L OCATED IN SOUTHWESTERN Africa, Namibia has an arid coastal strip formed by the Namib Desert. After many years of guerrilla warfare, Namibia achieved independence from South Africa in 1990. Despite the move away from apartheid, Namibia's economy remains reliant on the expertise of the small white population, a legacy of the previously poor education for blacks. Namibia is Africa's fourth largest minerals producer.

CLIMATE

WEATHER CHART

Namibia is almost rainless. The coast is usually shrouded in thick, cold fog unless the hot, very dry *berg* blows.

COMMUNICATIONS

 Windhoek Intl
258,373 passengers

 Has no fleet

THE TRANSPORT NETWORK

42,760 km (26,565 miles)		None
2382 km (1480 miles)		None

Large-scale industry is well served by road and rail. Plans exist to build a new harbour at Walvis Bay.

TOURISM

 213,000 visitors   Up 29% in 1992

MAIN OVERSEAS ARRIVALS

South Africa 50%
Germany 25%
UK 5%
Other 20%
% of total arrivals

Tourists contributed only 4% to GDP in 1991. A quarter are German, many of whom come to visit Windhoek's German sector. There are plans to limit tourists to 300,000 a year to preserve Namibia's fragile desert ecology.

Spitzkoppe, west of Karibib. *Unique scenery such as this is attracting increasing numbers of eco-tourists to Namibia.*

PEOPLE

 Ovambo, Kavango, English, Bergdama, German   2 people per km²

THE URBAN/RURAL POPULATION SPLIT

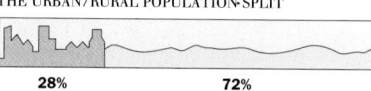

28%   72%

ETHNIC MAKEUP

Mixed 7%   White 7%
Black 86%

The largest ethnic group, the Ovambo, lives mostly in the north of the country. Whites – 60% of whom are Afrikaans-speakers – live mostly in Windhoek, which includes a large German community, living in comfortable, bourgeois, turn-of-the-century German houses. The strife between rival ethnic groups predicted at the time of independence in 1990 has not materialized, and Namibia has adapted well to a multiracial existence. Blacks, who are mostly subsistence farmers, have largely accepted the greater wealth of the white community.

Families are large in Namibia, and amongst the black community women have, on average, 6.5 children. The constitution supports sexual equality and positive discrimination in favour of women; few, however, have official jobs or own property.

POLITICS

Lower House 1994 Upper House 1995	President Samuel Daniel Nujoma

THE STATE OF THE PARTIES

National Assembly 72 members

4% Other

57% SWAPO   29% DTA   6% UDF   4% ACN

SWAPO = South West Africa People's Organization of Namibia **DTA** = Democratic Turnhalle Alliance **UDF** = United Democratic Front **ACN** = Action Christian National

National Council 26 members

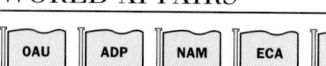

2 members are elected from among the members of each of the 13 regional councils

At independence from South Africa in 1990, Namibia switched from a system of apartheid based on ten separate homelands, to a state-wide, multiparty democracy. Since 1990, SWAPO, whose guerrilla wing fought for and won independence, has had control of the National Assembly. The Ovambo community in the north is SWAPO's main backer, although its centre-left stance also gives it the support of large numbers of state employees.

SWAPO has been criticized for not moving swiftly enough to end wealth inequalities. The land reform promised in 1990 has not materialized, and whites remain in control of most areas of the economy, whilst unemployment among blacks is high. SWAPO's main opposition comes from the centre-right DTA, a coalition of 11 parties which favours a free-market approach.

WORLD AFFAIRS

 OAU   ADP   NAM   ECA   ACP

Namibia joined the UN, OAU and Commonwealth within the first few months of independence. In 1992, agreement was reached on the disputed southern border with South Africa. In August 1993, South Africa also agreed to relinquish control of the enclave of Walvis Bay – Namibia's only deep-water port.

AID

 $184m (receipts)   Up 50% in 1991

The UN provides most aid. Germany is the main unilateral donor. 31% of aid is spent on education.

NAMIBIA

Total Area : 824 290 sq. km
(318 260 sq. miles)

LAND HEIGHT

2000m/6562ft
1000m/3281ft
500m/1640ft
200m/656ft
Sea Level

POPULATION

over 100 000
over 10 000
under 10 000

CHRONOLOGY

In 1915, South Africa took over the former German colony as a League of Nations' mandate known as South West Africa.

❑ **1950** South Africa refuses to give up the territory to the UN.
❑ **1966** Apartheid laws imposed. SWAPO begins armed struggle.
❑ **1968** Renamed Namibia.
❑ **1973** UN recognizes SWAPO.
❑ **1990** Independence.
❑ **1993** South Africa relinquishes Walvis Bay.

DEFENCE

 $47.44m

 Down 44% in 1990

Patrolling fishing stocks, which are frequently raided by Spanish and South African trawlers, is the main activity.

ECONOMICS

$2.1bn

3.40 South African rand

SCORE CARD

❑ WORLD GNP RANKING.......................138th
❑ GNP PER CAPITA $1240
❑ BALANCE OF PAYMENTS $30m
❑ INFLATION 11.9%
❑ UNEMPLOYMENT.................................40%

STRENGTHS

Varied mineral resources make Namibia the third wealthiest country in sub-Saharan Africa. Namibian waters encompass one of the world's richest offshore fishing grounds. Potential of Walvis Bay as transit point for Namibia's land-locked neighbours.

WEAKNESSES

Almost all manufactured goods have to be imported. Sensitivity to fluctuations in mineral prices. Lack of skilled labour; only 25% of Namibians participate in commercial economy.

IMPORTS / EXPORTS

Namibia has yet to publish official trade figures. South Africa remains the major source of imports and destination for exports

RESOURCES

New hydroelectric station will ensure self-sufficiency

Not an oil producer and has no refineries

7m sheep, 2m cattle, 68,000 asses

Uranium, lead, cadmium, diamonds, copper, zinc, silver

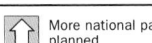

Namibia has the world's largest uranium mine, is the world's second largest lead producer, and the third largest producer of cadmium. Hydroelectric power has enormous potential; the Okavango River system carries a higher volume of water than all South Africa's rivers combined.

ENVIRONMENT

13% (2% partially protected)

More national parks planned

Illegal poaching and anthrax deposits are threatening the unique Namibian desert-adapted elephant (only 34 remain) and black rhino. Namibia has a unique, but fragile, desert ecosystem, much of which is protected. Government policy is generally sensitive to environmental issues (the annual seal-cull to protect fish stocks is an exception) and wishes to promote eco-tourists rather than mass-market developments.

MEDIA

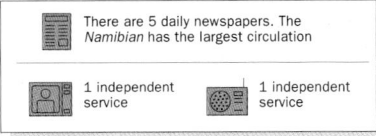
Since 1990, press freedom has been guaranteed under the constitution. Only minor criticism is tolerated in practice

PUBLISHING AND BROADCAST MEDIA

There are 5 daily newspapers. The *Namibian* has the largest circulation

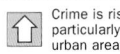
1 independent service

1 independent service

The Namibian Broadcasting Corporation transmits in 11 languages, including German and English.

CRIME

Namibia does not publish prison figures

Crime is rising, particularly in urban areas

350 people held by SWAPO before independence are still unaccounted for. Ostrich smuggling to the USA is common.

EDUCATION

 72%

High illiteracy rates among black adults, a legacy of apartheid, is the education system's main challenge.

HEALTH

 1 per 5008 people

 Respiratory, heart and intestinal diseases

A new health ministry is trying to balance the white-orientated health service. Most areas lack safe water.

WEALTH

Returning political exiles find employment, partly because whites do not like hiring former guerrillas

CONSUMER GOODS OWNERSHIP

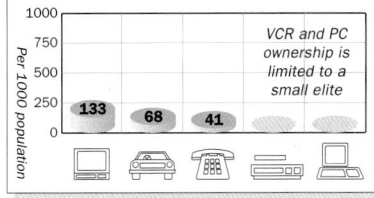

Whites still earn, on average, 20 times more than blacks. Mercedes are the most desirable status symbol.

WORLD RANKING

N

NAURU

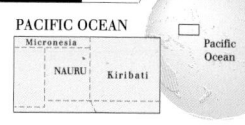

PACIFIC OCEAN

OFFICIAL NAME: The Republic of Nauru **CAPITAL:** *No official capital*
POPULATION: 9400 **CURRENCY:** Australian dollar **OFFICIAL LANGUAGE:** Nauruan

NAURU LIES IN the Pacific Ocean, 4000 km northeast of Australia. Formerly a British colony, Nauru was exploited for its phosphate deposits by the UK, Australia and New Zealand. Since independence in 1968, the phosphates industry has made Nauruan citizens amongst the wealthiest in the world. However, reserves are due to run out in 1995 and in the future, the proceeds of overseas investments will form the bulk of Nauru's income.

CLIMATE

WEATHER CHART

Nauru's tiny size means that rain clouds often miss the island; at times years pass without rain.

COMMUNICATIONS

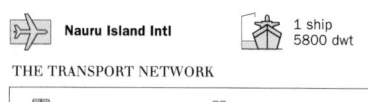

THE TRANSPORT NETWORK

27 km (17 miles)		None	
5 km (3 miles)		None	

Nauru operates its own airline with Boeing 737s piloted by Australians. The Nauru Steamship Line is Nauru's main link with the outside world. However, all external travel is very expensive. Nauru has no harbour, so ships taking phosphates aboard dock with engines still running on huge concrete caissons floating out at sea. Most Nauruans can afford cars. The single circular road is often littered with abandoned cars, such as Mercedes, as it is much cheaper for Nauruans to import new vehicles than attempt to repair existing ones. The number of car accident fatalities is one of the highest in the South Pacific.

TOURISM

MAIN OVERSEAS ARRIVALS

Nauru does not publish tourism figures by country of origin

Even if Nauru had any conventional tourist attractions, the enormous cost of getting there would dissuade most tourists from making the journey. The main feature of interest on the island is the bizarre lunar landscape created by over 80 years of phosphate extraction. There are no beaches on Nauru and only a few basic hotels.

NAURU

Total Area : 21.2 sq. km (8.2 sq. miles)

LAND HEIGHT
- 200m/565ft
- Sea Level

- Urban area
- Phosphate mineworks

PEOPLE

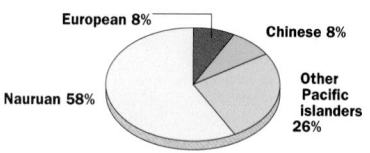

Nauruan, Kiribati, Chinese, Tuvaluan, English

429 people per km²

THE URBAN/RURAL POPULATION SPLIT

Nauru is 100% semi-urban

ETHNIC MAKEUP

European 8%
Chinese 8%
Other Pacific islanders 26%
Nauruan 58%

Indigenous Nauruans are a homogenous group. They do little of the tough work on the island, which is left to an imported labour force, mainly from Kiribati, who live in enclaves of male-only barracks and have few rights.

A society of just 9400, Nauru is mostly self-regulating. There is some generational tension between younger Nauruans, who go to Australia to study, but have little incentive to do well, and their parents, who fought hard for independence. As the phosphate runs out, an increasing feeling of pointlessness is gripping the young. Many see their future in Australia or New Zealand, but are wary of a drop in living standards and of losing the luxury of sovereignty. It was the latter which led Nauruans to reject the offer of resettlement on an island off the Australian Queensland coast.

POLITICS

1995

President Bernard Dowiyogo

THE STATE OF THE PARTIES

Parliament 18 members

All members are elected as independents

Hammer DeRoburt, Head Chief of Nauru, became the island's first president in 1968. He dominated the political structure until a vote of no confidence forced him to resign in 1989. He was replaced by Dowiyogo, who secured his continued term in office in the 1992 elections. The traditional chiefly leaders are still the dominant political figures. Nauru's Parliament is based on the British Westminster model. Members often switch between temporary, unstable groupings within it.

WORLD AFFAIRS

Comm   ESCAP   SPC   SPF

The case for compensation for phosphate exploitation brought by Nauru against the UK government was rejected in 1992 after the longest suit in British legal history. However, an Australian settlement in 1993 brought an immediate payment and a longer-term contribution totalling 107 million Australian dollars. Nauru's main concern is participation in the South Pacific Forum and the management of trust funds to support Nauruans when phosphate deposits run out.

AID

 Donations through the South Pacific Forum only   Not applicable

Nauru is neither an aid recipient nor donor, except as a member of the South Pacific Forum.

DEFENCE

 Australia responsible for defence   Not applicable

Nauru, which faces no outside threats, has no defence force. Australia, under a *de facto* arrangement, is responsible for the island's security.

ECONOMICS

  $90m   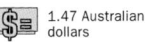 1.47 Australian dollars

SCORE CARD

❑ World GNP Ranking	187th
❑ GNP per Capita	$10,000
❑ Balance of Payments	$20m
❑ Inflation	Low inflation rate
❑ Unemployment	Minimal unemployment

Strengths
Considerable investments in Australian and Hawaiian property and hotels. Possible future as a tax haven.

Weaknesses
Phosphate, the only resource, is due to run out in 1995. Phosphate mining has left 80% of the island uninhabitable and uncultivable. Nauru has been prone to poor investments, such as backing the flop London musical *Leonardo* in 1993. Nauru's flagship Melbourne skyscraper, Nauru House, has developed 'concrete cancer' which is costing millions of dollars to repair.

IMPORT/EXPORTS

Nauru's only export commodity is phosphates, in which it trades with Australia and New Zealand. Almost all food, drinking water and manufactured goods are imported, mostly from Australia, New Zealand, the UK and Japan

RESOURCES

 29m kwh (capacity 10,000 kw)   Not an oil producer and has no refineries

 Pigs, chickens   Guano (phosphates)

Since 1888 Nauru has been exploited by the Germans, British, Australians, New Zealanders, and recently by Nauruans themselves, for its valuable phosphate reserves. Extraction, which took out most of the centre of the island, has occurred at a fast rate, and the deposits are due to run out in 1995. Nauru has no other resources. The island is entirely dependent on outside energy supplies and the cost of oil is 50% higher than the Pacific average as Nauru does not lie on any shipping routes. Most electricity is produced by small diesel generators.

ENVIRONMENT

 None   No prospect of making island cultivable

The main concern is possible fall-out from French nuclear test sites in the Pacific: Nauru lies downwind of these. Otherwise, ecological awareness is minimal. Nauruans accept that their source of wealth has effectively destroyed their island.

MEDIA

 Freedom of speech is protected by law

PUBLISHING AND BROADCAST MEDIA

There are no daily newspapers. The *Bulletin*, the *Young Post* and the *Observer* are published weekly	
No TV service	1 state-owned service

Nauru has no national TV broadcasting service; some overseas programmes are made available on video.

CRIME

 Nauru does not publish prison figures   Crime levels are rising slightly

Theft is almost non-existent. Assaults and dangerous driving as a result of drunkenness are the major problems.

Nauru is almost circular with a single, 19-km ring road. The overcrowded coastal strip is the sole habitable land.

EDUCATION

 99%

Many Nauruans attend boarding school in Australia from a young age. Few go on to university.

HEALTH

 1 per 700 people   Tuberculosis, vitamin deficiencies, diabetes

A diet of processed imported foods and widespread obesity are the major problems. One third of the population suffers from non-insulin-dependent diabetes. Industrial accidents are treated in Australia.

WEALTH

 Average white collar worker, 16,000 Australian dollars per year

CONSUMER GOODS OWNERSHIP

High levels of TV ownership   VCR and PC ownership at European levels

159   193

Nauru has one of the highest per capita incomes in the world. Wealth is fairly evenly distributed. Most Nauruans live in simple traditional houses and spend their money on luxury cars.

WORLD RANKING

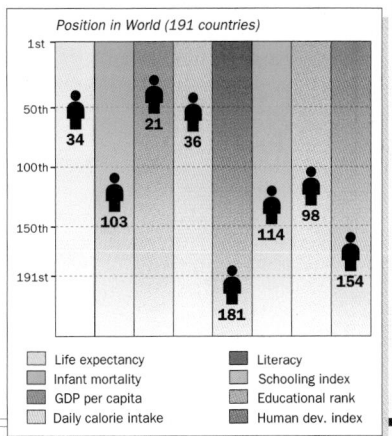

Position in World (191 countries)

34   21   36   103   114   98   181   154

- Life expectancy
- Infant mortality
- GDP per capita
- Daily calorie intake
- Literacy
- Schooling index
- Educational rank
- Human dev. index

N

NEPAL

SOUTH ASIA

OFFICIAL NAME: Kingdom of Nepal   CAPITAL: Kathmandu
POPULATION: 20.6 million   CURRENCY: Nepalese rupee   OFFICIAL LANGUAGE: Nepali

ON THE SHOULDER OF the southern Himalayas, Nepal is surrounded by India and China. It is one of the poorest countries in the world, and its largely agricultural economy is heavily dependent on the prompt arrival of the monsoon. Important new sources of income are now being developed, including hydroelectric power and tourism. In 1991, democratic elections were held for the first time since 1959, marking the end of a period of absolute rule by the king.

CLIMATE

WEATHER CHART

The warm July to October monsoon affects the whole country, causing flooding in the hot Terai plain, but generally decreases northwards and westwards. The rest of the year is dry, sunny and mild, except in the Himalayas, where valley temperatures in winter may average –10°C.

COMMUNICATIONS

Tribhuvan International, Kathmandu
800,000 passengers

Has no fleet

THE TRANSPORT NETWORK

7080 km (4399 miles)		None
52 km (32 miles)		None

Domestic flights link the main towns. There are paved roads in the south and in the Kathmandu valley; only one runs north to China. Two short stretches of railway cross into India.

Himalayan harvest. The steep mountainsides and easily-eroded soils mean that most fields are terraced. 90% of Nepalese are farmers.

TOURISM

255,000 visitors

Up 6% in 1990

MAIN OVERSEAS ARRIVALS

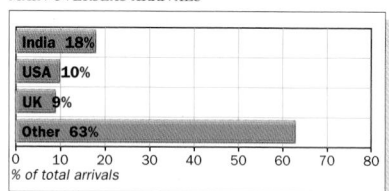

A serious conflict exists between the wish to preserve the environment and the desire for tourist revenue. Areas in the northwest were opened up to tourists in 1989, but degradation caused by 72,000 trekkers a year on popular routes forced the government to set up the Annapurna Conservation Project. Fuelwood cutting for tourists is said to have increased deforestation, and hence soil erosion, by 10%.

PEOPLE

Nepali, Maithilli, Bhojpuri

130 people per km²

THE URBAN/RURAL POPULATION SPLIT

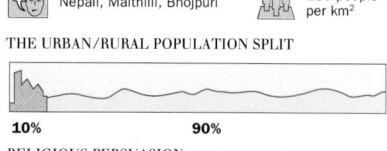

10%   90%

RELIGIOUS PERSUASION

Muslim 3%   Buddhist 5%
Other 2%

Hindu 90%

There are few ethnic tensions despite the variety of ethnic groups, including northerners, such as the Sherpas, the inhabitants of the Terai in the south and the Newars, mostly found in the Kathmandu valley. Women's subordinate position is enshrined in property and divorce laws; Hindu women are more restricted than Sherpas and Buddhists. Polygamy is practised in the hills.

POLITICS

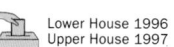

Lower House 1996
Upper House 1997

HM King Birendra Bir Bikram Shah Dev

THE STATE OF THE PARTIES

House of Representatives 205 members

8% Other

54% NCP   34% UCPN   4% UPF

NCP = Nepali Congress Party UCPN = United Communist Party of Nepal UPF = United People's Front Other = Nepali Sadbhavana Party, National Democratic Party

National Council 60 members

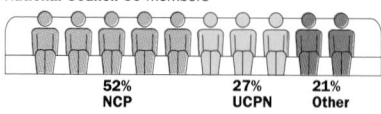

52% NCP   27% UCPN   21% Other

35 members elected by the House of Representatives, 15 chosen from the country's development zones, and 10 chosen by King Birendra

The end of absolute monarchy and the partyless *panchayat* system in 1990 allowed the NCP to take power in the 1991 elections. The main parties, even those on the left, are driven by allegiance to individual leaders rather than to different policies. Major issues include relations with India, especially concerning the Tanakpur Dam project, and how to handle both street agitation by the left, and the civil and military personnel from the old regime.

WORLD AFFAIRS

ESCAP   ADB   CP   NAM   SAARC

The NCP is friendly towards India, on which Nepal depends for the transit of much of its trade with the outside world. Nepal regards China as a potential threat; China suspects Nepal of being used as a base by Tibetan opposition groups.

AID

$453m (receipts)

Up 5% in 1991

Nepal's strategic position has made it a focus for powerful donors, including the USA, China, India, Japan and member states of the CIS.

DEFENCE

$33.19m

Up 8% in 1991

The army is small at 35,000 men. It has no tanks, combat aircraft or armed helicopters. The limited weaponry comes from the UK and India.

N

NEPAL
Total Area : 140 800 sq. km
(54 363 sq. miles)

POPULATION
over 100 000
over 10 000
under 10 000

LAND HEIGHT
6000m/19 686ft
4000m/13 124ft
2000m/6562ft
1000m/3281ft
500m/1640ft
200m/656ft
50m/164ft

CHRONOLOGY

The foundations of the Nepalese state were laid in 1769, when King Prithvi Narayan Shah conquered the region.

❏ **1816–1923** Establishment of quasi-British protectorate.
❏ **1959** First multiparty constitution.
❏ **1960** King Mahendra bans all political parties and suspends the constitution.
❏ **1962** *Panchayat* system launched.
❏ **1985** Nepal is a founder member of SAARC.
❏ **1989–1990** 'Trade and transit' dispute with India.
❏ **1990** Political parties reinstated.
❏ **1991** Multiparty elections.

ECONOMICS

 $3.5bn   46.30 Nepalese rupees

SCORE CARD

❏ WORLD GNP RANKING	120th
❏ GNP PER CAPITA	$170
❏ BALANCE OF PAYMENTS	$–181.3m
❏ INFLATION	9.1%
❏ UNEMPLOYMENT	5%

STRENGTHS
Self-sufficiency in food grains in most years. Great potential for hydroelectric power generation, although as yet little developed. Low debt level.

WEAKNESSES
Agricultural dependency; only 10% of GDP from manufacturing. Land-locked status. Low savings rate. Absence of active entrepreneurial class.

EXPORTS

Switzerland 8%
USA 28%
India 13%
Other 25%
Germany* 26%

IMPORTS

Japan 10%
Singapore 17%
Other 45%
India 28%

RESOURCES

739m kwh (capacity 230,000 kw)
Not an oil producer and has no refineries
6.3m cattle, 910,000 sheep, 548,000 pigs
Mica, lignite, copper, cobalt, iron

There are plans to develop the large, but barely exploited, hydro-power potential for domestic use and export.

ENVIRONMENT

8% (1% partially protected)
Two national parks threatened by large-scale HEP projects

Deforestation, including destruction of rhododendron forests, and the resulting soil erosion, is a serious problem. The native tiger is fast disappearing; skins are dumped by poachers who sell the bones to Chinese medicine makers.

MEDIA

Press freedom is guaranteed under the new constitution

PUBLISHING AND BROADCAST MEDIA

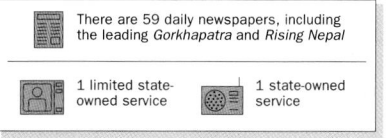
There are 59 daily newspapers, including the leading *Gorkhapatra* and *Rising Nepal*
1 limited state-owned service
1 state-owned service

The Nepal TV service began broadcasting in 1985 and 18% of the country now receives it. The press is mainly Kathmandu-based with low circulations. The *Sunday Despatch* is the paper most critical of government.

CRIME

Nepal does not publish prison figures
Up 11% in 1990

Petty theft and smuggling are the main problems. The legal provision for detention without trial is used and police suppression of demonstrations is often brutal.

EDUCATION

26%

Over 80% of boys attend school in Nepal, but still only a minority of girls. Nepal's literacy rate is among the lowest in the world.

HEALTH

1 per 20,978 people
Respiratory and diarrheal diseases, maternal deaths

There are about 100 *dharmi-jhankri* (faith healers) for every health worker. Maternal mortality is high, the result of harmful traditional birth practices; a re-education programme for midwives has been established.

WEALTH

Sawmill sawyer, 800 Nepalese rupees per month; yarn spinner, 2500-6000 Nepalese rupees per month

CONSUMER GOODS OWNERSHIP

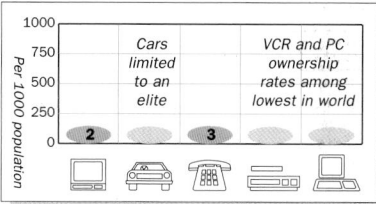
Cars limited to an elite
VCR and PC ownership rates among lowest in world

Nepal is one of the poorest countries in the world. Income per head is less than $200 a year.

WORLD RANKING

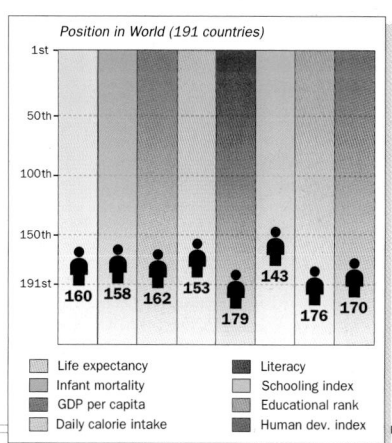

Position in World (191 countries)

160 158 162 153 179 143 176 170

Life expectancy | Literacy
Infant mortality | Schooling index
GDP per capita | Educational rank
Daily calorie intake | Human dev. index

NETHERLANDS

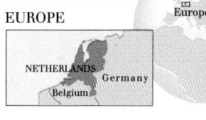

EUROPE

OFFICIAL NAME: Kingdom of the Netherlands **CAPITALS:** Amsterdam ,The Hague
POPULATION: 15.2 million **CURRENCY:** Netherlands guilder **OFFICIAL LANGUAGE:** Dutch **OVERSEAS TERRITORIES:** 2

THE NETHERLANDS is located at the delta of five major rivers in northwest Europe. The few hills in the eastern and southern part of the country fall into a flat coastal area, bordered by the North Sea to the north and west. This is protected by a giant infrastructure of dunes, dikes and canals, as 27% of the coast is below sea level. The Netherlands became one of the world's first confederative republics after Spain recognized its independence in 1648. Its highly successful economy has a long trading tradition and Rotterdam, its main port, is also the world's largest.

CLIMATE

WEATHER CHART

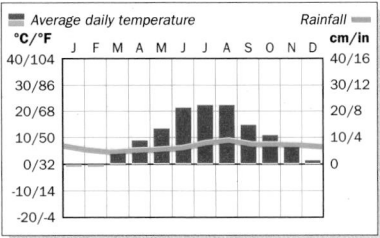

The Netherlands has a temperate climate, which is characterized by mild winters and cool summers. The country's coastal areas have the mildest climate, though northerly gales are fairly frequent, particularly in autumn and winter.

TOURISM

 6.2m visitors Up 7% in 1992

MAIN OVERSEAS ARRIVALS

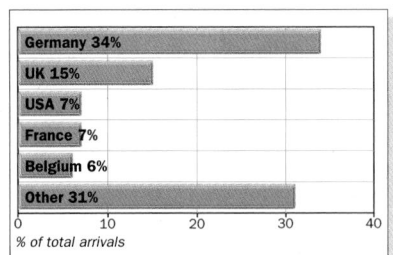

Germany 34%	
UK 15%	
USA 7%	
France 7%	
Belgium 6%	
Other 31%	

% of total arrivals

Tourism is a major business in the Netherlands. Visitors go mainly to Amsterdam, although cities such as Groningen and Maastricht are growing in popularity. Amsterdam caters for a diverse tourism market. Its world-famous museums include the Rijksmuseum, with its collection of Vermeers and Rembrandts. Amsterdam is also renowned as the sex capital of Europe. Its liberal traditions and red-light district draw millions every year.

COMMUNICATIONS

Schipol, Amsterdam
14.9m passengers

515 ships
4.51m dwt

THE TRANSPORT NETWORK

118,403 km (73,572 miles)	2045 km (1271 miles)
2828 km (1757 miles)	4832 km (3002 miles)

Rotterdam, the key transshipment port for northern Europe, is also the world's largest. It is currently expanding its container capacity. The government is also expanding Schipol airport; $15 billion has been committed to make it a hub of transport in Europe. There are plans to construct new high-speed track to allow the French TGV train to run from Brussels to Amsterdam.

In the past decade, the city has also become a centre for the European gay community. A thriving club scene and liberal drug laws have brought an increase in ravers from neighbouring countries. Rave trains from Brussels to the IT club carry thousands every week during the summer.

In spring and summer, the tulip fields and North Sea beaches attract large numbers of visitors.

Windmill at Baambrugge, *near Amsterdam. A century ago there were 10,000 in the country compared with today's 1000. A protective ring of 900 mills kept Amsterdam from flooding.*

PEOPLE

Dutch, Frisian

362 people per km²

THE URBAN/RURAL POPULATION SPLIT

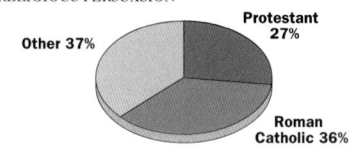

89%   11%

RELIGIOUS PERSUASION

Protestant 27%
Other 37%
Roman Catholic 36%

ETHNIC MAKEUP

Turkish 1% Other 2%
Moroccan 1%
Dutch 96%

The Dutch see their country as the most tolerant in Europe. This reflects a long history of welcoming refugees seeking religious and political asylum. In the 20th century, immigrants from former colonies have settled in the Netherlands and are fully accepted as citizens. The first wave came from Indonesia, followed by settlers from the Dutch colonies in the Caribbean and South America, Surinam and the Netherlands Antilles. The small Turkish community, however, does not enjoy full citizenship, but has guest worker status similar to that of its counterparts in Germany.

The tradition of tolerance is also reflected in liberal attitudes to sexuality. Dutch homosexuals have the same rights, including the same age of consent, as heterosexuals.

The state does not try to impose a particular morality on its citizens. Drug taking is seen in the Netherlands as a matter of personal choice.

Women enjoy equal rights but they are not well-represented at boardroom level.

POPULATION AGE BREAKDOWN

% of population by age group	0-14	15-64	65+		
	9%	10.2%	11.5%	12.7%	13.6%
	61%	62.5%	66.1%	69%	68%
	30%	27.3%	22.4%	18.3%	18.4%
	1960	1970	1980	1990	2000

POLITICS

Lower House 1998
Upper House 1995

HM Queen Beatrix
Wilhelmina Armgard

THE STATE OF THE PARTIES

Second Chamber 150 members

| 25% PvdA | 23% CDA | 21% VVD | 16% D66 | 15% Other |

PvdA = Labour Party **CDA** = Christian Democratic Appeal
VVD = People's Party for Freedom and Democracy
D66 = Democrats 66 **GL** = Green Front **Other** = Political
Reformed Party, Reformed Political Association, Reformist
Political Federation, Centre Democrats

First Chamber 75 members

| 36% CDA | 22% PvdA | 16% VVD | 16% D66 | 5% GL | 5% Other |

The Netherlands is a constitutional
monarchy. Legislative power is vested
in parliament. The monarch has only
nominal power.

MAIN POLITICAL ISSUES

The future of social welfare
Even after the cutbacks of
the 1980s, the Dutch still
have one of the most
generous welfare
systems in Europe.
Most political
parties now
accept that
current levels
of provision

*Queen Beatrix, who
acceded in 1980 and
rebuilt support for
the Dutch monarchy.*

*Wim Kok, won the
1994 elections and is
the first labour prime
minister since 1977.*

cannot be maintained indefinitely.
The debate is not whether to cut
welfare benefits, but by how much and
in which areas. The right-wing Liberal
party is advocating a minimal level of
provision, and the PvdA has suggested
cutbacks totalling $4 billion.

Political refugees
In recent years, an increasing number
of people have sought political asylum
in the Netherlands. There are fears that
unless immigration laws are tightened
there may be a rise in support for
extreme right-wing nationalist parties
in the country. The mainstream parties
have also begun to question whether
the economy can afford the costs of
housing refugees.

The fight against crime
The Dutch electorate has identified
rising crime as a major concern. The
prison system can no longer cope with
the growing number of detainees, and
many convicted criminals are being
released for want of space. None of the
parties has a programme for reversing
the trend.

PROFILE
Dutch politics is characterized by
coalitions and a high degree of
consensus. Most Dutch agree on the
social function of government and
readily accept relatively high taxes
and a generous social security system.
Political debate is more a question of
the stress and focus of policy than of
ideology. The CDA has traditionally led
two-party coalition governments,
either with the left-of-centre PvdA or
with the right-wing VVD. However, the
PvdA won the 1994 elections, although
both it and the CDA lost a significant
number of seats.

WORLD AFFAIRS

| EU | NATO | WEU | CSCE | Benelux |

The Netherlands has long been one of
the main advocates of the EU. It supports
both political and monetary integration,
but failed in its attempt to rush through
legislation enabling both during its
EU presidency in 1992. Internationally,
it has traditionally supported UK and
US foreign policy, and is a member
of NATO. The reunification of Germany
and consequent rise in German power
could see strong links with the
US being weakened.

AID

 $2.5bn (donations)   Down 3% in 1991

As a result of tight fiscal policies,
Dutch foreign aid has slightly
contracted over the past few years.
The Dutch government actively
pursues a policy to link foreign aid
and human rights. This led to a clash
with Indonesia which, as a former
colony, was one of the biggest
receivers of Dutch support. In 1993,
Indonesia turned down all Dutch aid,
accusing the Netherlands of
interfering in its internal affairs.

NETHERLANDS

Total Area : 37 330 sq. km
(14 410 sq. miles)

POPULATION

over 1 000 000	▣
over 500 000	◉
over 100 000	◎
over 50 000	○
over 10 000	●

LAND HEIGHT
100m/328ft
Sea Level
-100m/-328ft

N
0   40 km
0   40 miles

397

CHRONOLOGY

Suppression of Protestantism by the ruling Spanish Habsburgs led to the revolt of the Netherlands and the independence of the northern provinces as a republic in 1581.

- ❑ **1813** Dutch oust French after 30 years of French rule and choose to become a constitutional monarchy.
- ❑ **1815** United Kingdom of Netherlands formed to include Belgium and Luxembourg.
- ❑ **1830** Catholic southern provinces secede as Belgium.
- ❑ **1848** New constitution – ministers to be accountable to parliament.
- ❑ **1897–1901** Wide-ranging social legislation enacted. Development of strong trade unions.
- ❑ **1898** Wilhelmina succeeds to throne, so ending union with Luxembourg, where Salic Law is in force.
- ❑ **1914–1918** Dutch neutrality respected in First World War.
- ❑ **1922** Women fully enfranchised.
- ❑ **1940** Dutch attempt to maintain neutrality, but Germany invades. Fierce Dutch resistance.
- ❑ **1942** Japan invades Dutch East Indies.
- ❑ **1944–1945** 'Winter of starvation'.
- ❑ **1945** Liberation. International Court of Justice set up in The Hague.
- ❑ **1946** PVDA formed.
- ❑ **1946–1958** PVDA leads centre-left coalitions with CVP. Marshall Aid from USA speeds reconstruction.
- ❑ **1948** Queen Juliana takes throne.
- ❑ **1949** Joins NATO. Most of East Indies colonies gain independence as Indonesia.
- ❑ **1953** 2000 die in North Sea floods.
- ❑ **1957** Founder-member of EEC.
- ❑ **1960** Economic union with Belgium and Luxembourg comes into effect.
- ❑ **1973** PVDA wins power after 15 years spent mainly in opposition. Centre-left coalition, first ever majority of left-wing ministers.
- ❑ **1980** Two main opposition Protestant parties unite in CDA. Queen Beatrix accedes to throne.
- ❑ **1977–1981** CDA–VVD coalition.
- ❑ **1982** PVDA rejects deployment of US Cruise missiles in Netherlands. CDA–VVD centre-right coalition under Ruud Lubbers.
- ❑ **1989** VVD refuses to support finance for 20-year National Environment Policy (NEP). Elections. Lubbers' CDA–PVDA centre-left coalition.
- ❑ **1990** NEP introduced.
- ❑ **1992** Licensed brothels and euthanasia legalized.
- ❑ **1994** Elections. PVDA heads new coalition. Politically-conservative VVD holds balance of power.

DEFENCE

💲 $7.4bn   ⬇ Down 2% in 1992

Defence spending as % GDP   0 – 40
2.7%

DUTCH ARMED FORCES

🛡	913 main battle tanks (468 *Leopard* 1A4/ 445 *Leopard* 2)	60,800 personnel
🚢	5 submarines, 12 frigates and 4 destroyers	15,500 personnel
✈	188 combat aircraft (F-16A,-B)	12,000 personnel
🚀	None	

The Dutch military, which is part of NATO, is currently undergoing major restructuring. By the year 2000, it will have been transformed from an organization focusing on an anti-Soviet defence role into a rapidly-deployable, more flexible military force. The plans include a 44% reduction in personnel and the abolition of compulsory military service. Most of the reforms affect the army, which will be reduced from three to two divisions. The Netherlands has a large defence industry, specializing in submarines, weapons systems and aircraft. The air force is equipped with US F-16s, which were partly developed with the Dutch Fokker company.

ECONOMICS

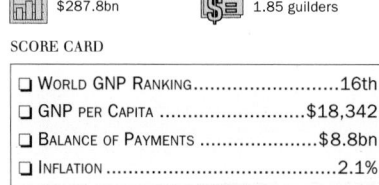

📊 $287.8bn   💲 1.85 guilders

SCORE CARD

- ❑ WORLD GNP RANKING..........................16th
- ❑ GNP PER CAPITA $18,342
- ❑ BALANCE OF PAYMENTS $8.8bn
- ❑ INFLATION 2.1%
- ❑ UNEMPLOYMENT................................7.8%

EXPORTS
- Italy 6%
- UK 10%
- France 10%
- Belgium and Luxembourg 14%
- Germany* 26%
- Other 34%

IMPORTS
- USA 8%
- France 8%
- UK 8%
- Belgium and Luxembourg 14%
- Germany* 25%
- Other 37%

STRENGTHS

Highly-skilled and educated workforce. Sophisticated infrastructure. Large number of blue-chip multinationals, including Philips and Shell. Strong currency, linked to the German Deutsch Mark. Low inflation. Tradition of high-tech innovation, including development of the music cassette and CD.

WEAKNESSES

Costly welfare system, resulting in high taxes and social insurance premiums; one third of national income spent on social security. High labour costs.

PROFILE

The Dutch economy is one of the most successful in Europe. Since the 16th century, trade has been of great importance. Today, imports and exports

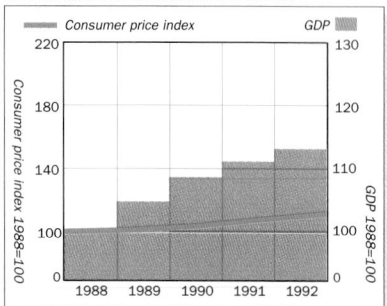

ECONOMIC PERFORMANCE INDICATOR

Consumer price index — GDP

Consumer price index 1988=100 / GDP 1988=100

1988 1989 1990 1991 1992

account for over 50% of GDP. Most goods travel through Rotterdam, the world's biggest port. In addition to high-tech sectors such as electronics, telecommunications and chemicals, the Netherlands has a successful agricultural industry. Productivity rates are high and agricultural products such as cheese, vegetables, meat and flowers are significant export earners.

NETHERLANDS : MAJOR BUSINESSES

- Amsterdam
- Groningen
- Utrecht
- 's-Gravenhage
- Enschede
- Arnhem
- Nijmegen
- Rotterdam
- Eindhoven
- Maastricht

🔌 Electronics		🛢 Gas refining	
💉 Pharmaceuticals		🛢 Oil refining	
⚙ Light engineering		⚗ Chemicals	
⚙ Heavy engineering		✳ Textiles	
✈ Aerospace industry			

0 — 50 km
0 — 50 miles

N

RESOURCES

71.9bn kwh
(capacity 17.4m kw)

53,900 b/d
(reserves
144,650,000 bbl)

13.8m pigs, 4.6m
cattle, 1.4m sheep,
64,000 horses

Natural gas, oil

ELECTRICITY GENERATION

Hydro 0.2% (120m kwh)

Thermal 94.8% (68.2bn kwh)

Nuclear 4.9% (3.5bn kwh)

Other 0.1% (50m kwh)

0　　20　　40　　60　　80　　100
% of total generation by type

There are large natural gas reserves in
the north. There is some oil production
from offshore drilling in the North Sea.

NETHERLANDS : LAND USE

Cropland
Forest
Pasture
Wetlands
Cattle
Pigs
Sugarbeet
Bulbs & flowers

Ijsselmeer

Ijssel

Waal
Maas

0　　50 km
0　　50 miles

ENVIRONMENT

9% (3% partially
protected)

National Environment
Policy adopted in
1990

ENVIRONMENTAL TREATIES

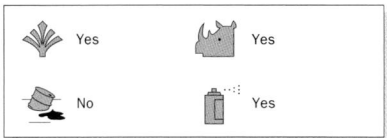

Yes

Yes

No

Yes

The Netherlands has a strong
environmental tradition, a legacy in
part of living in one of the most densely
populated states in the world. NGOs such
as Greenpeace are well supported and
the Green Party is well represented in
parliament. The Dutch recycle their
domestic rubbish and have a good
record of energy conservation.

The main concerns are halting
motorway building, and the proposed
high-speed TGV train. The government
plans that this will cross the green
heartland of the Netherlands, an area
known as the Randstad. It is being
strongly opposed by environmentalists,
who succeeded in halting a second
airport north of Rotterdam.

MEDIA

Freedom of press is guaranteed by the
constitution. The Netherlands has Europe's
most liberal laws on censorship

PUBLISHING AND BROADCAST MEDIA

There are 6 national dailies. The right-wing
De Telegraf has the largest circulation and is
the only one to offer sensationalist reporting

3 state-controlled
channels

5 state-controlled
stations

Intelsat V1 F1
Astra 1B

Over three quarters
of homes receive
cable TV

The media represents the whole social
and political spectrum. Newspapers are
aimed at the family and there is little
sensationalist reporting. Access to
cable TV is the highest in the world.

CRIME

5827 prisoners

Crime is rising

CRIME RATES

Murders
15　　*per 100,000 population*

Rapes
9　　*per 100,000 population*

Thefts
5552　　*per 100,000 population*

Liberal drugs laws make the
Netherlands a gateway for the
drugs trade. Several politicians
have suggested decriminalizing the
trade. Their aim is to reduce the crime
generated by the huge profits from the
business. However, such a measure
would not be acceptable to the
international community.

EDUCATION

99%

0　　*Education spending as % GNP*　　25
7.3%

THE EDUCATION SYSTEM

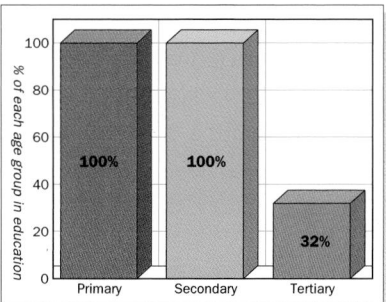

% of each age group in education

Primary 100%　　Secondary 100%　　Tertiary 32%

Apart from a few religious schools,
all education is state-run. Corporate
funding plays an important part in
university research.

HEALTH

1 per 414 people

Heart, cerebrovascular
and respiratory
diseases, cancers

0　　*Health spending as % GNP*　　25
6.2%

Dutch health care is almost entirely
funded by the state. High spending
ensures that it is among the best in
the world. However, there are fears
that the Dutch may have to accept
lower standards in future, particularly
as the population is ageing. Major
health problems are similar to those
in the rest of western Europe. There is
a higher incidence of AIDS. The Dutch
are active in research in this field.

WEALTH

Electronic fitter, 2248–2387 guilders per month;
journalist, 30,251–48,868 guilders per year

CONSUMER GOODS OWNERSHIP

Per 1000 population

1000
750
500　485　　371　　625
250　　　　　　　189
0　　　　　　　　　　36

The Netherlands is, per capita, one of
the richest nations in the world. The
wealthiest group are oil executives,
stock-market traders and businessmen.
A progressive taxation system and
extensive social welfare mean that
wealth is quite evenly distributed.
There is a small elite who have
considerable inherited wealth,
but extravagant displays of
wealth are rare.

Class does not play a big part in
Dutch society. Most citizens would
consider themselves middle class.
Immigrant communities are the
exception; they often live on the edges
of towns in deprived areas. The poorest
group are illegal immigrants.

WORLD RANKING

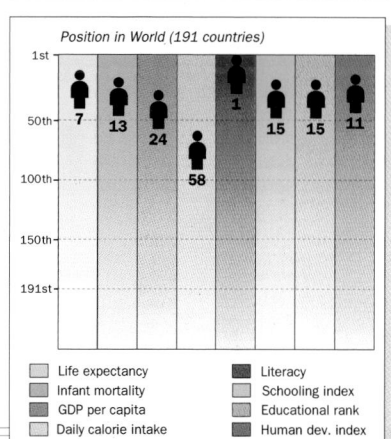

Position in World (191 countries)

1st
50th
100th
150th
191st

7　　13　　24　　58　　1　　15　　15　　11

Life expectancy
Infant mortality
GDP per capita
Daily calorie intake
Literacy
Schooling index
Educational rank
Human dev. index

N

NEW ZEALAND

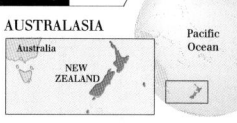

OFFICIAL NAME: The Dominion of New Zealand **CAPITAL:** Wellington
POPULATION: 3.5 million **CURRENCY:** New Zealand dollar **OFFICIAL LANGUAGE:** English **OVERSEAS TERRITORIES:** 3

LYING IN THE SOUTH PACIFIC, 1600 km southeast of Australia, New Zealand comprises the main North and South Islands, separated by the Cook Strait, and numerous smaller islands. South Island is the more mountainous; North Island contains hot springs and geysers, and the bulk of the population. The political tradition is liberal and egalitarian, and has been dominated by the National and Labour parties. Radical, and often unpopular, reforms since 1984 have restored economic growth, speeded up economic diversification and strengthened New Zealand's position within the Pacific Rim countries.

CLIMATE

WEATHER CHART

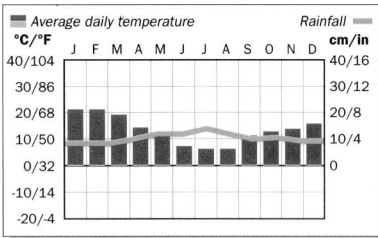

New Zealand's climate is generally temperate and damp, with an average temperature of 12°C. However, there are differences between the islands, which extend north–south nearly 2000 km. The extreme north is almost subtropical; southern winters are cold. New Zealand is windy. Wellington is particularly known for bouts of blustery weather that can last for days.

COMMUNICATIONS

 Auckland International
3.93m passengers

 25 ships
258,600 dwt

THE TRANSPORT NETWORK

93,278 km (57,960 miles)		None	
4040 km (2510 miles)		1609 km (1000 miles)	

Although both New Zealand's major islands are well served by transport services, the more populous North Island has a more extensive road and rail network than the South. Air and ferry services complement the land networks and provide links between the North and South Islands, as well as with the numerous smaller islands. Cargo ferry services are particularly important for remote populations in the Ross Dependency. Links with the Cook Islands, Niue and the Tokelau atolls, New Zealand's associated territories, are being improved.

TOURISM

 1.02 million

Up 5% in 1992

MAIN OVERSEAS ARRIVALS

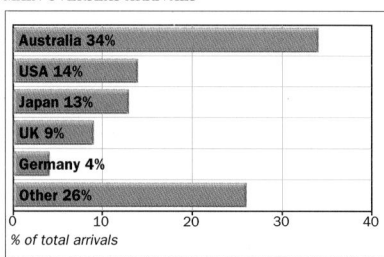

Australia 34%
USA 14%
Japan 13%
UK 9%
Germany 4%
Other 26%

% of total arrivals

New Zealand's prime attraction is its scenery. Unspoilt and, relative to the country's size, the most varied in the world, it offers mountains, fjords and lakes, glaciers, rainforests, beaches, boiling mudpools and geysers. Other attractions are the Maori culture, and outdoor activities such as river rafting, fishing, skiing, whale watching and bungee jumping, a local invention.

Tourists come mainly from the USA, Australia, the UK, Japan and Germany. Low-cost charter flights have helped boost visitor numbers to over one million a year. Tourism is now the largest single foreign-exchange earner, generating US$3 billion yearly. A new state tourist board has embarked on a high-profile campaign to treble visitors to three million by the year 2000.

***Mount Egmont**, an extinct volcano, is one of the numerous popular natural attractions of New Zealand's North Island.*

PEOPLE

English, Maori

13 people per km²

THE URBAN/RURAL POPULATION SPLIT

84%   16%

RELIGIOUS PERSUASION

Other Protestant 5%   Methodist 5%
Other 33%   Roman Catholic 15%
Anglican 24%   Presbyterian 18%

ETHNIC MAKEUP

Other (including Pacific Islander) 3%   Maori 9%
European 88%

New Zealand is a country peopled by migrants. The islands were first settled about 1200 years ago by the Maoris, as part of the Polynesian seaborne migrations. Today's majority European population is descended mainly from British migrants who settled after 1840. Recent arrivals include Asians from Hong Kong and Malaysia, and those who left Fiji following the 1987 coup.

Maoris today comprise 9% of the population. Their living and education standards are generally lower, and rates of unemployment higher, than average. Relations with the European-descended majority have been tense in recent years. The main cause has been the failure of the government to observe the terms of the 1840 Treaty of Waitangi, which protected Maori rights. In an effort to improve relations, the government reached a settlement of fishing claims with Maori leaders in 1992, and is now negotiating a settlement of land claims. New Zealand women were among the first in the world to get the vote. Today, they hold top jobs in business and politics.

POPULATION AGE BREAKDOWN

% of population by age group	0–14	15–64	65+

	1960	1970	1980	1990	2000
65+	8.6%	8.5%	10%	10.9%	11.3%
15–64	58.5%	59.8%	63.2%	66.4%	65.3%
0–14	32.9%	31.7%	26.8%	22.7%	23.4%

N

POLITICS

 1996

 HM Queen Elizabeth II

THE STATE OF THE PARTIES

House of Representatives 99 members

2%
NZ 1st

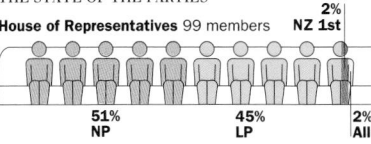

51%
NP

45%
LP

2%
All.

NP = National Party **LP** = Labour Party **All.** = Alliance
NZ 1st = New Zealand First Party

*James Bolger, NP
leader, and prime
minister since 1991.*

*Roger Douglas,
the creator of
'Rogernomics'.*

New Zealand is a single-chamber
parliamentary democracy within the
Commonwealth. The Cook Islands and
Niue are self-governing territories.

MAIN POLITICAL ISSUES

Electoral reform

New Zealand is to shift to a system of
proportional representation at the next
general election, due in 1996. Popular
endorsement of electoral reform in a
referendum in November 1993 reflects
widespread disillusionment with the NP
and LP, in particular over both parties'
about-turn on electoral promises
during the 1980s. The German-style
system, mixing constituency candidates
with those identified by party, will give
a much greater role to the smaller
parties, which received almost 30% of
the vote in the 1993 election.

PROFILE

Politics has been dominated by the NP
and the LP under the first-past-the-post
system. The period since 1984 has
been one of radical reform, first of
the economy under the LP and,
since 1990, of welfare under the
NP. Popular disaffection
hardened during this
period. NP and LP
dissidents formed two
main new parties, the
Alliance and the
New Zealand First
Party, which took
almost 30% of the
vote between them
at the 1993
election, and left
the NP with an
overall majority of
only one seat.

WORLD AFFAIRS

ANZUS   Comm   APEC   OECD   GATT

A majority of New Zealanders remain
strongly committed to the British crown
and the Commonwealth, but the UK no
longer plays a central role
in New Zealand's life.
The UK's involvement
in the EU has forced
New Zealand to
reorientate its trade and
foreign policy towards its
Pacific Rim neighbours,
especially Australia. The
1983 Closer Economic
Relationship (CER) treaty freed
trade between the two states.
Australia is now New Zealand's
largest trading partner, and even
closer links have been mooted in
the form of an eventual political
union. Relations with Asia are
growing in importance. Exports
to Japan are now second to
those to Australia and trading
relationships with other Asian
states are being secured. New
Zealand's anti-nuclear stance
has led to its exclusion from
key meetings of the ANZUS
pact. Relations with
France are still
recovering from the
1985 bombing of the
Greenpeace ship
Rainbow Warrior
by French agents
in Auckland
harbour.

AID

$100m (donations)

Up 47% between
1991 and 1993

Over half of New Zealand's overseas
aid is bilateral. Particular areas of focus
are the Pacific states and Pacific-wide
organizations. New Zealand is a major
supporter of the South Pacific Forum,
the University of the South Pacific
and the Pacific Environment
Programme. It also offers
scholarships allowing
overseas students to
study or train in
New Zealand.

NEW ZEALAND

Total Area : 268 680 sq. km
(103 730 sq. miles)

LAND HEIGHT

2000m/6562ft
1000m/3281ft
500m/1640ft
200m/656ft
Sea Level

POPULATION

over 500 000
over 100 000
over 50 000
over 10 000
under 10 000

N

0   100 km
0   100 miles

CHRONOLOGY

A former British colony, New Zealand became a dominion in 1907 and fully independent in 1947.

- ❏ **1962** Western Samoa gains independence.
- ❏ **1965** The Cook Islands become self-governing.
- ❏ **1972** Elections won by LP. Norman Kirk prime minister.
- ❏ **1973–1974** International oil crisis brings severe economic problems.
- ❏ **1974** Norman Kirk dies. William Rowling prime minister.
- ❏ **1975** Elections won by conservative NP party. Prime Minister Robert Muldoon introduces programme of economic austerity.
- ❏ **1976** Immigration cut by over 80%.
- ❏ **1978** Elections. NP retains power with reduced majority.
- ❏ **1981** Elections. NP wins.
- ❏ **1984** Trade-union legislation bans 'closed shops'. Government pledges ban on ships carrying nuclear weapons entering ports. Election returns LP. David Lange prime minister. Waitangi Tribunal restores Auckland harbour headland to Maori people.
- ❏ **1985** French agents sink Greenpeace ship *Rainbow Warrior* in Auckland harbour.
- ❏ **1986** USA suspends military obligations under ANZUS Treaty.
- ❏ **1987** Elections won by LP. Controversial privatization programme introduced. Legislation bans ships carrying nuclear weapons.
- ❏ **1989** Cabinet split. Lange resigns. Succeeded by Geoffrey Palmer.
- ❏ **1990** Palmer resigns because of unpopularity in polls. Replaced by Minister of Trade Michael Moore. LP defeated by NP in elections. James Bolger prime minister.
- ❏ **1991** Widespread protest at spending cuts. Two NP ministers resign.
- ❏ **1992** February, Sir Robert Muldoon resigns as minister in protest at government economic policy. April, France suspends nuclear tests in South Pacific. July, USA promises warships visiting New Zealand will no longer carry nuclear weapons. August, Waitangi Tribunal awards South Island fishing rights to Maoris. September, majority vote for electoral reform in referendum.
- ❏ **1993** May, *Jacques Cartier* first French naval ship to dock since 1985. November, elections. NP party returned with one-seat majority. As a result of referendum, proportional representation introduced for future elections.

DEFENCE

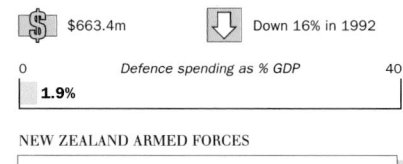

$663.4m   Down 16% in 1992

0   Defence spending as % GDP   40
1.9%

NEW ZEALAND ARMED FORCES

26 light tanks (26 *Scorpion*)	4800 personnel
4 frigates and 4 patrol boats	2400 personnel
41 combat aircraft (16 A-4K/5 TA-4K)	3700 personnel
None	

The security pact between Australia, New Zealand and the USA (ANZUS), the focus of New Zealand's defence policy since 1951, has been strained by New Zealand's refusal, since 1984, to allow nuclear warships into its ports. The USA suspended joint military exercises and preferential terms for arms purchase, forcing New Zealand to seek closer links with Australia. The 1992 announcement by the USA that its warships no longer carried nuclear weapons has paved the way for a return to more cordial relations.

Defence takes about 4.8% of government spending. The armed forces number 10,900 troops with an additional 8500 reserves.

ECONOMICS

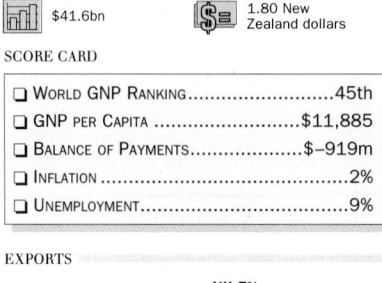

$41.6bn   1.80 New Zealand dollars

SCORE CARD

- ❏ WORLD GNP RANKING.........................45th
- ❏ GNP PER CAPITA $11,885
- ❏ BALANCE OF PAYMENTS...................$−919m
- ❏ INFLATION 2%
- ❏ UNEMPLOYMENT...................................9%

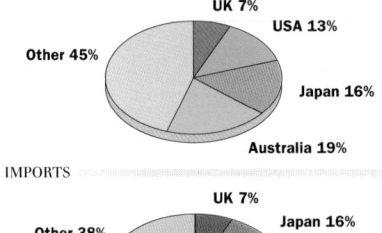

EXPORTS

- UK 7%
- USA 13%
- Other 45%
- Japan 16%
- Australia 19%

IMPORTS

- UK 7%
- Japan 16%
- Other 38%
- USA 18%
- Australia 21%

STRENGTHS
Modern agricultural sector; world's biggest exporter of wool, cheese, butter and meat. Rapidly expanding tourist sector. Manufacturing growing, with emphasis on high-tech. One of world's most open economies. Rapidly expanding trade links within Pacific Rim.

WEAKNESSES
Public debt two thirds of GDP, one of highest levels outside developing world. Persistent budget and balance of payments deficits. Continuing reliance on imported manufactured goods.

PROFILE
Since 1984, New Zealand has changed from being one of the most regulated to one of the most open economies in the world. Radical reforms, dubbed

ECONOMIC PERFORMANCE INDICATOR

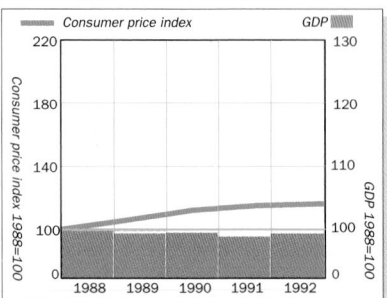

Consumer price index   GDP

Consumer price index 1988=100 / GDP 1988=100
1988 1989 1990 1991 1992

'Rogernomics' after LP Finance Minister Roger Douglas, have helped to restore growth, cut inflation to 2% and encouraged diversification into new markets and products. The huge public debt and poor levels of private investment, however, continue to hinder sustained recovery.

NEW ZEALAND : MAJOR BUSINESSES

- Auckland
- Nelson
- Napier
- Wellington
- Christchurch
- Dunedin

Brewing
Chemicals
Pulp & paper
Meat packing
Dairy products
Fruit processing
Wool processing
Light engineering
Telecommunications

0   200 km
0   200 miles

N

RESOURCES

30.2bn kwh (capacity 7.5m kw)

35,700 b/d (reserves 169,670,000 bbl)

55.2m sheep, 8.1m cattle, 407,000 pigs, 98,000 horses

Coal, oil, natural gas, iron, gold, silica sand

ELECTRICITY GENERATION

Hydro 73% (21.9bn kwh)

Thermal 21% (6.4bn kwh)

Nuclear 0%

Other 6% (1.8bn kwh)

% of total generation by type

New Zealand's rich pastures, a result of even rainfall throughout the year, have traditionally been its key resource. The sheep, wool and dairy products on which the country's wealth was built are still important, but farmers are also moving into new areas. The kiwi fruit is now a thriving export. Fisheries are a growth area.

New Zealand is well-endowed with energy resources. It has coal, oil, natural gas and huge hydroelectric potential.

NORTH ISLAND

NEW ZEALAND : LAND USE
- Cropland
- Forest
- Pasture
- High mountain regions
- Cattle
- Sheep
- Cereals

SOUTH ISLAND

0   200 km
0   200 miles

ENVIRONMENT

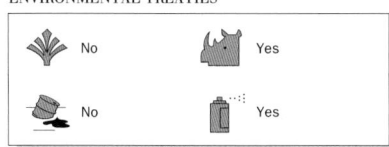

11% (1% partially protected)

Generally high environmental awareness

ENVIRONMENTAL TREATIES

No | Yes
No | Yes

New Zealand's isolation, small population and limited industry have helped to keep it one of the world's most pollution-free countries. Ozone depletion over Antarctica competes with nuclear power as the top domestic concern. New Zealand has been a leading opponent of French nuclear testing in the Pacific and has banned nuclear warships from its ports.

MEDIA

There is no censorship of the media

PUBLISHING AND BROADCAST MEDIA

There are 35 daily newspapers. The leading newspaper is the *New Zealand Herald*

2 state-owned, 1 independent service

1 state-owned, 22 independent services

Intelsat V F8

Cable TV is widely available

The Auckland-based *New Zealand Herald* is the only daily with a national circulation; the others are primarily local papers. A third state-owned TV station is being considered.

CRIME

3736 prisoners

Little overall change from year to year

CRIME RATES

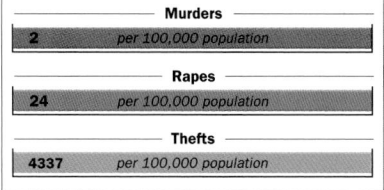

Murders
2 per 100,000 population

Rapes
24 per 100,000 population

Thefts
4337 per 100,000 population

Crime rates in New Zealand's urban areas have increased in recent years. However, overall, the country remains one of the world's safest and most peaceful places to live.

EDUCATION

99%

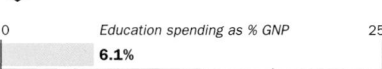

0   Education spending as % GNP   25
6.1%

THE EDUCATION SYSTEM

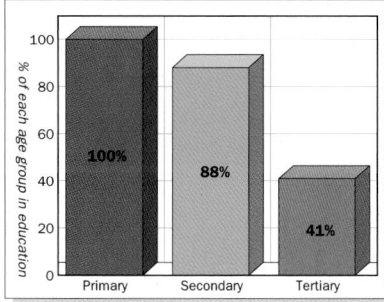

% of each age group in education

Primary 100%
Secondary 88%
Tertiary 41%

Education is compulsory between the ages of five and 16. Nearly 77% of 16-year-olds stay in full-time education. About 4% of pupils attend independent schools. The free state system is in the process of change: the government plans to give schools direct control over their finances.

HEALTH

1 per 373 people

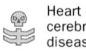

Heart and cerebrovascular diseases, cancers

0   Health spending as % GNP   25
6%

New Zealand has been a world leader in the provision of public health services. In 1936, it was the first country to introduce a full welfare state. Government efforts since 1991 to impose UK-style market systems on the health service have been very unpopular. Highly controversial charges for hospital beds had to be abolished in 1993 after widespread public protests.

WEALTH

Truck parts dealer, 20,000 New Zealand dollars per year; computer sales manager, 100,000 New Zealand dollars per year

CONSUMER GOODS OWNERSHIP

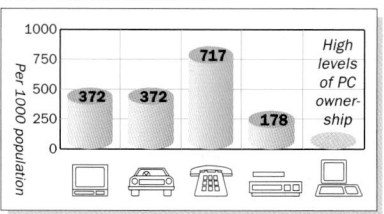

Per 1000 population

372   372   717   178

High levels of PC owner-ship

The decade since 1984 has been very difficult for New Zealanders, who are used to affluence within a generous welfare state. A rash of economic and social reforms has held back wages, raised unemployment and cut welfare benefits. Even so, average living standards are still high, and a strong egalitarian tradition means that wealth remains quite evenly distributed.

New Zealanders also enjoy one of the world's best qualities of life, in terms of access to basic necessities, and a pure, healthy urban and rural environment. Social mobility is fairly high. Wealthier people tend to spend their money on houses close to the water. Yachts are a major status symbol.

WORLD RANKING

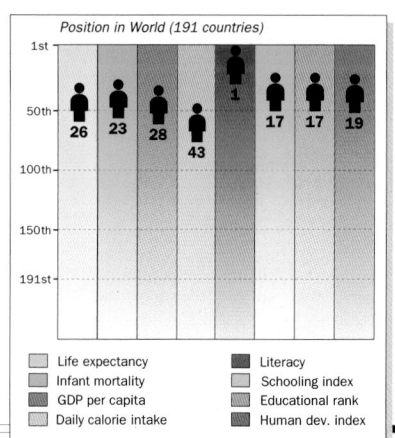

Position in World (191 countries)

1st
50th   26   23   28   43   1   17   17   19
100th
150th
191st

- Life expectancy
- Infant mortality
- GDP per capita
- Daily calorie intake
- Literacy
- Schooling index
- Educational rank
- Human dev. index

N

NICARAGUA

OFFICIAL NAME: Republic of Nicaragua **CAPITAL:** Managua
POPULATION: 4 million **CURRENCY:** New córdoba **OFFICIAL LANGUAGE:** Spanish

 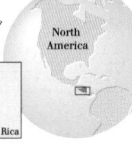

BOUNDED BY THE Pacific Ocean to the west and the Caribbean Sea to the east, Nicaragua lies at the heart of Central America. After more than 40 years of dictatorship, the Sandinista revolution in 1978 provoked eleven years of civil war, which almost destroyed the economy. Despite unexpectedly losing free elections in 1990, the Sandinistas remain a major political force in a country where poverty and unrest are rising.

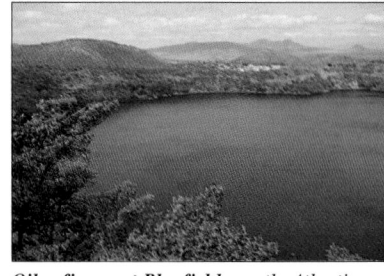

Oil refinery at Bluefields, on the Atlantic coast. Under the Sandinistas, most crude oil came from the former USSR, via Cuba.

CLIMATE

WEATHER CHART

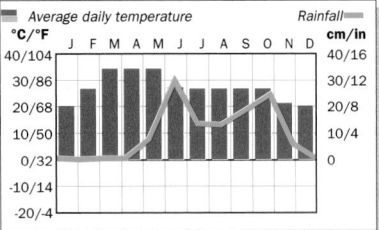

Nicaragua's climate is tropical and often violent. Hurricanes and earthquakes are an occasional threat.

COMMUNICATIONS

Augusto C Sandino Intl, Managua 225,725 passengers — 1 ship 1200 dwt

THE TRANSPORT NETWORK

15,287 km (9499 miles)	Pan-American Highway 384 km (239 miles)
321 km (199 miles)	2220 km (1380 miles)

Most roads are in the Pacific region and in poor condition. The Pan-American Highway provides a key external link.

TOURISM

145,872 visitors — Nicaragua is now actively promoting leisure tourism

MAIN OVERSEAS ARRIVALS

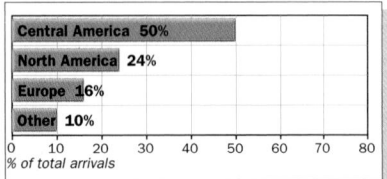

Central America 50%
North America 24%
Europe 16%
Other 10%

Nicaragua's tourist industry was always small. The civil war caused its near total collapse, although up to 100,000 'political tourists' visited the country every year to observe the effects of Sandinista reforms.

PEOPLE

Spanish, English Creole, Miskito — 32 people per km²

THE URBAN/RURAL POPULATION SPLIT

60%   40

ETHNIC MAKEUP

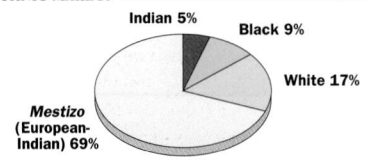

Indian 5%
Black 9%
White 17%
Mestizo (European-Indian) 69%

The Atlantic regions, which in 1987 achieved limited independence, are isolated from the more populous Pacific regions. The indigenous Miskito tribes and the descendants of Africans, brought over by Spanish colonists in the 18th century to work the plantations, are concentrated along the Atlantic coast, where English Creole is widely spoken. Almost 80% of the population live in poverty. Of these, some 20% are defined by the UN as extremely poor; between 1991 and 1992, Nicaragua's GDP per capita fell below Haiti's, normally the world's lowest. Half the population has no permanent employment and poverty has forced many women into prostitution.

POLITICS

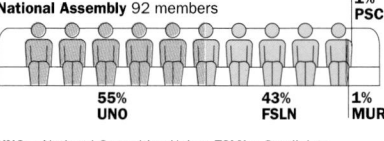

1996 — President Violeta Barrios de Chamorro

THE STATE OF THE PARTIES

National Assembly 92 members

55% UNO   43% FSLN   1% MUR   1% PSC

UNO = National Opposition Union **FSLN** = Sandinista National Liberation Front **MUR** = Revolutionary Unity Movement **PSC** = Social Christian Party

Nicaraguan politics are caught in a vice between right-wing pro-US parties and the left-wing Sandinistas, whose power base remains the army. Radical changes were expected after the 1990 electoral victory of Violeta Chamorro's UNO. However, her failure to revive the economy, and increasing reliance on Sandinista support, led to US threats to withhold aid. By 1993, the instability of the government was threatening a return to civil war.

NICARAGUA

Total Area : 130 000 sq. km (50 193 sq. miles)

POPULATION
- ⊙ over 500 000
- ◎ over 100 000
- ○ over 50 000
- ● over 10 000
- • under 10 000

LAND HEIGHT
- 1000m/3281ft
- 500m/1640ft
- 200m/656ft
- Sea Level

WORLD AFFAIRS

OAS CACM NAM GATT ECLAC

Nicaragua's most important, and most difficult, relationship has been with the USA. During the Sandinista years, the USA tried to overthrow the regime by providing military aid to the Contra rebels. Chamorro's 1990 election victory initially led to the resumption of US aid after years of blockade. The resurgent influence of the Sandinistas, however, led to US threats in 1993 to freeze $98 million of promised aid.

AID

 $826m (receipts)   Up 58% in 1991

The Nicaraguan economy is almost totally dependent on aid. The USA is the largest donor, but makes aid conditional on the end of Sandinista influence. Aid from the EU is more reliable. Large numbers of individually motivated foreign volunteers work in schools and hospitals.

DEFENCE

 $214.5m   Down 5% in 1992

Nicaragua's army was formed from the Sandinista forces that overthrew the Somoza regime. It grew to be the region's largest (134,000 troops) during the war with the Contras. By 1993, its numbers had fallen to 15,000. The USA has been pressing for the removal of General Humberto Ortega as leader of the Sandinista-controlled army as a condition for the resumption of full aid.

ECONOMICS

 $1.4bn   6.33 new córdobas

SCORE CARD

❏ WORLD GNP RANKING	147th
❏ GNP PER CAPITA	$350
❏ BALANCE OF PAYMENTS	$–695.4m
❏ INFLATION	432%
❏ UNEMPLOYMENT	14%

STRENGTHS
Very few. Coffee is the major export crop. Signs of cross-party support for an economic recovery programme.

WEAKNESSES
Hyperinflation, with regular devaluations. World prices for its main exports have all fallen sharply in recent years. Banana quotas with the EU are threatened by the GATT proposals. Opposition in USA to Sandinista influence in Nicaraguan politics limits access to the key US market. Growing trade deficit and failure of successive plans to stimulate exports.

EXPORTS

Belgium and Luxembourg 32%
USA 10%
Cuba 10%
Germany* 11%
Japan 17%
Other 20%

IMPORTS

France 4%
Spain 4%
Cuba 5%
CIS* 32%
Other 55%

RESOURCES

 1bn kwh (capacity 400,000 kw)
 Not an oil producer; refines 16,000 b/cd
 2m cattle, 680,000 pigs, 250,000 horses
 Gold, silver, lead, zinc

Nicaragua has no significant mineral resources and no oil. Lack of spare generator parts has led to longer and more frequent power cuts in Managua.

ENVIRONMENT

 2% (0.3% partially protected)
 No efforts to check deforestation

Deforestation and natural disasters, such as the earthquake that destroyed Managua in 1974, are major problems.

MEDIA

 The press is now relatively outspoken

PUBLISHING AND BROADCAST MEDIA

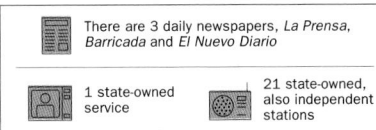

There are 3 daily newspapers, *La Prensa*, *Barricada* and *El Nuevo Diario*

1 state-owned service

21 state-owned, also independent stations

Radio is the most important medium. *Radio Mujer*, Central America's first station for women, went on air in 1992. *La Prensa*, the main daily newspaper, is owned by the Chamorro family.

CRIME

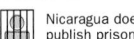 Nicaragua does not publish prison figures
 No official statistics, but the trend is up

Gun law still prevails in parts of the north, where gangs of ex-Contras and ex-Sandinistas control large areas.

CHRONOLOGY

Nicaragua became independent in 1838. Guerrilla forces, led by Gen Sandino, opposed the US marine presence in the early 1930s.

❏ **1935–1979** Somoza family in power.
❏ **1978** Sandinista revolution overthrows Anastasio Somoza II.
❏ **1979–1990** Civil war between Sandinistas and US-backed Contras.

EDUCATION

 57%

The Sandinista 'Literacy Crusade', which achieved dramatic results in the 1980s, has long since died away. The Jesuit-run University of Central America is one of two universities.

HEALTH

 1 per 1789 people
 Diarrheal, heart and cerebrovascular diseases, pneumonia

Life expectancy in Nicaragua rose from 50 to 64 years between 1960 and 1988. Real spending on health, however, fell by 71% between 1988 and 1993, with a consequent 15% rise in child mortality.

WEALTH

 Farm labourer, 240-300 new córdobas per month, plus meals and accommodation; top executive, 6000-12,000 new córdobas per month

CONSUMER GOODS OWNERSHIP

VCR and PC ownership is limited to a small elite

61 12 16

Wealthy Nicaraguans are based mainly in Miami. Some have returned under Chamorro as the 'new entrepreneurs'.

WORLD RANKING

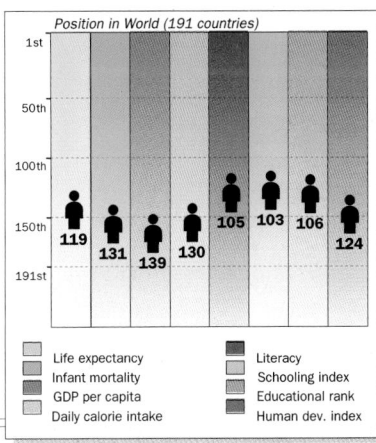

Position in World (191 countries)

1st
50th
100th
150th
191st

119 131 139 130 105 103 106 124

Life expectancy
Infant mortality
GDP per capita
Daily calorie intake
Literacy
Schooling index
Educational rank
Human dev. index

NIGER

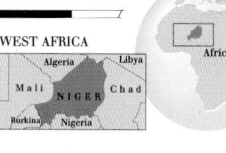
WEST AFRICA

OFFICIAL NAME: Republic of Niger   **CAPITAL:** Niamey
POPULATION: 8.3 million   **CURRENCY:** CFA franc   **OFFICIAL LANGUAGE:** French

LAND-LOCKED IN THE west of Africa, Niger is linked to the sea by the River Niger. The northern regions, the area around the Aïr mountains and particularly the vast uninhabited northeast have Saharan conditions. Niger experienced ten years of economic boom in the 1970s and 1980s, when the new uranium mines brought a budget surplus, but today most Nigeriens still live a harsh subsistence existence.

CLIMATE

WEATHER CHART

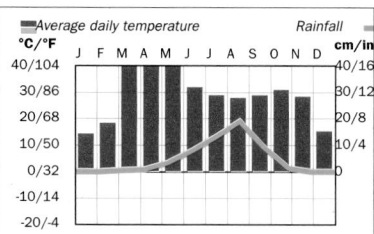

The Saharan north is virtually rainless. The south, in the Sahel belt, has an unreliable rainy season, preceded by a period of extreme daytime heat.

COMMUNICATIONS

 Niamey International 74,319 passengers   Has no fleet

THE TRANSPORT NETWORK

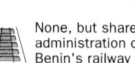

39,970 km (24,837 miles)	Trans-Sahara Highway 428 km (266 miles)
None, but shares administration of Benin's railway	300 km (186 miles)

Plans to extend the railway to Niamey from Parakou in Benin have been shelved. A bridge over the Niger, the country's second, is being built at Gaya.

TOURISM

 13,071 visitors   Down 14% in 1992

MAIN OVERSEAS ARRIVALS

France 28%	
Germany 7%	
USA 7%	
Other 58%	

% of total arrivals (0 10 20 30 40 50 60)

The Aïr mountains, southern Hausa cities, and Saharan Tuareg culture attract some tourists in spite of Niger's limited infrastructure and instability.

PEOPLE

 Hausa, Djerma, Fulani, Tuareg, Teda, French   6 people per km²

THE URBAN/RURAL POPULATION SPLIT

20%   80%

ETHNIC MAKEUP

Other 5%   Tuareg 8%
Fulani 9%
Hausa 56%
Djerma 22%

Considerable tensions exist between the Tuaregs in the north and the southern groups. The Tuaregs' sense of alienation from mainstream Nigerien politics has increased since the 1973 and 1983 droughts. Their herds decimated, many Tuaregs were forced away from their nomadic way of life to the towns. Northern Tuaregs responded to these pressures by mounting a low-key revolt.

A more subtle antagonism exists between the Djerma and Hausa groups. Until recently, the Djerma elite from the southwest dominated politics in Niger. Since 1993, however, control has passed to the Hausa majority.

Niger is essentially an Islamic society, having an 80% Muslim majority. Women have, on the whole, only limited rights and restricted access to education.

Testing boating poles in the market at Ayorou on the River Niger, the country's only major permanent watercourse.

POLITICS

 1998   President Mahamane Ousmane

THE STATE OF THE PARTIES

National Assembly 83 members

60% AFC   35% MNSD   5% Other

AFC = Alliance of the Forces of Change (composed of: CDS = Social Democratic Convention, PNDS = Niger Party for Unity and Democracy, ANDP = Niger Alliance for Democracy and Progress, PPN–RDA = Nigerian Progressive Party – African Democratic Rally, and two others)   **MNSD** = National Movement for a Development Society   **Other** = Democratic Union of Progressive Forces, Union of Democratic and Progressive Patriots

The death of the military dictator, President Seyni Kountché, in 1987, opened the way for the pro-democracy protests of 1990, led by students and the trades unions.

Amadou Cheiffou's interim government successfully contained a rearguard action by the military in 1992 and ran multiparty elections in 1993. The winning CDS and other parties have now forged a strong alliance (the AFC), but economic decline and a rebellion by the Tuaregs in the north are testing its permanence.

President Mahamane Ousmane is the first Hausa to lead the country.

WORLD AFFAIRS

 OAU   Ecowas   GATT   AfDB   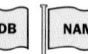 NAM

Relations with Libya and Algeria are sensitive, as Niger suspects they may be giving the Tuaregs support. The spillover into Niger of refugees loyal to Chad's ousted President Habré causes tension. Links with Nigeria will be strengthened now that Niger has a Hausa president.

AID

 $376m (receipts)   Down 4% in 1991

Almost all development is aid-funded. France is the principal donor, followed by the IMF and Arab funds, and a little from Ivory Coast and Nigeria.

DEFENCE

 $21m   Up 22% in 1989

Having withdrawn from politics, the military's role is now the active suppression of the Tuareg rebellion.

NIGER

Total Area : 1 267 000 sq. km
(489 188 sq. miles)

POPULATION   LAND HEIGHT

- ◎ over 100 000
- ○ over 50 000
- ● over 10 000
- · under 10 000

1000m/3281ft
500m/1640ft
200m/656ft
150m/492ft

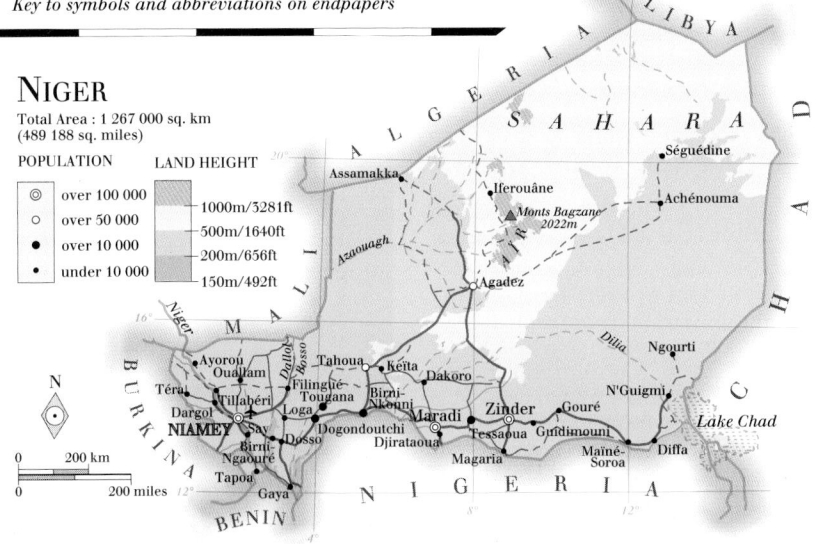

0   200 km
0   200 miles

CHRONOLOGY

The powerful Islamic Sokoto Empire dissolved as the French took Niger over between 1883 and 1901.

- ❏ **1958** Autonomous republic within French community.
- ❏ **1960** Independence. Hamani Diori's one-party PPN state.
- ❏ **1968** French open uranium mines.
- ❏ **1973** Drought; 60% of livestock die; no harvest for two years.
- ❏ **1974** Military coup. Gen Kountché bans political parties.
- ❏ **1976** First trade-balance surplus.
- ❏ **1984** New drought; River Niger dries up for first time in history. Uranium boom ends.
- ❏ **1987** Kountché dies. Gen Saibou eases transition to democracy.
- ❏ **1990** New constitution drawn up. Tuareg rebellion becomes serious.
- ❏ **1993** Democratic elections.

ECONOMICS

 $2.3bn   295.23 CFA francs

SCORE CARD

❏ WORLD GNP RANKING	135th
❏ GNP PER CAPITA	$280
❏ BALANCE OF PAYMENTS	$35m
❏ INFLATION	–7.8%
❏ UNEMPLOYMENT	47%

STRENGTHS

Vast uranium deposits; a few other minerals. Traditional Sahelian sense of community.

WEAKNESSES

Aid-dependent. Collapse of uranium prices in 1980s created large debt burden. Few other important minerals. Only 3% of land is cultivable. Crops are low-value. Frequent droughts.

EXPORTS

Spain 6%   Japan 6%
Other 8%
France 66%   Nigeria 14%

IMPORTS

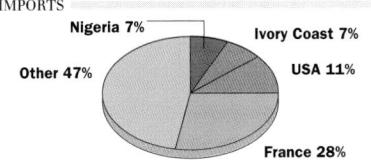

Nigeria 7%   Ivory Coast 7%
Other 47%   USA 11%
France 28%

RESOURCES

 163m kwh (capacity 600,000 kw)

 4m cattle, 4m sheep, 512,000 asses

Not an oil producer and has no refineries

Uranium, tin, gypsum, coal, salt, tungsten, iron, calcium

During the 1970s, Niger's uranium mines boomed, but output collapsed in

the 1980s when world prices slumped. Other mining is small-scale and oil reserves are not commercially viable. The uranium boom quadrupled electricity needs, half of which are now met by Nigeria's Kainji Dam on the River Niger.

ENVIRONMENT

 8% (7% partially protected)

Donor-funded afforestation programmes

Serious droughts are increasing the rate of desertification, the problem that overrides all others in Niger.

MEDIA

 The 1992 constitution guarantees freedom of expression, but there is still an official press

PUBLISHING AND BROADCAST MEDIA

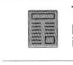 There is 1 daily newspaper, *Le Sahel*, published by the government, and a small, influential independent press since 1990

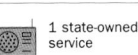 1 state-owned service   1 state-owned service

The BBC World Service's Hausa programming is more influential than local French short-wave radio.

CRIME

 Niger does not publish prison figures

Crime levels are fairly constant from year to year

Crime levels are low, though drought and Tuareg unrest have led to banditry. Smuggling to and from Nigeria is seen simply as part of the informal economy.

EDUCATION

 28%

Local languages are emphasized more strongly than in most francophone countries. School attendance is only 30%.

HEALTH

 1 per 38,500 people

Malaria, tuberculosis, meningitis, measles, malnutrition

In spite of progress in rural health care, immunization, malaria control and child nutrition are still limited.

WEALTH

 The Tuaregs are the lowest paid social group

CONSUMER GOODS OWNERSHIP

VCR and PC ownership is limited to an elite

59   5   2

Traditional egalitarianism in Sahelian life works against private enrichment, but uranium wealth is altering values.

WORLD RANKING

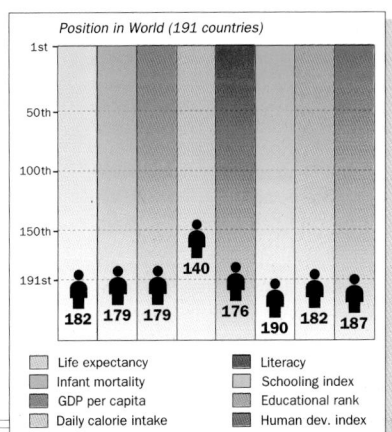

Position in World (191 countries)

182   179   179   140   176   190   182   187

- ◻ Life expectancy
- ◻ Infant mortality
- ◻ GDP per capita
- ◻ Daily calorie intake
- ◼ Literacy
- ◻ Schooling index
- ◻ Educational rank
- ◼ Human dev. index

N

NIGERIA

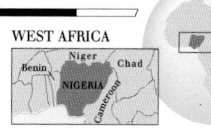

WEST AFRICA

OFFICIAL NAME: Federal Republic of Nigeria **CAPITAL:** Abuja
POPULATION: 90 million **CURRENCY:** Naira **OFFICIAL LANGUAGE:** English

AFRICA'S MOST POPULOUS state, Nigeria gained its independence from Britain in 1960. Bordered by Benin, Niger, Chad and Cameroon, its terrain varies from tropical rainforest and swamps in the south to savanna in the north. Nigeria has been dominated by military governments since 1966. A promised return to civilian rule was aborted in 1993 when the army refused to accept the results of presidential elections. Nigeria is OPEC's fourth largest oil producer, but it has experienced a fall in living standards since the 1970s, when it saw itself as the most dynamic African economy.

Village beneath Tengele Peak in Bauchi State. *A large proportion of Nigerians live from subsistence agriculture.*

CLIMATE

WEATHER CHART

	Average daily temperature												Rainfall	
°C/°F	J	F	M	A	M	J	J	A	S	O	N	D	cm/in	
60/150													60/24	
50/130													50/20	
40/104													40/16	
30/86													30/12	
20/68													20/8	
10/50													10/4	
0/32													0	

The south is hot, rainy and humid for most of the year. The arid north experiences only one, uncomfortably humid, rainy season from May to September. Its very hot dry season is marked by the dust-laden *harmattan* wind. The Jos Plateau and the eastern highlands are cooler than the rest of Nigeria. Forcados in the Niger delta gets most rain with 380 cm a year.

COMMUNICATIONS

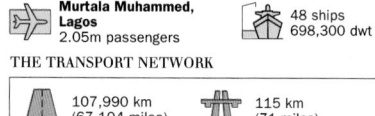

Murtala Muhammed, Lagos 2.05m passengers

48 ships 698,300 dwt

THE TRANSPORT NETWORK

107,990 km (67,104 miles)		115 km (71 miles)	
3505 km (2178 miles)		8575 km (5328 miles)	

Nigeria relies almost entirely on road transport. During the oil-boom years of the 1970s, new long-distance road links were built. Now that revenues have shrunk, maintenance is the major problem. The road accident rate is among the worst in the world. The small rail system, built for the once thriving bulk trade, is today very slow and badly maintained. Nigerian Airways' international operations have been privatized as a new corporation named Air Nigeria. The internal air market has shrunk since the prosperous years of the 1970s.

TOURISM

160,470 visitors

Down 47% in 1990

Nigeria has attempted to build a tourist industry, but with little success. Year-round tropical temperatures and poor infrastructure have limited its growth. The major deterrent to visitors, however, is crime. Travel can be hazardous, and Lagos has one of the world's highest crime rates.

MAIN OVERSEAS ARRIVALS

Benin	27%
Niger	26%
Ghana	14%
Togo	10%
Mali	3%
Other	20%

% of total arrivals

NIGERIA

Total Area : 923 770 sq. km (356 668 sq. miles)

POPULATION

▣	over 1 000 000
◉	over 500 000
◎	over 100 000
○	over 50 000
●	over 10 000
·	under 10 000

LAND HEIGHT

	2000m/6562ft
	1000m/3281ft
	500m/1640ft
	200m/656ft
	Sea Level

N

PEOPLE

 Hausa, English Creole, Yoruba, Ibo, English   96 people per km²

THE URBAN/RURAL POPULATION SPLIT

35%   65%

RELIGIOUS PERSUASION

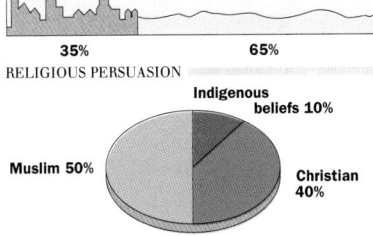

Indigenous beliefs 10%

Muslim 50%

Christian 40%

ETHNIC MAKEUP

245 (est) other ethnic groups 35%

Hausa-Fulani, Yoruba and Ibo 65%

In recent years, Nigeria has largely managed to contain the passions generated by the ethnic, religious and language differences that characterize its people. There is intense rivalry between the three main ethnic groups, as well as among the 245 smaller ones. Members of one group tend to blame those of another for their problems, rather than the broader political system. Religion is a particular source of tension. Outbreaks of communal violence, particularly in the north, are frequently attributable to clashes between Muslim fundamentalists and Christian proselytizers. Except in the Islamic north, women have traditionally possessed independent economic status. In recent years they have, however, been subjected to some prejudice in professional circles.

Lake Chad
amasak Baga
Ngala
uri

POPULATION AGE BREAKDOWN

%	■ 0–14	▨ 15–64			□ 65+
2.3%	2.4%	2.5%	2.5%	2.7%
52.3%	51.3%	50.9%	50.1%	51.3%
45.4%	46.3%	46.6%	47.4%	46%
1960	1970	1980	1990	2000

POLITICS

 Uncertain   General Sanni Abacha

THE STATE OF THE PARTIES
Provisional Ruling Council

The National Assembly was dissolved in November 1993 after the resumption of military rule. Government is now by a Provisional Ruling Council of senior military figures

Nigeria is a federation, currently of 30 states, controlled by a military dictatorship. The present regime assumed formal control in November 1993 – in the wake of the aborted August elections – after dissolving the National Assembly.

MAIN POLITICAL ISSUES

Corruption
International agencies have identified corruption as a major cause of Nigeria's debt levels. Bureaucrats commonly regard holding office as a source of lucrative kickbacks from the granting of contracts. This attitude is raising anti-government feeling.

Instability
There are fears, particularly amongst the Western-dominated business community, that popular resentment at the military's apparent determination to cling to power will create serious long-term political instability.

PROFILE
A programme to restore civilian government began in 1987 under President Babangida, but came to a halt in August 1993 when he annulled the results of the presidential election. Protests abroad and strikes at home persuaded Babangida to give up the presidency and a 'civilian' interim government was set up by the military.

However, the military soon resumed control under General Sanni Abacha. The interim government was swept away, along with the two political parties set up to fight the elections. General Abacha set up a Provisional Ruling Council and sacked state governors, replacing them with military officers. Political activity was banned.

General Ibrahim Babangida.
Nigeria's president from 1985 to 1993.

Moshood Abiola.
Won 1993 elections, but was prevented from taking power.

CHRONOLOGY

Before formal colonization by the British, begun only in 1861, Nigeria was a collection of African states owing their considerable wealth to trans-Saharan and transatlantic trade. During the 18th century the principle commodity was slaves: over 15,000 people were exported annually from the Bight of Benin and another 15,000 from the Bight of Biafra.

❏ **1885** George Goldie's Royal Niger Company given responsibility by the UK government for the British sphere of influence along the Niger and Benue rivers. British armed forces begin coercing local rulers into accepting British rule.

❏ **1897** West Africa Frontier Force (WAFF) established; subjugation of the north begins.

❏ **1898** The Royal Niger Company's charter revoked.

❏ **1900** British Protectorate of Northern Nigeria established.

❏ **1906** Lagos incorporated into the Protectorate of Southern Nigeria.

❏ **1914** Protectorates of Northern and Southern Nigeria joined to form colony of Nigeria.

❏ **1951** Elections. Nationalists win the Eastern, Western and Northern Regions.

❏ **1954** New constitution establishes federal system of government.

❏ **1957–1958** Constitutional conferences establish timetable for independence.

❏ **1960** Independence. Nigeria established as a federation.

❏ **1961** Northern part of UK-administered UN Trust Territory of the Cameroons incorporated as part of Nigeria's Northern Region.

❏ **1966** January, first military coup, led by Maj-Gen Ironsi. Leading politicians murdered, including Sir Tafawa Balewa, the federal prime minister. July, counter-coup mounted by group of northern army officers believing Ironsi was representing only Eastern Region interests. Ironsi murdered. Thousands of Ibo in Northern Region massacred.

❏ **1967–1970** Civil war. Lt-Col Ojukwu calls for secession of oil-rich east under the new name Biafra. Over one million Nigerians die before secessionists defeated by federal forces.

❏ **1970** General Gowon in power. New constitution creating 12 states from existing three.

❏ **1975** Gowon toppled in bloodless coup. Brigadier Murtala Mohammed takes power.

❏ **1976** Murtala Mohammed murdered in abortive coup. ▷

N

CHRONOLOGY continued

❏ **1978** Political parties legalized, on condition they represent national, not tribal, interests.

❏ **1979** Elections won by Alhaji Shehu Shagari and National Party of Nigeria (NPN), marking return to civilian government.

❏ **1983** September, elections won again by Shagari and NPN. December, military coup. Maj-Gen Mohammed Buhari heads Supreme Military Council.

❏ **1985** Maj-Gen Ibrahim Babangida takes over in bloodless coup, promising a return to democracy.

❏ **1992** Abuja becomes capital.

❏ **1993** August, postponed presidential election, won by Moshood Abiola, annulled by Babangida. International protest and strikes. Babangida resigns presidency; military sets up Interim National Government (ING) headed by Chief Adegunle Shonekan. November, ING dissolved. Military, headed by Gen Sanni Abacha, takes over. Provisional Ruling Council set up.

WORLD AFFAIRS

Nigeria's overseas ambitions have expanded and contracted with its oil revenues. The military government of the 1970s – when oil prices were high – saw itself as Africa's leading voice. It recognized the Marxist government in Angola, was a keen sponsor of ECOWAS, and strongly opposed apartheid in South Africa. With the fall in world oil prices after 1981, this ambition was trimmed. Relations with South Africa have been restored, now that political change there is under way.

The main foreign policy concern is Nigeria's key role in the ECOWAS force that invaded war-torn Liberia in 1990. Under Babangida, Nigeria also took the lead in planning for an African Common Market, with a target date of 2025. Nigeria now has one of the non-permanent African seats on the UN Security Council.

AID

 $262m (receipts)   Up 5% in 1991

Nigeria's debt rocketed with the 1981 drop in world oil prices and turned Nigeria from an aid donor into a major receiver of World Bank assistance. Several of the major aid agencies have expressed concern that the government may have understated its oil revenues to gain more aid.

DEFENCE

$255m   Up 27% in 1992

0 — Defence spending as % GDP — 40
0.8%

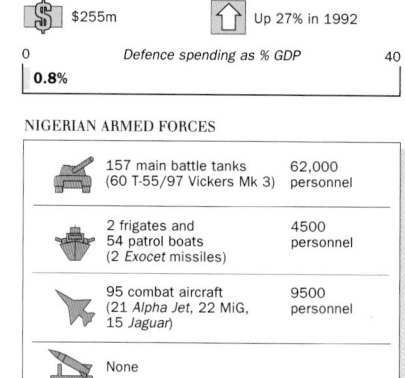

NIGERIAN ARMED FORCES

157 main battle tanks (60 T-55/97 Vickers Mk 3)	62,000 personnel	
2 frigates and 54 patrol boats (2 *Exocet* missiles)	4500 personnel	
95 combat aircraft (21 *Alpha Jet*, 22 MiG, 15 *Jaguar*)	9500 personnel	
None		

The defence establishment in Nigeria suffers from problems caused by corruption. During Babangida's rule (1985–1993), most of the air force's prestige jets were grounded as money for spare parts was diverted into senior officers' bank accounts. Soldiers' salaries have been steadily declining in real terms in recent years, barrack conditions have deteriorated and morale is low. However, the November 1993 restoration of military government by Defence Minister General Sanni Abacha – a key player in both the 1983 and 1985 coups – is likely to encourage expectations of improved conditions among the army rank and file.

ECONOMICS

$28bn   25.00 naira

SCORE CARD

❏ WORLD GNP RANKING...........................57th
❏ GNP PER CAPITA $311
❏ BALANCE OF PAYMENTS $1.49bn
❏ INFLATION 44.6%
❏ UNEMPLOYMENT....Widespread underemployment

EXPORTS

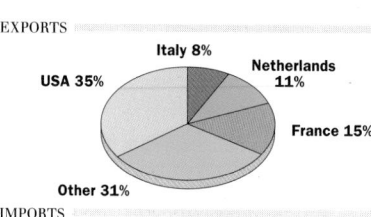

USA 35%
Italy 8%
Netherlands 11%
France 15%
Other 31%

IMPORTS

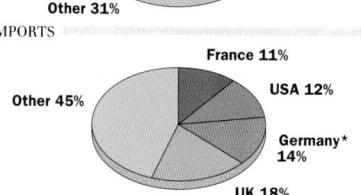

Other 45%
France 11%
USA 12%
Germany* 14%
UK 18%

STRENGTHS

One of world's top oil producers at 1.9 million b/d. Vast reserves of natural gas, still only partly exploited. Almost self-sufficient in food. Strong entrepreneurial class. Large domestic market of 90 million people.

WEAKNESSES

Over-dependence since the 1970s on oil, which accounts for 90% of export earnings and 80% of government revenue, and encourages massive state inefficiency. Advantages of a large domestic market mitigated by low per capita purchasing power and high unit transport costs. Entrepreneurs focus on trade rather than production. Only cocoa remains of Nigeria's traditional agricultural exports; it was once a major producer of tropical vegetables and fruit.

ECONOMIC PERFORMANCE INDICATOR

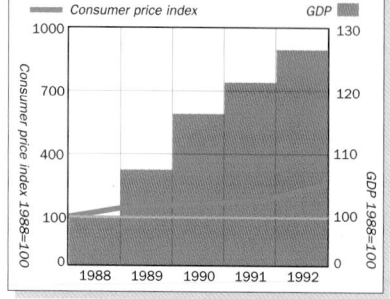

— Consumer price index   GDP

Consumer price index 1988=100
GDP 1988=100
1988 1989 1990 1991 1992

PROFILE

The economy has been characterized by massive government spending and the running up of debts which could not be serviced after the 1981 oil price fall. Led by the IMF, creditors want major cuts in spending – especially on loss-making public sector companies – and subsidies. Petrol subsidies alone are estimated to have cost $2.4 billion a year. Such changes are politically fraught, however. When petrol prices were raised 400% in November 1993, there were nationwide strikes.

NIGERIA : MAJOR BUSINESSES

Kaduna
Kano
Lake Chad
Shagamu
Lagos
Benin City
Warri
Port Harcourt

Oil
Textiles
Brewing
Manufacturing
Pharmaceuticals
Oil refining
Chemicals
Palm oil
Cement

0 — 200 km
0 — 200 miles   * significant multinational ownership

RESOURCES

9.9bn kwh
(capacity 4m kw)

1.9m b/d
(reserves
17,899,820,000 bbl)

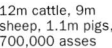
12m cattle, 9m
sheep, 1.1m pigs,
700,000 asses

Oil, natural gas, coal,
tin, iron, bauxite,
columbite, lead

Hydro 22% (2.2bn kwh)
Thermal 78% (7.7bn kwh)
Nuclear 0%
Other 0%

% of total generation by type

Oil has been Nigeria's main resource since the 1970s. Government policy is to increase output from 1.9 million b/d (7.5% of OPEC output) to 2.5 million b/d. Domestic demand is 300,000 b/d, much of it smuggled to neighbouring countries. Nigeria's vast gas deposits are still under-exploited. The state retains 60% control of the oil and gas industry. Shell is the main foreign shareholder, but most oil multinationals are represented.

Nigeria has sizeable iron ore deposits. These are not yet utilized in the state-run steel industry; imported ore is used instead. Bauxite deposits are also currently under-exploited. There are, however, plans for establishing an aluminium industry.

NIGERIA : LAND USE

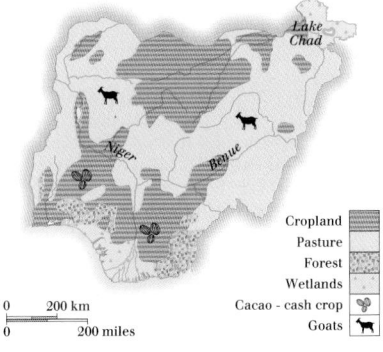

Lake Chad

Niger

Benue

0   200 km
0   200 miles

Cropland
Pasture
Forest
Wetlands
Cacao - cash crop
Goats

ENVIRONMENT

3% (1% partially
protected)

No progress in
controlling oilfield
pollution

ENVIRONMENTAL TREATIES

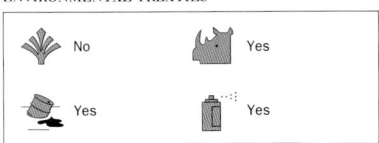

No

Yes

Yes

Yes

Oil industry pollution in the Niger delta is a major local concern. In 1992, Shell recorded 86 protest attacks against its plants. Before the discovery of a highly toxic cargo in Lagos in 1988, Nigeria was a regular dumping ground for dangerous European chemical waste.

MEDIA

Foreign journalists have been expelled for questioning corruption in government

Nigerians are avid newspaper readers and the press is traditionally one of Africa's liveliest. However, the new military regime has made clear its unwillingness to tolerate criticism. There are over 20 English-language current-affairs periodicals.

CRIME

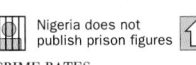
Nigeria does not
publish prison figures

Rising. One of the
highest crime rates
in the world

CRIME RATES

Murders
94   per 100,000 population

Rapes
Above regional average

Thefts
1256   per 100,000 population

The military government frequently uses *ad hoc* tribunals for politically sensitive cases. Nigeria has one of the highest crime rates in the world. Murder often accompanies even minor burglaries. Corruption pervades the bureaucracy; the provision of kickbacks to supporters is considered routine rather than a crime. Rich Nigerians live in high-security compounds, equipped with electric fencing and patrolled by armed guards.

EDUCATION

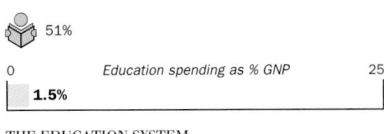
51%

0   Education spending as % GNP   25
1.5%

THE EDUCATION SYSTEM

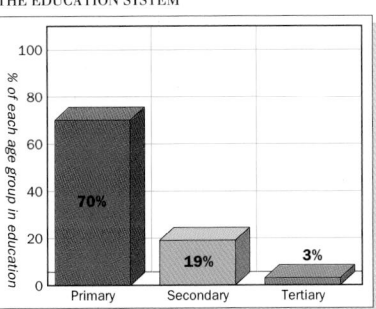

% of each age group in education

70%   Primary
19%   Secondary
3%   Tertiary

Education has suffered from the government's massive debt repayment burden. During the oil-boom years, Nigeria concentrated on creating 31 universities with prestigious medical and scientific schools. However, standards in primary education, which has not received the same level of investment, have fallen since the 1970s.

PUBLISHING AND BROADCAST MEDIA

There are 35 daily newspapers. The
largest is the *Daily Times*, published by
the government

1 state-controlled
service

1 state-controlled
service

Intelsat V1 F1

None

HEALTH

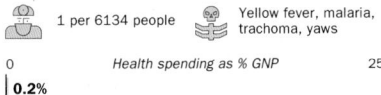
1 per 6134 people

Yellow fever, malaria,
trachoma, yaws

0   Health spending as % GNP   25
0.2%

The health service is concentrated in urban areas and mostly aimed at richer Nigerians. Modern medicine is not available to those living in rural areas. Health provision, with other public services, has suffered from the crisis in government revenues.

WEALTH

International company finance officer, 200,000
naira per year; polytechnic principal lecturer,
24,000–41,000 naira per year

CONSUMER GOODS OWNERSHIP

Per 1000 population

1000
750
500
250
0

PCs
limited
to an
elite

29   4   3   5

Nigerians with access to the rich pickings of political office spent on a massive scale during the oil-boom – on Maseratis, Mercedes and overseas education for their children. Much was financed by government loans. Habits have not changed with the fall in oil revenues: borrowing has simply grown.

WORLD RANKING

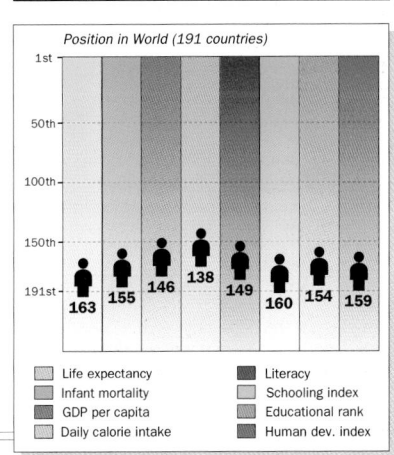

Position in World (191 countries)

1st
50th
100th
150th
191st

163   155   146   138   149   160   154   159

Life expectancy
Infant mortality
GDP per capita
Daily calorie intake

Literacy
Schooling index
Educational rank
Human dev. index

NORTH KOREA

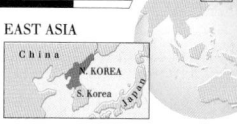

OFFICIAL NAME: Democratic People's Republic of Korea **CAPITAL:** Pyongyang
POPULATION: 22.6 million **CURRENCY:** Won **OFFICIAL LANGUAGE:** Korean

NORTH KOREA COMPRISES the northern half of the Korean peninsula and is separated from the US-dominated South at the 38th parallel. Much of the country is mountainous; the Chaeryŏng and Pyongyang plains in the southwest are the most fertile regions. Established as an independent communist republic in 1948, North Korea remains largely isolated from the outside world. Its economy, starved of development capital, is now facing severe difficulties.

CLIMATE

WEATHER CHART

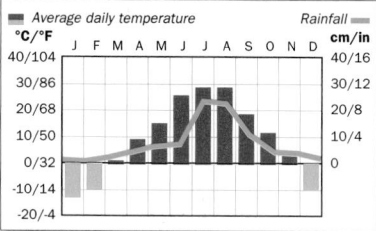

North Korea has a typically continental climate. Winters in the north can be extreme, with several months of snow.

COMMUNICATIONS

 Sunan, Pyongyang   71 ships 940,700 dwt

THE TRANSPORT NETWORK

 23,000 km (14,292 miles)   354 km (220 miles)

5045 km (3135 miles)   2253 km (1400 miles)

North Korea relies heavily on the antiquated railway network built by the Japanese during their occupation. The Pyongyang–Kaesŏng motorway, completed in 1992, is open only to very limited, officially-approved traffic.

TOURISM

 Tourism largely banned by government   Restrictions on tourism recently increased

MAIN OVERSEAS ARRIVALS

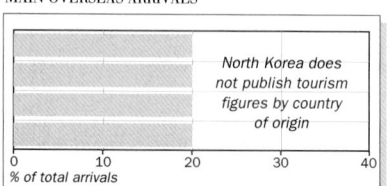

North Korea does not publish tourism figures by country of origin

0   10   20   30   40
% of total arrivals

The ban on Western tourists, who had been permitted to visit the country since 1985, was reimposed in 1993.

Rice paddy-field. The hot, wet summers are ideal for rice growing. Most farms are run as co-operatives.

PEOPLE

 Korean, Chinese   181 people per km²

THE URBAN/RURAL POPULATION SPLIT

60%   40%

ETHNIC MAKEUP

Korean 100%

North Korea operates a strict 'estates' system, by which the population is classed according to three categories: loyal, wavering and hostile. Inclusion in the first category is a prerequisite for advancement. Those deemed hostile – usually Christians and the children of landlords or of Koreans who fled to the South – have barely any rights. People live severely regulated lives. Divorce is non-existent and extra-marital sex highly frowned upon. Women form 57% of the workforce, but are also expected to run the home; it is not uncommon for them to rise at 4 am, and end their working day at 7 pm. From an early age, children are looked after by an extensive system of state-run crèches. The privileged lifestyle of the political elite – numbering only about 200,000 – is a source of considerable popular resentment.

POLITICS

Not applicable   President Kim Il Sung

THE STATE OF THE PARTIES

Supreme People's Assembly 687 members

100% KWP

KWP = Korean Workers' Party

The KWP, with a membership of some three million, is the only legal party and its influence is felt in all parts of North Korean life. Membership is essential for advancement. Kim Il Sung, the world's longest-serving political leader, presides over the party, carefully fostering his 'father of the proletariat' image. The main issue is the grooming of Kim Jong Il to take his father's place. To date, the personality cults and concentration of power in the two men have not been questioned, and the army has remained loyal to the regime. The death of the octogenarian Kim Il Sung could, however, provide a catalyst for political and economic change.

WORLD AFFAIRS

The worldwide collapse of communism has isolated North Korea. Its foreign policy is now in flux. In 1991, it joined the UN, and yet in 1992 and 1993 denied officials from the International Atomic Energy Agency (IAEA) access to suspected nuclear bomb manufacturing sites. In 1994, North Korea withdrew from the IAEA altogether. Similarly, talks have been held with South Korea about reunification, yet North and South Korean forces remain in a state of alert across the 38th parallel. The 1992 recognition of South Korea by China was a major blow to North Korea, resulting in a reduction in Chinese aid, and the implicit view from Beijing that South Korea would be the dominant partner in future.

AID

 $8m (receipts)   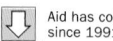 Aid has collapsed since 1991

Vital aid from the Soviet Union ended in 1991 and China ceased 'friendship supplies' in 1993. Despite official denials, the aid-dependent economy has suffered badly.

NORTH KOREA

Total Area : 120 540 sq. km (46 540 sq. miles)

POPULATION

over 1 000 000	⊡
over 100 000	◎
over 50 000	○
over 10 000	●

LAND HEIGHT

1500m/4920ft
1000m/3281ft
500m/1640ft
200m/656ft
Sea Level

CHRONOLOGY

North Korea (Korea north of the 38th parallel) was formed in 1948.

❑ **1950** Korean War, as North Korea invades the South. UN troops drive invasion back to 38th parallel.
❑ **1953** Armistice ends Korean War.
❑ **1958** Kim Il Sung establishes effective absolutism.
❑ **1993** Withdrawal from nuclear non-proliferation treaty.

EDUCATION

 95%

North Korea claims to have created over one million 'intellectuals'. Kim Il Sung, Pyongyang, is the only university.

HEALTH

 1 per 417 people   Heart diseases, cancers, digestive diseases

The free health service has raised life expectancy. The showpiece Pyongyang Maternity Hospital appears unused.

WEALTH

 The 20% or so of the population classified as 'hostile' live in remote areas, do the worst jobs and have little prospect of social advancement

CONSUMER GOODS OWNERSHIP

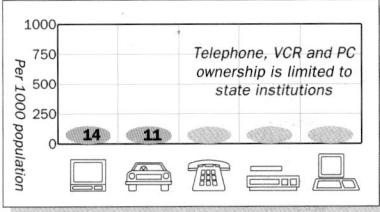

Telephone, VCR and PC ownership is limited to state institutions

An elite within the KWP lives well, with access to specialist shops and consumer goods such as VCRs. Both private car and telephone ownership are forbidden.

RESOURCES

 53.5bn kwh (capacity 9.5m kw)   Not an oil producer; refines 42,000 b/cd

 3.2m pigs, 1.3m cattle, 380,000 sheep   ◈ Coal, iron, lead, copper, zinc, tin, silver, gold, uranium

A shortage of electricity (blackouts are frequent) remains a major problem; a Chernobyl-type nuclear reactor remains half-built for want of Soviet aid. North Korea is relatively rich in metals, producing uranium for its nuclear programme. It is also the world's ninth largest silver producer.

ENVIRONMENT

0.5% (0.1% partially protected)   No access to state environmental information

Excessive use of fertilizers and unchecked pollution from heavy industry are the major problems.

MEDIA

 Total censorship. No foreign publications permitted. Radios have fixed dials

PUBLISHING AND BROADCAST MEDIA

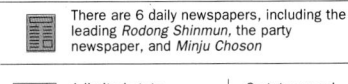

There are 6 daily newspapers, including the leading *Rodong Shinmun*, the party newspaper, and *Minju Choson*

1 limited state-owned service   2 state-owned services

North Korean TV consists mostly of musical shows praising the qualities of Kim Il Sung.

CRIME

North Korea does not publish prison figures   Low level of violent street crime

Corruption at all levels in dealings with the state is the major problem. The criminal code is weighted to protect the state against 'subversion', rather than the rights of the individual. North Korea has a very poor human rights record and a *gulag* of over 100,000 'subversives', where whole families are sent along with those accused and where torture is routine.

DEFENCE

 $2.8bn   Up 15% in 1992

North Korea is suspected of having a fast-track nuclear bomb programme. Its advanced arms industry supplies missiles to Iran, amongst others.

ECONOMICS

 $29.7bn   2.15 won

SCORE CARD

❑ WORLD GNP RANKING..........................54th
❑ GNP PER CAPITA $1390
❑ BALANCE OF PAYMENTS ... .*Closed economy;*
❑ INFLATION ....*.......does not publish*
❑ UNEMPLOYMENT ....*any figures*

STRENGTHS
Until 1970, North Korea had a higher GNP per capita than the South. Other than minerals, strengths are now few.

WEAKNESSES
GNP has been declining by 5% a year since 1990. The loss of Soviet and Chinese aid is a major blow.

EXPORTS/IMPORTS

North Korea's main trading partners are Russia, China and Japan

WORLD RANKING

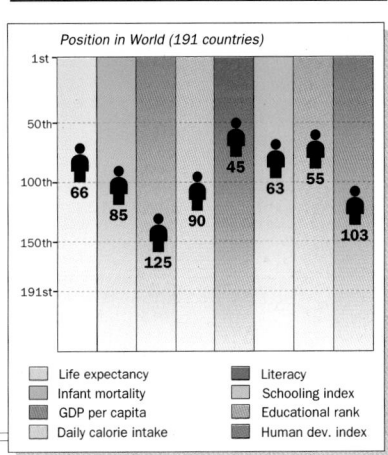

Position in World (191 countries)

Life expectancy		Literacy
Infant mortality		Schooling index
GDP per capita		Educational rank
Daily calorie intake		Human dev. index

NORWAY

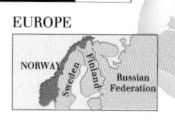

OFFICIAL NAME: Kingdom of Norway **CAPITAL:** Oslo **POPULATION:** 4.3 million
CURRENCY: Norwegian krone **OFFICIAL LANGUAGE:** Norwegian **OVERSEAS TERRITORIES:** 3

OCCUPYING THE WESTERN PART of Scandinavia, Norway borders Sweden, Finland and Russia to its east; its western coastline is characterized by numerous fjords and islands. Large oil and gas revenues have brought moderate prosperity. Gro Harlem Brundtland became the country's first woman prime minister in 1981. Despite the Europe-wide recession, Norway has managed to keep its unemployment rate below 6%. The duty of government to create conditions that enable every person to find work is enshrined in the constitution.

The village of Reine on Moskenesøya, 160 km inside the Arctic Circle in the Lofoten Islands. It is a popular destination for summer visitors.

CLIMATE

WEATHER CHART

The whole of Norway's west coast is kept ice-free by the warm Gulf Stream. It receives much more precipitation than the rest of the country; Bergen has a yearly average of 225 cm. Norway enjoys the highest mean temperatures in Scandinavia, but in winter the temperature in Oslo can drop to –25°C.

NORWAY

Total Area : 323 900 sq. km
(125 060 sq. miles)

LAND HEIGHT

2000m/6562ft
1000m/3281ft
500m/1640ft
200m/656ft
Sea Level

POPULATION

over 100 000 ◎
over 50 000 ○
over 10 000 ●
over 10 000 ·

COMMUNICATIONS

Fornebu Intl, Oslo
6.3m passengers

1194 ships
36.52m dwt

THE TRANSPORT NETWORK

88,800 km
(55,179 miles)

437 km
(272 miles)

4223 km
(2624 miles)

1577 km
(980 miles)

It has been impossible to extend rail links further than Bodø, inside the Arctic Circle. To reach Lofoten or Narvik and beyond, the most common form of transport is air. In 1988, Scandinavian Airlines Systems agreed that British Midland would take over some of its UK–Norway direct routes.

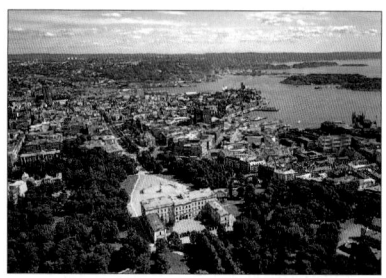

The royal palace, Oslo. This is situated near the national theatre, at one end of the Karl Johanisgate, the city's main thoroughfare.

TOURISM

 4.3m bed-nights. Norway does not record visitor numbers

 Up 9% in 1992

Norway is a popular destination with visitors from Sweden, Germany, Denmark, the UK and the USA. Its winter tourism industry is based on skiing and has been boosted by the location of the 1994 Winter Olympics in Lillehammer. Cruising along the fjords is popular with summer visitors. Areas within the Arctic Circle are a particular attraction in June, when tourists go in search of the midnight sun. Oslo has a reputation for good classical music and jazz. However, the strength of the

MAIN OVERSEAS ARRIVALS

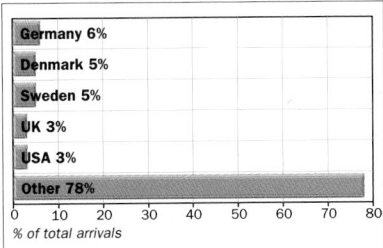

Germany 6%
Denmark 5%
Sweden 5%
UK 3%
USA 3%
Other 78%

0 10 20 30 40 50 60 70 80
% of total arrivals

krone and the high cost of living make Norway expensive.

PEOPLE

 Norwegian (*Bokmål* 'book language' and *Nynorsk* 'new Norsk'), Lappish

13 people per km²

THE URBAN/RURAL POPULATION SPLIT

75%   25%

RELIGIOUS PERSUASION

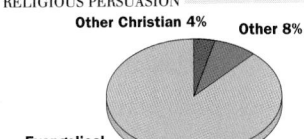

Other Christian 4%   Other 8%

Evangelical Lutheran 88%

ETHNIC MAKEUP

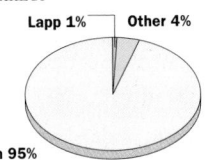

Lapp 1%   Other 4%

Norwegian 95%

Norway has a minimal immigrant population. Over the last few years there has been a small influx of European refugees; they have reportedly suffered some violent attacks from right-wing groups.

The family is traditionally close and nuclear. Men are expected to share responsibility for raising children.

Children frequently attend day schools from below the age of two years. Women in Norway enjoy considerable power and freedom. The prime minister is a woman, as are many other leading politicians.

Over half of marriages in Norway now end in divorce.

POPULATION AGE BREAKDOWN

%	0–14	15–64	65+		
11.1%	12.9%	14.8%	16.4%	15.8%
63%	62.6%	63%	64.8%	65.7%
25.9%	24.5%	22.2%	18.8%	18.5%
1960	1970	1980	1990	2000

POLITICS

 1997

 King Harald V

THE STATE OF THE PARTIES

Parliament 165 members

41% DNA	19% SP	17% H	8% KRF	8% SV	7% Other

DNA = Norwegian Labour Party **SP** = Centre Party
H = Conservative Party **KRF** = Christian Democratic Party
SV = Socialist Left Party **Other** = Progress Party, Liberal Party, Red Electoral Alliance

Norway is a constitutional monarchy, with a king as head of state and an elected parliament.

MAIN POLITICAL ISSUE

Membership of the EU

In 1994, terms for Norway's accession to the EU were agreed. The issue is divisive; over 60% of the electorate oppose joining on the grounds that membership will lead to a loss of control of national resources, notably fisheries and the offshore oil sector. However, government and industry support the move. A referendum is due in 1995. Some groups in parliament have threatened to ignore the result if it goes against EU membership.

PROFILE

Political decisions are based on a process of consensus-building between the government, parliament and the strong trade unions. The SP, which is against joining the EU, more than doubled its representation in the elections of September 1993, whereas the pro-EU Conservatives slipped badly, becoming the third party in parliament.

Gro Harlem Brundtland's DNA has retained power since 1990, after a decade of short-lived governments. Part of the reason is the personal respect she commands among most of the population. Her pro-whaling stance, which has damaged her international image, has been popular at home.

WORLD AFFAIRS

 EEA   NATO   OECD   CSCE   CE

Aside from its application for membership of the EU, the major foreign policy issue for Norway is ensuring the continuing security of its borders. As a member of NATO, Norway is concerned at the withdrawal of US military forces from Europe, especially as the Norwegian government remains unconvinced that Russia is politically stable. To strengthen its security, Norway became an associate member of the WEU in November 1992.

Norway has played peace-broker in a number of major international conflicts, notably in helping to progress towards a resolution of the Palestinian-Israeli dispute. It has also been directly involved in attempting to bring an end to the Bosnian conflict; the foreign minister, Thorvald Stoltenberg, was UN negotiator in the region in 1994.

The government is exasperated at its inability to control the ecological effects of acid rain, which is destroying its forests, and blames lax pollution controls in the UK, Germany and Russia for the problem.

King Harald V, *who succeeded his father King Olaf V in 1991.*

Gro Harlem Brundtland, *prime minister since 1990.*

N

CHRONOLOGY

Norway gained independence from the Swedish crown in 1905 and elected its own king, Håkon VII.

❑ **1935** DNA forms government.
❑ **1940–1945** Nazi occupation. Puppet regime led by Vidkun Quisling.
❑ **1945** DNA resumes power.
❑ **1949** Norway joins NATO.
❑ **1957** King Håkon dies. Succeeded by son, Olaf V.
❑ **1960** Norway member of EFTA.
❑ **1962** Norway unsuccessfully applies for EC membership.
❑ **1965** DNA electoral defeat by SP coalition led by Per Boten.
❑ **1967** Norway fails in second bid for EC membership.
❑ **1971** Prime Minister Per Boten resigns following disclosure of secret negotiations to join EC. DNA government, led by Bratteli. ➡

CHRONOLOGY *continued*

- ❑ **1972** EC membership rejected by the people in referendum by 3% majority. Bratteli resigns. Centre coalition government takes power. Lars Korvald prime minister.
- ❑ **1973** Elections. Bratteli returns to power as prime minister.
- ❑ **1976** Bratteli succeeded by Odvar Nordli.
- ❑ **1981** Nordli resigns owing to ill health. Gro Harlem Brundtland becomes Norway's first woman prime minister. Elections bring to power Norway's first Conservative Party (H) government for 53 years. Kare Willoch prime minister.
- ❑ **1983** H forms coalition with SP and KRF.
- ❑ **1985** Election. Willoch's H–SP–KRF coalition returned. Norway agrees to suspend commercial whaling.
- ❑ **1986** Industrial unrest involving over 100,000 workers over better pay and reduction in working week. Parliament rejects tax increase on petrol. Willoch resigns. Minority DNA government takes power with Brundtland as prime minister. Currency devalued by 12%.
- ❑ **1989** Brundtland's government resigns. H–KRF coalition in power. USSR agrees exchange of information after fires on Soviet nuclear submarines stationed off Norwegian coast.
- ❑ **1990** H–KRF coalition breaks up over closer ties with EU. Brundtland and DNA in power.
- ❑ **1991** Olaf V dies and is succeeded by son, King Harald V.
- ❑ **1992** Government declares commercial whaling will resume in 1993.
- ❑ **1993** Formal negotiations for Norway to join EU begin.

AID

 $1.2bn (donations)   Down 2% in 1991

Norway has been paying more than the UN development target of 0.7% of GNP in aid every year since 1975. Although Norway's ratio of aid to GNP declined from 1.17 to 1.14% in 1991, it remains the highest in the world.

The vast majority of Norway's bilateral aid donations goes to the least developed countries of south-eastern Africa, southern Asia and Central America. The Norwegian government also allocates funds to various multilateral assistance programmes. In 1991, some 20% of multilateral aid donations went through the UN and 34% through international development banks.

DEFENCE

 $3.5bn   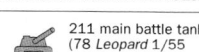 Up 1% in 1992

0   *Defence spending as % GDP*   40

3.2%

Norway spends just over 3% of GDP on defence, most of it on its conscript army of 22,800. It has been a full member of NATO since 1949, unlike its neighbours, Sweden and Finland. Norway's single overriding defence issue is the stability of Russia and the security of their common border.

NORWEGIAN ARMED FORCES

🛡	211 main battle tanks (78 *Leopard* 1/55 M-48A5/78 NM-116)	15,900 personnel
🚢	11 submarines, 5 frigates and 35 patrol boats	7300 personnel
✈	85 combat aircraft (F-16/F-5A)	9500 personnel
	None	

ECONOMICS

 $192.9bn   7.52 Norwegian kroner

SCORE CARD

- ❑ WORLD GNP RANKING..........................20th
- ❑ GNP PER CAPITA $44,000
- ❑ BALANCE OF PAYMENTS $4.9bn
- ❑ INFLATION 1.3%
- ❑ UNEMPLOYMENT..................................5.5%

EXPORTS

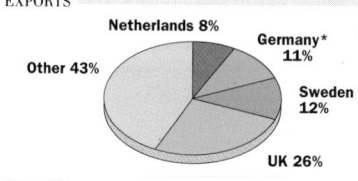

Netherlands 8%
Germany* 11%
Other 43%
Sweden 12%
UK 26%

IMPORTS

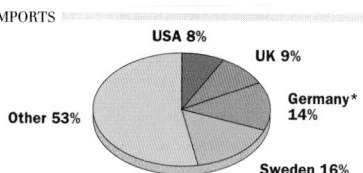

USA 8%
UK 9%
Germany* 14%
Other 53%
Sweden 16%

STRENGTHS

Western Europe's biggest producer and exporter of oil and natural gas. Mineral reserves. Hydroelectric power satisfies much of country's energy demands, allowing most oil to be exported. Large merchant-shipping fleet. Balance of payments surplus. Low inflation (1.3% in 1994) and unemployment compared to rest of Europe.

WEAKNESSES

Investment is still almost entirely directed at the oil industry. Over-dependence on oil revenue. Small home market and inaccessible geographical location. Harsh climate limits agriculture.

PROFILE

The state is interventionist by nature. In 1991 it stepped in to rescue most of the main commercial banks, which had been hit by bad loans. It began returning them to the private sector in 1994. The state also manages the distribution of offshore oil and gas

ECONOMIC PERFORMANCE INDICATOR

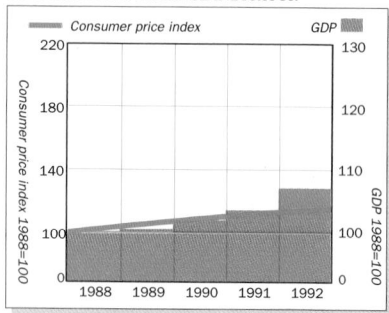

Consumer price index   GDP

licences, and maintains control of over 50% of these through its own company, Statoil.

Norway's immediate future prosperity is guaranteed by its lucrative offshore sector. However, despite a government jobs creation programme, unemployment is likely to remain higher than is traditionally acceptable. Continuing the strong regional policy of redirecting resources from the more prosperous south to the isolated north is likely to remain a priority, both for social and strategic reasons.

NORWAY : MAJOR BUSINESSES

Hammerfest
Tromso
Bodø
Trondheim
Höyanger
Bergen
Stavanger
Kristiansand
Larvik
Oslo

Aluminium smelting
Electrometallurgy
Printing & publishing
Fish processing
Copper mining
Shipbuilding
Textiles
Oil refining

0   200 km
0   200 miles

N

RESOURCES

121.6bn kwh (capacity 27.2m kw)

2.1m b/d (reserves 8,805,734,000 bbl)

2.2m sheep, 949,000 cattle, 697,000 pigs

Gas, oil, iron, pyrites, copper, lead, zinc

ELECTRICITY GENERATION

Hydro 99.6% (121.1bn kwh)

Thermal 0.4% (464m kwh)

Nuclear 0%

Other 0%

% of total generation by type

Norway is Europe's largest oil producer, with an output of some 2.1 million b/d; it also has sizeable gas reserves. Most of Norway's electricity is produced by hydro-power. In summer the HEP surplus is exported. Fish and forestry are traditionally significant sectors. With agriculture, they account for only 6% of the workforce and 3% of GDP, but to many Norwegians they are important enough to merit a rejection of EU membership. Salmon farms are especially efficient.

NORWAY : LAND USE

Cropland
Pasture
Forest
High mountain regions
Tundra
Cereals
Sheep

0   200 km
0   200 miles

ENVIRONMENT

13% (1% partially protected)

Decision to lift ban on whaling

ENVIRONMENTAL TREATIES

Yes

Yes

No

Yes

The government devotes considerable attention to preventing oil spills at sea, but is virtually powerless to halt the harmful effects of acid rain, which is damaging Norway's extensive forests. The UK, Germany and Russia have been identified as the main polluters. The north of Norway has suffered from radioactive contamination caused by the 1986 Chernobyl nuclear disaster. In 1993, Norway decided to lift a ban against fishing minke whales, arguing that the species was not threatened.

MEDIA

No government censorship

PUBLISHING AND BROADCAST MEDIA

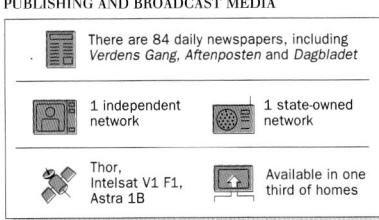

There are 84 daily newspapers, including *Verdens Gang*, *Aftenposten* and *Dagbladet*

1 independent network

1 state-owned network

Thor, Intelsat V1 F1, Astra 1B

Available in one third of homes

Norway has a diverse press. There are over 80 daily newspapers, with a combined circulation of over two million. *Verdens Gang* is the leading daily with a circulation of 365,000.

CRIME

2041 prisoners

Down 1% in 1990

CRIME RATES

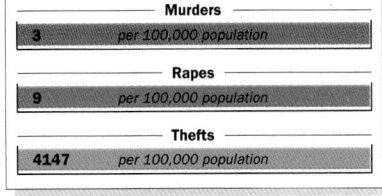

Murders

3   per 100,000 population

Rapes

9   per 100,000 population

Thefts

4147   per 100,000 population

Norway has low levels of crime, even by Scandinavian standards. Violent crime barely exists – the murder rate is a quarter of that of Finland or Sweden, and there are considerably fewer assaults and robberies.

EDUCATION

99%

0   Education spending as % GNP   25

7.5%

THE EDUCATION SYSTEM

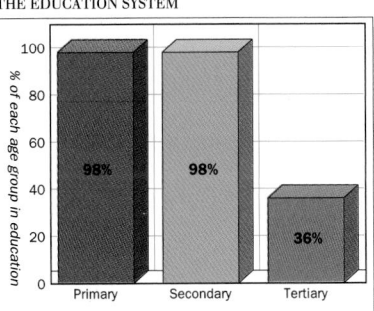

98%   Primary

98%   Secondary

36%   Tertiary

% of each age group in education

Most schools are run by the municipalities. Norway has a modern university system, with some 80,000 students attending higher education. There are four universities; specialized colleges include the Nordic College of Fisheries.

HEALTH

1 per 318 people

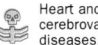

Heart and cerebrovascular diseases, cancers

0   Health spending as % GNP   25

4.5%

Norway's infant mortality rate is one of the lowest in the world and its life expectancy at birth one of the highest. Public health expenditure is, however, no higher than the OECD average, and it has a third of the number of hospital beds of neighbouring Finland.

Telemedicine (on-line remote audio and image diagnosis) began in 1988 and is developing fast. It allows remote northern hospitals to obtain specialist consultations without having to send patients to the regional hospital.

WEALTH

Carpenter, 90 Norwegian kroner per hour; bank teller, 14,824 Norwegian kroner per month

CONSUMER GOODS OWNERSHIP

423   403   730   198   22

Per 1000 population

In terms of income distribution, the Nordic countries are the most egalitarian in the world. The top 10% of Norway's population owns 21% of its wealth. (In Switzerland the comparable proportion of wealth would be 30%.) Homelessness and social deprivation are very rare. Recent refugees from the Bosnian conflict are the most disadvantaged group.

The discrepancy between men's and women's pay is greater than in either Sweden or Finland, although still well below the European average. Social provision was maintained even through the recession. Benefits are generous.

WORLD RANKING

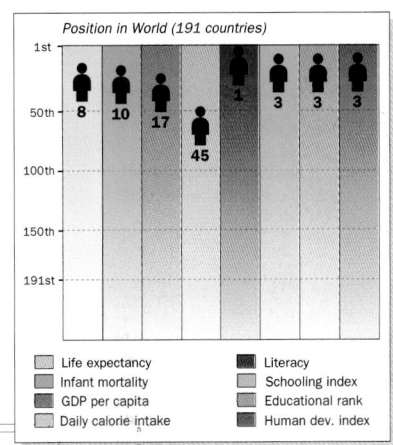

Position in World (191 countries)

1st
50th   8   10   17   45   1   3   3   3
100th
150th
191st

Life expectancy
Infant mortality
GDP per capita
Daily calorie intake
Literacy
Schooling index
Educational rank
Human dev. index

N

OMAN

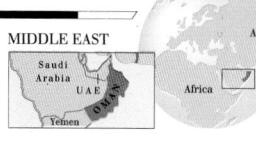

OFFICIAL NAME: Sultanate of Oman   **CAPITAL:** Muscat
POPULATION: 1.6 million   **CURRENCY:** Omani rial   **OFFICIAL LANGUAGE:** Arabic

S HARING BORDERS WITH Yemen, the United Arab
Emirates and Saudi Arabia, Oman is the second
largest country in the Arabian peninsula. It is the least
developed of the Gulf states. The most densely populated areas are the
northern coast and the southern Şalālah plain. Oil exports have given
Oman modest prosperity under a paternalistic Sultan, who defeated a
Marxist-led insurgency in the 1970s.

CLIMATE

WEATHER CHART

The north blisters under temperatures
that often climb above 45°C in summer.
The south has a monsoon climate.

COMMUNICATIONS

 Seeb Intl, Muscat
1.34m passengers

 4 ships
8100 dwt

THE TRANSPORT NETWORK

24,700 km (15,348 miles)		None
None		None

There are good roads to neighbouring
Gulf states, yet Oman's north–south
road was only completed in 1982.

TOURISM

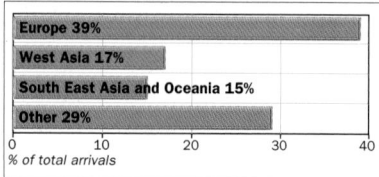 136,000 visitors   Up 8% in 1989

MAIN OVERSEAS ARRIVALS

Europe 39%	
West Asia 17%	
South East Asia and Oceania 15%	
Other 29%	

0   10   20   30   40
% of total arrivals

Until the late 1980s, Oman was closed
to all but business or official visitors.
The Sultanate's rich cultural heritage,
fine beaches and luxury hotels are now
enjoyed by thousands of Western
visitors a year.

PEOPLE

 Arabic, Baluchi   7 people per km²

THE URBAN/RURAL POPULATION SPLIT

11%   89%

RELIGIOUS PERSUASION

Other Muslim and Hindu 25%

Ibadi Muslim 75%

Native Omanis, who include Arab
refugees who fled Zanzibar in the
1960s, make up three quarters of the
population. Baluchis are the largest
foreign grouping. Expatriates
pose no threat to the regime
and Westerners enjoy
considerable freedom.
Although urban drift has taken
place, most Omanis still live on
the land, especially in the
south. Oman has a number of
distinct minorities; the most
numerous are the Jebalis in
Dhofar – nomadic herdsmen
who speak a language
which resembles
Ethiopian. Many Dhofaris
supported the Marxist-led
insurgents in the 1970s, but
they are now considered
loyal. Most Omanis are
Ibadi Muslims who
follow an
appointed
leader,
called
the
Imam.
Ibadism
is not
opposed to
freedom for
women, and
a few women
enjoy positions
of authority.

POLITICS

 Not applicable   Sultan Qaboos bin Said

THE STATE OF THE PARTIES

Consultative Council 60 members

The Sultan rules by decree on the advice of the cabinet and
the Consultative Council. The members of the Consultative
Council, one for each of the 59 districts and a speaker, are
chosen by the Sultan

Sultan Qaboos is an authoritarian but
paternalistic monarch, whose dynasty
traces its roots to the 18th century. In
addition to being head of state, he is
prime minister and minister for foreign
affairs, defence and finance. The
regime faces no serious challenge,
although Qaboos keeps a careful
eye on the religious right wing. In 1991,
he took the step of creating the
Consultative Council (*majlis al-shura*),
which gives a semblance of
democracy. The main political issues
include the planned privatization of
medium-sized government projects,
and the question of Oman's self-
defence capability.

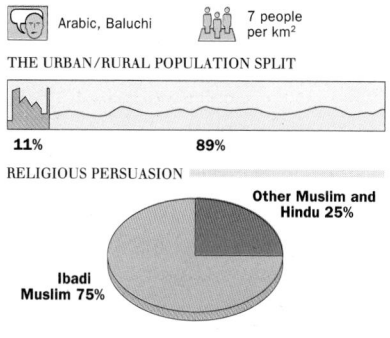

OMAN

Total Area : 212 460 sq. km
(82 030 sq. miles)

POPULATION

over 100 000 ○
over 50 000 ●
over 10 000 •

LAND HEIGHT

2000m/6562ft
1000m/3281ft
500m/1640ft
200m/656ft
Sea Level

WORLD AFFAIRS

Sultan Qaboos is unique in the Arab world, having supported the Camp David peace process and rejected any relationship with the PLO.

Traditionally supported by the West, Oman's foreign policies address interests in both Asia and Africa.

A watchtower above an oasis. Most of Oman is gravelly desert. The only large area of cultivation is the 20-km-wide Al Bāṭinah plain.

AID

 Less than $100m   Downward trend

Oman is a recipient of World Bank, US and UK overseas assistance. Agencies face difficulty in allocating aid to Oman as it has yet to hold a census. Oman itself donated aid to anti-communist causes in the 1970s.

DEFENCE

 $1.7bn   Up 16% in 1992

The defence forces and internal security together absorb 30–40% of government spending. The UK is the main supplier of equipment. During the 1991 Gulf War, Oman provided services and communications to US and UK forces. The army relies on Baluchi mercenaries to maintain full strength.

ECONOMICS

 $10.3bn   0.38 rials Omani

SCORE CARD

❑ WORLD GNP RANKING	76th
❑ GNP PER CAPITA	$6440
❑ BALANCE OF PAYMENTS	$1.1bn
❑ INFLATION	–6.6%
❑ UNEMPLOYMENT	0%

STRENGTHS

Oil industry, led by Royal Dutch Shell. Oman has benefited from staying out of OPEC and selling oil at spot prices without quotas. Rich waters off the Indian Ocean coast, with potential for sizeable fishing industry.

WEAKNESSES

Over-dependence on oil (90% of GNP); oil reserves, at some 4.5 billion barrels, are finite. Services sector less well-developed than in the United Arab Emirates. Reliance on foreign workers in all sectors of the economy.

EXPORTS

IMPORTS

RESOURCES

 5.3bn kwh (capacity 1.53m kw)   730,800 b/d (reserves 4,483,000,000 bbl)

 220,000 sheep, 136,000 cattle, 87,000 camels   Oil, natural gas, copper, chromite, marble, gypsum

Oman's policy of limiting oil production to conserve resources was abandoned in 1993 following a number of exploration successes.

ENVIRONMENT

 0.2% partially protected   Reintroduction of Arabian Oryx into wild

The over-pumping of ground water is becoming a pervasive problem; sea water is seeping into coastal aquifers in traditional irrigation areas.

MEDIA

 There is no public expression of criticism of the government as all press is censored

PUBLISHING AND BROADCAST MEDIA

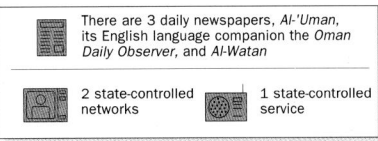

There are 3 daily newspapers, *Al-'Uman*, its English language companion the *Oman Daily Observer*, and *Al-Watan*

2 state-controlled networks   1 state-controlled service

Nothing critical of the government may be published in Oman. Foreign press is censored for the Omani market.

CRIME

 Oman does not publish prison figures   Crime levels are fairly constant

Reckless driving by young Omani males is a problem. A 'flying court' serves remote communities.

EDUCATION

 41%

Education has improved since Sultan Qaboos came to power, though rural illiteracy rates are still high.

HEALTH

 1 per 1040 people   Heart and cerebrovascular diseases, accidents

Muscat and Ṣalālah now have hospitals of a high standard. Rural areas are served by clinics.

WEALTH

 Many Omanis live off the land; some emigrate to seek work in other Gulf states

CONSUMER GOODS OWNERSHIP

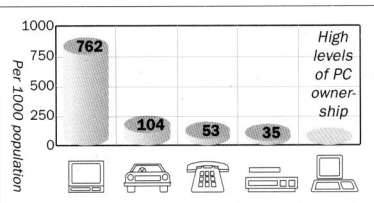

Omanis in urban areas enjoy the same high living standards as are found in other Gulf states. Among the rich, hunting trips to Pakistan are popular and a *khanjar*, a curved dagger, is a status symbol.

WORLD RANKING

O

PAKISTAN

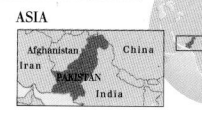

ASIA

OFFICIAL NAME: Islamic Republic of Pakistan **CAPITAL:** Islamabad
POPULATION: 124.8 million **CURRENCY:** Pakistani rupee **OFFICIAL LANGUAGE:** Urdu

ONCE A PART OF BRITISH INDIA, Pakistan was created in 1947 to answer the need for an independent and largely Muslim Indian state. Initially the new nation included East Pakistan, present-day Bangladesh, which became independent of Islamabad in 1971. Eastern and southern Pakistan, the flood plain of the River Indus, is highly fertile and produces cotton, the basis of the large textile industry.

Barren landscape in Kachhi, Baluchistan.
This area of Pakistan has some of the highest May to September temperatures in the world.

CLIMATE

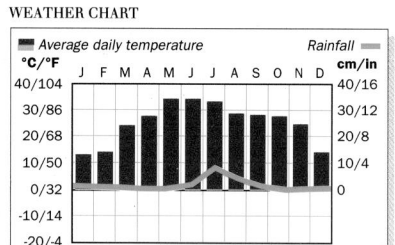

Temperatures can soar to 50°C in Sind and Baluchistan and fall to –20°C in the northern mountains.

COMMUNICATIONS

Karāchi International
4.94m passengers

29 ships
491,100 dwt

THE TRANSPORT NETWORK

111,432 km (69,241 miles)		340 km (211 miles)
12,620 km (7842 miles)		None

Basic infrastructure is to be given more priority, with less motorway building and more farm-to-market roads.

TOURISM

 423,800 visitors   Down 14% in 1990

MAIN OVERSEAS ARRIVALS

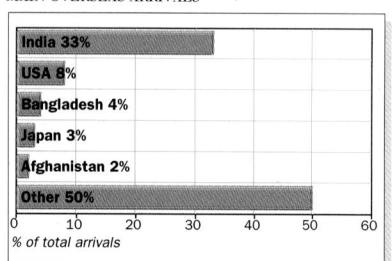

India 33%
USA 8%
Bangladesh 4%
Japan 3%
Afghanistan 2%
Other 50%

% of total arrivals

Relatively few tourists visit Pakistan, despite its rich cultural heritage and unspoilt natural beauty.

PEOPLE

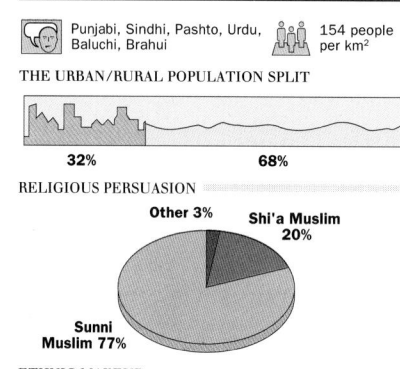

Punjabi, Sindhi, Pashto, Urdu, Baluchi, Brahui

154 people per km²

THE URBAN/RURAL POPULATION SPLIT

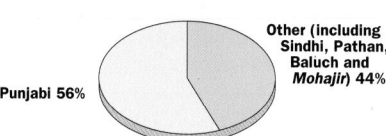

32%   68%

RELIGIOUS PERSUASION

Other 3%   Shi'a Muslim 20%
Sunni Muslim 77%

ETHNIC MAKEUP

Other (including Sindhi, Pathan, Baluch and *Mohajir*) 44%
Punjabi 56%

Punjabis account for 56% of the population, while Sindhis, Pathans and Baluch are also prominent. *Mohajirs* – Urdu-speaking immigrants from India at the time of partition – predominate in Karāchi and Hyderābād, Sind's main urban centres. Punjabi dominance of the army and bureaucracy, and the central government's distance from the smaller provinces, has spawned many separatist and autonomy movements. Pathans have frequently threatened to establish a homeland with ethnic kinsfolk over the border in Afghanistan. Tensions between the Baluch and Pathan refugees from Afghanistan sporadically erupt into violence, as do those between native Sindhis and immigrant *Mohajirs*.

The gap between rich and poor, as exemplified by the 'feudal' landowning class which dominates the ruling elite and their serfs, is considerable. Barring a massive education drive or an even less likely social revolution, it will not close. There is an expanding middle class of small-scale traders and manufacturers.

POPULATION AGE BREAKDOWN

	0–14	15–64	65+		
% of population by age group	4.2%	3.2%	2.9%	2.8%	3%
	51.9%	50.5%	52.7%	53.5%	54.8%
	43.9	46.3	44.4	43.7	42.2%
	1960	1970	1980	1990	2000

Although Islamic fundamentalists have only nine members in the National Assembly, an increase in Islamic influence has resulted in discrimination against minorities, tacitly condoned by the authorities. Laws on blasphemy, which carry a mandatory death sentence on conviction, are being increasingly invoked for political reasons.

The extended family is an enduring institution and ties between its members are strong, reflected in the dynastic and nepotistic nature of the political system. Although some women hold prominent positions, such as Prime Minister Benazir Bhutto, relatively few are allowed out to work by their religiously-conservative menfolk. Pakistan has one of the world's lowest ratios of females to males, implying widespread neglect and some female infanticide. Women's rights groups exist – however they are mainly urban-based and have made little impact.

POLITICS

1995   President Ghulam Ishaq Khan

THE STATE OF THE PARTIES

National Assembly 201 members

3%
PML–J

43%
PPP   36%
PML–N   2%
IJM   16%
Other

PPP = Pakistan People's Party   **PML–N** = Pakistan Muslim League (Nawaz)   **PML–J** = Pakistan Muslim League (Junejo) **IJM** = Islami Jamhoori Mahaz   **Other** = Awami National Party, Pakistan Islamic Front

Senate 87 members

The 87 members are elected by the 4 provincial legislatures

Pakistan is a multiparty democracy, with a president as head of state. The president has considerable power.

MAIN POLITICAL ISSUES

The army
Redefining the army's role is a major problem. The army has frequently intervened in politics, adding to instability. However, whatever reforms are put in place, these are unlikely to

significantly alter the military's considerable power behind the scenes.

Corruption
Recent cases of corrupt practices in government have made the Pakistani electorate increasingly critical of the existing political class. In future, government parties with clean images are likely to emerge.

Modifying the constitution
Pakistan's constitution is under review. The current administration wishes to alter it to increase parliament's power, and reduce the president's influence.

PROFILE
Pakistan is a weak democracy. The ruling parties tend to be fragile coalitions and have to rule in conjunction with the president and the army, both of whom regularly intervene in day-to-day politics. As in India, there is a large bureaucracy, which makes government inefficient. Even simple policies can therefore take years to implement. Islamic fundamentalism suffered a setback in the 1993 elections.

Benazir Bhutto, *serving a second term as prime minister.*

Nawaz Sharif, PML–N *leader and former prime minister.*

WORLD AFFAIRS

Comm   OAS   SAARC   GATT   CP

Pakistan's major concern is to avoid a fourth war with India over Kashmir. Pakistan supports the idea of a plebiscite for the largely Muslim Kashmiris, to decide whether they wish to be ruled by Islamabad or Delhi. India, which fears losing, opposes it. War nearly broke out in 1990, when Pakistan put its nuclear weapons on alert, the only means by which it can balance India's superior military power. The USA regards the region as a potential nuclear flashpoint.

Pakistan has so far resisted US pressure to end its nuclear weapons programme. The USA has in the past cut aid in response to Pakistan's refusal to abandon the nuclear option. Fears of Islamic fundamentalists gaining ground in Pakistan have led Washington to tone down its threats. In future it is more likely to support the current secular, and essentially pro-US, regime.

P

PAKISTAN

Total Area : 796 100 sq. km (307 374 sq. miles)

LAND HEIGHT

6000m/19 686ft	
4000m/13 124ft	
3000m/9843ft	
2000m/6562ft	
1000m/3281ft	
500m/1640ft	
200m/656ft	
Sea Level	

POPULATION

over 5 000 000	▣
over 1 000 000	▣
over 500 000	◉
over 100 000	◎
over 50 000	○
over 10 000	●

N

0   200 km

0   200 miles

Map labels: TAJIKISTAN, CHINA, HINDU KUSH, KARAKORAM RANGE, Gilgit, 8611m, Indus, JAMMU AND KASHMIR, AFGHANISTAN, Mingaora, Tarbela Reservoir, Khyber Pass, Kabul, Peshawar, Mardan, Wah, Nowshera, ISLAMABAD, Kohat, Kurram, Rawalpindi, POTWAR PLATEAU, New Mirpur, Chakwal, Jhelum, Kharian, Miānwali, Lala Musa, Gujrat, Sialkot, Wazirabad, Daska, Khushab, Gujranwala, Sheikhupura, Sargodha, Chiniot, Ravi, Lahore, Faisalabad, Jhang, Kasur, Leiah, Shorkot, Sahiwal, Okara, Kamalia, Dera Ismail Khan, Khanewal, Chichawatni, Pakpattan, Dera Ghazi Khan, Multan, Mandi Burewala, Muzaffargarh, Chishtian Mandi, SULAIMAN RANGE, KIRTHAR RANGE, Sibi, KACHHI, Bahawalpur, Ahmadpur East, Khanpur, Jacobabad, Shikarpur, Rahimyar Khan, Sadiqabad, Larkana, Kambar, Sukkur, Khairpur, INDIA, THAR DESERT, Nawabshah, SINDH, Tando Adam, Hyderabad, Nara, Indus, RANN OF KUTCH, Zhob, of the Indus, SEA

Rice paddy fields, with monsoon rains threatening from the Himalayas. Rice is Pakistan's second most valuable agricultural export after cotton.

CHRONOLOGY

From the 8th to the 16th centuries, Islamic rule extended to northwest and northeast India. The British East India Company annexed Punjab and Sind in the 1850s. They were ceded to the British Raj in 1857.

❑ **1906** Muslim League founded to demand independent Muslim state.

❑ **1947** Partition of India creating Muslim East and West Pakistan, divided by 1600 km of largely Hindu Indian territory, is accompanied by violence and large-scale migration of Muslims and Hindus. Ali Jinnah appointed first governor-general.

❑ **1947–1949** Conflict with India over ownership of Kashmir.

❑ **1949** Awami League (AL) founded. Seeks autonomy for East Pakistan.

❑ **1951** Liaqat Ali Khan, successor to Ali Jinnah, assassinated.

❑ **1956** Constitution establishes Pakistan as an Islamic republic. ➪

CHRONOLOGY *continued*

- ❏ **1958** Martial law imposed after several governments resign over electoral representation issues.
- ❏ **1960** Gen Muhammad Ayubb Khan elected president.
- ❏ **1970** Ayubb Khan resigns. Gen Agha Yahya Khan takes over. First direct elections. AL, led by Sheikh Mujibur Rahman, wins. West rejects East-led government. Civil war – India supports East.
- ❏ **1971** East splits away as Bangladesh. Zulfikar Ali Bhutto, leader of Pakistan People's Party (PPP) holding majority in the West, becomes Pakistan's president.
- ❏ **1972** Cease-fire line in Kashmir agreed with India.
- ❏ **1973** End of martial law. New constitution; Bhutto, now as executive prime minister, initiates 'Islamic socialism'.
- ❏ **1977** Riots after alleged electoral rigging. Coup puts Gen Zia ul-Haq in power.
- ❏ **1979** Bhutto executed. USSR invades neighbouring Afghanistan, so Zia regime gets US backing.
- ❏ **1985** PPP boycotts non-party elections for civilian government, but Zia holds onto real power.
- ❏ **1986** Bhutto's daughter, Benazir, returns from exile to co-lead PPP.
- ❏ **1988** Zia killed in air crash. Mrs Bhutto wins general elections.
- ❏ **1990** Ethnic violence in Sind. President dismisses Bhutto government on corruption charges. Replaced by anti-Bhutto coalition under Nawaz Sharif.
- ❏ **1991** Widespread protests against sending of 11,000 troops to support allies in Gulf War. Muslim *sharia* law incorporated in legal code.
- ❏ **1992** Violence worsens in Sind.
- ❏ **1993** Mrs Bhutto's PPP voted back into power.

AID

 High levels of aid   Relatively steady aid receipts

Pakistan is heavily dependent on aid, although the government has a long history of misdirecting aid payments. Aid intended for major projects has regularly been used to fund the current account deficit and regional governments have failed to match agreed funds on joint projects with overseas agencies. In 1990, the USA cut off aid in response to Pakistan's refusal to halt its nuclear programme. Chief multilateral donors are the World Bank, the IMF and the Asian Development Bank. In the absence of the USA, Japan and Germany are currently the main bilateral donors.

DEFENCE

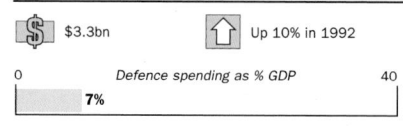

$3.3bn   Up 10% in 1992

Defence spending as % GDP 0 — 40
7%

PAKISTANI ARMED FORCES

1980 main battle tanks (150 M-47/280 M-48A5/ 50 T-54,-55)	515,000 personnel
6 submarines, 13 surface vessels and 25 patrol boats	20,000 personnel
352 combat aircraft (58 *Mirage* 5)	45,000 personnel
Capability undisclosed	

Defence spending ranks high in the government's priorities. Although it was budgeted to decline fractionally in real terms during 1993–1994, it still accounts for more than one third of current spending. The USA was the main arms supplier, until the severance of aid payments in 1990. The main procurement is now from France, the UK and China, although the likelihood is that supplies from the USA will resume in future. The army plays a major role in public life; in 1993, army chief Abdul Waheed forced the prime minister and president out of office. The army also provides covert support to Islamic fundamentalist *mujahideen* across the border in Afghanistan.

ECONOMICS

$46.7bn   30.10 Pakistani rupees

SCORE CARD

- ❏ WORLD GNP RANKING..........................41st
- ❏ GNP PER CAPITA $380
- ❏ BALANCE OF PAYMENTS....................$–1.9bn
- ❏ INFLATION 10.7%
- ❏ UNEMPLOYMENT................................6.3%

EXPORTS

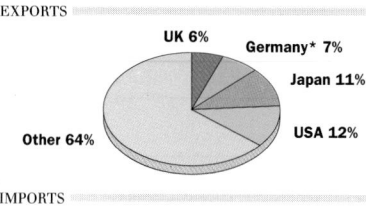

UK 6% · Germany* 7% · Japan 11% · USA 12% · Other 64%

IMPORTS

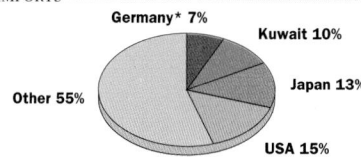

Germany* 7% · Kuwait 10% · Japan 13% · USA 15% · Other 55%

ECONOMIC PERFORMANCE INDICATOR

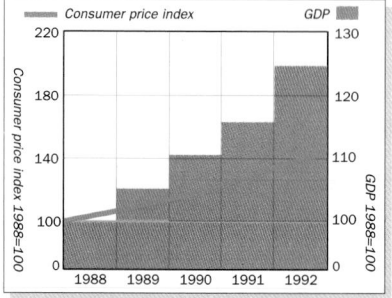

Consumer price index · GDP

STRENGTHS

Gas, water, coal, oil. Substantial untapped natural resources. Low labour costs. Potentially huge market. One of the world's leading producers of cotton and a major exporter of rice.

WEAKNESSES

Weather conditions cause considerable variation in annual production and sales of cotton and rice. Inefficient and haphazard government economic policies. Weak and overstretched infrastructure.

PROFILE

Pakistan has recently begun to tackle its considerable economic problems. Successive governments have reversed the nationalization policies instituted in the 1970s by President Bhutto. Under ex-prime minister Sharif, inefficiencies such as the need to license even small investment decisions, which could take years, began to be tackled. Private capital has been brought into previously state-only sectors such as banking, water and other utilities. However, approximately one third of the state budget is still allocated to military spending, and will as such remain a rein on development.

Despite its considerable economic potential, much of Pakistan's population lives below the poverty line.

PAKISTAN : MAJOR BUSINESSES

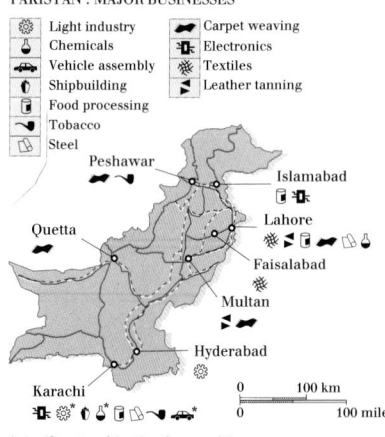

Light industry · Carpet weaving · Chemicals · Electronics · Vehicle assembly · Textiles · Shipbuilding · Leather tanning · Food processing · Tobacco · Steel

Peshawar · Islamabad · Lahore · Quetta · Faisalabad · Multan · Hyderabad · Karachi

0 — 100 km
0 — 100 miles

* significant multinational ownership

RESOURCES

43.9bn kwh
(capacity 9.14m kw)

75,800 b/d
(reserves
412,000,000 bbl)

28.3m sheep,
17.4m cattle,
3.1m asses

Oil, limestone, salt,
gypsum, silica sand,
natural gas, coal

ELECTRICITY GENERATION

Hydro 38% (16.9bn kwh)

Thermal 61% (26.7bn kwh)

Nuclear 1% (293m kwh)

Other 0%

0   20   40   60   80   100

% of total generation by type

Apart from cotton and rice, Pakistan's major resources are oil, coal, gas and water. The state hopes that the privatization of the utilities industries will reduce energy imports and shortages – peak electricity demand, for example, exceeds supply by 20%. Steps are being taken to attract more foreign investment in oil and gas exploration, extraction and distribution. Pakistan's current refining capacity of 150,000 b/d cannot meet the present 280,000 b/d demand, let alone the projected demand for 385,000 b/d by 1996.

PAKISTAN : LAND USE

0   100 km
0   100 miles

Cropland
Pasture
Forest
Desert
Wetlands
High mountain regions
Sugar cane
Wheat
Cattle

ENVIRONMENT

5% (3% partially protected)

2-year ban on logging

ENVIRONMENTAL TREATIES

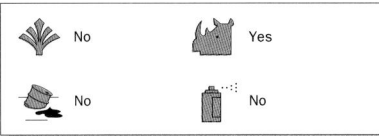

No   Yes

No   No

Revelations about large-scale illegal logging has led to a brief two-year ban. Green issues get little coverage; most concern is voiced by foreign NGOs.

MEDIA

No political censorship in theory

PUBLISHING AND BROADCAST MEDIA

There are 125 daily newspapers. The best-selling paper is *Jang*, published in Urdu

2 independent networks

1 independent network

Arabsat 1C   None

Journalists are often badly paid and therefore susceptible to financial and other inducements from politicians.

CRIME

44,640 prisoners

Crime levels at similarly high levels from year to year

CRIME RATES

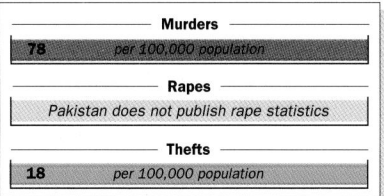

Murders
78   per 100,000 population

Rapes
Pakistan does not publish rape statistics

Thefts
18   per 100,000 population

Compared to similar Islamic states, Pakistan has a high incidence of murder, kidnapping, rape, robbery and drug trafficking. Corruption and

EDUCATION

35%

0   Education spending as % GNP   25
2.6%

THE EDUCATION SYSTEM

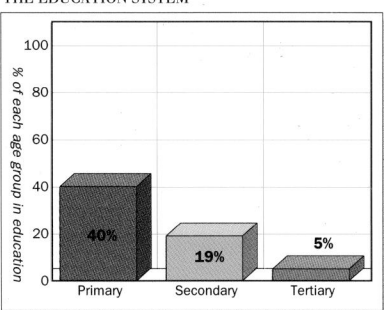

% of each age group in education

100
80
60
40
20
0

40%   19%   5%

Primary   Secondary   Tertiary

The Pakistani education system is heavily Islamicized, and weighted towards educating males. Of the 1.4 million children enrolled in primary schools in 1993, more than one million were boys. The 23 universities, 99 professional colleges and 675 arts and sciences colleges all have a heavy preponderance of arts students. Wealthy parents frequently choose to send their children abroad for higher education, mainly to colleges in the UK or USA.

the abuse of women (the latter usually unreported) are seen as the main causes for concern. Torture of prisoners and deaths in custody are frequent and the rape of women prisoners in police lock-ups is routine. The most dangerous area is Sind province, where the Mohajir Quami Movement was allowed to terrorize Karachi's residents until the army was deployed there in mid-1992. Heavily-armed *dacoits* (bandits) still hold sway in the interior. The British-based legal system is paralleled by a system of *sharia* courts, which have overriden elements of the civil code. Politically-motivated speedy trial courts also exist.

HEALTH

1 per 2127 people

Malaria, tuberculosis, diarrheal diseases

0   Health spending as % GNP   25
0.2%

The availability of doctors and hospital beds is among the lowest in the world. In addition, there is a shortage of equipment and medicines, and uncontrolled counterfeit drugs are common. Pakistan has a high incidence of heroin addicts.

WEALTH

The *Peshgi* system of bonded labour traps millions in virtual slavery – 5 million in the notorious brick industry. Debt often passes down the generations

CONSUMER GOODS OWNERSHIP

Per 1000 population

1000
750
500
250
0

VCR and PC ownership is limited to a small elite

16   6   8

Members of the bureaucratic and political elite tend to be extremely rich, the top military less so. Bonded labourers, often Christians or recent converts to Islam, form the underclass.

WORLD RANKING

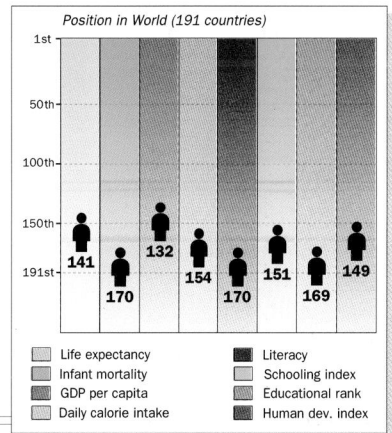

Position in World (191 countries)

1st
50th
100th
150th
191st

141   132   154   170   151   169   149
       170

Life expectancy
Infant mortality
GDP per capita
Daily calorie intake
Literacy
Schooling index
Educational rank
Human dev. index

P

PANAMA

OFFICIAL NAME: Republic of Panama   **CAPITAL:** Panama City
POPULATION: 2.5 million   **CURRENCY:** Balboa   **OFFICIAL LANGUAGE:** Spanish

PANAMA IS THE SOUTHERNMOST of the seven countries occupying the isthmus that joins North and South America. The rainforests of the Darien peninsula are some of the wildest areas left in the Americas. An elected government has held power since the US invasion of 1989. Panama's traditional economic strength is its banking sector. The USA is due to return control of the Panama Canal Zone to Panama in 2000.

Cruise liner on the Panama Canal. The canal takes 4800 km off the otherwise shortest sea route from the east coast of the USA to Japan.

CLIMATE

Panama has a humid tropical climate; rainfall is twice as heavy on the Caribbean coast as on the Pacific coast.

COMMUNICATIONS

Tocumen Intl, Panama City
898,000 passengers

3820 ships
79.31m dwt

THE TRANSPORT NETWORK

10,103 km (6278 miles)	Pan-American Highway 545 km (339 miles)
737 km (443 miles)	800 km (497 miles)

In tonnage, Panama has the world's second largest merchant fleet, 40% of it owned by the Japanese. 12,636 ocean-going ships used the 80-km Panama Canal in 1992. A bridge 117 m above it carries the Pan-American Highway.

TOURISM

289,602 visitors   Up 32% in 1991

MAIN OVERSEAS ARRIVALS

USA 23%
Colombia 16%
Costa Rica 12%
Other 49%

% of total arrivals

The bulk of tourism is from ships stopping at ports on the canal. A few eco-tourists visit the rainforests.

PEOPLE

Spanish, English Creole, Amerindian languages, Chibchan

31 people per km²

THE URBAN/RURAL POPULATION SPLIT

53%   47%

ETHNIC MAKEUP

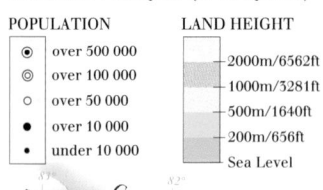

Indian 6%
White 10%
Black 14%
Mestizo (European-Indian) 70%

The northwest coast has a large black community, mostly descended from African immigrants who worked the plantations. The majority speaks English Creole rather than Spanish. About 6% of the population are Indians from three main tribes, the Cunas, Guaymies and Chocoes. Roman Catholicism and the extended family remain strong, although the Canal and US military bases have given society a cosmopolitan outlook.

PANAMA

Total Area : 77 080 sq. km (29 761 sq. miles)

POPULATION
- ⊙ over 500 000
- ◎ over 100 000
- ○ over 50 000
- ● over 10 000
- · under 10 000

LAND HEIGHT
- 2000m/6562ft
- 1000m/3281ft
- 500m/1640ft
- 200m/656ft
- Sea Level

POLITICS

1999

President Ernesto Pérez Balladares

THE STATE OF THE PARTIES

National Assembly 70 members

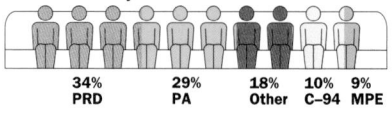

| 34% PRD | 29% PA | 18% Other | 10% C-94 | 9% MPE |

PRD = Revolutionary Democratic Party **PA** = Arnulfist Party
C-94 = Change 94 **MPE** = Papá Egoró Movement

In 1989, the USA sent 23,000 troops into Panama and arrested its ruler, General Manuel Noriega, for drug smuggling. US forces seized power from the military and gave it to civilian politicians. Noriega was arrested and is now serving a life sentence in the USA. The government of President Endara, installed in 1989, was criticized for its failure to halt corruption. The May 1994 presidential and congressional elections were won by Ernesto Balladares and the PRD, with the help of the British public relations firm, Saatchi and Saatchi. However, the PRD, Manuel Noriega's old party, fell short of a congressional majority. During the election campaign the PRD toned down its previously anti-US, left-wing views, while maintaining a populist stance.

WORLD AFFAIRS

The main priority is to maintain good relations with the USA. However, this has to be balanced against Panama's need to regain credibility with its Latin American neighbours, many of whom see President Endara, who took his oath of honour in a US military base in the Canal Zone, as little more than a US puppet.

AID

 $101m (receipts)   Up 9% in 1991

The USA is the largest donor. After the overthrow of Noriega in 1989, it provided a $480-million aid package.

DEFENCE

 Defence force disbanded in 1989   Not applicable

The National Guard and defence forces were disbanded following the 1989 US invasion and were replaced by a police force known as the *Fuerza Pública* – the Public Force. Panama is now allied militarily to the USA. The main defence issue is how to take over the policing of the Canal Zone.

ECONOMICS

 $5.8bn   1.00 balboas

SCORE CARD

❏ WORLD GNP RANKING	108th
❏ GNP PER CAPITA	$4414
❏ BALANCE OF PAYMENTS	$258m
❏ INFLATION	1.4%
❏ UNEMPLOYMENT	15.7%

STRENGTHS

Banking institutions, providing secrecy for investors. Financial, insurance and other services built around this sector. Banana and shrimp exports. Earnings from merchant ships sailing under the Panamanian flag.

WEAKNESSES

History of political instability continues to deter depositors and investors. Costs of extensive rebuilding following 1989 US invasion.

EXPORTS

IMPORTS

ENVIRONMENT

 17% (2% partially protected)   More state concern over debt problems than the environment

The wholesale destruction of Panama's rainforests is proceeding at an increasingly rapid rate, resulting in widespread soil erosion. The Panama Canal is silting up with soil washed down from deforested areas. In addition, large numbers of rare bird and animal species are under threat. There are international protests over plans for the expansion of the massive Cerro Colorado copper mine.

RESOURCES

 2.9bn kwh (capacity 990,000 kw)   Not an oil producer; refines 100,000 b/cd

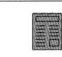 1m cattle, 202,000 pigs, 171,000 horses, 5000 mules   Copper, coal

Large copper deposits at Cerro Colorado have yet to be fully exploited. The government has stepped up hydroelectric production to reduce the country's dependence on oil imports; it claims 90% of power needs are now met in this way. Tropical hardwoods are being cut down at an alarming rate.

MEDIA

 Political censorship has become less pronounced. However, some newspapers critical of Endara have come under attack

PUBLISHING AND BROADCAST MEDIA

 There are 6 daily newspapers, including *La Prensa* and *La Estrella de Panamá*

 5 independent stations   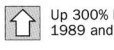 7 state-owned, 89 independent stations

A more independent press has flourished since Noriega's overthrow. The US forces' TV network is popular.

CRIME

 Panama does not publish prison figures   Up 300% between 1989 and 1993

Panama City and Colón in particular are notorious for high levels of violence and muggings.

EDUCATION

88%

Schooling is based on the US model. Provision for the urban poor, blacks and indigenous people is limited.

CHRONOLOGY

On independence from Spain in 1821, Panama was incorporated into Gran Colombia. Panama gained independence from Colombia with US support in 1903.

- ❏ **1903** USA buys concession for the construction of the Panama Canal.
- ❏ **1914** Canal opens to traffic.
- ❏ **1939** US protectorate status ended.
- ❏ **1968–1981** Administration of Colonel Torrijos Herrera.
- ❏ **1985** General Noriega indicted in USA on drug-trafficking charges.
- ❏ **1989** Noriega annuls presidential elections and remains in power. US invasion. Endara, thought to have won elections, made president.
- ❏ **1994** The PRD's Ernesto Balladares wins presidential election. PRD largest party in parliament.

HEALTH

 1 per 879 people   Cerebrovascular and heart diseases, accidents, violence

Primary health care is accessible to around two thirds of the rural population. The isolation of many villages hinders efforts to improve the system.

WEALTH

 Over half the population live in poverty

CONSUMER GOODS OWNERSHIP

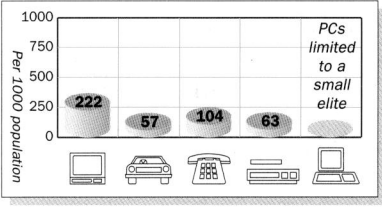

The wealthier members of society tend to be bureaucrats. Poverty is centred in the cities rather than rural areas.

WORLD RANKING

PAPUA NEW GUINEA

OFFICIAL NAME: The Independent State of Papua New Guinea **CAPITAL:** Port Moresby
POPULATION: 4.1 million **CURRENCY:** Kina **OFFICIAL LANGUAGES:** Pidgin English and Motu

THE MOST LINGUISTICALLY diverse country in the world, with approximately 750 languages, Papua New Guinea (PNG) achieved independence from Australia in 1975. The country occupies the eastern end of the island of New Guinea, and several other important groups of islands. Much of the country is still isolated, with most of the indigenous population living by hunter-gathering in the interior.

CLIMATE

WEATHER CHART

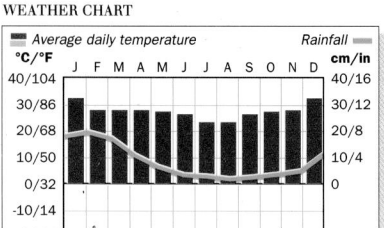

The unvarying heat of the lowlands decreases to snowfields on Mount Victoria. Rainfall is 200–500 cm a year.

COMMUNICATIONS

 Jacksons, Port Moresby
745,000 passengers

 39 ships
47,100 dwt

THE TRANSPORT NETWORK

19,736 km (12,264 miles)		None
None		10,940 km (6798 miles)

Plans exist to build a key road link between Port Moresby and the Lae–Mount Hagen road.

PAPUA NEW GUINEA

Total Area:
462 840 sq. km
(178 700 sq. miles)

POPULATION
◎ over 100 000
○ over 50 000
● over 10 000
• under 10 000

LAND HEIGHT
5000m/9843ft
2000m/6562ft
1000m/3281ft
500m/1640ft
200m/656ft
Sea Level

0 — 200 km
0 — 200 miles

Volcano. Papua New Guinea's 600 or so outer islands are mainly high, volcanic islands with fringing coral reefs.

TOURISM

 40,742 visitors   Down 17% in 1990

MAIN OVERSEAS ARRIVALS

Australia	46%
USA	11%
UK	8%
Other	35%

% of total arrivals

Tourism in PNG raises considerable ethical questions; the peoples of the interior are being pressured into performing for tourist groups.

PEOPLE

 Pidgin English, Papuan, English, Motu, 750 (est) native languages

 9 people per km²

THE URBAN/RURAL POPULATION SPLIT

16%   84%

RELIGIOUS PERSUASION

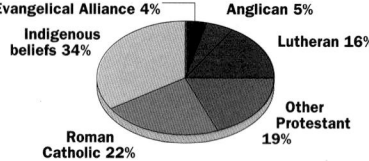

Evangelical Alliance 4%
Anglican 5%
Indigenous beliefs 34%
Lutheran 16%
Other Protestant 19%
Roman Catholic 22%

PNG has an extraordinary diversity of peoples, with around 750 different language groups and even more tribes. The key distinction is between the lowlanders, who have frequent contacts with the outside world, and the very isolated, but increasingly threatened, highlanders. Great tensions exist between highland tribes; anyone who is not a *wontok* (of one's tribe) is seen as potentially hostile. Vendettas can often last several generations.

POLITICS

 1997   HM Queen Elizabeth II

THE STATE OF THE PARTIES

National Parliament 109 members

20% PP	14% PDM	12% PAP	9% PPP	8% MA	37% Other

PP = Pangu (Papua New Guinea Unity) Pati **PDM** = People's Democratic Movement **PAP** = People's Action Party
PPP = People's Progress Party **MA** = Melanesian Alliance
Other = League of National Advancement, National Party

PNG's multiparty democracy operates on the British model, but the number of parties is such that allegiance is effectively to individuals. The most influential politicians are the PP elite, groomed for power by the Australians before independence. The main political issues concern the nature of local government, development, land rights and resource exploitation. Strong local traditions as well as communications problems make greater centralization difficult to implement. Political morality has declined in recent years – six ministers answered charges for misuse of public funds in June 1993.

WORLD AFFAIRS

The main concern is the status of Bougainville, where secessionist rebels are active. Bougainvillians are bitter that they benefit little from Panguna, the world's largest copper mine, forced to close by rebels in 1989.

AID

 $397m (receipts)   Down 5% in 1991

Australian aid accounts for 20% of the PNG state budget. Japan has provided technical assistance.

DEFENCE

 $46.03m   Fairly constant from year to year

Australia runs anti-submarine patrols throughout PNG's territorial waters and maintains military airfields inland.

ECONOMICS

 $3.9bn   0.97 kina

SCORE CARD

- World GNP Ranking........................117th
- GNP per Capita $950
- Balance of Payments...................$–466m
- Inflation 5.3%
- Unemployment...................................5%

STRENGTHS
Extensive copper resources, mainly controlled by the Australian Broken Hill group. Significant quantities of gold and other resources. Oil and gas reserves coming on-stream, and new gas discoveries being made in the highlands.

WEAKNESSES
Copper production disrupted by rebels. Lack of economies of scale in cash-crop markets such as coffee and copra. Political instability deters investors, as has failure to join ASEAN.

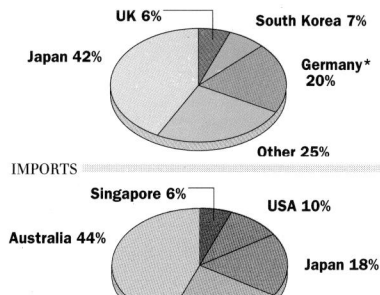

EXPORTS
UK 6%
South Korea 7%
Japan 42%
Germany* 20%
Other 25%

IMPORTS
Singapore 6%
USA 10%
Australia 44%
Japan 18%
Other 22%

RESOURCES

 1.8bn kwh (capacity 490,000 kw)   Reserves of 340,000,000 bbl

 2m pigs, 100,000 cattle, 3000 sheep, 1000 horses   Copper, gold, silver, natural gas, oil, chromite, cobalt

The world's largest copper mine, Panguna on Bougainville, has reserves of over 950 million tonnes. Ok Tedi in the Star Mountains is now the most productive mine. Porgera gold mine is one of the world's largest. Prospecting has revealed extensive oil and natural gas reserves.

ENVIRONMENT

 0.06% (0.05% partially protected)   Logging is on the increase

Some protection against development is provided by traditional PNG land laws, which attach a spiritual value to the land. Only 2% of land – mostly government-owned – is excluded from this system. The greatest problems are logging and heavy-metal pollution from the large mines.

MEDIA

 Freedom of speech is protected by law; the Bougainville uprising prompted limited censorship

PUBLISHING AND BROADCAST MEDIA

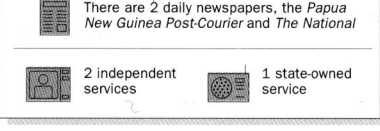

There are 2 daily newspapers, the *Papua New Guinea Post-Courier* and *The National*

2 independent services

1 state-owned service

Even the smallest, most isolated village has a transistor radio. Australian satellite TV can be received in Port Moresby and other major centres.

CRIME

 PNG does not publish prison figures   Up 1% in 1990

'Rascals' – organized gangs of thieves – are a problem. Set-piece axe battles occasionally occur between rival tribes.

EDUCATION

 52%

Until 1975, all education was supplied by religious missions. It is now state-funded with a university at Port Moresby.

HEALTH

 1 per 10,083 people   Malaria, pneumonia, diarrheal diseases

The health system has suffered badly from recent cutbacks. The barefoot doctor scheme, run mostly by women, has extended the net of state health care. Hospital services are only available in Port Moresby.

CHRONOLOGY

The British annexed the southeast and the Germans the southwest of the island of New Guinea in 1884.

- **1904** Australia takes over British sector; renamed Papua in 1906.
- **1914** German sector occupied by Australia.
- **1942–1945** Japanese occupation followed by Australian liberation.
- **1964** House of Assembly created, with elected indigenous majority.
- **1971** Renamed Papua New Guinea.
- **1975** Independence under Michael Somare, leader since 1972.
- **1983** Central government strengthened in attempt to stop mismanagement in provinces.
- **1985** State of emergency declared in Port Moresby as result of ethnic unrest.
- **1988** Secessionist Bougainville Revolutionary Army (BRA) starts campaign sabotaging mines.
- **1992** State offensive against BRA.

WEALTH

 Water board administration manager, 18,000 kina per year

CONSUMER GOODS OWNERSHIP

VCR and PC ownership is limited to a small elite

Most Papua New Guineans are poor. There is little notion of individual wealth and those who make money in the mines and on plantations tend to divide their wealth amongst their tribes. PNG has few cars; Japanese motorbikes and pickups are favoured.

WORLD RANKING

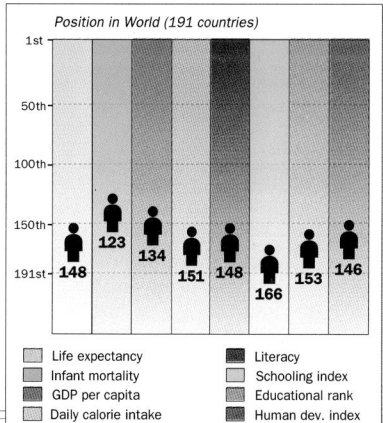

Position in World (191 countries)

Life expectancy
Infant mortality
GDP per capita
Daily calorie intake
Literacy
Schooling index
Educational rank
Human dev. index

P

PARAGUAY

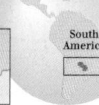

SOUTH AMERICA

OFFICIAL NAME: Republic of Paraguay **CAPITAL:** Asunción
POPULATION: 4.5 million **CURRENCY:** Guaraní **OFFICIAL LANGUAGE:** Spanish and Guaraní

LAND-LOCKED IN CENTRAL South America and a Spanish possession until 1811, Paraguay won large tracts of land from Bolivia in 1835. From then until the overthrow in 1989 of General Stroessner, South America's longest-surviving dictator, it experienced periods of anarchy and military rule. The River Paraguay divides the eastern hills and fertile plains, where 90% of people live, from the almost uninhabited Chaco in the west. Paraguay's economy is largely agricultural.

POLITICS

Lower House 1998
Upper House 1998

President Juan Carlos Wasmosy

THE STATE OF THE PARTIES

Chamber of Deputies 72 members

67% PC   26% PRLA   7% Other

PC = Colorado Party **PRLA** = Authentic Radical Liberal Party
Other = Revolutionary Febrerista Party, Radical Liberal Party, Christian Democrat Party

Senate 36 members

67% PC   28% PRLA   5% Other

CLIMATE

WEATHER CHART

Paraguay is subtropical with all parts experiencing floods and droughts, but the Chaco is generally drier and hotter.

COMMUNICATIONS

Silvio Pettirossi Intl, Asunción
320,000 passengers

12 ships
19,100 dwt

THE TRANSPORT NETWORK

23,606 km
(14,668 miles)

Pan-American Highway 700 km
(434 miles)

970 km
(603 miles)

3100 km
(1926 miles)

There are plans to privatize the airline and seek foreign investment to upgrade roads and the antiquated railways.

TOURISM

280,454 visitors

Up 1% in 1990

MAIN OVERSEAS ARRIVALS

Argentina 34%	
Brazil 21%	
Uruguay 7%	
Other 38%	

0   10   20   30   40
% of total arrivals

Tourism is low-level, except for large numbers of cross-border day-trippers from Brazil and Argentina, who flock to Ciudad del Este to buy cheap, mainly Far Eastern, electrical goods. It is hoped the Chaco will entice eco-tourists.

PEOPLE

Guaraní, Spanish

11 people per km²

THE URBAN/RURAL POPULATION SPLIT

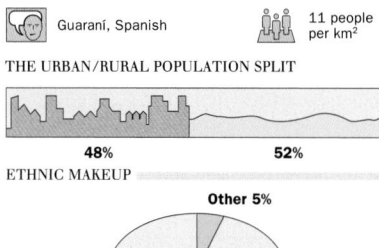

48%   52%

ETHNIC MAKEUP

Other 5%

Mestizo (European-Indian) 95%

Tensions in society are few as most Paraguayans are of combined Spanish and native Guaraní origin. The majority are bilingual, although outside the large cities, Guaraní is spoken almost exclusively. Most people live in the southeast. The vast and almost empty Chaco is home to two thirds of the small numbers of indigenous Indians, who legally own their lands, but do not have control of them in practice.

By the end of the 1980s, General Stroessner's failing health and grasp of affairs, disputes among the military elite about the succession, and economic discontent, brought General Rodríguez to power in 1989 in a one-night coup. His promise to bring in democracy was fulfilled in 1993 in the first free elections in 60 years of military rule. The PC, Stroessner's old ruling party, still received sufficient support to win both congressional and presidential elections. However, Guillermo Caballero Vargas, a leading businessman representing the PRLA and a chief exponent of free-market ideology, won half of Asunción's votes, suggesting his party may do even better in the next elections.

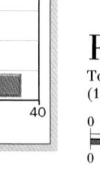

PARAGUAY

Total Area : 406 750 sq. km
(157 046 sq. miles)

0   100 km
0   100 miles

POPULATION
◎ over 100 000
○ over 50 000
● over 10 000
• under 10 000

LAND HEIGHT
1000m/3281ft
500m/1640ft
200m/656ft
Sea Level

P

WORLD AFFAIRS

OAS   LAES   ECLAC   RG   AG

Paraguay's main aims are integration in the MERCOSUR common market and improving relations with the USA.

AID

 $144m (receipts)   Up 157% in 1991

The World Bank and IMF are the chief providers (2% of GNP). NGO charities run small programmes in rural areas.

DEFENCE

 $60.59m   Up 38% in 1989

Under Stroessner, the 26,000-strong military had 42 generals and 245 colonels – a high ratio. As it was high-ranking officers who controlled political and economic life, their full disengagement is likely to be slow. In 1992, the army chief and others were retired in a car-smuggling scandal.

ECONOMICS

 $6.3bn   1794.96 guaraníes

SCORE CARD

❏ WORLD GNP RANKING	100th
❏ GNP PER CAPITA	$1400
❏ BALANCE OF PAYMENTS	$–622m
❏ INFLATION	14.6%
❏ UNEMPLOYMENT	5.1%

STRENGTHS
Electricity exporter – earnings cover oil imports. Self-sufficiency in wheat and other staple foodstuffs. Cotton (up to 50% of exports). Oilseeds, notably soya.

WEAKNESSES
Very high reliance on agriculture – 30% of GDP, 90% of exports, 45% of labour force. Has virtually no minerals. Land-locked and remote. Slow growth. Dependent on growth in neighbouring countries.

EXPORTS

IMPORTS

The Iguaçu Falls, on the border with Brazil and Argentina, are composed of over 20 cataracts, separated by rocks and tree-covered islands.

The Iguaçu Falls, on the border with Brazil and Argentina, are composed of over 20 cataracts, separated by rocks and tree-covered islands.

RESOURCES

 2.4bn kwh (capacity 5.8m kw)   Not an oil producer; refines 7500 b/cd

 8m cattle, 2.3m pigs, 449,000 sheep   Iron, manganese

The joint Paraguay–Brazil Itaipú HEP project has the world's largest generating capacity. Paraguay now has an exportable electricity surplus.

ENVIRONMENT

 3% (0.1% partially protected)   Government has no environmental safeguard policies yet

Apart from the destruction of forests for farming, the chief ecological worry is the smuggling abroad of endangered species, particularly parrots.

MEDIA

 The press is free in theory and banned newspapers have reopened, but there have been some recent instances of shootings and beatings of journalists

PUBLISHING AND BROADCAST MEDIA

 There are 6 daily newspapers, including *ABC Color, Hoy, La Tribuna* and *Ultima Hora*

 5 independent services   1 state-owned, 4 independent services

The media is generally sponsored by political parties. It flourished after the fall of Stroessner, publishing details of corruption and human rights abuses, but is no longer concentrating on investigative reporting.

CRIME

 Paraguay does not publish prison figures   Up 29% in 1990

Paraguay is the contraband capital of Latin America, with trade in everything from cars to cocaine. Jungle airstrips near Brazil provide a route for drugs.

EDUCATION

 90%

In 1989, an estimated 93% of children attended primary school, but only 24% secondary school. Provision is limited in remote rural areas.

HEALTH

 1 per 1007 people   Heart, respiratory and parasitic diseases, cancers

Only one third of the population has safe drinking water. Half of the country's hospital beds are located in Asunción.

WEALTH

 Kitchen assistant, 300,000 guaraníes per month

CONSUMER GOODS OWNERSHIP

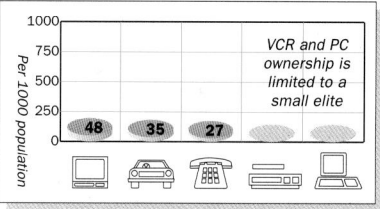

VCR and PC ownership is limited to a small elite

48   35   27

After 60 years of monopolizing lucrative state contracts, the top ranks of the military still control wealth.

WORLD RANKING

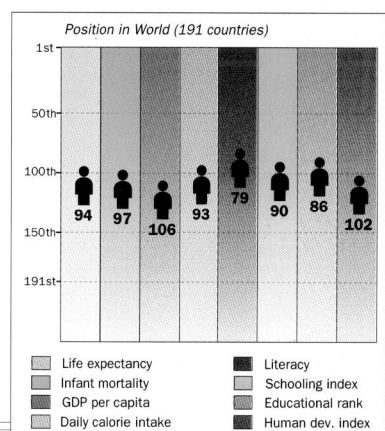

Position in World (191 countries)

94   97   106   93   79   90   86   102

Life expectancy	Literacy
Infant mortality	Schooling index
GDP per capita	Educational rank
Daily calorie intake	Human dev. index

P

PERU

SOUTH AMERICA

OFFICIAL NAME: Republic of Peru **CAPITAL:** Lima **POPULATION:** 22.5 million
CURRENCY: New sol **OFFICIAL LANGUAGES:** Spanish, Quechua and Aymará

LYING JUST SOUTH of the equator, on the Pacific coast of South America, Peru became independent of Spain in 1824. It rises from an arid coastal strip to the Andes, dominated in the south by volcanoes; about half of Peru's population live in mountain regions. Its border with Bolivia to the south runs through Lake Titicaca, the highest navigable lake in the world. In 1992, Peru agreed to allow land-locked Bolivia access to the Pacific port at Ilo; the two countries are developing it into a duty-free zone.

CLIMATE

WEATHER CHART

Peru has several distinct climatic regions. The arid or desert coastal region experiences the *garúa*, persistent low cloud and fog, giving Lima cool winters even though it is close to the equator. The temperate slopes of the Andes have large daily temperature ranges and one rainy season, whilst the tropical Amazon Basin receives year-round rains.

COMMUNICATIONS

 Jorge Chávez International, Lima 2.57m passengers

 35 ships 519,900 dwt

THE TRANSPORT NETWORK

 69,942 km (43,460 miles)

Pan-American Highway 2495 km (1550 miles)

2399 km (1491 miles)

 8600 km (5344 miles)

The government is resurfacing some of the road network (most is unpaved and subject to landslides during the rains), and rebuilding bridges destroyed in the guerrilla war with *Sendero Luminoso*. Work has begun on a transcontinental highway from Ilo, a free port on the Pacific, via Puerto Suárez in Bolivia, to the port of Portos in Brazil. The two rail networks, the Central and Southern, are as yet unconnected. The La Oroya–Huancayo line is the world's highest stretch of standard-gauge railway. River transport provides major access to Iquitos in Amazonia. There are over 130 airports.

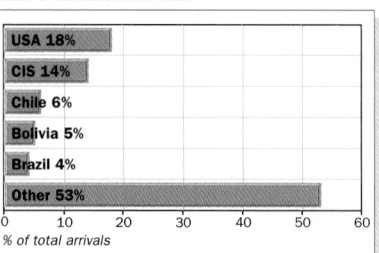

Spanish colonial church near Urubamba. The River Urubamba with its deep gorges was known as the Sacred Valley to the Incas.

TOURISM

 316,873 visitors

Down 5% in 1990. Still falling owing to political instability

MAIN OVERSEAS ARRIVALS

	% of total arrivals
USA	18%
CIS	14%
Chile	6%
Bolivia	5%
Brazil	4%
Other	53%

The five-day hike to Machu Picchu, the world-famous Inca city ruins in the Andes at the end of the 33 km *Camino Inca*, is the most popular trek in South America. The trail is also visited by thousands of day-trippers. Eco-tourism to lodges in the Amazon is growing. Whether this will promote conservation is disputed by some environmentalists. Many object that indigenous families are being forced to work, dance and produce handicrafts for tourists. The pre-Columbian areas cleared in patterns in the desert by the Nazca civilization (known as the Nazca lines) dating from the 2nd century BC, are another major attraction. However, Peru's recent political instability, visitors' fear of guerrilla activity and the relatively poor infrastructure limit tourist numbers.

PEOPLE

 Spanish, Quechua, Aymará

17 people per km²

THE URBAN/RURAL POPULATION SPLIT

70% 30%

RELIGIOUS PERSUASION

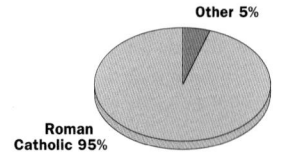

Other 5%
Roman Catholic 95%

ETHNIC MAKEUP

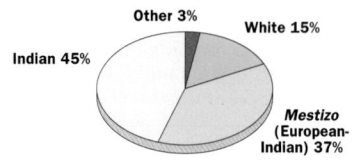

Other 3%
White 15%
Indian 45%
Mestizo (European-Indian) 37%

The majority of Peruvians are Indian or *mestizo*. The small group of Spanish descendants retain much of their hold on the economy, power and social standing. A few Chinese and Japanese live in the northern cities.

Most of Peru's three million Andean Indians live an existence completely detached from that of the urban residents of Lima and the coastal strip. They speak only their native Quechua and Aymará, and no Spanish. A further 250,000 Amazonian Indians live in the eastern lowlands. They, together with the small community of blacks (descendants of plantation workers), tend to suffer considerable discrimination in the towns.

The extended family remains strong. A part of traditional native Indian traditions, its role as a social bond was strengthened by Catholicism. In recent years, economic difficulties have raised its profile as the key social support system for most Peruvians. One result, however, is that society remains strongly patriarchal; feminism has had little impact in Peru.

POPULATION AGE BREAKDOWN

% of population by age group	0–14	15–64	65+
1950	3.5% / 54.9% / 41.6%		
1960	3.4% / 53.3% / 43.3%		
1970	3.5% / 52.5% / 44%		
1980	3.6% / 64.6% / 31.8%		
1990	3.8% / 58.6% / 37.6%		

POLITICS

 1995

 President Alberto Fujimori

President Fujimori. *His dismissal of parliament was widely approved.*

Leading novelist Mario Vargas Llosa, *who contested the presidency in 1990.*

THE STATE OF THE PARTIES

Democratic Constituent Congress 80 members

55%
NM–Cambio-90   **45%**
Other

NM–Cambio-90 = New Majority–Change-90   **Other** = Popular Christian Party, Independent Moralizing Front, Renovation, Democratic Left Movement

Peru is nominally a multiparty democracy in which the president holds executive power.

MAIN POLITICAL ISSUES

Sendero Luminoso

The *Sendero Luminoso* (Shining Path) guerrilla movement has been the main cause of Peru's recent political instability. Terrorist activity in the Andes, such as the murders of 60 members of the traditionally peaceful Ashaninka tribe in 1993, have made large areas of Peru ungovernable except by military rule. In 1992, Abimael Guzmán, *Sendero*'s leader, was captured, a propaganda victory for the government. However, the Maoist group have declared they will continue their activities. President Fujimori has staked his reputation on their defeat.

Democracy and the president's coup

In April 1992, President Fujimori, backed by the army, dismissed parliament, replacing it with an unelected Constituent Congress. He also introduced a new constitution allowing him to run again for election in 1995. To date, most Peruvians seem to have accepted his coup as being necessary for strong government. However, Fujimori has to realize his avowed goal of destroying terrorism if he is to maintain public support.

Privatization

As in the rest of Latin America, the government is selling state assets in an attempt to reduce the level of inflation and make industry more efficient. The aim is to encourage private investment in new equipment and management, in order to force increasingly uncompetitive Peruvian businesses to modernize.

PROFILE

Peru has been run by a Constituent Congress since 1992, following President Fujimori's coup.

Fujimori broke the long tradition of large parties dominating politics, by winning the 1990 presidential elections with a loose coalition. His success demonstrated the general disenchantment that most Peruvians feel for the politics of the past three decades. The failure of successive governments to deal with *Sendero Luminoso* and human rights violations by the army were key issues in securing Fujimori's election. They also explain why voters seemed happy to accept his coup.

Behind the scenes, the army and large private business concerns still have considerable influence in political affairs.

CHRONOLOGY

Francisco Pizarro's arrival in 1532 during a war of succession between two Inca rulers marked the beginning of the Spanish colonization of Peru, and the end of the Inca empire.

- ❑ **1821** Independence proclaimed in Lima after its capture by the Argentine liberator, José de San Martín, who had just freed Chile.
- ❑ **1824** Spain suffers final defeats at battles of Junín and Ayacucho by Simón Bolívar and Gen Sucre, the liberators of Venezuela and Colombia.
- ❑ **1836–1859** Peru and Bolivia joined in short-lived confederation.
- ❑ **1866** Peruvian–Spanish War.
- ❑ **1879–1884** War of the Pacific. Chile defeats Peru and Bolivia. Peru loses territory in south.
- ❑ **1908** Augusto Leguía y Salcedo's dictatorial rule.
- ❑ **1919** USA starts financing public works.
- ❑ **1924** Dr Víctor Raúl Haya de la Torre founds left-wing nationalist American Revolutionary Popular Alliance (APRA) in exile in Mexico.
- ❑ **1930** Leguía ousted. APRA moves to Peru as first political party.
- ❑ **1931–1945** APRA banned.
- ❑ **1939–1945** Moderate, pro-US civilian government.
- ❑ **1948–1956** Gen Manuel Odría in power. APRA banned again.
- ❑ **1956–1962** Civilian government.
- ❑ **1962–1963** Two military coups. ▷

PERU

Total Area :
1 285 220 sq. km
(496 223 sq. miles)

POPULATION

- ▣ over 1 000 000
- ◉ over 500 000
- ◎ over 100 000
- ○ over 50 000
- • under 50 000

LAND HEIGHT

- 4000m/13124ft
- 2000m/6562ft
- 500m/1640ft
- Sea Level

CHRONOLOGY *continued*

- ❑ **1963** Election of Fernando Belaúnde Terry. Land reform, but military used to suppress communist-inspired insurgency.
- ❑ **1968** Military junta takes over. Attempts to alleviate poverty. Large-scale nationalizations.
- ❑ **1975–1978** New right-wing junta.
- ❑ **1980** Belaúnde re-elected. Popular Action (AP) wins majority. Maoist guerrilla organization, *Sendero Luminoso* (Shining Path), begins armed struggle.
- ❑ **1981** Border war with Ecuador over Cordillera del Cóndor, which a 1942 protocol had given to Peru. Ecuador wants access to Amazon.
- ❑ **1982** Deaths and 'disappearances' start to escalate as army cracks down on guerrillas and narcotics.
- ❑ **1985** Electoral win for left-wing APRA under Alán García Pérez.
- ❑ **1987** Peru bankrupt. Guzmán's plans to nationalize banks blocked by new *Libertad* movement led by writer Mario Vargas Llosa.
- ❑ **1990** Over 3000 political murders. Alberto Fujimori, an independent, is elected president on anti-corruption platform. Economic austerity programme sends some food prices up 600%.
- ❑ **1991** Cholera epidemic.
- ❑ **1992** Fujimori suspends democracy in coup and establishes Constituent Congress.
- ❑ **1993** New constitution. Death penalty reintroduced.

P

WORLD AFFAIRS

Peru's most important relationship is with the USA, its main source of aid and the most influential power in Latin America. Co-operation with the USA also extends to the war on cocaine, although the policy of eradicating the crop in the Andean foothills has largely failed; Peruvian coca production has been rising rather than falling. Peru is keen to strengthen its regional links, and those with countries on the Pacific Rim, especially Japan.

AID

 $590m (receipts)   Up 49% in 1991

Aid provided by the USA has been mostly to help combat drugs. NGOs and Catholic charities have been active on a small scale in rural areas. The World Bank promised $42 million in 1994 to help with health projects in the Andean highlands.

DEFENCE

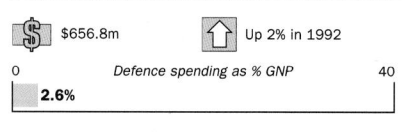

$656.8m   Up 2% in 1992

0   *Defence spending as % GNP*   40

2.6%

PERUVIAN ARMED FORCES

	300 main battle tanks (T-54/T-55)	75,000 personnel
	9 submarines, 6 destroyers and 4 frigates	22,000 personnel
	107 combat aircraft (13 *Canberra*/25 *Cessna*/ 24 *Mirage*)	15,000 personnel
	None	

The military, in power from 1968 to 1980, continues to exert a direct and powerful influence in politics. Many of Peru's Andean regions are under direct military rule, the only means by which the state can combat the terrorist activities of *Sendero Luminoso*. Rule in these regions can be brutal. Amnesty International has reported cases of whole villages being punished for allegedly siding with *Sendero Luminoso*. In the same way, *Sendero Luminoso* terrorizes villagers who side with the army.

Most arms procurement by the armed forces is from the USA. Recent budgetary problems have, however, left the army under-equipped.

ECONOMICS

$21.3bn   2.15 new soles

SCORE CARD

- ❑ WORLD GNP RANKING...........................63rd
- ❑ GNP PER CAPITA $950
- ❑ BALANCE OF PAYMENTS...................$–2.1bn
- ❑ INFLATION 57%
- ❑ UNEMPLOYMENT................................5.8%

EXPORTS

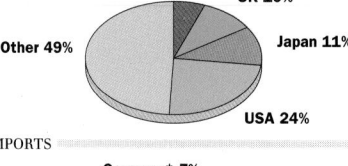

Germany* 6%
UK 10%
Japan 11%
Other 49%
USA 24%

IMPORTS

Germany* 7%
Argentina 7%
Italy 20%
Other 44%
USA 22%

ECONOMIC PERFORMANCE INDICATOR

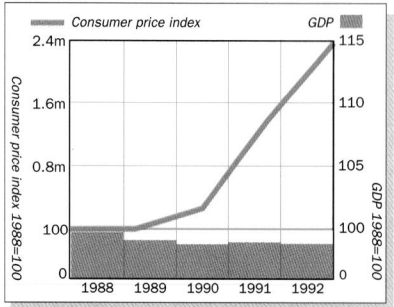

Consumer price index   GDP

the coca crop has not only damaged an important local economy, but also driven the growers into the hands of guerrilla groups such as *Sendero Luminoso*.

The thrust of state economic policy has changed radically since Peru's bankruptcy under the left-wing APRA administration of President Alan García. The Fujimori government is selling off state interests in everything from copper mining and oil exploitation to ports and roads, in one of the most radical and rapid privatizations in Latin America.

STRENGTHS

Abundant mineral resources, including oil. Rich fish stocks in the Pacific. Wide variety of climates allowing diverse and productive agriculture; cotton and coffee are important. Well-developed textile industry.

WEAKNESSES

Hyperinflation in the late 1980s destroyed confidence domestically and abroad. Foreign investors discouraged by political instability and terrorism. High levels of poverty exacerbate social tensions.

PROFILE

Wealth and economic activity in Peru is largely confined to the cities of the coastal plain. The inhabitants of the Andean uplands are subsistence farmers or coca producers. Disrupting

PERU : MAJOR BUSINESSES

Oil	
Oil refining	
Textiles	
Mining	
Fish processing	
Food processing	
Vehicle assembly	

0   400 km
0   400 miles

* significant multinational ownership

RESOURCES

 13.8bn kwh (capacity 4.1m kw)

 116,800 b/d (reserves 380,866,000 bbl)

12.9m sheep, 4m cattle, 2.3m pigs, 660,000 horses

 Oil, lead, zinc, silver, iron, gold, copper

ELECTRICITY GENERATION

Hydro 76% (10.5bn kwh)
Thermal 24% (3.3bn kwh)
Nuclear 0%
Other 0%

% of total generation by type

Peru is an important exporter of copper and lead. Further exploration is required to establish the true extent of its large oil reserves. The state oil concern, *PetroPeru*, is being privatized to attract new investment into the industry. The further development of hydroelectric power is a priority.

PERU : LAND USE

Cropland
Pasture
Forest
Desert
High mountain regions
Sugar cane - cash crop
Sheep

0   400 km
0   400 miles

ENVIRONMENT

 2% (0.1% partially protected)

No measures to prevent dolphin fishing

ENVIRONMENTAL TREATIES

Yes   Yes

No   No

Peru's environmentalists have long been concerned about coastal industrial pollution and the activities of its fishing industry. Overfishing of anchovies almost resulted in their extinction in the 1970s. Today, attention has switched to the rise in the number of dolphins being caught in drift nets – 3000 in 1992. Dolphin meat is being sold as a cheap alternative to pork and beef in Peruvian markets.

Concern has also turned to the coca industry. Environmentalists fear that Peru's and the USA's policy of using powerful air-sprayed herbicides to destroy the crop is adding to river pollution in the Andes.

MEDIA

 Press freedom is theoretically guaranteed. In practice, the media are expected to denounce terrorists and keep silent on human rights abuses

There are 45 daily newspapers. These include the conservative *El Comercio* and *El Expreso*, and the left-wing *La República*

1 state-owned, 2 main independent networks

3 state-owned, 2 main independent networks

Panamsat 1   None

Media freedom is severely restricted. Journalists and newspaper editors regularly receive death threats.

CRIME

 17,368 prisoners   Up 22% in 1990

CRIME RATES

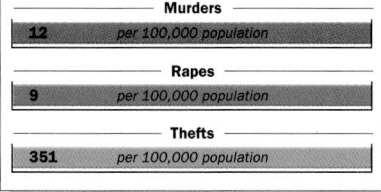

Murders
12   per 100,000 population

Rapes
9   per 100,000 population

Thefts
351   per 100,000 population

Random bombings, kidnappings and shoot-outs with security forces are still major problems in Peru. Main cities regularly have curfews and those who can afford it protect themselves with high-security homes and armed guards.

In the Andes, where *Sendero Luminoso* has been active, military law has suspended normal rights. Since 1980, over 25,000 have died as a result of guerrilla, and army, violence.

EDUCATION

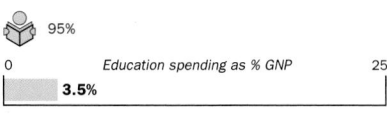 95%

0   *Education spending as % GNP*   25
3.5%

THE EDUCATION SYSTEM

% of each age group in education

Primary 97%
Secondary 65%
Tertiary 26%

Education is based on the US system. Spending has been declining. The state and private university system is accessible to a small minority.

HEALTH

 1 per 966 people

 Respiratory, heart, infectious and parasitic diseases

0   *Health spending as % GNP*   25
0.8%

Peru's public health system virtually collapsed in the late 1980s. In many areas primary care is now non-existent. Advanced treatment is available only to private patients in city clinics. Goitre, a thyroid abnormality, is widespread, with a 38% prevalence among children in mountain areas; in some regions the incidence may be as high as 90%. Infant mortality is rising, the result of increasing social deprivation, diarrheal diseases and tuberculosis. Malaria is once again widespread, and cholera returned in 1991, reaching epidemic proportions by 1994.

WEALTH

 Chemical industry machine operator, 45 new soles per week; journalist, 377 new soles per month

CONSUMER GOODS OWNERSHIP

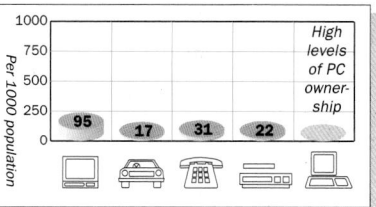

High levels of PC ownership

95   17   31   22

Per 1000 population

Most wealth and power in Peru is still held by old Spanish families. Indigenous peoples remain excluded from both. The wealthy in Peru live in a state of siege; a key status symbol is the number of armed guards and security cameras protecting family property. German cars – Mercedes or BMWs – are now more fashionable than American ones, whilst San Francisco and Miami have replaced Paris as fashionable destinations. The UN estimates that over 30% of Peruvians live below the poverty line.

WORLD RANKING

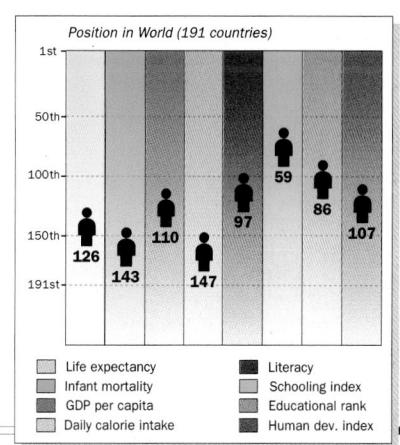

Position in World (191 countries)

1st
50th
100th
150th
191st

126
143
147
97
59
86
107

Life expectancy
Infant mortality
GDP per capita
Daily calorie intake
Literacy
Schooling index
Educational rank
Human dev. index

P

PHILIPPINES

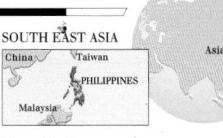
SOUTH EAST ASIA

OFFICIAL NAME: Republic of the Philippines **CAPITAL:** Manila
POPULATION: 65.2 million **CURRENCY:** Philippine peso **OFFICIAL LANGUAGES:** Filipino and English

LYING IN THE WESTERN Pacific Ocean, the Philippines is the world's second largest archipelago after Indonesia. It comprises 7107 islands, of which 4600 are named and 1000 inhabited. There are three main island groupings: the Luzon group, the Visayan group and the Mindanao and Sulu islands. Located on the Pacific 'ring of fire', the Philippines is subject to frequent earthquakes and volcanic activity. Since 1992, President Fidel Ramos has worked hard to bring political stability to the country. However, economic expansion continues to fall short of the Philippines' population-growth rate.

***Bohol Island** has over 1000 of these famous mounds, also known as 'the chocolate hills'.*

CLIMATE

WEATHER CHART

The Philippines is warm and humid all year. The rainy season lasts from June to October. Humidity falls from 85% in September to 71% in March.

COMMUNICATIONS

Nino Aquino Intl, Pasay City
6.44m passengers

834 ships
13.67m dwt

THE TRANSPORT NETWORK

161,709 km (100,486 miles)	None
805 km (500 miles)	3219 km (2000 miles)

Spending on transport infrastructure has fallen by over 40% since 1984. As a result, many main roads are in need of repair. Traffic jams in Manila are a growing problem and are holding back economic growth. Air transport is the only means of getting around the islands quickly.

In 1992, the state airline, Philippines Airlines, was privatized. It is planning to buy $1.2 billion-worth of new aircraft and to add to its regional route network. Subic Bay, the USA's largest overseas base until 1992, when the US navy decided to leave, has a prime strategic location, which the government is now exploiting. Opening onto the South China Sea, its deep natural harbour is being developed as a free port and enterprise zone. The Taiwanese are the biggest investors in this project.

TOURISM

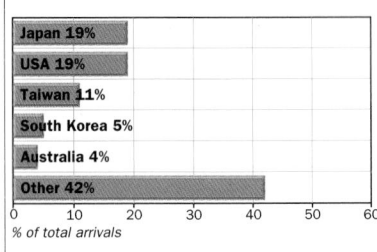

951,365 visitors

Down 48% between 1989 and 1991

MAIN OVERSEAS ARRIVALS

Japan 19%	
USA 19%	
Taiwan 11%	
South Korea 5%	
Australia 4%	
Other 42%	

% of total arrivals

Tourism remains a smaller business in the Philippines than in the NICs of South East Asia. The industry is still largely based around sex-tourism. However, business may suffer when an Australian law banning its citizens from sex-tourism holidays comes into effect. Many of the islands have tourism potential. Palawan, one of the least spoilt, retains most of its tropical rainforest and coral lagoons. The rice terraces of northern Luzon are another attraction.

PHILIPPINES

Total Area : 300 000 sq. km
(777 001 sq. miles)

POPULATION

over 1 000 000	
over 500 000	
over 100 000	

LAND HEIGHT

2000m/6562ft	
1000m/3281ft	
500m/1640ft	
200m/656ft	
Sea Level	

P

PEOPLE

 Filipino, Cebuano, Hiligaynon, Samaran, Ilocano, Bikol, English

 202 people per km²

THE URBAN/RURAL POPULATION SPLIT

43%   57%

The Philippines encompasses over 100 distinct ethnic groups. The majority of Filipinos are of Malay origin, and Christian. Most Christians belong to the Tagalog, Cebuano, Llocan, Longgo, Bicolano, Waray, Pampangueno or Pangasinense ethnic groups. They are concentrated on the main island, Luzon, and are a majority on Mindanao. Most Muslims also live on Mindanao, but many are also found in the Sulu archipelago. The Chinese minority, which was well established by 1603, have remained significant in business and trade. Over 120 Chinese schools have ensured that they have retained a distinct identity.

There are also a number of cultural minorities who practise animist

RELIGION PERSUASION

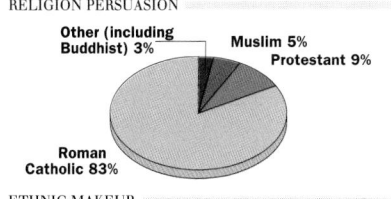

Other (including Buddhist) 3%
Muslim 5%
Protestant 9%
Roman Catholic 83%

ETHNIC MAKEUP

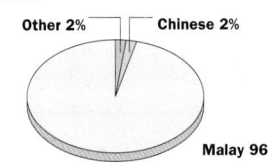

Other 2%   Chinese 2%
Malay 96%

religions. They include the Ifugaos, Bontocks, Kalingas and Ibalois on Luzon, the Manobo and Bukidnon on Mindanao, and the Mangyans on Palawan. Many of these groups speak Malayo-Polynesian dialects. Limited intermarriage with other peoples has meant that groups in the more remote regions have managed to retain their traditional ways of life.

POPULATION AGE BREAKDOWN

% of population by age group	■ 0–14	□ 15–64	□ 65+		
65+	3%	2.7%	2.8%	3.1%	3.6%
15–64	52.3%	51.9%	55.3%	57.2%	60.2%
0–14	44.7%	45.4%	41.9%	39.7%	36.2%
	1960	1970	1980	1990	2000

The Philippines is the only Christian state in Asia; over 80% of Filipinos are Roman Catholics and the Church is the dominant cultural force in the country. It opposes state-sponsored family planning programmes, designed to curb accelerating population growth, currently at 2% a year.

Women have traditionally played a prominent part in Filipino life. Inheritance laws give them equal rights to men. Many go into politics, banking and business, and in several professions women form a majority.

POLITICS

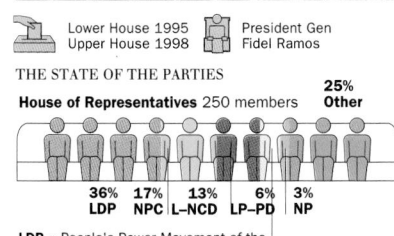

Lower House 1995
Upper House 1998
President Gen Fidel Ramos

THE STATE OF THE PARTIES

House of Representatives 250 members
25% Other

36% LDP | 17% NPC | 13% L–NCD | 6% LP–PD | 3% NP

LDP = People's Power Movement of the Democratic Philippines NPC = National People's Coalition L–NCD = Power of EDSA – National Union of Christian Democrats LP–PD = Liberal Party – Philippino Democratic Party – Laban NP = Nationalist Party

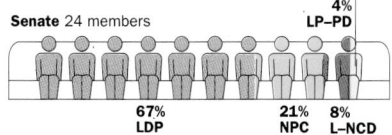

Senate 24 members
4% LP–PD
67% LDP | 21% NPC | 8% L–NCD

The Philippines is a multiparty democracy.

MAIN POLITICAL ISSUES

Power cuts

The 1986–1992 Aquino administration neglected investment in power stations. As a result, the Philippines suffers from widespread power cuts; in 1992 these occured on 258 of the 297 working days. The cuts are disrupting business and deterring foreign investment in the Philippines. Under the Electric Power Crisis Law of 1993, President Ramos was given extra powers to deal with the problem. New power station projects will no longer be subject to planning controls and the president is free to raise electricity prices by dictat.

Communist and Muslim separatists

Communist and Muslim separatists have been fighting Manila governments for over 25 years. Ten thousand armed confrontations with rebels have been recorded by the army during this period. Much of the support for secession has been fuelled by the failure of successive governments to curb poverty.

Since 1992, the Ramos government has been pursuing a peace process with all armed groups. The most powerful, the communist New People's Army (NPA), is in decline. Once regarded as a heroic army of the oppressed and as an alternative to traditional politics, it has split into factions. Some wish to achieve an accommodation with the government, while other wings still adhere to their Maoist leader, Jose Maria Sison, living in exile in Holland. The Ramos government is exploiting the divisions. Its peacemaking approach was boosted by the decision of Leopoldo Mabilangan, an NPA leader, to leave the organization. He was subsequently murdered by NPA agents.

PROFILE

Democracy was restored to the Philippines in 1986. Ferdinand Marcos, in power since 1965, was effectively deposed by an army coup headed by Fidel Ramos and Marcos's defence minister, Juan Ponce Enrile. Although Marcos claimed victory, both Ramos and Enrile declared Corazon Aquino the true winner of the 1986 elections

General Fidel Ramos, was elected president in 1992.

Imelda Marcos, wife of the former dictator Ferdinand Marcos.

and the USA decided to remove its backing for Marcos. Corazon Aquino's government succeeded in handing over power through fair elections in 1992, having survived seven coup attempts. Fidel Ramos, winner of the elections, is concentrating on achieving stability and economic growth. However, Ramos was elected on just 23% of the vote and is dependent on loose coalition arrangements in Congress. In 1994, however, opinion polls suggested 60% of the electorate approved of Ramos's performance.

WORLD AFFAIRS

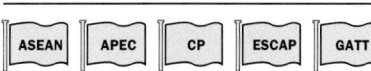

ASEAN | APEC | CP | ESCAP | GATT

Regional relationships are now paramount. The Philippines is keen to attract investment from booming ASEAN economies. The state took over US bases in 1992. US ships, however, still have rights of access to military installations in the country. Manila has established a claim to the Spratlys.

P

CHRONOLOGY

Ceded to the USA by Spain in 1898, the Philippines became self-governing in 1935. After Japanese occupation during the Second World War, the Philippines became an independent republic in 1946.

- ❑ **1965** Ferdinand Marcos, NP candidate, becomes president.
- ❑ **1969–1972** Marcos re-elected amid malpractice allegations.
- ❑ **1972** Marcos declares martial law. Opposition leaders arrested, National Assembly suspended, press censored.
- ❑ **1977** Ex-LP leader Benigno Aquino sentenced to death. Criticism forces Marcos to delay execution.
- ❑ **1978** Elections won by Marcos's new party, New Society (KBL). Marcos president and prime minister.
- ❑ **1980** Aquino allowed to travel to USA for medical help.
- ❑ **1981** Martial law ends. Marcos re-elected president by referendum. Malpractice alleged by opposition.
- ❑ **1983** Benigno Aquino shot dead at Manila airport on return from USA. Inquiry blames military conspiracy.
- ❑ **1986** USA forces Marcos to call a presidential election. Result disputed. Army rebels led by General Fidel Ramos, and public demonstrations, bring widow of Benigno Aquino, Corazon, to power. Marcos exiled to USA. Two coups crushed by troops loyal to Aquino.
- ❑ **1987** New constitution. Aquino-led coalition wins Congress elections. Coup crushed by Aquino's troops.
- ❑ **1988** Marcos and wife, Imelda, indicted on $100 million charge for embezzlement and racketeering.
- ❑ **1989** Marcos dies in the USA. Coup attempt fails.
- ❑ **1990** Imelda acquitted of fraud charges in the USA. Earthquake in Baguio City leaves 1600 dead.
- ❑ **1991** Mt Pinatubo erupts. US leaves Clark Air Base. Imelda Marcos returns to the Philippines.
- ❑ **1992** General Fidel Ramos wins presidential election. LDP secure most seats in parliament. US Navy leaves its bases in the Philippines.

AID

 Bilateral aid makes up the majority of aid receipts

 No significant variation from year to year

The Philippines' main bilateral aid donors are the USA and Japan. Large remittances are also received from Filipinos working overseas. In 1975, there were 40,000 OCWs (Overseas Contract Workers). By 1994, this had risen to 680,000. Many NGOs operate in the outlying islands.

DEFENCE

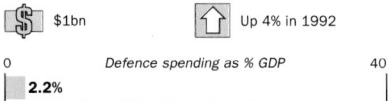

💲 $1bn

⬆ Up 4% in 1992

Defence spending as % GDP
0 — 40
2.2%

Subic Bay was the largest US base outside America and was used in both the Vietnam War and the 1991 Gulf War. The USA left Clark base in 1991, following the eruption of Mt Pinatubo, and Subic Bay in 1992. The military retains considerable political influence; Fidel Ramos is a former army general.

PHILIPPINE ARMED FORCES

🛡	41 light tanks (41 *Scorpion*)	68,000 personnel
🚢	1 frigate and 42 patrol boats	23,000 personnel
✈	49 combat aircraft (7 F-5-A/2 F-5-B/ 24 OV-10 *Broncos*)	15,500 personnel
	None	

ECONOMICS

💲 $46.1bn

💲 28.97 Philippine pesos

SCORE CARD

- ❑ WORLD GNP RANKING 42nd
- ❑ GNP PER CAPITA $707
- ❑ BALANCE OF PAYMENTS....................$–999m
- ❑ INFLATION 8%
- ❑ UNEMPLOYMENT.....................................9%

EXPORTS

Hong Kong 5% Netherlands 5%
USA 36%
Japan 20%
Other 34%

IMPORTS

Hong Kong 4%
Japan 17%
Other 58%
USA 21%

STRENGTHS
Economy now fully open to outside investment. Agricultural productivity rising. Remittances from Filipinos working overseas, estimated at $2 billion. Well-equipped ex-US military installations with economic potential, such as Subic Bay.

WEAKNESSES
Power failures limit scope for expansion. Rudimentary infrastructure, particularly transport. Low domestic savings rates make Philippines reliant on foreign finance. $30 billion debt.

PROFILE
In the 1950s, the Philippines was one of the strongest economies in Asia. Since then, it has fallen behind once much poorer nations such as Thailand, Malaysia and South Korea. Around 50% of the population live on the poverty line. It is this poverty that has fuelled many of the secessionist movements that have threatened the stability of successive governments.

ECONOMIC PERFORMANCE INDICATOR

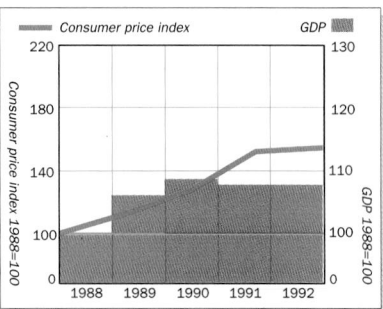

— Consumer price index   GDP ▨

The economy is undergoing slow reform. The Ramos administration aims to emulate the success of the other South East Asian NICs. Backed by the IMF, it is deregulating the economy to encourage foreign investment. It is also trying to trim the power of some of the large privately-run monopolies; a few families still control a major part of the economy. Long-term goals are to raise economic growth to double figures by 1998, raise the per capita income to $1000, as opposed to the current average of $750, and to reduce those affected by poverty to 30% of the population.

PHILIPPINES : MAJOR BUSINESSES

🍺 Brewing
👕 Garments
🧪 Chemicals
Electronics
⛏ Copper mining
🥫 Food processing
🚗 Vehicle assembly
💉 Pharmaceuticals
📡 Telecommunications

Baguio
San Fernando
Manila
Legaspi
Cebu
Cagayan de Oro
Davao
Lupon

0 — 200 km
0 — 200 miles

RESOURCES

26.3bn kwh (capacity 6.87m kw)

Reserves of 147,540,000 bbl; refines 278,450 b/cd

7.8m pigs, 1.7m cattle, 300,000 horses

Coal, copper, nickel, chromium, silver, manganese, gold

ELECTRICITY GENERATION

Hydro 24% (6.1bn kwh)

Thermal 56% (14.8bn kwh)

Nuclear 0%

Other 20% (5.5bn kwh)

0   20   40   60   80   100
% of total generation by type

The Philippines is the world's biggest supplier of refractory chrome. Copper is also a significant export. Many areas of the country have yet to be surveyed and estimates suggest 90% of mineral potential remains undeveloped. Oil production off Palawan began in 1979. The Philippines is the world's second biggest user of geothermal power after the USA. Almost 25% of electricity on Luzon is provided by this method. In 1989, timber exports were halted. However, illegal logging and slash and burn farming still cause deforestation.

ENVIRONMENT

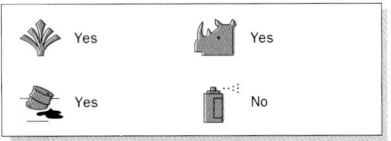

2% (1% partially protected)

Economic growth has precedence over ecological concerns

ENVIRONMENTAL TREATIES

Yes   Yes

Yes   No

The environment has become a major issue in the Philippines. Most of the tropical rainforest has been destroyed, except for pockets such as the island of Palawan. Fishermen have dynamited unique coral habitats, and continue to use cyanide and muro-ami techniques to increase the size of their catches.

The government has recognized the costs of environmental damage. Soil run-off is silting rivers and reducing the power generated by hydroelectric dams. Fast-depleting coral habitats reduce the attraction of the Philippines for tourists.

Logging has been banned, but enforcement is difficult; many loggers have their own private armies. In addition, continued use of slash and burn farming has aided deforestation.

MEDIA

The media practices self censorship and is inclined to be deferential to the government in power

PUBLISHING AND BROADCAST MEDIA

There are 30 daily newspapers. The most influential newspapers are the *Philippine Star* and the *Philippine Daily Globe*

1 state-owned, 4 independent networks

26 state-owned, 274 independent stations

Palapa B2-P Intelsat V F8

Cable TV is widely available in urban areas

The lifting of censorship following the election of Corazon Aquino in 1986 led to a burgeoning of the media. In addition to the national press, there are over 250 regional newspapers in local dialects. State TV broadcasts in English and Filipino. Four independent television stations serve Metro Manila.

CRIME

 14,525 prisoners   Down 8% in 1990

CRIME RATES

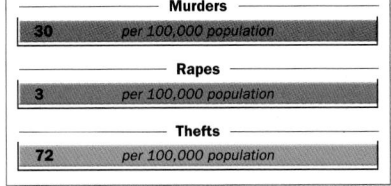

Murders

30   *per 100,000 population*

Rapes

3   *per 100,000 population*

Thefts

72   *per 100,000 population*

Crime rates are relatively high. Many shops have armed guards. The kidnapping of Chinese businessmen for ransom is a growing problem.

EDUCATION

 90%

0   *Education spending as % GNP*   25
2.9%

THE EDUCATION SYSTEM

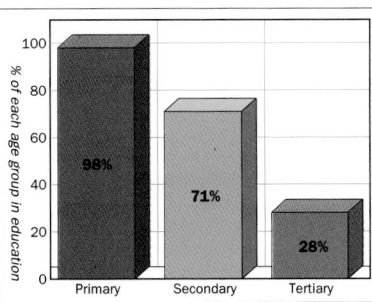

% of each age group in education

Primary 98%
Secondary 71%
Tertiary 28%

The Philippines has one of the highest literacy rates among developing countries. The education system is based on the US model, but characterized by many private schools. Sectarianism in education is common; the Chinese community has its own schools. Most colleges and universities are also run privately. The universities of San Carlos in Cebu city and Santo Tomas in Manila are Spanish colonial foundations, dating from 1595 and 1611 respectively.

PHILLIPINES : LAND USE

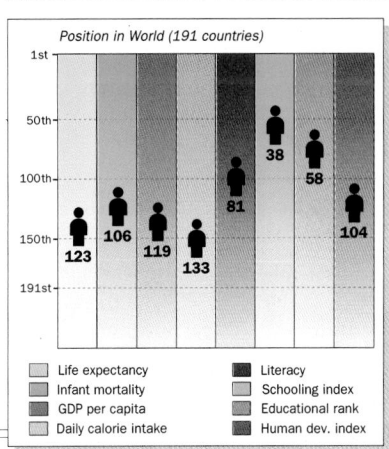

Cropland
Forest
Pigs
Sugar cane
Coconuts

LUZON

0   200 km
0   200 miles

MINDANAO

HEALTH

 1 per 6413 people

Respiratory and diarrheal diseases, tuberculosis

0   *Health spending as % GNP*   25
0.7%

Most general hospitals are privately run. Malaria, once a major problem, has been eradicated in all but remote areas.

WEALTH

 Miner, 2986 Philippine pesos per month; teacher, 3121 Philippine pesos per month

CONSUMER GOODS OWNERSHIP

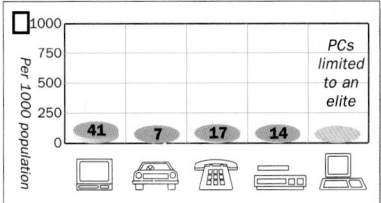

Per 1000 population

1000
750
500
250
0

41   7   17   14

PCs limited to an elite

Around 50% of Filipinos live on the poverty line. Wealth remains highly concentrated in a few Manila-based business families.

WORLD RANKING

Position in World (191 countries)

1st
50th
100th
150th
191st

123   106   119   133   81   38   58   104

Life expectancy   Literacy
Infant mortality   Schooling index
GDP per capita   Educational rank
Daily calorie intake   Human dev. index

P

POLAND

OFFICIAL NAME: Republic of Poland **CAPITAL:** Warsaw
POPULATION: 38.4 million **CURRENCY:** Zloty **OFFICIAL LANGUAGE:** Polish

LOCATED IN THE HEART OF EUROPE, Poland's low-lying plains extend from the Baltic shore in the north to the Tatry Mountains on its southern border with the Czech Republic and Slovakia. Since the Round Table Agreement of 1989, which led to the fall of the communist regime, Poland has undergone massive social, economic and political change. It is currently experiencing rapid economic growth. Its strategic location between western and eastern Europe and its developing market economy could make it a major player in European politics in the years to come.

CLIMATE

WEATHER CHART

Most of the country experiences a similar climate. Summers are hot, with heavy rainfall often accompanied by thunder. Winters are severe, with snow covering the ground on the southern mountains and for as much as 60–70 days in the east.

COMMUNICATIONS

 Okecie Intl, Warsaw

 251 ships
4.08m dwt

THE TRANSPORT NETWORK

363,116 km (225,636 miles)		257 km (160 miles)	
26,228 km (16,298 miles)		3997 km (2484 miles)	

Polish communications are in need of widespread upgrading to facilitate closer links with western Europe. Poland is uniquely located to capture east–west and north–south trading routes. The Gdańsk–Gdynia port complex is poised to become the centre of cross-Baltic trade and the Polish government is planning to build two east–west motorways. A new international airport has been built near Warsaw.

A much-needed improvement of the telecommunications network is beginning, with multinationals and Polish companies forming joint ventures to bring an optical fibre network to 125,000 households in southern Poland.

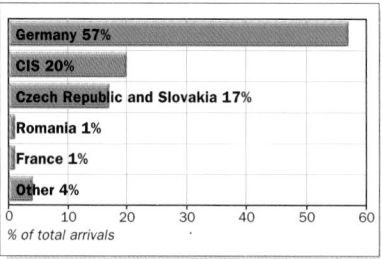

*The medieval administrative centre of **Lublin** lies in Poland's southeastern agricultural heartland.*

TOURISM

 18.2m visitors
 Up 221% in 1990

MAIN OVERSEAS ARRIVALS

Germany 57%	
CIS 20%	
Czech Republic and Slovakia 17%	
Romania 1%	
France 1%	
Other 4%	

% of total arrivals (scale 0–60)

Tourism in Poland has, until recently, been targeted towards domestic or eastern European tourists. Since 1989, however, some of the most visible signs of foreign investment have been in the hotel industry.

Despite considerable environmental problems, Poland is renowned for its skiing and hiking, especially in the Tatry Mountains. Kraków's medieval core has been preserved, while Toruń has restored its historic German Hanseatic buildings. Warsaw's historic centre has been meticulously reconstructed following its destruction in 1944.

Poznań has exploited its location between Warsaw and Berlin to create an international exhibition and business convention industry.

PEOPLE

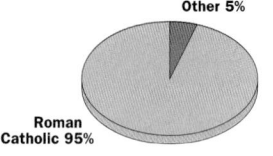 Polish

123 people per km²

THE URBAN/RURAL POPULATION SPLIT

62% — 38%

RELIGIOUS PERSUASION

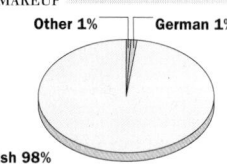

Other 5%
Roman Catholic 95%

ETHNIC MAKEUP

Other 1% — German 1%
Polish 98%

As a result of the readjustment of its borders agreed at the Yalta Conference in 1945, Poland has few ethnic minorities. The ethnic German minority in Silesia is becoming more self-assertive, especially over the region's environmental problems, and now has special representation in parliament. The Ukrainian minority make up only 0.7% of the population. The influx of Romanian gypsies trying to enter Germany through Poland, across the River Oder, has caused considerable hostility.

The main social conflict in democratic Poland has been that between liberal, secular tendencies, and the opposing influence of the Catholic Church.

Wealth disparities are not great. The growing wealth of the entrepreneurial class is causing tension between support for the free market and the egalitarian instinct inherited from 40 years of socialism.

Polish women are prominent policy makers. Hanna Suchocka was prime minister from 1992–1993. A woman currently heads the Central Bank.

POPULATION AGE BREAKDOWN

% of population by age group	0–14	15–64	65+		
65+	5.8%	8.2%	10.1%	10%	11.7%
15–64	60.8%	64.8%	65.7%	64.8%	66.9%
0–14	33.4%	27%	24.2%	25.2%	21.4%
	1960	1970	1980	1990	2000

POLITICS

 1997

 President Lech Wałęsa

THE STATE OF THE PARTIES

Parliament (*Sejm*) 460 members

| 37% SLD | 29% PSL | 16% UD | 9% UP | 9% Other |

SLD = Democratic Left Alliance **PSL** = Polish Peasant Party
UD = Democratic Union **UP** = Labour Union **S** = Solidarity
Other = Confederation for an Independent Poland, Non-party
Bloc in Support of Reforms, German minority organizations

Senate 100 members

| 37% SLD | 36% PSL | 10% S | 4% UD | 13% Other |

Since 1989, Poland has been a multiparty parliamentary democracy.

MAIN POLITICAL ISSUES

Coalition rule
Poland's emerging party system has been hindered by a superfluity of political factions and sustaining coalitions has proved difficult. Parties are required to have at least 5% of the vote in order to gain a seat and 8% to be eligible to join a coalition government.

Church–state relations
Building upon the legitimization of its authority in the martial law years, the Catholic Church has been outspoken in its views on social and political policy. Recent debates over abortion, worship in schools and values in the media have fuelled a heated dialogue over the proper role of the Church in public and private life.

PROFILE
A new post-Socialist constitution has yet to be drafted and government is currently operating under a revised version of the 1952 constitution. Under its provisions, the president has considerable power; this has led to a number of battles with the *Sejm* (parliament) over ultimate control. Frequent government changes have occured since 1989.

The 1993 elections saw the ousting of the DU, the offspring of Solidarity. Government is now in the hands of a coalition between the SLD and the PSL, both of which have their roots in

Lech Wałęsa, president since 1990. He was imprisoned under martial law.

Aleksander Kwasniewski, leader of the SLD, part of the ruling coalition.

Poland's communist past. The SLD, the successor to the Polish United Workers' Party (PUWP), supports continued economic reform. The PSL, under Prime Minister Waldemar Pawlak, represents the interests of the 30% of Poles who live off the land. This section has seen living standards decline sharply since 1989. The first months of this uneasy coalition saw Pawlak dismiss Deputy Finance Minister Stefan Kawalec over suspect share trading. Deputy Prime Minister and Finance Minister Marek Barowski then resigned in protest.

WORLD AFFAIRS

 CE V4 CSCE GATT   ECE

Poland has sought to strengthen its economic and security ties with the West. Its transition to a market economy depends upon trade links and eventual economic integration with western Europe. One of Poland's first acts as an independent nation was to apply for membership of the IMF. Developing economic and political links with the Baltics, Belarussia and the Ukraine is also seen as important.

P

POLAND

Total Area : 312 680 sq. km
(120 720 sq. miles)

POPULATION

▣	over 5 000 000
◉	over 1 000 000
◎	over 100 000
○	over 50 000

LAND HEIGHT

1000m/3281ft
500m/1640ft
200m/656ft
Sea Level

N

0   100 km

0   100 miles

CHRONOLOGY

Poland has Europe's second oldest written constitution. In 1795, it was partitioned between Austria-Hungary, Germany and Russia.

❏ **1918** Polish state recreated.

❏ **1921** Democratic constitution.

❏ **1926–1935** Pilsudski heads military coup. Nine years of authoritarian rule. Rising ethnic intolerance.

❏ **1939** Molotov-Ribbentrop pact. September, Germany invades and divides Poland with Russians.

❏ **1941** First concentration camps built on Polish soil.

❏ **1944** Warsaw Uprising: 200,000 killed in last stand against Nazis.

❏ **1945** Potsdam and Yalta Conferences set present borders and determine political allegiance to Soviet Union. ➪

CHRONOLOGY *continued*

- ❏ **1947** Communists manipulate elections to gain power. Opposition dissolved and exiled.
- ❏ **1949** Communist Party absorbs socialist coalition partners and forms Polish United Workers' Party.
- ❏ **1956** Protests in Poznań erupt into riots. More than 50 killed.
- ❏ **1970** Food price increases lead to strikes and riots in the Baltic port cities. Hundreds are killed.
- ❏ **1976** Government plans to raise food prices lead to protests. Government forced to back down.
- ❏ **1979** Pope John Paul II elected. Makes triumphal visit to Poland the next year.
- ❏ **1980** A series of strikes forces the government to negotiate with Solidarity. Resulting Gdańsk Accords grant the right to strike and to form free trade unions.
- ❏ **1981** General Wojciech Jaruzelski becomes prime minister.
- ❏ **1981–1983** Martial law. Solidarity forced into underground existence. Many of its leaders, including Wałęsa, are interned.
- ❏ **1983** Wałęsa awarded Nobel Peace Prize.
- ❏ **1986** Amnesty for political prisoners, but government refuses to negotiate with Solidarity.
- ❏ **1987** Referendum rejects government austerity programme.
- ❏ **1988** Industrial unrest leads to inconclusive government-Solidarity negotiations.
- ❏ **1989** PUWP agrees to hold talks with Solidarity, which is relegalized. Partially free elections are held. Solidarity candidates rout the PUWP. First postwar non-communist government formed.
- ❏ **1990** Swift transition to market economy begins. Wałęsa elected president.
- ❏ **1991** Free elections lead to fragmented parliament.
- ❏ **1992** Last Russian troops leave.
- ❏ **1993** Reformed communists form coalition government.
- ❏ **1994** Mass privatization programme implemented.

AID

 $8bn promised by the 24 top industrial nations   Aid is rising

Saddled with an enormous debt from the 1980s, Poland's most important foreign assistance was the cancellation of half of its debt by the Paris Club. A London Club agreement for commercial debt is still outstanding. The IMF, EBRD and EU have all taken an active role in supporting Poland's pioneering stabilization and reform programme.

DEFENCE

💲 $2.4bn   ⬇ Down 7% in 1992

0   *Defence spending as % GDP*   40
▨ **2.5%**

Since the demise of the Warsaw Pact, Poland has repeatedly stated its wish to join NATO, despite the West's hesitation. It recently signed the NATO-backed Partnership for Peace. Russia is a source for cut-price armaments and equipment for Poland's standing army, the largest in Europe after Russia's.

POLISH ARMED FORCES

🛡	2850 main battle tanks (2065 T-55/785 T-72)	194,200 personnel
🚢	3 submarines, 1 frigate, 1 destroyer and 20 patrol boats	19,300 personnel
✈	423 combat aircraft (221 MiG-21/ 37 MiG-23MF/104 Su-22)	83,000 personnel
	None	

ECONOMICS

🏢 $70.6bn   💲 17,239 zlotys

SCORE CARD

- ❏ WORLD GNP RANKING.........................34th
- ❏ GNP PER CAPITA $1838
- ❏ BALANCE OF PAYMENTS..................$−300m
- ❏ INFLATION 43%
- ❏ UNEMPLOYMENT................................15.7%

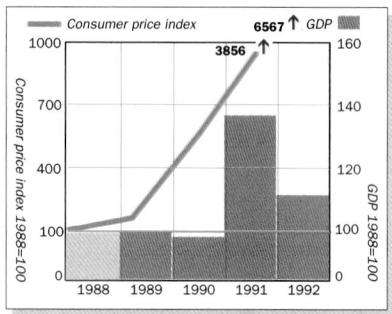

ECONOMIC PERFORMANCE INDICATOR

— Consumer price index   **6567** ↑ GDP ▨
1000   3856 ↑   160
700   140
400   120
100   100
0   0
1988 1989 1990 1991 1992

Consumer price index 1988=100 (left axis)
GDP 1988=100 (right axis)

EXPORTS
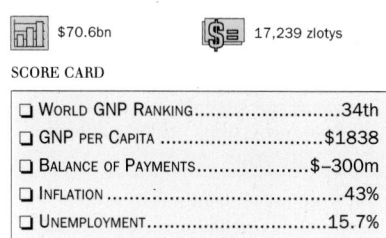

UK 7%
Germany* 15%
Other 57%
CIS* 21%

IMPORTS
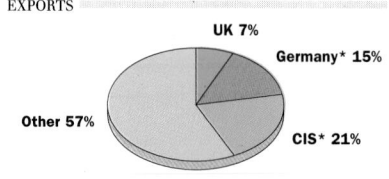

Austria 6%
Germany* 16%
Other 60%
CIS* 18%

STRENGTHS

Fastest economic growth in Europe in 1993. Steadfast implementation of economic reform since 1989 has encouraged growth of private sector. Ability to attract foreign investment. Mass privatization scheme, including the 600 largest state-owned industries, launched in 1994.

WEAKNESSES

Persistent high inflation. Outdated production plant. Need to compete for foreign investment with other former COMECON states.

PROFILE

Poland entered deep economic crisis in the 1980s, fuelled in part by high foreign debt levels. Following the change of government in January 1990, Finance Minister Leszek Balcerowicz implemented the Big Bang plan to bring about a swift transition to a market economy. Most prices were freed, trade was opened and the zloty was made convertible.

Although 40 years of communism have left considerable distortions in the economy, the framework necessary for a market economy is now being developed. The private sector now accounts for half of GNP and employs 60% of workers. Small businesses are flourishing in the previously neglected services sector. Stock and credit markets have opened and bankruptcy laws have been established. Share prices rose 900% in 1993.

Poland's economic growth and its 39 million domestic market make it attractive to foreign investors, which include companies such as Fiat, McDonalds and Proctor & Gamble.

POLAND : MAJOR BUSINESSES

Gdańsk
Warsaw
Szczecin
Białystok
Poznań
Wrocław
Łódź
Kraków

- ▨ Iron & steel
- 🔴 Coal mining
- Shipbuilding
- Electronics
- Textiles
- Engineering
- Chemicals
- Optics
- Vehicle assembly
- Pharmaceuticals

0   200 km
0   200 miles

RESOURCES

136bn kwh (capacity 30.7m kw)	Reserves of 42,208,000 bbl; refines 333,000 b/cd
18.8m pigs, 10.7m cattle, 4.4m sheep, 973,000 horses	Coal, copper, silver, sulphur, natural gas, lead, salt, iron ore

ELECTRICITY GENERATION

- Hydro 2% (3.3bn kwh)
- Thermal 98% (133bn kwh)
- Nuclear 0%
- Other 0%

0   20   40   60   80   100
% of total generation by type

Poland has significant quantities of coal, sulphur, copper, natural gas, silver, lead and salt. With the availability of cheap fuel from Russia at an end, Poland aims to reach self-sufficiency and eventually to export fuels. Coal supplies two thirds of electricity generation. The amounts of copper ores mined are too small to affect world markets.

POLAND : LAND USE

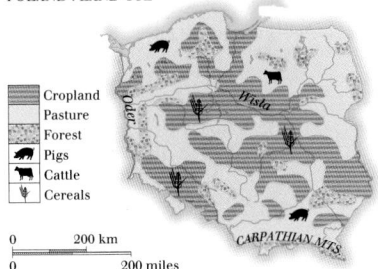

- Cropland
- Pasture
- Forest
- Pigs
- Cattle
- Cereals

0   200 km
0   200 miles

ENVIRONMENT

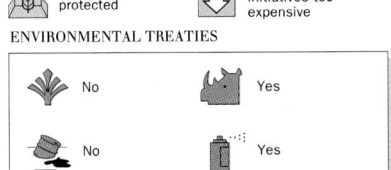

7% partially protected	Environmental initiatives too expensive

ENVIRONMENTAL TREATIES

	No		Yes
	No		Yes

Poland faces serious pollution problems from two generations of heavy industrialization. A third of Poles live in areas regarded as extremely polluted. In the southern region of Silesia, air, water and vegetation pollution are especially severe.

The metallurgical industry and thermal electric power stations are significant sources of air pollution. Sulpher dioxide readings in Kraków can exceed legal limits by 800 times.

Only 4% of Poland's rivers have water considered fit for human consumption; 75% had been declared biologically dead by the late 1980s. Any clean-up operation would be expensive.

MEDIA

Free, but broadcast media must by law reflect Christian values

Under martial law, Poland had a vigorous underground press and this energy has survived into democracy. The leading daily, *Gazeta Wyborcza*, began as Solidarity's paper. *Nie*, a satirical weekly, is edited by the former Communist Party spokesman, Jerzy Urban.

CRIME

40,321 prisoners	Levels are stable but likely to rise

CRIME RATES

Murders
3 per 100,000 population

Rapes
6 per 100,000 population

Thefts
1650 per 100,000 population

Smuggling is seen as the most significant crime problem. Warsaw is a main route for illicit as well as legal trade. Expensive cars are transferred eastwards to Russia and drugs westwards to Berlin. Smuggling is mostly undertaken by Poles and other eastern Europeans. In 1993, customs seized goods worth over $660,000.

EDUCATION

99%

0   Education spending as % GNP   25
4.6%

THE EDUCATION SYSTEM

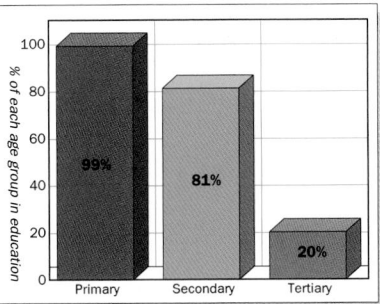

% of each age group in education
- Primary 99%
- Secondary 81%
- Tertiary 20%

The most contentious change is the expanded influence of the Catholic Church. Religious education is mandatory in all schools, and Church-run schools are now allowed. Traditionally based on the Russian system, Polish schools are reorientating themselves toward the French model.

Universities are of a high standard, especially in mathematics and philosophy. Business schools are training badly-needed managers.

	There are 7 national daily newspapers, including *Gazeta Wyborcza*, *Rzeczpospolita*, *Super Express* and *Zycie Warszawy*
	1 independent, several regional services
	2 independent, several regional services
	Thor Astra 1B Intelsat V1 F1
	Available in major cities

HEALTH

1 per 479 people	Heart and cerebrovascular diseases, cancers

0   Health spending as % GNP   25
4%

Medical care is provided free for workers and rural residents. Reform of the health system is being considered as the quality of health care is regarded as inadequate. Private health care is increasingly available in cities for those who can afford it.

WEALTH

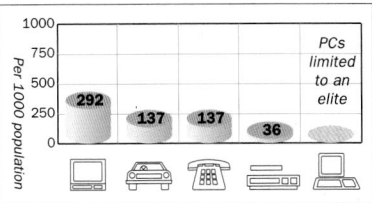

State employees are significantly worse off than those in the private sector

CONSUMER GOODS OWNERSHIP

Per 1000 population
- 292
- 137
- 137
- 36

PCs limited to an elite

Poland began its transition to a market economy with an extremely equitable distribution of income. After 1990, real wages in industry and agriculture fell from artificially high levels and the entrepreneurial class visibly increased its wealth. Growing wealth disparities have led to resentment from those who have not benefited from reforms.

WORLD RANKING

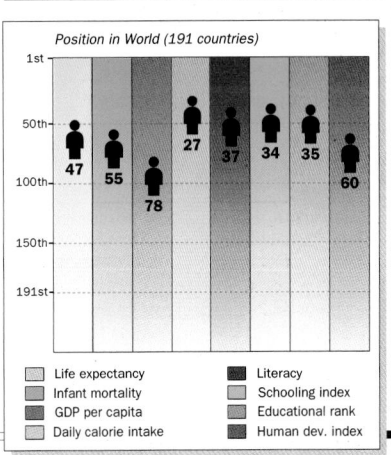

Position in World (191 countries)
- 47
- 55
- 78
- 27
- 37
- 34
- 35
- 60

1st
50th
100th
150th
191st

- Life expectancy
- Infant mortality
- GDP per capita
- Daily calorie intake
- Literacy
- Schooling index
- Educational rank
- Human dev. index

P

PORTUGAL

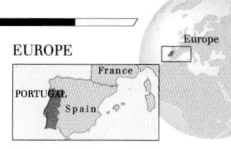

OFFICIAL NAME: Republic of Portugal   **CAPITAL:** Lisbon   **POPULATION:** 9.9 million
CURRENCY: Escudo   **OFFICIAL LANGUAGE:** Portuguese   **OVERSEAS TERRITORIES:** 1

PORTUGAL, WITH ITS long Atlantic coast, lies on the western side of the Iberian peninsular. The River Tagus divides the more mountainous north from the lower, undulating terrain to the south. In 1974, a bloodless military coup overthrew a long-standing conservative dictatorship. Democratic elections were held in 1975 and the armed forces withdrew from politics thereafter. The 1980s witnessed the implementation of a substantial programme of socio-economic modernization. Membership of the EU since 1986 has helped underpin this process.

Santa Marta de Penanguiao, a small village in the heart of Portugal's wine-producing region, which is centered on the Douro valley.

CLIMATE

WEATHER CHART

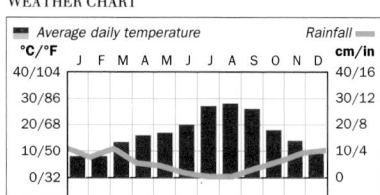

Portugal has a mild, Mediterranean climate, which is moderated by the influence of the Atlantic. Summers are hot and humid, while winters are relatively mild. Inland areas have more variable weather than coastal regions. Rainfall is generally higher in the mountainous north, while the central areas are more temperate. The southern Algarve region is predominantly dry and sunny.

COMMUNICATIONS

Portela de Sacavem, Lisbon
4.98m passengers

69 ships
897,200 dwt

THE TRANSPORT NETWORK

70,167 km (43,602 miles)	243 km (132 miles)
3549 km (2205 miles)	820 km (510 miles)

The Portuguese road system, which was formerly one of the least developed in Europe, has been extensively improved in recent years with grants from the EU. However, road links with Spain remain limited, despite a number of modernization schemes. Lisbon, the densely populated capital, continues to suffer from very heavy traffic congestion, which only a major new ring road will alleviate. The railway system is small but efficient. The national airline, TAP, is currently in economic difficulties.

TOURISM

8m visitors   Up 13% in 1990

MAIN OVERSEAS ARRIVALS

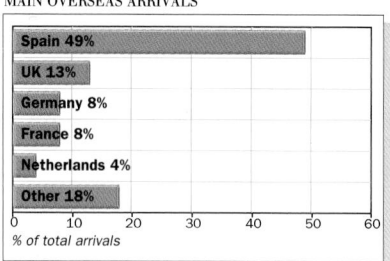

Spain 49%	
UK 13%	
Germany 8%	
France 8%	
Netherlands 4%	
Other 18%	

% of total arrivals

Since the 1960s, Portugal's popularity as a tourist destination has been linked to qualities which reflected its relatively poor economic development, such as low prices and little crime. Substantial economic growth has eroded some of its appeal, but tourism is likely to remain a major income-earner. The most popular destination is the Algarve, Portugal's southernmost province, followed by the western resorts of Figueira da Foz and the Tróia Peninsula. Visitors are also attracted by Portugal's architecture, notably that dating from the Manueline period (1490–1520), and handicrafts, such as ceramics, lace and tapestries. Portugal has some of Europe's finest golf courses.

PORTUGAL

Total Area : 92 390 sq. km (35 670 sq. miles)

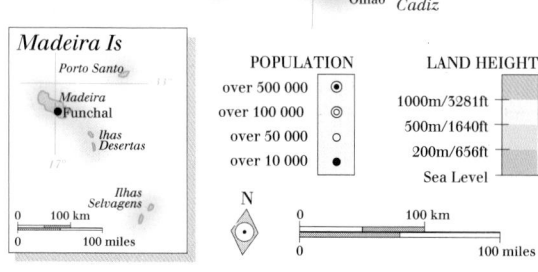

POPULATION		LAND HEIGHT
over 500 000	◉	1000m/3281ft
over 100 000	◎	500m/1640ft
over 50 000	○	200m/656ft
over 10 000	●	Sea Level

PEOPLE

Portuguese   107 people per km²

THE URBAN/RURAL POPULATION SPLIT

34%   66%

RELIGIOUS PERSUASION

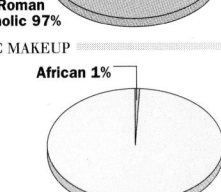

Protestant 1%   Other 2%

Roman Catholic 97%

ETHNIC MAKEUP

African 1%

Portuguese 99%

Portuguese society, once regarded as rather inward-looking, is now becoming increasingly integrated into the rest of Western Europe. Ethnic and religious tensions are limited. African immigrants, who come mainly from the former colonies, such as Angola, Mozambique and Guinea, have been assimilated into mainstream society with considerable ease.

As is true of other predominantly Catholic countries, the Church has lost much of its social influence in recent decades, a fact borne out by falling birth rates and more liberal attitudes to abortion and divorce. Nevertheless, with the exception of large urban areas, the north remains devoutly Catholic.

Family ties remain all-important. Women now have greater access to business and media jobs. Overall, democracy and rapid socio-economic change have tended to produce a more egalitarian society.

POPULATION AGE BREAKDOWN

%	☐ 0–14	☐ 15–64		☐ 65+	
	8%	9.2%	10.5%	12.9%	14.4%
	62.9%	62%	63.5%	65.8%	66.3%
	29.1%	28.8%	26%	21.3%	19.3%
	1960	1970	1980	1990	2000

(% of population by age group)

POLITICS

1995   President Mário Alberto Nobre Lopes Soares

THE STATE OF THE PARTIES

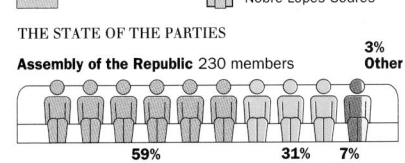

Assembly of the Republic 230 members   3% Other

59% PSD   31% PS   7% CDU

PSD = Social Democratic Party   **PS** = Socialist Party
CDU = Democratic Union Coalition (of which leading member is Portuguese Communist Party)   **Other** = Centre Democratic Party, National Solidarity Party

Portugal is a multiparty democracy.

MAIN POLITICAL ISSUES

Limiting pay rises
The government wishes to improve the state's weak financial position by keeping public sector pay rises below inflation. It proposed limiting wage rises to 2% – a cut in real terms. In 1994, the unions responded with a number of one-day strikes. The threat of rising unemployment, however, will limit demands for wage rises in the private sector.

Differences within the leadership
There have been a number of disputes between the president and the government. Prime Minister Cavaco's proposals to reform the military and to increase university fees have been opposed by President Mario Soares. Poor relations are likely to continue until the presidential elections of 1995.

PROFILE
Portugal has had almost a decade of centre-right government. Close links have developed between the ruling PSD and the civil service. There are fears that this could be undermining criticism of the government. However, the highly independent stance of President Mário Soares does provide an effective opposition voice. Soares frequently uses his power of veto to delay government legislation. This is in sharp contrast to the opposition PS and CDU; both parties faced serious internal problems following their defeat in the 1991 elections.

In spite of the recent recession, the PSD face few challenges to their continued hold on power. The electorate who voted them in on their sustained record of economic growth in 1991 will, according to opinion polls, give them another term in 1995.

Dr Mário Soares, *Portugal's socialist president since 1986, re-elected in 1991.*

Aníbal Cavaco Silva, *prime minister and leader of the centre-right PSD.*

WORLD AFFAIRS

EU   NATO   CSCE   GATT   OECD

Since 1986, Portugal's foreign policy has dealt almost exclusively with the consequences of membership of the EU, from which the country has greatly benefited. It is a committed member of NATO, though its relative strategic importance has declined as a result of Spanish membership. Relations with the former African colonies are occasionally turbulent and remain a high priority, as do those with Brazil. Relations with China over the return of Macao to the latter in 1999 are cordial.

AID

 $213 (donations)   Down 11% in 1991

Portugal became an aid donor only in the early 1980s. It currently earmarks just under than 0.2% of its GDP for aid to developing countries, mainly its former colonies in Africa. It is to provide $110 million to rebuild war-damaged power lines to the massive Cahora Bassa Dam in Mozambique, which has never been fully operational.

CHRONOLOGY

Portugal has existed as a nation state since the 11th century, although this was frequently challenged by Spain. Portugal reached its zenith in the 16th century, after which it entered a period of decline.

❑ **1703** Britain and Portugal sign the Methuen Treaty, facilitating the shipping of port to England.
❑ **1755** Earthquake destroys Lisbon.
❑ **1703** Joins coalition against revolutionary France.
❑ **1807** France invades; royal family flees to Brazil.
❑ **1808** British troops arrive under Wellington. Start of Peninsular War.
❑ **1810** French leave Portugal.
❑ **1820** Liberal revolution.
❑ **1822** King John VI returns and accepts first Portuguese constitution. His son Dom Pedro declares independence of Brazil.
❑ **1834** Dom Pedro returns to Portugal to end civil war and installs his daughter as Queen Mary II.
❑ **1856** First railway opens.
❑ **1872** First industrial strike.
❑ **1875–1876** Republican and Socialist parties founded.
❑ **1890** British ultimatum ends the land connection between Angola and Mozambique.
❑ **1891** Republican uprising in Porto.
❑ **1908** Assassination of King Carlos I and heir to the throne. ➪

P

CHRONOLOGY *continued*

- ❑ **1910** Abdication of Manuel II and proclamation of the Republic. Church and state separated.
- ❑ **1916** Portugal joins allied side in the First World War.
- ❑ **1917–1918** New Republic led by Sidónio Pais.
- ❑ **1926** Army overturns republic.
- ❑ **1928** Salazar joins government as finance minister. Economy improves significantly.
- ❑ **1932** Salazar appointed prime minister.
- ❑ **1933** Promulgation of the constitution of the 'New State', instituting right-wing dictatorship.
- ❑ **1936–1939** Salazar assists Franco in Spanish Civil War.
- ❑ **1939–1945** Portugal neutral during Second World War, but lets UK use air bases in Azores.
- ❑ **1949** Founder-member of NATO.
- ❑ **1955** Joins UN.
- ❑ **1958** Américo Thómas appointed president, following the fraudulent defeat of General Delgado.
- ❑ **1961** India annexes Goa. Guerrilla warfare breaks out in Angola, Mozambique and Guinea.
- ❑ **1970** Death of Salazar, incapacitated since 1968. Succeeded by Marcelo Caetano.
- ❑ **1971** Caetano attempts liberalization.
- ❑ **1974** Carnation Revolution – the left-wing Armed Forces Movement overthrows Caetano.
- ❑ **1975** Communist takeover foiled by moderates and Mário Soares's PS.
- ❑ **1974–1975** Portuguese possessions in Africa attain independence. Some 750,000 Portuguese expatriates return to Portugal. First democratic elections.
- ❑ **1975–1976** Indonesia seizes Portuguese possession of East Timor unopposed.
- ❑ **1976** General António Eanes elected president. New socialist constitution adopted. Mário Soares appointed prime minister.
- ❑ **1978** Period of non-party technocratic government instituted.
- ❑ **1980** Centre-right wins elections. General Eanes re-elected.
- ❑ **1982** Full civilian government formally restored.
- ❑ **1983** Soares becomes caretaker prime minister; PS is majority party.
- ❑ **1985** Cavaco Silva becomes prime minister. Minority PSD government.
- ❑ **1986** Soares elected president. Portugal joins EC.
- ❑ **1987** Cavaco Silva wins absolute majority in parliament. Agreement to return Macao to China in 1999.
- ❑ **1991** Soares re-elected president. Portugal begins talks to renegotiate US Azores air base treaty.

DEFENCE

$1.5bn   Up 3% in 1992

0   *Defence spending as % GDP*   40

2.2%

Portugal, a member of NATO since 1949, has a small but relatively modern navy. The army and air force are smaller and less efficient. Mounting opposition to military service is causing strains on these already semi-professional bodies. The USA is the major arms supplier. It has a strategic air base in the Azores.

PORTUGUESE ARMED FORCES

129 main battle tanks (43 M-47/86 M-48A5)	58,300 personnel
3 submarines, 11 frigates and 29 patrol boats	15,300 personnel
83 combat aircraft (A-7P/G-91R3/T1)	10,300 personnel
None	

ECONOMICS

$80bn   174.41 escudos

SCORE CARD

- ❑ WORLD GNP RANKING 33rd
- ❑ GNP PER CAPITA $8081
- ❑ BALANCE OF PAYMENTS...................$–600m
- ❑ INFLATION 6.5%
- ❑ UNEMPLOYMENT................................5.6%

EXPORTS

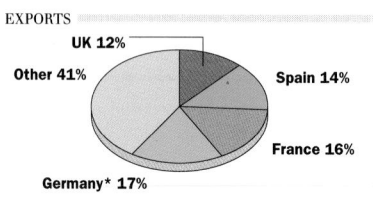

UK 12%
Other 41%
Spain 14%
France 16%
Germany* 17%

IMPORTS

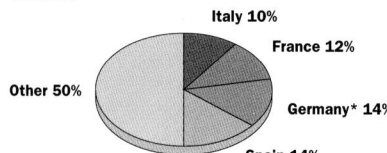

Italy 10%
France 12%
Other 50%
Germany* 14%
Spain 14%

STRENGTHS

Relatively low, though rapidly rising, labour costs. High rate of domestic and direct foreign investment, including a $3.3 billion Ford–Volkswagen vehicle-assembly plant near Lisbon, due to open 1995. Strong banking and tourism sectors. Tourism makes up 6% of GDP, the highest ratio in the EU; potential for further growth. Fast-track improvement of transport infrastructure under way. Good deep-water port at Lisbon. Wine, especially port. Tomatoes, citrus fruit, cork, sardines. Strong clothing and shoe manufacturing sectors.

WEAKNESSES

Large agricultural sector (5% of GDP, 10% of workforce) is most inefficient in EU. Outdated farming methods, small landholdings, low crop yields. Farm products outpriced by Spain. Large budget deficit (7% of GDP in 1993). Inflation higher than EU average. Rigid labour market. High dependence on imported oil.

ECONOMIC PERFORMANCE INDICATOR

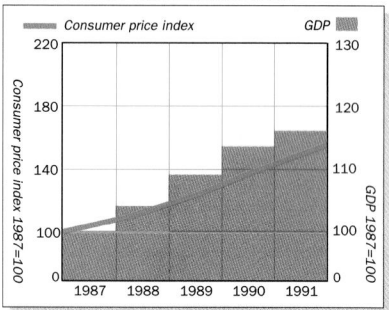

Consumer price index   GDP

Consumer price index 1987=100

GDP 1987=100

1987 1988 1989 1990 1991

PROFILE

EU membership in 1986 brought a sharp increase in foreign investment to Portugal. Exports rose dramatically until the economy went into recession in 1991.

Despite its improved economy, Portugal has some way to go to achieve convergence with its EU partners. With an inflation rate which is 3% greater than the EU average, monetary union is a distant prospect. The government is instituting a new economic plan, 'Quantum 2', which calls for budgetary and wage constraints, and industrial restructuring. Opinion polls in 1994 suggested 'Quantum 2' had the backing of the Portuguese electorate.

PORTUGAL : MAJOR BUSINESSES

Braga
Matosinhos
Porto
Aveiro
Lisbon
Setúbal
Faro

Steel
Wine
Textiles
Cement
Ceramics
Chemicals
Vehicle manufacture
Light engineering
Fish processing
Shipbuilding

0   100 km
0   100 miles

RESOURCES

28.5bn kwh (capacity 7.4m kw)

5.4m sheep, 2.3m pigs, 1.4m cattle, 170,000 asses

Not an oil producer; refines 294,000 b/cd

Limestone, granite, marble, copper

ELECTRICITY GENERATION

Hydro 33% (9.3bn kwh)

Thermal 67% (19.2bn kwh)

Nuclear 0%

Other 0%

% of total generation by type

Portugal has been plagued by a lack of natural resources, including water. Mining has historically been important, notably for wolfram, copper and tin. Industry has relied on small coal deposits and large oil imports. Portugal hopes to build HEP stations, and aims to pipe natural gas from Algeria by 1996.

PORTUGAL : LAND USE

Cropland
Pasture
Forest
Vineyards
Cereals
Sheep

0   100 km
0   100 miles

ENVIRONMENT

6% partially protected

Fast modernization balanced by new conservation concern

ENVIRONMENTAL TREATIES

Yes

Yes

No

Yes

The unrestricted development of tourist resorts in the Algarve and the huge investment in new harbour, road and bridge developments are having detrimental effects on natural habitats. EU agricultural grants for projects such as draining meadows, and monoculture afforestation, notably of *Eucalyptus* and *Pinus*, are degrading biodiversity. Much toxic waste is dumped on any available land as few official controls or infill sites exist. New waste management regulations are being planned.

MEDIA

There is full freedom from censorship and the press is entirely independent

PUBLISHING AND BROADCAST MEDIA

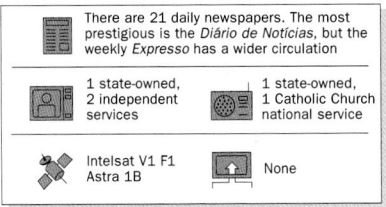

There are 21 daily newspapers. The most prestigious is the *Diário de Notícias*, but the weekly *Expresso* has a wider circulation

1 state-owned, 2 independent services

1 state-owned, 1 Catholic Church national service

Intelsat V1 F1 Astra 1B

None

Newspaper circulation figures are among the lowest in Europe and most papers have regional rather than national distribution. Radio and TV are therefore the main source of news, in part reflecting Portugal's low literacy rate. In 1992, two independent TV stations began broadcasting, breaking the state's monopoly. Most English-language footage is not dubbed.

CRIME

8181 prisoners

Up 9% in 1990

CRIME RATES

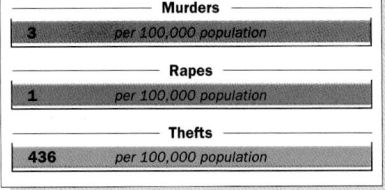

Murders
3   per 100,000 population

Rapes
1   per 100,000 population

Thefts
436   per 100,000 population

Compared to most West European countries, Portugal still enjoys a remarkably low crime rate. However, drug trafficking and related offences are rising.

EDUCATION

85%

0   Education spending as % GNP   25
4.9%

THE EDUCATION SYSTEM

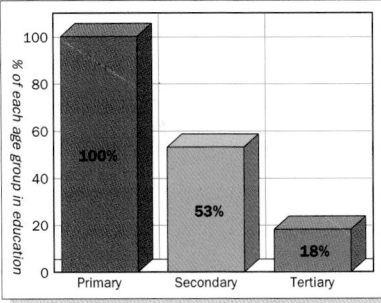

% of each age group in education

Primary 100%
Secondary 53%
Tertiary 18%

Free state education is available to all pupils between the ages of three and 15, although the pre-school stage up to the age of six is not compulsory. Middleclass parents rely heavily on the private sector. State universities are large and oversubscribed. There are several prestigious private universities.

HEALTH

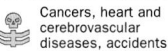

1 per 412 people

Cancers, heart and cerebrovascular diseases, accidents

0   Health spending as % GNP   25
3.5%

The public health system is free, but it suffers from underfunding. However, Portugal's larger urban hospitals are modern and well-equipped.

Private health care schemes are both affordable and good value for money. Over 40% of the population use the private system. In spite of high tobacco and wine consumption, the Portuguese are a healthy nation, with similar life expectancy rates to neighbouring Spain.

WEALTH

Shop assistant, 1.7m escudos per year; managing director, 11.3m escudos per year

CONSUMER GOODS OWNERSHIP

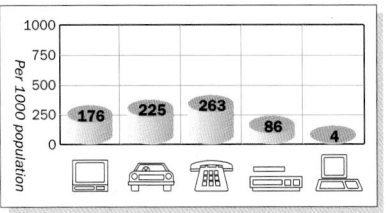

Per 1000 population

176   225   263   86   4

Wealth differentials in Portugal are smaller than in most EU countries. The bloodless military coup of 1974 led to many wealthy families transferring their assets abroad, or leaving Portugal altogether. The 1976 constitution enshrined socialist goals, and subsequent governments introduced limited wealth redistribution measures.

Many long-standing Portuguese families have seen the value of their assets fall with the dramatic drop in land prices since 1986. However, those with land with tourist development potential, such as golf courses, have made large profits. Much wealth generated by new businesses leaves Portugal as most are foreign-owned.

WORLD RANKING

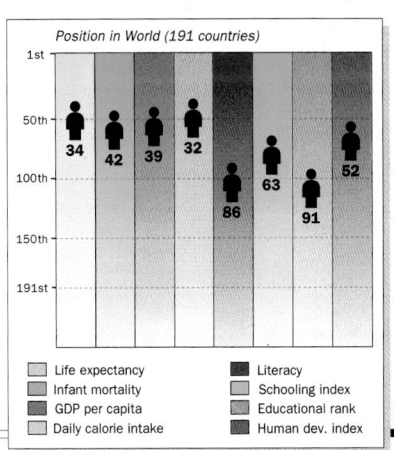

Position in World (191 countries)

1st

50th   34   42   39   32

100th   86   63   91

52

150th

191st

Life expectancy
Infant mortality
GDP per capita
Daily calorie intake
Literacy
Schooling index
Educational rank
Human dev. index

P

QATAR

OFFICIAL NAME: State of Qatar **CAPITAL:** Doha
POPULATION: 500,000 **CURRENCY:** Qatar riyal **OFFICIAL LANGUAGE:** Arabic

MIDDLE EAST

PROJECTING NORTH FROM the Arabian peninsula into the Persian Gulf, Qatar has land borders with Saudi Arabia and the United Arab Emirates, and a disputed sea border with Bahrain. Most of the country is flat, semi-arid desert. Qatar is a founder-member of OPEC and its plentiful oil and natural gas reserves make it one of the wealthiest states in the region. The country enjoys political stability under the rule of the 15,000-strong Al Thani clan.

CLIMATE

WEATHER CHART

The climate is hot and humid with midsummer temperatures reaching 44°C. Rainfall is rare.

COMMUNICATIONS

 Doha International 1.1m passengers (est)   23 ships 593,600 dwt

THE TRANSPORT NETWORK

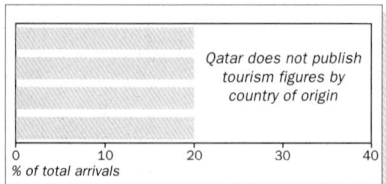

1500 km (932 miles)
None
None
None

A good road network links Qatar to its neighbours. A new international airport in Doha is scheduled for 1997.

TOURISM

Small-scale tourism Little variation from year to year

MAIN OVERSEAS ARRIVALS

Qatar does not publish tourism figures by country of origin

% of total arrivals

Qatar attracts several thousand European visitors a year, who enjoy unspoilt beaches, duty-free shopping, modern hotels and the desert hinterland. Alcohol is permitted in five-star hotels for non-Muslims.

PEOPLE

Arabic 36 people per km²

THE URBAN/RURAL POPULATION SPLIT

89% 11%

ETHNIC MAKEUP

Other 14%
Arab 40%
Iranian 10%
Pakistani 18%
Indian 18%

Only one in five Qataris is native-born. Most of the population are guest workers from the Indian subcontinent, Iran and the northern African countries. Expatriates enjoy a high standard of living and take no part in politics.

Qataris are followers of the Wahhabi interpretation of Sunni Islam and espouse conservative religious views. However, women are not obliged to take the veil and can hold driving licences. Expatriate Christians are allowed freedom to worship but not to promote Christianity.

Since the advent of oil wealth, the Qataris, who were formerly nomadic Bedouins, have become a nation of city-dwellers. Almost 90% of the population now inhabit the capital Doha and its suburbs. As a result, northern Qatar is dotted with depopulated and abandoned villages.

Doha, the capital. *Although desert covers the whole country, Qatar now grows most of its own vegetables by tapping ground water.*

POLITICS

Not applicable. Absolute rule by an Amir Amir Sheikh Khalifa bin Hamad Al Thani

THE STATE OF THE PARTIES

Qatar is an absolute monarchy and has no legislature. The Amir rules with the assistance of the Council of Ministers and the Advisory Council.

Qatar is a traditional emirate. Its government and religious establishment is dominated by Amir Sheikh Khalifa, who took power in a bloodless coup in 1972. His designated successor is his son, Sheikh Hamad. Although the Al Thani family has several sub-groups, the Amir and his immediate relatives are unchallenged.

The largely middle-class, pro-democracy movement has called for reform of the 35-member Advisory Council. The Amir's response has been to introduce more technocrats into the cabinet. However, he maintains a tight rein on finance, personally signing all government cheques over 250,000 Qatar riyals.

WORLD AFFAIRS

 OPEC AL GCC AFESD ESCWA

Qatar sided with Iraq in the Iran-Iraq War (1980–1988). However, during the Gulf War against Iraq (1990–1991), it hosted UN forces and its soldiers fought at the battle of Khafji. The Amir is keen to retain strong links with Western states, notably the UK and the USA. Within the quotas set by OPEC, Qatar has supported a moderate oil price. It has firmly resisted claims against its territory by Bahrain and has sought to strengthen ties with the Islamic Republic of Iran. In 1992, a ten-year defence agreement was signed with the USA, despite Saudi Arabia's disapproval. Qatar is a founder-member of the Gulf Co-operation Council, established in 1981 as an economic union with Saudi Arabia, Kuwait, the United Arab Emirates, Oman and Bahrain.

AID

 Qatar now gives minimal aid   Sharp fall in donations

Qatar was a generous aid donor to developing countries during the 1970s and early 1980s, but levels have fallen sharply as a result of lower oil prices.

QATAR

Total Area : 11 000 sq. km
(4247 sq. miles)

POPULATION
over 100 000 ◎
under 10 000 •

LAND HEIGHT
200m/1640ft
Sea Level

DEFENCE

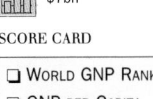 $934.1bn   Little variation in past year

The 9000-strong armed forces are too small to play a significant role in Qatari affairs, even in the event of political turmoil. A ten-year defence agreement with the USA provides for joint exercises, the stockpiling of American equipment and US access to bases.

ECONOMICS

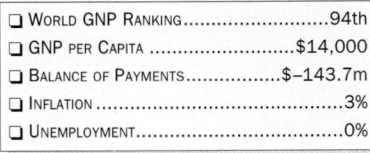 $7bn   3.63 Qatar riyals

SCORE CARD

- ❏ World GNP Ranking..........................94th
- ❏ GNP per Capita $14,000
- ❏ Balance of Payments.................$-143.7m
- ❏ Inflation 3%
- ❏ Unemployment.....................................0%

Strengths
A steady supply of crude oil and huge gas reserves, plus related industries. Modern infrastructure.

Weaknesses
Dependence on foreign workforce. All raw materials and most foods are imported. Virtually all water has to be desalinated. Government has large

RESOURCES

 4.6bn kwh (capacity 1.41m kw)   398,700 b/d (reserves 3,729,000,000 bbl)

2m chickens, 128,000 sheep, 78,000 goats   Oil, natural gas

Qatar has the third-smallest reserves of crude oil within OPEC but abundant reserves of gas, including the world's largest non-associated gas field, known as North Field.

ENVIRONMENT

 None   Most native game species exist only in zoos

The desert hinterland supports little plant or animal life. Oil pollution has damaged marine life. On land, game has been hunted out and most native species are extinct in the wild.

MEDIA

The press is subject to censorship

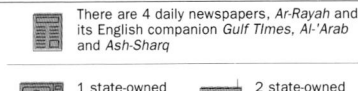
PUBLISHING AND BROADCAST MEDIA

There are 4 daily newspapers, *Ar-Rayah* and its English companion *Gulf Times*, *Al-'Arab* and *Ash-Sharq*

1 state-owned service   2 state-owned networks

There is total political censorship. The foreign media is also censored for good taste. Satellite TV channels are freely available.

CRIME

 6285 prisoners   Up 50% in 1990

Traditional Islamic punishments have deterred crime. However, drug trafficking is on the increase. The incidence of street crime is low.

EXPORTS

Singapore 3%   Brazil 9%
United Arab Emirates 3%
Japan 61%   Other 24%

IMPORTS
Germany* 7%   Italy 8%
UK 12%
Other 54%
Japan 19%

foreign reserves, but new industries depend on cementing agreements with foreign partners. Potential threat to security from Iraq and Iran makes some multinationals wary of investment.

EDUCATION

 76%

Education is free from primary to university level. The government finances students to study overseas.

HEALTH

 1 per 561 people   Heart, circulatory and infectious diseases, cancers

Primary health care is free to Qataris. Hospitals operate to Western standards of care and the government also funds treatment abroad.

WEALTH

 Poverty is very rare in Qatar

CONSUMER GOODS OWNERSHIP
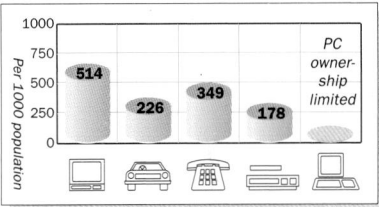
514, 226, 349, 178, PC ownership limited

Qataris have a very high income per capita. There is no income tax, public services are free and the government guarantees jobs for school-leavers. There are no exchange controls.

WORLD RANKING

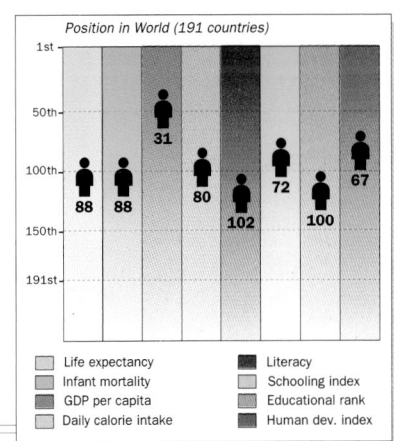
Position in World (191 countries)
88, 88, 80, 31, 102, 72, 100, 67

Life expectancy / Literacy
Infant mortality / Schooling index
GDP per capita / Educational rank
Daily calorie intake / Human dev. index

Q

ROMANIA

OFFICIAL NAME: Romania **CAPITAL:** Bucharest
POPULATION: 23.3 million **CURRENCY:** Leu **OFFICIAL LANGUAGE:** Romanian

ROMANIA LIES ON THE Black Sea coast, with the Danube as its southern border. The eastern Carpathian Mountains form an arc across the country, curving around the upland basin of Transylvania. Long dominated by the Ottoman, Russian and Hapsburg empires, Romania became an independent monarchy in 1878. After the Second World War, the monarchy was supplanted by a communist People's Republic, headed by Nicolae Ceauşescu from 1965. A revolution in 1989 resulted in Ceauşescu's execution. Romania is now a limited democracy, converting slowly to a free-market economy.

Village in northeastern Romania, in the foothills of the Carpathian Mountains, close to the border with Ukraine. Maize and wheat are Romania's main crops.

CLIMATE

WEATHER CHART

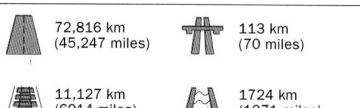

Romania has a continental climate with two growing seasons. Rainfall is generally moderate, with most falling in spring and early summer. Very heavy spring rains occasionally destroy new crops. Snow is frequent in winter, which can be bitterly cold.

COMMUNICATIONS

 Bucharest-Otopeni Intl   261 ships 4.13m dwt

THE TRANSPORT NETWORK

72,816 km (45,247 miles)		113 km (70 miles)	
11,127 km (6914 miles)		1724 km (1071 miles)	

Romania's outdated infrastructure remains a major obstacle to development. The EBRD and World Bank have subscribed $280 million to road improvement schemes. US interests have proposed increasing the regional role of the Black Sea port of Constanţa.

TOURISM

 6.28m visitors   Up 17% in 1992

MAIN OVERSEAS ARRIVALS

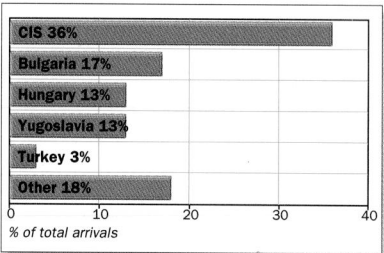

CIS 36%
Bulgaria 17%
Hungary 13%
Yugoslavia 13%
Turkey 3%
Other 18%

% of total arrivals

The Black Sea, Danube delta and Carpathian Mountains are the primary natural attractions, while Transylvania has a rich historical heritage. However, tourist facilities are generally poor. Under Ceauşescu, the need for foreign currency meant that tourists came before Romanians in accommodation priorities. Today, privatization of property and an acute housing shortage have reduced accommodation available to visitors. By 1992, tourism was no longer a net foreign exchange earner for Romania.

ROMANIA

Total Area: 237 500 sq. km
(91 700 sq. miles)

POPULATION
over 1 000 000 ⊡
over 100 000 ◎
over 50 000 ○

LAND HEIGHT
3000m/9843ft
2000m/6562ft
1000m/3281ft
500m/1640ft
Sea Level

PEOPLE

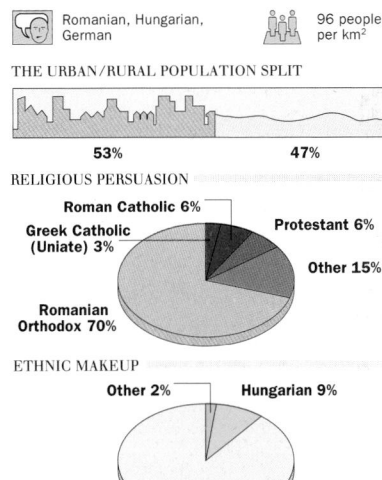

Romanian, Hungarian, German

96 people per km²

THE URBAN/RURAL POPULATION SPLIT

53%   47%

RELIGIOUS PERSUASION

Roman Catholic 6%
Greek Catholic (Uniate) 3%
Protestant 6%
Other 15%
Romanian Orthodox 70%

ETHNIC MAKEUP

Other 2%   Hungarian 9%
Romanian 89%

Since 1989, there has been a rise in Romanian nationalism, aggravated by the hardships brought by economic reform and accompanying austerity measures. The incidence of ethnic violence has also risen, particularly towards Gypsies and Hungarians. Ethnic Hungarians form the largest minority group in Romania. They are partly protected by the influence of the Hungarian state, whereas the Gypsies do not have any similar support and tend to suffer greater discrimination.

Romania's population is currently decreasing. This is due to rising emigration since 1989, mainly for economic reasons, and to a falling birth rate since the early 1990s. The latter trend is in sharp contrast to the 1980s, when the Ceauşescu regime enforced a 'pro-natalist' policy, by banning contraception and abortion. The government also imposed taxes on childless adults or on those with fewer than four children and obliged married women to have monthly fertility examinations. The birth rate accordingly rose. However, the population as a whole did not rise significantly due to an increase in Romania's mortality rate. Abortion was legalized in 1989; maternal death rates have recently declined.

POPULATION AGE BREAKDOWN

% of population by age group	0–14	15–64	65+		
	6.7%	8.6%	10.3%	10.3%	12.6%
	65.2%	65.4%	63.1%	66.3%	66.2%
	28.1%	26%	26.6%	23.4%	21.2%
	1960	1970	1980	1990	2000

WORLD AFFAIRS

CSCE   ECE   GATT   NAM   IBRD

While making efforts to remain on good terms with the former Soviet states, Romania is building closer links with western Europe. In 1993, it signed an association agreement with the EU.

Relations with Hungary are tense. Despite pressure from Budapest, Romania has resisted the demands of the Hungarian minority in Transylvania for greater autonomy.

After 1989, unification with Moldavia was a distinct possibility as Romanians are of the same ethnic group as Moldavians. However, the issue was quashed in 1993 when Moldavia voted for closer links with the CIS. Romania has followed UN policy on Yugoslavia, adhering to sanctions despite the negative effects on its own economy.

AID

Main donor is EBRD

Increasing aid from EBRD and IMF

There has been some delay in receiving IMF and World Bank aid. Romania does not wish to conform to IMF economic directives. Aid is being directed chiefly into mechanizing the privatized, but undercapitalized, agricultural sector and improving telecommunications.

POLITICS

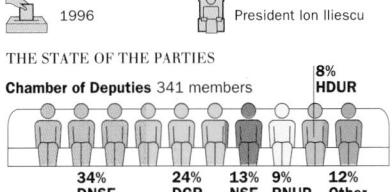

1996   President Ion Iliescu

THE STATE OF THE PARTIES

Chamber of Deputies 341 members

8% HDUR

34% DNSF   24% DCR   13% NSF   9% RNUP   12% Other

DNSF = Democratic National Salvation Front
DCR = Democratic Convention of Romania (composed of: Christian Democrat National Peasants' Party, Party of the Civic Alliance, National Liberal Party – Democratic Convention, National Liberal Party – Youth Wing, Romanian Social Democratic Party, Romanian Ecology Party)
NSF = National Salvation Front   **RNUP** = Romanian National Union Party   **HDUR** = Hungarian Democratic Union of Romania   **Other** = Greater Romania Party, Socialist Labour Party, Agrarian Democratic Party of Romania

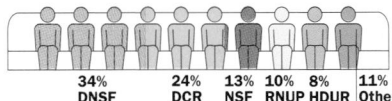

Senate 143 members

34% DNSF   24% DCR   13% NSF   10% RNUP   8% HDUR   11% Other

In 1991, Romania voted to become a multiparty democracy headed by a directly-elected president, who may not belong to any political party.

MAIN POLITICAL ISSUES

Economic performance

The poor performance of the economy has exerted pressure on the minority government. General strikes in early 1994 expressed popular discontent with falling living standards, and the seeming inability of the government to develop a coherent economic policy.

Ethnic tensions

Ethnic tensions are rising in Romania. The far right has made political gains and nationalism is increasingly accepted. In 1993, elements of the extreme right were advocating labour camps for ethnic minorities. Gypsies are becoming victims of violent, racially-motivated attacks.

PROFILE

Romania's 1989 revolution left an old communist elite in power. Unlike Poland, Hungary and Czechoslovakia, Romania did not have an organized group ready to introduce real democracy and with the skills necessary to create a vibrant market economy. Democracy is in place on the surface but political intimidation and ballot-rigging remain commonplace.

While many state assets have been privatized, most have remained in the hands of people tied to the ruling clique. The DNSF government retains the support of conservative groups, such as miners and rural workers.

President Ion Iliescu. He succeeded Ceauşescu and was re-elected in 1992.

Nikolae Vacaroiu, an economist who became prime minister in 1992.

R

CHRONOLOGY

Many of Romania's foreign policy tensions are the legacy of its long history of redrawn borders. Former territories are resisting reunification, not least on economic grounds.

❑ **1859** Unification of Moldavia and Wallachia forms basis of future Romania.
❑ **1878** Independence, but at cost of losing Bessarabia to Russia.
❑ **1916–1918** Enters First World War on Allied side. At end of war, gains substantial territory, including Transylvania from Hungary.
⇨

DEFENCE

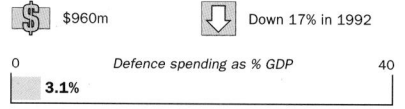

$960m   Down 17% in 1992

0   *Defence spending as % GDP*   40

3.1%

The military received limited funding under the Ceauşescu regime and troops were routinely deployed as cheap labour. Since the demise of the Warsaw Pact, Romania has not sought close ties with NATO. The weak economy means that military expenditure will fall further in future.

ROMANIAN ARMED FORCES

🚜	2875 main battle tanks (1059 T-34/756 T-55/ 30 T-72/ 456 TR-85)	161,000 personnel
🚢	1 submarine, 5 frigates 1 destroyer and 90 patrol boats	19,000 personnel
✈	486 combat aircraft (19 MiG-17/59 IAR-93/ 189 MiG-21/36 MiG-23)	20,000 personnel
	None	

ECONOMICS

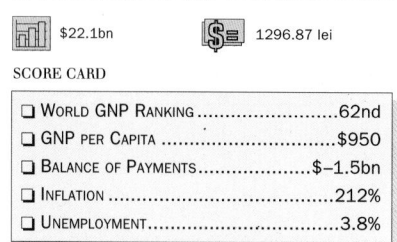

$22.1bn   1296.87 lei

SCORE CARD

- ❏ WORLD GNP RANKING 62nd
- ❏ GNP PER CAPITA $950
- ❏ BALANCE OF PAYMENTS...................$–1.5bn
- ❏ INFLATION 212%
- ❏ UNEMPLOYMENT..................................3.8%

ECONOMIC PERFORMANCE INDICATOR

EXPORTS

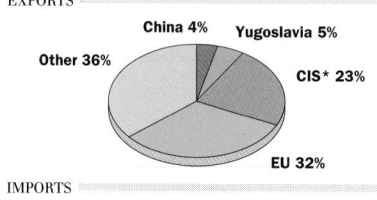

China 4%   Yugoslavia 5%
Other 36%
CIS* 23%
EU 32%

IMPORTS

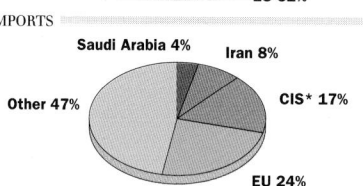

Saudi Arabia 4%   Iran 8%
Other 47%
CIS* 17%
EU 24%

STRENGTHS
Large number of foreign joint ventures. Tourism potential.

WEAKNESSES
Slow transition from centrally-planned to market economy. Delays in implementing economic reform. Low foreign investment levels. Large bureaucracy.

PROFILE
Few economic reforms have been undertaken in Romania compared with other former communist eastern European states. While all have suffered recession in the reform process, Romania's has been the most severe, and there appears to be little prospect of improvement in the near future. Pressure for reform is strongest in the chemical, petrochemical, metal, transport and food industries.

Only a small minority is doing well economically. Real wages have also fallen since the change of regime, and are continuing to do so. Farming began to be privatized in 1989 and by 1994, 80% of farmland was in private hands. It remains severely undermechanized. Agricultural processing is still under state control, and output levels have fallen, notably in meat products.

Romania was the first eastern European country to open its economy to foreign investment, allowing 100% foreign ownership from 1990. The number of joint ventures, 21,000, is the highest in eastern Europe, but most are small-scale. Foreign investment is hindered by bureaucracy and doubts about the country's stability. However, both imports and exports rose in 1993. The EU is now Romania's main trading partner.

ROMANIA : MAJOR BUSINESSES

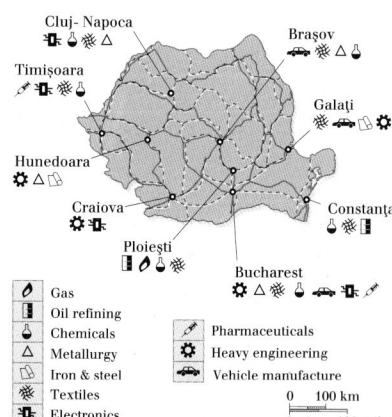

🔥	Gas	
🛢	Oil refining	
⚗	Chemicals	💉 Pharmaceuticals
△	Metallurgy	✿ Heavy engineering
🔩	Iron & steel	🚗 Vehicle manufacture
✳	Textiles	
🔌	Electronics	0 ———— 100 km 0 ———— 100 miles

RESOURCES

 64.3bn kwh (capacity 22.9m kw)

 138,300 b/d (reserves 1,588,754,000)

 16.2m sheep, 14.4m pigs, 6.4m cattle

Coal, salt, iron, natural gas, methane, bauxite, copper, lead, zinc, oil

ELECTRICITY GENERATION

Hydro 17% (11bn kwh)

Thermal 83% (53.3bn kwh)

Nuclear 0%

Other 0%

% of total generation by type

Romania has oil and gas reserves, but production is insufficient to meet domestic demand. Production from onshore fields fell during the 1980s as reserves were depleted and oil imports have risen substantially since 1989. Efforts are being concentrated on developing offshore reserves in the Black Sea and several drilling platforms are now in operation. Romania has opened up exploration and processing to foreign investors, including Middle Eastern and CIS companies.

The electricity supply is outdated and has been insufficient to meet national demand for the last 20 years. The development of a nuclear power industry has been scrapped because of the lack of available funds.

Deposits of other minerals are small and contribute little to export earnings.

ENVIRONMENT

 5% (4% partially protected)

 Rising public awareness, but no funds available

ENVIRONMENTAL TREATIES

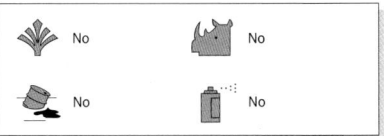

No   No

No   No

The south is the region with the most serious pollution problems. Cement plant and power-station emissions have been linked to respiratory diseases. The incidence of birth defects has risen in the vicinity of the artificial fibre plant at Suceava. Industrial water pollution is also a major problem, and aggravated by insufficient purification facilities. However, nature conservation is currently receiving more attention. The Danube delta has been identified as a site for a biosphere reserve.

MEDIA

 No restrictions on political reporting

PUBLISHING AND BROADCAST MEDIA

There are 36 daily newspapers, including *Curierul National, Ora, Tineretul Liber, România Liberă* and *Adevărul*

1 state-controlled, 1 independent service   1 state-controlled, 1 independent network

Arabsat 1B, Intelsat V1 F1   None

Restrictions were lifted on the press in 1989. The number of publications is now over 1600. The main dailies are *România Liberă* and *Adevărul*, as well as the tabloid *Tineretul Liber*. The broadcast media are still largely under government control, but the debut of the first independent TV station has provided viewers with an alternative news source.

CRIME

 41,300 prisoners   Up 31% in 1990

CRIME RATES

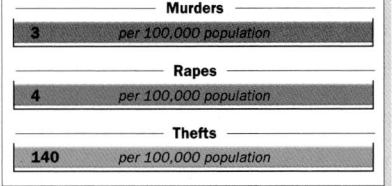

Murders

3   per 100,000 population

Rapes

4   per 100,000 population

Thefts

140   per 100,000 population

The black economy is the primary source of income for a third of the population. Levels of tax evasion are estimated to be among the highest in the world.

EDUCATION

 96%

0   Education spending as % GNP   25

2.1%

THE EDUCATION SYSTEM

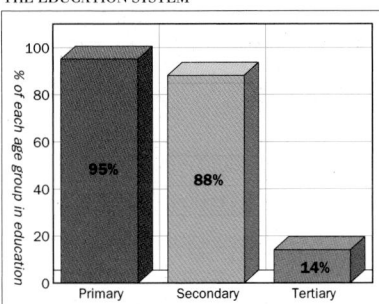

% of each age group in education

95% Primary   88% Secondary   14% Tertiary

Primary and secondary school attendance is 90%, lower than the European average. University enrolment is no longer restricted. The number of students in higher education has risen by nearly a third since 1989, temporarily alleviating high unemployment among young adults.

ROMANIA : LAND USE

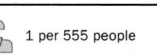

Cropland
Pasture
Forest
Wetlands
Potatoes
Cereals
Sheep

CARPATHIAN MOUNTAINS

Danube

0   100 km

0   100 miles

HEALTH

 1 per 555 people   Heart, cerebrovascular and respiratory diseases, cancers

0   Health spending as % GNP   25

2.5%

Romania's life expectancy is, jointly with Albania's, the lowest in Europe, at 71 years; in the worst polluted parts of Transylvania it is 61 years. Its TB rate is also the highest in Europe.

WEALTH

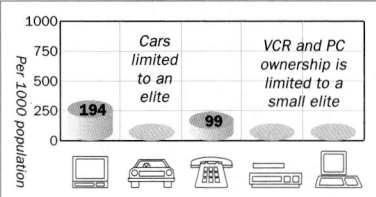 Coal miner, 19,349 lei per month; dentist, 9900 lei per month

CONSUMER GOODS OWNERSHIP

Per 1000 population

194   Cars limited to an elite   99   VCR and PC ownership is limited to a small elite

Wealth distribution has changed little since the fall of the Ceauşescu regime in 1989. The ruling ex-communist clique are still the richest group and determined to maintain their economic as well as political position.

WORLD RANKING

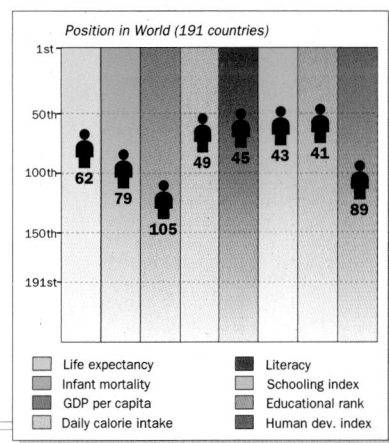

Position in World (191 countries)

1st
50th
100th
150th
191st

62   79   105   49   45   43   41   89

Life expectancy   Literacy
Infant mortality   Schooling index
GDP per capita   Educational rank
Daily calorie intake   Human dev. index

R

RUSSIAN FEDERATION

ASIA

OFFICIAL NAME: Russian Federation **CAPITAL:** Moscow
POPULATION: 148.7 million **CURRENCY:** Rouble **OFFICIAL LANGUAGE:** Russian

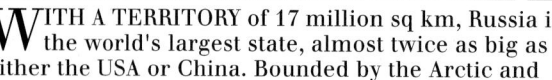

WITH A TERRITORY of 17 million sq km, Russia is the world's largest state, almost twice as big as either the USA or China. Bounded by the Arctic and Pacific Oceans on its northern and eastern coasts, it also has land boundaries with 13 countries. With the formal dissolution of the USSR in 1991, Russia became an independent sovereign state. Within the CIS, it maintains a traditionally dominant role in Central Asia and Eurasia. Ethnic Russians make up 80% of the population, but there are around 150 smaller ethnic groups, many with their own national territories within Russia's borders. The growth of regionalism is a major political issue. The situation is complicated by the fact that many of these territories are rich in key resources such as oil, gas, gold and diamonds.

The Kremlin, Moscow. Rebuilt in 1475 by Ivan the Great, who commissioned architects from Pskov and Italy, it is enclosed by walls 2.5km long and lies on the Moscow River.

CLIMATE

WEATHER CHART

Russia has a cold continental climate, characterized by two, widely divergent main seasons. Spring and autumn are very brief periods of transition between warm summers and freezing winters. The country is open to the influences of the Arctic and Atlantic to the north and west. However, mountains to the south and east prevent any warming effects from the Indian and Pacific Oceans filtering across. Severe winters characterize most regions. Winter temperatures vary suprisingly little from north to south, but fall sharply in eastern regions. The January temperature of –70°C recorded at Verkhoyansk in Siberia is the world record low outside Antarctica.

Housing in Moscow. Living conditions in major cities are cramped, with two families often sharing one small flat.

RUSSIAN FEDERATION

Total Area :
173 750 400 sq. km
(6 592 800 sq. miles)

POPULATION

■	over 5 000 000
▣	over 1 000 000
◉	over 500 000
◎	over 100 000
○	over 50 000
●	over 10 000

LAND HEIGHT

- 3000m/9843ft
- 2000m/6562ft
- 1000m/3281ft
- 500m/1640ft
- 200m/656ft
- Sea Level
- -200m/-656ft

0   500 km

0   500 miles

R

COMMUNICATIONS

Sheremetyevo, Moscow
9.31m passengers

1662 ships
13.98m dwt

THE TRANSPORT NETWORK

854,000 km
(530,066 miles)

None

87,090 km
(54,115 miles)

123,700 km
(76,865 miles)

Russia has a comprehensive transport network. Cities are served by good tram and bus systems and Moscow has one of the most impressive underground systems in the world. In rural areas, car ownership is still low and the population relies on an extensive bus service. However, since 1991, all systems have seen some decline. The railways, which were already declining in the Soviet era, are seriously overburdened and accidents and delays are increasing. About 20% of the railway track should be renewed annually owing to frost and other damage. Shortage of funds means this is no longer done. Roads are also deteriorating, especially in major cities, but inter-urban highways are also affected. Crime is growing on railways – notably the Trans-Siberian – and roads.

Since 1991, many new airlines have been set up as routes are privatized. However, Aeroflot, the previous state monopoly airline, is still the largest. Now called Russian International Airlines on overseas routes, it uses Boeing aircraft on flights from Moscow to London, Paris, Frankfurt, New York and Tokyo.

Standards on international routes are generally high. However, the safety record of internal routes is declining.

R

TOURISM

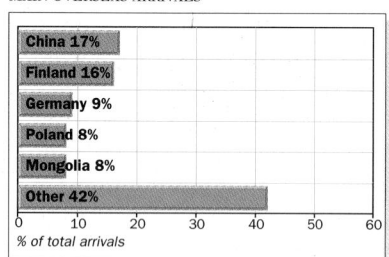

🧳 3m visitors

⬆ The number of visitors is increasing steadily

MAIN OVERSEAS ARRIVALS

China 17%
Finland 16%
Germany 9%
Poland 8%
Mongolia 8%
Other 42%

% of total arrivals

The privatization and break-up of *Intourist*, the previous monopoly tourist agency, has led to a vast expansion of tourism opportunities in Russia; each region is keen to earn hard currency and to attract rich visitors. At the luxury end of the market, trips from St Petersburg to Tashkent are now available on former President Brezhnev's official train. River trips down the Volga and visits to medieval monasteries are increasingly popular. Tourists can also experience life in a Russian forest, or fish for salmon in the Kola peninsula. The defence sector has opened up to tourism and now offers flights in MiG jets, or drives in T-84 Russian tanks.

Moscow and St Petersburg remain favourite destinations. Hotels in both cities tend either to cater for the well-off visitor, or to be of a basic standard. The St Petersburg region is also increasingly explored. Novgorod has many fine churches and the Pskov area is celebrated as the setting for many of Pushkin's works, including *Eugene Onegin* and *Boris Godunov*.

Many parts of Russia remain inaccessible to most tourists. The communist ban on foreigners visiting the Urals has only recently been lifted, but the area still has very few facilities. However, resorts such as Sochi on the Black Sea have experienced a building boom, including the 2500-room *Dagomys* Acapulco-style hotel complex.

PEOPLE

👤 Russian

👥 9 people per km²

THE URBAN/RURAL POPULATION SPLIT

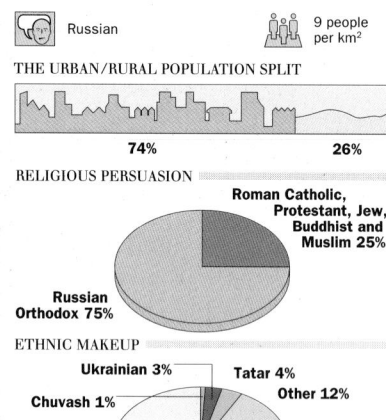

74%   26%

RELIGIOUS PERSUASION

Roman Catholic, Protestant, Jew, Buddhist and Muslim 25%

Russian Orthodox 75%

ETHNIC MAKEUP

Ukrainian 3%   Tatar 4%
Chuvash 1%   Other 12%

Russian 80%

In the former Soviet Union, Russians accounted for just over 50% of the population, but in Russia they are an overwhelming majority. Significant numbers of Russians still live in some of the neighbouring Central Asian republics, notably, in Ukraine and Latvia. However, a rise in nationalism throughout the former USSR has persuaded many central Asian Russians to return to Russia.

Within Russia there has also been some increase in ethnic tension. There are 57 nationalities with their own territories within the federation and 95 nationalities without a territory (although these groups make up only 6% of the population).

Social life in Russia has not changed significantly since the demise of communism. However, with the lifting of censorship, there has been a greater expression of sexuality as well as of political and religious views. Whilst there has been some increase in the availability of pornography and prostitution, this is mostly confined to major urban centres. There has been some revival of both the Russian Orthodox and Muslim faiths. However, Church attendance is still below Western levels. One marked change of which Russians speak is the growing importance attached to money. The mutual support systems of extended friendships are now in decline.

The position of women has changed little since the fall of communism. Many have suffered from the rise in unemployment, but this reflects the demise of many part-time or badly-paid jobs, rather than a gender-motivated change in Russian society. Most Russians' very modest living standards have been maintained and retail sales in Russia are rising. Compared with the West, unemployment remains low at an estimated 5% of the population.

POPULATION AGE BREAKDOWN

% of population by age group

The proportion of Russians over 65 is rising rapidly

1960   1970   1980   1990   2000

POLITICS

 Uncertain

 President Boris N Yeltsin

THE STATE OF THE PARTIES

State *Duma* 450 members

| 21% RC | 16% LDPR | 14% CPRF | 10% APR | 7% Y-B-L | 32% Other |

RC = Russia's Choice LDPR = Liberal Democratic Party of Russia CPRF = Communist Party of the Russian Federation APR = Agrarian Party of Russia Y-B-L = Yavlinsky-Boldyrev-Lukin bloc Other = Party of Russian Unity and Accord, Women of Russia, Democratic Party of Russia

Federal Council 178 members

2 members are elected to represent each of 89 regions and republics

Russia has a democratically-elected parliament under the leadership of an executive president.

MAIN POLITICAL ISSUES

Living standards

Russians are disillusioned at the failure of politicians to improve their living standards. The securities which used to underpin life – long-term employment, guaranteed housing and a basic diet – have been swept away. The decline has hit certain vulnerable groups – particularly the old – rather than the population as a whole. However, there are signs that conditions may be improving. Retail sales in Russia rose consistently in the 18 months to mid-1994.

Crime

Crime has risen alarmingly since the collapse of communism. It is no longer safe to walk the streets of St Petersburg or Moscow after dark. Bureaucratic corruption is now open and rising – officials demand payment for most services. Vladimir Zhirinovsky's promise to crush crime is a major reason behind his recent electoral success, particularly from the newly emerging middle class.

Disaffection with reform

Many Russians are disappointed with President Yeltsin's period in power and

President Yeltsin, backed the reformers who lost heavily in the 1993 elections

Vladimir Zhirinovksi, leader of the ultra-right Liberal Party

R

POLITICS *continued*

his attempts at reform. Mindful of the changing popular mood, parties no longer use the word 'reform' but speak of 'stabilization'.

Russia's loss of Great Power status

Under communism, Russians took a great pride in their country's role in the world. The collapse of the economy and Russia's withdrawal from a global role has badly dented this pride. For many Russians, accepting Western aid and technology is a reminder of Russia's loss of status. The result is that politicians such as Zhirinovsky, who are promising to restore Russia's prestige, are gaining popular support.

PROFILE

The elections of 1993 confirmed a shift in the popular mood in Russia away from the pro-Yeltsin, pro-Western reformers towards the New Right reform policies advocated by Vladimir Zhirinovsky's Liberal Party.

President Yeltsin dissolved the Congress of People's Deputies in October 1993 in order to break a deadlock in parliament which was impeding the government's programme. However, against Yeltsin's expectations, Russia's Choice lost votes whilst Vladimir Zhirinovky's Liberal Party saw a sharp increase in support. Following the elections, the key pro-Yeltsin reformers, Gaidar and Fyodorov, resigned. Yeltsin's loss of support in the *Duma* was clearly illustrated by the decision of Russian MPs to release the men behind the October 1993 attempted coup, in February 1994.

The rise of Zhirinovsky at the elections was significant. His Liberal Party's programme has been likened to that of the National Socialists in 1930s Germany. Zhirinovky is offering a New Right vision of Russia. He is not anti-reform, but proposes radical modernization. Much of his rhetoric attempts to inflame passions against ethnic minorities including the Azeris, Chechens and Armenians. He opposes Yeltsin's pro-Western stance. Zhirinovsky is emerging as a leading contender for the presidential elections of 1996.

Yegor Gaidar, one of the leading reformers in the Russian parliament

Defence Minister Grachev, effectively controls the Russian Army

The other significant change in 1993 was the increasingly aggressive attitude of the regions towards central government. The 89 regions in Russia are resentful that they do not have full control of their resources, while the former republics of the USSR now do. They also resented the Yeltsin-backed restrictions following the October 1993 coup attempt. Yeltsin's recent loss of influence could lead to the revival of a parliamentary debate on how a more federal Russia should work.

The future of Russian politics now depends on the ability of politicians to achieve economic growth. There was sharp change in policy following the elections. In 1994, the *Duma* decided to ignore strict IMF economic guidelines by increasing subsidies to the inefficient state sector. The policy is unlikely to be reversed before the elections of 1996.

WORLD AFFAIRS

During 1992 and 1993 Russia displayed little independent initiative in foreign affairs and allied itself closely to the USA. Its weak economy and a need for regular infusions of hard currency put it in no position to antagonize the Western powers and Japan.

However, since the 1993 elections, Russia has developed a more independent foreign policy. In February 1994, Russia brokered a withdrawal of Serbian heavy weapons around Sarajevo in Bosnia. This move brought Russia back again as a lead player in the Balkans, where Serbia is its traditional ally. Moscow also announced that its security guarantees to North Korea, should the South invade, remained in place. In March 1994, Russia disagreed with the USA on how to get the PLO-Israeli peace talks back on track after the Hebron massacre. This signalled an independent Russian Middle East policy for the first time since independence. During the Gulf War of 1990-91 Russia had been happy to follow the US line in the region. The expense of pursuing a global policy, however, has led to a total Russian withdrawal from Africa and the rest of the developing world.

Russia remains the overwhelmingly dominant partner in the CIS. It regards the successor states of the USSR as the 'near abroad' and maintains troops in most of them. The policy is motivated in part by the need to protect the many Russians living in these states. Many of the CIS regimes are run by ex-communists with close links with Moscow.

St Basil's Cathedral, Moscow. It was built in 1555-1561 to celebrate Ivan the Terrible's capture of the Tatar stronghold of Kazan. The exterior domes were decorated in the 1670s.

AID

 $1bn   Aid is rising

Russia has received about $1 billion from the IMF. However, failure to meet IMF economic criteria will restrict further loans. The EBRD has offered $300 million of credit; loans of up to $30,000 are on offer to small concerns. A similar fund invests in equities of newly-privatized companies.

DEFENCE

$ 29.1bn   Down 27% in 1993

0	Defence spending as % GDP	40
5%		

RUSSIAN ARMED FORCES

25,000 main battle tanks (T-54/-55, T-62, T-64A, T-72, T-80/-M9)	1m personnel	
2 carriers, 219 submarines, 29 cruisers, 24 destroyers, 114 frigates	300,000 personnel	
3600 combat aircraft (MiG 29, MiG 27, MiG 25, MiG-23, Su-27, Su-24)	170,000 personnel	
1204 ICBM, 52SSBN, 1700 APC, 100 ABM		

In 1991, Russia inherited armed forces of 2.7 million men, of which 2.1 million were within its borders. However, it proved incapable of affording such a large army. By 1994, the forces had fallen to 1.2 million. Draft dodging has also increased. In 1992, the army lost 35,000 officers and another 16,000 resigned in the first four months of 1993. Defence budgets have also been reduced. Spending on strategic nuclear forces is now limited to the physical protection of warheads. Early warning and space programmes have also been sharply reduced. The navy has been the worst affected, and Russia's northern and Pacific fleets are inactive and deteriorating fast. No agreement has yet been reached with the Ukraine over who owns the Black Sea fleet. The air force suffers from fuel shortages.

R

REGIONS

MOSCOW

Moscow

Botanical Gardens
Moscow Circus
Planetarium
Bolshoi Theatre
Revolution Square
Red Square
Kremlin
St. Basil's Cathedral
Tolstoy Museum
Tretyakov Art Gallery
Gor'kiy Park

0 ___ 5 km
0 ___ 5 miles

Moskva

☐ Built-up area ☐ Park or open land Major sites

Moscow, Russia's capital, administrative centre and the seat of parliament, has a population of 8,801,500. It is now the most Westernized of Russia's cities. In practice, it functions almost like an independent city state. Market reforms have proceeded faster in Moscow than in any other Russian city and, in the December 1993 local elections, Russia's Choice, the pro-reform party, won a majority in the city *Duma*. Privatization of housing, shops and enterprises has been swift, but this has led to a rapid increase in corruption and crime. According to its forceful mayor, Yury Luzhkov, the city is almost bankrupt as the Russian government has failed to pay Moscow 250 billion roubles in central grants. A new tax of 0.1% of turnover in the Moscow Inter-Bank Currency Exchange has been imposed to raise revenue, much to the annoyance of businessmen.

CHECHNYA

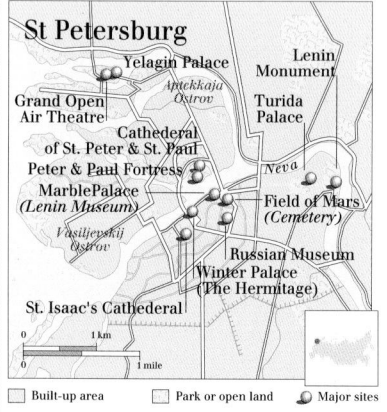

0 ___ 200 km
0 ___ 200 miles
KALMYKIA
Astrakhan'
STAVROPOL'
Stavropol'
CASPIAN SEA
KABARDINO-BALKARIA
CHECHNYA
Nal'chik
Groznyy
Vladikavkaz
Makhachkala
CAUCASUS
NORTH OSSETIA
DAGESTAN
GEORGIA
MOUNTAINS
TURKEY
ARMENIA
AZERBAIJAN

— Gas pipeline ⬦ Natural gas ⬧ Oilfields ⛏ Copper

Located in the southwest of the federation, Chechnya region is dominated by the Chechens, the largest of the North Caucasian nationalities. Half of Chechnya includes fertile plains. It is crossed by two rivers, the Terek and Sunja. To the south, the region is divided from Georgia by the Caucasus. Many Chechens were deported to Central Asia by Stalin following the war. They returned *en masse* in the 1960s. Their strong sense of regionalism is reflected in the fact that 98% use Chechen as their primary language. Chechnya has emphasized its aspiration to nationhood by appointing its own president and government, against Moscow's wishes.

ST PETERSBURG

St Petersburg

Yelagin Palace
Lenin Monument
Aptekkaja Ostrov
Grand Open Air Theatre
Turida Palace
Cathedral of St. Peter & St. Paul
Peter & Paul Fortress
Neva
Marble Palace (Lenin Museum)
Field of Mars (Cemetery)
Vasilievskij Ostrov
Russian Museum
Winter Palace (The Hermitage)
St. Isaac's Cathedral

0 ___ 1 km
0 ___ 1 mile

☐ Built-up area ☐ Park or open land Major sites

Built by Peter the Great in the 18th century to emulate European capitals, St Petersburg is still considered one of the most beautiful cities in Russia. Its magnificent Versailles-influenced architecture includes The Hermitage, home to one of the world's greatest art collections. It was the storming of its Winter Palace in 1917 which marked the start of the Revolution.

The city's various name changes reflect key periods in Russian history. In 1914, anti-German sentiment resulted in the more Slavic name of Petrograd. In 1924, the city became Leningrad, as a tribute to Lenin who died that year. In 1991, the restoration of St Petersburg was a snub to Russia's years under the Communist Party.

St Petersburg has faced greater problems than Moscow during its transition to a market economy. Its industry is dominated by companies supplying the defence sector.

KRASNOYARSK KRAI

Covering 14% of Russian territory, but with a population of only 3.1 million, Krasnoyarsk Krai is seeking greater autonomy from Moscow. The region has huge hydrocarbon and mineral reserves and wishes to establish greater control over the wealth that they produce. Over 60% of Siberia's oil and gas and a quarter of all Russian coal is found in the region. Krasnoyarsk Krai also accounts for most of Russia's nickel exports. Agriculture is a strong sector. With 3.3 million hectares of fertile arable land, the region is a net exporter of farming produce and has 18% of Russia's huge timber reserves.

Over 100 distinct nationalities live in Krasnoyarsk Krai. The majority are Russian. Nearly a third of the population lives in the capital, Krasnoyarsk, which began expanding in the 19th century following the discovery of gold in the region. The arrival of the Trans-Siberian railway and the relocation of industries to the city during the Second World War were a further boost.

In 1989, protests by the Krasnoyarsk residents managed to prevent the construction of the world's largest nuclear waste dump, which threatened to pollute the Yenisey River.

TYUMEN

Located in western Siberia Tyumen *Oblast* (region) has considerable economic potential. In October 1993, the region produced 19.2 million tonnes of oil, bucking the Russian trend for declining oil output. Natural gas output is also increasing.

Deutsche Bank has extended the region a DM1 billion ($650 million) credit package. The region planned to export one million tonnes of oil annually to Germany between 1993 and 1995. The credit was also to be used to develop consumer goods and agribusiness in the region. A further DM1 billion credit to develop the oil and gas industry is being negotiated.

Tyumen also possesses the huge Yamal peninsula gas deposits. Much of its production is already exported to western Europe through pipelines. Another pipeline (via Poland) is currently being built.

As Tyumen realizes its economic potential, so secession will become an increasingly popular prospect for the region. The state government is already in conflict with Moscow over how much of its economic and resource wealth must be delivered to the national treasury.

R

ECONOMICS

$479.5bn   624.03 roubles

SCORE CARD

☐ WORLD GNP RANKING	9th
☐ GNP PER CAPITA	$3218
☐ BALANCE OF PAYMENTS	Large deficit
☐ INFLATION	105%
☐ UNEMPLOYMENT	2.6%

EXPORTS

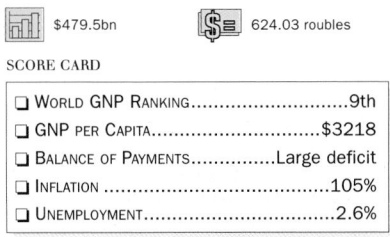

Japan 7%   USA 8%
Other 43%   UK 8%
China 12%
Germany* 22%

IMPORTS

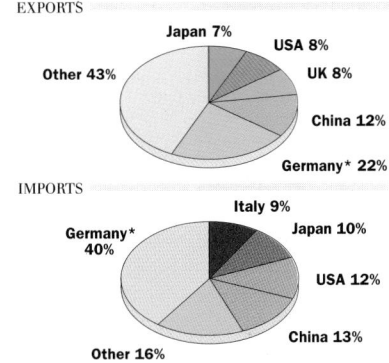

Italy 9%
Germany* 40%   Japan 10%
USA 12%
China 13%
Other 16%

ECONOMIC PERFORMANCE INDICATOR

$32 billion in Western bank accounts and the outflow of capital is estimated at $1 billion monthly. New commercial sector has to meet costs of its own security as police protection is now inadequate.

PROFILE

In 1988, President Gorbachev began a programme of introducing market principles to Russia's command economy. The result by 1991 was a fall in industrial output of 19%. Russian currency reserves were spent in an attempt to cover up the collapse and $10 billion was appropriated from Russian company deposits in the state bank. Foreign currency reserves fell to $21 million. By the end of 1991, the formal economy had almost collapsed and some estimates suggested output was down by 40%.

The next crop of reformers, backed by Yeltsin and led by Gaidar, liberalized prices. Massive inflation was the result, but goods and food were once again readily available. However, Russia's huge loss-making industrial concerns were not broken up. Many continue to supply goods for which there is little demand. The largest item of government spending remains the 10% of GDP spent on subsidies – a larger amount than on education and defence put together.

STRENGTHS

Huge natural resources; in particular hydrocarbons, precious metals, fuel, timber. Enormous engineering and scientific base. Some dynamic small joint-stock enterprises. Privatization is proceeding fast; by July 1994, it will embrace 60% of large-scale industry and agriculture. Huge potential for oil and natural gas.

WEAKNESSES

Many company directors are asset-stripping privatized companies. Most are adjusting to a market economy unwillingly. Many of the skills developed under communism are not relevant in a competitive economy. Lack of adequate legal infrastructure making establishing property rights and trading transactions difficult. Russian companies have an estimated

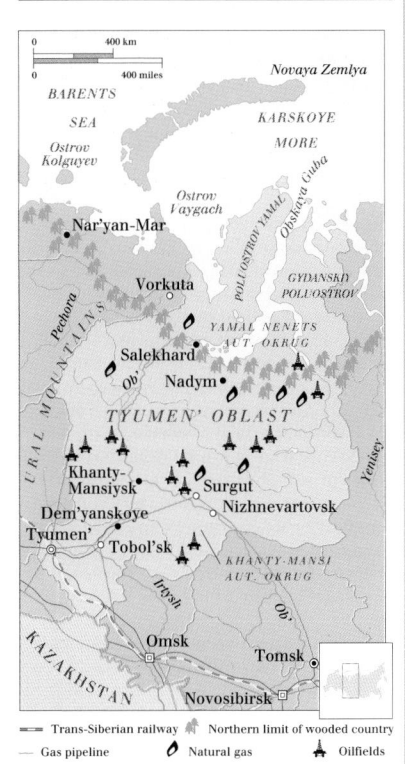

RUSSIAN FEDERATION : MAJOR BUSINESSES

R

457

CHRONOLOGY

The first Russian state (Rus) was in present day Ukraine. Occupation by the Tatars (1240–1480) left a mark on the Russian language and character. From the 17th century, rule was under the Romanovs.

- ❑ **1904–1905** Russian war against Japan; ends in defeat for Russia.
- ❑ **1905** Revolution.
- ❑ **1909–1914** Rapid expansion of economy.
- ❑ **1914** Enters First World War against Germany.
- ❑ **1917** February Revolution; abdication of Nicholas II. October Revolution; Bolsheviks take over with Lenin as leader.
- ❑ **1918** July, Nicholas II and family murdered.
- ❑ **1918–1920** Civil war.
- ❑ **1921** New Economic Policy; retreat from socialism.
- ❑ **1922** USSR established.
- ❑ **1924** Lenin dies. Struggle for leadership, eventually won by Stalin, follows.
- ❑ **1928** First Five-Year Plan begins; forced industrialization and collectivization.
- ❑ **1929** Trotsky is first banished to Kazakhstan, then deported to Turkey.
- ❑ **1936–1938** Show trials and campaigns against actual and suspect members of opposition. Millions sent to *gulags* in Siberia and elsewhere. Forced to do labour; purges widespread.
- ❑ **1939** Hitler-Stalin pact gives USSR Baltic states, eastern Poland and Bessarabia.
- ❑ **1941** Germany attacks USSR. Stalin unprepared. December, Battle of Moscow is first German defeat.
- ❑ **1943** February, great Soviet victory at Stalingrad.
- ❑ **1944–1945** Soviet offensive penetrates Balkans.
- ❑ **1945** January, Yalta agreement recognizes eastern and southeastern Europe as Soviet zone of influence; four power occupation of Germany. August, Potsdam agreement; intends Germany to be ruled as whole, but it quickly breaks up into east and west. USSR dominant European power.
- ❑ **1947** Cold War begins; Stalin on defensive and fears ideological penetration of Western and capitalist values.
- ❑ **1953** Stalin dies.
- ❑ **1956** Hungarian uprising against Soviet occupation. Moscow crushes uprising and reinstates Imre Nagy as Prime Minister. Krushchev's 'secret speech' attacking Stalin at Party congress. ▷

R

RESOURCES

 1015bn kwh (capacity 213m kw)

 8m b/d

 62.8m sheep and goats, 59.8m cattle, 39.2m pigs

 Coal, natural gas, gold, oil, diamonds

ELECTRICITY GENERATION

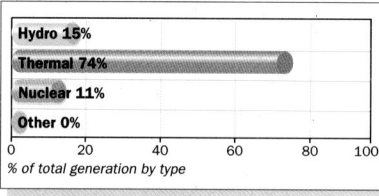

Hydro 15%
Thermal 74%
Nuclear 11%
Other 0%

0   20   40   60   80   100
% of total generation by type

RUSSIAN FEDERATION : LAND USE

- Cropland
- Forest
- Pasture
- Wetlands
- Tundra
- High mountain regions
- 🐄 Cattle
- 🌾 Cereals
- 🥔 Potatoes

URAL MOUNTAINS · SREDNE SIBIRSKOYE PLOSKOGOR'YE · Ob'

0   1000 km
0   1000 miles

ENVIRONMENT

 1% (of USSR)

 Few environmental protection laws are being passed

ENVIRONMENTAL TREATIES

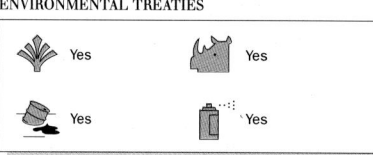

Yes   Yes
Yes   Yes

Awareness of Russia's environmental problems has risen sharply since the demise of communism. However, the resources, political will and know-how to tackle them are still lacking. While Russia now has an active green movement, it did not gain significant support at the 1993 general elections.

Each region has its own particular problems. The north suffers from the effects of nuclear dumping in the Barents Sea. Over 17,000 contaminated containers were dumped there by the Russian navy, including the old nuclear reactor from the icebreaker *Lenin*. Thousands of tons of chemical weapons have been dumped in the Baltic, although their exact location has not been revealed. The River Volga in Central Russia is so polluted and diverted by dam-building that many fish species are now extinct. The worst problems are probably in the Urals and the cities of European Russia. Chemical and heavy industrial plants still lack adequate protection. Most do not treat their effluents at all.

Russia is a leading world producer of oil, natural gas and electricity, among other resources. Confirmed reserves make Russia the world's leading country in terms of hydrocarbons, gold, precious metals, diamonds and timber.

Unlike some of the other republics of the ex-USSR, Russia has not opened its resources up to foreign concerns. It does not wish to lose any control to Western multinationals. They are consequently underexploited owing to a lack of investment and technology. Most of the major resources are also located in national territories such as Tatarstan and Sakha Yakutia in Siberia. The regions' desire for greater autonomy has turned the ownership of these resources into a delicate political issue.

MEDIA

 No political restrictions, though temporary censorship may occur

PUBLISHING AND BROADCAST MEDIA

The main newspapers are *Izvestiya, Rossiiskaya Gazeta, Komsomolskaya Pravda, Trud, Den, Nezavisimaya Gazeta*

2 state-owned, 1 independent network

3 state-owned networks

Arabsat 1C, Intelsat V F8

Cable is available in Moscow

Russians have traditionally been avid newspaper readers. This is reflected in the number of titles. In 1990, there were 4808 daily newspapers with a total circulation of 166 million copies compared to a population of 149 million. Since then, however, the number of titles has fallen dramatically, largely due to a rise in the cost of paper. The old state daily, *Pravda*, is barely surviving and is partly dependent on subsidies from the Greek Communist Party. After the October 1993 right-wing coup attempt many newspapers were banned. Most are now reappearing although often under new names. The regional and local press is also growing in importance. State TV is now the most important news source and less biased than under communism. It remains under the control of supporters of President Yeltsin. Many Russians now have satellite dishes and tune in to CNN and other Western channels.

CHRONOLOGY *continued*

- ❑ **1957** Krushchev consolidates power. Sputnik launched.
- ❑ **1961** April, Yuri Gagarin first man in space.
- ❑ **1962** October, Cuban Missile Crisis between USSR and USA brings world close to nuclear war.
- ❑ **1964** Krushchev ousted in coup, replaced by Leonid Brezhnev.
- ❑ **1975** Helsinki Final Act; confirms European frontiers as at end of Second World War. Soviets agree to human rights as legitimate concern of international community.
- ❑ **1979** Invades Afghanistan. Beginning of new Cold War.
- ❑ **1982** Brezhnev dies. Yuri Andropov takes over.
- ❑ **1984** Andropov dies and is succeeded by Chernenko.
- ❑ **1985** Chernenko dies. Gorbachev in power. Beginning of *perestroika*, era of new political thinking and the break-up of the USSR. First of summits with US President Reagan in Geneva, which lead to arms reduction treaties and détente between the superpowers. Nationality conflicts surface.
- ❑ **1988** Law of State Enterprises in operation. More power for enterprises; this leads to greater inflation and dislocation of economy.
- ❑ **1990** Gorbachev becomes president of the Soviet Union. First partly freely elected parliament (Supreme Soviet) meets.
- ❑ **1991** Boris Yeltsin elected president of Russia. August, attempted coup by right-wing elements against Gorbachev succesfully opposed by Yeltsin and Muscovites. CIS established; demise of USSR.
- ❑ **1992** Beginning of economic shock therapy; rapid price rises.
- ❑ **1993** September, Yeltsin decrees dissolution of Supreme Soviet. October, Yeltsin uses force to disband parliament. December, elections return conservative, anti-reform State *Duma*.

Tundra in Russia's far east. *Russia has some of the largest uninhabited tracts of land in the world.*

CRIME

 Russia does not publish prison figures
⬆ Rising dramatically

CRIME RATES

Rates for all types of crime are rising dramatically

Crime is now a formidable problem in Russia, and the police cannot keep up with its rise. Reported murders in the first nine months of 1993 rose to 33,798, up 47% on the previous year.

Most muders are the result of inter-gang violence. Muggings in the larger cities are sharply up. Corruption and mafia-style activity are also widespread. Protection rackets, prostitution, smuggling operations and drugs are the Russian mafia's sources of profit. Russian crime bosses are beginning to fund similar activities in Western Europe, using banks as fronts. In outlying areas, especially Siberia, Westerners are increasingly the victims of violent car theft. The rise in crime has become a major issue for most Russians. Parties such as Zhirinovsky's LDPR, who are promising to stamp crime out, are gaining popular support.

EDUCATION

 99%

0   *Education spending as % GNP*   25
7.9%

THE EDUCATION SYSTEM

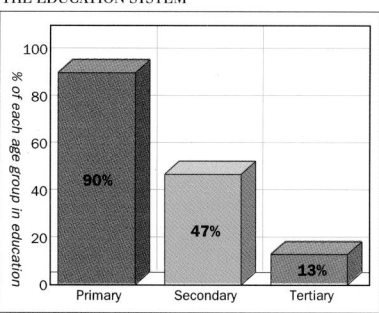

Russian education still follows the Soviet model. While there has been some attempt at historical revisionism, this has been hampered by a lack of funds to pay for new books. Many private lycées have sprung up – such as those run by the Orthodox Church – often offering courses in English and German. German, in particular, has made a come-back in Moscow as a key commercial language. Higher education is now underfunded. Prestigious institutions such as the Academy of Sciences have cut staff and research. Most academics now have to rely on extra-mural earnings.

HEALTH

 1 per 213 people
Heart, respiratory and cerebrovasculas diseases, cancers

0   *Health spending as % GNP*   25
Minimal health spending

Until 1991, state enterprises provided considerable health care for their employees. This is now disappearing as companies are privatized and seek to cut costs. Local authorities have few resources to take over these responsibilities. Bribing medical staff to obtain treatment is commonplace and there is a lack of pharmaceutical products and drugs. Hospital patients are normally fed by their relatives.

WEALTH

 It is estimated that 35% of the population now live below the poverty line

CONSUMER GOODS OWNERSHIP

Wealth disparities in Russia are increasing rapidly. A small minority of the population has made huge profits from marketization. About 10% are thought to have benefited in some way. There is a growing number of dollar millionaires who flaunt their wealth, especially in Moscow. Russia is now the biggest buyer of Rolls Royce cars, while BMWs, Mercedes and Volvos are relatively common in Moscow and St Petersburg. A considerable amount of wealth is now deposited abroad, however. There are now thousands of Russian offshore bank accounts; Northern Cyprus is a favourite location. The bosses of organized crime are Russian society's wealthiest group.

WORLD RANKING

R

RWANDA

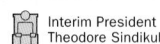

OFFICIAL NAME: Republic of Rwanda   **CAPITAL:** Kigali
POPULATION: 7.5 million   **CURRENCY:** Rwanda franc   **OFFICIAL LANGUAGES:** French, Kinyarwanda

LYING JUST SOUTH OF THE EQUATOR in east-central Africa, land-locked Rwanda is 1600 km from the nearest port. Its hillsides are covered in small family farms, reflecting Rwanda's position as Africa's most densely populated country. Since independence in 1962, ethnic tensions have dominated politics. In 1994, the death of the president in a plane crash led to a breakout of ethnic violence. Over 200,000 Rwandans died in the clashes.

CLIMATE

WEATHER CHART

Rwanda's climate is tropical, tempered by altitude. Two wet seasons allow for two harvests each year.

COMMUNICATIONS

 Grégoire Kayibanda, Kigali
52,000 passengers   Has no fleet

THE TRANSPORT NETWORK

13,173 km (8185 miles)		None
None		Lake Kivu

The road network is well developed. The international airport near Kigali was completed in 1986.

TOURISM

 52,000 visitors   Down 30% in 1991

MAIN OVERSEAS ARRIVALS

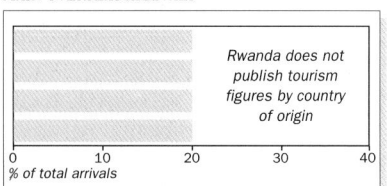

Rwanda does not publish tourism figures by country of origin

0 10 20 30 40
% of total arrivals

Rwanda is mainly a destination for wealthy wildlife enthusiasts. Top attractions are the mountain gorillas and Lake Kivu. The closure of some national parks because of security problems has hit visitor numbers.

PEOPLE

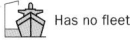 Kinyarwanda, French, Kiswahili   285 people per km²

THE URBAN/RURAL POPULATION SPLIT

8%   92%

ETHNIC MAKEUP

Twa pygmy 1%   Tutsi 14%

Hutu 85%

The Hutu and Tutsi are the main groups; the Twa pygmies, the original inhabitants, have been marginalized. For over 500 years, the cattle-owning Tutsi were politically dominant, oppressing the majority land-owning Hutu. In 1959, violent revolt led to a reversal of the roles. The two groups have since been waging a spasmodic war. Up to a third of the Tutsi are in exile and thousands were massacred in the 1960s and 1970s. Traditional family and clan structures are strong and give women fewer rights than men in areas such as property.

POLITICS

Uncertain   Interim President Theodore Sindikubgabo

THE STATE OF THE PARTIES

Transitional Parliament 19 members

Multiparty elections are scheduled to take place in 1995. The Hutu-dominated MRNDD (National Republican Movement for Development and Democracy) is controlling the transitional process

With the introduction of a new constitution in 1991, Rwanda attempted to come to terms with its ethnic divisions by moving towards a multiparty system. The changes were precipitated in 1990 by the invasion of a rebel army of exiled Tutsi, the FPR. There was also considerable international pressure on the ruling party, the Hutu-dominated MRNDD, to compromise with the Tutsi.

In 1992, a transitional coalition of the MRNDD and internal opposition parties was formed to negotiate peace with the FPR, before organizing elections. The extension of the coalition's mandate in 1993 pushed back the elections to 1995. However, all arrangements were thrown into turmoil by the death of the president in a plane crash. The FPR army mounted an attack to take control of the capital from government forces. Over 200,000 died in the conflict.

RWANDA

Total Area : 26 340 sq. km
(10 170 sq. miles)

POPULATION

over 100 000
over 10 000
under 10 000

LAND HEIGHT

3000m/9843ft
2000m/6562ft
1000m/3281ft

0   40 km
0   40 miles

WORLD AFFAIRS

 OAU | ECA | GATT | ACP | AfDB

The break-out of inter-ethnic violence in 1994 led to the collapse of the peace process. Hundreds of thousands fled into neighbouring Tanzania, creating a refugee crisis. Belgium sent forces to evacuate European nationals.

AID

 $351m (receipts)   Up 20% in 1991

The break-out of ethnic violence led to the suspension of all formal aid payments. Several UN aid workers were slaughtered by troops. Humanitarian agencies such as *Médécins sans Frontières* are active in the country.

DEFENCE

 $36.63m   Defence spending is rising

The army underpinned MRNDD power and is still under the latter's control. After the 1990 Tutsi invasion, it was expanded from 5000 to 35,000 troops.

ECONOMICS

$1.6bn   144.4 Rwanda francs

SCORE CARD

- ❑ WORLD GNP RANKING.........................144th
- ❑ GNP PER CAPITA $213
- ❑ BALANCE OF PAYMENTS..................$–34.1m
- ❑ INFLATION 9.5%
- ❑ UNEMPLOYMENT .....Few have formal employment

STRENGTHS
Currently none. Assuming peace, Rwanda produces coffee. Possible oil and gas reserves.

WEAKNESSES
Ethnic violence has suspended all economic activity. The 1610 km journey to both Kenyan and Tanzanian ports imposes high transport costs. Rwanda has few resources.

EXPORTS

UK 7%
Other 45%
Netherlands 11%
Germany* 18%
Belgium and Luxembourg 19%

IMPORTS

Germany* 8%
Other 46%
Japan 12%
Kenya 15%
Belgium and Luxembourg 19%

Terraced hillside. *As Rwanda is the most densely populated country in Africa, virtually all land suitable for agriculture is cultivated.*

RESOURCES

 176m kwh (capacity 60,000 kw)

 Not an oil producer and has no refineries

630,000 cattle, 367,000 sheep, 100,000 pigs

Tin, tungsten, gold, columbo-tantalite, beryl, methane

The Lake Kivu gas deposits are being explored with Zaire. The power grid is being expanded; only 20% of urban dwellers currently have electricity.

ENVIRONMENT

 12%

 Return of refugees will increase pressure on land

Population pressure, environmentally the biggest threat, is causing major problems, including soil erosion and forest loss. Tourism underpins the preservation of the mountain gorilla.

MEDIA

 There have been many instances of opposition journalists being harassed and arrested

PUBLISHING AND BROADCAST MEDIA

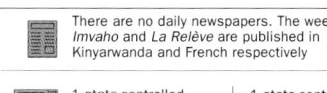

There are no daily newspapers. The weekly *Imvaho* and *La Relève* are published in Kinyarwanda and French respectively

1 state-controlled service   1 state-controlled service

The press in Rwanda operates in fear of reprisals by MRNDD and FPR agents. Journalists can 'disappear'.

CRIME

 Rwanda does not publish prison figures

 Down 33% in 1990.

Previously benefiting from a low crime rate, an orgy of inter-ethnic violence broke out in 1994 which left over 200,000 dead. Hundreds of thousands survived by fleeing the country.

EDUCATION

 50%

Schools are administered by the state and Christian missions. Primary education is officially compulsory, but only 60% of children attend; just 6% go on to secondary schooling.

CHRONOLOGY

The Hutu majority began to arrive in the 14th century; the warrior Tutsi in the 15th. From 1890, German and then Belgian colonizers acted to reinforce Tutsi dominance.

- ❑ **1962** Independence under Hutu-led government.
- ❑ **1960s** Tutsi revolt; massacres by Hutu; thousands of Tutsi in exile.
- ❑ **1973** Army head Gen Habyarimana takes power in bloodless coup.
- ❑ **1975** One-party state under MRNDD.
- ❑ **1990** Invasion by Tutsi FPR; MRNDD forced to move towards democracy.
- ❑ **1992–1993** Transitional coalition to negotiate peace. Elections planned.
- ❑ **1994** President Habyarimana dies in plane crash. Outbreak of ethnic violence between Tutsi and Hutu.

HEALTH

 1 per 33,170 people

 Malaria, measles, diarrheal diseases

A network of 34 hospitals and 188 health centres means the majority have easy access to care, but as treatment is rarely free, many cannot afford to use it.

WEALTH

 Most Rwandans live a subsistence existence

CONSUMER GOODS OWNERSHIP

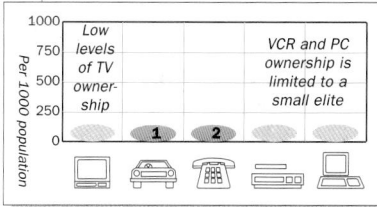

Low levels of TV ownership

VCR and PC ownership is limited to a small elite

Per 1000 population

Wealth is limited to the political elite. Most Rwandans are poor farmers; Twa pygmies and refugees are poorer still.

WORLD RANKING

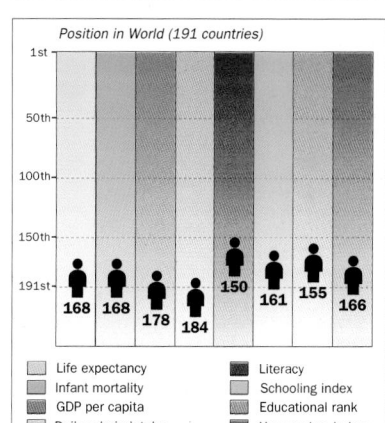

Position in World (191 countries)

168 | 168 | 178 | 184 | 150 | 161 | 155 | 166

- Life expectancy
- Infant mortality
- GDP per capita
- Daily calorie intake
- Literacy
- Schooling index
- Educational rank
- Human dev. index

R

St Kitts & Nevis

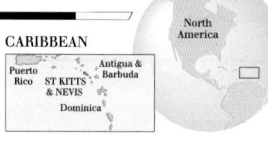

Official Name: Federation of Saint Christopher and Nevis   **Capital:** Basseterre
Population: 44,000   **Currency:** East Caribbean dollar   **Official Language:** English

ONE OF THE CARIBBEAN'S most popular tourist destinations, St Kitts and Nevis, a former British colony, lies at the northern end of the Leeward Islands chain. St Kitts is of volcanic origin; Mount Liamuiga, a dormant volcano with a crater 227 m deep, is the highest point on the island. Nevis is separated from St Kitts by a 3 km-wide channel and is the lusher but less developed of the two islands. In the 18th century its renowned hot and cold springs gave Nevis a reputation as 'the Spa of the Caribbean'.

PEOPLE

English, English Creole   153 people per km²

THE URBAN/RURAL POPULATION SPLIT

41%   59%

RELIGIOUS PERSUASION

Roman Catholic 7%
Moravian 9%
Anglican 33%
Other 22%
Methodist 29%

Most of the population is descended from Africans brought over in the 17th century; intermarriage has blurred other racial lines. There is opposition to government plans to grant citizenship to 3000 Hong Kong business executives in exchange for investment in the islands.

CLIMATE

WEATHER CHART

A combination of high temperatures, trade breezes, and moderate rainfall in summer account for St Kitts' typically Caribbean climate.

COMMUNICATIONS

 Golden Rock, Basseterre   1 ship 600 dwt

THE TRANSPORT NETWORK

 300 km (186 miles)   None

 58 km (36 miles)   None

Most roads on the islands skirt the coast, with just a few crossing through the interior. The government is planning to build a road to the isolated southern tip of St Kitts. The airport on St Kitts takes large jets; Nevis airport accepts only small propeller aircraft. Regular ferries connect both islands.

TOURISM

 75,789 visitors   Up 5% in 1990

MAIN OVERSEAS ARRIVALS

USA 39%
Canada 16%
US Virgin Islands 9%
Other 36%

0   10   20   30   40
% of total arrivals

Over the past 20 years, St Kitts has targeted the mass US tourist market. With improvements in communications, in particular plans to open up the southern peninsula of St Kitts island, the industry should continue to grow. Most visitors come for the beaches, the sun and the Caribbean mood, although in recent years safaris to see local wildlife and mineral springs have operated from isolated hotels in the hills. On St Kitts, the old Brimstone Hill fortress has been converted into a museum, as has the Nevis birthplace of Alexander Hamilton, one of the architects of the US constitution.

POLITICS

 1999   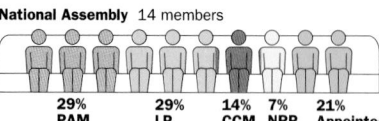 HM Queen Elizabeth II

THE STATE OF THE PARTIES

National Assembly   14 members

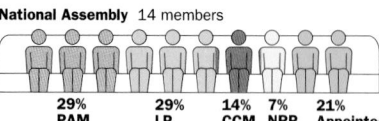

29% PAM   29% LP   14% CCM   7% NRP   21% Appointed

PAM = People's Action Movement   **LP** = Labour Party
NRP = Nevis Reformation Party   **CCM** = Concerned Citizens' Movement

Based on the British system, political funds are provided by urban professionals (for the PAM) and, unusually for the Caribbean, trade unions (for the LP). Political differences are those of style rather than policy, except for occasional calls for greater autonomy from the NRP.

St Kitts & Nevis

Total Area : 360 sq. km (139 sq. miles)

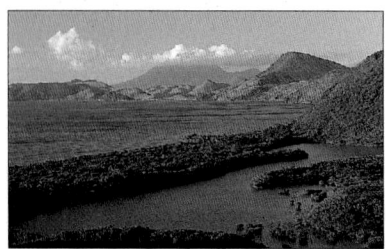

The southeastern peninsula of St Kitts, looking across to Nevis in the background, on a typical December evening.

LAND HEIGHT

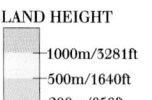

1000m/3281ft
500m/1640ft
200m/656ft
Sea Level

POPULATION

● over 10 000
• under 10 000

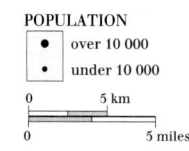

N

0   5 km
0   5 miles

Dieppe Bay Town
Parson's Ground
St. Paul's   Sadlers
Newton Ground   Tabernacle
Mt Liamuiga 1156m   Mansion
Molineux   Lodge
Sandy Point Town   Phillips   Cayon
Brimstone Hill   St Kitts
Middle Island   Parry's
Old Town Road   Upper Conaree
St Peter's   Golden Rock Airport
Challengers   Stoddart's
Boyd's   Kittitian Village
BASSETERRE

ATLANTIC OCEAN
CARIBBEAN SEA

Great Salt Pond
The Narrows
Newcastle
Cotton Ground
Nevis
Charlestown   Nevis Peak 985m
Bath   Fig Tree   Zion   Market Shop
Brown Hill

S

WORLD AFFAIRS

Maintaining preferential access to EU and US markets for its sugar is the main concern. St Kitts is not interested in the political union proposed by its Windward Islands neighbours.

AID

 $7m (receipts)   Up 17% in 1991

Aid, mostly from the USA, the EU and the UK, is very important, particularly project aid – such as the funding of the road to St Kitts' southern peninsula. Donors are also providing support for economic diversification.

DEFENCE

 Army duties under-taken by Volunteer Defence Force   Not applicable

An army existed for six years before it was disbanded to cut government expenditure in 1981. A small paramilitary unit remains within the police; it made a token appearance with US forces during the 1983 invasion of Grenada.

ECONOMICS

 $185m   2.70 East Caribbean dollars

SCORE CARD

- ❑ WORLD GNP RANKING........................180th
- ❑ GNP PER CAPITA $4200
- ❑ BALANCE OF PAYMENTS...................$–49.7m
- ❑ INFLATION 6.4%
- ❑ UNEMPLOYMENT....................................8%

STRENGTHS
Sugar industry, currently UK-managed, with preferential access to US and EU markets. Tourism, the source of recent growth, is set to expand further.

WEAKNESSES
Dependence on sugar cane industry, which is sensitive to fluctuating world market prices.

EXPORTS
IMPORTS

RESOURCES

 37m kwh (capacity 15,000 kw)
15,000 sheep, 5000 cattle, 4000 pigs
Not an oil producer and has no refineries
None

St Kitts has no strategic resources. Almost all energy has to be imported, mainly oil from Venezuela and Mexico. Sugar output is insignificant in world terms. New crops, such as Sea Island cotton on Nevis, are being introduced. Offshore fishing has potential.

ENVIRONMENT

 10%   New laws protecting monkeys

Hurricanes are the greatest environmental threat. The islands caught only the tail end of Hurricane Hugo in 1989, but it caused severe damage to the sugar crop and power supplies. As in the rest of the Caribbean, benefits from encouraging tourism must be set against potential ecological damage. The government has shown sensitivity, with strict preservation orders on the remaining rainforest and on indigenous monkeys.

MEDIA

 No political restrictions

PUBLISHING AND BROADCAST MEDIA

There are no daily newspapers. The two main weekly newspapers are *The Democrat* and the *Labour Spokesman*
1 state-owned station
1 state-owned, 2 independent stations

The media has little political independence, but this is not due to government interference. The funding for the two weekly newspapers is provided by the political parties.

CRIME

 St Kitts does not publish prison figures   Down 7% in 1988

The judicial system is based on British common law. The police force is trained by officers from London's Scotland Yard. Rape, burglary and armed robbery are the main concerns; murder is rare. In 1993, there were allegations that the political parties were arming their activists.

EDUCATION

 82%

Education is based on the old British 11-plus selective system and is mostly state-run. Students attend the regional University of the West Indies, or go on to colleges in the USA and UK.

CHRONOLOGY

A British colony since 1783 and part of the Leeward Islands Federation until 1956, St Kitts and Nevis achieved independence in 1983.

- ❑ **1932** St Kitts-Nevis-Anguilla Labour Party formed to campaign for independence.
- ❑ **1967** Internal self-government.
- ❑ **1980** Anguilla formally separates from St Kitts & Nevis.
- ❑ **1983** Independence from UK.
- ❑ **1989** Hurricane Hugo destroys sugar crop.

HEALTH

 1 per 1593 people   Heart and respiratory diseases, cancers

The government-run health service now provides rudimentary care on both St Kitts and Nevis. Doctors and other medical specialists train at the University of the West Indies. Some of the better-off use private doctors and health clinics for treatment.

WEALTH

 There is no great disparity of wealth on the islands, although urban professionals enjoy a higher standard of living than rural cane farmers

CONSUMER GOODS OWNERSHIP

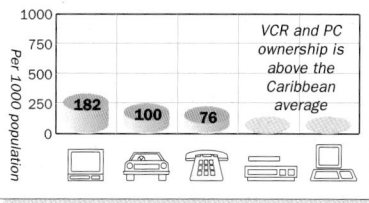
VCR and PC ownership is above the Caribbean average
182 100 76

Native professionals and civil servants have replaced expatriates over the past 20 years. They are now the best-paid group, but there are no great extremes of income. Status symbols include Japanese cars and satellite dishes.

WORLD RANKING

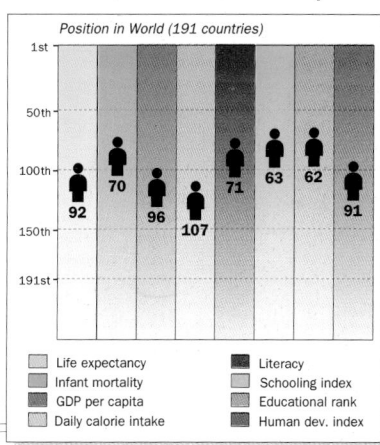
Position in World (191 countries)
92 70 96 107 71 63 62 91
Life expectancy / Infant mortality / GDP per capita / Daily calorie intake / Literacy / Schooling index / Educational rank / Human dev. index

S

ST LUCIA

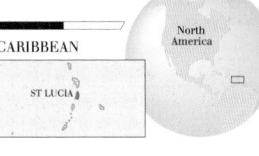
CARIBBEAN
ST LUCIA
North America

OFFICIAL NAME: Saint Lucia   **CAPITAL:** Castries
POPULATION: 153,000   **CURRENCY:** East Caribbean dollar   **OFFICIAL LANGUAGE:** English

ST LUCIA IS ONE OF THE MOST BEAUTIFUL islands of the Windward group of the Antilles. The twin Pitons, south of Soufrière, are one of the most striking natural features in the Caribbean. Ruled by the French and British at different times in its past, St Lucia retains the character of both. A multiparty democracy, it lives by banana growing and beach and cruise-ship tourism. Its unspoilt rainforest make it a popular eco-tourist destination.

CLIMATE

WEATHER CHART

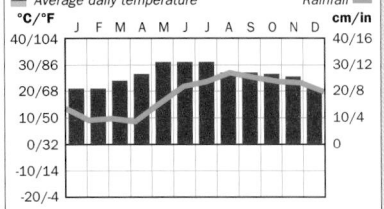

The dry season, from January to April, brings intense heat to sheltered parts of St Lucia. During the rainy season, short warm showers can be expected daily. Rainfall is highest in the mountains.

COMMUNICATIONS

 Hewanorra Intl, Vieux Fort
245,000 passengers

 2 ships
900 dwt

THE TRANSPORT NETWORK

970 km (603 miles)   None
None   None

There are no railways and roads are confined to the west and southeast coasts, making the mountainous interior inaccessible except on foot or mule. The main airport (Hewanorra International) accepts jumbo jets.

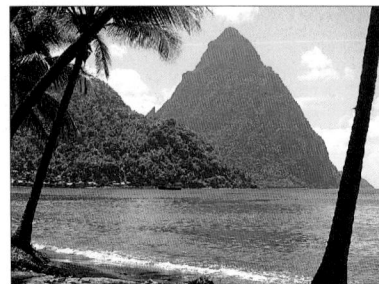

One of the twin Pitons south of Soufrière, marking the entrance to the Jalousie Plantation harbour.

TOURISM

 146,578 visitors   Up 5% in 1990

MAIN OVERSEAS ARRIVALS

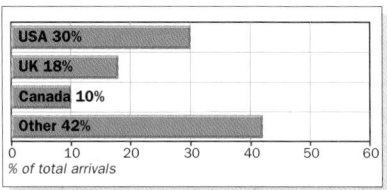

USA 30%
UK 18%
Canada 10%
Other 42%
% of total arrivals

Tropical beaches and typical Caribbean towns, such as Soufrière, have long made St Lucia a favourite Caribbean tourist destination. Eco-tourism into the island's rainforest and volcanic interior is growing, and with it local resistance to the over-development of the island.

PEOPLE

 English, French Creole   244 people per km²

THE URBAN/RURAL POPULATION SPLIT

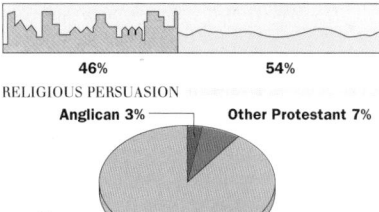

46%   54%

RELIGIOUS PERSUASION

Anglican 3%   Other Protestant 7%
Roman Catholic 90%

St Lucia now has a rich, tension-free racial mix of descendants of Africans, Carib Indians and European settlers. Despite relaxed attitudes, family life is still important to most St Lucians, many of whom are practising Roman Catholics. The nuclear family is the norm, but in rural districts, where women run many of the farms, absentee fathers are fairly common. In recent years, women have had greater access to university education and are moving into the legal, medical and financial professions.

POLITICS

1997   HM Queen Elizabeth II

THE STATE OF THE PARTIES

House of Assembly 17 members

65% UWP   35% SLLP

UWP = United Workers' Party   **SLLP** = St Lucia Labour Party

Senate 11 members

11 members appointed by the governor-general, including 6 appointed with the advice of the prime minister and 3 with the advice of the leader of the opposition

Politics has been dominated for the past decade by two brothers-in-law: John Compton, head of the UWP, and Julian Hunte, leader of the SLLP. The UWP favours the planned Windward Islands' federation. The SLLP opposes federation on the grounds that Compton will use it to retain power.

WORLD AFFAIRS

 Comm   Caricom   Lomé   ACP   CDB

St Lucia has traditionally backed US policy against left-wing regimes in the Caribbean, and openly supported the US invasion of Grenada in 1983. Relations with Washington have recently soured, however, following US pressure on the EU to remove its preferential treatment of bananas from the Caribbean. St Lucia cannot compete with cheaper fruit from South America. The other main issue is a proposed Windward Islands Federation with Dominica, Grenada and St Vincent, which will require ratification.

AID

 $20m (receipts)   Up 122% in 1991

The US, the EU, and, in particular, the UK are the main donors. Most aid is in the form of project loans.

DEFENCE

 Police force has special service unit for defence purposes   Not applicable

A police force of 500 is supported by a small paramilitary unit. Training is provided by the USA and the UK.

ST LUCIA
Total Area : 620 sq. km (239 sq. miles)

POPULATION
- ● over 10 000
- • under 10 000

LAND HEIGHT
- 500m/1640ft
- 200m/656ft
- Sea Level

RESOURCES

104m kwh (capacity 22,000 kw)

16,000 sheep, 13,000 cattle, 12,000 pigs

Not an oil producer and has no refineries

None

St Lucia has no mineral resources and imports most of its energy. Plans exist to develop geothermal energy from the hot springs in the volcanic interior.

ENVIRONMENT

2% partially protected

Decision to allow development on Jalousie Plantation

St Lucians are proud of their island and environmental questions arouse fierce debate. In recent years, the greatest controversy has surrounded the decision to allow a luxury hotel development on the ecologically important Jalousie Plantation, which encompasses the extraordinary twin Pitons and includes an important Amerindian archaeological site. The issue illustrates a key problem in St Lucia, where business pressures to develop tourism can outweigh vital environmental concerns. One notable conservation success has been the St Lucian parrot. In 1978, there were 150 birds; strict laws against the trade in parrots ensured that by 1992 numbers had risen to 400.

MEDIA

Generally free, although some government sensitivity about phone-in radio programmes

PUBLISHING AND BROADCAST MEDIA

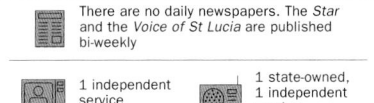

There are no daily newspapers. The *Star* and the *Voice of St Lucia* are published bi-weekly

1 independent service

1 state-owned, 1 independent service

The privately-owned press is free from government intervention. It is possible to receive TV programmes from US, Mexican and some Caribbean stations.

CRIME

1016 prisoners

Up 17% between 1985 and 1989

There are no particularly dangerous areas on the island. Murder is rare and burglary is regarded by the locals as a major crime. The police force is trained by the UK and the USA.

EDUCATION

 88%

Education is based on the British system. St Lucia has the most Nobel laureates per capita in the world – Sir Arthur Lewis (economics) and Derek Walcott (literature) are both St Lucians.

HEALTH

1 per 2429 people

Heart and respiratory diseases, cancers

Health care has improved since the 1960s. State hospitals are supplemented by private clinics.

WEALTH

Factory worker, 99 East Caribbean dollars per week; communications office worker, 380 East Caribbean dollars per week

CONSUMER GOODS OWNERSHIP

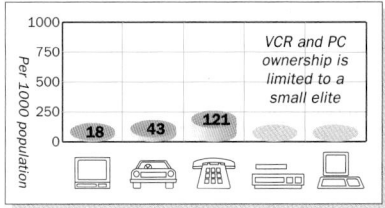

VCR and PC ownership is limited to a small elite

18   43   121

The big banana growers and hotel owners are the richest members of St Lucian society. Japanese cars are particularly favoured.

S

WORLD RANKING

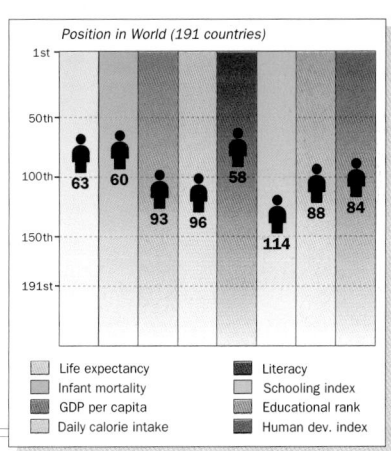

Position in World (191 countries)

63 60 93 96 58 114 88 84

- Life expectancy
- Infant mortality
- GDP per capita
- Daily calorie intake
- Literacy
- Schooling index
- Educational rank
- Human dev. index

ECONOMICS

 $456m*

 2.70 East Caribbean dollars

SCORE CARD

❏ WORLD GNP RANKING	164th
❏ GNP PER CAPITA	$2980
❏ BALANCE OF PAYMENTS	$–81.1m
❏ INFLATION	3.6%
❏ UNEMPLOYMENT	15%

STRENGTHS
Banana crop, currently with preferential access to EU, and tourism.

WEAKNESSES
Most tourist resorts foreign-owned; profits do not directly benefit St Lucia.

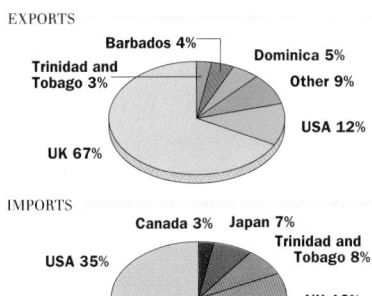

EXPORTS

- Barbados 4%
- Trinidad and Tobago 3%
- UK 67%
- Dominica 5%
- Other 9%
- USA 12%

IMPORTS

- Canada 3%
- Japan 7%
- USA 35%
- Trinidad and Tobago 8%
- UK 16%
- Other 31%

ST VINCENT & THE GRENADINES

OFFICIAL NAME: St Vincent and the Grenadines **CAPITAL:** Kingstown
POPULATION: 117,000 **CURRENCY:** East Caribbean dollar **OFFICIAL LANGUAGE:** English

AMONGST THE MOST ATTRACTIVE of the Windward Islands group, St Vincent and the Grenadines is renowned as the Caribbean playground of the international jet-set. Tourism and bananas are the economic mainstays, and St Vincent is also the world's largest arrowroot producer. St Vincent is mostly volcanic; the one remaining active volcano, La Soufrière, last erupted in 1979. The Grenadines are flat, mainly bare coral reefs.

CLIMATE

WEATHER CHART

Constant trade winds moderate St Vincent's tropical climate. Rainfall is heaviest during the summer months. Tropical depressions and hurricanes are likely between June and November.

COMMUNICATIONS

 Arnos Vale, Kingstown   595 ships 6.96m dwt

THE TRANSPORT NETWORK

1109km (689 miles)	None
None	None

The government plans to extend St Vincent's limited road network with coastal and interior roads. Also under construction is a shipyard and marina, financed by a German bank and the government. In 1992, an airport taking executive jets was completed on Bequia.

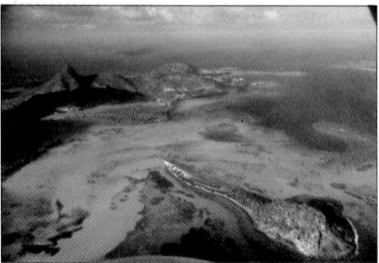

Aerial view of Union Island in the Grenadines chain. The government is developing the island as a major yachting centre.

TOURISM

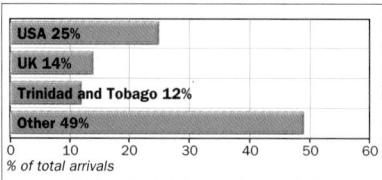
53,316 visitors   Up 3% in 1992

MAIN OVERSEAS ARRIVALS

USA 25%
UK 14%
Trinidad and Tobago 12%
Other 49%
% of total arrivals

Tourism is targeted at the jet-set and cruise-ship rather than the mass-market, and is concentrated on the Grenadines. Mustique, the most famous destination, is frequented by Mick Jagger and Princess Margaret among others. Union Island is developing as a playground for the yachting rich. On St Vincent, the pre-Columbian Amerindian petroglyphs at Layou are a major archaeological attraction.

PEOPLE

 English, English Creole   275 people per km²

THE URBAN/RURAL POPULATION SPLIT

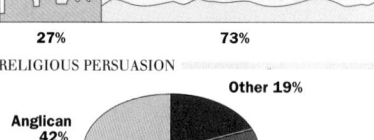
27%   73%

RELIGIOUS PERSUASION

Anglican 42%
Roman Catholic 19%
Methodist 20%
Other 19%

Family life on St Vincent is heavily influenced by the Anglican Church. Racial tensions are few, and intermarriage has meant that the original communities of descendants of African slaves, Europeans and the few indigenous Caribs can no longer be distinguished. Many locals fear that traditional St Vincent life is being threatened by the expanding tourist industry.

POLITICS

 1999    HM Queen Elizabeth II

THE STATE OF THE PARTIES

National Assembly 21 members

57% NDP	14% SVLP-MNU	29% Appointed

NDP = New Democratic Party **SVLP-MNU** = Saint Vincent Labour Party – Movement for National Unity

Prime Minister James Mitchell's NDP confirmed its political dominance with a clean sweep of seats at the 1989 elections. The opposition parties remain weak and short of funds; the top banana growers support the NDP. The main issue is the proposed Windward Islands Federation, which Mitchell favours. He has his eye on the federal presidency.

ST VINCENT & THE GRENADINES

Total Area : 340 sq. km
(131 sq. miles)

POPULATION
● over 10 000
● under 10 000

LAND HEIGHT
1000m/3281ft
500m/1640ft
200m/656ft
Sea Level

WORLD AFFAIRS

Usually excellent relations with Washington – St Vincent supported the US invasion of Grenada in 1983 – have been put under strain by the USA's efforts to pressurize the EU into deregulating its trade, which currently favours Caribbean banana growers.

AID

 $16m (receipts)   Up 78% in 1991

Aid is important in helping to stabilize the country's external finances. The USA and the EU are the main providers of project loans, the UK of grant aid.

DEFENCE

 $3.2m   No significant change from year to year

St Vincent has no army. A 500-strong police force, trained by the USA and UK, is part of the Windward and Leeward Islands' Regional Security System.

ECONOMICS

 $216m   2.70 East Caribbean dollars

SCORE CARD

❏ World GNP Ranking	176th
❏ GNP per Capita	$1845
❏ Balance of Payments	$–9.02m
❏ Inflation	5.8%
❏ Unemployment	40%

STRENGTHS
Bananas, with preferential access to the EU, and tourism. East Caribbean dollar provides currency stability. St Vincent is the world's largest producer of arrowroot starch.

WEAKNESSES
Little diversification. St Vincent is vulnerable to US moves to deregulate the world banana market.

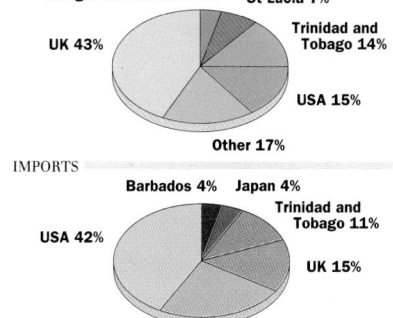

EXPORTS
Antigua and Barbuda 4%   St Lucia 7%
Trinidad and Tobago 14%
UK 43%
USA 15%
Other 17%

IMPORTS
Barbados 4%   Japan 4%
Trinidad and Tobago 11%
USA 42%
UK 15%
Other 24%

RESOURCES

 48m kwh (capacity 14,000 kw)
15,000 sheep, 9000 pigs, 7000 cattle
 Not an oil producer and has no refineries
 None

There is a hydroelectric plant on the Cumberland River. Virtually all other energy requirements have to be imported. Some of the Grenadines have no fresh water sources.

ENVIRONMENT

 21% (including marine and semi-protected areas)
 New airport on Bequia

Hurricanes are the main environmental threat; Hurricane Emily destroyed 70% of the banana crop in 1987. For years the inaccessibility of St Vincent and the Grenadines meant that tourism was a minor environmental threat. The attraction of islands such as Mustique was based on their untouched, idyllic landscape. Mustique remains well protected – building has been restricted to 30 houses and further development is limited as fresh water has to be shipped in. On Bequia, the new airport and the associated increase in visitors are seen as a mixed blessing. Commercial whaling is a contentious issue.

MEDIA

 Journalists and radio news editors have been subjected to government intimidation

PUBLISHING AND BROADCAST MEDIA

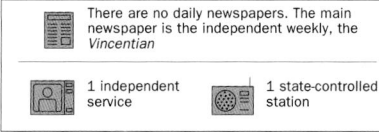
There are no daily newspapers. The main newspaper is the independent weekly, the *Vincentian*
1 independent service
1 state-controlled station

Only one of the four weekly papers is privately owned; the rest are published by political parties. Freedom of the press is written into the constitution.

CRIME

 281 prisoners   Down 3% in 1990

The judicial system on St Vincent is based on British common law. Rape and robbery are the main local concerns, although on the outlying islands both incidents are very rare.

EDUCATION

 85%

State schools follow the old British 11-plus selective system. There are a few private schools. University students go on to the regional University of the West Indies in Jamaica, although increasing numbers are also studying in the USA and the UK.

HEALTH

 1 per 3216 people   Heart and respiratory diseases, cancers

Doctors train at the University of the West Indies. The system is a mixture of state and private hospitals and clinics; facilities are scarcer on the Grenadines.

WEALTH

 Wealth is quite evenly dispersed, although large banana growers and established urban professionals tend to be more affluent

CONSUMER GOODS OWNERSHIP

VCR and PC ownership is limited to a small elite
Per 1000 population
79 50 85

Jet-set wealth is very much in evidence in the Grenadines, particularly on Union Island and Mustique. The local rich favour Jeeps and motor yachts.

WORLD RANKING

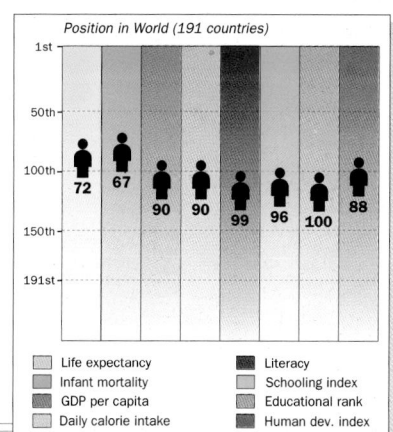
Position in World (191 countries)
72 67 90 90 99 96 100 88

Life expectancy | Literacy
Infant mortality | Schooling index
GDP per capita | Educational rank
Daily calorie intake | Human dev. index

S

467

SAN MARINO

OFFICIAL NAME: Republic of San Marino **CAPITAL:** San Marino
POPULATION: 22,000 **CURRENCY:** Italian lira **OFFICIAL LANGUAGE:** Italian

PERCHED ON THE SLOPES of Mount Titano in the Italian Appennines, San Marino is, after Nauru, the world's smallest republic. It has maintained its independence since the 4th century AD. The territory is divided into nine castles, or districts. One third of the San Marinese population lives in the northern town of Serravalle. Today San Marino lives by agriculture, tourism and limited industry. Italy effectively controls most of its affairs.

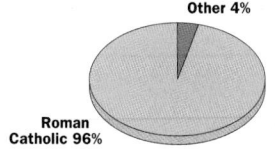

San Marino's second fortress, the Cesta, *built in the 13th century, dominates the republic from its highest pinnacle, 755 m above sea level.*

CLIMATE

WEATHER CHART

 Average daily temperature   Rainfall

```
°C/°F          J F M A M J J A S O N D        cm/in
40/104                                          40/16
30/86                                           30/12
20/68                                           20/8
10/50                                           10/4
0/32                                            0
-10/14
-20/-4
```

San Marino's Mediterranean climate is moderated by cool sea breezes and its height above sea level. In summer temperatures can reach 26°C, whilst in winter they fall to –7°C. Rainfall is more common in the winter months.

TOURISM

 2.73m visitors   Down 12% in 1992

Tourism is the mainstay of San Marino's economy, contributing 60% of government revenue. Tourist-related activities provide employment for 20% of the workforce, who cater for the three million visitors annually who come to sample its folklore and museums, and to explore the fortifications of Mount Titano.

The Titano fortresses of *la Rocca*, *la Cesta* and *Montale*, built during the Middle Ages, command superb views and are the main attractions. Many visitors to San Marino are day-trippers from Italy. The Republic's tourist

Religious procession. The official state religion of San Marino is Roman Catholicism, in contrast to Italy, which has no state religion.

COMMUNICATIONS

 None   Has no fleet

THE TRANSPORT NETWORK

237 km (147 miles)	None
None	None

The 24-km highway to Rimini, which has the closest airport, is San Marino's most important link. Congestion is a major problem, particularly during the annual *Mille Miglia* car rally. A funicular railway climbs the east side of Mount Titano. The railway to Rimini, closed since 1945, is being rebuilt.

industry is boosted by the close proximity of two international airports, in Rimini and Pisa.

Efforts have been made to attract business meetings and conferences with extensive publicity in the Italian media. There are plans for a new high-tech conference hotel.

The San Marino tourist bureau is also attracting thousands of sports enthusiasts to the republic by hosting a series of top international sporting events. In March, both the Rimini–San Marino marathon and the *Mille Miglia* veteran car meeting are held. May heralds the San Marino Grand Prix, when thousands of Formula One fans descend on the country. June, meanwhile, attracts more motor-racing fans for the World Motocross Championships.

MAIN OVERSEAS ARRIVALS

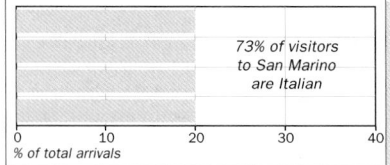

```
            0    10    20    30    40
% of total arrivals
```
73% of visitors to San Marino are Italian

PEOPLE

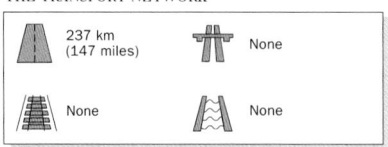 Italian   361 people per km²

THE URBAN/RURAL POPULATION SPLIT

90%   10%

RELIGIOUS PERSUASION

Other 4%
Roman Catholic 96%

San Marino is a tightly-knit society. Foreigners must have resided in the republic for at least 30 years to gain citizenship. Women gained the vote in 1960, but were able to stand for public office only in 1973. Twenty thousand San Marino citizens are resident abroad, mainly in Italy.

SAN MARINO

Total Area : 61 sq. km (24 sq. miles)

LAND HEIGHT	POPULATION
	• under 10 000
500m/1640ft	
200m/656ft	
above 175m/574ft	

Faletano
Dogana
Serravalle
Fiorina
Ventoso
Cailungo
Gualdicciolo
Acquaviva
Borgo
Maggiore
Domagnano
SAN MARINO
Monte Titano
739 m
Faetano
Murata
Chiesanuova
Montegiardino

```
0        4 km
0        4 miles
```

POLITICS

 1998

 Two Captains-Regent jointly hold office for a six month period

San Marino is a parliamentary democracy. The party system is parallel to Italy's, with regular coalition governments. The PDCS holds the majority of seats in the Great and General Council and governs in coalition with the PSS. The communists have been in decline since 1957.

WORLD AFFAIRS

 CE CSCE NAM

Foreign affairs are effectively decided by Italy, on which San Marino is entirely dependent. In 1992, San Marino acquired a seat at the UN.

AID

 Neither an aid donor or receiver

 Not applicable

San Marino does not receive aid. However, annual subsidies from Italy and free access to the Italian market are essential to the economy.

DEFENCE

 Combined Voluntary Military Forces

 Not applicable

San Marino has a small territorial army and fortification guards. There is no compulsory military service, but males aged 16–55 may be called up in a national emergency.

ECONOMICS

 $188m

 1712 Italian lira

SCORE CARD

- ❑ WORLD GNP RANKING........................179th
- ❑ GNP PER CAPITA $8545
- ❑ BALANCE OF PAYMENTS ....Within Italian total
- ❑ INFLATION 6.1%
- ❑ UNEMPLOYMENT................................4.3%

STRENGTHS
Tourism, providing 60% of government revenue. Light industry, notably mechanical engineering and clothing, with emphasis on sportswear and high-quality prestige lines.

WEAKNESSES
Need to import all raw materials.

EXPORTS/IMPORTS

Does not publish independent trade statistics; trade movements are included in the Italian totals

THE STATE OF THE PARTIES

Great and General Council 60 members

4% CR

43% PDCS   23% PSS   18% PDP   7% PDA   5% DM

PDCS = San Marino Christian Democrat Party
PSS = San Marino Socialist Party **PDP** = Democratic Progress Party **PDA** = Popular Democratic Alliance
DM = Democratic Movement **CR** = Communist Reformation

RESOURCES

 No electricity generation

 Not an oil producer and has no refineries

 Small numbers of cattle, pigs, sheep and horses

 None

San Marino has to import all its energy from Italy. It has no exploitable mineral resources now that the stone quarry on Mount Titano has been exhausted.

ENVIRONMENT

 None

 Farming demands threatening remaining indigenous woodland

Mount Titano is a unique limestone outcrop in the surrounding Italian plain and so has a very localized ecosystem.

MEDIA

 There is full freedom of expression

PUBLISHING AND BROADCAST MEDIA

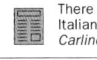 There are no daily newspapers. Regional Italian newspapers, especially *Il Resto del Carlino*, include coverage of San Marino

 1 state-owned service

 1 state-owned, 1 independent service

In 1993, a local TV station, *San Marino RTV*, began broadcasting. Sanmarinese can also receive Italian TV.

CRIME

 San Marino does not publish prison figures

 Little change from year to year

San Marino has a low crime rate. Justice, except in minor civil cases, is admnistered by the Italian legal system.

EDUCATION

 98%

The government spends 13% of the budget on education. Secondary school pupils can go on to Italian universities.

HEALTH

 1 per 375 people

 Heart diseases, cancers, accidents

San Marino's hospital provides a limited health service. Those people requiring difficult operations are normally taken to Rimini for treatment.

CHRONOLOGY

Founded in the 4th century, the Republic of San Marino became one of many medieval Italian city states. It refused to join the unified Italian state created in 1861.

- ❑ **1862** San Marino signs friendship treaty with Italy.
- ❑ **1914–1918** San Marino fights for Italy in the First World War.
- ❑ **1940** Supports Axis powers and declares war on the Allies.
- ❑ **1943** Declares neutrality shortly before Italy surrenders.
- ❑ **1960** Women obtain the vote.
- ❑ **1978** Coalition between San Marino Communist Party (PCS) and PSS – sole communist-led government in Western Europe.
- ❑ **1986** Financial scandals lead to a new PDCS–PCS government.
- ❑ **1988** Joins Council of Europe.
- ❑ **1990** PCS renames itself the Democratic Progress Party (PDP).
- ❑ **1992** San Marino joins the UN. The collapse of communism in Europe sees the PDCS–PDP alliance replaced by a PDSC–PSS coalition government.
- ❑ **1993** May, general election.

WEALTH

 Similar wealth levels to those in northern Italy

CONSUMER GOODS OWNERSHIP

High levels of VCR and PC ownership

752 680 326

Per 1000 population

Living standards are similar to those of northern Italy. The unemployment rate of 4% is below the Italian average.

S

WORLD RANKING

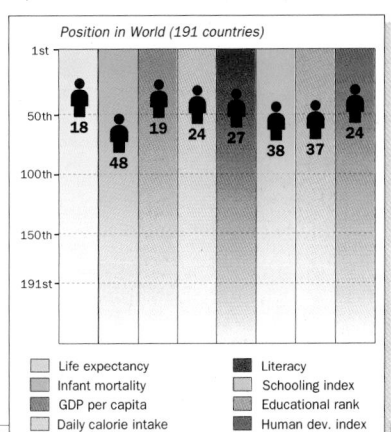

Position in World (191 countries)

18 48 19 24 27 38 37 24

- ◼ Life expectancy
- ◼ Infant mortality
- ◼ GDP per capita
- ◼ Daily calorie intake
- ◼ Literacy
- ◼ Schooling index
- ◼ Educational rank
- ◼ Human dev. index

SAO TOME & PRINCIPE

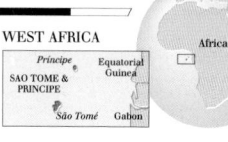

WEST AFRICA

OFFICIAL NAME: Democratic Republic of Sao Tome and Principe   **CAPITAL:** São Tomé
POPULATION: 124,000   **CURRENCY:** Dobra   **OFFICIAL LANGUAGE:** Portuguese

C OMPOSED OF the main islands of São Tomé and
Príncipe and surrounding islets, the republic of
Sao Tome and Principe is situated off the western coast of Africa. In
1975, a classic Marxist single-party regime was established following
independence from Portugal, but a referendum in 1990 resulted in a 72%
vote in favour of democracy. Sao Tome's main concerns are to rebuild
relations with Portugal and to seek closer ties with the EU and the USA.

CLIMATE

WEATHER CHART

The hot, humid islands straddle the
equator. Annual rainfall is 500 cm in
the southwest and 100 cm in the north.

COMMUNICATIONS

 São Tomé Intl
23,000 passengers (est)

 2 ships
1300 dwt

THE TRANSPORT NETWORK

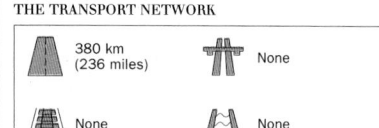

380 km (236 miles)	None
None	None

After years of neglect, road repairs
and the upgrading of São Tomé's
airport began in the late 1980s.

TOURISM

 Very limited tourism   Fairly constant from year to year

MAIN OVERSEAS ARRIVALS

Sao Tome and
Principe does not
publish tourism
figures by country
of origin

% of total arrivals

Tourism is still small-scale, attracting
wealthy Gabonese and Europeans.
Despite recent foreign investment,
tourism on a sizeable scale will take
decades to realize. The country's first
modern hotel opened in 1986.

PEOPLE

Portuguese Creole,
Portuguese

121 people
per km²

THE URBAN/RURAL POPULATION SPLIT

33%   67%

ETHNIC MAKEUP

Portuguese and Creole 10%

Black 90%

The population is entirely descended
from immigrants as the islands were
uninhabited when the Portuguese
arrived in 1470. As the Portuguese
settled, they imported Africans as slaves
to work the sugar and cocoa plantations.
The abolition of slavery in the 19th
century, and the departure of 4000
Portuguese at independence, has
resulted in a population which is 10%
Portuguese and Creole and 90% black
African, although Portuguese culture
predominates. Blacks run the political
parties. Society is well integrated and
free of racial prejudice. The main
conflicts relate to class or differing
ideologies. The extended family still
offers the best, if not the only, form of
social security. Women have a higher
status than in most other African
countries; many have attained
prominent positions in the professions.

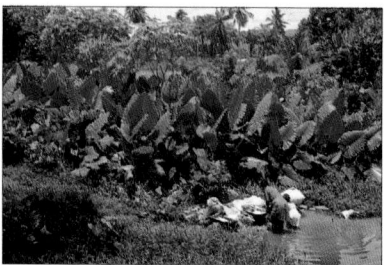

Lush vegetation on São Tomé. *The tropical
climate is slightly moderated by the cool
Benguela current.*

POLITICS

1995

President Miguel dos
Anjos da Cunha Lisboa
Trovoada

THE STATE OF THE PARTIES

National People's Assembly 55 members

60% PCD   38% MLSTP–PSD   2% CODO

PCD = Democratic Convergence Party
MLSTP–PSD = Movement for the Liberation of Sao Tome and
Principe – Social Democratic Party   **CODO** = Democratic
Opposition Coalition

In 1990, a new multiparty constitution
swept away the Marxist single-party
state that had existed since
independence in 1975. Elections in
1991 saw the PCD defeat the MLSTP–PSD,
the former ruling party, whose new
name reflects its change of ideology.
The next few years will show whether
or not the PCD dismantles socialism.
Most parties are now grouped around
personalities. Former leader, Pinto
da Costa, steered the way to
multipartyism. However, he withdrew
from the 1990 presidential elections,
leaving as sole candidate Miguel
Trovoada, who returned from
11 years' exile to stand successfully
as an independent. The most important
pressure groups in politics now are
the Roman Catholic Church (harassed
under Marxism) and the trade unions.
The main political concerns are to
uphold the multiparty system and
stimulate growth in the economy.

WORLD AFFAIRS

 OAU   ECA   CEEAC   AfDB   ACP

Sao Tome has achieved rapprochement
with Portugal and seeks to maintain
links with other ex-Portuguese
colonies, notably Angola. It has always
had close ties with Gabon and, while
not dropping its ex-communist links,
is seeking closer relations with other
CEEAC countries, France and the USA.

AID

 $48m (receipts)   Up 30% in 1991

Sao Tome has one of the highest
aid-to-population ratios in Africa.
Joining the Lomé convention in the
1970s has meant that Sao Tome has
found new sources of aid fairly easily
since the demise of communism
worldwide. The World Bank and
IMF are the main donors.

S

DEFENCE

 Defence budget not disclosed   Probably constant from year to year

Since independence, the armed forces have figured prominently in national life. They have put down several attempted coups, notably in 1978, after which 2000 Angolan troops plus Soviet and Cuban advisers were invited in, and in 1988. The national armed forces are still believed to number 2000, large for the size of the population. Aid donors are pressing for a reduction. With the collapse of the Eastern bloc, Sao Tome now receives military assistance from the USA.

ECONOMICS

 $37m   239.59 dobras

SCORE CARD

- ❑ WORLD GNP RANKING.........................191st
- ❑ GNP PER CAPITA $300
- ❑ BALANCE OF PAYMENTS...................$−26.3m
- ❑ INFLATION 25%
- ❑ UNEMPLOYMENT....Widespread underemployment

EXPORTS

Cameroon 3%
Other 3%
Germany* 51%
Portugal 13%
Netherlands 30%

SAO TOME & PRINCIPE

Total Area : 964 sq. km (372 sq. miles)

POPULATION
- ● over 10 000
- • under 10 000

LAND HEIGHT
- 1000m/3281ft
- 500m/1640ft
- 200m/656ft
- Sea Level

0   10 km
0   10 miles

Príncipe
Ilha Bombom
Santo António
Infante Dom Henrique
Ilha Caroço
Tinhosa Pequena
Tinhosa Grande
(continuation on same scale)

N
Ilha das Cabras
SÃO TOMÉ
Santana
Pico de São Tomé ▲ 2024m
São Tomé
Santa Cruz
Porto Alegre
Gulf of Guinea
Equator
Ilha das Rôlas

RESOURCES

 15m kwh (capacity 6,000 kw)   Not an oil producer and has no refineries

4000 cattle, 3000 pigs, 2000 sheep   None

Sao Tome has no mineral resources, although oil prospecting began in 1990. Almost all energy needs, apart from firewood, are met by oil imported from Angola. São Tomé is very fertile; cocoa estates are finally back to pre-1975 productivity and crop diversification is now a priority. Príncipe has better ports, but its wild scenery makes it more suitable for tourism than farming.

IMPORTS

Portugal 27%
Angola 11%
Belgium and Luxembourg 16%
Germany* 24%
Other 22%

STRENGTHS
Legacy of Portuguese-built infrastructure. Potential for tourism, agricultural and fisheries development. Ability to attract substantial aid.

WEAKNESSES
90% of export earnings from cocoa. Skilful diplomacy has attracted high levels of aid, although mismanagement of these funds has resulted in severe debt. Weak currency.

ENVIRONMENT

 None   No attempt to curb deforestation and soil erosion

Fish conservation, deforestation for fuel-wood and potential tourism expansion are the major issues.

MEDIA

 The press was strictly controlled until 1988, but censorship rules have now been relaxed

PUBLISHING AND BROADCAST MEDIA

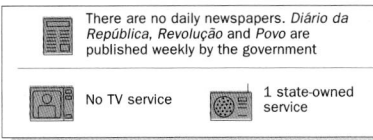

There are no daily newspapers. *Diário da República*, *Revolução* and *Povo* are published weekly by the government

No TV service   1 state-owned service

The strict censorship of the Marxist regime began to be relaxed in 1988. Radio ownership is high for Africa.

CRIME

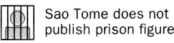 Sao Tome does not publish prison figures   Down 20% in 1988

Crime levels are fairly low owing to the tightly-knit nature of the community. Urban robbery is a problem.

EDUCATION

 57%

Education is compulsory for 6–12 year olds. All staff at the one technical and three secondary schools are foreigners.

HEALTH

 1 per 2819 people   Respiratory, diarrheal and parasitic diseases

Although health care is not free, Sao Tome has a better system of basic care than other ex-colonial African countries.

WEALTH

 Workers on the cocoa plantations form the poorest group

CONSUMER GOODS OWNERSHIP

VCR and PC ownership is limited to a small elite
No TV service
22   24

Wealth disparities are not conspicuous. There is a growing business class. Cocoa workers are the poorest group.

WORLD RANKING

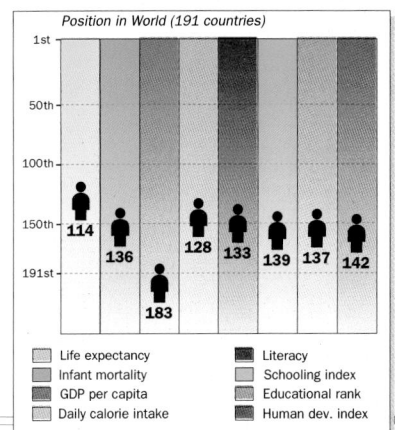

Position in World (191 countries)

114   136   128   133   139   137   142
183

- Life expectancy
- Infant mortality
- GDP per capita
- Daily calorie intake
- Literacy
- Schooling index
- Educational rank
- Human dev. index

S

SAUDI ARABIA

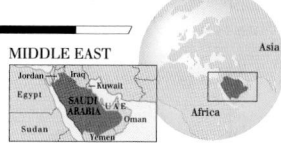

OFFICIAL NAME: Kingdom of Saudi Arabia **CAPITAL:** Riyadh
POPULATION: 15.9 million **CURRENCY:** Saudi riyal **OFFICIAL LANGUAGE:** Arabic

OCCUPYING MOST OF THE Arabian peninsula, Saudi Arabia covers an area as large as western Europe. Over 95% of its land is desert, with the most arid part, known as the 'Empty Quarter' or Rub al Khali, in the southeast. Saudi Arabia has the world's largest oil and gas reserves and major refining and petrochemicals industries. It includes Islam's holiest cities, Medina and Mecca, visited each year by two million Muslims performing the pilgrimage known as the *haj*. The Al-Saud family have been Saudi Arabia's absolutist rulers since 1932.

TOURISM

827,000 pilgrims   Up 8% in 1990

MAIN OVERSEAS ARRIVALS

Iran 16%
Egypt 10%
Turkey 10%
Pakistan 10%
Yemen 6%
Other 48%

% of total arrivals

Saudi Arabia does not encourage foreign tourism. Only Muslim pilgrims, business people and foreign workers are permitted entry. Non-Muslims are banned from the holy cities. Over two million Muslims perform the *haj* (pilgrimage) in the twelfth month of the Arabic year. Muslims are expected to carry out the *haj* at least once in their life, and strict quotas have had to be imposed to avoid massive overcrowding. Many choose Jiddah as a base from which to begin the pilgrimage. The *umra*, or little pilgrimage, has also become popular as it can be made at any time of year. The royal family has spent $2.5 billion in recent years on improving facilities at Medina and Mecca. Excellent scuba diving exists on the Red Sea, especially at Jīzān in the south of the country.

CLIMATE

WEATHER CHART

The kingdom's only reliable rainfall is in the southern Asir province, which makes agriculture there viable. The central plateau requires deep artesian wells to water crops. Inland, summer temperatures often soar above 48°C, but in winter, especially in the northwest, they may fall to freezing point.

SAUDI ARABIA

Total Area : 2 149 690 sq. km
(829 995 sq. miles)

POPULATION
- ⊡ over 1 000 000
- ⊙ over 500 000
- ◎ over 100 000
- ○ over 50 000
- ● over 10 000
- · under 10 000

LAND HEIGHT
- 3000m/9843ft
- 2000m/6562ft
- 1000m/3281ft
- 500m/1640ft
- Sea Level

COMMUNICATIONS

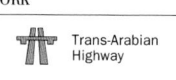 **King Abdul Aziz International, Jiddah** 3.65m passengers

 108 ships 1.25m dwt

THE TRANSPORT NETWORK

144,676 km (89,900 miles)   Trans-Arabian Highway

886 km (551 miles)   None

Since the advent of oil wealth in the 1970s, a modern transport infrastructure has been created, linking the main centres of population to the Gulf States, Jordan and Egypt.

Network of modern road junctions spread out across the landscape near Mecca.

PEOPLE

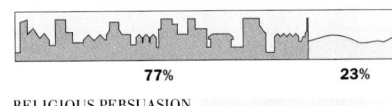

Arabic   7 people per km²

THE URBAN/RURAL POPULATION SPLIT

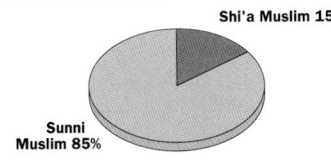

77%   23%

RELIGIOUS PERSUASION

Shi'a Muslim 15%

Sunni Muslim 85%

ETHNIC MAKEUP

Afro-Asian 10%

Arab 90%

The Saudis take their name from the ruling Al-Saud family. They were united by conquest between 1902 and 1932 by King Abd al-Aziz Al Sa'ud, who expelled the Turks.

The vast majority of Saudis are Sunni Muslims who follow the *wahhabi* (puritan) interpretation of Islam and embrace *sharia* (Muslim) law in their daily lives.

The politically-dominant Nejadi tribes from the central plateau around Riyadh are Bedouin in origin. The Hejazi tribes from southern and western Saudi Arabia, who have a more cosmopolitan, mercantile background, have largely been displaced from politics. In the eastern province there is a Shi'a minority of some 300,000, many of whom are employed in the oilfields.

Women are obliged to wear the veil, cannot hold driving licences and have no role in public life. They are effectively barred from the workplace except as teachers and nurses.

POPULATION AGE BREAKDOWN

%	■ 0–14		▢ 15–64		▢ 65+
	3.3%	3.2%	2.8%	2.6%	2.6%
	53.4%	52.3%	53%	52.1%	51.7%
	43.3%	44.5%	44.2%	45.3%	45.7%
	1960	1970	1980	1990	2000

% of population by age group

POLITICS

 Not applicable

 King Fahd ibn Abd al-Aziz as-Sa'ud

THE STATE OF THE PARTIES

Saudi Arabia is an absolute monarchy. The King rules with the assistance of an appointed Council of Ministers

Saudi Arabia is an absolute monarchy. A 60-man Consultative Assembly *(majlis ashoura)* is appointed by the King.

MAIN POLITICAL ISSUES

Questioning the ruling family

Following the 1991 Gulf War, a civil rights campaign emerged to challenge the authority of the ruling family, demanding closer adherence to Islamic values. The movement objected to the presence of US troops on Saudi territory and the consequent exposure to 'corrupt' Western culture; particular outrage was felt at the presence of women soldiers. The Sa'uds moved swiftly to quash the protest. Academics and civil servants behind the movement were imprisoned.

The religious establishment

The ruling family has the support of the religious establishment, led by the *ulema*, a convocation of Islamic scholars in *sharia* law. In the 1980s, King Fahd adopted the title Guardian of the Two Holy Shrines to emphasize his commitment to the defence of Islam. The King consults the Supreme Council of *Ulema* on moral and political issues. King Fahd has often suppressed his modernizing tendencies on the *Ulema*'s advice.

PROFILE

The royal family rules by carefully manipulating appointments in all sectors of government. Frequent changes of personnel within the armed forces ensure that officers do not build personal followings. All influential cabinet portfolios, apart from those of oil and religious affairs, are held by princes.

Absolutist rule means that domestic politics are virtually non-existent. The regime retains feudal elements: weekly *majlis*, or councils, are held where citizens can present petitions or grievances to leading members of the royal family. Large cash sums are often dispensed at these meetings.

The legitimacy of the regime is built on its adherence to Islamic values, and the backing of the *ulema*. It is the stress on Islam that colours Saudi life most. The 5000-strong *mutawa* (religious police) enforce the five-times-a-day call to prayer when businesses must close. During Ramadan the *mutawa* are especially active.

WORLD AFFAIRS

 AL   OPEC   NAM   ESCWA   GCC

Saudi Arabia's strategic importance is derived entirely from its oil reserves and worldwide investments. The Kingdom of Saudi Arabia is among the top ten trading partners of nearly every industrialized country in the world. Relations with the USA are particularly close. Although foreign reserves have fallen because of the cost of liberating Kuwait in 1991, the Saudis remain important institutional investors with significant amounts invested in the West.

The Saudi reaction to Iraq's invasion of Kuwait in 1990 demonstrated the Sa'uds' determination to maintain the current *status quo* in the Middle East. Saudi Arabia helped to persuade other Arab states of the need to evict Iraq from Kuwait. It gave sanctuary to the Kuwaiti royal family and offered its military bases to the Western allies. More Saudis fought in the UN's Operation Desert Storm than did troops from any other Arab country.

The guardian of Mecca, Saudi Arabia has immense importance as the spiritual centre for more than a billion Muslims all over the world.

AID

 $3.7bn (donations)   Up 315% in 1990

Through the Saudi Fund for Development, the kingdom makes generous loans and grants to other Arab and developing countries, mainly for infrastructure projects. Saudi Arabia promotes Islam through charitable foundations, especially in Africa, Asia and the former Soviet Union. The royal purse also supports scientific and medical research. Since the liberation of Kuwait in 1991, Saudi Arabia has given large sums to countries that supported the Allies, notably Egypt, Syria, Morocco and Turkey. In addition, the Saudi government substantially reimbursed the USA and UK for the cost of their expeditionary forces, as well as favouring companies from the Allied powers for reconstruction contracts.

King Fahd ibn Abd al-Aziz as-Sa'ud *acceded to the Saudi throne in 1982.*

Sheikh Muhammad Ali Aba al-Khail, *Saudi Arabia's Minister of Finance.*

S

CHRONOLOGY

The unification of Saudi Arabia under King Abd al-Aziz (Ibn Sa'ud) was achieved in 1932. The kingdom remains the only country in the world named after its royal family.

❏ **1937** Oil reserves discovered near Riyadh.

❏ **1939** Ceremonial start of oil production at Az Zahran.

❏ **1945** Abdel Aziz meets US President Roosevelt on *USS Quincy* in the Red Sea.

❏ **1953** King Sa'ud succeeds on the death of his father Abd al-Aziz.

❏ **1964** King Sa'ud abdicates in favour of his brother, Faisal.

❏ **1967** Saudi forces join with those of Jordan and Iraq against Israel during Six Day War.

❏ **1969** Air Force officers stage an abortive coup against King Faisal.

❏ **1973** Saudi Arabia imposes an oil embargo on Western supporters of Israel.

❏ **1975** King Faisal assassinated by a deranged nephew and is succeeded by his brother Khaled.

❏ **1979** Muslim fundamentalists led by Juhaiman Ibn Seif al-Otaibi seize the Grand Mosque in Mecca and proclaim a *Mahdi* (messiah) on the first day of the Islamic year 1400.

❏ **1981** Formation of Gulf Co-operation Council, with secretariat in Riyadh.

❏ **1982** King Fahd succeeds on the death of his brother King Khaled. Promises to create consultative assembly.

❏ **1986** Opening of King Fahd Causeway to Bahrain. Sheikh Yamani sacked as oil minister.

❏ **1987** Diplomatic relations with Iran deteriorate after 402 people die in riots involving Islamic fundamentalists at Mecca during the *haj* (pilgrimage).

❏ **1989** Saudi Arabia signs non-aggression pact with Iraq. Saudi Arabia brokers political settlement to Lebanese civil war.

❏ **1990** Kuwaiti royals seek sanctuary in Taif after Iraqi invasion.

❏ **1990–1991** US, UK, French, Egyptian and Syrian forces assemble in Saudi Arabia for Operation Desert Storm. Public executions are halted.

❏ **1991** Iraqis seize border town of Al Khafji, but are driven out by Saudi, US and Qatari forces.

❏ **1992** King Fahd pays for British girl Laura Davies to have heart transplant in USA.

❏ **1993** King Fahd appoints 60-man Consultative Assembly.

DEFENCE

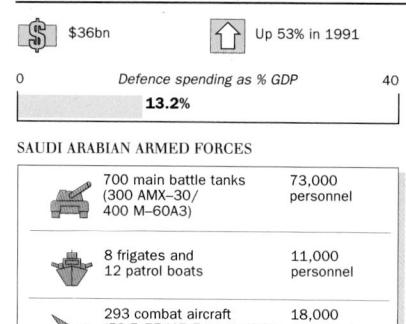

💲 $36bn   ⬆ Up 53% in 1991

0   *Defence spending as % GDP*   40
13.2%

SAUDI ARABIAN ARMED FORCES

🚙	700 main battle tanks (300 AMX–30/ 400 M–60A3)	73,000 personnel
🚢	8 frigates and 12 patrol boats	11,000 personnel
✈	293 combat aircraft (52 F–5E/45 *Tornado* IDS/ 24 *Tornado* ADV)	18,000 personnel
🚀	None	

The liberation of Kuwait increased the armed forces' prestige. Military equipment is purchased mostly from the USA, UK and France. Weapons systems are advanced and include *Patriot* missiles and AWACS early warning radar. However, skilled foreign personnel operate many of these: 1000 US Air Force troops are employed to keep AWACS flying. The air force is the elite branch of the military. It had one brief period of politicization in 1969 when officers attempts a coup. The paramilitary National Guard is drawn from tribal supporters of the Al-Sa'ud regime. Its commander-in-chief is the Crown Prince rather than the defence minister.

ECONOMICS

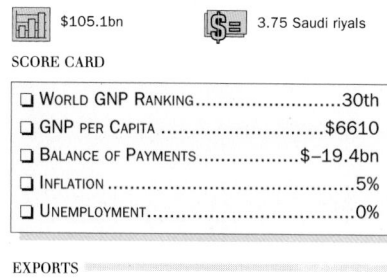

📊 $105.1bn   💲 3.75 Saudi riyals

SCORE CARD

❏ WORLD GNP RANKING	30th
❏ GNP PER CAPITA	$6610
❏ BALANCE OF PAYMENTS	$–19.4bn
❏ INFLATION	5%
❏ UNEMPLOYMENT	0%

EXPORTS

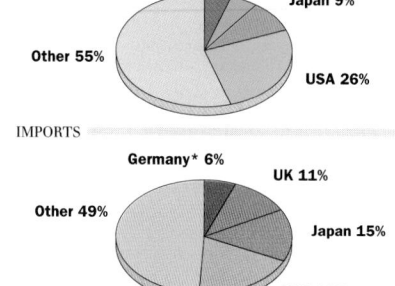

Singapore 5%   France 5%
Japan 9%
Other 55%
USA 26%

IMPORTS

Germany* 6%
UK 11%
Other 49%
Japan 15%
USA 19%

ECONOMIC PERFORMANCE INDICATOR

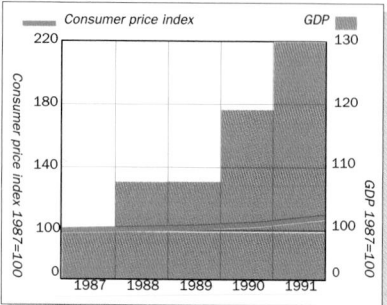

Consumer price index   GDP

Graph: Consumer price index 1987=100 (left axis, 0–220); GDP 1987=100 (right axis, 0–130); years 1987 1988 1989 1990 1991

STRENGTHS

Vast oil and gas reserves. World-class associated industries. Accumulated surpluses and steady current income. Large income from two million annual pilgrims to Mecca.

WEAKNESSES

Lack of skilled workers. Food production requires heavy subsidy. Most consumer items and industrial raw materials imported.

PROFILE

Since the 1970s, strenuous efforts have been made to shift the economy away from its dependence on oil exports and to provide employment for young Saudis. While most investment in oil is from the government, Saudi entrepreneurs have become more involved in secondary industries. Saudi financial markets are poorly developed, however, owing to religious inhibitions about paying or receiving interest. Saudi Aramco, the Middle East's largest employer, controls the national oil industry and has ambitious plans for new exploration. Large sums have been spent on giving Saudi Arabia a US-standard infrastructure, with the aim of providing the basis for a manufacturing economy. The economy, however, remains dependent on foreign workers.

SAUDI ARABIA : MAJOR BUSINESSES

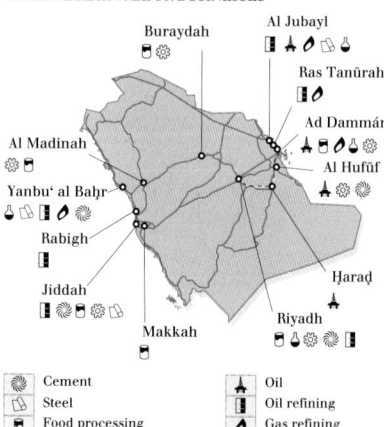

Buraydah   Al Jubayl   Ras Tanūrah   Ad Dammán   Al Hufúf   Al Madinah   Yanbu' al Bahr   Rabigh   Jiddah   Makkah   Riyadh   Haraḍ

🌀 Cement	🏭 Oil
🔩 Steel	⚙ Oil refining
🗄 Food processing	🔥 Gas refining
⚙ Light engineering	0 400 km
⚗ Petrochemicals/fertilizers	0 400 miles

S

RESOURCES

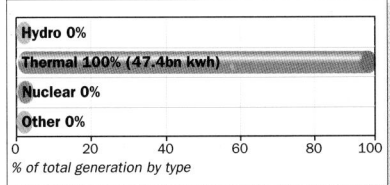

47.4bn kwh (capacity 18.5m kw)

8.38m b/d (reserves 257,842,000,000 bbl)

7.7m sheep, 405,000 camels, 250,000 cattle

Natural gas, limestone, gypsum, marble, clay, salt

ELECTRICITY GENERATION

Hydro 0%

Thermal 100% (47.4bn kwh)

Nuclear 0%

Other 0%

0   20   40   60   80   100
% of total generation by type

Home to the world's biggest oil and gas reserves, Saudi Arabia plays a key role in the global economy and is among the top ten traders of all the world's major industrialized nations.

SAUDI ARABIA : LAND USE

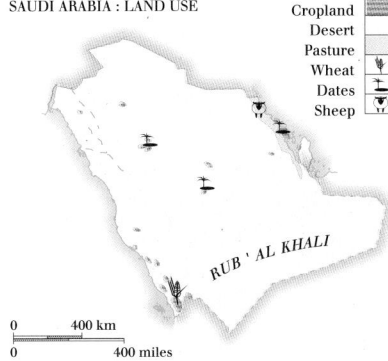

Cropland
Desert
Pasture
Wheat
Dates
Sheep

RUB ' AL KHALI

0   400 km
0   400 miles

ENVIRONMENT

9% partially protected

Little environmental legislation

ENVIRONMENTAL TREATIES

No

No

No

No

Pollution in the Gulf and Red Sea has threatened some wildlife and their habitats, as have hunters using high-velocity rifles and off-road vehicles. The government has taken steps to confine manufacturing to industrial estates. Environmental legislation is, nevertheless, poorly developed, although planning controls apply in the major cities.

MEDIA

Control of the media is achieved through the Ministry of Information, which controls the national news agency and the broadcasting services

PUBLISHING AND BROADCAST MEDIA

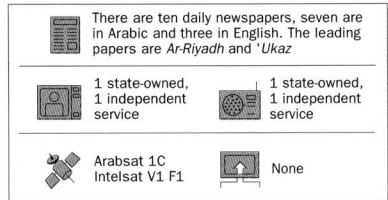

There are ten daily newspapers, seven are in Arabic and three in English. The leading papers are *Ar-Riyadh* and *'Ukaz*

1 state-owned, 1 independent service

1 state-owned, 1 independent service

Arabsat 1C Intelsat V1 F1

None

The government imposes total censorship and insists on strict morality in the Saudi press. In 1994, private citizens were banned from owning satellite dishes, reflecting the state's wish to keep CNN out of Saudi homes. Saudi publishers play a leading role in the Arabic media, however. *Sharq Al Awsat* (The Middle East) published in Saudi Arabia is considered one of the leading Arabic dailies. Saudi investors have bought the influential press agency United Press International.

CRIME

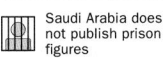

Saudi Arabia does not publish prison figures

Down 4% in 1990

CRIME RATES

Murders
0.6   per 100,000 population

Rapes
0.6   per 100,000 population

Thefts
58   per 100,000 population

Strict Islamic punishments – stoning for adultery, amputation for stealing and beheading for murder – deter crime. Amnesty International has condemned the high number of public executions.

EDUCATION

62%

0   Education spending as % GNP   25
7.6%

THE EDUCATION SYSTEM

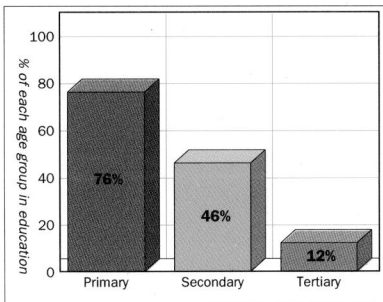

76% Primary
46% Secondary
12% Tertiary

In the 1950s, the then Crown Prince Faisal persuaded the religious establishment to give women equal opportunities in education. Much government money has gone into higher education and Islamic universities, though many Saudis still travel abroad to complete their studies.

HEALTH

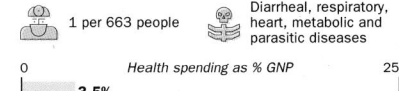

1 per 663 people

Diarrheal, respiratory, heart, metabolic and parasitic diseases

0   Health spending as % GNP   25
3.5%

In the 1970s, resources were committed to building a network of modern hospitals at the expense of primary health care. Large sums have been spent on Western expertise. The private sector has also been encouraged. Many Saudis are still sent overseas for treatment by the government, especially for transplant operations, which pose some ethical problems for religious leaders.

WEALTH

Top US surgeon (on contract), 267,023 Saudi riyals per year

CONSUMER GOODS OWNERSHIP

Higher than regional average

277   145   109   123

Saudi citizens are among the most prosperous in the world. The Al-Sa'uds have used their wealth to create a cradle to the grave welfare system. Ownership of TVs, telephones and VCRs is among the regions highest. The distribution of wealth is carefully controlled by the royal family through the *majlis* system. Petitioners attend weekly assemblies held by prominent royals and beg favours, which are usually granted. There is no stock market, although shares in public companies are traded privately. Many Saudis refuse to accept interest on deposits with banks, but Islamic banks offer profit-sharing investment schemes as an alternative.

S

WORLD RANKING

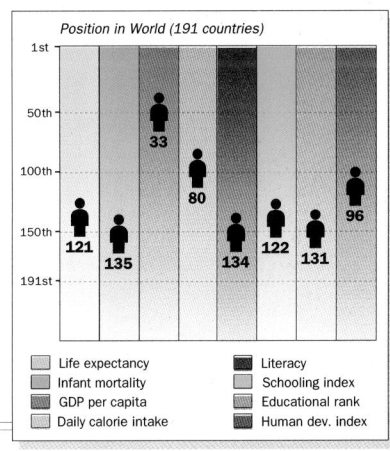

Position in World (191 countries)

1st
50th
100th
150th
191st

33
80
121
135
134
122
131
96

Life expectancy
Infant mortality
GDP per capita
Daily calorie intake
Literacy
Schooling index
Educational rank
Human dev. index

SENEGAL

OFFICIAL NAME: Republic of Senegal **CAPITAL:** Dakar
POPULATION: 7.7 million **CURRENCY:** CFA franc **OFFICIAL LANGUAGE:** French

WEST AFRICA
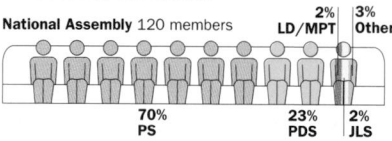
Africa

SENEGAL'S CAPITAL, Dakar, lies on the westernmost cape of Africa. The country is mostly low, with open savanna and semi-desert in the north and thicker savanna in the south. After independence from France in 1960, Senegal was ruled for 20 years by its first president, Léopold Senghor, who maintained a system of virtual single-party rule. Full multipartyism was introduced in the 1980s. Fishing and tourism are important industries.

CLIMATE

WEATHER CHART

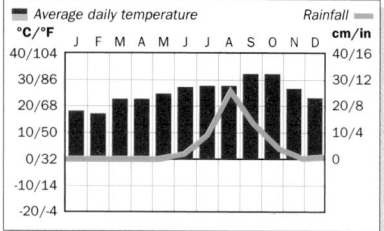

The coastal regions, which project into the path of the northern trade winds, are remarkably cool given their latitude.

COMMUNICATIONS

 Dakar-Yoff Intl
772,719 passengers

 6 ships
18,500 dwt

THE TRANSPORT NETWORK

| 13,850 km (8606 miles) | None |
| 1186 km (737 miles) | 900 km (559 miles) |

Dakar is too large a port for Senegal alone. It also serves the hinterland of Mali, southern Mauritania and Guinea. The key rail link to Bamako, Mali's capital, was built in the 1920s.

TOURISM

 233,512 visitors

 Down 5% in 1991

MAIN OVERSEAS ARRIVALS

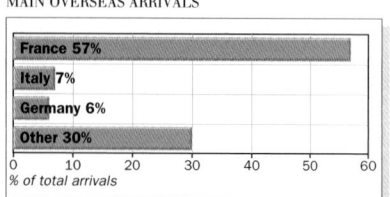

| France 57% |
| Italy 7% |
| Germany 6% |
| Other 30% |

% of total arrivals

In addition to French package tours to coastal resorts, tours for African-Americans to Gorée, an old slave island, are increasingly popular.

PEOPLE

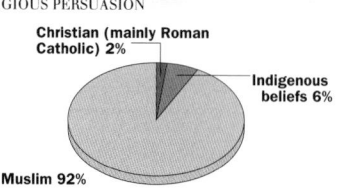
Wolof, Fulani, Serer, Diola, Malinke, Soninke, Arabic, French

37 people per km²

THE URBAN/RURAL POPULATION SPLIT

38%   62%

RELIGIOUS PERSUASION

Christian (mainly Roman Catholic) 2%

Indigenous beliefs 6%

Muslim 92%

Senegal has a fairly well-developed sense of nationhood, and intermarriage between groups has reduced ethnic tensions. Groups can still be identified regionally, however. Dakar is a Wolof area, the Senegal River is dominated by the Toucouleur, the Malinke mostly live in the east, and the Diola in Casamance. The Diola have felt excluded from the political process, and this has led to unrest in Casamance. A French-influenced class system is still prevalent and has become increasingly apparent in recent years.

POLITICS

1998

President Abdou Diouf

THE STATE OF THE PARTIES

National Assembly 120 members

| | 2% LD/MPT | 3% Other |
| 70% PS | 23% PDS | 2% JLS |

PS = Senegalese Socialist Party **PDS** = Senegalese Democratic Party **LD/MPT** = Democratic League/Movement for the Labour Party **JLS** = 'Let Us Unite' coalition **Other** = Independence and Labour Party, Senegalese Democratic Union – Renovation

Senegal is a multiparty democracy and freedom of association is respected. However, the PS has been in power since the 1950s, albeit under different names, and has spread its influence deep into the civil service, judiciary and local government, making opposition difficult. The main issue is the economy; the collapse of the AOF hit Senegal hard as it lost important markets, especially for Dakar's port. Other problems include the separatist movement in anti-Islamic Casamance, and discontent in the northeast, where drought and refugees from Mauritania are leading to tension.

WORLD AFFAIRS

OAU | Ecowas | AfDB | FZ | GATT

Senegal's most important relationship is with France, which provides high levels of aid; whether these will be maintained is Senegal's major concern. Relations with Mauritania have improved since tension was caused by the expulsion of 200,000 Mauritanians in 1989. A border dispute with Guinea-Bissau remains unresolved. Relations with the USA are good.

SENEGAL

Total Area : 196 720 sq. km (75 950 sq. miles)

POPULATION
- over 1 000 000
- over 100 000
- over 50 000
- over 10 000
- under 10 000

LAND HEIGHT
200m/656ft
Sea Level

AID

 $577m (receipts)   Down 27% in 1991

Senegal is one of the highest recipients of aid per capita in Africa, mostly from France, the EU and the World Bank. Aid receipts are used to import 400,000 tons of rice annually, but are also absorbed in administration costs, helping to finance the sizeable civil service. Senegal has given small aid donations to African liberation movements, including the ANC.

The mosque in Touba, religious capital of the Muslim Mouride sect, which was founded in 1887 in Senegal's groundnut-growing district.

DEFENCE

 $154.5m   Up 38% in 1991

Senegal receives protection from France, which maintains an important naval base at Dakar. By African standards the defence budget is small, and the army is not heavily involved in politics – Senegal has never had a coup. Senegal sent troops to Operation Desert Storm in 1991. Preventing assistance from Guinea-Bissau to Casamance separatists is the main current concern.

ECONOMICS

 $6.2bn   295.23 CFA francs

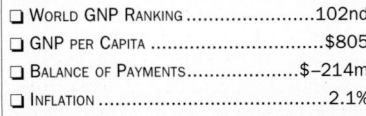

SCORE CARD

- ❑ WORLD GNP RANKING 102nd
- ❑ GNP PER CAPITA $805
- ❑ BALANCE OF PAYMENTS....................$–214m
- ❑ INFLATION 2.1%
- ❑ UNEMPLOYMENT....Widespread underemployment

STRENGTHS
Skilled workforce is highly educated and motivated. Dakar port linked to the interior by good French-built infrastructure. Also a conference venue.

WEAKNESSES
Few natural resources are exploited, other than groundnuts, phosphates

RESOURCES

 684m kwh (capacity 231,000 kw)   Not an oil producer; refines 22,600 b/cd

3.9m sheep, 2.7m cattle, 490,000 pigs   Phosphates, bauxite, salt, natural gas, marble, iron, copper

Senegal's electricity capacity is largely dependent on imported fuel; cheaper supplies are expected to become available soon from the Manantali dam in Mali. Initial explorations suggest oil reserves may exist off Casamance.

ENVIRONMENT

 11% (6% partially protected)   Damming of the Senegal River

The damming of the Senegal River has caused concern that traditional farming practices, which rely on seasonal floods, may be disrupted. Two major droughts in 1973 and 1983 led to the advance of the Sahara Desert in the west of the country.

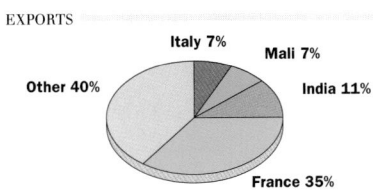

EXPORTS

- Italy 7%
- Mali 7%
- India 11%
- Other 40%
- France 35%

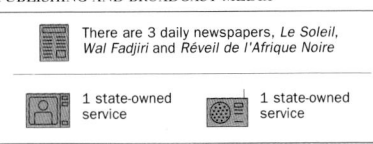

IMPORTS

- USA 5%
- Italy 7%
- Nigeria 8%
- Other 47%
- France 33%

and fish. The Gambia River remains unbridged, making access to the oil-rich Casamance region difficult.

MEDIA

 Opposition parties have limited access to the TV station. Together they are permitted 50% of viewing time; the rest goes to the ruling party

PUBLISHING AND BROADCAST MEDIA

There are 3 daily newspapers, *Le Soleil*, *Wal Fadjiri* and *Réveil de l'Afrique Noire*

 1 state-owned service   1 state-owned service

The independent media flourished with multipartyism. Senegal had the first satirical journal in Africa with the founding of *Le Politicien* in 1978.

CRIME

Senegal does not publish prison figures   Down 42% in 1990

Senegal has comparatively low crime rates, though levels are on the increase in Dakar and the surrounding shanty towns, where gangs are based.

CHRONOLOGY

France colonized Senegal, a major entrepôt from the 15th century, in 1890. Dakar was the capital of French West Africa.

- ❑ **1885** Gambia split off as British enclave within Senegal.
- ❑ **1960** Independence under socialist president Léopold Sédar Senghor.
- ❑ **1966** One-party state.
- ❑ **1976** Three-party system.
- ❑ **1981** Abdou Diouf president. Full multipartyism restored.

EDUCATION

 38%

Illiteracy is the major challenge faced by the system. There are two universities, at Dakar and St-Louis.

HEALTH

 1 per 16,909 people   Malaria, diarrheal diseases

Senegal's state health system is rudimentary. Rich Senegalese are well served by private clinics.

WEALTH

 Most Senegalese lead a subsistence existence

CONSUMER GOODS OWNERSHIP

VCR and PC ownership is limited to a small elite

- 35
- 9
- 8

Wealth disparities are considerable and poverty widespread. Those close to the government are the wealthiest group.

S

WORLD RANKING

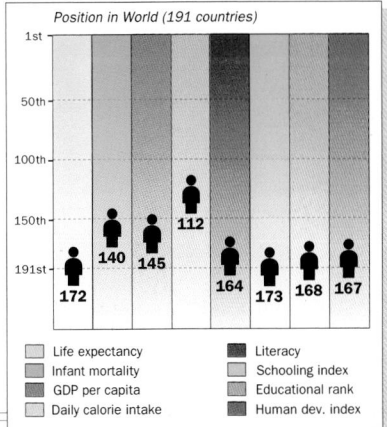

Position in World (191 countries)

- 112
- 140
- 145
- 172
- 164
- 173
- 168
- 167

- ☐ Life expectancy
- ☐ Infant mortality
- ☐ GDP per capita
- ☐ Daily calorie intake
- ☐ Literacy
- ☐ Schooling index
- ☐ Educational rank
- ☐ Human dev. index

SEYCHELLES

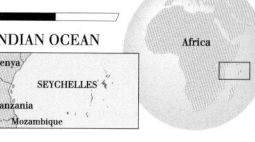

OFFICIAL NAME: Republic of the Seychelles **CAPITAL:** Victoria
POPULATION: 68,000 **CURRENCY:** Seychelles rupee **OFFICIAL LANGUAGE:** Creole

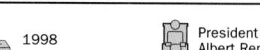

COMPRISING 115 ISLANDS in the Indian Ocean, the Seychelles support unique flora and fauna, including the giant tortoise and the world's largest seed, the *coco-de-mer*. Formerly a UK colony and then under one-party rule for 16 years, Seychelles became a multiparty democracy in 1993. The economy is reliant on tourism.

CLIMATE

WEATHER CHART

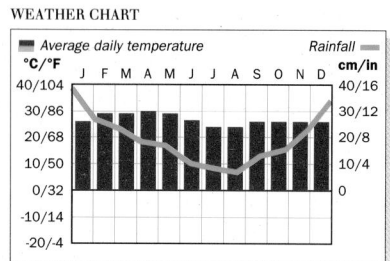

The islands have a tropical oceanic climate, with only small temperature variations.

COMMUNICATIONS

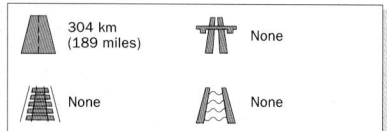

Seychelles Intl, Mahé
155,000 passengers

Has no fleet

THE TRANSPORT NETWORK

304 km (189 miles)	None
None	None

Transport policy is focused on building airstrips – nine islands now have them, improving roads on tourist islands and renewing the public transport fleet.

TOURISM

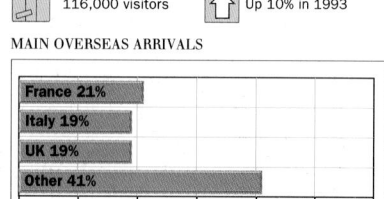

116,000 visitors   Up 10% in 1993

MAIN OVERSEAS ARRIVALS

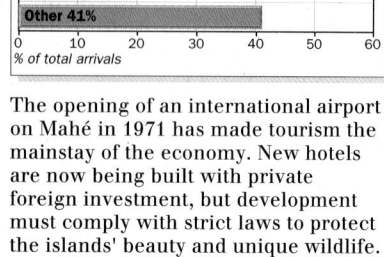

| France 21% |
| Italy 19% |
| UK 19% |
| Other 41% |

% of total arrivals

The opening of an international airport on Mahé in 1971 has made tourism the mainstay of the economy. New hotels are now being built with private foreign investment, but development must comply with strict laws to protect the islands' beauty and unique wildlife.

PEOPLE

French Creole, English, French

150 people per km²

THE URBAN/RURAL POPULATION SPLIT

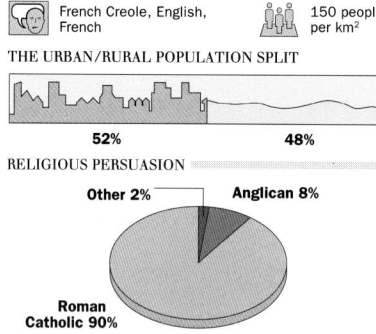

52%   48%

RELIGIOUS PERSUASION

Other 2%   Anglican 8%
Roman Catholic 90%

The Seychelles were uninhabited before French settlers arrived in the 1770s. Today, the population is markedly homogeneous as a result of intermarriage between different ethnic groups. The Creoles are the descendants of the French settlers and the Africans who were settled in the islands by subsequent British administrators.

There are small Chinese and Indian minorities. Almost 90% of Seychellois live on Mahé. Population growth has been very low, as about 1000 people a year have been emigrating. The new democracy may reverse this trend.

POLITICS

1998   President France Albert René

THE STATE OF THE PARTIES

National Assembly 33 members

82% SPPF   15% DP   3% UO

SPPF = Seychelles People's Progressive Front
DP = Democratic Party   **UO** = United Opposition

In 1993, the Seychelles returned to multiparty democracy after 16 years of one-party socialist rule under President René. As prime minister, he had seized complete power in a coup just one year after independence. Divisions within the opposition in the 1993 elections resulted in René being confirmed as president. His old party, renamed the SPPF, received the majority vote. In a major change of ideology and policy, the government has made wide-ranging social and economic reforms, including privatizations and the legalization

WORLD AFFAIRS

OAU   Comm   ACP   NAM   ECA

The Seychelles has pursued a non-aligned policy. However, its strategic location has encouraged competing world powers to seek its friendship. Trade accords exist with other Indian Ocean states.

SEYCHELLES

Total Area : 280 sq. km (108 sq. miles)

POPULATION
● over 10 000
· under 10 000

LAND HEIGHT
500m/1640ft
200m/656ft
Sea Level

AID

 $20m (receipts)   Down 43% in 1991

There is growing support for development projects from multilateral agencies, notably the EU and the Arab Development Fund. Bilateral aid, which used to be the main type of assistance, comes mostly from France and the USA. The UK, Australia and Japan are also sizeable donors.

DEFENCE

 $15.92m   Up 28% in 1991

Seychelles has a 1100-strong army, and a paramilitary guard of almost equal size. The latter includes a small coast guard made up of air and sea forces. The army, set up in 1977, was initially trained by Tanzania and Tanzanian troops were brought in for three years after a coup attempt in 1981. North Korea provided advisers until 1989.

ECONOMICS

 $380m   5.17 Seychelles rupees

SCORE CARD

❏ WORLD GNP RANKING	167th
❏ GNP PER CAPITA	$5588
❏ BALANCE OF PAYMENTS	$34.6m
❏ INFLATION	3.3%
❏ UNEMPLOYMENT	9%

STRENGTHS
Tourism. Fishing, especially shrimps and tuna: the latter is canned for export. Profitable re-export trade. Copra. Cinnamon. Tea.

WEAKNESSES
Growing trade and budget deficits in 1990s owing to drop in tourism following 1991 Gulf War, spending on hosting 1993 Indian Ocean Games and costs of four recent elections. High debt servicing costs. Reliance on food imports, especially for tourist industry. Copra production declining. Significant reliance on expatriate labour.

EXPORTS

IMPORTS

RESOURCES

One of the 40 central islands. These are mostly mountainous, with lush vegetation, and are the only granitic islands in the world.

 85m kwh (capacity 22,000 kw)   Not an oil producer and has no refineries

15,000 pigs, 2000 cattle   Guano, salt, granite, natural gas

The Seychelles has virtually no mineral resources. All mineral fuel is imported. It is used to generate the power on the three islands which have an electricity supply system. Natural gas finds have spurred oil exploration.

ENVIRONMENT

 95%   Strict state controls to conserve land and marine ecosystems

The Seychelles has been praised for its commitment to conservation. It is the sole country to possess two natural World Heritage sites.

MEDIA

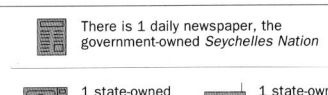 Freedom of expression has been permitted since 1992

PUBLISHING AND BROADCAST MEDIA

 There is 1 daily newspaper, the government-owned *Seychelles Nation*

 1 state-owned service   1 state-owned service

The state broadcasting company has been reorganized and is now ostensibly free of government control. Private periodicals are now permitted.

CRIME

 1060 prisoners   Up 4% in 1990

Violent crime is rare in the Seychelles. The main concern is the increasing rate of petty theft.

EDUCATION

57%

Private schools have been allowed since 1993. National Youth Service has been reduced from two years to one, but is still mandatory for entry to higher education.

HEALTH

 1 per 1404 people   Heart and cerebrovascular diseases, cancers

State health care is free. Private medicine is to be allowed for the first time under the government's new social legislation.

WEALTH

 Plantation worker, 9 Seychelles rupees per month; dentist, 23 Seychelles rupees per month

CONSUMER GOODS OWNERSHIP

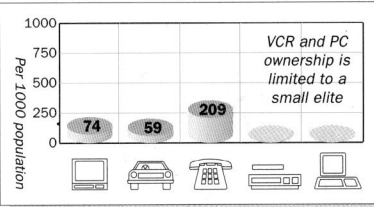

Living standards are the highest among OAU nations. There are no slums and the welfare system caters for all.

WORLD RANKING

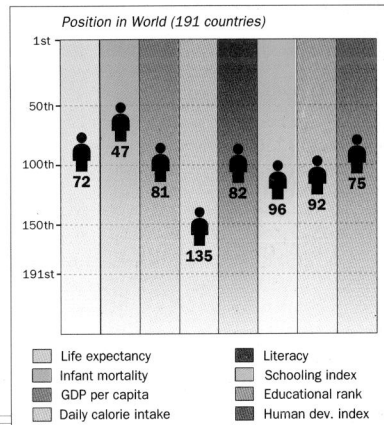

SIERRA LEONE

OFFICIAL NAME: Republic of Sierra Leone **CAPITAL:** Freetown
POPULATION: 4.4 million **CURRENCY:** Leone **OFFICIAL LANGUAGE:** English

THE WEST AFRICAN STATE of Sierra Leone was first colonized by the British in 1787 as a settlement for Africans freed from slavery. Bordered by Guinea and Liberia, its terrain rises from flat, coastal lowlands to mountains in the northeast. The military government that seized power in 1992 promised, but has yet to deliver, a swift return to civilian rule. One of the world's poorest countries, Sierra Leone's main export is diamonds.

CLIMATE

WEATHER CHART

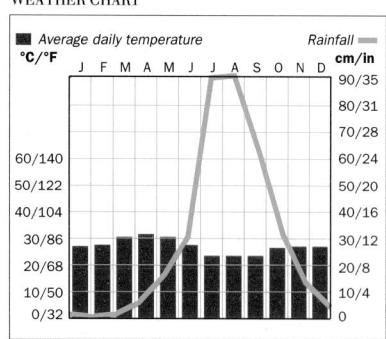

Rainfall on the coast can be as high as 500 cm a year, making Sierra Leone one of the wettest places in coastal West Africa. Humidity is consistently high – about 80% – during the rainy season. The dusty, northeasterly *harmattan* wind often blows during the hotter dry season from November to April. The northeastern savannas are drier, with 190–250 cm of rain a year, but are one of the hottest areas.

COMMUNICATIONS

Lungi International
84,547 passengers

6 ships
4500 dwt

THE TRANSPORT NETWORK

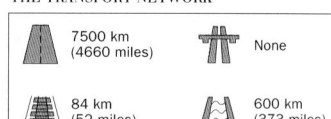

7500 km (4660 miles)	None
84 km (52 miles)	600 km (373 miles)

Little progress has been made in improving Sierra Leone's roads. The 300 km narrow-gauge railway was abandoned in 1971 as uneconomic, although 84 km of track still runs to the closed iron ore mines at Marampa. Having failed in 1987, Sierra Leone's national airline resumed flights – to Paris only – in 1991. The airport is across the estuary from the capital. The only link between the two is a limited ferry service.

TOURISM

89,334 visitors

Down 7% in 1992

MAIN OVERSEAS ARRIVALS

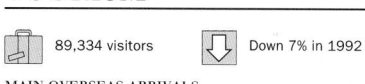

France 22%
North America 13%
UK 10%
Other 55%

% of total arrivals

Sierra Leone attracts few tourists, apart from occasional cruise-ship calls. Internal turmoil and instability mean that plans to develop tourism cannot progress at the moment. Among the chief potential attractions are the beaches along the Freetown peninsula, at present virtually undeveloped.

SIERRA LEONE

Total Area : 71 740 sq. km
(27 699 sq. miles)

LAND HEIGHT

1000m/3281ft
500m/1640ft
200m/656ft
Sea Level

POPULATION

◎ over 100 000
● over 10 000
• under 10 000

PEOPLE

Mende, Temne, Krio, English

59 people per km²

THE URBAN/RURAL POPULATION SPLIT

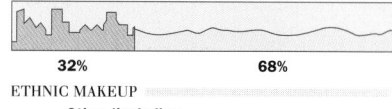

32% 68%

ETHNIC MAKEUP

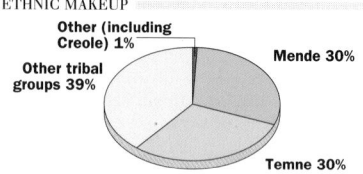

Other (including Creole) 1%
Other tribal groups 39%
Mende 30%
Temne 30%

Freetown, as its name suggests, was founded as a settlement for people freed from slavery. Its citizens' British and North American origins account for Sierra Leone's strongly anglicized Creole culture. Ethnic groups gained political control in 1951.

POLITICS

Uncertain

Capt Valentine Strasser

THE STATE OF THE PARTIES

House of Representatives

The legislature was dissolved following a coup in April 1992

The role of government is largely limited to maintaining the military and police. Its energy is now focused on suppressing rebel activity by Liberian troops, who entered the country in 1991, and Sierra Leonian rebels who have since joined them. The army chief, General Momoh, succeeded President Siaka Stevens on his retirement in 1985 and made moves to end Stevens' one-party system. However, a coup of junior army officers led by Captain Valentine Strasser halted the process. Strasser promised, but has yet to deliver, an early return to civilian rule.

WORLD AFFAIRS

    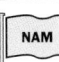

The main concern is that the civil war in neighbouring Liberia will create increasing instability in Sierra Leone.

AID

 $105m (receipts)   Up 62% in 1991

Sierra Leone has not been able to fulfil the terms of the aid package agreed with the IMF in 1989. Instead, funds have been diverted to cope with refugees from Liberia, internal migrants fleeing the rebellion in the southeast, and the near collapse of public services.

DEFENCE

 $5.15m   Defence spending is rising

After its last intervention in politics in 1968, the army resumed a central role in the 1992 coup. It has little credibility, however, as a fighting force.

ECONOMICS

 $625m   549.07 leones

SCORE CARD

❑ WORLD GNP RANKING	161st
❑ GNP PER CAPITA	$145
❑ BALANCE OF PAYMENTS	$–95m
❑ INFLATION	80.8%
❑ UNEMPLOYMENT	Endemic

STRENGTHS
Diamonds, although much of the output is smuggled out. Some bauxite and rutile production.

WEAKNESSES
Inefficient government, which has proposed a tax on imports by overseas charities working in Sierra Leone. Rebel fighting affects the most productive areas of the country, including diamond fields.

EXPORTS

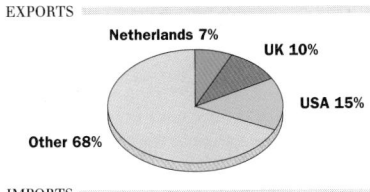

Netherlands 7%
UK 10%
USA 15%
Other 68%

IMPORTS

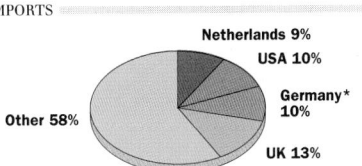

Netherlands 9%
USA 10%
Germany* 10%
Other 58%
UK 13%

RESOURCES

 224m kwh (capacity 130,000 kw)

 Not an oil producer; refines 10,000 b/cd

 330,000 cattle, 330,000 sheep, 50,000 pigs

 Diamonds, rutile, bauxite, gold, titanium

The large diamond deposits need fresh investment as areas currently being mined are becoming depleted. The southeast is the most fertile region.

ENVIRONMENT

 1% partially protected

 Attempt to establish university conservation course

Strain is being placed on the land and on other natural resources to support the growing population.

MEDIA

 Close government supervision of media. Journalists sometimes imprisoned

PUBLISHING AND BROADCAST MEDIA

 There are no daily newspapers. The *New Breed*, published by the government, has the largest circulation of the 11 weeklies

 1 state-owned service

 1 state-owned service

Freetown's Creole population is well served by the broad range of periodicals published there. The 1992 coup curbed rising press freedom.

CRIME

 Sierra Leone does not publish prison figures

 Crime is rising

Illegal diamond mining and smuggling is one of the most lucrative crimes, in which several government members have been implicated. Sierra Leoneans do not have confidence in the legal system. In December 1992, 26 people were executed for allegedly planning a coup, despite the fact that some were in jail at the time.

EDUCATION

 21%

Freetown has a long tradition of education and its university, Fourahbay College, became affiliated with Durham University in the UK in 1876. In recent times, its students have often been active in political dissent. Educational provision has deteriorated with the economic situation over the last decade.

HEALTH

 1 per 13,153 people

 Communicable diseases, malaria, malnutrition

Only traditional health care is available outside the capital. Average life expectancy is 41.5 years; only three other countries share such a low figure.

The main street, Kabala. *In 1993, Sierra Leone was second from bottom of the UN's Human Development Index.*

CHRONOLOGY

Freetown was founded in 1787 and became a British colony in 1808; the interior was annexed in 1896.

❑ **1961** Independence.
❑ **1968** Siaka Stevens prime minister.
❑ **1978** Single-party republic under Stevens. National bankruptcy.
❑ **1991** Liberian rebels invade Sierra Leone in protest at its participation in ECOWAS force in Liberia. Sierra Leonean rebels join the fighting.
❑ **1992** Army coup installs Captain Strasser. Executions after alleged counter-coup widely criticized.

WEALTH

 Most Sierra Leoneans lead a subsistence existence

CONSUMER GOODS OWNERSHIP

VCR and PC ownership is limited to a small elite

10 8 3

Per 1000 population

Most of the population is impoverished. Wealth is almost exclusively associated with political power and influence.

WORLD RANKING

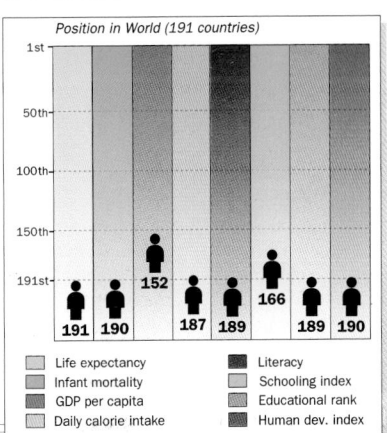

Position in World (191 countries)

191 190 152 187 189 166 189 190

Life expectancy	Literacy
Infant mortality	Schooling index
GDP per capita	Educational rank
Daily calorie intake	Human dev. index

S

SINGAPORE

South East Asia

OFFICIAL NAME: Republic of Singapore   **CAPITAL:** Singapore City
POPULATION: 2.9 million   **CURRENCY:** Singapore dollar   **OFFICIAL LANGUAGES:** Malay, Chinese, Tamil and English

A N ISLAND STATE linked to the southernmost tip of the Malay peninsula by a causeway, Singapore was largely uninhabited between the 14th and 18th centuries. In 1819, an official of the British East India Company, Stamford Raffles, recognized the island's strategic position on key trade routes and established Singapore as a trading settlement. Today, Singapore is still one of the most important entrepôts in Asia.

CLIMATE

WEATHER CHART

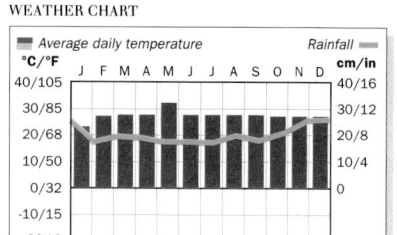

The only variations in the hot, wet and humid climate are the airless months of September and March, when the trade winds change direction.

COMMUNICATIONS

 Changi International 1.49m passengers   600 ships 15.45m dwt

THE TRANSPORT NETWORK

 2810 km (1746 miles)   102 km (63 miles)

 26 km (16 miles)   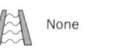 None

The Mass Rapid Transit System (metro), completed in 1991, is among the world's most efficient. Space for new roads has run out and monthly auctions are held to sell certificates entitling people to buy from a quota of new cars. The massive port at Pasir Panjang is being expanded on reclaimed land.

The financial centre. More than a quarter of Singapore's GDP is generated by financial and business services.

TOURISM

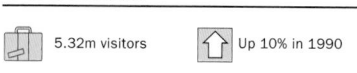 5.32m visitors   Up 10% in 1990

MAIN OVERSEAS ARRIVALS

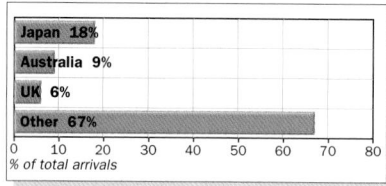

The Chinatown district is recognized as a picturesque tourist asset and its buildings are being restored. The other chief attractions are shopping and golf; Singapore has one of the highest densities of golf courses in the world.

PEOPLE

 Chinese, Malay, Tamil, English   4295 people per km²

THE URBAN/RURAL POPULATION SPLIT

100%

ETHNIC MAKEUP

Other 2%   South Asian 7%
Malay 15%
Chinese 76%

Singapore is dominated by the Chinese, who make up 76% of the community; the old English-speaking Straits Chinese and newer Mandarin-speakers are now well integrated. Indigenous Malays are generally the poorest group. Serious race riots erupted in the 1950s, but today there is little overt ethnic tension. There is a significant foreign workforce in Singapore; a recent labour shortage has forced the government to try to attract scientists from the CIS, Eastern Europe and Hong Kong. Society is highly regulated and government campaigns to improve public behaviour are frequent.

POLITICS

1996   President Ong Teng Cheong

THE STATE OF THE PARTIES

National Assembly 352 members

1% WP

95% PAP   4% SDP

PAP = People's Action Party   **SDP** = Singapore Democratic Party   **WP** = Workers' Party

Singapore is a multiparty democracy in name only. The People's Action Party (PAP) effectively controls all parts of the political process and much of the economy. Membership is almost a secret; the selection of members of parliament happens from above, rather than from grass-roots organizations.

The opposition faces severe restrictions – candidates are openly harassed and the government has threatened to cut grants to constituencies that vote for the opposition. Voters also suspect that their ballot papers can be identified. The PAP saw its share of the vote fall from 84% in 1968 to 61% in 1991, and there were signs that the party had lost support among the Chinese working class, its traditional backer. However, it is unlikely that the party, which has given Singaporeans one of the highest living standards in the world, will lose its grip on power.

WORLD AFFAIRS

ASEAN   ADB   APEC   GATT   NAM

Singapore's defence arrangements reflect its greatest fear – invasion by Malaysia. The government has been viewing the rise of Islam in the region with concern. Relations with Israel are close.

AID

 Singapore has no aid receipts or donations   Not applicable

Aid is simply not an issue in Singapore. The state does not provide aid to any states in South East Asia.

DEFENCE

 $2.1bn   Up 19% in 1991

Singapore is the most heavily armed state in the region. Defence accounts for 46% of current expenditure.

S

ECONOMICS

 $39.2bn

 1.61 Singapore dollars

SCORE CARD

- ☐ WORLD GNP RANKING...........................47th
- ☐ GNP PER CAPITA $12,310
- ☐ BALANCE OF PAYMENTS $2.9bn
- ☐ INFLATION 2.3%
- ☐ UNEMPLOYMENT.................................1.9%

STRENGTHS

Massive accumulated wealth – reserves are over $60 billion – derived from success as an entrepôt and centre of high-tech industries. Huge state enterprises, such as TAMESEK, with over 450 companies, have proved highly flexible in responding to market conditions. Singapore produces 50% of the world's computer disk drives. The world leader in new biotechnologies.

RESOURCES

 15.6bn kwh (capacity 3.4m kw)

 Not an oil producer; refines 1.03m b/cd

12,600 tonnes

Granite

Singapore has no strategic resources and has to import almost all the energy and food it needs. Its main resources, on which its wealth as a centre of commerce has been built, are its strategic position and its people.

ENVIRONMENT

4% partially protected

New clean city initiatives

There is a small green belt around the causeway. Singapore sees itself as a world leader in providing the perfect urban environment. There is no litter, thanks to instant heavy fines; chewing gum is banned by law.

SINGAPORE

Total Area : 620 sq. km (239 sq. miles)

EXPORTS

Other 43%

Thailand 7%

Hong Kong 7%

Japan 9%

Malaysia 13%

USA 21%

IMPORTS

Saudi Arabia 5%

Malaysia 14%

Other 45%

USA 16%

Japan 20%

WEAKNESSES

Dependence on Malaysia for water. All food and energy has to be imported. Skills shortages in some key areas, especially engineering. Lack of land restraining further development.

MEDIA

 The press is completely regulated

PUBLISHING AND BROADCAST MEDIA

There are 9 daily newspapers, including the leading *Singapore Straits Times* and *Business Times*

1 state-owned service

1 state-owned service

The government is very sensitive to any criticism that might reflect badly on Singapore as a business centre. The *Asian Wall Street Journal* was closed for a period for hinting at problems in the stock-exchange clearing system.

CRIME

6470 prisoners

Down 9% in 1990

Crime is limited and punishment can be severe. The Triads are no longer a problem; the main issue is intellectual piracy.

CHRONOLOGY

In 1819, Sir Stamford Raffles set up a trading post in the village of Singapore; by 1826 it was Britain's colonial centre in South East Asia.

- ☐ **1869** Suez Canal opens; start of Singapore's sustained trade boom.
- ☐ **1942–1945** Japanese occupation.
- ☐ **1959** Lee Kuan Yew and PAP elected. PAP in power ever since.
- ☐ **1965** Independence.

EDUCATION

 90%

Education is not a priority in Singapore, and industry suffers from skills shortages. Malays are effectively excluded from the single university.

HEALTH

1 per 753 people

Circulatory and respiratory diseases, cancers

Singapore has an efficient modern health system. Incentives exist aimed at preserving the extended family, so that the elderly are cared for at home.

WEALTH

Live-in maid, 500 Singapore dollars per month; experienced secretary, 5000 Singapore dollars per month

CONSUMER GOODS OWNERSHIP

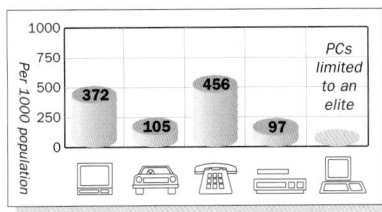

PCs limited to an elite

372 | 105 | 456 | 97

The Chinese and Indians live very well, although their party-allocated flats are not luxurious by Western standards. The Malays are the poorest group.

WORLD RANKING

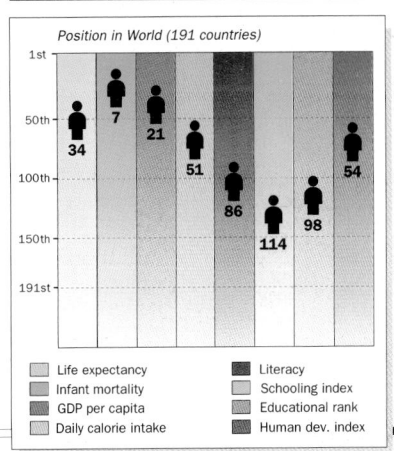

Position in World (191 countries)

34 | 7 | 21 | 51 | 86 | 114 | 98 | 54

- ☐ Life expectancy
- ☐ Infant mortality
- ☐ GDP per capita
- ☐ Daily calorie intake
- ☐ Literacy
- ☐ Schooling index
- ☐ Educational rank
- ☐ Human dev. index

S

SLOVAKIA

OFFICIAL NAME: Slovak Republic **CAPITAL:** Bratislava
POPULATION: 5.3 million **CURRENCY:** Slovak koruna **OFFICIAL LANGUAGE:** Slovak

SLOVAKIA IS BORDERED BY the Czech Republic, Austria, Poland, Hungary and the Ukraine. Southern lowlands contrast with the Carpathian mountain range, which extends along the Polish border. An independent democracy since 1993, Slovakia is the less-developed half of the former Czechoslovakia. It is facing difficulties in making its industry-based economy efficient.

Levoča, in northeastern Slovakia, dates from the 13th century and still retains its medieval street plan and town walls.

CLIMATE

WEATHER CHART

Slovakia has a continental climate. Snowfalls are heavy in winter, whilst summers are moderately warm.

COMMUNICATIONS

 Ivánka, Bratislava   Has no fleet

THE TRANSPORT NETWORK

17,737 km (11,021 miles)	191 km (119 miles)
3661 km (2275 miles)	172 km (107 miles)

Establishing transport links with Austria, the main route to central and western Europe, is vital. The horse and cart is still used in rural areas.

TOURISM

 750,000 visitors (est)   Up 30% in 1993

MAIN OVERSEAS ARRIVALS

Germany 19%
Poland 14%
Hungary 7%
Other 60%

% of total arrivals

The Tatra Mountains are popular with skiers, hikers and cavers. Most of the tourist industry has been privatized, but the government plans to retain partial control of Slovakia's many thermal-spring health spas.

PEOPLE

 Slovak, Hungarian, Czech 108 people per km²

THE URBAN/RURAL POPULATION SPLIT

77% 23%

RELIGIOUS PERSUASION

Orthodox Catholic 2%
Protestant 20%
Roman Catholic 50%
Other 28%

Slovaks dominate society, but 9% of the population is Hungarian, and there is a large Gypsy minority. Tension has increased between the Slovaks and Hungarians, particularly over the directive that Hungarians should adopt Slovak name endings. Before independence, many skilled Slovaks took senior jobs in Prague, but few have returned to help structure the new Slovakia. Roman Catholicism remains a powerful social force.

POLITICS

 1994 President Michal Kováč

THE STATE OF THE PARTIES

National Council of the Slovak Republic 150 members

49% MDS 20% PDL 12% CDM 10% SNP 9% C

MDS = Movement for a Democratic Slovakia **PDL** = Party of the Democratic Left **CDM** = Christian Democratic Movement **SNP** = Slovak National Party **C** = Coexistence (composed of: Hungarian Christian Democratic Movement, Coexistence, Hungarian People's Party)

The move to independence in 1993 was more a result of Czech than Slovak policies. Slovak leader Vladimír Mečiar was bargaining with Prague not for independence, but for more power within a federation. However, Klaus, the Czech leader, offered Slovakia continued membership of the federation on Czech terms or separation.

Slovakian politics are now in flux. Parties that once represented Slovak interests within Czechoslovakia are having to define new objectives in a mostly Slovak context. In 1994, Mečiar was ousted from the premiership in a no-confidence vote. He was criticized for being too dictatorial and for failing to address the growing economic problems. The Hungarian minority has its own parties, but the 300,000 Gypsies have no official representation.

WORLD AFFAIRS

 CE   CSCE   ECE

Relations with Hungary are strained over Slovakia's unilateral decision to complete the Gabcikovo Dam, and the treatment of the Hungarian minority in Slovakia. Slovakia is working to raise its international profile.

AID

 Significant receipts 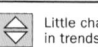 Little change in trends

Aid is of particular importance due to the lack of inward foreign investment. The IMF and EU are the main donors.

DEFENCE

 119.4m 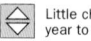 Little change from year to year

A new Slovak army, one third of the former Czechoslovak army, has been formed. Slovakia recently acquired some weapons from Russia, but lack of finance remains a major problem.

RESOURCES

 Over 50% of electricity is nuclear generated   Produces very small quantities of crude oil

 13.3m poultry, 576,000 pigs, 546,000 cattle   Coal, lignite, gas, oil, antimony, copper, iron, mercury, zinc

Slovakia is planning to export power from the massive Gabcikovo Dam on the River Danube.

S

SLOVAKIA

Total Area : 49 500 sq. km
(19 100 sq. miles)

POPULATION

over 100 000
over 50 000
over 10 000

LAND HEIGHT

2000m/6562ft
1000m/3281ft
500m/1640ft
200m/656ft
Sea Level

CHRONOLOGY

Formerly part of the Austro-Hungarian empire, Slovakia joined with the Czech Lands to form the Republic of Czechoslovakia in 1918.

- **1920** Treaty of Trianon sets Czechoslovakian borders.
- **1939–1945** Separate Slovak state under pro-Nazi Fr Jozef Tiso.
- **1945** Restoration of pre-war Czechoslovak state.
- **1947** Communists seize power.
- **1968** 'Prague Spring': brief period of political tolerance and reform, ended by Warsaw pact invasion.
- **1969** Federal system introduced.
- **1989** Demonstrations initiate process leading to democracy.
- **1990** Free multiparty elections.
- **1993** Jan 1, separate Slovak and Czech states established.

ECONOMICS

 10.1bn (est) $ 32.78 Slovak koruny

SCORE CARD

- World GNP Ranking...........................78th
- GNP per Capita $1910
- Balance of Payments ....Deficit
- Inflation ....21% (est)
- Unemployment...................................18%

STRENGTHS

Potential for tourism, particularly skiing in the Tatras, once hotel infrastructure is upgraded.

WEAKNESSES

Legacy of status as less developed part of Czechoslovakia. Loss of subsidies from Czech Republic. Narrow emphasis of economy on heavy engineering and arms manufacture; collapse of COMECON markets for these have hit Slovakia very hard. Unemployment high, since Slovak economy is not competitive in European markets. Lack of foreign investors. Many skilled Slovaks in areas such as banking and policy-making have remained in the Czech Republic.

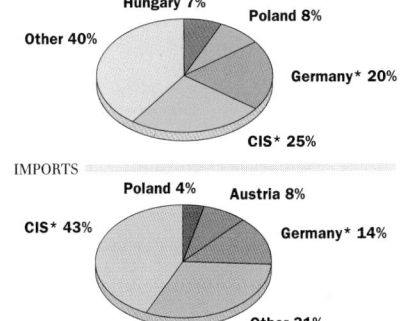

EXPORTS

Hungary 7%
Poland 8%
Other 40%
Germany* 20%
CIS* 25%

IMPORTS

Poland 4%
Austria 8%
CIS* 43%
Germany* 14%
Other 31%

ENVIRONMENT

 10%   Acid rain from power stations has damaged forests

Levels of industrialization are not as great, and pollution not as serious, as in the neighbouring Czech Republic.

MEDIA

 Press freedom is generally assured, though access is limited for minorities

PUBLISHING AND BROADCAST MEDIA

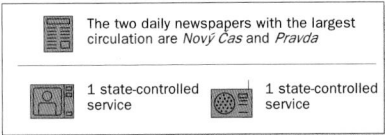

The two daily newspapers with the largest circulation are *Nový Čas* and *Pravda*

1 state-controlled service   1 state-controlled service

Hungarians, who make up 9% of the population, are now demanding access to the media; Gypsies have practically no media coverage.

CRIME

 Slovakia does not publish prison figures   Up 33% in 1993

The state is launching a major initiative to prevent Slovakia being used as a route by smugglers bringing uranium out of the Ukraine and Russia, Semtex explosives out of the Czech Republic and illegal drugs from the Far East.

EDUCATION

 93%

Schooling is reverting to the pre-1939 Slovakian traditions. Rural areas tend to be failed by the education system. There is a modern university in Bratislava.

HEALTH

 1 per 294 people   Cancers, heart and cerebrovascular diseases, accidents

The health service is limited, although of a higher standard than in most of the ex-COMECON states.

WEALTH

 Secretary, 4000 Slovak koruny per month; lawyer, 20,000 Slovak koruny per month

CONSUMER GOODS OWNERSHIP

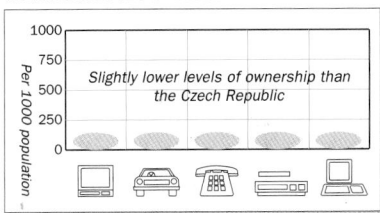

Slightly lower levels of ownership than the Czech Republic

A new elite is emerging, among whom Western goods are very popular. The rural workers are the poorest group.

WORLD RANKING

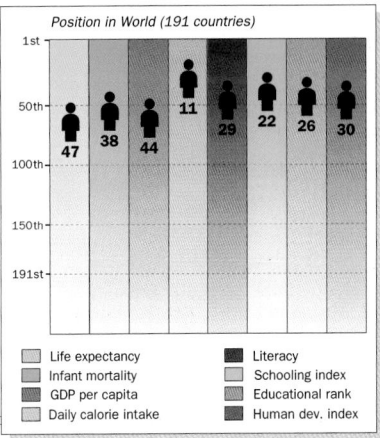

Position in World (191 countries)

47 38 44 11 29 22 26 30

- Life expectancy
- Infant mortality
- GDP per capita
- Daily calorie intake
- Literacy
- Schooling index
- Educational rank
- Human dev. index

S

SLOVENIA

OFFICIAL NAME: Republic of Slovenia **CAPITAL:** Ljubljana
POPULATION: 1.9 million **CURRENCY:** Tolar **OFFICIAL LANGUAGE:** Slovene

EUROPE

OF ALL THE FORMER Yugoslav republics, Slovenia has the closest links with western Europe. Located at the north-eastern end of the Adriatic Sea, this small, alpine country controls some of Europe's major transit routes. Its economy has been badly affected by the collapse of Yugoslavia, and it has struggled to develop economic ties with the West. Slovenia's transition to independence in 1991 avoided the violence associated with the break-up of Yugoslavia.

CLIMATE

WEATHER CHART

Slovenia's interior has a continental climate. Its small coastal region has a mild Mediterranean climate.

COMMUNICATIONS

 Ljubljana International

 2 ships
200 dwt

THE TRANSPORT NETWORK

 14,526 km
(9026 miles)

81 km
(50 miles)

1196 km
(743 miles)

None

Slovenia is strategically situated at some of Europe's major crossroads. In addition, its Adriatic ports provide Austria with its main maritime outlet.

TOURISM

 298,700 visitors

 Tourism has grown since 1991

MAIN OVERSEAS ARRIVALS

Former Yugoslavia 31%			
Italy 26%			
Austria 15%			
Other 28%			

% of total arrivals

Slovenia hopes 'village tourism' will bring visitors to rural towns and farms, as well as to its mountains and beaches. However, large numbers of tourists are still put off by the war in Bosnia.

PEOPLE

 Slovene, Serbo–Croatian

98 people per km²

THE URBAN/RURAL POPULATION SPLIT

49%   51%

ETHNIC MAKEUP

Serb 2% Other 3%
Muslim 1% Croat 3%
Slovene 91%

Slovenia is ethnically homogeneous; 91% are Slovene. There are also small communities of Italians and Hungarians. The Slovene language is sufficiently different from Serbo-Croatian to foster a separate identity from its Yugoslav neighbours. Slovenia has traditionally identified more with the alpine countries to the west than its Balkan neighbours. Access to Italy and Austria during the 1970s and 1980s encouraged a separatist movement. These factors, combined with a well-developed economy, aided Slovenia's relatively peaceful secession from the former Yugoslavia in 1991.

POLITICS

 1996

President Milan Kučan

THE STATE OF THE PARTIES

National Assembly 90 members

24% LDP	17% SCD	16% AL	13% SNP	11% SPP	19% Other

LDP = Liberal Democratic Party **SCD** = Slovenian Christian Democrats **AL** = Associated List **SNP** = Slovenian National Party **SPP** = Slovenian People's Party **Other** = Democratic Party of Slovenia, Greens of Slovenia, Social Democratic Party of Slovenia

National Council 40 members

22 members are elected and 18 are chosen by an electoral college to represent various interests

Following independence, a broad consensus on political reforms existed in Slovenia. This consensus has begun to evaporate. In December 1992, an LDP-led coalition government was elected, headed by Janez Drnovsek. His ability to transform Slovenia into a full market economy is being questioned. A major weakness is his government's dependence on the support of the largely ex-communist AL. The AL is using its influence to promote social policies with popular appeal that run contrary to Drnovsek's proposed reforms. Differences have also emerged among the coalition partners over the pace and impact of market reforms. The result is that economic and institutional change in Slovenia is proceeding slowly.

SLOVENIA

Total Area : 20 250 sq. km
(7820 sq. miles)

POPULATION

over 100 000	◎
over 50 000	○
over 10 000	●
under 10 000	·

LAND HEIGHT

1000m/3281ft
500m/1640ft
200m/656ft
Sea Level

0 25 km
0 25 miles

S

WORLD AFFAIRS

Slovenia has stated its intention to apply for membership of EFTA, the EU and GATT. Disputes with Croatia over fishing rights have now been settled.

AID

 Attraction of aid a major government concern

 Aid receipts have risen since independence

Recent agreements with the EU and the IMF have set up lines of credit. Aid is being targeted at infrastructural improvements and education projects.

DEFENCE

  $170m

 Spending has risen to protect Slovenian sovereignty

Slovene troops successfully held off federal Yugoslav army attacks following secession in 1991. A small air force is being developed.

ECONOMICS

 12bn (est)

 121.20 tolar

SCORE CARD

❑ WORLD GNP RANKING	72nd
❑ GNP PER CAPITA	6300
❑ BALANCE OF PAYMENTS	$764m
❑ INFLATION	22.9%
❑ UNEMPLOYMENT	13%

EXPORTS

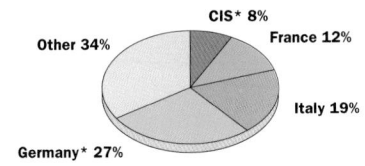

CIS* 8%
France 12%
Other 34%
Italy 19%
Germany* 27%

IMPORTS

Austria 10%
Other 37%
France 12%
Italy 16%
Germany* 25%

STRENGTHS
Competitive manufacturing industry. Prospects for growth in electronics industry. Well developed tourist sector. Czech demand for Slovenia's consumer goods exports. Well placed to supply ex-Yugoslavia when sanctions lifted.

WEAKNESSES
Rising real labour costs may stifle output growth. Highest wages in central Europe. Persistent wage pressures may fuel inflation. Rising unemployment. Privatization process has been slow.

Lake Bled in the Julian Alps, which lie astride the Slovenian–Italian border. The lake is a popular tourist destination.

RESOURCES

 12,669m kwh

 Not an oil producer; refines 14,700 b/cd

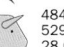 484,000 cattle 529,000 pigs 28,000 sheep

 coal, lignite, lead, zinc, uranium, silver, mercury

Slovenia has come under pressure from Austria to close the nuclear plant at Krško, which provides one third of Slovenia's power. It has deposits of brown coal and lignite, but they are difficult to extract and of poor quality.

ENVIRONMENT

 4%

  Some industrial pollution

Slovenes were in the vanguard of former Yugoslavia's environmental movement. Protecting the country's alpine ecology is a priority.

MEDIA

 The media is free from government interference

PUBLISHING AND BROADCAST MEDIA

There are 3 daily newspapers. The weekly magazine *Mladina* offers independent reporting and commentary

1 state-run service

1 state-run service

The Slovene-language media actively worked to undermine Yugoslav institutions during the secession crisis, reinforcing the sense of national identity.

CRIME

 Slovenia does not publish prison figures

 Low crime levels for region. Little change from year to year

Slovenia has traditionally been a transit point for drug smuggling into western Europe. The trade has declined since the UN imposed sanctions on Serbia.

EDUCATION

 99%

School is compulsory from 7 to 15 years, and standards are high. In 1992, there were over 30,000 students in tertiary education. The university at Ljubljana was founded in 1595.

CHRONOLOGY

Slovenia was part of the Austro-Hungarian empire until 1918. It was the first republic to secede from the Federal Republic of Yugoslavia.

- ❑ **1918** Slovenia joins Yugoslav kingdom.
- ❑ **1949** Tito's break with Moscow. Opens borders with the West.
- ❑ **1989** Parliament confirms right to secede. Calls multiparty elections.
- ❑ **1990** Control over army asserted, referendum approves secession.
- ❑ **1991** Independence declared. Yuogslav federal army attacks held off. EU-brokered cease-fire.
- ❑ **1992** EU recognizes Slovenia. First multiparty elections held. Milan Kučan elected president.
- ❑ **1993** Member of IMF and IBRD.

HEALTH

 1 per 523 people

 Cerebrovascular and heart diseases, cancers

National health care in Slovenia uses health centres and outpatient clinics to increase accessibility for patients.

WEALTH

 Slovenia has the highest wages among the former Yugoslav republics

CONSUMER GOODS OWNERSHIP

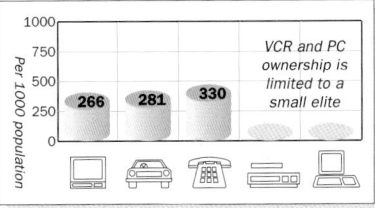

266   281   330

VCR and PC ownership is limited to a small elite

Per 1000 population

Slovenia was the most advanced and highly industrialized of the six Yugoslav republics. Average net monthly wages in 1993 were equivalent to $400.

S

WORLD RANKING

Position in World (191 countries)

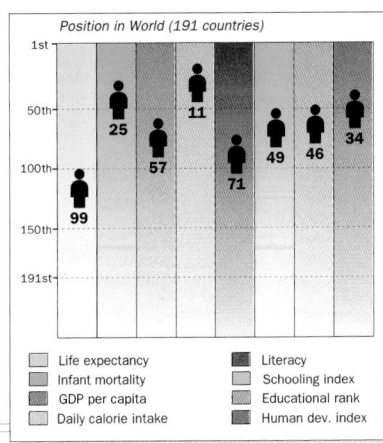

25   11   57   71   49   46   34   99

☐ Life expectancy	☐ Literacy
☐ Infant mortality	☐ Schooling index
☐ GDP per capita	☐ Educational rank
☐ Daily calorie intake	☐ Human dev. index

SOLOMON ISLANDS

OFFICIAL NAME: Solomon Islands **CAPITAL:** Honiara
POPULATION: 300,000 **CURRENCY:** Solomon Islands dollar **OFFICIAL LANGUAGE:** English

SCATTERED OVER 645,000 km², the Solomons archipelago consists of several hundred islands. Most of the population live on the six largest islands – Guadalcanal, Malaita, New Georgia, Makira, Santa Isabel and Choiseul. The Solomons have been settled since at least 1000 BC and the Spanish reached the islands in 1568. They gained independence from Britain in 1978. Most of the Solomons are coral reefs. Just 1% of the islands' land area is cultivable.

CLIMATE

WEATHER CHART

There is little variation in the humid, hot subtropical climate, but ferocious cyclones can occur in the rainy season.

COMMUNICATIONS

Henderson, Honiara 22,000 passengers

2 ships 600 dwt

THE TRANSPORT NETWORK

2152 km (1337 miles)		None
None		None

The airport on Guadalcanal was begun by the Japanese and completed by the USA during the Second World War. Most airfields are simple grass strips.

Unloading seed coconuts near Munda on New Georgia in the Solomons' southern chain of islands. Coconuts are by far the largest and most commercially important crop.

TOURISM

11,105 visitors Up 21% in 1991

MAIN OVERSEAS ARRIVALS

Australia	37%
New Zealand	14%
USA	9%
Other	40%

% of total arrivals

More tourists are expected now that Boeing 747 jets can land at the main airport. Guadalcanal, a key battle site of the Seond World War in the Pacific, has seen a decline in visitors in recent years. Outlying islands cater for visitors wishing to 'go native'.

PEOPLE

English, Pidgin English, Melanesian Pidgin

11 people per km²

THE URBAN/RURAL POPULATION SPLIT

9% 91%

RELIGIOUS PERSUASION

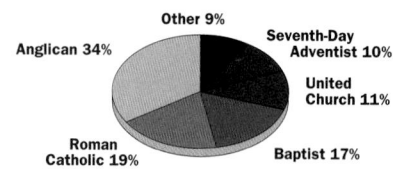

Anglican 34%
Other 9%
Seventh-Day Adventist 10%
United Church 11%
Baptist 17%
Roman Catholic 19%

Almost all Solomon Islanders are Melanesian. In 1957, large numbers of Gilbertese were resettled in the Solomons following a hurricane; a few stayed on and today form a small, distinct community. Over 50 dialects are spoken in the Solomons, a state of 326,000 people spread over 1600 km. As in other Melanesian island states, villagers are expected to share their wealth with their *wontoks*, or clan. Almost all islanders are nominally Christian. Most also maintain their traditional animist beliefs.

POLITICS

1997 HM Queen Elizabeth II

THE STATE OF THE PARTIES

National Parliament 47 members

8% LP 13% Other

45% GNUR 15% PAP 11% NAPSI 8% UP

GNUR = Group for National Union and Reconciliation
PAP = People's Alliance Party **NAPSI** = National Action Party of the Solomon Islands **LP** = Labour Party **UP** = United Party

The Solomons' parliament is based on the Westminster model. Unlike other Pacific states, there is no one class of chiefs which dominates the political process. It is prominent figures in village life – known locally as 'big men' – who stand as candidates. They are usually in parliament for just one term, as elections tend to result in a large turnover of members. Party arrangements within parliament are fluid and coalitions unstable. Women do not take part in the political process. How to reverse the decline in the economy is the main political issue.

SOLOMON ISLANDS

Total Area : 289 000 sq. km (11 158 sq. miles)

POPULATION		LAND HEIGHT	
over 10 000	●	1000m/3280ft	
under 10 000	•	500m/1640ft	
		Sea Level	

PACIFIC OCEAN
Papua New Guinea Nauru SOLOMON ISLANDS Tuvalu
Pacific Ocean

S

WORLD AFFAIRS

   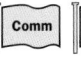 SPC

The main issue is the status of Bougainville in neighbouring Papua New Guinea (PNG). Geographically part of the Solomons, Bougainville, which includes the world's largest copper mine, became part of PNG as a result of an Anglo-German colonial deal. Honiara gives tacit support to the Bougainvillian secessionist groups.

AID

 $40m (receipts)   Down 9% in 1991

The refocusing of Australian aid payments away from the Pacific islands towards Asia has already affected the Solomons' economy. However, Australia has provided cyclone relief and helped restore airfields. Australian NGOs are active. Japan gives technical aid related to the fishing industry.

DEFENCE

 Australia responsible for defence   Not applicable

The Solomons has no armed forces. Australia provides *de facto* protection and two fast patrol boats which are used to protect fisheries from Taiwanese and Okinawan poachers. However, the huge distances which have to be covered mean that their effectiveness is limited.

ECONOMICS

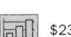 $234m   3.19 Solomon Islands dollars

SCORE CARD

- ❏ WORLD GNP RANKING........................173rd
- ❏ GNP PER CAPITA $780
- ❏ BALANCE OF PAYMENTS..................$−37.4m
- ❏ INFLATION 15.1%
- ❏ UNEMPLOYMENT ....some underemployment

EXPORTS

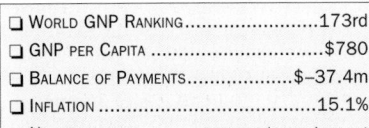

USA 7%
Other 31%
Thailand 12%
UK 14%
Japan 36%

IMPORTS

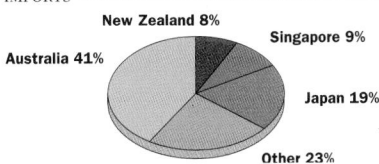

New Zealand 8%
Singapore 9%
Australia 41%
Japan 19%
Other 23%

STRENGTHS
Copra and timber. Survival of subsistence agriculture; Solomon Islanders are self-sufficient in food. Modest diversification of economy into oil palm and cocoa.

WEAKNESSES
Copra industry increasingly unproductive. Opposition to over-exploitation of timber. Dependence on imported energy. Location away from main Pacific sea and air routes.

RESOURCES

 30m kwh (capacity 10,000 kw)   Not an oil producer and has no refineries

 52,000 pigs, 13,000 cattle   Gold, copper, bauxite, lead, zinc, silver, cobalt, phosphates

Bauxite deposits have been discovered on Rennett Island. In addition, there are traces of gold and copper on Guadalcanal, but not in commercially exploitable quantities. Most energy has to be imported.

ENVIRONMENT

 None   Successful environmental campaigns

The environmental movement is strong in the Solomons. It persuaded the government that exploiting bauxite on Rennett would destroy the island. It is currently mounting a fierce campaign against the tropical timber industry.

MEDIA

 Minimal government interference

PUBLISHING AND BROADCAST MEDIA

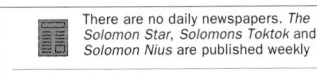

There are no daily newspapers. *The Solomon Star*, *Solomons Toktok* and *Solomon Nius* are published weekly

No TV service   1 independent service

The one radio station broadcasts in English and Pidgin. Islanders oppose TV as it would dilute their culture.

CRIME

 Solomon Islands does not publish prison figures   Crime rate rising

There has been a small increase in crime on Honiara. Most offences are drink-related.

CHRONOLOGY

Settled since before 1000 BC by Melanesian peoples, the Solomons became a British colony in 1893.

- ❏ **1900** Britain acquires northern Solomons from Germany. Copra industry established.
- ❏ **1942** Occupied by Japanese forces.
- ❏ **1943** Japan loses control to USA following fierce fighting.
- ❏ **1978** Independence from UK.
- ❏ **1986** Cyclone: massive damage.

EDUCATION

 60%

Education is modelled on the British system. Tertiary students go to the University of the South Pacific in Fiji.

HEALTH

 1 per 8812 people   Not available

The main hospital is in Honiara. Known as 'Number 9', it was built as a military hospital by the US army during the Second World War.

WEALTH

 Most islanders are subsistence farmers

CONSUMER GOODS OWNERSHIP

Has no TV service   VCR and PC ownership is limited to an elite

3   19

Solomon Islanders in government jobs are the wealthiest group. Outlying islands are extremely poor.

S

WORLD RANKING

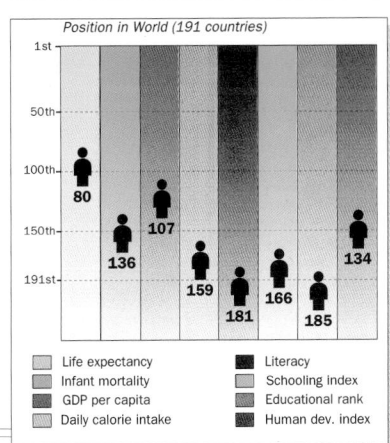

Position in World (191 countries)

80
107
136
159
181
166
185
134

- ☐ Life expectancy
- ☐ Infant mortality
- ☐ GDP per capita
- ☐ Daily calorie intake
- ■ Literacy
- ☐ Schooling index
- ☐ Educational rank
- ☐ Human dev. index

489

SOMALIA

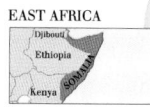
EAST AFRICA
Africa

OFFICIAL NAME: Somali Democratic Republic **CAPITAL:** Mogadishu
POPULATION: 9.2 million **CURRENCY:** Somali shilling **OFFICIAL LANGUAGES:** Somali and Arabic

OCCUPYING THE HORN of Africa, Italian Somaliland and British Somaliland were united in 1960 to form an independent Somalia. The land is semi-arid except in the more fertile south. Years of clan-based civil war have resulted in the collapse of central government. By 1992, drought and the conflict had created the worst mass starvation and refugee crisis ever to face the UN.

CLIMATE

WEATHER CHART

Somalia is very dry. The northern coast is very hot and humid, the eastern less so. The interior has some of the world's highest mean yearly temperatures.

COMMUNICATIONS

 Mogadishu International
 5 ships 12,800 dwt

THE TRANSPORT NETWORK

22,218 km (13,806 miles)	None
None	None

About 50% of Somalis are nomads for whom the camel is the principal means of transport. In 1990, the IDA agreed to repair the road network, but by 1994 no work had started on the seven-year project.

TOURISM

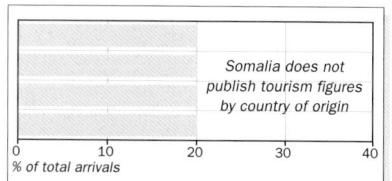
Urban and rural instability deters tourism

Not applicable

MAIN OVERSEAS ARRIVALS

Somalia does not publish tourism figures by country of origin

0 10 20 30 40
% of total arrivals

Aid workers, foreign journalists and UN peace-keepers are the only visitors. Land-mines are a hazard.

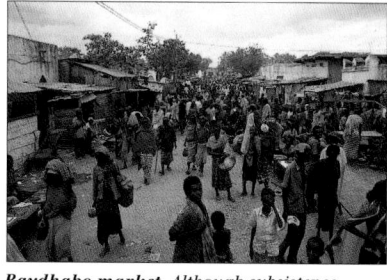
Baydhabo market. *Although subsistence farming supports most people, 2.8 million war refugees needed Red Cross food aid in 1992.*

PEOPLE

 Somali, Arabic, English, Italian
 12 people per km²

THE URBAN/RURAL POPULATION SPLIT

36%   64%

RELIGIOUS PERSUASION

Sunni Muslim 100%

The clan system is at the root of all social, political and commercial issues in Somalia. Shifting allegiances characterize its structure – a tendency stifled by Siad Barre's dictatorship but revived after his fall in 1991. His undermining of the traditional brokers of justice, the elders, contributed to the present power vacuum, while his persecution of the Issaqs led to Somaliland's secession in 1991. However, the entire population is ethnic Somali and national identity remains strong; widespread opposition to the US-led UN peace-keeping force reflects this.

POLITICS

Uncertain

Interim President Ali Mahdi Mohamed

THE STATE OF THE PARTIES

National Assembly 123 members

There has been no prospect of organizing new elections since the overthrow of Siad Barre, although an attempt has been made to draft a new democratic constitution

Somalia is no longer the undivided republic it was under its dictator, President Siad Barre. Civil war started in the north in the 1980s and spread as other opposition groups took up arms against his regime. He eventually fled the capital in early 1991. The subsequent civil war in the south and the self-proclaimed independence of Somaliland in the north in May that year have meant that the unitary state has effectively ceased to exist. In spite of UN intervention led by the USA, southern Somalia is almost entirely in the grip of warring clan factions and opportunist warlords. Chief among them are the two United Somalia Congress (USC) faction leaders, General Aideed, who was instrumental in ousting Siad Barre, and Ali Mahdi, who unilaterally declared himself president. Now that fighting has stopped in Somaliland, the region awaits international recognition.

SOMALIA
Total Area :
637 660 sq. km
(246 200 sq. miles)

POPULATION

over 1 000 000	⊡
over 100 000	◎
over 50 000	○
over 10 000	●
under 10 000	•

LAND HEIGHT

2000m/6562ft	
1000m/3281ft	
500m/1640ft	
200m/656ft	
Sea Level	

S

WORLD AFFAIRS

The central questions are whether the UN should extend its peace-keeping and humanitarian roles and effectively run the country, and whether self-declared Somaliland will gain international recognition, with borders in line with those of former British Somaliland. Even though fighting has stopped there, no help other than emergency aid is being provided because the region lacks official status.

AID

 $428m (receipts)   Up 1% in 1990

Mass starvation among the Somali population in 1991 finally prompted the UN into launching a large-scale humanitarian aid effort. US forces have been drafted in under the UN to protect aid convoys from attacks by armed gangs.

DEFENCE

 $18.05m   Down 61% in 1989

Somalia is awash with weapons supplied by both the USA and the former USSR during the Cold War.

ECONOMICS

 $835m   2615.58 Somali shillings

SCORE CARD

❑ WORLD GNP RANKING	160th
❑ GNP PER CAPITA	$100
❑ BALANCE OF PAYMENTS	*The formal*
❑ INFLATION	*economy has*
❑ UNEMPLOYMENT	*collapsed*

STRENGTHS
Very few. Export of livestock to Arabian peninsula resumed in the north. Inflow of money from Somalis living abroad. Growing market in stolen food aid.

WEAKNESSES
Every commodity, except arms, in extremely short supply. The south has little economic potential. Effects of drought include death of nomads' livestock herds.

EXPORTS

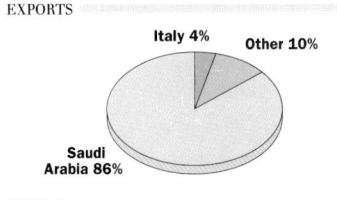

Italy 4%   Other 10%
Saudi Arabia 86%

IMPORTS

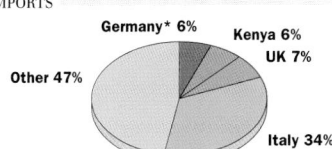

Germany* 6%   Kenya 6%   UK 7%
Other 47%   Italy 34%

declared Somaliland will gain international recognition, with borders in line with those of former British Somaliland. Even though fighting has stopped there, no help other than emergency aid is being provided because the region lacks official status.

RESOURCES

 230m kwh (capacity 60,000 kw)   Not an oil producer; refines 10,000 b/cd

 21.1m goats, 13.8m sheep, 6.8m camels   Salt, tin, zinc, copper, gypsum, manganese, uranium, iron

Commercially exploitable minerals remain untapped. Oil experts are confident of discovering large offshore reserves in the north.

ENVIRONMENT

 0.3% (partially protected)   Nomadic lifestyle by definition in tune with the environment

Human deprivation and starvation caused by the effects of drought and war on land and livestock outweigh all other ecological considerations.

MEDIA

 Following the overthrow of the Siad Barre regime, independent newspapers have been established

PUBLISHING AND BROADCAST MEDIA

There are no daily newspapers

No TV service   Several independent services

Two Radio Mogadishu stations run by the two main USC factions – Ali Mahdi's and General Aideed's – existed until US forces destroyed Aideed's. There are few newspapers as paper is currently in very short supply.

CRIME

 Somalia does not publish prison figures   Widespread breakdown in law and order since 1991

Armed clan factions (some, in remoter regions, engaged in family feuds rather than the war) and bandits rule large areas. Police forces exist in some cities but, with few resources, dare not risk confrontation with warlords. Muslim *sharia* law, now the *de facto* system, is run in a makeshift fashion by elders.

EDUCATION

 24%

The system collapsed during the civil war. There were reports of improvised open-air schools starting up again in urban areas in 1993. Somali has been a written language only since 1972.

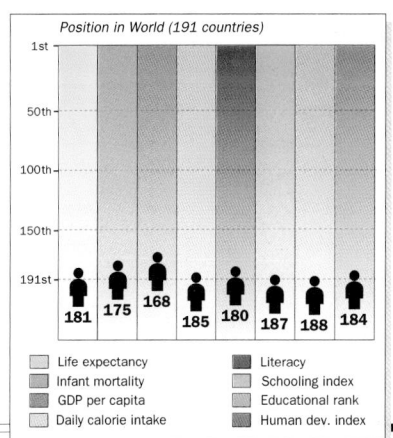

CHRONOLOGY

The lands of the Somalis became UK and Italian colonies in the 1880s.

- ❑ **1941–1950** UK rules both areas.
- ❑ **1960** Unification at independence.
- ❑ **1964** Somalia's claims to Ogaden leads to war with Ethiopia.
- ❑ **1969** Gen Siad Barre seizes power.
- ❑ **1977–1978** Attack on Ethiopia fails.
- ❑ **1981** Two opposition groups based in Ethiopia begin guerrilla war.
- ❑ **1987** Reconciliation with Ethiopia induces Somali National Movement group to occupy north.
- ❑ **1991** Siad Barre ousted. War degenerates into clan chaos. Mass starvation. Somaliland secedes.
- ❑ **1992** Warlords plunder food aid. US sends in military with UN backing.
- ❑ **1994** US troops withdrawn.

HEALTH

 1 per 4640 people   Diarrheal, communicable and parasitic diseases

The state-run system has collapsed entirely. A few very rudimentary facilities are run by foreign workers.

WEALTH

The subsistence existence of the nomads (the bulk of the population) contrasts with the Somali warlords' wealth, won by armed force

CONSUMER GOODS OWNERSHIP

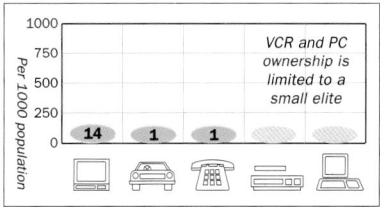

VCR and PC ownership is limited to a small elite

14   1   1

Rich pickings are available for bandits and warlords in the aid-stealing racket. In Somaliland, ministers survive from money sent by relatives living overseas.

S

WORLD RANKING

Position in World (191 countries)

181 175 168 185 180 187 188 184

❑ Life expectancy   ❑ Literacy
❑ Infant mortality   ❑ Schooling index
❑ GDP per capita   ❑ Educational rank
❑ Daily calorie intake   ❑ Human dev. index

SOUTH AFRICA

OFFICIAL NAME: Republic of South Africa **CAPITALS:** Pretoria, Cape Town, Bloemfontein
POPULATION: 37.4 million **CURRENCY:** Rand **OFFICIAL LANGUAGES:** 11 African languages, English, Afrikaans.

RICH IN NATURAL RESOURCES, South Africa comprises a central plateau, or *veld*, bordered to the south and west by the Drakensberg Mountains. After eight decades of white minority rule, and racial segregation under the apartheid policy since 1948, South Africa held its first multiracial, multiparty elections in 1994. The revolution in South Africa's politics began in 1990, when President F W De Klerk legalized black freedom groups and began dismantling apartheid. The African National Congress (ANC), under Nelson Mandela, is now the leading political movement.

Nelson Mandela, who became president of South Africa in April 1994.

F W De Klerk. He dismantled apartheid legislation during his presidency.

CLIMATE

WEATHER CHART

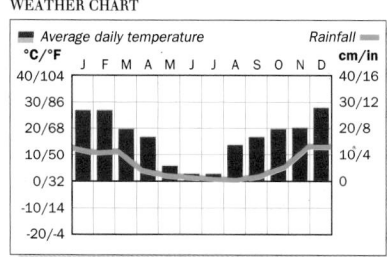

Despite the moderating effects of oceans on three sides, South Africa's warm temperate climate is dry; 65% of the country has less than 50 cm of rain a year. Drought is a periodic hazard.

COMMUNICATIONS

Jan Smuts International, Johannesburg
4.5m passengers

6 ships
200,500 dwt

THE TRANSPORT NETWORK

181,341 km (112,683 miles)		2040 km (1268 miles)
21,244 km (13,201 miles)		None

The further expansion of port capacity is a priority. Improvements to the road network are aimed in part at reducing accidents: South Africa has one of the world's worst road death rates.

Vineyard backed by the dramatic mountains of Cape Province. The lifting of trade sanctions has provided a major boost to the South African wine industry.

TOURISM

2.7m visitors

Up 58% in 1992

MAIN OVERSEAS ARRIVALS

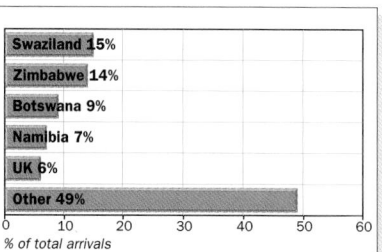

Swaziland 15%
Zimbabwe 14%
Botswana 9%
Namibia 7%
UK 6%
Other 49%

% of total arrivals

South Africa has a huge potential for tourism. Its attractions range from beaches to mountains, from prize-winning vineyards to internationally-renowned wildlife reserves. The Kruger National Park is perhaps the most diverse in the world, with 137 species of mammal and 450 species of bird. This potential, however, has yet to be fully realized. South Africa's isolation during the apartheid era kept tourist numbers down. Today, the key constraints on efforts to expand tourism are political uncertainty and the rising level of violent crime.

PEOPLE

Afrikaans, Zulu, Xhosa, Tswana, Sotho, Pedi, English, Swazi, Venda, Bushman

29 people per km²

THE URBAN/RURAL POPULATION SPLIT

60% 40%

RELIGIOUS PERSUASION

Methodist 6%
Zion Christian Church 5%
Roman Catholic 8%
Dutch Reformed 11%
Other 53%
Other Black Independent 17%

ETHNIC MAKEUP

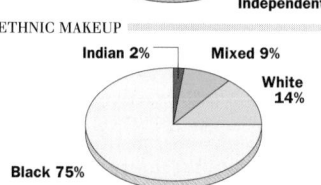

Indian 2% Mixed 9%
White 14%
Black 75%

Until 1991, the lives of South Africa's many ethnic groups were structured by apartheid, the system of racial segregation controlled by the white minority. The Dutch-descended Afrikaners dominated politics; the English-speaking whites the economy. The black majority was marginalized socially and politically.

The extended family has been undermined by regulations forcing men to migrate for work, leaving their wives and children in the rural areas. A small black middle-class has grown up, but most black South Africans are underemployed.

Ethnic tension remains high in the transition period following the dismantling of apartheid. This has led to demands for independent homelands by some Zulus and whites.

The decline of the male-dominated Afrikaner political culture will allow women, who already play an increasingly important economic role, to move to the centre of politics. Around 40% of ANC election candidates were female. The new constitution guarantees equality of the sexes.

POPULATION AGE BREAKDOWN

% of population by age group	0–14	15–64			65+
65+	3.9%	3.8%	4%	4.2%	4.5%
15–64	55.2%	55.2%	57.4%	58.7%	59.9%
0–14	40.9%	41%	38.6%	37.1%	35.6%
	1960	1970	1980	1990	2000

S

POLITICS

1998

President Nelson
Rolihlahla Mandela

THE STATE OF THE PARTIES

National Assembly 400 members

| 11% IFP | 2% FF |

| 63% ANC | 21% NP | 2% DP | 1% Other |

ANC = African National Congress **NP** = National Party
IFP = Inkatha Freedom Party **DP** = Democratic Party
FF = Freedom Front **Other** = Pan African Congress (PAC),
African Christian Democratic Party

Senate 90 members

10 members elected by each of 9 regional legislatures

South Africa became a multiparty
democracy following elections in 1994.

MAIN POLITICAL ISSUES

Maintaining unity

In April 1994, South Africa confounded
the proponents of violence and ethnic
division to hold peaceful elections
which brought its first multiracial
government to power. The challenge
facing the new ANC-dominated
administration is to ensure that, while
pursuing the aspirations of the black
majority, it does not
marginalize South Africa's
minorities. The white far

SOUTH AFRICA

Total Area : 1 221 040 sq. km
(471 443 sq. miles)

right and Chief Buthelezi's *Inkatha*
have the potential to resume violent
destabilization if they feel their
interests are not being addressed.

Role of the security forces

The loyalty of the security forces to the
new government is uncertain. There
was plenty of evidence, notably from
the 1994 Goldstone Commission, of
police and military involvement in pre-
election violence. A particular problem
for the police, long seen as the agents
of apartheid, is to evolve into a neutral
crime-prevention force.

PROFILE

The 1994 elections put an end to over
45 years of white rule by the NP. Its
leader, F W De Klerk, played a central
role with ANC leader Nelson Mandela
in the transition to multi-racial
democracy. The NP came second in the
polls but well behind the ANC, which
only just missed the two thirds majority
it needed to govern alone. The ANC
now dominates the Unity government.
Its main challenge, apart from
maintaining national unity, will be to
reconcile the demands of its
activists for jobs and better
living standards, whilst
encouraging foreign
investment.

WORLD AFFAIRS

| ECA | GATT | SACU | LORCS | IDA |

After several decades of political
isolation and economic sanctions, South
Africa is to be readmitted to the UN and
the Commonwealth. Its priority now is
to attract new international investors
and to encourage the return of the
many who disinvested during the
1980s. The end of apartheid brought an
end to hostility from its neighbours.
Improving relations with them and with
the non-aligned countries is also
important. Membership of the Southern
African Development Community (SADC)
is being discussed, although existing
members are concerned that South
Africa's economic domination of the
region could lead to it taking over the
organization. A regional security
alliance has also been mooted.
Evidence that rogue army and civilian
elements are involved with UNITA in the
renewed Angolan civil war has been an
embarrassment to the government.

POPULATION

over 1 000 000	⊡
over 500 000	◉
over 100 000	◎
over 50 000	○
over 10 000	●

LAND HEIGHT

| 2000m/6562ft |
| 1000m/3281ft |
| 500m/1640ft |
| Sea Level |

Note: *PWV*-Pretoria Witwatersrand-Vereeniging

AID

 $849 million (est) in 1993   Increasing with end of political isolation

South Africa was cut off from almost all aid, particularly from the World Bank and IMF, during the apartheid years. It is now trying to persuade donors to provide the massive financial aid needed to support reconstruction, in particular for job creation and social infrastructure programmes.

CHRONOLOGY

Until 1652, South Africa was peopled by Bantu-speaking groups and Bushmen. Then, Dutch settlers arrived. British colonizers followed in the 18th century.

❑ **1899–1902** Boer War with Britain.
❑ **1910** Union of South Africa set up as British dominion; white monopoly of power formalized.
❑ **1912** ANC formed.
❑ **1934** Independence.
❑ **1948** NP takes power; apartheid segregationist policy introduced.
❑ **1958–1966** Dr Hendrik Verwoerd prime minister. 'Grand Apartheid' policy implemented.
❑ **1959** Pan African Congress (PAC) formed in split from ANC.
❑ **1960** Sharpeville massacre. ANC, PAC banned. South Africa becomes republic; leaves Commonwealth.
❑ **1964** Nelson Mandela, a senior leader of the ANC, jailed.
❑ **1976** Soweto uprisings sparked by attempts to force black schools to teach Afrikaans; hundreds killed.
❑ **1978** P W Botha prime minister.
❑ **1984** New constitution: Indians and Coloureds get some representation. Growing black opposition.
❑ **1985** State of emergency introduced. International sanctions.
❑ **1989** F W De Klerk replaces P W Botha as president. Elections underline white conservative hostility to change.
❑ **1990** De Klerk legalizes ANC and PAC; frees Nelson Mandela.
❑ **1990–1993** International sanctions gradually withdrawn.
❑ **1991** Multiparty Convention for a Democratic South Africa (CODESA) begins negotiating new political structure.
❑ **1992** De Klerk wins whites-only referendum. June–August, 'Mass Action'; ANC breaks off talks over government veto on CODESA. September, talks resume. De Klerk and Mandela work together on transition process.
❑ **1993** Transitional timetable takes shape. Mandela and De Klerk win Nobel Peace Prize.
❑ **1994** April, multiracial elections.

DEFENCE

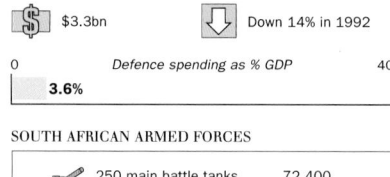 $3.3bn   ⬇ Down 14% in 1992

0	Defence spending as % GDP	40
3.6%		

SOUTH AFRICAN ARMED FORCES

🪖	250 main battle tanks (*Centurion/Olifant 2B*)	72,400 personnel
🚢	3 submarines and 9 patrol boats	4500 personnel
✈	259 combat aircraft (75 *Impala* II/12 *Cheetah* E 29 *Mirage* F-1AZ)	10,000 personnel
🚀	None	

The government is trying to turn the South African Defence Force (SADF), the enforcer of apartheid, into a body loyal to a multiracial government. The process has included cuts in defence spending, an end to the SADF's policy-making role and changes in top personnel. The possibility of a security alliance with South Africa's former opponents in the region has been proposed. A major test will be the integration of the armed wings of the ANC and PAC. Rogue SADF elements involved in political violence and former officers in the racist far-right may threaten the outcome of reform.

Sanctions encouraged a major arms industry. South Africa is now the world's twelfth leading arms exporter.

ECONOMICS

 $90.4bn   💲 3.06 rand

SCORE CARD

❑ WORLD GNP RANKING..........................31st
❑ GNP PER CAPITA $2520
❑ BALANCE OF PAYMENTS $2.7bn
❑ INFLATION 14.4%
❑ UNEMPLOYMENT.................................30%

EXPORTS

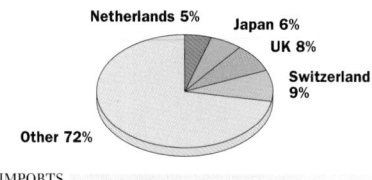

Netherlands 5%   Japan 6%   UK 8%   Switzerland 9%   Other 72%

IMPORTS

Japan 10%   USA 11%   Other 47%   UK 12%   Germany* 20%

STRENGTHS

Africa's largest and most developed economy; highly diversified with modern infrastructure. Strong financial sector for mobilizing investment. Growing manufacturing sector, at present accounting for 23% of GDP. Varied resource base, particularly of strategically important minerals.

WEAKNESSES

Risks of political instability deter foreign investment. Growth too low to provide resources to overcome deprivation among black majority. Black unemployment growing by 2.5% a year. High population growth.

PROFILE

South Africa has a large and diverse private sector, much of it controlled by multinationals. International

ECONOMIC PERFORMANCE INDICATOR

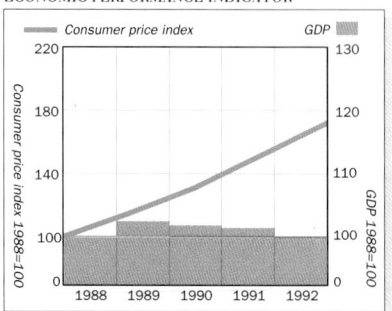

— Consumer price index   ▨ GDP

sanctions forced the government to play a central economic role through state corporations in the 1980s. This is now being reduced in a series of privatizations. The ANC has declared its intention to work with big business in order to revivify the economy and develop the townships.

SOUTH AFRICA : MAJOR BUSINESSES

🍴	Food processing	🏦	Banking & finance
🐟	Fish processing	⚙	Light engineering
📖	Publishing	✿	Heavy engineering
🛢	Oil refining	�car	Vehicle manufacture
⛏	Gold mining	💻	Hi-tech
🚚	Diamond mining	※	Textiles

* significant multinational ownership

0   300 km
0   300 miles

S

RESOURCES

 165bn kwh
(capacity 25.9m kw)

Not an oil producer;
refines 430,500 b/cd

30.9m sheep,
11.9m cattle,
1.5m pigs

Gold, coal, vanadium,
vermiciline, diamonds,
chromium, manganese

ELECTRICITY GENERATION

Hydro 0.5% (764m kwh)
Thermal 97% (159.8bn kwh)
Nuclear 2.5% (3.9bn kwh)
Other 0%

0　20　40　60　80　100
% of total generation by type

South Africa has some of the continent's
richest natural resources, in particular
minerals. Its dominance of the world
market in gold and diamonds was
central to its survival of sanctions
during apartheid. Over the past century,
47% of the world's gold has come from
South Africa. Today's output of 600-
tonnes-a-year accounts for 30% of the
world total. South Africa is the single
largest producer of manganese metal,
chrome ore, vanadium and vermiciline.

South Africa lacks oil reserves and
sanctions-busting was costly. Its huge
coal reserves are used to generate
87% of electricity and to make oil.
The priority is to bring the 80% of
black homes without electricity into
the national grid. Agriculture is varied.

SOUTH AFRICA : LAND USE

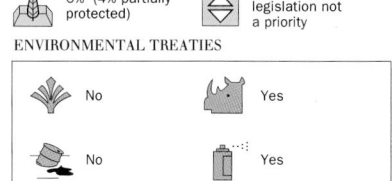

Cropland
Forest
Pasture
Desert
High mountain regions
Sheep
Maize
Fruit - cash crop

0　500 km
0　500 miles

ENVIRONMENT

 6% (4% partially
protected)

Environmental
legislation not
a priority

ENVIRONMENTAL TREATIES

	No		Yes
	No		Yes

Natural disasters, notably floods
and drought, are a hazard. The
main concern is protecting rich and
varied animal species. Environmental
measures could conflict in future
with the demands of economic growth.

MEDIA

 Censorship regulations imposed under apartheid
have been largely dismantled since 1990

PUBLISHING AND BROADCAST MEDIA

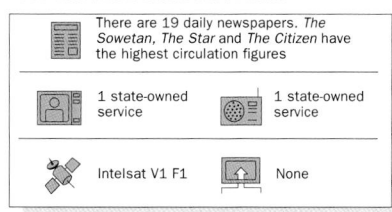

There are 19 daily newspapers. *The
Sowetan, The Star* and *The Citizen* have
the highest circulation figures

1 state-owned
service

1 state-owned
service

Intelsat V1 F1

None

The end of censorship is reflected in
the press, which ranges from far-left to
extreme-right. TV programming is now
more balanced and diverse.

CRIME

 11,000 prisoners　 Rapid rise in
violent crime

CRIME RATES

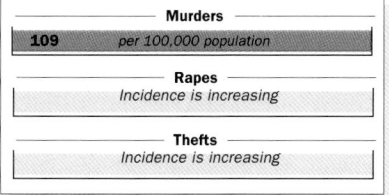

Murders
109　*per 100,000 population*

Rapes
Incidence is increasing

Thefts
Incidence is increasing

South Africa is the world's most
dangerous country (besides war zones),
with 40,000 murders a year. Despite its
high profile, political violence accounts
for only 10% of the total. The rise in
levels of murder, armed robbery and
muggings has led to a boom in the
personal security industry.

EDUCATION

 59%

0　　　*Education spending as % GNP*　　25
4.6%

THE EDUCATION SYSTEM

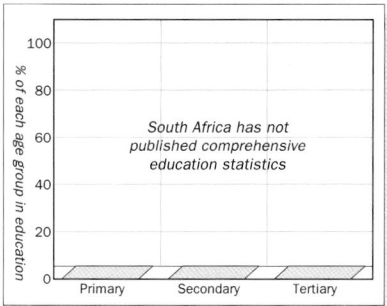

100
80
60
40
20
0

% of each age group in education

*South Africa has not
published comprehensive
education statistics*

Primary　Secondary　Tertiary

Education has been desegregated,
but most black children are still
restricted to underfunded schools.
Upgrading education is a priority
if employment prospects for blacks
are to meet their requirements.

HEALTH

 1 per 1340 people　 Heart, respiratory and
diarrheal diseases,
cancers, road deaths

0　　　*Health spending as % GNP*　　25
0.6%

Health services were desegregated in
1990, but have yet to be restructured
and expanded to give all people equal
access to care. The per capita figures
on provision of medical facilities hide
a strong bias towards whites and urban
areas, where 80% of doctors work. The
limited provision for rural black South
Africans, in particular, is reflected in
mortality figures. Out of every 1000
black children, 200 die before the age
of five, compared with the sub-Saharan
average of 165 per 1000.

WEALTH

 Salaries among whites are substantially
higher than among blacks

CONSUMER GOODS OWNERSHIP

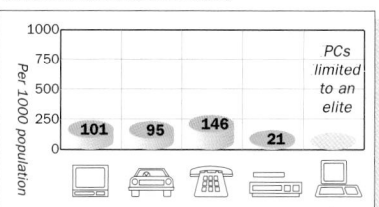

1000
750
500
250
0

Per 1000 population

*PCs
limited
to an
elite*

101　95　146　21

In South Africa, the black majority
is the poorest group. Wealth disparities
are marked. At the top, the white
elite enjoys one of the world's highest
standards of living, on a par with that
of California. In contrast, black living
standards are among Africa's poorest.
Half of black adults are unemployed.
Most blacks have been deprived of
decent housing, education and health
facilities. In between are the Asian
and mixed race communities, given
more privileges under apartheid's strict
racial hierarchy, and a very small black
middle class. Reducing these disparities
will be the new government's priority.

S

WORLD RANKING

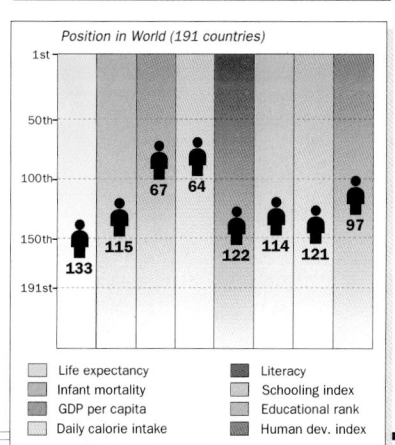

Position in World (191 countries)

1st
50th
100th
150th
191st

67　64　97
115　122　114　121
133

Life expectancy	Literacy
Infant mortality	Schooling index
GDP per capita	Educational rank
Daily calorie intake	Human dev. index

SOUTH KOREA

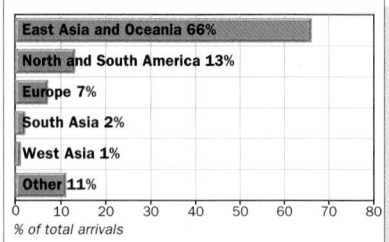

OFFICIAL NAME: Republic of Korea **CAPITAL:** Seoul
POPULATION: 44.2 million **CURRENCY:** Won **OFFICIAL LANGUAGE:** Korean

SOUTH KOREA OCCUPIES the southern half of the Korean peninsula in East Asia. Over 80% of its terrain is mountainous and two thirds is forested. Rice is the major agricultural product, grown by over 85% of South Korea's three million farmers. Most of the urban population lives along the coastal plains. Under US sponsorship, South Korea was separated from the communist North at the 38th parallel after the Second World War. In 1991, the two states discussed reunification. However, South Korea remains suspicious that the North may be planning a military take-over.

CLIMATE

WEATHER CHART

South Korea has four distinct seasons. Winters are dry and can be bitterly cold. Summers are hot and humid. The island of Cheju-do has a tropical climate.

COMMUNICATIONS

 Kimpo Intl, Seoul
21.33m passengers

645 ships
1.34m dwt

THE TRANSPORT NETWORK

55,778 km (34,659 miles)	1550 km (963 miles)
6456 km (4012 miles)	1609 km (1000 miles)

South Korea has a highly integrated transport policy. Massive investments have been made in all aspects of communications. In 1968, a nationwide motor expressway network was inaugurated. Mainly toll-based, it now joins most major urban centres. Air travel, an easy way to get around the mountainous interior, has expanded rapidly. Competition for Korean Air (KAL) has come with the licensing of a second airline, Asiana. The increase in air traffic has also brought forward plans to replace Kimpo International with a new airport.

South Korea has perhaps the world's best public transport system. Buses, trains, boats and planes are integrated in one timetable. All systems have a reputation for punctuality. A $14 billion high-speed rail link is being built between Seoul and Pusan.

TOURISM

2.96m visitors   Up 8% in 1990

MAIN OVERSEAS ARRIVALS

East Asia and Oceania 66%
North and South America 13%
Europe 7%
South Asia 2%
West Asia 1%
Other 11%

% of total arrivals

Overseas tourism to South Korea has increased ten-fold since 1969. Most visitors are Japanese, who come for the golf and Seoul's nightlife. Cheju-do is a favoured honeymoon destination. 13% of all tourists are visiting relatives; this would once have meant relations serving with the US army. Today, Los Angeles-based Korean-Americans make up the greatest proportion of visitors. However, despite the publicity generated by the 1988 Olympics, and the decision to make 1994 'Visit Korea Year', South Korea is still not seen in the West as a prime tourist destination.

SOUTH KOREA

Total Area : 99 020 sq. km
(38 232 sq. miles)

POPULATION

over 5 000 000
over 1 000 000
over 500 000
over 100 000
over 50 000
over 10 000
under 10 000

LAND HEIGHT

1000m/3281ft
500m/1640ft
200m/656ft
Sea Level

S

PEOPLE

 Korean, Chinese

 431 people per km²

THE URBAN/RURAL POPULATION SPLIT

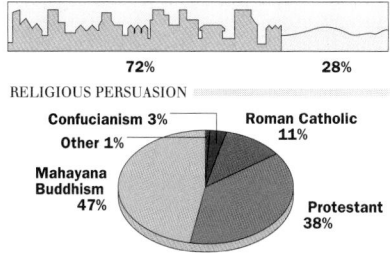

72% **28%**

RELIGIOUS PERSUASION

Confucianism 3%
Other 1%
Roman Catholic 11%
Mahayana Buddhism 47%
Protestant 38%

ETHNIC MAKEUP

Korean 100%

South Korea, like the North, is unusual in having been inhabited by one ethnic group for the last 2000 years. There is a tiny Chinese community, but this is diminishing as most emigrate to Taiwan. One result of economic growth has been an increase in illegal immigrants from the poorer Asian countries who take menial jobs that Koreans now refuse. Family life is a central and clearly-defined part of Korean society. Most Koreans can trace their ancestry back thousands of years. This is significant as those of the same surname group (rather than the same surname – 60% of Koreans are called Lee, Kim or Pak) may not marry. Pressure on housing has led to an increase in nuclear families, as city-centre flats do not have room for the traditional household of three generations. Women play a traditional role in society: it is still not respectable for those who are married to have a job.

POPULATION AGE BREAK DOWN

% of population by age group	■ 0–14	▨ 15–64	□ 65+

	1960	1970	1980	1990	2000
65+	3.3%	3.3%	3.8%	4.8%	6.4%
15–64	54.8%	54.7%	62.2%	69.5%	71.6%
0–14	41.9%	42%	34%	25.7%	22%

POLITICS

 1996

 Kim Young-Sam

THE STATE OF THE PARTIES

National Assembly 299 members

50% DLP **32% DP** **10% UNP** **8% Other**

DLP = Democratic Liberal Party **DP** = Democratic Party
UNP = Unification National Party **Other** = New Political Reform Party

Officially a democracy since its inception, in practice South Korea was ruled by military dictators until 1987, when the Sixth Republic established multiparty democratic politics.

MAIN POLITICAL ISSUES

Corruption
President Kim Young-Sam's anti-corruption programme has been popular with voters, and has succeeded in purging his enemies. Pushing the process too far, however, risks antagonizing the military and splitting his party.

The economy
South Korea's growth slowed to 4.8% in 1992 – poor by Korean standards. The debate is moving in favour of state intervention in the economy.

Faction-led parties
South Korea's political parties are highly factionalized and fragmented, and regroup often. Voters are beginning to demand unified parties that represent clearer ideological positions.

PROFILE
South Korea's politics changed radically in 1987 when President Roh Tae-Woo instituted a genuine transition to democracy, including, for the first time, direct elections for presidents, a parliament with enhanced powers and a free press.

In 1993, the first non-military leader in 30 years, Kim Young-Sam, became president. He quickly appointed a new head of the army staff, thereby establishing his independence from the military. Searching tax audits have also been used to embarrass political opponents. A reform drive in 1994 was aimed at rooting out malpractice in all areas of government.

Kim Young-Sam, *veteran democratic activist and president since 1993.*

Roh Tae-Woo, *a former general and president between 1988 and 1993.*

WORLD AFFAIRS

 APEC   OAS ADB   ESCAP   GATT

Since the 1950s, relations with North Korea have been the major concern of foreign policy. These remain unresolved. North Korea has recently shown a new willingness to consider reunification, while simultaneously, South Korea suspects, pursuing an aggressive nuclear programme. South Korea is also concerned that the North Korean economy may be about to suffer an East-German-style collapse, which would seriously increase the social and economic costs of union. Relations with China, once an important ally of North Korea, have improved and are being cemented by trade. Japan is also a major trading partner, although South Koreans harbour resentment over the 1910–1945 Japanese occupation.

AID

 $110m (donations)   Up 55% in 1992

Once a massive recipient of US aid, and then from 1965 of Japanese war reparations, South Korea has in recent years become an aid donor. Aid is primarily used to further foreign policy, such as the $3 billion sweetener to the CIS to promote good relations with Russia and Central Asia.

CHRONOLOGY

The Yi dynasty, founded in Seoul in 1392, ruled the kingdom of Korea until 1910. However, Korea became a vassal state of China in 1644.

❏ **1860** Korea reacts to French and British occupation of Peking by preventing Western influence.
❏ **1864–1907** Taewon'gun's rule. Korea remains the 'Hermit Kingdom'.
❏ **1894–1895** Social and religious revolt. Rebels defeat government, which invites Chinese help. Japanese seize power. Sino-Japanese War – Japanese win.
❏ **1896** King seeks Russian help.
❏ **1904–1905** Russo-Japanese War. Japan conquers Korea.
❏ **1910** Japan annexes Korea.
❏ **1919** Independence protests all over Korea violently suppressed.
❏ **1945** US and Soviet armies arrive. Korea split at 38°N. South comes under *de facto* US rule.
❏ **1948** Republic of South Korea created.
❏ **1948** Elections. Liberals' leader Dr Syngman Rhee becomes president. Leads increasingly authoritarian regime. ⇨

S

CHRONOLOGY *continued*

- **1950** Hostilities between North and South, each aspiring to rule a united Korea. North invades South sparking Korean War. US, with UN backing, enters on South's side, China on North's. In 1951, China takes Seoul, but is pushed back to 38°N. 600,000 die in South.
- **1953** Armistice.
- **1960** Syngman Rhee resigns in face of popular revolt.
- **1961** New military coup. Junta led by Park Chung-Hee.
- **1963** Pressure for civilian government. Park re-elected as president (also in 1967, 1971). Massive economic development in 1960s–1970s. All mineral resources in North Korea, so South concentrates on manufactures and huge export drive.
- **1965** Links restored with Japan.
- **1966** Sends 45,000 troops to fight for South Vietnam.
- **1972** Martial law stifles political opposition. New constitution with greater presidential powers.
- **1979** Park assassinated. Gen Chun Doo Huan, intelligence chief, leads coup. Kim Young-Sam, opposition leader, expelled from parliament.
- **1980** Chun chosen as president. Kim Dae-Jong and other opposition leaders arrested.
- **1985** Freer elections held. New Democratic Party (NDP), wins strong support.
- **1986** Car exports start.
- **1987** Domestic and international pressure for democracy. Roh Tae-Woo, Chun's chosen successor, elected president.
- **1988** Olympic Games in Seoul. Restrictions on foreign travel lifted.
- **1990** Government party and two opposition parties, including Kim Young-Sam's, merge to form DLP. Those opposed to merger form DP.
- **1991** South Korea joins UN. Reunification discussions with North Korea.
- **1992** Links with China established. Those with Taiwan severed.

Seoul lit up at night. The city is home to more than 10.5 million people – one quarter of South Korea's population. Seoul means 'capital'.

S

DEFENCE

$12.4bn   Up 15% in 1992

0   *Defence spending as % GDP*   40
3.8%

SOUTH KOREAN ARMED FORCES

	1800 main battle tanks (150 Type 88/400 M-47/950 M-48)	520,000 personnel
	4 submarines, 38 surface vessels and 81 patrol boats	60,000 personnel
	403 combat aircraft (48 F-16/142 F-5)	53,000 personnel
	None	

Since Kim Young-Sam came to power, the role of the military has been sharply downgraded. A campaign to root out corruption in arms procurement and investigations into past military involvement in politics have forced 40 generals to retire.

The main defence concern is the North Korean regime. South Korea has fewer troops, artillery and aircraft than the North, but it claims parity in having superior technology and the presence of 35,000 US troops permanently based on its territory. However, recent US computer simulations have questioned whether South Korea can resist an invasion by the North's one-million-strong army.

ECONOMICS

$293.7bn   807.15 won

SCORE CARD

- WORLD GNP RANKING..........................13th
- GNP PER CAPITA $6645
- BALANCE OF PAYMENTS....................$–4.5bn
- INFLATION 10.9%
- UNEMPLOYMENT................................2.3%

EXPORTS

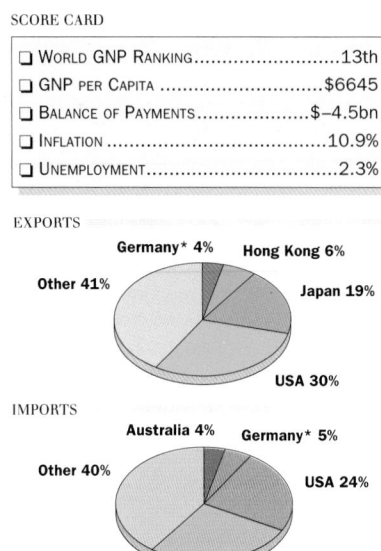

Germany* 4%   Hong Kong 6%
Other 41%   Japan 19%
USA 30%

IMPORTS

Australia 4%   Germany* 5%
Other 40%   USA 24%
Japan 27%

STRENGTHS

The world's most successful shipbuilder, with 45% of the market. Continuing benefits of highly valued yen which make Korean exports more competitive than Japan's. Strong demand from China for Korean goods, particularly cars.

WEAKNESSES

Workforce beginning to demand better working conditions. State sector is still a burden on the economy. Japanese plants in other South East Asian countries, particularly Indonesia, offering strong competition.

PROFILE

The first decades of the South Korean economic miracle were the result of centralized planning. Conglomerates known as *chaebol*, such as Samsung,

ECONOMIC PERFORMANCE INDICATOR

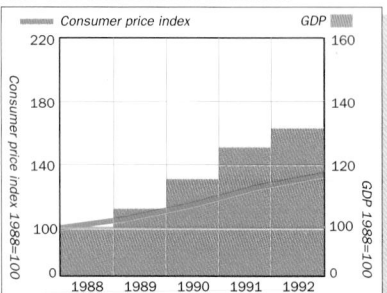

achieved impressive growth rates in strategic industries such as car manufacture, shipbuilding and semi-conductors. The three largest *chaebol* had sales of $180 billion. South Korea's workforce, well-educated but cheaper than Japan's, and cheap state credit, gave Korea a competitive edge. The government now aims to encourage foreign investment and to concentrate on smaller industries, which it sees as the key to maintaining current growth.

SOUTH KOREA : MAJOR BUSINESSES

Garments
Chemicals
Electronics
Iron & steel
Shipbuilding
Fish processing
Vehicle assembly
Telecommunications

RESOURCES

118.7bn kwh
(capacity 24.1m kw)

4.8m pigs,
2m cattle,
4000 horses

Not an oil producer;
refines 1.15m b/cd

Coal, iron, lead, zinc,
tungsten, gold,
graphite, fluorite

ELECTRICITY GENERATION

Hydro 5% (6.4bn kwh)
Thermal 50% (59.5bn kwh)
Nuclear 45% (52.9bn kwh)
Other 0%

0   20   40   60   80   100
% of total generation by type

South Korea has embraced nuclear power for generating electricity. Nine nuclear reactors are already in operation, with a combined generating capacity of nearly 8000 MW. One reactor a year is scheduled to come into production between 1991 and 1995. This will add a further 4740 MW of capacity to the national grid. South Korea has to import all its oil.

Agriculture remains a highly protected sector. Plans announced in 1994 to open up the rice market led to massive demonstrations in Seoul.

SOUTH KOREA :
LAND USE

Cropland
Pasture
Forest
Poultry
Rice
Cereals

0   50 km
0   50 miles

Cheju-do

ENVIRONMENT

8% (7% partially protected)

Environmental protection is not yet of primary concern

ENVIRONMENTAL TREATIES

Yes   No

No   No

Environmental groups in South East Asia have expressed concern at South Korea's fast-track nuclear power programme. The country's rapid industrialization and modernization has resulted in a number of environmental problems. Urban areas, particularly the capital Seoul, suffer from air pollution owing to the widespread use of low-grade coal for heating and industry. In rural parts, many rivers have been polluted by fertilizers and chemicals.

MEDIA

The media is free of direct governmental interference

PUBLISHING AND BROADCAST MEDIA

There are 65 daily newspapers. *Tong-A Ilbo* is the leading paper

1 state-owned, also independent services

1 state-owned, 100 independent services

Superbird B Intelsat V F8

Available in major cities

South Korea's media has been freed of most restrictions since the advent of full multiparty democracy. However, criticisms of the armed forces are still frowned upon and journalists tend to avoid the subject of the role of the military in society altogether. Caution also has to be exercised in reporting facts about North Korea. In the past, South Korean journalists who have made favourable mention of President Kim Il Sung's communist regime in North Korea have suffered harassment and intimidation.

CRIME

52,371 prisoners

Up 1% in 1986

CRIME RATES

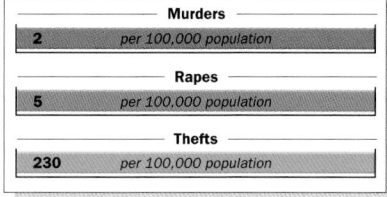

Murders
2   per 100,000 population

Rapes
5   per 100,000 population

Thefts
230   per 100,000 population

The government has begun to treat corruption as a crime. Otherwise, crime rates are relatively low and cases of violent crime uncommon. Since 1987, the internal security forces' operations have been restricted, although left-wing activists are still harassed. Striking workers and student demonstrators are subjected to tear gas and other methods of crowd control.

EDUCATION

96%

0   Education spending as % GNP   25
3.6%

THE EDUCATION SYSTEM

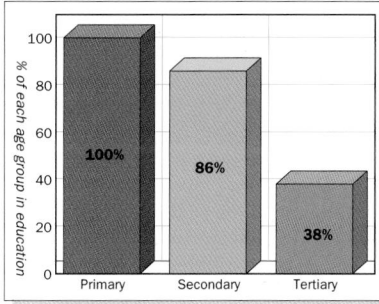

100% Primary
86% Secondary
38% Tertiary

% of each age group in education

South Korea embarked on a concentrated education programme in the 1950s. The high priority given to education contributed greatly to South Korea's subsequent economic success. Tertiary enrolment is 38%, one of the highest rates in the world.

HEALTH

1 per 1066 people

Cancers, heart and cerebrovascular diseases

0   Health spending as % GNP   25
0.4%

The health service has improved in line with economic growth and now offers most advanced treatments. Health indicators such as infant mortality and longevity have improved accordingly.

WEALTH

Secretary, 800,000 won per month; dentist, 3m won per month

CONSUMER GOODS OWNERSHIP

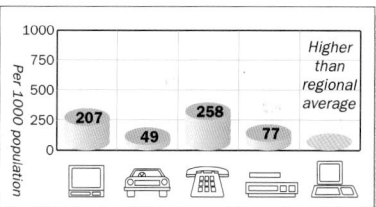

207   49   258   77

Per 1000 population

Higher than regional average

Most South Koreans have benefited from economic growth. However, the Cholla region remains the poorest.

S

WORLD RANKING

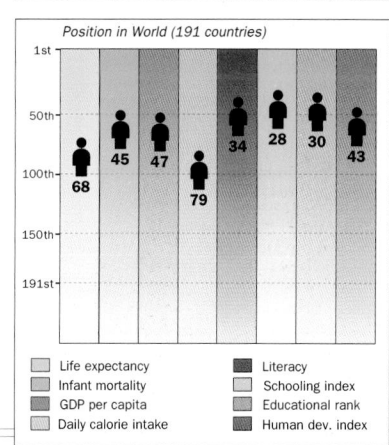

Position in World (191 countries)

1st
50th
100th
150th
191st

68   45   47   79   34   28   30   43

Life expectancy
Infant mortality
GDP per capita
Daily calorie intake
Literacy
Schooling index
Educational rank
Human dev. index

SPAIN

OFFICIAL NAME: Kingdom of Spain CAPITAL: Madrid POPULATION: 39.1 million
CURRENCY: Peseta OFFICIAL LANGUAGES: Spanish, Galician, Basque and Catalan

EUROPE

SITUATED IN SOUTHWESTERN EUROPE, Spain has a wet Atlantic and a dry Mediterranean coast. It is dominated by a central plateau drained by the Duero, Tagus and Guadiana rivers. Since the death of General Franco in 1975, Spain has managed a rapid and relatively peaceful transition to democracy under the supervision of King Juan Carlos I. In recent years, it has been governed by a succession of socialist administrations led by Felipe González. Since joining the EC in 1986, there has been an increasing devolution of power to the regions.

Alcaudete, Jaén Province, in the Andalusian mountains between Granada and the River Guadalquivir. The ruined castle is Moorish.

CLIMATE

WEATHER CHART

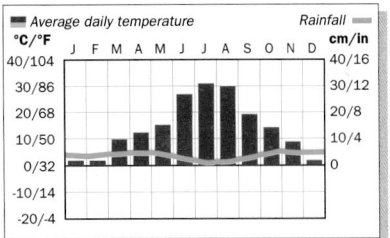

The central plateau, or *meseta*, endures an extreme climate. Coastal areas are milder, and wetter in the north than in the south.

COMMUNICATIONS

Barajas, Madrid
15.87m passengers

322 ships
3.98m dwt

THE TRANSPORT NETWORK

157,642 km (97,954 miles)	2286 km (1420 miles)
15,430 km (9588 miles)	1045 km (649 miles)

In 1992, Spain completed the *AVE*, a French *TGV*-style high-speed train linking Madrid and Seville. Spain's road accident rate remains high.

TOURISM

55.3m visitors

Upwards trend

MAIN OVERSEAS ARRIVALS

France 21%	
Portugal 21%	
Germany 14%	
UK 12%	
Netherlands 4%	
Other 28%	

% of total arrivals

Tourism accounts for 10% of Spain's GDP, and employs one in ten Spaniards. In 1989–1991, the industry made significant losses owing to competition from cheaper destinations. Spain is now concentrating on attracting higher-spending cultural tourists. Inland destinations, with their greater cultural, artistic and culinary appeal, are being promoted above beach resorts. The Olympics and Expo '92 provided a huge boost for Barcelona and Seville; tourism to both has risen sharply since.

PEOPLE

Spanish, Catalan, Galician, Basque

78 people per km²

THE URBAN/RURAL POPULATION SPLIT

78% 22%

RELIGIOUS PERSUASION

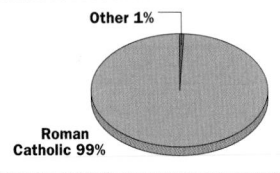
Other 1%
Roman Catholic 99%

ETHNIC MAKEUP

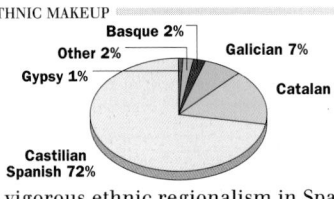
Basque 2%
Other 2%
Gypsy 1%
Galician 7%
Catalan 16%
Castilian Spanish 72%

A vigorous ethnic regionalism in Spain, suppressed under Franco, has been increasing as the influence of Spain's EU partners becomes more apparent. Further, Spain today has one of the lowest birth rates in Europe and the influence of the Catholic Church on personal behaviour has declined. However, many traditional features of Spanish life remain. Whilst attitudes to

POPULATION AGE BREAKDOWN

	1960	1970	1980	1990	2000
65+	8.2%	9.8%	10.7%	13.1%	15.2%
15–64	64.4%	62.3%	62.7%	66.8%	66.5%
0–14	27.4%	27.9%	26.6%	20.1%	18.3%

sexuality are now relaxed, Church-going remains popular. The divorce rate is extremely low and family ties remain strong, with young males living at home until their late 20s.

Economic growth from the 1970s led to a change in the composition of society. Spain began to attract substantial numbers of immigrants, mainly from Latin America and North Africa. However, the economic downturn in the early 1990s led to a rise in racial tensions and racism, a pattern echoed in France.

Spanish women are becoming increasingly emancipated. They have also become more influential in politics, currently making up 15% of the Spanish Congress, a higher proportion than in any other West European country.

S

POLITICS

1997

HRH King Juan Carlos I

THE STATE OF THE PARTIES

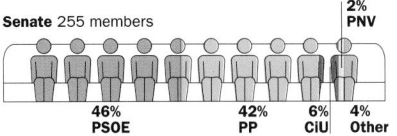

Congress of Deputies 350 members

5% CiU

46% PSOE | 40% PP | 5% IU | 4% Other

PSOE = Spanish Socialist Workers' Party **PP** = Popular Party
IU = United Left **CiU** = Convergence and Union
PNV = Basque National Party **Other** = Canary Islands
Coalition, United People, Republican Left of Catalonia,
Regionalist Party, Basque Solidarity, Valencian Union

Senate 255 members

2% PNV

46% PSOE | 42% PP | 6% CiU | 4% Other

Since 1978, Spain has been a semi-
federal, multiparty parliamentary
monarchy.

MAIN POLITICAL ISSUES

Power struggles in the PSOE

The power struggle between
renovadores (reformers) and *guerristas*
(followers of former Deputy Prime
Minister Alfonso Guerra) is threatening
to tear apart Spain's ruling party, the
PSOE, while preventing its leader, Felipe

González, from selecting a successor.
Having failed to win a working majority
in June 1993, González needs the
support of Catalan nationalists to see
through his economic reforms.

Increasing regionalism

Spain has 17 autonomous regions,
all vying for greater funds or
independence from Madrid. Many
have bypassed central government to
borrow their own funds on the
international money markets and are
close to breaching their legal debt
limits, set at 25% of revenue. The PSOE's
need for Catalan support in the *Cortes*
(parliament) will test the ability of the
centre to keep control. The Catalans
are demanding ever greater autonomy
and even a direct line to Brussels.

PROFILE

Spain has been dominated for the past
11 years by Felipe González's PSOE.
After such a long period in power,
however, the boundaries between party
and state have become blurred. The
Cortes cannot check executive power,
and political disputes are often left to
the judiciary. Ideological issues no
longer sharply divide the main parties,
and they hold similar views on
economic policy and EU membership.

Though hardly on the Italian scale,
political corruption – often related to
the financing of parties – has been a
problem, undermining voters' faith in
Spain's political system.

King Juan Carlos,
*who became head of
state on the death of
Gen Franco in 1975.*

**Felipe González
Márquez,** *prime
minister since 1982
and PSOE leader.*

WORLD AFFAIRS

GATT | NATO | WEU | CSCE

The Spanish government remains an
enthusiastic member of the EU in spite
of current difficulties. Spain is not
keen to enlarge the EU to include
Scandinavia or Central Europe, which
it sees as a threat to its own position
within the Union. Elsewhere, Spain
has sponsored an Ibero-American
Community of Nations (a Hispanic
Commonwealth), which held its third
summit meeting in Brazil in July 1993.
Anxious to establish itself as a
major international player, Spain has
contributed troops to the UN peace-
keeping force in the former Yugoslavia,
and aspires to a seat on the UN
Security Council.

CHRONOLOGY

United under Ferdinand and Isabella
in 1492, Spain became a dominant
force in Europe. A long period of
economic and political decline
followed, however. By the mid-19th
century, Spain lagged behind many
other European countries in stability
and prosperity.

❑ **1874** Constitutional monarchy
restored under Alfonso XII.
❑ **1879** Spanish Socialist Workers'
Party (PSOE) founded.
❑ **1881** Trade unions legalized.
❑ **1885** Death of Alfonso XII.
❑ **1898** Defeat in war with USA
results in loss of Cuba, Puerto Rico
and the Philippines.
❑ **1909** Barcelona's 'tragic week' of
anti-clerical riots.
❑ **1914–1918** Spain neutral in First
World War.
❑ **1921** Spanish army routed by
Berbers in Spanish Morocco.
❑ **1923** Coup by General Primo de
Rivera accepted by King Alfonso
XIII. Military dictatorship.
❑ **1930** General Primo de Rivera
dismissed by monarchy.

S

SPAIN

Total Area : 504 780 sq. km
(194 900 sq. miles)

POPULATION

over 1 000 000
over 500 000
over 100 000
over 50 000
over 10 000

LAND HEIGHT

3000m/9843ft
2000m/6562ft
1000m/3281ft
500m/1640ft
Sea Level

0   100 km
0   100 miles

Islas Canarias

La Palma
Santa Cruz de Tenerife
Lanzarote
Gomera
Las Palmas
Fuerteventura
Tenerife
Hierro
Gran Canaria

0   100 km
0   100 miles

CHRONOLOGY *continued*

- ❑ **1931** Second Republic proclaimed. Alfonso XIII flees Spain.
- ❑ **1933** Centre-right coalition wins general election.
- ❑ **1934** Asturias uprising quashed by army. Failure of attempt to form Catalan state.
- ❑ **1936** Popular Front wins elections. Right-wing military uprising against the Republic. Gen Franco subsequently appointed leader.
- ❑ **1939** Franco wins civil war which claims 300,000 lives.
- ❑ **1940** Franco meets Hitler, but does not enter Second World War.
- ❑ **1946** UN condemns Franco regime.
- ❑ **1948** Spain excluded from Marshall Plan.
- ❑ **1950** UN lifts veto.
- ❑ **1953** Concordat with Vatican. Spain grants USA military bases.
- ❑ **1955** Spain joins UN.
- ❑ **1959** Adoption of Stabilization Plan, prelude to rapid economic growth in the 1960s.
- ❑ **1962** Franco government applies for eventual membership of EEC.
- ❑ **1969** Gen Franco names Juan Carlos, grandson of Alfonso XIII, his successor.
- ❑ **1970** Spain signs preferential trade agreement with EEC.
- ❑ **1973** Prime Minister Carrero Blanco assassinated by Basque separatists. Succeeded by Arias Navarro.
- ❑ **1975** Death of Gen Franco. Proclamation of King Juan Carlos I.
- ❑ **1976** King replaces Arias Navarro with Adolfo Suárez.
- ❑ **1977** First democratic elections since 1936 won by Suárez's Democratic Centre Union.
- ❑ **1978** New constitution declares Spain a parliamentary monarchy.
- ❑ **1981** Leopoldo Calvo Sotelo replaces Suárez. King foils military coup. Calvo Sotelo takes Spain into NATO.
- ❑ **1982** Felipe González wins landslide victory for PSOE.
- ❑ **1986** January, Spain joins EC. March, González wins referendum on keeping Spain in NATO.
- ❑ **1992** Olympic Games held in Barcelona, Expo '92 in Seville.
- ❑ **1993** PSOE wins general election.

AID

 $1.2 billion (donations)　　 Up 219% between 1991 and 1993

Spain became a donor in 1977, and currently earmarks 0.4% of GDP for aid to developing countries (mainly in Latin America), slightly above average for western Europe.

DEFENCE

 $7.4bn　　 Down 10% in 1992

0　　　*Defence spending as % GDP*　　40
1.6%

Spain has a substantial, largely state-owned defence industry, which exports light weapons, ammunition and small aircraft to countries such as Indonesia and Chile. Spain is a co-partner with the UK, Germany, Italy and France in the EF-2000 fighter aircraft project.

SPANISH ARMED FORCES

🛡	838 main battle tanks (299 AMX-30/329 M-47E1/ 46 M-47E2/164 M-48A5E)	146,000 personnel
🚢	1 carrier, 8 submarines 15 frigates and 39 patrol boats	36,000 personnel
✈	207 combat aircraft (F-18 *Hornet*/RF-4C *Mirage* III/EE,-ED)	35,000 personnel
	None	

ECONOMICS

 $486.6bn　　 114.55 pesetas

SCORE CARD

- ❑ WORLD GNP RANKING.............................8th
- ❑ GNP PER CAPITA $12,455
- ❑ BALANCE OF PAYMENTS....................$–22bn
- ❑ INFLATION 5.3%
- ❑ UNEMPLOYMENT................................19.5%

EXPORTS

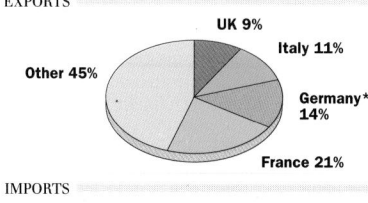

UK 9%
Italy 11%
Other 45%
Germany* 14%
France 21%

IMPORTS

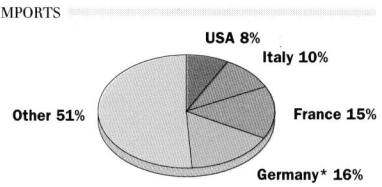

USA 8%
Italy 10%
Other 51%
France 15%
Germany* 16%

ECONOMIC PERFORMANCE INDICATOR

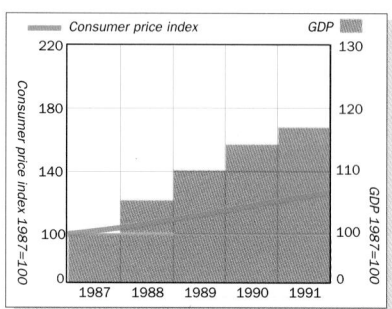

Consumer price index　　GDP

STRENGTHS

Spain's labour force is well qualified and relatively low labour costs are still an advantage, though less so than before. Improvements in transport and communications will continue to attract foreign investment. Potential for domestic growth is Spain's major asset.

WEAKNESSES

The massive foreign penetration of the Spanish economy and absence of Spanish multinationals pose long-term problems. Low investment in research and development, a rigid labour market (which trades unions are reluctant to reform), a concentration in declining industries and low productivity – notably in agriculture – are major weaknesses. Spain's percentage of economically-active people is lower than in the rest of the EU.

PROFILE

Since joining the EC in 1986, the government's main economic goal has been real convergence with the major European economies. This seemed possible in the period 1986–1991, when Spain enjoyed the highest investment-led output growth in the OECD. By 1991, GDP per capita stood at almost 80% of the EC average. In 1992, however, Spain plunged into recession along with its major trading partners. In 1992–1993, three devaluations of the peseta, by a total of 18%, just managed to keep it within the ERM.

Whatever happens to the EU, González remains committed to convergence, and is pinning his hopes on wage moderation, labour market reforms and increased productivity.

SPAIN : MAJOR BUSINESSES

🔲 Textiles	✿ Heavy engineering
Agribusiness	◎ Light engineering
Chemicals	Fish processing
Shipbuilding	
Vehicle manufacture	0　200 km
	0　200 miles

* significant multinational ownership

RESOURCES

 151bn kwh (capacity 43.3m kw)

 20,700 b/d (reserves 22,518,000 bbl)

 24.3m sheep, 16.7m pigs, 5.2m cattle

 Coal, oil, iron, uranium, mercury, fluorspar, gypsum

ELECTRICITY GENERATION

Hydro 17% (26.2bn kwh)
Thermal 47% (70.2bn kwh)
Nuclear 36% (54.3bn kwh)
Other 0%

% of total generation by type

Spain has always been thwarted by a lack of natural resources, including water, and is heavily dependent on imported oil and gas. Contrary to popular belief, food products such as fruit and vegetables constitute only 13% of its exports. Spain has one of the world's largest fishing fleets, but EU restrictions have reduced its catches.

SPAIN : LAND USE

Forest
Pasture
Cropland
Wetlands
High mountain regions
Sheep
Olives - cash crop
Citrus fruits
Vineyards

ENVIRONMENT

 7% partially protected

 Consciousness is rising. Highly active green NGOS

ENVIRONMENTAL TREATIES

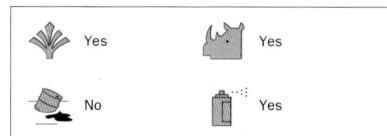

Yes   Yes
No   Yes

Although Spain paid little attention to environmental matters until very recently, public opinion is becoming increasingly demanding. A national tree-planting scheme has been initiated to reduce soil erosion, but its benefits have been offset by losses from increasingly-frequent intentional forest fires. Spain has more land with national park status than any other country in Europe and there are plans to double the number. However, rising visitor numbers and tourist developments inside the parks, as in the Coto Doñana wetlands in the south, are damaging their integrity. A large new dam project is threatening the habitat and hence the survival of Spain's last brown bears.

MEDIA

 Freedom of expression, though TV is vulnerable to government pressure

PUBLISHING AND BROADCAST MEDIA

There are 102 daily newspapers, including *ABC*, *Ya* and *El País*.

16 state-owned, also independent services

13 state-owned, 350 independent services

Intelsat V1 F1 Astra 1B

Extensive in all main cities

Despite the large number of daily newspapers, readership is among the lowest in Europe. Both public and private TV are popular. Radio is of a generally high standard.

CRIME

 29,344 prisoners

 Down 2% in 1990

CRIME RATES

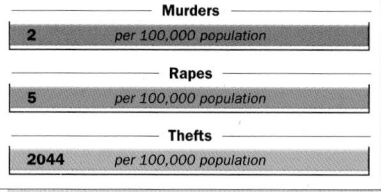

Murders
2   per 100,000 population

Rapes
5   per 100,000 population

Thefts
2044   per 100,000 population

Spain is a major crossroads in the world narcotics trade and drugs-related crime is rising. Rape is increasing (or reported more often), while property-related crime is stable.

EDUCATION

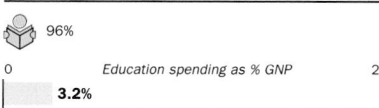 96%

0   Education spending as % GNP   25
3.2%

THE EDUCATION SYSTEM

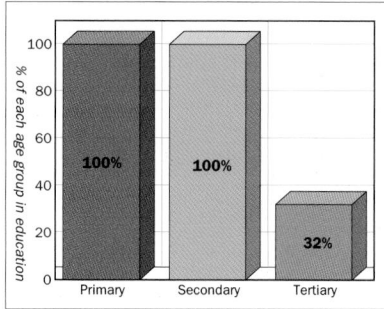

100%   100%   32%
Primary   Secondary   Tertiary

% of each age group in education

Primary and secondary schooling, 35% of it private but widely affordable, is effective. Universities, however, are over-subscribed. Most teaching is lecture-based. Bright students with parental funding and good English are increasingly completing their education abroad, often in the USA.

HEALTH

 1 per 288 people

 Heart, respiratory, cerebrovascular and digestive diseases

0   Health spending as % GNP .   25
4.2%

Public health care is high-quality and readily available, and public hospitals are generally considered to be better than private ones. In spite of very high tobacco and alcohol consumption, Spain has a healthy population, possibly due to its Mediterranean diet. The incidence of AIDS, however, is the second highest in Europe.

WEALTH

 Cleaner, 100,000 pesetas per month; company director, 1m pesetas per month

CONSUMER GOODS OWNERSHIP

389   294   396   121   8

Per 1000 population

In the late 1980s, it became fashionable in Spain to compete openly, make money and consume. The country's rapid economic growth at this time greatly enriched the professional and managerial classes. The latter became the best-paid, in real terms, in Europe. Some became media celebrities, such as the banker Mario Conde of Banesto, and began to rival footballers in popularity. In spite of high taxes, the rich became richer and more ostentatious. Spain quickly developed into an important market for luxury cars and yachts; a personal bodyguard also became a status symbol.

The recession of the early 1990s, however, changed attitudes, as Spain wasafflicted with one of the highest unemployment rates in Europe.

WORLD RANKING

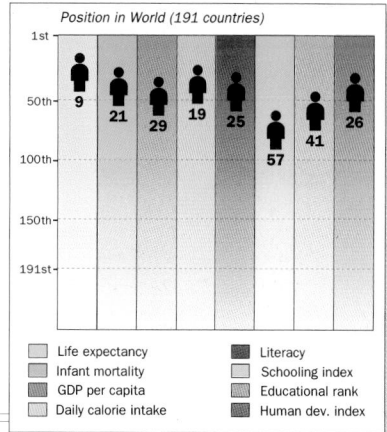

Position in World (191 countries)

9   21   29   19   25   57   41   26

Life expectancy
Infant mortality
GDP per capita
Daily calorie intake
Literacy
Schooling index
Educational rank
Human dev. index

S

SRI LANKA

OFFICIAL NAME: Democratic Socialist Republic of Sri Lanka **CAPITAL:** Colombo
POPULATION: 17.7 million **CURRENCY:** Sri Lanka rupee **OFFICIAL LANGUAGE:** Sinhalese

SOUTH ASIA

SEPARATED FROM INDIA by the Palk Strait, Sri Lanka comprises one large island and several coral islets to the northwest known as Adam's Bridge. The main island is dominated by rugged central uplands. The fertile plains to the north are dissected by rivers and bordered to the southeast by the Mahaweli Ganga River. Sri Lankan affairs are dominated by the conflict between the government and the Tamils, who are fighting for an independent state.

CLIMATE

WEATHER CHART

The climate is tropical, with afternoon breezes on the coast and cooler air in the highlands. The northeast is driest.

COMMUNICATIONS

✈ **Katunayake, Colombo**
1.52m passengers

🚢 32 ships
438,200 dwt

THE TRANSPORT NETWORK

75,263 km (46,766 miles)	🛣	None	
1944 km (1208 miles)		430 km (267 miles)	

Main roads are crowded and slow, but those to resorts are being improved. Air Lanka now flies non-stop to Europe.

TOURISM

🧳 297,888 visitors   ⬆ Up 61% in 1990

MAIN OVERSEAS ARRIVALS

Germany 24 %						
UK 11 %						
France 9 %						
Other 56 %						

0 10 20 30 40 50 60
% of total arrivals

Tourism, which halved between 1983 and 1989, is growing again, but hotels are rundown and in short supply. Buddhist centres such as Kandy are major attractions. Sri Lanka is a popular gay tourist destination.

PEOPLE

👥 Sinhalese, Tamil, Sinhalese-Tamil, English

👥 262 people per km²

THE URBAN/RURAL POPULATION SPLIT

21%   79%

ETHNIC MAKEUP

Burgher, Malay and Veddha 1%   Moor 7%
Tamil 18%
Sinhalese 74%

Ethnic tensions between the minority Tamils and majority Sinhalese erupted into civil war in 1983. The Tamils were the minority group favoured by the British colonists. When the British left, laws were passed to redress the balance by favouring the Sinhalese. The effect has been to make Tamils feel sidelined, and support for secessionism has grown. The conflict also has a religious dimension. Most Sinhalese are Buddhist, while Tamils are mostly Muslim or Hindu.

SRI LANKA

Total Area : 65 610 sq. km (25 332 sq. miles)

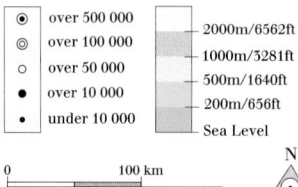

POPULATION
⊙ over 500 000
◎ over 100 000
○ over 50 000
● over 10 000
• under 10 000

LAND HEIGHT
2000m/6562ft
1000m/3281ft
500m/1640ft
200m/656ft
Sea Level

0 ___ 100 km
0 ___ 100 miles

N

POLITICS

🗳 1994   President Dingiri Banda Wijetunga

THE STATE OF THE PARTIES

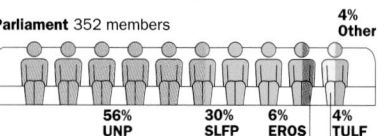

Parliament 352 members

4% Other

56% UNP   30% SLFP   6% EROS   4% TULF

UNP = United National Party **SLFP** = Sri Lankan Freedom Party **EROS** = Eelaam Revolutionary Organization of Students (renamed Eelaavour Democratic Front in 1990) **TULF** = Tamil United Liberation Front Alliance **Other** = Sri Lankan Muslim Congress, United Socialist Alliance

The Tamil-Sinhalese conflict colours all political debate. In 1983, civil war erupted between the Liberation Tigers of Tamil Eelam (LTTE or Tamil Tigers) and the government. The LTTE wants an independent state in the north and east. The government is committed to keeping Sri Lanka unified and has resisted federalism. The most recent peace efforts collapsed in 1990 and were followed by an army campaign in which 10,000 died. On 1 May 1993, President Ranasinghe Premadasa was assassinated. In 1993 and 1994 the army, which is growing in political influence, captured significant LTTE towns in the Jaffna peninsula.

WORLD AFFAIRS

Relations with India are paramount. The 1987 Indo–Sri Lankan accords led to Indian troops playing a peace-keeping role. They became embroiled in fighting the LTTE, however, and were forced to pull out. The LTTE is suspected of being behind the assassination of Indian president Rajiv Gandhi in 1992.

AID

 $814m (receipts)   Up 21% in 1991

Canada, the Netherlands and the UK have threatened to freeze aid unless Sri Lanka's human rights record improves.

DEFENCE

 $450.06m   Up 6% in 1991

Defeating the LTTE is the overwhelming concern. Sri Lanka's chief arms suppliers are the UK, India and China. The LTTE smuggles arms from India.

ECONOMICS

 $8.67bn   46.00 Sri Lanka rupees

SCORE CARD

❑ WORLD GNP RANKING	85th
❑ GNP PER CAPITA	$489
❑ BALANCE OF PAYMENTS	$−267.6m
❑ INFLATION	11%
❑ UNEMPLOYMENT	14.4%

STRENGTHS
The world's largest tea exporter. Export Processing Zones and state privatization programmes attracting foreign investment. Manufacturing now accounts for 60% of exports; in 1980 the figure was 15%. Tourism; potential for further growth.

WEAKNESSES
Civil war a drain on government funds and deters investors and many tourists.

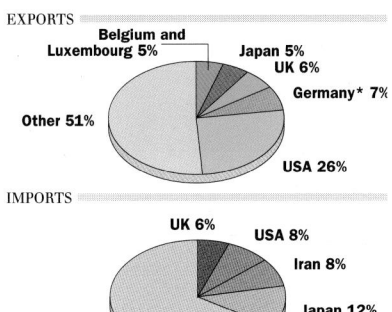

EXPORTS
Belgium and Luxembourg 5%
Japan 5%
UK 6%
Germany* 7%
Other 51%
USA 26%

IMPORTS
UK 6%
USA 8%
Iran 8%
Japan 12%
Other 66%

A peak in central Sri Lanka, close to the country's highest mountain, Pidurutalagala, which reaches 2524 m.

RESOURCES

 3.2bn kwh (capacity 1.29m kw)   Not an oil producer; refines 50,000 b/cd

 2m cattle, 94,000 pigs, 30,000 sheep, 1000 horses   Gemstones, graphite, iron, monazite, uranium, ilmenite

Sri Lanka has to import all its oil. Hydro-power supplies 75% of electricity; droughts are frequent and supplies can be erratic. Sri Lanka is keen to diversify power sources and is turning to coal-powered generation.

ENVIRONMENT

 12% (4% partially protected)   Deforestation is under control

Sri Lanka has successfully promoted national parks. The government is keenly aware of the benefits to tourism of a protected environment.

MEDIA

 Little press freedom due to Tamil–Sinhalese conflict. Government is able to enact emergency controls

PUBLISHING AND BROADCAST MEDIA

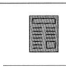 There are 16 daily newspapers, including the *Daily News*, *Davasa*, *Dinamina*, *Lankadipa* and *Dinapathi*

 2 state-owned services   1 state-owned service

The press is not critical of the government. Much is owned by the Sinhalese Lake House Group. Tamils have their own newspapers.

CRIME

 14,128 prisoners   Down 23% in 1990

Both the army and the LTTE have been accused of human rights abuses. The civil war has claimed at least 30,000 lives since 1983. LTTE members carry cyanide capsules in case of arrest.

EDUCATION

 88%

Sri Lanka has the highest literacy rate of any developing nation. Many Sri Lankans attend US universities.

HEALTH

 1 per 7255 people   Suicide, heart attacks, cancers, pneumonia, strokes

Years of high spending on health have resulted in an accessible, fee-free system. Ayurvedic medicine is popular.

WEALTH

 Plantation worker, 6 Sri Lanka rupees per hour; hotel receptionist, 16 Sri Lanka rupees per hour

CONSUMER GOODS OWNERSHIP

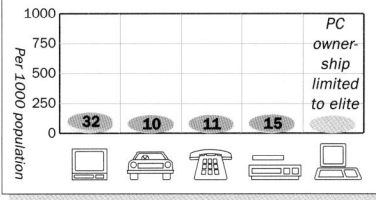

PC ownership limited to elite

32   10   11   15

Economic growth has created a new class of wealthy Sinhalese. Tamil tea workers are the poorest group.

WORLD RANKING

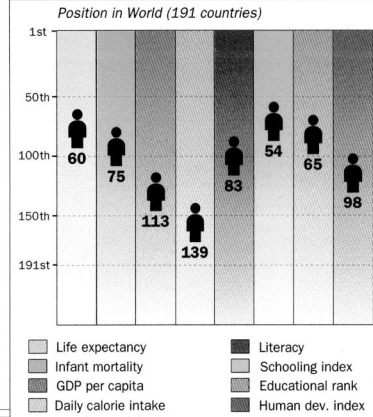

Position in World (191 countries)

60   75   113   139   83   54   65   98

Life expectancy | Literacy
Infant mortality | Schooling index
GDP per capita | Educational rank
Daily calorie intake | Human dev. index

S

SUDAN

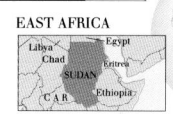

EAST AFRICA

OFFICIAL NAME: Republic of Sudan   CAPITAL: Khartoum
POPULATION: 26.7 million   CURRENCY: Sudanese dinar   OFFICIAL LANGUAGE: Arabic

BORDERING THE RED SEA, Sudan is the largest
country in Africa. Its landscape changes from desert
in the north to lush tropical in the south, with grassy plains and swamps
in the centre. Tensions between the Arab north and African south have
led to two civil wars since independence from British and Egyptian rule
in 1956. The second of these conflicts remains unresolved. In 1989, an
army coup installed a military Islamic fundamentalist regime.

*Camel caravan in the dry north. Periodic
drought coupled with war disruption mean
that Sudan requires large amounts of food aid.*

CLIMATE

WEATHER CHART

Sudan's northern half is hot arid desert
with constant dry winds. The rest has a
rainy season varying from two months
in the centre to eight in the south.

COMMUNICATIONS

✈ **Khartoum International**   7 ships 62,100 dwt

THE TRANSPORT NETWORK

20,000 km (12,427 miles)		None	
4725 km (2936 miles)		4068 km (2528 miles)	

The Port Sudan–Khartoum railway and
road are Sudan's most important links.
There are few other roads, but Iran is
financing a Rabak–Malakal highway.
Civil war has stopped all Nile shipping.

TOURISM

🏛 32,789 visitors   ⬆ Up 44% in 1990

MAIN OVERSEAS ARRIVALS

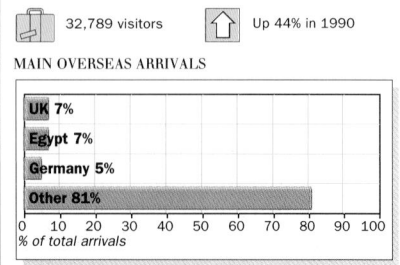

UK 7%
Egypt 7%
Germany 5%
Other 81%
% of total arrivals

Tourism has now almost ceased owing
to political unrest and civil war. Visitors
are mostly aid workers or on business.

PEOPLE

Arabic, Dinka, Nuer, Nubian,
Beja, Zande, Bari, Fur,
Shilluk, Lotuko   10 people per km²

THE URBAN/RURAL POPULATION SPLIT

22%   78%

RELIGIOUS PERSUASION

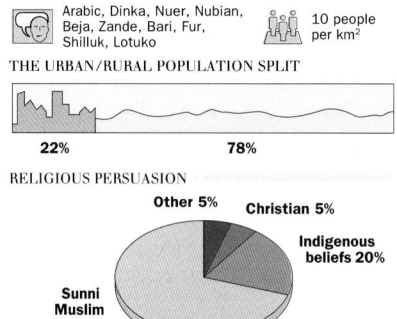

Other 5%   Christian 5%
Indigenous beliefs 20%
Sunni Muslim 70%

Sudan has a large number of ethnic
and linguistic groups. About two million
Sudanese are nomads. The major
social division, however, is between the
Arabized Muslims in the north and the
mostly African, largely animist or
Christian population in the south.
Attempts to impose Arab and Islamic
values throughout Sudan have been
the root cause of the civil war that has
ravaged the south since 1983. However,
the rebels have now split into two
factions, pitting southern Sudan's
small ethnic groups against the
Dinka, the south's largest
tribe. There are some non-
Arab groups in the north
and the densely-populated
Darfur region. Women
not wearing Islamic
dress can suffer
harassment or even
public flogging.

POLITICS

🗳 1995   👤 Lt-Gen Omar Hassan Ahmad al-Bashir

THE STATE OF THE PARTIES

National Assembly 300 members

A transitional government was appointed in 1992 to prepare
the country for elections

The military regime headed by General
al-Bashir took over in a coup in 1989. It
banned all political parties except the
the National Islamic Front (NIF), which
emerged as the force behind the coup.
Its leader, Dr Hassan al-Turabi, does
not hold ministerial office, but is
Sudan's most influential figure. A strict
policy of Arabization and Islamicization,
including *sharia* law, has been imposed,
but is ineffective in the southern areas
held by non-Muslim rebels. Dissent
elsewhere has been violently crushed.
Many opposition leaders are in exile.

SUDAN

Total Area : 2 505 5810 sq. km
(967 493 sq. miles)

0   400 km
0   400 miles

LAND HEIGHT

2000m/6562ft
1000m/3281ft
500m/1640ft
200m/656ft
Sea Level

POPULATION

◉ over 500 000
◎ over 100 000
○ over 50 000
● over 10 000
• under 10 000

S

WORLD AFFAIRS

Since Sudan's support for Iraq in the 1991 Gulf War, relations with the West have almost ceased and ties with the Arab world have deteriorated. Only Iran, Yemen and Libya maintain friendly relations.

AID

 $887m (receipts)   Up 8% in 1991

Sudan's only substantial bilateral aid comes from Iran. IMF funding ceased in 1990. Sudan depends on food aid.

DEFENCE

 $320m   Down 44% in 1990

The NIF controls the military and police and has its own paramilitary militia. Sudan's 68,000-strong army is engaged in fighting the two factions of the southern Sudanese People's Liberation Army, numbering up to 50,000 men.

ECONOMICS

 $7.2bn   13.01 Sudanese dinars

SCORE CARD

- ❑ WORLD GNP RANKING.........................93rd
- ❑ GNP PER CAPITA $269
- ❑ BALANCE OF PAYMENTS....................$–1.5bn
- ❑ INFLATION 200%
- ❑ UNEMPLOYMENT....Widespread underemployment

STRENGTHS
Cotton, gum arabic, sesame, sugar. Some gold mining.

WEAKNESSES
Low industrialization. Lack of foreign exchange for importing energy and spare parts for industry. Little transport infrastructure. Huge distances between towns. Civil war prevents exploitation of oil reserves. Drought. Alienation of Arab donors and investors.

EXPORTS

IMPORTS

RESOURCES

 1.33m kwh (capacity 500,000 kw)
Reserves of 300,000,000 bbl; refines 21,700 b/cd

20.5m cattle, 20m sheep, 2.8m camels
Oil, gas, gold, copper, gypsum, marble, mica, silver, chromium, zinc

Large oil and gas reserves were found in the south in the 1980s, but civil war has prevented their exploitation. The half-thermal, half-hydroelectric generating capacity is insufficient and week-long power cuts are frequent. Gold mining has expansion potential.

ENVIRONMENT

 4% (0.3% partially protected)   Desertification is increasing

Work on the Jonglei canal to straighten the White Nile was halted in 1986. If it was completed, environmentalists believe the world's largest swamp in the Sudd Plain would dry up, destroying wildlife and intensifying desertification.

MEDIA

 Tight government control of the media

PUBLISHING AND BROADCAST MEDIA

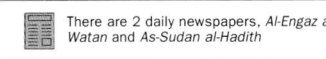

There are 2 daily newspapers, *Al-Engaz al-Watan* and *As-Sudan al-Hadith*

1 state-controlled service

1 state-controlled, 1 rebel-controlled service

The media were relatively free from 1985 to 1989, but all are now controlled by the government or the army.

CRIME

 Sudan does not publish prison figures   Up 10% in 1986

Anti-government dissent is often suppressed by violence, and torture by the security forces is widespread. In 1993, the UN condemned Sudan's poor human rights record.

EDUCATION

 27%

In 1991, measures were introduced to Islamicize education. Primary school children must have two years of Islamic religious instruction, and men wishing to enter university must first serve for a year in the NIF's People's Militia.

HEALTH

 1 per 9345 people   Infectious and parasitic diseases

As most health funds are tied to urban hospitals, health service standards in rural areas are basic. The civil war has led to an increase in communicable diseases, especially leishmaniasis.

CHRONOLOGY

Northern Sudan was taken by Egypt in 1821, the south by Britain in 1877.

- ❑ **1882** British invade Egypt.
- ❑ **1883** Muslim revolt in Sudan led by Muhammad Ahmed, the Mahdi.
- ❑ **1898** Mahdists defeated. Anglo-Egyptian condominium set up.
- ❑ **1955** Rebellion in south starts 17 years of civil war.
- ❑ **1956** Independence as republic.
- ❑ **1958–1964** Army runs Sudan.
- ❑ **1965** Civilian revolution, elections.
- ❑ **1969** Army coup led by Col Nimeri.
- ❑ **1971** Nimeri president.
- ❑ **1972** South gets limited autonomy.
- ❑ **1973** Sudanese Socialist Union (former communist) sole party.
- ❑ **1978** Supports Egypt–Israel peace.
- ❑ **1983** Southern rebellion resumes. *Sharia* law imposed. Nimeri's proposal that Sudan become a formal Islamic state is rejected.
- ❑ **1984** Devastating drought.
- ❑ **1986** Army coup restores civilian government.
- ❑ **1989** Gen al-Bashir takes over.
- ❑ **1991** *Sharia* penal code instituted. Sudan backs Iraq in Gulf War.

WEALTH

 Most of the population lives a subsistence existence

CONSUMER GOODS OWNERSHIP

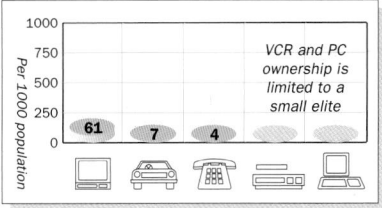

Wealth is limited to the NIF and southern rebel elites. Most of the population struggles to survive.

WORLD RANKING

S

SURINAM

SOUTH AMERICA

South America

OFFICIAL NAME: Republic of Surinam   **CAPITAL:** Paramaribo
POPULATION: 425,000   **CURRENCY:** Surinam guilder   **OFFICIAL LANGUAGE:** Dutch

LOCATED ON THE NORTH COAST of South America, Surinam is bordered by Guyana, French Guyana and Brazil. The interior is rainforested highlands; most people live near the coast. In 1975, after almost 300 years of Dutch rule, Surinam became independent. The Netherlands is still its main aid supplier, and home to one third of Surinamese. Multiparty democracy was restored in 1991, after almost eleven years of military rule.

Congested street in Paramaribo. It boasts 18th and 19th century Dutch architecture and the Caribbean's largest mosque.

CLIMATE

WEATHER CHART

Surinam's tropical climate is cooled by the trade winds. The temperature averages 27°C. Rainfall varies from 150 to 300 cm between coast and interior.

COMMUNICATIONS

Johann Pengel Intl, Paramaribo
175,000 passengers

7 ships
14,300 dwt

THE TRANSPORT NETWORK

9153 km (5687 miles)	None
157 km (98 miles)	5029 km (3125 miles)

The road network runs east–west and focuses on the coast and its immediate hinterland. Rivers provide the main north–south links. The vast interior relies on water or air transport.

TOURISM

20,700 visitors

Down 48% in 1989

MAIN OVERSEAS ARRIVALS

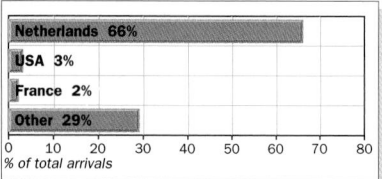

Netherlands 66%
USA 3%
France 2%
Other 29%

0 10 20 30 40 50 60 70 80
% of total arrivals

Tourism is undeveloped. Travellers outside Paramaribo are advised to carry their own hammock and food.

PEOPLE

Pidgin English (Taki-Taki), Dutch, Hindi, Javanese, Saramacca, Carib

3 people per km²

THE URBAN/RURAL POPULATION SPLIT

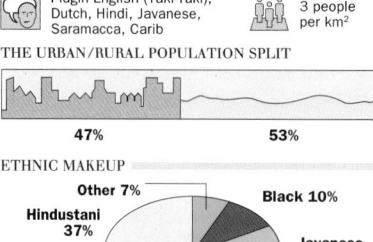

47%   53%

ETHNIC MAKEUP

Other 7%
Hindustani 37%
Black 10%
Javanese 15%
Creole 31%

About 200,000 Surinamese, one third of the ethnically diverse population, has emigrated since 1975. Of those still in Surinam, 90% live near the coast. The rest live in very scattered rainforest communities. About 7000 are native Amerindians. The remainder are *bosnegers* – the descendants of runaway African slaves. They fought the Creole-dominated government in the 1980s. Many Indians and Javanese work in farming.

POLITICS

1996

President Ronald Venetiaan

THE STATE OF THE PARTIES

National Assembly 51 members

59% NF   23% NDP   18% DA 1991

NF = New Front (composed of: NPS = Surinam National Party, VHP = Progressive Reform Party, KTPI = Party for National Unity and Solidarity, SPA = Surinam Labour Party) **NDP** = National Democratic Party **DA 1991** = Democratic Alternative 1991

Council of State 15 members

Representatives of trade unions, armed forces and elected political parties

The democratically-elected coalition that took power in 1991 is dominated by traditional, ethnically-based parties: the Creole NPS, the Indian VHP and the Indonesian KTPI. The opposition NDP is led by Desi Bouterse, former head of the military regime that ruled from 1980 to 1988. Bouterse was also the force behind the 1990 coup, which ended Surinam's first attempt to return to democracy, and is still a key political player.

ATLANTIC OCEAN

Nieuw Nickerie
Totness
Groningen
Calcutta
PARAMARIBO
Boskamp
Wageningen
Jenny
Nieuw Amsterdam
Galibi
Lelydorp
Onverwacht
Republiek
Paranam
Moengo
Albina
Pilgrimkondre
Apoera
Bitagron
Kwakoegron
Joden Savanne
Zanderij
Berg en Dal
Brokopondo
Kaaimanston
Brownsweg
Afobaka
Langatabbetje
Njoeng Jacobkondre
W.J. van Blommesteinmeer
Kabalebo Reservoir
Pokigron
Stoelmanseiland
Boti-Pasi
Ladoewani
Poeketi
Asidonhopo
Cottica
Juliana Top 1230m
Gran
Teboe Top
Intelewa
Alalapadu
Majoli
Appikalo

N

0   50 km
0   50 miles

BRAZIL

SURINAM

Total Area : 163 270 sq. km (63 039 sq. miles)

LAND HEIGHT
1000m/3281ft
500m/1640ft
200m/1640ft
Sea Level

POPULATI...
over
over
unde...

WORLD AFFAIRS

Relations with the Netherlands and the USA, Surinam's key aid and trading partners, have eased since the return to democracy in 1991. They were strained during the 1980s when both stopped aid in response to the military regime's human rights abuses. Integration into the Caribbean region and better links with India and Indonesia are priorities.

AID

 $40m (receipts)   Down 30% in 1991

The Netherlands is the largest donor. The economy was badly hit by aid suspensions from 1982 to 1988 over human rights abuses and after the 1990 coup. Humanitarian aid resumed in 1992. Other aid is still frozen.

DEFENCE

 $67m   Up 71% in 1990

Under Colonel Desi Bouterse, the army has played a dominant political role since 1980. Bouterse resigned as army head in 1992, but military intervention remains a threat. A six-year civil war against *bosneger* rebels ended in 1992.

ECONOMICS

 $1.6bn   1.79 Surinam guilders

SCORE CARD

❑ WORLD GNP RANKING	143rd
❑ GNP PER CAPITA	$3880
❑ BALANCE OF PAYMENTS	$31.9m
❑ INFLATION	30%
❑ UNEMPLOYMENT	16.5%

STRENGTHS

Bauxite. Rainforest potential, notably timber. Oil. Agricultural exports: rice, bananas, citrus fruits. Shrimp exports.

WEAKNESSES

Over-dependence on declining bauxite reserves and Dutch aid. Government failure to reform monetary system. Continued budget deficit is extending aid freeze and exacerbating associated economic recession. Net food importer.

EXPORTS

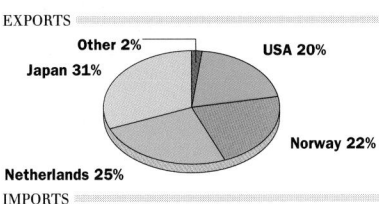

Other 2%
USA 20%
Japan 31%
Norway 22%
Netherlands 25%

IMPORTS

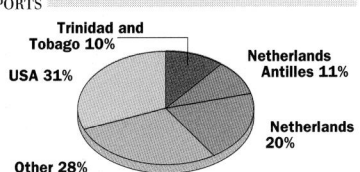

Trinidad and Tobago 10%
Netherlands Antilles 11%
USA 31%
Netherlands 20%
Other 28%

democracy in 1991. They were strained during the 1980s when both stopped aid in response to the military regime's human rights abuses. Integration into the Caribbean region and better links with India and Indonesia are priorities.

RESOURCES

 1.4bn kwh (capacity 420,000 kw)   Not an oil producer; refines 4700 b/cd

89,000 cattle, 25,000 pigs, 8,000 sheep   Bauxite, iron, manganese, copper, nickel, platinum, gold

Surinam is the world's sixth largest bauxite producer. Aluminium and bauxite account for over 75% of export earnings, but the sector has been hit by civil war and poor world prices. Oil production started in 1982, near Paramaribo. Exploitation of Surinam's rainforests has barely begun. Rice and fruit are the key agricultural products.

ENVIRONMENT

 4% partially protected   Economic growth has precedence over ecological concerns

Many of the 13 nature reserves were damaged in the civil war. *Bosneger* and Amerindian rainforest communities are becoming more militant in demanding control over their lands as commercial interest in the forests' potential grows.

MEDIA

 Censorship has eased since the return to democratic government in 1991

PUBLISHING AND BROADCAST MEDIA

There are 2 daily newspapers, *Ware Tijd* and *De West*

2 state-owned services   2 state-owned, 6 independent services

The radio stations broadcast in a number of languages. Dutch is used by the daily newspapers and TV stations.

CRIME

 Surinam does not publish prison figures   Relatively high crime levels from year to year

The human rights abuses associated with the military regime have largely ended. President Venetiaan has also tried to clamp down on cocaine and illegal arms smuggling, which became a major problem during the 1980s.

EDUCATION

 95%

Education is free and includes adult literacy programmes. There is a long tradition of higher education, but most graduates now live in the Netherlands.

HEALTH

 1 per 1798 people   Circulatory diseases, accidents, violence

Urban medical facilities are relatively good. In the interior, they are basic and provided largely by mission stations.

WEALTH

 Deep sea fisherman, 600–850 Surinam guilders per month; chemical industry foreman, 2890–4700 Surinam guilders per month

CONSUMER GOODS OWNERSHIP

VCR and PC ownership is limited to a small elite

Per 1000 population: 133   92   85

Living standards have fallen since 1982, due to the effects of aid suspension and civil war. Urban Creoles dominate the rich elite. Amerindians and *bosnegers* are the poorest groups.

WORLD RANKING

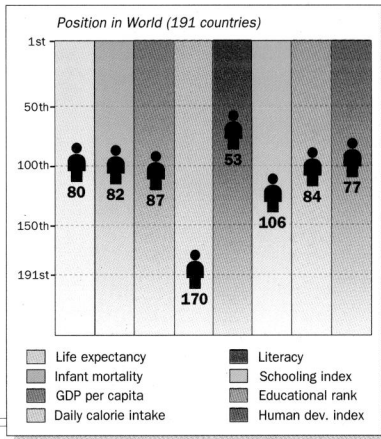

Position in World (191 countries)

80   82   87   53   106   84   77
170

Life expectancy	Literacy	
Infant mortality	Schooling index	
GDP per capita	Educational rank	
Daily calorie intake	Human dev. index	

S

SWAZILAND

SOUTHERN AFRICA

OFFICIAL NAME: Kingdom of Swaziland   **CAPITAL:** Mbabane
POPULATION: 800,000   **CURRENCY:** Lilangeni   **OFFICIAL LANGUAGES:** Siswati and English

 1968

THE TINY SOUTHERN AFRICAN kingdom of Swaziland, bordered on three sides by South Africa and to the east by Mozambique, comprises mainly upland plateaux and mountains. Governed by a strong hereditary monarch, Swaziland is a country in which tradition is being challenged by demands for modern multiparty government. King Mswati III, crowned in 1986, has overhauled the electoral process, but has still to legalize party politics.

CLIMATE

WEATHER CHART

Swaziland is temperate. Temperatures rise and rainfall declines as the land descends eastward, from high to low *veld*. The Low Veld is prone to drought.

COMMUNICATIONS

 Matsapa, Manzini
93,000 passengers

 Has no fleet

THE TRANSPORT NETWORK

2779 km (1727 miles)	None
370 km (230 miles)	None

A sharp rise in road traffic has led to a focus on road improvement schemes. The railway, which runs to Mozambique and South Africa, mainly carries exports.

TOURISM

 287,796 visitors   Up 3% in 1990

MAIN OVERSEAS ARRIVALS

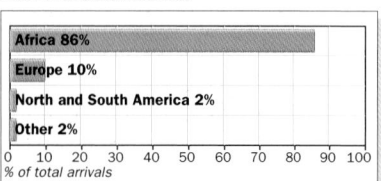
- Africa 86%
- Europe 10%
- North and South America 2%
- Other 2%

0 10 20 30 40 50 60 70 80 90 100
% of total arrivals

Swaziland's attractions are its game reserves, mountain scenery and, for the South Africans who make up more than 70% of tourists, its casinos.

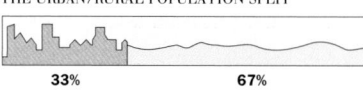

The outskirts of Mbabane. It lies on the High Veld, where traditional cattle farming has become more difficult owing to overgrazing.

PEOPLE

 Siswati, English, Zulu   46 people per km²

THE URBAN/RURAL POPULATION SPLIT

33%   67%

RELIGIOUS PERSUASION

Indigenous beliefs 40%

Christian 60%

Over 95% of the population belong to the Swazi ethnic group, making Swaziland one of Africa's most homogeneous states. It is also one of the most conservative, although it is now coming under pressure from urban-based modernizers. Its political system actively promotes Swazi tradition and is dominated by a powerful monarchy. Society is patriarchal and focused around the clan and chiefs. Both are also politically important. Polygamy is tolerated. Women farm and may vote, but have little economic or political power. The exception is the Queen Mother, the 'Great She Elephant', whose influence was demonstrated during the interregnum of the mid-1980s.

POLITICS

 1999   HM King Mswati III

THE STATE OF THE PARTIES

House of Assembly 65 members

55 members are elected by traditional communities, or Tinkhundla, from candidates nominated by the chiefs. 10 are appointed by the King

Senate 30 members

10 members are selected by the House of Assembly from among its own members, and 20 are appointed by the King

Politics is dominated by a strong executive monarchy, and rivalries within the royal Dlamini clan. The King's traditional advisers act as a counter to the cabinet. Constitutional reform introduced direct elections to the House of Assembly in 1993. There is growing pressure for the King to legalize political parties and move towards multiparty democracy.

SWAZILAND

Total Area : 17 360 sq. km (6703 sq. miles)

POPULATION
- ○ over 50 000
- ● over 10 000
- • under 10 000

LAND HEIGHT
- 1000m/3281ft
- 500m/1640ft
- 200m/656ft
- Sea Level

S

Key to symbols and abbreviations on endpapers

WORLD AFFAIRS

Swaziland's economic dependence on South Africa means good relations with the Republic are the top priority. It has had to balance membership of SADC with the need not to alienate Pretoria. A secret security pact was agreed with South Africa in 1982. With 134,000 Mozambican refugees, Swaziland is also keen to see peace in that country.

AID

 $48m (receipts)   Up 66% between 1989 and 1991

Balance of payments aid is important. Project aid has been targeted at the development of the Matsapha industrial estate, roads and social projects. Donors have generally looked favourably on Swaziland. The EU, Germany, the USA, the UK and the World Bank are important donors.

DEFENCE

 $12.68m   Up 12% in 1992

The Swaziland Defence Force numbers just 5000 troops. Although it does not play an overt political role, its loyalty is to the monarch and the *status quo*.

ECONOMICS

 $960m   3.40 emalangeni

SCORE CARD

☐ WORLD GNP RANKING........................156th
☐ GNP PER CAPITA $1200
☐ BALANCE OF PAYMENTS $25.3m
☐ INFLATION 13%
☐ UNEMPLOYMENT....Widespread underemployment

STRENGTHS
Economy quite diversified and buoyant; grew 4.5% a year during 1980s. Manufacturing 32% of GDP. Investment rules attractive. Sugar 33% of export earnings. Wood pulp. Debt service low: only 3.5% of export earnings in 1991.

WEAKNESSES
Sugar vulnerable to changes in world prices. Exports at risk through regional instability; most go through Mozambique. Dependence on South Africa for jobs, revenue, investment, electricity. Small plots of land and lack of land title hinder farm modernization. High population growth.

EXPORTS

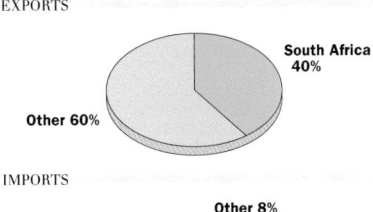

South Africa 40%
Other 60%

IMPORTS

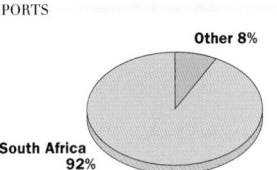

Other 8%
South Africa 92%

RESOURCES

 Over half of power supply imported from South Africa   Not an oil producer and has no refineries

 660,000 cattle, 33,000 sheep, 23,000 pigs   Coal, diamonds, gold, asbestos, cassiterite, iron, beryl

Swaziland's main export is sugar cane. Wood pulp, coal and asbestos are also exported. The HEP station at Lupholo-Ezulwim, completed in the 1980s, will reduce energy imports from South Africa.

ENVIRONMENT

 3% (partially protected)   Recognized as important for tourism

The main threat is land pressure owing to high population growth. In an effort to combat the problem, family planning programmes are being introduced.

MEDIA

 The media is strictly controlled. Editors must get permission before publishing sensitive articles

PUBLISHING AND BROADCAST MEDIA

There are 3 daily newspapers, *The Times of Swaziland*, *Tikhatsi Temaswati* and the *Swaziland Observer*

1 state-owned service   1 state-owned, 3 independent services

The Times of Swaziland and *Swaziland Observer* are independent, but the press is generally respectful of the monarch and the royal Dlamini clan.

CRIME

 Swaziland does not publish prison figures   Up 6% between 1988 and 1990

The crime rate is low, but rising. An influx of illegal weapons brought in by refugees has boosted armed crime.

EDUCATION

 68%

Education is not compulsory. Parents pay fees at all levels. Even so, primary enrolment is about 82%. Drop-out rates at secondary level are high.

CHRONOLOGY

Swaziland became a British protectorate in 1903.

☐ **1964** Limited self-government under King Sobhuza II.
☐ **1968** Independence.
☐ **1973** King bans political activity, repeals constitution.
☐ **1978** New constitution confirms King's executive, legislative control.
☐ **1982** King Sobhuza dies. Queen Mother becomes regent for Prince Makhosetive, aged 14. Power struggle between modernists and traditionalists in royal Dlamini clan.
☐ **1986** Prince Makhosetive crowned King Mswati III.
☐ **1992** King allows some electoral reform. Refuses to remove ban on political parties.
☐ **1993** Elections under new system.

HEALTH

 1 per 7971 people   Diarrheal and respiratory diseases

There is no national health service and the network of facilities is rudimentary. Health takes 7% of budget spending.

WEALTH

 Half the population lives below the UN poverty line

CONSUMER GOODS OWNERSHIP

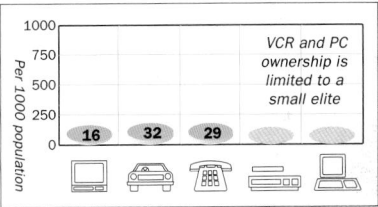

VCR and PC ownership is limited to a small elite

16 32 29

About 50% of Swazis live below the UN poverty line. The royal Dlamini clan enjoys Western luxuries and travel.

WORLD RANKING

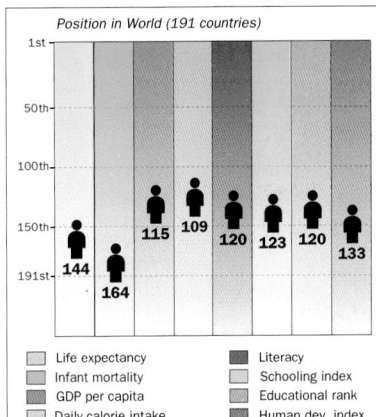

Position in World (191 countries)

144 164 115 109 120 123 120 133

Life expectancy / Literacy
Infant mortality / Schooling index
GDP per capita / Educational rank
Daily calorie intake / Human dev. index

S

511

SWEDEN

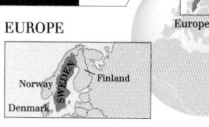

OFFICIAL NAME: Kingdom of Sweden **CAPITAL:** Stockholm
POPULATION: 8.6 million **CURRENCY:** Swedish krona **OFFICIAL LANGUAGE:** Swedish

Situated on the Scandinavian peninsula, between Norway and Finland, Sweden is a densely forested country with numerous lakes. The north of Sweden falls within the Arctic Circle. Much of the south is fertile and widely cultivated. Sweden has one of the most extensive welfare systems in the world, and is among the world's leading proponents of equal rights for women. Its economic strengths include high-tech industries and car production, including Volvo and Saab. Sweden settled terms for its accession to the EU in March 1994.

CLIMATE

WEATHER CHART

Sweden has a largely continental climate. The Baltic Sea often freezes in winter, making the east coast much colder than the west. Summers are cool everywhere, with temperatures varying suprisingly little between northern and southern regions.

COMMUNICATIONS

 Arlanda, Stockholm
14.82m passengers

 273 ships
3.35m dwt

THE TRANSPORT NETWORK

 133,673 km
(83,060 miles)

936 km
(582 miles)

 11,202 km
(6961 miles)

2052 km
(1275 miles)

Maintaining and improving transport links in Europe's fourth largest country is a key issue. Swedish governments have traditionally spent large sums on infrastructure. Transport spending is also seen as a way of boosting the economy as a whole. A new $20 billion programme was recently announced, which will finance road, rail and port development.

Sweden's biggest single transport project is a $5 billion bridge across The Sound. This will provide a road link to Denmark, and hence to the rest of Europe. A new rail link between Arlanda airport and Stockholm is also planned. By law, cars must travel with their headlights on at all times.

TOURISM

 6.1m bed-nights.
Sweden does not record visitor numbers

Up 3% in 1993

MAIN OVERSEAS ARRIVALS

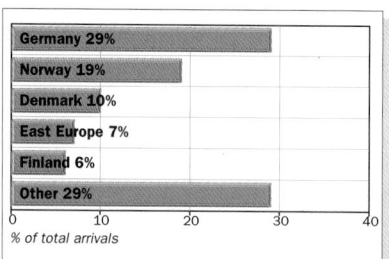

% of total arrivals

Sweden expanded rapidly as a tourist destination in the 1970s and 1980s. Stockholm, the capital, is renowned for its palaces. The international success of Abba in the 1970s boosted its vibrant nightlife. Visitors to the capital are typically young and affluent.

Although Sweden has fewer lakes than Finland, and lacks Norway's dramatic scenery, it still has a variety of natural attractions. The mountains of the 'Midnight Sun' lie north of the Arctic Circle, while the southern coast has many white sandy beaches. Visitors have also been attracted by the vast tracts of deserted landscape and the simple country communal living. Despite the relatively high cost of travel to Sweden, tourism now accounts for 5% of GDP.

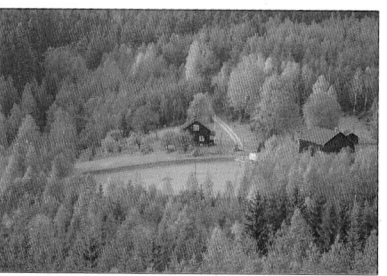

A crofter's holding in Darlana, Central Sweden, an area which is over 50% forested. The timber and paper industries account for almost 20% of Sweden's exports.

PEOPLE

Swedish, Finnish, Lappish

19 people per km²

THE URBAN/RURAL POPULATION SPLIT

84% 16%

RELIGIOUS PERSUASION

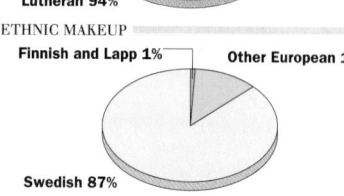

Pentecostal 1% Roman Catholic 2%
Other 3%
Evangelical Lutheran 94%

ETHNIC MAKEUP

Finnish and Lapp 1% Other European 12%
Swedish 87%

As in all of Scandinavia, the nuclear family forms the basis of society. The birth rate is low with, on average, less than two children per family. Marriage is declining, and cohabitation outside marriage is common.

Swedish society has an egalitarian tradition. The role of the state is seen as the provision of conditions allowing each individual, male or female, to gain economic independence through employment. Sweden's welfare system is also one of the most extensive in the world. However, in the early 1990s, recession reduced benefits, and mothers in particular face increasing difficulties with the closure of childcare facilities. Women make up nearly half of the workforce, one of the highest proportions in Europe.

Whilst Sweden has generous asylum laws, immigration is tightly controlled. Racial tensions are few, although there have been instances of right-wing attacks on Bosnian refugees.

A 15,000-strong minority of Sami (or Lapps) live in northern Sweden. Their traditional way of life is protected.

POPULATION AGE BREAKDOWN

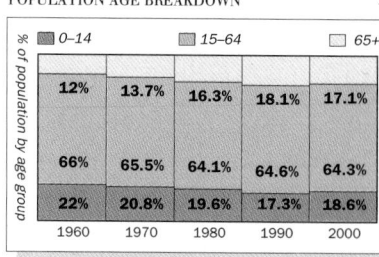

	0–14	15–64		65+	
% of population by age group	12%	13.7%	16.3%	18.1%	17.1%
	66%	65.5%	64.1%	64.6%	64.3%
	22%	20.8%	19.6%	17.3%	18.6%
	1960	1970	1980	1990	2000

S

POLITICS

1994   King Carl XVI Gustaf

THE STATE OF THE PARTIES

Parliament (Riksdag) 349 members

40% SDAP		23% MS	9% FP	9% CP	7% KdS	12% Other

SDAP = Social Democratic Labour Party   **MS** = Moderate Party   **FP** = Liberal Party   **CP** = Centre Party **KdS** = Christian Democratic Party   **Other** = New Democracy, Left Party, Green Party

Sweden is a constitutional monarchy with an elected parliament under the leadership of the prime minister.

MAIN POLITICAL ISSUES

EU membership
In March 1994, Sweden agreed terms to join the EU. A referendum will be held, although the result of this will not in law be binding on parliament. Opinion polls suggest a majority of Swedes will support membership.

High cost of the welfare state
The cost of Sweden's welfare system has brought about an enormous budget deficit, equivalent to 15% of GDP in 1993. The government has to steer a difficult course between raising taxes and cutting benefits.

PROFILE
Swedish politics has traditionally been split between the monolithic Social Democrats (SDAP) and trade unions on the left, and a host of moderate centre and right-wing parties. Since the 1930s, the Social Democrats have

governed every term with the exception of 1976–1982 and 1991–1994. 1991 marked a shift to the right in Swedish politics underlined by the rise of New Democracy, which won a remarkable 25 seats on a populist anti-immigration and anti-welfare platform. The SDAP remained the largest party in parliament, but the government was formed by a coalition of the MS, FP, CP and KdS.

Carl XVI Gustaf, ascended the throne in 1973. His role is purely ceremonial.

Carl Bildt, leader of the Moderate Party, became prime minister in 1991.

WORLD AFFAIRS

EEA   OECD   CSCE   NC   GATT

Sweden's main recent foreign policy concern has been obtaining membership of the EU; terms were agreed in 1994. Since the collapse of the Soviet Union, Sweden has also altered its traditionally neutral stance. Membership of the Western European Union and even NATO are being considered. This contrasts sharply with Prime Minister Olof Palme's period in office in the 1980s, when Sweden was a vociferous critic of the USA's antagonistic policy towards the USSR. In 1993–1994, Sweden participated in the UN peace-keeping force in former Yugoslavia.

AID

 $2.1bn (donations)   Up 5% in 1991

Sweden runs a very active development aid programme, to which 1% of GDP is allocated. The majority of bilateral aid goes to African countries.

CHRONOLOGY

Sweden's history has been closely linked to the control of the Baltic Sea and its highly profitable trade routes. Under the house of Vasa, Sweden became a major power, controlling much of the Baltic region. By the 18th century, however, Sweden's position had been eroded by its regional rivals, particularly Russia.

- ❏ **1814–1815** Congress of Vienna. Sweden cedes territory to Russia and Denmark. Period of 180 years of unbroken peace begins.
- ❏ **1844** Oscar I becomes king.
- ❏ **1859** Carl XV ascends the throne.
- ❏ **1865–1866** Minister of Justice Louis De Greer reforms the Riksdag into a bicameral parliament.
- ❏ **1872** Oscar II ascends the throne.
- ❏ **1905** Norway gains independence from Sweden.
- ❏ **1907** Gustav V becomes king.

SWEDEN

Total Area : 449 960 sq. km (173 730 sq. miles)

POPULATION

- ⊡ over 1 000 000
- ◎ over 100 000
- ○ over 50 000
- ● over 10 000

LAND HEIGHT

- 1000m/3281ft
- 500m/1640ft
- 200m/656ft
- Sea Level

S

CHRONOLOGY *continued*

- ☐ **1911** First Liberal government.
- ☐ **1914** Government resigns over defence policy.
- ☐ **1914–1917** Sweden remains neutral though it supplies Germany. Allied blockade.
- ☐ **1917** Food shortages. Conservative government falls. Nils Edén forms a Liberal government which limits exports contributing to German war effort.
- ☐ **1919** Universal adult suffrage.
- ☐ **1921** Finland gains Åland Islands, retribution for Sweden's war role.
- ☐ **1932** Severe recession. Social Democrat government under Per Hannsson elected.
- ☐ **1939–1945** Sweden neutral. Grants transit rights to German forces.
- ☐ **1945–1976** Continuing Social Democratic rule under Tage Erlander eschews 'Functional Socialism'. Establishes Sweden as world's most advanced welfare state, and one of the most affluent.
- ☐ **1950** Gustav VI Adolf becomes king.
- ☐ **1953** Nordic Council member.
- ☐ **1959** Founder member of EFTA.
- ☐ **1969** Erlander succeeded by Olof Palme as prime minister.
- ☐ **1973** Carl XVI Gustav on throne.
- ☐ **1975** Major constitutional reform. Riksdag becomes unicameral with a 3-year term. Role of monarchy reduced to ceremonial functions.
- ☐ **1976** SDAP lose power. Non-socialist coalition led by Thorbjörn Fälldin in government.
- ☐ **1978** Fälldin resigns over issue of nuclear power. Ola Ullsten prime minister.
- ☐ **1979** Fälldin prime minister again.
- ☐ **1982** Elections. SDAP form minority government. Palme prime minister.
- ☐ **1986** Palme shot dead. His deputy, Ingvar Carlsson, prime minister. Police fail to find assassin.
- ☐ **1989** Palme murder suspect acquitted.
- ☐ **1990** Carlsson introduces moderate austerity package. Cuts government spending, raises indirect taxes.
- ☐ **1991** July, Sweden applies to join the EU. September, SDAP remains largest party but is unable to form government; Carlsson resigns. October, Carl Bildt, leader of the Moderate Party (MS), forms coalition of non-socialist parties.
- ☐ **1992** Austerity measures succeed in reducing inflation. November, SDAP refuses to support further cuts in government expenditure.
- ☐ **1993** February, government begins negotiations for EU membership. MS coalition survives vote of no confidence.
- ☐ **1994** Terms of EU membership settled.

DEFENCE

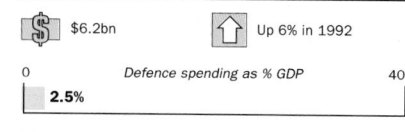

💲 $6.2bn	⬆ Up 6% in 1992

0 — *Defence spending as % GDP* — 40
2.5%

SWEDISH ARMED FORCES

🚜	885 main battle tanks (340 Strv-101/110 Strv-102,-104 *Centurior*)	43,000 personnel
🚢	12 submarines and 41 patrol boats	9500 personnel
✈	499 combat aircraft (79 AJ-37/18 SK-37/ 65 J-35/11 SK-35C)	7500 personnel
🚀	None	

Sweden maintains a sophisticated and powerful military force. Spending is concentrated on defence, reflecting Sweden's traditional need to protect its neutrality. Most weaponry, including Saab fighter jets and Bofor anti-aircraft guns, is supplied by its advanced home defence industry. Regular anti-submarine patrols are maintained in the Baltic and North Seas.

With the end of the Cold War, strategic priorities have changed. Sweden feels less bound to its neutral stance and is considering future membership of the Western European Union and even NATO. Mutual security co-operation agreements are also being discussed with the Baltic States.

ECONOMICS

📊 $218.9bn	💲 8.34 Swedish kronor

SCORE CARD

- ☐ WORLD GNP RANKING...........................19th
- ☐ GNP PER CAPITA $25,100
- ☐ BALANCE OF PAYMENTS....................$–4.9bn
- ☐ INFLATION 2.2%
- ☐ UNEMPLOYMENT..................................2.7%

EXPORTS

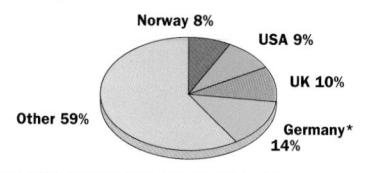

Norway 8%
USA 9%
UK 10%
Germany* 14%
Other 59%

IMPORTS

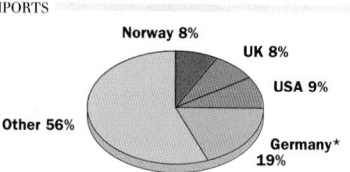

Norway 8%
UK 8%
USA 9%
Germany* 19%
Other 56%

STRENGTHS

Companies of global importance, including Ericsson, Saab, Volvo, Electrolux and SKF, the world's biggest roller bearing manufacturer. Highly developed and constantly updated infrastructure. Sophisticated technology. Skilled labour force is virtually bilingual in English.

WEAKNESSES

Uncompetitive labour costs, although this is beginning to change slowly. Highest taxation in the OECD, accounting for over 60% of GDP. Peripheral location, raising costs for producers and exporters.

PROFILE

The state plays a significant role in the economy, but tends to restrict its role to services and infrastructure.

ECONOMIC PERFORMANCE INDICATOR

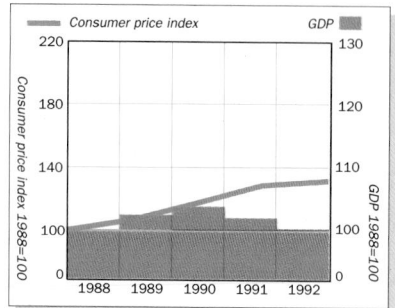

Consumer price index / GDP
Consumer price index 1988=100
GDP 1988=100
1988 1989 1990 1991 1992

Sweden's industrial giants have mostly been private-sector companies.

The early 1990s saw a shift in government economic policy. Some elements of the post-war consensus on the social role of government were abandoned in favour of measures designed to help business. However, the hoped-for result of greater growth was not achieved, and unemployment and the overall cost of welfare rose. Sweden's balance of payments deficit is now the highest in the OECD. The deficit will have to be financed by improved business performance and higher taxation.

SWEDEN : MAJOR BUSINESSES

- 🚗 Vehicle manufacture
- 📞 Telecommunications
- ⚡ Electrometallurgy
- ⛏ Iron ore mining
- 🔌 Electronics
- 📄 Pulp & paper
- ⚙ Engineering
- 🧪 Chemicals
- 🧵 Textiles

0 — 200 km
0 — 200 miles

Kiruna
Gällivare
Umeå
Gävle
Västerås
Stockholm
Norrköping
Linköping
Göteborg
Malmö

RESOURCES

146.5bn kwh (capacity 34.2m kw)

Not an oil producer; refines 427,500 b/cd

2.3m pigs, 1.7m cattle, 401,000 sheep

Iron, uranium, copper, lead, zinc, silver

ELECTRICITY GENERATION

Hydro 50% (73.1bn kwh)

Thermal 4% (5.2bn kwh)

Nuclear 46% (68.2bn kwh)

Other 0%

% of total generation by type

Sweden is rich in minerals, pig iron, copper and silver. While mining and quarrying account for only 0.3% of GDP, they underpin other industrial sectors. Despite its abundant uranium deposits, making up 80% of the European total,

ENVIRONMENT

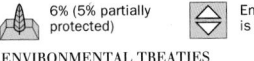

6% (5% partially protected)

Environmental policy is a high priority

ENVIRONMENTAL TREATIES

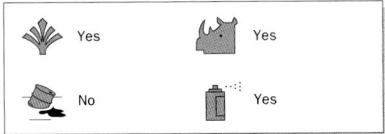

Yes   Yes

No   Yes

Since the Environment Protection Act of 1969, investment in environmental protection measures has totalled 20 billion kronor. Sweden has blamed the considerable acid-rain damage to forests and lakes on airborne sulphur dioxide from factories in western Europe. Swedish nuclear reactors are said to be very safe, with filtered venting systems designed to retain 90% of all radioactivity released in the event of a core meltdown.

MEDIA

Government censorship is non-existent

PUBLISHING AND BROADCAST MEDIA

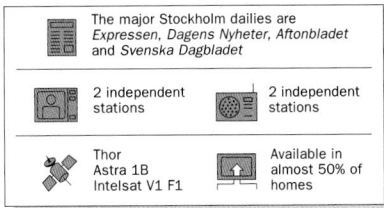

The major Stockholm dailies are *Expressen, Dagens Nyheter, Aftonbladet* and *Svenska Dagbladet*

2 independent stations   2 independent stations

Thor Astra 1B Intelsat V1 F1   Available in almost 50% of homes

Radical viewpoints are rarely expressed in the Swedish press. The influence of the major daily newspapers is largely confined to Stockholm, as the provinces have a strong press of their own. Six companies control almost all of Sweden's magazines. Political parties finance many newspapers.

Sweden has only four nuclear power stations. It is government policy that nuclear power should be phased out by the year 2010. As a result, Sweden is importing energy from Germany, some sourced from nuclear reactors.

SWEDEN : LAND USE

High mountain regions
Forest
Pasture
Cropland
Pigs
Barley

LAPLAND

0 200 km
0 200 miles

CRIME

4716 prisoners   Up 6% in 1990

CRIME RATES

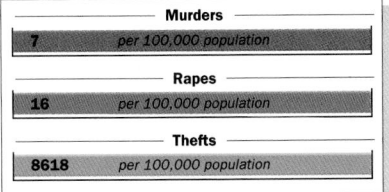

Murders
7   per 100,000 population

Rapes
16   per 100,000 population

Thefts
8618   per 100,000 population

Crime rates are below the European average, although they are the highest among Scandinavian countries. Assault, rape and theft are growing problems, especially in the cities.

EDUCATION

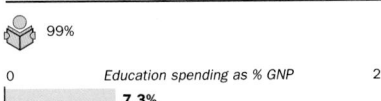

99%

0 Education spending as % GNP 25
7.3%

THE EDUCATION SYSTEM

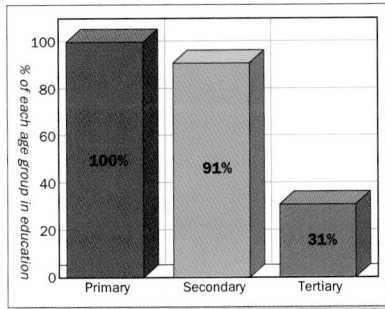

Primary 100%   Secondary 91%   Tertiary 31%

% of each age group in education

Coeducational comprehensive schools are the norm. The higher education system is freely available to most of the population, and many adults return to college to do further courses.

HEALTH

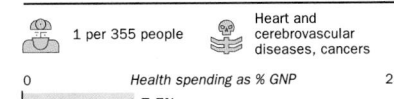

1 per 355 people   Heart and cerebrovascular diseases, cancers

0 Health spending as % GNP 25
7.5%

Sweden's health care system is comprehensive and of a universally high standard. Since 1991, it has been under review in an attempt to cut government spending. Almost 25% of surgical beds have been closed and 30,000 jobs cut. Sweden is now amongst the lowest spenders on health as a proportion of GNP in the OECD. Reforms in 1994 gave individuals the right to choose their own doctor, and allowed doctors and specialists to set up private practices.

WEALTH

Sawmill sawyer, 86 kronor per hour; accountant, 21,649 kronor per month

CONSUMER GOODS OWNERSHIP

471, 419, 940, 220, 22 (Per 1000 population)

Sweden has limited income disparities and Swedish executives are generally paid less than their counterparts in France, Germany and Italy. Social competition and a sense of hierarchy are limited compared to other European states or the USA. Despite some cuts in services, the welfare system still provides some of the best health, unemployment, and pension provision in Europe.

Swedes are keen overseas property buyers, particularly of villas in Italy and the south of France. Net overseas per capita investment remains among the highest in the world.

S

WORLD RANKING

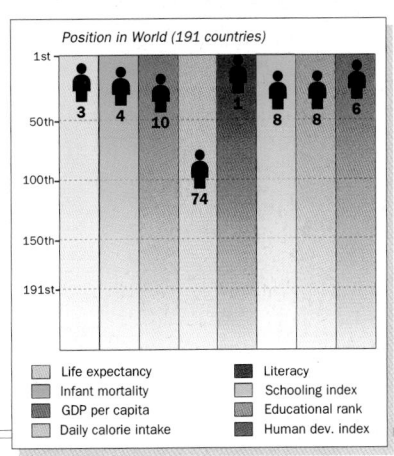

Position in World (191 countries)

3, 4, 10, 1, 8, 8, 6, 74

Life expectancy
Infant mortality
GDP per capita
Daily calorie intake
Literacy
Schooling index
Educational rank
Human dev. index

SWITZERLAND

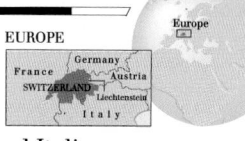

OFFICIAL NAME: Swiss Confederation   **CAPITAL:** Bern
POPULATION: 6.8 million   **CURRENCY:** Swiss franc   **OFFICIAL LANGUAGES:** German, French and Italian

SWITZERLAND LIES AT THE centre of western Europe geographically, but outside it politically. Sometimes called Europe's water tower, it is the source of western Europe's largest rivers: the Po, the Rhine, the Rhône and the Inn-Danube. Switzerland has managed to retain its neutral status through every major European conflict since 1815. It has also built one of the world's most prosperous economies. Whether or not to join the process of greater European political and economic integration is a central issue.

The Eiger in the Berner Oberland. In 1994, a referendum voted to ban all lorry transit traffic from the Swiss Alps as from 2004.

CLIMATE

WEATHER CHART

Average daily temperature / Rainfall
°C/°F   J F M A M J J A S O N D   cm/in
40/104 ... 40/16
30/86 ... 30/12
20/68 ... 20/8
10/50 ... 10/4
0/32 ... 0
-10/14
-20/-4

Temperature and weather vary enormously, not only with the seasons, but also because of the huge variations in altitude, and the country's location in the centre of Europe. On the plateau north of the Alps, where most of the population lives, summers are warm and winters dry, cool and often foggy. South of the Alps, it is considerably warmer and sunnier. Strong southerly winds, or *föhn*, can bring summer-like weather even in winter.

COMMUNICATIONS

 Kloten, Zürich
12.28m passengers

 24 ships
604,800 dwt

THE TRANSPORT NETWORK

71,099 km
(44,179 miles)

1515 km
(941 miles)

5208 km
(3236 miles)

1208 km
(751 miles)

Switzerland is a major European freight transit route. Pollution caused by lorries is a major concern. The NEAT project, approved in 1992, will provide two new high-speed rail lines linking Basel and Milan, on which lorries will be carried on trains. Estimates suggest it will cost three times as much to build as the Channel Tunnel.

TOURISM

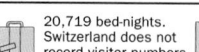 20,719 bed-nights. Switzerland does not record visitor numbers

 Down 3% in 1991

MAIN OVERSEAS ARRIVALS

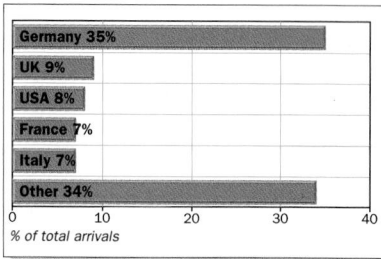

Germany 35%
UK 9%
USA 8%
France 7%
Italy 7%
Other 34%

0   10   20   30   40
% of total arrivals

Tourism is Switzerland's third largest industry. About 350,000 Swiss earn their living from it, and in 1992 tourism accounted for 6% of GNP. The Alps are the main attraction, drawing winter and summer tourists from around the world. However, several factors have led to the recent downturn in the industry. Warmer winters have resulted in a shorter skiing season. The rise in value of the Swiss franc has made Switzerland an expensive destination and Austria is offering tough competition.

SWITZERLAND

Total Area : 41 290 sq. km
(15 940 sq. miles)

POPULATION
over 100 000
over 50 000
over 10 000

LAND HEIGHT
3000m/9843ft
2000m/6562ft
1000m/3281ft
500m/1640ft
200m/656ft

[Map of Switzerland showing cities including Basel, Schaffhausen, Kreuzlingen, Frauenfeld, Arbon, Rorschach, Sankt Gallen, Herisau, Wil, Winterthur, Kloten, Baden, Aarau, Liestal, Delémont, Olten, Solothurn, Langenthal, Zürich, Uster, Horgen, Wädenswil, Stäfa, Jona, Zug, Baar, Grenchen, Biel, Rapperswil, Burgdorf, Einsiedeln, Schwyz, Luzern, La Chaux-de-Fonds, Neuchâtel, Bolligen, Muri, BERN, Köniz, Fribourg, Steffisburg, Chur, Davos, Thun, Spiez, Interlaken, Yverdon, Renens, Morges, Lausanne, Vevey, Pully, Montreux, Nyon, Monthey, Sion, Sierre, Brig, Bellinzona, Locarno, Lugano, Martigny, Genève. Surrounding countries: FRANCE, GERMANY, AUSTRIA, ITALY, LIECHTENSTEIN. Features: Lake Geneva, Lake Constance, Lake Maggiore, Rhine, Rhône, SWISS PLATEAU, BERNER OBERLAND, PENNINE ALPS, LEPONTINE ALPS, RHAETIAN ALPS, Dufourspitze 4634m, Eiger 3970m, Simplon Pass, Great St. Bernard Pass, Flüelapass, Passo del Bernina, Simplon Tunnel, San Bernardino Tunnel, Passo del San Gottardo]

S

PEOPLE

German, Swiss German, French, Italian, Romansch

160 people per km²

THE URBAN/RURAL POPULATION SPLIT

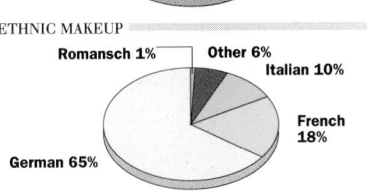

60%　　　　**40%**

RELIGIOUS PERSUASION

Other 8%

Roman Catholic 48%

Protestant 44%

ETHNIC MAKEUP

Romansch 1%　　Other 6%

Italian 10%

French 18%

German 65%

Switzerland is composed of distinct Italian-Swiss, French-Swiss and German-Swiss linguistic groups. About 40,000 in the canton of Grisons speak Romansch. The German-Swiss are in the majority. They are a tightly-knit community, with a dialect that is impenetrable to most outsiders. In recent years the three groups have grown further apart. The French-Swiss, in favour of joining the EU, are opposed by the German-Swiss. In Ticino, originally an Italian-Swiss canton, a political party has emerged to champion Italian-Swiss interests. There has also been a rise in tension between Swiss and guest workers. The fear that the Swiss are losing jobs to recent immigrants is commonly cited. Swiss society retains strong conservative elements. Two half-cantons granted women the vote in federal elections only in 1989 and 1990. Marriage rates are high and divorce less common than in most other European states.

POPULATION AGE BREAKDOWN

% of population by age group	■ 0–14	■ 15–64	□ 65+		
	10.1%	12.6%	13.8%	15%	16.3%
	65.7%	63.6%	66.5%	68.6%	66.9%
	24.2%	23.8%	19.7%	16.4%	16.8%
	1960	1970	1980	1990	2000

POLITICS

 1995

One of seven Federal Council members annually made president

THE STATE OF THE PARTIES

National Council 200 members

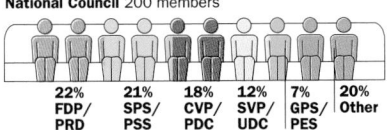

22% FDP/ PRD	21% SPS/ PSS	18% CVP/ PDC	12% SVP/ UDC	7% GPS/ PES	20% Other

FDP/PRD = Radical Democratic Party **SPS/PSS** = Social Democratic Party **CVP/PDC** = Christian Democratic People's Party **SVP/UDC** = Swiss People's Party **GPS/PES** = Green Party **LPS/PLS** = Liberal Party

Council of States 46 members

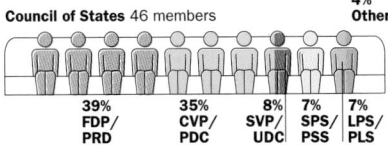

39% FDP/ PRD	35% CVP/ PDC	8% SVP/ UDC	7% SPS/ PSS	7% LPS/ PLS	4% Other

Switzerland is a federal democratic republic with 26 autonomous cantons.

Main Political Issues

Hard drugs

Public anxiety has been growing over the rise in drugs-related crime; Zürich, where most addicts and dealers congregate, has one of the biggest open drug scenes in Europe. The federal government decided to act in 1994, after the marginal right-wing SVP gained seats on Zürich's council. To the dismay of civil rights activists, tough new measures limiting the rights of asylum seekers were introduced. The aim was to make it harder for drug dealers from the former Yugoslavia to do business in Switzerland.

European integration

Almost all of the country's prominent politicians and business leaders favour joining the EU, but voters remain sharply divided. The Swiss are strongly attached to their decentralized style of government and fear that this would be lost within the EU. There are also fears that in a barrier-free Europe, Switzerland's high standards of living would fall because of a large influx of immigrants.

Profile

The same four-party coalition has been in power in Switzerland since 1959. This explains the consistency of Switzerland's domestic and foreign policies and the slow rate of political change. Politics has recently become more contentious, however, with voting patterns becoming more polarized. Divisive issues are those of drugs and membership of the EU. Both right-wing and green minority parties have recently gained more seats in parliament.

Switzerland's political system is unique in Europe. Important decisions are all made on the results of referenda. A petition of more than 100,000 signatures can also force a referendum on any issue.

WORLD AFFAIRS

EFTA　OECD　CE　CSCE　GATT

The basis of Switzerland's foreign policy remains its neutrality. Geneva has retained its position as a centre for many international organizations. The UN has its European headquarters there, and it is also home to the Red Cross. The city is often chosen as a site for diplomatic negotiations: the Camp David accords, START nuclear reduction treaties and attempts to resolve the conflict in former Yugoslavia were all negotiated in Geneva.

Switzerland has chosen not to join the process for closer European integration. It turned down membership of the EEA and voted at referendum in 1992 against joining the EU. Many believe, however, that the economic case for joining the union will become overwhelming once Switzerland's EFTA partners – Austria and the Scandinavian states – are members. Opponents of integration argue that Switzerland's seeming isolation will enhance its role as an international tax haven.

Otto Stich, *of the Social Democratic Party, president of Switzerland for 1994.*

Adolf Ogi, *of the Swiss People's Party, was president the previous year.*

S

CHRONOLOGY

The autonomy of the Swiss cantons was curtailed by the Habsburg Empire in the 11th century. In 1291, the three cantons of Unterwalden, Schwyz and Uri set up the Perpetual League to pursue Swiss liberty. Joined by other cantons, they succeeded in 1499 in gaining virtual independence. The Habsburgs retained a titular role.

❑ **1648** Peace of Westphalia ending 30 Years' War, in which Switzerland played no active part, recognizes full Swiss independence.
❑ **1798** Invaded by French.
❑ **1815** Congress of Vienna after Napoleon's defeat confirms Swiss independence and establishes its neutrality. Geneva and Valais join Swiss Confederation. ⇨

CHRONOLOGY *continued*

- ❑ **1848** New constitution – central government given more powers, but cantons' powers guaranteed.
- ❑ **1857** Joined by Neuchâtel.
- ❑ **1864** Henri Dumant founds International Red Cross in Geneva.
- ❑ **1874** Referendum established as important decision-making tool.
- ❑ **1888** Swiss Socialist Party founded.
- ❑ **1894** FDP/PRD founded.
- ❑ **1912** Conservative Party founded, later to become CVP/PDC.
- ❑ **1914–1918** Plays humanitarian role in First World War.
- ❑ **1917** Farmers and burghers found SVP/UDC.
- ❑ **1919** Proportional representation. Ensures future political stability.
- ❑ **1920s** New Swiss Communist Party gains little support.
- ❑ **1920** Joins League of Nations.
- ❑ **1939–1945** Neutral again. Refuses to join UN in 1945.
- ❑ **1959** Founder-member of EFTA. Present four-party coalition comes to power, taking over FDP/PRD dominance of government.
- ❑ **1967** Right-wing groups make electoral gains, campaigning to restrict entry of foreign workers.
- ❑ **1971** Most women granted right to vote in federal elections.
- ❑ **1984** Parliament approves application for UN membership. Dr Elisabeth Kopp is first woman minister (justice minister).
- ❑ **1986** Referendum rejects UN membership. New laws to restrict numbers of immigrants.
- ❑ **1987** Green Party wins its first two seats in parliament.
- ❑ **1988** Dr Kopp resigns over her alleged violation of secrecy of information laws.
- ❑ **1990** Dr Kopp acquitted. Case revealed that Public Prosecutor's office held secret files on 200,000 people. Violent demonstrations. State security laws amended.
- ❑ **1991** Large increase in attacks on asylum-seekers' hostels.
- ❑ **1992** Joins IMF and World Bank. Referendum votes against joining EEA (only French cantons and one German canton vote in favour).

AID

 $863m (donations)   Up 15% in 1991

Switzerland ranks fairly high among developed countries as an aid donor, with total disbursements amounting to 0.5% of the country's GDP in 1992. However, a large part, some 40%, of its aid is conditional on the recipients buying Swiss goods and services.

DEFENCE

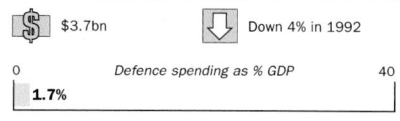

$3.7bn   Down 4% in 1992

0   *Defence spending as % GDP*   40
1.7%

SWISS ARMED FORCES

812 main battle tanks (275 Pz-87 *Leopard* 2/ 143 Pz-61/195 Pz-68)	565,000 personnel
None	
Air Corps (part of army) 242 combat aircraft (80 *Hunter* F-58/7 T-68)	60,000 personnel
None	

Switzerland has one of the largest armed forces in Europe. Military service and further training at intervals is compulsory for males, up to the age of 50. The army is organized so that 600,000 conscripts can be called up and armed in a few hours. The army still uses skis, bicycles and horses to protect the Alps. Bridges and tunnels are mined with explosives in accordance with a defence strategy drafted earlier this century. However, as in the rest of Europe, force numbers are being cut in response to the end of the Cold War. By 1995, the army will be two thirds its current size. Switzerland is also considering allowing its armed troops to join UN peace-keeping operations.

ECONOMICS

$225.9bn   1.50 Swiss francs

SCORE CARD

- ❑ WORLD GNP RANKING..........................17th
- ❑ GNP PER CAPITA $33,221
- ❑ BALANCE OF PAYMENTS $17bn
- ❑ INFLATION 3%
- ❑ UNEMPLOYMENT..................................5%

EXPORTS

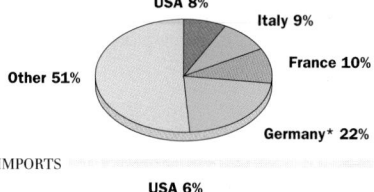

USA 8%
Italy 9%
France 10%
Germany* 22%
Other 51%

IMPORTS

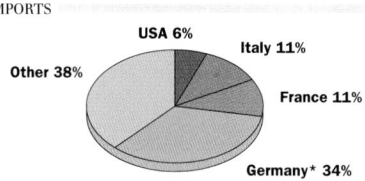

USA 6%
Italy 11%
France 11%
Germany* 34%
Other 38%

STRENGTHS

Highly skilled workforce. Reliable provider of services; key to strength of banking sector. Strong machine tools and precision engineering. Powerful chemicals and banking multinationals; banking secrecy laws attract foreign capital. Ability to innovate to capture mass markets, typified by Swatch watch and proposed Swatch car.

WEAKNESSES

Protected cartels result in many over-priced goods. Highly subsidized agricultural sector. 35% withholding tax on income earned in Switzerland by non-residents stifles direct foreign investment in business.

PROFILE

The Swiss economy is widely diversified, with 61% of GDP coming

ECONOMIC PERFORMANCE INDICATOR

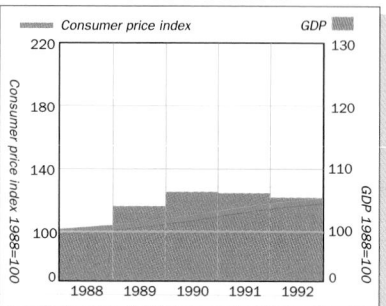

Consumer price index   GDP

from services and 26% from industry. The country has an outsized banking sector, thanks to its outstanding success in attracting capital for investment. Almost half of the world's investment capital placed outside the investor's own country is in Switzerland. It is also home to some large multinational enterprises.

SWITZERLAND : MAJOR BUSINESSES

❋ Textiles	⚙ Light engineering
🜂 Chemicals	✿ Heavy engineering
⚡ Electronics	✪ Research & development
⊙ Watch making	🅱 Banking & finance
⚕ Pharmaceuticals	
🖵 Consumer goods	

* significant multinational ownership

0   50 km
0   50 miles

RESOURCES

55.8bn kwh (capacity 16.3m kw)

Not an oil producer; refines 132,000 b/cd

1.9m pigs, 1.9m cattle, 371,000 sheep

Rock salt

ELECTRICITY GENERATION

Hydro 56% (30.9bn kwh)

Thermal 2% (1.8bn kwh)

Nuclear 42% (23.7bn kwh)

Other 0%

0   20   40   60   80   100

% of total generation by type

Switzerland is poor in natural resources, having no valuable minerals in commercially-exploitable quantities. Over half of its electricity comes from hydro-power, while five nuclear plants supply most of the rest. This allows spending on imported oil and coal to be kept to a minimum – they account for less than 4% of the total import bill. The Chernobyl accident inspired large-scale anti-nuclear-power demonstrations and a sixth plant was cancelled. However, a referendum approved continued use of existing plants.

SWITZERLAND : LAND USE

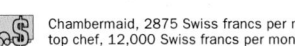

Cropland
Forest
Pasture
High mountain regions
Cattle
Vineyards

0   50 km
0   50 miles

ENVIRONMENT

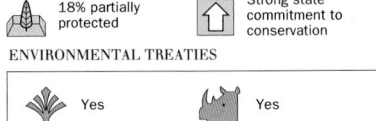

18% partially protected

Strong state commitment to conservation

ENVIRONMENTAL TREATIES

Yes

Yes

No

Yes

The Swiss are among the most environmentally conscious people in the world and are willing to back their convictions with money: the Basle–Milan tunnel plan was approved at referendum, despite the estimated $13.3bn cost. The planners aim to achieve a total ban on lorry transit traffic by 2004, although some argue that a ban will not be necessary as lorries travelling on trains will cut two hours off the Basle–Milan journey. The Swiss are keen recyclers and taxation is used to encourage this. A carbon dioxide tax was also proposed in 1994.

MEDIA

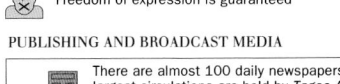

Freedom of expression is guaranteed

PUBLISHING AND BROADCAST MEDIA

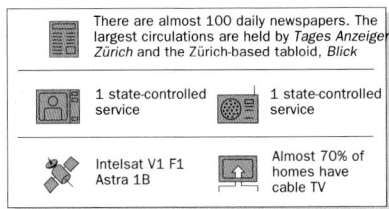

There are almost 100 daily newspapers. The largest circulations are held by *Tages Anzeiger Zürich* and the Zürich-based tabloid, *Blick*

1 state-controlled service

1 state-controlled service

Intelsat V1 F1 Astra 1B

Almost 70% of homes have cable TV

The Swiss media is broadly organized along regional lines and reflects the country's linguistic divisions. The state-owned German, French and Italian language TV and radio stations tend to focus on the interests of their specific communities. German, Italian and French satellite TV is widely available. Few newspapers have national coverage. *Tribune de Genève* and *Neue Zürcher Zeitung* are exceptions.

CRIME

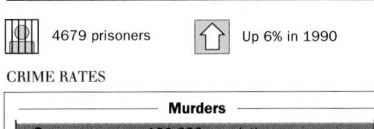

4679 prisoners

Up 6% in 1990

CRIME RATES

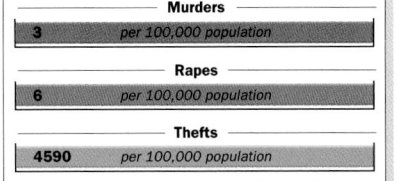

Murders
3   *per 100,000 population*

Rapes
6   *per 100,000 population*

Thefts
4590   *per 100,000 population*

Crime rates are low by international standards. However, muggings and burglaries are on the increase. Much of the growth is drugs-related. More cases of banking secrecy laws attracting laundered funds are coming to light.

EDUCATION

  99%

0   *Education spending as % GNP*   25
4.8%

THE EDUCATION SYSTEM

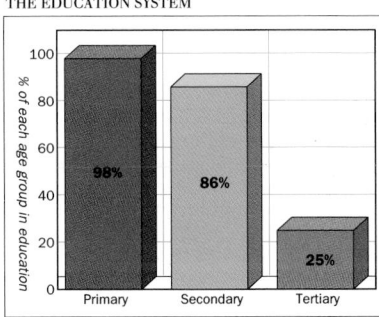

% of each age group in education

100
80
60
40
20
0

98%   86%   25%

Primary   Secondary   Tertiary

Most students after the age of 16 are encouraged to take up vocational studies. Training is thorough and is usually combined with three or four years' apprenticeship in the student's chosen field. The higher education institutions have the funds to attract top European academics. Zurich's Federal Technological Institute has gained an international reputation for its computer programming research.

HEALTH

1 per 584 people

Heart and cerebrovascular diseases, cancers

0   *Health spending as % GNP*   25
2.6%

The health system is among the most efficient and pioneering in the world. Health costs are covered by compulsory insurance schemes.

WEALTH

Chambermaid, 2875 Swiss francs per month; top chef, 12,000 Swiss francs per month

CONSUMER GOODS OWNERSHIP

Per 1000 population

1000
882
750
500   406   430
250   205
0   31

Switzerland is the world's wealthiest country – its per capita income is more than $33,000. Wages are relatively high although the cost of living is also well above the European average. Many workers choose to live in France and commute across the border. The land market is highly regulated.

S

WORLD RANKING

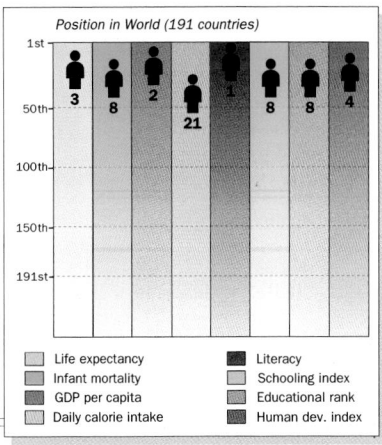

Position in World (191 countries)

1st
3   8   2   1   8   8   4
50th
21
100th
150th
191st

Life expectancy   Literacy
Infant mortality   Schooling index
GDP per capita   Educational rank
Daily calorie intake   Human dev. index

SYRIA

OFFICIAL NAME: Syrian Arab Republic **CAPITAL:** Damascus
POPULATION: 13.3 million **CURRENCY:** Syrian pound **OFFICIAL LANGUAGE:** Arabic

SYRIA SHARES BORDERS with Lebanon, Israel, Jordan, Iraq and Turkey. Many Syrians regard their country as an artificial creation of French colonial rule, which lasted from 1920 to 1946. They identify instead with a Greater Syria encompassing Lebanon, Jordan and Palestine. Since independence, Syria's foreign relations have been turbulent, although President Assad's authoritarian Ba'athist regime has brought a measure of internal stability.

CLIMATE

WEATHER CHART

The coastal climate is Mediterranean, with mild, wet winters and dry, hot summers. Away from the coast, the country is increasingly arid, with some desert areas. In the mountains, snow is common in winter. Most of the country receives less than 25 cm of rainfall a year and, away from the coast, rainfall is very unpredictable.

COMMUNICATIONS

Damascus International
1.5m passengers

94 ships
231,000 dwt

THE TRANSPORT NETWORK

29,682 km
(18,444 miles)

712 km
(442 miles)

1918 km
(1192 miles)

672 km
(418 miles)

The road network is adequate in the cities, but unreliable in rural areas, especially during the winter wet season. State-run and privately-owned bus services operate from Damascus and Aleppo to most towns. Roads are integrated with the railways, which carry over four million passengers a year and are vital to freight transport. Damascus is the main international airport and Latakia the main port.

PEOPLE

Arabic, French, Kurdish, Armenian, Circassian, Turkmen, Assyrian, Aramaic

72 people per km²

THE URBAN/RURAL POPULATION SPLIT

50%   50%

RELIGIOUS PERSUASION

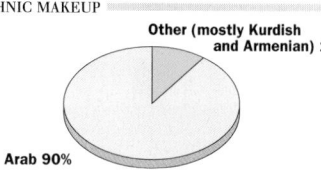

Christian 10%
Other Muslim 16%
Sunni Muslim 74%

ETHNIC MAKEUP

Other (mostly Kurdish and Armenian) 10%
Arab 90%

Most Syrians live within 100 km of the coast, where the largest cities are sited. About 90% are Muslim. They include the politically dominant Alawis, based in Latakia and Tartous provinces. There is also a sizeable Christian minority. In the west and north a mosaic of groups exists, including Kurds, Turkish-speaking communities and Armenians, the latter based in cities. Damascus, Al Qamishli and Aleppo have small Jewish communities, and there are three villages where Aramaic is spoken. In addition, some 300,000 Palestinian refugees have settled in Syria. Minorities were initially attracted to the ruling Ba'ath Party because of its emphasis on the state over sectarian interests. However, disputes between factions led to the Shi'a Muslim Alawis taking control, fostering resentment among the Sunni Muslim majority.

The emancipation of women, promoted by the Ba'ath regime in the late 1960s, has been carried forward under President Assad. His first woman cabinet minister was appointed in 1976.

TOURISM

562,000 visitors   Up 37% in 1990

MAIN OVERSEAS ARRIVALS

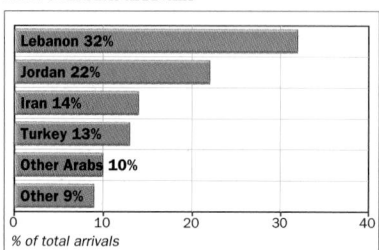

Lebanon 32%
Jordan 22%
Iran 14%
Turkey 13%
Other Arabs 10%
Other 9%

0   10   20   30   40
% of total arrivals

Years of political turbulence, allegations of human rights abuses committed by the Assad government and strict, complex, travel regulations retarded the development of tourism. However, just before the 1990–1991 Gulf War, Syria began to compete in popularity as a holiday destination with other Middle Eastern states. Modern hotels were built in most main cities and facilities improved to cater for growing numbers of Western visitors. Following the war, tourist numbers dropped sharply, but they are now gradually recovering. Syria's main attractions are the antiquities of Damascus – the oldest inhabited city in the world – and Aleppo and Palmyra, with their covered markets (*soukhs*), mosques and baths. Syria has a wealth of castles dating back to the Crusades and sites associated with the advent of Islam. In addition, there are as many as 3500 as yet unexcavated archaeological sites. Syria's Mediterranean coastline has fine beaches, and there are mountain resorts in Latakia.

The ancient city of Palmyra, in Syria's central region, possesses some of the Middle East's finest Classical monuments.

POPULATION AGE BREAKDOWN

% of population by age group	0–14	15–64	65+		
65+	3.8%	4.4%	3.2%	2.6%	2.6%
15–64	51.8%	46.7%	49.3%	49.1%	50.9%
0–14	44.4%	48.9%	47.5%	48.3%	46.5%
	1960	1970	1980	1990	2000

S

SYRIA

Total Area : 185 180 sq. km
(71 500 sq. miles)

LAND HEIGHT		POPULATION	
2000m/6562ft		over 500 000	⊙
1000m/3281ft		over 100 000	◎
500m/1640ft		over 50 000	○
200m/656ft		over 10 000	●
Sea Level		under 10 000	·

WORLD AFFAIRS

AL	OAPEC	CAEU	AMF	NAM

Following Egypt's 1979 accord with Israel, Syria sees itself as the major barrier to Israel's regional dominance. Syria has extended its influence over Lebanon (where it has achieved a high degree of control), Jordan and the Palestinians, as well as seeking alliances with North African states. The biggest single issue between Syria and Israel remains the occupation of the strategically vital Golan Heights, seized by Israel during the Six Day War in 1967. Under the 1993 Washington peace accord between Israel and the PLO, it was suggested that the Heights should become a demilitarized zone. Syria, however, insists on their return.

Syria faced international isolation in the 1980s because of the Assad government's alleged backing of terrorists. It regained a measure of respect in 1990 by securing the release of Western hostages in Lebanon from Shi'a militants. Assad followed up this diplomatic triumph by backing the Western allies in the 1990–1991 Gulf War, contributing troops to liberate Kuwait from Iraqi forces. Syria's involvement in the Gulf War was vital in legitimizing the action in the eyes of the Arab world. Syria has now emerged as a major ally of the West in containing Iraqi expansionism.

AID

$1.2bn (exceptional receipts)　　　Likely to return to low annual level

Syria has historically received little aid owing to its human rights record and substantial oil income. However, one-off payments totalling $2 billion in 1992 and $1.2 billion in 1993 were received after the Gulf War, mainly from Saudi Arabia and the Gulf states, but with contributions from the West and Japan.

POLITICS

 Uncertain

President Lt-Gen
Hafiz al-Assad

THE STATE OF THE PARTIES

People's Assembly 250 members

54% BP	3% SASUP	2% SUDP	36% Other
	3% ASUP	2% ASP	

BP = Ba'ath Party　**SASUP** = Syrian Arab Socialist Party
ASUP = Arab Socialist Unionist Party　**ASP** = Arab Socialist
Party　**SUDP** = Socialist Unionist Democratic Party
Other = Communist Party

Syria is, in practice, a single-party, national socialist state. Its military-backed leader since 1971 has been President Assad, a lifelong Ba'ath Party militant, dedicated to its campaign for Arab revival.

MAIN POLITICAL ISSUES

Human rights
The Syrian regime is under international pressure to improve its human rights record. Allegations of oppression of the country's Jews and opposition Sunni Islamic fundamentalists, and also of links with international terrorist groups are widespread. The EU has suspended aid payments until conditions improve.

Political pluralism
President Assad remains the dominant political figure and he and his military-backed regime, drawn mainly from the Shi'a Alawi grouping, keep a tight hold on power. Again under international pressure, Assad has made promises to permit more political parties, but they remain unfulfilled. Assad was sworn in for another seven-year term in 1992.

PROFILE
The Ba'athist military swept to power in 1963 with a vision of uniting all Arab nations under one, Syrian-dominated socialist system. The coup ended the power of city elites and promoted citizens from rural areas. The state became the main employer.

When Assad came to power in 1971, he consolidated the Ba'ath Party as the major political force. Unrest among Islamic militants was crushed, and Assad focused on foreign affairs in a bid to make Syria a major power.

Syria initially found a Ba'athist ally in Iraq, and the two countries embarked on a plan for union in 1978. Relations soon foundered amid mutual charges over interference in each other's internal affairs – to the extent that, alone among Arab nations, Syria backed Iran in the Iran–Iraq War.

President Assad, *who was elected for a fourth term of office in 1992.*

Mahmoud az-Zoubi, *who became prime minister of Syria in 1990.*

S

CHRONOLOGY

Complete independence from
France was achieved in 1946. From
1958–1961, Syria merged with Egypt
to form the United Arab Republic.

- ❏ **1963** Ba'athist military junta, the
  National Council of the
  Revolutionary Command, seizes
  power. Maj-Gen Amin al-Hafiz
  president.
- ❏ **1966** Military junta of radical
  Ba'ath Party members seizes
  power.
- ❏ **1967** Israel overruns Syrian
  positions above Lake Tiberias,
  seizes Golan Heights and occupies
  Quneitra. Syria boycotts Arab
  Summit and rejects compromise
  with Israel.
- ❏ **1970** Hafiz al-Assad seizes power
  in 'corrective coup'.
- ❏ **1971** Assad elected president for
  seven-year term.
- ❏ **1973** New constitution approved
  by plebiscite confirming Ba'ath
  Party as dominant force. War
  launched with Egypt against Israel
  to regain territory lost in 1967.
  Further territory lost to Israel.
- ❏ **1976** Syria intervenes militarily to
  quell fighting in Lebanon with a
  peace-keeping mandate from Arab
  League.
- ❏ **1977** Relations broken off with
  Egypt after President Sadat's visit
  to Jerusalem.
- ❏ **1978** National charter signed with
  Iraq for union. President Assad
  returned for second term.
- ❏ **1980** Membership of Muslim
  Brotherhood made capital offence.
  Treaty of Friendship with USSR.
- ❏ **1981** Israel formally annexes
  Golan Heights. Charter with Iraq
  collapses.
- ❏ **1982** Islamic extremist uprising in
  Hama crushed; thousands killed.
  Israel invades Lebanon; Syrian
  missiles in Bekaa Valley destroyed.
- ❏ **1985** Assad re-elected president.
  USA claims Syrian links to airport
  bombings at Rome and Vienna.
- ❏ **1986** Syrian complicity alleged in
  planting of bomb aboard Israeli
  airliner in London. EU, except for
  Greece, imposes sanctions.
- ❏ **1989** Diplomatic relations re-
  established with Egypt.
- ❏ **1990** Troops take part in
  Operation Desert Storm to liberate
  Kuwait from Iraqi forces. UK
  restores diplomatic relations after
  Syrian help in freeing Western
  hostages in Lebanon.
- ❏ **1991** Damascus Declaration aid
  and defence pact signed with Egypt,
  Saudi Arabia, Kuwait, the UAR,
  Qatar, Bahrain and Oman.
- ❏ **1992** Assad re-elected president.

S

DEFENCE

 $1.1bn   Down 24% in 1991

0   *Defence spending as % GDP*   40
8.1%

Having fought four wars against Israel
since 1948, Syria is the Arab world's
strongest military power after Egypt.
There is no political mechanism to
challenge the dominance of the
military. With more than 400,000
troops and nearly 50% of government
income spent on weapons, Syria is a
formidable power. The military is
mostly equipped with weapons
obtained from the former Soviet Union.
During the 1980s, Syrian forces
fought off a series of Israeli
encroachments in the region, and also
foiled Israeli attempts to control
Lebanon. Syria remains the power
Israel fears most.

SYRIAN ARMED FORCES

ECONOMICS

 $16.2bn   20.96 Syrian pounds

SCORE CARD

- ❏ WORLD GNP RANKING.........................66th
- ❏ GNP PER CAPITA $1218
- ❏ BALANCE OF PAYMENTS $1.8bn
- ❏ INFLATION ....40% (est)
- ❏ UNEMPLOYMENT ....Fairly low

EXPORTS

IMPORTS

ECONOMIC PERFORMANCE INDICATOR
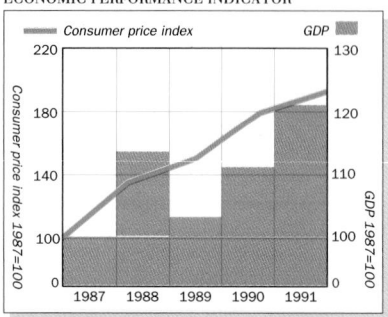

from the River Euphrates towards
fertile plains, rather than using it to
irrigate poorer land, led to a rise in
agricultural output. However, long-
term economic prospects remain
uncertain. The large public sector,
which employs 20% of the workforce,
makes little contribution to the
economy. State controls have inhibited
private enterprise and investment and
created a booming black market.
Turkey's plans to draw water from the
Euphrates threaten farming in Syria.

STRENGTHS
Exporter of crude oil – production
increasing as a result of new oil strikes.
Manufacturing base has grown.
Thriving agricultural sector.

WEAKNESSES
High defence spending is a major
drain on economy. Large black market.
High inflation. Economy dominated
by inefficient state-run companies.
Autocratic regime deters foreign
investment. High population growth.

PROFILE
Billions of dollars flowed into the
Syrian economy from the USA, Japan,
the EU, Saudi Arabia and other Gulf
states following the 1990–1991 Gulf
War. This cash injection, along with
increased oil revenue, led to rapid
growth. Also, a decision to divert water

SYRIA : MAJOR BUSINESSES

RESOURCES

10.6bn kwh
(capacity 3.7m kw)

531,100 b/d
(reserves
1,700,000,000 bbl)

13.9m sheep,
756,000 cattle,
177,000 asses

Phosphate, oil,
natural gas, iron

ELECTRICITY GENERATION

Hydro 45% (4.8bn kwh)

Thermal 55% (5.8bn kwh)

Nuclear 0%

Other 0%

0   20   40   60   80   100

% of total generation by type

Syria has large supplies of oil, mostly good quality light crude, which was discovered along the Euphrates in the 1980s. Gas was found in substantial quantities near Palmyra. Syria's other important minerals are phosphates and iron ore. Hydroelectric power satisfies most energy requirements. The manufacturing base is largely made up of oil-derived industries, including plastics and chemicals, textiles and food products. Cotton is the main cash crop, but fruit and vegetables are also grown. Livestock, especially sheep and goats, supports the rural economy.

SYRIA : LAND USE

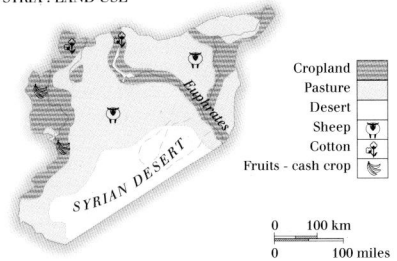

Cropland
Pasture
Desert
Sheep
Cotton
Fruits - cash crop

0   100 km
0   100 miles

ENVIRONMENT

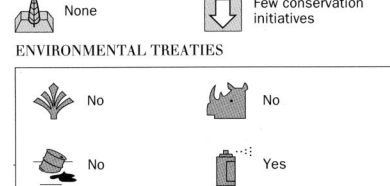

None

Few conservation initiatives

ENVIRONMENTAL TREATIES

No   No

No   Yes

The Assad regime's most expensive and controversial environmental project has been the Euphrates Dam, power station and irrigation network at Tabaqah. The dam's vast man-made reservoir, Lake Buḥayrat al Asad, engulfed some 300 villages and destroyed 25,000 hectares of fertile farm land. Syria's industrial programme has on occasion damaged the environment. A giant cement factory, built by the East Germans at Tartus in the mid-1970s, has been held responsible for polluting a valuable stretch of Mediterranean coastline.

MEDIA

 The media is under strict government control

Virtually all daily newspapers, which include the English language *Syria Times,* are state-owned or have government affiliations. Radio and TV, the news agency SANA, press distribution and advertising companies are also controlled by the regime. There is no freedom of information.

CRIME

 Syria does not publish prison figures   Up 30% in 1990

CRIME RATES

Murders

2   per 100,000 population

Rapes

1   per 100,000 population

Thefts

51   per 100,000 population

There is no truly independent judiciary. The powerful security services exercise arbitrary powers of arrest and detention. There are widespread reports of torture in custody. Politicians overthrown by President Assad in the 1970s are still held in the prison-fortress of Mezze in Damascus.

EDUCATION

 64%

0   Education spending as % GNP   25

4.1%

THE EDUCATION SYSTEM

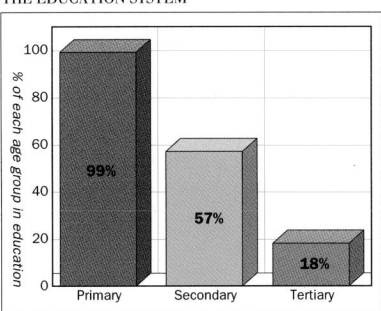

99% Primary
57% Secondary
18% Tertiary

% of each age group in education

A free and compulsory system of primary education for all was a priority of the Ba'ath Party when it came to power. Under Assad, co-education for boys and girls began in the cities and spread to rural areas. Higher education is provided by seven universities, notably at Damascus, Aleppo, Tishrin and Ḥimṣ. There are over 130,000 university students. Education ranks second – though by a considerable margin – to defence in government expenditure.

PUBLISHING AND BROADCAST MEDIA

Syria's major Arab newspapers are *Al-Ba'ath, Al-Thawra* and *Tishrin*

1 state-controlled service   1 state-controlled service

Arabsat 1C
Intelsat V1 F1   None

HEALTH

 1 per 1347 people   Heart, respiratory, digestive, infectious and parasitic diseases

0   Health spending as % GNP   25

0.4%

An adequate system of primary health care has been set up since the Ba'ath Party came to power. Treatment is free for those unable to pay. However, hospitals often lack modern equipment and medical services are in need of further investment.

WEALTH

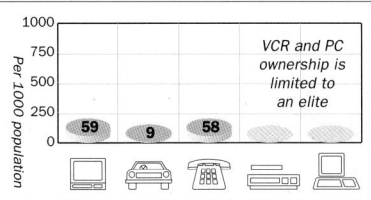 Very large gap between rich and poor

CONSUMER GOODS OWNERSHIP

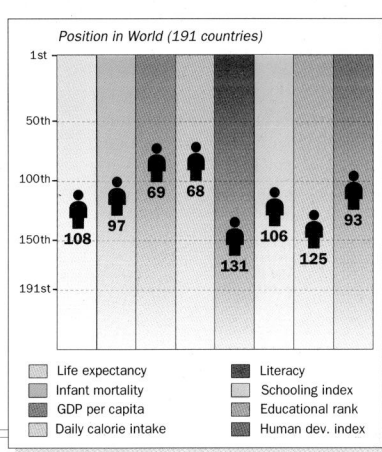

1000
750
500
250
0

Per 1000 population

VCR and PC ownership is limited to an elite

59   9   58

Syria is far from the equitable society that early Ba'ath Party thinkers envisioned. The gulf between rich and poor is widening. Syria's political elite, many of whom live in the West Malki suburb of Damascus, is more numerous and richer than ever before. Palestinian refugees and the urban unemployed make up the poorest groups.

S

WORLD RANKING

Position in World (191 countries)

1st
50th
100th
150th
191st

108   97   69   68   131   106   125   93

Life expectancy   Literacy
Infant mortality   Schooling index
GDP per capita   Educational rank
Daily calorie intake   Human dev. index

TAIWAN

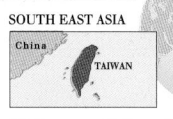

OFFICIAL NAME: Republic of China (Taiwan)   **CAPITAL:** Taipei
POPULATION: 20.8 million   **CURRENCY:** New Taiwan dollar   **OFFICIAL LANGUAGE:** Northern Chinese (Mandarin)

THE ISLAND REPUBLIC of Taiwan lies 130 km off the southeast coast of mainland China. Formerly known as Formosa, the Republic of China was established in 1949 by Chiang Kai-shek's Kuomintang (KMT), expelled from government in Beijing (then Peking) by the Communists under Mao. The KMT still claims to be the sole legitimate ruler of all China, whilst Beijing considers Taiwan to be one of its provinces. Taiwan island is dominated by a mountain region which runs north to south and covers two thirds of the island. The lowlands are highly fertile, cultivated mostly with rice, and densely populated. In 1986, Taiwan adopted democracy in place of *de facto* military rule. The KMT has been in power since 1949.

Wen Wu Temple, on the shores of Sun Moon Lake in the mountains of central Taiwan – a region famous for its many temples.

CLIMATE

WEATHER CHART

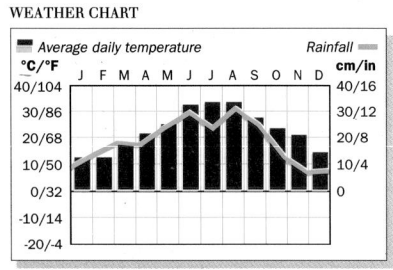

Taiwan has a tropical monsoon climate similar to that of the southern Chinese mainland. Typhoons from the South China Sea between July and September bring the heaviest rains.

COMMUNICATIONS

Chiang Kai Shek Intl, Taoyuan

239 ships
8.93m dwt

THE TRANSPORT NETWORK

20,042 km (12,453 miles)		North–South highway
4600 km (2858 miles)		None

Taiwan is implementing several major new transport infrastructure projects as part of the latest six-year economic plan. Metro and rapid transit systems are being built in Taipei and Kaohsiung. Several new roads are planned, including north–south and east–west cross-island highways. The plan is motivated by the fear that congestion will restrain future growth. Most urban Taiwanese currently ride motor scooters, but transport planners anticipate a sharp increase in car ownership over the next decade. The bicycle is not as popular in Taiwan as in mainland China. However, Taiwan is the world's biggest bicycle producer, exporting mostly to Europe and the USA.

TOURISM

1.93m visitors   Down 3% in 1990

MAIN OVERSEAS ARRIVALS

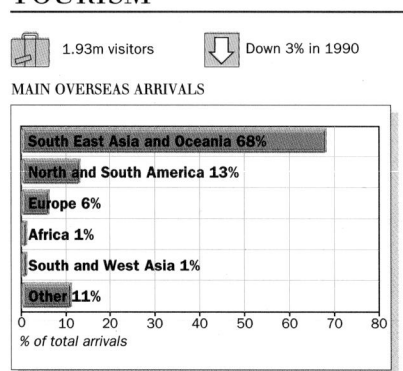

% of total arrivals

Taiwan is not a major tourist destination and has only recently begun to target tourists in the USA and Japan. As part of the most recent Six-Year Plan, hotels are being upgraded and tourist facilities at international airports are being improved. The major attraction is the Palace Museum in Taipei, which includes the massive treasure looted by the Nationalists from Beijing. Only 5% can be shown at any one time. Sex tourism is an important business in Taipei, which is second only to Bangkok. Sex establishments masquerade as barbers' shops.

PEOPLE

Amoy Chinese, Mandarin Chinese, Hakka Chinese   575 people per km²

THE URBAN/RURAL POPULATION SPLIT

66%   34%

RELIGIOUS PERSUASION

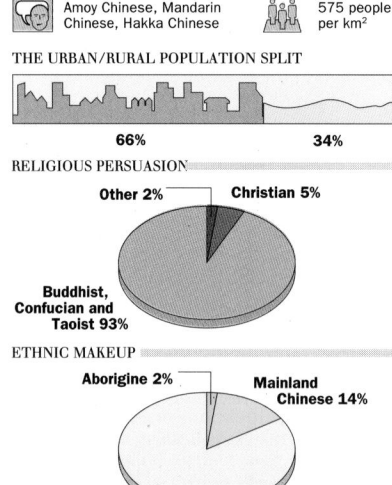

Other 2%   Christian 5%
Buddhist, Confucian and Taoist 93%

ETHNIC MAKEUP

Aborigine 2%   Mainland Chinese 14%
Indigenous Chinese 84%

Most Taiwanese are Han Chinese, descendants of the 1644 migration of the Ming dynasty from mainland China. The 100,000 Nationalists, who arrived in 1949, established themselves as a ruling class and monopolized the most prestigious jobs in the civil service.

This led to considerable resentment from the local inhabitants, but as the 1947 generation have aged, so local Taiwanese have entered the political process.

There is little ethnic tension in Taiwan, although the indigenous minorities who live in the eastern hills do suffer considerable discrimination.

As in the rest of South East Asia, the extended family is still important and provides a social security net for the elderly. However, the trend is towards European-style nuclear families, a result partly of housing shortages. Women are not well represented in the political process, but are prominent in business and the civil service.

POPULATION AGE BREAKDOWN

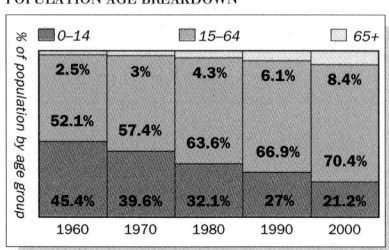

	0–14	15–64		65+
	2.5%	3%	4.3%	6.1%	8.4%
	52.1%	57.4%	63.6%	66.9%	70.4%
	45.4%	39.6%	32.1%	27%	21.2%
	1960	1970	1980	1990	2000

Key to symbols and abbreviations on endpapers

THE NATIONS OF THE WORLD: TAIWAN

POLITICS

Lower House 1995   President Lee Teng-hui

THE STATE OF THE PARTIES

National Assembly 405 members

| 79% KMT | 18% DPP | 3% Other |

KMT = National Party of China
DPP = Democratic Progressive Party

Legislative Yuan 161 members

| 63% KMT | 31% DPP | 6% Other |

Until 1986, Taiwan was effectively a one-party state. Today, it is a fully-functioning multiparty democracy.

MAIN POLITICAL ISSUES

Relations with China
Relations with China have a significant influence on Taiwanese domestic politics. Beijing has made clear its desire to see the Nationalists remain in power in Taiwan. It has threatened invasion should the DPP come to power. This has dissuaded many from voting for the DPP. Beijing objects to the DPP's policy of claiming independence from China, as against the Nationalists' claim to be the true government of the mainland. The Nationalists' policy sustains the idea that China is still a unitary state which includes Taiwan. The DPP's stance directly contradicts this. The issue is likely to dominate the 1995 elections.

Elective presidency
The president is currently elected by a caucus of the National Assembly. Suggestions that the office should be directly elected arose because, until 1992, the caucus was dominated by a

Li Yuan-zu, vice-president of Taiwan.

Lee Teng-hui, president since 1988, re-elected in 1990.

traditionalist gerontocracy from the generation of 1947. The caucus is now composed of much younger members, but most commentators believe the president will be directly elected by 1998. The effect will be to weaken the office of president and strengthen that of prime minister.

Corruption
Many voters associate corruption with democracy. Part of the reason is the open fraud which has surrounded elections, with candidates buying votes at polling booths. The issue is increasingly discussed in political debates.

PROFILE
Between 1949 and 1986, Chiang Kai-shek's KMT monopolized political power in Taiwan and ruled by strict martial law. In 1986, Gen Chiang Ching-kuo, Chiang Kai Shek's son and successor, decided to pave the way for democracy. Free multiparty elections were first held in December 1986.

WORLD AFFAIRS

Taiwan is diplomatically isolated. States wishing to do business with China cannot have relations with Taipei, which still claims to be the official government of the mainland as well as Taiwan. Taipei has to conduct its overseas relations via trade delegations rather than embassies and cannot gain representation at the UN. States which recently severed relations were Saudi Arabia in 1991 and South Korea in 1992. Just before becoming South Africa's leader, Nelson Mandela also stated his intention to do so.

Relations with the USA have been difficult since Washington was forced to recognize China at the UN in 1972. Taiwan effectively lost its status as a US client state, and the US 6th fleet was removed from the Taiwan Strait. US security guarantees to Taiwan have been ambiguous since.

China continues to recognize Taiwan only as a province of the mainland.

TAIWAN

Total Area : 36 179 sq. km (15 969 sq. miles)

POPULATION
over 1 000 000
over 500 000
over 100 000
over 50 000
over 10 000
under 10 000

LAND HEIGHT
3000m/9843ft
2000m/6562ft
1000m/3281ft
500m/1640ft
200m/656ft
Sea Level

T

525

AID

 Substantial donations to small Pacific states   LIttle change from year to year

Taiwan has a large aid fund devoted to small Pacific Island states. Aid donations are in practice an exchange for the fact that states such as Kiribati, Tuvalu and Tonga are among the few nations that have granted Taiwan diplomatic recognition. They have also represented Taiwan's interests in the UN since 1972, when it lost its seat following the US recognition of China.

CHRONOLOGY

Following the 1949 Communist revolution in China, Gen Chiang Kai-shek's nationalist KMT party sought refuge in the island province of Taiwan. The KMT saw the revolution as illegal and itself as the sole rightful Chinese government.

- ❑ **1971** People's Republic of China replaces Taiwan at UN and on UN Security Council.
- ❑ **1973** Taipei's KMT regime rejects Beijing's offer of secret talks on reunification of China.
- ❑ **1975** President Chiang Kai-shek dies. His son, Gen Chiang Ching-kuo becomes KMT leader. Dr Yen Chia-kan president.
- ❑ **1979** USA severs relations with Taiwan in favour of People's Republic of China. However, arms sales to Taiwan continue.
- ❑ **1981** Beijing's terms for reunification rejected.
- ❑ **1984** President Chiang re-elected.
- ❑ **1986** Political reforms: KMT allows other political parties in Taiwan, ends martial law and permits visits to Chinese mainland for 'humanitarian' purposes for first time for 38 years. In 1988, Chinese are allowed to visit Taiwan on same basis.
- ❑ **1988** Lee Teng-hui becomes president.
- ❑ **1989** April, KMT considers reconciliation with Beijing under the formula of 'one China, two governments'. June, ruthless suppression of student dissent by Communist regime ends rapprochement.
- ❑ **1990** Lee Teng-hui re-elected president. KMT formally ends state of war with People's Republic.
- ❑ **1991** DPP opposition draft alternative constitution for Taiwan as an independent state. Policy causes outrage among KMT regime and also in Beijing. KMT re-elected with large majority.
- ❑ **1993** Beijing proposes talks on reunification.

DEFENCE

 $9.7bn   ⬆ Up 5% in 1992

Defence spending as % GDP
0 — 40
5.4%

Taiwan, with a relatively small population, has the fifth largest army in the world. The main concern is a possible invasion from China. Taiwan is keen to buy the very latest air force technology. Worries about US loyalty have led Taipei to purchase French *Mirage* fighters in addition to their F-16s.

CHINESE ARMED FORCES

459 main battle tanks (309 M-48A5/150 M-48H)	260,000 personnel
4 submarines, 33 surface vessels and 93 patrol boats	30,000 personnel
486 combat aircraft (8 F-5B/215 -E/ 55 -F/32 TF-104G)	70,000 personnel
None	

ECONOMICS

 $162bn   26.63 New Taiwan dollars

SCORE CARD

- ❑ WORLD GNP RANKING 22nd
- ❑ GNP PER CAPITA $7990
- ❑ BALANCE OF PAYMENTS $12bn
- ❑ INFLATION 3%
- ❑ UNEMPLOYMENT................................1.4%

EXPORTS

Other 41% Hong Kong 13% Japan 14% USA 32%

IMPORTS
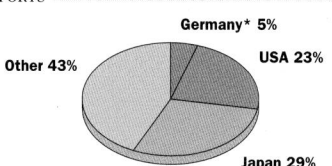
Germany* 5% USA 23% Other 43% Japan 29%

ECONOMIC PERFORMANCE INDICATOR

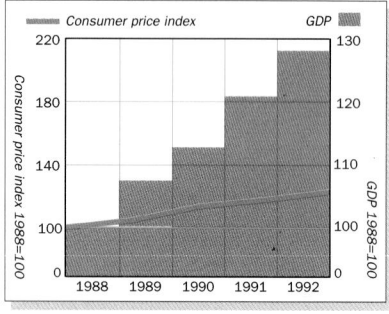

Consumer price index — GDP

PROFILE

Taiwan is one of the world's most successful economies. Its impressive growth rates, second only to Japan's, will probably not be sustained in the next decade, yet the economy is still expected to grow by 6%–7% a year. The economy retains a strong element of state direction, reflecting the KMT's Soviet economic training. All-embracing Six-Year Plans state targets to be achieved. Taiwan is now investing abroad and is responsible for over 60% of inward investment into China since 1990.

STRENGTHS

Highly educated and ambitious workforce, many US-trained and educated, with an inside knowledge of the US market. Manufacturing economy based on small companies which have proved extremely adaptable to changing market conditions. Track record of capturing major markets. Taiwan was successively the world's biggest TV producer, watch producer, PC producer and track shoe manufacturer. Economy in massive surplus, allowing it to invest in burgeoning South East Asian economies.

WEAKNESSES

Taiwan's small economic units lack the muscle of Japanese and Western multinationals; they are consequently unable to follow predatory pricing policies. Weak research and development: economy has no tradition of coming up with new products or creating new markets. Unresponsive banking system.

TAIWAN : MAJOR BUSINESSES

Hsin-chuang
T'ao-yüan   Taipei
Chung-li
Hsin-chu
T'ai-chung
Yüan-lin
T'ai-nan
Kao-hsiung

Textiles
Garments
Chemicals
Computers
Electronics
Fish processing

0 — 50 km
0 — 50 miles

T

RESOURCES

89.6bn kwh

Not an oil producer; refines 542,500 b/cd

77m chickens, 10.6m ducks, 8.6m pigs

Coal, copper, marble, dolomite, gold, silver

ELECTRICITY GENERATION

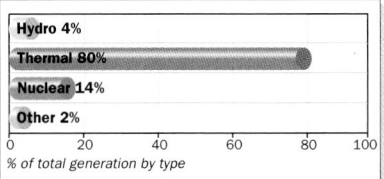

Hydro 4%
Thermal 80%
Nuclear 14%
Other 2%

% of total generation by type

Taiwan has few strategic resources and its minerals industry is not a significant foreign exchange earner. All oil supplies are imported, mostly from Saudi Arabia and Kuwait. The proportion of electricity generated by nuclear power is the highest in the world and Taiwan is a major buyer of South African uranium. Hydroelectric power is also an important sector. Taiwan's fishing industry is highly successful and is a major supplier to the huge Japanese market. Fishermen are often accused of plundering Atlantic fishing grounds.

Cho-shui

CHENG ANG SHAN MO

TAIWAN : LAND USE

Cropland
Forest
Pasture
Wetlands
Pigs
Rice

0   50 km
0   50 miles

ENVIRONMENT

8% (3% partially protected)

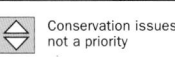

Conservation issues not a priority

ENVIRONMENTAL TREATIES

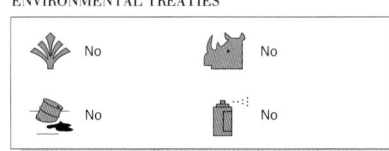

No   No
No   No

Environmental questions have not featured highly in Taiwan's dash for growth. Cities have grown fast without many planning controls and factories have few pollution laws to comply with. Taiwan's fishing industry has also been criticized for the use of long line techniques which trap dolphins, and for plundering other nations' fishing grounds without regard to stock levels.

MEDIA

Criticism of the government is discouraged

PUBLISHING AND BROADCAST MEDIA

There are 35 daily newspapers. The independent *Lienho Pao* has the largest circulation

3 state-controlled networks

33 state-controlled stations

Palapa B2-P, Intelsat V F8

In major cities

The rigid state control which used to exist over the media has been relaxed. Opposition parties now have access to the state media. Before the 1990s, press with simplified Chinese characters was banned, thus excluding all publications from the mainland. Taiwan has a large domestic TV and film industry.

CRIME

Taiwan does not publish prison figures

Little change from year to year

CRIME RATES

Most Taiwanese are highly conscious of crime. However rates are low by US or European standards

Since the end of martial law in 1986, most political prisoners have been released. Taiwan does not suffer from organized crime to the extent found in Hong Kong or Japan. Counterfeit CDs are a major business.

EDUCATION

92%

0   Education spending as % GNP   25
3.6%

THE EDUCATION SYSTEM

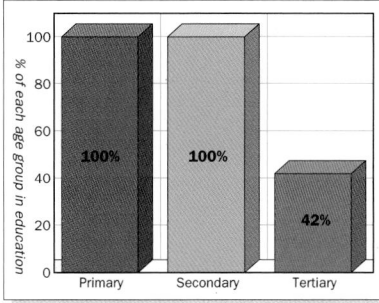

Primary 100%
Secondary 100%
Tertiary 42%

% of each age group in education

The education system is the same as that found on the mainland and inspired by 1922 reforms suggested to Beijing by Bertrand Russell and John Dewey. Attendance at tertiary level is one of the highest in the world. Schools have lavish facilities and equipment. Many Taiwanese study in the USA.

HEALTH

1 per 913 people

Cerebrovascular and heart diseases, hypertension

0   Health spending as % GNP   25
Higher than regional average

Most health provision in Taiwan is in the private sector. Taiwanese take out elaborate health insurance schemes and it is essential to prove cover before treatment is provided. Health facilities are on a par with the best in the world and Taiwanese enjoy a high life expectancy, similar to that in Sweden or Japan. The incidence of AIDS is in line with the South East Asian average.

WEALTH

Most Taiwanese are comfortably off

CONSUMER GOODS OWNERSHIP

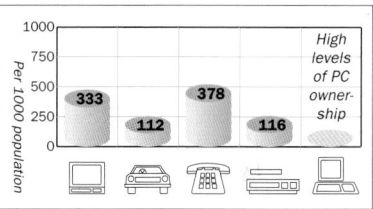

High levels of PC ownership

333   112   378   116

Per 1000 population

Until 1987, Taiwan had the largest cash reserves of any nation in the world. This reflected the closed nature of its markets and the success of the export economy. Taiwanese have shared in much of this wealth. Inequalities of income distribution are comparatively small, and a high degree of social cohesion has been achieved. In part, this is the result of the land reforms of the 1950s, which gave agricultural workers control of the land whilst compensating landowners and encouraging them to set up business in the cities. Today, most Taiwanese would describe themselves as middle class. Taiwan is perhaps the most consumerist society on earth; conspicuous consumption is celebrated.

WORLD RANKING

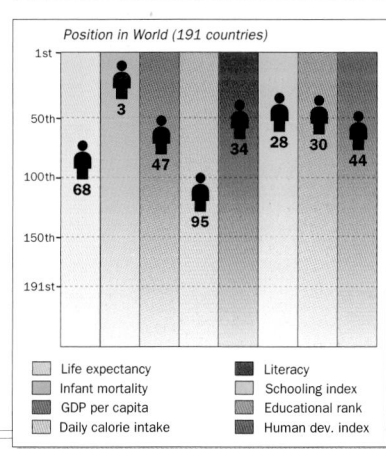

Position in World (191 countries)

1st
50th
100th
150th
191st

68   3   47   95   34   28   30   44

Life expectancy
Infant mortality
GDP per capita
Daily calorie intake
Literacy
Schooling index
Educational rank
Human dev. index

T

TAJIKISTAN

OFFICIAL NAME: Republic of Tajikistan **CAPITAL:** Dushanbe
POPULATION: 5.6 million **CURRENCY:** Rouble **OFFICIAL LANGUAGE:** Tajik

CENTRAL ASIA

TAJIKISTAN LIES ON the western slopes of the Pamirs in Central Asia. The Tajiks' language and traditions are similar to those of Iran rather than of Turkic Uzbekistan. Tajikistan decided on independence only when neighbouring Soviet republics declared theirs in late 1991. The republic has since been riven by armed conflict between the Communist government, backed by Russia and the Uzbeks, and Tajik Islamic rebels.

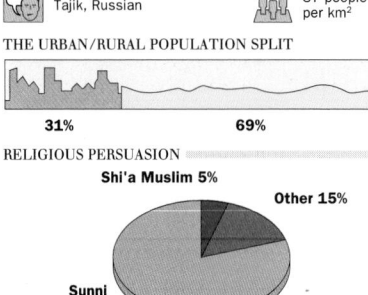
The Varzob Gorge, north of Dushanbe. Half of the country is over 3000 m above sea level.

CLIMATE

WEATHER CHART

(chart showing Average daily temperature and Rainfall; °C/°F axis from -20/-4 to 40/104; cm/in axis from 0 to 40/16; months J F M A M J J A S O N D)

Rainfall is low in the valleys. In mountainous areas, winter temperatures can fall below –45°C.

COMMUNICATIONS

 Dushanbe Intl   Has no fleet

THE TRANSPORT NETWORK

28,500 km (17,709 miles)		None
480 km (298 miles)		200 km (124 miles)

Tajikistan has good cross-border roads and well-maintained airfields, the result of its use as a staging post by Soviet forces during the Afghan War. The best way to visit the mountainous interior is by air.

TOURISM

 Almost no tourists   Little change from year to year

MAIN OVERSEAS ARRIVALS

(bar chart: % of total arrivals, 0 to 40)

Tajikistan does not publish tourism figures by country of origin

The conflict in Tajikistan makes travel almost impossible. Journalists from the West are often attacked.

PEOPLE

Tajik, Russian   37 people per km²

THE URBAN/RURAL POPULATION SPLIT

31%   69%

RELIGIOUS PERSUASION

Shi'a Muslim 5%
Other 15%
Sunni Muslim 80%

The main ethnic conflict in Tajikistan is between the Tajiks and Uzbeks – peoples of Persian and Turkic origin respectively. As in neighbouring Uzbekistan, however, Russians are discriminated against and their ranks have thinned from 400,000 in 1989 to around 200,000 today. By 1990, the 35,000-strong German minority had left. The struggle between Dushanbe-based Communists and the Islamic militants in the central and eastern regions has displaced over 60,000 refugees into Afghanistan, whose own Tajik population numbers over one million. Attempts to repatriate the refugees in 1993 failed.

TAJIKISTAN

Total Area : 143 100 sq. km (55 251 sq. miles)

POPULATION

- ◉ over 500 000
- ◎ over 100 000
- ○ over 50 000
- ● over 10 000
- • under 10 000

LAND HEIGHT

- 4000m/13 124ft
- 3000m/9843ft
- 2000m/6562ft
- 1000m/3281ft
- 500m/1640ft
- 200m/656ft

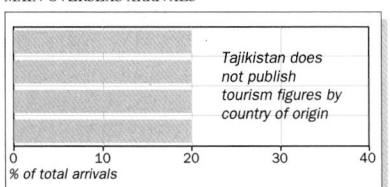

POLITICS

Uncertain   President Imamali Sharipovich Rahmonov

THE STATE OF THE PARTIES

Supreme Soviet 230 members

94% CPT   6% Other

CPT = Communist Party of Tajikistan
Genuine opposition was banned at the elections of 1990. Other main parties are the Democratic Party of Tajikistan, the Islamic Renaissance Party (IRP) and Rebirth

The Communist candidate won free presidential elections following independence in 1991. Nine months later, Dushanbe was taken over by a coalition of democrats and Muslims, but the capital was retaken by pro-government forces in December 1992. The presidency was abolished and the Chairman of the Supreme Soviet became head of state. In 1993–1994 the Communists began to regain control of the largely rebel east, but resistance continued from Afghanistan, despite the presence of 3500 Russian troops on the Tajik side of the border.

T

WORLD AFFAIRS

   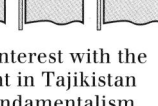

Russia has a common interest with the Communist government in Tajikistan in sidelining Islamic fundamentalism and lends military support; it provided border guards in 1993 to prevent cross-border incursions from neighbouring Afghanistan. Tacit support also comes from the USA, which is keen to limit the influence of Iranian-backed fundamentalists worldwide. The government does not stress the link with the USA, however, fearing that this may encourage Iran, and possibly Pakistan, to promote the Islamic fundamentalist IRP.

AID

 Precise figures not available, but mostly military aid

 Steep increases due to war with rebel forces

The government in Dushanbe is reliant on Russian and Uzbek military aid in its fight with the Afghan-based rebels.

DEFENCE

 $882.4m

 Steep increase due to war with rebel forces

The Tajik armed forces are weak; it is Russian forces who are winning the war against the rebels. The rebels are effectively cut off in the Fergana Valley. The only road bridge has been blown up by the government.

ECONOMICS

 $5.7bn

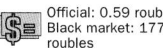 Official: 0.59 roubles Black market: 1770 roubles

SCORE CARD

❑ World GNP Ranking	109th
❑ GNP per Capita	$1020
❑ Balance of Payments	No formal economy
❑ Inflation	100%
❑ Unemployment	Only 40% in formal employment

STRENGTHS
Few, although Tajikistan has 14% of known world uranium reserves. Hydroelectric power has considerable potential. Carpet-making.

WEAKNESSES
Formal economy on verge of collapse. Dependence on barter economy. No central planning. Little diversification in agriculture; only 6% of land is arable. Skilled Russians leaving. Production in all sectors in decline.

EXPORTS

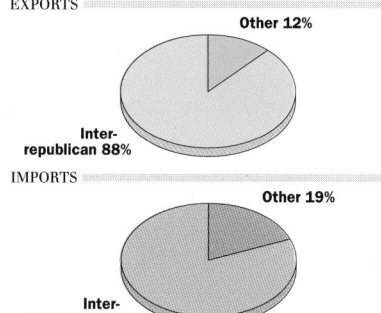

Other 12%

Inter-republican 88%

IMPORTS

Other 19%

Inter-republican 81%

Afghanistan. Tacit support also comes from the USA, which is keen to limit the influence of Iranian-backed fundamentalists worldwide. The government does not stress the link with the USA, however, fearing that this may encourage Iran, and possibly Pakistan, to promote the Islamic fundamentalist IRP.

RESOURCES

 HEP supplies 75% of domestic energy requirements

 3600 b/d

 3.4m sheep and goats, 1.4m cattle, 212,200 pigs

 Uranium, gold, iron, lead, mercury, tin

Tajikistan has one key resource – uranium – which accounted for 30% of the USSR's total production before 1990. The end of the nuclear arms race has reduced its value, however. Most of Tajikistan is bare mountain and just 6% of the land can be used for agriculture. Industry is concentrated in the Fergana Valley, close to the Uzbek border.

ENVIRONMENT

 1%

 No resources for environmental measures

Landslides are a problem, frequently cutting off villages. Excessive irrigation for cotton production has led to salination of the soil, with consequent reduced crop yields.

MEDIA

 Journalists who criticize the government may be risking their lives

PUBLISHING AND BROADCAST MEDIA

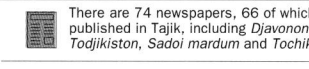 There are 74 newspapers, 66 of which are published in Tajik, including *Djavononi Todjikiston*, *Sadoi mardum* and *Tochikistoni*

 1 state-controlled service

 1 state-controlled service

The media are totally controlled by the Communist government. There have been a few cases of critical journalists dying in suspicious accidents.

CRIME

 Tajikistan does not publish prison figures

 Crime has been rising dramatically

Only very remote areas are free from violence perpetrated by armed gangs. Many political prisoners are still held in prison awaiting charges and trials.

EDUCATION

 Tajikistan does not publish literacy figures

The university at Dushanbe has been weakened by the departure of its Russian academics.

CHRONOLOGY

In the 19th century, Tajikistan was a collection of semi-independent principalities, some under Russian control, others under the influence of the Emirate of Bukhara.

- ❑ **1918** Bolsheviks take control of northern provinces of Tajikistan.
- ❑ **1921** Bolsheviks capture Dushanbe.
- ❑ **1925** Soviets gain control of whole of Tajikistan.
- ❑ **1940** Cyrillic script introduced.
- ❑ **1989** Tajik replaces Russian as official language. Arabic script taught in schools.
- ❑ **1991** Full independence from Moscow achieved.

HEALTH

 1 per 362 people

 Heart, cerebrovascular, respiratory, infectious and parasitic diseases

Tajikistan's health service has always been poor. The infant mortality rate before 1990 was one of the highest in the USSR.

WEALTH

 A minority are formally employed. Most Tajiks live by herding cattle

CONSUMER GOODS OWNERSHIP

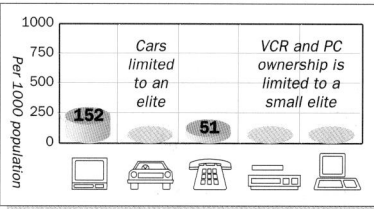

Cars limited to an elite

VCR and PC ownership is limited to a small elite

152

51

Around 87% of Tajiks live below the UN-defined poverty line. The war has made conditions even harder. The old Communist bureaucrats are still the wealthiest group.

WORLD RANKING

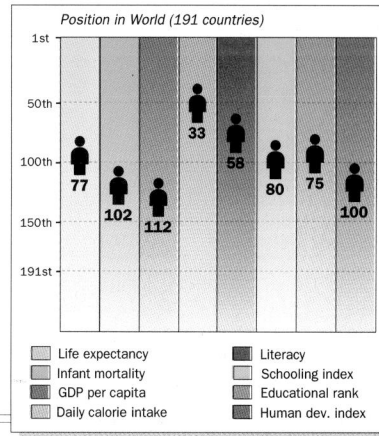

Position in World (191 countries)

77, 102, 112, 33, 58, 80, 75, 100

Life expectancy
Infant mortality
GDP per capita
Daily calorie intake
Literacy
Schooling index
Educational rank
Human dev. index

T

TANZANIA

EAST AFRICA

OFFICIAL NAME: United Republic of Tanzania **CAPITAL:** Dodoma
POPULATION: 27.8 million **CURRENCY:** Tanzanian shilling **OFFICIAL LANGUAGES:** English and Swahili

TANZANIA LIES BETWEEN KENYA and Mozambique on the East African coast. Formed by the union of Tanganyika and Zanzibar, Tanzania comprises a coastal lowland, volcanic highlands and the Great Rift Valley. It includes Mount Kilimanjaro, Africa's highest peak. Tanzania was led by the socialist Julius Nyerere from 1962 until his retirement in 1985. The trend in politics now is away from socialism and towards greater democracy.

Arusha National Park. *Lying within the Ngurdoto volcanic crater, the park has herds of buffaloes, rhinos, elephants and giraffes.*

CLIMATE

WEATHER CHART

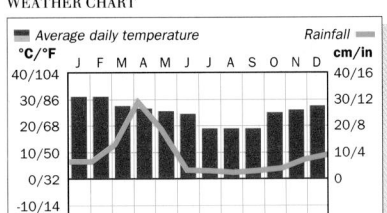

The coast and Zanzibar are tropical. The central plateau is semi-arid and the highlands are semi-temperate.

COMMUNICATIONS

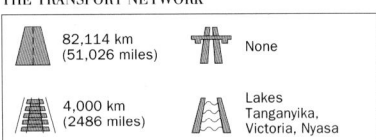

Dar es Salaam Intl
453,000 passengers

15 ships
45,200 dwt

THE TRANSPORT NETWORK

82,114 km (51,026 miles)		None
4,000 km (2486 miles)		Lakes Tanganyika, Victoria, Nyasa

The roads, railways and ports are being upgraded. An $870-million programme to improve 70% of Tanzania's trunk roads is due for completion in 1996.

TOURISM

186,000 visitors

Up 22% in 1991

MAIN OVERSEAS ARRIVALS

UK 9%	
Germany 6%	
USA and Canada 6%	
Other 79%	

% of total arrivals

One third of Tanzania is national park or game reserve. The Ngorongoro Crater and the Serengeti Plain are top attractions. Tourist numbers have risen sharply since 1990.

PEOPLE

Swahili, Sukuma, Chagga, Nyamwezi, Hehe, Makonde, Yao, Sandawe, English

29 people per km²

THE URBAN/RURAL POPULATION SPLIT

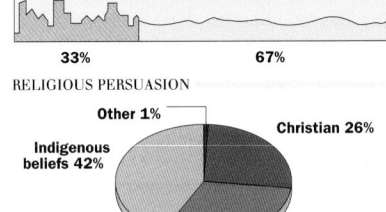

33%   67%

RELIGIOUS PERSUASION

Other 1%
Christian 26%
Indigenous beliefs 42%
Muslim 31%

For many Tanzanians the family is the focus of traditional rural life. About 99% belong to one of 120 small ethnic Bantu groups. The remaining 1% comprises Arab, Asian and European minorities. The use of Swahili as a *lingua franca* has helped make ethnic rivalries almost non-existent.

POLITICS

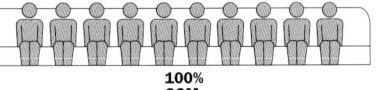

1995

President Ali Hassan Mwinyi

THE STATE OF THE PARTIES

National Assembly 291 members

100% CCM

CCM = Revolutionary Party of Tanzania

Now in voluntary retirement, Julius Nyerere was the dominant force in Tanzanian politics for 21 years. He founded the ruling party, the CCM, and his philosophy of African socialism guided Tanzania's development. Ali Hassan Mwinyi succeeded Nyerere as president in 1985, and as CCM chairman in 1990. He has overseen a gradual relaxation of socialist policies, and introduced reforms which are moving Tanzania towards multiparty elections. The key political problem is Zanzibar. Many Zanzibaris have never accepted the 1964 union of the island with Tanganyika and separatists are a growing force.

TANZANIA

Total Area
945 090 sq. km
(364 900 sq. miles)

POPULATION

over 1 000 000	▣
over 100 000	◎
over 50 000	○
over 10 000	●
under 10 000	•

LAND HEIGHT

3000m/9843ft	
2000m/6562ft	
1000m/3281ft	
500m/1640ft	
200m/656ft	
Sea Level	

T

WORLD AFFAIRS

 OAU Comm NAM SADC EADB

Tanzania plays a role in both eastern and southern Africa. An active member of the SADC, it was a base for the ANC during its anti-apartheid struggle. Relations with Kenya and Uganda have warmed since 1985 and there is talk of reviving the East African Community. A large influx of Burundian refugees has strained links with Burundi.

AID

 $1.1bn (receipts)   Down 6% in 1991

Tanzania is heavily dependent on aid to help offset a severe balance of payments deficit. Most aid is now linked to an IMF-backed economic reform programme. Infrastructure projects and the agricultural sector are the main recipients of aid.

DEFENCE

 $110.2m   Down 8% between 1987 and 1989

Defence accounts for 15% of budget spending. The armed forces are closely linked with the ruling CCM. There is a 100,000-strong citizens' reserve force.

ECONOMICS

 $2.5bn   475.19 Tanzanian shillings

SCORE CARD

❑ WORLD GNP RANKING	134th
❑ GNP PER CAPITA	$90
❑ BALANCE OF PAYMENTS	$−284m
❑ INFLATION	18.9%
❑ UNEMPLOYMENT	25%

STRENGTHS
Coffee, cotton, sisal, tea. Cloves from Zanzibar, the world's third largest producer. Diamonds. State commitment to reforms which have cut inflation and the budget deficit. Rise in inward investment. A return to positive growth.

WEAKNESSES
Growth still too low to increase per capita income. Shortage of foreign exchange. Poor credit and equipment limit agricultural development.

EXPORTS

IMPORTS

RESOURCES

 830m kwh   Not an oil producer; refines 17,000 b/cd

13m cattle, 5m sheep, 280,000 pigs   Natural gas, oil, iron, diamonds, gold, salt, phosphates, coal, gypsum, kaolin, tin

Agriculture, including livestock and forestry, is the key economic resource. It accounts for 60% of GDP and 80% of employment and exports. Forests cover 50% of Tanzania. More than 90% of energy demand is met from wood and charcoal. Hydro-power provides 70% of electricity and is being expanded. To reduce oil imports, which take 40% of export earnings, Tanzania is starting to exploit offshore gas at Songo Songo. Oil has been discovered off Pemba Island.

ENVIRONMENT

 14% (10% partially protected)   Growth in tourism poses long-term threat

The demand for fuelwood is a threat to forests. Tourism's demands have to be carefully balanced with those of delicate wildlife environments, like the Ngorongoro Crater and the Serengeti.

MEDIA

 Censorship is now minimal. There has been a great increase in the number of independent publishers

PUBLISHING AND BROADCAST MEDIA

	There are 3 daily newspapers, the *Daily News*, *Uhuru* and *Kipanga*
1 limited independent service	1 state-owned, 1 independent service

The daily press is state-owned. Much of the independent press is in Swahili. Only Zanzibar has TV.

CRIME

 Tanzania does not publish prison figures   Up 4% in 1990

Crime levels are low, although theft in Dar es Salaam has risen. Tanzania's human rights record is good.

EDUCATION

 89%

Primary education is free; secondary students pay fees. Only 50% of children attend primary and 4% secondary school, but adult literacy campaigns maintain high levels of literacy.

CHRONOLOGY

The mainland became the German colony of Tanganyika in 1884. The Sultanate of Zanzibar became a British protectorate in 1890.

- ❑ **1918** Tanganyika British mandate.
- ❑ **1961** Tanganyika independent.
- ❑ **1962** Nyerere becomes president.
- ❑ **1963** Zanzibar independent.
- ❑ **1964** Zanzibar signs union with Tanganyika to form Tanzania.
- ❑ **1977** One-party state. Mainland and Zanzibari parties form CCM.
- ❑ **1985** Nyerere resigns as president. President Mwinyi, former vice-president, begins relaxation of Nyerere's socialist policies.
- ❑ **1990** Nyerere resigns from CCM chair. Mwinyi becomes new chairman.
- ❑ **1992** Political parties allowed.

HEALTH

 1 per 19,775 people   Diarrheal and respiratory diseases, malaria

Basic medical care is provided by the state and Christian missions. Rural areas are served by local clinics.

WEALTH

 Most Tanzanians lead a subsistence existence

CONSUMER GOODS OWNERSHIP

The majority of Tanzanians are subsistence farmers. The wealthy elite is small, composed mainly of Asian and Arab business families.

WORLD RANKING

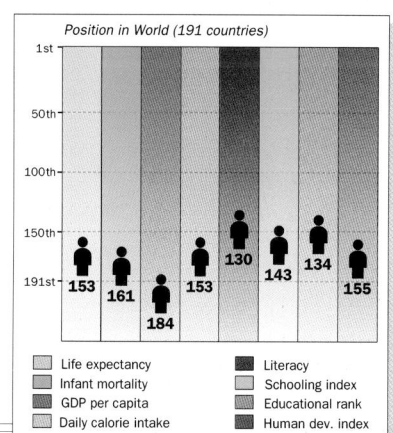

T

THAILAND

OFFICIAL NAME: Kingdom of Thailand **CAPITAL:** Bangkok
POPULATION: 56.1 million **CURRENCY:** Baht **OFFICIAL LANGUAGE:** Thai

SOUTH EAST ASIA

THAILAND LIES BETWEEN the Indian and Pacific Oceans in South East Asia. The north, the western border with Burma and the long Isthmus of Kra are mountainous. The central plain is the most fertile and densely-populated area, while the low northeastern plateau is the poorest region. Thailand has been an independent kingdom for most of its history and, since 1932, a constitutional monarchy with alternating military and civilian governments. Continuing rapid industrialization is resulting in massive congestion in Bangkok and a serious depletion of natural resources.

CLIMATE

WEATHER CHART

Thailand's tropical monsoon climate has three seasons – a hot sultry period, rains from May to October, and a dry, cooler season from November to March.

COMMUNICATIONS

Don Muang International, Bangkok
14.33m passengers

283 ships
1.28m dwt

THE TRANSPORT NETWORK

73,233 km (45,506 miles)		None
3755 km (2333 miles)		3701 km (2300 miles)

Bangkok suffers from huge traffic jams. An elevated railway and a highway to the airport are being built, but will have little impact on the problem. Good US-built roads run to the north and east. The Chao Phraya River carries most freight.

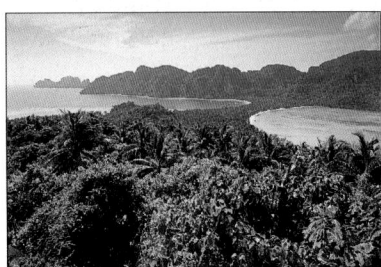

Island in the Andaman Sea. The over-development of Thailand's best-known resorts is pushing tourism into new, remoter locations.

TOURISM

5.7m visitors

Up 11% in 1993

MAIN OVERSEAS ARRIVALS

- Malaysia 14%
- Japan 11%
- Taiwan 8%
- UK 6%
- USA 6%
- Other 55%

% of total arrivals

Tourism is an important contributor to the Thai economy. Tourist numbers fell in the early 1990s as a result of both the worldwide recession and local over-development during the 1980s boom. Although the number of arrivals recovered in 1993, visitors are tending to seek the less developed resorts. Bangkok's hotel occupancy rates are still falling as yet more hotels are built. Pattaya beach resort has seen such uncontrolled development that sea pollution is now a serious problem, while opposition to the intrusion of large numbers of tourists is growing among northern hill tribes.

Although prostitution is illegal, Bangkok and Pattaya are centres for sex tourism, which thrives despite the state's embarrassment at its effect on Thailand's image. Japanese and German men are among the main clients, while Burmese girls are increasingly recruited as prostitutes. Child prostitution is also a major problem.

There has been a boom in golf tourism, especially among the Japanese. The large number of new golf courses which are under construction will make Thailand the largest golf destination in Asia. The vast amounts of water needed to maintain the courses is aggravating Thailand's serious water shortage.

PEOPLE

Thai, Chinese, Malay, Khmer, Mon, Karen, Miao

106 people per km²

THE URBAN/RURAL POPULATION SPLIT

23%   77%

RELIGIOUS PERSUASION

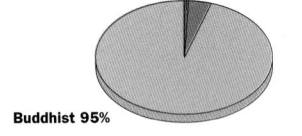

Other 1%
Muslim 4%
Buddhist 95%

ETHNIC MAKEUP

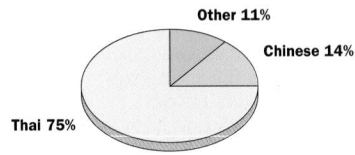

Other 11%
Chinese 14%
Thai 75%

There is little ethnic tension in Thailand and Buddhism is a great binding force. The majority of Thais follow Theravada Buddhism, although the reformist Asoke Santi Buddhist sect, which advocates a new moral austerity, is gaining influence. Its principles have been espoused by one of the leading opposition parties, the Palang Dharma (PD), led by the governor of Bangkok, which seeks to clean-up politics.

The far north and northeast are home to about 600,000 hill tribespeople with their own languages, and to permanently-settled refugees from Laos, mostly of the Hmong tribal group.

The large Chinese community is the most assimilated in South East Asia. Sino-Thais are particularly dominant in agricultural marketing. Most of Thailand's one million Muslim Malays live in the south. They feel stronger affinity with Muslims in Malaysia than with Thai culture, and this has given rise to a secessionist movement.

Women are important in business, but their involvement in national politics is limited.

POPULATION AGE BREAKDOWN

% of population by age group	0–14	15–64	65+
1960	44.7%	52.6%	2.7%
1970	46.2%	50.8%	3%
1980	40%	56.5%	3.5%
1990	32.7%	63.4%	3.9%
2000	26.5%	68.5%	5%

T

RESOURCES

 46.2bn kwh (capacity 9.72m kw)

 50,800 b/d (reserves 241,900,000 bbl)

5.3m cattle, 4.7m pigs, 156,000 sheep

Tin, lignite, gas, gems, oil, tungsten, lead, zinc, antimony, potash

ELECTRICITY GENERATION

Hydro 11% (5bn kwh)

Thermal 89% (41.2bn kwh)

Nuclear 0%

Other 0%

0   20   40   60   80   100
% of total generation by type

Thailand has minimal crude oil and has rejected the nuclear option in favour of speeding up development of its large natural gas fields. It also has significant lignite deposits for power generation. World demand for Thailand's tin has declined, but recent gold and copper finds offer new potential. Thailand has valuable gemstone deposits. It is also the world's biggest shrimp producer.

THAILAND : LAND USE

Cropland
Forest
Pasture
Cattle
Rubber - cash crop
Rice

0   200 km
0   200 miles

ENVIRONMENT

 11% (5% partially protected)

Increasing efforts to combat pollution and deforestation

ENVIRONMENTAL TREATIES

No   No
Yes   Yes

Deforestation, especially of the watersheds in the north, has led to the increasing severity of both floods and droughts. Particularly serious flooding in the south resulted in a total logging ban in 1988. Illegal logging still continues, however. Reafforestation projects, some criticized for using single quick-growing species, will not solve the national water shortage. There is evidence of growing official concern at pollution levels. The worst polluting factories are being forced to move out of Bangkok and no new factories may use CFCs.

MEDIA

 Criticism of the King is not tolerated

PUBLISHING AND BROADCAST MEDIA

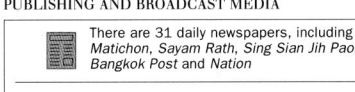

There are 31 daily newspapers, including *Matichon, Sayam Rath, Sing Sian Jih Pao, Bangkok Post* and *Nation*

5 state-controlled services

480 state-controlled stations

Intelsat V F8 Palapa B2-P

Cables were being laid in Bangkok in 1994

Newspapers now enjoy a high level of freedom in political reporting. Two of the five TV stations are run by the military. A fast expansion of cable-TV networks is planned.

CRIME

 73,296 prisoners

 Up 335% in 1990

CRIME RATES

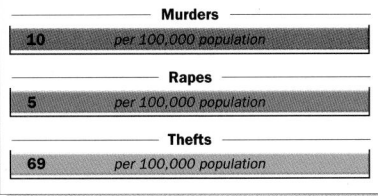

Murders
10   per 100,000 population

Rapes
5   per 100,000 population

Thefts
69   per 100,000 population

Political imprisonment has been almost non-existent since the early 1980s. There is some police involvement in crime, however, and extra-judicial killings and ill-treatment of prisoners in police detention are quite common.

The King has inspired an opium-substitution crop programme. The government has cracked down on music, software and video piracy.

EDUCATION

 93%

0   Education spending as % GNP   25

 3.2%

THE EDUCATION SYSTEM

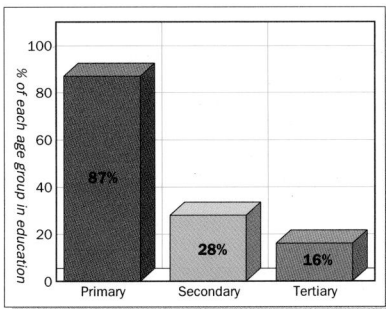

% of each age group in education

100
80
60   87%
40
20   28%   16%
0
Primary   Secondary   Tertiary

In 1993, the first steps were taken to make schooling compulsory for nine years instead of six.

HEALTH

 1 per 4843 people

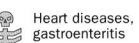 Heart diseases, gastroenteritis

0   Health spending as % GNP   25
1.1%

High-quality health care is heavily concentrated in Bangkok. Most of the 75% of the population who live in rural areas have access to primary health care. Trained personnel are aided by village health volunteers, monks, teachers and traditional healers. In 1993, the decision was taken to improve the skills of primary health workers, rather than increase the number of fully-trained doctors, as a means to improve rural health care.

The government operates a system whereby the poor can apply annually for a certificate entitling them to free health care. However, estimates suggest 30% of users can afford to pay.

High profile family planning programmes are slowing population growth and sex education programmes among prostitutes are aimed at combating the spread of AIDS.

WEALTH

 Employment of child labour is widespread

CONSUMER GOODS OWNERSHIP

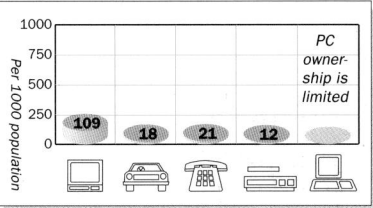

1000
750
500
250   109   18   21   12
0

Per 1000 population

PC ownership is limited

The government is trying to spread the great concentration of people and wealth from Bangkok to the provinces. The northeast in particular is very poor. The gap between rich and poor is greater in Thailand than in other industrializing South East Asian states.

WORLD RANKING

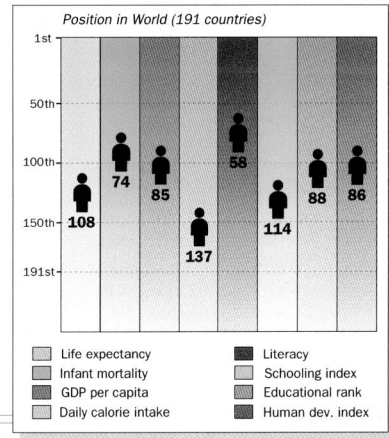

Position in World (191 countries)

1st
50th
100th
150th
191st

108   74   85   137   58   114   88   86

Life expectancy
Infant mortality
GDP per capita
Daily calorie intake
Literacy
Schooling index
Educational rank
Human dev. index

T

TOGO

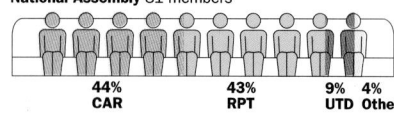

WEST AFRICA

Africa

OFFICIAL NAME: Togolese Republic   **CAPITAL:** Lomé
POPULATION: 3.8 million   **CURRENCY:** CFA franc   **OFFICIAL LANGUAGES:** French, Kabye and Ewe

TOGO IS SANDWICHED between Ghana and Benin in West Africa. A central forested region is bounded by savanna lands to the north and south. Togo exploits its position, and the port at Lomé, to act as an entrepôt for West African trade. The 1993 and 1994 elections were the first since independence.

CLIMATE

WEATHER CHART

Togo has a typical Gulf of Guinea climate – very hot and humid on the coast and drier inland.

COMMUNICATIONS

Tokoin, Lomé
168,981 passengers

21 ships
20,600 dwt

THE TRANSPORT NETWORK

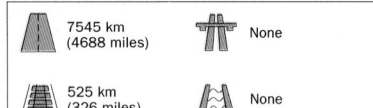

7545 km (4688 miles)		None
525 km (326 miles)		None

Improving the already good road network and Lomé's port facilities are priorities, given Togo's role as an entrepôt. The only railway runs from Lomé to Kpalimé.

TOURISM

 65,098 visitors
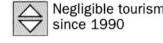 Negligible tourism since 1990

MAIN OVERSEAS ARRIVALS

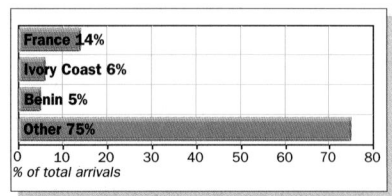

France 14%
Ivory Coast 6%
Benin 5%
Other 75%

% of total arrivals

There is some package tourism, mainly French and German, to coastal tourist villages and hotels built during the expansion programme of the 1980s. However, since 1990 most tourists have been deterred by the political crisis.

PEOPLE

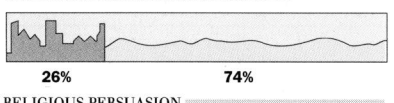

Ewe, Kabye, Gurma, French

62 people per km²

THE URBAN/RURAL POPULATION SPLIT

26%   74%

RELIGIOUS PERSUASION

Muslim 10%

Christian 20%

Indigenous beliefs 70%

A bitter divide has existed between north and south since before independence. Most southern resentment is directed towards a minority in the north, the Kabye people from the Kabye plateau, because of their domination of the military. The Kabye and other northerners in turn resent their own underdevelopment in contrast to the high development, especially educationally, of all southerners. The dominant southern group is the Ewe, who make up more than 40% of the population.

As elsewhere in Africa, the extended family is important and tribalism and nepotism are key factors in everyday life. Some Togolese ethnic groups, such as the Mina, have matriarchal societies. The 'Nana Benz', the market-women of Lomé market, who control the retail trade, have considerable private money. Politics, however, remains a male preserve.

Kabye cultivations near Kara, in northern Togo. The main food crops grown are cassava, yams and maize.

POLITICS

 1999

President Gen Gnassingbe Eyadéma

THE STATE OF THE PARTIES

National Assembly 81 members

44% CAR   43% RPT   9% UTD   4% Other

CAR = Action Committee for Renewal   **RPT** = Rally of the Togolese People   **UTD** = Togolese Union for Democracy **Other** = Union of Young Democrats, New Force Co-ordination

Politics has been dominated for two decades by General Gnassingbe Eyadéma, who took power at the head of a military government in 1967. The army is the main power broker, notably the small group of officers from Pya on the Kabye plateau.

A democracy movement has been gathering momentum since 1990, when serious rioting occured in Lomé. Many unofficial parties sprang up and were legitimized early in 1991, although since then they have been struggling against Eyadéma's efforts to claw back his power. Multiparty presidential elections held in 1993 confirmed Eyadéma in power. However, these were boycotted by some opposition candidates in protest at the exclusion from the elections of Gilchrist Olympio, an arch-opponent of Eyadéma and son of a former president. Legislative elections held early in 1994 saw a close contest between the CAR and Eyadéma's RPT. However, results in three constituencies have since been declared invalid, and further elections are scheduled for later in the year.

WORLD AFFAIRS

 OAU   Ecowas   FZ   ACP   GATT

The priority now is maintaining traditional links, especially with France, in spite of the crisis. For the past two years, Eyadéma's foreign policy has competed with that of the democratic forces seeking allies in Europe, the USA and West Africa.

AID

 $204m (receipts)   Down 15% in 1991

Development projects have suffered from recent aid suspensions by donors including the USA and the EU. Prior to this, Togo had a good record in project implementation, despite occasional cases of political interference.

T

TOGO

Total Area : 56 790 sq. km
(21 927 sq. miles)

POPULATION

over 100 000	◎
over 10 000	●
under 10 000	•

LAND HEIGHT

500m/1640ft	
200m/656ft	
Sea Level	

DEFENCE

 $47.44m   Down 5% in 1991

The military has an important role in
Togo, and spending on defence is high.
Modern equipment is supplied mainly
by France, Germany and the USA.
Potential intervention by Ghana is
regarded as a main defence issue.
France guarantees Togo's security
through a defence accord.

ECONOMICS

$1.6bn   295.23 CFA francs

SCORE CARD

- ❏ WORLD GNP RANKING........................145th
- ❏ GNP PER CAPITA $421
- ❏ BALANCE OF PAYMENTS......................$−97m
- ❏ INFLATION 3.3%
- ❏ UNEMPLOYMENT...................................2%

STRENGTHS

Efficient civil service. Ideal location for
role as entrepôt, based on Lomé port.
Proceeds of widespread smuggling.
Resourcefulness of entrepreneurs,
notably market women. Phosphate
deposits have the world's highest
mineral content. Self-sufficient in basic
foodstuffs. Diverse range of food crops.

RESOURCES

 41m kwh
(capacity
34,000 kw)

Not an oil producer
and has no refineries

 1.1m sheep,
433,000 pigs,
246,000 cattle

Phosphates, iron,
chromite, bauxite

Phosphates are Togo's most important
resource. Exploration for oil is under
way, but none has yet been found. The
Nangbeto Dam, constructed jointly with
Benin and opened in 1988, has reduced
dependence on Ghana for energy.

ENVIRONMENT

 11%   Few ecological
initiatives taken

Ecologists have been critical of the
transformation of nature reserves into
hunting grounds for the military elite.
Other problems include coastal erosion
around Aneho and desertification.

MEDIA

 The total censorship which existed prior to 1990
has eased. However, the new independent press
is subject to severe intimidaton

PUBLISHING AND BROADCAST MEDIA

 Daily newspapers include *Togo Presse*,
published by the government

1 state-owned
service   1 state-owned
service

With the arrival of the democracy
movement, a number of privately-
owned newspapers have sprung up.

CRIME

 Togo does not publish
prison figures   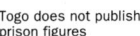 Theft on increase in
the capital

Togo is normally relatively peaceable.
However, crime has inevitably
increased during the recent periods of
unrest. Robberies, in particular, are on
the increase in the capital.

EXPORTS

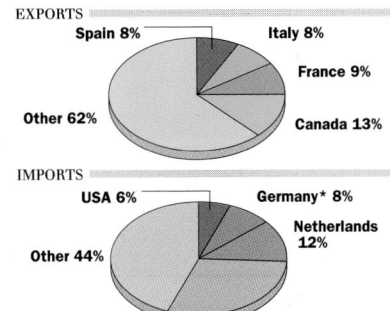

Spain 8%	Italy 8%
	France 9%
Other 62%	Canada 13%

IMPORTS

USA 6%	Germany* 8%
	Netherlands 12%
Other 44%	
	France 30%

WEAKNESSES

Smuggling-dependent economy could
easily be disrupted by border closure
with Ghana. Limited internal market
due to size of country. Lack of natural
resources.

EDUCATION

 43%

Schooling is based on the French
model. The university in Lomé has
over 4000 students.

HEALTH

 1 per 8700 people   Malaria, diarrheal,
infectious and
parasitic diseases

Togo's relatively well-structured health
care system is a reflection of its being a
favoured target of foreign aid.

WEALTH

 Agricultural worker, 16,500 CFA francs per
month; bank employee, 57,964 CFA francs
per month

CONSUMER GOODS OWNERSHIP

Considerable wealth disparities exist
between the political and business
classes, and Togolese who work the
land. Between these extremes, the
urban class is relatively prosperous.

WORLD RANKING

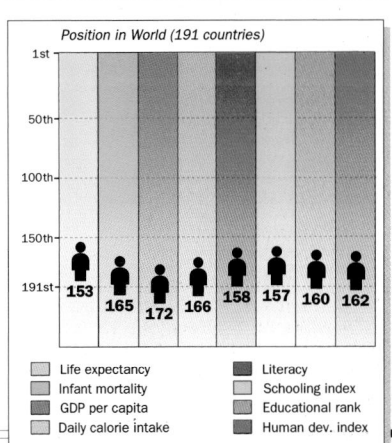

Position in World (191 countries)

Life expectancy	Literacy
Infant mortality	Schooling index
GDP per capita	Educational rank
Daily calorie intake	Human dev. index

T

537

TONGA

OFFICIAL NAME: Kingdom of Tonga **CAPITAL:** Nuku'alofa
POPULATION: 94,000 **CURRENCY:** Pa'anga **OFFICIAL LANGUAGE:** Tongan

LOCATED IN THE SOUTH PACIFIC northeast of New Zealand, Tonga is an archipelago of 170 islands. These are divided into three main groups, Vava'u, Ha'apai and Tongatapu. Tonga's easterly islands are generally low and fertile. Those in the west are higher and volcanic in origin. Tonga's economy is based on agriculture, especially coconut, cassava and passion fruit production. Politics is effectively controlled by the King.

CLIMATE

WEATHER CHART

Tonga has a tropical oceanic climate, with year-round temperatures ranging between 20°C and 30°C.

COMMUNICATIONS

Fua'amotu International, Tongatapu
67,000 passengers

8 ships
13,200 dwt

THE TRANSPORT NETWORK

433 km (269 miles)   None
None   None

Japanese and other foreign aid is currently financing a major port development at Nuku'alofa.

TOURISM

20,917 visitors   Down 1% in 1990

MAIN OVERSEAS ARRIVALS

New Zealand 25%
USA 23%
Australia 16%
Other 36%

0   10   20   30   40
% of total arrivals

Tonga's main attractions are its tropical beaches. Tourist arrivals, mainly from New Zealand and the USA, are expanding slowly. However, fears have been expressed that too many visitors may erode traditional Tongan culture.

Mountainous scenery typical of Tonga's westerly islands. Tonga's 170 islands are scattered over a wide expanse of the South Pacific. Only 45 are inhabited.

TONGA

Total Area : 750 sq. km
(290 sq. miles)

POPULATION
● over 10 000
● under 10 000

LAND HEIGHT
200m/656ft
Sea Level

PEOPLE

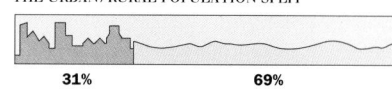

English, Tongan

132 people per km²

THE URBAN/RURAL POPULATION SPLIT

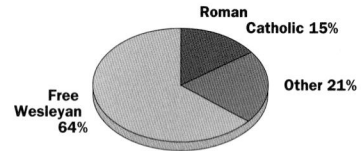

31%   69%

RELIGIOUS PERSUASION

Roman Catholic 15%
Other 21%
Free Wesleyan 64%

Tonga has strong ethnic ties with eastern Fiji and there has traditionally been considerable population movement between the two states. Tongans tend to see themselves as unique among Pacific islanders as they were never fully colonized and retain their monarchy.

Respect for traditional values and institutions remains high. Tongans are strong church-goers; the Wesleyan, Roman Catholic and Mormon churches are influential and often fund education. However, a new generation of Western-educated Tongans is querying some traditional attitudes.

POLITICS

1996

HM King Taufa'ahau Tupou IV

THE STATE OF THE PARTIES

Legislative Assembly 31 members

The Legislative Assembly comprises the King, the 12 members of the Privy Council, 9 hereditary nobles chosen by their peers and 9 elected members

The main power brokers in Tongan politics are the King, the noble establishment and the landowners. King Tupou IV effectively heads his government, frequently exercising kingly powers. The legislative assembly defers to his judgement and the King has taken the initiative in instigating several development projects. These initiatives, including recent talks on possible Libyan investment in oil exploration, are undertaken without reference to the government.

Younger Westernized Tongans are now increasingly questioning the role of the monarchy. When the current King dies, calls for change are likely to accelerate.

T

WORLD AFFAIRS

Tonga has historically fallen within New Zealand's sphere of influence. It is a member of the SPARTECA trade agreement, which includes Australia and New Zealand. Tonga is one of the few states in the region not to endorse the South Pacific Nuclear Free Zone.

AID

 Significant aid receipts

 Fairly constant

Aid finances major infrastructure projects; Australia, the USA, New Zealand, the EU and the ADB are major donors. Significant amounts were recently ploughed into oil exploration, but without success.

DEFENCE

 $2m

 Little variation from year to year

Tonga has a small defence force, which includes both regulars and reserves. 5% of the state budget is currently allocated to defence.

ECONOMICS

 $139m

 1.47 pa'anga

SCORE CARD

- ❏ WORLD GNP RANKING..........................184th
- ❏ GNP PER CAPITA $1500
- ❏ BALANCE OF PAYMENTS.....................$–1.4m
- ❏ INFLATION 10.6%
- ❏ UNEMPLOYMENT...................................13%

STRENGTHS
Range of subsistence agriculture. Commercial production of coconut, cassava and passion fruit.

WEAKNESSES
Off main shipping routes. Exports in direct competition with rest of South Pacific region. Many productive Tongans live abroad.

EXPORTS

IMPORTS

RESOURCES

 22m kwh (capacity 7000 kw)

 Not an oil producer and has no refineries

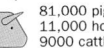 81,000 pigs, 11,000 horses, 9000 cattle

None

Tonga has no strategic or mineral resources. Electricity is generated from imported fuel, which is brought ashore in uneconomical 44-gallon units. Recent exploration has failed to identify any oil reserves.

ENVIRONMENT

 None

 Environmental issues not of particular concern

Tonga does not suffer from serious environmental problems, although it is occasionally afflicted by natural disasters, such as the 1982 typhoon. Commercial activity has made little impact on the environment.

MEDIA

 Censorship tends to be self-imposed. Outspoken slander or attacks on the King are not acceptable

PUBLISHING AND BROADCAST MEDIA

 There are no daily newspapers. Weeklies include the *Conch Shell* and the *Tonga Chronicle*

 No TV service

 1 independent service

There are five main newspapers. The *Conch Shell* has a circulation of around 10,000. The *Tonga Chronicle* is published by the government.

CRIME

 58 prisoners

 Rising levels of theft

Crime rates are generally low, partly due to the strong influence of the family. However, offences such as breaking and entering have increased with rising unemployment levels among young Tongans.

EDUCATION

 93%

Education is based on the Australian and New Zealand models and church participation in schools is high. The 'Atenisi Institute offers university level courses. A few students go on to the University of the South Pacific in Fiji.

HEALTH

 1 per 2790 people

 Heart, cerebrovascular and diarrheal diseases

Tonga has some modern health care facilities. However, patients have to be flown out to Australia or New Zealand for sophisticated surgery.

CHRONOLOGY

Originally discovered by the Polynesians, Tonga was visited by the Dutch in the 17th century and Captain Cook in the 18th. In the latter half of the 19th century, during the reign of King George Tupou I, the islands became a unified state after a period of civil war.

- ❏ **1875** First constitution established by King George Tupou I.
- ❏ **1900** Concern over German ambitions in region leads to signing of Treaty of Friendship and Protection with UK.
- ❏ **1918–1965** Reign of Queen Salote Tupou III.
- ❏ **1958** Greater autonomy from UK enshrined in Friendship Treaty.
- ❏ **1965** King Taufa'ahau Tupou IV accedes on mother's death.
- ❏ **1970** Independence within British Commonwealth.
- ❏ **1988** Treaty allowing US nuclear warships right of transit through Tongan waters signed.
- ❏ **1990** Court case starts against government over sale of passports to Hong Kong citizens.

WEALTH

 Remittances from Tongans living overseas are important for the local economy

CONSUMER GOODS OWNERSHIP

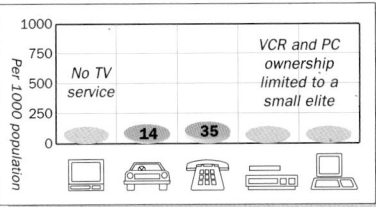

Tongans indulge in few ostentatious displays of wealth. The well-off provide financial support for relatives.

WORLD RANKING

TRINIDAD & TOBAGO

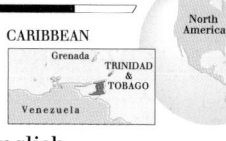

CARIBBEAN

OFFICIAL NAME: Republic of Trinidad and Tobago **CAPITAL:** Port-of-Spain
CURRENCY: Trinidad and Tobago dollar **POPULATION:** 1.3 million **OFFICIAL LANGUAGE:** English

THE TWO ISLANDS of Trinidad and Tobago are the most southerly of the Caribbean Windward Islands and lie just 15 km off the Venezuelan coast. They gained joint independence from Britain in 1962 and Tobago was given internal autonomy in 1987. The spectacular mountain ranges and large swamps are rich in tropical flora and fauna. Pitch Lake in Trinidad is the world's largest natural reservoir of asphalt.

CLIMATE

WEATHER CHART

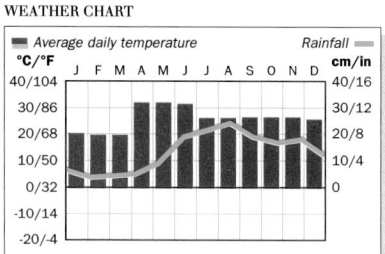

The islands are a little warmer than others in the Caribbean and escape the hurricanes, which pass by to the north.

COMMUNICATIONS

Piarco International, Port-of-Spain
1.31m passengers

10 ships
11,100 dwt

THE TRANSPORT NETWORK

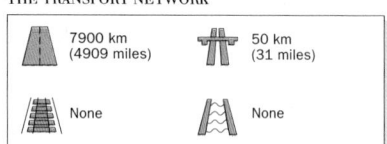

7900 km (4909 miles)

50 km (31 miles)

None

None

The road network is well developed. Trinidadians get around the islands in private taxis or by 'maxi-taxi', minibuses with set routes, which can be hailed at any point on the roadside.

TOURISM

194,021 visitors

No change in 1990

MAIN OVERSEAS ARRIVALS

USA 37%
Canada 13%
UK 10%
Other 40%

% of total arrivals

Trinidad's concentration on the oil sector meant that it was one of the last Caribbean states to develop its tourism potential. Tourism is concentrated on Tobago (said to be the model for the island in *Robinson Crusoe*) renowned for its wildlife, including over 500 species of butterfly.

TRINIDAD & TOBAGO

Total Area : 5130 sq. km (1981 sq. miles)

LAND HEIGHT
500m/1640ft
200m/656ft
Sea Level

POPULATION
over 50 000
over 10 000
under 10 000

PEOPLE

English Creole, English, Hindi, French, Spanish

241 people per km²

THE URBAN/RURAL POPULATION SPLIT

69%   31%

ETHNIC MAKEUP

Other 2%
Chinese 1%
Black 43%
Mixed 14%
South Asian 40%

Trinidad's South Asian community is the largest in the Caribbean, and holds on to its Muslim and Hindu inheritance. The open discussion of racial issues in Trinidad goes some way to dissipating latent tensions between black and South Asian Trinidadians.

POLITICS

1996

President Noor Mohammed Hassanali

THE STATE OF THE PARTIES

House of Representatives 36 members

58% PNM   36% UNC   6% NAR

PNM = People's National Movement **UNC** = United National Congress **NAR** = National Alliance for Reconstruction

Senate 31 members

16 members chosen by the prime minister, 6 by the leader of the opposition, and 9 by the president

Trinidad has lacked a major political figure since the death of Eric Williams, the autocratic PNM leader, who led the country to independence in 1962. After 29 years of PNM rule, politics has recently become fragmented, and dominated by the race issue. Black Trinidadians have clearly expressed their opposition to any South Asian Trinidadian becoming prime minister, a view strengthened by a 1990 coup attempt by the Black Muslim sect.

Tobago's white sand beaches, verdant landscape and natural anchorages have enabled it to develop a thriving tourist industry.

WORLD AFFAIRS

In 1994, Trinidad expressed a wish to improve economic ties with the Group of Three: Venezuela, Colombia and Mexico. This was a direct response to Mexico joining NAFTA. The major foreign policy issue is disputes with neighbouring Venezuela over sea boundaries, important for establishing both fishing and marine oil rights.

AID

 Minimal   Down from $18m (receipts) in 1990

Trinidad has a strong economy, and little need of aid. Minimal sums are received from the EU.

DEFENCE

 $74m   Up 25% between 1989 and 1992

Defence forces comprise a 2500-strong army and coastguard. The latter is used to patrol fishing grounds.

ECONOMICS

 $4.5bn   5.51 Trinidad and Tobago dollars

SCORE CARD

- WORLD GNP RANKING........................113th
- GNP PER CAPITA $3470
- BALANCE OF PAYMENTS..................$–16.7m
- INFLATION 16.5%
- UNEMPLOYMENT...................................22%

STRENGTHS
Oil, which accounts for 70% of export earnings. Gas is increasingly being exploited to support new industries, such as nitrogenous fertilizer manufacture. Tourism, particularly on Tobago, is being developed.

WEAKNESSES
The economy is still insufficiently diversified and highly sensitive to world oil price movements.

EXPORTS

IMPORTS

RESOURCES

 3.5bn kwh (capacity 990,000 kw)   136,500 b/d (reserves 572,600,000 bbl)

80,000 cattle, 70,000 pigs, 13,000 sheep   Oil, natural gas, natural asphalt

Oil and gas are Trinidad's major resources. Government policy is to continue increasing both production and refinery output.

ENVIRONMENT

 3% partially protected   Greater environmental consciousness

Spillages from oil tankers, which pose a serious threat to coastal conservation areas such as the Caroni Swamp with its 500 species of butterflies, are the major concern. Oil spills are also threatening some tourist beaches.

MEDIA

 No restrictions on political reporting

PUBLISHING AND BROADCAST MEDIA

 There are 4 daily newspapers, including the *Trinidad Express* and the *Trinidad Guardian*

 1 state-owned service 1 state-owned, 1 independent service

New TV and radio stations have sprung up since broadcasting licence rules were relaxed in 1992. Most TV programming is from US networks.

CRIME

 2387 prisoners   Down 3% in 1990

Crime in Trinidad is higher than in most of its Caribbean neighbours, and most towns have unsafe areas at night. A proposal to abolish the death penalty has been strongly opposed by locals.

EDUCATION

 96%

Education is based on the British 11-plus system. Most students go on to the University of the West Indies; Trinidad hosts the St Augustine campus. However, wealthy Trinidadians go to universities in the USA.

HEALTH

 1 per 1213 people   Cerebrovascular and heart diseases, cancers, diabetes

Oil wealth has given Trinidad a better public health service than most Caribbean states, and more private clinics, mainly serving the expatriate community. However, treatment delays are seen as a growing problem. 98% of the population have safe water.

CHRONOLOGY

Britain seized Trinidad from Spain in 1797 and Tobago from France in 1802. They were unified in 1888.

- **1956** Dr Eric Williams founds PNM and wins general elections: main support from blacks. Indian population supports opposition.
- **1961** Leaves West Indian Federation (joined 1958).
- **1962** Independence.
- **1970** Black Power demonstrations cause brief state of emergency.
- **1980** Tobago gets own House of Assembly; internal autonomy 1987.
- **1986** NAR coalition wins elections, but fails to halt economic decline.
- **1988** Baseo Panday dismissed from Cabinet; forms left-wing UNC.
- **1990** Premier taken hostage in failed fundamentalist coup.
- **1991** PNM elected back to power.

WEALTH

 Welder, 16 Trinidad and Tobago dollars per hour; government computer programmer, 2,640 Trinidad and Tobago dollars per month

CONSUMER GOODS OWNERSHIP

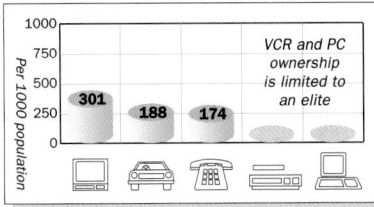

Wealth disparities between the affluent oil-rich business elite, many of whom are expatriate, and farm labourers are marked in Trinidad. During the oil-boom years of the 1970s, Trinidad was proportionately the world's biggest importer of Scotch whisky. Today, rural poverty in the interior, particularly among South Asian Trinidadian farmers, is a growing problem.

WORLD RANKING

TUNISIA

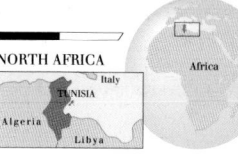

NORTH AFRICA

OFFICIAL NAME: Republic of Tunisia **CAPITAL:** Tunis
POPULATION: 8.4 million **CURRENCY:** Tunisian dinar **OFFICIAL LANGUAGE:** Arabic

NORTH AFRICA'S SMALLEST country, Tunisia lies sandwiched between Libya and Algeria. The populous north is mountainous, fertile in places and has a long Mediterranean coastline. The south is largely desert. Habib Bourguiba ruled the country from independence in 1956 until his downfall in a bloodless coup in 1987. Under President Ben Ali, the government has since been moving towards multiparty democracy, but faces a challenge from Islamic fundamentalists. Closer ties with the EU, Tunisia's main trading partner, are a priority. Manufacturing and the important tourism sector are expanding.

TOURISM

3.2m visitors   Up 15% in 1992

MAIN OVERSEAS ARRIVALS

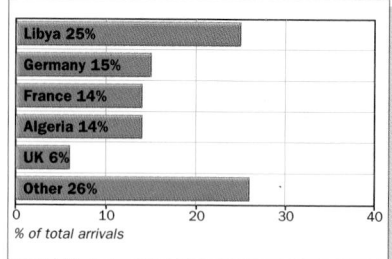

Libya 25%
Germany 15%
France 14%
Algeria 14%
UK 6%
Other 26%

% of total arrivals

Tourists have flocked to Tunisia since the 1960s, attracted by its winter sunshine, beaches, desert and Roman remains. One of the Mediterranean's cheapest package destinations, Tunisia attracts up to 1.8 million European visitors a year. However, numbers were hit in 1990–1991 by the Gulf War and the fear of attacks by Islamic militants. Tourism employs 190,000 people and is a focus of investment. Capacity has doubled since 1980 to 140,000 beds and is set to top 200,000 beds by the year 2000. However, concern about the environmental impact is growing.

CLIMATE

WEATHER CHART

Tunisia is hot in summer. The north is often wet and windy in winter. The far south is arid. The spring brings the dry, dusty *chili* wind from the Sahara.

COMMUNICATIONS

Habib Bourguiba, Monastir
1.72m passengers

28 ships
227,900 dwt

THE TRANSPORT NETWORK

29,183 km
(18,134 miles)

Highway from Tunis
to Carthage airport

2200 km
(1367 miles)

None

Tunisia has six international airports. A motorway from Tunis to Carthage airport opened in 1993. A light metro in Tunis and a rail link from Gafsa to Gabès are being built. The southern third of the country has few roads.

PEOPLE

 Arabic, French   50 people per km²

THE URBAN/RURAL POPULATION SPLIT

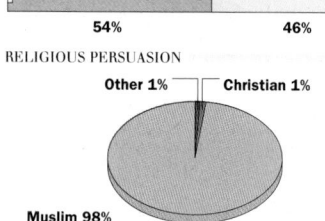

54%   46%

RELIGIOUS PERSUASION

Other 1%   Christian 1%

Muslim 98%

ETHNIC MAKEUP

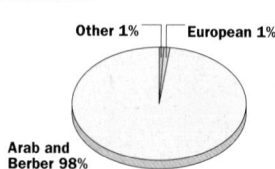

Other 1%   European 1%

Arab and Berber 98%

The population is almost entirely of Arab and Berber descent, although there are Jewish and Christian minorities. Many Tunisians still live in extended family groups, in which three or four generations are represented.

Tunisia has traditionally been one of the most liberal Arab states. The 1956 Personal Statutes Code of President Bourguiba gave women better rights than in any other Arab country. Further legislation has since given women the right to custody of children in divorce cases, made family violence against women punishable by law, and helped divorced women to get alimony. Family planning and contraception have been freely available since the early 1960s. Now Tunisia's population grows by only 16,000 a year. Women make up 25% of the total workforce and 35% of the industrial workforce. Company ownership by women is steadily increasing; politics, however, remains exclusively a male preserve.

These freedoms are threatened by the growth in recent years of Islamic fundamentalism, which also worries the mainly French-speaking political and business elite who wish to strengthen links with Europe.

The Ben Ali regime, although not as repressive as its predecessor, has been criticized for its actions against Islamic activists, in particular the banned *Al-Nahda* party. Amnesty International has detailed a number of human rights abuses, mainly against female members of *Al-Nahda*.

POPULATION AGE BREAKDOWN

	0–14	15–64	65+
% of population by age group			

	1960	1970	1980	1990	2000
65+	4.2%	3.8%	3.8%	4%	4.8%
15–64	52.5%	49.9%	54.5%	58%	62.2%
0–14	43.3%	46.3%	41.7%	38%	33%

Roman remains at the village of La-Kesra in Tozeur region, a low-lying area of oases in western central Tunisia.

POLITICS

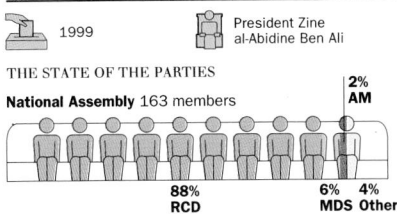

1999

President Zine
al-Abidine Ben Ali

THE STATE OF THE PARTIES

National Assembly 163 members

**2%
AM**

**88%
RCD**

**6%
MDS**

**4%
Other**

RCD = Constitutional Democratic Assembly   **MDS** = Social
Democratic Party   **AM** = *Attajidid Movement*
Other = Democratic Union, Popular Unity Party

Legally a multiparty democracy since
1988, Tunisia is still dominated by
the RCD and President Ben Ali.

President Ben Ali
*became head of
state in 1987.*

Dr Hamed Karoui,
*was appointed prime
minister in 1988.*

MAIN POLITICAL ISSUES

Fundamentalism
The RCD has clamped
down on Islamic
fundamentalists,
particularly the
outlawed *Al-Nahda*, or
Renewal Party. In 1991,
500 *Al-Nahda* members
were arrested
following a failed
coup, thought
to be inspired by
fundamentalists.
Its leader, Rachid
Gannouchi, is
now in exile.

Social reform
The RCD
sees social
programmes
aimed at
reducing
unemployment
as a way to
combat the
spread of
Islamic
militancy. The
expansion of
women's rights
is also likely
to continue,
balanced by
steps towards
Arabization.

PROFILE
President Ben Ali has made
strong efforts to draw
opposition parties into
government. The political system
has been liberalized with, for
example, the abolition of the life
presidency and state security court.
Press freedom has also been increased.
The aim of the 1994 election was to
form a national coalition against the
outlawed Islamic fundamentalists. A
complex proportional representation
system ensured an overwhelming
victory for the RCD, in addition to a
limted degree of political plurality.

TUNISIA

Total Area :
163 610 sq. km
(63 170 sq. miles)

Map of Tunisia showing cities including Bizerte, Menzel Bourguiba, Rass Jebel, Tabarka, Ariana, Carthage Airport, TUNIS, Bardo, La Marsa, La Goulette, Menzel Temime, Béja, Ben Arous, Hammam Lif, Mejerda, Jendouba, Nabeul, Hammamet, Zaghouan, Le Kef, Siliana, Sebkhet Kelbia, Kalaa Kebira, Monastir, Kesra, M'Saken, Sousse, Habib Bourigulba Airport, Kairouan, Jemmel, Moknine, Mahdia, Sebkhet de Sidi el Hani, El Jem, Kasserine, Jebel Chambi 1544m, Sidi Bouzid, Sebkhet el Gherça, Île Chergui, Île Kerkenah, Sfax, Île Gharbi, Gafsa, Sebkhet en Noual, Gulf of Gabès, Chott el Gharsa, Tozeur, Nefta, Chott el Fejaj, Houmt Souk, Île de Jerba, Gabès, Kebili, JEBEL TEBAGA, Golfe de Bou Grara, Zarzis, Chott el Jerid, Médenine, Bahiret el Bibane, Sebkhet el Melah, JEFFARA, Tataouine, GRAND ERG ORIENTAL, DAHAR, REMEL EL ABOID, ALGERIA, LIBYA

POPULATION

over 500 000	◉
over 100 000	◎
over 50 000	○
over 10 000	●
under 10 000	·

LAND HEIGHT

1000m/3281ft
500m/1640ft
200m/656ft
Sea Level

N

0   200 km
0   200 miles

WORLD AFFAIRS

AL   AMU   OAU   NAM   GATT

A foreign policy priority is to strengthen
contacts with the West, which have
generally been good because of
Tunisia's liberal economic and social
policies. Attention is focused on ties
with the EU, the main outlet for
Tunisia's agricultural exports.

Tunis has been host to the PLO since
the organization was expelled from the
Lebanon. Relations with other Arab
states, particularly Kuwait and Saudi
Arabia, were soured by Tunisia's
support for Iraq in the Gulf War. The
government would like to see them
restored to their former amicability.
There is concern over the possible
effects of the political success of
Islamic fundamentalism in
neighbouring Algeria. Relations with
Libya are improving, helped by the fact
that Tunisia has been turning a blind
eye to sanction-busters operating
through its territory.

CHRONOLOGY

Tunisia has been home to the Zenata
Berbers since earliest times and its
history is linked to the rise and fall of
the Mediterranean-centred empires.
Carthage (near present-day Tunis),
founded in the 9th century, became
the hub of a 1000-year Phoenician
trading empire which linked
European and African trading
networks. Tunisia was then
incorporated into the Roman,
Byzantine, Arab, Ottoman and,
finally, French empires.

❏ **1883** La Marsa Treaty makes
  Tunisia a French protectorate,
  ending its semi-independence. Bey
  of Tunis remains monarch.
❏ **1900** Influx of French and Italian
  settlers begins.
❏ **1920** Destour (Constitution) Party
  formed; calls for self-government.
❏ **1935** Habib Bourguiba forms Neo-
  Destour (New Constitution) Party.
❏ **1943** Defeat of Axis powers by
  British troops restores French rule.
❏ **1955** Internal autonomy. Bourguiba
  returns from exile.
❏ **1956** Independence. Bourguiba
  elected prime minister. Personal
  Statutes Code gives rights to
  women. Family planning introduced.
❏ **1957** The Bey is deposed. Tunisia
  becomes a republic with Bourguiba
  as first president.
❏ **1964** Neo-Destour becomes the only
  legal political party; changes its
  name to Destour Socialist Party
  (PSD). Moderate socialist economic
  programme is introduced.

T

CHRONOLOGY *continued*

- ❑ **1969** Agricultural collectivization programme, begun 1964, abandoned.
- ❑ **1974** Bourguiba becomes president for life. Trade unions disagree with PSD over economic policy.
- ❑ **1974–1976** Hundreds imprisoned for belonging to 'illegal organizations'.
- ❑ **1978** Trade union movement, UGTT, holds 24-hour general strike; over 50 killed in clashes. UGTT leadership replaced with PSD loyalists.
- ❑ **1980** Guerrillas attack Gafsa in western Tunisia; government forces quickly regain control. New prime minister Muhammed Mazli ushers in greater political tolerance.
- ❑ **1981** Elections. Opposition groups allege electoral malpractice after failing to win enough votes to entitle them to recognition as parties.
- ❑ **1984** Widespread riots after food price increases.
- ❑ **1986** General Zine al-Abidine Ben Ali becomes interior minister. Four Muslim fundamentalists sentenced to death.
- ❑ **1987** Fundamentalist leader Rachid Gannouchi arrested. Ben Ali becomes prime minister; takes over presidency after doctors certify Bourguiba senile. PSD becomes the RCD.
- ❑ **1988** Most political prisoners released. Constitutional reforms introduce multiparty system and abolish life presidency. Two opposition parties legalized.
- ❑ **1989** Elections. RCD wins all seats. Ben Ali president. Fundamentalists take 13% of vote. Gannouchi, now leader of banned Islamic *Al-Nahda* party, goes into exile.
- ❑ **1990** Tunisia backs Iraq over invasion of Kuwait. Clampdown on fundamentalists intensifies.
- ❑ **1991** Abortive coup blamed on *Al-Nahda*; over 500 arrests.
- ❑ **1993** Agreement on electoral reform paves way for opposition parties to participate equally with RCD in 1994 elections.

T

AID

 $322m (receipts)   Down 18% in 1991

France is the major single donor, providing 22% of bilateral aid. Italy, Germany, the World Bank and the African Development Bank are other important sources of assistance. Oil-rich Arab states, including Saudi Arabia and Kuwait, have suspended their aid programmes to Tunisia since 1990 because of its pro-Iraq stance in the Gulf War. Tunisia's total external debt is equivalent to 62% of GNP, making receipts crucial to its development.

DEFENCE

 $508.7m   Up 17% in 1992

0	Defence spending as % GDP	40
3.3%		

Despite its small size – 35,000 troops, 26,400 of them conscripts – the military holds the reins of power behind the scenes of the Ben Ali regime. The army is equipped with US weapons. Border security and potential instability in neighbouring Libya and Algeria are Tunisia's main defence concerns.

TUNISIAN ARMED FORCES

🛡	84 main battle tanks (54 M–60A3/30 M–60A1)	27,000 personnel
🚢	1 frigate and 14 patrol boats	4500 personnel
✈	38 combat aircraft (15 F–5E,–5F)	3500 personnel
🔪	None	

ECONOMICS

 $15.3bn   💲 1.04 dinars

SCORE CARD

❑ WORLD GNP RANKING	67th
❑ GNP PER CAPITA	$1820
❑ BALANCE OF PAYMENTS	$–675m
❑ INFLATION	5.4%
❑ UNEMPLOYMENT	15%

EXPORTS

Belgium and Luxembourg 7%
Other 30%
Germany* 15%
Italy 21%
France 27%

IMPORTS

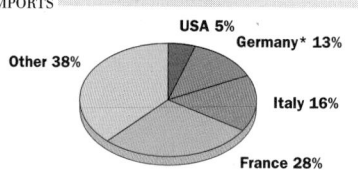

USA 5%
Germany* 13%
Other 38%
Italy 16%
France 28%

STRENGTHS
A well-diversified economy, despite limited resources. Tourism. Oil and gas exports. Manufacturing is expanding. European investment.

WEAKNESSES
Dependence on growth of drought-prone agricultural sector. Growing domestic energy demand on oil and gas resources.

PROFILE
Since it began a process of structural adjustment in 1988, supported by the IMF and World Bank, Tunisia has become an increasingly open, market-orientated economy. Helped by good harvests, real growth averaged almost 6% a year between 1989 and 1993. The budget deficit has been cut to under 2% of GDP, from around 4% in the late 1980s. Prices have been freed, most state companies privatized and import barriers reduced.

The government has also begun a search for foreign investment, which is

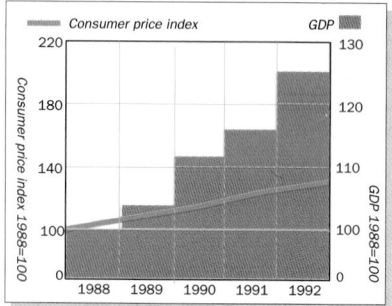

ECONOMIC PERFORMANCE INDICATOR

targeted to treble by 1996. High investment levels are essential if Tunisia is to reach its goal of providing an extra 313,000 jobs for young people over the next two years, let alone cutting the overall 15% unemployment rate. Another problem is the balance of payments, which relies on fluctuating tourism receipts to offset a trade deficit. The government must also balance the demands of growth with those of Tunisia's expanding middle class for better social provisions. Negotiations to increase trading opportunities with the EU, already Tunisia's main trading partner, have begun.

TUNISIA : MAJOR BUSINESSES

Oil
Wine
Chemicals
Phosphates
Textiles
Consumer goods
Leather tanning
Vehicle assembly

* significant multinational ownership

RESOURCES

ELECTRICITY GENERATION

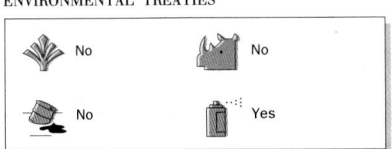

% of total generation by type

Tunisia is one of the world's leading producers of phosphates for fertilizers, mainly from mines near Gafsa. Oil and

TUNISIA : LAND USE

- Cropland
- Forest
- Pasture
- Wetlands
- Desert
- ⊙ Olives - cash crop
- Fruits
- Sheep

0 ——— 100 km
0 ——— 100 miles

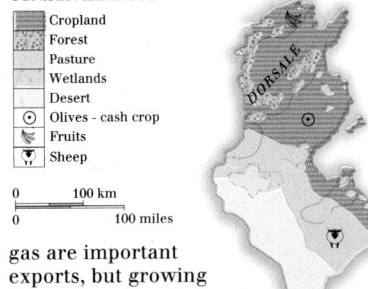

gas are important exports, but growing domestic energy demands mean Tunisia may be a net energy importer by 2000. Electricity is mainly thermal, with some hydro-power.

HEALTH

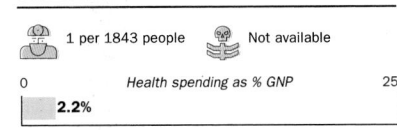

1 per 1843 people   Not available

0   *Health spending as % GNP*   25

2.2%

Well-developed family planning facilities have almost halved Tunisia's birth rate over the past 30 years. The population growth rate has dropped from 3.2% to 1.9% – the lowest in the region. The mortality rate has been more than halved, to around 48,000 a year, reflecting the extension of free medical services to over 70% of the population. Services lack sophistication, but an umbrella of primary care facilities covers all but the most isolated rural communities.

ENVIRONMENT

 0.3%   Mass tourism is an ecological threat

ENVIRONMENTAL TREATIES

No   No
No   Yes

Desertification is a serious problem in the largely arid central and southern regions. However, the dominant environmental issue is the rapid expansion of tourism since the 1980s. Large, insensitively designed hotel and resort developments, which do not fit in with the local architecture, are spoiling coastal areas such as the Isle of Jerba and Hammamet. Tourism is also making an impact on the fragile desert ecology of the south, previously protected by its isolated position.

MEDIA

 The press has enjoyed considerable freedom since 1987, but government still interferes at times

PUBLISHING AND BROADCAST MEDIA

There are 5 daily newspapers, *L'Action*, *al-Amal*, *La Presse de Tunisie*, *La Presse-Soir* and *As-Sabah*

1 state-owned service   1 state-owned service

Arabsat 1C   None

Reforms since the late 1980s have in theory increased press freedom in Tunisia, a country traditionally considered a source of liberal ideas in the Arab world. In practice, government restrictions remain. The foreign press is also occasionally banned, but the arrival of satellite TV from Europe has meant that people can receive a wide range of programmes in their homes.

CRIME

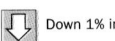 Tunisia does not publish crime figures   Down 1% in 1985

CRIME RATES

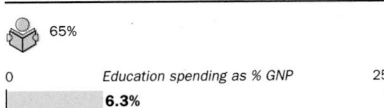

Murders
2 *per 100,000 population*

Rapes
8 *per 100,000 population*

Thefts
349 *per 100,000 population*

Street crime is unusual. Tunisia has a good human rights record. However, there were reports of the severe maltreatment of hundreds of Islamic fundamentalists, detained without trial by the authorities, following the abortive coup in 1991.

EDUCATION

 65%

0   *Education spending as % GNP*   25

6.3%

THE EDUCATION SYSTEM

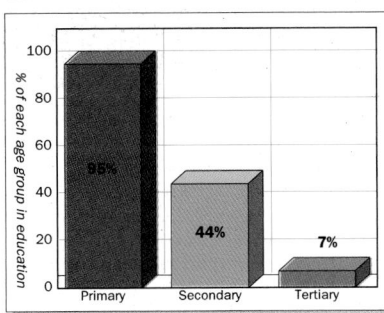

% of each age group in education

95% Primary
44% Secondary
7% Tertiary

Schooling is not compulsory, but about 80% of school-age children attend school. French is taught from the second year of primary school and is used almost exclusively in higher education. There are two universities.

WEALTH

 Waiter, 0.8 dinars per hour; journalist, 1.7 dinars per hour

CONSUMER GOODS OWNERSHIP

VCR and PC ownership is limited to a small elite

75   39   43

Per 1000 population

Today 7% of Tunisians are estimated to live in absolute poverty. In 1970 it was 30%. The poorest tend to live in the urban shanty towns, or *bidonvilles*. The Western-orientated elite has links to government or business. Social security covers sickness, old age and maternity, but not unemployment, currently at 15%. The government is concerned that unemployment is encouraging the spread of Islamic fundamentalism. Economic growth is its medium-term solution to the problem. Special projects are being set up in the most deprived urban areas to offset the worst effects of poverty.

WORLD RANKING

T

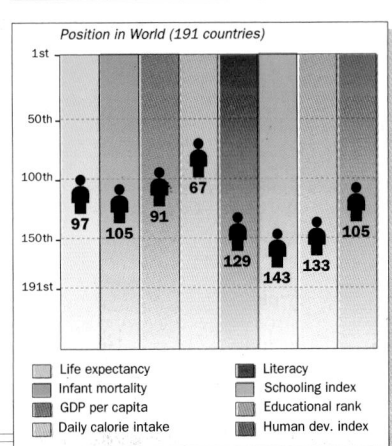

Position in World (191 countries)

1st
50th
100th
150th
191st

97   105   91   67   129   143   133   105

- Life expectancy
- Infant mortality
- GDP per capita
- Daily calorie intake
- Literacy
- Schooling index
- Educational rank
- Human dev. index

TURKEY

OFFICIAL NAME: Republic of Turkey   **CAPITAL:** Ankara
POPULATION: 58.4 million   **CURRENCY:** Turkish lira   **OFFICIAL LANGUAGE:** Turkish

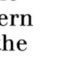

A SECULAR ISLAMIC STATE, Turkey occupies the peninsula of Asia Minor and the region of Eastern Thrace in Europe. It thus controls the entrance to the Black Sea, which is straddled by Turkey's largest city, Istanbul. The majority of Turks live in the western half of the country. The eastern and southeastern reaches of the Anatolia Plateau are Kurdish regions. Turkey's strategic location gives it significant influence in the Mediterranean, Black Sea and Middle East. Since the break-up of the USSR, Turkey has also been developing trading links with Central Asia.

The island of Akdamar, eastern Anatolia. Surrounded by Lake Van, the island is the site of the 10th-century Church of the Holy Cross.

CLIMATE

WEATHER CHART

 Average daily temperature   Rainfall

Coastal regions have a Mediterranean climate. The interior has cold, snowy winters and hot, dry summers.

COMMUNICATIONS

 Atatürk Intl, Ankara
10m passengers

 703 ships
6.88m dwt

THE TRANSPORT NETWORK

59,128 km (36,740 miles)		826 km (513 miles)
8439 km (5244 miles)		1200 km (746 miles)

The rail system is well-developed. Plans exist for a $4-billion rail tunnel under the Boğazi, and for a high-speed link between Istanbul and Ankara. More motorways are planned, including a road bridge across the Dardanelles.

TOURISM

 7.8m visitors

 Up 41% in 1992

As well as major classical sites such as Ephesus and Troy on the Aegean coast, Turkey is rich in antiquities of both the Ottoman and Byzantine periods. Istanbul is a magnet for shoppers, especially collectors of antiques and carpets. Southern Turkey has fine beaches. Tourism is a major foreign currency earner. Hotels are now being built to higher standards.

PEOPLE

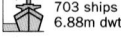 Turkish, Kurdish, Arabic, Circassian, Armenian, Greek, Georgian, Ladino

72 people per km²

THE URBAN/RURAL POPULATION SPLIT

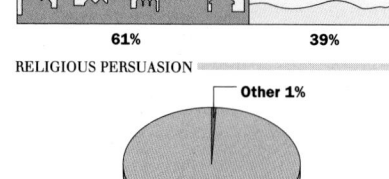

61%   39%

RELIGIOUS PERSUASION

Other 1%

Muslim (mainly Sunni) 99%

ETHNIC MAKEUP

Other 3%   Kurdish 17%

Turkish 80%

The Turks are racially diverse. Many are refugees or the descendants of refugees, often from the Balkans or other territories once under Russian rule. However, the sense of national identity is strong, rooted in a shared language and religion – the majority is Sunni Muslim, though there is a fast-growing Shi'a community in central Anatolia. The largest minority – 2.5 million – are the

POPULATION AGE BREAKDOWN

%	0–14	15–64	65+

	1960	1970	1980	1990	2000
65+	3.5%	4.4%	4.7%	4.2%	5.6%
15–64	55.2%	54.5%	56.1%	61.2%	62.6%
0–14	41.3%	41.1%	39.2%	34.6%	31.8%

Kurds, while some 500,000 people, mainly in the southeast, are Arabic speakers. Women have equal rights and Turkey's first woman prime minister came to power in 1993.

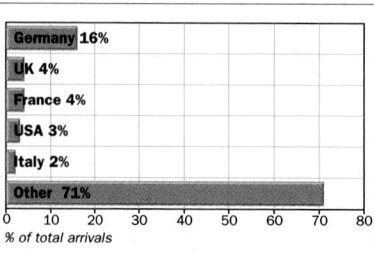

MAIN OVERSEAS ARRIVALS

Germany	16%
UK	4%
France	4%
USA	3%
Italy	2%
Other	71%

% of total arrivals

POLITICS

 1996

 President Süleyman Demirel

THE STATE OF THE PARTIES

National Assembly 450 members

| 39% DYP | 25% ANAP | 20% SHP/ HEP | 14% RP/ MÇP | 2% DSP |

DYP = True Path Party **ANAP** = Motherland Party
SHP = Social Democratic Populist Party **HEP** = People's
Labour Party **RP** = Welfare Party **MÇP** = Nationalist Labour
Party **DSP** = Democratic Left Party

By the 1982 constitution, Turkey is a multiparty republic with a national assembly elected every five years. The president serves a seven-year term and appoints the prime minister.

MAIN POLITICAL ISSUES

Islamic fundamentalism

In the municipal elections of 1994, the Islamic fundamentalist RP took 18% of the vote. The backers of the RP are mostly the poor of Turkey's urban slums. However, the RP's rise represents a growing challenge from below to the Westernizing secularist path that Turkey has been following since Atatürk's rule. Whether the fundamentalists can be contained within the democratic framework is now a central issue in Turkish politics.

Kurdish separatists

Turkey's southeastern region has been the scene of a bitter civil war since 1984. Kurdish secessionists are led by the Kurdistan Workers Party (PKK). Thousands have died in conflict with the Turkish army. The PKK agreed a cease-fire in 1993 and declared that they no longer wished for secession, but for recognition of Kurdish rights within Turkey. There is pressure on the government, which has spent $7 billion on containing the conflict, to reach a settlement.

PROFILE

In recent years, political parties have proliferated in Turkish politics. They encompass centre, right and left, social democrat and extremes of neo-fascists, socialists and Islamic radicals. Party distinctions are often highly artificial and frequently have more to do with personalities than politics.

With Süleyman Demirel's accession to the presidency in 1993, the leadership of the ruling centre-right DYP was won by ex-economics professor, Mrs Tansu Çiller, whose personal popularity helped the DYP to a narrow win in the 1994 elections. In practice, there is often little to distinguish the DYP from the second largest party, ANAP. The DYP draws its support mainly from the small towns of Anatolia and the Aegean, while ANAP is strongly supported by Istanbul's business community.

Under former Prime Minister Turgut Özal, Muslim fundamentalists were allowed a greater voice in politics. However, should their popularity increase to the point where Turkey's pro-Western secularism is threatened, the army could once more step in to run the government.

Mrs Tansu Çiller, prime minister since 1993 and committed free-marketeer.

Turgut Özal, who died in 1993, presided over several years of prosperity.

WORLD AFFAIRS

 NATO OECD CSCE CE GATT

With the end of the Cold War, Turkey's strategic value as NATO's first Western line of defence against the USSR has diminished. Turkey is now redefining its world role by exploring closer ties with neighbouring states. In 1992, Turkey hosted the first meeting of the Black Sea Economic Co-operation Region, involving Greece, Albania and several former Soviet republics. The government has also tried to mediate between Armenia and Azerbaijan.

As a base for operations against Iraq in the 1991 Gulf War, Turkey gave valuable assistance to the Western-led coalition, and was rewarded with economic aid. Membership of the EU, once a cherished goal, is now accepted as a distant prospect. Greece will oppose Ankara's membership as long as Turkey continues to occupy northern Cyprus. Trading links with the EU are close, however, and Turkey will join the EU customs union in 1995.

AID

 $1.6bn (receipts)   Up 30% in 1991

Turkey has a foreign debt of over $50 billion and is a net recipient of aid. The government received over $4 billion in grants and credits after the Gulf War, mainly from Saudi Arabia, Kuwait and Japan. Turkey supports peace between Israel and the Palestinians and has promised the West Bank $52 million in cash and credits.

TURKEY

Total Area : 779 450 sq. km (300 950 sq. miles)

LAND HEIGHT	POPULATION
3000m/9843ft	over 1 000 000
2000m/6562ft	over 500 000
1000m/3281ft	over 100 000
500m/1640ft	over 50 000
200m/656ft	over 10 000
Sea Level	under 10 000

T

CHRONOLOGY

Following the collapse of the Ottoman Empire and Turkey's defeat in the First World War, nationalist Mustafa Kemal Atatürk deposed the ruling sultan in 1922, declaring Turkey a republic in 1923.

❏ **1924** Religious courts abolished.

❏ **1928** Islam no longer the state religion.

❏ **1934** Women given the vote. Western-style surnames adopted.

❏ **1938** President Ataturk dies. Succeeded by Ismet Inonu.

❏ **1945** Turkey declares war on Germany and joins UN.

❏ **1947** Military assistance agreement signed with USA.

❏ **1952** Turkey admitted to Council of Europe and NATO.

❏ **1960** Army stages coup against ruling Democratic Party and suspends National Assembly.

❏ **1961** Fresh elections held after new constitution is approved by referendum. Party politics restored.

❏ **1963** Association agreement signed with EEC.

❏ **1974** After clashes between Greek and Turkish Cypriots, Turkish troops invade Cyprus and occupy northern part of the island.

❏ **1980** Armed forces overthrow the Demirel government's Justice Party and suspend party politics. Turkey under military rule for three years.

❏ **1982** New constitution enforced after referendum.

❏ **1983** General election won by Turgut Özal's Motherland Party.

❏ **1984** Ambassadors exchanged with 'Turkish Republic of Northern Cyprus'. Kurdish separatist PKK launch guerrilla war in southeast provinces.

❏ **1987** Turkey applies for full membership of EC.

❏ **1989** EC delays consideration of full membership until completion of single European market. Strained relations with Bulgaria over assimilation policy, which results in influx of 300,000 Turkish refugees.

❏ **1990** Allied powers permitted to operate air strikes against Iraq from Turkish bases. Escalating clashes between security forces and PKK.

❏ **1991** Iraqi Kurds, fleeing Iraqi army, try to cross Turkish border. Elections won by DYP, led by Süleyman Demirel.

❏ **1992** Turkey joins Black Sea alliance. Racist attacks on Turkish workers in Germany.

❏ **1993** Demirel elected president. Mrs Çiller becomes DYP leader and prime minister. Ceasefire with PKK breaks down and conflict resumes.

DEFENCE

💲 $4.2bn   ⬆ Up 16% in 1992

0   *Defence spending as % GDP*   40

3.1%

TURKISH ARMED FORCES

	3928 main battle tanks (523 M-47/1130 M-48A1 1980 M-48A5)	450,000 personnel
	12 submarines, 12 destroyers, 8 frigates and 47 patrol boats	52,300 personnel
	573 combat aircraft (F-16C,-D/F-5/F-4E/F-104)	58,000 Personnel
	None	

The army has, on occasion, intervened in Turkish politics (the last time was the 1980 military coup), and its leaders often determine the shape of governments. With 18 months' service compulsory for all males at the age of 20, Turkey is a sizeable military power. However, defence spending is slightly below average. Thanks to NATO membership, Turkey has access to Western arms suppliers. The air force flies F-16 fighters, while the navy has German-made frigates and the army is supplied with modern battle tanks. Over 20,000 troops have been deployed to fight Kurdish separatists based in northern Iraq and in Turkey's own southeastern provinces.

ECONOMICS

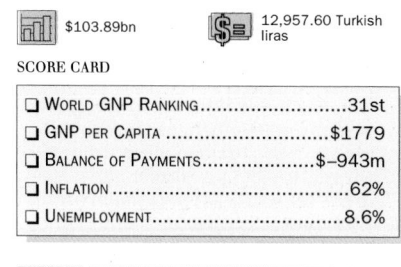

📊 $103.89bn   💹 12,957.60 Turkish liras

SCORE CARD

❏ WORLD GNP RANKING 31st
❏ GNP PER CAPITA $1779
❏ BALANCE OF PAYMENTS...................$–943m
❏ INFLATION 62%
❏ UNEMPLOYMENT................................8.6%

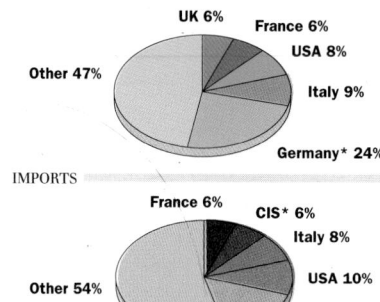

EXPORTS

UK 6%
France 6%
USA 8%
Other 47%
Italy 9%
Germany* 24%

IMPORTS

France 6%
CIS* 6%
Italy 8%
Other 54%
USA 10%
Germany* 16%

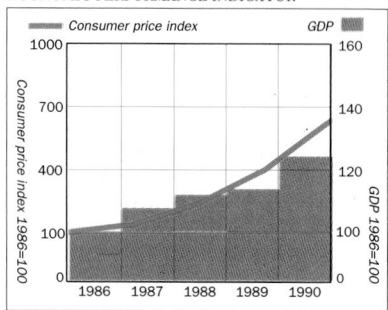

ECONOMIC PERFORMANCE INDICATOR

Consumer price index   GDP

Consumer price index 1986=100 — 1000, 700, 400, 100, 0

GDP 1986=100 — 160, 140, 120, 100, 0

1986 1987 1988 1989 1990

process of liberalization and increased competition began. The result was an unprecedented growth in exports. Turkey also has foreign currency reserves of $17 billion. However, the cost of rapid expansion has been high inflation, and government spending has not been brought under control. Public finances are also burdened by the loss-making state sector, low tax income and an annual population growth of 2.1%.

STRENGTHS

Liberalized economy resulted in the highest growth rate in the OECD in early 1990s. Self-sufficient in agriculture. Textiles, manufacturing and construction sectors competitive on world markets. Tourism industry.

WEAKNESSES

High inflation and unemployment. Many companies protected from external competition by high tariff barriers, due to come down when Turkey joins EU customs union in 1995. Shortage of investment capital. High costs of civil war with Kurds. Many sectors of state-owned economy making huge losses: $3 billion in 1993.

PROFILE

Turkey's economy began its dramatic growth in the early 1980s when a

TURKEY : MAJOR BUSINESSES

Istanbul   Ankara
Bursa   Kırıkkale
İzmit   Erzurum
Sivas
İsparta   Adana   Diyarbakır
İzmir   Mersin

Cement	Oil refining
Textiles	Iron & steel
Chemicals	Food processing
Electronics	Vehicle manufacture

0   200 km
0   200 miles

* significant multinational ownership

T

RESOURCES

 57.5bn kwh (capacity 16.3m kw)

 82,300 b/d (reserves 474,761,000 bbl)

 34.9m sheep, 13.1m goats, 11.8m cattle

Chromium, copper, borax, coal, natural gas, bauxite, iron

ELECTRICITY GENERATION

Hydro 40% (23.1bn kwh)

Thermal 60% (34.3bn kwh)

Nuclear 0%

Other 0%

% of total generation by type

In the mid-1980s Turkey launched the Southeastern Anatolian Projects. Harnessing the waters of the Euphrates and Tigris rivers, massive dams will allow the irrigation of 1.7 million hectares of land. Eighteen HEP stations will further increase Turkey's generating capacity.

Turkey produces oil in Garcan and Raman and some local refining takes place. The eastern Asian provinces are rich in minerals, such as chromium, of which Turkey is the world's largest producer.

TURKEY : LAND USE

0   200 km
0   200 miles

Cropland
Pasture
Forest
High mountain regions
Wheat
Tobacco - cash crop
Sheep

ENVIRONMENT

 0.4% (0.1% partially protected)

 Yacht-tourism threat to marine ecosystems in south and west

ENVIRONMENTAL TREATIES

No   No

No   No

Turkey's programme of dam-building on the Tigris and Euphrates has met with international condemnation, particularly from Syria and Iraq, whose rivers will suffer reduced flow rates as a result. Concern has also been expressed at plans to build a nuclear power plant. Much of the western coast has been spoiled by lack of planning and by uncontrolled tourist developments.

MEDIA

 Harsh laws inhibit freedom of expression

PUBLISHING AND BROADCAST MEDIA

There are 10 daily newspapers with national distribution. The leaders are the serious *Cumhuriyet* and the sensationalist *Hürriyet*

1 state-owned service   1 state-run service

Arabsat 1C, Intelsat V1 F1   None

The Turkish press is diverse, vigorous and largely privately-owned, but political debate is subject to censorship laws dating back to the 1980 military coup. Espousing the Kurdish cause is banned. Although Islam is the dominant religion, the media is not subject to the moral censorship found in the Gulf states. Almost all Istanbul newspapers are printed in Ankara and Izmir on the same day. Four have circulations of over 300,000 copies.

As an addition to programming offered by the state-owned Turkish Radio and Television Corporation, many Turks are now buying satellite dishes to receive foreign broadcasts.

CRIME

 51,800 prisoners

 Down 6% in 1990

CRIME RATES

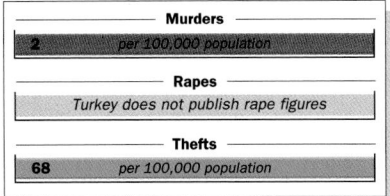

Murders

2   per 100,000 population

Rapes

Turkey does not publish rape figures

Thefts

68   per 100,000 population

Most crime levels are stable or falling slightly, although there has been an increase in drugs-related crime. The routine torture of prisoners by the police was an issue in the 1993 elections and the government intends to limit the force's powers.

EDUCATION

 81%

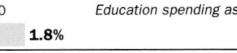

0   Education spending as % GNP   25

1.8%

THE EDUCATION SYSTEM

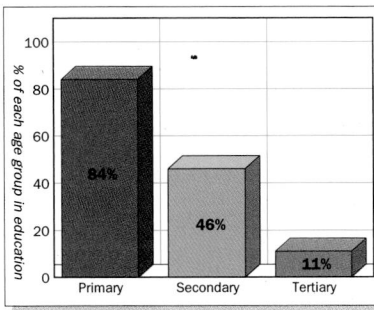

% of each age group in education

84% Primary
46% Secondary
11% Tertiary

On the formation of the Turkish republic, all educational establishments were nationalized. In 1928, a Turkish alphabet was introduced using Latin characters. Turkey spends 10% of its state budget on education – a relatively high figure. Engineering is usually the strongest faculty in Turkey's many universities.

HEALTH

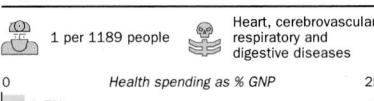 1 per 1189 people

Heart, cerebrovascular, respiratory and digestive diseases

0   Health spending as % GNP   25

1.5%

Turkey possesses an adequate national system of primary health care. By Western standards, however, hospitals are under-equipped.

WEALTH

 Tanner, 4535 Turkish liras per hour; chemical engineer, 2.53m Turkish liras per month

CONSUMER GOODS OWNERSHIP

Per 1000 population

PCs limited to an elite

174   25   117   44

The economic expansion of the 1980s has created a new class of wealthy entrepreneurs. High inflation has meant that many on fixed incomes have fared badly in the last decade, however. Many Turks chose to work abroad as guest workers in Germany and the Netherlands.

WORLD RANKING

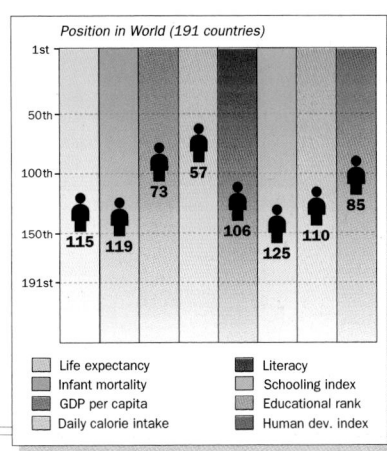

Position in World (191 countries)

1st
50th
100th
150th
191st

115   119   73   57   106   125   110   85

Life expectancy
Infant mortality
GDP per capita
Daily calorie intake
Literacy
Schooling index
Educational rank
Human dev. index

T

TURKMENISTAN

OFFICIAL NAME: Republic of Turkmenistan CAPITAL: Ashgabat
POPULATION: 3.9 million CURRENCY: Manat OFFICIAL LANGUAGE: Turkmen

CENTRAL ASIA

Asia

ORIGINALLY THE POOREST state among the former Soviet republics, Turkmenistan has adjusted better than most to independence, exploiting the market value of its abundant natural gas supplies. A largely Sunni Muslim area, Turkmenistan is part of the former Turkestan, the last expanse of Central Asia incorporated into Tsarist Russia. Much of life is still based on tribal relationships. Turkmenistan is isolated – telephones are rare and TV barely available.

CLIMATE

WEATHER CHART

Most of Turkmenistan is arid desert. Only 2% of the total land area is suitable for agriculture.

COMMUNICATIONS

Ashgabat

Has no fleet

THE TRANSPORT NETWORK

22,600 km (14,043 miles) / None
2120 km (1317 miles) / None

The road and rail links to Teheran will be the first to be upgraded. There are plans to modernize Ashgabat airport.

TOURISM

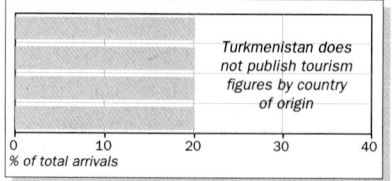

Levels of tourist arrivals low

Slight increase

MAIN OVERSEAS ARRIVALS

Turkmenistan does not publish tourism figures by country of origin

Most visitors are businessmen attracted by Turkmenistan's stability under President Niyazov. Turkmenistan may become a popular tourist destination in future; traditional Turkmen Muslim monuments are slowly being restored.

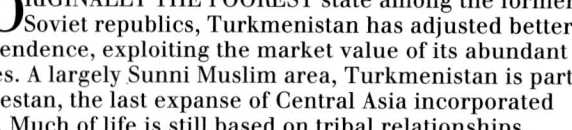

Kara Kum Canal zone: salt flats and the Kopetdag mountains on the Iranian border. The Kara Kum is Turkmenistan's largest desert.

PEOPLE

Turkmen, Uzbek, Russian

7 people per km²

THE URBAN/RURAL POPULATION SPLIT

45% 55%

RELIGIOUS PERSUASION

Other 5% Eastern Orthodox 10% Muslim 85%

Before Tsarist Russia annexed Turkmenistan in 1884, the Turkmen were a largely nomadic tribal people. The tribal unit remains strong – the largest tribes are the Tekke in the centre, the Ersary on the eastern Afghan border and the Yomud in the west. It is tribal conflicts among the Turkmen, rather than tensions with the two main minorities – Russians and Uzbeks – that are a source of strife. Paradoxically, this has meant that since independence from Moscow there has been less virulent nationalism than in other ex-Soviet republics. Since 1989, Turkmenistan has been rehabilitating its traditional language and culture, as well as reassessing its history. Islam is again central to the Turkmen, although few make the *haj* (pilgrimage) to Mecca and many continue to maintain a cult of ancestors.

POLITICS

Uncertain

President Gen Saparmurat Niyazov

THE STATE OF THE PARTIES

Parliament 50 members

Elections were last held in 1990. The Democratic Party of Turkmenistan (DPT), the former Communist Party, is the ruling party. The government-sponsored Peasants' Justice Party is the one other authorized party

People's Council

Comprises 60 elected members, the members of the Council of Ministers and others.

Officially, Turkmenistan became a multiparty democracy in 1990. As in other ex-Soviet states, however, the old Communist nomenklatura still controls the political process in practice: the Communists renamed themselves the Democratic Party of Turkmenistan in 1991. The DPT has maintained the communist suspicion of Islamic fundamentalism as promoted by Iran. President Niyazov has developed an extreme personality cult. He sustains his popularity with measures such as providing free electricity and water.

The main political concern is to prevent the social and nationalistic conflicts that have blighted other CIS republics. Broad policy is communist. Russian remains the bureaucratic language and gas revenues are still used to subsidize inefficient industry and agriculture.

WORLD AFFAIRS

CIS CSCE NACC IBRD

Turkmenistan is concentrating on establishing good relations with both Iran and Turkey. It needs investment from both countries, but wishes to avoid the Islamic fundamentalism promoted by the Iranians. President Niyazov opposes economic union with the CIS, fearing this would compromise Turkmenistan's control of its gas fields.

AID

Minimal receipts

Slight increase from year to year

Aid is mostly concentrated in the oil and gas industries and comes from Turkey, Iran, Switzerland and Germany.

T

POPULATION

over 100 000	◎
over 50 000	○
over 10 000	●
under 10 000	•

LAND HEIGHT

1000m/1640ft
500m/1640ft
200m/656ft
Sea Level
-200m/-656ft

TURKMENISTAN

Total Area : 488 100 sq. km (188 455 sq. miles)

0   200 km
0   200 miles

N

CHRONOLOGY

The nomadic peoples of Western Turkestan came under Russian imperial control from the 1850s.

❑ **1881** Russians found Ashkhabad (present-day Ashgabat).
❑ **1906** Mass colonization starts.
❑ **1924** Turkestan divided into five republics, including Turkmenistan.
❑ **1940** Cyrillic replaces Turkish.
❑ **1948** Earthquake destroys capital.
❑ **1991** Independence from USSR.

EDUCATION

 Literacy rate amongst lowest of ex-Soviet republics

The Turkmen language and literature (banned until 1987) are now on the syllabus. However, Russian schools still have the highest standards.

HEALTH

 1 per 274 people   Heart, cerebrovascular and respiratory diseases

Highly polluted water is a major health hazard; only 35% of the population have treated mains supply.

WEALTH

 The unemployed and the old form the poorest group. The extended family system and subsidies often prevent absolute poverty

CONSUMER GOODS OWNERSHIP

TV and radio ownership is limited to a small elite   *VCR and PC ownership is limited to a small elite*

67

The ex-Communist bureaucrats are still the richest group. They favour Japanese and Korean luxury goods.

DEFENCE

 $11bn    Little change in defence spending

Compared to other states in the region, Turkmenistan is reasonably stable. Its army is under joint control with Russia, on whom it is dependent for defence.

ECONOMICS

 $6.4bn   Official exchange rate not established

SCORE CARD

❑ WORLD GNP RANKING	98th
❑ GNP PER CAPITA	$1650
❑ BALANCE OF PAYMENTS	$2553m
❑ INFLATION	90%
❑ UNEMPLOYMENT	2.5%

STRENGTHS
Cotton and gas. Turkmenistan was the USSR's major supplier of cotton and supplied 12% of gas. Hard currency trading has meant that real prices are being paid for these commodities for the first time – under the USSR only 1% of profits returned to Turkmenistan.

WEAKNESSES
Cotton mono-culture means most food has to be imported. The least industrialized ex-Soviet state: most plant dates back to the 1920s.

EXPORTS/IMPORTS

Most imports and exports are still from and to Russia and other CIS republics. However, Turkmenistan is beginning to establish a wide range of Western contacts

RESOURCES

 15.8bn kwh   101,200 b/d

5.4m sheep and goats, 774,000 cattle   Potassium, sulphur, sodium sulphate

During the Soviet years most Turkmen agriculture was turned over to cotton – seen by Moscow as a strategic crop.

ENVIRONMENT

 2.3%   Greater awareness of environmental problems

The building of the Kara Kum Canal, hailed as a progressive move by Moscow in 1958, has drained 35% of the Aral Sea's water, leading to an increase in unproductive salinated soil.

MEDIA

 The government controls all media. Censorship is widespread

PUBLISHING AND BROADCAST MEDIA

There are 66 newspapers, including *Turkmenskaya iskra, Edebiyat ve sungat,* and *Novcha,* a weekly newspaper for children

1 state-controlled service   1 state-controlled service

Iranian and Afghan radio stations, beaming in Islamic programmes, are popular. TV is only available in cities.

CRIME

 Turkmenistan does not publish prison figures   Increasing levels of theft

Levels of crime are low compared with neighbouring ex-Soviet republics. Theft, however, is on the increase.

WORLD RANKING

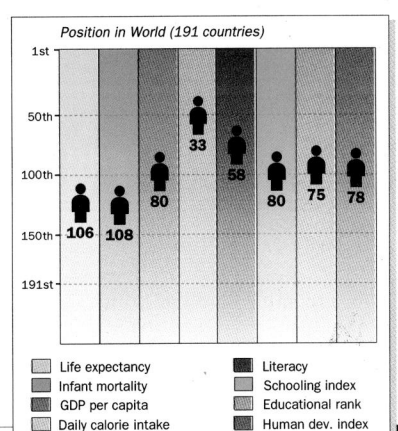

Position in World (191 countries)

☐ Life expectancy	☐ Literacy
☐ Infant mortality	☐ Schooling index
☐ GDP per capita	☐ Educational rank
☐ Daily calorie intake	☐ Human dev. index

T

TUVALU

OFFICIAL NAME: Tuvalu **CAPITAL:** Fongafale **POPULATION:** 9100
CURRENCIES: Australian dollar, Tuvaluan dollar **OFFICIAL LANGUAGE:** *No official language*

ONE OF THE WORLD'S SMALLEST, most isolated states, Tuvalu lies 1050 km north of Fiji in the central Pacific. A chain of nine coral atolls, 579 km long, it has a land area of just over 25 sq km. As the Ellice Islands, it was linked to the Gilbert Islands as a British colony until independence in 1978. Politically and socially conservative, Tuvaluans live by subsistence farming and fishing.

CLIMATE

WEATHER CHART

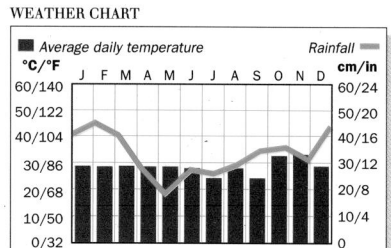

Although average humidity exceeds 90%, the climate is pleasantly warm. The mean annual temperature is 29°C. The October–March hurricane season brings many violent storms.

COMMUNICATIONS

 There is an airstrip on Funafuti atoll

5 ships 15,800 dwt

THE TRANSPORT NETWORK

8 km (5 miles)	None
None	None

A ferry links the atolls. There are air links with Kiribati and Fiji. Funafuti and Nukufetau have deep-water berths.

TOURISM

976 visitors

Up 45% in 1945

MAIN OVERSEAS ARRIVALS

Australia 13%								
New Zealand 7%								
USA 6%								
Other 74%								

0 10 20 30 40 50 60 70 80
% of total arrivals

Unspoiled and lapped by some of the world's warmest waters, these remote coral atolls have few visitors. Tourism plans focus around the recently paved airstrip, and Taiwanese investment in Tuvalu's only hotel, on Funafuti.

PEOPLE

 Tuvaluan, Kiribati, English

 364 people per km²

THE URBAN/RURAL POPULATION SPLIT

29% 71%

RELIGIOUS PERSUASION

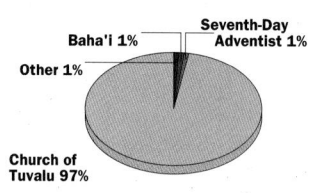

Seventh-Day Adventist 1%
Baha'i 1%
Other 1%
Church of Tuvalu 97%

Around 95% of Tuvaluans are Polynesian. Their ancestors came from Tonga and Samoa 2000 years ago. Nui atoll has Micronesian influences. There is an I-Kiribati community on Funafuti; many Tuvaluans who worked in Kiribati took local wives. All nine islands are inhabited. However, over 40% of the population now lives on Funafuti, pushing its population density to almost 1500 per km². Life is still communal, traditional and hard. Droughts are common and fresh water is precious. About 80% of people depend on subsistence farming, digging special pits out of the coral to grow most of the islands' limited range of crops. Fishing is also important, and Tuvaluans have a reputation as excellent sailors. Some 2000 Tuvaluans work overseas, many in Nauru's phosphate mines, others as merchant seamen.

Tuvalu's soil is porous, but sufficiently fertile to support coconut palms, pandanus and salt-tolerant plants. Fresh water supply is limited.

POLITICS

1997

HM Queen Elizabeth II

THE STATE OF THE PARTIES
Parliament 12 members

There are no political parties. All members are Independent candidates

The 12 MPs, elected every four years, are independents who work in loose political associations. The prime minister, an MP elected by Parliament, works with a cabinet of up to four other MPs. After the 1993 elections, MPs were evenly divided between the two men who had dominated politics for most of the post-independence period, Tomasi Puapua and Bikenibeu Paeniu. After a second general election, Puapua pulled out of the premiership contest. Paeniu was then defeated by Kamuta Laatasi, BP Oil's manager in Tuvalu. Day-to-day administration is in the hands of elected councils on each island.

WORLD AFFAIRS

 SPF   SPC   Comm   ACP   PSCAP

Agreements have been signed with Taiwan, Korea and the USA allowing their boats to exploit Tuvalu's fish-rich 1.2 million sq km exclusive economic zone in return for licensing fees. British criticism of the government's economic policy and Tuvaluan attacks on the pace of UK aid disbursements have strained relations with the former colonial power since 1990.

AID

 $7m (receipts)

 Steady aid receipts

With import costs over 400 times export earnings, aid is crucial to Tuvalu. Most importantly, in 1987, a trust fund was set up, with $A41 million in grants from Australia, New Zealand and the UK, to provide a regular income for Tuvalu. The first two are still major donors. The UK is reducing its aid as support from Taiwan and Japan grows.

DEFENCE

 There are no armed forces

 Not applicable

Tuvalu has no military. Internal security is the responsibility of the small police force.

T

ECONOMICS

 $46m

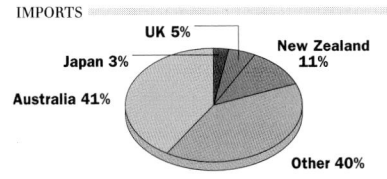 1.48 Australian dollars

SCORE CARD

- WORLD GNP RANKING........................191st
- GNP PER CAPITA $530
- BALANCE OF PAYMENTS ....Deficit
- INFLATION 8%
- UNEMPLOYMENT ....Low

STRENGTHS

Exclusive Economic Zone: a source of jobs, and income through fishing licence fees. Possible mineral potential. Regular income from trust fund. Sustainable subsistence economy.

WEAKNESSES

World's smallest economy. Physical

RESOURCES

 3m kwh

Not an oil producer and has no refineries

 11,000 pigs

None

Tuvalu's resource potential lies solely in the waters of its 1.2 million km² Exclusive Economic Zone (EEZ). Its rich fish stocks are being exploited mainly by foreign boats in return for licensing fees. However, Japan has donated fishing boats to Tuvalu and deep-water fishing is being developed. Hopes of valuable mineral reserves have been raised by the discovery of an undersea mountain in the EEZ. Solar energy is being developed to cut the use of petrol for power generation. Fuel accounts for about 14% of import costs.

TUVALU

Total Area : 26 sq. km (10 sq. miles)

POPULATION
- under 10 000

LAND HEIGHT
100m/328ft
Sea Level

0   100 km
0   100 miles

EXPORTS

Tuvalu does not publish export figures by country of destination

IMPORTS

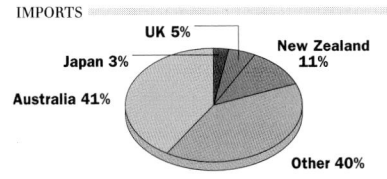

UK 5%
Japan 3%
New Zealand 11%
Australia 41%
Other 40%

isolation. Few exports: copra, stamps, garments. Few potential new income sources. Dependence on imports and aid. Remittances set to fall as Nauru phosphate mines nearly worked out.

ENVIRONMENT

 None

 Initiatives counterbalanced by population pressure

Efforts to protect the environmentally fragile atolls include reafforestation and solar energy projects. On Funafuti, population pressure is leading to overfishing in the atoll lagoon. The 'greenhouse effect' is a major concern since climate changes attributed to it are blamed for a steep rise in cyclone frequency. Any rise in sea levels induced by global warming would quickly drown the atolls.

MEDIA

 There is no censorship of the media

PUBLISHING AND BROADCAST MEDIA

There are no daily newspapers. *Sikuleo o Tuvalu* and *Tuvalu Echoes*, in Tuvaluan and English respectively, are published fortnightly

 No TV service

 1 independent service

Two fortnightly papers and a religious monthly, *Te Lama*, are the only publications. Many people have VCRs.

CRIME

 Tuvalu does not publish prison figures

Little change from year to year

Crime is minimal and the result mainly of alcohol-related violence, particularly at the weekends.

EDUCATION

 95%

Each island has a primary school. A secondary school and a marine training school are based on Funafuti. There are 20 state-funded students at the University of the South Pacific.

HEALTH

 1 per 1750 people

Malaria, diarrheal, infectious and parasitic diseases

Concerted efforts since independence to improve health care facilities and programmes have cut the incidence of communicable diseases. However, infant mortality rates remain high and life expectancy, at 59 years, is still well below the Pacific average of 71 years.

WEALTH

 Small wealth disparities

CONSUMER GOODS OWNERSHIP

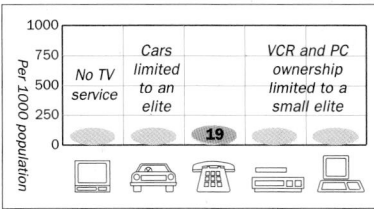

No TV service | Cars limited to an elite | VCR and PC ownership limited to a small elite

19

Although living standards are very low, traditional social support systems mean extreme poverty is rare. Most people rely on subsistence agriculture and fishing, supplemented by remittances from expatriate Tuvaluans.

WORLD RANKING

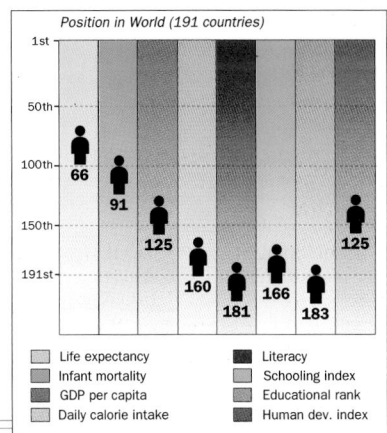

Position in World (191 countries)

66
91
125
160
181
166
183
125

Life expectancy
Infant mortality
GDP per capita
Daily calorie intake
Literacy
Schooling index
Educational rank
Human dev. index

553

UGANDA

EAST AFRICA

OFFICIAL NAME: Republic of Uganda **CAPITAL:** Kampala
POPULATION: 18.7 million **CURRENCY:** New Uganda shilling **OFFICIAL LANGUAGE:** English

A N EAST AFRICAN COUNTRY of fertile upland
plateau and mountains, Uganda has outlets to
the sea through Kenya and Tanzania. Its history from
independence in 1962 until 1986 was one of ethnic strife. Since 1986,
under President Museveni, peace has been restored and steps taken to
rebuild the economy and democracy.

Kampala, Uganda's capital. It lies in the country's most populated region close to Lake Victoria, the world's third largest lake.

CLIMATE

WEATHER CHART

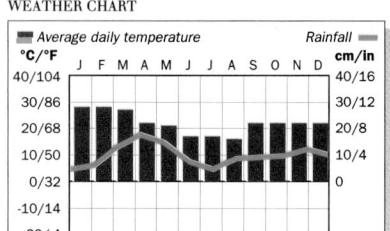

Altitude and the influence of Lake Victoria moderate Uganda's equatorial climate. Spring is the wettest period.

COMMUNICATIONS

 Entebbe International
122,000 passengers

2 ships
5900 dwt

THE TRANSPORT NETWORK

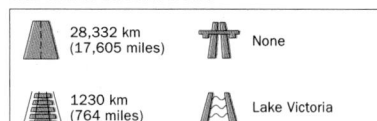

28,332 km (17,605 miles)	None
1230 km (764 miles)	Lake Victoria

The government is rebuilding the transport infrastructure with the help of international aid.

TOURISM

82,151 visitors

Up 11% in 1992

MAIN OVERSEAS ARRIVALS

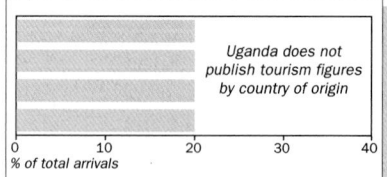

Uganda does not publish tourism figures by country of origin

0   10   20   30   40
% of total arrivals

The tourist industry is recovering with the return of stability. Visitors are mainly high-spending independent travellers. Major attractions are Uganda's lakes and mountains, notably the rugged Ruwenzori range, better known as the Mountains of the Moon.

PEOPLE

 Luganda, Nkole, Chiga, Lango, Acholi, Teso, Lugbara, English

80 people per km²

THE URBAN/RURAL POPULATION SPLIT

10%   **90%**

RELIGIOUS PERSUASION

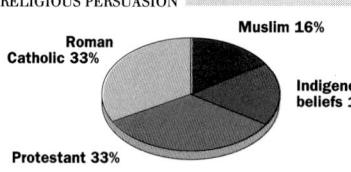

Roman Catholic 33%

Muslim 16%

Indigenous beliefs 18%

Protestant 33%

The predominantly rural population consists of 13 main ethnic groups. Traditional animosities, manipulated by ex-presidents Amin and Obote, underlay the ethnic conflict which has marred Uganda's history. Since 1986, President Museveni has worked hard for reconciliation. In 1993, he allowed the restoration of Uganda's four historical monarchies.

POLITICS

1995

President Lt–Gen Yoweri Kaguta Museveni

THE STATE OF THE PARTIES

National Resistance Council 278 members

The National Resistance Council is to remain as the legislative body until elections take place, following the expected drafting of a new constitution

Uganda is due to return to multiparty democracy in 1995. Since 1986, President Museveni has run a 'no-party democracy', with political parties represented in a broadly-based government, but banned from campaigning. Overcoming ethnic tension is now the main issue. In the 1970s and 1980s, ethnic conflict destroyed the economy and resulted in the death of almost one million Ugandans. The new constitution will involve a federal system with boundaries based on the old kingdoms. The hope in Uganda is that political parties will also broaden their traditional ethnically-based support and that the military, key power brokers in the past, will stay out of politics.

UGANDA

Total Area : 235 880 sq. km
(91 073 sq. miles)

POPULATION

over 100 000	◎
over 50 000	○
over 10 000	●
under 10 000	·

LAND HEIGHT

3000m/9843ft
2000m/6562ft
1000m/3281ft
500m/1640ft

N

0   100 km
0   100 miles

U

WORLD AFFAIRS

Relations with Sudan and Rwanda are strained. Internal conflicts in both countries have resulted in a large influx of refugees into Uganda. Occasional border tensions have led to incursions by the Zairean military. Relations with Tanzania and Kenya are improving; the three nations are discussing reforming the former East African Community.

AID

 $525m (receipts)   Down 5% in 1991

Aid receipts, mainly from the World Bank and the IMF, rose in the late 1980s, encouraged by Uganda's adoption of economic liberalization and private sector investment policies. Aid has focused on balance of payments support and the rehabilitation of the key transport sector.

DEFENCE

 $73.29m   Down 1% in 1991

Since 1986, the military's political role has been downgraded. The National Resistance Army, the official armed force, is being reduced in size and its ethnic base broadened. The pre-1986 army, dominated by northern Acholi and Langi groups, was responsible for many atrocities under Amin's rule. Security in border areas is the priority.

ECONOMICS

 $3.1bn   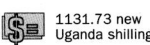 1131.73 new Uganda shillings

SCORE CARD

❑ World GNP Ranking	122nd
❑ GNP per Capita	$190
❑ Balance of Payments	$–118m
❑ Inflation	23.3%
❑ Unemployment	Widespread underemployment

STRENGTHS
Agriculture. Coffee brings in 93% of export earnings. Potential for more export crops. Road system is being repaired. Pro-investment policies.

WEAKNESSES
Recent ethnic conflict has left a generation lacking skills. Coffee vulnerable to world price fluctuations. High transport costs.

EXPORTS

IMPORTS

RESOURCES

 603m kwh (capacity 162,000 kw)

 Not an oil producer and has no refineries

 4.2m cattle, 1.8m sheep, 460,000 pigs

Copper, cobalt, tin apatite, magnetite, tungsten, gold

Mineral resources are varied but barely exploited. Uganda has sizeable copper deposits. The mines, closed under Obote, are now being reopened. Gold and cobalt mining is also due to resume and oil exploration is under way. Hydroelectric output is being expanded, notably at Owen Falls, with the aim of replacing 50% of oil imports.

ENVIRONMENT

 8% (4% partially protected)   Rising environmental awareness

Uganda's priority is economic reconstruction but ecological issues are not ignored. Construction of a huge hydroelectric power station at the Murchison Falls was cancelled recently, following strong local environmental objections to the choice of site.

MEDIA

 The press has been free since 1986. Comment likely to cause ethnic tension is banned

PUBLISHING AND BROADCAST MEDIA

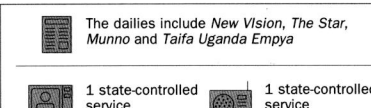

The dailies include *New Vision, The Star, Munno* and *Taifa Uganda Empya*

1 state-controlled service

1 state-controlled service

The 13 daily and weekly papers cover the political and religious spectrum; eight are published in English. Only the *New Vision* is government-controlled.

CRIME

 10,080 prisoners   Low levels; fairly stable from year to year

Crime levels are far lower than in neighbouring Kenya, although theft in Kampala is a growing problem. Uganda now has one of the best human rights records in Africa.

EDUCATION

 48%

Education is not compulsory and all schools charge fees. Only 10% of pupils go on to secondary school.

HEALTH

 1 per 22,291 people   Malaria, respiratory and diarrheal diseases, measles

The health system, badly hit by war and the loss of foreign personnel, is slowly being rebuilt. AIDS-related illness is a major problem in some areas.

WEALTH

 Most Ugandans live a subsistence existence

CONSUMER GOODS OWNERSHIP

VCR and PC ownership is limited to a small elite

Uganda has a small, but growing middle class. Those close to the government form the wealthiest group.

WORLD RANKING

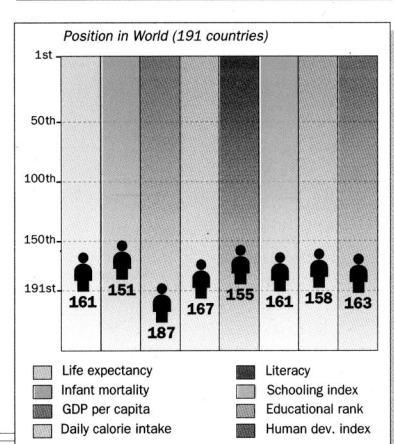

Position in World (191 countries)

U

UKRAINE

OFFICIAL NAME: Ukraine **CAPITAL:** Kiev
POPULATION: 51.9 million **CURRENCY:** Karbovanets **OFFICIAL LANGUAGE:** Ukrainian

UKRAINE IS BORDERED by seven states; to the south it lies on the Black Sea and the Sea of Azov. An independent Ukrainian state was established in 1918, but was overrun in the same year by Soviet forces from the east and Polish forces from the west. In 1991, Ukraine again became an independent state. The country has historically been divided between the nationally-conscious and Ukrainian-speaking west (which was not under Russian occupation until the Second Word War) and the east, which has a large ethnic Russian population.

View towards the Cathedral of the Assumption in Kharkiv. Many Ukrainian cities are equipped with elaborate tram networks.

CLIMATE

WEATHER CHART

Ukraine has a continental climate, with the exception of the southern coast of Crimea, which has a Mediterranean climate. There are four distinct seasons.

COMMUNICATIONS

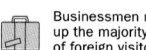 **Boryspiel Intl, Kiev**

🚢 2 ships
4800 dwt

THE TRANSPORT NETWORK

247,300 km
(153,665 miles)

None

22,730 km
(14,124 miles)

4400 km
(2734 miles)

Transport within major cities includes Soviet-style subway systems and tram networks. There are plans to improve the main highway linking Kiev and L'viv. The rail system is in need of extensive upgrading.

TOURISM

Businessmen make up the majority of foreign visitors

No significant change in tourism figures

MAIN OVERSEAS ARRIVALS

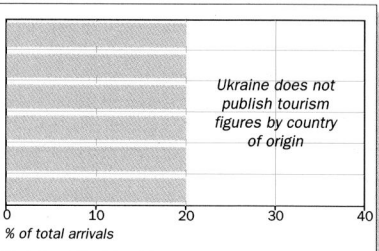

Ukraine does not publish tourism figures by country of origin

Among potential tourist attractions are warm resort areas in Crimea and the south, and the Carpathian Mountains. The government has maintained a highly regulated system of managing tourism. Western visitors are deterred by the expensive Soviet-style hotels they are required to use.

UKRAINE

Total Area : 603 700 sq. km (225 090 sq. miles)

POPULATION

- ▣ over 1 000 000
- ◉ over 500 000
- ◎ over 100 000
- ○ over 50 000
- ● over 10 000

LAND HEIGHT

- 2000m/6562ft
- 1000m/3281ft
- 500m/1640ft
- 200m/656ft
- Sea Level

0   100 km
0   100 miles

U

PEOPLE

 Ukrainian, Russian, Tartar   86 people per km²

THE URBAN/RURAL POPULATION SPLIT

67%   **33%**

RELIGIOUS PERSUASION

Ukrainian Orthodox is the dominant religion of the Ukraine. It has three branches, those under the Moscow and Kiev Patriarchates and the Autocephalous branch. There are also small Catholic, Protestant and Jewish groups

ETHNIC MAKEUP

Jewish 1%   Other 4%
Russian 22%
Ukrainian 73%

In the cities and countryside of western Ukraine, Ukrainians make up over 90% of the population. However, in several of the large cities of the east and south, Russians form a majority. The large Russian population in these areas is a legacy of 19th-century industrialization, and more recent migration during the Soviet-era. At independence, most Russians accepted Ukrainian sovereignty. However, tensions are now rising as both groups adopt more extremist nationalist policies.

In Crimea, relations between Russians, ethnic Ukrainians and Tartars are becoming increasingly tense. Crimea has a majority Russian population, but is also home to the Tartars, a Turkic-speaking people. The Tartars were deported *en masse* to the eastern USSR under Stalin in 1945. They have been returning to the region since 1990 and now compose roughly 10% of its population.

POPULATION AGE BREAKDOWN

The proportion of Ukrainians aged over 65 is rising
1960 1970 1980 1990 2000

Leonid Plyushch, *chairman of the Ukrainian parliament.*

President Leonid Kravchuk. *He tried to postpone democratic elections.*

WORLD AFFAIRS

 CIS   CSCE   BSEC   CBSS   ECE

The main foreign policy threat to Ukraine is Russia. Ukrainian commentators have expressed the fear that if the Crimea or pro-Russian regions in Ukraine demand unification with Russia, this could spark a civil war in Ukraine with the risk of Russian intervention. Alternatively, should extremist Russian nationalists, such as Vladimir Zhirinovsky, come to power in Moscow, it is possible they would try to incorporate Ukraine into Russia.

Ukraine's internal instability and the increasingly aggressive stance of Russia towards it has been a source of concern to the US government. The Clinton administration has demonstrated a growing willingness to support the state both politically and economically. Germany and other European states also support Ukraine as a buffer in Russia. However, it is unlikely that this support will extend to accepting Ukrainian EU membership.

POLITICS

 1998   Leonid Kravchuk

THE STATE OF THE PARTIES

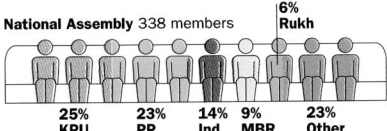

National Assembly 338 members   6% Rukh

25% KPU 23% PP 14% Ind. 9% MBR 23% Other

KPU = Ukrainian Communist Party PP = Party of Power Ind. = Independents MBR = Interregional Block for Reform Rukh = Ukrainian People's Movement Other = Ukrainian Socialist Party, Ukrainian Peasants Party, Congress of Ukrainian Nationalists, Ukrainian Republican Party, Crimean Communist Party, Ukrainian National Assembly, Ukrainian Democratic Party, New Wave

Ukraine has been a multiparty democracy since 1991.

MAIN POLITICAL ISSUES

Economic reform
Western and central Ukraine are generally more in favour of economic reform than the eastern regions, which prefer continued support for their subsidy-dependent economy. This division was illustrated by the strong showing of the communist and socialist parties in eastern regions in the 1994 elections.

Relations with Russia
Western Ukrainians are vehement in their opposition to closer ties with Russia, while such ties are supported by their eastern counterparts. In a referendum in March 1994, citizens in the Donetsk region voted for closer links with the CIS, and in favour of introducing Russian as a joint official language. Likewise, in Crimea, voters have demanded dual Russian–Ukrainian citizenship and closer economic integration.

Potential destabilization
Some commentators fear that the growing antagonism between nationalist and anti-nationalist groups could spark a civil war. Conflict could arise in Crimea, which is dominated by ethnic Russians. In 1994, the Crimean parliament issued another declaration of independence from Kiev. Kiev responded with an ultimatum, but failed to act on its threat. The situation remains unresolved. Tension is rising in other regions with large Russian minorities, such as the Donbass.

PROFILE
Ukraine has yet to develop a strong democratic party system. Individuals – generally local potentates, such as enterprise directors or collective farm chairmen – are very influential. Around 30 parties competed in the 1994 elections, while more than half of the candidates ran as independents. The dominant figure in politics since 1990 has been Leonid Kravchuk. A former ideologue for the Ukrainian Communist Party, he became president at independence in 1991.

CHRONOLOGY

In 1240, Kiev was conquered by the Mongols. The Ukrainian Cossacks later came under the domination of Lithuania, Poland and Russia.

❑ **1918** Independent Ukrainian state established in the aftermath of the collapse of Russian and Austrian empires. Brest-Litovsk Treaty signed with Germany.
❑ **1919** Red Army invades. Ukrainian Soviet Socialist Republic is proclaimed.
❑ **1920** Poland invades. Western Ukraine comes under Polish occupation.
❑ **1922** USSR founded; Ukrainian SSR is one of founder-members.
❑ **1922–1930** Cultural revival results from 'Ukrainianization' policy adopted by Lenin to pacify national sentiment.

U

CHRONOLOGY *continued*

- ❏ **1932–1933** 'Ukrainianization' policy reversed. Stalin's government induces man-made famine to eliminate Ukraine as source of opposition to his regime. Seven million die.
- ❏ **1939** Carpatho-Ukraine declares its independence from Slovakia. Soviet Union invades Poland and incorporates ethnic Ukrainian territories of Poland into the Ukrainian SSR.
- ❏ **1941** Germany invades USSR. Activities of Ukrainian nationalists suppressed by Germans. Seven and a half million Ukrainians die by end of Second World War.
- ❏ **1942** Nationalists form Ukrainian Insurgent Army, which wages war against both Germans and Soviets.
- ❏ **1954** Crimea ceded to Ukrainian SSR.
- ❏ **1972** Widespread arrests of intellectuals and dissidents by Soviet state. Shcherbitsky, a Brezhnevite, replaces moderate reformer Shelest as head of Communist Party of Ukraine (CPU).
- ❏ **1986** World's worst nuclear disaster takes place at Chernobyl nuclear power station north of Kiev.
- ❏ **1989** First major coalminers' strike in Donbass. Pro-Gorbachev Ivashko becomes head of CPU.
- ❏ **1990** July, Ukrainian parliament declares the Ukrainian SSR to be a sovereign state. Leonid Kravchuk replaces Ivashko as leader.
- ❏ **1991** January, Crimea declared an autonomous republic within Ukrainian SSR. August, government declares full independence, conditional on approval by referendum. December, over 90% of population approve move in referendum. CPU banned.
- ❏ **1993** Major strike in Donbass results in costly settlement, which exacerbates budget deficit and stimulates inflation. Karbovanets enters hyperinflation. CPU re-established at congress in Donetsk.
- ❏ **1994** First president of Crimea, Yuri Meshkov, elected on platform of Crimean independence and closer ties with Russia. March–April, first democratic elections in independent Ukraine take place.

AID

 Further aid is dependent on economic reform   No significant change

Ukraine has received assistance from Western countries in training a new administrative elite, and in modernizing telecommunications infrastructure.

DEFENCE

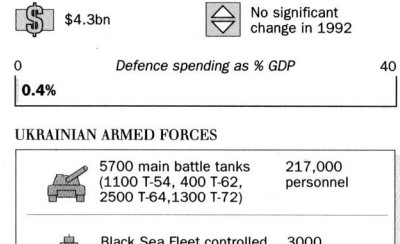

💲 $4.3bn   No significant change in 1992

0   *Defence spending as % GDP*   40
0.4%

UKRAINIAN ARMED FORCES

🛡️	5700 main battle tanks (1100 T-54, 400 T-62, 2500 T-64, 1300 T-72)	217,000 personnel
🚢	Black Sea Fleet controlled jointly with Russia	3000 personnel
✈️	900 combat aircraft (MiG-21, MiG-23, MiG-27)	171,000 personnel
🚀	166 ICBMs	

Ukraine is still a member of the CIS, but is consolidating its own forces because of fear about rising Russian willingness to intervene in other ex-Soviet republics. The main focus of defence spending is the modernization of weaponry. Ukraine has recently brought out a new version of the Soviet T-72 tank and is planning to update its fleet.

In late 1993, the Ukrainian parliament agreed to ratify the START-1 nuclear disarmament treaty. In March 1994, Ukraine transferred a number of nuclear warheads to Russia, in accordance with the agreement.

The long-smouldering dispute between Ukraine and Russia over control of the Black Sea Fleet has not yet been decisively resolved. Ukraine now seems likely to reverse its decision to give up ownership of the Fleet in return for debt relief from Russia. Further negotiations were held in 1994, but with little tangible result.

ECONOMICS

📊 $189.5bn   💲 18,231 karbovanets

SCORE CARD

- ❏ WORLD GNP RANKING..........................27th
- ❏ GNP PER CAPITA $2326
- ❏ BALANCE OF PAYMENTS.................Large deficit
- ❏ INFLATION 79.3%
- ❏ UNEMPLOYMENT......................................2%

EXPORTS

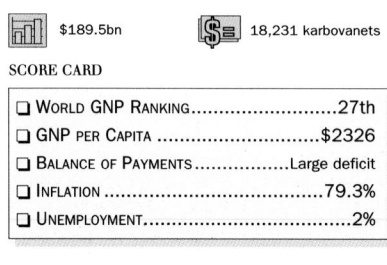

Other 18%
Soviet republics 82%

IMPORTS

Other 18%
Soviet republics 82%

ECONOMIC PERFORMANCE INDICATOR

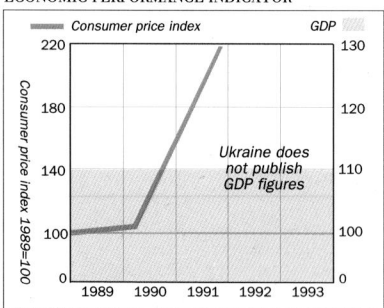

— Consumer price index   GDP

Ukraine does not publish GDP figures

(Consumer price index 1989=100, y-axis 0–220; GDP y-axis 0–130; x-axis 1989, 1990, 1991, 1992, 1993)

STRENGTHS
Well-educated workforce. Good public transport infrastructure within cities. Technological potential, especially in aerospace and computers; many research institutes in these areas. Long-term potential for extensive grain and food export. Minerals.

WEAKNESSES
Failure to reform centrally-planned economy following collapse of Soviet Union. Hyperinflation. Anti-reform political elites. Inefficient, subsidized manufacturing industries. Corruption.

PROFILE
While privatization of large enterprises has scarcely begun, there has been some privatization of small industries in the larger cities. Many traders and street vendors have sprung up in Kiev and other major cities. Agriculture, however, is still hindered by an entrenched collective farm system.

UKRAINE : MAJOR BUSINESSES

Kiev
Kharkiv
L'viv
Donets Basin
Odesa
Dnipropetrovs'k
Kherson
Kryvyy Rih

- 🗺️ Iron & steel
- Coal mining
- Engineering
- Iron ore mining
- Consumer goods
- Food processing
- Vehicle manufacture
- Chemicals
- Electronics
- Textiles

0   200 km
0   200 miles

RESOURCES

 251bn kwh

 Small-scale oil production

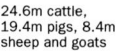 24.6m cattle, 19.4m pigs, 8.4m sheep and goats

Coal, iron, oil, natural gas, manganese, lignite, peat, mercury

ELECTRICITY GENERATION

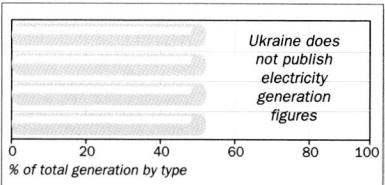

Ukraine does not publish electricity generation figures

0   20   40   60   80   100
% of total generation by type

Ukraine's most successfully exploited fuel resource is coal. Most coal is mined in the Donets'k basin or the Donbass, around Donets'k and Luhans'k. There are also smaller reserves in western Ukraine, in the L'viv-Volhynia coal basin. Production has, however, been declining since the 1970s, and the industry has been hit by strikes since 1989. In 1992, production stood at 134 million tons a year.

Production of natural gas has also been declining since the 1970s. There are some uranium deposits, but Ukraine does not yet have the facilities to produce fuel for its own nuclear reactors. Oil production has not been carried out on a large scale, although there are significant untapped reserves in the Donbass and in the Carpathian Mountains in the west.

UKRAINE : LAND USE

- Cropland
- Forest
- Pasture
- Cattle
- Wheat - cash crop
- Sugar beet

0   200 km
0   200 miles

ENVIRONMENT

 0.8%

Widespread contamination from Chernobyl incident

ENVIRONMENTAL TREATIES

No   No

No   No

As a result of the Chernobyl nuclear disaster – the worst nuclear accident in history – four millon Ukrainians now live in dangerously radioactive areas and 12% of arable land is contaminated. Children who live in areas with high radiation levels are sent by the state to summer camps in uncontaminated areas.

The government has now turned back to nuclear production because of the rising cost of Russian oil imports. In 1994, reactors from the Chernobyl plant were still being used to produce nuclear power.

Industrial pollution is widespread. Air pollution from coal and chemicals industries in the Donbass region remains particularly high.

MEDIA

 There is no tradition of investigative journalism

PUBLISHING AND BROADCAST MEDIA

Vechernyi Kyiv is among the most popular daily newspapers

1 state-run service   1 state-run service

Arabsat 1C   None

A number of independent, mass-circulation newspapers are now published. Local TV stations reflect regional political differences.

CRIME

 Ukraine does not publish prison figures

 Most crime is rising

CRIME RATES

Most types of crime have increased since the demise of the USSR

The deteriorating state of the economy, and a general breakdown in law and order following the collapse of the Soviet system, have led to a steady increase in crime rates. The police suffers from underfunding and has proved unable to control the increase. Corruption is now rampant in all areas of the economy. The mafia is thought to be even more influential in the Ukraine than in neighbouring Russia. Foreigners are targets for muggings.

EDUCATION

  96%

0   *Education spending as % GNP*   25
25%   *(includes health spending)*

THE EDUCATION SYSTEM

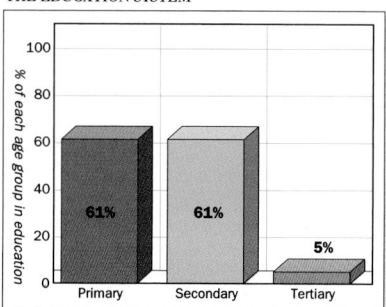

% of each age group in education

100
80
60   **61%**   **61%**
40
20   **5%**
0   Primary   Secondary   Tertiary

In eastern regions, most university teaching is in Russian; in western ones, in Ukrainian. Some schools in the west no longer teach Russian.

HEALTH

 1 per 288 people

Cerebrovascular and heart diseases, cancers

0   *Health spending as % GNP*   25
25%   *(includes education spending)*

The health ministry keeps a registry of all those affected by the Chernobyl disaster, including the 134,000 young army recruits who participated in the initial clean-up operation.

WEALTH

 In 1991, 41% of Ukrainians were living below the poverty line

CONSUMER GOODS OWNERSHIP

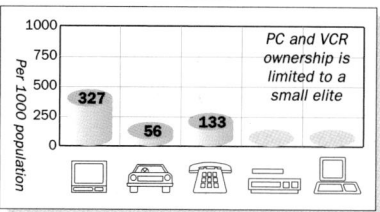

Per 1000 population

1000
750   *PC and VCR ownership is limited to a small elite*
500
327
250   56   133
0

Ukraine has a small well-off elite, which has grown rich from business, corruption or mafia activities.

WORLD RANKING

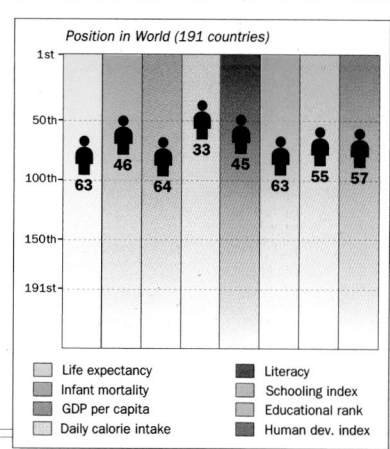

Position in World (191 countries)

1st
50th   46   33   45
100th   63   64   63   55   57
150th
191st

- Life expectancy
- Infant mortality
- GDP per capita
- Daily calorie intake
- Literacy
- Schooling index
- Educational rank
- Human dev. index

U

UNITED ARAB EMIRATES

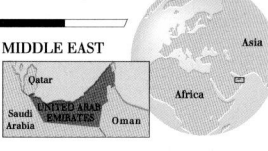

OFFICIAL NAME: United Arab Emirates **CAPITAL:** Abu Dhabi
POPULATION: 1.9 million **CURRENCY:** UAE dirham **OFFICIAL LANGUAGE:** Arabic

THE ARAB WORLD'S only working federation, the
United Arab Emirates (UAE) shares borders with
Oman, Saudi Arabia and Qatar, as well as a disputed maritime boundary
with Iran. The UAE is mostly semi-arid desert relieved by occasional
oases. The cities, watered by extensive irrigation systems, have lavish
greenery. The UAE's economic prosperity once relied on pearls, but it
is now a sizeable gas and oil exporter, and has a growing services sector.

CLIMATE

WEATHER CHART

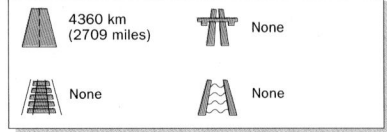

Although rainfall is minimal, summers
are humid. Sand-laden *shamal* winds
often blow in winter and spring.

COMMUNICATIONS

✈ **Abu Dhabi International**
1.01m passengers

🚢 92 ships
1.26m dwt

THE TRANSPORT NETWORK

4360 km (2709 miles)		None	
None		None	

The roads are good, though littered
with wrecked cars. Five of the seven
emirates have international airports.

TOURISM

🧳 345,000 visitors

📈 Tourism is increasing

MAIN OVERSEAS ARRIVALS

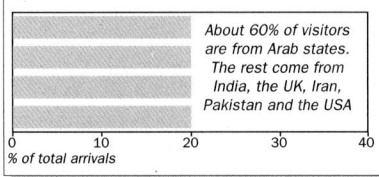

*About 60% of visitors
are from Arab states.
The rest come from
India, the UK, Iran,
Pakistan and the USA*

Until the mid-1980s, tourism was
minimal. Led by Dubai, the UAE
has now launched initiatives to attract
visitors during the Western winter for
sunshine, heritage, water sports, desert
safaris and duty-free shopping.

PEOPLE

👤 Arabic, Persian, Indian and
Pakistani languages, English

👥 19 people
per km²

THE URBAN/RURAL POPULATION SPLIT

78%   **22%**

ETHNIC MAKEUP

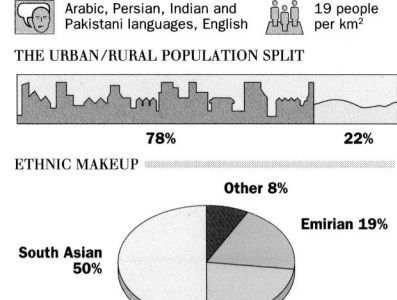

Other 8%
Emirian 19%
Other Arab 23%
South Asian 50%

UAE nationals are largely city dwellers,
with Abu Dhabi and Dubai the
dominant centres. They are
outnumbered by expatriates who
flocked to the country in the 1970s
during the oil boom; UAE nationals
make up one fifth of the population.

UAE citizens are mostly conservative
Sunni Muslims of Bedouin descent.
There is a Shi'a community in Dubai
with links to Iran. The Western
expatriate community is permitted a
virtually unrestricted lifestyle. Islamic
fundamentalism, however, is a growing
force among the young.

Poverty is rare in the UAE. The
government remains the biggest
employer. Women in theory enjoy
equal rights with men.

POLITICS

🗳 Not applicable

👤 President Sheikh Zayed
bin Sultan an-Nahyan

THE STATE OF THE PARTIES

Federal National Council 40 members

The 40 members are appointed by the emirates. There are
no political parties

Supreme Council of Rulers 7 members

The Supreme Council of Rulers, composed of the rulers of
the 7 emirates, has overall authority

The UAE's seven emirates – Abu Dhabi,
Dubai, Sharjah, Ras al Khaimah,
Ajman, Umm al Qaiwain and Fujairah –
are dominated by their ruling families.
The main personalities are the ruler of
Abu Dhabi and UAE President Sheikh
Zayed, and the Maktoum brothers who
control Dubai.

President Zayed has relaunched the
advisory Federal National Council in
response to criticism about the lack of
democracy. The growth of Islamic
fundamentalism is also a concern. The
freedoms granted to Westerners have
aroused some anger but, for economic
reasons, are unlikely to be withdrawn.

UNITED ARAB EMIRATES

Total Area : 83 600 sq. km (32 278 sq. miles)

POPULATION
◎ over 100 000
• under 10 000

LAND HEIGHT
1000m/3281ft
500m/1640ft
Sea Level

U

WORLD AFFAIRS

The UAE is well known as an advocate of moderation within the Arab world. It maintains close links with most OECD economies, especially the UK and the USA. In 1992, conflict flared when Iran seized control of three islands in the Strait of Hormuz. Attempts are being made to settle the dispute through diplomacy.

AID

 $588m (donations)   Down 34% in 1991

Once a generous donor to developing countries, the UAE's contributions have fallen because of weak energy prices.

DEFENCE

 $1.6bn   Up 3% in 1991

At 55,000, the UAE's forces are too small and too scattered among the emirates to pose a threat to the traditional rulers. Although they are well equipped, training is limited and manpower largely drawn from other Arab states and the Indian subcontinent. During the 1991 Gulf crisis, UAE air bases were used by UN forces for strikes against Iraq.

ECONOMICS

 $32.8bn   3.67 UAE dirhams

SCORE CARD

❏ WORLD GNP RANKING	52nd
❏ GNP PER CAPITA	$17,500
❏ BALANCE OF PAYMENTS	$4bn
❏ INFLATION	1.1%
❏ UNEMPLOYMENT	0.4%

STRENGTHS
Oil and gas reserves are the fourth biggest in OPEC. Service industries have been developed to support the economy when the wells run dry.

WEAKNESSES
Lack of skilled manpower. Most raw materials and foodstuffs have to be imported. Water resources scarce as ground water is depleted.

EXPORTS

Germany* 9%
USA 9%
UK 10%
Japan 14%
Other 58%

IMPORTS

Germany* 8%
USA 9%
UK 11%
Japan 18%
Other 54%

RESOURCES

 13.6bn kwh (capacity 4.66m kw)   2.3bn b/d (reserves 98,100,000,000 bbl)

 580,000 goats, 260,000 sheep, 115,000 camels   Oil, natural gas

The UAE is a major exporter of crude oil and natural gas; Abu Dhabi in particular has abundant reserves. Oil production is the largest economic sector and accounts for 89% of export revenue. Mīnā' Jabal 'Alī in Dubai is the world's largest man-made port and has attracted companies from 58 countries.

ENVIRONMENT

 None   Hunting has made the Arabian oryx extinct in the wild

Despite its harsh desert climate, the UAE has a rich variety of plant and animal life; rare species, however, are threatened by hunting.

MEDIA

 Western print media are censored for taste and political correctness

PUBLISHING AND BROADCAST MEDIA

There are 8 daily newspapers. The leading Arabic newspaper is *Al-Ittihad. Emirates News* is its English-language counterpart

1 state-owned, 2 independent services

2 state-owned, 1 independent service

Radio and TV are state-run; satellite TV is unrestricted. The privately-owned press follows censorship guidelines.

CRIME

 The UAE does not publish prison figures   Up 9% in 1987

Street crime and muggings are rare. However, Dubai has a reputation as a transit point for drugs.

An oasis village, inland from Fujairah, now accessible through a well-developed network of new highways.

EDUCATION

 68%

UAE citizens enjoy free education from nursery to university. The government funds overseas student scholarships.

HEALTH

 1 per 1619 people   Circulatory and respiratory diseases, cancers

A high-standard system of primary health care is in place for all UAE citizens, with hospitals able to perform most operations.

WEALTH

 Poverty is rare in the UAE

CONSUMER GOODS OWNERSHIP

UAE nationals have one of the highest incomes per head in the world. There is no income tax and oil revenues subsidize public services. Government policies encourage entrepreneurs.

WORLD RANKING

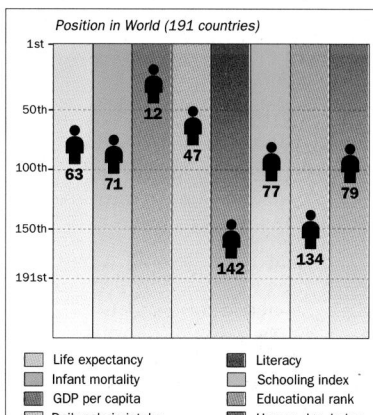

Life expectancy	Literacy
Infant mortality	Schooling index
GDP per capita	Educational rank
Daily calorie intake	Human dev. index

U

UNITED KINGDOM

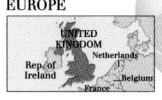

OFFICIAL NAME: United Kingdom of Great Britain and Northern Ireland **CAPITAL:** London
POPULATION: 57.7 million **CURRENCY:** Pound sterling **OFFICIAL LANGUAGE:** English **OVERSEAS TERRITORIES:** 15

LYING IN NORTHWESTERN EUROPE, the United Kingdom (UK) occupies the major portion of the British Isles. It includes the nations of England, Scotland and Wales, the constitutionally distinct region of Northern Ireland and several outlying islands. Its only land border is with the Republic of Ireland. The UK is separated from the European mainland by the English Channel and North Sea. To the west, lies the Atlantic Ocean. Most of the population lives in towns and cities and, in England, is fairly well scattered. The most densely populated region is the southeast. Scotland is the wildest region, with the Highlands less populated today than in the 18th century. The UK became a member of the EEC (later the EU) in 1973. Most of its trade is now with its European partners, although membership of the UN Security Council gives it a prominent role in international diplomacy.

PEOPLE

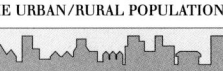
English, Welsh, Scottish, Gaelic

238 people per km²

THE URBAN/RURAL POPULATION SPLIT

89%   11%

RELIGIOUS PERSUASION

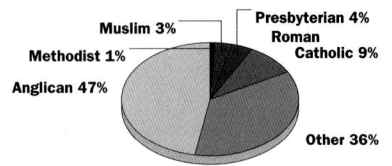

Muslim 3%
Methodist 1%
Anglican 47%
Presbyterian 4%
Roman Catholic 9%
Other 36%

ETHNIC MAKEUP

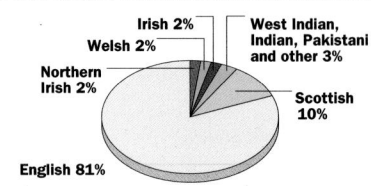

Irish 2%
Welsh 2%
Northern Irish 2%
West Indian, Indian, Pakistani and other 3%
Scottish 10%
English 81%

CLIMATE

WEATHER CHART

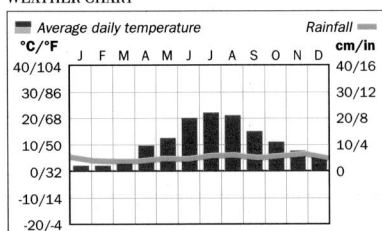

The UK has a generally mild, temperate, and highly changeable climate. Rain, regarded as synonymous with Britain's weather, is fairly well distributed throughout the year. The west is generally wetter than the east, and the south warmer than the north. The most extreme weather conditions occcur in the mountains of Scotland, Wales and northern England.

COMMUNICATIONS

Heathrow, London
42.65m passengers

447 ships
6.62m dwt

THE TRANSPORT NETWORK

356,517 km
(221,529 miles)

3093 km
(1922 miles)

16,583 km
(10,304 miles)

3200 km
(1988 miles)

Since the 1960s, Britain has built an extensive system of motorways, including the world's busiest ring road, the M25. The main link to Scotland is being upgraded to motorway standard. British Rail was reorganized in 1993 ready for its flotation on the stock market. In 1994, the Channel Tunnel opened, although Britain has yet to build a high-speed rail link to London.

TOURISM

18.5m visitors

Up 8% in 1992

MAIN OVERSEAS ARRIVALS

USA 15%
France 13%
Germany 12%
Ireland 8%
Netherlands 5%
Other 47%

% of total arrivals

Tourism is among the UK's most important industries and a growing source of employment. London, with its art galleries, theatres and historical buildings, remains the major destination. However, many visitors choose to by-pass the capital and head straight for the Roman splendours of Bath, Stratford-upon-Avon, medieval York or the Highlands of Scotland. Americans are the main visitors to the UK, although fear of terrorism and recession in the USA have recently dissuaded some from making the trip.

View of Oxford, *with the Clarendon Building and Sheldonian Theatre in the foreground. The 17th-century Sheldonian (right) was one of Sir Christopher Wren's first commissions.*

The UK is the 17th most populous state in the world. The Scottish and Welsh minorities are ethnically and culturally distinct. Both remain recognizable nations and the Scots retain their own legal and educational systems.

Britain's ethnic minorities account for less than 5% of the total population. Over 50% were born in Britain. The ethnic population is concentrated in the inner cities where there are problems of deprivation and social stress. Women in the Bangladeshi community in particular suffer from poor education and isolation from society. However, significant progress has been made in tackling racial disadvantage since the 1970s and there is very little support for racist politics.

Marriage is in decline in the UK. Over 30% of births now occur out of wedlock, compared with 12% in 1980. However, many of these births are to co-habiting couples. Around 17% of families with children under the age of 18 are one-parent families, compared with 6% in Italy and 25% in the USA.

POPULATION AGE BREAKDOWN

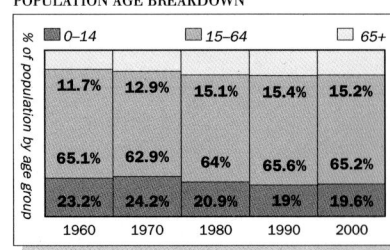

% of population by age group	0–14		15–64		65+
	11.7%	12.9%	15.1%	15.4%	15.2%
	65.1%	62.9%	64%	65.6%	65.2%
	23.2%	24.2%	20.9%	19%	19.6%
	1960	1970	1980	1990	2000

U

Black Mount, Rannoch Moor, in the Scottish Highlands. The Highlands are one of the UK's wildest regions.

CHRONOLOGY

Great Britain began the 20th century as one of the world's most advanced economies, backed by a massive trading empire.

- ❑ **1906** Reformist Liberal government.
- ❑ **1914** First World War begins.
- ❑ **1918** Armistice signals end of war. Cost to Britain: 750,000 dead.
- ❑ **1921** Southern Ireland becomes free state.
- ❑ **1926** General Strike.
- ❑ **1929** World stock market crash. Widespread unemployment.
- ❑ **1931** UK leaves gold standard and devalues pound.
- ❑ **1934** Arms spending increased in response to Hitler's rise to power.
- ❑ **1936** Edward VIII abdicates over marriage to Mrs Simpson.
- ❑ **1937** Neville Chamberlain prime minister.
- ❑ **1938** Chamberlain meets Hitler in Munich over Czech crisis and announces that threat of war with Germany has been averted.
- ❑ **1939** Germany invades Poland. UK declares war on Germany. Start of Second World War.
- ❑ **1940** Winston Churchill becomes prime minister. Battle of Britain. Bombing of London ('Blitz').
- ❑ **1941** USA joins Allies.
- ❑ **1942** UK victory at El Alamein.

UNITED KINGDOM

Total Area : 244 880 sq. km
(94 550 sq. miles)

POPULATION

over 5 000 000	⊡
over 500 000	◉
over 100 000	◎
over 50 000	○
over 10 000	●
under 10 000	·

LAND HEIGHT

1000m/3280ft
500m/1640ft
200m/656ft
Sea Level

U

563

CHRONOLOGY *continued*

- ❏ **1944** 6 June, D-Day launches invasion of German-occupied France.
- ❏ **1945** End of Second World War. War costs 330,000 British lives. LP government comes to power on social welfare platform.
- ❏ **1946** Government begins nationalization of Bank of England, railways, coal and utilities. Begins departure from former colonies.
- ❏ **1947** India granted independence.
- ❏ **1948** UK founder-member of UN Security Council. 'Austerity Olympics' held in London. National Health Service established.
- ❏ **1949** UK founder-member of NATO.
- ❏ **1956** Suez crisis. UK intervenes in Canal Zone but forced to withdraw by USA.
- ❏ **1957** US nuclear missiles accepted on UK soil.
- ❏ **1960** UK founder-member of EFTA.
- ❏ **1961** UK application to join EC rejected by French President De Gaulle.
- ❏ **1965** Winston Churchill dies.
- ❏ **1968** Abortion and homosexuality legalized.
- ❏ **1969** British troops sent into Ulster. Peace Wall between Protestant and Catholic communities erected.
- ❏ **1970** Age of majority cut to 18. CUP in power under Edward Heath. 8.8m work days lost in strike action.
- ❏ **1973** UK joins EEC. Oil crisis. Industry placed on three-day week following strikes by power workers and miners.
- ❏ **1974** LP government, under Harold Wilson, concedes miners' demands and strikes end. High inflation.
- ❏ **1975** Margaret Thatcher becomes CUP leader. Referendum ratifies EEC membership. First North Sea oil pipeline in operation.
- ❏ **1976** 'Cod War' with Iceland.
- ❏ **1979** CUP wins election.
- ❏ **1980** Anti-US Cruise missiles protests. Rising unemployment and inner city riots.
- ❏ **1981** CUP launch privatization programme.
- ❏ **1982** Unemployment three million. Argentina invades Falklands. Islands retaken by UK task force.
- ❏ **1983** Tax-cutting policies. CUP wins general election.
- ❏ **1985** Anglo-Irish Accord: attempt to resolve Ulster's 'troubles'.
- ❏ **1986** Financial services market deregularized ('Big Bang').
- ❏ **1987** CUP wins third election in a row. First black MP in Parliament.
- ❏ **1988** Pan-Am airliner blown up by terrorists over Lockerbie, Scotland.
- ❏ **1990** John Major takes over as CUP leader. UK joins Gulf War.
- ❏ **1992** CUP wins election.

POLITICS

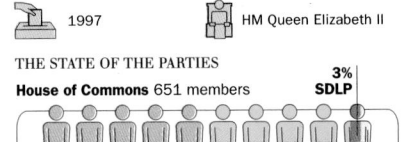

1997   HM Queen Elizabeth II

THE STATE OF THE PARTIES

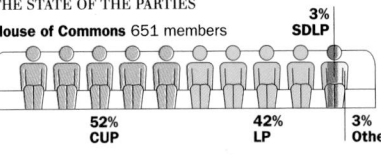

House of Commons 651 members

3% SDLP

52% CUP   42% LP   3% Other

CUP = Conservative and Unionist Party   **LP** = Labour Party
SDLP = Social and Liberal Democrats Party   **Other** = Ulster Unionists, Scottish National Party, Plaid Cymru

House of Lords 1199 members

The House of Lords is an unelected body of spiritual, judicial, hereditary and life peers appointed by the Queen. 39% are Conservative peers, 10% Labour peers, 5% Liberal Democrat peers, 23% are independent and 23% have an unspecified allegiance.

The UK is a multiparty democracy. The monarch holds no real power.

MAIN POLITICAL ISSUES

Europe
The question of whether the UK should pursue the goal of a Federal Europe has split the ruling CUP. The anti-EU faction is concerned that the EU is undemocratic and wasteful. The pro-EU faction believes that the UK has no choice but to follow the majority of European states who want federation, if it is to influence the nature of the UK's most important market.

The economy
There is now a broad consensus between the major parties on economic policy. The LP no longer believes in renationalizing privatized industries, and the CUP has toned down the pro-market rhetoric of the Thatcher years. However, the ruling CUP has been blamed for the recession and for raising taxes in 1994. Opinion polls suggest that both factors have led to a rise in support for the LP.

Health
The creation of an internal market in the National Health Service (NHS) has been opposed by doctors and voters. Many fear that the CUP may have plans to privatize the service. Most voters remain attached to the idea of an NHS which is free to all at point of use.

Northern Ireland
The Protestant and Catholic communities in Northern Ireland have suffered from sectarian conflict since the start of 'the troubles' in 1969. The Catholic community backs unification with the Irish Republic. The majority Protestant community wishes to remain part of the UK. Terrorism in the province by Catholic and Protestant groups continues. The Catholic Provisional Irish Republican Army (IRA)

Margaret Thatcher, *prime minister 1979– 1990; leader of the CUP 1975–1990.*

John Major, *leader of the CUP, became prime minister in 1990.*

John Smith, *LP leader from 1992, died suddenly of a heart attack in 1994.*

has also taken its campaign of terror to the British mainland. In 1994, the governments of the UK and Ireland attempted to bring all parties, including the IRA, to the negotiating table. However, many in both Catholic and Protestant camps will oppose any power-sharing arrangement.

PROFILE
Margaret Thatcher's 1979 election victory ushered in 15 years of CUP rule, and monetarist and privatization policies. The opposition LP lost four elections in a row, but moved to the political centre, abandoning policies of high taxation and renationalization.

In 1990, Margaret Thatcher was forced from office and replaced by John Major, who won the elections of 1992. Neil Kinnock resigned as LP leader and was replaced by John Smith.

However, by 1994, John Major's popularity had plummeted and the CUP lost heavily in local elections in May. LP leader John Smith died suddenly following a heart attack.

Vauxhall Cross, *a new post-modern office block by Terry Farrel on the River Thames. Farrel has had more influence on London's skyline than any architect since Wren.*

U

WORLD AFFAIRS

The UK owes much of its prominence in world affairs to its seat on the UN Security Council. However, since 1945, it has followed a largely US line in its foreign policy. It was a founder-member of NATO and maintained front-line troops in West Germany during the Cold War. In 1991, it was a major partner in UN Operation Desert Storm to evict Iraqi forces from Kuwait.

The UK signed the Maastricht Treaty in 1992, committing itself to eventual political and monetary union with its EU partners.

Relations with China over the hand-over of Hong Kong have been tense. Beijing has objected to British attempts to introduce democracy to the colony.

AID

 $3.2bn (donations)   Up 22% in 1991

Britain gives rather less aid than the European average. Its current donations of 0.3% of GNP are well below the target 0.7% for industrialized nations. Current policy is to freeze the aid programme until 1995 and to cut bilateral aid to countries in sub-Saharan Africa. Aid fell sharply during the 1980s. Three quarters goes to developing countries; India and Bangladesh are the biggest recipients.

Aid is not a highly politicized issue in the UK. However, the country is home to some prominent NGOs, including Oxfam. The Voluntary Service Overseas (VSO) organization sends people to share their skills in developing countries. In 1985, the Live Aid rock concert in London highlighted the plight of Ethiopia's devastating famine.

DEFENCE

 $41.2bn   Down 2% in 1992

0	Defence spending as % GDP	40
	4.2%	

BRITISH ARMED FORCES

1318 main battle tanks (426 *Challenger*/850 *Chieftain*/42 *Centurion*)	293,500 personnel	
2 carriers, 21 submarines 12 destroyers, 29 frigates and 27 patrol boats	61,100 personnel	
466 combat aircraft (120 *Tornado* GR-1/78 *Tornado* F-2,-3/53 *Jaguar*)	86,000 personnel	
SSBN (32 *Polaris* A-3TK)		

The UK's defence spending as a proportion of GNP is one of the highest in the OECD. However, as a response to the end of the Cold War, the 1990 Options for Change programme was implemented in 1993. The army and navy came in for the greatest cuts in personnel and equipment orders. The UK's independent nuclear deterrent was scaled down. The emphasis now is on creating rapid reaction forces and fulfilling the UK's UN commitments.

The UK is one of the world's leading arms exporters. Major buyers include Middle Eastern states and the booming economies of South East Asia.

ECONOMICS

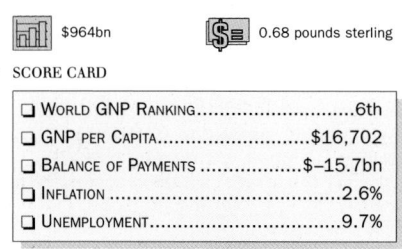 $964bn   0.68 pounds sterling

SCORE CARD

❏ WORLD GNP RANKING	6th
❏ GNP PER CAPITA	$16,702
❏ BALANCE OF PAYMENTS	$–15.7bn
❏ INFLATION	2.6%
❏ UNEMPLOYMENT	9.7%

EXPORTS

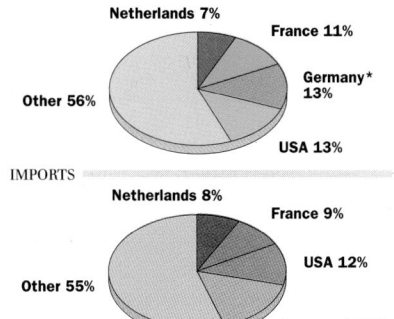

Netherlands 7%
France 11%
Germany* 13%
USA 13%
Other 56%

IMPORTS

Netherlands 8%
France 9%
USA 12%
Germany* 16%
Other 55%

STRENGTHS

World leader in financial services, pharmaceuticals and defence industries. Successful aerospace sector. Precision engineering and high-tech sectors, including telecommunications. Strong energy sector based on North Sea oil and gas production. Flexible working practices and lower wage rates than France, Germany or Scandinavia. The EU's largest recipient of inward investment. Strong multinational sector, with companies such as Glaxo, ICI, RTZ, BAT and Hanson.

WEAKNESSES

Decline of some key manufacturing sectors since 1970s, including cars and household goods. Much of industry still working with outmoded machinery. Past propensity for inflation. High levels of consumer and government debt. Quick-return mentality of many investment decisions does not create the culture to sustain long-term growth.

PROFILE

Manufacturing is still the largest sector

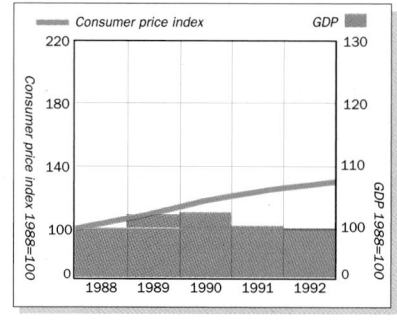

ECONOMIC PERFORMANCE INDICATOR

of the UK economy, although its importance has declined as the services and energy sectors have grown. During the 1980s, there was a sharp decline in heavy industries such as steel and engineering, located mostly in the Midlands and the North, while sectors such as financial services expanded rapidly in the south. A sharp recession led to a 2.5% decline in GDP in 1991. The subsequent revival was sluggish. By 1994, non-oil GDP was growing by 1.5% a year.

UNITED KINGDOM : MAJOR BUSINESSES

Oil & gas
Electronics
Computers
Engineering
Vehicle manufacture
Aerospace industry
Banking & finance
Iron & steel
Chemicals
Textiles
Whisky
Media

Inverness
Aberdeen
Glasgow
Edinburgh
Belfast
Liverpool
Newcastle upon Tyne
Middlesbrough
Manchester
Bacton
Birmingham
Derby
Cambridge
Swansea
London
Bristol
Oxford

0   200 km
0   200 miles

U

RESOURCES

319bn kwh (capacity 73.1m kw)

1.7m b/d (reserves 4,143,530,000 bbl)

124.4m chickens, 43.8m sheep, 12.1m cattle

Coal, limestone, natural gas

ELECTRICITY GENERATION

Hydro 2% (7.1bn kwh)

Thermal 77% (246.2bn kwh)

Nuclear 21% (65.7bn kwh)

Other 0%

0   20   40   60   80   100
% of total generation by type

The UK has the largest energy resources of any EU state. The country's energy position is bolstered by substantial oil and gas reserves offshore on the Continental Shelf in the North Sea. Drilled under difficult conditions, the oil is of a high grade. Revenues from taxes on oil companies have been a major contributor to government finances, averaging around $12 billion a year. The oil is expected to last at least until 2010.

Coal reserves are also sizeable, and at current rates could meet Britain's energy needs well into 2400. However, the privatization of the electricity industry resulted in the industry switching from coal to gas-fired power stations. The consequent fall in demand for coal has resulted in the closure of all but 14 pits.

The UK produces few other minerals in significant quantities. Tin workings in the West Country and gold mines in Wales and Scotland have mostly been mined out.

UNITED KINGDOM : LAND USE

Cropland
Pasture
Forest
High mountain regions
Sheep
Cattle
Fruit
Wheat

0   200 km
0   200 miles

ENVIRONMENT

19% partially protected

Increasingly active enviromental movement

ENVIRONMENTAL TREATIES

Yes

Yes

No

Yes

Environmental issues have come to the fore and are increasingly a political issue in the UK in the 1990s. Plans for the building of Thorp, a massive new nuclear reprocessing plant, have met with heated opposition. Sellafield, where the plant is due to be built, is already the largest single source of civil radioactive discharge in Europe. The UK's beaches have been condemned by the EU for their high levels of sewage pollution. Meanwhile, several road building projects are the focus of vigorous local opposition campaigns.

MEDIA

 No political restrictions

PUBLISHING AND BROADCAST MEDIA

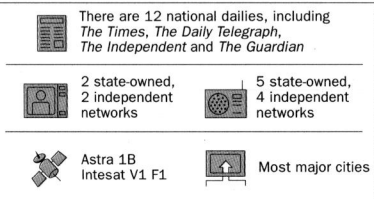

There are 12 national dailies, including *The Times*, *The Daily Telegraph*, *The Independent* and *The Guardian*

2 state-owned, 2 independent networks

5 state-owned, 4 independent networks

Astra 1B Intesat V1 F1

Most major cities

More newspapers are sold per capita in the UK than in any other European country. Newspapers are owned mostly by large media corporations, such as News International and, whilst free from censorship, tend to express right-of-centre political views. The arrival of satellite TV has led to plans for a deregulated market and increased competition for the highly protected British Broadcasting Corporation (BBC). The BBC's *World Service* remains an influential international news source.

The Welsh coal industry *has virtually disappeared. Wales now has the highest percentage of small business start-ups, relative to the population, of any part of the UK.*

CRIME

 52,169 prisoners

 Down 8% in 1990

CRIME RATES

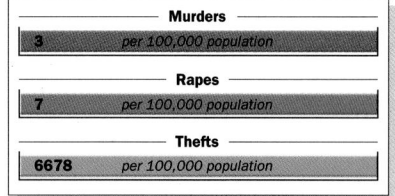

Murders
3   per 100,000 population

Rapes
7   per 100,000 population

Thefts
6678   per 100,000 population

Crime has risen sharply in the UK since the 1970s. The largest increase has been in burglary; car theft rates are the highest in Europe and higher than the USA's. Most crime is opportunistic and committed by young males. In the inner cities there is a growing problem fuelled by drug dependency.

The UK has one of the highest prison populations in Europe. CUP plans for tougher sentencing will result in a further increase in numbers by 2000.

EDUCATION

 99%

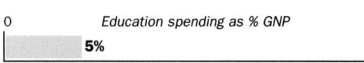

0   Education spending as % GNP   25
5%

THE EDUCATION SYSTEM

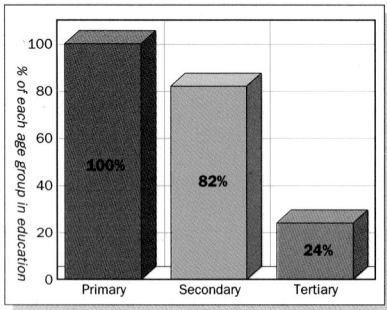

% of each age group in education

100
80
60
40
20
0

100%   Primary
82%   Secondary
24%   Tertiary

Once based on an elitist system of grammar schools, with membership decided by a competitive examination at the age of 11, the British state system underwent extensive reform in the 1970s and 1980s. Standards, however, declined sharply. The 1988 Education Reform Bill attempted to reverse falling standards by introducing a programme of required teaching. The state system is used by 94% of children. The rest attend private schools known as public schools. In Northern Ireland, many schools are segregated along religious (Catholic or Protestant) lines.

Compared with its EU partners, relatively few UK students proceed to tertiary education. Entry to university is highly competitive and dependent on grades achieved in the end of school A-level exams. Oxford and Cambridge are the most prestigious universities.

U

REGIONS
SCOTLAND

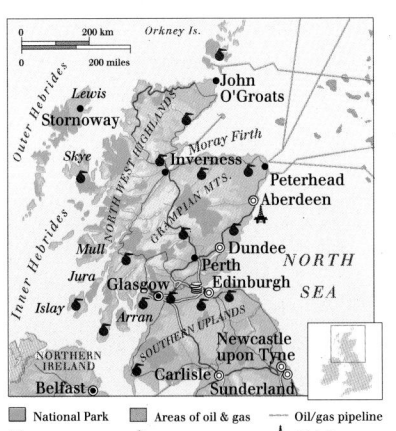

A LTHOUGH RULED FROM Westminster since 1707, Scotland is still very much a separate nation. It has its own legal and educational systems; its own church and banknotes. It is also one of the most pro-EU parts of the UK, believing closer integration would bring not only economic but also political benefits – notably devolution. Only a minority of Scots want independence, but most would like Scotland to have more control over its affairs. Mining and heavy industry are all but dead. Offshore oil helped fuel growth in the 1980s. New industry is proving hard to attract, a result of Scotland's peripheral positon in Europe.

■ National Park　■ Areas of oil & gas　— Oil/gas pipeline
🐚 Financial centre　◆ Areas with whisky distilleries　🏭 Oil industry

TYNESIDE

T YNESIDE IN NORTHEAST England is slowly emerging from decades of decline. Like neighbouring Wearside and Teeside, it depended on shipbuilding and heavy industry, and on a few large companies which employed successive generations of families. Today, little of that economic base is left, decimated by recession and by competition from cheaper producers. Instead, disused docks and derelict factory sites are being turned into business parks. Foreign investors have included prominent Japanese firms such as Nissan; Scandinavia and the EU are also well represented. A symbol of returning prosperity is Gateshead's huge Metro Centre – the UK's most profitable retail centre.

● American companies　★ Japanese companies　💻 Major sites
🏭 Shipbuilding industry　🚗 Motor industry　💻 Hi-tech industry　⚡ Electronics

LONDON

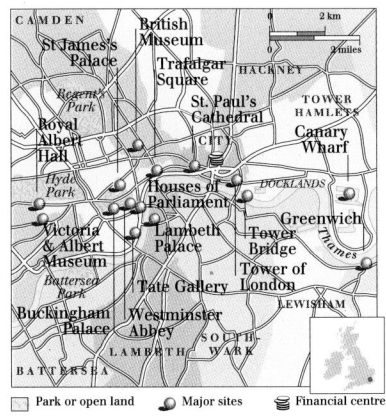

□ Park or open land　💻 Major sites　🐚 Financial centre

T HE FIRST OF THE WORLD'S mega-cities, the UK's capital today is home to 6.8 million people. London is the seat of government and dominates the country's political, financial and cultural life. The flight of industry to cheaper locations outside the capital means London depends mainly on service industries. Tourism and retail services are important, but the capital's $84 billion economy is underpinned by the financial sector.

Focused on the City of London, the site of the Roman city, this sector carries out 20% of all global banking transactions and is also the location of much international commodity trade. Following the deregulation of the market ('Big Bang') in the 1980s, the City expanded rapidly. Recession in the early 1990s, however, saw many job losses and dented profits.

Much of London was rebuilt in the 1980s and early 1990s, including the major East End development of Canary Wharf.

HEALTH

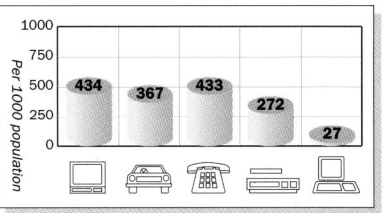

👤 1 per 1719 people　🫀 Heart, cerebrovascular and respiratory diseases, cancers

0 ——————— Health spending as % GNP ——————— 25
5.1%

The majority of health care is provided by the National Health Service (NHS) which is financed by central government and free to all residents. The system is efficient – the UK spends a smaller proportion of its GNP on health than Germany, France or Italy. However, the pressures of an ageing population are reflected in long waiting lists for non-essential operations.

WEALTH

💰 Dustman, 221 pounds sterling per week; accountant, 446 pounds sterling per week

CONSUMER GOODS OWNERSHIP

Per 1000 population: 434, 367, 433, 272, 27

Income inequality in the UK was higher in 1994 than in 1884, when records first began. In part, this is the result of the reductions in taxation for higher earners introduced under the Thatcher administration. The purchasing power of salaries rose sharply during the 1980s and early 1990s. However, in the same period unemployment tripled whilst the value of state benefits fell. The value of the old age pension has fallen sharply.

Wealth remains well-hidden in the UK. Considerable amounts are invested on the stock market, overseas, or in the Lloyds insurance market. A series of disastrous losses at Lloyds between 1991 and 1993 severely dented the fortunes of many investing families.

WORLD RANKING

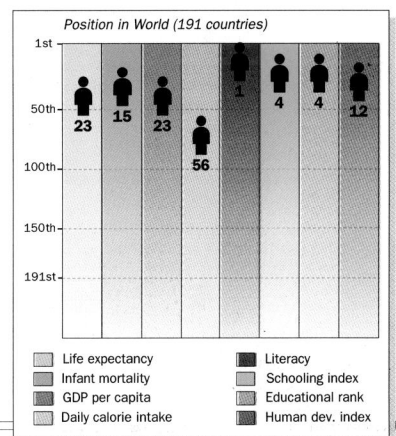

Position in World (191 countries)

1st, 50th, 100th, 150th, 191st

23　15　23　56　1　4　4　12

□ Life expectancy　■ Literacy
□ Infant mortality　□ Schooling index
□ GDP per capita　□ Educational rank
□ Daily calorie intake　■ Human dev. index

U

See also OVERSEAS TERRITORIES *p.616*

UNITED STATES

OFFICIAL NAME: United States of America   **CAPITAL:** Washington, DC
POPULATION: 255.2 million   **CURRENCY:** US dollar   **OFFICIAL LANGUAGE:** English   **OVERSEAS TERRITORIES:** 14

THE UNITED STATES COMPRISES 48 contiguous states, bounded by Canada and Mexico, and the outlying states of Alaska and Hawaii. Alone of the nations that encompass a great landmass, it is neither overpopulated (like China and India), underpopulated (like Australia), nor held hostage to extremes of climate or topography (like Russia and Brazil). The USA also stands apart from most other nations in that it is founded neither on ethnic unity nor within natural geographical boundaries, but instead on the appeal of some powerful ideas. Democracy and liberty, in both a political and an economic sense, continue to be the guiding lights of the USA – as they were for its founders over 200 years ago.

ALASKA

CLIMATE

WEATHER CHART

from November to April. The USA's weather is frequently dramatic. Tornadoes, cyclones, floods, thunderstorms and droughts are common.

Spanning a continent, and extending far into the Pacific Ocean in Alaska and Hawaii, the USA displays a full range of climatic conditions. Mean annual temperatures range from 29°C in Florida to –13°C in Alaska. Except for New England, Alaska and the Pacific North-West, summer temperatures are higher than in Europe. Southern summers are humid; in the southwest they are dry. Winters are particularly severe in the western mountains and plains and in the Midwest – where the Great Lakes freeze. The Atlantic northeast can experience heavy snow

The AT & T building, New York, a notable example of post-modern architecture by the influential US architect Philip Johnson.

HAWAII

COMMUNICATIONS

 John F Kennedy, New York
29.79m passengers

 502 ships
22.44m dwt

THE TRANSPORT NETWORK

6.37m km (3.96m miles)	84,361 km (52,419 miles)
270,312 km (167,964 miles)	41,009 km (25,482 miles)

The Mississippi–Missouri river system provided the USA's first transport network. Today, the USA has the world's cheapest, most extensive internal air network and also a good system of interstate highways. The rail network is poorly developed, by European standards, and carries mostly freight. Since Henry Ford began mass production in Detroit nearly 90 years ago, Americans have been wedded to the car. In 1919, Ford sold one million cars. Today, there are over 255 million cars in the USA. Many cities, such as Los Angeles, have come to depend on the car; the USA now accounts for more than half of the world's car journeys. Cheap petrol has underpinned this growth. In the long term, the prospect of dependence on oil imports, as domestic supplies run out could force a rethink of the car's role in society.

The Mittens, Monument Valley, Arizona.
These striking natural rock formations are created by erosion of red sandstone. The Valley is home to the Navajo people.

UNITED STATES

Total Area : 9 372 610 sq. km
(3 618 760 sq. miles)

POPULATION

over 5 000 000	⊡
over 1 000 000	⊡
over 500 000	◉
over 100 000	◎
over 50 000	○
over 10 000	●
under 10 000	·

LAND HEIGHT

3000m/9843ft	
2000m/6562ft	
1000m/3281ft	
500m/1640ft	
200m/656ft	
Sea Level	

U

TOURISM

 45.6m visitors   Up 2% in 1993

MAIN OVERSEAS ARRIVALS

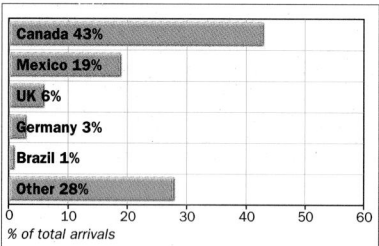

Canada 43%
Mexico 19%
UK 6%
Germany 3%
Brazil 1%
Other 28%

% of total arrivals

Tourism is an important industry, catering to ever-growing demand from both foreign visitors and Americans themselves. The number of overseas visitors has doubled in the past 15 years, reflecting the relative weakness of the dollar and the deregulation of air fares. Domestic tourism has expanded just as rapidly, as real incomes have risen. In 1993, over two billion trips were made within the USA.

The top tourist destinations include Florida's Disney World – with over 20 million visitors a year – Niagara Falls, Las Vegas, New York, San Francisco, LA and Hollywood, the Grand Canyon, New Orleans, Atlantic City and Washington. All the states have their attractions, however, and most court tourists. Tourism is a major generator of jobs, especially in areas of industrial decline, such as the northeast.

Tourism's rapid expansion has also brought some problems. The 367 parks and sites run by the National Parks Service (NPS) have been particular casualties. Visitor numbers have more than doubled since 1970, to a record 275 million in 1992. To try and reduce pressure on the most popular areas, NPS lands have been doubled in area since 1976, to 327,807 sq km. Even so, there is still bumper-to-bumper traffic in Yellowstone Park, and a seven-year waiting list for a raft ride down the Grand Canyon.

PEOPLE

 English, Spanish, Italian, German, French, Polish, Chinese, Tagalog, Greek   27 people per km²

THE URBAN/RURAL POPULATION SPLIT

75%   25%

RELIGIOUS PERSUASION

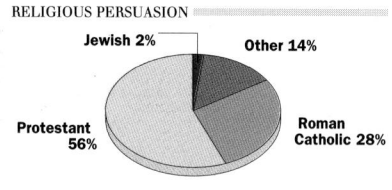

Jewish 2%
Other 14%
Protestant 56%
Roman Catholic 28%

ETHNIC MAKEUP

Other 4%
Black 12%
White (including Hispanic) 84%

Unlike Western Europe, the USA is experiencing a population boom. This is a consequence of the least understood, but arguably most important aspect of modern America – immigration.

Though the ideology of the 'melting pot' suggests that the USA has always been a country of immigrants, from the 1920s to the 1960s this was not the case. Fewer immigrants came to the USA in the 1950s than in the 1850s. However, since the mid-1960s, and especially since 1980, the USA has undergone an astonishing immigration boom. During the 1980s, probably ten million immigrants (legal and illegal) settled in the country, more than in any

other decade. The new immigrants are disproportionately drawn from Asia and Latin America. In the 1980s, more than two million immigrants came from Mexico alone.

Most of the available evidence suggests that Asians and Latinos assimilated into US society at the same rate as Poles and Italians did three generations ago. The critical variable for this is 'out-marriage' – the rate of marriage outside an ethnic group.

There is concern that the growth of immigration will marginalize the position of American blacks, who increasingly find they have to compete both politically and economically with the newer immigrants. In some communities, such as Los Angeles, this is already a source of tension.

For all the importance of immigration, though, it remains possible that by 2050 the majority of Americans (about 65%) will still be non-Latino whites. They are also likely to remain God-fearing. Americans are consistently shown to place a much higher premium on the value of religion than most other nationalities.

POPULATION AGE BREAKDOWN

% of population by age group	0–14	15–64	65+
	9.2%	9.8%	11.3%	12.6%	12.8%
	59.7%	61.9%	66.2%	66%	67%
	31.1%	28.3%	22.5%	21.4%	20.2%
	1960	1970	1980	1990	2000

POLITICS

 1996   President William Jefferson Clinton

THE STATE OF THE PARTIES

House of Representatives 435 members

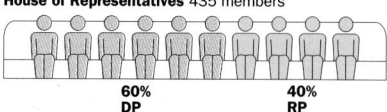

60% DP   40% RP

DP = Democratic Party   **RP** = Republican Party
There is also one independent member of the House of Representatives

Senate 100 members

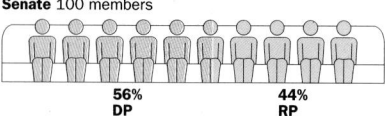

56% DP   44% RP

The USA has a federal democratic government. Under this system, many important issues are dealt with by the states. The federal government, for example, does not have a central role in education or urban development.

MAIN POLITICAL ISSUES

Crime, race and poverty

The USA has seen its crime rates soar for 20 years. At the same time parts of its cities have faced increasing social problems. The black community, who make up 60% of those living in poor districts, face particular problems. Both rates of criminality and crime victims are higher in the black community than in any other.

A priority over the next ten years will be finding a way of regenerating the cities where the poorest live. This is most likely to be achieved by a combination of new economic opportunities and programmes that give poor people more power over their own lives (for example, by self-management of public housing projects). If it fails in this effort, the country runs the risk of having a permanently disaffected section of the population living within its cities.

Health

The USA is wrestling with a health care system whose costs are increasing faster than private or public budgets can tolerate, and which gives patchy

***President Bill Clinton** was elected to office in November 1992.*

***Albert Gore Jr,** vice-president. He is a keen promoter of environmental issues.*

U

POLITICS *continued*

service to clients. The costs of health care are currently growing at twice the rate of the rest of the economy. The aim of the proposed legislation is to make health care free to all citizens at the point of access. However, there is considerable debate as to how this should be funded. According to the president's preferred option, employers would foot at least 80% of the bill of their employees' health costs. Regional bodies would be set up from which all but employees of the largest companies would choose from between at least three health care schemes. An alternative favoured by some liberal Democrats in Congress is the adoption of the Canadian model, under which costs are met out of direct taxation.

Foreign policy

In the post-Cold War world, the USA has to decide how and in what circumstances to project its unique power abroad. The USA is not by nature isolationist, but historically has required convincing in order to play the role of global policeman. As demands on US servicemen and logistics continue to grow, so will the domestic consequences of these demands.

The Clinton presidency

The Clinton administration has been beset by minor irritants, which commentators suggest are distracting the president. The president's personal life has been closely scrutinized by the press amidst a number of opportunistic lawsuits. A serious blow was the accusation of financial impropriety directed at Representative Dan Rostenkowski, a leading figure in the president's attempts to pass his health care programme.

PROFILE

In modern times, the Republican Party has dominated the presidency and the Democratic Party the Congress. The election of Bill Clinton at the end of 1992 was meant to end the resultant 'gridlock' between the executive and legislative branches. However, Congress has become such a power in its own right that it is at least as

Warren Christopher *holds the position of secretary of state.*

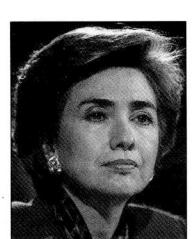

Hillary Clinton. *The First Lady is orchestrating health care reforms.*

important to the country's domestic agenda as Clinton.

In the 1950s and 1960s, some of the most momentous decisions in the country were in fact made in the Supreme Court. However, the big legal issues – such as ending racial discrimination – were taken long ago, and the Court is now retreating to a much less salient position in US politics.

A fundamental consensus on economic and foreign policy continues to exist between the USA's two main political parties.

WORLD AFFAIRS

The USA's attitude to international affairs has been coloured by two facts. Firstly, it is protected from the rest of the world by two great oceans. Secondly, its immediate neighbours – Canada and Mexico – have historically been benign. As a result, for much of its history the USA has enjoyed the luxury of being able to choose the extent of its involvement in the affairs of others.

For most of the first half of the 20th century it pursued an isolationist policy, becoming only reluctantly involved in the First and Second World Wars. After 1945, however, it swapped isolationism for involvement. The UN was headquartered in New York, and the USA took its seat on the Security Council. As leader of one side of the struggle between democracy and communism, the USA helped set up NATO, and subsequently played an active part in the defence of western Europe. For the USA, the Cold War was most immediate – and costly – in the Korean and Vietnam Wars. The heavy death toll and shock of defeat in Vietnam kept the USA out of military involvement overseas for over a decade. Instead, it concentrated on diplomacy – with particular success in China and the Middle East – and on supporting the opponents of left-wing regimes in the developing world, as in Nicaragua.

The collapse of the eastern bloc after 1989 has led to a renewed debate over foreign policy. In particular, as the only remaining superpower, the USA has to determine the scope of its foreign responsibilities in an era when its own survival is no longer threatened. At times in the early 1990s, it appeared set to take on the role of world policeman, taking a lead in the interventions in Kuwait and Somalia. However, as its subsequent problems in Somalia indicated – and lack of clear policy on Bosnia and Haiti confirmed – the USA is still uncertain about its role in the post-Cold War world.

Manhattan Island, *bounded by the Hudson and East Rivers. New York's two main clusters of skyscrapers are found in the financial district and in mid-town Manhattan.*

AID

 $9.4bn (donations)　 Down 17% in 1991

The USA gives proportionately little foreign aid, and such aid as it does give is perennially held hostage to special pleading in Congress. The lion's share goes to Israel and Egypt, although of late there has been substantial assistance to the countries of the former USSR and eastern Europe.

DEFENCE

 $277.2bn　　Down 2% in 1993

0	Defence spending as % GDP	40
5.1%		

AMERICAN ARMED FORCES

	15,629 main battle tanks (896 M-48A5/2, 155 M-60 A3/7, 422 M-1/M-1A1)	674,800 personnel
	110 submarines, 12 carriers, 45 destroyers, 83 frigates and 30 patrol boats	546,650 personnel
	3485 combat aircraft (F15, F15E, F16D/D, F-111, A-10, F-4G, F-117)	499,300 personnel
	25 SSBN (with 504 missiles)	

The enormous US military-industrial complex dates from the years since 1945. Before then, the armed forces were small in number, poorly equipped and rapidly dismantled at the end of wars. Defence spending has peaked three times since 1945: at the time of the Korean War in the 1950s, during the 1963–1973 Vietnam War and again in the defence build-up of 1979–1986.

A combination of the end of the Cold War and need to cut the budget deficit means defence spending has been cut in the 1990s. In real terms, it is now at its lowest level since 1945. This is having one unanticipated but troubling side effect. The armed forces are the area where blacks have found it easiest to gain top positions. As the military shrinks, so do the opportunities for black American advancement.

U

REGIONS

THE GREAT LAKES

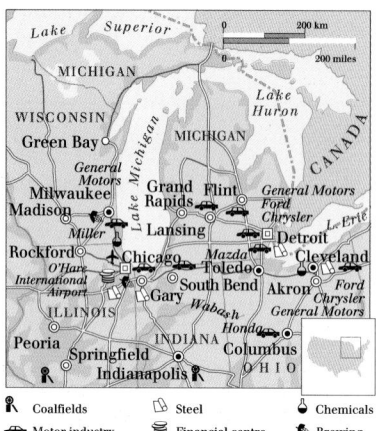

Coalfields — Steel — Chemicals
Motor industry — Financial centre — Brewing

WITH A total area of 244,754 sq km, Lakes Erie, Huron, Michigan, Superior and Ontario form the world's largest expanse of fresh water. The Great Lakes provide a natural transport system, which enabled the adjacent Midwest states to become the USA's leading industrial and agricultural area in the 19th century. Agriculture is still important, especially in Wisconsin and Minnesota; the Minneapolis grain exchange is the USA's largest strictly cash commodity market. The region's heavy industries have suffered badly since the early 1980s, hit by overseas competition and the shift towards the high-tech sector. Even so, Detroit, home of Ford, is still the USA's leading vehicle producer. Chicago, once known for its commodities markets and the Mob, is now one of the USA's leading cultural centres – and is still its transport hub.

SILICON VALLEY

Built-up area — Park or open land
Major university research centres — Hi-tech industry

LOCATED IN northern California, Silicon Valley has it origins in the years before the Second World War. By the early 1960s it had developed into a centre of high-tech innovation and entrepreneurialism. Home to scores of established companies – including Hewlett-Packard and Apple – Silicon Valley has lost little of its early spirit. It still generates many imaginative young enterprises. Hewlett-Packard has had recently to face stiff competition from newcomers, such as Sun Microsystems. Apple, too, has had to undertake significant restructuring to meet the demands of the 1990s market. Many Asian, European and Latin American immigrants have been drawn by the region's industry, which has a reputation for extracting the maximum from its workforce. Workers often have a stake in their company through share ownership. Local universities, in particular Stanford, have played an important role in developing the new technology on which the Valley thrives.

HOUSTON

The Texas Medical Center, Houston.
It is equipped with an array of up-to-the-minute high-tech facilities.

AMERICA'S fourth city, Houston has been the centre of the oil industry since 1901. However, oil is lessening in importance, as Houston, like the rest of Texas, turns to high-tech industries. In 1980, just 16% of its economy was not dependent on oil; today it is 40%. Houston has two main attractions for investors like computer giant Compaq: the Lyndon B Johnson Space Center, home to the space shuttle programme, and the Texas Medical Center, the world's largest medical complex. The resulting concentration of research facilities, scientists and engineers has enabled Houston to develop as a top applied and bio-technology centre.

THE SOUTH

IN THE 1940s, the South almost seemed to be another country. Thanks to abundant cheap labour, its agriculture was still tied to cotton. With a few exceptions, such as Birmingham, Alabama, industry had never taken root. The 'Jim Crow' laws epitomized a bitter racial division. The Second World War started a transformation process. Industry developed along the Gulf Coast, in towns such as Mobile. The cotton harvest was mechanized. Not least, the federal government extended its powers into the South in the battle to end legally sanctioned racial discrimination. Since the 1970s, the South has been one of the USA's fastest growing areas. Its population has increased by over 33% and many industries have invested. The core states of the 'Confederate' South, however, have done less well. In

NEW YORK

NEW YORK, the 'Big Apple', is the largest city in the USA and has been the gateway city for repeated waves of immigrants. During most of the first two centuries of the Republic, New York was its capital for everything but politics. It is a huge and in many ways still vibrant city, partly because it is currently experiencing a new influx of immigrants – this time from Asia and Russia. Its collar of suburbs has a population greater than that of Belgium. However, the extent of the city's decay is evident – more so in the outer boroughs than in Manhattan, where most of its tourist attractions are located. In terms of pop culture, art, sport, finance and recreation, New York has never loomed less large within the USA than it does now.

SEATTLE

THE MOST IMPORTANT city of the Pacific North-West, Seattle in Washington State has a dramatic location – bounded to the west by the Puget Sound and to the east by Lake Washington. The 1980s boom years saw large numbers of immigrants and new businesses attracted to the region. The latter included Microsoft, the world's leading software manufacturer. Yet, despite the arrival of a different style of industry, Boeing is still the largest employer in the Seattle area. With its new-found wealth, Seattle has swiftly changed from a backwater near America's northwest border with Canada into a cosmopolitan city. Its lively downtown area recently gained international fame as the birthplace of 'grunge' rock.

U

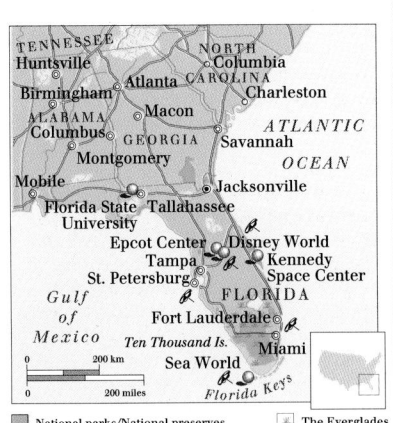

National parks/National preserves

National forests

☒ The Everglades

🚢 Major sites

✈ Tourism

addition, areas such as West Virginia, already among the poorest in the USA, stagnated and lost population.

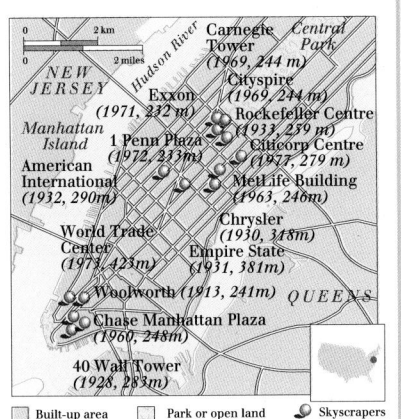

☐ Built-up area   ☐ Park or open land   🏢 Skyscrapers

Seattle

☐ Built-up area   ☐ County/state park   🚢 Major sites

🏭 High-tech industry   ⚓ Shipyards   ✈ Aerospace industry   🏭 Textiles

ECONOMICS

📊 $5686bn   💲 Not applicable

SCORE CARD

❑ WORLD GNP RANKING..........................1st
❑ GNP PER CAPITA...........................$22,475
❑ BALANCE OF PAYMENTS ....$–62.5bn
❑ INFLATION 3%
❑ UNEMPLOYMENT..................................7.4%

EXPORTS

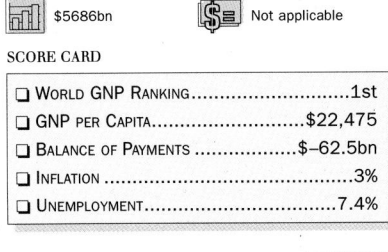

UK 6%   Mexico 7%   Japan 13%   Canada 21%   Other 53%

IMPORTS

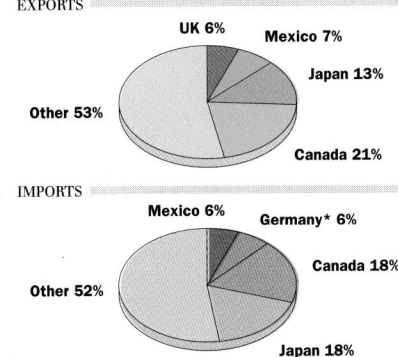

Mexico 6%   Germany* 6%   Canada 18%   Japan 18%   Other 52%

STRENGTHS

The world's largest economy. Wealth of natural resources, including energy, raw materials and foods. Strong high-tech base and world-leading research and development. Sophisticated service sector, as well as advanced and competitive manufacturing industry. World-class multinationals such as Ford, GM, Exxon. Global leader in computer software. Entrepreneurial business ethic. High quality of post-graduate education, especially related to application of high-tech to business. Global dominance of US culture a major boost to US manufactures.

UNITED STATES : MAJOR BUSINESSES

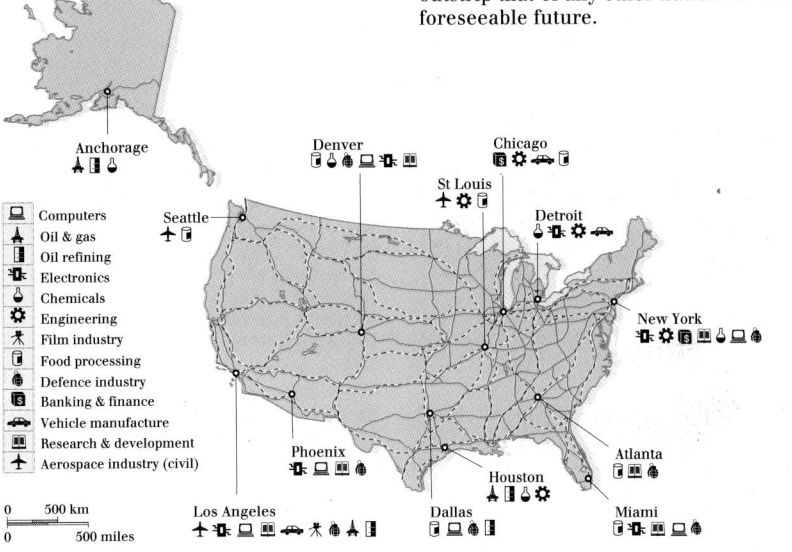

📺 Computers
⚒ Oil & gas
🔩 Oil refining
⚡ Electronics
🧪 Chemicals
⚙ Engineering
🏃 Film industry
🍴 Food processing
🛡 Defence industry
⑤ Banking & finance
🚗 Vehicle manufacture
🖥 Research & development
✈ Aerospace industry (civil)

0   500 km
0   500 miles

ECONOMIC PERFORMANCE INDICATOR

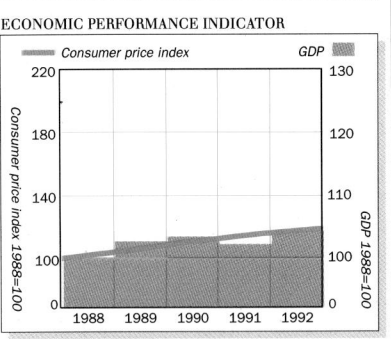

WEAKNESSES

Dramatic fall in manufacturing employment over last 20 years; though manufacturing sector has remained constant as a share of GDP. Post-war economic boom was built on low-skilled, high-waged employment in areas such as car industry. Tough competition from Japan, the rest of Asia and EU, particularly in future leading-edge technologies. Lower savings rate than many competitors. World's largest debtor nation.

PROFILE

In 1945, the USA accounted for about 50% of world output, in 1994 for about 25%. That is not, as Americans often think, a sign of failure, but a clear indication that the 1940s and 1950s were unusual years. The current total of 25% is about the same share of the world market that the USA claimed in 1914, when it was already the world's greatest economy.

The USA has become a great exporter, and continues to have both a stable political system and a uniquely strong combination of skilled labour and natural resources. Its economic potential will continue to outstrip that of any other nation for the foreseeable future.

U

CHRONOLOGY

At the beginning of the 17th century, British settlers began to establish colonies on the eastern seaboard. Following the American War of Independence, Britain recognized the independence of the 13 colonies in 1783. The Constitution of 1787 joined the original states to establish the USA. Following the victory of the northern states in the 1861–1865 Civil War, slavery was abolished throughout the USA. The latter half of the 19th century saw a series of conflicts in which native Americans were dispossessed of their land.

- ❏ **1917** Enters First World War.
- ❏ **1929** New York stock market collapse; economic depression.
- ❏ **1941** Japanese attack on Pearl Harbor. Enters Second World War.
- ❏ **1950–53** Korean War.
- ❏ **1954** Supreme Court rules racial segregation in schools is unconstitutional. Blacks, seeking constitutional rights, start campaign of civil disobedience.
- ❏ **1959** Alaska and Hawaii become 49th and 50th states of the USA.
- ❏ **1961** John F Kennedy becomes president. Promises to provide aid to South Vietnamese. Relations with Cuba deteriorate; US-backed invasion defeated at Bay of Pigs.
- ❏ **1962** Discovery of Soviet Missile bases on Cuba; serious threat of war with USSR averted.
- ❏ **1963** November, Kennedy assassinated. Lyndon Baines Johnson president. Effects on economy of increased defence and social expenditure begin to be felt.
- ❏ **1964** US involvement in Vietnam stepped up. Civil Rights Act gives blacks constitutional equality.
- ❏ **1968** Martin Luther King assassinated.
- ❏ **1969** Republican Richard Nixon takes office as president. Growing public opposition to Vietnam War.
- ❏ **1972** Nixon re-elected. Makes historic visit to China. Relations with USSR also improve.
- ❏ **1973** Withdrawal of US troops from Vietnam; 58,000 US troops dead by end of war.
- ❏ **1974** August, Nixon resigns following 'Watergate' scandal: revelation that his campaign team had organized break-in to DP headquarters. Replaced by Vice-President Gerald Ford.
- ❏ **1976** Democrat Jimmy Carter elected president.
- ❏ **1978** Conclusion of US-sponsored 'Camp David' agreement between Egypt and Israel.
- ❏ **1979** Seizure of US hostages in Tehran, Iran.

U

RESOURCES

3031bn kwh (capacity 775.4m kw)

7.2m b/d (reserves 24,682,000,000 bbl)

98.1m cattle, 55.5m pigs, 10.9m sheep, 5.32m horses

Phosphate, gypsum, oil, sulphur, lead, zinc, copper, gold

ELECTRICITY GENERATION

Hydro 10% (290.9bn kwh)

Thermal 70% (2145bn kwh)

Nuclear 19% (576.8bn kwh)

Other 1% (17.6bn kwh)

% of total generation by type

The USA has an abundance of natural resources, including oil, although the country is a net oil importer. There are massive deposits of coal in the Western states – where almost all mining is open-cast – and substantial mineral deposits in the mountains and intramontane basins.

Environmental concerns have prevented the development of new sources of nuclear power since the accident at Three Mile Island in 1979. Environmentalism has also forced the

timber industry to retreat from the Pacific North-West, especially from Washington State. It has moved to the south, where great stands of pine are harvested as if they were fields of wheat. The USA has harnessed hydroelectric power in the past; today, imports of hydro-power from Canada are commonplace.

By comparison with Western Europe, the USA is not intensively farmed. The huge size of farms in the Midwest and West has allowed both arable and livestock farming to be based upon a low-input for low-output model.

UNITED STATES : LAND USE

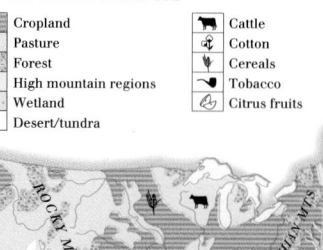

- Cropland
- Pasture
- Forest
- High mountain regions
- Wetland
- Desert/tundra
- Cattle
- Cotton
- Cereals
- Tobacco
- Citrus fruits

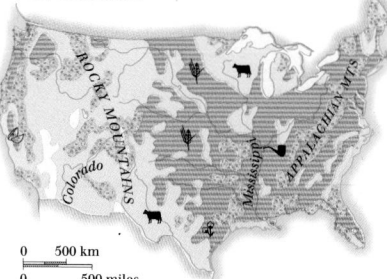

0   500 km
0   500 miles

ENVIRONMENT

11% (6% partially protected)

Political opposition to environmental causes

ENVIRONMENTAL TREATIES

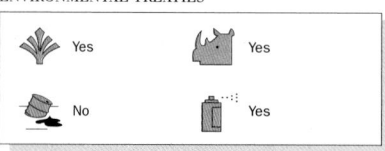

Yes

Yes

No

Yes

Although the USA came early to environmentalism, it has in some respects been overtaken by countries such as Germany. Food packaging is astonishingly wasteful and many cars are still 'gas-guzzlers'. As the suburban sprawl testifies, its wide open spaces have engendered a somewhat cavalier attitude to aspects of the environment.

To an extent which has not been true elsewhere, the ecological movement has been challenged politically. Protection necessarily involves the regulation of market activities; in the USA such a move is always contentious. The intramontane West is a battleground between those who want to maintain its beauty, and those who advocate 'wise use' – in practice this often means giving ranchers and miners free rein. Environmental teaching is, however, strong in schools.

MEDIA

Freedom of press guaranteed in constitution

PUBLISHING AND BROADCAST MEDIA

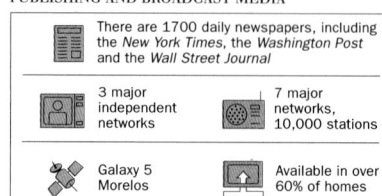

There are 1700 daily newspapers, including the *New York Times*, the *Washington Post* and the *Wall Street Journal*

3 major independent networks

7 major networks, 10,000 stations

Galaxy 5 Morelos

Available in over 60% of homes

Mass media as a phenomenon was born in the USA. No other society on earth has ever had anything quite like American network TV. And no other society has so easily moved into the world of multi-channel TV; homes with 50 or more channels are commonplace. Newspapers, however, are having a difficult time. With a few exceptions, newspapers are local, not national. They also tend to have very low cover prices and to gain most of their revenue from advertising. This business is under increasing threat from cable TV and other outlets. Many companies are exploring multimedia opportunities, investing in ways of providing on-line news, information and other services.

CHRONOLOGY *continued*

- ❏ **1980** Ronald Reagan wins elections for Republicans. Adopts tough anti-communist foreign policy.
- ❏ **1983** Military invasion of Grenada.
- ❏ **1985** Retaliatory air strikes against Libyan cities. Relations with USSR improve; first of three summits between Reagan and Mikhail Gorbachev.
- ❏ **1986** Iran-Contra affair revealed.
- ❏ **1987** Intermediate Nuclear Forces Treaty signed by USA and USSR.
- ❏ **1988** Republican George Bush, vice-president under Reagan, defeats Michael Dukakis in elections.
- ❏ **1989** Sending of 23,000 troops to Panama – to overthrow government and arrest General Noriega on drug-trafficking charges – condemned by UN Security Council.
- ❏ **1990** Normalization of relations with Nicaragua, following defeat of Sandinista government in elections. USA and six other nations agree to give aid to USSR to finance transition to market economy. USA takes leading role in international opposition to Iraqi invasion of Kuwait. NATO and Warsaw Pact group sign Treaty on Conventional Armed Forces in Europe.
- ❏ **1991** January, Operation Desert Storm launched against Iraq. Multinational forces include 43,000 US ground troops. USA and USSR sign START arms reduction treaty.
- ❏ **1992** Rioting in Los Angeles and other cities; brings to light the issue of disaffected black youth. Bush–Yeltsin summit agrees further arms reductions. Democrat Bill Clinton defeats Bush in election.
- ❏ **1993** USA participates in selective bombing of Iraqi missile sites. 24,000 US troops sent to Somalia to form part of US-led UN force. Reducing the large budget deficit and reforming health care among main objectives of new Clinton administration. US troops are withdrawn from Somalia.

***Snow-capped mountains rise from cattle pastures in Montana.** There are about 100 million head of cattle in the USA.*

CRIME

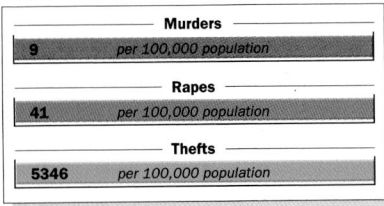
71,998 prisoners   Up 1% in 1990

CRIME RATES

Murders	
9	per 100,000 population

Rapes	
41	per 100,000 population

Thefts	
5346	per 100,000 population

The USA has seen a 20-year long crime wave. Violent crime – especially murder – is much more common than in other developed countries. This is the case even in relatively well-off parts of the country. Seattle, for example, which by US standards is a peaceful city, has a murder rate seven times that of Birmingham, England.

The rate of incarceration for drug crimes in the USA is much higher than in most Western countries – and the conditions worse. Capital punishment has made a strong comeback since the 1980s, especially in the South. Texas is the state that carries out most executions. Many of the liberal 'northern tier' states, by contrast, have abolished the death penalty.

EDUCATION

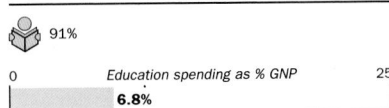
91%

0   *Education spending as % GNP*   25
6.8%

THE EDUCATION SYSTEM

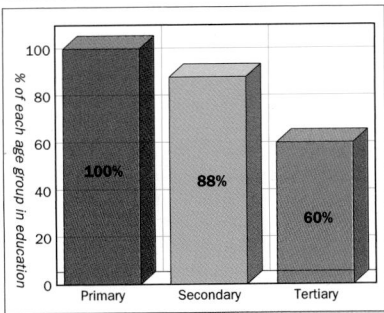

Education in the USA is primarily the responsibility of the state governments. A series of recent reports have been critical of standards in US high schools. Yet, all accept that US universities are world class.

Private education is a rapidly developing sector. Although the number of pupils in private education does not appear to have increased much in the last generation, this is misleading. While the number of Catholic private schools has shrunk, non-denominational fee-paying schools have been founded to take their place.

HEALTH

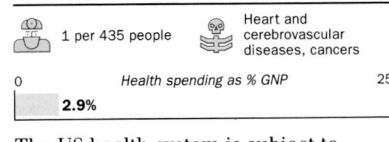
1 per 435 people   Heart and cerebrovascular diseases, cancers

0   *Health spending as % GNP*   25
2.9%

The US health system is subject to enormous disparities. At one level, sophisticated techniques are available to those with insurance (which they typically receive from their employer). The Texas Medical Center, in Houston, the epitome of high-tech medicine, has a budget equivalent to that of some small countries. On the other hand, infant mortality statistics in some parts of the country are at near-African levels.

Partly because of these disparities, reform has become a major political issue. But it has also been driven by the skyrocketing cost of care – the health sector now accounts for more than an eighth of the total economy.

WEALTH

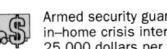
Armed security guard, 5 dollars per hour; in–home crisis intervention specialist, 25,000 dollars per year

CONSUMER GOODS OWNERSHIP

Between 1945 and 1973, all sectors of the population got richer. Since then, however, a new pattern has emerged. Those who finish high school have continued to see their standard of living increase, while those who did not have not seen an improvement for a generation. In a way that has not been seen for more than 50 years, the 'education effect' is leading to noticeable class divisions.

WORLD RANKING

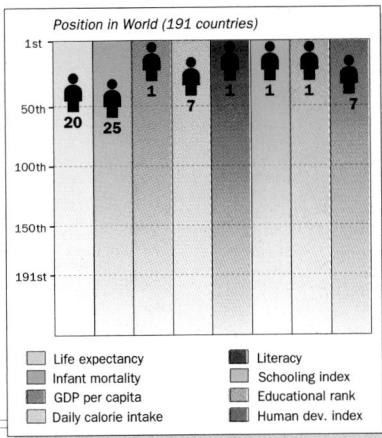

Position in World (191 countries)

- Life expectancy
- Infant mortality
- GDP per capita
- Daily calorie intake
- Literacy
- Schooling index
- Educational rank
- Human dev. index

URUGUAY

SOUTH AMERICA

OFFICIAL NAME: Eastern Republic of Uruguay   **CAPITAL:** Montevideo
POPULATION: 3.1 million   **CURRENCY:** New Uruguayan peso   **OFFICIAL LANGUAGE:** Spanish

URUGUAY IS SITUATED IN SOUTHEASTERN South America. Its capital, Montevideo, is an Atlantic port on the River Plate, lying across the river from Buenos Aires, Argentina's capital. Uruguay became independent in 1828, after nearly 150 years of Spanish and Portuguese control. Decades of liberal government ended in 1973 with a military coup that was to result in 12 years of dictatorship, during which 400,000 people emigrated. Most have since returned. Almost the entire lowlying landscape is devoted to the rearing of livestock, especially cattle and sheep. Uruguay is the world's second biggest wool exporter. Tourism and offshore banking now bring in substantial foreign earnings.

Uruguayan grasslands. Rich pasture covers three quarters of the country, ideal for cattle and sheep. Animals and animal products account for over one third of export earnings.

CLIMATE

WEATHER CHART

Uruguay has one of the most benign climates in the world. It is uniformly temperate over the whole country. Winters are mild, frost is rare and it never snows. Summers are generally cool for these latitudes and rarely tropically hot. The moderate rainfall tends to fall in heavy showers, leaving most days sunny.

COMMUNICATIONS

Carrasco, Montevideo
357,000 passengers

16 ships
151,200 dwt

THE TRANSPORT NETWORK

52,000 km
(32,312 miles)

None

3002 km
(1865 miles)

1250 km
(777 miles)

Uruguay's transport plans for the 1990s centre on privatization. The government has sold off its share in the national coach industry – there are extensive internal and international coach and bus services – and has closed down all passenger railway services. There is a plan to build a road tunnel from Montevideo to Buenos Aires under the River Plate, but this will take many years to complete.

TOURISM

 1.04m visitors

 Up 24% in 1989

MAIN OVERSEAS ARRIVALS

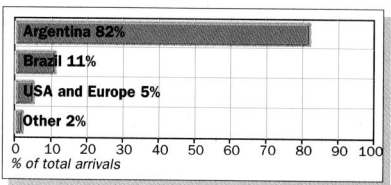
Argentina 82%
Brazil 11%
USA and Europe 5%
Other 2%
0 10 20 30 40 50 60 70 80 90 100
% of total arrivals

Most visitors to Uruguay travel through Montevideo to the sandy beaches near the River Plate estuary. Although the old Spanish fortifications of Montevideo have been destroyed, the city retains a colonial atmosphere. Punta del Este, 139 km east of the capital, Uruguay's major beach resort, is served by direct 737 flights from Buenos Aires.

PEOPLE

 Spanish

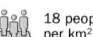 18 people per km²

THE URBAN/RURAL POPULATION SPLIT

86%   14%

RELIGIOUS PERSUASION

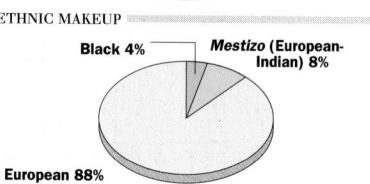
Protestant 2%
Jewish 2%
Other 30%
Roman Catholic 66%

ETHNIC MAKEUP

Black 4%
Mestizo (European-Indian) 8%
European 88%

Most Uruguayans are second or third generation European, mostly of Spanish or Italian descent. There are also some *mestizos* and a small minority of people descended from Africans or immigrants from Brazil, who live in or around the capital Montevideo or near the Brazilian border. All indigenous Amerindian groups became integrated in the *mestizo* population by the mid-19th century. The population's unusual degree of homogeneity – and the fact that it is small compared with the size of the country – mean that ethnic tensions are few. The birth-rate is low for Latin America.

The considerable prosperity derived from cattle ranching allowed Uruguay to become a welfare state long before any other Latin American country. In spite of Uruguay's serious economic decline since the end of the 1950s, there is still a sizeable, if less prosperous,

middle class. A clear sign of the country's economic and social deterioration during the years of military dictatorship was the unprecedented growth of shanty towns around Montevideo.

Although a Roman Catholic country, Uruguay is liberal in its attitude to religion and all forms are tolerated. Divorce is legal. Women are regarded as equal to men and have the vote. There is no capital punishment.

POPULATION AGE BREAKDOWN

% of population by age group	0–14	15–64	65+		
65+	8.1%	8.9%	10.5%	11.6%	12.7%
15–64	64%	63.2%	62.6%	62.6%	63.4%
0–14	27.9%	27.9%	26.9%	25.8%	23.9%
	1960	1970	1980	1990	2000

U

POLITICS

Lower House 1994
Upper House 1994

President Luis Alberto
Lacalle Herrera

THE STATE OF THE PARTIES

Chamber of Deputies 99 members

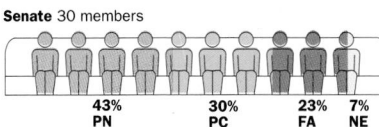

| 39% PN | 30% PC | 21% FA | 10% NE |

PN = National Party (*Blancos*) **PC** = Colorado Party
(*Colorados*) **FA** = Broad Front **NE** = New Space

Senate 30 members

| 43% PN | 30% PC | 23% FA | 7% NE |

Uruguay is a presidential multiparty
democracy.

MAIN POLITICAL ISSUES

Modernization and privatization

After 20 years of military dictatorship
and transitional government, Uruguay
is seeking the best way of modernizing
the state and state-run institutions. The
central political question is whether or
not privatization will help to reverse
economic decline.

The ageing population

Uruguay's long-established welfare
system is under strain from the
increasing proportion of elderly people
in the population. The emigration of
young workers to Europe and
Argentina is exacerbating the problem.

PROFILE

The elections of 1984 marked
Uruguay's return to democracy.
The winning Colorado (Liberal) Party
addressed some human rights issues,
but its attempts to reverse economic
recession met with fierce trade-union
opposition. The 1989 elections resulted
in an uneasy coalition between
the *Colorados* and the conservative
Blancos. Labour unrest has continued,
fuelled by popular anger over the
privatization of public companies. New
free-market economic policies are also
hampered by a law declaring that, if 25%
of the electorate agree, a referendum
must be held on new legislation.

**President Luis
Alberto Lacalle
Herrera**, *took office
in March 1990.*

**Dr Julio María
Sanguinetti**, *one of
the Colorado leaders
and former president.*

URUGUAY

Total Area : 177 410 sq. km (68 498 sq. miles)

LAND HEIGHT	POPULATION
200m/656ft	over 1 000 000 ◎
Sea Level	over 50 000 ○
	over 10 000 •
	under 10 000 •

0 —— 100 km

0 —— 100 miles

WORLD AFFAIRS

OAS Mercsr AG RG ECLAC

After many years of political isolation
and economic decline, Uruguay's chief
foreign-policy concern is achieving
regional integration with Argentina,
Brazil and Paraguay in MERCOSUR, the
common market of southern South
America. This should come into full
operation in 1996. Uruguay is already
part of a continental defence alliance
with other Latin American countries
and the USA. However, it has some
unresolved border problems with
Brazil. Uruguay allowed the UK to use
its ports during the Falklands conflict.

In 1991, Uruguay and the USA signed
a legal-assistance treaty to allow easier
access to the bank accounts of those
suspected of laundering the proceeds of
drug trafficking. This had increasingly
been carried out through Montevideo's
offshore banking sector.

AID

 $51m (receipts)

 Up 9% in 1991

Uruguay is a minimal recipient
of aid, and aid plays little part
in the Uruguayan economy.

CHRONOLOGY

The Spaniards were the first to
colonize the area north of the River
Plate. In 1680, the Portuguese also
founded a colony there, at Colonia
del Sacramento, so starting 150
years of rivalry between the colonial
powers for control of the territory.

❏ **1726** Spaniards found Montevideo.
By end of century, whole country is
divided into large cattle ranches.
❏ **1808** Montevideo declares
independence from Buenos Aires.
❏ **1811** Patriotic rancher and local
caudillo, José Gervasio Artigas,
fends off Brazilian attack.
❏ **1812–1820** Uruguayans, known as
Orientales ('Easterners', from the
eastern side of the River Plate)
fight wars against Argentinian and
Brazilian invaders. Brazil finally
takes Montevideo.
❏ **1827** Gen Lavallejo defeats
Brazilians with Argentine help.
❏ **1828** Seeing trade benefits that an
independent Uruguay would bring
as a buffer state between Argentina
and Brazil, Britain mediates and
secures Uruguayan independence.
❏ **1836** Start of large-scale European
immigration.

U

CHRONOLOGY *continued.*

- ❏ **1838–1865** *La Guerra Grande* civil war between *Blancos* (Whites, future conservative party) and *Colorados* (Reds, future liberals).
- ❏ **1865–1870** Colorado president, Gen Venancio Flores, takes Uruguay into War of the Triple Alliance against Paraguay.
- ❏ **1872** Peace under military rule. *Blancos* strong in country, *Colorados* in city.
- ❏ **1890s** Violent strikes by immigrant trade unionists against landed elite enriched by massive European investment in ranching.
- ❏ **1903–1907** Reformist Colorado, José Batlle y Ordóñez, president.
- ❏ **1911–1915** Batllé serves second term in office. *Batllismo* creates the only welfare state in Latin America with pensions, social security and free education and health service; also nationalizations, disestablishment of Church, abolition of death penalty.
- ❏ **1933** Military coup. Opposition groups excluded from politics.
- ❏ **1942** President Alfredo Baldomir dismisses government and tries to bring back proper representation.
- ❏ **1939–1945** Neutrality.
- ❏ **1951** New constitution replaces president with nine-member council. Decade of great prosperity follows until world agricultural prices plummet. Sharp drop in foreign investment.
- ❏ **1958** *Blanco* party wins elections for first time in 93 years.
- ❏ **1962** Tupamaros urban guerrilla group founded. Its campaign of terrorism continues until 1973.
- ❏ **1964** Large trade unions unite.
- ❏ **1966** Presidency reinstated. *Colorados* back in power.
- ❏ **1967** Jorge Pacheco president. Tries to stifle opposition to tough anti-inflation policies.
- ❏ **1973** Military coup. Promises to encourage foreign investment counteracted by denial of political freedom and brutal repression of the left. 400,000 emigrate.
- ❏ **1974** EEC bans meat imports.
- ❏ **1984** Military agrees to step down. Elections held.
- ❏ **1985** Dr Julio Sanguinetti (Colorado) president.
- ❏ **1986** Those guilty of human rights abuse granted amnesty.
- ❏ **1988** Drought: one million cattle die.
- ❏ **1989** Referendum endorses amnesty in interests of stability. Fully free elections won by Lacalle Herrera and *Blancos*. Attempt to include Colorado ministers fails.
- ❏ **1991** Signs MERCOSUR agreement.
- ❏ **1992** Referendum forces partial repeal of privatization plans.

DEFENCE

$260m

Fairly stable from year to year

0   *Defence spending as % GDP*   40

2.7%

The military withdrew from power in 1984 and has since respected civilian rule. However, secret right-wing groups linked to the military – a few members are said to be officers on active duty – have carried out terrorist attacks against the government. A law of 1986 virtually blocked investigations into 'disappearances', killings and torture during the dictatorship, but there is still public pressure to bring guilty officers to book. The defence

URUGUAYAN ARMED FORCES

17 light tanks (17 M-24/28 M-3A1)		17,200 personnel
3 frigates and 8 patrol boats		4500 personnel
37 combat aircraft (12 A37B/6 IA-58B)		3000 personnel
None		

budget is low; most equipment is bought from the USA and less sophisticated weaponry from Brazil.

ECONOMICS

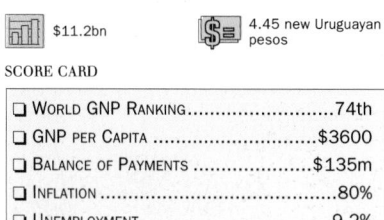

$11.2bn

4.45 new Uruguayan pesos

SCORE CARD

❏ WORLD GNP RANKING	74th
❏ GNP PER CAPITA	$3600
❏ BALANCE OF PAYMENTS	$135m
❏ INFLATION	80%
❏ UNEMPLOYMENT	9.2%

EXPORTS

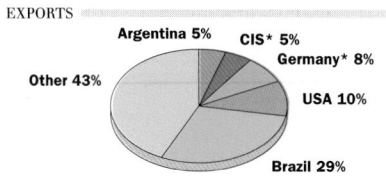

Argentina 5%   CIS* 5%
Germany* 8%
Other 43%
USA 10%
Brazil 29%

IMPORTS

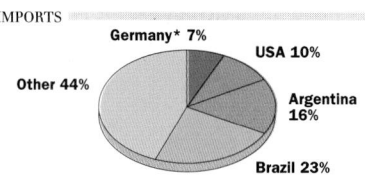

Germany* 7%
USA 10%
Other 44%
Argentina 16%
Brazil 23%

STRENGTHS

Substantial earnings as offshore banking centre. Buoyant tourism. Fertile grasslands. World's second biggest wool exporter.

WEAKNESSES

No oil or minerals except for agate, amethysts, unexploited gold deposits and small quantities of iron ore. Little progress in industrialization. Low world agricultural prices.

PROFILE

Uruguay is traditionally an agricultural economy. Three quarters of the country is rich pasture, supporting livestock. Much of the rest is given over to crops. Farming, which formerly brought great wealth to Uruguay, still employs about 15% of the labour force, accounting for about 10% of GDP. Livestock and animal products, especially meat and wool,

ECONOMIC PERFORMANCE INDICATOR

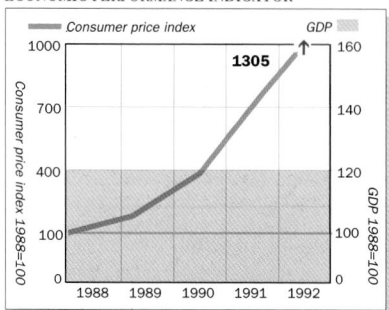

Consumer price index   GDP

1305

account for over one third of export earnings. In addition, manufacturing, which accounts for 25% of GDP, is farm-based. However, tourism has now overtaken both in terms of economic importance. Most economic activity – and half the population – is concentrated in Montevideo and its port. Much of the economy is still state-controlled, including all the largest companies. In 1992, voters rejected a large part of President Herrera's privatization programme in a referendum.

URUGUAY : MAJOR BUSINESSES

✿	Heavy engineering
⬛	Food processing
⬛	Oil refining
🐎	Wool spinning
🐄	Meat packing

Leather
Textiles

0   100 km
0   100 miles

RESOURCES

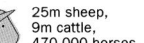 7.4bn kwh
(capacity 1.68m kw)

Not an oil producer;
refines 28,500 b/cd

25m sheep,
9m cattle,
470,000 horses

 Agate, amethyst,
gold, iron

Most of Uruguay is farmland, much of
it given over to cattle and sheep. Rice
is the country's only significant crop
on the world market. Mineral resources
may be considerable but, despite
optimistic geological surveys, are
yet to be exploited. Small quantities
of building materials and jewellery-
quality agate and amethysts are mined.

ENVIRONMENT

 0.2% (0.1% partially
protected)

Rising riverine
pollution

ENVIRONMENTAL TREATIES

No　　　　　Yes

No　　　　　No

Pollution of the country's two main
rivers, the Uruguay and the River Plate,
is of increasing concern.

MEDIA

 Full freedom of expression is guaranteed
by the constitution

PUBLISHING AND BROADCAST MEDIA

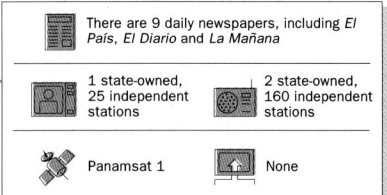

There are 9 daily newspapers, including *El
País*, *El Diario* and *La Mañana*

1 state-owned,
25 independent
stations

2 state-owned,
160 independent
stations

Panamsat 1　　　　None

The press is now relatively free. *El País*
supports the *Blancos* (PN), while *La
Manaña* backs the *Colorados* (PC).

CRIME

 1910 prisoners

 Up 29% in 1990

CRIME RATES

Murders
5 | per 100,000 population

Rapes
Below Latin American average

Thefts
Below Latin American average

Crime levels in Uruguay are low,
particularly compared with its
neighbours Brazil and Argentina.
Domestic theft is the main problem.
Bribery is not common.

ELECTRICITY GENERATION

Hydro 86% (6.4bn kwh)	
Thermal 14% (1bn kwh)	
Nuclear 0%	
Other 0%	

0　　20　　40　　60　　80　　100
% of total generation by type

Hydroelectric power generates 86%
of the country's electricity. Its export
offsets Uruguay's total dependency
on imported oil.

EDUCATION

 96%

0　　　*Education spending as % GNP*　　　25
3.1%

THE EDUCATION SYSTEM

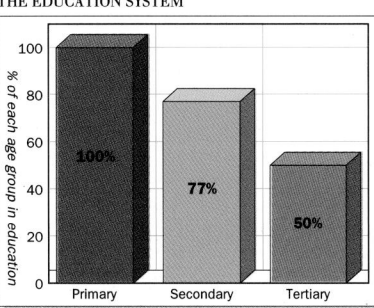

% of each age group in education

100% Primary
77% Secondary
50% Tertiary

Education is inspired by the French
lycée system. Up to secondary level
(12 years) it is paid for by the state,
and is compulsory for all children
between the ages of six and 14.
Uruguay boasts the highest literacy
rate (around 96%) in South America.
Both state and private schools follow
the same curriculum; private schools
are monitored by the government.
However, in poor rural areas, facilities
are rudimentary. Uruguay has two
state-funded universities. The children
of wealthy Uruguayans tend to
complete their studies in the USA.

HEALTH

 1 per 341 people

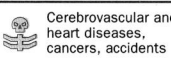 Cerebrovascular and
heart diseases,
cancers, accidents

0　　　*Health spending as % GNP*　　　25
1%

Most Uruguayans have easy access
to health services. The average life
expectancy of 72 years is the highest
in South America. Public services
cater for 40% of the population and the
private sector for the remaining 60%.
Despite opposition, the government
is attempting to privatize some
state medical establishments.

URUGUAY : LAND USE

Cropland
Pasture
Forest
Sheep
Cattle
Wheat

Uruguay
*Embalse del
Rio Negro*
Negro
Mirim Lake

0　　100 km
0　　100 miles

WEALTH

 Grain miller, 4860 new Uruguayan pesos per hour;
medical general practitioner, 20,400 new
Uruguayan pesos per hour

CONSUMER GOODS OWNERSHIP

Per 1000 population

1000
750
500
250
0

227　116　163　34

*PC
owner-
ship is
limited*

Uruguay possesses the social mobility
typical of countries created through
decades of large-scale immigration.
Many professionals come from modest
backgrounds. The wealthy tend either
to be landowners or are employed in
the financial sector. They still look
towards Europe, rather than the
USA, for luxury goods and the latest
fashions. They travel to Europe for
their holidays or visit Uruguay's
coastal resorts, such as Punta del Este.
The most common status symbol
is a Mercedes car.

The most deprived sections of
Uruguayan society are the urban poor
of Montevideo, a large proportion of
whom are of mixed African and
European descent, and the rural poor,
who have little or no land of their own.

WORLD RANKING

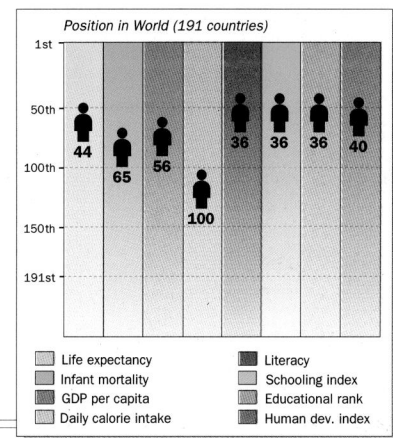

Position in World (191 countries)

1st
50th
100th
150th
191st

44　65　56　100　36　36　36　40

Life expectancy
Infant mortality
GDP per capita
Daily calorie intake
Literacy
Schooling index
Educational rank
Human dev. index

U

579

UZBEKISTAN

OFFICIAL NAME: Republic of Uzbekistan **CAPITAL:** Tashkent
POPULATION: 21 million **CURRENCY:** Som **OFFICIAL LANGUAGE:** Uzbek

S HARING THE ARAL SEA coastline with its northern neighbour, Kazakhstan, Uzbekistan has common borders with five countries, including Afghanistan to the south. It is the most populous Central Asian republic and has considerable natural resources. Uzbekistan contains the ancient Muslim cities of Samarkand, Bukhara, Khiva and Tashkent. The dictatorship of President Karimov has prevented the spread of Islamic fundamentalism.

CLIMATE

WEATHER CHART

Average daily temperature   Rainfall

Uzbekistan has a harsh continental climate. Summers can be extremely hot and dry. Large areas of the country are desert.

COMMUNICATIONS

 Tashkent Intl   Has no fleet

THE TRANSPORT NETWORK

73,100 km (45,422 miles)	None
3460 km (2150 miles)	1100 km (684 miles)

Uzbekistan has a well-developed transport system. An extensive network of buses serves country areas, while good Soviet-style systems of trolleybuses and trams operate in the major cities. Road and rail networks have, however, deteriorated since 1991, and are concentrated in the south and east. The national airline, the *Uzbek Khavo Yullan* (Uzbekistan Airways), is operated by a Pakistani company.

TOURISM

Small numbers of tourists   Little change from previous year

MAIN OVERSEAS ARRIVALS

Uzbekistan does not publish tourism figures by country of origin

% of total arrivals

Uzbekistan has considerable tourist potential. Bukhara, once a trading centre on the silk route, is famous worldwide for its architecture and carpet-making. To Muslims, it is second only to Mecca as a religious centre. Muslims unable to undertake the *haj* (pilgrimage) to Mecca can become *hajis* by visiting Bukhara seven times instead. The city of Samarkand was built in the 14th century by Tamburlaine, and is home to the monumental gateway of the Shir Dar Madrasa, which vies with India's Taj Mahal as one of the most beautiful buildings in the Islamic world.

UZBEKISTAN

Total Area : 1 138 910 sq. km
(439 733 sq. miles)

LAND HEIGHT   POPULATION

3000m/9843ft   ▣ over 1 000 000
2000m/6562ft   ◉ over 100 000
1000m/3281ft   ○ over 50 000
500m/1640ft   ● over 10 000
200m/656ft

CENTRAL ASIA

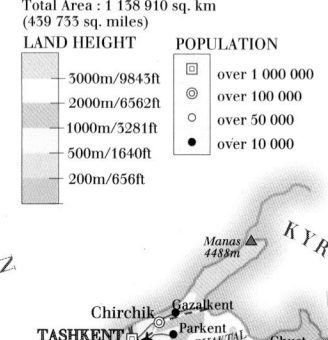

Mosque in Samarkand.
The city remained an Islamic stronghold, despite communist attempts at suppression, when Uzbekistan formed part of the Soviet Union.

PEOPLE

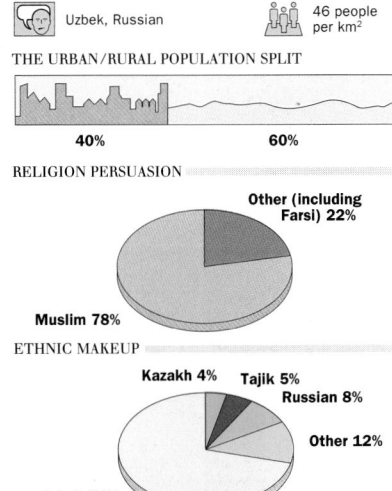

Uzbek, Russian

46 people per km²

THE URBAN/RURAL POPULATION SPLIT

40% 60%

RELIGION PERSUASION

Other (including Farsi) 22%

Muslim 78%

ETHNIC MAKEUP

Kazakh 4% Tajik 5%
Russian 8%
Other 12%
Uzbek 71%

Among ex-Soviet republics, Uzbekistan has a relatively complex make-up. In addition to the Uzbeks, Russians, Tajiks and Kazakhs, there are small minorities of Tatars and Karakalpaks. The proportion of Russians has been declining since the 1970s when net emigration of Russians began. Tensions among ethnic groups have the potential to create regional and racial conflict. The authoritarian nature of the Karimov leadership has so far prevented these antagonisms becoming violent. Incidents such as the 1989 and 1990 clashes between Meskhetian Turks and Uzbeks are rare. The removal of the Communist Party's leadership has meant that Uzbek society has reverted to traditional social patterns based on family, religion, clan and region, rather than on membership of the party. Independence has done little to alter the minor role of women in politics. Arranged marriages are still the custom in the countryside.

POPULATION AGE BREAKDOWN

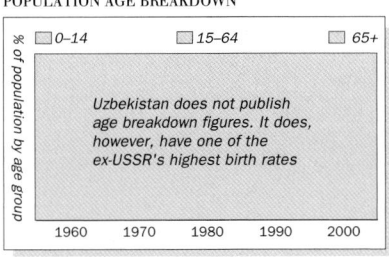

Uzbekistan does not publish age breakdown figures. It does, however, have one of the ex-USSR's highest birth rates

1960 1970 1980 1990 2000

POLITICS

 1994

 President Islam Karimov

THE STATE OF THE PARTIES

Supreme Soviet 500 members

The People's Democratic Party of Uzbekistan (the former Communist Party) is the ruling party. Elections to a new Supreme Assembly, due to replace the Supreme Soviet, are scheduled for 1994

Uzbekistan is effectively run by a presidential dictatorship.

MAIN POLITICAL ISSUES

Islamic fundamentalism
The civil war in neighbouring Tajikistan has made the Karimov leadership wary of Islamic fundamentalism taking hold in Uzbekistan. The Uzbek constitution stipulates the separation of Islam and the state, and Islam has been carefully kept out of politics.

Regionalism
Uzbekistan's high birth rate is placing pressure on limited agricultural resources. There have been calls for secession from some regions wishing to stop large numbers of people moving from poorer areas. In the Fergana Valley, one of the most densely populated regions, there have been a number of violent incidents.

PROFILE
President Karimov's People's Democratic Party of Uzbekistan has not been willing to devolve or share power. A constitution adopted in December 1992, a year after the country attained formal independence, appeared to allow for the development of multiparty politics along Western lines. However, it also gave the president greater powers than before. Karimov subsequently banned a number of opposition parties, including the nationalist *Birlik* (Unity) movement and the Islamic Renaissance Party. The only legal opposition party, *Erk* (Will), lost its licence with the Ministry of Justice in 1993.

Opposition is now almost entirely underground. Arbitrary imprisonment and even physical intimidation are being used against suspected enemies of the regime. Karimov's avoidance of overtly nationalist rhetoric gives him the support of the Russian minority.

Islam A. Karimov, first elected president in 1990; re-elected, by referendum, the following year.

WORLD AFFAIRS

 CIS   CSCE NACC

Unlike neighbouring Turkmenistan, Kyrgyzstan and Tajikistan, Uzbekistan has the resources to allow it to follow a relatively independent foreign policy. The Karimov leadership has used this to promote Uzbekistan as the leading central Asian state. It has established itself as the CIS powerbase in the region, and has even proposed a central Asian common market. The Silk Route used to run through Samarkand and Tashkent and, in a modern revival of the connection, Uzbekistan sees itself once more as a key link between Europe and China.

Relations with Turkey are also developing. Where Western companies have difficulty in sealing contracts in Uzbekistan, Turkish companies have been commissioned to build vital installations such as telecommunications. Many young Uzbeks are also being sent to Turkey to study business practice.

The crucial relationship, however, remains that with Russia, which has 100,000 troops stationed in the country. These are a key part of Karimov's ability to stay in power. Moscow backs him because it approves of his anti-nationalist approach to domestic politics.

CHRONOLOGY
Part of the great Mongol empire, present-day Uzbekistan was incorporated into the Russian Empire between 1865 and 1876. Russification of the area was superficial, and it was not until Soviet rule that significant Slav immigration occurred. A further influx of Slavs into Uzbekistan occurred during Stalin's programme of forced collectivization.

❏ **1917** Soviet power established in Tashkent.
❏ **1918** Turkestan Autonomous Soviet Socialist Republic (ASSR), incorporating present-day Uzbekistan, proclaimed.
❏ **1923–1941** Language changed four times, from Arabic alphabet to Latin, then based on Iranized Tashkent, and finally replaced by Cyrillic.
❏ **1924** Basmachi rebels who resisted Soviet rule crushed. Uzbek SSR founded (which, until 1929, included the Tajik ASSR).
❏ **1925** Repressive campaign against Islamic religion. All Muslim schools and mosques forced to close. Retains autonomous status.

U

CHRONOLOGY *continued*

- ❑ **1936** Karakalpak ASSR (formerly part of the Russian Soviet Federative Socialist Republic) incorporated into the Uzbek SSR.
- ❑ **1937** Akmal Ikramov, first secretary of the Uzbek Communist Party (CPUZ), and Prime Minister Faizulla Khodzhaev, purged by Stalin.
- ❑ **1941–1945** Industry and Slavs evacuated to Uzbekistan from war zone in eastern USSR during Second World War. Leads to considerable economic growth.
- ❑ **1959** Sharaf Rashidov becomes first secretary of CPUZ. Retains position until 1983.
- ❑ **1983** Yuri Andropov becomes president in Moscow. Begins campaign to root out corruption in government. CPUZ specially targeted. Massive corruption scandal uncovered in cotton procurement industry. The USSR's largest anti-corruption purge results in the replacement of 40 out of 65 party secretaries. In effect, an entirely new generation of Central Asian officials installed. Uzbekistan's managerial elite now the youngest in the USSR.
- ❑ **1989** First non-communist political movement, Unity Party (*Birlik*), formed but not officially registered. June, clashes between Meskhetian Turks and indigenous Uzbek population of Fergana Valley in eastern Uzbekistan; more than 100 dead. October, *Birlik* campaign leads to Uzbek being declared the official language.
- ❑ **1990** March, Islam Karimov becomes executive president of the new Uzbek Supreme Soviet. Sovereignty declared. Further inter-ethnic fighting in Fergana Valley. 320 killed.
- ❑ **1991** 31 August, independence proclaimed. September, Republic of Uzbekistan adopted as official name. October, Uzbekistan signs treaty establishing economic community with seven other former Soviet republics. November, Communist Party of Uzbekistan restructured as the People's Democratic Party of Uzbekistan (PDPU). Karimov remains its leader. December, Karimov confirmed in post of president with 86% of total votes. Uzbekistan joins the CIS.
- ❑ **1992** Price liberalization provokes student riots in Tashkent. New post-Soviet constitution adopted along Western democratic lines. All religious parties banned. September, Uzbekistan sends troops to Tajikistan to suppress violence and strengthens border controls.

AID

 $123m (receipts)   Likely to rise

A lack of commitment to economic stabilization or reform and the abuse of human rights have generally deterred bilateral aid donors. However, in 1993, the World Bank contributed $23 million and the EBRD $100 million to assist in the restructuring of small enterprises.

DEFENCE

 Low

 Currently stable, but likely to rise as national forces are established

0   Defence spending as % GDP   40

Uzbekistan does not publish defence spending figures

Uzbekistan has a 700-strong National Guard, which generally acts as the personal army of Karimov. The army is trained by Russian officers while the police are Turkish-trained. Russian troops are still based on Uzbek territory to protect the Russian minority and as part of Moscow's security strategy.

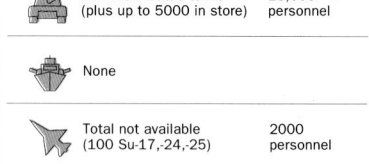

UZBEK ARMED FORCES

280 main battle tanks (plus up to 5000 in store)	15,000 personnel
None	
Total not available (100 Su-17,-24,-25)	2000 personnel
None	

ECONOMICS

 $28.26bn   20,000 Som

SCORE CARD

- ❑ WORLD GNP RANKING..........................55th
- ❑ GNP PER CAPITA $1346
- ❑ BALANCE OF PAYMENTS.....................$–60m
- ❑ INFLATION 600%
- ❑ UNEMPLOYMENT................................6.9%

EXPORTS/IMPORTS

Trade is overwhelmingly with the Russian Federation and neighbouring states of the former Soviet Union

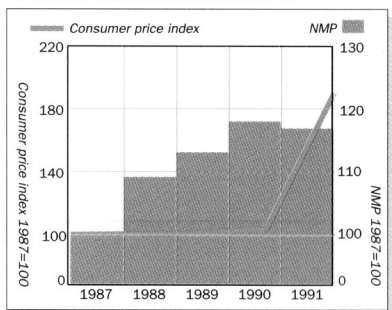

ECONOMIC PERFORMANCE INDICATOR

STRENGTHS

Gold: Uzbekistan was the USSR's second largest producer. Well-developed cotton market. Considerable unexploited deposits of oil and natural gas. Current production of natural gas makes significant contribution to electricity generation. Manufacturing tradition includes agricultural machinery and central Asia's only aviation factory.

WEAKNESSES

Dependent on Russia, Kazakhstan and at times the USA for grain, as Uzbekistan produces only 25% of its domestic requirements. Little progress on privatization. Very limited economic reform. Cotton production depends on massive, environmentally-damaging irrigation schemes.

PROFILE

Uzbekistan's economy remains predominantly agricultural. Tashkent became an industrial area following the evacuation of industry from the western USSR states during the Second World War. Privatization is unlikely to be speeded up while the ex-communists are in power. The gold sector, however, has been opened up to joint ventures with US companies. Uzbekistan also hopes that keen foreign interest in its unexploited energy resources will result in large investments.

UZBEKISTAN : MAJOR BUSINESSES

🌸 Textiles	
🧴 Fertilizers	
tm Silk weaving	
◢ Leather tanning	
🗂 Food processing	
⚙ Engineering	

0   200 km
0   200 miles

RESOURCES

 50.9bn kwh (capacity 11.9m kw)

 50,600 b/d

 8.8m sheep and goats, 4.2m cattle, 742,900 pigs

 Natural gas, coal, oil, gold, uranium, copper, tungsten, bauxite

As well as containing the world's largest single gold mine, at Murantau, Uzbekistan has large deposits of natural gas, petroleum, coal and uranium. An important oilfield was discovered in 1992 in the Namangan region and production will rise with further investment. Most gas production is currently used domestically, but gas could also become a strong export.

Cotton is the main focus of agriculture: Uzbekistan is the world's

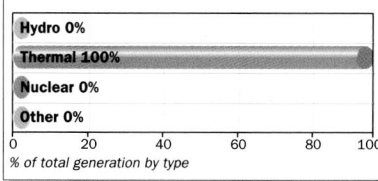
ELECTRICITY GENERATION

Hydro 0%
Thermal 100%
Nuclear 0%
Other 0%

0 — 20 — 40 — 60 — 80 — 100
% of total generation by type

fourth largest producer. A post-independence decision to diversify was reversed when the value of cotton as a commodity on the world market became clear. Fruit, silk cocoons and vegetables for Moscow's markets are also of rising importance.

UZBEKISTAN : LAND USE

ARAL SEA

KYZYL KUM

- Cropland
- Pasture
- Forest
- High mountain regions
- Desert
- Wetlands
- Sheep
- Cotton - cash crop

0 — 200 km
0 — 200 miles

ENVIRONMENT

 Minimal

 No major environmental initiatives under way

ENVIRONMENTAL TREATIES

No   No
No   No

Under Soviet rule, Uzbekistan's cotton industry became one of the largest in the world. The irrigation schemes required to sustain the crop were ill-conceived and have wreaked considerable environmental damage. Soil salination is now a major problem. The Aral Sea has also been seriously depleted, from a total area of 61,836 sq km in 1974, it is expected to decrease to 23,400 sq km by the year 2000. The almost indiscriminate use of fertilizers and pesticides to raise production has also heavily polluted many rivers.

MEDIA

 The media operates under tight political and religious censorship

PUBLISHING AND BROADCAST MEDIA

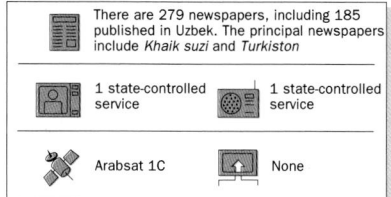
There are 279 newspapers, including 185 published in Uzbek. The principal newspapers include *Khaik suzi* and *Turkiston*

1 state-controlled service   1 state-controlled service

Arabsat 1C   None

Uzbekistan effectively has no independent media. The press supports the personality cult and policies of Karimov. All opposition press is censored. Expression of Islamic and nationalist opinion is also forbidden, and any journalists suspected of promoting such views are repressed. Russian-language newspapers imported from Moscow are censored.

CRIME

 Uzbekistan does not publish prison figures

 Crime is rising

CRIME RATES

All categories of crime are rising, especially in areas of high unemployment such as the Fergana Valley

A decline in living standards has meant a general increase in crime. Many of the rural population grow drug plants, particularly opium poppies, to supplement their falling incomes. Unofficial Islamic courts set up by disaffected young men in the Fergana Valley are an indication of growing Muslim opposition to the government.

EDUCATION

 Over 90%

0   *Education spending as % GNP*   25
7.9%

THE EDUCATION SYSTEM

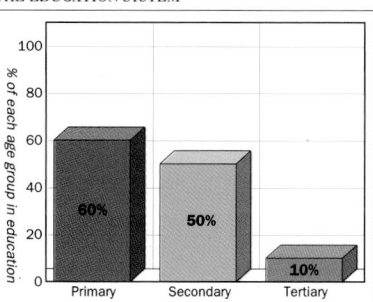

% of each age group in education

100
80
60 — **60%**
40   **50%**
20
0 — Primary — Secondary — Tertiary — **10%**

The system still follows the Soviet model, though some instruction is in Uzbek. In the late 1980s, a few ethnic Tajik schools appeared in large cities along with a university in Samarkand. They were virtually all closed down in 1992 as a result of a decline in relations between the leaderships of Uzbekistan and Tajikistan.

HEALTH

 1 per 275 people

Circulatory and respiratory diseases, accidents, cancers

0   *Health spending as % GNP*   25
Uzbekistan does not publish health spendng figures

The health service has been declining since the dissolution of the USSR. Some rural areas are not served at all. Serious respiratory diseases among cotton growers are increasing.

WEALTH

 There is a very large disparity of wealth between rich and poor

CONSUMER GOODS OWNERSHIP

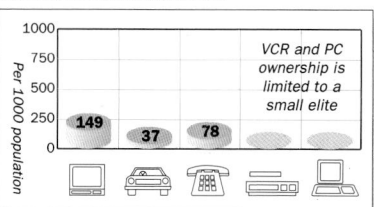

Per 1000 population

1000
750
500
250 — **149**   **37**   **78**
0

VCR and PC ownership is limited to a small elite

Former communists are still the wealthiest group as they retain control of the economy. Many rural poor live below the poverty line.

WORLD RANKING

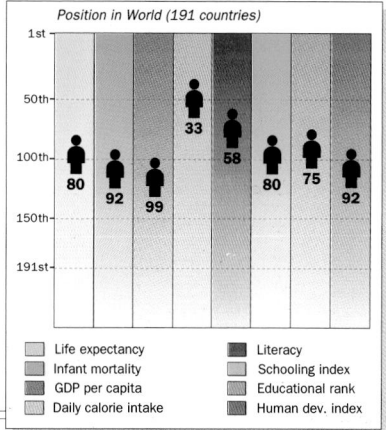

Position in World (191 countries)

1st
50th
100th
150th
191st

80   **92**   **99**   **33**   **58**   **80**   **75**   **92**

- Life expectancy
- Infant mortality
- GDP per capita
- Daily calorie intake
- Literacy
- Schooling index
- Educational rank
- Human dev. index

U

VANUATU

OFFICIAL NAME: Republic of Vanuatu   **CAPITAL:** Port-Vila
POPULATION: 163,000   **CURRENCY:** Vatu   **OFFICIAL LANGUAGES:** Bislama, English and French

PACIFIC OCEAN

AN ARCHIPELAGO strung out over 1300 km of the South Pacific, Vanuatu lies 1000 km west of Fiji. Mountainous and volcanic in origin, only 12 of the 82 islands are of significant size – Espiritu Santo and Malekula are the largest. The capital, Port-Vila, is on Éfaté. Formerly the New Hebrides – ruled jointly by France and Britain from 1906 – Vanuatu became independent in 1980. Politics since independence has been democratic but volatile.

CLIMATE

WEATHER CHART

The climate is tropical and hot. Rainfall and temperatures decrease north to south. Cyclones occur November–April.

COMMUNICATIONS

Frequent air and shipping services link the islands. State-owned Air Vanuatu flies to Australia and New Zealand.

TOURISM

 42,673 visitors   Up 22% between 1990 and 1992

MAIN OVERSEAS ARRIVALS

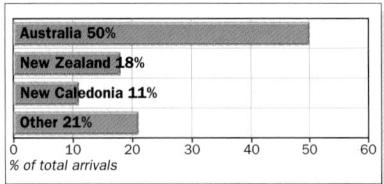

Tourism is the fastest-growing sector of the economy, accounting for 40% of GDP. There are plans to expand hotel capacity and international air links.

PEOPLE

Indigenous Melanesians, ni-Vanuatu, comprise 98% of the population. Of Vanuatu's 82 islands, 67 are inhabited, but 80% of people live on 12 main islands. The population is becoming more urbanized as one in eight ni-Vanuatu now lives in Port-Vila. However, 75% of of the population still live by subsistence agriculture.

Vanuatu is home to some of the Pacific's most traditional peoples and local social and religious customs are strong. With 105 indigenous languages, Vanuatu boasts the world's highest per capita density of languages. Bislama pidgin is the *lingua franca*.

Women have lower social status than men and bride price is still commonly paid. Many educated women refuse to marry because of loss of property rights. To boost equality, primary schools must now take 50% girls.

Vanuatu's *unspoilt beaches are one of the reasons for the upsurge in the tourist industry.*

POLITICS

1995   Acting-President Alfred Maseng

THE STATE OF THE PARTIES

Parliament 46 members

| 41% UMP | 22% VP | 22% NUP | 9% MPP | 6% Other |

UMP = Union of Moderate Parties   **VP** = Vanua'aku Party (Our Land Party)   **NUP** = National United Party
MPP = Melanesian Progressive Party

The government of Vanuatu was formerly shared by France and Britain. Political instability in the islands was one of the reasons which contributed to France's reluctance – not shared by the UK – to grant independence in 1980. The anti-French stance of the Vanua'aku Party (Our Land Party – VP), which governed from 1980–1991, was reinforced by French support for the short-lived secession of Espiritu Santo in 1980. Rivalries and splits in the VP culminated in a constitutional crisis in 1988, when President Sokomanu backed former VP secretary-general Barak Sope's efforts to oust Prime Minister Walter Lini. They failed and Fred Timakata became president. Lini's increasingly autocratic stance led to his dismissal by the VP in 1991.

Elections that year saw the victory of the opposition UMP. The UMP then formed a coalition with the NUP, set up by Lini, and began to repair relations with Paris. Strains in the coalition led to a stalemated election for a new president when Timakata's term ended in 1994. Parliamentary speaker Alfred Maseng became acting president.

WORLD AFFAIRS

 SPF   SPC   Comm   ACP   ESCAP

Vanuatu was the first South Pacific nation to gain full membership of the Non-Aligned Movement. Relations with Australia are close. Those with France have improved since 1991.

AID

 $48m (receipts)   Down 2% in 1991

Grant aid is equivalent to 30% of GDP, making Vanuatu Melanesia's most aid-dependent state. Leading donors include Australia, New Zealand, the UK and France. France cut aid twice in the 1980s after alleged interference in Vanuatu's internal affairs.

V

DEFENCE

 There are no military forces

 Not applicable

There is a small paramilitary force. Papua New Guinean troops helped to end the 1980 secessionist movement on Espiritu Santo under a defence agreement signed after independence.

ECONOMICS

 $193m

 122.86 vatu

SCORE CARD

❑ WORLD GNP RANKING	178th
❑ GNP PER CAPITA	$1184
❑ BALANCE OF PAYMENTS	$–17.1m
❑ INFLATION	4.3%
❑ UNEMPLOYMENT	Low rate

STRENGTHS

Expanding services sector, including tourism and offshore finance, now accounts for 68% of GDP. Subsistence farming and small-scale cash cropping give majority of population a livelihood. Low foreign debt. GDP increasing.

WEAKNESSES

Large trade and budget deficits. Heavy import–export duties – to compensate for no direct taxes – increase domestic prices and deter exports. Declining prices for two largest exports: copra and cocoa. Limited outlets for new crop exports.

EXPORTS
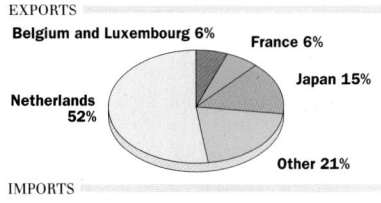
Belgium and Luxembourg 6%
France 6%
Japan 15%
Netherlands 52%
Other 21%

IMPORTS

Fiji 7%
Japan 9%
Australia 43%
New Zealand 10%
Other 31%

RESOURCES

 24m kwh (capacity 11,000 kw)

Not an oil producer and has no refineries

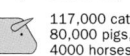 117,000 cattle, 80,000 pigs, 4000 horses

None

Vanuatu's main resources are its arable land – only 17% is utilized – and its forests and waters. These could be exploited by the tourist, timber and fishing industries. New export crops are being explored to offset declining copra and cocoa exports. Beef is of growing importance. Nuclear-power development was banned under 1983 legislation.

VANUATU

Total Area : 12 190 sq. km
(4707 sq. miles)

POPULATION
over 10 000 ●
under 10 000 ·

LAND HEIGHT

1000m/3281ft
500m/1640ft
200m/656ft
Sea Level

ENVIRONMENT

 None

No serious environmental imbalances

Logging is growing, but 75% of the rainforest remains. Population growth is high at 3.2% a year, but not yet a major problem. Introduced diseases and the labour trade reduced the population from some 500,000 in 1800 to 40,000 in 1920; it is still recovering.

MEDIA

 There is no censorship

PUBLISHING AND BROADCAST MEDIA
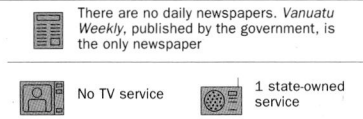
There are no daily newspapers. *Vanuatu Weekly*, published by the government, is the only newspaper

No TV service

1 state-owned service

The dour *Vanuatu Weekly* is published in the three official languages. There is also a monthly, *Pacific Islands Profile*.

CRIME

Vanuatu does not publish prison figures

Little change from year to year

Domestic violence is a problem, but otherwise Vanuatu is almost crime-free – unlike other Melanesian states.

CHRONOLOGY

In 1906, Britain and France set up the New Hebrides under joint rule.

❑ **1980** Secessionism on Espiritu Santo mars independence; Walter Lini of VP becomes prime minister.
❑ **1980–1991** VP retains power amid political infighting and instability.
❑ **1991** UMP forms coalition with NUP set up by Lini in split from VP.
❑ **1994** Electoral college fails to elect new president.

EDUCATION

 53%

The abolition of fees has helped to boost primary enrolment to 85%. Secondary enrolment is under 20%.

HEALTH

 1 per 8344 people

Heart diseases, cancers, malaria

A network of rural clinics and village health workers has helped to improve health levels. Nominal fees are charged.

WEALTH

 Wealth disparities are small among the indigenous population

CONSUMER GOODS OWNERSHIP
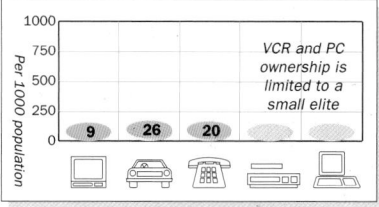
VCR and PC ownership is limited to a small elite
9 26 20

The dominance of subsistence farming and small-scale cash cropping has helped to prevent extreme poverty. The rich are mainly non-ni-Vanuatu.

WORLD RANKING

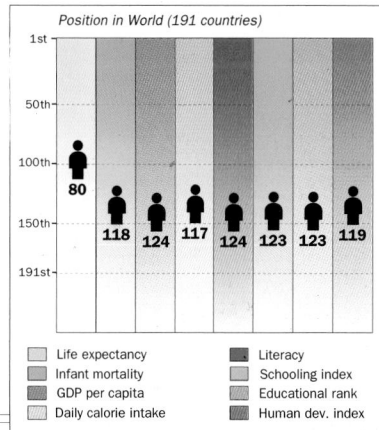
Position in World (191 countries)
80 118 124 117 124 123 123 119

Life expectancy / Infant mortality / GDP per capita / Daily calorie intake / Literacy / Schooling index / Educational rank / Human dev. index

V

VATICAN CITY

OFFICIAL NAME: State of the Vatican City   **CAPITAL:** *Not applicable*
POPULATION: 1000   **CURRENCY:** Lira   **OFFICIAL LANGUAGES:** Italian and Latin

THE VATICAN CITY lies close to the Tiber in central Rome and is a fully independent state. It also includes ten other buildings in Rome and the Pope's residence at Castel Gandolfo. As the Holy See, it is the seat of the Catholic Church, deriving its income from investments and voluntary contributions known as Peter's Pence.

CLIMATE

WEATHER CHART

Winters are mild, though November is particularly grey, and summers are hot.

COMMUNICATIONS

 Heliport for official visitors   Has no fleet

THE TRANSPORT NETWORK

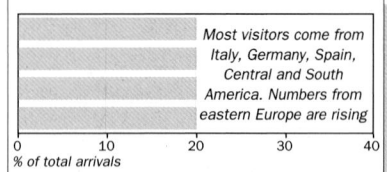

None	None
1 km (0.6 miles)	None

The railway is only used for carrying freight. Official visitors are transferred from Rome airport by helicopter.

TOURISM

The Vatican Museums can accommodate 20,000 visitors daily   Little change from year to year

MAIN OVERSEAS ARRIVALS

Most visitors come from Italy, Germany, Spain, Central and South America. Numbers from eastern Europe are rising

0   10   20   30   40
% of total arrivals

Almost all tourists who visit Rome visit the Vatican, while others come as pilgrims. Up to 100,000 hear the Pope's annual Easter Message in St Peter's Square. The Vatican's art collections are among the greatest in the world. Years of restoration work on the Sistine Chapel frescoes were completed in 1994.

PEOPLE

 Italian, Latin   2273 people per km²

THE URBAN/RURAL POPULATION SPLIT

100%

RELIGIOUS PERSUASION

Roman Catholic 100%

The Vatican has about 1000 permanent inhabitants, including several hundred lay persons, and employs a further 3400 lay staff. Citizenship can be acquired through stable residence and holding an office or job within the City. A citizen's family can gain residence only by authorization.

The Pope is spiritual head of almost 18% of the world's population. The countries with the largest number of Roman Catholics are Brazil, Mexico, Italy, the USA and the Philippines.

VATICAN CITY

Total Area : 0.44 sq. km (0.17 sq. miles)

The buildings and gardens of the Vatican City. St Peter's Basilica was built from 1506–1626 on the traditional site of St Peter's tomb.

POLITICS

On death of reigning Pope   His Holiness Pope John Paul II

THE STATE OF THE PARTIES

Sacred College of Cardinals 162 members

The Cardinals are divided into 3 orders, Bishops, Priests and Deacons

The Vatican City operates in the manner of an elected monarchy, as the reigning Pope has supreme executive, legislative and judicial powers, and holds office for life. He is elected by 120 members of the College of Cardinals, who vote until one candidate for the position of Supreme Pontiff achieves a two-thirds majority.

The administration of the Vatican City State, of which the Pope is temporal head, is conducted by the Pontifical Commission. The Holy See, which is the governing body of the Catholic Church worldwide and of which the Pope is spiritual head, is governed by the Roman Curia, the Church's administrative network. It is the Holy See that maintains diplomatic relations abroad. Pope John Paul II, elected in 1978, is the first non-Italian Pope since 1523.

WORLD AFFAIRS

The Vatican maintains a neutral stance in world affairs and has observer status in many international organizations. It has mediated in many conflicts, notably achieving the 1993 peace agreement in Mozambique. Pope John Paul II has travelled more extensively than any other Pope to promote peace, overcome religious and racial discrimination, support the rights of minorities, whether foreign or indigenous, and to spread Roman Catholicism. The Holy See now has diplomatic relations with Russia and other former Soviet-bloc nations, and in 1993 the Pope re-established the Catholic Church in previously atheist Albania.

AID

 Undisclosed   Undisclosed

Aid is donated through the Pope's Charities (The Holy Childhood Association, for example, distributes $15 million a year for children's causes), through funds donated for use at the Pope's discretion, and through religious orders acting under papal charter.

DEFENCE

 Ceremonial Swiss Guard only   No significant change from year to year

The Vatican is strictly neutral territory. Under the 1954 Hague Convention, it is recognized as 'a moral, artistic and cultural patrimony worthy of being respected as a treasure for all mankind'.

ECONOMICS

 Not applicable   1473.41 Italian lira

SCORE CARD

- ❏ WORLD GNP RANKING ....*The Vatican*
- ❏ GNP PER CAPITA.....................*does not have*
- ❏ BALANCE OF PAYMENTS...................*a national*
- ❏ INFLATION............................*economy in the*
- ❏ UNEMPLOYMENT.........................*usual sense*

STRENGTHS
Instituto per le Opere di Religione has assets of $3–$4 billion. Voluntary contributions from Catholics worldwide (Peter's Pence). Interest on investments. Gold reserves in Fort Knox, USA. Stamp and coin issues.

WEAKNESSES
Growing budgetary deficit (over $90 million): losses incurred by Vatican radio and newspaper, foreign Papal visits, high running costs of buildings, administration and diplomatic missions. Repayment of creditors from Banco Ambrosiano bankruptcy in 1982.

EXPORTS/IMPORTS

The Vatican produces no goods for export. All commodities are imported, mainly from Italy

RESOURCES

 None   None

 None   None

The Vatican imports all its energy. It has no farmland as its area is restricted to buildings and their formal gardens.

ENVIRONMENT

 None   Vatican has set up the St Francis Prize for the Environment

The Vatican is increasingly concerned about the need to balance development and conservation. In 1993, the Pope urged a gathering of scientists to press colleagues worldwide to inform people on the need to protect the environment.

MEDIA

 The Vatican regards freedom of expression as a fundamental human right. The Vatican's media promotes the Catholic Church's beliefs and views

PUBLISHING AND BROADCAST MEDIA

 There is one daily newspaper, *L'Osservatore Romano*, which is also published weekly in 5 European languages, and monthly in Polish

 1 state-owned service   1 state-owned service

The Vatican produces its own religious TV programmes, but has no transmitter. Its radio broadcasts in 37 languages.

CRIME

 There are no prisons in the Vatican City   Minimal crime levels

The only crime to have rocked the Vatican in recent years was the alleged implication of three of the Vatican Bank's officials in the Italian Banco Ambrosiano's fraudulent bankruptcy. Italy's Supreme Court ruled that Vatican affairs were beyond its jurisdiction.

EDUCATION

 100%

The University, founded by Gregory XIII, is renowned for its theological and philosophical learning. There are 79,141 primary and 31,406 secondary Catholic schools around the world.

CHRONOLOGY

The Vatican is located in Rome because tradition held that St Peter was buried on the site of the Church of Constantine, which was pulled down in the Renaissance to make way for the building of St Peter's Basilica. The Vatican has been the Pope's usual residence since 1417, when the pontiffs returned from Avignon in France at the end of the 39 years of Great Schism.

- ❏ **1870** Italy occupies Papal States – 41,500 sq km in central Italy.
- ❏ **1929** Lateran Treaty – Italy recognizes Vatican City as independent state.
- ❏ **1978** Cardinal Karol Wojtyła Pope.
- ❏ **1981–1982** Attempts on Pope's life.
- ❏ **1983** New Church legal code.
- ❏ **1984** Catholicism disestablished as Italian state religion.
- ❏ **1985** Catholic Catechism revised for first time since 1566.
- ❏ **1989** Pope appoints first bishop to Belorussia – the first in 60 years in the former Soviet Union.
- ❏ **1992** Formal acknowledgement that Galileo wrongly condemned.
- ❏ **1993** Chinese sanction first official publication of full Bible in Chinese.

HEALTH

 Pope's own doctor is in permanent residence at Vatican   Heart and cardiovascular diseases, cancers

The Catholic Church runs 5617 hospitals, 14,748 dispensaries, 774 leprosariums and 17,519 homes for the sick, the aged and orphans worldwide.

WEALTH

 Vatican employees earn salaries on a par with those in Rome

CONSUMER GOODS OWNERSHIP

The wealth of the Vatican is primarily that of the Church. Its art treasures may not be sold. It is not known how much personal wealth its citizens have.

WORLD RANKING

The Pope and his Vatican staff enjoy one of the highest standards of living in the world

V

VENEZUELA

OFFICIAL NAME: Republic of Venezuela   **CAPITAL:** Caracas
POPULATION: 20.2 million   **CURRENCY:** Bolívar   **OFFICIAL LANGUAGE:** Spanish

LOCATED ON THE northern coast of South America, Venezuela's vast central plain is drained by the Orinoco, while the Guiana Highlands dominate the southwest of the country. A Spanish colony until 1811, Venezuela was lauded as Latin America's most stable democracy. Recent political upheavals have, however, led to fears of instability. The country with one of the largest known oil deposits outside the Middle East still has much of its population living in shanty-town squalor.

Carlos Andrés Pérez, AD leader, who was deposed from the presidency in 1993.

Dr Rafael Caldera Rodríguez, who won the presidency for a second time in 1994.

CLIMATE

WEATHER CHART

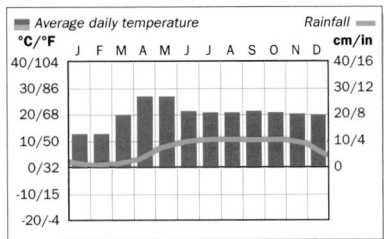

The hot Maracaibo coast is surprisingly dry, the Orinoco *Llanos* are alternately parched or flooded. Uplands are cold.

COMMUNICATIONS

Simón Bolívar, Caracas
6.48m passengers

75 ships
1.21m dwt

THE TRANSPORT NETWORK

100,571 km (62,494 miles)	Pan-American Highway 1290 km (802 miles)
542 km (338 miles)	7100 km (4412 miles)

A massive road-building programme in the 1960s was designed to serve the oil and aluminium industries. The French-designed Caracas metro is one of the world's most efficient. A new $1 billion, 80 km railway and port system is being built on Lake Maracaibo to service the expanding oil refining industry.

The Orinoco. Its huge Llanos (plains) *are grazed by five million cattle, which are herded down close to the river in the dry season.*

TOURISM

524,533 visitors

Up 27% in 1990

MAIN OVERSEAS ARRIVALS

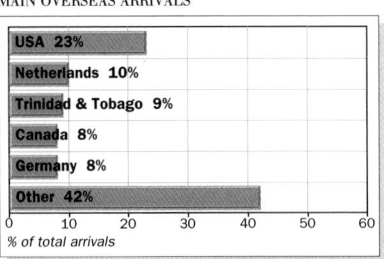

USA 23%
Netherlands 10%
Trinidad & Tobago 9%
Canada 8%
Germany 8%
Other 42%

% of total arrivals

Tourism is still a relatively minor industry in Venezuela, but one with enormous potential. Venezuela has many beaches that are the equal of any Caribbean island's, and a fascinating jungle interior. For many years, the high value of the bolívar made Venezuela an expensive destination but, after the devaluation of 1983, it became one of the cheapest in the Caribbean. Now the government is privatizing its state-run hotels and seeking to attract foreign investment.

PEOPLE

Spanish, Amerindian languages

21 people per km²

THE URBAN/RURAL POPULATION SPLIT

91%   9%

RELIGIOUS PERSUASION

Other 2%   Protestant 2%

Roman Catholic 96%

ETHNIC MAKEUP

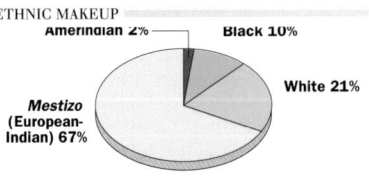

Amerindian 2%   Black 10%

White 21%

Mestizo (European-Indian) 67%

Venezuela is the most highly urbanized society in Latin America, with most of its population living in cities, mainly in the north of the country. Venezuela has traditionally been seen as Latin America's 'melting pot', with large-scale immigration from Italy, Portugal, Spain and all over Latin America. There is little of the white Hispanic aristocracy that survives in Colombia and Ecuador. The small number of

native Indians, such as the Yanomami, live in remote and inaccessible regions, and are often little touched by modern life. Most of the black population, descended from Africans brought over to work the cacao industry in the 19th century, live along the Caribbean coast.

Oil wealth has brought comparative prosperity, but life in the *barrios* (shanty towns), which sprawl over the hillsides around Caracas, is one of extreme poverty. Discontent peaked in the food riots of 1991, which forced the government to initiate poverty programmes. The oil boom accelerated change for women, who today find employment in all the professions. Politics, however, remains a masculine preserve. Oil wealth also brought Americanization – boxing and baseball are among the most popular sports.

POPULATION AGE BREAKDOWN

% of population by age group	0–14	15–64	65+		
65+	2.4%	2.9%	3.2%	3.7%	4.5%
15–64	51.5%	51.5%	55.7%	58%	63.1%
0–14	46.1%	45.6%	41.1%	38.3%	32.4%
	1960	1970	1980	1990	2000

V

VENEZUELA

Total Area : 912 050 sq. km
(352 143 sq. miles)

POPULATION

⊡ over 1 000 000
⊚ over 500 000
◉ over 100 000
○ over 50 000
● over 10 000

LAND HEIGHT

5000m/9843ft
2000m/6562ft
1000m/3281ft
500m/1640ft
Sea Level

– – – Projected Railway

POLITICS

Lower House 1999
Upper House 1999

President Dr Rafael
Caldera Rodríguez

THE STATE OF THE PARTIES

Chamber of Deputies 203 members

27% AD	27% COPEI	19% LCR	12% MAS	13% Con.	2% Other

AD = Democratic Action **COPEI** = Christian Socialist
Party **LCR** = The Radical Cause **Con.** = *Convergencia*
MAS = Movement Towards Socialism

Senate 53 members

34% AD	28% COPEI	17% LCR	11% MAS	10% Con.

Venezuela is a democracy, with
multiparty elections.

MAIN POLITICAL ISSUES

Corruption
Corruption, the issue which led to
the ousting of Carlos Andrés Pérez in
1993, has been a feature of Venezuelan
political life. Jaime Lusinchi, ex-
president and previous AD leader, was
more profligate than most, reputedly
squandering more than $8.5 billion
dollars buying political favours
in his last two years in office.

Trimming the state sector
For decades, Venezuelan governments
spent on a hugely wasteful scale,
with the assumption that petro-dollars
would keep flowing. The decline in
oil revenues has left the state unable
to fulfil its commitments without sharp
cutbacks, which will meet with fierce
resistance from the large numbers
of state employees.

PROFILE

Venezuela's democracy is looking more
fragile than a decade ago, in part due
to the failure of successive regimes to
tackle poverty. Three hundred died in
anti price-rise riots in Caracas in 1991,
and in 1992 the leader of an abortive
coup was declared a national hero by
barrio dwellers. In 1993, Carlos Andrés
Pérez, who had taken office in 1989 and
had grown increasingly unpopular for
his austerity measures, was deposed by
Congress on corruption charges which
have yet to be proven.

WORLD AFFAIRS

OPEC | GATT | OAS | NAM | ECLAC

Venezuela has traditionally been
seen as pro-US, since the USA was
the destination of most of its oil exports
and the source of its imports. There
was little reaction to the US removal
of Manuel Noriega from power in
Panama in 1989. Currently working
at easing US–Cuban relations,
Venezuela is also actively encouraging
Cuba to join the Organization of
American States.

Venezuela has disputed borders
with Colombia (fighting almost
erupted in 1987) and Guyana, its
much smaller neighbour, claiming
85,000 sq km of its oil, iron and gold-
rich territory.

CHRONOLOGY

Venezuela was the first of the
Spanish imperial colonies to
repudiate Madrid's authority under
the guidance of the revolutionary,
Simón Bolívar, in 1811.

❏ **1821** Battle of Carabobo finally
overthrows Spanish rule and leads
to consolidation of independence
within Gran Colombia (Venezuela,
Colombia and Ecuador).

❏ **1830** Gran Colombia collapses.
José Antonio Páez rules Venezuela;
coffee planters effectively in
control.

❏ **1870** Guzmán Blanco in power.
Attracts foreign investment to build
rail system.

❏ **1908** General Juan Vicente Gómez
dictator; oversees development of
oil industry.

❏ **1935** Vicente Gómez falls from
power. Increasing mass
participation in political process.

❏ **1945** Military coup overthrows
General Isías Medina Angarita.
Rómulo Betancourt of the
Democratic Action party (AD) takes
power as leader of a civilian-
military junta.

V

CHRONOLOGY *continued*

- ❏ **1948** February, AD wins elections, with novelist Rómulo Gallegos as presidential candidate.
- ❏ **1948** November, Gallegos overthrown in military coup. Marcos Pérez Jiménez forms government, with US and military backing.
- ❏ **1958** January, general strike. Admiral Wolfgang Larrázabal leads military coup deposing Jiménez government.
- ❏ **1958** December, free elections. Betancourt, newly returned from exile, wins presidential election as AD candidate. Anti-communist campaign mounted. A few state welfare programmes introduced.
- ❏ **1960** Movement of the Revolutionary Left (MIR) splits off from AD and begins anti-government activities.
- ❏ **1961** Venezuela becomes a founder member of OPEC.
- ❏ **1962** Communist-backed guerrilla warfare attempts repetition of Cuban revolution in Venezuela. Fails to gain support amongst the peasantry.
- ❏ **1963** Raúl Leoni (AD) elected president – the first democratic transference of power in Venezuelan history. Anti-guerrilla campaign continues.
- ❏ **1966** Unsuccessful coup attempt by supporters of former president, Pérez Jiménez.
- ❏ **1969** Elections. Dr Rafael Caldera Rodríguez of the Social Christian Party (COPEI) becomes president. Continues Leoni policies.
- ❏ **1973** Elections. Carlos Andrés Pérez wins back power for AD. Oil and steel industries nationalized. World oil crisis. Venezuelan currency peaks in value against the US dollar.
- ❏ **1978** Elections won by Dr Luis Herrera Campíns for COPEI. Disastrous economic programmes, and failure of huge Workers' Bank.
- ❏ **1983** Elections. AD victory under Jaime Lusinchi. Fall in world oil prices leads to cuts in state welfare schemes. Student and union unrest.
- ❏ **1988** Carlos Andrés Pérez wins elections for AD. Fails to deliver populist election promises.
- ❏ **1991** Caracas food riots; 300 dead.
- ❏ **1993** Carlos Andrés Pérez falls and is put on trial for corruption.

AID

 Minimal receipts   No change from year to year

Venezuela receives minimal aid; assistance from Germany and Spain is in the form of small NGO projects.

DEFENCE

 $1.6bn   Up 300% in 1991

0   *Defence spending as % GDP*   40
3.1%

The army is under-equipped and badly paid, with only 34,000 men including conscripts. Having been largely absent from politics for three decades, it regained prominence in the attempted coups of 1992, headed by relatively junior officers who identified with the squeeze on the middle classes.

VENEZUELAN ARMED FORCES

70 main battle tanks (AMX-30)	34,000 personnel
2 submarines, 6 frigates and 6 patrol boats	11,000 personnel
120 combat aircraft (10 F-5A/10 -B/19 T-2D/ 9 Mirage. Also F-16)	7000 personnel
None	

ECONOMICS

 $59.5bn   106.20 bolívares

SCORE CARD
- ❏ WORLD GNP RANKING..........................36th
- ❏ GNP PER CAPITA $2945
- ❏ BALANCE OF PAYMENTS..................$–3.4bn
- ❏ INFLATION 33.1%
- ❏ UNEMPLOYMENT................................8.4%

ECONOMIC PERFORMANCE INDICATOR

EXPORTS
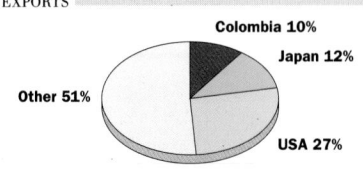
Colombia 10%
Japan 12%
Other 51%
USA 27%

IMPORTS
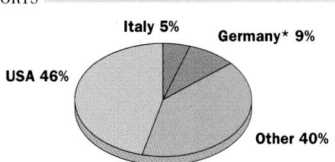
Italy 5%
Germany* 9%
USA 46%
Other 40%

STRENGTHS
The largest proven oil deposits outside the Middle East and CIS. Massive reserves of coal, bauxite, iron and gold. Successful development of new bitumen fuel, Orimulsion, produced in the Orinoco delta. Considerable foreign investment in all these sectors, led by US and giant Japanese concerns such as Mitsubishi. World's most efficient producer of high-grade aluminium.

WEAKNESSES
Huge, cumbersome state sector; despite some privatization, large areas of the state sector are still over-manned and inefficient. Poor public services, which, despite Venezuela's wealth during the oil-boom years, have been badly maintained. Major infrastructure renewal is now long overdue. Widespread tax evasion, and lack of political will to reform tax regime (Venezuela, thanks to large subsidies, has the lowest petrol prices in the world) dents government revenues.

PROFILE
Venezuela is an economic paradox. One of the strongest economies in Latin America, its government finances are in a poor state. A culture of non-accountability has been created due to years of politically motivated patronage in state-owned industries and government bureaucracies. A programme of privatization and cutting state spending has begun to tackle the problem, but too slowly to make a real impact. Conditions for the poor have not improved, and violent food riots in Caracas in 1991 highlighted their plight. This, along with fears of a military coup, has had the effect of deterring future investors.

VENEZUELA : MAJOR BUSINESSES

- Oil
- Rum
- Brewing
- Oil refining
- Ceramics
- Agribusiness
- Tobacco
- Engineering
- Metals
- Vehicle assembly

* significant multinational ownership

RESOURCES

 61bn kwh
(capacity 18.6m kw)

 2.29m b/d
(reserves
62,650,000,000 bbl)

13m cattle, 3m pigs,
523,000 sheep,
495,000 horses

Oil, bauxite, iron,
natural gas, coal, gold

ELECTRICITY GENERATION

Hydro 61% (37.2bn kwh)

Thermal 39% (23.8bn kwh)

Nuclear 0%

Other 0%

0   20   40   60   80   100
% of total generation by type

ENVIRONMENT

 31% (16% partially
protected)

 Ecology studies are
now part of the
school curriculum

ENVIRONMENTAL TREATIES

No   Yes

No   Yes

The destruction of the last remaining
rainforests and the oil pollution of Lake
Maracaibo are the main concerns.

MEDIA

 Attempts have been made to intimidate any
press which is critical of the government

PUBLISHING AND BROADCAST MEDIA

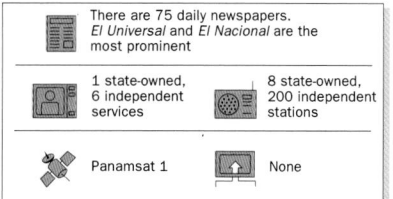

There are 75 daily newspapers.
El Universal and *El Nacional* are the
most prominent

1 state-owned,
6 independent
services

8 state-owned,
200 independent
stations

Panamsat 1   None

Most of the press is independent of
the main political parties. Venezuelan
soap operas vie with Mexican rivals
for dominance.

CRIME

 32,000 prisoners

 Up 4% in 1988

CRIME RATES

Murders
94   *per 100,000 population*

Rapes
Number of rapes increasing

Thefts
Number of thefts increasing

Venezuela is generally less violent than
neighbouring countries, though drugs-
related crime is on the increase. Cattle
smuggling to Colombia is rife.

Venezuela has a remarkable diversity
of resources. It has proven oil reserves
of 62 billion barrels, vast quantities of
coal, iron ore, bauxite and gold, and
cheap hydroelectric power. Huge
investment programmes are currently
under way to raise production in all
these sectors. Oil companies are also
increasing refining capacity. A $10-
billion refining expansion programme
is due for completion in 1996. The state
oil company, PDVSA, is also investing in
coal, particularly the Guanare fields, to
raise annual production from 1.5 to 20
million tonnes.

Venezuela has begun exploitation
of a new bitumen-based fuel from the
Orinoco, Orimulsion; commercially-
exploitable reserves are estimated at
270 billion barrels. The world's most
efficient producer of aluminium,
Venezuela aims to be the biggest by
the year 2000.

EDUCATION

 88%

0   Education spending as % GNP   25
4.2%

THE EDUCATION SYSTEM

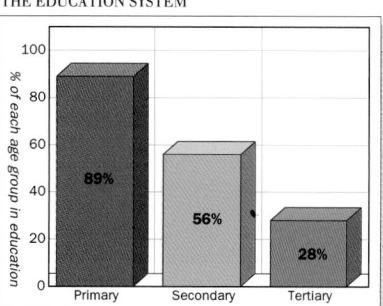

100

80

60
% of each age group in education

89%

56%

40

28%

20

0
Primary   Secondary   Tertiary

The state education system suffers
from a shortage of qualified teachers,
and from recent cuts in the state
education budget.

HEALTH

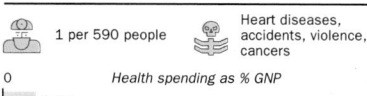 1 per 590 people

Heart diseases,
accidents, violence,
cancers

0   Health spending as % GNP   25
2.2%

The health service, although still
comparatively good, has suffered
along with other public services from
poor management in the 1970s and
1980s and the cuts introduced by
the Pérez government in the 1990s.

Most health care is concentrated
in the towns, and people from
indigenous communities often have to
travel long distances to receive
treatment. Venezuela has a reputation
for innovative plastic surgery.

VENEZUELA : LAND USE

Cropland
Pasture
Forest
Coffee - cash crop
Cattle

0   200 km
0   200 miles

WEALTH

 Miner, 276 bolívares per day; electronics
draughtsman, 17,000 bolívares per month

CONSUMER GOODS OWNERSHIP

1000

750

500
Per 1000 population

250

0

156   82   93   34

*Higher
than
South
American
average*

In 1973, when there were just 4.3
bolívares to the US dollar, Venezuela
was the world's biggest importer
of Chivas Regal Whisky and French
champagne, and it was cheaper to spend
the weekend in Miami than in Caracas.

Living standards have fallen since
the collapse in world oil prices.
However, wealth remains concentrated
amongst Venezuelans connected to the
government and a few industrialists.

The poorest section of society,
dependent on the welfare state, has
suffered particularly from austerity
measures introduced in an attempt
to cut the budget deficit. Recent moves
to tighten income tax collection (most
Venezuelans evade it) have hit
the salaried middle classes.

WORLD RANKING

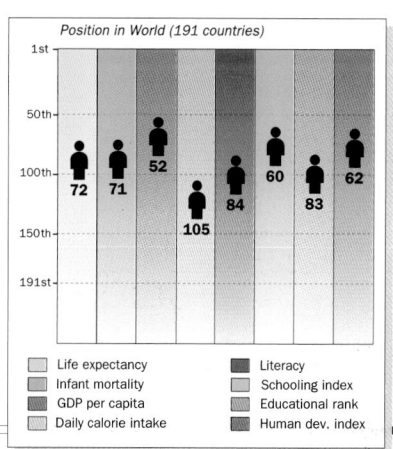

Position in World (191 countries)

1st

50th

100th

72   71   52   84   60   83   62

105

150th

191st

Life expectancy   Literacy
Infant mortality   Schooling index
GDP per capita   Educational rank
Daily calorie intake   Human dev. index

V

VIETNAM

SOUTH EAST ASIA

Asia

OFFICIAL NAME: Socialist Republic of Viet–Nam   **CAPITAL:** Hanoi
POPULATION: 67.8 million   **CURRENCY:** New dông   **OFFICIAL LANGUAGE:** Vietnamese

LOCATED ON THE EASTERN COAST of the Indochinese peninsula, over half of Vietnam is dominated by the heavily forested mountain range, the Chaîne Annamitique. The most populated areas, which are also the most intensively cultivated, are along the Red and Mekong rivers. Partitioned after the Second World War, the Communist north reunited the country after the world's longest 20th-century conflict, the 1962–1975 Vietnam War. Today, Vietnam is a single-party state ruled by the Communist Party. Since 1986, the regime has followed a liberal economic policy known as *doi moi* (renovation).

CLIMATE

WEATHER CHART

Vietnam has a sharply contrasting climate. The north has cool winters, while the south is tropical with even temperatures all year round. The central provinces are affected by typhoons. The most intensively cultivated areas are the deltas of the Red and Mekong rivers, which are respectively subject to drought and heavy flooding.

COMMUNICATIONS

 **Tan Son Naht Intl,
Ho Chi Minh City**   184 ships
597,300 dwt

THE TRANSPORT NETWORK

85,700 km (53,253 miles)		None	
2600 km (1616 miles)		17,702 km (11,000 miles)	

Rebuilding infrastructure destroyed during the war is still the priority. A key project is likely to be the reconstruction of Highway 1, linking Hanoi and Ho Chi Minh City (formerly Saigon). Ports and railways will also require rehabilitation, and construction has begun on two new port facilities, at Vung Tau in the south and Cai Lan in the north. Trains travel slowly in Vietnam, with an average speed of around 15 km an hour. The journey from Hanoi to Ho Chi Minh City takes three days.

TOURISM

 300,000 visitors   ⬆ Up 16% in 1991

MAIN OVERSEAS ARRIVALS

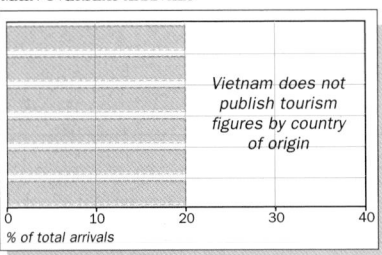

Vietnam does not publish tourism figures by country of origin

% of total arrivals

Russians, East Europeans and backpackers from the West made up the bulk of the 400,000 or so tourists Vietnam received each year during the 1980s. Other travellers were either on business, or overseas Vietnamese, *Viet Kie*, visiting relatives.

Since 1990, the government has opened the way to large-scale tourism. Massive investment is now going into hotels, and an official target of three million tourists a year by 2000 has been set. For the moment, Vietnam's appeal rests on its unspoilt Asian way of life and areas of spectacular natural beauty such as Ha Long Bay on the Red river delta. It is estimated that earnings from tourism in 1993 stood at $200 million.

Boats moored near Nha Trang. *A network connecting Vietnam's main ports provides an important internal communications link.*

PEOPLE

 Vietnamese, Chinese, Thai, Khmer, Muong, Nung, Miao, Yao, Jarai   202 people per km²

THE URBAN/RURAL POPULATION SPLIT

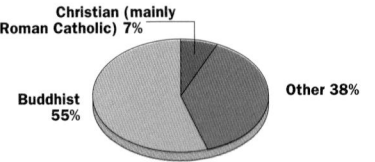

22%   78%

RELIGIOUS PERSUASION

Christian (mainly Roman Catholic) 7%

Other 38%

Buddhist 55%

ETHNIC MAKEUP

Chinese 4%   Other 6%

Thai 2%

Vietnamese 88%

Overseas Chinese constitute the largest minority group in Vietnam, and were subject to considerable discrimination in the early years of the Communist takeover. The Saigon Chinese, with their Taiwanese links, were viewed as corrupt bourgeoisie, while the northern Mountain Chinese were suspected as a fifth column for China's ambitions in Vietnam. Various other mountain minorities (*Montagnards*), who have a history of collaboration with the French and Americans and who continued armed resistance, were also sidelined by the regime in Hanoi. Today, the main source of tension is the resettling of lowlanders in mountain regions, which is putting pressure on limited farming and forest resources.

Women outnumber men, largely because of war deaths. They form a high proportion of the industrial workforce (during the war they were the majority), but have not received any greater political voice. There are still no women in the Politburo.

Family life is strong and is based on kinship groups within village clans.

POPULATION AGE BREAKDOWN

% of population by age group	■ 0–14	■ 15–64	□ 65+		
65+	4.2%	4.3%	4.8%	4.7%	5.1%
15–64	57.1%	51.9%	52.7%	56.8%	59.8%
0–14	38.7%	43.8%	42.5%	38.5%	35.1%
	1960	1970	1980	1990	2000

V

Le Duc Anh,
president since 1992.

Vo Van Kiet, *prime
minister of Vietnam.*

POLITICS

 1997   President Gen
Le Duc Anh

THE STATE OF THE PARTIES

National Assembly 395 members

Elections were last held in 1992, following a change in the
constitution of the same year.

Vietnam is a single-party communist
state.

MAIN POLITICAL ISSUES
Economic reform
Vietnam is attempting to
make the transition from
a centrally planned to a
market economy, without the
political liberalization that has
characterized the transition in
eastern Europe.

Resisting political reform
The founders of the Communist
Party have transferred power to
the younger generation, who
formed the vanguard in the
wars against the French and
Americans in the 1950s–1970s.
They are unwilling to give up
the power won by force of
arms by democratizing the
political process.

PROFILE
Politically, Vietnam still
operates according to a
traditional communist
system. The 13-
member Politburo,
elected by the 146-
strong Central
Committee, is
still the most
powerful
body. Power
filters down
to state-
enterprise
managers,
all of
whom are
members
of the Party.
However,
maintaining
the
Communist
Party's
legitimacy,
when the
central plank of
economic ideology
has been removed,
will not be easy.
There are already signs
of some multipartyists
pressing for reform.

WORLD AFFAIRS

Vietnam's economic liberalization has
led to improvements in its relationship
with the USA. In 1993, Washington
finally lifted its aid embargo, allowing
the World Bank to start investing in
reconstruction, and US companies to
bid for contracts. Relations with the ex-
colonial power, France, have also
improved; a French company is
upgrading Vietnam's telephone system.

The removal of Vietnamese troops
from neighbouring Cambodia in 1989
led to improved relations with China.
In 1992, the two countries resolved
their dispute over oil rights in the
South China Sea.

AID

 $190m   up 47% in 1990

The Vietnamese invasion of Cambodia
in 1978 halted all aid from China, Japan
and the West, with the exception of the
Scandinavian countries. Vietnam
turned to the Soviet Union, which
financed the large trade deficit until
1985. The USA resumed humanitarian
aid in 1992 and removed economic
restrictions in 1993. Aid now provides
for 89% of all capital expenditure.

CHRONOLOGY
From 1825, the brutal persecution of
the Catholic community, originally
converted by French priests in the
17th century, gave France the
excuse to colonize Cochin-China,
Annam and Tonkin, and then merge
them with Laos and Cambodia.

❑ **1920** *Quoc ngu* (Roman script)
replaces Chinese script.
❑ **1930** Ho Chi Minh founds
Indochina Communist Party.
❑ **1940** Japanese invade but tolerate
Vichy administration until 1945.
❑ **1941** Viet Minh resistance founded
in exile in China; aided by USA.
❑ **1945** Viet Minh take Saigon and
Hanoi. Emperor abdicates. Republic
with Ho Chi Minh as president.
❑ **1946** French (rearmed by UK)
re-enter. First Indo-China War.
❑ **1954** French defeated at Dien
Bien Phu. Vietnam divided at 17°N.
USSR supports North; USA arms
South. Communist opposition in
South secretly armed by North
down Ho Chi Minh Trail.
❑ **1960** Groups opposed to President
Diem's repressive regime in South
unite as Viet Cong.
❑ **1961** USA pours in military
advisers.

VIETNAM
Total Area : 329 560 sq. km
(127 243 sq. miles)

POPULATION
▣ over 1 000 000
◉ over 500 000
◎ over 100 000
○ over 50 000
● over 10 000
• under 10 000

LAND HEIGHT
2000m/6562ft
1000m/3281ft
500m/1640ft
200m/656ft
Sea Level

V

V

DEFENCE

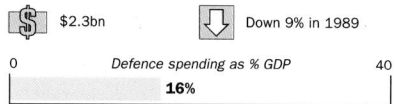

$2.3bn   Down 9% in 1989

0   *Defence spending as % GDP*   40
16%

Since the withdrawal from Cambodia in 1989 (only the Khmer Rouge suggests that the withdrawal has not occurred), the focus of defence spending has moved to the navy, a reflection of growing tensions in the South China Sea. Vietnam's 'volunteer force' in Laos has also been much reduced.

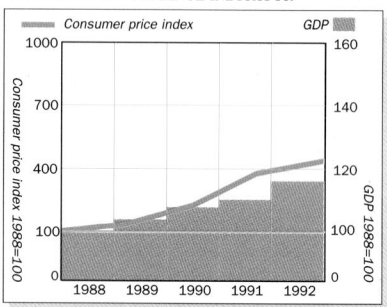

VIETNAMESE ARMED FORCES

1300 main battle tanks (T-34,-54,-55/T-62/ Ch Type-59/M-48A3)	70,000 personnel
7 frigates and 55 patrol boats	42,000 personnel
185 combat aircraft (20 Su-17/40 Su-22)	15,000 personnel
None	

ECONOMICS

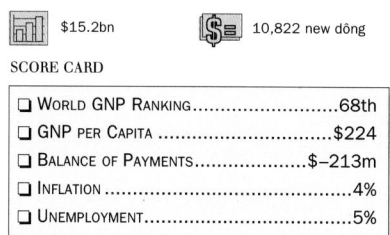

$15.2bn   10,822 new dông

SCORE CARD

- ❑ World GNP Ranking..........................68th
- ❑ GNP per Capita $224
- ❑ Balance of Payments...................$−213m
- ❑ Inflation 4%
- ❑ Unemployment....................................5%

ECONOMIC PERFORMANCE INDICATOR

— Consumer price index   ▨ GDP

Consumer price index 1988=100   *GDP 1988=100*

1988 1989 1990 1991 1992

EXPORTS ▨

- France 6%
- Singapore 8%
- Japan 36%
- Hong kong 10%
- Eastern Europe 11%
- Other 29%

IMPORTS ▨

- France 7%
- Japan 7%
- Singapore 33%
- Hong Kong 9%
- Eastern Europe 19%
- Other 25%

STRENGTHS
Diverse resource base. Location in East Asia. Much lower labour costs than second tier NICs such as Malaysia and Thailand.

WEAKNESSES
Weak economic institutions will make transition to a full market economy difficult. Enormous task of reconstruction after war; dependent on aid from the West, Japan and China.

PROFILE
Vietnam is already being billed by some commentators as the next Asian 'tiger'. The prospect is still distant, though the potential certainly exists. Mineral resources, located mostly in the north, and a resumption of Western aid to the capital-starved economy, are the foundations on which the adoption of a full market economy will be based. The major concerns are the need to develop the private sector and to maintain inflation at a tolerable level. It is now running at 4%, compared with 600% in

1987–1988. The tax net also needs to be widened if government finances are to be set on a proper footing.

Even before the collapse of the Soviet Union, there was a widespread acceptance in Vietnam that the centrally planned economy had problems. The encouragement of private enterprise began in 1988. Between 1988 and 1993, foreign investors proposed new projects worth over $6.8 billion. Exports, including rice, textiles and seafood, grew at 30% a year over the same period. In 1993, the economy grew by over 8.3%. The government has set a target of doubling Vietnam's GDP in the next decade.

VIETNAM : MAJOR BUSINESSES

- Hanoi
- Hai Phong
- Nam Đinh
- Đa Năng
- Quang Nam
- Biên Hoa
- Hô Chi Minh

Steel
Cement
Textiles
Brewing
Garments
Shipbuilding
Consumer goods
Vehicle manufacture
Oil & gas

0   300 km
0   300 miles
* significant multinational ownership

RESOURCES

 8.7bn kwh (capacity 1.32m kw)

 99,100 b/d (reserves 500,000,000 bbl)

 12.2m pigs, 3.2m cattle, 2.8m buffaloes

 Coal, oil, tin, zinc, iron, antimony, apatite, salt, bauxite

ELECTRICITY GENERATION

Hydro 62% (5.4bn kwh)
Thermal 38% (3.4bn kwh)
Nuclear 0%
Other 0%
% of total generation by type

Vietnam is the world's third largest exporter of rice, after Thailand and the USA. Oil production at 99,100 b/d is negligible by world standards, but sufficient to make it Vietnam's biggest export earner. Oil and gas exploitation is undertaken by VietSovPetro, a joint venture with Russia. However, Vietnam is linking up with new partners, including the Australian company BHP and British Gas. Mobil Oil is also signing new deals, having abandoned its interests in the face of advancing communist troops in 1975. Vietnam has considerable unexploited gas reserves in the South China Sea; gas from the only producing field currently has to be flared off.

Northern Vietnam has a surplus of electricity. A new power line will make this available to the South.

VIETNAM : LAND USE

Cropland
Pasture
Forest
Wetland
Rice
Rubber - cash crop
Pigs

0   300 km
0   300 miles

ENVIRONMENT

 3% (2% partially protected)

Environmental issues are not a priority

ENVIRONMENTAL TREATIES

No   No
No   No

Vietnam is still counting the massive environmental cost of the Vietnam War. Seven million tons of bombs were dropped, and the defoliant chemical Agent Orange was sprayed over 1.7 million hectares. In addition to the bridges, industrial zones and irrigation works destroyed, 50% of Vietnam's forests were seriously damaged and 5% wiped out. Continuing deforestation is now the major problem. Each year, 200,000 hectares are lost, with consequential soil erosion and flooding.

MEDIA

 Some political restrictions

PUBLISHING AND BROADCAST MEDIA

There are 4 daily newspapers, *Nhan Dan*, *Quan Doi Nhan Dan*, *Ha Noi Moi* and *Sai Gon Giai Phong*. All are state-owned

1 state-owned service   1 state-owned service

Palapa B2-P Intelsat V F8   None

Although the media is tightly regulated and all editors have to be Party members, criticism of the authorities is still possible. The weekly *Tuoi Tre* is known for its investigative reporting, and even *Nhan Dan*, the Party newspaper, has been known to expose laxity in the system, especially in the judiciary. The army daily, *Quan Doi Nhan Dan*, is the most hardline paper.

CRIME

 Vietnam does not publish prison figures

 Increase in petty theft

CRIME RATES

Rates of murder and rape remain fairly constant. Theft has risen slightly

The judicial system is based on the Soviet model. Although the education camps established after liberation have now closed, religious and political dissidents are still held without trial.

Petty theft from foreigners is a problem in the major cities. There has been a sharp rise in corruption since economic liberalization.

Religious tensions have given rise to recent disturbances. In one incident, supporters of the Buddhist minority clashed with the police in Hué.

EDUCATION

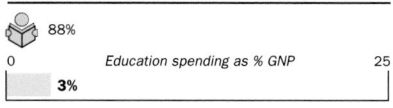 88%

0   Education spending as % GNP   25
          3%

THE EDUCATION SYSTEM

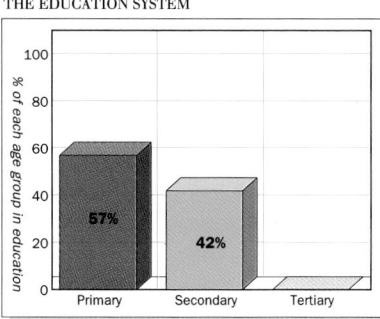

% of each age group in education

57%   42%

Primary   Secondary   Tertiary

Fees for education have recently been introduced, and enrolment is falling. Vietnamese universities have a strong liberal arts tradition.

HEALTH

 1 per 2882 people

Heart disease, cancers, malaria

0   Health spending as % GNP   25
          Minimal health spending

Vietnam's main medical achievements are the development of a vaccine for Hepatitis B, and the extraction of artemisinin (an anti-malarial drug) from the indigenous Thanh Hao tree.

WEALTH

 Wealth disparities are small

CONSUMER GOODS OWNERSHIP

Per 1000 population

Cars limited to elite   PC and VCR ownership is limited to a small elite

38   2

The Party remains the route to advancement. Ostentatious displays of wealth are still frowned upon.

WORLD RANKING

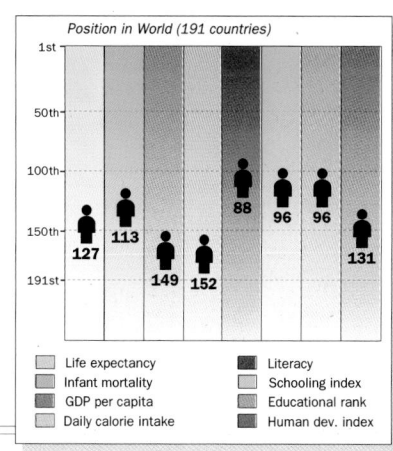

Position in World (191 countries)

1st
50th
100th   88   96   96
150th   127   113   131
          149   152
191st

Life expectancy   Literacy
Infant mortality   Schooling index
GDP per capita   Educational rank
Daily calorie intake   Human dev. index

V

WESTERN SAMOA

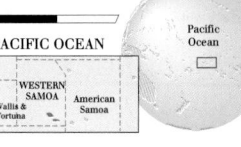

OFFICIAL NAME: Independent State of Western Samoa   **CAPITAL:** Apia
POPULATION: 169,000   **CURRENCY:** Tala   **OFFICIAL LANGUAGES:** Samoan, English

WESTERN SAMOA LIES IN THE HEART of the South Pacific, 2400 km north of New Zealand. Four of its nine volcanic islands are inhabited – Apolima, Manono, Sava'ai, the largest, and Upolu, home to 72% of the population. Rainforests cloak the mountains; vegetable gardens and coconut plantations thrive around the coasts. A German protectorate until 1914, Western Samoa was then administered by New Zealand until independence in 1962.

CLIMATE

WEATHER CHART

The climate is humid and temperatures rarely drop below 25°C. December to March is the hurricane season.

COMMUNICATIONS

Faleolo Apia
191,727 passengers

3 ships
5800 dwt

THE TRANSPORT NETWORK

2085 km
(1296 miles)

None

None

None

Apia port has been improved with Japanese aid. International links are mainly by air. Ferries provide inter-island connections.

TOURISM

39,414 visitors

Down 18% in 1991

MAIN OVERSEAS ARRIVALS

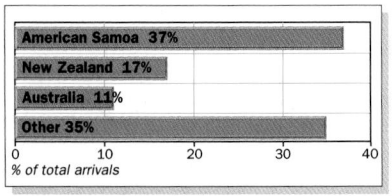

American Samoa 37%
New Zealand 17%
Australia 11%
Other 35%

0   10   20   30   40
% of total arrivals

Concern that the Samoan way of life would be disrupted has limited tourism development until recently. Efforts now to improve facilities reflect the need to increase national revenues.

PEOPLE

Samoan, English

60 people per km²

THE URBAN/RURAL POPULATION SPLIT

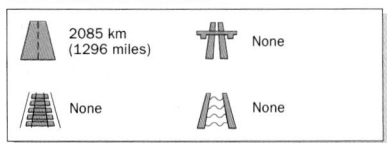

21%   79%

RELIGIOUS PERSUASION

Christian 100%

Ethnic Samoans – around 93% of the population – are the world's second largest Polynesian group, after the Maoris. The *fa'a Samoa*, Samoan way of life, is communal and formalized. Extended family groups, in which most people live, own 80% of the land, and are not permitted to sell it. Each family is headed by a *matai*, or elected chief, who looks after its political and social interests. Large-scale migration to New Zealand and the USA reflects a lack of jobs and the attractions of Western life. Conflict between the *fa'a Samoa* and modern life is strongest among the young, who have a high suicide rate.

WESTERN SAMOA

Total Area : 2840 sq. km (1097 sq. miles)

POPULATION
- over 10 000
- under 10 000

LAND HEIGHT
1000m/3281ft
500m/1640ft
200m/656ft
Sea Level

0   15 km
0   15 miles

POLITICS

1996

HH Malietoa
Tanumafili II

THE STATE OF THE PARTIES

Legislative Assembly 49 members

65%   33%   2%
HRPP   SNDP   Other

HRPP = Human Rights Protection Party
SNDP = Samoa National Development Party

The conservatism of the *fa'a Samoa*, reinforced by the Church's influence, has underpinned Western Samoa's political stability. Allegiance to the two main parties is quite fluid, and politics is as much to do with personalities as policies. Until 1990, only the 1800 elected chiefs, or *matai*, could vote for the 47 ethnic Samoan seats; the other two seats are elected by non-Samoans. Universal suffrage was introduced at the 1991 elections, although only *matai* may stand for the *fono*, or parliament. Following the elections, Fiame Naomi, a woman chief, became the country's first female cabinet minister.

WORLD AFFAIRS

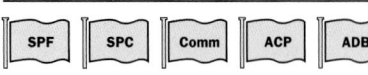

SPF   SPC   Comm   ACP   ADB

New Zealand is Western Samoa's main trading partner. However, a steady tightening of controls on Samoan immigrants has strained relations with Wellington, at times. Australia, the USA and EU are also important trading partners. Ties with Tokyo are growing, linked to Japanese investment.

AID

$52m (receipts)

Up 89% between 1989 and 1991

Australia, Japan, New Zealand and the EU are the main donors. With import costs 12 times export earnings and a heavy debt burden, aid is vital to the survival of the economy.

W

DEFENCE

 Western Samoa has no army and few police

 Not applicable

New Zealand looks after defence under a 1962 treaty. Internal order is mostly maintained by the chiefs, or *matai*.

ECONOMICS

 $152m

 2.60 tala

SCORE CARD

❏ WORLD GNP RANKING	182nd
❏ GNP PER CAPITA	$900
❏ BALANCE OF PAYMENTS	$–29.2m
❏ INFLATION	9.7%
❏ UNEMPLOYMENT	Underemployment

STRENGTHS

Light manufacturing growing; in 1992, it accounted for 75% of export earnings. Attracting foreign, especially Japanese, firms. Services growing rapidly since 1989 launch of offshore banking. Tropical agriculture; taro, coconut cream, cocoa, copra are main exports.

WEAKNESSES

Chronic balance of trade and payments deficits; dependence on aid and expatriate remittances. Declining agricultural exports. Clash between communal *fa'a Samoa* and donor pressure for market-style reforms.

EXPORTS

IMPORTS

RESOURCES

 46m kwh (capacity 19,000 kw)

 Not an oil producer and has no refineries

 55,000 pigs, 29,000 cattle, 7000 asses

 None

With no minerals, Western Samoa's main resources are its forests and tropical agriculture. The rainforests in lower lying areas are increasingly exploited for timber. Mahogany and teak plantations are being developed. The volcanic soils, particularly on Upolu, allow a wide range of staple and export crops to be grown. Two thirds of the population works in agriculture.

Apia, the capital, on Upolu, Western Samoa's second largest island. It has a central volcanic range of mountains and many rivers.

ENVIRONMENT

  None

 Rainforests are increasingly under threat from logging

Efforts to increase revenues are putting the environment under pressure – 80% of lowland rainforest has been replaced by plantations. Overhunting and loss of habitat have endangered rare species of fruitbat and pigeon. Foreign firms have proposed environmentally damaging projects such as waste disposal plants, but these have so far been rejected.

MEDIA

 Fairly open criticism of the government is possible

PUBLISHING AND BROADCAST MEDIA

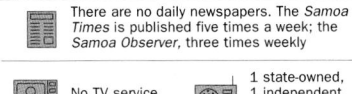

	There are no daily newspapers. The *Samoa Times* is published five times a week; the *Samoa Observer*, three times weekly	
No TV service		1 state-owned, 1 independent service

American Samoan TV, linking with the US networks, is widely received. A state-owned service is being set up.

CRIME

 Western Samoa does not publish prison figures

 Little change from year to year

Alcohol-related violence is a problem, at weekends, otherwise violent crime is almost unknown. Theft is increasing in urban areas.

EDUCATION

 98%

Education is based on the New Zealand system. School attendance is universal and literacy levels high. A university was established in 1988. Scholarships are available for study abroad.

HEALTH

 1 per 3685 people

 Heart and cerebro-vascular diseases, pneumonia, suicide

The Samoan preference for being big married well with traditional diets. Diabetes and heart disease are rising as people change to Western-style foods.

WEALTH

 Many in the private sector earn only the statutory minimum of 1.25 tala per hour

CONSUMER GOODS OWNERSHIP

VCR and PC ownership is limited to a small elite

One of the world's least developed nations according to the UN, Western Samoa has the lowest wage and highest unemployment rates in Oceania. As a result, emigration is high. Some 60,000 Samoans live in New Zealand, 50,000 in the USA and 10,000 in neighbouring American Samoa, where generous US support makes life much easier. Most people depend on subsistence farming and the remittances of relatives for their livelihood. Two thirds of those with a job work for the government.

WORLD RANKING

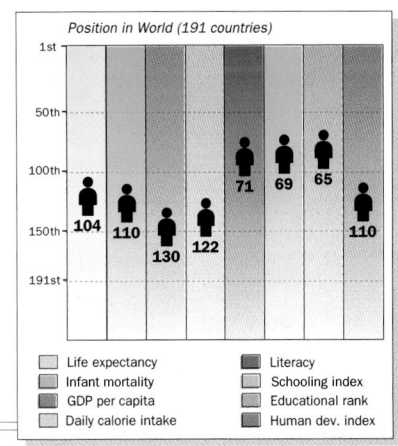

Position in World (191 countries)

☐ Life expectancy	☐ Literacy
☐ Infant mortality	☐ Schooling index
☐ GDP per capita	☐ Educational rank
☐ Daily calorie intake	☐ Human dev. index

W

597

YEMEN

MIDDLE EAST

OFFICIAL NAME: Republic of Yemen   **CAPITAL:** Sana
POPULATION: 12.5 million   **CURRENCY:** Yemen rial, Yemeni dinar   **OFFICIAL LANGUAGE:** Arabic

YEMEN IS LOCATED in southern Arabia between Saudi Arabia and Oman. The north is mountainous, with a fertile strip along the Red Sea. The south is largely arid mountains and desert. Yemen was formerly two countries, The Yemen Arab Republic in the north and The People's Democratic Republic of Yemen in the south, which united in 1990. The poorer south, with its capital in Adan, was the Arab world's only Marxist state after British rule ended in 1967. The north was run from Sana by successive military regimes, following a coup against the royalist imamate in 1962.

CLIMATE

WEATHER CHART

 Average daily temperature   Rainfall

The desert climate is modified by altitude, which affects temperatures by as much as 12°C. Rainfall increases in northwest and central Yemen.

COMMUNICATIONS

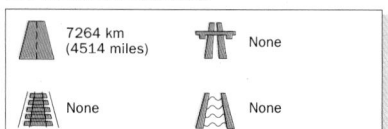

Sana International
624,000 passengers

7 ships
9700 dwt

THE TRANSPORT NETWORK

7264 km (4514 miles)		None	
None		None	

Adan's position at the entrance to the Red Sea makes it a key shipping port. The main cities are linked by adequate roads, but many rural areas are inaccessible. Sana and Adan are served by international airlines.

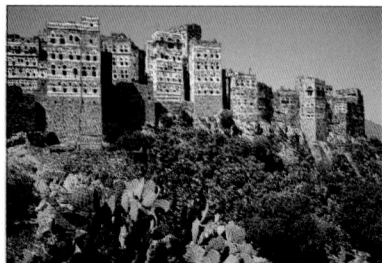

Hilltop village in northern Yemen, showing traditionally decorated, multi-storey houses built from mud bricks.

TOURISM

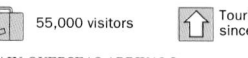

55,000 visitors

Tourism has risen since 1990

MAIN OVERSEAS ARRIVALS

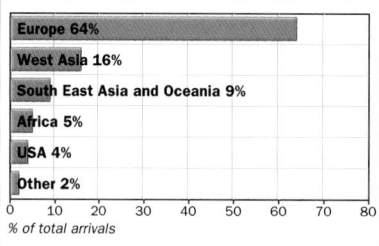

Europe 64%
West Asia 16%
South East Asia and Oceania 9%
Africa 5%
USA 4%
Other 2%

% of total arrivals

Believed to be the home of the legendary Queen of Sheba, Yemen attracts tourists interested in Arab society, architecture, archaeology and historical remains. The Romans called Yemeni Arabia *Felix* because of its fertile farmlands and dominance in the frankincense trade. Yemen was the second country, after Saudi Arabia, to convert to Islam.

Southern Yemen has been open to Western visitors only since 1990. Its run-down infrastructure and lack of hotels, especially on the coast, have hindered tourism. Sana, a walled medieval city, is the more interesting centre for tourists. It has impressive architecture, particularly tall stone and terracotta Arab houses, and the palaces of the former imamate. Despite being over 100 km from the capital, the Marib Dam, built in ancient times, is another major attraction.

German and French tourists were the first to travel in numbers to North Yemen, when specialist companies began to offer adventure holidays during the 1980s. Tourism is on the increase, despite growing reports of terrorism and kidnapping.

Tourists are subject to a ban on the consumption of alcohol, except in five-star hotels. Whisky and beer are available on the black market, which operates out of Djibouti.

PEOPLE

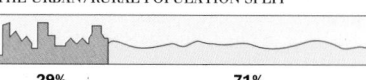

Arabic

22 people per km²

THE URBAN/RURAL POPULATION SPLIT

29%   71%

RELIGIOUS PERSUASION

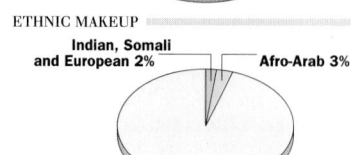

Christian, Hindu and Jewish 3%
Shi'a Muslim 42%
Sunni Muslim 55%

ETHNIC MAKEUP

Indian, Somali and European 2%
Afro-Arab 3%
Arab 95%

Yemenis are almost entirely of Arab and Bedouin descent, though there is a small, dwindling, Jewish minority. The majority are Sunni Muslims, of the Shafi sect. In the north, many people have close family in Saudi Arabia. Many Yemenis consider Saudi's Asir province to be part of Yemen.

Agriculture employs more than half the population. Many Yemenis sought jobs in Saudi Arabia and the Gulf states during the 1970s oil boom. More than one million worked in Saudi Arabia, most as manual labourers and farm hands. Their expulsion, a result of Yemen's support for Iraq's invasion of Kuwait in 1990, has raised unemployment within Yemen.

In rural areas and in the north, Islamic orthodoxy is strong and most women wear the veil. In the south, however, women still claim the freedoms they had under the Marxist regime, especially in urban areas.

Tension continues to exist between the south, led by the cosmopolitan city of Adan, and the more conservative north. Clashes have taken place between their former armies.

POPULATION AGE BREAKDOWN

%	0–14	15–64		65+
65+	3.1%	3%	2.6%	2.4%	2.4%
15–64	54%	53.4%	47.2%	48%	49.4%
0–14	42.9%	43.6%	50.2%	49.6%	48.2%
	1960	1970	1980	1990	2000

Y

YEMEN

Total Area : 527 970 sq. km
(203 849 sq. miles)

(map of Yemen with surrounding regions: SAUDI ARABIA, OMAN, RED SEA, GULF OF ADEN)

POPULATION

over 500 000	◉
over 100 000	◎
over 10 000	●
under 10 000	·

LAND HEIGHT

3000m/9843ft
2000m/6562ft
1000m/3281ft
500m/1640ft
200m/656ft
Sea Level

POLITICS

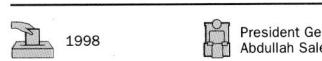

1998   President Gen Ali
Abdullah Saleh

THE STATE OF THE PARTIES

House of Representatives 301 members

40%	21%	19%	20%
GPC	YAR	YSP	Other

GPC = General People's Congress **YAR** = Yemeni Alliance
for Reform **YSP** = Yemeni Socialist Party **Other** = Arab
Socialist Ba'ath Party, Truth Party

Yemen is a multiparty democracy. The
president retains executive power while
the House of Representatives holds
legislative power.

MAIN POLITICAL ISSUES

Instability
The 1993 general election resulted in
a government of national unity being
formed. However, the merger of South
and North Yemen has been under
severe strain since then. Growing
animosity between the Yemen Socialist
Party (YSP), which formerly ruled in
Adan, and the conservative hierarchy
in Sana made full-blown civil war a
constant threat.

Saudi interference
In the run up to the elections, there
were bombings and attacks on leading
politicians. Since the Gulf War, political
relationships with Saudi Arabia have
been strained, raising suspicions that
the latter is funding northern dissidents.

PROFILE
The merger of North and South Yemen
in 1990 united Yemenis under one ruler
for the first time since 1735. President
Ali Saleh, who had had difficulty
controlling the north even before the
union with the socialist regime in Adan,
skilfully maintained unity. Then, in the
spring of 1994, tensions mounted
following an assassination attempt on a
political supporter of Saleh's, Hassan
Makki. Amid accusations from the
South that President Saleh was
attempting to overthrow Vice President
al-Baidh, the former leader of South
Yemen, civil war broke out. Most of the
fighting was centred in the south, in
particular around the port of Adan,
which became the scene of mass
evacuations by European workers. By
June 1994, the fighting had died down,
partly owing to Syrian influence, but
the situation remained extremely tense.

Ali Abdullah Saleh,
former North Yemen
president, now leader
of the unified Yemen.

Ali Salem al-Baidh,
vice-president and
former leader of
South Yemen.

CHRONOLOGY

From the 9th century AD the Zaydi
dynasty ruled Yemen, until their
defeat by the Ottoman Turks in
1517. The Turks were expelled by
the Zaydi Imams in 1636.

❑ **1839** Britain occupies Aden.
❑ **1918** Yemen secures independence.
❑ **1937** Aden made a Crown Colony,
the hinterland a Protectorate.
❑ **1962** Army coup. Imam deposed
and Yemen Arab Republic (YAR)
declared in the North.
❑ **1962–1970** Northern civil war
between royalists and republicans.
❑ **1963** Aden and Protectorate united
to form Federation of South Arabia.
❑ **1967** British troops leave Aden.
❑ **1970** South Yemen renamed the
People's Democratic Republic of
Yemen (PDYR). Republicans
victorious in the North.
❑ **1971** Civilian elections in the YAR.
❑ **1972** September, war between YAR
and PDYR. October, peace signed.
❑ **1974** Army coup in YAR.
❑ **1975** Sultan of Oman defeats PDYR-
backed revolt in Dhofar province.
❑ **1978** Lt-Col Ali Saleh YAR
president. Coup in PDYR. Radical
Abdalfattah Ismail in power.
❑ **1979** February, war breaks out.
March, peace. October, PDYR signs
20-year treaty with USSR.
❑ **1980** Ismail replaced by
moderate Ali Muhammed.

Y

CHRONOLOGY *continued*

- ❏ **1982** President of PDYR Ali Muhammed signs peace treaty with the Sultan of Oman.
- ❏ **1984** YAR signs 20-year co-operation treaty with USSR.
- ❏ **1986** January, coup attempt against President Muhammed in PDYR develops into civil war. Rebels take control of Adan. February, rebels install Haydar Al Attas as president. July, presidents of PDYR and YAR meet.
- ❏ **1987** Oil production starts in YAR.
- ❏ **1988** YAR holds elections for a consultative council, Muslim brotherhood gain influence.
- ❏ **1989** Unification process speeds up dramatically. June, telephone links established. July, PDYR publishes a programme of free-market reforms. November, YAR and PDYR sign agreement to unify the two states. December, constitution of unified Yemen published.
- ❏ **1990** January, restrictions on travel between YAR and PDYR end. Growing opposition to unification inside Yemen from fundamentalists against the secular constitution. May 22, unification of PDYR and YAR. Ali Saleh becomes president of the Republic of Yemen. August, Yemen criticizes Western response to the Iraqi invasion of Kuwait.
- ❏ **1991** Yemeni guest workers expelled by Saudi Arabia in retaliation for Yemen's position over the Iraqi invasion of Kuwait. Arab states boycott independence celebrations.
- ❏ **1992** Assassinations and political unrest delay elections until April 1993. Economic decline.
- ❏ **1993** April elections leave the ruling parties still in power. Islamic fundamentalists gain influence in President Saleh's government.

WORLD AFFAIRS

   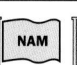 | ESCWA

Yemen's links with Saudi Arabia and the West have still not recovered from the support Yemen gave to Iraq during the Gulf War. Yemen's relationship with Oman has improved with the signing of a border agreement in 1992.

AID

 $313m (receipts)   Down 23% in 1991

Yemen receives limited backing from the World Bank and Western aid agencies. Aid from Gulf states depends on Yemen abandoning ties with Iraq.

DEFENCE

💲 $935m   ⬇ Down 12% in 1992

0   *Defence spending as % GDP*   40
13%

Following unification, mutual suspicion slowed down the integration of North and South Yemen's defence forces. Sporadic, bitter clashes have taken place, most notably in 1994. In the past, Soviet weapons were bought by both governments, although the north also possesses US arms.

YEMENI ARMED FORCES	
1275 main battle tanks (250 T-34/725 T-54,-55/ 250 T-62/50 M-60A1)	60,000 personnel
16 patrol boats (2 *Tarantul* I/6 Sov *Osa* II)	1500 personnel
101 combat aircraft (11 F-5E/111 Su-20, -22/188 MiG-21)	2000 personnel
None	

ECONOMICS

 $7.3bn   0.46 Yemeni dinars / 16.47 Yemen rials

SCORE CARD

- ❏ WORLD GNP RANKING..........................91st
- ❏ GNP PER CAPITA $585
- ❏ BALANCE OF PAYMENTS....................$–579m
- ❏ INFLATION 70%
- ❏ UNEMPLOYMENT...................................13%

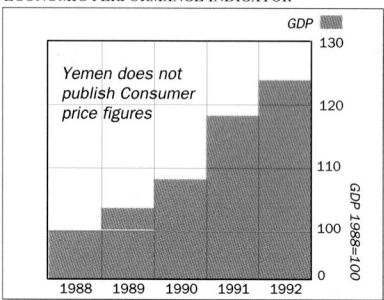

ECONOMIC PERFORMANCE INDICATOR

Yemen does not publish Consumer price figures

GDP — GDP 1988=100

EXPORTS

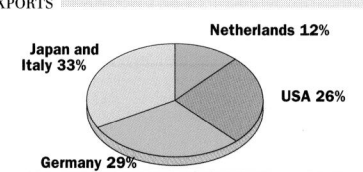

Japan and Italy 33% / Netherlands 12% / USA 26% / Germany 29%

IMPORTS

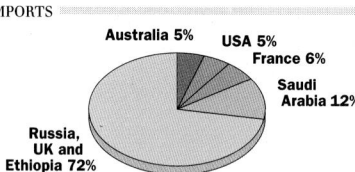

Australia 5% / USA 5% / France 6% / Saudi Arabia 12% / Russia, UK and Ethiopia 72%

STRENGTHS

Rising oil production. Salt mining. Deposits of copper, gold, lead, zinc and molybdenum. Industries include oil refining, chemicals food products.

WEAKNESSES

Political instability deters foreign investment. Well-organized black market undermines tax base. Large balance of payments deficit. Overall dependence on subsistence agriculture.

PROFILE

Yemen's unification in 1990 was designed to transform the economy. High expectations were placed on the exploitation of large oil and natural gas reserves, discovered in 1984. Exports of oil began in 1987. Plans were also made to encourage industrial investment around the port of Adan. Both these policies for regeneration suffered severe setbacks as a result of the 1990–1991 Gulf War. In addition, the expulsion of over one million Yemeni guest workers from Saudi Arabia imposed a huge burden on the economy and ended the flow of workers' remittances.

Economic crisis forced the government to reduce expenditure and subsidies on certain staple foods. This provoked widespread civil unrest and encouraged many farmers to switch from food crops, such as wheat, to growing the more profitable narcotic plant *qat*. As a result, Yemen has increasingly had to import foodstuffs.

In line with its free-market reforms, the government encouraged joint-venture deals with Western oil firms. Some companies were deterred by bandits, who stole equipment and kidnapped personnel for ransom. The evacuation of skilled foreign workers owing to an outbreak of civil war in 1994 will hit the economy hard.

YEMEN : MAJOR BUSINESSES

'Amrān* / Sana / Tarīm / Bājil / Al Mukallā / Ta'izz / Shuqrah / Adan / Zinjibār

Textiles / Cement / Salt mining / Oil refining / Food processing / Light engineering

0   100 km   0   100 miles

* significant multinational ownership

Y

RESOURCES

1.7bn kwh
(capacity
800,000 kw)

450,000 b/d
(reserves
4,000,000,000 bbl)

3.7m sheep,
1.2m cattle,
690,000 asses

Oil, natural gas, salt,
molybdenum, zinc,
gold, lead, copper

ELECTRICITY GENERATION

Hydro 0%

Thermal 100% (1.7bn kwh)

Nuclear 0%

Other 0%

0   20   40   60   80   100
% of total generation by type

There are considerable reserves of oil and gas. Crude oil production has reached 450,000 b/d. It would be more but for Western companies' reluctance to offend Saudi Arabia, whose relations with Yemen are strained. Despite attacks by bandits, exploration is continuing in many areas. Salt is the only other mineral that is commercially exploited at present, and its production continues to grow steadily.

The agricultural sector employs 55% of the working population and accounts for 22% of GDP. Cotton is grown as a cash crop. There is also some forestry and hunting for animal skins. Livestock and livestock products, such as dairy produce and hides, are the economic mainstays of the north.

Yemen's rich fishing grounds in the Arabian Sea have been developed. They now provide a major source of earnings, despite poor equipment.

YEMEN : LAND USE

RUB 'AL KHALI

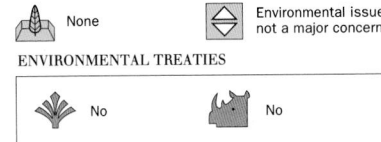

Cropland
Pasture
Desert
Cotton
Grapes
Sheep

0   100 km
0   100 miles

ENVIRONMENT

None

Environmental issues
not a major concern

ENVIRONMENTAL TREATIES

No

No

Yes

No

Yemen's low economic development has resulted in large untouched areas of land. However, game animals are under severe threat from hunters.

MEDIA

The media is under tight government control

PUBLISHING AND BROADCAST MEDIA

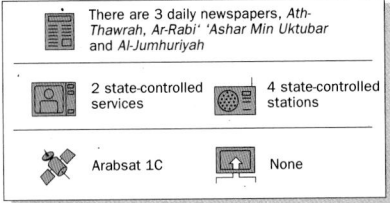

There are 3 daily newspapers, *Ath-Thawrah, Ar-Rabi' 'Ashar Min Uktubar* and *Al-Jumhuriyah*

2 state-controlled
services

4 state-controlled
stations

Arabsat 1C

None

CRIME

Yemen does not
publish prison figures

 Crime is rising

CRIME RATES

*Threat of civil war makes normal law
enforcement problematic*

Political assassinations have long been a feature of Yemeni life and continue to threaten political stability. Formal law enforcement does not often operate far outside the main cities. As a result, Western companies face the double risk of their personnel being kidnapped and their equipment being stolen by Bedouin raiding parties. To combat the latter, many vehicles have their roofs marked so that police can readily identify them from the air and, if necessary, track down thieves.

EDUCATION

 39%

0   *Education spending as % GNP*   25

6.1%

THE EDUCATION SYSTEM

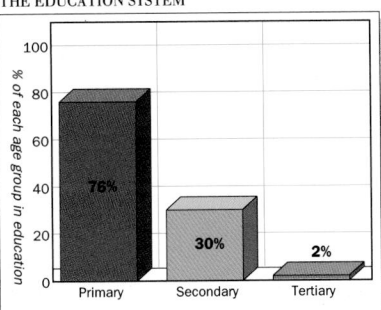

100
80
60
40
20
0

% of each age group in education

76%

30%

2%

Primary   Secondary   Tertiary

80% of the population have no formal classroom education. Schooling barely extends into the rural areas. Illiteracy is especially high among women: 75% cannot read or write. There are fewer than 10,000 students at Yemen's two universities – Sana and Adan. Yemen also has some technical colleges.

Yemen has a long, distinguished tradition of intellectual debate, but the press is poorly developed. The government keeps a tight control on the media and vets the entry of foreign journalists. TV and radio are state-controlled and have a limited range around the principal cities. Satellite TV is not generally available. The ownership of radio and TV receivers is low, with only a small minority of the population owning a TV.

HEALTH

1 per 5531 people

Diarrheal diseases,
tuberculosis, malaria,
bilharzia

0   *Health spending as % GNP*   25

1.5%

The major cities have an adequate primary health-care system. Rural areas are less well served. Yemen has only one doctor for every 5531 people. Infant mortality is high for the Middle East at 12%. Life expectancy is 52 years for men and 56 for women.

WEALTH

Most Yemenis lead a subsistence existence

CONSUMER GOODS OWNERSHIP

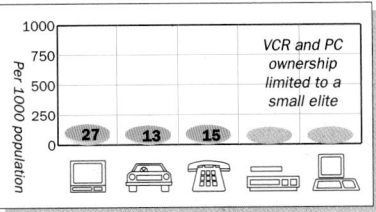

1000
750
500
250
0

Per 1000 population

*VCR and PC
ownership
limited to a
small elite*

27   13   15

Most Yemenis have experienced a reduced standard of living since Saudi Arabia expelled its Yemeni workers. The lack of jobs in other Gulf states has added to unemployment levels. Except for a small elite, the ownership of consumer goods is low.

WORLD RANKING

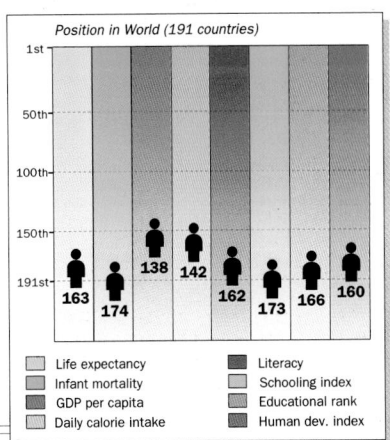

Position in World (191 countries)

1st
50th
100th
150th
191st

163   174   138   142   162   173   166   160

Life expectancy
Infant mortality
GDP per capita
Daily calorie intake

Literacy
Schooling index
Educational rank
Human dev. index

Y

YUGOSLAVIA (SERBIA & MONTENEGRO)

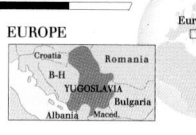

OFFICIAL NAME: Federal Republic of Yugoslavia **CAPITAL:** Belgrade
POPULATION: 10.4 million **CURRENCY:** Dinar **OFFICIAL LANGUAGE:** Serbo-Croatian

THE SELF-PROCLAIMED Federal Republic of Yugoslavia (FRY), comprising the republics of Serbia and Montenegro, lays claim to being the successor state to the former Yugoslavia. Serbia is vilified in the international community for its role in the ongoing conflict in the region and the FRY has been denied recognition by most countries. UN sanctions imposed in 1992 have taken a tremendous economic toll. Nationalism among the Hungarian minority in the autonomous region of Vojvodina and, in particular, among Albanians in Kosovo, is a further source of tension.

CLIMATE

WEATHER CHART

The climate is continental inland and Mediterranean along the Montenegrin coast. Summers are hot and springs rainy. Winters are cold, with heavy snowfalls. In July and August the average daily maximum in Belgrade is 28°C, while in January it is 3°C.

COMMUNICATIONS

Surcin, Belgrade
2.8m passengers

44 ships
1.5m dwt

THE TRANSPORT NETWORK

46,000 km
(28,584 miles)

350 km
(217 miles)

Extensive

River Danube
is the major
waterway

About one third of railways in the FRY are electrified. However, the important rail link to Greece, one of Serbia's main trading links, has been cut since 1993 as a result of international economic sanctions. Most goods are still available in the shops, but are brought into the country by illegal trade.

Roads in Serbia are manned by small groups of soldiers carrying AK47s. Yugoslavia issues transit visas relatively freely and travel on the main Budapest–Sofia highway through Serbia has resumed. Although Yugoslavia is fairly safe for foreign travellers and harrassment by the military is rare, most travellers choose to take longer routes through neighbouring countries.

TOURISM

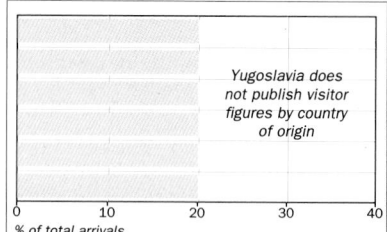

Very few – mainly people in transit or visiting relatives

Tourist industry collapsed in face of UN sanctions

MAIN OVERSEAS ARRIVALS

Yugoslavia does not publish visitor figures by country of origin

% of total arrivals

The former Yugoslavia's mountain scenery and beaches attracted over five million tourists a year before 1991.

Serbia has never been a centre of tourism. The Montenegrin coast, however, has renowned beaches. The imposition of UN sanctions means that foreign tourism has ceased. Montenegrin tourism is monopolized by Serbians, particularly by the political and criminal elements of the Serbian elite. The impact of recession and hyperinflation has kept the average Yugoslav holidaymaker away.

YUGOSLAVIA
(SERBIA & MONTENEGRO)

Total Area : 25 715 sq. km (9929 sq. miles)

POPULATION

over 1 000 000

over 100 000

over 50 000

LAND HEIGHT

2000m/6562ft
1000m/3281ft
500m/1640ft
200m/656ft
Sea Level

PEOPLE

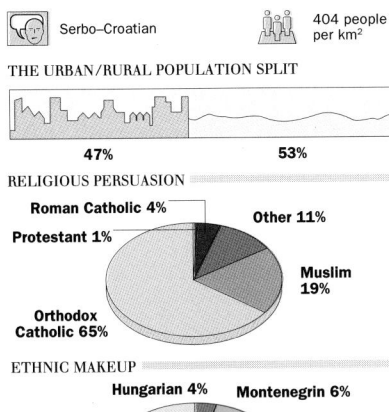

Serbo–Croatian

404 people per km²

THE URBAN/RURAL POPULATION SPLIT

47%   53%

RELIGIOUS PERSUASION

- Roman Catholic 4%
- Other 11%
- Protestant 1%
- Muslim 19%
- Orthodox Catholic 65%

ETHNIC MAKEUP

- Hungarian 4%
- Montenegrin 6%
- Other 13%
- Albanian 14%
- Serb 63%

The social order in the FRY is disintegrating. The professional classes have effectively been driven out of Serbia; 100,000 have left since the dissolution of federal Yugoslavia. The absence of a middle class is likely to be most strongly felt when sanctions are eventually lifted; the lack of educated and experienced professionals may affect the prospects for economic recovery.

An estimated two thirds of the population are currently living below a subsistence level. Many people are suffering from malnutrition; health problems are aggravated by bitingly cold winters. A modest estimate of a household's basic consumption needs costs three times the average wage. Unsupported pensioners are faring worst. At the end of 1993, real monthly pensions were a virtually worthless DM7 and pensioners in Belgrade were reported to be committing suicide at a rate of four a week.

POPULATION AGE BREAKDOWN

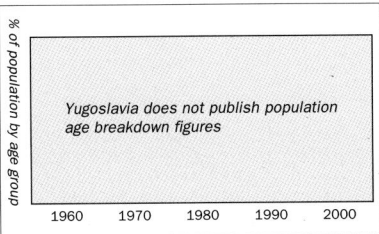

% of population by age group

Yugoslavia does not publish population age breakdown figures

1960   1970   1980   1990   2000

POLITICS

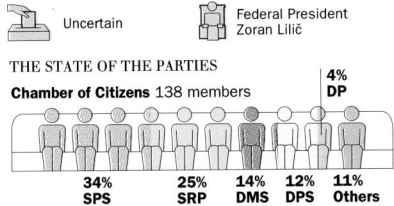

Uncertain

Federal President Zoran Lilić

THE STATE OF THE PARTIES

Chamber of Citizens 138 members

4% DP

34% SPS   25% SRP   14% DMS   12% DPS   11% Others

SPS = Socialist Party of Serbia   **SRP** = Serbian Radical Party
DMS = Democratic Movement of Serbia   **DPS** = Democratic Party of Socialists   **DP** = Democratic Party

Chamber of Republics 40 members

Comprised of 40 members from Serbia and Montenegro selected on a proportional basis to reflect the composition of Serbia's and Montenegro's republican legislatures

Serbia and Montenegro each have a single chamber democratically-elected parliament and a president. Each also contributes members to the bicameral Federal Assembly.

MAIN POLITICAL ISSUES

Inter-republican conflict

Montenegro has recently been showing greater independence from Serbia in decision making, in response to internal pressure and a need to secure its position within the Federal Republic. Serbia, in turn, has sought to undermine the authority of President Bulatović. In the summer of 1993, Serbia instigated a trade war with its smaller neighbour, focusing on energy and food. Montenegro responded with cuts in the exports of raw materials, such as aluminium, which are essential to Serbian industry, particularly the armaments sector.

Minority government in Serbia

The Serbian parliament remains unstable. In the 1993 elections, the Socialists enlarged their share of seats from 101 to 123, leaving them still three seats short of an absolute majority.

PROFILE

Serbia is the stronger political player and, as Serbian president, Milošević is at the centre of policy making. In Montenegro, the DPS government elected in 1992 formed a coalition with all but one of the other parties, despite having themselves received a clear majority.

Radoje Konić, who replaced Milan Panić as federal prime minister in 1993.

Slobodan Milošević, Serbian president and the FRY's major political influence.

WORLD AFFAIRS

UN economic sanctions against the FRY have isolated it from the international community, and foreign affairs centre on the states of the former Yugoslavia. The exact nature of the links with Bosnian Serbs is intentionally obscured, but it is widely accepted that Bosnian Serb troops receive considerable support from Serbia. An open declaration of support for integrating seized lands into a 'Greater Serbia' would destroy hopes of a peaceful settlement. Fighting continues over the region of Krajina, which is within Croatian territory, but is considered by President Milošević to be within the Serb sphere of influence. Slovenia and Serbia have disputed the division of federal Yugoslav property. The existence of a strong Hungarian minority in Vojvodina and the more explosive tensions which surround the Albanian minority in Kosovo complicate relations with the neighbouring states of Hungary and Albania.

AID

 Only humanitarian aid

 None likely until peace settlement

All aid has been suspended with other economic relations. It is unlikely that recovery from the economic devastation which the FRY has sustained will be possible without international assistance.

CHRONOLOGY

The Serbs were defeated by the Turks at the Battle of Kosovo in 1389. Parts of the region later came under the control of the Austrian Habsburg empire.

- ❏ **1878** Full independence gained by Serbia and Montenegro at Congress of Berlin.
- ❏ **1918** Joint Kingdom of Serbs, Croats and Slovenes created.
- ❏ **1929** King Alexander of Serbia assumes absolute powers over state; changes name to Yugoslavia.
- ❏ **1941** Germans launch surprise attack. Rival resistance groups: Chetniks (Serb royalist) and Partisans (communist, under Tito).
- ❏ **1945** Federal People's Republic of Yugoslavia founded with Tito as prime minister. Vojvodina and Kosovo provinces gain autonomy within Serbia.
- ❏ **1948** Tito breaks with Stalin.
- ❏ **1950** Workers' councils give employees voice on economy.

Y

CHRONOLOGY *continued*

- ❏ **1951** Farmers permitted to sell produce on free market.
- ❏ **1955** Detente between Yugoslavia and the USSR.
- ❏ **1973** April, economic co-operation agreement signed with West Germany. October, agreement of non-interference signed with Soviet Union. December, Croat nationalists purged from party leadership and government.
- ❏ **1974** New constitution decentralizes government. Vojvodina and Kosovo given status within Serbia.
- ❏ **1980** Tito dies. Succeeded by collective presidency.
- ❏ **1981** Unrest among Kosovo Albanians; state of emergency declared.
- ❏ **1985** Serbian intellectuals publish memorandum listing Serb grievances within Yugoslavia.
- ❏ **1986** Slobodan Milošević becomes leader of communist party in Serbia (SPS).
- ❏ **1987** Government wage freeze in attempt to combat inflation. Scandals lead to banking system crisis.
- ❏ **1988** Emergency party meeting proposes economic and social reforms. Belgrade protests against economic austerity. Mikulić government brought down over budget failure.
- ❏ **1989** Kosovo Albanians protest at presence of Serb police unit; crackdown leads to loss of autonomy for province. King Nicholas I reburied in Montenegro. 600th anniversary of Battle of Kosovo.
- ❏ **1990** December, Milošević and Socialist party victorious in elections in Serbia. Communists win presidency and dominate assembly in multiparty elections in Montenegro.
- ❏ **1992** EC recognizes breakaway republics of Croatia, Slovenia and Bosnia-Herzegovina. UN sanctions imposed. Ibrahim Rugova elected president of self-declared republic of Kosovo. Failure of Vance-Owen plan for Bosnia. Milošević defeats Prime Minister Milan Panić and is re-elected president, but Socialists lose absolute majority. Momir Bulatović wins Montenegrin presidency.
- ❏ **1993** Radical deputy Vuk Drasković arrested, but released after international protests. Ultra-nationalist Seselj calls successful vote of no confidence. Socialists improve parliamentary standing in December elections. New EU initiative in peace talks over Bosnia.

Y

DEFENCE

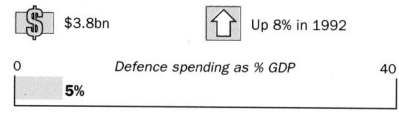

$3.8bn   Up 8% in 1992

0   *Defence spending as % GDP*   40

5%

SERBIAN ARMED FORCES

1000 main battle tanks (800 T-54-55/200 M-84)	100,000 personnel	
5 submarines, 4 frigates and 54 patrol boats	6000 personnel	
480 combat aircraft (98 MiG-21F/10 MiG-21U 18 MiG-29/12 *Galeb*)	29,000 personnel	
None		

The Serbian desire to reduce Bulatović's influence has resulted in the disestablishment of republican defence and foreign ministries in favour of the Serbian-controlled federal bodies. Montenegro has resisted the initiative.

The Serbian military has been the more visible actor in the conflict in former Yugoslavia. Serbia was traditionally the centre of armaments manufacture in the former republic. Its military hardware industry has enabled it to arm itself without being dependent upon imports. The need to create money to pay for domestically-produced weapons was a major factor in the crippling hyperinflation of 1993.

ECONOMICS

$13.5bn   Dinar on 1:1 par with the Deutsch Mark

SCORE CARD

- ❏ WORLD GNP RANKING..........................69th
- ❏ GNP PER CAPITA $1298
- ❏ BALANCE OF PAYMENTS ....Deficit
- ❏ INFLATION ....High
- ❏ UNEMPLOYMENT...................................25%

EXPORTS

> *Imports and exports have effectively been cut off as a result of UN sanctions*

STRENGTHS

Serbian machinery exports have found a niche selling their low-priced goods to their poorer neighbours despite sanctions. Even after adding the cost of sanctions-bending bribes, Serbian machines are still price-competitive.

WEAKNESSES

Virtual economic collapse following imposition of sanctions; effect on fuel supply particularly hard hitting. Severe disruption of food distribution networks, leading to shortages, a barter economy and widespread hunger.

PROFILE

Following the transition to a multiparty system, a short-lived reformist government began to implement privatization, fiscal reform and a reorganization of the banking sector. The war in Bosnia has since devastated these initiatives. Sanctions, which have cut off imports and exports, have decimated the emerging private sector as well as the state sector. The hyperinflation of 1992–1993 – inflation reached an hourly rate of 0.7% in December 1993 – pushed the economy to the verge of complete collapse.

ECONOMIC PERFORMANCE INDICATOR

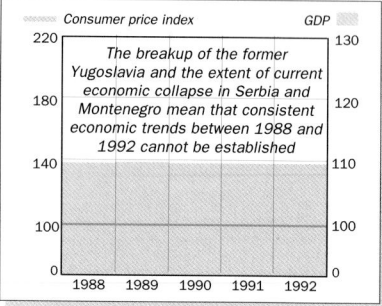

The breakup of the former Yugoslavia and the extent of current economic collapse in Serbia and Montenegro mean that consistent economic trends between 1988 and 1992 cannot be established

Consumer price index   GDP

Savings were rendered worthless and any incentive to invest in the economy was destroyed. Output levels in 1993 fell to a third of 1990 levels and Deutsch Marks assumed the position of almost legal tender. The 1994 stabilization plan is based on the creation of a 'super dinar' pegged to the Deutsch Mark. However, it will be difficult to implement without IMF backing or a cut in spending.

YUGOSLAVIA : MAJOR BUSINESSES

Pharmaceuticals	Light engineering
Textiles	Heavy engineering
Chemicals	Food processing
Metallurgy	
Electronics	

0   100 km
0   100 miles

RESOURCES

42m kwh (capacity 8.85m kw)

Some oil production

Cattle, sheep, goats

Coal, bauxite, iron, lead copper, zinc

ELECTRICITY GENERATION

Electricity is chiefly generated by thermal power stations

% of total generation by type

The FRY has attained self-sufficiency in coal and electricity production. The latter comes mainly from hydroelectric

ENVIRONMENT

3% (former Yugoslavia)

Environmental issues currently receive low priority

ENVIRONMENTAL TREATIES

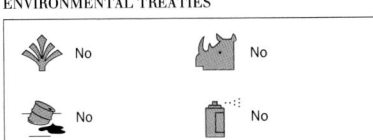

No   No

No   No

In Serbia, ecological awareness peaked in the late 1980s. The Ecological Forum sought to pursue the cross-border implications of pollution. Organized resistance in Montenegro to the Tara River dam project partially succeeded, in that the dam was moved upstream from a scenic canyon. The biosphere reserve at Durmitor National Park preserves unique wetlands.

MEDIA

Independent TV and radio stations have been targets of harassment and police raids

PUBLISHING AND BROADCAST MEDIA

The daily paper with the largest circulation is *Večernje Novosti*. Macedonia's is *Večer*

6 services   7 services

Intelsat V1 F1 Astra 1B   None

Public opinion continues to be shaped by the state-regulated broadcast media, on which most of the population is dependent for news coverage. There is also an independent press which provides news and commentary. Notable publications include *Vreme* and *Borba* in Serbia, and *Monitor* in Montenegro. *Tanjug*, the official news agency, was purged in 1991 to eliminate criticism of the regime. Independent TV and radio stations are only receivable in the Belgrade area.

or coal-fired plants. Vojvodina caters for one third of oil needs.

YUGOSLAVIA : LAND USE

Cropland
Forest
Pasture
High mountain regions
Pigs
Cereals

Danube

Drina

NORTH ALBANIAN ALPS

0   100 km
0   100 miles

ENVIRONMENT

CRIME

Serbia does not publish prison figures

No change in current high crime levels

CRIME RATES

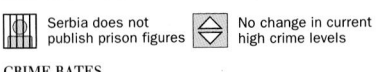

Civil disorder and the proliferation of weapons have led to a sharp rise in all categories of crime, including extortion

Economic crime, from currency trading to black market goods, has boomed. An estimated 40% of all economic activity takes place in the illegal market. Formerly on the main east–west smuggling route, Montenegro's drugs trade has been disrupted by sanctions. Fears exist that the Serbian militia will turn to mafia-type extortion operations.

EDUCATION

89%

0   *Education spending as % GNP*   25
Yugoslavia does not publish education spending figures

THE EDUCATION SYSTEM

Yugoslavia has not published new education enrolment figures. Education is theoretically compulsory between the ages of 7 and 15. Before the breakup of the former Yugoslavia, over 95% of children were in primary education and over 85% in secondary education.

% of each age group in education

Primary   Secondary   Tertiary

The education system is in crisis. Since the outbreak of war, some wealthy families have used hard currency earnings to send their children abroad to complete their secondary education. Literacy rates in Kosovo are below average for the FRY, at 82%. There are six universities and 37 colleges.

HEALTH

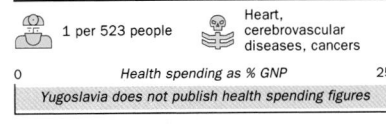

1 per 523 people

Heart, cerebrovascular diseases, cancers

0   *Health spending as % GNP*   25
Yugoslavia does not publish health spending figures

Isolation from former trading partners has affected the quality of the health service, despite the exemption of medicines and medical supplies from sanctions. Most medicines are unaffordable to the general population, and death rates among infants and the elderly have risen dramatically.

WEALTH

Average wage, US$12 per month

CONSUMER GOODS OWNERSHIP

Per 1000 population

High car owner-ship rate

VCR and PC ownership is limited to an elite

93   65

The country as a whole has been impoverished as a result of sanctions, but those who have managed to hang on to hard currency savings are at an advantage. Since the imposition of sanctions, real incomes have fallen to a tenth of what they were in 1990. Yet, food prices in Belgrade are higher than in much of western Europe. Many people were financially destroyed by the loss of their dinar savings in the bank collapses of 1992. Those who are presently amassing wealth are largely doing so by exploiting the chaos of war through the black market. One of the few areas of business expansion in recent years has been in exploiting markets for goods which were previously imported. The few rich buy sanctions-busting goods illegally imported from western Europe.

WORLD RANKING

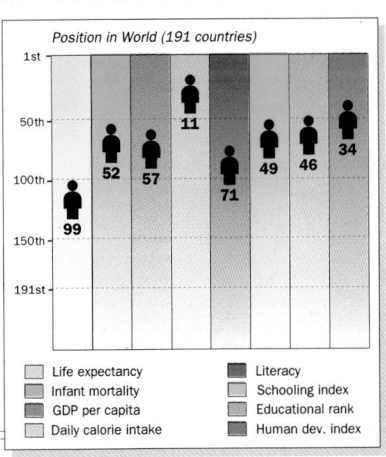

Position in World (191 countries)

1st
50th
100th
150th
191st

11
52   57   49   46   34
71
99

Life expectancy
Infant mortality
GDP per capita
Daily calorie intake

Literacy
Schooling index
Educational rank
Human dev. index

Y

605

ZAIRE

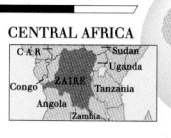

CENTRAL AFRICA

OFFICIAL NAME: Republic of Zaire **CAPITAL:** Kinshasa
POPULATION: 39.9 million **CURRENCY:** New zaire **OFFICIAL LANGUAGE:** French

L YING IN EAST-CENTRAL Africa, Zaire is one of the continent's largest countries. The rainforested basin of the Congo River occupies 60% of the country; its estuary provides Zaire's only sea access. The former Belgian Congo became independent in 1960 and was immediately plunged into civil war. President Mobutu took power in 1965, renamed the country Zaire and instituted an increasingly corrupt and unpopular regime. His reluctance to see through the transition to multiparty democracy, begun in 1990, has left Zaire with two governments and a disintegrating economy.

The Zaire River is navigable for 1600 km and provides one of the most convenient ways of travelling in the country.

CLIMATE

WEATHER CHART

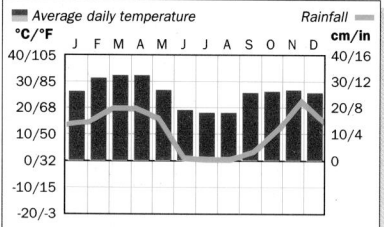

Zaire's climate is tropical and humid. Temperatures average 25°C and vary little through the year. Annual rainfall is around 150–200 cm; mountainous areas are wetter. The equator passes through the north of the country, causing marked regional variations. To its south, well-differentiated wet and dry seasons last from October–May and June–September respectively. North of the equator, a short dry season lasts from December to February; the rest of the year is wet.

COMMUNICATIONS

N'Djili, Kinshasa
525,000 passengers

2 ships
15,900 dwt

THE TRANSPORT NETWORK

145,000 km (90,100 miles)		None
4772 km (2965 miles)		15,200 km (9445 miles)

The Congo (known locally as the Zaire) and its many tributaries provide the main means of communication. Zaire's size and the fact that most of it is covered by dense rainforest have severely limited the development of road and rail networks. Many forest settlements are inaccessible except by air. Road maintenance, always poor, has virtually ceased outside the main towns since 1990, isolating even more settlements away from the main rivers.

TOURISM

51,422 visitors

Up 30% in 1989

MAIN OVERSEAS ARRIVALS

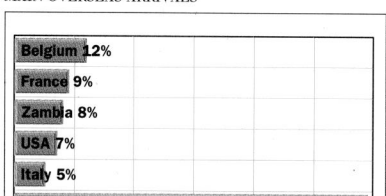

% of total arrivals

Zaire's attractions lie in its scenery, wildlife and the vibrant music of Kinshasa's many bands. Paramount is the Congo, 16 km wide in places and Africa's longest river after the Nile. President Mobutu's regime, however, has not encouraged tourism. Official restrictions on foreigners travelling around the country, combined with negligible tourism facilities outside the towns, have kept all but a few independent travellers away. Most of these have avoided Zaire since 1990 and the once-large number of business visitors has also collapsed.

PEOPLE

 Kiswahili, Tshiluba, Kikongo, Lingala, French

 17 people per km[2]

THE URBAN/RURAL POPULATION SPLIT

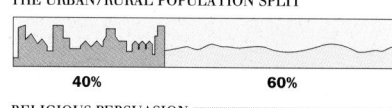

40%　　**60%**

RELIGIOUS PERSUASION

Kimbanguist 10%
Other 10%
Roman Catholic 50%
Muslim 10%
Protestant 20%

ETHNIC MAKEUP

Bantu and Hamitic 45%
Other 55%

Zaire is ethnically diverse, with more than 12 main groups and around 190 smaller ones. The majority are of Bantu origin, but there are also large Hamitic and Nilotic populations, mainly in the north and northeast. Zaire's original inhabitants, the forest Pygmies, today form a tiny and marginalized group. The population is very unevenly distributed. The Shaba mining area and major urban centres are densely populated, while the rainforests have a density of less than 3 people per km[2]. Those in remoter areas have always lived on the margins of the cash economy. Since 1990, however, hyperinflation has forced the majority into a subsistence lifestyle.

President Mobutu managed to contain ethnic tensions inherited from the colonial period during most of his rule. Since 1990, however, there have been outbreaks of ethnic violence and 'cleansing', notably in Shaba Kivu and Kasai provinces. Over 6000 people were reported to have been killed in clashes during 1993. Belgium has accused Mobutu of encouraging ethnic strife to delay democratic change.

POPULATION AGE BREAKDOWN

	0–14		15–64		65+
2.9%	**2.8%**	**2.8%**	**2.9%**	**2.8%**
53.1%	**52.9%**	**51.2%**	**49.8%**	**49.4%**
44%	**44.3%**	**46%**	**47.3%**	**47.8%**
1960	1970	1980	1990	2000

Z

ZAIRE

Total Area : 2 345 410 sq. km
(905 563 sq. miles)

POPULATION

▣	over 1 000 000
◉	over 500 000
◎	over 100 000
○	over 50 000
●	over 10 000
•	under 10 000

LAND HEIGHT

	2000m/6562ft
	1000m/3281ft
	500m/1640ft
	200m/656ft
	Sea Level

WORLD AFFAIRS

For almost 25 years, President Mobutu's anti-communism made Zaire one of the leading African allies of the West, and of the USA in particular. Western economic and military aid – which included sending troops to help suppress the 1977 and 1978 invasions by exiles based in Angola – played a critical role in sustaining his regime. In return, he guaranteed Western access to Zaire's mineral wealth and provided Angola's US-backed UNITA rebels with bases during the 1980s.

At the same time, however, Mobutu's political astuteness enabled him to maintain close ties with several communist states, notably China. Relations with African neighbours were more problematic, complicated by Mobutu's support for UNITA and for Morocco's annexation of Western Sahara. From 1984 to 1986, Zaire withdrew from the OAU in protest over its support of Western Saharan independence.

Since the late 1980s, the changing political situation in eastern Europe, combined with growing concerns about human rights abuses and corruption in Zaire, has led to a fundamental shift in attitudes to Mobutu. Most countries have stopped all but humanitarian aid since 1990. Belgium, France, the USA and EU, formerly Mobutu's closest allies, now view him as an embarrassment. Backing the High Council and its nominated government, led by Etienne Tshisekedi, they are involved in efforts to resolve the country's political crisis and persuade Mobutu to step down.

POLITICS

Uncertain	President Marshal Mobutu Sese Seko

THE STATE OF THE PARTIES

National Legislative Council 210 members

Zaire has two opposing governments. President Mobutu's administration is now opposed by a 435 member transitional legislature known as the High Council of the Republic (HCR). The HCR has appointed Etienne Tshisekedi as prime minister in opposition to the president and his government

President Mobutu Sese Seko has ruled Zaire since 1965.

MAIN POLITICAL ISSUE

Ending the political crisis

The fundamental problem facing Zaire is how to force President Mobutu to fulfil his 1990 promise of instituting a multiparty democracy. All his actions since have made clear his intention to hang on to power at all costs. He has refused to surrender control of the treasury and security forces, or accept the High Council and its government, and has set up a puppet alternative. This has combined to create a political vacuum in which violence flourishes while the economy falls apart.

PROFILE

From 1965 to 1989, President Mobutu's absolute rule combined repression with astute political manipulation. In 1990,

Etienne Tshisekedi, the High Council's choice as premier.

President Mobutu, who is under pressure to resign.

growing internal opposition and foreign pressure led him to announce moves to multiparty democracy. A National Executive Council, dominated by the Sacred Union coalition of opposition parties, was set up to negotiate a new constitution. In December 1992, it transformed itself into the High Council, a 435-member interim parliament which backed Etienne Tshisekedi as head of a transitional government. Rejecting this attack on his power, Mobutu set up his own government in 1993, headed by Faustin Birindwa. Tshisekedi has popular and international support; Mobutu controls the treasury and army.

AID

 $823m (receipts)

 Down 23% in 1990

Zaire's importance to the West during the Cold War brought it aid revenues on a large scale. Between 1970 and 1989, it received $8.3 billion in economic aid – including $1.1 billion from the USA and $6.9 billion from other OECD states – as well as large-scale military assistance. Changing political priorities led the USA to act on long-deferred problems of human rights abuses and misappropriation of aid by President Mobutu. In 1990, it suspended all but humanitarian aid; most other donors quickly followed suit. In 1992, the IMF declared Zaire 'non co-operative', ending any chances of rescheduling its $10 billion foreign debt. Aid will not be resumed until Mobutu goes and a new, democratic government is installed.

Z

CHRONOLOGY

Modern Zaire was the site of the Kongo and other powerful African kingdoms and a focus of the slave trade. Belgium's King Leopold II claimed most of the Congo basin after 1876.

❏ **1885** Congo Free State (CFS) founded as King Leopold's private fief; start of brutal colonization.
❏ **1908** Belgium takes over CFS after international outcry. Renamed Belgian Congo.
❏ **1960** Independence of Republic of Congo. Katanga (Shaba) province secedes. The UN intervenes.
❏ **1963** Katanga secession collapses.
❏ **1964** Belgian troops help crush new revolts in centre and east.
❏ **1965** General Joseph-Désiré Mobutu seizes power.
❏ **1970** Mobutu elected president; makes his Popular Revolutionary Movement (MPR) sole legal party.
❏ **1971** Country renamed Zaire.
❏ **1972** Africanization of names. Becomes Mobutu Sese Seko.
❏ **1977–1978** Two invasions by former Katanga separatists repulsed with Western help.
❏ **1982** Opposition parties set up Union for Democracy and Social Progress (UDPS).
❏ **1986–1990** Mobutu implements numerous cabinet reshuffles in face of growing popular unrest and foreign criticism of widespread human rights abuses.
❏ **1990** Belgium suspends aid after security forces kill democracy demonstrators. April, Mobutu announces transition to multiparty rule. UDPS legalized.
❏ **1991** Strikes, mass rallies continue. July, 130 opposition parties form Sacred Union coalition. August, National Conference (NC) convened. September, Belgian and French troops evacuate foreigners during rioting. UDPS leader Etienne Tshisekedi heads short-lived 'crisis government' formed by Mobutu.
❏ **1992** January. NC suspended. April. NC reconvenes and assumes sovereign powers. August, Tshisekedi made prime minister by NC. December, Mobutu sacks Tshisekedi who refuses to go; NC dissolves itself; elects 435-member High Council of the Republic (HCR).
❏ **1993** February, HCR endorses Tshisekedi. March, Mobutu appoints Faustin Birindwa as head of alternative government. October, compromise agreement on transitional constitution and government collapses when Mobutu faction refuses to accept Tshisekedi as interim premier.

DEFENCE

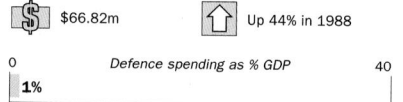

💲 $66.82m

⬆ Up 44% in 1988

0 — Defence spending as % GDP — 40
1%

Zaire's military has played a key role in keeping President Mobutu in power and has been responsible for widespread human rights abuses. The Israeli-trained presidential guard is the elite force. Ordinary troops, poorly equipped and poorly paid, have taken to rioting, looting and extortion.

ZAIREAN ARMED FORCES

🛡	60 main battle tanks (60 Ch Type-62/ 20 Ch Type-59)	26,000 personnel
🚢	4 patrol boats	13,000 personnel
✈	28 combat aircraft (7 Mirage 5M/1 -5DM)	1800 personnel
	None	

ECONOMICS

📊 $8.1bn

💰 249.00 new zaires

SCORE CARD

❏ WORLD GNP RANKING..........................89th
❏ GNP PER CAPITA $203
❏ BALANCE OF PAYMENTS ....Massive deficit
❏ INFLATION 4000%
❏ UNEMPLOYMENT.............................Very high

ECONOMIC PERFORMANCE INDICATOR

EXPORTS
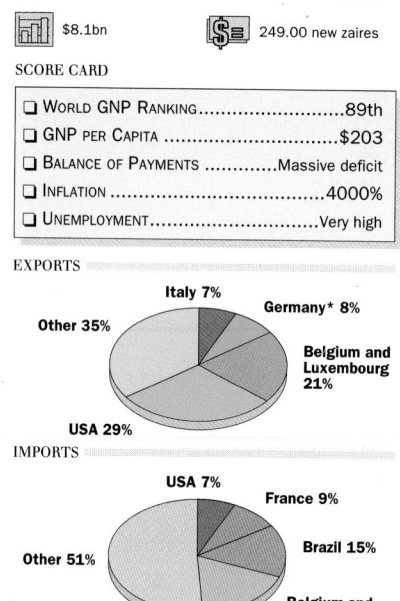
Italy 7%
Germany* 8%
Other 35%
Belgium and Luxembourg 21%
USA 29%

IMPORTS
USA 7%
France 9%
Other 51%
Brazil 15%
Belgium and Luxembourg 18%

STRENGTHS

Rich resource base. Minerals – notably copper, cobalt, diamonds – provide 85% of export earnings. Energy: oil; possibly Africa's largest hydro-power potential. Rich soil; much unutilized arable land. Trade surplus in normal years.

WEAKNESSES

Legacy of 25 years of mismangement and corruption: $10 billion foreign debt; withdrawal of crucial foreign aid; inadequate, disintegrating social and transport infrastructures; lack of food self-sufficiency. Political instability. Hyperinflation. Loss of export income. Withdrawal of foreign investment.

PROFILE

In the early 1990s, political instability, combined with the legacies of 25 years of mismanagement, had brought the economy near to collapse. Real GDP growth in 1990–1993 averaged –8% a year; in 1993 it topped –12%. The budget deficit is at record levels, in part due to hyperinflation which was not ended by the introduction of the new zaire – worth 3 million old zaires – in late 1993. Lack of spares and power cuts have closed many mines and halted most other industry. Strikes and riots over plummeting living standards have hastened the flight of foreign capital. Subsistence farming and petty trade keep most people going. But even if political stability is restored, Zaire's immediate outlook is grim. Resumption of large-scale aid and debt relief, essential to rebuild the economy, will depend on difficult reforms and paying off arrears to the IMF and other creditors. In the long term, Zaire's rich resources hold out hope of prosperity.

ZAIRE : MAJOR BUSINESSES

Kisangani
Mbandaka
Zaire
Kinshasa
Bukavu
Boma
Kananga
Mbuji-Mayi
Kolwezi
Likasi
Lubumbashi

🛢 Oil
✿ Textiles
⛏ Copper mining
⚒ Cobalt mining
🗄 Food processing
◉ Industrial diamonds
✸ Light engineering

0 — 200 km
0 — 200 miles

RESOURCES

 6.2bn kwh
(capacity 2.83m kw)

 3m goats,
1.5m cattle,
890,000 sheep

 26,200 b/d
(reserves
187,000,000 bbl)

Copper, diamonds, oil
cobalt, zinc, uranium,
manganese, tin, gold

ELECTRICITY GENERATION

Hydro 97% (6bn kwh)

Thermal 3% (155m kwh)

Nuclear 0%

Other 0%

% of total generation by type

With its huge mineral, agricultural and energy resources Zaire should be rich. Instead, mismanagement and, since 1990, political instability have reduced it to one of the world's poorest states. Copper, cobalt and diamonds provide almost 80% of export earnings. In the 1980s, Zaire was the world's largest cobalt exporter and second largest industrial diamond exporter. Since 1990, copper and cobalt output has collapsed and diamond smuggling is booming. Zaire has oil reserves, but its energy wealth lies in its HEP potential, which could supply much of Africa if fully exploited. Lack of maintenance has, instead, shut down many turbines and most urban areas face power cuts. Despite rich soils and the fact that 80% of people are involved in farming, Zaire is not self-sufficient in food.

ENVIRONMENT

  4%

Vast size of country means many ecosystems are intact

ENVIRONMENTAL TREATIES

No

Yes

Yes

No

The predominantly virgin rainforests covering over 60% of Zaire comprise almost 6% of the world's and 50% of Africa's remaining woodlands. They are home to important populations of several endangered species, including gorillas. Zaire's poor transport network has so far prevented large-scale commercial exploitation, but fuelwood clearance is a problem. The collapse since 1990 of many urban refuse and sewage disposal systems has led to major health and pollution problems.

MEDIA

 Press censorship has relaxed since 1990, but journalists critical of the regime still face harassment, including arrest

PUBLISHING AND BROADCAST MEDIA

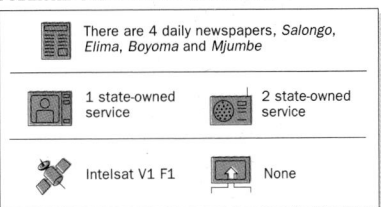

There are 4 daily newspapers, *Salongo*, *Elima*, *Boyoma* and *Mjumbe*

1 state-owned service

2 state-owned service

Intelsat V1 F1

None

In contrast to the broadcast media, the press is privately owned. Coverage of the opposition has widened since 1990, but press criticism of President Mobutu or the security forces is still generally muted. One newspaper's Kinshasa offices were burnt down in 1993 after it published a strongly anti-Mobutu article. Overtly critical journalists face arrest or other reprisals.

CRIME

 Zaire does not publish prison figures

 Violence and crime have risen rapidly since 1990

CRIME RATES

All types of crime are on the increase

Political crisis and economic collapse have exacerbated Zaire's long-standing problems of corruption and human rights abuses. Violence and crime of all kinds, including extortion, robbery, rape and murder, are on the increase. Many murders are attributed to the security forces and politically-linked death squads, as are the occasional 'disappearances'. Ethnic violence, suppressed after 1965, has resurfaced, particularly in the south.

EDUCATION

 60%

0   Education spending as % GNP   25

0.9%

THE EDUCATION SYSTEM

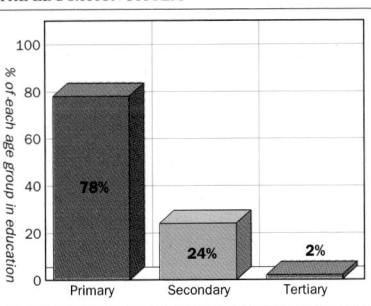

% of each age group in education

78% Primary

24% Secondary

2% Tertiary

State educational provision, like health care, is patchily distributed and has faced sharp budget cuts since 1980. As a result, about 70% of schooling is now provided by the Catholic Church.

ZAIRE : LAND USE

Cropland
Forest
Pasture
Wetlands
Cattle
Coffee
Palm oil - cash crop

0
0   200 miles

HEALTH

 1 per 13,540 people

Malaria, respiratory and diarrheal diseases

0   Health spending as % GNP   25

0.8%

State services, long underfunded, have virtually collapsed. Disease and death rates are rising, especially in rural areas. HIV/AIDS is a significant problem.

WEALTH

 A large majority of the population lives a subsistence existence

CONSUMER GOODS OWNERSHIP

Per 1000 population

1000
750
500
250
0

VCR and PC ownership is limited to a small elite

1   2   1

President Mobutu is one of the world's richest men, worth an admitted $50 million and an estimated $5 billion. Most Zaireans live in poverty.

WORLD RANKING

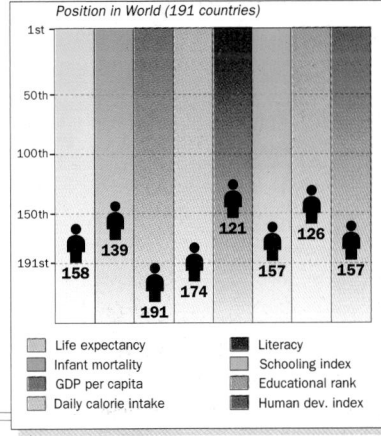

Position in World (191 countries)

1st
50th
100th
150th
191st

158   139   191   174   121   157   126   157

Life expectancy
Infant mortality
GDP per capita
Daily calorie intake

Literacy
Schooling index
Educational rank
Human dev. index

Z

ZAMBIA

SOUTHERN AFRICA
Africa

OFFICIAL NAME: Republic of Zambia   **CAPITAL:** Lusaka
POPULATION: 8.6 million   **CURRENCY:** Zambian kwacha   **OFFICIAL LANGUAGES:** English, Bemba and Nyanja

LYING IN THE HEART of southern Africa, Zambia is a country of upland plateaus, bordered to the south by the Zambezi River. Its economic fortunes are tied to the copper industry. Falling copper prices in the late 1970s, and then the growing inaccessibility of remaining reserves, have led to a severe decline in the economy. In 1991, Zambia achieved a peaceful transition from single-party rule to multiparty democracy.

CLIMATE

WEATHER CHART

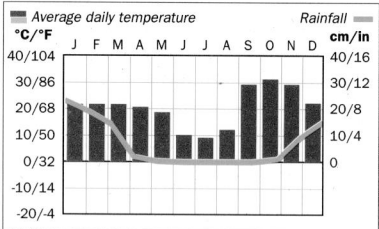

Zambia has a tropical climate, with rains from November to April. The southwest is prone to drought.

COMMUNICATIONS

 Lusaka International
590,000 passengers

 Has no fleet

THE TRANSPORT NETWORK

 37,360 km
(23,215 miles)

 None

 2164 km
(1345 miles)

 2250 km
(1398 miles)

The priorities are privatizing Zambia Airways and rehabilitating the rail and road networks. The poor state of rural roads hampers harvest collections and undermines food self-sufficiency plans.

TOURISM

 171,507 visitors   Up 22% in 1991

MAIN OVERSEAS ARRIVALS

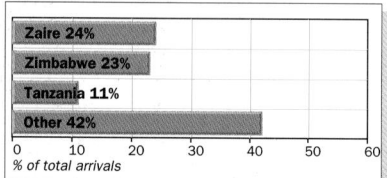

Zaire 24%
Zimbabwe 23%
Tanzania 11%
Other 42%
0   10   20   30   40   50   60
% of total arrivals

Wildlife, the Victoria Falls and white-water rafting on the Zambezi are Zambia's main attractions. Expansion plans are being hit by funding shortages.

PEOPLE

 Bemba, Nyanja, Tonga, Kaonde, Lunda, Luvale, Lozi, English

11 people per km²

THE URBAN/RURAL POPULATION SPLIT

50%   50%

RELIGIOUS PERSUASION

Indigenous beliefs 1%
Hindu 36%
Christian 63%

Although ethnically heterogeneous, with more than 70 different groups, Zambia has been less affected by ethnic tension than many African states. The largest ethnic group, about 18% of the population, is the Bemba, who live in the northeast and predominate in the central Copperbelt. Other major groups are the southern Tonga people, the eastern Nyanja, and the Lozi who live to the west.

Zambia is one of Africa's most urbanized countries with many third and fourth generation town dwellers in the Copperbelt, the main urban area. Urban life has done little to change the traditionally subordinate role of women in the family and politics. They are, however, increasingly involved in business and three women hold cabinet posts. The rural population lives mainly by subsistence farming.

Victoria Falls, known to Africans as Musi-o-Tunyi (*The Smoke That Thunders*). *Spray from the falls can be seen 30 km away.*

POLITICS

Lower House 1996

President Frederick Chiluba

THE STATE OF THE PARTIES

National Assembly 150 members

83% MMD   17% UNIP

MMD = Movement for Multiparty Democracy
UNIP = United National Independence Party

House of Chiefs 27 members

Composed of 27 chiefs representing 8 provinces

The 1991 defeat of Dr Kenneth Kaunda and the UNIP in the first multiparty elections for 19 years expressed popular discontent with the state of the economy and official corruption. President Chiluba and the MMD government have since made little headway in revitalizing the economy, despite socially painful reforms. There have also been renewed allegations of top-level corruption. In 1993, UNIP and MMD dissidents set up the National Party to challenge the dominant political position of the MMD.

WORLD AFFAIRS

 OAU   Comm   NAM   SADC   AfDB

Under President Kaunda, Zambia was one of Africa's leading opponents of the South African apartheid regime. The MMD is now seeking close links with reformed South Africa.

AID

 $884m (receipts)   Up 82% in 1991

Aid levels, mainly from the EU and the World Bank, are high. Most is used to support the restructuring of the economy away from the declining mining sector. Donors are concerned at levels of bureaucratic corruption and the need to strengthen democracy.

DEFENCE

 $213.4m   Up 15% in 1990

A large budget means the 24,000-strong armed forces are well equipped. Security on the border with Angola is the main defence concern.

ECONOMICS

 $1.8bn

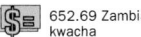 652.69 Zambian kwacha

SCORE CARD

- ❑ WORLD GNP RANKING.......................139th
- ❑ GNP PER CAPITA $210
- ❑ BALANCE OF PAYMENTS $1m
- ❑ INFLATION 155%
- ❑ UNEMPLOYMENT ...Widespread underemployment

STRENGTHS

Potential for self-sufficiency in food; also for export of wide range of crops. Arable land underutilized. Minerals, notably copper, cobalt and coal. Commitment of government to market-orientated reform.

WEAKNESSES

Dependence on copper for 80% of export earnings. Domestic reserves rapidly declining. Poor outlook for world copper prices. Shortage of finance for restructuring due to large deficit in balance of payments. Rescheduling payments on $7.6 billion debt take most export earnings. High inflation. Low productivity.

EXPORTS

China 7%
UK 7%
Japan 23%
Other 63%

IMPORTS

USA 9%
UK 15%
Other 57%
South Africa 19%

ZAMBIA

Total Area : 752 610 sq. km (290 563 sq. miles)

POPULATION

- ◉ over 500 000
- ◎ over 100 000
- ○ over 50 000
- ● over 10 000
- • under 10 000

RESOURCES

 7.8bn kwh (capacity 2.44m kw)

 2.8m cattle, 200,000 pigs, 85,000 sheep

Not an oil producer; refines 23,750 b/cd

Copper, cobalt, coal, zinc, lead, gold, emeralds, amethyst

Despite declining reserves, copper is still the key resource; Zambia is the world's fifth largest producer. It also has good hydro-power resources.

ENVIRONMENT

 8%

 Official involvement in conservation projects increasing

Drought is a recurrent hazard. Rhinos are almost extinct as a result of poaching. Revenues from legal hunting are being channelled into villages to encourage support for conservation.

MEDIA

 Little press censorship by government

PUBLISHING AND BROADCAST MEDIA

There are 3 daily newspapers, the Times of Zambia, the Daily Mail and the Daily Express

1 state-controlled service

1 state-controlled service

The state-owned Times and Daily Mail face increasing competition from independents like the Weekly Standard.

CRIME

 Zambia does not publish prison figures

 Rising rapidly since 1990

Cases of violent crime, burglary and rape are rising rapidly, particularly in major towns such as Lusaka and Ndola.

CHRONOLOGY

Former Northern Rhodesia was developed by Britain solely for its copper resources. Dr Kenneth Kaunda and the UNIP took power at Zambian independence in 1964.

- ❑ 1972 UNIP one-party government.
- ❑ 1980 Attempted coup fails.
- ❑ 1982-1991 Austerity measures introduced. Corruption scandals. Pressure for democracy grows.
- ❑ 1991 Democratically elected MMD government comes to power.

EDUCATION

 73%

Primary education is compulsory. New fees for secondary students will hit the already low attendance rate of 15%.

HEALTH

 1 per 8437 people

 Respiratory infections, diarrheal diseases, malaria

Austerity measures have resulted in health service cutbacks and a rise in the use of traditional medicines.

WEALTH

 Copper miner, 3880 Zambian kwacha per year; computer programmer in insurance, 196,982 Zambian kwacha per year

CONSUMER GOODS OWNERSHIP

VCR and PC ownership is limited to a small elite

25   9   12

Declining profits from copper mining mean that per capita GDP is $400 lower now than at independence in 1964.

WORLD RANKING

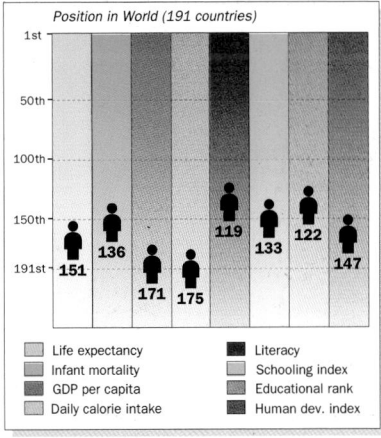

Position in World (191 countries)

151   136   171   175   119   133   122   147

- Life expectancy
- Infant mortality
- GDP per capita
- Daily calorie intake
- Literacy
- Schooling index
- Educational rank
- Human dev. index

LAND HEIGHT

1000m/3281ft
500m/1640ft
200m/656ft

0   200 km
0   200 miles

Z

ZIMBABWE

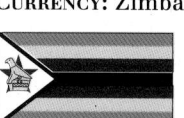

OFFICIAL NAME: Republic of Zimbabwe   **CAPITAL:** Harare   **POPULATION:** 10.6 million
CURRENCY: Zimbabwe dollar   **OFFICIAL LANGUAGE:** English

SITUATED IN SOUTHERN AFRICA, Zimbabwe is bordered by South Africa, Botswana, Zambia and Mozambique. The upland centre is criss-crossed by rivers, which flow into Lake Kariba and the Zambezi River. The Zambezi possesses Zimbabwe's most spectacular natural feature, the Victoria Falls. Formerly the British colony of Southern Rhodesia, the country achieved independence in 1980 after a struggle between the white minority, led by Prime Minister Ian Smith, and the black majority, represented by Robert Mugabe's and Joshua Nkomo's Patriotic Front (PF).

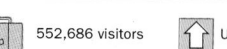

The Kariba Dam, which has created the vast Lake Kariba on the Zambezi River, lies on Zimbabwe's northwest border with Zambia.

CLIMATE

WEATHER CHART

Average daily temperature   Rainfall

COMMUNICATIONS

Harare International
1.02m passengers

Has no fleet

THE TRANSPORT NETWORK

85,237 km
(52,964 miles)

None

2745 km
(1706 miles)

None

Transport is a high government priority. Policies include developing and updating railways, and increasing the number of international air links.

Due to altitude, Zimbabwe is comparatively temperate for a country in the tropics; humidity is also low. The rainy season occurs between November and March. But, with the exception of the eastern highlands, rainfall is erratic and drought is common. Annual rainfall ranges from 140 cm in the Eastern Highlands to 40 cm in the Limpopo valley.

TOURISM

552,686 visitors

Up 27% in 1990

MAIN OVERSEAS ARRIVALS

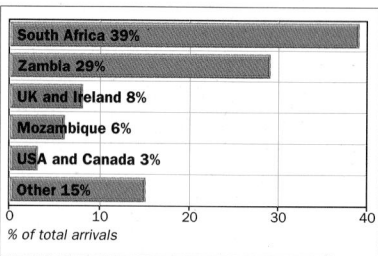

South Africa 39%
Zambia 29%
UK and Ireland 8%
Mozambique 6%
USA and Canada 3%
Other 15%

% of total arrivals

Tourists visit Zimbabwe for both cultural and safari holidays. The country's principal attractions are the Victoria Falls, the Kariba Dam and the many national parks. Great Zimbabwe ruins, near Masvingo, and World's View in the Matopo Hills, are of special interest. Action holidays are being developed, with canoeing trips and white-water rafting on the Zambezi, and trout fishing and climbing in the eastern highlands. Harare and Victoria Falls have conference facilities.
The government does not intend to make Zimbabwe a destination for mass-market tourism owing to fears of serious environmental damage. However, the lure of foreign exchange has encouraged the development of holiday complexes around Victoria Falls, such as Elephant Hills. Import controls relating to the tourist industry have been relaxed and prices deregulated. A two-tier pricing structure now prevails with locals paying less; foreigners must pay in hard currencies.

ZIMBABWE

Total Area : 390 580 sq. km
(150 800 sq. miles)

POPULATION

- ⊙ over 500 000
- ◎ over 100 000
- ○ over 50 000
- ● over 10 000
- · under 10 000

LAND HEIGHT

- 2000m/6562ft
- 1000m/3281ft
- 500m/1640ft
- 200m/656ft
- 180m/590ft

Z

PEOPLE

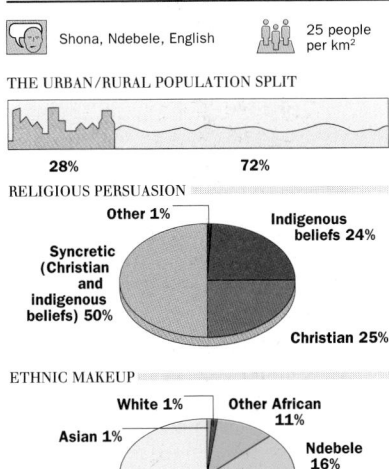

Shona, Ndebele, English

25 people per km²

THE URBAN/RURAL POPULATION SPLIT

28% 72%

RELIGIOUS PERSUASION

Other 1%
Indigenous beliefs 24%
Syncretic (Christian and indigenous beliefs) 50%
Christian 25%

ETHNIC MAKEUP

White 1% Other African 11%
Asian 1%
Ndebele 16%
Shona 71%

POPULATION AGE BREAKDOWN

% of population by age group	0–14	15–64		65+	
	2.9%	2.7%	2.6%	2.7%	2.8%
	50.6%	48.2%	49.6%	52.6%	53.2%
	46.5%	49.1%	47.8%	44.7%	44%
	1960	1970	1980	1990	2000

There are two main ethnic groups, the Ndebele (popularly known as the Matabele) in the north and the Shona (known as the Mashona) in the south. The Mashona outnumber the Matabele by about four to one. Europeans and Asians comprise 2% of the population.

Tension between the Matabele and the Mashona was rife in the 1980s. This was caused by the attempt of President Mugabe's ruling Zimbabwe African National Union (ZANU–PF), linked to the Mashona, to suppress the leading opposition party, the Zimbabwe African People's Union (ZAPU–PF), linked with the Matabele. The conflict was most intense in 1983, when the army killed 1500 Matabele. Tension abated following the Unity Accord of 1987 and the 1990 appointment of ZAPU-PF leader Joshua Nkomo as vice-president.

As a legacy of colonial rule, whites are still generally far more affluent than blacks. This imbalance has been somewhat redressed by government policies to increase black education and white-collar employment.

Families are large and almost half the population is under 15. Zimbabwean society is traditionally patriarchal, but the number of women managers is growing, and individuals, such as Sally Mugabe, late wife of the president, have achieved political prominence.

POLITICS

1995

President Robert Gabriel Mugabe

THE STATE OF THE PARTIES

House of Assembly 150 members

1%
ZANU-N

97%
ZANU-PF

2%
ZUM

ZANU-PF = Zimbabwe African National Union – Patriotic Front
ZUM = Zimbabwe Unity Movement **ZANU-N** = Zimbabwe African National Union – Ndonga

Zimbabwe is constitutionally a multiparty state. 80% of MPs are elected and serve five-year terms. Every six years, parliament elects the president, who is eligible for re-election.

MAIN POLITICAL ISSUES

Political repression
At independence, the PF was a coalition of ZANU, led by Robert Mugabe, and ZAPU, led by Joshua Nkomo. As ZANU-PF became more powerful, the coalition split and ZAPU-PF supporters resorted to guerrilla activity. This continued until 1987, when a unity agreement was signed with Nkomo, later made vice-president. With the main opposition party absorbed, Mugabe, now president, attempted to assert a one-party,

socialist state. These plans were abandoned in 1991 and other parties have since emerged. But repression continues: student dissension has been quashed and the civil service is closed to non-supporters of the ruling party.

Land redistribution
In an attempt to redistribute wealth from the white to the black community, the government introduced the Land Acquisition Act in 1992. This allowed the compulsory purchase of white-owned farmland. The Act provoked a storm of protest, including allegations of corruption, and was suspended.

PROFILE
The ruling ZANU-PF appears to have lost direction following the collapse of the eastern bloc and the end of apartheid in South Africa. The influence of its once-dominant leader, Robert Mugabe, is waning, but he has no clear successor.

Opposition parties include the Forum for Democratic Reform advocating an open, free-market society, and the United Front Party, an uneasy coalition of politicians from the pre-1980 period. These include Edgar Tekere, Reverend Sithole and Ian Smith.

Robert Mugabe, *elected prime minister in 1980 and president in 1987.*

Simon Muzenda, *senior vice-president. Joint vice-president is Joshua Nkomo.*

AID

 $393m (receipts)

 Up 16% in 1991

In January 1992, the IMF agreed the equivalent of $484 million to support an economic and financial reform programme. Zimbabwe is also to receive $117 million in grants, over five years, from the EU. Bilateral donors, including the UK, France, Germany, Denmark and the USA, intend their aid to be used to sustain the local economy and be directed at small farmers. However, the government directs much of it towards large industrial projects. In the 1980s, Zimbabwe sent food to help relieve famine in Ethiopia.

WORLD AFFAIRS

 OAU SADC Comm NAM GATT

Zimbabwe stresses close co-operation with its neighbours, in the context of SADC and the Preferential Trade Area for East and South Africa, and has consistently followed a policy of non-alignment. President Mugabe was

chairman of the Non-Aligned Movement from 1985 to 1989. His regime had an activist stance against South Africa and apartheid but, since the 1990 freeing of Nelson Mandela, relations have improved. However, a consistent policy is still evolving.

For ideological reasons and to maintain access to the sea via the Beira

corridor, the government began providing military assistance to the socialist Mozambican government against the RENAMO guerrillas in 1982. President Mugabe then played a major mediating role, resulting in a peace accord in August 1992. In 1993, 150 troops were sent to Somalia and training exercises began with the USA.

Z

CHRONOLOGY

In 1953, the British colony of Southern Rhodesia (Zimbabwe) became part of the Federation of Rhodesia and Nyasaland with Northern Rhodesia (Zambia) and Nyasaland (Malawi).

❑ **1959** African National Congress (ANC), led by Joshua Nkomo, banned.

❑ **1961** Nkomo forms ZAPU.

❑ **1962** ZAPU banned. Racial segregationist Rhodesian Front (RF) wins elections. Winston Field prime minister.

❑ **1963** African nationalists in Northern Rhodesia and Nyasaland demand dissolution of Federation. ZANU, offshoot of ZAPU, formed by Rev Sithole and Robert Mugabe.

❑ **1964** Ian Smith new RF prime minister. British conditions for independence, including majority rule, rejected. ZANU banned.

❑ **1965** May, RF re-elected. November, state of emergency declared (renewed every year until 1990). Smith makes unilateral declaration of independence. UK imposes economic sanctions. ANC, ZANU and ZAPU begin guerrilla war.

❑ **1970** Rhodesia declared republic.

❑ **1974** RF regime agrees ceasefire terms with African nationalists.

❑ **1975–1979** Intermittent negotiations between British government, the RF, and African nationalists to reach constitutional settlement.

❑ **1976** ZANU and ZAPU unite into Patriotic Front (PF).

❑ **1977** PF backed by 'frontline' African states: Mozambique, Tanzania, Botswana and Zambia.

❑ **1979** Internal settlement drafted by Ian Smith and moderate African nationalists. Rejected by PF.

❑ **1979** Constitution agreed.

❑ **1980** Independence. Following violent election campaign, Robert Mugabe becomes prime minister of ZANU-PF/ZAPU-PF coalition. Relations severed with South Africa.

❑ **1983–1984** Unrest in Matabeleland, ZAPU-PF's power base.

❑ **1985** Elections return ZANU-PF, with manifesto to create one-party state. Many ZAPU-PF members arrested.

❑ **1987** Unrest in Matabeleland. June, ban on ZAPU-PF. September, provision for white seats in parliament abolished. November, ban on ZAPU-PF lifted. December, ZANU-PF and ZAPU-PF sign unity agreement (merge in 1989). Mugabe elected president.

❑ **1990** Elections won by ZANU-PF. Mugabe re-elected president.

❑ **1991** Mugabe abandons plan for one-party state.

Z

DEFENCE

💲 $334m

⬇ Down 8% in 1991

Defence spending as % GDP
0   40
6.8%

ZIMBABWEAN ARMED FORCES

30 main battle tanks (30 Ch T-59/10 Ch T-69)		46,000 personnel
None		
36 combat aircraft (10 Hunter FGA-90/1 T-81)		2500 personnel
None		

The military appears to be under the complete control of President Mugabe, who is Commander-in-Chief of the armed forces. In the early 1980s, however, some soldiers deserted to fight government forces in the Matabele bush. They provided the nucleus of dissident movements that plagued the regime until the Unity Accord of 1987. Zimbabwe receives military aid and training from the UK and South Korea. Zimbabwe's policy of non-alignment means that it has entered into no formal military alliances. However, it has supported the Mozambican regime against RENAMO guerrillas and has also backed the US-led operation in Somalia.

ECONOMICS

📊 $5.4bn

💱 2.70 Zimbabwe dollars

SCORE CARD

❑ WORLD GNP RANKING 110th
❑ GNP PER CAPITA $509
❑ BALANCE OF PAYMENTS .... $–608m
❑ INFLATION 25.4%
❑ UNEMPLOYMENT .... 35% (est)

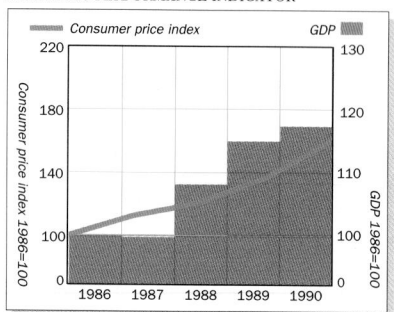

ECONOMIC PERFORMANCE INDICATOR

Consumer price index   GDP

EXPORTS

USA 6%
Germany* 8%
UK 10%
South Africa Customs Union 12%
Other 64%

IMPORTS

Germany* 9%
USA 9%
Other 44%
UK 12%
South Africa Customs Union 26%

STRENGTHS

The most broadly based African economy after South Africa. Sound infrastructure. Unrivalled international credit rating in sub-Saharan Africa, owing to careful policy of debt-servicing in 1980s. Virtual self-sufficiency in food and energy.

WEAKNESSES

Drought has hit agriculture, and also industry, owing to reduction in output of hydroelectric power. Large balance of payments and budgetary deficits. High inflation; unemployment over 30%. Belated moves towards market-orientated economy.

PROFILE

In the 1980s, the government's verbal commitment to socialist policies was in practice tempered by pragmatism. The main aim was to correct the imbalance between black and white incomes. In 1991, faced with growing balance of payments problems and a need to create jobs, the government embarked on a five-year structural adjustment programme which marked a radical reassessment of priorities. This move to a more market-orientated economy has had heavy social costs, pushing up unemployment and inflation, while leading to cuts in social welfare.

ZIMBABWE : MAJOR BUSINESSES

Tobacco	Agribusiness
Steel	Engineering
Textiles	Coal mining
Chemicals	Vehicle assembly
Footwear	
Gold mining	

RESOURCES

 9.6bn kwh (capacity 2.04m kw)

 Not an oil producer and has no refineries

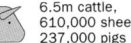 6.5m cattle, 610,000 sheep, 237,000 pigs

 Gold, coal, asbestos, nickel, copper, silver, iron, emeralds, lithium

ELECTRICITY GENERATION

Hydro 37% (3.5bn kwh)
Thermal 63% (6bn kwh)
Nuclear 0%
Other 0%

% of total generation by type

Almost 40% of Zimbabwe's electricity needs are met by hydro-power, notably from the Kariba Dam, jointly owned with Zambia. The state power company is seeking to maximize capacity and to undertake long-term development. In 1991, the government agreed to the construction of an extension facility at Kariba South, and a joint HEP station at Bartoka Gorge with Zambia. An oil pipeline from Beira, Mozambique, to Mutare is being extended to Harare. Coal mining is expanding at Hwange to exploit deposits of 400 million tonnes.

ENVIRONMENT

 8% (1% partially protected)

 Zimbabwe still suffers the after-effects of drought

ENVIRONMENTAL TREATIES

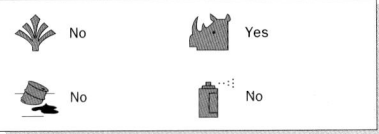

No

Yes

No

No

The 1991–1992 drought left half the population in need of drought relief, and used up 20% of public spending.

In communal areas, the land is suffering from overpopulation and overstocking. Deforestation, soil erosion and deterioration of wildlife and water resources are widespread.

Measures have been taken to protect the black rhinoceros, including moving animals to safer areas and combating poaching – patrols have killed 150 poachers since 1986. The government also supports a scheme for dehorning rhinos – the horn is the poachers' main target. In 1992, Zimbabwe argued that elephants no longer required special protection. However, the Convention on International Trade in Endangered Species disagreed. It claimed that much poaching still exists, and alleged collusion on the part of the army.

MEDIA

 There is no official censorship

PUBLISHING AND BROADCAST MEDIA

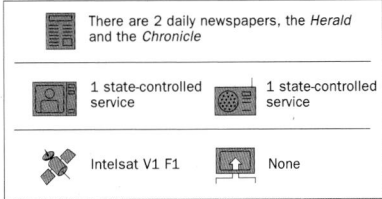

There are 2 daily newspapers, the *Herald* and the *Chronicle*

1 state-controlled service

1 state-controlled service

Intelsat V1 F1

None

The press is free, but the state has a controlling interest in the two main newspapers. There are, however, a great number of politically independent smaller newspapers and periodicals.

CRIME

 21,000 prisoners

 Up 15% in 1990

CRIME RATES

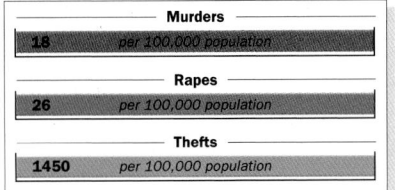

Murders
18 per 100,000 population

Rapes
26 per 100,000 population

Thefts
1450 per 100,000 population

Urban areas have a high incidence of murder and drugs-related offences. With the worsening economic climate, crime is increasing in rural areas. The secret service, the Central Intelligence Organization, has come in for international criticism for its alleged abuses of human rights.

EDUCATION

 67%

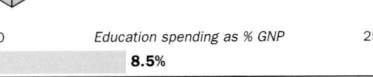

Education spending as % GNP
0   8.5%   25

THE EDUCATION SYSTEM

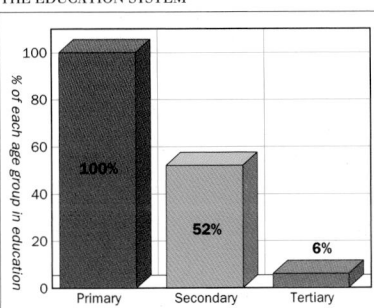

% of each age group in education

Primary 100%
Secondary 52%
Tertiary 6%

Education is compulsory. After reforms in 1991 and 1992, fees were introduced for primary and secondary education. Schooling is based on the British system and instruction is in English. The emphasis is now on vocational training to create a workforce with the skills in agriculture, medicine and engineering that Zimbabwe needs.

ZIMBABWE : LAND USE

Cropland
Pasture
Forest
Tobacco - cash crop
Maize
Cattle

Zambezi
Lake Kariba
MAFUNGABUSI PLATEAU
Sanyati
Sabi
Limpopo

0   200 km
0   200 miles

HEALTH

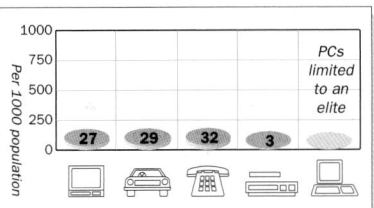 1 per 7180 people

Malnutrition, pneumonia, malaria, diarrheal diseases

Health spending as % GNP
0   3.7%   25

Free to those on less than a minimum wage, the health system is short of expertise and staff. The government has been slow to react to the spread of AIDS. In 1991, 28.5% of the workforce were reported to be HIV positive.

WEALTH

Bus driver, 600 Zimbabwe dollars a month; school teacher, 1500 Zimbabwe dollars a month.

CONSUMER GOODS OWNERSHIP

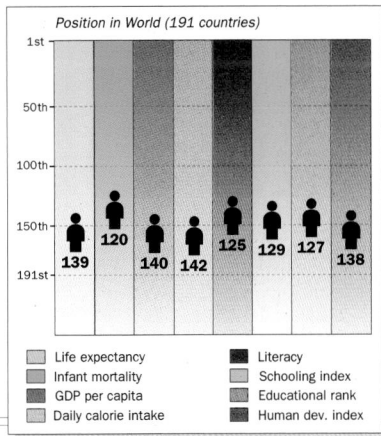

Per 1000 population

27   29   32   3

PCs limited to an elite

In the 1980s, 'Growth with Equity' policies lessened the gap between blacks and whites. Growth now has priority over wealth redistribution.

WORLD RANKING

Position in World (191 countries)

1st
50th
100th
150th
191st

139   120   140   142   125   129   127   138

Life expectancy
Infant mortality
GDP per capita
Daily calorie intake

Literacy
Schooling index
Educational rank
Human dev. index

Z

OVERSEAS TERRITORIES & DEPENDENCI

DESPITE THE RAPID process of decolonization since 1945 (pages 46-49), roughly 10 million people around the world still live under the protection of either France, Australia, Denmark, New Zealand, Norway, Portugal, UK, USA or the Netherlands. The continued existence of these territories from the colonial era is a result of either economic, historical or political reasons. Hong Kong, for instance, will revert to China in 1997 for historical reasons.

Others await political developments, such as referenda, which will determine their future status. Some territories are retained because of their strategic or economic importance. Finally, a large group of territories are considered too small, remote or weak to be able to survive as independent nations.

UNITED KINGDOM

The UK still has the largest number of overseas territories in the world. They are split into Crown colonies, Crown dependencies and dependent territories. The distinction between each is largely constitutional, since most sustain a large degree of local autonomy. Britain generally operates a policy of non-interference. If a territory expresses a constitutional desire for formal independence then it may have it, as long as it can form a viable independent country.

Svalbard
(to Norway)

BARENTS
SEA

Jan Mayen
(to Norway)

Faeroe Islands
(to Denmark)

NORWAY

NORTH
SEA

BALTIC SEA

Isle of Man
(to UK)

UNITED
KINGDOM

DENMARK

NETHERLANDS

Channel Islands:
Guernsey and Jersey
(to UK)

FRANCE

EUROPE

PORTUGAL

Gibraltar
(to UK)

MEDITERRANEAN SEA

ASIA

SEA OF
JAPAN

YELLOW
SEA

EAST
CHINA
SEA

AFRICA

ARABIAN
SEA

Hong Kong (to UK)
Macao
(to Portugal)
Paracel
Islands
(Disputed)

Northern Mariana
Islands (to US)

Guam (to US)

SOUTH
CHINA SEA

Spratly Islands
(Disputed)

Palau
(to US)

Ascension
(Administered by
St Helena)

British Indian
Ocean Territory
(to UK)

Mayotte (to France)

Cocos (Keeling) Islands
(to Australia)

JAVA SEA

ARAFURA
SEA

St Helena
(to UK)

Christmas Island
(to Australia)

Ashmore &
Cartier Islands
(to Australia)

Réunion (to France)

INDIAN
OCEAN

AUSTRALI

ATLANTIC
OCEAN

Europa
(Administered by Réunion)

Bassas da India
(Administered by Réunion)

Tristan da Cunha
(Administered by
St Helena)

Gough Island
(Administered by St Helena)

Amsterdam Island

St. Paul Island

French Southern &
Antarctic Territories
(France)

Crozet Islands

Kerguelen

Bouvet Island
(to Norway)

Heard & McDonald Islands
(to Australia)

*French Southern and Antarctic territories
are not included in the following section.
Any territories which involve an Antarctic
claim are not shown.*

NEW ZEALAND

New Zealand's government has no de
to retain any overseas territories.
However, the economic weakness of
dependent territory Tokelau and its
freely-associated states, Niue and the
Cook Islands, have forced New Zeala
remain responsible for their foreign
policy and defence.

OVERSEAS TERRITORIES AND DEPENDENCIES

◉	Australia	◉	Denmark	○	Portugal
○	New Zealand	◉	France	○	Disputed
◉	United Kingdom	◉	Netherlands		
◉	United States	○	Norway		

TED STATES OF AMERICA

rica's overseas territories have been seen as
egically useful, if expensive, links with its
kyards'. The US has, in most cases, given the
population a say in deciding their own status.
s, three former US administered UN Trust
ritories have been, or are being, granted full
reignty. A US Commonwealth territory has a
ter level of independence than that of an
corporated or external territory.

RCTIC OCEAN

BEAUFORT
SEA

Greenland
(to Denmark)

ATLANTIC
OCEAN

BERING
SEA

NORTH AMERICA

St Pierre & Miquelon
(to France)

UNITED STATES
OF AMERICA

Bermuda
(to UK)

Turks & Caicos Islands
(to UK)

Puerto Rico
(to US)

British Virgin Islands
(to UK)

Anguilla
(to UK)

Midway Islands
(to US)

Virgin Islands
(to US)

Guadeloupe
(to France)

CARIBBEAN
SEA

Netherlands Antilles
(to Neth)

Gulf of
Mexico

Cayman Islands
(to UK)

Johnston Atoll
(to US)

Montserrat
(to UK)

Navassa Island
(to US)

CARIBBEAN
SEA

Aruba
(to Neth)

Martinique
(to France)

ACIFIC OCEAN

Kingman Reef (to US)

Clipperton Island
(Administered by
French Polynesia)

French Guiana
(to France)

Palmyra Atoll
(to US)

Howland
s (to US)

Jarvis Island
(to US)

Tokelau (to NZ)

una
nce)

Cook Islands
(to NZ)

SOUTH
AMERICA

erican Samoa
(to US)

Niue
(to NZ)

French
Polynesia
(to France)

aledonia
ce)

Pitcairn Islands
(to UK)

folk Island
Australia)

NEW
ZEALAND

Falkland Islands
(to UK)

South Georgia and
South Sandwich Islands
(to UK)

FRANCE

French *Territoires d'Outre-Mer* are considered an
indivisible part of the French Republic. As a result,
France has developed economic ties, and stressed the
advantage of interdependence over independence, with
its overseas territories. A distinct hierarchy has been
developed. Overseas *départements*, officially part of
France, have their own governments. Territorial
collectivités are administered by a French-appointed
commissioner and a locally-elected council, whilst
overseas *territoires* have varying degrees of autonomy.

AMERICAN SAMOA

STATUS: Unincorporated territory of the USA **CLAIMED:** 1900
CAPITAL: Pago Pago **POPULATION:** 50,923 **DENSITY:** 240 per km²

AMERICAN SAMOA consists of five volcanic islands and two coral atolls in the southern Pacific Ocean. It has a tropical climate with an average annual rainfall of 500 cm. Typhoons and tropical storms are common from December to March.

Samoans are among the last remaining true Polynesians. *Fa'a Samoa,* meaning the Samoan way of life, still directs Samoan society. The extended family, the *aiga,* forms the base of Samoan life, with chiefs still holding a central role in government. This has created tension, however, with a younger generation attracted by the lifestyle of *fa'a America.* As a result, many young Samoans have emigrated to the USA. One fifth of all tuna consumed in the USA passes through Pago Pago's canneries, so employing 25% of the population. Recently, in an effort to diversify the economy, the American Samoan government has tried to encourage the development of other light industries and tourism.

ANGUILLA

STATUS: British dependent territory **CLAIMED:** 1650
CAPITAL: The Valley **POPULATION:** 8960 **DENSITY:** 93 per km²

ANGUILLA is situated at the northern end of the Leeward Islands, in the Caribbean. It has a sub-tropical climate, the heat and humidity being tempered by trade winds. In 1967 Anguillans refused to follow St Kitts and Nevis into independence, preferring instead to retain the economic stability that came with dependent status. Since then the People's Progressive Party, renamed the Anguilla National Alliance in 1980, has dominated politics. Its leader and Chief Minister, Emile Gumbs, has pursued a policy of developing the tourist sector and attracting foreign investment, particularly in the offshore banking industry. However stricter laws introduced in the 1990s forced a subsequent contraction in the sector. Lobster fishing continues to provide the majority of export earnings.

The island of Sombrero, 48 km north of Anguilla, is also part of the territory

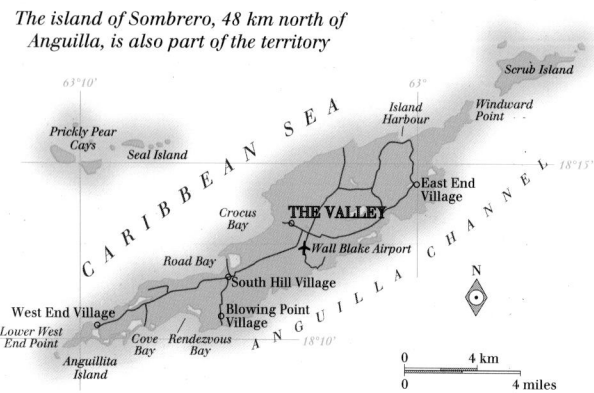

ARUBA

STATUS: Autonomous part of the Netherlands **CLAIMED:** 1643
CAPITAL: Oranjestad **POPULATION:** 62,365 **DENSITY:** 323 per km²

ONE OF THE SMALLEST islands in the Dutch Caribbean, Aruba lies 25 km off the coast of Venezuela. It has a tropical climate moderated by constant trade winds sweeping in from the Atlantic.

Formerly part of the Netherlands Antilles, Aruba became a separate dependency in 1986. However, as Aruba approaches independence in 1996, the Netherlands has voiced concern over the island's security and the danger of it becoming a base for drug-trafficking. Furthermore, the Aruban government, led by Nelson Oduber, has questioned the desirability of full independence, citing high unemployment and economic instability. For these reasons, the date of independence may well be postponed. The economy, formerly dependent on oil refining, has diversified, with tourism and offshore finance now the most important sectors. The oil refinery, which closed in 1985, was reopened at reduced capacity in 1990 by Coastal Oil of Texas.

Palm Beach, Aruba, also known as the Turquoise Coast, lies on the western side of the island. The beach stretches for 10 km and is the site of a low-rise beach resort.

ASHMORE & CARTIER IS.

STATUS: Australian external territory **CLAIMED:** 1978
CAPITAL: Not applicable **POPULATION:** None

LYING IN THE Timor Sea, the three Ashmore Islets and Cartier Island are separated by 60 km of water, and cover a land area of 5 sq km. They are governed from Darwin, capital of the Northern Territories, over 790 km to the west. Under an agreement with the Australian government, the sand and coral islands' waters are fished by Indonesians. However, reports of overfishing have led the government to monitor their activities. In 1983 Ashmore reef was made a nature reserve.

BAKER & HOWLAND IS.

STATUS: Unincorporated territory of the USA **CLAIMED:** 1856
CAPITAL: Not applicable **POPULATION:** None

THE UNINHABITED Baker and Howland Islands lie 2600 km southwest of Hawaii, in the Pacific Ocean. The USA's interest in the two coral islands centered on rich guano deposits, which were worked out by 1891. The islands were again inhabited between 1936 until 1942, becoming a stop for trans-Pacific flights. They are now a refuge for over a million birds.

LAND HEIGHT | above Sea Level | 200m/656ft | 500m/1640ft | 1000m/3281ft | 1500m/4572ft | above 2000m/6562ft

BERMUDA

STATUS: British Crown colony   **CLAIMED:** 1612

CAPITAL: Hamilton   **POPULATION:** 58,433   **DENSITY:** 1103 per km²

SITUATED OVER 900 km off the coast of South Carolina, USA, Bermuda consists of a chain of over 150 coral islands. The Gulf Stream, flowing between Bermuda and America's eastern seaboard,

keeps the climate mild and humid. Bermuda is racially mixed; some 60% of the population are of African origin, the rest are mostly of European extraction. Racial tension, which existed in the 1960s and 1970s, has declined in the face of a more representative electoral system which was established after a Royal Commission visited Bermuda in 1978.

Despite changes made to the constitution in 1979 all elections have been won by the moderate, conservative United Bermuda Party (UBP). Its leader, and the island's premier, John Swan, is an advocate of eventual independence from the UK. However, the electorate seems content to practise *de facto* independence. The UBP's prime current concerns are economic and environmental issues, as well as the growing problem of drug-trafficking. Despite its small size and few resources, Bermuda has one of the highest per capita incomes in the world. Tourism accounts for 55% of the island's GDP. Bermuda is a leading insurance market and also operates one of the world's largest flag-of-convenience shipping fleets.

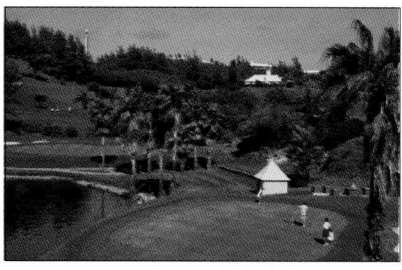

Bermuda has one of the highest densities of golf courses in the world. Eight courses have been developed in all.

BOUVET ISLAND

STATUS: Norwegian dependency   **CLAIMED:** 1927

CAPITAL: Not applicable   **POPULATION:** None

A VOLCANIC, ice-covered island in the South Atlantic Ocean, Bouvet lies 1600 km north of Antarctica. Because it lies north of the Antarctic Circle it is not covered by the Antarctic Treaty. A royal decree, issued in 1971, made the whole island a nature reserve. Bouvet Island regularly plays host to scientific expeditions from Norway.

BRITISH INDIAN OCEAN TERRITORY

STATUS: British dependent territory   **CLAIMED:** 1814

CAPITAL: Diego Garcia   **POPULATION:** 3400   **DENSITY:** 48 per km²

THE BRITISH Indian Ocean Territory, or Chagos Islands, lie in the middle of the Indian Ocean. The coral atolls, previously used for copra production, are now uninhabited, except for the US-UK military base on Diego Garcia – a vital link in US plans to ensure a strategic capability in the Persian Gulf. The UK has undertaken to cede the islands to Mauritius when they are no longer required for military purposes.

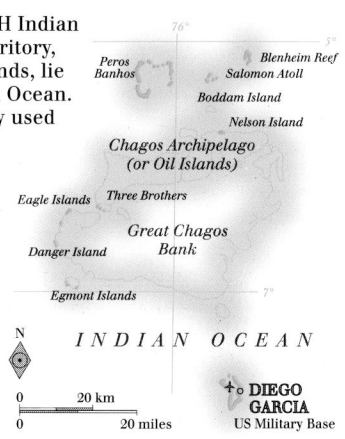

BRITISH VIRGIN ISLANDS

STATUS: British dependent territory   **CLAIMED:** 1672

CAPITAL: Road Town   **POPULATION:** 16,644   **DENSITY:** 109 per km²

AN ARCHIPELAGO OF 40 Caribbean islands, 15 of them inhabited, the British Virgin Islands lie at the eastern end of the Greater Antilles. The islands' tropical climate has encouraged the development of tourism, now the islands' major economic activity. The local government has also developed the Virgin Islands as an offshore tax haven. However, a number of scandals involving companies registered in the islands resulted in strict legislation, and a contraction of the sector in the 1990s. In recent years, a political issue has been the rise in illegal immigration.

CAYMAN ISLANDS

STATUS: British dependent territory **CLAIMED:** 1670
CAPITAL: George Town **POPULATION:** 25,355 **DENSITY:** 98 per km²

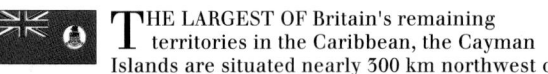

THE LARGEST OF Britain's remaining territories in the Caribbean, the Cayman Islands are situated nearly 300 km northwest of Jamaica. Convinced that the islands' economic prosperity is directly linked to the stability its dependent territory status gives, the islanders recently shelved plans to rewrite the constitution to give themselves greater autonomy from London. The islands are one of the world's largest offshore financial centres. Nearly 24,000 companies have been attracted by the lack of income tax and foreign-exchange controls. However, tourism underpins the economy providing 70% of GDP.

CHRISTMAS ISLAND

STATUS: Australian external territory **CLAIMED:** 1958
CAPITAL: Flying Fish Cove **POPULATION:** 1275 **DENSITY:** 9 per km²

SO NAMED because it was sighted on Christmas Day in 1643, the island lies in the Indian Ocean, some 300 km south of Java. It was inhabited by labour imported to mine rich phosphate deposits. As a result, the population is mostly Malay and Chinese. Since 1990, the islanders have enjoyed an economic boom. The mine – closed in 1987 – has been reopened and a tourist complex has been built.

COCOS (KEELING) ISLANDS

STATUS: Australian external territory **CLAIMED:** 1955
CAPITAL: West Island **POPULATION:** 647 **DENSITY:** 46 per km²

IN ALL, 27 coral atolls make up the Cocos (Keeling) Islands. They are situated in the Indian Ocean, roughly half way between Australia and Sri Lanka. The population is split between the European-dominated West Island and the Malays on Home Island. Coconuts are the sole cash crop and are grown throughout the atolls. The sale of postage stamps for foreign currency was stopped in the 1990s.

COOK ISLANDS

STATUS: Territory in free association with New Zealand **CLAIMED:**
CAPITAL: Avarua **POPULATION:** 18,547 **DENSITY:** 78 per km²

LYING 3500 KM NORTHEAST of New Zealand, the Cook Islands are a combination of 24 coral atolls and volcanic islands. The islands achieved self-government in 1965 and have adopted a diverse approach to their economy. Giant clam and pearl farming, and an ostrich farm, have been developed alongside tourism and banking. With the break-up of the ANZUS alliance in 1986, the Cook Islands declared their neutrality as doubts grew over New Zealand's ability to defend them. In 1991, the territory signed a friendship treaty with France which provided for French surveillance of its territorial waters.

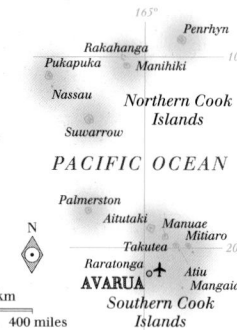

CORAL SEA ISLANDS

STATUS: Australian external territory **CLAIMED:** 1969
CAPITAL: Not applicable **POPULATION:** 3

THE TERRITORY OF THE Coral Sea Islands is a group of reefs and islands, scattered over an area of nearly one million sq km, off the east coast of Queensland, Australia. Uninhabited except for a manned weather station on Willis Island, the islands function as a large nature reserve. They provide sanctuary, in particular, to a number of rare seabirds and turtles.

FAEROE ISLANDS

STATUS: Self-governing territory of Denmark **CLAIMED:** 1380
CAPITAL: Tórshavn **POPULATION:** 47,310 **DENSITY:** 34 per km²

MIDWAY BETWEEN Scotland and Iceland in the North Atlantic, the Faeroe Islands have a moderate climate for their latitude – the result of the warm Gulf Stream current. Home rule since 1948 has given the Faeroese a strong sense of national identity – they voted against joining the EC with Denmark in 1973. In the face of international criticism, they have also continued their traditional cull of pilot whales and bottlenosed dolphins. Sheep farming is common, although fishing has had the strongest influence in shaping Faeroese society. As Denmark moves towards closer integration with the EU, which has a strict fisheries policy, internal pressure is growing for complete independence. However, as the islands' economy depends on Danish subsidies, this appears unlikely in the near future.

LAND HEIGHT ▢ above Sea Level ▢ 200m/656ft ▢ 500m/1640ft ▢ 1000m/3281ft ▢ 1500m/4572ft ▢ above 2000m/6562ft

FALKLAND ISLANDS

STATUS: British dependent territory   CLAIMED: 1832
CAPITAL: Stanley   POPULATION: 2121   DENSITY: 0.2 per km²

SITUATED IN THE South Atlantic Ocean, over 12,000 km from Britain, the Falkland Islands are influenced by the cold Antarctic current. The main islands of East and West Falkland and the hundreds of outlying islands have a cool, temperate climate with frequent strong winds.

The islands gained international renown with the Argentine invasion, and subsequent British recapture, in 1982. Since then, the British government has invested heavily in a 'Fortress Falklands' policy. A new runway and military base were built at Mount Pleasant to house an enlarged garrison. Sovereignty over the Falklands, however, continues to exert a negative influence on Anglo-Argentine relations. The islanders, for their part, are determined to maintain the *status quo*.

Since the Falklands war the economy of the islands has prospered. Falklanders invested heavily in schools, roads and tourism in a fresh drive for a strong identity. By 1987 the Falklands had become financially solvent due to the sale of fishing licences. However, sales of cheaper, less restrictive licences by Argentina forced a slump in fishing revenues. In addition, a fall in wool prices began to affect the living standards of the predominantly sheep-farming community. The islands' prospective fortunes were revived, and mass unemployment and emigration avoided, by the discovery of large oil reserves in their territorial waters. However, many islanders fear that the lure of oil will reawaken Argentina's desire to control the Falklands.

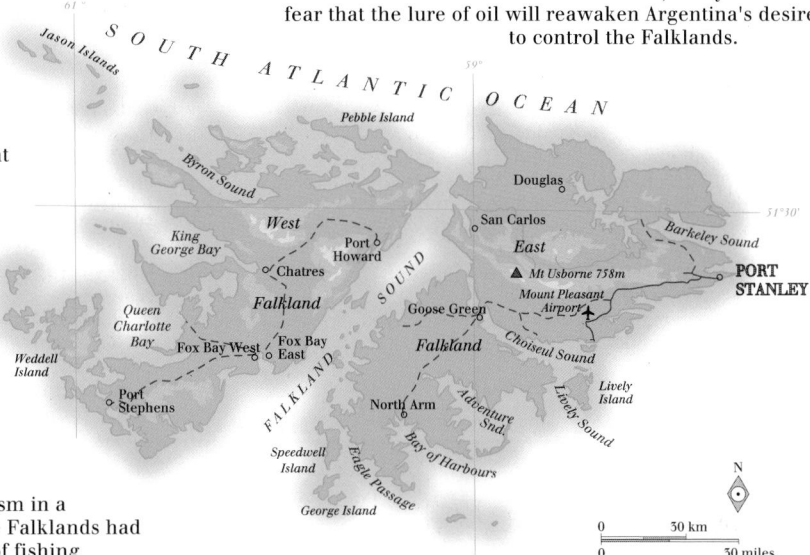

FRENCH GUIANA

STATUS: French overseas department   CLAIMED: 1817
CAPITAL: Cayenne   POPULATION: 114,808   DENSITY: 1 per km²

SANDWICHED BETWEEN Brazil and Surinam on the northeast coast of South America, French Guiana is South America's only remaining colony. A belt of coastal marsh, and an interior of equatorial jungle, combine in a location which was, for years, notorious for the offshore penal colony, Devil's Island. The rainforest is particularly rich in flora and fauna. It harbours over 400,000 species, including more different kinds of birds than the whole of Europe.

Concentrated near the coast, the population is ethnically mixed. There are some 5000 Indians and one of South America's largest group of bush negros, descended from escaped slaves.

A campaign for greater autonomy in the late 1970s and early 1980s led to limited decentralization of power to a regional council. The ruling Guianese Socialist Party (GSP) has maintained its hold on the regional council in the face of a divided opposition.

As French Guiana confronts growing economic and social instability, the people have become increasingly vocal in their condemnation of the French government's perceived indifference to their country's problems. Accordingly, the GSP has campaigned for greater autonomy from France in such important areas as transport, immigration, education and health.

As an overseas *département* of metropolitan France, French Guiana is also a region of the EU. Despite this the economy is heavily dependent on France for aid, food and manufactured goods. It has a number of valuable natural resources, and also tourist potential, but these are yet to be fully exploited, because of a lack of skilled labour, investment and an underdeveloped infrastructure. One asset, however, which has made French Guiana strategically important to France, is the European Space Agency rocket launch facility for the Ariane rocket at Kourou.

Kourou was selected for the launch of the Ariane rocket because of its equatorial site. The town has grown from 800 to 15,000 people.

 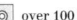

FRENCH POLYNESIA

STATUS: French overseas possession   **CLAIMED:** 1843
CAPITAL: Papeete   **POPULATION:** 199,031   **DENSITY:** 48 per km²

A MYRIAD of 130 South Pacific islands and coral atolls combine to form French Polynesia, in an area the size of Europe. The average annual temperature varies between 20ºC and 29ºC, with annual rainfall of over 150 cm. Nearly 75% of the population live on the main island of Tahiti. The Polynesian majority have seen their simple, self-sufficient economy transformed into one dependent on the French military and tourism. In particular, nuclear testing on Muroroa atoll created many jobs. Testing stopped in 1992, however, and unemployment has risen as a result. In addition, the French administration has developed the islands with little regard for local wishes. In response, the Polynesian majority has increased calls for greater autonomy, a reduction in tourism and a programme for rebuilding indigenous trade. However, the large minority of French expatriate workers oppose any change.

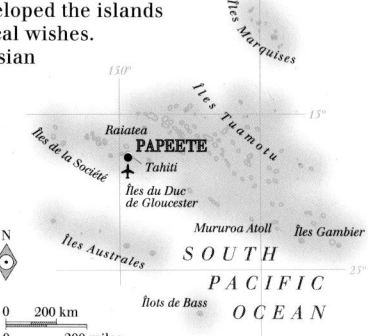

GIBRALTAR

STATUS: British Crown colony   **CLAIMED:** 1713
CAPITAL: Gibraltar   **POPULATION:** 28,074   **DENSITY:** 4319 per km²

G UARDING THE western entrance to the Mediterranean, Gibraltar has traditionally survived on military and marine revenues. However, as Britain has cut its defence spending so the UK's military presence on the Rock has declined. In response, Gibraltarians have developed a vibrant offshore banking industry, although 70% of employment still remains in the public sector. Politics is dominated by the issue of Gibraltar's relationship with Britain and Spain. As the UK's role diminishes, Gibraltar's chief minister, Joe Bossano, has called for independence under EU sponsorship. However, this seems unlikely while Spain continues to press for control over the Rock.

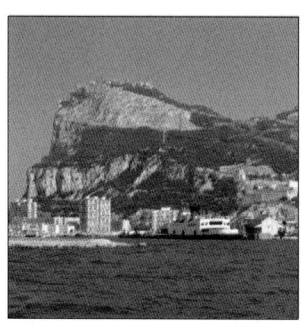

The Rock of Gibraltar. The British built 143 caves, 50 km of roads and as many km of tunnels for defensive purposes.

GREENLAND

STATUS: Self governing territory of Denmark   **CLAIMED:** 1380
CAPITAL: Nuuk   **POPULATION:** 55,385   **DENSITY:** 0.025 per km²

T HE WORLD'S LARGEST island, Greenland is situated in the North Atlantic and surrounded by seas that are either frozen or cooled by cold Arctic currents. The island has an Arctic climate and much of its land is permanently covered in ice. Granted home rule in 1979, Greenlanders are an independent people – a mix of Innuit and European in origin. Younger islanders are increasingly rejecting the traditional subsistence lifestyle by moving to towns. This move away from self-sufficiency, allied to a decline in the important fishing industry, has placed a heavy burden on Greenland's advanced welfare system.

GUADELOUPE

STATUS: French overseas department   **CLAIMED:** 1635
CAPITAL: Basse-Terre   **POPULATION:** 387,034   **DENSITY:** 217 per km

G UADELOUPE lies at the northern end of the Windward Islands in the Caribbean. It could become independent, but instead prospers from a developed infrastructure and large amounts of French and EU aid. However tensions are growing between the local population, who demand more autonomy, and the expatriate bureaucracy who impose the regulations of mainland France. Exports of the major cash crop, bananas, have been hit by the loss of special advantages under the Single European Act.

GUAM

STATUS: Unincorporated territory of the USA **CLAIMED:** 1898
CAPITAL: Agaña **POPULATION:** 133,152 **DENSITY:** 243 per km²

THE VOLCANIC ISLAND of Guam lies at the southern end of the Mariana Archipelago in the Pacific. Its tropical climate has encouraged tourism, although it lies in a region where typhoons are common. Guam's indigenous Chamorro people, who comprise just over half the population, dominate the island's political and social life. They are famous for a set of facial expressions, called 'eyebrow', which virtually constitutes a language of its own. The US military base, covering one-third of the island, has made Guam strategically important to the USA. Military spending and tourism revenues have given islanders a high living standard. The influx of American culture and *mores* has, however, threatened to upset Guam's social stability.

GUERNSEY

STATUS: British Crown dependency **CLAIMED:** 1066
CAPITAL: St Peter Port **POPULATION:** 58,867 **DENSITY:** 906 per km²

LYING 50 KM off the coast of France, Guernsey and its dependencies form the northwestern part of the Channel Islands. Some of the islands are too small for people to need cars, and life continues in an unhurried manner that has changed little through the centuries. The islanders guard this lifestyle with strict residential laws. Guernsey's mild climate has encouraged the development of tourism and market gardening as major industries.

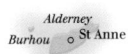

HEARD & MACDONALD IS.

STATUS: Australian external territory **CLAIMED:** 1947
CAPITAL: Not applicable **POPULATION:** None

SITUATED 4000 km southwest of Australia in the Indian Ocean, the Heard and Macdonald Islands are ice-covered, volcanic rock outcrops. Their principal use is for scientific research. In 1991 Heard Island's unique location – it offers direct access to the world's main oceans – led to it being chosen as the site of an experiment to monitor global warming using soundwaves.

ISLE OF MAN

STATUS: British Crown dependency **CLAIMED:** 1765
CAPITAL: Douglas **POPULATION:** 69,788 **DENSITY:** 122 per km²

LYING HALFWAY between England and Northern Ireland in the Irish Sea, the Isle of Man has been inhabited for centuries by the Celtic Manx people. Established by the Vikings in the ninth century, the Manx parliament, the Tynwold, has autonomy from the UK in a number of matters, including taxation. The islanders have used this independence to establish a thriving financial and business sector, which has aided employment as the traditional industries of agriculture and fishing decline. The Manx culture received a boost in 1993 when the local language, which was in danger of dying out, began being taught in the island's schools again. The Calf of Man is uninhabited and is administered as a nature reserve.

Isle of Man's TT motorbike race. Thousands of bikers come each year to see the island's famous Touring Trophy race. It is run on a 61 km circuit of the island.

JAN MAYEN

STATUS: Norwegian dependency **CLAIMED:** 1929
CAPITAL: Not applicable **POPULATION:** None

THE MOUNTAINOUS, volcanic island of Jan Mayen lies 900 km northwest of Norway, in the Arctic Ocean. The island's only resource is its rich fishing grounds. These were the subject of a long dispute with Greenland over fishing rights and possibly also oil and gas deposits. The International Court of Justice helped the two parties reach a compromise in 1993.

JARVIS ISLAND

STATUS: Unincorporated territory of the USA **CLAIMED:** 1856
CAPITAL: Not applicable **POPULATION:** None

A SMALL CORAL island, only 3 km long and one and a half km wide, Jarvis Island is located 2000 km south of Honolulu. It remains uninhabited, although scientists do occasionally visit. The island is managed primarily as a nesting, roosting and foraging site for seabirds and shorebirds.

JERSEY

STATUS: British Crown dependency   **CLAIMED:** 1066
CAPITAL: St Helier   **POPULATION:** 82,809   **DENSITY:** 713 per km²

THE BAILIWICK OF JERSEY, the largest of the Channel Islands, lies some 20 km from the coast of Normandy in France. The island has a mild climate owing to the Gulf Stream, fine beaches and more sunshine than anywhere in the British Isles.

Jersey has its own legislative and taxation systems which are a blend of the French and British versions. It also has one of the oldest legislative bodies in the world, the Jersey States Assembly. There are no political parties; members stand as independents. The islanders have used their autonomy from the UK to develop the economy as an offshore tax haven. Historically, agriculture has been Jersey's most important industry, with dairy cows its most famous export. Over the past 50 years, however, farming has been eclipsed by the rise of finance and tourism. The growth of these sectors, and rigid controls on the rights of residency, have ensured high living standards for most of the inhabitants. Jersey also plays host to a large Portuguese community who work in the island's tourist industry.

JOHNSTON ATOLL

STATUS: Unincorporated territory of the USA   **CLAIMED:** 1858
CAPITAL: Not applicable   **POPULATION:** 1375   **DENSITY:** 491 per km²

JOHNSTON ATOLL lies 1150 km southwest of Hawaii. The atoll consists of a coral reef, two highly-modified natural islands, Johnston and Sand, and two completely man-made islands, Akau and Hikina. The US military have drastically altered the islands and little of the original habitat remains. They have, in the past, been used for nuclear-weapons tests and storing nerve gases. However, the atoll is now used for a chemical-weapons disposal scheme by the US government. The islands are inhabited by US government personnel and civilian contractors who support the plant.

KINGMAN REEF

STATUS: Unincorporated territory of the USA   **CLAIMED:** 1856
CAPITAL: Not applicable   **POPULATION:** None

A barren, triangular reef, less than one metre in elevation, Kingman Reef lies 1500 km southwest of Hawaii. The reef is 14 km long and 8 km wide. Only the eastern end of it now remains above water. There is no land flora but it is rich in marine life. The reef is administered by the US Navy.

MACAO

STATUS: Special territory of Portugal   **CLAIMED:** 1557
CAPITAL: Macao   **POPULATION:** 355,693   **DENSITY:** 19,761 per km²

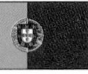

THE PORTUGUESE ENCLAVE of Macao is situated on the South China coast, at the mouth of the Pearl river. It comprises a small area of mainland and two nearby islands, linked to the mainland by bridge and causeway. A subtropical climate brings high humidity and the possibility of typhoons sweeping in from the South China Sea.

Macao is scheduled to become a Special Administrative Region of China in 1999. In contrast to the problems being experienced by the British in Hong Kong, Macao's preparations for Chinese sovereignty have been relatively smooth, not least because all Macanenes have been offered Portuguese passports. Tension has, however, developed between the skilled elite and the merchants who support China's takeover in 1999. In local legislative elections in 1992 the pro-China candidates secured half of the directly elected seats in the 23-seat assembly.

Macao has always suffered by comparison to Hong Kong, just 27 km to the east. Whilst Hong Kong has developed into an advanced capitalist economy, Macao is traditionally characterized by stagnation, corruption and bureaucratic inefficiency. However, the economy of Macao is now booming in the run-up to 1999. The government has been able to diversify the economy away from a dependency on gambling, although its casinos still lure hundreds of thousands of visitors a year. An international airport is being built on reclaimed land to aid economic development, and Macao is now a major centre for making cheap, finished goods for export. Its factories use cheap Chinese labour to produce anything from fireworks to artificial flowers.

Macao's skyline is dominated by large hotels and casinos which provide the territory with an important source of revenues.

LAND HEIGHT   above Sea Level   200m/656ft   500m/1640ft   1000m/3281ft   1500m/4572ft   above 2000m/6562ft

MARTINIQUE

STATUS: French overseas department   CLAIMED: 1635
CAPITAL: Fort-de-France   POPN: 359,579   DENSITY: 327 per km²

CHRISTOPHER COLUMBUS called Martinique 'The most beautiful country in the world'. It lies in the eastern Caribbean and is dominated by the dormant volcano Mont Pelée. The island is also situated in the Caribbean's hurricane belt and has therefore suffered an average of one natural disaster every five years. Nearly 90% of the population is of African or mixed ethnicity. However, economic power remains in the hands of the *Bekes* (descendants of white colonial settlers), who own most of the agricultural land. In addition, the bureaucracy is largely staffed by expatriates. This situation has led to outbreaks of violence and increased popular demands for more autonomy. The French government responded with some measures to increase the island's autonomy. However, the islanders are acutely aware that their high living standards are dependent on French subsidies. The economy relies on tourism and the production of sugar cane and bananas. EU reductions in subsidies has forced the island to diversify its economy.

MAYOTTE

STATUS: French territorial collectivity   CLAIMED: 1843
CAPITAL: Mamoudzou   POPULATION: 94,410   DENSITY: 253 per

PART OF THE Comoros archipelago, Mayotte lies some 8000 km from France, between Madagascar and the East African coast. The Mahorais are strongly in favour of maintaining their links with France, despite widespread poverty, endemic unemployment and a cost of living twice that of France. The main political movement has demanded that Mayotte be given the status of a French *département*. They hope that this would bring more aid to develop their largely agricultural economy. The expense involved has led France to oppose the idea. The French have, however, invested in an airport and port. It is hoped these will foster the growth of an up-market tourist sector.

MIDWAY ISLANDS

STATUS: Unincorporated territory of the USA   CLAIMED: 1867
CAPITAL: Not applicable   POPULATION: 453   DENSITY: 91 per km²

NAMED BECAUSE OF its position on the route between California, USA and Japan, Midway is a coral atoll at the western end of the Hawaiian islands. The scene of a major Second World War battle, the atoll comprises two large islands, totalling over four sq km, and several smaller ones. Midway functions as a naval air base and wildlife refuge. The population is limited to military personnel and civilian contractors.

MONTSERRAT

STATUS: British dependent territory   CLAIMED: 1632
CAPITAL: Plymouth   POPULATION: 11,852   DENSITY: 112 per km²

MONTSERRAT IS ONE of the Leeward Islands chain in the eastern Caribbean. Luxuriant flora and a tropical climate have made the island a tourist destination for the rich and famous. However, Montserrat's mountainous terrain, and hurricanes such as Hugo in 1989, have impeded its agricultural development. In response, the government has also developed the island as a financial and data-processing centre, although recent economic activity has been dominated by rebuilding infrastructure destroyed by Hugo. Independence, which dominated local politics in the late 1980s, fell into abeyance after the hurricane and a financial scandal involving local politicians.

*Monserrat.
Known as the Caribbean's 'emerald isle' because of its luxuriant flora and Irish heritage.*

NAVASSA ISLAND

STATUS: Unincorporated territory of the USA   CLAIMED: 1856
CAPITAL: Not applicable   POPULATION: None

AN UNINHABITED rocky outcrop, Navassa Island lies halfway between Cuba and Haiti, in the Caribbean. The island, also claimed by Haiti, is used by Haitians fishing the local waters. They also sometimes hunt the island's goats. Navassa has an automatic lighthouse which is run by the US Coast Guard.

NETHERLANDS ANTILLES

STATUS: Autonomous part of the Netherlands **CLAIMED:** 1816
CAPITAL: Willemstad **POPULATION:** 191,311 **DENSITY:** 239 per km²

THE NETHERLANDS Antilles are composed of two Caribbean island groups. Curaçao – the richest and wealthiest island – and Bonaire lie just off the Venezuelan coast, and Saba and St Eustatius and the Dutch part of St Maarten, lie 800 km to the north. The islands have caused the Dutch government, which gives $160 million in aid annually, a number of problems. These include financial scandals, arguments over the federation's future and – particularly on the four smaller islands – political instability and allegations of drug-trafficking. In 1993, the population of Curaçao opted to remain in the federation.

NEW CALEDONIA

STATUS: French overseas territory **CLAIMED:** 1853
CAPITAL: Nouméa **POPULATION:** 164,173 **DENSITY:** 9 per km²

NEW CALEDONIA, or as the indigenous Kanaks call it, Kanaky, is an island group 1500 km off the northeast coast of Australia. Tension between the Kanaks and the Caldoches, the francophile expatriate population, over socio-economic inequalities and independence, have resulted in a long history of political violence. By the 1988 Matignon Accord, the French government took over the administration of the territory for a year in order to introduce economic reforms and address Kanak grievances. Political prisoners were released and a referendum on independence promised for 1998. However, after the year was up, racial violence flared up and political resentments resurfaced. Nickel mining – the territory produces 25% of world output – tourism and agriculture have greatly enriched the economy, but there are considerable contrasts in living standards between rich and poor, with unemployment high among young Kanaks.

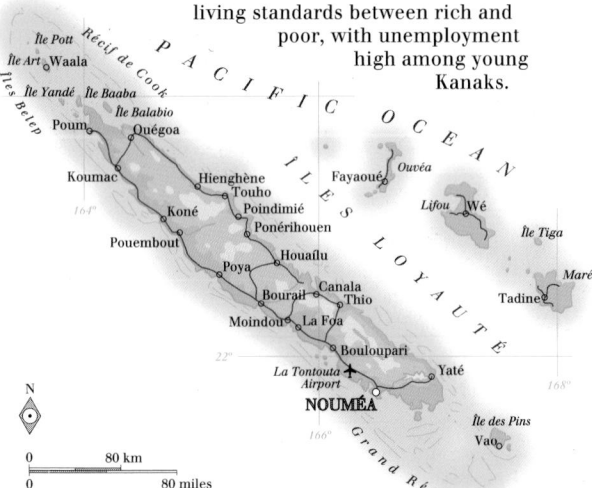

NIUE

STATUS: Territory in free association with New Zealand **CLAIMED:** [
CAPITAL: Alofi **POPULATION:** 2239 **DENSITY:** 9 per km²

THE WORLD'S largest coral island, Niue, lies 2100 km northeast of New Zealand. The subsistence economy produces a variety of tropical fruits, while tourism and the sale of postage stamps provide foreign currency. Despite the island's paradise image, nearly 10,000 Niueans, frustrated by the lack of job prospects on Niue, live in New Zealand. In the hope of stopping further emigration, New Zealand has invested heavily in the economy. However, inefficient use of aid and cyclone damage have held back growth.

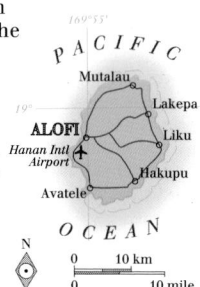

NORFOLK ISLAND

STATUS: Australian external territory **CLAIMED:** 1774
CAPITAL: Kingston **POPULATION:** 1912 **DENSITY:** 55 per km²

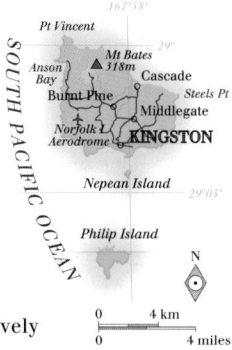

INHABITED by descendants of the *HMS Bounty* mutineers and more recent Australian migrants, Norfolk Island lies 1400 km east of Australia. The islanders speak a hybrid language, mixing West Country English, Gaelic and ancient Tahitian. They enjoy a fair degree of autonomy, and in 1991 rejected a plan to become part of the Australian federal state. Tourists, attracted by the climate and unique flora, have brought islanders a relatively high standard of living.

NORTHERN MARIANA IS.

STATUS: Commonwealth territory of the USA **CLAIMED:** 1947
CAPITAL: Saipan **POPULATION:** 43,345 **DENSITY:** 236 per km²

UNLIKE OTHER UN trust territories in the Western Pacific who opted for independence in 1987, the Northern Marianas preferred to retain links with the USA. However, local politicians have begun to question their new status. While US aid fuelled an economic boom during the 1980s, it failed to benefit the local Chamorro population. In addition, tourism has speeded the decline of the traditional subsistence economy.

Rota, Northern Marianas. The limestone outcrop of Wedding Cake Mountain overlooks the small village of Songsong.

LAND HEIGHT | above Sea Level | 200m/656ft | 500m/1640ft | 1000m/3281ft | 1500m/4572ft | above 2000m/6562ft

THE NATIONS OF THE WORLD: Overseas Territories

PALAU

STATUS: UN trust terr. administered by the USA   CLAIMED: 1947
CAPITAL: Koror   POPULATION: 16,386   DENSITY: 32 per km²

THE PALAU archipelago, a group of over 200 islands, eight of which are inhabited, is the last remaining UN trust territory in the Pacific administered by the USA. In 1993, after eight referenda, the Palauan people voted for independent statehood in free association with the USA. This compact, which had been held up by a local ban on the disposal of nuclear, chemical and biological weapons, will be enacted by February 1995. The economy operates on a subsistence level, the principal crops being coconuts and cassava. Revenue from fishing licences and tourism provide Palau with foreign currency. With a warm, if rainy, climate and outstanding coastlines, the tourism potential of Palau is considerable. However, the islands' isolation, and lack of facilities pose considerable problems for further tourism development.

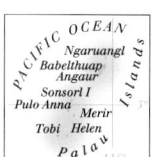

PALMYRA ATOLL

STATUS: Unincorporated territory of the USA   CLAIMED: 1898
CAPITAL: Not applicable   POPULATION: None

A PRIVATELY OWNED, uninhabited collection of 50 islets, Palmyra Atoll is situated some 1600 km southwest of Hawaii. Administered by the USA since 1898, the atoll is covered in dense vegetation, including coconut palms, which have prospered in its hot and humid climate. In 1990, an Hawaiian property developer took out a 75-year lease on Palmyra from its owners, the Fullard-Leo brothers. Plans exist to turn the atoll into a tourist and residential complex, which will promote a 'get away from it all' image.

PUERTO RICO

STATUS: Commonwealth territory of the USA   CLAIMED: 1898
CAPITAL: San Juan   POPULATION: 3.5 million   DENSITY: 396 per km²

THE MOST POPULOUS of the US overseas territories, Puerto Rico lies in the Caribbean between the Dominican Republic and the Virgin Islands. The island, which is split by a central mountain range, has a tropical climate which attracts growing numbers of

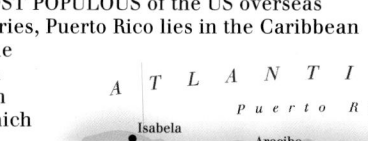

PARACEL ISLANDS

STATUS: Disputed   CLAIMED: Not applicable
CAPITAL: Woody Island   POPN: Unknown   DENSITY: Unknown

OCCUPIED BY CHINESE FORCES, but also claimed by Taiwan and Vietnam, the Paracel Islands are a small collection of coral atolls, situated some 400 km east of Vietnam, in the South China Sea. Subject to frequent typhoons and with a tropical climate, the Paracels are at the centre of a regional dispute over the vast reserves of oil and natural gas, which are believed to lie beneath its territorial waters. China has built port facilities and an airport on Woody Island to support its claim.

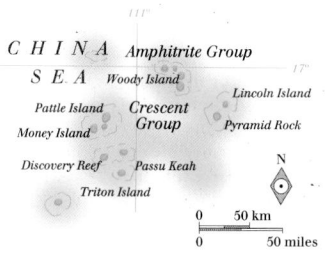

PITCAIRN ISLANDS

STATUS: British dependent territory   CLAIMED: 1887
CAPITAL: Adamstown   POPULATION: 52   DENSITY: 12 per km²

PITCAIRN, a group of volcanic South Pacific islands, is Britain's most isolated dependency. Pitcairn Island provided the last refuge for the HMS Bounty mutineers. Emigration continues to be a major problem for the Pitcairners, who depend on regular airdrops from New Zealand, and periodic visits by supply vessels. The economy operates by barter, fishing and subsistence farming. Postage stamps sales provide foreign currency earnings. Mineral exploitation could boost the economy in future.

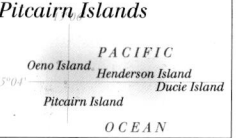

tourists. In 1993, the population voted by a narrow majority to maintain the current compromise between statehood and independence. The result was seen as a personal blow to governor Pedro Rossello, who campaigned to make Puerto Rico the USA's 51st state. The population has one of the highest living standards in the region. Tax relief, cheap labour, and its role as an export processing zone, have encouraged many businesses to the the island. As a result, industries – like electronics and petrochemicals – have overtaken agriculture as the major economic activity.

RÉUNION

STATUS: French overseas department   **CLAIMED:** 1638
CAPITAL: Saint-Denis   **POPULATION:** 597,828   **DENSITY:** 238 per km²

THE LARGE VOLCANIC island of Réunion, 800 km east of Madagascar, provides France with an important strategic presence – and a large military base – in the Indian Ocean. Its mountainous interior has forced the majority of the population to live along the coast. Socioeconomic differences between the poorer black community and the wealthier Indian and European groups raised ethnic tensions. These tensions were the cause of severe rioting in 1991. The French government responded with a series of measures, applicable to all overseas *départements*, to raise economic and social conditions to the level of those of France itself. Réunion's main crop is sugar cane.

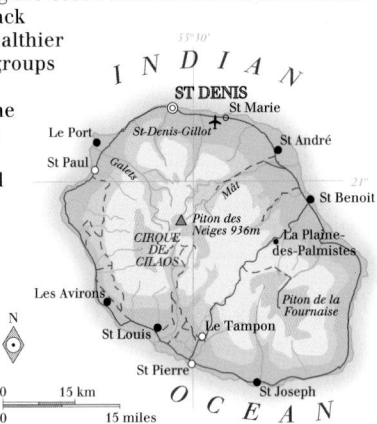

ST PIERRE & MIQUELON

STATUS: French territorial collectivity   **CLAIMED:** 1604
CAPITAL: St Pierre   **POPULATION:** 6392

ST PIERRE & Miquelon is a group of barren islands, just off the south coast of Newfoundland, Canada. The islands are surrounded by some of the world's richest fishing grounds. Their inhabitants have traditionally earned a living from fishing, and servicing foreign trawler fleets, off the coast. A long-running and sometimes bitter dispute between Canada and France over fishing and mineral rights was settled in 1992. The ruling, which was generally deemed to be in Canada's favour, has led the French authorities to diversify the economy by developing port facilities and encouraging tourism.

ST HELENA & DEPENDENCIES

STATUS: British dependent territory   **CLAIMED:** 1673
CAPITAL: Jamestown   **POPULATION:** 7000 (est)   **DENSITY:** 22 per km²

TOGETHER, the islands of St Helena, Tristan da Cunha and Ascension form Britain's main dependency in the South Atlantic. St Helena, the principal island, is the last remaining dependency to need budgetary aid from the UK. The island's main economic activities, fishing, livestock farming and the sale of handicrafts, are unable to support the population. As a result, underemployment is a major problem on St Helena. Opportunities seem to be better on its dependencies and many St Helenians have been forced to seek work on Ascension Island. Some were also employed building Mount Pleasant airport on the Falklands. No resident population is allowed on Ascension Island, which operates as a military base and communications centre. It is an integral part of the air-bridge supplying the Falklands. Tristan da Cunha, a volcanic island 2000 km to the south of St Helena, is inhabited by a small, closely-knit farming community.

SOUTH GEORGIA & SOUTH SANDWICH ISLANDS

STATUS: British dependent territory   **CLAIMED:** 1775
CAPITAL: Grytviken   **POPULATION:** Unknown

THE SOUTH Atlantic island of South Georgia, briefly occupied by Argentine forces during the Falklands War, has a small garrison at Grytviken and a British Antarctic Survey base. The volcanic South Sandwich Islands, 750 km to the southeast, are uninhabited. The territory is increasingly visited by eco-tourists, attracted by the abundant wildlife.

SPRATLY ISLANDS

STATUS: DISPUTED   **CLAIMED:** Not applicable
CAPITAL: Not applicable   **POPULATION:** Unknown

SCATTERED across a large area of the South China Sea, the reefs, islands and atolls that make up the Spratly Islands, have become one of South East Asia's most serious security issues. Claimed, all or in part, by China, Taiwan, Vietnam, Brunei, Malaysia and the Philippines, 44 of the larger islands now have garrisons from some of the claimant nations. The reasons for this interest, and the occasional skirmish, are twofold. Strategically, the islands control some of the world's most important shipping lanes. In addition, surveys suggest that some of the largest oil and gas reserves yet found lie in the Spratlys' territorial waters.

LAND HEIGHT ⬛ above Sea Level ⬛ 200m/656ft ⬛ 500m/1640ft ⬛ 1000m/3281ft ⬛ 1500m/4572ft ⬛ above 2000m/6562ft ⬜ Ice Cap

SVALBARD

STATUS: Norwegian dependency **CLAIMED:** 1920
CAPITAL: Longyearbyen **POPULATION:** 3116 **DENSITY:** 0.05 per km²

NINE ICE-COVERED Arctic islands, 650 km north of Norway, make up the territory of Svalbard. The population, mostly Norwegian and Russian coal miners – a 1920 treaty gives any country the right to exploit Svalbard's mineral resources – live in harsh conditions. However, falling coal reserves and the end of the Cold War have begun to test Norway's strong attachment with the islands.

TOKELAU

STATUS: New Zealand dependent territory **CLAIMED:** 1926
CAPITAL: Not applicable **POPULATION:** 1760 **DENSITY:** 167 per km²

ACCORDING TO A 1989 UN report, this island in the South Pacific will disappear under the sea in the 21st century unless action is taken to stop global warming. In 1990, in another blow for the islanders, a cyclone destroyed crops and wrecked Tokelau's infrastructure. The New Zealand government has, however, made efforts to spur development. A tuna cannery and the sale of fishing licences have raised revenue, and a catamaran link between the atolls has increased the islands' tourist potential. However, its small size and continued economic weakness still makes independence unlikely.

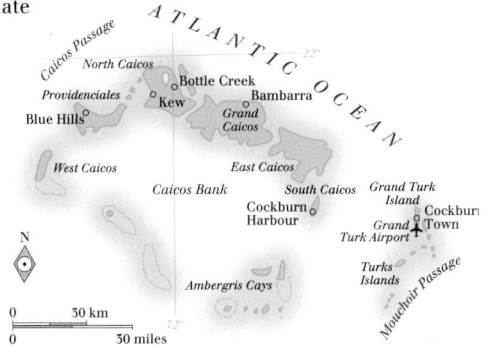

TURKS & CAICOS ISLANDS

STATUS: British dependent territory **CLAIMED:** 1766
CAPITAL: Cockburn Town **POPULATION:** 12,350 **DENSITY:** 29 per

SITUATED 40 km south of the Bahamas, the Turks and Caicos Islands is a group of 30 low-lying islands, eight of which are inhabited. Services dominate the economy, particularly tourism and offshore banking. Many skilled islanders seek work in the Bahamas. Haitian refugees form the poorest segment of society.

VIRGIN ISLANDS (US)

STATUS: Unincorporated territory of the USA **CLAIMED:** 1917
CAPITAL: Charlotte Amalie **POPN:** 101,809 **DENSITY:** 287 per km²

THE US VIRGIN Islands are a collection of 53 volcanic islands, just to the east of Puerto Rico. Most of the population – a mix of African and European ethnic groups – live on the main islands of St John, St Thomas and St Croix. Tourism is the principal industry, although St Croix has also used federal aid to develop industry. It has one of the world's largest oil refineries.

St Thomas, US Virgin Islands, is a major stop-off for Caribbean cruise ships. Tourists are attracted by the island's duty-free shopping.

WAKE ISLAND

STATUS: Unincorporated territory of the USA **CLAIMED:** 1898
CAPITAL: Not applicable **POPULATION:** 381 **DENSITY:** 59 per km²

FORMED BY the rim of an extinct underwater volcano, Wake Island's strategic importance has declined since the end of the Vietnam War. It is now used as an emergency airstrip for trans-Pacific flights, and as a stop-over for cargo planes.

WALLIS & FUTUNA

STATUS: French overseas territory **CLAIMED:** 1842
CAPITAL: Mata Uta **POPULATION:** 13,705 **DENSITY:** 50 per km²

UNLIKE FRANCE'S other overseas territories in the South Pacific, the inhabitants of the Wallis and Futuna have little desire for greater autonomy. The islands' subsistence economy produces a variety of tropical crops, while expatriate remittances and the sale of licences to Japanese and Korean fishing fleets provide foreign exchange. Futuna was hit by an earthquake in 1993.

3

GLOBAL ISSUES

WORLD POPULATION
HUNGER & DISEASE
THE WORLD ECONOMY
ETHNICITY AND THE NATION STATE
THE WORLD ENVIRONMENT
GLOBAL COMMUNICATIONS
SECURITY & DEFENCE
GLOBAL TOURISM
THE FINAL FRONTIERS

WORLD POPULATION

WORLD POPULATION, 5.4 billion people in 1992, is projected to rise to 8-10 billion people by 2025. It is estimated that population will stabilize at around 8-12 billion people after 2050. Despite a decline in total world fertility, population will increase in countries that are in the process of industrialization. There is little indication that fertility is set to decline in the least developed countries, presently comprising some 0.5 billion people. These densely populated regions of the world lack the infrastructure and resources needed to cope with growing populations. On the other hand, birth rates in the industrialized countries of Europe, in Japan and in the USA, have fallen to the point where they fail to replace deaths.

WORLD POPULATION DISTRIBUTION

POPULATION DENSITY PER SQUARE KILOMETRE

- Less than 10
- 10 - 49
- 50 - 99
- 100 - 299
- 300 - 1000
- More than 1000

CARIBBEAN

- BAHAMAS
- DOMINICA
- ANTIGUA & BARBUDA
- GRENADA
- GUADELOUPE (to France)
- ST KITTS & NEVIS
- ST LUCIA
- TRINIDAD & TOBAGO
- BARBADOS
- MARTINIQUE (to France)
- ST VINCENT & THE GRENADINES
- BERMUDA (to UK)

EUROPE

- FAEROE ISLANDS (to Denmark)
- ANDORRA
- LUXEMBOURG
- LIECHTENSTEIN
- SAN MARINO
- GIBRALTAR (to UK)
- MALTA
- MONACO

AFRICA

- CAPE VERDE
- SAO TOME & PRINCIPE

The crowded shanty towns of Rio de Janeiro.

OVERCROWDED CITIES

Mass migration from the countryside to urban centres has long been symptomatic of industrialization and rapid economic growth. This major shift in both rural and urban economic structures is normally matched by an inadequate distribution of available resources. The development of shanty towns around urban centres, such as Rio de Janeiro, is now a widespread problem, overtaxing municipal resources and services.

Asia is the most heavily populated region of the world.

REGIONAL POPULATION DISTRIBUTION

- North American 4.9%
- Australasia 0.45%
- Latin America & Caribbean 8.3%
- Middle East 4%
- Europe 13%
- Asia 55.8%
- Africa 13.3%

Figures show percentage of total world population

THE NETHERLANDS

The most densely populated country of Europe, the Netherlands, remains one of the wealthiest. Over the centuries, a balance between resources and population has been achieved which allows for a sustainable growth of the economy, of individual wealth and of living conditions. The pressure of a large population on very limited quantities of land has led to massive land reclamation projects in the Netherlands. From as early as the 16th century, land has been taken back from the sea – initially for agriculture, but also today for industrial plant and residential development.

The intensively farmed rural landscape of the Netherlands.

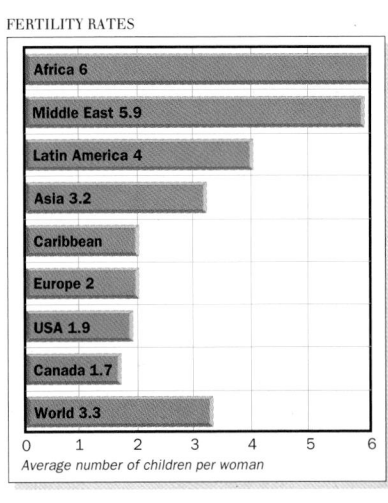

FERTILITY RATES

Africa 6	
Middle East 5.9	
Latin America 4	
Asia 3.2	
Caribbean	
Europe 2	
USA 1.9	
Canada 1.7	
World 3.3	

0 1 2 3 4 5 6
Average number of children per woman

Fertility has declined throughout the industrialized world and is highest in Africa.

RUSSIAN FEDERATION

KAZAKHSTAN

MONGOLIA

GEORGIA
ARM. AZERB.
UZBEKISTAN
KYRGYZSTAN
TURKMENISTAN
TAJIKISTAN

KEY

SYRIA
IRAQ
IRAN
AFGHANISTAN
JORDAN
KUWAIT
BAHRAIN
QATAR
UAE
SAUDI ARABIA
OMAN

CHINA

NORTH KOREA
SOUTH KOREA
JAPAN

PAKISTAN
NEPAL
BHUTAN
BANGLADESH
INDIA
BURMA
LAOS
THAILAND
VIETNAM
CAMBODIA

Hong Kong (to UK)
Macao (to Portugal)
TAIWAN

PACIFIC OCEAN

ERITREA
YEMEN
DJIBOUTI
ETHIOPIA
SOMALIA
UGANDA
KENYA
TANZANIA
SEYCHELLES
MALAWI
COMOROS
MOZAMBIQUE
MADAGASCAR
MAURITIUS
SWAZILAND
ESOTHO

MALDIVES
SRI LANKA

PHILIPPINES

BRUNEI
MALAYSIA
SINGAPORE

INDONESIA

PAPUA NEW GUINEA

SOLOMON IS

INDIAN OCEAN

AUSTRALIA

New Caledonia (to France)

NEW ZEALAND

PACIFIC OCEAN
○ FIJI
○ SOLOMON ISLANDS
○ VANUATU
○ WESTERN SAMOA
○ KIRIBATI
○ MICRONESIA
○ TONGA
○ NAURU

MIDDLE EAST
○ BAHRAIN

INDIAN OCEAN
○ COMOROS
○ SEYCHELLES
○ MALDIVES
○ MAURITIUS

ASIA
○ MACAO (to Portugal)
○ HONG KONG (to UK)
○ SINGAPORE

A nomadic goat-herder in north-west Somalia.

PASTORAL NOMADISM

Traditional ways of life, in which a balance between population numbers and natural resources had achieved equilibrium, are now under threat. Since the mid-1980s a succession of droughts in the Sahel and civil wars in Sudan, Ethiopia, Eritrea and Somalia have disrupted the traditional balance between population and resources in this region.

HUNGER AND DISEASE

THE RECENT PAST has seen an unparalleled increase in food production and availability. However, underlying global success there is marked regional inequality; drought, conflict and natural catastrophes can have disastrous effects on the ability of people to feed themselves. Current estimates are that nearly 800 million people, almost all in the developing countries, do not have enough food to meet their basic nutritional needs. A third of children in developing countries suffer growth faltering, mainly because of under-nutrition. Undernourished children are handicapped in their intellectual development, fall ill more easily and have lower physical productivity as adults.

WORLD INFANT MORTALITY

**INFANT MORTALITY RATE
PER THOUSAND LIVE BIRTHS**

- Less than 10
- 10 - 19.9
- 20 - 39.9
- 40 - 79.9
- 80 - 120
- More than 120

CARIBBEAN
- BARBADOS
- DOMINICA
- ST LUCIA
- TRINIDAD & TOBAGO
- ANTIGUA & BARBUDA
- BAHAMAS
- GRENADA
- ST KITTS & NEVIS
- ST VINCENT & THE GRENADINES

EUROPE
- ANDORRA
- LIECHTENSTEIN
- LUXEMBOURG
- MONACO
- MALTA
- SAN MARINO

AFRICA
- CAPE VERDE
- SAO TOME & PRINCIPE

**REGIONAL PREVALENCE OF
UNDERWEIGHT PRE-SCHOOL CHILDREN
IN DEVELOPING COUNTRIES**

- Sub-Saharan Africa 29.9%
- Near East / North Africa 13.4%
- South Asia 58.5%
- South East Asia 31.3%
- China 21.8%
- Middle America/Caribbean 15.4%
- S.America 7.7%

Under-nourishment is both an immediate and a long term problem, influencing the potential for future economic development in the regions affected.

POVERTY

Rural poverty, especially in Asia and Africa, is associated with hunger and malnutrition. People who are reduced to subsistence farming on unproductive land are most at risk. Their children are more likely to be under-nourished, and are prone to infections such as dysentery and respiratory and parasitic diseases. Improving the food supply is not the only solution: better access to health services, improved health education and sanitation, the promotion of breast feeding and immunization are all imporant priorities.

Poor soil, inadequate technology, lack of water control and infestation by pests are all problems afflicting farmers on marginal land in Asia.

CONFLICT

Conflict is increasingly a cause of hunger. In 1993-94, approximately 80% of food aid worldwide was being directed to relieve distress in man-made rather than natural disasters – in Somalia, Angola, Liberia, southern Sudan, Rwanda, Afghanistan and Cambodia. Breakdown of civil order and infrastructure in war zones makes food aid distribution hazardous and inadequate. Refugees are forced to become landless – cultivated land is neglected indefinitely, compounding the difficulties of recovery.

***The distribution** of food to refugees in war zones is often disrupted by the fighting. Food frequently disappears onto the black market, never reaching the starving.*

RUSSIAN FEDERATION

KAZAKHSTAN · MONGOLIA · NORTH KOREA · SOUTH KOREA · JAPAN · CHINA · GEORGIA · ARM. · AZERB. · UZBEKISTAN · KYRGYZSTAN · TURKMENISTAN · TAJIKISTAN · RKEY · SYRIA · IRAQ · IRAN · AFGHANISTAN · JORDAN · KUWAIT · PAKISTAN · NEPAL · BHUTAN · BAHRAIN · QATAR · UAE · BANGLADESH · SAUDI ARABIA · OMAN · INDIA · BURMA · LAOS · Hong Kong (to UK) · Macao (to Portugal) · TAIWAN · ERITREA · YEMEN · DJIBOUTI · THAILAND · VIETNAM · CAMBODIA · PHILIPPINES · ETHIOPIA · SOMALIA · MALDIVES · SRI LANKA · BRUNEI · MALAYSIA · SINGAPORE · UGANDA · KENYA · TANZANIA · SEYCHELLES · INDONESIA · PAPUA NEW GUINEA · SOLOMON IS · COMOROS · MALAWI · MOZAMBIQUE · MADAGASCAR · MAURITIUS · AUSTRALIA · New Caledonia (to France) · SWAZILAND · LESOTHO · NEW ZEALAND

PACIFIC OCEAN · FIJI · MICRONESIA · KIRIBATI · NAURU · SOLOMON ISLANDS · TONGA · VANUATU · WESTERN SAMOA · MIDDLE EAST · BAHRAIN · INDIAN OCEAN · SEYCHELLES · MAURITIUS · MALDIVES · COMOROS · ASIA · HONG KONG (U K) · SINGAPORE

A combination of war and famine in Ethiopia has brought starvation to catastrophic levels.

STARVATION IN AFRICA

Although food production in Africa has actually increased since the 1970s, per capita food production has fallen, and dependence on food imports and foreign aid has increased. In 1992, more than 40 million Africans were faced with the threat of famine, and nearly half of sub-Saharan Africa's population is facing food shortages.

THE WORLD ECONOMY

THE PATTERN OF THE GLOBAL ECONOMY frequently relates to an underlying equation, the relationship between population and available resources. Japan, for example, has a much 'bigger' economy than the former Soviet Union, or India or Latin America as a whole. Such imbalances occur because economies differ enormously in their living standards, the productivity of their agriculture and in the value of their markets. A close comparison of economic performance can be measured on a Purchasing Power Parity (PPP) basis, which tells us how much is produced and consumed in different countries when their prices are compared as exactly as possible.

NATIONAL ECONOMIC PERFORMANCE

PURCHASING POWER PARITY AS A
PERCENTAGE OF THE WORLD TOTAL

- Less than 0.4%
- 0.4 - 2.4%
- 2.5 - 4.9%
- 5 - 9.9%
- 10 - 20%
- More than 20%

In Mexico, *large influxes of tourists over the last two decades have transformed the local economy, generating jobs and foreign currency earnings.*

THE SERVICE SECTOR

During the last three decades the most rapidly growing sector of world trade is services – banking, insurance, tourism, accountancy, consultancy, films, music and other cultural services, airlines and shipping. Services account for 21% of world trade, almost equivalent to the volume of trade in food and raw materials.

WORLD TRADE

For most of the post-war period, trade has expanded more rapidly than the world economy – in 1991 global import trade alone accounted for $400 billion. Trade has acted as a dynamic influence in economics, helping to pull up growth. In 1992, manufactures made up around 57% of world trade, raw materials and food 22% and services 21%. Trade takes place predominantly between the rich countries of northern Europe, Japan and the USA.

Baltimore in Maryland *is a container port where large quantities of cargo are shipped to worldwide markets. Seaborne trade accounts for more than 80% of the total volume of world trade.*

PACIFIC RIM

The 'Four Dragons' of the Pacific Rim – South Korea, Taiwan, Hong Kong and Singapore – are high-growth areas, forging ahead with rapid export-led industrialization. Growth rates in the region over the last three decades have consistently been double or triple those of the USA or Western Europe. Low labour costs, stable governments and encouragement of foreign investment have all contributed to this spectacular growth.

South Korea *has become a major industrial power, specializing in shipbuilding, car manufacture, and high technology – computers and communications equipment.*

RUSSIAN FEDERATION

UZBEKISTAN

KEY

CHINA

SOUTH KOREA   JAPAN

IRAN

T

SAUDI ARABIA

INDIA

Hong Kong (to UK)

TAIWAN

PACIFIC

OCEAN

THAILAND

SINGAPORE

INDIAN

OCEAN

INDONESIA

AUSTRALIA

THE WORLD'S TOP EXPORTERS 1992

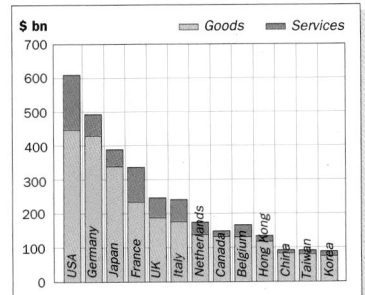

$ bn	□ Goods ■ Services
700	
600	USA
500	Germany
400	Japan
300	France
200	UK, Italy, Netherlands, Canada, Belgium, Hong Kong
100	China, Taiwan, Korea
0	

Manufactured goods *still dominate the export market, but service industries account for an increasingly large sector in the developed world.*

ETHNICITY AND THE NATION STATE

WITH THE END OF THE COLD WAR, long-standing alliances and conflicts based on ideological differences – ideas of 'left' and 'right' – have disappeared into the background. However, others based on some form of cultural identity or ethnicity, whether it is derived from language, religion, colour, clan, tribe or cultural tradition, have seemingly proliferated. Very few nation states can claim to have a homogenous identity. Almost all have minorities. In some cases, the alienation between the minority and majority can lead to a threatened break-up of nation states. In others, a sense of cultural identity spans several countries: it is known as 'pan-ethnicity.'

NATIONS WITHIN NATIONS

NATIONAL & ETHNIC CONFLICT

Countries with active secessionist movements

Intercommunal or ethnic violence

NATIONS BEYOND STATES

The peoples of the Jewish diaspora are linked by a sense of nationhood based on a combination of religious, racial and linguistic identity, despite their diverse origins. The Zionist movement has embraced black African *falashas* from Ethiopia, orthodox and atheist Jews, Hebrew-speakers, Russian-speakers and non-Hebrew speakers from the USA, as well as West Europeans (Ashkenazy) and North Africans (Sephardic).

Ethiopian Jews (falashas) were airlifted to the Jewish state of Israel in 1991 to escape the war in Ethiopia.

...ter protestants commemorate the ...glish victory against the Irish in ...0. The 'marching season' is often a ...ger for sectarian violence.

RELIGIOUS LOYALTIES

Religion can be a politically unifying force, as well as a source of friction with other religions and denominations. In the Irish Republic, Catholics make up the majority of the population, while Protestants dominate in Ulster. More than in any other country in western Europe, people's daily lives are shaped by their religion, and an acute sense of the roots of their differences has erupted in continuing inter-communal conflict.

Political posters in northern Spain keep Basque separatism on the political agenda. So far, the Spanish government has failed to deal with the question of Basque devolution.

PAN-ETHNICITY

Sometimes, groups which straddle different countries feel a sense of nationhood which cannot yet be realized in a nation state. There are many examples of ethnic minorities trying to secede, in many cases drawing sustenance from co-religionists or ethnic brethren across borders. In Europe, for example, the Basque people hope for a pan-ethnic Basque state within a federal EU. In West Asia, both the Kurds and the Palestinians aspire to national sovereignty.

RUSSIAN FEDERATION

...ORGIA

...KEY   AZERBAIJAN   TAJIKISTAN

IRAQ   IRAN   AFGHANISTAN

CHINA

...AN

YEMEN

DJIBOUTI

ETHIOPIA

SOMALIA

KENYA

...TANZANIA

MOZAMBIQUE

INDIA   BURMA

LAOS

CAMBODIA

SRI LANKA

PACIFIC

OCEAN

INDONESIA   PAPUA NEW GUINEA

PHILIPPINES

INDIAN

OCEAN

Iraq's Marsh Arabs have fallen victim to a campaign of 'ethnic cleansing'.

ETHNIC CLEANSING

Minority ethnic groups are frequently at risk because of their religious, cultural or linguistic differences. Extreme forms of persecution, forced relocation or genocide, known as 'ethnic cleansing', have recently been witnessed in Iraq, Iran, Bosnia and Rwanda.

THE WORLD ENVIRONMENT

EACH DAY 50 TO 100 SPECIES of plant and animal become extinct – it is now internationally recognized that conservation of the world's remaining wildlife and ecosystems is an urgent priority. In many countries, legislation is ensuring that land is protected from urbanization and agriculture – the two greatest threats to the environment. However, environmental protection legislation is much more apparent in the countries of the developed world. In the developing countries, pressure on land and resources creates more urgent priorities: environmental protection is often dependent on grants and aid from the developed world, and foreign currency-earners such as tourism take precedence over conservation.

GLOBAL CONSERVATION

PROTECTED LAND AS A PERCENTAGE OF TOTAL LAND AREA

- Less than 1%
- 1 - 4.9%
- 5 - 9.9%
- 10 - 20%
- More than 20%

CARIBBEAN
- BARBADOS
- GRENADA
- ST LUCIA
- TRINIDAD & TOBAGO
- BAHAMAS
- DOMINICA
- ANTIGUA & BARBUDA
- GUADELOUPE (Fr.)
- ST KITTS & NEVIS
- BERMUDA (U K)
- MARTINIQUE (Fr.)
- ST VINCENT & THE GRENADINES

EUROPE
- ANDORRA
- FAEROE ISLANDS (to Denmark)
- GIBRALTAR (to UK)
- LUXEMBOURG
- MALTA
- MONACO
- SAN MARINO
- LIECHTENSTEIN

AFRICA
- CAPE VERDE
- SAO TOME & PRINCIPE

The Los Angeles skyline is barely visible through a layer of smog.

AERIAL POLLUTION

By the year 2025, there will be an estimated 1000 million cars on the world's roads. Severe air pollution, partly caused by cars, is already having an impact. The burning of fossil fuel is responsible for the discharge of huge amounts of carbon dioxide into the atmosphere. The destruction of the rainforests, which absorb so-called 'greenhouse gases' such as carbon dioxide, leads to a build-up of gases in the atmosphere, which is believed to disrupt the global climate.

By 2030 only a fifth of the earth's original rainforest will remain.

DISAPPEARING RAINFORESTS

- Immediate threat 19%
- Irreplaceably lost 45%
- Future losses 18%
- Degraded forest 9%
- Pristine forest 9%

WATER RESOURCES

Global demand for water – for industrial, agricultural and domestic use – has increased five-fold since 1950. In many parts of the world, water resources are contaminated by industrial waste and pollution, while dams and irrigation schemes transform river and floodplain ecoystems. Localized drought, spread of water-borne diseases, and contaminated drinking water are all major problems.

The Aral Sea has shrunk by 60,000 sq km as a result of schemes to irrigate the cotton fields of Uzbekistan.

The tropical rainforests of Malaysia. Rainforests contain more than 20% of all the known natural species of plants and animals living on Earth.

RAINFOREST

It is thought that there are some 4.5 million plant and animal species, two-thirds of which are to be found in the tropics, with an abundance living in the equatorial rainforests. This diversity of plant and animal life is increasingly threatened by the destruction of the rainforest. Commercial logging and clearing forests for agriculture, ranching and mineral exploitation are destroying the rainforest at the rate of 160,000 square kilometres each year.

RUSSIAN FEDERATION

KAZAKHSTAN

MONGOLIA

GEORGIA
ARM. AZERB.
EY
SYRIA
IRAQ
JORDAN

UZBEKISTAN
KYRGYZSTAN
TURKMENISTAN
TAJIKISTAN
AFGHANISTAN

CHINA

NORTH KOREA
SOUTH KOREA

JAPAN

KUWAIT
BAHRAIN
QATAR
UAE
SAUDI ARABIA
OMAN

IRAN

PAKISTAN

NEPAL
BHUTAN
BANGLADESH

Hong Kong (to UK)
Macao (to Portugal)

TAIWAN

PACIFIC OCEAN

ERITREA
N
YEMEN
DJIBOUTI

INDIA

BURMA

LAOS

THAILAND
CAMBODIA

VIETNAM

PHILIPPINES

ETHIOPIA

MALDIVES

SRI LANKA

 NDA
KENYA

SEYCHELLES

BRUNEI
MALAYSIA
SINGAPORE

SOMALIA

ANZANIA

INDONESIA

PAPUA NEW GUINEA

SOLOMON IS

COMOROS

INDIAN

OCEAN

MALAWI
MOZAMBIQUE
MADAGASCAR
MAURITIUS

New Caledonia (to France)

AUSTRALIA

SWAZILAND
THO

NEW ZEALAND

PACIFIC OCEAN
FIJI
MICRONESIA
NAURU
SOLOMON ISLANDS
VANUATU
WESTERN SAMOA
TONGA
KIRIBATI

MIDDLE EAST
BAHRAIN

INDIAN OCEAN
COMOROS
MALDIVES
MAURITIUS
SEYCHELLES

ASIA
HONG KONG (to UK)
MACAO (to Portugal)
SINGAPORE

Sand dunes along the edges of the Sahara desert are encroaching on arable land.

MARGINAL LAND

One-third of the world's land area is subject to the risk of soil erosion and desertification – in the absence of other fuels, wood and charcoal burning destroys the forests, removing topsoils and hastening the encroachment of the desert. The onward march of desert can be halted by expensive tree-planting programmes and better land-management.

GLOBAL COMMUNICATIONS

WHEN ASKED what had caused the collapse of communism in eastern Europe, Polish President Lech Wałęsa pointed to a television set. 'It all came from there,' he said. Undoubtedly, the globalization of television and printed news has wrought dramatic changes in the world. In addition, a revolution in digital technology has created a truly global village.

Television viewers can now receive hundreds of channels by satellite, watch films and the latest news, shop, book tickets and access databanks. With the help of fibre-optic cables, the conduits of digital information, and increasingly compatible software, computer-users can now communicate across geographic borders.

GLOBAL SATELLITE TELEVISION COVERAGE

REGIONAL SATELLITE COVERAGE

- Low penetration
- Medium penetration
- High penetration

MAIN REGIONAL SATELLITES

- AUSSAT
- ARABSAT
- ASIASAT
- ASTRA
- Various

NORTH AMERICA

CENTRAL AMERICA

PACIFIC OCEAN

ATLANTIC OCEAN

UNITED KINGDOM

EUR

NOR AFRI

BRAZIL

SOUTH AMERICA

ATLANTIC OCEAN

SPACE AGE COMMUNICATIONS

Scores of communications satellites now circle the globe; not only have they transformed both television and telecommunications, they have radically altered our knowledge of the Earth, with both military and scientific applications. Access to satellite broadcasting means that people hitherto exposed only to material approved by their governments can now receive a broader and possibly more objective presentation.

Of the over 7000 man-made objects orbiting the Earth today, only some 500 are satellites.

GLOBAL VILLAGE

Since 1980, the number of television sets in the world neary tripled to one billion. Multimedia empires are currently competing for the vast satellite audiences (and lucrative advertising revenues) of the developing world. While there is resistance to the endless diet of Western popular culture broadcast by satellite, which is thought to corrupt traditional values, many governments are powerless to stop the spread of satellites.

A bicycle wheel on a Delhi rooftop picks up television signals. Used to makeshift technology, Indians are unwilling to pay for satellite.

GLOBAL BREAKDOWN OF INTERNET HOSTS

West Asia .33% South Asia .16%
Oceania 4.41%   North Asia 3.02%
Africa .5%   South America 0.26%
Europe 21.72%
Central America .23%
North America 69.37%

Total numbers of Internet hosts: 2.2 million

The 'information highway' enables information of all kinds – textual, graphical, still and moving pictures – to be transformed into computer language and transmitted through communications channels, (telephone lines, fibre optics) to a personal computer. Internet is an open access computer network with over 20 million users. A host is an exchange point at which a networked group of users may access the Internet. Some 80 countries are connected to the Internet.

MAIN METHODS OF RECEPTION

⊘ DTH (direct to home)

▢ CATV (via cable)

▲ General satellite receivership limited or banned

CENTRAL ASIA ⊘▢

NORTH KOREA ▲

JAPAN ▢

IRAQ ▲   IRAN ▲

MIDDLE EAST ⊘▢

SAUDI ARABIA ▲

CHINA ▲

SOUTH ASIA ⊘▢

PACIFIC OCEAN

SOUTH EAST ASIA ⊘▢

MALAYSIA ▲

SINGAPORE ▲   INDONESIA ▲

INDIAN OCEAN

AUSTRALASIA ⊘▢

SUB-SAHARAN AFRICA ⊘

170,000 pages of text can be fitted on one CD-Rom.

NEW TECHNOLOGY

The use of computers and digital technology to store, manipulate and publish information is transforming global media. Multimedia publishing on CD-Rom and the transmission of data through fax, modem and electronic mail links (the Internet) has made a global network of information available to the private home. This technology will radically alter the way in which we communicate, learn and think.

SECURITY AND DEFENCE

THE POST-COLD WAR PERIOD has produced a range of threats to the principal states of the international community. Ethnic conflict within states, mass migration and environmental hazards provide examples of new insecurities with potential for conflict of a very different sort from its Cold War counterpart. The spectacle of Yugoslavia's collapse into warring factions and the break-up of the Soviet Union were the most dramatic examples of the decline of the state as a source of security for its citizens and as a pillar of world order. Today, while orthodox diplomacy still has its place, recognition of the inability of the state to cope alone makes multi-lateral solutions imperative.

GLOBAL DEFENCE AND CONFLICT

DEFENCE BUDGET AS A PERCENTAGE OF
GROSS DOMESTIC PRODUCT

- Less than 2%
- 2 - 2.9%
- 3 - 5.9%
- 6 - 15%
- More than 15%
- Civil unrest since 1975
- International conflict since 1975
- Nuclear weapons capacity
- UN peacekeeping operation since 1985

A US marine keeps Somalis under close observation on the streets of Mogadishu.

UN INTERVENTION

Western governments are reluctant to intervene in conflict in the developing world fearing the prospect of becoming entangled in a protracted war. The 15 members of the UN Security Council often have difficulty in reaching unilateral decisions and taking decisive action swiftly enough. In recent conflicts in Somalia, Yugoslavia and Rwanda, UN peace-keeping forces became embroiled in the bloodshed. Nevertheless, at the end of February 1994, no fewer than 74,767 UN personnel, both peace-keepers and observers, were stationed around the globe.

THE ARMS RACE

After World War II, international power was concentrated in the hands of two superpowers, the USA and USSR, and their military and economic allies. Potential all-out conflict was effectively contained by the nuclear deterrent. Today, the collapse of the Soviet Union and the diminishing economic and political power of the USA have led to fundamental changes in the power balance. The developing economies of Asia and the Middle East now have nuclear capability.

An array of weaponry is paraded through the streets of Moscow on the anniversary of the Bolshevik October revolution.

GULF CONFLICT

In 1990, Iraq's President Saddam Hussein invaded the small oil-rich nation of Kuwait. This event led to rare accord amongst members of the United Nations Security Council, and troops were sent to the Gulf. The ensuing war (1990-1991) is a prime example of successful military intervention by the UN. However, the political objective was clear and limited: to drive the Iraqis out of Kuwaiti territory – defending one state against aggression by another.

The oil wells of Kuwait blazed for many months after the Gulf conflict, causing enormous environmental damage.

RUSSIAN FEDERATION

KAZAKHSTAN

MONGOLIA

GEORGIA
ARM. AZERB.
KEY
TURKMENISTAN
UZBEKISTAN
KYRGYZSTAN
TAJIKISTAN

NORTH
KOREA
SOUTH
KOREA
JAPAN

SYRIA
IRAN
JORDAN
IRAQ
KUWAIT
AFGHANISTAN
PAKISTAN
NEPAL
BHUTAN

CHINA

PACIFIC

OCEAN

BAHRAIN
QATAR
UAE
SAUDI
ARABIA
OMAN
BANGLADESH
INDIA
BURMA
LAOS
TAIWAN

ERITREA
YEMEN
THAILAND
VIETNAM
CAMBODIA
PHILIPPINES

DJIBOUTI
ETHIOPIA
SOMALIA
MALDIVES
SRI LANKA
BRUNEI
MALAYSIA
SINGAPORE

KENYA
TANZANIA
SEYCHELLES

INDONESIA
PAPUA
NEW GUINEA
SOLOMON
IS

COMOROS
MALAWI
MADAGASCAR
INDIAN
OCEAN
FIJI
New Caledonia
(to France)

MOZAMBIQUE
MAURITIUS
AUSTRALIA

SWAZILAND
LOTHO
NEW ZEALAND

PACIFIC OCEAN
◯ KIRIBATI
◯ MICRONESIA
◯ NAURU
◯ SOLOMON ISLANDS
◯ TONGA
◯ VANUATU
◯ WESTERN SAMOA
◯ FIJI

MIDDLE EAST
◯ BAHRAIN

INDIAN OCEAN
◯ COMOROS
◯ MALDIVES
◯ MAURITIUS
◯ SEYCHELLES

ASIA
◯ SINGAPORE

GLOBAL TOURISM

TOURISM IS THE WORLD'S biggest industry. In 1990 there were 425 million tourists worldwide; this number is expected to rise to 937 million by 2010. With improved transport, cheaper flights and increased leisure time, many of the countries of the developing world are rapidly becoming tourist meccas. Since the 1960s, mass tourism has become increasingly specialized, encompassing sporting and adventure holidays as well as ecological tours. Although the tourist industry employs 127 million people worldwide, the benefits of tourism are not always felt at a local level, where jobs are often low paid and menial. Unregulated growth of tourism is causing both environmental and social damage.

THE GLOBAL TOURIST INDUSTRY

TOURIST ARRIVALS IN THOUSANDS

- Less than 700
- 700 - 999
- 1000 - 2499
- 2500 - 4999
- 5000 - 9999
- 10,000 - 20,000
- More than 20,000
- Negligible tourism

EUROPE
- LUXEMBOURG
- MALTA

CARIBBEAN
- BAHAMAS

Even in the remote Himalayas, rubbish discarded by trekkers and mountaineers pollutes the landscape.

ENVIRONMENTAL DAMAGE

The rapid and unregulated growth of tourism in even the most distant corners of the world has had a severe environmental impact. Influxes of tourists put extra pressure on already inadequate infrastructures: rubbish piles up in beauty spots; beaches are polluted by sewage; mangrove swamps are destroyed; coral reefs are degraded. Where limited water supplies are diverted for tourist use, fragile ecosystems can be disrupted.

GLOBAL
TOURISM

ANNUAL TOURIST EARNINGS

Eastern Europe 1.11%
Southern Europe 19.55%
Western Europe 32.29%
Middle East 1.52%
Pacific 0.84%
Africa 1.76%
Australasia 2.01%
N America 21.24%
Asia 13.33%
Central America & Caribbean 3.88%
S America 2.47%

While western and southern Europe dominate the mass tourist market, the biggest growth area is in the southern hemisphere.

A TOURIST PARADISE?

The most remote corners of the world are now being penetrated by tourists in their quest for the exotic. In many parts of the developing world, tourism can be described as a form of 'neo-colonialism'; hotels and beaches are owned by multinational companies, and most of the profits are taken outside the country. Tourism frequently alienates local people from their own land, and has a negative impact on the local culture and environment.

The beautiful island of Phuket, Thailand, is being overtaken by tourist developments.

Tourists travel to the distant Antarctic, where they observe its rich wildlife.

ECO-TOURISM

Countries such as Belize, with their spectacular rainforest, have become a popular destination for nature lovers, or eco-tourists. Strenuous attempts are being made to preserve the environment on which national economies which are promoting eco-tourism depend.

THE FINAL FRONTIERS

RESPECT FOR NATIONAL SOVEREIGNTY and the international recognition of national boundaries is a principle central to the United Nations Charter. Nevertheless, there are over 60 disputed borders or territories in the world today; while many of these can be settled by peaceful arbitration, some are sources of international conflict. Ownership of valuable natural resources is a common reason for such disputes, although ethnic concerns provide frequent bloody flashpoints. The legacy of colonial mapmakers, notably in Africa, where inadequate knowledge and political pragmatism led to many arbitrary borders, has caused problems, while territorial acquisitions in long-settled wars can sour international relations.

INTERNATIONAL TERRITORIAL DISPUTES

DISPUTED TERRITORIES & BORDERS

- Countries involved in active territorial or border disputes
- Disputed borders
- Undefined borders
- Disputed territories
- Disputed maritime areas

The South Pole, now the site of the underground Amundsen-Scott scientific research station.

INTERNATIONAL AGREEMENT

The Antarctic Treaty of 1959 was a unique instance of international accord, in which the territorial claims made by the UK, Norway, France, Australia, New Zealand, Chile and Argentina were suspended. The continent was made a demilitarized zone, and set aside for international co-operation in scientific research. This principle has been put forward as a criterion for shaping space exploration.

OCCUPIED TERRITORY

After its creation in 1948, Israel expanded its territory to include the West Bank and Gaza Strip (1967), Sinai (1956, 1967-82) and the Golan Heights (1967). Israel has sustained a programme of settlement and administrative control in these occupied territories, claiming that the West Bank at least was an integral part of biblical Israel.

An Israeli settlement under construction on the West Bank.

MILITARY BORDERS

The partition of Korea along the 38°N parallel following the war of 1950-53 led to the creation of one of the world's few remaining 'military' borders. While the border itself was declared a DMZ (demilitarized zone) and administered by United Nations forces, the areas immediately to the north and south of the border zone are heavily fortified and constantly patrolled by armed troops while propaganda messages are broadcast over the barbed wire.

The border between North and South Korea follows an arbitrary demarcation line along the 38°N parallel.

RUSSIAN FEDERATION

KAZAKHSTAN

GEORGIA
ARM. AZERB.
EY
KYRGYZSTAN
TAJIKISTAN
SYRIA
LEBANON
IRAQ
AFGHANISTAN
IRAN
JORDAN
KUWAIT
BAHRAIN
QATAR
UAE
SAUDI ARABIA
PAKISTAN
INDIA

CHINA

NORTH KOREA
SOUTH KOREA
JAPAN

BANGLADESH
TAIWAN

LAOS
THAILAND
VIETNAM
PHILIPPINES

PACIFIC OCEAN

ETHIOPIA
SOMALIA
KENYA
NZANIA

MALAYSIA

INDONESIA

VANUATU

New Caledonia (to France)

COMOROS
British Indian Ocean Territory
MALAWI
MADAGASCAR
MAURITIUS

INDIAN OCEAN

The isolated Chinese occupying force on one of the Spratly Islands.

TERRITORIAL CLAIMS

Ambitious territorial claims are often advanced when the presence of rich mineral deposits is suspected. The Spratly Islands in the South China Sea, the site of potential oil and natural gas reserves, have been claimed by China, Vietnam, Taiwan, Brunei, Malaysia and the Philippines since a wartime claim by the Japanese was relinquished in 1951. All claimants have posted garrisons to the islands.

4

INDEX~ GAZETTEER

INTERNATIONAL ORGANIZATIONS

THIS LISTING PROVIDES definitions for all international organizations referred to, often by acronym, in the Atlas. (All political parties are defined under the Politics heading within each national entry.)

The definitions are followed by the date of establishment or foundation, an indication of membership where appropriate and a summary of the organization's aims and functions.

ABEDA
Arab Bank for Economic Development in Africa
established 1974
members – 18 Arab nations; promotes economic development

ACC
Arab Co-operation Council
established 1989
members – Egypt, Iran, Jordan, Yemen; promotes Arab economic co-operation

ADB
Asian Development Bank
established 1966
members – 36 Asian-Pacific nations, 16 non-regional members; encourages regional development

AfDB
African Development Bank
established 1963
members – 50 African nations, 25 non-African nations; encourages African economic development

AFESD
Arab Fund for Economic and Social Development
established 1968
members – 21 Arab nations; promotes social and economic development in the Arab world

AG
Andean Group
established 1969
members – Bolivia, Colombia, Ecuador, Peru and Venezuela (Panama is an associate member); promotes development through integration

AL
Arab League
established 1945
members – 21 Arab nations; forum to promote Arabic co-operation on social, political and military issues

AMF
Arab Monetary Fund
established 1976
members – 19 nations plus the PLO; promotes monetary and economic co-operation

AMU
Arab Maghreb Union
established 1989
members – Algeria, Libya, Mauritania, Morocco, Tunisia; promotes integration and economic co-operation among North African Arab states

ANC
African National Congress (originally the South African Native National Congress)
established 1912; political movement whose primary aim was to establish black majority rule in South Africa. Now the largest party in South African Parliament

ANZUS
Australia–New Zealand–United States Security Treaty
established 1951; implements trilateral security agreement

APEC
Asia-Pacific Economic Co-operation
established 1989
members – 15 Pacific Rim nations; promotes regional co-operation

ASEAN
Association of South East Asian Nations
established 1967
members – Brunei, Indonesia, Malaysia, Singapore, Thailand; promotes economic, social and cultural co-operation in non-communist countries of South East Asia

BBC
British Broadcasting Corporation
established 1922, given Royal Charter 1927; largest news broadcaster in the world. Renowned for its World Service broadcasts

BCCI
Bank of Credit and Commerce International
established 1972; Luxembourg-based bank that collapsed in 1992

BCIE
Central American Bank for Economic Integration
established 1960
members – Costa Rica, El Salvador, Guatemala, Honduras, Nicaragua; promotes economic integration and development in Central America

BDEAC
Central African States Development Bank
established 1975
members – Cameroon, Central African Republic, Chad, Congo, Equatorial Guinea, France, Gabon, Germany, Kuwait; furthers economic development

Benelux
Benelux Economic Union
established 1958
members – Belgium, Luxembourg, Netherlands; develops economic ties between member nations

BSEC
Black Sea Economic Co-operation Zone
established 1922
members – Albania, Armenia, Azerbaijan, Bulgaria, Georgia, Greece, Moldavia, Romania, Russia, Turkey, Ukraine; furthers regional stability through economic co-operation

CACM
Central American Common Market
established 1960
members – Costa Rica, El Salvador, Guatemala, Honduras, Nicaragua; furthers economic ties between members

CAEU
Council of Arab Economic Unity
established 1957
members – 11 Arab nations plus the PLO; encourages economic integration

Caricom
Caribbean Community and Common Market
established 1973
members – 13 Caribbean nations; fosters economic ties in the Caribbean

CBSS
Council of the Baltic Sea States
established 1992
members – Denmark, Estonia, Finland, Germany, Latvia, Lithuania, Norway, Poland, Russia, Sweden; promotes co-operation among Baltic Sea states

CDB
Caribbean Development Bank
established 1969
members – 20 Caribbean nations, 5 non-Caribbean nations; regional development

CE
Council of Europe
established 1949
members – 29 European nations; promotes unity and quality of life in Europe

CEEAC
Economic Community of Central African States
established 1983
members – 11 Central African nations; promotes regional co-operation and aims to establish Central African common market

CEI
Central European Initiative
established 1991 (evolved from Hexagonal Group)
members – Austria, Bosnia & Herzegovina, Croatia, Czech Republic, Hungary, Italy, Poland, Slovakia, Slovenia, Yugoslavia; promotes economic and political co-operation

CG
Contadora Group *see* RG

CIA
Central Intelligence Agency
established 1944
Agency in USA responsible
for external security

CILSS
Permanent Inter-state
Committee for Drought
Control in the Sahel
established 1973
members – Burkina, Cape
Verde, Chad, Gambia,
Guinea-Bissau, Mali,
Mauritania, Niger, Senegal;
promotes prevention of
drought and crop failure in
Sahel region

CIS
Commonwealth of
Independent States
established 1991
members – Armenia,
Belorussia, Kazakhstan,
Kyrgyzstan, Moldavia,
Russia, Tajikistan,
Turkmenistan, Ukraine,
Uzbekistan; promotes
inter-state relationships

Comm
Commonwealth (evolved
from British Empire)
established 1931
members – 48 nations;
develops relationships and
contacts between members

CP
Colombo Plan
established 1951
members – 26 nations;
encourages economic and
social development in Asia-
Pacific region

CSCE
Conference on Security and
Co-operation in Europe
established 1972
members – 52 nations;
organization which attempts
to reduce tensions associated
with the Cold War

CNN
Cable News Network
established 1980; worldwide
satellite-broadcast 24-hour
TV news channel

EADB
East African Development
Bank
established 1967
members – Kenya, Tanzania,
Uganda; encourages
economic development

EBRD
European Bank for
Reconstruction and
Development
established 1991
members – 58 nations; helps
transition of former
communist European states
to market economies

EC
European Community
see EU

ECA
Economic Commission for
Africa
established 1958
members – 52 nations;
regional commission of UN's
Economic and Social Council

ECE
Economic Commission for
Europe
established 1947
members – 44 nations;
regional commission of UN's
Economic and Social Council

ECLAC
Economic Commission for
Latin America and the
Caribbean
established 1948
members – 41 nations,
including those from outside
Latin America; regional
commission of UN's
Economic and Social Council

ECOWAS
Economic Community of
West African States
established 1975
members – 17 nations;
promotes closer regional
economic co-operation

EEC
European Economic
Community *see* EU

EFTA
European Free Trade
Association
established 1960
members – Austria, Finland,
Iceland, Norway, Sweden,
Switzerland; promotes
economic co-operation

ESCAP
Economic and Social
Commission for Asia and
the Pacific
established 1947 (as
Economic Commission for
Asia and the Far East)
members – 46 nations;
regional commission of UN's
Economic and Social Council

ESCWA
Economic and Social
Commission for Western
Asia
established 1973 (as
Economic Commission for
Western Asia)
members – Bahrain, Egypt,
Iraq, Jordan, Kuwait,
Lebanon, Oman, Qatar,
Saudi Arabia, Syria, UAE,
Yemen, PLO; regional
commission of UN's
Economic and Social Council

EU
European Union
established 1965; formerly
known as EEC (European
Economic Community) and
EC (European Community)
members – Belgium,
Denmark, France, Germany,
Greece, Ireland, Italy,
Luxembourg, Netherlands,
Portugal, Spain, UK; Austria
to join Jan 1995; Finland,
Norway and Sweden will join
in 1995, subject to national
referenda; seeks to
establish integrated
European common market,
and eventual federation

FLS
Front Line States
established 1975
members – Angola,
Botswana, Mozambique,
Namibia, Tanzania, Zambia,
Zimbabwe; group whose aim
was to achieve black
majority rule in South Africa

GATT
General Agreement on
Tariffs and Trade
established 1947
members – 104 nations; aims
to establish international
free trade through
multilateral trade
agreements

GCC
Gulf Co-operation Council
established 1981
members – Bahrain, Kuwait,
Oman, Qatar, Saudi Arabia,
UAE; promotes co-operation
in economic, political and
military affairs

G7
Group of 7
established 1985
members – Canada, France,
Germany, Italy, Japan, UK,
US; organization of the seven
major Western powers

HG
Hexagonal Group *see* CEI

IAEA
International Atomic Energy
Agency
established 1956
members – 115 nations;
promotes and monitors
peaceful use of atomic
energy

IBRD
International Bank for
Reconstruction and
Development (also known
as the World Bank)
established 1945
members – 117 nations; UN
agency providing economic
development loans

ICJ
International Court of Justice
established 1945
15 judges; primary judicial
organ of UN. All major legal
systems are represented

IDA
International Development
Association
established 1960
members – 147 nations; UN
agency providing loans for
low-income countries

IDB
Islamic Development Bank
established 1973
members – 45 nations;
promotes Islamic social aid
and development

IGADD
Inter-Governmental
Authority on Drought and
Development
established 1986
members – Djibouti, Ethiopia,
Kenya, Somalia, Sudan,
Uganda; promotes
co-operation on drought-
related matters

IMF
International Monetary Fund
established 1944
members – 175 nations;
UN agency concerned with
world monetary stability and
economic development

IWC
International Whaling
Commission
established 1946
members – 40 nations;
reviews conduct of whaling
throughout world.
Co-ordinates and funds
whale research

IOC
Indian Ocean Commission
established 1982
members – Comoros, France, Madagascar, Mauritius, Seychelles; promotes regional co-operation

IOC
International Olympic Committee
established 1894
members – 168 nations; promotes Olympic ideals and administers the Olympic games

LAES
Latin American Economic System
established 1975
members – 26 Latin American nations; promotes economic and social development through regional co-operation

LAIA
Latin American Integration Association
established 1980
members – Argentina, Bolivia, Brazil, Chile, Colombia, Ecuador, Mexico, Paraguay, Peru, Uruguay, Venezuela; promotes free regional trade

MERCOSUR
Southern Cone Common Market
established 1991
members – Argentina, Brazil, Paraguay, Uruguay; promotes economic co-operation

NACC
North Atlantic Co-operation Council
established 1991
members – 38 nations; forum for co-operation on political and security issues

NAFTA
North American Free Trade Agreement;
established 1994
members – Canada, Mexico, USA; free-trade zone

NAM
Non-Aligned Movement
established 1961
members – 103 nations; fosters political and military co-operation away from traditional Eastern or Western blocs

NASA
National Aeronautics and Space Administration
established 1958;
US government body that develops manned and unmanned space programmes

NATO
North Atlantic Treaty Organization
established 1949
members – Belgium, Canada, Denmark, France, Germany, Greece, Iceland, Italy, Luxembourg, Netherlands, Norway, Portugal, Spain, Turkey, UK, USA; promotes mutual defence co-operation

NC
Nordic Council
established 1952
members – Denmark, Finland, Iceland, Norway, Sweden; promotes cultural and environmental co-operation in Scandinavia

OAPEC
Organization of Arab Petroleum Exporting Countries
established 1968
members – Algeria, Bahrain, Egypt, Iraq, Kuwait, Libya, Qatar, Saudi Arabia, Syria, Tunisia, UAE; organization dealing with petrol and oil pricing for Arab world

OAS
Organization of American States
established 1948
members – 35 nations; promotes security, economic and social development in the Americas

OAU
Organization of African Unity
established 1963
members – 52 African nations; promotes unity and co-operation

OECD
Organization for Economic Co-operation and Development
established 1961
members – 24 nations; forum for economic development

OECS
Organization of Eastern Caribbean States
established 1981
members – Antigua & Barbuda, Dominica, Grenada, Montserrat, St Kitts & Nevis, St Lucia, St Vincent & the Grenadines; promotes political, economic and defence co-operation

OIC
Organization of the Islamic Conference
established 1969
members – 48 nations; furthers Islamic solidarity and co-operation

Opanal
Agency for the Prohibition of Nuclear Weapons in Latin America and the Caribbean
established 1967
members – 26 nations; promotes peaceful use of atomic energy

OPEC
Organization of Petroleum Exporting Countries
established 1960
members – Algeria, Gabon, Indonesia, Iran, Iraq, Kuwait, Libya, Nigeria, Qatar, Saudi Arabia, UAE, Venezuela; cartel aiming to co-ordinate oil prices

PLO
Palestine Liberation Organization
established 1964; seeks to create an independent Palestinian state

RG
Rio Group
established 1948 (evolved from Contradora Group)
members – Argentina, Bolivia, Brazil, Chile, Colombia, Ecuador, Mexico, Paraguay, Peru, Uruguay, Venezuela; forum for Latin American issues

SAARC
South Asian Association for Regional Co-operation
established 1985
members – Bangladesh, Bhutan, Maldives, Nepal, Pakistan, Sri Lanka; encourages economic, social and cultural co-operation

SACU
Southern African Customs Union
established 1969
members – Bophuthatswana, Botswana, Ciskei, Lesotho, Namibia, South Africa, Swaziland, Transkei, Venda; to promote co-operation in trade and customs matters among southern African states and homelands

SADC
Southern African Development Community
established 1992
members – Angola, Botswana, Lesotho, Malawi, Mozambique, Namibia, Swaziland, Tanzania, Zambia, Zimbabwe; promotes economic integration

SPARTECA
South Pacific Regional Trade and Economic Co-operation Agreement
established 1981
members – 15 nations; aims to redress unequal trade relationship of Australia and New Zealand with Pacific island economies

SPC
South Pacific Commission
established 1948
members – 27 nations; promotes regional co-operation in economic and social matters

SPF
South Pacific Forum
established 1971
members – 15 nations; develops regional political co-operation

UN
United Nations
established 1945
members – 184 nations; all countries in the world represented except Kiribati, Nauru, Switzerland (Observer status only) Taiwan, Tonga, Tuvalu, Vatican City (Observer status only); aims to maintain international peace and security and to promote co-operation over economic, social, cultural and humanitarian problems

GEOGRAPHICAL PLACE NAMES

UNDP
United Nations Development Programme
established 1965
members – 48 nations; provides technical assistance for economic development

UNHCR
United Nations Office of the High Commissioner for Refugees
established 1951
members – 46 nations; encourages humane treatment of refugees

UNESCO
United Nations Scientific and Cultural Organization
established 1945
members – 172 nations; encourages co-operation in education, science and culture

UNSC
United Nations Security Council
established 1945
members – China, France, Russia, UK, USA; 10 non-permanent members for 2 year terms; seeks to maintain international peace and security

UNTAC
United Nations Transitional Authority in Cambodia
established 1992
members – 31 nations; founded by UNSC to aid setting up of elections and maintenance of peace in Cambodia

WCL
World Confederation of Labour
established 1924 (as International Federation of Christian Trade Unions)
members – 94 nations; promotes trade union movements internationally

WEU
Western European Union
established 1954
members – Belgium, France, Italy, Germany, Luxembourg, Netherlands, Portugal, Spain, UK; organization for mutual defence and political union

WHO
World Health Organization
established 1946
members – 180 nations; UN agency specializing in health matters

THE CHOICES confronting a mapmaker when deciding which placename style to use on a map are surprisingly varied. The criteria adopted may be affected by a range of factors: the existence of foreign and native language forms of a place name (London, Londres, Londra), variant spellings used within the country itself (Gent, Gand) and the existence of completely different language forms for international features (the English Channel, La Manche).

In addition to these, political expedience, simple clarity and the use to which the published map may be put are all factors that need consideration.

The revision of place-name forms and spellings, which is a continuing administrative activity worldwide, adds a further dimension of complexity to the subject. Since the collapse of Soviet communism, for instance, place names in Russia have been altered to expunge traces of communist ideology (the most famous being the 1991 reversion of Leningrad to its pre-1914 name, St Petersburg). In many former Soviet republics, Russian names have been replaced with native language forms (notably in Ukraine, Belorussia, Georgia and Armenia).

Standardized Arabic forms and spellings have been instituted throughout most of the Arab world, although in some of the former French North African colonies, such as Algeria, the adoption of standardized Arabic names has been hindered by the persistent use of French forms in practice.

THE MAPS

The maps in the Nations of the World section of the Atlas have used the most up-to-date reference sources available to provide local name forms and spellings, that is to say those used within the country. In an age when international travel, on holiday or on business, is commonplace, this criterion seems the most appropriate.

English conventional forms have been used for all international features (such as sea areas between countries, and cross-border mountain ranges); for all country names (the Index~Gazetteer provides local forms and spellings, while commonly used alternative names, such as Burma/Myanmar are also made clear in the national A-Z entry) and for all capital cities. The Index~Gazetteer provides a fully cross-referenced system that will guide the reader the short distance from the English conventional 'Florence' to the local 'Firenze', as used on the maps.

English conventional forms also appear on all the maps in The World Today and Global Issues. These maps have not been indexed, as all contemporary places featured are more usefully and accurately identified on the national maps.

THE INDEX~GAZETTEER

The Index~Gazetteer lists all names that appear on the maps in the Nations of the World section of the Atlas. Physical features are defined as such, as are countries and those administrative or regional names included on the maps; all other names are those of population centres. Location is given by page number, then country, and is narrowed down by positional reference as N(orth), S(outh), E(ast), W(est) or C(entral), or combinations of these as appropriate.

Following each main entry name are given: variant spellings of the name most commonly found; its previous name or names; and such foreign-language forms of the name as are pertinent to modern history since 1940. This is the cut-off date generally adopted, permitting the inclusion of all place-name changes made during or after the Second World War. Exceptionally, name changes made in Russia and other countries of the former Soviet Union before 1940 are given, since many old names in these countries are now being restored.

The following pages provide a glossary of foreign geographical terms (656–657) that occur in the main entry names, and a comprehensive glossary of abbreviations (658) used in the Index~Gazetteer and throughout the Atlas.

GLOSSARY OF GEOGRAPHICAL TERMS

THE GLOSSARY FOLLOWING lists all geographical terms occurring on the maps and in main-entry names in the Index~Gazetteer. These terms may precede, follow or be run together with the proper element of the name; where they precede it the term is reversed for indexing purposes - thus Poluostrov Yamal is indexed as Yamal, Poluostrov.

KEY
Geographical term *Language*, Term

A

Å *Danish, Norwegian*, River
Alpen *German*, Alps
Altiplanicie *Spanish*, Plateau
Älv(en) *Swedish*, River
Anse *French*, Bay
Archipiélago *Spanish*, Archipelago
Arcipelago *Italian*, Archipelago
Arquipélago *Portuguese*, Archipelago
Aukštuma *Lithuanian*, Upland

B

Bahía *Spanish*, Bay
Baía *Portuguese*, Bay
Baḥr *Arabic*, River
Baie *French*, Bay
Bandao *Chinese*, Peninsula
Batang *Malay*, Stream
-berg *Afrikaans, Norwegian*, Mountain
Birket *Arabic* , Lake
Boğazı *Turkish*, Lake
Bucht *German*, Bay
Bugten *Danish*, Bay
Buḥayrat *Arabic*, Lake, reservoir
Buḥeiret *Arabic*, Lake
Bukit *Malay*, Mountain
-bukta *Norwegian*, Bay
bukten *Swedish*, Bay
Burnu *Turkish*, Cape, point
Buuraha *Somali*, Mountains

C

Cabo *Portuguese*, Cape
Cap *French*, Cape
Cascada *Portuguese*, Waterfall
Cerro *Spanish*, Mountain
Chaîne *French*, Mountain range
Chau *Cantonese*, Island
Chāy *Turkish*, River
Chhâk *Cambodian*, Bay
Chhu *Tibetan*, River
-chŏsuji *Korean*, Reservoir
Chott *Arabic*, Salt lake, depression
Ch'ün-tao *Chinese*, Island group
Chuôr Phnum *Cambodian*, Mountains
Cordillera *Spanish*, Mountain range
Costa *Spanish*, Coast
Côte *French*, Coast
Cuchilla *Spanish*, Mountains

D

Dağı *Azerbaijani, Turkish*, Mountain
Dağları *Azerbaijani, Turkish*, Mountains
-dake *Japanese*, Peak
Danau *Indonesian*, Lake
Đao *Vietnamese*, Island
Daryā *Persian*, River
Daryācheh *Persian*, Lake
Dasht *Persian*, Plain, desert

Dawḥat *Arabic*, Bay
Dere *Turkish*, Stream
Dili *Azerbaijani*, Spit
-do *Korean*, Island
Dooxo *Somali*, Valley
Düzü *Azerbaijani*, Steppe
-dwīp *Bengali*, Island

E

Embalse *Spanish*, Reservoir
Erg *Arabic*, Dunes
Estany *Catalan*, Lake
Estrecho *Spanish*, Strait
-ey *Icelandic*, Island
Ezero *Bulgarian, Macedonian*, Lake

F

Fjord *Danish*, Fjord
-fjorden *Norwegian*, Fjord
-fjørdhur *Faeroese*, Fjord
Fleuve *French*, River
Fliegu *Maltese*, Channel
-fljór *Icelandic*, River

G

-gang *Korean*, River
Ganga *Nepali, Sinhala*, River
Gaoyuan *Chinese*, Plateau
-gawa *Japanese*, River
Gebel *Arabic*, Mountain
-gebirge *German*, Mountains
Ghubbat *Arabic*, Bay
Gjiri *Albanian*, Bay
Gol *Mongolian*, River
Golfe *French*, Gulf
Golfo *Italian, Spanish*, Gulf
Gora *Russian, Serbian*, Mountain
Gory *Russian*, Mountains
Guba *Russian*, Bay
Gunung *Malay*, Mountain

H

Ḥadd *Arabic*, Spit
-haehyŏp *Korean*, Strait
Haff *German*, Lagoon
Hai *Chinese*, Sea, bay
Ḥammādat *Arabic*, Plateau
Hāmūn *Persian*, Lake
Hawr *Arabic*, Lake
Hāyk' *Amharic*, Lake
He *Chinese*, River
Helodrano *Malagasy*, Bay
-hegység *Hungarian*, Mountain range
Hka *Burmese*, River
-ho *Korean*, Lake
Hô *Korean*, Reservoir
Ḥolot *Hebrew*, Dunes
Hora *Belorussian*, Mountain
Hrada *Belorussian*, Mountains, ridge
Hsi *Chinese*, River
Hu *Chinese*, Lake

I

Île(s) *French*, Island(s)
Ilha(s) *Portuguese*, Island(s)
Ilhéu(s) *Portuguese*, Islet(s)
Irmak *Turkish*, River
Isla(s) *Spanish*, Island(s)
Isola (Isole) *Italian*, Island(s)

J

Jabal *Arabic*, Mountain
Jāl *Arabic*, Ridge
-järvi *Finnish*, Lake
Jazīrat *Arabic*, Island
Jazīreh *Persian*, Island
Jebel *Arabic*, Mountain
Jezero *Serbo-Croatian*, Lake
Jiang *Chinese*, River
-joki *Finnish*, River
-jökull *Icelandic*, Glacier
Juzur *Arabic*, Islands

K

Kaikyō *Japanese*, Strait
-kaise *Lappish*, Mountain
Kali *Nepali*, River
Kalnas *Lithuanian*, Mountain
Kalns *Latvian*, Mountain
Kang *Chinese*, Harbour
Kangri *Tibetan*, Mountain(s)
Kaôh *Cambodian*, Island
Kapp *Norwegian*, Cape
Kavīr *Persian*, Desert
K'edi *Georgian*, Mountain range
Kediet *Arabic*, Mountain
Kepulauan *Indonesian, Malay*, Island group
Khalîg, Khalīj *Arabic*, Gulf
Khawr *Arabic*, Inlet
Khola *Nepali*, River
Khrebet *Russian*, Mountain range
Ko *Thai*, Island
Kolpos *Greek*, Bay
-kopf *German*, Peak
Körfäzi *Azerbaijani*, Bay
Körfezi *Turkish*, Bay
Kõrgustik *Estonian*, Upland
Koshi *Nepali*, River
Kowtal *Persian*, Pass
Kūh(hā) *Persian*, Mountain(s)
-kundo *Korean*, Island group
-kysten *Norwegian*, Coast
Kyun *Burmese*, Island

L

Laaq *Somali*, Watercourse
Lac *French*, Lake
Lacul *Romanian*, Lake
Lago *Italian, Portuguese, Spanish*, Lake
Laguna *Spanish*, Lagoon, Lake
Laht *Estonian*, Bay
Laut *Indonesian*, Sea
Lembalemba *Malagasy*, Plateau
Lerr *Armenian*, Mountain

Lerrnashght'a *Armenian*, Mountain range
Les *Czech*, Forest
Lich *Armenian*, Lake
Liqeni *Albanian*, Lake
Lumi *Albanian*, River
Lyman *Ukrainian*, Estuary

M

Mae Nam *Thai*, River
-mägi *Estonian*, Hill
Maja *Albanian*, Mountain
-man *Korean*, Bay
Marios *Lithuanian*, Lake
-meer *Dutch*, Lake
Melkosopochnik *Russian*, Plain
-meri *Estonian*, Sea
Mifraz *Hebrew*, Bay
Monkhafad *Arabic*, Depression
Mont(s) *French*, Mountain(s)
Monte *Italian, Portuguese*, Mountain
More *Russian*, Sea
Mörön *Mongolian*, River

N

Nagor'ye *Russian*, Upland
Nahal *Hebrew*, River
Nahr *Arabic*, River
Nam *Laotian*, River
Nehri *Turkish*, River
Nevado *Spanish*, Mountain (snow-capped)
Nisoi *Greek*, Islands
Nizmennost' *Russian*, Lowland, plain
Nosy *Malagasy*, Island
Nur *Mongolian*, Lake
Nuruu *Mongolian*, Mountains
Nuur *Mongolian*, Lake
Nyzovyna *Ukrainian*, Lowland, plain

O

Ostrov(a) *Russian*, Island(s)
Oued *Arabic*, Watercourse
-oy *Faeroese*, Island
-øy(a) *Norwegian*, Island
Oya *Sinhala*, River
Ozero *Russian, Ukrainian*, Lake

P

Passo *Italian*, Pass
Pegunungan *Indonesian, Malay*, Mountain range
Pelagos *Greek*, Sea
Penisola *Italian*, Peninsula
Peski *Russian*, Sands
Phanom *Thai*, Mountain
Phou *Laotian*, Mountain
Pi *Chinese*, Point
Pic *Catalan*, Peak
Pico *Portuguese, Spanish*, Peak
Pik *Russian*, Peak
Planalto *Portuguese*, Plateau
Planina, Planini *Bulgarian, Macedonian, Serbo-Croatian*, Mountain range
Ploskogor'ye *Russian*, Upland
Poluostrov *Russian*, Peninsula
Potamos *Greek*, River
Proliv *Russian*, Strait
Pulau *Indonesian, Malay*, Island
Pulu *Malay*, Island
Punta *Portuguese, Spanish*, Point

Q

Qã' *Arabic*, Depression
Qolleh *Persian*, Mountain

R

Raas *Somali*, Cape
-rags *Latvian*, Cape
Ramlat *Arabic*, Sands
Ra's *Arabic*, Cape, point, headland
Ravnina *Bulgarian, Russian*, Plain
Récif *French*, Reef
Represa (Rep.) *Spanish, Portuguese*, Reservoir
-rettō *Japanese*, Island chain
Riacho *Spanish*, Stream
Riban' *Malagasy*, Mountains
Rio *Portuguese*, River
Río *Spanish*, River
Riu *Catalan*, River
Rivier *Dutch*, River
Rivière *French*, River
Rowd *Pashtu*, River
Rūd *Persian*, River
Rudohorie *Slovak*, Mountains
Ruisseau *French*, Stream

S

Sabkhat *Arabic*, Salt marsh
Şaḥrā' *Arabic*, Desert
Samudra *Sinhala*, Reservoir
-san *Japanese, Korean*, Mountain
-sanchi *Japanese*, Mountains
-sanmaek *Korean*,
Sarīr *Arabic*, Desert
Sebkha, Sebkhet *Arabic*, Salt marsh, depression
See *German*, Lake
Selat *Indonesian*, Strait
-selkä *Finnish*, Ridge
Selseleh *Persian*, Mountain range
Serra *Portuguese*, Mountain
Serranía *Spanish*, Mountain
Sha'ïb *Arabic*, Watercourse
Shamo *Chinese*, Desert
Shan *Chinese*, Mountain(s)
Shan-mo *Chinese*, Mountain range
Shaṭṭ *Arabic*, Distributary
-shima *Japanese*, Island
Shiqqat *Arabic*, Depression
Shui-tao *Chinese*, Channel
Sierra *Spanish*, Mountains
Sơn *Vietnamese*, Mountain
Sông *Vietnamese*, River
-spitze *German*, Peak
Štít *Slovak*, Peak
Stoeng *Cambodian*, River
Stretto *Italian*, Strait
Su Anbarı *Azerbaijani*, Reservoir
Sungai *Indonesian, Malay*, River
Suu *Turkish*, River

T

Tal *Mongolian*, Plain
Tandavan' *Malagasy*, Mountain range
Tangorombohitr' *Malagasy*, Mountain massif
Tao *Chinese*, Island
Tassili *Berber*, Plateau, mountain
Tau *Russian*, Mountain(s)
Taungdan *Burmese*, Mountain range
Teluk *Indonesian, Malay*, Bay
Terara *Amharic*, Mountain
Tog *Somali*, Valley
Tônlé *Cambodian*, Lake
Top *Dutch*, Peak
-tunturi *Finnish*, Mountain
Tur'at *Arabic*, Channel

V

Väin *Estonian*, Strait
-vatn *Icelandic*, Lake
-vesi *Finnish*, Lake
Vinh *Vietnamese*, Bay
Vodokhranilishche (Vdkhr.) *Russian*, Reservoir
Vodoskhovyshche (Vdskh.) *Ukrainian*, Reservoir
Volcán *Spanish*, Volcano
Vozvyshennost' *Russian*, Upland, plateau
Vrh *Macedonian*, Peak
Vysochyna *Ukrainian*, Upland
Vysočina *Czech*, Upland

W

Waadi *Somali*, Watercourse
Wādī *Arabic*, Watercourse
Wāḥat, Wâhat *Arabic*, Oasis
Wald *German*, Forest
Wan *Chinese*, Bay
Wyżyna *Polish*, Upland

X

Xé *Laotian*, River

Y

Yarımadası *Azerbaijani*, Peninsula
Yazovir *Bulgarian*, Reservoir
Yoma *Burmese*, Mountains
Yü *Chinese*, Island

Z

Zaliv *Bulgarian, Russian*, Bay
Zatoka *Ukrainian*, Bay
Zemlya *Russian*, Bay

GLOSSARY OF ABBREVIATIONS

THIS GLOSSARY provides a comprehensive guide to the abbreviations used in this Atlas, and in the Index~Gazetteer.

A
abbrev. abbreviated
ABM anti-ballistic missile(s)
ACP African, Caribbean and Pacific countries
AD admin. Anno Domini
Afr. Afrikaans
Alb. Albanian
ALCM air launched Cruise missile(s)
Amh. Amharic
anc. ancient
APC armoured personnel carrier(s)
approx. approximately
Ar. Arabic
Arm. Armenian
ASSR Autonomous Soviet Socialist Republic
Aust. Australian
Az. Azerbaijani
Azerb. Azerbaijan

B
bbl billion barrels
Basq. Basque
BC before Christ
b/cd barrels per calendar day
b/d barrels per day
Bel. Belorussian
Ben. Bengali
Ber. Berber
B-H Bosnia-Herzegovina
bn billion (one thousand million)
BP British Petroleum
Bret. Breton
Brig Brigadier
Brit. British
Bul. Bulgarian
Bur. Burmese

C
C central
C. Cape
°C degrees (Centigrade)
Cam. Cambodian
Cant. Cantonese
Capt Captain
CAR Central African Republic
Cast. Castilian
Cat. Catalan
Chin. Chinese
CIS Commonwealth of Independent States
CITES Convention on International Trade in Endangered Species of wild flora and fauna
cm centimetre(s)
Cmdr Commander
Col Colonel
Cro. Croat
Cz. Czech
Czech Rep. Czech Republic

D E
Dan. Danish
dept. department
dev. development
Dom. Rep. Dominican Republic
Dr Doctor
Dut. Dutch
dwt dead weight tonnage
E east
EC see EU
EEC see EU
EEZ Exclusive Economic Zone
ECU European Currency Unit
EMS European Monetary System
Eng. English
est estimated
Est. Estonian
EU European Union (previously European Community [EC], European Economic Community [EEC])

F G
°F degrees Fahrenheit
Faer. Faeroese
Fij. Fijian
Fin. Finnish
Fr Father
Fr. French
Fris. Frisian
ft foot/feet
FYRM Former Yugoslav Republic of Macedonia
FZ Franc Zone
g gram(s)
Gael. Gaelic
Gal. Galician
GDP Gross Domestic Product (the total value of goods and services produced by a country excluding income from foreign countries)
Gen General
Geor. Georgian
Ger. German
Gk Greek
GNP Gross National Product (the total value of goods and services produced by a country)

H I
Heb. Hebrew
HEP hydroelectric power
HH His/Her Highness
Hind. Hindi
hist. historical
HM His/Her Majesty
HMS His/Her Majesty's ship
HRH His/Her Royal Highness
HSH His/Her Serene Highness
Hung. Hungarian
I. Island
ICBM intercontinental ballistic missile(s)
Icel. Icelandic
in inch(es)
In. Innuit (Eskimo)
Ind. Indonesian

Intl International
Intl International
Ir. Irish
IRBM intermediate-range ballistic missile(s)
Is Islands
It. Italian
ITTA International Tropical Timber Agreement

J K L
Jap. Japanese
Kaz. Kazakh
kg kilogram(s)
Kir. Kirghiz
km kilometre(s)
km² square kilometre (singular)
Kor. Korean
Kurd. Kurdish
kw kilowatt(s)
kwh kilowatt hour(s)
L. Lake
Lao. Laotian
Lapp. Lappish
Lat. Latin
Latv. Latvian
Liech. Liechtenstein
Lith. Lithuanian
LNG liquefied natural gas
Lt Lieutenant
Lux. Luxembourg

M N
m million/metre(s)
Mac. Macedonian
Maced. Macedonia
Maj Major
Mal. Malay
Malg. Malagasy
Malt. Maltese
mi. mile(s)
Mong. Mongolian
Mt. Mountain
Mts Mountains
N north
Nep. Nepali
Neth. Netherlands
NGO Non-Governmental Organization
NIC Newly Industrialized Country
Nic. Nicaraguan
Nor. Norwegian
NZ New Zealand

P Q R
Pash. Pashtu
PC personal computer
Per. Persian
PNG Papua New Guinea
Pol. Polish
Poly. Polynesian
Port. Portuguese
prev. previously
Rep. Represa (Spanish, Portuguese for reservoir)
Rep. Republic
Res. Reservoir
Rev Reverend
Rmsch. Romansch
Rom. Romanian

Rus. Russian
Rus. Russian
Russ. Fed. Russian Federation

S
S south
SALT Strategic Arms Limitation Treaty
SCr. Serbo-Croatian
Serb. Serbian
Sinh. Sinhala
SLBM submarine-launched ballistic missile(s)
Slvk. Slovak
Slvn. Slovene
Som. Somali
Sp. Spanish
sq. square
SSBN nuclear-fuelled ballistic-missile submarine(s)
SSM surface-to-surface missile(s)
St., St Saint
START Strategic Arms Reduction Treaty
Strs. Straits
Swa. Swahili
Swe. Swedish
Switz. Switzerland

T U
Taj. Tajik
Th. Thai
Thai. Thailand
Tib. Tibetan
Turk. Turkish
Turkm. Turkmenistan
TV television
UAE United Arab Emirates
Uigh. Uighur
UK United Kingdom
Ukr. Ukrainian
UN United Nations
UNCLOS United Nations Convention on the Law of the Sea
Urd. Urdu
US/USA United States of America
USS United States ship
USSR Union of Soviet Socialist Republics
Uzb. Uzbek

V W X Y
var. variant
VCR video cassette recorder
Vdkhr. Vodokhranilishche (Russian for reservoir)
Vdskh. Vodoskhovyshche (Ukrainian for reservoir)
Vtn. Vietnamese
W west
Wel. Welsh
Yugo. Yugoslavia

INDEX

A

Akau *624* island of NW Johnston Atoll
Akdogan *see* Lysi
Aken *see* Aachen
Akhalts'ikhe *234* SW Georgia
Akharnaí *see* Acharnés
Akhisar *546* W Turkey
Akhmīm *202* *var.* Akhmîm. E Egypt
Akhna *see* Athna
Akhuryan *74* NW Armenia
Akiéni *230* E Gabon
Akita *304* Honshū, N Japan
Akjoujt *366* *prev.* Fort-Repoux.
  W Mauritania
Akkaraipattu *504* E Sri Lanka
'Akko *291* *Eng.* Acre. N Israel
Akmola *312* *prev.* Akmolinsk,
  Tselinograd, *Kaz.* Aqmola.
  N Kazakhstan
Akobo *215* river of Ethiopia and
  Sudan
Akonolinga *144* S Cameroon
Akordat *210* *var.* Agordat. C Eritrea
Akosombo Dam *242* dam of SE Ghana
Akranes *268* W Iceland
Åkrehamn *191* SW Norway
Akron *569* Ohio, NE USA
Akrotiri *187* UK air base in S Cyprus
Akrotiri Bay *187* bay of the
  Mediterranean Sea, to the S of Cyprus
Aksai Chin *162, 270* disputed territory
  of China and India
Aksaray *547* C Turkey
Aksay *312* NW Kazakhstan
Åksum *215* N Ethiopia
Aktash *580* *var.* Aktaš, *Uzb.* Oqtosh.
  S Uzbekistan
Aktau *312* *prev.* Shevchenko,
  Kaz. Aqtaū. W Kazakhstan
Akti *245* peninsula of NE Greece
Aktyubinsk *312* *Kaz.* Aqtöbe.
  NW Kazakhstan
Akure *408* SW Nigeria
Akurenan *208* *var.* Acurenan. S Río
  Muni, Equatorial Guinea
Akureyri *268* N Iceland
Akyab *see* Sittwe
Alabama *569* state of SE USA
Alacant *see* Alicante
Alah *435* river of Mindanao,
  S Philippines
Al Aḥmadī *322* E Kuwait
Alaïli Daḍḍa' *194* N Djibouti
Alai Range *325* *Rus.* Alayskiy Khrebet.
  Mountain range of SW Kyrgyzstan
Alajuela *172* C Costa Rica
Alakol', Ozero *312* *Kaz.* Alaköl. Lake
  of E Kazakhstan
Al 'Āl *310* NW Jordan
Alalapadu *508* S Surinam
Alamagan *626* island of C Northern
  Mariana Islands
Al 'Amārah *284* *var.* Amara.
  E Iraq
Alamikamba *404* E Nicaragua
Åland *221* *Fin.* Ahvenanmaa. Island
  group of SW Finland
Alaotra, Farihy *350* *var.* Farihin
  Alaotra, Lac Alaotra. Lake of
  E Madagascar
Al 'Aqabah *310* *var.* Aqaba, Akaba.
  SW Jordan
Al Arish *see* El 'Arîsh
Al Ashkharah *418* NE Oman
Alaska *568* non-contiguous state
  of USA, NW North America
Alaska Range *568* mountain range of
  Alaska, USA, NW North America
Älät *86* *Rus.* Alyat, Aljat,
  prev. Alyaty-Pristan'. SE Azerbaijan
Alausí *200* C Ecuador
Alaverdi *74* N Armenia
Alayh *see* Aaley
Alaykel' *325* *var.* Alajku.
  SW Kyrgyzstan
Al 'Ayn *560* *var.* Al Ain. E United Arab
  Emirates
Alayskiy Khrebet *see* Alai Range
Alazani *234* river of Azerbaijan and
  Georgia
Al Azimiyah *322* N Kuwait

Al 'Azīzīyah *339* NW Libya
Albacete *501* C Spain
Al Baḥrah *322* NE Kuwait
Al Baḥr al Mayyit *see* Dead Sea
Al Baḥrayn *see* Bahrain
Alba Iulia *448* *Ger.* Karlsburg,
  prev. Weissenburg,
  Hung. Gyulafehérvár. W Romania
Albania *56-57* officially Republic of
  Albania, *prev.* People's Socialist
  Republic of Albania, *Alb.* Shqipni.
  Country of S Europe divided into 26
  admin. units. (districts)
Albany *76* SW Australia
Albany *147* river of S Canada
Albany *569* New York, NE USA
Al Başrah *284* *var.* Basra. SE Iraq
Al Bāṭinah *418* *var.* Batinah. Coastal
  region of Oman and United Arab
  Emirates
Al Batrūn *see* Batroûn
Al Baydā' *339* *var.* Beida. NE Libya
Al Baydā' *599* *var.* Al Beida.
  SW Yemen
Alberdi *428* S Paraguay
Alberta *146* province of W Canada
Albert Edward Nyanza *see* Edward,
  Lake
Albert, Lake *554, 607*
  var. Albert Nyanza, Lac Mobutu Sese
  Seko. Lake of Uganda and Zaire
Albert Nile *554* river of NW Uganda
Albertville *see* Kalemie
Albi *225* S France
Albina *508* NE Surinam
Al Biqā' *see* El Beqaa
Al Birk *472* SW Saudi Arabia
Ålborg *190* *var.* Aalborg. Jylland,
  N Denmark
Alborz, Reshteh-ye Kuhhā-ye *281*
  Eng. Elburz Mountains. Mountains of
  N Iran
Ålborg Bugt *190* bay to the N of
  Jylland, Denmark
Al Budayyi' *91* NW Bahrain
Albuquerque *568* New Mexico,
  SW USA
Al Buraymī *418* *var.* Al Buraimi,
  Buraimi. NW Oman
Al Buraymī *560* *var.* Buraimi. Oasis of
  Oman and United Arab Emirates
Al Burayqah *339*
  var. Marsá al Burayqah. N Libya
Albury *77* SE Australia
Al Busaytīn *91* Jazirat al Muharraq,
  Bahrain
Al Buşayyir *447* *var.* Al Busayer.
  NW Qatar
Al Buzūn *599* E Yemen
Alcácer do Sal *442* W Portugal
Alcalá de Henares *500* C Spain
Alcalde Díaz *424* C Panama
Alcamo *295* Sicilia, S Italy
Alcántara, Embalse de *501* reservoir
  of W Spain
Alcaudete *501* S Spain
Alchevs'k *516* *prev.* Kommunarsk,
  Voroshilovsk. E Ukraine
Aldabra Atoll *478* Atoll of the Aldabra
  Group, SW Seychelles
Aldabra Group *478* island group of
  SW Seychelles
Aldan *453* river of E Russia
Aldanskoye Nagor'ye *453*
  Eng. Aldan Plateau. Highland plateau
  of E Russia
Alderney *623* island of N Guernsey
Al Djem *see* El Jem
Aleg *366* SW Mauritania
Alejandro Selkirk, Isla *159* island of
  Juan Fernández Islands, W Chile
Aleksandriya *see* Oleksandriya
Aleksandropol' *see* Gyumri
Aleksandrovsk *see* Zaporizhzhya
Aleksandrovsk-Sakhalinskiy *453*
  SE Russia
Aleksinac *602* SE Serbia, Yugoslavia
Alençon *225* NW France
Alep *see* Ḥalab
Aleppo *see* Ḥalab

Alert *147* Ellesmere Island, N Canada
Alessandria *294* *Fr.* Alexandrie.
  N Italy
Ålesund *414* *var.* Aalesund.
  SW Norway
A-le-t'ai *see* Altay
Aleutian Islands *568* island group of
  Alaska, USA
Alexander Range *see* Kirghiz Range
Alexandra *401* SW South Island, New
  Zealand
Alexandretta *see* İskenderun
Alexandretta, Gulf of
  see İskenderun Körfezi
Alexandria *202* *Ar.* Al Iskandarīya,
  El Iskandarīyah. N Egypt
Alexandria *448* S Romania
Alexandrie *see* Alessandria
Alexandroúpoli *245* *Turk.* Dedeagaç,
  Dedeagach. NE Greece
Al Fallūjah *284* *var.* Falluja. C Iraq
Al Faq' *560* *var.* Al Faqa. E United
  Arab Emirates
Al Farḍah *599* C Yemen
Al Fāshir *see* El Fasher
Al Fayyūm *see* El Faiyûm
Alfeiós *245* *prev.* Alfiós. River of
  S Greece
Alföld *264* *Eng.* Great Hungarian
  Plain. Plain of SE Hungary
Al Fuḥayḥīl *322* *var.* Fahaheel.
  E Kuwait
Al Fujayrah *see* Fujairah
Al Fuqahā *339* C Libya
Al Fuwayriṭ *447* *var.* Fuwairet.
  NE Qatar
Alga *312* NW Kazakhstan
Algeciras *500* SW Spain
Algena *210* N Eritrea
Alger *see* Algiers
Algeria *58-61* officially Democratic
  and Popular Republic of Algeria.
  Country of N Africa divided into 48
  admin. units (wilayat)
Al Ghārīyah *447* *var.* Al Ghariyeh.
  NE Qatar
Al Gharrāfah *447* E Qatar
Al Ghaydah *599* E Yemen
Alghero *295* Sardegna, W Italy
Al Ghuwayrīyah *447* N Qatar
Algiers *59* *var.* El Djazaïr, *Fr.* Alger.
  ❖ of Algeria, N Algeria
Al Haba *560* NE United Arab Emirates
Al Ḥabbānīyah *284* C Iraq
Al Ḥadd *418* *var.* Ras al Hadd.
  NE Oman
Al Ḥadd *see* Al Ḥidd
Al Haggounia *382* N Western Sahara
Al Ḥajarah *284* desert of S Iraq
Al Ḥajar al Gharbī *560* mountain
  range of Oman and United Arab
  Emirates
Al Hajarayn *599* C Yemen
Al Hamalah *91* NW Bahrain
Al Ḥammādah al Ḥamrā *339* desert
  region of NW Libya
Al Ḥamrīyah *560* *var.* Hamriya.
  NE United Arab Emirates
Al Harūj al Aswad *339* desert region
  of C Libya
Al Hasahisa *see* El Hasaheisa
Al Ḥasakah *521* *var.* El Haseke,
  Fr. Hassetché. NE Syria
Al Ḥawrah *599* S Yemen
Al Ḥidd *91* *var.* Al Ḥadd. Jazirat al
  Muharraq, Bahrain
Al Ḥijāz *472* coastal and highland
  region of NW Saudi Arabia
Al Ḥillah *284* *var.* Hilla. C Iraq
Al Hindīyah *284* *var.* Hindiya.
  C Iraq
Al Hoceima *382* *var.* Al Hoceïma,
  Alhucemas, *prev.* Villa Sanjurjo.
  N Morocco
Alhucemas *see* Al Hoceima
Al Ḥudaydah *599* *Eng.* Hodeida.
  W Yemen
Al Ḥufūf *472* *var.* Hofuf. NE Saudi
  Arabia
Al Ḥuşayḥişah *see* El Hasaheisa

'Alī *91* NW Bahrain
'Ali 'Addé *194* SE Djibouti
Aliákmonas *245* *prev.* Aliákmon. River
  of NW Greece
'Alī al Gharbī *284* E Iraq
Äli-Bayramlı *86* *Rus.* Ali-Bayramly,
  var. Ali Bajramly. SE Azerbaijan
Alibori *108* river of N Benin
Alicante *501* *Cat.* Alacant. SE Spain
Alice Springs *77* C Australia
Alima *176* river of C Congo
Alindao *154* S Central African
  Republic
Ali Qunayţirah *521* *var.* El Quneitra,
  Kuneitra. SW Syria
'Ali Sabieh *194* S Djibouti
A-li Shan-mo *525* mountain range of
  C Taiwan
Al Iskandarīya *see* Alexandria
Al Ismā'īlīyah *see* Ismā'ilîya
Al Ittiḥād *see* Madīnat ash Sha'b
Aliwal North *493* *Afr.* Aliwal-Noord.
  Eastern Cape, C South Africa
Al Jabal al Akhḍar *339* mountain
  range of NE Libya
Al Jabal al Akhḍar *418*
  var. Jabal Akhdar. Mountain range of
  NW Oman
Al Jabal ash Sharqi *see* Anti-Lebanon
Al Jafr *310* SW Jordan
Al Jaghbūb *339* NE Libya
Al Jahrah *322* *var.* Jahra, Al Jahrā'.
  C Kuwait
Al Jamīl *see* Al Jumayl
Al Jamm *see* El Jem
Al Jasrah *91* NW Bahrain
Aljat *see* Älät
Al Jawārah *418* E Oman
Al Jawf *472* *var.* Jauf. N Saudi Arabia
Al Jazīrah *284* physical region of Iraq
  and Syria
Al Jifārah *see* Jeffara
Al Jīzah *see* El Gîza
Al Jubayl *472* *var.* Al Jubail. NE Saudi
  Arabia
Al Jufayr *91* *var.* Al Juffair.
  NE Bahrain
Al Jumayl *339* *var.* Al Jamīl.
  NW Libya
Al Jumaylīyah *447* N Qatar
Al Junaynah *see* Geneina
Al Ka'aban *see* Madīnat al Ka'bān
Al Kahlil *see* Hebron
Al Kāmil *418* NE Oman
Al Karak *310* W Jordan
Al Khabb *560* E United Arab Emirates
Al Khābūrah *418* *var.* Khabura.
  N Oman
Al Khalīj al 'Arabī *see* Persian Gulf
Al Khāliş *284* C Iraq
Al Khaluf *see* Khalūf
Al Khārijah *see* El Khârga
Al Khārijīyah *91* NE Bahrain
Al Kharrārah *447* S Qatar
Al Khaşab *418* *var.* Khasab.
  Musandam Peninsula, N Oman
Al Khatt *560* *var.* Khatt. NE United
  Arab Emirates
Al Khaṭṭ *382* seasonal river of
  N Western Sahara
Al Khawr *447* *var.* Al Khaur, Al Khor.
  NE Qatar
Al Khīrān *322* SE Kuwait
Al Khubar *472* *var.* Al-Khobar.
  NE Saudi Arabia
Al Khums *339* *var.* Khoms, Homs.
  N Libya
Al Khuraybah *599* C Yemen
Al Khurţum *see* Khartoum
Al Khuwayr *447* *var.* Al Khuwair.
  N Qatar
Al Kir'ānah *447* *var.* Kharanah.
  SW Qatar
Alkmaar *397* NW Netherlands
Al Kūfah *284* S Iraq
Al Kufrah *339* *It.* Cufra. Oasis of
  SE Libya
Al Kūt *284* *var.* Kūt al 'Amārah,
  Kut al Imara. E Iraq
Al Kuwayt *see* Kuwait City

Allada *108* S Benin
Al Lādhiqīyah *521 Eng.* Latakia. W Syria
Allahābād *270* NE India
Allanmyo *135* W Burma
'Allâqi, Wâdi el *202 var.* Wādī al 'Allāqi. Dry watercourse of SE Egypt
All Awash Island *466* island of E St Vincent & the Grenadines
Allenstein *see* Olsztyn
Allentown *569* Pennsylvania, NE USA
Al Liwā' *560* oasis region of SW United Arab Emirates
All Saints *68* C Antigua, Antigua & Barbuda
Al Lubnān *see* Lebanon
Al Luḥayyah *599* W Yemen
Al Ma'āmīr *91* NE Bahrain
'Alma-Ata *312 Rus./Kaz.* Almaty. ❖ of Kazakhstan, SE Kazakhstan
Almada *442* W Portugal
Al Madīnah *472 Eng.* Medina. W Saudi Arabia
Al Mafraq *310 var.* Mafraq. N Jordan
Al Mahdīyah *see* Mahdia
Al Maḥmūdīyah *284 var.* Mahmudiya. C Iraq
Al Mahrah *599* mountains of E Yemen
Al Majma'ah *472* C Saudi Arabia
Al Mālikīyah *91* W Bahrain
Al Mālikīyah *521 var.* Dayrīk. NE Syria
Almalyk *580 Uzb.* Olmaliq. E Uzbekistan
Al Mamlakah *see* Morocco
Al Manādir *560 var.* Al Manadir. Desert region of Oman and United Arab Emirates
Al Manāmah *see* Manama
Al Manāṣif *521* mountains of E Syria
Al Manṣūrah *see* El Manṣûra
Al Maqta' *560* C United Arab Emirates
Al Marj *339 var.* Barka, *It.* Barce. NE Libya
Al Marsá *see* La Marsa
Almaty *see* Alma-Ata
Al Mawṣil *284 Eng.* Mosul. N Iraq
Al Mayādīn *521 Fr.* Meyadine. E Syria
Al Mazra' *310 var.* Al Mazra'ah. W Jordan
Almelo *397* E Netherlands
Almendra, Embalse de *501* reservoir of NW Spain
Almere *397* C Netherlands
Almería *501* S Spain
Al Mīnā' *see* El Mina
Al Minyā *see* El Minya
Al Miqdādīyah *see* Al Muqdādīyah
Almirante *424* W Panama
Al Mubarraz *472* NE Saudi Arabia
Al Mudawwarah *310* SW Jordan
Al Muḥammadīyah *91 var.* Umm aş Şabbān. Island of NW Bahrain
Al Muḥarraq *91 var.* Moharek, Muharraq, Jazirat al Muharraq. Bahrain
Al Mukallā *599 var.* Mukalla. SE Yemen
Al Mukhā *599 Eng.* Mocha. SW Yemen
Al Muknīn *see* Moknine
Al Munastīr *see* Monastir
Al Muqdādīyah *284 var.* Al Miqdādīyah. C Iraq
Al Mussayyib *284* C Iraq
Al Obayyid *see* El Obeid
Alofi *626* ❖ of Niue, W Niue
Alofi, Île *629* island of Île Futuna, N Wallis & Futuna
Alohungari *233* E Gambia
Alor, Kepulauan *276* island group of E Indonesia
Alor, Pulau *276* island of E Indonesia
Alor Setar *354 var.* Alur Setar, Alor Star. NW Peninsular Malaysia
Alost *see* Aalst
Alotau *426* SE Papua New Guinea
Aloupos *187 var.* Al 'Amārah. River of NW Cyprus
Alpen *see* Alps
Alpes *see* Alps

Alphen aan de Rijn *397* W Netherlands
Alphonse Group *478* island group of C Seychelles
Alpi *see* Alps
Alps *82, 225, 294, 516 It.* Alpi, *Fr.* Alpes, *Ger.* Alpen. Mountain range of C Europe
Al Qābil *418 var.* Qabil. NW Oman
Al Qaḍārif *see* Gedaref
Al Qāhirah *see* Cairo
Al Qal'ah al Kubrá *see* Kalaa Kebira
Al Qāmishlī *521 var.* Kamishli. NE Syria
Al Qaryah *91* NE Bahrain
Al Qaryāt *339* NW Libya
Al Qaṣr *310* W Jordan
Al-Qaşrayn *see* Kasserine
Al Qayrawān *see* Kairouan
Al Qubayyāt *see* Qoubaiyat
Al Qubbah *339* NE Libya
Al Quds *see* Jerusalem
Al Quṣayr *521 var.* El Quseir, *Fr.* Kousseir. W Syria
Al Quṭayfah *521 var.* Quṭayfah, Quteife, *Fr.* Kouteifé. SW Syria
Al Quwayrah *310 var.* Makhfar al Quwayrah, El Quweira. SW Jordan
Als *190 Ger.* Alsen. Island of S Denmark
Alsace *255* cultural region of NE France
Alsen *see* Als
Alt *see* Olt
Alta *414* NE Norway
Altai Mountains *380* mountain range of C Asia
Altay *162 Chin.* A-le-t'ai, *prev.* Ch'eng-hua, *var.* Chenghwa, *Mong.* Sharasume. Xinjiang Uygur Zizhiqu, NW China
Altay *380* W Mongolia
Altay, Respublika *453* autonomous republic of C Russia
Alt de la Coma Pedrosa, Pic *62* mountain of NW Andorra
Altkanischa *see* Kanjiža
Alto Molócuè *387* C Mozambique
Alto Paraná *see* Paraná
Alt-Schwanenburg *see* Gulbene
Altsohl *see* Zvolen
Altun Shan *162 var.* Altyn Tagh. Mountain range of Xinjiang Uygur Zizhiqu, NW China
Altyn Tagh *see* Altun Shan
Alu *see* Shortland Island
Al Ubayyiḍ *see* El Obeid
Al 'Udayd *560 var.* Al Odaid. W United Arab Emirates
Alūksne *330 Ger.* Marienburg. NE Latvia
Al 'Ulá *472* NW Saudi Arabia
Al 'Umarī *310* C Jordan
Al Uqṣur *see* Luxor
Al Wafrā' *322* SE Kuwait
Al Wāḥāt al Khārijah *see* El Wâhât el Khârga
Al Wajh *472* NW Saudi Arabia
Al Wakrah *447 var.* Wakra. E Qatar
Al Wukayr *447 var.* Al Wukair. E Qatar
Alyat *see* Älät
Alyaty-Pristan' *see* Älät
Alytus *344 Pol.* Olita. S Lithuania
Al Zubair *see* Az Zubayr
Amadora *442* W Portugal
Amakusa-shotō *304* island group to the W of Kyūshū, SW Japan
Amala *316* river of SW Kenya
Amami-Ō-shima *304* island of Amami-shotō, SW Japan
Amami-shotō *304* island group of Nansei-shotō, SW Japan
Amara *see* Al 'Amārah
Amarapura *135* C Burma
Amasia *74 Rus.* Amasiya, *var.* Amasija. NW Armenia

Amasya *547* N Turkey
Amatique, Bahía de, *250* bay of the Gulf of Honduras
Amaury *368* NE Mauritius
Amazon *121, 171, 431 Sp.* Amazonas. River of South America
Amazonia *120* physical region of C South America
Ambalangoda *504* SW Sri Lanka
Ambalavao *350* S Madagascar
Ambam *144* S Cameroon
Ambanja *350* N Madagascar
Ambato *200* C Ecuador
Ambatondrazaka *350* E Madagascar
Ambergris Cay *102* island of NE Belize
Ambergris Cays *629* island group of S Turks and Caicos Islands
Ambilobe *350* N Madagascar
Amblève *99* river of E Belgium
Ambo *see* Hāgere Hiywet
Amboasary *350* S Madagascar
Ambohidratrimo *350* C Madagascar
Ambon *276 prev.* Amboina. Ambon, C Indonesia
Ambositra *350* C Madagascar
Ambre, Ile d' *368* Island of NE Mauritius
Ambriz *64* NW Angola
Ambrym *585 var.* Ambrim. Island of E Vanuatu
'Amd *599* C Yemen
Ameland *397* island of Waddeneilanden, N Netherlands
American Samoa *618* unincorporated territory of the USA, Pacific Ocean.
Amersfoort *397* C Netherlands
Amherst *see* Kyaikkami
Amiens *225* N France
Amilḥayt, Wādī *418 var.* Wādī Umm al Ḥayt. Seasonal watercourse of SW Oman
Amindivi Islands *270* island group of Lakshadweep, SW India
Amioun *332 var.* Amyūn. N Lebanon
Amirante Islands *478 var.* Amirantes Group. Island of C Seychelles
Amlamé *537* C Togo
Amman *310 Ar.* 'Ammān. ❖ of Jordan, NW Jordan
Ammochostos *see* Gazimağusa
Ammochostos Bay *see* Famagusta Bay
Amnok *see* Yalu
Āmol *281 var.* Amul. N Iran
Amorgós *245* island of SE Greece
Amouli *618 var.* Tau. Tau, E American Samoa
Amourj *366* SE Mauritania
Ampara *504* E Sri Lanka
Amphitrite Group *627* island group of N Paracel Islands
'Amrān *599* W Yemen
Amrāvati *270 prev.* Amraoti. C India
Amritsar *270* N India
Amstelveen *397* W Netherlands
Amsterdam *397* ❖ of the Netherlands, C Netherlands
Amstetten *82* N Austria
Am Timan *156* SE Chad
Amu Darya *53, 528, 550, 580 Turkm.* Amyderya, *Uzb.* Amudaryo. River of C Asia
Amudat *554* E Uganda
Amul *see* Āmol
Amund Ringnes Island *146* island of Sverdrup Islands, N Canada
Amundsen Gulf *146* gulf of the Beaufort Sea, on the NW coast of Canada
Amundsen-Scott *66* US research station at the South Pole, Greater Antarctica, Antarctica
Amundsen Sea *66* sea of the Pacific Ocean, off Antarctica
Amur *163, 453 Chin.* Heilong Jiang. River of China and Russia
Amyderya *see* Amu Darya
Amyūn *see* Amioun
An Abhainn Mhór *see* Blackwater
Anaco *589* NE Venezuela

Anadolu Dağları *see* Doğu Karadeniz Dağlari
Anadyr, Gulf of *see* Anadyrskiy Zaliv
Anadyrskiy Zaliv *453 Eng.* Gulf of Anadyr. Gulf of Bering Sea, bordering NE Russia
Anáfi *245* island of SE Greece
Anaiza *see* 'Unayzah
Analalava *350* N Madagascar
Analamaitsa Plateau *350* plateau of NE Madagascar
Anambas, Kepulauan *276* island group to the NW of Borneo, W Indonesia
Anan *304* Shikoku, SW Japan
Anantapur *270* S India
Anápolis *121* S Brazil
Anarjokka *see* Inarijoki
Anatahan *626* island of C Northern Mariana Islands
Anatolia Plateau *546* plateau of C Turkey
Anatom *585 var.* Aneityum, *prev.* Kéamu. Island of S Vanuatu
An Bhearú *see* Barrow
An Bhóinn *see* Boyne
Anchorage *568* Alaska, USA
Ancona *295* C Italy
Andalucia *500-501* autonomous community of S Spain
Andaman Islands *270* island group of SE India
Andaman Sea *135, 276, 533* sea of Indian Ocean, to the SW of Burma and Thailand
'Andām, Wadi *418* seasonal desert watercourse of E Oman
Andapa *350* NE Madagascar
Andaung Pech *see* Bâ Kêv
Andenne *99* SE Belgium
Anderson Air Force Base *623* NE Guam
Andes *71, 112, 159, 171, 200, 431* mountain range of South America, running the entire length of the west coast
Andfjorden *414* fjord of NE Norway
Andijon *see* Andizhan
Andikíthira *245* island of S Greece
Andipsara *245* island of E Greece
Andizhan *580 var.* Andižan, *Uzb.* Andijon. E Uzbekistan
Andkhvoy *53* N Afghanistan
Andoany *350 prev.* Hell-Ville. N Madagascar
Andong *496 Jap.* Antō. E South Korea
Andong-ho *496* reservoir of E South Korea
Andorra *62-63* officially Principality of Andorra. Country of SW Europe divided into 7 admin. units (parishes)
Andorra la Vella *62* ❖ of Andorra, W Andorra
Andreas *623* N Isle of Man
Andreas, Cape *see* Apostolos Andreas, Cape
Andria *295* S Italy
Androna, Lembalemba Ambanin' *350 var.* Plateau de l'Androna. Plateau of N Madagascar
Ándros *245* island of SE Greece
Andros Island *88* island of W Bahamas
Andros Town *88* Andros Island, Bahamas
Andújar *501* SW Spain
Anegada *619* island of NE British Virgin Islands
Aného *537 var.* Anécho, *prev.* Petit-Popo. S Togo
Aneityum *see* Anatom
Ānew *see* Annau
An Fheoir *see* Nore
Anfile Bay *210* bay of the Red Sea to the E of Eritrea
Angara *453* river of C Russia
Angarsk *453* C Russia
Angaur *627* island of S Palau
Ånge *513* C Sweden

Arkansas *569* river of SC USA
Arkansas *569* state of SC USA
Arkhangel'sk *452* *Eng.* Archangel. NW Russia
Arklow *288* *Ir.* Inbhear Mór. E Ireland
Arles *225* SE France
Arlon *99* *Dut.* Aarlen, *Ger.* Arel. SE Belgium
Armagh *563* Northern Ireland, UK
Armathia *245* island of SE Greece
Armenia *171* W Colombia
Armenia *74-75* officially Republic of Armenia *prev.* Armenian Soviet Socialist Republic. Country of SW Asia divided into 39 admin. units (shrjaner)
Armidale *77* E Australia
Arnaouti, Cape *187* cape of W Cyprus
Arnhem *397* SE Netherlands
Arnhem Land *77* region of N Australia
Arno *294* river C of Italy
Arno *364* island of SE Marshall Islands
Aroab *391* SE Namibia
Aroe Islands *see* Aru, Kepulauan
Arop Island *426* *var.* Long I. Island of E Papua New Guinea
Arorae *320* island of the Gilbert Is, W Kiribati
Arp'a *74* river of Armenia and Azerbaijan
Arqalyk *see* Arkalyk
Ar Rahad *see* Er Rahad
Arraiján *424* C Panama
Arrak District *364* district of Majuro, SE Marshall Islands
Ar Ramādī *284* C Iraq
Ar Rams *560* NE United Arab Emirates
Ar Ramthā *310* N Jordan
Arran, Isle of *563* island of W Scotland, UK
Ar Raqqah *521* *Fr.* Rakka. N Syria
Arras *225* N France
Ar Rawḍah *599* S Yemen
Ar Rawḍatayn *322* N Kuwait
Ar Rayyān *447* *var.* Al Rayyan. E Qatar
Ar Rifā' al Gharbī *91* N Bahrain
Ar Rifā' ash Sharqī *91* NE Bahrain
Ar Riyāḍ *see* Riyadh
Ar Riyān *599* S Yemen
Arrö *see* Ærø
Ar Ru'ays *447* *var.* Ar Ruways, Al Ruweis, Ruwais. N Qatar
Ar Ru'ays *560* *var.* Ruwaisv, Ar Ruways, Ar Ruways. United Arab Emirates
Ar Rufayq *447* *var.* Al Rufaig. NW Qatar
Ar Rustāq *418* *var.* Rostak. N Oman
Ar Ruwayshid *310* NE Jordan
Ar Safad *see* Zefat
'Arta *194* SE Djibouti
Artashat *74* *var.* Artašat. S Armenia
Artemisa *182* NW Cuba
Artëm-Ostrov *see* Artyom
Artibonite *258* river of Haiti
Artigas *577* *prev.* San Eugenio, *var.* San Eugenio del Cuareim. N Uruguay
Art'ik *74* W Armenia
Art, Île *626* island of Îles Belep, W New Caledonia
Artois *225* cultural region of N France
Artsvashen *74* *var.* Bashkend. NE Armenia
Artvin *547* NE Turkey
Artyom *86* *Rus.* Artëm-Ostrov. E Azerbaijan
Arua *554* NW Uganda
Aruângua *see* Luangwa
Aruba *618* autonomous part of the Netherlands, Caribbean Sea
Aru, Kepulauan *276-277* *prev.* Aroe Islands. Island group to the SW of Irian Jaya, W Indonesia
Aruliho *488* NW Guadalcanal, Solomon Is
Årup *190* Fyn, SW Denmark
Arusha *530* N Tanzania

Aruwimi *607* river of NE Zaire
Arvand Rūd *see* 'Arab, Shaṭṭ al
Arvayheer *380* C Mongolia
Arvika *513* SW Sweden
Aryānah *see* Ariana
Asadābād *53* E Afghanistan
Asad, Buḥayrat al *521* reservoir of Syria
Asahi-dake *305* mountain of Hokkaidō, N Japan
Asahikawa *305* Hokkaidō, N Japan
Asamankese *242* SE Ghana
Asawa *596* Savai'i, Western Samoa
Āsbe Teferī *215* *var.* Asba Tafari. C Ethiopia
Ascension *628* dependent territory of St Helena, South Atlantic Ocean
Ascension *see* Pohnpei
Ascoli Piceno *295* C Italy
Aseb *see* Assab
'As 'Êla *194* SW Djibouti
Āsela *215* *var.* Aselle, Asella, Asselle. C Ethiopia
Asenovgrad *128* S Bulgaria
Aseri *212* *Ger.* Asserin. NE Estonia
Ashburton *401* C South Island, New Zealand
Ashdod *291* C Israel
Ashford *563* SE England, UK
Ashgabat *551* *prev.* Ashkhabad, Poltoratsk. ❖ of Turkmenistan, S Turkmenistan
Ashikaga *304* Honshū, SE Japan
Ashkhabad *see* Ashgabat
Ashmyany *104* NW Belorussia
Ashots'k *74* *prev.* Ghukasyan, *Rus.* Gukasyan. NW Armenia
Ashqelon *291* C Israel
Ash Shadādah *521* *var.* Ash Shaddādah, Shaddādī, Shedadi, Tell Shedadi. NE Syria
Ash Shahāniyah *447* *var.* Al Shahaniyah. C Qatar
Ash Shāmīyah *284* C Iraq
Ash Sharāh *310* *var.* Esh Sharā. Mountains of W Jordan
Ash Shaṭrah *284* SE Iraq
Ash Shawbak *310* *var.* Ash Shawbak an Nijil. W Jordan
Ash Shiḥr *599* SE Yemen
Ash Shişar *418* SW Oman
Ash Shuqayq *322* *var.* As Shageeg. Desert region of S Kuwait
Ashtarak *74* *var.* Aštarak. W Armenia
Ashton *466* Union I, St Vincent & the Grenadines
Asidonhopo *508* C Surinam
'Asi, Nahr al *see* Orantes
'Asi Oronte, Nahr al *see* Orantes
Asipovichy *104* *Rus.* Osipovichi. C Belorussia
'Askar *91* E Bahrain
Asmara *210* *Amh.* Asmera. ❖ of Eritrea, C Eritrea
Aspinwall *see* Colón
Aspropotamos *see* Acheloos
Assab *210* *Amh.* Aseb. SE Eritrea
Aş Şabirīyah *322* NE Kuwait
Aş Şabīyah *322* *var.* Sabyah. NE Kuwait
As Sabkhah *521* *var.* Sabkha. NE Syria
Aş Şafāwī *310* N Jordan
Aş Şafī *310* *var.* Safi. W Jordan
'Assa Gaïla *194* S Djibouti
As Sahlat al Ḥadrīyah *91* N Bahrain
Aş Şaḥrā' *see* Sahara
Aş Şaḥrā' al Gharbīyah *see* Sahara el Gharqīya
Aş Şaḥrā' al Lībīyah *see* Libyan Desert
Aş Şaḥrā' ash Sharqīyah *see* Sahara el Sharqīya
Assake *see* Leninsk
As Salimi *322* *var.* Salemy. W Kuwait
As Salīmīyah *322* E Kuwait
'Assal, Lac *194* lake of C Djibouti
As Salṭ *310* *var.* Salt. NW Jordan
As Salwá *447* *var.* Salwah, Salwa. SW Qatar

Assamaka *407* *var.* Assamakka. NW Niger
As Samāwah *284* *var.* Samawa. S Iraq
'Assâmo *194* S Djibouti
Aş Şarīḥ *310* NW Jordan
Assen *397* NE Netherlands
Asserin *see* Aseri
As Shageeg *see* Ash Shuqayq
As Sīb *418* N Oman
Assiout *see* Asyut
Assling *see* Jesenice
Assomption *478* island of the Aldabra Group, SW Seychelles
Aş Şubayḥīyah *322* S Kuwait
Aş Şufāl *599* S Yemen
As Sukhnah *521* *var.* Sukhne, *Fr.* Soukhné. C Syria
As Sulaymānīyah *284* *var.* Sulaimaniya, *Kurd.* Slēmānī. NE Iraq
As Sulayyil *472* C Saudi Arabia
As Suwaydā' *521* *var.* El Suweida, *Fr.* Soueida. SW Syria
As Suwayq *418* *var.* Suwaik. N Oman
As Suways *see* Suez
Astara *86* S Azerbaijan
Aštarak *see* Ashtarak
Asti *294* N Italy
Astipálaia *245* island of SE Greece
Astove *478* island of the Aldabra Group, SW Seychelles
Astrakhan' *452* SW Russia
Astrakhan-Bazar *see* Cälilabad
Astrida *see* Butare
Asturias *500* autonomous community of NW Spain
Asuisui, Cape *596* cape on the coast of Savai'i, Western Samoa
Asuncion *626* island of N Northern Mariana Islands
Asunción *428* ❖ of Paraguay, S Paraguay
Asunción Mita *250* SE Guatemala
Aswa *see* Achwa
Aswân *202* *var.* Aswān. SE Egypt
Aswân High Dam *202* dam of SE Egypt
Asyut *202* *var.* Assiout. C Egypt
Ata *538* island of SW Tonga
Atacama Desert *159* desert of N Chile
Atafu Atoll *629* island of NW Tokelau
Atakora, Chaîne de l' *108* *var.* Atakora Mountains. Mountain range of N Benin
Atakpamé *537* C Togo
Aṭār *366* C Mauritania
Atas, Pulu *see* South Island
Atbara *506* C Sudan *var.* Nahr 'Aṭbarah. River of NE Sudan
Atbara *506* *var.* 'Aṭbārah. NE Sudan
'Aṭbarah, Nahr *see* Atbara
Atbasar *312* N Kazakhstan
At-Bashy *325* *var.* At-Bashi, At-Baši. C Kyrgyzstan
Athabasca *146* *var.* Athabaska. River of W Canada
Athabasca, Lake *146* lake of W Canada
Athabaska *see* Athabasca
Athens *245* *Gk* Athína, *prev.* Athínai. ❖ of Greece, SE mainland Greece
Athi *316* river of S Kenya
Athienou *187* SE Cyprus
Athína *see* Athens
Athínai *see* Athens
Athlone *288* *Ir.* Áth Luain. C Ireland
Áth Luain *see* Athlone
Athna *187* *var.* Achna, Akhna, *Turk.* Düzce. E Cyprus
Ati *156* C Chad
Atiak *554* NW Uganda
Atitlán, Lago de *250* lake of W Guatemala
Atiu *620* island of Southern Cook Islands, S Cook Islands
Atlanta *569* Georgia, SE USA
Atlantic Ocean *66, 268, 563, 619* *var.* Atlantshaf. Ocean bounded to the W by the Americas, to the E by Europe and Africa and to the S by Antarctica

Atlantshaf *see* Atlantic Ocean
Atlas Mountains *382* mountain range of C Morocco
Atlas Saharien *59* mountain range of N Algeria
Atrak *281, 551* *Rus.* Atrek, *Turkm.* Etrek. River of Iran and Turkmenistan
Atrato *171* river of NW Colombia
Atrek *see* Atrak
Aṭ Ṭaff *560* desert region of C United Arab Emirates
Aṭ Ṭafīlah *310* W Jordan
Aṭ Ṭā'if *472* W Saudi Arabia
At Tall al Abyaḍ *521* *Fr.* Tell Abaid. N Syria
Attapu *327* *var.* Attopeu. SE Laos
Attersee *82* *var.* Kammersee. Lake of N Austria
At Tibnī *521* NE Syria
Attopeu *see* Attapu
At Turbah *599* SW Yemen
Atyrau *312* *prev.* Gur'yev. W Kazakhstan
Auch *225* SW France
Auckland *401* N North Island, New Zealand
Augier *465* S St Lucia
Augila *see* Awjilah
Augsburg *237* S Germany
Augusta *295* Sicilia, S Italy
Augusta *569* Maine, NE USA
'Aujā et Tahtā *292* E West Bank
Auki *488* NW Malaita, Solomon Is
Auliye-Ata *see* Zhambyl
Aur *364* island of E Marshall Islands
Aurich *236* NW Germany
Aurillac *225* S France
Aurine, Alpi *see* Zillertaler Alpen
Aurora *256* NW Guyana
Aurora *see* Maéwo
Aus *391* SW Namibia
Aussig *see* Ústí nad Labem
Austin *569* Texas, SC USA
Australes, Îles *622* island group of SW French Polynesia
Australia *76-81* officially Commonwealth of Australia. Country situated between the Indian and Pacific Oceans, divided into 8 admin. units (6 states and 2 territories)
Australian Alps *77* mountain range of SE Australia
Australian Capital Territory *77* territory of SE Australia
Austria *82-85* officially Republic of Austria, *Ger.* Österreich. Country of C Europe divided into 9 admin. units (states)
Ausuitoq *see* Grise Fiord
Auvergne *225* cultural region of SE France
Auxerre *225* N France
Avarua *620* ❖ of Cook Islands, Rarotonga, S Cook Islands
Avatele *626* S Niue
Avatele *626* S Niue
Aveiro *442* W Portugal
Avellino *295* S Italy
Aves, Islas les *589* island group of N Venezuela
Aveyron *225* river of S France
Avezzano *295* C Italy
Avignon *225* SE France
Avila *501* C Spain
Avilés *500* NW Spain
Avranches *224* NW France
Avuavu *488* SE Guadalcanal, Solomon Is
Awaaso *242* *var.* Awaso. SW Ghana
'Awāli *91* C Bahrain
Awara Plain *316* plain of NE Kenya
Awash *215* *var.* Hawash. River of C Ethiopia
Awbārī *339* W Libya
Awbārī, Şaḥrā' *339* desert of W Libya
Awjilah *339* *It.* Augila. NE Libya
Awled Djellal *see* Ouled Djellal
Axarfjördhur *see* Öxarfjördhur
Axel Heiberg Island *146* *var.* Axel Heiburg. Island of Sverdrup Islands, N Canada

Betsiboka *350* river of C Madagascar
Bette *339* *Fr.* Pic Bette, *It.* Picco Bette. Mountain peak of Chad and Libya
Bettembourg *346* S Luxembourg
Beuthen *see* Bytom
Beveren *99* N Belgium
Beverwijk *397* W Netherlands
Bexon *465* C St Lucia
Beyla *253* SE Guinea
Beylul *210* SE Eritrea
Beyneu *312* W Kazakhstan
Beyrouth *see* Beirut
Béziers *225* S France
Bezmein *see* Byuzmeyin
Bezwada *see* Vijayawāda
Bhāgalpur *271* NE India
Bhairab Bāzār *93* *var.* Bhairab. C Bangladesh
Bhairahawa *395* C Nepal
Bhaktapur *395* C Nepal
Bhamdoun *332* *var.* Bḥamdūn. C Lebanon
Bhamo *135* *var.* Banmo. N Burma
Bhangtar *110* SE Bhutan
Bharat *see* India
Bhawalpur *see* Bahāwalpur
Bheanntrai, Bá *see* Bantry Bay
Bheri *395* river of W Nepal
Bhimphedi *395* C Nepal
Bhojpur *395* E Nepal
Bhōpal *270* C India
Bhunya *510* *var.* Bunya. W Swaziland
Bhutan *110-111* officially Kingdom of Bhutan. Country of S Asia divided into 18 admin. units (districts)
Biabou *466* E St Vincent, St Vincent & the Grenadines
Biafra, Bight of *208, 408* *var.* Bight of Bonny. Bay of the Gulf of Guinea, on the coast of W Africa
Biak, Pulau *277* island to the NW of Irian Jaya, E Indonesia
Białystok *439* *Rus.* Belostok. E Poland
Biankouma *300* W Ivory Coast
Biarritz *224* SW France
Bibane, Bahiret el *543* lagoon of the Mediterranean Sea on the E coast of Tunisia
Bida *408* C Nigeria
Biel *516* *Fr.* Bienne. W Switzerland
Bielefeld *236* NW Germany
Bieler See *516* *Fr.* Lac de Bienne. Lake of W Switzerland
Bielitz-Biala *see* Bielsko-Biała
Biella *294* N Italy
Bielsko-Biała *439* *Ger.* Bielitz-Biala. S Poland
Biên Đông *see* South China Sea
Biên Hoa *593* S Vietnam
Bienne, Lac de *see* Bieler See
Bienvenue *621* SE French Guiana
Bíe, Planalto do *64* *var.* Bié Plateau. Plateau of C Angola
Bié Plateau *see* Planalto do Bíe
Big Bay *585* bay of the Pacific Ocean, off Espiritu Santo, C Vanuatu
Big Bend *510* SE Swaziland
Bigene *254* NW Guinea-Bissau
Bight, The *88* Cat I, Bahamas
Bignona *476* SW Senegal
Bihać *116* NW Bosnia & Herzegovina
Bijagós, Arquipélago dos *254* *var.* Bijagos Archipelago. Island group of W Guinea-Bissau
Bijeljina *116* NE Bosnia & Herzegovina
Bijelo Polje *602* E Montenegro, Yugoslavia
Bikaner *270* NW India
Bikar *364* island of N Marshall Islands
Bikini *364* island of NW Marshall Islands
Bilād Manaḥ *see* Manaḥ
Bilāspur *270* NE India
Biläsuvar *86* *Rus.* Bilyasuvar, *prev.* Pushkino, *var.* Puškino. S Azerbaijan
Bila Tserkva *556* *Rus.* Belaya Tserkov'. NW Ukraine

Bilauktaung Range *135, 533* *var.* Thanintari Taungdan. Mountain range of Burma and Thailand
Bilbao *501* *var.* Bilbo. N Spain
Bilbeis *202* *var.* Belbeis, Bilbays. N Egypt
Bilecik *546* NW Turkey
Biliran Island *435* island of E Philippines
Bilisht *57* *var.* Bilishti. SE Albania
Billings *568* Montana, NW USA
Billiton *see* Belitung, Pulau
Bilo Gora *181* mountains of N Croatia
Biloku *256* S Guyana
Biloxi *569* Mississippi, SE USA
Biltine *156* E Chad
Bilwi *see* Puerto Cabezas
Bilyasuvar *see* Biläsuvar
Bimbo *154* SW Central African Republic
Bimini Islands *88* *var.* Biminis. Island group of N Bahamas
Biminis *see* Bimini Islands
Binche *99* SW Belgium
Bindura *612* NE Zimbabwe
Binga, Monte *387* mountain of C Mozambique
Bingerville *300* SE Ivory Coast
Bin Ghalfān, Jazā'ir *see* Ḩalānīyāt, Juzur al
Bin Ghanīmah, Jabal *339* *var.* Jabal Bin Ghunaymah. Mountain range of C Libya
Bin Ghashīr *339* NW Libya
Bingol *547* E Turkey
Binkolo *480* C Sierra Leone
Bintang *233* river of Gambia and Senegal
Bintang *233* SW Gambia
Bintimani *480* mountain of NE Sierra Leone
Bint Jubayl *see* Bent Jbaïl
Bintulu *354* W Borneo, Malaysia
Bío Bío *593* river of C Chile
Bioko *144, 208* *prev.* Macías Nguema Biyogo, *Eng.* Fernando Po, *Sp.* Fernando Póo. Island of NW Equatorial Guinea
Birāk *339* W Libya
Birambo *460* W Rwanda
Birao *154* N Central African Republic
Biratnagar *395* E Nepal
Birch Grove *248* C Grenada island, Grenada
Bird Island *see* Vaches, Île aux
Bird Island *248* island to the NE of Grenada island, Grenada
Bird of Paradise Island *see* Little Tobago
Birdsville *77* C Australia
Birendranagar *395* *var.* Surkhet. W Nepal
Birgu *see* Vittoriosa
Birkenhead *563* NW England, UK
Birket Qârûn *202* *var.* Birkat Qārūn. N Egypt
Birkirkara *363* C Malta
Birmingham *563* C England, UK
Birmingham *569* Alabama, SE USA
Bîr Mogreïn *366* *var.* Bir Moghrein, *prev.* Fort-Trinquet. N Mauritania
Birnie Island *320* island of the Phoenix Is, C Kiribati
Birni-Ngaouré *407* SW Niger
Birni-Nkonni *407* SW Niger
Birsen *see* Biržai
Biruni *see* Beruni
Biržai *344* *Ger.* Birsen. NE Lithuania
Birżebbuġa *363* SE Malta
Biscay, Bay of *224, 501* *Fr.* Golfe de Gascogne, *Sp.* Golfo de Vizcaya. Bay of the Atlantic Ocean between W France and N Spain
Biscoftu *see* Debre Zeyit
Bishah, Wādī *472* dry watercourse of SW Saudi Arabia
Bishkek *325* *prev.* Frunze, Pishpek. ❖ of Kyrgyzstan, N Kyrgyzstan

Bishoftu *see* Debre Zeyit
Bishrī, Jabal *521* mountains of C Syria
Bisina, Lake *554* *prev.* Lake Salisbury. Lake of E Uganda
Biskra *59* *var.* Beskra. NE Algeria
Bismarck *569* North Dakota, NC USA
Bismarck Archipelago *426* island group of NE Papua New Guinea
Bismarck Sea *426* sea of the Pacific Ocean to the NE of Papua New Guinea
Bissagos Islands *see* Bijagós, Arquipélago dos
Bissau *254* ❖ of Guinea-Bissau, W Guinea-Bissau
Bissídiro *194* N Djibouti
Bissorã *254* W Guinea-Bissau
Bistriţa *448* *Ger.* Bistritz, *Hung.* Beszterce, *prev.* Nösen. N Romania
Bitagron *508* NW Surinam
Bitam *230* N Gabon
Bitlis *547* SE Turkey
Bitola *349* *prev.* Bitolj, *Turk.* Monastir. S FYR Macedonia
Bitter Lakes *202* lakes of NE Egypt
Biu *409* E Nigeria
Biumba *see* Byumba
Biwa-ko *304* lake of Honshū, C Japan
Biyagundi *210* SW Eritrea
Bizerte *543* *Eng.* Bizerta, *Ar.* Banzart. N Tunisia
Bizerte, Lac de *543* *Eng.* Lake Bizerta, *Ar.* Buḩayrat Banzart. Lake of N Tunisia
Bjala Slatina *see* Byala Slatina
Bjelovar *181* *Hung.* Belovár. N Croatia
Bjeshkët e Nemuna *see* North Albanian Alps
Björneborg *see* Pori
Blackburn *563* N England, UK
Black Drin *see* Drinit të Zi
Black Forest *236* *Ger.* Schwarzwald. Forested mountain range of SW Germany
Blackpool *563* NW England, UK
Black River *593* *var.* Sông Đa, *Chin.* Babian Jiang, *Fr.* Rivière Noire. River of China and Vietnam
Black River *303* SW Jamaica
Black Rock *97* W Barbados
Black Rocks *76* NW Australia
Black Sea *128, 546, 556* *Bul.* Cherno More, *Rom.* Marea Neagră, *Rus.* Chernoye More, *Turk.* Karadeniz, *Ukr.* Chorne More, *Eng.* Euxine Sea. Area of the Mediterranean Sea between W Asia and E Europe
Black Umbeluzi *see* Mubuluzi
Black Volta *132, 242, 300* *Fr.* Volta Noire, *var.* Borongo, Moun Hou. River of Ghana and Ivory Coast
Blackwater *288* *Ir.* An Abhainn Mhór. River of S Ireland
Blagoevgrad *128* *prev.* Gorna Dzhumaya. W Bulgaria
Blagoveshchensk *453* SE Russia
Blama *480* S Sierra Leone
Blanca, Bahía *71* bay of the Atlantic Ocean, to the E of Argentina
Blanca, Costa *501* coastal region of SE Spain
Blanchard *465* SE St Lucia
Blanchisseuse *540* N Trinidad, Trinidad & Tobago
Blanquilla, Isla *589* island of N Venezuela
Blantyre *353* SW Malawi
Blenheim *401* NE South Island, New Zealand
Blenheim Reef *619* reef of the Indian Ocean, N British Indian Ocean Territory
Bleus, Monts *607* mountains of Uganda and Zaire
Blida *59* *var.* El Boulaida. N Algeria

Bligh Water *218* area of water to the N of Viti Levu, N Fiji
Blitta *537* C Togo
Bloemfontein *493* Judicial capital of South Africa, Orange Free State, C South Africa
Blois *225* NW France
Blöndúos *268* N Iceland
Blowing Point Village *618* SE Anguilla
Bludenz *82* W Austria
Bluefields *404* SE Nicaragua
Blue Hill *628* W St Helena
Blue Hills *629* Providenciales, NW Turks and Caicos Islands
Blue Mountain Peak *303* mountain of E Jamaica
Blue Nile *215, 506* *var.* Bahr el Azraq, *Ar.* An Nīl al Azraq, *Amh.* Abay Wenz, *var.* Abai. River of Ethiopia and Sudan
Blumenau *121* S Brazil
Bo *480* S Sierra Leone
Boaco *404* C Nicaragua
Boa Esperança, Represa *121* NE Brazil
Boajibu *480* C Sierra Leone
Boali *154* SW Central African Republic
Boa Vista *120* NW Brazil
Boa Vista *152* island of E Cape Verde
Bobigny *225* N France
Bobo-Dioulasso *132* SW Burkina
Bobonong *118* E Botswana
Bobotov Kuk *602* mountain of SE Montenegro, Yugoslavia
Bobruysk *see* Babruysk
Boca de la Serpiente *see* Serpent's Mouth, The
Boca de Yuma *198* SE Dominican Republic
Bocage *465* NW St Lucia
Bocas del Dragón *see* Dragon's Mouths, The
Bocas del Toro *424* W Panama
Bochum *236* W Germany
Bococo *208* SW Bioko, Equatorial Guinea
Bocono *589* W Venezuela
Boda *154* SW Central African Republic
Bodaybo *453* E Russia
Boddam Island *619* island of N British Indian Ocean Territory
Bodden Town *620* Grand Cayman, W Cayman Islands
Bodegas *see* Babahoyo
Bodensee *see* Constance, Lake
Bodø *414* NE Norway
Bodrum *546* SW Turkey
Bodza *see* Buzău
Boé *254* *var.* Madina do Boé. SE Guinea-Bissau
Boende *607* NW Zaire
Boeroe *see* Buru
Boetica *196* SE Dominica
Boetoeng *see* Butung, Pulau
Boffa *253* W Guinea
Bogale *135* S Burma
Bogal, Lagh *316* *var.* Lak Boggal. Dry watercourse of N Kenya
Bogandé *132* C Burkina
Bogarfjördhur *268* E Iceland
Bogdanovka *see* Ninotsminda
Boggy Peak *68* mountain SW of Antigua, Antigua & Barbuda
Boghotu *see* Santa Isabel
Bogor *276* *Dut.* Buitenzorg. Java, C Indonesia
Bogotá *171* ❖ of Colombia, C Colombia
Bogra *93* N Bangladesh
Bogué *366* SW Mauritania
Bo Hai *163* *var.* Gulf of Chihli. Gulf of Yellow Sea, off NE China
Bohemia *188* historical and cultural region, W Czech Republic
Bohemian Forest *188, 237* *Ger.* Böhmerwald, *Cz.* Česky Les, Šumava. Forested mountain range of Czech Republic and Germany

Bohemian-Moravian Highlands
see Českomoravská Vysočina
Bohicon *108* S Benin
Böhmisch-Mährische Höhe
see Českomoravská Vysočina
Bohol *435* island of C Philippines
Bohol Sea *435* *var.* Mindanao Sea. Sea of the Pacific Ocean
Boise *568* Idaho, NW USA
Bois, Lac des Woods, Lake of the
Bois-le-Duc *see* 's-Hertogenbosch
Boji Plain *316* plain of E Kenya
Bokak *364* island of N Marshall Islands
Boké *253* W Guinea
Bo Kheo *see* Bâ Kêv
Bokhol Plain *316* plain of NE Kenya
Bokiba *see* Lengoué
Boknafjorden *414* fjord of SW Norway
Boko *176* S Congo
Boksburg *493* Pretoria-Witwatersrand-Vereeniging, NE South Africa
Bol *156* W Chad
Bolama *254* SW Guinea-Bissau
Bolama, Ilha de *254* island of Arquipélago dos Bijagós, SW Guinea-Bissau
Bolanos *623* mountain peak of S Guam
Bolans *68* SW Antigua, Antigua & Barbuda
Bolgatanga *242* N Ghana
Bolívar, Pico *589* mountain peak of the Cordillera de Mérida, W Venezuela
Bolivia *112-115* officially Republic of Bolivia. Country of South America divided into 9 admin. units (departments)
Bolligen *516* W Switzerland
Bologna *295* N Italy
Bolondo *208* W Río Muni, Equatorial Guinea
Bol'shevik, Ostrov *453* island of Severnaya Zemlya, N Russia
Bol'shoy Kavkaz *see* Greater Caucasus
Bol'shoy Lyakhovskiy, Ostrov *453* island of Novosibirskiye Ostrova, N Russia
Bolsón de Mapimí *370* mountain range of N Mexico
Bolton *563* N England, UK
Bolu *546* NW Turkey
Bolungarvík *268* NW Iceland
Bolzano *295* *Ger.* Bozen. N Italy
Boma *607* W Zaire
Bomassa *176* NW Congo
Bombay *270, 275* *Hind.* Mumbai. W India
Bomberai, Jazirah *276* peninsula of Irian Jaya, E Indonesia
Bombo *554* S Uganda
Bombom, Ilha *471* island to the N of Príncipe, Sao Tome & Principe
Bomi *336* W Liberia
Bomu *154, 607* *Fr.* Mbomou, *var.* M'Bomu, Mbomu. River of Central African Republic and Zaire
Bonaire *626* island of S Netherlands Antilles
Bonaire *589* island of the Netherland Antilles, Caribbean Sea
Bonao *198* C Dominican Republic
Bonaparte Archipelago *76* island group of NW Australia
Bondoukou *300* E Ivory Coast
Bône *see* Annaba
Bone, Teluk *276* bay of Laut Flores on the S coast of Celebes, E Indonesia
Bonga *215* SW Ethiopia
Bongolava *350* mountains of W Madagascar
Bongo, Massif des *154* *var.* Chaîne des Mongos. Mountainous region of Central African Republic
Bongor *156* SW Chad
Bongouanou *300* E Ivory Coast
Bongoville *230* E Gabon

Bon Grara, Golfe de *543* inlet of the Gulf of Gabès on the E coast of Tunisia
Bonifacio, Strait of *225* *Fr.* Bouches de Bonifacio, *It.* Bocche di Bonifacio. Strait of the Mediterranean Sea between the islands of Corse, France and Sardegna, Italy
Bonn *236* W Germany
Bonny, Bight of *see* Biafra, Bight of
Bonriki *320* Tarawa, W Kiribati
Bonthe *480* Sherbro I, Sierra Leone
Boosaaso *490* *var.* Bosaso, Bender Qaasim, *It.* Bender Cassim. N Somalia
Boothia Felix *see* Boothia Peninsula
Boothia, Gulf of *146* gulf of the Arctic Ocean between the Boothia Peninsula and Melville Peninsula, N Canada
Boothia Peninsula *146* *prev.* Boothia Felix. Peninsula of N Canada
Booué *230* NE Gabon
Bophuthatswana Bantustan 'self-governing homeland' comprising 8 non-contiguous territories of NC South Africa; created in 1977, abolished in 1994
Bopolu *336* NW Liberia
Boquete *424* *var.* Bajo Boquete. W Panama
Boraha, Nosy *see* Sainte Marie, Nosy
Borås *513* SW Sweden
Borborema, Planalto da *121* plateau of NE Brazil
Bordeaux *225* SW France
Borden Peninsula *147* peninsula of Baffin Island, N Canada
Bordergate *510* NE Swaziland
Bordhoy *620* *var.* Bordø. Island of NE Faeroe Islands
Bordj Bou Arreridj *59* N Algeria
Borgarnes *268* W Iceland
Borgholm *513* Öland, S Sweden
Borgo Maggiore *468* NW San Marino
Borikhan *327* *var.* Borikhane. C Laos
Borisov *see* Barysaw
Bor, Lagh *316* *var.* Lak Bor. Dry watercourse of NE Kenya
Borlänge *513* C Sweden
Borneo *276, 354-355* island of SE Asia divided between Brunei, two Malaysian states and part of Indonesia
Bornholm *190* island of E Denmark
Boromo *132* SW Burkina
Borongo *see* Black Volta
Borovo *181* NE Croatia
Borujerd *281* *var.* Burujird. W Iran
Börzsöny *264* mountain range of N Hungary
Bosanska Gradiška *116* N Bosnia & Herzegovina
Bosanski Brod *116* N Bosnia & Herzegovina
Bosanski Šamac *116* N Bosnia & Herzegovina
Boscobelle *97* NE Barbados
Bösing *see* Pezinok
Boskamp *508* N Surinam
Boskovice *128* SE Czech Republic
Bosna *116* river of N Bosnia & Herzegovina
Bosnia & Herzegovina *116-117* officially Republic of Bosnia and Herzegovina. Country of SE Europe
Bosporus *see* İstanbul Boğazı
Bossangoa *154* C Central African Republic
Bossembélé *154* C Central African Republic
Boston *569* Massachusetts, NE USA
Boteti *118* *var.* Botletle. River of C Botswana
Botevgrad *181* *prev.* Orkhanie, Orkhaniye. W Bulgaria
Bothnia, Gulf of *221, 513* *Fin.* Pohjanlahti, *Swe.* Bottniska Viken. Gulf of the Baltic Sea, between Finland and Sweden

Boti-Pasi *508* C Surinam
Botna *376* river of E Moldavia
Botoşani *448* NE Romania
Botrange *99* mountain of E Belgium
Botswana *118-119* officially Republic of Botswana. Country of southern Africa divided into 10 admin. units (districts)
Bottle Creek *629* North Caicos, N Turks and Caicos Islands
Bottniska Viken *see* Bothnia, Gulf of
Bottom, The *626* Saba, N Netherlands Antilles
Bouaflé *300* C Ivory Coast
Bouaké *300* *var.* Bwake. C Ivory Coast
Bouar *154* W Central African Republic
Bouca *154* C Central African Republic
Bouéni *625* SW Mayotte
Bouéni, Baie de *625* *var.* Bonéni Bay. Bay of the Mozambique Channel on the SW coast of Mayotte
Bouenza *176* river of S Congo
Boufarik *59* N Algeria
Bougainville Island *426* island of E Papua New Guinea
Bougie *see* Béjaïa
Bougouni *360* SW Mali
Bougouriba *132* river of SW Burkina
Boujdour *382* W Western Sahara
Boukoumbé *108* *var.* Boukombé. NW Benin
Boukra *382* C Western Sahara
Boulder *569* Colorado, SW USA
Boulogne-sur-Mer *225* *var.* Boulogne. N France
Bouloupari *626* S New Caledonia
Bouma *218* Taveuni, N Fiji
Boumango *230* SE Gabon
Boumba *144* river of SE Cameroon
Boumbé II *154* river of Cameroon and Central African Republic
Boûmdeïd *366* S Mauritania
Bouna *300* NE Ivory Coast
Boundiali *300* N Ivory Coast
Boungou *154* river of C Central African Republic
Bourail *626* C New Caledonia
Bourgas *see* Burgas
Bourg-en-Bresse *225* E France
Bourges *225* C France
Bourgogne *225* *Eng.* Burgundy. Cultural region of E France
Bourke *77* E Australia
Bournemouth *563* S England, UK
Boussé *132* C Burkina
Boussouma *132* C Burkina
Boutilimit *366* SW Mauritania
Bouton *465* W St Lucia
Bovec *486* *Ger.* Flitsch, *It.* Plezzo. NW Slovenia
Boven Kapuas, Pegunungan *354* mountain range of SW Borneo, Malaysia
Boyd's *462* S St Kitts, St Kitts & Nevis
Boyne *288* *Ir.* An Bhóinn. River of E Ireland
Boysun *see* Baysun
Bozen *see* Bolzano
Bozoum *154* W Central African Republic
Brač *181* *var.* Brach, *It.* Brazza. Island of S Croatia
Bradford *563* N England, UK
Braga *442* NW Portugal
Bragado *71* E Argentina
Bragança *442* *Eng.* Braganza. NE Portugal
Braganza *see* Bragança
Brahestad *see* Raahe
Brāhmanbāria *93* E Bangladesh
Brahmaputra *93,162, 271* *var.* Tsangpo, *Ben.* Jamuna. River of S Asia
Brăila *448* E Romania
Braine-l'Alleud *99* C Belgium
Branco *120* river of NW Brazil
Branco, Ilhéu *152* island of N Cape Verde
Brandberg *391* mountain of NW Namibia

Brande *190* Jylland, W Denmark
Brandenburg *237* C Germany
Brandon *146* S Canada
Brani, Pulau *483* island of S Singapore
Brasília *121* ❖ of Brazil, C Brazil
Braslaw *104* N Belorussia
Braşov *448* *prev.* Stalin, *Ger.* Kronstadt, *Hung.* Brassó. C Romania
Brasschaat *99* N Belgium
Brassey, Banjaran *355* *var.* Brassey Range. Mountain range of E Borneo, Malaysia
Brassey Range *see* Brassey, Banjaran
Bratislava *485* *Ger.* Pressburg, *Hung.* Pozsony. ❖ of Slovakia, SW Slovakia
Bratsk *453* C Russia
Bratskoye Vodokhranilishche *453* *Eng.* Bratsk Reservoir. C Russia
Braunau am Inn *82* *var.* Braunau. N Austria
Braunschweig *237* *Eng.* Brunswick. N Germany
Brava *see* Baraawe
Brava *152* island of SW Cape Verde
Brava, Costa *501* coastal region of E Spain
Bravo Del Norte *see* Grande, Río
Bray *288* *Ir.* Bri Chuallan. E Ireland
Brazil *120-125* officially Federative Republic of Brazil. Country of South America divided into 28 admin. units (26 states, 1 territory, 1 federal district)
Brazos *569* river of SW USA
Brazza *see* Brač
Brazzaville *176* ❖ of Congo, S Congo
Brčko *116* NE Bosnia & Herzegovina
Breda *397* SW Netherlands
Bregalnica *349* river of E FYR Macedonia
Bregenz *82* W Austria
Breidhafjördhur *268* bay of the Denmark Strait, on the coast of W Iceland
Bremen *236* NW Germany
Bremerhaven *236* NW Germany
Bremersdorp *see* Manzini
Brennero, Passo del *see* Brenner Pass
Brenner Pass *82, 295* *It.* Passo del Brennero, *Ger.* Brennerpass, *var.* Brenner Sattel. Mountain pass of Austria and Italy
Brerton *97* C Barbados
Brescia *294* N Italy
Breslau *see* Wrocław
Brest *104* *Pol.* Brześć nad Bugiem, *prev.* Brześć Litewski, *Rus.* Brest-Litovsk. SW Belorussia
Brest *224* NW France
Bretagne *224* *Eng.* Brittany. Cultural region of NW France
Brewerville *336* W Liberia
Brežice *486* *Ger.* Rann. E Slovenia
Brezno *485* *prev.* Brezno nad Hronom, *Ger.* Bries, *var.* Briesen, *Hung.* Breznóbánya. C Slovakia
Bria *154* C Central African Republic
Bribri *178* E Costa Rica
Bri Chuallan *see* Bray
Bride *623* N Isle of Man
Bridgetown *76* SW Australia
Bridgetown *97* ❖ of Barbados, SW Barbados
Bridgwater *563* SW England, UK
Brienzer See *516* lake of SW Switzerland
Brig *516* SW Switzerland
Brighton *563* SE England, UK
Brikama *233* W Gambia
Brindisi *295* S Italy
Brinstone Hill *462* NW St Kitts, St Kitts & Nevis
Brisbane *77* E Australia
Bristol *563* SW England, UK
Bristol Channel *563* inlet of the Atlantic Ocean, SW England, UK

British Columbia *146* province of SW Canada
British Guiana *see* Guyana
British Indian Ocean Territory *619* British dependent territory of the Indian Ocean. ❖ Diego Garcia
British North America *see* Canada
British Virgin Islands *619* British dependent territory of the Caribbean Sea. ❖ Road Town.
Brittany *see* Bretagne
Brizan *248* W Grenada island, Grenada
Brno *188* *Ger.* Brünn. SE Czech Republic
Bród *see* Slavonski Brod
Brodeur Peninsula *146* peninsula of Baffin Island, N Canada
Broken Hill *77* S Australia
Brokopondo *508* NE Surinam
Bromberg *see* Bydgoszcz
Brønderslev *190* Jylland, N Denmark
Brooks Range *568* mountain range of Alaska, USA
Broome *76* NW Australia
Brorup *190* Jylland, W Denmark
Broughton Bay *see* Tongjosŏn-man
Brown Hill *462* S Nevis, St Kitts & Nevis
Browns Town *303* N Jamaica
Brownsweg *508* C Surinam
Bruck an der Mur *82* *var.* Bruck. C Austria
Brufut *233* W Gambia
Brugge *99* *Fr.* Bruges. NW Belgium
Brunei *126-127, 354* officially Sultanate of Brunei, *Mal.* Negara Brunei Darussalam. Country on island of Borneo, SE Asia, divided into 4 admin. units (districts)
Brunei Bay *354* *var.* Teluk Brunei. Bay of the South China Sea
Brunei Town *see* Bandar Seri Begawan
Brünn *see* Brno
Brunswick *see* Braunschweig
Brusa *see* Bursa
Brussels *99* *Fr.* Bruxelles, *Dut.* Brussel, *Ger.* Brüssel. ❖ of Belgium, C Belgium
Brüx *see* Most
Bryansk *452* W Russia
Brześć Litewski *see* Brest
Brześć nad Bugiem *see* Brest
Bsharrī *see* Bcharré
Bua *353* river of C Malawi
Bu'aale *490* SW Somalia
Buada Lagoon *392* lagoon on the coast of Nauru
Buala *488* SE Santa Isabel, Solomon Is
Bū al Ḥīdān, Wādī *339* dry watercourse of C Libya
Buba *254* S Guinea-Bissau
Bubanza *138* NW Burundi
Bubaque *254* Ilha de Bubaque, Guinea-Bissau
Bubaque, Ilha de *254* island of SW Guinea-Bissau
Bubi *612* *var.* Bubye. River of S Zimbabwe
Būbīyan, Jazīrat *322* island of NE Kuwait
Buca *218* *prev.* Mbutha. Vanua Levu, N Fiji
Bucaramanga *171* N Colombia
Buchanan *336* *prev.* Grand Bassa. SW Liberia
Bucharest *448* *Rom.* Bucureşti. ❖ of Romania, S Romania
Budapest *264* ❖ of Hungary, N Hungary
Búdhardalur *268* W Iceland
Budweis *see* České Budějovice
Buea *144* SW Cameroon
Buena Vista *102* N Belize
Buena Vista *112* C Bolivia
Buena Vista *622* S Gibraltar
Buenos Aires *71* ❖ of Argentina, E Argentina

Buenos Aires *178* SE Costa Rica
Buenos Aires, Lago *71, 159* *Sp.* Lago General Carrera. Lake of Argentina and Chile
Buffalo *569* New York, NE USA
Buff Bay *303* E Jamaica
Bug *439, 556* *Ukr.* Zakhidnyy Buh, *Rus.* Zapadnyy Bug. River of E Europe
Buga *171* W Colombia
Bugala Island *554* island of Sese Islands, S Uganda
Buganda *138* NW Burundi
Bugarama *460* SW Rwanda
Bughotu *see* Santa Isabel
Buġibba *363* N Malta
Bugojno *116* C Bosnia & Herzegovina
Bugumya *460* SW Rwanda
Buin *426* Bougainville I, Papua New Guinea
Buitenzorg *see* Bogor
Bujumbura *138* *prev.* Usumbura. ❖ of Burundi, W Burundi
Buka Island *426* island of E Papua New Guinea
Bukakata *554* S Uganda
Bukasa Island *554* island of Sese Islands, S Uganda
Bukavu *607* *prev.* Costermansville. E Zaire
Bukeye *138* *var.* Bukaye. C Burundi
Bukhara *580* *var.* Bokhara, *Uzb.* Bukhoro. S Uzbekistan
Bukit Mertajam *354* NW Peninsular Malaysia
Bukit Panjang *483* area of C Singapore
Bukit Timah *483* area of C Singapore
Bükk *264* mountain range of NE Hungary
Bukoba *530* NW Tanzania
Bukum Kechil, Pulau *483* island of SW Singapore
Bukum, Pulau *483* island of S Singapore
Bula *254* W Guinea-Bissau
Bulawayo *612* *var.* Buluwayo. SW Zimbabwe
Bulembu *510* NW Swaziland
Bulgan *380* N Mongolia
Bulgaria *128-1231* officially Republic of Bulgaria, *prev.* People's Republic of Bulgaria. Country of E Europe divided into 8 admin. units (regions)
Buller *401* river of N South Island, New Zealand
Bulolo *426* SE Papua New Guinea
Bulungur *580* *prev.* Krasnogvardeysk, *Uzb.* Bulunghur. SE Uzbekistan
Bumba *607* N Zaire
Bumbah, Khalīj *339* *var.* Kalīj Bumbah. Gulf of the Mediterranean Sea, on the N coast of Libya
Bumbuna *480* C Sierra Leone
Bunbury *76* SW Australia
Bundaberg *77* E Australia
Bundoran *288* N Ireland
Bungoma *316* W Kenya
Bunia *607* *var.* Bunja. NE Zaire
Bunja *see* Bunia
Bunya *see* Bhunya
Buôn Ma Thuôt *593* *var.* Lac Giao. S Vietnam
Bur Acaba *see* Buurhakaba
Buraimi *see* Al Buraymī
Buraydah *472* *var.* Buraida. C Saudi Arabia
Burco *490* *var.* Burao, Bur'o. NW Somalia
Burdur *546* SW Turkey
Burē *215* NW Ethiopia
Burera, Lac *460* lake of N Rwanda
Būrewāla *see* Mandi Būrewāla
Burgas *128* *var.* Bourgas. E Bulgaria
Burgaski Zaliv *128* bay of the Black Sea on the E coast of Bulgaria
Burgdorf *516* NW Switzerland
Burgos *501* N Spain
Burgundy *see* Bourgogne
Burhou *623* island of N Guernsey

Burias Island *435* island of C Philippines
Buriram *533* E Thailand
Burkina *132-133* officially Burkina Faso, *prev.* Upper Volta. Country of West Africa divided into 30 admin. units (provinces)
Burlington *569* Vermont, NE USA
Burma *134-137* officially Burma, *var.* Myanmar. Country of SE Asia divided into 14 admin. units (7 states, 7 divisions)
Burnie *77* Tasmania, SE Australia
Burnt Pine *626* C Norfolk Island
Burrel *57* *var.* Burreli. C Albania
Burrell Boom *102* E Belize
Bursa *546* *prev.* Brusa, *var.* Brusa. NW Turkey
Būr Sa'īd *see* Port Said
Būr Sūdān *see* Port Sudan
Burtnieku Ezers *330* lake of N Latvia
Buru *276* *prev.* Boeroe. Island of Maluku, E Indonesia
Burujird *see* Borujerd
Burūm *599* SE Yemen
Burundi *138-139* officially Republic of Burundi, *prev.* Kingdom of Burundi. Country of Central Africa divided into 15 admin. units (provinces)
Bururi *138* SW Burundi
Buryatiya, Respublika *453* autonomous republic of C Russia
Busan *see* Pusan
Busengo *460* NW Rwanda
Buševa Planina *349* *var.* Baba. Mountain range of Greece and FYR Macedonia
Bushire *see* Bandar-e Bushehr
Busia *316* N Kenya
Busing, Pulau *483* island of SW Singapore
Busira *607* river of NW Zaire
Busoro *460* S Rwanda
Busuanga Island *435* island of W Philippines
Buta *607* N Zaire
Butahana *138* NW Burundi
Butare *460* *prev.* Astrida. S Rwanda
Butaritari *320* island of the Gilbert Is, W Kiribati
Butawal *see* Butwal
Butembo *607* NE Zaire
Butha Buthe *334* N Lesotho
Butiaba *554* NW Uganda
Butterworth *354* NW Peninsular Malaysia
Butuan *435* Mindanao, S Philippines
Butung, Pulau *276* *var.* Buton, *prev.* Boetoeng. Island to the SE of Celebes, C Indonesia
Butwal *395* *var.* Butawal. C Nepal
Buurgplaatz *346* mountain of N Luxembourg
Buurhakaba *490* *var.* Bur Hakkaba, *It.* Bur Acaba. SW Somalia
Buvuma Island *554* island of S Uganda
Büyükağrı Dağı *547* *Eng.* Mount Ararat, *var.* Great Ararat. Mountain of E Turkey
Büyükmenderes *546* river of SW Turkey
Büyükzap Suyu *see* Great Zab
Buzău *448* *Hung.* Bodza. SE Romania
Buzi *387* river of C Mozambique
Bwake *see* Bouaké
Bwiam *233* SW Gambia
Byahoml' *104* N Belorussia
Byala Slatina *128* *var.* Bjala Slatina. NW Bulgaria
Byaroza *104* SW Belorussia
Bydgoszcz *439* *Ger.* Bromberg. N Poland
Byelruskaya Hrada *104* *Rus.* Belorusskaya Gryada. Hilly region of N Belorussia
Byerazino *104* *Rus.* Berezina. River of C Belorussia

Byerazino *104* *Rus.* Berezino. C Belorussia
Bykhaw *104* *Rus.* Bykhov. E Belorussia
Byron Sound *621* area of the South Atlantic Ocean, NW Falkland Islands
Byrranga, Gory *453* mountain range of N Russia
Bystrovka *325* N Kyrgyzstan
Bytom *439* *Ger.* Beuthen. S Poland
Byumba *460* *var.* Biumba. N Rwanda
Byuzmeyin *551* *prev.* Bezmein. S Turkmenistan

C

Caacupé *428* S Paraguay
Caaguazú *428* SE Paraguay
Caála *64* *var.* Kaala, *Port.* Vila Robert Williams. C Angola
Caatinga, Serra da *121* mountain range of E Brazil
Caazapá *428* S Paraguay
Cabaiguán *182* C Cuba
Cabanatuan City *435* Luzon, Philippines
Cabhán *see* Cavan
Cabimas *589* NW Venezuela
Cabinda *64* *var.* Kabinda. Non-contiguous region, NW Angola
Cabinda *64* *var.* Kabinda, NW Angola
Cabora Bassa, Lake *see* Cahora Bassa, Lago de
Cabot Strait *147* strait connecting the Atlantic Ocean and Gulf of St. Lawrence, between Newfoundland and Nova Scotia
Cape Verde, Ilhas de *see* Cape Verde
Cabras, Ilha das *471* island to the N of São Tomé, Sao Tome & Principe
Cabras Island *623* island, W Guam
Čačak *602* C Serbia, Yugoslavia
Cacao *621* NE French Guiana
Cáceres *501* W Spain
Cachacrou *see* Scotts Head Village
Cacheu *254* *var.* Cacheo. W Guinea-Bissau
Cacheu *254* river of NW Guinea-Bissau
Cachimbo, Serra do *121* mountain range of C Brazil
Cacine *254* S Guinea-Bissau
Cacine *252* river of S Guinea-Bissau
Caconda *64* C Angola
Čadca *485* *Hung.* Csaca. N Slovakia
Cadiz *435* Negros, Philippines
Cádiz *500* SW Spain
Cádiz, Golfo de *442, 501* area of the Atlantic Ocean, on the SW coast of Spain
Caen *225* NW France
Caerdydd *see* Cardiff
Caerfyrddin *see* Carmarthen
Caergybi *see* Holyhead
Caernarfon *563* *var.* Caernarvon. N Wales, UK
Cagayan *435* river of Luzon, Philippines
Cagayan de Oro *435* Mindanao, Philippines
Cagayan Islands *435* island group of C Philippines
Cagliari *294* Sardegna, W Italy
Caguas *627* E Puerto Rico
Cahabón *250* river of C Guatemala
Cahora Bassa Dam *387* dam of NW Mozambique
Cahora Bassa, Lago de *387* *var.* Lake Cabora Bassa. Reservoir of NW Mozambique
Cahors *225* S France
Cahul *376* *Rus.* Kagul. S Moldavia
Caia *387* C Mozambique
Caibarién *182* C Cuba
Caicos Bank *629* undersea feature of the Atlantic Ocean

Castillos 577 SE Uruguay

Castlebar 288 W Ireland

Castle Bruce 196 NE Dominica

Castle Harbour 619 inlet of the North Atlantic Ocean, E Bermuda

Castletown 623 SE Isle of Man

Castries 465 ❖ of St Lucia, N St Lucia

Castro 159 Isla de Chiloé, W Chile

Castrovillari 295 SE Italy

Catacamas 260 C Honduras

Catacaos 431 NW Peru

Catalan Bay 622 var. Caleta. Bay of the Mediterranean Sea on the E coast of Gibraltar

Cataluña 501 autonomous community of N Spain

Catamarca see San Fernando del Valle de Catamarca

Catanduanes Island 435 island of E Philippines

Catania 295 Sicilia, S Italy

Catano 627 NE Puerto Rico

Catanzaro 295 SE Italy

Catedral, Cerro 577 mountain of S Uruguay

Catherine, Mount see Katherina, Gebel

Catholic Island 466 island of SW St Vincent & the Grenadines

Catió 254 S Guinea-Bissau

Cat Island 88 island of C Bahamas

Catuane 387 S Mozambique

Catumbela 64 W Angola

Cauca 171 river of N Colombia

Caucasia 171 NW Colombia

Caucasus 234, 452 Rus. Kavkaz. Mountain range of SE Europe and SW Asia, commonly taken as the boundary between Asia and Europe

Caura 589 river of E Venezuela

Căuşeni 376 Rus. Kaushany. E Moldavia

Causse du Kelifely see Kôsin' i Kelifely

Cauto 182 river of SE Cuba

Cavaia see Kavajë

Cavalla see Cavally

Cavally 300, 336 var. Cavalla. River of Ivory Coast and Liberia

Cavan 288 Ir. Cabháin. NE Ireland

Cave Hill 97 W Barbados

Caviana de Fora, Ilha 121 var. Ilha Cavinana. Island of N Brazil

Cawnpore see Kānpur

Caxamarca see Cajamarca

Caxias do Sul 121 S Brazil

Caxito 64 NW Angola

Cayambe 200 N Ecuador

Cayenne 621 ❖ of French Guiana, NE French Guiana

Cayey 627 SE Puerto Rico

Çayırova 187 var. Ayios Theodhoros. NE Cyprus

Cayman Brac 620 island, E Cayman Islands

Cayman Islands 620 British dependent territory of the Caribbean Sea. ❖ George Town.

Cayo see San Ignacio

Cayon 462 E St Kitts, St Kitts & Nevis

Cay Sal 88 islet of W Bahamas

Cazin 116 NW Bosnia & Herzegovina

Ceadâr-Lunga see Ciadîr-Lunga

Ceanannus Mór 288 NE Ireland

Ceará see Fortaleza

Cébaco, Isla 424 island of SW Panama

Cebollatí 577 river of E Uruguay

Cebu 435 Cebu, C Philippines

Cebu 435 island of C Philippines

Cedar Grove 68 N Antigua, Antigua & Barbuda

Cedar Rapids 569 Iowa, C USA

Cedros, Isla 370 island of NW Mexico

Ceelbuur 490 It. El Bur. C Somalia

Ceeldheere 490 var. Ceel Dheere, It. El Dere. E Somalia

Ceel Gaal 490 var. El Gal. NW Somalia

Ceel Xamurre see Jirriiban

Ceerigaabo 490 var. Erigabo, Erigavo. N Somalia

Cegléd 264 prev. Czegléd. C Hungary

Celaya 370 C Mexico

Celebes 276 Ind. Sulawesi. Island of C Indonesia

Celebes Sea 276, 355, 465 Ind. Laut Sulawesi. Sea of the Pacific Ocean, between N Indonesia and S Philippines

Čeleken see Cheleken

Celje 486 Ger. Cilli. C Slovenia

Celtic Sea 288, 563 Ir. An Mhuir Cheilteach. Sea of the Atlantic Ocean, between S Ireland and SW England, UK

Cenderawasih, Teluk 277 bay of the Pacific Ocean on the NW coast of Irian Jaya, E Indonesia

Central African Republic 154-155 abbrev. CAR. Country of Central Africa divided into 16 admin. units (prefectures)

Central Brāhui Range 421 mountain range of W Pakistan

Central China 167

Central, Cordillera 171 range of the Andes in W Colombia

Central, Cordillera 198 mountain range of C Dominican Republic

Central, Cordillera 435 mountain range of Luzon, N Philippines

Central, Cordillera 627 mountain range of C Puerto Rico

Central Group see Inner Islands

Central Island 316 island in Lake Rudolf, NW Kenya

Central Makrān Range 420 mountain range of W Pakistan

Central Range 426 mountain range of C Papua New Guinea

Central Siberian Plateau see Srednesibirskoye Ploskogor'ye

Centre de Flacq 368 E Mauritius

Centre Hills 625 mountain range, C Montserrat

Cephalonia see Kefallonía

Ceram see Seram

Ceram Sea see Seram, Laut

Cerfs, Ile aux 368 var. Isle aux Cerfs. Island of E Mauritius

Cernăuţi see Chernivtsi

Cërrik 57 var. Cerriku. C Albania

Cerro Chato 577 C Uruguay

Cerro de Pasco 431 C Peru

Cerrón Grande, Embalse 207 reservoir of N El Salvador

Ceru Colorado 618 S Aruba

Červen brjag see Cherven-Bryag

Cesena 295 N Italy

Cēsis 330 Ger. Wenden. NE Latvia

České Budějovice 188 Ger. Budweis. SW Czech Republic

Českomoravská Vysočina 188 var. Bohemian-Moravian Highlands, Ceskomoravská Vrchovina, Ger. Böhmisch-Mährische Höhe. Mountain range of S Czech Republic

Český Krumlov 188 SW Czech Republic

Český Les see Bohemian Forest

Céspedes 182 SE Cuba

Cess 336 var. Rivercess. S Liberia

Cestos 336 var. Cess. River of Liberia

Ceuta 382, 501 exclave of Spain, N Morocco

Cévennes 225 mountain range of SE France

Ceylon see Sri Lanka

Ceyhan 187 S Turkey

Chacachacare 540 island to the NW of Trinidad, Trinidad & Tobago

Chachapoyas 431 NW Peru

Chachoengsao 533 C Thailand

Chaclacayo 431 W Peru

Chaco see Gran Chaco

Chad 156-157 officially Republic of Chad, Fr. Tchad. Country of Equatorial Africa divided into 14 admin. units (prefectures)

Chã da Igreja 152 Santo Antão, N Cape Verde

Chad, Lake 144, 156, 407, 409 Fr. Lac Tchad. Lake of C Africa

Chadyr-Lunga see Ciadîr-Lunga

Chaeryŏng 413 SW North Korea

Chāgai Hills 420 mountain range of Afghanistan and Pakistan

Chaghcharān 53 C Afghanistan

Chagos Archipelago 619 var. Oil Islands. Island group of C British Indian Ocean Territory

Chaguanas 540 W Trinidad, Trinidad & Tobago

Chaguaramas 540 NW Trinidad, Trinidad & Tobago

Chagyl 551 NW Turkmenistan

Chahārborjak 53 SW Afghanistan

Chaillu, Massif du 230 C Gabon

Mongos, Chaîne des see Bongo, Massif des

Chainpur 395 W Nepal

Chai Wan 262 S Hong Kong

Chaiyaphum 533 N Thailand

Chakari 612 N Zimbabwe

Chake Chake 530 Pemba, E Tanzania

Chakwāl 421 NE Pakistan

Chalándri 245 prev. Khalándrion. SE Greece

Chalap Dalam 53 mountain range of W Afghanistan

Chalatenango 207 N El Salvador

Chalbi Desert 316 desert region of N Kenya

Chalchuapa 207 W El Salvador

Chalkída 245 Eng. Chalcis, prev. Khalkís. E Greece

Chalkidikí 245 prev. Khalkidhikí, Eng. Chalcidice. Peninsula of NE Greece

Challapata 112 SW Bolivia

Challengers 462 S St Kitts, St Kitts & Nevis

Châlons-sur-Marne 225 NE France

Chaman 421 NW Pakistan

Chambas 182 C Cuba

Chambéry 225 E France

Chambeshi 611 river of NE Zambia

Chambi, Jebel 543 mountain of W Tunisia

Chamouny 368 S Mauritius

Champagne 225 cultural region of NE France

Champasak 327 S Laos

Chañaral 159 N Chile

Chances Peak 625 mountain peak of S Montserrat

Chan Chen 102 N Belize

Chan-chiang see Zhanjiang

Chandīgarh 270 N India

Chandlers Falls 316 var. Chanlers Falls. Waterfall of C Kenya

Chāndpur 93 E Bangladesh

Changane 387 river of S Mozambique

Changara 387 W Mozambique

Changchun 163 prev. Hsinking. Jilin, NE China

Chang-hua 525 Jap. Shōka. W Taiwan

Changi 483 area of E Singapore

Chang Jiang 163 var. Yangtze Kiang. River of C China

Changkiakow see Zhangjiakou

Chang, Ko 533 island of C Thailand

Changsha 163 Hunan, S China

Chang-tien see Zibo

Changuinola 424 W Panama

Ch'angwŏn 496 S South Korea

Changyŏn 413 SW North Korea

Chaniá 245 Eng. Canea, prev. Khaniá. Crete, S Greece

Channel Islands 224 island group to the NW of France

Channel, The see English Channel

Channel Tunnel 563 tunnel between France and SE England, UK

Chanthaburi 533 C Thailand

Ch'ao-chou 525 var. Chaochow, Jap. Chōshū. SW Taiwan

Chao Phraya 533 river of C Thailand

Chaouèn 382 var. Chechaouèn, Chefchaouèn, Sp. Xauen. N Morocco

Chapada Diamantina 121 plateau of E Brazil

Chapala, Lago de 370 lake of SW Mexico

Chapelton 303 C Jamaica

Chaplin Bay 619 bay of the North Atlantic Ocean, W Bermuda

Chardonnières 258 SW Haiti

Chardzhev 551 prev. Chardzhou, var. Čardžou, prev. Leninsk, Turkm. Chärjew. E Turkmenistan

Chardzhou see Chardzhev

Ch'arents'avan 74 var. Čarencaven. C Armenia

Chari 156 var. Shari. River of C Africa

Chārīkār 53 NE Afghanistan

Charity 256 NE Guyana

Chärjew see Chardzhev

Charkhliq see Ruoqiang

Charleroi 99 S Belgium

Charleston 569 South Carolina, SE USA

Charleston 569 West Virginia, E USA

Charlestown 462 SW Nevis, St Kitts & Nevis

Charlestown 466 Canouan, St Vincent & the Grenadines

Charleville 77 E Australia

Charleville-Mézieres 225 NE France

Charlotte 569 North Carolina, SE USA

Charlotte Amalie 629 ❖ of Virgin Islands (US), S Saint Thomas Island

Charlotte Town see Gouyave

Charlottetown 147 Prince Edward Island, SE Canada

Charlotte Ville 196 SW Dominica

Charlotteville 540 N Tobago, Trinidad & Tobago

Charshangy 551 prev. Charshanga, Turkm. Charshangngy. SE Turkmenistan

Charsk 312 E Kazakhstan

Chartres 225 N France

Chateaubelair 466 NW St Vincent, St Vincent & the Grenadines

Châteauroux 225 C France

Chateaux, Pointe des 622 headland of E Guadeloupe

Châtelet 99 S Belgium

Chatham Island 401 island of Chatham Islands, E New Zealand

Chatham Islands 401 islands of E New Zealand

Chatkal Range 325, 580 Rus. Chatkal'skiy Khrebet. Mountain range of Kyrgyzstan and Uzbekistan

Chatres 621 West Falkland, W Falkland Islands

Chāttagām see Chittagong

Chattanooga 569 Tennessee, SE USA

Chatyrtash 325 var. Catyrtaš. E Kyrgyzstan

Châu Đôc 593 var. Chau Phu. SW Vietnam

Chauk 135 W Burma

Chaumont 224 NE France

Chau Phu see Châu Đôc

Chautara 395 C Nepal

Chaux 368 river of SE Mauritius

Chaves 442 N Portugal

Chbar 141 E Cambodia

Cheb 188 Ger. Eger. W Czech Republic

Chechaouèn see Chaouèn

Ch'e-ch'eng 525 S Taiwan

Che-chiang see Zhejiang

Chechnya, Respublika 452, 458 autonomous republic of SW Russia

Chech'ŏn 496 Jap. Teisen. N South Korea

Checker Hall 97 N Barbados

Cheduba Island 135 island of W Burma

Chefoo see Yantai

Chegutu 612 prev. Hartley. N Zimbabwe

Cheju *496 Jap.* Saishū. Cheju-do, South Korea
Cheju-do *496 prev.* Quelpart, *Jap.* Saishu. Island of S South Korea
Cheju Strait *496 var.* Chejuhaehyop, Cheju-Haehyop. Strait connecting the Korea Strait and Yellow Sea
Chek Chue *262 var.* Stanley. S Hong Kong
Chekiang *see* Zhejiang
Chek Lap Kok *262* W Hong Kong
Chek Mun Hoi Hap *262* NE Hong Kong
Cheleken *551 var.* Čeleken. W Turkmenistan
Chelkar *312* W Kazakhstan
Chelyabinsk *452* C Russia
Chemin Grenier *368* S Mauritius
Chemnitz *237 prev.* Karl-Marx-Stadt. E Germany
Chemulpo *see* Inch'ŏn
Ch'eng-chou *see* Zhengzhou
Chengchow *see* Zhengzhou
Chengdu *163 var.* Chengtu. Sichuan, SW China
Chenghsien *see* Zhengzhou
Ch'eng-hua *see* Altay
Chenghwa *see* Altay
Chenkaladi *504* E Sri Lanka
Cheoc Van, Baía de *624* bay of the South China Sea, S Macao
Cheom Ksan *see* Chôâm Khsant
Chepo *424* NE Panama
Cher *225* river of C France
Cherbourg *225* NW France
Cheren *see* Keren
Cherepovets *452* W Russia
Chergui, Chott ech *59* salt lake of NW Algeria
Chergui, Île *543 Ar.* Jazirat ash Sharqi. Island of E Tunisia
Cherikaw *104* E Belorussia
Cherkasy *556 Rus.* Cherkassy. C Ukraine
Cherne More *see* Black Sea
Chernivtsi *556 Rus.* Chernovtsy, *Rom.* Cernăuţi, *Ger.* Czernowitz. W Ukraine
Chernobil' *556 var.* Chernobyl. N Ukraine
Chernobyl *see* Chernobil'
Cherno More *see* Black Sea
Cherry Island *see* Anuta
Cherskiy *453* NE Russia
Cherskogo, Khrebet *453* mountain range of NE Russia
Cherso *see* Cres
Cherson *see* Kherson
Cherven-Bryag *128 var.* Červen brjag. NW Bulgaria
Chester *563* NW England, UK
Chetumal, Bahia *102 var.* Chetumal Bay. Bay of the Caribbean Sea
Chetumal Bay *see* Chetumal, Bahia
Cheung Chau *262* SW Hong Kong
Cheviot Hills *563* hills of England and Scotland, UK
Ch'ew Bahir *215 var.* Lake Stefanie. Lake of SW Ethiopia
Cheyenne *569* Wyoming, NW USA
Chhlong *see* Phumĭ Chhlong
Chhuk *see* Phumĭ Chhuk
Chhukha *110* SW Bhutan
Chia-i *525 var.* Chiayi, Kiayi, *Jap.* Kagi. W Taiwan
Chia-li *525 var.* Kiali, *Jap.* Kari. W Taiwan
Chia-mu-ssu *see* Jiamusi
Chiang-hsi *see* Jiangxi
Chiang Mai *533 var.* Chiengmai. NW Thailand
Chiang-su *see* Jiangsu
Chiat'ura *234* C Georgia
Chiba *304* Honshū, SE Japan
Chibuto *387* S Mozambique
Chicago *569* Illinois, C USA
Chichăwatni *421* E Pakistan
Chichicastenango *250* W Guatemala
Chichigalpa *404* W Nicaragua
Ch'i-ch'i-ha-erh *see* Qiqihar

Chiclayo *431* NW Peru
Chicoutimi *147* SE Canada
Chicualacuala *387* SW Mozambique
Chiemsee *237* lake of SE Germany
Chiesanuova *468* SW San Marino
Chih-fu *see* Yantai
Chihli *see* Hebei
Chihli, Gulf of *see* Bo Hai
Chihuahua *370* NW Mexico
Ch'ikhareshi *234* N Georgia
Chikwawa *353* SW Malawi
Chilanga *611* S Zambia
Chilaw *504* W Sri Lanka
Chile *158-161* officially Republic of Chile. Country of South America divided into 13 admin. units (12 regions and 1 metropolitan area)
Chile Chico *159* W Chile
Chilika Lake *270* lake of E India
Chililabombwe *611* C Zambia
Chi-lin *see* Jilin
Chillán *159* C Chile
Chilliwack *146* SW Canada
Chiloé, Isla de *159 var.* Isla Grande de Chiloé. Island of W Chile
Chilumba *353 prev.* Deep Bay. N Malawi
Chi-lung *525 var.* Keelung, *Jap.* Kirun. N Taiwan
Chilwa, Lake *353 var.* Lake Shirwa, *Port.* Lago Chirua. Lake of SE Malawi
Chimaltenango *250* W Guatemala
Chimanimani *612 prev.* Mandidzudzure, *prev.* Melsetter. E Zimbabwe
Chimbay *580 var.* Čimbaj, *Uzb.* Chimboy. NW Uzbekistan
Chimborazo *200* mountain of C Ecuador
Chimbote *431* W Peru
Chimboy *see* Chimbay
Chimishliya *see* Cimişlia
Chimkent *see* Shymkent
Chimoio *387* C Mozambique
China *162-169* officially People's Republic of China, *Chin.* Zhonghua Renmin Gonghe Guo, *var.* Chunghua Jen-min Kung-ho-kuo, *prev.* Chinese Empire (until January 1912). Country of E Asia divided into 30 admin. units (22 provinces, 5 autonomous regions, 3 province-level municipalities)
Chinan *see* Jinan
Chinandega *404* W Nicaragua
Chincha Alta *431* SW Peru
Chin-chiang *see* Quanzhou
Chin-chou *see* Jinzhou
Chinchow *see* Jinzhou
Chin-do *496 Jap.* Chin-tō. Island of SW South Korea
Chindwin *135* river of NW Burma
Ch'ing Hai *see* Qinghai Hu
Chinghai *see* Qinghai
Chingola *611* C Zambia
Ch'ing-shui *525 var.* Tsingshui, *Jap.* Kiyomizu. W Taiwan
Ching-Tao *see* Qingdao
Chinguetti *366* C Mauritania
Chinhae *496 Jap.* Chinkai. S South Korea
Chinhoyi *612 var.* Sinoia. N Zimbabwe
Chinhsien *see* Jinzhou
Chiniot *421* NE Pakistan
Chinit *141 var.* Chinit. River of C Cambodia
Chinju *496 Jap.* Shinshū. S South Korea
Chinkai *see* Chinhae
Chink Kaplankyr *551* ridge of NW Turkmenistan
Chinko *154* river of E Central African Republic
Chintheche *353 var.* Chinteche. N Malawi
Chin-tō *see* Chin-do
Chios *245 prev.* Khíos. Island of E Greece

Chíos *245 prev.* Khíos, *It.* Scio, *Turk.* Sakis-Adasi. Chios, E Greece
Chipata *611 prev.* Fort Jameson. E Zambia
Chipinge *612 prev.* Chipinga. E Zimbabwe
Chiponde *353* SE Malawi
Chiquimula *250* SE Guatemala
Chiquimulilla *250* S Guatemala
Chiradzulu *353* S Malawi
Chirang *110* S Bhutan
Chirchik *580 var.* Čirčik, *Uzb.* Chirchiq. E Uzbekistan
Chire *see* Shire
Chiredzi *612* SE Zimbabwe
Chirilagua *207* SE El Salvador
Chiriquí *424* W Panama
Chiriquí, Golfo de *424* gulf of the Pacific Ocean to the SW of Panama
Chiriquí Grande *424* W Panama
Chiriquí, Laguna de *424* lagoon of W Panama
Chiromo *353* S Malawi
Chirongui *625* S Mayotte
Chirripó Grande, Cerro *178* mountain of E Costa Rica
Chirua, Lago *see* Chilwa, Lake
Chirundu *612* N Zimbabwe
Chisenga *353* NW Malawi
Ch'i-shan *525 var.* Kishan, *Jap.* Kizan. SW Taiwan
Chishtiān Mandi *421* E Pakistan
Chisimaio *see* Kismaayo
Chişinău *376 var.* Kishinev. ❖ of Moldavia, C Moldavia
Chissioua Mtsamboro *625* island of NW Mayotte
Chita *453* C Russia
Chitipa *353 prev.* Fort Hill. NW Malawi
Chitose *305* Hokkaidō, N Japan
Chitré *424* S Panama
Chittagong *93 Ben.* Chāttāgām. SE Bangladesh
Chittagong Hills *93* hilly region of S Asia
Chitungwiza *612 prev.* Chitangwiza. NE Zimbabwe
Chiuta, Lake *353* lake of SE Malawi
Chivhu *612 prev.* Enkeldoorn. C Zimbabwe
Chixoy *250 var.* Río Negro, Salinas. River of Guatemala and Mexico
Chizarira Hills *612* hilly region of NW Zimbabwe
Chkalov *see* Orenburg
Chlef *59 prev.* El Asnam, Orléansville, *var.* Ech Cheliff, Ech Chleff. NW Algeria
Choa Chu Kang *483* area of W Singapore
Chôâm Khsant *141 prev.* Cheom Ksan. N Cambodia
Choiseul *465* SW St Lucia
Choiseul *488 var.* Lauru. Island of the W Solomon Islands
Choiseul Sound *621* area of the South Atlantic Ocean, E Falkland Islands
Cholo *see* Thyolo
Choluteca *260* S Honduras
Choluteca *260* river of S Honduras
Choma *611* S Zambia
Chomo Lhari *110* mountain of NW Bhutan
Chomutov *188 Ger.* Komotau. NW Czech Republic
Ch'ŏnan *496 Jap.* Tenan. W South Korea
Chon Buri *533* C Thailand
Chone *200* W Ecuador
Ch'ŏngch'ŏn *413* river of W North Korea
Ch'ŏngju *413* NE North Korea
Chŏngju *496 prev.* Chŏngup, *Jap.* Seiyu. SW South Korea
Ch'ŏngju *496 var.* Chŏngju. C South Korea
Chongqing *163 var.* Chungking, Ch'ung-ching, Yuzhou. Sichuan, SW China

Chongwe *611* E Zambia
Chŏnju *496 Jap.* Zenshū. SW South Korea
Chorne More *see* Black Sea
Chorzów *439 Ger.* Königshütte. S Poland
Chōsen-kaikyō *see* Korea Strait
Chōshū *see* Ch'ao-chou
Cho-shui Hsi *525* river of W and NE Taiwan
Chota Nagpur Plateau *270* plateau of NE India
Choybalsan *380* E Mongolia
Christchurch *401* E South Island, New Zealand
Christiana *303* C Jamaica
Christiania *see* Oslo
Christian, Point *627* headland of Pitcairn Island, S Pitcairn Islands
Christiansand *see* Kristiansand
Christianshåb *622 var.* Qasigianguit. W Greenland
Christiansted *629* Saint Croix, S Virgin Islands (US)
Christiansund *see* Kristiansund
Christmas Island *620* Australian external territory of the Indian Ocean. ❖ Flying Fish Cove.
Christmas Island *see* Kiritimati
Chrysochou Bay *see* Khrysokhou Bay
Chu *312 Kaz.* Shū. SE Kazakhstan
Chu *325 var.* Ču, *Kir.* Chüy. River of Kazakhstan and Kyrgyzstan
Chu *593* river of Laos and Vietnam
Chuădānga *93* W Bangladesh
Ch'uan-chou *see* Quanzhou
Chubek *see* Moskovskiy
Ch'u-chiang *see* Shaoguan
Chucunaque *424* river of E Panama
Chudskoye Ozero *see* Peipus, Lake
Chūgoku-sanchi *304* mountain range of Honshū, W Japan
Chuí *see* Chuy
Chukai *354 var.* Cukai. E Peninsular Malaysia
Chukchi Sea *453 Rus.* Chukotskoye More. Sea of Arctic Ocean between NE Asia and NW N America
Chukotskiy Poluostrov *453 Eng.* Chukchi Peninsula. Peninsula of NE Russia
Chulucanas *431* NW Peru
Chumphon *533* S Thailand
Chu-nan *525* NW Taiwan
Ch'unch'ŏn *496 Jap.* Shunsen. N South Korea
Chung-ang Shan-mo *525* mountain range of C Taiwan
Ch'ung-ching *see* Chongqing
Chung-ho *525* N Taiwan
Chung-hsing-hsin-ts'un *525* W Taiwan
Chung-hua Jen-min Kung-ho-kuo *see* China
Ch'ungju *496 Jap.* Chūshū. C South Korea
Ch'ungju-ho *496* reservoir of C South Korea
Chungking *see* Chongqing
Chung-li *525 Jap.* Chūreki. N Taiwan
Ch'ungmu *496* S South Korea
Chunya *530* SW Tanzania
Chuquícamata *159* N Chile
Chur *516 It.* Coira, *Rmsch.* Cuera, *Fr.* Coire. E Switzerland
Church Cay *466* cay of E St Vincent & the Grenadines
Churchill *146* C Canada
Church Village *97* SE Barbados
Chūreki *see* Chung-li
Chūshū *see* Ch'ungju
Chust *580 var.* Čust. E Uzbekistan
Chuuk Islands *375 var.* Hogoley Islands. Island group of C Micronesia
Chuvashskaya, Respublika *452* autonomous republic of W Russia
Chuy *577 var.* Chuí. SE Uruguay
Ciadîr-Lunga *376 var.* Ceadăr-Lunga, *Rus.* Chadyr-Lunga. S Moldavia

Ciceron *465* NW St Lucia
Cicia *218* *prev.* Thithia. Island of the Lau Group, E Fiji
Cidade Velha *152* Santiago, S Cape Verde
Ciego de Ávila *182* C Cuba
Ciénaga *171* N Colombia
Cienfuegos *182* C Cuba
Cieza *501* SE Spain
Çiftlik Dere *see* Aloupos
Cifuentes *182* C Cuba
Cikobia *218* *prev.* Thikombia. Island to the N of Vanua Levu, N Fiji
Cilacap *276* *prev.* Tjilatjap. Java, C Indonesia
Cill Airne *see* Killarney
Cill Choinnigh *see* Kilkenny
Cilli *see* Celje
Cill Mhantáin *see* Wicklow
Čimbaj *see* Chimbay
Cimişlia *376* *Rus.* Chimishliya. S Moldavia
Cina Selatan, Laut *see* South China Sea
Cincinnati *569* Ohio, NE USA
Ciney *99* SE Belgium
Ciotat *225* SE France
Čirčik *see* Chirchik
Cirebon *276* *prev.* Tjirebon. Java, C Indonesia
Cirque de Cilaos *628* mountain range of W Réunion
Cirquenizza *see* Crikvenica
Ciskei Bantustan 'self-governing homeland' comprising 2 non-contiguous territories of E Cape Province, South Africa; created in 1981, abolished in 1994
Citlaltépetl *370* *var.* Pico de Orizaba, Volcán Citlaltépetl. Mountain of SE Mexico
Citlaltépetl, Volcán *see* Citlaltépetl
Citron *621* NW French Guiana
Citron *368* river of NW Mauritius
Ciudad Arce *207* W El Salvador
Ciudad Bolívar *589* E Venezuela
Ciudad de Guatemala *see* Guatemala City
Ciudad del Este *428* *prev.* Puerto Presidente Stroessner. SE Paraguay
Ciudad de México *see* Mexico City
Ciudad de Panamá *see* Panama City
Ciudad Guayana *589* E Venezuela
Ciudad Juárez *370* NW Mexico
Ciudad Obregón *370* NW Mexico
Ciudad Ojeda *589* NW Venezuela
Ciudad Real *501* C Spain
Ciudad Trujillo *see* Santo Domingo
Ciudad Victoria *370* C Mexico
Civitavecchia *295* C Italy
Clarence *401* river of NE South Island, New Zealand
Clarence Island *66* island of South Shetland Islands, Antarctica
Clarence Town *88* Long Island, Bahamas
Clermont-Ferrand *225* C France
Clervaux *346* N Luxembourg
Cleveland *569* Ohio, NE USA
Clifden *288* W Ireland
Clifton *196* NW Dominica
Clifton *466* Union I, St Vincent & the Grenadines
Clonmel *288* *Ir.* Cluain Meala. S Ireland
Cluj-Napoca *448* *prev.* Cluj, *Hung.* Kolozsvár, *Ger.* Klausenburg. NW Romania
Clutha *401* river of SW South Island, New Zealand
Clyde, Firth of *563* estuary of the river Clyde, SW Scotland, UK
Coamo *627* S Puerto Rico
Coast Mountains *146* *Fr.* Chaîne Côtière. Mountain range of Canada and USA
Coast Range *568* mountain range of NW USA
Coast Ranges *568* mountain range of SW USA

Coatepeque *250* W Guatemala
Coatepeque, Lago de *207* lake of W El Salvador
Coatzacoalcos *370* *prev.* Puerto México. SE Mexico
Cobán *250* C Guatemala
Cobija *112* NW Bolivia
Cochabamba *112* C Bolivia
Cochin *270* *var.* Kochi. S India
Cockburn Harbour *629* South Caicos, E Turks and Caicos Islands
Cockburn Town *88* Great Exuma I, Bahamas
Cockburn Town *629* Grand Turk Island, SE Turks and Caicos Islands
Cockpit Country, The *303* physical region of NW Jamaica
Coco *404* *var.* Segovia. River of N Nicaragua
Coco *260* *var.* Wangkí, Segovia. River of Honduras and Nicaragua
Cocobeach *230* NW Gabon
Coco, Isla del *178* island of SW Costa Rica
Cocoli *see* Corubal
Cocos (Keeling) Islands *620* Australian external territory of the Indian Ocean. ❖ West Island
Cocos Island *623* island group of S Guam
Codrington *68* C Barbuda, Antigua & Barbuda
Codrington Lagoon *68* W Barbuda, Antigua & Barbuda
Coeroeni *see* Corantijn
Coëtivy *478* island of E Seychelles
Coffs Harbour *77* E Australia
Cogîlnic *376* *var.* Cogâlnic, *Rus.* Kogil'nik. River of SE Moldavia
Cognac *225* W France
Cogo *see* Kogo
Cohoha *see* Cyohoha-Sud Lac
Coiba, Isla de *424* island of SW Panama
Coihaique *159* *var.* Coyhaique. S Chile
Coimbatore *270* S India
Coimbra *442* W Portugal
Coin de Mire *368* *Eng.* Gunners Quoin. Island of N Mauritius
Coira *see* Chur
Coire *see* Chur
Coi, Sông *see* Red River
Cojutepeque *207* C El Salvador
Colchester *563* E England, UK
Coleraine *563* Northern Ireland, UK
Colesberg *493* Northern Cape, C South Africa
Colihaut *196* *var.* Kulihao. W Dominica
Collie *76* SW Australia
Collingwood Bay *426* bay of the Solomon Sea to the E of Papua New Guinea
Colmar *225* *Ger.* Kolmar. NE France
Cöln *see* Köln
Coloane *624* Coloane, S Macao
Coloane *624* island of S Macao
Cologne *see* Köln
Colomb-Béchar *see* Béchar
Colombia *170-173* officially Republic of Colombia. Country of South America divided into 32 admin. units (departments)
Colombo *504* ❖ of Sri Lanka, W Sri Lanka
Colón *182* NW Cuba
Colón *424* *prev.* Aspinwall. N Panama
Colón, Archipiélago de *see* Galapagos Islands
Colonia *see* Kolonia
Colonia del Sacramento *577* SW Uruguay
Colorado *178* river of NE Costa Rica
Colorado *569* river of Texas, SC USA
Colorado *569* river of SW USA
Colorado *568* state of SW USA
Colorados, Archipiélago de los *182* island group of NW Cuba

Colorado Springs *569* Colorado, SW USA
Columbia *568* river of NW USA
Columbia *569* South Carolina, SE USA
Columbia, District of *569* federal district of NE USA
Columbus *569* Georgia, SE USA
Columbus *569* Ohio, NE USA
Columbus Channel *540* channel connecting the Atlantic Ocean and Gulf of Paria
Colville Channel *401* channel linking the Bay of Plenty and Hauraki Gulf, N of North Island, New Zealand
Comarapa *112* C Bolivia
Comas *431* W Peru
Comayagua *260* W Honduras
Comendador *198* *prev.* Elías Piña. W Dominican Republic
Comer *see* Como, Lago di
Comilla *93* *Ben.* Kumillā. E Bangladesh
Commissioner's Point *619* headland of Ireland Island North, W Bermuda
Communism Peak *see* Pik Kommunizma
Como *294* N Italy
Comodoro Rivadavia *71* SE Argentina
Como, Lago di *294* *var.* Lario, *Eng.* Lake Como, *Ger.* Comer See. Lake of N Italy
Comoros *174-175* officially Federal Islamic Republic of the Comoros. Island group of the Indian Ocean, between Madagascar and the African mainland, divided into 3 admin. units (districts)
Comrat *376* *Rus.* Komrat. S Moldavia
Conakry *253* ❖ of Guinea, SW Guinea
Concepción *112* E Bolivia
Concepción *159* C Chile
Concepción *428* *var.* Villa Concepción. C Paraguay
Concepción *see* Riaba
Concepción de La Vega *see* La Vega
Conchos *370* river of NW Mexico
Concord *248* W Grenada island, Grenada
Concord *569* New Hampshire, NE USA
Concordia *71* E Argentina
Condado *182* C Cuba
Côn Dao *593* *var.* Con Son. Island of S Vietnam
Condroz *99* physical region of SE Belgium
Congo *64, 176, 607* *var.* Zaire, Kongo, Lualaba. River of C Africa
Congo *176-177* officially Republic of the Congo. Country of C Africa divided into 9 admin. units (regions)
Congo Basin *607* drainage basin of C Africa
Con, Loch *see* Conn, Lough
Connaught *288* province of W Ireland
Connecticut *569* state of NE USA
Conn, Lough *288* *Ir.* Loch Con. Lake of NW Ireland
Consolación del Sur *182* W Cuba
Constance, Lake *82, 236, 516* *Ger.* Bodensee. Lake of C Europe
Constanţa *448* *Ger.* Konstantza, *Turk.* Köstence, *var.* Küstendje, *Eng.* Constanza. SE Romania
Constantine *59* *Ar.* Qoussantîna, *var.* Qacentina, NE Algeria
Constantine *248* SW Grenada island, Grenada
Constantinople *see* Istanbul
Constant Spring *303* SE Jamaica
Constanza *198* C Dominican Republic
Contagem *121* SE Brazil
Contuboel *254* NE Guinea-Bissau
Cook Islands *620* territory in free association with New Zealand, Pacific Ocean. ❖ Avarua
Cook, Mount *401* *prev.* Aorangi. Mountain of W South Island, New Zealand
Cook, Récif de *626* reef of the Pacific Ocean, N New Caledonia

Cook Strait *401* *var.* Raukawa. Strait between North and South Islands of New Zealand, connecting the South Pacific Ocean and Tasman Sea
Cooper Creek *77* *var.* Barcoo, Cooper's Creek. River of C Australia
Cooper Island *619* island of SE British Virgin Islands
Copacabana *112* W Bolivia
Copenhagen *190* *Dan.* København. ❖ of Denmark, Sjælland, E Denmark
Copiapó *159* N Chile
Coppename *508* *var.* Koppename. River of C Surinam
Coppermine *146* *var.* Qurlurtuuq. NW Canada
Coquilhatville *see* Mbandaka
Coquimbo *159* N Chile
Corail *258* SW Haiti
Coral Harbour *147* Southampton Island, NE Canada
Coral Sea *77, 585, 426* sea of the Pacific Ocean between Australia and Papua New Guinea
Corantijn *256, 508* *var.* Coeroeni, Corentyne, Courantyne. River of Guyana and Surinam
Córdoba *71* C Argentina
Córdoba *501* *var.* Cordoba, *Eng.* Cordova. SW Spain
Cordova *568* Alaska, USA
Corentyne *see* Corantijn
Corfu *see* Kérkyra
Corinth *see* Kórinthos
Corinth *248* SE Grenada island, Grenada
Corinth, Gulf of *see* Korinthiakós Kólpos
Corinth, Isthmus of *see* Korínthou, Isthmós
Corinto *404* W Nicaragua
Coriole *see* Qoryooley
Corisco, Isla de *208* Island of SW Equatorial Guinea
Cork *288* *Ir.* Corcaigh. S Ireland
Cork Hill *625* W Montserrat
Corleone *295* Sicilia, S Italy
Cornellà de Llobregat *501* E Spain
Corner Brook *147* Newfoundland, E Canada
Corn Exchange *334* NW Lesotho
Corn Islands *see* Maíz, Islas
Cornwallis Island *146* island of Parry Islands, N Canada
Coro *589* *var.* Santa Ana de Coro. NW Venezuela
Corocoro *112* W Bolivia
Coromandel Peninsula *401* peninsula of NE North Island, New Zealand
Coronel Bogado *428* S Paraguay
Coronel Oviedo *428* SE Paraguay
Çorovodë *57* *var.* Çorovoda, Corovoda. SE Albania
Corozal *102* N Belize
Corrib, Lough *288* *Ir.* Loch Corrib. Lake of W Ireland
Corrientes *71* NE Argentina
Corriverton *256* E Guyana
Corriza *see* Korçë
Corse *225* *Eng.* Corsica. Island of SE France
Corsica *see* Corse
Cortés *178* SE Costa Rica
Corubal *254* *var.* Cocoli, Rio Grande. River of W Africa
Çorum *547* N Turkey
Corvallis *568* Oregon, NW USA
Corvo *442* *var.* Ilha do Corvo. Island of the Azores, Portugal
Cosenza *295* S Italy
Cosmolédo Atoll *478* atoll of the Aldabra Group, SW Seychelles
Cospicua *363* E Malta
Costa, Cordillera de la *589* *var.* Cordillera de Venezuela. Mountain range of N Venezuela
Costa Rica *178-179* officially Republic of Costa Rica. Country of Central America divided into 7 admin. units (provinces)

Costermansville *see* Bukavu
Cotagaita *112* S Bolivia
Côtière, Chaîne *see* Coast Mountains
Cotonou *108 var.* Kotonu. S Benin
Cotopaxi *200* active volcano of
  N Ecuador
Cotswold Hills *563* hills of
  W England, UK
Cottbus *237 prev.* Kottbus. E Germany
Cottica *64* E Surinam
Cotton Ground *462* NW Nevis, St Kitts
  & Nevis
Cotuí *198* C Dominican Republic
Coulibistri *196* W Dominica
Coupe, Cap *628* cape of the Atlantic
  Ocean on the coast of Miquelon,
  S Saint Pierre and Miquelon
Courantyne *see* Corantijn
Courcelles *99* S Belgium
Courland *see* Kurzeme
Courtrai *see* Kortrijk
Couva *540* W Trinidad, Trinidad
  & Tobago
Couvin *99* S Belgium
Cova Figueira *152* Fogo, S Cape Verde
Cove Bay *618* bay of the Caribbean
  Sea on the S coast of Anguilla
Coventry *563* C England, UK
Covilhã *442* E Portugal
Cox's Bāzār *93* S Bangladesh
Coyah *253* SW Guinea
Coyhaique *see* Coihaique
Cozumel, Isla de *370* island of
  SE Mexico
Cracow *see* Kraków
Cradock *493* Eastern Cape, S South
  Africa
Craiova *448* SW Romania
Cranbrook *146* SW Canada
Crane, The *97* SE Barbados
Crawley *563* SE England, UK
Créoles *368* river of SE Mauritius
Cres *181 It.* Cherso. Island of
  W Croatia
Crescent Group *627* island group of
  C Paracel Islands
Crete *see* Kríti
Créteil *225* N France
Crete, Sea of *245 Gk* Kritikó Pélagos.
  Area of the Mediterranean Sea,
  SE Greece
Creuse *225* river of C France
Crikvenica *181 It.* Cirquenizza.
  NW Croatia
Crimea *see* Krym
Cristóbal *424* N Panama
Cristóbal Colón, Pico *171* peak of
  N Colombia
Crna Gora *see* Montenegro
Crna reka *349* river of S FYR
  Macedonia
Crni Drim *see* Drinit të Zi
Črnomelj *486 Ger.* Tschernembl.
  S Slovenia
Croatia *180-181* officially Republic of
  Croatia, *SCr.* Hrvatska. Country of
  S Europe divided into 21 admin. units
  (provinces)
Crochu *248* SE Grenada island,
  Grenada
Crocker, Banjaran *355 var.* Crocker
  Range. Mountain range of C Borneo,
  Malaysia
Crocodile *see* Limpopo
Crocus Bay *618* bay of the Caribbean
  Sea on the W coast of Anguilla
Croia *see* Krujë
Cromer *563* E England, UK
Crooked Island *88* island of the
  E Bahamas
Crooked Island Passage *88* passage
  of the Atlantic Ocean between
  Crooked Island and Long Island,
  Bahamas
Crooked Tree *102* NE Belize
Crosby *623* C Isle of Man
Cross *408* river of Cameroon and
  Nigeria
Crossroads *288* N Ireland
Crotone *295* S Italy

Crucero Contramaestre *182* S Cuba
Cruz Bay *629* Saint John, E Virgin
  Islands (US)
Cruz del Eje *71* C Argentina
Csaca *see* Čadca
Csakathurn *see* Čakovec
Csáktornya *see* Čakovec
Csíkszereda *see* Miercurea-Ciuc
Cuamba *387* N Mozambique
Cuan Dhun Dealgan *see* Dundalk Bay
Cuando *64, 611 var.* Kwando. River
  of southern Africa
Cuango *see* Kwango
Cuan na Gaillimhe *see* Galway Bay
Cuanza *64 var.* Kwanza. River of
  Angola
Cuareim *577 Port.* Quaraí. River
  of Brazil and Uruguay
Cuba *182-185* officially Republic of
  Cuba. Country of the West Indies
  divided into 15 admin. units (14
  provinces and 1 special municipality)
Cubal *64* W Angola
Cubango *64 var.* Kuvango,
  Port. Vila Artuur de Paiva, Vila da
  Ponte. C Angola
Cubango *64, 118, 391 var.* Kavango,
  Kavengo, Kubango, Okavango,
  Okavanggo. River of Southern Africa
Cúcuta *171 var.* San José de Cúcuta.
  N Colombia
Cuddapah *270* S India
Cudjoehead *625* NW Montserrat
Cuenca *200* S Ecuador
Cuenca *501* C Spain
Cueno *294* N Italy
Cuera *see* Chur
Cuernavaca *370* S Mexico
Cueto *182* SE Cuba
Cufra *see* Al Kufrah
Cuiabá *121 prev.* Cuyabá. SW Brazil
Cuilapa *250* S Guatemala
Cuito *64 var.* Kwito. River of Angola
Culebra *627* Isla de Culebra,
  NE Puerto Rico
Culebra, Isla de *627* island of
  NE Puerto Rico
Culiacán *370* W Mexico
Culion Island *435* island of Calamian
  Group, W Philippines
Cumaná *589* NE Venezuela
Cumberland *466* river of W St
  Vincent, St Vincent & the Grenadines
Cumberland Peninsula *147*
  peninsula of Baffin Island,
  NE Canada
Cumbrian Mountains *563 var.* Lake
  District. Mountain range of
  NW England, UK
Cunene *64, 391 var.* Kunene. River
  of Angola and Namibia
Cunnamulla *77* E Australia
Curaçao *589, 629* island of the
  Netherland Antilles, Caribbean Sea
Curanilahue *159* C Chile
Curaray *200* river of Ecuador and
  Peru
Curepe *540* NW Trinidad, Trinidad
  & Tobago
Curepipe *368* C Mauritius
Curicó *159* C Chile
Curitiba *121 prev.* Curytiba.
  S Brazil
Curral Velho *152* Boa Vista, Cape
  Verde
Current *88* Eleuthera Island, Bahamas
Curuguaty *428* E Paraguay
Curzola *see* Korčula
Cusco *431 var.* Cuzco. SE Peru
Čust *see* Chust
Cutch, Gulf of *see* Kachch, Gulf of
Cuttack *270* E India
Cutting Camp *334* SW Lesotho
Cuxhaven *236* NW Germany
Cuyabá *see* Cuiabá
Cuyo East Passage *435* passage of the
  Sulu Sea between Cuyo Islands and
  Panay, Philippines
Cuyo Islands *435* islands of
  C Philippines

Cuyo West Passage *435* passage of
  the Sulu Sea between Cuyo Islands
  and Palawan, Philippines
Cuyuni *256* river of Guyana and
  Venezuela
Cuzco *see* Cusco
Čvrsnica *116* mountain of SW Bosnia
  & Herzegovina
Cyambwe, Lac *460* lake of E Rwanda
Cyangugu *460* SW Rwanda
Cyclades *see* Kyklades
Cymru *see* Wales
Cyohoha Sud, Lac *138, 460*
  var. Cohoha, Lac Tshohoha Sud.
  Lake of Burundi and Rwanda
Cyprus *186-187* officially Republic of
  Cyprus, *Gk* Kypros, *Turk.* Kıbrıs,
  Kıbrıs Cumhuriyeti. Country of
  E Mediterranean divided into 5
  admin. units (districts). Following
  Turkish invasion of 1974, northern
  sector became self-proclaimed state,
  officially Turkish Republic of
  Northern Cyprus (TRNC)
Cyrenaica *see* Barqah
Czechoslovakia *see* Czech Republic
  and Slovakia
Czech Republic *188-189 Cz.* Česká
  Republika, *prev.* constituent republic
  of Czechoslovakia. Country of
  C Europe divided into 7 admin. units
  (regions)
Czegléd *see* Cegléd
Czernowitz *see* Chernivtsi
Częstochowa *439 Ger.*
  Tschenstochau. S Poland

D

Dabakala *300* NE Ivory Coast
Dabola *253* C Guinea
Dabou *300* S Ivory Coast
Dąbrowa Górnicza *439* S Poland
Dacca *see* Dhaka
Dachau *237* S Germany
Dadanawa *256* SW Guyana
Daɗda 'to *194* N Djibouti
Dadeldhura *395 var.* Dandeldhura.
  W Nepal
Ḍaḍnah *560 var.* Dhadnah. NE United
  Arab Emirates
Daegu *see* Taegu
Daga *110* S Bhutan
Dagana *476* N Senegal
Dagden *see* Hiiumaa
Dagestan, Respublika *452*
  autonomous republic of SW Russia
Dagö *see* Hiiumaa
Dagupan *435* Luzon, N Philippines
Dahar *543* physical region of S
  Tunisia
Da Hinggan Ling *163 Eng.* Great
  Khingan Range. Mountain range of
  Nei Mongol Zizhiqu, NE China
Dahlak Archipelago *210* island group
  of E Eritrea
Dahlak Island *210* island of Dahlak
  Archipelago, E Eritrea
Dahm, Ramlat *599* desert region of
  NW Yemen
Dahomey *see* Benin
Dahra *see* Dara
Dahūk *284 var.* Dohuk, *Kurd.* Dihōk.
  N Iraq
Dai Island *488* of E Solomon Is
Dailekh *395* W Nepal
Daingin, Bá an *see* Dingle Bay
Dajabón *198* N Dominican Republic
Dakar *476* ❖ of Senegal, W Senegal
Dakoro *407* SW Niger
Đakovica *602 var.* Djakovica,
  Alb. Gjakovë. S Serbia, Yugoslavia
Đakovo *181 var.* Djakovo,
  Hung. Diakovár. NE Croatia
Dakshin *see* Deccan
Dalaba *253* W Guinea
Dalai Nor *see* Hulun Nur
Dalälven *513* river of SE Sweden

Dalandzadgad *380* S Mongolia
Đa Lat *593* S Vietnam
Dali *see* Dhali
Dalian *163 var.* Jay Dairen, Ta-lien,
  Rus. Dalny. Liaoning, NE China
Dallas *569* Texas, SC USA
Dallol Bosso *407* seasonal water-
  course of W Niger
Dalmā *560* island of W United Arab
  Emirates
Dalmacija *181 Eng.* Dalmatia.
  Cultural region of S Croatia
Dalmatia *see* Dalmacija
Dalny *see* Dalian
Daloa *300* C Ivory Coast
Dalvík *268* N Iceland
Damanhûr *202 var.* Damanhūr.
  N Egypt
Damara *154* S Central African
  Republic
Damasak *409* NE Nigeria
Damascus *521 var.* Esh Sham,
  Fr. Damas, *Ar.* Dimashq. ❖ of Syria,
  SW Syria
Damāvand, Qolleh-ye *281* mountain
  of N Iran
Dambulla *504* C Sri Lanka
Dame-Marie *258* SW Haiti
Damêrdjôg *194* E Djibouti
Damietta *see* Dumyât
Damongo *242* NW Ghana
Damoûr *332 var.* Ad Dāmūr.
  W Lebanon
Damphu *110* S Bhutan
Dampier *628* C Ascension Island
Damqawt *599 var.* Damqut. E Yemen
Dâmrei, Chuôr Phmun *141*
  Fr. Chaîne de l'Éléphant. Mountain
  range of SW Cambodia
Danakil Desert *210, 215 var.* Danakil
  Plain, Afar Depression. Desert region
  of Eritrea and Ethiopia
Danané *300* W Ivory Coast
Đa Nâng *593 prev.* Tourane.
  C Vietnam
Danav *see* Danube
Danborg *622* E Greenland
Dandeldhura *see* Dadeldhura
Dandong *163 var.* Tan-tung,
  prev. An-tung. Liaoning, NE China
Dänew *see* Deynev
Dangal *210* SE Eritrea
Dangara *528* W Tajikistan
Danger Island *619* island of W British
  Indian Ocean Territory
Dänglä *215 var.* Dangila. NW Ethiopia
Dangme *110* river of S Bhutan
Dang Raek, Phanom *141, 533*
  var. Phanom Dong Rak,
  Cam. Chuor Phmum Dângrêk,
  Fr. Chaîne des Dangrek. Mountain
  range of Cambodia and Thailand
Dangrak, Chaîne des *see* Dang Raek,
  Phanom
Dângrêk, Chuôr Phmun *see* Dang
  Raek, Phanom
Dangriga *102 var.* Stann Creek.
  SE Belize
Ḍank *418 var.* Dhank. NW Oman
Danlí *260* S Honduras
Danmark *see* Denmark
Danmark Havn *622* E Greenland
Danmarksstraedet *see* Denmark Strait
Danube *82, 128, 181, 237, 264, 448,*
  485, 556, 602 Bul. Danav,
  Hung. Duna, *Cz.* Dunaj, *Ger.* Donau,
  Rom. Dunărea. River of C Europe
Danube, Mouths of the *448*
  Rom. Delta Dunării. Delta of Romania
  and Ukraine
Danubian Plain *see* Dunavska
  Ravnina
Danyi-Apéyémé *537 prev.* Apéyémé.
  W Togo
Danzig *see* Gdańsk
Danzig, Gulf of *439 var.* Gulf of
  Gdańsk, *Gk* Danziger Bucht,
  Pol. Zatoka Gdańska,
  Rus. Gdan'skaya Bukhta. Gulf of the
  Baltic Sea, N Poland

Dapaong *537* N Togo
Dara *476 var.* Dahra. NW Senegal
Dar'ā *521 var.* Der'a, *Fr.* Déraa. SW Syria
Da Rang *593 var.* Ba. River of S Vietnam
Dardanelles *see* Canakkale Boğazı
Dar el Beida *see* Casablanca
Dar es Salaam *530* E Tanzania
Darfur *506 var.* Darfur Massif. Mountain range of W Sudan
Darganata *551 var.* Dargan-Ata. E Turkmenistan
Dargaville *401* NW North Island, New Zealand
Dargol *407* W Niger
Darhan *380* N Mongolia
Darien, Isthmus of *see* Panama, Isthmus of
Darién, Serranía del *424* mountain range of Colombia and Panama
Darjiling *271 prev.* Darjeeling. NE India
Darling *77* river of E Australia
Darling Range *76* mountain range of SW Australia
Darlington *563* N England, UK
Darmstadt *236* SW Germany
Darnah *339 var.* Derna. NE Libya
Daroot-Korgon *325 var.* Daraut-Kurgan. SW Kyrgyzstan
Darou Mousti *476* NW Senegal
Darrell Island *619* island of W Bermuda
Dartmoor *563* moorland of SW England, UK
Dartmouth *147* SE Canada
Daru *426* SW Papua New Guinea
Daru *480* SE Sierra Leone
Darvaza *551 Turkm.* Derweze. C Turkmenistan
Darvel Bay *see* Lahad Datu, Telukan
Darvel, Teluk *see* Lahad Datu, Telukan
Darwin *77* N Australia
Darwin, Isla *200* island of the NW Galapagos Is, Ecuador
Dashkhovuz *551 prev.* Tashauz, *var.* Tašauz, *Turkm.* Dashhowuz. N Turkmenistan
Dasht Kaur *420* river of SW Pakistan
Daska *421* NE Pakistan
Da, Sông *see* Black River
Dassa *108 var.* Dassa-Zoumé. S Benin
Datong *163 var.* Ta-t'ung. Shanxi, N China
Datu, Teluk *354* bay of the South China Sea, on the coast of Borneo, E Malaysia
Daua *316 Amh.* Dawa Wenz. River of E Africa
Daugava *see* Western Dvina
Daugavpils *330 Ger.* Dünaburg, *Rus.* Dvinsk. SE Latvia
Daule *200* W Ecuador
Daule *200* river of W Ecuador
Daurada, Costa *500 var.* Costa Dorada. Coastal region of E Spain
Davao *435* Mindanao, S Philippines
Davao Gulf *435* gulf of the Pacific Ocean
Davenport *569* Iowa, C USA
David *424* W Panama
Davis *66* Australian research station of Greater Antarctica, Antarctica
Davis Strait *147, 622* strait connecting the Atlantic Ocean and Baffin Bay, NE Canada between Baffin Island and Greenland
Davos *516* E Switzerland
Davyd-Haradok *104 Rus.* David Gorodok, *Pol.* Dawidgródek. S Belorussia
Dawa Wenz *see* Daua
Dawei *see* Tavoy
Dawidgródek *see* Davyd-Haradok
Dawra *382* NW Western Sahara
Dawson *146* NW Canada
Dawwah *418 var.* Dauwa. E Oman

Dayrah *560 var.* Deira. NE United Arab Emirates
Dayr az Zawr *521 var.* Deir ez Zor. E Syria
Dayrīk *see* Al Mālikīyah
Dayton *569* Ohio, NE USA
De Aar *493* Northern Cape, C South Africa
Deadman's Bay *628* bay of the South Atlantic Ocean on the SW coast of Tristan da Cunha
Dead Sea *291, 292, 310 Ar.* Al Baḥr al Mayyit, Baḥrat Lūṭ, *Heb.* Yam HaMelaḥ. Salt lake of SW Asia
Deadwood Plain *628* plain of N St Helena
Debar *349* W FYR Macedonia
Débo, Lac *360* lake of C Mali
Debre Birhan *215 var.* Debra Birhan. C Ethiopia
Debrecen *264 prev.* Debreczen, *Ger.* Debreczin. E Hungary
Debre Mark'os *215* NW Ethiopia
Debre Tabor *215* NW Ethiopia
Debre Zebīt *215* N Ethiopia
Debre Zeyit *215 var.* Debre Zeyt, *prev.* Bishoftu, *It.* Biscoftù. C Ethiopia
Deccan *270 Hind.* Dakshin. Plateau of C India
Děčín *188 Ger.* Tetschen. NW Czech Republic
Dedeagach *see* Alexandroúpoli
Dededo *623* N Guam
Dedeagaç *see* Alexandroúpoli
Dedoplistsqaro *234 Rus.* Dedoplis-Tskaro, *prev.* Tsiteli-Tskaro. SE Georgia
Dédougou *132* W Burkina
Deduru Oya *504* C Sri Lanka
Dedza *353* SW Malawi
Dee *563* river of NE Scotland, UK
Dee *563 Wel.* Dyfrdwy. River of N Wales, UK
Deep Bay *see* Chilumba
Deep Water Bay *see* Hau Hoi Wan
Değirmenlik *187 var.* Kythrea. N Cyprus
Dehiwala-Mount Lavinia *504* SW Sri Lanka
Deinze *99* W Belgium
Deira *see* Adh Dhayd
Deir el Balah *291, 292* C Gaza Strip
Deir el-Bahri *202* E Egypt
Deir ez Zo *see* Dayr az Zawr
Deirgeirt, Loch *see* Derg, Lough
Dej *448* NW Romania
Dekemhare *210* S Eritrea
Dékoa *154* C Central African Republic
Delagoa Bay *see* Maputo, Baía de
Delap District *364* district of Majuro, SE Marshall Islands
Delārām *53* SW Afghanistan
Delaware *569* state of E USA
Delčevo *349* NE FYR Macedonia
Delcommune, Lac *see* Nzilo, Lac
Delémont *516 Ger.* Delsberg. NW Switzerland
Delft *397* W Netherlands
Delft *504* island of NW Sri Lanka
Delfzijl *397* NE Netherlands
Delhi *270 Hind.* Dilli. N India
Délices *196* SE Dominica
Délices *621* C French Guiana
Delsberg *see* Delémont
Delvinë *57 var.* Delvina, *It.* Delvino. S Albania
Delvino *see* Delvinë
Demba *607* C Zaire
Dembéni *625* E Mayotte
Dembéni *174* S Grande Comore, Comoros
Dembī Dolo *215 var.* Dembidollo. W Ethiopia
Demerara *256* river of N Guyana
Denau *580 Uzb.* Denow. SE Uzbekistan
Dender *99 Fr.* Dendre. River of W Belgium
Dendre *see* Dender
Den Haag *see* 's-Gravenhage

Den Helder *397* NW Netherlands
Denis, Île *478* island of the Inner Islands, NE Seychelles
Denizli *546* SW Turkey
Denmark *190-193* officially Kingdom of Denmark, *Dan.* Danmark. Country of W Europe, divided into 14 admin. units (counties)
Denmark Strait *268, 622 var.* Danmarksstraedet. Strait between Greenland and Iceland
Dennery *465* S St Lucia
Denow *see* Denau
Denpasar *276 prev.* Paloe. Bali, C Indonesia
D'Entrecasteaux Islands *426* island group of SE Papua New Guinea
Denver *569* Colorado, SW USA
Der'a *see* Dar'ā
Deraa *see* Dar'ā
Dera Ghāzi Khān *421* C Pakistan
Dera Ismāīl Khān *421* N Pakistan
Ðeravica *602 var.* Durmitor. Mountain of N Montenegro, Yugoslavia
Derby *563* C England, UK
Derg, Lough *288 Ir.* Loch Deirgeirt. Lake of C Ireland
Dernière Rivière *465* NE St Lucia
Derrick *466* Bequia, St Vincent & the Grenadines
Derrière Morne *465* S St Lucia
Derrubado *152* N Boa Vista, E Cape Verde
Derry *see* Londonderry
Derventa *116* N Bosnia & Herzegovina
Derweze *see* Darvaza
Deryneia *see* Dherinia
Desaguadero *112* river of Bolivia and Peru
Desbarra *465* NE St Lucia
Desdunes *258* W Haiti
Desē *215 var.* Desse, *It.* Dessie. N Ethiopia
Desertas, Ilhas *442* island group of the Madeira Is, Portugal
Des Moines *569* Iowa, C USA
Desna *556* river of N Ukraine
Despoto Planina *see* Rhodope Mountains
Desroches, Île *478 var.* Desroches. Island of the Amirante Islands, C Seychelles
Desruisseaux *465* SE St Lucia
Dessau *237* C Germany
Dessie *see* Desē
Destêrro *see* Florianópolis
Dete *612 prev.* Dett. W Zimbabwe
Detroit *569* Michigan, NC USA
Deutsch-Brod *see* Havlíčkův Brod
Deutsche Bucht *see* German Bight
Deutschendorf *see* Poprad
Deutschland *see* Germany
Deva *448 Ger.* Diemrich, *Hung.* Déva. W Romania
Ðevđelija *see* Gevgelija
Deventer *397* E Netherlands
Devil's Island *621* island of N French Guiana
Devollit *57 var.* Devoll. River of SE Albania
Devon Island *146-147 prev.* North Devon Island. Island of Parry Islands, N Canada
Devonport *77* Tasmania, Australia
Deynev *551 prev.* Deynau, *Turkm.* Dänew. E Turkmenistan
Dezfūl *281 var.* Dizful. W Iran
Dhaalu Atoll *see* South Nilandhe Atoll
Dhahran *see* Az̧ Z̧ahrān
Dhaka *93 var.* Dacca. ❖ of Bangladesh, C Bangladesh
Dhali *187 var.* Dali. C Cyprus
Dhamar *599* W Yemen
Dhanbād *270* NE India
Dhankuta *395* E Nepal
Dharan *395 var.* Dharan Bazar. E Nepal
Dheere Laaq *490 It.* Lach Dera. Seasonal river of SW Somalia

Dhekelia *187 var.* Dekeleia. UK Air base, SE Cyprus
Dherinia *187 var.* Deryneia. E Cyprus
Dhiarizos *187 var.* Diarizos. River of SW Cyprus
Dhībān *310* NW Jordan
Dhofar *see* Z̧ufār
Dhráma *see* Dráma
Dhún na nGall, Bá *see* Donegal Bay
Dhuudo *490 It.* Uadi Dudo. Seasonal river of NE Somalia
Dhuusa Marreeb *490 var.* Dusa Marreb, *It.* Dusa Mareb. C Somalia
Diafarabé *360* C Mali
Diakovár *see* Ðakovo
Diamond Island *248* island to the N of Grenada island, Grenada
Diana's Peak *628* mountain of C St Helena
Diangounté-Kamara *360* W Mali
Diapaga *132* E Burkina
Diarizos *see* Dhiarizos
Dibā *560 var.* Dibā al Ḥiṣn, Dibba. NE United Arab Emirates
Dicle *see* Tigris
Diébougou *132* SW Burkina
Diego Garcia *619* island of S British Indian Ocean Territory
Diego Garcia *619* ❖ of British Indian Ocean Territory, Diego Garcia, S British Indian Ocean Territory
Diégo-Suarez *see* Antsirañana
Diekirch *346* C Luxembourg
Diéma *360* W Mali
Diemrich *see* Deva
Ðiên Biên *593 var.* Dien Bien Phu. NW Vietnam
Dieppe *225* N France
Dieppe Bay Town *462* N St Kitts, St Kitts & Nevis
Diffa *407* SE Niger
Differdange *346* SW Luxembourg
Digne *225* SE France
Digul *277 var.* Digoel. River of Irian Jaya, E Indonesia
Dihōk *see* Dahūk
Dijlah *see* Tigris
Dijon *225* NE France
Dikhil *194* SW Djibouti
Dīla *215 var.* Dilla. S Ethiopia
Dilbeek *99* C Belgium
Dilia *407 var.* Dillia. River of SE Niger
Dilijan *74 Rus.* Dilizhan, *var.* Diližan. NE Armenia
Di Linh *593* S Vietnam
Dilli *see* Delhi
Dillia *see* Dilia
Dillikot *395* W Nepal
Dilling *506 var.* Ad Dalanj. C Sudan
Dilolo *607* S Zaire
Dimashq *see* Damascus
Dimbokro *300* S Ivory Coast
Dimitrovgrad *128* S Bulgaria
Dimitrovo *see* Pernik
Dimlang *408 var.* Vogel Peak. Mountain of E Nigeria
Dimona *291* S Israel
Dinagat Island *435* island of E Philippines
Dinājpur *93* NW Bangladesh
Dinan *224* NW France
Dinant *99* S Belgium
Dinara *181* mountain of S Croatia
Dinara *116, 181* mountain range of Bosnia & Herzegovina and Croatia
Dinaric Alps *181* mountain range of Bosnia & Herzegovina and Croatia
Dindigal *270* S India
Dingle Bay *288 Ir.* Bá an Daingin. Bay of the Atlantic Ocean, SW Ireland
Dingli *363* SW Malta
Dingli Cliffs *363* cliffs of SW Malta
Dinguiraye *253* C Guinea
Dion *253* river of S Guinea
Dioro *360 var.* Dyero. SW Mali
Diourbel *476* W Senegal
Dipayal *395* W Nepal
Dipkarpaz *187 var.* Rizokarpaso. NE Cyprus

Fajãzinha *152* Fogo, S Cape Verde
Fakaofo Atoll *629* island of
  SE Tokelau
Fako *144* active volcano of
  W Cameroon
Falaba *480* N Sierra Leone
Falam *135* NW Burma
Falciano *468* NE San Marino
Fale *553* islet of Nukufetau, Tuvalu
Falealupo *596* Savai'i, Western Samoa
Falelima *596* Savai'i, Western Samoa
Falémé *360, 476* river of W Africa
Faleshty *see* Fãleşti
Fãleşti *376* *Rus.* Faleshty.
  NW Moldavia
Falevai *596* Upolu, Western Samoa
Falkat *210* seasonal river of N Eritrea
Falkirk *563* C Scotland, UK
Falkland Islands *71, 621*
  Sp. Islas Malvinas. British dependent
  territory of the South Atlantic Ocean.
  ❖ Port Stanley.
Falkland Sound *621* strait of the
  South Atlantic Ocean between East
  Falkland and West Falkland, Falkland
  Islands
Falluja *see* Al Fallūjah
Falmouth *68* S Antigua, Antigua
  & Barbuda
Falmouth *303* NW Jamaica
Falster *190* island of SE Denmark
Falun *513* C Sweden
Famagusta *see* Gazimağusa
Famagusta Bay *187*
  var. Ammochostos Bay, Gazimağusa
  Körfezi. Bay of the Mediterranean
  Sea, on the E coast of Cyprus
Fandriana *350* C Madagascar
Fang-liao *525* SW Taiwan
Fanling *262* N Hong Kong
Fanning Island *see* Tabuaeran
Fano *295* N Italy
Fan Si Pan *593* mountain of
  NW Vietnam
Faraday *66* UK research station
  of Antarctic Peninsula, Antarctica
Faradofay *see* Tôlañaro
Farafangana *350* SE Madagascar
Farafenni *233* NW Gambia
Farāh *53* W Afghanistan
Farāh Rūd *53* river of W Afghanistan
Farallon de Medinilla *626* island of
  C Northern Mariana Islands
Farallon de Pajaros *626* island of
  N Northern Mariana Islands
Faranah *253* S Guinea
Faraulep *375* atoll of C Micronesia
Farghona *see* Fergana
Fargo *569* North Dakota, NC USA
Farīdābād *270* N India
Farīdpur *93* C Bangladesh
Farim *254* NW Guinea-Bissau
Farm *625* river of E Montserrat
Farmington *568* New Mexico, SW USA
Faro *144* river of Cameroon and
  Nigeria
Faro *442* S Portugal
Farquhar Atoll *478* atoll of the
  Farquhar Group, S Seychelles
Farquhar Group *478* island group of
  S Seychelles
Fars, Khalīj-e *see* Persian Gulf
Farvel, Kap *622* var.
  Uummannarsuaq. Cape on the
  S coast of Greenland
Fass *233* W Gambia
Fastiv *556* NW Ukraine
Fatala *253* river of W Guinea
Fatick *476* W Senegal
Fatoto *233* E Gambia
Fatua, Pointe *629* var. Pointe Nord.
  Headland of Île Futuna, N Wallis
  & Futuna
Fatutaka *488* var. Mitre I. Island of
  E Solomon Islands
Faxaflói *268* bay of North Atlantic
  Ocean, on SW coast of Iceland
Faya *156* N Chad
Fayaoué *626* Ouvéa, Îles Loyauté,
  N New Caledonia

Fayetteville *569* Arkansas, SC USA
Faylakah *322* var. Failaka Island.
  Island of E Kuwait
Fazao, Monts du *537* mountain range
  of W Togo
Fazzān *339* *Eng.* Fezzan. Cultural
  region of W Libya
Fdérik *366* prev. Fort-Gouraud.
  NW Mauritania
Feabhai, Loch *see* Foyle, Lough
Fédala *see* Mohammedia
Fehmarn *237* island of N Germany
Fehmarnbelt *237* strait connecting
  Kieler Bucht and Mecklenburger
  Bucht, between Denmark and
  Germany
Feira de Santana *121* prev. Feira.
  E Brazil
Feistritz *82* river of SE Austria
Fejaj, Chott el *543* salt lake of
  C Tunisia
Feldkirch *82* W Austria
Félegyháza *see* Kiskunfélegyháza
Felidhu Atoll *358* atoll of C Maldives
Fénérive *see* Fenoarivo Atsinanana
Feng-lin *525* *Jap.* Hōrin. E Taiwan
Feng-shan *525* *Jap.* Hōzan.
  SW Taiwan
Fengtien *see* Shenyang
Fengtien *see* Liaoning
Feng-yüan *525* var. Toyohara,
  Jap. Hōgen. W Taiwan
Feni *93* E Bangladesh
Fennern *see* Vändra
Fenoarivo Atsinanana *350*
  prev. Fénérive. NE Madagascar
Fens, The *563* wetlands of E England,
  UK
Ferdinand *see* Montana
Fergana *580* prev. Novyy Margilan,
  Uzb. Farghona. E Uzbekistan
Fergana Valley *528* physical region
  of C Asia
Fergusson Island *426* var. Kaluwawa.
  Island of SE Papua New Guinea
Ferizaj *see* Uroševac
Ferkessédougou *300* N Ivory Coast
Ferlo *see* Vallée du Ferlo
Fernandina, Isla *200* island of
  W Galapagos Is, Ecuador
Fernando de la Mora *428* S Paraguay
Fernando de Noronha *121* island of
  E Brazil
Fernando Po *see* Bioko
Ferrara *295* N Italy
Ferrol *500* prev. El Ferrol del
  Caudillo. NW Spain
Ferryville *see* Menzel Bourguiba
Ferto-tó *see* Neusiedler See
Fès *382* *Eng.* Fez. N Morocco
Fethiye *546* SW Turkey
Feyzābād *53* var. Faizabad.
  NE Afghanistan
Fezzan *see* Fazzān
Fianarantsoa *350* C Madagascar
Fianga *156* SW Chad
Fichē *215* *It.* Ficce. C Ethiopia
Fielding *401* S North Island,
  New Zealand
Fier *57* var. Fieri. SW Albania
Fierzës, Liqeni i *57* lake of
  N Albania
Fig Tree *462* S Nevis, St Kitts
  & Nevis
Figueira da Foz *442* W Portugal
Figueres *501* E Spain
Figuig *382* var. Figig. E Morocco
Fiji *218-219* officially Sovereign
  Democratic Republic of Fiji, *Fij.* Viti.
  Country of the Pacific Ocean divided
  into 4 admin. units (divisions)
Filadelfia *178* W Costa Rica
Filingué *407* W Niger
Fimi *607* river of W Zaire
Finke *546* SW Turkey
Finland *220-223* officially Republic of
  Finland, *Fin.* Suomen Tasavalta.
  Country of N Europe divided into
  12 admin. units (11 provinces and
  1 autonomous region)

Finland, Gulf of *212, 221, 452*
  Fin. Suomenlahti, *Swe.* Finska Viken,
  Est. Soome Laht, *Rus.* Finskiy Zaliv.
  Gulf of the Baltic Sea, N Europe
Finnmarksvidda *414* physical region
  of NE Norway
Fins *418* NE Oman
Finskiy Zaliv *see* Finland, Gulf of
Fiorina *468* NE San Marino
Firenze *294* *Eng.* Florence. NW Italy
Fischbacher Alpen *82* mountain
  range of E Austria
Fish *391* *Afr.* Vis. River of S Namibia
Fishguard *563* *Wel.* Abergwaun.
  W Wales, UK
Fiskeræsset *622*
  var. Qeqertarsuatsiaat, S Greenland
Fiume *see* Rijeka
Five Islands Village *68* W Antigua,
  Antigua & Barbuda
Fizuli *see* Füzuli
Fjerritslev *190* Jylland, NW Denmark
Fläming *237* hill region of
  NE Germany
Flanders *99* *Dut.* Vlaanderen,
  Fr. Flandres. Cultural region of
  W Belgium
Flat Island *628* island of NE Spratly
  Islands
Flatts Village *619* C Bermuda
Flensburg *236* N Germany
Flessingue *see* Vlissingen
Flinders *77* river of N Australia
Flinders Island *77* island of
  SE Australia
Flinders Ranges *77* mountain range
  of S Australia
Flin Flon *146* SW Canada
Flint *569* Michigan, NC USA
Flint Island *320* island of the Line Is,
  E Kiribati
Flitsch *see* Bovec
Floréal *368* C Mauritius
Florence *see* Firenze
Florencia *171* SW Colombia
Flores *250* N Guatemala
Flores *276* island of Nusa Tenggara,
  C Indonesia
Flores *442* island of the Azores,
  Portugal
Flores, Lago de *see* Petén Itza, Lago
Flores, Laut *276* *Eng.* Flores Sea.
  Sea of the Pacific Ocean,
  C Indonesia
Floreşti *376* *Rus.* Floreshty.
  N Moldavia
Florianópolis *121* prev. Destêrro.
  S Brazil
Florida *182* SE Cuba
Florida *260* W Honduras
Florida *569, 573* state of SE USA
Florida *577* S Uruguay
Floridablanca *171* NE Colombia
Florida Islands *488* group of islands
  of C Solomon Is
Florida, Straits of *88, 182* strait
  connecting the Atlantic Ocean and
  Gulf of Mexico
Flórina *245* var. Phlórina. N Greece
Flüelapass *516* mountain pass of
  E Switzerland
Flushing *see* Vlissingen
Fly *426* river of Indonesia and Papua
  New Guinea
Flying Fish Cove *620*
  ❖ of Christmas Island
Fnjóská *268* river of C Iceland
Foa *538* island of Ha'apai Group,
  Tonga
Foča *116* SE Bosnia & Herzegovina
Focşani *448* E Romania
Foggia *295* S Italy
Fogo *152* island of SW Cape Verde
Fogo'one, Pointe *629* headland of
  Île Uvea, S Wallis & Futuna
Foix *225* S France
Folkestone *563* SE England, UK
Fomboni *174* N Mohéli, Comoros
Fon *253* mountainous region of
  E Guinea

Fond St. Jean *196* S Dominica
Fongafale *553* var. Funafuti.
  ❖ of Tuvalu, Funafuti, Tuvalu
Fonseca, Gulf of *207, 260, 404* gulf
  of the Pacific Ocean, on the W coast
  of Central America
Fontvieille *378* SW Monaco
Fonuafo'ou *538* island of Nomuka
  Group, W Tonga
Fonualei *538* island of N Tonga
Foochow *see* Fuzhou
Forécariah *253* SW Guinea
Forestière *465* N St Lucia
Forlì *295* N Italy
Formentera *501* island of the Islas
  Baleares, E Spain
Formosa *71* NE Argentina
Formosa Bay *see* Ungama Bay
Formosa, Ilha *254* island of
  Arquipélago dos Bijagós, SW Guinea-
  Bissau
Formosa, Serra *121* mountains of
  C Brazil
Formosa Strait *see* Taiwan Strait
Forssa *221* SW Finland
Fortaleza *112* N Bolivia
Fortaleza *121* prev. Ceará. NE Brazil
Fort-Archambault *see* Sarh
Fort-Bayard *see* Zhanjiang
Fort-Cappolani *see* Tidjikja
Fort Charlet *see* Djanet
Fort Collins *569* Colorado, SW USA
Fort-Crampel *see* Kaga Bandoro
Fort-Dauphin *see* Tôlañaro
Fort-de-France *625* ❖ of Martinique,
  W Martinique
Fort-Foureau *see* Kousséri
Fort George *see* Grande Rivière, La
Fort-Gouraud *see* Fdérik
Forth *563* river of C Scotland, UK
Fort Hall *see* Murang'a
Forth, Firth of *563* estuary of the river
  Forth, E Scotland, UK
Fort Hill *see* Chitipa
Fortín General Diaz *428* W Paraguay
Fortín General Eugenio Garay
  see General Eugenio A. Garay
Fort Jameson *see* Chipata
Fort Johnson *see* Mangochi
Fort-Lamy *see* N'Djamena
Fort Lauderdale *569* Florida, SE USA
Fort-Liberté *258* N Haiti
Fort Manning *see* Mchinji
Fort McMurray *146* W Canada
Fort-Repoux *see* Akjoujt
Fort Rosebery *see* Mansa
Fort Saint John *146* W Canada
Fort Saskatchewan *146* SW Canada
Fort-Shevchenko *312*
  W Kazakhstan
Fort-Sibut *see* Sibut
Fort Smith *146* W Canada
Fort Smith *569* Arkansas, SC USA
Fort-Trinquet *see* Bîr Mogreïn
Fort Victoria *see* Masvingo
Fort Wayne *569* Indiana, C USA
Fort William *563* UK
Fort Worth *569* Texas, SC USA
Fougamou *230* C Gabon
Foulenzem *230* NW Gabon
Foumban *144* NW Cameroon
Foumbouni *174* S Grande Comore,
  Comoros
Fourchue, Île *622* island of
  N Guadeloupe
Fournaise, Piton de la *628* mountain
  of SE Réunion
Four Roads *540* NW Trinidad,
  Trinidad & Tobago
Fouta Djallon *253* var. Futa Jallon.
  Mountainous region of C Guinea
Foveaux Strait *401* strait between
  South Island and Stewart Island,
  New Zealand
Fox Bay East *621* West Falkland,
  W Falkland Islands
Fox Bay West *621* West Falkland,
  W Falkland Islands
Foxe Peninsula *147* peninsula
  of Baffin Island, NE Canada

Gedaref *506 var.* Al Qaḍārif, El Gedaref. E Sudan
Gedser *190* Falster, SE Denmark
Geel *99* NE Belgium
Geelong *77* SE Australia
Gege *510* SW Swaziland
Geghama Lerrnashght'a *74 Rus.* Gegamskiy Khrebet. Mountain range of C Armenia
Geita *530* NW Tanzania
Gëkdepe *551 prev.* Geok-Tepe, *Turkm.* Gökdepe. SW Turkmenistan
Gela *295* Sicilia, S Italy
Gelang *see* Geylang
Geleen *397* S Netherlands
Gelib *see* Jilib
Gelsenkirchen *236* W Germany
Gemena *607* NW Zaire
Genalē Wenz *see* Juba
Geneina *506 var.* Al Junaynah, Ajjinena. W Sudan
General Bernardo O'Higgins *66* Chilean research station of Antarctic Peninsula, Antarctica
General Carrera, Lago *see* Buenos Aires, Lago
General Eugenio A. Garay *428 var.* Fortín General Eugenio Garay, *prev.* Yrendagüé. NW Paraguay
General J.F. Uriburu *see* Zárate
General Machado *see* Camacupa
General Santos *435* Mindanao, S Philippines
Gênes *see* Genova
Geneva, Lake *225, 516 Fr.* Lac Léman, *var.* Le Léman, Lac de Genève, *Ger.* Genfer See. Lake of France and Switzerland
Genève *516 Eng.* Geneva, *Ger.* Genf, *It.* Ginevra. SW Switzerland
Genk *99 var.* Genck. NE Belgium
Gennargentu, Monti del *295* mountain of Sardegna, W Italy
Genova *294 Eng.* Genoa, *Fr.* Gênes. N Italy
Genova, Golfo di *294 Eng.* Gulf of Genoa. Gulf of the Ligurian Sea, on the W coast of Italy
Genovesa, Isla *200* island of N Galapagos Is, Ecuador
Genshū *see* Wŏnju
Gent *99 Eng.* Ghent, *Fr.* Gand. NW Belgium
Geokchay *see* Göyçay
Geok-Tepe *see* Gëkdepe
Georga, Zemlya *452 Eng.* George Land. Island of Zemlya Frantsa-Iosifa, N Russia
George *493* Western Cape, S South Africa
George Island *621* island of S Falkland Islands
George, Lake *554* lake of SW Uganda
George Land *see* Zemlya Georga
Georgenburg *see* Jurbarkas
George Town *88* San Salvador, Bahamas
George Town *354 var.* Penang, Pinang. NW Peninsular Malaysia
George Town *620* ❖ of Cayman Islands, Grand Cayman, W Cayman Islands
Georgetown *628* ❖ of Ascension Island, W Ascension Island
Georgetown *233* E Gambia
Georgetown *256* ❖ of Guyana, NE Guyana
Georgetown *466* NE St Vincent & the Grenadines
Georgeville *102* W Belize
Georgia *569* state of SE USA
Georgia *234-235* officially Republic of Georgia, *Geor.* Sak'art'velo, *Rus.* Gruziya, *prev.* Georgian SSR, *Rus.* Gruzinskaya SSR. Country of E Europe divided into 65 admin units (raioni)
Georgi Dimitrov, Yazovir *128* reservoir of C Bulgaria

Georg von Neumayer *66* German research station of Greater Antarctica, Antarctica
Gera *237* C Germany
Geral de Goiás, Serra *121* mountain range of E Brazil
Geraldton *76* W Australia
Gereshk *53* SW Afghanistan
Gerlachovský Štít *485 var.* Gerlachovka, *Ger.* Gerlsdorfer Spitze. Peak of Poland and Slovakia
German Bight *236 Ger.* Deutsche Bucht, *Dut.* Duitse Bocht. Bay of the North Sea
German East Africa *see* Tanzania
German Southwest Africa *see* Namibia
German Ocean *see* North Sea
Germans Bay *625* bay of the Caribbean Sea on the SW coast of Montserrat
Germany *236-241* officially Federal Republic of Germany, *Ger.* Deutschland. Country of Western Europe divided into 16 admin. units (Länder)
Germering *237* S Germany
Germiston *493 var.* Pretoria-Witwatersrand-Vereeniging, NE South Africa
Getafe *501* C Spain
Gevgelija *349 var.* Đevdelija, Djevdjelija, *Turk.* Gevgeli. SE FYR Macedonia
Geylang *483 var.* Gelang. River of SE Singapore
Geylegphug *110* S Bhutan
Ghadāmis *339 var.* Rhadames. NW Libya
Ghana *242-243* officially Republic of Ghana. Country of W. Africa divided into 10 admin. units (regions)
Ghanongga *see* Ranongga
Ghanzi *118* W Botswana
Ghap'an *see* Kapan
Gharbi, Île *543 Ar.* Jazirat al Gharbi. Island of E Tunisia
Ghardaïa *59* N Algeria
Gharsa, Chott el *543 var.* Shaṭṭ al Gharsah. Salt lake of W Tunisia
Gharyān *339* NW Libya
Ghāt *339 var.* Gat. W Libya
Ghawdex *see* Gozo
Ghawdex, Il-Fliegu ta' *363 Eng.* North Comino Channel. Strait of Mediterranean Sea between Gozo and Kemmuna, NW Malta
Ghayathi *560* W United Arab Emirates
Ghazal *156 var.* Soro. Seasonal river of C Chad
Ghazalkent *see* Gazalkent
Ghaznī *53* E Afghanistan
Ghazzah *see* Gaza
Ghelīzâne *see* Relizane
Ghent *see* Gent
Gherra, Sebkhet el *543* salt flat of NE Tunisia
Ghijduwon *see* Gizhduvan
Ghilizane *see* Relizane
Ghimbi *see* Gīmbī
Ghochas *see* Gochas
Ghukasyan *see* Ashots'k
Ghūrīān *53* W Afghanistan
Ghuwayfāt *560 var.* Gheweifat. W United Arab Emirates
Giahel, Uadi *see* Jaceel
Giamame *see* Jamaame
Giants Castle *493* mountain of Lesotho and South Africa.
Gibeon *391* S Namibia
Gibraltar *501, 622* British Crown Colony, to the S of Spain
Gibraltar, Bay of *622 var.* Bahía de Algeciras. Bay of the Atlantic Ocean on the W coast of Gibraltar
Gibraltar Harbour *622* W Gibraltar

Gibraltar, Strait of *382, 501, 622 Sp.* Estrecho de Gibraltar. Strait connecting the Atlantic Ocean and Mediterranean Sea, between Gibraltar and Morocco
Gibson Desert *76-77* desert of W Australia
Gifu *304* Honshū, C Japan
Giggiga *see* Jijiga
Gihororo *138* C Burundi
Gijón *501* NW Spain
Gikongoro *460* SW Rwanda
Gilbert Islands *182* island group of W Kiribati
Gilf Kebir Plateau *202 Ar.* Haḍabat al Jilf al Kabīr. Plateau of SW Egypt
Gilgit *421* river of N Pakistan
Gilolo *see* Halmahera
Gīmbī *215 It.* Ghimbi. W Ethiopia
Gimie, Mount *465* mountain of C St Lucia
Gimma *see* Jīma
Ginda *210* C Eritrea
Ginevra *see* Genève
Ginger Island *619* island of SE British Virgin Islands
Giohar *see* Jawhar
Giran *see* I-lan
Girardot *171* C Colombia
Giraudel *196* S Dominica
Girba, Khashm el *506 var.* Khashm al Qirbah, Khashim Al Qirba. E Sudan
Girgenti *see* Agrigento
Girne *187 var.* Keryneia, Kyrenia. N Cyprus
Girón *171* N Colombia
Girona *501* E Spain
Girsun *547* NE Turkey
Gisagara *460* S Rwanda
Gisborne *401* E North Island, New Zealand
Giseifu *see* Ŭijŏngbu
Gisenyi *460 var.* Gisenye. NW Rwanda
Gishyita *460* W Rwanda
Gissar *528* W Tajikistan
Gissar Range *528, 580 Rus.* Gissarskiy Khrebet. Mountains of Tajikistan and Uzbekistan
Gissarskiy Khrebet *see* Gissar Range
Gisuru *138 prev.* Kisuru. E Burundi
Gitanga *138 prev.* Kitanga. S Burundi
Gitarama *460* C Rwanda
Gitega *138 prev.* Kitega. C Burundi
Giulie, Alpi *see* Julian Alps
Giurgiu *448* S Romania
Give *190* Jylland, W Denmark
Giyon *215 var.* Wehso. C Ethiopia
Giza *see* El Gîza
Gizhduvan *580 var.* Gizhduvan, *Uzb.* Ghijduwon. S Uzbekistan
Gizo *488* New Georgia Is, Solomon Is
Gjakovë *see* Đakovica
Gjirokastër *57 var.* Gjirokastra, *prev.* Gjinokastër, Gjinokastra, *It.* Argirocastro, *Gk* Argyrokastron. S Albania
Gjoa Haven *146* King William Island, N Canada
Gjøvik *414* S Norway
Gkreko, Cape *see* Greco, Cape
Glåma *see* Glomma
Glanvilles *68* E Antigua, Antigua & Barbuda
Glanvillia *196* NW Dominica
Glasgow *563* W Scotland, UK
Glazoué *108* S Benin
Glendale *612* NE Zimbabwe
Glenties *288* N Ireland
Glina *181* NE Croatia
Glittertind *414 var.* Glittertinden. Mountain of S Norway
Gliwice *439 Ger.* Gleiwitz. S Poland
Głogów *439 Ger.* Glogau. W Poland
Glomma *414 var.* Glommen, Glåma. River of S Norway
Gloucester *563* C England, UK
Glover Island *248 var.* Ramier I. Island to the S of Grenada island, Grenada

Glubokoye *see* Hlybokaye
Gmundner See *see* Traunsee
Gnaviyani Atoll *see* Fuammulah
Goascorán *207* river of El Salvador and Honduras
Goascorán *260* river of SW Honduras
Goat Island *68* island to the N of Barbuda, Antigua & Barbuda
Goba *215 var.* Gobba. S Ethiopia
Gobabis *391* E Namibia
Gobi *163, 380* desert of China and Mongolia
Goce Delčev *see* Gorna Oryakhovitsa
Gochas *391 var.* Ghochas. SE Namibia
Go Công *593* S Vietnam
Godāveri *270* river of C India
Godhavn *622 var.* Qeqertarsuaq, W Greenland
Göding *see* Hodonín
Gödöllő *264* N Hungary
Godoy Cruz *71* W Argentina
Godwin Austen, Mount *see* K2
Goedgegun *see* Nhlangano
Goelette, Passe a la *628* channel of the Atlantic Ocean, to the E of Miquelon, Saint Pierre and Miquelon
Goeree *397* island of SW Netherlands
Goes *397* SW Netherlands
Goettingen *see* Göttingen
Gogounou *108* N Benin
Goiânia *121 prev.* Goyania. S Brazil
Gökdepe *see* Gëkdepe
Gokwe *612* N Zimbabwe
Gol *414* S Norway
Golan Heights *291* disputed territory of SW Syria
Gold Coast *77* E Australia
Gold Coast *243* coastal region of W Africa
Golden Bay *401* bay on the coast of N South Island, New Zealand
Golden Valley *612* N Zimbabwe
Goldingen *see* Kuldīga
Golfito *178* SE Costa Rica
Gollel *see* Lavumisa
Golmud *162 var.* Golmo, *Chin.* Ko-erh-mu. Qinghai, W China
Golungo Alto *64* NW Angola
Goma *607* NE Zaire
Gombe *408* E Nigeria
Gomel' *see* Homyel'
Gomera *501* island of Islas Canarias, SW Spain
Gómez Palacio *370* NW Mexico
Gonaïves *258* W Haiti
Gonâve, Golfe de la *258* gulf of the Caribbean Sea to the W of Haiti
Gonâve, Île de la *258* W Haiti
Gonder *215 var.* Gondar. NW Ethiopia
Gondomar *442* NW Portugal
Goodenough Island *426 var.* Morata. Island of SE Papua New Guinea
Good Hope *196* E Dominica
Good Hope, Cape of *493 Afr.* Kaap die Gooie Hoop. Coastal feature of SW South Africa
Goodlands *368* NE Mauritius
Goose Bay *see* Happy Valley-Goose Bay
Goose Green *621* East Falkland, C Falkland Islands
Gopālpur *93* N Bangladesh
Gorakhpur *270* NE India
Gorce Island *476* island of W Senegal
Gore *401* S South Island, New Zealand
Goré *156* S Chad
Gorē *215* W Ethiopia
Gorey *624* E Jersey
Gorgān *281 var.* Gurgan. N Iran
Gori *234* C Georgia
Goris *74* SE Armenia
Gorki *see* Horki
Gor'kiy *see* Nizhniy Novgorod
Görlitz *237* E Germany
Gorlovka *see* Horlivka
Gorna Dzhumaya *see* Blagoevgrad
Gorna Oryakhovitsa *128 var.* Gorna Orjahovica. N Bulgaria
Gornji Milanovac *602* C Serbia, Yugoslavia

Himeji *304* Honshū, C Japan
Himora *215* *var.* Humera. NW Ethiopia
Ḩimş *521* *var.* Homs. W Syria
Hînceşti *376* *var.* Hânceşti, *prev.* Kotovsk. C Moldavia
Hinche *258* C Haiti
Hindenburg *see* Zabrze
Hindiya *see* Al Hindīyah
Hindu Kush *53, 421* *Per.* Hendū Kosh. Mountain range of C Asia
Hingol *420* river of SW Pakistan
Hinson Bay *619* bay of the North Atlantic Ocean, C Bermuda
Hinson Island *619* island of W Bermuda
Hirmil *see* Hermel
Hirosaki *304* Honshū, N Japan
Hiroshima *304* Honshū, W Japan
Hirschberg in Riesengebirge *see* Jelenia Góra
Hirtshals *190* Jylland, N Denmark
Ḩisbān *310* NW Jordan
Ḩisb, Sha'īb *284* *var.* Sha'ib Hasb. Dry watercourse of S Iraq
Hitachi *304* Honshū, SE Japan
Hitra *414* *prev.* Hitteren. Island of W Norway
Hitteren *see* Hitra
Hiu *585* Torres Islands, N Vanuatu
Hjälmaren *513* *Eng.* Lake Hjalmar. Lake of S Sweden
Hjalmar, Lake *see* Hjälmaren
Hjørring *190* Jylland, N Denmark
Hkakabo Razi *135* mountain of Burma and China
Hlathikulu *510* *var.* Hlatikulu. S Swaziland
Hlohovec *485* *prev.* Frakštát, *Ger.* Freistadtl, *Hung.* Galgóc. W Slovakia
Hlotse *334* *var.* Leribe. NW Lesotho
Hlybokaye *104* *Rus.* Glubokoye. N Belorussia
Ho *242* SE Ghana
Hoa Binh *593* N Vietnam
Hoang Liên Sơn *593* mountain range of China and Vietnam
Hoani *174* NW Mohéli, Comoros
Hobart *77* Tasmania, Australia
Hobro *190* Jylland, NW Denmark
Hobyo *490* *It.* Obbia. E Somalia
Hô Chi Minh *593* *var.* Ho Chi Minh City, *prev.* Saigon. S Vietnam
Hodeida *see* Al Ḩudaydah
Hódmezővásárhely *264* SE Hungary
Hodonín *188* *Ger.* Göding. SE Czech Republic
Hoë Karoo *see* Northern Karoo
Hoeryŏng *413* NE North Korea
Höfdhakaupstadhur *see* Skagaströnd
Hofei *see* Hefei
Hofsá *268* river of E Iceland
Hofsjökull *268* glacier of C Iceland
Hofuf *see* Al Hufuf
Hōgen *see* Feng-yüan
Hoggar *see* Ahaggar
Hogoley Islands *see* Chuuk Islands
Hohenems *82* W Austria
Hohes Venn *see* Hautes Fagnes
Hohe Tauern *82* mountain range of W Austria
Hohhot *163* *var.* Huhehot, *prev.* Kweisui. Nei Mongol Zizhiqu, N China
Hôi An *593* *prev.* Faifo. C Vietnam
Hoihow *see* Haikou
Hoima *554* W Uganda
Hojancha *178* W Costa Rica
Hokitika *401* W South Island, New Zealand
Hokkaidō *305, 309* island of N Japan
Hokkō *see* Pei-kang
Hokō *see* P'ohang
Hoktemberyan *74* *Rus.* Oktemberyan. SW Armenia
Holbæk *190* Sjælland, E Denmark
Holetown *97* *prev.* Jamestown. W Barbados
Holguín *182* SE Cuba

Holhol *194* SE Djibouti
Holland *see* Netherlands
Hollandia *see* Jayapura
Hólmavík *268* NW Iceland
Holmsland Klit *190* fjord of Jylland, W Denmark
Holon *291* C Israel
Holonga *538* Uta Vava'u, Tonga
Holot Haluza *291* historic site of S Israel
Holstebro *190* Jylland, W Denmark
Holsteinsborg *622* *var.* Sisimiut. SW Greenland
Holyhead *563* N Wales, UK
Homa Bay *316* W Kenya
Homāyūnshahr *see* Khomeynīshahr
Hombori Tondo *360* mountain of E Mali
Home Island *620* island of C Cocos Islands
Homenau *see* Humenné
Homonna *see* Humenné
Homs *see* Ḩimş
Homs *see* Al Khums
Homyel' *104* *Rus.* Gomel'. SE Belorussia
Honan *see* Henan
Hondo *102, 370* river of Central America
Honduras *260-261* officially Republic of Honduras. Country of C America divided into 18 admin. units (departments)
Honduras, Gulf of *102, 250* gulf of the Caribbean Sea to the E of Central America
Hønefoss *414* S Norway
Hông Gai *593* *var.* Hongay. N Vietnam
Hong Kong *262-263* dependent territory of UK, due to revert to China in 1997
Hong Kong Island *262* island of S Hong Kong
Hongwŏn *413* E North Korea
Hongze Hu *163* *var.* Hung-tse Hu. Lake of E China
Honiara *488* ❖ of the Solomon Islands, N Guadalcanal, Solomon Islands
Honolulu *568* Oahu, Hawaii, USA
Honshū *304* island of C Japan
Honte *see* Westerschelde
Hoogeveen *397* NE Netherlands
Hoogezand *397* NE Netherlands
Hooker, Cape *493* cape of Marion Island, S South Africa
Hoorn *397* NW Netherlands
Hope Town *88* Great Abaco, Bahamas
Horgen *516* N Switzerland
Hōrin *see* Feng-lin
Horki *104* *Rus.* Gorki. NE Belorussia
Horlivka *556* *Rus.* Gorlovka. E Ukraine
Hormuz, Strait of *281, 418, 560* *var.* Strait of Ormuz, *Per.* Tangeh-ye Hormoz. Strait connecting the Persian Gulf and Arabian Sea
Hornád *485* *Ger.* Hernad, *Hung.* Hernád. River of Hungary and Slovakia
Horn, Cape *159* cape of S Chile
Horog *see* Khorog
Horoshiri-dake *305* mountain of Hokkaidō, N Japan
Horowupotana *504* NE Sri Lanka
Horqueta *428* C Paraguay
Horsburgh Atoll *358* atoll of N Maldives
Horsburgh Island *620* *var.* Pulu Luar. Island of C Cocos Islands
Horsens *190* Jylland, C Denmark
Horseshoe Bay *619* bay of the North Atlantic Ocean, W Bermuda
Horsham *77* SE Australia
Hørsholm *190* Sjælland, E Denmark
Hortobágny-Berettyó *264* river of E Hungary
Horten *414* S Norway
Hosa'ina *215* *var.* Hosseina, *It.* Hosanna. SW Ethiopia

Hose, Penunungan *354* *var.* Hose Mountains. Mountain range of Borneo, E Malaysia
Hotan *162* *var.* Khotan, *Chin.* Ho-t'ien. Xinjiang Uygur Zizhiqu. NW China
Hot Springs *569* Arkansas, SC USA
Hotte, Massif de la *258* highlands of SW Haiti
Houaïlu *626* C New Caledonia
Houmt Souk *543* *var.* Djerba, Ḩawmat as Sūd, Jerba. Île de Jerba, Tunisia
Houndé *132* SW Burkina
Houston *569* Texas, SC USA
Hovd *380* W Mongolia
Hoverla *556* *Rus.* Gora Goverla. Mountain of W Ukraine
Hövsgöl Nuur *380* lake of N Mongolia
Howe, Cape *77* cape on the SE coast of Australia
Howakil Bay *210* bay of the Red Sea to the E of Eritrea
Howrah *see* Hāora
Hōzan *see* Feng-shan
Hradec Králové *188* *Ger.* Königgrätz. E Czech Republic
Hrazdan *74* *Rus.* Razdan. C Armenia
Hrazdan *74* *Rus.* Razdan, Zanga. River of C Armenia
Hrodna *104* *Rus.* Grodno. W Belorussia
Hron *485* *Ger.* Gran, *Hung.* Garam. River of C Slovakia
Hseuh Shan *525* mountain of N Taiwan
Hsi-an *see* Xi'an
Hsiang-t'an *see* Xiangtan
Hsi Chiang *see* Xi Jiang
Hsin-chu *525* NW Taiwan
Hsin-chuang *525* *var.* Sinchwang, *Jap.* Shinshō. N Taiwan
Hsing-K'ai Hu *see* Khanka, Lake
Hsi-ning *see* Xining
Hsinking *see* Changchun
Hsin-tien *525* *var.* Sintien, *Jap.* Shinten. N Taiwan
Hsin-yang *see* Xinyang
Hsin-ying *525* *var.* Sinying, *Jap.* Shinei. W Taiwan
Hsu-chou *see* Xuzhou
Hsüeh-shan Shan-mo *525* mountain range of N Taiwan
Huacho *431* W Peru
Huainan *163* *var.* Hwainan. Anhui, E China
Hua-lien *525* *var.* Hwalien, *Jap.* Karen. E Taiwan
Huallaga *431* river of N Peru
Huambo *64* *Port.* Nova Lisboa. C Angola
Huancavelica *431* SW Peru
Huancayo *431* C Peru
Huang Hai *see* Yellow Sea
Huang He *163* *Eng.* Yellow River. River of C China
Huánuco *431* C Peru
Huanuni *112* W Bolivia
Huaral *431* W Peru
Huascarán, Nevado *431* mountain of W Peru
Huaraz *431* *var.* Huaráz. W Peru
Hubei *163* *var.* Hupei. Province of C China
Hubli *270* SW India
Huddersfield *563* N England, UK
Hudson *569* river of NE USA
Hudson Bay *147* bay of the Atlantic Ocean, NE Canada
Hudson Strait *147* strait connecting the Atlantic Ocean and Hudson Bay
Hue *593* C Vietnam
Huehuetenango *250* W Guatemala
Huelva *500* SW Spain
Huesca *501* NE Spain
Hughenden *77* NE Australia
Huhehot *see* Hohhot
Hŭich'ŏn *413* C North Korea
Huizen *397* C Netherlands
Huksan-kundo *496* *var.* Huksan-chedo. Island group of SW South Korea

Hull *see* Kingston-upon-Hull
Hull *147* SE Canada
Hullo *212* Vormsi, Estonia
Hulun Nur *163* *Chin.* Hu-lun Ch'ih, *prev.* Dalai Nor. Lake of Nei Mongol Zizhiqu, NE China
Ḩulwan *see* Ḩelwân
Humacao *627* E Puerto Rico
Humaitá *428* S Paraguay
Humber *563* river of NE England, UK
Humenné *485* *Ger.* Homenau, *Hung.* Homonna. E Slovakia
Humera *see* Himora
Húnaflói *268* bay of the Norwegian Sea on the N coast of Iceland
Hunan *163* province of S China
Hundested *190* Sjælland, E Denmark
Hunga Ha'apai *538* island of the Nomuka Group, W Tonga
Hungary *264-267* officially Republic of Hungary, *Hung.* Magyarország, *prev.* Hungarian People's Republic. Country of C Europe divided into 19 admin. units (counties)
Hunga Tonga *538* island of the Nomuka Group, W Tonga
Hŭngnam *413* E North Korea
Hung-tse Hu *see* Hongze Hu
Huntington *569* West Virginia, E USA
Huntsville *569* Alabama, SE USA
Hunyani *see* Manyame
Huon Gulf *426* gulf of the Solomon Sea, to the E of Papua New Guinea
Huo-shao Tao *see* Lan Yü
Hupei *see* Hubei
Hurghada *202* E Egypt
Huron, Lake *147, 589* lake of Canada and USA
Hurunui *401* river of NE South Island, New Zealand
Húsavík *620* Sandoy, C Faeroe Islands
Húsavík *268* NE Iceland
Ḩuşayn, Dawḩat al *447* *var.* Dauhat al Husein. Inlet of the Gulf of Bahrain on the NW coast of Qatar
Ḩūth *599* NW Yemen
Huwâr *447* island of SE Bahrain
Huwwâra *see* Hawwârah
Hvammstangi *268* N Iceland
Hvannadalshnúkur *268* mountain of S Iceland
Hvar *181* *It.* Lesina. Island of S Croatia
Hvíta *268* river of W Iceland
Hvolsvŏllur *268* SW Iceland
Hwach'ŏn-chŏsuji *see* P'aro-ho
Hwainan *see* Huainan
Hwange *612* *prev.* Wankie. W Zimbabwe
Hwang-Hae *see* Yellow Sea
Hyargas Nuur *380* lake of W Mongolia
Hyderābād *270* *Hind.* Hyderabad. C India
Hyderābād *421* *var.* Haidarabad. S Pakistan
Hyères *225* SE France
Hyères, Îles d' *225* island group of SE France
Hyesan *413* NE North Korea
Hyūga *304* Kyūshū, SW Japan
Hyvinge *see* Hyvinkää
Hyvinkää *221* *Swe.* Hyvinge. S Finland

I

Ialomiţa *448* river of SE Romania
Ialpug *376* *Rus.* Yalpug. River of S Moldavia
Iaşi *448* *Ger.* Jassy. NE Romania
Ibadan *408* SW Nigeria
Ibagué *171* C Colombia
Ibar *602* river of SW Serbia, Yugoslavia

Ibarra *200 var.* San Miguel de Ibarra. N Ecuador
Ibb *599* W Yemen
Ibbenbüren *236* NW Germany
Ibenga *176* river of N Congo
Ibérico, Sistema *501 var.* Cordillera Ibérica, *Eng.* Iberian Mountains. Mountains of NE Spain
Ibiza *see* Eivissa
Ibo *see* Sassandra
Iboundji *230* C Gabon
Ibrā' *418* N Oman
Ibrī *418* NW Oman
Irbīl *see* Arbīl
Ibusuki *304* Kyūshū, SW Japan
Içá *120* river of NW Brazil
Ica *431* SW Peru
Iceflavik *see* Keflavík
İçel *see* Mersin
Iceland *268-269* officially Republic of Iceland, *Icel.* Ísland. Country of the North Atlantic Ocean divided into 8 admin. units (regions)
Ichinomiya *304* Honshū, C Japan
Ichinoseki *304* Honshū, N Japan
Idah *408* S Nigeria
Idaho *568* state of NW USA
Idaho Falls *568* Idaho, NW USA
Idensalmi *see* Iisalmi
Idfu *202 var.* Idfū, Edfu. SE Egypt
Idi Amin, Lac *see* Edward, Lake
Idlib *521* NW Syria
Idrija *486 It.* Idria. W Slovenia
Idzhevan *see* Ijevan
Iecava *330* C Latvia
Ieper *99 Fr.* Ypres. W Belgium
Ifalik *375* atoll of C Micronesia
Ife *408* SW Nigeria
Iferouâne *407* N Niger
Iferten *see* Yverdon
Iganga *554* SE Uganda
Igarka *453* N Russia
Igatimí *see* Ygatimí
Iglau *see* Jihlava
Iglesias *294* Sardegna, W Italy
Igló *see* Spišská Nová Ves
Ignalina *344* E Lithuania
Iguaçu, Salto do *121 Sp.* Cataratas del Iguazú, *prev.* Victoria Falls. Waterfall of Argentina and Brazil
Iguetti, Sebkhet *366* salt lake of N Mauritania
Ihavandippolhu Atoll *358 var.* Ihavandiffulu Atoll. Atoll of N Maldives
Ihema, Lac *460* lake of Burundi and Rwanda
Ihosy *350* S Madagascar
Iida *304* Honshū, C Japan
Iijoki *221* river of C Finland
Irbīl *see* Arbīl
Iisalmi *221 Swe.* Idensalmi. C Finland
Ijebu-Ode *408* SW Nigeria
Ijevan *74 Rus.* Idzhevan, *var.* Idževan. N Armenia
IJssel *397 var.* Yssel. River of C Netherlands
IJsselmeer *397 prev.* Zuider Zee. Lake of N Netherlands
Ikare *408* SW Nigeria
Ikaría *245* island of SE Greece
Ikast *190* Jylland, W Denmark
Ikeja *408* SW Nigeria
Ikerre *408 var.* Ikerre-Ekiti. SW Nigeria
Iki *304* island to the NW of Kyūshū, SW Japan
Ikom *408* S Nigeria
Ikopa *350* river of N Madagascar
Ila *408* W Nigeria
Ilam *395* W Nepal
I-lan *525 Jap.* Giran. NE Taiwan
Ile *see* Ili
Ilebo *607 prev.* Port Francqui. W Zaire
Ilesha *408* SW Nigeria
Ilha Solteira, Represa de *121* reservoir of S Brazil

Ili *312 Kaz.* Ile. River of China and Kazakhstan
Iligan *435* Mindanao, S Philippines
Ilirska Bistrica *486* SW Slovenia
Il'jaly *see* Yylanly
Illapel *159* C Chile
Illiassa *233* NW Gambia
Illinois *569* state of C USA
Ilobasco *207* C El Salvador
Ilobu *408* W Nigeria
Iloilo *435* Panay, C Philippines
Ilopango, Lago de *207* volcanic lake of C El Salvador
Ilorin *408* W Nigeria
İluh *see* Batman
Il'yaly *see* Yylanly
Imatong Mountains *506* mountains of S Sudan
Imatra *221* SE Finland
Imeni 26 Bakinskikh Komissarov *see* Bakı Komissarı
Imilili *382* W Western Sahara
İmişli *86 Rus.* Imishli, Imišli. C Azerbaijan
Imja-do *496* island of SW South Korea
Imola *295* N Italy
Imperatriz *121* NE Brazil
Imperia *294* N Italy
Impfondo *176* NE Congo
Imphāl *271* E India
Ina *304* Honshū, C Japan
Inakona *488* S Guadalcanal, Solomon Is
In Aménas *59 var.* I-n-Amenas, In Amnas. E Algeria
Inárajan *623* SE Guam
Inarijärvi *221 Swe.* Enareträsk, *Lapp.* Aanaarjävri. Lake of N Finland
Inarijoki *221 Nor.* Anarjokka. River of Finland and Norway
Inawashiro-ko *304* lake of Honshū, N Japan
Inbhear Mór *see* Arklow
Inch'ŏn *496 prev.* Chemulpo, *Jap.* Jinsen. NW South Korea
Inchope *387* C Mozambique
Incles *62* river of NE Andorra
Independence *102* SE Belize
Inderagiri *see* Indragiri
India *270-275* officially Republic of India, *Hind.* Bharat. Country divided into 32 admin. units (25 states and 7 union territories)
Indiana *569* state of C USA
Indianapolis *569* Indiana, C USA
Indian Desert *see* Thar Desert
Indian Ocean *66, 620* ocean bounded to the W by Africa, to the E by Australia and to the S by Antarctica
Indigirka *453* River of NE Russia
Indonesia *276-279* officially Republic of Indonesia, *Ind.* Republik Indonesia, *prev.* United States of Indonesia, Dutch East Indies, Netherlands East Indies. Country of SE Asia divided into 25 admin. units (24 provinces and 1 autonomous district)
Indonesian Borneo *see* Kalimantan
Indore *270* NW India
Indragiri *276 var.* Inderagiri. River of Sumatra, W Indonesia
Indre *225* river of C France
Indus *270, 421* river of S Asia
Indus, Mouths of the *421* river delta of S Pakistan
Infante Dom Henrique *471* SE Príncipe, Sao Tome & Principe
Ingolstadt *237* S Germany
Inguri *see* Enguri
Ingushetiya, Respublika *452* autonomous republic of SW Russia
Ingwavuma *see* Nggwavuma
Inhambane *387* S Mozambique
I-ning *see* Yining
Inírida *171* river of E Colombia
Inis *see* Ennis
Inland Sea *304 var.* Seto Naikai. Sea of the Pacific Ocean between Honshū and Shikoku, W Japan

Inn *82, 237* river of C Europe
Inner Channel *102 var.* Main Channel. Inlet of W Caribbean Sea
Inner Hebrides *563* island group of NW Scotland, UK
Inner Islands *478 var.* Central Group. Island group of NE Seychelles
Inner Mongolian Autonomous Region *see* Nei Mongol Zizhiqu
Innsbruck *82* W Austria
Inrin *see* Yüan-lin
In Salah *59 var.* I-n-Salah. C Algeria
Insein *135* S Burma
Intelewa *508* S Surinam
Interlaken *516* SW Switzerland
Inthanon, Doi *533* mountain of NW Thailand
Intipucá *207* SE El Salvador
Inuvik *563* N Canada
Invercargill *401* SW South Island, New Zealand
Inverness *563* N Scotland, UK
Inyanga *see* Nyanga
Inyangani *612* mountain of E Zimbabwe
Inyazura *see* Nyazura
Ioánnina *245 var.* Janina, Yannina. W Greece
Iolotan' *see* Ëloten
Ionian Islands *see* Iónioi Nísoi
Ionian Sea *57, 245, 295 Gk* Iónio Pélagos, *It.* Mar Ionio. Area of the Mediterranean Sea, between Italy and SE Europe
Ionio, Mar *see* Ionian Sea
Iónioi Nísoi *245 Eng.* Ionian Islands. Island group of W Greece
Iori *234* river of Azerbaijan and Georgia
Íos *245* island of SE Greece
Iowa *569* state of C USA
IpeI *see* Ipoly
Ipiales *171* SW Colombia
Ipoh *354* W Peninsular Malaysia
Ipoly *264, 485 Slvk.* IpeI, *Ger.* Eipel. River of Hungary and Slovakia
Ippy *154* C Central African Republic
Ipswich *77* E Australia
Ipswich *563* E England, UK
Iqaluit *147 prev.* Frobisher Bay. Baffin Island, NE Canada
Iquique *159* N Chile
Iquitos *431* N Peru
Irákleio *245 Eng.* Candia, *prev.* Iráklion. Crete, S Greece
Iran *280-283* officially Islamic Republic of Iran, *prev.* Persia. Country of SW Asia divided into 24 admin. units (provinces)
Iran, Pegunungan *355 var.* Iran Mountains. Mountain range of Borneo, Indonesia and Malaysia
Iran, Plateau of *281* plateau of C Iran
Irapuato *370* C Mexico
Iraq *284-287* officially Republic of Iraq, *Ar.* 'Irāq. Country of SW Asia divided into 18 admin. units (governorates)
Irbe Strait *212 Est.* Kura Kurk, *prev.* Irbe Väin, *Latv.* Irbes Šaurums. Strait connecting the Baltic Sea and Gulf of Riga
Irbid *310* N Jordan
Ireland Island North *619* island of W Bermuda
Ireland Island South *619* island of W Bermuda
Ireland, Northern *see* Northern Ireland
Ireland, Republic of *288-289* officially Republic of Ireland, Éire. Country of W Europe divided into 26 admin. units (counties)
Ireng *256 var.* Maú. River of Brazil and Guyana
Irgalem *see* Yirga 'Alem
Iri *496 Jap.* Riri. W South Korea
Irian *see* New Guinea

Irian Jaya *276-277 Eng.* West Irian, *prev.* Dutch New Guinea. Province of W Indonesia
Iringa *530* C Tanzania
Iriomote-jima *304* island of Sakishima-shotō, SW Japan
Iriri *121* river of N Brazil
Irish Sea *288, 563, 623 Ir.* Muir Eireann. Sea of the Atlantic Ocean between Ireland and UK
Irkeshtam *325 var.* Irkeštam. SW Kyrgyzstan
Irkutsk *453* C Russia
Irmak *547* river of N Turkey
Iroise *224* area of the Atlantic Ocean to the NW of France
'Irqah *599* SW Yemen
Irrawaddy *135 var.* Ayeyarwady. River of C Burma
Irrawaddy, Mouths of the *135* delta area of SW Burma
Irrsee *82* lake of N Austria
Irtysh *312, 452 Kaz.* Ertis. River of Kazakhstan and Russia
Irun *501* N Spain
Iruñea *see* Pamplona
Isabela *627* NW Puerto Rico
Isabela, Isla *200* island of SW Galapagos Is, Ecuador
Isachsen *146* Ellef Ringnes Island, N Canada
Ísafdhardjúp *268* inlet of the Atlantic Ocean, NW Iceland
Isangel *585* Tanna, Vanuatu
Isa Town *see* Madīnat 'Īsá
Isalo, Tangorombohitr' *350* mountains of SW Madagascar
Ischia, Isola d' *295* island of S Italy
Ise *304* Honshū, C Japan
Isefjord *190* fjord of Sjælland, E Denmark
Isembe *138 var.* Shembe. S Burundi
Isère *225* river of SE France
Iseyin *408* W Nigeria
Isfara *528* N Tajikistan
Ísfjördhur *268* NW Iceland
Isha Baydhabo *see* Baydhabo
Isherton *256* S Guyana
Ishigaki-jima *304* island of Sakishima-shotō, SW Japan
Ishikari *305* river of Hokkaidō, N Japan
Ishim *312 Kaz.* Esil. River of Kazakhstan and Russia
Ishinomaki *304* Honshū, N Japan
Ishkashim *528* S Tajikistan
Ishurdi *93* W Bangladesh
Isidoro Noblia *577* NE Uruguay
Isiolo *316* C Kenya
Isiro *607* NE Zaire
Iskeçe *see* Xánthi
İskele *187 var.* Trikomo. E Cyprus
İskenderun *547 Eng.* Alexandretta. S Turkey
İskenderun Körfezi *547 Eng.* Gulf of Alexandretta. Gulf of the Mediterranean Sea
Iskŭr *128* river of NW Bulgaria
Iskŭr, Yazovir *128* reservoir of W Bulgaria
Islāmābād *421* ❖ of Pakistan, NE Pakistan
Island Harbour *618* bay of the Caribbean Sea on the N coast of Anguilla
Islay *563* island of Inner Hebrides, W Scotland, UK
Isle *225* river of SW France
Ismâ'ilîya *202 var.* Al Ismā'īlīyah, *Eng.* Ismaila. N Egypt
Isna *202 var.* Isnā, Esna. SE Egypt
Isoka *611* NE Zambia
Isonzo *see* Soča.
Ispahan *see* Eşfahān
İsparta *547* SW Turkey

Kalundborg *190* Sjælland, C Denmark
Kalungwishi *611* river of N Zambia
Kalutara *504* SW Sri Lanka
Kaluwawa *see* Fergusson Island
Kalyān *270* W India
Kama *607* E Zaire
Kamai *156* N Chad
Kamaishi *305* Honshū, N Japan
Kamakwie *480* NW Sierra Leone
Kamālia *421* NE Pakistan
Kamanjab *391* NW Namibia
Kamarān *599* island of W Yemen
Kamarang *256* W Guyana
Kamativi *612* W Zimbabwe
Kambar *421* *var.* Qambar.
  SW Pakistan
Kambara *see* Kabara
Kamchatka, Poluostrov *453*
  Eng. Kamchatka Peninsula. Peninsula
  of NE Russia
Kamchiya *128* *var.* Kamčija. River of
  E Bulgaria
Kamenets-Podol'sk *see* Kam"yanets'-
  Podil's'kyy
Kamenets-Podol'skiy
  see Kam"yanets'-Podil's'kyy
Kamenica *349* NE FYR Macedonia
Kamenskoye *see* Dniprodzerzhyns'k
Kamina *607* S Zaire
Kamishli *see* Al Qāmishlī
Kamloops *146* SW Canada
Kammersee *see* Attersee
Kamnik *486* *Ger.* Stein. C Slovenia
Kamo *74* C Armenia
Kamp *82* river of N Austria
Kampala *554* ❖ of Uganda, S Uganda
Kampar *354* W Peninsular Malaysia
Kampar *276* river of Sumatra,
  W Indonesia
Kampo *see* Ntem
Kampong Batang Duri *126*
  NE Brunei
Kampong Benutan *126* C Brunei
Kampong Bukit Sawat *126* C Brunei
Kampong Bunut *126* N Brunei
Kâmpóng Cham *141*
  prev. Kompong Cham. S Cambodia
Kâmpóng Chhnăng *141* C Cambodia
Kampong Jerudong *126* N Brunei
Kâmpóng Khleăng *141*
  prev. Kompong Kleang.
  NW Cambodia
Kampong Kuala Abang *126* C Brunei
Kampong Kuala Balai *126* SW Brunei
Kampong Labi *126* S Brunei
Kampong Labu *126* NE Brunei
Kampong Lumut *126* N Brunei
Kampong Paring *126* N Brunei
Kampong Parit *126* N Brunei
Kâmpóng Saôm *141*
  var. Kompong Som,
  prev. Sihanoukville. SW Cambodia
Kâmpóng Saôm, Chhâk *141*
  Fr. Baie de Kompong Som. Bay of the
  Gulf of Thailand on the SW coast of
  Cambodia
Kâmpóng Spoe *141*
  prev. Kompong Speu. S Cambodia
Kampong Sukang *126* C Brunei
Kampong Tanajor *126* C Brunei
Kampong Teraja *126* S Brunei
Kâmpóng Thum *141*
  prev. Kompong Thom. C Cambodia
Kâmpôt *141* S Cambodia
Kampuchea *see* Cambodia
Kamsar *253* W Guinea
Kam"yanets'-Podil's'kyy *556*
  Rus. Kamenets-Podol'skiy,
  prev. Kamenets-Podol'sk. W Ukraine
Kanacea *218* *prev.* Kanathea. Taveuni,
  N Fiji
Kanacea *218* island of the Lau Group,
  E Fiji
Kananga *607* *prev.* Luluabourg.
  SW Zaire
Kanazawa *304* Honshū, C Japan
Kanazi *460* SE Rwanda
Kandahār *53* *var.* Qandahār.
  S Afghanistan
Kandavu *see* Kadavu

Kandé *537* NE Togo
Kandi *108* N Benin
Kandrian *426* New Britain, E Papua
  New Guinea
Kandy *504* C Sri Lanka
Kaneohe *568* Oahu, Hawaii, USA
Kanevskoye Vodokhranilische
  see Kanivs'ke Vodoskhovyshche
Kang *118* C Botswana
Kangar *354* NW Peninsular Malaysia
Kangaroo Island *77* island of
  S Australia
Kangaruma *256* C Guyana
Kangchenjunga *271*
  var. Kanchenjunga. Mountain of
  NE India
Kanggye *413* N North Korea
Kanghwa-do *496* *Jap.* Kōka-tō. Island
  of NW South Korea
Kangnŭng *496* *Jap.* Kōryō. NE South
  Korea
Kango *230* NW Gabon
Kanibadam *528* N Tajikistan
Kani, Baie de *625* *var.* Kani Bay. Bay
  of the Mozambique Channel on the
  SW coast of Mayotte
Kanivs'ke Vodoskhovyshche *556*
  Rus. Kanevskoye Vodokhranilische.
  Reservoir of C Ukraine
Kanjiža *602* *prev.* Stara Kanjiža,
  Ger. Altkanischa,
  Hung. Magyarkanizsa, Ókanizsa.
  N Serbia, Yugoslavia
Kankan *253* E Guinea
Kankesanturai *504* N Sri Lanka
Kan-kô *see* Han
Kankossa *366* S Mauritania
Kanli Dere *see* Pedhieos
Kanmaw Island *135* *var.* Kettharin I,
  Kisseraing. Island of S Burma
Kano *408* N Nigeria
Kanombe *460* C Rwanda
Kanoya *304* Kyūshū, SW Japan
Kānpur *270* *prev.* Cawnpore. N India
Kanra-san *see* Halla-san
Kansas *569* state of C USA
Kansas City *569* Kansas, C USA
Kant *325* C Kyrgyzstan
Kantipur *see* Kathmandu
Kanton *320* *var.* Abariringa, Canton I,
  prev. Mary I. Island of the Phoenix Is,
  C Kiribati
Kanyaru *see* Akanyaru
Kanye *118* S Botswana
Kao *538* island of W Tonga
Kao *538* mountain of Kao, Tonga
Kaôh Nhêk *141* E Cambodia
Kao-hsiung *525* *var.* Kaohiung,
  Jap. Takao. SW Taiwan
Kaolack *476* *var.* Kaolak. W Senegal
Kaolak *see* Kaolack
Kaolan *see* Lanzhou
Kaoma *611* W Zambia
Kao-p'ing Hsi *525* river of C Taiwan
Kapan *74* *var.* Ghap'an. *Rus.* Kafan.
  SE Armenia
Kapchorwa *554* E Uganda
Kapenguria *316* W Kenya
Kapfenberg *82* C Austria
Kapingamarangi *375* atoll of
  S Micronesia
Kapiri Mposhi *611* C Zambia
Kapiti Island *401* island to the
  S of North Island, New Zealand
Kapka, Massif du *156* mountains
  of E Chad
Kaposvár *264* SW Hungary
Kaproncza *see* Koprivnica
Kapsabet *316* W Kenya
Kapsukas *see* Marijampolė
Kapuas *276* *prev.* Kapoeas. River of
  Borneo, C Indonesia
Kapuas Mountains *276, 354*
  Ind. Pegunungan Kapuas Hulu.
  Mountain range of Indonesia and
  Malaysia
Kara *537* *var.* Lama-Kara.
  NE Togo
Karaba *460* SW Rwanda
Kara-Balta *325* NW Kyrgyzstan

Karabil', Vozvyshennost' *551* region
  of SE Turkmenistan
Kara-Bogaz-Gol, Zaliv *551*
  NW Turkmenistan
Kara-Bogaz-Gol, Proliv *551*
  Turkm. Garabogazköl Bogazy. Strait
  of the Caspian Sea, on the NW coast
  of Turkmenistan
Karabük *547* N Turkey
Karachayevo-Cherkesskaya SSR *452*
  autonomous republic of
  SW Russia
Karāchi *421* S Pakistan
Karadeniz *see* Black Sea
Karadeniz Boğazi *see* İstanbul Boğazi
Karaferiye *see* Véroia
Karaganda *312* *Kaz.* Qaraghandy.
  C Kazakhstan
Karaitivu *504* N Sri Lanka
Karaj *281* NW Iran
Karak *see* Al Karak
Kara-Kala *see* Garrygala
Karaklin *see* Vanadzor
Karakol *325* *var.* Karakolka.
  E Kyrgyzstan
Karakol *325* *prev.* Przheval'sk,
  var. Prževalsk. NE Kyrgyzstan
Karakoram Range *270, 421* mountain
  range of C Asia
Karakose *547* NE Turkey
Kara-Kul' *325* *Kir.* Kara-Köl.
  W Kyrgyzstan
Karakul' *580* *Uzb.* Qorakŭl.
  S Uzbekistan
Karakul' *528* E Tajikistan
Karakul', Ozero *528* lake of
  E Tajikistan
Karakumskiy Kanal *551*
  Turkm. Garagum Kanaly. Canal of
  SE Turkmenistan
Karakumy *551* *Eng.* Kara Kum,
  Turkm. Garagum, *var.* Qara Qum.
  Desert region of C Turkmenistan
Karaman *547* S Turkey
Karamay *162* *var.* Karamai,
  Chin. K'o-la-ma-i. Xinjiang Uygur
  Zizhiqu, NW China
Karamea Bight *401* area of the
  Tasman Sea, on the NW coast
  of South Island, New Zealand
Kara-Say *325* E Kyrgyzstan
Karasburg *391* S Namibia
Kara Sea *see* Karskoye More
Karasjok *414* N Norway
Kara Su *see* Mesta, Néstos
Karatau *312* *Kaz.* Qarataū.
  S Kazakhstan
Karatsu *304* Kyūshū, SW Japan
Karavastasë, Laguna e *57*
  var. Kënet' e Karavastas, Kravasta
  Lagoon. Lagoon of W Albania
Karawang *276* *prev.* Krawang. Java,
  C Indonesia
Karawanken *82* *Slvn.* Karavanke.
  Mountain range of C Europe
Karbalā' *284* *var.* Kerbala. C Iraq
Kardítsa *245* C Greece
Kärdla *212* *Ger.* Kertel. Hiiumaa,
  Estonia
Kareliya, Respublika *452*
  autonomous republic of NW Russia
Karen *see* Hua-lien
Kari *see* Chia-li
Kariba *612* N Zimbabwe
Kariba Dam *612* dam at NE end of
  Lake Kariba, on Zambezi river,
  NW Zimbabwe
Kariba, Lake *611, 612* reservoir of
  Zambia and Zimbabwe
Karibib *391* C Namibia
Karimama *108* N Benin
Karimata, Selat *276* strait connecting
  Laut Jawa and the South China Sea,
  E Indonesia
Karisimbi, Volcan *460* *var.* Mount
  Karisimbi. Mountain of Rwanda and
  Zaire
Karkaralinsk *312* E Kazakhstan
Karkar Island *426* island of NE Papua
  New Guinea

Karkinits'ka Zatoka *556*
  Rus. Karkinitskiy Zaliv. Gulf of the
  Black Sea, S Ukraine
Karleby *see* Kokkola
Karl-Marx-Stadt *see* Chemnitz
Karlö *see* Hailuoto
Karlovac *181* *Ger.* Karlstadt,
  Hung. Károlyváros. N Croatia
Karlovo *128* *prev.* Levskigrad.
  C Bulgaria
Karlovy Vary *188* *Ger.* Karlsbad,
  var. Carlsbad. W Czech Republic
Karlsbad *see* Karlovy Vary
Karlskrona *513* S Sweden
Karlsruhe *236* *var.* Carlsruhe.
  SW Germany
Karlstad *513* SW Sweden
Karlstadt *see* Karlovac
Karmi 'él *291* N Israel
Karnali *395* *var.* Kauriala. River of
  W Nepal
Karnobat *128* E Bulgaria
Karoi *612* N Zimbabwe
Károlyváros *see* Karlovac
Karonga *353* N Malawi
Karonje, Mount *138* mountain of
  W Burundi
Karpasia *187* *var.* Karpas Peninsula.
  Peninsular of NE Cyprus
Karpaten *see* Carpathian Mountains
Kárpathos *245* island of SE Greece
Karpaty *see* Carpathian Mountains
Karrānah *91* N Bahrain
Kars *547* NE Turkey
Karshi *580* *var.* Karši, *prev.* Bek-Budi,
  Uzb. Qarshi. S Uzbekistan
Karskoye More *453* *Eng.* Kara Sea.
  Sea of Arctic Ocean, bordering
  N Russia
Kartala *174* mountain of Grande
  Comore, Comoros
Kartung *233* W Gambia
Kārūn *281* river of W Iran
Karungu Bay *316* bay of Lake
  Victoria, to the SW of Kenya
Karuzi *138* C Burundi
Karviná *188* *Ger.* Karwin. E Czech
  Republic
Karzakkān *91* NW Bahrain
Kas *547* SW Turkey
Kasai *64, 607* *var.* Kassai, Cassai.
  River of Angola and Zaire
Kasama *611* N Zambia
Kasan *580* *Uzb.* Koson.
  S Uzbekistan
Kasane *118* N Botswana
Kasari *212* river of W Estonia
Kasbegi *see* Qazbegi
Kaschau *see* Košice
Kasese *554* SW Uganda
Kashaf Rūd *281* river of NE Iran
Kāshān *281* NW Iran
Kashgar *see* Kashi
Kashi *162* *Uigh.* Kashgar. Xinjiang
  Uygur Zizhiqu, NW China
Kashiwa *304* Honshū, SE Japan
Kashiwazaki *304* Honshū, N Japan
Käsmark *see* Kežmarok
Kasongo *607* E Zaire
Kaspi *234* C Georgia
Kaspiyskoye More *see* Caspian Sea
Kaspiy Tengizi *see* Caspian Sea
Kassa *see* Košice
Kassai *see* Kasai
Kassala *506* *var.* Kassalā, Kasala.
  E Sudan
Kassándra *245* peninsula of
  NE Greece
Kassel *236* *prev.* Cassel. C Germany
Kasserine *543* *var.* Al-Qaşrayn.
  W Tunisia
Kassikaityu *256* river of S Guyana
Kastamonu *547* N Turkey
Kastsyukovichy *104* E Belorussia
Kasugai *304* Honshū, C Japan
Kasulu *530* W Tanzania
Kasumiga-ura *304* lake of Honshū,
  SE Japan
Kasungu *353* C Malawi
Kasupe *see* Machinga

Kikila, Lac *629* lake of Île Uvea, S Wallis & Futuna
Kihnu Island *212* island of SW Estonia
Kikládhes *see* Kyklades
Kikori *426* river of C Papua New Guinea
Kikwit *607* W Zaire
Kilchu *413* NE North Korea
Kili *364* island of S Marshall Islands
Kilien Mountains *see* Qilian Shan
Kilifi *316* SE Kenya
Kilima *138* N Burundi
Kilimanjaro *530* mountain of NE Tanzania
Kilingi-Nõmme *212* *Ger.* Kurkund. S Estonia
Kilinochchi *504* N Sri Lanka
Kilis *547* S Turkey
Kilkee *288* W Ireland
Kilkenny *288* *Ir.* Cill Choinnigh. SE Ireland
Kilkís *245* N Greece
Kilkoch *288* E Ireland
Killarney *288* *Ir.* Cill Airne. SW Ireland
Kilmarnock *563* W Scotland, UK
Kilosa *530* C Tanzania
Kilwa Masoko *530* SE Tanzania
Kimbe *426* New Britain , Papua New Guinea
Kimberley *493* Northern Cape, C South Africa
Kimberley Plateau *76* plateau of NW Australia
Kimch'aek *413* *prev.* Sŏngjin. E North Korea
Kimch'ŏn *496* C South Korea
Kimhae *496* SE South Korea
Kimito *221* *Swe.* Kemiö. Island of SW Finland
Kimje *496* SW South Korea
Kinabatangan *354* river of NE Borneo, Malaysia
Kinabalu, Gunung *354* mountain of N Borneo, Malaysia
Kindamba *176* S Congo
Kindia *253* SW Guinea
Kindu *607* C Zaire
Kineshma *452* W Russia
King George Bay *621* bay of the South Atlantic Ocean, W Falkland Islands
King George Land *66* island of South Shetland Islands, Antarctica
King Island *77* island of SE Australia
King Island *see* Kadan I
Kingissepp *see* Kuressaare
King's Lynn *563* E England, UK
King's Mills *623* SW Guernsey
Kingston *147* SE Canada
Kingston *303* ❖ of Jamaica, E Jamaica
Kingston *626* ❖ of Norfolk Island, S Norfolk Island
Kingston upon Hull *563* *var.* Hull. NE England, UK
Kingstown *466* ❖ of St Vincent & the Grenadines, SW St Vincent
King William Island *146* *var.* King William. Island of N Canada
Kinihira *460* N Rwanda
Kinkala *176* S Congo
Kinneret-Negev Conduit *291* canal of S Israel
Kinsale *625* SW Montserrat
Kinshasa *607* *prev.* Léopoldville. ❖ of Zaire, W Zaire
Kintampo *242* C Ghana
Kinyeti *506* mountain of S Sudan
Kipushi *607* SE Zaire
Kirakira *488* San Cristobal I, Solomon Islands
Kirambo *460* N Rwanda
Kirdzhali *see* Kŭrdzhali
Kirehe *460* SE Rwanda
Kirghizia *see* Kyrgyzstan
Kirghiz Range *325* *Rus.* Kirgizskiy Khrebet, *prev.* Alexander Range. Mountain range of Kazakhstan and Kyrgyzstan

Kirghiz Steppe *312* plain of W Kazakhstan
Kiribati *320-321* officially Republic of Kiribati. Country of the Pacific Ocean
Kırıkhan *547* S Turkey
Kırıkkale *547* C Turkey
Kirin *see* Jilin
Kirinyaga *316* *var.* Mount Kenya. Extinct volcano of C Kenya
Kiritimati *320* *var.* Christmas I. Island of the Line Is, E Kiribati
Kiriwina Islands *426* *var.* Trobriand Is. Island group of SE Papua New Guinea
Kirkenes *414* NE Norway
Kirklareli *547* NW Turkey
Kirkmichael *623* W Isle of Man
Kirkpatrick, Mount *66* mountain of Greater Antarctica, Antarctica
Kirkûk *284* *var.* Karkūk. N Iraq
Kirkwall *563* Orkney Islands, N Scotland, UK
Kirman *see* Kermān
Kirov *452* *prev.* Vyatka. W Russia
Kirovabad *see* Gäncä
Kirovakan *var.* Vanadzor
Kirovohrad *556* *prev.* Kirovo, Zinov'yevsk, Yelizavetgrad. C Ukraine
Kirşehir *547* C Turkey
Kīrthar Range *421* mountain range of S Pakistan
Kirun *see* Chi-lung
Kiruna *513* N Sweden
Kirundo *138* *var.* Kirundu. N Burundi
Kiryū *304* Honshū, SE Japan
Kisangani *607* *prev.* Stanleyville. NE Zaire
Kishan *see* Ch'i-shan
Kishinev *see* Chişinău
Kishiwada *304* Honshū, C Japan
Kishorganj *93* NE Bangladesh
Kisii *316* SW Kenya
Kisitwe *138* N Burundi
Kiskörei-víztároló *264* reservoir of E Hungary
Kiskunfélegyháza *264* *prev.* Félegyháza. C Hungary
Kiskunhalas *264* *prev.* Halas. S Hungary
Kismaayo *490* *var.* Kismayu, Chisimayu, *It.* Chisimaio. S Somalia
Kisoro *554* SW Uganda
Kisseraing *see* Kanmaw Island
Kissidougou *253* S Guinea
Kistna *see* Krishna
Kisumu *316* *prev.* Port Florence. W Kenya
Kisuru *see* Gisuru
Kita *360* W Mali
Kitab *580* *Uzb.* Kitob. SE Uzbekistan
Kitakami *304* Honshū, N Japan
Kitakyūshū *304* Kyūshū, SW Japan
Kitale *316* W Kenya
Kitami *305* Hokkaidō, N Japan
Kitanga *see* Gitanga
Kitchener *147* S Canada
Kitega *see* Gitega
Kitgum *554* N Uganda
Kíthira *245* island of S Greece
Kíthnos *245* island of SE Greece
Kitinen *221* river of N Finland
Kitob *see* Kitab
Kitobe *138* N Burundi
Kit Stoddart's *462* SE St Kitts, St Kitts & Nevis
Kittitian Village *462* SE St Kitts, St Kitts & Nevis
Kitui *316* S Kenya
Kitwe *611* *var.* Kitwe-Nkana. C Zambia
Kitzbühler Alpen *82* mountain range of W Austria
Kiunga *426* W Papua New Guinea
Kivalo *221* physical region of C Finland
Kiviõli *212* NE Estonia
Kivoga *138* C Burundi

Kivu, Lac *see* Kivu, Lake
Kivu, Lake *460, 607* *Fr.* Lac Kivu. Lake of Rwanda and Zaire
Kivumba, Lac *460* lake of E Rwanda
Kiyev *see* Kiev
Kiyevskoy Vodokhranilishche *see* Kyyivs'ke Vodoskhovyshche
Kiyomizu *see* Ch'ing-shui
Kiyumba *460* C Rwanda
Kizan *see* Ch'i-shan
Kizyl-Arvat *var.* Gyzylarbat
Kizyl-Kaya *551* *var.* Kizyl-Kaja, Gyzylgaya. NW Turkmenistan
Kjølen *see* Kölen
Kladno *188* NW Czech Republic
Klagenfurt *82* S Austria
Klaipėda *344* *Ger.* Memel. NW Lithuania
Klaksvík *620* Bordhoy, N Faeroe Islands
Klang *see* Kelang
Klarälven *513* river of SW Sweden
Klatovy *188* W Czech Republic
Klausenburg *see* Cluj-Napoca
Klein Bonaire *626* island to the W of Bonaire, S Netherlands Antilles
Klerksdorp *493* North West, N South Africa
Klirou *187* W Cyprus
Ključ *116* NW Bosnia & Herzegovina
Klosterneuburg *82* NE Austria
Kloten *see* Switzerland
Kluang *see* Keluang
Klyuchevskaya Sopka *453* Mountain of NE Russia
Knezha *128* *var.* Kneža. NW Bulgaria
Knin *181* S Croatia
Knittelfeld *82* C Austria
Knox Atoll *see* Narikrik
Knoxville *569* Tennessee, SE USA
Knud Rasmussen Land *622* physical region of N Greenland
Kōbe *304* Honshū, C Japan
København *see* Copenhagen
Kobenni *366* S Mauritania
Koblenz *236* W Germany
Kobryn *104* *Rus.* Kobrin. SW Belorussia
Kocaeli *see* İzmit
Kočani *349* NE FYR Macedonia
Kočevje *486* *Ger.* Gottschee. S Slovenia
Kōchi *see* Cochin
Kochi *304* Shikoku, SW Japan
Kochkor *see* Kochkorka
Kochkorka *325* *Kir.* Kochkor. NE Kyrgyzstan
Koddiyar Bay *504* bay of the Indian Ocean, on the NE coast of Sri Lanka
Kodiak *568* Alaska, USA
Koedoes *see* Kudus
Koeln *see* Köln
Ko-erh-mu *see* Golmud
Koes *391* SE Namibia
Koetai *see* Mahakam
Kofarnikhon *528* *prev.* Ordzhonikidzeabad. W Tajikistan
Kofinou *see* Kouklia
Koforidua *242* SE Ghana
Køge *190* Sjælland, E Denmark
Kogil'nik *see* Cogîlnic
Kogo *208* *var.* Cogo, *prev.* Puerto Iradier. SW Equatorial Guinea
Kogon *253* river of W Guinea
Kogon *see* Kagan
Kŏgŭm-do *496* island of S South Korea
Kohāt *421* N Pakistan
Kohtla-Järve *212* NE Estonia
Kohŭng *496* S South Korea
Koilabas *395* W Nepal
Koimbani *174* E Grande Comore, Comoros
Koindu *480* E Sierra Leone
Koi Sanjaq *284* *var.* Kūysanjaq, Koysanjaq. N Iraq

Kŏje-do *496* *Jap.* Kyōsai-tō. Island of S South Korea
Kokand *580* *var.* Khokand, *Uzb.* Qŭqon. E Uzbekistan
Kŏka-tŏ *see* Kanghwa-do
Kokchetav *312* *var.* Kökshetaū. N Kazakhstan
Kokemäenjoki *221* river of SW Finland
Kök-Janggak *see* Kok-Yangak
Kokkina *187* *var.* Erenköy. W Cyprus
Kokkola *221* *Swe.* Karleby, *prev.* Gamlakarleby. W Finland
Koko Nor *see* Qinghai Hu
Kokshaal-Tau *325* *Rus.* Khrebet Kakshaal-Too. Mountain range of China and Kyrgyzstan
Kökshetaū *see* Kokchetav
Kokstad *493* Kwazulu Natal, E South Africa
Kok-Yangak *325* *var.* Kok-Jangak, *Kir.* Kök-Janggak. SW Kyrgyzstan
Kolahun *336* N Liberia
K'o-la-ma-i *see* Karamay
Kola Peninsula *see* Kol'skiy Poluostrov
Kolda *476* S Senegal
Kolding *190* Jylland, W Denmark
Kölen *513* *Nor.* Kjølen. Mountains of N Sweden
Kolenté *253* river of Guinea and Sierra Leone
Kolga Laht *212* bay of the Gulf of Finland, on the coast of N Estonia
Kolguyev, Ostrov *452* Island of NW Russia
Kolhāpur *270* SW India
Kolhumadulu Atoll *358* *var.* Kolumadulu Atoll, Thaa Atoll. Atoll of S Maldives
Kolia *629* Île Futuna, N Wallis & Futuna
Koliba *253* river of NW Guinea
Kolín *188* *Ger.* Kolin. C Czech Republic
Kolkasrags *330* *prev.* Cape Domesnes. Cape of NW Latvia
Kolkhozabad *528* *var.* Kolhozabad, *prev.* Kaganovichabad, Tugalan. SW Tajikistan
Kolmar *see* Colmar
Köln *236* *var.* Koeln, *prev.* Cöln, *Eng.* Cologne. W Germany
Kolokani *360* W Mali
Kolombangara *488* *var.* Nduke. New Georgia Is, Solomon Islands
Kolonia *375* *var.* Colonia. ❖ of Micronesia, Pohnpei, Micronesia
Kolonjë *see* Ersekë
Kolonyama *334* NW Lesotho
Kolozsvár *see* Cluj-Napoca
Kolpa *486* *SCr.* Kupa, *Ger.* Kulpa. River of S Slovenia
Kol'skiy Poluostrov *452* *Eng.* Kola Peninsula. Peninsula of NW Russia
Koltur *620* island of C Faeroe Islands
Kolumadulu Atoll *see* Kolhumadulu Atoll
Kolwezi *607* S Zaire
Kolyma *453* river of NE Russia
Kolyma Lowland *see* Kolymskaya Nizmennost'
Kolymskaya Nizmennost' *453* *Eng.* Kolyma Lowland. Lowland region of NE Russia
Kolymskiy, Khrebet *453* *Eng.* Kolyma Range. Mountain range of NE Russia
Komanit, Liqeni i *57* lake of N Albania
Komárno *485* *Ger.* Komorn, *Hung.* Komárom. SW Slovakia
Komárom *see* Komárno
Komati *510* river of SE Africa
Komatsu *304* Honshū, C Japan
Kombissiri *132* *var.* Kombissiguiri. C Burkina

Kome Island *554* island of S Uganda
Komi, Respublika *452* autonomous republic of NW Russia
Komló *264* SW Hungary
Kommunarsk *see* Alchevs'k
Kommunizma, Pik *528*
  Eng. Communism Peak, *prev.* Stalin Peak, Garmo Peak. Mountain of E Tajikistan
Komoé *300* river of E Ivory Coast
Komono *176* SW Congo
Komorn *see* Komárno
Komotau *see* Chomutov
Komotiní *245* *Turk.* Gümülcine, Gümüljina. NE Greece
Kompong Kleang *see* Kâmpóng Khleang
Kompong Som *see* Kâmpóng Saôm
Kompong Speu *see* Kâmpóng Spoe
Kompong Thom *see* Kâmpóng Thum
Komsomol *see* Komsomol'sk
Komsomolets, Ostrov *453* island of Severnaya Zemlya, N Russia
Komsomol'sk *551* *Turkm.* Komsomol. SE Turkmenistan
Komsomol'sk-na-Amure *453* SE Russia
Komusan *413* NE North Korea
Kondoa *530* C Tanzania
Koné *626* W New Caledonia
Köneürgench *see* Këneürgench
Kông *141, 327* river of Cambodia and Laos
Kông, Kaôh *141* *prev.* Kas Kong. Island of SW Cambodia
Kong Christian IX Land *622* physical region of SE Greenland
Kong Christian X Land *622* physical region of E Greenland
Kong Frederik VIII Land *622* physical region of NE Greenland
Kong Frederik VI Kyst *622* physical region of SE Greenland
Kongju *496* *Jap.* Kōshū. W South Korea
Kong Karls Land *629* island group of SE Svalbard
Kongo *see* Congo
Kongoloto Lafanga *553* islet of Nukufetau, Tuvalu
Kongoloto Motulalo *553* islet of Nukufetau, Tuvalu
Kongoussi *132* N Burkina
Kongsberg *414* S Norway
Kongsvinger *414* S Norway
Königgrätz *see* Hradec Králové
Königshütte *see* Chorzów
Konispol *57* *var.* Konispoli. S Albania
Köniz *516* W Switzerland
Konjic *116* S Bosnia & Herzegovina
Konkämäälv *see* Konkämäeno
Konkämäeno *221* *Swe.* Konkämäälv. River of N Europe
Konkouré *253* river of W Guinea
Konotop *556* N Ukraine
Konrei *627* N Palau
Konsankoro *253* SE Guinea
Konstantza *see* Constanţa
Konstanz *236* S Germany
Kontagora *408* NW Nigeria
Kon Tum *593* *var.* Kontum. S Vietnam
Konya *547* *prev.* Konia. C Turkey
Kopaonik *602* mountain range of C Serbia, Yugoslavia
Kópavogur *268* W Iceland
Koper *486* *It.* Capodistria. SW Slovenia
Köpernick *237* NE Germany
Kopetdag, Khrebet *551*
  Turkm. Kopetdag Gershi, *Per.* Koppeh Dāgh. Mountain range of W Turkmenistan
Kophinou *187* S Cyprus
Kophinou *see* Kouklia
Koplik *57* N Albania
Koppeh Dāgh *see* Kopetdag Khrebet
Koppename *see* Coppename
Koprivnica *181* *Ger.* Kopreinitz, *Hung.* Kaproncza. NE Croatia

Köprülü *see* Titov Veles
Köprülü Rezevuar *see* Kouklia Reservoir
Korat *see* Nakhon Ratchasima
Korat Plateau *533* plateau of NE Thailand
Korçë *57* *var.* Korça, *prev.* Koritsa, *It.* Corriza, *Gk* Korytsa. SE Albania
Korčula *181* *It.* Curzola. Island of S Croatia
Korea Bay *163, 413* bay of Yellow Sea, off the coast of E Asia
Korea Strait *496*
  Kor. Taehan-haehyŏp, *Jap.* Chōsen-kaikyō. Channel connecting the East China Sea and the Sea of Japan, E Asia
Korhogo *300* N Ivory Coast
Koribundu *480* S Sierra Leone
Korinthiakós Kólpos *245* *Eng.* Gulf of Corinth. Gulf of the Ionian Sea, C Greece
Kórinthos *245* *Eng.* Corinth. S Greece
Korínthou, Isthmós *245*
  Eng. Isthmus of Corinth. Narrow strip of land joining Pelepónnisos and SE Greece
Koritsa *see* Korçë
Kōriyama *304* Honshū, N Japan
Korla *162* *Chin.* K'u-erh-lo. Xinjiang Uygur Zizhiqu, NW China
Kormakiti, Cape *187*
  var. Korucam Burnu. Cape of NW Cyprus
Koro *218* island to the SE of Vanua Levu, C Fiji
Korogwe *530* E Tanzania
Korolevu *218* Viti Levu, W Fiji
Koror *627* ❖ of Palau, C Palau
Kőrös *see* Križevci
Körös *264* river of E Hungary
Koro Sea *218* sea of the Pacific Ocean, C Fiji
Korosten' *556* NW Ukraine
Koro Toro *156* C Chad
Korovou *218* Viti Levu, W Fiji
Korsør *190* Sjælland, S Denmark
Kortrijk *99* *Fr.* Courtrai. W Belgium
Korucam Burnu *see* Kormakiti, Cape
Koryakskoye Nagor'ye *453*
  Eng. Koryak Range. Mountain range of NE Russia
Kōryō *see* Kangnŭng
Kos *245* island of SE Greece
Kosan *413* SE North Korea
Kosciusko, Mount *77* mountain of SE Australia
Koshikijima-rettō *304* island group to the W of Kyūshū, SW Japan
Kōshū *see* Kongju
Košice *485* *Ger.* Kaschau, *Hung.* Kassa. E Slovakia
Kôsin'i Kelifely *350* *var.* Causse du Kelifely. NW Madagascar
Kosŏng *413* SE North Korea
Kosovo *602* *prev.* Autonomous Province of Kosovo and Metohija. Region of S Serbia, Yugoslavia
Kosovska Mitrovica *602*
  prev. Titova Mitrovica, *prev.* Mitrovica, *Alb.* Mitrovicë. S Serbia, Yugoslavia
Kosrae *375* *prev.* Kusaie. Island of E Micronesia
Köstence *see* Constanţa
Kosti *506* *var.* Kūstī. C Sudan
Koszalin *439* *Ger.* Köslin. NW Poland
Kota *270* *prev.* Kotah. NW India
Kota Bharu *354* N Peninsular Malaysia
Kota Kinabalu *355* *prev.* Jesselton. N Borneo, Malaysia
Kota Kota *see* Nkhotakota
Kotel'nyy, Ostrov *453* island of Novosibirskiye Ostrova, N Russia
Kotido *554* NE Uganda
Kotka *221* S Finland
Kotlas *452* NW Russia
Kotonu *see* Cotonou

Kotovsk *see* Hînceşti
Kottbus *see* Cottbus
Kotte *see* Sri Jayawardenapura
Kotto *154* river of C Africa
Kotu Group *538* island group of W Tonga
Kouandé *108* NW Benin
Kouango *154* S Central African Republic
Koubia *253* NW Guinea
Koudougou *132* C Burkina
Kouffo *108* river of S Benin
K'ou-hu *525* W Taiwan
Kouilou *176* river of S Congo
Kouklia *187* *var.* Kophinou, Kofinou. SW Cyprus
Kouklia Reservoir *187*
  var. Köprülü Rezevuar. Reservoir of E Cyprus
Koulamoutou *230* C Gabon
Koulikoro *360* SW Mali
Koulountou *253, 476* river of Guinea and Senegal
Koumac *626* W New Caledonia
Koumandou *253* SE Guinea
Koumra *156* S Chad
Koundâra *253* NW Guinea
Koungheul *476* C Senegal
Koupéla *132* C Burkina
Kouri *187* river of S Cyprus
Kourou *621* N French Guiana
Kouroussa *253* C Guinea
Kousseir *see* Al Quşayr
Kousséri *144* *prev.* Fort-Foureau. NE Cameroon
Koûta Boûyya *194* SW Djibouti
Kouteifé *see* Al Quţayfah
Koutiala *360* S Mali
Kouvola *221* S Finland
Kouyou *176* river of C Congo
Kovel' *556* NW Ukraine
Kovno *see* Kaunas
Kowkcheh *53* seasonal river of NE Afghanistan
Kowloon *262* *Chin.* Jiulong. SW Hong Kong
Kowno *see* Kaunas
Kowŏn *413* E North Korea
Kowtal-e Khaybar *see* Vākhān, Kūh-e
Kowt-e 'Ashrow *53* E Afghanistan
Kōya, Zē-i *see* Little Zab
Koysanjaq *see* Koi Sanjaq
Kozan *547* S Turkey
Kozáni *245* N Greece
Kozara *116* mountain range of NW Bosnia & Herzegovina
Kozhikode *see* Calicut
Kpagouda *see* Pagouda
Kpalimé *537* *var.* Palimé. SW Togo
Kpandu *242* E Ghana
Krâchéh *141* *prev.* Kratie. E Cambodia
Kragujevac *602* C Serbia, Yugoslavia
Krainburg *see* Kranj
Kra, Isthmus of *135, 533* strip of land joining Malay Peninsula to Thailand, and separating the Andaman Sea and Gulf of Thailand
Kraków *439* *Eng.* Cracow, *Ger.* Krakau. S Poland
Krâlănh *141* NW Cambodia
Kralendijk *626* Bonaire, S Netherlands Antilles
Kraljevo *602* *prev.* Rankovićevo. C Serbia, Yugoslavia
Kranj *486* *Ger.* Krainburg. NW Slovenia
Kranji Reservoir *483* reservoir of W Singapore
Krapina *181* river of N Croatia
Krasnodar *452* *prev.* Yekaterinodar. SW Russia
Krasnogor *see* Kallaste
Krasnogvardeysk *see* Bulungur
Krasnovodsk *551* W Turkmenistan
Krasnovodskiy Zaliv *551*
  Turkm. Krasnowodsk Aylagy. Gulf of the Caspian Sea, on the W coast of Turkmenistan
Krasnoyarsk *453* C Russia
Krasnoyarsk Krai *459* administrative region of C Russia

Krasnyy Luch *556*
  prev. Krindachevka. E Ukraine
Kraszna *264* river of Hungary and Romania
Kratie *see* Krâchéh
Kratovo *349* NE FYR Macedonia
Kraulshavn *622* *var.* Nuussuaq. NW Greenland
Krâvanh, Chuŏr Phnum *141*
  Eng. Cardamom Mountains, *Fr.* Chaîne des Cardamomes. Mountain range of SW Cambodia
Kravasta Lagoon *see* Karavastasë, Laguna e
Krawang *see* Karawang
Kremenchuk *556* *Rus.* Kremenchug. C Ukraine
Kremenchuts'ke Vodokhovyshche *556* *Rus.* Kremenchugskoye Vodokhranilische. Reservoir of C Ukraine
Krems an der Donau *82* N Austria
Kretinga *344* *Ger.* Krottingen. NW Lithuania
Kreuz *see* Križevci
Kreuzlingen *516* NE Switzerland
Kribi *144* SW Cameroon
Krichev *see* Krychaw
Krindachevka *see* Krasnyy Luch
Krishna *270* *prev.* Kistna. River of C India
Kristiansand *414* *prev.* Christiansand. SW Norway
Kristianstad *513* S Sweden
Kristiansund *414* *prev.* Christiansund. SW Norway
Kríti *245* *Eng.* Crete. Island of S Greece
Kritikó Pélagos *see* Sea of Crete
Kriva Palanka *349* NE FYR Macedonia
Krivoy Rog *see* Kryvyy Rih
Križevci *181* *Ger.* Kreuz, *Hung.* Kőrös. NE Croatia
Krk *181* *It.* Veglia. Island of NW Croatia
Krnov *188* *Ger.* Jägerndorf. E Czech Republic
Krŏng Kaôh Kŏng *141* SW Cambodia
Kronstadt *see* Braşov
Kroonstad *493* Orange Free State, C South Africa
Krottingen *see* Kretinga
Krško *486* *prev.* Videm-Krško, *Ger.* Gurkfeld. E Slovenia
Kruševac *602* C Serbia, Yugoslavia
Krugersdorp *493*
  Pretoria-Witwatersrand-Vereeniging, NE South Africa
Krujë *57* *var.* Kruja, *It.* Croia. C Albania
Krung Thep *see* Bangkok
Krung Thep, Ao *533* bay within Gulf of Thailand
Kruševo *349* SW FYR Macedonia
Krušné Hory *see* Erzgebirge
Krychaw *104* *Rus.* Krichev. E Belorussia
Krym *556* *var.* Crimes. Peninsula and region of SE Ukraine
Kryvyy Rih *556* *Rus.* Krivoy Rog. SE Ukraine
Ksar el Kebir *382* NW Morocco
Kuala Belait *126* W Brunei
Kuala Dungun *354* *var.* Dungun. E Peninsular Malaysia
Kuala Kangsar *354* W Peninsular Malaysia
Kuala Lumpur *354* ❖ of Malaysia, W Peninsular Malaysia
Kuala Pilah *354* SW Peninsular Malaysia
Kuala Terengganu *354*
  var. Kuala Trengganu. NE Peninsular Malaysia
Kuang-chou *see* Guangzhou
Kuang-hsi *see* Guangxi
Kuang-tung *see* Guangdong
Kuang-yuan *see* Guangyuan
Kuantan *354* E Peninsular Malaysia
Kuba *see* Quba

La Habana *see* Havana
Lahad Datu, Telukan *355 var.* Teluk Darvel, Darvel Bay. Bay of the Celebes Sea, on the NE coast of Borneo, Malaysia
La Haye *see* 's-Gravenhage
Laḥij *599 var.* Laḥj, *Eng.* Lahej. SW Yemen
Lahore *421* NE Pakistan
Lahti *221 Swe.* Lahtis. S Finland
Laï *156 var.* Behagle. S Chad
Laibach *see* Ljubljana
Lai Châu *593* NW Vietnam
Lai Chi Van *624* inlet of the South China Sea, SW Macao
Lainioälven *513* river of N Sweden
Laisholm *see* Jõgeva
Laitokitok *see* Oloitokitok
Lakamti *see* Nek'emtē
Lakeba *218 prev.* Lakemba. Island of the Lau Group, E Fiji
Lakeba Passage *218* channel of the Pacific Ocean E Fiji
Lake District *see* Cumbrian Mountains
Lakepa *626* NE Niue
Lakhnau *see* Lucknow
Lakota *300* S Ivory Coast
Lak Sao *see* Ban Lakxao
Lakshadweep *270 Eng.* Laccadive Islands. Island group to the SW of India
Lakshām *93* E Bangladesh
Lakshmipur *93* S Bangladesh
La Laguna *501* Islas Canarias, SW Spain
Lāla Mūsa *421* NE Pakistan
Lalëzit, Gjiri i *57 var.* Gji i Lalzës. Gulf of the Adriatic Sea, SW Albania
La Libertad *250* N Guatemala
La Libertad *207* SW El Salvador
La Libertad *200* W Ecuador
Lalitpur *395* C Nepal
Lālmanir Hāt *93* N Bangladesh
La Louvière *99* SW Belgium
la Maçana *62* W Andorra
Lama-Kara *see* Kara
La Manche *see* English Channel
La Marsa *543 var.* Al Marsá. N Tunisia
La Matepec *see* Santa Ana, Volcan de
Lambaré *428* S Paraguay
Lambaréné *230* W Gabon
Lambi *488* N Guadalcanal, Solomon Is
Lami *218* Viti Levu, W Fiji
Lamía *245* C Greece
Lamin *233* W Gambia
Lamiti *218* Gau, C Fiji
Lamma Island *262* island of S Hong Kong
Lamotrek *375* atoll of C Micronesia
Lampang *533 var.* Muang Lampang. NW Thailand
Lamu *316* SE Kenya
Lanao, Lake *435 var.* Lake Sultan Alonto. Lake of Mindanao, S Philippines
Lanbi Island *135 prev.* Sullivan I. Island of S Burma
Lancang Jiang *see* Mekong
Lancaster *563* NW England, UK
Lancaster Sound *147* stretch of water between Baffin Island and Devon Island, NE Canada
Lance aux Epines *248* S Grenada island, Grenada
Lanchow *see* Lanzhou
Landes *224* cultural region of SW France
Landing Bay *625* bay of the Caribbean Sea on the SE coast of Montserrat
Landsberg *see* Gorzów Wielkopolski
Landshut *237* SE Germany
Langabou *537* C Togo
Langar *see* Lyangar
Langatabbetje *508* E Surinam
Langeland *190* island of S Denmark

Langenthal *516* NW Switzerland
Langjökull *268* glacier of C Iceland
Langkawi, Pulau *354* island to the NW of Peninsular Malaysia
Langlade *628* physical region of Miquelon, S Saint Pierre and Miquelon
Langlade, Isthme de *628* isthmus of Miquelon, C Saint Pierre and Miquelon
Lang Sơn *593* N Vietnam
Languedoc *225, 228* cultural region of SE France
Länkäran *86 Rus.* Lenkoran'. S Azerbaijan
Lansing *569* Michigan, NC USA
Lantau Island *262* island of SW Hong Kong
Lantau Peak *262* mountain of Lantau Island, Hong Kong
Lan Yü *525 var.* Huo-shao Tao, *Eng.* Orchid Island. Island of SE Taiwan
Lanzarote *501* island of Islas Canarias, SW Spain
Lanzhou *163 var.* Lanchow, *prev.* Kaolan. Gansu province, C China
Lao Cai *593* NW Vietnam
Laojunmiao *see* Yumen
Laon *225* N France
La Oroya *431* C Peru
Laos *326-329* officially Lao People's Democratic Republic. Country of SE Asia divided into 16 admin. units (provinces, khouèng)
La Palma *501* island of Islas Canarias, SW Spain
La Palma *424* E Panama
La Palma *207* N El Salvador
La Paz *260* SW Honduras
La Paz *112 var.* La Paz de Ayacucho. ❖ of Bolivia, W Bolivia
La Paz *577* S Uruguay
La-Perouse Strait *305* strait connecting the Sea of Japan and Pacific Ocean between Sakhalia, SE Russia and Hokkaidō, N Japan
Lapithos *see* Lapta
La Plaine *196* SE Dominica
La Plaine-des-Palmistes *628* E Réunion
Lapland *221, 414, 513 var.* Lappland, *Fin.* Lappi. Cultural region of N Europe, extending over the N of Finland, Norway and Sweden, and the Kola Peninsula of NW Russia
La Plata *577* estuary of Argentina and Uruguay
La Plata *71* E Argentina
La Pointe *see* Pointe Michel
La Pointe *465* E St Lucia
Lappeenranta *221 Swe.* Villmanstrand. SE Finland
Lappland *see* Lapland
Lapta *187 var.* Lapithos. NW Cyprus
Laptev Sea *see* Laptevykh, More
Laptevykh, More *453 Eng.* Laptev Sea. Sea of Arctic Ocean, bordering N Russia
L'Aquila *295 var.* Aquila, Aquila degli Abruzzi. C Italy
Larache *382 prev.* El Araïche. NW Morocco
La Resource *465* S St Lucia
La Ressource *465* NE St Lucia
Large Island *248* island to the S of Carriacou, Grenada
Largo, Cayo *182* island of SW Cuba
L'Ariana *see* Ariana
Larieu *196* N Dominica
Lario *see* Como, Lago di
La Rioja *71* NW Argentina
La Rioja *501* autonomous community of N Spain
Lárisa *245 var.* Larissa. E Greece
Lārkāna *421* SW Pakistan
Larnaca *187 var.* Larnaka, Larnax. SE Cyprus

Larnaca Bay *187 var.* Larnaka Gulf. Bay of the Mediterranean Sea, to the SE of Cyprus
La Rochelle *224* W France
La Roche-sur-Yon *224* W France
La Romana *198* SE Dominican Republic
Larvik *414* S Norway
Larvotto *378* N Monaco
La-sa *see* Lhasa
Lascahobas *258* SE Haiti
Lascano *577* SE Uruguay
Las Cruces *568* New Mexico, SW USA
La Selle *see* Selle, Pic de la
La Serena *159* N Chile
La Seyne-sur-Mer *225* SE France
Las Heras *71* W Argentina
Lashio *135* NE Burma
Lashkar Gāh *53* SW Afghanistan
La Sila *295* mountain range of S Italy
Las Minas, Cerro *260* mountain of W Honduras
La Soie *see* Wesley
La Soufrière *466* mountain of N St Vincent, St Vincent & the Grenadines
Las Palmas *501 var.* Las Palmas de Gran Canaria. Islas Canarias, SW Spain
La Spezia *294* N Italy
Las Piedras *577* S Uruguay
Las Tablas *424* S Panama
Lastoursville *230* E Gabon
Las Tunas *182* SE Cuba
Las Vegas *568* Nevada, W USA
Lata *488* E Nendö, Solomon Islands
Latacunga *200* C Ecuador
Latagle *330 Eng.* Latgalia. Region of SE Latvia
Latakia *see* Al Lādhiqīyah
Late *538* island of the Vava'u Group, Tonga
Latina *295* S Italy
La Tortuga, Isla *589* island of N Venezuela
La Trinité *625* E Martinique
Latvia *330-331* officially Republic of Latvia, *Latv.* Latvija, Latvijas Republika, *Ger.* Lettland, *prev.* Latvian SSR, *Rus.* Latviyskaya SSR. Country of NE Europe divided into 26 admin. units (rajons)
Laudat *196* S Dominica
Lau Group *218* island group of E Fiji
Lauis *see* Lugano
Launceston *77* Tasmania, SE Australia
La Unión *159* C Chile
La Unión *207* SE El Salvador
Laurentian Plateau *147 var.* Canadian Shield. Plateau of E Canada
Lauru *see* Choiseul
Lausanne *516* SW Switzerland
Lautaro *159* C Chile
Lautoka *218* Viti Levu, W Fiji
Laut, Pulau *276 var.* Laoet. Island to the SE of Borneo, C Indonesia
Laval *147* SE Canada
Laval *224* NW France
Lava, la *621* river of French Guiana and Surinam
Lavant *82* river of S Austria
La Vega *198 var.* Concepción de La Vega. C Dominican Republic
L'Aventure *368* NE Mauritius
Lavumisa *510 prev.* Gollel. S Swaziland
Lawa *508* river of French Guiana and Surinam
Lawdar *599* SW Yemen
Lawton *569* Oklahoma, SC USA
Laxey *623* E Isle of Man
Layjūn *599* C Yemen
Laylá *472 var.* Laila. C Saudi Arabia

Layou *196* river of W Dominica
Layou *466* W St Vincent, St Vincent & the Grenadines
Lazarus Island *see* Sakijang Pelepah, Pulau
Laz Daua *see* Laas Dawaco
Lazovsk *see* Sîngerei
Leal *see* Lihula
Leamhcán *see* Lucan
Leava *629* Île Futuna, N Wallis & Futuna
Lébamba *230* S Gabon
Lebanon *332-333* officially Republic of Lebanon, *Ar.* Al Lubnān. Country of SW Asia divided into 5 admin. units (governorates)
Lebap *551* NE Turkmenistan
Lebombo Mountains *493, 510* mountain range of southern Africa
Le Cap *628* peninsula of N Saint Pierre and Miquelon
Le Cap *see* Cap-Haïtien
Le Carbet *625* NW Martinique
Lecce *295* S Italy
Lecco *294* N Italy
Lech *82* river of Austria and Germany
Leduc *146* SW Canada
Lee *288 Ir.* An Laoi. River of S Ireland
Leeds *563* N England, UK
Leeuwarden *397 Fris.* Ljouwert. N Netherlands
Leeuwin, Cape *76* cape on the SW coast of Australia
Léfini *176* river of SE Congo
Lefka *187 var.* Lefke. W Cyprus
Lefkada *245 prev.* Levkás, *var.* Leucas, *It.* Santa Maura. Island of W Greece
Lefke *see* Lefka
Lefkoniko *see* Geçitkale
Lefkoşa *see* Nicosia
Lefkosia *see* Nicosia
Le François *625* E Martinique
Leganés *501* C Spain
Legaspi *435 var.* Legzpi. Luzon, N Philippines
Leghorn *see* Livorno
Legnica *439 Ger.* Liegnitz. W Poland
Le Havre *225* N France
Leiah *421* NE Pakistan
Leicester *563* C England, UK
Leiden *397 prev.* Leyden. W Netherlands
Leie *99 Fr.* Lys. River of Belgium and France
Léim an Bhradáin *see* Leixlip
Leinster *288* province of E Ireland
Leipzig *237 Pol.* Lipsk. C Germany
Leivádia *245 prev.* Levádhia. SE Greece
Leixlip *288 Ir.* Léim an Bhradáin. E Ireland
Leizhou Bandao *163 var.* Luichow Peninsula. Peninsula of S China
Lejone *334* N Lesotho
Lek *397* river of SW Netherlands
Lékana *176* W Congo
Le Kef *543 var.* Al Kāf, El Kef. NW Tunisia
Lékéti *176* river of W Congo
Lékéti, Monts de le *176 var.* Monts de la Leketi, Mont de la Lékéti. Mountain range of W Congo
Lékila *230* E Gabon
Lékoni *230* E Gabon
Le Lamentin *625* C Martinique
Le Lorrain *625* NE Martinique
Lélouma *253* W Guinea
Lelydorp *508* N Surinam
Lelystad *397* C Netherlands
Le Mans *225* NW France
Lemberg *see* L'viv
Lemdiyya *see* Médéa
Lemesos *see* Limassol
Le Morne Rouge *625* N Martinique
Le Moule *622* NE Guadeloupe
Lempa *207* river of El Salvador and Honduras

Lü Tao *525* island of SE Taiwan
Lūt, Baḥrat *see* Dead Sea
Lūt, Dasht-e *281 var.* Kavīr-e Lūt.
   Desert region of E Iran
Luton *563* C England, UK
Luts'k *556 Rus.* Lutsk, *Pol.* Łuck.
   NW Ukraine
Lüttich *see* Liège
Luud, Waadi *490 It.* Uadi Lhut.
   Seasonal river of N Somalia
Luuq *490 It.* Lugh Ganana.
   SW Somalia
Luvironza *see* Ruvironza
Luxembourg *346* ❖ of Luxembourg
Luxembourg *346-347* officially Grand
   Duchy of Luxembourg,
   var. Lëtzebuerg. Country of
   W Europe divided into 3 admin.
   units (districts)
Luxor *202 Ar.* Al Uqşur. E Egypt
Luz, Costa de la *501* coastal region
   of SW Spain
Luzern *516 Fr.* Lucerne.
   C Switzerland
Luzon *435* island of N Philippines
L'viv *556 Rus.* L'vov, *Pol.* Lwów,
   Ger. Lemberg. W Ukraine
Lyallpur *see* Faisalābād
Lyangar *580 var.* Ljangar,
   Uzb. Langar. SE Uzbekistan
Lycksele *513* N Sweden
Lydda *see* Lod
Lyepyel' *104 Rus.* Lepel'. N Belorussia
Lyme Bay *563* bay of S England, UK
Lyon *225 Eng.* Lyons E France
Lys *see* Leie
Lysi *187 var.* Akdoğan. C Cyprus
Lyublin *see* Lublin
Lyublyana *see* Ljubljana

M

Ma'ān *310* SW Jordan
Maanselkä *221* mountain range of
   NE Finland
Maardu *212 Ger.* Maart. N Estonia
Maarianhamina *see* Mariehamn
Maarmovilik *622* W Greenland
Ma'arrat an Nu'mān *521* NW Syria
Maarssen *397* C Netherlands
Maart *see* Maardu
Maas *see* Meuse
Maasmechelen *99* NE Belgium
Maastricht *397* S Netherlands
Maaza Plateau *202* plateau
   of NE Egypt
Mabalane *387* S Mozambique
Mabanda *230* S Gabon
Mabouya Island *248* island to the
   W of Carriacou, Grenada
Macao *624 var.* Macau. Special
   territory of Portugal, SE China.
   ❖ Macao
Macapá *121* N Brazil
Macará *200* S Ecuador
Macarsca *see* Makarska
MacArthur *see* Ormoc
Macas *200* S Ecuador
Macassar *see* Ujungpandang
Macau - Taipa Bridge *624* bridge
   between Macao & Taipa islands,
   C Macao
Macdonnell Ranges *77* mountain
   range of C Australia
Macedonia *348-349* officially the
   Former Yugoslav Republic of
   Macedonia, *abbrev.* FYR Macedonia,
   Mac. Makedonija. Country of
   SE Europe divided into 34 admin.
   units (opcine)
Maceió *121* E Brazil
Macenta *253* SE Guinea
Macgillicuddy's Reeks *288*
   var. Macgillicuddy's Reeks
   Mountains, *Ir.* Na Cruacha Dubha.
   Mountain range of SW Ireland
Machakos *316* S Kenya
Machala *200* SW Ecuador

Machaneng *118* SE Botswana
Machanga *387* SE Mozambique
Machaze *387* SW Mozambique
Machile *611 var.* Machili. River of
   SW Zambia
Machinga *353 var.* Kasupe, Kasupi.
   S Malawi
Machiques *589* NW Venezuela
Macia *387 var.* Vila de Macia.
   S Mozambique
Macías Nguema Biyogo *see* Bioko
Mackay *77* NE Australia
Mackay, Lake *77* salt lake of
   C Australia
Mackenzie *146* river of NW Canada
Mackenzie Mountains *146* mountain
   range of NW Canada
Macleod, Lake *76* lake of
   W Australia
Macomer *294* Sardegna,
   S Italy
Macon *569* Georgia, SE USA
Mâcon *225* E France
Macouba *625* N Martinique
MacRitchie Reservoir *483* reservoir
   of C Singapore
Macroom *288* SW Ireland
Macuelizo *260* W Honduras
Ma'dabā *310 var.* Mādabā.
   NW Jordan
Madagascar *350-351* officially
   Democratic Republic of Madagascar,
   Malg. Madagasikara, *prev.* Malagasy
   Republic. Country of SE Africa
   divided into 6 admin. units
   (provinces)
Madan *128* S Bulgaria
Madang *426* E Papua New Guinea
Madanīyīn *see* Médenine
Mādārīpur *93* S Bangladesh
Madeira *442 var.* Ilha de Madeira.
   Madeira Is, Portugal
Madeira *120* river of Bolivia and
   Brazil
Madeira, Arquipélago da *see* Madeira
   Islands
Madeira Islands *442 Port.*
   Arquipélago da Madeira. Island
   group to the W of Portugal
Madina do Boé *see* Boé
Madīnat al Abyār *339* NE Libya
Madīnat al Ka'bān *447*
   var. Al Ka'aban. N Qatar
Madīnat ash Sha'b *599*
   prev. Al Ittiḥād. SW Yemen
Madīnat ash Shamāl *447*
   var. Madīnat el Shamal. N Qatar
Madīnat ath Thawrah *521* N Syria
Madinat el Shamal *see* Madīnat ash
   Shamāl
Madīnat Ḩamad *91 var.* Hamada
   Town, Hamad. W Bahrain
Madīnat 'Īsá *91 var.* Isa Town.
   N Bahrain
Madīnat Khalīfa *447* E Qatar
Madingo-Kayes *176* S Congo
Madingou *176* S Congo
Madison *569* Wisconsin, NC USA
Madiun *276 prev.* Madioen. Java,
   C Indonesia
Madlangampisi *510* N Swaziland
Madona *330 Ger.* Modohn. E Latvia
Madras *273* S India
Madre de Dios *112, 431* river of
   Bolivia and Peru
Madrid *501* ❖ of Spain, C Spain
Madriu, Riu *62* river of S Andorra
Madura *276 prev.* Madoera. Island to
   NE of Java, C Indonesia
Madurai *270 prev.* Madura. S India
Maebashi *304* Honshū, SE Japan
Mae Name Khong *see* Mekong
Mae Nam Khong *see* Mekong
Mae Nam Moi *see* Thaungyin
Mae Nam Ping *533* river of
   NW Thailand
Maéwo *585 prev.* Aurora. Island of
   C Vanuatu
Mafa'a, Pointe *629* headland of Île
   Alofi, N Wallis & Futuna

Mafeteng *334* W Lesotho
Mafia *530* island of E Tanzania
Mafou *253* river of C Guinea
Mafraq *see* Al Mafraq
Mafraq *560* C United Arab Emirates
Mafungabusi Plateau *612* plateau of
   C Zimbabwe
Mafut *560* NE United Arab Emirates
Magadan *453* NE Russia
Magadi *316* SW Kenya
Magadi, Lake *316* lake of SW Kenya
Magallanes *see* Punta Arenas
Magallanes, Estrecho *see* Magellan,
   Strait of
Magangué *171* N Colombia
Magaria *407* S Niger
Magat *435* river of Luzon,
   N Philippines
Magburaka *480* C Sierra Leone
Magdalena *171* river of C Colombia
Magdalena *112* N Bolivia
Magdeburg *237* C Germany
Magelang *276* Java, C Indonesia
Magellan, Strait of *71, 159*
   Sp. Estrecho de Magallanes. Strait
   connecting the S Atlantic and
   S Pacific Oceans between Tierra del
   Fuego and mainland South America
Magerøya *414 var.* Magerøy. Island of
   NE Norway
Maggiore, Lake *294, 516 It.* Lago
   Maggiore. Lake of Italy and
   Switzerland
Magh Ealla *see* Mallow
Maglaj *116* N Bosnia & Herzegovina
Magnitogorsk *452* C Russia
Mago *218 prev.* Mango. Island of the
   Lau Group, E Fiji
Magta' Laḥjar *366* SW Mauritania
Māgura *93* W Bangladesh
Magwe *135 var.* Magway. W Burma
Magyarkanizsa *see* Kanjiža
Magyarország *see* Hungary
Magyaróvár *see* Mosonmagyaróvár
Mahafaly, Lembalemban' *350*
   var. Plateau Mahafaly. Plateau of
   SW Madagascar
Mahaicony Village *256* E Guyana
Mahajamba *350* seasonal river
   of N Madagascar
Mahajanga *350 prev.* Majunga.
   N Madagascar
Mahajilo *350* seasonal river of
   C Madagascar
Mahakali *395* river of India and Nepal
Mahakam *276 var.* Kutai, Koetai.
   River of Borneo, C Indonesia
Mahalapye *118 var.* Mahalatswe.
   SE Botswana
Maḥallah al Kubrá *see* El Mahalla el
   Kubra
Mahamba *510* SW Swaziland
Mahanādi *270* river of E India
Mahanoro *350* E Madagascar
Maha Sarakham *533* NE Thailand
Mahaut *196* W Dominica
Mahavavy *350* seasonal river of
   N Madagascar
Mahaweli Ganga *504* river of C Sri
   Lanka
Mahdia *543 var.* Al Mahdīyah,
   Mehdia. NE Tunisia
Mahdia *256* C Guyana
Mahé *478* island of NE Seychelles
Mahébourg *368 var.* Mahebourg.
   SE Mauritius
Mahenge *530* SE Tanzania
Mahia Peninsula *401* peninsula of
   E North Island, New Zealand
Mahina *360* W Mali
Mahiyangana *504* E Sri Lanka
Maḥmūd-e Rāqī *53* NE Afghanistan
Mahmudiya *see* Al Maḥmūdīyah
Mahou *360* S Mali
Mährisch-Ostrau *see* Ostrava
Mährisch-Schönberg *see* Šumperk
Maiana *320* island of the Gilbert Is,
   W Kiribati

Maicao *171* N Colombia
Mai Ceu *see* Maych'ew
Mai Chio *see* Maych'ew
Maiduguri *409* NE Nigeria
Mailand *see* Milano
Maimāna *see* Meymaneh
Main *236* river of C Germany
Main Camp *320* Kiritimati, E Kiribati
Main Channel *624* channel of the
   Pacific Ocean, S Johnston Atoll
Main Channel *see* Inner Channel
Mai-Ndombe, Lac *607 prev.* Lac
   Léopold II. Lake of W Zaire
Maine *569* state of NE USA
Maine *225* cultural region of
   NW France
Maïné-Soroa *407* SE Niger
Mainland *563* Shetland, NE UK
Mainland *563* Orkney, NE UK
Maintirano *350* W Madagascar
Mainz *236 Fr.* Mayence. SW Germany
Maio *152 var.* Vila de Maio. Maio,
   S Cape Verde
Maio *152* island of SE Cape Verde
Maiquetía *589* N Venezuela
Maissade *258* N Haiti
Maisur *see* Mysore
Maitland *77* E Australia
Maíz, Islas *404 var.* Corn Islands.
   Island group of E Nicaragua
Maizuru *304* Honshū, C Japan
Majardah, Wādī *see* Mejerda, Oued
Majimbini, Réserve Forestière de
   625 forest reserve of C Mayotte
Majoli *508* S Surinam
Majorca *see* Mallorca
Majunga *see* Mahajanga
Majuro *364* atoll of SE Marshall
   Islands
Majuro District *364* district of Majuro,
   SE Marshall Islands
Makamba *138* S Burundi
Makarska *181 It.* Macarsca.
   SE Croatia
Makasar *see* Ujungpandang
Makasar, Selat *276 Eng.* Makassar
   Strait. Strait connecting the Celebes
   Sea and Laut Flores, C Indonesia
Makassar Strait *see* Makasar, Selat
Makay, Tangorombohitr' i *350*
   var. Massif du Makay. Mountains
   of SW Madagascar
Makeni *480* C Sierra Leone
Makgadikgadi *118 var.* Makarikari
   Pans. Saltpans of NE Botswana
Makhachkala *452 prev.* Petrovsk-Port.
   SW Russia
Makharadze *see* Ozurget'i
Makhfar al Quwayrah
   see Al Quwayrah
Makin *320* island of the Gilbert Is,
   W Kiribati
Makira *see* San Cristobal
Makiyivka *556 Rus.* Makeyevka,
   prev. Dmitriyevsk. E Ukraine
Makkah *472 Eng.* Mecca. W Saudi
   Arabia
Makō *see* Ma-Kung
Makó *264* SE Hungary
Makogai *218* island to the NE of Viti
   Levu, C Fiji
Makokou *230* NE Gabon
Makona *253* river of S Guinea
Makoua *176* C Congo
Makran Coast *281* coastal region of
   SE Iran
Ma-Kung *525 var.* P'eng-hu,
   Jap. Makō. Island of W Taiwan
Makunudhoo Atoll *358*
   var. Makunudu Atoll. Atoll of
   N Maldives
Makurazaki *304* Kyūshū,
   SW Japan
Makurdi *408* C Nigeria
Makuti *612* N Zimbabwe
Makwate *118* SE Botswana
Mala *see* Malaita
Malabo *208 prev.* Santa Isabel.
   ❖ of Equatorial Guinea, N Bioko
Malacca *see* Melaka

Margate *493* Kwazulu Natal, SE South Africa
Margherita, Lake *see* Ābaya Hāyk'
Margherita Peak *554, 607* mountain of Uganda and Zaire
Margilan *580 var.* Margelan, *Uzb.* Marghilon. E Uzbekistan
Mārgow, Dasht-e- *53* desert of SW Afghanistan
Mari *187* S Cyprus
Marianao *182* NW Cuba
Marías, Islas *370* Island of W Mexico
Maria-Theresiopel *see* Subotica
Máriatölgyes *see* Dubnica nad Váhom
Mar'ib *599* W Yemen
Maribo *190* Lolland, S Denmark
Maribor *486 Ger.* Marburg. NE Slovenia
Marid *560* NE United Arab Emirates
Marie Byrd Land *66* physical region of Greater Antarctica, Antarctica
Marie-Galante *622* island of SE Guadeloupe
Mariehamn *221 var.* Maarianhamina. Aland, Finland
Mariel *182* NW Cuba
Marienburg *see* Alūksne
Mariental *391* S Namibia
Marigot *622* St. Martin, N Guadeloupe
Marigot *196* NE Dominica
Marigot de Baïla *476* river of SW Senegal
Mariguana *see* Mayaguana
Marijampolė *344 prev.* Kapsukas. S Lithuania
Marília *121* S Brazil
Marinduque Island *435* island of C Philippines
Maringá *121* S Brazil
Marins, Île aux *628* island of SE Saint Pierre and Miquelon
Marion Island *493* island of Prince Edward Islands , S South Africa
Ionio, Mar *see* Ionian Sea
Maripasoula *621* W French Guiana
Mariscal Estigarribia *428* NW Paraguay
Marisule Estate *465* N St Lucia
Maritsa *128, 245 var.* Marica, *Gk* Évros, *Turk.* Meriç. River of SE Europe
Mariupol' *556 prev.* Zhdanov. SE Ukraine
Mariy El, Respublika *452* autonomous republic of W Russia
Märjamaa *212 Ger.* Merjama. W Estonia
Marjayoun *332 var.* Marj 'Uyūn. S Lebanon
Marka *490 var.* Merca. S Somalia
Marka *353* S Malawi
Market Shop *462* SE Nevis, St Kitts & Nevis
Markounda *154 var.* Marcounda. NW Central African Republic
Marlánské Lázně *188* W Czech Republic
Marmara Denizi *546 Eng.* Sea of Marmara. Sea to the NW of Turkey
Marmaris *546* SW Turkey
Marne *225* river of NE France
Marneuli *234* S Georgia
Maro *156* S Chad
Maroantsetra *350* NE Madagascar
Maromokotro *350* mountain of N Madagascar
Marondera *612 var.* Marandellas. NE Zimbabwe
Maroni *505, 621 Dut.* Marowijne. River of French Guiana and Surinam
Maros *see* Mureş
Marosvásárhely *see* Târgu Mureş
Maroua *144* N Cameroon
Marovoay *350* NW Madagascar
Marowijne *see* Maroni
Marqūbān *91* NE Bahrain
Marquises, Îles *622* island group of N French Polynesia

Marrakech *382 var.* Marakesh, *Eng.* Marrakesh, *prev.* Morocco. W Morocco
Marrupa *387* N Mozambique
Marsa *363* C Malta
Marsá al Burayqah *see* Al Burayqah
Marsabit *316* N Kenya
Marsala *295* Sicilia, S Italy
Marsaxlokk *363* SE Malta
Marsaxlokk Bay *363* inlet on the SW coast of Malta
Marseille *225 prev. Eng.* Marseilles. SE France
Marshall *336* W Liberia
Marshall Islands *364-365* officially Republic of the Marshall Islands. Country of the Pacific Ocean divided into 33 admin. units (districts)
Marsh Harbour *88* Great Abaco, Bahamas
Martaban *135* SE Burma
Martadi *395 var.* Bajura. W Nepal
Martigny *516* SW Switzerland
Martigues *225* SE France
Martin *485 prev.* Turčiansky Svätý Martin, *Ger.* Sankt Martin, *Hung.* Turócszentmárton. NW Slovakia
Martinique *625* French overseas department of the Caribbean Sea.
❖ Fort-de-France.
Martinique Passage *196 var.* Dominica Channel, Martinique Channel. Passage connecting the Atlantic Ocean and Caribbean Sea between Dominica and Martinique
Martuni *74* E Armenia
Marungu *607* mountain range of SE Zaire
Mary *551 prev.* Merv. SE Turkmenistan
Maryborough *77* E Australia
Mary Island *see* Kanton
Maryland *569* state of E USA
Marzūq *see* Murzuq
Masai Steppe *530* grassland of NW Tanzania
Masaka *554* SW Uganda
Masākin *see* M'saken
Masally *see* Massilı
Masampo *see* Masan
Masan *496 prev.* Masampo. S South Korea
Masasi *530* SE Tanzania
Masatepe *404* SW Nicaragua
Masaya *404* S Nicaragua
Masbate *435* island of C Philippines
Mascara *59 var.* Mouaskar. NW Algeria
Maseru *334* ❖ of Lesotho, W Lesotho
Mas-ha *292* W West Bank
Mashava *612 prev.* Mashaba. SE Zimbabwe
Mashhad *281 var.* Meshed. NE Iran
Māshkel *281, 420 var.* Rūd-i Māshkel, Māshkīd. River of Iran and Pakistan
Māshkel, Hāmūn-i *420* salt marsh of Iran and Pakistan
Māshkīd *see* Māshkel
Mashtagi *see* Mastağı
Masīlah, Wādī al *599* dry watercourse of E Yemen
Masindi *554* SW Uganda
Masinga Reservoir *316* reservoir of C Kenya
Masirah, Gulf of *see* Maşīrah, Khalīj
Maşīrah, Jazīrat *418 var.* Masirah, Masira. Island of E Oman
Maşīrah, Khalīj *418 var.* Gulf of Masirah. Bay of the Arabian Sea, E Oman
Masis *74* SW Armenia
Masjed Soleymān *281 var.* Masjed-e Soleymān, Masjid-i Sulaimān. W Iran
Masjid-i Sulaimān *see* Masjed Soleymān
Maskall *102* NE Belize

Maskanah *521 var.* Meskene. N Syria
Maskin *418 var.* Miskin. N Oman
Mask, Lough *288 Ir.* Loch Measca. Lake of W Ireland
Ma *593* river of Laos and Vietnam
Massa *294* N Italy
Massachusetts *569* state of NE USA
Massacre *196* W Dominica
Massawa *210 Amh.* Mits'iwa. E Eritrea
Massawa Channel *210* channel of the Red Sea between Dahlak Archipelago and mainland Eritrea
Massenya *156* SW Chad
Massif Central *225* plateau region of C France
Massilı *86 Rus.* Masally. S Azerbaijan
Massoukou *230 var.* Masuku, *prev.* Franceville. E Gabon
Maştağa *86 Rus.* Mastaga, *var.* Maştaga, Mashtagi. E Azerbaijan
Masterton *401* S North Island, New Zealand
Masuda *304* Honshū, W Japan
Masunga *118* NE Botswana
Masvingo *612 prev.* Nyanda, *prev.* Fort Victoria. SE Zimbabwe
Mât *628* river of NE Réunion
Matacawa Levu *218* island of the Yasawa Group, NW Fiji
Matadi *607* W Zaire
Matagalpa *404* C Nicaragua
Matale *504* S Sri Lanka
Matam *476* NE Senegal
Matamoros *370* E Mexico
Matanzas *182* NW Cuba
Matara *504* S Sri Lanka
Mataró *501* E Spain
Mataura *401* river of SW South Island, New Zealand
Matautu *596* Upolu, Western Samoa
Matá 'Utu *629 var.* Mata Uta.
❖ of Wallis & Futuna, Île Uvea, S Wallis & Futuna
Matela's *334* W Lesotho
Matelot *540* NE Trinidad, Trinidad & Tobago
Matiguas *404* C Nicaragua
Matina *178* E Costa Rica
Matit *57 var.* Mat. River of C Albania
Mato Grosso, Planalto de *121* plateau of C Brazil
Matopos *612* SW Zimbabwe
Matosinhos *442 prev.* Matozinhos. NW Portugal
Mátra *264* mountain range of N Hungary
Maţraḩ *418 var.* Mutrah. NE Oman
Matrûh *202 var.* Maţrūḩ. NW Egypt
Matsapha *510 var.* Matsapal, Mtsapa. C Swaziland
Matsieng *334* W Lesotho
Matsue *304* Honshū, W Japan
Matsumato *304* Honshū, C Japan
Matsusaka *304* Honshū, C Japan
Matsuyama *304* Shikoku, SW Japan
Matthews Ridge *256* N Guyana
Matthew Town *88* Great Inagua, Bahamas
Mattsee *82* lake of N Austria
Matuku *218* island to the SE of Viti Levu, N Fiji
Maturín *589* NE Venezuela
Mauga Silisili *596 var.* Mount Silisili. Mountain of NW Western Samoa
Maug Islands *626* island group of N Northern Mariana Islands
Maui *568* island of Hawaii, USA, C Pacific
Maun *118* C Botswana
Mauren *342* NE Liechtenstein
Maurice *see* Mauritius
Maú *see* Ireng

Mauritania *366-367* officially Islamic Republic of Mauritania, *Ar.* Mūrītānīyah. Country of W Africa divided into 12 admin. units (regions)
Mauritius *368-369* officially Republic of Mauritius, *Fr.* Maurice. Country of Indian Ocean divided into 9 admin. units (districts)
Mavrovsko Ezero *349* lake of W FYR Macedonia
Mawlaik *135* NW Burma
Mawlamyine *see* Moulmein
Mawr, Wādī *599* dry watercourse of NW Yemen
Mawson *66* Australian research station of Greater Antarctica, Antarctica
Mayaguana *88* Island of S Bahamas
Mayaguana Passage *88* passage between Crooked I and Mayaguana, Bahamas
Mayagüez *627* W Puerto Rico
Mayagüez, Bahia *627* bay of the Caribbean Sea on the W coast of Puerto Rico
Mayaluka *510* SE Swaziland
Maya Mts *102* mountain range of Belize and Guatemala
Mayarí *183* SE Cuba
Maych'ew *215 var.* Mai Chio, *It.* Mai Ceu. N Ethiopia
Maydī *see* Midī
Mayence *see* Mainz
Mayenne *225* river of NW France
Mayli-Say *345 Kir.* Mayly-Say. W Kyrgyzstan
Mayly-Say *see* Mayli-Say
Maymyo *135* N Burma
Mayoko *176* SW Congo
Mayor Pablo Lagerenza *see* Capitán Pablo Lagerenza
Mayotte *625* French territorial collectivity of the Indian Ocean.
❖ Mamoudzou.
May Pen *303* S Jamaica
Mayreau *466* island of SW St Vincent & the Grenadines
Mayumba *230* S Gabon
Mazabuka *611* S Zambia
Mazagan *see* El Jadida
Mazār-e Sharif *53* N Afghanistan
Mazaruni *256* river of N Guyana
Mazatenango *250* SW Guatemala
Mazatlán *370* W Mexico
Mažeikiai *344* NW Lithuania
Mazirbe *330* NW Latvia
Mazowe *612 prev.* Mazoe. NE Zimbabwe
Mazowe *612 var.* Mazoe. River of Mozambique and Zimbabwe
Mazra'at Turaynā *447 var.* Traina Garden. S Qatar
Mazury *439* region of NE Poland
Mazyr *104 Rus.* Mozyr'. SE Belorussia
Mba *see* Ba
Mbabane *510* ❖ of Swaziland, NW Swaziland
Mbacké *see* Mbaké
Mbagne *366* SW Mauritania
Mbaïki *154 var.* M'Baiki. SW Central African Republic
Mbakaou, Lac de *144* lake of C Cameroon
Mbaké *476 var.* Mbacké. W Senegal
Mbala *611 prev.* Abercorn. NE Zambia
Mbalabala *612 prev.* Balla Balla. SW Zimbabwe
Mbale *554* E Uganda
Mbalmayo *144 var.* M'Balmayo. S Cameroon
Mbalo *488* SE Guadalcanal, Solomon Is
Mbam *144* river of NW Cameroon
Mbandaka *607 prev.* Coquilhatville. NW Zaire
Mbanga *144* W Cameroon
M'Banza Congo *64 Port.* São Salvador do Congo. NW Angola

Mílos *245* island of SE Greece
Mil'skaya Step' *see* Mil Düzü
Milton Keynes *563* C England, UK
Milwaukee *569* Wisconsin,
  NC USA
Milyang *see* Miryang
Mimongo *230* C Gabon
Mīnā' 'Abd Allāh *322* *var.* Mina
  Abdulla. E Kuwait
Mīnā' al Aḥmadī *322* *var.* Mina
  Ahmadi. E Kuwait
Mīnā' Jabal 'Alī *560* NE United Arab
  Emirates
Minas *577* S Uruguay
Mīnā' Sa'ūd *322* *var.* Mīnā' Su'ūd.
  SE Kuwait
Minas de Corrales *577* N Uruguay
Minas de Matahambre *182* W Cuba
Minatitlán *370* SE Mexico
Minbu *135* W Burma
Minch, The *563* strait of the Atlantic
  Ocean, between Outer Hebrides and
  Scotland
Mincivan *86* *Rus.* Mindzhivan.
  SW Azerbaijan
Mindanao *435* island of S Philippines
Mindanao Sea *see* Bohol Sea
Mindelo *152* *var.* Porto Grande.
  São Vincente, N Cape Verde
Mindoro *435* island of C Philippines
Mindoro Strait *435* strait connecting
  South China Sea and Sulu Sea
Mindouli *176* S Congo
Mindživan *see* Mincivan
Mingäçevir *86* *Rus.* Mingechaur
  var. Mingečaur. C Azerbaijan
Mingäçevir Su Anbarı *86*
  Rus. Mingechaurskoye
  Vodokhranilishche. Reservoir
  of NW Azerbaijan
Mingala *154* SE Central African
  Republic
Mingãora *421* *var.* Mingora, Mongora.
  N Pakistan
Mingechaurskoye Vodokhranilishche
  see Mingäçevir Su Anbarı
Ming-Kush *see* Min-Kush
Minho *see* Miño
Minicoy Island *270* island of
  Lakshadweep, SW India
Min-Kush *325* *Kir.* Ming-Kush.
  C Kyrgyzstan
Minna *408* C Nigeria
Minneapolis *569* Minnesota, NC USA
Minnesota *569* state of NC USA
Miño *442, 500* *Port.* Minho. River of
  Portugal and Spain
Minorca *see* Menorca
Minot *569* North Dakota, NC USA
Minsk *104* ❖ of Belorussia,
  C Belorussia
Minto Reef *375* atoll of C Micronesia
Minvoul *230* N Gabon
Minwakh *599* N Yemen
Miquelon *628* N Saint Pierre and
  Miquelon
Miquelon *628* island of N Saint Pierre
  and Miquelon
Miquelon, Cap *628* cape of the
  Atlantic Ocean on the coast of
  Miquelon, N Saint Pierre and
  Miquelon
Miragoâne *258* SW Haiti
Miranda de Ebro *501* N Spain
Mirbāṭ *418* *var.* Marbat. SW Oman
Mirebalais *258* C Haiti
Miri *354* NW Borneo, Malaysia
Mirim Lagoon *121, 577* *var.* Lake
  Mirim. Lagoon of Brazil and
  Uruguay
Mirim, Lake *see* Mirim Lagoon
Mirnyy *453* C Russia
Mirnyy *66* CIS research station of
  Greater Antarctica, Antarctica
Mirpur *see* New Mirpur
Mirs Bay *262* *Cant.* Tai Pang Wan.
  Bay to the NE of Hong Kong
Mirtóo Pelagos *245* *Eng.* Mirtoan
  Sea. Area of the Mediterranean Sea,
  S Greece

Miryang *496* *var.* Milyang
  Jap. Mitsuō. SE South Korea
Misery, Mount *see* Liamuiga, Mount
Miskito Coast *see* Mosquito Coast
Miskitos, Cayos *404* island group of
  NE Nicaragua
Miskolc *264* NE Hungary
Misool, Pulau *276* island of Maluku,
  E Indonesia
Miṣrātah *339* *var.* Misurata.
  N Libya
Mississippi *569* river of C USA
Mississippi *569* state of SE USA
Missoula *568* Montana, NW USA
Missouri *569* river of NC USA
Missouri *569* state of C USA
Misurata *see* Miṣrātah
Mitau *see* Jelgava
Mitchell *77* river of NE Australia
Mitiaro *620* island of Southern Cook
  Islands, S Cook Islands
Mitilíni *245* *var.* Mytilene. Lésvos,
  E Greece
Mito *304* Honshū, SE Japan
Mitre Island *see* Fatutaka
Mitrovica *see* Kosovska Mitrovica
Mitrovicë *see* Kosovska Mitrovica
Mitsamiouli *174* N Grande Comore,
  Comoros
Mits'iwa *see* Massawa
Mitsoudjé *174* SW Grande Comore,
  Comoros
Mitsuyō *see* Miryang
Mitú *171* SE Colombia
Mitumba, Monts *607* *var.* Chaîne des
  Mitumba, Mitumba Range. Mountain
  range of E Zaire
Mitzic *230* N Gabon
Miyako *305* Honshū, N Japan
Miyako-jima *304* island of
  Sakishima-shotō, SW Japan
Miyakonojō *304* Kyūshū,
  SW Japan
Miyazaki *304* Kyūshū,
  SW Japan
Miyoshi *304* Honshū, W Japan
Mizdah *339* *var.* Mizda.
  NW Libya
Mjøsa *414* *var.* Mjøsen. Lake of
  SE Norway
Mkhondvo *510* *var.* Mkondo.
  River of South Africa and
  Swaziland
Mladá Boleslav *188*
  Ger. Jungbunzlau. N Czech Republic
Mlanje *see* Mulanje
Mljet *181* *It.* Meleda. Island of
  S Croatia
Mmabatho *493* North West,
  N South Africa
Mmathethe *118* S Botswana
Mnjoli Dam *510* reservoir of
  NE Swaziland
Mo *414* NE Norway
Moa *480* river of W Africa
Moa *183* SE Cuba
Moabi *230* SW Gabon
Moala *218* island to the SE of Viti
  Levu, S Fiji
Moamba *387* SW Mozambique
Moanda *230* SE Gabon
Moba *607* E Zaire
Mobaye *154* S Central African
  Republic
Mobile *569* Alabama, SE USA
Moca *198* N Dominican Republic
Moçambique *387* island and
  settlement of NE Mozambique
Moçâmedes *see* Namibe
Moce *218* island of the Lau Group,
  E Fiji
Mocha *see* Al Mukhā
Mochudi *118* S Botswana
Mocímboa da Praia *387* *var.* Vila de
  Mocímboa da Praia. N Mozambique
Môco *64* *var.* Serra Môco, Morro de
  Môco. Mountain of W Angola
Mocoa *171* SW Colombia
Mocuba *387* E Mozambique
Modena *294* NW Italy

Mödling *82* NE Austria
Modohn *see* Madona
Modriča *116* N Bosnia & Herzegovina
Moe *77* SE Australia
Moen *see* Weno
Möen *see* Møn
Moena *see* Muna, Pulau
Moengo *508* NE Surinam
Moers *236* W Germany
Moesi *see* Musi
Moeskroen *see* Mouscron
Mogadishu *490* *Som.* Muqdisho,
  It. Mogadiscio. ❖ of Somalia,
  S Somalia
Mogador *see* Essaouira
Mogilëv *see* Mahilyow
Mogotón, Pico *404* mountain of
  NW Nicaragua
Mohales Hoek *334* SW Lesotho
Mohammadia *59*
  var. El Mohammaidia. NW Algeria
Mohammedia *382* *prev.* Fédala.
  NW Morocco
Moharek *see* Al Muḥarraq
Mohéli *174* *var.* Mwali. Island of
  Comoros
Mohn *see* Muhu
Moihani *174* S Mohéli, Comoros
Moindou *626* C New Caledonia
Mõisaküla *212* *Ger.* Moiseküll.
  S Estonia
Moïssala *156* S Chad
Moka *368* C Mauritius
Mokhotlong *334* NE Lesotho
Mokil *375* atoll of E Micronesia
Moknine *543* *var.* Al Muknīn.
  NE Tunisia
Mokp'o *496* *Jap.* Moppo. SW South
  Korea
Mokra Gora *602* mountain range
  of SW Serbia, Yugoslavia
Mokwa *408* W Nigeria
Moldau *see* Vltava
Moldavia *376-377* officially Republic
  of Moldova, *var.* Moldova,
  prev. Moldavian SSR,
  Rus. Moldavskaya SSR. Country of
  E Europe divided into 40 admin.
  units (districts)
Molde *414* SW Norway
Moldotau, Khrebet *325* mountain
  range of C Kyrgyzstan
Moldova *see* Moldavia
Molepolole *118* S Botswana
Môle-St-Nicolas *258* NW Haiti
Molineux *462* NE St Kitts, St Kitts
  & Nevis
Möll *82* river of S Austria
Mölndal *513* SW Sweden
Molodechno *see* Maladzyechna
Molodeczno *see* Maladzyechna
Molodezhnaya *66* CIS research
  station of Greater Antarctica,
  Antarctica
Molokai *568* island of Hawaii, USA,
  C Pacific
Molopo *118, 493* seasonal river
  of southern Africa
Molotov *see* Severodvinsk
Molotov *see* Perm'
Moloundou *144* SE Cameroon
Moluccas *see* Maluku
Molucca Sea *see* Maluku, Laut
Mombasa *316* SE Kenya
Môn *see* Anglesey
Møn *190* *prev.* Möen. Island of
  SE Denmark
Mona, Canal de la *198, 627* channel
  connecting the Atlantic Ocean and
  Caribbean Sea, between Dominican
  Republica and Puerto Rico
Monaco *378-379* officially Principality
  of Monaco. Country of W Europe
  divided into 4 admin. units (quarters)
Monaco *see* München
Monaghan *288* *Ir.* Muineachán.
  NE Ireland
Monagrillo *424* S Panama
Mona, Isla *627* island of SW Puerto
  Rico

Monapo *387* NE Mozambique
Monaragala *504* SE Sri Lanka
Monastir *543* *var.* Al Munastīr.
  NE Tunisia
Monastir *see* Bitola
Mönchengladbach *236*
  prev. München-Gladbach.
  W Germany
Monchy *465* N St Lucia
Monclova *370* N Mexico
Moncton *147* SE Canada
Mondego *442* river of N Portugal
Mondsee *82* lake of N Austria
Money Island *627* island of W Paracel
  Islands
Monfalcone *295* N Italy
Mongar *110* E Bhutan
Mongo *156* C Chad
Mongolia *380-381* country of NE Asia
  divided into 21 admin. units
  (18 provinces, 3 cities)
Mongomo *208* E Río Muni, Equatorial
  Guinea
Mongora *see* Mingãora
Mongos, Chaîne des *see* Bongo,
  Massif des
Mongouge *465* SW St Lucia
Mongoumba *154* SW Central African
  Republic
Mongu *611* W Zambia
Mönh Hayrhan Uul *380* mountain
  of W Mongolia
Moni *187* S Cyprus
Monkey Bay *353* SE Malawi
Monkey River Town *102* SE Belize
Mono *108, 537* river of Benin and
  Togo
Monopoi *295* E Italy
Monos *540* island to the NW of
  Trinidad, Trinidad & Tobago
Mon Repos *465* E St Lucia
Monrovia *336* ❖ of Liberia,
  W Liberia
Mons *99* *Dut.* Bergen.
  SW Belgium
Montana *568-569* state of NW USA
Montana *128* *prev.* Mikhaylovgrad,
  var. Mihajlovgrad, Mikhailovgrad,
  prev. Ferdinand. NW Bulgaria
Montauban *225* S France
Montbéliard *225* NE France
Mont Blanc *225, 294* *It.* Monte Bianco.
  Mountain of France and Italy
Mont-de-Marsan *225* SW France
Monteagudo *112* S Bolivia
Monte-Carlo *378* NE Monaco
Monte Cristi *198* NW Dominican
  Republic
Monte Croce Carnico, Passo di
  see Plöcken
Montegiardino *468* SE San Marino
Montego Bay *303* NW Jamaica
Montelindo *428* river of
  C Paraguay
Montenegro *602* *Serb.* Crna Gora.
  Republic of Yugoslavia
Monte Plata *198* C Dominican
  Republic
Montepuez *387* N Mozambique
Montería *171* NW Colombia
Montero *112* C Bolivia
Monterrey *370* N Mexico
Montes Claros *121* SE Brazil
Montevideo *577* ❖ of Uruguay,
  S Uruguay
Montgomery *569* Alabama,
  SE USA
Montgomery *see* Sāhīwāl
Monthey *516* SW Switzerland
Montijo *442* W Portugal
Montpelier *569* Vermont,
  NE USA
Montpellier *225* S France
Montréal *147* *Eng.* Montreal.
  SE Canada
Montreux *516* SW Switzerland
Montserrat *625* British dependent
  territory of the Caribbean Sea.
  ❖ Plymouth
Montsinéry *621* NE French Guiana

Monywa *135* NW Burma
Monza *294* N Italy
Monze *611* S Zambia
Moora *76* W Australia
Moose Jaw *146* SW Canada
Moosonee *147* SE Canada
Moppo *see* Mokp'o
Mopti *360* C Mali
Moqor *53* SE Afghanistan
Moquegua *431* SE Peru
Morales *250* E Guatemala
Moramanga *350* E Madagascar
Morant Bay *303* E Jamaica
Morata *see* Goodenough Island
Moratuwa *504* SW Sri Lanka
Morava *602* *var.* Velika Morava. River of C Serbia, Yugoslavia
Morava *188, 485* *Ger.* March. River of C Europe
Moravia *188* cultural region of E Czech Republic
Moravská Ostrava *see* Ostrava
Morawhanna *256* N Guyana
Moray Firth *563* inlet of Atlantic Ocean, NE Scotland, UK
Mordovskaya SSR *452* autonomous republic of W Russia
Moree *77* E Australia
Morehead *426* SW Papua New Guinea
Morelia *370* C Mexico
Moreno *112* N Bolivia
Morfou *see* Güzelyurt
Morfou Bay *see* Morphou Bay
Morges *516* SW Switzerland
Morghāb, Daryā-ye *53* river of Afghanistan and Turkmenistan
Morija *334* W Lesotho
Morioka *304* Honshū, N Japan
Morne Aux Frégates *196* E Dominica
Morne Diablotins *196* mountain of N Dominica
Morne Raquette *196* W Dominica
Morne Seychellois *478* mountain of Mahé, NE Seychelles
Morne Trois Pitons *196* mountain of C Dominica
Morocco *see* Marrakech
Morocco *382-385* officially Kingdom of Morocco, *Ar.* Al Mamlakah. Country of N Africa divided into 37 admin. units (provinces and prefectures)
Morogoro *530* E Tanzania
Moro Gulf *435* area of the Sulu Sea
Morombe *350* SW Madagascar
Morón *182* C Cuba
Morón *71* E Argentina
Mörön *380* N Mongolia
Morondava *350* W Madagascar
Moroni *174* ❖ of Comoros, W Grande Comore, Comoros
Morotai, Pulau *276* island of Maluku, E Indonesia
Moroto *554* NE Uganda
Morphou *see* Güzelyurt
Morphou Bay *187* *var.* Morfou Bay, Güzelyurt Körfezi. Bay of the Mediterranean Sea, on the NW coast of Cyprus
Morris *625* S Montserrat
Morro de Môco *see* Môco
Mors *190* island of NW Denmark
Moruga *540* S Trinidad, Trinidad & Tobago
Morvan *225* physical region of NE France
Morvant *540* NW Trinidad, Trinidad & Tobago
Morwell *77* SE Australia
Moscow *452* *Rus.* Moskva. ❖ of Russia, W Russia
Mosel *225, 236, 346* *Fr.* Moselle. River of W Europe
Moselle *see* Mosel
Moshi *530* NE Tanzania
Mosjøen *414* N Norway
Moskovskiy *528* *prev.* Chubek. SW Tajikistan
Moson *see* Mosonmagyaróvár
Mosoni-Duna *264* river of NW Hungary

Mosonmagyaróvár *264* *prev.* Moson, Magyaróvár, *Ger.* Wieselburg. NW Hungary
Mosquito Coast *260, 404* *var.* Miskito Coast, *Sp.* La Mosquitia. Coastal region of E Central America
Mosquitos, Golfo de *424* gulf of the Caribbean Sea to the N of Panama
Moss *414* S Norway
Mossâmedes *see* Namibe
Mosselbaai *493* *Eng.* Mossel Bay. Western Cape S South Africa
Mossendjo *176* SW Congo
Mossoró *121* NE Brazil
Most *188* *Ger.* Brüx. NW Czech Republic
Mosta *363* *var.* Musta. C Malta
Mostaganem *59* *var.* Mestghanem. NW Algeria
Mostar *116* S Bosnia & Herzegovina
Mosul *see* Al Mawşil
Mota *585* Banks Islands, N Vanuatu
Motaba *176* river of N Congo
Motagua *250* river of Guatemala and Honduras
Mota Lava *585* Banks Islands, N Vanuatu
Mothae *334* NE Lesotho
Motherwell *563* C Scotland, UK
Motjane *510* NW Swaziland
Motril *501* S Spain
Motueka *401* river of NE of South Island, New Zealand
Motulalo *553* islet of Nukufetau, Tuvalu
Motulua *553* islet of Nukufetau, Tuvalu
Motumua *553* islet of Nukufetau, Tuvalu
Mouaskar *see* Mascara
Moucha, Îles *194* islands in the Gulf of Aden, C Djibouti
Mouchoir Passage *629* passage of the Pacific Ocean, SE Turks and Caicos Islands
Moudjéria *366* SW Mauritania
Mouila *230* C Gabon
Mould Bay *146* Prince Patrick Island, N Canada
Moulèngui Binza *230* S Gabon
Moulhoulé *194* N Djibouti
Moulins *225* C France
Moulmein *135* *var.* Mawlamyine. SE Burma
Moulmeingyun *135* SW Burma
Mouloud *194* SW Djibouti
Moulouya *382* seasonal river of NE Morocco
Moun Hou *see* Black Volta
Mounana *230* S Gabon
Moundou *156* SW Chad
Moŭng Roessi *141* *var.* Moung. W Cambodia
Mount Barclay *336* W Liberia
Mount Darwin *612* NE Zimbabwe
Mount Friendship *97* SW Barbados
Mount Gambier *77* SE Australia
Mount Hagen *426* C Papua New Guinea
Mount Isa *77* C Australia
Mount Lebanon *see* Liban, Jebel
Mount Magnet *76* W Australia
Mount Maunganui *401* C North Island, New Zealand
Mount Moorosi *334* SW Lesotho
Mount Moritz *248* SW Grenada island, Grenada
Mount Rose *248* NE Grenada island, Grenada
Mourdi, Dépression de *156* desert lowland of E Chad
Mouscron *99* *Dut.* Moeskroen. W Belgium
Moussa 'Ali *194* mountain of NW Djibouti
Moussoro *156* W Chad
Moya *174* SW Anjouan Comoros
Moyale *215* S Ethiopia
Moyale *316* N Kenya

Moyamba *480* W Sierra Leone
Moyen Atlas *382* *Eng.* Middle Atlas. Mountain range of N Morocco
Moyeni *334* *var.* Quthing. SW Lesotho
Moyo *554* NW Uganda
Moyobamba *431* NW Peru
Moyuta *250* S Guatemala
Mozambique *386-389* officially Republic of Mozambique, *prev.* People's Republic of Mozambique, Portuguese East Africa. Country of East Africa divided into 10 admin. units (provinces)
Mozambique Channel *174, 350* *var.* Canal de Mozambique, Canal de Moçambique, Lakandranon' i Mozambika. Strait of the Indian Ocean, between Mozambique and Madagascar
Mozambique Island *see* Moçambique
Mozyr' *see* Mazyr
Mpama *176* river of C Congo
Mpanda *530* W Tanzania
Mpanga, Lac *460* lake of E Rwanda
Mphaki *334* S Lesotho
Mpigi *554* S Uganda
Mpika *611* NE Zambia
Mporokoso *611* N Zambia
Mpulungu *611* N Zambia
Mpwapwa *530* C Tanzania
Mqocha *353* NW Malawi
M'Rémani *174* S Anjouan, Comoros
M'Saken *543* *var.* Masakin. N Tunisia
Msida *363* C Malta
M 'Sila *59* N Algeria
Mtoko *see* Mutoko
Mtsamboro *625* N Mayotte
Mtsamgamouji *625* W Mayotte
Mtsapa *see* Matsapha
Mtwara *530* SE Tanzania
Mu'a *538* Tongatabu, Tongatapu Group, Tonga
Mualama *387* E Mozambique
Mualo *see* Messalo
Muang Ham *327* NE Laos
Muang Hinboun *327* S Laos
Muang Kalasin *see* Kalasin
Muang Kap *327* S Laos
Muang Khammouan *327* *var.* Thakhek. S Laos
Muang Không *327* S Laos
Muang Khôngxédôn *327* *var.* Khong Sedone. S Laos
Muang Khon Kaen *see* Khon Kaen
Muang Lampang *see* Lampang
Muang Loei *see* Loei
Muang Lom Sak *see* Lom Sak
Muang Nakhon Sawan *see* Nakhon Sawan
Muang Namo *327* N Laos
Muang Nan *see* Nan
Muang Pakxan *327* *var.* Pak Sane. C Laos
Muang Phalan *327* S Laos
Muang Phin *327* S Laos
Muang Phitsanulok *see* Phitsanulok
Muang Phôn-Hông *327* C Laos
Muang Phrae *see* Phrae
Muang Roi Et *see* Roi Et
Muang Samut Prakan *see* Samut Prakan
Muang Sing *327* NW Laos
Muang Vangviang *327* C Laos
Muang Xaignabouri *327* *var.* Sayaboury. W Laos
Muang Xay *327* *var.* Muong Sai. N Laos
Muang Xépôn *327* *var.* Sepone. SE Laos
Muar *354* river of S Peninsular Malaysia
Muar *354* *prev.* Bandar Maharani. S Peninsular Malaysia
Muara Besar, Pulau *126* island of N Brunei
Mubende *554* SW Uganda
Mucojo *387* N Mozambique

Mudanjiang *163* *var.* Mu-tan-chiang. Heliongjiang, NE China
Mudon *135* SE Burma
Mueda *387* NE Mozambique
Muenster *see* Münster
Mufulira *611* C Zambia
Muğan Düzü *86* *Rus.* Muganskaya Step'. Physical region of S Azerbaijan
Mugera *138* C Burundi
Mugesera, Lac *460* lake of E Rwanda
Mugi *304* Shikoku, SW Japan
Mugla *546* SW Turkey
Muharraq *see* Al Muḩarraq
Muḩarraq, Jazīrat al *91* island of N Bahrain
Muhazi, Lac *460* lake of E Rwanda
Muhinga *see* Muyinga
Muh, Sabkhat al *521* salt-flat of S Syria
Muhu *212* *Ger.* Mohn, Moon. Island of W Estonia
Muhu Väin *see* Väinameri
Muineachán *see* Monaghan
Muir Bhreatan *see* St. George's Channel
Muir Eireann *see* Irish Sea
Mukacheve *556* W Ukraine
Mukalla *see* Al Mukallā
Mukden *see* Shenyang
Muksu *528* river of NE Tajikistan
Mukungwa *460* river of NW Rwanda
Mulaku Atoll *358* *var.* Meemu Atoll. Atoll of C Maldives
Mulanje *353* *var.* Mlanje. S Malawi
Mulhacén, Cerro de *501* mountain of SE Spain
Mulchén *159* C Chile
Mülheim *236* *var.* Mulheim an der Ruhr. W Germany
Mulhouse *225* *Ger.* Mülhausen. NE France
Mulifanua *596* Upolu, Western Samoa
Mulin'u, Cape *596* cape of Savai'i, Western Samoa
Mulitapu'ili, Cape *596* cape on the S coast of Upolu, Western Samoa
Mullaittivu *504* *var.* Mullaitivu. NE Sri Lanka
Muller, Pegunungan *276* *Dut.* Müller-gerbergte. Mountain range of Borneo, C Indonesia
Mullingar *288* C Ireland
Mull, Isle of *563* island of Inner Hebrides, W Scotland, UK
Multān *421* E Pakistan
Mumbai *see* Bombay
Mumbwa *611* C Zambia
Mummatalah, Ra's al *91* *var.* Ra's al Mamtalah. Cape of SW Bahrain
Munamägi *see* Suur Munamägi
Muna, Pulau *276* *prev.* Moena. Island to the SE of Celebes, C Indonesia
München *237, 241* *Eng.* Munich, *It.* Monaco. S Germany
Munch'ön *413* SE North Korea
Munda *488* New Georgia, C Solomon Islands
Mundal Lagooon *504* lagoon of W Sri Lanka
Mu Nggava *see* Rennell
Mungla *93* S Bangladesh
Mungwa *138* C Burundi
Mungwi *611* NE Zambia
Munia *218* island of the Lau Group, E Fiji
Munich *see* München
Munini *460* SW Rwanda
Munshiganj *93* C Bangladesh
Munster *288* province of S Ireland
Münster *236* *var.* Muenster. NW Germany
Muntinglupa *435* Luzon, N Philippines
Muong Sai *see* Muang Xay
Muonioälv *see* Muoniojoki
Muoniojoki *221, 513* *Swe.* Muonioälv. River of Finland and Sweden
Muqdisho *see* Mogadishu

Mur *82, 486 SCr.* Mura. River of C Europe
Mura *see* Mur
Muragarazi *see* Malagarasi
Murai Reservoir *483* reservoir of NW Singapore
Muramba *138* NE Burundi
Murambi *460* C Rwanda
Muramvya *138* C Burundi
Murang'a *316 prev.* Fort Hall. SW Kenya
Murata *468* S San Marino
Murchison Falls *554 var.* Kabalega Falls. Waterfall of NW Uganda
Murcia *501* autonomous community of SE Spain
Mureş *448 var.* Mureşul, *Hung.* Maros, *Ger.* Muresch. River of Hungary and Romania
Murehwa *612 var.* Murewa. NE Zimbabwe
Muresch *see* Mureş
Murgab *551 var.* Murghab. River of SE Turkmenistan
Murgab *528* E Tajikistan
Murgap *551 prev.* Murgab. SE Turkmenistan
Muri *516 var.* Muri bei Bern. W Switzerland
Murilo *375* atoll of N Micronesia
Mūrītānīyah *see* Mauritania
Müritz *237 var.* Müritzee. Lake of NE Germany
Murmansk *452* NW Russia
Muroran *304* Hokkaidō, N Japan
Muroto *304* Shikoku, SW Japan
Murray *77* river of SE Australia
Murray, Lake *426* lake in swamp region of W Papua New Guinea
Murrumbidgee *77* river of SE Australia
Murska Sobota *486 Ger.* Olsnitz. NE Slovenia
Murua Island *426 var.* Woodlark I. Island of SE Papua New Guinea
Murupara *401* SE North Island, New Zealand
Mururoa Atoll *622 var.* Moruroa. Atoll of French Polynesia
Murzuq *339 var.* Marzūq, Murzuk. W Libya
Murzuq, Ḥammādat *339* plateau of W Libya
Muş *547* E Turkey
Mūša *344* river of N Lithuania
Musaffah *560* C United Arab Emirates
Musä'id *339* NE Libya
Musala *128 prev.* Stalin Peak. Mountain of W Bulgaria
Musan *413* NE North Korea
Musandam Peninsula *418 Ar.* Ra's Musandam, *var.* Ras Masandam. Peninsular of N Oman
Musay'id *447 var.* Umm Sa'īd. SE Qatar
Muscat *418 Ar.* Masqaṭ. ❖ of Oman, N Oman
Muscat and Oman *see* Oman
Musema *138* C Burundi
Musenyi *138* W Burundi
Mushin *408* SW Nigeria
Musi *276 prev.* Moesi. River of Sumatra, W Indonesia
Musoma *530* N Tanzania
Mussau Island *426* island of NE Papua New Guinea
Mustafa-Pasha *see* Svilengrad
Mustique *466* island of C St Vincent & the Grenadines
Mustvee *212 Ger.* Tschorna. E Estonia
Mutalau *626* N Niue
Mutambara *138* SW Burundi
Mu-tan-chiang *see* Mudanjiang
Mutare *612 prev.* Umtali. E Zimbabwe
Mutoko *612 prev.* Mtoko. NE Zimbabwe
Mutorashanga *612 prev.* Mtorashanga. N Zimbabwe

Mutsamudu *174* NW Anjouan, Comoros
Muyaga *138* C Burundi
Muyaga *138* E Burundi
Muyebe *138* C Burundi
Muyinga *138 var.* Muhinga. NE Burundi
Muy Muy *404* C Nicaragua
Muynak *580 var.* Mujnak, *Uzb.* Mŭynoq. NW Uzbekistan
Muyunkum, Peski *312* desert region of S Kazakhstan
Muzaffargarh *421* E Pakistan
Muzarabani *612* N Zimbabwe
Mvuma *612 prev.* Umvuma. C Zimbabwe
Mvurwi *612 prev.* Umvukwes. N Zimbabwe
Mwali *see* Mohéli
Mwanza *530* NW Tanzania
Mwanza *353* SW Malawi
Mweka *607* C Zaire
Mwenda *611* N Zambia
Mwene-Ditu *607* S Zaire
Mwenezi *612* river of S Zimbabwe
Mwenezi *612 prev.* Nuanetsi. S Zimbabwe
Mweru, Lake *607, 611 Fr.* Lac Moero. Lake of Zaire and Zambia
Mweru Wantipa, Lake *611* lake of N Zambia
Mwombezhi *611* river of W Zambia
Myanaung *135* SW Burma
Myanmar *see* Burma
Myaungmya *135* SW Burma
Myingyan *135* C Burma
Myitkyina *135* N Burma
Myitnge *135* river of NE Burma
Mykines *620* island of W Faeroe Islands
Mykolayiv *556 Rus.* Nikolayev. S Ukraine
Mymensingh *93 prev.* Nasirābād. N Bangladesh
Myŏngch'ŏn *413* NE North Korea
Mýrdalsjökull *268* glacier of S Iceland
Mysore *270 var.* Maisur. S India
My Tho *593* S Vietnam
Mytilene *see* Mitilíni
Mývatn *268* lake of C Iceland
Mzimba *353* NW Malawi
Mzuzu *353* N Malawi

N

Naas *288 Ir.* Nás Na Riogh, An Nás. E Ireland
Nabatiyé *332 var.* Nabatiyet et Tahta, An Nabaṭīyah at Taḥtā. SW Lebanon
Nabavatu *218* Vanua Levu, N Fiji
Naberezhnyye Chelny *452 prev.* Brezhnev. W Russia
Nabeul *543 var.* Nābul. N Tunisia
Nabgha *560* NE United Arab Emirates
Nabīh aş Şalīḩ, Jazīrat an *91 var.* Nabih Saleh, Nabīh Salīḥ. Island of NE Bahrain
Nabī Shu'ayb, Jabal an *599* mountain of W Yemen
Nablus *291, 292 Heb.* Shekhem. N West Bank
Nabouwalu *218* Vanua Levu, N Fiji
Nacala *387* NE Mozambique
Nacaome *260* S Honduras
Na-Chii *see* Nagqu
Nachingwea *530* SE Tanzania
Na Cruacha Dubha *see* Macgillicuddy's Reeks
Nacula *218 prev.* Nathula. Island of the Yasawa Group, NW Fiji
Nadi *218 prev.* Nandi. Viti Levu, W Fiji
Nador *382 prev.* Villa Nador. NE Morocco
Nadur *363* Gozo, Malta
Naduri *218 prev.* Nanduri. Vanua Levu, N Fiji

Nadym *452* N Russia
Næstved *190* Sjælland, SE Denmark
Nafūsah, Jabal *339* mountain range of NW Libya
Naga *435 prev.* Nueva Caceres. Luzon, N Philippines
Nagano *304* Honshū, C Japan
Nagaoka *304* Honshū, N Japan
Nagarote *404* SW Nicaragua
Nagasaki *304* Kyūshū, SW Japan
Nāgercoil *270* S India
Nagorno-Karabakh *86* former autonomous region of SW Azerbaijan
Nagoya *304* Honshū, C Japan
Nāgpur *270* C India
Nagqu *162 Chin.* Na-Ch'ii, *prev.* Hei-ho. Xizang Zizhiqu, W China
Nagua *198* N Dominican Republic
Nagybánya *see* Baia Mare
Nagybecskerek *see* Zrenjanin
Nagykanizsa *264 Ger.* Grosskanizsa. SW Hungary
Nagykőrös *264* C Hungary
Nagymihály *see* Michalovce
Nagysurány *see* Šurany
Nagyszeben *see* Sibiu
Nagyszombat *see* Trnava
Nagytapolcsány *see* Topolčany
Nagyvárad *see* Oradea
Naha *304* Nansei-shotō, SW Japan
Naḥal Elisha *292* E West Bank
Nahariyya *291* N Israel
Nahiçevan' *see* Naxçıvan
Furāt
Urdunn *see* Jordan
Nairai *218* island to the E of Viti Levu, C Fiji
Nairobi *316* ❖ of Kenya, S Kenya
Naitaba *218 prev.* Naitamba. Island of the Lau Group, E Fiji
Naitamba *see* Naitaba
Naivasha *316* SW Kenya
Naivasha, Lake *316* lake of SW Kenya
Najaf *see* An Najaf
Najafābād *281* W Iran
Najd *472 var.* Nejd. Region of C Saudi Arabia
Najin *413* NE North Korea
Najrān *472* S Saudi Arabia
Naju *see* Kumsong
Nakadōri-jima *304* island of Gotō-rettō, SW Japan
Nakamura *304* Shikoku, SW Japan
Nakasongola *554* W Uganda
Nakatsu *304* Kyūshū, SW Japan
Nakatsugawa *304* Honshū, C Japan
Nakfa *210* N Eritrea
Nakhichevan' *see* Naxcivan
Nakhodka *453* SE Russia
Nakhon Pathom *533* C Thailand
Nakhon Phanom *533* NE Thailand
Nakhon Ratchasima *533 var.* Korat. E Thailand
Nakhon Sawan *533 var.* Muang Nakhon Sawan. W Thailand
Nakhon Si Thammarat *533* S Thailand
Nakskov *190* Lolland, S Denmark
Naktong *496 var.* Nakdong, *Jap.* Rakutō-kō. River of South Korea
Nakuru *316* W Kenya
Nāl *421* river of W Pakistan
Nalayh *380* C Mongolia
Nal'chik *452* SW Russia
Nam *413* river of C North Korea
Nam *496* river of S South Korea
Namaacha *387* S Mozambique
Namacurra *387* E Mozambique
Namak, Daryācheh-ye *281* lake of W Iran
Namak, Kavīr-e *281* desert region of NE Iran
Namanga *316* S Kenya
Namangan *580* E Uzbekistan

Namatanai *426* New Ireland, Papua New Guinea
Nam Ðinh *593* N Vietnam
Namen *see* Namur
Namhae-do *496 Jap.* Nankai-tō. Island of S South Korea
Namib Desert *391* coastal desert region of W Namibia
Namibe *64 Port.* Moçâmedes, *var.* Mossâmedes. SW Angola
Namibia *390-391* officially Republic of Namibia, *prev.* South-West Africa, German Southwest Africa. Country of Southern Africa divided into 13 admin. units (districts)
Namoluk *375* island of SE Micronesia
Namonuito *375* atoll of NW Micronesia
Namorik *364* island of S Marshall Islands
Nampa *568* Idaho, NW USA
Namp'o *413* SW North Korea
Nampula *387* NE Mozambique
Namsos *414* C Norway
Namu *364* island of C Marshall Islands
Namuka-i-lau *218* island of the Lau Group, E Fiji
Namur *99 Dut.* Namen. SE Belgium
Namutoni *391* N Namibia
Namwŏn *496 Jap.* Nangen. S South Korea
Namyit Island *628* island of S Spratly Islands
Nan *533 var.* Muang Nan. N Thailand
Nanaimo *146* Vancouver Island, SW Canada
Nanao *304* Honshū, C Japan
Nanchang *163* Jianxi, SE China
Nan-ching *see* Nanjing
Nancy *225* NE France
Nanda Devi *270* mountain of N India
Nandaime *404* S Nicaragua
Nandi *see* Nadi
Nanduri *see* Naduri
Nanga Eboko *144* C Cameroon
Nangbéto, Retenue de *537* reservoir of C Togo
Nangen *see* Namwŏn
Nan Hai *see* East China Sea and South China Sea
Nan-hsi *525* SW Taiwan
Nanjing *163 var.* Nanking, Nan-ching. Jiangsu, E China
Nankai-tō *see* Namhae-do
Nanning *163 prev.* Yung-ning. Guangxi, S China
Nanortalik *622* S Greenland
Nansei-shotō *304* island group to the SW of Kyūshū, SW Japan
Nanshan Island *628* island of E Spratly Islands
Nansio *530* NW Tanzania
Nanterre *225* N France
Nantes *224* W France
Nanthi Kadal Lagoon *504* lagoon of N Sri Lanka
Nan-t'ou *525* W Taiwan
Nanuku Passage *218* channel of the Pacific Ocean between the Lau Group and Taveuni, NE Fiji
Nanumaga *553 prev.* Nanumanga. Coral atoll of NW Tuvalu
Nanumea *553* coral atoll of NW Tuvalu
Nan Wan *525* bay of the South China Sea, S Taiwan
Nanyang *163* Henan, C China
Nanyuki *316* C Kenya
Naogaon *93* NW Bangladesh
Napier *401* SE North Island, New Zealand
Naples *see* Napoli
Napo *200, 431* river of Ecuador and Peru
Napoli *295 Eng.* Naples, *Ger.* Neapel. S Italy
Nāra *421* irrigation canal of S Pakistan

Nara *304* Honshū, C Japan
Narathiwat *533* S Thailand
Narayani *395* river of C Nepal
Narbada *see* Narmada
Narbonne *225* S France
Nare's Strait *622* strait of NW Greenland
Narew *439* river of E Poland
Narganá *424* NE Panama
Narikrik *364* *prev.* Knox Atoll. Atoll of SE Marshall Islands
Narmada *270* *var.* Narbada. River of C India
Narok *316* SW Kenya
Närpes *221* *Swe.* Närpiö. SW Finland
Narrows, The *462* channel connecting the Atlantic Ocean and Caribbean Sea, between Nevis and St Kitts
Narsingdi *93* C Bangladesh
Nartës, Gjol i *see* Nartës, Liqeni i
Nartës, Liqeni i *57* *var.* Gjol i Nartës. Lake of SW Albania
Naruto *304* Shikoku, SW Japan
Narva *212* *prev.* Narova. River of Estonia and Russia
Narva *212* NE Estonia
Narva Bay *212* *Est.* Narva Laht, *Rus.* Narviskiy Zaliv. Bay of the Gulf of Finland
Narva Reservoir *212* *Est.* Narva Veehoidla. Reservoir of Estonia and Russia
Narvik *414* NE Norway
Nar'yan-Mar *452* *prev.* Dzerzhinskiy, *prev.* Beloshchel'ye. NW Russia
Naryn *325* E Kyrgyzstan
Naryn *325* river of Kyrgyzstan and Uzbekistan
Nasau *218* Koro, C Fiji
Nāshik *270* *prev.* Nāsik. W India
Nasho, Lac *460* lake of E Rwanda
Nashville *569* Tennessee, SE USA
Näsijärvi *221* lake of SW Finland
Nasirābād *see* Mymensingh
Nâsir, Buḥeiret *202* *var.* Buḥayrat Nāṣir, *Eng.* Lake Nasser. Lake of Egypt and Sudan
Nasiriya *see* An Nāṣirīyah
Nás Na Riogh *see* Naas
Nassau *88* ❖ of Bahamas, New Providence, Bahamas
Nassau *620* island of Northern Cook Islands, N Cook Islands
Nasser, Lake *see* Nâsir, Buheiret
Nata *118* NE Botswana
Natal *121* E Brazil
Nathula *see* Nacula
Natitingou *108* NW Benin
Natl *310* *var.* Nitil. NW Jordan
Nator *93* W Bangladesh
Natron, Lake *530* lake of Kenya and Tanzania
Natuna Besar, Pulau *276* island of Kepulauan Natuna, W Indonesia
Natuna, Kepulauan *276* island group to the NW of Borneo, W Indonesia
Nau *528* NW Tajikistan
Naujoji Akmenė *344* NW Lithuania
Nā'ūr *310* NW Jordan
Nauru *392-393* officially Republic of Nauru, *prev.* Pleasant Island. Island country of the Pacific Ocean divided into 14 admin. units (districts)
Naushahra *see* Nowshera
Nausori *218* Viti Levu, Fiji
Navabad *528* W Tajikistan
Navaga *218* W Koro, W Fiji
Navahrudak *104* *Rus.* Novogrudok, *Pol.* Nowogródek. W Belorussia
Navangar *see* Jāmnagar
Navapolatsk *104* *Rus.* Novopolotsk. N Belorussia
Navarra *501* autonomous community of N Spain
Naviti *218* island of the Yasawa Group, NW Fiji
Navoalevu *218* NE Vanua Levu, N Fiji

Navoi *580* *Uzb.* Nawoly. S Uzbekistan
Navua *218* Viti Levu, W Fiji
Nawābganj *93* NW Bangladesh
Nawābshāh *421* S Pakistan
Nawmah, Ra's *91* *var.* Ra's Noma. Cape of SW Bahrain
Nawoly *see* Navoi
Naxçıvan *86* *Rus.* Nakhichevan', *var.* Nahičevan'. SW Azerbaijan
Náxos *245* island of SE Greece
Nayau *218* island of the Lau Group, E Fiji
Nazareth *see* Naẓerat
Nazca *431* S Peru
Naze *304* Nansei-shotō, SW Japan
Naẓerat *291* *Eng.* Nazareth. N Israel
Nazerat 'Illit *291* N Israel
Nazilli *546* SW Turkey
Nazrēt *215* *var.* Adama, Hadama. C Ethiopia
Nazwá *418* N Oman
Nchelenge *611* N Zambia
Ncheu *see* Ntcheu
Nchisi *see* Ntchisi
Ncue *208* N Río Muni, Equatorial Guinea
Ndaghamcha, Sebkra de *see* Te-n-Dghâmcha, Sebkhet
N'Dalatando *64* *Port.* Vila Salazar. NW Angola
Ndali *108* C Benin
Ndélé *154* N Central African Republic
Ndendé *230* S Gabon
Ndeni *see* Nendö
Ndindi *230* S Gabon
N'Djamena *156* *var.* Njamena, *prev.* Fort-Lamy. ❖ of Chad, W Chad
Ndjolé *230* C Gabon
Ndoki *176* river of N Congo
Ndola *611* C Zambia
Ndora *138* NW Burundi
Ndrhamcha, Sebkha de *see* Te-n-Dghâmcha, Sebkhet
Nduindui *488* S Guadalcanal, Solomon Is
Nduke *see* Kolombangara
Neagh, Lough *563* lake of Northern Ireland, UK
Neapel *see* Napoli
Nébeck *see* An Nabk
Nebitdag *551* W Turkmenistan
Nebk *see* An Nabk
Neblina, Pico da *120* mountain of NW Brazil
Nebraska *569* state of C USA
Neckar *236* river of SW Germany
Necochea *71* E Argentina
Nederland *see* Netherlands
Neder-Rijn *397* *Eng.* Lower Rhine. River of C Netherlands
Nefasit *210* C Eritrea
Nefta *543* *var.* Naftah. W Tunisia
Neftezavodsk *see* Seydi
Negara Brunei Darussalam *see* Brunei
Negēlē *215* *var.* Negelli, *It.* Neghelli. S Ethiopia
Negev *see* HaNegev
Neghelli *see* Negēlē
Negomane *387* *var.* Negomano. N Mozambique
Negombo *504* SW Sri Lanka
Negotino *349* C FYR Macedonia
Negril *303* W Jamaica
Negro, Rio *120, 171* river of N South America
Negro, Río *see* Sico
Negro, Río *577* river of Brazil and Uruguay
Negro, Río *see* Chixoy
Negros *435* island of C Philippines
Neiafu *538* Uta Vava'u, Vava'u Group, Tonga
Neiba *198* SW Dominican Republic
Neiges, Piton des *628* mountain of C Réunion
Neily *178* SE Costa Rica

Nei Mongol Zizhiqu *163* *Eng.* Inner Mongolian Autonomous Region, *prev.* Nei Monggol Zizhiqu. Autonomous region of N China
Neiva *171* W Colombia
Nek'emtē *215* *var.* Nakamti, Lakamti, Lekemti. W Ethiopia
Nelson *146* river of C Canada
Nelson *401* N South Island, New Zealand
Nelson Island *619* island of N British Indian Ocean Territory
Nelspruit *493* Eastern Transvaal, NE South Africa
Néma *366* SE Mauritania
Neman *104, 344* *Bel.* Nyoman, *Lith.* Nemunas, *Ger.* Memel, *Pol.* Niemen. River of NE Europe
Německý Brod *see* Havlíčkův Brod
Nemunas *see* Neman
Nenagh *288* S Ireland
Nendeln *342* C Liechtenstein
Nendö *488* *var.* Ndeni, Santa Cruz Is, Solomon Islands
Nepal *394-395* officially Kingdom of Nepal. Country of Asia divided into 5 admin. units (regions)
Nepalganj *395* W Nepal
Nepean Island *626* island of C Norfolk Island
Neretva *116* river of S Bosnia & Herzegovina
Neris *344* *Bel.* Viliya, *Pol.* Wilja. River of Belorussia and Lithuania
Neskaupstadhur *268* E Iceland
Ness, Loch *563* lake of N Scotland, UK
Néstos *128, 245* *Turk.* Kara Su, *Bul.* Mesta. River of Bulgaria and Greece
Netanya *291* C Israel
Netherlands *396-399* officially Kingdom of the Netherlands, *var.* Holland, *Dut.* Nederland. Country of W Europe divided into 12 admin. units (provinces)
Netherlands Antilles *589, 626* *prev.* Dutch West Indies. Autonomous part of the Netherlands, Caribbean Sea.
Netherlands East Indies *see* Indonesia
Netrakona *93* N Bangladesh
Netze *see* Noteć
Neubrandenburg *237* NE Germany
Neuchâtel *516* *Ger.* Neuenburg. W Switzerland
Neuchâtel, Lac de *516* *Ger.* Neuenburger See. Lake of W Switzerland
Neuenburger See *see* Neuchâtel, Lac de
Neugradiska *see* Nova Gradiška
Neuhäusl *see* Nové Zámky
Neumarkt *see* Târgu Mures
Neumarktl *see* Tržič
Neumünster *237* N Germany
Neunkirchen *82* E Austria
Neuquén *71* SE Argentina
Neusatz *see* Novi Sad
Neusiedler See *82, 264* *Hung.* Fertő-tó. Lake of Austria and Hungary
Neusohl *see* Banská Bystrica
Neustadt *see* Baia Mare
Neustadtl *see* Novo Mesto
Neutra *see* Nitra
Neu-Ulm *237* S Germany
Nevada *568* state of W USA
Nevers *225* C France
Nevis *462* island of the Lesser Antilles which, with St Kitts, forms the independent state of St Kitts & Nevis
Nevis Peak *462* mountain peak of C Nevis, St Kitts & Nevis
Nevşehir *547* C Turkey
Newala *530* SE Tanzania
New Amsterdam *256* E Guyana
New Britain *426* island of E Papua New Guinea

New Brunswick *147* province of SE Canada
New Bussa *408* W Nigeria
New Caledonia *626* French overseas territory of the Pacific Ocean ❖ Nouméa
Newcastle *77* E Australia
Newcastle *462* N Nevis, St Kitts & Nevis
Newcastle upon Tyne *563* NE England, UK
New Delhi *270* ❖ of India, N India
Newfield *68* SE Antigua, Antigua & Barbuda
Newfoundland *147* *Fr.* Terre-Neuve. Island of S E Canada
Newfoundland *147* province of E Canada
New Georgia *488* island of the New Georgia Is, W Solomon Is
New Georgia Islands *488* island group of W Solomon Is
New Guinea *277, 426* *Dut.* Nieuw Guinea, *Ind.* Irian. Large island of W Pacific Ocean, divided administratively into the Indonesian state of Irian Jaya and the independent country of Papua New Guinea
New Halfa *see* Halfa el Gadida
New Hampshire *569* state of NE USA
New Haven *569* Connecticut, NE USA
New Hebrides *see* Vanuatu
New Ireland *426* island of NE Papua New Guinea
New Jersey *569* state of E USA
Newman *76* W Australia
New Mexico *568-569* state of SW USA
New Mīrpur *421* *prev.* Mīrpur. NE Pakistan
New Orleans *569* Louisiana, SC USA
New Plymouth *401* SW North Island, New Zealand
Newport *563* S Wales, UK
Newport News *569* Virginia, E USA
New Providence *88* island of C Bahamas
New River *256* river of SE Guyana
New River *102* river of N Belize
New Ross *288* SE Ireland
Newry *563* Northern Ireland, UK
New Sandy Bay Village *466* N St Vincent, St Vincent & the Grenadines
New Siberian Islands *see* Novosibirskiye Ostrova
New South Wales *77* state of SE Australia
Newton Ground *462* NW St Kitts, St Kitts & Nevis
Newtownabbey *563* Northern Ireland, UK
New Winthorpes *68* N Antigua, Antigua & Barbuda
New York *569* state of NE USA
New York *569, 573* New York, NE USA
New Zealand *400-403* country of the Pacific Ocean, divided into 14 admin. units (regions)
Nezhyn *556* N Ukraine
Ngabé *176* SE Congo
Ngadda *409* river of NE Nigeria
Ngala *409* NE Nigeria
Ngangerabeli Plain *316* plain of SE Kenya
Ngaoundéré *144* *var.* N'Gaoundéré, N'Gaundere. N Cameroon
Ngara *530* NW Tanzania
Ngarama *460* N Rwanda
Ngardmau *627* C Palau
Ngaruangl *627* island of N Palau
Ngatik *375* atoll of E Micronesia
Ngau *see* Gau
N'Gaundere *see* Ngaoundéré

Geographical Terms and Abbreviations on pages 656-658 / ❖ = *capital of*

Nggamea see Qamea
Nggatokae 488 island of the New Georgia Islands, W Solomon Islands
Nggwavuma 510 var. Ingwavuma. River of South Africa and Swaziland
N'Giva 64 var. Ondjiva Port. Vila Pereira de Eça. S Angola
Ngo 176 SE Congo
Ngogolo 510 C Swaziland
Ngoko 144, 176 river of Cameroon and Congo
Ngorongoro Crater 530 crater and conservation area of N Tanzania
Ngororero 460 W Rwanda
Ngounié 230 river of Congo and Gabon
Ngouoni 230 E Gabon
Ngourti 407 E Niger
Ngozi 138 N Burundi
N'Guigmi 407 SE Niger
Ngulu 375 atoll of W Micronesia
Ngum 327 river of C Laos
Nguna 585 island of C Vanuatu
Ngundu 612 S Zimbabwe
N'Gunza see Sumbe
Nguru 408 NE Nigeria
Ngwempisi 510 river of South Africa and Swaziland
Ngweze see Katima Mulilo
Nhacra 254 W Guinea-Bissau
Nhamundá 120 var. Yamundá, Jamundá. River of NW Brazil
Nha Trang 593 SE Vietnam
Nhlangano 510 prev. Goedgegun. SW Swaziland
Niagara Falls 147 SE Canada
Niagassola 253 var. Nyagassola. NE Guinea
Niamey 407 ❖ of Niger, SW Niger
Niamtougou 537 N Togo
Niandan 253 river of E Guinea
Niangay, Lac 360 lake of E Mali
Nianija Bolon 233 river of Gambia and Senegal
Niantanina 253 E Guinea
Niari 176 river of S Congo
Nias, Pulau 276 island to the W of Sumatra, W Indonesia
Niassa, Lago see Nyasa, Lake
Nicaragua 404-405 officially Republic of Nicaragua. Country of Central America divided into 16 admin. units (departments)
Nicaragua, Lago de 404 var. Gran Lago. Lake of S Nicaragua
Nicastro 295 S Italy
Nice 225 It. Nizza. SE France
Nicholls Town 88 Andros I, Bahamas
Nickerie 508 river of NW Surinam
Nicobar Islands 270 island group to the SE of India
Nicosia 187 var. Lefkosia, Turk. Lefkoşa. ❖ of Cyprus, C Cyprus
Nicoya 178 W Costa Rica
Nicoya, Península de 178 peninsula of W Costa Rica
Nictheroy see Niterói
Nidaros see Trondheim
Niedere Tauern 82 mountain range of C Austria
Niefang 208 var. Sevilla de Niefang. NW Río Muni, Equatorial Guinea
Niemen see Neman
Niéri Ko 476 river of SE Senegal
Nieuw Amsterdam 508 N Surinam
Nieuwegein 397 C Netherlands
Nieuwkoop 397 W Netherlands
Nieuw Nickerie 508 NW Surinam
Niğde 547 C Turkey
Niger 108, 253, 360, 407, 408, river of W Africa
Niger 406-407 officially Republic of Niger. Country of West Africa divided into 7 admin. units (departments)
Nigeria 408-411 officially Federal Republic of Nigeria. Country of West Africa divided into 20 admin. units (19 states and 1 federal capital Territory)

Niger, Mouths of the 408 delta of the river Niger, on the S coast of Nigeria
Niigata 304 Honshū, N Japan
Niihama 304 Shikoku, SW Japan
Niihau 568 island of Hawaii, USA, C Pacific
Niimi 304 Honshū, W Japan
Nijmegen 397 Ger. Nimwegen. SE Netherlands
Nikki 108 E Benin
Nikolainkaupunki see Vaasa
Nikolayev see Mykolayiv
Nikol'skiy 312 C Kazakhstan
Nikol'sk-Ussuriyskiy see Ussuriysk
Nikopol' 556 SE Ukraine
Nikšić 602 W Montenegro, Yugoslavia
Nikumaroro 320 var. Gardner I. Island of the Phoenix Is, C Kiribati
Nikunau 320 island of the Gilbert Is, W Kiribati
Nile 202, 506 Ar. Nahr an Nīl. River of N Africa
Nile Delta 202 delta of N Egypt
Nil, Nahr an see Nile
Nilphāmāri 93 NW Bangladesh
Nimba, Monts 253 var. Nimba Mountains. Mountain range of W Africa
Nimba, Mount 300, 336 mountain of W Africa
Nimba Mountains see Nimba, Monts
Nîmes 225 SE France
Nimwegen see Nijmegen
Ningbo 163 var. Ning-po, prev. Ninghsien. Zhejiang, E China
Ning-hsia see Ningxia
Ninghsien see Ningbo
Ning-po see Ningbo
Ningxia 163 Chin. Ningxia Huizu Zizhiqu, Eng. Ningsia Hui Autonomous Region, var. Ning-hsia. Autonomous region of N China
Ninotsminda 234 prev. Bogdanovka. S Georgia
Ninove 99 C Belgium
Niokolo Koba 476 river of SE Senegal
Niono 360 C Mali
Nioro 360 var. Nioro du Sahel. W Mali
Nioro du Rip 476 SW Senegal
Niort 225 W France
Nippon-kai see Japan, Sea of
Niquero 182 S Cuba
Nirin see Erh-lin
Niš 602 Eng. Nish. E Serbia, Yugoslavia
Nişāb 599 var. Anşāb. SW Yemen
Nisporeni 376 Rus. Nisporeny. W Moldavia
Nissan Islands see Green Islands
Nissum Bredning 190 inlet of North Sea on the NW coast of Denmark
Nistru see Dniester
Niterói 121 prev. Nictheroy. SE Brazil
Nitil see Natl
Nitra 485 Ger. Neutra, Hung. Nyitra. River of SW Slovakia
Nitra 485 Ger. Neutra, Hung. Nyitra. SW Slovakia
Niuafo'ou 538 var. Niuafoo. Island of NW Tonga
Niuatoputapu 538 var. Niuatobutabu, prev. Keppel Island. Island of N Tonga
Niuatui 553 islet of Nukufetau, Tuvalu
Niue 626 territory in free association with New Zealand, Pacific Ocean
Niulakita 553 var. Nurakita. Coral atoll of S Tuvalu
Niutao 553 coral atoll of NW Tuvalu
Nizāmābād 270 C India
Nizhnevartovsk 452 C Russia
Nizhniy Novgorod 452 prev. Gor'kiy. W Russia
Nizhniy Pyandzh 528 var. Nižnij Pjandž. SW Tajikistan

Nizhnyaya Tunguska 453 Eng. Lower Tunguska. C Russia
Nizza see Nice
Njaba see N'ja Kunda
Njaiama 480 E Sierra Leone
N'ja Kunda 233 var. Njaba. NW Gambia
Njamena see N'Djamena
Njardhvík 268 SW Iceland
Njazidja see Grande Comore
Njoeng Jacobkondre 508 C Surinam
Njombe 530 S Tanzania
Njoro 316 W Kenya
Nkanini 510 W Swaziland
Nkata Bay see Nkhata Bay
Nkayi 176 var. N'Kayi, prev. Jacob. S Congo
Nkhata Bay 353 var. Nkata Bay. N Malawi
Nkhotakota 353 var. Kota Kota, Nkota Kota. C Malawi
Nkonfap 408 S Nigeria
Nkongsamba 144 var. N'Kongsamba. W Cameroon
Nkumekie 208 C Río Muni, Equatorial Guinea
Nkundla 510 W Swaziland
Nkusi 554 river of W Uganda
Nmai Hka 135 var. Me Hka. River of N Burma forming a headstream of the Irrawaddy river
Noākhāli 93 prev. Sudharam. S Bangladesh
Noboribetsu 304 Hokkaidō, N Japan
Nogal, Uadi see Nugaal
Noire, Rivière 368 river of SW Mauritius
Noire, Rivière see Black River
Noirmoutier, Île de 224 island of W France
Nokia 221 SW Finland
Nokou 156 W Chad
Nokoué, Lac 108 lake of S Benin
Nola 154 SW Central African Republic
Nólsoy 620 island of E Faeroe Islands
Noma, Ra's see Nawmah, Ra's
Nomuka 538 island of the Nomuka Group, Tonga
Nomuka Group 538 island group of W Tonga
Nomwin 375 atoll of C Micronesia
Nông Hèt 327 E Laos
Nong Khai 533 NE Thailand
Nonouti 320 island of the Gilbert Is, W Kiribati
Nonsan 496 Jap. Ronzan. W South Korea
Nonsuch Island 619 island of E Bermuda
Noord 618 N Aruba
Noord-Beveland 397 island of SW Netherlands
Noordoewer 391 S Namibia
Noordpunt 626 headland of Curaçao, W Netherlands Antilles
Noordzee see North Sea
Nor Achin see Nor Hachn
Nor Ačin see Nor Hachn
Nord 622 N Greenland
Nordaustlandet 629 island of NE Svalbard
Norddeutsches Tiefland 236-237 Eng. North German Plain. Plain of N Germany
Nordfriesische Inseln 236 Eng. North Frisian Islands. Island group of NW Germany
Nordhausen 237 C Germany
Nordishavet see Arctic Ocean
Nord, Massif du 258 mountainous region of N Haiti
Nord, Mer du see North Sea
Nord-Pas de Calais 228 administrative region of N France
Nordsee see North Sea
Nordsjøen see North Sea
Nordsøen see North Sea
Nordtiroler Kalkalpen 82 mountain range of W Austria

Nore 288 Ir. An Fheoir. River of SE Ireland
Norfolk 569 Virginia, E USA
Norfolk Island 626 Australian external territory of the South Pacific Ocean. ❖ Kingston
Norge see Norway
Nor Hachn 74 var. Nor Hachyn, Rus. Nor Achin, var. Nor Ačcin. C Armenia
Nor Hachyn see Nor Hachn
Noril'sk 453 N Russia
Norman 569 Oklahoma, SC USA
Normanby Island 426 island of SE Papua New Guinea
Normandie 225 Eng. Normandy. Cultural region of N France
Normandie, Collines de 225 hilly region of NW France
Norman Island 619 island of S British Virgin Islands
Norrköping 513 S Sweden
Norseman 76 SW Australia
Norskehavet see Norwegian Sea
Norsup 585 Malekula, Vanuatu
North Albanian Alps 57, 602 SCr. Prokletije, Alb. Bjeshkët e Nemuna. Mountain range of Albania and Yugoslavia
Northam 76 SW Australia
Northampton 563 C England, UK
North Andaman 135, 270 island of the Andaman Is, E India
North Battleford 146 SW Canada
North Bay 147 SE Canada
North Caicos 629 island of NW Turks and Caicos Islands
North Carolina 569 state of SE USA
North Channel 563 strait of Atlantic Ocean, between Northern Ireland and Scotland, UK
North Comino Channel see Ghawdex, Il-Fliegu ta'
North Dakota 569 state of NC USA
North Devon Island see Devon Island
Northern Territory 77 territory of N Australia
North East China 167
North East Point 620 headland on the NE coast of Christmas Island
Northeast Providence Channel 88 channel between Eleuthera I and Great Abaco I, Bahamas
Northern Cape 493 province of W South Africa
Northern Cook Islands 620 island group of N Cook Islands
Northern Cyprus, Republic of see Cyprus
Northern Dvina see Severnaya Dvina
Northern Forest Reserve 196 nature reserve of N Dominica
Northern Ireland 568 var. the Six Counties. Political division of UK
Northern Karoo 493 var. High Veld, Afr. Hoë Karoo. Plateau region of W South Africa
Northern Mariana Islands 626 Commonwealth territory of the USA, Pacific Ocean. ❖ Garapan.
Northern Rhodesia see Zambia
Northern Sporades see Vor eioi Sporades
Northern Transvaal 493 province of NE South Africa
North Frisian Islands see Nordfriesische Inseln
North German Plain see Norddeutsches Tiefland
North Huvadhu Atoll 358 var. Gaafu Alifu Atoll. Atoll of S Maldives
North Island 401 northernmost of the two main islands that comprise New Zealand
North Keeling Island 620 island of NW Cocos Islands

North Korea *412-413* officially Democratic People's Republic of Korea. Country of E Asia divided into 12 admin. units (9 provinces, 3 independent municipalities)

North Maalhosmadulu Atoll *358 var.* North Malosmadulu Atoll, Raa Atoll. Atoll of N Maldives

North Miladummadulu Atoll *358* atoll of N Maldives

North Nilandhe Atoll *358 var.* Faafu Atoll. Atoll of C Maldives

North Point *628* headland on the N coast of Ascension Island

North Saskatchewan *146* river of SW Canada

North Sea *236, 563 Dan.* Nordsøen, *Nor.* Nordsjøen, *Fr.* Mer du Nord, Dut. Noordzee, *Ger.* Nordsee, *prev.* German Ocean. Sea of the Atlantic Ocean, between mainland Europe and Britain

North Siberian Lowland *see* Severo-Sibirskaya Nizmennost'

North Siberian Plain *see* Severo-Sibirskaya Nizmennost'

North Sound *620* area of the Caribbean Sea, Grand Cayman, W Cayman Islands

North Taranaki Bight *401* area of the Tasman Sea, to the W of North Island, New Zealand

North Uist *563* island of Outer Hebrides, NW Scotland, UK

North Union *466* E St Vincent, St Vincent & the Grenadines

North West *493* province of N South Africa

North West Bluff *625* headland on the N coast of Montserrat

North West Highlands *563* mountain range of N Scotland, UK

North West Point *620* headland on the NW coast of Christmas Island

Northwest Providence Channel *88* channel of Atlantic Ocean, between Grand Bahama Island and Bimini Islands, Bahamas

Northwest Territories *146-147, 151* territory of N Canada

Norton *612* NE Zimbabwe

Norway *414-417* officially Kingdom of Norway, *Nor.* Norge. Country of N Europe divided into 19 admin. units (counties)

Norwegian Sea *268, 414 var.* Norske Havet, Norskehavet. Area of Arctic Ocean between Iceland, Greenland and Norway

Norwich *563* E England, UK

Nösen *see* Bistriţa

Noshiro *304* Honshū, N Japan

Nosop *118, 391 var.* Nossob, Nossop. River of southern Africa

Nossob *see* Nosop

Nossop *see* Nosop

Noteć *439 Ger.* Netze. River of NW Poland

Noties Sporádes *see* Dodekánisos

Notodden *414* S Norway

Notsé *537* S Togo

Nottingham *563* C England, UK

Nouâdhibou *366 prev.* Port Étienne. W Mauritania

Nouakchott *366* ❖ of Mauritania, SW Mauritania

Noual, Sebkhet en *543 var.* Sabkhat an Nawâl. Salt flat of C Tunisia

Nouméa *626* ❖ of New Caledonia, S New Caledonia

Nouna *132* W Burkina

Nouvelle France *368* S Mauritius

Nová Dubnica *485* W Slovakia

Nova Gorica *486* W Slovenia

Nova Gradiška *181 Ger.* Neugradiska, *Hung.* Újgradiska. NE Croatia

Nova Iguaçu *121* SE Brazil

Nova Kakhovka *556* SE Ukraine

Nova Lamego *see* Gabú

Nova Lisboa *see* Huambo

Novara *294* N Italy

Nova Scotia *147* province of SE Canada

Novaya Sibir', Ostrov *453* island of Novosibirskiye Ostrovo, N Russia

Novaya Zemlya *452* island group of N Russia

Nova Zagora *128* C Bulgaria

Nové Mesto nad Váhom *485 Ger.* Waagneustadtl, *Hung.* Vágújhely. W Slovakia

Nové Zámky *485 Ger.* Neuhäusl, *Hung.* Érsekújvár. SW Slovakia

Novgorod *452* NW Russia

Novi Sad *602 Ger.* Neusatz, *Hung.* Újvidék. N Serbia, Yugoslavia

Novogrudok *see* Navahrudak

Novokazalinsk *312 Kaz.* Zhangaqazaly. SW Kazakhstan

Novokuznetsk *453 prev.* Stalinsk. C Russia

Novolazarevskaya *66* CIS research station of Greater Antarctica, Antarctica

Novo Mesto *486 Ger.* Rudolfswert, *prev.* Neustadtl. SE Slovenia

Novopolotsk *see* Navapolatsk

Novo Redondo *see* Sumbe

Novosibirsk *453* C Russia

Novosibirskiye Ostrova *453 Eng.* New Siberian Islands. Island Group of N Russia

Novo Urgench *see* Urgench

Nový Jičín *188* SE Czech Republic

Novyy Margilan *see* Fergana

Novyy Uzen' *312 Kaz.* Zhangaözen. W Kazakhstan

Nowogródek *see* Navahrudak

Nowshera *421 var.* Naushahra. NE Pakistan

Nowy Sącz *439* S Poland

Noyemberyan *74* N Armenia

Nsanje *353* S Malawi

Nsawam *242* SE Ghana

Nsok *208 var.* Nsoc, Nsork. SE Río Muni, Equatorial Guinea

Nsoko *510* SE Swaziland

Nsuta *242* SW Ghana

Ntcheu *353 var.* Ncheu. S Malawi

Ntchisi *353 var.* Nchisi. C Malawi

Ntem *144, 208 prev.* Campo, *var.* Kampo. River of Cameroon and Equatorial Guinea

Ntomba, Lac *607 var.* Lac Tumba. Lake of NW Zaire

Ntoum *230* NW Gabon

N'Tsaoueni *174* NW Grande Comore, Comoros

Ntusi *554* SW Uganda

Nuanetsi *see* Mwenezi

Nubian Desert *506* desert of NE Sudan

Nu Chiang *see* Salween

Nu'eima *292* E West Bank

Nueva Caceres *see* Naga

Nueva Concepción *250* SW Guatemala

Nueva Gerona *182* Isla de la Juventud, Cuba

Nueva Helvecia *577* SW Uruguay

Nueva Loja *200* NE Ecuador

Nueva Ocotepeque *260* W Honduras

Nueva Palmira *577* SW Uruguay

Nueva San Salvador *207 prev.* Santa Tecla. SW El Salvador

Nuevitas *182* E Cuba

Nuevo Laredo *370* N Mexico

Nuevo Rocafuerte *200* E Ecuador

Nugaal *490 It.* Uadi Nogal. Seasonal river of N Somalia

Nui *553* coral atoll of W Tuvalu

Nu Jiang *see* Salween

Nukha *see* Şäki

Nuku *629* Île Futuna, N Wallis & Futuna

Nuku' alofa *538* ❖ of Tonga, Tongatabu, Tongatapu Group, Tonga

Nukuatea *629* island of Île Uvea, S Wallis & Futuna

Nukufetau *553* coral atoll of C Tuvalu

Nukulaelae *553 var.* Nukulailai. Coral atoll of E Tuvalu

Nukuloa *629* island of Île Uvea, S Wallis & Futuna

Nukunonu Atoll *629* island of C Tokelau

Nukuoro *375* atoll of SE Micronesia

Nukus *580* W Uzbekistan

Nullarbor Plain *76-77* plateau of S Australia

Numan *409* E Nigeria

Numazu *304* Honshū, SE Japan

Nume *208* W Río Muni, Equatorial Guinea

Nuoro *294* Sardegna, W Italy

Nuquí *171* W Colombia

Nurakita *see* Niulakita

Nurata *580 Uzb.* Nurota. SE Uzbekistan

Nuratau, Khrebet *580* mountains of E Uzbekistan

Nurek *528* W Tajikistan

Nurmes *221* E Finland

Nürnberg *237 Eng.* Nuremberg. S Germany

Nurota *see* Nurata

Nusa Tenggara *276 Eng.* Lesser Sunda Islands. Island group of C Indonesia

Nusaybin *547* SE Turkey

Nuşayrīyah, Jabal al *521* mountains of W Syria

Nuuk *622 var.* Godthåb. SW Greenland

Nuwara Eliya *504* S Sri Lanka

Nyaake *336* SE Liberia

Nyabarongo *460* river of W Rwanda

Nyabisindu *460* SW Rwanda

Nyabugogo *460* river of C Rwanda

Nyagassola *see* Niagassola

Nyahururu *316* W Kenya

Nyainqêntanglha Shan *162* mountain range of Xizang Zizhiqu, W China

Nyala *506* W Sudan

Nyalikungu *530* N Tanzania

Nyamapanda *612* NE Zimbabwe

Nyanda *see* Masvingo

Nyanga *612 var.* Inyanga. E Zimbabwe

Nyanga *176, 230* river of Congo and Gabon

Nyanza-Lac *138* S Burundi

Nyarutovu *460* NW Rwanda

Nyasa, Lake *353, 387, 530 var.* Lake Malawi, *Port.* Lago Niassa, *prev.* Lago Nyassa. Great lake of E Africa

Nyasaland *see* Malawi

Nyasvizh *104* W Belorussia

Nyaunglebin *135* S Burma

Nyazura *612 prev.* Inyazura. E Zimbabwe

Nyenyen *336* C Liberia

Nyeri *316* C Kenya

Nyika *316* plain of SE Kenya

Nyika Plateau *353 var.* Nyika Uplands. Plateau of N Malawi

Nyíregyháza *264* NE Hungary

Nyiri Desert *316* desert region of SE Kenya

Nyitra *see* Nitra

Nykøbing *190* Sjælland, E Denmark

Nykøbing-Falster *190 var.* Nykøbing. Falster, S Denmark

Nyköping *513* SE Sweden

Nylstroom *493* Northern Transvaal, NE South Africa

Nyoman *see* Neman

Nyon *516* SW Switzerland

Nyong *144* river of SW Cameroon

Nyslott *see* Savonlinna

Nzambi *176* S Congo

Nzega *530* NW Tanzania

Nzérékoré *253* SE Guinea

Nzi *300* river of C Ivory Coast

Nzilo, Lac *607 var.* Barrage de Nzilo, *prev.* Lac Delcommune. Lake of SE Zaire

Nzwani *see* Anjouan

O

Oahu *568* island of Hawaii, USA, C Pacific

Oakland *568* California, W USA

Oamaru *401* S South Island, New Zealand

Oaxaca *370 var.* Oaxaca de Juárez. S Mexico

Ob' *452-453* river of C Russia

Oban *563* W Scotland, UK

Obando *see* Puerto Inírida

Obbia *see* Hobyo

Obdorsk *see* Salekhard

Oberhausen *236* W Germany

Oberpahlen *see* Põltsamaa

Obihiro *305* Hokkaidō, N Japan

Obo *154* E Central African Republic

Obock *194* E Djibouti

Obskaya Guba *453* bay of Karskoye More, N Russia

Obuasi *242* C Ghana

Ocaña *171* N Colombia

Occidental, Cordillera *112* range of the Andes in Bolivia and Chile

Occidental, Cordillera *171* range of the Andes in W Colombia

Occidental, Cordillera *431* range of the Andes in W Peru

Ocean Falls *146* W Canada

Ocean Island *see* Banaba

Och'amch'ire *234 Rus.* Ochamchira. W Georgia

Ocho Rios *303* N Jamaica

Ocotal *404* NW Nicaragua

October Revolution Island *see* Oktyabr'skoy Revolyutsii, Ostrov

Oda *242* SE Ghana

Ōdate *304* Honshū, N Japan

Odawara *304* Honshū, SE Japan

Oddur *see* Xuddur

Ödenburg *see* Sopron

Odendaalsrus *493* Orange Free State, C South Africa

Odenpäh *see* Otepää

Odense *190* Fyn, S Denmark

Oder *188, 237, 439 Cz./Pol.* Odra. River of C Europe

Oderhaff *237, 439 var.* Stettiner Haff, *Pol.* Zalew Szczeciński. Bay of the Baltic Sea, on the N coast of Germany and Poland

Odesa *556 Rus.* Odessa. S Ukraine

Odienné *300* NW Ivory Coast

Ôdôngk *141* S Cambodia

Oeno Island *627* island of NW Pitcairn Islands

Ofanto *295* river of S Italy

Offa *408* W Nigeria

Offenbach *236 var.* Offenbach am Main. SW Germany

Offenbach am Main *see* Offenbach

Offenburg *236* SW Germany

Ofu *618* island of Manua Islands, E American Samoa

Ogaden *215* arid plateau of SE Ethiopia

Ōgaki *304* Honshū, C Japan

Ogasawara-shotō *304 Eng.* Bonin Islands. Island group to the SE of Honshū, SE Japan

Ogbomosho *408* W Nigeria

Ogden *568* Utah, SW USA

Ogea Driki *218* island of the Lau Group, E Fiji

Ogea Levu *218* island of the Lau Group, E Fiji

Ogooué *176, 230* river of Congo and Gabon

Ogou *537* river of E Togo

Ogražden *349* mountain range of Bulgaria and FYR Macedonia
Ogre *330* *Ger.* Oger. C Latvia
Ogulin *181* N Croatia
Ohau, Lake *401* W South Island, New Zealand
Ohio *569* river of NC USA
Ohio *569* state of NE USA
Ohobela *334* N Lesotho
'Ohonua *538* 'Eua, Tongatapu Group, Tonga
Ohře *188* *Ger.* Eger. River of Czech Republic and Germany
Ohrid *349* *var.* Ochrida. SW FYR Macedonia
Ohrid, Lake *57, 349* *var.* Lake Ochrida, *Alb.* Liqeni i Ohrit, *Maced.* Ohridsko Ezero. Lake of Albania and Macedonia
Oiapoque *121, 621* *var.* Oyapok, Oyapock. River of Brazil and French Guiana
Oil Islands *see* Chagos Archipelago
Oise *225* river of N France
Oistins *97* S Barbados
Ôita *304* Kyūshū, SW Japan
Ojos del Salado, Nevado *159* mountain of N Chile
Okahandja *391* C Namibia
Okakarara *391* N Namibia
Ókanizsa *see* Kanjiža
Okāra *421* E Pakistan
Okarem *551* *Turkm.* Ekerem. W Turkmenistan
Okavango *see* Cubango
Okavango Delta *118* large wetland area of N Botswana
Okaya *304* Honshū, C Japan
Okayama *304* Honshū, W Japan
Okazaki *304* Honshū, C Japan
Okeechobee, Lake *569* lake of Florida, SE USA
Okhotsk, Sea of *453* *Rus.* Okhotskoye More. Sea of Pacific Ocean, bordering E Russia
Oki *304* island to the N of Honshū, W Japan
Okinawa-shotō *304* island group of Nansei-shotō, SW Japan
Oklahoma *569* state of SC USA
Oklahoma City *569* Oklahoma, SC USA
Okondja *230* E Gabon
Okovanggo *see* Cubango
Okoyo *176* W Congo
Okpara *108* river of Benin and Nigeria
Oktemberyan *see* Hoktemberyan
Oktyabr'skoy Revolyutsii, Ostrov *453* *Eng.* October Revolution Island. Island of Severnaya Zemlya, N Russia
Okushiri-tō *304* island to the W of Hokkaidō, N Japan
Ólafsfjördhur *268* N Iceland
Ólafsvík *268* W Iceland
Olaine *330* C Latvia
Olanchito *260* C Honduras
Öland *513* island of S Sweden
Olavarría *71* E Argentina
Olbia *294* Sardegna, W Italy
Oldenburg *236* NW Germany
Old Fort Point *625* headland on the S coast of Montserrat
Old Harbour *303* S Jamaica
Old Road *68* SW Antigua, Antigua & Barbuda
Old Road Town *462* W St Kitts, St Kitts & Nevis
Olëkminsk *453* C Russia
Oleksandriya *556* *Rus.* Aleksandriya. C Ukraine
Olenëk *453* *var.* Olenyok. N Russia
Oléron, Île d' *224* island of W France
Ólgiy *380* W Mongolia
Olhão *442* S Portugal
Olimarao *375* atoll of C Micronesia
Olimar Grande *577* *var.* Olimar. River of E Uruguay
Ólimbos *see* Ólympos

Olinda *121* E Brazil
Olita *see* Alytus
Olmaliq *see* Almalyk
Olmütz *see* Olomouc
Olocuilta *207* SW El Salvador
Oloitokitok *316* *var.* Laitokitok. S Kenya
Olomouc *188* *Ger.* Olmütz. SE Czech Republic
Olongapo *435* Luzon, N Philippines
Olosega *618* island of Manua Islands, E American Samoa
Olsnitz *see* Murska Sobota
Olsztyn *439* *Ger.* Allenstein. N Poland
Olt *448* *Ger.* Alt. River of S Romania
Olten *516* NW Switzerland
O-luan Pi *525* *var.* Cape Olwanpi. Cape on the S coast of Taiwan
O-luan-pi *525* S Taiwan
Olympia *568* Washington, NW USA
Ólympos *245* *Eng.* Mount Olympus, *prev.* Ólimbos. Mountain of N Greece
Olympus, Mount *187* *var.* Troodos, Olympos. Mountain of C Cyprus
Olympus, Mount *see* Ólympos
Omagh *563* Northern Ireland, UK
Omaha *569* Nebraska, C USA
Oman *418-419* officially Sultanate of Oman, *prev.* Muscat & Oman. Country of SW Asia divided into 3 admin. units (governorates)
Oman, Gulf of *281, 418, 560* *Ar.* Khalīj 'Umān. Gulf of the Arabian Sea
Omaruru *391* C Namibia
Omba *see* Aoba
Omboué *230* W Gabon
Omdurman *506* *var.* Umm Durmān. C Sudan
Om Hajer *210* W Eritrea
Ōmiya *304* Honshū, SE Japan
Omo Wenz *215* river of SW Ethiopia
Omsk *452* C Russia
Ōmuta *304* Kyūshū, SW Japan
Ondangwa *391* *var.* Ondangua. N Namibia
Ondava *485* river of NE Slovakia
Ondjiva *see* N'Giva
Ondo *408* SW Nigeria
Öndörhaan *380* E Mongolia
One and Half Degree Channel *358* channel of the Indian Ocean, S Maldives
Oneata *218* island of the Lau Group, E Fiji
Onega, Lake *see* Onezhskoye Ozero
Onezhskoye Ozero *452* *Eng.* Lake Onega. Lake of NW Russia
Onga *230* E Gabon
Ongjin *413* SW North Korea
Oni *234* N Georgia
Onilahy *350* river of SW Madagascar
Onitsha *408* S Nigeria
Ono *218* island to the S of Viti Levu, SW Fiji
Ono-i-lau *218* island to the S of the Lau Group, SW Fiji
Onomichi *304* Honshū, W Japan
Ononte *see* Orantes
Onotoa *320* island of the Gilbert Is, W Kiribati
Onslow *76* W Australia
Onsŏng *413* NE North Korea
Ontario *146-147* province of S Canada
Ontario, Lake *147, 569* lake of Canada and USA
Ontong Java Atoll *488* *prev.* Lord Howe Island. Atoll of N Solomon Is
Onverwacht *508* N Surinam
Ooma *320* Banaba, W Kiribati
Oos-Londen *see* East London
Oostende *99* *Fr.* Ostende, *Eng.* Ostend. NW Belgium
Oosterhout *397* SW Netherlands
Oosterschelde *397* *Eng.* Eastern Scheldt. Inlet of the North Sea, on the coast of SW Netherlands

Opava *188* *Ger.* Troppau. E Czech Republic
Opole *439* *Ger.* Oppeln. SW Poland
Oporto *see* Porto
Oppdal *414* S Norway
Oppeln *see* Opole
Opuwo *391* NW Namibia
Oqtosh *see* Aktash
Oradea *448* *prev.* Oradea Mare, *Ger.* Grosswardein, *Hung.* Nagyvárad. NW Romania
Oral *see* Ural'sk
Oran *59* *var.* Ouahran, Wahran. NW Algeria
Orange *77* SE Australia
Orange Free State *493* province of C South Africa
Orange Mouth *see* Oranjemund
Orangemund *see* Oranjemund
Orange River *334, 391, 493* *Afr.* Oranjerivier. River of southern Africa
Orange Walk *102* N Belize
Orango, Ilha de *254* island of Arquipélago dos Bijagós, SW Guinea-Bissau
Orangozinho, Ilha de *254* island of SW Guinea-Bissau
Oranjemund *391* *var.* Orangemund, *Eng.* Orange Mouth. S Namibia
Oranjestad *626* St Eustatius, N Netherlands Antilles
Oranjestad *618* ❖ of Aruba, W Aruba
Orantes *332, 521* *var.* Ononte, Orontes, *Ar.* Nahr al 'Āşī, *var.* Nahr al 'Āşī Oronte, Nahr el Aassi. River of SW Asia
Orany *see* Varėna
Orapa *118* C Botswana
Orcadas *66* Argentinian research station of Greater Antarctica, Antarctica
Orchid Island *see* Lan Yü
Orchila, Isla le *589* island of N Venezuela
Ordino *62* NW Andorra
Ordu *547* N Turkey
Ordubad *86* SW Azerbaijan
Ordzhonikidze *see* Yenakiyeve
Ordzhonikidze *see* Vladikavkaz
Ordzhonikidzeabad *see* Kofarnikhon
Orealla *256* E Guyana
Örebro *513* S Sweden
Oregon *568* state of NW USA
Orem *568* Utah, SW USA
Orenburg *452* *prev.* Chkalov. W Russia
Orense *see* Ourense
Orestiáda *245* *prev.* Orestiás. NE Greece
Öresund *see* Sound, The
Øresund *see* Sound, The
Oreti *401* river of S South Island, New Zealand
Orgeyev *see* Orhei
Orhei *376* *var.* Orheiu, *Rus.* Orgeyev. N Moldavia
Orhon Gol *380* river of N Mongolia
Oriental, Cordillera *112* range of the Andes in C Bolivia
Oriental, Cordillera *171* range of the Andes in C Colombia
Oriental, Cordillera *431* range of the Andes of C Peru
Orikum *57* *var.* Oriku. SW Albania
Orinoco *171, 589* river of Colombia and Venezuela
Oristano *294* Sardegna, W Italy
Orizaba, Pico de *see* Citlaltépetl
Orkhanie *see* Botevgrad
Orkney *563* islands of NE UK
Orlau *see* Orlová
Orléanais *225* cultural region of N France
Orléans *225* N France
Orléansville *see* Chlef
Orlová *188* *Ger.* Orlau, *Pol.* Orlowa. SE Czech Republic
Ormoc *435* *var.* MacArthur. Leyte, E Philippines
Ormsö *see* Vormsi

Ormuz, Strait of *see* Hormuz, Strait of
Örnsköldsvik *513* NE Sweden
Oro *413* E North Korea
Orodara *132* SW Burkina
Orol Dengizi *see* Aral Sea
Oroluk *375* atoll of C Micronesia
Oron *408* S Nigeria
Orona *320* *var.* Hull I. Island of the Phoenix Is, C Kiribati
Oronoque *256* river of SE Guyana
Orontes *see* Orantes
Oroszháza *264* SE Hungary
Orotina *178* W Costa Rica
Orsha *104* NE Belorussia
Orsk *452* C Russia
Ørsta *414* SW Norway
Ortoire *540* river of S Trinidad, Trinidad & Tobago
Orto-Tokoy *325* *var.* Orto Tokoj. N Kyrgyzstan
Orūmīyeh *281* *prev.* Rezāīyeh, Urmia. NW Iran
Orūmīyeh, Daryācheh-ye *281* *prev.* Daryācheh-ye Rezā'īyeh, *Eng.* Lake Urmia. Lake of NW Iran
Oruro *112* W Bolivia
Orvieto *295* C Italy
Oryakhovo *128* *var.* Orjahovo. NW Bulgaria
Oryokko *see* Yalu
Ōsaka *304, 309* Honshū, C Japan
Osa, Península de *178* S Costa Rica
Ösel *see* Saaremaa
Osh *324* *var.* Oš. SW Kyrgyzstan
Oshakati *391* N Namibia
Oshawa *147* SE Canada
Oshikango *391* N Namibia
Oshogbo *408* W Nigeria
Osijek *181* *Hung.* Eszék, *Ger.* Esseg. NE Croatia
Osipenko *see* Berdyans'k
Osipovichi *see* Asipovichy
Öskemen *see* Ust'-Kamenogorsk
Ösling *346* physical region of N Luxembourg
Oslo *414* *prev.* Christiania. ❖ of Norway, S Norway
Oslofjorden *414* fjord of S Norway
Osmaniye *547* S Turkey
Osnabrück *236* NW Germany
Osogovski Planini *349* *var.* Osogovske Planine. Mountain range of Bulgaria and FYR Macedonia
Oss *397* S Netherlands
Ossa, Serra de *442* mountain range of SE Portugal
Ostee *see* Baltic Sea
Ostend *see* Oostende
Ostende *see* Oostende
Österbotten *see* Pohjanmaa
Östermyra *see* Seinäjoki
Österreich *see* Austria
Östersund *513* C Sweden
Ostfriesische Inseln *236* *Eng.* East Frisian Islands. Island group of NW Germany
Ostrava *188* *Ger.* Mährisch-Ostrau, *prev.* Moravská Ostrava. E Czech Republic
Ostrobothnia *see* Pohjanmaa
Ostrov *188* NW Czech Republic
Ostrowiec Świętokrzyski *439* E Poland
Ostyako-Voguls'k *see* Khanty-Mansiysk
Ōsumi-shotō *304* island group of Nansei-shotō, SW Japan
Osumit *57* *var.* Osum. River of SE Albania
Otago Peninsula *401* peninsula of SE South Island, New Zealand
Otaru *304* Hokkaidō, N Japan
Otavalo *200* N Ecuador
Otavi *391* N Namibia
Otepää *212* *Ger.* Odenpäh. SE Estonia
Oti *108, 242, 537* river of W Africa
Otjinene *391* NE Namibia

Otjiwarongo *391* N Namibia
Otra *414* river of SW Norway
Otranto, Strait of *57, 295* It. Canale d'Otranto. Strait connecting the Adriatic Sea and Ionian Sea, between Albania and Italy
Otrokovice *188* SE Czech Republic
Õtsu Yokkaichi *304* Honshū, C Japan
Ottawa *147* ❖ of Canada, SE Canada
Ottawa *146* Fr. Outaouais. River of SE Canada
Otterup *190* Fyn, C Denmark
Otu Tolu Group *538* island group of SE Tonga
Otztaler Alpen *82* It. Alpi Venoste. Mountain range of Austria and Italy
Ou *327* river of N Laos
Ouaddi *194* SW Djibouti
Ouâd Nâga *366* SW Mauritania
Ouagadougou *132* var. Wagadugu. ❖ of Burkina, C Burkina
Ouâhayyi *194* river of Djibouti and Somalia
Ouahigouya *132* NW Burkina
Ouahran *see* Oran
Ouaka *154* river of C Central African Republic
Oualâta *366* SE Mauritania
Ouallam *407* var. Oualam. W Niger
Ouanary *621* E French Guiana
Ouanda Djallé *154* NE Central African Republic
Ouani *174* N Anjouan, Comoros
Ouara *154* river of E Central African Republic
Ouargla *59* var. Wargla. NE Algeria
Ouarkziz *382* seasonal river of SW Morocco
Ouarzazate *382* S Morocco
Ouazzane *382* N Morocco
Oubangui *see* Ubangi
Ouchan *623* E Isle of Man
Oued Zem *382* C Morocco
Ouégoa *626* N New Caledonia
Ouéléssébougou *360* var. Ouolossébougou. SW Mali
Ouémé *108* river of C Benin
Ouessant, Île d' *224* Eng. Ushant. Island of NW France
Ouèssè *108* var. Ouéssé. E Benin
Ouésso *176* NW Congo
Ouham *154, 156* river of Central African Republic and Chad
Ouidah *108* Eng. Whydah, var. Wida. S Benin
Oujda *382* NE Morocco
Oujeft *366* C Mauritania
Ould Yenjé *366* S Mauritania
Ouled Djellal *59* var. Awled Djellal. N Algeria
Oulu *221* Swe. Uleåborg. C Finland
Oulujärvi *221* Swe. Uleträsk. Lake of C Finland
Oulujoki *221* Swe. Uleälv. River of C Finland
Oumé *300* SW Ivory Coast
Oum er Rbia *382* river of C Morocco
Oumm ed Droûs Telli, Sebkhet *366* salt lake of N Mauritania
Ounasjoki *221* river of N Finland
Ounianga Kébir *156* NE Chad
Ountivou *537* E Togo
Ouolossébougou *see* Ouéléssébougou
Our *346* river of W Europe
Ourense *500* Cast. Orense. NW Spain
Ourthe *99* river of E Belgium
Ouse *see* Great Ouse
Ouse *563* river of N England, UK
Outaouais *see* Ottawa
Outer Hebrides *563* var. Western Isles. Island group of NW Scotland, UK
Outer Islands *478* island group of C and SW Seychelles
Outjo *391* N Namibia

Ouvéa *626* island of Îles Loyauté, NE New Caledonia
Ovalau *218* island to the NE of Viti Levu, C Fiji
Ovalle *159* N Chile
Ovan *230* NE Gabon
Overflakkee *397* island of SW Netherlands
Overhalla *414* C Norway
Ovgos *187* river of NW Cyprus
Oviedo *500* NW Spain
Owando *176* C Congo
Owen Falls Dam *554* dam of S Uganda
Owen Stanley Range *426* mountain range of SE Papua New Guinea
Owerri *408* S Nigeria
Owia *466* N St Vincent, St Vincent & the Grenadines
Owo *408* SW Nigeria
Öxarfjördhur *268* var. Axarfjördhur. Fjord of NE Iceland
Oxbow *334* N Lesotho
Oxford *563* C England, UK
Oyama *304* Honshū, N Japan
Oyapock *see* Oiapoque
Oyapok *see* Oiapoque
Oyem *230* N Gabon
Oyo *408* W Nigeria
Oyo *176* C Congo
Oyster Island *135* island of W Burma
Ozama *198* river of S Dominican Republic
Ózd *264* NE Hungary
Özgön *see* Uzgen
Ozurget'i *234* prev. Makharadze. W Georgia

P

Paama *585* island of C Vanuatu
Paarl *493* Western Cape, SW South Africa
Pābna *93* W Bangladesh
Pacaraima, Serra *121, 256* var. Pakaraima Mountains. Mountain range of N South America
Pa'chao Tao *525* island group of W Taiwan
Pachna *see* Pakhna
Pachuca *370* var. Pachuca de Soto. C Mexico
Pacific Ocean *66, 253, 304-305, 618, 623* world's largest ocean bounded by Asia and Australia to the W, the Americas to the E and Antarctica to the S
Padang *276* Sumatra, W Indonesia
Paderborn *236* NW Germany
Padma *93* name of the Ganges in Bangladesh, *see* Ganges
Padova *295* Eng. Padua. N Italy
Paektu-san *413* Chin. Baitou Shan. Mountain of China and North Korea
Pafos *see* Paphos
Pag *181* It. Pago. Island of C Croatia
Pagan *626* island of C Northern Mariana Islands
Pager *554* river of NE Uganda
Paget Island *619* island of E Bermuda
Pago *see* Pag
Pagon, Bukit *126* mountain of SE Brunei
Pago Pago *618* ❖ of American Samoa, Tutuila, W American Samoa
Pagouda *537* var. Kpagouda. NE Togo
Pahang *354* var. Syngei Pahang. River of C Peninsular Malaysia
Pai-ch'eng *see* Baicheng
Paide *212* Ger. Weissenstein. C Estonia
Päijänne *221* lake of S Finland
Pailin *141* W Cambodia
Paine, Cerro *159* mountain of S Chile
Paisance *see* Piacenza

Pais Vasco *501* autonomous community of N Spain
Pakambaru *276* Sumatra, W Indonesia
Pakaraima Mountains *see* Pacaraima, Serra
Pakch'ŏn *413* W North Korea
Pakhna *187* var. Pachna. SW Cyprus
Pakin *375* atoll of E Micronesia
Pakistan *420-423* officially Islamic Republic of Pakistan. Country of Asia divided into 4 admin. units (provinces)
Pak Lay *327* W Laos
Pakokku *135* W Burma
Pākpattan *421* E Pakistan
Pak Sane *see* Muang Pakxan
Pāksey *93* W Bangladesh
Pakwach *554* NW Uganda
Pakxé *327* var. Pakse. S Laos
Pal *62* W Andorra
Pala *156* SW Chad
Palapye *118* SE Botswana
Palau *627* var. Balau. UN trust territory, administered by the USA, Pacific Ocean. ❖ Koror
Palauli *596* Savai'i, Western Samoa
Palauli Bay *596* bay of Pacific Ocean off Sava'i, SW Western Samoa
Palawan *435* island of W Philippines
Palawan Passage *435* passage of the South China Sea, between Spratly Islands and Palawan, Philippines
Paldiski *212* prev. Baltiski, Eng. Baltic Port, Ger. Baltischport. NW Estonia
Palembang *276* Sumatra, W Indonesia
Palencia *501* NW Spain
Palermo *295* Fr. Palerme. Sicilia, S Italy
Palimé *see* Kpalimé
Palk Strait *270, 504* strait connecting the Bay of Bengal and Gulf of Mannar, between India and Sri Lanka
Palma *501* var. Palma de Mallorca. Mallorca, E Spain
Palma *387* N Mozambique
Palmar *178* SE Costa Rica
Palma Soriano *182* SE Cuba
Palm Beach *618* NW Aruba
Palmeira *152* Sal, NE Cape Verde
Palmer *66* US research station of Antarctic Peninsula, Antarctica
Palmerston *620* island of Southern Cook Islands, S Cook Islands
Palmerston North *401* S North Island, New Zealand
Palmetto Point *68* SW Barbuda, Antigua & Barbuda
Palmira *171* W Colombia
Palmyra *see* Tudmur
Paloe *see* Denpasar
Palu *276* Celebes, C Indonesia
Pamandzi *625* Petite-Terre, E Mayotte
Pamir *528* river of Afghanistan and Tajikistan
Pamirs *528* mountain range of C Tajikistan
Pampa Aullagas, Lago *see* Poopó, Lago
Pampas *71* flatlands of South America
Pampeluna *see* Pamplona
Pamplemousses *368* NW Mauritius
Pamplona *501* var. Pampeluna, Basq. Iruñea. N Spain
Pamplona *171* NE Colombia
Pana *230* S Gabon
Panadura *504* SW Sri Lanka
Panagyurishte *128* var. Panagjurište. W Bulgaria
Pānāji *270* SW India
Panama *424-425* officially Republic of Panama. Country of Central America divided into 10 admin. units (9 provinces, and 1 special territory)
Panamá, Bahía de *424* bay to the S of Panama
Panama Canal *424* shipping canal linking the Caribbean Sea to the Pacific Ocean, passing through C Panama

Panama City *424* Sp. Panamá, var. Ciudad de Panama. ❖ of Panama, C Panama
Panamá, Golfo de *424* gulf of the Pacific Ocean to the S of Panama
Panama, Isthmus of *424* prev. Isthmus of Darien, Sp. Istmo de Panamá. Narrow strip of land, between North America and South America
Panamá, Istmo de *see* Panama, Isthmus of
Panay *435* island of C Philippines
Panay Gulf *435* gulf of the Sulu Sea
Pancevo *602* Ger. Pantschowa, Hung. Pancsova. N Serbia, Yugoslavia
Panda *387* S Mozambique
Pandan, Selat *483* strait connecting Strait of Malacca and South China Sea
Pandan Reservoir *483* reservoir of SW Singapore
Pandaruan *126* river of NE Brunei
Pan de Azúcar *577* S Uruguay
Pandėlys *344* var. Pandelis. NE Lithuania
Pandivere Kõrgustik *212* var. Pandivere Kõrgendik. Plateau of NW and NE Estonia
Pando *577* S Uruguay
Panevėžys *344* NE Lithuania
Panfilov *312* SE Kazakhstan
Pangai *538* Lifuka, Hai'pai Group, Tonga
Pangani *530* E Tanzania
Pangani *530* river of NE Tanzania
Pangar *144* river of C Cameroon
Pangkalpinang *276* Pulau Bangka, W Indonesia
Panguma *480* E Sierra Leone
Panguna *426* Bougainville I, Papua New Guinea
Pangutaran Group *435* island group of Sulu Archipelago, SW Philippines
Panhame *see* Manyame
Paniai, Danau *276* lake of Irian Jaya, E Indonesia
Panj *53* Rus. Pyandzh. River of Afghanistan and Tajikistan
Panjang, Pulu *see* West Island
Pano Lefkara *187* S Cyprus
Pano Panayia *187* var. Pano Panagia. W Cyprus
Pano Platres *187* SW Cyprus
Pantanal *120, 125* swamp region of SW Brazil
Pantelleria *295* island to the SW of Sicilia, S Italy
Pantschowa *see* Pancevo
Pánuco *370* river of C Mexico
Panzhihua *163* prev. Dukou var. Tu-k'ou. Sichuan, SW China
Panzós *250* E Guatemala
Pao-chi *see* Baoji
Paoki *see* Baoji
Paola *363* E Malta
Paola *295* S Italy
Pao-shan *see* Baoshan
Pao-ting *see* Baoding
Pao-t'ou *see* Baotou
Paotow *see* Baotou
Pápa *264* W Hungary
Papakura *401* N North Island, New Zealand
Papatoetoe *401* NW North Island, New Zealand
Papayes *368* river of W Mauritius
Papeete *622* Tahiti, W French Polynesia
Paphos *187* var. Pafos. W Cyprus
Papua, Gulf of *426* gulf of the Coral Sea, to the S of Papua New Guinea
Papua New Guinea *426-427* officially Independent State of Papua New Guinea, prev. Territory of Papua and New Guinea. Country of the SW Pacific divided into 19 admin. units (provinces)

Põltsamaa *212 var.* Pyltsamaa. River of C Estonia
Põlva *212 Ger.* Pölwe. SE Estonia
Pomeranian Bay *237, 439 Pol.* Zatoka Pomorska, *Ger.* Pommersche Bucht. Bay of the Baltic Sea, on the coasts of Germany and Poland
Pomio *426* New Britain, Papua New Guinea
Pommersche Bucht *see* Pomeranian Bay
Pomona *102* E Belize
Pomorie *128 var.* Pomoriye. E Bulgaria
Pomorska, Zatoka *see* Pomeranian Bay
Ponape *see* Pohnpei
Ponce *627* S Puerto Rico
Pondicherry *270* S India
Ponérihouen *626* C New Caledonia
Ponferrada *501* NW Spain
Pongo *506* river of S Sudan
Ponta Delgada *442* São Miguel, Azores, Portugal
Ponta Grossa *121* S Brazil
Pontevedra *501* NW Spain
Pontianak *276* Borneo, C Indonesia
Pontian Kechil *354 var.* Puntian Kecil, Pontian Kecil. S Peninsular Malaysia
Pontoise *225* N France
Pontypridd *563* S Wales, UK
Ponziane, Isole *295* island of C Italy
Pooh San *620* NE Christmas Island
Poole *563* S England, UK
Poona *see* Pune
Pooneryn *504* N Sri Lanka
Poopó, Lago *112 var.* Lago Pampa Aullagas. Lake of W Bolivia
Popayán *171* SW Colombia
Popomanaseu, Mount *488* mountain of S Guadalcanal, Solomon Islands
Popondetta *426* SE Papua New Guinea
Popovo *128* N Bulgaria
Poprad *485 Ger.* Deutschendorf, *Hung.* Poprád. NE Slovakia
Poprad *485 Ger.* Popper, *Hung.* Poprád. River of Poland and Slovakia
Pori *221 Swe.* Björneborg. SW Finland
Porirua *401* S North Island, New Zealand
Porlamar *589* Isla de Margarita, Venezuela
Porsangen *414* fjord of N Norway
Porsgrunn *414* S Norway
Portachuelo *112* C Bolivia
Portage la Prairie *146* S Canada
Portalegre *442* E Portugal
Port Alfred *493* Eastern Cape, S South Africa
Port Antonio *303* E Jamaica
Port Augusta *77* S Australia
Port-au-Prince *258* ❖ of Haiti, S Haiti
Port Blair *270* S Andaman, SE India
Port-Bouët *300* SE Ivory Coast
Port d'Envalira *62* zigzag pass of E Andorra
Port-de-Paix *258* N Haiti
Port Dickson *354* SW Peninsular Malaysia
Port Elizabeth *466* Bequia, St Vincent & the Grenadines
Port Elizabeth *493* Eastern Cape, S South Africa
Port Erin *623* SW Isle of Man
Port Étienne *see* Nouâdhibou
Port Florence *see* Kisumu
Port Francqui *see* Ilebo
Port-Gentil *230* W Gabon
Port Harcourt *408* S Nigeria
Port Hedland *76* NW Australia
Port Howard *621* West Falkland, C Falkland Islands
Portimão *442 var.* Vila Nova de Portimão. S Portugal

Port Láirge *see* Waterford
Portland *569* Maine, NE USA
Portland *568* Oregon, NW USA
Portland Bight *303* bay of Caribbean Sea
Portland Point *628* headland on the SW coast of Ascension Island
Port Laoise *288 Ir.* Portlaoighise, Portlaoise, *prev.* Maryborough. C Ireland
Port Lincoln *77* S Australia
Port Loko *480* W Sierra Leone
Port-Louis *622* N Guadeloupe
Port Louis *368 var.* Port-Louis. ❖ of Mauritius, NW Mauritius
Port Lyautey *see* Kénitra
Port Macquarie *77* E Australia
Port Maria *303* N Jamaica
Port Mathurin *368* Rodrigues, Mauritius
Port Morant *303* E Jamaica
Portmore *303* SE Jamaica
Port Moresby *426* ❖ of Papua New Guinea, SE Papua New Guinea
Porto *442 Eng.* Oporto. NW Portugal
Porto Alegre *121 prev.* Pôrto Alegre. S Brazil
Porto Alegre *471* S São Tomé, Sao Tome & Principe
Porto Alexandre *see* Tombua
Porto Amélia *see* Pemba
Portobelo *424 var.* Porto Bello, Puerto Bello. N Panama
Porto Edda *see* Sarandë
Porto Exterior *624* harbour of NE Macao
Port-of-Spain *540* ❖ of Trinidad & Tobago, NW Trinidad, Trinidad & Tobago
Porto Gole *254* C Guinea-Bissau
Porto Grande *see* Mindelo
Porto Interior *624* harbour of NW Macao
Porto-Novo *108* ❖ of Benin, S Benin
Porto Santo *442 var.* Ilha do Porto Santo. Island of the Madeira Is, Portugal
Porto Torres *295* Sardegna, W Italy
Porto Velho *120 prev.* Pôrto Velho. W Brazil
Portoviejo *200 var.* Puertoviejo. W Ecuador
Port Pirie *77* S Australia
Port Refuge *620* strait of the Indian Ocean between Horsburgh Island and Direction Island, C Cocos Islands
Port Royal *303* SE Jamaica
Port Said *202 Ar.* Bur Sa'îd. N Egypt
Port St Mary *623* S Isle of Man
Portsmouth *563* S England, UK
Portsmouth *196 var.* Grande-Anse. NW Dominica
Port Stanley *621* ❖ of Falkland Islands, East Falkland, Falkland Islands
Port Stephens *621* West Falkland, W Falkland Islands
Port Sudan *506 var.* Bûr Sûdân. NE Sudan
Port Swettenham *see* Kelang
Port Talbot *563* S Wales, UK
Portugal *442-445* officially Republic of Portugal. Country of W Europe divided into 18 admin. units (districts)
Portuguese East Africa *see* Mozambique
Port-Vila *585 var.* Vila. ❖ of Vanuatu, Éfate, Vanuatu
Porvenir *159* Tierra del Fuego, Chile
Porvenir *112* NW Bolivia
Posadas *71* NE Argentina
Posen *see* Poznań
Posŏng *496* river of S South Korea
Poste de Flacq *368* river of E Mauritius
Postojna *486 Ger.* Adelsberg, *It.* Postumia. SW Slovenia
Pöstyén *see* Piešťany
Potaro *256* river of C Guyana

Potchefstroom *493* North West, N South Africa
Potenza *295* S Italy
Potgietersrus *493* Northern Transvaal, NE South Africa
Pot House *97* E Barbados
Po Toi Island *262* island of S Hong Kong
Potoru *480* S Sierra Leone
Potosí *112* S Bolivia
Potsdam *237* NE Germany
Potters Village *68* C Antigua, Antigua & Barbuda
Pott, Île *626* island of Îles Belep, W New Caledonia
Pottuvil *504* SE Sri Lanka
Potwar Plateau *420* plateau of NE Pakistan
Poudre d'Or *368* NE Mauritius
Pouembout *629* W New Caledonia
Poum *626* W New Caledonia
Pout *476* W Senegal
Poutasi *596* Upolu, Western Samoa
Poûthĭsăt *141 var.* Pursat. River of W Cambodia
Poûthĭsăt *141 prev.* Pursat. W Cambodia
Po Valley *294* valley of N Italy
Považská Bystrica *485 Ger.* Waagbistritz, *Hung.* Vágbeszterce. NW Slovakia
Povoaçao de Hác-Sá *624* Coloane, S Macao
Povoaçao de Ká-Hó *624* Coloane, S Macao
Povoaçao de Sai Sa *624* Taipa, C Macao
Povoaçao de Samka *624* Taipa, C Macao
Póvoa de Varzim *442* NW Portugal
Powell, Lake *568* reservoir of SW USA
Poya *626* C New Caledonia
Poyang Hu *163* lake of E China
Poyan Reservoir *483* reservoir of W Singapore
Poza Rica *370 var.* Poza Rica de Hidalgo. C Mexico
Poznań *439 Ger.* Posen. W Poland
Pozo Colorado *428* C Paraguay
Pozsega *see* Slavonska Požega
Pozsony *see* Bratislava
Prábis *254* W Guinea-Bissau
Præstø *190* Sjælland, SE Denmark
Prague *188 Cz.* Praha, *Ger.* Prag. ❖ of Czech Republic, NW Czech Republic
Praia *152* ❖ of Cape Verde, Santiago, S Cape Verde
Praia Grande, Baia da *624* bay of the South China Sea, N Macao
Praslin *478* island of the Inner Islands, NE Seychelles
Praslin *465* E St Lucia
Prato *294* N Italy
Preguiça *152* São Nicolau, N Cape Verde
Prenjas *see* Përrenjas
Preparis Island *135* island of SW Burma
Přerov *188 Ger.* Prerau. SE Czech Republic
Presidente Prudente *121* S Brazil
Prešov *485 Ger.* Eperies, *var.* Preschau, *Hung.* Eperjes. NE Slovakia
Prespa, Lake *57, 245, 349 Alb.* Liqen i Prespës, *Mac.* Prespansko Ezero, *Gk* Límni Megáli Préspa, *var.* Limni Prespa. Lake of SE Europe
Prespës, Liqen i *see* Prespa, Lake
Pressburg *see* Bratislava
Prestea *242* SW Ghana
Preston *563* NW England, UK
Pretoria *493* ❖ of South Africa. Pretoria-Witwatersrand-Vereeniging, NE South Africa

Pretoria-Witwatersrand-Vereeniging *493* province of NE South Africa
Préveza *245* W Greece
Prey Vêng *141* S Cambodia
Priboj *602* W Serbia, Yugoslavia
Příbram *188* W Czech Republic
Prickly Pear Cays *618* island group of NW Anguilla
Prieska *493* Northern Cape, C South Africa
Prievidza *485* C Slovakia
Prijedor *116* NW Bosnia & Herzegovina
Prilep *349 Turk.* Perlepe. S FYR Macedonia
Prince Albert *146* SW Canada
Prince Edward Island *147* province and island of SE Canada
Prince Edward Island *493* island of the Prince Edward Islands, S South Africa
Prince Edward Islands *493* island group of S South Africa
Prince George *146* W Canada
Prince Island *see* Príncipe
Prince of Wales Island *see* Pinang, Pulau
Prince of Wales Island *146* island of N Canada
Prince Patrick Island *146* island of Parry Islands, N Canada
Prince Rupert *146* W Canada
Prince Rupert Bay *196* bay of the Caribbean Sea, to the NW of Dominica
Princes Town *540* SW Trinidad, Trinidad & Tobago
Príncipe *471 var.* Príncipe Island, *Eng.* Prince Island. Island to the N of São Tomé, Sao Tome & Principe
Pripet *104* river of S Belorussia
Pripet Marshes *104,* forested and swampy region of Belorussia and Ukraine
Priština *602* S Serbia, Yugoslavia
Privas *225* SE France
Privigye *see* Prievidza
Priwitz *see* Prievidza
Prizren *602 Alb.* Prizreni. S Serbia, Yugoslavia
Probištip *349* N FYR Macedonia
Probolinggo *276* Java, C Indonesia
Progreso *577* S Uruguay
Prome *135 var.* Pyè. SW Burma
Promissão, Represa de *121* reservoir of S Brazil
Proskurov *see* Khmel 'nyts'kyy
Prostějov *188 Ger.* Prossnitz. SE Czech Republic
Provadiya *128 var.* Provadija. E Bulgaria
Provence *225* cultural region of SE France
Providence *569* Rhode Island, NE USA
Providence *97* S Barbados
Providence Atoll *478 var.* Providence. Atoll of the Farquhar Group, S Seychelles
Providenciales *629* island of NW Turks and Caicos Islands
Provo *568* Utah, SW USA
Prudhoe Bay *568* Alaska, USA
Prune Island *466* island of SW St Vincent & the Grenadines
Prut *376, 448, 556 Ger.* Pruth. River of E Europe
Pruth *see* Prut
Pruzhany *104* SW Belorussia
Pryazova'ks Vysochyna *556* mountain range of SE Ukraine
Prychornomors'ka Nyzovyna *556* mountain range of S Ukraine
Prydniprovs'ka Nyzovyna *556* mountain range of NE Ukraine
Prydniprovs'ka Vysochyna *556* mountain range of NW Ukraine
Przemyśl *439* SE Poland
Przheval'sk *see* Karakol
Pskov *452 Ger.* Pleskau. W Russia

Pskov, Lake 212 *Est.* Pihkva Järv, *Rus.* Pskovskoye Ozero. Lake of Estonia and Russia
Ptsich 104 *Rus.* Ptich'. River of C Belorussia
Ptuj 486 *Ger.* Pettau. NE Slovenia
Pua'a, Cape 596 cape on the coast of Savai'i, NW Western Samoa
Pu'apu'a 596 Savali'i, Western Samoa
Pucallpa 431 C Peru
Puch'ŏn 496 *prev.* Punwŏn. NW South Korea
Pudasjärvi 221 C Finland
Puebla 370 *var.* Puebla de Zaragoza. S Mexico
Pueblo 569 Colorado, SW USA
Pueblo Nuevo Tiquisate 250 *var.* Tiquisate. SW Guatemala
Puente Alto 159 C Chile
Puerto Acosta 112 W Bolivia
Puerto Aisén 159 S Chile
Puerto Armuelles 424 W Panama
Puerto Ayacucho 589 SW Venezuela
Puerto Bahía Negra 428 N Paraguay
Puerto Baquerizo Moreno 200 San Cristobal I, Galapagos Is.
Puerto Barrios 250 E Guatemala
Puerto Bello *see* Portobelo
Puerto Berrío 171 N Colombia
Puerto Busch 112 *var.* Puerto General Busch. SE Bolivia
Puerto Cabello 589 N Venezuela
Puerto Cabezas 404 *var.* Bilwi. NE Nicaragua
Puerto Carreño 171 E Colombia
Puerto Casado 428 C Paraguay
Puerto Cooper 428 C Paraguay
Puerto Cortés 260 NW Honduras
Puerto El Carmen de Putumayo 200 *var.* Putumayo. NW Ecuador
Puerto el Triunfo 207 S El Salvador
Puerto Inírida 171 *var.* Obando. E Colombia
Puerto Iradier *see* Kogo
Puerto La Cruz 589 NE Venezuela
Puerto Lempira 260 E Honduras
Puertolland 501 SW Spain
Puerto Maldonado 431 E Peru
Puerto México *see* Coatzacoalcos
Puerto Montt 159 C Chile
Puerto Natales 159 S Chile
Puerto Padre 182 SE Cuba
Puerto Pinasco 428 C Paraguay
Puerto Plata 198 *var.* San Felipe de Puerto Plata. N Dominican Republic
Puerto Presidente Stroessner *see* Ciudad del Este
Puerto Princesa 435 Palawan, W Philippines
Puerto Príncipe *see* Camagüey
Puerto Rico 627 Commonwealth territory of the USA, Caribbean Sea
Puerto Rico Trench 627 undersea feature of the Caribbean Sea, N Puerto Rico
Puerto San José 250 *var.* San José. S Guatemala
Puerto Suárez 112 E Bolivia
Puerto Vallarta 370 W Mexico
Puerto Varas 159 C Chile
Puerto Viejo 178 NE Costa Rica
Puertoviejo *see* Portoviejo
Pujehun 480 S Sierra Leone
Pukaki, Lake 401 lake of C South Island, New Zealand
Pukapuka 620 island of Northern Cook Islands, N Cook Islands
Pukch'ŏng 413 E North Korea
Pukë 57 *var.* Puka. N Albania
Pukekohe 401 NW North Island, New Zealand
Pukhan 496 river of North Korea and South Korea
Pula 181 *prev.* Pulj, *It.* Pola. W Croatia
Pulangi 435 river of Mindanao, S Philippines
Pulap 375 atoll of C Micronesia
Pulau 277 river of Irian Jaya, E Indonesia

Pulau Tekong Reservoir 483 reservoir of E Singapore
Pul-i-Khumri *see* Pol-e Khomrī
Pully 516 SW Switzerland
Pulusuk 375 island of C Micronesia
Puluwat 375 atoll of C Micronesia
Puna, Isla 200 island to the SW of Ecuador, in the Gulf of Guayaquil
Punakha 110 C Bhutan
Punata 112 C Bolivia
Pune 270 *prev.* Poona. W India
Punggol 483 area of NE Singapore
Púngoè 387 *var.* Pungue, Pungwe. River of C Mozambique
Punkudutivu 504 island of N Sri Lanka
Puno 431 SE Peru
Punta Arenas 159 *prev.* Magallanes. S Chile
Punta Chame 424 C Panama
Punta del Este 577 S Uruguay
Punta Gorda 102 S Belize
Puntarenas 178 W Costa Rica
Punta Santiago 228 S Bioko, Equatorial Guinea
Punto Fijo 589 NW Venezuela
Punwŏn *see* Puch'ŏn
Purari 426 river of C Papua New Guinea
Puri 270 E India
Purmerend 397 NW Netherlands
Pursat *see* Poŭthĭsăt
Purus 120 river of Brazil and Peru
Pusan 496 *var.* Busan, *Jap.* Fusan. SE South Korea
Pusat Gayo, Pegunungan 276 mountain range of Sumatra, W Indonesia
Pushkino *see* Biläsuvar
Pu-tai 525 W Taiwan
Putorana, Plato 453 mountain range of N Russia
Puttalam 504 W Sri Lanka
Puttalam Lagoon 504 lagoon of W Sri Lanka
Putumayo 171, 431 river of NW South America
Putumayo *see* Puerto El Carmen de Putumayo
Puyo 200 C Ecuador
Pyandzh 528 *var.* Panj. River of Afghanistan and Tajikistan forming a headstream of the Amu Darya
Pyandzh 528 *var.* Pjandž. SW Tajikistan
Pyapon 135 S Burma
Pyarnu *see* Pärnu
Pyinmana 135 C Burma
Pyltsamaa *see* Põltsamaa
Pyongyang 413 *Kor.* P'yŏngyang. ❖ of North Korea, SW North Korea
Pyramiden 629 Spitsbergen, W Svalbard
Pyramid Rock 627 island of E Paracel Islands
Pyrenees 62, 224-225, 501 *Sp.* Pirineos, *Fr.* Pyrénées. Mountain range of SW Europe
Pyu 135 S Burma
Pyuntaza 135 S Burma
Pyuthan 395 W Nepal

Q

Qabatiya 292 N West Bank
Qâbis *see* Gabès
Qacentina *see* Constantine
Qafşah *see* Gafsa
Qahremānshahr *see* Bākhtarān
Qala' en Nahl 506 *var.* Qala' an Nahl. E Sudan
Qalali 91 Jazirat al Muharraq, Bahrain
Qalansīyah 599 NW Suqutra, Yemen
Qalāt *see* Kalāt
Qal'at Bīshah 472 SW Saudi Arabia
Qal'eh-ye Now 53 *var.* Qala Nau. NW Afghanistan

Qalīb ash Shuyūkh 322 *var.* Jleeb al Shuyoukh. C Kuwait
Qalīb, Shiqqat al 322 *var.* Shagat al Jleeb. Desert region of NW Kuwait
Qamar, Ghubbat al 599 bay of Arabian Sea, E Yemen
Qamar, Jabal al 418 mountain range of SW Oman
Qambar *see* Kambar
Qamea 218 *prev.* Nggamea. Island to the E of Taveuni, N Fiji
Qandahār *see* Kandahār
Qaraghandy *see* Karaganda
Qaraoun, Lac de 332 *var.* Buḩayrat al Qir'awn. Lake of S Lebanon
Qara Qum *see* Karakumy
Qarataū *see* Karatau
Qardho 490 *It.* Gardo. N Somalia
Qareh Chāy 281 river of NW Iran
Qarkilik *see* Ruoqiang
Qarshi *see* Karshi
Qartaba 332 *var.* Qarţabā. N Lebanon
Qatar 446-447 officially State of Qatar. Country of SW Asia divided into 9 admin. units (municipalities)
Qaţţâra, Monkhafad el 202 *var.* Munkhafad al Qaţţārah, *Eng.* Qattara Depression. Arid desert basin of NW Egypt
Qazaqstan *see* Kazakhstan
Qazax 86 *Rus.* Kazakh. W Azerbaijan
Qazbegi 234 *Rus.* Kazbegi. NE Georgia
Qazimämmäd 86 *Rus.* Kazi-Magomed. SE Azerbaijan
Qazvīn 281 *var.* Kazvin. NW Iran
Qena 202 *var.* Qina. E Egypt
Qena, Wâdi 202 *var.* Wādī Qinā. Seasonal river of E Egypt
Qeshm 281 *var.* Jazīreh-ye Qeshm, Qeshm Island. Island of S Iran
Qezel Owzan 281 river of NW Iran
Qibilī *see* Kebili
Qilian Shan 162 *var.* Kilien Mountains. Mountain range of W China
Qingdao 163 *var.* Tsintao, Ching-Tao, Ch'ing-tao. Shandong, E China
Qinghai 162 *var.* Chinghai, Tsinghai. Province of W China
Qinghai Hu 162 *var.* Tsing Hai, Ch'ing Hai *Mong.* Koko Nor. Lake of W China
Qing-Zang Gaoyuan 162 *Eng.* Plateau of Tibet. Plateau of Xizang Zizhiqu, W China
Qiqihar 163 *prev.* Lungkiang, *var.* Tsitsihar, Ch'i-ch'i-ha-erh. Heilongjiang, NE China
Qir'awn, Buḩayrat al *see* Qaraoun, Lac de
Qirba, Khashim Al *see* Girba, Khashm el
Qiryat Ata 291 N Israel
Qiryat Gat 291 C Israel
Qiryat Motzkin 291 N Israel
Qiryat Shemona 291 N Israel
Qishn 599 SE Yemen
Qishon, Naḩal 291 river of N Israel
Qīzān *see* Jīzān
Qizilqum *see* Kyzyl Kum
Qom 281 *var.* Qum, Kum. NW Iran
Qomolangma Feng *see* Everest, Mount
Qomul *see* Hami
Qondūz *see* Kunduz
Qondūz, Daryā-ye 53 seasonal river of NE Afghanistan
Qorakŭl *see* Karakul'
Qormi 363 C Malta
Qornet es Saouda 332 mountain of NE Lebanon
Qoryooley 490 *It.* Coriole. SW Somalia
Qoubaiyat 332 *var.* Al Qubayyāt. NE Lebanon
Qoussantîna *see* Constantine
Quang Ngai 593 E Vietnam
Quan Long *see* Ca Mau
Quanzhou 163 *var.* Ch'uan-chou, *prev.* Chin-chiang, *var.* Tsinkiang. Fujian, SE China

Quaraí *see* Cuareim
Quarles, Pegunungan 276 mountain range of Celebes, W Indonesia
Quarnero *see* Kvarner
Quartier Militaire 368 C Mauritius
Quatre Bornes 368 W Mauritius
Quatre Bornes 478 Mahé, Seychelles
Quatre, Isle à 466 island of C St Vincent & the Grenadines
Quba 86 *Rus.* Kuba. N Azerbaijan
Queanbeyan 77 SE Australia
Québec 147 SE Canada
Québec 147, 151 province of SE Canada
Quebo 254 S Guinea-Bissau
Queen Charlotte Bay 621 bay of the South Atlantic Ocean, W Falkland Islands
Queen Charlotte Islands 146 *Fr.* Îles de la Reine-Charlotte. Island group of SW Canada
Queen Charlotte Sound 146 area of the Pacific Ocean between the Queen Charlotte Islands and Vancouver Island, SW Canada
Queen Elizabeth Islands 146 *Fr.* Îles de la Reine-Élisabeth. Island group of N Canada
Queen Mary's Peak 628 mountain of C Tristan da Cunha
Queen Maud Gulf 146 gulf of the Arctic Ocean on the coast of N Canada
Queen Maud Land 66 physical region of Greater Antarctica, Antarctica
Queensland 77, 81 state of N Australia
Queenstown 483 area of S Singapore
Queenstown 493 Eastern Cape, S South Africa
Queguay Grande 577 river of W Uruguay
Quelimane 387 E Mozambique
Quelpart *see* Cheju-do
Queluz 442 W Portugal
Quepos 178 S Costa Rica
Que Que *see* Kwekwe
Querétaro 370 C Mexico
Quesada 178 N Costa Rica
Questelles 466 SW St Vincent, St Vincent & the Grenadines
Quetta 421 NW Pakistan
Quezaltenango 250 *var.* Quetzaltenango. W Guatemala
Quezaltepeque 207 C El Salvador
Quibdó 171 W Colombia
Quillacollo 112 C Bolivia
Quilpué 159 C Chile
Quimper 224 W France
Quinhámel 254 W Guinea-Bissau
Quiniluban Group 435 island group of C Philippines
Quissico 387 S Mozambique
Quito 200 ❖ of Ecuador, N Ecuador
Qum *see* Qom
Qŭnghirot *see* Kungrad
Qŭqon *see* Kokand
Qurayn, Ra's al 91 cape of SE Bahrain
Qurayyāt 418 *var.* Qurayat, Quraiyat. NE Oman
Qurlurtuuq *see* Coppermine
Quş 202 *var.* Qūş. E Egypt
Quthing *see* Moyeni
Quy Nhon 593 *var.* Quinhon. SE Vietnam
Qvareli 234 *Rus.* Kvareli. E Georgia
Qyteti Stalin *see* Kuçovë
Qyzylorda *see* Kzyl-Orda

R

Raab *see* Rába
Raab *see* Győr
Raahe 221 *Swe.* Brahestad. W Finland
Ra'ananna 291 C Israel
Rába 82, 264 *Ger.* Raab. River of Austria and Hungary
Rabat 363 W Malta
Rabat 382 ❖ of Morocco, NW Morocco

Ruvironza *138 var.* Luvironza. River of C Burundi
Ruvubu *138 var.* Ruvuvu. River of C Burundi
Ruvuma *387, 530 Port.* Rovuma. River of Mozambique and Tanzania
Ruwais *see* Ar Ru'ays
Ruwaisv *see* Ar Ru'ays
Ruwenzori *554* mountains of Uganda and Zaire
Ruya *612* river of Mozambique and Zimbabwe
Ruyigi *138* C Burundi
Ružomberok *485 Hung.* Rózsahegy, *Ger.* Rosenberg. N Slovakia
Rwamagana *460* E Rwanda
Rwamatamu *460* W Rwanda
Rwanda *460-461* officially Republic of Rwanda, *prev.* Ruanda. Country of Central Africa divided into 10 admin. units (prefectures)
Rwanyakizinga, Lac *460* lake of NE Rwanda
Rwasanga *138* C Burundi
Rweru *138, 430 var.* Lac Rugwero. Lake of Burundi and Rwanda
Rwesero *138* C Burundi
Rwesero *460* SW Rwanda
Ryazan' *452* W Russia
Rybinskoye Vodokhranilishche *452 Eng.* Rybinsk Reservoir. Reservoir of W Russia
Rybnik *439* S Poland
Rybnitsa *see* Rîbniţa
Rykovo *see* Yenakiyeve
Rysy *439* mountain of S Poland
Rzeszów *439* SE Poland

S

Saale *237* river of C Germany
Saarbrücken *236 Fr.* Sarrebruck. SW Germany
Sääre *212* Saaremaa, Estonia
Saaremaa *212 var.* Saare, Sarema, *Ger.* Ösel, *var.* Oesel. Island of W Estonia
Saaristomeri *221* strait connecting the Gulf of Bothnia and Gulf of Finland
Saartuz *528* W Tajikistan
Saati *210* E Eritrea
Saatlı *86 Rus.* Saatly. C Azerbaijan
Saatta *210* NW Eritrea
Sab *141* river of S Cambodia
Saba *626* island of N Netherlands Antilles
Šabac *602* NW Serbia, Yugoslavia
Sabadell *501* E Spain
Sabana, Archipiélago de *182* island group of N Cuba
Sabana de la Mar *198* E Dominican Republic
Sabanalarga *171* N Colombia
Sabaneta *198* NW Dominican Republic
Sab'atayn, Ramlat as *599* desert region of C Yemen
Sabaya *112* S Bolivia
Şābērī, Hāmūn-e *53 var.* Sīstān, Daryācheh-ye. Lake of Afghanistan and Iran
Sabhā *339* W Libya
Sabi *233* E Gambia
Sabi *see* Save
Sabinal, Cayo *182* island of NE Cuba
Sabirabad *86* C Azerbaijan
Sabkha *see* As Sabkhah
Sabkhat al Mūh *520* river of S Syria
Sabyah *see* Aş Şabīyah
Sabzevār *281* NE Iran
Sacavém *442* W Portugal
Sachs Harbour *146* Banks Island, NW Canada
Sacramento *568* California, W USA
Sada *625* W Mayotte
Sá da Bandeira *see* Lubango
Şa'dah *599* NW Yemen

Sadaï *194* river of NE Djibouti
Sa Đec *593* S Vietnam
Sādiqābād *284* SE Pakistan
Sa'dīyah, Hawr as *284* lake of E Iraq
Sadlers *462* N St Kitts, St Kitts & Nevis
Sado *304* island to the W of Honshū, N Japan
Safāqis *see* Sfax
Safi *382* W Morocco
Safi *see* Aş Şafi
Safīd Khers, Kūh-e *53* mountain range of NE Afghanistan
Safīd Kūh *53* mountain range of NW Afghanistan
Safim *254* W Guinea-Bissau
Saga *304* Kyūshū, SW Japan
Sagaing *135* C Burma
Saganthit Island *135 var.* Sakanthit, *prev.* Sellore I. Island of S Burma
Sagarmatha *see* Everest, Mount
Sagay *435* Negros, C Philippines
Sagua la Grande *182* C Cuba
Saguia al Hamra *382* river of N Western Sahara
Saham *310 var.* Sahm. N Jordan
Sahara *156, 339, 360, 366, 407 Ar.* Aş Şahrā'. Vast desert area of N Africa
Sahara el Gharqīya *202 var.* Aş Şahrā' al Gharbīyah, *Eng.* Western Desert. Desert of C Egypt
Sahara el Sharqīya *202 var.* Aş Şahrā' ash Sharqīyah, *Eng.* Eastern Desert. Desert of E Egypt
Sāhīwāl *421 prev.* Montgomery. E Pakistan
Šahrisabz *see* Shakhrisabz
Saïda *332 var.* Şaydā. W Lebanon
Saïda *59* NW Algeria
Saidpur *93* NW Bangladesh
Saigon *see* Hô Chi Minh
Saiki *304* Kyūshū, SW Japan
Sai Kung *262* E Hong Kong
Sail Rock *466* islet of S St Vincent & the Grenadines
Saimaa *221* lake of SE Finland
Saint Albert *146* SW Canada
St. André *628* NE Réunion
St. Anne *623* Alderney, N Guernsey
St. Ann's Bay *303* N Jamaica
St Aubin *624* S Jersey
St Austell *563* SW England, UK
St. Barthélémy *622* island of N Guadeloupe
St. Benoit *628* E Réunion
Saint-Brieuc *224* NW France
St. Catherine, Mt *248* mountain C Grenada island, Grenada
St. Catherine Point *619* headland of E Bermuda
Saint Catherines *147* SE Canada
Saint-Chamond *225* E France
Saint Croix *629* island of S Virgin Islands
St. David's *248* SE Grenada island, Grenada
St. David's Island *619* island of E Bermuda
St Denis *628* ❖ of Réunion, N Réunion
Ste Anne *625* SE Martinique
Ste. Anne *622* E Guadeloupe
Saint-Élie *621* N French Guiana
Ste. Rose *622* W Guadeloupe
Saintes *225* W France
Saint-Étienne *225* E France
St Eustatius *626* island of C Netherlands Antilles
St. François *622* E Guadeloupe
Saint-Gall *see* Sankt Gallen
St-Georges *621* E French Guiana
St. George *619* St. George's Island, N Bermuda
St. George's *248* ❖ of Grenada, SW Grenada
St. George's Channel *288, 563 Ir.* Muir Bhreatan. Channel connecting the Celtic Sea and Irish Sea

St. George's Harbour *619* bay of E Bermuda
St. George's Island *619* island of E Bermuda
St. Giles Islands *540 prev.* Melville Islands. Islands to the NE of Tobago, Trinidad & Tobago
St Helena *628* British dependent territory of the South Atlantic Ocean ❖ Jamestown
St. Helena Bay *493* bay of Atlantic Ocean, of coast of W South Africa
St Helier *624* ❖ of Jersey, S Jersey
St John *624* N Jersey
St John *623* C Isle of Man
Saint John *147* SE Canada
St. John *336* river of Guinea and Liberia
Saint John Island *629* island of NE Virgin Islands
St John's *625* N Montserrat
St John's *182* C Cuba
Saint John's *147* Newfoundland, E Canada
St. John's *68* ❖ of Antigua & Barbuda, NW Antigua
St. John's Island *see* Sakijang Bendera, Pulau
St. Johnston Village *68* C Antigua, Antigua & Barbuda
St. Joseph *628* S Réunion
St Joseph *196* W Dominica
St. Joseph *540* SE Trinidad, Trinidad & Tobago
St Julian's *363* N Malta
St Kilda *563* island of NW Scotland, UK
Saint Kitts *462* island of the Lesser Antilles, which, with Nevis, forms the independent state of St Kitts & Nevis
Saint Kitts and Nevis *462-463* officially Federation of Saint Christopher and Nevis. Country of the West Indies
Saint-Laurent, Golfe du *see* Saint Lawrence, Gulf of
St.-Laurent-du-Maroni *621* NW French Guiana
Saint Lawrence *147 Fr.* Fleuve Saint-Laurent. River of SE Canada
Saint Lawrence, Gulf of *146* Gulf of the Atlantic Ocean, SE Canada
Saint-Lo *224* NW France
St. Louis *628* SW Réunion
St Louis *623* Marie-Galante, S Guadeloupe
St Louis *569* Missouri, C USA
Saint-Louis *476* NW Senegal
St-Louis-du-Nord *258 var.* St-Luis du Nord. N Haiti
Saint Lucia *464-465* independent island state of the Caribbean
Saint Lucia Channel *465* channel connecting the Atlantic Ocean and Caribbean Sea
St. Lucia, Lake *493* lake of Kwazulu Natal, E South Africa
Saint Malo *224* NW France
Saint-Malo, Golfe de *224* gulf of the English Channel to the NW of France
St-Marc *258* W Haiti
St-Marc, Canal de *258* channel of the Caribbean Sea between Île de la Gonâve and W Haiti
Sainte Marie, Nosy *350 var.* Nosy Boraha. Island of NE Madagascar
Ste Marie *625* NE Martinique
St. Marie *628* NE Réunion
St Martin *626* island of N Netherlands Antilles
St. Martin *622* island of N Guadeloupe
St. Martins *97* SE Barbados
Saint-Nazaire *224* W France
St.-Nicolas *see* Sint-Niklaas
St. Patricks *97* S Barbados
St Paul *628* NW Réunion
St. Paul *569* Minnesota, NC USA
St. Paul *336* river of Guinea and Liberia

St. Paul's *462* NW St Kitts, St Kitts & Nevis
St. Paul's Bay *363* area of the Malta Channel
Saint Paul's Bay *see* San Pawl il Baħar
St Paul's Point *627* headland of Pitcairn Island, S Pitcairn Islands
St Peter Port *623* ❖ of Guernsey, C Guernsey
St Peters *462* SE St Kitts, St Kitts & Nevis
St Petersburg *569* Florida, SE USA
Saint Petersburg *452, 458 var.* Sankt-Peterburg, *prev.* Leningrad, Petrograd. NW Russia
St. Philips *68* SE Antigua, Antigua & Barbuda
Saint-Pierre *628* ❖ of Saint Pierre and Miquelon, SE Saint Pierre
Saint Pierre *628* island of SE Saint Pierre and Miquelon
St. Pierre *628* SW Réunion
St Pierre *625* NW Martinique
St. Pierre *478* island of the Farquhar Group, Seychelles
Saint Pierre and Miquelon *628* French territorial collectivity of the Atlantic Ocean ❖ Saint-Pierre
St. Sampson *623* S Guernsey
Saint Sauveur *196* E Dominica
Saint Thomas Island *629* island of W Virgin Islands
Saint Thomas Island *see* São Tomé
St.-Trond *see* Sint-Truiden
Saint Vincent *466* island of the Lesser Antilles which, with the Northern Grenadines forms the independent state of St Vincent & the Grenadines
Saint Vincent and the Grenadines *466-467* country of the West Indies
St Willibrordus *626* Curaçao, S Netherlands Antilles
Saipan *626* island of S Northern Mariana Islands
Saishū *see* Cheju
Sajama, Nevado *112* mountain of W Bolivia
Sakaide *304* Shikoku, SW Japan
Sakākah *472* N Saudi Arabia
Sakalua *553* islet of Nukufetau, Tuvalu
Sakanthit *see* Saganthit Island
Sakarya *see* Adapazarı
Sakarya *546* river of NW Turkey
Sakata *304* Honshū, N Japan
Sakchu *413* W North Korea
Sakété *108* S Benin
Sakhalin, Ostrov *453* island of SE Russia
Sakha, Respublika *452 var.* Respublika Yakutiya. Autonomous republic of E Russia
Şäki *86 Rus.* Sheki, *var.* Šeki, *prev.* Nukha. NW Azerbaijan
Sakijang Bendera, Pulau *483 prev.* St. John's Island S Singapore
Sakijang Pelepah, Pulau *483 prev.* Lazarus Island S Singapore
Sakis-Adasi *see* Chíos
Sakishima-shotō *304* island group of Nansei-shotō, SW Japan
Sakon Nakhon *533* NE Thailand
Sakra, Pulau *483* island of SW Singapore
Sakskøbing *190* Lolland, SE Denmark
Sal *152* island of NE Cape Verde
Šaľa *485 Hung.* Sellye. SW Slovakia
Sala Ban Thin *327* C Laos
Salacgrīva *330* N Latvia
Salado *182* river of SE Cuba
Salaga *242* C Ghana
Sala'ilua *596* Savai'i, Western Samoa
Salala *336* C Liberia
Şalālah *418* SW Oman
Salamá *250* C Guatemala
Salamanca *370* C Mexico
Salamanca *500* NW Spain
Salamat *156* river of S Chad
Salamīyah *521 var.* Selemia. W Syria

San Miguel *200* river of Colombia and Ecuador
San Miguel de Ibarra *see* Ibarra
San Miguel de Tucumán *71 var.* Tucumán. N Argentina
San Miguel, Golfo de *424* inlet of the Gulf of Panama to the S of Panama
San Miguelito *424* C Panama
Sannār *see* Senna
San Nicolas *618* S Aruba
San Nicolás de los Arroyos *71* E Argentina
Sanniquellie *336* NE Liberia
San Pablo *435* Luzon, N Philippines
San Pablo *424* river of SW Panama
San Pablo *112* S Bolivia
San Pablo *102* N Belize
San Pawl il Bahar *363* *Eng.* Saint Paul's Bay. NW Malta
San Pedro *428* SE Paraguay
San Pedro *250* river of Guatemala and Mexico
San Pedro *102* NE Belize
San-Pédro *300* S Ivory Coast
San Pedro Carchá *250* C Guatemala
San Pedro del Durazno *see* Durazno
San Pedro de Lloc *431* NW Peru
San Pedro de Macorís *198* SE Dominican Republic
San Pedro Sula *260* NW Honduras
San Rafael *178* NW Costa Rica
San Rafael *207* C El Salvador
San Rafael *71* W Argentina
San Rafael del Moján *589* NW Venezuela
San Rafael del Sur *404* SW Nicaragua
San Ramón *178* C Costa Rica
San Ramón *577* S Uruguay
San Remo *294* N Italy
San Salvador *207* ❖ of El Salvador, SW El Salvador
San Salvador *88 prev.* Watlings I. Island of E Bahamas
San Salvador, Isla *see* Santiago, Isla
San Salvador de Jujuy *71 var.* Jujuy. N Argentina
Sansanné-Mango *537 var.* Mango. N Togo
San Sebastián *627* NW Puerto Rico
San Sebastián *501 var.* Donostia. N Spain
Sansenhō *see* Samch'ŏnpŏ
San Severo *295* S Italy
Santa Ana *207* NW El Salvador
Santa Ana, Volcan de *207 var.* La Matepec. Volcanic peak of W El Salvador
Santa Ana de Coro *see* Coro
Santa Bárbara *260* W Honduras
Santa Caterina *626* Curaçao, S Netherlands Antilles
Santa Clara *182* C Cuba
Santa Coloma *62* SW Andorra
Santa Comba *see* Uaco Cungo
Santa Cruz *178* W Costa Rica
Santa Cruz *471* SE São Tomé, Sao Tome & Principe
Santa Cruz *112* *var.* Santa Cruz de la Sierra. C Bolivia
Santa Cruz *303* SW Jamaica
Santa Cruz, Isla *200* island of C Galapagos Is, Ecuador
Santa Cruz de El Seibo *see* El Seibo
Santa Cruz del Sur *182* S Cuba
Santa Cruz de Tenerife *501* Islas Canarias, SW Spain
Santa Cruz Islands *488* island group of E Solomon Is
Santa Elena *102* W Belize
Santa Fe *71* NE Argentina
Santa Fé *182 var.* La Fe. Isla de la Juventud, Cuba
Santa Fé *424* W Panama
Santa Fe *568* New Mexico, SW USA
Santa Isabel *see* Malabo
Santa Isabel *488 Poly.* Boghotu. Island of the C Solomon Islands
Santa Isabel *250 var.* Cancuén. River of N Guatemala

Santa Isabel, Pico de *see* Basilé, Pico de
Santa Lucía *577* S Uruguay
Santa Lucía Cotzumalguapa *250* SW Guatemala
Santa Luzia *152* island of N Cape Verde
Santa Maria *442* island of the Azores, Portugal
Santa Maria *178* S Costa Rica
Santa Maria *121* S Brazil
Santa Maria *152* Sal, NE Cape Verde
Santa Maria, Isla *200* island of S Galapagos Is, Ecuador
Santa Maria Island *585* Banks Islands, N Vanuatu
Santa Marta *171* N Colombia
Santa Maura *see* Lefkada
Santana *471* NE São Tomé, Sao Tome & Principe
Santander *501* N Spain
Sant' Antioco *294* Sardegna, W Italy
Santarém *442* W Portugal
Santarém *121* N Brazil
Santa Rita *623* SW Guam
Santa Rosa *200* SW Ecuador
Santa Rosa *71* C Argentina
Santa Rosa de Copán *260* W Honduras
Santa Rosa de Lima *207* E El Salvador
Santa Tecla *see* Nueva San Salvador
Santiago *see* Grande de Santiago
Santiago *159* ❖ of Chile, C Chile
Santiago *500 var.* Santiago de Compostela. NW Spain
Santiago *198 var.* Santiago de los Caballeros. NW Dominican Republic
Santiago *152 var.* São Tiago. Island of S Cape Verde
Santiago *424* SW Panama
Santiago de Cuba *182* SE Cuba
Santiago de Guayaquil *see* Guayaquil
Santiago del Estero *71* C Argentina
Santiago, Isla *200* *var.* Isla San Salvador. Island of C Galapagos Is, Ecuador
Santiago Maior *152* Santiago, S Cape Verde
Santi Quaranta *see* Sarandë
Sant Joan de Caselles *62* NE Andorra
Sant Julià de Lòria *62* SW Andorra
Sant Miguel d'Engolasters *62* C Andorra
Santo *see* Espiritu Santo
Santo André *121* S Brazil
Santo Antão *152* island of N Cape Verde
Santo António *152* Maio, S Cape Verde
Santo António *471 var.* São António. N Príncipe, Sao Tome & Principe
Santo Domingo *182* C Cuba
Santo Domingo *198* *prev.* Ciudad Trujillo. ❖ of Dominican Republic, S Dominican Republic
Santo Domingo de los Colorados *200* NW Ecuador
Santon *623* SE Isle of Man
Santos *121* S Brazil
Santo Tomás *207* SW El Salvador
Santo Tomás de Castilla *250* E Guatemala
Santuari de Méritxell *62* C Andorra
San Vicente *207* C El Salvador
San Vito *178* SE Costa Rica
Sanyati *612* river of N Zimbabwe
São Bernardo do Campo *121* S Brazil
São Domingos *254* W Guinea-Bissau
São Filipe *152* Fogo island, S Cape Verde
São Francisco *121* river of E Brazil
São Jorge *442* island of the Azores, Portugal
São José do Rio Preto *121* S Brazil
São José dos Campos *121* S Brazil
São Luís *121* NE Brazil
São Manuel *120-121 var.* Teles Piras. River of W Brazil

São Marcos, Baía de *121* bay of the Atlantic Ocean, on the coast of N Brazil
São Miguel *442* island of the Azores, Portugal
Saona, Isla *198* island of SE Dominican Republic
Saône *225* river of E France
São Nicolau *152* island of N Cape Verde
São Paulo *121, 125* S Brazil
São Pedro *152* São Vincente, N Cape Verde
São Pedro do Rio Grande do Sul *see* Rio Grande
São Salvador *see* Salvador
São Salvador do Congo *see* M'Banza Congo
São Simão, Represa de *121* reservoir of S Brazil
São Tiago *see* Santiago
São Tomé *471 Eng.* Saint Thomas. Island of S Sao Tome & Principe
São Tomé *471* ❖ of Sao Tome & Principe, NE São Tomé
Sao Tome & Principe *470-471* officially Democratic Republic of Sao Tome and Principe, *Port.* São Tomé e Príncipe. Country of W Africa divided into 7 admin. units (districts)
São Tomé, Pico de *471* mountain of São Tomé, Sao Tome & Principe
São Vicente *121* S Brazil
São Vicente *152* island of N Cape Verde
Sapele *408* S Nigeria
Sapitwa *353* mountain of S Malawi
Saponé *132* C Burkina
Sappemeer *397* NE Netherlands
Sapporo *304* Hokkaidō, N Japan
Sapta Koshi *395* river of India and Nepal
Sār *91* NW Bahrain
Šara *349* mountain range of FYR Macedonia and Yugoslavia
Sara Buri *533* C Thailand
Saragossa *see* Zaragoza
Saragt *551 prev.* Serakhs, *var.* Serahs. S Turkmenistan
Sarajevo *116* ❖ of Bosnia & Herzegovina, SE Bosnia & Herzegovina
Saran' *312* C Kazakhstan
Sarandë *57 var.* Saranda, *It.* Porto Edda, *prev.* Santi Quaranta. S Albania
Sarandí del Yí *577* C Uruguay
Sarandí Grande *577* S Uruguay
Sarangani Islands *435* island group of SE Philippines
Saratov *452* W Russia
Saravan *327 var.* Saravane. SE Laos
Sarbhang *110* S Bhutan
Sardegna *294 Eng.* Sardinia. Island of W Italy
Sardinia *see* Sardegna
Sargodha *421* NE Pakistan
Sarh *156 prev.* Fort-Archambault. S Chad
Sārī *281* N Iran
Sarigan *626* island of C Northern Mariana Islands
Sarikol Range *528* *Rus.* Sarykol'skiy Khrebet. Mountain range of China and Tajikistan
Sarimbun Reservoir *483* NW Singapore
Sariwŏn *413* SW North Korea
Sark *623* island of SE Guernsey
Sarpsborg *414* S Norway
Sarrebruck *see* Saarbrücken
Sarstoon *102, 250 var.* Sarstún. River of Belize and Guatemala
Sarstún *see* Sarstoon
Sarthe *225* river of NW France
Saruhan *see* Manisa
Sarykol'skiy Khrebet *see* Sarikol Range
Sary-Tash *325 var.* Sary-Taš. SW Kyrgyzstan

Sasebo *304* Kyūshū, SW Japan
Saseno *see* Sazan
Saskatchewan *146* river of C Canada
Saskatchewan *146* province of C Canada
Saskatoon *146* SW Canada
Sasolburg *493* Orange Free State, C South Africa
Sassandra *300* S Ivory Coast
Sassandra *300 var.* Ibo. River of S Ivory Coast
Sassari *294* Sardegna, W Italy
Sasstown *336* SE Liberia
Sataua *596* Savai'i, Western Samoa
Satawal *375* island of C Micronesia
Satawan *375* atoll of C Micronesia
Sātkhira *93* SW Bangladesh
Satpura Range *270* mountains of C India
Satu Mare *448 Hung.* Szatmárnémeti. NW Romania
Satunan-shotō *304* island group of Nansei-shotō, SW Japan
Sau *see* Sava
Sauce *see* Juan L. Lacaze
Saudhárkrókur *268* N Iceland
Saudi Arabia *472-475* officially Kingdom of Saudi Arabia. Country of SW Asia divided into 13 admin. units (provinces)
Saül *621* C French Guiana
Saulkrasti *330* N Latvia
Sault Sainte Marie *147* S Canada
Sauma, Pointe *629* headland of Île Alofi, N Wallis & Futuna
Saûmâtre, Étang *258* lake of SE Haiti
Saurimo *64* *Port.* Vila Henrique de Carvalho. NE Angola
Sauteurs *248* N Grenada island, Grenada
Sava *116, 181, 486, 602 Eng.* Save, *Hung.* Száva, *Ger.* Sau. River of SE Europe
Savai'i *596* island of NW Western Samoa
Savalou *108* S Benin
Savan Island *466* island of S St Vincent & the Grenadines
Savannah *569* Georgia, SE USA
Savannakhét *327* S Laos
Savanna-la-Mar *303* W Jamaica
Savave *553* islet of Nukufetau, Tuvalu
Save *387, 612 var.* Sabi. River of Mozambique and Zimbabwe
Savè *108* SE Benin
Savissivik *622* NW Greenland
Savona *294* N Italy
Savonlinna *221 Swe.* Nyslott. SE Finland
Savusavu *218* Vanua Levu, N Fiji
Savu Sea *see* Sawu, Laut
Savute *118* river of N Botswana
Sawdā', Jabal *472* mountain of SW Saudi Arabia
Sawdā, Jabal as *339* mountain range of C Libya
Sawdirī *see* Sodiri
Sawhaj *see* Sohâg
Şawqirah *418* SE Oman
Şawqirah, Ghubbat *see* Suqrah Bay
Sawu, Laut *276 Eng.* Savu Sea. Sea of the Indian Ocean, C Indonesia
Say *407* SW Niger
Sayaboury *see* Muang Xaignabouri
Sayat *551* E Turkmenistan
Sayhūt *599* E Yemen
Saylac *490 var.* Zeila. NW Somalia
Saynshand *380* S Mongolia
Say 'ūn *599 var.* Saywūn. C Yemen
Sazan *57 It.* Saseno. Island of SW Albania
Scaldis *see* Scheldt
Scarborough *563* NE England, UK
Scarborough *540* S Tobago, Trinidad & Tobago
Scarborough *97* S Barbados
Scebeli *see* Shebeli
Schaan *342* W Liechtenstein

Sissek *see* Sisak
Sīstān, Daryācheh-ye *281*
    var. Hāmūn-e Şāberī,
    Daryācheh-ye Hāmūn. Lake of E Iran
Sisters, The *248* islands N of Grenada
    island, Grenada
Siteki *510* *var.* Stegi. E Swaziland
Sithoniá *245* peninsula of NE Greece
Sitobela *510* S Swaziland
Sitona *210* SW Eritrea
Sitrah *91* *var.* Sitra. Island of
    NE Bahrain
Sittang *135* *var.* Sittoung. River of
    C Burma
Sittard *397* S Netherlands
Sitten *see* Sion
Sittwe *135* *prev.* Akyab. W Burma
Siuna *404* NE Nicaragua
Sivas *547* C Turkey
Sivers'kyy Donets' *see* Donets
Six Counties, the *see* Northern Ireland
Siyäzän *86* *Rus.* Siazan'.
    NE Azerbaijan
Sjælland *190* *Ger.* Seeland,
    Eng. Zealand. Island of E Denmark
Skadar *see* Shkodër
Skadarsko Jezero *see* Scutari, Lake
Skagaströnd *268*
    prev. Höfdhakaupstadhur. N Iceland
Skagen *190* Jylland, N Denmark
Skagerrak *190, 414, 513*
    var. Skagerak. Area of the Baltic Sea
Skalica *485* *Hung.* Sellye. W Slovakia
Skeleton Coast *391* coastal region of
    NW Namibia
Skellefteå *513* NE Sweden
Skellefteälv *513* river of N Sweden
Skien *414* S Norway
Skikda *59* *prev.* Philippeville.
    NE Algeria
Skíros *245* island of E Greece
Skive *190* Jylland, NW Denmark
Skjálfandafljót *268* river of C Iceland
Skjern *190* Jylland, W Denmark
Skjern Å *190* river of W Denmark
Skon *141* S Cambodia
Skopje *349* *prev.* Skoplje,
    Turk. Üsküb. ❖ of FYR Macedonia,
    N FYR Macedonia
Skoplje *see* Skopje
Skövde *513* S Sweden
Skrunda *330* W Latvia
Skúvoy *620* island of C Faeroe Islands
Skye, Isle of *563* island of W Scotland,
    UK
Slagelse *190* Sjælland, SE Denmark
Slaney *288* *Ir.* An tSláine. River of
    SE Ireland
Slatina *see* Podravska Slatina
Slatina *448* S Romania
Slave Coast *537* coastal region of
    W Africa, Atlantic Ocean
Slavonska Požega *181* *prev.* Požega,
    Hung. Pozsega. NE Croatia
Slavonski Brod *181* *prev.* Brod,
    Hung. Bród. E Croatia
Slavyansk *see* Slov"yans'k
Sléibhte Chill Mhantáin
    see Wicklow Mountains
Slēmānī *see* As Sulaymānīyah
Sliema *363* N Malta
Sligo *288* *Ir.* Sligeach. N Ireland
Sliven *128* *var.* Slivno. E Bulgaria
Slobozia *448* SE Romania
Slobozia *376* *Rus.* Slobodzeya.
    E Moldavia
Slonim *104* *Rus.* Slonin. W Belorussia
Slovakia *484-485* officially Slovenská
    Republika, *prev.* constituent republic
    of Czecholsovakia. Country of
    C Europe divided into 4 admin.
    regions (kraj)
Slovenia *486-487* officially Republic
    of Slovenia, *Slvn.* Slovenija.
    Country divided into 62 admin.
    units (občina)
Slovenské Rudohorie *485*
    Ger. Slowakisches Erzgebirge,
    var. Ungarisches Erzgebirge.
    Mountain range of C Slovakia

Slov"yans'k *556* *Rus.* Slavyansk.
    E Ukraine
Słupsk *439* *Ger.* Stolp. N Poland
Slutsk *104* C Belorussia
Smallwood Reservoir *147* lake of
    S Canada
Smarhon' *104* NW Belorussia
Smederevo *602* *Ger.* Semendria.
    N Serbia, Yugoslavia
Smila *556* C Ukraine
Smith's Island *619* island of
    E Bermuda
Smithson Bight *620* bay of the Indian
    Ocean on the S coast of Christmas
    Island
Smolensk *452* W Russia
Smolyan *128* *var.* Smoljan,
    prev. Pashmakli. SW Bulgaria
Smyrna *see* İzmir
Snaefell *623* mountain of C Isle of Man
Snake *568* river of NW USA
Sneeuw-gebergte
    see Maoke, Pegunungan
Sněžk *188* *Ger.* Schneekoppe.
    Mountain of N Czech Republic
Snow Mountains
    see Maoke, Pegunungan
Snug Corner *248* SW Grenada island,
    Grenada
Snuŏl *141* E Cambodia
Soacha *171* C Colombia
Sobaek-sanmaek *496* mountain range
    of S South Korea
Sobat *506* river of Ethiopia and Sudan
Sobradinho, Represa de *121*
    var. Barragem de Sobradinho.
    Reservoir of E Brazil
Soča *295, 486* *It.* Isonzo. River of Italy
    and Slovenia
Socabaya *431* SE Peru
Sochi *452* SW Russia
Société, Îles de la *622* island group of
    W French Polynesia
Socotra *see* Suquţrá
Soc Trăng *593* *var.* Khanh,
    Hung. S Vietnam
Sodankylä *221* N Finland
Södertälje *513* SE Sweden
Sodiri *506* *var.* Sawdirī, Sodari.
    C Sudan
Sodo *215* *var.* Soddo, Soddu.
    SW Ethiopia
Soekaboemi *see* Sukabumi
Soela Väin *212* strait of Baltic Sea,
    between the islands of Hiiumaa and
    Saaremaa, W Estonia
Soembawa *see* Sumbawa
Soerabaja *see* Surabaya
Soerakarta *see* Surakarta
Sofala, Baía de *387* Bay of Indian
    Ocean, off Mozambique
Sofia *350* seasonal river of
    NW Madagascar
Sofia *128* *var.* Sofija, *Bul.* Sofiya.
    ❖ of Bulgaria, W Bulgaria
Sogamoso *171* C Colombia
Sognefjorden *414* fjord of
    SW Norway
Sohâg *202* *var.* Sawhaj. C Egypt
Sŏjosŏn-man *413* inlet of Korea Bay ,
    on W coast of N Korea
Sokch'o *496* N South Korea
Söke *547* SW Turkey
Sokhumi *234* *Rus.* Sukhumi.
    NW Georgia
Sokodé *537* C Togo
Sokoto *408* NW Nigeria
Sokoto *408* river of NW Nigeria
Sola *414* SW Norway
Solapur *270* *var.* Sholapur.
    SW India
Sol, Costa del *501* coastal region of
    S Spain
Soldeu *62* NE Andorra
Soledad *589* E Venezuela
Soledad *171* N Colombia
Soleure *see* Solothurn
Soligorsk *see* Salihorsk
Solimões *121* local name for a stretch
    of the Amazon river, NW Brazil

Solin *181* *It.* Salona. S Croatia
Solingen *236* W Germany
Sollum, Gulf of *202*
    Ar. Khalīj as Sallūm. Gulf of the
    Mediterranean Sea, NW Egypt
Solokov *188* NW Czech Republic
Sololá *250* W Guatemala
Solomon Islands *488-489*
    prev. British Solomon Islands
    Protectorate. Country of the South
    Pacific Ocean divided into 7 admin.
    units (provinces)
Solomon Sea *426, 488* sea of the
    Pacific Ocean, to the E of Papua
    New Guinea
Solothurn *516* *Fr.* Soleure.
    NW Switzerland
Solway Firth *563* arm of the Irish Sea,
    W UK
Solwezi *611* NW Zambia
Solyn *see* Thessaloníki
Soma *233* C Gambia
Somalia *490-491* officially Soomaaliya,
    prev. Somaliland Protectorate, Italian
    Somaliland. Country of E Africa
    divided into 16 admin. units (regions)
Sombor *602* *Hung.* Zombor.
    NW Serbia, Yugoslavia
Somerset *619* Somerset Island,
    W Bermuda
Somerset Island *619* island of
    W Bermuda
Somerset Island *146* island of
    N Canada
Somerset Nile *see* Victoria Nile
Someş *264, 448* *Hung.* Szamos,
    Ger. Samosch. River of Hungary and
    Romania
Somme *225* river of N France
Somosomo *218* Taveuni, N Fiji
Somotillo *404* NW Nicaragua
Somoto *404* NW Nicaragua
Soná *424* SW Panama
Sonaco *254* NE Guinea-Bissau
Sonda des Vieques *627* bay of the
    Caribbean Sea, E Puerto Rico
Sønderborg *190* *Ger.* Sonderburg.
    Als, S Denmark
Søndre Strømfjord *622*
    var. Kangerlussuaq. SW Greenland
Songea *530* S Tanzania
Songhua Jiang *see* Sungari
Sŏngjin *see* Kimch'aek
Songkhla *533* *Mal.* Singora.
    S Thailand
Sŏngnam *496* *var.* Seongnam.
    NW South Korea
Songnim *413* SW North Korea
Songo *387* NW Mozambique
Songt'an *496* NW South Korea
Sông Tiên Giang *see* Mekong
Songwe *353* river of Malawi and
    Tanzania
Sonmiāni Bay *421* bay of the Arabian
    Sea, on the S coast of Pakistan
Sonsonate *207* W El Salvador
Sonsori Islands *627* island group of
    Palau
Soochow *see* Suzhou
Soomaaliya *see* Somalia
Soome Laht *see* Finland, Gulf of
Sop Hao *327* NE Laos
Sopron *264* *Ger.* Ödenburg.
    NW Hungary
Sôp Xai *327* NE Laos
Sórd Choluim Chille *see* Swords
Soria *501* N Spain
Soriano *577* W Uruguay
Soro *see* Ghazal
Sorø *190* Sjælland, SE Denmark
Soroca *376* *Rus.* Soroki. N Moldavia
Sorocaba *121* S Brazil
Sorol *375* atoll of W Micronesia
Soroti *554* C Uganda
Sørøya *414* *var.* Sørøy. Island of
    N Norway
Sŏsan *496* *Jap.* Zuisan.
    W South Korea

Sosnowiec *439* *Ger.* Sosnowitz.
    S Poland
Sota *108* river of NE Benin
Sotavento, Ilhas de *152* southernmost
    of the two main island groups
    comprising Cape Verde
Sotouboua *537* C Togo
Souanké *176* NW Congo
Soubré *300* S Ivory Coast
Soueida *see* As Suwaydā'
Soufrière *196* S Dominica
Soufrière *465* W St Lucia
Soufrière Hills *625* mountain range,
    E Montserrat
Souillac *368* S Mauritius
Souk Ahras *59* NE Algeria
Soukhné *see* As Sukhnah
Sŏul *see* Seoul
Sound, The *513* *Swe.* Öresund,
    Nor. Øresund. Strait between
    Denmark and Sweden, connecting
    the Baltic Sea and Kattegat
Soûr *332* *var.* Şūr. SW Lebanon
Sousse *543* *var.* Sūsah. N Tunisia
South Africa *492-495* officially
    Republic of South Africa. Country of
    southern Africa, divided into 9 admin.
    units (provinces)
Southampton *563* S England, UK
Southampton Island *147* island of
    N Canada
South Andaman *270* island of the
    Andaman Islands, SE India
South Australia *77* state of S Australia
South Bend *569* Indiana, C USA
South Caicos *629* island of C Turks
    and Caicos Islands
South Carolina *569* state of SE USA
South Carpathians *see* Carpaţii
    Meridionali
South China Sea *354, 435, 483, 525,*
    593 *Ind.* Laut Cina Selatan,
    Chin. Nan Hai, *Vtn.* Biên Đông.
    Sea of the Pacific Ocean
South Comino Channel
    see Malta, Il-Fliegu ta'
South Dakota *569* state of NC USA
South East China *166* region of
    SE China
South East Head *628* headland on the
    E coast of Ascension Island
Southeast Island *629* Tagula Island
Southend-on-Sea *563* SE England,
    UK
Southern Alps *401* mountains of
    N South Island, New Zealand
Southern Cook Islands *620* island
    group of S Cook Islands
Southern Uplands *563* mountain
    range of S Scotland, UK
South Hill Village *618* C Anguilla
South Huvadhu Atoll *358*
    var. Gaafu Dhaalu Atoll. Atoll of
    S Maldives
South Island *620* *var.* Pulu Atas.
    Island of SE Cocos Islands
South Island *401* southernmost of
    the two main islands that comprise
    New Zealand
South Island *316* NW Kenya
South Korea *496-499* officially
    Republic of South Korea,
    Kor. Taehan. Country of E Asia
    divided into 9 admin. units
    (provinces)
South Maalhosmadulu Atoll *358*
    var. Baa Atoll. Atoll of N Maldives
South Miladummadulu Atoll *358*
    atoll of N Maldives
South Nilandhe Atoll *358*
    var. Dhaalu Atoll. Atoll of C Maldives
South Orkney Islands *66* island group
    to the NE of Antarctic Peninsula,
    Antarctica
South Point *628* headland on the
    S coast of Ascension Island
South Point *620* headland on the
    S coast of Christmas Island
South Rukuru *353* river of
    NW Malawi

South Saskatchewan *146* river of SW Canada

South Shetland Islands *66* island group to the W of Antarctic Peninsula, Antarctica

South Sound *619* Virgin Gorda, E British Virgin Islands

South Taranaki Bight *401* area of the Tasman Sea, SW of North Island, New Zealand

South Town *620* Little Cayman, C Cayman Islands

South Uist *563* island of Outer Hebrides, NW Scotland, UK

South West Bay *628* bay of the South Atlantic Ocean on the SW coast of Ascension Island

Sowa *118* var. Sua. NE Botswana

Soweto *493* Pretoria-Witwatersrand-Vereeniging, NE South Africa

Soyang-ho *496* reservoir of N South Korea

Sozh *104* river of NE Europe

Spain *500-503* officially Kingdom of Spain, *Sp.* España. Country of SW Europe divided into 18 admin. units (autonomous communities, comprised of 50 provinces)

Spalato *see* Split

Spaldings *303* C Jamaica

Spanish Point *68* S Barbuda, Antigua & Barbuda

Spanish Town *619* Virgin Gorda, E British Virgin Islands

Spanish Town *303* SE Jamaica

Spanish Wells *88* Eleuthera I, Bahamas

Spartanburg *569* South Carolina, SE USA

Spárti *245* *Eng.* Sparta. S Greece

Speedwell Island *621* island of S Falkland Islands

Speery Island *628* island of SW St Helena

Speightstown *97* N Barbados

Spence Bay *146* N Canada

Spencer Gulf *77* gulf of S Australia

Spey *563* river of NE Scotland, UK

Spice Islands *see* Maluku

Spiez *516* W Switzerland

Spijkenisse *397* SW Netherlands

Spīn Būldak *53* S Afghanistan

Spišská Nová Ves *485* *Ger.* Zipser Neudorf, *Hung.* Igló. E Slovakia

Spitak *74* NW Armenia

Spitsbergen *629* island of NW Svalbard

Spittal an der Drau *82* var. Spittal. S Austria

Split *181* *It.* Spalato. S Croatia

Spokane *568* Washington, NW USA

Spot Bay *620* Cayman Brac, NE Cayman Islands

Spratly Island *628* island of Spratly Islands

Spratly Islands *628* Disputed island group of the South China Sea

Spree *237* river of E Germany

Springfield *569* Illinois, C USA

Springfield *569* Massachusetts, NE USA

Springfield *569* Missouri, C USA

Spring Garden *256* NE Guyana

Springs *493* Pretoria-Witwatersrand-Vereeniging, NE South Africa

Springs *248* SW Grenada island, Grenada

Srbija *see* Serbia, Yugoslavia

Srê Âmbĕl *141* SW Cambodia

Srebrenica *116* E Bosnia & Herzegovina

Sredna Gora *128* mountain range of Bulgaria

Srednesibirskoye Ploskogor'ye *453* *Eng.* Central Siberian Plateau, *var.* Central Siberian Uplands. Large upland area of C Russia

Sreng *141* river of NW Cambodia

Srêpôk *141* river of Cambodia and Vietnam

Sri Jayawardenapura *504* prev. Kotte. Suburb of Colombo and admin. ❖ of Sri Lanka, W Sri Lanka

Sri Lanka *504-505* officially Democratic Socialist Republic of Sri Lanka, *prev.* Ceylon. Country of South Asia divided into 25 admin. units (districts)

Srimongal *93* E Bangladesh

Srīnagar *270* N India

Ssu-ch'uan *see* Sichuan

Ssu-p'ing *see* Siping

Ssu-p'ing-chieh *see* Siping

Stacklen *see* Strenči

Stadskanaal *397* NE Netherlands

Stäfa *516* NE Switzerland

Stalin *see* Braşov

Stalin *see* Varna

Stalinabad *see* Dushanbe

Stalingrad *see* Volgograd

Stalino *see* Donets'k

Stalin Peak *see* Kommunizma, Pik

Stalin Peak *see* Musala

Stalinsk *see* Novokuznetsk

Stampriet *391* S Namibia

Stamsund *414* NE Norway

Stange *414* S Norway

Stanislav *see* Ivano-Frankivs'k

Stanke Dimitrov *see* Dupnitsa

Stanley *see* Chek Chue

Stanley Pool *176*, *607* var. Pool Malebo. Expanded section of the Congo river between Congo and Zaire

Stanleyville *see* Kisangani

Stann Creek *see* Dangriga

Stanovoy Khrebet *453* mountain range of E Russia

Stara Kanjiža *see* Kanjiža

Stara Planina *see* Balkan Mountains

Stara Zagora *128* C Bulgaria

Starbuck Island *320* island of the Line Is, E Kiribati

Staten Island *see* Estados, Isla de los

Station Hill *97* SW Barbados

Stavanger *414* SW Norway

Stavropol' *452* prev. Voroshilovsk. SW Russia

Stavropol' *see* Tol'yatti

Steels Point *626* headland of E Norfolk Island

Stefanie, Lake *see* Ch'ew Bahir

Steffisburg *516* W Switzerland

Stegi *see* Siteki

Stein *see* Kamnik

Steinamanger *see* Szombathely

Steinkjer *414* C Norway

Steirisch *82* mountain range of C Austria

Stendal *237* C Germany

Stende *330* NW Latvia

Stepanakert *see* Xankändi

Step'anavan *74* N Armenia

Sterlitamak *452* W Russia

Stettin *see* Szczecin

Stettiner Haff *see* Oderhaff

Stewart Island *401* island to the S of South Island, New Zealand

Steyr *82* N Austria

Stif *see* Sétif

Štip *349* E FYR Macedonia

Stirling *563* C Scotland, UK

Stjørdal *414* C Norway

Stockerau *82* NE Austria

Stockholm *513* ❖ of Sweden, SE Sweden

Stockton-on-Tees *563* NE England, UK

Stoelmanseiland *508* E Surinam

Stoke-on-Trent *563* C England, UK

Stolp *see* Słupsk

Stonyhill Point *628* headland on the S coast of Tristan da Cunha

Stony Tunguska *see* Podkamennaya Tunguska

Stóra Dimun *620* island of S Faeroe Islands

Storbælt *190* *Eng.* Great Belt, var. Store Bælt. Channel between Fyn and Sjælland Denmark

Store Heddinge *190* Sjælland, E Denmark

Støren *414* C Norway

Storfjorden *629* area of the Greenland Sea, S Svalbard

Stornoway *563* Isle of Lewis, Outer Hebrides, NW Scotland, UK

Strakonice *188* SW Czech Republic

Stralsund *237* N Germany

Stranraer *563* SW Scotland, UK

Strasbourg *225* *Ger.* Strassburg. NE France

Strǎşeni *376* var. Strasheny. C Moldavia

Strassburg *see* Strasbourg

Stratford-upon-Avon *563* C England, UK

Strenči *330* *Ger.* Stacklen. NE Latvia

Streymoy *620* var. Strømø. Island of N Faeroe Islands

Strickland *426* river of W Papua New Guinea

Strimón *245* var. Strimon, Strimónas. River of Bulgaria and Greece

Struer *190* Jylland, W Denmark

Struga *349* SW FYR Macedonia

Struma *128* *Gk* Strimon, var. Strymon. River of Bulgaria and Greece

Strumeshnitsa *see* Strumica

Strumica *349* E FYR Macedonia

Strumica *349* var. Strumitsa, *Bul.* Strumeshnitsa. River of Bulgaria and FYR Macedonia

Strumitsa *see* Strumica

Strymon *see* Struma

Stuart Peak *493* mountain of Central Marion Island, South Africa

Stubbs *466* SE St Vincent, St Vincent & the Grenadines

Studen Kladenets, Yazovir *128* reservoir of Bulgaria

Stuhlweissenburg *see* Székesfehérvár

Štúrovo *485* prev. Parkan, *Hung.* Párkány. S Slovakia

Stuttgart *236*, *241* SW Germany

Stykkishólmur *268* W Iceland

Sua *see* Sowa

Su-ao *525* *Jap.* Suō. NE Taiwan

Subic Bay *434* bay of South China Sea, Luzon, N Philippines

Subotica *602* *Hung.* Szabadka, *Ger.* Maria-Theresiopel. N Serbia, Yugoslavia

Suceava *448* *Ger.* Suczawa. NE Romania

Suchow *see* Suzhou

Sucre *112* ❖ (judicial & legal) of Bolivia, S Bolivia

Suczawa *see* Suceava

Sud, Canal de *258* channel of the Caribbean Sea between Île de la Gonâve and Haiti

Sudan *506-507* officially Republic of Sudan, *prev.* Anglo-Egyptian Sudan. Country of NE Africa divided into 9 admin. units (states)

Sudan *132* physical region of C Africa, composed of desert region, plains and grassy steppes

Sudbury *147* S Canada

Sudd *506* swamp region of S Sudan

Suddie *256* NE Guyana

Sudeten *188*, *439* var. Sudetenland, Sudetes, Sudetic Mountains, *Cz./Pol.* Sudety. Mountain range of Czech Republic and Poland

Sudharam *see* Noākhāli

Suduroy *620* var. Suderø. Island of S Faeroe Islands

Suðuroyarfjørdhur *620* strait between Suðuroy and Sandoy, C Faeroe Islands

Sudong, Pulau *483* island of SW Singapore

Sudostroy *see* Severodvinsk

Sue *506* river of S Sudan

Sue Wood Bay *619* bay of the North Atlantic Ocean, C Bermuda

Suez *202* *Ar.* As Suways, var. El Suweis. NE Egypt

Suez Canal *202* *Ar.* Qanāt as Suways. Canal of NE Egypt

Suez, Gulf of *202* *Ar.* Khalīj al 'Aqabah. Gulf of the Red Sea, to the NE of Egypt

Sūf *310* NW Jordan

Sugar Loaf *248* var. Levera Island. N of Grenada island, Grenada

Şuḩār *418* var. Sohar. NW Oman

Sühbaatar *380* N Mongolia

Suigen *see* Suwŏn

Suir *288* *Ir.* An tSiúir. River of S Ireland

Sukabumi *276* prev. Soekaboemi. Java, C Indonesia

Sukagawa *304* Honshū, N Japan

Sukarnapura *see* Jayapura

Sukarno, Puntjak *see* Jaya, Puncak

Sukhne *see* As Sukhnah

Sukhumi *see* Sokhumi

Suki *506* E Sudan

Sukkertoppen *622* var. Maniitsoq. SW Greenland

Sukkur *421* S Pakistan

Sukuta *233* W Gambia

Sulaimaniya *see* As Sulaymānīyah

Sulaimān Range *421* mountain range of C Pakistan

Sula, Kepulauan *276* prev. Xulla Islands, Soela. Island group to the E of Celebes, E Indonesia

Sulawesi *see* Celebes

Sulawesi, Laut *see* Celebes Sea

Sulby *623* N Isle of Man

Sullana *431* NW Peru

Sullivan Island *see* Lanbi Island

Sultan Alonto, Lake *see* Lanao, Lake

Sulu Archipelago *435* island group of SW Philippines

Sulu Sea *355*, *435* sea of the Pacific Ocean, to the NE of Borneo, Malaysia

Sulyukta *325* *Kir.* Sülüktü. SW Kyrgyzstan

Sumatera *see* Sumatra

Sumatra *276* var. Sumatera. Island of W Indonesia

Šumava *see* Bohemian Forest

Sumba *620* Suðuroy, S Faeroe Islands

Sumba *276* prev. Soemba, *Eng.* Sandalwood Island. Island of Nusa Tenggara, C Indonesia

Sumba, Selat *276* strait of the Indian Ocean between Sumba and Sumbawa, C Indonesia

Sumbawa *276* prev. Soembawa. Island of Nusa Tenggara, C Indonesia

Sumbawanga *530* W Tanzania

Sumbe *64* *Port.* Novo Redondo. W Angola

Sumbuya *480* S Sierra Leone

Šumen *see* Shumen

Sumisu-jima *304* island to the SE of Honshū, SE Japan

Šumperk *188* *Ger.* Mährisch-Schönberg. E Czech Republic

Sumpul *207* river of Honduras and El Salvador

Sumqayıt *86* *Rus.* Sumgait. E Azerbaijan

Sumy *556* NE Ukraine

Sunan *413* NW North Korea

Sunch'ŏn *413* SW North Korea

Sunch'ŏn *496* *Jap.* Junten. S South Korea

Sunda, Selat *276* strait connecting Indian Ocean and Laut Jawa between Java and Sumatra, W Indonesia

Sunderland *563* NE England, UK

Sundsvall *513* C Sweden

Sungai Seletar Reservoir *483* reservoir of N Singapore

Sungari *163 Chin.* Songhua Jiang. River of NE China
Sun Koshi *395* river of E Nepal
Suntar-Khayata, Khrebet *453* mountain range of NE Russia
Sunyani *242* W Ghana
Sunzu *611* mountain NE Zambia
Suō *see* Su-ao
Suomenlahti *see* Finland, Gulf of
Suomenselkä *221* physical region of C Finland
Suŏng *141* SE Cambodia
Superior de Tristaina, Estany *62* lake of NW Andorra
Superior, Lake *147, 569 Fr.* Lac Supérieur. Lake of Canada and USA
Sup'ung-ho *413* reservoir of China and North Korea
Sūq 'Abs *see* 'Abs
Sūq ash Shuyūkh *284* SE Iraq
Suqrah Bay *418* Bay of the Arabian Sea, SE Oman
Suquṭrā *599 Eng.* Socotra. Island of SE Yemen, off the Horn of Africa
Şūr *418* NE Oman
Surabaya *276 prev.* Surabaja, Soerabaja. Java, C Indonesia
Surakarta *276 prev.* Soerakarta. Java, C Indonesia
Šurany *485 Hung.* Nagysurány. SW Slovakia
Sūrat *270* W India
Surat Thani *533* S Thailand
Sûre *346* river of W Europe
Sure, Lagh *316* dry watercourse of NE Kenya
Surin *533* E Thailand
Surinam *368* S Mauritius
Surinam *508-509* officially Republic of Surinam, *var.* Suriname. Country of Central America divided into 8 admin. units (provinces)
Surinam *97* E Barbados
Surkhet *see* Birendranagar
Surkhob *528* river of C Tajikistan
Şurmān *339* NW Libya
Surt *339 var.* Sidra, Sirte. N Libya
Surt, Khalīj *339 var.* Gulf of Sirte, Gulf of Sidra. Gulf of the Mediterranean Sea, off N coast of Libya
Sūsah *see* Sousse
Susana *254* W Guinea-Bissau
Susuman *453* Ostrov Sakhalin, E Russia
Sutlej *421* river of India and Pakistan
Suure-Jaani *212 Ger.* Gross-Sankt-Johannis. C Estonia
Suur Munamägi *212 var.* Munamägi. Mountain of SE Estonia
Suur Väin *212* strait of the Baltic Sea, between the mainland and the island of Muhu, W Estonia
Suva *218* ❖ of Fiji, Viti Levu, W Fiji
Suwa *210* SE Eritrea
Suwarrow *620* island of Northern Cook Islands, N Cook Islands
Suwayhān *560* E United Arab Emirates
Suways, Qanāt as *see* Suez Canal
Suwŏn *496 var.* Suweon, *Jap.* Suigen. NW South Korea
Suzhou *163 var.* Soochow, Su-chou, Suchow, *prev.* Wuhsien. Jiangsu, E China
Suzuka *304* Honshū, C Japan
Svalbard *629* Norwegian dependency of the Greenland Sea
Svätý Kríž nad Hronom *see* Žiar nad Hronom
Svay Chék *141* river of Cambodia and Thailand
Svay Riĕng *141* SE Cambodia
Svendborg *190* Fyn, S Denmark
Sverdlovsk *see* Yekaterinburg
Sverdrup Islands *146* island group of N Canada

Sveti Nikole *349 prev.* Sveti Nikola. C FYR Macedonia
Svetlogorsk *see* Svyetlahorsk
Svetozarevo *602 prev.* Jagodina. C Serbia, Yugoslavia
Svilengrad *128 prev.* Mustafa-Pasha. SE Bulgaria
Svínoy *620 var.* Svinø. Island of NE Faeroe Islands
Svishtov *128 var.* Svištov. N Bulgaria
Svitavy *188* E Czech Republic
Svyetlahorsk *104 Rus.* Svetlogorsk. SE Belorussia
Swabian Jura *see* Schwäbische Alb
Swakopmund *391* W Namibia
Swallow Islands *488* small island group within Santa Cruz Is, E Solomon Is
Swan *76* river of SW Australia
Swansea *563 Wel.* Abertawe. S Wales, UK
Swatow *see* Shantou
Swaziland *510-511* officially Kingdom of Swaziland. Country of southern Africa divided into 4 admin. units (districts)
Sweden *512-515* officially Kingdom of Sweden, *Swe.* Sverige. Country of Scandinavia divided into 24 admin. units (läns)
Swedru *see* Agona Swedru
Swetes *68* S Antigua, Antigua & Barbuda
Swift Current *146* SW Canada
Swindon *563* C England, UK
Swiss Plateau *516 Ger.* Schweizer Mittelland. Plateau of W Switzerland
Switzerland *516-519* officially Swiss Confederation, *Ger.* Schweiz, *It.* Svizzera. Country of C Europe divided into 26 admin. units (cantons)
Swords *288 Ir.* Sórd Choluim Chille. E Ireland
Syaphrubesi *395 var.* Syabrubensi. C Nepal
Sydney *77, 81* SE Australia
Sydney *147* Cape Breton Island, SE Canada
Sydney Island *see* Manra
Syktyvkar *452 prev.* Ust'-Sisol'sk. NW Russia
Sylhet *93* NE Bangladesh
Syowa *66* Japanese research station of Greater Antarctica, Antarctica
Syracuse *569* New York, NE USA
Syracuse *see* Siracusa
Syr Darya *312, 528, 580 Rus.* Syrdar'ya, *Kaz.* Syrdariya, *Uzb.* Sirdaryo. River of C Asia
Syrdar'ya *see* Syr Darya
Syria *521-523* officially Syrian Arab Republic, *Ar.* Suriyah. Country divided into 13 admin. units (governorates)
Syriam *135* S Burma
Syrian Desert *284, 310, 521 Ar.* Bādiyat ash Shām. Desert of SW Asia
Syvash, Zatoka *556* inlet of the Sea of Azov
Szabadka *see* Subotica
Szamos *see* Someş
Szatmárnémeti *see* Satu Mare
Szczecin *439 Ger.* Stettin. NW Poland
Szczeciński, Zalew *see* Oderhaff
Szechuan *see* Sichuan
Szeged *264 Ger.* Szegedin. SE Hungary
Székesfehérvár *264 Ger.* Stuhlweissenburg. W Hungary
Szekszárd *264* S Hungary
Szenice *see* Senica
Szentes *264* SE Hungary
Szeping *see* Siping
Szered *see* Sered
Sziszek *see* Sisak

Szlatina *see* Podravska Slatina
Szolnok *264* C Hungary
Szombathely *264 Ger.* Steinamanger. W Hungary
Sztálinváros *see* Dunaújváros

T

Tabac *368* river of S Mauritius
Tabaqah *521* N Syria
Tabaquite *540* C Trinidad, Trinidad & Tobago
Tabarka *543 var.* Tabarqah. NW Tunisia
Tabasará, Serranía de *424* mountain range of W Panama
Tabasco *see* Grijalva
Tabernacle *462* NE St Kitts, St Kitts & Nevis
Tabiteuea *320* island of the Gilbert Is, W Kiribati
Tablas Island *435* island of C Philippines
Table Hill Gordon *68* SE Antigua, Antigua & Barbuda
Tabligbo *537* SE Togo
Tábor *188* SW Czech Republic
Tabora *530* W Tanzania
Tabou *300 var.* Tabu. S Ivory Coast
Tabrīz *281* NW Iran
Tabuaeran *320 var.* Fanning Island. Island of the Line Is, E Kiribati
Tabūk *472* NW Saudi Arabia
Tabwémasana *585* mountain of Espiritu Santo, W Vanuatu
Täby *513* SE Sweden
Ta-chia Hsi *525* river of W Taiwan
Ta-cho-shui *525* E Taiwan
Tacloban *435* Leyte, E Philippines
Tacna *431* SE Peru
Tacoma *568* Washington, NW USA
Tacuarembó *577* N Uruguay
Tacuarembó *577* river of C Uruguay
Tacurupucú *see* Hernandarias
Tademaït, Plateau du *59* plateau of C Algeria
Tadine *626* Maré, Îles Loyauté, E New Caledonia
Tadjoura *194* E Djibouti
Tadjoura, Golfe de *194* inlet of the Gulf of Aden, E of Djibouti
T'aebaek-sanmaek *496* mountain range of North Korea and South Korea
Taedong *413* river of C North Korea
Taegu *496 var.* Daegu, *Jap.* Taikyū. SE South Korea
Taehan-haehyŏp *see* Korea Strait
Taejŏn *496 Jap.* Taiden. C South Korea
Tafahi *538* island of N Tonga
Tafí Viejo *71* NW Argentina
Taftlund *190* Jylland, SW Denmark
Taga *596* Savai'i, Western Samoa
Taganrog, Gulf of *556 Ukr.* Tahanroz'ka Zatoka, *Rus.* Taganrogskiy Zaliv. Gulf of the Sea of Azov, SE Ukraine
Tagarzimat *382* W Western Sahara
Tagiura *see* Tājūrā'
Tagliamento *295* river of N Italy
Tagtabazar *551 prev.* Takhta-Bazar. SE Turkmenistan
Taguasco *182* C Cuba
Taguatinga *121* C Brazil
Tagula Island *426 prev.* Southeast I. Island of SE Papua New Guinea
Tagum *435* river of Mindanao, S Philippines
Tahanroz'ka Zatoka *see* Taganrog, Gulf of
Tahat *59* mountain of SE Algeria
Tahiti *622* island of W French Polynesia
Tahoua *407* W Niger

Taia *480* river of C Sierra Leone
Taiama *480* C Sierra Leone
T'ai-chung *525 Jap.* Taichū. W Taiwan
Taiden *see* Taejŏn
Taieri *401* river of S South Island, New Zealand
Taihoku *see* Taipei
T'ai-hsi *525* W Taiwan
Tai Hu *163* lake of E China
Taikyū *see* Taegu
T'ai-nan *525 Jap.* Tainan. SW Taiwan
Tai O *262* W Hong Kong
Taipa *624* Taipa, C Macao
Taipa *624* island of C Macao
Taipa - Coloane Causeway *624* bridge between Taipa and Coloane islands, S Macao
Tai Pang Wan *see* Mirs Bay
Taipei *525 Chin.* T'ai-pei, *Jap.* Taihoku. ❖ of Taiwan, N Taiwan
Taiping *354* NW Peninsular Malaysia
Tai Po *262* N Hong Kong
T'ai-tung *525 Jap.* Taitō. SE Taiwan
Tai Van *624* bay of the South China Sea, S Macao
Taiwan *524-527* officially Republic of Taiwan. Country of E Asia divided into 16 admin. units (counties)
Taiwan Strait *163, 525 var.* Formosa Strait, *Chin.* T'ai-wan Hai-hsia. Strait connecting East China Sea and South China Sea, between Taiwan and China
Taiyuan *163 var.* T'ai-yuan *prev.* Yangku. Shanxi, N China
Ta'izz *599* SW Yemen
Tajarḥī *339* SW Libya
Tajikistan *528-529* officially Republic of Tajikistan, *Rus.* Tadzhikistan, *Taj.* Jumhurii Tojikiston *prev.* Tajik S.S.R. Country of C Asia divided into 3 admin. units (2 oblasts, 1 autonomous region)
Tajo *see* Tagus
Tajrīsh *281* NW Iran
Tajumulco, Volcán *250* mountain of W Guatemala
Tājūrā' *339 var.* Tagiura, NW Libya
Tak *533 var.* Rahaeng. W Thailand
Taka *364* island of N Marshall Islands
Takamaka *478* Mahé, Seychelles
Takamatsu *304* Shikoku, SW Japan
Takao *see* Kao-hsiung
Takaoka *304* Honshū, C Japan
Takapuna *401* NW North Island, New Zealand
Takasaki *304* Honshū, SE Japan
Takefu *304* Honshū, C Japan
Takêv *141* S Cambodia
Takhiatash *580 Uzb.* Takhiatosh. W Uzbekistan
Takhiatosh *see* Takhiatash
Ta Khmau *141* S Cambodia
Takhta-Bazar *see* Tagtabazar
Takhtakupyr *580 var.* Tahtakupyr, *Uzb.* Takhtaküpir. NW Uzbekistan
Takikawa *305* Hokkaidō, N Japan
Taklimakan Shamo *162* Desert of Xinjiang Uygur Zizhiqu, NW China
Takutea *620* island of Southern Cook Islands, S Cook Islands
Tala *577* S Uruguay
Talamanca, Cordillera de *178, 424* mountain range of Costa Rica and Panama
Talara *431* NW Peru
Talas *325* NW Kyrgyzstan
Talaud, Kepulauan *276* island group to the NE of Celebes, E Indonesia
Talawakele *504* S Sri Lanka
Talca *159* C Chile
Talcahuano *159* C Chile
Taldy-Kurgan *312 Kaz.* Taldyqorghan. SE Kazakhstan
Ta-lien *see* Dalian
T'alin *74 prev.* Verin T'alin. W Armenia

Tocantins *121* river of N Brazil
Tocumen *424* C Panama
Tocuyito *589* NW Venezuela
Todos os Santos, Baía de *121* bay of the Atlantic Ocean, on the E coast of Brazil
Tōen *see* T'ao-yüan
Tofua *538* island of Ha'apai Group, Tonga
Toga *585* Torres Islands, N Vanuatu
Togo *536-537* officially Republic of Togo, *prev.* French Togoland. Country of West Africa divided into 5 admin. units (regions)
Tohoun *537* SE Togo
Tokar *506* var. Ṭawkar. NE Sudan
Tokat *547* N Turkey
Tŏkchŏk-kundo *496* island group of NW South Korea
Tŏkch'ŏn *413* C North Korea
Tokelau *629* New Zealand dependent territory of the Pacific Ocean
Tŏketerebes *see* Trebišov
Tokmak *325* Kir. Tokmok. N Kyrgyzstan
Tōkō *see* Tung-kang
Tokoroa *401* C North Island, New Zealand
Toktogul *325* W Kyrgyzstan
Toku *538* island of N Tonga
Tokuno-shima *304* island of Amami-shotō, SW Japan
Tokushima *304* Shikoku, SW Japan
Tokuyama *304* Honshū, W Japan
Tokwe *612* river of SE Zimbabwe
Tokyo *304, 309* var. Tōkyō.
❖ of Japan, Honshū, SE Japan
Tôlañaro *350* prev. Faradofay, Fort-Dauphin. S Madagascar
Tolbukhin *see* Dobrich
Toledo *112* W Bolivia
Toledo *435* var. Toledo City. Cebu, Philippines
Toledo *569* Ohio, NE USA
Toledo Settlement *102* SE Belize
Toliara *350* var. Toliary, *prev.* Tuléar. SW Madagascar
Tolmin *486* Ger. Tolmein. W Slovenia
Tolo Harbour *262* NE Hong Kong
Tolo, Teluk *276* bay of Laut Banda on the E coast of Celebes, C Indonesia
Tolsan-do *496* island of S South Korea
Toluca *370* var. Toluca de Lerdo. C Mexico
Toluca de Lerdo *see* Toluca
Tol'yatti *452* prev. Stavropol'. W Russia
Toma *132* W Burkina
Tomakomai *305* Hokkaidō, N Japan
Tomanivi *218* var. Mount Victoria. Mountain of Viti Levu, W Fiji
Tomás Gomensoro *577* N Uruguay
Tombali *254* river of SW Guinea-Bissau
Tombeau *368* river of NW Mauritius
Tombouctou *360* Eng. Timbuktu. N Mali
Tombua *64* Port. Porto Alexandre. SW Angola
Tominé *253* river of W Guinea
Tomini, Teluk *276* prev. Teluk Gorontalo. Bay of Laut Maluku on the E coast of Celebes, C Indonesia
Tomsk *453* C Russia
Tomur Feng *see* Pobedy, Pik
Tönder *190* Jylland, SW Denmark
Tonga *538-539* officially Kingdom of Tonga, Friendly Islands. Country of the Pacific Ocean divided into 3 admin units.
Tongatapu *538* island of Tongatapu Group, Tonga
Tongatapu Group *538* island group of S Tonga
Tong Fuk *262* SW Hong Kong
Tonghae *496* NE South Korea
Tong-hae *see* Japan, Sea of
Tonghua *163* Jilin, NE China

Tongjosŏn-man *413* prev. Broughton Bay. Bay of the Sea of Japan on the E coast of North Korea
Tongking, Gulf of *163, 593* Chin. Beibu Wan, Vtn. Vinh Bắc Bô. Gulf of the South China Sea, SE Asia
Tongsa *110* C Bhutan
Tongue of the Ocean *88* strait between Exuma Cays and Andros I, Bahamas
Tônlé Sap *141* Eng. Great Lake. Lake of W Cambodia
Tonosí *424* S Panama
Tønsberg *414* S Norway
Toowoomba *77* E Australia
Topeka *569* Kansas, C USA
Topľa *485* Hung. Toplya. River of NE Slovakia
Toplya *see* Topľa
Topolčany *485* Hung. Nagytapolcsány. W Slovakia
Topolya *see* Bačka Topola
Toraigh *see* Tory Island
Torbeck *258* SW Haiti
Torghay *312* W Kazakhstan
Torino *294* Eng. Turin. N Italy
Torneälv *513* river of NE Sweden
Tornio *221* Swe. Torneå. NW Finland
Torniojoki *221* Swe. Torneälven. River of Finland and Sweden
Torola *207* river of El Salvador and Honduras
Toronto *147, 151* S Canada
Tororo *554* E Uganda
Toros Dağları *see* Taurus Mountains
Torquay *563* SW England, UK
Torre del Greco *295* S Italy
Torrejón, Embalse de *501* reservoir of W Spain
Torrelevega *501* N Spain
Torrens, Lake *77* salt lake of S Australia
Torreón *370* N Mexico
Torres Islands *585* Fr. Îles Torrès. Island group of N Vanuatu
Torres Strait *77, 426* strait connecting the Arafura Sea and Coral Sea, between Australia and the island of New Guinea
Torsa *110* river of SW Bhutan
Tórshavn *620* var. Thorshavn. ❖ of Faeroe Islands, Streymoy, N Faeroe Islands
Torteval *623* SW Guernsey
Tortoise Islands *see* Galapagos Islands
Tortola *619* island of C British Virgin Islands
Tortosa *501* E Spain
Tortue, Île de la *258* var. Tortuga I. Island of N Haiti
Tortue, Montagne *621* mountain range of C French Guiana
Toruń *439* Ger. Thorn. C Poland
Tõrva *212* Ger. Törwa. S Estonia
Tory Island *288* Ir. Toraigh. Island of N Ireland
Torysa *485* Hung. Tarca. River of NE Slovakia
Toscano, Archipelago *294* var. Tuscan Archipelago. Island group of C Italy
Tosco-Emiliano, Appennino *294* mountain range of C Italy
Tōsei *see* Tung-shih
Toshkent *see* Tashkent
Toteng *118* C Botswana
Totness *508* N Surinam
Totonicapán *250* W Guatemala
Totota *336* C Liberia
Totoya *218* island to the SE of Viti Levu, S Fiji
Tottori *304* Honshū, W Japan
Touba *300* W Ivory Coast
Touba *476* W Senegal
Touboro *144* NE Cameroon
Toubkal, Jebel *382* mountain of W Morocco
T'ou-ch'eng *525* NE Taiwan

T'ou-ch'ien Hsi *525* river of NW Taiwan
T'ou-fen *525* NW Taiwan
Tougan *132* W Burkina
Tougana *407* SW Niger
Touggourt *59* NE Algeria
Tougué *253* NW Guinea
Touho *626* Île Balabio, E New Caledonia
Toukoto *360* W Mali
Toulon *225* SE France
Toulouse *225* S France
Toumodi *300* C Ivory Coast
Tou-nan *525* W Taiwan
Toungoo *135* S Burma
Tourane *see* Đa Năng
Tournai *99* Dut. Doornik. W Belgium
Tours *225* NW France
Tovar *589* W Venezuela
Tovuz *86* Rus. Tauz. W Azerbaijan
Towada *304* Honshū, N Japan
Townsville *77* NE Australia
Towraghondī *53* NW Afghanistan
Towuti, Danau *276* lake of Celebes, C Indonesia
Toyama *304* Honshū, C Japan
Toyohara *see* Feng-yüan
Toyohara *see* Yuzhno-Sakhalinsk
Toyohashi *304* Honshū, C Japan
Toyonaka *304* Honshū, C Japan
Toyota *304* Honshū, C Japan
Tozeur *543* var. Tawzar. W Tunisia
Tqibuli *234* Rus. Tkibuli. W Georgia
Tqvarch'eli *234* Rus. Tkvarcheli. NW Georgia
Trabzon *547* Eng. Trebizond. NE Turkey
Trafalgar *196* S Dominica
Tráighlí *see* Tralee
Traiguén *159* C Chile
Traina Garden *see* Mazra'at Turaynā
Traisen *82* river of NE Austria
Trakai *344* SE Lithuania
Tralee *288* Ir. Tráighlí. SW Ireland
Trang *533* S Thailand
Tranqueras *577* N Uruguay
Trans-Alaska pipeline *568* oil pipeline of Alaska, USA
Transantarctic Mountains *66* mountain range of Antarctica
Transkei *Bantustan 'self-governing homeland' of E Cape Province, South Africa; created in 1963, abolished in 1994*
Transylvania *448* cultural region of NW Romania
Transylvanian Alps *see* Carpaţii Meridionali
Trant's Bay *625* bay of the Caribbean Sea on the E coast of Montserrat
Trapani *295* Sicilia, S Italy
Trâpeăng Vêng *141* C Cambodia
Traralgon *77* SE Australia
Trasimeno, Lago *295* var. Lake of Perugia, Ger. Trasimenischersee. Lake of C Italy
Träskända *see* Järvenpää
Traù *see* Trogir
Traun *82* river of N Austria
Traun *82* N Austria
Traunsee *82* var. Gmundner See, Eng. Lake Traun. Lake of N Austria
Trautenau *see* Trutnov
Tra Vinh *593* var. Phu Vinh. S Vietnam
Travnik *116* C Bosnia & Herzegovina
Trbovlje *486* Ger. Trifail. C Slovenia
Treasury Islands *488* island group of W Solomon Is
Třebíč *188* Ger. Trebitsch. S Czech Republic
Trebinje *116* S Bosnia & Herzegovina
Trebišov *485* Hung. Tŏketerebes. E Slovakia
Trebizond *see* Trabzon
Trebnje *486* SE Slovenia
Treinta y Tres *577* E Uruguay
Trelew *71* SE Argentina

Trenčín *485* Ger. Trentschin, Hung. Trencsén. W Slovakia
Treng *141* prev. Treng. NE Cambodia
Trent *563* river of C England, UK
Trento *294* Eng. Trent, Ger. Trient. N Italy
Trenton *569* New Jersey, E USA
Tres Arroyos *71* E Argentina
Treskavica *116* mountain range of SE Bosnia & Herzegovina
Três Marias, Represa *121* reservoir of SE Brazil
Treviso *295* N Italy
Trial Farm *102* N Belize
Triangle *612* S Zimbabwe
Tricaorno *see* Triglav
Trichinopoly *see* Tiruchchiráppalli
Trichūr *270* S India
Trient *see* Trento
Trier *236* W Germany
Triesen *342* SW Liechtenstein
Triesenberg *342* SW Liechtenstein
Trieste *295* Slvn. Trst. N Italy
Trieste, Gulf of *295* It. Golfo di Trieste, Slvn. Tržaški Zaliv, Croat. Tršćanski Zaljev. Gulf to the SW of Slovenia
Trifail *see* Trbovlje
Triglav *486* It. Tricaorno. Mountain of NW Slovenia
Tríkala *245* prev. Trikkala. C Greece
Trikomo *see* Iskele
Trincomalee *504* NE Sri Lanka
Třinec *188* Ger. Trzynietz. SE Czech Republic
Trinidad *112* N Bolivia
Trinidad *540* island of the West Indies which, with Tobago, forms Trinidad & Tobago
Trinidad *577* SW Uruguay
Trinidad and Tobago *540-541* officially Republic of Trinidad and Tobago. Country of the West Indies divided into 6 admin. units (counties)
Trinité, Montagnes de la *621* mountain range of C French Guiana
Triolet *368* NW Mauritius
Trípoli *245* prev. Trípolis. S Greece
Tripoli *332* var. Trâblous, Ṭarābulus. N Lebanon
Tripoli *339* Ar. Ṭarābulus al-Gharb. ❖ of Libya, NW Libya
Tristan da Cunha *628* dependent territory of St Helena, South Atlantic Ocean
Tristao, Îles *253* islands to the W of Guinea
Triton Island *627* island of S Paracel Islands
Trivandrum *270* var. Thiruvananthapuram. S India
Trnava *485* Ger. Tyrnau, Hung. Nagyszombat. W Slovakia
Trobriand Islands *see* Kiriwina Islands
Trogir *181* It. Traù. S Croatia
Troía Peninsula *442* peninsula of W Portugal
Trois-Rivières *147* SE Canada
Trojan *see* Troyan
Trollhättan *513* SW Sweden
Tromsø *414* NE Norway
Trondheim *414* prev. Nidaros, Trondhjem, Ger. Drontheim. C Norway
Trondheimsfjorden *414* fjord of SW Norway
Troodos *see* Olympus, Mount
Troodos Mountains *187* var. Troödos. Mountain range of C Cyprus
Troppau *see* Opava
Trou-du-Nord *258* N Haiti
Troumaka *466* NW St Vincent, St Vincent & the Grenadines
Troyan *128* var. Trojan. NW Bulgaria
Troyes *225* NE France
Tršćanski Zaljev *see* Trieste, Gulf of
Trst *see* Trieste
Truc Giang *see* Bên Tre

Trucial Coast *560* coastal region of the United Arab Emirates
Trucial States
   see United Arab Emirates
Trujillo *260* N Honduras
Trujillo *431* NW Peru
Trujillo *589* NW Venezuela
Trung Phân *593 prev.* Annam. Cultural region of Vietnam
Trunk Island *619* island of C Bermuda
Truro *563* SW England, UK
Trutnov *188 Ger.* Trautenau. NE Czech Republic
Tržaški Zaliv *see* Trieste, Gulf of
Tržič *486 Ger.* Neumarktl. NW Slovenia
Trzynietz *see* Třinec
Tsabong *see* Tshabong
Tsaghkahovit *74* W Armenia
Tsamkong *see* Zhanjiang
Tsangpo *see* Brahmaputra
Tsaratanana, Tangorombohitr' i *350 var.* Massif du Tsaratanana. Mountains of N Madagascar
Tsarigrad *see* Istanbul
Tsaritsyn *see* Volgograd
Tschakathurn *see* Čakovec
Tschenstochau *see* Częstochowa
Tschernembl *see* Črnomelj
Tschorna *see* Mustvee
Tselinograd *see* Akmola
Tseng-wen Hsi *525* river of SW Taiwan
Tsetserleg *380* W Mongolia
Tseung Kwan O *262 Eng.* Junk Bay. E Hong Kong
Tsévié *537* S Togo
Tshabong *118 var.* Tsabong. SW Botswana
Tshane *118* C Botswana
Tshaneni *510* NE Swaziland
Tshangalele, Lac *see* Lufira, Lac de Retenue de la
Tshela *607* W Zaire
Tshikapa *607* SW Zaire
Tshohoha Sud, Lac *see* Cyohoha Sud, Lac
Tshuapa *607* river of C Zaire
Tsinan *see* Jinan
Tsing Hai *see* Qinghai Hu
Tsinghai *see* Qinghai
Tsingtao *see* Qingdao
Tsing Yi *262* W Hong Kong
Tsingyuan *see* Baoding
Tsinkiang *see* Quanzhou
Tsiroanomandidy *350* C Madagascar
Tsiteli-Tskaro *see* Dedoplistsqaro
Tsitsihar *see* Qiqihar
Tskhinvall *457* C Georgia
Tsna *104* river of S Belorussia
Tsodilo Hills *118* mountain range of NW Botswana
Tsoelike *334* SE Lesotho
Tsu *304* Honshū, C Japan
Tsuchiura *304* Honshū, SE Japan
Tsuen Wan *262* W Hong Kong
Tsugara-kaikyō *304* strait connecting the Sea of Japan and Pacific Ocean, between Hokkaidō and Honshū, N Japan
Tsumeb *391* N Namibia
Tsumkwe *391* NE Namibia
Tsuruga *304* Honshū, C Japan
Tsuruoka *304* Honshū, N Japan
Tsushima *304* island group to the W of Honshū, W Japan
Tsushima Strait *304 var.* Korea Strait. Strait connecting the Sea of Japan and East China Sea, between South Korea and Japan
Tsuyama *304* Honshū, W Japan
Tuamotu, Îles *622* island group of N French Polynesia
Tuasivi *596* Savai'i, Western Samoa
Tuban, Wādī *559* dry watercourse of S Yemen
Tubmanburg *336* NW Liberia
Ṭubruq *339 Eng.* Tobruk. *It.* Tobruch. NE Libya

Tucker's Town *619* E Bermuda
Tuckum *see* Tukums
Tucson *568* Arizona, SW USA
Tucumán *see* San Miguel de Tucumán
Tucupita *589* E Venezuela
Tucuruí, Represa de *121* reservoir of N Brazil
Tudmur *521 var.* Tadmur, *Eng.* Palmyra. C Syria
Tuen Mun *262* W Hong Kong
Tugalan *see* Kolkhozabad
Tuira *424* river of SE Panama
Tukangbesi, Kepulauan *276* island group to the SE of Celebes, C Indonesia
Tu-k'ou *see* Panzhihua
Tūkrah *339* NE Libya
Tukums *330 Ger.* Tuckum. W Latvia
Tukuyu *530* S Tanzania
Tula *618* Tutuila, W American Samoa
Tula *452* W Russia
Tulaghi *488* Florida I. Solomon Islands
Tulcán *200* N Ecuador
Tulcea *448* E Romania
Tuléar *see* Toliara
Tuli *see* Thuli
Tulkarm *291, 292* NW West Bank
Tulle *225* S France
Tulsa *569* Oklahoma, SC USA
Tulsipur *395* W Nepal
Tuluá *171* W Colombia
Tumaco *171* SW Colombia
Tumareng *256* NW Guyana
Tumatumari *256* C Guyana
Tumba, Lac *see* Ntomba, Lac
Tumbes *431* NW Peru
Tumen *441 Rus.* Tumyntszyan. River of China and North Korea
Tumpat *354* N Peninsular Malaysia
Tumuc-Humac Mountains *121 Port.* Serra Tumuc-Humac. Mountain range of N South America
Tumuc-Humac, Serra *see* Tumuc-Humac Mountains
Tunapuna *540* N Trinidad, Trinidad & Tobago
Tunduru *530* S Tanzania
Tundzha *128 var.* Tundža. River of Bulgaria and Turkey
Tungabhadra *270* river of S India
Tung-kang *525 var.* Tung-chiang, *Jap.* Tōkō. SW Taiwan
Tung Lung Chau *262 var.* Tung Lung Island. Island of SE Hong Kong
T'ung-shan *see* Xuzhou
Tung-shih *525 Jap.* Tōsei. W Taiwan
Tung-t'ing Hu *see* Dongting Hu
Tunis *543 var.* Tūnis. * of Tunisia, NE Tunisia
Tunis, Golfe de *543* gulf of the Mediterranean Sea on the NE coast of Tunisia
Tunisia *542-545* officially Republic of Tunisia. Country of North Africa divided into 23 admin. units (governorates)
Tunja *171* C Colombia
Tương Đương *593* NW Vietnam
Tupiza *112* S Bolivia
Turan Lowland *551, 580 var.* Turan Plain, *Rus.* Turanskaya Nizmennost'. Plain of Turkmenistan and Uzbekistan
Ţurayf *472* N Saudi Arabia
Turbat *420* W Pakistan
Turčiansky Svätý Martin *see* Martin
Turda *420* NW Romania
Turgel *see* Türi
Tŭrgovishte *128 var.* Tărgovište, *prev.* Eski Dzhumaya. NE Bulgaria
Turgutlu *546* W Turkey
Türi *212 Ger.* Turgel. C Estonia
Turin *see* Torino
Turkana, Lake *215, 316 Eng.* Lake Rudolf. Lake of E Africa

Turkestan *312 Kaz.* Türkistan. S Kazakhstan
Turkestan Range *528 Rus.* Turkestanskiy Khrebet. Mountain range of NW Tajikistan
Turkestanskiy Khrebet *see* Turkestan Range
Turkey *546-549* officially Republic of Turkey, *Turk.* Türkiye Cumhuriyeti. Country of W Asia divided into 73 admin. units
Turkish Republic of Northern Cyprus *see* Cyprus
Turkmenistan *550-551* officially Republic of Turkmenistan, *prev.* Turkmenskaya Soviet Socialist Republic. Country divided into 4 admin. units (oblasts)
Turkmenskiy Zaliv *551 Turkm.* Türkmen Aylagy. Inlet of the Caspian Sea, on the W coast of Turkmenistan
Turks and Caicos Islands *629* British dependent territory of the Atlantic Ocean
Turks Islands *629* island group of SE Turks and Caicos Islands
Turku *221 Swe.* Åbo. SW Finland
Turkwel *316* seasonal river of NW Kenya
Turmero *589* N Venezuela
Turneffe Islands *102* islands of E Belize
Turnhout *99* NE Belgium
Turning Basin *624* undersea feature of the Pacific Ocean, NW Johnston Atoll
Turnov *188* N Czech Republic
Turnu Severin *see* Drobeta-Turnu Severin
Turócszentmárton *see* Martin
Turquino, Pico *182* mountain of SE Cuba
Turrailba *178* E Costa Rica
Tursunzade *528 prev.* Regar. W Tajikistan
Turtkul' *580 prev.* Petroaleksandrovsk, *Uzb.* Türtkül. W Uzbekistan
Turtle Islands *480* island group of SW Sierra Leone
Tuscaloosa *569* Alabama, SE USA
Tuscan Archipelago *see* Toscano, Arcipelago
Tuscany *299* region of Italy
Tuticorin *270* S India
Tutong *126* NW Brunei
Tutong *126* river of C Brunei
Tutrakan *128* N Bulgaria
Tutuila *618* island of W American Samoa
Tutume *118* E Botswana
Tuvalu *552-553 prev.* The Ellice Islands. Country of the Pacific Ocean
Tuvana-i-colo *218* island to the S of the Lau Group, SE Fiji
Tuvana-i-ra *218* island to the S of the Lau Group, SE Fiji
Tuva, Respublika *452* autonomous republic of C Russia
Tuvuca *218 prev.* Tuvutha. Island of the Lau Group, E Fiji
Ţuwayq, Jabal *472* mountain range of C Saudi Arabia
Tuxtla Gutiérrez *370 var.* Tuxtla. SE Mexico
Tuy Hoa *593* SE Vietnam
Tuz Khurmātū *284* N Iraq
Tuzla *116* NE Bosnia & Herzegovina
Tvøroyri *620 var.* Tverå. Suðuroy, S Faeroe Islands
Twante *135* S Burma
Tweed *563* river of SE Scotland, UK
Twin Falls *568* Idaho, NW USA
Twizel *401* C South Island, New Zealand
Tychy *439 Ger.* Tichau. S Poland

Tynda *453* E Russia
Tyne *563* river of NE England, UK
Tyneside *567*
Tyrnau *see* Trnava
Tyrol *see* Tirol
Tyrrhenian Sea *295 It.* Mare Tirreno. Area of the Mediterranean Sea
Tyumen' *452, 459* C Russia
Tyup *325 var.* Tjup. NE Kyrgyzstan
Tzekung *see* Zigong

U

Uaco Cungo *64 var.* Waku Kungo, *Port.* Santa Comba. C Angola
UAE *see* United Arab Emirates
Uamba *see* Wamba
Uanle Uen *see* Wanlaweyn
Ubangi *154, 176, 607 Fr.* Oubangui. River of C Africa
Ubarts' *104* river of Belorussia and Ukraine
Ubayyiḍ, Wādī al *284* dry watercourse of SW Iraq
Ube *304* Honshū, W Japan
Uberaba *121* S Brazil
Uberlândia *121* S Brazil
Ubin, Pulau *483* island of NE Singapore
Ubon Ratchathani *533* E Thailand
Ucar *86 Rus.* Udzhary. C Azerbaijan
Ucayali *431* river of C Peru
Uchkuduk *580 var.* Učkuduk, *Uzb.* Uchquduq. C Uzbekistan
Udine *295* N Italy
Udmurtskaya, Respublika *452* autonomous republic of W Russia
Udon Thani *533* N Thailand
Udzhary *see* Ucar
Ueda *304* Honshū, C Japan
Uele *607 var.* Welle. River of N Zaire
Ufa *452* W Russia
Ugāle *330* NW Latvia
Uganda *554-555* officially Republic of Uganda. Country of E Africa divided into 4 admin. units (regions)
Ugum *623* river, S Guam
Uherské Hradiště *188 Ger.* Ungarisch-Hradisch. SE Czech Republic
Úhlava *188 Ger.* Angel. River of W Czech Republic
Uíge *64 Port.* Vila Marechal Carmona, Carmona. NW Angola
Uiha *538 var.* 'Uiha. Island of the Ha'apai Group, Tonga
Ŭijŏngbu *496 Jap.* Giseifu. NW South Korea
Uis *391* NW Namibia
Uitenhage *493* Eastern Cape, S South Africa
Ujae *364* island of W Marshall Islands
Ujelang *364* island of W Marshall Islands
Újgradiska *see* Nova Gradiška
'Ujman *see* Ajman
Ujungpandang *276 prev.* Makasar, Macassar. Celebes, C Indonesia
Ujung Salang *see* Phuket
Újvidék *see* Novi Sad
UK *see* United Kingdom
Ukerewe *530* island of NW Tanzania, situated at the S of Lake Victoria
Uki Island *488* island of E Solomon Is
Ukmergė *344* E Lithuania
Ukraine *556-559* officially Republic of Ukraine, *Ukr.* Ukrayina, *Rus.* Ukraina, *prev.* Ukrainian Soviet Socialist Republic, Ukrainskaya S.S.R. Country of E Europe divided into 25 admin. units (24 regions and 1 republic)
Uku-jima *304* island of Gotō-rettō, SW Japan
Ula *104 Rus.* Ulla. River of N Belorussia
Ulaangom *380* NW Mongolia

Ulan Bator *380 var.* Ulaanbaatar. ❖ of Mongolia, C Mongolia

Ulan-Ude *453 prev.* Verkhneudinsk. C Russia

Ulawa Island *488* island of E Solomon Is

Uleåborg *see* Oulu

Uleälv *see* Oulujoki

Uleträsk *see* Oulujärvi

Uli *312* NW Kazakhstan

Uliastay *380* W Mongolia

Ulithi *375* atoll of W Micronesia

Ulla *see* Ula

Ullapool *563* N Scotland, UK

Ulm *237* S Germany

Ulonguè *387 var.* Ulongwé. NW Mozambique

Ulsan *496 Jap.* Urusan. SE South Korea

Ulster *563* province of Ireland, mostly included within Northern Ireland, UK

Ulúa *260* river of NW Honduras

Uluru *77 var.* Ayers Rock. Rocky outcrop of C Australia

Ulverstone *77* Tasmania, Australia

Ul'yanovsk *452 prev.* Simbirsk. W Russia

Uman' *556* C Ukraine

Umanak *622* W Greenland

'Umān, Khalīj *see* Gulf of Oman

Umatac *623* SW Guam

Umboi *426 var.* Rooke I. Island of E Papua New Guinea

Umbro-Marchigiano, Appennino *295* mountains of C Italy

Umeå *513* NE Sweden

Umeälv *513* river of NE Sweden

Umm al Ḥayt, Wādī *see* Amilḥayt, Wādī

Umm al Qaiwain *560 Ar.* Umm al Qaywayn. NE United Arab Emirates

Umm an Na'sān *91* island of W Bahrain

Umm aş Şabbān *see* Al Muḥammadīyah

Umm as Samim *418* seasonal desert lake of W Oman

Umm Bāb *447* W Qatar

Umm Durmān *see* Omdurman

Umm Ruwaba *506 var.* Umm Ruwābah, Um Ruwāba. C Sudan

Umm Sa'īd *see* Musay'īd

Umm Şalāl 'Alī *447 var.* Umm Silal Ali. NE Qatar

Umm Şalāl Muḥammad *447 var.* Umm Silal Mohammed. E Qatar

Umtali *see* Mutare

Umtata *493* Eastern Cape, SE South Africa

Umvukwes *see* Mvurwi

Umvuma *see* Mvuma

Umzingwani *612* river of S Zimbabwe

Una *116, 181* river of Bosnia & Herzegovina and Croatia

'Unayzah *472 var.* Anaiza. C Saudi Arabia

Ungama Bay *316 var.* Formosa Bay. Bay of the Indian Ocean to the SE of Kenya

Ungarisches Erzgebirge *see* Slovenské Rudohorie

Ungarisch-Hradisch *see* Uherské Hradiště

Ungava Bay *147* bay of the Labrador Sea, E Canada

Ungava, Péninsule d' *147* peninsula of E Canada

Ungheni *376 Rus.* Ungeny. W Moldavia

Ungvár *see* Uzhhorod

Union *248* NW Grenada island, Grenada

Union Island *466* island of SW St Vincent & the Grenadines

United Arab Emirates *560-561 prev.* Trucial States, *abbrev.* U.A.E. Country of SW Asia comprised of 7 admin units (states)

United Kingdom *562-567* officially United Kingdom of Great Britain and Northern Ireland, *abbrev.* UK. Country of NW Europe comprising England (86 admin. units -47 counties, 6 metropolitan counties, 32 London boroughs and the City of London), Wales (8 admin. units - counties), Scotland (12 admin. units - 9 regions, 3 island authorities) and Northern Ireland (26 admin. units - districts)

United States of America *568-575* officially United States of America, *abbrev.* USA. Country of North America divided into 51 admin. units (50 states, 1 federal district)

Uno *254* Ilha de Uno, Guinea-Bissau

Uno, Ilha de *254* island of SW Guinea-Bissau

Uoleva *538* island of the Ha'apai Group, Tonga

Uozu *304* Honshū, C Japan

Upaar Lagoon *504* lagoon of E Sri Lanka

Upala *178* NW Costa Rica

Upata *589* E Venezuela

Upernavik *622* W Greenland

Upington *493* Northern Cape, W South Africa

Upolu *596* island of SE Western Samoa

Upper Bann *563* river of Northern Ireland, UK

Upper Conaree *462* E St Kitts, St Kitts & Nevis

Upper Hutt *401* S North Island, New Zealand

Upper Lough Erne *563* lake of Northern Ireland, UK

Upper Mortlocks *375* island group of C Micronesia

Upper Peirce Reservoir *483* reservoir of C Singapore

Upper Volta *see* Burkina

Uppsala *513* SE Sweden

Ural *312, 452 Kaz.* Zayyq. River of Kazakhstan and Russia

Ural Mountains *452 var.* Ural'skiy Khrebet, Ural'skiye Gory. Mountain range of W Russia

Ural'sk *312 Kaz.* Oral. NW Kazakhstan

Ura-Tyube *528* NW Tajikistan

Uréparapara *585* Banks Islands, N Vanuatu

Urfa *see* Şanlıurfa

Urgench *580 var.* Urgenč, *prev.* Novo Urgench, *Uzb.* Urganch. W Uzbekistan

Urgut *580* SE Uzbekistan

Urlings *68* SW Antigua, Antigua & Barbuda

Urmia *see* Orūmīyeh

Urmia, Lake *see* Orūmīyeh, Daryācheh-ye

Urmston Road *262* W Hong Kong

Uroševac *602 Alb.* Ferizaj. S Serbia, Yugoslavia

Uruapan *370 var.* Uruapan del Progreso. SW Mexico

Urubamba *431* river of C Peru

Uruguay *71, 121, 577 Port.* Uruguai. River of S South America

Uruguay *576-579* officially Oriental Republic of Uruguay. Country of South America divided into 19 admin. units (departments)

Urukthapel *627* island of C Palau

Ürümqi *162 var.* Urumchi, Wu-lu-mu-ch'i, *prev.* Ti-hua. Xinjiang Uygur Zizhiqu , NW China

Urusan *see* Ulsan

USA *see* United States of America

Uşak *546 prev.* Ushak. W Turkey

Usakos *391* C Namibia

Usborne, Mount *621* mountain of East Falkland, E Falkland Islands

Ushant *see* Ouessant, Île d'

Ushuaia *71* S Tierra del Fuego, Argentina

Usk *563 Wel.* Wysg. River of S Wales, UK

Üsküb *see* Skopje

Usmas Ezers *330* lake of W Latvia

Usol'ye-Sibirskoye *453* C Russia

Ussuriysk *453 prev.* Voroshilov, Nikol'sk-Ussuriyskiy. SE Russia

Ust'-Abakanskoye *see* Abakan

Uster *516* NE Switzerland

Ustica, Isola de *295* island of S Italy

Ústí nad Labem *188 Ger.* Aussig. NW Czech Republic

Ustinov *see* Izhevsk

Ust'-Kamchatsk *453* NE Russia

Ust'-Kamenogorsk *312 Kaz.* Öskemen. E Kazakhstan

Ust'-Sisol'sk *see* Syktyvkar

Ustyurt Plateau *312, 580 Uzb.* Ustyurt Platosi. Plateau of Kazakhstan and Uzbekistan

Usulután *207* SE El Salvador

Usumacinta *250, 370* river of Guatemala and Mexico

Usumbura *see* Bujumbura

Usutu *see* Lusutfu

Utah *568* state of SW USA

Utamboni *208 var.* Temboni. River of Equatorial Guinea and Gabon

'Uta Vava'u *538* island of the Vava'u Group, Tonga

Utena *344* E Lithuania

Utirik *364* island of N Marshall Islands

Utrecht *397* C Netherlands

Utsunomiya *304* Honshū, SE Japan

Uttaradit *533 var.* Utaradit. N Thailand

Utuado *627* C Puerto Rico

Utupua *488* island of the Santa Cruz Is, E Solomon Is

Uvea, Île *629* island of S Wallis & Futuna

Uvs Nuur *380* lake of NW Mongolia

Uwajima *304* Shikoku, SW Japan

Uyo *408* S Nigeria

Uyuni *112* W Bolivia

Uzbekistan *580-583* officially Republic of Uzbekistan. Country of C Asia divided into 12 admin. units (oblastey)

Uzgen *325 Kir.* Özgön. W Kyrgyzstan

Uzhhorod *556 Rus.* Uzhgorod, *Cz.* Užhorod, *Hung.* Ungvár. W Ukraine

Užice *602 var.* Titovo Užice. W Serbia, Yugoslavia

V

Vaal *493* river of C South Africa

Vaasa *221 prev.* Nikolainkaupunki, *Swe.* Vasa. W Finland

Vác *264 Ger.* Waitzen. N Hungary

Vaches, Île aux *478 var.* Bird Island. Island group of the Inner Islands, N Seychelles

Vacoas *368* W Mauritius

Vadar *245 prev.* Axios. River of Greece and FYR Macedonia

Vadile *see* Vatili

Vadodara *270 prev.* Baroda. W India

Vaduz *342* ❖ of Liechtenstein, W Liechtenstein

Vágar *620 var.* Vågø. Island of W Faeroe Islands

Vágbeszterce *see* Považská Bystrica

Vágújhely *see* Nové Mesto nad Váhom

Vágur *620 var.* Våg. Sudhuroy, S Faeroe Islands

Váh *485 Ger.* Waag, *Hung.* Vág. River of W Slovakia

Väike-Emajõgi *212* river of S Estonia

Väinameri *212 prev.* Muhu Väin. Area of Baltic Sea, off the coast of W Estonia

Vaitogi *618* Tutuila, W American Samoa

Vaitupu *553* coral atoll of C Tuvalu

Vakhah *528 var.* Vahš. SW Tajikistan

Vākhān, Kūh-e *53 Per.* Kowtal-e Khaybar. Mountain range of C Asia

Vakhsh *528 var.* Vahš. River of SW Tajikistan

Valdecañas, Embalse de *501* reservoir of W Spain

Valdez *568* Alaska, USA

Valdia *see* Weldiya

Valdivia *159* C Chile

Valence *225* SE France

Valencia *501 Cat.* València. Autonomous community of NE Spain

Valencia *589* NW Venezuela

Valencia, Golfo de *501* area of the Mediterranean Sea, E of Spain

Valera *589* NW Venezuela

Valga *212 Ger.* Walk. S Estonia

Valkeakoski *221* SW Finland

Valladolid *501* NW Spain

Valle de la Pascua *589* C Venezuela

Valledupar *171* N Colombia

Vallée de Mboun *476* river of C Senegal

Vallée du Ferlo *476 var.* Ferlo. River of N Senegal

Vallegrande *112* C Bolivia

Vallenar *159* N Chile

Valletta *363 prev.* Valetta. ❖ of Malta, E Malta

Valley *97* C Barbados

Valley, The *618* ❖ of Anguilla, E Anguilla

Vallgrund *221* island of W Finland

Valmiera *330 Ger.* Wolmar. NE Latvia

Valona *see* Vlorë

Valona, Bay of *see* Vlorës, Gjiri i

Valparaíso *159* C Chile

Valsayn *540* NW Trinidad, Trinidad & Tobago

Van *547* E Turkey

Vanadzor *74 prev.* Kirovakan. N Armenia

Vanard *465* NW St Lucia

Vana-Vändra *see* Vändra

Vancouver *146* SW Canada

Vancouver Island *146* island of SW Canada

Vanda *see* Vantaa

Vanderbijlpark *493* Pretoria-Witwatersrand-Vereeniging, NE South Africa

Vändra *212 prev.* Vana-Vändra, *Ger.* Fennern. C Estonia

Vänern *513 Eng.* Lake Vaner, *prev.* Lake Vener. Lake of SW Sweden

Vangaindrano *350* S Madagascar

Van Gölü *546 Eng.* Lake Van. Lake of E Turkey

Vangunu *488* island of the New Georgia Is, Solomon Is

Vanikolo *488 var.* Vanikoro. Island of the Santa Cruz Is, E Solomon Islands

Vanimo *426* NW Papua New Guinea

Van, Lake *see* Van Gölü

Vannes *224* W France

Vantaa *221 Swe.* Vanda. SW Finland

Vanua Balavu *218 prev.* Vanua Mbalavu. Island of the Lau Group, E Fiji

Vanua Lava *585* Banks Islands, N Vanuatu

Vanua Levu *218* island of N Fiji

Vanuatu, Republic of *584-585* officially Republic of Vanuatu, *prev.* New Hebrides. Country of the Pacific Ocean divided into 11 admin. units (districts)

Zhlobin *104* E Belorussia
Zhob *421* river of C Pakistan
Zhodino *see* Zhodzina
Zhodzina *104 Rus.* Zhodino.
 N Belorussia
Zhytkavichy *104* SE Belorussia
Zhytomyr *556 Rus.* Zhitomir.
 NW Ukraine
Žiar nad Hronom *485*
 var. Svätý Kríž nad Hronom,
 Ger. Heiligenkreuz,
 Hung. Garamszentkereszt.
 W Slovakia
Zia Town *336* E Liberia
Zībāk *53* NE Afghanistan
Zibo *163 var.* Zhangdian, Chang-tien.
 Shandong, E China
Zielona Góra *439*
 Ger. Grünberg in Schlesien.
 W Poland
Zienzu *336* C Liberia
Zigong *163* Tzekung. Sichuan,
 SW China
Ziguinchor *476* SW Senegal
Zilah *see* Zalău
Žilina *485 Hung.* Zsolna, *Ger.* Sillein.
 NW Slovakia
Zillah *339* C Libya
Zillenmarkt *see* Zalău
Ziller *82* river of W Austria
Zillertaler Alpen *82 It.* Alpi Aurine,
 Zillertal Alps. Mountain range
 of Austria and Italy
Zilupe *330 Ger.* Rosenhof.
 E Latvia
Zimbabwe *612-615* officially Republic
 of Zimbabwe, *prev.* Rhodesia
 (1964-1979) part of Central African
 Federation (1953-1963). Country of
 Africa divided into 8 admin. units
 (provinces)
Zimmi *480* S Sierra Leone
Zinder *407* S Niger
Ziniaré *132* C Burkina
Zinjibār *599* SW Yemen
Zinov'yevsk *see* Kirovohrad
Zion *462* E Nevis, St Kitts & Nevis
Zipaquirá *171* C Colombia
Zipser Neudorf *see* Spišská Nová Ves
Zitundo *387* S Mozambique
Ziway Hāyk' *215 var.* Lake Zway.
 Lake of C Ethiopia
Ziyamet *187 var.* Leonarisso.
 NE Cyprus
Zlatarsko Jezero *602* lake of
 SW Serbia, Yugoslavia
Zlaté Moravce *485*
 Hung. Aranyosmarót. SW Slovakia
Zletovo *349* NE FYR Macedonia
Zlín *188 prev.* Gottwaldov.
 SE Czech Republic
Zlīṭan *339 var.* Zlīṭān. N Libya
Znaim *see* Znojmo
Znojmo *188 Ger.* Znaim,
 S Czech Republic
Zóbuè *387* NW Mozambique
Zoetermeer *397* W Netherlands
Zólyom *see* Zvolen
Zomba *353* S Malawi
Zombor *see* Sombor
Zongo *607* N Zaire
Zonguldak *546* NW Turkey
Zorzor *336* N Liberia
Zou *108* river of S Benin
Zouar *156* N Chad
Zouérat *366 var.* Zouérate, Zouîrât.
 N Mauritania
Zrenjanin *602 prev.* Petrovgrad,
 Veliki Bečkerek,
 Ger. Grossbetschkerek,
 Hung. Nagybecskerek. N Serbia,
 Yugoslavia
Zsily *see* Jiu
Zsolna *see* Žilina
Zsupanya *see* Županja
Zueila *see* Zuwaylah
Zuénoula *300* C Ivory Coast
Zufār *418 Eng.* Dhofar. Administrative
 region of SW Oman
Zug *516* C Switzerland

Zugdidi *234* W Georgia
Zugspitze *237* mountain of Austria
 and Germany
Zuid *508* river of SW Surinam
Zuid-Beveland *397* island of
 SW Netherlands
Zuider Zee *see* IJsselmeer
Zuisan *see* Sŏsan
Zumbo *387 var.* Zumbu.
 NW Mozambique
Županja *181 Hung.* Zsupanya.
 NE Croatia
Zürich *516 Eng.* Zurich.
 N Switzerland
Zürichsee *516 Eng.* Lake Zurich.
 Lake of NE Switzerland
Żurrieq *363* S Malta
Zurūd, Wādī *see* Zeroud, Oued
Zuwārah *339* NW Libya
Zuwaylah *339 var.* Zawīlah,
 It. Zueila. SW Libya
Zvishavane *612 prev.* Shabani.
 S Zimbabwe
Zvolen *485 Ger.* Altsohl,
 Hung. Zólyom. C Slovakia
Zvornik *116* E Bosnia & Herzegovina
Zway, Lake *see* Ziway Hāyk'
Zwedru *336* E Liberia
Zwickau *237* SE Germany
Zwijndrecht *397* SW Netherlands
Zwolle *397* NE Netherlands
Zyryanovsk *312* E Kazakhstan

ACKNOWLEDGEMENTS

DORLING KINDERSLEY would like to express their thanks to the following individuals, companies and institutions for their help in preparing this atlas:

ADDITIONAL CARTOGRAPHY
Advanced Illustration (Congleton, UK)
Andrew Bright
Cosmographics (Watford, UK)
Malcolm Porter
Swanston Publishing (Derby, UK)
Andrew Thompson

DESIGN
Boyd Annison, Icon Solutions (Chesham, UK) *for Macintosh consultancy and chart templates*
Bruno Maag, Dalton Maag (London, UK) *for font consultancy and production*

RESEARCH AND REFERENCE
Dr D Alkhateeb, Organization of Petroleum Exporting Countries (OPEC, Vienna, Austria)
Amnesty International (London, UK)
Caroline Blunden
CNN International (New York, USA)
Dataquest Europe SA (Paris, France)
CSL Davies
Department of Trade and Industry Export Market Information Centre (London, UK)
The Flag Institute (Chester, UK)
Foreign and Commonwealth Office (London, UK)
Alexander Fyges-Walker
Christel Heideloff, Institute of Shipping Economics and Logistics (Bremen, Germany)
International Bank for Reconstruction and Development (World Bank, Washington, DC, USA)
International Committee of the Red Cross (ICRC, Geneva, Switzerland)
International Civil Aviation Organization (ICAO, Montreal, Canada)

International Criminal Police Organization (INTERPOL, Lyon, France)
International Institute for Strategic Studies, for information from *The Military Balance* (London, UK)
Institute of Latin American Studies, University of London (London, UK)
Intermediate Technology Development Group (Rugby, UK)
Chris Joseph, United States Travel and Tourism Administration (USTTA, London, UK)
Latin American Bureau (London, UK)
Patrick Mahaffey, Ohio European Office (Brussels, Belgium)
Peter Mansfield
Robert Minton-Taylor
National Meteorological Library and Archive (Bracknell, UK)
Oil and Gas Journal (Houston, Texas)
Organization for Economic Cooperation and Development (OECD, Paris, France)
Penal Reform International (London, UK)
Matt Ridley
Screen Digest (London, UK)
William Smith, Chicago Sun-Times (Chicago, USA)
Tourism Concern (London, UK)
United Nations Crime Prevention and Criminal Justice Branch (UNCPC, Vienna, Austria)
United Nations Development Programme (UNDP, New York, USA)
United Nations Environment Programme (UNEP, Nairobi, Kenya)
United Nations Food and Agriculture Organization (UNFAO, Rome, Italy)
United Nations International Labour Organization (UNILO, Geneva, Switzerland)
United Nations Population Fund (UNFPA, New York, USA)
Westminster Reference Library (London, UK)
World Conservation Monitoring Centre (Cambridge, UK)
World Health Organization (WHO, Geneva, Switzerland)
World Tourism Organization (Madrid, Spain)

The many embassies, High Commissions, airports, national information and tourist offices in London and around the world.

PICTURE CREDITS

t=top, b=below, a=above, l=left, r=right, c=centre

Adams Picture Library: 482bl. Ancient Art & Architecture Collection: 38bcr, 39cra, 39bl, 41tc, 45br; G. Tortoli 39tr. G. Andrews: 426ca. Arcaid: P. Mauss Esto 568bc. Aspect Picture Library Ltd.: D. Bayes 338bl; K. Naylor 606tr; F. Nichols 276tr; B. Seed 386ca. Associated Press: 215bcr, 588tr, 603bcl; AFP 383 bcr. Australian High Commission: 78br. Belgian Embassy: 99bcr. Bridgeman Art Library: (artist: J-M Nattier) Hermitage, St. Petersburg 40bcr; ('Bonaparte Crossing The Alps', artist: J.L. David) Lauros-Giraudon, Chateau de Malmaison 42bcr; National Maritime Museum 41br; (artist: G. de Castro) Private Collection 42bcl. D. Doug Bryant Stock Photos: 429tc; B. Augustin 404tr. Camera Press: 129bcr, 613cr; H. Andrews 599bcr; L. Brook 401tcl; T. Charlier 449cbr, 577bl; F. Goodman 625cbr; A. Pucciano 71cr; S. Smith 215bcl. J. Allan Cash Ltd.: 49tl, 82ca, 92bc, 122br, 125tl, 144tr, 147tr, 164tr, 211tr, 261tc, 280tr, 292br, 311cra, 316bl, 351tc, 354ca, 406bc, 408tr, 421cb, 422tr, 423bc, 556bc. Bruce Coleman Ltd.: 466bl; M. Berge 564tr; B&C Calhoun 150bc; G. Cubitt 64tr, 214bc; P. Davey 186bc; B. Fogden 430ca; J. Fry 477tc; J. Jurka 512bc; Dr. M.P. Kahl 70tr; G. Langesbury 232bc; O. Langrand 558tr; L. Lee Rue 67tl; K. Maj 438ca; L.C. Marigo 251tc; S. Prato 244bc; F. Prenzel 80tc; K. Taylor 481tr. Colorific!: J. Howard 505bl; J. Polleross/JB Pictures 54br; M. Rogers 506tr. Colorific!/Black Star: M. Kreiner 48cl; S.Tucci 135bl. Compix: 320tr, 355tc, 393bc; J. Leach 488ca; B. McGrath 510ca; J. Thomas 552bc. Comstock Ltd. : 170bc, 298tl, 505tc; T.Eigeland 567tc; G.L. Scarfiotti 446bc. Cuban Embassy: 185bcl. James Davis Travel Photography: 62cla, 117bc, 120bl, 121tl, 127tl, 190ca, 220bc, 302bc, 347tl, 358tr, 369ca, 379tl, 396bc, 400bc, 461tc, 462bl, 464bl, 468tr, 520bc, 528tr, 556tr, 571tr, 598bl, 619cr, 636cbl; Prisma 198tr; S. Thingeyjar 269tc; World View/Fotothek 155tc. ET Archive: 38bcl; (artist: N.Dance) 45cr; ("Halt of Boer Family" artist: S. Daniel) 43bl; (artist: D. Gregory) 45tcl. Embassy of the Islamic Republic of Iran: 281tcl. Embassy of the People's Democratic Republic of Laos: 326bcr, 326br. Embassy of Peru: 431tl. Mary Evans Picture Library: 41cra, 41bcl. Chris Fairclough Colour Library: 45cr, 343tl, 542br. J. Guest: 140ca, 592bc. Robert Harding Picture Library: 52tr, 156ca, 197tl, 243tc, 252bl, 265tr, 284tr, 308bl, 324bc, 419tc, 434tr, 448tr, 452tr, 479tc, 597tc; P. Craven 224tr; F. Dubes 124bl; Explorer 345tc; Explorer/Roy 86tr; R. Frerck/Odyssey 370tr; Gascoine 580bl; R. Harding/C. Martin 241bl, G. Hellier 189tr, 484tr; D. Hughes 229bc; C. Martin 256br; Photri 194ca; R. Rainford 565tl; C. Rennie 550ca; G. Roli 414tr; Rosehaven Management Ltd. 629cr; J. Ross 353bc; Sassoon 110cb, 254cl; A. Woolfitt 90bc. Paul Harris Photography: 459bl. High Commission for India: 272cb, 272cbr, 272br. High Commission for The People's Republic of Bangladesh: 92cla. Hulton Deutsch Collection: 44br, 45br, 47br. Robert Hunt Library: 47tc. Hutchison Library: 112ca, 337tc, 566bc, 612tr; R. Francis 530tr; J.G. Fuller 626br; B. Gerard 251bc; J. Henderson 256ca; A. Hill 610bc; M. Macintyre 558ca; T. Page 490ca; C. Pemberton 182tr; Penn 635tl; L. Taylor 452bl. The Image Bank: M. Beebe 181cl; G. Jung 546tr; T. Madison 163br; M.E. Newman 296tr; C.M. Pasdzior 564br; A. Rippy 162tr; G.A. Rossi 622bl; H. Sund 463tr; P. Trummer 202tr. Images Colour Library: 394bl. Impact Photos Ltd.: J. Arthur 492tcr; P. Cavendish 435tc; B. Edwards 420tr, 421cr; A. le Garsmeur 580cca, 649cra; R. Lubbock 206tr; G-J. Norman 322tr; C. Penn 554tr. Japan Information & Cultural Centre: 306tr, 306cb, 306cbr. David King Collection: 49cra.

Magnum Photos Ltd.: H. Cartier-Bresson 47cra; H. Gruyaert 639tr; J. Hillelson Agency 649tc; C. Steele-Perkins 641cbl. Mexican Embassy: 371bc, 371bcr. NASA: 49br. Network: M. Goldwater 643tl; J. Jordan 645cr. New Zealand High Commission: 401tl. Novosti Press Agency: 105cbr. Office of the Leader of the Opposition, Australia: P. West 78cbr. PA News: 415c; AFP 55tr, 587bcl; AFP/M. Clement 543tr; AFP/M. Shoraf 521br. Panos Pictures: N. Cooper 102tr, 655cra; M. French 259tc; R. Giling 508tr; J. Hartley 132bc, 655bc; D. Hulcher 326tr; S. Sprague 112bl, 138tr; B. Tobiasson 301bc. N. Peck: 182bl. Picturepoint Ltd.: 109tc, 208tr, 470bc, 618c. Popperfoto: 45cra, 46br, 49bl, 205bcr; AFP/Armand 48br; EPA 113cr; Official U.S. Air Force Photo 49cr. Reuters Television: 105cbl, 122tcl, 272cb, 272bc, 473br, 557tr. Rex Features Ltd.: 92cra, 135bcl, 148cbr, 148bc, 164br, 221tr, 226cbr, 258cbr, 245tr, 265bcr, 265bcl, 296cbr, 306bc, 312bcl, 555bcl, 409bcl, 421tr, 423tr, 449cb, 454bcr, 455bcl, 492tr, 497bcl, 501tr, 513tcr, 513tr, 525tr, 564tr, 564cra, 571bcl, 581bcr, 599bcl, 638bl; Sipa-Press 55tc, 59bl, 59bcl, 71tc, 99bcl, 158tr, 164bcl, 164bcr, 185bcr, 245tcr, 277bcr, 285c, 290br, 387cbl, 397tcl, 415cr, 454br, 455bl, 553tcr, 603bcr, 621bl, 659tl, 644cbl. Ann Ronan At Image Select: 36bc. Royal Danish Embassy: 191tcr, 191tr. Royal Geographical Society: R. Mear 646cbl. Royal Thai Embassy: 553tr. Science Photo Library: D. Parker 50tr; Dr. D. Millar 648cbl; Novosti Press Agency 641tc. Harry Smith Collection: 40cbl. Embassy of The Socialist Republic of Vietnam: 593tl, 593tcl. South-American Pictures: J. Berrange 178br; P. Dixon 424tr; T. Morrison 576tr. Spanish Embassy: 501tcr. Sovfoto/Eastfoto: 649clb. Frank Spooner Pictures: 47cbl, 296bcl, 317tcr, 577bcl; Amin-Camera Pix 317tr; L. Anticoli 296cbl; Arnaud 129bc; W. Christopher 170tcr; A. Denize 559tcr; A. Duclos 158tcr, 281tcr; K.J. Eddy 85cbl; C. Hires 521bcr, 639bcl; P. Perrin 285cr; C. Poulet 623cr; Reglain 141tcr; N. Sagansky 607cr; A. Sassaki 122tr, 122cra; Versele-Deville 226bc. Frank Spooner Pictures/Gamma: 85cbr, 226cb; K. Al Arab 543tc; C. Angel 171tcr, 588tcr, 590tr; F. Apesteguy 473cb; F. Arthur 443bcr; J.C. Aunos 290bcr; V. Brynner 421tcr, 423tcr; L. Chaperon 238cbl; R. Gaillarde 443bcr; B. Iverson 203bcl; Iliona-Figaro Magazine 89tc; N. Jallot 376tr; Jasmin 645tc; E. de Keerle 459tcr; K. Kuukka 221tcr; Loviny 141tcr; A. Movan 277bcl; Najer 555bcr; Photo News 607cl; P. Piel 258bcr; E. Vandeville 171tr; C.H. Vioujard 583bcl; Xinhua 164bl. Frank Spooner Pictures/Liaison: Anderson 497bcr; T. Arthur 570br; B. Asoto 455cr; Ferry 451tcl; Halstead 113c; Markel 571bl, 615c; Peterson 409bcr; B. Stern 213tr. Frank Spooner Pictures/Stills: Ponopresse 148ecb. Tony Stone Images: 155bc, 174tr, 414br, 498bl; G. Allison 575bl; D. Armand 148tr; O. Benn 69tc, 249tr; K. Biggs 640cbl; M. Brooke 134tr; J. Callahan 262ca; A. Cassidy 274br; P. Chesley 374ca; J. Cornish 289bc; S. Egan 500tr, 516tr; R. Evans 128tr; R. Everts 585tr; D. Hanson 532bl; A. Kearney 158bc, H. Kurihara 240bc; G. Pease 657tc; J. Pragen 586tr; F. Prenzel 584bc; S. Rothfeld 561tc; D. Schultz 44bl; A. Smith 350ca; R. Smith 78tr; 201tl; D. Stone 516tr; P. Tweedie 552bc; C. Waite 562bc. Swiss Embassy: 517c, 517cr. Sygma: Baldev 412tr; R. Reuter 468bl. Taipei Representative's Office in the U.K.: 525tcr, 525tr. TASS: Itar 512bcr. Telegraph Colour Library: 76tr; Ford Motor Co. Ltd. 46cbl. J. Tempest: 219tc, 561cb. Texas Medical Center: 572bl. Topham: A. Azakir 559tr. Travel Photo International: Fotoworld 362bl. Trip: C. Bowman 239br, 241tl; T. Goodman 255tc; V. Shuba 104ca; V. Sidoropolev 512tr; G. Spenceley 348tr. Viva: M. Franck 74tr. S. Wheat: 647cra. R. Woods: 271tl, 273br. World Pictures: 59cla, 294br, 404ca, 524tr, 653tl. Zefa: 56bc, 96bl, 176ca, 492bl, 540bc, 590bl, 647cbl; Damm 657cr; Everts 602ca; F. Lanting 118tr; H. Lutticke 491tc; Smith 624br; Streichan 258bl, 241c; Sunak 588bl.

KEY TO SYMBOLS, ICONS & ABBREVIATIONS

A LL SYMBOLS AND ICONS used in the Atlas are illustrated and defined here. A fuller explanation can be found on pages 9, 10 and 11. Other detailed references include: the list of International Organizations (pages 652–655), the Glossary of Geographical Terms (pages 656–657) and the Glossary of Abbreviations used in the Atlas (page 658).

Abbreviations most regularly used throughout the Atlas are listed below.

bbl	billion barrels
b/cd	barrels per calendar day
b/d	barrels per day
bn	billion (one thousand million)
°C	degrees Celsius (Centigrade)
cm	centimetres

SWITCHES

yellow infill = conditions apply;
grey infill = conditions do not apply

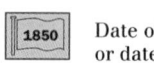 Date of independence or date current borders established

 Multiparty democracy

 Convertible currency

 Net aid receiver

 Net aid donor

 No significant aid donations or receipts

 Net energy importer

 Net energy exporter

 Compulsory military service

 Death penalty currently in use

 Full social security provisions

 Unemployment benefit only

 Free health service only

COMMUNICATIONS

 Main international airport

 Merchant fleet, total tonnage

 Extent of national road network (kilometres/miles)

 Extent of motorways or major national highways (kilometres/miles)

 Extent of commercial rail network (kilometres/miles)

 Extent of inland waterways navigable by commercial craft (kilometres/miles)

TOURISM

 Total number of tourists per year

 Trend indicators: increase/no variation/decrease in tourism over previous year

PEOPLE

 Main languages spoken (including official language)

 Population density (per km²)

POLITICS

 Date of next election

 Head of state

WORLD AFFAIRS

 Membership of international organizations

 Non-membership of additional international organizations

UN and World Bank membership is assumed

AID

 Total aid donations or receipts in US$

 Trend indicators: increase/no variation/decrease in aid over previous year

DEFENCE

 Annual defence budget in US$

 Trend indicators: increase/no variation/decrease in defence spending over previous year

 Army: equipment and personnel

 Navy: equipment and personnel

 Air force: equipment and personnel

 Nuclear capability: armaments

ECONOMICS

 Average exchange rate against the US$ over the last year

 Gross National Product (GNP) in US$